THE OXFORD COMPANION TO AUSTRALIAN LITERATURE

WILLIAM H. WILDE
JOY HOOTON
BARRY ANDREWS

Melbourne
OXFORD UNIVERSITY PRESS
Oxford   Auckland   New York

OXFORD UNIVERSITY PRESS AUSTRALIA

Oxford   New York
Athens   Auckland   Bangkok   Bombay
Calcutta   Cape Town   Dar es Salam   Delhi
Florence   Hong Kong   Istanbul   Karachi
Kuala Lumpur   Madras   Madrid   Melbourne
Mexico City   Nairobi   Paris   Singapore
Taipei   Tokyo   Toronto

and associated companies in
Berlin   Ibadan

OXFORD is a trade mark of Oxford University Press

National Library of Australia
Cataloguing-in-Publication data:

Wilde, W.H. (William Henry).
The Oxford companion to Australian literature.

2nd ed.
ISBN 0 19 553381 X.

1. Australian literature—Dictionaries. I. Hooton, Joy W. (Joy
Wendy), 1935–   . II. Andrews, Barry G. (Barry Geoffrey),
1943–1987. III. Title. IV. Title; Australian literature.

A820.9

Edited by Venetia Nelson
Typeset by Abb-typesetting Pty Ltd, Victoria
Printed by Brown Prior Anderson Pty Ltd, Victoria
Published by Oxford University Press,
253 Normanby Road, South Melbourne, Australia

PREFACE

The Oxford Companion to Australian Literature is a reference work which we hope will be of interest to the general reader as well as of use of students of Australian literature and related fields. Central to the book are the alphabetical entries on authors and literary works, and clearly there has been selection and weighting in the preparation of these entries: not every Australian author has been included, and some have been discussed in far greater detail than others. But we have taken a broad definition of 'author' (including entries, for example, on historians, critics and journalists) and of 'literary work', and the varied length of entries is only partly the result of our judgements on relative importance: for example, for some authors information has been difficult to discover, the plots of some novels are more conducive to summary than others, and for contemporary writers we have aimed to be conservative in coverage on the grounds that the output of those writers and the assessment of them is likely to undergo significant change. While we decided very early that to exclude living authors would be absurd in a Companion to a national literature as young as Australia's, we have not included many contemporary critics, except where they are also creative writers (e.g. Michael Wilding) or where their reputation has been established over a significant period (e.g. A.A. Phillips). For the author entries our aim has been to supply basic biographical and publishing information (including, with major authors, some critical studies of them) and generally also some measure of description and appreciation. We have been highly selective in our coverage of literary characters, including mainly characters who are of special significance (e.g. Lawson's Joe Wilson) or who can be firmly linked with a historical personage.

The second major group of entries encompasses the literary, historical and other cultural contexts within which Australian authors and their writings can be placed. Our notion of literary context has been broad enough to permit entries on literary journals, series, awards, societies and movements; on libraries, publishers and cultural organisations; on aspects of closely associated fields (e.g. cinema, broadcasting, the theatre, Australian English); on overseas writers who either visited Australia (e.g. Trollope, Stevenson) or exercised significant influence in Australian cultural history (e.g. Dickens, Shakespeare); and on other topics. By historical and other cultural contexts is meant those aspects of Australian life and history about which readers unfamiliar with Australia might need basic information (e.g. the Eureka Stockade or the Heidelberg School) or which might be encountered in the reading of Australian literature and need explanation: places, people, events, idioms and so on. Some of these have produced an extensive creative literature of their own (e.g. the phenomenon of bushranging) and most are at least alluded to somewhere in Australian writing. Such entries have been consciously focused towards Australian literature: thus the entry on the turf deliberately provides only very basic information about the development of horse-racing and associated activities in Australia, and emphasises instead the kinds of connections between the turf and Australian literature through information on the poems and stories on the subject, the writers involved in horse-racing, and so on.

In a work of this scope and magnitude it is inevitable that we have been much indebted to the work of others, ranging from standard reference works such as E. Morris Miller's bibliography of Australian literature and the *Australian Dictionary of Biography* to specialist studies of individual authors. It is impossible to list all the works consulted in the preparation of the *Companion*, but we have included entries on many of the standard reference works and mentioned specialist studies in other entries; despite these inclusions, it is essential that we offer a general acknowledgement to all those who have written on Australian literature and its contexts. We are grateful to the writers who are the subject of entries who responded to our request for biographical and publishing information, generously supplying in many cases more information than we were able to use; for additional help over a wide range of enquiries we are also grateful to the staff of the Australian Council for the Arts, the Community Arts Board, the Fellowship of Australian Writers, the Literature Board and the universities of Sydney and New England; and to Philip Butterss, Chris Cunneen, C.B. Christesen, Ros Pesman Cooper, Robert Darby, Peter Dennis, Robert Dingley, Livio Dobrez, Suzanne Edgar, Paul Eggert, Patricia Excell, Cliff Hanna, J.P. Hardy, Josie Hilliger, Ian Jones, Val Kent, Brian Kiernan, Elaine Lindsay, Roger McDonald, Mungo Ballardie MacCallum, Russell McDougall, Humphrey McQueen, John McQuilton, Brian Matthews, John Meredith, Craig Munro, Margaret O'Hagan, W.S. Ramson, John Robertson, Ken Stewart, Anne Summers, Alrene Sykes, G.P. Walsh and James Wieland. We would also like to acknowledge the informative assistance provided by the late Dorothy Green and Alrene Sykes for the 1985 edition. Considerable effort has been made to check the accuracy of the facts included in the *Companion*, although it must be pointed out that in some areas of Australian literature and literary history — Australian theatre history is a case in point — the definitive studies are only now emerging; we welcome any suggestions and corrections for future revisions and editions. The accuracy of the work of the 1985 edition was greatly enhanced by the efforts of Sandra Burchill, research assistant in the Department of English at Duntroon throughout the project, who did much research and performed many routine tasks of checking and filing; for other research assistance we were grateful to Patricia Dobez early in the project and Kay Walsh towards the end. Research assistance for the second edition was funded by a small Australian Research Council grant, for which we are grateful. Kay Walsh's efforts as research assistant for the second edition have been invaluable and indeed crucial in achieving its completion by the publishing deadline. Margaret McNally's cheerful and efficient assistance in the technical production of the book and her firm control of the computer's master copy is also gratefully acknowledged as is the initial research assistance by Frances Dixon. We thank Professor Bruce Bennett, head of the Department of English at University College, Australian Defence Force Academy, and Professor Harry Heseltine, rector, for their support and co-operation. Much of the project was researched at the National Library of Australia, where we were dependent on the range of services provided by the library and where the staff displayed extraordinary tolerance of the inordinate number of submitted call-slips. The bulk of the enormous amount of typing and retyping of entries, lists of headwords and cross-references for the first edition was performed by Trish Middleton in the days before computers; Bev Stuckey also assisted towards the end of the project. Our sincere thanks go to all of these helpers at the Canberra end of the project; at the publishing end we were fortunate in having Frank Eyre as copy editor for the first edition and Venetia Nelson for the second. The first edition owed much to the support and encouragement of James Hall and David Cunningham, while Peter Rose has been unfailingly enthusiastic and supportive during the writing of the second. During the writing of the first edition, the support and interest of our colleagues in the Department of English at Duntroon extended beyond a tolerance of our obsessions to a willingness each to contribute a significant entry. Some colleagues who subsequently joined us at University College, the Australian Defence Force Academy, have also contributed entries. Individual entries contributed by colleagues, which are signed at the foot of the entry, include those by Sandra Burchill, Adrian Caesar, Ros Pesman Cooper, Frances Dixon, Jeff Doyle, David Headon, Harry Heseltine, Doug Jarvis, John Laird, Elizabeth Lawson, Trish Middleton, Bruce Moore and Kay Walsh.

The writing of the second edition was greatly handicapped by the tragic loss of Barry Andrews, who died shortly after the first edition was published. We have made every effort, however, to retain his quintessential qualities of humour and relish for the absurd as well as the fruits of his exceptional scholarship and wide-ranging interests. The second edition represents a substantial revision and expansion of the first, reflecting the appearance of new writers, the more recent work of established writers, the findings of recent research and scholarship and general changes in Australia's cultural context. Last, we should like to thank our families and friends, especially Viv Hooton, Ena Wilde and Robyn Andrews, for their continued tolerance of our obsessive commitment to what has been a long haul.

W.H.W
J.H
B.A

STYLE

In this work the surnames of authors (e.g. **BARRY, Clive**) and other persons (e.g. **BARRY, Dan**) are printed in bold capitals at the head of articles, with given names in bold upper and lower case; the titles of literary works and newspapers in upper- and lower-case bold italics (e.g. ***Boomerang, Bring Larks and Heroes***); the titles of items within books in bold roman, in quotation marks (e.g. **'Man from Snowy River, The'**); and other entries, including the names of characters, in bold roman (e.g. **Canadian Exiles, Cabbage Tree, Beck, Martin**). Other aspects of our style should be apparent for such matters as the deletion of the definite article in head-words for newspapers and organisations, and the use of quotation marks on a headword which is treated as a *word* (e.g. **'Drover'**). There are, however, one or two matters that perhaps need comment or emphasis. Our two most difficult problems were to decide on an effective policy regarding the use of 'q.v.' and the citations of plays. With the former, we have used the cross-reference indicator 'q.v.' selectively rather than automatically, and as a general rule only when a reading of the entry referred to by 'q.v.' will, in our judgement, enhance the entry under consideration; readers are encouraged to use the *Companion* to see if an item not covered by a 'q.v.' is nevertheless the subject to an entry. With plays the problems are whether to give priority to date of performance or publication, and when to italicise the titles of plays, given that plays are not always separately published. Our final decision was to italicise all plays which have been published, whatever the form of publication (e.g. published separately, published as part of a volume of plays, or published within journals), and only to use quotation marks for unpublished plays. For many published plays we have given, where these are known to us, the dates of performance and publication, and we have tried to make clear, where only one date is given, which one it is; where doubt exists, readers are encouraged to turn to the entry on the individual play or its author. Among other decisions of policy, the titles of films and television series have been italicised; known dates of publication which differ from the date on the title page have been preferred for a few works (e.g. *Quintus Servinton, The Hermit in Van Diemen's Land* and *The Escape of the Notorious Sir William Heans*, qq.v); titles and subtitles (e.g. those beginning with *Or*) have been standardised so that all words have been capitalised apart from articles, conjunctions and prepositions; and better-known pseudonyms have been preferred in the headwords for some authors, although the appropriate cross-references are supplied. The cut-off date for inclusion of material is the end of 1993, although in some instances 1994 material has been included.

ABBREVIATIONS

The following abbreviations have been generally adopted, but are not used where the full name is of major significance to an entry:

ABC	Australian Broadcasting Commission
AC	Companion of the Order of Australia
ACT	Australian Capital Territory
ADB	*Australian Dictionary of Biography*
AIF	Australian Imperial Force
ALS	Australian Literature Society
ALS	*Australian Literary Studies*
AM	Member of the Order of Australia
ANA	Australian Natives' Association
ANU	Australian National University
AO	Officer of the Order of Australia
APG	Australian Performing Group
A&R	Angus and Robertson
ASAL	Association for the Study of Australian Literature
BBC	British Broadcasting Corporation
BEM	British Empire Medal
CAE	College of Advanced Education
CLF	Commonwealth Literary Fund
CMG	Companion of the Order of St Michael and St George
CSIRO	Commonwealth Scientific Industrial and Research Organization
DBE	Dame of the Order of The British Empire
FAW	Fellowship of Australian Writers
FRGS	Fellow of the Royal Geographical Society
MBE	Member of the Order of The British Empire
MHR	Member of the House of Representatives
NIDA	National Institute of Dramatic Art
NSW	New South Wales
NZ	New Zealand
OAM	Medal of the Order of Australia
OBE	Officer of the Order of The British Empire
OUP	Oxford University Press
POW	prisoner of war
PNG	Papua New Guinea
QC	Queen's Counsel
RAAF	Royal Australian Air Force
RAF	Royal Air Force
RAN	Royal Australian Navy
RN	Royal Navy
RSL	Returned Services League
SA	South Australia
SBS	Special Broadcasting Service
SF	Science Fiction

ABBREVIATIONS

TAFE	(Department of) Technical and Further Education
UN	United Nations
UQP	University of Queensland Press
USA	United States of America
VC	Victoria Cross
WA	Western Australia
WAAAF	Women's Auxiliary Australian Air Force
WEA	Workers' Educational Association

A

ABBOTT, J.H.M. (John Henry Macartney) (1874–1953), born Haydonton, NSW, was working as a jackeroo when his first contribution was accepted by the *Bulletin* in 1897. He served in the Boer War, an experience which produced both *Tommy Cornstalk* (1902), an early example of Australian war writing which presents the Australian soldier in a way similar to the Anzac (q.v.) legend, and *Plain and Veldt* (1903). In London after the war Abbott worked as a freelance writer and journalist and published *An Outlander in England* (1905) and *Letters from Queer Street* (1908), a moving account of London poverty. Back in Australia, Abbott was a prolific contributor of articles, series and serials to the *Bulletin*, the *Lone Hand* and many other journals. His historical fiction, which presented a particular view of colonial society, included *The Governor's Man* (1919), *Castle Vane* (1920), *Ensign Calder* (1922) and *Sydney Cove* (1923). Other historical works by Abbott were *The Story of William Dampier* (1911), *Ben Hall* (1934), *The Newcastle Packets and the Hunter Valley* (1943), *Out of the Past* (1944) and *Red O'Shaughnessy* (1946). Historical figures such as Lachlan Macquarie and William Bligh appear in his fiction.

ABC Weekly, the journal of the Australian Broadcasting Commission, was published 1939–59, when it was superseded by the *TV Times*. Chiefly a descriptive outline of national and commercial radio programmes (later including television), it also carried articles of broad cultural interest.

ABDULLAH, Mena (1930–), of Indian extraction, was born at Bundarra in northern NSW. She contributed short stories to the *Bulletin* and several of the *Coast to Coast* collections and to Louise Rorabacher's *Two Ways Meet* (1963). She collaborated with Ray Mathew (q.v.) to produce a collection of stories, *The Time of the Peacock* (1965). Most of the twelve stories in the collection are narrated by the small Indian girl Nimmie, who weaves together the sometimes sad, sometimes happy, strands of a mixed Indian-Australian life. The Indian family, bound together by an intense love, cope with a poignant situation of exile that is tempered by hope for the future and joy in each other in the present. Well-known stories are 'Because of the Rusilla', in which an Indian lad, insulted by an Australian boy and bereft of his beloved 'rosella', has his happiness restored by the gift of a kettle that sings like a bird; 'Grandfather Tiger', in which a little Indian girl creates an *alter ego*, the Tiger, who advises her how to combat the discrimination she meets at her first Australian school; and 'A Long Way', in which a mother walks from her village to Karachi to send a knitted jumper to her student son in Australia. *The Time of the Peacock* has often been reprinted. Recently the stories have been sensitively interpreted by Yasmine Gooneratne in the multicultural critique, *Striking Chords* (1992, ed. Sneja Gunew and Kateryna O'Longley). Mena Abdullah recently retired after forty years' service with CSIRO.

A'BECKETT, Sir, William (1806–69), born London, had a career in law and literature before coming to Australia in 1837. He was appointed resident judge of Port Phillip in 1845 and chief justice of the newly created Supreme Court of Victoria in 1852. A'Beckett, who had published a book of verse in England at the age of 18, edited the weekly *Literary News* in NSW in 1837, published *Lectures on the Poets and Poetry of Great Britain* in 1839, contributed articles to the *Port Phillip Herald* under the pseudonym 'Malwyn', wrote a poem on Ludwig Leichhardt in that newspaper (later reprinted in Edmund Finn's *The Chronicles of Early Melbourne*, 1888), and published a long verse narrative, *The Earl's Choice*, in 1863. He was the great-grandfather of Martin Boyd (see Boyd Family).

Aboriginal and Islander Identity, see *Identity*

Aboriginal Arts Committee (Aboriginal and Torres Strait Islanders Arts Committee), one of two major committees of the Australia Council (q.v.), was formed by the Minister for the Arts, Tourism and Territories in 1989 to replace the Aboriginal Arts Board, which had been established in 1973 and made one of the seven arts boards of the Australia Council in 1975. Chairperson Lin Onus and Aboriginal representatives from around Australia were given the task of undertaking a policy and structural review of the previous Aboriginal Arts Board, while maintaining its funding and support programmes. The Aboriginal Arts Committee has its own three specialised art-form committees – Performing Arts, Literature and Visual Arts/Craft – each comprising practitioners from these fields. The Australia Council also appoints representatives from the Aboriginal Arts Committee to all three art-form boards of the Council itself, thus ensuring Aboriginal representation within those boards and the possibility of funding Aboriginal arts from them. The focus of the Aboriginal Arts Board is on the development and nurturing of contemporary Aboriginal artistic and cultural expression, building on the preservation of cultural traditions and artistic techniques of the past. Community arts officers funded by the Aboriginal Arts Committee and employed by Aboriginal community committees organise workshops, festivals and residences in all art-forms and advise artists and writers on such matters as copyright and recording contracts. Typical of funded organisations are the Aboriginal Dance Theatre in Redfern, Sydney, Brisbane's Contact Youth Theatre, the Sydney-based Bangarra Dance Theatre and the Kyana Aboriginal Cultural Festival in Perth. An increasing number of writing fellowships and grants is offered annually to Aboriginal writers in addition to those funded by the Literature Board of the Australia Council.

Aborigine in White Australian Literature. Reflections on Aborigines in the literature before European invasion/settlement in 1788 were mostly unfavourable. William Dampier saw them as 'the miserablest People in the World'; Captain James Cook said they appeared 'to be the most wretched people upon Earth', though he was impressed by their tranquil, seemingly untainted nomadic lifestyle; Sir Joseph Banks described them as 'naked, treacherous, and armed with Lances, but extremely cowardly'. Governor Arthur Phillip, however, who had a closer and longer acquaintance with them than these earlier commentators, was so impressed by the bearing of some of the Port Jackson Aborigines that he named the cove where he met them, Manly (q.v.) Cove.

David Collins, in *An Account of the English Colony in New South Wales* (1798), indicated that by the end of April 1788 spasmodic violence had broken out between the Aborigines and the settlers. Watkin Tench, in *A Complete Account of the Settlement at Port Jackson in New South Wales* (1793), felt that the attacks by Blacks were in retaliation for convicts having stolen their fishing tackle and weapons. The convict population, overwhelmingly male, also targeted Aboriginal women, who were regularly attacked, raped and sometimes killed. Aboriginal men reacted to these severe provocations only to be labelled with the 'violent savage' stereotype (an image which would suit the propaganda purposes of the European population for at least the next 150 years). The cycle of violence between White and Black became established. By the time the Colony's first newspaper, the *Sydney Gazette and New South Wales Advertiser*, appeared in 1803 violent clashes were occurring only on the outskirts of the settlement, particularly up the Hawkesbury River, and the 'civilised' settlement Aborigine was becoming the butt of colonial ridicule. Early *Gazette* references, reflecting White contempt, lampooned Aboriginal people, thus creating a further stereotype, the 'ignoble savage': an ugly, comic figure whose image persisted until well into the twentieth century as a counterpoint to the notion of the violent savage. Barron Field, who arrived in Sydney in 1817, noted the growth of a hapless Aboriginal subculture in his *Geographical Memoirs on New South Wales* (1825).

In the earliest poetry emanating from the Colony the Aborigines were portrayed more as objects of curiosity (like the other strange Antipodean fauna) than as individual human beings. The 'sable race' existed in that early poetry as an awestruck backdrop to the energetic scenes of British colonising. Michael Massey Robinson voiced the conventional evangelising sentiments of the time by wishing to repair 'their youth neglected and their age untaught'. The only poem with any significant Aboriginal theme was Charles Tompson's 'Black Town', written as a comment on the government's establishment of the hamlet of Black Town for the purpose of civilising the natives. It expresses platitudinous pity ('poor restless wand'rers of the woody plain') for the Aborigines, who lived in ignorance of the benefits of Christianity, but it reveals no understanding at all of Aboriginality.

With the spread of exploration and settlement, contact between Europeans and the outlying nomadic Aborigines intensified. Killings increased accordingly, especially of Aboriginal men outnumbered and outgunned by a relentless invader. The development of the overland route from Sydney to Adelaide and the increasing movement of settlers and travellers set off prolonged hostilities with the Aborigines along the Murray River. Reports of these encounters ironically reinforced in the minds of the invader the stereotype of the violent, treacherous savage. Sir Thomas Mitchell's expeditions had so much trouble with the Blacks that he described them as 'implacably hostile and shamelessly dishonest', and his frustration culminated in a concerted attack on them at Mount Dispersion in May 1836, one of several organised White massacres in the 1830s. Edward John Eyre, however, regarded Aborigines as human beings, not merely ugly and violent primitives, as his sensitive relationship with his Black companion Wylie indicated. In 1838 the Myall Creek massacre (q.v.), following upon the Pinjarra massacre in WA (1834) and the Mount Dispersion incident, brought Aboriginal people into the centre of controversy in Australia. The trial and ultimate hangings of seven White men for the Myall Creek murder of twenty-eight Aborigines was passionately debated in the columns of the colonial newspapers of the day. Much White opinion was outraged at the idea that White men should die for killing Aborigines, who were seen as a threat to White society. The *Sydney Morning Herald* urged the authorities to 'protect the White settler, his wife and children, in remote places, from the filthy, brutal cannibals of New Holland'. Not all writers, however, showed the same antagonism. In the Swan River settlement the *Perth Gazette* published a sympathetic account of Aboriginal culture by R.M. Lyon in 1833, entitled 'A Glance at the manners and language of the Aboriginal inhabitants of Western Australia', together with an extensive Aboriginal vocabulary. The Rev. John Dunmore Lang delivered a sermon in the Scots Church, Sydney, in November 1838 entitled 'National Sins the Cause and Precursor of National Judgements', which suggested that the drought and influenza epidemic afflicting the colony were at least in part due to the Aborigines 'waging unequal warfare with their civilized aggressors'. Said Lang: 'Yes, brethren, every district of this land of our adoption has been defiled with the blood of these innocents . . .' The *Inquirer* (WA) published a series of articles by William Nairne Clark in 1842 defending Aboriginal people against the accusation of racial inferiority.

One of the earliest novels to feature Aboriginal characters was *Alfred Dudley: Or, the Australian Settler* (1830), published anonymously but attributed to Sarah Porter. Alfred Dudley, successful in acquiring wealth in the colony, attempts to reconstruct in the Antipodes the lost family estate of Dudley Park in England. Dudley's inclusion of the Aborigines in the transplanted English community reveals an early, and rare, spark of optimism in fiction about the possible union of the two races. In *Tales of the Colonies: Or, The Adventures of an Emigrant* (1843) and *The Bushranger of Van Diemen's Land* (1846) Charles Rowcroft outlines the experiences of the settlers against a backdrop of natural hazards which included bushrangers and Aborigines. The notorious Black man Mosquito is featured and many instances of butchery are included to confirm the image of the violent savage. Although overly sensational, melodramatic, and inaccurate in his shallow fictional portrait of the Blacks, Rowcroft did emphasise perceived positives such as the capacity for tracking, tribal customs and habits, and the essentially mild nature of Aboriginal culture. *The Bushranger of Van Diemen's Land*, which depicts a White woman in the hands of the Aborigines, guardedly introduces topics such as sexual harassment and miscegenation, topics which were to be explored more fully by later writers. Thomas McCombie's *Arabin: Or, The Adventures of a Colonist in New South Wales* (1845) contains a separate, concluding section, 'Essay on the Aborigines of Australia'. The two chief fictional works of the 1840s were Alexander Harris's *The Emigrant Family: Or, The Story of an Australian Settler* (1849) and James Tucker's *Ralph Rashleigh*, written in the 1840s but not published in full until 1952. Harris's novel contains stories of depredations by the Blacks, including an attack by 'myalls' (a common name, in the genre of pioneer/settler fiction, for wild natives) on a cottage where a White family is sheltering, and there are some suggestions of cannibalism. Harris discusses Black–White relationships at length, and through his protagonist, Reuben Kable, comments that such relationships must, in the isolated pioneer environment, be settled on an individual basis – 'Every man must be his own constable who goes to the extreme verge of civilization, and the retribution enforced must be palpable, prompt and decisive'. His assessment that the aggression of the Blacks was the natural result of ill feeling because of the invasion of their territory is balanced by his typical White settler conviction of his own right to the land in question – 'who will say that the invasion is an improper one?' Harris's earlier work, *Settlers and Convicts: Or, Recollections of Sixteen Years' Labour in the Australian Backwoods* (1847), purportedly non-fiction but not always factual, also deals with Black–White relationships and is highly critical of the existing situation. The dilemma in which the sensitive settler found himself is well portrayed in *Settlers and Convicts*. On the one hand Harris voices an impassioned plea for the protection of the White settler and for the government to abandon its policy of compelling settlers to take away their workmen's guns, thus encouraging attacks by the Aborigines. On the other hand he acknowledges that the rapaciousness of the squatters and

their wholesale appropriation of the land had led to resentment from the Aborigines, whose own nature was free from avarice. Harris is scornful of the missionary efforts to Christianise the Blacks – 'there seems something intrinsically absurd in the nation which is robbing another of its land and its means of subsistence soliciting that other to adopt its religion'. In Tucker's *Ralph Rashleigh*, the relationship between the two 'lowest' elements of Australian society, the escaped convict and the Aborigine, is developed. The convict is despised by the Aborigine, who sees him as the scum of White society, yet the convict, because he is White, regards the Black with contempt. Ralph Rashleigh, the escaped convict of Tucker's novel provides, especially in its account of Rashleigh entering and leaving the Black community, the best contemporary record of Aboriginal society, customs and law.

In conjunction with the increased flow of fiction from the 1840s onwards, there was a constant supply of non-fictional accounts of life in the Australian colonies. Most of those works included descriptive, and sometimes amateurish, ethnographic accounts of the Aborigines. G.H. Haydon's *Five Years' Experience In Australia Felix* (1846) includes some commentary on Benbo, a well-known Melbourne Aborigine, and his later, more fictional, *The Australian Emigrant* (1854) continues the Benbo story, presenting the 'civilised' Aborigine as an object of amused, scornful White tolerance, much as Barron Field had done with the Sydney native Bungaree (q.v.) thirty years earlier. In *A Visit to the Antipodes: with Some Reminiscences of a Sojourn in Australia* (1846), E. Lloyd ('A Squatter') wrote of the difficulties of setting up a station. Among the problems he examined was the presence of the Aborigines who, by their adoption of a constant threatening posture, added the psychological burden of fear to the isolated settler's already difficult existence. In WA, race relationships became troubled after the opening of pastoral settlements north of the Swan River. There were the same ingredients for violence and hostility that had been present in the eastern colonies, as the Pinjarra massacre of 1834 indicates. A notable WA contemporary account was Edward Landor's satirical *The Bushman: Or, Life in a New Country* (1874).

In the second half of the nineteenth century the Aboriginal presence in literature was much more marked. The poet Charles Harpur, who had viewed with satisfaction the Myall Creek executions of 1838, later wrote 'An Aboriginal Mother's Lament', a poem sympathetic to the Aborigines, based on the massacre. His longer poem, 'Ned Connor', tells of a White stockman wantonly killing an Aborigine who has led him to safety through the bush. The stockman, Ned Connor, falls victim to a mysterious illness and dies after seeing a vision of the dead Aborigine. Harpur saw the White stockman's act as a violation of the natural moral order and the poem was his indictment of the practice of casual White brutality towards the Aborigine. In Harpur's best-known frontier poem, 'The Creek of the Four Graves' (q.v.), where four White men are murdered by tribal Aborigines into whose territory they have come in search of pasture and water for their herds, there is no assessment of guilt or innocence on either side. The event itself is seen only as part of the frontier condition and general context of man's inhumanity to man. Henry Kendall's early Aboriginal poems 'Aboriginal Death Songs' (1862) invest the Black man with the charisma of the noble savage. Such songs as 'Kooroora', 'Ulmarra' and 'Urara' dwell on tribal battles, heroic deeds, grief-stricken Aboriginal women and desolate landscapes. His much-anthologised 'The Last of His Tribe' (q.v.) pictures the final stages in the destruction of the Aboriginal tribes but avoids the question of culpability. Kendall later joined in the popular literary pastime of lampooning the Aborigine and his tasteless skits such as 'Black Lizzie', 'Black Kate' and 'Jack the Blackfellow' were typical of the contemptuous and derisive mockery of Aboriginal people that had begun with the Sydney *Gazette* at the turn of the century. Kendall and fellow poet James Brunton Stephens (q.v.) vied with each other for leadership in this poetry of ridicule – it was Kendall's boast that he could 'out-Blackfellow Stephens'. George Gordon McCrae's (q.v.) two poems 'Mamba ('The Bright Eyed'): An Aboriginal Reminiscence' and 'The Story of Balladeadro' (both 1867) were a significant addition to the poetry on Aboriginal themes, in that they were genuine attempts to understand and represent Aboriginal myth. McCrae's belief that a better understanding of Aboriginality would come through knowledge and appreciation of Aboriginal myth and legend can be seen, with hindsight, to have been soundly based; in modern times myth and legend have provided a bridge between Aboriginal culture and White consciousness.

The stream of memoirs and reminiscences continued undiminished in the second half of the nineteenth century. The writers, usually erstwhile squatters, government officials and public figures, reflected, often from the heightened imagination of their twilight years, on the lively colonial times they had lived through. The squatters had the closest and most prolonged contact with the Aborigines, a contact that inevitably entailed dispossession and violence. The constant search for land further out meant that the far-flung squatter runs kept impinging on hitherto-untouched Aboriginal areas. As Alexander Harris had indicated, the frontier White man's safety lay in constant vigilance and merciless retribution. For him the only absolute solution to the racial problem lay in extermination of the Blacks. On established runs, after the frontier had moved on, a changed pattern of relationships developed. The Aborigines who survived became a source of cheap labour; Aboriginal women were frequently coerced into sexual roles for White males; and in time a *modus vivendi* evolved, with the Aborigines existing as a dispossessed but patronised minority within the station framework. Squatter literature reveals some close personal relationships between Black and White in this secondary stage of settlement, e.g. W.A. Brodribb's *Recollections of an Australian Squatter* (1883) and E.M. Curr's *Recollections of Squatting in Victoria Then Called the Port Phillip District (from 1841 to 1851)* (1883). Along with numerous observations on the Aborigines, Curr included a lively

account of the Crown Lands commissioners and their methods of settling the 'frequent difference which occurred between the original lords of the soil and the Anglo-Saxon *parvenus*'. One such method was for the commissioner to appear before the Aborigines 'sabre in hand, surrounded by his troops industriously loading and discharging their carbines'. Not all White justice was so summarily dispensed, but Curr's account indicates the way in which the scales of justice were tipped against the Aboriginal people in the outlying areas. Similar reminiscent writings reflecting the racial situation include the works of George Fletcher Moore, the early pioneer settler of WA. His memoirs, *Diary of Ten Years Eventful Life of an Early Settler in Western Australia* (1884), which included an Aboriginal vocabulary, showed a genuine desire to understand the Black culture. Richard Cannon, a surgeon who visited the remote Cape York area in 1863, in HMS *Salamander*, was horrified, as his *Savage Scenes from Australia* (1885) reveals, by the typical frontier brutality which attached as little significance to the life of an Aboriginal person as to that of an animal. Additional reminiscent works include 'Rolf Boldrewood's *Old Melbourne Memories* (1884), Mrs Dominic D. Daly's *Digging, Squatting, and Pioneering Life* (1887), John Phillips's ('A Pioneer') *Reminiscences of Australian Early Life* (1893), James Kirby's *Old Times in the Bush of Australia* (1895), Thomas Bride's edition of *Letters from Victorian Pioneers* (1898) and Constance Campbell Petrie's *Tom Petrie's Reminiscences of Early Queensland* (1904). Judith Wright's *The Generations of Men* (q.v., 1959), although written in the twentieth century, was compiled from family diaries and letters going back to the nineteenth century. It contains many reflections on the Aborigines, the most illuminating of which are the puzzled ponderings of May Wright (the poet's grandmother) on the possibility of Aborigines having souls. The story of the Tasmanian Aborigines is related in a series of contemporary semi-historical works by James Bonwick: *Daily Life and Origin of the Tasmanians* (1870), *The Last of the Tasmanians; Or, The Black War of Van Diemen's Land* (1870) and *The Lost Tasmanian Race* (1884). In *Friendly Mission: The Tasmanian Journals and Papers of George Augustus Robinson 1829–1834* (1966, edited by N.J. Plomley), a personal and contemporary account of the destruction of the Tasmanian tribes is given.

The second half of the nineteenth century witnessed a number of attempts to document the Aborigines in semi-scientific and ethnographic works. Often the writers were no more than well-intentioned laymen and their observations often a mixture of fact, fancy and speculation. Yet this growing interest in Aboriginality, even at the informed amateur level, was the forerunner of later substantial sociological enquiries and investigations. With Alfred William Howitt and Lorimer Fison, true anthropological studies of the Aborigine began. Their joint work, *Kamilaroi and Kurnai* (1880), and Howitt's *Native Tribes of South-East Australia* (1904), constitute the first scientific studies of Aboriginal social relationships. Their successors, W.B. Spencer and F.J. Gillen, published many works, among them *The Native Tribes of Central*

Australia (1899) and *The Northern Tribes of Central Australia* (1904). A later revision, *The Arunta: A Study of a Stone Age People* (1927), provided the impetus for the extensive ethnological investigation into the Aborigine that came in the twentieth century.

The fiction of the second half of the nineteenth century included only occasional attempts at a sensitive investigation of racial contact and very little questioning of the accepted Aboriginal stereotypes. In Henry Kingsley's *The Recollections of Geoffry Hamlyn* (1859), the Aborigines are mostly presented as stock figures of savagery, one of the traditional hazards of pioneer life. However, Charles de Boos's novel *Fifty Years Ago: An Australian Tale* (1867) begins by presenting the customary stereotype of racial contact (violence and counter-violence) but ends with a strong indication that new approaches to the racial problem are possible and desirable. The massacre by the Maroo tribe of the family of the White settler George Maxwell is followed by vengeance plotted and systematically carried through in the James Fenimore Cooper tradition. Maxwell comes to regret his obsession with vengeance, that way being little better than the way of the 'myalls' who killed his family. The Aboriginal chief, Macomo, comes to understand the crime he has committed and moves to an awareness of the 'civiliser's' human and moral values, of which he had no comprehension at the beginning. The original violence of the Black is portrayed as the impulsive, semi-instinctive action of the primitive when confronted with the threat of the White man. When not cast in the role of hunter, that is, when surrounded and facing death, 'the Aboriginal' is seen as a heroic though pitiable figure. The novel seems to suggest that the White man is superior to the Black only in the lucky accident that he has had the benefit of civilisation to develop a higher consciousness. De Boos's sympathetic observations, coupled with his imaginative and sensitive analysis, produced an interpretation of Aboriginality highly unusual for the time. 'Rolf Boldrewood' incorporated all the Aboriginal stereotypes in his fiction. Having experienced, as a squatter in western Victoria in the 1840s, the worst period of racial violence, he clearly found it difficult, even fifty years later, to eliminate from his consciousness the image of the pervasive Aboriginal threat – which had to be eliminated if the Whites were to live free of intimidation. An attempt to view the racial problems ambivalently occurs in his 'The Squatters's Dream' (1875) where the characters Guy Waldon and Redgrave measure the choice between peace through coexistence or peace through extermination. The first alternative is shown to be illusory and moral judgement an irrelevant luxury when, in White opinion, conflict is inevitable because of the perceived savage nature of the Aborigine. 'Boldrewood' gave himself the opportunity of presenting a meaningful account of Black–White contact by introducing the massacre site of Murdering Lake, but ended, as in *Old Melbourne Memories* (1884), by indulging in nostalgic recreations of the stock idealised figures of dignified Aboriginal male and winsome Aboriginal girl; in *Robbery Under Arms* (1888), Warrigal embodied much of what 'Boldre-

wood' innately felt about the Aborigines. Rosa Praed lived as a child in the 1850s in isolated Queensland. She was 6 years old when the Aboriginal massacre of the Fraser family occurred on nearby Hornet Bank (q.v.) station. That massacre produced a considerable current of fear and prejudice, some of it sexually based. In many of her novels and in the factual-fiction *My Australian Girlhood: Sketches and Impressions of Bush Life* (1902), she draws on her childhood closeness to and affection for the station Blacks, but on the whole she was vague and ill-informed about the Aborigines. In her fictional work *Fugitive Anne* (1902), the Aborigine Kombo is an enigmatic presence, symbolising the White woman's sexual unease about the Black man.

In *Lady Bridget in the Never-Never Land* (1915), the racial problem is at the centre of the confrontation between misguided English philanthropy in the guise of Lady Bridget and hard-headed squatter realism in the form of McKeith, whose family has been massacred by Blacks. In Simpson Newland's *Paving the Way* (1893), the inevitability of Aboriginal extinction is envisaged. In spite of their natural virtues of determination, bushcraft and courage (as illustrated in the death of the noble Murray River leader) the Aborigines are seen to be unable to withstand the power of the White man. Once physically defeated, detached from their own powerful social mores and forced into close contact with White society (rum, tobacco, disease), the Aborigines are depicted as degenerating into the degradation that is summed up in the ignoble savage stereotype. Newland conveys that degradation by his use of Aboriginal English, intending by this to suggest the impurity of race.

In the last years of the nineteenth century, the Australian press of the period adopted a deeply conservative, often racist position. The *Bulletin* (9 June 1883) quoted from the Queensland newspaper the *Northern Miner*, which deplored the 'holy howling' over the wholesale killing of male Aborigines and the sexual use of the females, then went on to offer its own solution to the Aboriginal problem:

> Gather them all together on an immense reserve in North-Western Australia ... Let them have no rum and no religion, but fight and frolic in their own way. And by the time the Whites would be closing upon them, they would have reduced their own numbers so much by internal quarrels that the boundary line of their reservation could be shifted inwards far enough to allow four or five 'runs' in the space vacated. So the process of closing in could go on until the last survivors, two or three in number, were frozen out altogether. Some showman by that time could make a good thing of taking them around the other colonies and exhibiting them as curiosities. This is the way to let the Black race die out easily and naturally. The present efforts to ameliorate their conditions only result in killing them out sooner, and making their lives miserable while they do last ... the relentless logic of the history of all our past dealings with the natives is summed up concisely in the dictum of the *Northern Miner* – 'the nigger must go'.

On 17 December 1887, the radical *Boomerang* made the following pronouncement:

The Australian nigger is generally regarded as about the lowest type of human creature about ... There are some splendid points about the Black and one in which he is far ahead of the Chinkie. He'll die out, and the Chinkie won't.

The turn of the century provided no magic line of demarcation after which the representation of Aboriginal people in literature improved dramatically. The nationalism and radicalism of the 1890s, which spilled over enthusiastically into Federation, scarcely bothered to acknowledge the country's Black inhabitants. They were excluded by the Constitution – 'the Aborigine shall not be counted' – and the stories and poems of Henry Lawson and A.B. Paterson, and the novel *Such Is Life* of Joseph Furphy, paid only the briefest (in the latter case, somewhat vicious) attention to their presence. New attitudes, however, gradually evolved, slowly at first but more rapidly after the Second World War as the race paranoia of the White population began to modify. Protection of the Aborigines against maltreatment and exploitation began to be embodied in parliamentary legislation. Queensland's *Aborigines Protection and Presentation of Sale of Opium Act* (1897) was followed by similar Acts in WA (1905), NSW (1909) and SA (1911). Yet oppressive legislation such as the *Native Administration Act* of WA and the *Queensland Aborigines and Torres Strait Islanders Act*, which enforced minority status on Aboriginal people, remained on the statutes. There was little progress towards political and social justice for Aborigines in the early decades of the century. A government-sponsored massacre of Aboriginal people, the Coniston Massacre north-west of Alice Springs, occurred as late as 1928. Aboriginal protests in 1938 against the sesquicentenary of European visionary settlement largely failed to gain sympathy from the White population. As late as 1961 the conservative government of Robert Menzies blocked full voting rights for Aborigines; however, the Australian community's growing awareness of the appalling conditions under which many Aboriginal people lived became the catalyst for change in the later 1960s and 1970s. That progress is reflected in the setting up of the Australian Institute of Aboriginal Studies in 1964, the establishment of a Centre for Research into Aboriginal Affairs at Monash University in 1964, the sponsoring in 1964 of the series *Aborigines in Australian Society* by the Social Sciences Research Council of Australia, the referendum to remove discriminating clauses against Aborigines from the Commonwealth Constitution in 1967, the establishment of the federal government's Department of Aboriginal Affairs in 1972, the establishment of the National Aboriginal Conference in 1978, and the Aboriginal Development Commission. On the cultural side there was positive discrimination in favour of Aboriginal people by the Australia Council and considerable impetus given to Aboriginal art by the establishment of the Aboriginal Arts Board (later Committee) (q.v.).

The scientific and anthropological works of the pioneer investigators Howitt and Fison, Spencer and Gillen were followed by numerous other studies, notable among which were A.P. Elkin's (q.v.) *The Australian Aborigines* (1938), T.G.H. Strehlow's (q.v.) *Aranda Traditions* (1947), J.W. Bleakley's *The Aborigines of Australia* (1961), Ronald and Catherine Berndt's (q.v.) *Aboriginal Man in Australia* (1965) and *The World of the First Australians* (1964, revised edition 1981), Marie Reay's (ed.) *Aborigines Now* (1964), A.R. Pilling and R.A. Waterman's *Diprotodon to Detribalization* (1970) and W.E.H. Stanner's many works on Aboriginal religion. In the light of all this new knowledge the long-held popular image of Aboriginal people as sub-human gradually faded. The years of the Whitlam Government (1972–75) might be regarded as the watershed period. After 1975 there was no possibility of White Australia retreating into the insularity of the past.

Throughout this century White awareness of Aboriginality has also been enhanced by Aboriginal myth and legend. The publication of Catherine Langloh Parker's (q.v.) *Australian Legendary Tales* (1896) and *More Australian Legendary Tales* (1898) began a European popularisation of Aboriginal tribal stories and songs. In the 1930s the Jindyworobak (q.v.) desire to present Aboriginal lore as potentially important to White Australians, in the hope that they might establish an equivalent affinity with the Australian landscape, helped inspire the work of Roland Robinson (q.v.) whose numerous volumes include *Legend and Dreaming* (1952), *The Feathered Serpent* (1956), *Aboriginal Myths and Legends* (1966) and *The Nearest the White Man Gets* (1989). The contribution in the 1940s and 1950s of W.E. (Bill) Harney (q.v.), like that of Roland Robinson, cannot be underestimated. Volumes such as *Brimming Billabongs* (1947), *Content to Lie in the Sun* (1958) and *Grief, Gaiety, and the Aborigines* (1961) did much to educate White Australia about the mysteries and wonder of Aboriginal mythology. More recently, and significantly, Aboriginal writers and speakers such as Oodgeroo Noonuccal (Kath Walker), Dick Roughsey, Robert Layton, Daisy Utemorrah and Paddy Japaljarri Sims have effectively re-established the rightful Black claim to custodianship. Books such as Charles Mountford's *The Dreamtime Book* (1973), visually impressive yet obviously aiming to find a place on the coffee tables of White Australia, appear destined to disappear completely. The Australia that begot them is gone.

Fiction-writers who included Aboriginal people at the turn of the century were few. Jeannie Gunn's (q.v.) two stories *The Little Black Princess* (1905) and *We of the Never-Never* (1908) are classic examples of the patronising but totally short-sighted approach of many well-intentioned Australians towards the Aborigine. In her tales of Elsey station and the 'Never-Never' the 'station' Aborigine is depicted as a cross between a backward but lovable child and an awkward, shambling domestic pet. The 'outsiders' or 'wild niggers', however, are subjected to the atrocities of the 'nigger hunts', briefly and dispassionately described by Mrs Gunn, where the pastoralists (such as her husband, the 'Maluka'), ride out in response to the killing of their cattle 'with rifles unslung and revolvers at hand'. The recent publication of Aboriginal testimony material relating to the Elsey area has necessitated a stringent reassessment of the nature of Mrs Gunn's pastoral idyll. English biologist E.L. Grant Watson (q.v.) produced the first worthwhile fictional treatment of the Aboriginal people in this century. Watson spent most of 1910–11 with fellow biologist Radcliffe Brown and with Daisy Bates (q.v.) among the Kimberley Aborigines and in the Bernier Island isolation hospital for diseased Blacks from the North-west. His story 'Out There', an account of the eternal triangle (White man with Black woman and White woman), ends in affirmation of the White–Black relationship and a recognition of the harmony and sense of purpose in Aboriginal life. 'Out There' decries the pervasive stigma attached to the White men who decide to 'go Black'. In Watson's novels, e.g. *The Desert Horizon* (1923), the problem of White accommodation to the vast isolated North-west is examined, and the relevance and importance of Aboriginal people stressed. In the mid-1920s several major clashes, such as the Onmalmeri massacre in the Kimberley (1926) and Coniston, led to a concerted demand for new attitudes to Aboriginal people and a stop to the continued killing of indigenous people in the North and North-west of the continent.

Against this background of wide national debate on the Aboriginal question two professional writers, Vance Palmer and Katharine Susannah Prichard (qq.v.), introduced new dimensions into the particularly sensitive area of Black–White sexual relations. Looking back on the 1920s in *Laughter, Not for a Cage* (1956), Miles Franklin (q.v.) stated that 'one of the greatest [literary themes] demanding treatment' was 'Black velvet' (q.v.) . The White man's sexual use of Aboriginal women had long been tacitly recognised as an acceptable behaviour pattern in the isolated outback, where White women were few, but that acceptance had always insisted that such miscegenation was merely a casual consorting with no deep underlying emotional attachment. Both Palmer and Prichard presented a much more complicated view of interracial sexuality. In Palmer's *The Man Hamilton* (1928), the White man Hamilton chooses life on the station with his Aboriginal 'wife' and son rather than the love of the White governess; by contrast, in *Men Are Human* the White character Boyd discards the pregnant 'half-caste' Josie and prefers the White woman Barbara. By some ironic nemesis Boyd is trampled to death by cattle and Josie bears his stillborn son. Between Palmer's two novels came Prichard's *Coonardoo* (q.v.), after which no return to the simplicity of the original 'Black velvet' stereotype was possible. Between station-owner Hugh Watt and Aboriginal girl Coonardoo there develops a physical and spiritual affinity, although Watt, unable to reject his White conditioning about miscegenation, tragically rejects Coonardoo and the chance of happiness. Some contemporary opinion was scandalised by *Coonardoo*. S.H. Prior refused to publish Palmer's *Men are Human* in 1929 because 'the disastrous experience with *Coonardoo* shows us that the Australian public will not stand stories based on a White man's relations with an Aborigine'. *Coonardoo* was part of a continuing attempt (which included the short stories 'Happiness' and 'The

Cooboo' and the later play, *Brumby Innes*) by Prichard to interpret, often compassionately and always imaginatively, the poetic essence of Aboriginality, and to present something of the quality and integrity that she believed to be possible in racial relationships. Jessie Litchfield, in *Far-North Memories* (1930), a novel contemporaneous with those of Prichard and Palmer yet based on significantly more experience of the North than the latter two could muster between them, has one of her characters sum up the reality of the pastoral enterprise this way:

> Fully nine out of every ten murders in the North have been due, directly or in part, to unauthorised interference with gins. Not all the true facts ever get into print, of course, but those who have been privileged to peep behind the scenes know more than the general public can ever know, or will ever want to know.

In the past sixty years the early literary stereotypes of the Aborigine have gradually faded. Contemporary practice has been to place the Aboriginal people in the centre of the literature of social protest, either out of genuine concern for Aborigines as an underprivileged minority or because an Aboriginal character can enable the novel readily to address particular social or political issues. In more recent literature the chief themes have been interracial sexual relationships, contemporary racial prejudice, White guilt about the past, the assertion of Black identity, and territorial rights. The theme of interracial sexuality, begun in *Coonardoo*, was continued by many writers. In Mary Durack's *Keep Him My Country* (q.v., 1955) the young White station-owner, Stan Rolt, ultimately achieves serenity through recognising that his relationship with the native girl, Dalgerie, has linked him indissolubly to the land itself. The primal relationship between the land and Aboriginality is widened to include the White man, and the union between Black and White and the spirit of the land itself is seen as beneficial to all three. In novels such as F.B. Vickers's *The Mirage* (1955), Gavin Casey's *Snowball* (1958), Randolph Stow's *To The Islands* (1958), Donald Stuart's *Yaralie* (1962) and Dymphna Cusack's *Black Lightning* (1964) the problems that follow emotional involvements between Black and White are honestly and sensitively examined. The starting-point for the modern novel of social protest featuring Aboriginal characters is Xavier Herbert's *Capricornia* (q.v., 1938), a work which grew out of an earlier unpublished novel, 'Black Velvet'. *Capricornia* is a novel of social protest (as 'Black Velvet' seems to have been). Its opening chapter, 'The Coming of the Dingoes', records the arrival of Europeans in Capricornia (the Northern Territory) and their impact on hitherto-uncorrupted Aboriginal life:

> All over the land were bone-piled spots where lazy Aborigines were taught not to steal a Whiteman's bullocks ... Most Aborigines who had been born in freedom preferred to do their starving in the bush. And all the while the Nation was boasting to the world of its Freedom and Manliness and Honesty. Australia Felix!

Capricornia is a devastating indictment of such customary White rationalisations of the treatment of Aboriginal people as the need to civilise and Christianise the Black, and the benefits to them of benevolent White despotism. It particularly attacks the White usurpation of Aboriginal territory, the callousness, hypocrisy and cant of official attitudes (both government and religious) and the inhumanity of the White attitudes to the 'half-caste' (the tragic Naw-Nim – no name) who is alienated from both parent races. The 'half-caste' theme, a reflection in literature of the 'assimilation' era, recurred throughout the 1940s, 1950s and 1960s in novels such as T.A.G. Hungerford's war novel *The Ridge and the River* (1952), Nene Gare's *The Fringe Dwellers* (1961), Leonard Mann's *Venus Half-Caste* (1963) and Raymond Aitchison's *The Illegitimates* (1964). In Herbert's later novel *Poor Fellow My Country* (q.v., 1975), his self-proclaimed *magnum opus*, where the theme of modern Australia as a shiftless, materialistic and spiritually devastated society is dominant, he returns to his indictment of the nation's shameful treatment of Aboriginal people. His considerable knowledge of and affinity for Aboriginal customs and lore make that massive work a significant expression of protest on their behalf. Other examinations and expressions of White guilt for Australia's history of racialism range from Judith Wright's poetry, e.g. 'Nigger's Leap, New England', 'Bora Ring' and 'At Cooloolah', to Heriot's exorcism of guilt and subsequent spiritual regeneration in Randolph Stow's *To the Islands*. Thomas Keneally's *The Chant of Jimmie Blacksmith* (based on the story of Jimmy Governor, q.v. 1972), a sensational account of tyranny and bigotry finally driving an Aboriginal out of the ignoble into the violent stereotype, has (largely through the impact of the film of the novel) finally awakened many Australians to the reality of Australian racism. In addition to Keneally's novel, Peter Mathers's *Trap* (1966) and David Ireland's *Burn* (1974) illustrate the theme of violence against established society by the 'outsider' of that society. Patrick White uses an Aboriginal character, Alf Dubbo, to reinforce the wider theme of social alienation in *Riders in the Chariot* (1961). Official racism is featured in F.B. Vickers's novel *The Mirage*, where the repressive race laws of WA produce tragedy in the lives of a young 'half-caste' and his bride. Richard Beilby's *The Brown Land Crying* (1975), a novel about an Aboriginal community in WA, indicates how underprivilege in the form of poverty, police brutality and restrictive taboos lead to total social immobility and utter deprivation for the Aborigines involved. Donald Stuart's concern in *The Driven* (1961) and *Yaralie* (1962) is to predict that the final solution to racial conflict lies in racial integration. His belief, expressed in *Yaralie*, is that the combination of the remarkable qualities of both races – the 'forward-thrusting attributes' of the White and the 'wise love of the country' of the Black – will produce a people especially suited for the vast outback of Australia.

White writers over the last fifteen years have continued to address the difficult issue of Black–White relations in this country, though they now noticeably avoid the simplistic generalisations about race of the past. A new seriousness exists, a desire to create the work of art with honesty and fair-dealing. Two of the most interesting plays of recent years are Tony Strachan's *State of Shock* (1986) and Northern Territorian Gordon Francis's *God's Best Country* (1987). They are radically different offerings. Strachan's play is based on the true story of Alwyn Peter, a Queensland Aborigine charged with murder in 1979, and it is the result of the author's interviews with Peter, his defence counsel, family and friends; Francis, in Herbertian mode, deals with the fight between Blacks and Whites for a Kimberley station. Two of the more interesting and quite different books written for children are Bruce Pascoe's *Fox* (1988), the sensitive story of a young boy who discovers his Aboriginality while escaping the law, and Diana Kidd's ambitious *The Fat and Juicy Place* (1992), a story told by a young Koori boy, Jack, to his escapee pet lizard. Jack manages to confirm his ties with his culture, the land and his dead father. Kidd researched the project carefully with Koori people and her book was endorsed by the New South Wales Aboriginal Education Consultative Group.

There has also been considerable variety in recent fiction (for adults) by White writers incorporating Aboriginal themes, ranging from those works exploiting an urban milieu, such as Victor Kelleher's *Wintering* (1988) and Justin D'Ath's *The Initiate* (1989), to adventure yarns such as Peter Corris's Cliff Hardy novel *White Heat* (1981), Ian Moffitt's *Death Adder Dreaming* (1988) and Jon Cleary's *Pride's Harvest* (1991). Bill Green's political spoof set in 1996, *Cleaning Up* (1993), adds to this variety. Perhaps the four most notable works by White writers in the last decade have been Kate Grenville's *Joan Makes History* (1988), Rodney Hall's *The Second Bridegroom* (1991), Thomas Keneally's *Flying Hero Class* (1991) and David Malouf's *Remembering Babylon* (1993). None of the writers would agree with Nene Gare, who suggested in the early 1960s in reference to her novel *The Fringe Dwellers* (1961) that slipping into what she felt were the feelings of Aborigines was as natural as breathing. Thirty years on, after the 1967 referendum, the Aboriginal Tent Embassy, Land Rights and Mabo, such artistic certainty by a White writer is no longer possible. The issues are too sensitive, too slippery. Thus, Rodney Hall in *The Second Bridegroom* has his protagonist, an escaped convict last century, travel for nearly two years with local Aborigines. These 'Men', as they are called, help him to view the country through their eyes. Once back in the White settlement he no longer sees fences and roads, but barriers or intrusions. It is, as the critic Helen Daniel has said, 'a profound shift of vision and language'. In *Flying Hero Class*, a plane *en route* to Frankfurt is hijacked by Palestinian terrorists. Since the passengers include the Aboriginal Barramatjara Dance Troupe, Keneally cleverly exploits the cultural possibilities of the situation. Aboriginality, past and present, interacts with a range of contemporary Western mores and attitudes. *Remembering Babylon*, like Hall's novel, deals with a White man who has lived with Aborigines midway through last century. We view Aboriginal culture through the eyes of Gemmy Fairley, a teenager who spent some years among the Blacks, only to return to a Queensland settlement. As with *The Second Bridegroom*, we are on the outside looking in. Aboriginal people hold the secrets to belonging, to feeling at one with the earth and the Australian continent.

The past two decades have seen the emergence of an extraordinary body of Aboriginal writing/testimony in English (q.v.). Not all of this material is literature of social protest, but given the long silence during the many decades of invasion/settlement by Whites during which Aboriginal people were obviously unable to speak for themselves in print, it would have been remarkable if their own first utterances had not been highly critical of past attitudes and situations. The main concerns of the new Aboriginal literature have been the spiritual and physical alienation and deprivation of Aboriginal and Torres Strait Islander people throughout colonial and modern times, the search for identity, the insistence on basic human rights for present-day Aborigines, the demand for land rights and the assertion of Aboriginal sovereignty. Oodgeroo Noonuccal, Aboriginal poet and conservation writer, indicates through the title of her first volume of poetry, *We Are Going* (1964), the doom of Aboriginal people if drastic changes are not immediately made in White attitudes. She sees it as her responsibility to record the aspirations and frustrations of her people; her message is that Aborigines deserve a place in Australian society equal to that of the White man, but without the forfeiture of their own identity and culture. *We Are Going* is typical of a number of the works of the emergent first group of Aboriginal writers – including Kevin Gilbert, Jack Davis and Mudrooroo (Colin Johnson) – whose lives were shaped during the grim decades of 'assimilation'. Davis (q.v.), a WA Aboriginal poet and playwright and editor of the Aboriginal magazine *Identity* (q.v.) 1973–79, sees land rights as the key to Aboriginal regeneration. Kevin Gilbert, whose play *The Cherry Pickers* (qq.v.), about Aboriginal seasonal workers was produced in 1971, has published several significant protest works which reflect the Aboriginal crisis through Aboriginal eyes. *Because a White Man'll Never Do It* (1973) advocates Aboriginal land rights and total Aboriginal community development, the latter not through the 'reservation' concept, but through the concept of a 'Black Israel' which would bring a resurgence of racial pride. His later collection of interviews with Aborigines, the superb *Living Black* (1977), makes clear to contemporary White Australians the sense of injustice and depression felt by Aboriginal people from the slums of Redfern to outback Queensland, and attempts to stimulate White consciences to the acceptance of basic justice for all Australians, Black and White. Gilbert's introduction to *Inside Black Australia* (1988) and his monumental yet ignored *Aboriginal Sovereignty – Justice, The Law and Land* (1988) are at once searing indictments of the barbarity of the European invasion and documents intent on discussing the necessity of Aboriginal sovereignty and a just treaty. Gilbert has always been the most provocative and political of Aboriginal writers – Mudrooroo has called him 'the strongest, toughest and most political of all' – and his works have over the years challenged Aboriginal writers in all parts of the country. Similar political

writings include Cheryl Buchanan's *We Have Bugger All!* (1974) and *Black Power in Australia* (1975), a debate on Aboriginal issues by Aboriginal Senator Neville Bonner and Bobbi Sykes. Two waves of Aboriginal writers have now created a literature which is vital to the health and standing of Australian literature generally. These contributors include, in addition to Gilbert, Davis, Oodgeroo and Mudrooroo, writers of the quality of Robert Merritt, Gerald Bostock, Dick Roughsey, Bobbi Sykes, Lionel Fogarty, Archie Weller, Faith Bandler, Bill Rosser, Ruby Langford Ginibi, Sally Morgan and Bill Neidjie. Other writers include Richard Walley, Graeme Dixon, Eva Johnson and Glenyse Ward.

From an abundance of recent historical and sociological writing on Aboriginal people, the following are noteworthy: C.D. Rowley's *The Destruction of Aboriginal Society* (1970), *Outcasts in White Australia* (1970), *The Remote Aborigines* (1970), *A Matter of Justice* (1978) and *Recovery – the Politics of Aboriginal Reform* (1986); Richard Broome's *Aboriginal Australians: Black Response to White Dominance 1788–1980* (1982), which traces the Aboriginal response to White settlement and domination from initial resistance and destruction to the recent push for 'self-determination'; Noel Loos's *Invasion and Resistance: Aboriginal–European Relations on the North Queensland Frontier 1861–1897* (1982), a carefully researched regional history; Garth Nettheim's *Victims of the Law: Black Queenslanders Today* (1982), which reviews Queensland's Aborigines Act of 1971 to 1979 and the Torres Strait Islanders Act of 1971 to 1979; Colin Tatz's six essays in *Aborigines and Uranium and Other Essays* (1982), which discuss human rights and race relations; Michael Howard's (ed.) *Aboriginal Power in Australian Society* (1982); Lyndall Ryan's *The Aboriginal Tasmanians* (1981); Judith Wright's *The Cry for the Dead* (1981), which highlights (in part) the contest for the land between Black and White in pioneer times, along with *We Call for a Treaty* (1985) and the provocative collection of essays (1976–90) *Born of the Conquerors* (1991); *Race Relations in Australia: A History* (1982) by A.T. Yarwood and M.J. Knowling, which traces the history of racialism (not only towards the Aborigines) in Australia from the beginnings to the present day; Henry Reynolds's *The Other Side of the Frontier* (1981), which sets out Aboriginal reactions to the White invasion, along with *Frontier* (1987), *The Law of the Land* (1987), *Dispossession – Black Australians and White Islanders* (1989) and *With the White People* (1990); Diane Bell's *Daughters of the Dreaming* (1983, rev. edn 1993); N.G. Bullin's *Our Original Aggression: Aboriginal Populations of Southeastern Australia, 1788–1850* (1983); John Cribben's re-creation of the Coniston story, *The Killing Times* (1984); James Miller's other-side-of-the-frontier history, *Koori – A Will to Win: The Heroic Resistance, Survival and Triumph of Black Australia* (1985); Ann McGrath's *'Born in the Cattle': Aborigines in Cattle Country* (1987); A. Marcus's *Blood from a Stone* (1988); the Jeremy Beckett-edited *Past and Present: The Construction of Aboriginality* (1988); Peter Read's *A Hundred Years War, The Wiradjuri People and the State* (1988); Bain Attwood's *The Making of the Aborigines* (1989);

D.J. Mulvaney's *Encounters in Place – Australian and Aboriginal Australians 1606–1985* (1989); Scott Bennett's *Aborigines and Political Power* (1989); *Going It Alone: Prospects for Aboriginal Autonomy* (1990), edited by Robert Tomkinson and Michael Howard; Kevin Keefe's *From the Centre to the City: Aboriginal Education, Culture and Power* (1992); and Roger Milliss's exhaustive *Waterloo Creek* (1992).

W.H. WILDE AND DAVID HEADON

Aboriginal Publications Foundation, established in 1971, produces the quarterly magazine *Identity* (q.v.). Managed by a national committee of Aborigines and Torres Strait Islanders, the Foundation's other functions include the publication of writings by and for Aborigines, the organisation of training and the provision of scholarships and financial aid for Aborigines with potential in literature and the creative arts, and the appropriate recognition of distinguished creative achievements by Aborigines.

Aboriginal Song and Narrative in Translation.
Aboriginal song and narrative, traditionally oral literature, are much more complex and diverse than one might assume from the evidence of the so-called 'myths and legends' which are often published for the general reading public. These 'myths and legends' have usually been subjected to synthetic treatment, and are almost invariably presented in a vacuum – wrenched from and without any account of the cultural contexts in which they were originally performed. Outside the Aboriginal world, songs and narratives in Aboriginal languages have been accessible only to a specialised group of anthropologists, linguists and ethnomusicologists, and although recordings of Aboriginal songs and music are now available it is unlikely that texts solely in Aboriginal languages will ever become accessible to the wider public in any meaningful way by such means (although the Central Australian Aboriginal Media Association plays an important role in disseminating the work of oral performers to Aboriginal communities, and there have been some encouraging developments towards the inclusion of Aboriginal studies in school curricula). The living tradition of oral literature, which is part of the cultural achievement of the people who lived in this land for over 40 000 years before being dispossessed by White settlers, is closed to the wider public except through translation. Apart from the usual losses which occur in translation from one language to another, the translation of Aboriginal literature presents special difficulties: in the shift from oral delivery to the written word, aspects of dramatic presentation (such as music, dance, mime, gesture, tone, pace and so on), which are part of the meaning of the songs, are inevitably lost; many of the songs are composed in a highly stylised poetic *koiné* which differs in important ways from the language of common speech (for example, everyday words may have special symbolic associations and even different meanings when used in song, or the songs may include archaic linguistic forms); and the content and the form of the songs and narratives vary according to the cultural and social contexts in which they are performed. It needs to be stressed that this is a living tradition, even if much has been lost. The Australian Institute of Aboriginal and Torres Strait Islander Studies in Canberra has an important collection of manuscripts and recordings, and is actively engaged in collecting and publishing this material.

The myths of the Aboriginal religions vary from area to area, but one common factor is the concept of the 'Alcheringa' or 'Dreamtime', which refers in part to that time in the past when mythic heroes or totemic ancestors moved through the country and were responsible for the shaping of the land, the creation of people, the institution of rituals and the establishing of cultural values, but which refers equally to the present, since these mythic beings continue to live on in spiritual form and exert their influence on the people and the environment. The myths enshrine a history, a code of cultural ideals and laws, and an ontology; and central to all these is the sacred bond between the land and everything that exists within it. The literature that embodies these myths is therefore also sacred. There are, however, degrees of sacredness, which depend on such factors as the occasion of the performance, and the sex, age and social status of the performers. For example, songs associated with initiation rites, with fertility and increase rites and with the commemorative re-enactment of events that took place in the Dreamtime may be limited to certain categories of initiated men and therefore be classified as sacred-secret. Other songs and narratives may be classified as sacred but non-secret (or public), and therefore may be made known to a wider section of the community. This non-secret material often deals with the same myth that occurs in the sacred-secret songs, or with sections of it, but there are significant differences both in the levels of interpretation and in form (including the relative sophistication of the melodic line). At the other end of the scale the distinction between sacred and secular is not always clear-cut: there are narratives of various kinds including 'secular' versions of the sacred myths, children's songs and stories, and songs and stories about contemporary and topical events. Nor is the distinction between song and narrative always clear-cut: there is straightforward narrative, narrative interspersed with songs, forms of narrative whose rhythms so vary from the rhythms of everyday speech that they verge on song, songs with narrative links, song-cycles with narrative links, and songs by individual composers which deal with topical issues. Since the most sacred songs are assumed to have come down from the past unchanged, they are to a large extent 'fixed'; less sacred songs, the songs of individual composers and, of course, narratives, are more susceptible to variation in performance. The style of songs also varies from region to region: for example, in Central Australia and western Arnhem Land the individual songs that make up the song-cycles are typically short, and much of their effect depends on the symbolic and associative significance of key words which are repeated with variations, whereas in north-eastern Arnhem Land the individual songs are longer and more elaborate, and include rich descriptive detail.

These factors (and there are others) suggest why translation without detailed explanatory information (including proper acknowledgement to the owners of the songs and narratives) is an entirely inadequate way of presenting this material.

Many narrative myths and legends were collected by the early anthropologists, but their concern was primarily with content as a springboard to anthropological theorising rather than with the aesthetic and style of oral narrative. Outside the specialist area, Catherine Langloh Parker's (q.v.) *Australian Legendary Tales* (1896) began a tradition of popular retellings of myths, legends and stories by non-Aborigines, retellings which are usually synthetic and non-contextual. This tradition continues, with Alan Marshall's (q.v.) *People of the Dreamtime* (1952) and A.W. Reed's (q.v.) *Myths and Legends of Australia* (1965) being representative of it. Closer to the spirit of the oral narratives are Bill Harney's (q.v.) collection of camp-fire stories, *Tales from the Aborigines* (1959), and Roland Robinson's (q.v.) *The Man Who Sold His Dreaming* (1965) and *The Nearest the White Man Gets* (1989). A significant early exception to the 'popular-synthetic' approach is the work of Ursula McConnel, who from 1927 onwards collected narratives which treat of the institution of religious cults by totemic ancestors in the Cape York area of northern Queensland. Many of these were published in various numbers of *Oceania* between 1930 and 1950, with transcriptions, literal translations, free translations and accounts of the kinship and totemic systems of the people. These narratives, along with others from the same area, were published in *Myths of the Mungkan* (1957) in their free English versions, where once again McConnel stresses the importance of viewing such narratives in their cultural contexts and discusses the difficulties involved in translating from an oral to a written medium. In this tradition too is A. Capell's collection of ten myths connected with the culture heroes Gagamara and Gumbar from the Garadjeri people in WA (*Mankind*, 1949); Capell provides transcriptions, interlinear translations, freer translations and interpretative notes. C.H. and R.M. Berndt's report on fieldwork in the Ooldea region (see below) gives many narratives with translations and commentary, including an interesting sampling of women's stories concerned with such topics as hunting, betrothal, initiation, pregnancy, birth, and death. C.H. Berndt (*Oceania*, 1952) gives a 'play-story' from the Milingimbi region which is told chiefly to children and young adults; it relates the adventures of two brothers, Balangu and Damburu, in a way that directly and indirectly enforces accepted social values. C.H. Berndt's *The Land of the Rainbow Snake* (1979) gives translations to a number of children's stories collected from women informants in the Gunwinngu language of western Arnhem Land, which provides an insight into the way children are introduced to myths and legends in a relatively simplified form. C.G. von Brandenstein, in *Narratives from the North-West of Western Australia in the Ngarluma and Jindjiparndi Languages* (1970), gives sixty narratives with translations on a variety of subjects ranging from the traditional to the topical. The studies outlined above have been pub-lished under the names of the compilers and translators, although in general due acknowledgement is given to the informants. Thus in *The Land of the Rainbow Snake* Berndt gives the names of the main teller after each story (including Mangurug, Ngalmidul, Mareiiga, Hannah Gadjibunda and Dorcas Ngalgindali), and von Brandenstein lists the narratives under the names of the narrators: R. Churnside, W. King, Waljbira (Bulbul), Cobbin Dale and D. Bobby-Kiagi. More recently, collections of stories by the one narrator have been published in translation, as with *Milbi: Aboriginal Tales from Queensland's Endeavour River* (1980), told by Tulo Gordon and translated by J.B. Haviland. This contains narratives which explain the formation of features of the landscape and the origins of local plant and animal life, and which impart moral lessons; the translations attempt to convey something of the narrative style of the originals. Interesting material continues to appear in specialist journals. Luise Hercus, 'Tales of Ngadu-dagali (Rib-bone Billy)' (*Aboriginal History*, 1977), gives a number of Wangganguru narratives (with interlinear gloss and freer translation), including a story of a massacre in the Clifton Hills area in the later nineteenth century. The massacre has been otherwise obliterated from history, and this narrative indicates the importance of Aboriginal oral history in recovering the past. Jack Butler and Peter Austin, '*The Earthquake* and *Halley's Comet*: Two Jiwarli Texts' (*Aboriginal History*, 1986), similarly illustrate the way historical events become part of oral history. *This Is What Happened: Historical Narratives by Aborigines* (1986), ed. Luise Hercus and Peter Sutton, is a fine example of the way oral narrative can be made accessible to a wider audience. This book contains thirty-three stories by twenty-five narrators in twenty-two languages (thereby helping to dispel the notion that there is a single Aboriginal language – when in fact up to 260 Aboriginal languages have been identified, each usually as distinct from one another as English is from German). The stories were told orally by the 'authors' and usually tape-recorded and transcribed by linguists. There are literal interlinear glosses and then a freer translation. The emphasis in many of the stories is on early contact with non-Aboriginals, and there is detailed information about the tellers as well as background and explanatory notes.

Some of the earliest transcriptions and translations of songs appear in the mid-nineteenth century (often in private journals), including those by Mrs Eliza Hamilton Dunlop (q.v.) (which appeared in various newspapers, including the *Sydney Morning Herald*, in the 1830s and 1840s). G. Taplin, in *The Native Tribes of South Australia*, ed. J. Woods (1879), gives two short songs from the Nirrinjeri people, one of which is an exoteric song that compares the smoke and steam which issue from a train with the water that blows from a spouting whale. A.W. Howitt, in *Notes on Songs and Song Makers of Some South Australian Tribes* (1887), gives 'Wenberi's Song', 'Mragula's Song', 'Kurburu's Song', and 'Umbara's Song' (with information about their composers), a short song about elopement, a charm, and some children's songs. Howitt stressed the importance of collecting such songs before they are lost, but his warning was not taken up seriously for almost another fifty years, at a time when the cultures which produced them had been even further eroded. In *Oceania* (1933), however, T.G.H. Strehlow, in his 'Ankotarinja, an Aranda Myth', provides a methodological model for the recording and translation of such songs. Strehlow gives the text and translation of the eighteen verses of the 'Song of Ankotarinja', provides a full account of the myth to which the song alludes, and describes in detail the ritual of which the song is an integral part. He also discusses difficulties of translation and explores the complex style of the original, pointing out how, in song, everyday words are often rearranged according to traditional verse patterns, explaining some differences between speech-accent and verse-accent, and noting how the quality and quantity of vowels are often altered in singing. Strehlow continued his study of Aranda songs in *Aranda Traditions* (1947) and in his most important work, *Songs of Central Australia* (1971). Included in this work are transcriptions and translations of over 2000 lines of verse, detailed accounts of the metrical, rhythmic, and verbal structures of the originals, full information about the occasions when they were sung and the purposes they were intended to achieve, and discussion of the differences between the song and narrative versions of myth. There are some secular songs of a kind that are sung at camp gatherings (the true 'corroborees'), but Strehlow classifies most of his material as sacred: charms, songs performed during totemic increase ceremonies, songs which commemorate the deeds of totemic ancestors, initiation songs, songs celebrating the totemic homeland, and songs concerned with death. Other important contributions, though not as detailed as Strehlow's, have been made by anthropologists such as N.B. Tindale and E.A. Worms, but the work which ranks in significance with Strehlow's is the combined research of Catherine H. Berndt and Ronald M. Berndt (qq.v.). Their account of fieldwork in the Ooldea region of western SA (*Oceania*, 1942–45) includes texts, translations and discussions of a number of short songs, both esoteric and exoteric. A collection of 144 children's songs from the same area (*Mankind*, 1952–54) demonstrates that even these songs have their own highly stylised poetic conventions (for example, the use of words which do not appear in everyday speech), and that they cannot be appreciated or understood without a knowledge of their cultural context. In *Sexual Behaviour in Western Arnhem Land* (1951) there is an interesting collection of eighty-nine 'gossip' songs, the compositions of contemporary songmen who, while not mentioning names, compose songs about topical issues, especially marital behaviour, which have been gleaned from overheard conversation – although the songmen claim they receive them in dreams. C.H. Berndt (*Oceania*, 1905) gives a selection of songs from Bathurst and Melville Islands, which are sung by women at the death of a husband or near relative. Most important, however, are R.M. Berndt's translations of six song-cycles and a collection of secular songs from the Yirrkalla area in northeastern Arnhem Land. Although the published

material amounts to only about a fifth of that which Berndt collected in the area (much of it in the period 1946–47), it offers an instructive insight into the function of song in this society and into the beauty and power of the song. *Djanggawul* (1952) is a free poetic translation of the Djanggawul song-cycle (188 songs, 1921 lines in the translation), the most sacred of the song-cycles in this area. There are detailed explanatory notes on the songs, an account of the complete myth and its local variants, and a description of the rituals which the myth sanctions. The song-cycle describes the events which occurred as the Djanggawul (a collective name for three ancestral beings, Two Sisters and a Brother) journeyed from the spirit home of the Bralgu, off the Arnhem Land coast, to the region of Milimgimbi. They brought with them sacred emblems, and the two perpetually pregnant Sisters created the ancestors of the present-day Aborigines. The main theme is fertility, expressed in the importance of human sexuality and its culmination in childbirth, and in the inextricable relationship between human sexuality and fecundity in the wider natural world. One of the interesting features of the myth is that the Sisters originally possessed the sacred emblems and therefore were the controllers of ritual; but the sacred emblems were stolen by men, thus explaining the contemporary social and ritual roles of men and women, while at the same time emphasising the fact that woman is the source of the sacred. In *Kunapipi* (1951) Berndt gives an account of a religious cult which is widespread over the Northern Territory, but which is a recent import into the Yirrkalla area, where it has become associated with more established mythology. Kunapipi is one of the sacred names of the Great Mother or Fertility Mother who is responsible for the cycle of reproduction and fertility in the human, animal and natural worlds (in particular the coming of the north-west monsoon). Since the cult is a recently introduced one, the style of song differs from the Djanggawul song-cycle: the individual songs are short, made up of a few key words which are suggestive and associative, and which are repeated with variations. The study includes 129 sacred Kunapipi songs, and forty-seven secular songs (which differ in rhythm from the sacred songs, and which are sung, for example, in the main camp before the sacred rituals). Comparisons are made with 118 Kunapipi songs from outside the Yirrkalla area. The 'Wonguri-Mandjikai Song Cycle of the Moon-Bone' (*Oceania*, 1948; see also 'Buladelah-Taree Holiday Song Cycle'), made up of thirteen songs (181 lines in Berndt's free translation), is a non-secret sacred cycle which has as its background the myth of the death and rebirth of the moon, which pattern is seen as a reflection of the cyclical process of the seasons and indeed of all life. The 'Wuradilagu Song-Cycle' in *The Anthropologist Looks at Myth*, ed. J. Greenway (1966), is similar in status to the Moon-Bone Cycle, and has as its background the mythical actions of a spirit being (or beings) from the Groote Eylandt area called Wuradilagu, who is not a sacred being although associated with features of the local landscape. It is made up of eighteen songs (166 lines in Berndt's translations), and in common with the other cycles it celebrates the bond between human beings and other living creatures, and between all living things and natural phenomena – in this case, the coming of the south-east wind after the north-west monsoonal season. *Love Songs of Arnhem Land* (1976) contains two song-cycles which are the least sacred of those noted so far (but which nevertheless have sacred overtones), and a collection of secular love songs. The song-cycles are characterised by much sexually frank and erotic imagery, and through association with mythic symbolism they relate human sexuality to fertility in the wider natural world, demonstrating that 'sexual union is an eternal principle in nature which is reflected in universal fertility and natural continuity' (Berndt). The 'Goulburn Island Cycle', made up of twenty-six songs (312 lines in translation), Berndt describes as a manifestation of the 'social face of love': human beings engage in sexual activity, but this activity has significance and meaning primarily in the relationship between it and parallel forces in the natural world, in particular the arrival of the monsoonal rains which revitalise the land. The 'Rose River Cycle' is made up of twenty-six songs (382 lines), and although it shares many features with the 'Goulburn Island Cycle' its emphasis is on the ritual aspects of sexuality (symbolised in the cycle by the non-local rites of defloration, subincision and ritual coitus), which have their parallels and consequences in the wider natural world – specifically in the coming wet season and more generally in the cyclical pattern of the seasons. The 'Djarada' is a collection of sixty-five self-contained songs (all very short, indicating their non-local origin) which deals with sexual and love matters in a directly personal way, largely divorced from mythological significance. *A World That Was: The Yaraldi of the Murray River and the Lakes, South Australia* (1993) brings together the results of fieldwork which the Berndts conducted in the 1940s. It is a detailed study of all aspects of Yaraldi society, and includes texts and translations of various clan songs.

Apart from the work of the Berndts, other significant studies of song include D.J. Turner's *Tradition and Transformation* (1974) which includes a series of mortuary songs from Groote Eylandt; and *Taruru: Aboriginal Song Poetry from the Pilbara* (1974) by C.G. von Brandenstein and A.P. Thomas. The latter work is a collection of eighty tabis (individually composed songs as distinct from communal songs), from the north-west of WA, with explanatory notes about the songs and information about the composers (where known). The collection includes songs dealing with the honour of dead relatives and the heroic deeds of the past, topical songs dealing with love and other social relationships, and responses to the White man's technology. Although the songs were all composed within the preceding fifty years and usually deal with topical events, they still use the highly stylised poetic diction which is characteristic of the more traditional songs. Tamsin Donaldson (*Aboriginal History*, 1978) cites a number of contemporary songs, including a poem by a teenager, David Marrputja Munungurr, in the Yolngu language of north-eastern Arnhem land. The text describes pelicans journeying along loading

their pouches with fish, but at the same time it is an account of a journey in a Toyota car called 'Pelican'.

A significant development has been the availability of recordings on LP disc and cassette, with accompanying texts and translations. In 1967 Alice Moyle produced *Songs from the Northern Territory: Companion Booklet* to accompany five LP discs of songs from a number of areas at the 'top end'. Margaret Clunies Ross and Stephen A. Wild provide a companion booklet, *Djambidj: An Aboriginal Song Series from Northern Australia* (1982), for the recording of a performance of the songs by Frank Gurrmanama and Frank Malkorda. This is a 'group of thematically related songs, which have as their subjects the actions and characteristics of spirit beings (*wangarr*) who were active and creative in the Dreamtime and who are still believed to exist and inhabit the estates of Djambidj-owning clans' (p. 3). *Songs of Aboriginal Australia* (1987), ed. Margaret Clunies Ross, Tamsin Donaldson, and Stephen A. Wild, a collection of essays on various aspects of Aboriginal song (including texts with translations), has accompanying cassettes. Similar is the companion book (by Margaret Clunies Ross and Johnny Mundrugmundrug) to the cassette, *Goyulan: The Morning Star: An Aboriginal Clan Song Series from North Central Arnhem Land* (1988). *Songs of Central Australia. Alyawarra Music: Songs and Society in a central Australian community* (1986), by Richard B. Moyle (with the help of Slippery Morton, Alyawarra interpreter), gives detailed descriptions and analyses of performance, including texts, translations, and accompanying disc.

In recent years translations of Aboriginal oral poetry have appeared in many anthologies of Australian literature. This tradition began with *The Collins Book of Australian Poetry* (1981) ed. Rodney Hall. Hall opens his anthology with Berndt's translation of the 'Wonguri-Mandjikai Song Cycle of the Moon-Bone' and includes other translations from various sources. The tradition continues in anthologies such as: *The New Oxford Book of Australian Verse* (1986), ed. Les A. Murray; *The Orange Tree: South Australian Poetry To The Present Day* (1986), ed. K.F. Pearson and Christine Churches; *Two Centuries of Australian Verse* (1988) ed. Mark O'Connor; *The Macmillan Anthology of Australian Literature* (1990), ed. Ken Goodwin and Alan Lawson; *North of the Ten Commandments* (1991), ed. David Headon. These anthologies vary greatly in the kind of contextualising they provide for their Aboriginal material, and a glance at the 'Acknowledgements' pages of each anthology provides interesting insights into the issue of post-colonial appropriation, since 'acknowledgement' is often to the translator rather than to the owner of the song. Even so, these anthologies and the responses to them indicated that there was a desire in the wider community to gain some knowledge of Aboriginal song. It was partly in response to this perceived desire that R.M.W. Dixon and Martin Duwell produced the anthology, *The Honey-Ant Men's Love Song and Other Aboriginal Song Poems* (1990). The book is divided into four sections: 'Some Dyirbal Songs', 'A Central Australian Men's

Love Song', 'Some Anbarra Songs', 'Some Wangkan-gurru Songs', translated respectively by R.M.W. Dixon, Stephen A. Wild, Margaret Clunies Ross, and Luise A. Hercus. The songs (from fifteen performers) are given in the Aboriginal languages with page-facing translations. There are concise introductions to the material, comments on performance, and the performers are given proper recognition.

Works such as Berndt's *Love Songs of Arnhem Land*, the Dixon-Duwell anthology and the Hercus-Sutton anthology indicate that in spite of the great difficult-ies, and in spite of the continuing theoretical and social dilemmas concerning appropriation, it is possible to present Aboriginal oral song and narrative in trans-lation to a wider audience – in ways which, twenty years ago, would have seemed inconceivable.

BRUCE MOORE

Aboriginal Writing/Testimony in English, a relatively recent phenomenon in Australian literature, began with David Unaipon's *Native Legends* (1929), the first book published by an Aborigine in Australia, and re-emerged with Kath Walker's (see Noonuccal, Oodgeroo) successful first book of poetry *We Are Go-ing* (1964). A small but steady flow of books followed in the years up to the publication of Kevin Gilbert's (q.v.) *Living Black* (1977), a landmark work. In a 1975 statement Kath Walker, while reflecting on the 'as-similated' Aboriginal literature of the past, anticipated 'an exciting time ahead'. Certainly the commercial success of *Living Black*, along with a more sympathetic and informed Australian public and increasingly vig-orous Aboriginal politicking, resulted in an abundance of publications in the 1980s and beyond. Aboriginal literature now includes poetry, fiction, drama, autobi-ography and biography, Aboriginal myth and legend (particularly stories for children), transcribed testi-mony material, life history, and political, sociological and educational writing. Significant Aboriginal and Islander writers/speakers include, in addition to Oodgeroo and Kevin Gilbert, Jack Davis, Mudrooroo (Colin Johnson), Robert Merritt, Dick Roughsey, Bobbie Sykes, Lionel Fogarty, Archie Weller, Faith Bandler, Elsie Roughsey, Bill Rosser, Ruby Langford Ginibi, Daisy Utemorrah, Sally Morgan and Bill Neidjie. Oodgeroo, Davis, Gilbert, Mudrooroo, Weller, Ginibi and Morgan, in particular, now have bodies of work which demand the contemporary White critic's attention: Oodgeroo as the respected matriarchal figure; Davis as arguably Australia's most challenging dramatist in plays such as *Kullark* (per-formed 1979, publ. 1982) and the trilogy *The Dreamers* (performed 1981, publ. 1982), *No Sugar* (performed 1985, publ. 1986) and *Barungin – Smell the Wind* (1989); Mudrooroo as the post-colonial theorist's de-light; Weller as novelist and author of some of our finest short stories; Ginibi as the most outspoken of the 'life history' writers in English; and Sally Morgan as the author of the highly successful yet controversial *My Place* (1987). Indeed, throughout 1993–94 the re-spected journal *Australian Historical Studies* gave prominence to a literary/cultural debate about the worth, even validity, of Morgan's autobiographical

enterprise. She has become, as one writer said, 'some-thing of a Nyungar tall poppy'. The rapidly increasing significance of Aboriginal writing, both as Fourth World literature and as a seminal area of Australian literature, has encouraged a new wave of writers including Bob Maza, Eva Johnson, Richard Walley, Jimmy Chi, Graeme Dixon, Alf Taylor, Bill Dodd, John Wilson, Sam Watson, Doris Pilkington (Nugi Garimara), Philip McLaren, John Burke, Glenyse Ward, Margaret Brusnahan and Kim Scott.

Aboriginal autobiographies include, in the 1970s, *Moon and Rainbow* (1971) by Dick Roughsey; *Lamilami Speaks* (1974) by the Reverend Lazarus Lamilami; *A Bastard Like Me* (1975) by Charles Perkins; *If Everyone Cared* (1977) by Margaret Tucker; *My People's Life: An Aboriginal's Own Story* (1976) by Jack Mirritji; and *There's More to Life* (1979) by Roy Simon (Koori Dhou-lagarle). Autobiographical publications over the last fifteen years include *Mum Shirl: An Autobiography* (1981) by Shirley C. Smith; *To My Delight – a Grandson of the Gumbangarri* (1987) by Bill Cohen; *My Place* (1987); Glenyse Ward's companion volumes *Wander-ing Girl* (1988) and *Unna You Fullas* (1991); *Somebody Now* (1989) by Ellie Gaffney; *Me and You: The Life Story of Della Walker* (1989) by Della Walker; *Son of Alyandabu – My Fight for Aboriginal Rights* (1991) by Joe McGinness; *A Boy's Life* (1991) by Jack Davis; *Learning the Ropes* (1992) by Keith B. Saunders; *When the Pelican Laughed* (1992) by Alice Nannup; Rosemary van den Berg's interesting construction of her father Thomas Corbett's story *No Options No Choice! The Moore River Experience* (1994); and Evonne Goolagong-Cawley's *Home! The Evonne Goolagong Story* (1993), a lavish volume published by Simon & Schuster and clearly designated for the international market. Publisher interest in the biographies of well-known Aborigines such as Harold Blair, Sir Douglas Nicholls, Lionel Rose, Evonne Goolagong, Reg Saunders and Senator Neville Bonner – possibly reflecting a more paternal era – has noticeably waned in recent years; token interest has been replaced by a recognition of the changing nature of Black–White relations in this country and the irrepressible desire of the Aboriginal community to present its perspective, its side of the frontier.

Hence the real growth area in Aboriginal publi-cations has been not so much in works conforming to the traditional European literary genres as in political writings and life histories. The first cluster of such volumes – Gilbert's *Because a White Man'll Never Do It* (1973) and *Living Black* (1977), Cheryl Buchanan's *We Have Bugger All! The Kulaluk Story* (1974) and the Neville Bonner–Bobbie Sykes debate *Black Power in Australia* (1975) – helped to promote other works such as those of Bill Rosser: *This Is Palm Island* (1978, and dedicated 'To all my brothers and sisters who have suffered under the tyranny of the Queensland Abor-iginal Act'), *Dreamtime Nightmares – Biographies of Aborigines under the Queensland Aborigines Act* (1985), *Up Rode the Troopers – The Black Police in Queensland* (1990) and *Return to Palm Island* (1994). Of *Up Rode the Troopers*, reviewer Judith White said: 'With this new book he [Rosser] has made a remarkable contribution to Australia's national literature. It is a story burning to be told. And it is told in the way the history of the nineteenth century should be told, going behind the official myths to reveal the truth'. Other overtly political works of Aboriginal literature include Mary Coe's *Windradyne – a Wiradjuri Koorie* (1986, and dedicated to her father, 'a Wiradjuri Warrior [who] taught us to remember our past and make our future'), Faith Bandler's *Turning the Tide* (1989) and the edited collections of oral testimony material *Long Time, Olden Time – Aboriginal Accounts of Northern Territory History* (1991) and *North of the Ten Commandments – a Collection of Northern Territory Literature* (1991).

The burgeoning field of 'life history' is now a well-established genre, the most interesting and certainly the most controversial of all the genres of Aboriginal literature. Life history works which have followed Jimmie Barker's *The Two Worlds of Jimmie Barker – the Life of an Australian Aboriginal 1900–1972* (1977, as told to Janet Mathews) include *Gularabulu* (1983) by Paddy Roe; Elsie Roughsey's *Reasons for Not Forgetting* (1984) and *An Aboriginal Mother Tells of the Old and the New* (1984); *Warumungku Watikirli* (1984); Marnie Kennedy's *Born a Half-Caste* (1985; 1990); *This is What Happened – Historical Narratives by Aborigines* (1986); *Raparapa* (1987), comprising the transcriptions of lively, at times humorous conversations with nine Fitzroy River Aboriginal cattlemen, edited by Paul Marshall and published in the United States as *Outback Cowboys*(!); *Survival in Our Own Land* (1988; 1992); *Reaching Back – Queensland Aboriginal People Recall Early Days at Yarrabah Mission* (1989); *Women at the Centre* (1990); *Ingelba and the Five Black Matriarchs* (1990), edited by Patsy Cohen and Margaret Somerville; Barbara Cummings's *Take This Child . . . from Kahlin Compound to the Retta Dixon Children's Home* (1990); *Growing Up Walgett* (1990); *Being Aboriginal* (1990); *Boigu – Our History and Culture* (1991); *Over My Tracks* (1993); *Sort of a Place Like Home* (1993); and *Kaytetye Country* (1993), compiled and edited by Grace Koch. Black–White partnership enterprises include the Paddy Roe/Stephen Muecke/Krim Benterrack volume *Reading the Country* (1984); *Jilji. Life in the Great Sandy Desert* (1990) and *Yinti: Desert Child* (1992), by Pat Lowe and Jimmy Pike; *Yorro Yorro – Spirit of the Kimberley* (1993), by David Mowaljarlai and Jutta Malnic; and Sandra Le Brun Holmes's *Yirawala – Painter of the Dreaming* (1992). The wealth of material available in the land rights claim books and the mini-biographies in the 'Talking History' section of *Land Rights News* only add to this new and extraordinarily rich field.

Development of the life history genre has occurred so quickly that it is only recently that some of the ethical and practical implications of translation/transcription have been discussed. Literary criticism, not for the first time, has been left far behind. Yet some commentators are making a genuine effort to answer the difficult questions raised by the sudden rise to prominence of Aboriginal literature, among them Mudrooroo, Bobbi Sykes, Bob Hodge, Stephen Muecke, Veronica Brady, David Headon, Bruce Shaw, Adam Shoemaker, Jackie Huggins, Judith

Wright and Peter Read. These attempts have stimulated, in Read's words, 'lively and sometimes acrimonious debate'. In her review of the Susan Maushart-edited *Sort of a Place Like Home*, Huggins presents a more extreme Aboriginal view, but one which must be addressed, and answered:

> When engaging in dialogue there is an inherent danger when non-Aboriginal people transcribe the speech patterns of Aboriginal people. I have never seen an acceptable transformation and often find this feeble attempt offensive. Non-Aboriginal writers tend to exaggerate which verges on patronising interpretations and language. Speaking for is not the same as speaking with. While it is vital to give Aboriginals voice, whose voice is it?

His considerable experience with the practice of gathering testimony prompts non-indigenous historian Peter Read to ask questions of more practical import:

> Aboriginal pastoral station English should be presented in a reader-friendly form. Should it be a literal transcription, be sold with a copy of the original tape, rendered into standard English or, the latest advance, set out as a line of blank verse complete with separators and stress marks? Each has its advantages and drawbacks.

Non-indigenous anthropologist Bruce Shaw has been wrestling with the particular problems posed by transcription for a number of years in several volumes reflecting his fieldwork, which present the wonderful life histories of a range of East Kimberley Aboriginal men: *My Country of the Pelican Dreaming – the Life of an Australian Aborigine of the Gadjerong, Grant Ngabidj, 1904–1977* (1981), *Banggaiyerri – the Story of Jack Sullivan* (1983), *Countrymen – the Life Histories of Four Aboriginal Men* (1986) and *When the Dust Come in Between – Aboriginal Viewpoints in the East Kimberley Prior to 1982* (1992). By his own admission 'tampering with the original expressiveness' of the taped conversations, Shaw defends his 'relatively extensive' role as editor /translator because he feels it 'unrealistic to expect the general reader to wade through 200 pages written in the original style'. Perhaps he is right. The controversy continues.

Numerous books edited by or written by non-indigenous Australians avoid any extensive discussion of the ethical implications of transcription/translation, yet they still make a notable contribution to the field. Among the best are Frank Hardy's *The Unlucky Australians* (1968); John Cribbin's *The Killing Times* (1984); *Fighters and Singers – the Lives of Some Australian Aboriginal Women* (1985); Steve Hawke's award-winning *Noonkanbah – Whose Land, Whose Law* (1989); Deborah Bird Rose's *Hidden Histories* (1991) and *Dingo Makes Us Human* (1992); and the Pamela Lyon/Michael Parsons work *We Are Staying: the Alyawarre Struggle for Land at Lake Nash* (1989), which details the precise nature of Aboriginal representation and politicking at Lake Nash. Other works written or compiled by non-indigenous Australians which add to this overtly political literature include *Black Viewpoints: the Aboriginal Experience* (1975), ed. Colin Tatz;

Wreck Bay: an Aboriginal Fishing Community (1981; 1990) by Brian Egloff (with members of the Wreck Bay community); Erich Kolig's *The Noonkanbah Story* (1987); D.J. Mulvaney's *Encounters in Place – Outsiders and Aboriginal Australians 1606–1985* (1989); Diane Bell's *Daughters of the Dreaming* (1983, 1993); Nonie Sharp's two incisive Torres Strait volumes *Footprints Along the Cape York Sandbeaches* (1992) and *Stars of Tagai – the Torres Strait Islanders* (1993); and Stuart Rintoul's *The Wailing: a National Black Oral History* (1993). While the title of the latter volume has upset some, it nevertheless gathers together an excellent range of Aboriginal speakers. It adds 'new voices to old voices'.

The collection, interpretation and publication of Aboriginal myths and legends have for many years occupied both Black and White writers. Representative early samples of this genre are Wilf Reeves's *The Legends of Moonie Jarl* (1964); Sylvia Cairns's *Uncle Willie Mackenzie's Legends of the Goundirs* (1967); Oodgeroo Noonuccal's *Stradbroke Dreamtime* (1972); Dick Roughsey's *The Giant Devil Dingo* (1973) and *The Rainbow Serpent* (1975); Nancy Sheppard's *Alitji in the Dreamtime* (1975); *Joe Nangan's Dreaming: Aboriginal Legends of the North-West* (1976); Narritjan Maymuru's *The Milky Way* (1979); Kormilda Community College's (Darwin) *Djugurba: Tales from the Spirit Time* (1974) and *Visions of Mowanjum – Aboriginal Writings from the Kimberley* (1980). Since 1980, the more serious commitment to the rendering of Aboriginal mythology has resulted in works such as the Warlukurlangu Artists' *Kuruwarri: Yuendumu Doors* (1987) and Robert Layton's *Uluru: an Aboriginal History of Ayers Rock* (1986; 1989). Children's literature, too, has recently witnessed far greater Aboriginal involvement in the rendition of Aboriginal stories. Decades of non-indigenous appropriation of this genre are over. The striking entry of the Aboriginal publishing house Magabala Books (Broome) and the Aboriginal Studies Press (Canberra) into the field of indigenous literature has rejuvenated it. Each is producing splendid volumes, marked by meticulous attention to detail and the integrity of the story-telling. In the last five years published Magabala titles include *The Story of Crow* (1988) of the Nyul Nyul people of Western Australia; *Jalygurr – Aussie Animal Rhymes* (1987) of the Yawuru people of Broome; the award-winning tale *Bip – the Snapping Bungaroo* (1990) by Narelle McRobbie; Daisy Utemorrah's book of children's poems *Do Not Go Around the Edges* (1990), which won the Australian Multicultural Children's Book Award, and *Moonglue* (1993); *The Arguing Edibles* (1992); the collaborative story *Tjarany-Roughtail: the Dreaming of the Roughtail Lizard and Other Stories Told by the Kukatja* (1992); and Anne Abednego Gela's Torres Strait legend *Gelam – The Man from Moa* (1993). Other adventurous Magabala commissionings include John Wilson's *Lori* (1989); *The Dream* (1991) by Rae Harris and Beryl Harp; Selena Solomon's *Dabu – the Baby Dugong* (1992) and Mary Charles's *Winin – Why the Emu Cannot Fly* (1993). Aboriginal Studies Press titles include May O'Brien's *The Legend of the Seven Sisters – a Traditional Aboriginal Story from Western Australia* (1990) and the visually stunning *Wunambi the Water*

Snake (1991). Special mention must be made of ASP's encouragement of the Western Regional Aboriginal Land Council's collective work *The Story of the Falling Star* (1989), told by Elsie Jones. This was a project conceived in part as an adult literacy tool; it is also a marvellous children's story, linking past and present Aboriginal generations in the NSW town of Wilcannia. *The Story of the Falling Star* topped the list of best-selling Australian children's books and received no less than three awards in the annual Australian Book Publishers Association Design Awards: Book of the Year, Children's Book of the Year and Highly Commended in the paperback category.

The most useful survey of Aboriginal literature is Adam Shoemaker's *Black Words, White Page – Aboriginal Literature 1929–1988* (1989), supplemented by the bibliographic volumes *Black Australia* (1978; 1985) by Marji Hill and Alex Barlow. The most incisive commentary is provided by the range of contributors to *Aboriginal Writing Today* (1985), edited by Jack Davis and Bob Hodge, and *Connections – Essays on Black Literatures* (1988), edited by Emmanuel S. Nelson. Mudrooroo Narogin's *Writing from the Fringe – a Study of Modern Aboriginal Literature* (1990) provides some insights but it, like the Bob Hodge/Vijay Mishra critical work, *Dark Side of the Dream – Australian Literature and the Post Colonial Mind* (1991), suffers from a surfeit of generalisations, rash statements and culpably obscure expression. Both books fail to recognise their responsibilities to an intelligent and interested readership beyond the academy. Their focus is too narrow.

The major anthologies are *Us Fellas – an Anthology of Aboriginal Writing* (1987), collected by Colleen Glass and Archie Weller; *Inside Black Australia – an Anthology of Aboriginal Poetry* (1988), edited by Kevin Gilbert and 'Dedicated to Aboriginaland'; and *Paperbark – a Collection of Black Australian Writings* (1990), edited by Jack Davis, Stephen Muecke, Mudrooroo (Narogin) and Adam Shoemaker. The most noticeable point about the 'Contents' list of *Paperbark* is not who is in it, but who is absent. The explanation for the absence of writers such as Kevin Gilbert, Bobby Merritt, Lionel Fogarty, Bobbi Sykes, Louise Corpus, Faith Bandler and Robert Walker, to mention only the most significant, stems at least in part from the sponsorship of *Paperbark* by the National Bicentennial Aboriginal and Torres Strait Islander Program. Gilbert flatly refused on principle any Bicentennial money, 'blood money' as he put it. Nevertheless, the Introduction to *Paperbark* is excellent – both trenchant and iconoclastic. It challenges European notions of literature. 'In a broader sense', the editors maintain, 'writing is definable as any sort of meaningful inscription, and in the case of Aboriginal Australia this would include sand paintings and drawings ... as well as engravings ... body markings, paintings as well as engravings on bark or stone'. *Paperbark* includes letters, Jimmy Pike's distinctive graphics, a small amount of oral testimony material, songs, political addresses and even an excerpt from Jimmy Chi's Black musical *Bran Nue Dae*; with all this variety the collection by its very nature undermines the established and necessarily limiting genres of Western literature. The editors' most instructive comments refer to the first National Aboriginal Writers' Conference (Murdoch University, 1983). They maintain that:

> This conference consolidated the political basis for Aboriginal literature, a literature or a set of writings which has never been divorced from the Aboriginal struggle for economic freedom, legal recognition and reforms of basic living conditions. It is as if aesthetic questions have taken a back-seat compared to the politics of literature. Put another way, if one accepts the proposition that all literatures are political expressions, then Aboriginal literature is one of those which has not yet succumbed to the rhetorical ploy of saying that 'politics gets in the way of literature'. It asserts the contrary: literature is one of the ways of getting political things done.

It is certain that Aboriginal writers will maintain their political focus for many decades yet.

Three presses now exist to assist individual Aboriginal writers and help Aboriginal communities to preserve their histories and traditions: Magabala, originally established in April 1987 by the Kimberley Aboriginal Law and Culture Centre with the assistance of Bicentennial funding; the Aboriginal Studies Press, the publishing arm of the Australian Institute of Aboriginal and Torres Strait Islander Studies in Canberra; and the Institute for Aboriginal Development Inc., of Alice Springs. In addition, non-indigenous publishing houses such as Fremantle Arts Centre Press, Allen & Unwin, Currency, Heinemann, Hyland House and the University of Queensland Press have markedly increased their commitment to Aboriginal publications. In a media release early in 1990, UQP launched their 'Black Australian Writing' series, intended to 'open new and exciting opportunities in Black writing . . .' and to complement UQP's David Unaipon Award, established in 1988 to commemorate the achievements of David Unaipon (1873–1967) and presented annually to a previously unpublished Aboriginal and Torres Strait Islander writer. The inaugural winner was Graeme Dixon for his volume of political poems *Holocaust Island* (1990). Subsequent winners have been Doris Pilkington (Nugi Garimara) for *Caprice: A Stockman's Daughter* in 1990; Bill Dodd for *Broken Dreams* in 1991; Philip McLaren for *Sweet Water – Stolen Land* in 1992; and John Burke for *Bridge of Triangles* in 1993.

DAVID HEADON

Aboriginalities was the title of a column which ran in the *Bulletin* from 15 October 1887 until control of the journal passed from the Prior family to Consolidated Press in 1960. For much of its life the column comprised paragraphs about bush life and people supplied by contributors. C.H. Bertie edited *Aboriginalities from the Bulletin* (1913), which was illustrated by Lionel Lindsay.

Academy Editions of Australian Literature is a series of scholarly critical editions of major Australian literary works. The project is sponsored by the Australian Academy of the Humanities and funded by the Australian Research Council. Begun in 1992, the project is directed at the Australian Scholarly Editions Centre at the University College, Australian Defence Force Academy, Canberra, where the director is Associate Professor Paul Eggert. The project is a national co-operative venture with its Editorial and Advisory Boards and editors of individual volumes drawn from many Australian universities. Among the proposed titles and editors are *His Natural Life* by Marcus Clarke (Lurline Stuart), *Robbery Under Arms* by 'Rolf Boldrewood' (Robert Dixon), *An Australian Girl* by Catherine Martin (Rosemary Foxton), *Complete Poems* of Charles Harpur in two volumes (Michael Ackland and Elizabeth Perkins), *Complete Poems* of John Shaw Neilson (Cliff Hanna), *The Recollections of Geoffry Hamlyn* by Henry Kingsley (Stanton Mellick and Patrick Morgan), *The Complete Poems* of Mary Gilmore (Jennifer Strauss) and *Australian Plays 1834–1926* (Richard Fotheringham). The *Academy Editions Newsletter* is published annually (No. 1 in July 1992, No. 2 in May 1993) to summarise progress and to inform writers and scholars of the project. The Australian Scholarly Editions Centre also combines with the National Library of Australia to publish a joint bibliography series. The first volume, *Australian Autobiographical Narratives: Volume 1: to 1850*, by Kay Walsh and Joy Hooton, was published in 1993

Acolyte, The, a novel by Thea Astley (q.v.), was published in 1972 and won the 1973 Miles Franklin Award (q.v.). Set mainly in southern Queensland, it is an obliquely developed study of a blind, egocentric musician, Holberg, seen through the eyes of Paul Vesper, his disciple and factotum. Holberg's blindness, personality and possible genius arouse a mixture of compassion, fascination and dependence in all those drawn into his orbit, including Vesper, who has abandoned an engineering career to serve him. A versatile master in the manipulation of others, Holberg manages for the most part to conceal his ruthless self-centredness. Eventually, however, by a slow process of several years' cumulative perceptions, Vesper penetrates the truth and violently rejects him.

ADAM-SMITH, Patsy (1924–) grew up in Victorian country districts, where her father worked as a fettler on the railway and her mother was station-mistress-cum-postmistress at numerous small, isolated towns. She served with the VADs in the Second World War; was a radio operator (the first woman to be so articled) on an Australian trading ship 1954–60; was an Adult Education Officer in Hobart, 1960–67; and was appointed manuscripts field officer in the State Library of Victoria in 1970. Her autobiographical (to the beginning of the Second World War) *Hear the Train Blow*, described by Kenneth Slessor as 'a minor classic', was published in 1964, an expanded and illustrated edition appearing in 1981. Her long list of other published works includes *Moonbird People* (1965), about the inhabitants of the Furneaux Islands in Bass Strait and their annual harvesting of the migratory shearwater petrels; *There Was a Ship*, the story of her years on the Australian coast (1967, republished in 1977 as *Trader to the Islands* and in a composite volume with *Moonbird People* in 1983); *Tiger Country* (1968); *No*

Tribesman (1971); *The Anzacs* (1978), which gives a fresh and vivid account of Australia's participation in the First World War and which shared the 1978 *Age* Book of the Year Award; *Outback Heroes* (1981), which finds heroism in the lives of such diverse personalities as Daisy Bates and the squatter-explorer Nat Buchanan, and in such types as the mailman and minister of religion in the outback and the workers on the Overland Telegraph Line; *The Shearers* (1982), a parallel volume to *The Anzacs*; *Australian Women at War* (1984), stories of women in wartime in factory, farm and the services, accompanied by splendid historical photographs; *Heart of Exile* (1986), about the seven Irish political exiles sent to Tasmania in 1848; *Pity of War* (1991); and *Prisoners of War: From Gallipoli to Korea* (1992) which won the 1993 National Book Council Order of Australia Book Prize, awarded triennially. Patsy Adam-Smith's abiding interest, however, stemming from her great affection for her railwayman father and from her childhood experiences when the family's annual fortnight holiday was spent on continuous (and free) train travel, is the Australian railways. In addition to *Hear the Train Blow*, she has written *The Rails Go Westward* (1969), *Across Australia by Indian Pacific* (1971), *The Desert Railway* (1974), *Romance of Australian Railways* (1973–74) and *When We Rode The Rails* (1983); and she has edited *Folklore of the Australian Railwaymen* (1969). Her interest in history is also evident in *Hobart Sketchbook* (1968), *Tasmania Sketchbook* (1971), *Port Arthur Sketchbook* (1971), *Launceston Sketchbook* (1973), *Islands of Bass Strait* (1978) and *Victorian and Edwardian Melbourne from Old Photographs* (1979). She was made OBE in 1980 for her services to literature.

ADAMS, A.H. (Arthur Henry) (1872–1936), born in NZ, graduated from Otago University and tried law and journalism before coming to Australia, where he became secretary to the theatrical entrepreneur J.C. Williamson. In 1900 he left for China to cover the Boxer Rebellion, and after some further visits to London, Australia and NZ returned to Australia and established himself as a leading journalist, editing, in succession, the Red Page of the *Bulletin*, the *Lone Hand* and the Sydney *Sun*. His verse, which includes the collections *Maoriland: And Other Verses* (1899), *London Streets* (1906) and *The Collected Verses of Arthur H. Adams* (1913), avoids the rawness of the contemporary Australian ballads but also lacks their verve and intensity. Of his novels, which include *Tussock Land* (1904), *Galahad Jones* (q.v., 1910), *A Touch of Fantasy* (1911), *The Knight of the Motor Launch* (1913), *Double Bed Dialogues* (1915, under the pseudonym 'Henry James James'), *Grocer Greatheart* (1915), *The Australians* (1920), *Lola of the Chocolates* (under the pseudonym 'James James') and *A Man's Life* (1929), *Galahad Jones* and *The Australians* are the best. Australia, or more often Sydney, frequently figures in his work as a partly known rather than a fully felt landscape and although both his fiction and poetry are crafted to a degree, the tone of his work oscillates between romantic sentimentality and cynicism or worldly wisdom. Nevertheless, his fiction is often enlivened by whimsical

characterisation, gentle irony and a lively writing style. Adams also wrote several full-length plays and a number of one-acters, few of which, though often witty and socially pertinent, achieved commercial production. His most significant published plays include *The Wasters, Galahad Jones* and *Mrs Pretty and the Premier* (qq.v.), which comprise *Three Plays for the Australian Stage* (1914).

ADAMS, David (1908–) was born at Bringelly, on the outskirts of Sydney in the Camden–Cowpastures area (now Camden), with which his family had long been associated. He had been associated with the *Bulletin* in 1927 when he was an assistant to the financial editor on the 'Wild Cat' section of that magazine while completing a diploma in accountancy. He was appointed a director of the *Bulletin* in 1934 and revived and expanded the famous 'Business, Robbery, Etc.' column, which became well known in the 1930s for its exposure of investment malpractices, especially in Sydney, and during and after the Second World War persistently expressed the paper's concern about the long-term national economic and financial problems. In 1948 he became editor of the *Bulletin*, at the age of 39 the youngest editor since J.F. Archibald, a position he held until 1961. Adams's other notable literary achievement was the discovery and editing of *The Letters of Rachel Henning* (see Henning, Rachel) which, illustrated by Norman Lindsay, was first serialised in the *Bulletin* 1951–52.

ADAMS, Francis (1862–93) was born at Malta, son of an army surgeon and well-known novelist, Bertha Jane Grundy Adams. Educated in England, Adams studied languages in Paris with a diplomatic post in mind but was compelled by tuberculosis to come to Australia in 1884. In 1887 he turned to journalism and leader-writing with the *Brisbane Courier* and with William Lane's radical weekly, the *Boomerang*; he also became a prolific contributor of poems, short fiction and critical articles to the *Bulletin*. Although initially enthusiastic about Australia ('a true republic'), in 1890 Adams returned ('mind-sick of Australia') to England where in 1893, with his health much deteriorated, he committed suicide.

Although he spent less than six years in Australia, Adams's influence was considerable, for he brought a sophisticated intellect, born partly of his European experiences and background, to contemporary Australian social, cultural and political problems. His major effect was on the developing radicalism of the day. His intensely radical collection of poetry, *Songs of the Army of the Night* (1888), violent in its outbursts against privilege, oppression and exploitation of the poor and lowly, encouraged radicalism in this country by predicting a successful democracy here. The local scene was further scrutinised in the prose works, *Australian Essays* (1886) and *The Australians* (1893), the latter contrasting the two Australias, the lush, populated, coastal fringe and the dry, sparsely peopled interior. In a judgement that expressed a belief close to the heart of the developing nationalism of the time, Adams assessed the bushman as 'the one powerful and unique national type yet produced in Australia'. Many of the stories in his volume, *Australian Life* (1892), take up the theme of outback life, indicating in otherwise ordinary adventure stories, something of its praiseworthy, though idiosyncratic, nature. Of his other fiction, both *John Webb's End* (1891) and *The Melbournians* (1892) indicate the impact of Australia on his literary creativity, while *A Child of the Age* (1894) is partly autobiographical. Interest in Francis Adams has remained high since the 1890s and continues to increase, a recognition not so much of his own creative writing as of the impact of his intellectual modernity and revolutionary zeal, qualities which helped to sound the death knell of colonialism in Australia. Adams is the subject of Clive Turnbull's biographical essay, *These Tears of Fire* (1949), which was included in *Australian Lives* (1965).

ADAMS, Glenda (1940–), born Sydney, was educated at the University of Sydney, where she studied Indonesian and other languages, and became intrigued by other cultures. After graduation she went to Indonesia on a small scholarship to study language and literature and taught Indonesian at the University of Sydney for a period before going to New York in 1964. She partly ascribes her taste for travel, which is shared by her characters and was encouraged in childhood by her family's frequent moves within Sydney, to the restlessness which is an 'Australian tradition'; her early attempts at writing were encouraged by her mother, whose own struggles to keep the family out of financial trouble fostered independence in her children. Australian society in the 1960s was still discouraging for women and Adams was not alone in the determination to travel, which was not just 'a getting of culture' but 'meant an important personal liberation, mental and physical . . . a getting of freedom, a real growing up'. In New York she was encouraged to pursue her vocation as a writer after becoming a student at the Graduate School of Journalism at Columbia University. Marriage to a Californian, followed by the birth of a daughter and two years in Europe, prevented her return and it was not until she had been living for seven years in New York, surviving as a single mother by teaching fiction-writing workshops at Sarah Lawrence College and Columbia, that she felt the need to reclaim her Australian past, which was the staple of all her stories and novels, in a physical sense. After several visits to Australia in the 1980s, she returned to live in Sydney in 1990. She has published two collections of short stories, *Lies and Stories* (1976) and *The Hottest Night of the Century* (1979, which includes seven from *Lies and Stories*); and three novels, *Games of the Strong* (1982), *Dancing on Coral* (1987, which won the Miles Franklin Award and a NSW State Premier's Award) and *Longleg* (1990, which won the *Age* Book of the Year Award). She has also written for television.

Several of the fourteen stories of *The Hottest Night of the Century* concern family and school life in Australia; the later stories are influenced by the experimental form and heavy symbolism of some contemporary American fiction. *Games of the Strong* is a complex novel with strong overtones of the classic Orwellian '1984'; narrated by Neila, who lives in the 'Complex', another name for a police state which has exiled dissidents, including writers, to the Island, it is the story of her efforts to undermine the system from within. Rising to the position of Acting Minister of Information, she discovers that her duplicitous position has unanticipated ambivalences and that her enemies are not only elusive but include her lover and even her own unsuspected motives. Drawn into causing the deaths of numerous people, Neila becomes both an agent of corruption and its opponent in this totalitarian environment where nothing is necessarily as it seems. *Dancing on Coral*, set in Australia and the USA of the 1960s, might be interpreted as a response to Christina Stead's *For Love Alone*. Lark Watter, restless in the provincial environment of her childhood and attracted to her Jonathan Crow (the American, Tom Brown), leaves for New York by German freighter, accompanied by the unpleasant Donna Bird, daughter of a world famous anthropologist and cultural imperialist. The novel takes its title from a central incident when the captain of the freighter puts the girls ashore on a coral reef and witnesses their distress as the tidal waters rise. A subversion of the traditional male *bildungsroman* such as *Portrait of the Artist as a Young Man, Dancing on Coral* concludes with Lark's separation from husband and potential lover 'in the space of [her] baby's afternoon nap' and her discovery of independence. Play is central to this novel, which comically satirises the hollowness of some familiar political attitudes and manipulations, although it is itself a deeply political book subversive of both latter-day imperialism and masculinism. Beginning in Sydney of the post-war years and partly set in Europe, *Longleg* is the story of the unremarkable William Badger from childhood to middle age and his long adjustment to his early abandonment by his mother; his unsuccessful, part-painful and part-comic search for the woman to replace the lost feminine ideal, accompanied by his more successful discovery of self, becomes the means for Adams to explore complex issues concerning identity and meaning.

ADAMS, Nancy (1890–1968), granddaughter of the famous educationalist, Alexander Morrison (principal of Scotch College, Melbourne, from 1857 to 1903), was born in Melbourne, grew up in that city and in England, married a well-known Melbourne wine merchant and was for many years a noted member of Melbourne's social establishment. Her historical novel, *Saxon Sheep* (1961), traces the history of the Templeton and Forlong families who brought the first Saxon merino sheep to Australia. Her autobiographical *Family Fresco* (1966) is a remarkably detailed account of a generation that was loyal in its adherence to old British traditions but genuinely proud of its Australian character.

ADAMS, Phillip (1939–), born Maryborough, Victoria, has had a wide-ranging career in advertising, television, journalism and the film industry in Australia. Columnist for the *Australian*, he has also written columns for or contributed to the Melbourne *Age*, *Sydney Morning Herald*, *Bulletin*, Adelaide *Advertiser*, Brisbane *Courier-Mail*, London *Financial Times* and *New York Times*. He has chaired or been a member of numerous advisory bodies on the Australian media and the performing arts, including chairman of the Australian Film Commission (1983–90), chairman of the Commission for the Future (1985–90), chairman of the Film, Radio and Television Board (1972–75), foundation member of the Australia Council (1972–75), president of the Victorian Council of the Arts (1982–86) and member of the Australian Children's Television Foundation (1981–87). He was instrumental in the establishment of the Experimental Film Fund and Australian Film Development Corporation and the Film School. His numerous awards include the Raymond Longford Award (1981), the Australian Arts Award conferred at the Henry Lawson Festival (1987), several Film Festival Awards and two gold medals in international competition. He was made AM in 1987, Senior Anzac Fellow in 1981 and is a Fellow of the Royal Society of Arts. He has produced such films as *The Adventures of Barry McKenzie, Don's Party, The Getting of Wisdom* and *We of the Never Never*. His publications include *Adams with Added Enzymes* (1975, his observations on the advertising industry), *The Unspeakable Adams* (1977), *More Unspeakable Adams* (1979), *Uncensored Adams* (1981), *The Inflammable Adams* (1983), and *Adams versus God* (1985). Truda Olson published a bio-bibliography, *Phillip Adams: A Reference Guide to his Life and Work* (1986).

ADAMSON, Bartlett (1884–1951), born Ringarooma in north-eastern Tasmania, was a journalist with the *Sunday News* and *Smith's Weekly* in Sydney from 1919 to 1950. His smoothly lyrical poetry includes *Twelve Sonnets* (1918); *These Beautiful Women* (1932); *Bringer of Light: An Allegorical Fantasy* (1945), a long poem on a romantic medieval theme that was judged in the *Bulletin's* Red Page (16 January 1964) to be 'a swoon of romantic nonsense' with versification 'unusually capable'; *Comrades All and Other Poems for the People* (1945), which attests to Adamson's political attitudes (he was a member of the Communist Party); and *For Peace and Friendship* (1952), a posthumous selection from his poetry. His fiction includes *Mystery Gold* (1925), a story of hidden treasure in the South Seas, and *Nice Day for a Murder and Other Stories* (1944), many of which relate to bushranging derring-do. An influential member of the FAW, Adamson challenged that organisation's conservative attitudes. He was president three times over a twenty-year period. Len Fox gave the address, *Bartlett Adamson*, published in 1963, to commemorate his achievements.

ADAMSON, Robert (1943–), born Sydney of Scottish and Irish ancestry, spent his boyhood in Neutral Bay and the environs of the Harbour but often visited the Hawkesbury River district where his paternal grandfather was a fisherman. Boyhood unruliness, culminating in several semi-criminal misdemeanours, sent him to the Gosford Boys' Home for juvenile offenders and he was seldom out of corrective institutions until his mid-twenties. He educated himself while in gaol and developed an interest in poetry. After he became part of the Sydney literary scene in the late 1960s, Adamson was instrumental in the rise of the so-called New Australian Poetry (q.v.), editing Grace Perry's magazine, *New Poetry*, and establishing Prism Books where such poetry was published. For more than two decades he has been an influential literary personality, successfully combining careers in writing, editing and publishing. He was editor-director, with Dorothy Hewett, of Big Smoke Books, editing, designing and publishing several collections of Hewett's poetry as well as his own. He launched Paper Bark Press to publish Hewett's *Alice in Wormland* (1987); Paper Bark (Adamson's wife, photographer, Juno Gemes, and writer, Michael Wilding, are also part of the Press, which has published the work of Terry Gillmore and Tim Thorne and Adamson's own *The Clean Dark*), has been praised for its quality design and presentation.

Adamson now lives on the Hawkesbury River ('I doubt I could live without the river') close to where he spent his time as a boy, fishing with his grandfather and exploring the river environment. Adamson's books of poetry include *Canticles on the Skin* (1970), *The Rumour* (1971), *Swamp Riddles* (1974), *Theatre I-XIX* (1976), *Cross the Border* (1977), *Where I Come From* (1979), *Selected Poems* (1977, for which many of the earlier poems were rewritten and which won the Grace Leven Prize for Poetry), *The Law at Heart's Desire* (1982), *The Clean Dark* (1989) and *Selected Poems 1970–1989* (1990).

The Clean Dark has been Adamson's chief poetic triumph, winning the NSW and Victorian State Literary Awards and the National Book Council's Banjo Award. He also published *Zimmer's Essay* (1974) in collaboration with Bruce Hanford, an experimental fictional work, which, partly narrative, partly discursive and with a concluding poetry section, critically examines the prison experience. His autobiographical collection of prose and poetry, *Wards of the State*, was published in 1992.

Recognised as one of Australia's best contemporary poets, Adamson has recorded in his poetry the depths and achievements of his personal and professional life. His early poetry (*Canticles of the Skin* and *Swamp Riddles*) recounts reform school, prison and drug experiences and highlights the growing importance to him of the Hawkesbury River and its landscape. Both themes recur in much of his later poetry. Adamson's links with the American Black Mountain poets, particularly Robert Duncan, and his revolutionary ambitions for Australian poetry led to 'The Rumour', a complex poem which, in terms of experimental form and preoccupation with the craft of poetry, can now be seen as one of the foundation stones of post-modernism in Australian poetry. It has been seen, too, as 'a manifesto of the new romanticism' (James Tulip), the 'romantic' label being one that has long attached to Adamson. Some of the later volumes such as *Where I Come From* and *The Law at Heart's Desire* are autobiographically based, recording painful periods of Adamson's boyhood as well as the destructive break-up of his first marriage. *The Clean Dark* celebrates the Hawkesbury as his soul-country. The river's physical and spiritual influences coalesce:

> The river / is like a blank page
> you enter it / differently: shape
> it as you would
> a new thought / first vaguely
> with phrases / then sentences
> until finally / its language
> starts talking

The Clean Dark, among the most significant volumes of poetry of the late 1980s, also contains poems critical of both political and community apathy about the environment, violence and intolerance e.g. 'Canticle for the Bicentennial Dead', 'Wild Colonial Boys', 'Phasing Out the Mangroves', 'Remembering Posts', 'No River No Death'. Among the more personal poems are those that recall lost friends such as Robert Duncan and Francis Webb, others with new hope ('Songs for Juno'), and yet others with the inescapable Adamson burden of old griefs and uneasy memories ('The Difference Looking Back', 'Dreaming Up Mother', 'What's Slaughtered's Gone').

Wards of the State, while autobiographically based, is not the complete key to the enigma of Adamson's early life but it does, more so than the rest of his writings, reveal something of the detail of the experiences of reform school, prison and young manhood. Adamson has always had to contend with the publicly perceived image of *persona* in lieu of person. It is unlikely that *Wards of the State* will change that situation. He has also edited (with Manfred Jurgensen) the anthology *Australian Writing Now* (1988).

ADAMSON, Walter (1911–   ), born Königsberg, Germany, came to Australia in 1939 and worked at various jobs until he joined the Australian Army in 1944 as an Italian language interpreter. In 1949 he went to Bolivia, where he taught English, but returned to Australia in 1953. Since 1969 he has been a full-time writer, contributing short stories, poems and articles to Australian and German magazines and newspapers. His publications include two fictionalised accounts of his experiences of Australia published in German in 1973 and 1974, one of which was translated by Sonja Delander and published in Australia in 1984, titled *Australia of All Places*; a novel, *The Institution* (published in Germany in 1974 and in translation in Australia in 1976); a collection of light verse, *Adamson's Three Legged World* (1985); and a collection of short stories, *The Man with the Suitcase* (1989).

ADELAIDE, Debra (1958–   ), born Sydney, has compiled a substantial bibliography of Australian women's writing 1795–1990 (1991) and edited both an influential collection of critical essays on colonial women's writing, *A Bright and Fiery Troop* (1988) and Dymphna Cusack's autobiography, *A Window in the Dark* (1991). With Laurie Bookluck she co-authored the novel, *Headlines* (1993).

Adelaide Observer, see **Observer** (1)

Adelaide Punch, see **Melbourne Punch**

Adelaide Review, begun in 1984 and sponsored by South Australian business organisations and the SA Government's Department of the Arts and the Literature Board of the Australia Council, has a circulation of about 35 000 (it is distributed free in SA). Published monthly (fortnightly in 1987), it is edited by Christopher Pearson and offers, in addition to original literature, sections on film, theatre, dance and music as well as wide-ranging commentary on all facets of cultural life in SA.

Admella, a steamship, was wrecked on a reef off Cape Northumberland in SA on 6 August 1859. Contemporary accounts of the shipwreck and the ensuing efforts to save the crew and passengers include Samuel Mossman's *Narrative of the Shipwreck of the Admella* (1859), Philip Barry's *The Wreck of the Admella: A Metrical Narrative* (1859), George French Angas's *The Wreck of the Admella and Other Poems* (1874), as well as sundry poems, e.g. Adam Lindsay Gordon's 'From the Wreck'. Ian Mudie published *Wreck of the Admella* in 1966; in it he disposes of the legend that Gordon himself took part in the ride described in 'From the Wreck'.

'Advance Australia Fair', see **National Anthem**

Advancement of Spencer Button, The, a novel by 'Brian James' (q.v.), was published in 1950. Spencer Button, the son of a dim-witted struggling farmer of Wombat Creek, NSW, and a mother ambitious for gentility, rises from his inauspicious rural beginnings to be headmaster of Simmons Street (Fort Street), one of Sydney's most important high schools. After education at the nearest town, Selkirk (Mudgee), Spencer begins at fifteen as a pupil-teacher at a Sydney primary school, takes his degree and then alternates between the 'Celestial City' and the necessary 'pilgrim's progress' in the country at such places as Barden (Broken Hill) and Brushwood (Grafton). Dogged by his uncultured relatives and increasingly ashamed of his unfashionable mother, Spencer marries Susie Sparrow, a girl who shares his ambitions but whose life-denying nature becomes increasingly obvious. The well-planned arrival of a son, Carlyle, does little to reanimate their marriage. An earlier romantic relationship with a Selkirk girl, Winnie Ogg, culminates in a nightmarish way after Winnie takes to prostitution and is finally drowned; a later love affair with a member of his staff at Brushwood is prevented from having extensive consequences by Spencer's innate preference for safety. Other potentially destructive experiences, such as the First World War, pass Spencer by, although his brother, Graham, is a victim. Of his numerous relatives, the most memorable is Aunty May, a little woman of amazing activity, who is obsessed with physical illness and addicted to a comic style of verbal shorthand. Interwoven with Spencer's career are a multitude of minor destinies, from Mr Wren, the part-time farmer and teacher of a small school, who battles inspectors and droughts with equal ferocity, to the innocuous Mr Cyril Finger, who opts for the Salvation Army, to Mr Foll, who dies after his son's disgrace makes his years of sacrificial teaching pointless. The background of the novel consists of a panorama of the general life of NSW from the 1890s to the 1940s and a more detailed picture of the specific life of the State's educational system; particularly striking are 'James's' descriptions of the daily life and characteristics of country and city schools and the perennial trials of the schoolteacher, from angry parents to eccentric headmasters and the rivalries of colleagues.

Adventures in Queensland (1879) by 'Australian' (F.A. Blackman), one of Queensland's most significant early works, is a combination of history, fiction and guidelines for immigrants. Strongly pro-squatter, Blackman describes the settlement of the area west of Maryborough in the 1840s and 1850s; his callous attitude to the Aborigines is typical of the period.

Adventures of a Guardsman, a convict memoir by Charles Cozens, was published in 1848. One of the few accounts of transportation life by a gentleman convict, it records the early life and adventures of Cozens, his enlistment in the Royal Horse Guards, his court-martial for threatening a superior officer, and his years (1840–46) in NSW where he worked as a constable, clerk and census collector in the Monaro district, Yass, Sydney and elsewhere. *Adventures of a Guardsman* is critical of the convict system but expresses admiration for the governor of the colony, Sir George Gipps.

Advertiser, the best-known Adelaide morning daily newspaper, began publication in 1858 as the *South Australian Advertiser* (its title until early in 1899). It was founded by John Henry Barrow, editor 1858–73. In 1931 it incorporated its long-standing rival, the *Register*. Sir (John) Langdon Bonython (1848–1939) began the lengthy association of the Bonython family (q.v.) with the *Advertiser* when he gained employment on it in 1864; he bought into the newspaper from the 1870s, became editor in 1884 and proprietor in 1893, and retained personal control until his retirement in 1929. The *Advertiser* then became a public company (although the Bonython family retained an interest), which is now controlled by the Melbourne newspaper group, Herald and Weekly Times Ltd. Editors after Bonython include Sir Frederick Dumas (1929–53). In its early days the *Advertiser* was associated with conservative pastoral interests, but under Bonython identified more with SA middle-class and small business interests.

Advocate, a weekly Catholic newspaper, with local and overseas items of Irish Catholic interest and some literary material was published 1868–1990.

'AFFERBECK LAUDER', see **MORRISON, A.A.**

AFFORD, Max (1906–54), born Parkside, Adelaide, was a reporter and feature writer with the Adelaide *News* (1929–32) and subsequently joined the drama staff of the ABC after his play 'Colonel Light the Founder' won the 1936 SA Centenary Drama Competition. Between 1929 and 1954 he wrote more than sixty radio and stage plays and radio serials, most of which remain unpublished. His play 'The Flail of God' was the first play by an Australian writer broadcast on Australian radio (19 July 1932). Three of his stage plays were published in the posthumous volume, *Mischief in the Air* (1974); they were the title play, *Mischief in the Air*, which was performed in Sydney in 1944; *Lady In Danger* (1944), which was first performed in Sydney in 1942 and on Broadway in 1944; and *Awake My Love*, a revised version of 'Colonel Light the Founder', performed in 1936. Two of his radio plays, *Lazy in the Sun*, about Australia's hedonistic unawareness of the problems of the world, and *Consulting Room*, about an attempted suicide by a couple who face the imminent death of the wife from cancer, were also published in the *Mischief in the Air* volume. Afford's radio serials included such popular favourites as 'First Light Fraser' (624 episodes), 'Danger Unlimited' (624 episodes), 'Digger Hale's Daughters' (416 episodes), 'Hagen's Circus' (800 episodes) and 'Stranger Come In' (400 episodes). He adapted Jon Cleary's novel *The Sundowners* (1952) for radio serialisation and wrote his own mining town serial, 'Silver Ridge', which ran from 1952 to 1953. His remarkable success as a radio dramatist was due to his exciting plots, realistic characterisation and mastery of the technical requirements of radio drama. A successful writer also of detective and 'thriller' fiction, Afford published six novels, *Blood on His Hands* (1936), *Death's Mannikins* (1937), *The Dead are Blind* (1937) and *Owl of Darkness* (1942), which were all republished in White Circle Crime Club editions in London, and *Sinners in Paradise* (1951) and *An Ear for Murder* (1951), published in Sydney.

AFTERMAN, Allen (1941–), born Los Angeles, USA, a graduate in arts and law, was associated with the La Mama (q.v.) poetry workshops and lectured in law at the University of Melbourne before resigning in 1973 to become a full-time writer. Afterman has published two books of poetry, *The Maze Rose: Poems, 1970–1973* (1974) and *Purple Adam: Poems 1974–1979* (1980); much of the latter volume stems from Afterman's reaction to the genocide of the Jews in Europe and the Aborigines in Tasmania.

AFTERMAN, Susan (1947–), born Dandenong, Victoria, was educated at the University of Melbourne and has worked as an architect in Australia, England and Israel. She has published two collections of poetry, *Rites* (1979, under the name Susan Whiting) and *Rain* (1987).

Age, published in Melbourne since 1854, was a liberal daily of world standard before 1900 and remains today one of Australia's leading newspapers. Founded by John and Henry Cooke, it was run as a co-operative venture, 1854–56; in 1856–57 and 1859–60 it was owned by Ebenezer and David Syme (q.v.), in 1857–59 by Ebenezer, and in 1860–1908 it was under David's control. After his death the *Age* remained within the family until the Syme company became a public one in 1948. In 1983 control of the *Age* passed to the Fairfax (see John and J.G. Fairfax) chain, which had acquired a 50 per cent interest in the newspaper in 1970. After the Fairfax group went into receivership in 1990 the *Age* passed (1991) into the hands of Charles Black's Tourang consortium. A selection of early *Age* editorials and articles was published as *The Australian Thunderer* (1971); the newspaper's battles with the *Argus* (q.v.) at that time are referred to in Henry Kingsley's *The Hillyars and the Burtons* (1865), where the *Age* becomes the *Mohawk*. A.L. Windsor, a much-admired figure in Australian journalism, was editor 1871–1900, when Alfred Deakin and Charles Henry Pearson were prominent contributors; other editors have included G.H.F. Schuler (1901–26), L.V. Biggs (1926–39), Sir Harold Campbell (1939–59), E.K. Sinclair (1959–66), Graham Perkin (1966–75), Lyle Turnbull (1975–77), Greg Taylor (1978–80), Creighton Burns (1981–89), Michael Smith (1989–93) and Adam Kohler (1993–). Other staff have included Charles Bright, J.E. Neild, Philip Mennell, Roy Bridges, Benjamin Hoare (leader writer 1890–1914), George Johnston and C.E. Sayers. The *Age* has given regular coverage to literature by way of book reviews and articles.

Age Book of the Year Awards, two in number, are presented annually, one for a work of imaginative writing, the other for a non-fiction work, which are of outstanding literary merit and express Australia's identity or character. Winners have included David Foster's *The Pure Land* and C.M.H. Clark's *A History of Australia*, vol. 3 (both 1974); Thea Astley's *A Kindness Cup* (1975); A.D. Hope's *A Late Picking* and Hugh Stretton's *Capitalism, Socialism and the Environment* (both 1976); Graham Freudenberg's *A Certain Grandeur* (1977); Christopher Koch's *The Year of Living Dangerously* and Patsy Adam-Smith's *The Anzacs* (both 1978); Roger McDonald's *1915* (1979); David Ireland's *A Woman of the Future* and Murray Bail's *Homesickness* (both 1980); Eric Rolls's *A Million Wild Acres* and Blanche d'Alpuget's *Turtle Beach* (both 1981); David Malouf's *Fly Away Peter* and Geoffrey Serle's *John Monash: A Biography* (both 1982); Elizabeth Jolley's *Mr Scobie's Riddle* and Lloyd Robson's *A History of Tasmania* (both 1983); Nicholas Hasluck's *The Bellarmine Jug* and John Rickard's *H.B. Higgins* (1984); Peter Carey's *Illywhacker* and Chester Eagle's *Mapping the Paddocks* (both 1985); Joan London's *Sister Ships and Other Stories* and Garry Kinnane's *George Johnston: A Biography* (both 1986); Jessica Anderson's *Stories from the Warm Zone* and Robert Hughes's *The Fatal Shore* (both 1987); Frank Moorhouse's *Forty-seventeen* and Robin Gerster's *Big-noting* (both 1988); Elizabeth Jolley's *My Father's Moon* and Marsden Hordern's *Mariners Are Warned* (both 1989); Gwen Harwood's *Blessed City* and Glenda Adams's *Longleg* (both 1990); Brian Castro's *Double-Wolf* and David Marr's *Patrick White* (both 1991); Marion Halligan's *Lovers' Knots* and Ruth

Park's *A Fence Around the Cuckoo* (both 1992); Elizabeth Jolley's *The Georges' Wife* and Janet McCalman's *Journeyings* (both 1993). In 1993 a poetry award in honour of Dinny O'Hearn was inaugurated; it went to John Tranter's *At the Florida*.

AITCHISON, Ray (1923–), born Sydney, served with the AIF in the Second World War, and was a journalist with the *Daily Telegraph* (1945–48) and the ABC (1948–70). He was executive director of the Australian Confederation of Apparel Manufacturers 1970–84 and director of the Australian Clothing Export Council 1978–86. He published two novels, *The Illegitimates* (1964), a long and episodic story about the part-Aboriginal O'Shannon family, which traces their attempts to establish themselves in White Australian society by methods that vary with the personalities of the individuals themselves; and *Contillo* (1966). In 1970 he published *From Bob to Bungles*, a view of the political scene and its personalities in the 1960s, encompassing the period from the retirement of Sir Robert Menzies to the downfall of Sir John Gorton and his succession by Sir William McMahon. Aitchison has written two books on Australia's historical and contemporary relationship with America, *Americans in Australia* (1972), also published with the title *Thanks to the Yanks?* and *The Americans in Australia* (1986). He edited *Looking at the Liberals* (1974).

AITKIN, Don (1937–), born Sydney, was professor of politics at Macquarie University, Sydney (1971–79), professor of political science at the ANU (1980–88), and chairman of the Australian Research Council 1988–90, before becoming vice-chancellor of the University of Canberra in 1991. He has written several books on Australian politics, a biography of Sir Michael Bruxner (1969), and has edited the diaries of Peter Howson (1984), which give a detailed picture of Australian federal politics from 1963 to 1972. His one novel, *The Second Chair* (1977), set in 'Phillip' University, Sydney, combines sexual, political and academic intrigue.

AKHURST, W.M. (William Mower) (1822–78) arrived as a migrant in Adelaide in 1849, with two plays at Cremorne Gardens, London, to his credit. Initially a journalist in Adelaide and Melbourne, he became music and drama critic on the Melbourne *Herald* and a leading figure in Melbourne's theatrical world. From the 1850s until he returned to London in 1871 he wrote numerous stage pieces: dramas, pantomimes, extravaganzas and burlesques. During the 1860s he was the life-force of Melbourne's pantomime productions, devising a piece every year for the Theatre Royal, most of them designed and executed by the scenic artist John Hennings, and several written specially as a vehicle for George Coppin. His Australian dramatic work, mostly a mixture of traditional English material and colonial topicalities, includes 'Quite Colonial' (1853), 'The Rights of Woman' (1854), 'The Magician's Daughter' (1855), 'Coppin in Cairo' (1858), 'We've Taken Gardiner' (1862), 'Romance and Reality or the Digger in London' (1854),

Gulliver on his Travels (1866), *King Arthur: or, Lancelot the Loose* (1868), *Tom, Tom, the Piper's Son* (1868), *Harlequin Robinson Crusoe* (1868), *Paris the Prince and Helen the Fair* (?1868), *Harlequin Jack Sheppard* (1869), *The Battle of Hastings* (1869), and *The House That Jack Built* (1869). The last, a pantomime allegory, celebrating and partly satirising Victoria's sudden prosperity during the gold rush, is his most original work. In London from 1871 to 1877 he produced another sixteen pieces, including nine pantomimes and four dramas. He decided to return to Australia in 1878 but died at sea.

Alcheringa, see **Jindyworobak Movement**

ALDEN, John, see **Shakespeare and Australia**

ALDOUS, Allan (1911–), born Leederville, Perth, began writing plays in WA before going to England in 1935. There three of his radio plays were produced by the BBC, 'Timothy Thimble's Boat'(1938), 'Dancing Red Earth' (1939) and 'Game as Ned Kelly' (first produced 1939 and subsequently frequently revived). In the Second World War he served with the AIF in New Guinea and the Solomon Islands as a drama specialist with Army Education. A prolific writer of children's fiction, Aldous was particularly successful with the McGowan series of five novels, beginning with *McGowan Climbs a Mountain* (1945). His other children's fiction included two Colin McKee books (1948), *Quitters Can't Win* (1946) and *Doctor with Wings* (1960). Other plays by Aldous were 'Western Gateway', produced for the 1966 Festival of Perth and the first authentic *son et lumière* presentation in Australia, and 'Cook of the Endeavour', produced in 1970 for the Cook Bicentenary celebrations. Aldous also wrote a booklet titled *Theatre in Australia* (1947), which is largely an account of the limitations of past and contemporary Australian drama.

ALDRIDGE, James (1918–), born White Hills, Victoria, worked briefly on the staffs of the Melbourne *Herald* and *Sun* (1937–38) before pursuing a successful journalistic career in England, where he has remained apart from occasional visits to Australia. A war correspondent in the Second World War, Aldridge is a leading fiction-writer. His first three novels, *Signed with Their Honour* (1942), *The Sea Eagle* (1944) and *Of Many Men* (1946), are stories of men in battle in Greece, Crete, Egypt, Finland and Russia. *The Diplomat* (1950), published in twenty-five languages and a bestseller in Russia, established Aldridge as an important political novelist with Marxist persuasions. A story of the Anglo-American-Russian dispute over Iran and Iranian oil, *The Diplomat* combines a complicated political theme with an analysis of human motives. Other political novels by Aldridge, which are sometimes criticised as being vehicles for their author's political views rather than fiction, include *Heroes of the Empty View* (1954); *The Last Exile* (1961), encompassing the whole story of British rule in Egypt while focusing on the last days of British influence there and the Suez Canal crisis; *A Captive in the Land* (1962); and *The Statesman's Game* (1966). *My Brother*

Tom (1966), one of Aldridge's few works concerned with Australia ('I can't escape Australia and don't want to'), concerns religious factions (Protestant and Catholic) in an Australian country town. His other novels include *I Wish He Would Not Die* (1957), a wartime story set in Egypt and the Western Desert; *A Sporting Proposition* (1973); *Mockery in Arms* (1974); *The Untouchable Juli* (1975); *The True Story of Lilli Stubeck* (1984, set in the Depression years in a small town on the Murray River); and *The True Story of Lola MacKellar* (1992), set in the same region. He has also written a book of short stories, *Gold and Sand* (1960); a play, 'The 49th State', produced in London in 1946; non-fiction, *Living Egypt* (1969) and *Cairo* (1969); and several books for children, including *The True Story of Spit MacPhee*, which won the NSW Premier's Award for children's fiction in 1986.

ALEXANDER, Alan (1941–), born Strabane, Northern Ireland, emigrated from Belfast to WA in 1965. With the assistance of two writing fellowships from the Literature Board and part-time teaching, Alexander has managed to support himself as a writer. He has published four books of verse: *In the Sun's Eye* (1977) and *Scarpdancer* (1982) reflect his response to new experiences and the beauty of the new land, the limestone area of WA's south coast and the wonderful shining granite of the Darling scarp. *Northline* (1987) celebrates, with photographs by Victor France, the inner-city area of Northbridge, an area rich in local history but now made equally rich by its colourful cosmopolitan ambience. The staid, rundown urban scene is now permeated with multicultural essences from Italy, Greece, Vietnam, Yugoslavia, Chile, Poland – as poems such as 'Zagreb Mick', 'Visitors', 'The Birth', 'Thelma Cutting Sandwiches' and 'Morning Till Night' affectionately indicate. Important in the evocative poems is the presence of one, she of the 'slim Norse head', who has much to do with the poet falling in love with Northbridge. *Principia Gondwana* (1992), the title's use of the ancient name of the great continent of which Australia was once considered a part, indicating the poet's linkage of past and present into a single universe of being, continues Alexander's skilful evocation of people and places in dramatically restrained and controlled verse. Figures from WA's history, both Aboriginal and White, inhabit a landscape that Alexander continues to muse on lovingly. 'Night of the Whales' was used as a theme poem by Rodney Waterman at the Contemporary Music Concert at the International Festival in Melbourne and at the Academy of Performing Arts in Perth. It was set to music by Glyn Marillier of Edith Cowan University.

Alfred Dudley, see **Aborigine in White Australian Literature**

Alien Son, a series of fictionalised autobiographical sketches of childhood by Judah Waten (q.v.), was first published in 1952 and has been reprinted frequently. The narrator's parents, Russian Jews, settle in a small WA town just before the First World War. The new land appears incomprehensible and alien, especially to the mother, who clings resolutely to the old culture; for the more sanguine father, 'business' projects prove disappointing and he resorts to hawking bottles from a horse-drawn cart. He soon realises, however, that they 'belong to this new earth. It has sucked us in whether we know it or not', and for his son Australia offers exciting new experiences. As the narratives chronologically develop the story of the family's adjustment, a vivid general picture of immigrant life in Australia emerges. Striking individuals include Hirsch, a lonely old hawker who dreams of settling in Palestine; Mrs Hankin, a formidable Jewish mother in search of a suitable husband for her daughter; Mr Smutkevitch, a severe Jewish father who nevertheless loses his sons to the new culture; Lily Samuels, an Aboriginal girl; and Mr Finnan, a militant waterside worker, who becomes a hero to the young narrator. Most memorable of all is the portrait of the strong-willed mother, immersed in 'passionate dreams of the past'. Resigned to her husband's lack of success in this land in which she will always be an alien, she nevertheless fanatically pursues her goal of a good education for her children.

Alive, see **WRIGHT, Judith**

All About Books, originally titled *All About Books for Australian and New Zealand Readers*, was published in Melbourne 1928–38. It resumed publication in 1961 and after August 1963 was incorporated in the journal, *Ideas*. The early series had affiliations with book-publishing interests but devoted a two-page section in each edition to Australian books; that section was conducted by Nettie Palmer and, later, F.T. Macartney.

All That Swagger, a novel by Miles Franklin (q.v.), won the S.H. Prior Memorial Prize for 1936 and was published that year both in book form and serially in the *Bulletin*. The novel's hero, Irish immigrant Danny Delacy, is modelled upon Miles Franklin's paternal grandfather, Joseph Franklin, and the exploits and adventures of four generations of Delacys on the land around the headwaters of the Murrumbidgee River follow roughly the fortunes of the Franklin family from 1833 to 1933. 'Fearless Danny's' story begins in 1833 by the Shannon in County Clare when he and his Johanna elope and take ship for the Antipodes. In Sydney, discovering that land grants had ceased in 1831, Danny sets out as a hired man for Bandalong, one of the most remote stations, far beyond the already-populated Goulburn plains, past Lake George, Gounderu (Gundaroo) and the Limestone Plains. Always the mountains further south beckon Danny 'as the Lorelei', so after a spell of hired labour to accumulate fifty head of cattle and a dozen horses he finally makes his way to a valley that the Aborigines call Burrabinga. As the seasons pass, the station, Burrabinga, is carved out of virgin land and Johanna produces sons and daughters who go to school in Sydney and become the second Delacy generation. Significant Australian events dot the narrative, conveying a sense of historical continuity – the gold rushes, the Robertson and Duffy Land Acts, free selection, self-government, the

Boer War. From its cohesive opening the narrative falls away (especially after the first generation) into a discursive series of episodes and events, broken only by the favourite Miles Franklin device of 'possuming' or yarning – meandering, conversational reflections on the rapidly changing scene. Generations merge, each leaving its imprint on the others. Themes become interwoven, the focus of attention shifting easily from one to another. The novel's canvas becomes crowded with more and more participants as the century gradually moves to its ending in the modern day (1933) when the fourth generation Brian Delacy, aviator, lifting his plane into the Murrumbidgee sky, glimpses in his mind's eye 'the spectral forms of bullock transport and receding Delacys moving against ancient unfamiliar apparitions on the palimpsest of Time'.

All the Rivers Run (1978), by Nancy Cato (q.v.), was published simultaneously in America, England and Australia as a composite of three earlier novels, *All the Rivers Run* (1958), *Time, Flow Softly* (1959) and *But Still the Stream* (1962). Chosen by the Literary Guild as its first choice for its members (which guaranteed a pre-publication sale of more than 25 000 copies), *All the Rivers Run* was seen by its publishers as a rival to Colleen McCullough's *The Thorn Birds*. Philadelphia (Delie) Gordon, aged 13, sole surviving member of her family from the wreck of the *Loch Tay*, joins her Aunt Hester, Uncle Charles and her cousin, Adam, at the little Snowy Mountains township of Kiandra. From her uncle, a shiftless fossicker for gold, she first learns of the Murray, the great river that carries the Snowy water to the sea. When Uncle Charles has a lucky find the family buys land at Echuca on the Murray and Delie's infatuation with the river begins. With money from her parents' estate she buys a part share in a riverboat owned by the seaman, Tom, her rescuer from the *Loch Tay* disaster. Her cousin, Adam, her first love, dies in an accident and Delie goes to live in Echuca, earning a living through her artistic talent. There she meets Brenton Edwards, Tom's partner on the boat *Philadelphia*. Delie goes briefly to Melbourne to study art (her drawing master is Frederick McCubbin) but contracts tuberculosis and returns to Echuca, where she marries Brenton Edwards and accompanies him on the *Philadelphia* on the endless round of riverboat trading. As the years pass Delie has six children, her husband is incapacitated in an accident, and later dies from a stroke. She takes over his role on the *Philadelphia*, raises her family, has lovers, and ends her days living by the river at Goolwa. A mammoth novel, *All the Rivers Run* spans the years 1899 to 1956, encompassing the Boer War and the two world wars, and providing, with the river as the central figure, a romantic and nostalgic view of Australia's pioneer past. A television mini-series of the book was shown in 1983.

ALLAN, J.A. (James Alexander) (1889–1956), born and educated in Melbourne, was a former editor of the *Victorian Historical Magazine* and heraldic adviser to the Royal Australian Navy. He published verse, *A Wineshop Madonna* (1911) and *Revolution* (1940); prose,

The Old Model School (1934) and *Men and Manners in Australia* (1945); and a historical work, *The History of Camberwell* (1949).

ALLEN, Sir Carleton Kemp (1877–1966), brother of Leslie Holdsworth Allen (q.v.), born at Carlton, Melbourne, went from the University of Sydney to Oxford, where he studied law and was elected Eldon Law Scholar in 1913. After distinguished service in the First World War he returned to Oxford where, in 1929, he was appointed professor of jurisprudence and, from 1931, second warden of Rhodes House. His chief publications were *Bureaucracy Triumphant* (1931), *Law and Orders* (1945), *The Queen's Peace* (1953), *Law and Disorders* (1954) and *Aspects of Justice* (1958). He also wrote fiction, *The Judgment of Paris* (1924) and *Oh! Mr Leacock!* (1925).

ALLEN, David (1936–) was born in Birmingham, England, spent some years teaching drama in English schools and from 1966 to 1970 worked as an education officer in Uganda, where he also helped to found a theatre company. In 1972, after studying under Hugh Hunt, he came to Australia to lecture in drama at the Salisbury College of Advanced Education. Co-founder of Troupe, Adelaide's alternative professional theatre company, for which he directed and wrote plays, he has worked as a full-time writer for radio, film and television since December 1979. His plays, which have been produced in Australia, England and America, include 'Behold the Gay Marsupial', 'Florrie', 'The Night We Blitzed the Bridge', 'Madness', *Gone with Hardy* (published in *Theatre Australia*, 1978), 'Joseph Conrad Goes Ashore' (1980), *Don't Listen to Gouger* (published in *Opinion*, 1978), 'Meat', 'Dickinson', 'Down, Down at Dingley Dell', *Karen* (1983), 'Tina's Troupers', *Upside Down at the Bottom of the World* (1981), *Cheapside* (1984), 'Manila Yellow' (1985), *Slamm, Decco, Steff & George* (1985) 'Pommies' (1986), *Modest Expectations* (1990), 'Native Tongue' (1991) and, with Doreen Clarke (q.v.), 'Coppin & Co.' (1982). As some of the titles of his plays demonstrate, Allen's plays are often centred on literary figures of the past; *Upside Down at the Bottom of the World*, first produced in 1979 by the Nimrod Company, is based on D.H. Lawrence's stay in Australia and his novel *Kangaroo*; *Modest Expectations* explores what might have happened to Dickens had he visited Australia. Allen has won several awards including the Victorian Premier's Award for *Cheapside* and three Awgies.

ALLEN, L.H. (Leslie Holdsworth) (1879–1964) was born at Maryborough, Victoria, studied English and classics at the University of Sydney and completed a Ph.D. at the University of Leipzig in 1907. He held lecturing positions at the University of Sydney and Sydney Teachers' College before becoming professor of English at the Royal Military College, Duntroon, in 1918. From 1931 to 1951 he was sole lecturer in English and Latin at the Canberra University College, later the ANU. He became a member of the Commonwealth Book Censorship Advisory Committee in 1933 and was chairman of the Literature Censorship

Board from 1937. His poetry, which reflects his classical interests, has a deft lyric touch. It consists of *Phaedra and Other Poems* (1921), *Araby and Other Poems* (1924) and *Patria* (1941). 'Patria', title poem of the last volume, is a series of nine sonnets which reflect on the future of Australia. Allen also published a book of children's poetry, *Billy-Bubbles* (1920); a volume of prose sketches (with six poems) *Gods and Wood-things* (1913); and translations of three plays by the German dramatist Friedrich Hebbel.

Alma Mater, a Melbourne University journal, began publication in July 1895, carrying university news, articles of literary interest and original creative material (short fiction and poetry). From April 1899 its subtitle was *An Illustrated Australasian University Newspaper*. It ceased in 1902.

Almanacs were issued in Australia from the early days of European settlement and, in the first half of the nineteenth century in particular, were an important adjunct to newspapers in disseminating information within the colonies as well as overseas (e.g. among intending immigrants). Most almanacs were produced by colonists already associated with publishing, whether mainly as printers (e.g. George Howe), newspaper editors (e.g. Henry Melville), stationers (e.g. John Sands), or booksellers (e.g. James Tegg). Characteristically, they comprised not only a calendar of months and days (with ecclesiastical dates, other anniversaries and basic astronomical information noted) but also an increasing amount of miscellaneous material: several statistical tables (tides, weights and measures, ready reckoners); directories of the civil and military establishments, traders and pastoralists; digests of land, police, telegraphic and postal regulations and lists of fees; agricultural reports, rural calendars, and gardening advice; historical reviews, chronologies, and diaries of events; coastal and rural itineraries; and special articles. It was not unusual for a publisher to issue several works with overlapping information. In 1843, for example, James Tegg published *Tegg's Handbook for Emigrants*, *Tegg's Commercial Sheet Almanac*, *Tegg's New South Wales Daily Memorandum Book and Pocket Companion*, and *Tegg's New South Wales Pocket Almanac and Remembrancer*.

The first Australian almanac was George Howe's *New South Wales Pocket Almanack and Colonial Remembrancer* (1806), which he issued annually until his death in 1821, when it was continued as the *Australasian Pocket Almanack*, the *Australian Almanack* and under other titles (1822–35). The *N.S.W. Calendar and General Post Office Directory* (1832–46), a publication from the *Sydney Herald* office and *Tegg's New South Wales Pocket Almanac and Remembrancer* (1836–44) were two other important Sydney almanacs of the 1830s. In Hobart four prominent newspaper editors or proprietors produced almanacs in the 1820s and 1830s: Andrew Bent, who issued the *Van Diemen's Land Pocket Almanack* (later the *Tasmanian Almanack*) in 1824–30; James Ross, whose almanac was issued 1829–36 under various titles, most commonly with the *Hobart Town Almanack* or (*Ross's*) *Hobart Town*

Almanack somewhere in the title, but in 1833–34 as the *Van Diemen's Land Almanack and Hobart Town Annual*; William Gore Elliston, who took over from Ross as government printer and issued *Hobart Town Almanacks* in 1837–38; and Henry Melville, who issued his almanacs as the *Van Diemen's Land Almanack* in 1831–33 and as the *Van Diemen's Land Annual* in 1834–37. In the other colonies the later appearance of almanacs reflects their later development: in Victoria an early printing firm published *Kerr's Melbourne Almanac, and Port Phillip Directory* in 1841–42; in SA the *Royal South Australian Almanack and General Directory* commenced publication in 1839 and was issued for several decades, sometimes as the *South Australian Almanac*; in the same State the *Adelaide Almanack* (known also as *Boothby's Adelaide Almanack*) ran from 1864 to 1883; in WA two *Western Australian Almanacks* were published from 1842 until at least the end of the 1840s; and in Queensland, *Pugh's Almanac* was published under several titles, 1859–1927.

To varying degrees, the early colonial almanacs combined elements of the calendar, the diary, the gazetteer, the directory and the yearbook. Although this comprehensiveness of information was retained in later years, consumers after 1860 were increasingly catered for by publications focused more firmly on one of the elements; for example, by the business and postal directories of John Sands and his partners in Melbourne, Sydney and Adelaide; by specific manuals such as *S.W. Silver & Co. Australian Grazier's Guide* (1879, 1881), written by 'Rolf Boldrewood'; or by diaries like the Letts diary for 1883–84, from which Tom Collins amplifies entries in *Such is Life* (q.v., 1903). The importance to Australian literature of almanacs and their offshoots, however, goes beyond 'Boldrewood's' involvement in the preparation of a pastoralists' handbook, or Furphy's use of a diary to establish an aleatory mode of narration. They are important sources of information about Australian authors and cultural institutions, and the early almanacs in particular, prized among collectors of Australiana, are important in publishing history for the part they played in the activities of pioneering printers and the opportunities they provided for individual editors and contributors.

Some of the special articles, particularly in the Tasmanian almanacs of the 1820s and 1830s, are significant both as specimens of early Australian descriptive and historical prose, and as sources for subsequent Australian authors; the *Hobart Town Almanacks* of Ross and Elliston, for example, contain several articles that were used by Marcus Clarke in *Old Tales of a Young Country* and *His Natural Life*.

ALOMES, Stephen (1949–), born Hobart and educated at the University of Tasmania and the ANU, teaches Australian Studies at Deakin University. He is the author of *A Nation At Last?* (1988), an analysis of the changing character of Australian nationalism from 1880 to 1988; he has also edited with Bob Bessant, *Visions of Australia* (1987), with Dirk den Hartog, *Post Pop: Popular Culture, Nationalism and Postmodernism*

(1991) and with Catherine Jones, a collection of historical documents, *Australian Nationalism* (1991).

ALTMAN, Dennis (1943–) was educated at the University of Tasmania and Cornell University, New York and is a reader in politics at La Trobe University. Well known as an activist of the Gay Movement, his intellectual contribution has been likened to that of Germaine Greer's to feminism. His books include *Homosexual: Oppression and Liberation* (1971), *Coming Out in the Seventies* (1979), *Rehearsals for Change: Politics and Culture in Australia* (1980), *The Homosexualisation of America: The Americanisation of the Homosexual* (1982) and *AIDS and the New Puritanism* (1986). He has also written a study of the politics of postage stamps, *Paper Ambassadors* (1991) and a novel, *The Comfort of Men* (1993).

American Association of Australian Literary Studies (AAALS), was established at Columbia University, New York, in 1986. In 1987 its journal, *Antipodes* (q.v.), was launched to replace the Association's *Newsletter* which was begun in 1985 to stimulate interest in the formation of AAALS.

Americans, Baby, The, the second prose collection by Frank Moorhouse (q.v.), was published in 1972; reprinted several times since then, it helped significantly to establish Moorhouse's reputation as a writer of short fiction. *The Americans, Baby* reprints one of the stories in *Futility and Other Animals* (1969) and like that work is a 'discontinuous narrative', set mainly within the Sydney alternative subculture of the 1960s. The major, but not dominant, character is Becker, an American Coca-Cola executive who feels isolated in Australia and who forms a relationship with the unstable Terri McDowell, daughter of George McDowell of *The Electrical Experience* (q.v.); dismissed from his position as a result of the liaison, he ends up working as a jazz pianist. There are six Becker stories among the twenty which comprise *The Americans, Baby*; of the remainder, several focus on the shifting relationships of a group of university students and fellow radicals. The fragility of personal relationships (for example, in the failure of sexuality to bond people) and the estrangement and isolation of most of Moorhouse's characters are major themes in the collection, which is also notable for the satiric portrait of radical movements in stories like 'The American Poet's Visit'.

AMIET, William (1890–1959), born near Geelong, Victoria, practised law in various parts of Queensland and from 1920 in Mackay. A contributor of literary articles and reviews over many years to the Mackay *Mercury* (he was spoken of with respect and pleasure by Nettie Palmer), Amiet published numerous works including a book of his newspaper articles, *Scrambled Scrutinies* (1949). In *The Practice of Literary History* (1936) he discusses methods of presenting the history of literature and looks at the relationship of literary history to biography, criticism and history.

AMOS, Robert (1920–), Austrian by birth, fled to China when the Nazis took over Austria and was a civilian internee of the Japanese in Shanghai during the Second World War. He came to Australia in 1949, joined CSIRO as a research chemist and then became editor of publications. His play *When the Grave Diggers Come* (co-winner of the Sydney Journalists' Club drama competition of 1961) was staged in 1963 at the Emerald Hill Theatre, Melbourne. It concerns a group of emigrants, mostly white Russians, in an Asian city awaiting the communist takeover of the city. Amos wrote numerous plays for television and radio, chief of which are 'A Game of Numbers', 'A Country for Proud People', 'Wind from the Icy Country' and 'Survival in the Service'.

Anapress, see **Australian Natives' Association**

Ancestor Game, The (1992), a novel by Alex Miller (q.v.), won the 1993 Miles Franklin Award and the 1993 Commonwealth Writers Prize. Set in Melbourne in the mid-1970s, it interweaves the stories of three contemporary 'Australians': Lang Tsu, born 1927 in China of Chinese parents and now, aged about 50, an art teacher at a Melbourne school; Gertrude Spiess, daughter of a German father (Dr August Spiess) and a Chinese mother, born 1946 at St Kilda and now about 30 and a senior lecturer in drawing at Prahran College of Advanced Education; and Steven Muir, the narrator of much of the book, son of a Scottish father and Irish mother, also teaching at the age of 39 in the same Melbourne school. In modern Australia, where 'folk reside beyond the reach of history', where 'extra-territoriality is the status quo' and where 'the displaced are in place', these three both propose and illustrate the thesis that ancestry is irrelevant, that the fixed identity conferred by race and background is much less important than individuality. The three, however, appear to exist in an often trivial void.

It is the near ancestry of Lang Tsu that dominates the novel. In 1848 his great-grandfather, orphaned at the age of 10 and denying both his traditional ancestry and his name, sold himself as an indentured labourer and left Amoy to become a shepherd on a Ballarat station in the district of Port Phillip. Captain Larkins of the ship *Nimrod* that took him to the new land, gave him a new name, Feng. 'To be renamed is to be reborn', said the Captain. 'I shall call you Feng, the Phoenix. Is that not a fine name for one who is reborn?' Feng became friendly with two other shepherds, misfits and dispossessed like himself – an Aboriginal boy named Dorset and a 42-year-old Irishman, Patrick Nunan. When Dorset was murdered by White settlers because he failed to lead them to a Koori warrior, whom they were hunting, Feng and Patrick tried to give him a decent burial but each time they attempted to dig his grave they found the ground full of gold nuggets. Their fortunes won, they went to Melbourne, where Feng married Patrick's daughter, Mary, and set up the Phoenix Co-operative Society of Victoria, which went on to gain the lucrative monopoly on the trade of bringing Chinese gold-seekers to Australia. Feng divided his time between Australia, establishing with Mary his Chinese-Australian family of nine girls, and China, where he made another Chinese marriage and had a son, Feng II. In 1876 he built the great mansion, 'Coppin Grove', in the Melbourne suburb of Kew, where he died in 1908. Feng II, a practical man, who had no interest in Australia or his stepfamily there, lived out his life in China and had a son, Feng III, (the third Phoenix). Feng III was born in 1886 as Feng Chien-hsing and became a successful, arrogant, self-willed Shanghai capitalist, so obsessed with Western attitudes that he, too, dismissed his Chinese ancestry and changed his name to C.H. Feng. Married twice to Chinese women, who failed to produce a son, he ultimately succeeded in his desire for an heir in his marriage to Lien (Lotus), only child of Huang Yu-hua, the venerable literary painter of Hangzhou. Lien and her father encapsulated all the traditions of China that Feng III despised. His son, Lang Tsu (the art teacher of the Melbourne school), was educated in traditional Chinese ways under his mother's guidance until 1937 when, at the age of 10 and with the Japanese about to sack Shanghai, he was sent to Australia, there to make connection with his aunt, Mrs Halloran (granddaughter to Feng I and Mary Nunan). He was accompanied to Australia by the expatriate German, Dr August Spiess, who had lived in Shanghai and who had delivered Lang Tsu at birth. Educated in Australia and prevented from returning to China (he had shown no such inclination) because of the rule of Mao Tse Tung, Lang Tsu continued to live in Australia in the now dilapidated 'Coppin Grove'.

The other two protagonists, Steven Muir and Gertrude Spiess, have histories which are much less dramatic, but each adds a further dimension to the theme of rootlessness in modern Australian society, Steven being unable to find satisfaction in either of his Celtic backgrounds (his mother accused him of 'a lack of ancestral pride') and Gertrude, the daughter of a man who 'was only ever at home in exile'.

Throughout the complex and intricate novel which moves into and out of traditional linear development, there is an ambivalent assessment of ancestry. For much of the time ancestry is rejected: by Feng I, who shrugs it off as he departs for Australia; by Feng III, who despises it as sentimental; by Feng IV (Lang Tsu), who says before destroying his grandfather's sacred book of the ancestors, that he wishes to break 'the stranglehold of the ancestors, those dead who will not die, but who persist in asserting an influence upon the living'; and by Dr Spiess, who asserts that 'boundaries . . . exist to be transgressed' and that nobody belongs 'anywhere real'. The way in which the three protagonists are portrayed in the novel, however, could imply that the shedding of ancestry has hidden penalties. In the enigmatic final chapter, when Steven discovers that Gertrude has taken editorial liberties in translating her father's diaries, there are subtle indications that like the translations, the novel itself is an elaborate *trompe-l'oeil*. One of the most impressive of contemporary Australian novels, *The Ancestor Game* is provocative and challenging.

ANCHEN, J.O., see **Criticism**

ANDERSON, Don (1939–), born Sydney, teaches at the University of Sydney. A regular columnist for the *Sydney Morning Herald*, he has published selections from his column and articles and reviews for other journals and newspapers in *Hot Copy* (1986) and *Real Opinions* (1992). He has also edited *Enchanted Apartments, Sad Motels* (1989), a collection of American writing, and *Transgressions: Australian Writing Now* (1986), a collection of Australian short fiction intended to subvert the 'unexamined realist orthodoxy' of the genre in Australia and to carry on a dialogue with Frank Moorhouse's anthology, *The State of the Art* (1983).

ANDERSON, Ethel (1883–1958), born Leamington, England, of Australian parents, was educated in Sydney before marrying a British officer serving with the Indian Army. After living for some years in India and England, she returned in 1924 to Australia, where her husband served on the staff of three State governors and the governor-general. Her published works include two volumes of poetry, *Squatter's Luck* (1942) and *Sunday at Yarralumla* (1947); two collections of essays, *Adventures in Appleshire* (1944) and *Timeless Garden* (1945); and three collections of short stories, *Indian Tales* (1948), *At Parramatta* (1956) and *The Little Ghosts* (1959). *The Best of Ethel Anderson*, edited by J.D. Pringle (1973), is a selection from her previous collections. Although she saw herself as primarily a poet, it is her prose work that is most distinctive. *Indian Tales* and *The Little Ghosts*, drawn from her experience of India and its history, illustrate her wry humour, ironic wit, quick observation and spare, precisely worked style. Although dated in some of their social attitudes, they richly evoke the flavour of Indian life. *At Parramatta* is an even more assured collection; set in the country near Parramatta at the time of the Crimean War, the stories form a sequence with some plot development and recurring characters. In both her short fiction and essays her lyrical power is striking, although in the latter it has more scope. *Adventures in Appleshire*, which draws on her reminiscences of England, and the more varied collection, *Timeless Garden*, reflect her diverse interests and distinctive personality. Bethia Foott's biography of her parents, Ethel and Austin Anderson, *Ethel and the Governor-General: A Biography of Ethel Anderson (1883–1958) and Brigadier General A.T. Anderson (1868–1949)*, was published in 1992.

ANDERSON, Hugh (1927–), born Elmore, Victoria, has had a long teaching and administrative career with the Victorian Education Department and has been one of Australia's most prolific writers. He has published over sixty titles in Australian history, biography, literary criticism, folklore, folk-song and balladry, and bibliography. His publications include such critical and bibliographical works as *A Guide to Ten Australian Poets* (1953); *Frank Wilmot (Furnley Maurice): A Bibliography and a Criticism* (1955, with Barbara Ramsden); *Shaw Neilson: An Annotated Bibliography and Check List, 1889–1956* (1956); *Christopher John Brennan: A Comprehensive Bibliography with Annotations* (1959, with Walter Stone); *Bernard O'Dowd (1866–1953): An Annotated Bibliography* (1963); *The Singing Roads: A Guide to Australian Children's Authors and Illustrators* (1965, 1969); *The Poet Militant: Bernard O'Dowd* (1969); and *John Shaw Neilson* (1972, with L.J. Blake). Anderson's interest in Australian folk-song and balladry is reflected in his compilation of *Colonial Ballads* (1955, an enlarged and revised edition published in 1970 as *The Story of Australian Folksong*), and in such publications as *Botany Bay Broadsides* (1956), *Songs of Billy Barlow* (1956), *Goldrush Songster* (1958), *Farewell to Old England: A Broadside History of Early Australia* (1964) and *Folk Songs of Australia and the Men and Women Who Sang Them* (1967, with John Meredith). His work on Charles Thatcher (q.v.), *The Colonial Minstrel* (1960), is a detailed biography of Thatcher's Australasian career with liberal quotations from Thatcher's favourite songs. He also wrote a biography, *George Loyau: The Man Who Wrote Bush Ballads* (1991) and published the anthology *On the Track with Bill Bowyang* (1991). His historical works include *Out of the Shadow: The Career of John Pascoe Fawkner* (1962); *Eureka: Victorian Parliamentary Papers, Votes and Proceedings, 1854–1867* (1969), *Victoria: From Discovery to Federation* (1974), *Saltwater River History Trails* (1984) and *Victorian Squatters* (1983, with Robert Spreadborough). Since retiring in 1982 Anderson has been Managing Editor of a small publishing firm specialising in history and folklore. A visitor to China on several occasions, he has become interested in Chinese writing and has published *A Wind Across the Grass* (1985), a translation of stories by three Chinese writers and a bibliography, *Australian Writing Translated into Chinese 1954–1988*, compiled with Ma Zuyi and Chen Zhengfa (1989).

ANDERSON, Jessica (1916–) was born in Brisbane but has lived most of her life in Sydney, apart from a few years in London. Although she only began to write novels at the age of 40, she had previously written short stories for newspapers and drama scripts for radio, especially adaptations of novels by Henry James and Charles Dickens. Her novels are *An Ordinary Lunacy* (1963); *The Last Man's Head* (1970); *The Commandant* (1975); *Tirra Lirra by the River* (1978), which won the Miles Franklin Award and the Australian Natives' Association Literary Award; *The Impersonators* (1980), which also won the Miles Franklin Award and the NSW Premier's Award and was republished in 1985 in the USA titled *The Only Daughter*; and *Taking Shelter* (1989). She has also published a collection of short stories, *Stories from the Warm Zone* (1987), which won the *Age* Book of the Year Award.

A compressed style, delicate irony, narrative control and dramatic dialogue are characteristics of all Anderson's novels, reflecting her admiration for writers such as Henry James, Evelyn Waugh and, especially, Henry Green. *An Ordinary Lunacy* combines penetrating observation of a sophisticated segment of Sydney society with exploration of an obsessive passion; *The Last Man's Head*, ostensibly a crime novel, has moral and psychological subtleties that lift it out of that category; *The Commandant*, a historical novel based on the life of Captain Patrick Logan, commandant of the Moreton Bay penal settlement 1826–30, is a vivid account given a new, partly feminist perspective in that it is centred on the experience of Logan's young sister-in-law. But it is in *Tirra Lirra by the River*, *The Impersonators*, *Taking Shelter* and *Stories from the Warm Zone* that Anderson's professed aim of 'poetic brevity' is most fully achieved. *Tirra Lirra by the River* is a retrospective, carefully structured account of one woman's life. Nora Roche, now in her seventies, returns to her childhood home in Queensland after many years first in Sydney and then in London; confined to bed by severe illness, she begins to turn her 'globe of memory', rediscovering key incidents and people in her life and attempting, like the Lady of Shallott, to come to terms with her lonely tower. Sociological observation is not the novel's primary concern, but it also presents an intimate picture of life in suburban Australia between the wars. *The Impersonators*, set in Sydney in the 1970s, is a complicated and ambitious study of an Australian family, although once again it deals with the rediscovery of Australia by an expatriate woman; the theme is money and the impersonations that its pursuit imposes on people, especially on women. *Taking Shelter* is partly a study of the fragility of relationships and the difficulties, consolations and traps of various forms of 'shelter' in the society of the mid-1980s; bringing together the experiences of a group of people, all living in Sydney of 1986 and of diverse ages and needs, the novel explores themes of dislocation, commitment, self-determination and imprisonment. *Stories from the Warm Zone* juxtaposes a group of semi-autobiographical stories of childhood in Brisbane of the 1920s and a contrasting group of stories set in 1980s Sydney; densely layered, both sets illustrate Anderson's characteristic, intricately textured patterns masked by a deceptively simple surface. Both have an understated feminist theme, the first group charting the *rite de passage* of the child Bea as she grows in understanding different, largely gendered ways of knowing, and the second group focusing on women who need to retrieve possession of what is left of their lives. Elaine Barry has written the study *Fabricating the Self: the Fictions of Jessica Anderson* (1992).

ANDERSON, John (1893–1962), born Lanarkshire, Scotland, had a distinguished academic career in Great Britain before occupying the Challis Chair of Philosophy at the University of Sydney, 1927–58. Instigator of the Sydney Freethought tradition, Anderson exercised great influence over several generations of Sydney students, writers and intellectuals, an influence that continued to be widely expressed into the 1960s in the attitudes of writers and thinkers such as Donald Horne, Dorothy Green and Peter Coleman and in journals such as the *Observer, Quadrant* and *Nation*. The Sydney Freethought group split radically in the 1950s over attitudes to the Cold War and, apart from small enclaves, Andersonianism is no longer a force in Sydney's intellectual life. Anderson's early publications were *Education and Politics* (1931) and *Some*

Questions in Aesthetics (1932); a collection of forty of his major papers was published posthumously in 1962 as *Studies of Empirical Philosophy*. He was for some years editor of the then *Australasian Journal of Psychology and Philosophy* (now the *Australian Journal of Philosophy*) and published in its pages several of his most influential essays, 'Art and Morality' (1941), 'The Servile State' (1943) and 'Education for Democracy'. Of importance also was his introduction to W.H.C. Eddy's (ed.) *Prospects of Democracy* (1945). *Art and Reality*, a collection of thirty-five of his essays on aesthetics and literature, was published in 1982, edited by Janet Anderson, Graham Cullum and Kimon Lycos. An analysis of Andersonianism and its influence in Sydney is given in John Docker's *Australian Cultural Elites* (1974); A.J. Baker wrote *Anderson's Social Philosophy* (1979).

ANDERSON, Dame Judith (1898–1992), born Adelaide, made her stage debut at the Theatre Royal, Sydney, in 1915 and her screen debut in 1933 in the film *Blood Money*. Acclaimed in a long career in America, Europe and Australia, Judith Anderson appeared in important stage productions of *Mourning Becomes Electra, Macbeth* and *Medea* and in films such as *Rebecca, Laura* and *Cat on a Hot Tin Roof*. Acknowledged as a fine Shakespearean actress in particular, she was made DBE in 1960 and AC in 1991.

ANDERSON, Maybanke Susannah (1845–1927), born England, accompanied her family to Sydney in 1855. In 1867 she married E.K. Wolstenholme, a timber merchant, and in the next eleven years had seven children, only three of whom survived childhood. Wolstenholme proved to be an alcoholic who later deserted her and in the early 1880s she resorted to establishing a school, Maybanke College, to support her family. Respected for its modern teaching methods, and academic achievements, the College also benefited from Maybanke's public activities. Vice-president of the Womanhood Suffrage League of NSW and president 1893–96, she was a member of the Women's Literary Society, which had strong feminist convictions, and founded the Australasian Home Reading Union, which aimed to establish study circles in country areas. In 1894 she began publishing *Woman's Voice*, a newspaper which canvassed a broad range of feminist issues and was sold all over NSW with outlets in Victoria and NZ. Lack of finance forced her to abandon it after eighteen months. Although she sold Maybanke College in 1898, she continued to play a prominent role as an educationist and feminist. She had divorced Wolstenholme in 1892 and in 1899 married Sir Francis Anderson, professor of philosophy at Sydney University and continued her public activities and writing on feminist issues. Her biography by Jan Roberts, *Maybanke Anderson: Sex, Suffrage and Social Reform* (1993), is also a revealing account of the community of feminists in Sydney of the 1890s, including such women as Rose Scott, Lady Mary Windeyer, Margaret Windeyer, Louisa Macdonald, Dora Montefiore and Dorette MacCallum.

ANDREONI, Giovanni (1935–), born Grossetto, Italy, left Italy in 1962, worked as a teacher in Tasmania (1962–63) and was at the University of WA (1964–68). He worked in NZ, 1968–73, returning to Australia to lecture at the University of New England. Before arriving in Australia, Andreoni had published a book of short stories, *Sedici Notti d'Insonnia (Sixteen Nights of Insomnia*, 1962). His later works include the semi-autobiographical novel, *Martin Pescatore (Martin Fisherman*, 1967), set in both Italy and Australia; in the second part of the novel the WA outback makes a considerable impact on the protagonist's spiritual and literary development. He has also written 'Abo Bianco', poems on the Australian outback, published in *Quaderni 4* (1971), and a book of short stories, *La Lingua degl'Italiani d'Australia e Alcuni Racconti (The Language of Italian-Australians and Some Stories*, 1978).

ANDREWS, Barry Geoffrey (1943–87), born Sydney, taught English at University College, University of New South Wales. With W.H. Wilde and Joy Hooton he co-authored *The Oxford Companion to Australian Literature* (1985), and was also the author of a critical study of 'Price Warung' (1976). He edited 'Price Warung's' *Tales of the Convict System* (1975), was associate editor of *The Oxford Literary Guide to Australia* (1987) and with W.H. Wilde compiled *Australian Literature to 1900: A Guide to Information Sources* (1980). University College sponsors an annual lecture in his honour, partly funded by a trust fund established in 1987 to commemorate his contribution to Australian literature.

ANDREWS, J.A. (John Arthur) (1865–1903), born Bendigo, was educated in Melbourne and was a public servant for four years before his dismissal for insubordination in 1886. Soon after, he became active in the Melbourne Anarchists Club, and continued espousing the anarchist cause in pamphlets and public platforms after moving to NSW in 1891. Imprisoned twice in 1894–95, he edited *Anarchy* (1891–92) and published a magazine, *The Revolt* (1893–94), before returning to Victoria, although he was in Sydney again in 1897–99 reporting for the *Australian Worker* and the *Australian Workman*; he also wrote for *Melbourne Punch* and the *Bulletin* in the late 1880s, was briefly editor of the *Australian* (1888) and *Tocsin* (1902), and was a reporter for newspapers in Yea (1890) and Mudgee (1894). As 'Sebastian Bach' or under his own name, Andrews published three small volumes of verse, *Temple Mystic* (1888), *Teufelswelt* (1896) and *Poems of Freedom* (?1905); he may also have been the author of a fourth volume, *Apollyon*, suppressed during the 1890s.

'Andy's Gone With Cattle', a poem by Henry Lawson (q.v.), laments the departure of a member of a selection family to go overlanding cattle. It was first published in October 1888 in the *Australian Town and Country Journal*, which also published the sequel, 'Andy's Return'. Some of the best-known lines of the poem are not Lawson's but are revisions by David McKee Wright when the poem was being prepared for publication in Lawson's *Selected Poems* (1918). The Andy of 'Andy's Gone With Cattle' (which is also in the repertoire of Australian folk-singers) is not the Andy of Lawson's poem, 'Middleton's Rouseabout', which traces the rise to wealth through thrift and hard work of a stolid rouseabout. J. Anthony King published an illustrated version of 'Andy's Gone With Cattle' in 1985.

ANGAS Family, a notable pioneering family of SA, was headed by George Fife Angas (1789–1879), who was born at Newcastle-on-Tyne. He was instrumental in the establishment of the colony of SA by providing, through the South Australian Company, several vessels to transport settlers, especially German Lutheran families, to the colony from 1836 onwards. In 1851 he came to SA and settled at Angaston, the township site selected by his agent, Charles Flaxman, in the Barossa Valley. Thereafter he served the new colony industriously, being the Barossa's representative in the Legislative Council from 1851 until his retirement from public life in 1866. George Fife Angas is the subject of a biography by Edwin Hodder (1891). He is prominently treated in Hodder's *The History of South Australia from Its Foundation to the Year of Its Jubilee* (1893) and in A. Grenfell Price's *Founders & Pioneers of South Australia* (1929). George Fife Angas's fourth child and eldest son was George French Angas (1822–86). Born at Newcastle-on-Tyne, George French showed an early interest in natural history; at the age of twenty he published *A Ramble in Malta and Sicily in the Autumn of 1841* (1842). He arrived in Australia in 1844 and toured extensively until 1846 both here and in NZ, recording his journeys in watercolour drawings. In 1847 he published *South Australia Illustrated* and *The New Zealanders Illustrated*, together with the illustrated two-volume account of his travels, *Savage Life and Scenes in Australia and New Zealand*. On a second trip to Australia in 1851 he visited the gold diggings at Bathurst, publishing in that year *Six Views of the Gold Field of Ophir* and *Views of the Gold Fields of Australia*. His later publications included *Australia, A Popular Account* (1865). George Fife Angas's fifth child, John Howard Angas (1823–1904), was, like his father, a renowned pastoralist, politician and philanthropist. The family's influence has continued to be exerted in SA pastoral and commercial interests to the present time.

Angry Penguins (1940–46), a quarterly journal of literary, artistic, musical and general cultural interest, was sponsored initially by the Adelaide University Arts Association but became an independent enterprise in its third number, published in Melbourne by Reed and Harris. Chiefly edited by Max Harris and John Reed (qq.v.), *Angry Penguins* was a self-consciously modernist magazine which coincided with a radical movement in Australian art and became a rallying point for artists and writers who had otherwise diverse interests; they included the artists Sidney Nolan, Albert Tucker, John Perceval, Danila Vassilieff, Joy Hester and Arthur Boyd and the writers Peter Cowan, Geoffrey Dutton and Harry Roskolenko.

Nolan, Tucker and Roskolenko in particular were involved in the magazine's production and publication. Rejecting all political creeds and influenced by the anarchist theories of Sir Herbert Read, *Angry Penguins* and its 1946 monthly supplement, *Angry Penguins Broadsheet*, attempted to present art as an organic whole, producing articles on cinema, jazz, the visual arts and literature. At the same time it attempted to link the Australian writer and artist to the European modernist movement, often publishing work by contemporary overseas writers such as Karl Shapiro and Dylan Thomas. Max Harris, who contributed a large range of material to the magazine, was particularly opposed to the nationalist socialism of such magazines as *Australian New Writing* and attacked what he saw as 'the tired and mediocre nationalism which passed for poetry, the pedestrian bush whackery which gave Australia a novel of unequalled verbal dullness'. Subject to inevitable 'excesses and absurdities', as Harris later admitted, and fatally attracted to any writing which presented itself as *avant garde*, *Angry Penguins* failed to survive the Ern Malley hoax (q.v.). Alister Kershaw has written reminiscences of *Angry Penguins* and the hoax in *Hey Days* (1991) and the journal's history and impact are extensively discussed in Richard Haese's *Rebels and Precursors* (1981), and in Michael Heyward's *The Ern Malley Affair* (1993).

ANGUS, D.M. (David Mackenzie) (1851–1901), born Caithness-shire, Scotland, worked in Edinburgh as apprentice to a bookseller before being forced by tuberculosis to come to Australia in 1882. He was employed in the Sydney branch of the Melbourne bookseller and publisher George Robertson (1) (q.v.) where he met another George Robertson (2) (q.v.) with whom, in 1886, he formed the famous bookselling and publishing firm Angus & Robertson (q.v.). In 1899 Angus retired through ill health and returned to Scotland. He, and Angus & Robertson, are discussed in J.R. Tyrrell's (q.v.) *Old Books, Old Friends, Old Sydney* (1952) and in G.A. Ferguson's (q.v.) *Some Early Australian Bookmen* (1978).

Angus & Robertson (A & R), one of Australia's earliest and most important bookselling and book-publishing firms, came into existence in January 1886 as a partnership between David Mackenzie Angus and George Robertson (2) (qq.v.). Angus and Robertson had both arrived in Australia from Scotland in 1882 and worked in the Sydney branch of the Melbourne bookseller and publisher, also named George Robertson (1). In 1884 Angus set up his own bookshop at 110 Market Street, Sydney, later taking George Robertson (2) as partner. The rapid success of its retail bookselling saw the firm expand into the adjoining Market Street premises; in 1890 it moved to 89 Castlereagh Street, where for more than sixty years it was Sydney's best-known bookshop. Angus's chief concern was with the sale of educational books, while Robertson developed a particular interest in the collection and sale of Australiana; one of his main customers was David Scott Mitchell (q.v.), whose collection of Australiana became a major factor in the later establishment of Syd-

ney's Mitchell Library (q.v.). The partnership ended in 1900, Angus returning to England where he died soon after from tuberculosis. The business was converted in 1907 into a public company with George Robertson (2) as its managing director. After his death in 1933, Walter Cousins became its head; he was succeeded by Robertson's grandson, George Ferguson. In 1970 A & R became a subsidiary of Ipec Insurance and the business was relocated in Pitt Street, Sydney. In 1978 the bookshop division was sold to Gordon and Gotch.

Angus & Robertson's illustrious Australian publishing history, largely inspired by George Robertson (2), began in 1888 with the appearance of two books of verse, *A Crown of Wattle* by H. Peden Steel and *Sun and Cloud on River and Sea* by 'Ishmael Dare' (Arthur Jose), and a reprint of an important piece of Australiana, *Facsimile of a Proposal for a Settlement on the Coast of New South Wales, by Sir George Young* (1785). Its halcyon period began in 1895 when it published A.B. Paterson's *The Man from Snowy River and Other Verses*, followed in 1896 by Henry Lawson's *While the Billy Boils* and *In the Days When the World was Wide and Other Verses*. The first catalogue of publications of A & R was circulated in 1895, the first separate catalogue of purely Australian publications ever issued. The long list of Australian writers later published by A & R includes Victor Daley, Will Ogilvie, James Brunton Stephens, Louise Mack, C.J. Dennis, Norman Lindsay, Mary Gilmore, Ion Idriess and Frank Clune. During the First World War Dennis's *The Songs of a Sentimental Bloke* (1915) was one of A & R's major successes. The 1920s saw the publication of *The Australian Encyclopaedia* while the *Official History of Australia in the War of 1914–1918* was distributed by and bore the imprint of A & R. Notable children's books from A & R include Lindsay's *The Magic Pudding* (1918), Dorothy Wall's *Blinky Bill* series, and May Gibbs's *Gumnut Tales*. The firm's natural science list of publications began with Neville Cayley's *What Bird Is That?* in 1931. In 1923 George Robertson (2) took over a small printing house, Eagle Press, which became Halstead Press (q.v.), the chief printing arm of the firm. After the takeover of A & R in 1970 Halstead Press was sold and the publishing division (now separated from the bookshop), under Richard Walsh, who was managing director 1972–86, was relocated at Cremorne, Sydney. Thereafter, although it maintained some publishing of quality fiction, non-fiction and poetry, it concentrated on the mass market. In 1981 it became part of the News Limited group. In 1985 it purchased the US book distributor Salem House. In 1989, as one of the period's many mergers, takeovers and conglomerations, producing large publishing bureaucracies, A & R merged with William Collins, thus becoming the Australian trade publishing imprint of the giant multinational conglomeration, HarperCollins. A & R has, however, continued to play a conspicuous role as publisher of quality Australian writing, e.g. the A & R Modern Poets Series and the Imprint Series, which specialises in reviving previously published works. It continues to provide incentives also for promising Australian writers, e.g. in 1993 it awarded the first A &

R Bookworld Prize ($10 000) for a first book of fiction by an unpublished writer.

Much of the earlier history of Angus & Robertson and the men associated with it, such as F.V. Wymark, is included in James Tyrrell's (q.v.) *Old Books, Old Friends, Old Sydney* (1952) and *Postscript: Further Bookselling Reminiscences* (1957), and George Ferguson's (q.v.) *Some Early Australian Bookmen* (1978). In 1910 Henry Lawson (who is alleged to have interpreted A & R as 'Anguish and Robbery') wrote a verse tribute to George Robertson (2) and A & R, *The Auld Shop and the New* (1923).

Annals of Australian Literature (1970), compiled by Grahame Johnston (q.v.), lists, by yearly entries, noteworthy Australian books from 1789 to 1968 in alphabetical order of authors and with an accompanying abbreviation to indicate genre. The listing was expanded and updated to 1988 by Joy Hooton and Harry Heseltine in a second edition published in 1992. Side columns to the yearly entries contain such ancillary information as authors' birth and death dates; the founding and duration of newspapers and periodicals; visits or books by notable writers from overseas; books written in Australia in languages other than English; some books on non-Australian subjects by authors whose other works are in the main column; books written abroad by authors now settled in Australia; and English classics referring to Australia.

Annual Catalogue of Australian Publications, see **Australian National Bibliography**

Anoli the Blind, a psychological melodrama by Sydney Tomholt (q.v.), was published in his collection *Bleak Dawn and Other Plays* (1936) and included in the London anthology *The Best One-Act Plays of 1936*. Set in an isolated part of northern Queensland, the drama, which concentrates on the embittered emotions of three Italians, the blind but powerful Anoli Ferari, his common-law wife Rose and her lover Antonio, moves to a violent conclusion.

'ANSTRUTHER, Gilbert' (Russel S. Clark) (1909–   ), born Carcoar, NSW, was author of *An End to Tears* (1946), an account of the war years in Hong Kong, and a successful writer of popular fiction, all published under the pseudonym 'Gilbert Anstruther'. His fiction includes *Three Went West* (1939), *To Hell with Love* (1943), *The Wench Was Wicked* (1944), *Fishes Also Make Love* (1944), *God Glanced Away* (1945), *The Anstruther Three-Story Omnibus* (1946), *The Ladies Came Undressed* (1947), *Move Over, Honey* (1949) and the more recent *Look Dad They're Hanging Grandpa* (1968), *Grandma Came Across on a Raft* (1969) and *The Anstruther (Captain) Cook Book* (1970), all of which are ironic creative myths about the founding of Australian culture.

Anthologies. The earliest attempts to sample Australian writing in anthologies include Isaac Nathan's *The Southern Euphrosyne and Australian Miscellany* (1848), which contains 'original Anecdote, Poetry and Music'; *The Australian Souvenir for 1851* (1851), which contains stories, essays and poems; and W.H.H. Yarrington's *Prince Alfred's Wreath* (1868), which, with its selections from Henry Kendall, J. Sheridan Moore, W.M. Adams and others, is the first approximation to later verse anthologies. In 1869 William H. Williams introduced a form of anthology with his Christmas 'annuals' for holiday reading; his *Illustrated Australian Annuals* for 1869–70 and 1870–71 contain a medley of verse, short fiction and sketches, mostly by Australian writers. The 'annual' rapidly became a popular anthological device; well-known examples include *The 'Vagabond' Annual* (1877), by John Stanley James; *Hash* (1877) by Garnet Walch; *The Antipodean* (1893, 1895, 1897) by George Essex Evans and others; and *The Golden West* (1906–46) by R.C. Spear. One of the earliest examples of the anthology that comprises selections taken from a newspaper, magazine or journal is *Punch Staff Papers* (1872), a collection of short fiction, sketches and verse by members of the staff of *Sydney Punch*; among the contributors were D.H. Deniehy, Henry Kendall, G.G. McCrae, Garnet Walch and Richmond Thatcher. The first significant anthology to combine selections *and* criticism was G.B. Barton's *Poets and Prose Writers of New South Wales* (q.v., 1866); Barton used extracts from the writings of Deniehy, W.B. Dalley, W.C. Wentworth, Charles Harpur, Henry Kendall, J.L. Michael and others to illustrate and substantiate his critical commentary.

The centenary of the colony in 1888 produced two busy anthologists, Douglas Sladen and Arthur Patchett Martin, who took advantage of the historic moment to promote Australian literature; their critical discrimination was, however, somewhat overruled by their enthusiasm and hampered by their lack of awareness of the new spirit of nationalism that was already affecting Australian writing. Sladen's first anthology, *Australian Ballads and Rhymes* (1888), was a selection of 'Poems inspired by Life and Scenery in Australia and New Zealand'; it was reissued in the same year with a critical introduction and in an enlarged edition, titled *A Century of Australian Song*. With the help of contributions and suggestions gained from canvassing in the press, Sladen published an even wider selection, *Australian Poets, 1788–1888* (1888). In all, he published the work of more than eighty poets; inevitably many were undeserving of recognition and were discarded by later anthologists. Sladen's sins were also of omission. Much of Adam Lindsay Gordon is missing, the *Bulletin* writers are excluded, as are Ada Cambridge, Victor Daley, Mary Hannay Foott and John Farrell. Martin, who had edited an earlier anthology, *An Easter Omelette in Prose and Verse* (1879), drew upon Australian writers resident in England for a collection of stories and sketches, *Oak-Bough and Wattle-Blossom* (1888); contributors included Rosa Praed, Sladen, Philip Mennell and Martin himself. His wife, Harriette Anne Martin, compiled similar anthologies, *Under the Gum Tree* (1890) with contributions from Praed, Jessie Couvreur and Hume Nisbet, and *Volcanic Gold* (1890); she also edited the first all-women collection, *Coo-ee: Tales of Australian Life by Australian Ladies* (1891). Philip Mennell added *In Australian Wilds*

(1889), a similar collection of largely undistinguished short fiction, and Lala Fisher made a selection of writings by Australians in England, *By Creek and Gully* (1899).

Ignored by Sladen and Martin, the *Bulletin* proceeded to publish its own miscellanies; in 1890 J.F. Archibald in collaboration with F.J. Broomfield compiled *'A Golden Shanty': Australian Stories and Sketches in Prose and Verses by 'Bulletin' Writers*. Those represented include Henry Kendall, Victor Daley, Edward Dyson, A.B. Paterson, John Farrell and Henry Lawson; the fact that only Kendall appears in Sladen and Martin shows how lacking in literary discrimination the earlier anthologies were. Further *Bulletin* collections were *The Bulletin Story Book* and *The Bulletin Reciter*, both edited by A.G. Stephens in 1901; in 1920 Bertram Stevens selected and edited *The 'Bulletin' Book of Humorous Verse and Recitations*.

The first half of the twentieth century brought a continuous stream of anthologies of all kinds, some of which can now be seen as significant landmarks in Australian literary history. Bertram Stevens edited *An Anthology of Australian Verse* in 1906; from it came *The Golden Treasury of Australian Verse* (1909), the first collection that could be said to be truly reflective of Australian sentiment and attitude. Stevens produced other minor anthologies such as *Bush Ballads* (1908), *The Australian Birthday Book* (1908), *A Book of Australian Verse for Boys and Girls* (1915); and he collaborated with George Mackaness to produce *The Children's Treasury of Australian Verse* (1913) and *Selections from Australian Poets* (1913). The selections are characteristically Australian not only in content (Australian life, landscape and events) but also in their simple, direct and sometimes rugged style. Mackaness, an anthologist of other genres also, returned to verse anthologies twenty years later with *The Wide Brown Land* (1934), chosen by himself and his daughter Joan: perhaps the most famous of all Australian verse anthologies, it took its title from a phrase in Dorothea Mackellar's poem, 'My Country' (q.v.), and was often reprinted. Douglas Stewart continued the title with his 1971 anthology. A significant milestone was reached in verse anthologies in 1918 when Walter Murdoch (q.v.) edited the first *Oxford Book of Australasian Verse*; when the second edition was published in 1923 'Oxford' was omitted from the title. Murdoch's original selection did not please all critics but it was more wide ranging than most of those published earlier and less emphatic on Australian content than the 1913 anthology of Stevens and Mackaness. Murdoch's third edition (1945) was the subject of considerable criticism in *Southerly* (1946); the fourth edition, titled *A Book of Australian and New Zealand Verse* (1950), was edited jointly by Murdoch and Alan Mulgan; Judith Wright's *A Book of Australian Verse* (1956, second edition 1968), ultimately replaced the Murdoch Oxford anthologies. Another well-received verse anthology of the early twentieth century was Percival Serle's *An Australasian Anthology (Australian and New Zealand Poems)* (1927). Serle was assisted by 'Furnley Maurice' and R.H. Croll, both of whom were established critics; the combination produced a comprehensive and well-balanced selection and was accompanied by an account of the development of Australian and NZ poetry. The third edition of Serle's anthology (1946) added a short and rather unsatisfactory section on contemporary verse. Another significant anthologist of this period was J.J. Stable (q.v.), professor of English at the University of Queensland, who compiled *The Bond of Poetry* in 1924. It combined English and Australian poems because Stable felt that poetry provided a bond that might keep nationalistic Australians linked to their British heritage. *The Bond of Poetry* remained a popular school text for many years, more so than Stable's later anthology, *The High Road of Australian Verse* (1929). One of the earliest movements towards the regional collection of verse was Stable's *A Book of Queensland Verse* (1924, with A.E.M. Kirwood), which was published in conjunction with the Brisbane centenary and illustrated the development of verse in Queensland. A verse anthology that stood deliberately apart from the nationalistic collections of this period was *Poetry in Australia 1923* (1923), edited by Jack Lindsay and Kenneth Slessor, with a preface by Norman Lindsay that decried nationalism in literature. Compelled to accept the 'accident' of geographical location and thus label its poetry 'Australian', the anthology is not representatively Australian in a general sense; its contributors were chosen largely to illustrate the Lindsay and *Vision* insistence on internationalism in literature and the importance of language in creative thought. Much of the selected poetry came from Hugh McCrae, Jack Lindsay and Kenneth Slessor, all of whom wrote at that time in accord with *Vision* attitudes. A notable specialised anthology of the period was Louis Lavater's *The Sonnet in Australasia* (1926), a collection of about 225 sonnets by more than 100 Australian poets. The occasional annual selection of the poetry of the period, e.g. *Australian Poetry Annual 1920–21* (1921), chosen from contributions to the magazine *Birth* (q.v.), was the forerunner of the poetry magazines that proliferated after the middle of the century and of such annual selections of verse as *Australian Poetry* (q.v.), published by Angus & Robertson and which ran 1941–73 (and revised later) with a different editor for each volume. Most of *Australian Poetry*'s editors were established poets/critics, e.g. Douglas Stewart, R.D. FitzGerald, Kenneth Slessor and Judith Wright, and the annual selections were, at least until the 1960s, conventional and predictable. Notable among the specialised verse anthologies of the first half of the century were those published by the Jindyworobaks (q.v.). They ran 1938–53, included only poetry that satisfied the Jindyworobak criteria, and were edited by notable poets of the movement, e.g. Rex Ingamells, Flexmore Hudson, W. Hart-Smith, Ian Mudie and Roland Robinson.

Although less prolific than verse anthologies, prose collections in the first half of the twentieth century were no less significant. In addition to the *Bulletin* anthologies already mentioned, other early collections of note were the stories reprinted from the *Sydney Mail*, *Red Kangaroo and Other Stories* (1907); Donald McLachlan's *Austral Garden: An Anthology of Australian Prose* (1922), which contained chapters from novels and extracts of non-fiction as well as short stories; *Australian Short Stories* (1928), edited by Mackaness; *An Australian Story Book* (1928), selected by Nettie Palmer and restricted to stories written in the twentieth century; and *Adventures in the Bush: Australia's Story* (1931), edited by Herbert Strang. Most prominent in these early anthologies are Barbara Baynton, Henry Lawson, 'Louis' Becke, Edward Dyson, Ernest Favenc, Vance Palmer, Katharine Susannah Prichard and Ethel Turner. In 1941 *Coast to Coast* (q.v.), an anthology of the year's best stories, was first published; it ran annually 1941–48, and biennially 1949–70, with a final issue in 1973. *Coast to Coast* was revived in 1986 with Kerryn Goldsworthy as editor. Early collections of Australian essays include *Essays, Imaginative and Critical* (1933), compiled by Mackaness and John D. Holmes, and *Australian Essays* (1935), selected by G.H. Cowling and 'Furnley Maurice'. Notable essayists represented are Marcus Clarke, John le Gay Brereton, Walter Murdoch and Ernest Scott.

Drama and literary criticism also appeared in anthology form in the first part of the twentieth century. Collections of one-act plays include *Eight Plays by Australians* (1934) and *Five Plays by Australians* (1936), both published by the Dramatists' Club of Melbourne; *Best Australian One-Act Plays* (1937), edited by William Moore and T. Inglis Moore; and Leslie Rees's *Australian Radio Plays* (1946). In somewhat similar vein to G.B. Barton's critical anthology of the previous century are Colin Roderick's *The Australian Novel* (1945) and *20 Australian Novelists* (1947), where critical and biographical commentary accompany excerpts from such writers as A.H. Adams, 'Rolf Boldrewood', Marcus Clarke, Henry Kingsley, Jessie Couvreur and others of the more modern period.

After the Second World War poetry anthologies came in four main categories: general anthologies that gave a selection from colonial times to the present; those which attempted a periodic update of the contemporary scene prior to 1968; those which specifically illustrated the 'New Australian Poetry' (q.v.) which dated from 1968; and those which reflected sectional interests or illustrated particular types and periods of poetry. The general anthologies, largely a continuation of similar types published earlier in the century, include Judith Wright's *A Book of Australian Verse* (1956, rev. edn 1968), Geoffrey Dutton's *Australian Verse from 1805* (1976) and Rodney Hall's *The Collins Book of Australian Poetry* (1981). Most of those attempting an up-to-date view of poetry in the period up to 1968 convey their intention by using the word 'modern' in their titles; they include H.M. Green's *Modern Australian Poetry* (1946, rev. edn 1952); R.G. Howarth, Kenneth Slessor and John Thompson's *The Penguin Book of Australian Verse* (1958, titled *Modern Australian Verse* in 1961), which was replaced by Harry Heseltine's *The Penguin Book of Australian Verse* (1972); Douglas Stewart's *Modern Australian Verse* (1964), which is the second volume of the two-volume *Poetry in Australia*; Rodney Hall and Thomas Shapcott's *New Impulses in Australian Poetry* (q.v., 1968), which concerns itself with the poetry of the 1960s but which

appeared before the 'New Australian Poetry' had fully developed; David Campbell's *Modern Australian Poetry* (1970), which was also compiled before 1968 and which closes with the work of Geoffrey Lehmann, the only poet in the anthology who was born in the 1940s; Dennis Robinson's *Those Fabled Shores: Six Contemporary Australian Poets* (1972), which contains only the work of the mainstream poets, Slessor, Hope, Wright, James McAuley, Stewart and FitzGerald; and Thomas Shapcott's *Contemporary American and Australian Poetry* (1976), which includes some post-1968 poetry but which continues to emphasise the older representatives of contemporary Australian poetry, i.e. Hope, Wright, McAuley, Campbell, Gwen Harwood, Blight and others. The 'New Australian Poetry', which came after 1968, has been given almost blanket coverage, chiefly by the myriad poetry magazines that are a striking phenomenon of the modern literary scene, and to a lesser extent by more formal anthologies. The latter include Shapcott's *Australian Poetry Now* (1970), which is the companion to and extension of David Campbell's *Modern Australian Poetry* and which focuses on the poets who were on the verge of the new movement, e.g. Michael Dransfield, Robert Adamson, John Tranter and Roger McDonald; Robert Kenny and Colin Talbot's *Applestealers* (q.v., 1974), a collection specifically stated to represent the 'renaissance in Australian poetry'; John Tranter's *The New Australian Poetry* (1979), which includes selections from twenty-four poets of 'Australian poetry's most exciting decade', e.g. Bruce Beaver (one of the seminal poets of the 'renaissance'), Dransfield, Adamson, Rae Desmond Jones, Nigel Roberts, Jennifer Maiden, Vicki Viidikas and John Forbes; Heseltine's *The Penguin Book of Modern Australian Verse* (1981), which includes both new and somewhat older writers, e.g. many born in the 1920s and 1930s; and two important attempts to assist the development of the then contemporary poetry, the Paperback Poets (q.v.) series of UQP which culminated in two paperback poetry anthologies (1974, 1981) and Angus & Robertson's Poets of the Month (q.v.) series. Robert Gray and Geoffrey Lehmann's *The Younger Australian Poets* (1983) brings the poetry scene up to date at that time, thereby relegating the 1968 revolution to history. The same two also produced *Australian Poetry in the Twentieth Century* (1992), a radically new overall approach to the poetry of the second Australian century.

Increasingly in recent years the anthology has been used as a device to espouse causes, highlight philosophies and attitudes, illustrate particular literary movements, types of writing and groups of writers, and draw attention to particular periods, places and regions. The feminist movement is represented by such collections as *Mother I'm Rooted* (1975), an anthology of Australian women poets edited by Kate Jennings; *Hecate's Daughters* (1978), verse and prose edited by Carole Ferrier; *Stories of Her Life* (1979), edited by Sandra Zurbo; *The True Life Story of . . .* (1981) and *Frictions* (1982), prose anthologies edited respectively by Jan Craney and Esther Caldwell and by Anna Gibbs and Alison Tilson; and *The Half-Open Door* (1982), accounts of the lives and careers of sixteen modern Australian women, edited by Patricia Grimshaw and Lynne Strahan. A similar collection of interviews (with Susan Mitchell) was *Tall Poppies* (1984). The success of the feminist movement in the 1970s and 1980s led to numerous further anthologies of women's writing, e.g., *And So Say All of Us* (1984), ed. Pearlie McNeill and Marie McShea (short stories); *The Penguin Book of Australian Women Poets* (1986), ed. Susan Hampton and Kate Llewellyn; *Happy Endings: Stories by Australian and New Zealand Women 1850s –1930s* (1987), ed. Elizabeth Webby and Lydia Wevers; and *The Babe is Wise* (1987), ed. Lyn Harwood, Bruce Pascoe and Paula White (short stories). It was the Bicentenary (1988), however, which turned this trickle of all-women anthologies into a flood. The Bicentenary year saw such collections as *200 Australian Women: A Redress Anthology*, ed. Heather Radi; *Angry Women*, ed. Di Brown, Heather Ellyard and Barbara Polkinghorne; *Room to Move*, ed. Suzanne Falkiner; the Redress Press Anthology of Women's short stories; and *Eclipsed: Two Centuries of Australian Women's Fiction*, ed. Connie Burns and Marygai McNamara. Some did not make it through the presses in that hectic year, e.g. *Eight Voices of the Eighties* (1989), ed. Gillian Whitlock; *Feeling Restless* (1989), ed. Connie Burns and Marygai McNamara; *Kiwi & Emu* (1989 – NZ and Australian women writers), ed. Barbara Petrie. Somewhat different was *Moments of Desire* (1989), ed. Susan Hawthorne and Jenny Pausacker, an anthology of fiction, prose and poetry exploring women's sensuality. Later all-women collections included *Speaking with the Sun* (1991), ed. Stephanie Dowrick and Jane Parkin (new stories by both NZ and Australian women), *Heroines* (1991), ed. Dale Spender, and *Life Lines: Australian Women's Letters and Diaries 1788–1840* (1992), ed. Patricia Clarke and Dale Spender.

The experience of war had produced earlier anthologies such as C.E.W. Bean's *The Anzac Book* (1916) and Ian Mudie's *Poets at War* (1944). Modern variations on traditional war anthologies include the anti-war collection *We Took Their Orders and Are Dead* (1971), a protest against the Vietnam War compiled by Shirley Cass, Ros Cheney, David Malouf and Michael Wilding; and Geoff Page's *Shadows from Wire* (1983), which demonstrates, by juxtaposing modern reactions to the First World War with actual war photographs, the irony of the initial response to the war. Recent war anthologies include John Laird's *The Australian Experience of War* (1988) and *On All Fronts: Australian Stories of World War II* (1989). The reaction to the experience of incarceration is collected in two volumes of poetry, *Poems from Prison* (1973), edited by Rodney Hall, and *Walled Gardens* (1978), poems from NSW prisons, published by the aptly named Ball & Chain Press. The experiences of the immigrant in Australia are the theme of Louise Rorabacher's group of short stories, *Two Ways Meet* (1963); Nancy Keesing's edition of Jewish stories, *Shalom* (1978); *Voci Nostre (Our Voices)* (1979), an Italo-Australian anthology edited by G.L. Abiuso, M. Giglio and V. Borghese; Manfred Jurgensen's verse and prose anthology, *Ethnic Australia* (1980), the work of twenty-four writers whose native language is not English; *Tradition* (1982), edited by R.F. Holt; *Pomegranates: A Century of Jewish Australian Writing* (1988), ed. Gael Hammer; *Beyond the Echo* (1988), ed. Sneja Gunew and Jan Mahyuddin, an anthology of women's multicultural writing with a considerable feminist flavour; *On the Fence* (1985), featuring the work of Ukrainian writers in English with their experiences both in the 'homeland' country and in Australia; and *Homeland* (1991), ed. George Papaellinas, twenty-five writers expressing their idea of 'homeland'. Regionalism provides a constant impulse to anthologising and never so much as in the Bicentenary period: recent examples include the WA collections *Soundings* (1976) ed. Veronica Brady; *Quarry* (1981), ed. Fay Zwicky; *Summerland: A West Australian Sesquicentenary Anthology* (1979), ed. Alec Choate; *Portrait: A West Coast Collection of Short Fiction and Poetry* (1986), ed. B.R. Coffey and Wendy Jenkins, which celebrates a decade of publishing by Fremantle Arts Centre (q.v.) Press; *Celebrations: A Bicentennial Anthology of Fifty Years of Western Australian Poetry and Prose* (1988), ed. Brian Dibble, Don Grant and Glen Phillips; *Wordhord: A Critical Selection of Contemporary Western Australian Poetry* (1989), ed. Dennis Haskell and Hilary Fraser, a collection of poetry written in the 1980s; and the twin Bicentenary anthologies, *Margins: A West Coast Collection of Poetry, 1829–1988* (1988), ed. William Grono, and *Impressions: West Coast Fiction 1829–1988* (1989), ed. Peter Cowan. SA anthologies include *Dots Over Lines* (1981), a collection of recent poetry from that state; *Unsettled Areas: Recent Short Fiction* (1986), ed. Andrew Taylor; *The Orange Tree* (1986), ed. K.F. Pearson and Christine Churches, an anthology of SA poetry from its beginnings to the present, which borrows its title from John Shaw Neilson's famous poem, although Neilson was only a South Australian until the age of 10; and *The Inner Courtyard* (1990), ed. Anne Brewster and Jeff Guess, a collection of contemporary SA love poetry. Queensland was represented quite early in the century by Stable and Kirkwood's *A Book of Queensland Verse* (1924), then by the *Queensland Centenary Anthology* (1959), ed. R.S. Byrnes and Val Vallis, later by *Place and Perspective* (1983), ed. Barry O'Donohue, collecting the works of thirty Queensland poets, and the twin anthologies *North of Capricorn: An Anthology of Prose* (1989), ed. Des Petersen and Stephen Torre, and *North of Capricorn: An Anthology of Verse* (1988), ed. Elizabeth Perkins and Robert Handicott. The Northern Territory's own collections include *Latitudes: New Writing from the North* (1986), ed. Susan Johnson and Mary Roberts; *North of the Ten Commandments* (1991), ed. David Headon, an anthology of various types of Territory writing; and the companion volumes of the Northern Territory Writers' Groups, *Life Beyond the Louvres* (1989) and *Bugs and Bliss* (1991). Tasmanian poetry was collected in *Effects of Light: The Poetry of Tasmania* (1986), ed. Vivian Smith and Margaret Scott; the Australian Capital Territory's anthologies include *Canberra Tales* (1988), where seven ACT women writers weave stories with a Canberra setting, and *The Poetry of Canberra* (1990), ed. Phillip Mackenzie. Gippsland (the 'soul-country' of Eve Langley) is the base for *Shadow and Shine* (1988), ed. Patrick Morgan, and the Hunter Valley of NSW has various collections including Norman Talbot's *Hunter Valley Poets* (1973) and Ross Bennett's *This Place: Poetry of the Hunter Valley* (1980).

Typical of specific period anthologies has been the return to colonial writing in such collections as T. Inglis Moore's *From the Ballads to Brennan* (1964), Brian Elliott and Adrian Mitchell's *Bards in the Wilderness: Australian Colonial Poetry to 1920* (1970), G.A. Wilkes's *The Colonial Poets* (1974), *Colonial Voices* (1989), ed. Elizabeth Webby, containing letters, diaries, journalism and other accounts of nineteenth-century Australia, *The Poet's Discovery: Nineteenth Century Australia in Verse* (1990), ed. R.D. Jordan and Peter Pierce, an anthology arranged by colony, *The Penguin Book of Australian Ballads* (1993), ed. Philip Butterss and Elizabeth Webby and *The Penguin Book of Nineteenth Century Australian Literature* (1993), ed. Michael Ackland.

A narrowing of the focus to inspect the most important decade of the nineteenth century – the Nineties – is made in Leon Cantrell's collection of writings from that decade, *The 1890s* (1977). A similar narrowing is seen in the somewhat frenetic efforts of anthologists to capture the character of the literature being written in the immediate here and now – i.e. contemporary literature, e.g., *Transgressions: Australian Writing Now* (1986), ed. Don Anderson, with its emphasis on the innovative and experimental; *Contemporary Australian Poetry* (1986), ed. Dimitris Tsaloumas; *The Tin Wash Dish* (1989), an anthology edited by John Tranter of the poetry entered in the ABC/ABA Bicentennial competition; *Expressway* (1989), ed. Helen Daniel, an anthology of short fiction offering a contemporary view of Australia; *Contemporary Australian Poetry* (1990), ed. John Leonard; *The Australian Anthology of New Poets* (1989); *Picador New Writing* (1993), ed. Robert Dessaix and Helen Daniel; and Penguin's ceaseless battle, using the term 'modern' on several occasions over the decades, to be the first with the latest, *The Penguin Book of Modern Australian Poetry* (1991), ed. John Tranter and Philip Mead. And there are plenty of anthologies which continue to give not a narrow but an overall view, e.g. (among many) *Two Centuries of Australian Poetry* (1988), ed. Mark O'Connor; *The Heritage of Australian Poetry* (1984), ed. Geoffrey Dutton; *The New Oxford Book of Australian Verse* (1986, expanded 1991), ed. Les Murray, which extends from Aboriginal songs to modern verse; *The Penguin Best Australian Short Stories* (1991), ed. Mary Lord; and *The Macmillan Anthology of Australian Literature* (1990), ed. Ken Goodwin and Alan Lawson, which, with its 629 pages, is about the largest, though undoubtedly not the last word in complete anthologies.

Readily identifiable thematic groups of anthologies in recent decades include the book of erotic verse *Within the Hill* (1975), ed. Alan Gould and others; *The Oxford Book of Australian Love Poems* (1993), ed. Jennifer Strauss; the humorous collections *Comic Australian Verse* (1972), ed. Geoffrey Lehmann; *Robust, Ribald and Rude Verse in Australia* (1972), ed. Bill Wannan; *The Penguin Book of Australian Satirical Verse* (1986), ed. Philip Neilsen; *The Illustrated Treasury of Australian Humour* (1988), ed. Michael Sharkey; *The Flight of the Emu: Contemporary Light Verse* (1990), ed. Geoffrey Lehmann; and *The Oxford Book of Australian Light Verse* (1991), ed. R.F. Brissenden and Philip Grundy; the nationally oriented Wannan collections, *The Wearing of the Green* (1965) and *The Heather in the South* (1966); David Stewart's *Voyager Poems* (1960); and David Martin's book of left-wing verse, *New World, New Song* (1955).

Black Writing is contained in *Australian Aboriginal Literature: An Anthology* (1987), ed. Adam Shoemaker, *Inside Black Australia* (1988), ed. Kevin Gilbert, a collection of Aboriginal poetry, and *Paperbark: A Collection of Black Australian Writings* (1990), ed. Jack Davis et al. Science fiction is indebted to well-known writer Damien Broderick, who has edited *The Zeitgeist Machine* (1977), *Strange Attractions* (1985) and *Matilda at the Speed of Light* (1988). Les Murray collated the important and popular *Anthology of Australian Religious Poetry* (1986). Symptomatic of the changes in public perception in recent times is the ready acceptance of gay and lesbian anthologies, e.g., *Edge City on Two Different Plans* (1983), ed. Margaret Bradstock, Gary Dunne et al., a collection of poems, songs and fiction from forty-three gay/lesbian writers; *The Exploding Frangipani* (1990), ed. Cathie Dunsford and Susan Hawthorne, featuring Australian and NZ lesbian writing; *Travelling on Love in a Time of Uncertainty* (1991), ed. Gary Dunne, a book of contemporary Australian gay fiction; *Falling for Grace: an Anthology of Australian Lesbian Fiction* (1993), ed. Roberta Snow and Jill Taylor; and *Australian Gay and Lesbian Writing* (1993), ed. Robert Dessaix. Reminscences of childhood are the theme of *In the Half Light* (1988), ed. Jacqueline Kent, and *Australian Childhood: An Anthology* (1991), ed. Gwyn Dow and June Factor. The growing popularity of crime fiction in Australia is reflected in recent anthologies of crime and mystery short fiction, *Sand on the Gumshoe* (1989), ed. David Latta, and two edited by Stephen Knight, *Dead Witness* (1989) and *More Crimes for a Summer Christmas* (1991). The best Australian air stories are brought together in *On a Wing and a Prayer* (1989), ed. Terry Gwynn-Jones; the best travel stories in *Home and Away* (1987), ed. Rosemary Creswell; and the most ardent expressions of romance in *The Language of Love* (1991), ed. Pamela Allardice, which is an anthology of Australian love letters, love poetry and prose.

Literary societies and groups have compiled anthologies of the writings of their members: Wesley Milgate and Imogen Whyse produced the Poetry Society of Australia's first anthology in 1956; Nancy Keesing's *Transition* (1970) is a collection of the ASA; *Square Poets* (1971) groups the work of the Queensland FAW, as does *Breakaway* (1980) for the WA branch of the FAW, Barry Bannister's *Walk a Different Way* (1979) for the Darwin FAW and *Island Authors* (1971) for the Tasmanian Branch. *Tuesday Night Live* (1993), ed. Jeri Kroll and Barry Westburg, contains the work of eighty Friendly Street (q.v.) poets of SA. Selections from literary journals and newspapers have been gathered together in periodical collections, e.g. *Austro-verse*

(1952) from *Austro-vert; An Overland Muster* (1965), selected by Stephen Murray-Smith from *Overland 1954–64; On Native Grounds* (1968), selected by C.B. Christesen and *The Temperament of Generations* (1990), by Jenny Lee, Gerald Murnane and Philip Mead from *Meanjin; The Vital Decade* (1968), chosen by Geoffrey Dutton and Max Harris from *Australian Letters; Poems from the Age 1967–79* (1979), edited by R.A. Simpson; and *Quadrant: Twenty-Five Years* (1982), selected by Peter Coleman, Lee Shrubb and Vivian Smith. Compatible groups of poets have been brought together in such volumes as Judith Green et al. *Four Poets* (1962), Vincent Buckley's *Eight by Eight* (1963), Alexander Craig's *Twelve Poets 1950–1970* (1971), and Michael Dugan's *The Drunken Tram: Six Young Melbourne Poets* (1972). Poetry and short stories submitted to competitions are frequently collected; examples of such anthologies are those associated with the Mattara Spring Festival (q.v.), the C.J. Dennis and the Harold Kesteven poetry competitions, and the Henry Lawson festivals at Grenfell, NSW.

In the second half of the twentieth century, there has been an intensive gathering of Australian folksongs and ballads (q.v.), tall tales and folklore; Bill Wannan (q.v.) has been the most assiduous compiler of the last, having published many collections. A.B. Paterson's 1905 edition of *Old Bush Songs* was the forerunner of a host of similar modern collections of ballads and folk-songs by such writers as Vance Palmer, Will Lawson, Douglas Stewart, Nancy Keesing, John Meredith, John Manifold, Russel Ward, Hugh Anderson and Ron Edwards.

The increased attention paid to Australian literature by recent generations of scholars and students has led to a proliferation of critical writing. Notable among the collections of important critical statements are *Australian Literary Criticism* (1962) edited by Grahame Johnston; *The Literature of Australia* (q.v., 1964, rev. edn 1976), edited by Geoffrey Dutton; *Literary Australia* (1966) by Clement Semmler and Derek Whitelock; *Twentieth Century Australian Literary Criticism* (1967) by Semmler; *The Writer in Australia* (1969) by John Barnes; *The Australian Nationalists* (1971) by Chris Wallace-Crabbe; *Bards, Bohemians, and Bookmen* (1976) by Leon Cantrell; and *The Penguin New Literary History of Australia* (1988) under the general editorship of Laurie Hergenhan.

Antipodean: An Illustrated Annual, The (1893–97)

was edited by George Essex Evans and John Tighe Ryan, the third volume being edited by A.B. Paterson although the original editors are named on the title page. In addition to poetry and short fiction by well-known contemporary writers (e.g. Paterson's 'The Geebung Polo Club' and Henry Lawson's 'The Bush Undertaker'), the annuals contained critical and descriptive articles (e.g. 'The Australian Drama' and 'Australian Scenery').

Antipodes, meaning literally 'having feet opposed', emerged in English at the end of the fourteenth century to describe those who dwelt on opposite sides of the globe. It then came to mean the diametrically opposite regions of the earth, as in Shakespeare's *Much Ado About Nothing*, where Benedick, anxious to avoid Beatrice, offers to 'go on the slightest errand now to the Antipodes'. Early references to the Antipodes, which were sometimes imagined as a Utopia, were to the eastern as well as the southern hemispheres, but in 1800 the Antipodes Islands, just over 700 kilometres south-east of NZ, were so named by British seamen because they were diametrically opposite Greenwich; in the nineteenth century 'Antipodes', 'Antipodean' and other derivatives were applied more generally to Australia and NZ, again from a British perspective. The Christmas pantomimes of Australian colonial playwrights sometimes showed a consciousness of the Antipodes, e.g. Garnet Walch's *Hey Diddle Diddle* (1879) has as characters the Longest Day and the Shortest Night, 'subject to reverse in the Antipodes'; *The Antipodean* was an illustrated annual published in Melbourne 1893, 1895, 1897. A popular colloquialism derived from the concept of Antipodes is 'down under' (q.v.); Geoffrey Dutton's book of poems *Antipodes in Shoes* (1958) derives its title from a line in Andrew Marvell's poetry.

Antipodes: A North American Journal of Australian Literature,

established in 1987 with Robert Ross as editor is the official journal of AAALS, the American Association of Australian Literary Studies. Published twice a year, it is supported in part by the Literature Board of the Australia Council and the Information and Cultural Relations Branch of the Department of Foreign Affairs and Trade. Each issue contains a selection of previously unpublished poetry and fiction by both acclaimed and new Australian writers. Interviews with writers are also regularly published. *Antipodes* has an extensive book reviews section and a comprehensive bibliography of Australian writing as well as critical essays on topics such as 'Australian/American Literary Connections', 'Australian Literature in an International Context' and 'Women's Writing in Australia'.

Antithesis, a journal of contemporary theory, criticism and creative writing produced by postgraduate students in English at the University of Melbourne, was first published in August 1987, edited by Michelle de Kretser, Helene Nevola and Sara White.

Anzac, originally an acronym, has become one of the words most closely identified with Australia. It originated during the First World War, when the Cairo headquarters of General William Birdwood (later Baron Anzac and Totnes) became cluttered with dispatch boxes bearing the words 'Australia and New Zealand Army Corps'; this title was abbreviated to 'A&NZAC' when an administrative stamp was cut which became known as the Anzac stamp. Soon after – and definitely by January 1915 – 'Anzac' was used as a planning code word suggested to, and adopted by, Birdwood to describe the Australian forces, which he commanded. Early in the Gallipoli (q.v.) campaign, Birdwood named the cove where the first landings of Australian troops took place, Anzac Cove; in time any

Australian or NZ soldier who served at Gallipoli became known as an Anzac, while the Anzacs came to refer, as in Patsy Adam-Smith's *The Anzacs* (1978), to Australian troops serving anywhere in the First World War. The term itself has been widely used in Australian writing. Emily Coungeau's fantasy play *Princess Mona* (?1916) has Mona wearing a coronet forming the letters Anzac, which is a present from her five sons who have died in the war; the last scene has her pronounce Anzac as the name of the new capital city of Australia. Soldier poets and memoirists have frequently adopted Anzac as a pseudonym (e.g. R.W. Jones, J.P. O'Donnell) or used it in the titles of their works (e.g. *An Anzac Areopagus and Other Verses* (1923) by George Black, and *Five Months at Anzac . . .* (1916) by J.L. Beeston). War correspondent and historian C.E.W. Bean (q.v.), who compiled *The Anzac Book: Written and Illustrated in Gallipoli by the Men of Anzac* (1916), titled the first two volumes of the history of Australia's role in the First World War *The Story of Anzac* (1921, 1924) and his one-volume abridgement of that history *Anzac to Amiens* (1946). The Anzac experience and its treatment form a significant part of Australian war literature (q.v.). Phrases such as the 'Anzac spirit' and the 'Anzac tradition' have become synonymous with courage, loyalty, mateship, and to a lesser degree with the rugged and cheerful insouciance and individualism said to be characteristic of the Australian soldier. By contrast, the recent ironic use (during and since the Second World War) of the phrase 'big, bronzed Anzac' indicates a debunking of the original concept of the physical and mental excellence of the average Australian male. Anzac Day (25 April) has been a public holiday in Australia and NZ since about 1920 and falls on the anniversary of the inception with the First landing at Gallipoli in 1915; from its unofficial inception in 1916 until the end of the Second World War, its focus was Gallipoli itself and the First World War. It has since become the annual day of remembrance for those who participated in all the conflicts in which Australia has been involved. Anzac Day and its place in the Australian tradition are examined in Alan Seymour's play *The One Day of the Year* (q.v., 1962). See also Gallipoli.

Anzac Muster, An (1915) is a collection of soldiers' tales of the Gallipoli campaign by 'William Baylebridge' (q.v.). Using the Chaucerian device of a band of story-tellers, 'Baylebridge' has nine Gallipoli veterans each tell three tales, one tale each on three successive Saturday night gatherings on a Queensland cattle station. 'Baylebridge's' tales are markedly different from the usual boisterous Australian 'digger' stories.

APAIS, see **Australian Public Affairs Information Service**

Applestealers (1974), selected and introduced by Robert Kenny and Colin Talbot (qq.v.), is a collection of what was termed the 'New Australian Poetry' (q.v.). In the editors' prefaces the volume is said to represent 'what can be considered a renaissance in Australian poetry, which took place from about 1968'. In addition to the selection of poetry, *Applestealers* includes notes on the Poetry Workshops at La Mama (q.v.); a statement on the origin and development of 'the new poetry in Australia' movement by Kris Hemensley (q.v.); and a chronological check-list of the mini magazines of the period 1968–71, with brief notes on those poetry magazines extant in 1974.

ARABANOO was the first Aborigine captured by Captain Arthur Phillip as an experiment in learning the language of the Aborigines and ultimately winning their confidence. Taken at Manly Cove on 31 December 1788, Arabanoo grew reconciled to his captivity and became a celebrity in the settlement. He died of smallpox in May 1789. An account of his activities is in Watkin Tench's *A Complete Account of the Settlement at Port Jackson* (1792). He is fictionally represented in Eleanor Dark's *The Timeless Land* (1941).

Arabin: Or, the Adventures of a Colonist in New South Wales (1845), the first novel of Thomas McCombie (q.v.), is a combination of melodramatic romance and moral tale illustrating the rewards of perseverance and patient industry in the pioneering situation. The humble-born, hard-working Godfrey Arabin wins prosperity and a worthy bride, but the highborn, lazy, dissolute Willis meets a violent end. Although fictional, *Arabin* belongs to the emigrant guidebook literature popular at the time. More a treatise on colonisation than a novel, it discusses the mysterious grandeur of the bush, the concept of the bushman and the worth of the colonial-bred or currency (q.v.) inhabitant *vis-à-vis* the aristocratic immigrant. Its final chapter, 'An Essay on the Aborigines', mixes description of the lifestyle of the Blacks with questions about the morality of their treatment by White society. A stage adaptation of *Arabin* by J.M. McLachlan, titled 'Arabin: Or, the Adventures of a Settler', was presented in Sydney in 1849.

ARCHER Family included the brothers Charles (1813–62), John (1814–57), David (1816–1900), William (1818–96), Archibald (1820–1902), Thomas (1823–1905) and Colin (1832–1921), who were all involved in pioneering pastoral ventures in northern Queensland in the decades 1840–70. Thomas, who was agent-general for the State during most of the period 1872–90, published pamphlets on the history, resources and prospects of Queensland (1881, 1882) and an autobiography, *Recollections of a Rambling Life* (1897), which describes his pioneering experiences in Australia and his adventures on the Californian goldfields. *Recollections of a Rambling Life* was reprinted in 1988 with additional chapters by Murdoch Wales dealing with Thomas's subsequent life after about 1852, the period covered by the original *Recollections*. His son was William (1856–1924), a leading London dramatist, critic, and translator of Ibsen's plays.

ARCHER, Robyn (1948–) was born in Adelaide, the daughter of Lykke Smith, a club entertainer and comedian. A television personality at the age of 15,

Archer graduated from Adelaide University and worked as a secondary schoolteacher before becoming a full-time actor, singer, writer and musician. Well known as an interpreter of Bertolt Brecht's songs, she has also produced two albums of her own songs, many of which pithily express her strong feminist and political convictions. She has written two plays, 'Il Magnifico', which deals with Lorenzo de Medici, and 'The Conquest of Carmen Miranda', and numerous cabaret shows which she has performed with outstanding success. These include 'Kold Komfort Kaffee', 'Side Show Alley', 'Tonight: Lola Blau', 'Robyn Archer at Large', 'A Star is Torn', 'Le Chat Noir', 'Cafe Fledermaus', and 'A Pack of Women'. 'A Star is Torn' is her best-known show; performed in Australia from 1979 and in London 1982–83, it is a one-woman interpretation of thirteen women singers as diverse as Janis Joplin, Bessie Smith, Judy Garland, Billie Holiday and Edith Piaf. Archer has produced books based on her shows, *The Pack of Women* (1986, with Diana Simmonds), *A Star is Torn* (1986) and *Cafe Fledermaus* (1990). She has also published a children's book, *Mrs Bottle Burps* (1983).

ARCHIBALD, J.F. (1856–1919), was born near Geelong, Victoria, the son of an Irish-born policeman; baptised John Feltham Archibald, he adopted the Christian names Jules François in the 1870s and revised his family history in accord with his Francophilia. He was educated in Warrnambool, where as a youth he became an apprentice in the printing trade. His first paragraphs were written for the *Hamilton Spectator* and the *Port Fairy Gazette* and in 1875 he left for Melbourne to try journalism. Disappointed in his hopes of securing a position on the *Argus* he became a public servant from 1876 until he was retrenched early in 1878, when he went to Queensland for a clerkship in an engineering firm. During his time there he had a few months on the Palmer River diggings; it was his 'one real experience of Australian frontier life' (Sylvia Lawson) and imbued him with a deep concern for the bush worker, the 'lone hand' who was central to the bush ethos of the *Bulletin* (q.v.) under his editorship.

In 1879 Archibald went to Sydney where he worked for the *Evening News* and *Hansard*. In 1880, with John Haynes (q.v.), he started the journal which eventually became nationally famous as the radical *Bulletin*. The first issue in January 1880 was dominated by Archibald's account of the hanging of the Wantabadgery bushrangers and established the reformist zeal of the journal. After a stormy first year, in which the *Bulletin's* survival was constantly threatened, Archibald and Haynes lost control of the journal to W.H. Traill (q.v.) although, after spending six weeks in Darlinghurst gaol over a libel action, they returned as salaried staff and from 1883 shared joint ownership with Traill when the Bulletin Newspaper Company was constituted. In the same year Archibald paid his only visit to England, where he struggled for a living after his bank failed. What he saw confirmed the Anglophobia which was the obverse of his republican nationalism and which found expression not only in the *Bulletin's* boycott of the 1888 centenary of settlement but also in Archibald's willingness – against his natural inclination for the 'boiled-down' contribution – to serialise F.J. Donohue's and 'Price Warung's revisionist writings about Australia's convict past.

In 1886 Traill left with the *Bulletin* on a sound footing, and thus began the decade and a half in which Archibald put his stamp on the journal. As a journalist he had several great gifts, not the least of which was his ability to recognise talent in others: through him William Macleod, James Edmond and A.G. Stephens (qq.v.) were enticed on to the staff and given the freedom to make their individual contributions to the *Bulletin's* success. Second, he encouraged writers and artists throughout Australia: although the achievements of Stephens as literary editor cannot be overlooked, it was Archibald, a good judge of folk-writing, who 'discovered' Henry Lawson, A.B. Paterson, 'Louis' Becke, 'Price Warung' and others, and who showed in letters and interviews and in the famous correspondence column that the journal was interested in all *Bulletin* contributors and cared about their welfare. His third great gift was as a sub-editor, a 'soler and heeler' of paragraphs who did much to establish the characteristic tone of the *Bulletin*, the brightness and sharpness of its prose in caption, column and leader. As editor Archibald worked obsessively, neglecting his wife Rose, whom he had married in 1885. After 1900 his nervous energy exhausted itself and in 1903 Edmond became editor of the *Bulletin* while Archibald busied himself planning the monthly *Lone Hand*. In 1906 he had a spectacular mental collapse and was admitted to Callan Park Asylum; he was finally discharged, fully recovered, in 1910. He sold his interest in the *Bulletin* in 1914 to S.H. Prior although just before his death in 1919 he returned to journalism to help establish the fledgeling *Smith's Weekly* (q.v.), which had some of the impact on the Australian reading public in the 1920s and 1930s that the *Bulletin* had had in the 1890s. His estate of nearly £90 000 provided Sydney with the Archibald Fountain in Hyde Park; Australian art with the Archibald Prize; and Australian journalism with a massive contribution to the benevolent fund of the Australian Journalists' Association. Sylvia Lawson's incisive study of Archibald and the *Bulletin, The Archibald Paradox*, which is also a significant cultural study, was published in 1983; it won the NSW Premier's Award for non-fiction.

ARDEN, George (?1820–54) arrived in Australia from England in 1838, settled in Melbourne, and at the age of 18 launched the weekly *Port Phillip Gazette*. He is credited with having written the first poem on Melbourne and having published (with Thomas Strode) in 1840, *Latest Information with Regard to Australia Felix*, the first book published in Melbourne. In 1843 he also published the short-lived (two monthly issues) *Arden's Sydney Magazine of Politics and General Literature* with articles on general, local and literary topics.

Arena (1), a small Melbourne weekly magazine carrying short fiction and sketches together with literary and theatrical reviews (Catherine Helen Spence was a contributor), was published 1900–4 and was edited by C.H. Chomley. In its final year of publication it was titled *Arena-Sun*.

Arena (2), a Victorian Marxist quarterly journal of criticism and discussion, was published 1963–92. It occasionally published articles on literature and aesthetic theory.

Arena Magazine, published initially in October 1992 and with a planned six issues annually, is produced by the editors of *Arena* (2) which ceased publication with its hundredth issue. *Arena Journal*, a twice-yearly internationally oriented scholarly periodical, is also published by *Arena* (2) editors. Both magazine and journal are committed to the Left's vision of a better world.

ARGLES, Theodore Emile ('The Pilgrim', 'Harold Grey') (?1851–86), born London, was well known in Sydney, as both writer and bohemian, in the later 1870s and early 1880s. Under several pseudonyms (e.g. 'Harold Grey', 'A (The) Pilgrim', 'The Moocher') he wrote sensational and satiric prose and verse about low-life Sydney and other subjects. In 1877 eight issues of the *Pilgrim*, his satiric periodical pamphlet, were published; it contained a sequence of articles on 'Sydney Cafés after Midnight'. The *Pilgrim* was revived intermittently in 1878 in two series, *Another Pilgrim* (nine issues) and the *Pilgrim* (nine issues, although the first issue was titled *Harold Grey's Sensational Weekly Pamphlet*). The second 1878 series satirised John Stanley James. In 1879 Argles edited *Common Cause* in Adelaide, published one issue of a Melbourne *Pilgrim*, and wrote a reply to an anonymous satire of him, titled *Pilgrim: A Weakly Sensational Pamphlet*. Among his other publications were *Sum Punkins* (1878), a series of poems and stories ostensibly read by the patients and staff of a Sydney asylum as they gather together over Christmas; the autobiographical *My Unnatural Life* (1878); *Scenes in Sydney by Day and Night* (?1878); and the verse satire *The Devil in Sydney* (1878), whose targets included several prominent journalists. Employed on the staff of the *Evening News*, Argles contributed spicy society gossip (some of which proved libellous), theatrical criticism and topical verse to the early *Bulletin*. His legendary escapades with Victor Daley included one in which they ran foul of the *Bulletin's* editor, W.H. Traill, after each appeared in turn in Traill's office to ask for money to pay for the other's funeral.

Argus, a Melbourne daily newspaper published 1846–1957, was described by R.E.N. Twopeny in *Town Life in Australia* (1883) as 'the best daily paper published out of England'. Among the literary identities associated with it were Marcus Clarke, Charles de Boos and John Stanley James ('The Vagabond'), whose *Vagabond Papers*, on Melbourne's social and public life, were first published in the *Argus* in 1876. The great rival of the *Age*, the *Argus* is represented in Henry Kingsley's *The Hillyars and the Burtons* (1865) as the *Palmerston Sentinel*; W.M. Akhurst's 1855 pantomime,

The Magician's Daughter, has a scene depicting the *Argus* office; and Fergus Hume's *The Mystery of a Hansom Cab* (1886) opens with an *Argus* murder report. Before its demise in 1957 the *Argus* carried a literary section as part of its weekend review. John Feely compiled a five-volume index to the *Argus* for 1846–59 (1942–65); the newspaper also published a half-yearly index 1910–49. Among early proprietors of the *Argus* was Edward Wilson (q.v.); George Higinbotham edited the newspaper 1856–59, as did F.W. Haddon 1867–98 and Sir Edward Cunningham 1906–28. Notable staff or contributors included Julian Howard Ashton, Hugh Buggy, J.F. Hogan, Sir Walter Murdoch, and Frederick Sinnett.

ARMOUR, John (1889–1954), born Warragul, Victoria, served with the Australian Inland Mission (1918–20) and had a long and distinguished career in the Presbyterian ministry in Queensland, Victoria and NSW. His publications include *The Spell of the Inland* (1923), a descriptive narrative of life in Central Australia; *Burning Air* (1928), an adventure story set also in Central Australia; *Century Sandy* (1936, revised in 1938 as *The Road to El Dorado*); and *The Story of Christianity* (1952).

ARMSTRONG, Millicent (1888–1973), born Sydney, graduated with first-class honours in English from the University of Sydney, before serving as a nurse in France during the First World War. She was awarded the Croix de Guerre for her bravery in rescuing soldiers under fire in 1918. She began to write and to stage plays during the war as an entertainment for the wounded. On her return she took up a farming block at Gunning, NSW, in the Returned Soldiers' Settlement Scheme. Her play *Drought* (1934), possibly written out of her experience on the land and performed in London, won a prize in an international drama competition in 1934, as well as the 1923 Rupert Brooke Prize. *At Dusk* was published in *Best Australian One-Act Plays* (1937). Her unpublished plays include 'Fire' (1923), which won a *Daily Telegraph* drama competition prize, 'Nina' (1936), 'Windward' (1937) and 'The Moon Sets' (1958); *Thomas* and *Penny Dreadful* were published in 1958 (together with *Drought*) in a volume titled *Plays in One Act*.

'Army of the Rear, The' is, like 'Faces in the Street', one of the early Henry Lawson (q.v.) poems which established his reputation as radical writer; it was first published in the *Bulletin* in 1888 as 'Song of the Outcasts' and under its better-known title in 1910. 'The Army of the Rear' is the legion of the poor and the outcasts of society, whom Lawson images marching towards revolution at the end of the poem.

Arna, the journal of the University of Sydney Arts Society, began in 1918 and appeared irregularly; it was incorporated into *New Literature Review* (q.v.) in 1975. Several subsequently well-known writers contributed to *Arna*, including A.D. Hope, Muir Holburn, Charles Higham, Vincent Buckley, Bernard Smith, John Croyston, Bruce Beaver, Donald Horne, Harold

Stewart, James McAuley, Geoffrey Lehmann, Les Murray and Clive James.

ARNEIL, Stan, see **War Literature**

ARNOLD, Josie (1941–), born Walwa, Victoria, and educated at the University of Melbourne, teaches at the Swinburne Institute of Technology and has written numerous English textbooks. She has published an autobiography, *Mother Superior, Woman Inferior* (1985), which describes the impact on her childhood of Catholicism and the wartime death of her father, and has edited with Lurline Stuart, *Letters Home 1939–1945* (1987), a collection of correspondence by Australian men and women serving overseas in the Second World War. As Josie Stainsby, she published a collection of verse in 1982, *Love Laughing Among the Trees*.

ARNOLD, Thomas (1823–1900), second son of Thomas Arnold, the great English headmaster, and brother of the poet Matthew Arnold, emigrated to NZ in 1848 and then went to Hobart in 1850, where he was appointed inspector of schools for Van Diemen's Land. In 1850 he married Julia Sorell, granddaughter of Colonel William Sorell, Lieutenant-Governor of Van Diemen's Land 1817–1823. Following considerable and arduous labours for education in the colony (1850–56) Arnold returned to England, ultimately filling the Chair of English Language and Literature at University College, Dublin (1882). Among his many publications was a book of reminiscences, *Passages in a Wandering Life* (1900), which gives a picture of life in Van Diemen's Land in the 1850s. Of the three surviving children born to the Arnolds during their time in Australia, the eldest, Mary Augusta, born in 1851, was to win fame as the novelist, Mrs Humphrey Ward. A second daughter, Julia Frances, born in England, married Leonard Huxley and became the mother of Julian and Aldous. Arnold's experiences during this period are described in P.A. Howell's *Thomas Arnold the Younger in Van Diemen's Land* (1964).

ARONSON, Linda (1950–), born London, has worked in Sydney since 1973 as a professional writer for stage, film, radio and television and as scriptwriting consultant at the Australian Film and Television School. She has written stage plays, 'Lonely for My Garden' (1975), *The Fall Guy* (1976, also published in *Theatre-Australia*, 1977), 'Elegy for a Boy Musician' (1977), 'Endangered Species' (1979), 'Invitation to Eternity' (1982), *Reginka's Lesson* (1989), *Dinkum Assorted* (1989) and 'A Night with Robinson Crusoe' (1990); radio plays, 'Cafe in a Side Street' (1980, adapted from 'Lonely for My Garden') and 'Closing Down'; and film scripts, *Kostas* (1978, screened at Cannes in 1980) and *Until It's Over* (1981). *Reginka's Lesson* won the Sydney Theatre Company's Short Play competition in 1985 and the Australian Elizabethan Theatre Trust Bicentennial Play Award in 1986. Aronson has also won two Awgies for her writing for film.

Around the Boree Log and Other Verses (1921) by 'John O'Brien' (q.v.) is a book of ballad-like poems dealing mainly with the vicissitudes of Irish-Australian Catholic rural communities. The characteristics of good nature, obstinacy and religious faith traditionally associated with the Irish permeate such well-known and popular verses as 'The Old Bush School', 'Ten Little Steps and Stairs', 'Tangmalangaloo', 'At Casey's after Mass', and 'Said Hanrahan' (q.v.).

Arrow, see ***Dead Bird***

Art in Australia, published quarterly in Sydney from 1916 to 1942, with the exception of 1930 when it was published six times, appeared in four series, 1916–21, 1922, 1922–40, 1941–42. Founded by Sydney Ure Smith and edited initially by him and Bertram Stevens, then Leon Gellert, *Art in Australia* was the leading journal on art, music and literature during its existence, attracting significant contributions from the leading cultural figures of the day, e.g. Norman, Lionel and Jack Lindsay, Kenneth Slessor, A.G. Stephens, Katharine Susannah Prichard, Hugh McCrae, Leslie Rees, Zora Cross and Mary Gilmore. Its numerous special numbers featured the work of, for example, Hans Heysen, Lionel Lindsay, Daryl Lindsay, George Finey, Hugh McCrae and Thea Proctor.

ARTHUR, Sir George (1784–1854), born Plymouth, England, was an army officer before becoming a colonial administrator, serving as lieutenant-governor of Van Diemen's Land (1824–36) and Upper Canada (1837–41) and as governor of Bombay (1842–46). Highly efficient and authoritarian, Arthur viewed Van Diemen's Land as an 'Extensive Gaol to the Empire' where strict conditions should apply. He established the secondary punishment centre at Port Arthur (q.v.), from which John Rex escapes in *His Natural Life*, refined the system of assignment (see Transportation), and defended his methods in two pamphlets, *Observations upon Secondary Punishment* (1833) and *Defence of Transportation* (1834) (both written in reply to Richard Whately), and in voluminous dispatches, some of which are included in the *Historical Records of Australia* (q.v.).

The severity of Arthur's views meant that he had little time for civil liberties and that almost from the day of his arrival he met opposition from some free settlers and most pressmen. He fought strenuously to control the press by prosecution and legislation, introducing licensing provisions in 1827, which were disallowed in England in 1828; among his opponents were Andrew Bent, Robert Murray, Henry Melville, Gilbert Robertson, and Evan Henry Thomas (qq.v.). Apart from the attacks in the contemporary press, there are unflattering portraits of Arthur in David Burn's play *The Bushrangers* (q.v.), which was probably why Burn excluded it from his *Plays and Fugitive Pieces* (1842); in Henry Melville's *The History of the Island of Van Diemen's Land* (1835); in 'Price Warung's' story 'A Day with Governor Arthur' (*Tales of the Old Regime*,

1897); in the broadsides which celebrated Arthur's recall; and in some of the reminiscences of the Canadian exiles transported to Van Diemen's Land after the rebellions of 1837–38 (e.g. Caleb Lyon called him 'the bloody Robespierre of the Revolution'). Other works in which Arthur appears (not always specifically identified) include Roy Bridges's *By His Excellency's Command* (1910); J.B. Cooper's *Leg-Bail* (1918); Horace B. Pithouse's *The Luck of 1825* (1922); *The Hermit in Van Diemen's Land* (1830); *Quintus Servinton* (1831) by Henry Savery, whose lenient treatment by Arthur was criticised; and Catherine Shepherd's radio play 'Arthur of Van Diemen's Land', broadcast on ABC radio in the 1940s. Among studies of Arthur, A.G.L. Shaw's *Sir George Arthur* (1980) is a comprehensive biography, and E. Morris Miller's *Pressmen and Governors* (1952), Joan Woodberry's *Andrew Bent and the Freedom of the Press in Tasmania* (1972) and James Bonwick's *Early Struggles of the Australian Press* (1890) discuss his relationship with the press.

Artlook, a monthly newsletter published 1975–83 by a Perth (WA) group known as the Nine Club, was founded and edited by Helen Weller. Intended as a means of disseminating information and opinions on the arts in WA, it contained critical reviews and articles, as well as short stories and poetry.

Arts, the journal of the Sydney University Arts Association, appeared for three issues in 1956. In 1958 it recommended publication, with the subtitle *Proceedings of the Sydney University Arts Association*, which was changed to *Journal of the Sydney University Arts Association* in 1967.

Arts Council of Australia is an organisation linking nine bodies which operate within the area of community arts. The six Australian States, the ACT and the Northern Territory each has an autonomous arts council (e.g. the Queensland Arts Council; the Arts Council of Australia, Tasmania Division) which is represented on the board of a federal Arts Council of Australia. This body is also autonomous and in 1978–83 was the largest client of the Community Arts Board (q.v.) of the Australia Council. In those years the Community Arts Board's allocation to the Arts Council of Australia was distributed to the federal division, mainly for national and co-ordinating activities, and to the State and territory organisations, which are also funded from the respective State governments and from private sources. In 1983 a new policy was announced which increased decentralisation and provided for direct Community Arts Board allocations to the State and territory organisations. The State Arts Councils have numerous regional branches (more than 300 in 1994).

The various Arts Councils traditionally have helped to provide performing arts experiences for schools and for communities outside metropolitan centres; in recent years exhibitions, festivals, summer schools and workshops have more regularly come within their ambit. The Arts Council movement had its origin in the Council for the Encouragement of Music and the Arts (CEMA), modelled on an equivalent British organisation and formed in 1943 by the singer Dorothy Helmrich; it was centred in NSW, where an arts council, sometimes called the Arts Council of Australia in the 1950s, was established in 1946. Arts Councils were formed soon after in some other States and territories (e.g. SA in 1946, Tasmania in 1951), but lack of adequate funding prevented development until the 1960s. In 1966 the Arts Council of Australia, first proposed in the 1940s, was established, receiving its first funds from the Australian Council for the Arts (q.v.) in 1969. In 1973 the last State or territory arts council, the WA Arts Council, was established, following those in Victoria (1971), the Northern Territory (1967), SA (reformed in 1965 after lapsing in 1952), ACT (reformed 1962 after lapsing in 1952), and Queensland (1961).

ASCHE, Oscar (1871–1936), actor, producer, manager and writer, was one of the leading Australian theatrical personalities of the early decades of the twentieth century. Born Geelong, Victoria, Asche studied acting in Norway and London, made his stage debut in London in 1893, became a notable Shakespearean actor and with his wife Lily Brayton, with whom he formed the Asche-Brayton Company, toured Australia on two occasions (1909–10, 1912–13). Brayton refused to join him on his third tour of Australasia 1922–24, which recaptured some of the successes of his previous tours but ended abruptly after his contract with J.C. Williamson's was terminated. Two of Asche's greatest successes were *Chu Chin Chow* (1921), his only published play, which ran for a record five-year season from 1916, and *The Maid of the Mountains*, (1917), which he produced. He wrote two novels, *The Saga of Hans Hansen* (1930) and *The Joss Sticks of Chung* (1930), and an autobiography (1929).

ASHBOLT, Allan (1921–), born Melbourne, has had a wide-ranging career in radio, television and political journalism. He came into prominence in 1946 as co-founder, with the actor Peter Finch, of the Mercury Theatre, Sydney. From 1951 to 1957 he was drama critic and book reviewer for the *Sydney Morning Herald*. In his career with the ABC (1954–77) he was a talks and documentary producer, foreign correspondent and head of special projects. His publications include *An American Experience* (1966), an unsparingly critical assessment of such features of American life and government as the segregation of society by race, religion and money, the public scandals, organised crime, imbalance of the American economy, and American foreign policy; and *An Australian Experience: Words from the Vietnam Years* (1974), which is an extended commentary on war and racism, nationalism and imperialism, conscription and conscience, socialism and class consciousness, all in an Australian context.

ASHTON, Julian Howard (1877–1964), the artist, born in London, son of Julian Rossi Ashton (q.v.), accompanied his parents to Australia in 1878. Following a liberal education in music, art and literature, he turned to journalism as a career although he published short fiction in the *Bulletin* under the pseudonym 'Hassan' from 1904 onwards. Over many years he was a general reporter, music critic and literary and art reviewer on the *Sydney Morning Herald, Argus*, Sydney *Sun, Sunday Sun* and *Guardian* and *Art in Australia*, rising eventually to be editor of the *Sun* in 1924. From 1926 he reverted to associate editor, which allowed him to resume his literary and art criticism and leader-writing. He won the Sydney sesquicentenary prize for landscape painting in 1938 and was president of the Royal Art Society, 1940–45.

ASHTON, Julian Rossi (1851–1942), born Surrey, England, came to Australia with his wife Eliza Ann Pugh and son Julian Howard Ashton (q.v.) in 1878 to work as an illustrator on David Syme's *Illustrated Australian News*. In 1881 he joined the *Australasian Sketcher* and in 1883 moved to Sydney to work on the *Picturesque Atlas of Australasia* and later on the *Bulletin*. An active professional artist, Ashton was president of the Art Society of New South Wales (1887–92) and president of the Society of Artists (1897–98), the two organisations amalgamating in 1903 to become the Royal Art Society of New South Wales. His own art school, which was variously known as the Sydney Art School and (from 1935) the Julian Ashton Art School, enjoyed a considerable reputation, numbering among its students the later well-known artists Elioth Gruner, J. J. Hilder, Sydney Ure Smith and William Dobell. A gifted teacher and artist, Ashton's achievements included the painting *Evening, Merri Creek* (1882), claimed by him to be the first *plein air* painting done in Australia. He won the Sydney sesquicentenary prize for a watercolour in 1938; painted numerous portraits of prominent Australians (e.g. Sir Henry Parkes); was awarded the Society of Artists' Medal for distinguished services to Australian art in 1924; and was made CBE in 1930. He contributed numerous articles to *Art in Australia* and published his reminiscences, *Now Came Still Evening On*, in 1941. *The Julian Ashton Book* was published in his honour in 1920.

Aspect: Art and Literature, a Sydney magazine edited since its inception by Rudi Krausmann (q.v.), was published 1975–89. It contained interviews, prose, poetry, articles and comments on art and literature.

Aspinall, Arvie is the central character in Henry Lawson's (q.v.) first major series of stories, written in 1892. The best-known story in the sequence is 'Arvie Aspinall's Alarm Clock', in which Arvie, who has been given an alarm clock so that he can get to work on time at Grinder Brothers railway coach factory, does not hear the alarm go off because he has died of a fever during the night. The other stories in the sequence, which depict the squalor and misery of the urban poor, are 'Two Boys at Grinder Bros', in which friendship grows between the sensitive Arvie and the larrikin of the shed, Bill Anderson, after it is discovered that they have both lived in the tenements of Jones's Alley; 'A Visit of Condolence', in which Bill visits the Aspinall home, discovers Arvie's death and shows a rough humanity to the bereaved mother; and 'Jones's Alley', in which Bill, meeting Mrs Aspinall some years later after she has lost a court case against her slum landlord, helps her smuggle her possessions at night out of the rented home. Lawson's 'A Fragment of Autobiography' and other sources reveal that the Aspinall stories were largely informed by his experiences at Hudson Brothers coach factory in the 1880s. The name Aspinall, however, came from a family living at New Pipeclay twenty years before: the death of the 9-year-old Thomas Aspinall, who fell down a mine shaft in 1865, was a source for 'His Father's Mate'. In *While the Billy Boils* (1896), which includes three stories from the city sequence, Arvie Aspinall is the first of the children marked present at the bush school in 'An Echo from the Old Bark School'.

Association for Commonwealth Language and Literature Studies (usually known by its acronym, ACLALS) aims to encourage and stimulate the writing, reading and study of what was formerly known as Commonwealth literature (i.e. new literatures in English). An Association whose widespread membership mainly comprises teachers and writers, ACLALS was the brainchild of A.N. Jeffares, professor of English at the University of Adelaide 1951–56 and later at the Universities of Leeds and Stirling; it was formally constituted during a Commonwealth literature conference held at the University of Leeds in 1964. From 1968 the chairmanship of ACLALS and the editorship of the *ACLALS Bulletin* (1965–), which has evolved from a newsletter into primarily a critical journal, became rotating offices; since 1971 they have been located for three-year terms in the region hosting the ACLALS conference at the end of that triennial period. The regionalisation of ACLALS has been further consolidated by the establishment of branch organisations, the chairman of each having membership of the ACLALS executive. In 1971 the European branch (EACLALS) was established, followed by organisations in Canada (CACLALS) in 1972; the South Pacific (SPACLALS) in 1975; and others in India, the West Indies and elsewhere, each with the appropriate cacophonous acronym. The regional organisations have held regular meetings and conferences and have published bulletins such as EACLALS's *Commonwealth Newsletter*, later the journal *Kunapipi* (1979–) and SPACLALS's *Span* (1975–). The conference volumes and other publications of ACLALS and its constituent organisations represent an impressive body of critical writing in which Australian literature has been placed in a context of new literatures in English; ACLALS has also encouraged Commonwealth writers through the provision of visiting fellowships, literary competitions and the like. In 1975–81 SPACLALS was centred at the University of Queensland; other Australian universities with an active interest in Commonwealth literature/new literatures in English include Flinders University, where the Centre for Research in the New Literatures in English (1977–) produces the *CRNLE*

Reviews Journal and organises conferences which accommodate Australian topics; Macquarie University, where a New Literatures in English unit was established in 1982; and the University of Wollongong, where the New Literatures Centre produces *New Literatures Review*. The *Journal of Commonwealth Literature* arose from the Leeds interest in Commonwealth literature and has been published since 1965; its annual bibliography includes an Australian section which complements the *Australian Literary Studies* bibliography and it also regularly publishes criticism on Australian literature. Another overseas journal on new literatures in English in which Australian literature is regularly discussed is *World Literature Written in English* (*WLWE*, 1967–).

Association for the Study of Australian Literature (ASAL), was founded in 1977 and formally constituted at its inaugural conference at Monash University in May 1978; its patrons are A.D. Hope and Judith Wright (qq.v.) and its life members, to 1992, are C.B. Christesen, Mary Lord, Judith Wright, Thea Astley, Peter Cowan, Rosemary Dobson, Gwen Harwood, Eric Irvin, Ken Stewart, Julian Croft and Ian McLaren. The Association, which has a nationwide and overseas membership, includes among its aims the study and encouragement of Australian literature and literary culture, particularly through the interaction of Australian writers with teachers and students. Among its activities are the holding of a yearly conference and the publication of a newsletter, *Notes & Furphies* (q.v.). ASAL has incorporated the Australian Literature Society (q.v.) and now administers the ALS Gold Medal, as well as the Walter McRae Russell, the Mary Gilmore and the A.A. Phillips Awards. Among the important publications it has sponsored are *The Oxford Literary Guide to Australia* (1987, revised 1993), the *Penguin New Literary History of Australia* (1988) and the *Macquarie Dictionary of Australian Quotations* (1990).

ASTLEY, Thea (1925–), born Brisbane, was educated at the University of Queensland and taught in schools in Queensland and NSW until 1967, and at Macquarie University, Sydney, 1968–80. Her published works include the novels *Girl with a Monkey* (1958), *A Descant for Gossips* (1960, dramatised for ABC television in 1983), *The Well Dressed Explorer* (q.v., 1962), *The Slow Natives* (q.v., 1965, winner of the Moomba Award), *A Boat Load of Home Folk* (1968), *The Acolyte* (q.v., 1972), *A Kindness Cup* (1974), *An Item from the Late News* (1982), *Beachmasters* (1985, winner of the Australian Literature Society Gold Medal), *It's Raining in Mango* (1988, winner of the inaugural Steele Rudd prize and of the Fellowship of Australian Writers Award), and *Reaching Tin River* (1990); and the collection of short stories *Hunting the Wild Pineapple* (1979). She has also published two linked novellas, *Vanishing Points* (1992); some uncollected verse and short stories; a critical study, *Three Australian Writers* (1979); and edited an anthology of short stories (1971). Her other prizes include the Miles Franklin Award on three occasions (for *The Well Dressed Explorer*, *The Slow Natives* and *The Acolyte*), the *Age* Book

of the Year Award in 1975 (for *A Kindness Cup*), and the Townsville Foundation for Australian Literary Studies Award (for *Hunting the Wild Pineapple*). In 1989 she won the Patrick White Award, in 1990 a NSW State Literary Award; she was made AO in 1992, having been previously made AM, and has been granted an Hon D.Litt by Queensland University.

Astley's first novel appeared a decade before women writers began to make a large impact on Australian writing and two decades before the efflorescence of the 1980s. This, combined with her sceptical view – specifically of the condition of Australian women in the context of a general scepticism about the human potential for good, comparable in bleakness to Barbara Baynton's – has set her apart to some extent. Notwithstanding her numerous awards and acknowledged position as a significant and powerful senior writer, she is sometimes perceived as less of a committed feminist than some of her younger colleagues. Astley herself sees the difference as one of generational change, in that her novels reflect pre-feminist cultural attitudes to women as lacking the interest and adult seriousness of men. Another factor in her comparative neglect may have been her idiosyncratic, image-encrusted style, although Astley has stressed that like Gerard Manley Hopkins she uses metaphors in an attempt 'to get to the exact nature of something . . . to get at the essence of a thing'. The complexities of her ambivalent relationship with northern Queensland and with Catholicism, both of which are strongly present in her work, colour her distinctive apprehension of the contemporary Australian social environment. No longer a practising Catholic, she describes herself as grateful for the experience of growing up in the Catholic Church which 'stimulates the metaphor glands, heightens the sense of suffering, gives a meaning to guilt'. Characteristically witty, with a keen eye for egoistic pretension and exploitation and a rich talent for social comedy, she frequently writes from the point of view of the vulnerable misfit, the unspectacular outsider, destined if not for tragedy then at least for failure. For the self-conscious, hyperperceptive individuals on whom she concentrates, life is necessarily isolated, an unequal, doomed, tragi-comic struggle for identity and integrity. From Elsie Ford of *Girl with a Monkey* to Paul Vesper of *The Acolyte*, to Belle of *Reaching Tin River*, she develops related but increasingly complex studies of desperate attempts to preserve the self in the face of disintegration. Violence is endemic to her world, if it is more often psychic than physical, and her narratives are often freighted with an increasing burden of impending, irreversible disaster, an unremitting progression to the point where the push for power or its abuse reaches a critical level. Implicitly she chips away at national myths such as mateship, rural solidarity, the 'fair go', egalitarianism and the notion of a homogeneous national (male) identity. Occasionally she revives characters from previous novels, so that background characters in one become central in another. Opposed to the hyperperceptive outsiders she presents a vast range of shallow insiders, those who are safely encased in an armour of insensitivity, malice and vanity. The representations of small-town life in *A Descant for Gossips* and *A Kindness Cup* are particularly striking pictures of general malicious stupidity, although Astley's studies of such putrescent microcosms of bigotry imply their affinity with larger cultures, as the name of one of them, All-but, indicates. *The Well Dressed Explorer* and *The Acolyte*, on the other hand, are consummate studies of two very different, voracious egotists who generate a wide destruction by preying on all around them. Satire is often lined with compassion, however, an element Astley herself has emphasised, describing her novels as 'a plea for charity – in the Pauline sense, of course – to be accorded to those not ruthless enough or grand enough to be gigantic tragic figures, but which, in their own way, record the same *via crucis*'.

Beachmasters is Astley's most international and anti-imperialist novel, focusing on an abortive revolution on a Pacific Island ruled by a British-French condominium; combining pathos and comedy, the novel exposes the absurdity of the revolution without trivialising its significance. *It's Raining in Mango*, less intricately plotted than Astley's other novels, spans four generations of a North Queensland family from the 1860s to the 1980s. Each chapter concentrates on the point of view of one of the characters of the Laffey family from the gregarious patriarch, Cornelius Laffey, to his great-grandson, Reever. Taking in a great span of Australian history, Astley skilfully blends individuals' histories and tragedies with pictures of Aboriginal dispossession and slaughter, economic depression, war, the exploitation of women, prostitution, incest, suicide, and the drug culture. An Aboriginal family, which shares this representative Queensland history and the Laffeys' lives, also participates in their wry philosophy and contributes to the tough humour which sometimes moderates the novel's underlying tone of anger. *Reaching Tin River*, set in various outback towns between Brisbane and Cairns from the 1950s to the 1970s, combines witty satire of male pretensions and acute socio-historical analyses of Queensland with a young girl's quest for identity and meaning. The daughter of an absent trumpet-playing American, Huck, and Bonnie, once an indifferent drummer in a two-woman band and now a self-absorbed hippy, Belle suffers an uncertain childhood in boarding school and rooming houses. Unable to centre her life, either in the unfortunate marriage she makes or in her relationship with her parents, Belle finds a temporary form of meaning in her obsessive research into the life of the late Gaden Lockyer, smallholder, politician and embezzler. As Belle's obsession leads her to the point of insanity, Astley is led unusually and boldly to the surreal. The short stories of *Hunting the Wild Pineapple*, narrated by Keith Leverson, who appears as his younger self in *The Slow Natives* when he lost a leg, and is now in his own words 'a monopod self-pitier', are among Astley's funniest, most artfully artless writing, ranging from acute satire to poignant pathos. The linked stories of *Vanishing Points* present quintessential Astley misfits, a disenchanted academic, Mac, in *The Genteel Poverty Bus Company* and an alienated, discarded housewife, Julia, in *Inventing the Weather*, both of whom confront

a massively insensitive successful entrepreneur, Clifford Truscott, the focus for the linking theme of loss and exploitation; regarding Australia as 'a cosmic jumble-sale through which he might pick up the most incredible bargains', Clifford transforms the Queensland coastline into 'tenement joy stalags'; he meets a temporary but ineffective retribution when Julia re-writes the story of her abandonment for more pliant secretaries by leaving him with the children, but his vulgarity and aggression are finally a physical match for Julia's spiritual double, Mac, if not a moral one. Astley was made a Creative Fellow of the Australia Council in 1993.

ASTON, Tilly (1873–1947), born Carisbrook, Victoria, was blind from the age of 6 years. She became a teacher of the blind in Melbourne, was a founder of the library of the Victorian Association of Braille Writers (1894) and was, for many years, president of Victoria's Association for the Advancement of the Blind. She wrote several books of verse and prose, of which *Old Timers* (1938) contains pen pictures of gold-rush characters, and an autobiography, *Memoirs of Tilly Aston* (1946).

Athenaeum: A Journal Specially Devoted to the Encouragement of Australian Literature, Science and Art, a brief-lived (1875–76) weekly journal, carried short stories, poetry, literary and theatrical reviews; it was edited by H.W.H. Stephen and P.J. Holdsworth, and included Henry Halloran, G.G. McCrae and James Brunton Stephens among its contributors.

ATKINSON, Hugh (?1924–), born Parkes, NSW, was educated at the University of Sydney and was both a conscientious objector and an RAAF serviceman during the Second World War. He spent four years in India, the setting for his first novel, *The Pink and the Brown* (1957), before returning to Australia, where he worked in advertising and journalism. In 1963, a Commonwealth Literary Fund fellowship enabled him to move to the Channel Islands; subsequently he lived in London, France, Majorca, Malta and elsewhere before returning again to Australia in 1977. He holds an Emeritus Fellowship from the Literature Board of the Australia Council. Atkinson has written film scripts and short stories as well as many novels: *The Pink and the Brown, Low Company* (1961), *The Reckoning* (1965, also published in 1977 as *Weekend of Shadows*, its film title, and *Weekend to Kill*), *The Games* (1967), *Johnny Horns* (1971), *The Most Savage Animal* (1972), *The Man in the Middle* (1973), *Crack-Up* (1974), *Unscheduled Flight* (1976), *The Manipulators* (1978, released in the USA as *Big Money*), *Billy Two-Toes' Rainbow* (1982), *The Longest Wire* (1982), *Grey's Valley: The Legend* (1986) and *The Jumping Jeweller of Lavender Bay* (1992). His most commercially successful novel, *The Games* (1967), focuses on the seamy politics of the Olympic movement and has as one of its main characters a part-Aborigine, Sunny Pintubi, who wins an Olympic marathon; the novel was filmed in the USA. Of his other novels, several of which are sensational exposés of the chicanery of governments or multinationals (e.g. *The Most Savage Animal, The Man in the Middle, The Manipulators*), *Low Company* chronicles Sydney bohemian life at the end of the 1950s; *The Reckoning*, which won the Xavier Prize for literature, is a study of violence in a small mining community in NSW in the 1930s; *Billy Two-Toes' Rainbow* explores multiracial tensions among opal-miners at Coober Pedy; *The Longest Wire* is a fictionalised account of the building of the Overland Telegraph line between Adelaide and Darwin; *Grey's Valley* is an attempt to make something of a folk-legend out of the story of a family of early settlers who grow apples in a fertile valley – 'Grey's Valley' – in outback NSW. *Grey's Valley* was reprinted in 1991 in *A Twist in the Tale* with two other novellas, 'The Burial of Robinson Crusoe' and 'The Language of Flowers'. Different in every way is Atkinson's *The Jumping Jeweller of Lavender Bay* (1992), published as a short story in *Coast to Coast 1958*, whose hero rides the ferry to work each morning, leaping from wharf to ferry. During that leap he gets a momentary glimpse of 'Paradise'. The leaps get bigger week by week until finally Pratt the jeweller leaps right into 'Paradise'. As 'Hugh Geddes', Atkinson also wrote *The Pyjama Girl Case* (1978), a study of a sensational murder of the 1930s.

ATKINSON, James (1795–1834), born Oldbury, England, arrived in Australia in 1820, became principal clerk in the Colonial Secretary's office and took up 1500 acres of land in the Bong Bong district. Back in England in 1825, he wrote *An Account of the State of Agriculture & Grazing in New South Wales* (1826), one of the first comprehensive accounts of farming in the colony. His daughter was the novelist and naturalist Louisa Atkinson.

ATKINSON, Louisa (Caroline Louisa Waring, Louisa Calvert) (1834–72), was born at the family property, Oldbury, near Berrima, NSW. Encouraged as a child by her mother, she later trained herself as a natural historian and became a skilled collector and illustrator of botanical specimens, fauna and birds. Between 1853 and 1872 her popular illustrated articles on natural history appeared regularly with the signature 'LA' (from 1869, 'LC') in the *Illustrated Sydney News*, *Sydney Morning Herald* and *Sydney Mail* as well as in the *Horticultural Magazine*. As 'An Australian Lady' she wrote six novels notable for their close observation of colonial life from a domestic point of view. The first two of these, *Gertrude The Emigrant: A Tale of Colonial Life* (1857) and *Cowanda, the Veteran's Grant* (1859) share their action between pastoral, Sydney city and goldfields life and were published by J. R. Clarke of Sydney. Four later novels were serialised in the *Sydney Mail* and the *Sydney Morning Herald* between 1861 and 1872. One of the earliest Australian writers and the first native-born woman to fictionalise Australian domestic, pastoral and bush life, Louisa Atkinson was also distinguished by having named for her those botanical specimens she identified for European science. Her novels, *Debatable Ground, or the Carlillawarra Claimants*, (1861, 1992), *Myra* (1864, 1983) and *Tom*

Hellicar's Children (1871, 1983), have been recently republished in Canberra by Mulini Press and Books on Demand. A modern scholarly edition of *Gertrude The Emigrant: A Tale of Colonial Life* (1857), edited by Elizabeth Lawson for the Colonial Texts Series of University of New South Wales Press, will appear shortly. *Cowanda, the Veteran's Grant* (1859) and the last novel, *Tressa's Resolve* (1872) have never been republished. Mulini Press has also published two collections of Atkinson's natural history journalism, *A Voice from the Country* (1978) and *Louisa Atkinson, Excursions from Berrima and a Trip to Manaro and Molonglo in the 1870s* (1980). *Excursions from Berrima*, introduced by Lionel Gilbert, has a foreword by Atkinson's granddaughter, Janet Cosh. Patricia Clarke has written the biography *Pioneer Writer: The Life of Louisa Atkinson: novelist, journalist, naturalist* (1990), and her life and achievement are discussed in Elizabeth Lawson's 'Louisa Atkinson, Naturalist and Novelist' in *A Bright and Fiery Troop*, ed. Debra Adelaide (1988), and *Louisa Atkinson: The Distant Sound of Native Voices* (1989).

ELIZABETH LAWSON

ATKINSON, Rupert (1881–1961), born Bendigo, Victoria, and educated in Australia and England, was left comfortably off after his father's death and then led a leisurely life as a man of letters. A close friend of the poet Hugh McCrae, Atkinson published numerous volumes of lyric, narrative and philosophical verse, including *The Shrine of Desire* (1906), *Wayside Poets* (1913), *A Modern Magdalene* (1913, reprinted as *The Renegades* in 1921), and *A Flagon of Song* (1920), the last being a selection from previously published work together with some new poems. His series of twenty 'Melbourne Sonnets' gives some local flavour to his verse. Atkinson also wrote several plays including *A Nocturne* (1919), an intriguing two-act verse-drama about a murder committed by a drunken man who can only recollect the incident when under the influence of alcohol, *Each Man a Multitude* (1923), a prose play in three acts, and some one-acters.

Atlas, a weekly journal published in Sydney 1844–48, carried literary reviews, original poetry, articles on literary topics and a considerable dash of satire, especially from William Forster. One of its leading figures was Robert Lowe (q.v.). Liberal in stance, the *Atlas* was originally the organ of the squatting interests against Governor Gipps. It published Forster's 'The Devil and the Governor', 17 May 1845.

'Atlas, The', a group of five poems by Kenneth Slessor (q.v.), was published in *Cuckooz Contrey* (1932). The individual poems of the sequence, 'The King of Cuckooz', 'Post-Roads', 'Dutch Seacoast', 'Mermaids' and 'The Seafight', have no continuity or overall theme. Disconnected scraps from Slessor's omnivorous reading interests, they reveal his delight in the odd and exotic.

ATTIWILL, K.A. (Kenneth Andrew) (1906–60), born Adelaide, was a journalist on the Adelaide *Register*, the *Sun* and *Herald* (both Melbourne) and the *Daily*

Sketch (London) before becoming a POW of the Japanese in the Second World War. His novels, which draw on his experiences in journalism, at war and at sea, include *Horizon* (1930), *Steward!* (1932), *Thirteen Sailed Home* (1935, with J.O.C. Orton), *Reporter!* (1933), *Big Ben* (1936), *The Rising Sunset* (1957) and *The Singapore Story* (1959). Resident in England for most of the latter part of his life, Attiwill was also a successful playwright. He was married to Evadne Price (q.v.).

AUCHTERLONIE, Dorothy, see **GREEN, Dorothy**

AUMLA, the journal of the Australasian Universities Language and Literature Association (q.v), formerly Australasian Universities Modern Languages Association, is a journal of literary criticism, philology and linguistics. *AUMLA* was first published in August 1953 and appeared annually until May 1956, thereafter twice annually. *AUMLA* was edited by R.T. Sussex until 1979. Later editors have included I.H. Smith, John Hay and Margaret Burrell.

Aunt's Story, The, a novel by Patrick White (q.v.), was published in 1948. In three parts, it narrates the life of Theodora Goodman, an outwardly unattractive spinster, and her solitary quest for ultimate lucidity. The first phase, beginning and ending with her mother's death, deals retrospectively with her life and inner experience till middle age. Brought up on a run-down family property, Meroë, Theodora is surrounded by people who fail to understand her: her pretty but superficial sister Fanny, and Frank Parrott, whom Fanny marries; her mother; her school friend Violet Adams; and her suitor, Huntly Clarkson. Only with her father, her niece Lou, and in a few other fleeting experiences such as those with an old reprobate acquaintance of her father, whom she later calls 'The Man Who Was Given His Dinner' and a Greek cello player, Moraïtis, is Theodora able to experience the fierce intensity she discovers in the natural world. The second section of the novel, titled 'Jardin Exotique', finds Theodora in a dreary European hotel, surrounded by people whose intrusion into her consciousness is expressed in a fragmented, expressionistic way. They include two faded spinsters, the Demoiselles Bloch; Wetherby, a failed Englishman and poet, who is engaged in a passionately destructive affair with the wife of a German count, the decadent Lieselotte; Mrs Rapallo, an American lady whose most prized possession is her fantasy of a titled daughter; Sokolnikov, an exiled Russian general; and Katina Pavlou, a young girl who is ignored by her parents and travels Europe accompanied by an English companion. Through her testing relationships with these people and their fantasies, Theodora achieves a new appreciation of the 'otherness' of others and a fresh perspective on her past relationships. This section ends with a fire at the hotel in which some of the residents die. The brief concluding section finds Theodora on a train in America's Middle West. Unpredictably leaving the train, she makes her way to an isolated farmhouse, where she is briefly cared for by a family, the Johnsons. The end of her quest is achieved the next day in the mountains when she meets Holstius, an emanation from her psyche, who suggests that there is little to choose 'between the reality of illusion and the illusion of reality'. Integration can only be achieved by acceptance of life's irreconcilable dualities, joy and sorrow, illusion and reality, life and death. Theodora is finally led away by the Johnsons and a doctor who remarks that 'lucidity . . . isn't necessarily a perpetual ailment'.

AUROUSSEAU, Marcel (1891–1983), born Woollahra, Sydney, of French and Irish parentage, graduated from the University of Sydney with the University Medal in geology and became a lecturer in geology at the University of WA. After distinguished service in the First World War he joined the Carnegie Institute in Washington (1920–23), and later went to Europe to spend time on writing, his growing love. He published *Highway into Spain* (1930), an account of his journey on foot from Paris to Madrid in 1926. A period with the Royal Geographical Society in London led to his compilation of an *Index to Supplements* (1936) to the *Geographical Journal*, an important work of bibliographical reference. During the Second World War he led a small expert group producing numerous gazetteers (the first in 1942) on foreign countries for the Allied forces. A member of the council of the Hakluyt Society, he assisted in the preparation of the indexes to the edition of Captain James Cook's *Journals*, edited by J.C. Beaglehole for the Hakluyt Society, 1955–67. In 1956 he returned to Australia, was president of the Geographical Society of NSW (1959–61) and was a member (1964–68) of the National Committee for Geography of the Australian Academy of Science. Aurousseau's major contribution to Australian writing was his editing of *The Letters of F.W. Ludwig Leichhardt* (1968).

Aussie: The Australian Soldiers' Magazine, originally printed in the field by the AIF printing section in France, began publication in January 1918 and ceased in 1931. Published monthly (but irregularly at times), it changed its title to *Aussie: The Cheerful Monthly* from the April 1920 issue. It contained poetry, short fiction, cartoons, an 'Aussie dictionary', and articles on Australian writers in a series 'Aussie Verse and Verse-Writers' by its long-term editor, Phillip Lawrence Harris. Writers discussed in short articles for general readers included Barcroft Boake, E.J. Brady, John le Gay Brereton, John Farrell, Henry Kendall, Henry Lawson and Roderic Quinn.

'Australaise, The' was originally submitted by C.J. Dennis (q.v.) as an entry in a national song competition conducted by the *Bulletin* in 1908. Christened the 'Blanky Australaise' by the judge, because of the many blank spaces for the great Australian adjective 'bloody' to be inserted ('blessed' or 'blooming' were later suggested by Dennis for folk genteel), it won a prize of a guinea and was predicted to 'win its way to every heart in the back-blocks'. In 1913 an expanded version (from four to seven verses) was published in Dennis's *Backblock Ballads and Other Verses.* In 1915 it was reprinted as a leaflet for the Australian soldiers, to whom it was dedicated as a marching song. With a mixture of irony and sincerity typical of him, Dennis suggested that the song be sung to the tune of 'Onward Christian Soldiers'. It was adopted as a recruiting song in 1951 during the Korean War and was selected in 1968 as the official regimental march of the Seventh Battalion of the Royal Australian Regiment.

Australasia (1823), a poem by William Charles Wentworth (q.v.), was an entry in the Chancellor's Gold Medal poetry competition at Cambridge in 1823 on the subject of Australasia. With his opening apostrophe, 'Land of my birth!', Wentworth made clear his special position in relation to the topic. The poem attempts to project a distinctively Australian viewpoint and, with its prophecy of future greatness, is one of the first outbursts in Australian literature of nationalistic pride. Although sometimes marred by the customary inflated rhetoric of the public poem of the day, *Australasia* has been praised for its well-planned structure and its vigorous, eloquent, if rugged, verse.

Australasian, which was formed in 1864 by a merger of three Melbourne weeklies and subsequently incorporated *Bell's Life in Victoria* and the *Australasian Sketcher with Pen and Pencil*, was the weekend companion to the *Argus*; in 1946 it became the popular magazine the *Australasian Post*. Notable literary features of the *Australasian* were its columns 'Essayist' and 'The Traveller', and Marcus Clarke's 'Lower Bohemia' series of 1869. Marcus Clarke also published, in the *Australasian, Old Tales of a Young Country* (intermittently in 1870–71) and *The Peripatetic Philosopher* (1867–70), under the pseudonym 'Q'. Among its other well-known contributors were 'Rolf Boldrewood', Ada Cambridge, Louisa Anne Meredith, J.E. Neild, Catherine Helen Spence and Jessie Couvreur.

Australasian Book News and Library Journal, published monthly 1946–48, and edited by George Farwell with Eve Pownall as children's editor, listed books published in Australia and contained book reviews and other literary articles.

Australasian Book Society, a publishing company with a limited liability incorporated in Victoria and owned by its members, was registered in 1952; it was wound up in 1981. Its purpose was to publish 'manuscripts reflecting the life struggles and militant traditions' of the Australian people. Its first publication, with Bill Wannan as secretary-manager, was Ralph de Boissiere's novel of West Indian life, *Crown Jewel* (1952), no suitable Australian manuscript then being available. The Society's political stance was predominantly left, but its relationships with the Communist Party of Australia were never smooth. Some of its notable publications were *The Tracks We Travel* (1953, 1961, 1965, 1976), four short-story collections edited successively by Stephen Murray-Smith, Jack Beasley

and Leslie Haylen (twice); Judah Waten's novel *The Australian* (1954); Dorothy Hewett's novel *Bobbin Up* (1959); John Manifold's cultural history *Who Wrote the Ballads?* (1964); and the memorial tribute to Dame Mary Gilmore in 1965. The Society was active in many fields, e.g. during Ian Turner's period as secretary it commissioned William Dobell's controversial portrait of Dame Mary Gilmore and initiated and participated in the Australian Book Fairs. A full list (to 1978) of the Society's publications and considerable information about the Society is in Jack Beasley's *Red Letter Days* (1979). *Readers and Writers* was the Society's intermittent newsletter.

Australasian Critic: A Monthly Review of Literature, Science and Art, was a short-lived (1890–91) attempt by its editors, Professors T.G. Tucker, W. Baldwin Spencer and E.E. Morris, to institute a regular and systematic review of the arts in Australia.

Australasian Home Reader, which had a wide reading circle during the 1890s and was edited by E.E. Morris and Robert Garran, ran 1892–97 when it was superseded by the *Year Book of the Australasian Home Reading Union*.

Australasian Journal of Psychology and Philosophy, a quarterly journal begun in Sydney in 1923, changed its title to the *Australian Journal of Philosophy* after 1947. It embraced a wide area of interest – psychology, philosophy, education, sociology and literature. Its literary content was especially significant in the 1930s. See also Anderson, John.

Australasian Post, an illustrated weekly published since 1946, is a continuation of the *Australasian* (q.v.). A popular magazine and standard reading material in Australian barbers' shops, it has little literary merit; but, like the early *Bulletin*, its cartoons and other features have helped to consolidate the image of the bush within the Australian consciousness.

Australasian Sketcher with Pen and Pencil, a monthly published in Melbourne 1873–89, had a marked literary content in its early years (short stories, sketches, reviews) but later became an illustrated news magazine with Adelaide and Brisbane editions. It was incorporated into the *Australasian* (q.v.) after 1889.

Australasian Universities Language and Literature Association (AULLA) came into being in 1950 at a congress held in Melbourne, largely through the efforts of A.R. Chisholm and R.H. Samuel. Originally called Australasian Universities Modern Languages Association, which was open to the modern languages staff of Australian universities, it aimed at the advancement of modern languages study and research in Australia. Its journal, which publishes literary criticism and studies in philology and linguistics, is *AUMLA* (q.v.). The Association holds an annual congress, the articles and reports from which are usually published.

Australia (1). The name 'Australia' derives from the Latin word *australis*, meaning 'southern', and was originally applied to all regions existing, or thought to exist, south of the equator. The terms *continens australis* and *terra australis* were in use from about the sixteenth century to apply to the undiscovered landmass thought to exist in the southern oceans. Pedro Fernandez de Quiros (see *Captain Quiros*) in 1606 named an island of the New Hebrides group (which he believed to be part of the great southern continent) 'Austrialia del Espiritu Santo'. In 1692 Gabriel de Foigny, writing under the pseudonym 'Jacques Sadeur', published a novel in whose title the terms *la terre Australe* and *Australiens* occur; the English translation of his novel used the words 'Australia' and 'Australians'. The eighteenth century saw plentiful use of 'Australia' or equivalent terms. Captain James Cook, however, believing that the Australian east coast where he had made landfall in 1770 had no connection with de Quiros's Austrialia continent, called the land New Wales, later New South Wales, and New South Wales was the name applied by the British government to the penal colony established by Captain Arthur Phillip at Botany Bay in 1788. From about 1786 everything east of the 135° meridian of longitude was called New South Wales and everything west of the meridian, New Holland. In James Wilson's *A Missionary Voyage* (1799) the names 'Greater Australia' and 'Lesser Australia' were used; and Matthew Flinders (often erroneously considered to be the first to use 'Australia') spoke in his *A Voyage to Terra Australis* (1814) of his wish to have called the book *Voyage to Australia*, a wish that was thwarted by the influence of Sir Joseph Banks. The charts published in connection with Flinders's voyages used the name 'Australia'; when those charts reached the Colony in 1817 the governor, Lachlan Macquarie, adopted the name for official use, writing in a dispatch in December 1817, 'I hope [Australia] will be the name given to this country in future'. When Macquarie was buried in Scotland in 1824, 'Australia' was written on his tomb. Macquarie's 'official' poet, Michael Massey Robinson, had already used the term in his 'Ode for His Majesty's Birthday', published in the *Sydney Gazette* in 1815; and in 1819 Barron Field published *First Fruits of Australian Poetry*, the first book of verse to include 'Australian' in its title. In 1821 a literary magazine titled the *Australian Magazine* appeared, and in the same year the first scientific association formed in the colony was established as the Philosophical Society of Australasia. 'Australia' and 'Australasia' were virtually interchangeable terms; W.C. Wentworth's Cambridge poem of 1823 was titled *Australasia* and it ended with the well-known lines 'And Australasia float with flag unfurled/A New Britannia in another world!' Wentworth's 1819 history, *A Statistical, Historical and Political Description of the Colony of New South Wales*, was changed in the third edition (1824) to *A Statistical Account of the British Settlements in Australasia*. After Wentworth returned to the Colony from England in 1824 he established with Robert Wardell the newspaper *Australian*, which was a rival to the *Sydney Gazette* which, incidentally, used 'Advance Australia' on its masthead. The impetus

to use 'Australia' thus came almost entirely from the Colony itself and there was noticeable reluctance by the authorities in England to follow the colonial lead. In colonial writing the word was used with increasing regularity from the 1820s onwards, e.g. Phillip Parker King's *Narrative of a Survey of the Intertropical and Western Coasts of Australia* (1827), Robert Dawson's *The Present State of Australia* (1830), Charles Sturt's *Two Expeditions into the Interior of Southern Australia* (1833), R.M Martin's *History of Australasia* (1836) and W.B. Ullathorne's *The Catholic Mission in Australasia* (1837). The early colonial poet Charles Harpur, in his poem 'The Emigrant's Vision', portrayed the goddess of the south wearing a helmet on which was engraved the word 'Australia'; in the same poem he proclaimed:

> Tis the Shiloh of freedom expected so long:
> Tis the evergreen land of Australia.

Fellow colonial poet Henry Kendall frequently attached to his early verses the initials NAP, 'Native Australian Poet'.

'Australia' was officially used for the new colonies of WA and SA, founded in 1829 and 1836 for free settlers; the Act of 1829 establishing the Swan River colony spoke of 'His Majesty's Settlement in Western Australia'. The Commonwealth of Australia, constituted by an Act of the imperial parliament 9 July 1900, was inaugurated 1 January 1901. 'Australasia' is now used as a joint term for Australia and NZ.

Australia (2), an eight-volume descriptive work published 1874–76, was the nineteenth-century equivalent of the modern coffee-table book. Its text was written by E. Carton Booth and it was illustrated by leading contemporary artists, e.g. J. Skinner Prout and Nicholas Chevalier. Booth also wrote *Another England: Life, Living, Homes and Homemakers in Victoria* (1869), a work describing Victorian society in the post-gold period.

Australia (3), a seminal history by Sir Keith Hancock (q.v.), was first published in 1930. The history, which moves from the efforts of Australia's White settlers to conquer the land to the development of sectional conflict and the growth of democracy and nationalism, prefigures a number of themes taken up by subsequent historians and cultural studies; particularly influential have been Hancock's analyses of the national character and the role of rural values and egalitarianism in Australian society. Writers who have subsequently developed similar themes include Brian Fitzpatrick, Russel Ward, Robin Gollan, Craig McGregor, Vance Palmer, Donald Horne, C. Hartley Grattan, J.D. Pringle and A.A. Phillips.

'Australia' (4), a sonnet by Bernard O'Dowd (q.v.), is the introductory poem to the volume *Dawnward?* (1903). With its well-known opening line, 'Last seathing dredged by sailor Time from Space' and its questioning of the destiny of Australia, the sonnet is one of the best-known and most-anthologised of O'Dowd's works.

'**Australia**' (5), a poem written by A.D. Hope (q.v.) in 1939, was first published in 1943 and has frequently been anthologised. In a mood of cool appraisal, the poet dwells on the country's isolation, philistinism and cultural deprivation In the last two stanzas, however, he accepts this 'Australian desert of human mind' as home in the hope that 'Such savage and scarlet as no green hills dare/ Springs in that waste', and that 'still from the deserts the prophets come'. The last quotation provided Geoffrey Serle with the title of his historical study of Australian culture, *From Deserts the Prophets Come* (1973).

Australia & New Zealand Weekly, see **British Australasian**

Australia Council is a statutory authority operating under the Australia Council Act 1975. It replaced the Australian Council of the Arts which was established in 1973 under the Whitlam government. Earlier systems of government patronage such as the Arts Council and the Commonwealth Literary Fund had been assisting Australian writers since 1908. The 1975 Act was amended in 1991 to change slightly the composition of the Council and its Boards by including members representing broad community interests at the expense of government representatives. The minister, however, remains the final authority, being now empowered to give written direction to the Council regarding the performance of its functions and the exercise of its powers. At present the Council comprises fourteen (14) members including a chairperson and a general manager. With the exception of the general manager, appointments are part-time and are made by the governor-general. Members are selected with the intention of ensuring relevant expertise in the arts and in regional, gender, and non-English-speaking backgrounds and ensuring also Aboriginal community representation. Operating within the Council's structure are three art-form boards (Literature, Performing Arts and Visual Arts/Crafts) and two major committees (Aboriginal Arts and Community Cultural Development). The three boards and two major committees decide on the Council's major arts support programmes, which are then managed by the administrative units attached to each of them – i.e. the Literature Unit manages the Literature Board unit and so on. In the administrative structure under the general manager the Strategic Development Unit manages the Council's several arts support functions, while the Corporate Services Unit co-ordinates the Council's administrative and operating systems. The Council is presently housed in Redfern, Sydney.

Currently the Council is funded in excess of $60 million annually, over $50 million being expended on direct financial support for arts activities. More than 600 artists and 1600 organisations have thus far been supported by the Council, which has made almost 50 000 grants since its establishment. Its most prestigious individual grants are its Australian Artists Creative Fellowships ($50,000 a year for three or more years) and Emeritus Fellowships (Pensions), which provide a specified amount for life. Creative Fellow-

ships, instituted in 1989, were awarded to (among others) Les Murray, Frank Moorhouse, Jack Davis, Robyn Archer, Eric Rolls and John Tranter. Emeritus Fellows include Hugh Atkinson, John Blight, C.B. Christesen, Dame Mary Durack, Harold Stewart and Judith Wright.

The Council's work is based on two principles – 'arm's length', which attempts to ensure that decisions on arts support are distanced from political considerations; and 'peer review', in which policy decisions and grants selections are made by fellow artists and community representatives of those being assessed. The 'peer review' principle has been both supported and criticised; those who object to it point to the possibility of 'cronyism'. Broadly the Council's functions are to promote excellence in the arts in Australia, to promote the appreciation, understanding and enjoyment of the arts among Australians, to foster the expression of a national Australian identity by means of the arts and to promote the knowledge and appreciation of Australian arts in the world at large.

H.C. Coombs, a significant figure in the formation of arts policy in Australia in the 1950s and 1960s was the first chairperson of the Australia Council. His successors to 1994 have been Peter Karmel, Geoffrey Blainey, Timothy Pascoe, Donald Horne, Rodney Hall and Hilary McPhee.

Australia Felix was the name given by Major Thomas Mitchell (q.v.), in *Three Expeditions into the Interior of Eastern Australia* (1839), to the land which he discovered on his expedition in 1836 from Portland to the Murray River near Albury, i.e. much of present-day central Victoria. It was frequently used in titles of literary, historical, geographical and biographical works in the nineteenth century, e.g. *Australia Felix Monthly Magazine* (1849) and Richard Howitt's *Impressions of Australia Felix* (1845).

Australia First, an extreme nationalist movement which P.R. Stephensen and W.J. Miles (qq.v.) were instrumental in founding, was formally established in Sydney in October 1941; Stephensen was its foundation president and its membership included C.W. Salier and Ian Mudie. Australia First was isolationist and chauvinist; strongly anti-English, anti-Semitic and anti-communist, it expressed some sympathy for the Japanese and German governments. In March 1942, following the arrest in Perth of four people charged with conspiracy to assist Japan, who had Australia First material in their possession, sixteen people suspected of being Australia First members or sympathisers were arrested in Sydney, including Stephensen, Salier and the poet Harley Matthews. Their internment was criticised at a subsequent inquiry (1944–45) as an infringement of civil liberties; most of the internees were released in 1942, but Stephensen remained in detention until the end of the Second World War. In Xavier Herbert's *Poor Fellow My Country* (q.v., 1975), Australia First is critically portrayed as 'Australia Free'; the movement is also the subject of Bruce Muirden's *The Puzzled Patriots* (1968). Muirden's book is a history of the generation and decline of the movement from the founding of the *Publicist* in 1936 until Stephensen's death almost thirty years later. It includes the collaboration between Stephensen and Miles in their efforts to get a hearing for their particular brand of nationalism. It suggests that they were misdirected by Miles and describes the final political structure erected by Stephensen (without the backing of Miles) which lasted only five months and led to their internment.

Australia in the War of 1939–45, the official history, edited by Gavin Long (q.v.), consists of twenty-two volumes arranged in five series (Army, Navy, Air, Civil and Medical) published between 1952 and 1977. Volumes I to VII of the first series (Army) include *To Benghazi* (1952) by Gavin Long, *Greece, Crete and Syria* (1953) by Gavin Long, *Tobruk and El Alamein* (1966) by Barton Maughan, *The Japanese Thrust* (1957) by Lionel Wigmore, *South-West Pacific Area – First Year* (1959) by Dudley McCarthy, *The New Guinea Offensives* (1961) by David Dexter, and *The Final Campaigns* (1963) by Gavin Long. G. Hermon Gill wrote the two-volume account of the part played by the Royal Australian Navy (1957 and 1968), which forms the second series. The third series (Air) includes *Royal Australian Air Force, 1939–1942* by Douglas Gillison (1961), *Air War against Japan 1943–1945* by George Odgers (1957), *Air War against Germany and Italy 1939–1943* (1954) and *Air Power over Europe 1944–1945* (1963) by John Herington. The fourth series (Civil) includes *The Government and the People 1939–41* and *The Government and the People 1942–45* (1955, 1970) both by Sir Paul Hasluck, *War Economy 1939–1942* (1955) by S.J. Butlin and *War Economy 1942–45* (1977) by Butlin and C.V. Schedvin, and *The Role of Science and Industry* (1958) by D.P. Mellor. Allan S. Walker wrote the four volumes of the fifth series (Medical). A concise one-volume history by Gavin Long, *The Six Years War*, was published in 1973.

Australia in Western Imaginative Prose Writings 1600–1960 (1967), edited by Werner P. Friederich, is a combination of anthology and literary history. It contains commentaries on the works of non-Australian writers about Australia from the time of its discovery to the period after the Second World War. Among those anthologised are the Portuguese-Spanish explorer Pedro Fernandez de Quiros; the Frenchman de Brosses; the English writers Henry Kingsley, Anthony Trollope and D.H. Lawrence; the Italian Raffaello Carboni; the German Friedrich Gerstaecker; the Frenchman Paul Wenz; and the Swiss Esther Landolt.

Australia Poetry series, begun in 1992 by Heinemann Australia with Jamie Grant as editor, published poets Alan Gould, Peter Kocan and Les Murray in 1992. Later volumes include work by Grant, Kate Jennings, Hal Colebatch and Robert Gray.

'Australia to England', the poem by John Farrell (q.v.) to celebrate Queen Victoria's Diamond Jubilee, was published in the *Daily Telegraph* 22 June 1897, as

'Ave Imperatrix'. With slight alterations and under its new title the poem was reprinted in the same year as a booklet. Highly regarded at the time, the poem is a patriotic expression of hopes for Australia's future and an acknowledgement of the great achievements of the mother country.

Australia, Visited & Revisited (1853, facsimile 1974), by Samuel Mossman and Thomas Banister, is basically 'a narrative of recent travels and odd experiences in Victoria and New South Wales', and was intended to lay before the public a work that would be useful to those intending to hazard their fortunes in 'The Australian Gold Colonies' and be interesting to the general reader. The goldfields at Mount Alexander, the Turon, Bathurst, Louisa Creek and Braidwood are described, as are pastoral pursuits and life on sheep and cattle stations. Mossman also wrote *A Voice from Australia* (1852), *The Gold Region of Australia* (1852), *Railways in Victoria* (1857), *Narrative of the Shipwreck of the 'Admella'* (1859), *Our Australian Colonies* (1866), *Heroes of Discovery* (1868) and *New Japan* (1873); and edited *General Gordon's Private Diary of His Exploits in China* (1885).

Australia Week-End Book began in 1942 and was published annually until 1946. It was edited by Sydney Ure Smith (q.v.) and Gwen Morton Spencer; notable among its contributors were Marjorie Barnard, Alan Marshall, D'Arcy Niland, Jon Cleary and Eleanor Dark.

Australian (1), founded by W.C. Wentworth (q.v.) and Robert Wardell, helped produce a free press in NSW. It ran 1824–48 and serialised novels by Charles Dickens and other English authors; its contributors included Henry Halloran, Charles Harpur, Richard Howitt and Charles Tompson. Wardell (1793–1834) was admitted to the Bar in 1821 and came to NSW on the same ship as Wentworth in 1824; he subsequently established a successful law practice.

Australian (2), was established in 1964 by Rupert Murdoch as a national daily newspaper, with Maxwell Newton as foundation editor. Robert Brissenden was its first literary editor and David Campbell its first poetry editor; later Rodney Hall was poetry editor for eleven years from 1967, and Katharine Brisbane its national (1967–74) and Sydney (1978–80) theatre critic.

Australian: a Monthly Magazine, which ran 1878–81, carried short fiction, poetry and serials. Its contributors included Henry Halloran, Richmond (Dick) Thatcher, A. Patchett Martin and John Stanley James ('The Vagabond'); it professed to be 'national in our views, national in our politics, national in our relations to all public and social questions'.

Australian Academy of the Humanities (based in Canberra), a body established under Royal Charter in 1969, succeeded the Australian Humanities Research Council (q.v.). It constitutes one of the nation's four learned Academies, which are recognised by the Department of Employment, Education and Training as advisory bodies on educational and research matters. The Academy aims to advance knowledge of and the pursuit of excellence in the Humanities. Its general disciplinary areas include Archaeology, Asian Studies, Classical Studies, English and European Languages and Literatures, the Fine Arts, History, Linguistics and Philology, Philosophy, Prehistory, and Religious Studies.

Election to the fellowship takes place at the annual general meeting, following nomination to Council through the nine electoral sections. The fellowship in 1992 numbered 223, comprising fellows, senior fellows, honorary and overseas fellows. The Academy is funded primarily through an annual grant from the federal government, fellowship fees, and sale of publications.

The Academy convenes an annual symposium, publishes the papers of these symposia, and issues annual volumes of *Proceedings.* Sponsored lectures are the Annual Lecture and the Sir Keith Hancock Lecture. It also assists publications within the humanities through a grants scheme, and offers short-term travelling fellowships to assist with research visits abroad. The Max Crawford Medal is awarded for distinction in research by a younger scholar.

It has sponsored several long-term projects, currently the Academy Editions of Australian Literature (q.v.), which aims to produce a series of scholarly critical editions of major Australian literary works. The editions will provide reliable texts suitable for republication in student and popular editions, as well as serving as a future rich resource of textual and contextual information. Among the Academy's fellows are A.D. Hope (a foundation fellow), Judith Wright and C.B. Christesen.

Australian Accent (1958), by John Douglas Pringle (q.v.), is an impressionistic, sometimes humorous, analysis of Australian culture and society, with particular emphasis on the urban environments of Sydney and Melbourne and the political and cultural scenes. The book was illustrated by George Molnar, then cartoonist of the *Sydney Morning Herald.*

Australian & New Zealand Studies in Canada (1989–), edited by Thomas E. Tausky, is a semi-annual journal which publishes articles and reviews in the fields of literature and the related arts in Australia and NZ.

Australian Author, the quarterly magazine of the Australian Society of Authors (q.v.), superseded *Broadside* in 1969, the latter having been since 1963 a printed broadsheet of literary news available to members of the Society. Editors of the *Australian Author/Broadside* have included Barrie Ovenden, Nancy Keesing, Gavin Souter, Colin Simpson, Bill Larkins, Robert Pullen and Dominic O'Grady.

Australian Band of Hope Review and Children's Friend, a temperance journal, published short stories, sketches, moral tales and poetry; Charles Harpur and Henry Kendall were contributors. Published fortnightly 1856–61, it was known also as the *Band of Hope Journal and Australian Home Companion* and as the *Australian Home Companion and Band of Hope Journal.*

Australian Bibliography: A Guide to Printed Sources of Information by D.H. Borchardt (q.v.), then chief librarian of La Trobe University, Melbourne, was published first in 1963, with subsequent editions in 1966, 1976 and 1979. A comprehensive treatment of Australian reference works, the *Bibliography* offers an annotated commentary on libraries and library catalogues, encyclopaedias and general reference works, general and subject bibliographies (the latter divided into the social sciences, the humanities and the pure and applied sciences), bibliographies of geographic regions, sources of biographical information, government publications and the bibliographical scene.

Australian Book Publishers Association (ABPA) was formed in 1949 from a merger of two smaller associations of publishers, the New South Wales Publishers Association and the Victorian Publishers Association. The aims of the ABPA include the fostering of original publishing in Australia and encouragement of the highest standards of writing, editing and manufacture of books in Australia. Its chief areas of activity include copyright, the fostering of governmental and public understanding of the book-publishing industry in Australia, the monitoring of members' interests in regard to book bounty, duties, tariffs and taxes, and liaison with other book trade organisations, e.g. the National Book Council, the Australian Society of Authors and the Australian Copyright Council. The initial president of ABPA was W.H. Cousins of Angus & Robertson. George Ferguson (q.v.), largely instrumental in the founding of ABPA, was president 1950–56 and 1959–60. During his term of office ABPA's annual Book Design Awards were inaugurated. ABPA in conjunction with the Literature Board, administers the Beatrice Davis (q.v.) Award inaugurated in 1992.

Australian Book Review (ABR) has been the title of two journals. The first, published from Adelaide (1961–74, monthly to 1971, then quarterly), was edited by Max Harris and Rosemary Wighton. The second, published by the National Book Council with the assistance in recent years from the Literature Board of the Australia Council, the Victorian Ministry for the Arts and Telecom Australia, began in 1978. It was edited by John McLaren until 1986, followed by Kerryn Goldsworthy and then by Louise Adler. Since 1989 it has been edited by Rosemary Sorensen. The original series also included an annual children's book and educational supplement (1961–70).

Australian Books in Print, an annual publication, includes (in addition to Australian books in print) lists of literary societies and associations, literary prizes and awards, names and addresses of Australian publishers, their representatives and agents, and those of overseas publishers who have representatives or agents in Australia. It was first published in 1956. It is available also on microfiche and CD ROM and is updated monthly.

Australian Books on Demand, published by the Mulini Press, Canberra (Victor Crittenden), are editions of early Australian writings, especially nineteenth-century works which have not normally been available to readers, book collectors and libraries. Titles available by 1993 were *Annabella Boswell's Other Journal 1848–1851*, John Lang's *Lucy Cooper*, Louisa Atkinson's *Debatable Ground*, Charles De Boos's *Mark Brown's Wife*, Eliza Winstanley's *For Her Natural Life: A Tale of the 1830s*, Ellen Davitt's *Force and Fraud* and Rosa Praed's *The Bond of Wedlock*. Victor Crittenden's title for the series stems from the fact that he prints only a few copies of each book and binds them in either paperback or hardback when they are required, i.e. on demand. Of particular value to students and researchers, these texts, usually not the major works of the writers chosen, add to the accumulated knowledge of those writers and are usually of social and historical interest. The Mulini Press also publishes a series of broadsheets listing Australian nineteenth-century literature in print and *Bibliographica Historica Australiae*, a series of books and pamphlets about the Book (writing, publishing and other aspects) in Australia and a Colonial Poets series which includes the poetry of Henry Halloran, George I. MacDonald, Charles Harpur, Eliza Dunlop, Henry Kendall, Barron Field and Fidelia S.T. Hill.

Australian Bookseller & Publisher, founded by D.W. Thorpe in 1921, is a monthly publication still emanating from D.W. Thorpe Pty Ltd, publishers of trade journals and reference books. Originally (1921–25) titled the *Australasian Stationery and Fancy Goods Journal*, and later with other titles, the *Bookseller* split into two in 1971, its other half becoming the *Australian Newsagent and Stationer*. The *Bookseller* contains a list of Australian books published in the previous month (cumulated in Thorpe's *Australian Books in Print*), news of the Australian bookselling and publishing trade and short reviews of forthcoming books.

Australian Broadcasting Corporation, formerly Australian Broadcasting Commission, the national broadcasting service, known also as the 'ABC' and more colloquially as 'Aunty', was established in 1932, nine years after commercial radio broadcasting had begun in Australia with a sealed-set system. Under this system organisations were licensed to broadcast by the Postmaster-General, listeners paid a licence fee to the federal government and a subscription fee to a designated station, and each wireless set was sealed so that it could only operate on the wavelength of the station receiving the subscription. Sealed sets were abandoned in 1924 in favour of A and B class stations, both operating under government licence, with the A class stations (which included 2FC, 2BL and 3LO, all later part of the ABC network) to be financed mainly from licence fees and the B class stations from advertising revenue. The problem with this second system – its concentration of broadcasting services in city areas – led in 1927 to the establishment of a Royal Commission which recommended that the Postmaster-General's department operate the A class stations (at that stage two in Sydney and Melbourne, one each in the other State capitals) but let the programming services out to private companies under contract. In 1929 the contract went to the Australian Broadcasting Company, a combination mainly of theatre and cinema interests. Although in the three years of the Company's operation there were substantial developments in programming, the establishment of stations outside metropolitan areas and the relaying of items between stations, the J.H. Scullin government decided in 1930 that broadcasting should be brought under public control; that decision was implemented in 1932 by the government of Scullin's successor, Joseph Lyons.

Under the first Australian Broadcasting Commission Act, the Commission – originally five members, increased to seven in 1948, nine in 1967, and eleven in 1976 – took over the existing A class stations, with the B class stations continuing to develop commercial radio. The Commission's technical services were to be provided by the Postmaster-General's department (the transmitters remained in the hands of the PMG throughout the history of the ABC, although radio studio services were handled by the ABC from 1964 and by parallel television services from the outset); its funds came from a proportion of the licence fee paid by listeners (although in 1944–45 it received its first supplementary grant and from 1948 a direct government appropriation); it was not allowed to broadcast advertisements (a provision which remains); and it was entrusted to provide adequate and comprehensive programmes and encourage local talent. Initially the Postmaster-General, the minister responsible for the ABC, could 'direct the Commission to broadcast, or refrain from broadcasting, any specified material', although a 1942 Act stipulated notice in writing of intention to use these powers and the reporting of their use in the Commission's annual report. The extent of political interference and related issues of autonomy and bias are themes of some longevity in commentary on the ABC, as also are the extent to which it has been (or should have been) 'highbrow', 'middlebrow' or 'lowbrow', the degree of its neglect of rural listeners, and its relationship (competing with or complementary to) commercial broadcasting. Discussion of some of those issues intensified after the introduction of television to Australia in 1956, which brought profound changes to the operations of the Commission. The enormous developments in communications since the establishment of the ABC, e.g. the improvement of lines to Perth and Hobart in the early days of radio, videotape, coaxial cables and satellites after television was introduced, the introduction of FM radio in 1976, have helped to make the ABC more truly a national broadcasting service, while always maintaining some regionalisation. These developments have also made necessary the extensive legislative revision and updating of the early broadcasting acts (major broadcasting bills were enacted by the federal parliament in 1942, 1948, 1956, 1976 and 1983), the establishment of various broadcasting committees outside but encompassing the ABC (e.g. the Australian Broadcasting Control Board of 1948–76) and the periodic committees of review of the Commission itself. One such committee, the Dix Committee of 1979–81, produced a report which was the basis of the federal government's decision to dissolve the Australian Broadcasting Commission and establish (on 1 July 1983) the Australian Broadcasting Corporation (with eight members) in its place, under Geoffrey Whitehead as managing director, a position taken by David Hill in 1987, now in his second term of office.

The main spheres of broadcasting operation of the ABC have been in the areas of music (53 per cent of the ABC's activities in its first year), news, current affairs, sport, drama and other features, education, and youth and rural broadcasts; and in many of these activities Australian writers and critics have been significant. A.B. Paterson expressed interest in being one of the initial commissioners; he was not appointed, but Ernestine Hill (1942–44) and David Williamson (1978–79) served terms on the Commission; Williamson was a contemporary of Dame Leonie Kramer (q.v.), a commissioner in 1977–81 before her appointment as chairman (1982–83). Among long-term employees of the Commission were the critic and biographer Clement Semmler (q.v.), who retired in 1977 after thirty-five years (the last thirteen as deputy general manager); the poet and anthologist John Thompson (q.v.), who joined in 1939 and was associated for many years with the cultural radio programme 'Quality Street', which ran from 1946 to 1973 and was narrated in its first year by Peter Finch; the dramatist, novelist and journalist Mungo MacCallum (q.v.), who produced the ABC's first night of television; and the writer and theatre historian Leslie Rees (q.v.), who played a significant role in the development of the ABC's tradition of radio drama. Other appointments were held by the poet and critic Dorothy Green, who helped implement the ABC's independent news services; the playwrights Ron Blair, Tony Morphett and Bob Ellis; the novelists Roger McDonald and Christopher Koch; the travel writer Colin Simpson, who prepared the 'Australian Walkabout' series in 1947–49 before leaving to write in the same subject area; and many others. Regular radio broadcasters have included Walter Murdoch, Vance and Nettie Palmer, H.M. Green, A.D. Hope, who was 'Anthony Inkwell' for a time on the famous children's programme 'The Argonauts' (1941–72), and Douglas Stewart, who gave the 1977 Boyer lectures on the *Bulletin*. Frank Hardy and Cyril Pearl were ABC television panellists. On the opening nights of both ABC radio and television a play was included in the programme. Although on each occasion the work broadcast was by an English writer (a symptom of the Commission's models and influences), the work of Australian writers has been significantly represented in each medium. In general terms – and leaving aside the countless features and talks programmes such as

'Quality Street' and its successors, 'Sunday Night Radio 2' and 'Radio Helicon', which have all had a significant literary component – Australian writers have been represented in three ways: by dramatic works (single plays and series) written especially for radio or television; by dramatic adaptations (again, single plays or series of already published material – often novels); and by readings rather than dramatic adaptations of already published material (again, often novels, as in the serialisation of Miles Franklin's *All That Swagger* in 1942 and the readings on ABC morning radio of Lennie Lower's *Here's Luck* in 1982 and Eve Langley's *The Pea Pickers* in 1983). Two pioneers in the first category were Max Afford (q.v.), whose 'The Flail of God' was the first play by an Australian writer broadcast on Australian radio (19 July 1932), and Edmund Barclay, who wrote the first ABC radio serial, 'As Ye Sow', which ran for nine months (January–September 1937) and like many successors in radio and television took early Australian history as its subject. Both Afford and Barclay were employed on contract by the Commission, although it was more usual for writers to be freelance. Among their contemporaries and successors in the field of radio drama (which was given impetus by several ABC competitions and drama weeks in the 1930s and 1940s) were Alexander Turner, George Landen Dann, Charles Porter, Betty Roland, Catherine Shepherd, Gwen Meredith (the creator and writer of two famous long-running serials, 'The Lawsons', 1944–49, and 'Blue Hills', 1949–76), Dymphna Cusack, Dulcie Deamer, Catherine Duncan, Colin Thiele, Ruth Park, D'Arcy Niland, Coral Lansbury, Vance Palmer, Jessica Anderson, Oriel Gray, Rex Rienits, George Farwell, Eleanor Witcombe, Peter Kenna, Kay Keavney, Hal Porter, Sumner Locke-Elliott and Douglas Stewart, whose *The Fire on the Snow* (q.v.), broadcast first in 1941, is a famous Australian radio play, and whose *Ned Kelly* and *The Golden Lover* were also broadcast by the ABC in 1942 and 1943. Several of these writers wrote mainly outside broadcasting, but Dann, Porter, Shepherd, Duncan, Lansbury, Gray and Meredith are among those who established their reputations in radio. Some, like Gray, Keavney, MacCallum and Rienits, who wrote *Stormy Petrel* (1960), the first ABC television serial, made the transition successfully to television; other ABC television playwrights of note have been Locke-Elliott, Peter Yeldham, Alan Seymour, and Ray Lawler, who were all also successful in television overseas; Colin Free, who wrote for the successful series *Contrabandits*, *Delta*, *Over There* and *Learned Friends*; Barbara Vernon, who created *Bellbird* (1967–79), television's equivalent of 'Blue Hills'; Pat Flower, Michael Boddy, Phillip Grenville Mann and Tony Morphett.

Some of these writers were responsible for the dramatic adaptations of previously published material, the second major way in which Australian writers have been represented on ABC radio and television. Innumerable Australian poems, plays, stories and novels have been dramatically adapted for or broadcast on ABC radio. Among notable television series or serials based on Australian novels are George

Johnston's *My Brother Jack* in 1965, D'Arcy Niland's *Dead Men Running* in 1971, the Norman Lindsay festival (adaptations of six novels) in 1972, Frank Hardy's *Power Without Glory* in 1976, Kylie Tennant's *Ride on Stranger* in 1979, Eleanor Dark's *The Timeless Land* and Sumner Locke-Elliott's *Water Under the Bridge* in 1980, Alan Marshall's *I Can Jump Puddles* in 1981, Roger McDonald's *1915* in 1982, Thea Astley's *A Descant for Gossips* in 1983, and Locke-Elliott's *Edens Lost* in 1989. Several of these series have been repeated on commercial television, which has also represented the work of Australian writers in its own series, e.g. *His Natural Life* (q.v.) in 1983. Some commentators have criticised the shift from single plays, whether adaptations or not, to series and serials. In 1986 the ABC introduced 'The Book Program', its first regular literary T.V. programme whose orientation was mainly towards Australian books, writers and publishing. It ran for only two series, 1986–87. ABC Radio has the long-running 'The Book Report', while Radio National has 'Books and Writing' and a book review programme, 'First Edition'. In 1992, the 60th anniversary of the ABC, several fine dramatic series were written and performed for ABC television, e.g. *Brides of Christ* and *Leaving Liverpool*; in 1993 *The Seven Deadly Sins*.

The ABC figures prominently in the many studies of Australian communications and the media (e.g. Sandra Hall's *Supertoy: 20 Years of Australian Television*, 1976). More specialist in focus are various memoirs or studies by ex-ABC employees and commissioners, including J.R. Darling's *The ABC and the Community* (1962), M.F. Dixon's *Inside the ABC* (1975), Ellis Blain's *Life with Aunty* (1977), B. McCallum's *Tales Untold: Memories of an ABC Publicity Officer* (1978), Richard Harding's *Outside Interference: The Politics of Australian Broadcasting* (1979), Clement Semmler's *The ABC: Aunt Sally and Sacred Cow* (1981) and *Pictures on the Margin: Memoirs* (1991), which includes some of his reminiscences of thirty-five years with the ABC, and Ida Elizabeth Jenkins's *Good Rowing!* (1983). There have been two major histories, Alan Thomas's study of the early years, *Broadcast and Be Damned* (1980), and K.S. Inglis's *This is the ABC: The Australian Broadcasting Commission 1932–83* (1983). The ABC has also made its own contribution to Australian literature through publishing activities which range from journals such as the *ABC Weekly* and *24 Hours* (which began as a programme guide in 1976 but now stands as an arts magazine in its own right, edited since 1990 by Suzy Baldwin) to books based on series, including *Australian Writers Speak* (1942), *Current Books Worth Reading* (1941–55), *Todays Books* (1956–63), *Todays Writing* (1963–64), *Books for Comment* (1963–69), John Thompson's *On Lips of Living Men* (1962) and *Five to Remember* (1964), and Douglas Stewart's *Writers of the Bulletin* (1977). *News Not Views: The ABC, the Press and Politics 1932–1947* (1993) by Neville Petersen is the first of a scheduled three-volume sociological history of ABC News.

Australian-Canadian Studies, a twice-yearly journal, began publication at La Trobe University in 1983 and in 1986 came under the sponsorship of ACSANZ (the Association for Canadian Studies in Australia and New Zealand), and under the editorship of Gillian Whitlock and Malcolm Alexander of Griffith University. Originally subtitled 'an interdisciplinary social science review', it was later subtitled 'a journal for the humanities & the social sciences', reflecting its shift to literary issues. *Australian-Canadian Studies* is currently edited by Gerry Turcotte of the New Literatures Research Centre at the University of Wollongong.

Australian Capers: Or, Christopher Cockle's Colonial Experience, a novel by John Richard Houlding (q.v.), was first published in 1867; it is also known by the title of the 1913 edition, *Christopher Cockle's Australian Experiences*. A cautionary tale of the misadventures of a 'new chum' (q.v.) in the colonies, *Australian Capers* opens with the birth of Christopher Cockle, the son of a wealthy London fishmonger and alderman; the surname-occupation pun is characteristic of Houlding, as is his comic use of dialect and exaggerated metaphor. At twenty, attracted by news of the gold discoveries, Christopher sets sail for Australia but falls victim *en route* to seasickness, drink, tobacco, gambling and his own naivety. On arrival he tours Melbourne, where he is inadvertently left in charge of a runaway cab and is locked up in the watchhouse after a drunken spree, before disembarking at Sydney. He takes rooms in a hotel where he meets Mr Fitz-Chowse Slyver, a swindler who relieves Christopher not only of money but also of the papers by which he can be impersonated. After further difficulties in Sydney, Christopher travels up-country to Kickadingo to stay with his uncle, where his new chum *gaucheries* are revealed when he puts both charges down one barrel of a double-barrelled shotgun; while returning home he meets a young woman, Julia Doveskin, at whose house he takes up lodging and to whom he becomes engaged. On his return from another visit to the country, this time to the kindly Mr Todd, Christopher surprises Julia entertaining a sailor; he goes on a binge, suffers a bout of delirium tremens, and attempts suicide. He is rescued by the support of his uncle Nicholas, Mr Todd and Tim Rafferty, a rough-diamond steward on the boat to Australia who has defended Christopher when his family in England, deceived by Slyver's duplicities, had thought the worst of his conduct. Converted to Christianity at the end of the novel, Christopher settles down to become a clerk. The best of Houlding's books, *Australian Capers* is interspersed with homiletic and other tales recounted by the people Christopher meets. A gently satirical picture of the new chum, it contains some shrewd observations of city life and of colonists.

Australian Council for the Arts was established in 1968 to take over from the Australian Elizabethan Theatre Trust the task of advising the federal government and distributing its subsidy in the area of the performing arts. In 1973 its functions were expanded in order to implement the policies of the government of E.G. Whitlam for the enlargement and consolidation of federal government support to the arts. As a consequence, literature and arts other than the performing arts, which had previously attracted separate government support (e.g. through the Commonwealth Literary Fund) were also brought within the jurisdiction of the Australian Council for the Arts, which became the Australia Council (q.v.) after legislation creating that statutory authority was passed in 1975.

Australian Cultural Elites: Intellectual Traditions in Sydney and Melbourne (1974), a provocative study by John Docker (q.v.), suggests that the different cultural histories of Australia's major cities, Sydney and Melbourne, have produced fundamentally conflicting views of the relationship between Australia's European inheritance of ideas, ideologies and assumptions and the new 'Australian' experience and social environments. Australian culture itself is not unified and monolithic; it contains alternative and varied traditions which are versions, in Australia, of major European cultural arguments, exemplified by Docker as 'social optimism versus social pessimism, varieties of romanticism, pluralism, anarchism, libertarianism, liberal humanism, theories of social intervention, and the role of intellectuals in society'. In two parts, 'A Sydney Literary Tradition', and 'Sydney and Melbourne', *Australian Cultural Elites* discusses, for example, the roles of Christopher Brennan, the Norman Lindsay-Kenneth Slessor Artist-Aristocracy, A.D. Hope, Patrick White, John Anderson and the Sydney Freethought tradition, and the influence of *Meanjin* and *Southerly* in their respective home cities. It concludes by offering a view of the impact of the Vietnam War on Australian cultural life.

Australian Cultural History, published annually since 1981, originated from the Australian Academy of the Humanities and the History of Ideas Unit, RSSS, ANU, with S.L. Goldberg and F.B. Smith. From 1989 it was published by the School of History, University of New South Wales, edited by David Walker. It deals specifically with themes raised by the preceding annual conference, themes associated with the history of culture in Australia. Literary and publishing features are often included.

Australian Dictionary of Biography (ADB) has been published in twelve volumes organised alphabetically within three periods (1788–1850, 1851–90 and 1891–1939). The *ADB* treats significant Australian identities and personalities, including many writers. Based at the Australian National University, Canberra, the *ADB* has had several general editors – Douglas Pike (volumes 1–5), Bede Nairn (6), Bede Nairn/Geoffrey Serle (7–10), Geoffrey Serle (11) and John Ritchie (12). A four-volume series covering the period 1940–80 has commenced, volume 13, A–De, under the editorship of Ritchie, appearing in 1993.

'Australian Dream' is a phrase that has been used to describe the hopes and anticipations that have been traditionally held by Australians for themselves and their country. Those hopes and anticipations have varied with the changing circumstances and patterns of Australian life from the first settlement in 1788 through the colonial period to nationhood. Components of the dream have included liberty, equality and fraternity (the last given a particular Australian flavour by the creed of mateship), Utopianism, the ethos of the bush, democratic humanism, nationalism and radicalism. Writers who have been significant in the creation of the dream include W.C. Wentworth, Charles Harpur, Henry Kendall, John Dunmore Lang, Daniel Deniehy, William Lane, W.G. Spence, John Farrell, Mary Gilmore, Henry Lawson, A.B. Paterson, Bernard O'Dowd, Miles Franklin, E.J. Brady, Randolph Bedford, Alfred Deakin, Henry Bournes Higgins, R.D. FitzGerald, Brian Penton and Les Murray. Ian Turner compiled an anthology, *The Australian Dream* (1968); T. Inglis Moore traces the chronological variations of the dream in *Social Patterns in Australian Literature* (1971).

Australian Elizabethan Theatre Trust, first proposed by H.C. Coombs (q.v.), was formed in 1954 to provide assistance to theatre and later the other performing arts. It was funded initially by private sources but subsequently secured increasing government aid and became a combination of private entrepreneur and the agency through which federal government support was dispensed to the performing arts. After the formation of the Australian Council for the Arts in 1968 it continued with its entrepreneurial functions and administered, through the Australia Council, the orchestras of the Australian Ballet Foundation and the Australian Opera. It played a significant part in establishing performing arts companies in opera, ballet, drama and music; helped to found NIDA (see National Institute of Dramatic Art) and administered the Elizabethan Theatre in Sydney. Its publications included *Theatre Spectrum* (1969–71), *Elizabethan Trust News* (1971–76) and *Theatrescope* (1976). In the late 1980s the Trust ran into financial difficulties and went into liquidation in 1991.

Australian Encyclopaedia, first projected by Angus & Robertson in 1912 as a biographical and historical record of Australia, was published in its inaugural edition in 1925 in two volumes, edited by A.W. Jose and H.J. Carter. A second edition was published in 1958 in ten volumes, edited by A.H. Chisholm and Bruce Pratt. In 1962 Angus & Robertson sold the *Australian Encyclopaedia* to the Grolier Society of Australia. Five reprintings of the 1958 edition, with minor alterations, were made under the editorship of Bruce Pratt between 1962 and 1972. A third edition, edited by Pratt in six volumes, was published in 1977, revised in 1979 and reprinted in 1981. The third edition contains 1700 biographies of notable Australians, many of whom are literary figures, and contains many entries on geographical features and historical events that are also significant in Australian literature. An expanded fourth edition of twelve volumes, with new cross-reference and index systems, and produced by an editorial board headed by Sir Harold White with Richard

Appleton as editor-in-chief, was published in 1983. In 1987 the *Encyclopaedia* was purchased by the Australian Geographic Society which published a fifth edition in 1988, under Richard Appleton as editor-in-chief. The 1988 edition is in nine volumes and contains 400 new articles and a new introductory section, 'Australia and the World'. Angus & Robertson returned to the encyclopaedia field with *The Australian People* (1988), one of the many works inspired by the Bicentenary. Other Australian encyclopaedias include *Encyclopaedia of Australia* (1968) by Andrew and Nancy Learmonth and *The Penguin Australian Encyclopaedia* (1988), edited by Sarah Dawson.

Australian English is a term used to describe the form of English spoken and written in Australia. Like other national varieties of English, it shares much of its vocabulary and pronunciation with the parent form, but historical, social and environmental factors mean that it has developed distinctive features of its own. This distinctive component of the English spoken and written in Australia has itself been called Australian English or something similar, as in E.E. Morris's dictionary, *Austral English* (1898), and W.S. Ramson's *Australian English. An Historical Study of the Vocabulary 1788/1898* (1966) where it is suggested that 'For all practical purposes, Australian English consists of the additions to British English'. The narrower usage has declined somewhat, however, and in reference to the vocabulary of Australian English it is now as common to use terms like 'Australianisms' to describe the distinctively Australian component of the lexicon; 'Australianism' was used in this way at least as far back as the 1890s. The spoken English of Australians is referred to by a variety of terms, including Australian pronunciation, Australian speech, the Australian accent and spoken Australian English.

English began to be established in Australia with the arrival of the First Fleet in 1788. Because of the penal nature of the original British settlement, there existed initially a distinction between the language of the military administrators – what Ramson has called 'polite English' – and the more 'vulgar' language of convicts, e.g. the thieves' slang of James Hardy Vaux (q.v.), and the language of some early immigrants. It was from the latter linguistic group, and well before the end of transportation, that a new speech developed among the Australians born and raised in the colonies, a speech still noted for its homogeneity; in other words, although there is a range of pronunciation in Australia, it is determined by social rather than regional factors. The 'mixing-bowl' theory advanced by A.G. Mitchell, J.R.L. Bernard and some others to account for the evolution of Australian speech has three main ingredients. First, because the earliest settlers came from all parts of Britain, a distinctive speech evolved, initially among colonial children, from the mixture of dialects spoken, with London English the most important influence. Second, the urban origins of a significant proportion of the settlers, together with the fact that they were overwhelmingly British, were factors in the standardisation of the new speech.

Third, regional homogeneity is explained by the re-creation of the new speech again and again in 'germinal centres' of the colonies (i.e. in different parts of the colonies, as settlement spread).

That the first distinctively Australian speech derived from the convicts and other humble settlers means that from the outset Australian speech bore, in Bernard's words, a 'halo of attributes which necessarily alienated it from many ... other speakers of English'. Thus from the 1820s until recently Australian English has been criticised both inside the country (notably among educated Australians adopting as their model, standard English, what is called 'Received Pronunciation' or 'RP') and outside it (notably among RP speakers in England). In 1946 A.G. Mitchell listed as the commonest criticisms that Australian speech was ugly, lazy, slovenly, nasal, drawling, unclear, Cockney, monotonous and flat. Some of the criticisms can be linked with differences between Australian speech and other forms of spoken English – the notion of flatness, for example, derives from the fact that the tonal range of Australian speech is smaller than that of RP – but others (for example, nasality) have no basis in fact; and even the assimilations and elisions which characterise 'Strine' (q.v.) are commonly found in other varieties of English. Fundamentally, spoken Australian English is no worse or no better than other varieties, and the criticisms made of it are substantially value judgements based on taste and association.

Nevertheless, Bernard has suggested that some speakers of Australian English have felt the need to upgrade their speech, and that this is one reason for the evolution of what is recognised as three main styles or types of pronunciation: Broad Australian (the form closest to the distinctive Australian speech which emerged early in the nineteenth century, and the one most commentators have in mind when they are critical of Australian speech); Cultivated Australian (a minority form, the prestige dialect in the minds of its speakers, valued as closer to the prestige dialects of England and the USA and that followed by some broadcasters); and General Australian (the form, spoken by the majority of Australians, which lies between Broad and Cultivated). These varieties share distinctive phonetic and prosodic characteristics but exist on a spectrum, with Cultivated Australian closest to RP and Broad Australian furthest away; Australian speakers have the capacity to use sounds from across the spectrum and to move between categories. It follows that the distinctive features of Australian English are to be found most clearly within the Broad Australian. In general, and in comparison with RP, spoken Australian English is narrower in tonal range, and slower in rhythm because of a more even stress pattern, e.g. Australians give more equal weight to their vowels in 'Sunday' than other English speakers. Speech at the Broad Australian end of the spectrum also tends to be marked by assimilation and elision. Apart from these prosodic features, the major differences occur in the vowels and diphthongs: Australian vowels are closer, i.e. made with higher tongue positions, and some are more frontal, i.e. made more towards the front of the mouth. As well as these phonetic differences between Australian English and RP in the quality of what is essentially the same sound, some Australian English vowels and diphthongs are pronounced in such a way that they move towards (and for some Broad Australian speakers become) other sounds – or at least are heard as other sounds by other English speakers, hence the numerous stories of Englishmen hearing 'mite' when an Australian has said 'mate'. Among other noticeable features, there is a greater use of the indeterminate or neutral vowel in Australian English than in other varieties; many speakers of Australian English choose quite different vowels or diphthongs from RP speakers in pronouncing words like 'chance'; and Australians make greater use of truncated forms, e.g. 'footy', 'schoolie'.

Like Australian speech, the vocabulary of Australian English is noted for its homogeneity, despite the kind of regional variety that makes it difficult for a New South Welshman when he asks for 'scallops' instead of 'potato cakes' in Melbourne, or for a 'schooner' instead of a 'pint' of beer in Adelaide. That Australians until recently have overwhelmingly used British or American dictionaries is a measure of the extent to which Australian English shares its vocabulary with the parent form and with other national varieties; yet there have been significant additions to British English, particularly in colloquial usage and occupational vocabularies (e.g. shearing) which derive from the unique history of Australia and from other factors. Four historical periods have been identified in the development of the lexicon of Australian English: the colonial period from 1788 to about 1850 (i.e. the end of transportation and the beginning of the gold rushes, when the first settlers were responding to their new environment); the gold-rush period, which is characterised by more diverse immigration which had a consequential effect on the expansion of the vocabulary (for example, in increasing influence from America); the nationalist period from the 1890s until after the First World War, when journals like the *Bulletin* fostered a sense of national identity and some of its most popular writers (e.g. Henry Lawson, 'Steele Rudd') extensively employed Australian idioms; and the modern period, particularly since the Second World War, in which developments in communications have been significant in bringing Australian English closer to other national varieties, at the same time as playwrights such as Jack Hibberd and satirists such as Barry Humphries (qq.v.) have exploited the potential of indigenous idiom. Within and sometimes straddling these chronological boundaries, significant influences on the development of Australian idiom include the convict system, the rural character of nineteenth-century Australia, the war experiences of Australians, and the importance of sport and other leisure activities. In general Australianisms have been created in three main ways: by borrowing from Aboriginal, Australian pidgin, other languages and other national varieties of English (e.g. 'cooee', 'bush', 'squatter', qq.v.); by the extensions and new meanings given to existing English words (e.g. 'wattle', q.v., and the compounds deriving from 'stock'); and by the survival of words, notably slang and dialect words (e.g. 'bowyang', 'larrikin', 'billy', qq.v.), which have had a longer life or more general use in Australia, sometimes to such an extent that they are popularly thought to be Australian creations. The last two processes often overlap.

Throughout the nineteenth century, numerous comments on colonial idiom and pronunciation were made by government officials, visitors and travellers, explorers, newly-arrived settlers and established residents: for example (among many who could be cited), James Backhouse, David Collins, Peter Cunningham, Barron Field, Friedrich Gerstaecker, Richard and William Howitt, David McKenzie, John MacGillivray, Louisa Anne Meredith, T.L. Mitchell, Samuel Mossman, G.C. Mundy, Charles Rudston Read and Alexander Tolmer. The published writings of these observers have been major sources, along with unpublished journals and diaries, contemporary newspapers and the work of early creative writers such as Alexander Harris, for later historians and lexicographers of Australian English. At the end of the century, at a time of increased national awareness, the first studies of Australian pronunciation and the first word lists, glossaries and dictionaries of Australianisms began to appear. The first detailed account of Australasian pronunciation was by Samuel McBurney, a Glasgow-born principal of a Geelong ladies' college who in 1887 travelled extensively in eastern Australia and NZ examining singers in schools; he made extensive notes as he went on his examinees' pronunciation of sample words, and his observations form the basis of the analysis of Australasian pronunciation included in A.J. Ellis's *On Early English Pronunciation* (1887). In the same period were published the anonymous *Sydney Slang Dictionary* (?1882), the German scholar Karl Lentzner's *Dictionary of the Slang-English of Australia and of Some Mixed Languages* (1892), based partly on residence in Australia, and Cornelius Crowe's *The Australian Slang Dictionary* (1895).

These dictionaries are all limited in coverage and reliability, including words that did not have either a currency or a distinctive usage in Australia. Nonetheless, they attest to an interest in collecting Australian idioms, particularly informal idioms, which has continued to the present day; the most important collector until recent times is Sidney Baker (q.v.), whose *The Australian Language* (1945) and other publications remain indispensable reference tools. Apart from his work, there have been many twentieth-century vocabularies and dictionaries, even leaving aside the glossaries of slang and colloquial terms included in dictionaries of folklore, e.g. by Bill Wannan, or literary works which extensively employ Australian popular idiom, from C.J. Dennis's *The Songs of a Sentimental Bloke* (1915) to Hibberd's *A Stretch of the Imagination* (1973). The most important dictionary of informal usage is G.A. Wilkes's scholarly *A Dictionary of Australian Colloquialisms* (1978, revised 1985 and 1990), a historical dictionary which supplies illustrative quotations taken mainly from printed sources; others include Baker's *A Popular Dictionary of Australian Slang* (1941) and *The Barracker's Bible* (1983) by Jack Hibberd and Garrie Hutchinson, a witty treatment of Australian sporting slang. A second group of works either combines commentary and glossary, e.g. Baker's *The Drum: Australian Character and Slang* (1959), or remains focused on Australian slang and colloquial usage without including any consolidated word list, e.g. Bill Hornadge's *The Australian Slanguage* (1980) and Nancy Keesing's *Lily on the Dustbin: Slang of Australian Women and Families* (1982). These popular publications are all mainly confined to the distinctively Australian informal part of Australian English, the Australianisms; even the Wilkes *Dictionary of Australian Colloquialisms*, by far the most important of those listed, has been renamed a *Dictionary of Colloquial Australianisms* by one of its reviewers. Another group of vocabularies and dictionaries, however, incorporates Australian slang within a wide lexical context. W.H. Downing's *Digger Dialects* (1919, updated in 1990 by the Australian National Dictionary Centre), the first record of Australian service slang, includes words current elsewhere in English, and Australian material is incorporated, with Baker as a major source, in the several slang dictionaries of Eric Partridge, notably *Slang To-Day and Yesterday* (1933, 4th edn 1970), *A Dictionary of Slang and Unconventional English* (1937, 7th edn 1970), and *A Dictionary of the Underworld* (1950, 3rd edn 1968) and Gary Simes's more specific *A Dictionary of Australian Underworld Slang* (1993). The most important early contribution to the lexicography of Australian English, however, was a work which has been criticised for its scant treatment of colloquial vocabulary: *Austral English: A Dictionary of Australasian Words, Phrases and Usages* (1898, reprinted 1968, 1971, 1972), by E.E. Morris (q.v.), an Indian-born Englishman who came to Australia in 1875 to take up a Melbourne headmastership and was appointed professor of English, French and German in 1883. Begun as a by-product of work for the *Oxford English Dictionary*, *Austral English* is strongest in its coverage of Aboriginal, Maori and scientific words, particularly in the attention given to flora and fauna, and includes quotations which illustrate the history of the words included. As a historical dictionary of Australianisms it was complemented by the Wilkes dictionary and ultimately replaced by the *Australian National Dictionary* (see Australian National Dictionary Centre) prepared by a team of lexicographers at the Australian National University under the direction of W.S. Ramson and published in 1988, the bicentenary of English settlement in Australia. The *Australian National Dictionary* is the first comprehensive, historically based record of the 10 000 words which make up the Australian contribution to the English language. The preparation of the *Australian National Dictionary* benefited not only from the attention paid by Baker, Wilkes and others to informal Australian English, but also from a range of other research: more broadly based studies of Australian vocabulary, research into specialist vocabularies and studies of other aspects of Australian English (e.g. phonetics). Historically (before the establishment of the Australian National Dictionary Centre in Canberra), the most important centre for research was the University of Sydney where A.G. Mitchell was both student and professor of English; among his several publications was *The Pronunciation of English in Australia* (1946) the first systematic account of Australian pronunciation. Among later students were Arthur Delbridge, J.R.L. Bernard, R.D. Eagleson, J.S. Gunn, and Ramson, all of whom have made significant contributions to knowledge about Australian English phonetics and lexicography; all were on the staff and part of the Australian Language Research Centre of the university but several have furthered Australian English research at other institutions, e.g. Delbridge and Bernard at Macquarie University, Ramson at the ANU. The 1960s saw several important studies: Ramson's *Australian English*; revised editions of Baker's *The Australian Language* (1966) and Mitchell's *The Pronunciation of English in Australia* (1966, with Delbridge, who earlier collaborated on *The Speech of Australian Adolescents* 1965); *The English Language in Australia and New Zealand* (1966) by G.W. Turner, who like several other scholars of Australian English (Ramson, Baker, Grahame Johnston) was originally from NZ; studies of migrant varieties of Australian English, e.g. Michael Clyne's *Transference and Triggering* (1967), Aboriginal languages, and Australian place-names.

Research has continued from the 1970s to the 1990s, although the last decade has been probably more notable for the emergence (as well as the dictionaries of Australianisms already mentioned) of general Australian English dictionaries, i.e. dictionaries which give due weighting both to Australianisms and to the standard English basis of Australian English. Before 1976 general dictionaries used in Australia were predominantly English or American ones such as the various *Oxford* and *Webster's*, although editions with a supplement of Australasian words were published periodically. The first of these was Joshua Lake's dictionary of Australasian words, published in the Australasian edition of *Webster's International Dictionary of the English Language* (1898) and also in the separately published *The Australasian Supplement to Webster's International Dictionary* (1898). Later supplements include Mitchell's 'A Supplement of Australian Words' in a 1952 edition of *Chambers' Shorter English Dictionary*, R.W. Burchfield's 'A Supplement of Australian and New Zealand Words' in the 1969 edition of *The Pocket Oxford Dictionary of Current English*, and George Mackaness's 'A Selective Dictionary of Australian & New Zealand Words and Phrases' in several Collins dictionaries, including *Collins New English Dictionary* (1956), ed. Alexander H. Irvine. Just as Lake's supplement was incorporated into the body of *Webster's*, so many other general dictionaries without Australian supplements have included Australian words, e.g. the *Oxford English Dictionary*. Nineteen seventy-six, however, saw the publication of both the *Heinemann Australian Dictionary*, compiled in conjunction with a team at La Trobe University with all words 'written in standard Australian' but limited in its usefulness and the far more important *Australian Pocket Oxford Dictionary*. Edited by Grahame Johnston, the *Australian Pocket Oxford* was based on the 1969 *Pocket Oxford Dictionary of Current English*, but with each entry 'scrutinized for its application to Australian conditions' it went much further than previous English dictionaries of comparable size in covering Australian vocabulary, idiom and, to a lesser extent, pronunciation. A second edition of the *Australian Pocket Oxford* by George Turner was published in 1984 and a third edition by Bruce Moore in 1993. In 1979 a new *Collins Dictionary of the English Language* was published in an 'Australian edition', with introductory material on Australian English by G.A. Wilkes. Although it includes Australian words and usages it is an international dictionary, with an identical word list for the Australian, American, English and other editions; its offshoots, however, the *Gem* and the *Pocket* (both 1981 second edition 1992, edited by W.A. Krebs) and the *Concise* (1982, edited by Krebs and Wilkes) with a second edition in 1992 titled *The Collins Concise Dictionary* containing a further 15 000 entries on people, places and institutions, are 'Australianised' in a comparable way to the *Australian Pocket Oxford*. Finally, there is the monumental *Macquarie Dictionary* (1981, second edition 1992, computerised 1993), prepared at Macquarie University with Arthur Delbridge as editor-in-chief; modified from the *Encyclopedic World Dictionary* it in turn has been the parent dictionary for the *Concise* (ed. Delbridge and Bernard), *Budget, Pocket* (1982, ed. David Blair) and *Handy* (1983, ed. Ramson) *Macquarie*. The *Macquarie Dictionary* goes much further than its immediate predecessors in the precedence it gives to Australian pronunciation and definitions. Thus the 'i' and 'y' sounds in 'capacity' are rendered respectively as the neutral vowel and to rhyme with 'sea' in the *Macquarie;* in the *Collins* and the *Australian Pocket Oxford* the international or more standard English 'i' (as in 'sit') is given for both. Similarly, a special Australian usage of a word is given precedence over a special British or American usage, as in 'lay-by' or 'colonial'. Reviews of the *Macquarie* have welcomed the comprehensiveness of its coverage of Australian idiom and vocabulary, although its dropping of such labels as 'Aust.' means, paradoxically, that its readers have no way of knowing which of its words are Australianisms. Research and publication continue. Stephen Murray-Smith's *Right Words: A Guide to English Usage in Australia* (1987) contributes to the discussion on the way the English language is used (and misused) in Australia; other works include *Exploring Australian English* (1987) by Wilkes, *Glancing Blows: Life and Language in Australia* (1987) by playwright Alex Buzo, and *Modern Australian Usage* (1993) by Nicholas Hudson. Peter Collins and David Blair edited *Australian English: The Language of a New Society* (1989), a collection of essays on subjects ranging from vocabulary and syntax to linguistic geography, the history of particular dialects and the origins of the Australian accent. From the Australian National Dictionary Centre came, in 1989, *Australian Words and Their Origins*, which gives the meanings, origins and pronunciation of those words which were coined in Australia, which have wider currency here than elsewhere or which have special significance in Australian history. The Centre also published in 1992 the *Concise* version of the 1988 *Australian National Dictionary*, the *Concise* edited by Joan Hughes, associate editor of the Centre.

Australian Feminist Studies (1985–   ), a twice-yearly publication edited by Susan Magarey, publishes articles and reviews in the fields of feminist research and women's studies courses.

Australian Girl, An, a novel by Catherine Martin (q.v.), was published anonymously in 1890, although the 1894 edition used Martin's pseudonym, 'Mrs Alick MacLeod'. Stella Courtland, an exceptionally well-educated and spirited girl of independent attitudes, is the youngest member of a large, prosperous and happy family. With her deeply religious widowed mother, she lives on one of the family's properties, Fairacre, in SA. Stella's brothers and sisters look forward to marriage as an agreeable destiny, but Stella is far from sanguine about the institution; she has similar, strong ideas about most of the conventional religious attitudes professed by their neighbours. Fascinated by the life of the Aborigines, sensitive to the sufferings of the rural poor and drawn by the beauties of the bush, she prefers the natural pleasures of station life to the trivial pursuits of the city. Her doubts about marriage are reinforced by the misfortunes of her friend Cicely Mowbray, who has left her alcoholic husband, and contribute to her reluctance to marry Edward Ritchie, a childhood friend who has passionately courted her for several years. Ritchie, a well-connected squatter, has one sister, Laurette, a social climber whose ambitions have been furthered to some extent by her marriage to a dissolute member of the British aristocracy, the Hon. Talbot Tareling. Aware that she feels only a mild affection for Ritchie, Stella is further alienated from him by his inability to share her intellectual interests. At times, however, she feels that it is her inevitable destiny to be his wife. The engagement of her clergyman brother, Cuthbert, appears to threaten one of her closest relationships and to strengthen the likelihood of her own marriage. Meanwhile her aspirations for a real friendship with a member of the opposite sex have been encouraged by a brief meeting with Anselm Langdale, an English doctor with German connections and a man 'devoted to ideas and not jostled up with the meanness of ordinary life'. During a visit to her brother's station in Victoria, she meets Langdale again, and forms a close friendship with him which deepens into love. Langdale is suddenly recalled to England, but before he leaves they become informally engaged. Prevented by circumstances from telling Stella of his previous disastrous marriage and his wife's death, Langdale leaves a letter containing the facts of the past with Laurette in Melbourne. Intent on furthering her brother's desires, since in this way she solves some of her financial difficulties, Laurette conceals the fact of Langdale's visit, partly destroys his letter and inserts a false one implying that his wife is still alive. Anguished by the news, Stella agrees to marry Ritchie but discovers shortly afterwards to her horror and disgust that he is an alcoholic. They visit Europe where Stella meets Anselm again and learns the truth. She becomes ill, falling into a mental apathy that is close to insanity, but recovers with Anselm's moral support. Tempted to renounce her marriage, she undergoes a profound religious experience during a service held by Cardinal Newman, which convinces her that she must set aside her personal happiness and find common cause with suffering humanity. *An Australian Girl* was republished in 1988 in Allen & Unwin's series, *Australian Women Writers: The Literary Heritage*.

Australian Highway, the monthly journal of the Workers' Educational Association of Australia, was published in Sydney 1919–69; it contained literary articles, sketches, short stories and book reviews.

Australian Humanities Research Council, an organisation which aimed to promote knowledge in and awareness of the humanities, was formally constituted in 1956, two years after an interim council had been established through, in particular, the efforts of Brian Elliott and A.N. Jeffares of the University of Adelaide. Originally comprising twenty-six members, the Council was enlarged through the regular election of fellows and honorary fellows. One of its first achievements was the survey *The Humanities in Australia*, published in 1959 under the editorship of A. Grenfell Price. Among its other publications were occasional papers, monographs and a *Report* which was published annually until the Council was replaced by the Australian Academy of the Humanities (q.v.) in 1969.

Australian Journal (weekly 1865–69, monthly 1869–1962), originating in Melbourne and published for much of its life by A.H. Massina & Company, was one of the few Australian magazines to satisfy popular taste for a prolonged period. During the editorship of Marcus Clarke (1870–71) it announced a policy of publishing only original fiction set in the colonies or which treated colonial life or subjects of colonial interest. Best known for its serialisation (1870–72) of the original version of Marcus Clarke's *His Natural Life*, of *Chidiock Tichborne* (1874–75), and of Charles de Boos's *Fifty Years Ago* (1869–70), it also published works by Charles Harpur, Ada Cambridge, 'Rolf Boldrewood' and James Skipp Borlase. An attractive feature was its profile of 'Australian Characters' such as 'The Shearer', 'The Stockman', 'The Bullock Driver' and so on during the 1860s.

Australian Journal of Cultural Studies, published in Australia 1983–87, was replaced by *Cultural Studies*, published in rotation in Australia, UK and the USA. Australian content was highest in the period 1983–87.

Australian Journalists' Association (AJA) was formed in Melbourne in 1910. Before then there had been organisations of journalists in most capital cities and some provincial centres, e.g. the Victorian Reporters Association (formed 1889), the Bendigo Press Association (1901), the Melbourne Press Bond (1906), and the NSW Institute of Journalists (1907), but most of these were more social than concerned with better-

ing the conditions of journalists. The driving force behind the establishment of the AJA was B.S. Baxter Cook (1877–1968) who, as a member of the staff of the *Herald* in Melbourne, had reported the passing of the Commonwealth Conciliation and Arbitration Act (1904). He convened the meeting which formed the AJA in order to seek registration under the Act. In 1911 branches were formed in the other States, in most cases from a nucleus of the existing social organisations, though there was some opposition in NSW from the Writers and Artists Union, which T.D. Mutch had formed in 1910 for a similar industrial purpose; Mutch, however, was later active in the AJA. In 1911 registration was granted and in 1917 the first award was granted, based on a system of grading journalists which survives today. The AJA embraces other newspaper workers such as photographers and artists as well as journalists who work for government and in other places outside newspapers. It is a federal organisation with eight districts, one in each of the six States and in the ACT, as well as a NSW provincial district. Among the awards it administers are the Montague Grover Award for cadet journalists and, since 1956, the W.G. Walkley Awards; winners of the Walkley Award have included Craig McGregor, Anne Summers and Keith Willey. Apart from B.S. Baxter Cook, foundation members of the AJA included Benjamin Hoare, Percy Lindsay and Sir Keith Murdoch in Victoria, W.A. Woods (Walter Head) in Tasmania and, in NSW, F.J. Broomfield and H.M. Green who helped in the merging of the NSW Institute of Journalists with the AJA and was a delegate to the first national conference in 1912. Another significant figure in Australian literature to have been involved with the AJA was Brian Penton, who fell foul of the organisation's code of ethics while editor of the *Daily Telegraph* in the 1940s.

Australian Left Review, published bi-monthly since 1966, superseded the *Communist Review*. A Marxist journal devoted to promoting socialist ideas, it carries political, economic, historical and literary articles as well as book reviews. Its contributors include literary figures e.g. Dorothy Hewett, Judah Waten and Victor Williams. In 1992 it became *ALR Magazine*.

Australian Legend, The (1958, 2nd edn 1966 and illustrated edn 1978), is an influential account of the Australian national *mystique*, its origins and development, by Russel Ward (q.v.). Ward's analysis of the national self-image as egalitarian, collectivist, anti-authoritarian and practical, and his thesis that the ethos first grew up among the bush workers of the Australian pastoral industry, have been much debated. Writers who have contributed to the debate include Michael Roe in *Meanjin* (1962 and 1973), J.M. Ward in *The Pattern of Australian Culture* (1963), Coral Lansbury in *Arcady in Australia* (1970), Vincent Buckley in *Prospect* (1959), Sean Glynn in *Urbanisation in Australian History 1788–1900* (1970), Humphrey McQueen in *A New Britannia* (1970), Ronald Lawson in *Brisbane in the 1890s* (1973), Leon Cantrell in *The*

1890s (1970), Graeme Davison, Stuart Macintyre, David Walker and J.B. Hirst in *Historical Studies* (1978) and John Docker in *The Nervous Nineties* (1991). Roe, Lansbury and Docker in particular have offered alternative theses; Roe argues that the legend was derived from European romantic writers of the eighteenth and nineteenth centuries and transferred to Australia by urban, literary and contemplative men; Lansbury maintains that the legend derives from the rural idyll created in English literature of the 1850s by such writers as Charles Dickens and Bulwer-Lytton, and was transferred to non-industrial Australia, where it was taken up by literary Australians, while Docker asserts the impact of American culture on the developing nationalism of late nineteenth-century Australia. Ward has frequently replied to his critics and has re-examined his thesis in *Historical Studies* (1978).

Australian Letters, a SA quarterly founded by Geoffrey Dutton, Max Harris and Bryn Davies, appeared 1957–68. The editorial team consisted of Dutton and Harris throughout its history, Davies 1957–64 and Rosemary Wighton 1963–68. Cosmopolitan and urbane in tone, the periodical was less consciously political than *Overland, Meanjin* or *Quadrant*, less literary and academic than *Southerly* or *Australian Literary Studies* and less regional than *Westerly*. One of its distinctive features, a keen interest in art, was reflected in its covers, which carried reproductions of original drawings or paintings specially executed by Australian artists, and in a series of nineteen artist-poet collaborations. These included such striking partnerships as Russell Drysdale and David Campbell, Donald Friend and Douglas Stewart, Leonard French and James McAuley, and Sidney Nolan and Randolph Stow. Contributors to *Australian Letters* also included Patrick White, Randolph Stow, Judith Wright, Barry Oakley, Peter Mathers and Hal Porter. Many of its best contributions are reprinted in the anthology, *The Vital Decade* (1968), selected by Geoffrey Dutton and Max Harris. The annual verse anthology, *Verse in Australia* (1958–61), also appeared under its auspices

Australian Library Journal, the journal of the Library Association of Australia (formerly the Australian Institute of Librarians), began publication in July 1951. A quarterly, the *Australian Library Journal* is the successor to the much earlier and short-lived *Library Records of Australasia* (1901–2), the organ of the then Library Association of Australasia. Although primarily concerned with Library Association matters, the present journal carries information on recent publications in Australian literature.

Australian Literary Studies (ALS), largely the inspiration of James McAuley who played a significant role in the journal's establishment and maintenance until his death in 1976, began publication in 1963 from the University of Tasmania under the editorship of L.T. Hergenhan (q.v.); in 1975 the journal transferred to the University of Queensland. *ALS*, a half-yearly journal concerned exclusively with Australian litera-

ture, has no particular political affiliation or critical canon. Although devoted to both scholarly and critical studies of Australian literature, its chief interest has lain in the field of literary history; its contribution, for example, to the study of Australian literature of the nineteenth century has been considerable. Two valuable features of *ALS* have been its annual bibliography of Australian literature, compiled in the first years by the arduous research of individuals but maintained later from records of the Fryer Library of the University of Queensland; and the section entitled 'Notes and Documents', where small but significant research discoveries, especially in the biographical and bibliographical fields, are recorded. Among the special issues of *ALS* is (15, 2) Giovanna Capone (ed.) *European Perspectives: Contemporary Essays on Australian Literature*, the essays being by overseas critics and scholars. To mark the thirtieth year of *ALS* a cumulation of it annual bibliographies, *The ALS Guide to Australian Writers: A Bibliography 1963–1990*, edited by Martin Duwell and Laurie Hergenhan, was published in 1992.

Australian Literature: A Reference Guide (1977), by Fred Lock and Alan Lawson, is a guide to the reference sources, both Australian and non-Australian, useful for a study of Australian literature. With the E. Morris Miller and F.T. Macartney (qq.v.) bibliographies of Australian literature and other works as its starting-points, it includes sections on bibliographical aids, other reference sources such as encyclopaedias and dictionaries, periodicals and guides to periodicals, literary studies, and Australian libraries holding significant Australian literature material. It also has an authors' section which describes and evaluates bibliographical information on forty Australian authors. The second edition (1980) revises and updates the original, and includes a new section listing organisations concerned with the study of Australian literature.

Australian Literature Database (AUSTLIT), produced jointly by the Department of English and the Library of the University College of the University of New South Wales at the Australian Defence Force Academy in Canberra, was launched in August 1988 (with over 100 000 individual references) by E.G. Whitlam. The Database began under Professor Graham Johnston at the English Department, Faculty of Military Studies of the Royal Military College, Duntroon and was built up by the preparation of such Faculty of Military Studies publications as Joy Hooton's bibliography of A.D. Hope (1979), Barry Andrews and Bill Wilde's *Australian Literature to 1900: a Guide to Information Sources* (1980, in the Gale Information Guide Library Series, USA) and in Bill Wilde, Joy Hooton and Barry Andrews's *Oxford Companion to Australian Literature* (1985). Late in 1985 Professor Harry Heseltine, then of the English Department, and Mr Lynn Hard, the Academy Librarian, completed arrangements for the conversion of the Department's files to an online database on the Library's computer. AUSTLIT now comprises the largest Australian literature database in Australia and is updating continuously. Access to AUSTLIT on a national basis for schools and Australian and overseas universities and tertiary institutions is available and the database is now available on CD ROM.

Australian Literature from Its Beginnings to 1935: A Descriptive and Bibliographical Survey of Books by Australian Authors in Poetry, Drama, Fiction, Criticism and Anthology with Subsidiary Entries to 1938 was compiled by E. Morris Miller (q.v.) and published in two volumes in 1940. Sir John Quick (q.v.), working in collaboration with such researchers as F.J. Broomfield and Miller, had initiated the bibliographical work but it was left unfinished when Quick died in 1932. Miller undertook to complete the task, although in fact he had to begin the work again and revise its plan and scope. Volume I includes a descriptive, chronological survey of poetry to 1935, arranged by State, and followed by a chronological, extensively annotated bibliography of poetry, with entries to 1938; a chronological survey of drama for the same period, followed by a similar bibliography; and a descriptive survey of novelists and novels until 1899. Volume II includes a continuation of the fiction survey to 1935, followed by a chronological bibliography of fiction; a historical introduction to Australian criticism, followed by an extensive bibliography, which includes work on classical, modern and English as well as Australian literature, biography, essays, travel writings, philology, anthologies and translation; an appendix listing non-Australian authors of novels associated with Australia; and three exhaustive indexes, a subject index to the fiction entries, a general name-subject index and a general index of Australian authors. Although inaccuracies and critical absurdities can be found in *Miller*, as it is familiarly known, it is still an indispensable reference work, especially for the period 1850–1937, and contains a wealth of detailed, general information in its annotations and indexes. In response to a continuing demand, a facsimile edition was published in 1975. A second edition of *Australian Literature*, condensed, revised and rearranged by Frederick T. Macartney (q.v.), was published in 1956. As the full title *Australian Literature: A Bibliography to 1938 by E. Morris Miller, Extended to 1950, Edited with a Historical Outline and Descriptive Commentaries by Frederick T. Macartney* suggests, Macartney extended the work to 1950, wrote his own descriptive commentaries and included an introductory/historical survey. He also replaced Miller's unwieldy systems of arrangement with an alphabetical order, pruned much of the biographical material, corrected some of the inaccuracies and omitted much information that he regarded as non-literary. When some reviewers of the second edition objected to the narrowed scope, Macartney published a trenchant riposte, titled *An Odious Comparison* (1956), in his Bulldozer Booklets series. Most students of Australian literature would probably agree that although *Miller and Macartney* (as the second edition is known) does not replace *Miller*, it is also an indispensable reference work.

Australian Literature Society (ALS) was founded in 1899 in Melbourne (where it remained based), its twin objects being the study of Australian literature and the encouragement of writers in Australia. The president in 1900 was 'Rolf Boldrewood' whose successors included H.G. Turner, Bernard O'Dowd (whose *Poetry Militant* was delivered as a presidential address in 1909), Percival Serle and Victor Kennedy; other prominent writer/members were F.T. Macartney, 'Furnley Maurice', and Nettie Palmer. The Australian Literature Society's Gold Medal (sometimes called the Crouch Gold Medal after its benefactor, Colonel R.A. Crouch) was originally awarded to the best novel published in the previous year, although from 1937 poetry and other literary forms were entitled to consideration. The first winner, in 1928, was Martin Boyd for *The Montforts;* subsequent winners included 'Henry Handel Richardson' (1929), Vance Palmer (1930), Eleanor Dark (1934, 1936), Xavier Herbert (1939), Patrick White (1941, 1955, 1965), R.D. FitzGerald (1938), Randolph Stow (1959), Herz Bergner (1948), Vincent Buckley (1962), John Morrison (1963), Clem Christesen (1966), Alexander Buzo (1972) and Francis Webb (1973). In 1982 arrangements were completed for the incorporation of the Australian Literature Society within the Association for the Study of Australian Literature (q.v.) which now administers and awards the ALS Gold Medal and the new award, the Dr Walter McRae Russell Award (for an outstanding recent work of literary scholarship by a young or unestablished author) named in honour of the president of the Australian Literature Society during the last quarter century of its existence. In 1983 the Gold Medal was awarded under the new arrangement to David Malouf, winner on the last occasion (1974) on which it was awarded. Other winners include former president of ASAL, Brian Matthews, and noted poet Peter Porter. Among the publications of the Australian Literature Society was the magazine *Corroboree* (1921–22). The first minute book of the ALS, titled *'Twixt Heather and Wattle*, which provides a record of the Society in the years 1899–1903, was edited in 1990 by Susan Radvansky and Patricia Alsop.

Australian Literature to 1900: A Guide to Information Sources (1980), compiled by Barry G. Andrews and William H. Wilde, is a bibliographical guide. The first part offers an annotated list of bibliographies and bibliographic guides, reference works, literary history and criticism, Australian English, nineteenth-century journals and anthologies. The second part provides a bibliographical, biographical and critical guide to sixty-six individual nineteenth-century Australian writers. The third part is a guide to selected non-fiction prose, including writings on exploration, transportation, travel and description, history and biography, and literary and theatrical autobiographies and reminiscences. Its companion volumes are *Modern Australian Poetry, 1920–1970* (1979) by Herbert C. Jaffa and *Modern Australian Prose* (1980) by A. Grove Day.

Australian Little Magazines, 1923–1954 (1964), by John Tregenza, lists forty-nine periodicals with details of their frequency of publication, their usual content, their editors and chief contributors.

Australian Magazine, the first Australian periodical, was published monthly 1821–22. Edited by Ralph Mansfield (q.v.) and published first by George Howe and then by his son, Robert, the *Australian Magazine* carried local news, articles on religious topics, fiction and poetry. Other magazines to bear this title appeared in 1835, 1838, 1859 and 1899; the 1899 *Australian Magazine* was edited by A.W. Jose and included among its contributors C.J. Brennan, J. le Gay Brereton and Roderic Quinn.

Australian Mercury was a journal conducted by P.R. Stephensen (q.v.) which ran for one issue, that of July 1935. Over half the issue was devoted to an editorial essay which became the first part of Stephensen's influential *The Foundations of Culture in Australia* (q.v., 1936).

Australian Monthly Magazine was published 1865 to August 1867 under its original title, then changed to the *Colonial Monthly*, its title until its demise in 1870. It was owned for a time, and edited (1867–69), by Marcus Clarke; in its pages are some of Clarke's first contributions to Australian literary journalism. Strongly nationalist in sentiment (although less so than the *Australian Journal*) the *Australian Monthly* carried evaluative articles on Australian writing, e.g. 'Australian Fiction' (March 1866) and 'National Poetry' (August 1867). Contributors included H.G. Turner, G.G. McCrae, Adam Lindsay Gordon and Henry Kendall.

Australian National Bibliography, a publication of the National Library of Australia, Canberra, commenced in January 1961, replacing the *Annual Catalogue of Australian Publications* published 1937–61, covering 1936–60. Its rate of publication has varied, as has its arrangement, but it currently comprises three parts (Classified Sequence; Author, Title and Series Index; and Subject Index) and lists books, serials, pamphlets, government publications and printed music published in Australia within the current and the preceding two years. Overseas publications by Australians or with Australian subject content are included. It is issued monthly as a classified list with an author and title index and cumulated in an annual volume. Cumulations are also published on microfiche for the periods January–April, January–August and January–December.

Australian National Dictionary Centre was established in 1988 with the twin purposes of conducting research into Australian English and providing OUP's Australian dictionaries with editorial expertise. Jointly funded by the ANU and OUP, Australia, the Centre's editor until 1994 was W.S. Ramson and its associate editor, Joan Hughes; its present editor is Bruce Moore. The Centre takes its name from the *Australian National Dictionary* (*AND*), a dictionary of Australianisms compiled on historical principles which was prepared at the ANU between 1978 and 1988 and published in 1988. A second edition of *AND* is planned for 1998. The Centre has also published *The Australian Oxford Paperback Dictionary* (1989), *Australian Words and Their Origins* (1989), *Digger Dialects* (1990), *Aboriginal Words in English: Their Origin and Meaning* (1990), *Australian Writers' and Editors' Guide* (1991), *The Australian Reference Dictionary* (1991) and the *Concise Australian National Dictionary* (1992). See also Australian English.

Australian Natives' Association, founded in Melbourne in 1871, had the twin aims of promoting the welfare and advancement of Australia and providing mutual aid for its members. It stemmed from the earlier Victorian Natives' Society and branches of the Association now operate in all Australian States. Among its vigorously pursued causes were federation, women's suffrage, the one-man-one-vote principle, a minimum wage, an adequate Australian defence capability, conservation of natural resources, Aboriginal welfare and a policy of 'buy Australian-made'. Well-known members of the Association included Sir Edmund Barton, Alfred Deakin and Sir Robert Menzies. The ANA Literature Award (first awarded 1978) is made annually for a work of sustained quality and distinction with an Australian theme (winners have included Jessica Anderson, Frank Hardy, Glen Tomasetti, Rodney Hall, Laurie Clancy, Roger Millis, John Bryson and Janette Turner Hospital); similar awards are made in art and science and poetry. ANA conducts regular poetry, short-story and essay competitions in the various States. Its publications have included the *Australian Native* (1882–83), the *National Australian* (1885–86), the *Australian* (1887–96) and *Advance Australia* (1897–1919). The *ANA Journal* has been its organ in NSW, *Our Australia* and *Cooee* in Queensland, *Our Australia* in SA, *ANA Advocate* in WA and *Anapress* in Victoria. It shows its interest in Australian writers in many other ways, e.g. it provides for the maintenance of Adam Lindsay Gordon's grave in Brighton Cemetery, Melbourne. Brian Fitzpatrick published *Australian Natives' Association 1871–1961* (1961), B.J. Kelleher, *Australian Natives' Association* (1963) and J.E. Menadue, *A Centenary History of the Australian Natives' Association 1871–1971* (1971)

Australian New Writing, anthologies of prose and verse, were issued annually from 1943 to 1946. Involved in editing the anthologies were Katharine Susannah Prichard, George Farwell, Bernard Smith and Ken Levis.

Australian Outlook, the journal of the Australian Institute of International Affairs, began publication (originally quarterly, then three times a year) in 1947. It superseded the *Austral-Asiatic Bulletin* which had appeared bi-monthly 1937–42. Its main focus was socio-political and its area of interest primarily Australasia and South-East Asia. It carried book reviews and some articles of literary and cultural interest. After

December 1989 it was continued by the *Australian Journal of International Affairs*.

Australian Performing Group (APG) was a company formed from actors' workshops at Melbourne's La Mama theatre in the late 1960s. In 1970 the Group established itself at Carlton, an inner suburb of Melbourne, in an old building in Drummond Street which had once housed a pram factory and which became known as the Pram Factory theatre. Generally anti-establishment, politically and socially (the group's cultural hero was Chairman Mao, whose portrait adorned the walls of the Pram Factory), the Group was opposed to 'conventional, conservative and commercial theatre', which it saw as catering for 'middle-brow, middle-class and middle-aged tastes'. Plays which found a ready acceptance by the Group were generally freewheeling, radical, physically expressive, verbally uninhibited and Australian in origin and content; some contemporary international plays and some classics were, however, also performed. At first an informal grouping, the APG became more structured in a legal sense after 1972, although it continued to be a democratic co-operative in all aspects of administration and production. It later received some sponsorship from the Australia Council and the Victorian Ministry for the Arts. One of the focal points of the 1970s resurgence in Australian drama, the APG gave strong encouragement to the work of such playwrights as Jack Hibberd, Barry Oakley, John Romeril, John Timlin, Kerry Dwyer, David Williamson, Barry Dickins, Garrie Hutchinson and Phil Motherwell, and to such actors as Graeme Blundell, Max Gillies, Bruce Spence and Evelyn Krape. Well-known plays which were first produced by the Group include David Williamson's *The Removalists* and *Don's Party*, Jack Hibberd's *White with Wire Wheels*, *Dimboola* and *A Stretch of the Imagination*, Barry Oakley's *The Feet of Daniel Mannix* and *Beware of Imitations*, John Romeril's 'The Golden Holden Show', *Chicago, Chicago* and *I Don't Know Who to Feel Sorry For*. Several vaudeville-type shows were worked up by the Group as a whole, often focusing on a general theme such as uranium-mining, unemployment and the status of women; 'Betty Can Jump' was one of the most striking of the feminist plays produced by APG, but the women members of the collective, dissatisfied with their perceived role in the collective, helped to initiate the Melbourne Women's Theatre Group (q.v.) which was separate from the APG. Popular entertainments developed by the APG included 'The Hills Family Show', 'Soapbox Circus', 'Waltzing Matilda', 'Circus Oz' and 'How Grey Was My Nurse'. The Group also frequently played a creative role in workshopping the plays of authors, John Romeril's in particular undergoing numerous adaptations inspired by the actors. In 1980 the Pram Factory was sold by the lessees of the building (it is now a supermarket) and the APG disbanded in 1981; its last production was John Blay's 'The Bed Bug Celebration' in September 1981. In the words of Graeme Blundell (who 'survived' the Pram Factory) 'the APG was an actors' laboratory, with a craving for practical investigation and theory'.

Australian Pocket Library was a series of austerity paperbacks published with the help of the then Commonwealth Literary Fund during the economic restrictions imposed by the Second World War. The Pocket Library series mostly comprised re-issues of books (fiction, poetry, essays) by well-known Australian writers, e.g. C.J. Dennis, A.B. Paterson, Henry Lawson, Vance Palmer.

Australian Poetry was a series of annual anthologies of Australian poetry published by Angus & Robertson 1941–73. Distinguished writers and critics were invited to edit the anthologies, which contained the individual editor's choice of the outstanding Australian poetry published in the previous year. The series began with *Australian Poetry 1941*, edited by Douglas Stewart. Ensuing volumes were edited by: R.D. FitzGerald (1942), H.M. Green (1943), R.G. Howarth (1944), Kenneth Slessor (1945), T. Inglis Moore (1946), Frederick T. Macartney (1947), Judith Wright (1948), Rosemary Dobson (1949–50), Kenneth Mackenzie (1951–52), Nan McDonald (1953), Ronald McCuaig (1954), James McAuley (1955), A.A. Phillips (1956), Hal Porter (1957), Vincent Buckley (1958), Nancy Keesing (1959), A.D. Hope (1960), Leonie Kramer (1961), Geoffrey Dutton (1962), G.A. Wilkes (1963), Randolph Stow (1964), John Thompson (1965), David Campbell (1966), Max Harris (1967), Dorothy Auchterlonie (1968), Vivian Smith (1969), Rodney Hall (1970), Chris Wallace-Crabbe (1971), R.F. Brissenden (1972), J.M. Couper (1973). A subsequent work *Australian Poetry* (1986) was edited by Vivian Smith. Penguin Australia began a later Australian Poetry series edited by Judith Rodriguez.

Australian Poetry Now (1970), an anthology of Australian poetry selected largely from the late 1960s, was edited with an explanatory preface by Thomas Shapcott (q.v.). The anthology is chronologically arranged but since its purpose and emphasis are 'discovery', the older and/or better-known poets, such as Bruce Beaver, Bruce Dawe, Chris Wallace-Crabbe, Les Murray and Geoffrey Lehmann are given only token representation. The anthology is, in the main, representative of 'the New Australian Poetry' (q.v.) and gives a selection of poems that were (at the time of publication) experimental in form and theme.

Australian Public Affairs Information Service: A Subject Index to Current Literature (APAIS) (1945–), issued monthly except December and cumulated annually, is a subject index to current literature on the social sciences and the humanities appearing in Australian journals. Also listed selectively are feature articles in Australian newspapers, chapters in monographs, pamphlets and conference proceedings, and items in overseas publications relating to Australia. APAIS is available as a computer searchable database.

Australian Quarterly, published since 1935 by the Australian Institute of Political Science, began in March 1929 under the auspices of the Constitutional

Association of NSW. It carries a wide range of articles on Australian politics, international relations, literature, education, art and drama. From 1967 its title has been *AQ: the Australian Quarterly*.

Australian Rip Van Winkle and Other Pieces, An, a sketch-book imitation of Washington Irving by William Gosse Hay and published in 1921, comprises ten stories; of these, three focus on the explorations of Thomas Livingstone Mitchell, three (including the title story) deal with other Australian subjects, and three deal with significant women in English history, Lady Hamilton, Mary Stuart, and Jonathan Swift's Stella.

Australian Rules, the only football game unique to Australia, is the dominant code in Victoria, Tasmania, SA and WA but takes second place to rugby league in NSW and Queensland, though it has adherents there as well. A spectacular, fast-moving game played with an oval ball between teams of eighteen men, it features both kicking and handling. If Australian rules differs from soccer (eleven a side) in allowing the ball to be handled, the essential difference between it and rugby league (thirteen a side) and rugby union (fifteen a side) is that the last two are games based on the ball being progressed by being carried by players and passed between them, whereas the ball is mainly progressed in Australian rules by team-mates kicking it to each other. Among other significant differences, apart from scoring methods, is the absence of an 'offside' rule in Australian rules.

Australian rules has contributed richly to the lexicon of Australian English (q.v.) and numerous Australian writers have written about the game, notably Bruce Dawe in 'Life-Cycle' (q.v.) and other poems, Alan Hopgood and David Williamson in their plays *And the Big Men Fly* (1969) and *The Club* (1978), and Barry Oakley in his novel *A Salute to the Great McCarthy* (1970). Leonie Sandercock and Ian Turner collaborated in a study of Australian rules, *Up Where Cazaly? The Great Australian Game* (1981); the title derives from the phrase, 'Up there Cazaly' which greeted the high leaps to mark (catch) the ball of a famous Australian rules player, Roy Cazaly. The phrase became a rallying call for Australian soldiers during the Second World War and became entrenched in the idiom of Australian English. Graeme Atkinson, who has recorded many statistics of the game, has also published *All You Ever Wanted to Know about Australian Football* (1982).

Australian Science Fiction Review, see **Science Fiction**

Australian Short Stories (1982–   ), an illustrated quarterly journal of short fiction, published by Pascoe Publishing and edited by Bruce Pascoe (co-edited recently by Lyn Harwood), has, by virtue of its format and price, and the very fact of its continuing existence,

played a major role in the revival of the Australian short-story. The journal relies on the tried and tested formula for popular short fiction – brevity, realism, traditional narrative structure and an intention of entertaining and stimulating the reader. Two Collectors' Editions have been published – *The Early Years* and *Australian Short Stories 19–22* (1988), the latter to commemorate the journal's first twenty-five issues.

Australian Society: A Magazine of Social Issues (1982–92), subtitled 'A Magazine of Social Issues', began as a fortnightly publication in 1982 (a monthly from February 1983). It was edited until 1985 by Peter Temple, after that date by Peter Browne and Mark Carter (the latter until 1990). Concerned with a wide range of social, economic and political matters, it frequently included reviews of creative and critical writing and articles and general cultural issues. In March 1992 it was succeeded by *Modern Times*.

Australian Society of Authors (ASA) was founded in 1963 to promote and protect the professional interests of creators of literary, dramatic or musical material, i.e. all those who in Australia or NZ write for publication as opposed to performance. The Society has published *The Australian and New Zealand Writers Handbook* (1975) and *Australian Book Contracts* (1983) by Barbara Jefferis. Its journal is the *Australian Author* (q.v.). The work of the Society is outlined in *A Writer's Rights: The Story of the Australian Society of Authors 1963–1983* by Deirdre Hill (1983).

Australian Stage, The: A Documentary History (1986), edited by Harold Love, is a historical survey of the theatre in Australia.

Australian Studies, a journal published under that title for the first time in 1988 and edited by Martin Gray of Stirling University, Scotland, succeeded the *BASA Magazine* as the twice-yearly publication of the British Australian Studies Association. *Australian Studies* was launched at the 'Australia Towards 2000' conference held in Lincoln, England in July 1988.

Australian Studies Centres have in recent years been set up in most Australian universities and in many universities overseas to study aspects of Australian society and culture, especially Australian history and literature. South Australia, Queensland and WA were to the forefront in the establishment of centres in this country but of the more recent, those by the University of Melbourne, Monash University and the University of New England have been particularly active. The Australian Centre, established in Melbourne in 1989, with Chris Wallace-Crabbe as director, has, as its charter, a high-profile public and academic role in promoting research into an understanding of all aspects of Australian society and culture. The Centre for Australian Language and Literature Studies, established at the University of New England in 1990, under Dr Shirley Walker as director, has the more specific aim of conducting external degree courses in Australian Language and Literature for Australian and overseas students as well as satisfying local community interest in Australian writing, especially of New England writers. The National Centre for Australian Studies at Monash University has compiled the *International Directory of Australian Studies* which lists all undergraduate and postgraduate courses with Australian content offered by universities outside Australia as well as giving details on Australian studies centres. One of the first centres, the Australian Studies Centre of the University of Queensland, was established in 1979 as a separate interdisciplinary centre but is currently based in the English Department, its director being Professor L. Hergenhan who was its foundation director 1979–82. Dr Richard Nile, formerly deputy director of the Robert Menzies Centre for Australian Studies, University of London and foundation director at both the Australian Studies Centre at Eotvos Lorand University (Budapest) and the Lajos Kossuth University (Debrecen), is now deputy director of the ASC at St Lucia with responsibility for the Centre's expanding teaching programme and other allied activities. The Sir Robert Menzies Centre for Australian Studies in London and the British Australian Studies Association (which publishes the journal *Australian Studies*) co-ordinate much of the activity in Australian Studies in the UK, while the European Association of Studies on Australia, which was formed in 1989, aims to promote the teaching of Australian Studies in countries such as Poland, Portugal, Hungary, Denmark, Italy, Belgium, Spain, Ireland and Germany. The inaugural conference of EASA was held in Berne in 1991. In Japan Australian Studies units exist at Seikei and Keio Universities in Tokyo and at Nanzan University, Nagoya. The Australian Studies Association of China (ASAC) was formed in 1990 with Professor Hu Wenzhong of Beijing Foreign Studies University as Chairman. There are several Australian Studies Centres in American universities. One of the first established was at Pennsylvania State University in 1982 under Professor Henry Albinski. Pennsylvania State has links with Australia through Bruce Sutherland who spent a year in Australia as a Fulbright Scholar in 1951 and was thereafter an enthusiastic supporter of Australian literature in America. The University of Texas (Professor Joseph Jones of that institution published widely on Australian writing) has an Australian Studies Centre as does the University of Oregon. An Australian Studies Centre was set up in Indonesia in 1990.

Australian Town and Country Journal, also known as the *Town and Country Journal*, was published 1870–1919. Its editors included Samuel Bennett (1870–79), Walter J. Jeffery (1893–1906) and A.B. Paterson (1907–8). The weekly companion of the *Evening News*, it provided a constant publication outlet for Australian writers for half a century. Among its best-known contributors were Henry Kendall, 'Louis' Becke, Ethel Turner, Henry Lawson and 'Rolf Boldrewood'.

Australian Tradition, the journal of the Folk Lore Society of Victoria (founded 1955, with Alan Marshall as its first president) and the Victorian Bush (later Folk) Music Club, began publication in 1960 as a roneoed bulletin under the title of *Gumsuckers' Gazette*. It became increasingly sophisticated and in 1964 changed its name to *Australian Tradition;* over the next decade it was published mainly three times a year, the final issue (December 1975) consisting of an index to the journal under both titles. Edited by the folklorist Wendy Lowenstein, *Australian Tradition* reflected the revival of interest in Australian folk-song and ballad (q.v.) which gathered pace in the 1950s. It carried the words and music of songs, reports of the activities of folk-music and folklore societies, recitations, reminiscences, book and record reviews, and articles or notes on the provenance and transmission of songs, on Australian idiom, and on other aspects of the Australian folk tradition. Contributors included folklorists such as John Meredith, Bill Wannan, Alan Scott, Edgar Waters and Wendy Lowenstein; among the Australian authors whose lyrics became songs published in *Australian Tradition* are Henry Lawson and Dorothy Hewett.

Australian Tradition: Studies in a Colonial Culture, The (1958, revised 1966) is a significant collection of essays and commentaries, mainly on Australian writing, by A.A. Phillips (q.v.). The 1958 edition includes essays on Henry Lawson and Joseph Furphy as well as Phillips's well-known 'The Cultural Cringe' (q.v.). The revised 1966 edition added 'Lawson Revisited', 'The Short Stories of Vance Palmer', and 'Barbara Baynton and the Dissidence of the Nineties', essays which reflect Phillips's response to some of the new understandings and perspectives of Australian literature that had arisen during the period between the editions. A 1980 reissue of the 1966 edition includes an introduction by H.P. Heseltine, which appraises Phillips's critical stance on Australian literature, especially in the light of the objections that arose from the late 1950s onwards against the nationalist-democratic theories of the origin and development of Australian literature advanced by Phillips, Vance Palmer and others. Such theories are, as Heseltine states, 'based on the translation of the bush ethos into the social-democratic code of mateship, and the effort to express that code in an adequate aesthetic form'.

Australian/Vogel National Literary Award, offered annually since 1980, is awarded to the writer (under 35) of the best unpublished manuscript of fiction, Australian history or biography each year. Winners of the award have been Paul Radley for *Jack Rivers and Me* in 1980, Tim Winton for *An Open Swimmer* and Chris Matthews for *Al Jazzar* (jointly) in 1981, Brian Castro for 'Solitude' and Nigel Krauth for 'The Jolly Swagman Affair' (jointly) in 1982, Jenny Summerville for *Shields of Trell* in 1983, Kate Grenville for *Lilian's Story* in 1984, no award in 1985, Robin Walton for *Glace Fruits* (1986), Jim Sakkas for *Ilias* (1987), Tom Flood for *Oceana Fine* (1988), Mandy Sayer for *Mood Indigo* (1989), Gillian Mears for *The Mint Lawn* (1990),

Andrew McGahan for *Praise* (1991), Fotini Epanomitis for *The Mule's Foal* (1992) and Helen Demidenko for 'The Hand that Signed the Paper' (1993).

Australian Week-End Review, a fortnightly review of books originating from Melbourne under the editorial direction of G.B. Allan and Bertram Higgins, ran for twenty-one issues 1950–51.

Australian Women's Book Review, the only Australian review devoted specifically to women's books, began publication in Melbourne in 1989 and appears quarterly.

Australian Women's Weekly, the concept of G.W. (George) Warnecke and owned initially by Frank Packer and E.G. Theodore, first appeared 8 June 1933 in Sydney. Warnecke, the *Weekly*'s foundation editor, remained with it until 1939; he was followed by a succession of women editors, Alice Jackson, Esme Fenton, Dorothy Drain, Ita Buttrose and Dawn Swain. Committed to 'an unswerving Australian outlook' so that it would be welcome 'in every Australian home from the outback to the industrial suburbs', the *Weekly* has maintained a remarkably high circulation. It spread to Victoria (September 1933), Queensland (October 1933), SA (March 1934), Tasmania (June 1935) and WA (October 1936). Although the *Weekly* has made some attempt to debate women's issues it has always emphasised the fulfilment to be gained from marriage and motherhood and it was quick to follow government policy on the replacement of women by men in the work-force after the Second World War. Its notable women journalists included (in addition to the editors named) Etta Cowen, Saide Parker, Ruth Preddey, Phyllis Duncan-Brown, Jessie Tait, Louise Mack, Jean Williamson, Kay Keavney, Anne Matheson, Mary Hordern and Adele Shelton Smith. Regular literary features of the *Weekly* have included book, film and drama reviews, lift-out fiction supplements, short fiction, serials, and poetry. Profusely illustrated, the *Weekly* has been well served by artists such as W.E. Pidgeon ('WEP'), Virgil Reilly and Wynne W. Davies; its most notable humorists have been L.W. (Lennie) Lower and Ross Campbell; and its most celebrated and enduring comic strip has been 'Mandrake the Magician'. For many years the *Weekly* made no definite attempt to encourage Australian writing; its 'full-length, lift-out' novel supplements (about 250 condensed novels), which were a regular feature from 1934 to 1940, were mostly imported English light romances, as were its regularly appearing short stories and serials. Frank Dalby Davison's *Forever Morning* and Henrietta Drake-Brockman's *The Disquieting Sex* were two Australian exceptions. Notable among its poetry contributors was Mary Gilmore; she provided the *Weekly* with many poems, two of note during the Second World War being the patriotic pieces 'No Foe Shall Gather Our Harvest' and 'Singapore'. Belatedly recognising the Australian writer, the *Weekly* conducted a fiction competition in 1942; it received more than 1000 manuscripts. In 1975 the familiar large-size *Weekly* was replaced by a smaller, more conventional size; in 1982 it belied, but kept, its traditional title, becoming a monthly publication. Denis O'Brien compiled a lively biography, *The Weekly*, in 1982.

Australian Worker, the longest-running Australian labour movement newspaper, grew out of the *Hummer*, which was founded in 1891 by Arthur Rae and W.W. Head as the weekly organ of the Wagga branch of the Amalgamated Shearers Union. In 1892 the *Hummer* changed its name to the *Worker* and became the NSW edition of the well-established Brisbane *Worker*. The following year it moved to Sydney and resumed an independent existence; remaining under the control of the Almalgamated Shearers Union (later the Australian Workers' Union), it changed its name to the *Australian Worker* (the present title) in 1913 and incorporated other labour newspapers including the *Australian Workman* in 1897 and the *Westralian Worker* in 1913. A weekly for most of its life, the *Australian Worker* has had a number of prominent Australian writers on its staff: William Lane (1900), E.J. Brady (1904–5), Henry Boote (1914–43) and Frank Moorhouse were all editors; Mary Gilmore ran its women's page from 1908 to 1931; and T.D. Mutch and R.J. Cassidy were prominent staff writers before the Second World War. Its most famous contributor during the 1890s (see Nineties) was Henry Lawson, who had some of his best work published there and moved from contributor to provincial editor and then briefly to salaried writer. Later contributors included Roderic Quinn and John Shaw Neilson.

Australian Workman was a Sydney labour movement newspaper which was established during the great maritime strike of 1890 and ran, mainly as a weekly, until 1897; for most of that time it was the official organ of the Trades and Labour Council. As well as labour news, it published short stories, serial fiction and poetry, sometimes reprinted from other sources (e.g. work by Henry Kendall). E.J. Brady was its editor in 1892, and was succeeded by two other literary figures, 'Price Warung' in 1893 and (Sir) Frank Fox in 1893–95.

Australian Writers (1896), by Desmond Byrne, deplores in its introduction the lack of enthusiasm by readers and critics for colonial writing, and provides analytical essays on Marcus Clarke, Henry Kingsley, Ada Cambridge, Adam Lindsay Gordon, 'Rolf Boldrewood', Rosa Praed and Jessie Couvreur.

Australian Writers, a series designed to replace and update the Australian Writers and Their Work (q.v.) series, began in 1992 with the publication of three titles, *James McAuley* by Lyn McCredden, *Peter Porter* by Peter Steele and *A.D. Hope* by Kevin Hart, followed in 1993 by *David Malouf* by Ivor Indyk and *Gerald Murnane* by Imre Salusinszky and in 1994 by *Gwen Harwood* by Stephanie Trigg and *Christina Stead* by Jennifer Gribble. Planned titles in the series include *Martin Boyd* by Jim Davidson, *Bruce Dawe* by Peter Koch, *Helen Garner* by Kerryn Goldsworthy, *Elizabeth Jolley* by Elizabeth Webby, *Henry Lawson* by Kay

Schaffer, *Les Murray* by Paul Kane, *Kenneth Slessor* by Adrian Caesar, *Patrick White* by Simon During, *Judith Wright* by Jennifer Strauss. Published by OUP and under the general editorship of Chris Wallace-Crabbe, the new series is more expansive than its smaller predecessor and, written by a new generation of academic critics, seeks to reflect recent developments in cultural outlook and literary theory.

Australian Writers and Their Work, a series published by Lansdowne Press until taken over by OUP in 1966, was initially edited by Geoffrey Dutton and later by Grahame Johnston (qq.v.). The series was designed to offer a concise (about fifty pages) but informative introduction to the main Australian writers.

Australian Writers Guild, founded in Sydney in 1961 as a 'trade union for script writers' of television, radio, screen and stage, publishes a monthly journal, *Viewpoint*, and presents Awgie Awards annually to members for the best scripts for film, stage, radio and television.

Australian Writers Speak (1942) is a booklet of nine scripts prepared for the ABC's series 'Literature and Life in Australia' by the Fellowship of Australian Writers (q.v.). Topics discussed during this formative period of Australian literary development included 'Our Literature' by Marjorie Barnard, the relationship between author and reader by Vance and Nettie Palmer, the working-class element in Australian literature by Jean Devanny, the difficulties and achievements of Australian dramatists by Leslie Rees, and the impact of Australian writers on the national life by Katharine Susannah Prichard and Gavin Casey. There were also attempts to answer the questions 'What is Literature?' by Frank Dalby Davison and 'Need Australian Writers Write about Australia?' by Norman Bartlett.

Australiana Facsimile Editions (AFE) and **South Australiana Facsimile Editions** (SAFE) were two historical facsimile series published by the Libraries Board of SA. The AFE series included seventy-four titles numbered 1–206 (with many numbers not used) and published 1962–79; among the titles published were journals of explorers (e.g. Matthew Flinders, James Cook, John Oxley, E.J. Eyre, Ludwig Leichhardt), descriptive and historical works (e.g. by David Collins, Raffaello Carboni, W.B. Ullathorne) and some SA titles (e.g. works by George French Angas and Catherine Helen Spence). The SAFE series ran 1962–69, though most of its sixty-five titles (nos 1–91, with numbers not used) were published in 1962; it included works on the foundation and early settlement of SA, exploration, local history, European–Aboriginal contact, almanacs and other SA material.

'AUSTRALIE', see **MANNING, Emily**

Australopaedia, The (1988), ed. Joan Grant, designer Keith Robertson, is subtitled *How Australia Works after 200 Years of Other People Living Here*. One of the Bicentenary special publications, aimed at the younger audience, it tells first of the origins of Australia and proceeds to give informative details on all facets of Australian life, past and present. The Aborigines and ethnic groups are given full recognition.

Austrovert, edited by B.W. Muirden (q.v.), was published irregularly (ten numbers) 1950–53. Planned as 'a half-way mark' between academic and popular discussion of writers, *Austrovert* ran a series of critical and biographical articles on established Australian authors. A selection of poetry from its pages was published as *Austroverse* (1952).

Awards, see **Literary Awards**

Awful Australian, The (1911), by Valerie Desmond, is an amusing and critical account of Australia from an early twentieth-century perspective. It contains chapters such as 'The Australians at Shirk' and 'The Australian's Parasitical Tendencies'. A response was *The Real Australian* (1912) by Malcolm C. Donald.

Awgie Awards, see **Australian Writers Guild**

Ayers Rock, a giant monolith, orange-brown in colour, rises to a height of 335 metres out of the plains about 40 kilometres south of Lake Amadeus in the south-west of the Northern Territory. Sacred to Aborigines who have left rock paintings in its caves, Ayers Rock (named 'Uluru' by the Aborigines) is associated with their legends of the Dreaming. First recorded in 1872 by explorer Ernest Giles but named by William Gosse, the first White man to visit it, in honour of Sir Henry Ayers, then premier of South Australia, the Rock has been more important in Australian art than in literature. W.E. 'Bill' Harney, at one time curator of the Ayers Rock reservation, told the Aboriginal story of the rock in his *Tales from the Aborigines* (1959). C.P. Mountford (q.v.) wrote *Ayers Rock* (1965), which examines the association of the monolith with Aboriginal myth and art. Ayers Rock was officially handed back to the Aborigines by the federal government in 1983. It assumed new significance in Australian culture in 1980 after a 9-week-old baby, Azaria Chamberlain, disappeared from her parents' tent during a camping holiday in the area. The Chamberlains, who steadfastly maintained that a dingo had taken the child, came under suspicion, and Lindy Chamberlain, convicted of murder in 1982, served over three years in prison before fresh evidence added credibility to her story and she was released. Her conviction was quashed in 1988. The case, which was hotly debated for several years, is described in John Bryson's (q.v.) *Evil Angels* (1985), produced as a film in 1988.

B

'Backblocks Shearer, The' is an Australian folk-song in which a shearer, identified in the last verse as 'Widgigoweera Joe' (an alternative title for the song), first laments that he has never become a 'gun' shearer and then vows to improve his technique until he wins a shearing contest at a country show. The concluding lines of the song,

> Instead of Deeming, you will hear
> Of Widgigoweera Joe,

may date the composition of the song to around 1892, when the murderer, Frederick Deeming, was much in the news. An informant of Russel Ward has suggested that the song was written by a shearer named Bill Tulley at Howlong station in the Riverina. A similar but more characteristically confident shearer's song is 'The Ryebuck Shearer'. In this song the singer demonstrates through several verses his superiority to his fellow shearers and the extent to which he is a 'ryebuck' (i.e. gun or masterful) shearer.

BACKHOUSE, Elizabeth (1917–), born Northam, WA (of Yorkshire ancestry), served in the WAAAF in the Second World War and then went to England, where, for several years, she was with Korda Films. She returned to Australia in 1951. She has written numerous novels, several of which are lively detective thrillers, *In Our Hands* (1942), *The Sky Has Its Clouds* (1944), *Day Will Break* (1946), *Leaves in The Wind* (1946), *A Wreath for the Party* (1954), *Death Came Uninvited* (1957), *The Mists Came Down* (1959), *The Night Has Eyes* (1961), *The Web of Shadows* (1960), *Death of a Clown* (1962) and *Death Climbs a Hill* (1963). She has also written stage plays, e.g. 'The Thin Line' produced in 1968, 'Mirage', in 1972 and 'The Fourth Picture', 1974, as well as scenarios for ballets (KAL, 1979) and a television play, 'The Olive Tree' (1975), which has been screened in Australia and the USA. *Against Time and Place* (1990), which unravels her family history after migration to Australia, is also valuable as social history. Mainly the story of the women in the family, *Against Time and Place* is an affectionately told, modest and engaging work, which has been ranked with such successes as Facey's *A Fortunate Life* and Sally Morgan's *My Place*.

BACKHOUSE, James (1794–1869), born Durham, England, arrived at Hobart Town in 1832 as a Quaker missionary with a particular interest in the welfare of the convicts. From 1832 to 1838, in company with George Washington Walker, he evangelised through Tasmania, NSW and the Moreton Bay district. His experiences are recorded in A *Narrative of a Visit to the Australian Colonies* (1843), a work which contains considerable information on the convicts and Aborigines and on the botany of the colonies. Extracts from his letters from Van Diemen's Land and NSW were published in London in pamphlet form (1838–41) by the Society of Friends. Sarah Backhouse wrote *Memoir of James Backhouse* (1870).

BADHAM, Charles (1813–84), born Shropshire, England, and renowned as one of the leading Greek scholars of his day in Europe, became professor of classics at the University of Sydney in 1867. Intensely interested in the problems of tertiary education in the colony, Badham strongly espoused the introduction of evening classes at the University of Sydney. He was the first president of the board of trustees of the Free Public Library, later the Public Library of NSW. An important textual critic, he wrote widely on Plato and Euripides. His *Speeches and Lectures Delivered in Australia* were published in 1890 through subscriptions by former students and other admirers.

Bagman's Gazette was an imaginary newspaper circulating among the 'bagmen' of the Australian outback. It was a rich source of rumour and gossip, the expression 'According to the Bagman's Gazette' inevitably casting doubt on the accuracy of the information being supplied. 'The Drover's Guide' is the equivalent for the droving fraternity. Henry Lawson tends to use the word 'bagman' to mean a commercial traveller, but a bagman was usually a mounted itinerant, with anything from one to a dozen horses. Sometimes shearer, sometimes drover or even general rouseabout, he often concealed a 'cutter' (a racehorse in disguise) among his horses and won an occasional bet from unsuspecting station workers. Tom Ronan's autobiography (1966) is titled *Once There Was a Bagman*.

BAIL, Murray (1941–), born Adelaide, though living mainly in Australia has spent some time in other countries including India (1968–70) and England and Europe (1970–74); in London he wrote for the journals *Transatlantic Review* and the *Times Literary Supplement*. In 1975 he published *Contemporary Portraits and Other Stories* (republished 1986 as *The Drover's Wife and Other Stories*), short fiction that varies between the experimental and the conventional and is, in the main, sardonic and dominated by the strain of absurdity that, for Bail, characterises contemporary life. His story, 'The Drover's Wife', prefaced by an insert of Russell Drysdale's painting of the same name, treads satirically on hallowed Henry Lawson ground; his most effective pieces, however, are the surrealistic

'Cul de Sac' and 'Paradise', and some sections of the 'Heubler' sequence beginning 'At least one person who . . .'. *Homesickness*, a novel published in 1980, won the National Book Council Award and shared the *Age* Book of the Year Award. It relates the experiences of thirteen Australians who, travelling in that modern phenomenon the 'package tour' (itself a target for satire), visit Africa, England, Ecuador, New York and Moscow. The tourists include a zoologist; an oversexed dentist and his none too accommodating wife; a woman and her blind husband; another colourless couple; two fairly thoughtful, unattached males; a youngish, male 'ocker'; a wealthy spinster and two actresses, one ageing, the other younger and more naive. There is the usual interaction among individuals within the group – petty jealousies, attempts to impress and an occasional outburst of furtive sex – but the group develops an interesting collective personality that comes to dominate the novel. Tourism, a contemporary mode of perception, compartmentalises the world into a succession of museums. The museums (interpreted satirically or as part of the Absurd) include the Museu (the 'm' had fallen off the sign in a windstorm) of Handicrafts in Africa which contains old lawnmowers, used toothpaste tubes, and a sodawater syphon; the Corrugated Iron Museum of Yorkshire; and a Museum of Legs in Quito; and Central Park in New York (a giant zoo) where the tourists watch from a spectator gallery such behavioural patterns as muggings and pack rapes. The group, too, exhibits certain behaviour patterns characteristic of Australians and these are set in ironic contrast with the cosmopolis through which they haphazardly wander. Bail, who is interested in painting and was a trustee of the Australian National Gallery for five years, wrote a monograph (1981) on the artist Ian Fairweather. Bail's long literary silence after *Homesickness* was finally broken with another triumph, the novel *Holden's Performance* (1987), which won the 1988 Victorian Premier's Award for fiction. Bail attributed the lengthy period between his two novels to a failed work which he finally abandoned, to his slowness (he seldom writes more than 200 words a day), and to his resolve that his work should be original and significant.

Holden's Performance could well be the title of a road test of Australia's own family car and the analogy is deliberate. 'Australia is full of men like Holden, who perform like cars. It's appalling', Bail told one interviewer. The story narrates the progress of Holden Shadbolt who was born in Adelaide in 1933 and who, while in adolescence, came under the influence of his Uncle Vern, a proofreader of the Adelaide *Advertiser*, whose own life revolved around the 'truths' that reside in the printed word of newspapers. Holden, in one of Bail's many bizarre metaphors, digested those 'truths' himself by mixing pulped newsprint into his icecream and spreading it on his toast. To embark on his journey to maturation, the literal-minded Holden went to Manly, Sydney, then advanced an unspectacular career by acting as a bouncer at a cinema, a chauffeur to, and minder of, politicians, and a bodyguard of the Prime Minister before going off to America where such skills are even more in demand. Holden's progress ('performance') mirrors the mechanical and mindless values of Australian society as they might have been inferred from newsreels and newspaper headlines through the 1950s and 1960s. Holden is a skilfully drawn character in that he has no real character at all; he is Bail's version of the archetypal, venial and ordinary Australian of those decades, 'unable to view the world critically or understand it'. The supporting cast is a rich and bizarre mix – from the politicians (whom Bail appears to loathe) such as Sid Hoadley, Frank McBee and Colonel Light to Uncle Vern who continues to send Holden proofsheets of the *Advertiser*, the repositories of all wisdom. A wry, clever, amusing and disturbing book, *Holden's Performance* places Bail among the acknowledged chroniclers of modern Australians and their social milieu. *Longhand: A Writer's Notebook*, published by Bail in 1989, is, on the surface, a diary account of his activities and thoughts while he was overseas in the late 1960s and 1970s, but it is also a quite personal account of the author, evasive and revealing at the same time. One of his literary editors felt that there was too much First Person, Singular, in the book, but few readers would agree. Bail also edited *The Faber Book of Contemporary Short Stories* in 1988. He is one of the subjects of Helen Daniel's *Liars: New Australian Novelists* (1988).

BAILEY, Bert (1868–1953) was the actor who became famous for his portrayal of Dad, the patriarch of the Rudd family (q.v.), on stage and screen. Born in Auckland, NZ, Bailey entered vaudeville in the 1880s and had a notable success when he co-authored with Edmund Duggan the bush melodrama 'The Squatter's Daughter' (staged 1907), in which there is a portrait of Ben Hall and his gang. Versions of the melodrama were filmed in 1910 and 1933; it also forms the basis of a novel by Hilda Bridges (1922). In 1912 Bailey and Duggan presented *On Our Selection* (q.v.), their adaptation of the stories of 'Steele Rudd' (q.v.). Remarkably popular, *On Our Selection* was performed repeatedly until 1929 and was successfully revived in 1979 with additional material by George Whaley. The Bailey-Duggan script of *On Our Selection* was used in the sound film version of *On Our Selection* (1932), in which Bailey starred. Closely identified with the role of Dad, Bailey was also successful in two plays adapted by 'Steele Rudd' from his books, and made three further films which owed less to 'Rudd' than to Bailey and collaborators such as Duggan and Ken Hall: *Grandad Rudd* (1935), *Dad and Dave Come to Town* (1938) and *Dad Rudd M.P.* (1940). He also produced a stage adaptation of C.J. Dennis's *The Sentimental Bloke* in 1922, taking the part of Ginger Mick. Bailey and Duggan's *On Our Selection*, edited by Helen Musa, was published in 1984.

BAILEY, Mary (1792–?), born Halstead, Essex, as Mary Walker, married an Anglican clergyman, William Bailey, in 1832 and followed him to Hobart in 1844 after he was convicted of an illegal financial transaction and transported. A poet with a keen interest in the classics, she had previously published religious and other poetry including *The Months and Other Poems* (2nd edn, 1833), *Reflections upon the Litany of the Church of England* (1833), and *Musae Sacrae: a Collection of Hymns and Sacred Poetry* (1835). In Hobart she regularly published verse and erudite translations in the *Colonial Times* between 1844 and 1850, and as 'Mary' or 'M.B.' contributed both verse and prose to the *Hobarton Guardian* in 1847 when her husband was its editor. Nothing is known of Mary Bailey's life after 1850, although in 1855 William Bailey left for Sydney, where he became involved in religious and other controversy, married again and died in 1879.

BAILLIE, Allan, see *The Oxford Companion to Australian Children's Literature* (1993), pp. 37–8.

BAKER, Candida (1955–   ), born London, worked in the theatre and first visited Australia with the Royal Shakespeare Company in 1975. She subsequently emigrated and is now an Australian citizen living in Sydney. She has published a novel, *Women and Horses* (1990), and three influential collections of interviews with Australian writers, *Yacker* (1986), *Yacker 2* (1987) and *Yacker 3* (1989). She is married to Robert Drewe (q.v.).

BAKER, Kate (1861–1953) was born in Ireland, came to Victoria as a child, and was a teacher in the Victorian Department of Education 1881–1913. In 1886 she met Joseph Furphy, with whom she formed a friendship that lasted until Furphy's death in 1912. For the next four decades she was Furphy's 'gallant standard-bearer'; indefatigable in her efforts to promote his works and secure his reputation, she published his poems at her own expense (1916), arranged for the reissue of *Such is Life* (q.v., 1917) and for the first publication in book form of *Rigby's Romance* (1921), addressed literary societies and assembled the material used in Miles Franklin's *Joseph Furphy: The Legend of a Man and His Book* (1944). For her services to Furphy in particular, and to Australian literature in general, she was made OBE in 1937. John Barnes's *The Order of Things: A Life of Joseph Furphy* (1990) examines the relationship between Baker and Furphy and also to some extent Miles Franklin.

BAKER, Sidney John (1912–76), born and educated in NZ, became interested in Australasian English when questioned about his own idiom while in England in the late 1930s. Although hampered by multiple sclerosis for most of his last thirty years, he was an enthusiastic pioneer of the study of NZ and Australian English (q.v.), particularly the study of idiom and its relationship to national character and folklore; his several books, which include extensive word lists, have proved invaluable sources for later studies. His major work was *The Australian Language*, first published in 1945 and revised in 1966; a 1953 supplement to the first edition was titled *Australia Speaks*. His other publications include *New Zealand Slang* (1940); *A Popular Dictionary of Australian Slang* (1941); *Australian Pronunciation* (1947); *The Drum: Australian Character and Slang* (1959); a novel, *The Gig* (1958); a

study of Matthew Flinders, *My Own Destroyer* (1962); *The Ampol Book of Australiana* (1963); and contributions to encyclopaedias (e.g. the 1958 edition of the *Australian Encyclopaedia*), cultural surveys (e.g. A.L. McLeod's *The Pattern of Australian Culture*, 1963) and dictionaries (e.g. the slang dictionaries of Eric Partridge).

Balcony, a quarterly journal of literature and the arts, ran for six issues 1965–67. It began under the sponsorship of the Sydney University Arts Seminar Society. Contributors included James McAuley, Rodney Hall, Michael Wilding and Frank Moorhouse. *Balcony* was intended as a counter to the then Leavisite journal, *Melbourne Critical Review*.

BALDERSON, Margaret, see *The Oxford Companion to Australian Children's Literature* (1993), p. 39.

'Ballad of Bloodthirsty Bessie, The', a poem by Ronald McCuaig (q.v.), was first published in the *Bulletin* (19 September 1951) and was later used as the title poem for McCuaig's *The Ballad of Bloodthirsty Bessie and Other Poems* (1961). Sometimes cited as an example of an especially macabre brand of humour, said to be Australian in character, McCuaig's poem tells of the stratagems used by a farmer near Sydney to keep himself in cheap labour and his amorous daughter, Bessie, in lovers. When the exhausted labourers ultimately try to leave, the farmer pushes them off a nearby cliff, at the bottom of which Bessie waits to finish them off with an axe. Seventeen farmhands end up in graves along the creek. A spying trooper is similarly dispatched and nine investigating soldiers are made drunk by the farmer, who pours rum on them and sets them alight. Bessie objects to this wholesale squandering of such valuable amatory material:

> 'Oh, father, I say it is cruel
> Oh, father, I say it's unfair:
> You're using my sweethearts as fuel
> And doing me out of my share'.

She approaches her father menacingly, axe in hand. Thrusting sentimentality sternly behind him, he 'out with a pistol and shot her/ Through the heart for the first and last time'.

BALLANTYNE, Colin Sandergrove (1908–88) was born in Adelaide and from the late 1920s was a strong influence in SA theatre. Actor, producer and playwright, he produced numerous plays including five major productions for the Adelaide Festival and was instrumental in the establishment of the Adelaide Theatre Group's Sheridan Theatre. Chairman of the SA Theatre Company 1972–78, he was an active force in the SA division of the Arts Council of Australia. From 1966 to 1974 he was federal director of the combined Arts Councils of Australia and from 1974–77 federal president. From 1979 to 1987 he was the founding chairman of the Performing Arts Collection of SA. With his wife Gwenneth, an actor and drama teacher, Ballantyne trained numerous future stars including Keith Michell, Leslie Dayman, Tom Brown, and his daughter, Elspeth Ballantyne. He was also a photographer and made several documentary films for the federal government. His own plays include *The Ice-Cream Cart*, a one-act drama about the adjustment of a Turkish couple to Australia, published in *Australian One-Act Plays: Book Two*, ed. Greg Branson (1962); 'Between Gunshots' (1963); 'Harvest'; 'Here Take My Picture'; and 'Pacific Rape', a free-verse drama about Western infiltration into the Pacific, produced in 1970. He was made CMG in 1971.

BALLANTYNE, Gina (1916–), born Adelaide, published several volumes of verse which gave expression to Jindyworobak (q.v.) sentiments, e.g. *Phantom* (1942), *Vision* (1942) and *Vagrant* (1943). She won the C.J. Dennis Memorial Prize in 1942 and edited the 1945 *Jindyworobak Anthology*.

Ballarat, from the Aboriginal 'Balla-arat', meaning 'elbow place', situated 110 kilometres north-west of Melbourne, is one of Victoria's major provincial cities. The Ballarat area was opened up as a pastoral district in 1837 but, with the influx of population following the discovery of gold in August 1851, a township was surveyed in December of that year. In 1852 the system of deep lead mining exposed 'buried rivers of gold' and Ballarat became Victoria's most active goldfield, with a population of 12 660 miners in 1854. It was on Bakery Hill, Ballarat, that the Eureka Stockade (q.v.) incident occurred, 3 December 1854. Ballarat was prominent in the goldfields literature of the second half of the nineteenth century, e.g. J.A. Patterson's *The Gold Fields of Victoria in 1862* (1862) and W.H. Thomas's *Life at the Gold Mines of Ballarat* (1885), and in the many writings on Eureka. Individual works on Ballarat include the important early history by W.B. Withers, *The History of Ballarat* (1870); *Ballarat and Vicinity* (1894) by W. Kimberly; *History of Ballarat* (1935) by Nathan Spielvogel; *Some Ballarat Pioneers* (1935) by R. Gay; and *One Hundred Years, 1838–1939, Ballarat* (1939), ed. W.H. Rees. The Ballarat goldfields continue to be discussed in more recent works such as Geoffrey Serle's *The Golden Age* (1963); J.H.W. McGeorge's *Buried Rivers of Gold* (1966); H.J. Stacpoole's *Gold at Ballarat* (1971); and Jan Neil and M.C. Sayers's *Ballarat, from Bullion to Begonias* (1973). The most comprehensive history of gold-rush Ballarat is Weston Bate's *Lucky City* (1978). Ballarat and events on the diggings provide an important background in such fictional works as *Australia Felix* (1917) from 'Henry Handel Richardson's' trilogy *The Fortunes of Richard Mahony* (1930), and Eric Lambert's novel *Ballarat* (1962). Adam Lindsay Gordon kept a livery stable at Ballarat in 1868 and rode in steeplechase races on its picturesque Dowling Forest course. Norman Lindsay, who was born at Creswick near Ballarat, based his trilogy *Saturdee* (1933), *Redheap* (1930), and *Halfway to Anywhere* (1947) on town life of the area; his novel *The Cousin from Fiji* (1945) is also set there.

Ballarat Punch, see ***Melbourne Punch***

Balmain, a Sydney suburb, was named after William Balmain (1762–1803), assistant surgeon to John White in the First Fleet and principal surgeon and magistrate at Norfolk Island in 1791 and in Sydney 1795–1801. Balmain was granted 222 hectares of land in the area now bearing his name. The grant was later sold and the land subdivided to become originally a fashionable Sydney suburb (literary patron, N.D. Stenhouse, living there in the 1850s), then a working-class area, and in recent years a gathering-place of writers and artists. The annual Balmain poetry and prose competitions contributed to the rise of the 'New Australian Poetry' (q.v.) in the late 1960s. Frank Moorhouse's *Days of Wine and Rage* (1980) depicts cultural life in Balmain in the 1970s. Balmain has been less significant as a literary and cultural area since the 1980s.

BALODIS, Janis (1950–), born Tully, North Queensland, is the son of post-war immigrants from Latvia. He worked briefly as a primary school teacher before joining the Queensland Theatre Company as assistant stage manager in 1974 and later working at the E.15 Acting School in London, as tutor and director. In 1980 his play 'Backyard' was produced at the Nimrod Theatre and was followed by 'Beginning of the End' (1982), 'Happily Never After' (1982), 'Summerland' (1984), *Too Young for Ghosts* (1985), which won a Victorian Premier's Award in 1986, 'Heart for the Future' (1988) and *Wet & Dry* (1991). In 1988 he became associate director of the Melbourne Theatre Company. *Too Young for Ghosts* is a bold treatment of the immigrant experience in Australia, intertwining the European memories and reactions to Australia of a group of Latvian migrants working on the North Queensland canefields in the late 1940s with those of the members of Leichhardt's expedition in 1845. *Wet & Dry* uses stark imagery to explore the contemporary experience of sex, love and parenthood; 'Heart for the Future', set in the year 2000 in the Nullarbor Desert, is a technically ambitious play, which is similarly concerned with questions of identity and choice.

Banana-bender, a current colloquialism for a Queenslander, replaced 'bananalander' in the 1970s. Both words derive from the fact that Queensland was, at least from the 1890s, known as 'Bananaland'. The usage survives in, for example, the title of Hugh Lunn's study of Queensland society, *Behind the Banana Curtain* (1979). A play by Barry Dickins, *The Banana Bender*, was produced in 1980 and published 1981.

BANCKS, J.C. (James Charles) (1889–1952) was born at Enmore, Sydney, and brought up at Hornsby amid a family he remembered as a 'living comic strip'. He became a full-time artist with the *Bulletin*, for which, from 1914, he drew cartoons and caricatures; and in 1921 he began drawing 'Us Fellers', a colour comic strip for the Sydney *Sun*. 'Us Fellers' soon came to centre on the prepubescent larrikin Ginger Meggs (q.v.). The phenomenal success of the strip made Bancks the highest-paid black-and-white artist of his era. Bancks drew several other strips and panels, collaborated with his first wife Jessie Nita (Tait) on the musical comedy 'Blue Mountain Melody' (performed 1936), and was also a newspaper columnist.

BANDLER, Faith (1920–   ) was born at Tumbulgum, Murwillumbah, NSW, the daughter of Wacvie Mussingkon (Peter Mussing), a Hebridean islander who was brought to Australia by slave traders in 1882 to work on the Queensland canefields. In lyrical prose, which recaptures the atmosphere of the Tweed Valley of northern NSW, when it was farmed for bananas by Kanaka-descended families, she has written her father's story in the novels *Wacvie* (1977) and *Marani in Australia* (1980, with Len Fox), and her brother's story in *Welou, My Brother* (1984). She has been strongly identified with the struggle for Aboriginal rights, having served for many years on the executive of the Federal Council for the Advancement of Aboriginals and Torres Strait Islanders, and as director in NSW of the 1967 referendum campaign, which led to equal citizenship for Aborigines under the Australian Constitution. Her other writing includes *Turning the Tide* (1988), an account of contemporary Aboriginal wretchedness and the struggle to overcome it, and *The Time Was Ripe* (1984, with Len Fox), a history of the Aboriginal people in Australia. She was made AO in 1984.

BANFIELD, E.J. (Edmund James) (1852–1923), born Liverpool, England, came to Australia as a child; his wide experience as a journalist included a period on the *Townsville Daily Bulletin*, 1882–97. After a severe illness he settled on Dunk Island off the Queensland coast, where he remained until his death. His placid but purposeful existence there led to several books about his experiences: *Confessions of a Beachcomber* (1908), *My Tropic Isle* (1911), *Tropic Days* (1918) and *Last Leaves from Dunk Island* (1925). Michael Noonan wrote a biography of Banfield, *A Different Drummer* (1983), and edited a collection of his writings, *The Gentle Art of Beachcombing* (1989).

BANISTER, Thomas, see *Australia, Visited & Revisited*

BANJO AWARDS, see **National Book Council**; **Literary Awards**

'BANJO, The', see **PATERSON, A.B.**

BANKS, Sir Joseph (1743–1820), who has been called 'the Father of Australia', was born in London and began to devote himself to natural science soon after coming into his inheritance in 1764. In 1766, the year he was elected to the Royal Society, he made his first expedition, collecting specimens from Newfoundland and Labrador, and in 1768 he and a staff of eight joined the *Endeavour* under Captain James Cook on its voyage to the South Seas. The naturalists made collections and observations in South America, Tahiti, NZ and on the eastern coast of Australia (April–August 1770); at Stingray Bay such a variety of specimens was collected that the spot was renamed Botany Bay (q.v.). The expedition returned in 1771; thereafter

Banks retained his interest in Australia and became the acknowledged authority on NSW after the Colony was settled in 1788. The correspondent and confidant of governors, immigrants, missionaries, explorers and scientists, all of whom continued to send back specimens to England, he was a famous patron of science, president of the Royal Society (1778–1820) and a principal in the establishment of the Royal Gardens at Kew. He published little in his lifetime, but *The Endeavour Journal of Joseph Banks*, edited by J.C. Beaglehole, was published in 1962 and Banks's *Florilegium*, which reproduces engravings of botanical species from illustrations commissioned by Banks during the *Endeavour* voyage, was published in 1988. The Sydney suburb of Bankstown, Cape Banks at Botany Bay, and the plant genus Banksia are among his other memorials. Biographies of Banks include those written by J.H. Maiden (1909), Edward Smith (1911), H.C. Cameron (1952), Charles Lyte (1980), Patrick O'Brian (1987) and H.B. Carter (1988). Carter has written widely on Banks, including in 1987 a biographical and bibliographical guide. Brian Adams in *The Flowering of the Pacific* (1986) has written an account of the 1768–71 voyage, illustrated by colour plates from Banks's *Florilegium*.

'Banks of the Condamine, The', one of the few Australian folk-songs (see Folk-Song and Ballad) that take as their subject the relationship between men and women, begins with a shearer's announcement to his love that he is leaving to join 'the Sydney shearers/ On the banks of the Condamine' (River). He rejects his girl's request that she accompany him, on the grounds that the squatters have banned women from the shearing sheds and that her constitution would be too delicate. After rejecting her further request that he stay at home and take up a selection, the shearer departs with the promise that he'll return after the season is completed. The version of the folk-song included in some editions of A.B. Paterson's *Old Bush Songs* is entitled 'Banks of the Riverine'; there are other versions in which the departing bush worker is a horse-breaker or stockman rather than a shearer. 'The Banks of the Condamine' is an anonymous composition dating from the 1860s (after the passing of the Selection Acts) but clearly derives from 'The Banks of the Nile', an English broadside ballad of the earlier nineteenth century, in which the dialogue is between a girl and a soldier departing for the Egyptian front. 'The Banks of the Nile' itself probably borrows from an eighteenth-century song, 'High Germany', which is also in the form of a dialogue between a soldier and his lover, the difference being that it is the girl who refuses the soldier's entreaties that she accompany him.

'Bannerman of the Dandenong', a popular and much-anthologised ballad by Alice Werner (1859–1935), is a sentimental tale of bush heroism and mateship. Bannerman and his mate are caught in a bushfire while on their way to the latter's wedding. Bannerman insists that his mate take Bannerman's faster horse. The mate escapes and Bannerman dies in the fire.

BANNING, Lex (1921–65), born Sydney, was, despite the disablement of cerebral palsy, a graduate of the University of Sydney and editor of *Arna*. He worked as a freelance journalist, writer for film and radio, librarian of the Mosman Spastic Centre (1954–62) and book reviewer for the *Sydney Morning Herald*. His first volume of poems, *Everyman His Own Hamlet* (1951), is a rueful indictment of the disillusioning experiences of life against which the only recourse is the poet's art. *The Instant's Clarity* (1952), as the title suggests, offers a momentary hope, but in *Apocalypse in Springtime* (1956) the mood of the title poem (which is perhaps Banning's best-known poem and which was read at his funeral) is again one of nihilism and despair. Highly regarded by fellow writers, and a considerable influence on the Sydney literati of the day, Banning is a poet of intellect and passion, neither of which is concealed by his characteristic sardonic mask. Both his published and unpublished verse have been revived by the 1987 *There Was a Crooked Man: The Poems of Lex Banning*, in which Richard Appleton supplies a biographical memoir and Alex Galloway an introduction to the poetry.

'BANNISTER, S.F.' is the composite pseudonym of wife and husband, Sally and Frank Bannister. Both were born in England, experienced the problems of growing up in poor conditions and developed strong radical attitudes at an early age – attitudes that persisted in their life in Australia – Sally, for example, becoming absorbed in the feminist cause. Their chief works are the novels *God's Own Country* and *Tossed and Blown* (both 1953), which concern an adventurous Australian character named Steve.

BARANAY, Inez (1949–), born Naples, Italy, of Hungarian parents, was brought to Australia in 1950. She has worked as a freelance journalist, editor, schoolteacher and scriptwriter and from 1987 to 1989 was a member of the Immigration Review Panel of the Department of Immigration, Local Government and Ethnic Affairs. In 1992 she worked in Papua New Guinea for a provincial Women's Council as an Australian Volunteer Abroad. She has contributed to numerous anthologies and periodicals and has published three novels, *Between Careers* (1989), *Pagan* (1990) and *The Edge of Bali* (1992), and a collection of short fiction, *The Saddest Pleasure* (1989). *Between Careers*, the story of Vita who invents a call-girl, Violet, as an alter ego, questions the social construction of sex; *Pagan*, set in Sydney's King's Cross of the 1950s, explores the personality of Eveleen Warden (Rosaleen Norton), known as the 'Witch of the Cross', from a range of perspectives and voices; *The Edge of Bali* traces the different experiences of three visitors to Bali and their individual constructions of place.

BARANGAROO was the wife of the Aborigine Bennelong (q.v.). She is mentioned in Watkin Tench's *A Complete Account of the Settlement at Port Jackson* (1793) and is fictionally presented in Eleanor Dark's *The Timeless Land* (1941).

BARBALET, Margaret (1949–), born Adelaide, grew up in Tasmania and has lived for some years in Canberra. She has written three novels, *Blood in the Rain* (1986), *Steel Beach* (1988), and *Lady, Baby, Gypsy, Queen* (1992), and two histories, *The Adelaide Children's Hospital: 1875–1976* (1975) and *Far from a Low Gutter Girl* (1983), a study of female state wards in South Australia from the 1880s to the 1940s. She has also written numerous short stories, a book for children, *The Wolf* (1991), and contributed to the collection *Canberra Tales* (1988). *Blood in the Rain* traces the life story of Jessie Sheldon from her SA childhood in foster homes during the First World War after she was deserted by her mother at the age of 4, to her own experience as a young mother in the economic depression twenty years later. The men she has loved, from her father to her lover, prove either inadequate or temporary, but Jessie learns to rely on her own rich resources. *Steel Beach* is narrated by an academic, Jeffrey Casswell, whose long-standing research on the Australian experience of D.H. Lawrence (q.v.) takes him to Thirroul on the NSW south coast. Fate provides him with two gifts, a literary discovery and the return of his girl-friend Jaco, but he proves unequal to the human challenges they offer. *Lady, Baby, Gypsy, Queen* narrates the emotional and physical odyssey of a woman who is suddenly widowed and slowly comes to terms with retrospective knowledge of the past.

BARCALDINE, a town in central Queensland, west of Rockhampton, played an important role in the Shearers' Strike of 1891. The shearers set up an armed camp at Barcaldine, flew the Eureka flag above it and sang Henry Lawson's 'Freedom on the Wallaby' with its well-known threat that if the shearers were denied justice 'blood should stain the wattle'. The strike camp at Barcaldine lasted only a few months, collapsing in June 1891 because of lack of funds. In 1991, the centenary of the Shearers' Strike, the Australian Labor Party held its own centenary celebrations in Barcaldine, the centrepiece being an old eucalypt, 'The Tree of Knowledge', under which the striking shearers met in 1891. Barcaldine is now widely regarded as the birthplace of the Australian Labor Party.

Barcoo, The is the name of an outback district and of a river in Queensland. Explorer E.B.C. Kennedy discovered in 1847 that the river named by Sir Thomas Mitchell in 1836 as Victoria River was, in reality, the upper part of Cooper's Creek, and he renamed that part of it the Barcoo River. The Barcoo district was used by A.B. Paterson as the setting for his poem 'The Bush Christening'. 'Barcoo' also became widely used to signify any vague outback malaise; among the variants were Barcoo Rot, Barcoo Spew and Barcoo Vomit. Barcoo Rot indicated a mild type of scurvy brought about by lack of fresh vegetables in the outback diet and by excessive use of tinned meat, damper and tea; a sign of Barcoo Rot (as mentioned in Donald Stuart's novel *Yaralie*) was a shiny pink patch of skin on the back of the hand. Barcoo Spew and Barcoo Vomit (stomach upsets) were sometimes caused by tainted food and sometimes, in the case of shearers, by excessive sweating and prolonged bending. Phil Mowbray (the whaler, 'Scotty the Wrinkler') was the *Bulletin's* expert on Barcoo Rot. Barcoo Rot is a character in Henry Lawson's *Send Round the Hat* sequence of stories.

Bards in the Wilderness: Australian Colonial Poetry to 1920 (1970), edited (with an introduction) by Brian Elliott and Adrian Mitchell, is an extensive anthology that focuses on the growth of indigenous Australian poetry throughout the colonial period which, the editors suggest, has 'a kind of terminus' about 1920. The wide-ranging selection begins with Aboriginal poetry, extracts from English poets writing about the distant colony and anonymous early balladry, and includes not only the major colonial poets but also lesser-known figures.

Barefooted Bob, see *Buln-Buln and the Brolga, The*; *Such is Life*

Barjai, a progressive literary magazine for youth, originated in June 1943 from the senior classes of Brisbane High School, edited by Laurence Collinson and Barrett (Barrie) Reid. After the fifth issue its original title, *Senior Tabloid*, was changed to *Barjai*. It ceased publication in 1947.

BARKER, Captain Collet (1784–1831), born Middlesex, England, entered the British Army in 1806 as an ensign and was promoted lieutenant in 1809 and captain in 1825. After service in Sicily, in the Peninsular War and in Ireland, he was posted to Sydney in 1828 and appointed commandant of the settlement at Fort Wellington on Raffles Bay. From 1829 to 1831 he had command of the penal settlement at King George Sound and on the return voyage to Sydney explored the eastern shore of Gulf St Vincent. From Yankalilla Bay he went overland with a party to Encounter Bay where he was speared to death by hostile Aborigines while swimming the Murray mouth. An unusually enlightened penal commandant, particularly skilled in conciliating Aborigines, he was highly regarded by both his superiors and peers. He is commemorated by various memorials, and by Mount Barker, in the Mount Lofty ranges and the township Barker, north of Albany. His journals 1828–1831, meticulously edited and annotated by John Mulvaney and Neville Green and titled *Commandant of Solitude*, were published in 1992. They are reminiscent of the First Fleet annals of David Collins and Watkin Tench, particularly valuable for their reflection of relations between Aborigines and White settlers.

BARKER, Jimmie, see *Two Worlds of Jimmie Barker, The*

BARLEE, Charles Haynes, editor of the magazine *Sydney Once a Week* (1878), also published an emigration pamphlet, *Queensland, Australia* (1868), and wrote *Humorous Tales and Sketches of Colonial Life* (1893).

Barlow, Billy, see '**Billy Barlow in Australia**'

BARNARD, Marjorie (1897–1987), born and educated in Sydney, graduated in 1920 with first-class honours in history from the University of Sydney. There she met Flora Eldershaw (q.v.), her future collaborator under the joint pseudonym 'M. Barnard Eldershaw' (q.v.), and was strongly influenced by George Arnold Wood, then professor of history. Later friendships of importance were with Vance and Nettie Palmer, Frank Dalby Davison, Jean Devanny and Miles Franklin. Unable to take up a graduate Oxford scholarship, Barnard worked as a librarian at Sydney Technical College, resigning in 1935 to write full-time. The next few years were the most productive and politically involved of her life. She joined the FAW and met Frank Dalby Davison, who became her lover and with whom she and Flora Eldershaw formed a close association known as 'the triumvirate'. By 1937 four of the five 'M. Barnard Eldershaw' novels had appeared and Barnard began a series of independent publications, mostly short stories, historical monographs and articles. She also contributed to three historical studies, a collection of critical essays and other work by 'M. Barnard Eldershaw' before returning to librarianship at the CSIRO from 1942 to 1950. In 1986 she received an honorary D.Litt. from the University of Sydney. Although the publication in 1947 of the novel *Tomorrow and Tomorrow* (q.v.) marked the end of the collaboration with Flora Eldershaw, she remained an active historical and short-story writer, reviewer and literary critic. Her writings, apart from those in collaboration, are *The Ivory Gate* (1920), a group of thirteen children's stories; *The Persimmon Tree and Other Stories* (1943), most of which had first been published in *Home*; two histories, *Macquarie's World* (1941) and *A History of Australia* (1962); five minor historical studies, *Australian Outline* (1943), *The Sydney Book* (1947), *Sydney: The Story of a City* (1956), *Australia's First Architect: Francis Greenway* (1961), and *Lachlan Macquarie* (1964); and a substantial critical study of Miles Franklin (1967). A selection of Barnard's correspondence is included in the collection *As Good As a Yarn With You* (1992), edited by Carole Ferrier.

It is impossible to assess the relative importance of the contributions by Barnard and Eldershaw to their joint works, but it seems likely, on the grounds of their differing circumstances, styles and personalities, that Barnard contributed most to the actual writing and Eldershaw most to the organisation and shaping. The ambitious anti-Utopian novel *Tomorrow and Tomorrow*, however, is essentially Barnard's, described by her in an interview as 'the sum of anything I could do or say' and as 'an essay in perspectives . . . a dramatisation of the forces at work in our society'. The novel was published in its uncensored form and with its full title, *Tomorrow and Tomorrow and Tomorrow*, in 1984. Barnard's own short stories are ironic, carefully structured studies of inward, mostly feminine, experience. Their understated effects are seen at their best in such stories as 'The Persimmon Tree' and 'Dry Spell'. As a historian Barnard writes from a wide perspective in a clear, figurative style. *Macquarie's World* is a colourful, convincing picture of Sydney from 1810 to 1821. The more ambitious and substantial *A History of Australia* combines grasp of detail and breadth of vision; although as an academic work it has attracted some criticism, its popularity with the general reader has resulted in a second edition and several reprintings. The same conscious artistry enlivens her minor historical articles and monographs. Her independent contribution as a literary critic, mostly in the pages of *Meanjin* and *Southerly* from the late 1940s to the early 1960s, is a distinguished one. Particularly noteworthy is her review of Patrick White's fiction in *Meanjin* (1956), the first extended appreciation by an Australian critic. Other substantial achievements are her entry on Australian literature for the 1950 edition of *Chambers's Encyclopaedia* and her personally knowledgeable study of Miles Franklin. She was made AO in 1980 for her services to literature and won the Patrick White Literary Award in 1983.

BARNES, John, see **Criticism; FURPHY, Joseph**

Barranugli, one of Patrick White's fictional Australian suburbs and akin to Sarsaparilla, is expressive, as its title suggests, of the suburban ugliness that White deplores. It features in his novels *Riders in the Chariot* (1961) and *The Solid Mandala* (1966), and in several of the short stories collected in *The Burnt Ones* (1964).

BARRETT, Charles ('Donald Barr') (1879–1959), born Hawthorn, Victoria, joined the staff of the Melbourne *Herald* in 1906 and spent much of his life writing on Australian natural history. He was assistant editor of *Emu*, the journal of the Royal Australasian Ornithologists' Union 1910–16, and edited the *Victorian Naturalist* 1925–40. Barrett wrote (sometimes under the pseudonym 'Donald Barr') more than sixty books on the Aborigines, the flora, fauna and landscape of Australia, and on such natural wonders as the Barrier Reef and the Nullarbor Plain, which he frequently visited. He edited anthologies of prose and verse, e.g. *The Swagman's Note-Book* (1943); wrote *Across the Years* (1948), a commentary on early Australian books; and published several collections of essays, e.g. *From a Bush Hut* (1942) and *Wanderer's Rest* (1946). Barrett was also the editor of *Pals*, 'the Australian Paper for the Australian Boy', which ran from 1920 to 1927. A bibliography of his work is included in Ian F. McLaren's index to *The Weekly Times Annual 1911–1934* (1986).

BARRETT, Robert, see **Crime Fiction**

Barrier Daily Truth, a Broken Hill labour newspaper, commenced publication in 1898 as the *Barrier Truth* and became a daily (the first labour movement daily in Australasia) under its present title in 1908. Joseph Furphy's *Rigby's Romance* was serialised in the newspaper in 1905–6.

BARRINGTON, George (?1755–1804) was an Irish-born pickpocket of great style and eloquence, who fleeced the rich of London in the 1770s and 1780s. Several times acquitted, he was eventually arrested for a racecourse theft in 1790 and transported for seven years to NSW, where by 1792 his good conduct had won him a conditional pardon, which was made absolute in 1796, the year of his appointment as chief constable at Parramatta. As well known in his heyday as earlier criminals such as Jonathan Wild and Jack Sheppard had been in theirs, Barrington was the subject of numerous contemporary newspaper articles, pamphlets, broadsides and chapbooks, including *The Genuine Life and Trial of George Barrington* (1790), *Memoirs of George Barrington* (1790) and *The Life of George Barrington* (1792). Barrington wrote neither these nor the subsequent publications associated with his name, including *Biographical Annals of Suicide* (1803), *Barrington's New London Spy* (1804, 1805, etc.) and several works which incorporated his Australian experiences: e.g. *A Voyage to New South Wales* (1795), *A Voyage to Botany Bay* (1795), *A Sequel to Barrington's Voyage to New South Wales* (1800) and *The History of New South Wales* (1802). *The History of New South Wales* was the first of the Barrington books to contain the 'Barrington Prologue', the lines (long thought to have been spoken at the opening of the first Australian theatre in Sydney in 1796) which begin:

> From distant climes o'er wide-spread seas we come,
> Though not with much eclat or beat of drum,
> True patriots all; for be it understood,
> We left our country for our country's good.

Subsequent research has established, however, that the author of the Prologue was not Barrington but the Englishman Henry Carter, who never visited Australia. As well as the English hack writers who exploited Barrington's name for decades, several Australian authors wrote about his career, including John Lang in *Botany Bay* (1859), Marcus Clarke in *Old Tales of a Young Country* (1871) and Roy Bridges in *Mr. Barrington* (1911).

BARRY, Clive (1922–), born Sydney, served in the Second World War, then became a district education officer in Kenya in the mid-1950s. In 1961 he was appointed UN representative in the Congo. Barry has published three novels, two of which, *The Spear Grinner* (1963) and *Fly Jamskoni* (1969), use the same central character, Hector Reed, an Australian, and the same imaginary African state, Jamskoni. In *The Spear Grinner* Jamskoni, before independence, is an anarchic state preyed upon by officials such as the Ostrich, the District Commissioner's office boy. In *Fly Jamskoni* Reed returns to the small, newly independent state as a UN officer. Nothing has changed – the Ostrich, now minister of aviation, still controls the country and the chief gangster of *The Spear Grinner* has now become the new superintendent of police. Barry's other novel, *Crumb Borne* (1965), examines the microcosm of a POW camp, drawing to some degree, as do the African novels, on his own experience and background. A vivid stylist with a capacity for dry humour, Barry exploits the bizarre and incongruous to produce interesting, if slight, narratives.

BARRY, Dan (1851–1908), born Dublin, Ireland, as John Ringrose Atkins, was educated in Melbourne, where his lawyer father was friendly with Redmond Barry; the connection may have provided him with the stage name he took from the 1870s. Barry's greatest success as a theatre manager came at the turn of the century. Although his own acting style was understated, he specialised in producing sensational Australian melodramas and adaptations of Shakespeare. His production of 'The Kelly Gang' in 1898 was perhaps among his most popular, although he had a flair for producing topical plays and unacknowledged adaptations of the work of other dramatists. He was best known for his outback tours.

BARRY, J.A. (John Arthur) (1850–1911), born Torquay, England, came to Australia in 1870 after an apprenticeship as a seaman, to participate in the Palmer gold rush. He later spent some years in itinerant outback occupations alternating with periods in the coastal trade. While he was in England in 1893 he published *Steve Brown's Bunyip and Other Stories*, a popular collection of tales that had earlier appeared in Australian and English journals. He joined the Sydney *Evening News* in 1896 and also wrote regularly for the *Australian Town and Country Journal*. His other published fiction, based on his adventures at sea and in the outback, included *In the Great Deep* (1896), *The Luck of the Native-Born* (1898), *Against the Tides of Fate* (1899), *A Son of the Sea* (1899, partly autobiographical), *Red Lion and Blue Star with Other Stories* (1902), *Sea Yarns* (1910) and *South Sea Shipmates* (?1914). He also wrote a historical work, *The City of Sydney* (1902).

BARRY, Sir John Vincent (1903–69), born Albury, NSW, the son of a painter and decorator of Irish descent, was an eminent lawyer and judge. Appointed to the Supreme Court of Victoria in 1947, he led the Australian delegations to the first and Second United Nations Congresses for the Prevention of Crime and Treatment of Offenders in 1955 and 1960. His interest in convict history resulted in two biographies, *Alexander Maconochie* (1958) and *The Life and Death of John Price* (1964).

BARRY, Sir Redmond (1813–80) was an Irish-born lawyer who settled in Melbourne in 1839 and became a judge of the Supreme Court of Victoria in 1852. During a long career on the Bench he presided over many important trials, including those of the prominent Eureka rebels and of Ellen and Ned Kelly (q.v.). He had a reputation for severity as a judge but was a leading figure in Melbourne intellectual and cultural life and, for 'Garryowen', was 'the most remarkable personage in the annals of Port Phillip'. One of the founders of the University of Melbourne, he was equally important in making the Melbourne Public Library, in the nineteenth century, one of the great libraries of the world. As president of the trustees, Barry was influential in Marcus Clarke's appointment to the Library in 1870. His death just days after Ned Kelly's execution – and after Kelly had promised at the trial to meet Sir Redmond in the beyond – lost Clarke

a possible ally in his quest for appointment to the public librarianship in 1881.

BARTLETT, Norman (1908–   ), born England, grew up in WA and graduated from the University of WA before working as a journalist and serving with the RAAF in Europe and New Guinea during the Second World War. After the war he worked for the *Sunday Daily Telegraph* and the *Sunday Telegraph* as literary editor and leader writer and from 1954 to 1973 was a press attaché and information counsellor in Australian diplomatic posts in Bangkok, New Delhi, Tokyo and London. In retirement he gained a Ph.D. in history from the Australian National University. Bartlett has published two dramatised histories, *The Pearl Seekers* (1954), which deals with Australia's pearling industry, and *The Gold-Seekers* (1965), an account of the Victorian gold rush and the Eureka Stockade; a collection of his literary sketches and articles for newspapers and journals, *Australians Are Different* (1988); a travel book about Thailand, *Land of the Lotus Eaters* (1959); and a commissioned account of the main events in Australian and American history 1776–1976, *Australia and America through Two Hundred Years* (1976). He has also edited *With the Australians in Korea* (1954) and *Australia at Arms* (1955), collections of reminiscences of war experiences.

BARTLETT, Stephen, see **'SLADE, Gurney'**

BARTLEY, Nehemiah (1830–94), born London, arrived in Hobart in 1849 and after periods of seafaring, gold-digging and overlanding sheep, became a commercial agent and landowner in Queensland. A notable Brisbane eccentric, in his later years he wrote *Opals and Agates* (1892), the reminiscences of his early Queensland experiences, and *Australian Pioneers and Reminiscences* (1896), ed. J.J. Knight.

BARTON, Charlotte, see *Mother's Offering to Her Children, A*

BARTON, Sir Edmund (1849–1920), brother of G.B. Barton (q.v.), was born and educated in Sydney and was a lawyer before entering the NSW parliament in 1879. Speaker of the Legislative Assembly 1883–87, he was nicknamed 'Toby Tosspot' by the *Bulletin*. He was prominent in the Federation movement in the 1890s and became in 1901 the first prime minister of the Commonwealth of Australia. After his defeat in 1903 he became judge of the High Court of Australia. A biography by John Reynolds was published in 1948.

BARTON, George Burnett (1836–1901), born Sydney, elder brother of Sir Edmund Barton, was called to the bar in England in 1860. He became editor of the *Sydney Punch* in 1864 and was reader in English literature at the University of Sydney 1865–68. In 1868 he went to New Zealand to edit the *Otago Daily Times*, then practised law in Dunedin and Christchurch before returning to Sydney in the early 1880s. In 1887 he was appointed to bring out a fifteen-volume edition of the *History of New South Wales from the Records* but lost favour with the government and left the project after completing only one volume, *Governor Phillip, 1783–1789* (1889). A keen federationist and protectionist, Barton wrote 'Historical Sketch of Australian Federation' which appeared in the *Yearbook of Australia*, 1891, and edited, in the year he died, the *Werriwa Times*, a protectionist newspaper published in Goulburn. In a memorial assessment the *Bulletin* described Barton as 'the first purely literary man produced by New South Wales'. The most substantial proof of that commendation lay in his wide-ranging and notable contributions to a variety of journals and newspapers, e.g. 'The Status of Literature in New South Wales', *Centennial Magazine* (1889–90), and in his publication in 1866 of *Literature in New South Wales* and *The Poets and Prose Writers of New South Wales* (qq.v.).

BARTON, Robert Darvall (1843–1924), born Boree, NSW, grazier and uncle of the poet A.B. Paterson, was the author of *Reminiscences of an Australian Pioneer* (1917). Barton's mother, Emily Mary Barton (1817–1909), grandmother of A.B. Paterson, also published poetry. Her shipboard diary of the voyage to Australia appeared in 1985 as *The Diary of Miss Emily Darvall 1839–1840*.

BASEDOW, Herbert (1881–1933), born Kent Town, Adelaide, studied anthropology and medicine and became an outstanding contemporary authority on the Aborigines. His publications include *The Australian Aboriginal* (1925) and *Knights of the Boomerang: Episodes from a Life Spent Among the Native Tribes of Australia* (1935).

BASS, George (1771–1803), born Aswarby, Lincolnshire, joined the Royal Navy as a surgeon's mate at the age of 18. With Matthew Flinders (q.v.) he sailed in HMS *Reliance* on its voyage taking Governor Hunter to NSW in 1795. In 1795–96 Bass, Flinders and a boy, William Martin, explored the coastline adjacent to the Port Jackson settlement in two small boats, both named *Tom Thumb*. His major explorations, however, were the 1797–98 voyages down the far south coast of NSW and through the strait (named Bass Strait in his honour by Governor Hunter) that separates the mainland from Tasmania. Bass's journal of the first voyage (December 1797–February 1798) was published as *Journal of a Whaleboat Voyage* in 1986; the journal of his later 1798 voyage, in the company of Flinders, is quoted in David Collins's *An Account of the English Colony in New South Wales* (1798, 1802); it gives a meticulous account of the geology, geography, flora and fauna of the area explored. The Bass Strait voyage and the earlier *Tom Thumb* voyages are described in Flinders's *Voyage to Terra Australis* (1814). Bass spent his few remaining years in somewhat fruitless trading ventures to the NSW colony, the Pacific Islands and South America. His ship, *Venus*, disappeared on one such venture in 1803. K.M. Bowden published *George Bass, 1771–1803* in 1952.

BASSETT, Marnie (Lady Flora Marjorie Bassett) (1889–1980) was born in Melbourne into a distinguished academic family. Her published works include *The Governor's Lady* (1940), the story of Mrs Philip Gidley King, the first woman to come to Australia as a governor's wife; *The Hentys* (1954), an account of the pioneering Henty family (q.v.); *Realms and Islands* (1962), an account of the world voyage of Rose de Freycinet 1817–20; and *Behind the Picture: HMS Rattlesnake's Australia–New Guinea Cruise, 1846–1850* (1966), an account said to have been inspired by a watercolour sketch (hence the title) by marine artist Oswald Brierly of HMS *Rattlesnake* anchored off Cape York. The *Rattlesnake's* cruise is used to unite many slightly related events – the disastrous E.B. Kennedy expedition in the Cape York Peninsula; the rescue of White woman Barbara Thompson after her five years as a prisoner of the Prince of Wales Island Aborigines; the career of Benjamin Boyd; and the abortive defence settlement at Port Essington in what is now the Northern Territory. Marnie Bassett also published *Letters from New Guinea 1921* (1969), letters written during a three-months' visit she paid to New Guinea just after the Australian civil administration was established in 1921. They are interesting for the insight they give into the preoccupations of the contemporary administrators. In 1985 a work she had been preparing at the time of her death, *Henry Fyshe Gisborne*, was published, together with reminiscences of her parents and her childhood in Melbourne. She received honorary D.Litt. degrees from Monash University (1968) and the University of Melbourne (1974), and was a foundation fellow of the Australian Academy of the Humanities.

Batavia, a Dutch trading vessel under the command of Captain Pelsart (Pelsaert), ran on to the Wallabi reefs of the Abrolhos Islands off the coast of WA in June 1629. In the ensuing weeks some of the crew murdered a number of the survivors and attempted to make off with the *Batavia* to go pirating on the high seas. They were thwarted by the timely arrival of a rescue ship from the East Indies. The crew and passengers of the *Batavia* are the first known White inhabitants of Australia. The wreck of the *Batavia* and the events which followed are at the centre of Ernest Favenc's novel *Marooned on Australia* (?1896), Malcolm Uren's narrative *Sailormen's Ghosts* (1940), Douglas Stewart's radio play *Shipwreck* (1947), Henrietta Drake-Brockman's novel *The Wicked and the Fair* (1957) and Robert Close's *The Voyage Continues* (1969). A detailed, factual account of the *Batavia* is in Drake-Brockman's *Voyage to Disaster* (1963). *Islands of Angry Ghosts* (1966) by Hugh Edwards (q.v.), who led the expedition that discovered the wreck of the *Batavia* and salvaged the remains of her cargo, recounts both sagas, the original story of the *Batavia* and the twentieth-century recovery of the wreck. The *Batavia* story continues to exert its fascination on modern writers, e.g. Lee Knowles's 'Batavia Incident' in *Cool Summer* (1977); Hal Colebatch's 'Batavia' Suite' (1979), in *Outer Charting* (1985); Mark O'Connor's poem sequence 'The *Batavia*' in *Selected Poems* (1986). Nicholas

Hasluck's *The Bellarmine Jug* (1984) has the *Batavia* affair as a starting-point for a story about international espionage. Of interest also in children's books, it features in Deborah Lisson's *The Devil's Own* (1990) and Gary Crew's *Strange Objects* (1990). The Australian National Maritime Museum has issued (1993) *The Voyage of the Batavia* by Francis Pelsaert, the second in its Australian Maritime Series. The museum's volume includes a facsimile of the 1647 printing of Pelsaert's journal, a translation of the original Dutch text, an essay on the background of the voyage and ten facsimile engravings.

BATES, Daisy (1859–1951), the legendary 'Kabbarli' (grandmother/wise woman/friend) of the Aborigines, was born Daisy May O'Dwyer in Tipperary, Ireland. She was sent by her guardians to Australia in 1883 because she was thought to have tuberculosis. On 13 March 1884 at Charters Towers, Queensland, she married an Edwin Henry Murrant, said by Margaret Carnegie and Frank Shields in *In Search of Breaker Morant* (1979) to have been Harry Harbord ('Breaker') Morant; she parted from him almost immediately because of his unstable character. Less than a year later (17 February 1885) she went through a marriage ceremony at Nowra, NSW, with cattleman, Jack Bates. She left Bates to return to England in 1894, where she worked as a journalist until she returned to Perth in 1899. By 1901 she was at the Trappist Aboriginal Mission at Beagle Bay near Broome, and in 1904 she was back in Perth, having been appointed by the WA government to research the languages of the Aborigines of WA, soon extended to other aspects of their culture. During 1910–11 she was with the Radcliffe Brown expedition on the hospital islands, Dorré and Bernier, off Carnarvon in WA. From 1912 to 1945, with brief periods of ill health intervening, she lived among the Aboriginal tribes but always maintained fastidious Edwardian standards of dress and decorum at various camps on the fringes of the Nullarbor. She worked assiduously to document Aboriginal customs and lore and to badger governments and authorities into programmes of racial reform. She wrote almost 300 newspaper and journal articles on her experiences and on the Aboriginal situation, publishing her autobiography, 'My Natives and I', as a newspaper serial, and as *The Passing of the Aborigines* (written with the help of Ernestine Hill), in 1938. In 1940 her vast Aboriginal collection was deposited in the National Library, which published her anthropological study, *The Native Tribes of Western Australia*, edited by Isobel White, in 1985. Her anthropological observations have in modern times received only minimal scientific approval, and her attitude and approach to the Aboriginal question have continued to arouse considerable controversy. There is no doubt that, by adopting methods not then common in anthropological research, in living with communities for extended periods and sharing their everyday lives, gaining acceptance into their kinship systems, Daisy Bates was able to document details of Aboriginal life, as remembered by old people before it was affected by Europeans, and during her many years of daily contact, with considerable depth and understanding. But her attitudes were coloured by prevailing theories of evolutionism and social Darwinism, which saw Aboriginal society 'fading away' naturally in the path of a superior European civilisation, and by her personal prejudices of class, race and gender. Although she has received widespread approbation among the White community, who placed her among such notable humanitarians as Caroline Chisholm, Elizabeth Fry and Florence Nightingale, and awarded her the CBE in 1934, some current Aboriginal opinion maintains that patronising and well-intentioned amateurs such as she delayed the development of effective welfare programmes. Her biography, *Daisy Bates* by Elizabeth Salter, was published in 1971; an opera, *The Young Kabbarli* (1972), written by Maie Casey to music by Margaret Sutherland, celebrates some of her exploits. Aboriginal legends collected by her, *Tales Told to Kabbarli* and Ernestine Hill's tribute, *Kabbarli: A Personal Memoir of Daisy Bates*, were published respectively in 1972 and 1973. The Sydney Dance Company staged Barry Moreland's dance-drama, *Daisy Bates*, in 1982. John Aitken wrote the play 'Daisy Bates and the Dancer' (1990); Allan Curtis's *Kabbarli* (1985) juxtaposes Daisy Bates and her work with Black activist movements of the 1970s and 1980s.

BATESON, Charles (1903–74), born Wellington, NZ, came to Australia in 1922. A notable journalist, he was a war correspondent in Europe and Italy during the Second World War and editorial manager of Mirror Newspapers in Australia 1960–66. One of Australia's most prolific maritime historians, Bateson published *The Convict Ships, 1787–1868* (1959), an account of the voyages of the convict ships and the administrative system under which they were selected, manned, provisioned and dispatched. His other major published works include *Gold Fleet for California* (1963), *Patrick Logan: Tyrant of Brisbane Town* (1966), *The War with Japan* (1968), *Australian Shipwrecks* (1972), and *Dire Strait: A History of Bass Strait* (1973).

BATEY, Peter (1933–), born Benalla, Victoria, and educated at the University of Melbourne, was a foundation member of the Melbourne Theatre Company, of which he was later associate director. He has also been resident director of the National Theatre of WA, artistic director of the SA Theatre Company, director of the Victorian Arts Council, director/manager of the Canberra Repertory Company and director/executive producer of Reg Livermore's solo productions. He wrote the popular musical plays 'The No-Hopers' (1961); 'Adelaide Happening' (1971); 'From Smike to Bulldog', an entertainment based on the letters of Arthur Streeton; 'Ecstasies', a rock opera; and 'Songs My Mother Didn't Teach Me', a dramatic biography for the stage.

Bathurst, one of the major cities of central western NSW, is situated on the Macquarie River about 200 kilometres from Sydney. After the crossing of the Blue

Mountains in 1813, Governor Lachlan Macquarie travelled in 1815 to the site of the present city, which he named Bathurst in honour of the secretary of state for the colonies, Earl Bathurst. The town was gazetted in 1833 and boomed from 1851, when gold was discovered at nearby Summer Hill Creek. Significant in bushranging history as a result of the gold discoveries, Bathurst became the headquarters of Cobb & Co. (q.v.) in the 1860s. When the gold rushes subsided it became the centre of a prosperous primary-producing district and, subsequently, a noted educational centre. The history of Bathurst in the gold-rush era is outlined in Geoffrey Blainey, *The Rush That Never Ended* (1963); Bernard Greaves (ed.) *The Story of Bathurst* (1961) covers a wider historical span. Among writers to have lived or worked in Bathurst are William Derricourt, Nat Gould, George Black, 'Price Warung', and A.W. Jose; several of Gould's sporting novels have Bathurst scenes, as also does 'Grant Hervey's' *An Eden of the Good* (1934), written while 'Hervey' was an inmate of Bathurst gaol. Other literary connections with Bathurst include Gordon Neil Stewart's historical novel *House of Bondage* (1975), which is focused on Stewart's Bathurst ancestors, and D'Arcy Niland's *Walkabout* article (31, 1965), 'Our First Inland City'.

BATMAN, John (1801–39), born Rose Hill (Parramatta), went in 1821 to Tasmania, where he took up a small farming property. He formed an association of fourteen Tasmanian settlers (later the Port Phillip Association) to search for grazing land in the unexplored Port Phillip district, and sailed in the *Rebecca*, landing at Indented Head on the Geelong side of Port Phillip Bay, 29 May 1835. From the Aborigines he purchased almost a quarter of a million hectares of land in return for blankets and other gifts and utensils. At a point on the Yarra River near where Melbourne now stands, Batman's diary of 8 June 1835 noted 'This will be the place for a village'. Although Governor Bourke refused to sanction the land deal, an influx of settlers soon established the first Port Phillip settlement. *The Settlement of John Batman in Port Phillip from His Own Journal* was published posthumously in 1856. James Bonwick's biography *John Batman, the Founder of Victoria* was published in 1867; subsequent studies include C.P. Billot's biography (1979) and *John Batman and the Aborigines* (1987) by Alistair Campbell. In Xavier Herbert's *Capricornia* (1938), Melbourne is represented as Batman; Robert Close's novel *Eliza Callaghan* (1957) features Batman's courtship of Eliza.

BATTARBEE, Rex (1893–1973), born Warrnambool, Victoria, was severely wounded in the First World War and became a commercial artist (1924–27) before devoting himself to watercolour painting. He travelled and painted extensively in the outback, especially in Central Australia where, in the late 1930s and early 1940s, he worked with some of the Aranda Aborigines at the Hermannsburg mission. Astonished and inspired by their aptitude, Battarbee fostered the development of the Hermannsburg school of watercolourists, whose best-known representative was Albert Namatjira. He became Namatjira's teacher and

mentor, arranging a solo exhibition for him in Melbourne in 1938, and working with him in the documentary film *Namatjira the Painter*. Battarbee published two works on Aboriginal art, *Modern Australian Aboriginal Art* (1951) and *Modern Aboriginal Paintings* (1971, with Bernice Battarbee).

Battlers, The, a novel by Kylie Tennant (q.v.) first published in 1941, shared the S.H. Prior Memorial Prize, and the Australian Literature Society's Gold Medal, and is her most popular work. The 'battlers' are the nomad unemployed, last remnants of the Depression, who in 1939 were still tramping the roads. The central characters are Snow, a morose, middle-aged, solitary wanderer, who is fleeing the poor 'cocky' life he had known as a boy; and Dancy the Stray, a 19-year-old girl waif from Sydney's slums. Dirty, toothless and starving, Dancy is the first and the most remarkable of a group of outcasts who attach themselves to Snow. Although unattractive, frail and beset with terrors, Dancy has sensitivity, spirit, wit and a richly macabre imagination. Other close adherents of the group include Duke, a yodelling busker, and the fat, parasitic, pseudo-genteel, Miss Phipps. As Snow's 'mob' roams the country in pursuit of the dole stations or work, it becomes absorbed in the larger crowd of nomads, who also live aimlessly and desperately at the edge of existence, pushed aside by the rest of 'respectable' society but sustained by a sense of fellowship, dogged will to survive and resilient humour. Individuals who stand out include the Apostle, ex-minister and half-madman, half-saint; the Tyrell family and their companion Thirty Bob; and the political activists Burning Angus, Dogger and Snake. Striking and animated as these people are, the immense and indifferent land dwarfs them and defines both the futility and the heroism of their struggle.

BATTYE, J.S. (James Sykes) (1871–1954), born Geelong, Victoria, was appointed chief librarian of the Victoria Public Library in Perth, WA, in 1895 and from 1912 until his death was general secretary of the amalgamated library, museum and art gallery. His keen personal interest in the history of WA is reflected in his establishment in 1923 of the Public Records Committee of WA (later the State Archives Board); his writing and compiling the *Cyclopedia of Western Australia* (1912–13), *The History of the North West of Australia* (1915), and *Western Australia: A History* (1924); and his role in establishing the Royal WA Historical Society in 1926. Pro-chancellor of the University of WA 1931–36 and Chancellor 1937–43, Battye is commemorated by the J.S. Battye Library of Australian History, established as an adjunct to the State Reference Library of WA in 1956.

BAUME, Eric (1900–67), born Auckland, NZ, of German-Jewish ancestry, came to Australia in 1923 after a meteoric rise in NZ journalism, having been editor, at the age of 22, of the largest provincial newspaper, the *Timaru Herald*. His successful Australian journalistic career began with a period as news editor of the *Daily Guardian;* he was later editor of the *Sunday*

Sun, the *Truth* and *Daily Mirror*, and deputy editor-in-chief of Truth Newspapers Ltd 1949–52. He spent ten years in England (1939–49) representing *Truth* and *Daily Mirror*; he scooped the world press with his forecast of the German invasion of Russia and went as a war correspondent to the Second Front invasion of Europe. It was, however, after the war as a controversial radio and television commentator that he became a household name in NSW. His well-known (loved and hated) radio programmes, ombudsman-like in style and parish-pump in theme, were 'I'm On Your Side' and 'This I Believe'. He chaired, often abrasively, the television discussion programme 'Beauty and the Beast'. In 1966 he was made OBE for his services to journalism. More the master of the spoken than the written word, Baume was nevertheless a prolific writer. He wrote a mixture of fictional, autobiographical and documentary works including *Tragedy Track* (1932), *Half-Caste* (1933), *Burnt Sugar* (1934), *I Lived These Years* (1941), *I've Lived Another Year* (1942), *Sydney Duck* (1944), *Five Graves at Nijmegen* (1945), *Ponty Galler* (1947), *Devil Lord's Daughter* (1948), *Unrehearsed Incident* (1948, short stories) and *The Mortal Sin of Father Grossard* (1953). *Five Graves at Nijmegen* is Baume's only work with some literary claims; the remainder reflect impatience and lack of care. A.E. Manning wrote the biographical account *Larger Than Life* (1967).

BAXTER, Anne (1923–85), born Indiana, USA, and a well-known American film star, lived in Australia for three years after she married American cattleman Randolph Galt, who owned a large station, Giro, in the Barrington Tops area of NSW. Her account of that experience, *Intermission* (1976), is a perceptive look at both the marriage and the Australian environment and is notable for its keen appraisal of Australian customs, manners and landscape.

BAXTER, Annie Maria, see **DAWBIN, Annie Maria**

BAXTER, John (1939–), born Sydney, is a film historian, biographer and novelist, was publicity director of the Australian Commonwealth Film Unit 1968–70 and lecturer in film and theatre in Britain and the USA 1970–80. Among his numerous publications on the cinema are *The Australian Cinema* (1970), *Science Fiction in the Cinema* (1970), *Sixty Years of Hollywood* (1973), *Filmstruck: Australia at the Movies* (1986), and a portrait of Ken Russell, titled *An Appalling Talent* (1973). He edited *The Pacific Book of Australian Science Fiction* (1968), *Australian Science Fiction* (1975) and *The Second Pacific Book of Science Fiction* (1971). He has also written scripts for several films, including the experimental *After Proust*, was co-editor, until its demise, of the Australian magazine *Film Digest*, and has written several novels including *The Hermes Fall* (1978), *The Black Yacht* (1982), and *Bondi Blues* (1993).

Bay of Noon, The, a novel by Shirley Hazzard (q.v.), was published in 1970. Time is handled as a series of subtly linked perspectives on past, present and future so that the following chronological scheme is revealed only in stages. Jenny, the narrator, a girl in her early twenties, born in England, has been deprived of a sense of home by her evacuation to South Africa during the Second World War and by the loss of her mother. When she perceives that her close relationship with her brother Edmund has become part of a convenient triangle after his marriage to a nondescript Englishwoman, Norah, Jenny applies for a clerical position with the NATO establishment at Naples. She finds her occupation sterile and boring, but Italy alters her life dramatically. She becomes intimate with a beautiful, sensitive Italian girl, Giaconda, who is involved in a relationship with a middle-aged film director, Gianni. Giaconda's past has been marked by tragedy; the war visited ostracism and physical suffering on her family, caused the death of her mother and later of her father, a distinguished scholar, and took the life of her artist lover Gaetano in a land-mine accident. Gianni has retrieved her from this wreckage and for this reason she clings to him even though he often seems self-centred and cruel. Jenny also becomes friendly with an English scientist, Justin Tulloch, although he prevents their relationship from becoming intimate by keeping it at a humorous level. During the Neapolitan summer Jenny falls severely ill and only belatedly discovers that Giaconda has left for Spain with Justin. Gianni, in his anguish, turns to Jenny for comfort. They become lovers but it is clear that they both desire the return of Giaconda and, after protecting Jenny on a journey to Genoa, where she is to board a ship for the USA and a new position, Gianni hastens, with Jenny's blessing, to rejoin Giaconda. Justin disappears from their lives until years later Jenny learns of his death in a plane accident. After several years in the USA Jenny revisits Italy, conscious that 'like the dye they had injected into my veins, the country coloured my essence, illuminated my reaction to everything else. Here, literally, I had come to my senses'.

BAYER, Louis (1858–1907), born Germany, studied at Tubingen University before arriving in Australia in 1873. He lived mainly at Camperdown and Warrnambool in the Western District of Victoria, where he earned his living as an orchestral musician and music teacher, meanwhile making a reputation as the composer and author of numerous operas. Australian in setting, with one exception, they dealt with the lives of ordinary people and were enthusiastically received by Western District audiences, although only the published lyrics of three and the reviews of individual productions have survived. His operas included 'Federation' (1887), 'Muutchaka; or, The Last of his Tribe' (1888), 'Dora; or The Trapper's Bride' (1893) and 'The Golden West' (1907). 'The Golden West', which celebrated the Victorian dairying industry to the extent of including live cows on stage, was subsequently published but is no longer extant. The first of the nineteenth century playwrights to attempt to represent contemporary everyday Australian life, Bayer wrote the text, lyrics and music for each opera, assembled and trained the orchestras and organised their tours of regional towns.

BAYLDON, A.A. (Arthur Albert Dawson)
(1865–1958), born Leeds, England, arrived in Brisbane
in 1889 and contributed to the flood of bush balladry
of the 1890s. A typical *Bulletin* poet, Bayldon reflected
the ambivalent attitude of the day towards the outback
and bush life; sometimes pessimistically depicting the
hardships of that life, at other times caught up in the
enthusiastic Arcadian vision of A.B. Paterson. His
books of poetry include *Poems* (1897), *The Western
Track and Other Verses* (1905), *The Eagles: Collected
Poems* (1921), a further *Collected Poems* (1932), and
Apollo in Australia and Bush Verses (1944). His only
published work of fiction was *The Tragedy behind the
Curtain and Other Stories* (1910); a novel and some various other works remain unpublished.

**'BAYLEBRIDGE, William' (Charles William
Blocksidge)** (1883–1942), born Brisbane, adopted the
name Baylebridge from about 1925. He lived in England 1908–19, publishing numerous limited editions
of poetry and working in Intelligence during the First
World War. He was assisted financially at this time by
his mother's half-sister Grace Leven (Celia Grace
Leven); in her memory he later established the annual
Grace Leven Poetry Prize. He returned to Australia in
1919 but became an increasingly isolated figure in the
Australian literary scene. Although critics such as
H.M. Green and T. Inglis Moore have classed 'Baylebridge' as one of Australia's few philosophical and
intellectual poets, others such as F.T. Macartney have
seen him as a literary larcenist. He remains one of the
more puzzling and enigmatic of Australian writers,
the pages of his verse seldom turned by modern
readers. In prefaces to several of his works he protested
against the philistinism and cultural inertia of contemporary Australian society. His chief works (reprinted
under the terms of his will in a memorial edition as
Salvage: Collected Works of William Baylebridge, 1964)
include *Love Redeemed* (1934), love sonnets; *This Vital
Flesh* (1939), the application of his philosophy of vitalism to Australian nationalism; and *An Anzac Muster*
(q.v., 1921), short fiction centred on the Gallipoli campaign of 1915. Robin Gerster in *Big-noting: the Heroic
Theme in Australian War Writing* (1993), sees *An Anzac
Muster* as a deliberate attempt by Baylebridge to mythologise Gallipoli.

BAYNTON, Barbara (1857–1929), who claimed to
have been born in 1862 after the elopement of her
mother, Penelope Ewart, with an Indian army officer
named Kilpatrick, may have been the daughter of a
carpenter, John Lawrence, and his wife Elizabeth, and
was born in Scone, NSW. Penne Hackforth-Jones
(great granddaughter of Baynton) in *Barbara Baynton:
Between Two Worlds* (1989) maintains that Baynton's
father was named Kilpatrick but took the name John
Lawrence and lived with Baynton's mother, Elizabeth
Lawrence, after her arrival in Australia in 1840.
Brought up on the Liverpool Plains, Barbara Baynton
married a selector, Alexander Frater, in 1880, and bore
him three children. In 1887 he ran off with his wife's
niece; Barbara moved to Sydney, divorced him in 1890
and the next day married Thomas Baynton, a retired

surgeon who moved in literary and academic circles. It
was not until the 1890s that she began to write; her
first story was published in the *Bulletin* in 1896. In
1902–3 she visited London, where *Bush Studies* (q.v.,
1902) was published, and after her husband's death in
1904 she alternated residence between Australia and
England, becoming well known as a literary hostess
and as a collector of antiques and furniture. In 1921 she
married the fifth Lord Headley, a colourful engineer,
sportsman and president of the Muslim Society; they
separated soon after. As Lady Headley, Baynton continued to divide her time between Australia and England until her death.

Baynton's movement through society obviously led
her to distort the facts of her early life and first marriage; yet this part of her past informs her fiction,
which depicts the horrors of bush life and confirms
Australia as the 'windblown, shimmering, shifting,
awful waste,/ Fringed by a broken edge of green and
grey' that she wrote about in the poem 'To My
Country'. The malevolence of the bush is insisted
upon throughout her work; so is the suffering of her
female characters, who are consistently seen as the victims of predatory, brutal men. In *Bush Studies*,
'Squeaker's Mate' tells of a woman whose back is
broken by a falling tree and who is left neglected by
the man she has nurtured and protected; in 'Billy Skywonkie' a woman endures a nightmarish ride from a
railway siding to a bush station only to be refused
employment as housekeeper because of her colour;
and in 'The Chosen Vessel' (q.v.) a young mother left
alone in a bush hut is raped and murdered by a passing
swagman. Of the other *Bush Studies*, 'Scrammy 'And'
and 'A Dreamer' are similar tales of terror, and 'Bush
Church' presents the inadequacies of religion as a
comfort against fear and loneliness. Baynton's output
was small, but in both *Bush Studies* and her short novel
Human Toll (q.v., 1907) her grim realism, which is
authenticated by the accumulation of detail and by the
accuracy of the idiom her characters use, offers a
powerful alternative to the romantic pictures of bush
life. *Barbara Baynton* in the Portable Australian
Authors series was edited by Sally Krimmer and Alan
Lawson in 1980. She is one of the writers discussed by
Thea Astley in *Three Australian Writers* (1979).

'Beach Burial', a poem by Kenneth Slessor (q.v.) first
published in 1944, is set in the period when Australian
soldiers were fighting in the Western Desert near El
Alamein. The poem describes the hasty burial of
seamen washed ashore from the naval battles of
the Mediterranean. A fine poem, which reflects the
futility of war, it expresses the bewildered pity of
battle-hardened troops as they perform rough-and-
ready but deeply tender last rites over the sodden,
nameless corpses.

BEACH, Eric (1947–   ), born NZ, came to Australia in 1972 and has written plays, verse and short
stories. Active in the Performance Poetry scene, his
published works are *Saint Kilda Meets Hugo Ball* (1974),
In Occupied Territory (1977), *A Photo of Some People in a*

Football Stadium (1978), and *Hey Hey Brass Buttons* (1990).

BEADELL, Len (1923–), born Pennant Hills, Sydney, has had a long career in surveying and mapping in outback Australia and Papua-New Guinea. His books are mainly concerned with his surveying life and projects. They include *Too Long in the Bush* (1965), *Blast the Bush* (1967), *Bush Bashers* (1971), *Still in the Bush* (1975), *Beating about the Bush* (1976), *Outback Highways* (1979, a compendium of the five previous books) and *End of an Era* (1983). He holds the BEM and OAM.

BEAGLEHOLE, J.C. (John Cawte) (1901–71), born Wellington, NZ, became one of his country's foremost historians and a leading figure in its literary, historical and community life. The recipient of numerous awards and honours, Beaglehole was made CMG in 1958 and awarded the Order of Merit in 1970, the latter after the publication of his work on Captain James Cook (q.v.). His most notable historical publications were *Exploration of the Pacific* (1934), *The Journals of Captain James Cook* (1955, 1961, 1967), *The Endeavour Journal of Joseph Banks* (1962) and *The Life of Captain James Cook* (1974).

BEAN, C.E.W. (Charles Edwin Woodrow) (1879–1968), born Bathurst, NSW, was educated in England at Clifton College and at Oxford, and was called to the Bar in 1903. After returning to Australia in 1904 he taught briefly, travelled on the country legal circuit as an assistant (1905–7), and wrote of his impressions in a series of articles published by the *Sydney Morning Herald*, June–July 1907. In 1908 he joined that newspaper as a reporter and was sent in 1909 to western NSW to gather material for a series of articles on the wool industry. Those articles, titled 'The Wool Land', formed the basis of *On the Wool Track* (1910), one of the classic accounts of outback Australian life. The book traverses the 'red country' – the land of the western rivers (the Namoi, Bogan, Culgoa, Warrego, Paroo and Darling) and the land of the great sheep runs where four stations on the Darling and Paroo made one property of three and a quarter million acres and ran along 280 miles of the winding rivers. Along Bean's wool track passes a procession of squatters, shearers, rouseabouts, boundary-riders, swagmen, bullock teams, flocks of sheep, plagues of rabbits and many varieties of natural and human disasters. Bean's travels also produced his historical and social documentary of the Darling River, *The Dreadnought of the Darling* (1911), an account of his trip down the river on a small paddle-steamer. From 1910 to 1912 Bean was in London, reporting for his paper on the ships being built for the Royal Australian Navy. Those reports formed the basis of his publication *Flagships Three* (1913). In the First World War he was appointed official war correspondent with the Australian forces and was at Gallipoli, where he was wounded. In 1916 he edited *The Anzac Book*, a collection of contributions by Australian soldiers on Gallipoli, which includes his own photographs, drawings and verse. *The Anzac*

Book was a considerable influence on the rise of the Anzac legend. His observations on the war in the trenches, *Letters from France*, were published in 1917 and his hopes for the post-war future, *In Your Hands, Australians*, in 1918. In 1919 he began *The Official History of Australia in the War of 1914–1918* (q.v.); the first two volumes, *The Story of Anzac*, were published in 1921 and 1924. He also wrote four other volumes dealing with the war in France and edited the remainder of the *History*. The last of the twelve-volume work was published in 1942; Bean's own single-volume abridgement of the series, *Anzac to Amiens*, was published in 1946. During the Second World War he was occupied in creating the Commonwealth Archives and planning the National War Memorial in Canberra. Bean's later writings include *Here, My Son* (1950), a history of the independent schools of Australia, and *Two Men I Knew* (1957), the two men being 'the founders of the AIF', Sir William Bridges and Sir Cyril Brudenell White. Highly respected as a military historian, Bean was awarded the Chesney Gold Medal of the Royal United Service Institution in 1930, and honorary doctorates from the University of Melbourne in 1931 and the ANU in 1959. Throughout his life an enthusiastic nationalist, Bean did much, through his *Official History*, to establish the Anzac (q.v.) legend. *Gallipoli Correspondent: The Frontline Diary of C.E.W. Bean*, compiled by Kevin Fewster, was published in 1983, as was a biographical account of Bean's war years, *Gallipoli to the Somme* by Dudley McCarthy. *Making the Legend: The War Writings of C.E.W. Bean* (1991), ed. Dennis Winter, is a selection from Bean's *Official History*, his diaries and letters. David Kent in *Historical Studies* (April 1985) discusses Bean's selective editing of *The Anzac Book* to exclude anything which might tarnish the image of the Anzac soldier; Robin Gerster's *Big-noting: the Heroic Theme in Australian War Writing* (1993) also draws attention to the tendency to lionise the Anzac digger in much creative and historical war writing.

BEASLEY, Jack (1921–), born Merewether, NSW, was an apprentice electrical fitter at the BHP steelworks in Newcastle 1936–41, worked in his trade throughout the war years, part of the time at sea. A functionary of the Communist Party of Australia (1948–51) he became associated with the Australasian Book Society (q.v.) in 1959, spent about fifteen years in retail trade advertising and promotion (1963–77) and in 1977 resumed his interest in the Book Society. His publications include *Socialism and the Novel: A Study of Australian Literature* (1957); a short story anthology, *The Tracks We Travel* (1961); *The Rage for Life: The Work of Katharine Susannah Prichard* (1964); *Red Letter Days: Notes from Inside an Era* (1979); a novel, *Widdershins* (1986); *Journal of an Era* (1988); and a further book on Prichard, *A Gallop of Fire* (1993), which attempts to correlate her work with her life. *Red Letter Days* contains a comprehensive account of the history of the Australasian Book Society and discusses in detail the work and personalities of such Australian writers as Alan Marshall, Frank Hardy, Judah Waten, Mary Gilmore and Leslie Haylen.

Widdershins (the title meaning 'going backwards' or 'swimming against the tide') is the story of Jeff Conway, born into a working-class family in Newcastle in the 1920s. After the Depression and the war he becomes involved in trade union and Communist Party affairs, but from the mid-1950s to the 1970s the Communist Party fortunes deteriorate in Australia and Conway's working and domestic life goes down with it. Remarkably accurate in its feeling for men like Conway committed to the cause of radicalism, the novel is at times as much documentary as fiction. It is a highly radical political novel, one of a rare breed in Australian writing.

BEATTY, Bill (1902–72), born Sydney, was an accomplished pianist who studied at the NSW Conservatorium of Music, worked for the ABC (1941–50) and appeared in public and in radio recitals in Australia and overseas. His chief love, however, was Australiana – folklore, legends, traditions, customs, and oddities of every kind. He ranged the Australian outback, gathering material for his profusion of published works, which began in 1941 with *This Australia: Strange and Amazing Facts* and which include *Amazing Australia* (1943), *Australian Wonders* (1945), *'Come a Waltzing Matilda': Australian Folk Lore and Forgotten Tales* (1954), *A Treasury of Australian Folk Tales and Traditions* (1966), *Around Australia with Bill Beatty* (1966) and *Tales of Old Australia* (1966).

BEAVER, Bruce (1928–   ) was born Manly, Sydney, where he spent much of his youth and where, after many nomadic years, he now lives. Beaver's childhood and adolescence, as revealed by his own frequent comments and in his autobiographical *As It Was* (1979), were unsettled and unhappy. He took refuge as a boy in the fantasy world of comics, radio serials and movies, and later became absorbed in books. From the age of 17 he had several periods of psychiatric treatment for manic-depressive psychosis. It was at that time that he said he came under the influence of poetry – Pound, Eliot, Yeats, Brennan, Lowell, Auden, Graves, Williams and Frank O'Hara. He lived and worked for a time on his uncle's farm on the south coast of NSW, spent six years as chainman for a surveyor in northern NSW and was at various times radio programme arranger, clerk and proofreader before settling on freelance journalism and writing as a career. He spent six months on Norfolk Island, a place he detested, in 1958 and lived in NZ from 1958 to 1962, an experience that he enjoyed.

Beaver published his first volume of poetry, *Under the Bridge*, in 1961. His later publications are *Seawall and Shoreline* (1964), *Open at Random* (1967), *Letters to Live Poets* (q.v., 1969), *Lauds and Plaints: Poems, 1968–1972* (1974), *Odes and Days* (1975), *Death's Directives* (1978), *As It Was* (1979), *Selected Poems* (1979), *Headlands, Prose Sketches* (1986), *Charmed Lives* (1988) and *New and Selected Poems 1960–1990* (1991). Beaver has also written ten novels, including *The Hot Spring* (1965) and *You Can't Come Back* (1966). Based on the experiences of a gang of railway fettlers, *You Can't Come Back* takes an abysmal view of the Australian working man's life and

of the working man himself. Throughout his first three volumes of poetry, and with considerable success in individual poems such as 'Camp Shift', 'Seawall and Shoreline', 'Chainman's Diary' (winner of the 1964 *Poetry Magazine* Award), 'The Killers' and 'The Cranes of Auckland', Beaver pursues his search for an understanding of his disturbed life, maintaining a preoccupation with 'the celebration and lamentation of existence' that carries through into his first major collection, *Letters to Live Poets*. Written in 1966 under the spur of an illness that convinced Beaver he had only a couple of months of rationality left, *Letters to Live Poets* represents his attempt 'to make one clear readable statement before I stopped writing altogether'. In the form of the *livre composé*, the thirty-four separate poems piece together the jigsaw of existence and assess the worth of that existence. Influenced by Whitman's *Leaves of Grass* and Brennan's *Poems 1913*, *Letters to Live Poets* ranges over the experiences of Beaver's childhood, his adolescence with its periodic bouts of mental illness, and his present middle age, attempting a 'spiritual, intellectual and emotional autobiography' set against the striking natural landscape and monotonous suburbia of seaside Manly. *Letters to Live Poets* won the Grace Leven Prize for Poetry, the Poetry Society of Australia Prize and the Captain Cook Bicentennial Prize for Poetry, all in 1970. *Lauds and Plaints*, by contrast with the hasty creation of *Letters to Live Poets*, was slowly (1967–72) and lovingly built. An extension of *Letters to Live Poets* ('the spirit of the body of *Letters*'), *Lauds and Plaints* turns from the poet's self-obsession to an awareness of others, for example the young man who kills himself jumping from a roof, the old Manly fisherman, Albert Fry, and Arthur Stace (Sydney's 'Mr Eternity'). The technical liberation that Beaver had celebrated in *Letters* ('My thoughts [once] ticked iambically in ten syllables') is complete in *Lauds and Plaints*, where visual and syntactical experimental forms (the shedding of punctuation and the unbridled rhetoric) complement the exultation that Beaver felt as a release from the pessimism of so much of *Letters to Live Poets*. The poems praise ('Lauds') those with largeness of spirit and blame ('Plaints') those lesser spirits, whose life vision never transcends the materialism of daily existence. *Odes and Days*, written by Beaver during a period spent at Grace Perry's Berrima house, comprises fifteen odes, eight addressed to himself or the house and seven addressed (as biographical sketches) to the composers Beethoven, Mahler and Delius and to the poets Holderlin, Brennan, Rilke and Hesse. The 'Days', which form a type of verse journal, are the forty-seven shorter poems of the second part of the book. Many of them, freed from Beaver's compulsive philosophising, record and rejoice in natural sights and sounds and contain some of his most attractive lyricism. *Death's Directives*, twenty poems in which Death variously suggests, reminds, advises or lays down directives to the poet about life, are the most relaxed of Beaver's poetry. The near genial tone and the absence of tension reflect, perhaps for the first time in the whole body of Beaver's poetry, an affirmation of life and a mental and emotional confidence. *As It*

Was, the autobiographical prose poem which Beaver for a long time felt unable to write, confirms by the fact of its existence that affirmation and confidence. The *New and Selected Poems 1960–1990* selects from four decades of Beaver's poetry and emphasises again the considerable scale of his achievements. There are few poems from the early volumes but an impressive reminder of the most significant of his work from *Letters to Live Poets*, *Lauds and Plaints* and *Odes and Days*.

Headlands conveys in prose poems his sometimes sardonic but basically affectionate reactions to and reflections on the people he has known and the places he has been in Australia and NZ. *Charmed Lives* contains a verse biography of Rainer Maria Rilke, two sections of more personal poems, 'Silhouettes' and 'Solos' and a concluding section, 'Tiresias Sees'. In scope and power *Charmed Lives* is the equal of Beaver's *Odes and Days* and confirms his stature as one of Australia's most important poets. An original and idiosyncratic writer, a fine exponent of the prose-poetry form and one of the earliest Australian poets to explore the possibilities of confessional poetry of the life studies genre, Beaver through his own work and in his role as adviser and contributing editor to *Poetry Australia* was an important influence in the 1970s rise of the 'New Australian Poetry' (q.v.). He was awarded the Patrick White Literary Award in 1982, the Christopher Brennan Award in 1983, both in recognition of the sustained distinction of his work, and was made AM in 1991 as a tribute to his contribution to Australian literature.

BÉCHERVAISE, John (1910–), born Malvern, Victoria, led three Australian expeditions to Antarctica 1952–60 and taught at Geelong Grammar School where he was director of studies 1962–72. Béchervaise has published numerous books on Antarctica, Australian mountains and rivers, the Victorian goldfields, the University of Melbourne and towns like Castlemaine and Ballarat. He was awarded the MBE, the Queen's Polar Medal, the Gold Medal of the Royal Geographical Society, and an honorary D.Litt. from Deakin University. His many books include *ANARE: Australia's Antarctic Outposts* (1957, with Phillip Law), *The Far South* (1961, revised as *Antarctica: The Last Horizon* (1979), *Blizzard and Fire* (1963) and *Australia: World of Difference* (1967, winner of the Con Weickhardt Award).

BECK, Ian (William) (1946–) has had a variety of occupations – storeman, salesman, labourer – and is currently a sub-editor. Beck has published two books of short stories, *The Diver's Reluctance to Ascend* (1986) and *Jumping the Chasm* (1990), both of which have been praised for their technical competence and stylish prose. Many of Beck's stories present an almost wholly male perspective on interpersonal relationships, e.g. 'The Diver's Reluctance to Ascend', 'The Return of the Shadow' and 'Harvesting'. 'The Writer at Work' is a fine account of the self-imposed exile of the writer.

Beck, Martin is the villain and one of the chief characters in Alexander Harris's novel *The Emigrant Family* (q.v., 1849). The 1852 edition was titled *Martin Beck: Or the Story of an Australian Settler*. The son of convict parents of Black American origin, Beck is an outsider in his native land because of his colour; his avarice is largely an attempt to compensate for his lowly social position. He turns bushranger and is later shot dead.

BECKE, 'Louis' (George Lewis) (1855–1913) was born Port Macquarie, NSW, and educated in Sydney. At 14 he sailed for America and began the series of adventures that provided the basis of his writing; for long periods during the next twenty-five years he travelled and traded in the Pacific, alleging among his experiences a spell as supercargo to the legendary 'Bully' Hayes (q.v.), arrest and acquittal for piracy, and several shipwrecks. In 1893, back in Sydney, he met the explorer Ernest Favenc, who introduced him to J.F. Archibald; under Archibald's tutelage he began to turn out stories of the Pacific and Australia for the *Bulletin* and other journals. Although some of Becke's best early writings went into 'Rolf Boldrewood's' *A Modern Buccaneer* (q.v.) in 1893, his reputation was established with the publication of *By Reef and Palm* (1894), *His Native Wife* (1895) and *The Ebbing of the Tide* (1896). In 1896 he moved to England, where he enjoyed the patronage of the Earl of Pembroke and was something of a celebrity; he subsequently lived in Ireland and France and visited Jamaica, America and NZ before returning to Sydney in 1909, where he died in poverty four years later. In all, Becke wrote thirty-five books, several in collaboration with Walter Jeffery (q.v.). His forte was the short story or sketch in which he drew on his experiences, so that for his readers the Pacific became real as well as romantic. He gave credit for his emergence as a writer to Archibald, who 'taught me the secrets of condensation and simplicity of language' and helped fashion his spare prose style. His departure from Australia and Archibald's influence is part of the reason why his best books are the early collections, *By Reef and Palm* and *The Ebbing of the Tide;* like 'Steele Rudd' he became a formula writer. The best of his dozen or so novels are *A First Fleet Family* (1896) and *The Mutineer* (1898), both written in collaboration with Jeffery, and the heavily autobiographical *The Adventures of Louis Blake* (1909); he also wrote descriptive and scientific prose, and was one of the first admirers of Henry Melville. Envied by Joseph Conrad and compared in his lifetime with Rudyard Kipling and Robert Louis Stevenson, Becke is generally catalogued among the *Bulletin* 1890s school by critics of Australian literature but has a considerable reputation overseas. A. Grove Day's study, *Louis Becke*, was published in 1966; Grove Day also edited *South Sea Supercargo* (1967).

BEDFORD, Jean (1946–), born Cambridge, England, was brought up in the country in Victoria and has been a journalist and teacher. She was literary editor of the *National Times* 1980–82 before taking up the Australian/American Stanford Writing Scholarship in 1982. Bedford has published two collections of short stories, *Country Girl Again* (1979), reissued in 1985 with additional stories, and, with Rosemary Creswell (q.v.), *Colouring In* (1986); and the novels *Sister Kate* (1982), *Love Child* (1986), *A Lease of Summer* (1990), *Worse Than Death*, in collaboration with Tom Kelly (1991), *To Make a Killing* (1992) and *If With a Beating Heart* (1993). *Country Girl Again*, a discontinuous narrative, traces the growth of Anne, from her childhood in rural Victoria to marriage and possible motherhood. The collection, which paints a bleak, unillusioned picture of rural life and its stifling or destructive effects on the lives of women, also deals sensitively with the seductions of older, pre-feminist social patterns and with the complexities facing contemporary women. In the original collection's last story the wheel has turned full circle and Anne is once more trapped in the country after finding sexually liberated Fitzroy almost as limiting as her childhood home. *Colouring In*, a seamless blending of talents, focuses on the lives of two women, the best friends Iris and Sal, both divorced and living in Sydney. A frank picture of the pressures and pleasures of urban life for the single woman, the collection also celebrates women's friendship and what is seen as their characteristic habit of conversationally colouring themselves in 'and their friends and their lovers, endlessly'. *Sister Kate* is a fresh feminist perspective on the Ned Kelly legend and the male myth of the hero. Beginning when Kate Kelly, Ned's sister, is 12, the novel presents the familiar story from her point of view and deals with the tragic outcome of her love for Joe Byrne; Kate, who never recovers from the shock of Byrne's violent death, is ultimately as much a victim of the Kelly gang as Aaron Sherritt. *Love Child*, set partly in England and partly in Australia, has a similar determinist theme in its concentration on the extended effects of a tyrannical domestic patriarch and his daughter's unfortunate wartime marriage. New Guinea, two years before independence, is the setting of *A Lease of Summer*, which explores the violent sexual, racial and political oppositions created by antithetical cultures. *Worse Than Death* and *To Make a Killing* are crime novels (see Crime Fiction) in which the private eye is a woman, Anna Southwood. *If With a Beating Heart* is a novel about Claire Claremont, stepsister to Mary Shelley and lover to Lord Byron, and her turbulent life.

BEDFORD, Randolph (1868–1941), born Sydney, tramped across outback NSW at 16, taking such bush jobs as rabbiter, fencer and Murray River paddle-steamer hand. He settled into journalism in the late 1880s, working variously for newspapers in Bourke, Broken Hill, Adelaide and Melbourne. He founded the *Clarion*, a mining and literary journal (1897–1909), and accumulated wealth through gold-mining ventures in WA. In 1901–4 he was in Europe, where his first novels, *True Eyes and the Whirlwind* (1903) and *The Snare of Strength* (1905), both largely autobiographical, were published. His *Bulletin* travel notes were published as *Explorations in Civilization* (1914). Bedford's later life was occupied by his writings, his grandiose mining and pastoral speculations, and politics; he was

a member of the Queensland Legislative Council 1917–22, and of its Legislative Assembly 1923–41. A prolific and racy writer, Bedford published five novels, countless short stories, poetry, travel, descriptive and autobiographical works, and the play, 'White Australia: Or, The Empty North' which was staged in Melbourne in 1909. His short story 'Fourteen Fathoms by Quetta Rock' has been much anthologised, but his most significant work is the autobiographical *Naught to Thirty-Three* (q.v., 1944). A man of large appetites, Bedford had a reputation as a raconteur, broadcaster and bohemian, was a celebrated *Bulletin* and *Lone Hand* contributor and was a vocal and militant supporter of an Australia that was White, socialist and republican.

BEDFORD, Ruth (1882–1963), born Petersham, Sydney, published lyric verse, e.g. *Sydney at Sunset and Other Verses* (1911) and *The Learner and Other Verses* (1937); fiction (in collaboration with Dorothea Mackellar), e.g. *The Little Blue Devil* (1912) and *Two's Company* (1914); and children's verse, e.g. *Rosycheeks & Goldenhead* (1913) and *Hundreds and Thousands* (1934). She also wrote *Think of Stephen, A Family Chronicle* (1954), a delightful account of the family of Sir Alfred Stephen. A minor classic in the social history genre, *Think of Stephen* re-creates the life of an upper-middle-class professional family in Sydney in the middle of the nineteenth century. She also wrote several plays including 'At the Inn', 'Fear', 'The Girls from the Marsh Croft', 'Hide the Thimble', 'Murder Next Door', 'Pear's Soap' and 'Postman's Knock'.

BEDFORD, William (?1781–1852) was born in England and arrived in Van Diemen's Land in 1823 as that colony's second Anglican minister. Popular with successive administrators though not with some settlers and most convicts, Bedford had a reputation for moral earnestness and financial extravagance. He is savagely portrayed as the avaricious hypocrite, Parson Ford, in a dozen or so stories of 'Price Warung', and his practices parallel those of the sanctimonious minister, Meekin, in Marcus Clarke's *His Natural Life*. He is also one of the first colonists Simon Stukeley meets in *The Hermit in Van Diemen's Land* (1830) and is a minor figure in William Gosse Hay's *The Escape of the Notorious Sir William Heans* (1919).

BEEBY, Sir George (1869–1942), born Sydney, was a pupil-teacher, a solicitor, a Labor member of the NSW parliament (1907), and afterwards a State and federal judge. Beeby was editor and manager of the *Bowral Free Press* in 1892 and the *New England Democrat* in 1894. In 1923 he published *Concerning Ordinary People*, a book of six plays, one of which, *Point O' View*, reflected his knowledge of industrial relations and the law. *In Quest of Pan* (1924) is a satiric and somewhat bawdy play; he also wrote the novel *A Loaded Legacy* (1930) and a number of short stories.

BEILBY, Richard (1918–   ), born in Malacca, Malaysia, of Australian parents, came to WA in 1929. In the Second World War he served in the AIF in the campaigns of North Africa, Greece, Crete and New Guinea. Since then he has worked in the building trades, has been a part-time union organiser, an insurance salesman and, since 1970, a full-time novelist. Two of his novels are set in Greece, *The Sword and the Myrtle* (1968) at the time of Thermopylae, and *No Medals for Aphrodite* (1970) at the time of the German invasion in 1941, when two Australian soldiers attempt to slow the German advance by blowing up a road. *Gunner* (1977, published as *Retreat*), also a war novel, is set in Crete during the German assault. It highlights the unlikely relationship that develops between the Australian digger Gunner Lewis and the young officer ('the boy-bastard') Lieutenant Whiteside. Beilby also published *The Bitter Lotus* (1978). His chief novel, however, is *The Brown Land Crying* (1975) in which he examines the dilemma of the part-Aborigine living in the modern White urban environment of Perth and torn between the traditional ties of race and tribe and the need for recognition by, and status in, the White community of which he is perforce a part.

BELFIELD, Francis, one of Australia's earliest playwrights, published *Retribution: Or, the Drunkard's Curse* (1849); it was performed at the Queen's Theatre, Melbourne in 1849 and was later reprinted (?1872) as *The Bottle: Or, the Drunkard's Curse*. He also published *The Rebel Chief* (1850).

'Bell Birds', the much-anthologised Henry Kendall (q.v.) lyric poem, was first published in the *Sydney Morning Herald*, 25 November 1867. The poet hears, in imagination, the chiming notes of the bellbirds of his youth and re-creates in rich pictorial phrases the typical bellbird (and Kendall) landscape of 'channels of coolness', 'dim gorges' and 'cool wildernesses'. Like Wordsworth with his 'sensations sweet', Kendall is sustained by his recollections of natural beauty amid the ugliness of later years in the 'city and alleys'.

BELL, Diane (1943–), previously professor of Australian studies at Deakin University and now Henry R. Luce Professor, College of the Holy Cross, USA, has written *Daughters of the Dreaming* (1983, 2nd edn 1993), an influential study of the roles of women in tribal Aboriginal society which revises many of the findings of male anthropologists, as well as several other anthropological studies. She is also the author of *Generations: Grandmothers, Mothers and Daughters* (1987), which is based on interviews with numerous women across Australia and explores the cultural and social links between generations of Australian women. She is co-editor of *Religion in Aboriginal Australia* (1984) and, with Pam Ditton, co-author of *Law: The Old and the New. Aboriginal Women in Central Australia Speak Out* (1980).

Bellbird is the name given to two species of Australian birds: the crested bellbird and the bell-miner. The latter species is responsible for the well-known, persistent chiming sound heard in cool, moist areas along the eastern coast. The bellbird and its bell-like notes have been immortalised in Henry Kendall's poem 'Bell Birds', but other poets have also been fascinated by it: e.g. Charles Harpur, who discusses it in the notes to his poem 'The Kangaroo Hunt or a Morning in the Bush', and P.J. Holdsworth, who wrote of it in 'The Valley of the Popran'. *Bellbird* (the name of a fictitious country town) was a popular ABC television serial in 1967–79.

'BELLERIVE', see TISHLER, Joseph

Bell's Life in Sydney (1845–?71), *Bell's Life in Victoria and Sporting Chronicle* (1857–68) and *Bell's Life in Adelaide and Sporting Chronicle* (1861–62) were sporting journals. They were modelled on *Bell's Life in London and Sporting Chronicle* (1822–86), which in turn exploited the popularity of *Bell's Weekly Messenger*, a London periodical founded by John Bell (1745–1831). The Australian *Bell's* each focused on sport and politics and carried both local and overseas literary material. A distinctive feature of *Bell's Life* was the verse forecast of important races, as exemplified by Adam Lindsay Gordon's 'Hippodromania', originally published in *Bell's Life in Victoria*, which unsuccessfully predicted the results of the 1866 and 1867 Melbourne Cups.

BENBO, see Aborigine in White Australian Literature

Bendigo, one of the chief cities of central northern Victoria, came into being in 1841 as a goldfields town on a sheep station known as Ravenswood, which had been taken up by Charles Sherratt in 1840. Popularly known as Bendigo (after a Ravenswood Aboriginal stationhand), the town was officially called Sandhurst until 1891. Discontent on the goldfields of Ballarat and Bendigo led to the Eureka Stockade (q.v.); an account of the troubles at Bendigo is given in Geoffrey Serle's *The Golden Age* (1963). The Bendigo goldfields are described in many of the numerous historical and travel books of the period, e.g. George Wathan's *The Golden Colony* (1855), Ellen Clacy's *A Lady's Visit to The Gold Diggings of Australia, in 1852–53* (1853), William Howitt's *Land, Labour and Gold* (1855) and Samuel Mossman's *The Gold Regions of Australia* (1852). Charles Thatcher, the 'Colonial Minstrel', was known as 'The Bard of Bendigo'. Histories of the city include George Mackay's *History of Bendigo* (1891) and *Annals of Bendigo* (1912) and, more recently, Frank Cusack's *Bendigo – A History* (1973), Jan Neil's *Bendigo, the Golden Age Retraced* (1973), and A.V. Palmer's *The Gold Mines of Bendigo* (1976). James Devaney's novel *Washdirt* (1946) is set in the Bendigo goldfields; the poet William Gay (q.v.), lived and wrote in Bendigo in the late 1890s.

BENNELONG (Banneelon), the second Aborigine to live in the Port Jackson settlement (Arabanoo was the first), was captured, with another Aborigine, Colbee (q.v.), by Lieutenant William Bradley on instructions from Captain Arthur Phillip at the end of 1789. He became a well-known identity of the settlement; Bennelong Point, where the Sydney Opera House now stands, is named after him. In 1792

Bennelong and an Aboriginal boy, Yemmerrawannie, were taken to England by Phillip; Bennelong returned to Australia in 1795 but Yemmerrawannie died in England. An account of Bennelong's activities is in Watkin Tench's *A Complete Account of the Settlement at Port Jackson* (1793) and a fictional portrait of him is given in Eleanor Dark's *The Timeless Land* (1941). Michael Boddy wrote 'The Cradle of Hercules' (1974), a play about Phillip and Bennelong; Joan Phipson's children's story *Bennelong* was published in 1975; E.O. Schlunke wrote the poem 'Bennelong Returns to Heaven', in which he portrays Bennelong's later reaction to the White colonisation of Australia. Barry Conyngham's opera *Bennelong* (1987) was commissioned by the Australian Bicentennial Authority and performed in Australian capital cities in 1988. Bennelong appears as a character in Eric Willmot's novel *Pemulwuy* (1987).

BENNETT, Bruce, see **Criticism**; *Westerly*; **Anthologies**

BENNETT, George (1804–93), born Plymouth, England, wandered the Pacific 1828–35, writing many papers on natural history, as a result of which he was made a fellow of the Linnean Society of London and a member of the Zoological Society. He visited Australia in 1829 and 1832, publishing *Wandering in New South Wales, Batavia, Pedir Coast, Singapore and China* (1834). Back in Sydney in 1836 he developed a successful medical practice, became a leading figure in the Australian Museum and published *Gatherings of a Naturalist in Australasia* (1860).

BENNETT, Ross, see **Hunter Valley Poets**

BENNETT, Samuel (1815–78), born Cornwall, England, came to Australia in 1841 to work as a printer on the *Sydney Herald*. In 1859 he resigned to become part-owner of the rival *Empire* (q.v.); he later became proprietor of the *Evening News* and the *Australian Town and Country Journal*. Bennett's *The History of Australian Discovery and Colonisation* (1865) was a significant early history of Australian exploration. His daughter Rose, who later married John Henniker Heaton, is the 'Rose Lorraine' of Henry Kendall's love poetry. Bennett was attacked in the satiric pamphlets of Theodore Argles ('The Pilgrim').

BENNETT, Stefanie (1945–), born Townsville, Queensland, followed a brief formal education by working as a factory hand, saleswoman, hairdresser, graphic artist, rock musician, reader/editor with various journals, and tutor at the Institute of Modern Languages, James Cook University. Among her publications are *Blackbirds of Superstition* (1973), *Madam Blackboots* (1974), *Five Poets* (1974), *Poems from the Paddy Wagon* (1975), *The Medium* (1976, prose and poetry), *Tongues and Pinnacles* (1976), *The Tenth Lady* (1977), *The Leaf, the Lion, the Lariat* (1992), and the novel *Stefan* (1978). With Joanne Burns and Ruth Fordham, Bennett contributed to the collection *Radio City 2 a.m.* (1976) and with R.G. Hay and Anne Lloyd to *Three North Queensland Poets* (1990).

BENT, Andrew (1790–1851), pioneering Tasmanian printer and publisher, was born in London, convicted of burglary in 1810, and arrived in NSW in 1812 under a sentence of transportation for life. He soon became government printer in Van Diemen's Land and was, in 1816, the first publisher of the *Hobart Town Gazette* (q.v.). In 1824–25 Bent came into conflict with the new lieutenant-governor, George Arthur (q.v.), over leading articles by Evan Henry Thomas in the *Gazette* and letters written for it by Robert Lathropp Murray; eventually he was imprisoned for libel. After Arthur pirated his *Gazette* title, Bent renamed his newspaper the *Colonial Times* and later ran the *Colonial Advocate* (1828) and *Bent's News* (1836–39), which he began in Hobart and continued in Sydney; subsequently he was a hotelier and cedar merchant on the NSW north coast. An important figure in the fight for the freedom of the press in Australia, Bent became known as the 'Tasmanian Franklin' and like Franklin published a series of early almanacs. He also published Thomas Wells's *Michael Howe* (1818), the first private book or pamphlet published in Tasmania, and *The Hermit in Van Diemen's Land* (q.v., 1830), the first volume of Australian essays, for which he was prosecuted for libel. Bent figures largely in most studies (e.g. by E. Morris Miller and James Bonwick) of the earlier Tasmanian press, in biographies and studies of Arthur, and in Joan Woodberry's *Andrew Bent and the Freedom of the Press in Van Diemen's Land* (1972).

BERGNER, Herz (1907–70), born Poland, published a book of short stories, *Houses and Streets*, in Poland in 1935. He migrated to Australia in 1938 and in 1941 published another collection of stories, *The New House*, which reflected both the new Australian environment and the difficulties that faced the immigrant Jews. His first novel, written in Yiddish (as were all his books) and translated into English by Judah Waten, was *Between Sky and Sea* (1946); the story of a group of Jewish refugees whose ship is denied landing by the other countries of the world, it won the Australian Literature Society Gold Medal for 1948. In 1950 a further novel, *A City in Poland*, dealing with his Polish experience, was published and in 1955 another collection of short stories, *The House of Jacob Isaacs*. In 1960 his novel *Light and Shadow*, about the Jewish experience in Australia as seen through the eyes of the migrant Zeling family, won the Zwi-Kessel Prize as one of the world's best Jewish books published in that year; it was translated from the Yiddish by Alec Braizblatt with a foreword by Alan Marshall. *Where the Truth Lies* (1965), a further collection of twenty-two stories on Jewish life in Australia, also won the Zwi-Kessel Prize.

BERNDT, Ronald M. (1916–90) and **Catherine H.** (born Auckland, NZ, 1918–94), both had distinguished academic and professional careers in anthropology, and had considerable influence on the development of Australian anthropology and on

Aboriginal welfare. Both obtained higher degrees at the University of Sydney and the London School of Economics and were awarded honorary D.Litt. by the University of WA, where Ronald Berndt was appointed foundation professor of anthropology in 1963. From 1941 they carried out field research together in many parts of Aboriginal Australia and in the Eastern Highlands of Papua New Guinea.

Focusing on traditional and changing societies, they maintained a division of labour, Ronald working with men on social organisation, myth and ritual, Catherine working on the status of women, marriage and family, religion and oral literature. They published separately as well as in collaboration a large number of books and articles. Their major works include *The World of the First Australians* (1964), *Man, Land and Myth in North Australia* (1970), *The Barbarians* (1971), *The Aboriginal Australians: The First Pioneers* (1982), *Australian Aboriginal Art: A Visual Perspective* (1982), *Social Anthropology and Australian Aboriginal Studies* (1988, with R. Tonkinson) and *A World That Was: The Yaraldi of the Murray River and the Lakes, South Australia* (1993, with John E. Stanton). From the commencement of their research and writing they were concerned with Aboriginal song-poetry and oral literature, and were responsible for translating and publishing a substantial body of such material in various anthropological journals and books; *Djanggawul* (1952) and *Love Songs of Arnhem Land* (1976) are examples. Of special importance are several translated Aboriginal stories for children, e.g. *Land of the Rainbow Snake* (1981). Their translation of the Wonguri-Man-jikai Moon-bone Song was used by Les Murray as the basis for his poem 'The Bulahdehah-Taree Holiday Song Cycle' (q.v.). They also edited an anthology of Aboriginal myths and legends, *The Speaking Land* (1989), about 200 myths and stories translated from the vernacular languages of 50–60 storytellers from parts of Central Australia and Arnhem Land collected during their periods with the Aborigines. Robert Tonkinson and Michael Howard edited *Going It Alone? Prospects for Aboriginal Autonomy* (1990), a series of essays in honour of the Berndts. The first part contains tributes to and biographical information on them; the second part contains ten anthropological essays on the Aborigines and their prospects of autonomy. There is also a select bibliography of the Berndts' work. Foundation members of the Australian Institute of Aboriginal Studies, they were made AO in 1987.

Berrima, 140 kilometres south-west of Sydney on the Hume Highway, is one of NSW's most historic towns. Sir Thomas Mitchell camped on the site in 1829 and Australia's oldest gaol and oldest licensed inn are both in the town; Starlight and Dick Marston escape from Berrima gaol in 'Rolf Boldrewood's' *Robbery Under Arms* (1888). Berrima has other literary connections: with Louisa Atkinson, who was born at nearby Oldbury in 1834; with Grace Perry, who lived there and wrote *Black Swans at Berrima* (1972), a long lyric sequence, and *Berrima Winter* (1974); and with Bruce Beaver, who wrote some of his *Odes and Days* (1975) while living there. Other writers associated with Berrima have been Gwen Meredith, Ronald McKie and Maslyn Williams.

BERTIE, C.H. (Charles Henry) (1875–1952), born Lyonsville on the Clarence River, NSW, joined the Sydney Municipal Council in 1899 as a junior in the city survey office and ultimately rose to be the Council's chief clerk. In 1909 he was appointed first librarian of the new Sydney Municipal Library and later established within it the first public lending library for children in Australia. An indefatigable member of the Royal Australian Historical Society and a regular contributor to its *Journal and Proceedings*, Bertie became one of Sydney's most important collectors of Australiana; his collection is one of the most substantial in the Mitchell Library. Bertie's numerous publications include *The Early History of the Sydney Municipal Council* (1911), *Story of Old George Street* (1920) and *Old Colonial By-Ways* (1928). He did much of the preliminary work for the inaugural edition of the *Australian Encyclopaedia* (1925–26); wrote *The Story of the Royal Hotel & the Theatre Royal, Sydney* (1927); and arranged for the first publication of *Ralph Rashleigh* in 1929.

BEVERIDGE, Judith (1956–), born London, came to Australia as a small child. She has worked as a teacher of creative writing and a library assistant. Her poetry has appeared in numerous periodicals and anthologies and in one collection, *The Domesticity of Giraffes* (1987). Rich in complex imagery, Beveridge's poetry is remarkable for its individual, sharply engraved perceptions and stylish language. *The Domesticity of Giraffes* won the Mary Gilmore Award and Premier's Awards from both Victoria and NSW.

BEYNON, Richard (1927–), born Carlton, Melbourne, went to England in 1947 and worked as an actor for stage, film and television, appearing in productions with such well-known artists as Peter Ustinov, Joan Greenwood and Richard Attenborough. On a visit to Australia in 1956 he entered his play *The Shifting Heart* (q.v., 1960) in the Playwrights' Advisory Board competition and won first prize. First produced in Sydney at the Elizabethan Theatre in 1957, and subsequently produced in New York and London, the play also won third prize in the London *Observer* competition of 1957 and an AJA award. A popular text for schools, it has continued to be produced in Australia. Beynon has subsequently worked mainly for the BBC as script editor and producer on such popular television series as *Rebecca*, *My Cousin Rachel*, *Madam Bovary*, *Fame is the Spur*, *Z Cars*, *Softly Softly*, *The Duchess of Duke Street* and *Lord Peter Wimsey*. He has also written for radio, has published a play, *Epitaph for Two Faces*, in a selection he edited with H.G. Fowler, *Next Act!* (1964), and in 1958 won a Thames television award for his television play 'Time and Mr Strachan'. His other publications include the stage plays *Summer Shadows* (1986), a study of a working-class family in Prahran in the 1920s, and *Simpson J. 202* (1991), on one of the heroes of Gallipoli; and another collection of plays edited with H.G. Fowler, *First Act* (1966). One of the group of plays which seemed to herald a renaissance of Australian drama in the 1950s, *The Shifting Heart* is, like Ray Lawler's *Summer of the Seventeenth Doll*, a naturalistic study of a tense domestic situation. Concerned with the uneasy relationship between Australians and European immigrants, it is perhaps the best known of a series of plays dealing with cultural conflict, which includes Oriel Gray's *Burst of Summer* (1959), J.P. McKinney's 'The Shadows We Cast' (n.d.), Barbara Vernon's *The Multi-Coloured Umbrella* (1961), Anthony Coburn's *The Bastard Country* (1963) and Alexander Buzo's *Norm and Ahmed* (1969). Occasionally criticised on the grounds of ethnic stereotyping and sentimental avoidance of the xenophobic problem it raises, *The Shifting Heart* has strong elements of pathos and humour and several suspenseful situations which ensure its theatrical effectiveness.

Bibliographies of Australian Writers, a series published by the Libraries Board of SA, began in 1966 with Janette H. Finch's bibliographies of Patrick White and Hal Porter. Other authors covered in the series include Catherine Helen Spence (1967), A.D. Hope (1968), Judith Wright (1968), Randolph Stow (1968), Ian Mudie (1970), R.D. FitzGerald (1970) and C.J. Dennis (1979). After the series was discontinued the bibliographies were updated in *Index to Australian Book Reviews* (q.v.).

Bibliography of Australia, the standard bibliography of printed material relating to Australia and published between 1784 and 1900, was compiled by Sir John Ferguson (q.v.) and published in seven volumes 1941–69. The first four volumes chronologically (and comprehensively) cover the period 1784–1850 and include books, pamphlets, broadsides and periodicals relating to, but not necessarily published in, Australia; the last three volumes alphabetically (and more selectively) cover the period 1851–1900 and exclude certain classes of printed material, notably periodicals and 'belles-lettres as covered by Morris Miller and F.T. Macartney'. In 1975 the National Library of Australia (q.v.) acquired the copyright to Ferguson's *Bibliography*, parts of which had become collectors' items. In 1977 it published a facsimile edition and in 1986 an *Addenda* to volumes I to IV, 1784–1850, which lists items omitted from those volumes, some corrections to original entries, and many additional locations for bibliography items. Ferguson's *Bibliography* has been recognised as one of the world's great national bibliographies, an indispensable tool for Australian historians; its usefulness for students of nineteenth-century Australian literature, however, is limited by the omission of poetry, drama and fiction published after 1850.

Bibliography of Australian Literature is currently under preparation at the National Centre for Australian Studies at Monash University, Melbourne. Edited by John Hay and John Arnold, the project aims to record all creative writing published in book or pamphlet form by Australian authors. The project is supported by a National Advisory Committee and working parties in each State, as well as the Association for the Study of Australian Literature (ASAL).

Bibliography of Australian Poetry 1935–1955, compiled by Sue Murray, was published in 1992 by D.W. Thorpe in association with the National Centre for Australian Studies at Monash University.

Biblionews and Australian Notes & Queries, the journal of the Book Collectors' Society of Australia, began publication in 1947 and was edited by Walter Stone until his death in 1981. Originally titled *Biblionews*, it was distributed as a monthly newsletter to members until March 1964. A second, more substantial but irregular series, titled *Biblionews and Australian Notes & Queries*, ran 1966–72; a third series began quarterly publication in 1976. The periodical, which includes much useful miscellaneous bibliographical and biographical material, also publishes lists of important accessions to the Mitchell Library.

Big Toys, a play by Patrick White, first produced in 1977, was published in 1978. Set in a luxurious penthouse apartment with a panoramic view of Sydney's skyline, it deals with the brief relationship between Ritchie Bosanquet, a successful QC, Mag, his 'utterly chic' wife, originally the daughter of a hawker, and Terry Legge, a working-class Marxist of Irish Catholic extraction. The Bosanquets, for whom life has become a stylish, sterile game, regard Terry as a welcome diversion. Mag, nostalgically attracted by his working-class cachet, seduces him; Ritchie is partly interested in him for his past connection with his client, Sir Douglas Stannard, and because he arouses his latent homosexuality. The Bosanquets' link with the general corruption in high places, which has some unspecified connection with uranium-mining and looks forward to the 'explosion . . . the biggest, gaudiest toy that ever escaped from a child's hand', threatens to involve Terry. But he finally rejects the toy, a Ferrari car, that Ritchie offers him as payment and leaves the Bosanquets to the dull sterility of their possessions and each other.

BIGGE, J.T. (John Thomas) (1780–1843), born in Northumberland, England, was selected in 1819 as a commissioner to inquire into conditions in the colony of NSW. Bigge's subsequent reports, *Report of the Commissioner of Inquiry into the State of the Colony of New South Wales* (1822), *On the Judicial Establishments of New South Wales and Van Diemen's Land* (1823) and *On the State of Agriculture and Trade in the Colony of New South Wales* (1823), although sometimes inaccurate and received with hostility by Governor Lachlan Macquarie, provide a detailed picture of the Colony at the time. Bigge and his reports are discussed in John Ritchie's *Punishment and Profit* (1970); he also appears as a character in Alexander Buzo's play *Macquarie* (1971).

'BILL BOWYANG', see **VENNARD, Alexander Vindex**

'Bill the Bullock Driver', one of Henry Kendall's (q.v.) best-known and most-anthologised poems, published in the *Australian Town and Country Journal* in 1876, is an ironic portrait of one of the stock figures of Australian outback life and literature. While Kendall applauds the sturdy independence and easygoing nature of the teamster, he also subtly criticises his parochialism and insensitivity to the natural wonders that surround him.

'Bill, the Ventriloquial Rooster', a humorous story by Henry Lawson, was written in 1893 and included in *On the Track* (1900). One of the Jack Mitchell yarns, the story records the misfortunes of the Mitchell family rooster, Bill, who is unwittingly ventriloquial and believes his own crow is that of a challenging bird. Bill defeats a rooster from the adjoining selection but its owner, Page, borrows another bird, Jim, which Bill believes is the original challenger. In the ensuing fight Bill pursues Jim vigorously until exhausted, whereupon Jim turns on Bill and gives him a hiding; disgusted with himself, Bill dies. The autobiographical bases for part of the story are confirmed by Lawson's 'A Fragment of Autobiography'.

'Billabong', a word of Aboriginal origin, means a waterhole which fills in flood time from the overflow of a river or creek and is then cut off from the main stream as the floodwaters recede. The word occurs frequently in Australian folk-song and ballad, poetry and fiction; its best-known use is in the song 'Waltzing Matilda' (q.v.) in which the jolly swagman, referred to in other places as a 'billabong whaler', is camped by a billabong when a jumbuck comes there to drink. Charles Fenner's *Bunyips and Billabongs* (1933) and W.E. Bill Harney's *Brimming Billabongs* (1948) reflect the popularity of 'billabong' as a title. Mary Grant Bruce (q.v.) wrote a popular Billabong series of stories for children about station life in north-eastern Victoria.

BILLETER, Walter (1943–), born Sierre, Switzerland, came to Australia in 1966. He has written *Sediments of Seclusion* (poetry, 1973), *Dreamrobe Embroideries and Asparagus for Dinner* (with John Jenkins, 1974), *Australian Novemberies* (prose, 1978) and *Radiotalk: 10 Pieces for Magnetic Tape* (1979). He has also published translations of German writers (e.g. Konrad Bayer and Paul Celan). In 1974 he co-founded with John Jenkins the magazine *etymspheres*, and in 1977 he co-edited with Kris Hemensley and Robert Kenny the anthology *3 Blind Mice*.

Billy (Billy-can), a tin can used for making tea, was an essential item of bush equipment, especially for swagmen. 'Boiling the billy' has long been part of Australian bush life and the period spent waiting for it to boil is usually a time for leisurely comradeship and yarning, as Henry Lawson indicates by using *While the Billy Boils* as the title for his 1896 volume of short stories. Suggested origins of 'billy' include the French word *bouilli*, from the French canned soup used on the goldfields; the Aboriginal word *billa*, meaning 'creek'

hence water; and the Scottish word, 'billypot', meaning cooking utensil. William Howitt in *Land, Labour and Gold* (1855), Samuel Lemaitre in *Song of the Goldfields* (1861) and E.S. Sorenson in *Life in the Australian Backblocks* (1911), date the word from the goldfields of the 1850s; but James Lester Burke, in *The Adventures of Martin Cash* (1870), suggests that it was in use in the penal settlement of Norfolk Island in the 1840s. Usually referred to affectionately, as in 'My Old Black Billy' by Edward Harrington, 'To a Billy' by James Lister Cuthbertson, 'The Old Black Billy an' Me' by Louis Esson, and in songs such as 'With My Swag All on My Shoulder', the billy was treated less nostalgically by other writers (of whom Lawson is one), who saw it as the unromantic symbol of hard times, the badge of the out-of-luck, down-at-the-heel itinerants of the bush. Billy Tea, the name of a brand of tea that has been popular in Australia for many years, has some links with 'Waltzing Matilda' (q.v.).

'Billy Barlow in Australia' is a folk-song (sometimes called 'Billy Barlow') which recounts the unfortunate experiences of an immigrant from London, who endures most of the hazards of colonial life in both town and bush, e.g. rapacious Sydney merchants who sell him poor stock, attacks by bushrangers and Aborigines when he moves up-country, and eventual arrest for debt. A typical example of new chum literature, 'Billy Barlow in Australia' was written by Benjamin Griffin and first performed by him as a concert piece in Maitland in 1843. In composing the song (which was a source for James Tucker's *Jemmy Green in Australia*, q.v.), Griffin provided an antipodean context for a character who had been the subject of an earlier series of British street ballads which were so popular that street singers impersonated Billy Barlow in selling their wares. The several sequels to 'Billy Barlow in Australia' are collected with it in Hugh Anderson's *Songs of Billy Barlow* (1956). Billy Barlow was one of George Selth Coppin's (q.v.) most popular stage characters.

BINGHAM, Colin (1898–1986), born Townsville, Queensland, had a long and distinguished career as a journalist and administrator in the newspaper world; he was leader-writer on the *Sydney Morning Herald* 1949–57, associate editor 1957–60 and editor 1961–65. His publications include *Marcinelle and Other Verses* (1925), which includes Bingham's University of Queensland Prize poems (1920, 1923, 1924), *A Book of Verse* (1929), *Men and Affairs* (1967), *The Affairs of Women* (1969), *Decline of Innocence and Other Poems* (1970), *National Images and Other Poems* (1979) and *Wit and Wisdom: A Public Affairs Miscellany* (1982). His autobiography, *The Beckoning Horizon*, was published in 1983.

BINGHAM, Geoffrey (1919–), born Goulburn, NSW, was a POW in Changi during the Second World War and was ordained an Anglican priest in 1953. A regular contributor of short stories to Australian journals (e.g. thirty-four of his stories were published in the *Bulletin* 1939–83), Bingham has published several collections of short fiction including *To Command the Cats* (1980), *Angel Wings* (1981), *The Translation of Mr. Piffy* (1982), *The Concentration Camp* (1983) and *Three Special Stories* (1983). He also wrote *Bright Bird & Shining Sails* (1981), a fantasy illustrated by the artist Pro Hart, and *Harps, Viols and Goodly Guitars* (1981), a collection of verse. In 1991 he published a novel, *Tall Grow the Tallow-Woods*, incorporating his wartime experiences and their impact on his life after the war.

BIRD, Carmel (1940–), born Launceston, Tasmania, was educated at the University of Tasmania and lived for a period in Europe and the USA before settling in Melbourne. Bird's fiction blends real and surreal, mundane and macabre with inventive irony, reflecting her perception of Tasmania itself as an 'ironic' island, whose picturesque surface masks deep secrets and is haunted by the ghosts of Aborigines and convicts. She has published two novels, *Cherry Ripe* (1985) and *The Bluebird Cafe* (1990), and four collections of short stories, *Births, Deaths and Marriages* (1983), *The Woodpecker Toy Fact* (1987), *Woodpecker Point* (1988) and *The Common Rat* (1993). She has also written a guide for writers, *Dear Writer* (1988), and edited a collection of short stories, *Relations* (1991). A witty writer with a wide but always highly original tonal range, Bird raises what is often potentially dour or even sinister or horrific to something approaching comedy. Disease, deaths and violence are staples in her fictional world, which has similarities with Barbara Hanrahan's in Gothic sensuality and feminist irony, although Bird's deadpan humour is a distinctive, determining element. The stories of *Woodpecker Point*, for instance, focus on the common emotion of sibling jealousy which has the uncommon consequence of a dual death, on marital infidelity and the sterility of close relationships, on failed lives, murder, madness and extreme domestic violence; the stories of *The Common Rat* are linked by common themes of death, madness and crime. Bird's approach to these themes, however, is both detached and involved, a search for pattern which may have simply the satisfaction of art or approach a more essential truth, which may represent meaning or just the arbitrary effect of language. As the semi-autobiographical narrator of 'The Woodpecker Toy Fact' comments after describing her childhood inference of a special meaning in 'Toy Fact', a result of her ignorance that a toy factory's shop sign was truncated, and her subsequent search for imaginatively significant facts, 'trapping them, bright birds in flight, planets in amber', the quest offers either the possibility of metaphysical discovery or aesthetic production: 'I am still uncertain as to whether I will ultimately discover The Toy Fact, and so complete the pattern, or whether, by placing the final Fact I will produce The Toy Fact.' She is fascinated by the power of memory and the capacity of mundane scenes, incidents and sensations to trigger it into life as well as by the truth-telling power of fiction and its ability to mine and represent the past more effectively than the single-minded pursuit of documentary fact. As she has commented in an article titled 'Fact or Fiction', 'Life is

a crude inventor; fiction will only be convincing if it is more artful than life'; she has also described herself as 'interested in the play between fact and fiction, interested in the moment when the metamorphosis takes place, when the grub of fact becomes the butterfly of fiction'. Finely observed details – snails crawling over old love-letters, a grandmother's patchwork quilt, the solemn brown eyes of a cow – are often the hinges of her short fiction, the points at which external sketch and first-person reminiscence blend in epiphanies of insight. Some of her stories, such as 'The Woodpecker Toy Fact' are as much demonstrations of the art of fiction-making as they are themselves fictions, although artful play and seriousness exist side by side as do gloom and joy. *The Bluebird Cafe* is set partly in Copperfield, a once prosperous mining town in north-west Tasmania, but now a ghost town, inhabited by a single inhabitant, Bedrock Mean. Bedrock mourns the disappearance of Loveleygod, her perfectly formed but stunted daughter, conceived in an incestuous relationship with her brother Carillo, whose fate resembles that of several real-life Australian children who have mysteriously disappeared. Meanwhile, at Launceston, Copperfield is replicated in the 'Historic Museum Village of Copperfield', a theme park under an immense crystalline dome. Here Virginia O'Day, now a successful New York novelist and playwright, who has returned to her birthplace, finds her memories of childhood both stimulated and distorted. Underlying the novel's quirky semi-Gothic surface is a polemical concern with the commercial destruction of the Tasmanian landscape and with the isolationist attitudes of its inhabitants.

Birdsville Track, one of Australia's early and most hazardous overland stock routes, runs for about 500 kilometres between Marree in SA and the outback town of Birdsville in south-western Queensland. The track is featured in Francis Ratcliffe's *Flying Fox and Drifting Sand* (1948) and George Farwell's *Land of Mirage* (1951), and its history is outlined in Jocelyn Burt's *The Birdsville Track* (1971). Douglas Stewart's poem sequence *The Birdsville Track* (1955) describes his experiences on the track in 1954 and celebrates some of its well-known landmarks and identities.

BIRDWOOD, Field Marshal William (1865–1951) was born in India. After service in India and the Boer War he was appointed general officer commanding the Australian and NZ Army Corps and led them at Gallipoli and in France; he was involved in the coining of the term 'Anzac' (q.v.). He published the memoirs *Khaki and Gown* (1941), *In My Time* (1946).

BIRKBECK, Henry Angel (1850–82), born Mexico, came to Queensland as a boy of 12 after a brief schooling in England. He published *Cupid and Psyche* (1875), a classical epic in ten books in the style of *Paradise Lost*.

BIRKETT, Winifred (1897–1966), born North Sydney, published poetry, *Edelweiss and Other Poems* (1932), and fiction, *Three Goats on a Bender* (1934),

Earth's Quality (1935) and *Portrait of Lucy* (1938). *Three Goats on a Bender* is an amusing story of three women living in a house at Camden; *Earth's Quality*, a substantial novel thought highly of by contemporary critics, deals with the influence of an Australian pastoral property on the lives of three generations of the Weldon family; *Portrait of Lucy* tells of the happy outcome of a marriage between a man and his orphaned ward.

BIRNIE, Richard (1808–88), born London, arrived in Perth in 1854 as advocate-general and magistrate of territories but after an unsuccessful legal career in WA and Victoria became a columnist ('The Essayist') on the *Australasian* in 1870. A prominent literary figure in Melbourne and a member of the literary society, the Cave of Adullam, Birnie published *Essays: Social, Moral and Political* (1879).

Birth: A Little Journal of Australian Poetry appeared, mostly monthly, 1916–22. A slight journal (usually only four pages), it began as the personal venture of William Mitchell, who edited the first few issues, and became the journal of the Melbourne Literary Club. Several well-known Australian poets featured in its pages and two small annuals (1920 and 1921) were published. Other editors of the magazine were, in succession, Gilbert Wallace, Bernard O'Dowd, Nettie Palmer, Frederick Macartney and Frank Wilmot; Louis Lavater was also involved in its production.

BIRTLES, Dora (1903–94), born Dora Toll at Newcastle, NSW, was educated at the University of Sydney. In 1923 Bert Birtles, Dora's future husband, then a non-degree evening student and subsequently the author of a book on Greek political history, was expelled from the university after one of his love poems, considered overly explicit by the Proctorial Board, was published in *Hermes*. Dora, who also had a poem on a related theme in the same issue, was rusticated for two years. Dora Birtles was a teacher before sailing in 1932 in the cutter *Gullmarn* from Newcastle to Singapore; living abroad for the next five years, she visited the Far East, Scandinavia, Russia and most European countries. She published travel books, short stories and poetry, but is best known as a writer for children. Her publications include *North-West by North: Journal of a Voyage* (1935, reprinted 1985), based on the cutter voyage; *The Overlanders* (1946), the book of the Australian film made in that year; *Australia in Colour* (1946); *Pioneer Shack* (1947), a well-known children's novel, which, set in Newcastle, uses the well-tried formula of children employing their wits to retrieve family situations that adults have allowed to get out of control; and *Bonza the Bull* (1944), in which a similar retrieval of family fortunes occurs when Bonza wins first prize at the Sydney Show.

BJELKE-PETERSEN, Marie (1874–1969), born near Copenhagen, Denmark, came to Tasmania with her parents in 1891. Her brother Hans established the Bjelke-Petersen Physical Culture School in Hobart; Marie became an instructor there and taught physical culture in Hobart schools. Forced to abandon that career because of illness, she turned to writing. Three short sketches, religious in tone, were published as *The Mysterious Stranger* (1913), *Before an Eastern Court* (1914) and *Muffled Drums* (1914). Her first novel, *The Captive Singer* (1917), based on a guide who sang at the Marakoopa Caves in Tasmania, was a conspicuous financial success. Her other novels, sentimental, romantic and florid in language, included *Dusk* (1921), *Jewelled Nights* (1923), *The Immortal Flame* (1919 and 1926), *The Moon Minstrel* (1927), *Monsoon Music* (1930), *The Rainbow Lute* (1932), *The Silver Knight* (1934) and *Jungle Night* (1937). More appreciated as a novelist in the USA and England than in Australia, she was awarded the King's Jubilee Medal for literature in 1935.

'Black Bonnet', a poem by Henry Lawson (q.v.), was first published in the *Lone Hand* in 1916; one of Lawson's most worked-over compositions, it was extensively revised after a detailed correspondence between Lawson and George Robertson in 1917 and revised again by David McKee Wright (q.v.) for inclusion in his edition of *Selected Poems of Henry Lawson* (1918). A tribute to Australian pioneer women (more specifically bush pioneers in the original version), 'Black Bonnet' pictures an old woman on her walk to church, her memories as she sits through the service, her talk with the local children after the service, and her return home where in dignity and contentment she resumes her domestic routine. Lawson's memories of his own grandmother Harriet Winn went into the writing of the poem (just as Robertson's recollection of 'my Mother' stimulated his involvement in the revisions), although he also revealed that his models at the time of composition were a great-aunt and a neighbour at Blues Point, North Sydney.

BLACK, George Mure (1854–1936), born Edinburgh, migrated to Australia about 1877 to work on a Gippsland station as a bookkeeper. He soon moved to NSW and by 1889 was sub-editor on the *Bulletin*. Active in the emerging labour movement of the 1890s, Black edited the *Australian Workman* 1891–92 and was a member of the NSW parliament 1891–98. He then resumed a journalistic career, editing the *Barrier Truth* (1898), the *Australian Worker* (1900–4) and the *National Advocate* (1908) before returning to the NSW Legislative Assembly 1910–17; during 1917–36 he was a member of the Legislative Council. One of the Labor Party's first historians, Black wrote *History of the NSW Labor Party* (1910), expanded 1926–29 into the seven-part *A History of the NSW Political Labor Party*. Among his other publications was *An Anzac Areopagus and Other Verses* (1923).

'Black Stump, The' is an expression figuratively denoting the boundary line between civilisation and the remote outback. It is most commonly used in the phrase 'this side of the Black Stump', e.g. in Xavier Herbert's *Poor Fellow My Country* there is a reference to 'the biggest mug this side of the Black Stump'. Various suggestions have been made as to the locality of the original Black Stump, e.g. that it once stood on the site of the government stock tank between Gunbar and Crow's Nest Tank in south-western NSW. 'Duke' Tritton in *Time Means Tucker* (1964) states that it had been the name of a wine shanty near Coolah in north-eastern NSW. The Black Stump is a landmark in 'Rolf Boldrewood's' *Robbery Under Arms* (1888) and it has been suggested that the term may have originated from its use in that novel. *Beyond the Black Stump* (1956) is the title of a novel by Nevil Shute.

'Black Velvet' is the colloquial term used to indicate the sexual attraction of the Aboriginal woman for the White male. Indulgence in black velvet, a common practice in outback areas where White women were often unavailable, was tacitly condoned as an inevitable phenomenon of frontier life. It is featured in such diverse writing as W.A. Cawthorne's *The Kangaroo Islanders: A Story of South Australia before Colonization* (1926), Ernest Favenc's story 'The Parson's Blackboy', Vance Palmer's novel *The Man Hamilton* (1928), Katharine Susannah Prichard's novel *Coonardoo* (1929), Frank Dalby Davison's story 'Further West', G. Herbert Gibson's 'A Ballad of Queensland' (also known as 'Sam Holt'), Mary Durack's novel *Keep Him My Country* (1955), and Henrietta Drake-Brockman's play *Men Without Wives* (1955). The first version of Xavier Herbert's *Capricornia* (1938) was titled 'Black Velvet'. See also Aborigine in White Australian Literature.

'Black Velvet Band, The', also known as 'The Girl With the Black Velvet Band' and 'The Black Ribbon Band', is a folk-song in which a convict recalls the circumstances of his transportation to Van Diemen's Land. As an apprentice in Dublin (Tralee and London in other versions of the song), he meets a young girl whose hair is tied with a black velvet band; she picks a gentleman's pocket but slips the proceeds into the apprentice's hand when the crime is discovered. 'The Black Velvet Band' is claimed as an Australian folk-song and was part of the repertoire of Blind Billy Huntingdon, but clearly derives from Ireland, where it is still sung in a longer version than that known in Australia. The brevity of the main Australian version is characteristic of the Irish-to-Australian process of transmission.

Blackbirding was the name given to the practice of kidnapping indigenous people from the Pacific Islands for labour in the sugar-cane industry of Queensland and for pearl diving in the Torres Strait. The first such people (usually referred to as kanakas) introduced into Australia were 140 Tanna Islanders from the New Hebrides, imported by Benjamin Boyd in 1847. After many notorious blackbirding atrocities, the Pacific Islanders Protection Act was passed in 1872. Other Acts followed and from 1892 stringent regulations were imposed on the import of Islanders. Recruiting ceased in 1904 and many were repatriated, although those who had married in Australia or had lived here for twenty years were allowed to remain if they so chose. Accounts of blackbirding are given in T. Dunbabin's *Slavers of the South Seas* (1935) Hector Holthouse's

Cannibal Cargoes (1969) and E.W. Docker's *The Blackbirders* (1970). Faith Bandler has written the story of her father, a New Hebridean Islander, who was brought to Australia to work on the Queensland sugar-cane fields in 1883, in *Wacvie* (1977) and *Marani in Australia* (1980). Peter Corris wrote an historical work on blackbirding, *Passage, Port and Plantation* (1973).

Black-Ey'd Susan (1829), by the English writer Douglas Jerrold, was the first professionally produced play in Australia, performed in Sydney at Barnett Levey's (q.v.) Theatre Royal in 1832.

BLADEN, Peter (1922–), born Subiaco in Perth, WA, served in the RAN in the Second World War, and is a graduate of the University of WA and the University of Melbourne (MA). He published *The Old Ladies at Newington* (1953), a long poem which won first prize in the Commonwealth Jubilee literature competition in 1951. The poem gives a perceptive treatment of Australia's past and present as seen during the visit of a charitable group to the Newington state home for aged women in Sydney. It also develops the theme of human subjection to decay and death and thus a need for sympathy and understanding of those who are nearing that state. As 'L. Bladen' he published *Selected Poems* (1945); he has also written *Masque for a Modern Minstrel* (1962), *Island Trilogy* (1970) and *Adelaide Sonnets: A Biography of the City* (1975). In 1984 Bladen went to Turkey to live and has continued to write (although not publish) fiction, poetry and autobiographical works.

Blaiklock Memorial Lectures is a series of annual Australian literature lectures inaugurated in 1971 at the University of Sydney as the result of a gift by Lady Gallegan to commemorate both her father, Herbert Blaiklock, and the poet Henry Kendall. The series began with A.D. Hope's 'Henry Kendall: A Dialogue with the Past'. Subsequent lectures have been given by Manning Clark, Rosemary Dobson, G.A. Wilkes, James McAuley, Thea Astley, R.F. Brissenden, Peter Quartermaine, Walter Stone, Leonie Kramer, H.P. Heseltine, T.T. Reed, Robin Grove, David Malouf, Michael Wilding, Vivian Smith, Fay Zwicky, Glenda Adams, Ken Stewart, Elizabeth Jolley and Adrian Mitchell. The lectures are usually printed annually in *Southerly*. Leonie Kramer edited the collection *Blaiklock Memorial Lectures 1971–1981* (1981).

BLAINEY, Geoffrey (1930–), professor of economic history at the University of Melbourne 1968–76, Ernest Scott professor of history at the University of Melbourne 1976–88 and chairman of the Australia Council 1977–81, is one of Australia's most active economic and social historians. His most significant publications (now provided as a trilogy, *A Vision of Australian History*) are *The Tyranny of Distance* (1966), *Triumph of the Nomads* (1975) and *A Land Half Won* (1980). The three books give a comprehensive account of Australian history from the discovery and settlement of the continent by Aborigines 40 000 years ago to the end of the colonial era, i.e. the end of the nineteenth century. *The Tyranny of Distance* comprises three sections: a study of how Australia's geographic location affected her growth to about 1860; a history of transport since 1850; and a survey of Australia's foreign relations. As the title suggests, distance is proposed as the major influence on both the direction and the scope of Australian development, both the distance of Australia from other parts of the world and distance within Australia itself. *Triumph of the Nomads* reassesses the accepted theories of the humanisation of this continent by the Aborigines and speculates on the structure and motivation of Aboriginal society in the distant past. *A Land Half Won* is a history of White settlement in Australia from the early Dutch and Portuguese voyages of discovery and the establishment of the convict colony at Port Jackson to 1900, by which time the struggle was partly over, the 'land half won'. Blainey's other major published works include *The Peaks of Lyell* (1954), a history of the Mount Lyell region and its mining industry; *The Rush That Never Ended* (1963), a general history of Australian mining; *The Steel Master* (1971), a biography of the industrial magnate Essington Lewis; *The Causes of War* (1973); *Our Side of the Country*, a history of Victoria (1984); *All for Australia* (1984); *The Great Seesaw: A New View of the Western World 1750–2000* (1988); *A Game of Our Own: The Origins of Australian Football* (1990) and *Blainey, eye on Australia* (1991). The ABC produced a sociological and historical series, *The Blainey View*, based on Blainey's interpretation of Australian life and history, in 1982. Blainey's controversial views on modern immigration appear in *All for Australia* (1984). A denunciation of those views is contained in *Surrender Australia?* (1985), a criticism of Blainey by eleven scholars and historians of the day. In 1988 at the UN he became the first historian to receive the Encyclopaedia Britannica Prize for 'excellence in the dissemination of knowledge'. Among numerous awards won by his writings are the Australian Literature Society's Gold Medal for *The Rush That Never Ended* and the Captain Cook Bicentenary Prize for Biography for *The Steel Master*. Emeritus Professor of the University of Melbourne, he has also been made an AO.

BLAIR, David (1820–99), born Ireland, arrived in Australia in 1850 to train under John Dunmore Lang as a Presbyterian minister. After breaking with Lang he settled into radical journalism and politics, mainly in Melbourne; twice member of the Victorian parliament, he wrote for the *Empire* and the *Sydney Morning Herald* and had a long career as leader-writer for the *Age*. Prominent in Melbourne literary and intellectual circles, Blair was the author of an important early history, *The History of Australasia* (1878), and of *Cyclopaedia of Australasia* (1881).

BLAIR, Ron (1942–), born Sydney and educated at Christian Brothers, Lewisham, and Sydney University, was closely associated with the founding of the Nimrod Street Theatre. He has worked as an actor, producer, writer and play-reader for the ABC, and as an assistant artistic director of the SA Theatre Company. Blair collaborated with Michael Boddy, Marcus Cooney and the actors in writing and producing the entertainment 'Biggles', which marked the opening of Nimrod, and was one of the writers of its Christmas 1971 show, 'Hamlet on Ice'. His first independent dramatic piece, *Flash Jim Vaux*, a ballad opera dealing with the life of the convict James Hardy Vaux, was produced in 1971 and published in 1989. His other plays include 'Kabul' (1973), *President Wilson in Paris* (first produced 1973, published 1974), *The Christian Brothers* (first produced 1975, published 1976), 'Owning Things' (1974), *Mad, Bad and Dangerous to Know* (published *Quadrant* 1976), 'Perfect Strangers' (1976), 'The Political Bordello or How Waiters Got the Vote' (1977), *A Place in the Present* (first produced 1977, published 1985), *Marx* (1983) and *Last Day in Woolloomooloo* (1983), a later version of 'Owning Things'. He has also collaborated with Nick Enright in 'Servant of Two Masters' and has edited the two collections *Popular Short Plays for the Australian Stage* (both 1985). Blair's work is varied, ranging from the large-scale satirical revue to the free-ranging chronicle play such as 'Kabul', which centres on the massacre of a British garrison in Kabul in 1841, and to the one-man shows, *Mad, Bad and Dangerous to Know* (a study of Byron) and *The Christian Brothers* (his best-known play, a representative re-creation of a day in a 1950s-style Roman Catholic school). Despite its simple chronological action and single actor, *The Christian Brothers* is a complex play; evoking the old-fashioned authoritarianism, religious paranoia, bigotry, dedication, love, unconscious frustrations and pathos of a representative brother, the play sounds the same note of familiarity for Australian audiences as Peter Kenna's *A Hard God*, Barry Oakley's *A Lesson in English* and the film *The Devil's Playground* (1976). *President Wilson in Paris*, which shared an Awgie for the best Australian stage-play in 1973, is part historical play and part macabre thriller. First produced in 1978, *Marx* won the Awgie for the best stage play of that year.

BLAKE, Leila, born and brought up in England, came to Australia in 1950 and has worked as actor and director in both England and Australia. She is also a playwright. She started the first Australian theatre-in-the-round in Sydney in 1954 (the Intimate Theatre) and was co-founder of the Claremont Theatre. One of her one-act plays, 'Fair Go', was first produced in 1974 and another, *Prey*, first produced in 1974, is included in the collection, *Can't You Hear Me Talking to You?* (1978), ed. Alrene Sykes. Her other plays include 'I Love, You Love' (1974), 'The Stirrer' and 'Feminine Plural: The Women of Shakespeare and Wilde', a successful one-woman show which she has performed in Australia, Asia and the USA.

BLAKERS, George Theodore (1828–1912), born Germany, arrived in Australia in 1849. His account of his experiences during the first fifteen years after his arrival, written for his sister and friends in Germany 1888–89, was first published in 1986 titled *A Useless Young Man? An Autobiography of Life in Australia, 1849–64*. After a brief period in Sydney, Blakers took passage on a ship to America, but was diverted on the way and spent two years in the Pacific Islands, mainly in Hawaii. Returning to Australia in 1851, he tried his luck at the diggings, and later worked in a wide variety of occupations, including surveyor, timber-getter, sawyer, goldfields trooper, storekeeper and electoral officer. Undertaking numerous journeys in NSW, he encountered a variety of hazards and on several occasions barely escaped with his life. In 1864, after his left hand was severely injured in a fight with an Aborigine, he trained as a teacher, and was still so employed at the time of writing. Blakers is reserved about some of his private life, especially about his first marriage in 1861, but gives a colourful picture of his youthful self, emerging as a man of courage, resource and principle. His narrative is also a vivid account of conditions in the colony in the 1850s–1860s.

BLAMEY, Sir Thomas (1884–1951), born Lake Albert near Wagga Wagga, NSW, served with distinction in the First World War (on Gallipoli and in France) and in 1942 became commander-in-chief of the Australian military forces in the Second World War. A controversial figure, extraordinarily unpopular with the Australian troops he commanded but grudgingly admired for his aggressive competence, Blamey has been the subject of several biographical works, including John Hetherington's (ed.) *Blamey, Controversial Soldier* (1973) and *Thomas Blamey* (1974). He is also the subject of Kenneth Slessor's scathing poem 'An Inscription for Dog River', and has parallels with General Starkey in Thomas Keneally's novel *The Cut-Rate Kingdom* (1980).

BLAND, William (1789–1868), born London, trained in medicine and became a naval surgeon. As a result of a duel Bland was transported for seven years to NSW, where he had a stormy career, being sentenced to twelve months' imprisonment (1818–19) for publishing 'pipes' lampooning Governor Lachlan Macquarie. As medical practitioner, philanthropist, political reformer, promoter of education and enthusiastic transportationist, Bland was a considerable force in the colony. He edited the exploration journals of W.H. Hovell and Hamilton Hume (qq.v., 1831).

Blast was the title of Wyndham Lewis's brief-lived satirical magazine published in England 1914–15. Reborn in 1987 in Canberra, *Blast*, a quarterly, is published by Bill Tully, Ann Nugent and Craig Cormick. It is partly supported by the ACT Government through its Arts Development Board.

BLAXLAND, Gregory (1778–1853), born Kent, England, came to Australia in 1806 as a free settler. Blaxland is remembered for his participation in the expedition with W.C. Wentworth and William Lawson that crossed the Blue Mountains in 1813. His account of the expedition, *A Journal of a Tour of Discovery across the Blue Mountains in New South Wales*, was published in 1823. There were several later editions, some based on variant transcripts of the journal, as is the version included in George Mackaness's *Fourteen Journeys over the Blue Mountains of New South Wales 1813–1841* (1950–51). Blaxland appears as a character in Eleanor Dark's novel, *No Barrier* (1953).

BLAY, John Charles (1944–), born Parramatta, NSW, has lived in Sydney and Bermagui and is a freelance writer with numerous radio plays to his credit, e.g. 'Vinegar Hill', 'Journeys of Aubrey D', 'Great Village Dream', 'Jazz Singer', 'Fleet'. He has also written the play *Bedbug Celebration* (1981), an autobiographical semi-documentary *Part of the Scenery* (1984) and *Trek Through the Back Country* (1987). He won the Farmer's Poetry Prize in 1969 and in 1982 the Parks Writers Award, jointly sponsored by the Literature Board and the National Parks and Wildlife Service.

Bleak Dawn, a play by Sydney Tomholt (q.v.), was published in 1936; it probes the twisted relationship between the drunken, bullying Jim Stanford and his ex-wife, Emily, exposing the destructive power of their emotional ties.

BLIGH, William (1754–1817), born Plymouth, England, sailed under the command of Captain James Cook on the latter's third voyage in 1776, fought against the French in the American Revolutionary War and in 1783–87 served on merchant ships. In 1787 he was given command of HMS *Bounty* to procure breadfruit plants in Tahiti. On 30 April 1789, soon after leaving Tahiti, the crew mutinied under the leadership of Fletcher Christian and cast off Bligh with eighteen of his men in a small open boat. Bligh skilfully navigated the boat 5822 kilometres to Timor in six weeks, charting part of the 'North-East coast of New Holland' *en route.* Although the persistent legend that his tyrannical personality was the main cause of the mutiny immediately established itself, Bligh was acquitted by a court-martial and the general evidence suggests that he was not an excessively harsh commander. An abridged account of his first expedition, *A Voyage to the South Sea*, was published in 1792 and an unabridged version, *Bligh and the Bounty*, in 1936. From 1795 to 1802 Bligh fought in several actions, including Copenhagen in 1801, where he earned the praise of Nelson. In 1805 he was appointed, with the influence of Sir Joseph Banks, governor of NSW, in succession to Philip G. King; he arrived in Sydney in 1806. His vigorous attempts to control the liquor trade, the currency system and the use of convicts by free settlers led to strong opposition from interested sections. His arrest of John Macarthur on a charge of sedition led to the Rum Rebellion, an insurrection of the NSW Corps led by Major George Johnston; Bligh was 'arrested' in January 1808, although he appears to have had passive support from a large number of private settlers. Until February 1809, when he agreed to return to England aboard HMS *Porpoise*, Bligh remained in confinement in Sydney. Once on board the *Porpoise*, he took command and sailed instead to Hobart, where he remained until January 1810 and the arrival of Colonel Lachlan Macquarie's regiment in Sydney. Bligh spent the next four months in Sydney gathering evidence for the forthcoming trial of John-ston in London, where the incidental charges against Bligh were investigated and disproved. A courageous and competent naval officer, navigator and cartogra-pher, Bligh possessed numerous skills as an adminis-trator although his quick temper, abusive language and rigid adherence to instructions handicapped him in the last role.

Of the numerous biographies of Bligh and accounts of the *Bounty* mutiny, the most substantial are Geof-frey Rawson's *Bligh of the Bounty* (1930), Owen Rutter's *Turbulent Journey* (1936), H.V. Evatt's *Rum Rebellion* (1938), George Mackaness's *The Life of Vice-Admiral William Bligh* (1931, 2nd edn 1951), Arthur Hawkey's *Bligh's Other Mutiny* (1975), Kenneth S. Allen's *That Bounty Bastard* (1976), Gavin Kennedy's *Bligh* (1978), and Glynn Christian's *Fragile Paradise* (1982). Ross Fitzgerald and Mark Hearn examined the controversial events surrounding the coup against Bligh in New South Wales in *Bligh, Macarthur and the Rum Rebellion* (1989). Bligh's journals and those of his fellow officers aboard *Bounty* have been tapped by Douglas Oliver for *Return to Tahiti: Bligh's Second Bread Fruit Voyage* (1988). Paul Brunton edited *Awake Bold Bligh!: William Bligh's Letters describing the Mutiny on HMS Bounty* (1989). Fictional versions of the *Bounty* mutiny have been numerous and are included in *The Mutineer* (1898) by 'Louis' Becke and Walter J. Jeffery, *Joan of the Pilchard* (1930) by Mary Gaunt, and *Man Against the Sea* (1934) and *Mutiny on the Bounty* (1961) by C.B. Nordhoff and J.N. Hall. Other fic-tional representations of the Bligh story are included in J.H.M. Abbott's *The Governor's Man* (1919), Roy Bridges's *The Fires of Hate* (1915), Eleanor Dark's *Storm of Time* (1948), and Bill Collett's *The Last Mutiny* (1993). J.M. Couper's *The Book of Bligh* (1969) is the major poetic examination of Bligh and his actions, although William Beard published a poem on the sub-ject, *Valiant Martinet* (1956). The first stage presen-tation of Bligh's story was 'The Pirates: Or, the Calamities of Captain Bligh', a 'naval overture' of the late eighteenth century, which has been followed by *Governor Bligh* (1930) by Doris Egerton Jones, *The House That Jack Built* (1950) by George Farwell, 'Governor Bligh' (1955) by Brian Medlin, and 'The Man Who Shot the Albatross' (1971) by Ray Lawler. *Stormy Petrel*, a radio serial of over sixty episodes by Rex Rienits, was popular in the 1940s and 1950s and became the first Australian television series; the Bligh episode in the *Behind the Legend* television series (1973) was written by Thomas Keneally. Films include *The Mutiny of the Bounty* (1916), produced by Raymond Longford; *In the Wake of the Bounty* (1933), produced by Charles Chauvel; and *Mutiny on the Bounty* (1935) by MGM, with Charles Laughton as Bligh and Clark Gable as Fletcher Christian. The most innovative study of Bligh and his myth is Greg Dening's *Mr Bligh's Bad Language: Passion, Power and Theatre on the Bounty* (1992), winner of the Victorian Premier's Nettie Palmer Award for non-fiction in 1993; a multi-layered reconstruction of the characters and events through a close examination of the physical, social and psychological circumstances of the protagonists,

Dening's study shows the mythologising of the mutiny in English, American and Polynesian cul-ture.

BLIGHT, John (1913–), born Unley, SA, has spent most of his life in Queensland. During the 1930s De-pression he tramped the Queensland coast in search of work, settling in 1939 to an accountant's job in Bundaberg. After the war he became part-owner of a group of timber mills in the Gympie district but in 1968 he gave up those interests to return to Brisbane where, since 1973, he has been a full-time writer. Blight's first poetry appeared in the *Bulletin* in 1939, his first collection, *The Old Pianist*, being published in 1945. His other volumes of poetry are *The Two Suns Met* (1954), *A Beachcomber's Diary* (1963), *My Beach-combing Days* (1968), *Hart: Poems* (1975), *Selected Poems 1939–1975* (1976), *Pageantry for a Lost Empire* (1978), *The New City Poems* (1980), *Holiday Sea Sonnets* (1985) and *Selected Poems 1939–1990* (1992). *A Beachcomber's Diary* won the Myer Award for the best Australian book of verse in 1964, the *Selected Poems* won a National Book Council Literary Award in 1976, and in the same year he gained the Patrick White Literary Award. He was awarded the Dame Mary Gilmore Medal in 1965, the Grace Leven Prize for poetry in 1977, and the Christopher Brennan Award in 1980.

The Old Pianist sees Blight, in fellow poet Bruce Beaver's phrase, 'a reluctant lyrist', celebrating the 'mean, bounteous land' of Queensland, assessing both its landscape and its people. In *The Two Suns Met*, where he continues to explore his own Queensland and more general Australian experiences, Blight's innovations in punctuation and syntax, his staccato, idiomatic phrasing and ironic complexity, produce poetry which diverges considerably from the conven-tional poetry of the day. With the two 'Beachcomber' volumes (each of ninety sonnets) that explore every-thing marine 'from the periwinkle to the whale' and search for universal meanings in the everyday life of the sea, Blight established a reputation as Australia's leading poet of the sea. *Holiday Sea Sonnets* is his third book of sonnets about the sea. In the sardonic poem 'His Best Poems are About the Sea', in *Hart*, he rejects the inference that he is no other kind of poet. The best of the 'Beachcomber' sonnets include 'Death of a Whale', 'A Child's Essay about the Sea', 'The Beach-comber', 'Mud' and 'The Volutes'. Although not usually regarded as a confessional poet, Blight pro-duces in his substantial volume *Hart* some individual and introspective poetry. Many of the brief poems are intensely personal statements, while others ('A Day', 'Racialism', 'Bricks') reflect on the total human con-dition. Other themes of the collection are urban life, especially the high-rise culture ('The New City Series'), women's beauty and the sexuality of old men. Similar themes persist in *Pageantry for a Lost Empire* where, in the title poem and in others such as 'Tenant at Number 9', the flight of time, the pathos of age and the disappointment of life itself are highlighted. Blight has long been regarded highly by fellow writers as the Patrick White Literary Award of 1976 indicates. He has been the holder of a Literature Board

Emeritus Fellowship since 1984 and in 1987 was made AM for services to literature and education.

Bliss (1981), a novel by Peter Carey (q.v.), won the 1981 Miles Franklin Award. Harry Joy, aged 39 and the moderately successful owner of an advertising agency, suffers a severe heart attack and dies for nine minutes. Sure of the love of his wife, Bettina, and the well-being of his two children, David and Lucy, Harry has previously insulated himself from pain and anxiety, relying on his natural charm and his talent as a Good Bloke to smooth his way both publicly and privately. He has also had a facile gift for retelling the romantic stories of his globe-trotting father, which have had an unexpected impact on Bettina, who yearns to be part of the sophisticated world of New York; on David, who is determined to be wealthy; and on Lucy, who is attracted to communism. Compelled by his fear of impending heart surgery to contemplate the afterlife, Harry is convinced, once he has survived the operation, that he has entered Hell. He discovers a series of unpleasant truths including David's avarice and involvement with the drug trade; Bettina's infidelity with Joel, his partner; David and Lucy's incestuous relationship; and his agency's connection with carcinogenic products. Disgusted with his family, Harry moves into the Hilton Hotel where he lives in style on credit and meets the woman he is to love passionately, the sexually generous and vibrantly alive Honey Barbara. From the rural community of Bog Onion Road, Honey has come to the city to sell the community's crop of marijuana and to make money by selling her body. Meanwhile Harry's apparent irresponsibility and his attempts to abandon the profitable account of Krappe Chemicals result in his family's decision to have him committed to an asylum. The authorities at first mistakenly seize Harry's colleague Alex Duval from the Hilton and, once he is also captured and incarcerated, Harry finds that Alex has stolen his identity in order to escape from a disastrous marriage. Eventually reborn as Harry Joy after Alex's ruse has been discovered, Harry buys his way out of the asylum with Bettina's help and looks forward to living with Honey in her community. Bettina, however, has secured his release on condition that he help her in her long-held ambition to design and sell commercials; and both he and Honey join the Joy family at their Palm Avenue home, now also containing Joel and Lucy's lover Ken. Honey's energy is eventually sapped by the unhealthy aspects of modern city life, by the tangled problems of the Joy family and Harry's rapid moral deterioration, and she leaves for home. Bettina's remarkably successful career is cut short by her discovery that she has fallen victim to the city's cancer epidemic. Her suicide, in an explosion that also causes the death of several others, is followed by Joel's suicide and David's departure for Colombia; there he is eventually executed in a style that seems to correlate with the romances of his grandfather. Harry leaves for the Bog Onion community where, after some initial difficulties, he gains acceptance. Rejected by Honey for five years, he finally wins her, fathers two more children, leads a satisfying if obscure life and dies for the third time at 75 when a branch of a tree falls on his head. The feature film *Bliss* was screened in 1985.

Blocks and Tackles, see **MURRAY, Les**

BLOCKSIDGE, Charles William, see **'BAYLEBRIDGE, William'**

BLOOM, Norma (1924–), born Melbourne, has lived in England and NZ, but since 1960 has resided in Hobart. Widely represented in NZ and Australian literary journals and poetry anthologies, she has had two books of verse published: *The Larger View* (1972) and *When I See You* (1978). Her play, 'Ruby', was performed in several Victorian country towns in 1973.

'BLUEBUSH', see **BOURKE, J.P.**

BLUNDELL, Graeme (1945–), born Melbourne, first became involved in student theatre in 1963 at the University of Melbourne while studying to be a teacher. He moved to the Melbourne Theatre Company in 1966, making his first professional appearance in 1967 in 'Private Yuk Objects' by Alan Hopgood. He then became one of the founders of the Australian Performing Group (q.v.). From 1969 onwards he acted in film and television in such productions as *2,000 Weeks*, *The Naked Bunyip*, *The Box*, *Stork*, *Mad Dog Morgan*, *Don's Party*, *Power Without Glory*, *The Odd Angry Shot*, *The Best of Friends*, and *The Year My Voice Broke*. His most spectacular success was, however, in the sex romps *Alvin Purple* (1973) and *Alvin Rides Again* (1974); *Alvin Purple* appeared also as an ABC series in 1973 but was taken off air by the chairman, Sir Henry Bland. Blundell has also been active as a director (e.g. *Dimboola*, *Norm and Ahmed*, *Dad and Dave*) and founder of various production companies (e.g. Hoopla Theatre Foundation, Stable Productions, its film-making branch and the Playbox Theatre Company). After moving to Sydney in 1985 he founded Kinselas Productions with Tony Cranes. Blundell is the editor of *Plays* (1970, early plays by Alexander Buzo, Jack Hibberd and John Romeril).

BLUNDEN, Godfrey (1906–), born Melbourne, was a journalist in several Australian States before going to America and later to England. He has been a newspaper correspondent in many of the world's capital cities including Moscow, Paris, New York and London. His Second World War dispatches were published in the London *Evening Standard* and he was, for some years, an associate editor of *Time* magazine. His chief Australian novel is *No More Reality* (1935); set in the small Australian township Hobbleton, the novel is an exuberant though sardonic view of the characters and mores of the typical Australian small community. Blunden's other novels include *The Time of the Assassins* (1953), *A Room on the Route* (1947) and *The Looking Glass Conference* (1956). With *Charco Harbour* (1968) he ventured into historical fiction; it deals with the James Cook expedition to observe the transit of Venus at Tahiti in 1768 and particularly the period of seven weeks spent by Cook in Charco Harbour after the *Endeavour* had run on to a reef. In 1969 Blunden edited *Norman Lindsay Watercolours*, a new edition of the 1939 *The Norman Lindsay Watercolour Book*. In 1954 he compiled *The Land and People of Australia*.

BOAKE, Barcroft (1866–92) was born in Sydney, son of an immigrant Irish photographer. After an education better than was usual for the time, he decided to work in the bush, first (in 1886) as assistant to a surveyor in the Snowy River country, later as boundary-rider and drover. He believed bush life to be 'the only life worth living' and preferred droving to all other occupations, but he felt compelled by difficult family circumstances to return to Sydney in 1891. Taciturn and brooding by nature, and easily disposed to pessimism and depression, Boake failed to cope with the personal and financial difficulties facing him and his family. He disappeared on 2 May 1892 and his body, hanging by the neck from a stockwhip, was found eight days later in scrub at Middle Harbour, Sydney. His suicide recalled that of his poetic idol Adam Lindsay Gordon, twenty-two years earlier. Boake believed that there was 'a romance, though a grim one' in the story of outback life and that belief is well illustrated in his most notable poem, 'Where the Dead Men Lie' (q.v.), the title poem of his only book of poetry, published in 1897 by A.G. Stephens under the pseudonym 'Surcingle'. Boake's attacks on the absentee landlords and ruthless banking systems that exploited the hard-working, long-suffering bushmen were in line with the customary radical complaints of the time, but his obsession with the tragedy and despair associated with bush life set him apart from most contemporary bush balladists, whose stance was more light-hearted and ironic. The grimness of his vision, however, links him with Barbara Baynton and Henry Lawson. Clement Semmler's *Barcroft Boake: Poet of the Stockwhip* was published in 1965.

'BOAKE, Capel' (Doris Boake Kerr) (1895–1945), born Sydney, niece of the poet Barcroft Boake, published the novels *Painted Clay* (1917), *The Romany Mark* (1923), *The Dark Thread* (1936) and *The Twig Is Bent* (1946). Her poetry was published as *Selected Poems of Capel Boake* (1949), and she collaborated with Bernard Cronin (q.v.) in *Kangaroo Rhymes* (1922) under the pseudonym 'Stephen Gray'. Except for *The Romany Mark*, her novels are set in Melbourne, where she lived for most of her life; *The Twig Is Bent* re-creates such significant events of the 1850s as the gold rushes, the establishment of Victoria as a separate colony and the Eureka Stockade. *Painted Clay*, republished by Virago in 1986, is based on Doris Kerr's experiences of work as a shop assistant and typist.

Bobbin Up, a novel by Dorothy Hewett (q.v.), was first published in 1959 and subsequently translated into several foreign languages. Unified by setting and theme, it describes the disparate experiences, problems and values of a group of fourteen women employed in a Sydney spinning mill. They contend with grinding poverty and are made memorable by their courage, endurance and comradeship.

Bobwirridirridi, see *Poor Fellow My Country*

BODDY, Michael (1934–), born in England and educated at Cambridge University, came to Australia in 1959 and spent three years in Tasmania before joining the Emerald Hill Theatre in Melbourne. In 1965 he won the Erik Award for theatre work and moved to Sydney, where he worked as writer, actor and director in theatre, film, television and radio until 1974. He wrote 'Biggles' with Ron Blair and Marcus Cooney for the opening of the Nimrod Street Theatre in 1970 and, with Ron Blair and the original cast, 'Hamlet on Ice' in 1971, but is best known for his collaboration with Bob Ellis in the popular musical play, *The Legend of King O'Malley* (q.v., 1974), which seemed to mark a renaissance in Australian drama. First produced in 1970 by the National Institute of Dramatic Art (where Boddy lectured in the history of theatre, 1969–70) at the Jane Street Theatre, and based on the life of an extraordinary Labor politician of the early years of this century, King O'Malley, the play is a series of music-hall sketches linked by song, dance and mime. Boddy collaborated with Marcus Cooney in 'Cash' (1972), based on the life of the bushranger Martin Cash, and has also written 'The Last Supper Show' (1972); 'The Cradle of Hercules' (1974), a chronicle play about Arthur Phillip and Bennelong; 'Lust for Power' (1977), a music-hall melodrama; and 'Crushed by Desire' (1978), an Australian melodrama set on the goldfields. A pioneer in Theatre in Education, he has written 27 TIE plays. He is married to the artist Janet Dawson Boddy, who won the 1973 Archibald Prize for her portrait of him. Since 1974 Boddy has combined farming and running the Bugle Press at Binalong, NSW, has published seven books, produces a bi-monthly newsletter, and has been a regular columnist in the national press on food, consumer afairs, natural history and farming. He now writes mainly fiction.

Bohemia: The All-Australian Literary Magazine, published by the Melbourne Bread and Cheese Club (q.v.), ran in its first series 1939–40; the second series ran 1945–67. Although usually traditional and patriotic in stance, *Bohemia* published the work of such younger writers of the time as Max Harris and Gavin Casey. An earlier journal, also called *Bohemia*, with items of theatrical, social and general interest, was published 1890–92.

Bohemians of the Bulletin (1965) is a collection of reminiscences and drawings by Norman Lindsay (q.v.) of people he knew at the turn of the century. Mostly literary figures connected with the *Bulletin*, they include J.F. Archibald, A.G. Stephens, J.H.M. Abbot, A.B. Paterson, James Edmond, Livingston Hopkins, Bernard O'Dowd, Randolph Bedford, Hugh McCrae and Louis Stone.

BOL, Lorna, born Sydney, graduated as a commercial artist before training as an actor with the New Theatre. In 1973 she moved to Queensland, where she became associated with La Boite theatre and began a career as a playwright. Her plays include *Treadmill* (1978), *They Had to Go* in *Five Warana One-Act Winners* (1984) and *But I'm Still Here* (1986).

'BOLDREWOOD, Rolf' (Thomas Alexander Browne) (1826–1915), born London, arrived in Australia in 1831. His father, Sylvester Brown ('Boldrewood' added the *e* to his own surname in the 1860s), settled first in Sydney, where he engaged in whaling and built the stone mansion after which the suburb of Enmore is named. In 1838 he overlanded cattle to Port Phillip, speculated in land and started a ferry service. He was ruined in the depression of the early 1840s and Thomas saw himself as the means of repairing the family's fortunes. In 1844 he took up a run in western Victoria, where he prospered as a livestock-breeder and potato-grower over the next fifteen years. The run was named Squattlesea Mere – taken, like his pseudonym, from his favourite author, Sir Walter Scott. In 1862 he sold Squattlesea Mere to buy a sheep station on Lake Boga, near Swan Hill; the move marked the start of a decade of misfortune. In 1863 he was forced to sell the Lake Boga property at a considerable loss, and although he moved in 1864 to another sheep station near Narrandera he was driven off by drought in 1869. 'Boldrewood' moved to Sydney with his family until 1871, when he was appointed police magistrate at Gulgong, a rapidly expanding gold-mining town in central western NSW. The office of goldfields commissioner, added to his duties in 1872, brought him some unpopularity with local miners and the press, although he earned respect for his work on the Bench and became prominent in community affairs; in 1871 he presided over a luncheon for the visiting novelist Anthony Trollope. In 1881 'Boldrewood' left Gulgong to become police magistrate at Dubbo (where a centenary dinner in 1982 honoured his presence in the town) and from there moved to similar positions in Armidale (1884–85) and Albury (1885–95). After his retirement from the public service he returned with his family to Melbourne, and as a successful author entered the society in which his family had been prominent in the 1830s and 1840s; a stalwart of the Melbourne Club, he did much of his later writing there.

'Boldrewood' had articles published in the *Cornhill Magazine* in 1866 and 1868 but it was not until he was living in Sydney in 1870 and began having contributions accepted by the newly established *Australian Town and Country Journal* that he began writing seriously; like his hero, Scott, he wrote in part to pay off his debts. An early *Australian Town and Country Journal* series of articles was republished in 1983 as *Shearing in Riverina*. During the 1870s 'Boldrewood' had seven novels serialised in the same journal; the second, 'The Squatter's Dream' (q.v., 1875), was revised and issued as *Ups and Downs* in 1878 and as *The Squatter's Dream* in 1890. By 1881 he was a moderate success, but his reputation was firmly established by the serialisation of his bushranging adventure *Robbery Under Arms* (q.v.) in the *Sydney Mail* 1882–83. *Robbery Under Arms* was published in London in 1888 and then in revised form by Macmillan in 1889; the great popu-

larity of the 1889 edition made his name in England and the USA as well as in Australia and led Macmillan to publish seventeen more 'Boldrewood' books (1890–1905). Of these, *A Colonial Reformer* (q.v., 1890), *The Miner's Right* (q.v, 1890), *My Run Home* (1897) and *Babes in the Bush* (1900) had been first published as *Australian Town and Country Journal* serials during the Gulgong years; and *A Sydney-Side Saxon* (1891), *Nevermore* (q.v., 1892), *The Crooked Stick* (1895), *The Sphinx of Eaglehawk* (1895), *The Sealskin Cloak* (1896) and *Plain Living* (1898) were first published as serials in other journals in the 1880s. The remaining Macmillan works are *A Modern Buccaneer* (q.v., 1894), which brought 'Boldrewood' a charge of plagiarism from 'Louis' Becke (q.v.); two romances with a pastoral or mining setting, *The Ghost Camp* (1902) and *The Last Chance* (1905); *War to the Knife* (1899), an adventure set in NZ; and *A Romance of Canvas Town* (1898) and *In Bad Company* (q.v., 1901), which reprinted some of 'Boldrewood's shorter contributions to the press. Earlier he had written *Old Melbourne Memories* (1884) and was the anonymous author of two agricultural manuals, each published by a London firm of colonial outfitters as *S.W. Silver & Co's Australian Grazier's Guide* (1879, 1881), the only books not published under his pseudonym. As 'Mrs Rolf Boldrewood' his wife wrote *The Flower Garden in Australia* (1893); as 'Rose Boldrewood' his daughter published the novel *The Complications at Collaroi* (1911). His pseudonym survives today in the Rolf Boldrewood Short Story Award given by the Eaglehawk Dahlia and Arts Society.

Politically conservative, 'Boldrewood' advocated throughout his life and work a belief in good breeding and education, individual enterprise, and honesty; that many of the heroes of his novels have these qualities in abundance and are also English gentlemen has encouraged some critics to dismiss him as an Anglophile writing for an English audience. In fact he had no small commitment to Australia, where virtually all his work was first published: he recognised the potential of the country and he believed Australians to be the equal of the English in everything save perhaps breeding. Yet equally clearly he looked beyond Australia in his reading, and from Scott he inherited not only a pseudonym but also a literary form. Most of his seventeen novels are romances, some with a pastoral setting, and are characteristically marred by stilted dialogue and selfconscious literariness that plumbs the depths in *A Sealskin Cloak* and *War to the Knife*. 'Boldrewood' wrote best when informed by his experience rather than by his imagination, as in some of the short pieces in *Old Melbourne Memories* and *In Bad Company*, in the strongly autobiographical *The Squatter's Dream*, or in *The Miner's Right*, which is rich in the details of mining life which he saw at first hand at Gulgong. His most enduring work, however, is *Robbery Under Arms*, which is often grouped with *His Natural Life* (1874) and *The Recollections of Geoffry Hamlyn* (1859) as the three classics of colonial Australian fiction. Whether by accident or design, 'Boldrewood' chose as his narrator Dick Marston, a poorly educated colonial worker, who tells in the vernacular the story of his and his family's bushranging past as part of Starlight's (q.v.) gang. The colloquial voice establishes in the novel an authentic tone which is confirmed by the historical foundation for most of the major incidents; other virtues of *Robbery Under Arms* are the pace and tightness of its plot and the vivid realisation of some of its characters. H.M. Green thought Dick Marston 'perhaps the first thoroughly Australian character in fiction'; certainly the contrast between the Marston and Barnes families on the one hand, and the Byronic hero Starlight and the insufferably responsible George Storefield on the other, helps explain the survival of *Robbery Under Arms* alone of 'Boldrewood's' work. The contrast also points to the ambivalence about Australia and England that characterises all his writing. Alan Brissenden edited the UQP collection *Rolf Boldrewood* in 1979 and the earlier 1973 OUP monograph. P.H. McCarthy wrote *Starlight: The Man and the Myth* (1972).

BOLTON, Alec (1926–), born Drummoyne, Sydney, served in the RAN in the latter part of the Second World War. Graduating BA from the University of Sydney, he joined Angus & Robertson where he worked with Beatrice Davis and Rosemary Dobson (q.v.), marrying the latter in 1951. In 1960 he left A&R to work with Ure Smith but returned to A&R to become their London editor in 1966. In 1971 he became director of publications at the National Library of Australia and in 1972 established Brindabella Press as a leisure-time occupation. From the press (which he renamed Officina Brindabella 1985–92 because Brindabella Press had already been registered as a business name) has come a steady stream of impressive publications, e.g. Rosemary Dobson's *Three Poems on Water Springs, Greek Coins: A Sequence of Poems* and *The Continuance of Poetry: Twelve Poems for David Campbell*, James McAuley's *Time Given* and Les Murray's *The Idyll Wheel*. In 1987 Bolton left NLA to operate Brindabella Press (reverting to that title when it became vacant in 1992) full-time. The story of Brindabella Press, with a list of Bolton's publications, is in *A Licence to Print* (1993) in the Friends of the National Library of Australia series, text by Michael Richards.

BOLTON, G.C. (Geoffrey Curgenven) (1931–), born Perth, was professor of history at Murdoch University from 1973 until seconded in 1982 to be first head of the Sir Robert Menzies Centre for Australian Studies in London. Since 1989 he has been professor of Australian history and head of the History Department at the University of Queensland. His many writings include *Alexander Forrest* (1958); *A Thousand Miles Away: A History of North Queensland to 1920* (1963); *Dick Boyer: An Australian Humanist* (1967), the biography of Sir Richard Boyer; *A Fine Country to Starve In* (1972), a re-creation of the 1930s Depression years in WA; and *Spoils and Spoilers: Australians Make Their Environment 1788–1980* (1981), a comprehensive account of the so-called love-hate relationship which Australians have with the land. General editor of the *Oxford History of Australia*, he wrote Volume 5 (1942–88) of that history, thus adding to his reputation as one

of Australia's most accomplished historians. He edited (1991) the first volume of the journals of Archdeacon J.R. Wolleston. He delivered the 1992 Boyer Lectures, *A View from the Edge: An Australian Stocktaking*, an analysis of Australian history that refutes commonly held assertions of anti-authoritarianism and inbuilt inferiority in the national psyche. He is an Officer of the Order of Australia (AO).

BOLTON, Ken (1949–), born Sydney, formerly editor of *Magic Sam* and currently *Otis Rush*, and involved in a small press venture, Little Esther Books, has written numerous books of poetry, both singly and in collaboration. His own works include *Four Poems* (1977), *Blonde & French* (1978), *Christ's Entry into Brussels: Or, Ode to the Three Stooges* (1978), *Two Sestinas* (1980), *Talking To You: Poems 1979–81* (1983), *Notes for Poems* (1984), *Blazing Shoes* (1984), *Two Poems (A Drawing of the Sky)* (1990) and *Sestina to the Centre of the Brain* (1991). With John Jenkins he has written *Airborne Dogs* (1988); *The Ferrara Poems* (1989), a hectic, mostly joyous account of a group of Australian (or Australian-minded) tourists having a riotous vacation in Italy; and *The Gutman Variations* (1992). Bolton's *Selected Poems 1975–1990* appeared in 1992, a summary to that point of his considerable poetic talents and achievements. Some poems are complemented by diary comments and observations that throw light on the creative process itself. He won the Wesley Michel Wright Poetry Prize in 1990.

BOND, Grahame (1943–), born Sydney, graduated in architecture from the University of Sydney but developed a taste for writing satirical sketches for revues. These sketches appeared in such revues as 'Drip Dry Dreams' (1970) and 'Filth' (1971) and the pantomime 'Hamlet on Ice' (1971). He created the bizarre pantomime character Aunty Jack and wrote *The Aunty Jack Show* (1971–72) and *Wollongong the Brave* (1974) for ABC television. He also created 'Flash Nick from Jindavick' (1973) and 'Captain Bloody' (1984), and wrote and performed 'Little Big Show' (an Aunty Jack special) for London Weekend TV in 1978. *Boy's Own McBeth* (written in collaboration with Jim Burnett) was produced in Sydney in 1979 and published in 1980.

BONWICK, James (1817–1906), born Lingfield, England, was educated in London and began a career in teaching in 1833. In 1841, pledged to the Nonconformist and temperance causes, he arrived in Hobart and ran schools in Tasmania until he left for Adelaide in 1850. In 1852 he was briefly on the Victorian goldfields before moving to Melbourne to become proprietor of the Australian *Gold Digger's Monthly Magazine*; after that he was a lecturer, land agent and schools inspector (1856–59) until a coaching accident caused his retirement in 1859. During the 1860s and 1870s he alternated teaching and writing in Australia with periodic visits to England, where he was a lecturer and emigration agent, and in the early 1880s began searching London for source material relating to early Australia. From 1883 to 1902 he was engaged mainly in transcribing documents for several Australian State governments; most of the material is now in the Mitchell Library and formed the basis, insufficiently acknowledged at the time, for the *Historical Records of New South Wales* and the *Historical Records of Australia* (q.v.). After his retirement he completed *An Octogenarian's Reminiscences* (1902). The 'Bonwick Transcripts', as they came to be known, were a huge endeavour which laid the foundation for later documentation and writing of Australian history, but, quite apart from them, Bonwick's output was prodigious. He wrote over sixty works covering a wide range of subjects: history, biography, geography, education (in which he was something of a pioneer in teaching practices), anthropology and fiction. Perhaps the most significant, apart from his autobiography and the emigration novel *The Tasmanian Lily* (1873), were the historical works *Discovery and Settlement of Port Phillip* (1856), *The Bushrangers* (1856), *A Sketch of Boroondara* (1858), *Curious Facts of Old Colonial Days* (1870), *First Twenty Years of Australia* (1882) and *Port Phillip Settlement* (1883); the early biographies of William Buckley (1856) and John Batman (1867); the travel narrative *Western Victoria: Its Geography, Geology, and Social Condition* (1858); three studies of the Tasmanian Aborigines, *Daily Life and Origin of the Tasmanians* (1870), *The Last of the Tasmanians* (1870) and *The Lost Tasmanian Race* (1884); and a significant sketch of colonial newspapers, *Early Struggles of the Australian Press* (1890). The recent reissue of a number of Bonwick volumes is evidence that several remain useful reference works and others interesting specimens of their genres.

BONYTHON Family of SA has had among its prominent members Sir (John) Langdon Bonython (1848–1939), who came to SA as a boy of 6. At 16 he joined the Adelaide *Advertiser* (q.v.) as a reporter; by 1879 he was rich enough from mining speculation to buy a share of the newspaper; by 1893 he was sole proprietor. He edited the *Advertiser* 1884–1929, being 81 years old when he relinquished control and the paper became a public company. In a wide-ranging public and commercial career that made him one of the wealthiest and most influential figures in SA, one event of literary significance was his part in establishing the Commonwealth Literary Fund and his chairmanship of its central committee, 1908–29. His son Sir (John) Lavington Bonython (1875–1960), an eminent figure in civic affairs and in the commercial world of SA, was associated with his father in the family newspaper empire; he also edited the *Saturday Express* 1912–30. Sir Lavington Bonython's third son, Hugh Reskymer (Kym) Bonython, whose autobiography *Ladies' Legs and Lemonade* was published in 1979, established major commercial art galleries first in Adelaide and later in Sydney. E.G. Bonython has published *History of the Families of Bonython* (1966).

Book Collectors' Society of Australia began as an informal group of bibliophiles who gathered every week in the 1940s in Gilmour's Bond Street Bookshop, Sydney. Regular members were Walter Stone, H.F. Chaplin, F. Malcolm, S.L. Lanarch, D.J. Farrell, E.G. Boreham and C.D. Berckelman. In 1944, at the suggestion of Berckelman, the group established a formal society. Walter Stone was an office-bearer of the Society for many years and also edited its journal, *Biblionews and Australian Notes & Queries.*

Book Lover, a monthly literary review, was published by H.H. Champion 1899–1921, although it did not appear between February 1919 and February 1920. The magazine carried creative literature, chiefly poetry, together with book reviews, literary commentaries and reports of the activities of the Melbourne Literary Club and the Melbourne Repertory Society. A notable event was its publication in December 1916 of 'Furnley Maurice's' poem 'To God: From the Weary Nations'.

Book of the Bush, The (?1898), by George Dunderdale and illustrated by J. Macfarlane, contains, as its subtitle indicates, 'many truthful sketches of the early colonial life of squatters, whalers, convicts, diggers, and others who left their native land and never returned'. The most remarkable of Dunderdale's stories is that of a Scotsman, Macdonnell of Glengarry, who tries to set up a fiefdom in the remote bush and is known throughout the country as 'Lord Glengarry'.

'Book Show, The', presented as a half-hour weekly show on SBS television by the late Dinny O'Hearn and Andrea Stretton, began in 1988 and, unlike several similar short-lived programmes on ABC television, has (to 1993) survived. Interviews are screened with both Australian and overseas writers. O'Hearn, who died in 1993, is commemorated by an award in the *Age* Literary Awards; John Tranter (q.v.) won the first award with *At the Florida.*

Bookfellow, planned as early as 1895 by A.G. Stephens (q.v.) as a magazine in which the literary contents of the Red Page could be elaborated, appeared monthly, January–May 1899 under the auspices of the *Bulletin;* thereafter until 1906 it was incorporated in the Red Page. In 1907 Stephens, having left the *Bulletin,* briefly revived the *Bookfellow* as a separate weekly, but it lapsed when he became leader-writer for the *Evening Post* in Wellington, NZ. Back in Australia in 1909, he revived the *Bookfellow* (1911), which led a precarious monthly existence until 1925, apart from the period March 1916 to November 1919, when it was suspended because of the war. In addition to being the leading, and sometimes the only, purely literary magazine of the period, the *Bookfellow* consistently encouraged the Australian book trade, carrying many booksellers' and publishers' advertisements. In its pages was published a wide variety of Australian poetry, together with some of the best literary comment of the day. Under its imprint Stephens published volumes of verse by C.H. Souter, James Hebblethwaite, John Shaw Neilson and others.

Bookman of the Year Award was awarded by the National Book Council 1974–79 to a person who had made a substantial contribution to the promotion of books. Winners were printer and publisher, Bob Cudgley (1974); editor, author, printer and publisher, Walter Stone (1975); publisher's editor Beatrice Davis (1976); bookseller Cedric Pearce (1977); booksellers Marcie and Harry Muir (1978); editor, librarian and bibliophile Austin McCallum (1979).

Books for Comment, scripts of an ABC series of radio talks on Australian and overseas books, ran August 1963 to December 1969. Reviewers included contemporary writers and critics, e.g. Flexmore Hudson, Cecil Hadgraft, George Farwell and Leonie Kramer. Similar earlier series were *Current Books Worth Reading* (irregularly 1941–55), *Todays Books* (October 1956–63) and *Todays Writing* (August 1963 to January 1964). A.D. Hope and Vance Palmer were regular contributors to the earlier series.

Boomerang (1887–92) was a radical Brisbane weekly founded by William Lane and Alfred Walker; after Lane's departure at the end of 1890 it was edited by Gresley Lukin. Two notable staff members were Henry Lawson, who wrote 'Country Crumbs', a summary of news from the provincial press, and A.G. Stephens. Lawson's attitude towards his retrenchment from the *Boomerang* is recorded in his poem 'The Shame of Going Back'. The demise of the *Boomerang* is often thought to have inspired 'The Cambaroora Star' (q.v.), but although Lawson called his poem 'the *Boomerang's* own epitaph' he linked 'The Cambaroora Star' more firmly with the *Republican* (q.v.). There were several earlier, less significant journals called the *Boomerang* (Melbourne, 1861 and 1894; Sydney, 1877).

BOOTE, H.E. (Henry Ernest) (1865–1949), born Liverpool, England, became apprenticed to a printer after leaving school at the age of 10, and emigrated to Australia in 1889. He soon became involved in the emerging labour movement and edited the *Bundaberg Guardian* (1894–96), the *Gympie Truth* (1896–1902) and the Brisbane *Worker* (1902–11), the last for the Australian Labour Federation, a trade union organisation. In 1911 he moved to Sydney to join the *Australian Worker*, which he edited 1914–43, exercising considerable influence in the labour movement. Active in artistic, music, library and literary circles, Boote wrote four volumes of verse, two works of fiction, two books of essays selected from his newspaper articles, and numerous political pamphlets; of these the most important are his essays *A Fool's Talk on Various Subjects* (1915) and *Tea with the Devil and Other Diversions* (1928); the political novel *The Human Ladder* (1920); and the satiric allegory *The Land of Wherisit* (1919).

BOOTHBY, Guy (1867–1905), born Adelaide and educated in Australia and England, became private secretary to the mayor of Adelaide before returning to live in England in 1894. He became a highly successful novelist creating a magician character, Dr Nikola, around whom he wove a popular fictional series. Australian settings are frequently used in his fiction,

mainly to add colour to his exciting romance and adventure stories. Between 1894 and 1907 about fifty books of fiction by Boothby were published; of them *In Strange Company* (1894), *A Lost Endeavour* (1895), *The Marriage of Esther* (1895), *Sheilah McLeod: A Heroine of the Backblocks* (1897), *The Curse of the Snake* (1902), *Connie Burt* (1903) and *The Race of Life* (1906) have significant Australian connection. Boothby's travels in Australia before his return to England are recorded in *On the Wallaby: Or, Through the East and Across Australia* (1894). Paul Depasquale wrote *Guy Boothby: His Life and Work* (1982), and *Guy Boothby: The Science Fiction Connection* (1985).

BORCHARDT, D.H. (Dietrich Hans) (1916–), born Hanover, Germany, went in 1939 to NZ, where he was a university librarian. He moved to the University of Tasmania in 1950 as deputy librarian and was later librarian (1953–64). From 1965 until his retirement in 1981, he was chief librarian at La Trobe University, the main library of which was named after him. A compiler of many bibliographical works and check-lists, Borchardt published *Australian Bibliography: A Guide to Printed Sources of Information* (1963, with subsequent editions 1966, 1976 and 1979), and edited, with Victor Crittenden, *Australians, A Guide to Sources* (1987) and, with Wallace Kirsop, *The Book in Australia* (1988). He was foundation editor of the professional journal *Australian Academic and Research Libraries* 1970–84. Since 1987 he has edited *Reference Australia*, an occasional series of essays on sources for Australian Studies. In 1979 he received the H.C.L. Anderson medal and was made AM in 1982. *Australian Academic Libraries in the Seventies*, edited by Harrison Bryan and John Horacek (1984), was published in his honour.

BORG, Sonia (1931–), also known as Sonia Fankhanel, was born in Vienna, Austria, and has been an actor, scriptwriter, script editor and associate producer for cinema and television in Australia since 1962. As scriptwriter for Crawford Productions she was involved in the beginnings of Australian television drama. Her screenplays include *Storm Boy* (1976), for which she received a Penguin Award, and *Blue Fin* (1979); her television dramas include episodes of *Rush*, *Homicide*, *Division 4* and *Matlock*, and adaptations of *Power Without Glory* and *I Can Jump Puddles*, as well as the play *Alinta*, which also won a Penguin Award, and *Ratbag Hero*. In 1982 she collaborated with Hyllus Maris in *Women of the Sun* (q.v.), a television series about the Aborigines. She is a Member of the Order of Australia (AM).

Borker, Billy is the humorous 'bar-fly' and spinner of tall yarns in three collections written by Frank Hardy (q.v.). The yarns formed a popular television series in 1964.

BOSI, Pino (1933–), born Italy of an Italian father and an Austrian mother, arrived in Australia in 1951. He worked at a variety of occupations before taking a position with the paper *La Fiamma* in Sydney. He has continued to work for the Italo-Australian press, becoming editor of *Il Globo* and *Settegiorni* and founding and editing the magazine *Australia Ieri Oggi Domani*, published since 1984. He has also worked in radio and television and associated ethnic organisations both as a reporter and administrator. A Knight Commander of the Italian Republic, he has been made AM and has won several international awards for his writing. He has published extensively in both Italian and English, his English publications including *The Checkmate and Other Stories* (1973); the verse collections, *I'll Say Good Morning* (1974) and *Thirteen Continents and a Rocket-Magi Lost* (1988); the biography *Blood Sweat and Guts* (1971); the autobiography *Farewell Australia* (1972); the socio-historical studies *Who is Afraid of the Ethnic Wolf* (1986) and *On God's Command: Italian Missionaries in Australia* (1989), and the children's book *Peoples of Australia: the Italians* (1983). His writing in Italian includes a novel, *Australia Cane* (1971), dealing with the experiences of an Italian immigrant in Australia in the 1950s.

BOSTOCK, Gerald (1942–), born Grafton, NSW, was a seasonal worker before joining the army and serving in Malaya and Borneo. After leaving the army he became interested in the history and welfare of his Aboriginal people. In 1972 he helped establish the Black Theatre in Sydney and has since been involved in various aspects of drama and film production. His important play 'Here Comes the Nigger' (q.v.) was performed in Sydney in 1976. He has also published poetry, *Black Man Coming* (1980, see Aboriginal Writing/Testimony in English), and co-produced, with Alex Morgan, the film *Lousy Little Sixpence* (1983), a documentary about the lives of the Aboriginal people in NSW in the early part of this century. The film's title comes from the amount that an Aboriginal girl house-servant was entitled to receive as her week's wages from the White family for whom she worked. His poem 'Black Children' became a catchcry of the Aboriginal political movement.

BOSWELL, Annabella (1826–1916), born Annabella Innes, at Bathurst, lived in several parts of NSW. After her father's death she moved with her mother and sister in 1843 to Port Macquarie and Lake Innes House, the home of her uncle, Major Archibald C. Innes, the police magistrate for the area. She married Patrick Boswell in 1856 and moved to Scotland in 1864 but always retained warm memories of her early years in Australia, publishing two collections of reminiscences, *Some Recollections of My Early Days Written at Different Periods* (1908), and *Further Recollections of My Early Days in Australia* (1911). Revealing accounts of domestic life in early Australia, they give a particularly attractive picture of life at Lake Innes. *Annabella Boswell's Journal*, edited by Morton Herman, and first published in 1965, is an abridged version of her first publication, focusing on Boswell's descriptions of the house at Lake Innes. *Further Recollections of My Early Days in Australia* was republished by Mulini Press in 1992, titled *Annabella Boswell's Other Journal 1848–1851*.

Botany Bay, an inlet on the eastern coast of Australia just south of Sydney, was the site of the first landing by Captain James Cook 29 April 1770; originally Stingray Bay, it was renamed because of the profusion of botanical specimens collected there by Sir Joseph Banks and his assistants. Botany Bay figured on the London stage even before the arrival of the First Fleet, and although in January 1788 Governor Phillip found Botany Bay unsuitable for settlement and moved the First Fleet to Port Jackson (Sydney Harbour), Botany Bay became, particularly in the nineteenth century, a term referring to the penal colony of NSW in particular, as in the folk-song 'Botany Bay' (q.v.), and to the Australian colonies in general, as in the title of John Lang's collection of stories, *Botany Bay* (1859), in many cartoons, and later in Mary Gilmore's poem 'Old Botany Bay'. A number of related phrases derived from 'Botany Bay', including 'Botany Bay Dozen' (a punishment of twenty-five lashes), 'Botany Bay Disease' (insanity, from its prevalence among prominent early colonists of NSW) and 'Botany Bay Rothschild' (Samuel Terry, an early colonial capitalist). Barron Field's poem 'Botany Bay Flowers' was included in his *First Fruits of Australian Poetry* (1819).

'Botany Bay' is, along with 'Click Go the Shears' and 'The Wild Colonial Boy', one of the most popular Australian folk-songs. Several songs bearing the title 'Botany Bay' have survived; the best-known one (which begins 'Farewell to Old England for ever') is the lament of a male convict who has been transported to Botany Bay, although the warning embodied in the text is made less sombre by the jauntiness of the melody. The words in this version of 'Botany Bay' owe much to an early nineteenth-century English broadside about transportation, 'Farewell to Judges and Juries', but the song derives directly from a comic song in the burlesque drama *Little Jack Shepherd* which was performed in London in 1885 and in Melbourne a year later. The origins of the song are discussed in Hugh Anderson's *Farewell to Old England* (1964).

BOULT, Jenny (1951–), born England, came to Australia in 1966. Co-editor with Kate Veitch of *Pearls: Writing by South Australian Women* (1979–80), and *After the Rage* with Tess Brady (1983), she has published several volumes of verse: *The Hotel Anonymous* (1980), *Handbaggery* (1982), *The White Rose and the Bath* (1984) and *Flight 39* (1986), and a play, *Can't Help Dreaming* (1981). *The Hotel Anonymous* shared the Anne Elder Poetry Award for 1981. *'I' is a versatile character* (1986), her first book of prose, contains several impressive stories e.g., 'no room at the top' and the title story. Boult has had wide experience in readings in schools, prisons, nursing homes and with community groups.

BOURAS, Gillian (1945–), born Melbourne, has worked as a schoolteacher in Melbourne and as a teacher of English as a second language. In 1980 she went to live in Greece with her Greek husband and has written two autobiographical accounts of her experience there, *A Foreign Wife* (1986) and *A Fair Exchange* (1991).

Bourke, one of the chief towns of north-western NSW, is situated on the Darling River. The Bourke region was explored by Charles Sturt in 1829 and in 1835 Thomas Mitchell erected a stockade which he named Fort Bourke (after Sir Richard Bourke, then governor of NSW) as a protection against the Aborigines. The present township was laid out in 1862 about 11 kilometres south-west of Mitchell's fort. Bourke has legendary associations with the outback. Henry Lawson set out from Bourke in 1892 on his tramp around the outback, an experience that led to a number of his best-known stories and poems. Stories like 'Send Round the Hat' and the poem 'Bourke' emphasise how central to Lawson's perception of mateship and outback life were his experiences at the back o' Bourke. The phrase 'Back o' Bourke', indicating extreme remoteness, occurs in Will Ogilvie's poem 'At the Back o' Bourke', which concludes nostalgically,

> It's the bitterest land of sweat and sorrow
> But if I were free I'd be off tomorrow
> Out at the Back o' Bourke.

The phrase, still in general use, occurs also in Alexander Buzo's play *The Front Room Boys* (1970). Noted folklorist Bill Wannan published *Tales from Back o' Bourke* (1957). Bourke has also lent its name to other picturesque phrases, e.g. a 'Bourke shower' which indicates not a welcome shower of rain but a dust storm.

BOURKE, John Philip ('Bluebush') (1860–1914), born Peel River diggings, NSW, was a schoolteacher who turned gold-digger who in 1894 went off to the WA diggings. Under the pseudonym 'Bluebush' he wrote ballads and lyric poems that were published in such WA newspapers as the Kalgoorlie *Sun* and the Perth *Sunday Times*. One of a group of popular versifiers writing in the west in the 1890s and at the turn of the century – others were E.G. Murphy ('Dryblower'), Julian Stuart ('Saladin') and Francis Ophel ('Prospect Good') – Bourke recorded, with vigour and realism, experiences in the outback and in the mines. His poems were collected into a volume, *Off the Bluebush: Verses for Australians, West and East*, edited by A.G. Stephens in 1915; Stephens had already, in a *Bulletin* review, 'The Manly Poetry of Western Australia' (1910), praised Bourke and his contemporaries for writing 'the most virile' poetry in Australia at the time.

BOWEN, Stella (1895–1947), born Adelaide, received some training in art by studying with Margaret Preston before leaving for England in 1914. She enrolled at the Westminster School of Art, where she was taught by Walter Sickert. In London she became friendly with numerous writers including Ezra Pound, T.S. Eliot, Arthur Waley, W.B. Yeats and Ford Madox Ford. She lived with Ford for nine years from 1919, at first in Sussex and then in France. Their daughter, Esther Julia Madox, was born in 1920. In Paris, where they were friendly with such writers as Hemingway, Pound, Joyce and Stein, Ford began the *Transatlantic review* and Bowen painted landscapes, still life and portraits on commission. After the collapse of her relationship with Ford, she had a successful visit to the United States in 1932 but found living in Paris economically impossible and was forced to return to London where she wrote art reviews for the *News Chronicle* and taught students. She maintained her portrait painting, completing portraits of many well-known writers and individuals during the course of her life. Appointed the second woman war artist by the Australian government in 1944, she made numerous paintings and drawings of RAAF bomber crews based in England. After the war she was keen to return to Australia but was denied both pension and rehabilitation rights and passage on a troopship. Her autobiography, *Drawn From Life* (1941), is a revealing account of the difficulties faced by the woman artist and contrasts her unusual experiences as a member of the literary and artistic world of Paris in the 1920s and 1930s with her conventional childhood in Adelaide.

ROSLYN PESMAN COOPER

Bowyang is a piece of string or a strap tied around the trouser leg below the knee to allow freedom of movement, to prevent the bottom of the trouser from dragging, or to keep the full weight of the trouser off the belt or braces. Bowyangs were popular on the goldfields and among selectors in the second half of the nineteenth century; the term was thought to have derived from the two words 'bowie' and 'Yankee' (American miners on the diggings often wore a bowie knife strapped to their legs), although the derivation accepted now is from the English dialect word 'bowy-yanks' for the leather leggings worn by agricultural labourers. Bowyangs are seldom now worn in Australia, but the term has survived in twentieth-century Australian English, usually to indicate rustic naivety. This usage probably derived from C.J. Dennis's 'Letters from the Bush', a series of misspelt letters in the Melbourne *Herald* purporting to be written by the 'Dad and Dave' farmer Ben Bowyang to his son in the city; 'Ben Bowyang' subsequently became a popular comic strip (sometimes known as 'Gunn's Gully'), which was drawn by Daryl Lindsay, Alex Gurney and others. The connection between bowyangs and rural life was consolidated by the recitation booklets brought out by 'Bill Bowyang' in the 1930s, although the contemporary journal *Bowyang* (1979–) is more general in focus and publishes articles on politics, history, literature, art and other subjects.

Boy in the Bush, The (1924), a novel written by D.H. Lawrence and Mollie Skinner (qq.v.) in collaboration, recounts the adventures of Jack Grant, a young English immigrant who establishes a life for himself on the land in the WA outback in the 1880s. Lawrence, who met Mollie Skinner while he was in Australia in 1922, took her unpublished novel 'The House of Ellis', transformed it ('the only thing was to write it all out again, following your MS almost exactly, but giving a unity, a rhythm, and a little more psychic development than you have done'), and had it published. In particular, he dramatically modified the character of Jack and totally altered the last two chapters. Accounts of the collaboration are given in Frieda Lawrence's autobiography *Not I, But the Wind* (1935), in Mollie Skinner's autobiography *The Fifth Sparrow* (1972) and in the critical edition of the novel edited by Paul Eggert (1990) in the Cambridge Edition of Lawrence's Letters and Works.

BOYD, A.J. (William Alexander Jenyns) (1842–1928), born in France of Scottish parents, came to Australia in 1860 and took up a small selection at Oxley Creek in southern Queensland. From 1866 to 1897 Boyd was mainly a farmer and schoolteacher; he then became editor of the *Queensland Agricultural Journal*, a position he held for the next twenty-five years. Boyd's minor publications included *Queensland* (1882), an immigration handbook; *The Earth's History for Boys* (1889), a poetic *aide-memoire* for schoolboys studying geology; and *Some Fragments of Old Sydney* (1898). His major work was *Old Colonials* (1882), a collection of shrewd observations of life in northern Queensland in the latter half of the nineteenth century. *Old Colonials* contains thirty-five anecdotal sketches; some describe familiar bush characters such as the stockman, the shepherd, the drover, the cockatoo farmer and the swagman; others offer insight into contemporary events such as the gold discoveries, into contentious issues such as the presence of the Chinese on the diggings, and into the relationships between the White settlers and the Aborigines. Many of the sketches had appeared under Boyd's pseudonym 'Old Chum' in the *Queenslander* in 1875–76.

BOYD, Arthur (1920–), the son of the potter and sculptor Merric Boyd and a nephew of the novelist Martin Boyd, was born at Murrumbeena, Victoria. He studied at the National Gallery School in Melbourne but was chiefly taught by his parents and grandfather, Arthur Merric Boyd. In the pre-war years he painted numerous landscapes, but by 1941 was producing his first distinctive figurative works. Closely associated with Sidney Nolan, Albert Tucker and John Perceval, he was greatly influenced by the ideas of John Reed (q.v.). Boyd's first retrospective exhibition was held in Sydney in 1950 and in the same year he visited Central Australia, which resulted in his famous 'Love, Marriage and Death of a Half-Caste' series. He has since drawn on biblical stories, Aboriginal ballads, Shakespearean drama, the Australian landscape and religious legend. He lived in London 1959–78, establishing an international reputation as painter, ceramicist and theatrical set designer, but returned to Australia in 1978 to live near the Shoalhaven River in NSW. Boyd has collaborated with the poet Peter Porter in several works including *Jonah* (1973), *The Lady and the Unicorn* (1975), and *Mars* (1989), and has illustrated a collection of poetry by A.D. Hope, *The Drifting Continent* (1979). Boyd received the Britannica Australia Award in 1979, was made OBE in 1970 and AO in 1979. In 1993 he donated his property on the Shoalhaven to the nation as a centre for the visual and performing arts.

BOYD, Benjamin (?1803–51), born London, became a stockbroker and successful businessman. Convinced that the use of steamships on regular coastal runs would be both profitable to himself and of benefit to the Australian colonies, he sought in 1840 the use of numerous harbours on the Australian coast and the right to buy land adjacent to them. He arrived at Port Jackson in his schooner, *Wanderer*, in July 1842, having been preceded by four steamships carrying the supplies for his operations. His coastal steamers were soon engaged on regular schedules to Twofold Bay on the NSW south coast and to Hobart Town. Within a few years Boyd and his business associates controlled or owned more than three million acres in the Port Phillip, Monaro and Riverina areas. Twofold Bay became established as the port through which the agricultural and pastoral products of the Monaro district were shipped to Sydney, and Boyd Town, of which some buildings still exist, became its township; at East Boyd a whaling station was established. Boyd, having overreached himself financially, unsuccessfully sought to repair his fortunes on the Californian goldfields. In 1851 he set out in *Wanderer* to cruise the Pacific and establish, if the opportunity arose, a 'Papuan Republic or Confederation'. In October 1851 at Guadalcanal in the Solomon Islands he went ashore to shoot game and was never seen again. The captain of the *Oberon*, one of the two ships sent to search for Boyd in 1854, returned with a skull which was finally proved to be that of a native. An account of Boyd and his varied activities is given in Francis Webb's poem *A Drum for Ben Boyd* (q.v., 1948). He is also mentioned in Hugh McCrae's edition of *Georgiana's Journal* (1934). J. Webster published *The Last Cruise of the 'Wanderer'* (?1863) and H.P Wellings wrote *Benjamin Boyd in Australia, 1842–1849* (1936). Marion Diamond wrote the biography *The Sea Horse and the Wanderer: Ben Boyd in Australia* (1988).

BOYD Family has a distinguished history in the arts both in Australia and Europe. The family was founded in Australia by Captain John Theodore Boyd (1825–91), military secretary to an early governor of Victoria, who migrated from Ireland in 1860 and had earlier eloped with Lucy Martin, an heiress of Spanish ancestry. One of their sons, Arthur Merric Boyd (1862–1940), became well known as a painter, mainly in watercolour, and three of the children of Arthur Merric Boyd's marriage to Emma Minnie à Beckett (1858–1936) (also a talented painter and granddaughter of Sir William à Beckett, q.v.) had distinguished careers. They were the potter (William) Merric Boyd (1888–1959), the landscape artist (Theodore) Penleigh Boyd (1890–1923) and the novelist Martin Boyd (q.v.). Merric's children are all recognised artists; his sons are the painter Arthur Boyd (q.v., 1920–), sculptor Guy Boyd (1923–88) and potter and painter David Boyd (1925–), and his daughters are painter and potter Lucy Beck (1915–) and Mary Nolan (1926–), formerly Perceval, who is a painter and a photographer.

Many of Merric Boyd's grandchildren are also established artists, such as Arthur's children Polly, Jamie and Lucy Ellen, painters; Lucy's son Robert Beck, a potter; Guy's daughter Lenore, a sculptor and potter; David's daughters Amanda, Lucinda and Cassandra, painters; and Mary's children Matthew and Celia Perceval, who are painters. Robin Boyd's son Penleigh is an architect. Patricia Dobrez and Peter Herbst compiled *The Art of the Boyds: Generations of Artistic Achievement* (1991).

BOYD, Martin (1893–1972) was born in Lucerne, Switzerland, but his early years were spent in Victoria. The Boyd family (q.v.), a distinguished one with a long history in Australia and roots in England, Ireland and Spain, has in the past conferred on its members an inheritance which transcends country and owes as much to European cultural tradition as to Australia. In Martin Boyd's fiction this inheritance was to emerge in an independence of thought and aristocratic, anti-bourgeois values, a strong sense of the past and tradition, an interest in heredity, and a complex, dual allegiance to Australia and Europe. In response to an interest in 'poetic religion', Boyd first studied theology but later turned to architecture. In the First World War he joined an English regiment and served in France 1915–18, first in the infantry and then in the flying corps. The experience had a permanent effect on his attitudes to war and Britain's governing classes, determining his anti-authoritarianism and commitment to a 'qualified pacifism'. His privately published verse collection *Retrospect* (1920) expresses his post-war restlessness and alienation. After a stay in Australia he returned to Europe in 1921, where he did some newspaper work, made another unsuccessful attempt at a religious vocation by joining a Franciscan community in the Church of England, and began his career as a fiction-writer. His first three novels, *Love Gods* (1925), *Brangane: A Memoir* (1926) and *The Montforts* (1928), appeared under a pseudonym, 'Martin Mills'. They were followed by *Dearest Idol* (1929, under the pseudonym 'Walter Beckett'), *Scandal of Spring* (1934), *The Lemon Farm* (1935), *The Painted Princess* (1936), *The Picnic* (1937), *Night of the Party* (1938), *Nuns in Jeopardy* (1940), *Lucinda Brayford* (q.v., 1946), and *Such Pleasure* (1949). In 1948 he returned to Australia to restore his grandfather's house near Berwick but ill health and other difficulties intervened and he left for England in 1951, finally settling in Rome in 1957. There he completed his best-known work, the series of novels now referred to as the Langton tetralogy: *The Cardboard Crown* (1952), *A Difficult Young Man* (1955), *Outbreak of Love* (1957) and *When Blackbirds Sing* (1962) (qq.v.). His other works include a lighter novel, *The Tea-Time of Love* (1969); two autobiographies, *A Single Flame* (1939) and *Day of My Delight* (1965); and a 'subjective travel book', *Much Else in Italy* (1958). A week before his death in Rome after a long illness he was received into the Roman Catholic Church.

Boyd's first major work was *The Montforts*, winner of the first Australian Literature Society's Gold Medal and an ambitious attempt to chronicle the history of his mother's family in Victoria from the 1850s to the end of the First World War. The novel's emphasis on heredity, the reflection of social change, the ironically detached juxtaposition of English and Australian attitudes as well as some characters and incidents, anticipate his later works. In his next five novels, which are lighter works, he turns away from his Australian experience. *Nuns in Jeopardy*, which approaches religious allegory with its typed characters and metaphysical theme, is in form an anomaly in his fiction, although characteristic in its preoccupation with the nature of man and the place of evil. *Lucinda Brayford*, which made a strong impression overseas, returns to his family's history but in a more leisurely and expansive manner. Although the novel is interesting as social history, Boyd's main concern is with the individual and the possibility of spiritual fulfilment. Lucinda, who is the novel's focus (although the destiny of her son Stephen dominates in the latter part), embodies Boyd's conception of the aristocratic principle in her natural pleasure-seeking response to life and beauty. The four movements of the novel which trace the consecutive stages of Lucinda's outward tragic defeat by circumstance, also describe her spiritual growth and final victory. Contrasting with Lucinda and the saintly Stephen is a diverse array of individuals, many of whom have lost touch with real civilisation in their pursuit of power, money or position.

Boyd's most striking achievement is the Langton tetralogy in which he again takes up the Australian material, although now more obviously influenced by his renewed contact with the Graeco-Christian tradition in Italy. The subject of the four novels is the history of the Langton family over more than eighty years, narrated mainly by one of its mature members, Guy Langton, and illuminated by the lives of three main characters: Alice, Guy's grandmother; Diana, his aunt; and Dominic, his brother. Guy is involved as both narrator and character; his birth is a determining event in *The Cardboard Crown*, although most of the action occurs before it; *A Difficult Young Man* spans his childhood and youth, and he is a self-preoccupied young man in *Outbreak of Love*. In the first two novels particularly, this narrative perspective contributes to the complexity of Boyd's re-creation of the past. The external destinies of Alice in *The Cardboard Crown* and Diana in *Outbreak of Love* reflect the processes of disintegration within the family as new bourgeois, materialist forces make themselves felt. Nevertheless both women remain exceptional figures of steadfast integrity. Dominic, the troubled young man who is the subject of *A Difficult Young Man* and *When Blackbirds Sing*, reflects even more acutely the disparity between personal and social morality. Boyd sees all three central characters as aristocrats, in that they try to live by natural, inner ideals rather than by external valuations. Contrasting with them are individuals like Aunt Baba, Cousin Sarah and Colonel Rodgers who follow only the dictates of their misguided society, whether English or Australian. The detached social satire of Boyd's representation of Australian and English life before 1914, his evocation of place and of time passing are generally admired, although his narrowness of social range has also been criticised.

Boyd's remaining non-fiction works illuminate his preoccupations and fictional method. *Much Else in Italy* develops his religious and aesthetic ideas in a lively and idiosyncratic manner. His two autobiographies are remarkably similar and demonstrate his fiction's dependence on fact. Both reveal Boyd as a religious man without a calling, a lover of order who disliked institutionalised authority and an admirer of the aristocratic way who rejected the Establishment of his day. Brenda Niall's *Martin Boyd, A Life* (1988) is a substantial biography, preceded by her extensive bibliography *Martin Boyd* (1977).

BOYD, Robin (1919–71), born Melbourne, became a leading figure in Australian architecture as professional practitioner, writer, critic and lecturer. During his distinguished career he was awarded the Gold Medal of the Royal Australian Institute of Architects (1969) and the honorary degree of D.Litt. from the University of New England (1967); he was made CBE in 1971. He published twelve books, the most important of which were *Australia's Home* (1952), *The Australian Ugliness* (1960), *The Walls Around Us* (1962) and *Living in Australia* (1970).

Boyer Lectures were inaugurated in 1959 under the title ABC Lectures, but the series was renamed the Boyer Lectures in 1961 as a memorial to Sir Richard Boyer who, as chairman of the ABC, had been largely responsible for the introduction of the original series. Since 1959 the ABC has each year invited a prominent Australian to present the results of his work and thinking on major social, scientific or cultural issues in a series of radio talks; these talks are published by the ABC. The series includes Robin Boyd's *Artificial Australia* (1967), W.E.H. Stanner's *After the Dreaming: Black and White Australians – An Anthropologist's View* (1968), Sir Keith Hancock's *Today, Yesterday and Tomorrow* (1973), C.H. Manning Clark's *A Discovery of Australia* (1976), Douglas Stewart's *Writers of the Bulletin* (1977), Bernard Smith's *The Spectre of Truganini* (1980), M.D. Kirby's *The Judges* (1983), Shirley Hazzard's *Coming of Age in Australia* (1984), Helen Hughes's *Australia in a Developing World* (1985), T.M. Fitzgerald's *Between Life and Economics* (1990), Fay Gale's *Changing Australia* (1991), and Geoffrey Bolton's *A View from the Edge: An Australian Stocktaking* (1992). In 1993 seven Aborigines – Mandaway Yunupingu, Dot West, Ian Anderson, Getano Lui Jnr, Helen Corbett, Jeanie Bell and Noel Pearson, each gave a lecture.

BOYES, George Thomas William Blamey (1786–1853), born Portsea, England, had an unsettled youth and irregular education which he supplemented by voracious reading and study of science and the arts. In 1809 he joined the Commissariat Department of the army and from 1810 to 1815 served under Wellington in the Peninsular war. He married Mary Ediss in 1818 and in 1823 travelled alone to Sydney, after his financial affairs collapsed and he was forced to accept an appointment as assistant-commissary general in NSW. In November 1826 when the commissariat in Van Diemen's Land was separated from that of NSW, Boyes was transferred to Hobart Town, where he was appointed auditor of civil accounts. In Australia he cultivated his gift for painting and established a career as a dedicated public servant. In 1832 he returned to England to reclaim his family, returning to Hobart Town in 1834. In 1842–43 he acted as colonial secretary following the dismissal of John Montagu. A keen observer of society, and occasionally described as an Australian Pepys, Boyes committed his private, often satirical thoughts to his extensive journal and letters to his wife. Peter Chapman has edited the first volume of his diaries and letters 1820–32 (1985).

Boys in the Island, The, a novel by Christopher Koch (q.v.), was published in 1958 (revised 1974). Set mainly in Tasmania, it deals with the childhood and adolescence of a boy, Francis Cullen. From the age of 6 the boy has a dream of a 'web of horizons', of a paradisal future that will somehow enlarge his being. He pursues the dream through his experiences at school, through his relationship with his larrikin mates Lewie Mathews and Jake Brodie, and through his love affair with a country girl, Heather Miles. After this last relationship crumbles he responds to the lure of Melbourne, whence Lewie and Jake have already gravitated. Their anarchic life in the city culminates in a car crash after a three-day drinking bout. One man is killed, Francis is injured and returns to Tasmania having finally abandoned his dream. Another friend, Shane Noonan, who also runs away to Melbourne with similar aspirations, commits suicide rather than face the death of his romantic vision.

Boys Who Stole the Funeral, The (1980) by Les Murray (q.v.) is subtitled 'a novel sequence' and has been variously described by Murray as 'a novel in poetry', 'a verse play' and 'a verse movie . . . because of its filmic construction'. Essentially it is a narrative in verse made up of 140 separate sonnets, some formal Petrarchan, others irregular in form and structure; some serious, even portentous in tone, others ironic, even tongue-in-cheek. The narrative tells how two young city men, Kevin Stace Forbutt, 'unemployed for speaking proudly under pressure', and former university student, Cameron Reeby, 'nicknamed Ratchet, for his prospects', steal the body of Kevin's great-uncle, Clarrie Dunn, from a city funeral parlour and take it by car for burial to the isolated farming community of Dark's Plain on the north coast of NSW where Clarrie was born. Throughout the drive north and later in 'Dunn's country', snatches of conversations and flashbacks reveal many facets of the characters' lives and attitudes: Cameron Reeby's violent altercation with feminists at the university and his later fracas with one of them, Noeline Kampff; Clarrie Dunn's nostalgia for his birthplace; the unbridgeable gap in attitudes and values between the Bush and City, exemplified by the contrast between Kevin and his father, Stacey Forbutt; Stacey's infidelity to Kevin's mother, which the son has discovered; Kevin's dissatisfaction with city life ('Sydney? It's a building site now') and his yearning for a meaningful life and occupation, 'not just employment'. After they arrive at the farm of Athol Dunn, Clarrie's nephew, the corpse is placed in the smokehouse ('he'll be on the turn tonight') then prepared ('rock salt and bagging needles and sheets') for the burial. Organisation of the funeral passes to the matter-of-fact ('It must not be let grow dramatic') postmistress Beryl Murchison, and the district, now accessory to the fact, seethes with a conspiratorial sense of community. As the funeral ceremony ends the police arrive and the two funeral-stealers escape into the bush. They hide out in a shack on the postmistress's farm and take a job driving a truck loaded with beef for illegal sale in Newcastle. Cameron Reeby is shot and killed by a policeman who stops their meat run and recognises them as the funeral-stealers. Kevin wanders into the bush and, dazed with shock and grief at his mate's death, falls into a coma. He is confronted by a vision of two figures from Aboriginal legend, Njimbin and Birroogun, the latter's name varying from the pure Aboriginal to the Irish-Australian 'Berrigan', illustrating the blend of both Black and White in early Australia. Kevin is put through a series of initiations and instructions and (in echoes of Aboriginal ritual) his soul is renewed by the 'crystal of Crystals'. He listens to 'the blood-history of the continent' and eats from the Common Dish carried by the spirit of Clarrie Dunn. Kevin is free to choose whether he eats or not from this dish but he is not free (nor is anyone) to merely taste in theory the 'work, agony, laughter' in it. It has to be 'body and soul'. As Kevin eats, his reaction deepens: 'It's – ordinary. It's – subtle. It is – serious.' He wakes from the coma with the vision's final injunction in his mind:

> 'Go back now, find your true work,
> Now you can be trusted with it.
> Go back. Keep faith with the battlers' food'.

Kevin, reborn after the vision, and again a part of the bush-inspired masculine world that is at the heart of Australia's nationalist democratic legend, makes his life with the rural 'battlers' of Dark's Plain on a part of Beryl Murchison's farm that was to have been Clarrie Dunn's. Cameron had been destroyed because he had never completely freed himself from the values of the city. *The Boys Who Stole the Funeral* is notable for its absorbing narrative, intricate symbolism, and innovatory technique. It expresses Murray's admiration for the mores and values of both legendary rural Australia and earlier Aboriginal culture.

BOZIC, Sreten, see **'WONGAR, B.'**

BRADDON, Russell (1921–), born Sydney, was posted to Singapore in 1942 with the Australian Army shortly after graduating from the University of Sydney. For four years he was a prisoner of the Japanese in Changi and on the notorious Burma–Thailand railway. He vividly describes his experiences in his controversial best-selling book, *The Naked Island* (1952); rewritten later as a three-act play (published in 1961), *The Naked Island* was produced in Australia and Britain. *End of a Hate* (1958) describes some of Brad-

don's experiences after his release from Changi and his initiation into the profession of writing via scriptwriting for a friend's (Piddington's) telepathic act produced by the BBC. From 1949 Braddon has been mainly resident in Britain. He has written numerous novels, including *When the Enemy Is Tired* (1968), *End Play* (1972), produced as a film with an Australian setting in 1976, and *The Finalists* (1977). Novels which draw on his Australian experience are *Out of the Storm* (1956), *The Year of the Angry Rabbit* (1964, produced as a film titled *Night of the Lepus*), *When the Enemy Is Tired* (1968) and *The Finalists* (1977). He has also written documentary and historical accounts and biographies, including *Cheshire, V.C.* (1954), *Nancy Wake* (1956), *Joan Sutherland* (1962), *Thomas Baines and the North Australian Expedition* (1986) and *Images of Australia* (1988), based on his series for television. He has sold the film rights also for *End of a Hate* and *Joan Sutherland*; *Nancy Wake* was produced as a TV mini-series in 1987 and he has written several other TV scripts, including *Cowra Breakout* (co-author).

BRADLEY, John (1944–), born and educated in Brisbane, lived for some years in Canada but returned in 1972 to Queensland, where he teaches English. He has written several plays one of which, *Irish Stew*, first performed in 1979, is included in *Three Political Plays* (1980), ed. Alrene Sykes. His other plays include 'Logan' (1985), 'Noah's Paradise' (1990) and 'Rosy Apples Need Shining' (1990), the last winning the award for the Best New Play of 1990.

BRADLEY, William (1757–1833), came to Australia in the First Fleet as first lieutenant of HMS *Sirius* and surveyed, with Captain John Hunter, the Port Jackson and Broken Bay areas; Bradley's Head on the northern shore of Sydney Harbour is named after him. In 1790 he surveyed Norfolk Island while compelled to remain there because of the wreck of the *Sirius*. Considerable information on the Aborigines and on the flora and fauna of the colony is contained in his journal *A Voyage to New South Wales*, which was first published in 1969 from the original manuscript.

BRADSHAW, Jack (1846–1937), born Dublin, arrived in Australia in 1860 and was a swagman and small-time confidence man in the outback before graduating to bank robbery. Arrested after a Quirindi robbery in 1880, he spent most of the next twenty years in prison. Released at the turn of the century, he became known as a topical balladeer, a Domain orator and a sensational chronicler of crime. Bradshaw's first publications were the autobiographical *The Quirindi Bank Robbery* (?1899) and *Twenty Years' Experience of Prison Life in . . . New South Wales* (?1899), but his best-known work was *The True History of the Australian Bushrangers* (?1924), in which he claimed personal acquaintance with Dan Morgan, Ned Kelly and others. A bitter opponent of the prison system, Bradshaw hawked his broadsheet poems and paperback books, which had several, sometimes combined, editions on the streets of Sydney and in the larger country towns of NSW.

BRADSHAW, Richard (1938–   ), born and educated in Sydney, began to tour as a puppeteer in 1969 working with shadow puppets. Well known overseas, he has performed at puppet theatres and international festivals throughout Europe and America. In 1976–83 he was artistic director of the Marionette Theatre of Australia. *Bananas* and *The Fourth Wall*, his first plays for actors, were published in 1976. He is married to drama historian, Margaret Williams. He was awarded the OAM.

BRADSTOCK, Margaret, born Melbourne, grew up in Bendigo, Mt Beauty and Cooma, and lectures in English at the University of New South Wales. She has published poetry and short stories in numerous periodicals, as well as a poetry collection, *Flight of Koalas* (1992). With Louise Wakeling (q.v.) and others she edited the collection *Edge City on Two Different Plans* (1983) and with Wakeling, *Words from the Same Heart* (1988); and collaborated with her in an edition of Ada Cambridge's autobiography *Thirty Years in Australia* (1989) and a biography of Cambridge, *Rattling the Orthodoxies* (1991). Wakeling and Bradstock have also published a joint collection of their poetry, *Small Rebellions* (1984).

BRADY, E.J. (Edwin James) (1869–1952), born Carcoar, NSW, was the son of an Irishman who came to Australia from America, where he had fought in the Civil War. Brady first worked as a shipping clerk on the Sydney wharves, thereby forming that strong link with ships and sailors that inspired his taste for sea shanties and ballads of the days of sail. Thereafter he followed, for brief periods, a variety of occupations in many places. As journalist, feature-writer, dramatic reporter and editor he was connected with the *Australian Workman*, the *Australian Worker*, the *Bull-Ant*, the *Arrow*, the *Native Companion* and the *Grip*. Accounts of his wanderings are contained in two travel books: *The King's Caravan: Across Australia in a Wagon* (1911), the story of his journey from Parramatta to Townsville in 1899–1900; and *River Rovers* (1911), the story of his trip in an open boat down the Murray River from Albury. The impressions gathered from his many experiences are contained in *Australia Unlimited* (1918), a survey of Australia's resources and potential. Brady settled finally on the Victorian east coast at Mallacoota (where Henry Lawson spent some time with him) and while living a simple outdoor life there continued to write, invent and plan prodigiously. Much of this can be gleaned from his entertaining autobiography 'Life's Highway', published in instalments in *Southerly* 1952–55. Brady's poetry, which first appeared in the *Bulletin* in 1891, was published in four main collections, *The Ways of Many Waters* (q.v., 1899), *Bush-land Ballads* (1910), *Bells and Hobbles* (1911) and *Wardens of the Seas* (1933). It is as a writer of sea ballads that Brady has his particular niche in Australian literary history, but his literary talents were varied: he also wrote children's books, economic treatises, a biography, many short stories and a semi-fictional book on his father's adventures.

BRADY, Matthew (1799–1826) was a celebrated early Tasmanian bushranger, who had been sentenced to transportation for stealing in 1820. In 1823 he was sent to the newly established penal settlement at Macquarie Harbour, from where he escaped in 1824. He remained free for two years, staging a daring capture of the township of Sorell and at one stage posting his own reward for the apprehension of the lieutenant-governor of the colony, George Arthur. Popular legend has Brady using violence only in self-defence, and he was treated sympathetically by contemporary writers: e.g. by David Burn (q.v.) in *The Bushrangers* (performed 1829) and *Vindication of Van Diemen's Land* (1840), and by 'Pindar Juvenal' in *The Van Diemen's Land Warriors* (1827) in which Brady captures his would-be captors and sends them home to Launceston. Richard Butler's biographical novel *And Wretches Hang* was published in 1977.

BRAHE, William, see **BURKE and WILLS**

BRAIM, T.H. (Thomas Henry) (1814–91), born Doncaster, Yorkshire, studied divinity at Cambridge and went to Tasmania in 1835. He was a headmaster in Hobart and Sydney before his ordination to the Anglican priesthood in 1849; he returned to England in 1865. Braim edited the *New South Wales Magazine* in 1843 and published two significant works, *A History of New South Wales* (1846) and the emigrant guidebook *New Homes* (1870).

BRAND, Mona (1915–   ), born Sydney, worked during the Second World War as an industrial social-welfare worker. She was a research officer with the Department of Labour and National Service 1945–48, travelled and worked in Europe 1948–54 and lived in Hanoi 1956–57, where she assisted with the teaching of English. In 1958 she returned to Sydney. Her plays, which deal frequently with controversial, political topics and which reflect her dedication to socialism, appeared from 1948, mainly before left-wing New Theatre audiences, until in 1963 *Our 'Dear' Relations* won first prize in the New South Wales Arts Council drama festival. Since then her revues and more conventional dramas for adults and children have found a wider audience. Her two-act satire 'Going, Going, Gone' (1968) in particular found the same sort of popular acceptance as Bob Ellis's and Michael Boddy's *The Legend of King O'Malley* (1970). Much of her early dramatic work gained a wider popularity overseas (especially in socialist countries) than in Australia. Her published writing includes three collections of poetry, *Wheel and Bobbin* (1938), *Silver Singing* (1940) and *Lass in Love* (1946); *Daughters of Vietnam*, a collection of five novellas and five poems published in Vietnam in 1958; *Strangers in the Land* in *Two Plays about Malaya* (1954); *Mona Brand: Plays* (1965), published in Moscow in English and comprising *Strangers in the Land*, *No Strings Attached* and *Better a Millstone*; *Here Under Heaven* (1969), comprising *Barbara*, *Our Dear Relations* and *Here Under Heaven*; *Flying Saucery* (1981), three plays for children; *Here Comes Kisch!* (1983); and *For Richer For Poorer* (1989). Her unpublished plays and revues include 'Down Under Chelsea', 'First Aid' (1940), 'Out of Commission' (1955), 'Hold the Line' (1960), 'Come All Ye Valiant Miners' (1965), 'On Stage Vietnam', with Pat Barnett (1967), 'Going, Going, Gone' (1968), 'Ghost of Grey Gables' (1972), 'And a Happy New Year' (1976), 'The Pirates of Pal Mal' (1977) and 'Three Secrets' (1980). Brand has also written educational books for schools, and scripts for television and radio. She is married to the poet and writer Len Fox.

BRAY, J.J. (John Jefferson) (1912–), born Adelaide and admitted to the Bar in 1933, had a distinguished career as chief justice of South Australia 1967–78. Steeped in classical learning, Bray is, nevertheless, a man of modern times. He writes both of the classical and modern world, possessing the elegance and erudition of a scholar and the ironic wit and cool detachment of a perceptive observer of his own times. A member of Adelaide's Friendly Street (q.v.) since its beginnings in 1975, Bray dedicated his 1990 volume of poetry, *Seventy Seven*, 'To my colleagues, the Friendly Street Poets/For comradeship, example and survival'. His published works include verse – *Poems* (1962), *Poems 1961–1971* (1972), *Poems 1972–1979* (1979), *The Bay of Salamis and Other Poems* (1986), *Satura: Selected Poetry and Prose* (1988), *Seventy Seven* (1990), and *Tobacco: A Valedictory* (1990). He has also written a play, *Papinism* (1955), and *The Emperor's Doorkeeper* (1988), a collection of his speeches and addresses on academic occasions during his chancellorship. His poetry is usually a mix of contemporary verse and translations and adaptations from Greek mythology and other sources. *Seventy Seven*, for example (the title indicating his age at publication), has a section 'Recent Poems', a brief (five poems) section of European translations from French and German writers, and a lengthy section of adaptations from Greek writers (with some biographical notes) such as Archilochus, Alcaeus and Theognis. 'Recent Poems' reflects his characteristic personal tone: warmly humorous as in the two Ant pieces; acidic as in his retort to strident feminists ('In all public and social areas you are accepted as gender-free citizens,/ Behave as if you are'); impressively descriptive as in 'Winter Night'; and cleverly epigrammatic, as in his warning about rash promises ('Let all your awkward promises, . . . / Be metaphorical and imprecise'), betoken the man as well as the poet.

Satura – Selected Poetry and Prose won the SA Festival Award for Literature in 1990; the Award now named in his honour is an attempt to recognise Bray's long and distinguished contribution to Australian culture. He was made Companion of the Order of Australia in 1979.

Bread and Cheese Club was an all-male society formed in Melbourne in 1938 with twelve original members to foster a knowledge and love of Australian literature, art and music and to cultivate an Australian sentiment. Its co-founder and first president was J.K. Moir (q.v.); its monthly journal was *Bohemia* (q.v.). It published the work of Australian writers, e.g. Chris-

tina Mawdesley's *The Corroboree Tree: and Twelve Shorter Poems of Melbourne's Early Days of Settlement* (1944) and Kathleen Dalziel's *Known and Not Held* (1941). P.I. O'Leary compiled the anthology *The Bread and Cheese Book* (1939) containing poems by Australian writers, e.g. Roderic Quinn, E.J. Brady, J. Shaw Neilson, Mary Gilmore and others. Henry William Malloch, foundation member and secretary of the club and first editor of *Bohemia*, published *A Brief History of the Bread and Cheese Club* (1940) and *Fellows All: The Chronicles of the Bread and Cheese Club* (1943).

'BREAKER, THE', see **MORANT, Harry Harbord**

'BREE NARRAN', see **WILLIS, William Nicholas**

BREEN, B.A. (Barry Andrew) (1938–), born St Arnaud, Victoria, is a teacher in the Victorian Education Department. He has published two books of verse, *Behind My Eyes* (1968), *inter im* (1973, a tiny pamphlet); several anthologies for schools and a book of short stories, *Flop & Mick & John & Me* (1976). The quietly emphatic diction, easy informal style and sincerity, compassion, and sensitivity of Breen's poetry combine to make it appealing and accessible. *Behind My Eyes* includes numerous poems which reflect his teaching experiences e.g. 'To Let Her Think Shadows', 'The Gang-Gang Boy', 'Problem Children' and 'The Retard'. Others mirror the sadness that life brings, e.g. 'Widow', 'Point of Focus' and 'Requiescat'. Some, such as 'End of a Journey', portraying the Jews going to the gas chambers, and 'Oppenheimer', about the discovery of nuclear power and the results thereof, make effective narratives. The five comic sections 'Fragments of O'Flaherty' shared the *Poetry Magazine* Award for 1967.

BRENNAN, Anne (1898–1929), born Sydney, the daughter of Christopher Brennan (q.v.), is recalled in numerous autobiographies and reminiscences of Sydney's bohemian life in the 1910s and 1920s. Barred from the family home in 1917 because of her wayward behaviour, she turned to prostitution for a period. Her intense relationship with her father is described in Axel Clark's 1980 biography and she is recalled in the autobiographies of Jack and Ray Lindsay and Dulcie Deamer (qq.v.).

BRENNAN, C.J. (Christopher John) (1870–1932), was born in Sydney, eldest son of Irish Catholic immigrants. He was educated at St Ignatius College (Riverview) and at the University of Sydney, where he studied classics and philosophy and graduated in 1892. In that year he won a travelling scholarship to the University of Berlin, where he intended to study philosophy. He was distracted from his original intention to obtain a doctorate by a love affair with Anna Werth (daughter of his German landlady), by the cultural life and institutions of Berlin and by the attraction of French symbolist writers, particularly Mallarmé. Returning to Sydney in 1894 Brennan gained a position in the Public Library and began to write poetry that differed markedly from the prevailing balladry and nationalist-radical verse of the day. He married Anna Werth in Sydney in 1897. During the next decade Brennan was disappointed many times in his efforts to secure an academic appointment at the University of Sydney. His jibes about the conservative reactions of some University senate members to the sexual nature of his poetry, his anti-British attitude in the Boer War controversy and his reputation for intemperate habits and behaviour led to his being passed over for numerous lecturing positions. In 1909 he was finally given a permanent lecturing position in modern literature and in 1920, in spite of a stormy career studded with many differences of opinion between himself and the University authorities, he was appointed associate professor in German and comparative literature. His contemporary and friend, John le Gay Brereton, then professor of English, underlined the brilliant scholarship and intellectual capacity of Brennan by indicating that he could have filled with distinction any of the University chairs in philosophy, classics, literature or languages. Some contemporary opinions stress Brennan's remarkable charisma and unpredictability as a teacher and his contribution to the intellectual life of the University. His domestic life, however, grew increasingly strained, especially after the addition to his household of his German mother-in-law, and after the birth of his children, of whom there were four by 1907. With the gradual failure of the marriage that had begun with such romantic expectations on his part, Brennan turned to Sydney café society where, e.g. in the Casuals Club (q.v.) and in the group known as 'les Compliqués' (q.v.), he became a notorious figure. His ebullience, wit and dominating personality made him a legend in the city's bohemian circles but to his wife and children he was often a ranting, drunken bully. In 1922 he formed a tender relationship with Violet Singer ('Vie'), a lively, fun-loving woman nearly twenty years his junior, with whom he lived until she was killed by a tram in 1925. The open scandal surrounding his affair with Violet Singer and the University's dissatisfaction with what they saw as his degenerate behaviour and irresponsible conduct led to his dismissal in June of that year. The alcoholism and poverty of his remaining years were occasionally alleviated by the attempts of friends and former students to rehabilitate him. In 1931 he was awarded a Commonwealth Literary Fund pension of £1 a week. Following a period of ill-health he gave up alcohol and returned before his death to his Catholic faith, which he had neglected since his early university days.

Brennan's first collection of verse was a booklet stereographed by himself (eight copies) entitled *XVIII Poems: Being the First Collection of Verse and Prose by Christopher Brennan* (1897). In the same year he also published *XXI Poems: (1893–1897) Towards the Source*. This booklet met a mixed critical reception: praise from friendly reviewers in *Freeman's Journal* and *Hermes* and from A.G. Stephens in the *Bulletin* Red Page, but contemptuous dismissal (e.g. 'musical, meaningless words to an accompaniment of equally futile and meretricious pessimism') from other critics.

In 1903, with the help of John le Gay Brereton, he prepared several copies of a manuscript edition of poems written in response to the Boer War. Titled *XV Poems* it was not published until Harry F. Chaplin's 1953 edition *The Burden of Tyre: Fifteen Poems by C.J. Brennan*. Brennan was opposed to the Boer War and Australia's role in it; in common with many, he felt sympathy for the Boers and saw Britain ('Tyre') as an overbearing imperial power, prostituting herself to commerce. He denounced Christianity, which sanctioned the conquest and exploitation of the Boers, as the immoral, ideological support of the imperialist system. It was probably because of its stringent attack on Great Britain that the poems remained unpublished during Brennan's lifetime. Brennan's chief volume, titled *Poems* but usually referred to as *Poems (1913)*, was published in December 1914. It incorporates revisions of material published in both of the 1897 booklets and many earlier poems. It is made up of three major sections – 'Towards the Source', 1894–97; 'The Forest of Night', 1898–1902; 'The Wanderer', 1902, and two concluding segments, 'Pauca Mea' and 'Epilogues'. *Poems (1913)*, although long a source of bewilderment to readers, has been largely interpreted and explained by the analysis and commentary of such writers as A.R. Chisholm and G.A. Wilkes (qq.v.). Wilkes was responsible for the interpretation of the poems as corresponding to Mallarmé's concept of the *livre composé* (i.e. the book of verse which, although made up of many separate individual pieces, is conceived and executed as a whole). With the publication in 1980 of Axel Clark's biography of Brennan, much of *Poems (1913)* can be seen to be biographically based. *Poems (1913)* has the overall theme of man's search for Eden, a paradisal state. The opening section, a mainly lyrical prelude, 'Towards the Source', has thirty individual poems that recall the courtship of Brennan and Anna Werth in Berlin and reveal him as the impatient, expectant lover who is confident that the consummation of their love in marriage will achieve his Eden. Extravagantly expressed and highly embellished, these lyrical attempts (e.g. 'A Prelude', 'We Sat Entwined', 'Autumn', 'Deep Mists of Longing') to invest his love with an ethereal, paradisal quality are not highly regarded. In the second section 'The Forest of Night' (originally conceived as 'The Book of Lilith'), the search for Eden, apparently unsuccessful in the love affair of 'Towards the Source' (as the linking poem 'Luminary', written only four months after his marriage, clearly shows), is pursued into the deepest regions of the poet's inner self and into myth and legend where other searches for the paradisal state are recorded. The second cycle opens with the twelve-poem series 'The Twilight of Disquietude' and reveals the poet tormented by his 'vast and impotent' dreams. 'The Quest of Silence', which follows, explores the mythology and legendry of the past. At the centre of 'The Forest of Night' is the figure of Lilith, in Hebrew tradition 'Lady of Night', an ambivalent figure who is both the source of man's longing yet a source also of malignity which brings apprehension and horror. In Jewish legend Lilith is Adam's mate before Eve but is forsaken by Adam. Her revenge on Adam is to destroy his capacity for contentment in his new life and to instil in him a torturing vision of a lost paradise, which she represents, for which he is fated to yearn eternally but never attain. The essence of Lilith, a powerful concept containing within it Brennan's recognition of the dualistic view of man's divided nature, is conveyed in the thirteenth part with the lines beginning 'She is the night'. 'The Shadow of Lilith' section ends also in failure of the quest for the paradisal state. The concluding lines of 'The Wanderer' (the last of the major sections of *Poems (1913)*) sum up Brennan's life more aptly than any complex appraisal could do:

> I am the wanderer of many years
> Who cannot tell if ever he was king
> Or if ever kingdoms were.

'The Wanderer' abandons the quest for Eden through the Absolute and with an air of resolution turns to the Actual, the life-experience of the material world. 'Disabused of illusory hope' (Clark) he appears to accept that Eden, as he dreamed it, is unattainable. With that acceptance comes the calm of resignation.

> I feel a peace fall in the heart of the winds
> and a clear dusk settle, somewhere, far in me.

Such a peace never really settled on Brennan's life, but 'The Wanderer' does signal the poetic, if not the actual, end of his exhaustive search. Brennan's only other collection of poetry was *A Chant of Doom and Other Verses* (1918), the title poem, a violent denunciation of Germany's role in the First World War, having first been published in the *Lone Hand*, 1 August 1916. He wrote some love lyrics during the period he lived with Violet Singer. The tenderness and certainty of poems such as 'Midnight' and 'Because She Would Ask Me Why I Loved Her', indicate how important that relationship was to him. His critical works include 'German Romanticism: A Progressive Definition', which appeared in the *Modern Language Review of New South Wales* in January 1920; 'Studies in French Poetry', a planned series of sixteen articles for the *Bookfellow* in 1920, only six of which were completed; and 'Symbolism in Nineteenth Century Literature', a series of University Extension lectures, later published in *The Prose of Christopher Brennan* (1962), edited by A.R. Chisholm and J.J. Quinn. For a long time only dimly understood, yet reverenced the more because of that inaccessibility, Brennan is one of the first legendary figures in Australian literature. Unresponsive to, and seemingly uninfluenced by, the forces of nationalism and radicalism that dominated the contemporary Australian scene, he was a literary enigma standing apart from his own social and literary milieu, finding instead an intellectual affinity with European interest in philosophy and human psychology, and a literary affinity with the French symbolist writers. Although virtually unknown and unrecognised outside Australia, he is clearly part of the international mainstream of writing that gave rise to poets such as T.S. Eliot and William Butler Yeats. Axel Clark's 1980 study is a substantial Brennan biography; other important works on Brennan include A.R. Chisholm's *Christopher Brennan: The Man and His Poetry* (1946) and G.A.

Wilkes's *New Perspectives on Brennan's Poetry* (1953). Terry Sturm edited *Christopher Brennan* (1984), in the Portable Australian Authors series, which draws on the whole range of Brennan's writing including his literary criticism and theory, his autobiographical writing and his letters. *Poems (1913)* was republished in 1992 (a facsimile edition in 1972 by Wilkes) with an introduction by poet, Robert Adamson (q.v.).

'BRENNAN, D.', see **LAMBERT, Eric**

BRENNAN, Niall (1918–), born Melbourne and a freelance writer since 1942, has published numerous works on politics, moral philosophy and biography as well as several small volumes of verse. His two chief biographies are those of Archbishop Daniel Mannix (1964) and John Wren (1971). His other works include *The Ballad of a Government Man* (1944, a satire on public servants), *The Making of a Moron* (1953, social philosophy), *A Hoax Called Jones* (1961, memoirs), *The Politics of Catholics* (1975, historical and political issues), *Vice Versa: Verses and Poetry* (1975, poetry), *Tales from the Australian Mountains* (1979, tales, history and memoirs) and *Damien Parer, War Photographer* (1991). *Man Upon His Mountain*, a story based on an unresolved double murder in Wonnangatta Valley at the turn of the century, won a 1976 prize awarded by the FAW and was published in 1984.

'BRENT OF BIN BIN' was the pseudonym under which Miles Franklin (q.v.) wrote a series of six novels dealing with Australian station and rural life from the 1850s to the 1920s. The opening novel of the series, *Up the Country* (1928), roughly dated about the year of the great floods, 1852, is a saga of several squatting families whose complicated interrelationships, set against the backdrop of the Monaro (q.v.) region of southern NSW, produces a confused, almost chaotic narrative. The novel's narrative is aptly described by the author's own term 'possuming', a word used to describe the seemingly frenzied and uncoordinated movements of possums in the branches of a tree. *Ten Creeks Run* (1930), which moves the stories a generation further on (1880s–1890s), has an ambivalence to sex that leads to improbabilities of plot and character, marring an otherwise compelling story and an emotional evocation of the loveliness of the countryside. Chronologically, *Cockatoo* (1954) follows, set in the period 1890s–1900. It concerns the lives of the small farmers and selectors, descendants of the earlier squatters, and in particular the destiny of Ignez Milford who, dissatisfied with the sterility of a future life at Oswald's Ridges, follows Miles Franklin's own example of escape into a larger, more satisfying world through her writing and emigration to America. *Gentlemen at Gyang Gyang* (1956) reverses the story of *Cockatoos*; Bernice Gaylord, a successful artist, returns disillusioned to Australia, marries Peter Poole (great-grandson of James Poole of the first novel) and finds happiness. The final novel of the series (published third in 1931), *Back to Bool Bool*, completes the cycle, returning far-flung descendants of the original families to Bool Bool for reunion celebrations. In spite of its web of intricate human relationships and rather repetitive plot the closing novel provides a strong value judgement in favour of Australia from those who have sought their fulfilment in a variety of ways in a variety of places. The remaining novel, *Prelude to Waking* (1950), is, according to its title and its prefatory comment, intended as a prelude to the series but has little real connection with the chronicle novels. The pseudonym (originally 'Brand of Bin Bin' but changed by a typing error to 'Brent') was said to represent a kindly, elderly gentleman (perhaps a composite of Miles's father John Franklin and the novelist Joseph Furphy) writing from his experience of Australian bush life. The identity of 'Brent of Bin Bin' caused lively speculation in the early 1930s and was not completely established until the 1950s. Franklin's motive in using the pseudonym is usually attributed to the embarrassment she had experienced from the publication of *My Brilliant Career* (q.v.) in her own name, while her correspondence with Mary Fullerton about the pseudonym indicates her overwhelming fear of intrusions upon her privacy.

BRERETON, John le Gay (1) (1827–86), born Yorkshire, came to Australia in 1859 as a doctor and practised in Sydney. Father of John le Gay Brereton (2) (q.v.), he published the volumes of poetry, *The Travels of Prince Legion* (1857), *Poems* (1865), *The Goal of Time* (1883) and *Beyond* (1886). His prose works included *One Teacher: One Law* (1883) and *Genesis and the Beatitudes* (1887).

BRERETON, John le Gay (2) (1871–1933), born Sydney, son of John le Gay Brereton (1), had a long association with the University of Sydney as student, librarian and, finally, professor of English literature. Well known for his charm and his interest in the writers who sought his advice (he was a close friend of Henry Lawson, q.v.) he was an unusual academic for the time, never divorcing himself from the world of men outside the University. His own scholarship is evident in such a work as *Writings on Elizabethan Drama* (1948), collected by R.G. Howarth. His charming though slight lyric poetry includes *The Song of Brotherhood* (1896), *Sea and Sky* (1908) and *Swags Up!* (1928). He published two whimsical collections of essays and reminiscences: *Landlopers* (1899), which records his wanderings along the coast and in the mountains near Sydney, and *Knocking Round* (1930), which contains anecdotal reminiscences and occasional references to writers like Christopher Brennan and Henry Lawson. With Brennan and under the direction of Louisa MacDonald, the first principal of the Women's College of Sydney University, Brereton composed *A Mask* in 1913 to celebrate the twenty-first anniversary of the Women's College. The *Mask*, a pageant of famous women, was presented again in 1932 and in 1982, the centenary of the college. R.D. FitzGerald (Brereton's nephew) has an account of Brereton in *Of Places and Poetry* (1976); H.P. Heseltine wrote *John le Gay Brereton* (1965).

BRETT, Doris (1950–), born Melbourne, sister of Lily Brett (q.v.) and participant in the post-war Melbourne environment depicted in the latter's poetry and stories, is a clinical psychologist who has written on parenting skills in the *Annie Stories* (1986) and on cooking in *Doris Brett's Australian Bread Book* (1984). Her first book of verse, *The Truth about Unicorns* (1984), won the Anne Elder Award and the Mary Gilmore Award. A psychological novel, *Looking for Unicorns* (1992), takes the reader into a somewhat weird medical world, in which the psychologists are somewhat less stable than their patients.

BRETT, Lily (1946–), born at the end of the Second World War in a displaced persons' camp in Germany, had Jewish parents who survived the Holocaust. She migrated with her parents to Australia in 1948 and spent her girlhood in Melbourne. Determined to understand more fully the horrors which, as a child, she had been only vaguely aware of in her parents' past, she went as a young woman to Poland to visit her parents' old home and Auschwitz itself. Of her childhood she wrote, 'I have walked through Melbourne as though it were Warsaw', and of her alter ego, Lola Bensky, in her stories 'Lola felt that she had been born with a backlog of sadness'. Brett has published two books of fiction, *Things Could be Worse* (1990) and *What God Wants* (1991), and four books of poetry, *The Auschwitz Poems* (1986), which won the Victorian Premier's Literary Award in 1987; *Poland and Other Poems* (1987), a group of fourteen poems from the 'Poland' section of that book having won the 1986 Mattara Poetry Prize; *After the War* (1990), and *Unintended Consequences* (1992), the last two being less dominated by the Holocaust although its presence is never very far away. The best, the most poignant, of her poetry is linked to her mother's experiences in the ghetto and in Auschwitz. Brief poems, with even briefer lines (often of only a single word), distil the essence of the all-enveloping terror of those times:

> It was/ a frantic life
> nothing/ remained/ the same
> from/ minute/ to minute
> there/ was/ no peace
> there/ was/ no rest
> there/ was/ no rhythm
> there/ was/ no sense
> there/ was/ no life.

They depict the horrors of Auschwitz: the regular selections for the gas chambers, the nauseating sight of naked bodies covered with 'made to measure layers of sleek, shiny, white lice', the scorched flesh of those driven to suicide on the electrified fences, the methodical piling of bodies in the pits to ensure that they burned 'with a minimum of fuss and fuel', and then there is the final evidence, when one of the camps was liberated, of the destruction of a race of people, '38,000 pairs of men's shoes, 13,964 carpets, and 836,255 dresses'. The poems move back in time from Auschwitz to the innocent days before the war, then on to a new life in Australia, where the parents' anxieties about the past are carried over into their behaviour in the present – the fear of again being hungry ('the cupboards groaned/ the fridge shrieked') and the need for security ('four locks on the front door'). Lily Brett's visit to Poland (in *Poland and Other Poems*) conveys her hostility to a population that cared too much for its own security to bother about the Jews. She visits Lodz and the streets that still contain the buildings (some of which her great grandfather built) where her parents lived and from where they were 'emptied into the ghetto'. Ghetto tales about 'potato peel patties' and 'The Excrement Cart' are interwoven with more contemporary poems (in 'Kaddish for My Mother') describing in minute physical detail her mother's slow death from cancer. In *After the War* Jerusalem and Israel are the focus as are the scenes from a Jewish childhood in Melbourne. With a keen eye for detail, Brett conjures up a vivid picture of post-war Melbourne and its suburbs. *Unintended Consequences* also includes painful poems about the suffering of her parents and her own repressed anxieties as well as poems about her present life, including reflections on her life in New York (where she now resides).

Brett's short fiction is characterised by Jewish drollness and wry entertaining dissection of the Jewish character. *Things Could Be Worse* concerns the Bensky family (the Bretts) but other Jewish families, the Borgs, Ganzs, Pekelmans from *Things Could Be Worse* and the Brots, the Schoers and Ella Tennenbaum from *What God Wants*, including husbands, wives, sons, daughters and black sheep children with gay connections, pass in and out of stories about communal visits to the cinema on Saturday evenings, dinner parties on Sundays, gossip sessions, shopping binges. Many of the stories record Brett's own personal adventures, e.g. into, out of, and into marriage again, as well as her continuing attempt to come to grips with the past (Lola Bensky has more than a thousand books about the Holocaust). There are occasional reminders of that past, e.g. Genia Buckbinder was the only survivor of Auschwitz of an extended family of eighty-seven Buckbinders; Shumek Greenbaum survived the last desperate days of the war by cooking and eating the liver of a dead friend. Lily's mother (Renia Bensky) is the dominating figure of the stories as she was of the poems. But the central woman of the stories, a vain, often irritating, ordinary Jewish mother and wife, seems incompatible with the devastated, tragic persona of the poems. Survival and a resumption of normal life appear to have turned her back into an ordinary, venial human being. Lily Brett's husband, David Rankin, a prominent Australian painter who has won many important art prizes, including the 1983 Wynne Prize, has illustrated the books, movingly and poignantly in the case of the Holocaust poems. *What God Wants* won the 1992 Steele Rudd Award.

BRICKHILL, Paul (1916–91), born Melbourne, began work as a copy-boy with the Sydney *Sun* and became one of its feature writers before serving in the RAAF during the Second World War. He was a prisoner of war in Germany for two years; his wartime experiences provided the material for his first book, *Escape to Danger* (1946). After the war he was an Aus-

tralian newspaper correspondent in England, Europe and the USA, returning to Australia in the 1950s. Other war books followed: *The Great Escape* (1950), the story of 'X organization', the escape network in the camp, Stalag Luft III; *The Dam Busters* (1951), the story of 617 Squadron and its attacks on the German network of dams in the Ruhr valley; *Escape or Die* (1952); and *Reach for the Sky* (1954), the story of Douglas Bader. *The Dam Busters* became a world bestseller, a radio feature and a film; *The Great Escape* and *Reach for the Sky* were also filmed. Brickhill also wrote *The Deadline* (1962), a novel about a young Australian who becomes involved in a murder campaign conducted by Algerian terrorists.

BRIDE, T.F. (Thomas Francis) (1849–1927), born Cork, Ireland, came to Australia as an infant, had a brilliant career as a law student and became librarian of the Public Library in Melbourne in 1881; one of his rivals for the position was Marcus Clarke. In 1895 he was appointed curator of estates of deceased persons, retiring to private life in 1909. During his term as librarian he edited *Letters from Victorian Pioneers*, a collection of colonial reminiscences presented to Lieutenant-Governor Charles La Trobe for his own proposed book of reminiscences which was never published. La Trobe returned the letters to Victoria in 1872; they were finally published in 1898.

Bridge, The, a magazine published quarterly by the Australian Jewish Quarterly Foundation, began in 1964 and ceased in 1972. It contained Jewish history, creative writing and book reviews; its contributors included David Martin, Herz Bergner, Walter Stone, Frank Moorhouse, C.B. Christesen, Randolph Stow and Leslie Rees.

BRIDGES, Hilda (1881–1971), sister of Roy Bridges (q.v.), was born in Sorell, Tasmania. She wrote about twenty books of light fiction 1922–50, often under male pseudonyms. They include *The Squatter's Daughter* (1922, a novel adapted from the play by Bert Bailey and Edmund Duggan), *House of Storms* (1931), *Chinese Jade* (1933), *Distant Fields* (1936) and *Men Must Live* (1938). She also wrote children's books, e.g. *Bobby's First Term* (1924) and *The House of Make Believe* (1928) and many stories and serials for popular magazines, e.g. the *Australian Woman's Mirror*.

BRIDGES, Roy (1885–1952), born Hobart, joined the staff of the Melbourne *Age* in 1909 and was associated with that newspaper for almost twenty years before retiring to Tasmania in 1933 to live with his sister Hilda Bridges (q.v.) on the old family property, Wood's Farm, in the Sorell district. Most of Bridges's books are connected with the early history of Tasmania although some are set in Victoria. He wrote about forty adventure novels 1909–50, which have contrived plots and stereotyped characters. Among the best known are *The Barb of an Arrow* (1909); *Mr. Barrington* (1911), which gives a fictional account of the well-known convict George Barrington (q.v.) in London; *The Immortal Dawn* (1917), a series of Anzac character sketches; *These Were Thy Merchants* (1935), *The House of Fendon* (1936) and *Sullivan's Bay* (1937), three novels dealing with the early Port Phillip settlement; *Green Butterflies* (1923), which begins a series of books about the Richmond–Sorell district of Tasmania from the convict period, e.g. *Negrohead* (1930), *Trinity* (1931), *Cloud* (1932) and *The League of the Lord* (1950). Bridges also wrote *That Yesterday Was Home* (1948), which is partly autobiographical and contains some of the history of Wood's Farm. D.H. Borchardt and B. Tilley compiled *The Roy Bridges Collection in the University of Tasmania* (1956).

BRIGGS, Ernest (1905–67), born Sydney, was a radio broadcaster in Brisbane, where he also wrote music and art reviews for the Brisbane *Courier Mail*. He published two volumes of meditative lyrics, *The Merciless Beauty* (1943) and *The Secret Listener* (1949). The 'merciless beauty' is that of the pure mind; the seven metaphysical-style poems of the volume emphasise the permanence of the mind of man in contrast with the transience of material things. The poems of a third volume, *The Timeless Flowers* (1952), are chiefly translations or derivations from the Chinese.

BRIGHT, Charles (1832–1903), born probably Liverpool, England, came to Australia to join the Victorian gold rush at Ballarat but was soon back in Melbourne, where he joined the *Argus* as a reporter and later wrote for the *Herald*. Significant in Melbourne intellectual life in the second half of the nineteenth century, he was editor (1859–64) of the *Examiner and Melbourne Weekly News* and of *Melbourne Punch* (1863–66). He contributed also to the *Spectator*, a free-trade journal; to Marcus Clarke's *Humbug* and in later life to the *Age*. He edited (1856–59) the popular literary weekly *My Note Book*, his contributors including R.H. Horne and J.E. Neild. Married to leading spiritualist and feminist Annie Bright, he is portrayed in her autobiographical novel *A Soul's Pilgrimage* (1907).

'Brighten's Sister-in-Law' is both a poem and a story by Henry Lawson (q.v.) in which the narrator's sick son is nursed through a fever by the sister-in-law of a shanty keeper, to whom the narrator has been guided by the vision of a woman he sees in the branches of a tree. When the poem was published in 1889 the narrator was a carrier and his son Harry a schoolboy with seven brothers and sisters; in the prose version, which forms part of the Joe Wilson (q.v.) sequence, the narrator is Joe and his son, Jim, is an only child of three years.

Brindabella, see FRANKLIN, Miles

Brindabella Press, see BOLTON, Alec

Bring Larks and Heroes, Thomas Keneally's (q.v.) third novel, was published in 1967 and won the Miles Franklin Award for that year. Its protagonist is Phelim Halloran, a corporal in the marine detachment guarding the prisoners in a penal colony at 'the world's worse end'; the novel records the effect on the individual conscience of a repressive and authoritarian society. Although an Irish Catholic dragooned into the military service of the Protestant English, Halloran feels bound to live within a society to which he has given an oath of allegiance, until a series of incidents reveals the brutality and corruption of the 'System' and makes moral evasion impossible; these incidents include the flogging to the point of death of a convict on suspicion of his involvement in an Irish uprising, the execution of a convict artist wrongly accused of rape, the bureaucratic bungling which victimises a convict at the end of his sentence, and the savage quelling of an uprising. Under the influence of the convict Robert Hearn, who presents the view of an alternative society informed by the ideas of the Enlightenment and the French and American revolutions, Halloran steals the stores of the starving colony to help victual an American whaler; he is assisted by Ann Rush, a convict servant with whom, in the absence of a priest, he has contracted a secret marriage validated by their oaths to each other. Betrayed by an accomplice, Terry Byrne, Halloran and Ann are executed.

BRINSMEAD, Hesba, see *The Oxford Companion to Australian Children's Literature* (1993), p. 67.

Brisbane Courier, the oldest Queensland newspaper, began publication as a weekly, the *Moreton Bay Courier*, in 1846; its founder, Arthur Sydney Lyon, established other early Queensland newspapers including the *Moreton Bay Free Press*, the *North Australian* and the *Darling Downs Gazette*. James Swan, an early partner of Lyon, became proprietor of the *Moreton Bay Courier* in 1848; subsequent owners included Theophilus Pugh (1859–63), under whom the newspaper became a daily, titled the *Courier*, in 1861, Thomas Blackett Stephens (1864–73), Gresley Lukin (1873–80) and Charles Hardie Buzacott. The *Courier* became the *Brisbane Courier* in 1864 and ran until 1933, when it merged with the *Daily Mail* (1903–33) to form the *Courier-Mail*. This newspaper was under the control of Sir Keith Murdoch and John Wren until sold to the Herald and Weekly Times group after Murdoch's death in 1952. Among editors of the *Brisbane Courier* were William Wilkes (1848–56), Charles Lilley, Lukin, F.W. Ward (1894–98), C. Brunsdon Fletcher (1898–1903) and J.J. Knight (1906–16); staff or contributors significant in Australian literature include W.H. Traill in the 1870s and Nettie Palmer and Brian Penton in the 1920s. David Rowbotham was literary editor of the *Courier Mail* 1980–87.

BRISBANE, Katharine (1932–), born Singapore, was educated in WA, where she worked on the *West Australian* as reporter and theatre critic (1954–59). She was national theatre critic 1967–74 and Sydney theatre critic 1978–80 for the *Australian* and has written extensively on Australian drama in books and periodicals. She has edited *Entertaining Australia* (1991), an illustrated history of the performing arts in Australia, published to coincide with the twentieth anniversary of Currency Press (q.v.), which she founded in 1971 with her husband Philip Parsons for the publication of the work of Australian playwrights.

Brisbane Water, the north-east arm of Broken Bay about 40 kilometres north of Sydney, was explored by Governor Arthur Phillip in 1788 and was named after Governor Sir Thomas Brisbane in 1825; on it is situated such well-known resorts as Gosford, Woy Woy and Ettalong Beach. Henry Kendall (q.v.) recuperated there from alcoholism in 1872 and wrote a long description of the area, 'Arcadia in Our Midst', for the *Australian Town and Country Journal*, 27 February and 6 March 1875. Three of his poems are set against the Brisbane Water background, 'The Voice in the Wild Oak', 'Narrara Creek' and 'Mooni', the last two using well-known Brisbane Water place-names. Charles Swancott wrote *The Brisbane Water Story* (1953–55).

BRISSENDEN, R.F. (Robert Francis) (1928–91), born Wentworthville, Sydney, was educated at the universities of Sydney and Leeds. He joined the ANU (then the Canberra University College) as a lecturer in English in 1953. He also held teaching and research positions at several Australian and overseas universities. At the time of his early retirement through ill health in 1985 he was reader in English at the ANU. He was a member of the Literature Board of the Australia Council 1977–78 and its chairman 1978–81. Associate editor of *Meanjin Quarterly* (1959–64) and first literary editor of the *Australian* (1964–65), Brissenden edited the anthologies *Southern Harvest* (1964, short stories) and *Australian Poetry 1972* (1972). He was elected a member of the Australian Academy of the Humanities in 1976 and was made AO in 1982 for his services to literature. In addition to critical work on English and Australian literature (e.g. *Virtue in Distress*, 1973, on eighteenth century English literature) he published several books of poetry, *Winter Matins* (1971), *Elegies* (1974), *Building a Terrace* (1975), *The Whale in Darkness* (1980) and *Sacred Sites* (1990). He also wrote *Gough and Johnny Were Lovers: Songs and Light Verse Celebrating Wine, Friendship and Political Scandal* (1984) and was preparing *The Oxford Book of Australian Light Verse* (1991), in which he collaborated with Philip Grundy, at the time of his death. *Winter Matins* reveals Brissenden to be a romantic, even sensual, poet, strongly attracted to natural physical beauty, certainly of the sea (he loved the NSW South Coast) but also of bush landscapes. Most of his personal love poems in this early volume might more appropriately be called 'love-making' poems e.g. 'Another Place, Another Time', 'Winter Matins', 'Dream' and 'Isolde's Song'. His love also of the 'wet, salt sea-smell' runs throughout several poems. He is inspired by the sea partly through his own love of the classics:

> the same sea
> sang round the rocks
> On which Ulysses drove
> His battered wrecks
> And told his lies, while love
> Herself was born
> In the sea-foam

Ulysses's return home is also recorded in a twentieth-century version, an indication that modern and classical times both absorbed Brissenden's creative energies. He was equally at home in everyday culture as his poem 'Verandahs', which recalls the simpler, more agreeable aspects of traditional Australian country life, demonstrates. From *The Whale in Darkness*, 'Verandahs' takes its place with the popular poetry of Paterson, Lawson, Dorothea Mackellar, Kenneth Slessor, David Campbell and Judith Wright. Brissenden's final volume, *Sacred Sites*, sees him at his most skilful. In many ways his own epitaph, published shortly before he died, *Sacred Sites* recalls significant places and events in his life, e.g. his boyhood memories of a father who read Masefield to him and of the friends he made while at high school in Cowra. The series 'A Country Childhood' lingers lovingly over his own 'sacred sites' – 'The Pepper Tree', where he fed bread to the soldier bird, 'The Moreton Bay', where he first began to understand the magic of life revealed by the ripening body of his young girl playmate; 'The Fig Tree' where he sat viewing the world below him. Other 'sacred sites' were in the Greek Islands (the sonnet series 'Leros, 1982') and Aboriginal sacred sites ('Rock Climbers: Uluru, 1985' and 'South Coast Midden'). Brissenden's belief that both Black and White Australians now truly share the land is revealed in his poems. Intimations of mortality are ever present, and the rapidly deteriorating body and the restrictions it imposes are both bitterly resented and philosophically accepted. After his retirement Brissenden began to write crime fiction. *Poor Boy* (1987) and its sequel, *Wildcat* (1991), which introduce the somewhat bumbling journalist-hero, Tom Caxton and the as-yet, and probably, now, never-to-be caught villain, Tiburzi, are compelling, realistically written 'thrillers'.

The tributes that followed Bob Brissenden's death recognised that Australian literature had lost one of its best-liked and most human faces. In 1993 David Brooks, one-time student and long-time friend, edited, with an introduction, *Suddenly Evening: The Selected Poems of R. F. Brissenden*.

Britannica-Australia Award, see **Encyclopaedia Britannica Australia Awards**

British Australasian, an Anglo-Australian weekly which catered for expatriates living in England and for investors, intending immigrants and others interested in the Australian colonies and New Zealand, began publication in London in 1884. In 1924–40 it was known as the *British Australian and New Zealander*, but reverted to its original title in 1941, and in 1948 became the *Australian & New Zealand Weekly;* from 1943 until it ceased publication in 1969 it was a magazine. For most of its life the *British Australasian* carried Australian business, political and sporting news as well as information about Australasian visitors to the United Kingdom and reports of activities in the United Kingdom (e.g. meetings of the Royal Colonial Institute) of relevance to Australasia. Two important editors were Philip Mennell (1892–1905) and Charles Henry Chomley (1908–42); Chomley published literary supplements in which he included the work of his circle of ex-Australian writers and artists, among them his nephew Martin Boyd.

Broad Arrow, The, a novel written by Caroline Leakey (q.v.) under the pseudonym 'Oline Keese', was first published in 1859; there were several later editions, including one in 1886 revised by Mrs Townshend Mayer which omitted three chapters of the original. Subtitled *Some Passages in the History of Maida Gwynnham, A Lifer*, *The Broad Arrow* opens with the innocent Maida in prison, having been seduced and then tricked into forgery by the caddish Henry Norwell. Wrongly convicted also of infanticide, she is transported to Van Diemen's Land where she becomes a servant in the Evelyn household and struggles to reconcile her pride and sense of worth with the degradation she endures. At the end of the novel she is converted to a Christian's acceptance of her situation but dies soon after. Her death is discovered by Norwell, who has come repentant to the colony after the revelation of his perfidy has led to his wife's death in England. Broken by his sins, Norwell ends his days in a local asylum. Within this melodramatic frame *The Broad Arrow* is a social and domestic novel offering a picture of Tasmanian society during transportation, based on Leakey's experiences in the colony between 1848 and 1853 and centred on the household of George Evelyn, his wife, his brother, the Reverend Herbert Evelyn, and the minister's daughter Emmeline and visiting niece Blanche D'Urban. The paradoxes of colonial attitudes towards 'Home' are shrewdly observed, but the main focus of the narrative is on the convict system, in particular on the contrast between the Christian fortitude advocated by Herbert Evelyn and the harsh realities of convict life which he recognises and which lead George Evelyn to temper his humane instincts with a rational, hard-headed approach to the management of convict servants. The emphasis in *The Broad Arrow* is on the humiliations of convict life rather than on the horrors; an anti-System novel which was read by Marcus Clarke, it played its part in creating the legend that the convicts were more sinned against than sinning.

Broadcaster, a WA weekly published 1934–55, included items of literary and historical significance (e.g. articles on bushrangers and the goldfields) and fiction serials (e.g. Katharine Susannah Prichard's *Black Opal*).

Broadsides or, as they were sometimes called, broadsheets were a popular way of spreading the news in Australian towns and cities in the period before the widespread circulation of the daily newspapers. Hawkers of broadsides, often referred to as 'chapmen', 'ballad singers', 'flying stationers' or 'patterers', would carry their supply of printed sheets through the streets, attracting the crowds by their lively 'spiel' about the subject of the broadside – the latest murder, horror, tragedy, war, battle, death or remarkable event. Broadsides were also used to carry the words of ballads or songs and for the issue of proclamations and government orders. Printed on only one side of the paper, the broadsides could be posted on fences and walls for better communication of their contents; they thus anticipated the modern poster. Geoffrey C. Ingleton's *True Patriots All* (1952) includes typical Australian broadsides from the first half of the nineteenth century.

BRODERICK, Damien (1944–), born Melbourne, graduated in 1966 from Monash University where he had been co-editor of the student newspaper, *Lot's Wife* (q.v.), and holds a Ph.D. from Deakin University in the comparative semiotics of science and literature. He had a brief but varied career in journalism before becoming a full-time writer, chiefly of science fiction (q.v.). Now one of the leading Australian exponents of SF, although antagonistic to the limiting nature of such a label (Broderick is more inclined to call it 'speculative' than 'science'), Broderick has been widely represented in Australian and overseas SF anthologies and has published many works of science fiction, *A Man Returned* (1965), *Sorcerer's World* (1970), *The Dreaming Dragons* (1980), *The Judas Mandala* (1982), *Transmitters* (1984), *The Black Grail* (1986) *Striped Holes* (1988), *The Dark Between the Stars* (1991) and *The Sea's Furthest End* (1993). *The Dreaming Dragons* was runner-up in the worldwide John W. Campbell Memorial Prize for science fiction. With Rory Barnes, a colleague from Monash student days, Broderick wrote the SF novel *Valencies* (1983). He has edited three collections of Australian science fiction, *The Zeitgeist Machine* (1977), *Strange Attractors* (1985) and *Matilda at the Speed of Light* (1988). Of his own fiction, *The Judas Mandala* (which has a feminist heroine) portrays the problems of interaction between man and the dominating machine world of the seventh millennium and includes a portrayal of Sydney of the year 2009. *The Black Grail* (of which a first version appeared in 1970) is mostly 'sword and sorcery', while *Striped Holes*, which is not too easily understood by non-SF devotees, includes considerable parody of earlier SF. *The Dark Between the Stars* consists of ten short stories and novellas first published between 1964 and 1988, prefaced by some autobiographical musings. Among the stories are 'All My Yesterdays' with Lazarus still seeking solutions to his eternal wanderings; 'The Magi', where a Jesuit priest's belief is challenged on a distant planet; 'A Tooth for Every Child', which presents some extraordinary possible medical advances and 'Coming Back', where there is a reversal of time and its personal impact on the researcher. *Transmitter* and *Striped Holes* were adapted for radio presentation. He has also published a study of the links between parapsychology and the popular gambling game, Tattslotto, *The Lotto Effect* (1992), and has written *The Architecture of Babel: Discourses of Literature and Science* (1994).

Broderick has been described as 'the enfant terrible' of Australian SF, taking the genre to the utmost limits of its imaginative potential.

BRODNEY, Spencer (Leon Brodzky) (1883–1973), born Melbourne, spent most of his life abroad working as editor and journalist. In 1904 he founded the Australian Theatre Society in Melbourne with the object of producing Australian plays of merit; after his departure for London the Society, renamed the Playgoers' Club, dwindled into a play-reading social gathering and around 1909 ceased to exist. Inspired by the efforts of Louis Esson and the Pioneer Players, Brodzky later completed a provocative and spirited three-act play, *Rebel Smith*, published in New York in 1925 but not produced by the Pioneer Group.

BRODRIBB, W.A. (William Adams) (1809–86), born London, went to Hobart in 1818 but from 1835 was a squatter in south-western NSW (one homestead being on the present site of Gundagai), in the Gippsland area, in the Monaro district, and then on huge runs (up to 1165 square kilometres) in outback NSW. His reminiscences of a long and successful career on the land are contained in his *Recollections of an Australian Squatter* (1883).

BRODZKY, Leon, see **BRODNEY, Spencer**

BRODZKY, Maurice (1847–1919), born in East Prussia, migrated to Australia in 1871 after service in the French army during the Franco-Prussian War. He taught for some years after his arrival, then became a journalist with the Sydney *Evening News*, the Melbourne *Age* and the Melbourne *Herald*. In 1885 he began his own journal, *Table Talk*, a weekly compendium of literature, the arts, political and social affairs. Brodzky was sued for libel in 1902 and lost *Table Talk*, which continued (under the aegis of the Melbourne *Herald*) until 1939. He went to San Francisco where he became editor of a weekly, the *Wasp*, and later worked as a journalist in London and New York. He published two small books, *Genius, Lunacy and Knavery* (1876), the story of an unprincipled doctor, and *Historical Sketch of the Two Melbourne Synagogues* (1877).

BROINOWSKI, Alison (1941–), born Adelaide, has worked as a diplomat in the Department of Foreign Affairs and Trade and has lived in numerous overseas countries including Japan, Burma, Iran, the Philippines and South Korea. Her publications include a novel, *Take One Ambassador* (1973), and *The Yellow Lady* (1992), a history of Australian ideas about Asia and the Pacific from pre-colonial times to the present, including the recorded impressions of painters, novelists, sculptors, film-makers, composers and other artists.

BROINOWSKI, Robert (1877–1959), born Balwyn, Victoria, became a Commonwealth public servant, rising to be clerk of the Senate 1939–42. Active in Melbourne literary circles, he was secretary of the Repertory Theatre Club and a member of the Melbourne Literary Club. He was editor of the poetry page in *Stead's Review* and launched the *Spinner* (1924–27), which published Australian poetry. After his retirement in 1942 he was a reviewer for the *Sydney Morning Herald*.

Broken Hill, a mining city situated almost on the western border of NSW, is much closer to Adelaide than to Sydney and has been linked more closely, both commercially and culturally, with SA than with NSW. Charles Sturt discovered the Barrier region in 1844; noting a break in the range at one point, he named the area 'Broken Hill'. Charles Rasp, a boundary rider, discovered outcrops of ironstone in the area in 1883; from his discoveries emanated the Broken Hill Proprietary Company (BHP) in 1885 to exploit the rich silver, lead and zinc deposits later found there. BHP remains one of Australia's most important industrial giants and the city of Broken Hill one of Australia's most colourful mining and frontier communities. The nearby township of Silverton (silver town) grew up in the 1880s on the site of a rich silver field, Umberumberka. Mary Gilmore was a young schoolteacher there 1887–89; her association with the working-class people of the area stimulated her radical attitudes. The *Silver Age*, a newspaper that originated from Silverton in 1884, published some of her early poetry. Other literary personalities associated with Broken Hill include A.A.G. ('Smiler') Hales, who was a journalist with the *Broken Hill Times* and the *Barrier Miner* (1886–90); C.J. Dennis, who worked at odd jobs in the mines and wrote a poem, 'A Ballad of the Barrier'; Ion Idriess, who attended the Broken Hill School of Mines and worked in an assay office there; and Joseph Furphy, whose novel *Rigby's Romance* (1946) was serialised in the Broken Hill newspaper the *Barrier Truth*, 1905–6. R.H.B. Kearns, who rose to be chief accountant of North Broken Hill Ltd, wrote a historical series beginning with *Broken Hill 1883–1893* (1973), followed by three other volumes, 1974, 1975 and 1976. Geoffrey Blainey wrote *The Rise of Broken Hill* (1968), Brian Kennedy *Silver, Sun and Sixpenny Ale: A Social History of Broken Hill 1883–1921* (1978) and Barry Ellis *Broken Hill 1883–1983* (1983). Kenneth Cook's novel *Wake in Fright* (1961) appears to be set in Broken Hill. A visual and historical account of Broken Hill is contained in the paintings of Sam Byrne who lived his whole life there (1883–1978) and whose career is described in Ross Moore's *Sam Byrne: Folk Painter of the Silver City* (1985). W.A. Howard's *Barrier Bulwark: The Life and Times of Shorty O'Neil* (1990), while describing the evolution of the Barrier Industrial Council and the Strike of 1891–92 also contains a considerable amount of Broken Hill history.

Typical of the anecdotes about fortunes won and lost in the early days of Broken Hill is the story of cattleman, Sidney Kidman, who sold four steers to James Poole, one of the original members of the Broken Hill syndicate, for a fourteenth share of the initial lease. Kidman, unimpressed by the area's prospects, sold the share for £150; within three years it was worth one and a quarter million pounds.

Broken Melody, The, F.J. Thwaites's (q.v.) first novel, was published in 1930 and has been reprinted many times. The novel chronicles the misadventures and eventual triumph of Ted Jenkins, a member of a pioneer Riverina family who is expelled for drug addiction from his school in Sydney. He returns to the family station, Nullabean, where he restores himself to health until ordered from home by his father when the truth emerges about his expulsion. Back in Sydney under an assumed name and again a drug addict, Ted is rescued from despair by a young woman, Carmol Blythe, who, towards the end of the novel, leaves him a substantial legacy after she is accidentally killed. With Carmol's assistance he again breaks his addiction, secures a job as a club cellist, and after moving to Thursday Island because of his health is discovered by a visiting concert pianist, Fay Le Bretton; she sponsors him to England, where he makes a brilliant debut at the Albert Hall playing 'The Broken Melody' on a stage festooned with gum trees and wearing a white silk shirt, breeches, leather leggings and riding boots. After further success in Europe and the USA he returns to Australia, purchases drought-stricken Nullabean and is reconciled with his father and Nibs, the girl from the adjoining property. Thwaites's most successful novel, *The Broken Melody* was followed in 1935 by *The Melody Lingers*, which takes the story of the Jenkins family into the next generation. Dale Jenkins, the son of Ted and Nibs, is sent down from Sydney University for desecrating the Cenotaph in a drunken spree and has to endure privation in London and Colombo before being rescued by an old friend and restored to his family. The epigraph to *The Melody Lingers* dedicates the novel to the first Riverina Jenkins, Francis, 'my great-great grandfather'; this places Thwaites in the next generation after Dale Jenkins, although *The Melody Lingers* also carries an assurance that the characters in the novel are fictitious.

BROOKE, G.V. (Gustavus Vaughan) (1818–66), born Dublin, had established himself on the British and American stage when he was engaged by George Selth Coppin early in 1855 for an Australasian tour. He arrived with a company which included Fanny Cathcart, and played major Shakespearean roles in Melbourne and Sydney and on provincial tours both before and after going into partnership with Coppin in 1856. In 1859 he broke with Coppin but failed on his own account as manager and entrepreneur, partly through the drinking problem which was also an important factor in his deterioration as an actor when he returned to England in 1861. He made numerous farewell appearances both in Australia in the 1850s and England in the 1860s, and was *en route* back to Australia under engagement again to Coppin when he was drowned in the Bay of Biscay. Several contemporary accounts of the shipwreck were published in Australia and a biography of Brooke by W.J. Lawrence was published in 1892.

BROOKES, Herbert (1867–1963), born Sandhurst (Bendigo), Victoria, played a leading role for many years in Victorian cultural and community affairs. Brookes held appointments with the Commonwealth Board of Trade (1918–28) and the Tariff Board (1922–28) and was Australian commissioner-general to the USA. He was a foundation commissioner of the ABC (1932–39), edited *Liberal* (1911–14), the journal of the People's Liberal Party, and actively promoted the

Protestant newspaper *Vigilant*. He also edited *The Federal Story* (1944) by Alfred Deakin, his father-in-law. His son-in-law, Rohan Rivett, published *Australian Citizen: Herbert Brookes* (1965).

BROOKES, Dame Mabel (1890–1975), born Melbourne, won esteem for a lifetime of patriotic, social and charitable work. She was made CBE in 1933 and DBE in 1955 and was awarded an honorary D.Litt. by Monash University in 1967. She published fiction, *Broken Idols* (1917), *On the Knees of the Gods* (1918) and *Old Desires* (1922), as well as historical, documentary and autobiographical works, e.g. *Crowded Galleries* (1956), *St. Helena Story* (1960), *Riders of Time* (1967) and *Memoirs* (1974).

BROOKS, David (1953–), born Canberra, graduated from the ANU in 1974, before completing postgraduate studies at the University of Toronto, 1976–79. He has since taught in English departments at the University of WA, the ANU and the University of Sydney. While a student Brooks was involved in a small publishing venture, Open Door Press, and was North American editor for *New Poetry* 1976–80. In 1980 he edited *New South* (published in Canada), a small booklet of Australian poetry of the late 1970s which included R.F. Brissenden's 'Verandahs' as well as two of Brooks's own early poems. He also published *Five Poems* (1981) and *The Cold Front* (1983), the latter winning the Anne Elder Award for Poetry. Brooks's major impact as a writer came with his highly acclaimed short fiction, *The Book of Sei and Other Stories* (1985, republished in 1988 as *The Book of Sei*) and *Sheep and the Diva* (1990). The short stories stamp Brooks as a seeker for perfection in language. The intuition that in such perfection lies the ultimate satisfaction and exhilaration for the writer came to Brooks in his student days:

> I found myself less excited by the information I had put down . . . than I was about the shape and movement of a paragraph, the rhythms of sentences, the games of cat-and-mouse that one found oneself involved in with one's subject, one's text, one's hypothetical reader . . . the excitement, the freedom of that writing is its own reason, its own excuse.

That excitement lies barely suppressed beneath the surface of Brooks's carefully structured prose. Like his model Calvino, Brooks adopts a cool poise in an attempt to disguise, or at least restrain, the exhilaration that such language brings to him. Yet narrative or subject is also important to him. His best writing is usually on the extreme boundaries of fiction – metafiction – while the realistic, natural world with its normal time and place settings are deserted in favour of an invented, fantastic world whose exotic, even bizarre character is its own fiction. The title stories, 'The Book of Sei', 'Sheep', 'The Diva', and 'The Garden' and 'The Family of the Minister' are outstanding. 'The Book of Sei' tells of a man crossing the mythical Sei Mountains in the tenth century seeking shelter at nightfall in the cottage of a weaver (a shadowy, beautiful woman). The night passes in love-making but the beautiful woman never reappears. Brooks agrees that the story is 'a kind of sexual bestiary' but it is also an expression of the intangibility of fantasy itself. 'Sheep' is a tale of a miracle of recurring sheep that bring survival and credibility to a shepherd, a miracle that must vanish if rational explanations are allowed to surface. 'The Diva' tells of an old man's memories of a singer whose voice brought meaning to the lives of her listeners and the life of her country, but that one morning fell silent and was never heard again. 'The Garden' is an extraordinary story of a garden and its maker whose lives and fortunes follow a similar pattern of growth, decay and renewal, while 'The Family of the Minister' is a macabre account of the revenge Nature takes on the family of a man who attempts to oppress the environment. Brooks has also published a book of essays, *The Necessary Jungle* (1990), which discusses 'poetry and poetics, advertising, the definition of literature, the perception and construction of gender, the ideas of pornography and excess', and provides, in 'The Blood of José Arcadio', a key to his own writing credo. He has edited *Suddenly Evening, the Selected Poems of R. F. Brissenden* (1993) and *Selected Poems by A.D. Hope* (1992).

BROOKSBANK, Anne (1943–), born Melbourne, has written television documentaries and dramas, stage plays and film scripts. With her husband Bob Ellis (q.v.) she wrote the stage play *Down Under* (1977), first produced in 1975, and *Mad Dog Morgan* (1976), a novel based on the film by Philippa Mora. She also wrote *Green Room* (1976), performed in Perth in 1976, and was co-author of the feature film *Maybe This Time* (1980). Her other novels are *On Loan* (1985), *Archer* (1985), both of which are based on her scripts for television, and *All My Love: the Lost Romance of Mary Gilmore and Henry Lawson* (1991), a fictionalised representation of the relationship between the two writers. She has won five Awgies and various overseas awards.

BROOME, Lady Mary Anne (Mary Anne Barker) (1831–1911), born Spanish Town, Jamaica, was educated in England and, after marrying for the second time in 1865, went to NZ where her first book, *Station Life in New Zealand* (1870), won praise for its vivid account of pioneering life. In 1882 her husband, after whom the port of Broome is named, became governor of WA; her account of their experiences in that colony was published as *Letters to Guy* (1885), her elder son, Guy, having remained at school in London. Her final work (she had earlier written novels, children's books, cookery books and edited travel books) was *Colonial Memories* (1904). *Remembered with Affection*, edited by Alexandra Hasluck (1963), is a new edition of *Letters to Guy*.

BROOMFIELD, F.J. (Frederick John) (1860–1941), born Hampshire, England, was brought to Australia in 1868. For more than three decades from the 1880s he had wide experience as a journalist. As sub-editor on the *Bulletin*, Broomfield reputedly accepted Henry Lawson's first contribution and helped prepare the *Bulletin's* famous anthology, *A Golden Shanty* (q.v., 1890). He also wrote for the *Freeman's Journal*, the *Sydney Mail*, the *Brisbane Courier* and the *Australian Worker*, edited the *Centennial Magazine*, the *Elector* and the *Golden Fleece*, and was employed on the *Picturesque Atlas of Australia* and as a government journalist. His creative work included several published songs and contributions to anthologies of prose and verse, but his major contributions to Australian literature were his encouragement of contemporaries like Lawson, John Farrell and Victor Daley, and his great assistance to Sir John Quick and later E. Morris Miller in the compilation of the pioneering bibliographical work, *Australian Literature From Its Beginnings to 1935* (q.v., 1940). Broomfield was a flamboyant *Bulletin* bohemian and a central figure in the Dawn and Dusk Club (q.v.) and the Century Club, the latter a meeting place for artists, journalists, writers and others ('the best wits and the soundest brains in Sydney') from 1887 onwards.

BROPHY, Kevin (1949–), a teacher of developmental psychology and a tutor in the English Department of the University of Melbourne, is co-editor of the small literary magazine *Going Down Swinging*, a frequent reviewer of books and a well-known identity in literary circles in Melbourne. He is particularly interested in performance poetry and fiction. He has written three novels, *Getting Away With It* (1982), *Visions* (1989) and *The Hole through the Centre of the World* (1991). The central characters of *Getting Away With It* are a young couple, the narrator and Mary, who leave their somewhat vague but apparently well-paid jobs in the country to find freedom and excitement in the city. They are pursued by the shadowy Inspector Grundler of the Middle Western Bureau, whose task it is to report upon them monthly. In the city the two go through a series of trivial/boring encounters with others as trivial/boring as themselves. *Visions* has, as its narrator, Margaret, whose ambition is to live like a saint. Life has no such plans for her, nor do the males who enter her life, especially Scar (Oscar) the boy who formulates his plans for her at puberty. Margaret manages to enter a convent, but her 'saintliness' proves too much for her religious supervisors, who return her to normal life where most of her acquaintances believe that she has 'a fever of the mind or something. Hysteria'. Margaret marries Scar believing that that is the suffering Jesus intended for her. She pursues her 'vision' to its ultimate – 'your life will be connected with His cross. You are to be an image of His crucified life'. With *The Hole through the Centre of the World* Brophy continues with both larger-than-life characters, e.g. Erno Gaasland, the science-obsessed Perfect Chair salesman, and those with no life at all, e.g. his son, Martin. Both are remarkably successful creations. Erno and his obsessions batter their way through a narrative that is believable and absorbing when it deals with the tragically serious, that is the death of the little boy, Daniel, and its destructive effect on Erno, his wife, Val and Martin, and is equally believable and absorbing when it deals (with blatant tongue-in-cheek) with the farcical, e.g. the Chair-selling expedition to China. Throughout his fiction

Brophy appears to have been seeking the right mix of fantasy and realism, signally achieved in *The Hole through the Centre of the World*. His first book of verse, *Replies to the Questionnaire on Love* (1992), reveals Brophy's intuition that poetry should appeal to an audience. Some poems deal with the personal – imponderables found in marriage, and parenthood – while others are concerned with social problems.

'BROWN, Carter' (Alan Geoffrey Yates) (1923–85), born London, served in the Royal Navy in the Second World War and came in 1948 to Australia where he began, almost immediately, to write for the thriving pulp fiction market, turning out an endless stream (six books a year) of mystery stories, westerns, romances, science fiction and horror stories under a variety of pseudonyms including 'Paul Valdez' and 'Tex Conrad'. As 'Peter Carter Brown' (later 'Carter Brown' because it suited the American market) he began in 1950 a series of mystery stories, which by his own vague count stood at upward of 150 titles, many of which have sold 200 000 copies in the USA alone. 'Carter Brown's' staple is a combination of mystery, violence, sex and snappy dialogue. His fictional hard-drinking heroes are Al Wheeler, Rick Holman and Danny Boyd; typical titles are *Tomorrow Is Murder*, *Ice-Cold Nude*, *Blonde on the Rocks*, *No Blonde is an Island* and *Lady is Available*. 'The Carter Brown Mystery Theatre', an Australian radio series 1956–58, was devoted to his works, and an Australian musical, 'The Stripper', based on his book, was performed by the Sydney Theatre Company in 1982. His autobiography, *Ready When You Are, CB!*, was published in 1983.

BROWN, Edwin Tylor (1889–1957), educated at the University of Melbourne, travelled extensively in Europe and India. He published two collections of essays on various subjects, some literary, *Excursions and Enquiries* (1935) and *Not Without Prejudice* (1955), as well as books reflecting his travel experiences and political beliefs, *Curry and Rice* (1937), *Bread and Power* (1940), *The Sovereign People* (1954) and *This Russian Business* (1933).

BROWN, Eliza and **Thomas** arrived in the Swan River colony in 1841 and took up land at York, Grassdale. Eliza Brown's letters to her father, William Bussey, back in Oxfordshire, during the period 1840–51 offer one of the most comprehensive accounts of life in the colony. Their descendant Peter Cowan edited *A Faithful Picture; The Letters of Eliza and Thomas Brown at York in the Swan River Colony 1841–1852* (1977).

BROWN, Lyn (1918–), born Fairfield, NSW, graduated MA from the University of Sydney in 1940. Editor, librarian and language teacher, she has also published poetry: *Late Summer* (1970), *Jacaranda and Illawarra Flame* (1973) and *Going Home at Night* (1979).

BROWN, Max (1916–), born Invercargill, NZ, was educated in Melbourne and has worked as a journalist there and in Sydney, Perth and country towns in NSW and WA; he has also worked as a teacher, labourer and film publicist. He served in the RAAF during the Second World War and used his severance pay to write *Australian Son* (1948), a highly regarded and sympathetic biography of Ned Kelly. He has subsequently published the novels *Wild Turkey* (1958), which focuses on making a film about Australia by a Hollywood company, and *The Jimberi Track* (1966), as well as *The Black Eureka* (1976), which focuses on the 1946 strike by Aboriginal station hands in the Pilbara region of WA, fictionalised in Donald Stuart's *Yandy* (q.v., 1959).

BROWN, Pamela (1948–), born Seymour, Victoria, has held tutoring and lecturing positions in Newcastle and Sydney, was playwright-in-residence in 1989 at Performance Space, and works at the Badham Library, University of Sydney, and as a writer as well as a lecturer in film-making. She has published, over twenty years, numerous books of poetry, prose and drama. Her books include *Sureblock* (1972), *Cocabola's Funny Picture Book* (1973), *Automatic Sad* (1974), *Cafe Sport* (1979), *Correspondences* (1979), *Country & Eastern* (1980), *Small Blue View* (1982), *Selected Poems 1971–1982* (1984), *Keep it Quiet* (1987), *New and Selected Poems* (1990) and *This World, This Place* (1991). She has also published a play (and radio play), *As Much Trouble As Talking* (1988) and an earlier radio play, *And That Is Very Interesting* (1984). Her poems, often brief, enigmatic and epigrammatic, chart the terrain traversed by the newly freed woman of the 1960s, the search for identity and fulfilment that begins with gusto and optimism, wavers into doubt and misery and ends in resolution and wry self-acceptance. Brown's poems are 'a fever chart' (her friend, Kate Jennings's description) of a fearless, honest attempt to cope with and make sense of the often illusory freedom of the feminist decades. John Tranter's view that her *New and Selected Poems* 'have the flavour of Gertrude Stein sung to a blues guitar' catches the tough, brave poignancy of much of her writing. *Keep It Quiet*, her first book of prose (twenty-seven pieces) shows the poet's sensitivity to language and emotion but is, as customary with Pamela Brown, searingly critical. She describes her prose pieces as 'snapshots of conditions. Incidents of emotion. Episodes of a long running serial. Chronicles of a transition which is never completed.'

BROWNE, Thomas Alexander, see 'BOLDREWOOD, Rolf'

BRUCE, Mary Grant (1878–1958) was born and educated at Sale in the Gippsland district of Victoria, and began writing as a young child. After thrice winning the essay competition of the Melbourne Shakespeare Society she settled into journalism in Melbourne. Employed on the staff of the *Age* to run, as 'Cinderella', the children's page of the *Leader* (q.v.), she contributed short stories, articles on a wide variety of subjects, and serials not only to the *Age* and the

Leader but also to *Woman's World*, *Woman* (both of which she temporarily edited), *Lone Hand*, *Pastoralist's Review*, *Table Talk* and other journals. In 1905–7 *A Little Bush Maid* was serialised in the *Leader*; published as a book in 1910, it inaugurated the Billabong series of children's books, which ran until 1942 and made Bruce one of the best-known Australian authors of her time. Sales of her work have been estimated at two million copies. Bruce went to England in 1913 and wrote for the *Daily Mail;* in 1914 she married her second cousin, George Bruce, who wrote two novels and many angling pieces. They spent most of the war in Ireland before returning to Victoria, where Mary resumed journalism in Melbourne and renewed contacts there with other women writers. In 1927 the Bruces settled in Ireland but following the accidental death of one of their two sons lived on the Continent and at Bexhill-on-Sea in Sussex until 1939, when they again settled in Victoria. In 1949 George Bruce died, and in 1954 Mary, visiting England for the centenary of her publisher, Ward, Lock & Company (whose 'stable' had also included her contemporary and competitor, Ethel Turner) moved once more to Bexhill, where her last years were spent.

In all, Mary Grant Bruce published thirty-seven children's novels 1910–42, usually at the rate of one a year; a book of Aboriginal legends, *The Stone Age of Burkamukk* (1922); a collection of radio talks, *The Power Within* (1940); and an enormous amount of journalism, short fiction and poetry, most of it uncollected. A selection of her journalism, autobiographical writing and uncollected short stories, *The Peculiar Honeymoon*, was published in 1986 edited by Prue KcKay. The special subject of her fiction was the re-entered bush world of her childhood, most memorably re-created for her readers in the Utopian portrait of Billabong, a fictional station in northern Victoria, home of David Linton, his two children Jim and Norah (Mrs Linton died after Norah's birth), Jim's friend Wally Meadows (who comes on holidays soon after the series starts and stays on to marry Norah), the homestead staff, various hired hands and periodically appearing Linton relatives. In *A Little Bush Maid*, the first of the fifteen Billabong books, David Linton is about 40 and his children about 15 and 11 respectively. They remain so in the next two novels, but the First World War forces a change in the timeless, static nature of existence at Billabong: Jim and Wally go to the Front (*From Billabong to London*, 1915; *Jim and Wally*, 1916; *Captain Jim*, 1919), and after the war the courtship of Wally and Norah (*Billabong's Daughter*, 1924) is followed by their marriage (*Billabong Adventures*, 1927) and first child (*Bill of Billabong*, 1931). In contrast to the feminine, urban world created by Ethel Turner, Bruce's Billabong is masculine, emphasising such virtues as independence, resourcefulness, a love of adventure (Billabong is both a sanctuary and the centre of many crises), hard work, honesty and mateship, mateship encompassing even the relationship between Wally and Norah. Although Bruce drew on other traditions (e.g. Jim is the schoolboy-brother hero familiar in children's domestic fiction), she also meant her small stock of characters to be seen as typical bush Australians. Her popularity made Jim and Norah Linton as significant in the development of an Australian mythology as the Little Boy from Manly, Ginger Meggs, Dad and Dave, and the characters in Gwen Meredith's *Blue Hills*. Brenda Niall's *Seven Little Billabongs* (1979) compares the fictional worlds of Bruce and Ethel Turner; Alison Alexander's *Billabong's Author* (1979) is a biography.

'Brumby' is a word of uncertain origin. It may have derived from a Major James Brumby, who reputedly left behind a number of horses when he returned to England in the early years of the settlement; they ran wild and became known as Brumby's horses. Another possible source was from a Major William Brumby, who was a noted horse-breaker in the nineteenth century. A.B. Paterson, who wrote a poem, 'Brumby's Run', believed it sprang from the Aboriginal word *booramby*, meaning 'wild'. The *Bulletin*, 21 March 1896, suggested it came from Baramba, the name of a property in the Burnett district of Queensland. Will Ogilvie wrote a poem, 'The Brumby Stallion', and Katharine Susannah Prichard created a rather wild character, Brumby Innes, in her play of that name.

BRYANT, William (1757–91) and **Mary** (1765–?), convicts in the First Fleet, married at Port Jackson in February 1788. On 28 March 1791 the Bryants and seven other convicts escaped in a small boat, making a hazardous voyage to Koepang in Timor, about 5200 kilometres in ten weeks. Taken back into custody, they were being returned to England when William died. Mary was pardoned in 1793. Literature on the William and Mary Bryant saga includes 'Louis' Becke and Walter Jeffery, *A First Fleet Family* (1896), Geoffrey Rawson, *The Strange Case of Mary Bryant* (1938), C.H. Currey, *The Transportation, Escape and Pardoning of Mary Bryant* (1963), and Anthony Scott Veitch, *Spindrift: The Mary Bryant Story* (1980). Mary Bryant is a character in Thomas Keneally's novel *The Playmaker* (1987) and in the play which it inspired, *Our Country's Good* (1988) by Timberlake Wertenbaker. A narrative of the escape by one of the convicts involved, James Martin, was published under the title *Memorandoms* (1937).

BRYNING, Frank, see **Science Fiction**

BRYSON, John (1935–), born Melbourne of Polynesian and Scottish ancestry, has been racing car driver, pilot, lawyer and company director. He was a member of the Literature Board of the Australia Council, later its deputy chairman and acting chairman, as well as chairman of the Community Arts Board of the Australia Council. He was secretary of the Australian Performing Group (q.v.) at the Pram Factory in Melbourne. He turned to writing in 1978 and published a collection of short stories, *Whoring Around* (1981), which examines, ironically, the moralities of the middle class. His non-fiction account of the Azaria Chamberlain case, *Evil Angels* (1985), won several awards in Australia and overseas, including the Victorian Premier's Award and the British Crime

Writer's Golden Dagger. It was published overseas as *A Cry in the Dark* and was made into a Fred Schepisi/Meryl Streep film in 1988. A contributor for many years to newspaper feature pages and literary supplements, Bryson published *Backstage at the Revolution* (1988), a collection of his journalistic writings.

BUCHANAN, A.J. (Alfred Johnson) (1874–1941), journalist and lawyer, was on the staff of the Melbourne *Age* and was editor of the Brisbane *Daily Mail.* His publications include the novels *Bubble Reputation* (1906), *She Loved Much* (1907), *Where Day Begins* (1911) and *The Modern Heloise* (1912). *Where Day Begins* is a fictionalised version of the Harry Harbord Morant ('The Breaker') saga. Buchanan also wrote *The Real Australia* (1907), which contains chapters on the literary figures Adam Lindsay Gordon, Victor Daley, Henry Lawson and Louise Mack.

BUCHANAN, Nat (1826–1901), born Dublin, arrived in Australia in 1837. One of the early overlanders, he joined William Landsborough in 1837 in establishing vast runs in the Thomson River country of western Queensland. He made a succession of overlanding trips: in 1878 to stock the Glencoe station in the Northern Territory; in 1880 with 20 000 cattle, again to Glencoe; and in 1883 with 4000 cattle to the Ord River in the Kimberleys. He died owning only a small farm on Dungowan Creek near Tamworth, NSW. Buchanan's feats as bushman and overlander are recorded in C. Fetherstonhaugh's *After Many Days* (1918), G. Buchanan's *Packhorse and Waterhole* (1933), Ernestine Hill's *The Territory* (1951), Mary Durack's *Kings in Grass Castles* (1959) and D.S. McMillan (ed.) *Bowen Downs, 1863–1963* (1963).

BUCKLEY, Samuel ('Frank Blair') (1886–1950), born Strathpine, Queensland, served in the AIF in the First World War and taught in Queensland. His published poetry includes *They Shall Not Pass and Other Poems* (1943) and *'Neath Sunny Skies* (1944); he also wrote a novel, *Digger Sea Mates* (1929), under the pseudonym 'Frank Blair'.

Buckley Family, comprising the Waterloo veteran Major James Buckley, his wife Agnes and their son Sam, is one of the three families whose fortunes are chronicled in Henry Kingsley's *The Recollections of Geoffry Hamlyn* (q.v., 1859). Distinguished but impoverished members of the English gentry, the Buckleys succeed gloriously as pastoralists in Australia and eventually return to the ancestral home of Clere. Sam's comment towards the end of the novel, 'I don't want to be young Sam Buckley of Baroona. I want to be the Buckley of Clere', is often quoted as evidence of Kingsley's Anglocentricism, which led Joseph Furphy to object to the unrealistic portrayal of Australia in *Geoffry Hamlyn* and to present an alternative history of the Buckley fortunes in Chapter VI of his novel *Such is Life.* There it is reported that 'Hungry Buckley' has lost his property Baroona to the banks and has died, his son has gone to gaol for embezzlement, and his

daughter, Maud, after three husbands, has become housekeeper at Runnymede station.

BUCKLEY, Vincent (1925–88) was born in Romsey, a small Victorian country town. Of Irish Catholic lineage (seven of his great-grandparents were Irish), he had a strong sense of identity with Irish culture, demonstrated by his long involvement in Australian Catholic intellectual life, his interest in Irish Republican politics and his love for Ireland itself, where he spent considerable time in his later years. In 1969 he founded the Committee for Civil Rights in Ireland. He was educated at a Jesuit college in Melbourne and at the universities of Melbourne and Cambridge. He was Lockie Fellow at the University of Melbourne 1958–60, and from 1967 held a Personal Chair in Poetry there. As poet, critic, academic and editor, Buckley was influential (especially in Melbourne) in the late 1950s and 1960s, when he was the central figure of a group of university poets and intellectuals with a distinctive philosophy of literature.

Buckley's volumes of poetry are *The World's Flesh* (1954), *Masters in Israel* (1961), *Arcady and Other Places* (1966), *Golden Builders* (1976), *The Pattern* (1979), *Late-Winter Child* (1979), *Selected Poems* (1981) and *Last Poems* (1991). He also published the critical works *Essays in Poetry: Mainly Australian* (1957), *Poetry and Morality* (1959), *Henry Handel Richardson* (1961) and *Poetry and the Sacred* (1968). He edited *Australian Poetry 1958*, *The Campion Paintings, by Leonard French* (1962), *Eight by Eight* (q.v., 1963), a poetry anthology, and *The Faber Book of Modern Australian Verse*, which appeared in 1991, after his death. From 1958 to 1964 he edited the magazine *Prospect*, and in 1961–63 he was poetry editor of the *Bulletin*, during which period (but not, according to Buckley, through his own editorial prejudices) the domination of the *Bulletin*'s pages by the then 'mainstream' poets was broken and a new set of poets came into prominence. Buckley's autobiographical *Cutting Green Hay* was published in 1983. Subtitled 'Friendships, movements and cultural conflicts in Australia's great decades' (Buckley refers to 1945–1965), it is both a social history and a personal statement. Buckley also published *Memory Ireland: Insights into the Contemporary Irish Condition* (1985), cultural analysis with an autobiographical flavour.

The poems of Buckley's first volume, *The World's Flesh*, the title referring to the body of Christ which sustains and nourishes the world, are essentially, if sometimes subtly and ambivalently so, poems of love – religious love, familial love and love of nature and of places. The complex ten-poem sequence 'Land of No Fathers' takes up, in its links with de Quiros, the voyager theme, relating it to Buckley's people, celebrating them and their pioneer endeavours. The second volume, *Masters in Israel*, taking its title from the Gospel of St John, contains better-known Buckley poems: 'Late Tutorial', 'Reading to My Sick Daughter' and 'Impromptu for Francis Webb' – all of which reflect largely on the poetic process – and 'In Time of the Hungarian Martyrdom' and 'Sinn Fein: 1957', which are Buckley's personal views of past and contemporary political and historical events. Buckley later judged the poetry of these first two volumes as glib, falsely spontaneous and couched in smooth, soft rhythms, 'not fit to express the things I was groping to express'. Other critics saw it as over-rhetorical, extrovert and too obviously didactic in stance. *Arcady and Other Places*, more moderate in tone and flexible in style, saw Buckley achieve some measure of the 'hardness in phrasing' that he desired so long as it was not inconsistent with the 'rhythmic impulse' that he believed to be the essence of poetry. The volume begins with the seven-part 'Stroke' (q.v., perhaps the earliest illustration of the influence on Buckley of the 'life studies' genre then popular in American poetry), which reveals, behind its terse language and often brutally frank description, the pathos of the final encounter between a father and son who had never in the course of their lives really 'learned to touch'. *Arcady and Other Places* has five other sections: poems with the familiar religious and family backgrounds; eight translations from Catullus; and 'Eleven Political Poems', satirical verses on the expediency of politics and certain of its practitioners. Ten years later Buckley published *Golden Builders*. Its opening sequence, 'Northern Circle', is a series of seven 'postcard' poems recording his experiences in Canada. They illustrate the other side of modern globetrotting, the boredom and loneliness that engulf the single traveller. 'Gunsynd', 'Jumps Jockey' and 'Kilmore Races' reflect Buckley's well-known fascination with the turf. 'Golden Builders' (q.v.), a 27-poem sequence set in Melbourne, examines the problems that modern city life poses for the human spirit. Despite the constant assault of the din, squalor and ugliness of the city, human resilience is seen to triumph. Buckley's innovations in the shape and spacing of the verses on the page, in the use of lower-case lettering and in the free-running speech rhythms, make *Golden Builders* his most technically adventurous work. *The Pattern* (1979) begins with a series of poems on Ireland which merge long-past historical events, such as the massacre at Smerwick in 1580 (Edmund Spenser and Sir Walter Raleigh were reputedly present), and more recent happenings (such as the internment of Patrick Shivers in the present 'trouble') with contemporary Irish life, with the vividly evoked Irish landscape and with the reflections of the visiting Irish-Australian poet who seeks that part of himself that has its roots in Ireland. Ireland, 'the source country', flows imperceptibly into Australia, the Irish poems giving way to those with Australian settings – and the 'pattern' is demonstrated. While in Ireland writing these poems Buckley was awarded the 1977 Dublin Prize, a quinquennial award by the University of Melbourne for an outstanding contribution to art, music, literature or science. *Late-Winter Child* (1979) moves back to the personal world of man and wife, celebrating the birth to Buckley and his younger second wife of a daughter. *Late-Winter Child* reinforces the impression from his early poetry that Buckley, although sometimes accused of a certain academic detachment and lack of commitment, is a sensitive love poet. *Selected Poems* (1981) combine the poems of his first six volumes. *Last Poems* (1991), which won the Adelaide Festival of the Arts John Bray Award for

Poetry, is a memorable work, setting the seal on Buckley's substantial achievements. Edited, with a foreword, by his wife Penelope, *Last Poems* reveals more about Buckley than all his earlier works and read together with *Cutting Green Hay*, provides a remarkable picture of the complete Buckley – poet, patriot, husband, father, intellectual and warm, volatile, compassionate individual. *Last Poems* has two parts, 'A Poetry Without Attitudes' and 'The Watch's Wheel – Pieces and Songs'. 'A Poetry Without Attitudes' contains many poems that Buckley intended for his next volume, which he proposed to call 'A General Order for the Night'. 'The Watch's Wheel' is more or less a 'workshop' collection of pieces, poems, songs, some complete, others in draft form. *Last Poems* has many childhood memories, poems about a present that has been shaped by his past, poems of love, poems about Ireland and poems of serenity in the face of approaching death. There is also still evident the typical biting criticism of a world where brutality, greed and injustice continue to flourish.

Cutting Green Hay is an absorbing account of Buckley's own life, from boyhood in Romsey, through school and student days on to his years as poet and teacher. Interwoven with the autobiographical picture is a fascinating study of the culture and society of the time, including the Catholic university apostolate movement and other controversial social and political events. More than an autobiography, *Cutting Green Hay* is a chronicle of the 1950s and 1960s in Australia, and in Melbourne in particular.

Buckley's published critical works began with *Essays in Poetry: Mainly Australian* (1957) which encompass individual poets (Kenneth Slessor, R.D. FitzGerald, A.D. Hope, Judith Wright and James McAuley), contemporary left-wing Australian poetry (especially John Manifold, John Thompson and Laurence Collinson), and the new generation of poets who were emerging in the *Bulletin*. By dismissing, or at least devaluating, such traditionally accepted influences as nationalism, radicalism and vitalism on the development of Australian literature, Buckley set up an alternative canon which, though controversial at the time, has proved to be significant and influential. The Vincent Buckley Poetry Prize, alternating between Australian and Irish poets, and instituted in Buckley's memory, was awarded for the first time in 1993. It was won by Lisa Gorton for a group of poems, 'Tidings'.

BUCKLEY, William (1780–1856), born Cheshire, England, was sentenced to transportation for life for having received a stolen roll of cloth. He was taken in the convict ship *Calcutta* with David Collins's colonising expedition to Port Phillip in 1803 and there absconded with two fellow convicts who were never heard of again. Buckley was befriended by the Watourong tribe of Aborigines who believed him to be 'Murrangurk', a reincarnation of a dead chieftain of the tribe, and he lived with them until 1835. On his return to White civilisation he was pardoned and became a government interpreter. Accounts of his life as a 'white blackfellow' have been given by John

Morgan in *The Life and Adventures of William Buckley* (1852), by James Bonwick in *William Buckley, the Wild White Man, and His Port Phillip Black Friends* (1856) and by W.T. Pyke in *Buckley, the Wild White Man* (1889). Craig Robertson published the biographical *Buckley's Hope* (1980), the title stemming from the phrase 'Buckley's Hope' (sometimes 'Buckley's Chance'), meaning little or no hope and reflecting the pessimistic view of Buckley's prospects of survival. The phrase is, however, linked by some to the Melbourne store of Buckley & Nunn. Barry Hill (q.v.) wrote the long verse sequence *Ghosting William Buckley* (1993).

BUCKMASTER, Charles (1951–72), born Gruyere, Victoria, was closely involved in his brief life with the drug subculture of the 1960s and with the hostility of his generation towards the perceived materialism and sterility of Australian life. A strong supporter of the 'New Australian Poetry' movement, Buckmaster participated in the poetry workshops of La Mama and edited the small magazine *The Great Auk* which helped to disseminate the new poetry. He published two volumes of poetry, *Deep Blue and Green* (1970) and *The Lost Forest* (1971); before his suicide he is alleged to have burned many of his unpublished manuscripts. Buckmaster's poetry reflects both his enthusiasm for the traditional Australian Arcadia under threat and his repugnance at the shallow artificiality of some modern values. A collected edition, gathered from his surviving papers, was edited by Simon Macdonald in 1989. It reinforces the belief that in Buckmaster's early death Australia lost a potentially significant lyric talent. A small press, Wildgrass, inaugurated the Charles Buckmaster Poetry Prize in 1985.

BUDDEE, Paul (1913–   ), born WA, was a concert flautist by the age of 14 and while teaching in WA conducted a large choir (1935–40) and organised singing broadcasts for schools (1946–50). He served in the AIF in the Second World War, publishing *Stand To and Other Poems* in 1943. After the war he combined a successful teaching career with active participation in civil and community affairs; he was president of the WA branch of FAW (1947–49). Buddee received a WA Citizenship Award in 1977 for his service to the State in Art, Culture and Entertainment and the OAM in 1989 for his service to music, children and literature. He is a life member of the FAW (WA). A prolific writer of children's books and historical fiction, Buddee created the Air Patrol series, the Ann Rankin Pony stories, the Peter Devlin Outback series and the Jim Meredith series. He also wrote *The Escape of the Fenians* (1972), a story of the journey in 1876 by Irish patriots from the USA to rescue Irish political prisoners from the Fremantle gaol. His *The Escape of John O'Reilly* (1973) is a companion volume. Buddee's other writings include *Airways: The Call of the Sky* (1978), the story of Australian civil aviation, and *Fate of the Artful Dodger* (1984), an account of the boy convicts transported from Parkhurst Prison on the Isle of Wight to Australia and NZ between 1842 and 1852. Buddee's meticulous research has produced an

interesting narrative accompanied by notes and illustrations, a valuable addition to the overall body of convict literature. An offshoot of his Parkhurst research was *Legacy of Love, Jud Mudbury, Parkhurst Boy* (1991).

BUGGY, Hugh (1896–1974), born Seymour, Victoria, joined the Melbourne *Argus* in 1917 and in a career extending over half a century became one of Australia's best-known reporter-journalists, covering many of the nation's major (and sometimes bizarre) criminal, sporting and political events. He is said, for example, to have coined the word 'bodyline' to describe the intimidatory bowling that caused a furore in the 1930s. He was a journalist with the *Argus*, the Melbourne *Sun News-Pictorial*, the *Evening Sun*, the Sydney *Sun*, the Melbourne *Herald* and the *Truth*. He 'ghosted' *Story of the Southern Cross Trans-Pacific Flight* (1928) for the aviators Charles Kingsford-Smith and Charles Ulm; wrote *Pacific Victory* (1946), a history of Australia's part in the war against Japan; compiled *Hugh Buggy's Murder Book* (?1953), a selection from the murder trials he had covered as a reporter; and wrote *The Real John Wren* (1977), a rebuttal of Frank Hardy's *Power Without Glory* (1950).

'Buladelah – Taree Holiday Song Cycle, The', a long poem in thirteen sections by Les Murray (q.v.), published in his volume of poetry *Ethnic Radio* (1977), won the C.J. Dennis Memorial poetry competition for 1976. The 'Holiday Song Cycle', claimed by Murray to be the first poem written by a White man in an Australian Aboriginal metre (derived essentially from music – clapsticks and didgeridoo – and dance), is based thematically and structurally on R.M. Berndt's translation of the Wonguri-Mandjikai song, 'The Moon-bone Song', from north-eastern Arnhem Land. Murray uses as his 'spirit country' the mid-north-coast countryside of NSW between Buladelah and Taree, renowned for its coastal strip of popular beaches and seaside resorts and its lush hinterland of dairy farms. To accord with the Aboriginal Moon-bone song, which illustrates harmony and total communication between all living creatures in an intimately known and coherent environment, Murray introduces into his north-coast world the annual migration of holiday-makers at Christmas time, many of whom are families returning to their ancestral places – the farms, rural villages and seaside towns from which they sprang a generation or so ago. There they recover or, in the case of the younger ones, discover, by communion with the bush, the mountains, the sea and by contact with their parents and grandparents, the origins of their being. The first section describes the pleasurable preparations in the country for the annual influx of visitors. In the second section the holiday-crammed Pacific Highway, which runs through the district, is described (ironically according to Murray but with inspired effect) as the 'great fiery but all-giving Rainbow Snake, writhing over the country and throwing out deadly little offshoots of excitement into the districts up back roads'. After their arrival in 'that country of the Holiday' the returnees rediscover many half-forgotten things, the poem's capitalising of seemingly commonplace things ('Wood Duck's Nest', 'Cattlecamp') bestowing on them a totemic significance. The cycle goes on to celebrate holiday activities and the animals, birds, topography, and events of the 'spirit country'. Murray's belief that place-names are an essential way for people to encapsulate the spirit of place and to link themselves with that spirit is manifested in the song-cycle's numerous place-names; some come from the Aboriginal ('Kiwarric', 'Bucca Wauka', 'Krambach'), others are associated with the White inhabitants and events of the district ('the place of Bingham's ghost', 'the place of the Plough Handles'). Murray sees the latter nomenclature as the White equivalent of the Aboriginal habit of naming from the spirit of place. The eleventh section describes the children establishing affinity with ancestral things: they bite into the old-fashioned summer fruits (china pear, quince and persimmon) of the abandoned 'fruit trees of the grandmothers' and absorb 'the taste of former lives, of sawdust and parlour song, the tang of manners'. In the final section the whole holiday experience is crystallised and evaluated; having gazed for a week or two 'at their year's worth of stars', the holiday-makers prepare to return to their ordinary concerns.

BULCOCK, Emily (1877–1969), born Tinana near Maryborough, Queensland, was an older sister of the novelist Vance Palmer. A schoolteacher and later a regular writer for Brisbane and southern newspapers, she was a life member of the Queensland Authors' and Artists' Association. She wrote several books of verse, *Jacaranda Blooms* (1923), *From Quenchless Springs* (1945) and *From Australia to Britain* (1961). Remembered particularly for her verses celebrating important national occasions, she remains somewhat underrated as a poet. At her best she displays a sensitive perception of life and nature, imaginative imagery and a firm control of poetic form and structure.

Bull-Ant, a Melbourne literary weekly containing short fiction, poetry, sketches, theatrical reviews and cartoons, was edited by its part-owner, Edward George Dyson, and ran 1890–92, although its title was changed to *Ant* from April 1891 to June 1892. Dyson wrote material for it under the pseudonym 'Silas Snell'.

BULL, J.W. (John Wrathall) (1804–86), born Kent, England, arrived in Australia with his family in 1838. After he took up farming he invented a mechanical means of harvesting wheat. His book of reminiscences, *Early Experiences of Colonial Life in South Australia* (1878), first appeared in the South Australian *Chronicle;* a revised, expanded edition was published in 1884.

Bulletin, the most famous and most significant Australian weekly periodical, was founded 31 January 1880 by J.F. Archibald and John Haynes (qq.v.); it took its title from the San Francisco *Bulletin.* In the first year it suffered crises over printing, advertising

revenue and libel actions, and in January 1881 published a leader by W.H. Traill (q.v.) on larrikinism at the Clontarf picnic grounds. The proprietors of the picnic grounds wrote protesting their innocence, Haynes composed a cheeky rejoinder, and a libel action ensued which led to the imprisonment of Archibald and Haynes for failure to pay legal costs. By then Traill had control of the *Bulletin;* although he allowed Archibald and Haynes each to purchase a quartershare when the Bulletin Newspaper Company was constituted in 1883, he remained editor and proprietor until he sold out in 1886. In 1887 Archibald and William Macleod (q.v.) became joint owners, Archibald as editor and Macleod as business manager and later managing director. In subsequent years principal members of the literary and artist staff of the *Bulletin* such as Livingston Hopkins (q.v.) were permitted to buy 25 per cent of shares but Macleod remained in financial control until 1927, when he sold out to the family headed by S.H. Prior (q.v.), who had purchased 25 per cent of Archibald's holding in 1914. Prior edited the *Bulletin* 1915–33, following Archibald (1886–1903) and James Edmond (q.v., 1903–15). Subsequent editors included John Webb (1933–48), David Adams (1948–61) and, after the *Bulletin* was sold in 1960 by the Prior family to Australian Consolidated Press and changed direction towards a news magazine format, Donald Horne (1961–62, 1967–72). From an initial circulation of 3000 it now sells in excess of 80 000 copies.

Traill played a significant part in consolidating the *Bulletin* by improving its appearance, by developing its political and economic policy, and by securing the services of Hopkins and Phil May (q.v.), who did much to establish the *Bulletin*'s reputation in the field of black-and-white art. Prominent among subsequent cartoonists and illustrators were Norman and Lionel Lindsay, Will and Ambrose Dyson, David Low, D.H. Souter, Alf Vincent, Frank Mahony, George Lambert, Percy Leason and Ted Scorefield. The heyday of the journal is traditionally reckoned as the Archibald years and particularly the 1890s (see Nineties), when Archibald had the assistance of A.G. Stephens (q.v.) as editor (1896–1906) of the Red Page (q.v.) and Edmond as expert financial journalist as well as Macleod's sound business sense. Just as Archibald needed the support of the varied talents of these men, so the key to the *Bulletin*'s success was not its innovations so much as its blend of ingredients: neither the first radical or humorous weekly in Australia, nor the first to seek an Australian audience and contributors, it was the first to combine these elements into an attractive whole. During the early days the *Bulletin* had a somewhat negative creed, economically and racially isolationist, politically and culturally anti-British; it was, in Vance Palmer's words, a 'waspish little guerilla', striking out at antiquated values. But by the 1890s it had positive attitudes as well, promoting itself as the 'premier literary journal' with an 'Australian national policy'. It advocated republicanism, a democratic franchise, land taxation, state education, penal reform and 'A United Australia and Protection against the World'. It denounced sectarianism, foreign titles, the Chinese, and Imperial Federation.

A significant part of the programme was the cultural chauvinism fostered among its writers and artists, who confronted readers with villains (John Bull, Fatman, Johnny Chow) and heroes (The Little Boy from Manly, q.v., the idealised bushman) stereotyped according to the *Bulletin* philosophy. The bushman appeared in many costumes – one week as the Lone Hand fighting Fatman in a 'Hop' cartoon; on another page as the Man from Snowy River or the Man from Ironbark in an A.B. Paterson poem; next as Steelman or Mitchell in a Henry Lawson story; later as one of 'Steele Rudd's' selection battlers. Whatever the guise, he was a distinctive 'Australian', a product of the bush environment to which Archibald encouraged his writers to turn, urging them all the while to write in an equally distinctive 'no nonsense' way. 'Shun superfluous adjectives', Archibald advised a contributor in 1894, 'stick to sturdy nouns'. The results included hard-bitten paragraphs about up-country life packed into such columns as 'Plain English' and 'Aboriginalities' (q.v.); the bush ballads which were often strikingly illustrated; and the famous *Bulletin* yarn, with its emphasis on originality, brevity, realism and dramatic force.

That the *Bulletin* cultivated the bush did not necessarily guarantee enduring literature or mean that there was a consensus about what the 'bush' itself meant, as the famous *Bulletin* debate (q.v.) shows. Similarly, the *Bulletin's* bush ethos and its contribution to the emergence of literary nationalism has sometimes been overemphasised, with the result that the diversity of interests, attitudes and opinions expressed in the journal has been underestimated; Stephens, for example, was as much an internationalist as a nationalist critic. Similarly, the endeavours of earlier colonial writers and journals have been somewhat undervalued. But it remains true that the *Bulletin* did great service for Australian literature by encouraging local writers and artists, providing a regular outlet for their work. Backing up its policies with practical help, it paid its contributors, advised them in the correspondence column and instituted a publishing programme which included the anthologies '*A Golden Shanty*' (1890), *The Bulletin Reciter* (1901) and *The Bulletin Story Book* (1901); '*Steele Rudd's*' *On Our Selection* (1899) and Joseph Furphy's *Such is Life* (1903); and, in subsequent years, novels by Louis Stone, Norman Lindsay, Kylie Tennant and Brian Penton. The literary contributors to the *Bulletin* comprise a roll-call of Australian poets and writers of fiction since 1880. Some of them, notably G.A. Taylor, A.W. Jose, Randolph Bedford (qq.v.) and Norman Lindsay, left reminiscences which either established or confirmed the reputation of the journal before the First World War. Equally significant are the writings of *Bulletin* staff members or their families: Archibald's and Traill's 'The Genesis of the *Bulletin*' (*Lone Hand*, May–December 1907), Haynes's 'Early *Bulletin* Memories' (*Newsletter*, April–December 1905), Dorothy June Hopkins's *Hop of the 'Bulletin'* (1929), A.C. Macleod's *Macleod of 'The Bulletin'* (1931), Douglas Stewart's (q.v.) *Writers of the Bulletin* (1977), and the commemorative numbers of the *Bulletin* in 1930, 1950 and 1980.

Patricia Rolfe has written a history of the *Bulletin*, *The Journalistic Javelin* (1980) and Sylvia Lawson *The Archibald Paradox* (1983), a significant study of Australia's colonial culture and the role of the *Bulletin*, as well as a biography of Archibald.

The *Bulletin's* contribution to Australian literature did not end with the departure of Archibald and Stephens early in the twentieth century. Under Edmond, Mary Gilmore, Louis Esson, C.J. Dennis and 'John O'Brien' first appeared in its pages; under Prior there were contributions by the youthful Kenneth Slessor, Jack Lindsay and Vance and Nettie Palmer; under Webb the S.H. Prior Memorial Prize for fiction was awarded 1935–46; under Adams, assisted by Stewart as editor of the Red Page (1940–61), its writers included Judith Wright, Rosemary Dobson, Ronald McCuaig, 'Brian James', Hal Porter and David Campbell. But there was more than a measure of truth in Archibald's prediction, when the *Bulletin* was a 'clever youth', that it would become a 'dull old man'. Part of the reason may be that many of its prominent staff stayed so long: W.H. East, the *Bulletin's* printer, was there for forty-nine years, Macleod for forty-one, Adams for thirty-four, Prior for thirty, Edmond for twenty-nine, Webb for twenty-eight. The *Bulletin* became increasingly conservative and its policies, some of which had not changed since the turn of the century, increasingly anachronistic. The slogan 'Australia for the White Man', which replaced 'Australia for the Australians' in 1908, was only removed from the masthead in 1960. After a brief resurgence during the Second World War, sales dropped steadily until the format was changed under the new proprietors. As a news magazine the *Bulletin* has made an insignificant contribution to Australian literature in the last two decades, although from 1980 to 1985 it carried a quarterly literary supplement edited by Geoffrey Dutton, after the success of the centenary issue, 29 January 1980.

Bulletin Debate began as a rather contrived argument in verse between Henry Lawson and A.B. Paterson and then widened into a full-scale controversy that involved numerous well-known writers, including John le Gay Brereton, Francis Kenna, Edward Dyson, A.G. Stephens, Henry Cargill ('The Dipso'), Joseph Furphy and James Brunton Stephens. At issue was the real nature of Australian life (at first in the outback, but ultimately in the whole country) and the responsibility of writers to interpret it truthfully. In literary terms it was the traditional argument between romance and realism. The debate began with Lawson's poem 'Borderland', later titled 'Up the Country', published in the *Bulletin* (9 July 1892). Lawson's outback was not a landscape of shining rivers and sunlit plains peopled by folk-heroes living happy, carefree lives. It was a callous land, inhabited by gaunt, haggard men and women, broken by the never-ending battle against natural disasters, voracious banking systems and unsympathetic absentee landlords. Paterson replied with 'In Defence of the Bush' (23 July 1892). He evaded Lawson's issue of literary honesty and dismissed his criticism with the jibe that

Lawson had better stick to the city for he would 'never suit the bush'. Then followed (6 August 1892) Lawson's 'In Answer to 'Banjo' and Otherwise', later titled 'The City Bushman', and Paterson's 'Defence of the Bush' (1 October 1892), later titled 'An Answer to Various Bards'. Lawson's 'Poets of the Tomb' (8 October 1892) widened the discussion to include the role of literature in reforming the total Australian society and was followed (18 November 1893) by 'Some Popular Australian Mistakes', a list of romantic fallacies concluding with a rough handling of the mythical Australian outback folk-hero ('the real native outback bushman is narrow-minded, densely ignorant, invulnerably thick-headed'). Lawson's twenty-three facts and concluding summary are now recognised as an important early statement on Australian literary realism. Three years later Lawson began his crusade again. In the *Bulletin* (27 February 1897) he declared the 'bush bard' to be 'blinded to the Real', and in further articles, '"Pursuing Literature" in Australia', 'Crime in the Bush' and 'If I Could Paint', continued, often in the face of considerable hostility and in spite of personal attacks on his integrity, to insist on truth. The weakness of Lawson's attitude lay in his failure to recognise, or at least to admit, that literary nationalism, with its idealisation of the outback life, had helped to usher Australia out of colonialism and had made a significant contribution to the development of a national pride, a fact made evident by the huge sales of Paterson's *The Man from Snowy River and Other Verses*. What is obvious now, with the benefit of almost a century's hindsight, is that Lawson's insistence on realism instead of romance was, in the light of literary movements then in full force throughout the world, an inevitable step forward in Australian literature. What is equally clear is that his own stories of outback life settled the issue far more decisively than the doggerel verses of the 'Debate' and the angry outbursts in the *Bulletin* columns.

'Bullocky', a poem by Judith Wright (q.v.), links the bullock-driver in his pioneer role of unlocking the land with Moses, leading his people into the promised land. In a dramatic switch to the present, the poem shows the long-dead bullocky and his teams continuing to nourish the land – 'the plough strikes bone beneath the grass'. The poem indicates that the continuing fruitfulness and progress of the country depend upon the past as much as the present; that Australia of the future will be shaped by its traditions and history. In recent times Judith Wright has forbidden the use of 'Bullocky' in anthologies because it has generally been considered to be a eulogy of the pioneers, many of whom (she felt) had despoiled the land and almost destroyed the Aboriginal people.

Bullocky was the term applied to the drivers of the bullock wagons that were for many years the sole means of transporting supplies and essentials between the settlements and the outback. Usually of dour or phlegmatic disposition but capable of legendary powers of swearing when his beasts faltered, the bullocky was a vital factor in the opening of the country.

His pioneering role is emphasised in Judith Wright's poem 'Bullocky' (q.v.) and in the anecdotes of Mary Gilmore's *Old Days, Old Ways* (1934). Joseph Furphy's novel *Such is Life* (q.v., 1903) is centred on bullock-drivers and the way of life they represented. The bullocky is featured by many other writers, e.g. Alexander Harris, Henry Kendall, Henry Lawson, Will Ogilvie, C.J. Dennis and Katharine Susannah Prichard, usually in affectionate but occasionally in critical tones. Charles Thatcher revealed the disasters that could happen when the bullocky had to curb his language, in the song 'The Lady and the Bullock Driver' (1861). Well-known traditional bullocky songs include 'Bullocky-Oh', 'The Bullockies' Ball', 'The Old Bullock Dray' and 'Holy Dan'. It is in the bullocky's song 'Nine Miles from Gundagai' that the famous dog on the tuckerbox story has its origin. After a procession of woes ('the team got bogged, the axle snapped in two') the final indignity is added when 'the dog sat (?) on the tuckerbox, nine [five] miles from Gundagai'. L.G. Braden wrote *Bullockies*, an illustrated history, in 1968; Arthur Cannon's *Bullocks, Bullockies and Other Blokes* (1983) is a lively account of ten years' bullock-driving in the Gippsland and Mallee areas between the wars; Olaf Ruhen wrote the documentary work, *Bullock Teams* (1980), and Malcolm J. Kennedy *Hauling the Roads: a History of Australia's Working Horses and Bullocks* (1992).

Buln-Buln and the Brolga, The is a long story by Joseph Furphy (q.v.) which formed part of the original version of *Such is Life* (q.v., 1903); it was deleted during the revision of *Such is Life*, and was itself revised and elaborated by Furphy in 1904–5. First published in 1948, it was republished with other Furphy stories in 1971 as *The Buln-Buln and the Brolga and Other Stories*. The narrator of *The Buln-Buln and the Brolga*, Tom Collins (q.v.), is in Echuca to meet a representative of the Melbourne firm for which he works when he receives a telegram announcing the arrival of his childhood friend Fred Falkland-Prichard and his family; Fred is the buln-buln or lyrebird (pheasant-type bird native to Australia) of the title, so called because he is an inveterate liar, as Tom demonstrates when he reminisces about his childhood. *En route* to the station to meet the Falkland-Prichards, Tom meets Barefooted Bob, the brolga or 'native companion' (a species of crane also native to Australia) of the title, so called because of his physique and rough manners. Barefooted Bob strikes up a friendship with Fred and the bulk of *The Buln-Buln and the Brolga* consists of the yarns each swaps with the other during that day and night; Fred's stories get taller and taller but Bob accepts them as truth. *The Buln-Buln and the Brolga* is much slighter than *Such is Life* but raises some of the same issues, particularly the significance of the individual's perception of reality. It also contains a humorous account of Bob's visit to a performance of *Hamlet* in Melbourne which is similar to the better-known visit by the Sentimental Bloke and Doreen to a performance of *Romeo and Juliet*. In the discussion of Fred's English background Furphy parodies 'Rolf Boldrewood's' *The Miner's Right* (q.v., 1890).

BULWER-LYTTON, Edward George Earle Lytton (1803–73), first Lord Lytton, the English novelist and secretary for the colonies 1858–59, never visited Australia but included Australian episodes in his novel *The Caxtons* (1849), which reflect Bulwer-Lytton's perception of the imperial relationship and the state of Britain. The 'philosophy of colonising' which the heroes take with them to Australia includes the notion that British values must be transplanted to the new country lest it grow up to be 'a strange motley chaos of struggling democracy, an uncouth livid giant, at which the Frankenstein may tremble'. At the same time, however, the novel implies that Australia should develop a new identity free of the evils which taint Britain's past: Australia may thus be 'destined . . . from the sins and sorrows of a civilisation struggling with its own elements of decay, to renew the youth of the world, and transmit the great soul of England through the cycles of Infinite Change!' In depicting Pisabtratus Caxton's recuperation of his fortunes in an Arcadian Australia, Bulwer-Lytton was informed by the work of Saumel Sidney (q.v.) and the idealisation of the colony often found in the 'guidebook' genre.

BUNGAREE (Bongaree, Boungaree), of the Broken Bay tribe, was one of the first Aborigines (Arabanoo was the first) to have extended contact with the White settlement at Port Jackson. A well-known figure in the colony for over thirty years, he accompanied many expeditions and voyages of discovery (e.g. Matthew Flinders in HMS *Norfolk)* acting as intermediary with other Aborigines. Accounts of Bungaree and other Aborigines whose characters disintegrated after prolonged exposure to White influence are in Barron Field's *Geographical Memoirs on New South Wales* (1825), Robert Dawson's *The Present State of Australia* (1830), and Richard Sadlier's *Aborigines of Australia* (1883). John Lang wrote 'Bungaree, King of the Blacks', a story in *All the Year Round*, 21 May 1859, published also in *Australian Home Companion* of that year. Ernestine Hill mentions him in *My Love Must Wait* (1941). A portrait of him (c.1826) by Augustus Earle is in the Australian National Gallery.

Bunyip, a monster of Aboriginal mythology with a huge body covered with fur, is said to live in swamps, lagoons and billabongs from which it emerges on moonlit nights to prey on humans, especially women and children. Zoologists believe the Aboriginal legend may have originated in the occasional appearances of seals in coastal and inland streams and rivers. Numerous accounts of the bunyip are given in nineteenth-century literature of travel and description, e.g. in E. Lloyd's *A Visit to the Antipodes* (1846), William Westgarth's *Australia Felix* (1848) and G.C. Mundy's *Our Antipodes* (1852). It is mentioned also in Joseph Furphy's *Such is Life* and 'Steele Rudd's' *On Our Selection* and is the subject of the well-known title story of J.A. Barry's collection *Steve Brown's Bunyip* (1893); Ella Airlie's pantomime 'The Bunyip' was staged in Sydney in 1916. The bunyip has persisted in modern Australian writing, e.g. in Charles Fenner's *Bunyips and Billabongs* (1933), Charles Barrett's *The Bunyip and*

other *Mythical Monsters and Legends* (1946) and in 'Brian James's' short story 'The Bunyip of Barney's Elbow' (q.v., 1946). One of the best known of the 'species' is the Dynevor Bunyip (mentioned in Ernestine Hill's writings) which was said to inhabit the Dynevor Lakes in the Thargomindah district of south-western Queensland. A notable use of the word 'bunyip' was in 'Bunyip Aristocracy', used derisively in 1853 by Daniel Deniehy to ridicule W.C. Wentworth's suggested colonial peerage. Norman Lindsay created a koala character, Bunyip Bluegum, in his famous book for children, *The Magic Pudding* (1918).

'Bunyip Aristocracy', see **DENIEHY, D.H.**; **Squatter**; **WENTWORTH, W.C.**

'Bunyip of Barney's Elbow, The', a short story by 'Brian James' and set in the Henry Lawson country near Mudgee, was first published in the *Bulletin* (15 May 1946) and reprinted in 'James's' collections *The Bunyip of Barney's Elbow* (1956) and *The Big Burn* (1965). Mick Cullen's Wild Cat Hotel (named after his first wife), at the foot of Barney's Elbow in the Sandy Ridges close to the NSW township of Summerlea (Mudgee), acquires a brief interstate fame after spine-chilling cries of unknown origin are heard in the surrounding hills. A party of Summerlea 'sports', which includes Mr Simpson Butler, the local Member, 'a sprinkling of young fellows from the Grey Box and beyond – Doolans, Ryans, Rosens, Wenns, Wotts', van-loads of hunters and a representative from the *Western Argus*, sets out in unsuccessful pursuit of the bunyip-like monster. Reunited at the hotel that evening and miraculously unharmed by their own indiscriminate shooting, they hear once again the terrifying cry of the 'yahoo' but fail to respond to its challenge. Although the failure of their expedition continues to be a jest in the neighbourhood, 'the Yahoo was never heard again . . . gone to join the Bunyip and other impossible terrors'.

BURCHETT, Wilfred (1911–83), born Melbourne, left Australia in 1936 and became involved in negotiating the release of Jews from Germany in the immediate pre-war years. Returning from Europe early in 1939, he was sent by a group of Australian newspapers to report on war preparations in Central and South-East Asia. He joined the staff of the London *Daily Express* in Chungking in 1941 and spent the war reporting on the Asian-Pacific area. One of his greatest journalistic 'scoops' was 'The Atomic Plague', the first eye-witness account by a Western journalist of the aftermath of the Hiroshima atom bomb. After the war he worked for the *Daily Express* in Berlin and returned to Australia in 1950, lecturing for the campaign against nuclear armaments and against the proposed banning of the Communist Party in Australia. He went to China as a correspondent, thence to Korea to cover the cease-fire talks; his visit to an Allied POW camp in North Korea led to a furore in Australia, charges of treachery, a court case for defamation (which he lost) and the withdrawal of his Australian passport (returned in 1972 by the Whitlam Labor government). Later in Moscow, Hanoi, Phnom Penh, Paris and Bulgaria, Burchett consolidated his links with the communist world, always maintaining his lack of interest in communist ideology as such, while avowing a lifelong interest in and support of national independence movements. One of Australia's most controversial and most experienced international journalists, Burchett wrote more than twenty books, *At the Barricades* (1980) being his autobiography. His published works include *Pacific Treasure Island* (1941), *Bombs over Burma* (1944), *China's Feet Unbound* (1952), *This Monstrous War* (1953), *North of the 17th Parallel* (1955), *Come East, Young Man* (1962), *The Furtive War* (1963), *Vietnam North* (1966), *Again Korea* (1968), *Vietnam Will Win!* (1968), *Passport* (1969), *China: The Quality of Life* (1976) and *Catapult to Freedom* (1978). An account of Burchett's political activities is in *The Exile* by Roland Perry, published in 1988. *Passport* contains much information about his early life which is not in *At the Barricades*.

BURCHILL, Elizabeth (1908–) trained as a nurse in Melbourne before serving with the Australian Inland Mission at Innamincka. She subsequently nursed in a variety of places including Labrador, Thursday Island, New Guinea, Darwin and Central Africa and served in the Spanish Civil War and with the Australian Army Nursing Service in the Middle East in the Second World War. After discharge in 1946 she became an announcer with the local radio station at Shepparton but in 1950 returned to nursing, both in Australia and the USA. She has published several autobiographies including *Labrador Memories* (1947), *Innamincka* (1960), *New Guinea Nurse* (1962), *Thursday Island Nurse* (1972) and *The Paths I've Trod* (1981). She has also written *Australian Nurses Since Nightingale 1860–1990* (1992).

BURKE AND WILLS. The Burke and Wills expedition, the most costly exploration of its time in terms of money spent (£60 000) and lives lost (seven), originated when the Royal Society of Victoria, supported by the Victorian government, decided to snatch from J. McDouall Stuart and the colony of SA the honour of making the first south–north crossing of the Australian continent. Abundantly provisioned, the expedition left Melbourne in August 1860 under the leadership of the inexperienced Robert O'Hara Burke (1821–61), an Irish-born superintendent of police; others in the party included the German naturalist Ludwig Becker (q.v.) and the surveyor and meteorologist William John Wills (1834–61), who was promoted to second-in-command after Burke fell out with the camel-master. Burke reached Menindee on the Darling River in October and Cooper's Creek six weeks later; in both places he divided his party, taking Wills, John King (1841–72) and Charles Gray with him on the final haul to the Gulf of Carpentaria, which was reached in February 1861. On 21 April Burke, Wills and King staggered back into Camp LXV at Cooper's Creek on the very day the party left behind there under the command of William Brahe had departed for Menindee. Burke decided to try for

Mount Hopeless, north-west of Menindee, leaving a message of his plans at Camp LXV in case Brahe returned. Brahe did so but did not find the message and departed again for Menindee; Burke, Wills and King were too weak to get beyond the reaches of Cooper's Creek, and by the time A.W. Howitt's search party arrived in September 1861 only King had survived. The remains of Burke and Wills were returned to Melbourne for burial in January 1863; a monument to them, one of the many memorials in Victoria and overseas, was later erected outside the Victorian parliament house. The royal commission appointed to inquire into the disaster apportioned blame among the death-or-glory Burke, those commanding his back-up parties, and the expedition's organising committee; none was attached to Wills, whose journal formed the basis of *A Successful Exploration through the Interior of Australia* (1863), prepared for publication by his father. Although successful in completing a south–north crossing, Burke's expedition was virtually worthless as exploration; the search parties led by McKinlay, Landsborough and Howitt were much more useful in advancing geographical knowledge. Burke and Wills have long been enshrined in Australian folklore, and have captured the imagination of a number of Australian artists and writers. Becker and William Strutt left contemporary sketches of the early parts of the expedition; later artists attracted to the story include Sir John Longstaff, whose famous painting of the return to Camp LXV is familiar to generations of Australian schoolchildren, and Sidney Nolan. Frank Clune's *Dig* (1937), often reprinted, did much to publicise the Burke and Wills legend in the twentieth century although it has been superseded as the standard popular account by Alan Moorehead's *Cooper's Creek* (1963), titled *The Real Story of Burke and Wills* when republished in 1985. The poets Henry Kendall in 'The Fate of the Explorers, Burke and Wills' (1861), R.H. Horne in 'Australian Explorers' (1863), Adam Lindsay Gordon in 'Gone' (1867), Catherine Martin in 'The Explorers' (1874), Margaret Thomas in 'Death in the Bush' (1888) and Ken Barratt in 'Burke and Wills' (1946), helped to develop an heroic dimension to the disaster. In the 1940s Colin Thiele's 'Burke and Wills', a radio verse-play, uses King as narrator; Bill Reed's (q.v.) later play, *Burke's Company* (1969), takes up the question of Brahe's responsibility, while Burke's culpability is addressed in Philip Mead's poem, 'W.J. Wills to R. O'Hara Burke 1861' (1980). Tom Bergin, a zoologist and veterinarian who retraced the Burke and Wills expedition in a modern attempt to discover the reasons for the disaster, wrote *In the Steps of Burke & Wills* (1981). The most complete account is Tim Bonyhady's *Burke and Wills: From Melbourne to Myth* (1991), which examines for the first time fourteen boxes of manuscripts from the Exploration Committee, untouched since 1874, and interprets the retrospective, cultural mythologising of the two explorers. A diary left by Hermann Beckler, medical officer and botanical collector of the exploration adds a further dimension to the criticism of Burke. Edited by Stephen Jeffries, it was published in 1994 as *A Journey to Cooper's Creek*.

BURKE, Colleen (1943–), born Sydney of Irish Catholic background, graduated BA from the University of Sydney in 1974 and has worked variously as a clerk, research assistant, community worker and creative writing tutor. Active in poetry workshops, community writing groups and folk-music concerts, she was editor (1974–75) of the *Cornstalk Gazette*, magazine of the NSW Folk Federation, and was involved in establishing the Australian National Folk Trust 1974–75. She has published several books of verse, *Go Down Singing* (1974), *Hags, Rags & Scriptures* (1976, with two other women poets), *The Incurable Romantic* (1979), *She Moves Mountains* (1984) and *The Edge of It* (1992). A city girl – 'I was born and bred at Bondi under the smell of surging surf and sewage' – Burke writes of herself, her milieu ('asphalt days'), social justice, political outrages (e.g. the Irish question, nuclear testing) and the wonder of nature. Her simple, often vernacular, poems are saved from triteness by her capacity for fine images and skilled crafting. She has also written a biography of Marie Pitt (q.v.), *Doherty's Corner* (1985).

BURKE, James Lester (c.1820–79) was born in Ireland and served as a soldier in India before his conviction there of insubordination in 1847; sentenced to transportation, he arrived in Hobart in 1848 and eventually received a conditional pardon in 1859. Burke was the author, although only acknowledged as the editor, of *The Adventures of Martin Cash* (1870), one of the best-selling studies of the Tasmanian bushranger; he may also have 'ghosted' *A Burglar's Life* (1893), the memoir of a well-known convict, Mark Jeffrey. *A Burglar's Life* was edited in 1968 with an introduction by W. & J. E. Hiener. Those editors suggest James Lester Burke as the author.

BURKE, Janine (1952–), born Melbourne, graduated from the University of Melbourne in 1974 and lectured in art history at the Victorian College of the Arts 1977–82. A founding member of the feminist art journal *Lip*, she has written art criticism for numerous journals and has organised exhibitions of historical and contemporary Australian art for State and regional galleries. She has written the first history of women artists, *Australian Women Artists, 1840–1940* (1980) and a biographical/critical study of the artist Joy Hester (1983); some of her essays on women's art in the 1970s were published in 1990 titled *Field of Vision*. Burke is also a fiction-writer and has published three novels, *Speaking* (1984), *Second Sight* (1986) and *Company of Images* (1989). *Second Sight* won the Victorian Premier's Award for fiction in 1987. *Speaking* charts the inner and outer experiences of four contrasting women of the 1970s against a background of the rise and fall of student activism and the changing nature of the feminist movement; *Second Sight*, a first person narrative, describes a journey from grief to a new sense of purpose and self; mingling fantasy, myth and allegory, it is concerned with ways of seeing and coming to terms with reality. *Company of Images*, set in Melbourne's artistic community, is a witty, varied study of a range of individuals presented in a fragmentary but cumulative way and seen largely through the eyes of five women. *Janine Burke* (1987), edited by Jim Davidson, includes extracts from her work, an interview and a bibliography.

BURN, David (?1799–1875) was born in Scotland and followed his mother, the first woman to be granted land in Van Diemen's Land, to Hobart in 1826. Until 1845 he combined residence in Hobart with visits to Britain, participated in colonial affairs, and wrote widely on colonial life and politics. In 1845 he left Tasmania for NSW and in 1847 went to NZ, where he edited several newspapers. His travel and descriptive accounts include *A Picture of Van Diemen's Land* (first published 1840–41), *Vindication of Van Diemen's Land* (1840), *An Excursion to Port Arthur in 1842* (first published 1842) and *Narrative of the Overland Journey of Sir John and Lady Franklin and Party from Hobart Town to Macquarie Harbour 1842* (first published 1843). Burn is chiefly remembered for his play *The Bushrangers* (q.v.). Staged at the Caledonian Theatre, Edinburgh, in 1829 with his nautical farce *Our First Lieutenant*, the play was not published or performed in Australia until 1971. His other plays include *Sydney Delivered* (q.v., 1845) and several literary-historical dramas, mainly in verse with European settings, published in his *Plays, and Fugitive Pieces, in Verse* (1842).

BURNELL, F.S. (Frederick Spencer) (1880–?), born Sydney, was special correspondent for the *Sydney Morning Herald* with the New Guinea expedition in 1914 and compiled an illustrated account of that action, *How Australia Took German New Guinea* (1914), and an expanded version of the same, *Australia versus Germany: The Story of the Taking of German New Guinea* (1915). He also wrote several travel books and two volumes of verse, *Before Dawn and Other Poems* (1912) and *A Sallet of Songs* (1920).

BURNS, D.R. (David Robert) (1925–93) taught English at the University of NSW and wrote two novels, *Mr Brain Knows Best* (1959) and *Early Promise* (1975); and a critical study, *The Direction of Australian Fiction 1920–1974* (1975).

BURNS, Joanne (1945–), born Sydney, is a teacher and has published several volumes of poetry, *Snatch* (1972), *Ratz* (1973), *Adrenalin Flicknife* (1976), *Radio City 2 a.m.* (1976, with Stephanie Bennett and Ruth Fordham), *On a Clear Day* (1992); three books of prose, *Correspondences* (1979, with Pamela Brown), *Ventriloquy* (1981) and *Blowing Bubbles in the 7th Lane* (1988) ; and a book of children's stories, *Alphabatics* (1976). *On a Clear Day* (Burns would discard the capitals) was short-listed for the National Book Council Turnbull Fox Phillips Award for poetry. It is a collection of brief, anecdotal pieces of prose-poetry that examines with some acerbity the mores of modern middle-class existence and takes a somewhat cynical view of those who are enmeshed in that existence and the society that keeps them there. Nor does she spare herself in the process. Burns sees her poems (or her prose, since she sees no real distinction between the two) as performance pieces and they often have the characteristics – short, sharp lines and punchline conclusions – that performance requires. Her use of lower case and the prose form is, she maintains, a device to make poetry more humble, in accordance with her belief that the vernacular is best fitted to express complexities and ironies.

BURSTALL, Betty, see **La Mama**

BURSTALL, Tim (1929–), born Stockton-on-Tees, England, was educated at Geelong Grammar and Melbourne University. His name first appeared in 1960 with the success of his short film *The Prize*, which led to a Harkness Fellowship to study filmmaking in the USA 1965–67. His first feature film, *2000 Weeks* (1968), was followed by *Stork* (1971), *Alvin Purple* (1973), *Petersen* (1974), *End Play* (1975), *Eliza Fraser* (1976) and *The Last of the Knucklemen* (1979). He has also written and directed documentary and short films and mini-series for television and in 1973 formed his own company, Hexagon Films. In the 1980s he directed *Attack Force Z* (1981) and *Naked Country* (1984). His wife Betty Burstall founded La Mama.

BURY, Thomas ('Tom Touchstone') (1838–1900), born Dublin, came to Australia in 1854 during the gold rushes. He wrote under his pseudonym for the *Ballarat Courier* from the late 1870s until his death. His weekly column, 'Cornerisms', touched on most of the moral, philosophical, artistic and social questions of the day. He was a significant influence on the poet Bernard O'Dowd.

'Bush' is a term which probably derives from the Dutch word 'bosch', and was used as early as 1800. By the 1820s it was in common use to denote the unsettled areas of the Colony and, more specifically, as the Australian equivalent of the English words 'woods' or 'forest'. Although many early settlers disliked and feared the bush, it did not go completely unpraised. Barron Field's *First Fruits of Australian Poetry* (1819) and *Geographical Memoirs on New South Wales* (1825) are enthusiastic about the flora of the bush. Charles Tompson, born in the colony, spent much of his youth in the bush settlements around Windsor and Penrith and sees the bush, in his *Wild Notes, from the Lyre of a Native Minstrel* (1826), through the sympathetic eyes of a 'currency lad'. Early complaints about the sombreness of the bush were strengthened by the many tragedies that befell the explorers and pioneers in their efforts to chart and settle it. Charles Harpur and Henry Kendall write of such tragedies in 'The Creek of the Four Graves' and 'The Glen of the Whiteman's Grave'. Harpur, also a 'currency lad' bred in the spectacular Hawkesbury valley, writes of the bush with affectionate awe in 'Lost in the Bush', 'A Bush Fire' and 'Dawn and Sunrise in the Snowy Mountains'. Kendall suggests both the loneliness and the loveliness of the bush in poems such as 'Death in the Bush', 'Morning in the Bush', 'September in Australia', 'Bellbirds' and 'Arcadia in Our Midst', the last a prose description of the Brisbane Water area. The bush was

also the background for many of the journals, reminiscences and memoirs of early colonial life. Typical of a host of such works ranging over more than half a century are H.W. Haygarth's *Recollections of Bush Life in Australia* (1848), James Armour's *The Diggings, the Bush and Melbourne* (1864), Mrs James Foott's *Sketches of Life in the Bush* (1872), James Kirby's *Old Times in the Bush of Australia* (1895) and George Dunderdale's *The Book of the Bush* (1898). Similarly, much of the fiction of early colonial times is set in the bush, e.g. Charles Rowcroft's *Tales of the Colonies* (1843), Alexander Harris's *The Emigrant Family* (1849), Louisa Atkinson's *Gertrude the Emigrant* (1857), William Howitt's *Tallangetta* (1857), Henry Kingsley's *The Recollections of Geoffry Hamlyn* (1859), Rosa Praed's *The Head Station* (1885) and 'Rolf Boldrewood's' *Robbery Under Arms* (1888), the last subtitled 'A Story of Life and Adventure in the Bush and in the Goldfields of Australia'. In her autobiographical *My Australian Girlhood: Sketches and Impressions of Bush Life* (1902), Rosa Praed reminisces, 'I never smell the pungent aromatic scent [of gum trees] ... without falling again under the grim spell of the bush.' When Marcus Clarke, in his preface in the 1876 edition of Adam Lindsay Gordon's *Sea Spray and Smoke Drift*, describes the dominant note of the Australian bush as one of 'weird melancholy' and the bush itself as 'funereal, secret, stern', he is reflecting the view that persisted for most of the first century of White settlement; that view persists, half a century further on, in D.H. Lawrence's *Kangaroo* (1923), whose keynote is 'the terror of the bush'. With the 1890s and the upsurge of nationalism and through the influence of the *Bulletin* and the works of A.B. Paterson, Henry Lawson, Joseph Furphy, 'Steele Rudd', Bernard O'Dowd and Miles Franklin (to name only the major figures) the bush (now often capitalised, The Bush) comes to be viewed as a major shaping instrument of the Australian national spirit and outlook. The bulk of the literature 1890–1914 is bush-inspired, and bush values, as illustrated in that literature, are accepted as Australian values. Observers who recognise this particular significance of the bush include Francis Adams, who finds 'all that is genuinely characteristic in Australia and Australians springing from this heart of the land [the bush]' (*The Australians*, 1893); the French writer Emile Saillens, who believes that 'the bush has its history which is that of Australia – the bush is not a fixed place, it is a state of things' ('Le Bush Australien et Son Poete', 1910); and C.E.W. Bean, who is sure that in the bush is 'the core of Australia' (*On The Wool Track*, 1909). An almost inevitable extension of this assessment of the bush was the development of the mystique of the bush, a sense that it was a sacred, inspiriting power, influencing for good both individual and nation. Voiced earlier in Kendall's 'To a Mountain', which echoes the pantheism of Wordsworth, this mystique is expressed by O'Dowd in *The Bush* (1912) but is present also in 'Furnley Maurice's' poem 'The Gully', and to some degree in the poetry of John Shaw Neilson, Douglas Stewart and Roland Robinson. It exists also in the Jindyworobak (q.v.) movement and is expressed in such works as 'Henry Handel Richardson's' *The Fortunes of Richard*

Mahony (1930), Eleanor Dark's *The Timeless Land* (1941), Mary Durack's *Keep Him My Country* (1955), Patrick White's *Voss* (1957) and Randolph Stow's *To the Islands* (1958), and in more recent times in Les Murray's *The Boys Who Stole the Funeral* (1980) and Geoffrey Lehmann's *Ross' Poems* (1978). Not that the bush is glorified by all writers, as the *Bulletin* Debate (q.v.) on literary realism in the early 1890s reveals. While there are contrary views on the merits of the bush and bush life, there is, with the exception of Barbara Baynton, reasonable unanimity on the qualities of the bush people. There were, of course, examples in the bush of the flotsam and jetsam of humanity (Lawson's Sweeney and Jimmy Woods) but the bushman stereotype emerges as a rugged, versatile individualist, cheerful, laconic, philosophical in the face of hardship, independent in his own troubles but generous and loyal to his mates and others who need help. Such a stereotype is partly glimpsed as early as Adam Lindsay Gordon's 'The Sick Stockrider' and in Gordon's philosophy of 'kindness in another's trouble, courage in your own'. The literature of the nationalist 1890s has many such figures; typical in some or all respects are Lawson's Joe Wilson, 'Steele Rudd's' Dad, and Miles Franklin's Danny Delacy.

In a less complex fashion than O'Dowd and the Jindyworobaks, a host of other Australian writers used the bush (and bush life) as the theme or as the setting in their work, e.g. Katharine Susannah Prichard, Miles Franklin as 'Brent of Bin Bin', Vance Palmer, Frank Dalby Davison, Kylie Tennant, Jon Cleary, Tom Ronan, D'Arcy Niland, Olga Masters and, at times, Patrick White. The travel and descriptive works of Ion L. Idriess, following on from earlier writers such as Mrs Aeneas Gunn and C.E.W. Bean, popularised the bush and were, in turn, followed by others such as Myrtle Rose White, William Hatfield and Ernestine Hill. Louis Esson, seeking a valid indigenous drama in the early twentieth century, went as W.B. Yeats had suggested to a particularly Australian source – the bush. His plays *Dead Timber* (1920), *The Drovers* (1923) and *Mother and Son* (1923) employ bush settings and laconic bush idiom. The tragic aspects of the bush, developed in Esson, reappear in Vance Palmer's *The Black Horse* (1924), Sydney Tomholt's *Anoli the Blind* (1936), Millicent Armstrong's *Drought* (1932) and Betty Roland's *The Touch of Silk* (1942).

There has been a significant correlation between the visual and literary interpretations of the bush. Artist J.W. Lewin (1770–1819) accompanied Governor Macquarie over the Blue Mountains to Bathurst, the first major breaching of the bush's inviolability. In his watercolours (e.g. *Cox's River* and *Springwood*) the bush is freed from the artificiality of both earlier writers and painters. Artists of the mid-century, e.g. William Strutt (1825–1915), with their grim interpretations of the bush provide suitable parallels to the melancholy poetry of Adam Lindsay Gordon and the equally melancholy stories of Marcus Clarke. Of the later Heidelberg School, Frederick McCubbin's *The Lost Child* (1886) and *Bush Burial* (1890) retain much of the elemental sense of doom and tragedy associated with Marcus Clarke's view of the bush, but Tom

Roberts's *Shearing the Rams* (1890) and *The Breakaway* (1891) convey the dynamic energy of bush life and activities associated with the 1890s. Russell Drysdale's 1941 Riverina paintings contain the same realistic appraisal of the bush as is seen in the Henry Lawson stories.

From the bush has come a multitude of expressions, several of which reflect the townsman's patronising attitude towards his bush cousin, e.g. 'bushwhacker', a naive, country type; 'bush carpenter', one who builds in a rough-and-ready fashion; 'bush week', the time of the year when the bush cousin comes to town and is ripe for plucking; 'bush baptist', one who is of very doubtful religious persuasion; and 'bush lawyer', one who will argue his rights in any and every situation. 'Bushed', which originated about the 1850s, meant 'lost in the bush' but now is used as a general colloquial expression to indicate a state of perplexed indecision. 'The Bushman's Bible' was the *Bulletin* and 'the Bushman's Clock' was, according to C.E.W. Bean in *On the Wool Track*, the kookaburra, the noisiest bird in the bush. 'Sydney (Melbourne) or the Bush' indicates an 'all or nothing' decision, which results in the 'big time' (Sydney or Melbourne) or obscurity (the bush). *Intruders in the Bush: The Australian Quest for Identity* (1982), edited by John Carroll assembles the views of certain Australian historians, sociologists and critics to challenge the legend of the bush and the bushman.

Bush Ballads and Galloping Rhymes (1870) is the second and more important of the collections of poetry of Adam Lindsay Gordon (q.v.). Best-known poems are the opening verses, 'A Dedication' (q.v.); narratives such as 'From the Wreck', 'How We Beat the Favourite' and 'The Romance of Britomarte'; the character sketch 'The Rhyme of Joyous Garde'; and Gordon's most significant poem, 'The Sick Stockrider' (q.v.). The contents scarcely substantiate the impression given by the title of an overwhelming Australian flavour to this Gordon collection.

'Bush Christening, A', a poem by A.B. Paterson in the *Bulletin* 16 December 1893, and published in *The Man from Snowy River and Other Verses* (1895), is a rollicking account of how the traditional Irish preoccupations, whisky and religion, come together in the unique christening ceremony of the lad, Maginnis Magee. Probably taken by Paterson from the bush oral tradition where such tales thrive, the poem has been linked by Lucy Sussex to an anonymous story, 'Peggy's Christening', in the *Colonial Monthly*, April 1868, a quarter of a century before Paterson's poem. Paterson used the Irish Catholic community as the basis of many similar bush verses, e.g. 'Father Riley's Horse', 'Gilhooley's Estate' and 'Mulligan's Mare'.

Bush Studies, a collection of six stories by Barbara Baynton (q.v.), was published in 1902; it included Baynton's best-known stories, 'Squeaker's Mate', 'Scrammy 'And', 'Billy Skywonkie' and 'The Chosen Vessel'. The collection was issued in another edition in 1917 under the title *Cobbers*, with two new stories added and the others revised.

Bush, The (1912), by Bernard O'Dowd (q.v.), is one of the most important expressions of nationalist-radical sentiment in Australian literature. O'Dowd's most attractive poem, it forecasts future greatness for Australia once the ideals of radicalism are transplanted from the 'grottos of decrepitude' of the Old World into the eagerly waiting, green sanctuary of the Australian Bush.

'BUSHMAN, A', see **SIDNEY, Samuel**

Bushman's Bible was a common nickname of the *Bulletin* before the First World War. It is used, for example, in Randolph Bedford's autobiographical *Naught to Thirty-Three* (1944).

Bushranger in Australian Literature. The term 'bushranger', which is still used in Australia to describe a manipulative or exploitative person (e.g. a club golfer who arranges his form in such a way as to gain maximum advantage of his handicap is called a 'bushranger' or 'burglar'), originally meant someone with an official task in the bush; thus it was a compound of 'bush' and 'ranger'. From this origin the word broadened to cover anyone skilled in bushcraft (i.e. a 'bushman'); deteriorated to describe a runaway convict attempting to survive in the bush; and then acquired its most common meaning, a person who evaded the law by living in the bush and committing robbery and related crimes (e.g. arson, murder, the stealing of horses), usually in partnership with others in a bushranging 'gang'. As well as 'bushranging' and other derivatives, the bushranging phenomenon introduced into or consolidated within Australian English such words and phrases as 'duffing', 'bush telegraph', 'bail up', 'stick up' and 'game as Ned Kelly'.

Bushrangers operated periodically from 1789, when Black Caesar, a First Fleet convict, first took to the bush, until 1880 when Ned Kelly (q.v.), the most famous Australian bushranger, was hanged in Melbourne. Apart from isolated instances such as the activities of 'Moondyne Joe' (q.v.) in WA and Alpin McPherson (q.v.), 'The Wild Scotchman', in Queensland, bushranging was confined to the south-eastern part of Australia – to the colonies of NSW, Tasmania and Victoria. Three main periods of activity are usually identified; the first, longest but most intermittent, encompasses the convict bushrangers up to 1850, particularly in the period 1820–50. The most prominent mainland bushranger in this period was John Donohoe (q.v.), an early Australian folk-hero whose exploits near Sydney in the late 1820s are the subject of the 'Bold Jack Donahoe' cycle of ballads and inspired Charles Harpur's early play *The Bushrangers* (q.v., 1853). In the same decade that Donohoe operated near Sydney, Matthew Brady (q.v.) in Tasmania staged several daring attacks on property before his death in 1826. Brady was treated sympathetically by early writers, notably David Burn in his play *The Bushrangers* (q.v., performed 1829) and 'Pindar Juvenal' in *The Van Diemen's Land Warriors* (q.v., 1827), but some other Tasmanian bushrangers had deserved reputations for violence. They included Michael Howe

(q.v.); the cannibal Alexander Pearce or Pierce, a convict escapee from Macquarie Harbour who was the model for Gabbett (q.v.) in Marcus Clarke's *His Natural Life* (1874); and, at least for part of his career, Martin Cash (q.v.).

The defiance of authority which marked the careers of Donohoe, Brady and Howe was met by intermittent government legislation, beginning in 1800 with the outlawing of robbers and stock thieves and culminating in this period in a harsh Bushranging Act of 1830, which gave the authorities in NSW wide powers of seizure and arrest. This Act, bitterly resented by many settlers and discussed in Alexander Harris's *Settlers and Convicts* (1847), was still in force at the start of the second wave of bushranging activity, the twenty years following the discovery of gold in 1851. The increase in activity was caused by a combination of factors, including the isolation of the various goldfields and the inadequacy of the police force. Perhaps the best-known bushrangers of the 1860s were Ben Hall, Frank Gardiner and Johnny Gilbert (qq.v.), who several times operated together in western NSW and had sympathisers beyond their immediate circle. Among other well-known bushrangers whose careers broadly coincided with theirs were the Clarke brothers, the evil Dan Morgan and the exotically named 'Captain Thunderbolt', 'Captain Moonlite' and 'Captain Starlight' (qq.v.); earlier 'Captain Melville' had had brief notoriety in Victoria before his death in detention in 1857. Despite some spectacular successes – e.g. the Eugowra gold robbery which was used by 'Rolf Boldrewood' in *Robbery Under Arms* (1888) and *The Miner's Right* (1890) – most of the bushrangers, in this period as in others, died young and violently: Morgan, Gilbert and Hall were all killed in 1865, and by 1870, when Thunderbolt was hanged, bushranging had been more or less brought under control. The 1870s were quiet until near the end of the decade, when in 1878 the Kelly gang was outlawed and began its defiance of governments on both sides of the Murray River which lasted until the siege of Glenrowan in 1880.

Kelly's convict connections, like those of Hall and Melville and all the bushrangers before 1850, indicate that to insist upon a firm division of bushranging history into distinct periods can disguise important links between many of the bushrangers. For example, bushranging was very often a response by those affected directly by the cruelty, weakness or corruption of government and other forms of authority. Thus, in the early period, most convict bushrangers were escaping from cruel masters or gaolers; after the discovery of gold the encouragement offered by an incompetent or corrupt police force (attested to by as respectable a writer and citizen as Louisa Anne Meredith) to a 'wild colonial boy' like Frank Gardiner was compounded by the injustice some settlers, including the Kellys and the Halls, felt at the unequal distribution of land. The Kellys and the Halls were from selection (q.v.) stock and their activities have something of the dimension of social banditry and agrarian protest. Again, despite the cold-blooded murderousness of such as 'Mad Dog' Morgan, others had deserved reputations for bravery (e.g. Donohoe), dash and pluck (e.g. Kelly), chivalry (e.g. Hall), bravado (e.g. Gardiner) or cheek (e.g. Brady) which consolidated support from some settlers and confirmed their placement within a larger highwayman/outlaw, Robin Hood/Dick Turpin/Jesse James tradition. The preponderance of bushrangers by the name of 'Captain' is evidence that some agreed with this romantic image of themselves.

The extent of the sympathy for many bushrangers has made them important figures in Australian folklore who are sometimes seen to embody national characteristics, e.g. in enacting deeply ingrained antagonisms towards authority and the police. Although some commentators have viewed them less favourably, seeing in the cockiness and flashness of bushrangers early manifestations of larrikin and ocker behaviour, favourable entries on bushranging figure prominently in Australian folklore compendiums. There is a bushranging section in most Australian folklore and ballad anthologies; virtually all the bushranging songs and ballads (e.g. 'The Death of Ben Hall', 'How Gilbert Died', 'The Streets of Forbes') are sympathetic to their subjects. Among numerous general bushranging histories are Frank Clune's *Wild Colonial Boys* (1948), *A Pictorial History of Australian Bushranging* (1966) by Tom Prior, Bill Wannan and Harry Nunn, who have each also written separately on the subject, and *Stand and Deliver: 100 Australian Bushrangers 1789–1901* (1991) by Allan M. Nixon; earlier studies include Charles White's *History of Australian Bushranging* (1902), George Boxall's *The Story of the Australian Bushranger* (1899) and Jack Bradshaw's (q.v.) *The True History of the Australian Bushrangers* (?1924). Most of these works have been written for a popular market, although Russel Ward's *The Australian Legend* (1958) is one of several works which place bushranging within the Australian tradition. Bushrangers' own memoirs are few (for obvious reasons) but *'Guilty Wretch That I Am', Echoes of Australian Bushrangers* (1984), edited by Ken Byron, contains the Death Row memoirs of Richard Burgess and provides a remarkable insight into life and crime in early colonial times.

For all the importance of the bushranger in Australian folklore and in studies of the Australian tradition, the bushranging phenomenon has produced a creative literature significant as much for its quantity as its quality. The bushranging plays of Burn, Harpur and Henry Melville (q.v.) have historical importance as early Australian plays; drawing on the stage tradition of the outlaw protagonist, they are also significant in confirming the links between bushranging and convict literature evident in folk-songs like 'Jim Jones at Botany Bay' and novels like *Ralph Rashleigh* (written in the 1840s). In addition, Harpur's play displays an ambivalence about the bushranger which characterises stage portrayals later in the nineteenth century; the ambivalence derives from the intersection of the melodrama (which demanded the triumph of virtue over vice) with the folklore tradition (overwhelmingly sympathetic), and was partly resolved by the emergence of both good and bad bushrangers and police. The government licensing of plays in NSW

resulted in few bushranging plays in the period 1840–70, but the bushranger emerged again in the 1870s as one of the heroes – despite condemnation by some newspaper critics – of the Australian melodrama which flourished into the twentieth century. The most popular of all bushranging plays was the Alfred Dampier and Garnet Walch adaptation of *Robbery Under Arms* (q.v., 1888), first staged in 1890 with 'Rolf Boldrewood' in the audience, but its success was rivalled by some of the numerous Kelly plays staged during the gang's activities and after Ned's execution. Other bushranging plays focused on Midnight, Thunderbolt, Gardiner, Hall and Gilbert; apart from these, the bushranger was a stock character in more broadly based plays such as George Darrell's *The Sunny South* (first staged 1884).

Beyond the colonial stage, the nineteenth-century bushranging plays can be placed within what one commentator on Kelly has called the 'media tradition' treatment of bushrangers, which remains ambivalent towards the bushranger, because, although influenced by folklore, it is concerned also to harness the abundant potential for sensation, excitement, adventure or romance. Within the media tradition can be placed some of the films made before a ban on the making of bushranging films was instituted in the NSW police department in 1912 – seven such films had been made the previous year – and a clutch of novels centred on individual outlaws, fictitious and real. Examples of the former include Charles Rowcroft's *Mark Brandon*, E.W. Hornung's *Captain Stingaree* and Gavin Holt's *Captain Scarlet*; examples of the latter include novels by Hume Nisbet, Nat Gould, Thomas Walker and Roy Bridges about Howe, and by Carlton Dawe, Ambrose Pratt, Hilda Bridges and Launcelot Booth about Hall or the Hall/Gardiner gang. Ambivalence is also to be found in the most famous bushranging novel of all, 'Boldrewood's' *Robbery Under Arms*, which is both a cautionary tale about how crime doesn't pay and a novel which enjoys the dash of Captain Starlight, the efficiency of Ben Marston and the discomfort of Sir Ferdinand Morringer, Starlight's police opponent. Part of the appeal of *Robbery Under Arms* stemmed from 'Boldrewood's' ability to incorporate familiar elements from the experiences of several bushrangers, e.g. the easy identification of Wall, Hulbert, Moran and Lardner with Hall, Gilbert, Morgan and Gardiner. Wall and Lardner reappear in 'Boldrewood's' *The Miner's Right* (1890). The contrast between this novel, in which bushranging is an incidental ingredient to provide colour or excitement in a goldfields romance, and *Robbery Under Arms*, which can be catalogued more accurately as a bushranging novel, is similar to the contrast not only between *The Sunny South* and the stage adaptation of *Robbery Under Arms*, but also between other bushranging novels (e.g. the works by the media tradition novelists already mentioned) and a larger body of fiction with a bushranging element. The latter include Alexander Harris's *The Emigrant Family* (1849), John Lang's *The Forger's Wife* (1855), Henry Kingsley's *The Recollections of Geoffry Hamlyn* (1859), William Gosse Hay's *Strabane of the Mulberry Hills* (1929), several of the sporting (as distinct from bushranging) novels of Nat Gould and Arthur Wright, and an even larger number of children's novels. There are some children's novels, however, which deal explicitly with bushrangers, including William Howitt's A *Boy's Adventures in the Wilds of Australia* (1854) and Judith Wright's *Range the Mountains High* (1962).

The fact that Australian creative writers have been concerned to exploit rather than to explore the phenomenon of bushranging has produced many plays and novels which have mainly historical interest, one or two exciting adventures of which *Robbery Under Arms* is justifiably the best known, and a handful of fine ballads and later poems (e.g. Francis Webb's 'Morgan'); these can be put alongside the paintings of Tom Roberts and Sidney Nolan. To these works should be added the novels by David Martin and Randolph Stow, *The Hero of Too* and *Midnite* (qq.v., both 1967), which satirise the bushranging legend, and Douglas Stewart's 1941 play *Ned Kelly* (q.v.), which explores the 'deep national significance' Stewart felt was embedded in the Kelly story.

Bushranger of Van Diemen's Land, The, see **Aborigine in White Australian Literature**; **ROWCROFT, Charles**

Bushrangers, A Play in Five Acts, and Other Poems, The (1853), was one of the two major works published by Charles Harpur (q.v.) in his lifetime. Although *The Bushrangers* first appeared in full in 1853, Harpur worked on the melodrama intermittently, publishing part of it in 1835 with the title 'The Tragedy of Donohoe' (*Sydney Monitor*) and leaving a final manuscript version entitled 'Stalwart the Bushranger' (dated 1867). Incongruously dependent on Elizabethan models and weakly constructed, the play nevertheless has some dramatic and literary merit and is interesting for Harpur's ambivalent treatment of the bushranger hero/villain. *Stalwart the Bushranger*, with original extracts from 'The Tragedy of Donohue' was published in 1987, edited by Elizabeth Perkins, and was performed for the first time in 1988.

Bushrangers: Or, Norwood Vale, The, a play by Henry Melville (q.v.) staged in Tasmania in 1834 and published in the *Hobart Town Magazine* in the same year, was the first dramatic piece with an Australian theme presented and published by an author resident in Australia. A melodrama of little literary merit, it consists of thirteen tableaux and deals with an attack by bushrangers on a settler's home.

Bushrangers, The, a three-act play in prose by David Burn (q.v.), was presented at the Caledonian Theatre, Edinburgh, in 1829 and was the first Australian drama to be performed on stage. It remained unpublished and unperformed in Australia until 1971. Although of little literary merit, the play has action and colour and is interesting for its innovative treatment of a familiar theme in Australian literature, the romanticising of the rebel (in this case the bushranger Matthew Brady,

q.v.) and for its incidental revelation of life in colonial Tasmania.

But the Dead Are Many, a novel by Frank Hardy (q.v.), was published in 1975. The story of John Morel, born in 1917 and a leading member of the Communist Party of Australia after a dedicated Catholic youth, the novel has a complex structure, explicitly analogous to a musical fugue. Subjects, incidents, individuals, themes, relationships and experiences are constantly counterpointed so that past and present merge and time proceeds vertically rather than chronologically. Morel's story emerges from several chapters of autobiography and a note that he bequeaths after his suicide at the age of 50 to his close friend and alter ego, Jack. Convinced that an understanding of Morel's suicide will uncover personal, psychological and general ideological truths, Jack combines Morel's notes with his own extensive researches, interviews and recollections. As Morel's history gathers shape, personal crises such as the death of his father, his decision to leave the Catholic seminary and his hunger strike in the 1940s merge with public events, and private relationships are tainted with the tense, unresolved ambivalences of the political movement. Morel's story becomes not just an individual history but a reflection of the conflicts within the international communist movement from the 1930s to the 1960s and of the ever-widening gap between ideal and real. Morel's relationship with his wife Penelope, his Russian mistress Anna, his colleagues such as the party hack Trevor Duncan, his best friend Jack, and, above all, with his memory of the old Bolshevik Buratakov, whose Stalinist trial he witnessed, reflect his futile quest for harmony and integrity in an increasingly tangled, baffling environment. Afflicted with an acute sense of duality and inadequacy, Morel seeks to find a final transcendence in suicide, which he hopes will transform his memory and resolve the inevitable dichotomy in life between ideal and blemished selves; suicide becomes an act

> not of self-destruction but of self-preservation, an attempt to confront the meaning of death by making it part of life, an attempt to synthesise the unresolvable paradox of life and death by thwarting the life-denying forces which make actual living impossible . . . suicide is an attempt to equate the identity of the self as experienced by the self and the self as experienced by others, an attempt to establish the interconnection between the living and the dead.

Butcher Shop, The (1926), a novel by Jean Devanny (q.v.), was published in England and went through six printings by 1931, after which it was not republished until 1981, when it reappeared with an introduction and notes by Heather Roberts and an account by Bill Pearson of its banning in NZ in 1926 and Australia in 1929. Grounds for its censorship were its emphasis on sexuality, its depiction of the brutality of life in rural NZ and its expressions of socialism in a country that in the 1920s would have been appalled by the idea of a socialist form of government and society. Feminism and socialism are central to the novel. Devanny perceives woman's bondage as rooted in the family; it is because the males in the story (husband and lover) both conform, albeit unconsciously, to the view that the married woman is her husband's property, that the final tragedy occurs. Set on Maunganui station in the King Country of the North Island of NZ, the novel advances placidly through the first ten years of married life of Margaret and Barry Messenger, owners of the station. Physically beautiful, intellectually aware and comfortably situated, they appear to be a perfect match. However, with the arrival of the Scots overseer, Glengarry, Margaret realises the full impact of her sexuality and while Barry is away the two become lovers. The three then live for some time in a precarious relationship. Barry, who notes the attraction between Margaret and Glengarry, does not suspect the extent of the affair, while Glengarry, who is at first torn with jealousy, comes to like and respect Barry so much that he finally decides not to continue the affair because Margaret is his friend's wife. He thus denies Margaret the very individuality she seeks and confirms her sense of herself as merely property. Threatened by Glengarry's decision, Margaret reveals their full liaison to Barry, who drowns himself in a dam. The now-unbalanced Margaret cuts the throat of the sleeping Glengarry, claiming that she has revenged 'the Margarets of the world' and that 'never again shall man claim property rights in me'. A couple from England, Ian and Miette Longstair, have been a contributing factor to the tragedy, both with their disturbing socialist attitudes and Miette's sexual approaches to Glengarry which have inflamed Margaret's jealousy. The violence of NZ rural life, objected to by the censors, is characterised by such things as lamb-killing, the killing of cats for their skins, the mutilation of a dog, the decapitation of a drunken rabbiter by his mate and the oral castration of lambs. Devanny explains the novel's title by affirming that it is the woman who is butchered in life.

BUTLER, Richard (1925–   ), born and educated in Liverpool, England, served in the RAF and then taught in England and Australia (1963–74) before becoming a full-time writer, literary consultant and professional actor. His novels include *Fingernail Beach* (1964), *South of Hell's Gate* (1967), *Sharkbait* (1970) *The Buffalo Hook* (1974), *Lift-Off at Satan* (1978) and several based on Australian historical subjects: *The Men That God Forgot* (1975), *And Wretches Hang* (1977, on Matthew Brady), *A Blood-Red Sun at Noon* (1980) and *The Devil's Coachman* (1981). He has also written television, film and radio scripts, historical texts for schools, and novels associated with TV series and films, e.g. *Against the Wind* (1978), *The Sullivans* (1980), *Eureka Stockade* (1983) and *Coolangatta Gold* (1984).

BUTTROSE, Larry (1952–   ), born Adelaide, was a journalist with the ABC 1970–75 and has since been a freelance writer. In 1971 he founded *Dharma* with Stephen Measday; he was co-editor of *Real Poetry* 1977–78, and of *Number Three Friendly Street Poetry Reader* (1979). He has published two books of verse,

One Step Across the Rainbow (1974) and *Random Leaves* (1976), and two more substantial collections, *The Leichhardt Heater Journey* (1982) and *Learning Italian* (1986), which illustrate his capacity to combine thematic depth and subtlety with colloquial idiom. He has also written plays, *Pallas* (1987) and *Kurtz* (1990), and a book of travel reminiscences, *The King Neptune Day & Night Club* (1992).

BUZACOTT, Martin (1958–   ), born Queensland, was educated at Macquarie University and the University of Wales. His first novel, *Charivari* (1987), is a picaresque story of a disreputable young man, David Badger, as revealed by various witnesses of his actions, newspaper and court reports and diaries, supposedly compiled and edited by a taxation clerk, fascinated with his subject. His second novel, *Narrenschiff* (1988), follows the life of Seth Sajewski from the time that he witnessed the fire-bombing of Dresden as a child and lost his mother. His life of extremes is periodically relieved by an elaborate fantasy in which he sails through time and place on board 'a ship of fools'.

BUZO, Alexander (1944–   ), born Sydney, the son of an Albanian civil engineer and an Australian mother, was brought up and educated in Armidale, NSW, and at the International School in Geneva. He graduated from the University of NSW in 1965. The play which first brought Buzo to national notice was *Norm and Ahmed* (first produced in 1968, published 1969), largely because of the prosecutions for obscenity that followed its productions in Brisbane and Melbourne. 'The Revolt' (1967), his first play, remains unpublished. *Norm and Ahmed* was followed by the comedy *Rooted* (q.v., 1969; published 1973), the first of his plays to receive overseas productions, *The Front Room Boys* (q.v., 1969; published 1970), and *The Roy Murphy Show* (1971, published 1973), a farce which draws on the clichés and familiar rituals of a television football panel for its hilarious effects. In 1972–73 Buzo was resident playwright with the Melbourne Theatre Company and during this time produced *Macquarie* (1972, published 1971), his first historical drama and his first serious study of a complex individual; *Tom* (1972, published 1975); and 'Batman's Beach Head' (1973), a free adaptation of Ibsen's *An Enemy of the People*. He was awarded the Australian Literature Society's Gold Medal in 1972 for *Tom* and *Macquarie*. His next play, *Coralie Lansdowne Says No* (q.v., 1974), was followed by *Martello Towers* (1976), *Makassar Reef* (1978, published 1979), 'Vicki Madison Clocks Out' (1979), *Big River* (1980, published 1985), 'Duff' (1981), *The Marginal Farm* (1983, published 1985), 'Sting Ray' (1988) and 'Shellcove Road' (1989). Buzo has also written plays for radio and has contributed to film and television scripts.

An inveterate collector of solecisms, malapropisms, tautologies and mixed metaphors and an acute recorder of social stereotypes and their transitions, Buzo has published a series of satirical collections and analyses: *Tautology* (1980), and its successor, *Tautology Too* (1981), are compilations of attributed verbal redundancies; *Glancing Blows: Life and Language in Australia*

(1987) and *The Young Person's Guide to the Theatre and Almost Everything Else* (1988) mingle witty cultural comment, analysis of verbal habits, idiosyncrasies and traditions and autobiography; *Meet the New Class* (1981), dedicated to 'Bali and vulnerability', explores the languages and attitudes of the 'New Class people', those born post-1945 who have been 'over-educated to a new level of discontent'. The sporting world has provided Buzo with much of his farcical material and in *The Longest Game* (1990), edited with Jamie Grant (q.v.), he pays tribute to the Australian passion for cricket. Buzo has drawn on the same resources of parody and verbal wit in his two novels *The Search for Harry Allway* (1988) and *Prue Flies North* (1991). A series in that both have the same heroine, they combine social satire, detective fiction and picaresque adventure.

Buzo's plays were first seen as similar to those of David Williamson in their satiric treatment of Australian society although concentrating on Sydney's mores rather than Melbourne's. In his early work the focus is more on the dehumanising characteristics of the society that oppresses its individuals than on the individuals themselves, whether it is general Australian society as in *Norm and Ahmed* or the world of a large corporation as in *The Front Room Boys*. In plays such as *Rooted, Tom, Coralie Lansdowne Says No* and *Martello Towers*, he has been seen as wittily exposing the hollowness of the new generation of educated, prosperous and permissive Australians. Buzo has frequently stressed, however, that his plays are fiction not documentary sociology, and his later work in particular reveals a concern with the human predicament that is universal and existential, and only incidentally Australian. Nearly all his main characters, however witty their dialogue and comic their situation, are engaged in a serious struggle to find purpose, value and stability in an alien, amoral and meaningless world. *Macquarie*, which centres on Macquarie's career as governor of NSW from 1810 to 1822, explores the impact of a corrupt society on the ideals of a liberal humanist; *Martello Towers*, ostensibly a light, witty comedy of manners, describes the renewed marital commitment of Edward and Jennifer Martello in the face of generally fragmented, 'free' and tenuous relationships; *Makassar Reef*, set in the torpid, tropical port of Ujung Padang, explores the search for stability in love, the ennui, shifting bonds and compromises that life forces on an odd but representative assortment of people. Often admired for their verbal brilliance and their satiric wit, Buzo's plays also depend heavily on a more serious subtext, which is both romantic and sad and demands sensitive skills on the part of actor and producer. This characteristic is even more marked in his latest plays, *Big River* and *The Marginal Farm*. *Big River* is set in

Australia of 1900 and *The Marginal Farm* in Fiji of the 1950s and 1960s, but both are penetrating studies of the experience of radical transition, and reminiscent of Chekhov in their suggestions of subtextual action. A subtle stylist with a strong sense of structural balance, Buzo is both traditional and innovative in his approach, a mix which some of his critics have found difficult to accept. John McCallum's *Buzo* (1987) is a critical study of his work for the stage.

BYLES, Marie Beuzeville (1900–79), born Ashton-on-Mersey, England, was brought to Australia in 1911 and was educated at the Presbyterian Ladies College, Pymble, and at the University of Sydney. With one other woman, Sibyl Gibbs, she graduated LLB, in 1924, despite the opposition of male students and became the first woman to be admitted to practice in NSW. In 1929 she set up her own practice. A pacifist and feminist, she was also a keen bush walker and mountaineer and climbed in Europe, India, China and Burma. She published several books which reflect her travels and philosophy, *By Cargo Boat and Mountain* (1931), *Footprints of Gautama the Buddha* (1957), *Journey into Burmese Silence* (1962), *The Lotus and the Spinning Wheel* (1963) and *Paths to Inner Calm* (1965). In 1985 Gillian Coote produced a film on her life and achievements.

BYRNE, Desmond, see *Australian Writers*

BYRNE, Joe, see *Ned Kelly*

BYRNES, Robert Steel (1899–1979), born Goldsborough, Victoria, was educated at the University of Sydney and served with the AIF in the First World War before working as an administrator for the Presbyterian Church of Queensland. He was State and federal president of the Fellowship of Australian Writers and for twenty years a member of the Queensland Literature Board of Review. He was made MBE in 1964. Two collections of his poetry were published, *Endeavour and Other Poems* (1954) and *The Light of Setting Suns* (1980), and with Val Vallis he edited *The Queensland Centenary Anthology* (1959).

bystander, a biannual literary magazine emanating from the monthly Monday night readings in Lower Hawthorn Town Hall (Melbourne), began publication in 1993 with an editorial panel headed by John Irving who has been prominent for some years in writing workshops and community poetry readings. Contributors to the first issue included Kristin Henry, Alex Skovron, Mal Morgan, R.A. Simpson and Chris Wallace-Crabbe. There were interviews with poets Ken Smeaton and Kevin Hart.

C

Cabbage Tree, a tall palm with large leaves, is found in the coastal areas of eastern Australia. In early colonial times its leaves were used to make the cabbage-tree hat, which came to be something of a symbol of nationalistic feeling. A well-known song, 'The Cabbage Tree Hat', allegedly written by C.A. Flower, was popular from the 1880s. The so-called Cabbage Tree Mobs, the precursors of the later larrikin pushes, were gangs of young rowdies, usually native-born and wearing cabbage-tree hats, who roamed the streets of Sydney in the 1840s and 1850s. They are described in G.C. Mundy's *Our Antipodes* (1852) and are mentioned in many of the reminiscences of the period, e.g. James T. Ryan's *Reminiscences* (1894) and Charles MacAlister's *Old Pioneering Days in the Sunny South* (1907).

Caddie, a Sydney Barmaid (1953), an autobiographical work published anonymously but edited by Dymphna Cusack (q.v.), is the poignant story of a young woman (identified in some catalogues as Mrs Henry Elliott), who leaves her adulterous husband and attempts to fend for herself and her two small children in the 1930s Depression. The book pays tribute also to the generous-hearted slum dwellers of inner Sydney, whose kindness and charity help her in her struggle. Both the book and the Australian film, *Caddie*, produced in 1976 with Helen Morse in the title role, effectively re-create the inner Sydney environment of the time.

CADDY, Caroline (1944–), born WA during the Second World War, went to the USA in infancy. There are echoes in her poetry of that phenomenon of the war years – American father and Australian mother. She returned to WA, still a schoolgirl, and has travelled through much of that State, living both in the northern and southern areas. She worked for some time in a travelling dental unit and now lives on a small farm on the south coast. She has published the poetry collections *Singing at Night* (1980), *Letters from the North* (1985), *Beach Plastic* (1989, winner of the 1990 WA Literary Week Award for poetry) and *Conquistadors* (1991, winner of the 1992 NBC Banjo Award for poetry). Caddy's poetry highlights the WA physical landscape, the title poem series, 'Letters from the North', for example, reflecting the demanding climate and topography of the northern iron ore country:

Sometimes there is only heat, sometimes only wind.
I have stopped expecting definite rivers or mountains.

Other poems deal with beach and seascapes and with the life found there, such as the pelicans:

They preen
practise sawing each other in half

Her poems also range widely over personal experience – childhood in America and the family characters that live in her memory, the voyage back to Australia, school in Australia where she was looked on as a Yank, love that is love, neither surrender nor submission. Her wit, humour, sense of the absurd, crisp and shrewd assessments of events and situations and sensitive, if austere, description all add up to a considerable poetic talent. The density and intensity of her language are accentuated by her favourite devices of fragmented lines and staccato phrases, often brought together in a final, elucidating image.

CAFFYN, Kathleen ('Iota') (1853–1926), wife of Stephen Mannington Caffyn (q.v.), usually wrote under the pseudonym 'Iota'. She was born in Ireland and came to Australia in 1880, returning to England in 1892. Of her seventeen novels, mainly written after the death of her husband in 1896, only the first, *A Yellow Aster* (1894), was written in Australia and only two, *A Comedy of Spasms* (1895) and *Dorinda and Her Daughter* (1910), have any connection with Australia. Her success as a novelist was due to the strong romantic and sexual element in her books and to her skill in characterisation.

CAFFYN, Stephen Mannington (1850–96), born Sussex, England, migrated in 1880 with his wife Kathleen Caffyn (q.v.) to Australia, where he worked as government health officer in Sydney and Wollongong before moving in 1883 to private medical practice in Melbourne. In addition to publishing numerous medical pamphlets, he wrote for the *Bulletin*, *Centennial Magazine* and other journals. He published two novels, *Miss Milne and I* (1889), and *A Poppy's Tears* (1890).

Cake Man, The (1978), a play by Aboriginal dramatist Robert Merritt (q.v.), was performed at the National Black Theatre, Redfern, Sydney, in 1975 and at the World Theatre Festival in Colorado, USA, in 1982. A television version of the play was produced by the ABC in 1977. The play's title has its origin in the story told by Ruby, the Aboriginal mother on the mission at Cowra, NSW, to her son, Pumpkinhead, about the mythical, half-blind cake man, who will one day be able to see little Black boys as clearly as he seems to see little White boys and will give the Black boys their overdue rewards. The White man's salving of his conscience for Aboriginal mistreatment is suggested by the play's White character, the Civilian, who offers cakes and goodies to the poverty-stricken Black family. The more important themes of the play lie in the presentation of the poor conditions suffered by mission Aborigines, the warm affection existing within the Aboriginal family and the male members' loss of self-respect and dignity. Brian Syron has been associated with Merritt in the success of *The Cake Man*; he has co-directed the play and has played the role of the husband, Sweet William.

CALDER, James Erskine (1808–82), born Buckinghamshire, England, arrived in Van Diemen's Land at the age of 21 as an assistant surveyor. His appointment as surveyor-general in 1859 reflected his achievements in opening up and surveying the island. In addition to many articles on the early history of the colony and numerous official reports, Calder published *The Woodlands . . . of Tasmania* (1874), *Some Accounts of the Wars, Extirpation, Habits &c of the Native Tribes of Tasmania* (1875) and a parliamentary paper in 1901 on the Aboriginal languages of Tasmania.

CALDWELL, Grant (1947–) graduated with a commerce degree from the University of Melbourne and taught, before travelling abroad. In 1975 he was imprisoned for six months in Tangiers for attempting to smuggle hashish. His impressions of that experience are contained in *Malabata* (1991), the title being the name of the prison. A writer since his release, he has published *The Screaming Frog that Ralph Ate* (1979), *The Bells of Mr Whippy* (1982), *The Nun Wore Sunglasses* (1984), *The Revolt of the Coats* (1988), and *The Life of a Pet Dog* (1992). Described as a 'post-modernist fabulist', Caldwell is frequently ironic, sympathising always with those who draw the shortest straws in the game of life, the battlers, the deprived, the perplexed, the lonely, the misfits. His simple, effective poetry often carries a sociological and political sting in its tail.

CALDWELL, Robert ('Andrew Cochrane') (1843–1909), born near Ardrossan, Scotland, came to Australia in 1849 and was a farmer and Methodist lay preacher. In 1884 he became a member of the SA House of Assembly. He published nine volumes of verse 1874–1908, including *A Vision of Toil* (1875), *The Australian Year* (1876), *In Our Great North-West* (1894), *The Pioneers* (1898) and *Adam Gowrie: Or, the Australian Farmer* (1903).

CALDWELL, Zoe (1933–), born Melbourne, an internationally famous actor and director, began training for a life in the theatre after an education at the Methodist Ladies College. At 18 she began to act with the Union Theatre Repertory Company, at 24 she left for England to study with the Royal Shakespeare Company and has since acted frequently in theatres in England, America, Canada and Australia. She received her first Tony Award for her role in a play by Tennessee Williams in 1966 and her second for her starring role two years later in *The Prime of Miss Jean Brodie*. In 1977 she co-directed *An Almost Perfect Person*

for a Broadway production and has since directed several other plays. Two of her most exacting roles have been Medea in the play by Euripides, which earned her a third Tony Award and was first performed in 1982, and her presentation of Lillian Hellman in the one-woman show *Lillian* in 1985–86. Caldwell has won numerous other awards for her acting and in 1970 was made OBE.

CALTHORPE, Mena (1905–), born Goulburn, NSW, taught in small country schools and later did secretarial and clerical work. She published three novels, *The Dye House* (1961), which was translated into German and Czech, *The Defectors* (1969) and *The Plain of Ala* (1989). *The Dye House* (highly regarded and short-listed for the Miles Franklin Award) creates the atmosphere of a seedy Sydney factory where the workers' lives are a tedious humdrum in an oppressive environment. *The Defectors* exposes the power struggle in the world of trade unions and the Labor Party. *The Plain of Ala* traces four generations of the Field family in Ireland and Australia.

Calverton, Archie, a character in George Johnston's novel *Clean Straw for Nothing* (q.v., 1969), is a fictionalised study of the actor Peter Finch (q.v.).

'Cambaroora Star, The', a poem by Henry Lawson (q.v.) about the rise and fall of a goldfields newspaper, was first published in the *Boomerang* in 1891. As the result of a reference in '"Pursuing Literature" in Australia' (q.v.), the *Cambaroora Star* has usually been identified as the *Boomerang* itself, which ceased publication four months later, but Lawson's 'A Fragment of Autobiography' specifies the *Republican* (q.v., 1887–88), which he contributed to and nominally edited while it was under the management of his mother, Louisa Lawson.

CAMBRIDGE, Ada (1844–1926), born and raised in Norfolk, England, had published moral tales and verse which reflected her strong religious feelings by the time she married a young curate, George Frederick Cross, in 1870. Three weeks after their wedding the couple left for Victoria, where Cross served as an Anglican minister at Wangaratta, Yackandandah, Ballan, Coleraine, Sandhurst (Bendigo) and Beechworth, before moving to Williamstown in 1893. Two of their children died during this period and another son was to die in 1902 at the age of 24; *Thirty Years in Australia* (q.v., 1903), Cambridge's first volume of autobiography, describes the vicissitudes of her experiences in rural Victoria as a clergyman's wife and her establishment of a writing career; a companion volume, *The Retrospect* (1912), deals mainly with her early years and her reactions to England during her first return visit in 1908. In 1912 she returned again to England after her husband's retirement, but following his death in 1917 moved back to Victoria.

By 1871 Cambridge was contributing short sketches and poems to the *Australasian* and the *Sydney Mail*, but her first significant work was the serial 'Up the Murray' in the *Australasian* (1875), a novel which initiated some of the themes she was to continue to pursue. For the next twenty years she contributed numerous serials mainly to the *Australasian*, but also to the *Sydney Mail* and the *Age*. Of the serials contributed to the *Australasian*, six were published as books: *In Two Years' Time* (1879, serialised 1878), *A Mere Chance* (1882, serialised 1880), *The Three Miss Kings* (1891, serialised 1883), *A Marriage Ceremony* (1893, serialised 1884–85 as 'Mrs Carnegie's Husband'), *A Humble Enterprise* (1896, serialised 1891 as 'The Charm That Works') and *Not All in Vain* (1892, serialised 1890–91). Of her other novels which were published as books, *A Marked Man* (1890) was serialised in the *Age* 1888–89 titled 'A Black Sheep' and *A Little Minx* (1889) in the *Sydney Mail* in 1885; *A Woman's Friendship*, a novella serialised in the *Age* in 1889, was not published in book form until 1988, edited by Elizabeth Morrison. Cambridge's other published novels, some of which established an English as well as Australian reputation, were *My Guardian* (1878), *The Devastators* (1890), *Fidelis* (1895), *Materfamilias* (q.v., 1898), *Path and Goal* (1900), *Sisters* (1904), *A Platonic Friendship* (1905), *A Happy Marriage* (1906), *The Eternal Feminine* (1907) and *The Making of Rachel Rowe* (1914). Cambridge also contributed numerous short stories, poems and essays to the *Australasian, Sydney Mail, Australian Journal, Bulletin* and *Atlantic Monthly*. One collection of her short stories appeared in 1897, *At Midnight and Other Stories*, and she also published five collections of verse, *Hymns on the Litany* (1865), *Hymns on the Holy Communion* (1866), *The Manor House and Other Poems* (1875), *Unspoken Thoughts* (1887, republished in 1988, edited by Patricia Barton) and *The Hand in the Dark* (1913).

Until the late 1970s Cambridge, with Jessie Couvreur and Rosa Praed (qq.v.), was dismissed as extraneous to the nationalist tradition which asserted itself in the 1890s. Perceived as a writer of Anglo-Australian romance fiction, she was criticised by later commentators for the contrivances and triviality of her plots, her narrow social focus (many of her novels are set among the pastoral aristocracy or within Melbourne society), and her British bias which permits many of her heroines to marry Englishmen of good breeding. Such an assessment not only ignores the importance of marriage and its organisation for colonial women, but also does less than justice to the delight Cambridge sometimes found in the Australian landscape, to the realistic and sometimes satirical view which she offers of colonial society and to her informed and often radical treatment of courtship, romantic love, marriage and parenting. The heroines of her serials are characteristically sensitive newcomers, who come into conflict as did Cambridge herself, particularly when she began to write fiction, with the middle-class guardians of respectability, among them materialistic matriarchs and defenders of country town hierarchies; her later more substantial novels continue to explore the proper bases for marital choice, although the exploration is combined with such other themes as exile, the nature of sexual passion and the alternatives to organised religion. Recent feminist studies in particular have reinterpreted Cambridge as a radical writer, who was preoccupied with the 'injustices of human arrangements' in Victorian society and rejected or questioned many of its conventions and customs. *Unspoken Thoughts*, described by A.G. Stephens as immediately withdrawn from publication because of George Cross's disapproval of its unorthodox content, was in fact not withdrawn until five years later; nevertheless both *Unspoken Thoughts* and the contemporaneous *A Marked Man* express most explicitly Cambridge's intense questioning and even rebellion against the system.

Her major novels include *A Marked Man,* in which the hero, Richard Delavel, periodically escapes from the consequences of a disastrous marital choice to a bush retreat modelled on the artists' camp Cambridge visited during her Sydney sojourn; *The Three Miss Kings,* where the contrivances of a conventional romantic plot (three sisters acquiring suitable husbands) are relieved by Cambridge's sardonic view of *nouveau riche* vulgarity and her acute presentation of Melbourne during the Great Exhibition of 1880; *Not in Vain,* in which the heroine defies convention to wait for her fiancé, imprisoned for defending her honour, only to find on his release that he no longer loves her; *A Marriage Ceremony* and *Fidelis,* which both include as major characters a disfigured and isolated artist; *A Little Minx,* which exposes the provincialism and religious bigotry of a small town; and *Materfamilias,* a grandmother's chronicle of her marriages and motherhood, in which Cambridge's ironic representation of her narrator permits a satirical exposé of the dehumanising effects of traditional feminine roles. *Thirty Years in Australia* and several of Cambridge's novels have been reprinted in the 1980s, although much of her work remains inaccessible for the general reader. Two biographies have also been published, *Rattling the Orthodoxies* (1991) by Margaret Bradstock and Louise Wakeling and *Ada Cambridge* (1991) by Audrey Tate.

CAMPBELL, David (1915–79), born Ellerslie, the family property near Adelong in the Monaro district of NSW, was educated in Australia and at Cambridge, where his tutor was the well-known scholar E.M.W. Tillyard. In the Second World War he served with distinction as a pilot in the RAAF; after the war he lived on various properties in the Canberra area, dividing his time between a farming life and a career as a poet. In 1964 he became poetry editor of the *Australian*; he edited *Australian Poetry 1966* and *Modern Australian Poetry* (1970).

His first volume of poetry, *Speak with the Sun* (1949), is strongly Australian in tone. The poem 'Harry Pearce' forms a triptych with two other celebrated 'teamster' poems, Henry Kendall's 'Bill the Bullock Driver' and Judith Wright's 'Bullocky'. The first volume also contains his well-known war poem 'Men in Green'. *The Miracle of Mullion Hill* (1956), with 'The Speewah Picnics', 'The Westing Emu' and the title poem itself, shows Campbell's continued interest in balladry and the tall tale, but the meditative lyrist is evident in two of his best poems, 'Night Sowing' and 'Who Points the Swallow?' In *Poems* (1962) his characters and poetic landscapes are still

Australian but have lost much of their parochial quality, taking on a universality that provides the basis for more mature, philosophical meditations. 'On Frosty Days', 'Winter Hills', 'Pallid Cuckoo' and 'Bindweed and Yellowtails', all from 'Cocky's Calendar', the twelve-poem sequence devoted to the countryman's life, are fresh and original nature lyrics with roots in the pastoral tradition. *The Branch of Dodona and Other Poems, 1969–1970* (1970) uses the Jason and Medea legend to offer a biting commentary on modern life and attitudes. *Devil's Rock and Other Poems, 1970–1972* (1974) begins with the biographical sequence *Starting from Central Station* (published separately in 1973), includes a tribute to Kenneth Slessor and contains 'Letters to a Friend', memories of pleasant activities shared with Douglas Stewart. The title poem, 'Devil's Rock and Other Carvings', is a series of brief, imaginative glimpses into the Aboriginal past. After the colloquial narrative and dramatic sequence entitled *Deaths and Pretty Cousins* (1975), came the collection *Words with a Black Orpington* (1978); its cameo nature lyrics, seriocomic travel verses, fragments from Sappho, and love poetry (whether the lusty 'Portrait of a Lady' or the tender 'Soundings') reveal Campbell adopting the free-ranging attitudes and experimental techniques characteristic of the poetry of the 1970s. In his final volume, *The Man in the Honeysuckle* (1979), he explores the relationship between physical science, Taoism and poetry.

Campbell published two volumes of short stories: *Evening under Lamplight* (1959), childhood impressions of homestead life on a sheep station, and *Flame and Shadow* (1976). The stories were republished, with a foreword by David Malouf, in 1987 as *Evening Under Lamplight: Selected Stories of David Campbell*. With Rosemary Dobson and Natalie Staples he published *Moscow Trefoil* (1975) and *Seven Russian Poets* (1979), translations of Russian poetry; and with artist Keith Looby he produced *The History of Australia* (1976). Campbell received numerous awards in recognition of his poetry – the Henry Lawson Australian Arts Award in 1970, the Patrick White Literary Award in 1975, the NSW Premier's Prize in 1980 for *The Man in the Honeysuckle* and FAW's Christopher Brennan Award in 1980. *Poetry Australia* (December 1981), edited by Leonie Kramer, is a special David Campbell edition; it contains, in addition to numerous appreciations of one of Australia's most accomplished lyric poets, some unpublished poems and significant biographical material. *A Tribute to David Campbell* (1987), edited by Harry Heseltine, contains a series of papers given at a Campbell seminar at the Department of English, Royal Military College, Duntroon in 1985. Writers include Rosemary Dobson, Chris Wallace-Crabbe, Joy Hooton, R.F. Brissenden and Leonie Kramer. Campbell's *Collected Poems*, edited by Leonie Kramer, was published in 1989.

Campbell Howard Collection of Australian Plays in Manuscript is held at the Dixson Library at the University of New England, Armidale, NSW. The collection was made by A.C.M. (Campbell) Howard (1906–84), who was lecturer in music at the Armidale Teachers' College (1928–47), inspector of schools (1947–54), assistant director of adult education at the University of New England (1955–70), and acting director of University Extension (1970–72). For his service to education he was awarded the BEM. The Campbell Howard Collection contains more than 300 manuscripts of plays by both well-known and lesser-known Australian writers and covers the period from 1920 to the present. A check-list of the collection, *Australian Plays in Manuscript*, was published in 1984.

CAMPBELL, Jean (1901–84), born Melbourne, was a prolific writer of light novels, the first of which was *Brass and Cymbals* (1933), set in Melbourne in the first two decades of the twentieth century. It deals with a Jewish family, which faces disintegration as the children gradually relinquish their Jewish background. *Greek Key Pattern* (1935) deals with a Greek family in Melbourne in a somewhat similar vein. Other novels, many of which have tangled personal relationships, include *Lest We Lose Our Edens* (1935), *The Red Sweet Wine* (1937) and *The Babe Is Wise* (1939).

CAMPBELL, Marion (1948–) teaches English and comparative literature at Murdoch University and is a graduate of the universities of WA and Provence. She has written plays, 'Dr Memory in the Dreamhouse' (1990) and 'Understudies: Part 1' (1990); and two novels, *Lines of Flight* (1985) and *Not Being Miriam* (1988). Campbell is well versed in contemporary cultural and literary theories, although her work is by no means slavishly post-modernist; deploying, on the one hand, the insights of post-structuralist theorists into the non-representational nature of language and of French feminists into the construction of the female psyche, she is sensitive, on the other, to the political implications and unstated patriarchal assumptions of some contemporary theorising. Rita Finnerty, the first-person/third-person narrator of *Lines of Flight*, is an Australian artist working in France. As an Australian, an artist and a woman, she is cast in the role of outsider, which can be as liberating as it is periodically imprisoning. In quest of herself as artist and as woman, Rita undergoes various confrontations with male narcissism and in some relationships conforms temporarily to the roles which have been traditionally inscribed for her gender. Concerned with perspective in various senses, including the bias of the male gaze as it has determined value in art, *Lines of Flight* is a challenging novel which subverts reader expectations at almost every level, including the post-modernist expectation of a non-linear narrative and a fragmented central self. Particularly striking are Campbell's innovative use of language, her zest for comedy and the imaginative energy which propels the narrative notwithstanding the novel's thin plot. *Not Being Miriam* is constructed of various strands, which represent the lives of a group of tenuously related women. The strands of the story concern Bess, a drama teacher who would rather have been an actor; Lydia, the German-born wife of one of Bess's colleagues, Harry; Bess's

Aunt Mamie; and the most economically and educationally deprived of the group, Elsie, Bess's next-door neighbour. Betrayal is a major theme, ranging from the massive betrayal of the Jewish Holocaust to Harry Grogan's betrayal of his wife to the betrayal of Bess's needs as a mother, all destined to be dramatically revenged by Bess's courageous defence of Elsie. The early stories rapidly chart moments from Bess's childhood and adolescence, her marriage to an Italian and life with her son before he is taken away by her estranged husband. Her growing closenesss to Harry Grogan introduces Grogan's wife Lydia. Splintering the narrative between the women's individual experiences and switching unpredictably from one to the other, Campbell unites them by means of myth and imagery. Elsie, a victim of her deprived past and her abused present, finds some relief in seeing herself as the second Mrs de Winter of Daphne Du Maurier's novel *Rebecca*; Bess's aunt Mamie models herself on Katerina Kepler, the witch mother of Johannes Kepler; Bess herself is Ariadne, the eternal Other Woman, dark-haired and seductive. Miriam, the first wife of Elsie's husband, who keeps her blown-up photograph hanging in his closet, is the ideal woman, whose unattainable perfection, defined according to the male gaze, looms implicitly over all the women. Playing once again with the instabilities of language, Campbell uses a kaleidoscopic structure and a fractured syntax to explore ways of seeing and cultural projections of reality. Sensitive as her novels are to issues of fictionality, they are also alert to the political realities and the power structures which underlie both notions of gender and of art.

CAMPBELL, Ross (1910–82), born Kalgoorlie, WA, was educated at Melbourne University and won a Rhodes Scholarship to Oxford. Back in Australia, he joined the staff of the Sydney *Daily Telegraph*, staying with that paper until the Second World War in which he served in the RAAF. After the war he joined the *Sydney Morning Herald* as a feature-writer, then transferred to Consolidated Press, writing articles and reviews for its stable of publications, the *Daily Telegraph*, *Sunday Telegraph*, *Australian Women's Weekly* and *Bulletin*. A selection of those articles was published by Campbell in two small books, *Daddy Are You Married?* (1962) and *Mummy, Who Is Your Husband?* (1964); a further selection of longer, more sophisticated articles from his *Bulletin* writings appeared as *She Can't Play My Bagpipes* (1970). The first two books tell of the vicissitudes of Campbell, Mrs Campbell, Theodora, Lancelot, Little Nell and Baby Pip in Oxalis Cottage. Intent after his Oxford days on being a 'dag' (an Australian humorist), Campbell became part of a long line of ironic Australian writers. His writings, and those of contemporaries such as Leon Gellert, Alexander Macdonald and Cyril Pearl, represented a particular type of humour, one in which a keen intelligence provided a sophisticated and lively set of ideas combined with a satirical scrutiny of contemporary Australian society. Campbell's autobiography, *An Urge to Laugh*, was published in 1981.

CAMPION, Edmund (1933–), born Sydney, graduated from the University of Cambridge after being ordained as a priest in 1961. After a curacy in several Sydney parishes he lectured at the Catholic Institute, Sydney. He edited *Lord Acton and the First Vatican Council* (1975) and published *John Henry Newman* (1980), *Rockchoppers: Growing up Catholic in Australia* (1982) and *Australian Catholics* (1987), which is subtitled 'The Contribution of Catholics to the Development of Australian Society'. He also edited the anthology *Living Here: Short Stories from Australasia 1938–1988* (1988). He has since 1975 been editor of *Studies in the Christian Movement*. *Rockchoppers*, often personal in tone and occasionally autobiographical, is largely a series of essays about the state of Catholic culture in Australia, and the history of Catholicism locally and internationally. The title, a derivation from the initials RC, is also a derogatory Protestant reference to Irish-Australian Catholic convict origins. Campion is a character in Jill Neville's novel *Last Ferry to Manly* (1984).

CAMPION, Sarah ('Mary Alpers') (1906–), born Mary Rose Coulton, Eastbourne, and brought up in Cambridge, England, became from the 1930s journalist, novelist, traveller and political activist. Her five English novels of the 1930s show an increasing concern for pre-war Europe and, drawing on her experience teaching English in Germany to Berliner Jews in 1936–37, with the plight of the German Jews in particular, an interest carried over into *Mo Burdekin*. After accompanying her elderly parents to South Africa to escape pre-war Cambridge in 1938, Campion visited NZ and arrived in Sydney in February 1939 for the crucial eight-month Australian visit which produced her six 'Australian' novels and ended abruptly with the outbreak of war. Two months working in Sydney were followed by Campion's six fascinated months on the Atherton Tableland which produced most notably her Queensland trilogy, *Mo Burdekin* (1941), *Bonanza* (1942) and *The Pommy Cow* (1944), a historical sequence centred in the Queensland gold rush and shearers' strike of the 1890s and the Queensland involvement in the Boer War. Using unabashed bush nationalist modes this lively novel sequence interweaves a racy comic realist narrative, lyrical natural description and unexpected pathos with a strong satirical vein and, in *The Pommy Cow*, suffragist interest with a trenchant indictment of the South African war. Failing in her attempt through the 1940s to return to Australia, Campion nonetheless wrote the successful crime fiction and 'lurid melodrama' *Dr Golightly* (1946), which transfers the infamous career of Scottish surgeon, confidence trickster and murderer Dr Edward William Pritchard (1825–65) to colonial Adelaide (convicted of poisoning his wife, Pritchard was executed before an estimated crowd of 100 000; *Dr Golightly*'s 'Pritchard' narrative includes a grotesque colonial hanging). Campion's other Australian novels were *Turn Away No More* (1940) and *Come Again* (1951). Her biography of her father, Cambridge medieval scholar George Gordon Coulton, *Father: A* portrait of *G.G. Coulton at home, etc.* (1948), achieved acclaim and contemporary notoriety as an exposé of a late Victorian patriarch in England. *National Baby* (1949), an autobiographical advocacy of the new British National Health system, confirms the breadth and pragmatism of Campion's social and political concern. In early 1952 Sarah Campion settled with her infant son and then husband, writer Antony Alpers, in NZ and did not revisit Australia until 1959 when she was deeply disappointed by the country's perceived 'Americanisation'. She made some subsequent visits as late as the 1980s but never returned to fiction-writing, 'Australian' or otherwise. She has lived in Auckland since the 1950s, writing as a journalist, social historian, and political activist especially concerned with the anti-racism and nuclear disarmament movements. In 1964 with Walter Scott she visited China as a delegate from the New Zealand–China Friendship Society. Critical essays on Campion's work have been published by John McKellar in *Southerly* (1950) and Elizabeth Lawson (*LiNQ*, 1987). *Mo Burdekin* was republished with an introduction by Elizabeth Lawson in 1990 in the Penguin Australian Women's Library Series.

ELIZABETH LAWSON

Canadian Exiles is a name given to a group of about 200 men, also known as the Canadian Patriots, transported to Australia after the failure of rebellions in Canada in 1837–38. The Canadian Exiles comprised in fact two distinct groups: the rebels from Upper Canada (now the province of Ontario, then under the governorship of Sir George Arthur) consisted mainly of British Canadians and Americans and were sent to Tasman's Peninsula in Van Diemen's Land; the rebels from Lower Canada (now the province of Quebec) were French Canadians and were sent to Sydney. Some of the patriots were harshly treated and all felt their exile keenly, although within five years of their arrival most had won pardons or effected escapes. Like earlier political prisoners they were relatively well-educated convicts and several left memoirs of their Canadian and Australian experiences, which form part of Australian convict literature (see Convict in Australian Literature). William Gates's *Recollections of Life in Van Dieman's* [sic] *Land* (1850), Daniel D. Heustis's *A Narrative of the Adventures and Suffering of Captain Daniel D. Heustis and His Companions* (1847), Caleb Lyon's *Narrative and Recollections of Van Dieman's* [sic] *Land, during a Three Years' Captivity of Stephen S. Wright* (1844), Robert Marsh's *Seven Years of My Life* (1847), Linus W. Miller's *Notes of an Exile to Van Dieman's* [sic] *Land* (1846), Samuel Snow's *The Exile's Return* (1846) and Benjamin Wait's *Letters from Van Dieman's* [sic] *Land* (1843) are reminiscences of convicts from Upper Canada. The experiences of the Lower Canadian prisoners are documented by Leon Ducharmé's *Journal of a Political Exile in Australia*, François Xavier Prieur's *Notes of a Convict of 1838 (published in translation by George Mackaness in 1944 and 1949 respectively)* and by the prison diary of François-Maurice Lepailleur, *translated by F.M. Greenwood in Land of a Thousand Sorrows* (1980).

Canberra Times, founded by Thomas Mitchell Shakespeare (1873–1938), published its first issue 3 September 1926; in 1928 it became a daily. It was controlled by T.M. Shakespeare and his sons A.T., C.J. and J.W. Shakespeare, until it was sold to John Fairfax and Sons Ltd in 1964. In 1989 it was purchased by Kerry Stokes. It carries regular literary columns, organises an annual National Short Story competition sponsored by the Commonwealth Bank, and publishes prize-winning entries from each year's competition. In 1983 it co-sponsored the first National Word Festival. In March 1994 it introduced a twice-yearly supplement, the *Reader*, offering a mix of reviews, articles, interviews and extracts from contemporary writing.

CANNON, Michael (1929–), born Brisbane, has spent his working life as a journalist and historian in Melbourne, Sydney and London and is at present chief editor of the *Historical Records of Victoria* (q.v.). He has written many works centred on Australian life, past and present, including *The Land Boomers* (1966, 2nd edn titled *Land Boom and Bust* 1972); the best-selling series *Australia in the Victorian Age*, comprising three volumes, *Who's Master? Who's Man?* (1971), *Life in the Country* (1973) and *Life in Cities* (1975); *An Australian Camera 1851–1914* (1973); *That Damned Democrat: John Norton, An Australian Populist, 1858–1916* (1981); *Australia: A History in Photographs* (1983, republished in 1993 as *Black Land, White Land*), *Australia: Spirit of a Nation* (1985), *Who Killed the Koories?* (1990), *Old Melbourne Town Before the Gold Rush* (1991), and *Melbourne After the Gold Rush* (1993). Cannon's wide historical interest in Australia is also reflected in his editing of e.g. *The Vagabond Papers* (1969), *Victoria's Representative Men at Home* (1977), *Vagabond Country: Australian Bush and Town Life in the Victorian Age* (1981), *The Victorian Goldfields, 1852–3: An Original Album* (S.T. Gill) (1982), and volumes I–VI of *Historical Records of Victoria* (1981–91). His *Who's Master? Who's Man?* won the FAW Barbara Ramsden Award in 1971.

'Canticle, The', a poem in four parts by Francis Webb (q.v.), was published in Webb's volume *Birthday* (1953). In notes to the poem Webb maintains that St Francis of Assisi had provided, in his *Canticle to the Sun* written at Assisi in the garden of the Minoresses of San Damiano shortly before his death, 'a great hymn of devotion, a rewarding personal document, and fine poetry'; excerpts from *Canticle to the Sun* are used in Webb's poem. Webb builds up the character of St Francis by observations from those in contact with him and by indicating the changes wrought in them through his influence. The first such observer is the leper, whose bitter sense of rejection by God and society is transformed to joy and peace through St Francis's loving embrace and cure of his putrefying body. St Francis's father (the cloth merchant, Pietro di Bernadone), the Jongleur, the Wolf of Gubbio, whom St Francis called 'brother', and the Knight and the Serf, are others regenerated through the saint's influence. The fourth part emphasises the veneration in which

St Francis, the 'second Christ', is held by his devoted followers and concludes with a reference to the stigmata of Christ, which are said to have appeared on St Francis's body in the latter part of his life.

CAPPIELLO, Rosa Raffaella (1942–) came to Australia in 1971 from Naples and worked in various Sydney clothing factories, often facing unemployment and discrimination. In 1981 she published, in Italian, a novel titled *Paese Fortunato*, which won the 1981 Premio Calabria prize. Before coming to Australia, Cappiello had written another novel, *I Semi neri* (*The Black Seeds*) (1977). *Paese Fortunato* was translated into English by Gaetano Rando and published in 1984 titled *Oh Lucky Country*; in 1985 it won the Ethnic Book Prize in the NSW Premier's Literary Awards. Unremittingly angry and scatological, the novel is partly autobiographical, in Cappiello's own words, 'a tragi-comic interpretation extracted from the primitive and stagnant chaos of the migrant experience'. Received warmly in Italy, the novel aroused protests in Australia from sections of the Italian community, dismayed by the language, the explicit presentation of heterosexual and homosexual activity and concentration on the exploitation of women workers in migrant-run Sydney factories. The novel is a scathing indictment of Australian attitudes, especially of the nation's philistinism, but it is also a denunciation of the old country, which has imposed migration on the migrant, of its remnants in the host country, which exploit newly arrived compatriots, and of the rigid patterns of male dominance in both cultures. At the novel's close, the group of immigrant women from different backgrounds, whose experiences are its subject, are in much the same case as at their arrival; there is no escaping the trap of poverty and 'difference'. Drawing on European traditions, especially the *commedia dell'arte* and a Neapolitan folk tradition of caricature, Cappiello delights in subversion and comic disruption: 'Through writing I often feel the exhilarating sensation of breaking with society, and disrupting its rules, regulations and mediocre values.' Much of this freedom is achieved by an exuberant use of language in a virtuoso performance, which counters to some extent the powerlessness and plotless lives of its central characters.

Capricornia, a novel by Xavier Herbert (q.v.), was published in 1938 (republished in 1990 in the A & R Imprint series with an introduction by Mudrooroo), when it won both the Commonwealth sesquicentenary literary competition and the Australian Literature Society's Gold Medal. The story of the writing, editing and publication of the novel is a celebrated and, so far as the editing is concerned, controversial episode in Australian literary history. In a talk given at the Adelaide Festival in 1962, Herbert recalled that *en route* to England in 1930 he wrote a 'tough little book' called 'Black Velvet', seemingly focused on sexual relations between European men and Aboriginal women, which he failed to place with publishers. Disenchanted with England and about to leave for Africa, he was persuaded by Sadie Norden, later his wife, to

remain and rewrite 'Black Velvet'. What emerged over the next two years was a much longer work in which the toughness of 'Black Velvet' was softened by Herbert's sense of 'the loveliness of the land I'd left' and his feeling that the people 'were really comical, not so bad as mad, as aren't we all?' Herbert returned to Australia with the first draft of *Capricornia*; in 1933 he met P.R. Stephensen (q.v.), who urged him to revise the novel and acted as adviser during the revision in which its half-million words were reduced by half. The extent of Stephensen's assistance was the subject of some dispute between the two men, but it seems clear that even if Stephensen did not actually write any part of the novel he made suggestions which Herbert adopted. Stephensen started typesetting in 1934 but his company went into liquidation before *Capricornia* could be published. After three years, during which Herbert had tried to place the novel with other publishers, Stephensen accepted *Capricornia* for publication with the press of the *Publicist* (q.v.) and not only completed printing in time to enter it in the sesquicentenary competition but also promoted it enthusiastically. Angus & Robertson, which had twice rejected *Capricornia*, accepted it finally in 1938 and has published the many editions and reprints since then which attest to its popularity.

In 1933 Stephensen urged Herbert 'to keep the story of *Capricornia* strictly to Norman's life, deleting everything extraneous'. Although in its final form the novel retains a large cast of characters (more than a hundred) and a broad chronological sweep (from the mid-1880s to about 1930), the story of Norman Shillingsworth and his family occupies an important part of the foreground. Arriving in Capricornia (a fictional name for the Northern Territory) in 1904 with his brother Oscar, Mark Shillingsworth soon becomes part of the flotsam and jetsam of Port Zodiac (Darwin) society. Dismissed from the public service for drunkenness, Mark forms a brief relationship with an Aboriginal woman and fathers a son, whom he deserts and who acquires the name of Naw-Nim (no name), later Norman, and after killing a Chinese storekeeper, disappears from view until the second half of the novel. Oscar, the respectable contrast to Mark, marries and tries to establish himself on a Capricornian cattle station, Red Ochre, but is deserted by his wife and eventually returns for a time to Batman (Melbourne) accompanied by his daughter Marigold and foster son Norman, who has been sent to him after Mark's desertion. Before their departure Oscar rejects the plea of a former employee, Peter Differ, to see to the welfare of his daughter Constance; Constance Differ is placed under the 'protection' of Humbolt Lace, a Protector of Aborigines, who seduces her and then marries her off to another man of part-Aboriginal descent. Forced into prostitution, Constance is dying of consumption when discovered by a railway fitter, Tim O'Cannon, one of the few inhabitants of Capricornia who treat the Aborigines with humanity. After Connie's death Tim takes her daughter, Tocky, into his household; after Tim's own death in a railway accident she is sent to the native compound at Port Zodiac and then to a mission station.

Hearing news in 1928 of an economic boom in Capricornia, Oscar returns to his station, where he is joined by Marigold and Norman, who has grown to manhood believing himself to be the son of a Javanese princess and a soldier killed in the First World War. Soon after he discovers part of the truth about his identity – that his mother was Aboriginal – Norman meets his father, now a railway construction boss working under the name of Jack Ramble. Their reconciliation is not completed until after Ramble disappears again and Heather Shay, Norman's aunt and Mark's former lover, reveals Ramble's secret. The discovery of the truth about his past is the first stage of Norman's education in Capricornia; in response to his discoveries, he embarks on a series of journeys to discover his true, part-Aboriginal self. On his second journey, which takes place after Oscar has died, he meets and wanders in the wilderness with Tocky, who has escaped from the mission station. Their interlude is interrupted when Tocky, while separated from Norman, shoots Frank McLash, a fugitive from the police, in self-defence. Tocky does not tell Norman of the killing and after their return to civilisation Norman is arrested and stands trial for Frank's murder. Mark, too, once his identity becomes known beyond his own circle, stands trial for the original murder of the Chinese storekeeper. At the end of the novel both are acquitted, Heather and Mark are married, and Norman returns to Red Ochre where he finds the body of Tocky and their child in a water tank in which she had taken refuge from the authorities.

Like *Poor Fellow My Country*, Herbert's later novel about the Northern Territory, *Capricornia* is a sprawling, swashbuckling work teeming with incident and with 'mad' characters. A major focus is the indictment of civilisation in this part of Australia, particularly the violent treatment meted out to the Aborigines (as well as the Chinese) by the pioneering Europeans, whose racism is responsible for the tragedies of Connie Differ and Tocky O'Cannon and for the ambivalent status in society of people of mixed descent such as Norman. In exposing the institutions of White society (e.g. religion, the law, civil administration) as hypocritical, corrupt and inefficient, Herbert has recourse to heavy irony, e.g. in the capitals which signal the clichés of his Dickensian and satirically named characters: thus the legal profession is represented by Judge Caesar Bightit, the prosecutor is Thumscrough and the solicitors Nawratt and Nibblesom. Yet it does an injustice to the vitality of *Capricornia* to see it as simply a novel of social protest that encompasses class as well as race. Herbert has written that 'the greatest feeling expressed' in the novel is 'my love of this good earth'. The abundance of nature is emphasised but so is its fickleness and the danger it holds for the isolated Europeans who fail to adapt to its changing moods and demands. Although the element of chance in human affairs is an important ingredient in Capricornian life, so is human culpability for the disasters that befall characters like Tim O'Cannon. The rhythm of the seasons is one of the ways *Capricornia* is shaped; others are the search for identity and the quest to belong, which encompass not only individuals like Norman

and Tocky but also whole societies. The journey (hence the importance of trains) is a dominant motif in a novel that combines comedy and tragedy and, like many other saga-chronicles of the 1920s and 1930s (e.g. *Landtakers* and *All That Swagger),* offers a radical view of Australia's development. Louis Nowra's (q.v.) play *Capricornia* (1988) is based on Herbert's novel.

'Captain Dobbin', a poem by Kenneth Slessor (q.v.) in *Cuckooz Contrey* (1932), is based partly on a Captain Bayldon, retired sea captain and uncle of Slessor's first wife Noela, and owes some of its picturesque detail to Herman Melville's *Omoo*. The poem describes an eccentric old seaman, who is enshrined in his cottage by the harbour the treasures of his seafaring days. Slessor's colourful description of the exotic places and incidents that live in the old captain's memory and his contrast of those with the cold, alienating contemporary scene point to his own commitment to the romantic past. A fine piece of characterisation with the Slessor penchant for lavish and colourful imagery, 'Captain Dobbin' is one of his major poems.

Captain Quadring (1912), William Gosse Hay's (q.v.) third novel, is set in Manalia (Hay's name for Australia in his early novels), where the ex-convict Henry Fairservice, whose aliases in the novel are first Mr Meadstone and then Captain Quadring, comes to restore order at a quarry worked by convicts, which is near land held by his brother Andrew. The brothers have become bitter enemies in England and, after believing he has killed Henry Fairservice in a fight at Quadring quarry, Andrew has fled to Tasmania. The brothers are eventually reconciled (although Henry is killed at the end of the novel by vengeful convicts) through the endeavours of the saintly Elizabeth Beckworth, who has taken over the Fairservice family home.

Captain Quiros (1964), James McAuley's (q.v.) narrative poem describing the expeditions of the Portuguese explorer Pedro Fernandez de Quiros (1563–1614) in his search for the Great South Land, is an important contribution to the voyager (q.v.) theme in Australian literature. In 'The Inception of the Poem' the long-held fascination of the theme for McAuley is revealed:

> Then suddenly, unbidden, the theme returns
> That visited my youth; over the vast
> Pacific with white wake at their sterns,
> The ships of Quiros on their great concerns
> Ride in upon the present from the past!

The first part of the poem, 'Where Solomon was Wanting', records through the narrator, Belmonte, the voyage of Alvaro de Mendana in 1595 to Santa Cruz Island near the Solomon Islands with Quiros as navigator; the establishment of the abortive settlement at Graciosa Bay; the murder of the native chieftain Malope; and the forced withdrawal of the expedition. The second part, 'The Quest for the South Land', recounts Quiros's own expedition to establish the New Jerusalem in the South Seas. He comes to an island in the New Hebrides, which he names La Australia del Espiritu Santo (Southern Land of the Holy Spirit). A river to the west of the anchorage is named Jordan and a site is selected for a city to be called New Jerusalem. Quiros's great plan fails, not because of any defect on his part, but because no man can bring about the millennium – 'The New Jerusalem . . . shall never be Christ's bride save in eternity.' The third part, 'The Times of the Nations', presents Quiros's dying vision of the unveiling of the Great South Land (Australia) by the Dutch explorers and Bougainville and Cook; the formation of the initial colony 'under the shadow of harsh penal law'; and its growth to nationhood 'fortunate and free'. De Quiros is also the subject of a play, 'The Quest', by Louis Esson and of a television opera by Peter Sculthorpe in 1982.

Captain Swift, a play with slight Australian content by Charles Haddon Chambers (q.v.), was first produced in London in 1888 with Herbert Beerbohm Tree in the name role and published in 1902. It is chiefly memorable for originating the phrase 'the long arm of coincidence', used by the title character, a bushranger.

CARBONI, Raffaello (1817–75) was born Urbino, Italy, spent a restless youth in which he studied at Urbino University, joined the Young Italy movement, was wounded in the rebellion of 1848–49, and was forced into exile in Germany and then London. He arrived on the Ballarat goldfields in 1853 and became a member of the miners' central committee supervising the events leading to the Eureka Stockade (q.v.) but was a spectator when the stockade was attacked, 3 December 1854. He was charged with treason for his role in the Eureka incident but was acquitted with the other participants. His account of the revolt, *The Eureka Stockade*, was published as by 'Carboni Raffaello' late in 1855 and was sold personally by Carboni at the site of Eureka on the first anniversary of the attack. A modern edition (1942) has an introduction by H.V. Evatt, who asserts that 'it is impossible to deny him greatness as writer and historian'. Although that is excessive praise, Carboni's book has gained recognition, in spite of its eccentric structure and florid style, as a vivid and reliable account of the Eureka events, as well as a remarkably sound analysis of the underlying causes of those events. Carboni left Australia in January 1856 after becoming a naturalised British subject and travelled widely for several years. He returned to Italy to participate in the Risorgimento, and in later years was a busy but unacknowledged dramatist and composer. Carboni's long allegorical poem 'Gilburnia', dealing with Eureka and the diggings, was discovered in 1980 by A.D. Pagiaro in Rome. Carboni and the Eureka Stockade are the subjects of John Romeril's play 'Carboni' (1980). He appears in other literature about Eureka, e.g. in Louis Esson's play *The Southern Cross* (1946) and in E.V. Timms's juvenile novel *The Red Mask* (1927). Desmond O'Grady wrote the biography *Raffaello! Raffaello!* (1986), which uncovered previously unknown facts.

Cardboard Crown, The, a novel by Martin Boyd (q.v.) published in 1952, is the opening work of a tetralogy in which Boyd depicts the fortunes of the Langton family, living between two hemispheres and two cultures. With the aid of her diaries and a relative's reminiscences, Guy Langton reconstructs the history of his grandmother Alice from the 1850s to the turn of the century, her marriage to Austin Langton and their life in Australia and England. The narrative centres on Austin's adultery with a cousin, Hetty Mayhew, who bears him four sons, and on Alice's friendship with Aubrey Tunstall, a cultured Italianate Englishman living in Rome. Alice invests her favourite daughter Diana with her aspirations towards European civilisation, although Diana's marriage to an impecunious Australian musician and the financial crash of the 1890s erode the family's aristocratic expectations and way of life.

Careful, He Might Hear You, a semi-autobiographical novel by Sumner Locke Elliott (q.v.), was published in 1963 and won the Miles Franklin Award that year. Immediately successful, it was translated into six languages and selected by *Reader's Digest* Book Club; produced as a film in 1983 directed by Carl Schultz, it won the award for best Australian film. Set in 1930s Sydney, the novel traces the relationship between a small boy (nicknamed 'PS' by his mother, the writer Sinden Marriott, who had died at his birth) and his aunt, Vanessa. Brought up from birth by his impoverished but loving Aunt Lila and her husband, George, PS has been impressed with the legend of his talented and charming mother, referred to as 'Dear One' by Lila. He has never met his father, Logan Marriott, an alcoholic ex-journalist who is incapable of affecting his destiny. Two other aunts, the perennially girlish Vere and Agnes who suffers from a religious mania, care for him intermittently. The stability of his childhood is threatened when Vanessa, the aunt who has lived with the family's wealthy Cousin Ettie for many years, arrives from England and attempts to gain sole custody. PS is sent to an expensive but unpleasant school, instructed in good manners and provided with an elegant home, clothes and friends. His instinctive resistance to Vanessa's attempts to appropriate him, heightened by a visit from his father, culminates in his refusal to return after a weekend with Lila. Meanwhile the grounds are suggested of Vanessa's prickly insecurity and the inadequacies of her relationship with her parents and sisters and with Logan Marriott. After a protracted legal battle, PS is assigned to Vanessa by an insensitive judge. Incarcerated once again in her unfriendly house, he engages in an effective game of passive resistance. Vanessa's confidence is progressively undermined and finally crumbles when she witnesses his cruelly accurate imitation of her at a children's party. She decides to give him up, experiences a new sense of peace and freedom, but is drowned in a ferry accident on her way to Lila. After her funeral PS is reconciled to her memory and determines to follow her last advice to him, to be himself. Refusing to be categorised any longer as a postscript, he demands to be known by his real name, Bill.

CAREW, Elsie (1895–1971), born Auckland, NZ, had by her account a Cinderella-type existence as a child before setting out at 19 for an independent life in Australia. In her lonely and rather unusual life she spent long periods at the Salvation Army's Sydney People's Palace, where she died; she had a failed marriage, occasional bouts of travel including a trip to Moscow, and a penchant for writing esoteric verse and prose which she kept in tattered notebooks. Made known to Australian readers through the interest of Nancy Keesing, who wrote *Elsie Carew: Australian Primitive Poet* (1965), she still remains something of an enigma; her visionary experiences and dry perceptions on the follies of modern humanity are conveyed in direct and aphoristic verse. *The Passing Pageant: Poems and Prose by Elsie Carew* was published in 1970.

CAREY, Gabrielle (1959–), born Sydney, has been a street singer, farmer, journalist, youth worker, typist, and radio producer. She first came into prominence with the co-authorship with Kathy Lette of *Puberty Blues* (q.v., 1979), a frank account of the surfie culture of the 1970s from a girl's viewpoint. At the age of 17 she formed a comedy act with Lette, the Salami Sisters, which became immensely popular. Carey has also written an account of her relationship with Terry Haley, a long-term inmate of Parramatta gaol, and her fight to have him released, *Just Us* (1984); and the story of her search for spiritual meaning in her encounter with the cultures of Ireland and Mexico and the implications of this search for her relationship with her father, Alex Carey, *In My Father's House* (1992). A left-wing academic, prominent in the 1970s, especially in the protest movement against Australian participation in the Vietnam War, Alex Carey was a profound influence on his daughter, growing closer to her in their correspondence while she was in Mexico. After the birth of her daughter Gabrielle Carey returned to Australia to see her father only to discover that he had committed suicide the day before she returned; *In My Father's House* is a coming to terms with this tragedy and also an exploration of different cultural responses to death. *Just Us* has been produced for television and a popular film was made of *Puberty Blues* in 1981.

CAREY, Peter (1943–), born Bacchus Marsh, Victoria, where his father was a car salesman, was educated at Geelong Grammar and Monash University. At Monash he studied science but became interested in writing and joined an advertising agency, where his colleagues included Morris Lurie and Barry Oakley. He later worked in advertising in London (1968–70), moved to Sydney in 1974 and now lives in Manhattan, New York. His expatriate experience has not affected his concern with Australia: 'Being away from it, I've never been less able to separate myself from it.' He has also emphasised his continuing concern with Australian history: 'What you end up wanting to talk about is Australian history . . . You've grown out of that soil – out of the soil that starts with a convict economy, a concentration camp, genocide and all of that. You're the echo of a defeat culture. All my narratives can only end in failure.'

His first three novels are unpublished although part of an early book, titled *Contacts,* appeared in the anthology *Under Twenty Five* (1966). His short stories, some of which first appeared in such periodicals as *Overland, Tabloid Story, Stand, Nation Review* and *Meanjin,* have been published in two collections, *The Fat Man in History* (1974) and *War Crimes* (1979), which won a NSW Premier's Literary Award in 1980. A collection, published in London in 1980 and titled *The Fat Man in History*, contains some stories from both collections as does *Exotic Pleasures* (1980). He has also published the novels *Bliss* (q.v., 1981), which won the Miles Franklin Award in 1981, a NSW Literary Award and the NBC Banjo Award in 1982; *Illywhacker* (1985), which won the *Age* Book of the Year Award, the FAW Barbara Ramsden Award and the NBC Banjo Award in 1985, and the Vance Palmer Prize for Fiction in 1986; *Oscar and Lucinda* (1988),which won the Townsville Foundation for Australian Literary Studies Award and the Booker Prize in 1988, the Miles Franklin Award and the NBC Banjo Award in 1989 and the SA Festival Award in 1990; and *The Tax Inspector* (1991). Carey has also contributed to the short-story collection *The Most Beautiful Lies* (1977), edited by Brian Kiernan, and collaborated in the screenplay of *Bliss* (with Ray Lawrence in 1985) and of *Until the End of the World* (with Wim Wenders in 1991). The film *Bliss* won three Australian Film Institute Awards in 1985, including best feature film. The screenplay by Carey and Ray Lawrence was published in 1985.

An accessible and popular writer, who takes pride in his appeal to a wide audience and believes firmly 'in the possibility of popular art that's good art in anybody's terms', Carey has been described as a fabulist similar to such overseas writers as Jorge Luis Borges, Gabriel García Márquez and Donald Barthelme, although his fiction is distinctive and not derivative. Surrealism and realism blend in most of his stories to create a compelling, often nightmarish world which is mysterious and serious, fantastic yet real. Common to most of his stories are a sardonic sense of comedy and a relish for the macabre, a matter-of-fact tone, a controlled treatment of suggestive, seemingly bizarre detail and a narrator whose character is as ambiguous and shadowy as his experience is immediate and compelling. Underlying Carey's surrealism is a keen sense of what he sees as the absurd paradoxes and contradictions of contemporary life, of the problematic nature of ordinary reality. Many of his characters are social failures, such as the unemployed man in 'Peeling'; or dispossessed, as the young man Crabs is dispossessed of physical stature and car parts in the story of that title; or victims of insane institutions, such as the soldier in 'Windmill in the West', who is ordered at all costs to guard an indeterminate area for an indeterminate reason, or the shepherd class 3 in 'Life and Death in the South Side Pavilion', who is futilely employed by his faceless 'Company' to prevent horses from falling into an unenclosed tank. Most of his individuals are powerless against an exterior force of some kind, whether it is small-town prejudice as in 'American Dreams', the 'Committee' ruling the world in

'The Fat Man in History', or the new dictators, the corrupt and corrupting Fastalogians in 'The Chance'. Occasionally, as in the brilliantly suggestive story 'War Crimes', the victim forces himself to rise above his degrading status only to be irretrievably debased by the vicious means he chooses. Carey has described his characters as 'victims of a way of living', people who have 'come to accept their nightmares', embodiments of his own 'fainthearted optimism and strong pessimism'. Frequently their absurd experiences are a metaphor of the mindless destructiveness of contemporary, technological society. Stories such as 'Crabs', which starts with the realistic setting of a drive-in cinema and ends with the transformation of an inadequate young man into a perfectly functioning machine (a tow-truck), and 'The Fat Man in History', which deals with the dilemma of a fat man after the revolution has declared obesity to be subversive, satirise recognisable, reductive trends in modern society. Others such as 'War Crimes', 'Conversations with Unicorns' and 'The Chance' suggest the conditions that combine to create alienation and frustration.

Bliss, Carey's schematically conceived novel which deals with the life of Harry Joy, an advertising man who dies three times and is resurrected on each occasion to new hellish or heavenly experience, combines light and black comedy, incisive social satire and a poetic, futuristic vision. A stylish satire on modern living, it includes visionary and allegorical elements like his short stories, although it stops short of science fiction. Herbert Badgery, the narrator and illywhacker of the novel of that title, is an accomplished liar, spieler and salesman. Founded on Mark Twain's famous statement that Australian history does not read like history but 'like the most beautiful lies', this large, wide-ranging, picaresque novel is implicitly concerned with one of the nation's most basic lies, that the land was *terra nullius* when the European settlers arrived. Claiming to be 139 when the novel opens and rejoicing in his history of being 'a terrible liar', Herbert takes his story back to 1861 and forward into the present when he has become a largely unwilling resident of his son Charles's establishment in Sydney, the Best Pet Shop in the World. The novel is also self-consciously preoccupied with lying in its concern with the processes of writing, the inevitable element of fiction-making in every human attempt to tell the truth, and the power of fiction to transform and illuminate bald fact. Carey's interest in fictionality extends to history, which he sometimes presents in alternative, 'fantastic' versions, implicitly suggesting the constructed quality of all 'objective' historical narrative and the partiality of all explanations of events. Charles's obsession with the truth, for instance, in *Illywhacker* makes him a bad salesman, because 'the truth, told thus, makes him a bad punter'. Following Badgery's relationships with Phoebe McGrath, the mother of his son Charles, and later with Leah Goldstein, the book concentrates on the fortunes of Charles in its third section, presenting his pet shop as a kind of zoo, a symbol of contemporary Australia, as the various temporary houses that Badgery builds express the national predilection for physical and mental struc-

tures which will represent home in a landscape that continues to be alien. Interested in the human capacity to construct meaning rather than in meaning itself, Carey explores the various life stories his characters create to console experience and constitute community. Allegory, however, is muted in *Illywhacker*, absorbed in Carey's versatile ability to create character, place and striking incident.

Oscar and Lucinda is a bold attempt to wed the nineteenth century with the twentieth, drawing briefly on the historical relationships and world views of George Eliot and G.H.Lewes and providing an alternative version of Edmund Gosse's *Father and Son*, as well as recalling Eliot's *Mill on the Floss*. Like Gosse, Oscar is afflicted with a father who is a marine biologist as well as a leader of the Plymouth Brethren sect; his eccentric religious pursuits include an obsession with his son's soul, but unlike Gosse, Oscar early seeks his own salvation by choosing alternative parents and by providing for his own education by pursuing a successful career as a gambler. His gambling predilection is shared by the woman who is to become belatedly his companion/lover, Lucinda Leplastrier, and is like himself in her unconventionality, energy and conviction of a lonely destiny. These attributes are brought to the fore in her attempts to invest in and run a glassworks in Sydney. After a brief interlude as vicar of an Anglican parish at Randwick, Oscar is ousted by the scandal the pair's relationship and gambling arouses and undertakes the gamble which will cost him his life, an attempt to transport a prefabricated glass church across unexplored back country to a small settlement in the far north of the country on the Bellinger River. Both gambling and glass become potent symbols, the first expressive of the pair's idealistic attitudes to their spiritual, material and emotional destinies, the second of the paradoxical strength/fragility of their individual ways of being in the world. Confronted with a colonial society which is brutal, materialist and inherently violent, evils which predominate during Oscar's journey with the church and culminate in his killing of the vicious leader of the expedition, Jeffris, the idealistic vision of the lovers is fatally fractured. Described by one reviewer as 'a comic version of *Voss* with Laura/Lucinda driving her lover out into the wilderness to prove himself', and as 'one of the finest Victorian novels of the twentieth century', *Oscar and Lucinda* projects Carey's perception of Australian society as historically grounded in violence and forces antithetical to the spiritual.

The Tax Inspector moves into an Australia set slightly into the future, and into a decayed corrupt outer Sydney, whose streets are infested with packs of feral children with 'lighter fuel breath' and precocious appetites for violence, with homeless individuals inhabiting concrete pipes on a burnt-out K-Mart lot. Maria Takis, the tax inspector who is also in the final stages of pregnancy and in semi-flight from her Greek origins, is the agent and catalyst for Carey's exposure of a city starkly divided into the dispossessed and the grotesquely wealthy. Compressed into four days, the action ostensibly turns on the fortunes of the Catchprice car company, threatened with ruin by a tax audit, although the novel's themes expand to include family violence, the origins of psychopathological behaviour and its links with community degeneration symbolised by abuse of the tax system. The novel's conclusion is one of the most violent in Carey's fiction, although ostensibly it is an affirmation of life at the end of a series of destructive stories spanning several generations. Studies of Casey's work include Karen Lamb's *Peter Carey: The Genesis of Fame* (1992), and Anthony J. Hassall's *Dancing on Hot Macadam: Peter Carey's Fiction* (1994).

CARLETON, Caroline (?1820–74) migrated from England to Australia in 1839. She wrote 'The Song of Australia' (1858) and *South Australian Lyrics* (?1860), the latter the first recorded book of verse published by a woman in SA.

CARLON, Patricia (1927–), born Wagga Wagga, NSW, has written numerous books, chiefly romantic fiction under the pseudonym 'Barbara Christie', and crime and thriller novels largely under her own name or as 'P. Scot Bernard'. Of the latter the best known are *Circle of Fear* (1961), *Danger in the Dark* (1962), *The Unquiet Night* (1965), and two republished (1992–93) in the Wakefield Crime Classics, *The Souvenir* (first published 1970), and *The Whispering Wall*. First published in 1969 in Britain by Hodder & Stoughton in the King Crime series, *The Whispering Wall* was a considerable success. A suspense story, it has a central character Sarah Oatland, who overhears a murder plotted by tenants who have taken over part of her house. Patricia Carlon has also published many articles (often using the pseudonym 'Patricia Bernard'), short stories and serials.

CARMICHAEL, Grace Jennings (1867–1904), born Ballarat, spent her childhood in the Gippsland area – there is a plaque to her memory in Orbost – and then trained as a nurse in Melbourne. She published prose sketches, *Hospital Children* (1891), and *Poems* (1895). After a tragic marriage she was left destitute in London, where she died in 1904. Her surviving three sons were rescued from the Northampton workhouse six years later and returned to Australia after some Australian writers called for funds to be raised on their behalf. Ian F. McLaren published *Grace Jennings Carmichael: from Croajingolong to London: with an Annotated Bibliography* (1986).

Carringbush, the setting of Frank Hardy's novel *Power Without Glory* (q.v., 1950), is the Melbourne suburb of Collingwood. The fictitious name was subsequently adopted by the Collingwood council for the local library.

CARRINGTON, Tom (1843–1918), born London, is reputed to have taken drawing lessons from the caricaturist George Cruikshank; his early work imitated John Tenniel, the illustrator of Lewis Carroll. He came as a gold-seeker to Australia in the 1860s and in 1866 began a long association as a cartoonist with *Melbourne Punch*, in which he virulently satirised the

politician Graham Berry in the late 1870s. He also drew for *Adelaide Punch* and produced a notable series on the capture of Ned Kelly (q.v.) for the *Australasian Sketcher* in 1880. He was on the staff of the *Australasian* and the *Argus* after his departure from *Melbourne Punch* in 1887. A founder of the Yorick Club (q.v.), Carrington was the best political cartoonist in Australia before the advent of the *Bulletin*: he developed his own line and successfully bridged the transition from wood to process engraving. With the journalist John Eville he published an adaptation and localisation of John Strachan's pantomime *Humpty Dumpty (Who Sat on a Wall), or, Harlequin King Arthur* (1874).

CARROLL, John Richard (1945–) has been a teacher and publisher's representative and now is a full-time writer, mainly of adventure and mystery fiction. He has regularly reviewed crime fiction for the *Australian Book Review* in its 'Guilt Edge' section. His books are *Token Soldiers* (1983), a novel from the viewpoint of an ordinary soldier about the Vietnam war; two thrillers, *Catspaw* (1988) and *Tropic of Fear* (1990); and *No Way Back* (1992), a novel about a psychotic detective, which is closely modelled on American forms of the genre in its treatment of language and sex.

CARTER, Paul (1951–), born England, came to Australia in the 1980s after spending periods in Spain and Italy. He was the editor of the *Age Monthly Review* 1986–91. He has written two studies of early responses to Australia, *The Road to Botany Bay: An Essay in Spatial History* (1987) and *Living in a New Country: History, Travelling and Language* (1992). Concentrating mainly on explorers' journals, Carter analyses various patterns, especially naming patterns, in which the interpretations of landscape and the imaginative appropriation of Australia as a previously unknown space were determined by the cultural baggage the explorers and early settlers brought from Europe. Applying the analytical techniques of structuralism, and combining the disciplines of history, philosophy and literary criticism, Carter uses explorers' journals, accounts and even maps as texts with significant grammars capable of explication. He has also written *The Sound In-Between. Voice, Space, Performance* (1992), a study of in-between speech in colonial race relations and the contemporary relations between immigrants and established Australians.

CARTER, Robert (1945–), born Australia, studied psychology at Macquarie University. Before becoming a full-time writer he was a patrol officer in Papua New Guinea, a teacher and an educational psychologist and school counsellor. He won National Short Story awards in 1983 and 1985 and the Angus & Robertson Writer's Fellowship in 1985 with the manuscript of *The Sugar Factory* (1986), a psychological novel about an adolescent who is wrongly diagnosed as a problem child and placed in the company of disturbed teenagers in a 'halfway house', where disaster ensues. His other books are *The Pleasure Within* (1987, short stories), and *Prints in the Valley* (1989).

The latter is set in the 1960s, the story moving between the suburbs of Sydney and tropical Papua New Guinea, entwining several originally disparate lives: Alec, a confused school psychologist; Anik, a sophisticated French woman; Jack, her son; and Koam, a girl from PNG. A compelling story-teller, Carter creates suspense and tension which provide him with the opportunity to examine, often remorselessly, the behaviour of his characters.

CASEY, Gavin (1907–64), born Kalgoorlie, WA, grew up in a gold-mining environment on which he drew in his later writings. During the 1930s Depression he worked in the Kalgoorlie mines and began his long experience as a journalist by reporting the Kalgoorlie news for the Perth *Mirror*. By 1936 he was publishing short stories in the *Australian Journal* and the *Bulletin*. He won the *Bulletin* short-story prize in successive years with 'Rich Stew' and 'Mail Run East'. In 1942 and 1943 he published his two chief collections of short stories, *It's Harder for Girls* (which won the S.H. Prior Memorial Prize and was republished in 1973 as *Short Shift Saturday and Other Stories)* and *Birds of a Feather*. Short-story fiction was Casey's forte; such stories as 'A Job in the Mill', 'That Day at Brown Lakes', 'It's Harder for Girls' and 'Short Shift Saturday' are accepted as among the finest Australian examples of the genre. As a short-story writer he has often been compared with Henry Lawson. In his stories of the goldfields (as with Lawson's of the bush) there is, beneath the easy yarning style and gently melancholy tone, a consistent emphasis on hardship that is tempered, for the male at least, by the conviviality ('beery good-fellowship' in the eyes of one critic) of mates. In 1945 Casey went to New York to administer the Australian News and Information Service; later he worked for the Australian News and Information Bureau in Canberra and Sydney. A gregarious personality, Casey became a popular member of Sydney's journalistic scene. His novels include *Downhill Is Easier* (1945), which illustrates the fatal ease of a gradual slide into crime; *The Wits Are Out* (1947), a light-hearted but perceptive and occasionally critical account of a beer party and its participants; *City of Men* (1950), the saga of two generations of the Willard family on the goldfields; *Snowball* (1958), a study of Black–White relations in the country town of Gibberton; *Amid the Plenty* (1962), an account of the Mayhew family who struggle through adverse times; and *The Man Whose Name Was Mud* (1963), which returns to a goldfields setting and is one of Casey's most interesting character studies. With Ted Mayman he wrote a documentary about Kalgoorlie, *The Mile That Midas Touched* (1964). An interesting alternative view of Casey's ethos of mateship in both life and work is that given by his first wife, Dorothy Casey-Congdon, in *Casey's Wife* (1982); her account of their marriage would seem to vindicate the theory that in the male-dominated Australian environment it was certainly 'harder for girls'.

CASEY, Lady Maie (1892–1983), born Melbourne as Maie Ryan, was the wife of Baron Casey of Berwick.

She published three autobiographical accounts, *An Australian Story 1837–1907* (1962), a history of four generations of her family in Australia; *Tides and Eddies* (1966), an account of her early married life; and *Rare Encounters* (1980), reminiscences of several distinguished individuals; an account of Nellie Melba's life, *Melba Revisited* (1975); and two volumes of verse, *Verses* (1963) and *From the Night* (1976). She also edited, with others, *Early Melbourne Architecture 1840 to 1888* (1953) and wrote the libretto for the musical *The Young Kabbarli* (1972).

CASEY, Richard Gavin Gardiner (Baron Casey of Berwick, Victoria, and the City of Westminster) (1890–1976), a distinguished Australian soldier, politician and statesman, was governor of Bengal, India, 1944–46. Created a life peer, Lord Casey was governor-general of Australia 1965–69. His writings include *An Australian in India* (1947), *Friends and Neighbours* (1954), the autobiographical *Personal Experience, 1939–1946* (1962), and *The Future of the Commonwealth* (1963). In *Australian Father and Son* (1966) he writes about his grandfather, Cornelius Gavin Casey (1811–96), and his father, Richard Gardiner Casey (1846–1913). T.B. Millar edited *Australian Foreign Minister: The Diaries of R.G. Casey 1951–60* (1972). His wife Maie Casey (q.v.) tells of her husband and their life together in *Tides and Eddies* (1966). W.J. Hudson and Jane North edited *My Dear P.M.: R.G. Casey's Letters to S.M. Bruce 1924–1929* (1980) and Hudson wrote the biography *Casey* (1986).

CASH, Deirdre, see 'ROHAN, Criena'

CASH, Martin (1808–77), born Enniscorthy, Ireland, was transported to NSW in 1827 for housebreaking. He worked out his seven-year sentence in assignment in the Hunter Valley before going to Van Diemen's Land in 1837 to avoid charges of cattle-duffing. In 1839 he was convicted of larceny and sentenced to seven years' imprisonment; over the next five years he made several escapes from Port Arthur, and in 1843 was the leader of a bushranging gang sometimes called 'Cash & Co'. After his arrest Cash was sentenced to death, but his sentence was commuted to transportation for life. He spent 1844–54 on Norfolk Island, a reformed character, and soon after his return to Tasmania received a ticket of leave; conditionally pardoned in 1856, he lived in NZ for four years before returning to Tasmania, where he was a farmer and an affectionately regarded old identity. In 1870 his autobiography, *The Adventures of Martin Cash,* edited and also probably written by James Lester Burke, was published in Hobart by the *Mercury*. That first 1870 edition contains 'The Ballad of Martin Cash', attributed usually to Francis MacNamara ('Frank the Poet') but attributed to Burke by Philip Butterss in 1992. The book went through several editions and was a source of Marcus Clarke's account of John Rex's escape from Port Arthur in *His Natural Life* (1874). Discussed in most histories of bushranging in Australia, Cash is the subject of Frank Clune's *Martin Cash: The Last of the Tasmanian Bushrangers*

(1955) and of 'Cash', a play by Michael Boddy and Marcus Cooney, which inaugurated the Tasmanian Theatre Company in 1972. Cash and his gang are also a threat in William Hay's novel *Strabane of the Mulberry Hills* (1929).

CASSIDY, Robert John ('Gilrooney') (1880–1948), born Coolac, NSW, worked in various bush occupations before joining the *Australian Worker*, then the *Barrier Truth* and the *Worker* again in 1912. Under the pseudonym 'Gilrooney' he published bush ballads, *The Land of the Starry Cross and Other Verses* (1911); a novel, *Chandler of Corralinga* (1912); and *The Gipsy Road and Other Fancies* (1919), a book of humorous prose sketches and verse.

'Cast-lron Canvasser, The', a short story by A.B. Paterson (q.v.), was published in *Three Elephant Power and Other Stories* (1917). One of the most humorous Australian stories, it tells of a mechanical book-seller devised to counter the treatment bush folk mete out to travelling salesmen, and its attempt to sell an atlas to the giant Scot, Macpherson.

Castlereagh River, discovered by George Evans, a member of John Oxley's 1818 expedition, and explored by Charles Sturt in 1829 to its junction with the Darling River, was named after Lord Castlereagh, then secretary of state for the colonies. It flows through the wool country of central northern NSW, its course marked by such outback towns as Coonabarabran, Gilgandra, Gulargambone and Coonamble. The Castlereagh is A.B. Paterson country, his famous 'land of lots of time along the Castlereagh': in his poem 'The Travelling Post Office' an old man sends a letter addressed to his drover son, 'care of Conroy's sheep along the Castlereagh'; and in his 'Shearing at Castlereagh' the quality of the wool grown on the Castlereagh is stressed. Not everything remains idyllic, however, on Paterson's Castlereagh, for his poem 'A Bushman's Song', which later became a popular bush song with the title 'Travellin' down the Castlereagh', expresses the radical and racist sentiments typical of the bushman's philosophy in the 1890s. In the poem the true bushman is forced 'further out' once the Castlereagh pastoral idyll has been corrupted by 'scab' Chinese labour and 'the little landlord god'.

CASTRO, Brian (1950–), born Hong Kong, taught English and French in Australia and France 1972–79 before becoming a full-time writer. In addition to short stories in various journals he has published the novels *Birds of Passage* (1983), which was the joint winner of the *Australian*/Vogel Literary Award of 1982, *Pomeroy* (1990), *Double-Wolf* (1991), which won the *Age* Book of the Year Award, and *After China* (1992), winner of the Vance Palmer Award for fiction in 1993. *Birds of Passage*, set in both the mid-nineteenth century and the present day, links the experiences of two characters – Shan, a Chinese who takes part in the Australian gold rushes, and Seamus, his mixed-race descendant – in such a way as to suggest that ancestry bridges the gulf interposed by time and changing cultures. *Double-Wolf*, set partly in contemporary Katoomba, moves between different times and places, including pre-revolution Russia and turn-of-the-century Austria and Germany, to question the origins of Freud's influence on twentieth-century culture and the truth of his interpretations of dreams. Central to the novel is the life of Sergei Wespe, the Wolf-man of one of Freud's most famous cases and an important contributor to his theory of infantile sexuality. Self-consciously post-modernist, the novel is preoccupied with contemporary notions of truth and fiction, reason and unreason and the instability of language. *Pomeroy*, ostensibly a spy thriller and alternating between first- and third-person narrators, uses the genre to speculate on the relationship between existence and language. A short but labyrinthine novel, *After China* ranges widely in time and place to explore the experience of mutability and the persistent human desire for story, correction and closure. At one level the story of the relationship between a Chinese architect and a woman writer dying of cancer, at another *After China* deals with the seductive illusions of story-telling itself. The novel's 'story' persistently attempts to escape linearity by emerging in the form of discontinuous anecdotes and recollections and moving between past and present and first- and third-person narration.

Casuals Club, an informal association of literary figures, artists and *bons vivants* founded in Sydney in 1906 by R.F. Irvine, lasted until 1922. Its members met fortnightly for conversation, convivial company and at times rowdy entertainment. Among its notable members were Christopher Brennan, Arthur H. Adams, John le Gay Brereton, Lionel Lindsay, Julian Ashton and Bertram Stevens. It was in the Casuals Club that Christopher Brennan gained the reputation for bohemianism that made him the leading figure of the Sydney café society of the day. Brennan came, in time, to dominate the Casuals Club, which afforded a group of disciples the chance to admire his oratory, scholarship, wit and outrageous behaviour.

CATALANO, Gary (1947–), born Brisbane and educated in Sydney, has been art critic for the *Age* since 1985 and has combined that career with writing several major books on Australian art and art criticism including *The Years of Hope: Australian Art and Criticism 1959–1968* (1981), *The Bandaged Image: A Study of Australian Artists' Books* (1983), and *An Intimate Australia: The Landscape and Recent Australian Art* (1985). His reputation as one of Australia's finest prose stylists gained from his critical writings has been confirmed in his purely literary works, including five books of poetry beginning with *Remembering the Rural Life* (1978), the title taken from a long personal poem dominating the volume. *Heaven of Rags: Forty Poems 1978–1981* (1982) sets most of its brief poems in normal verse lines but in section four uses the prose poem device of sentences and paragraphs, a technique which increasingly interested Catalano, *Fresh Linen* (1988) being composed entirely of prose poems, some of which were repeated from *Heaven of Rags*. In his *Heaven of Rags* Catalano would have 'all things aged, beaten and torn ... stained with sweat and dirt and basking in the glory that only comes of use'. There are, in *Heaven of Rags*, some informal and witty travel poems, 'Postcards for Peter', and a group of poems that marvel at the intricate mechanisms and procedures of photography. *Slow Tennis* (1984), *The Empire of Grass* (1991), which won the Grace Leven Prize for Poetry in 1992, and *Selected Poems 1973–1992* (1993) are his other poetry volumes. The 'Empire of Grass' is the Earth itself, the permanent Empire that remains greater than all the passing empires that man has endeavoured to place upon it. The presence of the artistic imagination is important in Catalano's poems, as is a nostalgia for the Australia depicted in Les Murray's 'weatherboard cathedral' and 'vernacular republic'. The occasionally sardonic and quizzical side of Catalano is seen in some grimy glimpses of the less pleasant side of cohabitation. Catalano often moves from depicting mundane (but useful) objects such as an old cup, or hat, or pair of boots to imaginative flights of fancy – from spoons to a flight of birds, from a row of decapitated toadstools to a vision of 'a group of refugees pausing at the edge of the abyss'. His imagery is often simple but striking, e.g. the writer regularly burning the contents of his waste-paper basket watches his 'old or abandoned thoughts perish once more'; or the vision of Hell is 'a landscape of torn and broken books' out of which each of us comes in turn to piece together an autobiography, a story that can only be known when, regretfully, complete and irreparable. The image that best encapsulates his writing is that contained in his own title, *Fresh Linen*. It is wholesome, elegant and attractive. Catalano has also published *The Woman Who Lives Here and Other Stories* (1983), a book of five short stories and sixteen 'sketches', the latter dealing with some of his boarding house experiences.

CATALDI, Lee (1942–), born Sydney of Italian and Australian parents, was educated at the Friends School, Hobart, and the University of Sydney. She later studied at Oxford University, lectured at Bristol University and became attracted to Marxism. From 1963 she worked as a teacher and linguist at Lajamanu School in the Northern Territory, producing books in the Warlpiri language and collecting and transcribing Warlpiri narratives. She has published two collections of poetry, *Introduction to a Marxist Lesbian Party* (1978), winner of the Anne Elder Poetry Award, and *The Women Who Live on the Ground* (1990). Other awards that Cataldi has won include the Northern Territory Red Earth Poetry Award and the Australian Human Rights Award. Cataldi writes a stripped-down, minimalist poetry, in which line variation is as important as vocabulary; wry, elliptical and often satirical when she writes of White culture and its inability to understand Aboriginal attitudes, she develops more sustained rhythms in those poems which deal directly with Black experience.

'Catalpa, The', also known as 'The Escape of the *Catalpa*' and 'The Ballad of the *Catalpa*', is an Australian folk-song which celebrates the daring escape of several Irish political prisoners from WA in 1876. A triumph for the Fenian movement, the escape was organised in America by John Boyle O'Reilly (q.v.) and others, who purchased the *Catalpa*, a New Bedford whaler used to transport the prisoners back to America. The escape, during which the *Catalpa* had to hoist the American flag to avoid being boarded off Fremantle, is the subject of Z.W. Pease's *The Catalpa Expedition* (1897), Sean Luing's *Fremantle Mission* (1965), Paul Buddee's *The Escape of the Fenians* (1971), and George Russo's radio drama 'Voices from the Tomb', published in *Race for the Catalpa* (1986), and is discussed in most studies of O'Reilly. There was sympathy for the prisoners among the citizens of Perth at the time of the escape and the song which celebrated the escape became popular enough to be banned by the embarrassed authorities.

CATCHPOLE, Margaret (1762–1819), born Suffolk, England, arrived in Australia in 1801 under a life sentence after having been twice sentenced to death, first for horse-stealing and then for escaping from Ipswich gaol. In the Colony she led an industrious and productive life; pardoned in 1814 she remained in Australia, keeping a small store at Richmond and becoming a well-known and much-appreciated citizen of that district. Her letters (now in the Mitchell Library) to her uncle and aunt in Suffolk and to her former mistress, Mrs John Cobbold, are an excellent account, in somewhat erratic spelling and syntax, of contemporary colonial life and events. The letters, distorted and rewritten, were used by Richard Cobbold as the basis of his *The History of Margaret Catchpole* (1845) and a number of them were published in Helen Heney's compilation *Dear Fanny* (1985). *The True Story of Margaret Catchpole* by G.B. Barton, was published in 1924 and a novel, *Margaret Catchpole,* by G.G. Carter in 1949.

CATHCART, Fanny (1833–80) arrived in Australia (where she reached her professional maturity as an actor) in 1855 with G.V. Brooke. During the next decade she was the leading actress in Australia, with Joseph Jefferson and Barry Sullivan as well as with Brooke. In 1855 she married Robert James Heir, a juvenile lead in Brooke's company, and after his death married George Darrell in England, with whom she toured extensively in Australasia and America in the 1870s. Her brother, James Faucitt Cathcart (1828–1902), was an actor who was discovered by Charles Kean and worked with him throughout the 1850s and 1860s. He accompanied Charles and Ellen Kean on their Australian tour of 1863–64; in Melbourne they played in opposition to Barry Sullivan, whose leading lady was Fanny. After Charles Kean retired in 1867, James played supporting roles to Sullivan for some years in London and America. He returned to Australia in 1879, where he performed in Shakespearean and other roles for George Musgrove, George Rignold and J.C. Williamson.

CATHELS, William, see **FURPHY, Joseph**

Catholic Magazine, published quarterly 1888–91 and monthly 1892–1920, had various titles. As a quarterly it was the *Catholic Magazine*; as a monthly both *Austral Light and Sword of St. Michael* (1892–99) and *Austral Light: A Catholic Magazine* (1900–20). In addition to Irish Catholic news and information it carried fiction, poetry, sketches and articles on literary topics.

CATO, Nancy (1917–   ), born Adelaide, was a cadet journalist on the Adelaide *News* 1936–41 and an art critic on the same newspaper 1957–58; since then she has been a freelance writer. Active in literary affairs, she edited the 1950 *Jindyworobak Anthology,* co-edited *Southern Festival* (1960), and has been involved in the SA branch of the FAW (1956–64) and ASA (1963–64). Her most important work is her trilogy of historical novels set against the background of the Murray River, *All the Rivers Run* (1958), *Time, Flow Softly* (1959) and *But Still the Stream* (1962). These were re-written and combined into a single best-seller, *All the Rivers Run* (q.v., 1978) and screened as a TV series in 1983. She has also published *Forefathers* (q.v., 1983), another long historical novel which traces the fortunes of three Australian families through seven generations. Her other prose works include *Green Grows the Vine* (1960), a novel about an irrigation settlement on the banks of the Murray but not linked with the trilogy; *The Sea Ants, and Other Stories* (1964); *North-West by South* (1965); *Brown Sugar* (1974); *Mister Maloga* (1976, republished 1993), which is the life story of Daniel Mathews, who with his wife Janet established a mission station for Aborigines near Echuca (later called Cummeragunja) last century; *The Lady Lost in Time* (1986), a fictional reconstruction of the life of Mary Beale, an important seventeenth-century English painter; *A Distant Land* (1988); *The Heart of the Continent* (1989), another family saga, this time of two young women who qualify as nurses in Adelaide in 1911 and pursue their careers in outback SA; and *Marigold* (1992), the story of a 17-year-old girl, a cadet reporter on the *Standard* in Adelaide in the 1930s, who pursues an early form of feminism by passing up the conventional life of marriage and a family for travel and adventure. The Murray River has a place also in her poems; 'Paddle Steamer', for example, emphasises the majesty of 'the endless river' in comparison with the humans who exploit it. Her two volumes of poetry, *The Darkened Window* (1950) and *The Dancing Bough* (1957), show her to be a lyrist with a capacity for serious, sometimes sombre, themes; *The Dancing Bough*, for example, is concerned with the twin forces that threaten existence – nuclear weapons that can destroy the world's order and loveliness, and the more persistent enemy, Time. In 1984 she was made AM and received an honorary D.Litt. from the University of Queensland, and in 1988 was granted the Alice Award by the Society of Women Writers.

CATTS, Dorothy (1896–1961), born Beecroft, NSW, was the second wife of union secretary, politician and businessman James Howard Catts (1877–1951). She edited and published (with her husband) the *Australian Home Budget*; published fiction, including *Dawn to Destiny* (1946) and *Cornerstone* (1947); and wrote biographies, *James Howard Catts MHR* (1953) and *King O'Malley* (1957).

CAVENAGH, George (1808–69), born India, arrived in Australia in 1825 and after various ventures joined the staff of the *Sydney Gazette* in 1833 and became its editor in 1836. By 1840 he was in Melbourne, where he founded the *Port Phillip Herald.* He also printed the first Melbourne almanac (1841–42).

Cave of Adullam was an eccentric, bohemian literary society founded by Marcus Clarke in Melbourne in 1869. It took its name from the Old Testament (1 Samuel 22: 1–2): 'David therefore departed thence, and escaped to the cave, Adullam . . . And every one that was in distress, and every one that was in debt, and every one that was discontented gathered themselves unto him.' The word 'Adullamites' had been applied in 1866 in England to a group of Liberal members of the House of Commons who were opposing certain aspects of franchise reform then being canvassed in the Franchise Bill. The club appears in fictional guise, 'the honourable and exclusive Society of Native Companions', in Clarke's *'Twixt Shadow and Shine* (1875).

CAWTHORNE, W.A. (William Anderson) (1825–97), born England, came to SA in 1841. He wrote 'The Islanders' in 1854; a significant account of Black–White relationships in SA, it was published first in the *Illustrated Adelaide Post*, which Cawthorne published 1867–74, and then in 1926 as *The Kangaroo Islanders: A Story of South Australia before Colonization 1823.* Cawthorne also wrote *The Legend of Kupirri, or the Red Kangaroo: An Aboriginal Tradition of the Port Lincoln Tribe* (1858), a work that concerned the customs, tradition and lore of that tribal group. His biographical sketch of SA's first mineralogist, Johann Menge (1788–1852), was published in 1859.

CECIL, Lord Robert (Arthur Talbot Gascoyne) (1830–1903), third Marquis of Salisbury, travelled throughout the colonies recording in his diaries many pertinent and lively comments about life in Australia. A portion of his diaries was edited by Ernest Scott as *Lord Robert Cecil's Gold Fields' Diary* (1935, 1945). He was prime minister of England at the time of Australian Federation.

'Cell, The', a play by Robert Wales set in a convent of an order that cares for delinquent girls, was produced in Adelaide and Sydney in 1966 and subsequently on ABC and BBC television. Part naturalistic drama and part thriller, 'The Cell' explores the tensions, frustrations, conflicting ambitions and internal politics of a claustrophobic community. 'The Grotto' (1962), another play by Wales, who came to Australia in 1946 and subsequently worked for the ABC, focuses on the feuds of a southern European family living in Sydney.

Celtic Twilight, see **DALEY, Victor**

Centennial Magazine, largely devoted to literary topics and carrying original fiction, poetry and literary criticism, ran monthly 1888–90. Its contributors included most of the well-known contemporary writers, e.g. Francis Adams, 'Rolf Boldrewood', G.B. Barton, George Gordon McCrae, Louisa Meredith and Catherine Helen Spence.

CHABRILLAN, Céleste de (1824–1909), born Paris, had a colourful career as a dancer ('La Mogador') and courtesan before marrying the impecunious Lionel, Comte de Chabrillan, who vainly tried his luck on the Victorian goldfields in 1852 and later returned to Australia in a semi-official consular post in Melbourne. Céleste's scarlet diary-memoirs, *Adieux au Monde*, were published just before the Chabrillans reached Australia. Of her other numerous writings, the main one with an Australian background is the novel *Les Voleurs d'Or* (1857), a violent story set in Victoria in the gold-rush days. It was translated by Lucy and Caroline Moorehead and published in 1970 as *The Gold Robbers*. An account of her life, *Daughter of Paris* by Charlotte Haldane, was published in 1961.

CHAMBERS, Charles Haddon (1860–1921), born and educated in Sydney, left Australia to live in England in 1882. He achieved substantial success in the light drama of high-society manners then popular in London, writing fourteen full-length plays of which only one, *Captain Swift* (q.v., 1902), first produced in 1888, has any Australian content. *Thumbnail Sketches of Australian Life* (1891) is his only other publication of Australian interest.

CHAMPION, Henry (1859–1928), born Poona, India, first came to Australia in 1890, an established socialist with a background of militancy and an amply demonstrated capacity for the organisation and motivation of the radical forces in society through his public speeches and writings. On a second visit, which extended from 1894 until his death, he set out to lead the socialist movement in Australia. He helped found the Fabian Society and formed the Social Democratic Federation of Victoria and the National Anti-Sweating League. He was prominent in the Victorian Socialist Party 1906–9 and was actively involved in co-operative socialist business and farming ventures. By 1909 prolonged illness and bitter factional disputes had forced him out of politics. His literary activities were mainly allied to his politics. He published *The Root of the Matter: Being a Series of Dialogues on Social Questions* (1895); conducted the *Champion* (1895–97), a weekly propagandist journal; and edited the *Socialist* (1908). With his wife he conducted the Book Lovers' Library for over thirty years and in 1899 founded the monthly literary journal *Book Lover*, which ran until 1921. He also founded the Australasian Authors' Agency in 1906 and published numerous works by Australian writers, e.g. Dorothea Mackellar, Martin Boyd and Marjorie Barnard.

CHANDLER, A. (Arthur) Bertram (1912–84), born Aldershot, England, spent most of his young manhood sailing the world in tramp and passenger steamers. He emigrated to Australia in 1956 and commanded vessels of Australia and NZ. During a spell in New York during the Second World War he was encouraged to indulge his liking for science fiction by John W. Campbell, who edited the SF journal *Astounding*. Initially Chandler wrote short stories but began writing novels in the 1950s, largely due to his wife's encouragement. The final thirty years of his life saw the publication in the USA and numerous other countries of nearly fifty science fiction novels, many of which are robust adventure stories involving Commander Grimes and the 'Rim Worlds' sector of space. Among his best-known works are *Rendezvous on a Lost World* (1961), *The Rim of Space* (1961), *Beyond the Galactic Rim* (1963), *Into the Alternate Universe* (1964), *Space Mercenaries* (1965), *The Empress of Outer Space* (1965), *The Road to the Rim* (1967), *The Rim Gods* (1968), *The Dark Dimensions* (1971), *The Inheritors* (1972), *The Far Traveller* (1977), *Star Courier* (1977), *Star Loot* (1981) and *The Wild Ones* (1984). On a different theme is *Kelly Country* (1983), a fantasy novel which reveals what might have happened if Ned Kelly (q.v.) had triumphed at Glenrowan. Acknowledged as the Grand Old Man of Australian Science Fiction, Chandler won four Ditmar annual Science Fiction Awards in Australia as well as awards in the USA and Japan. A much-lauded guest of honour at science fiction conventions all over the world, including the World Science Fiction Convention at Chicago in 1982, Chandler was a Fellow of the British Interplanetary Society. The A. Bertram Chandler Award was inaugurated in Australia in his honour and has been won by Van Ikin (1992), Mervyn Binns (1993) and George Turner.

CHANDLER, Alfred ('Spinifex') (1852–1941), born Geelong, was a journalist with the Hamilton *Spectator* and the *Register* in Adelaide, where he established *Quiz*, a satirical weekly, and published two books of verse, *A Bush Idyl* (1886) and *Songs of the Sunland* (1889). In 1894 he went to the goldfields of WA, where he played an important role in the rapidly developing newspaper scene; he edited the *Goldfield Courier*, the first newspaper in Coolgardie, the *Golden Age*, the *Coolgardie Miner* and the Perth *Sunday Times*, and was associated with the monthly magazine *Leeuwin*. With William Siebenhaar he published *Sentinel Sonnets* (1919), a book of war poetry; his other volume of verse is *'Beauty' and Other Poems: A Selective Anthology from the Author's Previous Books and Manuscripts* (1935).

Channel Country, a large area of south-western Queensland extending into the corners of SA and NSW, is drained by the Georgina and Diamantina Rivers and Cooper's Creek. Important in the pastoral expansion of Australia in the latter part of the nineteenth century, the Channel Country was the scene of the pastoral exploits of Sir Sidney Kidman and the Durack family. Burke and Wills (q.v.) perished at

Cooper's Creek in 1861. It is featured in Ion Idriess's *The Cattle King* (1936), Mary Durack's *Kings in Grass Castles* (1959), Frank Clune's *Dig* (1937) and Alan Moorehead's *Cooper's Creek* (1963).

Chant of Jimmie Blacksmith, The, Thomas Keneally's (q.v.) seventh novel, was published in 1972 and filmed in 1978. A fictional re-creation of the experiences of Jimmy Governor (q.v.), the novel chronicles the rejection by the part-Aboriginal Jimmie Blacksmith, of his Black heritage and his attempt to become part of European society by embracing its institutions, including marriage to the White girl Gilda. The indignities and injustices Jimmie suffers at the hands of a succession of White employers culminate in his mistreatment by the Newby family, who try to break up his marriage and use Gilda's refusal to leave Jimmie and the arrival at their property of Jimmie's uncle Tabidgi Jackie Smolders and brother Mort as an excuse to cut off rations. Assisted by Tabidgi, Jimmie murders the Newby women and their governess and the party flees the district. The second half of the novel records the pursuit of Jimmie and Mort, who leave the others, by police and vigilantes; during the pursuit further murders are committed, a schoolteacher, McCreadie, is taken hostage, Mort is shot and Jimmie taken prisoner. The context of Jimmie's execution in May 1901, just after Federation and during the Boer War, gives a historical dimension to the racism which Jimmie has tragically confronted.

Chantic Bird, The, a novel by David Ireland (q.v.), published in 1968, won the Adelaide *Advertiser*'s literary competition in 1966. The novel focuses on the narrator, an anonymous teenage boy and extreme anarchist who oscillates between murderous violence and protective care for his 'family', especially his 'brother' Stevo and the girl Bee who cares for them. Despite the savagery of his behaviour, his perspective as outsider illuminates the suffocating drabness of ordinary, adult, law-abiding, suburban life.

Chapel Perilous, The, a play by Dorothy Hewett (q.v.), was first performed in Perth in 1971, arousing a storm of protest and approval, and was published in 1972. The life of Sally Banner from age 15 to 61 is the play's subject. A self-absorbed heroine in constant search for a commitment that will bring 'a sense of immortality', she confronts the conventions and taboos of her society as boldly and hazardously as Sir Lancelot confronts the knights guarding the Chapel Perilous in Malory's Arthurian tales. Persistently judged and condemned by her contemporaries and a series of older authority figures, and frequently betrayed by her lovers, Sally finally makes a tormented journey back to 'that lonely place/ where I began'. Fast-moving and expressionistic, with diverse effects and moods, the play ranges from burlesque to lyrical to satirical, evoking Hewett's ambivalent attitude to her heroine.

CHARLWOOD, Don (1915–   ), born Hawthorn, Melbourne, worked on the land at Nareen in western Victoria during the 1930s Depression years and served in the RAAF during the Second World War. After the war he worked for thirty years in air-traffic control. His published works include *No Moon Tonight* (1956), memoirs of thirty bombing operations over Germany in 1942–43; *All the Green Year* (1965), a novel of adolescence set in the Victorian town of Frankston, where Charlwood spent much of his boyhood; *An Afternoon of Time* (1966), a book of ten short stories tracing the experiences of growing up, and based to some degree on Charlwood's time at Nareen; *Take-Off to Touchdown* (1967), the story of air-traffic control in Australia; *Wrecks and Reputations* (1977), an account of the loss of the sailing ships *Schomberg* and *Loch Ard* off the Victorian coast; *Settlers Under Sail* (1978), which depicts shipboard life on the early sailing vessels; *Flight and Time* (1979), another small volume of eleven short stories most of which are autobiographically based, seven being stories of wartime or civil flying; and *The Long Farewell* (1981), largely based on diaries which early nineteenth-century emigrants kept on their long sea voyage to Australia. The last-named won the 1982 NSW Premier's Ethnic Literary Award. Charlwood's hindsight account of his life and attitudes up to his participation in the Second World War is *Marching As To War* (1990). The second volume of his memoirs, *Journeys into Night* (1991), deals with his wartime experiences, culminating in his return to Australia after an operations tour over Germany. *Journeys into Night* won the 1992 Victorian FAW Herb Thomas Literary Award and the Christina Stead Award.

CHATWIN, Bruce (1940–89), born Sheffield, England, joined the art auction firm Sotheby's while still in his teens and earned rapid promotion but left to study anthropology. He eventually became a journalist, travelling to remote corners of the world for the London *Sunday Times*. His publications include the travel book *In Patagonia* (1977), which won the Hawthornden Prize and the E.M. Forster Award, and the novels *The Viceroy of Ouidah* (1980), *On the Black Hill* (1983) and *Utz* (1988); an individual study of Aboriginal nomadism, *The Songlines* (1987); and a collection of essays, *What Am I Doing Here* (1989). *The Songlines* was inspired by T.G. Strehlow's *Songs of Central Australia* but makes no claims to ethnography itself, concentrating rather on the implications for general human culture of the instinct of wandering.

CHAUNCY, Nan (1900–70), see *The Oxford Companion to Australian Children's Literature* (1993), pp. 91–2.

CHAUVEL, Charles (1897–1959), born Warwick, Queensland, formed his own film company in 1923, producing two silent films. In 1928 he and his wife Elsa (1898–1983), actor and scriptwriter, went briefly to America to study the making of sound films. His first sound film, *In the Wake of the Bounty* (1933, filmed at Pitcairn Island), began the career of Errol Flynn. Chauvel's later successes include *Heritage* (1935), a generalised view of Australian history; *Forty Thousand Horsemen* (1940), starring Chips Rafferty and based on the campaigns of the Australian Light Horse in the First World War; *Sons of Matthew* (1948), a pioneering saga set in south-eastern Queensland; *The Rats of Tobruk* (1944), about the famous siege of the Second World War, and *Jedda* (1955), the tragic story of a young Aboriginal girl. The Chauvels, a successful husband and wife team, also made the notable television series *Walkabout* for the BBC. Elsa Chauvel wrote the autobiographical *My Life with Charles Chauvel* (1973), and the Chauvels' daughter, Susanne Chauvel Carlsson, has written *Charles & Elsa Chauvel* (1989). *Featuring Australia* (1991), by Stuart Cunningham, is a study of Charles Chauvel's work as a film-maker.

CHAUVEL, Sir **Harry** (1865–1945), uncle of Charles Chauvel and father of writer Elyne Mitchell, was born Tabulam, NSW, and spent most of his adult life as a soldier, rising to the rank of general in 1929, the first Australian to attain that rank. He served in both the Boer War and the First World War; in the latter he was at Gallipoli and in 1917 commanded the Desert Mounted Corps. His biography, *Chauvel of the Light Horse* (1978), was written by A.J. Hill. Elyne Mitchell's *Chauvel Country* (1983) gives details of her father's childhood on the Clarence River at Tabulam.

Cheery Soul, A is the title of a short story and a play by Patrick White (q.v.). The short story, first published in 1962, is included in his collection *The Burnt Ones* (1964); the play, first produced in 1963, is included in his collection *Four Plays* (1965). Miss Docker, a tactless, destructive but invincible and even pathetic do-gooder, is the central figure of both.

Cherry Pickers, The, a play by Kevin Gilbert (q.v.), staged in Sydney 1971, deals with a group of Aboriginal fruit-pickers preparing to work on the year's cherry crop. They are delayed by the non-appearance of Johnollo, one of their number, who turns out to have been killed in an accident, and by a disease that has affected the cherry trees. The delay is the device which allows the play's themes to be presented; these include the close relationship that exists between the Aborigines and nature, the White man's lack of affinity with and his despoiling of nature, the Aborigines' concern for tribal traditions but their inability to incorporate those traditions into their lives, and the White man's inability to understand Aboriginal life. An extended, more polemical version was published in 1988 for the Bicentenary. It contains a prologue in mock-heroic verse about the Aboriginal character at the time of the founding of the Colony and details some of the destructive activities of the first settlers.

CHEVALIER, Nicholas (1828–1902) was a Russian-born artist who studied in Switzerland and worked in London before arriving in Australia in 1855. He became the first prominent cartoonist for the newly established *Melbourne Punch*, for which he drew for six years; he later worked for the *Illustrated Australian News* and continued as a landscape painter in oils and watercolour. Chevalier married in Australia and his home was a centre of cultural and intellectual life in Melbourne until his departure in 1869 for London. Melvin N. Day has written *Nicholas Chevalier, Artist* (1981).

CHI, Jimmy grew up in Broome, WA, in the 1960s and with the five-man band Kuckles composed a musical based on his experience of forced assimilation into White culture, *Bran Nue Dae*. Premièred at the Festival of Perth in February 1990, the musical became a hit and subsequently travelled extensively interstate. In September 1990 it was staged in Broome in the old Sun Pictures cinema where audiences were once segregated. *Bran Nue Dae* was published in 1991.

CHIDLEY, William James (?1860–1916) was an eccentric whose sexual and social theories brought him into trouble with the authorities, particularly in the period 1911–16. A proponent of vegetarianism, the open air, unrestrictive clothing, and sexual intercourse 'in the Spring . . . between true lovers only', Chidley ran foul of the Melbourne police when he began to sell copies of his work *The Answer* (1911), which was regularly revised and reprinted and is included in Bill Hornadge's *Chidley's Answer to the Sex Problem* (1971). He moved to Sydney where, characteristically clad only in a short white tunic, he was regularly fined for offensive behaviour and several times committed to mental asylums. His case was debated in the NSW parliament and a Chidley Defence Committee was formed in 1916; his supporters included J. le Gay Brereton, H.H. Champion, T.D. Mutch and Dowell O'Reilly. In 1899 Chidley sent the manuscript of his autobiography, 'The Confessions of William James Chidley', to Havelock Ellis, who included extracts in *Studies in the Psychology of Sex* (1897–1910); the autobiography was published in full in 1977 as *Confessions of William James Chidley*, ed. Sally McInerney. The Chidley case raised issues of personal freedom and the power of legal authorities to commit people to asylums, issues which are the focus of the plays by Alma de Groen, *Chidley* (performed in 1976 and published in *Theatre-Australia*, 1977), and George Hutchinson, *No Room for Dreamers* (produced 1979 and published 1981).

'Child in the Dark, and a Foreign Father, A', a story by Henry Lawson (q.v.), was written in 1902 and included in *Triangles of Life* (1913). The story records the return home to his farm on New Year's Eve of a poor carpenter, who discovers that his three children and the household chores have been neglected by his neurotic and slatternly wife; after cleaning up and attending to his family during the night, the workman returns to his trade next morning. The setting of the story (Pipeclay), the fact that the foreign father's name is Nils, and the tension between the parents, suggest that the story is autobiographical.

CHILDE, Vere Gordon (1892–1957), born Sydney, had a brilliant scholastic record at the universities of Sydney and Oxford but his strongly held socialist, pacifist and anti-conscription beliefs prevented his securing an academic appointment in the conservative universities of Australia after his return from England in 1917. In 1918 he taught briefly in Maryborough, Queensland, where P.R. Stephensen was a pupil, and in 1919–21 was private secretary to the NSW Labor politician John Storey; he returned to England as a research officer in the NSW agent-general's office, but was dismissed in 1922 after a change of government. The following year *How Labor Governs*, a pessimistic view of the difficulties faced by working-class politicians working within a parliamentary system, was published; thereafter Childe's attention was focused on the fields of archaeology, prehistory and anthropology. In a career that saw him librarian of the Royal Anthropological Institute (1925–27) and professor of archaeology at the universities of Edinburgh (1927–46) and London (1946–57), he published about twenty books and many papers; the best known were his much-revised and republished *The Dawn of European Civilization* (1925) and two works written primarily for the general public, *Man Makes Himself* (1936) and *What Happened in History* (1942). Two studies of Childe have been published, *Prehistorian*, by Sally Green (1981) and *Gordon Childe: Revolutions in Archeology* by Bruce G. Trigger (1980).

Children of the Bush, a collection of twenty-three stories and sketches by Henry Lawson (q.v.), was first published in London in 1902; most of the stories date from the late 1890s and early 1900s, although some were written as early as 1894. In 1907 the first part of *Children of the Bush*, including 'Send Round the Hat', other Bourke stories and several more in which Jack Mitchell is the dominant character, was published as *Send Round the Hat*; the second part, including several Eurunderee stories and three in which the central character is Peter McLaughlin, 'Christ of the Never Never', was published, also in 1907, as *The Romance of the Swag*.

Children of the Dark People, a popular children's novel with adult appeal by Frank Dalby Davison (q.v.), was first published in 1936, illustrated by Pixie O'Harris. It narrates the adventures of two Aboriginal children, Nimmitybelle and Jackadgery, separated from their tribe by the evil purposes of a witch-doctor, but saved by the spirits of the bush, especially Old Mr Bunyip, guardian spirit of the land. Although the story's fantastic elements make no pretensions to represent tribal lore, it is true to the Aboriginal way of life and reflects Davison's understanding of outback Australia.

Children's Book Council of Australia came into being in 1958 largely through the efforts of an earlier Children's Book Council, established in Sydney in 1947. The Council presents annual Children's Book of the Year (q.v.), Picture Book of the Year and Junior Book awards. Its quarterly publication is *Reading Time*; it published a booklet in 1980, *The Children's Book Council in Australia 1945–1980*. It mounts a promotional campaign for Australian children's books

each year, centred on its annual award winners. The Nan Chauncy Award is given every five years by the Council to a person who has made an outstanding contribution to Australian children's literature.

Children's Book of the Year Award was first presented by the Australian Book Society in 1946 but from 1950 has been administered by the Children's Book Council of Australia (q.v.). The winners have been: 1946, *Karrawingi the Emu* by Leslie Rees; 1948, *Shackleton's Argonauts* by Frank Hurley; 1949, *Whalers of the Midnight Sun* by Alan Villiers; 1951, *Verity of Sydney Town* by Ruth C. Williams; 1952, *The Australia Book* by Eve Pownall; 1953, shared by *Good Luck to the Rider* by Joan Phipson and *Aircraft of Today and Tomorrow* by J.H. and W.D. Martin; 1954, *Australian Legendary Tales* by K. Langloh Parker; 1955, *The First Walkabout* by Norman B. Tindale and H.A. Lindsay; 1956, shared by *The Crooked Snake* by Patricia Wrightson and *Wish and the Magic Nut* by Peggy Barnard; 1957, *The Boomerang Book of Legendary Tales*, edited by Enid Moodie Heddle; 1958, *Tiger in the Bush* by Nan Chauncy; 1959, shared by *Devils' Hill* by Chauncy and *Sea Menace* by John Gunn; 1960, *All the Proud Tribesmen* by Kylie Tennant; 1961, *Tangara* by Chauncy; 1962, shared by *The Racketty Street Gang* by L.H. Evers and *Rafferty Rides a Winner* by Joan Woodberry; 1963, *The Family Conspiracy* by Phipson; 1964, *The Green Laurel* by Eleanor Spence; 1965, *Pastures of the Blue Crane* by H.F. Brinsmead; 1966, *Ash Road* by Ivan Southall; 1967, *The Min-Min* by Mavis Thorpe Clark; 1968, *To the Wild Sky* by Southall; 1969, *When Jays Fly to Barbmo* by Margaret Balderson; 1970, *Uhu* by Annette Macarthur-Onslow; 1971, *Bread and Honey* by Southall; 1972, *Longtime Passing* by Brinsmead; 1973, *Family at the Lookout* by Noreen Shelley; 1974, *The Nargun and the Stars* by Wrightson; 1976, *Fly West* by Southall; 1977, *The October Child* by Eleanor Spence; 1978, *The Ice Is Coming* by Wrightson; 1979, *The Plum-Rain Scroll* by Ruth Manley; 1980, *Displaced Person* by Lee Harding; 1981, *Playing Beatie Bow* by Ruth Park; 1982, *The Valley Between* by Colin Thiele; 1983, *Master of the Grove* by Victor Kelleher; 1984, *Little Fear* by Wrightson; 1985, *The True Story of Lilli Stubeck* by James Aldridge; 1986, *The Green Wind* by Thurley Fowler; 1987, *All We Know*, by Simon French; 1988, *So Much to Tell You* by John Marsden; 1989, *Beyond the Labyrinth* by Gillian Rubinstein; 1990, *Came Back to Show You I Could Fly* by Robin Klein; 1991, *No Such Country* by Gary Crew; 1992, *The House Guest* by Eleanor Nilsson; 1993, *Looking for Alibrandi* by Melina Marchetta. There were no awards in 1947, 1950 and 1975.

Children's Literature, see **Anthologies**; **Children's Book Council of Australia**; **Children's Book of the Year Award**; **Muir, Marcie**

Chinese in Australian Literature. The idea of introducing Chinese coolie labour into Australia can be found as early as Edward Gibbon Wakefield's *A Letter from Sydney* (1829); in 1848, less than a decade after transportation of convicts to NSW ceased, the first consignment of Chinese workers (all males) arrived. The establishment in 1854 of a select committee on Asiatic labour in NSW reflected the rapidly growing unpopularity of the Chinese presence. With the development of the goldfields, however, Chinese numbers increased dramatically: 10 000 on the Victorian diggings in 1855, 25 000 by 1857; 1700 at the newly discovered Palmer River goldfields in Queensland in 1875, 17 000 (compared with 1400 Europeans) by 1877. The earliest agitation against the Chinese goldminers was at Bendigo in July 1854, a disturbance that resulted in Victorian legislation imposing a tax of £10 on every Chinese immigrant. Shipping owners, unwilling to lose their profitable cargo, evaded the Victorian tax by landing the Chinese at Twofold Bay in southern NSW or at Guichen Bay in SA. From those points the hapless immigrants trekked to the diggings; an account of them in a procession 2 miles long, each one with a pole and two baskets 'winding across the plain like a long black mark', is given in J. Chandler's *Forty Years in the Wilderness* (1893).

Anti-Chinese riots occurred on the Buckland River goldfield in eastern Victoria, 4 July 1857. The anonymous song 'Dick the Digger: A Tale of the Buckland', published in J. Small's *The Colonial Songster* (?1884), reflects the White digger's hostility:

> For pick, pick it made him sick
> To think that he was getting daily, a
> Heap of these accursed Chinese
> And he cried 'They'll ruin Australia'.

A similar song is Charles Thatcher's 'The Chinamen'. The Lambing Flat riots of June 1861, described in George E. Boxall's *The History of the Australian Bushrangers* (1899) and Frank Clune's *Wild Colonial Boys* (1948), are the subject of Mary Gilmore's poem 'Fourteen Men':

> Fourteen men
> Chinamen they were
> Hanging on the trees
> In their pig-tailed hair.

After Lambing Flat, with its alleged 'lynchings' denied by official reports, the NSW government in 1861 enacted the Chinese Immigration Bill, inspiring the jubilant response of the White diggers:

> Rule Britannia! Britannia rules the waves
> No more Chinamen will enter New South Wales

In September 1873 the Clunes (Victoria) riots occurred when cheap Chinese labour was brought in to break strikes. This practice, later used in the shearing troubles of the 1890s as A.B. Paterson's poem 'A Bushman's Song' suggests, led to the use of the contemptuous words 'leprosy' and 'scab' to indicate Chinese and later all strike-breakers; both words were linked to the White man's irrational fear that the Chinese harboured exotic infectious diseases. A light-hearted evocation of the Chinese on the Victorian goldfields is Edward Dyson's story 'A Golden Shanty' (q.v.), in which Michael Doyle and his 'strongly anti-Chinese' mongrel dog finally outwit the Chinese fossickers, who are attempting to demolish his Shamrock Hotel for the rich gold bricks with which it was built. Henry

Lawson, who frequently included Chinese in his stories, was less inclined to be critical of them, as his opening remarks in the story 'Ah Soon', published in *Lone Hand,* 1911, indicate: 'I never knew or heard of a Chinaman who neglected to pay his debts, who did a dishonest action, or who forgot a kindness to him or his, or was not charitable when he had the opportunity.'

When it was possible to obtain gold only by the costly quartz-crushing process, those Chinese miners who did not return to their own country were absorbed peacefully into the life of the Australian community, mainly as market gardeners, fruit hawkers, laundry operators, storekeepers and bush cooks. Cheon in Mrs Aeneas Gunn's *We of the Never-Never* (1908), and James Brunton Stephens's 'My Chinee Cook' and 'My Other Chinee Cook', are examples of the patronising and sometimes racist perceptions of the Chinese in later literature.

Anti-Chinese legislation was periodically enforced and periodically allowed to lapse in all Colonies, but in 1880–81 an intercolonial conference resulted in uniform legislation in all the eastern Colonies. An immigration Act of 1901, incorporating the so-called White Australia Policy, almost entirely debarred Asiatics from entering Australia. Despite this apparent safeguard, White fear of the 'yellow peril' continued, finding literary expression in such plays as Randolph Bedford's 'White Australia: Or, the Empty North' (1909), which pointed to the danger of foreign occupation; and F.R.C. Hopkins's *Reaping the Whirlwind* (1909), 'an Australian patriotic drama for Australian people'. Similar works, both factual and fictional, that incorporate the presence of the Chinese include James Murdoch's *Felix Holt Secundus* (1892), William Craig's *My Adventures on the Australian Goldfields* (1903), Joyce Vincent's *The Celestial Hand* (1903), R.A. Kent's *A Chinese Vengeance* (1909), Hilda Bridges's *Our Neighbours* (1922) and H. Haverstock Hill's *Golden Harvest* (1919). The Chinese presence is also obvious in David Martin's fiction, *The Hero of Too* (1960) and *The Chinese Boy* (1973), and in Helen Heney's *The Chinese Camellia* (1953). Brian Castro's novel *Birds of Passage* (1983) records some of the experiences of a Chinese gold-miner in Australia in the gold-rush days. Alex Miller's *The Ancestor Game* (1992) links the making of a fortune on the Australian goldfields to the establishment of a family dynasty, located both in Australia and China. After the restrictions imposed in the 1901 Act, Chinese numbers declined markedly, from 50 000 in 1888 to less than 10 000 in 1934. Important sociological and historical works on the Chinese in Australia include Persia Campbell's *Chinese Coolie Emigration to Countries within the British Empire* (1923), Arthur Huck's *The Chinese in Australia* (1967), C.Y. Choi's *Chinese Migration and Settlement in Australia* (1975), Jean Gittins's *The Diggers from China* (1981), Kathryn Cronin's *Colonial Casualties: Chinese in Early Victoria* (1982), David Horsfall's *March to Big Gold Mountain* (1985), Morag Loh's *Dinki-di, the Contributions of Chinese Immigrants and Australians of Chinese Descent to Australia's Defence Forces and War Efforts 1899–1988* (1989), Eric Rolls's *Sojourners* (1992) and Alison

Broinowski's *The Yellow Lady* (1992). Ian McLaren's *The Chinese in Victoria* (1985) is an anthology of official reports and documents from colonial Victoria. Lionel Welsh's small work *Vermilion and Gold* (1984) is one of the few works to praise the patience and industry of the Chinese. It deals with the lives and achievements of the Chinese in Ballarat in the nineteenth century.

CHISHOLM, A.R. (Alan Rowland) (1888–1981), born Bathurst, NSW, had a distinguished academic career in Australia, France and Germany, was head of the school of French at the University of Melbourne 1921–56 and gained an international reputation as a critic of French poetry. He edited the brief-lived *Modern Language Review of New South Wales*, 1920–21. A strong supporter of Australian literature, Chisholm was chiefly interested in the poetry of Christopher Brennan. His lectures on Brennan were published as *Christopher Brennan: The Man and His Poetry* (1946); he also published, with J.J. Quinn, the first comprehensive editions of Brennan's verse and prose (1960, 1962); edited the *Selected Poems of Christopher Brennan* (1966); and wrote *A Study of Christopher Brennan's 'The Forest of Night'* (1970). He edited the poems of John Shaw Neilson in 1965 and 1973, and wrote two autobiographical books, *Men Were My Milestones* (1958) and *The Familiar Presence* (1966), which helped to document Australian cultural history. Long associated with *Meanjin* as a member of its editorial committee, Chisholm was honoured in May 1959 in a special number of *AUMLA*.

CHISHOLM, A.H. (Alexander Hugh) (1890–1977), born Maryborough, Victoria, worked on the staff of the Maryborough *Advertiser* before transferring to the Brisbane *Daily Mail* in 1915. His subsequent experience as a journalist included editorship of the Melbourne *Argus*, the *Australasian* and the Sydney *Sunday Pictorial*. A keen naturalist – he gave his recreation as 'idling in green places' – he edited the *Victorian Naturalist* (1939–48) and wrote numerous naturalist works including *Bird Wonders of Australia* (1934), *Australian Wild Life* (1966) and *The Joy of the Earth* (1969). He was editor of *Who's Who in Australia* (1947); editor-in-chief of the *Australian Encyclopaedia* (1958); and wrote *The Making of a Sentimental Bloke: A Sketch of the Remarkable Career of C.J. Dennis* (1946). He edited *Selected Verse of C.J. Dennis* (1950); E.J. Banfield's *The Confessions of a Beachcomber* and *Last Leaves from Dunk Island* (first published 1908, 1925); and John White's *Journal of a Voyage to New South Wales* (first published 1790). In 1958 he was made OBE and in 1940 received the Australian Natural History Medallion.

CHISHOLM, Caroline (1808–77), born near Northampton, England, arrived in Australia in 1838 with her husband and family, settling at Windsor. Deeply concerned at the plight of immigrants who could find no employment because of the rural depression, she persuaded Governor Gipps to support her establishment of a Female Immigrants' Home and her scheme to disperse the immigrants into employment in the interior of the Colony. The report of her first year's activities was published as *Female Immigration Considered, in a Brief Account of the Sydney Immigrants' Home* (1842). She travelled to England in 1846 to promote her colonisation scheme, which she furthered by publishing *Emigration and Transportation Relatively Considered* (1847). *The ABC of Colonization* (1850) explains her Family Colonization Loan Society, formed in 1849, and criticises existing colonisation schemes. By the time Chisholm returned to Australia in 1854 the Society had sent out more than 3000 immigrants. Her humanitarian interests continued in spite of ill health and needy circumstances. She returned to England in 1866; her grave at Northampton bears the inscription 'The emigrant's friend!' Robert Lowe wrote a poem, 'To Mrs. Chisholm', and Henry Kendall wrote 'Caroline Chisholm'; George Landen Dann published a play, *Caroline Chisholm*, in 1943 and she is the subject of Lola Irish's novel *Streets of Dust* (1993). Biographical works on her include Eneäs Mackenzie's *Memoirs of Mrs Caroline Chisholm* (1852), Margaret Kiddle's *Caroline Chisholm* (1950), Mary Hoban's *Fifty-One Pieces of Wedding Cake* (1973) and Joanna Bogle's *Caroline Chisholm: The Emigrant's Friend* (1993). It is possible that she was partly the model for Charles Dickens's Mrs Jellaby of *Bleak House*, although Dickens also supported and made use of her views on emigration.

CHOATE, Alec (1915–   ), born High Barnet, England, came to Australia at the age of 7. He served in the AIF 1940–45 in the Middle East and the Pacific, then spent thirty years (1945–75) as a surveyor in the Public Service. Choate, well disposed towards the Jindyworobak affinity with the land, had his early poetry published in that movement's anthologies immediately after the war. Co-editor of the WA anthology *Summerland* (1979), Choate has also written three books of verse, *Gifts upon the Water* (1978), *A Marking of Fire* (1986) and *Schoolgirls at Borobudur* (1990). He was awarded the Tom Collins Poetry Prize in 1976 and the Patricia Hackett Prize in 1989 for the outstanding poetry contribution to *Westerly* in the 1988 Bicentennial issue of that magazine. His third volume, written in retirement, is characteristic of all his poetry – good-natured, pleasantly sentimental and appreciative of the good things that life, nature, friendship, art and literature can offer. From *Schoolgirls at Borobudur*, the poem 'The Flute Girl' recalls his experiences of war in Syria, Libya, Egypt and Borneo, while the title poem records the poet's interaction with the two extremes – a group of schoolgirls and the classical wonder of Borobudur.

CHOMLEY, C.H. (Charles Henry) (1868–1942), born Sale, Victoria, uncle of Martin Boyd, graduated in law and was admitted to the Bar in 1891 but settled on the land in 1893 with a group of friends and relatives in the King River valley in north-east Victoria. Ill health took him in 1900 back to Melbourne, where he edited *Arena*, an illustrated weekly, until its demise in 1904. Chomley published fiction including *Tales of Old Times: Early Australian Incident and Adventure*

(1903), *The Flight of the Black Swan* (1903), *Mark Meredith: A Tale of Socialism* (1905) and, with R.L. Outhwaite, *The Wisdom of Esau* (1910). He also wrote *The True Story of the Kelly Gang of Bushrangers* (1900) and a number of works on economics, trade and law. From 1908 until his death, Chomley edited the *British Australasian* (q.v.) in England.

'Chosen Vessel, The', Barbara Baynton's (q.v.) first story, was published in the *Bulletin* in 1896 as 'The Tramp'; it was revised and included in *Bush Studies* (1902) and *Cobbers* (1917) under the title 'The Chosen Vessel'. Reminiscent of Henry Lawson's 'The Drover's Wife', it tells of the terror of a young wife left with her baby in a bush hut as she awaits attack by a swagman who has called there during the day. The sound of hoofbeats causes her to flee the house for assistance, but the horseman is a young Catholic who is on his way to record an election vote against the wishes of his mother and the local priest. He interprets the 'white-robed figure' crying 'For Christ's sake!' as a vision from God and gallops madly away, leaving the woman to be raped and murdered by the swagman.

CHRISTESEN, C.B. (Clement Byrne) (1911–), born Townsville, was educated at the University of Queensland, then became a publicity officer for the Queensland government and later a journalist on the Brisbane *Courier* and the *Telegraph*. He worked briefly for the London *Times* and the *New York Times* before returning to Brisbane, where in 1940 he founded the literary magazine *Meanjin* (q.v.), moving with it to Melbourne early in 1945. Christesen's first publication was a tourist guide, *Queensland Journey* (1937). Subsequently he published four volumes of verse, *North Coast* (1943), *South Coast* (1944), *Dirge and Lyrics* (1945) and *Having Loved* (1979); edited the anthologies *Australian Heritage* (1949), *Coast to Coast 1953–54* (1955) and *On Native Grounds* (1967), a selection from *Meanjin*'s first twenty-five years; and edited *The Gallery on Eastern Hill* (1970). A selection of his own short fiction and poetry, *The Hand of Memory,* was published in 1970. In 1990 he published another book of stories, *The Troubled Eyes of Women,* which includes some earlier stories from *The Hand of Memory*. Although his lyrical verse and spare short stories have a modest reputation, Christesen is best known for his tireless promotion and encouragement of Australian writing, particularly as editor for thirty-four years of *Meanjin,* which he transformed from the little poetry magazine of 1940 into a major Australian cultural journal significant in the development of Australian literary criticism. Active also as broadcaster, writer of radio features and University Extension and CLF lecturer, he has been honoured by the gold medal of the Australian Literature Society (1965), the Britannica-Australia Award (1970), the first gold medal of the Foundation for Australian Literary Studies (1980), and an honorary D.Litt. from Monash University (1975). He was made OBE in 1962 and is an Emeritus Fellow of the Literature Board of the Australia Council. His work as editor is discussed in Lynne Strahan's *Just City*

and the Mirrors (1984) and in Jenny Lee et al. (eds), *The Temperament of Generations* (1990).

Christopher Brennan Award, formerly known as the Robert Frost Prize, is given by FAW to a poet whose sustained work achieves distinction. Recipients of the award have included R.D. FitzGerald, Judith Wright, A.D. Hope, Douglas Stewart, Gwen Harwood, Rosemary Dobson, John Blight, Vincent Buckley, Bruce Beaver, Bruce Dawe, Les Murray, William Hart-Smith, Peter Porter, Harold Stewart, Roland Robinson, Chris Wallace-Crabbe, Elizabeth Riddell. It was also awarded posthumously to Francis Webb, James McAuley and David Campbell.

Christopher Columbus (1948) by William Hart-Smith (q.v.) is part of the voyager (q.v.) theme in Australian poetry. The sequence of forty-two poems begins in antiquity with its comfortable certainty that 'The world is flat/ And that's that' but moves rapidly to the late medieval world and 'the Brothers Columbus, Mapmakers of Lisbon'. The series encompasses Columbus's first voyage to the New World, his triumphant return to Spain, his second voyage and the discovery of the tragedy of the colony he left at La Navidad, the initial enchantment of the New World spoiled by the European taints of disease and greed, the founding of the city of Isabella, his final voyages and the decay of his great dream.

Chronicle, the weekly companion of the *Advertiser*, was published in Adelaide 1858–1975. Originally titled the *South Australian Weekly Chronicle*, it became the *South Australian Chronicle* (sometimes the *South Australian Chronicle and Weekly Mail*) in 1868 and the *Chronicle* in 1895; in 1931 it incorporated the *Observer*. A literary supplement, titled the *Wallet*, was published in the *Chronicle* in 1864–65.

CHURCH, Hubert (1857–1932), born Hobart, Tasmania, spent lengthy periods in both England and NZ before settling in 1923 in Melbourne, where he was well known in literary circles. A poet of elegance and restraint, Church published *The West Wind* (1902), a *Bulletin* booklet republished in the anthology *A Southern Garland* (1904); *Poems* (1904); *Egmont* (1908); and *Poems* (1912), a selection from the earlier volumes with ten additional poems. He also wrote a novel, *Tonks: A New Zealand Yarn* (1916).

CILENTO Family, well known for diverse achievements, includes Sir Raphael West Cilento (1893–1985), Lady Phyllis Dorothy Cilento (1894–1987) and their daughter, actor and writer Diane Cilento (1934–). Lady Cilento published numerous books on nutrition, child care and birth control and was medical columnist of the Brisbane *Courier-Mail*, her column 'Medical Mother' running for about half a century. Her autobiography, *Lady Cilento M.B. B.S.: My Life,* was published in 1987 when she was 92. Diane Cilento has followed a successful career on stage and in films since 1953, has been a television film producer and has published two novels, *The Manipulator* (1968) and *Hybrid* (1970).

Cinema and Australian Literature. The first film made in Australia was of the Melbourne Cup of 1896, and just over a decade later a feature-film industry had evolved before equivalent developments in England and the USA. Claims have been advanced for considering *Soldiers of the Cross* (1900) as the first full-length film made in the world and for *The Story of the Kelly Gang* (1906), one of the six Ned Kelly films, as the first feature film. The most productive and the most nationalistic period for the Australian cinema was 1906–14, when films about convicts and bushrangers were particularly popular. In 1911, for example, films which focused on the exploits of Captains Midnight and Starlight, Frank Gardiner and Dan Morgan were screened and Ben Hall was the subject of no fewer than three treatments. Since those early days the Australian cinema has had to fight overseas competition and distribution domination, particularly from Hollywood, but has intermittently flourished. There have been three significant periods: the years just after the First World War, when Raymond Longford (q.v.), at the height of his powers, made naturalistic adaptations of *The Sentimental Bloke* and *On Our Selection*, which are regarded as classics of film-making and consolidated myths about Australian larrikins and pioneers embodied in those works; the 1930s, when Ken Hall's (q.v.) Cinesound Company had a number of commercial successes including a far different *On Our Selection* (1932) which, with three Rudd family spin-offs, helped to popularise Dad and Dave as rural hayseeds; and the years from 1970 when, after three decades in the doldrums, the Australian cinema has undergone a renaissance and films like *Picnic at Hanging Rock* (1975), *Breaker Morant* (1980), *Gallipoli* (1981), *Strictly Ballroom* (1991) and *The Piano* (1993) have won critical acclaim both in Australia and overseas.

Almost from its inception the Australian cinema established firm links with Australian writing and writers. *On Our Selection* is not the only Australian literary work to have been filmed more than once: so also were *Robbery Under Arms* (1907, 1920, 1957; Alfred Dampier's stage adaptation of the novel was also filmed in 1911 as *Captain Starlight*); *For the Term of His Natural Life* (1908, 1927; another treatment in 1911 was titled *The Life of Rufus Dawes* and starred Longford as the convict Gabbett); *The Mystery of a Hansom Cab* (1911, 1924); *The Pioneers* (1916, 1926); *The Sentimental Bloke* (1916, 1932); and adaptations of the stories of Henry Lawson (1921, 1924, 1957). Among other well-known literary works to have been filmed are *The Double Event* (1911), *The Sick Stockrider* (1913), *Moondyne* (1913), *The Sunny South* (1913), *Struck Oil* (1919), *How McDougall Topped the Score* (1924), *Around the Boree Log* (1925), *Seven Little Australians* (1929), *Red Sky at Morning* (1944), *Summer of the Seventeenth Doll* (1959), *Age of Consent* (1969), *Wake in Fright* (1971), *Picnic at Hanging Rock* (1975), *The Great McCarthy* (1975), *The Getting of Wisdom* (1977), *The Mango Tree* (1977), *Dot and the Kangaroo* (1977), *The Chant of Jimmie Blacksmith* (1978), *Monkey Grip* (1981), *We of the Never-Never* (1982), *The Year of Living Dangerously* (1982), *Careful, He Might Hear You* (1983), *Bliss* (1985), *Kangaroo* (1985), *For Love Alone* (1985), *The Fringe Dwellers* (1986) and *The Everlasting Secret Family* (1987). Popular novelists to have attracted the attention of film-makers include Ambrose Pratt, Marie Bjelke-Petersen, Beatrice Grimshaw, Dorothy Cottrell, Miles Franklin, Ronald McKie, 'Gurney Slade', F.J. Thwaites, Ion Idriess, Jon Cleary, D'Arcy Niland, Frank Hardy, Thomas Keneally, John O'Grady, Helen Garner and Peter Carey. In general it is only recently that Australian writers established outside the cinema have become involved in that medium, although Hugh McCrae played Adam Lindsay Gordon in *The Life's Romance of Adam Lindsay Gordon* (1916), Arthur Wright had several of his racing and mining novels filmed and wrote the scripts for several others, and E.V. Timms and Douglas Stewart wrote briefly for films. In the last twenty years Frank Moorhouse (*Between Wars*, 1974, *The Everlasting Secret Family*, 1987), Hal Porter (*Libido*, 1973), Thomas Keneally (*Libido*, 1973, *The Chant of Jimmie Blacksmith*, 1978), Jack Hibberd (*Dimboola*, 1978), John Romeril (*The Naked Bunyip*, 1970; *Bonjour Balwyn*, 1971; and *The Great McCarthy*, 1975), Peter Carey (*Bliss*, 1985), and Helen Garner (*The Last Days of Chez Nous*, 1992) are examples of the many Australian writers who have written film scripts, but David Williamson's involvement has been perhaps the most extensive. Six of his plays, *Stork* (1971), *The Removalists* (1975), *Don's Party* (1976), *The Club* (1980), *Travelling North* (1986) and *Emerald City* (1988), have been filmed and he has written or collaborated on numerous screenplays for other Australian films, including *Peterson* (1974), *Eliza Fraser* (1976), *Gallipoli* (1981) and *The Year of Living Dangerously* (1982). Williamson, Romeril and Keneally have played 'bit' parts in films, continuing the tradition of Marion Marcus Clarke who played Lady Devine in the 1927 version of her father's *For the Term of His Natural Life*, having earlier prevented *His Convict Bride* (1919) being titled *For the Term of Her Natural Life*. Henry Lawson also made a brief appearance as a bushman yarning around a camp-fire at the start of the film of *While the Billy Boils* in 1921. Among studies of the Australian cinema, John Baxter's *The Australian Cinema* (1970), Hal Porter's *Stars of Australian Stage and Screen* (1965), Eric Reade's *The Australian Screen* (1976) and *History and Heartburn: The Saga of Australian Film 1896–1978* (1979), Andrew Pike and Ross Cooper's *Australian Film 1900–1977* (1980), John Tulloch's *Legends of the Australian Screen* (1980), *The New Australian Cinema*, ed. Scott Murray (1980) all discuss the relationship between Australian literary works and Australian films, a subject which is also the focus of Brian McFarlane's *Words and Images* (1983), Bruce Molloy's *Before the Interval: Australian Mythology and Feature Films 1930–1960* (1990), which recalls many of the important book-to-film transferences and *Australian Film Index: A Guide to Australian Films Since 1900* (1992), and David Myers's *Bleeding Battlers from Ironbark* (1987, 2nd edn 1992). More recent general works on the Australian film scene include William K. Halliwell's *The Filmgoers' Guide to Australian Films*

(1985), Susan Dermody and Elizabeth Jacka's two-volume *The Screening of Australia* (1987, 1988) and *The Imaginary Industry* (1988), Sandra Hall's *Critical Business: The New Australian Cinema in Review* (1985), Graeme Turner's *National Fictions* (1986), Brian McFarlane's *Australian Cinema 1970–1985* (1987), and *New Australian Cinema* (1992, 2nd edn 1993), and *The Australian Screen* (1989), edited by Albert Moran and Tom O'Regan. *Don't Shoot Darling! Women's Independent Film-making in Australia* (1987), edited by Annette Blonski, Barbara Creed and Freda Freiberg, exposes the historical limitations which women film-makers have experienced. *Cinema Papers*, the most important of current Australian film journals, began its series in 1974. Other journals associated with the film industry have been the *Australian Journal of Screen Theory* and its virtual successor, *Continuum* (q.v.).

CLACY, Ellen (1830–?), the author of a collection of short stories and sketches, titled *Lights and Shadows of Australian Life* (1854), accompanied her brother to the Victorian goldfields in 1852–53 and wrote one of the liveliest accounts of daily life there, *A Lady's Visit to the Gold Diggings of Australia in 1852–53, written on the spot by Mrs Charles Clacy* (1853). Ellen Clacy had a gift for vivid, detailed description and dramatic narrative which differentiates her story from that of more prosaic visitors; highpoints of her account include a description of a sudden storm in which she suffered a sprained ankle, the story of Harriette Walters, a young woman who found herself alone and almost penniless in Melbourne and took refuge from the city's perils by disguising herself as a man, their party's adoption of an orphan girl after the death of her grandfather, and an encounter with bushrangers who were defeated in their intentions by the fact that the party's travelling money was hidden in the lining of Ellen's dress. These aspects as well as the book's information about gold-mining and its prospects made it an instantaneous success in England; it was republished in 1963, edited by Patricia Thompson.

Clanalder Sennachie (1963–75), originated by John J. Alderson, was the journal (monthly, then quarterly) of the Clanalder Archives. The Clanalder Archives house material of local history, anthropology and folklore interest from an area of Victoria bounded on the south by Ballarat, on the north by Inglewood, on the east by Bendigo and on the west by St Arnaud. The archives date back into the nineteenth century but serious collection began from 1942. 'Sennachie' is an old Scottish word meaning 'historian'.

CLANCHY, John (1943–), born Melbourne, was educated at the University of Melbourne and taught in Victorian schools before moving to Canberra to head the Communication and Study Skills Centre at the ANU. He has written several non-fiction books as well as poetry, short stories and plays and has published a collection of stories, *Lie of the Land* (1985); a collection of three novellas, *Homecoming* (1989); and a novel, *Breaking Glass* (1992). His short stories have won several awards including the Commonwealth Literature & Language Studies (Europe) Prize, and the National and State of Victoria Short Story Awards. Wide-ranging in the choice of narrators, characters and settings, Clanchy's stories are subtle, sharply observed and well-orchestrated studies of such familiar experiences as travelling in a Third World country, coming to terms with a failed relationship, confronting the disappointment of a family future on the land, and remembering the rigours and absurdities of a rigid Irish Catholic education. The three novellas of *Homecoming* are united in their concentration on themes of love, self-deception, hypocrisy and infidelity, although otherwise dissimilar. *Breaking Glass* is the story of a lapsed Catholic and failed husband, James Dunne, who, in an attempt to understand his life, writes a novel which angers his twin sister, Bernadette; correctly perceiving the novel as autobiographical, Bernadette fails to penetrate the underlying insecurity of its aggressive masculinism.

CLANCY, Laurie (1942–), born Melbourne, was educated by the Christian Brothers and then at Melbourne University and has since taught in the English departments at Melbourne and La Trobe universities. In 1975 he published his first novel, *A Collapsible Man*, which traces the life of the narrator, Paul O'Donohue, through his Catholic education to university and on to a bohemian existence which culminates in a period in a sanatorium; the novel shared the National Book Council Award for fiction in 1975. Clancy has also published two collections of short stories, *The Wife Specialist* (1979) and *City to City* (1989); critical studies of Xavier Herbert (1981) and Vladimir Nabokov (1984); *A Reader's Guide to Australian Fiction* (1992), which discusses selected authors; and a further novel, *Perfect Love* (1983). Clancy's stories, largely autobiographical in content and ironic in tone, deal partly with childhood, with the milieu and mores of Carlton academics, and with life in the USA from a visiting Australian's point of view. *Perfect Love* is a family chronicle which focuses mainly on Nora Lloyd, a good Catholic working-class girl whose life from 1901 to 1951 is representative of her time, place and social position.

'Clancy of the Overflow', a poem by A.B. Paterson (q.v.), was first published in the Christmas 1889 number of the *Bulletin* under the pseudonym 'The Banjo'. A great favourite with Australians, the poem established Clancy as one of Australia's best-known folk-heroes. The poem records the writer's distaste for city life as well as hymning the great outdoors; it pictures Clancy's carefree existence amid 'the vision splendid of the sunlit plains extended' and 'the everlasting stars'. A phrase from the poem, 'a thumbnail dipped in tar', has come to be used in modern times as a derogatory label for both the bush ballad genre and the unsophisticated, bucolic view of Australia which produced and encouraged it.

Clara Morison (1854), a novel written by Catherine Helen Spence (q.v.) and subtitled A *Tale of South Australia during the Gold Fever*, was one of the first novels about the Australian colonies written by a woman. Spence sent the manuscript to England with a letter to the publishers indicating the authenticity of its characters, events and backgrounds – 'the domestic life represented in my tale is the sort of life I have led – the people are such as I have come in contact with – the letters from the diggings are like those I have seen – so that it may be considered a faithful transcript of life in the Colony.'

The heroine, Clara Morison, and her sister Susan, orphaned by the death of their father, come under the care of their uncle in Edinburgh. Nineteen-year-old Clara is sent to the Colony of SA, supposedly to be taken into the family of a merchant, Mr Campbell, before gaining a position as governess. She arrives in Adelaide to find Mr Campbell's wife has died and the merchant neither able nor especially anxious to do much about her welfare. After unsuccessful attempts to become a governess she goes into service, surviving such a shock to her fragile, well-bred system by her determination and courage. Her situation is ameliorated somewhat when she is taken into the home of a relative, where she falls in love with Charles Reginald, an up-country squatter whom she meets on her arrival in Adelaide. Reginald is engaged to a girl in England who has no intention of coming to live in the colonies. After many vicissitudes the engagement is broken and Charles and Clara marry.

Highly thought of by the early critic Frederick Sinnett, *Clara Morison* is an important Australian literary landmark rather than a notable work of literature. It is a domestic novel with considerable soul-searching by its heroine and many wrong turnings and culs-de-sac which a word of explanation could have set right. Particular Australian interest is provided by the novel's portrayal of the conditions on the diggings and the effects of gold fever in the Colony.

CLARE, Monica (1924–73), born Dareel, Queensland, was the daughter of Ron McGowan, an Aboriginal shearer, and an English mother. After the birth of her younger brother the family lived in various towns on the upper Darling but when the children were 7 and 5 their mother died in childbirth. Their father attempted to keep his family together but in 1931 the Child Welfare Department placed them in institutions in Sydney, where they endured loneliness and an education in racial inferiority. In 1932 they were accepted as foster children by farmers on the Hawkesbury and began a much happier period, although they were removed once more to the city and institutional life before their education was completed. Separated from her brother and father, who had made unsuccessful attempts to contact her, Clare was placed with a succession of families as a domestic servant until she was of an age to be released by the Department. Clare subsequently became an energetic activist in the cause of the Aboriginal people, was secretary of the South Coast Illawarra Tribe and a delegate to several conferences of the Federal Council for the Advancement of Aborigines and Torres Strait Islanders. Clare wrote a fictionalised account of her childhood titled *Karobran* (1978), possibly the first

novel by an Aboriginal woman. It was edited by Jack Horner with assistance from Mona Brand after Monica Clare's death.

Clarion, a Melbourne monthly mining and literary journal, launched by Randolph Bedford (q.v.), ran 1897–1909. An ardent Australian nationalist, Bedford used the *Clarion* to carry his message of White Australian, socialist republicanism. The magazine's notable contributors included the writers Hugh McCrae, John Shaw Neilson, Edward Dyson and Louis Esson, and the artists Will Dyson and Norman Lindsay. Dyson's multicoloured political cartoons were a feature of the *Clarion*'s covers in its last years.

CLARK, Manning (Charles Manning Hope) (1915–1991), born Sydney, was educated at the universities of Melbourne and Oxford. He taught at Geelong Grammar School (1940–43) before joining the staff of the University of Melbourne; in 1949 he was appointed foundation professor of history at Canberra University College, and was professor of history at the ANU from 1960. He retired in 1980 but remained a visiting fellow until his death. Clark's first articles were on French topics but increasingly he came to focus his attention on Australian history and culture; a 1943 contribution to the 'Letters to Tom Collins' (q.v.) series in *Meanjin* was his first publication in this area. Clark established a scholarly reputation in the 1950s with his collections of documents (*Select Documents in Australian History*, 2 vols, 1950–55; *Sources of Australian History*, 1957) and with his contribution to the dismantling of the convict legend (see Transportation), but it was the publication of his multi-volumed *A History of Australia* which made him Australia's most widely read but also most controversial historian. The six volumes of his *History* were published 1962, 1968, 1973, 1978, 1981, 1987, taking the story of Australia from 1788 to 1935, with Volume 6 containing a six-page epilogue to 1945. Michael Cathcart produced a condensed, single-volume version of the *History*, in 1993. The interplay of the forces of Protestantism, Catholicism and the Enlightenment in nineteenth-century Australia is an important theme in the *History*, which is informed by Clark's idealism and by a pessimism about Australian society influenced in part by the extended years of conservative political rule after the Second World War and by the dismissal of the Whitlam government in 1975. Clark has sometimes been criticised for his pessimism as well as for alleged factual inaccuracies in the *History*, the state of 'moral hypertension' in which many of his historical personages operate, and his 'apocalyptic' prose style. A strong defence has been mounted emphasising Clark's imagination, vision and the magnitude of his achievement and reminding his detractors of his insistence that his is a personal view of Australia's development. His prose style has also not been without its admirers. Fellow historian Geoffrey Blainey describes it as 'stately prose' well suited to 'the difficult art of narrative'.

Although Clark's reputation derives primarily from his historical writing, which includes the popular *A Short History of Australia* (1963, revised and illustrated 1986), his other works have attracted attention; in particular the sombre biographical portrait *In Search of Henry Lawson* (1978, republished in 1985 as *Henry Lawson: The Man and the Legend*) provoked vigorous criticism, notably by Colin Roderick, and spirited defences of Clark by Patrick White, Xavier Herbert and others. The view that Australia is Lawson 'writ large' is restated in the fifth volume of *A History of Australia*, in which Lawson is a central character; among other creative writers who significantly shaped Clark's response to Australian history are Joseph Furphy, 'Henry Handel Richardson', James McAuley, Martin Boyd, Bernard O'Dowd and Douglas Stewart. Clark's own contribution to Australian literature includes not only the study of Lawson but also two volumes of autobiographical short stories, *Disquiet and Other Stories* (1969), and a collected edition (1986 which adds two new stories); and an edition of *Settlers and Convicts* (1953) which encouraged a renewed interest in its then-unknown author, Alexander Harris. In addition Clark wrote *Meeting Soviet Man* (1960), the product of a 1958–59 visit to Russia by a FAW delegation comprising Clark, James Devaney and Judah Waten; *A Discovery of Australia* (1976), which reprints Clark's ABC Boyer Lectures for that year; and *Occasional Writings and Speeches* (1980), which reprints the 'Letter to Tom Collins', essays on Ned Kelly and Barry Humphries; and a tribute to David Campbell. In 1988 the musical *Manning Clark's History of Australia*, which intertwines Clark's biography and Australian history, and was scripted by Tim Robertson, Don Watson and others, was produced in Melbourne. In the last two years of his life Clark published the autobiographical volumes *The Puzzles of Childhood* (1989) and *The Quest for Grace* (1990). The first volume is largely concerned with his father, an Anglican clergyman from a working-class background, and his mother, who had more distinguished origins, claiming descent from the Rev. Samuel Marsden (q.v.). The incompatibility of his parents and their apparent insensitivity to his intellectual and emotional needs contributed to what Clark saw in retrospect as an unfulfilled and quietly unhappy boyhood. *The Quest for Grace* concerns Clark's student years set largely against the University of Melbourne and the city itself, represented as conservative, intellectually and socially snobbish and obsessed with sport. The end of *The Quest for Grace* sees Clark, his apprenticeship as a historian having barely ended, about to embark on his monumental Australian history. The account of how he wrote the six-volume history is contained in the posthumously published *A Historian's Apprenticeship* (1992), edited by Clark's wife Dymphna and son Sebastian. It contains his explanation of his approach to writing history and his disavowal of the discipline as a social science, dependent on statistics and data tables. In his own words he began to see history as tragedy with failure the inevitable fate of the individual, even if society could be viewed as progressive. In the broadest sense history is itself epic, but an epic made up of many individual tragedies.

Clark was one of Australia's few high-profile intellectuals and academics. A familiar figure with his broad-brimmed bush hat, spare beard and slightly severe, melancholy expression, he was at the forefront of many national, environmental and cultural movements, most of which were progressively radical in spirit and tone. Volume 6 of his *History* won the NBC Banjo Award for 1988; *The Puzzles of Childhood* won the FAW Christina Stead and Herb Thomas Awards in 1989. He was made AC in 1975. Stephen Holt's *Manning Clark and Australian History* (1982) traces Clark's life and intellectual evolution between 1915 and 1963.

CLARK, Mavis Thorpe, see *The Oxford Companion to Australian Children's Literature* (1993), p. 97.

CLARK, Ralph (1755–94), an officer in the marines, volunteered for duty at Botany Bay in an attempt to gain promotion and sailed in HMS *Friendship* in the First Fleet. Clark's detailed and frank diary, kept assiduously 1787–92, is a source of information about shipboard life during the voyage to Botany Bay and the daily routine of the Colony, especially the convict settlement at Norfolk Island where Clark was stationed 1790–91. *The Journal and Letters of Lt. Ralph Clark 1787–1792*, edited by Paul G. Fidlon and R. J. Ryan, was published in 1981. Clark is a character in Thomas Keneally's novel *The Playmaker* (1987) and in the play which it inspired, *Our Country's Good* (1988) by Timberlake Wertenbaker.

CLARK, Robert (1911–), born Darjeeling, India, came to Australia as a boy and was educated in Adelaide, where he practised as a solicitor. He is now retired and is a full-time writer. He won the 1956 *Sydney Morning Herald* prize for poetry for 'The Dogman' and has been widely represented in Australian anthologies. Co-editor of *Verse in Australia* 1958–61 and *No. 8 Friendly Street Poetry Reader* (1984) he wrote the significant introduction on Max Harris in Harris's poems *A Window at Night* (1967). His own publications of verse are *The Dogman and Other Poems* (1962), *Segments of the Bowl* (1968), *Thrusting into Darkness* (1978) and *Walking to Bethongabel* (1986). A traditional poet concerned especially with language, most of his work is lyrical and meditative.

CLARK, Ross (1953–), born in the Darling Downs region of Queensland, has worked as a bookseller, teacher, editor and freelance writer. He has published verse in numerous periodicals and anthologies and in three collections, *Chameleon* (1982), *With Fires on Every Horizon* (1986), and *Still Waiting for the Thunder* (1992). Co-editor of *The Border Issue*, he is also editor and publisher of the SweetWater Poets series and has edited the collections *Lightning Lyrics* (1983, with Peter Burton and Audrey Heck) and *Turns of Phrase* (1988, with Lawrie Ryan). Concerned with continuity and the problems of understanding the past, Clark's accessible, sometimes whimsical poetry is strongly evocative of Brisbane.

CLARK, William Nairne (1804–54), born Perthshire, Scotland, emigrated in 1830 to WA, where he practised as a lawyer, edited the *Inquisitor* in 1833 and established the *Swan River Guardian* in 1836. His accomplishments include the killing of a Major George Johnson, an associate on the *Inquisitor*, in a duel in 1831 (Clark was acquitted of murder) and the publication of the first book in the Swan River Colony. In many newspaper articles Clark defended the Aboriginal people. He later left WA for Tasmania.

CLARKE, Coralie (1909–72) was born in Perth and educated at the University of WA. There she sub-edited the student magazine, the *Black Swan*, which was edited by her future husband Leslie Rees. Some of her one-act plays were printed in the *Black Swan*, including 'Shielded Eyes', produced in 1930 with Paul Hasluck in the main role. In 1931 she and Rees were married in London, where they lived until 1936. During this time she contributed numerous articles to the *West Australian* under the pseudonym 'Boronia'. After their return to Australia she wrote extensively for radio and was an occasional broadcaster. As well as short stories for children and travel articles, she wrote a verse elegy, *Silent His Wings* (1946), for her brother who was killed in the Second World War, and four travel books in collaboration with Leslie Rees, *Spinifex Walkabout* (1953), *Westward from Cocos* (1956), *Coasts of Cape York* (1960) and *People of the Big Sky Country* (1970). Her play for children, *Wait Till We Grow Up*, is included in *Australian Youth Plays* (1948) edited by Leslie Rees.

CLARKE, Donovan (1907–87), born Bristol, England, had a long career as schoolmaster and academic, poet and literary critic. Particularly interested in Australian colonial poetry, he wrote on the Henry Kendall–Charles Harpur relationship and edited a selection of Harpur's poetry in 1963. He also published two volumes of poetry, *Ritual Dance* (1940) and *Blue Prints* (1942).

CLARKE, Doreen (1928–), born Manchester, England, came to Australia in 1958. Since the production of her first play, *Roses in Due Season* (performed 1978, published 1982), she has worked in the theatre or in projects connected with the theatre. Her other published plays include *Bleedin' Butterflies* (1982), *Farewell Brisbane Ladies* (1982), and *Give 'em Chips* (1985). Unpublished but performed plays include 'Missus Queen' (1979), 'The Sad Songs of Annie Sando' (1981) and 'Salt and Vinegar' (1982), plays dealing with life in the SA satellite city of Elizabeth and, with David Allen, 'Coppin & Co' (1982).

CLARKE, Marcus (1846–81), born Kensington, London, was educated at Highgate, where Gerard Manley Hopkins and his brother Cyril were contemporaries and close friends. He had expectations of a substantial inheritance and a Foreign Office career but those hopes were dashed at 16 by the sudden illness of his father, a Chancery lawyer, and the discovery that his financial affairs were in disarray. One of Clarke's

uncles had been governor of WA, another was a judge in Ararat, and a cousin, Captain Andrew Clarke, had been Victorian surveyor-general and a member of parliament, and had recently returned to England; it was Andrew who arranged Clarke's emigration to Australia in 1863 armed with some £800 and several letters of introduction.

Clarke began to write for the Australian press soon after arrival in Melbourne, but his first employment was in the Bank of Australasia; in 1865 he left Melbourne to spend two years working on sheep stations in the Wimmera district of Victoria. During his time there he contributed to the *Australian Monthly Magazine* under the pseudonyms 'Mark Scrivener' and 'Q'; later it became the *Colonial Monthly* (q.v.) and serialised his first novel, *Long Odds* (q.v.), in 1868–69. In 1867 he returned to Melbourne and was soon writing for the *Argus* and the *Australasian*, where the popular series 'The Peripatetic Philospher' (q.v.) was published 1867–70; together with the 'Lower Bohemia' (q.v.) sketches, theatre criticism and other writings, 'The Peripatetic Philosopher' helped to establish Clarke as a leading Melbourne journalist, a reputation he held till his death. His efforts as an editor and publisher were less successful: brief periods with the *Colonial Monthly* (1868–69), the *Humbug* (q.v., 1869–70) and the *Australian Journal* (q.v., 1870–71) were unprofitable and contributed to the first of his bankruptcies in 1874. This period also established Clarke's reputation as a bohemian, a leading member of Melbourne's café society: witty, urbane, brilliant, he was one of the founders of the Yorick Club (q.v.) in 1868 and moved easily in theatrical circles. His published plays include the pantomimes *Goody Two Shoes* (1870) and *Twinkle, Twinkle Little Star* (1873); the comedy *Reverses* (1876, first performed 1979); the operetta *Alfred the Great* (1879); the satire, *The Happy Land* (q.v., 1880); and *A Daughter of Eve* (first published in 1986). In 1869 he married the actor Marian Dunn.

In 1870 Clarke was sent by the *Argus* management to Tasmania to research the convict past. The immediate literary consequences were the series of historical articles published in the *Australasian* (1870–71) as 'Old Stories Retold' by 'Q', and collected in 1871 as *Old Tales of a Young Country* (q.v.); and Clarke's most famous work, *His Natural Life* (q.v.), which was serialised in the *Australian Journal* in 1870–72 and revised for its first publication in book form in 1874. Soon after his return from Tasmania he found employment at the Public Library in Melbourne, first as secretary to the trustees and then from September 1873 as sub-librarian. Two months later his association with the *Argus* group ceased after a squabble over Clarke's report in the rival *Herald* of the 1873 Melbourne Cup. As well as *The Peripatetic Philosopher* and *Old Tales of a Young Country*, the *Argus* and *Australasian* years had resulted in three newspaper columns and in the short stories published 1870–73 and included in *Holiday Peak and Other Tales* (1873) and *Four Stories High* (q.v., 1877).

In comparison with the immensely productive years 1869–74 Clarke was subsequently less prolific, partly because of his work at the Public Library and partly because he was involved in the management of a country property for his cousin. But he still found time to write for the theatre; to publish two novels, *Chidiock Tichbourne* (1893, serialised 1874–75) which traded on the Tichborne controversy but is not about Australia, and *'Twixt Shadow and Shine* (1875), and begin a third ('Felix and Felicitas'); to prepare the commentary accompanying *Photographs of Pictures in the National Gallery, Melbourne* (1875), part of which became a famous preface to the 1876 edition of Adam Lindsay Gordon's *Sea Spray and Smoke Drift*; to write the pamphlet *The Future Australian Race* (1877); and to contribute to a variety of newspapers and periodicals including the *Age*, the *Leader*, the *Melbourne Review* and *Victorian Review* in Melbourne, and the *Daily Telegraph* and *Notes and Queries* in London. A *Victorian Review* article in 1879 by Clarke on the role of the church in society led to a reply by the Bishop of Melbourne; Clarke wrote a rejoinder and the controversy was collected and published as *Civilization Without Delusion* (1880). His resulting unpopularity with officialdom, increased by his involvement in *The Happy Land*, a satire on the Berry government of the day, was instrumental in his failure to become public librarian in 1881. He had fallen into financial difficulties again; when he was not appointed he was pressed for payment, made bankrupt a second time, collapsed amidst the strain and died within a week, leaving his wife and six children destitute. His friend Hamilton Mackinnon prepared *The Marcus Clarke Memorial Volume* (1884) to help the family, and *The Austral Edition of the Selected Works of Marcus Clarke* (1890); parts of the latter were reissued as *Stories of Australia in the Early Days* (1897), *Australian Tales* (1896) and *Australian Tales of the Bush* (1897). Other Clarke volumes published soon after his death include the two stories *The Mystery of Major Molineux and Human Repetends* (1881) and *Sensational Tales* (1886). Significant publications on Clarke include Brian Elliott's biography *Marcus Clarke* (1958); L.T. Hergenhan's selection of journalism *A Colonial City* (1972); the bibliographies by Samuel Rowe Simmons (1975, ed. Hergenhan) and Ian McLaren (1982); and the volume on Clarke in the Portable Australian Authors Series (1976), ed. Michael Wilding, who has also edited a collection of Clarke's short stories (1983) and written a monograph revaluing Clarke's achievements (1977).

For years Clarke was remembered as the popular author of one major work, *His Natural Life*, a convict novel of immense proportions and power although regarded as somewhat flawed by melodramatic excesses. Since Clarke's death it has been reprinted frequently, reserialised, dramatised, filmed, abridged, anthologised and translated. Modern scholarship and criticism, however, and the increasing availability of Clarke's other writings have resulted not only in a reconsideration of *His Natural Life* itself – Michael Wilding, for example, sees the plot coincidences less as naturalistic absurdities than as a mechanism for exploring psychological levels of character – but also in a revaluation of Clarke's achievement. Although *His Natural Life* remains his most important work, he was amazingly versatile and made significant contributions to colonial literary culture as novelist, short-story writer, historian, critic, journalist, dramatist, poet and editor. As a historian, particularly in *Old Tales of a Young Country*, he helped to create the romance of the Australian past, as had Cooper and Hawthorne for American literature and Scott for English literature. As a short-story writer he ranged from realism to the Gothic to fantasy and preceded Henry Lawson in opening up the bush to Australian readers. As a critic he took part, as *Civilization Without Delusion* shows, in the great questions of the day and wrote perceptively about American, English and European literature (Balzac was his favourite author and a major influence) as well as about his contemporaries. As a journalist he continued, in the 'Lower Bohemia' sketches, the investigative tradition of Henry Mayhew, while *The Peripatetic Philosopher* and his other series derived their success from the skilful blend of satire, irony and characterisation which created the Clarke style.

CLARKE, Patricia (1926–), born Melbourne, was a journalist for thirty years in Melbourne and Canberra, where she worked for the Australian News and Information Bureau and for the ABC. She has written several books on colonial women, including *The Governesses: Letters from the Colonies 1862–1882* (1985), *A Colonial Woman: The Life and Times of Mary Braidwood Mowle 1827–1857* (1986), *Pen Portraits: Women Writers and Journalists in Nineteenth Century Australia* (1988), *Pioneer Writer: The Life of Louisa Atkinson* (1990) and *Tasma: the Life of Jessie Couvreur* (1994). With Dale Spender she compiled and edited *Life Lines: Australian Women's Letters and Diaries 1788–1840* (1992).

CLARKE, Peg, see **Feminism and Australian Literature**

CLARKE, W.B. (William Branwhite) (1798–1878), born Suffolk, England, was an Anglican clergyman, schoolteacher, experienced geologist and published poet before he arrived in Australia in 1839. He was headmaster of the King's School at Parramatta before his appointment to a North Sydney ministry in 1846. His geological explorations revealed gold in the Colony as early as 1841 but Governor Gipps, alarmed at the specimen of gold shown him in 1844, is reported to have said, 'Put it away, Mr Clarke, or we shall all have our throats cut.' After the discovery of gold by Edward Hammond Hargraves in 1851, Clarke became the government's scientific adviser on the goldfields. His publication *Plain Statements and Practical Hints Respecting the Discovery and Working of Gold in Australia* (1851) became known as 'The Prospector's Bible'; he also published *Researches in the Southern Gold Fields of New South Wales* (1860). A tireless contributor of scientific articles to newspapers and journals, Clarke deserved the title 'Father of Australian Geology', as in James Jervis's biography (1944).

CLAY, H.E. (Henry Ebenezer) (1844–96), born Cheshire, England, migrated in 1858 to WA, where he worked as a government clerk. His volume of verse

Two and Two: A Story of the Australian Forest, with Minor Poems of Colonial Interest (1873) was the first separate publication of poetry in WA. His other works include *Westralian Poems* (1907), *Poems* (1910) and the proclamation song, *Rouse Thee Westralia* (1890). Although he wrote in a conventional English poetic style, Clay included such colonial ingredients as kangaroos, sheep, wild dogs, bushfires, and life on the diggings.

Clean Straw for Nothing, a novel by George Johnston (q.v.), was published in 1969 and won the Miles Franklin Award. The middle volume of Johnston's semi-autobiographical trilogy, which includes *My Brother Jack* (q.v., 1964) and *A Cartload of Clay* (1971), it narrates the experience of David Meredith from 1945 to the 1960s. Looking back at the kaleidoscope of the past, Meredith searches for the reasons for his sense of failure. After leaving his first wife to marry Cressida Morley, he abandons Melbourne for Sydney, then Sydney for London, and finally London and his career as a journalist for life as a creative writer on a Greek island. Freedom, however, proves elusive: his hopes of writing a great novel disintegrate, his health is ruined and material worries threaten his hopes for his children. His relationship with Cressida, deteriorating even in London, almost collapses after her affair with an American, Jim Galloway, in 1959. Although they are helped by their friends, especially Tom Kiernan (a study of Sidney Nolan) and Archie Calverton (a study of Peter Finch), Meredith returns to Australia in 1964 with the sense that he will always be an alien 'because there is no-one you will ever really know, not even yourself.'

CLEARY, Jon (1917–), born Sydney, the eldest of seven children, left school at 15. He worked at various occupations in the textile industry, as a film cartoonist, salesman, laundryman, bushworker and commercial artist. He served in the Australian army 1940–45 in the Middle East and New Guinea. From 1945 he has been a full-time writer apart from two periods as a journalist with the Australian News and Information Bureau. In 1946 he married Joy Lucas, who, as Joy Cleary, wrote *Strike Me Lucky* (1959). Cleary has lived abroad for extensive periods in the USA, England, Spain, Italy and Austria and has travelled widely to research his novels. His books, published in numerous foreign countries, have a wide overseas audience and have been produced as films on several occasions. Cleary's novels are *You Can't See Round Corners* (q.v., 1947), *The Long Shadow* (1949), *Just Let Me Be* (1950, reissued 1990 as *You, The Jury*), *The Sundowners* (q.v., 1952), *The Climate of Courage* (1954, also titled *Naked in the Night*), *Justin Bayard* (1955, also titled *Dust in the Sun*), *The Green Helmet* (1957), *Back of Sunset* (1959), *North from Thursday* (1960), *The Country of Marriage* (1962), *Forests of the Night* (1963), *A Flight of Chariots* (1963), *The Fall of an Eagle* (1964), *The Pulse of Danger* (1966), *The High Commissioner* (1966), *The Long Pursuit* (1967), *Season of Doubt* (1968), *Remember Jack Hoxie* (1969), *Helga's Web* (1970), *Mask of the Andes* (1971, also titled *The Liberators*), *Man's Estate* (1972, also titled *The Ninth Mar-*

quess), *Ransom* (1973), *Peter's Pence* (1974), *The Safe House* (1975), *A Sound of Lightning* (1976), *Vortex* (1977), *High Road to China* (1977), *The Beaufort Sisters* (1979), *A Very Private War* (1980), *The Faraway Drums* (1981), *The Golden Sabre* (1981), *Spearfield's Daughter* (1982), *The Phoenix Tree* (1984), *City of Fading Light* (1985), *Dragons at the Party* (1987), *Now and Then, Amen* (1988), *Babylon South* (1989), *Murder Song* (1990), *Pride's Harvest* (1991), *Dark Summer* (1992), and *Bleak Spring* (1993), the last two being the ninth and tenth in the Scobie Malone series. He has also published two collections of short stories, *These Small Glories* (1946) and *Pillar of Salt* (1963). He has written scripts for television, radio and film for production in Australia, the USA and England, and has had stories published in several of the world's leading magazines. Novels which have been filmed include *You Can't See Round Corners*, *The Sundowners*, *Justin Bayard*, *The Green Helmet*, *The High Commissioner*, *Helga's Web* (as *Scobie Malone*) and *High Road to China*. Cleary won first prize in the ABC's 1944 competition for radio drama, second prize in the *Sydney Morning Herald*'s novel competition of 1946, the Australian section prize in the World Short Story contest of the *New York Herald Tribune* in 1950, the Gold Medal of the Australian Literature Society for the best Australian novel of 1950 (*Just Let Me Be*) and the Mystery Writers Edgar Award of 1975.

Although Cleary's novels have varied settings, ranging from Bhutan to the USA to New Guinea, several of them are set in Australia, most notably *You Can't See Round Corners*, *The Long Shadow*, *The Sundowners*, *Justin Bayard*, *Back of Sunset*, *Helga's Web*, *Dragons at the Party* and *Babylon South*. In others, Australian characters frequently appear and with Scobie Malone, the Sydney detective who figures in *Helga's Web*, *The High Commissioner* and *Ransom*, Cleary has come close to creating the Australian Maigret. A popular adventure writer with a talent for gripping action, atmosphere and convincing dialogue, Cleary frequently evokes the psychological subtleties and moral complexities of personal relationships.

'Click Go the Shears', one of the best-known Australian folk-songs, was probably written in the early years of the twentieth century and derives from the English song 'Ring the Bell, Watchman'. It offers a picture of shearing life in the days of the blade shears, and each of its several verses focuses on a typical inhabitant of the shearing shed and his activities: the old shearer, the boss, the new chum, the boy supplying tar to seal a wound caused by the shears, the spree after the shearing season is over. The chorus,

> Click go the shears boys, click, click, click
> Wide is his blow and his hands move quick
> The ringer looks around and is beaten by a blow
> And curses the old snagger with the bare [blue]-bellied 'joe'.

refers to the sound of the shears, the shearing style of the ringer or fastest shearer, and his chagrin when his tally is bettered by a snagger, a shearer who works roughly. Robert Ingpen published a fine illustrated version of 'Click Go the Shears' in 1985.

CLIFT, Charmian (1923–69) was born at Kiama, NSW. During the Second World War she served in the Australian Women's Army Service as an anti-aircraft gunner and edited a magazine for the Army Ordnance Corps. On demobilisation she worked as a journalist for the Melbourne *Argus*. She married George Johnston (q.v.) in 1947 and accompanied him to London in 1950 and to Greece in 1954. After the Johnstons returned to Australia in 1964, Charmian Clift turned to freelance journalism. She contributed a popular weekly column to the *Sydney Morning Herald* and also wrote regularly for the Melbourne *Herald* and for various other magazines and newspapers. She wrote three novels with George Johnston: *High Valley* (1949), which won first prize in the 1948 literary competition of the *Sydney Morning Herald*, *The Big Chariot* (1953) and *The Sponge Divers* (1955), the last published in the USA with the title *The Sea and The Stone* (1955); two other novels, *Walk to the Paradise Gardens* (1960) and *Honour's Mimic* (1964); and two accounts of the Johnston family's experiences in Greece, *Mermaid Singing* (1956) and *Peel Me a Lotus* (1959). Of the 240 essays which she contributed to the Melbourne *Herald* and the *Sydney Morning Herald*, 107 were collected in the anthologies *Images in Aspic* (1965) and *The World of Charmian Clift* (1970, both edited by George Johnston; a 1987 edition includes an introduction by Martin Johnston). Her remaining essays were published in two collections, *Trouble in Lotus Land* (1990) and *Being Alone with Oneself* (1991, both edited by Nadia Wheatley). *The Strong Man from Piraeus* (1984), edited by Garry Kinnane, contains four stories by Clift and seven by Johnston, written in the 1950s and earlier. Clift also adapted Johnston's novel *My Brother Jack* (q.v.) for televison. His study of Cressida Morley in that novel and in *Clean Straw for Nothing* (q.v., 1969) and *A Cartload of Clay* (1971) is loosely based on her life and his reactions to her early death; Garry Kinnane's biography of Johnston (1986) is also densely informative on Clift and the Johnstons' family life. One of their sons was the poet Martin Johnston (q.v.). A fluent writer with a range of tones and a congenial wit, Charmian Clift found her natural bent in the essay, where she moves easily from concerned discussion of national issues to nostalgic, personal reminiscence of people or places, to humorous reflection on social practices or everyday experiences.

CLOSE, Robert (1903–), born Camberwell, Melbourne, became an apprentice at the age of 14 on a sailing ship and after six years' exuberant adventures gave up the sea when he failed his second mate's ticket because of colour-blindness. With his one career ambition lost, Close drifted through a series of unsatisfactory occupations such as shipping clerk, vacuum-cleaner salesman and accounts collector with the Melbourne *Truth*. Incipient tuberculosis, employment difficulties during the Depression, and an unhappy marriage also contributed to his bleak view of life at the time. After six months of sanatorium care

in 1936 his tuberculosis was cured and he was successful in having short stories published. In 1945 he published his first novel, *Love Me, Sailor* (q.v.). It deals with the voyage of a windjammer and the chaos caused on board ship by its sole passenger, a neurotic nymphomaniac. The first edition sold out in a few weeks but the novel was then banned and Close and his publishers, Georgian House, were charged with 'obscene libel'. After two trials and in a blaze of publicity and controversy, Close was found guilty and sentenced to three months' gaol and a fine of £100. The gaol sentence was quashed on appeal but the fine increased to £150. In 1950 Close, divorced and 'tired of living in an atmosphere of parochial suburbanism', left Australia to live in France, where the French edition, *Prends-moi, Matelot*, was a best-seller. Close's second novel, *The Dupe* (1947), written to prove that he did not have to rely on sex to win literary acclaim, is also set on a windjammer but contains no female characters and no sexuality. *The Dupe* is the story of a young seaman apprentice, who loses his indentures by missing his ship because of a drunken spree and attempts to regain his lost prestige by pretending responsibility for the murder of the ship's brutal first mate. As with *Love Me, Sailor*, Close's knowledge of the sea and sailing ships is impressive; his portrait of the young man, Carson, is also superior to that of Ella, the central figure in the earlier novel. After *The Dupe*, Close published an autobiographical account of his seafaring days, *Morn of Youth* (1948), and after arriving in Europe, wrote an autobiographical novel, 'Not of Salt Nor Earth', but withdrew it before publication. In 1977 his autobiography up to the point of his gaol sentence was published as *Of Salt and Earth*. His next novel, *Eliza Callaghan* (1957), described by the *New York Times* as 'a realistic historical novel, replete with sex, booze, violence and malevolence', is based on the courtship of John Batman and the young Irish girl of the title. Later less significant novels by Close are *With Hooves of Brass* (1961), set in the Victorian timber country; *She's My Lovely* (1962), with an American setting; and *The Voyage Continues* (1969), a fictional reconstruction of the wreck of the *Batavia* off the west coast of Australia in 1629, with the events leading up to it and its tragic sequel. Close's significance in Australian literary history is largely due to the extraordinary events attached to *Love Me, Sailor*, but his ability to construct a realistic narrative set against the background of life on a sailing ship is considerable.

Cloudstreet (1991), a novel by Tim Winton (q.v.) and winner of both the NBC Banjo Award for fiction in 1991 and the Miles Franklin Award in 1992, is the story of the 'sandwich' families, the Lambs and the Pickleses, set mainly in Perth, WA, from the later years of the Second World War to the late 1960s. The Pickleses are the father, Sam, whose whole life is focused on Luck, 'the shifty shadow of God', and who has lost the fingers of his right hand in a wartime accident; his wife Dolly, 'a damn goodlooking woman', whose accommodating nature makes her welcome among the sailors who frequent the busy wartime port of Geraldton, where the Pickleses live when the story begins; his children, Ted and Chub, and daughter, Rose. Left £2000 and an old derelict Perth mansion (No. 1 Cloud Street) by Dolly's brother, who dies of a heart attack while fishing, Sam loses the money in an afternoon at the races then takes possession of 'Cloudstreet'. Ultimately he divides it roughly into two, letting half of it to another rural family, also driven by catastrophe to the city. They comprise Lester and Oriel Lamb, their six children, Hattie, Elaine, Red (girls), Mason (nicknamed 'Quick' because he isn't), Samson (called 'Fish') and the baby, Lon. Fish's brain damage is the family's catastrophe, caused by his submersion several minutes under water by the family's fully laden prawning net. Those submerged minutes have created, in what is left of Fish's mind, images of peace and tranquillity that draw him constantly to water. Cloudstreet's own aura is grim and unhappy, restless and disturbed spirits haunting its gloomy rooms. It had been used as a place to 'educate' young Aboriginal girls taken by force from their families. So miserable were they that they frequently tried to run away or commit suicide, one succeeding with ant poison. The busy Lambs, led by Oriel, turn their half of the house into a thriving food shop, but they lack contentment, pursued always by a sense of guilt over Fish's accident. The harmony of the Pickleses is constantly disturbed by the behaviour of the still promiscuous and now alcoholic Dolly and by the poverty that results from Sam's gambling. Rose, the one steadying influence, passes through adolescence in an ever-increasing anorexic daze that is only relieved when at 16 she gets a job as telephonist in a department store and begins to make a life for herself away from Cloudstreet. Gradually but inevitably the lives of the two families merge. A string of crises – Sam's rescue by Lester from the bookies, Rose's anorexia, boys from both families getting involved in 'shotgun' weddings – provides growing common ground and a clannish sense. Rose marries Quick and with the birth of their child, Wax Harry, the union between the families is complete. Cloudstreet, too, is cleansed of its unhappy past by the birth of the child and Fish, now a grown man but still a child, takes advantage of a few minutes of lax supervision on a family picnic to rediscover the wonderful world beneath the water that he had so long desired. No plot summary of Cloudstreet can begin to illustrate its extraordinary richness of character, incident, dialogue, humour, pathos, imagination and sensitivity. It seems certain to establish itself as one of Australia's best novels.

CLOW, Robitt Jon (1876–1952), born Melbourne, was a minister of the Churches of Christ in Victoria, SA and Queensland in the early part of this century. He published two plays, The Cause of Kelly (1919) and The Dewmah, subtitled The Collected Literature of the Australian Aborigine as Told in Native Drama (1949); fiction, The Pillar of Salt: A Story of Station Life (1903); verse, Vive la Australe (1910) and Australie ... Three Poems (1910); and miscellaneous works including Among the Chief Colonials (1921), The Pacific Empire: An Authentic History of the Venerable James Clow (1929), The

Book of the Ages: A Centennial Story of Melbourne and Adelaide (1937) and The Royal Charter (1938).

Club, The, a play by David Williamson (q.v.), first performed in 1977, was published in 1978 and produced as a film in 1980. Set in the committee room of a top Melbourne Australian rules football club (perceived as Collingwood by many) and surveyed by the ranged photographs of the club's past heroes, it comically enacts familiar competing tensions between six of its members. The personal rivalries between Ted Parker (the president), Jock Riley (the vice-president, ex-player and ex-coach) and Laurie Holden (ex-player and dedicated coach) have their roots in the club's past history and are exacerbated by the current pressure to revive its declining fortunes. They are manipulated by Gerry Cooper, the new-breed administrator who ignores tradition and practises the 'logic of pragmatism'. Players are no longer men but marketable commodities, and committee members and coaches are equally subject to the demands of football as an entertainment industry. Danny Rowe, the player who lives for the game but is almost expendable, and Geoff Hayward, the brilliant but uncommitted new 'purchase', watch and barrack the game of power politics from the sidelines.

CLUNE, Frank (1893–1971), born and educated in Sydney, got his first job, selling newspapers, at the age of 7. At 15 he left home and for the next five years led an adventurous life on sea and land in Australia, France, Belgium, the USA and Canada. He returned to Australia in 1913, enlisted in the AIF in 1915 and was wounded at Gallipoli; invalided home, he resumed a vagabond's existence and was in turn a fireman, recruiting sergeant, concert balladist, steward, vaudevillian and mousetrap salesman before settling into the practice of accountancy after his marriage in 1923. A decade later, while convalescing from an ulcer attack, he wrote an account of his earlier wanderings. Published as Try Anything Once (1933), the book launched Clune on a writing career that produced over sixty books 1934–71. During much of this period, when he was one of Australia's best-selling authors, he had the services of P.R. Stephensen (q.v.) as collaborator; Stephensen is acknowledged as co-author of The Viking of Van Diemen's Land (1954) and The Pirates of the Brig 'Cyprus' (1962), and as 'literary collaborator' in other volumes (e.g. in the preface to Wild Colonial Boys, 1948). On the evidence, Clune provided the travel diaries, historical research and other raw material for his books, which were mostly written by Stephensen, especially in the 1940s and 1950s.

Clune regularly catalogued his works under several headings: autobiography (Try Anything Once; Pacific Parade, 1945; Try Nothing Twice, 1946; Korean Diary, 1955); biography (some dozen titles including studies of varying length on the bushrangers 'Captain Melville', 'Captain Starlight' and Martin Cash; the adventurers Edward Hammond Hargraves, 'Bully' Hayes, Jorgen Jorgenson, 'Chinese' Morrison and Louis de Rougemont; and the mass murderer Deeming); history (a similar number of titles including Wild Colonial

Boys; *Bound for Botany Bay*, 1964; *The Norfolk Island Story*, 1967; and *The Scottish Martyrs* (1969); exploration (notably *Dig*, 1937, a narrative of the Burke and Wills expedition); historical novels *(Dark Outlaw*, 1945, a study of the bushranger Frank Gardiner, reprinted as *Gunman Gardiner*, 1951, and *King of the Road*, 1967; and *Ben Hall the Bushranger*, 1947); adventure (e.g. *The Red Heart*, 1944); and travel (more than two dozen volumes including *Rolling down the Lachlan*, 1935; *Roaming Round the Darling*, 1936; *Prowling Through Papua*, 1942; *Tobruk to Turkey*, 1943; *High-ho to London*, 1948; *Somewhere in New Guinea*, 1951; *Roaming Round Europe*, 1954; *Flight to Formosa*, 1958; *Journey to Kosciusko*, 1964; *Journey to Pitcairn*, 1966). Such distinctions, however, camouflage important overlaps in Clune's work: for example, there is little difference apart from scale between his historical novels, histories, biographies and exploration studies, which all focus on sensational personalities or historical incidents and in which Clune characteristically takes liberties with the evidence, as in the reporting of invented conversations. Clune's prose is racy, journalistic and immediate, an appealing amalgam of alliteration, cliché, colourful image and title which has its parallel in the writing of journalists such as John Norton and Cyril Pearl. Although Clune's Cold War travel books are politically conservative, his historical writing reflects his Irish Catholic background and shows sympathy for some Australian underdogs, notably bushrangers such as Ben Hall and Ned Kelly and the Scottish martyr Thomas Muir. Apart from the personal appeal of *Try Anything Once*, which went through several editions in its first decade, his importance in Australian literature is mainly as a historical populariser – on radio as well as in books – who introduced successive generations to some of the legendary figures of Australia's past, notably in the often-reprinted *Dig*, *King of the Road*, *Wild Colonial Boys*, and *The Kelly Hunters* (1954) as well as in *Rascals, Ruffians and Rebels of Early Australia* (1987). One such reader was the novelist Thomas Keneally, whose interest in the Jimmy Governor story, aroused by Clune's 1959 volume on the Aboriginal mass-murderer, led eventually to the novel *The Chant of Jimmie Blacksmith* (q.v., 1972).

Coast to Coast, an anthology of Australian short stories, was published annually 1941–48 and biennially 1949–70. The final anthology in the series appeared in 1973. The editors of the individual volumes were: Cecil Mann (1941), Beatrice Davis (1942), Frank Dalby Davison (1943), Vance Palmer (1944), Douglas Stewart (1945), 'M. Barnard Eldershaw' (1946), Don Edwards (1947), Brian Elliott (1948), Nettie Palmer (1949–50), Ken Levis (1951–52), C.B. Christesen (1953–54), H. Drake-Brockman (1955–56), Dal Stivens (1957–58), Cecil Hadgraft (1959–60), Hal Porter (1961–62), Leonie Kramer (1963–64), Clement Semmler (1965–66), A.A. Phillips (1967–68), Thea Astley (1969–70) and Frank Moorhouse (1973). *Coast to Coast: Recent Australian Prose Writing* (1986) was edited by Kerryn Goldsworthy.

Cobb & Co. The first mention of public road transport in Australia was a notice in the *Sydney Gazette*, May 1803, by one Henry Cable that he proposed 'to run a Common Stage Machine from Sydney to Parramatta and Hawkesbury'. By 1814 regular weekly services by 'Common Stage Cart' ran for passengers from Sydney to Parramatta, Windsor and Richmond; in 1821 the Colony's first regular coach service began along the road to Parramatta and extended in the 1830s across the Blue Mountains to Bathurst, with an overnight stay at the present township of Wentworth Falls. Before the gold-rush period there were few coach services in the Port Phillip district, but an overland service for mail and passengers existed between Sydney and Melbourne, following roughly the route of the present Hume Highway. With the discovery of gold in 1851 in both NSW and Victoria an army of 'diggers', many from overseas, surged to the goldfields; their demands – and those of eager entrepreneurs, tourists, and harassed governments who had to set up administrations on the fields – for fast, reliable transport led to the emergence of Australia's most famous pioneering transport company, Cobb & Co. In 1853 American-built Concord coaches, well tested on the Californian goldfields in 1850, arrived in Australia; with them came four young Americans, Freeman Cobb, John Murray Peck, James Swanton and John B. Lamber, the first two of whom had been employees of the well-known American express companies Adams & Co. and Wells, Fargo & Co. One version of the origin of Cobb & Co. suggests that the four formed a small carrying company (named Cobb & Co.) plying between Melbourne and Sandhurst (Bendigo) which, after a very wet 1853 Victorian winter, they converted to a coaching service. A different account suggests they began the carrying service in the names of the two American express companies, but after their suggestion of a change to coach service had been rejected by the parent companies they resigned to start their own service between Melbourne and the goldfields at Forest Creek (now Castlemaine) and Bendigo. They were financially assisted by American entrepreneur George Francis Train (q.v.), who had also arrived in Australia in 1853. By 1856 Freeman Cobb had sold his coaching interests and returned to America; the name Cobb & Co., however, was retained by the new owners and came in time to be used by numerous other coaching firms, many of whom had little or no connection with the original Cobb & Co. The impression thus gained of a massive network of coaching routes which by the 1880s traversed the whole country, all part of a single Cobb & Co. empire, is somewhat erroneous. By 1861 the name of Cobb & Co. had become a legend in Victoria. In 1862, then owned by a syndicate headed by another American, James Rutherford, Cobb & Co. extended into NSW, running first between Bathurst and Sydney and later opening up numerous other routes. A factory was established at Bathurst to build the company's coaches and Rutherford lived there until his death in 1911; he helped to establish the Bathurst *National Advocate* in 1889. In 1865 the Cobb & Co. Queensland services were inaugurated; the Cobb & Co. tradition of serving the frontier was maintained by its pioneering of the service to the Gympie goldfields. In 1866 Cobb & Co. coaches were running in SA. By 1883 it was possible to travel on a coach named Cobb & Co. (but not necessarily part of the original company) from the Gulf of Carpentaria to SA, the most extensive system of coach routes in the world. At its peak Cobb & Co. itself harnessed over 6000 horses a day and served more than a hundred separate routes in NSW and Victoria alone. Cobb & Co. coaches were 'bailed up' by bushrangers on thirty-six separate occasions; and it gave to Australian legend such famous driver-figures as 'Cabbage Tree Ned' Devine (1833–1908), who was paid £1000 a year, and George Adams, later the founder of Tattersall's lottery. By the turn of the century, with the advent of the railway, and later with the coming of the motor car, Cobb & Co. lost its importance as the country's chief source of transport. By 1913 Cobb & Co. coaches had ceased running in NSW, and in 1924 in Queensland the last commercial Cobb & Co. coach journey was made.

Although newspapers and journals of the 1850s gave considerable publicity to the advent of the coaching days, the first clear signs of a Cobb & Co. legend were in Thomas McCombie's *Australian Sketches* (1861). Anthony Trollope's *Australia and New Zealand* (1873) added to that growing legend by describing the coach journeys of his Australian tour and expressing his admiration for the Cobb & Co. drivers. Some old bush songs dating from as early as the 1870s (e.g. 'The German Girls') have direct reference to Cobb & Co. From the 1890s, however, the ubiquitous Cobb & Co. coach featured widely in verse and story that celebrated the final conquest of 'the tyranny of distance' and the opening of the land. Will Ogilvie's poem 'Cobb & Co.', and Henry Lawson's 'The Lights of Cobb & Co.' appeared in the *Bulletin* in 1895 and 1897 respectively, Lawson's poem conveying the excitement of travelling by coach to the goldfields in those halcyon times. Other Lawson poems, nostalgic and sentimental like 'The Roaring Days', 'The Last Review' and 'The Old Bark School', describe coaching incidents and mention Cobb & Co. by name; there are also references to the firm in such Lawson stories as 'The Shanty Keeper's Wife', 'Payable Gold', 'Brighten's Sister-in-Law', 'The Buck Jumper', 'The House That Was Never Built', 'Getting Back on Dave Regan' and 'The Horses'. Other poems and stories to celebrate coaching exploits are 'Salt' (A.S. Allison), 'The Braidwood Coach' (Guy Eden), and 'The Coachman's Yarn' and 'The Western Road' (both by E.J. Brady). Will Lawson's novel *When Cobb & Co. Was King* (1936) deals with the adventures of a youth who became a coach-driver in the 1860s. In *Robbery Under Arms* (1888) 'Rolf Boldrewood' expresses the impact of Cobb & Co. with the comment 'the Yankee came and showed us what cross-country coaching was'. Australian artists Tom Roberts and Lionel Lindsay have immortalised Cobb & Co. in their work, Roberts with his famous oil painting *Bailed Up*, and Lindsay with an etching of a Cobb & Co. coach which was used on the Cobb & Co. commemorative stamp issued in 1955. The Cobb & Co. history and legend

have inspired such works as William Lees's *A History of the Coaching Firm of Cobb & Co.* (1917), E.J. Aisbett's *Men of Cobb & Co.* (1940), N. Rutherford's *A Brief Account of Cobb & Co.* (1963), Joan E.L. Rutherford's *Cobb & Co.* (1971), Margaret Jean Jennings's *Cobb & Co.* (1972) and K.A. Austin's *The Lights of Cobb & Co.* (1967, republished in 1977 as *A Pictorial History of Cobb & Co.*).

COBB, Chester (1899–1943), born and educated in Sydney, was a journalist until he came into an inheritance in 1921 and left for England. He published two novels, *Mr Moffatt* (1925) and *Days of Disillusion* (1926), in both of which he drew on his Australian experiences. He is significant as the first Australian-born novelist to employ the 'stream of consciousness' technique in his work.

COBLEY, John (1914–89) was the author of a series of books relating to the First Fleet and the first twelve years of White settlement in Sydney. They included *Sydney Cove 1788* (1962, a de luxe edition in 1987 illustrated by paintings of the early settlers), *Sydney Cove 1789–90* (1963), *The Convicts 1788–1792* (1964), *Sydney Cove 1791–92* (1965), *The Crimes of the First Fleet Convicts* (1970), *Sydney Cove 1793–1795* (1983), *Sydney Cove 1795–1800* (1986), and *The Crimes of the Lady Juliana convicts, 1790* (1989). The *Sydney Cove* series aimed to chronicle events up to publication in 1803 of the first Australian newspaper, the *Sydney Gazette*.

COCHRANE, George Henry, see 'HERVEY, Grant'

'Cockatoo' is a word of Malay origin for a crested parrot, of which there are several varieties distinctive to Australia; but the word has two additional Australian usages and once had a third, meaning a convict from Cockatoo Island in Sydney Harbour, which is now obsolete. A cockatoo, first, is a sentinel keeping watch for people engaged in an unlawful activity, e.g. convicts in road gangs in the nineteenth century who wanted to sleep rather than work, and two-up players in the twentieth century seeking to avoid the police; the usage derives from the long-held belief that feeding cockatoos post a sentry to warn of approaching danger. The second meaning of cockatoo, a small farmer, emerged around 1850, was pejorative in the nineteenth century and probably derived from the small farmer's practice, particularly after the Selection (q.v.) Acts, of settling or perching on parts of a squatter's run. Other suggested derivations relate to the 'scratching' of the land by selectors, their departure to a new district after a few years, their (enforced) thrift and their meagre harvests because of the ravages of the cockatoos themselves. A number of compounds have developed from cockatoo (which has also been used as a verb) or from the diminutive 'cocky' (commonly used from the 1880s): 'stringybark cockatoo' (the poorest small farmer of all, whose soil was so thin it could only nourish the stringybark gum tree), 'cockatoo fence' and 'cockatoo gate' (both improvised from rough materials), 'cocky's friend' and 'cocky's string' (fencing wire), 'cocky's joy' (golden syrup, a popular Australian treacle), 'boss cocky' (someone usually assertive and enjoying the exercise of authority), and 'cow cocky' or 'spud cocky' (referring to the main source of income). There is some evidence that 'cocky' is undergoing elevation, e.g. in the fact that the word is now often used to mean any kind of farmer, not necessarily one with a small holding. *Vanishing Vistas* (1984) by Dougal Ramsay is an illustrated salute to the now virtually extinct species. There are numerous folk-songs and ballads about the trials of the cocky (e.g. the anonymous 'The Stringybark Cockatoo', 'Cockies of Bungaree' and 'The New England Cocky'), but the most extensive treatment in Australian literature is in 'Steele Rudd's' famous series *On Our Selection* (q.v.).

COCKERILL, George (1871–1943), born Bendigo, Victoria, spent a lifetime in journalism culminating in his editorship of the Sydney *Daily Telegraph* 1926–28. His memoirs were published in 1944 as *Scribblers and Statesmen*. He also wrote fiction: *Down and Out: A Story of Australia's Early History* (1912), *The Convict Pugilist* (1912) and *In Days of Gold* (1926).

COEN, Margaret, see **STEWART, Douglas**

COLBEE (Colebee), an Aborigine captured with Bennelong as part of Captain Arthur Phillip's plan to win the confidence of the Aborigines, escaped from captivity within a week but became a well-known identity around the First Fleet settlement. An account of his activities is in Watkin Tench's *A Complete Account of the Settlement at Port Jackson* (1793) and he appears as a character in Eleanor Dark's *The Timeless Land* (1941).

COLE, E.W. (Edward William) (1832–1918), the most amazing bookseller in the history of Australian publishing, was born in Kent, England, and arrived as a gold-rush immigrant to Australia in 1852. He sold lemonade and speculated in land on the goldfields, rowed down the Murray River taking photographs and ran a pie-stall in Melbourne before the refusal of publishers to handle the manuscript of his *The Real Place in History of Jesus and Paul* (1865) led him to open his own bookshop in the Eastern Market, Melbourne, in 1865. The business flourished and in 1873 he opened the first Cole's Book Arcade; in 1883 it found a permanent base in Bourke Street, where it eventually ran through to Little Collins Street. Cole's Book Arcade was as much bazaar as bookshop, with a huge rainbow over the door and such features inside as funny mirrors, slot machines, live monkeys, talking birds and brightly dressed staff; the public was encouraged to browse as long as they liked without being pressed to buy. The arcade was phenomenally successful, allowing Cole to establish more orthodox branches interstate and to publish pamphlets on public questions and miscellanies such as *Cole's Funny Picture Book* (1879–), *Cole's Fun Doctor* (1886), and *Cole's Intellect Sharpener* (?1890); the miscellanies sold widely, the *Funny Picture Book* achieving more than a million

sales to 1984. A prominent Book Arcade employee was 'Furnley Maurice' (q.v.), who rose from messenger boy to manager before the business, which needed Cole's entrepreneurial ingenuity and goodwill, was wound up in 1929. Cole Turnley's affectionate pictorial biography, *Cole of the Book Arcade*, was published in 1974. Cole also published C.J. Dennis's first book of verse, *Backblock Ballads*, in 1913.

COLE, Tom (1906–), born England, came to Australia at the age of 17 and worked in outback Queensland and the Northern Territory as a stockman, drover and horse-breaker before establishing a coffee plantation in New Guinea. A celebrated hunter of crocodiles and buffalo who has been described as 'a real life Crocodile Dundee', he drew on his experience in New Guinea for his short-story collection, *Spears and Smoke Signals* (1966). He has also published two autobiographies, *Hell West and Crooked* (1988) and *The Last Paradise* (1990); a collection of reminscences, *Crocodiles and Other Characters* (1992) and selections from his letters and diaries 1923–34, *Riding the Wildman Plains* (1992).

COLEBATCH, Hal (1948–), born Perth, WA, the son of Sir Hal Colebatch (1872–1953), a prominent WA newspaper proprietor and politician, has been a lawyer, journalist and editor. He has published several volumes of poetry, *Spectators on the Shore* (1975), *In Breaking Waves* (1979), *Coastal Knot* (1980), *Outer Charting* (1985), *The Earthquake Lands* (1990), and *The Stonehenge Syndrome* (1993). He has also written fiction, *Souvenir* (1981), and radio drama. As the titles of his volumes of poetry suggest, Colebatch has an abiding interest in the sea and is a keen yachtsman and a maritime historian. One of his notable poems is 'Crowhurst', the story of the lone yachtsman Donald Crowhurst, lost at sea in a round-the-world yacht race. In Colebatch's poetry the sea is a potent force, one against which man has to summon all his dexterity and courage in order to survive, yet a source too of a code of honour that enriches those who spend much of their time in contact with it. A firm traditionalist, Colebatch has a strong regard for long-established poetic values – clarity, coherence, classical forms and formal verse structures. His poetry examines the age-old questions of human need and experience, weighing those against existing and often sterile philosophical and political practices. Something of his traditional outlook is apparent in his study *Return of the Heroes: The Lord of the Rings, Star Wars and Contemporary Culture* (1990), where he deplores the collapse of traditional Western values in the uneasy 1960s and 1970s and the subsequent rise of nihilism and the cult of the anti-hero. For Colebatch the struggle between good and evil in Tolkien and 'Star Wars' is the path the world should follow, where the old values of courage, honour and chivalry oppose and defeat apathy, evil and tyranny. Colebatch's small novel *Souvenir* deals with a writers' workshop on the small Eden Island off the coast of WA. Set in the early 1970s, it is a mixture of light-hearted farce and more sinister events, with the writers mixed up with yachtsmen who have made the neglected island their own.

COLEBROOK, Joan, born Joan Heale, grew up in the 1920s on the Atherton Tableland of north Queensland, where her father was a pioneering dairy farmer. She attended the University of Queensland and worked as a freelance writer until she married and moved to London. In the last years of the Second World War she moved to the USA, where she has continued to live apart from periods of travel and some return visits to Australia. She has written articles for the *New Yorker*, *Commentary* and the *New Republic* and three novels, *All That Seemed Final* (1941), *The Northerner* (1948), which centres on the life of a pioneering family in north Queensland of the 1920s, and *The Cross of Latitude* (1968); extracts from a travel journal kept from 1964–69 and originally published in *Commentary*, which deal with the threat posed by communism to democratic societies, *Innocents of the West* (1979); and an account of her childhood and youth in Australia, *A House of Trees* (1987). An extremely vivid re-creation of the natural landscape of the tropical north in the 1920s and 1930s, *A House of Trees* is a frank account of the difficulties and joys of Colebrook's childhood, which is also sensitive to the contradictions inherent in her family's observance of English, middle-class conventions and attitudes in an isolated, exotic environment not too far removed from its violent past.

COLEMAN, Peter (1928–), born Melbourne, has combined careers in politics, public administration and literature. One-time leader of the parliamentary Liberal Party in NSW, he was federal member for Wentworth until 1986. He was editor of the *Bulletin* 1964–67 and has been co-editor of *Quadrant* since 1967. With Lee Shrubb and Vivian Smith he edited *Quadrant: Twenty Five Years* (1982). His publications include *Obscenity, Blasphemy, Sedition: Censorship in Australia* (1962); *Cartoons of Australian History* (1967, compiled with Les Tanner); *The Heart of James McAuley* (1980); *The Real Barry Humphries* (1990); and a political history, *The Liberal Conspiracy: the Congress for Cultural Freedom and the Struggle for the Mind of Post-War Europe* (1989), which has been widely reviewed overseas. He also edited the collection of essays *Australian Civilization* (1962).

COLLIER, James (1846–1925), born Dunfermline, Scotland, became a leader-writer and reviewer for the *Scotsman* and spent a decade working with Herbert Spencer on his sociological works. He came to Australia in 1895 from NZ, where he was parliamentary librarian at Wellington (1885–95) and where he compiled the bibliography *The Literature Relating to New Zealand* (1890). In Australia he published widely in journals on sociological and colonisation subjects but his main works were *Sir George Grey* (1909) and *The Pastoral Age in Australasia* (1911); the latter discusses some of the books written on bush life.

COLLINGRIDGE, George (1847–1931), born Oxfordshire, England, and educated in France in architecture, painting and wood engraving, came to Australia in 1879 to join the *Illustrated Sydney News* and later the *Australian Town and Country Journal* and the *Sydney Mail*. With his brother Arthur (1853–1907) he launched the short-lived *Australian Art* in 1888, the first such journal in Australia. His chief passion was the history of maritime discovery involving Australia; his major work was *The Discovery of Australia* (1895, revised 1906 as *The First Discovery of Australia and New Guinea*) based on the so-called Dieppe maps, in which he espoused the Portuguese claim to have charted most of Australia by 1530. Among his other published works are children's books, *Alice in One Dear Land* (1922) and *Through the Joke in Class* (1923), and travel reminiscences, *Round and Round the World* (1925–27) and *Pacifika, the Antediluvian World* (1928–30), which places the lost civilisation of Atlantis in the Pacific.

COLLINS, Dale (1897–1956), born Balmain, Sydney, became a reporter with the Melbourne *Herald* and contributed stories to *Table Talk* and the *Bulletin*. In 1922 he accompanied American millionaire A.Y. Gowen on a world tour in his yacht *Speejacks*, an experience that provided Collins with the material for his travel book *Sea-Tracks of the Speejacks Round the World* (1923) and the novel *Ordeal* (1924), which became a best-seller and later a film, *The Ship from Shanghai*. In the period 1923–48 Collins lived in England but travelled widely gathering material for the many romantic novels about shipboard life and Oceanian places, including Australia, that appeared under his own name or under his pseudonyms, 'Michael Copeland' and 'Stephen Fennimore'; the latter was also used in his books for children. He returned to Australia to live in 1948. In addition to *Ordeal*, his novels included *The Haven* (1925), *The Sentimentalists* (1927), *Vanity under the Sun* (1928), *Idolaters* (1929), *Rich and Strange* (1930), *Jungle Maid* (1932), *Lost* (1933), *Vulnerable* (1933) and *The Mutiny of Madam Yes* (1935). *Race the Sun* (1936) is set in the new medium of air travel while *The Fifth Victim* (1930) is, like his first novel *Stolen or Strayed* (1922), a crime novel. *Bright Vista* (1946) and *Victoria's My Home Ground* (1951) are autobiographically based.

COLLINS, David (1756–1810), born London, joined the Marine Corps at 14. After an active service life in which he participated in the War of American Independence, he was retired in 1783 but accepted appointment in 1786 as deputy judge-advocate of the impending expedition to Botany Bay. On his arrival with the First Fleet, Collins became responsible to the governor for the Colony's entire legal establishment; in June 1788 he was also made secretary to the governor. So keen was his sense of duty to the new colony that it was not until 1797 that he returned to England. Because of his exceptional knowledge of colonial affairs he was appointed lieutenant-governor of the proposed new settlement to be established at Port Phillip. Unimpressed by the prospects in that area, which he reached in October 1803, he transferred his expedition to Van Diemen's Land, where he established Hobart Town. An account of that settlement is given in Marjorie Tipping's *Convicts Unbound* (1988). After six frustrating years of trying to make the settlement flourish in the face of appalling local conditions and neglect from the Colonial Office in London, he died in Hobart.

Collins's *An Account of the English Colony in New South Wales* (1798, 1802) was the most complete and optimistic account of the settlement to emerge in its first decade. Although he had indicated in his private correspondence that he saw the Colony as 'a Place of Banishment for the Outcasts of Society', he claimed that the object of his long and detailed *Account* was to dissuade Englishmen from viewing the Colony with 'odium and disgust'. He revealed a humanitarian interest in the Aborigines, blaming the convicts rather than the natives for the violent racial clashes that occurred in the early months of the settlement. C.R. Collins wrote *Saga of Settlement: A Brief Account of the Life and Times of Lieutenant-Colonel David Collins* (1957). The house where Collins died forms part of the setting of William Hay's novel *The Escape of the Notorious Sir William Heans* (1919).

COLLINS, Liz (Vera Elizabeth) (1921–), a freelance travel-writer and critic for newspapers and magazines in Sydney, has published two novels as Betty Collins, *The Copper Crucible* (1966) and *The Second Step* (1972); her short stories have been published in Australia, England and Germany as well as in three collections in the former USSR.

'Collins, Tom' was, at the end of the nineteenth century, a slang term for a mythical bush rumour-monger. The expression was obviously known to Joseph Furphy (q.v.), who adopted 'Tom Collins' as his pseudonym from 1892 and also made Collins an important character in *Such is Life* (1903), *Rigby's Romance* (1946), and *The Buln-Buln and the Brolga* (1948, qq.v.). By coincidence the term 'Tom Collins' was replaced by 'furphy' (q.v.), not because of Joseph Furphy's adoption of the pseudonym but because his brother's water carts came to be known as 'furphies' and gossip was exchanged around them during the First World War.

COLLINSON, Laurence (1925–86), born Yorkshire, England, was brought to Australia in infancy and returned to England to live in 1964. He worked as a freelance writer for radio, newspapers and magazines; as a secondary teacher; and as actor, director and writer for Australian little theatres. He published four collections of verse, *Poet's Dozen* (1953), *The Moods of Love* (1957), *Who is Wheeling Grandma?* (1967) and *Hovering Narcissus* (1977); a novel, *Cupid's Crescent* (1973); three plays, *Friday Night at the Schrammers* in *Australian One-Act Plays Book Two*, ed. Greg Branson (1962), *A Slice of Birthday Cake* in *Eight Short Plays* (1965) and *Thinking Straight* in *Homosexual Acts* (1975); and a children's book (1968). Of his numerous unpublished plays for stage, radio and television the best known in Australia is the stage play 'The Selda Trio',

produced in Melbourne in 1961 and London in 1974. Collinson also contributed to the poetry collection *Eight by Eight* (1963) and was one of the editors of the magazine *Barjai*.

Although Collinson, a Marxist, was criticised on publication of *The Moods of Love* for his treatment of social and political issues, he was always more concerned with love and its disappointments, and with what he termed 'the self-destruction that pervades our personal and social lives', than with political themes. His interest in the formal aspects of poetry is especially reflected in his later verse, which is compressed and tightly structured. The same concern with love, the limitations of conventional morality and the 'admass' culture can be found in his plays.

'Colonial' is a word which in Australia refers to the period between 1788, when the first British colony, NSW, was established, and 1901, when NSW and the other five colonies were federated to form the Commonwealth of Australia; thus a 'colonial' was an inhabitant of one of those colonies (particularly one whose allegiance was to the colony rather than Britain), and 'colonial architecture' is the architecture of the period. Compounds derived from 'colonial' include 'colonial goose (duck)', a boned and stuffed shoulder or leg of mutton, from the prevalence of mutton in the colonial period; 'my colonial oath', where 'colonial' is a euphemism for 'bloody', the Great Australian Adjective; and 'colonial experience(r)' (q.v.).

'Colonial Experiencer' was a phrase particularly used in the nineteenth century to describe a young, well-connected Englishman sent out to gain work experience in Australia. Enough colonial experiencers proved themselves new chums (q.v.) for the terms to be almost synonymous. The new chum's colonial experience is an important feature of nineteenth-century Australian drama, as in W.M. Akhurst's 'Colonial Experience' (1854) and Walter Cooper's *Colonial Experience* (1979, first performed 1868).

Colonial Literary Journal and Weekly Miscellany of Useful Information, edited by James Reading and Francis Sandoe, appeared weekly in Sydney 1844–45. One of the earliest magazines to use illustrations, it included poetry, short stories, sketches and literary reviews and notices. Among its contributors were Charles Harpur and Daniel Deniehy.

Colonial Monthly, successor to the *Australian Monthly Magazine*, was published 1867–70. For its first year it was edited by Marcus Clarke, and published in serialised form his novel *Long Odds* (two monthly instalments of which were written by G.A. Walstab), 1868–69. Three significant critical articles on Australian literature (a general account of the relationships between literature and national character, and separate analyses of Henry Kendall and Charles Harpur) appeared in the issues December 1868 to February 1869. Contributors included David Blair, J.E. Neild, Adam

Lindsay Gordon, R.H. Horne, Henry Kendall, James Smith and Julian Tenison-Woods.

Colonial Reformer, A (1896), a novel by 'Rolf Boldrewood' (q.v.), was first published as a serial in the *Australian Town and Country Journal*, 1876–77. It chronicles the experience in Australia of the Buckinghamshire gentleman new chum (q.v.) Ernest Neuchamp, who is guided to success by a banker, Paul Frankston, and a squatter, Abstinens Levison, whom 'Boldrewood' modelled on James Tyson. Another character in the novel, the Reverend Herbert Heatherstone, is based on Cuthbert Fetherstonhaugh (q.v.).

Colonial Texts Series. Under the general editorship of Professor Harry Heseltine, the English Department of University College, the Australian Defence Force Academy (ADFA), through the University of New South Wales Press publishes a series (the Colonial Texts Series) of critical editions of little-known and otherwise inaccessible works of nineteenth-century Australian fiction. The published volumes include Ada Cambridge's *A Woman's Friendship* by Elizabeth Morrison (this novel had previously only appeared in serial form), Mary Theresa Vidal's *Bengala: Or Some Time Ago* by Susan McKernan (now Lever), and N. Walter Swan's *Luke Mivers' Harvest* by Harry Heseltine.

Colonial Times and Tasmanian Advertiser was a journal that grew out of the battle for the freedom of the press in Tasmania, which was centred on the disputes between Andrew Bent and the lieutenant-governor of Van Diemen's Land, George Arthur (qq.v.). Incensed by criticism of his administration in Bent's *Hobart Town Gazette* in 1824–25, Arthur pirated Bent's title for his own newspaper, so that from June until August 1825 there were two *Hobart Town Gazettes* published in Hobart. Bent then changed the title of his journal to the *Colonial Times and Tasmanian Advertiser*, which he ran until 1830, although publication was briefly suspended after Bent was refused a licence under Arthur's new press legislation in 1827. In 1829 the *Colonial Times* serialised *The Hermit in Van Diemen's Land*, for which Bent was prosecuted for libel. The following year he sold the newspaper to Henry Melville; other prominent journalists associated with the proprietorship or editorship of the paper were John Macdougall, R.L. Murray, Thomas Richards and Henry Savery. The *Colonial Times* incorporated the *Tasmanian and Austral-Asiatic Review* (see *Tasmanian*) in 1845 and was itself incorporated into the *Mercury* in 1857.

Colonist, a Sydney weekly journal with some literary content, was published 1835–40; a regular contributor was John Dunmore Lang. A more general Launceston journal also named the *Colonist*, subtitled *A Weekly Journal for Town and Country*, ran 1888–91.

Come In Spinner, a novel by Dymphna Cusack and Florence James (qq.v.), was published in 1951, having won the *Daily Telegraph* novel competition in 1948.

The 1951 edition, published by Heinemann, is an abridged one after massive cuts were demanded by the *Daily Telegraph* which eventually resiled from its original commitment to publish the novel. In 1988 the complete edition of *Come In Spinner*, reworked by Florence James from the original manuscript, was published. Set in Sydney during the Second World War, the novel gives a vivid picture of the impact of American forces on the city and traces the fortunes of a group of girls, most of whom work in the beauty salon of the Hotel South-Pacific. They include Deborah Forrest, a masseuse whose husband Jack is with the Australian forces in New Guinea, and whose daughter Luen lives with Deborah's motherly sister Nolly. For Deborah the war has presented new opportunities in the form of remarriage with the wealthy but considerably older Angus McFarland. Resentful of Jack's decision to resume their life of poverty in the country after the war and of his assumption that she will automatically follow where he leads, she eventually accepts Angus. Claire, the manager of the salon, has a long-standing relationship with a weak but good-looking Englishman, Nigel, and looks forward to the time when they will have saved enough to marry. When Nigel loses their savings by gambling, she considers ending their relationship, but soon realises that he is necessary to her happiness. The most lively, self-sufficient girl of the group, Guinea Malone, breezily circumvents all sexist and class barriers although her deep feeling for her first love, Kim, is at first frustrated by his immature chauvinism. Guinea eventually gains love on her terms and Nolly appears to have found fulfilment in her large family. Dallas MacIntyre, a surgeon whose professional life has flourished in the absence of men, is another who finds life satisfying. But others succumb to the emotional and physical dangers of wartime Sydney; they include Guinea's younger sister Monnie, who is trapped into a brief life in a brothel, and Mary Parker, who is in the Australian Women's Army Service and is the mistress of an American soldier and dies as the result of an abortion. The more conventional losses of war are reflected in the life of Val, whose husband is posted as missing shortly after their marriage. Contrasting with these destinies are the aimless, exploitative existences of several wealthy women, such as Mrs D'Arcy-Twyning and her obnoxious daughter Denise, and the overweight society matron, Mrs Dalgety. *Come In Spinner* was produced as a mini-series by ABC television in 1989.

Comic Australian Verse (1972, retitled *The Flight of the Emu: Contemporary Light Verse*, 1990), edited by Geoffrey Lehmann, begins with an anonymous epitaph on a headstone at St Matthew's cemetery, Windsor, NSW, and concludes with three poems by Bruce Dawe. Lehmann notes the importance of humorous verse as a literary form in the nineteenth century and its relative demise in modern times. The *Bulletin* is the chief source of his nineteenth-century selections; A.B. Paterson, W.T. Goodge and Joseph Tishler ('Bellerive') are his chief representatives from the early twentieth century; later poets represented are A.D. Hope,

Douglas Stewart, Kenneth Slessor, Ronald McCuaig and Bruce Dawe.

Comment, A, a magazine devoted to experimental writing, was published irregularly in Melbourne 1940–47. Australian contributors included Max Harris, Alister Kershaw, Muir Holburn and Arthur Ashworth; the work of prominent overseas avant-garde writers, e.g. Harry Roskolenko and Karl Shapiro, was also featured.

Commonwealth: An Annual of Australian Art & Literature, The was published 1901–2 by A.C. Rowlandson. George Essex Evans's acrostic poem 'The Commonwealth' was used on the opening page of the first edition. The magazine made a brief reappearance in 1907–8 as *Rowlandson's Success.*

Commonwealth Literary Fund, the first systematic federal government initiative in support of the arts, was established by the Alfred Deakin government in 1908; its model was the Royal Literary Fund (UK) and its original allocation was £500. For its first thirty years the CLF, as it came to be known, was administered by a central committee comprising representatives from NSW, SA and Victoria with advisers in the other States, and awarded pensions to sick and distressed authors and their families, the families of authors who had died poor, and literary men doing good work but 'unable on account of poverty to persist in that work'. In 1939, after agitation by the former prime minister, J.H Scullin, and by the FAW, the budget of the fund, then £1500, was trebled and this enabled the fund eventually to embrace four additional activities: the award of annual fellowships and other grants to writers; assistance to publishers through a guarantee against loss on Australian literary works approved by the fund; assistance to literary journals such as *Meanjin*, *Southerly*, *Overland* and *Quadrant*; and the promotion of Australian literature, notably through annual lectures in the universities (1940–64) and lectures in regional centres. The broadening in scope of the CLF was accompanied by a change in administrative structure: the central committee was replaced by a parliamentary committee comprising initially the prime minister, R.G. Menzies, the leader of the Opposition, John Curtin, and Scullin, and eventually a representative of the three major political parties in the federal parliament; and by an advisory board which included writers, academics and, later, publishing interests. Sir Langdon Bonython, Sir Mungo MacCallum (q.v.), Sir A. Grenfell Price, Vance Palmer, T. Inglis Moore, Douglas Stewart and Geoffrey Blainey had significant terms in the administration of the CLF, which had increased its budget to $300 000 by the time its functions were taken over by the Literature Board (q.v.) in 1973. In its first thirty years the CLF could do little more than ameliorate the lot of writers and their dependants who had fallen on hard times; in its second phase it played a significant part in the development of Australian literature through its scheme of fellowships and through its publishing and promotional activities. A brief history of the CLF by Grenfell Price, *Helping Literature in Australia*, was published in 1967.

Commonwealth Poetry Prize, an annual award, is administered jointly by the Commonwealth Institute and the National Book League. It is awarded for a first published book of poetry in English from a country other than the United Kingdom. Australian winners of the prize, first awarded in 1972, included Phillip Salom (1981), Peter Goldsworthy (1982) and Julian Croft (1985).

Commonwealth Writers Prize was established in 1987 to encourage literary writing and publishing in English from all the Commonwealth countries. While not of great significance in Australia where a widespread system of grants and prizes exists to encourage writers, the Commonwealth Writers Prize is important in the less developed countries in fostering local talent. The prizes are sponsored by the Commonwealth Foundation which is based in London but the administration of the Prizes moves from region to region on a two-yearly basis, e.g. the University of Wollongong administered the awards in 1989–90, Canada in 1991–92 and Singapore 1993–94. Prizes are awarded in several regions, Australia competing in the South East Asia and South Pacific region. Australian winners include Robert Drewe, Thea Walsh, Andrew McGahan and Alex Miller, the latter's novel *The Ancestor Game* winning the overall Best Book Award in 1993.

Communist Review (1934–66), the main policy organ of the Communist Party of Australia and an important record of the shifts in debate on the relationship between party politics and literature, attracted articles and creative work from numerous writers of the Left. They included Katharine Susannah Prichard, George Farwell, Alan Marshall, Betty Roland, John Morrison, Nettie Palmer, Frank Hardy, Jack Beasley, Jean Devanny, Miles Franklin and Judah Waten. Banned in May 1940, the magazine continued to appear irregularly, recommencing continuous publication in 1942.

Community Arts Board, one of the seven arts boards of the Australia Council (q.v.), was established in 1977; before that community arts came within the ambit of the Council's own programmes. The Board's annual allocation was distributed in support of multi-arts programmes (including literature), implemented by community arts organisations; in 1978–83 its largest grant went to the Arts Council of Australia (q.v.) but it also supported organisations and individuals catering for the needs of regional, ethnic, suburban and disadvantaged communities. The Community Arts Board has been replaced by the Community Cultural Development Committee (q.v.).

Community Cultural Development Committee (CCDC), one of the two major Committees of the Australia Council (q.v.), replaced the Community Arts Board, established in 1977 as one of the seven arts boards of the Council. The CCDC aims to encourage and assist communities from different cultures and backgrounds to help shape Australia's cultural identity and assists communities to obtain the resources they need to develop their own culture. The CCDC works with local government, trade unions and migrant organisations to further its objectives.

Compass, the journal of the Melbourne University literature club, was published irregularly 1956–63. Originally intended as a workshop journal publishing experimental undergraduate creative writing, *Compass* included among its early contributors now-established figures such as Chris Wallace-Crabbe and Bruce Dawe. Among its editors have been the poets Wallace-Crabbe, Clive Faust and Andrew Taylor.

Compliqués, Les, a club for literati and intellectuals, originated in Sydney during the First World War. It met for lunch and French conversation at Paris House in Phillip Street, a well-known Sydney restaurant of the day. A notable member of the group was Christopher Brennan.

COMPTON, Jennifer (1949–), born NZ, came to Australia in 1973. Her play *Crossfire*, also produced as 'No Man's Land' (1976), shared first place with John Romeril's *The Floating World* in a 1974 Newcastle play-writing competition and was first produced in 1975. Her other plays include *They're Playing Our Song*, first produced in 1975 and included in the collection *Can't You Hear Me Talking to You?* (1978) ed. Alrene Sykes, and *Julia's Song*, published in *Australasian Drama Studies* (1992). She has also written radio plays, poetry and short stories and has won several awards for her work for radio.

Concrete Poetry conceives of the poem as ideogram, as an instantly assimilable, visually ordered text in which the word stands both as physical spatial object and as a plurality of simultaneous meanings. Said to have originated with the publication of *Konstellationen* in 1953 by the Bolivian-born Swiss poet Eugen Gomringer, concrete poetry was evident in Australia in the 1960s (e.g. Dennis Douglas's *Relating*, 1968) but became more widespread in the 1970s through the growth of the little magazines. The all-concrete magazine *Born to Concrete* evolved in 1975 from *Fitzrete,* which was an all-concrete issue of *Fitzrot* (1975–77), which itself had developed as an outlet for concrete poetry under the leadership of Peter Oustabasidis ('ΠΟ', q.v.). Other modernist magazines and journals, e.g. *Dharma, Magic Sam, New Poetry, The Saturday Club Book of Poetry, SCOPP* and *Your Friendly Fascist*, have published concrete poetry. Australian poets, e.g. Oustabasidis, Peter Murphy, Garrie Hutchinson, B.A. Breen, Alex Selenitsch and Peter Taylor, have published concrete poetry volumes or sections of volumes. The first issue of *Mixed Concrete Poetry* appeared in 1993.

Condamine River, discovered by Allan Cunningham in 1827 and named after T. de la Condamine,

aide-de-camp to Governor Darling, flows through south-eastern Queensland. It is linked in the traditional song 'The Banks of the Condamine' (q.v.) with male-oriented, outback life. Cattle- and horse-bells made at the township of Condamine were hung around the necks of stock; the expression 'to lay the Condamine on' thus meant to put the bell on stock inclined to wander. Mary Gilmore, in *The Tilted Cart* (1925), indicated that it was a cruel practice, for the note of the Condamine bell was so penetrating that it often made the animal deaf. The drover-poet Jack Sorenson wrote a poem 'Condamine Bells'; the bells are also mentioned in Vance Palmer's *Men Are Human* (1930). John Joseph Jones compiled *'Condamine Bells': Songs and Stories of the Australian Outback* (1961). K. Emmerson wrote *A History of the Condamine 1856–1963* (1963).

CONDER, Charles (1868–1909), born London, came to Australia in 1883. In 1885 he obtained a position on the *Illustrated Sydney News*. In 1888 with Tom Roberts, Frederick McCubbin and Arthur Streeton, Conder formed the well-known Heidelberg School (q.v.) of Australian painting. Biographical works on Conder include Frank Gibson's *Charles Conder* (1914), J.K.M. Rothenstein's *Life and Death of Conder* (1938), Ursula Hoff's *Charles Conder* (1972), and *Charles Conder* (1989) by Sarah Wheatley. Charles Brydon, the painter in Kathleen Caffyn's novel *A Yellow Aster* (1894), is based on Conder.

Condolences of the Season (1971), the first selected volume of Bruce Dawe's (q.v.) poetry, was chosen by the author from the four earlier volumes, *No Fixed Address* (1962), *A Need of Similar Name* (1965), *An Eye for a Tooth* (1968) and *Beyond the Subdivisions* (1969); it also contains nineteen new poems. An extraordinarily popular collection, *Condolences of the Season* was reprinted annually 1971–80, except in 1974. It contains many of Dawe's best-known poems: 'Public Library, Melbourne', 'Enter Without So Much as Knocking', 'Happiness Is the Art of Being Broken', 'Any Shorter and I'd Have Missed It Altogether', 'The Not-so-good Earth', 'Life-Cycle', 'A Victorian Hangman Tells His Love', 'Homecoming', 'Homo Suburbiensis' and 'Weapons Training'.

CONDON, Matthew (1962–), educated at the University of Queensland and the Goethe Institute, Bremen, is a reporter for the *Sun-Herald*, having previously worked for the Brisbane *Courier-Mail* and the *Gold Coast Bulletin*. He has published two novels, *The Motorcycle Café* (1988) and *Usher* (1991). Set in Brisbane from the 1920s to the 1980s, *The Motorcycle Café* is a collection of reminiscences of a dead man, George Baker, brought together by his grandson, who also discovers his notebook; recovering the various sides of his grandfather, who was a motorcycle fanatic, photographer, poet, husband, father, mate and platonic lover, is also a discovery of self for the grandson. *Usher*, also set mainly in the Brisbane area, charts the rise and fall of T. Nelson Downs, a would-be entrepreneur and owner-usher of an ancient cinema on the Gold Coast, who overreaches himself in the world of commerce and corruption. The novel opens with his suicide, an event his son attempts to understand, reinterpreting his father's career and its connection with a changing Queensland as he travels America. A story of a father–son relationship, the novel is also an inventive, humorous satire on Queensland under the premiership of Jo Bjelke-Petersen.

Conference-ville, a novella by Frank Moorhouse (q.v.), was published in 1976. A work which reflects Moorhouse's interest in the social dynamics of the conference, *Conference-ville* explores the Australian intellectual subculture as it chronicles the personal and group experiences of the narrator (characteristically self-doubting yet self-aware) when he attends and presents a paper on the mass media at a conference early in 1976. Among the other participants are James McAuley, Frank Hardy and Stephen Murray-Smith.

Congewoi Correspondence, The (1874) purports to be the letters of a Hawkesbury farmer, John Smith, 'edited' by Charles de Boos (q.v.); in fact Smith was a character created in the Sydney press by de Boos in 1862. *The Congewoi Correspondence* comprises three series of letters, the first two satirising members of the NSW parliament in office in 1862 and 1870, and the last consisting of Smith's impressions of the Duke of Edinburgh's visit to Sydney in 1868. The letters were originally published in the *Sydney Mail* and the *Sydney Morning Herald.* The humour of the volume derives from Smith's uneducated dialect and comic misspellings, which have been seen as an early form of 'Strine' (q.v.). Possible models for Smith are Sam Slick, a Nova Scotian character created in 1835 by the Canadian writer T.C. Haliburton, and the 1860s American frontier humorist-philosopher 'Artemus Ward' (C.F. Browne).

CONIGRAVE, Sarah (1841–1940), born England, the daughter of Charles Price a well-known SA pioneer, came to Australia in 1853. The family settled on Hindmarsh Island, encountering numerous hardships in the early years. Sarah Conigrave's autobiography, first published in 1916 titled *Reminiscences of the Early Days. Personal Incidents on a Sheep and Cattle Run in South Australia*, is a lively, humorous account of their difficulties which also gives an insight into the life of large families of the period. One of the attractions of the account is the revelation of the author's unconventional, confident personality and her passion for the landscape of her youth.

CONNELL, Robert William (1944–), born Sydney, is professor of sociology at Macquarie University and has written several books on Australian culture, class attitudes and gender relations. They include *Ruling Class, Ruling Culture* (1977), *Class Structure in Australian History* (1980, with T.M. Irving), *Making the Difference* (1982, with others), *Which Way is Up?* (1983), and *Gender and Power* (1987); with G.M. Dowsett he edited *Rethinking Sex* (1992).

CONNOLLY, Roy (1893–1966), a journalist, born Queensland, wrote an important pastoral novel, *Southern Saga* (1940). It traces the history of station life in the 1850s in the Burnett district of Queensland, and portrays the difficulty that a city-bred girl of fashion has in adapting to the harsh, unglamorous outback life. As it works towards a conventional happy ending, *Southern Saga* gives a full account of the activities and vicissitudes of pioneer pastoral life.

CONRAD, Joseph (1857–1924), the Polish-born English novelist, made several brief visits to Australia (1879, 1880, 1887 and 1892). In *Mirror of the Sea* (1906) he records his impressions of Sydney – its people, pleasures, personalities and especially its harbour ('one of the finest, most beautiful, vast and safe bays the sun ever shone upon'). Scattered throughout his novels and in his short story 'Because of the Dollars' are Australian references, usually expressing his 'affection for that young continent'. From his third voyage to Australia (1887) came the experiences which gave rise to the story *The Shadow Line* (1917) and which are echoed in 'The Secret Sharer' (1910) and 'The Planter of Malata' (1914). David Allen has written a play, 'Joseph Conrad goes Ashore'.

CONRAD, Peter (1948–), born Tasmania and educated there and at Oxford University, where he lectures, has written numerous works of literary and musical criticism including the *Everyman History of English Literature* (1985). His autobiographical writings are *Down Home: Revisiting Tasmania* (1988) and *Where I Fell to Earth: A Life in Four Places* (1990), those four places being (after Tasmania) Oxford, London, New York and Lisbon. He has also written a novel, *Underworld* (1992).

Conrad's *Down Home* has been described as one of the best non-fiction works ever written about Tasmania, defining what C.J. Koch has described as 'The Tasmanian Problem'. Some reviewers, however, have resisted the book's negative representation of the island. Perceiving his birthplace as fundamentally 'funereal', a place of ghost towns and graveyards, Conrad claims to have been aware of living on the edge of the earth; paradoxically the sense of displacement and existential anguish was made more not less acute by the island's imitation of things English and by the 1950s ideology of Empire. In his situation of physical and psychological windswept desolation, English literature provided a 'windbreak', allowing him to 'piece together' his own 'unassailable fort of paper'. *Where I Fell to Earth*, by contrast, celebrates the diversity and cultural life of his acquired homes, from the dreaming spires of Oxford to the street theatre of London and New York, to the uninhibited Latin life of Lisbon.

Contempa, a Melbourne illustrated magazine of poetry and prose, was published in two series. The first series of ten undated issues (1972–75) aimed 'to publish and encourage nascent writers, and where possible present them alongside more accomplished writers', and was edited by Phillip Edmonds and Robert Kenny. The second series (1978–) is also edited by

Edmonds, who has written fiction, *Scientists Discover* (1977) and *Big Boys* (1978). Contempa Publications, also founded in 1972 by Kenny, Edmonds and Michael Dugan, has published works by contemporary writers such as Dugan, Colin Talbot, B.A. Breen, Walter Billeter, John Jenkins and Ken Taylor.

Continuum, a journal of cultural studies based at Murdoch University (the Centre for Research in Culture and Communication), WA, funded by the Australian Film Commission replaced the *Australian Journal of Screen Theory* which wound up in 1985. Its first issue (1987) was *Australian Film in the 1950s*. Gradually the emphasis has broadened towards a journal of cultural studies with a particular interest in screen.

Conversations is a series of audio tape interviews of Australian literary figures by Suzanne Hayes of the Adelaide TAFE. They are (in order) Peter Carey, Christopher Koch, Frank Moorhouse, Michael Wilding, Ian Moffitt, Frank Wilmot, Barbara Hanrahan, Judith Rodriguez, Helen Garner, Elizabeth Jolley, Thomas Keneally, Morris West, Tim Winton, Peter Kenna, Betty Roland, David Holman, Stephen Sewell, Sumner Locke Elliott, David Campbell, Rosemary Dobson, Tom Shapcott, Rodney Hall, Shaun Gurton, Rodney Fisher, David Pownall, Graeme Murphy, Janet Vernon, John Garden, Jonathan Taylor, Tony Strachan, Nigel Triffit, Geoffrey Dutton, A.D. Hope, Bruce Dawe.

Convict in Australian Literature. Transportation (q.v.) of convicts to the Australian colonies began in 1787, when the First Fleet (q.v.) left England for NSW, and continued until 1868 when the *Hougoumont* arrived in WA, numbering among its convict passengers John Boyle O'Reilly (q.v.), first WA novelist. In the eighty-one years of transportation approximately 160 000 convicts were sent to Australia, 80 per cent after 1820. They dominated the demography of the colonial settlements for more than fifty years, and although it was clear well before the discovery of gold in 1851 that Australia had a future other than as a giant gaol, the convict experience was crucial in the development of the Australian consciousness and has been of major significance to historians and creative writers.

Transportation has also been of interest to writers overseas, which is not surprising given the British and Irish origins of the convicts, the decline in the eighteenth and nineteenth centuries of punishment as spectacle, and the corresponding rise of punishment through imprisonment; thus Marcus Clarke's *His Natural Life* (q.v., 1874), the most famous novel about the 'System', as it came to be called, is the product of a century which produced *Crime and Punishment*, *Little Dorrit* and *Les Misérables*. The famous lines

> True patriots all; for be it understood
> We left our country for our country's good

were written to amuse an English coterie by the journalist Henry Carter, who never set foot in Australia. Nor did Robert Southey, the author of 'Botany Bay Eclogues' (1794); 'William Thomas Moncrieff', the author of the play *Van Diemen's Land* (q.v., performed in London 1830); or Charles Dickens, who has convict characters in some of his novels. Southey's poem is significant both for the use of the 'Botany Bay' (q.v.) tag for NSW, and for the lamentation of the convict Elinor at her exile from England. The elegiac mood and the sense of exile are important ingredients in a street literature written for an English, Irish and Scottish audience throughout the transportation period; some of the songs, ballads, broadsides and later music-hall adaptations reached Australia to become part of local folk-song and ballad (q.v.). Other overseas writers who became interested in the Australian convicts include penal reformers such as Charles Reade (q.v.), investigators of the plight of the urban poor such as Henry Mayhew, and journalists seemingly interested only in the sensational potential of the transportation material, such as George Augustus Sala (q.v.). The willingness of Reade and Mayhew to include Australian material even though their main interest was in reforming English prisons or in exposing the condition of the London working class is complemented by such novels as *Ralph Rashleigh* (q.v., 1952) and *The Broad Arrow* (q.v., 1859), which for significant parts of their narratives are set in the streets of London or in the prisons and hulks preceding transportation. The voyage to the penal settlement produced a body of writing that establishes a link between convict literature and the voyager theme in Australian poetry and prose. There are voyage sections in most memoirs of convicts (who kept collective journals on some ships), and in many convict novels (e.g. *His Natural Life*). In addition, the voyage is the focus of reminiscences of officials employed aboard the ships (e.g. the surgeon Colin Arrott Browning, author of *The Convict Ship* (1844) and *England's Exiles* (1847)); several strongly worded complaints by convicts about their treatment by those officials (see Scottish Martyrs); and several novels and plays written after the cessation of transportation (e.g. William Gosse Hay's *Stifled Laughter*, 1901, Jill Shearer's play *Catherine*, 1977, Thomas Keneally's *Passenger*, 1979).

Despite the overseas interest in transportation, the Australian contribution to convict literature remains dominant; and given transportation as the major reason for the First Fleet settlement, all early Australian writing in a broad sense forms part of convict literature: the diaries, annals and journals kept by the officers of the NSW Corps; official documents such as the *New South Wales General Standing Orders* (q.v., 1802), the first Australian 'book'; the dispatches and enclosures forwarded by successive governors to the Colonial Office and included in the *Historical Records of New South Wales* and the *Historical Records of Australia* (qq.v.); and the early newspapers and other publications printed and edited by convicts and emancipists such as George Howe and Andrew Bent. Studded throughout this historical material, which was a source for later writers such as 'Price Warung' (q.v.), are references to some convicts (e.g. Michael Massey Robinson, Edward Geoghegan, Henry Savery and

James Tucker) who became known in Australian literature.

In the narrower sense, however, convict literature begins with the convict memoirs, which were sometimes 'ghosted' or invented (e.g. the publications associated with George Barrington, q.v.) and start to trickle from colonial and English presses after 1810. The end of transportation did not mean the end of these memoirs, for Mark Jeffrey's *A Burglar's Life* was published in 1893 and there have been recent publications (e.g. Thomas Cook's horrendous *The Exile's Lamentations*, 1978) in the historically conscious 1970s and 1980s. The memoirs usually conform to three sometimes overlapping formulae. The rogue's picaresque adventure is exemplified by the *Memoirs* of the sleazy entertainer James Hardy Vaux (q.v.), who is significant as probably the only convict thrice transported to Australia and whose autobiography, the first full-length one written in the Colony, includes a slang vocabulary which is an important source for the study of Australian English. The second and largest group of memoirs, but the least distinguished as literature, comprises the moral tales, sometimes mere pamphlets, of the child of respectable parents who is led astray by bad companions, suffers great physical hardship and emotional anguish during transportation, but returns to the native land to issue a suitable warning to recalcitrant youth. Third, there are the memoirs written by the political prisoners dispatched by an offended English government through its legal system to Australia from Scotland, Ireland, Wales and even England itself (e.g. the Scottish Martyrs, John Mitchel, John Frost, the Canadian Exiles, George Loveless, qq.v.). The political prisoners were largely literate, well-educated men and their memoirs are significant because of their disproportionate number – only about 1000 political prisoners were transported to Australia – and because they form part of other national literatures.

Whether for motives of sensation, instruction or protest, the memoirs characteristically assert the innocence or underplay the culpability of the writer, as well as accentuating his suffering in Australia. The guiltless, suffering convicts of the memoirs helped to establish the legend, which has much credence still, that the convicts were 'more sinn'd against than sinning'. Another influence on the development of this legend was the transportation songs and ballads, which reached Australia or were modified or composed here. Where the cause of transportation is stated, the most common offence is poaching (e.g. 'Jim Jones at Botany Bay') and even when the offenders are from the cities they have often been tricked into crime (e.g. 'The Black Velvet Band', q.v.). In Australia the dismal experiences of the convict are highlighted so that the songs become protest songs, lamentations of the downtrodden (e.g. 'Van Diemen's Land'), occasionally mixed with the threat of revolt (e.g. 'Jim Jones at Botany Bay' and 'Moreton Bay', q.v.). In fact there were not many acts of open rebellion by convicts in Australia, although Vinegar Hill (q.v.) has produced a literature and 'A Convict's Tour to Hell' (q.v.) stands as a form of literary revenge for all downtrodden convicts. The fact that 'Bold Jack

Donahoe' is one of the heroes of 'A Convict's Tour to Hell' and of 'Jim Jones at Botany Bay' confirms the link in much early Australian literature between the convict and the bushranger (see Bushranger in Australian Literature). For example, in the first Australian play performed overseas, David Burn's *The Bushrangers* (q.v., performed 1829, published 1971), Matthew Brady and his associates are designated 'Convicts and Bushrangers' and Burn bitterly attacks the penal administration of Governor Arthur (q.v.); Mark Brandon, the protagonist of Charles Rowcroft's *The Bushranger of Van Diemen's Land* (1843), is an escaped convict (like most early bushrangers); and *Ralph Rashleigh* has an important interlude in which Ralph is the unwilling member of a bushranging gang of escaped convicts. These works were all written before 1850, yet the links between convict and bushranging literature continued to be forged after the cessation of transportation, e.g. in Ned Kelly's reference to 'Moreton Bay' in the Jerilderie Letter.

Ralph Rashleigh, almost certainly written in 1845–50 by the convict James Tucker, is a text which links not only convict and bushranging literature but also convict fiction and the convict memoirs; indeed it was presented as a convict memoir when first published in abridged form in 1929. Two other major novels which are informed by their authors' experiences as convicts are Savery's *Quintus Servinton* (q.v., 1831) and O'Reilly's *Moondyne* (q.v., 1879). Although in structure each corresponds to a different memoir formula – *Ralph Rashleigh* to the picaresque, *Quintus Servinton* to the moral tale and *Moondyne* to the socio-political protest – they are alike in that each is a kind of 'literary wish fulfilment': *Ralph Rashleigh*, in that it projects a convict's attempt to come to terms with and free himself physically and spiritually of the effects of transportation; *Quintus Servinton*, in the loyalty offered to the recalcitrant Quintus by his wife Emily, which contrasts with the desertion of Savery by his wife after she saw at first hand his real situation in Australia; and *Moondyne*, in the idealised portrait of the convict-turned-gentleman, Wyville, who succeeds in reforming a system about which O'Reilly felt so strongly.

The confrontation with the issue of penal reform which occurs in *Moondyne*, a major theme also in Caroline Leakey's *The Broad Arrow*, looks back to the great debates about transportation in the years after 1820. Among the issues were the questions of whether the labourers of the Colony should be convicts or freemen and, particularly in the 1830s, whether transportation, which had become more 'systematised' following the reports of J.T. Bigge (q.v.), should itself be abolished. In a period which also saw fundamental press liberties secured in NSW and Van Diemen's Land, a polemical prose literature emerged in which the convicts became ambivalent figures. At one extreme, they were 'branches lopp'd for their rottenness from the tree of British freedom', as James Mudie called them in *The Felonry of New South Wales* (1837); at the other, they were innocent exiles undergoing *The Horrors of Transportation* (1838), as William Bede Ullathorne titled his anti-System treatise. Stern defences of transportation were offered by some writers (e.g. George Arthur), but a seemingly greater proportion of writers either opposed the continuation of transportation or desired its reformation. Some writers (e.g. John Dunmore Lang, q.v.) argued for the abolition of transportation mainly from a concern for the moral welfare of free settlers or from a belief in the future of the colonies, but most abolitionists or reformers were sympathetic to convict suffering, including James Backhouse, Alexander Maconochie, Henry Melville, W.B. Ullathorne (qq.v.) and, perhaps most influential of all the opponents of transportation, Richard Whately (q.v.), whose writings provoked replies not only from Arthur but also from Arthur's own critic, David Burn. The significant amount of anti-transportation material published in 1837–38 is linked with the exhaustive review of transportation undertaken in those years by a select committee of the British parliament. The committee's report and minutes of evidence, usually called the Molesworth Report after its chairman, Sir William Molesworth (1810–55), is a famous specimen of convict literature which confirms the brutalities which the System perpetrated at its worst. Like other parliamentary papers concerned with transportation, and the polemical writings of crusaders such as Whately, these publications became sources to be tapped by later writers, e.g. Marcus Clarke in *His Natural Life* or 'Price Warung', who used Whately's reference to Norfolk Island as an 'Isle of Death' as the title for his last series of stories. The Molesworth Report helped to abolish transportation to NSW; subsequent attempts to revive it provided the occasions for such writings as Charles Harpur's 'The Proposed Recurrence of Transportation', William Forster's satire 'The Genius and the Ghost', and other poems. Transportation continued, however, and led to the swamping of Tasmania with convicts in the 1840s and in the same period to the use of Norfolk Island and Port Arthur (q.v.) as penitentiaries for long-term or colonially reconvicted prisoners. The high proportion of Tasmanian convicts helps to explain why the island is the setting for much of the literature written about the convicts. The use of Port Arthur and Norfolk Island led to the worst excesses of transportation, particularly after the recall of Maconochie from Norfolk Island and his replacement by Joseph Childs (the model for 'Warung's' archvillain Commandant Scragge) and John Price (q.v.), the model for Maurice Frere in *His Natural Life*. Norfolk Island and Tasman's Peninsula as natural paradises turned into man-made hells, and the desire of many convicts to commit capital crimes in order to earn their freedom from a 'worse than death' existence (as Dawes seeks to do under Frere), became literary commonplaces from the 1840s.

The 'prose of controversy', as H.M. Green termed the polemical literature about transportation, largely ended with the cessation of transportation to the eastern colonies. In ensuing decades, the first important colonial histories were written by G.B. Barton, David Blair, William Howitt, Thomas McCombie, George Rusden, John West, William Westgarth (qq.v.) and others. With the notable exception of West's *History of Tasmania* (1852), which contains a savage indict-

ment of transportation, the convicts are conspicuously absent from these histories; the desire to avoid embarrassing those of convict or gaoler descent, and the desire to emphasise colonial progress have been advanced as the reasons. It was in – and partly because of – this climate of silence that convict literature became more and more the province of the creative writer, particularly in fiction and drama. Most importantly, it was the period which saw the publication of the major anti-System novels and stories – *The Broad Arrow*, *His Natural Life*, *Moondyne* and 'Warung's' *Tales of the Convict System* (1892), *Tales of the Early Days* (1894), *Tales of the Old Regime* (1897) and *Tales of the Isle of Death* (1898) – which by their popularity helped to consolidate the convict legend within the Australian consciousness. *His Natural Life*, it has been claimed, was to be found in every cottage in Australia; *The Broad Arrow* and *Moondyne* each went through several editions *(Moondyne* at the rate of one a year in its first dozen years), and 'Warung' was the most prolific contributor of stories to the *Bulletin* in the 1890s. These works are in part the fictional equivalents of the contributions to the prose of controversy by the abolitionists of the 1830s. Whatever questions they explore beyond transportation, they are texts which explicitly confront the System and condemn it; as Clarke writes in his preface to *His Natural Life*, the novel is intended to demonstrate the 'inexpediency of again allowing offenders against the law to be herded together in places remote from the wholesome influence of public opinion'. 'Warung' went further than Clarke in insisting on the accuracy of his historical interpretation of convictism to strengthen the political message of his stories, which were written in support of the republican anti-English stance of the *Bulletin* and its editor, J.F. Archibald. For Archibald, as much as for 'Warung', the legacy of the past could be detected in the sustained brutality of the penal code and in the corruption endemic in politics and business life in the 1880s and 1890s. A second group of novels, published 1850–1900, focuses on but exploits rather than confronts or condemns transportation. In this tradition of fiction, which encompasses John Lang's (q.v.) *Botany Bay* (1855) and *The Forger's Wife* (1859), James Hebblethwaite's *Castle Hill* (1895), and E.W. Hornung's *The Rogue's March* (1896), the interpretation offered of the System seems less important to a reader than the author's desire to harness the potential for excitement, romance or adventure inherent in the subject.

In drama, convicts gave the first theatrical performance in Australia *(The Recruiting Officer*, 1789), briefly ran the first theatre in 1796, and conducted the activities of the Emu Plains theatre from the 1820s to the 1840s (as *Ralph Rashleigh* depicts). The government licensing of plays in NSW resulted in few convict or bushranging plays in the first decades after the cessation of transportation, but in the 1870s the convict emerged in the Anglo-Australian melodramas of George Darrell and later in the repertoires of Alfred Dampier and Dan Barry (qq.v.); in 1882 Barry was arrested in Sale as a prison escapee when he dressed up as a convict to advertise a performance. The melodrama tradition emphasised the triumph of virtue over vice; the necessity to reconcile this tradition with the emerging convict legend probably explains why the convict as villain is increasingly replaced on the stage from the 1870s onwards by the convict who has been wrongly convicted or transported, as in Darrell's first Australian play, 'Transported for Life' (performed 1877), and in the many stage adaptations of *His Natural Life*, an outstanding theatrical success from the 1880s into the 1920s. As well, in many melodramas not specifically about transportation, the convict or ex-convict became one of the stock characters alongside his cousins the bushranger, the new chum and the remittance man (qq.v.). This second use of the convict, as a character who is an incidental part of the fabric of colonial society and history, can be placed within a literary tradition stretching back to the fiction of Charles Rowcroft and Alexander Harris. Both authors have convict characters or explicitly discuss the issue of transportation, e.g. Rowcroft in *Tales of the Colonies* (1843), Harris in *Settlers and Convicts* (1847) and *The Emigrant Family* (1849), the last dedicated to Maconochie in admiration of his work in penal reform. Yet both are also catalogued as 'guide-book' novelists interested more in the emigrant's total experience than specifically in any one of those experiences; indeed, *Tales of the Colonies* is less significant in convict literature than in the study of the Aboriginal in Australian literature. If Harris and Rowcroft can be said to have inaugurated a tradition, then between 1850 and 1900 it is continued in other fictional works. These works include emigration novels (e.g. Henry Kingsley's *The Hillyars and the Burtons*, 1865); the first generation of historical novels and romances to look back on the early period of Australian history and embrace the convict experience as part of a broader historical sweep (e.g. Mary Vidal's *Bengala: Or Some Time Ago*, 1860; Charles de Boos's *Fifty Years Ago*, 1867; Eliza Winstanley's *Twenty Straws*, 1864); and an increasing number of popular works in which convictism is only one of a number of staple or sensational ingredients (e.g. Carlton Dawe's *The Golden Lake*, 1891). There are also novels which make use of ex-convict characters for the purposes of plot construction (e.g. Hume Nisbet's sensational *Dr Bernard St. Vincent*, 1889); or character motivation (as in *Robbery Under Arms*, 1888, where Ben Marston, an old lag, is naturally inclined towards cattle-duffing); or to distinguish between English and Australian types (as in *The Recollections of Geoffry Hamlyn*, 1859).

The inevitable overlap between these traditions of convict fiction is demonstrated by the fact that to a significant extent they all embrace the melodramatic, a consequence of the System's concern with the extremes of human behaviour. Yet for all the blurring of distinctions, it is possible to consider the convict in Australian literature after 1900 in terms of the three major traditions. Thus the Lang tradition (the literary works which focus on the convict experience but which are less concerned with interpreting that experience than in mining its narrative, dramatic, sensational or other literary potential) is continued in literally dozens of novels, many intended for a popular market. These include William Hay's early romances

(*Stifled Laughter*, 1901; *Herridge of Reality Swamp*, q.v., 1907) and even, arguably, *The Escape of the Notorious Sir William Heans* (q.v., 1919); several of the New South Wales Bookstall Company's 'pulps' (e.g. Roy Bridges's *The Barb of an Arrow*, 1909, and *Mr. Barrington*, 1911; J.B. Cooper's *Leg-Bail*, 1916; Ambrose Pratt's *Her Assigned Husband*, 1916; and James Devaney's *The Currency Lass*, 1927); and several recent works, among them Richard Butler's *The Men That God Forgot* (1975) and *Against the Wind* (1978), Colin Free's *Vinegar Hill* (1978), Yoram Gross's children's book *The Little Convict* (1979) and Frank Baron Kreffl's projected trilogy *Con, Vic* and *Ted* (1979) (equals 'convicted'). The tradition incorporates some of the radio plays of the 1940s and is paralleled by many of the early silent films including adaptations of *His Natural Life* (1908, 1911, 1927), *It Is Never Too Late to Mend* (1911) and *Moondyne* (1913), and by some of the film and television series of the 1970s and 1980s (*Journey Among Women, Against the Wind, For the Term of His Natural Life*).

If the Lang tradition has continued, the Rowcroft–Harris tradition (in which the convict experience forms only an intrinsic or incidental part of the subject matter or themes of the work) has positively flourished. The novels that form part of such a tradition can be numbered not in dozens but in hundreds, and include several multi-volume historical sagas which embrace the transportation period. A notable example, and one of the major achievements in Australian historical fiction, is Eleanor Dark's trilogy *The Timeless Land* (q.v., 1941), *Storm of Time* (1948) and *No Barrier* (1953), which has been greatly admired for the imaginative entrance it permits into the early days of settlement. Among other series are the Hobart–Richmond series of Roy Bridges, a group of six novels published 1927–33 which offer an interpretation of Tasmanian society from the 1830s to the 1850s, Doris Chadwick's children's trilogy, *John of the 'Sirius'* (1955), *John of Sydney Cove* (1957) and *John and Nanbaree* (1962); and Vivian Stuart's recent romances. The single-volume novels which encompass the transportation period range from the more 'respectable' historical novels such as J.H.M. Abbot's *The Governor's Man* (1919), *Castle Vane* (1920), *Ensign Calder* (1922) and *Sydney Cove* (1923), 'M. Barnard Eldershaw's' *A House Is Built* (1929), Helen Simpson's *Under Capricorn* (1937), 'G.B. Lancaster's' *Pageant* (1933), Nancy Cato's *North-West by South* (1965), and Patrick White's *A Fringe of Leaves* (1976) and *Voss* (1957); to the historical romances such as Catherine Gaskin's *Sara Dane* (1954) and Ernestine Hill's *My Love Must Wait* (1941); down to the followers of Carlton Dawe using convictism as an ingredient for a mass-market concoction (e.g. Nat Gould in *King of the Ranges*, 1902). The Rowcroft–Harris tradition has also lived on in several radio plays and in the historical costume dramas seen so often on Australian television (e.g. Rex Rienits's *Stormy Petrel* in 1960).

The third and most important tradition, the Clarke tradition (comprising the major literary works which in 1850–1900 explicitly confronted the System), has undergone an interesting modification in the twentieth century. As the convict period has receded further into the past, twentieth-century writers have focused their attention less on an indictment of the System (although that is one of the purposes of David Hennessey in his 1913 novel *The Outlaw*, and Stuart Macky in his convict plays) than on the exploration of its meaning for and beyond contemporary Australian society. The general direction to be taken was signposted in the stories of 'Warung', who in the 1890s was preoccupied with the legacy of the past. Similarly preoccupied, though in the 1930s, was Brian Penton (q.v.), whose polemical *Think or Be Damned* (1941) set out to dispel some national myths, and who in *Landtakers* (q.v., 1934) and *Inheritors* (1936) embarked on a revaluation of Australian history in which the convict experience is seen as significant in the development of the national psyche. In another historically conscious age, the 1970s, Ron Blair's 'Flash Jim Vaux' stands as one of the earliest plays in which the local melodramatic tradition of the late nineteenth century was revived, but with a difference: plays like 'Flash Jim Vaux' are satiric slices of history designed not merely to return their audience to the past but also to look sideways at the contemporary political scene. If the tone of 'Flash Jim Vaux' is consistently light-hearted, that mood is conspicuously absent from R.D. FitzGerald's poem 'The Wind at Your Door' (q.v., 1958). The poem explores FitzGerald's response to his discovery that an ancestor, Martin Mason, was a penal official in attendance at a particularly brutal flogging of a convict who shared the poet's surname. The conclusion he reaches is to accept that the convict and the ancestor, the brutalised and the brutaliser, are both victims of the System. FitzGerald's major source, the 1838 memoirs of Joseph Holt, was used for a similar purpose by Thomas Keneally in *Passenger*. Holt, 'the one who would not watch' the flogging in 'The Wind at Your Door', is also one of the 'gentry from the aft cabins' on board the *Minerva* in Keneally's novel. The journey of the *Minerva* to Australia provides Keneally with an important metaphoric parallel for the modern journey of his main passenger, Sal FitzGerald's foetus-narrator, towards birth. The foetus identifies himself with another passenger on the *Minerva*, Maurice Fitz-Gerald, who is not only the victim of 'The Wind at Your Door' but also the ancestor of Sal's husband. Through the foetus/FitzGerald identification Keneally establishes the same kind of link between the present and the past that is explored in 'The Wind at Your Door' and also in his more explicitly convict novel *Bring Larks and Heroes* (1967), which Keneally has described as a 'parable for the present'. The protagonist of *Bring Larks and Heroes*, Phelim Halloran, is an outsider destroyed by a society whose 'systems' – civil, military and religious – do not adequately serve the needs of the individual. The point of the parable, several commentators have suggested, is the spiritual emptiness of Australian society, which has developed an effective machinery for crushing individual initiative.

Although it might be tempting to see as evolutionary the process by which writers like Penton, Blair, FitzGerald and Keneally have moved Australian literature away from a confrontation with the histori-

cal phenomenon of transportation and towards an appropriation of its symbolic or metaphoric possibilities, these possibilities inherent in the System have always been present. *His Natural Life* does more than merely confront and condemn the System: it also, and more broadly, explores man's capacity for evil. Similarly, one reason why some convict novels are difficult to classify according to any single tradition is partly because such classifications do not accommodate their thematic, metaphoric and stylistic complexity; Hal Porter's richly textured *The Tilted Cross* (q.v., 1961) and the mixture of contrived romance, historical costumery and subtle exploration of evil that comprises *The Escape of the Notorious Sir William Heans* are two such texts. Among more recent novels, Patrick White's *A Fringe of Leaves* is surprisingly considered as a convict novel even though White in his own way is as opportunistic in his use of the convict experience as any NSW Bookstall novelist; in the words of L.T. Hergenhan *(Unnatural Lives: Studies in Australian Fiction about the Convicts*, 1983) White's convicts provide an 'ambience of imprisonment' and are a reference point in relation to which Ellen Roxburgh's attempt to effect a spiritual escape is measured. Similarly, the convict system is recalled in a novel about modern Systems, David Ireland's *The Unknown Industrial Prisoner* (1971), in which the workers have marks on their legs where the irons have chafed their ancestors.

Finally, it is impossible either to say how Australian literature would have been different without the convict experience, or to quantify the effect of that experience on the Australian creative imagination. What can be said is that alienation, exile, imprisonment, the search for freedom and the legacy of the past are all recurring themes in convict literature and perhaps, partly because of this, important themes in Australian literature generally. A guide to the literary depiction of convicts in such works as *Geoffry Hamlyn, His Natural Life, Moondyne* and *Voss* (qq.v.) is given in A.W. Baker's *Death is a Good Solution: The Convict Experience in Early Australia* (1984). The experience of women convicts is examined in part of Katrina Alford's *Production or Reproduction: An Economic History of Women in Australia 1788–1850* (1984) and in Portia Robinson's *The Women of Botany Bay* (1993). A new historical perception of Australia's convict past is offered in Stephen Nicholas (ed.) *Convict Workers* (1988) while Robert King's interpretation and translation of Alexandro Malaspina's report, *The Secret History of the Convict Colony* (1990), investigates the notion that the Australian colony was not settled because England wanted a gaol in the South Seas but because she wanted a position of commercial and political advantage that the colony might offer in the struggle for supremacy among the European powers. Robert Hughes's (q.v.) *The Fatal Shore* (1987) differs strongly from King's interpretation, seeing Britain's motivation springing from a desire to rid itself of the elements that threatened its society based largely on wealth and privilege. Hughes sees the convict settlement as an eighteenth-century example of the 'Gulag', the vast concentration camp that became familiar in the twentieth century. An epic work, *The Fatal Shore* is by far the most complete account of the Convict System.

Convict Oath is the oath of allegiance between convicts which begins

> Hand to hand
> On Earth, in Hell,
> Sick or Well
> On Sea on Land
> On the Square, ever.

Much quoted by historians as evidence of mateship, it first appeared in 'Price Warung's' (q.v.) story 'The Liberation of the First Three', in which three convicts kill three other convicts with whom they have been chained; in the sequel, 'The Liberation of the Other Three', the irony is completed when the three survivors kill each other. Although the Convict Oath may have been 'Warung's' invention, there is evidence to suggest that it came to him through oral tradition.

Convict Once (1871) is a long narrative poem by James Brunton Stephens (q.v.). It has an intricate, melodramatic plot which revolves around a beautiful *femme fatale* – a 'convict once' but now a governess – who becomes romantically involved with several men but dies before disaster overtakes all concerned. Heavily ornate, and outmoded in its elevated literary tone, the poem at times conveys an impressive air of gravity and grace. Highly valued by contemporary critics, who regarded it as Stephens's most significant literary work, it has been largely ignored in recent years.

'Convict's Tour to Hell, A', a long witty poem in rhyming couplets, was written by 'Frank the Poet' (see MacNamara, Francis) probably in 1839 at Stroud, NSW. Modelled on the satires of Jonathan Swift, who attended school in Kilkenny (where MacNamara committed the offence which led to his transportation), 'A Convict's Tour to Hell' chronicles Frank's tour of the underworld, where he discovers that notorious penal administrators such as Captain Logan and Governor Darling are suffering the kind of hellish punishments that they inflicted on the convicts. At the end of the poem, just after Frank is admitted into Heaven, he awakens to find that he has been dreaming. There is evidence that 'A Convict's Tour to Hell', which is also known as 'The Convict's Dream' and 'Frank's Tour of Hell', was popular among the more incorrigible convicts. Parts of the poem are quoted in 'Price Warung's' (q.v.) story of the chain gangs, 'The Ross Gang "Yarner"-Ship'.

CONWAY, Jill Ker (1934–), born Hillston, NSW, left Australia in 1960 for the USA, where she completed a doctorate in history at Harvard. From 1964 to 1975 she taught at the University of Toronto, where she was vice-president 1973–75. She was the first woman president of Smith College, Massachusetts, in 1975–85 and has been visiting scholar at the Massachusetts Institute of Technology since 1985.

The author of several books on the historical experience of American women, she is a director on numerous company boards and in 1976 was named by *Time* magazine as one of its twelve women of the year. In 1989 she published a widely acclaimed autobiography of her early years, *The Road from Coorain*. Coorain was the name of the immense drought-ridden property in western NSW where Conway grew up. The property was so isolated that she was 7 before she saw another girl, but her early years before drought destroyed the family's hopes were idyllic; by the time she was 7 her brothers were away at boarding school and she became her father's station hand, working desperately with him in the losing battle to save their stock. Her father's death in 1944 in a mysterious accident which might have been suicide was succeeded by her mother's heroic efforts to save the property, although she was eventually persuaded to leave Coorain for Sydney. There Conway attended the prestigious girls' school Abbotsleigh, where she proved to be intellectually precocious owing to her habit of voracious reading at Coorain, but also socially inept, contemptuous of rules and indifferent to hierarchies. Meanwhile her mother worked at two jobs and gradually restocked Coorain, which eventually became a paying proposition, providing the family with a comfortable living. Ironically, however, the succeeding years for Conway's mother were filled with bitterness, as she failed to adjust to opportunities in the city, and became steadily more emotionally dependent on her children. The death of one of her sons in a car accident exacerbated this dependency and Conway became increasingly aware that a destiny as dutiful daughter awaited her. At the University of Sydney her studies prospered, culminating in the University Medal for history, but she became disenchanted with Australian scholarship, aware that both right and left historians were hostages to British imperialism. In an attempt to escape from the various intellectual and emotional traps surrounding her, she applied for a traineeship in Foreign Affairs but was refused on the grounds that she would soon marry and was forced to recognise the fact that her 'sex rendered [her] merits invisible'. The discovery reinforced her conclusion that she must leave Australia and after a period teaching history at the University, she enrolled in the doctoral programme at Harvard. A revealing account of the difficulties faced by Australian women of Conway's generation, *The Road from Coorain* is also a valuable sociological representation of life in outback Australia and post-war Sydney.

CONWAY, Ronald Victor (1927–), formerly senior lecturer in applied psychology at RMIT and senior consulting psychologist for twenty-five years at St Vincent's Hospital, Melbourne, has written several works on Australian society and especially on the Australian male character. He published a trilogy of such books, *The Great Australian Stupor* (1971, revised 1985); *Land of the Long Weekend* (1978), which won the FAW Australian Natives Association Literary Award; and *The End of Stupor?* (1984), which sees some hope of national fulfilment, biologically and socially, in a union of science and religion. He has also written the autobiographical *Conway's Way* (1988), and *Being Male: A Guide for Masculinity in a Time of Change* (1985), *The Rage For Perfection* (1991) and *The Rage for Utopia* (1993). He was awarded the OAM.

'Coo-ee', a penetrating shout used by those in the bush to denote their own whereabouts or to seek an indication of the whereabouts of others, has become a recognised feature of Australian bush life. Daniel Southwell, an officer in the First Fleet, in a letter 27 July 1790, referred to an expression 'coe' used by the Aborigines meaning 'come hither'. Governor Hunter in the vocabulary of the Port Jackson Aborigines given in his *An Historical Journal of the Transactions at Port Jackson* (1793) spells the word 'cowee'. The Aborigines appear to have derived the expression from the call of the koel cuckoo, sometimes termed the 'cooee bird'. Peter Cunningham in *Two Years in New South Wales* (1827) indicates that the call was then in general use among the White settlers. The word has been used in the titles of numerous Australian books and anthologies in order to indicate an Australian flavour, e.g. *Cooee: Tales of Australian Life by Australian Ladies* (1891) by Harriette Anne Martin; *Coo-oo-ee: A Tale of Bushmen from Australia to Anzac* (1916) by J.B. Cooper; and *The Coo-ee Call: Dedicated to the Men in Khaki* (1917) by M.W. James. 'Cooee: Or, Wild Days in the Bush Forty Years Ago' (1906) was a popular stage melodrama by E.W. O'Sullivan. Henry Lawson uses 'cooee' to superb effect in the opening verse of his poem 'Jack Cornstalk':

I met with Jack Cornstalk in London today,
He saw me and coo-eed from over the way.
The solemn-faced Londoners stared at Long Jack,
At his hat, and his height, and the breadth of his back.
Then he coo-eed again (and his voice was not low)
And – there's not room to coo-ee in London, you know.

Although the expression 'within cooee' meant literally to be within shouting distance (more than 3 kilometres on a still night) of the place or person desired and is used in that sense in Lawson's poem 'The Shanty on the Rise' and in 'Henry Handel Richardson's' *The End of a Childhood* (1934), it also has a metaphorical meaning, i.e. close to but not exactly on the mark; its rather derisory antithesis, 'not within cooee', means to be widely astray in judgement.

COOK, Captain James (1728–79), born at Marton-in-Cleveland, near Middlesbrough, Yorkshire, lived much of his young life at Staithes and Whitby, in close proximity to the sea. Briefly an apprentice shopkeeper, he became indentured at 15 on the coal ships of John Walker of Whitby. He entered the Royal Navy as an able seaman in 1755, served in the Seven Years' War and, as master of HMS *Pembroke*, participated in the siege of Louisburg and the survey of the St Lawrence River that facilitated General Wolfe's capture of Quebec. Promoted to lieutenant in 1768, he was given command of HMS *Endeavour* in an expedition to Tahiti to observe the transit of the planet Venus and then to search for the Great South Land, the unknown continent (see Terra Australis) of the southern seas.

Between October 1769 and March 1770, Cook charted the coast of NZ. His decision to sail westward from NZ led to landfall at Point Hicks (now Cape Everard) on the Australian coast. Sailing northward, he reached Botany Bay (28 April 1770) and on 22 August 1770 at Possession Island, off the northern tip of Cape York Peninsula, named the whole of the east coast 'New South Wales' and took possession of it for Britain. Promoted to captain, Cook returned to search for the Great South Land in a second voyage (1772–75) with the ships *Resolution* and *Adventure*, and by circumnavigating the globe at high southern latitudes confirmed that no southern continent other than New Holland existed. On his third voyage (1776–80), again in the *Resolution*, while attempting to find a passage from the Pacific to the Atlantic, Cook was killed by Hawaiian islanders at Kealakekua Bay. Contemporary accounts of Cook's voyages include John Hawkesworth's *An Account of the Voyages Undertaken by the Order of His Present Majesty for Making Discoveries in the Southern Hemisphere* (1773), Sydney Parkinson's *A Journal of a Voyage to the South Seas, in His Majesty's Ship, the Endeavour* (1773), G. Forster's *A Voyage Round the World in His Britannic Majesty's Sloop, Resolution, Commanded by Captain James Cook, During the Years 1772,3,4 and 5* (1777). Cook is the subject of numerous studies including Arthur Kitson's *Captain James Cook* (1907), G. Arnold Wood's *The Voyage of the Endeavour* (1926), R.T. Gould's *Captain Cook* (1935), Hugh Carrington's *Life of Captain Cook* (1939), John R. Muir's *The Life and Achievements of Captain James Cook* (1939), C. Lloyd's *Captain Cook* (1952), G.M. Badger's *Captain Cook* (1970), J.V.S. Megaw's (ed.) *Employ'd As a Discoverer* (1971), Gavin Kennedy's *The Death of Captain Cook* (1978), Jillian Robertson's *The Captain Cook Myth* (1981) and Gananath Obeyesekere's *The Apotheosis of Captain Cook* (1992). The most substantial work on Cook is, however, that of J.C. Beaglehole, who edited *The Journals of Captain Cook* in three volumes (1955, 1961, 1967) and wrote *Cook the Writer* (1970) and *The Life of Captain James Cook* (1974).

Popular with poets, Cook was the subject of two sonnets by Barron Field in the *Sydney Gazette*, 22 March 1822, celebrating the unveiling of a tablet to commemorate the landing at Botany Bay in 1770, and he is mentioned in W.C. Wentworth's *Australasia* (1823). The newly established University of Sydney selected 'Cook, Meditating on Australia's Future' as the subject for a prize poem in 1859 (won by William Yarrington and published 1908). Henry Kendall wrote four sonnets about Cook at Botany Bay, including the poetic re-creation of the first landing, 'The Spot Where Cook Landed'. Roland Robinson ('Captain Cook') and Alan Frost ('Elizabeth to James Cook, August 1770') have also written poems on Cook, but the most important are Kenneth Slessor's 'Five Visions of Captain Cook' (q.v.) and Alan Gould's 'The Great Circle' in *Years Found in Likeness* (1988). K.J. Prunty published *On a Picture of Captain James Cook R.N.: Selected Poems* (1979) and Lance Banbury, *Captain James Cook: A Poetical Drama* (1981). Fictional treatments of Cook include Godfrey Blunden's *Charco Harbour* (1968), while in Henry Kingsley's *The Hillyars and the*

Burtons (1865) part of the narrative is set in the Australian colony of Cooksland. A Cook tableau was included in Garnet Walch's pantomime *Hey Diddle Diddle* (1878), and in 1888 Alfred Dampier staged John Petry's 'The Life and Death of Captain Cook', a winner of a drama prize to celebrate the centenary. The imaginative impact of Cook's voyages is the subject of the collection of essays edited by Walter Veit, *Captain James Cook, Image and Impact* (1972). Cook is commemorated in Australia by numerous places bearing his name – mountains, rivers, towns, streets, lighthouses – by a variety of statuary, by having his father's Yorkshire cottage transferred to Melbourne's Fitzroy Gardens, and by James Cook University at Townsville. He was also honoured in 1970 by the Cook Bicentenary literary competitions in Australia. The impact of Cook's voyages on contemporary European thought is examined in *Imagining the Pacific. In the Wake of the Cook Voyages* (1992) by Bernard Smith (q.v.), who also compiled, with Rudiger Joppien, *The Art of Captain Cook's Voyages* (3 vols, 1985–88).

COOK, Kenneth (1929–87), born Sydney, worked at first as a journalist but turned to full-time writing in 1960, shortly before the publication of his best-known novel, *Wake in Fright* (1961). A gripping account of a young teacher's nightmarish experience in an outback town of NSW, *Wake in Fright* was produced as a film in 1971. His musical stage play *Stockade*, which centres on the Eureka Stockade, was first produced in 1971 and published in 1975. Fast-moving and interspersed with songs, *Stockade* is more sombre in mood and less of a spectacular entertainment than similar productions, e.g. *The Legend of King O'Malley*; central to the play is an extended debate on the question of the rule of law versus individual rights and the validity of violence. *Stockade* was produced as a film in 1971 and has been shown on television. Cook also published numerous novels, television plays, film scripts, documentaries and short stories, and as director of his own company produced, wrote and appeared in numerous films, mostly for children's television. His novels include *Chain of Darkness* (1962), *Stormalong* (1963), *Wanted Dead* (1963), *The Wine of God's Anger* (1968), *Eliza Fraser* (1976), *The Man Underground* (1977) and *The Film Makers* (1983, with Kerry Cook).

Coolgardie, a town in WA about 600 kilometres east of Perth, was the scene of a rich gold discovery in September 1892. It is featured in David Carnegie's *Spinifex and Sand* (1898) and its part in the gold rushes is described in Malcolm Uren's *Glint of Gold* (1948). Coolgardie is the leaping-off point for M.J. O'Reilly ('Mulga Mick') in his poem 'The Adams River Rush'; E.G. Murphy ('Dryblower'), one of the first employees of William Clare's newspaper the *Coolgardie Miner*, tells of the conditions on the Coolgardie field, especially the presence of so many 'faceless' men, in the poem 'The Smiths'; and Dorham Doolette ('The Prodigal') wrote the ballad 'The Old Coolgardie Road'. In J. Arthur Barry's *The Luck of the Native Born* (1899), Coolgardie is the background for the adventures of his hero, Ned Linton. Richard Donald Lane

wrote *The Romance of Old Coolgardie* (1929), a novel which is a mixture of historical fact and fiction; Norma King wrote the historical *Early Days around Coolgardie* (1975). The 'Coolgardie Safe' was standard equipment of the prospector in the desert; it used percolating water to keep food cool.

'Coolibah' (also spelt coolabah, koolibah and coolybar) is the Aboriginal name for a eucalypt tree common in the Australian inland. It was on a coolibah that Brahe carved the word 'Dig' to inform Burke and Wills that their stores were buried there. It was under the shade of a coolibah in A.B. Paterson's 'Waltzing Matilda' that the 'Jolly Swagman' camped, and 'in the shade where the coolibahs grow' that the Dying Stockman wished to be buried.

COOMBS, H.C. (Herbert Cole) (1906–), born Kalamunda, WA, had a distinguished career as an economist, culminating in his appointments as governor of the Reserve Bank of Australia (1960–68) and chairman of its Board (1960–68). Active in Aboriginal affairs and the arts, he founded the Australian Elizabethan Theatre Trust (q.v.), was chairman of the Australian Council of the Arts (1968–74) and of the Australian Council of Aboriginal Affairs (1968–76). His publications include *Other People's Money* (1971), *The Fragile Pattern* (1970, the Boyer Lectures for that year), and several works in support of the Aboriginal cause, e.g. *Kulinma – Listening to Aboriginal Australians* (1978), *Towards a National Aboriginal Conference* (1986). His autobiography, *Trial Balance* (1981), records Coombs's commitment to public service over four decades. He was voted Australian of the Year, 1972, and has received an honorary LL D from the ANU, the universities of Melbourne and Sydney and an honorary D.Litt. from the University of WA. Since his retirement he has been a visiting fellow at the Centre for Resource and Environmental Studies at the ANU. He was chancellor of that University 1968–76.

COOMBS, Margaret, born Mudgee, NSW, studied arts at the University of Sydney, graduating with an MA in government. She has lived in England for extensive periods, including eighteen months travelling with traditional circuses. She has contributed stories and articles to literary magazines, newspapers and anthologies and has written two novels, *Regards to the Czar* (1988) and *The Best Man for This Sort of Thing* (1990). *Regards to the Czar* follows the experiences of Helen Diamond, from her childhood as a doctor's daughter in Narramundi, when she is indoctrinated in the middle-class ideology of gender, to her ultimate struggle to become free and autonomous. The best man for this sort of thing in the novel of that title is a Harley Street psychiatrist, who attempts to cure Helen Ayling's post-natal depression. Her efforts to counter his patronising dismissal of her as a living, feeling individual lead her into an obsessive quest for attention which she mercilessly and sometimes comically interprets nineteen years later.

Coonardoo (1929), a novel by Katharine Susannah Prichard (q.v.), deals with the deep emotional relationship between White man Hugh Watt and Aboriginal girl Coonardoo, who have been friends since childhood. Raised by his mother, Bessie Watt, on Wytaliba, a cattle station in north-west WA, Hugh is sent south to be educated before returning to manage Wytaliba. After the death of his mother he is rescued from his obsessive grief by the love of Coonardoo, who ultimately bears his son. Repelled by the ugly, casual attitude of White males towards sexual relationships with Aboriginal women, Hugh cannot bring himself to allow the natural feelings that he and Coonardoo share for each other to develop to their mutual satisfaction. In an attempt to solve his moral dilemma he marries a White girl from the south but several years later she discovers the secret of Coonardoo's son, Winni, and uses it as an excuse to leave the outback life she loathes. Coonardoo's tribal husband, Warieda, dies and, partly out of his still strong desire for her and partly to save her from other tribal husbands, Hugh acknowledges Coonardoo as his woman. His White 'morality', however, continues to prevent him living with her. After the White man Sam Geary forces himself upon Coonardoo while Hugh is away, Hugh, furiously jealous, beats Coonardoo and banishes her from Wytaliba. As the years pass, she drifts into a life of shame among the boats of the pearling fleet around Broome. The seasons go from bad to worse and Hugh loses Wytaliba to his enemy, Sam Geary. Coonardoo, wasted by disease, returns to the deserted Wytaliba to die. Highly controversial and offensive to many in the 1930s, *Coonardoo* threw new light on the taboo subject of Black–White sexual relationships.

COOPER, Walter (1842–80), born Liverpool, NSW, was actor, journalist, playwright, lawyer and, briefly, member of parliament. Although handicapped by an unstable temperament, financial problems and scandal, Cooper was a popular playwright who successfully exploited the colonial perspective, especially in his comedy *Colonial Experience* (1868, first published 1979, edited by Eric Irvin). In 1870 his first sensation drama, 'Sun and Shadow', was staged, followed by 'Foiled: Or Australia Twenty Years Ago' (1871), *Hazard* (1872, reprinted 1987 edited by Dennis Davison) and 'Fuss' (1880), all enjoying longer than usual runs. Cooper also presented some of these plays successfully in American cities in 1872–73.

Cooper's Creek, which skirts the eastern side of Queensland's Channel Country (q.v.), runs through south-western Queensland into SA and on infrequent occasions (e.g. 1949–50, 1973) its floodwaters have reached Lake Eyre. Cooper's Creek was discovered by Charles Sturt in 1845 and named after Charles Cooper, SA's first chief justice. Extraordinary confusion surrounded the original identification of the much-interrupted stream, but north from its junction with the Thomson River it is now known as the Barcoo (q.v.) and south from the junction, Cooper's Creek. Linked in the history of Australian exploration with the Burke and Wills (q.v.) expedition, the Cooper is featured in such accounts as Frank Clune's *Dig* (1937) and Alan Moorehead's *Cooper's Creek* (1963). The Cooper's Creek area was also important in Australia's pastoral expansion in the mid-nineteenth century. The account of its opening by the Durack and Costello families in the 1870s is given in Mary Durack's *Kings in Grass Castles* (q.v., 1959). After Burke and Wills and the Duracks, the Cooper's most celebrated personality is probably A.B. Paterson's Clancy of the Overflow (q.v.), whose romanticised life as a drover 'down the Cooper where the western drovers go' has stirred nostalgia and envy in many an Australian heart.

COPPEL, Alec, an actor and writer for stage and radio, published three plays, *I Killed the Count* (1938), *The Captain's Paradise* (1961) and *The Gazebo* (1962); and four books of light fiction, *A Man about a Dog* (1947), *Mr Denning Drives North* (1950), *The Last Parade* (1953), and *Tweedledum and Tweedledee* (1967). His other plays include 'Believe It or Not', 'Cadenza', 'The Joshua Tree' and 'Mr Smart Guy'.

COPPIN, George Selth (1819–1906), born Sussex, England, was one of the earliest significant figures of the nineteenth-century Australian stage to have had extensive theatrical experience before coming to Australia. The son of itinerant English performers, Coppin made his debut as an infant and performed mainly in the English provinces and Ireland before emigrating to Australia in 1843, performing first in Sydney. In 1845–46 he toured Hobart, Launceston, Melbourne and Adelaide, where he was based 1846–51, and expanded his interests into hotels, racehorses and other business. Insolvent in 1851, Coppin repaired his fortunes as a theatrical performer on the Victorian goldfields; after repaying his creditors in full in Adelaide he left for England, where he had some success as a comedian – Billy Barlow was one of his notable roles – and engaged G.V. Brooke (q.v.) for an Australian tour. Later performers who toured under Coppin's management were Joseph Jefferson, Charles and Ellen Kean (q.v.), and J.C. Williamson (q.v.). Back in Melbourne in 1854, Coppin was in partnership with Brooke 1856–59 and 1860–61 and despite another financial crisis in 1863 remained one of the major figures of the Melbourne and Australian stage until his retirement early in the 1880s. He had many other business interests and was also active in politics as a member of the Victorian Legislative Council or Legislative Assembly for much of the period 1858–95. Coppin is the subject of a biography by Alec Bagot, *Coppin the Great* (1965), which is also informative on early Australian theatre.

Coralie Lansdowne Says No, a play by Alexander Buzo (q.v.) first produced in 1974, was published the same year. Set in a large modern house perched high above the sea in the Bilgola–Palm Beach area north of Sydney, the action turns on the predicament of Coralie Lansdowne, a vibrant, satirically witty former art teacher now looking after the house of a wealthy

American ex-lover. Daunted by her approaching thirtieth year, Coralie ponders her future and the three different men who pursue her, none of whom seems to offer the 'high-flying' role that she had always anticipated would be hers. Unpredictably, she finally compromises by marrying the outsider, the outwardly unprepossessing Stuart Morgan, since with him she has a better chance of retaining her authentic self.

CORBETT, Nancy (1944–), born Canada, has lived in Australia since 1973. She has written two novels, *Floating* (1988) and *Heartland* (1989). Moving between contemporary Sydney and eighteenth-century Japan, *Floating* is a boldly imaginative novel which presents a fresh perspective on the historical oppression of women. *Heartland* is set in a post-nuclear Australia which consists of gender-separate societies, the women (Womanright), with their five tribes (Earthwomen, Starwomen, Whalewomen, Memory-women and the Daughters of Light) inhabiting the Queensland coast, with the men in their own area (Phoenix) on the west coast of the continent. Continuation of both groups is provided by a sperm bank controlled by the women, who raise the female children while the male children are sent off to Phoenix, but problems arise when the sperm bank becomes faulty. Corbett is also co-editor of the collection of women's poetry *Up From Below: Poems of the 1980s* (1987).

CORENO, Mariano (1939–), born Frosinone, Italy, arrived in Australia in 1956. He has published five collections of poetry in Italian and has won several awards in Italy. In 1965 he began to write poetry in English, after encouragement by Judith Wright, and has published his poems in numerous anthologies and periodicals as well as in one collection, *Yellow Sun* (1980).

'Cornstalk' was originally used early in the nineteenth century to denote a colonial-born, White Australian, as opposed to those born overseas; the word derived from the physique of the colonial-born, who were thought to be taller and fairer than the European-born and had thus flourished like the Indian corn brought to Australia. With the spread of settlement 'cornstalk' narrowed in meaning to apply to someone born in NSW as distinct from the other colonies (cf. 'croweater', 'sandgroper'), as in Henry Lawson's poem 'Jack Cornstalk'. Synonyms for 'cornstalk' in its original sense included 'currency' and 'native' (qq.v.). There was a 'Jack Cornstalk' series in the *Australian Star* in 1899, and the word itself was sometimes used in titles and for pseudonyms, e.g. *Land of Australia: Songs and Verses by Samuel Cornstalk* (1913) by F.S. Walker. Daniel Healey ('Whaks Li Kell') wrote *'The Cornstalk' His Habits and Habitat* (1893), a mixture of satirical prose and verse, and J.H.M. Abbott, in *Tommy Cornstalk* (1902), related some of the Australian soldiers' experiences in the Boer War. Many Australian stage characters in the nineteenth century bore the name Cornstalk.

CORRIS, Peter (1942–), born Stawell, Victoria, was an academic historian (Ph.D. from ANU and earlier degrees from the University of Melbourne and Monash University) and literary editor of the *National Times* (1979–80) before becoming a full-time writer. He is presently Australia's most successful and popular exponent of the crime fiction genre. His Cliff Hardy crime series (Hardy is his private investigator) began with *The Dying Trade* (1980) and has pursued an inexorable path through to (by February 1994) seventeen other Hardy books – *White Meat* (1981), *The Marvellous Boy* (1982), *The Empty Beach* (1983, serialised on radio and made into a film), *Heroin Annie* (1984, short stories), *Make Me Rich* (1985), *The Big Drop* (1985, short stories), *Deal Me Out* (1986), *The Greenwich Apartments* (1986), *The January Zone* (1987), *Man in the Shadows* (1988, a novella and four short stories), *O'Fear* (1990), *Wet Graves* (1991), *Aftershock* (1991), *Beware of the Dog* (1992), *Burn and Other Stories* (1993), *Matrimonial Causes* (1993) and *Casino* (1993). Cliff Hardy is probably the best-known character in contemporary Australian fiction. Born and bred in Sydney and a veteran of the Malaya Emergency, Hardy lives in Glebe, 'one of those places where if you can't see a pub by looking both ways down the street you must be standing outside one' (*The Dying Trade*). His Private Investigator office is in St Peter's Lane, Darlinghurst. Nearby are most of the Hardy essentials for work and play – a pub, a betting shop (the TAB), a fast-food takeaway and a post office. His close knowledge of Sydney affords him quick access (except for occasional eccentric behaviour from his dilapidated old Falcon car) to wherever his Private Eye talents are required. Given total choice in the matter Hardy would probably prefer to gravitate between Glebe, Darlinghurst and Bondi but he has, in pursuit of the dollar, ventured occasionally into more salubrious localities such as Vaucluse, Bellevue Hill, the North Shore and once, but only once, even Melbourne. In the stories of the early 1980s Hardy freely satisfied his quintessential male appetite for women, drinking, smoking, gambling. A dozen years on an older, wiser Hardy follows a less self-destructive regimen but the seedy, hard-bitten sleuth is essentially much the same as before, maintaining in the midst of his cynicism and world-weariness a stubborn streak of uprightness and moral integrity that continues to surprise and sometimes dismay him. Corris's story themes are wide-ranging: family hostilities and quarrels (*The Dying Trade*, *The Marvellous Boy*); racial tensions, drugs and corruption in the prize-fight game (*White Meat*); big-time corruption (*The Empty Beach*); political corruption (*The Greenwich Apartments*); financial duplicity (*Make Me Rich*); nuclear espionage (*The January Zone*); missing persons (*Wet Graves*); tracking down a murderer (*Aftershock*). The success of the Cliff Hardy series has clearly been responsible for the remarkable upsurge of crime fiction throughout Australia in the late 1980s and early 1990s.

An obsessive writer (1000–2000 words every day of the year), Corris has not been content with one series. The *Pokerface* series, begun with that title in collaboration with Bill Garner in 1985 and produced as an

ABC drama series, has Federal Security Agency's Ray ('Creepy') Crawley as its none too attractive central character. The series includes (to 1993) *The Baltic Business* (1988), *The Kimberley Killing* (1988), *The Cargo Club* (1990), *The Azanian Action* (1991), *The Japanese Job* (1992), and *The Time Trap* (1993). ASIO-style spy stories, the *Pokerface* books are mostly set against a background of actual world events and are more physically violent and sexually explicit than the Cliff Hardy stories.

A third Corris series re-creates the events of Hollywood of the 1940s, supposedly discovered in a set of tape recordings of that era. Another seedy, inept type is the central character, this time an expatriate octogenarian Australian, Richard Kelly Browning. The scenario consists mostly of gangsters, bootleggers, movie personalities engaged in corruption-rampant cinematic-type behaviour. The series includes *'Box Office' Browning* (1987), *'Beverly Hills' Browning* (1987), *Browning Takes Off* (1989), *Browning in Buckskin* (1991), *Browning P.I.* (1992) and *Browning Battles On* (1993). A fourth series may well be in the offing if *Set Up* (1992) with its new character Luke Dunlop, a found-guilty-of-corruption ex-cop, is any indication. Corris's 'word-factory' (as it has been called) continues in full production.

Corris has also written two books based on boxing, *Lords of the Ring* (1980, a history of prize-fighting in Australia) and *The Winning Side* (1984, fiction). *The Gulliver Fortune* (1989), Corris's large (405 pages) and successful historical novel with its myriad of sub-plots and intertwining actions is a family saga which begins properly with the voyage of pornographic publisher John Gulliver and his family from England to Australia. Catastrophe strikes their ship, *Southern Maid*, and the Gullivers are scattered far and wide. The story then centres on a modern-day search for the Gulliver descendants who have become heirs to a Turner painting, 'Harwich Seascape'. Corris has also written *Naismith's Dominion* (1990), a fictional account of a struggle for power in the British Jeremiah Islands Protectorate in the South Pacific in the 1920s. He collaborated with the late Professor Fred Hollows, whom he much admired, in the latter's autobiography.

A skilled writer in all the genres he has attempted, Corris is pre-eminent as an exponent of crime fiction, where he has demonstrated a remarkable ability to create and maintain credibility of character, dialogue and ambience and to devise and manipulate exciting and realistic action.

Corroboree, see **Australian Literature Society**

'Corroboree' is the term for an Aboriginal ceremonial dance accompanied by song. The dancers are usually painted with clay in traditional designs. Music is provided by clapping sticks and the didgeridoo. The circle of dancers in the corroboree is known as the bora ring; Judith Wright's poem 'Bora Ring', regrets the loss of the corroboree in modern times. One of the earliest instances of the corroboree in Australian literature is in David Burn's play *The Bushrangers* (performed 1829), where a 'corobbora' is mentioned.

Cosme, see **New Australia**

Cosmos Magazine, which contained a considerable amount of literary material, both creative writing (stories, sketches, poetry) and review articles, ran monthly in Sydney 1894–99, after which it was incorporated into the monthly *Southern Cross* 1898–1900. Its contributors included G.B. Barton, Edward Dyson, Ernest Favenc and 'Price Warung'.

Cotters' England, a novel by Christina Stead (q.v.), was published in London in 1967 and in New York in 1966 with the title *Dark Places of the Heart*. The two titles reflect the novel's dual political-personal theme. Set in working- and middle-class England of the early 1950s and written almost wholly in dialogue with a cumulative rather than a chronological plot form, the story centres on Nellie Cook, née Cotter, a domineering woman from the industrial north. Loquacious, excitable, histrionic, Nellie is a compelling study of unconscious corruption, a coarse-grained egoist who manipulates the emotions of her relatives and friends. A vociferous champion of the underdog, she works for a socialist newspaper and is married to a trade union organiser although, like her husband, she is a political charlatan. The past effects of her influence, apparent in the stunted lives of her sister Peggy and brother Tom, are dramatically acted out in a grotesque scene in a Palace of Mirrors. It is clear that she has a stifled incestuous relationship with Tom, and lesbian undercurrents also affect her connections with the various women who are drawn to her Islington house. They reach a tragic culmination in the suicide of her protégée, Caroline.

COTTON, John (1801–49), born London, arrived in Australia in 1843. His account of the voyage was published as *Journal of a Voyage in the Barque, 'Parkfield'* (1845). Cotton soon became a substantial squatter, occupying about 60 square miles by 1846. His correspondence with his brother William in England is of historical significance and was published by George Mackaness in 1953. His great-granddaughter, Maie Casey, wrote of him in *An Australian Story 1837–1907* (1962).

COTTRELL, Dorothy (1902–57), born Picton, NSW, contracted infantile paralysis as a child and was thereafter confined to a wheelchair. The separation of her parents led to a rather chaotic girlhood, part of which she spent on stations in Queensland. She attended classes at the Royal Art Society of NSW and became a competent black-and-white artist. At 18 she went to live at Ularunda station near Morven, Queensland, and married the station bookkeeper in 1922. Her first novel, *The Singing Gold*, serialised in the American *Ladies Home Journal* in 1927 and in the *Sydney Mail* in 1928, was published in book form in 1928. Set in pastoral Queensland and Dunk Island off the Queensland coast, *The Singing Gold* is a warm, unsophisticated story of young love. It takes its title from the ground lark, an attractive small golden bird which flourishes in the open Queensland grasslands.

Royalties from *The Singing Gold* enabled the Cottrells to go to America; they returned to Australia only briefly 1954–56. In the USA Dorothy became a successful journalist and writer, especially of short fiction on Australian themes. She published *Earth Battle* (1930, titled *Tharlane* in America); less charming and less successful than *The Singing Gold*, *Earth Battle* draws a grim picture of the struggle between man and the environment in western Queensland. A later novel, *The Silent Reefs* (1953), a tale of mystery and adventure set in the Caribbean, was serialised in the *Saturday Evening Post* and filmed in 1959. She also published two children's books, *Winks: His Book* (1934) and *Wilderness Orphan* (1936).

COUANI, Anna (1948–), born Sydney of Greek and Polish descent, was educated at the University of Sydney and teaches art and English at secondary level. Founder of the small-press publishing companies Magic Sam and Sea Cruise Books, she was a founding member of the Sydney women writers' group 'No Regrets'. She has published stories and prose poems in numerous periodicals and anthologies and in four collections, *Italy* (1977), *Were All Women Sex-Mad?* (1982), *The Train* (1983, published with Barbara Brooks's *Leaving Queensland*) and, with Peter Lyssiotis, *The Harbour Breathes* (1989), short-listed in the 1990 Victorian Premier's Literary Awards. She has also co-edited *Island in the Sun* 1 (1980), *Island in the Sun* 2 (1981), *Telling Ways: Australian Women's Experimental Writing* (1988) and *Angry Women* (1989). Preoccupied with what lies beneath the surface of everyday life, Couani's prose poems explore the disjunction between the apparent inconsequentiality of mundane happenings, images, gestures/expressions and their deep, hidden and even inexpressible personal consequences. Skilfully evoking the casual absorption of painful experience in external society, Couani exposes the disjunction between personal feeling and impersonality, between so-called rationality and impulse, recording sensations of alienation, dissociation, failures of relationship and general social malaise. Underlying all her work is a keen interest in the links between personal attitudes and public power structures, in the inexorable, insidious influence of politics on everyday living; as one of her narrators comments, people's behaviour can be explained 'in terms of power both attributed and actual, personal and public'.

COUNGEAU, Emily (1860–1936), born Essex, England, came to Australia in 1887. She published several books of verse, including *Stella Australis* (1914), *Rustling Leaves* (1920), *Palm Fronds* (1927) and *Fern Leaves* (1934). Her verse drama *Princess Mona* (1916) is a fantasy in which a pageant of Anzac is featured.

COUNIHAN, Noel (1913–86), born Albert Park, Melbourne, went to the National Gallery Drawing School at night while working by day in a Flinders Lane warehouse. Counihan exhibited his first drawings in a Melbourne restaurant in 1933, as a result of which he gained a job as a newspaper cartoonist with the Melbourne *Argus*. His cartoons of the 1930s Depression, in which he often used the nude human figure to depict social injustice, are among his best known. Following a career as a political cartoonist for newspapers, mostly those with radical tendencies, he turned in 1941 to painting, winning the major prize in 1945 in the 'Australia at War' art competition exhibited at the National Gallery of Victoria. A socialist-realist painter, Counihan deplored through his art the Vietnam War, urban poverty, racism and human suffering. Two literary personalities he depicted are Henry Lawson and Alan Marshall. *Noel Counihan: Caricatures* (1985) contains a fine introduction by Vane Lindesay. Bernard Smith wrote the definitive work on Counihan, *Noel Counihan: Artist and Revolutionary* (1993).

Count Your Dead (1968), subtitled *A Novel of Vietnam,* was written by professional Australian soldier John Rowe (q.v.), who served for a year in the Vietnam War. The novel, centred on the village of Dong Tuy, earmarked for destruction because it is suspected of harbouring Viet Cong, presents a realistic picture of the jungle war and concerns the relationship between two officers who disagree on the pacification programme of the area.

COUPER, J.M. (John Mill) (1914–), born Dundee, Scotland, came in 1951 to Australia, where he lectured in education and English at the universities of Queensland and NSW and Macquarie University. Couper has published several volumes of verse, *East of Living* (1967), *The Book of Bligh* (1969), *In From the Sea* (1974), *The Lee Shore* (1979) and *Canterbury Folk* (1984); he also published two children's books, *The Thundering Good To-Day* (1970) and *Looking for a Wave* (1973). *East of Living* has four sections: 'Cape Catastrophe', which tells of the drowning in the Great Australian Bight of the master and several of the crew of Matthew Flinders's ship the *Investigator*; a series of sonnets addressed to Mark Alexander Boyd (1563–1601), a Scottish poet with whom Couper, exiled in Australia, feels he shares experiences of love, life and nostalgia for home; 'Catterline', in which a born loser ultimately achieves self-respect and a resolution of his place in the scheme of things; and 'East of Living', which reflects Couper's own intellectual, cultural and spiritual estrangement in Australia and his attempt to come to terms with the situation. *Canterbury Folk*, continues Couper's predilection for both the sonnet form and for translations of the classics while again achieving his usual high quality of language and thought. *The Book of Bligh* is a contribution to the voyager theme (q.v.) in Australian writing, recounting the mutiny on the *Bounty* and the epic voyage of Bligh and his crew in a small boat to Timor. It also makes moral and psychological judgements on the Bligh story, contrasting the integrity and selfless sense of service displayed in those events with the hedonism of modern man. *In from the Sea* is more emphatically personal, with the values instilled in Couper's early life and upbringing in Scotland in obvious collision with the new Australian attitudes and environment.

Courier-Mail, see *Brisbane Courier*

Courland Penders, an old derelict family estate, is the setting for a sequence of poems by Michael Dransfield (q.v.). The imaginary house, introduced in Dransfield's *Streets of the Long Voyage* (1970) in the poem 'Portrait of the Artist as an Old Man', is further described in 'Courland Penders: Going Home', 'Tapestry at Courland Penders', 'Library, Courland Penders', 'Birch Trees, Courland Penders' and 'Courland Penders: Reminiscences'. The obsession with vanished glory indicates the romantic strain in Dransfield.

COURTIER, Sidney Hobson (1904–74), born Kangaroo Flat, Victoria, worked as a schoolteacher in rural Victoria and Melbourne. He was the author of twenty-six crime novels, set in various parts of Australia and mostly published in London. They include *Gold for My Fair Lady* (1951), *The Mudflat Million* (1955), *One Cried Murder* (1956), *Now Seek My Bones* (1957), *Come Back to Murder* (1957), *Death in Dreamtime* (1959), *Gently Dust the Corpse* (1960), *Let the Man Die* (1961), *Mimic a Murder* (1964), *A Corpse Won't Sing* (1964), *Murder's Burning* (1967), *No Obelisk for Emily* (1970), *Ligny's Lake* (1971), and *A Window in Chungking* (1975).

Cousin from Fiji, The, a novel by Norman Lindsay (q.v.), was first published in 1945. Set in Ballarat, Victoria, in the 1890s, it describes the comically unsettling effects of Cecilia Bellairs and her 18-year-old daughter Ella, recently arrived from Fiji to live with their relations the Domkins. The romantic adventures of Cecilia and Ella as they successfully elude Ballarat's strait-laced conventions structure the story, although there is a range of memorable characters. These include the outwardly respectable Uncle George, torn between two mistresses and threatened with financial ruin; the indomitable Grandma Domkin, who combines senility and licence to farcical effect; and her intimate, old Miss Biddlecombe, still manically obsessed with romantic pursuit. By means of these and other characters, Lindsay presents a vivid contrast between the surface tedium of small-town religiosity and the comic excitement of its secret sexual life.

COUVREUR, Jessie ('Tasma') (1848–97) was born Jessie Huybers at Highgate, London, the eldest daughter of an Anglo-French mother and a father of Dutch extraction, and came to Australia when her family migrated to Tasmania in the early 1850s. The opening sequence of *Not Counting the Cost* (1895) is evidently based on her childhood in and near Hobart. In 1867 she married Charles Fraser; they settled on the land in the Kyneton district in Victoria, but the marriage was a failure and after long periods of separation (Jessie spent much of 1873–83 in England and Europe) they were divorced in 1883. In 1880 she embarked on a series of very successful lectures on Australia, delivered initially to the Geographical Society in Paris and later in the French provinces, Holland and Belgium. Returning to Europe, Jessie married in 1885 Auguste Couvreur, a Belgian journalist and politician. She was thereafter based in Brussels, succeeding her husband as Brussels correspondent of the London *Times* after his death in 1894.

Writing usually as 'Tasma', Couvreur began her literary career in 1877 with a contribution to *The 'Vagabond' Annual* and over the next few years had short stories, travel articles and other pieces published in the *Australasian*, the *Melbourne Review* and other annuals; before her divorce she helped to support herself in Europe by freelance journalism. Her major fiction, however, was written after 1885. *Uncle Piper of Piper's Hill* (q.v., 1889), her first and best novel, portrays middle-class society in colonial Melbourne; its characterisation, humour, and analysis of the interaction between the genteel but impoverished Cavendish family newly arrived from England, and their hosts the Pipers, won praise in England as well as Australia. Couvreur's later novels – *In Her Earliest Youth* (1890), *The Penance of Portia James* (1891), *A Knight of the White Feather* (1892), *Not Counting the Cost* (1895), and *A Fiery Ordeal* (1897) – may reflect contemporary interest in the problems of sexuality and marriage but are also informed by her experience of Charles Fraser: they characteristically portray heroines in Australia or England as the victims of husbands who to varying degrees are weak, boorish, egotistical, alcoholic, brutal and dishonest. Couvreur also wrote *A Sydney Sovereign and Other Tales* (1890), which reprints stories originally published in the *Australasian* in the 1880s, and had work included in the Anglo-Australian anthologies of A.P. Martin and others. Previously grouped with other women writers, such as Rosa Praed and Ada Cambridge, as writing outside the nationalist tradition established by the *Bulletin*, Couvreur has recently been rediscovered by feminist critics. Her work is discussed by Margaret Harris in *A Bright and Fiery Troop*, edited by Debra Adelaide (1988), and she is the subject of a biography by Patricia Clarke (1994).

COVE, Michael (1946–), born London, came in 1971 to Australia, where he has written for film, radio, stage and television. His stage plays include 'Fields of Offering', 'Gingerbread House', 'Running Away', *Dazzle*, 'Duckling', 'Convict Cakewalk', 'Kookaburra', 'Jesters', 'Mariner', *The Gift* (published in *Biala*, 1977), 'Happy Landings', *Family Lore* (published in *Theatre-Australia*, 1976 and in *Popular Short Plays for the Australian Stage. Volume 1* (1985) selected by Ron Blair) and, with Ron Blair, 'Too Early to Say'. *Dazzle* was published in the collection *Can't You Hear Me Talking to You?* (1978), ed. Alrene Sykes.

COWAN, Peter (1914–), born in Perth into a family long established in WA, spent most of the 1930s working as an itinerant labourer in rural areas before becoming a student at the University of WA in 1938. After serving with the RAAF in the Second World War, he became a teacher of English and geography at Scotch College. In Melbourne in the war years he was one of the group of artists and writers associated with the *Angry Penguins* (q.v.) movement. Some of Cowan's earliest stories appeared in *Angry Penguins*,

Direction and the *Ern Malley Journal*. His first collection was published by Reed and Harris and he has remained committed to the innovative, modernist ideals that underlay that movement. In 1964 he became a senior tutor at the University of WA, where he is now an honorary research fellow. He has published seven short-story collections, *Drift* (1944), *The Unploughed Land* (1958), *The Empty Street* (1965), *The Tins* (1973), *New Country* (1976), *Mobiles* (1979) and *Voices* (1988); another collection, *A Window in Mrs X's Place* (1986), was culled from earlier ones and edited by Bruce Bennett. Cowan has also written four novels, *Summer* (1964), *Seed* (1966), *The Color of the Sky* (1986), and *The Hills of Apollo Bay* (1989); two biographies, *A Unique Position – A Biography of Edith Dircksey Cowan 1861–1932* (1978), an account of his grandmother, the first woman member of an Australian parliament, and *Maitland Brown* (1988), a study of an influential, controversial WA personality which is also a historical account of life in the Colony in the latter half of the nineteenth century. Co-editor of *Westerly*, he has also edited or co-edited eight collections of short fiction and editions of writings by his ancestors, *A Colonial Experience – Perth and York 1839–1888* (1978) and *A Faithful Picture: The Letters of Eliza and Thomas Brown at York in the Swan River Colony 1841–1852* (1977).

Both in his short stories and novels, Cowan's central theme is isolation. The physical isolation imposed by the WA bush dominates his early work, although in *Seed* and his later stories he also contemplates the frustration and boredom of suburbia, the emotionally impoverished and fragmentary lives of middle-class Australians. His concern with the spiritual emptiness of Australian life is similar to Patrick White's, but he lacks White's satire and range, meanwhile expressing a more intense regional consciousness. A conservationist before the issue became fashionable, he has been preoccupied with the land from the first and is particularly sensitive to the relationship between the immensity of place and the human need to find a home. Hemingway is an acknowledged influence, although the influence is more a matter of prose rhythms, language and dramatisation than content, Cowan's subject matter owing nothing to the American. As sensitive to nuance as Chekhov, and as interested in silence and the power of the unspoken as Pinter, he characteristically avoids external dramatic events, concentrating on the drama of his characters' inner lives. If the carefully worked texture of his understated but concentrated prose rises to moments of lyrical intensity, the overall effect is one of seeming impassivity or subdued disengagement; mirroring the austerities of the WA landscape, his spare craft relies on minute subtle effects, the delicate interplay of colours and shapes, juxtapositions and echoes reminiscent of poetry or music to project emotion, to interpose the play of ironies and suggest a tentative form. Cowan's vision of human nature and the possibilities of relationship and communication has always been bleak, but an increasing scepticism about the state of contemporary Australia and especially the effects of commercial greed and environmental neglect can be detected in his later fiction. The stories of *Mobiles*, for instance, written as an interrelated group and supported by black-and-white photographs, expose a tougher, coarser emotional environment. The stories of *Voices* are the most minimalist in Cowan's work, abandoning punctuation and all external distractions in favour of the characters' internal failed or failing attempts at communication. *The Hills of Apollo Bay*, set in Perth and Melbourne and moving in time from the recent present to the pre-war and war years, emulates the spatial effects of painting and the reconciling effects of music, the art which 'encompasses everything, admits everything, all the contradictions of the world, even brutality, sadness and consolation. Yet it affirms that everything somehow is right.' The title of *The Color of the Sky* is taken from Stephen Crane's story *The Open Boat*, where four shipwrecked men intent on survival are unaware of the sky's colour as they concentrate on the waves; expressive of what Cowan has described as 'the fragmentary nature of today's living', the metaphor also suggests the gulf between the characters' consciousness of the need for meaning and pattern and their inability to discover them. Cowan was made AM in 1987 and received the Patrick White Award in 1992.

COWLING, G.H. (George Herbert) (1881–1946), born Leeds, England, was professor of English at the University of Melbourne 1928–43. An authority on Shakespeare, Milton and Blake, whose texts he edited, Cowling also wrote on other English literary figures. With Victorian poet 'Furnley Maurice', he compiled the significant anthology *Australian Essays* (1935). It was Cowling's critical article on Australian literature in the *Age* 16 February 1935 that partly led to Rex Ingamells's statement of Jindyworobak attitudes, *Conditional Culture* (1938), and it was also criticised by P.R. Stephensen.

COX, Erle (1873–1950), born Melbourne, was one of Melbourne's best-known journalists, working on the staff of the Melbourne *Argus*, the *Australasian* and later the *Age*. He published three novels: *Out of the Silence* (1925), a fantasy in which an Australian station-owner finds on his property an underground treasure house of remarkable works of art, craft and machinery which indicate the existence here of an older, superior civilisation; *Fool's Harvest* (1939), in which Cox, picturing Australia invaded by an oriental power, attempts to shake the country out of its lethargy as the Second World War approaches; and *The Missing Angel* (1947), which records the transformation, with the help of the Devil, of the strait-laced, sober young Melbourne wowser Tydvil Jones into a boisterous hedonist.

COX, William (1764–1837), born Dorset, England, arrived in NSW in 1800 and succeeded John Macarthur as paymaster of the NSW Corps. Cox was commissioned by Governor Lachlan Macquarie in 1814 to make the road across the Blue Mountains; the journal that he kept while making the road was published as *A Narrative of Proceedings of William Cox* (1888). It was republished in 1901 in *Memoirs of William Cox*, which includes some biographical details.

COYLE, William, see **KENEALLY, Thomas**

COZENS, Charles, see *Adventures of a Guardsman*

CRAIG, Ailsa (1917–), born Sydney, was educated at the University of Sydney and at universities in West Germany. She worked mainly as a teacher and journalist, was sub-editor of the *Australian Women's Weekly* 1950–51, the London correspondent for the *Sydney Morning Herald* 1954–57 and at various periods sub-editor, assistant editor, news editor and feature writer for *Woman's Day* 1957–76. The author of short stories and radio plays and of the long-running radio serial 'The Intruder' (1949), she also wrote the series 'Life With the Middletons' in *Woman's Day* which ran from the 1950s; a novel, *If Blood Should Stain the Wattle* (1947); and edited *Australia Album: the Past in Pictures* (1974). In 1966 she won the Walkley Award for the best magazine story.

CRAIG, Alexander (1923–), born Malvern, Victoria, studied at the universities of Melbourne and Iowa and served with the AIF in New Guinea, before teaching English at Macquarie University where he became director of literary craftsmanship. He has published three volumes of verse, *Far-Back Country* (1954), *The Living Sky* (1964) and *When No-One is Looking* (1977); and edited *Twelve Poets 1950–1970* (1971). Craig's poetry is included in numerous anthologies, including *Eight by Eight* (1963), *Poetry in Australia* (1964) and *The Penguin Book of Australian Verse* (1972).

Cranky Jack, a character who occasionally appears in the Rudd family books, is a bush 'hatter' (q.v.) whose arrival at the selection is narrated in 'Cranky Jack', a story in *On Our Selection* (1899). Engaged by Dad Rudd at no wages, Cranky Jack is a willing worker but subject to delusions of paranoia; on one occasion when chasing a snake that he is convinced is the Devil, he recoils in horror from his own image, which he sees in a mirror and thinks is his father. Locked away because he terrifies Mother Rudd, Jack escapes, smashes the mirror and becomes a docile worker for the family again. The story has been seen as a dramatic and psychologically coherent comment on the decline in familial relationships because of the rigours of selection life. 'Cranky Jack' in the book version combines the stories 'Jack or Cranky Jack' (*Bulletin*, 1897) and 'His Father' (*Bulletin*, 1899).

CRAWFORD, Eugénie, see **McNEIL, Eugénie**

CRAWFORD, R.M. (Raymond Maxwell) (1906–91), born Grenfell, NSW, was professor of history at the University of Melbourne 1937–71 and chairman of the Australian Humanities Research Council 1966–68. His role as an influential teacher and his contribution to Australia's intellectual life are recognised in a special edition of *Historical Studies* (1971). His published works include *The Study of History* (1939), *Ourselves and the Pacific* (1941), *Australia* (1952), *An Australian Perspective* (1960) and *'A Bit of a Rebel': The Life and Work of George Arnold Wood* (1975). He was made OBE in 1971.

'Creek of the Four Graves, The', one of Australia's earliest narrative poems, was published by Charles Harpur (q.v.) in *The Bushrangers, A Play in Five Acts, and Other Poems* (1853). Its story of a group of settlers murdered by natives is presented with individuality and force. Set in the Hawkesbury district and the Blue Mountains, the poem combines a realistic narrative with effective description of the local Australian scene.

Creeve Roe (1947), a collection of Victor Daley's (q.v.) radical and satiric verse, was edited by Muir Holburn and Marjorie Pizer. The title (also Daley's pseudonym) is taken from the Red Branch Knights of Conchubar, one-time kings of Ulster. Most of the poems had been published earlier in the *Bulletin* and the *Tocsin*, a labour weekly which was edited in the 1890s by fellow radical Bernard O'Dowd. One of Daley's best-known satirical poems (mainly on A.G. Stephens) is 'Narcissus and Some Tadpoles', published in the *Bulletin* (19 April 1899).

CRESWELL, Rosemary (1941–), born Sydney, has worked in a variety of occupations including a period as a teaching fellow at the University of Sydney and is now a literary agent. She has published short stories in numerous periodicals and in two collections, *Colouring In* (1986, with Jean Bedford) and *Lovers and Others* (1989), and has edited a volume of stories by contemporary Australian writers which deal with the experience of travel, *Home and Away* (1987). With Carol Manners she has collaborated in crime fiction under the joint pseudonym 'Ruth Clarement'. See Crime Fiction.

CREW, Gary, see *The Oxford Companion to Australian Children's Literature (1993), pp. 112–13.*

CRICK, Donald (1916–), born Sydney, has combined creative writing with such occupations as farm and factory worker, clerk, insurance representative, publisher, and book reviewer for the *Australian* and the *Sydney Morning Herald*. He has published five novels, *Bikini Girl* (1963), *Martin Place* (1964), *Period of Adjustment* (1966), *A Different Drummer* (1972) and *The Moon to Play With* (1981). *Period of Adjustment*, the first Australian novel, in the opinion of its author, to deal specifically with class distinctions and values in Australian society, won the Dame Mary Gilmore Centenary Prize in 1965. *The Moon to Play With*, a satirical comedy, won the Rigby 1980 Anniversary Award.

Crime Fiction, like its companion genre science or speculative fiction, has not been prominent, historically, in Australian literature. Regarded by most literary critics as writing of a 'sub-literary level' (Edmund Wilson's judgement), crime fiction has seldom been included in any country's mainstream literature. Yet it continues to be widely read and appreciated in almost every country. In the USA and Britain the early to mid-nineteenth century saw the rise of the first major crime and detection writers (in English) such as Edgar Allan Poe, Wilkie Collins and (later) Arthur Conan Doyle and such detective/investigator creations as Nick Carter and Sherlock Holmes. With the exception of Fergus Hume's *The Mystery of a Hansom Cab* (q.v., 1886), Australia had little of worth to exhibit in crime fiction in the same period. Lucy Sussex, examining the early achievements of Australian women crime fiction writers, points to Mary Fortune, who wrote, as 'W.W.' or 'Waif Wanderer', about 500 detective stories in the *Australian Journal* 1866–1909, and to Ellen Davitt (sister-in-law of Anthony Trollope), who wrote the murder mystery *Force and Fraud* (1865), but these writers are not of the quality of their contemporaries overseas. Similarly, the success of American crime fiction writers through the 1930s–1950s, such as Raymond Chandler, Erle Stanley Gardner, Dashiell Hammett, 'Ellery Queen' and 'Mickey Spillane', had really no equivalent in Australia, although 'Carter Brown' wrote about 150 mystery/violence stories which come close to belonging to the crime fiction genre and Paul McGuire published a dozen or more murder stories in the 1930s. Arthur Upfield's stories, centred on the part-Aboriginal detective Napoleon Bonaparte ('Bony'), quite clearly belong to the genre as do Jon Cleary's slightly later Scobie Malone novels. Upfield was the first foreign writer to be admitted as a full member of the Mystery Writers' Guild of America, and Jon Cleary was later (1975) to win the Mystery Writers Edgar Allan Poe Award. Michael Tolley and Peter Moss are currently editing for Wakefield Press of SA a series of 'forgotten' or 'neglected' Australian 'crime classics' from roughly the first half of the twentieth century. Whether *The Whispering Wall* and *The Souvenir* by Patricia Carlon (q.v.), *The Misplaced Corpse* and *Sinners Never Die* by A.E. Martin (q.v.), *A Hank of Hair* and *Beat Not the Bones* (which won the inaugural Edgar Allan Poe Award in 1952) by Charlotte Gay, *Vanishing Point* by Pat Flower (q.v.), *The Secret of the Garden* by Arthur Gask (q.v.), and S.H. Courtier's *Ligny Lake*, the early titles in the series, are truly 'classics' of crime fiction is doubtful. Tolley, assisted by Adela Love and Robin Eaden, is also compiling a bibliography of crime in Australasian fiction which will not only provide a complete account of the genre in this country but will record each and every crime ever *mentioned* in Australasian fiction. Tolley's newsletter, aptly titled *The Body Dabbler* (34 issues to mid-1994), records the progress of the bibliography.

The Wakefield Crime Classics, valuable as they will be to remind readers and critics of the authors included in the series, are unlikely to convince them that this work represents a once-lost golden age of Australian crime fiction now rediscovered. There is some evidence, however, that such a golden era did begin in 1980 with the publication of Peter Corris's (q.v.) first novel in the Cliff Hardy series, *The Dying Trade*, a series that has (to the end of 1993) stretched to eighteen titles and made Hardy the best-known character in contemporary Australian fiction. The achievements of Peter Corris are noted elsewhere in this *Companion* but the tremendous upsurge in crime fiction writing that accompanied the Cliff Hardy series must, in part at least, be attributed to Corris's success. Many outstanding contemporary crime fiction writers are women. Marele Day, like Corris, finds Sydney a rich and suitable setting for crime stories, *The Case of the Chinese Boxes* (1990) being set in Sydney's inner-city Chinatown and suburban Asian Cabramatta. Day's 'private-eye' is a lively creation, Claudia Valentine, a 'part-time' mother, whose children spend much of their time with their father in Queensland. Day's other novels, *The Life and Crimes of Harry Lavender* (1988) and *The Last Tango of Dolores Delgado* (1992, winner of the 1993 American Shamus Crime Fiction Award), confirm her position among the leading group of contemporary crime-writers. Susan Geason, literary editor of the Sydney *Sun-Herald* since 1992 and the author of several do-it-yourself 'Preventing Crime' books, has written several racy and entertaining crime novels, *Shaved Fish* (1990), *Dogfish* (1991), *Swordfish* (1993) and *Sharkbait* (1993), titles catching the surname of her new-to-the-game 'private-eye' Syd Fish, an inept ex-journalist and politician-minder. Jennifer Rowe, editor of the *Australian Women's Weekly* and successful children's books writer (as 'Emily Rodda'), has adopted the crime fiction mode with conspicuous success in *Grim Pickings* (1987), *Murder by the Book* (1989), *Death in Store* (1991), *The Makeover Murders* (1992) and *Stranglehold* (1993). Rowe's creation Verity Birdwood ('Birdie') is an ABC researcher and amateur detective, who solves mysteries in the reasoned Agatha Christie manner rather than in the more violent ways of her counterparts in other books. Jan McKemmish has been successful with *A Gap in the Records* (1985), a creative, spy-cum-detection thriller set in Australia after the Second World War, and *Only Lawyers Dancing* (1992), a skilful attempt to lift the literary level of crime fiction by, among other methods, varying the formula of using a bumbling/inept/violent/sleazy/seedy professional 'private-eye', her sleuths being a lawyer and a photographer, both female. Jean Bedford (q.v.), author of several other well-known works such as *Country Girl Again*, has written two crime fiction novels involving her 'private-eye' Anna Southwood, *Worse Than Death* (1991) and *To Make a Killing* (1992). Kerry Greenwood, a self-confessed long-time devotee of the genre, has written five books for her splendid creation, the glamorous young 1930s up-market 'flapper', the Hon. Phryne Fisher, who sleuths with style through Melbourne in *Cocaine Blues* (1989), *Flying Too High* (1990), *Murder on the Ballarat Train* (1991), *Death at Victoria Dock* (1992) and *The Green Mill Murder* (1993). Gabrielle Lord, a script-writer (e.g. TV's *Last Resort*) as well as a novelist with several topical thrillers to her credit, including *Fortress* (1980), *Tooth and Claw* (1983), *Jumbo* (1986), and the speculative fiction eco-thriller *Salt* (1990), uses two women, a lawyer, Cass Meredith, and a part-Aboriginal nicknamed Seal, to head a team investigating sexual perversion in the crime thriller *Whipping Boy* (1992). Other crime fiction works by women include Claire McNab's *Cop Out* (1991) and *Off Key* (1992) and 'Melissa Chan's'

Too Rich (1991) and *One Too Many* (1993), with lesbian sleuths; Brenda Walker's *Crush* (1991), set in Perth and a solid swipe at the masculine nature of the genre; well-known poet Jennifer Maiden's well-plotted and skilfully narrated psychological thriller *Play With Knives* (1990); 'Ruth Clarement's' (Carol Manners and Rosemary Creswell) *To Sleep To Die* (1989) and *Drop Dead Minister* (1991); 'Catherine Lewis's' and Judith Guerin's two popular books of intrigue, *Unable by Reason of Death* (1989) and *Not in Single Spies* (1992); and Finola Moorhead's *Still Murder* (1991) (winner of the 1992 Victorian Premier's Award for Fiction), which uses the crime fiction genre not only to tell a compelling mystery tale but also to explore changing patterns of male–female attitudes, especially as these attitudes are reflected in her characters, the detective Margot Norman of the National Crime Authority in NSW, and the 'betrayed' Vietnam 'warrior' Peter Larsen. Delys Bird edited in 1993 *Killing Women*, a collection of articles by many prominent Australian crime fiction writers.

Male writers of crime fiction have been equally numerous in the 1980s and early 1990s, some of them experts in other literary fields, e.g. the late R.F. Brissenden (q.v.) who satisfied, in retirement, a lifelong urge to write thrillers, producing the well-plotted and racily written *Poor Boy* (1987) and *Wildcat* (1991). A planned third book in the series may well have allowed hero Tom Caxton to prevail finally over the villain, Tiburzi. Garry Disher (q.v.), a skilled exponent of the short story, is seen by many as Corris's nearest rival. His incipient crime series, begun with *Kickback* (1991), *Paydirt* (1992) and *Deathdeal* (1993), has as its central character the cold, menacing professional thief Wyatt, who bears a seemingly charmed, if totally charmless, life in the world of organised crime that he inhabits. David Foster (q.v.), one-time research scientist and multi-award-winning novelist, has, among his wide-ranging, idiosyncratic works, the detective novel *Dog Rock* (1985), whose narrator and central character is the postman-turned-detective D'Arcy D'Oliveres. Amusing but serious, *Dog Rock* is an effective detective story that exposes, along with the villainy, social injustice and class hostility. Steve Wright, English-born, uses an English detective, Barry Donovan, in his three enjoyable crime fiction books *Love, Avalon* (1990), *A Drop in the Ocean* (1991) and *A Break in the Traffic* (1992). Ken Methold, playwright, scriptwriter and author of numerous educational texts, uses the wry, dry, stubborn ex-Queensland policeman Alec McIntyre as his 'private-eye' on the Gold Coast in *Death by Defamation* (1991). Methold also wrote *Moonlight over the Estuary* (1989) and *Sherlock Holmes in Australia* (1991).

Robert G. Barrett, who has booming sales figures while more sophisticated writers fail to attract readers, reaches back into his own personal experience to write tough, violent, sexual thrillers at the centre of which is his good-hearted bruiser Les Norton, who metes out a kind of rough justice as he thumps his way through life. Experienced journalist and novelist Ian Moffitt, who has been assessed as Australia's John Le Carré, began his thriller mysteries with *The Colour Man*

(1983) and has also written *Blue Angels* (1987), a psychological thriller leading back to the Second World War, and *Gilt Edge* (1991). Max Gill's *Count Down for Murder* (1992), set in the desert around Woomera and Coober Pedy, won first prize in the 1992 Tom Howard mystery novel contest, while Paul Mann's *Season of the Monsoon* (1992) investigates a series of murders of homosexuals in Bombay, India, linking those present-day murders to the son of a similar serial killer of the 1930s.

Denis Freney's *Larry Death* (1991) deliberately parodies Cliff Hardy with his 'private-eye' of the title. The ranks of crime and thriller mystery fiction include Richard Cassidy (also a film and television writer), whose first novel is *White Collar* (1992) about computer crime; Kel Richards (an ABC broadcaster), who writes biblical 'whodunits', e.g. *The Case of the Vanishing Corpse* (1990) and *The Case of the Secret Assassin* (1992); John Sligo, who has written numerous and varied thrillers under the pseudonym 'Tom Beauford'; J.R. Carroll, whose *No Way Back* (1992) and *Out of the Blue* (1993), portray a homicidal, sexually fixated, over-the-edge cop, Detective Sergeant Dennis Gatz, who is the counterpart of countless TV cops both in America and recently in Australia. Other notable and successful writers in a long list are Richard Hall with *Spy's Revenge* (1987), *Costello* (1989) and *Bailey* (1991), Martin Long with his Gaslight Mystery series set in Sydney in the 1880s, Robin Wallace-Crabbe ('Robert Wallace') with his Essington series, 'Tom Howard' (John Howard Reid) with his mystery novels beginning with *The Health Farm Murders* in 1985, John Baxter, who, with *Bondi Blues* (1993), has unleashed a new P.I., Noakes, a hard-boiled ex-con, and Debra Adelaide and Laurie Bookluck, who have introduced Aboriginal detectives, Sergeant Tathra and her gay partner, Constable Pat Temple, in *Headlines* (1993).

Other indications of this upsurge of interest in crime fiction (in addition to the Wakefield Press series) include the 1992 National Word Festival presenting as its chief overseas literary guest the British crime fiction writer P.D. James, and the emergence in October 1990 of the crime, mystery and detective fiction magazine *Mean Streets*, edited by Stuart Coupe and Julie Ogden, which offers crime enthusiasts interviews with leading crime fiction writers, reviews and extracts from newly published works. So regular is the output of such works that *Australian Book Review* has, since 1991, allowed a special crime fiction section, 'Guilt Edge', in almost every issue with reviewers such as Philip Bryan and John Carroll assessing each month's publications. Several popular anthologies have also appeared, including *Sand on the Gumshoe* (1989), edited by David Latta, *Dead Witness* (1989), edited by Stephen Knight, and *Crosstown Traffic* (1993), compiled by Stuart Coupe, Julie Ogden and Robert Hood Stephen. Knight has compiled four annual anthologies for Allen & Unwin, *Crimes for a Summer Christmas*; Jennifer Rowe is to take over that editorship in 1994. Crime fiction and science fiction, with their large and regular sales, are, it would seem, subsidising the publication of the less popular, more traditional literary genres. What has to be emphasised, however, is that crime fiction is no longer the escapist whodunit writing of a generation ago. The themes of crime fiction have become increasingly complex with corporate crime, political corruption, international commercial espionage having taken over from simple murder and bank robbery. Often, in recent times, the investigators of crime have become the moral heroes and heroines of the day. The solving of crime has become the arena of high tech, and the cop on the beat, the P.I. sitting all night in the car on the corner, have been consigned to literary history.

Critic (1), an Adelaide weekly which ran 1897–1924 when it was succeeded by the *Gossip*, carried, especially in its later years, literary articles, poetry and news of books and authors. C.J. Dennis was briefly its editor (c.1904). Various other journals entitled *Critic* were published earlier, e.g. 1843 (Sydney), 1862–63 (Adelaide), 1873 (Sydney), 1883 (Melbourne), 1889 (Windsor, NSW) and 1892–93 (Hobart).

Critic (2), a mainly monthly journal published by the Literary Society of the University of WA in Perth, ran 1961–70. Its contributors included many significant literary personalities of WA, e.g. Gavin Casey, Henrietta Drake-Brockman, Mary Durack, J.K. Ewers, Dorothy Hewett and Randolph Stow.

Criticism. The beginnings of literary criticism in Australia are inextricably bound up with the early history of magazine publishing in the colonies. As Frank S. Greenop's *History of Magazine Publishing in Australia* (1947) makes clear, the early decades of the nineteenth century are strewn with short-lived journals, some of which at least made a gesture towards disseminating literary views and information. The first magazine published in NSW, the *Australian Magazine*, appeared in 1821 under the editorship of the Rev. Ralph Mansfield as *A Compendium of Religious, Literary, and Miscellaneous Intelligence*; it laid greater stress, however, on religious than on literary matters. The *Australian Quarterly Journal* paid equally slight attention to literature from its inception in Sydney in 1828; the *Hobart Town Magazine*, produced 1833–34 by Henry Melville, was rather livelier in tone and content. Meagre as it was, most of the literary material that found its way into the early colonial magazines was largely derived from and concerned with English writing; a good deal of it, indeed, was reprinted from English sources.

As early as 1838 James Martin, then only 18, published his *Australian Sketch Book*, a collection of essays, one of which, 'The Pseudo-Poets', was an unflattering account of some Australian versifiers. In spite of Martin's *Sketch Book* most of the still rudimentary criticism of colonial writers appeared in magazines or newspapers of the day. In 1855–56 the *Month* caused some stir in Sydney largely by virtue of the controversial style of Frank Fowler (q.v.), a young visitor to the Colony, and by the contributions of 'Peter Possum' (Richard Rowe). In 1856 the *Leader* began publication as the weekly companion of the *Age*, to be followed in 1864 by the *Australasian* produced in the office of the *Argus*. These were early examples of the close connec-

tion between criticism and journalism which continued in Australia to the end of the nineteenth century and beyond. A Sydney counterpart to the *Australasian* was the *Sydney Mail*, which had a close association with the *Sydney Morning Herald*. Almost contemporaneously with these ventures, there were attempts to reproduce in Australia the success of the London *Punch*. *Melbourne Punch* appeared in 1855, the first Sydney *Punch* in 1856, and for the rest of the century there were sporadic attempts to emulate the British journal.

In the 1860s much of the liveliest literary discussion was centred in Melbourne, and especially within such groups as the Yorick Club and the Cave of Adullam, some of whose leading members are recollected in Hugh McCrae's *My Father and My Father's Friends* (1935). *Melbourne Punch*, for instance, included among its founding writers R.H. Horne, Marcus Clarke and Frederick Sinnett. Sinnett is especially notable for his essay *The Fiction Fields of Australia* (q.v., 1966), first published in two instalments in the *Journal of Australasia* in 1856. This early conspectus of the Australian novel included comments on *Clara Morison* (1854), *The Emigrant Family* (1849) and *Tales of the Colonies* (1843), as well as taking up the general problem of developing a native literature in a derivative culture, an issue which has continued to exercise Australian criticism ever since. Some of Sinnett's remarks about the thinness of the social materials on which fiction might be based quite remarkably foreshadow Henry James's more celebrated remarks in his *Hawthorne* (1879) of more than twenty years later.

While Melbourne was developing a lively literary community, Sydney was also discovering new ways of supporting cultural activity. The University of Sydney was founded in 1852, and soon began to help the fostering of the arts, which before that time had rested largely on the efforts of individual patrons like Nicol Drysdale Stenhouse. In the 1850s, furthermore, a revived Mechanics' School of Arts provided another forum for literary discussion and debate. Yet it was not until 1864 that there appeared what Cecil Hadgraft (q.v.) has described as the 'first piece of literary criticism published in Australia as a separate work'. William Walker's *Australian Literature* was first given as a public lecture in the Windsor School of Arts, 20 July 1864. Restricting his survey to NSW, Walker argued that, while no great Australian author had yet appeared, 'Australia certainly has a literature, though it is a circumscribed one'. In support of his case, he gave some account of magazine publication in the colony as well as of historical writing and verse.

Two years later G.B. Barton produced *The Poets and Prose Writers of New South Wales* (q.v., 1866), among the first examples of a kind of work – the chronological review of the national achievement in creative literature – that has consistently attracted the attention of Australian critics. In association with his survey, Barton compiled a companion work, *Literature in New South Wales* (q.v., 1866). By the late 1860s, too, the time was ripe for the appearance of another mode of criticism by which to interpret a literary tradition already more than half a century old. J. Sheridan

Moore's *Life and Genius of J.L. Michael* (1868), in its own right a minor study of a minor poetaster, nevertheless initiated a kind of critical activity important to the repertoire of any culture. Sheridan Moore began contributing to literary journalism in Sydney at much the same time as Marcus Clarke was writing for the Melbourne newspapers. Clarke collected some of his journalistic pieces in *The Peripatetic Philosopher* (1869); several of his more explicitly critical essays, e.g. on 'Balzac and Modern French Literature' and 'Charles Dickens', are included in *A Colonial City, High and Low Life: Selected Journalism of Marcus Clarke* (1972), edited by L.T. Hergenhan.

Probably the best-known single piece of Clarke's critical prose is, however, his introduction to the posthumous edition of A.L. Gordon's *Sea Spray and Smoke Drift* (1876). In spite of propagating much misinformation about Australia's 'trees without shade' and 'flowers without perfume', Clarke's essay made three significant contributions to the stock of critical ideas about Australian writing: it stressed the gothic element in the Australian literary imagination, identified the response to landscape as an abiding issue, and lavished high praise on Gordon. From the year of Gordon's death (1870) at least until the end of the nineteenth century, Australian critics consistently placed him at the head of their country's roll of poets. Arthur Patchett Martin, for example, included some highly laudatory remarks about Gordon in his *Fernshawe* (1882), as did Francis Adams in *The Australians: A Social Sketch* (1893). Gordon was the only poet allotted a complete chapter in Desmond Byrne's *Australian Writers* (q.v., 1896), while Martin repeated his praise in *The Beginnings of Australian Literature* (1898) at the same time as he assigned Marcus Clarke an equivalent place in fiction. *The Beginnings of Australian Literature* was originally delivered as a lecture in London, 27 March 1898, and in their *The Development of Australian Literature* (1898) H.G. Turner and Alexander Sutherland identify Martin and Douglas Sladen as prime movers in developing a London awareness of Australian writing. By 1898, however, significant forces were generating a critical response to Australian writing on its own soil. The best known of these was the Sydney weekly the *Bulletin,* founded in 1880. From 1894 to 1906 the literary voice of the *Bulletin* was A.G. Stephens (q.v.), who instituted the paper's famous Red Page on 29 August 1896. Stephens's personal self-confidence, critical astuteness and wide knowledge of literature gave the *Bulletin* an influence and importance in literary matters probably unmatched by any Australian weekly before or since. Stephens himself was arguably the first great critic to have been produced by Australian society. He certainly assisted the careers of virtually every important writer of his generation, e.g. Joseph Furphy through the acceptance of *Such is Life* (1903), as well as providing a forum for wide-ranging, often competing, critical ideas and attitudes. The writers of the 1890s did not, nevertheless, have to depend entirely on the *Bulletin* for periodical publication. The latter years of the century were as rich in ephemeral magazines as any earlier decade. Eighteen eighty-eight was an ap-

propriate year for the *Centennial Magazine* to appear in Sydney; it was followed two years later by the *Australasian Critic* (1890); in 1899 the *Australian Magazine* carried work by Christopher Brennan and John le Gay Brereton among others; the *Antipodean* appeared in Melbourne 1893–97. During the 1890s also, several collections of essays appeared, some carrying pieces on Australian writers and writing. In 1893 C.H. Pearson published *National Life and Character* and in 1896 *Reviews and Critical Essays*. A.H. Carney's *Land of the Dawning* (1894) combined *belles-lettres* with some critical comment, while A.G. Stephens rounded out his *Bulletin* years with *The Red Pagan* (1906). The closing years of the century were also marked by some efforts to provide reliable texts of major writers. Charles Harpur had been poorly served by the posthumous edition of his *Poems* (1883), but in 1886 Alexander Sutherland made a more successful attempt to present an accurate text of Henry Kendall's verse. Douglas Sladen's anthology *A Century of Australian Song* (1888) offered a practical signpost to achievement in poetry, but among the most characteristic critical work of the 1890s were historical surveys of the kind exemplified by Barton's earlier studies. Among these, Desmond Byrne's *Australian Writers* offers a sensible and moderate account of Australian literary achievement up to the time of its publication. Turner and Sutherland's *The Development of Australian Literature* is a better-known work of the same kind. Nearly all the nineteenth-century historians of Australian literature, however, pick out the same writers for praise and attention: among the poets, Harpur, Kendall, Gordon, J. Brunton Stephens; among the novelists, Clarke, 'Rolf Boldrewood', Henry Kingsley. If any theoretical theme pervades their judgements, it is likely to be that voiced by Barton in 1866 in the opening pages of his *Literature of New South Wales*: 'What *is* Australian Literature?' Variations on the same question have continued to dominate a large proportion of Australian criticism up to the present time.

During the 1890s questions about the nature and limits of truly Australian writing were answered largely but not entirely in nationalistic terms: genuinely Australian work was that which, written by the native-born, expressed a recognisably Australian subject matter in an essentially Australian way. There were, to be sure, countervailing views. Christopher Brennan expressed some of his personal enthusiasms in a series of seven *Bulletin* articles on 'The Newer French Poetry' (1899), while A.G. Stephens himself had an impressive acquaintance with contemporary English and European writing. Recent scholarship, furthermore, has suggested that European theories about fictional realism, among others, were quite deeply assimilated into the critical ideas and literary expression of the time.

Brennan was a classical scholar as well as a student of contemporary French and German literature, and his years as associate professor of German and comparative literature at the University of Sydney (1920–25) gave him a platform for the exercise of his scholarship. The University of Sydney has enabled a number of scholar-critics to develop areas and kinds of interest which might otherwise have been difficult to cultivate in Australia. The Sydney tradition of English Renaissance scholarship and criticism is especially noteworthy; it is exemplified by such figures as Mungo MacCallum, J. le Gay Brereton, A.J.A. Waldock, R.G. Howarth, Wesley Milgate, H.J. Oliver and G.A Wilkes. Similar traditions of scholarly and critical specialisation can be associated with the other Australian universities, of which the excellence in French studies in the University of Melbourne, fostered by A.R. Chisholm's long occupancy of the chair (1921–57), is a good example.

Balancing the growing cosmopolitan awareness of Australian criticism at the end of the nineteenth century was an understandable and necessary concern for some of the grass-roots elements of the indigenous literary culture. A.B. Paterson's collection of *Old Bush Songs* (1905) was an important recognition that since 1788 Australia had developed a rich folk literature which needed to be incorporated into critical interpretation of the country's culture. In the twentieth century the need met by Paterson's collection has been served by Bill Wannan's several anthologies, by Douglas Stewart and Nancy Keesing's *Australian Bush Ballads* (1955) and *Old Bush Songs* (1957), as well as by collections and historical research by writers like John Manifold, Hugh Anderson and John Meredith (see also Folk-Song and Ballad).

It is often said that Australian literature and culture generally went through a trough in the period between Federation and the First World War. The same point might be made of literary criticism. Several phenomena, however, can be noted which indicate that critical activity was not completely stagnant. After breaking with the *Bulletin,* Stephens edited *The Bookfellow.* Another important magazine, the *Lone Hand,* was joined in 1915 by the *Triad* which had originated in NZ and which appeared, under a variety of editors and towards the end of its existence as the *New Triad,* until 1928. In the years after 1901 Stephens also wrote a number of brief lives of poets with whom, for the most part, he had been personally acquainted. Even in 1897 he had contributed a memoir to Barcroft Boake's posthumous *Where the Dead Men Lie.* His later work in this vein includes *Victor Daley* (1905), *Henry Kendall* (1928) and *Chris. Brennan* (1933).

During the post-Federation period the mode of belletristic criticism was maintained in T.G. Tucker's *The Cultivation of Literature in Australia* (1902) and Archibald T. Strong's *Peradventure* (1911). Probably Australia's best-known practitioner of the graceful essay, not uncommonly applied to literary appreciations, was Walter Murdoch (q.v.), whose *Collected Essays* came out in 1938. Bertram Stevens's *An Anthology of Australian Verse* (1906) added to the list of representative selections, while in 1909 Bernard O'Dowd produced *Poetry Militant,* an example of a kind of criticism comparatively rare in Australian writing: the practitioner's manifesto of what should be the aims and methods of his art. O'Dowd, who had corresponded with Walt Whitman in his youth, argues for a set of democratic, egalitarian values in large measure derived from the American poet, and demands a deliberately didactic

poetry to put them into effect. Norman Lindsay's *Creative Effort* (1920) resembles *Poetry Militant* in being an artist's passionate statement of the nature and purposes of his art, but in almost nothing else. Where O'Dowd had promulgated the values of a democratic literature, Lindsay was unashamedly élitist, taking his stand on the special value of the artist's energy, talent, will. *Creative Effort* was the first full-scale expression of that Nietzschean element in Australian literary thought which has subsequently attracted a good deal of attention, most thoroughly in Noel Macainsh's *Nietzsche in Australia* (1970). Lindsay's ideas did not have to wait fifty years, however, before they filtered into many areas of Australian culture. The force of his personality had an enormous effect on poets like R.D. FitzGerald, Kenneth Slessor, Douglas Stewart and 'Seaforth' Mackenzie. It was an obvious element in the best-known literary magazine of the 1920s, the shortlived *Vision* (1923–24) edited by Frank C. Johnson, Kenneth Slessor and Jack Lindsay, Norman's son. In spite of its notoriety, *Vision* was only one among many 'little magazines' which appeared and disappeared in the years between the two world wars. The magazines most important to the history of criticism in that period and beyond are dealt with in John Tregenza's *Australian Little Magazines 1923–1954* (1964).

Book-length criticism during the 1920s continued to serve much the same ends as those established in the 1890s: the provision of a coherent historical account of Australian writing within the framework of nationalist democratic values. Zora Cross's *Introduction to the Study of Australian Literature* (1922) conforms to this pattern, as does Nettie Palmer's (q.v.) *Modern Australian Literature* (1924). Of particular interest to this article are those figures whom Nettie Palmer considers to have made a genuine contribution to Australian criticism. They include Arthur Adams, Hilary Lofting, David McKee Wright, Frank Morton, T.G. Tucker and Walter Murdoch. Throughout her life Nettie, along with her husband Vance Palmer (q.v.), spared no effort in advancing the cause of Australian writing and Australian writers, especially those who, like Joseph Furphy and 'Henry Handel Richardson', had been unjustly neglected. Even by the end of the 1920s the Palmers were established as the leading partnership in Australian writing, critical as well as creative. For them and their contemporaries the generation of the 1890s was far enough in the past to be susceptible of idealisation as the fountainhead of all that was best in the Australian literary tradition. This historiographical enterprise was reinforced by such works of first-hand reminiscence as George Taylor's *Those Were the Days* (1918) and A.W. Jose's *The Romantic Nineties* (1933). By 1930 one of the most significant results of this trend in criticism was the general acceptance of Henry Lawson as the representative Australian writer, *par excellence.*

In a number of ways 1930 proved to be a fulcrum year in the history of Australian literary criticism. In that year, for instance, J. le Gay Brereton published *Knocking Round,* combining *belles-lettres* with personal recollection. In the same year F.J. Broomfield consolidated Lawson's reputation with his *Henry Lawson and*

His Critics, which was followed in 1931 by a work in similar vein, the set of essays edited by Brereton and Bertha Lawson under the title of *Henry Lawson by His Mates*. Nineteen thirty also saw the appearance of H.M. Green's *An Outline of Australian Literature*, the first comprehensive critical survey to 1928, and H.A. Kellow's *Queensland Poets*. A shrewd critic, and headmaster of Rockhampton Grammar School, Kellow made a substantial addition to the regional study of Australian writing. Since Kellow's book, it is possible to discern something like a tradition of such studies, including Cecil Hadgraft's *Queensland and Its Writers* (1959), Paul Depasquale's *A Critical History of South Australian Literature 1836–1930* (1978) and Bruce Bennett's *The Literature of Western Australia* (1979). If, on the one hand, 1930 witnessed the consolidation of a tradition of critical interpretation and assessment going back something like half a century, it also saw the rise of some new elements in Australian critical thought. John Anderson, professor of philosophy at the University of Sydney, had strong interests in literature and criticism as well as in philosophy. He expressed some of the former in a series of talks given to the Sydney University English Society. His topics in 1930 included 'Realism and Some of Its Critics' and 'Ulysses'. Anderson's concern for modernism in literature was certainly not unique, but it is worth noting that his defence of James Joyce in particular relates him to several distinguished Joycean commentators who came to prominence much later; S.L. Goldberg in *The Classical Temper* (1961), Clement Semmler in *For the Uncanny Man* (1963) and Clive Hart with his *Concordance to Finnegans Wake* (1963).

Even in the 1930s, however, native-born Australian critics as well as the Scot, John Anderson, were keenly aware of literary movements overseas. Although a committed nationalist, Vance Palmer was nevertheless widely acquainted with contemporary English, European and American writing. Randolph Hughes's 1935 monograph *Christopher Brennan: An Essay in Values* makes an analysis of the Australian poet the occasion for an attack on Australian provincialism. P.R. Stephensen was an enthusiast, at first hand, for D.H. Lawrence, his books and ideas. After returning home from Europe in 1932, Stephensen made a contribution of a somewhat different kind to Australian critical attitudes. *The Foundations of Culture in Australia* (q.v., 1936) argues the necessity of building a local culture out of local experience rather than materials derived at second hand from England and Europe. Two years later Rex Ingamells and Ian Tilbrook extended Stephensen's thesis in *Conditional Culture* (1938) which provided, in turn, the basic doctrines of the Jindyworobak movement (q.v.). The Jindyworobaks never commanded the allegiance of more than a section of the literary community. Yet they crystallised much of the critical feeling of the 1930s, especially the steady advance in the belief that a national literature could and should be created out of indigenous experience expressed in that form of the English language which had grown up through 150 years of antipodean usage. Out of that ambience came several important surveys, among them 'M. Barnard Eldershaw's' *Essays in Aus-*

tralian Fiction (q.v., 1938), which included among its subjects Frank Dalby Davison, Leonard Mann, Christina Stead and Eleanor Dark. Another overview of fiction was J.O. Anchen's *The Australian Novel: A Critical Survey* (1940). Anchen's study opens with a brief history of Australian criticism, selecting for particular praise Barton, Byrne, Turner and Sutherland and Tucker from the nineteenth century; Zora Cross, Nettie Palmer, H.M. Green, P.R. Stephensen and 'M. Barnard Eldershaw' in the twentieth. A book of rather greater importance than Anchen's also appeared in 1940: E. Morris Miller's *Australian Literature* (q.v.). A bibliographic compilation, it was revised and extended by F.T. Macartney in 1956 and remains a fundamental reference work.

The wartime years of the 1940s produced in criticism, as in so much of Australian life, a heightened and vigorous activity. Some of it represented an implicit acknowledgement of the message of Miller's bibliography: that there was a need to consolidate the factual bases of interpretation and judgement. The need was in part met by a series of literary biographies: Vance Palmer's *A.G. Stephens: His Life and Work* (1941) and *Frank Wilmot* (1942), Miles Franklin and Kate Baker's *Joseph Furphy* (1944), James Devaney's *Shaw Neilson* (1944) and Nettie Palmer's *Henry Handel Richardson* (1950). At the same time other commentators continued the process of assessment. Tom Inglis Moore's *Six Australian Poets* (1942) offered accounts of Hugh McCrae, Shaw Neilson, Bernard O'Dowd, 'William Baylebridge', Christopher Brennan and R.D. FitzGerald. Brian Elliott collected a number of his essays in *Singing to the Cattle* (1947). Douglas Stewart, literary editor of the *Bulletin* 1939–61, published *The Flesh and the Spirit* (1948), the lead essay clearly announcing Stewart's affinity with Norman Lindsay. In 1944 H.M. Green's *Fourteen Minutes* put into print a series of radio talks on Australian poets, recognising the possibilities of a further medium for critical discourse which was most fully exploited by Vance Palmer in his regular book reviews for the ABC. C.B. Christesen's (q.v.) anthology *Australian Heritage* (1949) indicated through its title its emphases and principles of selection. Christesen's contribution to and influence on Australian literary criticism began in Brisbane in 1940 when he founded *Meanjin Papers*. Later to shift to Melbourne and to change its name to *Meanjin Quarterly*, *Meanjin* soon became a major force in the literary life of the country. With a democratic temper and a bias distinctly Australian, the journal not only maintained its own point of view; it offered a forum for some of the most sophisticated and professional criticism to have been written in Australia. By his unfailing commitment to the development of Australian literature and culture, together with his flair for discovering writers of major talent, Christesen proved himself to be the most gifted literary editor in Australia since A.G. Stephens. In 1967 he published some of the most distinguished contributions to *Meanjin* under his editorship in *On Native Grounds*. *Southerly* (q.v.), the other leading journal of the 1940s, was born a little earlier than *Meanjin* – in 1939 as the organ of the Sydney branch of the English Association. Not so exclusively concerned with indigenous writing as *Meanjin*, *Southerly* nevertheless regularly found space for local creative and critical work. First edited by R.G. Howarth and later by Kenneth Slessor, Walter Stone, G.A. Wilkes and Elizabeth Webby, it remains an important arena for literary discussion. One other well-known magazine came into existence in the early years of the Second World War: Max Harris's (q.v.) *Angry Penguins*, first issued in Adelaide in 1941, was rendered notorious in 1944 as host to the Ern Malley hoax (q.v.) poems. Where *Southerly* was eclectic and *Meanjin* vigorously Australian, *Angry Penguins* was modernistic and cosmopolitan. Between them, the three magazines exemplify the range, spirit and variety of Australian literary culture in the 1940s. During the 1940s Colin Roderick began his long career as critic, historian and editor. *In Mortal Bondage* (1948) is a biography of Rosa Praed, but Roderick's most substantial contribution to Australian literary scholarship has been as an editor of Henry Lawson.

The kind of historical research demonstrated in these volumes runs through the 1950s, sometimes intersecting with critical evaluation, sometimes remaining parallel and separate. The concern for research, furthermore, was intensified by the noticeable growth in academic attention to Australian literary studies. Before the 1950s isolated individuals in university English departments, Hadgraft in Brisbane, Elliott in Adelaide, Inglis Moore in Canberra, had taken a serious professional interest in Australian writing. It was not until the middle of the century, however, that a major institutional commitment became apparent in the universities. An early manifestation of this phenomenon was G.A. Wilkes's *New Perspectives on Brennan's Poetry* (1952). The product of postgraduate research, *New Perspectives* was a very thorough exegesis of a body of verse whose symbolic difficulties had hitherto largely defied penetration. Wilkes's unravelling of *Poems (1913)* pointed the way to a wide-ranging academic enquiry into the sources, materials, affinities and techniques of Australian literature. The universities provided only one part of the critical effort of the 1950s. Major metropolitan dailies like the *Sydney Morning Herald* and the Melbourne *Age*, joined later by the national daily the *Australian*, continued through their literary pages to disseminate information and opinion. Hugh Anderson added to the growing store of bibliographical information with his *Guide to Australian Poets* (1953) and *Frank Wilmot* (1955). The bibliophile Walter Stone maintained publication of his *Biblionews*. Many established writers expressed their views in books of criticism, among them James Devaney's *Poetry in Our Time* (1952), Miles Franklin's *Laughter, Not for a Cage* (1956) and Frederick T. Macartney's *Australian Literary Essays* (1957). Leslie Rees, for many years a leading producer of radio drama with the ABC, wrote *Towards an Australian Drama* (1953), one of the first books on the subject. Later revised and expanded as *A History of Australian Drama* (1973, 1978, and 1987) it remains an important reference work. The 1950s were further marked by the entry into the field of some new literary journals which soon made their mark. *Australian Let-*

ters, edited by Max Harris, Geoffrey Dutton and Bryn Davies, was devoted more to creative than critical work. A selection of some of its best material was brought out in 1968 under the title *The Vital Decade*. *Overland* (q.v.), first issued in 1954 under the editorship of Stephen Murray-Smith, was radical on social and political issues, more catholic in the range of fiction, verse and criticism it accepted. A sampling from its first ten years of publication appeared in 1965 as *An Overland Muster*. *Quadrant* (q.v.), founded in 1956 by James McAuley, adopted a political attitude almost the exact opposite of *Overland*'s, although it was similarly willing to print a wide range of literary material. Nineteen fifty-eight was an especially important year for Australian criticism, bringing with it at least three books of major consequence. Russel Ward's *The Australian Legend*, although essentially a work of history, illustrated, through its heavy dependence on bush songs and ballads, the close nexus between historical and literary studies in Australia. *The Penguin Book of Australian Verse*, edited by John Thompson, Kenneth Slessor and R.G. Howarth, was one of the several collections of poetry which have helped to form Australian taste. This Penguin anthology was replaced in 1972 by a new selection made by Harry Heseltine. Finally in 1958 A.A. Phillips published *The Australian Tradition* (qq.v.). The essays brought together in this volume were drawn from the best Phillips had written in the previous ten years or so, many of them for *Meanjin*. They included close analyses like 'The Craft of Lawson' and 'The Craft of Furphy', along with more general commentaries such as 'The Democratic Theme' and a piece which has given Australian criticism some of its permanent currency, 'The Cultural Cringe' (q.v.). Printed within the covers of a single book, work of this calibre established Phillips as one of the major critics of the mid-century. In the year following *The Australian Tradition* Vincent Buckley (q.v.) brought out his *Essays in Poetry, Mainly Australian* (1959), which views its material from a quite different standpoint from Phillips. Suspicious of both the democratic account of Australian writing and what he termed the 'vitalism' of the Lindsay school, Buckley, in pieces like 'The Image of Man in Australian Poetry', looked for a spiritual dimension to his culture. Cecil Hadgraft's *Australian Literature: A Critical Account to 1958* (1960), on the other hand, falls more readily into the ambience of Phillips and Ward. For many years a member of the English department of the University of Queensland, Hadgraft carried out much pioneering work in Australian literary history. His own historical overview is commonsensical, engaging and free of distorting dogma. His large contribution to Australian literary scholarship was recognised on the occasion of his retirement when a collection of essays, *Bards, Bohemians, and Bookmen* (1976), was edited by Leon Cantrell.

The permanent commitment of the universities to Australian literary studies was marked by the appointment in 1962 of G.A. Wilkes to the Chair of Australian Literature at Sydney University, the first in the country. He was succeeded in 1968 by Leonie Kramer, editor of *The Oxford History of Australian Literature*

(1981) and the author of several studies on 'Henry Handel Richardson'. A further indication of the increasing professionalisation of Australian criticism was the establishment in 1963 of *Australian Literary Studies* (q.v.), a journal devoted, under the editorship of L.T. Hergenhan, exclusively to the scholarly and critical study of Australian writing. Its annual bibliographies and reports on research in progress, along with its wide-ranging articles and reviews, offer a useful index to the state of the discipline. In the 1960s and 1970s the growth of a body of professional criticism was further assisted by the activities of a number of publishing houses: the Australian Writers and their Work series, for instance, initiated by Lansdowne Press and taken over by OUP; UQP's Portable Australian Authors series, the Australian Literary Reprints, facsimile texts of nineteenth-century works from Sydney University Press; or the many play texts from Currency Press. The increased availability of previously inaccessible titles was matched by the provision of fuller and more reliable texts of major authors, e.g. T.T. Reed's edition of Kendall (1966) or the editions of Brennan's *Verse* (1960) and *Prose* (1962) by A.R. Chisholm and J.J. Quinn. Comprehensive interpretations of various aspects of literary history were offered by Brian Elliott in *The Landscape of Australian Poetry* (1967) and Tom Inglis Moore in *Social Patterns in Australian Literature* (1971). Other important reference works came from Grahame Johnston and John Barnes. Johnston's *Annals of Australian Literature* (1970) followed his earlier selection, *Australian Literary Criticism* (1962); Barnes collated some major literary documents in *The Writer in Australia,* ranging from Sinnett's *The Fiction Fields of Australia* to Judith Wright's 'The Upside-down Hut'. The flow of literary biographies was maintained by Clement Semmler's *The Banjo of the Bush* (1966), James Normington-Rawling's *Charles Harpur: An Australian* (1962), Hugh Anderson's *Poet Militant: Bernard O'Dowd* (1968) and Jack Beasley's account of Katharine Susannah Prichard, *The Rage for Life* (1964). Two general histories were especially characteristic of the critical achievement of the 1960s. In 1964 Geoffrey Dutton edited *The Literature of Australia* (q.v.), recruiting a panel of writers to provide broad surveys of the chief literary genres, together with specialist studies of leading individual figures. Three years earlier (1961) a quite different kind of conspectus had appeared in H.M. Green's two-volume *History of Australian Literature* (q.v.). Unlike Dutton's co-operative venture, this was the culmination of a lifetime's effort of an individual who had been intimately involved in many of the episodes he chronicled. Green's two volumes encompass an extraordinarily comprehensive survey of every department and level of literary activity, including criticism. His thoroughness, sympathetic common sense and unique relation to his material make Green's *History* a major work unlikely ever to be duplicated. R.F. Brissenden's 1966 study, *Patrick White,* was characteristic of its time in a different way, in its response to a writer who had imposed himself as the giant of contemporary Australian writing. From the early 1960s on, Australian criticism responded with markedly increased understanding

and frequency to the body of White's creative literature, especially his fiction. Brissenden was a poet as well as an academic critic, and the 1960s saw the production of several important critical works by leading creative writers. The tradition of the artist-critic goes back in Australia through figures like Stewart, Slessor and FitzGerald to Lindsay and Brennan, even to Kendall and Harpur. In the 1960s it was notably represented by Judith Wright's *Preoccupations in Australian Poetry* (1965) and A.D. Hope's *Australian Literature 1950–62* (1963). Hope had taken part in some of the livelier polemical debates of the 1940s, conducting skirmishes with Arthur Phillips and Max Harris among others. It was not, however, until comparatively late in his career that he brought together his critical writings into a number of substantial volumes: *The Cave and the Spring* (1965), *Native Companions* (1974), *The Pack of Autolycus* (1978) and *The New Cratylus* (1979). Especially in *The New Cratylus* he embarks on a kind of consideration quite rare in Australian critical prose, speculation by a creative artist about the sources and processes of his own imagination. The uniquely stimulating and personal brand of criticism sometimes commanded by the practising writer is further exemplified in Les A. Murray's *The Peasant Mandarin* (1974) and in many of the judgements of Chris Wallace-Crabbe, whose *Melbourne or the Bush* (1974) is a representative work. D.R. Burns, a novelist and university teacher, combined the strengths of both callings in his lively *The Directions of Australian Fiction 1920–1974* (1975), while Nancy Keesing brought together the work of several hands in *Australian Postwar Novelists* (1975). Her title reflects the widely held view that the most challenging Australian literature is increasingly to be found towards the more recent end of its time span, leaving the work of the colonial writers as the domain of research scholars and cultural historians.

One mark of the increasing professionalism of criticism through the 1980s and early 1990s was its further concentration in the universities. As the intellectual perspectives on Australian writing became more varied and complex throughout the period, so the proportion of practising critics located in university literature and humanities departments became larger. The literary supplements of the metropolitan dailies like the Melbourne *Age*, the *Sydney Morning Herald*, and the *Australian* nevertheless maintained a healthy tradition of non-academic commentary, as well as offering space to some of the livelier academic writers. Don Anderson, for instance, of Sydney University, wrote a regular weekly column for the *Sydney Morning Herald*, a good deal of his literary journalism being collected in *Hot Copy* (1986). A number of literary journals were produced independently of the universities. The most substantial new periodicals to appear in this period, however, were by and large produced within or supported by university English departments – Melbourne University's *Scripsi*, for example, which first appeared in 1981, or *Meridian*, which commenced publication in 1982 under the sponsorship of the La Trobe University English department.

There was often a perceived connection between the more conservative assessments of Australian writing and some of the well-established academic scholars. At the beginning of the 1980s the *Oxford History of Australian Literature* (1981), edited by Leonie Kramer, attracted the particular disapproval of the younger critics for what was seen to be its authoritarian, élitist stance. What, indeed, might be described as a critical 'generation gap' was vigorously delineated in John Docker's account of Australian literary culture at the time – *In a Critical Condition*, published in 1984. John McLaren's *Australian Literature: An Historical Introduction* (published toward the end of the decade in 1989) although far less controversial than the *Oxford History*, was still the product of another academically trained and employed critic. The first edition of this *Companion*, which appeared in 1985, was also the product of three tenured academics. Representing that more inclusive sense of literature which underpinned a great deal of the criticism of the period, the *Companion* gained immediate acceptance as an indispensable reference tool for anyone with an interest in Australian writing, whether professional or amateur.

The comprehensive survey, however, was by no means the pre-eminent form of Australian criticism during the 1980s. Just as characteristic was the extension of the range of theoretical discourses which had begun to emerge in the 1970s. Not surprisingly, post-colonial theory rose to a position of prominence in an increasingly multicultural and self-reliant Australia. An important text in this regard was *The Empire Writes Back: Theory and Practice in Post-Colonial Literature* (1989) by Bill Ashcroft, Gareth Griffiths and Helen Tiffin. The three authors were less concerned to interpret Australian writing according to their own theoretical predilections than to acclimatise those predilections within the Australian intellectual environment. A more direct application of the theory to Australian literary history is to be found in *The Dark Side of the Dream* (1991) by Bob Hodge and Vijay Mishra.

Developing multiculturalism produced a variety of critical voices speaking to or for a range of ethnic communities – European and, as the decade wore on, Asian. Sneja Gunew, among others, sought to provide an integrated account of the significant non-Anglo-Celtic elements in contemporary Australian writing, through bibliographical listings or in collaboration with other commentators such as Ian Reid (*Not the Whole Story*, 1984) or Kateryna Longley (*Striking Chords*, 1992). In some of her work Gunew linked her multicultural interests with her feminist concerns. Her *Feminist Knowledge: Critique and Construct* (1990) relates her to other feminist theorists and critics active during the 1980s. At the beginning of the period Beatrice Faust published *Women, Sex, and Pornography* (1980), a study followed in 1983 by Dale Spender's *Feminist Theorists* (1983), and in 1985 by Carole Ferrier's *Gender, Politics and Fiction: Twentieth Century Australian Women's Novels*. Elizabeth Grosz, in such works as *Jacques Lacan: A Feminist Introduction* (1990) made further significant contributions to feminist writing. In *Stories of Herself when Young* (1990)

Joy Hooton moved both feminist theory and the autobiographical genre into a new dimension of understanding.

Post-colonial and feminist theorising, together with the analysis of European and Asian elements in contemporary Australian writing, certainly helped to define the contours of literary criticism in the 1980s. Just as important was the increasing attention being paid to Aboriginal writing. Thus Jack Davis and Bob Hodge edited *Aboriginal Writing Today* in 1985; Stephen Muecke's *Textual Spaces: Aboriginality and Cultural Studies* of 1992 demonstrated not only the sharper focus on Australia's indigenous people but equally the increasing convergence of literary criticism and cultural studies. Two other important books were Adam Shoemaker's *Black Words White Page: Aboriginal Literature from 1929 to 1988* (1989) and Mudrooroo's *Writing from the Fringe: A Study of Modern Aboriginal Literature* (1990).

At the same time as Australian writers and critics were becoming more aware of and responsive to the nation's cultural and ethnic diversity, they were also becoming more attuned to its regional variety. It was no longer felt to be good enough to represent Australian literature as a single undifferentiated geographical phenomenon. Thus Bruce Bennett insisted on the importance of local coloration in Australian writing in works such as *Wide Domain: Western Australian Themes and Images* (1979, with William Grono), *Place, Region and Community* (1985), and *An Australian Compass* (1991). Other regions of the continent also attracted the kind of localising interest which was summed up in the *Oxford Literary Guide to Australia*, first published in 1987 under the editorship of Peter Pierce.

While new critical emphases were developing in Australia (often mirroring or responsive to European or American developments) some of the older forms of commentary and interpretation continued to flourish. In 1984 John Colmer, for instance, published a critical account of the fiction of Patrick White, Australia's only Nobel Laureate in literature; this was followed in 1991 by David Marr's highly acclaimed biography of White. Tony Hassall's *Strange Country* (1986) offered a clear-headed guided to the work of Randolph Stow. In 1981 Rosemary Dobson spoke with a practitioner's voice of *The Continuance of Poetry*, while another practitioner, Andrew Taylor, offered his *Reading Australian Poetry* in 1987.

No single year of the decade was better calculated to focus Australians' growing awareness of the many-faceted nature of their contemporary culture than the bicentennial year, 1988. The range and complexity of the popular response to the celebration of 200 years of European occupation of the Australian continent were mirrored in the diversity of critical writing which appeared in 1988. Kevin Gilbert's anthology *Inside Black Australia* provided compelling evidence of the quantity and quality of contemporary Aboriginal writing. Debra Adelaide's *A Bright and Fiery Troop* not only reinstated some of Australia's nineteenth-century women writers, but also exemplified the wider scholarly effort to recapture ever more facets of the country's literary past. At the same time Jack Beasley's *Journal of an Era* demonstrated that more immediate history was not without its interest and unresolved conflicts. Ann Curthoys's *For and Against Feminism* was a clear reminder of the significant impact of feminist theory on contemporary Australian criticism. Meaghan Morris's *The Pirate's Fiancée* proved that some of the liveliest and sharpest criticism was still being written outside university departments.

Perhaps, however, no single book more completely captured the critical temper of the decade than one whose publication was clearly designed to coincide with the bicentennial year – the *Penguin New Literary History of Australia*, produced by a team of writers under the general editorship of Laurie Hergenhan and Bruce Bennett. The sweep of its concerns, its practical perspectives, its theoretical framework – all demonstrated as plainly as possible the enormous changes Australian criticism had undergone since the original Penguin *Literature of Australia* was published in 1964 under the editorship of Geoffrey Dutton. In the intervening years it had been thoroughly theorised, had learned to take full advantage of an ever more supportive scholarly infrastructure, had grown immeasurably in the professionalism of its practices and procedures. If it had forsaken anything, it was perhaps the exercise of evaluative judgement. Nevertheless, as the critics of the 1980s and 1990s scanned the horizons of their broadened domain, they did so, by and large, with a discerning gaze.

H.P. HESELTINE

CRITTENDEN, Victor (1925–), educated in Sydney, London and Toronto, was formerly librarian at the University of Canberra and has compiled and edited numerous bibliographies, indexes and guides to reference sources; these include *Australians, a Guide To Sources* (1987, with D.H. Borchardt) and *A Bibliography of the First Fleet* (1981). The director of Mulini Press, he has also republished several nineteenth-century novels with valuable introductions (see Australian Books on Demand).

CRNLE Reviews Journal, see **Association for Commonwealth Language and Literature Studies**

CROFT, Julian (1941–), born Newcastle, NSW, is associate professor of English and communication studies at the University of New England. Keenly interested in Australian literature, he helped in the establishment of the Association for the Study of Australian Literature (ASAL), whose journal *Notes & Furphies* he co-edited for many years. He has written a study of the Welsh poet T. Harri Jones who taught him as a student, and *The Life and Opinions of Tom Collins: A Study of the Works of Joseph Furphy* (1991), which won the ASAL Walter McRae Russell Award. Croft has published the volumes of poetry, *Breakfasts in Shanghai* (1984, winner of the Asia-Pacific section of the Commonwealth Poetry Prize in 1985), which reviews 'the tugs and buffets of the years', savouring

all life's experiences, even the seemingly commonplace; *Confessions of a Corinthian* (1991), in which poems of boyhood experiences give way to nostalgic recollections of the north coast and the tablelands of NSW and dismay at the mass migration of people to those areas, ruining their once-pristine beauty; and, with Michael Sharkey, *Loose Federation* (1979). As the title of *Confessions of a Corinthian* suggests, Croft is himself a classicist; critics have placed him in the company of such traditional Australian poets as Kenneth Slessor, R.D. FitzGerald (on whom he has written), A.D. Hope and David Campbell. His novel *Their Solitary Way* (1985), which won a Best First Book Award in 1985, is the story of the failing marriage of an Australian and his Swiss wife, told in separate versions emphasising the innate incompatibilities of the two.

CROGGON, Alison (1962–), born South Africa, came to Australia at the age of 7, was educated at Ballarat and worked as a cadet journalist on the Melbourne *Herald*. Since 1985 she has been a freelance journalist and a Melbourne theatre critic for the *Bulletin*. Her poetry, published in Australian and overseas journals, was performed at La Mama in 1988 as a theatrical presentation (*NOTES*). Awarded a Victorian Council for the Arts Poetry Fellowship in 1989, she became poetry editor of *Overland Extra* and is poetry editor of the literary art poster *Modern Writing*. Her first collection of poems, *This is the Stone*, was published in 1991 in Penguin's *The Australian Poetry Series* (a shared volume with Fiona Perry's *Pharaohs Returning*). An intimately personal volume traversing a range of women's experience, *This is the Stone* is a sensitive, intelligent and deeply emotional collection. Its final series 'Quickening', with its sections 'Family Notes', 'Love Poems', 'Domestic Art' and 'Howl', is highly impressive.

CROLL, R.H. (Robert Henderson) (1869–1947), born Stawell, Victoria, combined a long career on the administrative staff of the Victorian Education Department with an unusually active participation in literary, artistic, bushwalking and educational organisations. One of Melbourne's best-known men of letters and a prolific contributor of verse and prose to Australian newspapers and journals, Croll published numerous works including *By-products: A Book of Verses* (1932), *The Open Road in Victoria* (1928), *Along the Track* (?1930), *Tom Roberts* (1935), *Wide Horizons: Wanderings in Central Australia* (1937) and *I Recall: Collections and Recollections* (1939). He edited *Collected Poems of John Shaw Neilson* (1934), *Smike to Bulldog* (1946, letters of Sir Arthur Streeton to Tom Roberts), and collaborated with Percival Serle and 'Furnley Maurice' to produce *An Australasian Anthology* (1927).

CRONIN, Bernard Charles (1884–1968), born Ealing, Middlesex, England, came to Australia as a child in 1890 and was later a jackeroo in Gippsland, northern Victoria and Tasmania. He worked briefly as a government clerk in Melbourne, then freelanced as a journalist before joining the *Herald* in the 1930s.

During the Second World War he was a publicity censor in Victoria and WA and later taught creative writing at Melbourne Technical College as well as contributing regular items to the Melbourne *Sun*. In 1920 Cronin helped found the Old Derelicts Club for indigent authors and artists. He also founded the Quill Club in 1933 and was made a life member in 1961 of the International PEN Club. A prolific writer of light fiction, Cronin wrote about thirty novels; several one-act plays including the radio play *Stampede*, represented in *Best Australian One-Act Plays* (1937); short fiction and poetry. Two of his best novels are *Bracken* (1931) and *The Sow's Ear* (1933), in both of which aspects of Australian life are critically examined. His other novels include *The Coastlanders* (1918), *Timber Wolves* (1920), *Bluff Stakes* (1922), *Salvage* (1923) and *Red Dawson* (1927), all of which are derived from Cronin's rural experiences in Tasmania, as is *The Sow's Ear*. The northern areas of Australia are the setting for *White Gold* (1927), *Dragonfly* (1928) and *The Treasure of the Tropics* (1928). Cronin used various pseudonyms, 'Wallace Dixon', 'Hugh Bohun', 'Eric North' and 'Denis Adair'.

Crooked Mick, see **Speewah**

CROSS, Stan (1888–1977) was the artist responsible for a 1930s cartoon famous in Australia, 'For gorsake stop laughing – this is serious!' (q.v.). Born Los Angeles, Cross arrived in Australia with his parents in 1892 and was well known for his work on *Smith's Weekly*, which published his comic strips 'You and Me' (renamed 'The Potts' when taken over by another artist) and later 'Dad and Dave' (q.v.), a visual adaptation of the radio serial of that name. A superb draughtsman, Cross was also responsible for 'Wally and the Major' which, with 'Bluey and Curley', was tremendously popular during the Second World War. 'Wally and the Major' began as 'The Winks' in the Melbourne *Herald* in 1940 but later that year, to give the strip a wartime flavour, Cross took Mr Winks and Wally Higgins into the army, Mr Winks becoming Major Winks in July 1940; later Pudden Benson was added to 'Wally and the Major' as the major's batman and often stole the scene. The major has been compared in attitude, temperament and efficiency with Captain Mainwaring of the British television series *Dad's Army*. After Cross's retirement in 1970, 'Wally and the Major' was continued by Carl Lyon.

CROSS, Zora (1890–1964), born Brisbane, was for much of her life a freelance journalist, contributing regularly to the *Worker* and writing freelance for the *Australian Woman's Mirror* and the *Bulletin* and other publications. A remarkable woman much in advance of her time, she had a rather chaotic personal life, her long *de facto* relationship with David McKee Wright scandalising the Sydney literary establishment of the day. She published several volumes of frank love poetry in which she explored her reactions to the experience of love, sexuality and motherhood. They were *A Song of Mother Love* (1916), *Songs of Love and Life* (1917) and *The Lilt of Life* (1918). She also wrote *The City of Riddle-me-ree* (1918), children's verses which illustrate her lyric gift, and *Elegy on an Australian Schoolboy* (1921), an impressive poem in which she mourns the death of her young brother, John Skyring Cross, in the First World War. She published several works of fiction: *Daughters of the Seven Mile: The Love Story of an Australian Woman* (1924), a romance set against the background of the Queensland bush; *The Lute-Girl of Rainyvale: A Story of Love, Mystery and Adventure in North Queensland* (1925), accurately described by the subtitle; and *This Hectic Age* (1944), in which a country girl has problems coping with the sophisticated milieu of Sydney. Zora Cross also wrote a pamphlet, *An Introduction to the Study of Australian Literature* (1922), now dated and superficial, but valuable at the time. Other novels by Cross appeared in serial form, including *The Victor* (1933) and *Moonstone Luck* (1930), both in the *Sydney Morning Herald*. Cross also collaborated with Wright in a novel originally titled 'Julian the Apostle', commended in the *Bulletin* Prize Story Competition of 1928. The novel was subsequently serialised in the *Sydney Morning Herald* (1930), titled *Luta of Lutetia* and ascribed only to David McKee Wright.

Crouch Gold Medal, see **Australian Literature Society**

Crow, of which there are several varieties, is a large bird of the genus *Corvus* with black plumage and a mournful, monotonous call. It is native to the bushlands of eastern, western and southern Australia. An omnivorous feeder and skilful scavenger, it prefers a meat diet, usually of small bush animals, but it also preys on helpless livestock, especially sheep and lambs, a practice that makes it unpopular with farmers. Its sombre appearance, doleful cry and repulsive habit of feeding on carrion have combined to represent it in Australian literature as a harbinger of tragedy and death, an integral part of the 'weird melancholy' that Marcus Clarke saw as the distinctive feature of the Australian bush. So marked a feature is the crow of the lonely outback environment that G. Herbert Gibson ('Ironbark'), in his advice 'How to Write an Australian Novel', stressed the need for its presence,

> Have a drawin' of a station
> And another illustration
> Of a carcass, with a crow upon a fence.
> There is nothing so expressive
> Of the sadness of our solitude immense
> ... As a carcass and a crow upon a fence.

The ceaseless conflict between crow and man has been widely illustrated in Australian writing. In Henry Lawson's 'The Drover's Wife' the crow is seen as one of the numerous predators against which the hard-pressed people of the outback have to battle. In Lawson's story 'A Hero in Dingo Scrubs' and Mary Gilmore's poem 'The Crows Kept Flyin' Up', helpless human beings are targets for the cruel but cowardly bird. Barcroft Boake sees the crow as an omen of disaster:

Crows are flying, hoarsely crying
Burial service o'er the dying –
Four Harbingers of Death.

A.B. Paterson refers to them as 'grim sextons of the Overland'. Barbara Baynton's tragic story 'The Chosen Vessel' sees them thwarted in their attempt to inflict the final indignity on the raped and murdered woman. The well-known folk-song 'The Dying Stockman' (q.v.) reiterates in its chorus the bushman's last wish to be buried out of their reach. Stories of crows preying upon helpless livestock are equally common. In Barbara Baynton's 'Billie Skywonkie' the infuriated rouseabout tells of their 'scoffin' out' the eyes of the tottering, drought-weakened sheep. Dowell O'Reilly's story 'Crows' depicts a young ewe with one eye picked out and her dead lamb with both eyes gone and kidneys torn out. Countryman and poet David Campbell has a similar grisly scene in 'The Kidney and the Wren'. In E.G. Moll's poem 'During Drouth' there is a sense of the perverse irony of nature in the Australian enviroment where drought, an enemy to most living things, is a benefactor to the carrion-eating crows, providing them with a feast in the midst of famine. Dislike of the crow has led to derogatory use of its name, e.g 'crow' is a slang term for a female, especially if ugly or old, and was also used contemptuously for female Aborigines. To 'cop the crow' or 'draw the crow' is to get the poorest or least attractive of a set of alternatives. 'Stone the crows!' is an exclamation of exasperation or disgust, largely because stoning the crows was the ultimate exercise in futility. The term 'croweater' is used as a derisory comment on the imagined primitivism of the inhabitants of SA. An area of extreme remoteness, heat, aridity and general unattractiveness can be described as a place where 'the crows fly backwards' to keep the dust, the wind or the sun out of their eyes. The eternal, exasperating presence of the crows is reflected in such jokes as: Horseman to Cocky: 'How far is it to Bilga, mate – as the crow flies?' Cocky: 'Struth I dunno! The flamin' crows never leave here.'

CROYSTON, John (1933–), born Enfield, Sydney, spent most of his career with the ABC as director, producer and editor. His own work includes *23 Poems* (1953, with Julian Woods); a verse drama, 'The Hills Shall Fly'; several plays including *The Runaway*, published in Brian Fitzsimmons's collection *Sight and Sound* (1969); numerous scripts for the TV series 'Certain Women' and 'Behind the Legend'; and translations and adaptations of *Lysistrata* and *Medea*.

CUE, Kerry (1952–), born Melbourne, grew up there and at Kyneton, where her father was the police sergeant. She studied maths and chemistry at the University of Melbourne and worked as an industrial chemist and as a teacher before successfully exploiting her talent for comedy. She has written numerous humorous books, including *Crooks, Chooks, & Bloody Ratbags* (1983), *Another Bloody Ratbag Book* (1986) and *My Ratbag Relations* (1989), all based on her family's experiences at Kyneton; *Hang on to your Horse's Doovers*

(1987), a comic study of Australian eating habits; *Born to Whinge* (1988), an 'unreliable' guide for parents; *Life on a G-String* (1991), an irreverent guide to fashion; *Kerry Cue's Worser Homes and Gardens* (1990), an exposé of Australia's real homes and gardens; and the *Girls' Own Guide to Ego Maintenance* (1993). She has also written for television, for a range of newspapers and periodicals as well as several books for children. *Crooks, Chooks, & Bloody Ratbags* won a prize for humour in 1982 in a literary contest promoted by Rigby Ltd during the Adelaide Festival.

'CULOTTA, Nino', see **O'GRADY, John**

Cultural Cringe was an expression first used by A.A. Phillips (q.v.) as the title of an essay in *Meanjin* (1950) and subsequently included in his *The Australian Tradition* (1958). The expression implies Australian cultural self-depreciation and subservience to European culture.

CUMPSTON, Amy (1921–), born Melbourne, has been a writer for television and director of the International Theatre Forum. She has published poetry, *Human, My Race* (1955), *Borrow the Spring* (1961), *The Towers of Earth: Poems of the Blue Mountains* (1969); and drama, *This Fatal Island* (1973) and *Woodrow Wilson* (1973). As Amy MacGrath she has published the verse collections *Australia My Home* (1991) and *Canberra, Home* (1992), and a fictionalised study of Kublai Khan, *Free From All Curses* (1983). Her other plays include 'Mary, Queen of Scots', 'Eldorado', 'Chinese Gordon', 'The Dragon Throne', 'Crusade', 'Kublai Khan', 'Sir Walter Raleigh' and 'The Swagman'.

CUNNINGHAM, Peter (1789–1864), born Dumfries, Scotland, became a surgeon in the Royal Navy; between 1819 and 1828 he made five voyages to NSW as surgeon-superintendent in convict transports. In 1825 he took up land on the Hunter River and in 1827 published *Two Years in New South Wales*, a combination of memoirs, experiences and information for intending immigrants. In 1830 he returned to England and in 1841 published a further work, *Hints for Australian Emigrants*, in which he urged the use of irrigation for farming in dry areas, he himself having been driven from his Hunter River property in 1830 by a severe drought.

CUNNINGTON, Vivian (1921–), born Toowoomba, Queensland, served with the AIF in the Second World War, conducted an electroplating business 1946–67 and has since been a freelance writer. A prolific writer of short fiction, Cunnington has published *Big Fat Tuesday* (1963, short stories), *A Change of Key* (1975, verse and short stories), *Naked at the Typewriter* (1977, poems and prose pieces) and a novel, *Jack Bones* (1978). At his best in brief humorous sketches of people, Cunnington made a considerable impression with *Big Fat Tuesday* (a literal translation of 'Mardi Gras'), the stories of which are unpretentious and illustrate Cunnington's talent as a raconteur.

CURLEWIS, Jean (1899–1930), collaborated with her mother, Ethel Turner (q.v.), in *The Sunshine Family: A Book of Nonsense for Girls and Boys* (1923); she also wrote five books for children and edited the children's column of the *Daily Telegraph* before her early death from tuberculosis. A more romantic and less humorous writer than her mother, she made Sydney's beaches and waterways the setting of several of her novels. In *The Ship That Never Set Sail* (1921), a representative Curlewis novel, Sydney Harbour suggests to the heroine the romance and adventure she yearns for but fails to find in real life; *Drowning Maze* (1922) describes the adventures of high-school boys on Pittwater; and *Beach Beyond* (1923), which deals partly with the thrills and perils of surfing, has an imaginary beach as an idyllic background.

CURR, E.M. (Edward Micklethwaite) (1820–89), born Hobart, was the son of Edward Curr (1798–1850), merchant and landowner who wrote *An Account of the Colony of Van Diemen's Land* (1824); Curr junior was educated in England and returned to Australia at the age of 19. He managed a series of runs in Victoria, many of them in tribal Aboriginal areas. His later life, mostly connected with pastoral activities, alternated between Victoria, NZ and Queensland and he wrote voluminously on matters pertaining to the land. His chief work was *Recollections of Squatting in Victoria* (1883), which contained his reminiscences of squatting life and reflected his keen and unusually humanitarian interest in the Aborigines. He also compiled and partly wrote a four-volume collection of observations entitled *The Australian Race* (1886–87).

'Currency', a word with special Australian meanings during the nineteenth century, was first used thus in Governor Macquarie's time to denote the promissory notes issued by Sydney merchants at a time when sterling coinage was in short supply; its usage was soon extended to include those born in the Australian colonies, as in 'currency lads' and 'currency lasses', to distinguish them from 'sterling', those born in England. The latter distinction was originally something of an insult (given that the currency notes had been valued at less than their sterling equivalents) but became more and more a jest between European Australians, and in the 1830s sporting contests were regularly held in NSW between 'currency' and 'sterling'. 'Cornstalk' and 'native' (qq.v.) were contemporary synonyms for 'currency'; it is used also in the *Currency Lad,* a newspaper which articulated the interests of the 'Cornstalks' in 1832–33, and in *The Currency Lass,* the title both of a play (performed 1844) by Edward Geoghegan and of a novel (1927) by James Devaney.

Currency Lass, The, a musical comedy by Edward Geoghegan (q.v.), probably the earliest surviving, professionally produced play with a local setting, was first performed in Sydney in 1844 and published in 1976. Although flawed by stilted mannerisms and typed characters, the play has colour and is interesting for its reflection of the division in colonial society between expatriate and native-born, and for its idealisation of the latter.

Currency Press, initiated in 1971 by wife-and-husband team Katharine Brisbane (q.v.) and the late Philip Parsons, contributed greatly to the 1970s renaissance of Australian drama by its publication and promotion of Australian dramatists. Currency Press is, or was, responsible for producing several separate drama series: *Modern Drama*, edited by Katharine Brisbane, which made available the newest work of established playwrights such as David Williamson, Patrick White, Alex Buzo, John Romeril, Louis Nowra and Peter Kenna, as well as the work of newer writers; *National Theatre*, edited by Philip Parsons, which presented important older plays in well-annotated texts with critical biographical and social comment; *Double Bills*, edited by Frank Bladwell, which comprised short plays in pairs (e.g. *The Christian Brothers* by Ron Blair and *A Lesson in English* by Barry Oakley) designed to capture aspects of Australian life; *Australian Screen*, edited by Sylvia Lawson, which comprised critical and historical studies of aspects of film and television in Australia, published in joint imprint with the Australian Film Institute; and the *Current Theatre*, devoted exclusively to modern Australian drama. Although most of these series are now discontinued, Currency Press continues to be the major publisher of Australian drama.

CURREY, C.H. (Charles Herbert) (1890–1970), born Ulmarra, near Grafton, NSW, was long associated with history and the teaching of it in NSW, and was president of the Royal Australian Historical Society 1954–58. His publications include *Modern British History* (1931), *The Story of Man* (1947), *The British Commonwealth since 1815* (1951), *The Irish at Eureka* (1954), *The Transportation, Escape, and Pardoning of Mary Bryant* (1963), *Sir Francis Forbes* (1968) and *The Brothers Bent* (1968).

CURTHOYS, Ann (1945–) was educated at the University of Sydney and Macquarie University. Professor of social history at the University of Technology, Sydney, she has co-edited several influential, historical studies of Australia's socio-political culture; with Susan Eade and Peter Spearritt, *Women at Work* (1975), with Andrew Markus, *Who Are Our Enemies? Racism and the Australian Working Class* (1978), with John Merritt, *Australia's First Cold War 1945–1953* (1984 and 1986), with Michael J. Roache, *Not the Bicentennial* (1986), and, with A.W. Martin and Tim Rowse, *Australians from 1939* (1987). Active in the women's movement since 1970, she has published a collection of essays on the position of women and the feminist movement, *For and Against Feminism* (1988).

CUSACK, Dymphna (1902–81), born Wyalong, NSW, was educated at the University of Sydney and worked as a teacher until chronic illness forced her to retire in 1944. Her published writings include twelve novels: *Jungfrau* (1936), *Pioneers on Parade* (1939, written in collaboration with Miles Franklin), *Come In Spinner* (q.v., 1951, written in collaboration with Florence James and winner of the 1948 Sydney *Daily Telegraph* competition), *Say No to Death* (1951), *Southern Steel* (1953), *The Sun in Exile* (1955), *Heatwave in Berlin* (1961), *Picnic Races* (1962), *Black Lightning* (1964), *The Sun is Not Enough* (1967), *The Half-Burnt Tree* (1969) and *A Bough in Hell* (1971); eight plays: *Red Sky at Morning* (q.v., 1942), *Morning Sacrifice* (1943), *Three Australian Three Act Plays (Comets Soon Pass, Shoulder the Sky, Morning Sacrifice)* (1950), *The Golden Girls* (1955), *Shallow Cups* in *Eight Plays by Australians* (1934) and *Pacific Paradise* in *Theatregoer* (1963); three travel books: *Chinese Women Speak* (1958), *Holidays Among the Russians* (1964) and *Illyria Reborn* (1966); and two children's books: *Four Winds and a Family*, with Florence James (1947), and *Kanga-Bee and Kanga-Bo* (1945). In 1953 she edited and introduced *Caddie, the Story of a Barmaid*, produced as a film, *Caddie*, in 1976. In 1991 Cusack's account of her experiences as a high-school teacher in NSW from the late 1920s, *A Window in the Dark*, was published, edited by Debra Adelaide. Cusack was awarded the Elizabeth II Coronation Medal (1953) and was made AM in 1981 for her contribution to Australian literature. Translated into numerous languages and especially popular with the former socialist bloc, her books have been published in thirty-four countries. Her biography, *Dymphna* (1975), was written by her husband Norman Freehill, with her co-operation.

Although Cusack never belonged to a political party, she was preoccupied with social injustice of all forms: *Jungfrau*, runner-up in the 1935 *Bulletin* competition, deals frankly with sexual matters; *Come In Spinner* is an unillusioned study of wartime Sydney; *The Sun in Exile* is a bitter denunciation of racism; *Picnic Races* gives a light-hearted but critical picture of Australia's rural background; *The Half-Burnt Tree* deals partly with the Vietnam War and partly with Aboriginal problems; *Heatwave in Berlin* treats of the survival of fascism in post-war Germany; and *A Bough in Hell* focuses on the problems of alcoholism. Similar preoccupations inform her published and unpublished plays, many of which have been produced on stage, radio and television both in Australia and overseas. *Pacific Paradise*, a particularly popular play which deals with the issue of nuclear weapons, has been published and performed in China and in numerous overseas countries; 'Eternal Now', which won a prize in the 1946 Playwrights Advisory Board (q.v.) competition, was televised by the BBC in 1954 with the title *Stand Still Time*; *The Golden Girls*, produced several times by

the ABC, was staged in England and won a British Arts Council grant in 1955; a dramatised version of *Heatwave in Berlin* was produced in Moscow and several other socialist countries; *Red Sky at Morning* was produced as a film in 1944, and *Come In Spinner* as a television series in 1989.

CUTHBERTSON, James Lister (1851–1910), born Glasgow, Scotland, came to Australia in 1875 and taught at Geelong Grammar School for most of the period 1875–96. His *Grammar School Verses* appeared in 1879 and his slim book of poetry, *Barwon Ballads*, in 1893; a memorial edition of his poems, *Barwon Ballads and School Verses*, edited by E.T. Williams, was published in 1912. His poem 'The Australian Sunrise' has been frequently anthologised. A dedicated schoolmaster who helped to meld English school ways and methods to the Australian character and environment, Cuthbertson made a deep impression on the Geelong Grammar School where his memory is still revered.

CUTLACK, F.M. (Frederick Morley) (1886–1967), born Sussex, England, came to SA in 1891. After some early journalistic experience in Australia he served in France in the First World War, then became an assistant to C.E.W. Bean on *The Official History of Australia in the War of 1914–1918*. He returned to Australia, joined the *Sydney Morning Herald* in 1920 and wrote volume 8 of the official history, *The Australian Flying Corps in the Western and Eastern Theatres of War, 1914–1918* (1923). He was associate editor of the *Sydney Morning Herald* 1937–47. His other publications include *The Manchurian Arena* (1934), *War Letters of General Monash* (1934) and *Breaker Morant* (1962), an attempted vindication of Harry Harbord Morant, whom he met in 1899 and whose execution in South Africa in 1902 he believed to be a miscarriage of justice.

Cyprus, a government brig carrying convicts from Hobart Town to Macquarie Harbour, was seized by the convicts in Recherche Bay, Tasmania, in August 1829. One of the more dramatic events in Australia's convict history, the seizure of the *Cyprus* was dramatised on the London stage and a ballad sympathetic to the convicts, 'Seizure of the *Cyprus Brig* in Recherche Bay', was written by Frank MacNamara (q.v.). The full story of the incident is in Frank Clune and P.R. Stephensen, *The Pirates of the Brig Cyprus* (1962), and it is represented fictionally in Marcus Clarke's *His Natural Life* (1874).

D

DABBS, Jennifer (1938–), born Orange, NSW, grew up in Melbourne. She has worked as a teacher, journalist, singer, bank clerk, receptionist, publican, associate systems engineer in the computer industry and teacher of professional writing and has contributed short stories to numerous anthologies and periodicals. She has published a novel about growing up Catholic in the 1950s, *Beyond Redemption* (1987), and a novel for children based on a screenplay by Michael Aitkens and Jackie McKimmie, *Top-Enders* (1988).

Dad and Dave, two of Australia's most famous rural inhabitants, began life in the *Bulletin* in 1895 as father and son of the Rudd family in the first of 'Steele Rudd's' (qq.v.) selection sketches. In *On Our Selection* (q.v.) and other early 'Rudd' books, the Rudds were battlers, the harshness of their pioneering life emphasised rather than its humour. A younger son, Joe, rather than Dave, was the 'galoot' of the family. In time, however, Dad and Dave emerged as comic characters and were finally transformed into generic Australian 'hayseeds' – laconic, unsophisticated and slow-witted, occasionally putting one over a new chum (q.v.) but more usually the victims of their own dullness or of the sharp practices of 'city slickers' when they came to town.

The transformation of Dad and Dave was due partly to 'Rudd', who responded to the popularity of his work by making the Rudd family more farcical in his later sketches. But equally responsible were 'Rudd's' illustrators, who may in turn have influenced his change of direction: e.g. a drawing of Dave as a yokel by Norman Lindsay, first published in *Our New Selection* in 1903, clearly influenced the portrayal of Dave by Fred McDonald in the stage (1912) and sound film (1932) adaptations of *On Our Selection*, and also the portrayal by Tal Ordell in Raymond Longford's (q.v.) silent film version (1920), which was closer in mood to the original. A third factor was 'Rudd's' loss of control over what he had created. He had no part either in the stage adaptation of *On Our Selection*, which was phenomenally successful, or in the four Rudd films made in 1932–40 which starred McDonald and Bert Bailey (q.v.); and he died before the commencement of 'Dad and Dave', the radio serial produced by George Edwards which ran for over 2000 episodes 1937–51. The popularity of the radio serial consolidated the phrase 'Dad and Dave' in Australian idiom and confirmed the characters as bush stereotypes. The serial also introduced Mabel as Dave's sweetheart, placed Snake Gully on the map of mythical Australia alongside the Black Stump, and spawned yet another metamorphosis, the comic strip 'Dad and Dave' drawn by Stan Cross in *Smith's Weekly*. For their part the proprietors of *Smith's Weekly* encouraged a backblocks theme (sometimes called 'Dad and Dave' humour) for its single-panel cartoons.

The heyday of Dad and Dave was in the 1930s and 1940s: *Smith's Weekly* ceased publication in 1950 and the radio serial a year later, although it had a number of repeats and there was a 'Dad and Dave' television series (1972) scripted by Ralph Peterson. The stereotypes survive in such comic strips as 'Gunn's Gully', and Dad and Dave survive in countless bar-room jokes, in which Dave rather than Dad is the rural idiot and Mabel alternates between being as slow-witted as her sweetheart and sexually more sophisticated. The fact that recent reprints of *On Our Selection* and *Our New Selection* have themselves been titled *Dad and Dave* illustrates the extent of the transformation of 'Rudd's' original creations.

Dad in Politics and Other Stories, a series of sketches by 'Steele Rudd' (q.v.), was published in 1908. In the chronicle of the Rudd family (q.v.), *Dad in Politics* precedes *Back at Our Selection* (1906). Dad is persuaded to stand for parliament, unexpectedly wins, is soon embroiled in feuds and suspensions when he takes his seat, and resigns in disgust to return to the selection. *Dad in Politics*, which resulted in 'Rudd' being barred from the Queensland parliamentary press gallery, is a key volume in the movement towards a farcical presentation of Dad, which characterised the later Rudd volumes and stage and screen adaptations of them; it obviously influenced the film, *Dad Rudd M.P.* (1940), starring Bert Bailey (q.v.) and made after 'Rudd's' death. The other stories in the volume include two of particular biographical interest, 'The Selection Where I Was Reared' and 'How I Wrote *On Our Selection*'.

DADSWELL, Mary (1943–) grew up in Sale, Victoria, and has lived and travelled in various countries in Europe and the USA. She graduated B.Litt. from the ANU, Canberra, where she now lives, and has worked as a nurse, teacher/librarian, proofreader, jazz piano teacher and as the director of Canberra's first gallery for art photography. Her short stories and poems have appeared in newspapers, periodicals and anthologies and have won various awards including the FAW John Shaw Neilson Poetry Award, and have been published in one collection, *Circles of Faces* (1987).

Daily Mail, see ***Brisbane Courier***

Daily Telegraph, a morning daily newspaper, began publication as the *Sydney Daily Telegraph* on 1 July 1879, struggled in its first years but survived to become the great rival of the *Sydney Morning Herald*. A supporter of free trade, political democracy and private property, the *Daily Telegraph* 'scooped' the world in 1884 with its announcement of the German annexation of northern New Guinea, but is probably best remembered before 1900 for its opposition to Federation in the referenda of 1898–99; in the twentieth century it had a long tradition of opposition to the Labor Party. Notable editors of the newspaper included Frederick Ward (1884–90, 1903–14), John Farrell (1890), Lachlan Brient (1890–1901), Thomas Heney (1924–26) and Brian Penton (1941–51); Farrell and Penton also occupied other staff positions, as did Lennie Lower, Frank Moorhouse and Kenneth Slessor among other prominent Australian authors. A *Daily Telegraph* company ran the newspaper for over forty years from 1884, but by 1927 it had been taken over by Sun Newspapers, later Sir Hugh Denison's (q.v.) Associated Newspapers; subsequently the *Telegraph* was rejuvenated when brought under the control (1936–72) of Frank Packer and E.G. Theodore of Consolidated Press, and after 1972 was owned by Rupert Murdoch's News Limited. The *Tribune* (1882–89), a weekly 'companion' of the *Daily Telegraph*, was less successful in this role than the *Sydney Mail* and the *Australian Town and Country Journal* with their parent dailies (the *Sydney Morning Herald* and *Evening News* respectively), but the *Tribune*'s twentieth-century equivalent, the *World's News* (1901–?55) and the *Sunday Telegraph* (1939–), have had longer and more prosperous lives. In 1990 the *Daily Telegraph* became the *Telegraph-Mirror* when it incorporated the recently defunct evening newspaper the *Daily Mirror*.

DALEY, Victor ('Creeve Roe') (1858–1905), born County Meath, Ireland, came to Australia at the age of 20. For several years he roamed southern Australia as an itinerant journalist, but from 1882 began to establish himself as a popular lyric poet, contributing to *Punch*, *Freeman's Journal* and the *Bulletin*. In 1898 he published his first book of verse, *At Dawn and Dusk*; the Sydney literary coterie used the title for their bohemian Dawn and Dusk Club (q.v.). With fellow poet Roderic Quinn he was part of the so-called 'Celtic Twilight', a small enclave of lyrical romanticism amid the intense nationalistic-radical writing and the noisy bush balladry that dominated the literary scene of the day. Although he, too, was a radical poet his chief poetic love was 'the shining shallows' of the lyric. After his early death from tuberculosis, several further volumes of his poetry were published – *Poems* (1908, a miniature edition), *Wine and Roses* (1911, ed. Bertram Stevens), *Creeve Roe* (q.v., 1947), a selection of his radical verse edited by Muir Holburn and Marjorie Pizer, and *Victor Daley* (1963), edited by H.J. Oliver. A.G. Stephens wrote the biography *Victor Daley* (1905).

DALLEY, J.B. (John Bede) (1876–1935), born Rose Bay, Sydney, son of William Bede Dalley, was called to the Bar in England in 1901. After an accident caused deafness, Dalley became a journalist, editing the Bathurst *National Advocate* 1906–7, then joining the *Bulletin* where, by 1911, he was a leader-writer and a contributor of short stories, verse, and witty, ironic paragraphs. After the First World War, in which he served in the AIF and during which he contributed to *Aussie*, he rejoined the *Bulletin*, edited *Melbourne Punch* in 1924 and was then representative of the Melbourne *Herald* in London. As a novelist Dalley perceptively satirised the upper-class life of Sydney of the 1920s. His novels are *No Armour* (1928), *Max Flambard* (1928) and *Only the Morning* (1930).

DALLEY, W.B. (William Bede) (1831–88), born Sydney, the son of convict parents, attended Sydney College, was admitted to the Bar in 1856 and capped a long parliamentary career by being the first Australian to become a member of the Privy Council (1887). In 1865 he became editor and part-proprietor of the *Freeman's Journal* and wrote for the *Sydney Morning Herald* and Sydney *Punch* to which he contributed a number of satirical biographical sketches of notable contemporary political figures. Although a successful barrister, Dalley lost two important cases – his defence of the bushranger Frank Gardiner in 1864 and of H.J. O'Farrell for the shooting in 1868 of the Duke of Edinburgh. In 1884 he published *Speeches on the Proposed Federal Council for Australasia*. His contemporary literary reputation is indicated by his presence in G.B. Barton's *The Poets and Prose Writers of New South Wales* (1866).

D'ALPUGET, Blanche (1944–), born Sydney, daughter of Lou d'Alpuget, a well-known Sydney journalist, worked as a journalist before her marriage which took her overseas for nine years. She spent four years in Indonesia and one in Malaysia. Her first novel, *Monkeys in the Dark* (1980), is set in Indonesia in 1966 and centres on Alexandra Wheatfield, a young journalist attached to the Australian Embassy at Djakarta, and her ambivalent reactions to the problems of life in Indonesia. *Turtle Beach* (1981), which won the *Age* Book of the Year Award, the SA government's biennial Award for literature and the PEN Golden Jubilee Award for fiction in Sydney and was produced as a film in 1992, also concerns an Australian journalist, Judith Wilkes. In spite of her husband's displeasure, Judith obtains an assignment to Malaysia to cover the arrival in that country of Chinese refugees from Vietnam. Although the novel is primarily concerned with Judith Wilkes's own emotional problems, culminating in her separation from her patronising, selfish husband, other characters to create interest are Minou, said to have been a Saigon bar-girl but now Lady Hobday, second wife of the Australian high commissioner to Malaysia, and Ralph Hamilton, Australian immigration officer in Kuala Lumpur. The novel's long-delayed climax comes with the disclosure of the horrors of the refugee island of Bidong and Minou's suicide so that her refugee relatives may reach safety. D'Alpuget's third novel, *Winter in Jerusalem* (1986), centres on the return of the protagonist

Danielle Green to her birthplace, Jerusalem, in 1983 at the time of the Israeli incursion into Lebanon. Engaged to write a film script about Eleazar, leader of the zealots, she is also in search of her estranged father. A crowded novel in terms of characters and events, it represents vividly the contradictions, tensions and distinctive physical landscape of Israel. *White Eye* (1993), d'Alpuget's fourth novel, is set mainly in outback NSW, apart from some episodes in Thailand and Sydney. At a remote biotechnological research establishment in NSW, John Parker, a scientist, is developing a vaccine for a highly contagious bacterium (called White Eye because of the film of thick white matter which coats the eyes of its victims). Convinced that the disease will be a way of regaining control of an over-populated world, Parker intends to use White Eye to cause mass deaths or mass sterilisations. Parker's principal adversary is the wildlife activist Diana Pembridge. Although the novel's action and catalogue of murders resembles the thriller genre, d'Alpuget's concerns are complex moral ones, including ethical questions about biotechnology, animal experimentation and trafficking in wild life. An underlying issue, meanwhile, is that of freedom, especially the freedom to love on a new basis of equity after the feminist revolution in relations between the sexes. D'Alpuget also wrote *Mediator* (1977), a biography of Sir Richard Kirby, who was the chief judge of the Conciliation and Arbitration Commission for seventeen years. In researching *Mediator* she became interested in one of its background figures, Robert (Bob) Hawke, then president of the Australian Council of Trade Unions and prime minister of Australia 1983–91. In 1982 she published the biographical work *Robert J. Hawke*, which won the NSW Premier's Award for non-fiction. Based extensively on interviews, the work is a frank psycho-biography. In 1993 d'Alpuget visited Croatia as a representative of Austcare and subsequently helped to raise support for Bosnian women severely affected by war.

'DALY, Rann', see **PALMER, Vance**

DALZIEL, Kathleen (1881–1969), born Kathleen Walker at Durban, South Africa, came to Australia at the age of 6 and lived in an isolated area of north-west Tasmania, where her parents were farmers. After her marriage she lived in Victoria and regularly contributed verse to the *Bulletin* after receiving encouragement from J.F. Archibald. Later she contributed to several American, English and Australian anthologies and periodicals, but continued to publish regularly in the *Bulletin*. Her verse appeared in one collection, *Known and Not Held* (1941).

DAMPIER, Alfred (1847–1908), born Horsham, Sussex, acted in a provincial company headed by Henry Irving before coming to Australia in 1873; in 1877 he formed his own company which included his wife, Katherine Russell, and his daughters Lily and Rose. He specialised in producing the spectacular, nationalistic melodramas that were the staple of colonial audiences and provided a fruitful field for local

playwrights. Dampier wrote several melodramas himself including 'The Nihilists' (1880, with 'Julian Thomas'), 'Marvellous Melbourne' (q.v., 1889, with J.H. Wrangham and possibly others), 'This Great City' and 'The Scout' (both 1891, with Garnet Walch) and 'To the West' (1896, with Kenneth Mackay). He also presented popular versions of Australian novels, adapting Marcus Clarke's *His Natural Life* in 1886 with 'Thomas Somers' as collaborator; and, with Walch, 'Rolf Boldrewood's' *The Miner's Right* in 1891. The most popular was his 1890 adaptation with Walch of 'Boldrewood's' *Robbery Under Arms*, which he took to London in 1894.

DAMPIER, William (1652–1715), born Somerset, England, spent his early manhood trading and privateering in both the Atlantic and Pacific Oceans. In 1688 he spent about three months on the north-western coast of Australia (New Holland) in the area of King Sound. His account of his voyages in the Pacific (1686–91), published in 1697 as *A New Voyage Round the World*, led to his commanding an English naval expedition in 1699 to explore further in New Holland and New Guinea. He cruised the WA coast from Shark Bay to Roebuck Bay (named after his ship), before going on to discover New Britain. His later voyages included one in 1702 in which Alexander Selkirk (Daniel Defoe's Robinson Crusoe) was marooned on Juan Fernandez from one of Dampier's ships. Dampier's writing created a new vogue in travel literature at the time; his publications, in addition to the 1697 work, being *A Supplement to the Voyage Round the World* (1699), *A Voyage to New Holland in the Year 1699* (1703, 1709) and *Captain Dampier's Vindication of His Voyage to the South Seas in the Ship St. George* (1707). Dampier's narratives of his voyages were edited by John Masefield in 1906, and biographical studies of him were written by J.H.M. Abbott (1911), W.H. Bonner (1934), Joseph C. Shipman (1962) and Christopher Lloyd (1966). Leslie R. Marchant's *An Island Unto Itself: William Dampier and New Holland* (1988) reproduces Dampier's descriptions of New Holland from various sources. Alan Chester's novel *The Cygnet Adventure* (1984) is based on Dampier's voyages in the *Cygnet* 1686–91 including his period in NW Australia.

Dandaloo, a small country town about 50 kilometres due west of Narromine, NSW, is presented in two A.B. Paterson (q.v.) poems, 'An Idyll of Dandaloo' and 'An Evening in Dandaloo', as the archetypal bush town where 'life's total sum' is 'sleep, diversified with rum'. Dandaloo's chief pride is its annual race meeting, where a combination of extraordinary decisions by the race judge and tampered weighing scales usually results in Dandaloo money staying in local pockets rather than filling the pockets of the city slickers who deem the Dandaloonies to be easy pickings.

DANN, George Landen (1904–77), born Sandgate, Queensland, wrote numerous plays for stage, radio and television. Two of his full-length plays have been published, *Caroline Chisholm* (1943) and *Fountains Beyond* (1944); the latter deals in an enlightened and sympathetic way with the problems faced by Aborigines in Australian society, as did Dann's earlier, controversial drama 'In Beauty It Is Finished' (1931). His other plays include 'Days of Roses', 'The Giant', 'The Green Trees', 'Monday Morning', 'Oh, The Brave Music', 'Rainbows Die at Sunset', 'Resurrection at Matthewtown', 'No Incense Rising' which won first place in two play-writing competitions in 1937, 'Wild Bells', 'The Orange Grove', 'Funerals for Fieldmice' and 'Ha Ha, Among the Trumpets'. An annual George Landen Dann award of $5000 is made to a Queensland playwright.

DANN, Max (1955–), born Melbourne, left school to become a carpenter but has written prolifically and successfully for young readers as well as being a scriptwriter for film and television. Mann won the *Age* Short Story Award in 1983 and the Children's Book Council's Junior Book of the Year Award in 1984 for *Bernice Knows Best* (1983). His many children's books include *Adventures with My Worst Best Friend* (1982), *Going Bananas* (1983), *Ernest Pickle's Remarkable Robot* (1984), *One Night at Lottie's House* (1985), *The Lonely Hearts Club* (1987, with Robin Klein), *Dusting's Disasters* (1989), *Dusting in Love* (1990), and *Jason Prince* (1992). He also wrote an adult work of fiction, *The Onion Man* (1988) and contributed to the screen plays *The Big Steal* (1989) and, with Andrew Knight, *Spotswood* (1992). For TV he wrote *Not Suitable for Adults* (1984), *The Fast Lane* (1986, two episodes), *Worst Best Friends* (1986, six episodes), and contributed to *Fast Forward* (1988–90).

DARCY, Les (1895–1917), born Stradbroke, near Maitland, NSW, became a boxing champion in Australia but went to the USA in 1916 at the time of the conscription controversy in Australia and in circumstances that led to his being branded as a shirker of his duty to his country. Unable to gain an opportunity to establish himself as a boxer in America, Darcy fell ill and died. Darcy's undoubted boxing prowess and his untimely death have established him, like Phar Lap, as an Australian folk-hero. A number of sentimental verse tributes to Darcy (e.g. by Jack Bradshaw) were composed soon after his death. W. Lawless wrote the contemporary *The Darcy Story* (1919) and Raymond Swanwick the later biographical study, *Les Darcy: Australia's Golden Boy of Boxing* (1965). Darcy is portrayed in Frank Hardy's *Power Without Glory* (1950) as Lou Darby; Monk O'Neill reminisces about him in Jack Hibberd's play *A Stretch of the Imagination* (1973); and Hibberd's celebration of him, *The Les Darcy Show* (published 1976), was first performed in 1974. The Darcy myth also had a great influence on D'Arcy Niland, who was working on a Darcy biography when he died.

D'ARCY-IRVINE, Gerard Addington (1862–1932), born London, went with his family to NZ before moving to Goulburn, NSW, where his father conducted a school. He entered the Anglican ministry and was consecrated coadjutor bishop of Sydney in 1926. In 1899 he published his first verse collection, *Poems*, followed by *Additional Poems* in 1901 and a further collection, *Poems*, in 1903. In 1905 an illustrated edition of his work was produced and it was later reprinted and enlarged. His final volume, *Analects*, appeared in 1923. D'Arcy-Irvine preached at Henry Lawson's funeral.

'DARE, Ishmael', see **JOSE, Arthur Wilberforce**

DARK, Eleanor (1901–85), the only daughter of the writer Dowell O'Reilly (q.v.), was born and educated in Sydney. After a brief period of employment as a stenographer, in 1922 she married Dr Eric Payten Dark, a general practitioner and writer on physiotherapy and sociological medicine. In 1923 the Darks moved to the Blue Mountains town of Katoomba where they remained, apart from lengthy visits 1951–57 to their citrus and nut farm in Queensland. They also made an extended visit to the USA in 1937. Eleanor Dark's earliest writings, short stories and verse, were contributed from 1921 to a range of magazines including the *Bulletin*, *Home* and *Triad*, mostly under the pseudonym 'Patricia O'Rane' or 'P. O'R.'. *Slow Dawning*, her first novel, was completed in 1923 though it failed to find a publisher until 1932. Her other novels are *Prelude to Christopher* (1934), *Return to Coolami* (1936), *Sun across the Sky* (1937), *Waterway* (1938), *The Little Company* (q.v., 1945), *Lantana Lane* (1959) and the historical trilogy, *The Timeless Land* (q.v., 1941), *Storm of Time* (1948) and *No Barrier* (1953). Dark's short stories, as yet uncollected, continued to appear until 1946 and she also contributed some historical and travel articles to journals and anthologies. Most of the latter reflect her keen appreciation and knowledge of the Australian landscape. She was awarded the Australian Literature Society's Gold Medal in 1934 and 1936, and in 1978 received the Australian Society of Women Writers' Alice Award. In 1977 she was made AO. Some of her later novels have been translated into other languages and in October 1941 *The Timeless Land* was selected as Book of the Month in the USA. One of Australia's best-selling serious novelists for twenty years, Dark has received little attention in recent times, although a dramatised version of her historical trilogy was produced by the ABC in 1980. Varuna, the Darks' family home, has been restored as a writers' centre and donated to the Eleanor Dark Foundation.

A writer of formidable intellectual powers and technical subtlety, Dark had distinctive skills which found their fullest scope in her novels. Stylistically influenced by major European writers of the 1920s and 1930s, especially in her psychological focus and use of timeshifts, she rapidly developed a characteristic narrative technique. Concerned always to represent the inward experience of reality as well as its objective shape, she most characteristically used the interior monologue. A novelist of ideas, particularly receptive to the power of cultural myths, she was personally committed to a socialist philosophy that stopped short of ideological dogma. Striking features of her novels include her deep love of the land, insight into the needs of women, respectful understanding of Aboriginal culture and awareness of the destructive effects of Western civilisation. Her feminist concerns are already apparent in *Slow Dawning*; the story of a young woman doctor's search for happiness in both personal life and career, the novel is remarkable for its technical control and authentic representation of life in an Australian country town. *Prelude to Christopher*, a more complex work, reveals a deep interest in heredity and abnormal psychology; the action, compressed into four days, is the critical culmination of a series of events in the past which are gradually and suspensefully revealed to explain the motives of the main characters. This is the first of her novels in which Dark's expressed concern to record life 'as an endless present moment, moving snail-wise through time, carrying the past and future on its back' rather than as a 'steady onward march', finds full expression. *Return to Coolami*, which deals mainly with the interrelationship of four people on a 300-mile journey by car through NSW, is a dramatic unfolding of the dynamic emotions of ordinary, likeable people. In *Sun across the Sky* the action is restricted to a single day of crisis and turns upon the relationship between three different men: Gormley, a philistine, power-hungry capitalist; Denning, a humane, vitalist doctor; and Kavanagh, a craggy poetic genius whose spirit dominates the book and who is based on Dark's memory of C.J. Brennan. Unobtrusively but deftly structured, the novel is shaped by opposing ideas of life and sterility. *Waterway*, a lengthy novel which features a number of the characters from *Sun across the Sky* and is similarly restricted to a single day culminating in violent tragedy, includes a broader statement of Dark's general ideas. A densely characterised novel distinguished by descriptions of its Sydney Harbour setting, its action consists mainly of a diverse, inward drama. With *The Little Company*, Dark returned to a more conventional novel form. Darker and more pessimistically determinist than her earlier work, it is concerned with various forms of failure and deals with a number of broad issues such as war and pacifism, education, feminism and religious and political attitudes. *Lantana Lane*, more a light-hearted collection of loosely united short stories and essays than a novel, was inspired by the Darks' experience of farming in Queensland. Humorously affectionate in tone, it offers some memorable pictures of Queensland rural life. Dark is best known, however, for her historical trilogy which traces the development of the European settlement in Australia 1788–1814. Based on extensive research, the trilogy is true to the events of history, although enlivened by the novelist's imaginative treatment of the inward life of the participants. As its title suggests, the underlying theme of *The Timeless Land*, which deals with the first five years of White settlement, is the spiritual dichotomy between the age-old, relatively timeless continent of Australia and the time-governed, new 'civilisation' of Europe. The experiences of and the relationship between Bennelong and Governor Phillip, both representative of and yet distanced from their respective cultures, contain the central conflict. Striking features of the novel include a wide range of well-realised individuals, both White and Black, convict and free; a consistently sympathetic presentation of the culture of the Aborigines; lyrical descriptions of the Australian landscape; and a style that moves easily from epic to comic and graphic. Unillusioned in its attitude to Western civilisation, the novel has been praised as a landmark in Australian historical fiction and an important work for all students of the first period in Australian history or of general ethnic conflict. There is no reduction in tone in the massive, solidly detailed *Storm of Time*, which covers the governorships of Hunter, King and Bligh; the novel is also an incisive analysis of the dynamic interplay of interests in the new society. The same flair for description, characterisation and detail enlivens *No Barrier*, which takes the story up to the crossing of the Blue Mountains. Some of Dark's correspondence with other women writers is included in the collection *As Good as a Yarn With You* (1992), edited by Carole Ferrier.

Darling Downs, one of Queensland's most fertile pastoral and agricultural areas, watered by the Condamine River and its tributaries, is situated about 160 kilometres west of Brisbane. Discovered in 1827 by explorer and botanist Allan Cunningham, and named after Sir Ralph Darling, then governor of NSW, the Darling Downs district was settled in the 1840s by squatters such as the Leslie brothers who established the Canning Downs station near the present township of Warwick, one of the chief urban centres of the area. The regional capital of the Darling Downs is Toowoomba; it grew into a township in the 1840s because it was on the wagon route to Brisbane. Toowoomba's famous literary sons include A.G. Stephens, 'Steele Rudd', George Essex Evans (q.v.) and, in more recent times, Bruce Dawe (q.v.). *Downs Images*, a selection of essays, stories and poems by twenty-one Downs writers, was published in 1981. D.B. Waterson wrote *Squatter, Selector and Storekeeper: A History of the Darling Downs 1859–93* (1968). Nancy Bonnin edited *Kate Hume on the Darling Downs* (1987), a revised edition of an earlier book of letters of an original Toowoomba resident.

DARLING, Sir James (1899–   ), born Tonbridge, England, became headmaster of Geelong Grammar School in Victoria in 1929. He served on the Universities Commission 1942–51, was foundation president of the Australian College of Education in 1959 and chairman of the ABC 1961–67. A selection of his speeches and sermons, *The Education of a Civilized Man*, appeared in 1962, and a selection of his Saturday leaders for the *Age*, *Reflections for the Age*, edited by James Minchin and Brian Porter, in 1991. *Richly Rewarding*, his autobiography, was published in 1978.

DARLING, Sir Ralph (1772–1858) was governor of NSW 1825–31. He introduced extensive financial and administrative reforms in the Colony and encouraged exploration, but had a reputation for autocracy in a time of change. Darling tried unsuccessfully to legislate to control the press and was criticised in verse and editorials published in the *Australian* and the *Sydney Monitor*; he also opposed Barnett Levey's (q.v.) attempts to establish a colonial theatre and banned the singing of the John Donohoe (q.v.) ballads. The Darling River and the Darling Downs, which were discovered during his term of office, were named after him; so was the 'Darling necklace', an iron collar which imprisoned two soldiers, Sudds and Thompson, in a controversial punishment in 1826. Darling appears briefly in 'Price Warung's' story of 1820s Sydney society, 'Marie Antoinette's Fandango' (1891). Brian H. Fletcher wrote the biography *Ralph Darling: A Governor Maligned* (1984).

Darling River, named after Sir Ralph Darling, governor of NSW 1825–31, is a major part of the great inland river system that runs from Queensland through NSW to Victoria and SA. The Darling has its source near Stanthorpe in Queensland, where it is known as the Severn, and flows under various names – the Dumaresque, the Macintyre, the Barwon – until, from the junction of the Barwon and Culgoa Rivers, it flows as the Darling, joining the Murray River at Wentworth in south-western NSW. Exploration of the Darling Basin began with Allan Cunningham in 1827; in 1828 Charles Sturt and Hamilton Hume reached the spot on the river where Bourke now stands. Settlement followed in the wake of exploration and by the latter decades of the century the Darling region had been carved up into gigantic runs. The pastoral occupation of the Darling is described in C.E.W. Bean's *On the Wool Track* (1909). The use of the river for transport and commerce is discussed in Bean's *The Dreadnought of the Darling* (1911) and Ian Mudie's *Riverboats* (1961). F.M. Browne's poem 'The Last of the Darling Dreadnoughts' captures the atmosphere of the riverboat era. Henry Lawson, sent by J.F. Archibald of the *Bulletin* to Bourke in 1892 to collect material for outback stories, spent laborious months tramping the environs of the Darling; his poems 'Song of the Darling River' and 'Bourke', together with his story 'The Darling River', capture much of the area's atmosphere. The Darling has given its name to the toxic plant the Darling pea, which poisons cattle, and the phrase is applied to humans who, exhibiting strange symptoms of moodiness or eccentricity, are said to 'have the Darling pea'. The river's name is also used in such outback humorisms as a 'Darling shower', i.e. a clap of thunder, two drops of rain and a dust-storm; a 'Darling sandwich', i.e. a goanna between two layers of bark; and a 'Darling pie', i.e. baked rabbit and bindi-eyes.

DARRELL, George (1841–1921), born Bath, England, with the name George Frederick Price, came to Australia in 1865 and joined the NZ gold rush in the same year. He spent little time as a digger, having quickly discovered his interest in the theatre, and achieved some success as an actor at Dunedin. He returned to Melbourne in 1868 to act at the Theatre Royal and at the same time changed his name to Dar-

rell. In 1870 he married the well-known actor Fanny Cathcart (q.v.), who had already influenced his career, and for the next ten years toured with her in NZ, Australia and the USA. During this time he also formed his own company, for which he wrote numerous plays, and acquired a reputation as an actor, playwright, manager, producer and entrepreneur. After the death of Fanny in 1880, he continued to tour extensively in Australia and overseas, often accompanied by his second wife, the young actor Christine Peachey, whom he married in 1886 and who died in 1892. In addition to these personal tragedies, his career was curbed by an accident in 1884 and by illness in 1887, but was not severely checked until the 1890s when the growth of the J.C. Williamson company offered strong competition and the economic depression affected the size of audiences. By 1905 his career was virtually over, his later productions having failed and his acting skills finding few openings, and in 1921 he committed suicide. Of the numerous plays written by Darrell, possibly as many as fifty-eight, most retained the traditional elements of melodrama, although they had a distinctive topical and lively Australian flavour including a range of stock colonial types and featuring both expatriate nostalgia and robust good humour. Apart from *The Sunny South* (q.v., 1883), his only extant play, his most popular productions were 'Man and Wife' (1871), 'The Trump Card' (1874), 'Transported for Life' (1876), 'Back from the Grave' (1878), 'The Forlorn Hope' (1879) and 'The Naked Truth' (1883). Most of these were original although Darrell occasionally wrote adaptations of English and Australian novels, including one of Fergus Hume's *The Mystery of a Hansom Cab*, produced in 1888. He also wrote a novel, *The Belle of the Bush* (1916). Darrell's career is the subject of Eric Irvin's *Gentleman George* (1980).

DARWIN, Charles (1809–82), the famous English naturalist and evolutionary theorist, visited Australia briefly in HMS *Beagle* in 1836 in the course of his five-year voyage round the world. Darwin contributed the third volume in the official record of the voyage, which includes his impressions of Australia and was initially titled *Journal and Remarks* and published in May 1839. The volume proved to be so popular that it was republished three months later as a separate book titled *Journal of Researches into the Geology and Natural History of the Various Countries visited by HMS Beagle*. In 1845 a second edition appeared which omitted some sections of the 1839 *Journal* and introduced some new material. The personal diary he kept on the voyage and drew on for the 1839 and 1845 *Journals* was first published in full in 1933, titled *Charles Darwin's Diary of the Voyage of H.M.S. 'Beagle'*, edited by Nora Barlow. *Charles Darwin in Australia* (1989) by F.W. and J.M. Nicholas draws on several sources including the rough notes he made in the field, his geological and zoological diaries, his personal diary, his contribution to the official record of 1839 and his revisions in 1845, and his correspondence. The volume is illustrated by paintings by Augustus Earle and Conrad Martens, who were Darwin's shipmates during an earlier stage of the voyage. Darwin appears in 'Price Warung's' story

'Absalom Day's Promotion' and in 'Grant Hervey's' novel *An Eden of the Good* (1934).

DAVEY, Jack (1910–59), one of Australia's earliest and best-known radio and television entertainers, was born in Auckland, NZ, and came to Australia in 1934. His book *Hi, Ho! Everybody!*, the title being the famous opening remark of his programmes, was published in 1945. Lew Wright published *The Jack Davey Story* (1961).

DAVID, Mary Edgeworth (1888–1987), born Maitland, NSW, was the youngest daughter of Sir William Edgeworth David, the eminent geologist and Antarctic explorer, and the author of his biography, *Professor David* (1937). After her father accepted the chair of geology at the University of Sydney the family moved to the city, where the two girls were educated privately and divided their time between Sydney and the Blue Mountains. Mary Edgeworth David's autobiography *Passages of Time* (1975) gives an intimate picture of her late Victorian-Edwardian childhood, dominated by the strong personality of her mother and the growing prestige of her father, but which was unusually free both physically and intellectually because of her parents' unconventional values and emphasis on independence. The first part of *Passages of Time* is largely devoted to the author's parents, whose public activities drew on her energies as an unmarried daughter living at home. The death of her beloved sister was a major blow, although the role of aunt provided some consolations. The latter part, dealing with her work as a small farmer from the late 1940s, celebrates her discovery of a separate destiny. An interesting representation of Australian life from the 1900s to the 1940s within a certain academic, public-spirited milieu, *Passages of Time* is not unlike Vera Brittain's autobiographies in its representation of the condition of women before and after the First World War.

DAVIDSON, Jim, see *Meanjin*

DAVIDSON, Robyn (1950–), born Miles, Queensland, has worked at several occupations after a childhood in western Queensland and Nambour. In 1977 she made a solitary trek with four camels across the Gibson desert and subsequently wrote the story of her experiences, *Tracks* (1980), which became an international best-seller and won the Thomas Cook Travel Book of the Year Award in 1981. She has subsequently lived in New York and London, returning periodically to Australia. She has also written a novel, *Ancestors* (1989); a collection of articles on her travels, *Travelling Light* (1989); and contributed an account of her 1950s childhood and reactions to a changing Australia, 'The Mythological Crucible', to *Australia. Beyond the Dreamtime* (1987).

DAVIES, Alan Fraser (1924–87), born Wangaratta, Victoria, was professor of politics at the University of Melbourne and published numerous sociological and political works including *Policies for Progress* (1954), *Australian Democracy* (1958), *Private Politics* (1961), *Aus-*

tralian Society (1965, edited with Sol Encel), *Images of Class* (1967) and *Skills, Outlooks and Passions* (1980); the last is a psychoanalytic contribution to the study of politics. Davies also published a volume of short stories, *A Sunday Kind of Love* (1961).

DAVIES, Eliza, born Eliza Arbuckle in Paisley, Scotland, made two visits in the 1830s and 1850s–1870s to Australia, where she encountered extraordinary adventures according to her substantial autobiography, *The Story of an Earnest Life* (1881). Her story includes an account of Sturt's disastrous 1839 expedition, which she accompanied, and her subsequent work with G.F. Angas in education. Written in heightened prose and packed with dramatic events and crises, *The Story of an Earnest Life* is both a historically informative account and a revealing exposé of a paranoid personality.

DAVIES, John (1813–72), born London, came to Australia at the age of 18, having been sentenced to transportation for seven years for fraud. An audacious and energetic character, Davies became a reporter for the *Port Phillip Gazette* in 1842 and in 1852 in Hobart, in partnership with George Auber Jones, published the *Hobarton Guardian*, which was incorporated in 1854 with the *Hobarton Mercury*. Davies became its sole proprietor, absorbing several other Tasmanian newspapers and establishing it as a daily by 1858. The *Mercury* was taken over by his sons, John George Davies and Charles Ellis Davies, in 1871. John Davies, an amateur actor, was also part-proprietor of the Theatre Royal, Hobart.

DAVIES, Julian (1954–), born Melbourne, is a potter, artist and writer working in the rapidly developing cultural centre (artists' retreat) of Braidwood in the southern highlands of NSW. He has written two successful novels, *Revival House* (1991) and *Love Parts* (1992). *Revival House* – the title refers both to the revival cinemas of America in which old movies are shown and the religious establishments common in Australia – deals with the experiences of a young Australian art historian doing graduate studies in New York. He stays at the house of an old family friend, Moishe Feinbaum, in the New York seaside suburb, Island City. Much of the novel concerns his obsession with the dead millionaire industrialist Henry Clay Frick, whose art collection is housed in the Frick Museum in New York. The story of Frick interweaves with the young academic's own experiences in New York. His affair with Moishe's wife Elizabeth leads to the break-up of the Feinbaum family, but the affair was probably unconsciously engineered by Moishe to secure his own release. *Love Parts*, also concerned with men's attitude to women, is the story of a love triangle – father and son Max and David Hawthorne, who live together in 'intimate friction' and their mysterious new neighbour, the attractive Ashland Eichmann. When she disappears the two men set out to find her (which they never do) but in the process they find, for the first time, a more satisfactory relationship with each other.

DAVIES, Lloyd (1922–), a civil liberties lawyer, graduated from the University of WA in 1948 after serving with the AIF 1941–46. He has published two collections of short stories, *Past Master* (1980) and *The Lawyer and the Rhine Maiden* (1989), a novel, *Cult and Countercult* (1984), and an account of his libel actions against his ex-wife Dorothy Hewett (q.v.) and other parties, *In Defence of My Family* (1986).

DAVIES, Rowland (Lyttleton Archer) (1837–80), born Longford, Tasmania, the son of an archdeacon, studied engineering in England and pursued his profession in Tasmania, NZ and Victoria. He was also one of Australia's earliest poets although he preserved few of his manuscripts. Writing in the tradition of Wordsworth and the Victorian poets, he attempted with some success to express his affinity for the Australian landscape, though he failed to reach the same heights as Harpur and Kendall. A selection of his poetry was published in 1884, titled *Poems and Other Literary Remains*, edited with a biographical sketch by Charles Tomlinson.

DAVIS, Arthur Hoey, see 'RUDD, Steele'

DAVIS, Beatrice (1909–92), born Bendigo, Victoria, became in 1937 the first full-time general editor employed by Angus & Robertson (q.v.). She was closely associated with many important Australian writers during the thirty-six years she occupied that position. They included Hugh McCrae, Norman Lindsay, Miles Franklin, Xavier Herbert, Douglas Stewart, Hal Porter, Eve Langley and Thea Astley. She edited *Coast to Coast* in 1942 and compiled the anthologies *Short Stories of Australia: The Moderns* (1967) and *The Illustrated Treasury of Australian Verse* (1984). From 1973 to 1986 she was editor in NSW for Thomas Nelson and was a judge of the Miles Franklin Award for fiction from 1957 until her death. She was elected Bookman of the Year in 1977. She was made MBE in 1965, AM in 1981 and received an honorary D.Litt. from the University of Sydney in 1992. The inaugural Beatrice Davis Editorial Fellowship established in her honour (it sends the successful editor to New York to work in a publishing house) was won by Roseanne Fitzgibbons of UQP, the second was won by Sue Hines of Reed Books. Anthony Barker wrote a memoir, *One of the First and One of the Finest* (1991), the title aptly summing up the general estimate of her major contribution to the publishing of Australian literature over more than half a century.

DAVIS, Jack (1917–) born Perth, into the Nyoongah people of the south-west of WA and into a large family, was brought up at Yarloop. His mother, who had been forcibly removed from her own family to be brought up by White people, never received an education and her tribal roots were only discovered belatedly and fortuitously by Davis. At 14 Davis went to the Moore River Native Settlement, ostensibly to learn farming, but the Settlement, which subsequently became the basis of two of his plays, *The Dreamers* and *No Sugar*, had more resemblance to a prison camp than to

an educational institution. After nine months he returned home, but his father's death shortly afterwards resulted in the family's break-up and Davis left to embark on varied experiences as a stockman, boxer and horse-breeder. He first began to learn the language and culture of his people while living on the Brookton Aboriginal Reserve, and later became an activist for the Aboriginal people. From 1967 to 1971 he was director of the Aboriginal Centre in Perth, first chairman of the Aboriginal Lands Trust in WA in 1971 and managing editor of the Aboriginal Publications Foundation 1972–77. He was also joint editor of *Identity* 1973–79.

Davis's first book of poetry, *The First-Born and Other Poems* (1970), contains an introductory autobiographical sketch and an appendix of Bibbulmun tribal words. The title poem, a nostalgic *cri de coeur* for the 'dark proud race', indicates in its opening line, 'Where are my first-born said the brown land, sighing', the innate Aboriginal gentleness and melancholy. Other poems that reveal Davis's yearning for the past include 'The Drifters' and 'Desolation', the latter echoing the sense of loss so predominant in Aboriginal verse. His strongest protest poem, 'Whither?', portrays the typical Aboriginal life from optimistic youth to disillusioned age, a life characterised by a succession of withheld or withdrawn basic human rights. His best-known individual poem is possibly 'Yadabooka', the story of a tribal Aborigine who was sentenced by White law to life imprisonment for a ritual killing that was sanctioned by Aboriginal law. 'Integration', with its message 'This is ours together/ This nation', is a plea for Black–White union in attempting to resolve racial problems. Davis's other volumes of verse are *Jagardoo: Poems from Aboriginal Australia* (1978), *John Pat and Other Poems* (1988) and *Black Life* (1992).

He has also written short stories and acquired a reputation as a leading playwright. His first play, *Kullark* (1979), written to mark the sesquicentenary celebrations in WA and successfully staged there, focuses upon three episodes in the race-relations history of that State – the Nungar (Nyoongah) tribe during the years 1829–30, a Black family in the Moore River district of the 1930s, and a contemporary Aboriginal family. The same treatment of the Aborigine by White society, repeated at the three intervals during a century and a half, creates a cyclical effect of injustice that leads to a fatalistic pessimism. That pessimism and despondency can only be broken, the play indicates, by a change in Aboriginal cultural self-perception. His next play, *The Dreamers* (1982), narrates the story of a family cut off from its tribal and cultural past and consigned to Perth's lowest social level. The most authoritative character, Old Worrun, based on an influential individual in Davis's youth and played by himself in the first performance of *The Dreamers*, relates his memories of his own and his people's maltreatment. Meanwhile the realistic surface of the play is disrupted by the intrusion of different time-levels, reminding the audience of the earlier rich culture which White settlement had nearly extinguished. *No Sugar* (1985), Davis's next play, focuses on a central incident in the life of his people, the 1933 evacuation of a large camp of people including the Millimurra family to the Moore River Native Settlement. A loosely structured play, designed for a dispersed setting on an open stage, it has been performed in Canada and Britain. *Barungin: Smell the Wind* (1988), Davis's response to the Bicentennial celebrations, takes his Nyoongah family to the 1980s and focuses on the links between historical killings and massacres and contemporary deaths of Aborigines while in custody. *The Dreamers, No Sugar* and *Barungin* have also been performed as a a trilogy, with the title *The First Born*; opening with *No Sugar*, the trilogy thus traces Aboriginal history by following the story of one family over sixty years to the present. Davis has continued his interest in the life of the family in his latest play, *In Our Town* (1992), and has written two plays for children, *Honey Spot* (1987) and 'Moorli and the Leprechaun' (1988). He has also written an autobiography of his childhood, *A Boy's Life* (1991), and, with Stephen Muecke, Mudrooroo and Adam Shoemaker, edited *Paperbark, a Collection of Black Australian Writings* (1990). *Jack Davis. A Life-Story* (1988) by Keith Chesson was narrated by Davis and recorded and arranged by Chesson. Davis has won numerous awards and honours. In 1977 he was awarded the BEM for services to the Aborigines and for his writings, in 1980 the Patricia Weickhardt Award for an Aboriginal writer, and in 1985 was made AM, was elected Citizen of the Year in WA and won the Sidney Myer Performing Arts Award. In 1988 he won the BHP Pursuit of Excellence Award for Literature and the Arts, and the Dick Roughsey Award, and in the same year *The First Born* trilogy won the Green Room Award for best production. He has also received honorary doctorates from the University of WA and Murdoch University. In 1992 *No Sugar* won the $10 000 RAKA (Ruth Adeney Koori Award).

DAVIS, Norma (1905–45), born Glenore, Tasmania, began her writing career by publishing verse in the *Woman's Mirror* under such pseudonyms as Norelda, Glenarvon, Malda, Malda Norris and Normalda as well as her own name. She also contributed to the *Bulletin, Meanjin, Poetry* and *Jindyworobak Anthology* and published two collections before her early death from cancer, *Earth Cry* (1943) and *I, the Thief* (1944). Davis's poetry, which reflects her passion for the Tasmanian bush and resembles that of Shaw Neilson in sensitivity and delicacy, won praise from such critics as Douglas Stewart, H.M. Green and E. Morris Miller.

DAVISON, Frank Dalby (1893–1970), born Hawthorn, Melbourne, was christened Frederick Douglas but began to use the names Frank Dalby after 1931 to distinguish himself from his father, Frederick Davison (q.v.). After leaving school at 12, he worked on farms in Victoria, acquiring a wealth of rural experience that he later used in his short stories. In 1909 the Davison family moved to the USA, where Frank was apprenticed to the printing trade, worked for some time in New York and tried his hand at writing. He travelled widely in North America and in the West Indies, the latter experience proving useful for his travel book *Caribbean Interlude* (1936). He enlisted enthusiastically in the First World War and served with the British cavalry in France, returning to Australia in 1919. Throughout these years of travel his nostalgia for home quickened his appreciation of the Australian bush. There followed four years of hard farming in southern Queensland, brought to a close by drought and debt, a period of working in his father's real estate business in Sydney and involvement in his father's journal the *Australian*, later *Australia*, 1923–25. The *Australian* published several of his short stories and serialised versions of his two novels, *Man-Shy* (q.v.) and *Forever Morning*. In 1931 both novels were published separately in cheap editions by Frederick Davison, *Man-Shy* winning the Australian Literature Society Award. *The Wells of Beersheba* (q.v.), an account of the Australian Light Horse in Palestine 1914–18, appeared in 1933. During a trip to Queensland in 1934 Davison was shocked by the destruction of the natural environment by developers; his book *Blue Coast Caravan* (1935) was written as a response, and *Children of the Dark People* (1936) has a conservationist theme. He became active in the FAW, working with Marjorie Barnard and Flora Eldershaw to put forward progressive political views, taking strong stands on issues such as censorship and civil liberties. At this time he was writing reviews for the *Bulletin*, which also published a number of his short stories, revised for the collection *The Woman and the Mill* (1940). In 1944 he married for the second time and in 1951 bought a small farm north of Melbourne, 'Folding Hills', where he lived for his last two decades. *Dusty* (q.v., 1946) and his collection of shorter works in one volume, titled *The Road to Yesterday* (1964), seemed to set the seal on his reputation as a writer of animal stories and a sensitive interpreter of Australian bush life in the tradition of Henry Lawson, Joseph Furphy and Vance Palmer. The publication of the massive novel *The White Thorntree* (q.v., 1968), however, a book that had taken twenty-two years to write, seemed a major change in direction, requiring a new, more difficult assimilation of his talent.

Apart from the novels *Man-Shy* and *Dusty*, Davison's most popular works are his short stories. The fourteen stories grouped under the heading 'Queensland' in *The Road to Yesterday* are an imaginatively coherent whole, evoking a way of life that is particular in time and place but more representative in its reflection of human motives, frustrations, hopes and disillusionments. The theme of sexuality as a subterranean, potentially destructive force, a continuing preoccupation for Davison, as *The White Thorntree* shows, runs through several of the stories including 'The Woman at the Mill', 'Return of the Hunter', 'Further West' and 'Blood Will Tell'. Others such as 'Tank-Sinkers', 'Nobody's Kelpie' and 'Soldier of Fortune' deal sensitively with the important minutiae of human relationships in a landscape where relationships are sparse. 'The Good Herdsman' and 'A Letter from Colleen' express unsentimentally the pathos of old age. Throughout the stories the common implication of all things animate in a tragic, endless recurrence is indirectly probed. A posthumous collection, *The Wells of Beersheba and Other Stories* (1985), includes material not previously published. Two book-length accounts of Davison's work have been published, by Hume Dow (1971) and Louise E. Rorabacher (1979); Owen Webster in *The Outward Journey* (1978) deals with his early life and writing. Davison appears as Knarf in 'M. Barnard Eldershaw's' novel *Tomorrow and Tomorrow* (1947). His relationship with Marjorie Barnard is partly illuminated in the collection of correspondence by women writers of the 1930s and 1940s, *As Good as a Yarn With You* (1992), ed. Carole Ferrier.

DAVISON, Frederick (1868–1942), born Mount Buninyong near Ballarat, was printer, publisher, editor, journalist, fiction-writer and the father of Frank Dalby Davison (q.v.). His energetic nationalism, which included a keen interest in Australian literature, found expression in the organ of the Australian Natives' Association, *The Advance Australia*, which he edited 1897–99. After an unsuccessful sojourn in the USA (1909–17) and service with the First AIF in France, he continued his efforts in two journals he founded, the *Australian Post* (1920–21) and the *Australian*, later *Australia* (1923–25). These depended heavily on contributions from his son Frank and other members of the Davison family. During the 1930s Depression, he turned the family's energies to publishing and produced cheap editions of Frank Davison's novels, *Man-Shy* and *Forever Morning*, in 1931. He also wrote several works of fiction, including *Storm Bradley – Australian* (1932), *Duck Williams and His Cobbers* (1939), and *Public Enemy No. 1* (1940).

DAVISON, Liam (1957–), born Melbourne, teaches creative writing. His short stories have been widely published and have received several awards in short-fiction competitions, including the FAW (Victoria) competition (1979), the Caulfield Festival Competition (1988), the *Canberra Times* competition (1983) and the Judah Waten competition (1988). He has published two novels, *The Velodrome* (1988) and *Soundings* (q.v., 1993), winner of the 1993 NBC Banjo Award, and a collection of short stories, *The Shipwreck Party* (1989). Sculpting his narratives with meticulous care, Davison writes a spare, compressed prose with evocative effects. His major work is the novel *Soundings* (1993), which is set in a watery milieu as is so much of his writing. A study of three particular periods in the history and development of Westernport Bay in Victoria, *Soundings* is a sombre novel including a range of misfortunes and hardships and experiences of isolation and unhappiness. It is a powerful work that has added considerably to Davison's growing reputation as a writer of fiction. In the stories of *The Shipwreck Party*, refracted through an underwater perspective, meaning shifts as inevitably and as impersonally as the tides as individuals come upon disturbing truths, insights and revelations; at a party on a sinking ship, a guest

discovers a strange secret floating below decks, a boy looking through the Greenwich telescope discovers his mother in a love affair. Like William Buckley, the lonely convict of 'The Left Man', confronted with a snake which is threatening yet disconcertingly aloof, and even more threateningly confronted with the knowledge of his total separation from White society, these events and revelations change the situation and strike fear into the flesh. Restrained and yet confident, Davison's prose teases the reader with unexplained or half-explained mysteries.

DAVITT, Ellen (1812–79), born Ellen Heseltine at Hull, England, married Arthur Davitt, an educationist, in 1845 and accompanied him to Melbourne in 1854 to manage a new Model School. Well educated and strong-minded, Ellen Davitt was appointed as superintendent and her husband as principal. Running the school was fraught with political in-fighting, resulting in the Davitts' discharge. After Arthur Davitt's death from tuberculosis in 1860, Ellen continued to teach and began a new career as a public speaker and writer. Her first work, 'Edith Travers', has not yet been traced, but her serial, the murder mystery *Force and Fraud*, which appeared in the *Australian Journal* (1865), has been recovered and published by Mulini Press in 1993. It was followed by several novel-length serials and novellas, including 'Black Sheep', 'Uncle Vincent', 'Past and Future' and 'The Wreck of the Atlanta'. After apparently pursuing a career in journalism, Ellen tried teaching again from 1874 as first assistant teacher at Kangaroo Flat, near Bendigo. This position proved to be a difficult one and she was forced to resign, subsequently facing extreme indigence when her claims for compensation were refused. She was a sister-in-law of Anthony Trollope, although she appears to have had little connection with him during her lifetime.

DAWBIN, Annie Maria (Annie Maria Baxter) (1816–1905), born Devon, England, as Annie Maria Hadden, came to Australia as the 17-year-old bride of Lieutenant Andrew Baxter, whose regiment was stationed in Van Diemen's Land. From 1834 to 1851, in a steadily deteriorating marriage, she accompanied Baxter over much of the Colony – to Sydney and Port Macquarie as a soldier's wife, to the Macleay River in NSW and the Port Fairy district in western Victoria as a pastoralist's wife. A second marriage, after her husband's suicide in 1855, to Robert Dawbin was marked by further disappointments and unsuccessful ventures in Victoria, England and NZ. In 1873 she published *Memories of the Past by a Lady in Australia*, memories drawn from the diaries which she had maintained over thirty-two years and which give not only a revealing picture of the society of the Colony in the years 1834–65 but also a remarkable self-portrait of one of Australia's pioneer women. Lucy Frost has drawn on the diaries in *A Face in the Glass: the Journal and Life of Annie Baxter Dawbin* (1992). The Baxters and their run Yambuck, at Port Fairy, are described by 'Rolf Boldrewood' in *Old Melbourne Memories* (1884).

DAWE, Bruce (1930–), born Geelong, Victoria, left high school at 16, a dissatisfied and uninterested student. A variety of briefly held jobs followed until he completed adult matriculation at night classes in 1953 and began a university course in 1954. Although he left the University of Melbourne after a year, that period had a significant influence on his developing literary interests. Of particular importance was his association with Philip Martin (q.v.), whose continuing friendship and literary expertise have been acknowledged by Dawe as important in his own development as a poet. He was also associated with *MUM* (*Melbourne University Magazine*), *Compass* and *Farrago*, in the last of which he published the 'Joey Cassidy' stories. After a period as factory worker in Sydney and postman in Melbourne, he joined the RAAF. During his service (1959–68) he published two volumes of poetry, married a Toowoomba girl (Gloria) and completed his first degree (he now holds an MA and Ph.D.). In 1971 he became a teacher at Toowoomba's Downlands College, in 1972 a lecturer at the Darling Downs Institute of Advanced Education and was associate professor of literary studies at the University College of Southern Queensland at Toowoomba 1990–93. Dawe has written prolifically. His poetry volumes are *No Fixed Address* (1962); *A Need of Similar Name* (1965, the Myer Award for Poetry); *An Eye for a Tooth* (1968, the Sidney Myer Charity Trust Award for Poetry); *Beyond the Subdivisions* (1969); *Heat-Wave* (1970); *Condolences of the Season: Selected Poems* (1971); *Just a Dugong at Twilight: Mainly Light Verse* (1975); *Sometimes Gladness: Collected Poems 1954–1978* (the 1979 Grace Leven Prize for Poetry; second and third editions in 1983 and 1988); *Towards Sunrise: Poems 1979–1986* (1986) and *This Side of Silence* (1990). He has also written short fiction, *Over Here Harv! and Other Stories* (1983), which is a collection of the 'Joey Cassidy' and other stories; edited the poetry anthology *Dimensions* (1974) and selected and edited Old and New Testament parables, Rabbinic, Hindu, Buddhist and Islamic parables in *Speaking in Parables* (1987). Ken Goodwin collected Dawe's prose writings – essays, letters, radio broadcasts and interviews – as well as critical articles about him and his poetry in *Essays and Opinions* (1990). Goodwin also wrote *Adjacent Worlds: A Literary Life of Bruce Dawe* (1988). There are two recordings of Dawe reading from his own poetry, 1971 and 1983. Among his many awards are the Patrick White Award in 1980 and the FAW Christopher Brennan Award in 1983. He was made AO in 1992 for his contribution to Australian literature, especially poetry.

In a CLF lecture in 1964 Dawe regretted the lack of 'social awareness' in contemporary Australian poetry. His own poetry, by contrast, is one of unremitting social concern; it criticises governments, regimes, institutions and modes of life which oppress and deprive; its concern is for individuals, 'the lost people in our midst for whom no one speaks', and for modern man in general, 'homo suburbiensis', for whom happiness and meaning in life are mostly withheld. The early poems berate totalitarianism in 'Only the Beards are Different' and 'The Not-so-good Earth'; the church

(Dawe was a convert to Roman Catholicism) in 'The Decay of Preaching'; and the self-centred insularity and nationalism of Australia in '"A" is for Asia' and 'Burial Ceremony. Hungary 1956–62'. Dawe's chief criticism, however, is for the oppressive force of modern life – 'one of the main things I would say . . . about this awkward proposition known as Life, is that it can be a bit of a bastard.' Life's brevity and meaninglessness are at the heart of 'Enter Without So Much As Knocking' and 'Any Shorter and I'd Have Missed It Altogether'; its pettiness is illustrated in 'Two Ways of Considering the Fog', 'Beatitudes' and in the masterly evocation of Melbourne football mania, 'Life-Cycle' (q.v.); its unrelenting pressure is exposed in 'Slow Coach' and 'Leasehold'; and its victims are categorised in 'No Fixed Address' (alcoholics), 'Happiness Is the Art of Being Broken' (the aged), 'Good Sport' (the ugly), 'Homecoming' (q.v., the casualties of war) and 'The Family Man' (the casualty of domesticity). The totality of human bondage, and Dawe's somewhat rueful recognition that it is a situation beyond mending, are illustrated in the closing words of 'Homo Suburbiensis'. Man's offering to the insatiability of life is all that he has to give: 'time, pain, love, hate, age, war, death, laughter, fever.'

The later poems show that, over three decades, Dawe has neither mellowed nor lost any of his crusading zeal. There are many simple, affectionate poems ('Katrina's Wedding' with its demonstration of a father's love) and compassionate poems where his sympathy is still for the unhappy individual who faces crises, great or small (the Kurdish rebel about to be shot, the mother whose daughter has been abducted, neighbours facing illness and death). The keynote to his later poetry can be found in the Epigraph to *This Side of Silence*, dedicated to 'those students around the world who have fought to free their countries from oppression', recalling Woodrow Wilson's axiom, 'the history of liberty is the history of resistance'. Many poems continue to illustrate the need to fight wherever liberty is at risk, and greed, corruption and the lust for power work against the common good, e.g. the students' struggle for democracy in Tiananmen Square; the world's battle against communism, strikingly triumphant with the fall of the Berlin Wall; the 'green' movement's fight to preserve the land; the need for vigilance against such political corruption as Queensland long experienced. His love of the land makes his own conservation poems both sensitive and appealing; nowhere is that better illustrated than in 'When First the Land Was Ours', where he links humanity and nature in the one great scheme of things:

> For we are part of the shimmering web
> that binds the vast and small,
> and what is done to a single strand
> has meaning to it all

Yet the bitter aftertaste left by contemporary crudities and excesses remains predominant, as the final poem of *This Side of Silence* reveals:

As typical of these times I would include
a dirty needle and rip-top can,
pebbled glass from a windscreen, some spent cartridges,
a singlet noose fresh from a prisoner's neck,
a pamphlet proving
pornography is love, a flash of tears
from battered women (laced with children's blood) . . .

And as a final parting shot at those who indifferently preside over such sordid disasters he cites

> a press release
> from the Bureau of Statistics showing
> things are getting better all the time.

Paradoxically Dawe's poetry is mostly neither sombre nor pessimistic. Humour, usually satirical, introduces a light tone, attractively mingling the serious and the droll. His early poems are invariably brief, succinct and pertinent, 'one-shot' poems that say only as much as they need to. Sometimes they end without the ultimate confrontation, but with a poetic shrug of the shoulders that, in characteristically Australian fashion, implies a laconic acceptance of things as they are. The later poems are less philosophic, much more trenchant, more damning and less humorously tolerant. The later Dawe sees more that is disturbing and, with the passing of time, fewer possibilities of improvement to humanity's overall condition. His articulate and readily understood response to situations and themes is expressed in speech cadences that combine the brashly colloquial of the spoken Australian language (and 'slanguage') with subtle and deftly placed lyricism. His success in blending these apparent incongruities of language is his most remarkable technical achievement. But his achievement as a poet goes far beyond mere technique. As David Headon comments on *This Side of Silence*:

> Bruce Dawe has thumbed his nose at contemporary literary fashion, preferring instead to write as a kind of contemporary prophet within the long and honoured tradition of poetry of commitment ... His poetry simply and eloquently reinforces what's right in a world of confused moral distinctions and Post-Modernist torpidity.

DAWE, Carlton (1865–1935), born Adelaide, published three volumes of verse and two works of fiction including *The Golden Lake* (1891), an adventure story based on the search for a cave of gold in Australia, before settling permanently in England from 1892. He then became a prolific writer of popular fiction (romance, mystery, crime) with more than seventy books published over forty years. His experience of Australia is drawn on mainly in his earlier novels, which include *Mount Desolation* (1892), where he uses a bank robbery based on an incident from the exploits of the Kelly gang; *The History of Godfrey Kinge* (1893), a story of English disinheritance and colonial rehabilitation; *The Emu's Head* (1893), a search for treasure hidden by a bushranger; *The Pilgrims* (1894), set in a gold-mining town in Victoria; and *The Confessions of a Currency Girl* (1894), a transportation story. In his book *The Nervous Nineties* (1991), John Docker discusses *The Golden Lake* as a Lemurian novel.

Dawes, Rufus, see *His Natural Life*

Dawn, The, the first Australian journal for women, was edited by Louisa Lawson (q.v.) and ran as a monthly 1888–1905. Boycotted by male printers in its early days because of Lawson's policy of employing women where possible, the *Dawn* had a reformist and feminist outlook, and contained articles on social issues such as divorce reform and women's suffrage as well as news items, fiction and poetry. Significant contributors included Lawson herself, sometimes writing as 'Dora Falconer', and the self-titled 'female bachelor', Rose Soley. Olive Lawson, Louisa Lawson's great-granddaughter, has edited excerpts from the *Dawn* 1888–95, titled *The First Voice of Australian Feminism* (1990). Patricia Clarke's *Pen Portraits* (1988) includes an account of the founding and running of the *Dawn*.

Dawn and Dusk Club, a convivial society of artists and writers, was established in Sydney after the publication of Victor Daley's (q.v.) first book of verse, *At Dawn and Dusk* (1898), and named in honour of that work. The 'Symposiarch' or chief Dawn and Dusker was Daley himself; other notable members of the club of *bon vivants* were F.J. Broomfield (at whose house the first meeting is said to have been held), Norman Lindsay, Henry Lawson, Bertram Stevens and Randolph Bedford. The rules of the club were allegedly printed in Chinese; the only person allowed to interpret them was supposedly Jim Philp, who could not read Chinese. G.A. Taylor's *'Those Were the Days'* (1918) contains details of the club's membership.

Dawnward? (1903), Bernard O'Dowd's (q.v.) first volume of poetry, speculates on the prospects of freedom, equality and fraternity in Australia and ponders the nation's future direction – 'To Failure's midnight sea or Dawnward?' The numerous inflammatory personified poems, e.g. 'Prosperity', 'Hate', 'Compromise' and 'Proletaria', heap abuse upon such enemies of society as 'Vested Rights', 'Mammon', 'Bacchantic Trade' and 'Lamias of Caste'. *Dawnward?* satisfied the radical tenets of O'Dowd's *Poetry Militant* (q.v.) but with its baffling maze of personification and allusion and its mesmerising 'fourteener' stanza it met a puzzled and unsympathetic reception from readers and literary critics of the day.

DAWSON, A.J. (Alec John) (1872–1951), born England, came to Australia as an apprentice on a sailing ship. He deserted his ship in Melbourne and remained in Australia for several years before returning to England. Author of more than twenty fictional works and numerous works of non-fiction including war memoirs, Dawson drew only incidentally on his Australian experiences. In his book of short stories, *Mere Sentiment* (1897), four of the twelve pieces have Australian settings. *The Record of Nicholas Freydon* (1914), purporting to be the autobiography of an Englishman who was brought to Australia as a boy, captures something of the atmosphere of the bush.

DAY, A. Grove, see *Modern Australian Prose, 1901–75*

DAY, Marele, see **Crime Fiction**

DAY, Sarah (1958–), born Lancashire, England, grew up in Hobart. She has been an English teacher and a teacher of English as a foreign language, both in Sydney and at the University of Tasmania. She has published three books of poetry: *A Hunger to be Less Serious* (1987), which won the Anne Elder Award for a first volume of poetry, *A Madder Dance* (1991) in the Australian Poetry series, and *Sarah Day* (1990) in The Pamphlet Poets series of the National Library of Australia.

'DAY, William', see **DERRICOURT, William**

Daybreak, a novel by Vance Palmer (q.v.), was published in 1932. Set in a small Victorian town in the 1920s, its action is compressed into twelve hours. The central figure, a fruit farmer, Bob Rossiter, has reached a turning point in his close relationship with Harry Sievright, another farmer and his ex-commanding officer. Sievright, who is suffering from severe psychological stress induced by the war and is subject to jealous fantasies about his wife Jean and Rick Lennard, the district doctor, wants Rossiter to abandon his farm and join him in a search for gold. Meanwhile Rossiter's wife Mary is in hospital expecting the baby they have long hoped for. In addition, there has been a lock-out at the local sawmill and Lysaght, a labour agitator, is anxious for Rossiter to persuade the local orchard workers to support the mill hands in their claims. Although the novel centres on Rossiter's self-liberation from a tangle of conflicting loyalties, it includes a wide range of distinctive, dramatically conceived personalities and is a convincing socio-political study of small-town life. The action culminates in the death of Sievright in an apparent shooting accident, the birth of Rossiter's son, the ending of the lock-out and the completion of Rossiter's moral growth to full self-acceptance.

Dead Bird: A Journal Devoted to Sport and the Drama, a sensational weekly journal containing short fiction and verse together with sporting and theatrical news, ran 1889–91. It continued under the title *Bird o' Freedom* 1891–96, then as *Arrow: Sport and Play* 1896–1912 and as *Saturday Referee and Arrow* 1912–16; it was then incorporated into the *Referee* (q.v.).

'Dead Heart' was a phrase coined by J.W. Gregory in his book *The Dead Heart of Australia* (1906), to describe the desolate region between Lake Eyre and the Simpson Desert. The term was retained by C.T. Madigan in *Crossing the Dead Heart* (1946), his account of the first scientific expedition across the Simpson Desert in 1939. Madigan's earlier book, *Central Australia* (1936), gives an account of expeditions in the area in the 1930s. The phrase is still in general use to describe the most arid areas of the centre of the continent.

Dead Men Rising, a novel by Kenneth Mackenzie (q.v.), was first published in London in 1951 under his pseudonym, 'Seaforth Mackenzie'. Based on an outbreak of Japanese prisoners of war from a camp at Cowra, NSW, in 1944, which Mackenzie witnessed, the novel was not published in Australia until 1969, and copies of the London publication were withheld from circulation in Australia. Rather than attempting to probe the psychology of the Japanese, the novel concentrates on the general boredom of garrison life and the individual experiences of some of those who are involuntarily involved, from the camp commandant to the half-Japanese interpreter Orloff. The love story of Corporal Sargent and his girl Cathie, which comes to a tragic end when Sargent is killed in the outbreak, takes up a large proportion of the story.

Dead Timber, a play by Louis Esson (q.v.) which was first produced in 1911 and published in the same year, gives a grim but starkly impressive picture of Australian rural life. The action takes place on a Gippsland selection and deals with a family plagued by a range of farming disasters and personal bitternesses, culminating in the suicide of the father.

DEAKIN, Alfred (1856–1919), one of the important figures in Australian political history, was born and educated in Melbourne, where he was admitted to the Bar in 1877. After experience as a teacher and as a journalist for the *Age*, as well as in the law, he entered politics in 1879. A member of the Victorian parliament for over twenty years, he was a minister in 1883–86 and joint leader of the coalition government in 1886–90. Active in the Federation (q.v.) movement during the 1890s, he moved to the federal (national) parliament in 1901 and was Australian prime minister 1903–4, 1905–8 and 1909–10. Throughout his term in the federal parliament (1901–13) he wrote a regular letter on Australian subjects, which was published anonymously in the London *Morning Post*; a selection of the million or so words he sent to the *Morning Post* was published in 1968 as *Federated Australia*, ed. J.A. La Nauze.

Deakin had wide literary interests and wrote prolifically on English poetry and drama in the 1870s. He subsequently destroyed many of his early manuscripts, which included verse dramas, dramatic narratives and studies of Shakespeare and Wordsworth, although he had occasional poems published; his verse drama *Quentin Massys* (q.v., 1875) is credited as the first volume of verse by a native Victorian, and *A New Pilgrim's Progress* (1877) is an allegory written in forty-nine sittings at a time when Deakin believed himself to be a medium. In the 1880s and 1890s Deakin wrote several reports on irrigation which were published separately; later narratives of his early involvement in Victorian politics and in the Federation movement were published after his death as *The Crisis in Victorian Politics, 1879–1881* (1957, ed. J.A. La Nauze and R.M. Crawford), and *The Federal Story* (1944, ed. H. Brookes; 1963, ed. J.A. La Nauze). Even more important for Australian literature was his understanding of and sympathy for the problems of Australian writers.

During his career in Victorian politics he was active on behalf of writers and their families in need (e.g. he helped to provide for Marcus Clarke's widow), and as prime minister he responded to the call of Henry Bournes Higgins and was instrumental in the foundation of the CLF in 1906–8. A long-standing friend of later years was the essayist Walter Murdoch; letters between the two, many of them on literary topics, were published in 1974 as *Walter Murdoch and Alfred Deakin on Books and Men*, ed. J.A. La Nauze and Elizabeth Nurser. Murdoch's *Alfred Deakin* (1923) was the standard account of Deakin before the appearance of La Nauze's comprehensive biography *Alfred Deakin* (1965). A biography which relates Deakin's intense religious beliefs to his public life is A.C. Gabay's *The Mystic Life of Alfred Deakin* (1992). He is also partly the subject of Stuart Macintyre's study *A Colonial Liberalism: The Lost World of Three Victorian Visionaries* (1991), and the subject of Kylie Tennant's radio play *Tether a Dragon* (performed and published 1952).

DEAMER, Dulcie (1890–1972), born Christchurch, NZ, actor, freelance journalist, dramatist and writer of fiction, was a well-known figure in Sydney bohemian and literary society in the 1920s and 1930s. She published a book of short stories, *In the Beginning: Six Studies of the Stone Age and Other Stories* (1909), the title story of which won a *Lone Hand* short fiction competition in 1907. Her novels include *The Suttee of Safa: A Hindoo Romance* (1913), *Revelation* (1921, set in Jerusalem during the life of Jesus), *The Street of the Gazelle* (1922), *The Devil's Saint* (1924), and *Holiday* (1940), which deals with the persecution of the early Christians. Her two volumes of poetry are *Messalina* (1932), the first section, 'Nine Women', comprising portraits of classical or historically significant women; and *The Silver Branch* (1948), elaborately phrased verses. Deamer also wrote plays performed in Sydney, including 'That by Which Men Live' (1936), 'Victory' (1938), *The Heart of a Woman*, *In the Mind of a Child* and *In the Soul of a Man* (the last three all published in the 1930s). She is represented in *Best Australian One-Act Plays* (1937) by *Easter*, a morality play dealing with death. Deamer's unpublished autobiography, 'The Golden Decade', is informative on the literary circles of Sydney in the 1920s and 1930s and she is a major figure in Peter Kirkpatrick's *The Sea Coast of Bohemia* (1992).

DEAN, Geoffrey (1930–), born Hobart, has had numerous occupations – sailor, salesman, carpenter, farmer, house-painter and editor – but is now retired. Most of his occupations were transient, allowing him to pursue his chief interest of writing. He has published fiction: *Strangers' Country and Other Stories* (1977), *Cold Dead Monday and Other Australian Stories* (1985), *Summerbird and Other Stories* (1989) and is one of the contributors to *Personal Best 2* (1991). For TV he wrote *The Town that Died* (1988). His short stories have won him the FAW State of Tasmania Short Story Awards, 1964–65; the FAW State of Victoria Short Story Award, 1981; the Victorian Premier's Literary Award, 1985 and the Northern Territory Literary Award 1985. 'Strangers' Country', the title story of his first book, is the familiar tale of a woman starved of love by her insensitive husband, turning to the romantic stranger, the 'Iti' worker doing some fencing on the farm and bringing with him the aura of romantic, far-off places ('la bell' Italia!'). 'Handout', set in Edmonton, Canada, is the story of scrounging meals and beds and the odd day's work in difficult recession times. Other Dean stories concern young love, a mother's attempt to instil different values into her children from those held by her husband, the wanton killing of an eagle finally compensated for by the saving of another, a father looking for his missing daughter, and an old sea captain tossed ashore like a piece of flotsam.

DE BOISSIÈRE, Ralph (1907–), born Trinidad in the West Indies, emigrated to Australia in 1948 after experiencing persecution in Trinidad for his political activities. He has since worked in various capacities, e.g. salesman, car assembler and clerk, while writing novels and plays. *Crown Jewel* (1952), the first book published by the Australasian Book Society is de Boissière's story of the Trinidadians' struggle to establish social justice and culminates in the island's riots of 1937. Its sequel, *Rum and Coca-Cola* (1956), set during the American presence in the island in the Second World War, enlarges on the urban proletariat's struggle for their rights in that period. *No Saddles for Kangaroos* (1964) is set in a Melbourne car-manufacturing firm and continues the theme that trade union action is the remedy for social and economic injustice.

DE BOOS, Charles (1819–1900), born London, came to Australia in 1839 after fighting in Spain during one of the Carlist wars and tried farming in the Hunter district of NSW before turning to journalism. He worked on the *Monitor* and the *Sydney Gazette* before joining the *Argus* to write about the Victorian goldfields. By 1856 he was the *Sydney Morning Herald*'s correspondent on the NSW goldfields and later its parliamentary reporter; his weekly column 'The Collective Wisdom of New South Wales' (1867–73) is a lively and informative account of political affairs in the days before Hansard. In 1862 he created for the *Sydney Morning Herald* the character 'John Smith' whose satirical 'letters' became *The Congewoi Correspondence* (q.v., 1874). In 1870 de Boos's evidence to the royal commission on the goldfields led to his appointment as mining warden and police magistrate (posts in which he was considerably criticised) on the NSW diggings. His chief literary work was the novel *Fifty Years Ago: An Australian Tale* (q.v., 1867). Although somewhat overlooked by critics, *Fifty Years Ago* successfully brings together several strands of early Australian life – convicts, settlers, bushrangers and Aborigines. De Boos's other novels include *Mark Brown's Wife*, published in the *Sydney Mail* in 1871, which gives a violent picture of life on the goldfields and was published as a monograph, edited by Victor Crittenden in 1992, and *The Stockman's Daughter*, serialised anonymously in the *People's Advocate* (1856).

Set in the region of Bungendore and Lake George in the pre-gold-rush era, *The Stockman's Daughter* is a bushranging story which anticipates many of the later themes and stock situations and characters in colonial fiction.

DE BRUNE, Aidan (1879–?1944), born Montreal, Canada, was a journalist in London but wandered the world before coming to Australia. His many popular novels of mystery and adventure include *The Carson Loan Mystery* (1926), *The Dagger and Cord* (1927) and *The Shadow Crook* (1930). Involved in the establishment of the FAW in Sydney in 1928, de Brune also wrote *Fifty Years of Progress in Australia 1878–1928* (1929).

DE GARIS, C.J. (Clement John) (1884–1926), born North Melbourne, was one of Australia's most flamboyant entrepreneurs. He was associated with the dried-fruit industry at Mildura, land ventures in WA, oil exploration, the theatre, the publishing industry and land subdivisions in outer Melbourne. He made and lost several fortunes, faked one suicide but carried out the real thing when he gassed himself in his home in 1926. The proprietor and founder of the provincial newspaper the *Sunraysia Daily*, for which he often wrote articles and stories, De Garis was also the author of a war drama, *Ambition Run Mad* (1914), an autobiographical novel, *The Victories of Failure* (1925), and a musical comedy, 'F.F.F.', staged in Perth and Melbourne. In 1920 he founded the C.J. De Garis publishing house which ran a literary competition 1920–21 and published eight books before its demise in 1922. *Rigby's Romance*, submitted in the 1921 competition by Kate Baker as part of her plan to resurrect the writings of Joseph Furphy, was published by De Garis in an abridged edition in 1921.

DE GROEN, Alma (1941–   ), born NZ, came to live in Australia in 1964, spent some years in Europe and Canada, and returned here in 1973. Her plays include *The Joss Adams Show* (first produced in 1970, published 1977), 'The Sweatproof Boy' (1972), which was later shortened and titled *Perfectly All Right* (1977), 'The After-Life of Arthur Cravan' (1973), *Going Home* (produced 1976, published 1977), *Chidley* (published in *Theatre-Australia*, 1977), *Vocations* (produced 1982, published 1983), *The Rivers of China* (produced 1987, published 1988), and *The Girl Who Saw Everything* (1993). She has also written for television, film and radio and was awarded an Awgie in 1985 for her television adaptation of Glen Tomasetti's novel *Man of Letters*. *The Rivers of China* won both the NSW and Victorian Premiers' Awards for best play. De Groen has dealt with a range of subjects, from marital relationships (*Going Home*) to the battered-baby syndrome (*The Joss Adams Show*) to the social challenges posed by eccentric individuals such as William James Chidley, a propagandist on the subjects of food, dress and sex, and Arthur Cravan, nephew of Oscar Wilde. All her plays are concerned with women or artists and attempt to draw the audience into the dramatic situation by challenging assumptions based on gender

difference. She strives for a blending of form and content that has the same integration as a painting and which she terms 'theatrical quietism'. In her earliest plays, such as *The Joss Adams Show* and 'The After-Life of Arthur Cravan', she attempted to express meaning by unconventional, visual and structural means as much as by dialogue. *Perfectly All Right*, whose central character is a woman confined to home and housework, and *Going Home*, a study of the problems of a group of alienated Australians living in Canada, appeared to be located in the tradition of naturalism, but De Groen's later plays suggest that her intentions have always been to transcend and transform the 'real'. *Vocations*, which depends on a divided set, explores the relationships between two couples as a means to challenging patriarchal structuring of male/female possibilities. *The Rivers of China* interweaves two distinctive narratives, one covering the last months of Katherine Mansfield's life from early 1922 to her death in January 1923 and the other, set in the 1980s, presenting a feminist dystopia, where women have replaced men as patriarchs. Mansfield's experiences in the last three months of her life when she was treated by Georgei Gurdjieff are a metaphor for women's general experience of being in the world without a history.

DE HAAS, Rudolf (1870–?), born Germany, was a Lutheran pastor who spent three years in Australia at Charters Towers. He wrote three novels in German based on his Australian experience, *Among Australian Gold Diggers* (1922), a semi-autobiographical account of everyday life in his parish, *Mirage* (1924), the story of a German immigrant and his double adjustment, to Australia and to a new sense of self, and *The Revenge of the Australian* (1928), a tale of adventure in the style of Fenimore Cooper.

'Dedication, A' is the opening poem of Adam Lindsay Gordon's (q.v.) final volume *Bush Ballads and Galloping Rhymes* (1870). The dedication was to English novelist G.J. Whyte-Melville, whose popular adventure novels appealed to Gordon. The chief interest in Gordon's lines is his reluctant admission that Australia, to which he had been exiled, had helped to inspire his verse. Despite his well-known but inaccurate claim that Australia is a land 'where bright blossoms are scentless/ And songless bright birds', Gordon makes, in the lines beginning 'In the Spring, when the wattle gold trembles', one of his rare acknowledgements of the land's natural beauty.

DEEBLE, R.J. (Russell John) (1944–   ), born Melbourne, has published several books of verse including *War Babies and Other Poems* (1965), *A Trip to Light Blue* (1968), *High on a Horse with Wax Wings* (1969), *You* (1970), *Just Before Eyelight* (1979), *A Poem That Wants to Be Painted* (1979) and *Aqualine and Other Poems* (1980).

DELMER, Frederick Sefton (1864–1931), born Hobart, studied at Melbourne University but failed to graduate although he won numerous medals and prizes. In Melbourne he formed lasting friendships with Arthur Streeton, and G.W.L. Marshall-Hall (qq.v.), before leaving for Europe 1894–96 where he studied art and literature and became friendly with Herman Grimm, the eldest son of Wilhelm Grimm. Back in Melbourne in 1896 Delmer made his living as a teacher, an occupation he detested, meanwhile contributing travel stories and reviews to the *Bulletin* and *Alma Mater*. A brief period teaching in Sydney, where he made the acquaintance of Chris Brennan, was followed by further travel in Europe, and appointments as lecturer first at the University of Königsberg and then at Berlin University. In Europe he occasionally made contact with Tom Roberts (q.v.) and his family. He was interned during the First World War, but was released in 1915 and from 1917 to 1919 acted as the *Daily Mail*'s correspondent in Switzerland. Delmer's remaining years were spent as a journalist, translator and interpreter in Germany and Italy, where he made the acquaintance of Ezra Pound. As well as numerous reviews and articles, Delmer published a popular history of English literature (1910) and a translation of Gustav Frenssen's novel *Jörn Uhl* (1905). John Fletcher published an account of Delmer's life and a bibliography in 1991.

'DE LOGHE, Sydney', see **LOCK, Frederick Sydney**

DENIEHY, D.H. (Daniel Henry) (1828–65), was born in Sydney of emancipist Irish parents. His intellectual potential was recognised in childhood by his parents and teachers and he was well educated by colonial standards. In adolescence he visited England and the Continent with his parents to further his education and after his return to Australia in 1844 was articled to solicitor and literary patron N.D. Stenhouse, being admitted as a solicitor in 1851. His growing literary and political interests at this time are indicated by the lectures he gave on literary subjects in 1851–53 at the Sydney Mechanics' School of Arts and by his radical speeches at public meetings on the political controversies of the day. One of his memorable satirical speeches was his ridicule in 1853 of W.C. Wentworth's suggestion of a colonial peerage, dubbed by Deniehy a 'bunyip aristocracy'. As a member of parliament in 1857–60 he made effective parliamentary speeches on land and immigration matters and on electoral reform. Disillusioned by politics and lacking a clear purpose in life, he began drinking heavily. In 1862 he went to Melbourne, where he edited the *Victorian*, but returned to Sydney to resume his legal practice after the paper closed in 1864. He died from head injuries following a fall in Bathurst 22 October 1865. His death was widely mourned, the more so because it was felt that his enormous promise had not been adequately fulfilled. Deniehy's creative writing was meagre. He published a short story, 'Love at First Sight', in the *Colonial Literary Journal* in 1844 and some youthful verses in *Heads of the People*. He later contributed verse to the *Empire* and the *Freeman's Journal*. The best evidence of his wit and intellect lies in his wide-ranging speeches, lectures, critical articles and essays. A selection of these is included in Elvera A. Martin's *The Life and Speeches of Daniel Henry Deniehy* (1884). The only widely known Deniehy creation is the prose satire *How I Became Attorney-General of New Barataria* (1860), written to ridicule the appointment of L.H. Bailey as attorney-general in the second Cowper ministry of 1859, and first published that year in the *Southern Cross*, which Deniehy had established. Although rather dated by modern standards, the *New Barataria* piece is a good example of the literary satire popular in the Colony in the mid-nineteenth century. It is reproduced in the anthology *The Unsparing Scourge: Australian Satirical Texts 1845–1860* (1988), edited by Vincent O'Sullivan. Because of the sparse nature of his published literary works any modern judgement of Deniehy must take account of the golden opinions he won from such contemporaries as Stenhouse, Dalley, Charles Harpur, G.B. Barton and R.H. Horne. A biography of Deniehy by Cyril Pearl, *Brilliant Dan Deniehy: A Forgotten Genius*, was published in 1972, and *Daniel Deniehy: A Portrait with Background*, by Gerald Walsh, in 1988.

DENISON, Sir Hugh (1865–1940), born Forbes, NSW, was a cousin of the collector of Australiana Sir William Dixson. He was born Hugh Robert Dixson but changed his surname in 1907 to avoid confusion with his uncle, Sir Hugh Dixson, with whom he established a tobacco business partnership in 1902. In 1910 he formed Sun Newspapers Ltd, which later took over publication of the *Sunday Sun* and the *Sun*, formerly the *Australian Star*. In 1927 Denison acquired the *Daily Telegraph Pictorial*, formerly the *Daily Telegraph*, and when in 1929 he combined with the Samuel Bennett (q.v.) group to form Associated Newspapers and also bought the *Daily Guardian* and *Sunday Guardian*, he controlled eight Sydney newspapers. A programme of rationalisation over the next two years saw the eight become three, one morning daily, one afternoon daily and one Sunday newspaper: the *Sunday News*, *Sunday Guardian* and *Sunday Pictorial* were incorporated into the *Sunday Sun*, the *Daily Guardian* and the *Daily Pictorial* were amalgamated into a revamped *Daily Telegraph*, and the *Evening News* (q.v.) ceased publication to avoid competition with the *Sun*. Denison's managing director of the *Daily Telegraph* in 1931–33 was R.C. Packer, whose son, Frank Packer, gained control of the newspaper in 1936. One of the significant figures in Australian newspaper proprietorship between the wars, Denison was also interested in developments in radio and was the founder in 1938 of Macquarie Broadcasting Services.

DENNIS, C.J. (Clarence Michael James) (1876–1938), born Auburn, SA, spent much of his boyhood in the care of four maiden aunts. He worked briefly as a solicitor's clerk, was a journalist on the Adelaide weekly the *Critic* (q.v.), filled in as barman at his father's hotel in Laura and then drifted off to become an odd-jobman about the mines of Broken Hill. Returning to Adelaide, he later became editor of the *Critic* and in 1906 commenced the short-lived satirical journal the *Gadfly* (q.v.). In 1908 after a miserable period in Melbourne as a freelance journalist, he went with the artist Hal Waugh to Toolangi, an isolated timber settlement not far from Healesville north-east of Melbourne. At Toolangi, living in a tent and later in a timber-getter's hut, he worked hard at his writing, mainly, in his own words, 'to fend off the blues'. In 1913 he published through Cole's Book Arcade of Melbourne his first book of verse, *Backblock Ballads and Other Verses*, with a cover designed by the cartoonist David Low. The book was not successful so Dennis went off on a spree to Sydney, working there on the union journal the *Labour Call*, but was back in Melbourne early in 1915. From four verse stories of 'The Sentimental Bloke' in the *Backblock Ballads* he conceived the idea of a separate series, and late in 1915 *The Songs of a Sentimental Bloke* (q.v.) was published with an explanatory glossary 'for the thoroughly genteel'. Dennis's story of the young larrikin, Bill, who is enticed from his life with the 'push' to domestic bliss on a berry farm with his 'ideal bit o' skirt', Doreen, rapidly became popular, bringing fame and affluence to its creator. It sold more than 60 000 copies in Australia in less than eighteen months. A sequel dealing with the adventures of Ginger Mick, the Bloke's friend and 'best man', titled *The Moods of Ginger Mick*, was published in October 1916. In an inspired move Dennis had Ginger Mick answer the 'Call of the Stoush' and go off to 'the flamin' war' as so many young Australians had done. The book, and Mick, went straight to the hearts of the Australian soldiers serving overseas and the pocket editions of both *The Sentimental Bloke* and *Ginger Mick* were treasured possessions of many homesick diggers. In 1917, the year that Dennis married Olive Herron, he published the very different work *The Glugs of Gosh*, a satire on such pretentious community figures as lord mayors, councillors and petty government officials.

Dennis tried to repeat the Bloke and Ginger Mick formula with *Doreen* (1917), which looked at the lovers of *The Sentimental Bloke* in their married roles; and with *Digger Smith* (1918), the adventures of one of Mick's mates on Gallipoli who returned to Australia, not to the slums of Collingwood where he had been born but to the freshness and beauty of the Australian bush. But the public's love affair with the racy, vernacular verse was over. An attempt in 1924 to revive the passion with *Rose of Spadgers*, the saga of Ginger Mick's girl-friend of bygone days, also failed. Dennis's other works include the 'Australaise' (q.v.), a marching song (1908); the verse narrative *Jim of the Hills* (1919), a timber-getter's story told with only a smattering of exaggerated colloquialisms; a revised and enlarged *Backblock Ballads and Later Verses* (1918); *A Book for Kids* (1921), a whimsical mixture of verse and prose; and *The Singing Garden (1935)*, prose and verse which reflect Dennis's long-sustained devotion to the landscape around Arden, his home at Toolangi. From 1922 until his death he held the highly unusual position of staff poet with the Melbourne *Herald*. His many contributions of prose and verse to the *Herald* include 'Epistles to Ab', a series of letters from a farmer to his son in the city; the 'Ben Bowyang' series; and the 'Miss Mix' series, snippets from the gossipy but deadly accurate pen of a country town seamstress.

After Dennis's death enthusiastic eulogies saluted him as Australia's national poet, one who had captured much of the essential Australian spirit. Prime Minister Joseph Lyons referred to him as the 'Robbie Burns of Australia'. Much of that adulation evaporated as the years passed and Dennis's ingenious verse came to be looked on as a literary curiosity, an idiosyncratic expression of the intense nationalism that gripped Australia from the 1890s until after the First World War. Some Australians found the Bloke and Ginger Mick nationally embarrassing and thus ignored them, while even well-disposed readers were puzzled by the extraordinary and exaggerated idiom and were doubtful about the authenticity of the central characters, larrikins with hearts of gold. The well-publicised Dennis centenary (1976), which was accompanied by a successful musical version of *The Sentimental Bloke* for television, and the later stage performances of John Derum, *More Than a Sentimental Bloke* (published in book form in 1990), have sparked a revival of interest in his work. Its ability to convey the quality of 'wit' in down-to-earth Australian humour makes it an integral part of this country's folk-literature. But there is more to it than that. Beneath its seemingly trite and banal surface there is, at times, a pathos, an appreciation of the foibles of human nature and a sophistication of thought that explores some of the complex issues of life. Henry Lawson, well qualified to judge talent and achievement in this area of literature, paid Dennis a significant tribute in the foreword to the first edition of *The Songs of a Sentimental Bloke*, when he echoed the Bloke's own words – 'I dips me lid.' Dennis was commemorated by the C.J. Dennis Award, an annual award (from 1976) provided by the Victorian government and administered by the Victorian branch of the FAW for a book about Australian natural history. Recently the C.J. Dennis Award has been for poetry and is one of the Victorian Premier's annual literary awards. A.H. Chisholm published the biography *The Making of a Sentimental Bloke* (1946); 'Margaret Herron' (Dennis's wife Olive), *Down the Years* (1953); I.F. MacLaren, *C.J. Dennis* (1961); and G.W. Hutton, *C.J. Dennis, the Sentimental Bloke* (1976). Barry Watts edited *The World of the Sentimental Bloke* (1976), which contains A.H. Chisholm's 'The Remarkable Career of C.J. Dennis' and articles by such associates of Dennis as David Low and R.H. Croll, together with excerpts from *The Sentimental Bloke* and *The Moods of Ginger Mick*. The first film of *The Sentimental Bloke* was the Raymond Longford 1919 production. A special screening of that film was given at the Cannes International Film Festival in 1987. Dennis wrote the screen play for F.W. Thring's 1932 film of *The Sentimental Bloke*.

DENTON, Kit (1928–   ), born in England, grew up in the East End of London. After serving with the British Army and as a broadcaster with the British Forces Network in Germany, he migrated to Australia, where he tried gold-mining at Kalgoorlie and numerous other occupations. He was an announcer with the ABC 1951–65, and has worked extensively as a freelance writer and producer/director of commercial films and documentaries for television and radio.

He has published a collection of short stories, *Burning Spear* (1990), and four novels, *The Breaker* (1973), *The Thinkable Man* (1976), *Fiddlers Bridge* (1986) and *Red on White* (1991). *The Breaker*, based on the life of Harry Harbord Morant (q.v.), was the basis of Bruce Beresford's popular film about Morant (1980), and both film and book romanticise his life and death. Denton subsequently wrote a more negative, factual account of Morant's case, culled from official records and newspaper reports, *Closed File* (1983). Denton's other publications include a collection of sketches and reminiscences, *A Walk Around My Cluttered Mind* (1968), an illustrated account of the Gallipoli campaign, *Gallipoli Illustrated* (1981), and two Time-Life books on the Boer and First World Wars, *For Queen and Commonwealth* (1987) and *Gallipoli: One Long Grave* (1986). His son, Andrew Denton, is a well-known TV personality.

Department, The, a play by David Williamson (q.v.), was first performed in 1974 and published in 1975. Set in the engineering department of a college of advanced education, the play consists of a staff meeting called by the head of the department, Robby, a consummate power-broker. The characters, instantly recognisable as types of any institution, include Hans, the departmental clown; Peter, its kept radical; the vindictive, prickly Al; Myra, the intruder from humanities; the irrelevant, apologetic Bobby, who can only teach one outdated course; and the independent, indispensable mechanic, Gordon. Overhanging the familiar frictions, power struggles and rituals is a scandal about a costly water tank, erected by mistake on the mezzanine floor, that no one dares fill. As the academics wrangle, Gordon fills the tank without disaster and the play ends as Robby reassesses his tactical position.

DEPASQUALE, Paul (1938–), born Lockleys, Adelaide, of Italian parents, was a teacher 1959–70 and since 1974 has been a bookseller and publisher. He has published short stories, *In the Land of the Devil's Promise* (1962) and *Angelo* (1979); and verse, *The Will to Dream* (1968, with Janeen Samuel), *A Lonely, Venturesome Outgoing* (1969), *The Mad Priest Meditates* (1982), *The Dying Dago's Dance of Death* (1982), *The Mad Priest Foams with Rage* (1983), *The Dying Dago Dances Again* (1984) and *Love Songs for Vernon Knowles* (1985). His historical/critical publications include *The Writing of Plays in South Australia to 1950* (1977), *A Critical History of South Australian Literature 1836–1930* (1978), *The Life and Work of Vernon Knowles* (1979), *Guy Boothby: His Life and Work* (1982), *The Life and Work of Tarella Quin* (with Judith Crabb, 1981), *Sherlock Holmes and Doctor Nikola* (1982), *Courage Corporate: Adelaide Songs of World War One* (1983), and *Guy Boothby: the Science Fiction Connection* (1985); and the critical pamphlets *Patrick Eiffe* (1980) and *Flexmore Hudson* (1981). Depasquale has also edited *Labor's Bard: the Broken Hill Poems of Tom Black* (1985) and *Selected Poems of Paul McGuire* (1980).

DERHAM, Enid (1882–1941), born Hawthorn, Melbourne, was educated at the universities of Melbourne and Oxford and held lecturing appointments in the department of English at Melbourne. A lyric poet, she published *The Mountain Road and Other Verses* (1912); a posthumous selection, *Poems* (1958), reveals her to be a poet of hitherto unsuspected emotional intensity.

DERRICOURT, William (1819–?), born Kings Norton, England, was a convict whose reminiscences, 'Old Convict Times to Gold-Digging Days', were serialised under the pseudonym 'William Day' in the Sydney newspaper the *Evening News* in 1891. Prepared for publication by 'Louis' Becke, the reminiscences were then published in book form as *Old Convict Days* (1899). *Old Convict Days* vividly chronicles Derricourt's experiences as a convict at Port Arthur and elsewhere, as well as his life following the completion of his sentence: bushworker, gold-digger, bushranger, prisoner again and finally selector near Bathurst, where he was still living when 'Old Convict Times to Gold-Digging Days' completed its run in the *Evening News*.

Descant, see **Drylight**

Desiderata, subtitled A *Guide to Good Books*, was a SA magazine of book reviews published by the bookselling firm of F.W. Preece; it ran for a decade, 1929–39. Almost entirely confined to critical reviews and articles by named contributors, *Desiderata* was a useful guide to then current Australian and world literature. Contributors included Randolph Bedford, Norman and Lionel Lindsay, 'M. Barnard Eldershaw', Mary Gilmore, Hugh McCrae, Rex Ingamells, Kylie Tennant and 'Seaforth Mackenzie'.

Design: An Australian Review of Critical Thought, edited by Patrick I. O'Leary (q.v.) and published in Melbourne, appeared for three issues in 1940. Writers who contributed to the journal included James Devaney, P.R. Stephensen, Martin Haley, Rex Ingamells, Mary Finnin and Max Harris.

DESMOND, Arthur (?1859–?1926), born NZ, came to Sydney in 1892 after being an active radical in NZ. In Sydney he became a leading figure in socialist and radical circles, publishing the magazine *Hard Cash* in 1893–94, which attacked capitalism. In 1893–94 he also published the vitriolic journal *Standard Bearer* and contributed poetry in 1894 to the socialist magazine *New Order*. He left Australia for the USA in 1895 and later published, as 'Ragnar Redbeard', *Survival of the Fittest* (1896). Desmond is purported to have been a strong influence on the radicalism of Henry Lawson.

DESSAIX, Robert (1944–) was adopted as a baby and grew up on Sydney's lower north shore. He lectured in Russian literature and language at the University of NSW and the ANU for nearly twenty years before leaving for Sydney, where he worked in the theatre and at the ABC. In 1989 he moved to Melbourne. Well known for his literary journalism, and since 1985 as producer and presenter of the weekly

ABC Radio programme 'Books and Writing', he is the editor of the Oxford anthology *Australian Gay and Lesbian Writing* (1993) and, with Helen Daniel, of *Picador New Writing* (1993). In 1994 he published a remarkable autobiography, *A Mother's Disgrace*, which describes his subsequent tracing of his natural mother, his discovery of an alternative sexuality after twelve years of marriage, and his personal philosophy.

DEZSERY, Andras (1920–), born Budapest, Hungary, arrived in Australia in 1949. After obtaining a doctorate in public administration and political science from Pazmany Peter University, he worked as a journalist, as press secretary and later editor-in-chief of a news centre which published in three languages, and of the newspaper *Lanyok Utja*. He was a war correspondent in the Second World War and in Australia worked in a rubber factory and then as a cleaning contractor. In 1975 he established Dezsery Ethnic Publications, later Dezsery Publications, which published migrant writing in various languages and bilingual editions. Active in ethnic and community affairs he was awarded the OAM in 1986. He has published a novel, *The Amphibian*, in Hungarian in 1980, translated into English in 1981, and three collections of short stories, one of which, *Neighbours* (1980), has been translated into English. He has also contributed short stories to numerous anthologies both in Australia and in Hungary and is the editor of the anthology *English and Other Than English* (1979) and the periodical *Vitezek Lapja*.

DEVANEY, James (1890–1976), born Bendigo, Victoria, was educated in Sydney, at St Joseph's College, where he entered the Marist Brothers juniorate in 1904. He took his final vows in 1915. He was a teacher in several Australian States and NZ and a tutor on outback stations before severe tuberculosis led to his departure from the order in 1921 and sent him permanently to Queensland to full-time writing and journalism. From 1924 to 1943 he published a weekly column of nature notes for the Brisbane *Courier-Mail* under the pseudonym 'Fabian'. For years a leading literary figure in Queensland, he was president of the Queensland Authors' and Artists' Association (later the FAW) and gave CLF lectures on Australian literature in 1947.

Devaney's unpretentious, traditional lyric poetry, well regarded by contemporary critics, began with the volume *Fabian* (1923), written during a period of ill health and religious doubts. The chief poem, 'The Lost Love', reflects his mood of the time, personal disquiet and a loss of delight in the natural world. *Earth Kindred* (1931) reveals the delight regained, the disquiet gone. *Dark Road* (1938), a privately printed edition of twenty-five copies which is now extremely rare, consists of six deeply personal poems written in tribute to his wife, his nurse during his tubercular illness in Diamantina hospital. From his later volumes, *Debutantes* (1939), *Where the Wind Goes* (1939) and *Freight of Dreams* (1946), Devaney selected the bulk of the verses chosen for his *Poems* (1950), a volume of wistful, pensive, melodious lyrics. Devaney also wrote

fiction, *The Currency Lass* (1927), *The Vanished Tribes* (1929), a collection of short stories focusing on Aboriginal myths and tribal adventures, and *Washdirt* (1946), a novel of the Bendigo goldfields. He wrote a play, *The New Law* (1955), his version of the Gospel story. His critical credo, *Poetry in Our Time* (1952), with its emphasis on the maintenance of recognisable form and rhythm and the need for beauty and lucidity, was seen by some as reactionary, but it embodied all that Devaney stood for. A friend and mentor of John Shaw Neilson (q.v.) in his final years, Devaney wrote the biographical *Shaw Neilson* (1944) and edited *Unpublished Poems of Shaw Neilson* (1947).

DEVANNY, Jean (1894–1962), born Jean Crook at Ferntown in the South Island of NZ, married miner and radical Hal Devanny when she was 17. She and her husband were active in the NZ labour movement before coming to Australia in 1929 and joining the Communist Party of Australia. She was expelled from the organisation during 1940–44 for reasons unspecified, but later hinted at (though never substantiated) as including sexual impropriety. Her expulsion was probably connected with her feminist attitudes, forthright personality, and suspicions about her writing activities. She was prominent in the party as agitator and orator until she left it in 1950. She spent most of her Australian life in north Queensland, where she played a leading role in Popular Front activities and helped to form the Writers' League (later the Writers' Association) and the Queensland branch of the FAW. Ill health and an increasing desire to develop her craft as a writer led her, in her last years, away from political activities into journalism and writing on Queensland local and natural history.

Before leaving NZ she published four novels, *The Butcher Shop* (q.v., 1926), *Lenore Divine* (1926), *Dawn Beloved* (1928) and *Riven* (1929); and a book of short fiction, *Old Savage and Other Stories* (1927). *The Butcher Shop* (published in Germany as *Die Herrin*) was banned in NZ, Australia, Boston and Nazi Germany, on the grounds of its feminist and socialist attitudes, emphasis on sexuality and depiction of brutality in rural NZ life. Sensational, undisciplined and highly coloured, *The Butcher Shop* is nevertheless a remarkable novel for its time, especially as a feminist examination of the role of women in the family situation. Three other novels with NZ settings are *Bushman Burke* (1930), *Devil Made Saint* (1930) and *Poor Swine* (1932). After her arrival in Australia, Devanny wrote a further fourteen novels, four of which remain unpublished, and several works of non-fiction: *By Tropic Sea and Jungle* (1944), *Bird of Paradise* (1945) and *Travels in North Queensland* (1951). Her first novel set in Australia is *Out of Such Fires* (1934), based on her experiences as a domestic on a sheep station in western NSW. *Sugar Heaven* (1936), which was translated into Russian, deals with the 1935 strike on the Queensland canefields. Dulcie, the novel's heroine, begins as a naive, passive girl but develops into an ardent political activist. The novel contains some interesting details of the 1935 strike, in particular the part that Weil's Disease, a plague spread by rats, played in the discontent of the cane-cutting communities. Something of a literary curio, the novel is now ranked as one of the earliest and most significant of the socialist-realist Australian novels. Devanny's other literary projects include an uncompleted trilogy about the sugar industry, of which only the first volume, *Cindie* (1949), was published. *Cindie* opens in the 1890s on the Queensland canefields and deals largely with the changes that occur as Kanaka labour is repatriated. Among her other novels are *All for Love* (1932), *The Virtuous Courtesan* (1935), *The Ghost Wife* (1935), *Paradise Flow* (1938), *The Killing of Jacqueline Love* (1942) and *Roll Back the Night* (1945). *Paradise Flow* is also the title of a play by Devanny, discovered and edited by Carole Ferrier in 1985. In most of her fiction Devanny draws attention to the need for women to struggle against sexual and class oppression. Her hitherto unpublished autobiography, *Point of Departure*, was edited by Carole Ferrier in 1986, and she is one of the subjects of Drusilla Modjeska's *Exiles at Home* (1981). Devanny is prominent in Errol O'Neill's play *Popular Front* (1988). Some of her letters to other women writers, including Katharine Susannah Prichard, are included in the collection edited by Carole Ferrier, *As Good as a Yarn with You* (1992).

Development of Australian Literature, The (1898), by Henry Gyles Turner and Alexander Sutherland, is one of the pioneering works of Australian literary criticism. Biographical essays on colonial literary figures, Adam Lindsay Gordon, Henry Kendall and Marcus Clarke, are prefaced by Turner's essay 'A General Sketch of Australian Literature', said by its author to be an attempt to define the growth and current position of Australian literature.

DIAMOND, Dick (?–1989), the author of *Reedy River* (q.v., 1970), the popular Australian musical based on the shearers' strike of 1891, also wrote sketches for vaudeville, plays for radio and television, and a novel about the war between Vietnam and France, *The Walls Are Down*, published in Hanoi in 1958. *Reedy River* was first produced by the New Theatre, Melbourne, in 1953 and has had frequent revivals.

Diary of a New Chum, by Paul Wenz (q.v.), was published under his pseudonym, 'Paul Warrego', in 1908. A largely humorous account of some of Wenz's first experiences in Australia, it describes his reactions to the climatic extremes and hardships of the outback; to the varied activities he engages in as jackeroo, from boundary-riding to cutting Bathurst burrs; to the various bush characters he meets, such as swagmen, itinerant salesmen, rabbiters, selectors, Aborigines and Chinese cooks; and to the practical jokes that are inevitably visited on the 'new chum' (q.v.). The account is enlivened by the narrator's vivid descriptions of the bush landscape, by his feeling for the animals of the outback, and by his fiction of flight from a recklessly incurred engagement back home. The narrative concludes with ten points of advice, which include the recommendations to 'keep an angelic temper and a live imagination, for you will have to see jokes' and, when hearing a snake or Murray cod yarn, to 'multiply the breadth by the length and divide by ten'. *Diary of a New Chum* was republished with some of Wenz's stories, letters and unpublished material, translated and edited by Maurice Blackman, in 1990.

DIBDIN, Charles Alexander was presumably born in England and was resident in Sydney in the 1840s. Little is known of his life and background, although his grandfather, Charles Dibdin, was a well-known playwright, actor and composer and other members of his family had theatrical experience. Dibdin himself was employed as a prompter at the Royal Victoria Theatre. Two plays by Dibdin and possibly a third were performed in Sydney in the early 1840s: 'The Queer Client; or The Avenger' (1842), a three act adaptation of a tale in Dickens's *Pickwick Papers*, *Billy Barlow*, also known as *The Barlow Family* (1843), and the more doubtful 'Humphrey Clinker' (1844?), an adaptation of Smollett's novel. Written as a vehicle for George Coppin (q.v.) *Billy Barlow* was probably an attempt to capitalise on the popularity of the ballad (see 'Billy Barlow in Australia'); the play was published with introduction by Maryanne Dever in *Australasian Drama Studies* (1989).

DICK, Charlotte Isabel (1881–1959), born Tasmania, published several novels set there: *The Veil of Discretion* (1920), which has the well-tried plot of governess marrying squatter; *Huon Belle* (1930), which is also concerned with the vicissitudes of an orphaned girl immigrant in Tasmania; *Wild Orchard* (1945), a story of early Tasmania; and *Country Heart* (1946). Her volume *Garden Peace and Christmas Tales* (1927) combines verse and prose.

DICK, William (1937–), born Yarraville, Victoria, grew up in the Melbourne suburb of Footscray (Goodway in *A Bunch of Ratbags*). He worked first as a furniture upholsterer, then in a variety of temporary occupations while pursuing a career as a writer, part of which has been as a television scriptwriter (e.g. *Bellbird*). His first published work, the semi-autobiographical novel *A Bunch of Ratbags* (1965), is set in the slum world of Melbourne; it conveys a realistic picture of the harsh poverty and aimless violence of that environment and narrates the gradual movement away from it of the central character, Terry Cooke, who is saved by a decent girl and a brush with the law. A successful musical adaptation of the novel, with lyrics and music by Don Battye and Peter Pinne, was staged in Melbourne in 1966. Dick also wrote the novels *Naked Prodigal* (1969) and *The Pope and the President* (1972).

DICKENS, Charles (1812–70) had several connections with Australia and Australian literature. He established his reputation with *The Posthumous Papers of the Pickwick Club* (1837) which, like *Nicholas Nickleby* (1839), has a character who is transported to Australia. The *Papers* proved widely popular in colonial Australia, where Pickwick parties were held, an Australian imitation was advertised (*Tobias Twickenham*) and the first pirated edition of the original was published in Hobart in 1838. Although in later works Dickens continued to transport occasional characters to Australia (e.g. Uriah Heep in *David Copperfield*) he increasingly came to regard the colonies as a land of opportunity both for convicts and for immigrants. Thus in *David Copperfield* the Micawbers, Peggotty, Emily and others emigrate and succeed in Port Middlebray (Melbourne), and in *Great Expectations* Pip's benefactor, the convicted felon Magwitch, makes his fortune on the land. An Australian tradition that Miss Havisham in *Great Expectations* is based on the Sydney eccentric Eliza Emily Donnithorne (?1826–86), who was jilted in 1856 and thereafter never left her house at Newtown in Sydney, is possibly correct but difficult to verify. Dickens's view of Australia, discussed in Coral Lansbury's (q.v.) controversial *Arcady in Australia* (1970), seems to have developed as a result of his meetings with Caroline Chisholm and his awareness of Samuel Sidney's (q.v.) encouraging writings about the colonies. The first issue in 1850 of the Dickens journal *Household Words* carried an approving exposition of Chisholm's emigration schemes, and subsequent numbers of the journal carried contributions by J.G. Lang (q.v.) as well as Sidney, who dedicated his *Gallops and Gossips in the Bush of Australia* (1854) to Dickens. Dickens was less impressed with Caroline Chisholm's domestic skills and possibly based Mrs Jellaby of *Bleak House* on his memory of a visit to her house. Extracts from both *Household Words* and the later journal, *All the Year Round*, were regularly printed in Australian newspapers; similarly, Dickens's novels were not only widely sold and serialised in Australia but also dramatised. In 1841 Dickens, wearying of English society, thought that he might emigrate to Australia. Two of his sons, Alfred D'Orsay Tennyson Dickens (1845–1912) and Edward Bulwer Lytton Dickens (1852–1902), in fact did so, the latter becoming a member of the NSW parliament in 1889–94; their careers are discussed in Mary Lazarus's *A Tale of Two Brothers* (1973). Henry Lawson, in 'A Fragment of Autobiography' and in the long poem 'With Dickens' (*When I Was King*, 1905), expresses his love for and wide knowledge of Dickens. Among modern authors, Barry Oakley in *The Ship's Whistle* (1979) portrays the relationship between Dickens and Kate Horne, the wife of R.H. Horne, during Horne's absence in Australia, David Allen in *Modest Expectations* (1990) explores what might have happened to Dickens had he visited Australia, and Barry Dickins reinterprets *A Christmas Carol*, providing it with a Melbourne setting in his play *A Dickins' Christmas* (1992).

DICKINS, Barry (1949–), born Reservoir, Victoria, was a member of the La Mama theatre and poetry group of the early 1970s; in 1975 his first play, 'Ghosts', was presented at La Mama. A full-time writer, Dickins contributes to numerous newspapers and is a regular columnist for the *Sun News-Pictorial* and various Melbourne newspapers. Twelve of his plays have been published: *The Banana Bender* (1981), *The Death of Minnie* (1981), *Lennie Lower* (1982), *One Woman Shoe* (1984), *The Horror of the Suburban Nature Strip* (1984), *Beautland* (1985), *The Bridal Suite* [with]

Mag and Bag (1985), *The Golden Goldenbergs* (1986), *Royboys* (1987), *The Fool's Shoe Hotel* (1987) and *A Dickins' Christmas* (1992). His unpublished plays include 'Only an Old Kit Bag' (1976), 'The Rotten Teeth Show' (1977), 'The Greenroom', 'Reservoir by Night', 'The Ken Wright Show' (1980), 'The Interrogation of Angel' (1981) and 'A Couple of Broken Hearts' (1983). He has also written two novels, *The Crookes of Epping* (1984) and *Ron Truffle. His Life & Bump-Out* (1988); a collection of football stories, *You'll Only Go In for Your Mates* (1991); two books of autobiographical fiction, *The Gift of the Gab* (1981) and *I Love to Live* (1991); reminiscences of his grandmother, *My Grandmother* (1989); a selection of his journalism, *What the Dickins!* (1985) and *Post Office Restaurant and Other Stories* (1992), a collection of stories, vignettes and extended observations. A zany, self-deprecating humorist, firmly located in the traditions and rituals of his native Melbourne, Dickins has a gift for poetic fantasy and for comically transforming mundane city life. His inventive powers are seen at their most extravagant in his plays, many of which are short pieces written for small, intimate theatres, where their flexible structures, lunatic characters and direct relations with the audience can be best exploited.

Dictionary of Australian Biography, see **SERLE, Percival**

Dictionary of Australian Colloquialisms, A, see **Australian English**

DIESENDORF, Margaret (1912–93), born and educated (MA, D.Phil.) in Vienna, Austria, came to Australia in 1939. A gifted linguist, educationist, translator, editor and creative writer, she played an active role in the Sydney literary scene for several decades and later in Canberra; she was, for example, associate editor of *Poetry Australia* (q.v.) in 1967–81 and during that time was also associate editor of the American magazine *Creative Moment*. She received the Pacific Books Publishers 'Best Poems' Awards for 1972 and 1973 and the Borestone Mountain Poetry Award for 1974 and 1976. Widely featured in anthologies and journals, she published *Light: Poems by Margaret Diesendorf* (1981) and *Holding the Golden Apple* (1991), a collection of love poems, in which love takes a myriad forms and is directed at many objects. Tributes to her are Gwen Harwood's 'Three Poems to Margaret Diesendorf', Grace Perry's 'Translation' and Philip Grundy's 'To a Trilingual Poet'. She translated the work of Rilke into English, of A.D. Hope into French, of Grace Perry into German as well as other works, e.g. Rosemary Dobson's *Child with Cockatoo* into French.

Difficult Young Man, A, a novel by Martin Boyd (q.v.), the second in a tetralogy dealing with the Langton family, was published in 1955. The narrator, Guy Langton, recounts the history of his family during the turn-of-the-century period, concentrating on his elder brother Dominic. A passionate individual, invested with a dark inheritance from the Spanish side of the family, Dominic frequently finds it impossible to reconcile his personal sense of honour with the prevailing social morality. A series of incidents reveals his 'difficult' nature: he is expelled from school; walks naked at night and allegedly seduces his Aunt Baba's maids; rides his horse to death; and is found worshipping in a Hellenic mood his half-dressed cousin, Helena Craig. His behaviour causes his parents, Steven and Laura, to uproot their family and move to England. There Dominic experiences two curious relationships, one with a retired Colonel Rodgers and the other with Sylvia Tunstall, the daughter of Lord Dilton. His engagement to Sylvia, seen by some as a brilliant match, is broken off because of Sylvia's snobbery. Once again in Australia, Dominic elopes with his childhood sweetheart Helena on the eve of her wedding to a wealthy grazier.

'Digger' was in use as a term in Australia before 1850 but it came to prominence with the gold discoveries, the 'diggers' being those who rushed to 'the diggings' (the goldfields) to make their fortune. The term is encountered in the titles of such early works as David Mackenzie's *The Gold Digger* (1852) and James Bonwick's *Notes of a Gold Digger, and Gold Diggers' Guide* (1852); in the words of songs such as 'The Broken-Down Digger', a fragment of which is in Charles MacAlister's *Old Pioneering Days in the Sunny South* (1907, but including reminiscences from the 1830s on), and 'The Palmer Days' with its refrain 'I see the diggers as they go with dreams of wealth untold'; and in the sketch-book of contemporary artist S.T. Gill, published as *Sketches of the Victorian Gold Diggings and Diggers as They Are* (1852). The rebellious miners at Ballarat were also referred to as the 'diggers' in contemporary official and unofficial reports of Eureka. In George Dunderdale's *The Book of the Bush* (1898), 'diggers' is used in the subtitle with such other Australian types as 'squatters' and 'convicts'. Although there is some indication that the term persisted in bush life from the goldfields period until the First World War, it did not return to prominence until the Gallipoli campaign of 1915. The Australian and NZ soldiers adopted 'digger' because it described their lifestyle on the Gallipoli cliffs (to the ironic question of 'What's your present occupation?' the reply in unison by the troops was 'Digging, digging, always bloody well digging') and because it carried with it the rebellious flavour of Eureka, defiance of authority being seen as part of the Anzac character. War historian C.E.W. Bean, however, suggests that it originated among members of the Anzac Corps on the Somme front, June–August 1917; as on Gallipoli, the word 'digger' carried so rich an implication of the Anzac infantryman's own view of his functions and character that it spread like wildfire through the AIF. 'The Digger's Song', written during the First World War, carries typical 'digger' sentiments – contempt of the frontline soldier for the pompous, regulation-bound headquarters' soldier ('brave men are dying for bastards like you' and 'Lord Gort awarded the digger a V.C. and two bars/ For giving the corporal a kick in the a . . .').

'Digger' or 'A Digger' was adopted as a pseudonym by several minor war memoirists; C.J. Dennis published *Digger Smith* (1918), the experiences of a Gallipoli veteran; and the soldiers' magazine *Aussie* published a selection of sketches by soldiers as *Digger Aussieosities* (192?). Politician W.M. Hughes, who often wore the Australian soldier's slouch hat during the patriotic public occasions of the war, was popularly known as 'The Little Digger'. Since the First World War 'digger' has continued as the regular synonym for the Australian soldier and is widely used to apply colloquially to the Australian male in general; the friendly, colloquial diminutive 'dig' still retains the flavour of 'mate'.

DILKE, Sir Charles Wentworth (1843–1911), was born into a well-connected English family and at an early age mixed with distinguished statesmen and writers. After studying law at Cambridge, he travelled extensively, spending some time in Australia and NZ and writing an account of his travels on his return, *Greater Britain* (1868). Although the book contains factual errors, it includes one of the most observant accounts of Australia by a traveller from overseas. An international bestseller, the book was frequently reprinted, six editions appearing in three years. Dilke subsequently had a successful career in British politics, but was debarred from high office after 1886 when he was cited in a divorce case. Geoffrey Blainey has edited an abridged version of *Greater Britain* (1985).

Dimboola, an outstandingly popular play by Jack Hibberd (q.v.), was first produced by the Australian Performing Group in 1969 and published in 1974. Subtitled *A Wedding-Reception Play*, it has proved popular with theatre-restaurants, has been more widely produced than any other play in Australia and has also been staged in London, in the USA and in several European countries. Dimboola, a small town in western Victoria, has also produced and welcomed the play, although Hibberd denies that it is based on any particular reception there. The wedding reception of Morris (Morrie) and Maureen (Reen) McAdam has all the familiar, if exaggerated, attributes of a country ritual. Held in the church hall, which has been decorated 'beaut' in green and orange, the reception is provided with music by Lionel Driftwood and the Pile Drivers and is enlivened by several scheduled entertainments such as a tapdance by Astrid, the flower girl, to the tune of 'Animal Crackers in My Soup', and the traditional speeches. For the audience, however, a variety of unscheduled entertainments proves more comic, such as a strident quarrel between Shirl, the 'experienced' bridesmaid, and Dangles, the best man; the irreverent, scatological clowning of two uninvited local drunks, Mutton and Bayonet; an outbreak of Protestant–Catholic animosity; the total alcoholic collapse of the Catholic priest, Father O'Shea; and several brief, amicable fights between both male and female guests. The disapproval of Leonardo Radish, a reporter from the *Mildura Trumpet* (and a caricature of a well-known theatre critic, Leonard Radic), is quenched by his physical removal from the scene.

'Dingo' was an Aboriginal name (see also 'Warrigal') for the wild dog which roamed the Australian bush and which was believed to have originated from domesticated dogs that accompanied the first Aborigines to the Australian continent. Recorded by such early voyagers as Jan Carstensz and William Dampier, the dingo is described as 'the dog of New South Wales' in *The Voyage of Governor Phillip to Botany Bay* (1789) and in John White's *Journal of a Voyage to New South Wales* (1790). Colonial poets such as Charles Harpur and Henry Kendall saw the dingo as part of the hazardous pioneer environment. It and its 'blood polluted dens' form the backdrop to the murder of the settlers in Harpur's 'The Creek of the Four Graves' and Kendall's 'The Glen of Arrawatta', and it is hunted down in Adam Lindsay Gordon's 'The Sick Stockrider'. Because the dingo's attacks on the pioneers' precious sheep and cattle were perpetrated with cunning and stealth, the word 'dingo' came into colloquial use also as a term of contempt to denote cowardice and treachery in humans. The dingo has had a more attractive presence in children's literature, featured in such stories as H.G. Lamond's *White Ears the Outlaw: The Story of a Dingo* (1949), John Kiddell's *The Day of the Dingo* (1955) and Elyne Mitchell's *Jinki, Dingo of the Snows* (1970). The celebrated murder trial of Lindy and Michael Chamberlain which followed the disappearance of their baby, Azaria, at Ayers Rock in 1980, led to numerous theories and counter-theories on the viciousness of the dingo, e.g. James Simmonds's *Azaria – Wednesday's Child* (1982).

Diogenes, the journal of the Literary Society of the University of Tasmania, was published annually 1955–65. It carried original poetry and short fiction as well as critical articles and expositions.

Direction, published in four issues 1952–55, 'devoted exclusively to the encouragement of a youthful and vigorous literature in Australia, honest criticism and discussion', was edited by L.H. Davison. Contributors included Max Harris, Judith Wright, James McAuley, A.D. Hope, Vivian Smith, Brian Elliott, Vincent Buckley, Barry Oakley, Bruce Dawe and Evan Jones.

DISHER, Garry (1949–), born Burra, SA, holds a Master's degree in history and is a full-time writer and a teacher of creative writing. He lived and worked for a time in England, Europe and Africa but has lived in Melbourne since 1974. In 1978–79 he held the Australian Creative Writing Fellowship at Stanford University, California, and in 1987 won the Angus & Robertson Writers' Fellowship. He has been highly successful in his attempts at various literary genres. He has written three books of short stories: the first, *Approaches* (1981), is a series of episodes in the lives of members of an Australian family, ranging from diggers' experiences in the First World War to the Vietnam moratorium marches and later experiences in America and Africa. One of the stories in *Approaches* is a version of the later children's book *The Bamboo Flute* (1992). *The Difference to Me* (1988) is perhaps his finest

short fiction; 'Amateur Hour' won the 1986 National Short Story Award, 'Poor Reception' the Alan Marshall Award and 'Dead Eye' the Henry Lawson Award. *Flamingo Gate* (1991) is a collection of six stories and a novella, mostly concerned with the people in the townhouse group bearing the book's name. The novella is in the thriller mode. A lawyer, Maslen, the trouble-shooter for a corporation which is systematically polluting the urban environment, becomes obsessed with a serial killer who uses a disguise as an older woman to get involved with women returning to their cars in supermarket car parks, then hacks them to death with an axe. Maslen discovers that the killer is methodically carving out a cross on the suburban map of Melbourne and believes he is able to predict where the final attack will occur. He is prevented, however, from being present at the climax by a traffic jam largely brought about by another of his corporation's accidents. Disher's two novels are *Steal Away* (1987) and *The Stencil Man* (1988). *Steal Away* explores the ordinary life of ordinary Robert Saxby, who never deviates from the path dictated to him by fate – marriage to a wealthy girl, fatherhood, career as an academic, desertion by his wife and the passing up of numerous opportunities of adding significance and meaning to his life, opportunities that, as he comes to celebrate his own son's coming of age, he realises he has allowed to 'steal away'. *The Stencil Man* is the story of the internment during the Second World War of Martin Linke, a German, resident in Australia for seventeen years. Interned, with others, at Tatura in Victoria, he sends home drawings to his children who live with his ex-wife's sister. Finally he escapes but only the war's end will secure both his physical and mental release. Disher's thrillers, *Kickback* (1991), *Paydirt* (1992) and *Deathdeal* (1993), present the professional thief Wyatt, who inhabits a brutal Melbourne world of organised crime. More violent than the usual run of Australian crime fiction, Disher's thrillers are in the contemporary American mould. His children's book *The Bamboo Flute*, partly autobiographical, recounts the loneliness of a young lad growing up in a family caught in the rural depression of the 1930s. Highly praised, and winner of the NBC Younger Readers Book of the Year Award in 1993, it is more a child's story for adults than a story for children. *Ratface* (1993) tells of the escape of three children from an oppressive religious sect.

In all Disher's writing there is evidence of a remarkable, understated craftsmanship. Exact language, pruned to an absolute spareness, carries the narratives of the short fiction and the novels with effortless ease. Precise and economical though his style is, it is often subtly spiced with sensitive observation and imaginative insight. Disher has also edited the anthologies *Personal Best* (1989 and 1991), in which Australian writers choose their own best short stories and comment on both the stories and the writing process itself and *The Man Who Played Spoons* (1987), and several historical works and creative writing manuals.

Dissent: A Radical Quarterly, a quarterly emanating from the University of Melbourne Students'

Representative Council and Dissent Publications, was published 1961–78 with an editorial committee that included Chris Wallace-Crabbe and Brian Buckley. *Dissent*, an independent forum for the discussion of social, cultural, economic and political issues, published book reviews, some poetry and short fiction. Its special-subject editions included topics such as education, women's issues and abortion.

DIXSON, Miriam (1930–), born Melbourne and at present associate professor of history at the University of New England, Armidale, NSW, is a well-known feminist writer whose central interest as a writer concerns issues of cultural identity from a historical and psychoanalytic viewpoint. Her publications include *The Real Matilda* (1976, revised 1984), a work on 'woman and identity in Australia', and *Greater than Lenin?: Lang and Labor 1916–1932* (1977), which reflects her interest in the Australian labour movement.

DIXSON, Sir William (1870–1952), born Sydney, was an engineer in Scotland 1889–96, then returned to Australia where, while making a business fortune, he became a keen collector of Australian rare books, manuscripts and art works. He donated his collection to the State of NSW and the government of the day built the Dixson wing of the NSW Public Library to house it in 1929. He donated the great bronze doors of the library's main entrance, dedicating them to the memory of David Scott Mitchell. He also set up the William Dixson Foundation to reproduce and translate manuscripts and rare books relating to Australia and the Pacific. The Dixson Library of the University of New England bears his name in recognition of his generosity in helping its establishment 1937–39. *Treasures of the State Library of New South Wales* by Anne Robertson, which describes the Dixson and Mitchell collections, was published in 1988.

DOBELL, Sir William (1899–1970), born Newcastle, NSW, into a poor family, studied art in Sydney before leaving for London and Europe in 1929. In London he developed his particular forte, the genre painting which epitomises a common trait or tendency. Paintings which belong to his London period include *The Charlady*, *Mrs South Kensington*, *Irish Youth*, *The Red Lady* and *Boy at the Basin*. In 1939 he returned to Australia and became established as a leader of a vigorous wartime Sydney movement, painting such celebrated portraits as *The Billy Boy*, *The Strapper*, *Scotty Allan*, *The Cypriot* and *Cement Worker*. He won the 1943 Archibald Prize with a controversial portrait of his colleague Joshua Smith, which led to a celebrated court case. Dobell, who subsequently won the Archibald Prize in 1948 and 1959 and the Wynne Prize in 1948, painted several well-known portraits of Australian writers including Brian Penton, Frank Clune and Mary Gilmore – the last-named being also one of his most controversial. His story of an experience in London, embodied in his painting *The Dead Landlord* (1936), was the starting-point of Patrick White's play *The Ham Funeral* (1965). Dobell's work is examined in

James Gleeson's *William Dobell* (1964, revised 1969 and 1981); a biography by Brian Adams, *Portrait of an Artist: A Biography of William Dobell*, was published in 1983.

DOBSON, Rosemary (1920–), born Sydney, joined the publishing firm Angus & Robertson during the Second World War, working as editor and reader with Beatrice Davis, Douglas Stewart and Nan McDonald. She has also been an art historian and teacher. She has published numerous books of poetry: *In A Convex Mirror* (1944); *The Ship of Ice* (1948); *Child with a Cockatoo* (1955); *Cock Crow* (1965); *Selected Poems* (1973, a further edition in 1980); *Three Poems on Water Springs* (1973); *Greek Coins: A Sequence of Poems* (1977); *Over the Frontier* (1978); *The Continuance of Poetry* (1981); *The Three Fates and Other Poems* (1984); *Collected Poems* (1991) and *Untold Lives* (1992). Her poetry has also been featured in the Australian Poets series (1963) and in the Australian National Library's Pamphlet Poets series (1990). Her other publications include anthologies, *Songs for All Seasons: 100 Poems for Young People* (1967); *Australian Voices, Poetry and Prose of the 1970s* (1975) and *Sisters Poets I* (1979); *Moscow Trefoil* (1975, translations with David Campbell and Natalie Staples of the Russian poets Anna Akhmatova and Osip Mandelstam); *Seven Russian Poets* (1979, with David Campbell, versions or imitations of poems from the Russian); *Summer Press* (1987), a novel for young adults; radio scripts, essays and articles on various writers and artists and two critical works, *Focus on Ray Crooke* (1971) and *A World of Difference: Australian Poetry and Painting in the 1940s* (1973). A selection of her poems, *L'Enfant en Cacatoès*, translated by Louis Dautheuil and Margaret Diesendorf, was published in 1967 in the series *Autour du Monde*.

The love of art, antiquity and mythology are in Dobson's poetry from the beginning. Endymion, Botticelli, Mars, Prometheus, Daphne, van Eyck, Brueghel, Icarus, Raphael, Giotto, Calvi, Vermeer are but some of her early passing parade of artists and mythical figures. In *Child with a Cockatoo* there is a group of fifteen 'Poems from Paintings' (her favourite device is poems in series) and of them 'Paintings' emphasises her conviction of the supremacy of Art over Time:

> Climate of stillness: though I hear
> No sound that falls on mortal ear
> Yet in the intricate, devised
> Hearing of sight these waves that break
> In thunder on a barren shore
> Will foam and crash for evermore
>
> And you, grave Florentine, who turn
> And look at me with eyes that burn,
> I hear you asking – 'What is Time
> Since Art has conquered it? I speak
> Five hundred years ago. You hear.
> My words beat still upon your ear.'

Many of her poems – 'Still Life', 'Young Girl at a Window', 'Over the Hill', 'In a Cafe', 'Painter of Antwerp' – are themselves word paintings, capturing moments of existence frozen in time. Personal experiences – family ties, wife and motherhood – take precedence in *Cock Crow*, with 'Child of Our Time', 'Out of Winter', 'Annunciations', 'To Meet the Child' and 'To a Child', for example, being sensitive and deeply poetic expressions of maternal love. 'Cock Crow', the title poem, portrays the dilemma of divided loyalties – those owed to others and that owed to oneself. Self appears, briefly, likely to prevail:

> And walking up and down the road
> Knew myself, separate and alone,
> Cut off from human cries, from pain
> And love that grows about the bone

It is only a momentary resolution. The daughter–mother 'love that grows about the bone' has the final claim.

In the sequence 'The Devil and the Angel' Dobson displays a deft touch of whimsy and fantasy with the Devil and an angel competing for the souls of those departing from this life. There is a similar captivating jauntiness in 'The Sailor: May 1960', which tells of a sailor, tired of the seafaring life, shouldering his oar and marching inland, across the Great Divide, through many a 'one-horse town' and on across the vast inland stock routes until finally he is asked 'What's that, mate, tied up on your back?' There he stays, his journey ended. Ruefully the poet proposes making a similar journey with a gun on her shoulder.

Several of Rosemary Dobson's smaller books of poetry have been published by her husband Alec Bolton's (q.v.) Brindabella Press – Officina Brindabella – *Three Poems on Water Springs*, *Greek Coins: A Sequence of Poems*, *The Continuance of Poetry* and *Untold Lives*. *Greek Coins* comprises twenty four-line poems each of which sets out 'a visual idea which could be contained within a circle – that is, within the coin-sized four line stanza'. The poems, accompanied by her own line drawings, reflect her attachment to Greek themes, love of antiquity and admiration for the wisdom and perception of the Greek traveller Pausanias, who wrote a guide to Greece in the second century AD. *Over the Frontier* contains a section 'Poems from Pausanias', which includes the Greek Coins poems. *The Continuance of Poetry* (1981) contains another small series, twelve poems written after the death of fellow poet David Campbell (q.v.). Simple, restrained poems, they recall pleasant times of friendship, returning often to the belief that those shared moments live still, in memory and in the continuing presence of Campbell's poetry. *The Continuance of Poetry* is contained also in *The Three Fates and Other Poems*, as is another poem of friendship, 'A Letter to Lydia', which moves beyond the personal to echo again Dobson's love of the classical past and the ancient lands, Greece and Crete. There is, in her later poetry, the occasional measured glance at approaching death and a sharper awareness of mortality but her joy and wonder at the treasure still to be gleaned from art, poetry, the loveliness of nature and the continuing miracle of life are undiminished. While there is life there is direction and purpose.

> Learn still; take, reject,
> Choose, use, create,
> Put past to present purpose. Make.

The *Collected Poems*, chosen from her earliest ('I have stood by the poet that I was') to her latest volumes, brings together about 200 poems written over half a century. They represent, as has been aptly said, 'a lifework of love and dedication to the craft of writing'. If that craftsmanship has often led to her classification as a poet's poet, the unassuming tone, lucid style and honest, direct presentation of her work make her also a reader's poet. Recognition of Rosemary Dobson's poetry has accumulated over many years. She won the *Sydney Morning Herald* Award for Poetry in 1948 for 'The Ship of Ice', the FAW Christopher Brennan Award in 1978, the Patrick White Award in 1984, the Grace Leven Poetry Prize in 1984 and shared the Victorian Premier's Literary Award in 1985, the last two with *The Three Fates*. She was made an honorary life member of the Association for the Study of Australian Literature and AO in 1987 for her outstanding contribution to Australian literature.

DOCKER, John (1945–), born Sydney, has degrees from the universities of Sydney and Melbourne and a Ph.D. from the ANU. He has taught at various universities in NSW and at the then Canberra College of Advanced Education. He has published several important analyses of Australian culture and literature, including *Australian Cultural Elites: Intellectual Traditions in Sydney and Melbourne* (q.v., 1974), and *In a Critical Condition: Reading Australian Literature* (1984). The former examines the different cultural histories of the two major Australian cities and the resultant contrasting views of the relationship between Australia's inherited European and indigenous colonial cultures. The latter examines the history and practice of the teaching of literature in Australian universities, ranging the radical nationalists (the Palmers, A.A. Phillips, Russel Ward, Geoffrey Serle, Stephen Murray-Smith) against the Australian New Critics and Leavisites (Wilkes, Buckley, Heseltine, Kramer, Cantrell). Largely composed of journal articles and conference papers from 1971 to the 1980s, *In a Critical Condition* argues that students of Australian literature throughout the 1960s and 1970s were unduly influenced by contemporary literary theories promoted by Australian universities. Docker has also written *The Nervous Nineties* (1991), which views that decade from various perspectives. He examines Louisa Lawson's the *Dawn*, the *Bulletin* and the period's utopian and fantasy literature (e.g. Edward Bellamy, William Lane, H. Rider Haggard) as well as Lawson's short stories and Joseph Furphy's *Rigby's Romance*, and defines the impact of American culture on late nineteenth-century Australia. He has also edited, with Susan Dermody and Drusilla Modjeska, *Nellie Melba, Ginger Meggs and Friends: Essays in Australian Cultural History* (1982).

Dog on the Tuckerbox, see **Gundagai**

DOMAHIDY, András (1920–   ), born Romania into the landed gentry, gained his doctorate in law at Budapest University before serving in the Hungarian Hussars. From 1945 to 1947 he farmed what was left of the family estate at County Szatmár but was forced from the land by growing communist pressure. In 1950 he migrated to Australia, where he worked at first in a factory and as a clerk and later as a librarian with the University of WA. In 1966 he graduated BA from the same university. An outstanding novelist in Hungarian, he has published a trilogy, *Indian Summer* (1969), *Shadows and Women* (1979), and *Peacock on a Plate* (1991), and a collection of short fiction, *Dragonflies* (1989). *Shadows and Women* has been translated by Elizabeth Windsor and published in 1989. *Indian Summer* won the Lehel Prize in 1969. A lyrical novel, *Shadows and Women* contrasts experience in pre-war Hungary and Transylvania and post-war Australia.

DONOHUE, Frank ('Arthur Gayll') (?–1908) published fiction, *A Sheaf of Stories for the Centenary Year* (1888) and *The History of Botany Bay* (1888), which originally appeared in the *Bulletin*. He also published *Stray Leaves* (1883), relating to Henry Kendall and Daniel Deniehy.

DONOHOE, John (?1806–30), born Dublin, Ireland, was convicted in 1823 of intention to commit a felony, sentenced to transportation and arrived in NSW in 1825. At the end of 1827 he committed his first robberies on the roads outside Sydney, was captured and sentenced to death, but escaped from custody and for over two years headed a bushranging gang that operated mainly in the Nepean area. In September 1830 he was killed in a shoot-out with soldiers and police near Campbelltown. Donohoe's defiance of authority, his sympathy for the convict and emancipist poor (who helped to protect him) and his personal daring in urging the police to fire on him during the exchange which led to his death, won him many admirers: in 'Jim Jones at Botany Bay' the convict narrator announces his intention of taking to the bush and joining the 'brave bushrangers . . . Jack Donohoo and Co.', and in 'A Convict's Tour to Hell' (q.v.) a knowledge of Donohoe helps 'Frank the Poet' gain admission to Heaven. 'Bold Jack Donahoe' (sometimes spelt 'Donahue', 'Donohue', 'Donohoo' and 'Donahoo' as well as the original 'Donohoe') became one of the first bushrangers (q.v.) depicted in Australian literature, notably in Charles Harpur's play *The Bushrangers* (q.v., 1853), titled 'The Tragedy of Donohoe' when extracts were first published in the *Sydney Monitor* in 1835. Donohoe was also an early hero of Australian folklore, his exploits celebrated in several songs and ballads, one of which he may have written himself. Texts of the Donohoe cycle of ballads, which were banned as treason songs by the penal authorities in the 1830s and are known in Ireland, are provided in John Meredith's *The Wild Colonial Boy: Bushranger Jack Donahoe, 1806–30* (1982), which also discusses the links between the 'Bold Jack Donahoe' songs and 'The Wild Colonial Boy' (q.v.) songs. John Manifold's poem 'The Afterlife of Bold Jack Donahue'

pictures Donohoe as a president of the company of folk heroes enjoying an idyllic afterlife until he is ready to lead an attack on the corrupt rich of Australia.

Don's Party, a popular play by David Williamson (q.v.), was first performed in 1971 by the Australian Performing Group, published in 1973 and later made into a film. A group of eleven people, mostly in their early thirties, materially well established although mostly committed Labor voters, attend a party on the night of the 1969 federal election. As the evening progresses, the various sexual expectations of the participants are frustrated, usually farcically. Meanwhile the party degenerates into drunkenness and the couples scrutinise their tired marriages and the discrepancy between youthful aspirations and present bourgeois reality. The fortunes of the Labor Party simultaneously decline, although virtually unnoticed by the party-goers.

Dorchester Labourers, see **LOVELESS, George**

DORRINGTON, Albert ('AD', 'Alba Dorian') (?1874–1953), born London, came to Australia in his youth and travelled widely until 1895 when he settled in Sydney. A frequent contributor to the *Bulletin* in the 1890s, often under the pseudonyms 'AD' and 'Alba Dorian', he published a book of short stories, *Castro's Last Sacrament and Other Stories* (1900), then collaborated with A.G. Stephens in a romantic novel, *The Lady Calphurnia Royal*, which was serialised in the *Bookfellow* in 1907 and published in book form in 1909. Disgruntled with his lack of recognition from local critics, Dorrington returned to England in 1907 and thereafter published a further thirteen works of fiction, some of which have an Australian background. They include *And the Day Came* (1908); *Children of the Cloven Hoof* (1911), a novel of pastoral life; *A South Sea Buccaneer* (1911), in which Bully Hayes figures; and *Our Lady of the Leopards* (1911). *The Lady Calphurnia Royal* deals with an exotic female character whose bizarre career extends from Paris to the French penal colony of Noumea and into outback Australia. His best-known short story is 'A Bush Tanqueray'. A popular novelist, whose pen was guided mainly by commercial opportunism, Dorrington relied chiefly on sensational plots filled with mystery and romance.

DOWNES, Marion Grace (?–1926), was the author of four novels, *Swayed by the Storm* (1911), *A Brave Bush Girl* (1912), *Flower o' the Bush* (1914) and *In the Track of the Sunset* (1919); and two volumes of poetry, *Wayside Songs for Women* (1921) and *Wayside Songs* (1927). Her verse, largely on religious themes and expressing the conventional attitudes of the period, was published in journals both in England and Australia and won an appreciative audience. The same attitudes are projected in her novels, which are mainly love stories, although they are competently written and relatively dramatic and fast-moving.

'Down Under', a colloquial term for Australia and sometimes applied also to NZ, was in existence at least by the end of the nineteenth century. The term, seldom used by Australians themselves, implies a northern-hemisphere perspective of Australia and clearly derives from the notion of the Antipodes (q.v.). The popular song 'Down Under', sung during the successful challenge for the America's Cup in 1983, is an example of a modern usage.

DOWRICK, Stephanie (1947–), born NZ, lived 1967–82 in London, where, with Naim Atallah, she founded a feminist publishing house, The Women's Press. In 1981 she came to Australia where she turned to fiction-writing. Her first novel, *Running Backwards Over Sand* (1985), follows the experiences of Zoe Delighty, a NZ-born girl whose life changes dramatically following the death of her mother and her own flight to London, where she discovers love and finally a new sense of self. Dowrick has also edited with Jane Parkin a collection of stories by NZ and Australian writers, *Speaking with the Sun* (1991), and a study of identity based on psychosynthesis and object-relations theory, *Intimacy and Solitude* (1991).

DOWSE, Sara (1938–), born Chicago, USA, grew up in New York and Los Angeles, and studied arts at the University of California. Writing, acting and film-making were part of her early experience as her mother was an actor, her father a lawyer who dealt with actors and her stepfather a writer. In 1958 she came to Australia, settling first in Sydney, where she studied at the University of Sydney and then in Canberra. She has worked in publishing and journalism, as head of the women's affairs section of the Prime Minister's department 1974–77 and as a teacher at the ANU. She is now a full-time writer. She has published three novels, *West Block* (1983), *Silver City* (1984) and *Schemetime* (1990) and contributed to the collection of short stories *Canberra Tales* (1988). *West Block*, titled after one of Canberra's earliest office buildings, is based on Dowse's experiences as a public servant, although it is not narrowly autobiographical; the narrative consists of five loosely linked stories all set within the Prime Minister's department. The first story focuses on the career of a top public servant; the second deals with the uranium negotiations of 1977; the third looks back to the liberation of Saigon in 1975; the fourth deals with a single father's acceptance of fatherhood; and the final tale concerns the women's affairs unit and its downgrading in 1977 which led to Dowse's resignation from her position. Presenting a rare picture of the public service as a human enterprise, Dowse explores the drama of decision-making and negotiation and the links between private lives and public actions; the novel also sensitively reflects the frustrations encountered by feminists during the 1970s and the unresolved anomalies within the women's movement. *Silver City* is based on the screenplay of that title directed by Sophia Turkiewicz and released in 1984. *Schemetime*, set in Los Angeles during the Vietnam years, follows the career of an Australian film-maker whose life intersects with four Americans.

In all these various lives, which Dowse describes in absorbing detail, external events are less important than internal revolutions, while the kaleidoscopic narrative interweaves film, dream and 'reality'.

DRAKE, Mary (1912–), born Sydney, began writing professionally in the 1950s and has since been a successful and prolific writer of short stories, many of which have been published in Australian and overseas magazines. She has written the novel *Murder is Like Caviar* (1978) and two books of reminiscences, *Come Away with Me* (1969) and *The Trees Were Green* (1984) as well as two plays, 'The Waiting Room', produced in Queensland and 'The Couch', produced in Sydney.

DRAKE-BROCKMAN, Henrietta (1901–68), born Perth, spent considerable time with her husband, Geoffrey Drake-Brockman, in outback WA. Her impressions of those colourful pioneering times are recorded in articles she wrote under the pseudonym 'Henry Drake' for the *West Australian*. A considerable force in the literary community of WA over many years, she played a major role in the establishment of the State branch of FAW in 1938 and was also a long-serving member of the advisory committee of *Westerly*. Her novels are *Blue North* (1934), set against the background of the pearling industry at Broome; *Sheba Lane* (1936), also in Broome, but no longer the raw frontier town; *Younger Sons* (1937), a historical novel, which portrays the development of the colony and the struggles of the early settlers; *The Fatal Days* (1947), set during the American servicemen's 'invasion' of Australia during the Second World War; and *The Wicked and the Fair* (1957), a fictional account of the events surrounding the wreck of the *Batavia*, which she explores more fully and authentically in *Voyage to Disaster: The Life of Francisco Pelsaert* (1963). Her short fiction is represented in her collection of stories *Sydney or the Bush* (1948). Drake-Brockman also wrote with success for the theatre in the late 1930s and 1940s. Her first play, *The Man from the Bush* (1934, published in *Eight Plays by Australians*), examines the contrasting ethics of the privileged and the poor during the Depression years; her chief dramatic work, however, is *Men Without Wives and Other Plays* (1955), which contains *Men Without Wives* (first published 1938), *Hot Gold*, *Dampier's Ghost* (first published 1937) and *The Blister*. The title play, which won the NSW sesquicentenary competition of 1938, is set in the remote north-west of WA and is concerned with the difficulties of a newly married woman in adjusting to life in the harsh environment of an outback station. The interaction of character and environment (the favourite device of both Drake-Brockman's fiction and drama) leads in the end to a mood of optimism, expressed by the play's strongest character, Ma Bates – 'the land looks after those who love it.' *Hot Gold* uses the contemporary Kalgoorlie scene (gold, gambling, romance) to depict interplay and complexity of character. Drake-Brockman's other plays are *Order for the Day* in *Southerly* (1942) and *The Lion Tamer* (1948), a comedy about expatriate Australians successfully using their Antipodean wit in a London society situation. Drake-Brockman was co-editor, with Walter Murdoch, of *Australian Short Stories* (1951) and edited the 1957 edition of *Coast to Coast* as well as *West Coast Stories* (1959). She also edited *Australian Legendary Tales* (1953) by Mrs K. Langloh Parker and wrote the critical monograph, *Katharine Susannah Prichard* (1967). Her husband gives much of the background to her life and work in his autobiographical *The Turning Wheel* (1960).

DRANSFIELD, Michael (1948–73), born Sydney, educated at Sydney Grammar School and, briefly, at the University of Sydney, worked intermittently on several newspapers and was for a time a government clerk. His short, restless adult life was spent largely in bohemian areas of Sydney (Balmain, Paddington, Darlinghurst), in the country at Cobargo and Candelo, NSW, or wandering over eastern Australia from Queensland to Tasmania. Failing to discover a meaningful role for himself in conventional society, Dransfield vainly sought an alternative in the drug culture. After a motor-cycle accident in April 1972 his health deteriorated and he died, aged 24. Dransfield published three volumes of poetry, *Streets of the Long Voyage* (1970), *The Inspector of Tides* (1972) and *Drug Poems* (q.v., 1972). A further collection largely prepared by him, *Memoirs of a Velvet Urinal*, was published posthumously in 1975. About 600 other poems, collated and edited by Rodney Hall, were brought together in two volumes, *Voyage into Solitude* (1978, poems from the period 1969–71) and *The Second Month of Spring* (1980, poems from 1972). Dransfield's *Collected Poems* was also edited by Hall in 1987. First published in the late 1960s in the underground magazines that arose in criticism of the conservative nature of Australian poetry, Dransfield's talented verse soon became a regular feature of more established newspapers and journals. The consistent themes of his poetry include protest against the quality of contemporary Australian life, especially the monotony and regimentation of an urban existence; the drug culture and the addiction process; life's fragility; loneliness; the importance of human relationships; and the clash between an innate romantic spirit and the ugliness of contemporary life. *Streets of the Long Voyage*, his first and perhaps his most effective body of verse, won the University of Newcastle special Award for a work of literature by an Australian writer under 30. It contains the 'Courland Penders' (q.v.) group of poems; important drug poems such as 'Overdose', 'Fix' and 'Bum's Rush' (see *Drug Poems*); protest poems such as 'Lamentations' and 'That Which We Call a Rose'; and love poems such as 'Parthenogenesis', 'July with Her' and 'Dread Was'. Despite his view of himself as a radical figure, and some unconventional use of punctuation, typography and drug culture jargon, Dransfield's technique was only superficially *avant-garde*. In fact the influence of poets such as Tennyson and Swinburne is clearly seen in his work, both in structure and sensibility; his innovation was, in Geoff Page's words, his 'distinctly personal combination of certain traditional elements'. The best of his poetry combines lyrical beauty with a directness of expression and emotional honesty, as in 'That Which We Call a Rose' –

'I dremt of next week perhaps then we would eat
    again sleep
in a house again
perhaps we would wake to find humanity where
    at present
freedom is obsolete and honour a heresy. Innocently
I dremt that madness passes like a dream'.

Dransfield's later poetry is uneven in quality. Reluctant to revise his verse, he preferred to rely on his first inspiration, and is quoted as saying 'I operate on feelings, not thoughts'. Critics have also been irritated by his focus on stock counter-culture complaints; protest poems such as 'Endsong' and 'Prosperity' in *The Inspector of Tides* rail against pollution, commerce, urban ugliness and insensitive governments. In a slightly patronising fashion, Dransfield distanced himself from other, established 'Official Poets' who also voiced their dismay, but, he felt, merely in 'genteel iambics'. *Drug Poems*, which contains poems from earlier volumes, is both an insight into the process of addiction and an acknowledgement of the isolation and despair that face the addict. The final volume, *The Second Month of Spring*, consists mainly of poems written in the last few months of his life. They are angry and tragic expressions of his desperate attempts to survive the forces engulfing him. As a poet who expressed the anger and disillusionment of many of his generation, Dransfield's status as an anti-establishment cult figure was enhanced by his untimely death. His relatively small body of work, however, is sufficient to establish him as a gifted poet with an important place in the main-stream of Australian poetry. Livio Dobrez published *Parnassus Mad Ward: Michael Dransfield and the New Australian Poetry* (1990).

Dream and Disillusion: A Search for Australian Cultural Identity (1976) by David Walker examines the lives and times of Vance Palmer, Louis Esson, 'Furnley Maurice' and Frederick Sinclaire, and their efforts to establish both a distinctively Australian culture and a national literature.

Dreamtime, see **Aboriginal Song and Narrative in Translation**; **Jindyworobak movement**

DREWE, Robert (1943–   ), born Melbourne and educated in WA, began a journalistic career with the *West Australian* in 1961. He was literary editor of the *Australian* (1971–74) and has also written for the *Age* and the *Bulletin*. He won the Walkley Award for journalism in 1976 and 1981 and in 1990 the Commonwealth Writers Prize for SE Asia and the Pacific. Drewe has published four novels, *The Savage Crows* (1976), *A Cry in the Jungle Bar* (1979), *Fortune* (1986, winner of the NBC Banjo Award in 1987), and *Our Sunshine* (1991); and two collections of short stories, *The Bodysurfers* (1983) and *The Bay of Contented Men* (1989). *The Bodysurfers* has been dramatised for film, radio, television and stage; Drewe has also written a play, 'South American Barbecue', which was staged 1990–91, and edited *The Picador Book of the Beach* (1993).

The Savage Crows (its title being a colonial term for the Aborigines) carries two stories in tandem: that of the complex nineteenth-century figure George Augustus Robinson, who was involved in the oppression of the Tasmanian Blacks; and that of the present-day Stephen Crisp who, confronting an increasing sense of alienation, vainly attempts to escape his immediate dilemma by investigating Robinson's relations with his Aboriginal 'protégés'. Seemingly disparate, the inner lives of both men are alike in a deep but indefinite conviction of guilt. *A Cry in the Jungle Bar* is based on the experiences of a beefy ex-footballer Australian, the tragi-comic Dick Cullen, who is working in Manila as an agricultural scientist for the UN. Well-meaning and earnest, Cullen is inept and unsuccessful in both his personal and his professional lives; he typifies especially the blundering Australian caught in an Asian experience he is totally unequipped to either understand or handle. *Fortune* is superficially an adventure story about a modern explorer, Don Spargo, who combs the WA coastline for shipwrecks, and finds the remains of a Dutch merchant ship, *Fortyn*, in 1957, only to lose it again until 1962. The story of Spargo and of those most directly affected by his discovery is related in a carefully dispersed way, partially mediated by the journalist-narrator's meditations on the state of Australia, especially in the 1960s, and the roles played by the media and by lawyers, entrepreneurs, developers, speculators and bureaucrats. *Our Sunshine*, focusing on the last thirty-six hours of Ned Kelly's freedom as he waited at Glenrowan, is a distinctive reappraisal of the Kelly myth. Presenting Kelly as one 'whose story outgrew his life', who was finally more driven by events and attitudes than driving, Drewe uses the familiar story to question the power of myth, the possibility of attaining objective truth and the power and responsibility of the press. The beach and its associated life-style is the background of *The Bodysurfers*, which explores the shifts in relationships in a large middle-class Australian family over three generations. Solitary, half-comprehending, well-meaning but unlucky, Drewe's characters are dismayed and confused by their lack of success in relationships. The short stories of *The Bay of Contented Men*, set variously in Australia, the USA, Hong Kong and Japan, are similarly concerned with moments of crisis, changes of life, failed or failing marriages. Like the engineer of one of the stories, many of the characters are conscious of living at 'the angle of repose' in that their lives seem at the point of tilting into disaster. Drewe paints a bleak, sometimes sinister world, in which children drown, foreign doctors are persecuted to the point of death and Kamikaze pilots are selected because of their youth, but the tone of his narratives often verges on black comedy.

DREYER, Marien (1911–80), born Mornington, Victoria, lived mainly in Kings Cross, Sydney, where she became a well-known figure in bohemian circles and an effective activist on local issues. Deprived of the chance of becoming an actor by the loss of a leg, she worked as a stenographer before turning to full-time freelance journalism in the 1940s. She wrote short stories, plays and radio scripts as well as numerous articles for magazines and newspapers, and a column, 'Marien's Day', for the magazine *New Idea*. One of her plays, 'Bandicoot on a Burnt Ridge', produced in 1965, won the 1962–63 Journalists' Club Award. Her other plays include *The Hard Way Back* (1953), 'Coffee for Sixpence', 'Don't Forget Barney', 'Hangover', 'No Need for Tinkers', 'A Touch of the Dark', 'Wish No More', 'Return of the Tinker' and 'Marien Dreyer's World', which includes three short plays, 'Charles Was There', 'The Power of a Woman' and 'Too of a Kind'.

'Drover' (see also 'Overlander') is a Middle English noun stemming from an Old English verb 'to drove', i.e. to drive herds of cattle or flocks of sheep to market. The drover is the less glamorous cousin of the overlander; droving was the mundane, day-to-day process of moving mainly small groups of sheep and cattle over relatively short distances; overlanding was on a more epic scale; vast distances were often traversed and stock moved by the thousands. The occupations are to some extent interchangeable and both could be included under the more general heading of 'stockman', the latter term involving the overall handling rather than the mere moving of stock. The most famous literary drover is A.B. Paterson's Clancy of the Overflow, whose 'vision splendid' of the droving life confirmed the idyll, first envisioned in Adam Lindsay Gordon's 'The Sick Stockrider', of carefree stockmen 'sitting loosely in the saddle all the while'. Paterson's Saltbush Bill poems present the other version of the drover, the grass-stealer, whose ruses to allow his travelling sheep to graze on the squatters' best runs confirmed him as the outback's most skilled artist in sharp practices. Henry Lawson created two well-known drovers, the unfortunate Harry Dale of 'The Ballad of the Drover', and Andy who went with cattle and came safely home in 'Andy's Return'. Lawson also wrote the poem 'The Drover's Sweetheart', and the stories 'A Droving Yarn' and 'The Drover's Wife' (q.v.), the latter a famous Australian short story. Paterson further contributed to the droving legend with his nostalgic poems 'In the Droving Days', 'The Travelling Post Office' and 'With the Cattle'. Other well-known droving verses are Harry Morant's 'West by North Again', Will Ogilvie's 'The Last Muster' and 'From the Gulf', G.H. Gibson's 'A Ballad of Queensland', Roland Robinson's 'The Drovers', David Campbell's 'Droving' and Thea Astley's 'Droving Man'. Donald Stuart's novel *The Driven* (1961) and Louis Esson's play *The Drovers* (1920) are also notable representations of the droving theme. Droving and stockman songs and ballads are plentiful. Douglas Stewart and Nancy Keesing include a section, 'The Stockmen of Australia', in their volume *Old Bush Songs* (1957). Best known of the droving stockman songs are 'The Sandy Maranoa' and 'The Dying Stockman'. Documentary and historical works on droving include Mary

Durack's *Kings in Grass Castles* (1959), H.M. Barker's *Droving Days* (1966), Keith Willey's *The Drovers* (1981), Mary Durack, Hugh Sawrey et al., *The Stockman* (1984), an illustrated, somewhat romantic semi-history of the stockman and his role in Australian history, Marie Mahood's *The Australian Stockman* (1988), and *The Romance of the Stockman* (1993), published by Viking O'Neil but with no author or editors named, a brief attribution indicating that the book had come from material gathered by historian R.M. Younger. P.R. Gordon compiled *A Drover's Guide* in 1893; from it stemmed the colloquial expression 'The Drover's Guide' to indicate an anonymous source of outback rumours. An early Australian film, *The Drover's Sweetheart*, was produced in 1911.

Drovers, The, a one-act play by Louis Esson (q.v.) first produced in 1923 by the Pioneer Players (q.v.), was published in 1920 and is often described as an Australian classic. The simple plot, which relates the death of Briglow Bill, a drover injured in a stampede and left to die by his mates who are bound to drive the cattle on to water, has an austere and terse inevitability, reflecting the grimness of life in the bush.

'Drover's Wife, The', one of Henry Lawson's (q.v.) best-known stories, was first published in the *Bulletin* in 1892. It recounts the experiences of an outback woman left alone with her four children in an isolated hut; her husband has been away droving for six months. Near sunset one day a snake disappears under the house; the woman puts her children to bed in the kitchen, and as she awaits its reappearance she recalls incidents which confirm the drabness, tragedy and struggle of her life. As dawn approaches the snake emerges and is killed by the woman with the assistance of Alligator, the family dog.

'The Drover's Wife' has been justly admired for its ruthlessly realistic portrayal of pioneering life, although the courage and stoicism of the unnamed woman temper Lawson's pessimism. Much anthologised and also filmed, it inspired a famous painting by Sir Russell Drysdale (q.v.). The story has been variously parodied and revised in several contemporary versions. Murray Bail's (q.v.) story, published in 1975 in *Contemporary Portraits*, is centred on Drysdale's painting and is ostensibly narrated by the drover's wife's first husband, a dentist, who outlines the circumstances of her desertion of him and questions the 'reality' of Drysdale's interpretation. Frank Moorhouse's (q.v.) hilarious 'The Drover's Wife', published in 1980 in the centenary *Bulletin*, is narrated by an Italian student of Australian literature and satirises both the bush ethos of writers like Lawson and the responses of academics to those writers. Barbara Jefferis's 'The Drover's Wife', also published in the *Bulletin* in 1980, is narrated by the woman herself and offers a feminist answer not only to males like Lawson, Drysdale, Bail and Moorhouse, whose 'errors' she corrects, but also to journals like the *Bulletin* which during the 1890s only told 'how half the world lives'. Anne Gambling's 'The Drover's De Facto', published in *Latitudes* (1986), rewrites the woman protagonist as

well-educated but romantic, attracted by the drover's (now a truck-driver) bush background and physical brawn. When her dream of a bush idyll fails and the 'drover's' presence becomes more of a burden and a threat than his absence, she abandons him and decides to change the topic of her thesis. Damien Broderick has also rewritten the story from the point of view of the dog in 'The Drover's Wife's Dog', in *The Dark Between the Stars* (1991). Elaine Zinkhan in *Australian Literary Studies* (1984) suggests that Lawson drew on his mother Louisa Lawson's story 'Australian Bush-Woman' (1889), omitting her feminist analysis of the situation. Parallels have also been found between Lawson's story and Katherine Mansfield's 'The Woman at the Store' (1911). Kay Schaffer in *Debutante Nation: Feminism Contests the 1890s* (1993) discusses the various interpretations and reworkings of the story, as well as the film *Serious Undertakings* by Helen Grace, which uses the story to question the idea of an authentic national culture.

Drug Poems (1972), a collection by Michael Dransfield (q.v.), gives an insight into the drug culture. Poems such as 'Bum's Rush', 'Fix', 'Overdose', 'Jam' and 'Getting Out' comment on many aspects of the drug experience – the isolation of the addict, the need for the 'fix', the terror of withdrawal and the difficulty of returning to normality.

Drum for Ben Boyd, A, a major poem in fifteen sections by Francis Webb (q.v.), was published in the *Bulletin* in three weekly segments in July 1946, then as a separate publication with illustrations by Norman Lindsay in 1948, when it was awarded the Grace Leven Prize for poetry. Indebted in its form and structure to Kenneth Slessor's 'Five Visions of Captain Cook', Webb's poem attempts a composite picture of Benjamin Boyd (q.v.), the enterprising Scottish merchant-entrepreneur who sought his fortune in maritime and pastoral activities in NSW in the 1840s. Boyd's arrival at Port Jackson in his yacht *Wanderer* in 1842 is pictured in the third part of the sequence. In turn, Boyd is assessed by the Norwegian boat-builder, Jan Strindberg; by an envious journalist who bewails the fact that Boyd will 'grind out a fortune, rule this blasted colony/ While I sit here rotting slowly between editions'; by Sir Oswald Brierly who accompanied him to Australia in the *Wanderer*; by a disgruntled whaler at Twofold Bay who ruefully reflects on 'Mr Blasted Boyd [who] owns us all'; by a Papuan who becomes a victim of Boyd's blackbirding activities; by a colonial politician who likes the aura of power and aristocratic tradition that surrounds Boyd; by a Monaro squatter who deplores Boyd's misuse of the land; by the captain of the *Oberon* who is sent to unravel the mystery of Boyd's death at Guadalcanal in the Solomon Islands; and, finally by John Webster who accompanies Boyd on his last voyage of self-aggrandisement around the Pacific.

'DRYBLOWER', see **MURPHY, E.G.**

Drylight, a literary journal published by the Students Representative Council of the Sydney Teachers' College, appeared annually 1955–67 and in 1971 and 1974. Integrating literature, music and art, *Drylight* was a lively and informative journal in whose pages appeared items from many well-known Australian literary personalities of the day. *Descant*, the annual of the Sydney Teachers' College Literary Club, appeared 1948–50.

DRYSDALE, Sir Russell (1912–81), one of Australia's best-known artists, was born at Bognor Regis, England, and settled in Australia in 1923. His paintings are notable for their depiction of the harshness of the outback landscape and for their interpretation of the difficult lives of the settlers and Aborigines of the area. He won the Wynne Prize in 1947, the Melrose Prize in 1949 and the Britannica Australia Award in 1965. In 1957 he toured central Australia and WA, an experience that was rich in artistic results and which led to the publication, in collaboration with A.J. Marshall, of *Journey Among Men* (1962). Joseph Burke introduced *The Paintings of Russell Drysdale* (1951); studies of Drysdale include Geoffrey Dutton's *Russell Drysdale* (1964), Lou Klepac's *The Life and Work of Russell Drysdale* (1983) and Jenni Boddington's *Drysdale: Photographer* (1987). Drysdale was knighted in 1969.

'Duffing', a slang term for livestock-stealing, probably derives from an English slang word, 'duff', which meant to fake old things for new, e.g. clothes, jewellery. A cattle-duffer either stole unbranded cattle (a practice referred to as 'poddy-dodging' when calves were involved) and put his own brand on them or changed the brands already there. Livestock-duffing gave rise to an extended vocabulary dealing with the practice, e.g. 'duffing yard', a secluded corral in the bush where stolen cattle were yarded and branded; and 'plant', the secluded spot itself, where the cattle were hidden. The practice of duffing was especially rife in squatting times before the use of fencing wire; it is often mentioned in nineteenth-century Australian fiction, e.g. in Alexander Harris's *The Emigrant Family* (1849) and 'Rolf Boldrewood's' *Robbery Under Arms* (1888), the latter using the famous Harry Redford duffing incident in 1870, as well as in later semi-historical writing such as S.H. Roberts's *The Squatting Age in Australia 1835–1847* (1935) and Margaret Kiddle's *Men of Yesterday* (1961). Cattle-duffing has been immortalised in one of Australia's best-known folksongs, 'The Eumerella Shore' (q.v.). The Redford incident and its use by 'Boldrewood' is discussed in P.H. McCarthy's *Starlight: The Man and the Myth* (1972).

DUFFY, Sir Charles Gavan (1816–1903), born Monaghan, Ireland, migrated to Melbourne in 1855 after a stormy political career in Ireland. He was soon involved in colonial politics, where he was active in land reform and was premier of Victoria briefly in 1871. He helped found the Catholic journal the *Advocate* in 1868, having been involved with an earlier Irish Catholic weekly, the *Victorian* (1862–64). After his retirement from politics in 1880 he lived in France. In addition to numerous important works on Irish history, the most popular of which was *Young Ireland* (1880), he wrote *My Life in Two Hemispheres* (1898), which includes a record of his activities in Victoria. He was knighted in 1873 and made KCMG in 1877. Leon O'Broin wrote *Charles Gavan Duffy, Patriot and Statesman* (1967). Members of Sir Charles Gavan Duffy's family, e.g. his son, Sir Frank Gavan Duffy (1852–1936) and his grandson, Sir Charles Leonard Gavan Duffy (1882–1961), achieved distinction in Australian legal and political life. Duffy appears briefly as Dempsey in Henry Kingsley's novel *The Hillyars and the Burtons* (1865).

DUGAN, Michael Gray (1947–), born Melbourne, has been involved with books and writing all his adult life, editing the *Australian School Librarian* (1968–69) and acting as consultant to Jacaranda Press and Oldmeadow Booksellers in the 1970s during which he edited the *Australian Library News* and was founder and co-editor of *Bookmark*. Latterly consultant to Penguin Books and the Australian Institute of Multicultural Affairs, of which he was publications editor 1983–86, he now writes full-time. He was closely associated with the rise of the 'New Australian Poetry' (q.v.), produced the small magazine *Crosscurrents*, was involved in Contempa (q.v.) Publications with Robert Kenny and Phillip Edmonds, and edited *The Drunken Tram: Six Young Melbourne Poets* (1972) and, with John Jenkins, *The Outback Reader* (1975), a collection of contemporary and experimental short fiction. He has written and edited numerous children's books, has been the children's book reviewer for the *Age*, and editor of the children's magazine *Puffinalia*. He has contributed to and edited many children's books, both fictional and factual, several plays and numerous radio scripts. Among his many publications are *Missing People* (1970), *Clouds* (1975), *Nonsense Places* (1976), *Dragon's Breath* (1978), *Dingo Boy* (1980), *Melissa's Ghost* (1986), *The Maltese Connection* (1988), *The Highjacked Bathtub* (1988) and *The Wombats' Party* (1990).

DUGDALE, Joan (1943–), born Orkney Islands, has been a producer for ABC radio and information officer with the Australian Council of Churches and is now a full-time writer. Her two well-regarded novels are *Struggle of Memory* (1991) and *The Gripping Beast* (1993). Fiction based on fact, *Struggle of Memory* is the story of Otto Gluck, German-born but naturalised Australian, who married an Australian girl, Miriam, and had three Australian children before the First World War. Suspected, largely because of an intemperate tongue, of being an active German sympathiser, Gluck was interned in the war, his business taken over and his assets impounded. After the Armistice he was 'denaturalised' (i.e. his Australian citizenship was revoked) and he was deported to Germany, not to be readmitted to Australia until 1926. He committed suicide in 1925. This destruction of an innocent man and his family provides a poignant and absorbing narrative. *The Gripping Beast* is also a story of transformation. Ursula Kenning, senior Australian public servant, widowed, 50, and on the point of mental breakdown, travels to Norway, then to the Orkney Islands and on to the English Lake District, recovering her family ancestry. By contrast with Alex Miller's *The Ancestor Game* (qq.v.), where ancestry is rejected by most of the characters, Ursula benefits greatly from the rediscovery of her heritage. Joan Dugdale has also written *Radio Power: A History of 3ZZ* (1979) and *City Bitten Country Shy* (1989).

DUGGAN, Edmund (?1862–1938), born County Waterford, Ireland, came to Australia as a child and became a professional actor in his early twenties. He was known as a comedian but is more significant for his stage adaptation in 1891 of *For the Term of His Natural Life* and for his collaborations, sometimes under the joint pseudonym of 'Albert Edmunds', with Bert Bailey (q.v.). Their successes included 'The Squatter's Daughter' (1907), 'The Man from Out Back' (1909), 'On Our Selection' (q.v., 1912) and 'The Native Born' (1913). Duggan's work on his own account included 'The Democrat' (1891), a Eureka play later staged as 'Eureka Stockade' (1897), and 'My Mate' (1911), in which there are excerpts from the writings of Adam Lindsay Gordon. He also played Dad in a stage version of *The Rudd Family* in 1928. Hilda Bridges's novel *The Squatter's Daughter* (1922) is based on Duggan and Bailey's play.

DUGGAN, Laurie (1949–), born South Melbourne, graduated from Monash University, lectured at Swinburne College (1976) and Canberra College of Advanced Education (1983) and was art critic for the *Times on Sunday* (1986–87). He went on the Australia Council and Department of Foreign Affairs reading tour of the USA in 1987 and spent a year (1990) at the Australian Centre of the University of Melbourne. He has written film scripts but his chief publications have been poetry: *East: Poems 1970–1974* (1976) which won the Anne Elder Poetry Award, the title poem 'East' having won the Poetry Society of Australia Award in 1971; *Under the Weather* (1978); *Adventures in Paradise* (1982); *The Great Divide* (1985); *The Ash Range* (1987); *The Epigrams of Martial* (1989, winner of the Wesley Michel Prize); *All Blues* (1989, a pamphlet of poems published in London) and *Blue Notes* (1990), which contains some of the poems from *All Blues*. *The Ash Range* won the 1988 Victorian Premier's Award; a historical anthology celebrating Gippsland, the home of Duggan's forebears, it gathers together in a poetry/prose schema many documents such as diaries, letters, maps, journal extracts, newspaper clippings and articles containing the history and legendry of Gippsland. *Blue Notes*, Duggan's latest poetry collection, contains four sections, 'All Blues', 'Trans-Europe Express', 'Dogs' and 'More Blues', all widely varied in form and theme. There are also translations of the Italian Futurist poets and a concluding nine-part poem, 'The Front', which deals in part with the art of making poetry or music in the face of 'prevailing imagery'. In earlier days Duggan was associated with the magazines *New Poetry*, *Surfers Paradise* and *Three Blind Mice*, and confesses that it was the Ern Malley poems

which initiated him into the excitement of post-modernism. In 1994 he was appointed poetry editor of *Meanjin*.

DUGON, Nora (1925–), born Northern Ireland, came to Australia in the 1930s. She has written numerous plays for stage and radio, sometimes writing for the latter under the name of Nora Shaw. Her plays include *Can't You Hear Me Talking to You?* in the collection of that title edited by Alrene Sykes (1978), *The Waiting Room* in *Malice Menace and Malevolence, 3 Sinister One-Act Plays* (1984), 'Memories of an Irish Childhood', and *What's it Like to be Living?*, the latter in *Five Warana One-Act Winners* (1984). She has also contributed short stories to anthologies and magazines and has written two novels, *Lonely Summers* (1988) and *Clare Street* (1990).

DUKE, Jas. H. (James Hercot) (1939–92), born Ballarat, where his father was a teacher, became a laboratory assistant for the Department of Supply, then was a technical officer at the Melbourne and Metropolitan Board of Works. Such seemingly conservative occupations belied the real Jas. H. Duke, who left Australia in revolt against the Vietnam War (living in Brighton, England 1970–72) and, radically oriented through his Irish ancestry, kept up, on his return, a constant barrage of criticism in his writing against governments and governmental institutions, greedy and corrupt professionals and an uncaring society. A cult figure in the performance poetry milieu, Duke, beefy, bald and bearded, began, as he said, as 'a timid person with a stutter', but was converted by his anger and indignation into 'a bellowing bull, noted for my vehemence and intensity'. An ardent advocate of a change of direction for Australian poetry in the late 1960s poetry revolution, Duke published the best of his own poetry in *Poems of War and Peace* (1987), an impressive if esoteric work which, in mostly anecdotal verse, examines aspects of the Second World War and the shortcomings of contemporary society. It also contains a section of 'Concrete' (q.v.) poems, another of translations, and some extracts from *Destiny Wood*, a novel which Duke wrote in England but did not publish until 1978 in Australia. *Destiny Wood*, a deliberate concoction of fantasy and realism, is loosely based on the adventures of its central character, Jim Arch. Published in a limited edition of 250 copies, *Destiny Wood* has attracted little critical attention. After his accidental death in 1992 a CD of Duke in performance poetry mode (claimed to be Australia's first poetry CD) was launched by fellow poet Alan Wearne, who balances one picture of Duke, as mad scientist and way-out poet, with his assessment as 'learned, committed and passionate'.

DUNCAN, Catherine (1915–), born Launceston, Tasmania, was a well-known stage and radio actor of the 1930s and 1940s, as well as a playwright. She later worked as a film-maker and in 1945 joined the Australian National Film Board. Her plays include 'The Sword Sung', winner of the Sydney New Theatre League competition in 1937; *Sons of the Morning* (1946), which won the 1945 Playwrights' Advisory

Board competition; *Some New Moon* (1961) in the Derwent series of one-act plays which she edited; and 'We the Living'. She also wrote, for radio, her verse play *Path of the Eagle*, which is included in *Australian Radio Plays* (1946, ed. Leslie Rees), winning an ABC award in 1943.

DUNCAN, W.A. (William Augustine) (1811–85), born Aberdeenshire, Scotland, was a bookseller and publisher in Aberdeen before emigrating to NSW in 1837. In 1839 he founded the Catholic newspaper the *Australasian* (later *Sydney*) *Chronicle*, and after losing control of it established *Duncan's Weekly Register* (1843–45); Charles Harpur and Henry Parkes contributed to both journals and Duncan published Harpur's first major collection, *Thoughts, A Series of Sonnets* (1845). In 1846 Duncan became a public servant, working in the customs service in Moreton Bay, 1846–59 and Sydney, 1859–81. He wrote a number of pamphlets and other works on religion, education, politics and history.

Dunciad Minor, a lengthy, mock-heroic satire in the eighteenth-century manner by A.D. Hope (q.v.) published in 1970, is based on an earlier, mainly unpublished work of 1950 titled 'Dunciad Minimus'. In 1950 when both Hope and A.A. Phillips took part in a series of radio broadcasts titled 'Standard Works I'd Like to Burn', Phillips's denunciation of Alexander Pope presented Hope with an ideal opportunity to write a modern *Dunciad*. Arthur Phillips, presented by Hope as descended from the infamous Ambrose Philips, is only nominally the butt of the satire, the main brunt of which is borne by modern literary criticism in general. Witty and lively and equipped with the required superstructure of footnotes, the poem is both an amusing *jeu d'esprit* and a serious criticism of academic pedantry. In 1978 Hope and Phillips became joint patrons of the Association for the Study of Australian Literature.

DUNDERDALE, George (1822–1903), born Lancashire, England, worked as a school-teacher in the USA before joining the gold rush to Australia in 1853. He was later a clerk of courts and a customs officer in the Victorian Western District and Gippsland. His experiences of early colonial life, especially in Gippsland, are related in *The Book of the Bush* (q.v., 1898). He also wrote *Prairie and Bush* (1891), the title reflecting his interest in the two continents North America and Australia.

DUNLOP, Eliza Hamilton (1796–1880), born County Armagh, Ireland, arrived in Australia in 1823 accompanied by four of her children and her second husband, David Dunlop, who was police magistrate and protector of the Aborigines at Wollombi and Macdonald River until 1847. A literary figure of considerable standing in her period, Eliza Dunlop had previously published poetry in Irish newspapers such as the *Dublin Penny Journal* and in Australia published lyrics in such newspapers as the *Australian*, the *Sydney Gazette*, the *Sydney Morning Herald*, the *Sydney Stan-*

dard, the *Atlas* and the *Maitland Mercury*; some were collected and titled 'The Vase', a manuscript which remains unpublished. Sympathetic to the plight of the Aborigines and interested in their culture, Dunlop was the first Australian poet to attempt transliterations of Aboriginal songs and poetry, and she carried out valuable research into Aboriginal languages. Her best-known poem is 'The Aboriginal Mother', a response to the Myall Creek massacre, which was first published in the *Australian* on 13 December 1838 and is one of several which were set to music by Isaac Nathan. It is reprinted in a selection of her poetry titled *The Aboriginal Mother and Other Poems* (1981).

DUNN, Max (1895–1963), born Dublin and educated in Scotland, France and America, came to Australia in 1924, having served in the First World War. An impressive intellectual with a somewhat obscure background, Dunn played numerous roles in the Melbourne scene in the years before and during the Second World War. He was a psychotherapist, a journalist with the *Argus*, *Smith's Weekly* and other papers and magazines, a publisher and a poet. His books of poetry include *Random Elements* (1943), *No Asterisks* (1944), *Time of Arrival* (1947), *Portrait of a Country* (1951), *The Journey of Diornos* (1953) and *The Mirror and the Rose* (1954). The poem 'The Journey of John Donne', which had appeared in *Time of Arrival*, was republished in 1952. A collection of his translations from the Chinese, *The City of Wide Streets by the Friendly River: Leaves of Jade: Poems from Dragon Land*, was also published in 1952. The best of his poetry is in *Portrait of a Country* and *The Mirror and the Rose*. The former, which reflects Dunn's views of the Australian environment, has been described as a kind of Australian *Waste Land*; the latter is a collection of eleven poems ('Reflections'), concerned with love, life and death, the rose and the mirror being the key symbols. His work is represented in the anthology *Eight by Eight* (1963). In 1955 Dunn became a Buddhist priest; he celebrated his ordination with the publication of the booklet *Into the Radiance*, which consisted of one short poem, one line of which was printed on each page of the booklet.

DUNSTAN, Keith (1925–), born Melbourne, served in the RAAF before becoming a journalist in 1946; a columnist with the *Courier-Mail* in Brisbane 1954–58 and the *Sun News-Pictorial* in Melbourne 1958–84, he began to write for the *Age* and the *Sydney Morning Herald* in 1985; he has also worked as a correspondent in London, New York and on the west coast of the USA. Dunstan has written numerous books including *Supporting a Column* (1966), which amusingly reflects on his life as a daily columnist; *No Brains at All* (1990), an autobiography which takes its title from a kindly comment by his former science teacher; *No Brains on Tuesday* (1991), a collection of his articles for the *Age* and the *Sydney Morning Herald*; and *A Day in the Life of Australia* (1989), a bicentennial publication which draws together the events on key days throughout the 200 years of Australia's European history. Dunstan's reputation as a witty and perceptive analyst of Australian life has been extended by such books as *Wowsers* (1968) and *Knockers* (1972, an updated edition 1992), which are accounts of those traditions in Australia; *Sports* (1973), which discusses the sporting obsessions of Australians; *Ratbags* (1979), which chronicles the careers of two dozen Australian eccentrics including Barry Humphries, E.W. Cole, H.D. McIntosh and Xavier Herbert; and *Saint Ned* (1980), a contribution to the literature of the Ned Kelly centenary.

DURACK, Dame Mary (1913–), of the pastoralist Durack family (see *Kings in Grass Castles*), was born in Adelaide and spent her very early life in the Kimberley region of WA. She was educated in Perth, then returned to the Kimberleys where she and her younger sister Elizabeth (1915–) helped to run the family company properties during the 1930s Depression. The sisters collaborated in publishing *All-About: The Story of a Black Community on Argyle Station, Kimberley* (1935), Mary supplying the text and Elizabeth the illustrations. Mary and Elizabeth produced a number of books for children: *Chunuma* (1936), *Son of Djaro* (1940), *The Way of the Whirlwind* (1941), *The Magic Trumpet* (1946), *Kookanoo & Kangaroo* (1963) and *To Ride a Fine Horse* (1963). Mary was on the staff of WA Newspapers Ltd 1937–38, where as the columnist 'Virgilia' she wrote for country women and children. Since 1938 she has been a prolific freelance writer. Her most significant literary works are the novel *Keep Him My Country* (q.v., 1950), the story of an idyllic relationship between White station-owner Stan Rolt and native girl Dalgerie, which brings Rolt into a spiritual union with the land itself; *Kings in Grass Castles* (1959), which traces the saga of the Durack family from their emigration from Ireland in the middle of the nineteenth century to the death of Mary's grandfather, the legendary pastoralist Patsy Durack, in 1898; and *Sons in the Saddle* (1983), the sequel to *Kings in Grass Castles*, which continues the Durack family saga through to the time of her father, Michael ('MP') Durack. Mary Durack's other writings include further children's books, e.g. *The Courteous Savage: Yagan of Swan River* (1964), *An Australian Settler* (1964, in Australia titled *A Pastoral Emigrant*), *The Ship of Dreams* (1968, a two-act play) and *Tjakamarra: Boy Between Two Worlds* (1977). Her other historical writings include *The Rock and the Sand* (1969), which deals with missionary activities in WA; *Swan River Saga* (1975), a play about the experiences of pioneer WA woman Eliza Shaw; *To Be Heirs Forever* (1976), Eliza Shaw's biography; and *The Aborigines in Australian Literature* (1978). She co-authored *The Land Beyond Time* (1984) and *The Stockman* (1984). In recognition of her achievements Mary Durack was made OBE in 1966, DBE in 1978 and AC. She was awarded an honorary D.Litt. from the University of WA in 1978. She is a foundation fellow of Curtin University in WA and is presently an emeritus fellow of the Literature Board of the Australia Council. Elizabeth Durack CMG, internationally recognised for her artistic representation of the WA outback and its Aboriginal

people, is the subject of *The Art of Elizabeth Durack* (1981) with introduction by Patrick Hutchings.

Dusty, a novel by Frank Dalby Davison (q.v.), first published in 1946 and winner of the *Argus* novel competition, is second only to his *Man-Shy* in popularity. The main protagonist is a half-breed dog, offspring of a wild dingo bitch and a red kelpie working dog. The dog's divided personality, reflected in his response to the call of the wild coupled with his yearning for the quiet domestic life of the farm, creates tensions that finally destroy him. No simple animal story, the novel has human relevance, illustrating the unity of all nature in cyclical change and the universal tension between conformism and rebellion. An Australian film, *Dusty*, was screened in 1983.

DUTTON, Geoffrey (1922–), was born at Kapunda, SA, where his great-granduncle founded that State's first stud sheep station in 1838. He was educated at the University of Adelaide before enlisting in the RAAF in 1941 as a flying instructor. During the 1940s Dutton was associated with the *Angry Penguins* (q.v.) group. Close friends included the poets Donald Kerr, Paul Pfeiffer, Max Harris and Alister Kershaw, and the painters Arthur Boyd and Sidney Nolan. The cover of his first book of poetry was designed by Sidney Nolan and he has continued to work closely with artists. He studied at Oxford 1946–49. After spending the early 1950s travelling extensively, he lectured in English at the University of Adelaide 1955–62. He was editor of Penguin Australia 1961–65 and in 1965 founded, with Brian Stonier, the paperback publishing firm Sun Books. He was joint founder and editor of the periodicals *Australian Letters* and *Australian Book Review*; was one of the editors of the annual poetry anthology *Verse in Australia* (1958–61); edited the *Australian Writers and Their Work* series 1962–66; and the *Bulletin*'s quarterly literary supplement 1980–85. Active in the Australian Council for the Arts 1968–70, and in other cultural organisations, he was made AO in 1976.

A versatile writer, Dutton has published nine collections of verse, *Night Flight and Sunrise* (1944), *Antipodes in Shoes* (1958), which was awarded the Grace Leven Prize, *Flowers and Fury* (1962), *Poems Soft and Loud* (1967), *Findings and Keepings* (1970), which is mainly a substantial collection from the preceding volumes, *New Poems to 1972* (1972), *A Body of Words* (1977), *Selective Affinities* (1985) and *New and Selected Poems* (1993); five novels, *The Mortal and the Marble* (1950), *Andy* (1968), *Tamara* (1970), *Queen Emma of the South Seas* (1976) and *Flying Low* (1992); a collection of short stories, *The Wedge-Tailed Eagle* (1980); two critical studies, *Patrick White* (1961) and *Walt Whitman* (1961); a full-length biography of Kenneth Slessor (1991); three substantial historical biographies, *Founder of a City* (1960), *The Hero as Murderer: The Life of Edward John Eyre* (1967) and *Australia's Last Explorer: Ernest Giles* (1970); several works of art appreciation, *The Paintings of S.T. Gill* (1962), *Russell Drysdale* (1964) and *White on Black* (1974, winner of the L.C. Weickhardt prize in 1978); two books of art and literary history,

The Innovators (1986) and *Snow on the Saltbush* (1984); three travel books, *A Long Way South* (1953), *Africa in Black and White* (1956) and *States of the Union* (1958); three novels for children, *Seal Bay* (1966), *Tisi and the Yabby* (1965) and *Tisi and the Pageant* (1968); and a book of verse for young people, *On My Island* (1967). His work as an editor has been equally varied and includes the influential collection of critical essays *The Literature of Australia* (1964, 2nd edn 1976); two anthologies of verse, *Australian Poetry 1962* (1962) and *Australian Verse from 1805* (1975), and two of verse and prose, *Modern Australian Writing* (1966) and, with Max Harris, *The Vital Decade* (1968); two collections of essays on republicanism, *Australia and the Monarchy* (1966) and *Republican Australia?* (1977), and one on censorship in Australia (1970); a collection of photographs 1901–14 in the *Australia Since the Camera* series; an edition of Havelock Ellis's *Kanga Creek* (1989); a selection of Henry Lawson's writing, *The Picador Henry Lawson* (1991); and a selection of autobiographical accounts of rural childhoods, *Country Childhoods* (1992). He has also written numerous uncollected critical essays, articles and reviews and published translations of the Russian poets Yevgeny Yevtushenko and Bella Akhmadulina. His less ambitious publications include several 'coffee-table' books of which the most significant are *A Taste of History* (1978) and *Patterns of Australia* (1980).

Dutton's early poetry, self-consciously modernist and experimental, has given way to an easy reflective lyricism marked by a strong visual element. He has written some topical and satiric poems but his most characteristic are those celebrating the joys of love, the beauties of the natural scene or the pleasures of friendship. Some of his best work is found in his more sustained autobiographical poems such as 'The Smallest Sprout' and 'Abandoned Airstrip, Northern Territory', where the tone is part-elegiac and part-humorous. An urbane and uninhibited prose writer, Dutton is a versatile novelist. *The Mortal and the Marble*, an Anglo-Australian novel, is partly the story of a young marriage and partly a study of national differences. *Andy* is a lively, picaresque tale of a wartime flying instructor; *Tamara* is a deeply felt love story set mainly in Russia; *Queen Emma of the South Seas* is an exotic, historical tale based on the life of an extraordinary Samoan-American woman who built a vast trading empire in the Pacific. *Flying Low* is a revised version of *Andy*, deleting some characters and episodes, adding others and providing a different ending.

DWIGHT, Henry Tolman (?1823–71), born London, migrated to Melbourne in 1855 with a large stock of second-hand books which enabled him to open a bookshop in 1857 in Bourke Street of that city. By 1862 his stock had grown to 60 000 volumes. Dwight's shop became a regular meeting-place of the Melbourne literary coterie that included Adam Lindsay Gordon, Henry Kendall, Marcus Clarke, George Gordon McCrae and R.H. Horne. Dwight published works by Horne, McCrae, Thomas McCombie and

others. Ian McLaren compiled the bibliography *Henry Tolman Dwight: Bookseller and Publisher* (1989).

DWYER, J.F. (James Francis) (1874–1952), born Camden Park, NSW, became a contributor of verse and short fiction to the *Bulletin* under J.F. Archibald while serving a prison sentence 1899–1902. He left Australia in 1906 and became a prolific short-story writer and novelist in the USA and France. Of his ten novels, most of which are tales of mystery and adventure, *The White Waterfall* (1912) and *O Splendid Sorcery* (1930) have some connection with Australia. He also published a collection of short stories, *Breath of the Jungle* (1915), and an autobiographical work, *Leg Irons on Wings* (1949).

'Dying Stockman, The' is a lugubrious Australian folk-song which chronicles the last wishes of a stockman as he lies dying, his head supported by a saddle. His requests, communicated to his two mates, begin with the words of the chorus:

> Wrap me up with my stockwhip and blanket,
> And bury me deep down below,
> Where the dingoes and crows can't molest me,
> In the shade where the coolibahs grow.

The song was included as an anonymous composition in A.B. Paterson's pioneering collection, *Old Bush Songs* (1905), but claims have been made (*Australian Tradition*, September 1968) for Horace Alfred Flower's authorship while he was a bank manager in Queensland in 1892. More certainly the song derives, as Hugh Anderson has explained in *The Dying Stockman* (1954), from the English sentimental song 'The Tarpaulin Jacket'; Anderson traces parallels between 'The Tarpaulin Jacket' and an earlier English song, 'Rosin the Beau', although American melodies have also been associated with 'The Dying Stockman'. The popularity of 'The Dying Stockman' is attested to by the many close parallels and parodies about dying shearers, bagmen, aviators, gunners, bargehands, fettlers and so on. Part of the reason for its popularity may well lie in its parallels with Adam Lindsay Gordon's earlier literary ballad 'The Sick Stockrider', although it is also one of the relatively few traditional Australian songs given currency in the twentieth century by hillbilly singers such as Tex Morton. More recently, Rolf Harris's popular song 'Tie Me Kangaroo Down, Sport', clearly belongs to the 'Dying Stockman' tradition, despite the unsentimental response to the last request of Harris's stockman:

> 'Tan me hide when I'm dead, Fred,
> Tan me hide when I'm dead;'
> So we tanned his hide when he died, Clyde,
> And that's it hangin' in the shed!

DYMOCK, William (1861–1900), born North Melbourne, came to Sydney as a boy and began in the book trade in 1878 working for, among others, George Robertson (1) (q.v.). In the early 1880s he established his own bookshop, known as Dymock's Book Arcade by 1884 when situated in Pitt Street, Sydney. In 1890 he moved to 428 George Street, where the business still operates. In 1896 he took over William Maddock's circulating library with Maddock as manager and advertised his shop as 'the largest Book shop in the world', with more than a million books. A bookseller rather than a publisher, William Dymock was the first native-born Australian to launch and maintain a successful bookselling venture. He is among the personalities discussed in George Ferguson's *Some Early Australian Bookmen* (1978).

DYSON, Ambrose Arthur, see DYSON, Will

DYSON, Edward

DYSON, Edward (1865–1931) was born at Morrison near Ballarat, Victoria, son of a mining engineer. He moved with his family about the goldfields during childhood and grew up familiar with life both in the bush and on the diggings. In adolescence he worked in odd jobs about the Victorian mines, then was a miner in Tasmania and a factory worker in Melbourne before turning to journalism and freelance writing. Throughout a long career as a writer he contributed short stories and novels of bush life, the diggings and the *Bulletin*, the *Age* and *Melbourne Punch* under a variety of pseudonyms. His *métier* was the short story, his novels being little more than a series of simply connected sequential events. His best-known story, a classic among Australian goldfields tales, was 'A Golden Shanty' (q.v.). In the *Fact'ry 'Ands* (1906) stories he departs from the traditional 'slum' literature portrayal of human misery to emphasise the bizarre and comic side of slum life. His large output of fiction included the short-story collections *Below and On Top* (1898), *Benno and Some of the Push* (1911) and *Spats' Fact'ry* (1914), and the novels *The Gold-Stealers: A Story of Waddy* (1901) and *In the Roaring Fifties* (1906). Dyson's collection of verse, *Rhymes from the Mines and Other Lines* (1896), although very much the balladist's usual concoction of irony and humour, pathos and comedy, is singular in that it reflects the life and environment of the underground miner.

DYSON, Will (1880–1938), born Alfredton near Ballarat, Victoria, was a younger brother of the writer Edward Dyson (q.v.). In 1903 he became a caricaturist with the Adelaide *Critic* and in 1906 illustrated his brother's book of stories *Fact'ry 'Ands*. In 1908 he drew coloured cartoons for the covers of Randolph Bedford's journal *Clarion*. In 1912 he was appointed chief cartoonist of the *Daily Herald* in London and became extremely popular through his championing of the working man and his satirical tilts at pomposity and greed. His most famous cartoon depicted Woodrow Wilson, Lloyd George and Orlando of Italy leaving the Versailles peace treaty in a self-congratulatory mood while in the background was a child (labelled '1940 Class') weeping. By 1925 Dyson was back in Australia, his cartoons appearing in the Melbourne *Herald*, *Punch* and *Table Talk*. On the termination of his contract with the *Herald* he returned to England, where he died while working again for the *Daily Herald*. Australia's most trenchant satirical cartoonist, Dyson published *Cartoons* (1914), *Kultur Cartoons* (1915) and a volume, *Australia at War*, the last from his work as an Australian official war artist (he was twice wounded) in the First World War. He also published a small volume, *Poems: In Memory of a Wife* (1919), after his wife, Ruby, sister of Norman Lindsay and a talented black-and-white artist, died in the influenza epidemic of 1919. In 1933 he published *Artist among the Bankers*, a hostile commentary on the commercial world. Will Dyson's elder brother, Ambrose Arthur Dyson (1876–1913), a cartoonist for the Adelaide *Critic* 1898–1903, was similarly employed on the *Bulletin* 1903–6, and contributed drawings to numerous other newspapers and journals including the *Gadfly*, the *Clarion*, *Table Talk* and the Sydney *Worker*. Ambrose is credited with the first artistic portrayal of the Australian larrikin. Ross McMullin wrote *Will Dyson: Cartoonist, Etcher and Australia's Finest War Artist* (1984).

E

EAGLE, Chester (1933–), born Bendigo, grew up on a Riverina sheep property and was educated at Melbourne Grammar and at the University of Melbourne. He has worked as a teacher and administrator in technical and further education institutions in Victoria. He has written five novels, *Who Could Love the Nightingale?* (1973), *Four Faces, Wobbly Mirror* (1976), *At the Window* (1984), *The Garden Gate* (1984) and *Victoria Challis* (1991); two volumes of autobiography, *Mapping the Paddocks* (1985), which won the *Age* Book of the Year Award for non-fiction in 1985, and *Play Together, Dark Blue Twenty* (1986); and 'an evocation of Gippsland', where he lived for twelve years, *Hail and Farewell!* (1971), reissued as *House of Trees* in 1987. *Mapping the Paddocks* is an elegiac description of a rural boyhood in a period and a family of firm values, changed for ever by the event of Hiroshima which closes the book; mapping the paddocks refers to Eagle's childhood attempt to discover a pattern in the movements of sheep across a field, an activity which he reproduces in his narrative's movement through time and space in search of meaning. *Play Together, Dark Blue Twenty* re-creates his experiences at Melbourne Grammar from 1946 to 1951, exploring in retrospect the school's ideology of elitism; as *Hail and Farewell!* demonstrated, Eagle is particularly gifted in evoking a sense of place, and in this autobiography it is the claustrophobic, forcing system of a public school for boys which emerges with convincing power. Eagle's novels, mainly cerebral love stories, have been less well received than his autobiographies and his regional study.

Ear in a Wheatfield, a poetry magazine edited by Kris Hemensley (q.v.) 1972–76, began as an extension of *Earth Ship*, a small literary journal that Hemensley had produced in England in 1970–72. It was succeeded by *The Merri Creek, or Nero* (1977–), a section of which was entitled 'H/Ear'.

'EAST, Michael', see **WEST, Morris**

Echo, see **FAIRFAX, John**

EDEN, Charles Henry (1839–1900), born England, came to Moreton Bay in 1863 and tried various occupations, including digging for gold, before being appointed a police magistrate and sub-collector of customs in 1868. He was dismissed from those posts in 1870 and returned to England where he later wrote sixteen novels and numerous travel books; two of the latter, *Australia's Heroes* (1875) and *The Fifth Continent* (1877), relate to Australia. His chief Australian work

was the autobiographical *My Wife and I in Queensland* (1872), a disenchanted and highly coloured account of his altogether undistinguished Australian experience.

EDEN, Guy E. Morton (?1864–1954), elder son of Charles Henry Eden (q.v.), wrote numerous works of fiction of which *The Cry of the Curlew: A Yarn of the Bush* (1892) and *He Went Out with the Tide* (1896) are set in Australia. He also wrote *Bush Ballads and Other Verses* (1907).

EDGAR, Suzanne (1939–), born Adelaide, graduated from the University of Adelaide and in 1963 moved to Canberra, where she has worked in adult education, as a teacher of women's studies at the ANU and, since 1976, as an editor at the *Australian Dictionary of Biography*. One of the seven contributors to the short-story collection *Canberra Tales* (1988), she has published a collection of her stories, some of which appeared previously in newspapers and journals, *Counting Backwards* (1991).

EDMOND, James (1859–1933), born Glasgow, Scotland, migrated in 1878 to NZ and to Australia in 1884. While on the staff of the Rockhampton *Morning Bulletin* he contributed financial comments to the Sydney *Bulletin* and in 1886 joined the latter, becoming associate editor in 1890, financial editor in 1892, and initiator of the well-known 'Wild Cat' column dealing with financial matters. He also contributed short stories, sketches, dramatic criticism and a column, titled 'The Brickbat'; his pseudonym for some of this writing was 'Titus Salt'. He was editor 1903–14; under his influence the *Bulletin* retained and even expanded its nationalistic outlook but dropped much of its earlier republican emphasis. Edmond exercised some influence on the shaping of the Australian constitution and Australian federal politics through his *Bulletin* editorials advocating protectionism, immigration control and centralist control of education and transport. His *Bulletin* leaders were published as *A Policy for the Commonwealth* (1900) and some of his humorous writings were collected as *A Journalist and Two Bears* (1913), illustrated by Norman Lindsay.

EDMONDS, Phillip (1949–), born Epping, Sydney, was educated in Melbourne, attending Monash University. Edmonds was deeply involved in the rise of the New Australian Poetry (q.v.), editing the magazine *Contempa* and publishing contemporary poetry through Contempa Publications. Edmonds has taught creative writing and is a freelance journalist, writer and historian. He has published several books of short fiction – *Big Boys* (1978), *Everybody used to Know Each Other* (1987), *Locals* (1989) and *Don't Let Me Fall* (1991). Most of the stories are vignettes, characters caught and impaled on words as revealing as 'still' camera shots; events are merely glanced at, hinted at, while their effect on the people caught in them is captured in precise and definitive language. Many of the excerpts, especially in *Don't Let Me Fall*, reveal more about the author than the events they relate.

'EDMUNDS, Albert', see **DUGGAN, Edmund**

Education of Young Donald, The, an autobiography by Donald Horne (q.v.), was published in 1967. The first section, titled 'Primary, 1927–1933', deals with his early life in Muswellbrook, a small town in NSW, and compellingly evokes the general flavour of Australian life between the wars. Horne records the town's clearly defined social system, ranging from the 'Old Families' to the scroungers and outcasts, and his own family's niche in the lower-middle ranks (his father was a schoolteacher). Also memorable are his descriptions of the town's religious divisions and varied social activities which engaged everyone in a 'demanding bustle of pleasure'. Nostalgic descriptions of frequent visits to Sydney, where his maternal grandparents lived, heighten the impression of a golden age. In the second section, titled 'Secondary, 1934–1938', which deals with his experiences at high school and the family's move to Sydney, the mood darkens. In the city the family lives in a withdrawn way, threatened by the father's growing mental disorder which culminates in a breakdown. Horne, unable to identify himself with his family, school or suburb, takes refuge partly in fantasy and partly in his intellectual growth. The last section, titled 'Tertiary, 1939–1941', covers Horne's experiences at the University of Sydney and his association with such figures as John Anderson, A.D. Hope, James McAuley, Oliver Somerville, Harold Stewart and Ronald Dunlop. This section is both an effective realisation of an important intellectual milieu and a frank study of a young man's reaction to heady new influences.

EDWARDS, Don (1905–63), born Sydney, became a teacher and from 1945 was also literary critic for the *Sydney Morning Herald*. He published a book of short stories, *High Hill at Midnight* (1944), with recurring themes of marital problems and unemployment during the 1930s depression. His novel *The Woman at Jingera* (1948) is an expansion of his short story 'The Woman from the Bend', about the narrator's fascination with a strange woman of the bush.

EDWARDS, George (1886–1953), born Harold Parks, SA, had a career as a comic actor and dancer in vaudeville and films before moving into radio in 1931, when he changed his name. For two decades he dominated the production of comic and dramatic serials, which were popular on commercial radio during that period. Perhaps the best known was 'Dad and Dave' (q.v.), which ran for over 2000 episodes 1937–51 and

was one of the last metamorphoses of *On Our Selection* (q.v.). *Ralph Rashleigh*, Edwards's last serial (1953), was another work of Australian literature to attract his attention. A man of wide ventriloquial gifts, Edwards played more than six characters in a single scene, sometimes doubling that number in an episode, and was widely known as 'The Man with a Thousand Voices'. His fourth and last wife was Coral Lansbury (q.v.).

EDWARDS, Hugh (1933–), born Perth and educated in Victoria, was a journalist with the *West Australian* 1953–68 and has since been a full-time writer. His best-known books are those dealing with wrecks of Dutch ships off the Australian coast, e.g. the *Batavia* (q.v.), the *Zeewyk* and the *Gilt Dragon*. His *Islands of Angry Ghosts* (1966) is an important addition to the large body of literature about the ill-fated *Batavia*; *The Wreck on the Half-Moon Reef* (1970) is the story of the *Zeewyk*, wrecked in 1727. A skilled diver, Edwards carried out much of the hazardous exploratory work for both books. His interest in wrecks led to the compilation of *Australian and New Zealand Shipwrecks and Sea Tragedies* (1978); his interest in sharks to the editing of *Sharks and Shipwrecks* (1975), a collection of seventeen stories. His other books, including books for adolescents, include *Captain William Bligh R.N.* (1972), *The Triumphs and Tragedies of Pearl Divers of Australia* (1972), *Skin Diving* (1975), *Tiger Shark* (1976), *Sea Lion Island* (1977), *The Pearl Pirates* (1977), *Sim, the Sea Lion* (1981), *The Crocodile God* (1982) and a history of Broome, WA, *Port of Pearls* (1983). With Aboriginal writer Joe Nangan he compiled *Joe Nangan's Dreaming* (1976), a collection of twenty illustrated Aboriginal legends.

EDWARDS, Ron (1930–), born Geelong, Victoria, is an artist, writer and publisher who has been active for many years in the field of Australian folklore. In 1950 he founded the Galley Press, which became the Rams Skull Press in 1952. The Press specialises in books on Australian folklore and published the series *Bandicoot Ballads* (1951–55) and *Black Bull Chapbooks* (1954–57), illustrated by Edwards and including John Manifold and Hugh Anderson as authors. Edwards's major folk-song collections are *The Overlander Songbook* (1971) and *The Big Book of Australian Folk Song* (1976), which both incorporate material published in smaller compilations; his *200 Years of Australian Folk Song* (1988) is an index, by title and first line, to some 2000 folk songs published in eighty-six sources. He has also written or compiled *The Australian Yarn* (1977), *Yarns and Ballads* (1981), *Australian Traditional Bush Crafts* (1975), *Skills of the Australian Bushman* (1979); other publications include sketch-books, some of which reflect his recent interest in Eastern calligraphy, and chapbooks on Australian folklore topics. A bibliography of Ron Edwards is included in *The Rams Skull Press. A Listing of Its Publications Up to This Date* (1991).

EE TIANG, Hong (1933–), born in Malacca of Chinese background, arrived in Australia in 1975 as a political exile and teaches at the WA College of Education. He became an Australian citizen in 1977. One of Malaysia's best-known poets, he has published three collections, *I of the Many Faces* (1960), *Lines Written in Hawaii* (1973) and *Myths for a Wilderness* (1976) and has contributed to anthologies in Australia. With Bruce Bennett and Ron Shepherd he edited the collection of essays, *The Writer's Sense of the Contemporary* (1982).

EGAN, Greg (1961–), born Perth, was educated at the University of WA. He has written numerous short stories, published mainly in England, and two novels, *An Unusual Angle* (1983) and *Quarantine* (1992), both in the genre of speculative fiction.

EGGLESTON, Sir **Frederic** (1875–1954), born Melbourne, trained as a lawyer and combined his legal practice with public work and writing for the local and British press on Australian politics. He served in the First World War before standing for election for the Victorian parliament, and holding several ministerial offices 1924–27. After he left government he wrote prolifically for newspapers, and published a major biography of George Swinburne (1931). In 1933 he was appointed first chairman of the Commonwealth Grants Commission, a position he held until 1941 and which was followed by ambassadorial postings to China and the USA. An innovative thinker, he wrote a bold, theoretical approach to the social sciences, *Search for a Social Philosophy* (1941), a collection of reminiscences, *Reflections of an Australian Liberal* (1952), his only best-selling book, and other works of political analysis, *State Socialism in Victoria* (1932) and *Reflections on Australian Foreign Policy* (1957). Warren G. Osmond, who has written Eggleston's biography (1985), argues that among other achievements Eggleston occupied a strategic position in the history of Australian political beliefs and ideas, generalising and articulating 'what is arguably the core of the Australian political tradition – Deakinite Liberalism'.

1890s, see **'Nineties'**

EIPPER, Chris, (1950–), born Woolooma in the Hunter Valley of NSW, graduated from the University of Sydney with a Ph.D. in anthropology. A senior lecturer at La Trobe University, he has published two books associated with his fieldwork in Ireland, *Ruling Trinity* (1980) and *Hostage to Fortune* (1989), and two works of fiction, *Dieback* and *Shadowing Secrets* (both 1990). *Shadowing Secrets* is a fast-moving and well-written thriller, set in Sydney with a cast of ruthless entrepreneurs, intelligence agents, mercenaries and questioning journalists. *Dieback* is a well-realised if gloomy story of the disintegration of a family and of a way of life, that of a small-time ordinary farming family who grow up, outgrow the farm and go off to seek their separate, inevitably ordinary, destinies, leaving behind the three whom only death will release: the father, who will take as much refuge in alcohol as his ever-diminishing means will allow; the mother, who is facing a bleak future with breast cancer; and the crippled narrator, who will be left to make his own gesture, an attempt to break out of the glass bubble (the louvred sleep-out) in which he has been imprisoned.

Eisenbart, Professor, an enigmatic creation of the poet Gwen Harwood (q.v.), has been interpreted as a 'mask' through which the poet expresses certain anarchic or anti-Establishment views, and as a persona which allows her to reflect ironically on the human condition. Eight Professor Eisenbart poems form the second part of Gwen Harwood's *Poems* (1963), although several of them had appeared earlier in *Meanjin* (1956, 1959). In 'Prize-Giving', the first poem in the series, Eisenbart, an ageing nuclear physicist, attends a girls' school speech night to present the prizes and is there bewitched by a girl pianist with titian hair who plays Mozart with extraordinary passion and skill. The remaining poems, in which she has become his mistress, demonstrate such facets of their relationship as her maturity and wisdom compared with his erratic megalomania and his gradual acquisition, largely through her influence, of self-knowledge.

'Ek Dum', see **ELLIS, M.H.**

ELDER, Anne (1918–76), born Auckland, NZ, lived in Australia from the age of 3. As Anne MacKintosh she was a noted ballet-dancer with the Borovansky Ballet Company. She published her first book of poetry, *For the Record*, in 1972; a second volume, *Crazy Woman and Other Poems*, highly commended in the National Book Council awards for 1977, was published posthumously in 1976. *For the Record* contains some fine individual poems, especially those with deep personal associations for the poet, e.g. 'Midnight', which concerns her mother, and 'Journey to the North', with its immense joy in homecoming after an absence; and the sequence 'Four Elegies for the Death of Women'. A new selection of her work, *Small Clay Birds*, including some previously unpublished poems, was edited by Lynette Wilson in 1988. The Anne Elder Trust Fund Award for poetry is administered by the Victorian branch of FAW and is awarded annually to the best first book of poetry published. First awarded in 1977, it was won by Laurie Duggan for *East* and Graeme Curtis for *At Last No Reply*. The 1978 award went to Lee Cataldi for *Invitation to a Marxist Lesbian Party*; 1979 to Les Harrop for *The Hum of the Old Suit*; 1980 to Richard Lunn for *Pompeii Deep Fry*; 1981 to Jenny Boult for *The Hotel Anonymous* and Gig Ryan for *The Division of Anger*; 1982 to Kate Llewellyn for *Trader Kate and the Elephants* and Peter Goldsworthy for *Reading from Ecclesiastes*; 1983 to David Brooks for *The Cold Front*; 1984 to Doris Brett for *The Truth about Unicorns*; 1985 to Stephen Williams for *A Crowd of Voices*; 1986 to Jan Owen for *Boy with a Telescope*; 1987 to Sarah Day for *A Hunger to be Less Serious*; 1988 to Alex Skovron for *The Rearrangement*; 1989 to Mark Miller for *Conversing with Stones*; 1990 to Jean Kent for *Verandahs*.

ELDERSHAW, Flora (1897–1956), born Sydney and brought up on a sheep station in the Riverina, graduated in 1918 from the University of Sydney, where she met Marjorie Barnard (q.v.). Their collaboration under the pseudonym 'M. Barnard Eldershaw' (q.v.) produced five novels and various other writings. After teaching in Sydney 1921–40 she joined the Department of Reconstruction in Canberra, then transferred to Melbourne in 1943 to the Department of Labour and National Service. In 1948 she entered private practice as an industrial consultant. Active in the Sydney branch of the FAW, she was president in 1935 and 1943. With Frank Dalby Davison she was significant in the expansion of the CLF and was an active member of its Advisory Board 1939–53. She was also a member of the Women's Advisory Council. Some of her most important friendships were with Vance, Nettie and Aileen Palmer, Katharine Susannah Prichard, Frank Dalby Davison and T. Inglis Moore. More active in public life than Barnard, she achieved fewer independent publications. Two of her addresses to the English Association were published in 1931 and 1935; the first, titled *Contemporary Australian Women Writers*, is the more significant. In 1936 she edited the *Australian Writers' Annual* for the FAW and in 1938 *The Peaceful Army* (reprinted in 1988), an anthology of essays and poems by women in honour of Australia's sesquicentenary in which prominent women writers such as Mary Gilmore, Miles Franklin, Eleanor Dark, Kylie Tennant and Helen Simpson are represented. Some of her correspondence with other women writers is contained in the collection *As Good as a Yarn With You*, ed. Carole Ferrier (1992).

'ELDERSHAW, M. Barnard' was the pseudonym adopted by Flora Eldershaw and Marjorie Barnard (qq.v.) for their works of collaboration, published 1929–47. Although it is impossible to assess the relative importance of their contributions, it seems likely that the lion's share of the writing fell to Barnard but that Eldershaw played an important role in the conceptual and shaping stages. The last novel published under the joint pseudonym was *Tomorrow and Tomorrow*. Writings published by 'M. Barnard Eldershaw' are five novels, *A House is Built* (q.v. 1929), *Green Memory* (1931), *The Glasshouse* (1936), *Plaque with Laurel* (1937) and *Tomorrow and Tomorrow* (1947), republished in its full, uncensored version as *Tomorrow and Tomorrow and Tomorrow* in 1983; three histories, *Phillip of Australia* (1938), *The Life and Times of Captain John Piper* (1939) and *My Australia* (1939); and a significant collection of critical essays, *Essays in Australian Fiction* (q.v. 1938). They also wrote several short stories, other general critical and historical essays, a radio drama, *The Watch on the Headland*, published in *Australian Radio Plays* (1946), and edited a collection of short stories, *Coast to Coast 1946* (1947). A collection of the unpublished stories of 'M. Barnard Eldershaw', *But Not For Love*, was published in 1988, edited by Robert Darby.

The novels of the collaboration have met varying receptions. *A House is Built*, a study of one family's fortunes in nineteenth-century Sydney, shared first prize in the 1928 *Bulletin* novel competition. The combination of a well-realised historical background and varied individual characters assured the novel an immediate and lasting popularity in England and Australia. *Green Memory*, also set in nineteenth-century Sydney, has been less popular; with *The Glasshouse* the novelists moved to contemporary times and life aboard an ocean vessel. *Plaque with Laurel*, a more complex novel, has the unusual background of a three-day conference of the Australian Writers' Guild in Canberra.

ELDRIDGE, Marian (1936–), born Victoria, has worked as a teacher at secondary level and in adult education. A contributor to the collection *Canberra Tales* (1988), she has published two collections of her short stories which have appeared in numerous journals and newspapers, *Walking the Dog* (1984) and *The Woman at the Window* (1989), and a novel, *Springfield* (1992). In 1981 she won the *Canberra Times* National Short Story Award. The stories in *Walking the Dog* explore the various ways in which people encounter passion or adjust to changed relationships and feelings; stylish and witty, they deal with the everyday world and belong to a traditional genre of story-telling in their avoidance of post-modernist preoccupations with issues of fictionality. The stories of *The Woman at the Window* concentrate on a range of personalities and regions, although they are uniform in their subtle exploration of human engagements with the challenges of other people and other circumstances. *Springfield* is set in Victorian farming country and focuses on the relationship between two people damaged by life, Gita, who is recovering from a drug dependency, and Angus Springfield, a Vietnam veteran still haunted by the war; delicately crafted, the novel explores the inner lives of the characters with sensitivity and suspense, setting them in a natural landscape which is intimately known and evoked. Eldridge won the 1992 ACT Literary Award ($15 000), enabling her to complete a selection of short stories titled 'The Greening of Alvie Skerritt', Skerritt being a character who had appeared in her earlier collections.

Electrical Experience, The, Frank Moorhouse's (q.v.) third 'discontinuous narrative', was published in 1975 and won the National Book Council Award for fiction for that year. Comprising nineteen stories which are interspersed with more than twenty fragments, *The Electrical Experience* focuses on T. George McDowell, a manufacturer of soft drinks in a NSW south-coast town; most of the stories recount significant moments in his life though not in chronological order. Although McDowell becomes a successful businessman partly because he is able to adapt to change, symbolised by his acceptance of electricity, *The Electrical Experience* establishes the gulf between his generation and that of his unstable daughter, Terri, an important character in *The Americans, Baby* (q.v., 1972). Among the other inhabitants of his town are Irving Bow, the central character in the 'Pacific City' section of *The Everlasting Secret Family and Other Secrets* (q.v. 1980), and Dr Trenbow, the protagonist of the film *Between Wars* (1974). The ironic detachment with which a past ethos is established, partly by the fragments of 1930s folklore and history, is balanced by Moorhouse's sympathy towards and understanding of the central character.

ELISHA, Ron (1951–), born Jerusalem, Israel, came to Melbourne with his family in 1953. He graduated in medicine from the University of Melbourne and has worked as a general practitioner. His earliest play, *In Duty Bound* (1983), was first produced in Melbourne in 1978. Its story of a young Jewish doctor prevented from marrying a Gentile by family opposition, and its criticism of the barriers of racial and religious prejudice aroused considerable controversy, especially in Jewish circles. Elisha's subsequent drama centres on the individual issue of what it is to be Jewish but includes the larger issues of good and evil. *Einstein* (1986), which was first produced in 1981, won Awgies for best stage play and most outstanding script and was taken by the Melbourne Theatre Company on its tour of the USA in 1982; the play takes the form of a debate between three selves of the famous physicist: as 'Professor' at the age of 76 when he faces death, as the middle-aged 'Einstein' after 1919 after his theories were confirmed and he achieved world fame, and as the younger 'Albert', after 1905 and his discovery of the formula $E = MC^2$. Interpreting Einstein as scientific genius, lofty moralist and emotionally inadequate human being and comparing him with another Jewish lawgiver, Moses, Elisha portrays him as finally betrayed and self-betrayed by political exigencies. *Two* (1985), set in 1948 in a cellar in a German town, contains only two characters, Chaim, a rabbi who survived the Holocaust, and Anna, a woman who becomes his student in Hebrew in order to migrate to Israel. Although Anna emerges as an ex-member of the SS, who shares Chaim's Auschwitz past and is related to him as torturer to victim, the play's action demonstrates the inseparable nature of good and evil and humankind's universal dark potential. *The Levine Comedy* (1987) is preoccupied with similar large issues (in this case the destructive effects of misguided hope) but is a more populated play which draws on traditional Jewish humour to disguise its tragedy and attempts to subvert audience apathy by surrealistic effects. *Safe House* (1989) traces the disillusionment of a Russian economist who migrates to a safe new life in Australia in the 1950s but who finds, thirty years later, that he is still an alien. Elisha's most anomalous play to date is *Pax Americana* (1990), a satirical panorama of post-McCarthy America which exposes the defective optimism and false myth-making of public life. *Esterhaz* (1990), set in 1772 in the Austro-Hungarian court of Crown Prince Nicolaus Esterhazy, uses that microcosm and the experience of Haydn to explore the perennial 'normality' of evil. Elisha's unpublished plays include 'Still Life', 'Gropius', 'Pigtails', and 'Ecumenical Gestures'; he has also written for television, radio and film.

Elizabethan Theatre Trust, see **Australian Elizabethan Theatre Trust**

ELKIN, Adolphus Peter (1891–1979), born West Maitland, NSW, was professor of anthropology at the University of Sydney 1934–56. A fellow of the Social Science Research Council of Australia and a member of the Australian Institute of Aboriginal Studies, Elkin was a much-honoured anthropologist, receiving the Royal Society of NSW, James Cook, Mueller and H.E. Gregory medals. He was made CMG in 1966. His publications include *The Australian Aborigines* (1938), *Aboriginal Men of High Degree* (1946) and *The Aboriginal Australians* (1961). His son, Peter Kingsley Elkin (1924–), who edited *Australian Poems in Perspective* (1978), became professor of English at the University of New England in 1972. Tigger Wise wrote the biography *The Self-Made Anthropologist: a Life of A.P. Elkin* (1985).

ELLIOTT, Brian (1910–91), born and educated in Adelaide, was on the staff of the University of Adelaide 1940–75, first as lecturer in English and then as reader in Australian literary studies 1961–75. He is reputed to have been the first to suspect the nature of the Ern Malley hoax (q.v.). Instrumental in the founding of the Humanities Research Council of Australia, he was made AM in 1976. Elliott was the author of the novel *Leviathan's Inch* (1946), but his major contribution to Australian literature was as essayist (*James Hardy Vaux*, 1944; *Singing to the Cattle*, 1947); critic (*The Landscape of Australian Poetry*, 1967); biographer (*Marcus Clarke*, 1958); and editor (*Coast to Coast*, 1948; *Bards in the Wilderness*, 1970; *Adam Lindsay Gordon*, 1973; *The Jindyworobaks*, 1979). A collection of essays and poems from many well-known Australian writers and critics was compiled as a public tribute to Elliott on his seventy-fifth birthday in 1986. Titled *Mapped but Not Known: The Australian Landscape of the Imagination*, it was edited by P.R. Eaden and F.H. Mares.

ELLIOTT, Sumner Locke (1917–91), the son of the writer Sumner Locke (q.v.), who died soon after his birth, and Henry Logan Elliott, a freelance journalist, was born in Sydney. Brought up by several aunts he was the subject of a fierce battle for custody that was determined when he was 10. On leaving school he became an actor and writer for radio and joined the Independent Theatre, which produced seven of his plays: *Interval* (produced in 1939, published in 1942), 'The Cow Jumped Over the Moon' (1939), 'The Little Sheep Run Fast' (1940), 'Goodbye to the Music' (1942), 'Your Obedient Servant' (1943), 'The Invisible Circus' (1946) and *Rusty Bugles* (q.v. 1948). *Buy Me Blue Ribbons*, produced at the Empire Theatre, New York, in 1951 and published in 1952, was also produced by the Independent in 1953. During the Second World War Locke Elliott served in the Australian Army, spending six months at a remote ordnance camp at Mataranka in the Northern Territory, an experience which he drew on for *Rusty Bugles*. In 1948 he left for the USA before the first production of *Rusty Bugles* and missed both the play's outstanding success and the public storm over the censorship of its language. In the USA he worked for CBS and NBC, eventually becoming one of the best-known writers for television. Of the fifty or more plays that he wrote for television at least one, 'The Grey Nurse Said Nothing' (1959), has acquired the status of a classic. Two plays for theatre, both produced on Broadway, *Buy Me Blue Ribbons* and 'John Murray Anderson's Almanac' (1953), were less successful. In 1955 he became an American citizen.

Apart from a brief visit in 1950, Locke Elliott did not return to Australia until 1974. The visit stirred memories of his youth, which he had already drawn on for his successful autobiographical novel *Careful, He Might Hear You* (q.v. 1963) and for *Edens Lost* (1969), and resulted in further novels with Australian settings, *Water under the Bridge* (q.v. 1977), *About Tilly Beamis* (1985), *Waiting for Childhood* (1987) and *Fairyland* (1990). *Careful, He Might Hear You* won the Miles Franklin Award, was subsequently translated into six languages, was selected by the *Reader's Digest* Book Club and was filmed in 1983. *Water Under the Bridge* was produced as an Australian television serial in 1980; *Edens Lost*, produced by Margaret Fink, was also made into a television serial in 1988 and screened in Britain and Australia. Locke Elliott's other novels, apart from *Going* (1975), a work of science fiction, are set in the USA; they are *Some Doves and Pythons* (1966), *The Man Who Got Away* (1972) and *Signs of Life* (1981). *Radio Days*, a collection of short stories which revive memories of Australian radio of the 1930s and 1940s, introduced by Sharon Clarke, was published in 1993. In 1977 he won the Patrick White Literary Award.

For Australian readers the outstanding feature of Locke Elliott's work is the re-creation of the distinctive flavour of the national life of the 1930s and 1940s. *Rusty Bugles*, which he later described as a documentary rather than a play, was the most popular production with Australian audiences since *On Our Selection* (1912). A mirror of the unspectacular daily life of the ordinary soldier, it represents the deprivation, boredom, irritations, loneliness, disappointments, wartime loves and griefs familiar to many of its first audiences. At the same time Locke Elliott's exploitation of the comic possibilities of the vernacular and his critical attitude to aspects of the Australian legend foreshadowed what was to be a continuing preoccupation in Australian drama and was shortly to emerge in Lawler's *Summer of the Seventeenth Doll* (1957) and Seymour's *The One Day of the Year* (1962).

His Australian novels illustrate even more fully his powers of convincing sociological re-creation, his psychological insight and diversity of range from comedy to pathos. *Careful, He Might Hear You*, a carefully structured novel with an intricate time-scheme, is presented to a large extent from a child's perspective. As the boy's unusual emotional experience propels him rapidly to a precocious maturity, he becomes increasingly aware of life's ambivalences. *Edens Lost* turns on the theme of sophisticated corruption versus guileless innocence, which is also one of the themes of his more ambitious novel *Water under the Bridge*. Set mainly in mid-1930s Sydney, it deals with several interrelated but diverse destinies, some of which are drawn from Locke Elliott's memories of news stories of the period. Of the book's numerous memorable

characters, the most striking and the most illustrative of Locke Elliott's simultaneous detachment and sympathy is the central character's aunt and surrogate mother, the ageing ex-chorus-girl Shasta Davies. But Sydney itself is also a loved and hated protagonist; in this stagnant, blandly suburban environment which constantly exalts the mediocre at the expense of the talented and the idealistic, the Harbour Bridge images the unachieved possibilities of creativity and communication. *Waiting for Childhood* draws on the history of his mother's family and includes a character, Sidney, based on his mother. Against a background of Australia before the First World War, it is an account of the different destinies of a family of seven children who lose both parents. *Fairyland*, a semi-autobiographical novel which takes the narrator, Seaton Daly, to early adulthood, describes Daly's difficult adjustment to his homosexuality, his career as a writer, his move to America and quest for love. Like earlier novels by Locke Elliott, it gives a vivid picture of 1930s Sydney.

ELLIS, Bob (1942–), born Lismore, NSW, has worked as a writer and production assistant for the ABC. Television and film critic and columnist for various journals and newspapers, including *Nation*, *Nation Review*, the *National Times*, *Theatre Australia* and the *Sydney Morning Herald*, he has written plays for radio, television and film and has won many AFI, Awgie and Sammy awards. His published plays include the musical extravaganza *The Legend of King O'Malley* (q.v. 1974), which he wrote with Michael Boddy and which was first produced with great success in 1970; and a more naturalistic play, *Down Under* (1977), written with his wife Anne Brooksbank and first produced in 1975. He has also written 'The James Dossier' (1975), a musical based on the life of Francis James (1918–92), the controversial Australian editor and journalist who was a prisoner in China 1969–72; with Richard Hall, 'The Duke of Edinburgh Assassinated: Or, the Vindication of Henry Parkes' (1971); and, with Chris McGill, the film script for *Fatty Finn*, the 1980 version of the classic silent film about Fatty Finn (q.v.) *The Kid Stakes*. Ellis also wrote a children's tie-in to the film *Fatty Finn* (1980). His other publications include the novel *Mad Dog Morgan* (1976), written with Anne Brooksbank and based on the film by Philippa Mora; *Two Weeks in Another Country: A Journal of the 1983 British Election* (1983); *The Things We Did Last Summer* (1983), a narrative of four weeks during the 1983 Australian election; *Letters to the Future* (1987) and *The Inessential Ellis* (1992), selections from his journalism; *The Hewson Tapes* (1993), a fictional secret history of Australia's contemporary politics; and, with John Hepworth, *Top Kid* (1985) and *The Paper Boy* (1985), novels based on teleplays for children.

ELLIS, Havelock (1859–1939), born Surrey, England, spent four years teaching in Australia 1875–79; a year of that time was spent in a small school at Sparkes Creek deep in the bush near Scone, NSW. That year, lonely in terms of human contact, was rich and rewarding in terms of Ellis attaining self-knowledge. His novel *Kanga Creek*, written in his late twenties but published forty-three years later in 1922, tells of his experiences at Sparkes Creek and adds a central fictitious romantic episode purportedly based on his love for the novelist Olive Schreiner. Geoffrey Dutton edited, with an introduction, a later edition of *Kanga Creek* in 1989 which includes selections from his correspondence, poems, and reviews of the novel. Ellis's later career in England saw the publication of his major works, *Studies in the Psychology of Sex* (1897–1910), and *Impressions and Comments* (1914–24). His autobiography, *My Life*, which recounts his time in Australia, was published in 1940. Houston Peterson wrote the biography, *Havelock Ellis: Philosopher of Love* (1928), which also contains the most complete bibliography of Ellis's writings.

ELLIS, M.H. (Malcolm Henry) (1890–1969), born Narine, Queensland, grew up in the Queensland bush; his account of those early times and experiences was published in the *Bulletin* in 1965. He entered journalism in Brisbane and later joined the Sydney *Daily Telegraph*. Aged 42 he joined the *Bulletin* where, in a career of thirty-three years, he became well known as a feature writer on historical and political affairs, usually under the pseudonym 'Ek Dum'. During the Second World War 'Ek Dum' published accounts of battles and campaigns in which Australian troops were involved, remarkably accurate considering they were written at second hand. Ellis is best known for his writing on early Australian history, e.g. the biographies *Lachlan Macquarie* (1947), for which he won the Harbison-Higinbotham Award in 1948, *Francis Greenway* (1949) and *John Macarthur* (1955). His interest in colonial literature is reflected in his exchanges with Colin Roderick in the *Bulletin* (1952–53) about the authorship of the convict novel *Ralph Rashleigh* (q.v.). He was involved in planning the *ADB*. Recognition of his journalistic and historical writings came when he was made CMG in 1956 and when he later received an honorary doctorate from the University of Newcastle.

ELLISTON, W.G. (William Gore) (1798–1872), born Bath, England, was the son of the English actor and theatre manager Robert William Elliston (1774–1831), who in 1828 composed an ode for his son's projected departure for Australia and after his arrival had the playwright 'William Moncrieff' write the extravaganza *Van Diemen's Land* (q.v. performed 1830). Briefly engaged in business pursuits, Elliston was a schoolmaster in 1833–37 before taking over from James Ross as government printer and proprietor of the *Hobart Town Courier* and publisher of the *Hobart Town Almanack*; after his retirement from the press in 1848 he was prominent in civic affairs.

Elocution of Benjamin Franklin, The, a one-actor play by Steve J. Spears (q.v.), was first produced in 1976, has been widely staged in Australia, and was produced in London in 1978 and in New York and San Francisco in 1979. Gordon Chater, a well-known Australian actor, appeared in all productions. The play was published in 1977 in *Drag Show* with Peter Kenna's *Mates*. The protagonist of the play, a middle-aged transvestite and speech therapist, Robert O'Brien, reveals in a private monologue and in his telephone conversations both the ordinary human nature of his life and his reciprocated feelings for one of his pupils, the dissolute 12-year-old Benjamin Franklin. The relationship remains innocent but O'Brien is harassed by his Toorak neighbours and by Act III, which takes place eight years later, he has become the helpless, tormented inmate of a mental hospital.

'Emancipist' is a word regularly used in nineteenth-century Australia and by modern historians to designate an ex-convict, both one who completed his term of sentence and one whose good conduct earned a conditional or absolute pardon. The emancipists formed a significant group in a colonial society and their struggles with the 'pure merinos' (free settlers), particularly in the period 1810–50, is a significant theme in the history of NSW and Tasmania. George Howe, the first Australian printer, sentenced to transportation for life in 1799 but conditionally pardoned in 1803, is an example of an emancipist; others include Michael Massey Robinson, Mary Reibey and Francis Greenway. 'Price Warung's' 'The Pure Merinoes' Ball' and 'Marie Antoinette's Fandango' humorously re-create the emancipist–pure-merino tensions of the 1820s.

EMERSON, Ernest Sando ('Milky White') (1870–1919), whose father was a first cousin of the American poet Ralph Waldo Emerson, was born in Ballarat, Victoria, and became a journalist with the *Brisbane Courier* and a freelance writer and journalist. He published *A Shanty Entertainment* (1904, bush stories and poems) and *An Australian Bird Calendar* (1909, illustrated by Norman Lindsay).

EMERY, John (1947–), born Cairns , has been a lecturer in media sociology and literature, has written prolifically for film and television and is now a freelance writer. Growing up in New Guinea he learned from his father much of the lore of the early White settlement times in that country and became well acquainted with the tribespeople and their customs. His novel *The Sky People* (the natives' name in the early days for the White men), published in 1984, deals with the Australian administration of northern New Guinea after the First World War and especially in the 1930s. An account of the experiences of several patrol officers, it is an exciting mix of violence, fear and sexuality, highlighting the differences between the two opposing cultures – White and native. Emery has received numerous awards including the Commonwealth Bank National Short Story of the Year Award in 1974 for 'Rape' and an Awgie in 1983 for the TV mini-series *Chase through the Night*. His book of short stories, *Summer Ends Now* (1980), contains nineteen pieces, including 'Rape'; 'The First Day of Spring', which formed the basis of his screenplay, *Backroads*, filmed by Philip Noyce; 'Caravan Park', also filmed by Noyce; 'The Parable of the Storyteller', broadcast on radio; 'Pine Gap', a derisive account of CIA paranoia; and 'Out from Mount Hagen', a story with a New Guinea setting. He has also written the novel *Freedom* (1982); scripts for the screen, *The Coming* (1981), *Freedom* (1982), *Fever* (1987), *Strangers* (1990) and *The Cutting Edge* (1991); and for television various episodes of *Possession* (1983). His writing reveals a considerable talent for characterisation and the establishment of atmosphere and setting.

Emigrant Family: Or, The Story of an Australian Settler, The (1849), a novel by Alexander Harris (q.v.) but ascribed on the title page to 'the author of *Settlers and Convicts*', was titled in an 1852 edition *Martin Beck: Or, The Story of an Australian Settler*. Although it is a fictional account of the adventures of the Bracton family in the Australian colony, Harris stresses in his preface the authenticity of the events narrated and the background to them. The novel has several major plots, all reasonably successfully interwoven; they include the experiences of the Bracton family in establishing themselves on the land in the Colony, the adventures of the 'Australian', Reuben Kable, and the machinations of the American Negro Martin Beck (q.v.). Harris's elevation of Beck to the title of the second edition indicates the importance he attached to that malign, and maligned, outsider, who seeks to gain wealth and power in order to compensate for the inferior position his colour creates for him in colonial society. Numerous sub-plots include the exploits of Willoughby Bracton, who strikes out for himself in the new land; the affairs of John Thomas, the stubborn ticket-of-leave bullock-driver; the fortunes of the Moses family, Jewish storekeepers at Ghiagong; and the development of various romantic relationships, Reuben Kable–Catherine Bracton, Willoughby Bracton–Mary Kable and Mr Hurley–Marianna Bracton. As a background to the sometimes repetitive plot and the meanderings of the romances there is much compensatory colonial colour. Harris provides many interesting local details, e.g. Australian eating habits (steak and damper), the ceremony of boiling the billy, and includes descriptions of bush huts, bullock-driving, cattle-stealing, an Australian Christmas, bushfires, scabby sheep, depredations of bushrangers and attacks by Blacks. At various points the narrative pauses to discuss such colonial problems as land reform, the brutalities of the convict system and the inadequacy of official attitudes towards the Aborigines. Although marred by its melodramatic events, *The Emigrant Family* is an important work of early colonial fiction.

'Emigrant Mechanic, An', see **HARRIS, Alexander**

Emigrant's Guide to Australia, The (1853), by John Capper, was typical of the many guidebooks written in England for sale to intending migrants to the Australian colonies. Capper's *Emigrant's Guide* was an enlarged version of a work published in 1852 as *Philips' Emigrants' Guide*. The guidebooks and hand-books informed immigrants about the geography and climate of Australia, prospects of employment and how to win a living on the land or on the goldfields. Full of well-meaning advice, sometimes based on the briefest personal experience of the writer (and occasionally on none at all) the guidebooks were a lucrative source of revenue for English publishers.

Empire, a liberal-radical newspaper, was founded by Henry Parkes (q.v.) in 1850; it began as a weekly, but soon became a daily and was the main rival of the *Sydney Morning Herald* between the death of the *Australian* in 1848 and the birth of the *Daily Telegraph* in 1879. Publication of the *Empire* was suspended in 1858 after Parkes ran into financial difficulties; the newspaper was revived the following year by Samuel Bennett and was incorporated into the *Evening News* in 1875. Significant contributors included Daniel Deniehy, William Forster, Frank Fowler, Henry Kendall and Charles Harpur.

Encyclopaedia Britannica Australia Awards, also known as the Britannica Australia Awards, were given 1964–73 to recognise outstanding achievement in Australia and to recognise Australian–American links. Sponsored by the *Encylopaedia Britannica* company, the awards were presented in the fields of the arts, education, literature, medicine and science 1964–67, and in the arts, science and humanities 1968–73. Winners in the literature or humanities area included Judith Wright (1964), R.D. FitzGerald and A.D. Hope (1965), Hal Porter and Randolph Stow (1966), Douglas Stewart (1968), C.B. Christesen (1970) and James McAuley (1972). No award was made for literature in 1967, when Christina Stead was rejected on the grounds that she had ceased to be Australian.

Endeavour Press, see **STEPHENSEN, P.R.**

ENGLAND, E.M. (Edith Mary) (1899–1979), born Townsville, Queensland, was a prolific contributor of verse and prose to a variety of Australian and overseas journals. Her publications include fiction, *The Sealed Temple* (1933), *Tornado and Other Stories* (1945), *Where the Turtles Dance* (1950), *House of Bondage* (1950) and *Road Going North* (1952, with Ray Albion); and verse, *The Happy Monarch and Other Verses* (1927) and *Queensland Days* (1944).

English Association (Sydney Branch), which is affiliated with the parent English Association (London, 1906–), was founded in 1923 and until 1944 was known as the Australian English Association. It has aimed since its inauguration to foster the recognition, study and teaching of English language and literature, with the additional objective since 1949 of encouraging the study of Australian literature. Prominent among its activities are the annual public lectures for matriculation students and the sponsorship of the journals *Southerly* (q.v.) and *Sydney Studies in English* (1975–). There have been other Australian branches of the English Association, e.g. in Melbourne,

Adelaide and Townsville. The last-named published *North* (1963–68).

ENRIGHT, Nicholas (1950–), born Maitland, NSW, was educated at the University of Sydney after which he spent a year with the Nimrod Street Theatre before joining the Melbourne Theatre Company in 1973 as their first trainee director. From 1975–77 he studied playwriting with Israel Horovitz at New York University, was assistant director at the SA State Theatre Company 1978–81 and was head of acting at NIDA 1983–84. In addition to being director, actor and musician he has published *The Maitland & Morpeth String Quartet* (1980), a long humorous children's poem which has been made into a film; *On the Wallaby* (1982), a musical about the 1930s Depression era; *Daylight Saving* (1990), a modern comedy of manners which won two Awgies, and *St James Infirmary* (1993), a study of a young man's resistance to his Catholic upbringing which is inconsistent with his opposition to the Vietnam War. His other performed plays include 'Variations' (1982, winner of the NSW Premier's Award) about the changing roles of women within the family; 'First Class Women', about the treatment of women convicts in the days of the first settlement; 'Summer Rain' (1983, substantially revised for a professional production in 1989), about an acting troupe stranded in a small bush town at Christmas; 'Mongrels' (1991); and 'A Property of the Clan' (1993), which won a Golden Awgie. He has also written the book and lyrics for three musicals with the composer Terence Clarke, including the popular 'The Venetian Twins' (1979), adapted from Goldoni's comedy, and has translated and adapted the work of Beaumarchais, Molière and Euripides. With George Miller he wrote the screenplay *Lorenzo's Oil* (1993), which won him a nomination for an Oscar in the American Academy Awards.

EPANOMITIS, Fotini (1969–), who is an MA from Curtin University, WA, was born the year her family migrated to Australia from Greece. She has lived most of her life in Perth but spent a year back in Greece on her grandparents' farm. Her first novel, *The Mule's Foal* (1992), won the *Australian*/Vogel Award. Set in a nameless Greek village, *The Mule's Foal* is less a story than a series of fable-like incidents, in the author's own words, 'a lot like a tapestry where you get all the historical periods going at once, backwards and forwards'. The characters range from the unusual to the bizarre – the ugly children, Vaia and Theodosios, who marry and have a child, conceived in the one night they spend together; the child itself, a 'gorilla' baby, who grows up to be Yiorgios the Apeface; the parents of Theodosios, Meta and Stefanos, Meta, a child bride who bears fourteen children and becomes so strong that she can tear a wild boar apart with her hands; the Blind Traveller; Pourthitsar the matchmaker; Mirella (the narrator of much of the book) who keeps the village whorehouse, the focus of the place, and Agape of the Glowing Face, one of the whores. The aura of fable (links have also been suggested with the genre magic realism) stems both

from language of a biblical spareness and from the author's awareness of Greek customs, attitudes, outlook and history. The rituals of the village (e.g. deformed infants being left to be eaten by pigs) appear primitive and even bestial, but the horrors and grotesqueries (gorilla babies and the like) always seem vaguely unreal, as if transported from a Greek version of some 'black' fairy tale.

EPSTEIN, June (1918–), born Perth, WA, has had a distinguished career as a musician and writer with outstanding service to the cause of music education. She has also written scripts and plays for radio and television. Her community work for people with disabilities and her services to music education were recognised in 1986 with the award of the OAM. She has written several biographies, e.g. *Mermaid on Wheels: The Story of Margaret Lester* (1967), *No Music by Request: A Portrait of the Gorman Family* (1980); *A Golden String: The Story of Dorothy J. Ross* (1981); numerous children's books, e.g. *Boy on Sticks* (1979), *The Friends of Burramys* (1981, award for the best children's book by the Royal Zoological Society of NSW), *The Ice-Cream Kids* (1984), *Scarecrow and Company* (1984, winner of Adelaide Writer's Week Award), *Blue Serpent* (1986) and many shorter books for younger children. She has also published songs and music, anthologies for children, a textbook, *Enjoying Music with Young Children* (1973, 1986) and an autobiography, *June Epstein – Woman with Two Hats* (1988).

ERCOLE, Velia ('Margaret Gregory') (1903–78), born White Cliffs, NSW, experienced life in a country town (Grenfell, NSW) before becoming a journalist with the Sydney *Sun*. Her first novel, *No Escape* (1932), winner of the *Bulletin* novel competition, concerns the experiences of an Italian family in a small NSW country town in 1905. Leo Gherardi (modelled on Ercole's Italian father, Quinto Ercole), an Italian political emigrant, takes up a medical practice in Banton with his wife Teresa and son Dino, intending to return to Italy as soon as practicable. Teresa, unable to accommodate to her new and hated environment, commits suicide and Leo ultimately marries an Australian, Olwen Ferrars, has another son and participates in the First World War as an army doctor; these events conspire to turn him into an Australian in spite of himself. In a second novel, *Dark Windows* (1934), Julie Purvis, daughter of an Australian father and French mother, goes to France to live after her father's death. Ultimately convinced of her inability to bridge the gulf between the two worlds with their widely differing traditions, manners and cultures, she returns to the familiarity of Australia. As 'Margaret Gregory' (Gregory was her married name) and living in England, Velia Ercole published numerous popular romances, e.g. *Marriage Made on Earth* (1939), *Marriage by Ordeal* (1941) and *This Life to Live* (1944).

ERICKSEN, Ray (1919–), born Springvale, Victoria, graduated from the University of Melbourne and served with the Australian Army in the Second

World War. After a career as a historian at the University of Melbourne 1947–69, he became a full-time writer. His publications include the travel book *West of Centre* (1972) and *Cape Solitary* (1975, winner of the National Book Council's Australian Book of the Year); the latter is his account of an attempt to live alone in an isolated environment. His biography of the explorer Ernest Giles (q.v.), published in 1978, also won a National Book Council Award.

Ern Malley Hoax. The Autumn 1944 issue of *Angry Penguins* (q.v.) contained *The Darkening Ecliptic*, sixteen poems supposedly written by a recently deceased mechanic/insurance salesman named Ern Malley and sent to Max Harris (q.v.), co-editor of *Angry Penguins*, by Ethel Malley, the sister of Ern Malley. On 25 June 1944 the Sydney *Sunday Sun* magazine section 'Fact' carried the news that the Ern Malley poems were a hoax, written by James McAuley and Harold Stewart (qq.v.). A statement by the co-authors in 'Fact' explained that their action stemmed from their anxiety over what they saw as 'the gradual decay of meaning and craftsmanship in poetry'. McAuley and Stewart believed that the avant-garde poetry of the day was 'insensible of absurdity and incapable of ordinary discrimination'. To put that belief to the test they compiled Ern Malley's 'life-work' in an afternoon with the aid of any books that lay within reach: the *Concise Oxford Dictionary*, a collection of Shakespeare's plays, a *Dictionary of Quotations*, Ripman's *Rhyming Dictionary* and an American report on the drainage of swamps where mosquitoes bred. In their words, 'We opened books at random, choosing a word or a phrase haphazardly. We made lists of these and wove them into nonsensical sentences. We misquoted and made false allusions.' The Ern Malley hoax was featured in the world press and a lively discussion ensued as to the literary merit of the concocted verses, which had been highly acclaimed by many literary experts of the day. The discussion was temporarily silenced by the action of the SA police in prosecuting Harris for the publication of 'indecent advertisements' in the form of some of the Ern Malley poems. A marathon trial followed and Harris was fined £5. More important than the hoax itself was the effect that it had on the development of Australian poetry. The vigorous and legitimate movement for modernism in Australian writing, espoused by many writers and critics in addition to the members of the Angry Penguins group, received a severe setback and the conservative element was undoubtedly strengthened. The Ern Malley controversy continued throughout the following two decades; Harris's views on it are given in the introduction to *Ern Malley's Poems* (1960), and in 'Angry Penguins and After', *Quadrant* (1963); James McAuley's attitude is given in 'The Ferment of the Forties' in *A Map of Australian Verse* (1975). Ian Kennedy Williams wrote *Malarky Dry* (1990), a fictional account of the hoax. *The Poems of Ern Malley* with commentaries by Max Harris and Joanna Murray-Smith was published in 1988, and the *Collected Poems of Ern Malley* with commentaries by Albert Tucker, Max Harris and Colin Wilson in 1993. *The Ern Malley Affair* by Michael Heywood, with an introduction by Robert Hughes, was also published in 1993.

Ern Malley's Journal, a journal of six numbers (1952–55) edited in Adelaide by Max Harris, John Reed (qq.v.) and Barrett Reid, took its name from the 'poet' Ern Malley (see Ern Malley Hoax). Less extreme than the earlier *Angry Penguins* (q.v.), *Ern Malley's Journal* reflected the editors' continuing interest in modernist literature and art.

Escape of the Notorious Sir William Heans and the Mystery of Mr. Daunt, The, William Gosse Hay's (q.v.) best-known novel, was published in 1919 although 1918 best is the date given on the title page of the first edition. First published in England, where it was well received, it was republished in Australia in 1955 in an edition which stimulated renewed interest in Hay, although his mannered, dense style and melodramatic plots have been savagely attacked by some critics. *The Escape of the Notorious Sir William Heans* is a historical romance focused on Tasmania in the late 1830s and early 1840s. Its protagonist, an Irish baronet who has been transported for abduction, is befriended by a distant cousin, Matilda Hyde-Shaxton, and her husband. Despite his privileges as a gentleman convict and the efforts of the Hyde-Shaxtons to assist him, the proud Heans feels his reduced position in society keenly, frequents tavern society and plans to escape the island on board a ship he has purchased. He enlists the assistance of Matilda, with whom he has fallen in love, but although Matilda acts as a go-between before the escape is attempted, she refuses Heans's entreaty that she elope with him. Their conversation is overheard both by Captain Paul Hyde-Shaxton and by Heans's nemesis, the penal official Mr Daunt, whose own attachment to Matilda is one of the reasons for his relentless surveillance of the baronet.

The second of the novel's three books opens a year later with Heans, his escape detected, now the assigned servant of an ex-convict, Charles Oughtryn, whose house was formerly the residence of the first governor, David Collins. Heans's fall is reflected not only in his lowly position as a groom, teaching Oughtryn's half-blind daughter Abelia to ride, but also in the sinister people among whom he is forced to work, notably the tormented soldier Joseph Spafield. As Heans unravels Spafield's past and the secrets of the house, he learns that Spafield, a 'murderer's murderer', was responsible for the death of the young stone-cutter Walter Surridge, whose narrative confessing to the murder of Collins (a Hay invention), and implicating Spafield in his own death, Heans finds in the caves near the house. Heans, still watched carefully by Daunt, plans again to escape, but this time is thwarted by his concern for Abelia, who he believes is under threat from Spafield; in a fight in the caves, Spafield is killed. Heans's selflessness in protecting Abelia is a significant stage in his moral rehabilitation, although equally significant in this section of the novel has been his defence of Matilda's honour against the scandal-mongering of Daunt, who has perpetrated the rumour that Matilda used her husband's money to help

Heans's first escape attempt. During a theatrical entertainment at Oughtryn's house on the day of the fight between Heans and Spafield, Captain Hyde-Shaxton challenges Daunt to a duel but Daunt dies of a heart attack just before revealing to Heans information 'deeply to his advantage'. The nature of this information is part of the mystery surrounding Daunt as signalled in the title, although the extent and nature of his evil and the exact reasons why he relentlessly pursues Heans are equally mysterious. Having achieved moral freedom through his defence of Matilda and Abelia, Heans achieves physical freedom in the brief final part of the novel when he is helped to escape from Port Arthur to Dieppe in France by Hyde-Shaxton and by Conapanny, the Aboriginal lover of Walter Surridge.

The Escape of the Notorious Sir William Heans is an elaborately patterned, carefully written novel, influenced by Walter Scott in its exploration of the romance of the past, reminiscent of Nathaniel Hawthorne in its exploration of Heans's fall and regeneration, and demanding of its readers as a consequence of Hay's abdication of authorial omniscience and the piecemeal way evidence is presented. R.G. Howarth called it Australian literature's 'most successful period novel'. Although some commentators dispute that judgement, the novel does introduce historical personages such as Sir John Franklin, William Bedford and Henry Savery, and captures the texture of Tasmanian society during Franklin's rule as lieutenant-governor, e.g. in its depiction of the machinery of patronage in a penal colony, the aftermath of the destruction of Tasmanian Aboriginal society and in the presentation of the faction fights between Franklin and his colonial secretary John Montagu.

'Essay on Memory', a long meditative poem by R.D. FitzGerald (q.v.), was published in the Sydney Morning Herald 9 April 1938, having won the sesquicentenary prize for poetry. It was also published in FitzGerald's Moonlight Acre (1938) and later in Forty Years' Poems (1965). The intellectual content of the poem stems in part from the writings of the philosopher A.N. Whitehead. Rain images, FitzGerald's symbol for memory, dominate the poem, which was conceived while he was surveying the mountains of Veivatuloa in Fiji. Presenting memory as the total past – more than the past of an individual, or a people, or a nation, or a civilisation – the poem insists that it should activate the life of the present; the past influences the present and the present individual, for every individual is a composite of everyone and everything that has gone before him – 'we are the substance of their thought'. It also suggests (FitzGerald's abiding principle) that individual lives, perishable though they are, are made meaningful both in themselves and for the future by action. The themes of the poem, the continuing core of existence and meaning in the universe and the implications of this for individual lives, are solidly held in the logical structure of the poem and illuminated by effective, if complex, imagery.

Essays in Australian Fiction, a group of seven critical essays by 'M. Barnard Eldershaw' (q.v.), was published in 1938. One of the earliest extended pieces of modern criticism and written when publishing opportunities were meagre, it is still fresh and mostly valid. The collection includes one essay on Katharine Susannah Prichard and Henry Handel Richardson and individual essays on Frank Dalby Davison, Vance Palmer, Leonard Mann, Martin Boyd, Christina Stead and Eleanor Dark. The essay on Boyd, although still valuable, restricts itself to The Montforts, and time has made others less comprehensive, especially those on Dark and Mann.

ESSON, Louis (1879–1943), born Edinburgh, Scotland, was brought to Australia in childhood. He was brought up with his uncle, the painter Ford Paterson, and mixed with writers and artists in his youth. For most of his working life he was a freelance journalist, writing for such periodicals as the Bulletin, the Socialist, Table Talk and the Lone Hand, where he was able to give vent to his artistic-socialist ideals and iconoclastic wit. He travelled widely 1915–21 and became deeply impressed by the work of the Irish dramatists at the Abbey Theatre, Dublin, especially by his meetings and correspondence with W.B. Yeats. In 1921–22 Esson made a concerted effort to put Yeats's advice into action by collaborating with Vance Palmer and Stewart Macky in the formation of the Pioneer Players (q.v.). His second wife was Dr Hilda Bull, who continued to promote his theatrical aims after his death and who was the financial mainstay of the family after Esson was afflicted with a nervous illness in the 1930s.

Esson's plays were published in several collections: Three Short Plays, which includes The Woman Tamer, Dead Timber and The Sacred Place (1911); The Time is Not Yet Ripe (1912); Dead Timber and Other Plays, which includes The Drovers (q.v. 1920); The Southern Cross and Other Plays, which includes The Southern Cross, Mother and Son and The Bride of Gospel Place (1946, ed. Hilda Bull); and The Woman Tamer (1976). Andeganora is included in Best Australian One-Act Plays (1937), and an anthology of Esson's writing edited by Hugh Anderson, Ballades of Old Bohemia (1980), includes The Sacred Place, Dead Timber, The Woman Tamer and Vagabond Camp as well as verse, stories and articles. His unpublished plays include 'The Battler' (1922), 'Australia Felix' (1926), 'The Quest' and 'Shipwreck' (1928). Vance Palmer published a volume of reminiscences and some of Esson's letters in Louis Esson and the Australian Theatre (1948). Esson also published two collections of poetry, Bells and Bees (1910) and Red Gums (1912), as well as numerous uncollected short stories. Often described as the first Australian playwright to achieve distinction for plays with Australian settings, Esson was in fact a naturally cosmopolitan, urbane and witty writer. He suppressed this gift in favour of nationalistic folk themes and poetic realism. Although his more extended efforts are flawed by weak construction and confused characterisation, he produced some fine short 'bush' plays of which The Drovers is the best. He is a character in Nigel Krauth's play Muse of

Fire (1985). The Victorian Premier's Literary Awards includes a Louis Esson Award for drama.

'Euabalong Ball, The' is an Australian folk-song which celebrates a dance at the bush hamlet of Euabalong on the Lachlan River in NSW. The humour of the song derives from the parallels drawn between the appearance and activities of the bucolic participants and the sheep and cattle with which they normally work; thus the shearers are 'stringy old wethers', the 'sheilas' are 'weaners' or 'two-tooths', and during the dancing

> There was bucking and gliding,
> pigrooting and sliding,
> When they varied the gait,
> there was couples colliding.

'The Euabalong Ball' was possibly adapted by A.L. Lloyd from an earlier song, 'The Wooyeo Ball', written by 'Vox Silvis' (?Rob Webster) and published in a history of Temora in 1888. The printed original reports a lively but not uproarious dance focused on the squatters and jackeroos rather than the pastoral workers. John Manifold, in *Who Wrote the Ballads?* (1964), speculates that the 'Euabalong Ball' adaptation represents not only an oral-transmission improvement of the original but also a proletarianisation by bush workers of a jackeroo homestead song.

'Eumerella Shore, The' is a well-known folk-song about the 'duffing' (q.v.) of cattle; there are a number of variant texts and titles including 'The Eumeralla Shore', 'The Numerella Shore' and 'The Neumerella Shore'. The references to free selection and Sir John Robertson make it clear that the 'Eumerella' district referred to is that in the NSW Monaro region, where there is a river known as the Numerella, and not the Eumerella River in south-eastern Victoria. It is less certain whether the song is the sarcastic lament of a squatter who feels his cattle will be stolen as a result of the Robertson Lands Acts or the boasts of a selector at the increased opportunities for 'duffing' as a result of the same Acts. 'Cockatoo Jack' is sometimes given as the author of the song, which was in print in the early 1860s.

Eureka Stockade is the title given to the clash that occurred on Bakery Hill, Ballarat, 3 December 1854, between rebellious miners, mainly from the Ballarat diggings, and soldiers and police of the Victorian government. Contributing factors to the Eureka incident were the discriminatory arrogance of the goldfields authorities towards the miners, the licence-fee system and the notorious licence hunts, the corruption and ineptitude of the Ballarat goldfields administration, the lack of political rights for the miners, and the presence on the diggings of considerable numbers of disaffected Irish and American nationals. On 29 November 1854 the rebel Eureka flag, the Southern Cross, was raised on Bakery Hill; on 30 November Peter Lalor (q.v.) and 500 miners swore on that flag of independence to fight for their rights; on 1 December the miners' 'Declaration of Independence' was publicly

proclaimed on Bakery Hill; on 2 December the Stockade, enclosing an acre of ground, was completed; on 3 December a force of 270 soldiers and police attacked the stockade and dispersed its 150 defenders. Within ten minutes, five soldiers and thirty miners were dead or dying and the incident itself was over, but its repercussions have long continued to be felt in Australian politics, history and literature. The official version of Eureka is contained in Sir Charles Hotham's 'Despatches to the Secretary of State for the Colonies, 1851–54'. Contemporary accounts of Eureka by the participants include Raffaello Carboni's (q.v.) *The Eureka Stockade* (1855), Peter Lalor's 'Statement on the Ballarat Rebellion' (*Age* and *Argus*, 10 April 1855) and Frederick Vern's 'Colonel Vern's Narrative' (*Age*, 15 January 1855). Later personal reminiscences include J. Lynch's 'The Story of the Eureka Stockade' (*Austral Light*, October 1893 to March 1894); H.R. Nicholls's 'Reminiscences of the Eureka Stockade' (*Centennial Magazine*, May 1890); and Frank Skurray's 'Some Memories of the Eureka Stockade' (*Steele Rudd's Magazine*, January 1905).

In almost every general study of the Australian goldfields in the past century writers have described, analysed, pondered over and pontificated on Eureka. Studies of particular significance include W.B. Withers's *The History of Ballarat* (1870), H.G. Turner's *Our Own Little Rebellion – the Story of Eureka* (1913), R.S. Ross's *Eureka! Freedom's Fight of '54* (1914), Clive Turnbull's *Eureka: The Story of Peter Lalor* (1946), C.H. Currey's *The Irish at Eureka* (1954), Robin Gollan's *Radical and Working Class Politics* (1960), Geoffrey Serle's *The Golden Age* (1963), Geoffrey Blainey's *The Rush That Never Ended* (1963), Richard Butler's *Eureka Stockade* (1983) upon which the television series was based, John Molony's *Eureka* (1984) and the popular history *Massacre at Eureka* (1992) by Bob O'Brien.

Eureka, with its colour and drama, has also provided a rich lode for creative writers, but no great work of fiction, poetry or drama has so far been produced. The first fictional account of Eureka appeared in 1870–72 in the original serial version in the *Australian Journal* of Marcus Clarke's *His Natural Life*, but the goldfields section was omitted from the novel when it was published in 1874. Clarke's account owes much to Raffaello Carboni's earlier eye-witness version and to W.B. Withers's *The History of Ballarat*, which had just been published. Edward Dyson's novel *In the Roaring Fifties* (1906) is centred on Eureka and gives a faithful if melodramatic version of the incident. In *Australia Felix* (1917), the first part of Henry Handel Richardson's trilogy *The Fortunes of Richard Mahony* (1930), the rebellion is assessed by Dr Mahony, who tends the wounded and dying on Bakery Hill, as futile 'straws against the wind', but the novel brings out the united determination of the diggers to oppose the oppressive administration. Leonard Mann's novel *Human Drift* (1935) portrays the conflicts that occurred within the ranks of the participants and examines the roles of the various national groups. Eric Lambert wrote two Eureka novels, *The Five Bright Stars* (1954) and *Ballarat* (1962). Other fictional works which include Eureka are J.M. MacDonald's *Roll-Up: A Tale of the Eureka*

Riots (1901), John Sanders's *The Call of the Southern Cross* (1915), Mollie Skinner's *Black Swans* (1925), George Cockerill's *In Days of Gold* (1926), E.V. Timms's *Red Mask* (1927), and Nathan Spielvogel's *An Affair at Eureka* (1930).

The outburst of egalitarianism, republicanism and democratic fervour that characterised the 1890s had some of its roots in Eureka. The radical nationalists of that decade were scarcely more than a generation removed from their counterparts the Stockade diggers, as is indicated by Henry Lawson's story 'An Old Mate [i.e. a Eureka mate] of Your Father's'; by his words 'It is thirty-six years this December' in his poem 'The Fight at Eureka Stockade'; by his 'Eureka (A Fragment)', which was inspired by Peter Lalor's death in 1889; by Mary Gilmore's childhood reminiscence 'Here comes a Eureka man!' and her poem 'The Men of Eureka'; and by Victor Daley's 'A Ballad of Eureka'. Anti-imperialist Francis Adams brought the Eureka flag to the centre of national attention in the 1880s with his poem 'Fling out the Flag', written for the newly formed Australian Labour Federation. There it has certainly stayed. It was raised in 1891 by the striking shearers at Barcaldine, Queensland, and Lawson was moved to applaud that gesture with his lines from 'Freedom on the Wallaby', 'So we must fly a rebel flag/ As others did before us'. He had in 1887 expressed much the same sentiments in his 'Flag of the Southern Cross', and E.J. Brady had also taken up the flag of independence in his poem 'The Flag of the South', as Helen Palmer later did in her 'Ballad of Eureka'. In modern times the Eureka flag and Billy Bluegum have become rallying symbols for those Australians of republican persuasion and for those who feel, with H.V. Evatt, that 'Australian Democracy was born at Eureka'. Len Fox wrote *Eureka and Its Flag* (1973).

Playwrights have attempted, with limited success, to present the chaos of Eureka in drama and on stage. Edmund Duggan's 'Eureka Stockade' (staged in 1891 as 'The Democrat') was performed at the Adelaide Theatre Royal in 1897. Duggan follows the Eureka events accurately but includes nationalist sentiments ('This flag is destined to wave over free and united Australia') more typical of the 1890s than of the mid-century goldfields. E.W. O'Sullivan's 'The Eureka Rebellion' (1907) also echoes the sentiment of the author's own times rather than of Eureka's by having Peter Lalor quote 'a new Britannia in another world' from W.C. Wentworth's *Australasia*. Of many other Eureka plays, those of significance are Louis Esson's *The Southern Cross* (1946); Leslie Rees's 'Lalor of Eureka', which won a Melbourne New Theatre Prize in 1939; Leslie Haylen's *Blood on the Wattle* (1948), a crowded and confused drama; Richard Lane's radio play in free verse, 'Eureka Stockade'; Kenneth Cook's *Stockade* (1975), one of the more successful theatre attempts on the subject; and John Romeril's 1980 production 'Carboni'. Films of Eureka include *The Loyal Rebel* (1915), *Eureka Stockade* (1949) and *Stockade* (1971). In 1992 the Eureka Commemorative Society launched at Sovereign Hill in Ballarat 'Blood on the Southern Cross', an automated sound-and-light production recreating the events of Eureka; in a single year it had ticket sales of a million dollars. A television series was shown in 1984. An extensive bibliography of Eureka literature is contained in *Historical Studies: Eureka Supplement* (1954).

Eurunderee, located about 6 kilometres north of Mudgee in central western NSW, was called New Pipeclay at the time gold was discovered there in 1863; its name was changed to Eurunderee around the time a school was established in 1876 for the children of the selectors who had remained in the area after the diggings petered out. The most celebrated inhabitant of Eurunderee was Henry Lawson, who lived there for most of his first fifteen years (1867–82). Lawson's experiences in and recollections of Eurunderee, both as a 'Roaring Days' gold community and as the home of struggling selectors, was an important source for numerous poems, e.g. 'Eurunderee', 'The Free Selector's Daughter', 'The Shanty on the Rise', and stories, e.g. 'His Father's Mate' and the school stories in *While the Billy Boils* (1896). The original Eurunderee School, lovingly rebuilt and refurbished by the members of the local historical society, was reopened as a Lawson museum in 1989.

EVANS, George Essex (1863–1909), born London, came to Australia in 1881. He tried farming then turned briefly to teaching, and later journalism as agricultural editor of the *Queenslander*. In 1888 he joined the public service, ultimately becoming district registrar at Toowoomba. His first volume of poetry, *The Repentance of Magdalene Despar*, was published in 1891. Two other volumes are *Loraine and Other Verses* (1898) and *The Secret Key and Other Verses* (1906). In 1901 he won £50 for his 'Ode for Commonwealth Day'. The *Collected Verse of George Essex Evans* was published as a memorial edition in 1928. His best-known individual poem, a great favourite in the first half of this century and frequently anthologised, is 'The Women of the West', a tribute to the women of the outback. His 'An Australian Symphony' is still considered highly as a patriotic poem, but in his other verse romantic themes predominate. More highly thought of in Queensland than elsewhere, Evans was undoubtedly a better poetic craftsman than many of his contemporaries among the bush balladists, but he failed to win the same popularity. His major narrative works, e.g. 'Magdalene Despar', although competent and enthusiastic, have lapsed into obscurity. In Toowoomba, where he worked and died, there is a monument to him and an annual George Essex Evans pilgrimage. Henry A. Tardent wrote *The Life and Poetry of George Essex Evans* (1913).

EVANS, George William (1780–1852), born Warwickshire, England, came to Australia in 1802 and after the crossing of the Blue Mountains in 1813 was employed by Governor Lachlan Macquarie to extend and exploit the crossing. He guided the governor's party on its tour to the Bathurst plains in 1815 and accompanied John Oxley on his explorations in 1817–18. From 1818 until his resignation in 1825 Evans was a government surveyor in Tasmania. He published *A Geographical, Historical and Topographical Description of Van Diemen's Land* (1822). Sketches by Evans of early Sydney and Hobart are in the Dixson Gallery of the State Library of NSW. A.K. Weatherburn wrote *Australia's Interior Unveiled* (1987), a revision of *George William Evans, Explorer*, published in 1966.

EVANS, Matilda Jane ('Maud Jeanne Franc') (1827–86), born Surrey, England, came to Australia with her family, Henry and Elizabeth Ann Congreve, sister Emily and two younger brothers in 1852. Her mother died on the voyage and her father shortly after arrival. At first a governess, she later opened her own school at Mount Barker. In 1860 she married the Rev. Ephraim Evans, and became responsible for his two children from his first marriage and her own two infant sons after he died in 1863. With the help of a public subscription she was able to open a school, which she continued to run until 1868, when she became a deaconess in the Baptist Church and devoted herself to writing. She published fourteen novels and numerous short stories and articles. Her fiction, with its ringing moral message and its inspiration from the scriptures, was mainly for young people, with whom it was highly popular. Her first novel, *Marian: Or, The Light of Some One's Home* (1859), deals with bush life, as do many others, e.g. *Emily's Choice* (1867) and *John's Wife* (1874). A collected edition of her Australian tales was published in 1888. Her two sons were Henry Congreve Evans (1861–99), who became chief of staff of the Adelaide *Advertiser* and the creator of *Quiz*, a social and political weekly; and William James Evans (1863–1904), who collaborated with her in the volume of short stories *Christmas Bells* (1882) and who wrote *Rhymes without Reason* (1898).

EVATT, H.V. (Herbert Vere) (1894–1965), born East Maitland, NSW, capped a brilliant university record in law at the University of Sydney with the award of LL D in 1924. Made KC in 1929, he was appointed justice of the High Court in 1930. He resigned in 1940 to win the federal seat of Barton for the Labor Party. In the wartime Curtin ministry he was attorney-general and minister for external affairs; in the Chifley ministry he became deputy prime minister. He was Australia's chief representative at the newly formed United Nations Organization and was president of the General Assembly 1948–49; he left politics in 1960 to become chief justice of NSW. Evatt published books on Australian history, politics and law; they included *Rum Rebellion* (1938) and *Australian Labour Leader* (1940), whose subject was W.A. Holman. Allan Dalziel wrote *Evatt, the Enigma* (1967); Kylie Tennant, *Evatt: Politics and Justice* (1970); Alan Renouf, *Let Justice Be Done* (1983); and Peter Crockett, *Evatt: A Life* (1993). Evatt is Dr Bert Effort in Barry Oakley's play *The Feet of Daniel Mannix* (1975).

Evening News, the first penny newspaper in NSW, was established by Samuel Bennett (q.v.) in 1867; it incorporated the *Empire* in 1875, and remained under the control of the Bennett family until the public company Samuel Bennett Ltd was formed in 1918. In 1929 this company merged with that of Sir Hugh Denison (q.v.) to form Associated Newspapers, which controlled both the *Sun* and the *Evening News* as afternoon dailies until the latter ceased publication in 1931. Although periodically ridiculed as the *Snooze* and the *Noose* by the *Bulletin* and other competitors, the *Evening News* was a technically innovative, middlebrow newspaper which outsold other metropolitan dailies for significant periods of its life, e.g. the 1880s and 1890s. Its editors included William Ridley (1873–78), James Alexander Hogue (1884–94) and A.B. Paterson (1903–6); Walter Jeffery was manager and editor 1906–22. Among notable staff were Theodore Argles ('The Pilgrim'), whose dismissal by Samuel Bennett led to *The Devil in Sydney* (1878), in which Argles caricatured the Bennetts; John Haynes, a sub-editor in 1879, when he secured J.F. Archibald a position as reporter before they founded the *Bulletin*; John Norton, a star reporter in the 1880s; and J.D. FitzGerald, Alex Montgomery and Will Lawson. *The Evening News 1867–1926* (1926) is a company history.

Everage, Edna, a character created by Barry Humphries (q.v.), made her stage debut in 1955 and became a central persona in Humphries's satirical presentation of Australian life. An 'average' (hence 'Everage') housewife from Moonee Ponds in Victoria, married to Norm ('normal') Everage and the mother of three children, Edna originally articulated the prejudices and pretensions of the suburban middle class. In 1965, in the show 'Excuse I' she first induced her audiences to wave gladioli at the end of the performance – an Edna trademark, which signalled that the audience as well as Edna herself was becoming the target of Humphries's satire. In the 1970s, after her creation as DBE in the film *Barry McKenzie Holds His Own* (1974), and possibly as a consequence of Humphries's domicile overseas, Edna became an international jet-setter. Although dubbed 'Suburbia's La Stupenda' and the 'Moonee Ponds Megastar', she is increasingly a celebrity in her own right, a cult figure rather than a satirical portrait of suburban momism. She is the 'author' of *Dame Edna's Coffee Table Book* (1976) and *Dame Edna's Bedside Companion* (1982) as well as the autobiography *My Gorgeous Life* (1989) and has 'made' many gramophone records.

Everlasting Secret Family and Other Secrets, The, a collection of stories and notes by Frank Moorhouse (q.v.), was published in 1980. It consists of four sequences linked by an association in each between sexuality and secrecy. The first, 'Pacific City', focuses on the secret world of Irving Bow, a cinema proprietor in the township where T. George McDowell, the central character of *The Electrical Experience* (q.v. 1975), has his soft-drink business; the sequence records Bow's sexual dalliances with the children of the town and his association with its other outsiders who, like Bow, are spiritual exiles. 'The Dutch Letters', the second sequence, consists mainly of the Second World War letters of a Dutch family, discovered and divulged by the narrator when he occupies a student's room during a conference; it emerges at the end of the sequence that the student is the child Dirk, whose castration is recorded in the letters between his parents. The third sequence, 'Imogene Continued', is set at the time of the same conference, during which an academic, Cindy (a recurring character in Moorhouse's fiction), is raped by an Aboriginal delegation; the sequence records her reaction to this and that of the narrator, her former lover. The final and title sequence is the erotic memoir of a homosexual.

EWART, Ernest Andrew ('Boyd Cable') (1878–1943), born India, served in the Boer War, migrated to Australia where he lived a nomadic existence, contributing to the *Bulletin* and *Lone Hand*, and was a newspaper correspondent in the First World War. His numerous fictional works include some that arose out of his war experiences, e.g. *Between the Lines* (1915), *Action Front* (1916), *Front Lines* (1918) and *The Old Contemptibles* (1919); in the last he claims to have originated the phrase 'Old Contemptibles' and explains its derivation. He also wrote books for children, including *Mates* (1929) and *The Wrist Watch Castaways* (1929).

EWERS, J.K. (John Keith) (1904–78), born Subiaco, WA, was a schoolteacher in WA 1924–47, thereafter living by his writing. Foundation president of the WA branch of the FAW (1938–39), he was made a life member in 1967. Ewers published poetry, fiction, history and works of literary criticism and social analysis. His two books of verse were *Boy and Silver* (1929), the narrative of a boy and a kangaroo, and *I Came Naked* (1976), philosophical comments on life. His novels began with *Money Street* (1933), moulded from a series of short stories; his second novel, *Fire on the Wind* (1935), is based on the experiences of the Ewers family in the Gippsland bushfire in 1898. *Men Against the Earth* (1946) and *For Heroes to Live In* (1948) are set in the WA wheat belt. His short stories include the children's works *Tales from the Dead Heart* (1944), about the life and legends of the Aborigines, and *Written in Sand* (1947), as well as the whimsical adult collection *Harvest and Other Stories* (1949). *With the Sun on My Back* (1953), an autobiographical account of Ewers's travels in northern Australia, won a prize in the Commonwealth Jubilee literary competition. His general works include *The Story of the Pipe Line* (to Coolgardie) (1935) and *The Western Gateway* (1948), about the city of Fremantle. His books of social commentary and literary criticism include *The Great Australian Paradox* (1939), a patriotic address he gave to the FAW in Perth at the beginning of the Second World War; *Tell the People!* (1944), an application of the social philosophy of Joseph Furphy to Australia's problems of the day; and *Creative Writing in Australia* (1945), an early survey of Australian literature. His biography of the explorer Charles Sturt, *Who Rides on the River?*, was published in 1956. He edited *Modern Australian Short Stories* (1965) and, with Deirdre Watson, *Take 23: Short Stories round the World* (1971). Very much a favourite son of his home state and one of its first writers to gain Australia-wide recognition, Ewers is

the subject of *The Ultimate Honesty: Recollections of John K. Ewers 1904–1978* (1982), published by the WA branch of the FAW and edited by Peter Bibby. His autobiography, *Long Enough for a Joke*, was published in 1983.

Examiner and Weekly Melbourne News, published 1857–64, contained a wide selection of literary articles including serials. Its drama critic was J.E. Neild writing as 'Christopher Sly'. In 1864 it was incorporated into the *Australasian*.

'Exequy, An' by Peter Porter (q.v.) from *The Cost of Seriousness* (1978), forms, with 'The Delegate', the crux of the volume. It displays his ability to blend artistic and deeply personal responses, the traditional and the contemporary. 'An Exequy' is modelled in metrics and theme on Bishop King's poem on the untimely death of his young wife, and explores with 'The Delegate' new avenues of the art of poetry. The poem states that the 'cost of seriousness' is death, implying at once that it is his pursuit of poetry, his seriousness, which has robbed both him and his wife of her life, and moreover that his art is insufficiently alive to console the feelings aroused, feelings not only of loss but of guilt. In 'The Delegate' the wife's ghost is speaking to the poet; it seems she has been sent ahead and is reluctantly reporting and advising him on the afterlife. The images she uses are not comforting and disrupt his attempted consolings, leaving him with more shame and guilt and the 'punishment of remembrance'. In these poems, as in others in the volume, Porter's preoccupations with the landscape of the mind turns to the inability of art, particularly his, to offer any more than a public expression of feeling. The paradox is that in poetry which is so private in its source of feeling Porter is able, by earnestly questioning in language textured with artistic allusions, to convince the reader while he himself is left unconvinced.

JEFF DOYLE

Eye of the Storm, The, a novel by Patrick White (q.v.), was published in 1973 and awarded the Nobel Prize for Literature. The last days of Elizabeth Hunter, a wealthy, dominant and once beautiful socialite, are the novel's subject. Now in her eighties, bedridden and half-blind, Mrs Hunter lies in her opulent Sydney mansion, still profoundly affecting all those around her. As her memories of the past and the memories of others are counterpointed with present events, both at her bedside and in the outer world, a comprehensive picture of Mrs Hunter's quest for transcendent meaning emerges. Crucial experiences in her life include her relationship with her husband Alfred, especially during his last illness, and a vision of 'glistening peace' fifteen years earlier when she lived through a cyclone on a tropical island. Her perception of her inclusion in the unity of being, perhaps as 'a flaw at the centre of this jewel of light', has shaped both her subsequent life and her act of dying. Those who are most affected by her intense authenticity of being include Arnold Wyburd, her lawyer; two of her nurses, as antithetical as their names suggest, Sister de Santis and Sister Manhood; and her cook, Lotte Lippmann, an ex-cabaret performer from Berlin. The psychological drama is heightened and unified by the return of her two middle-aged children, Dorothy and Basil, from Europe, their co-operation in an effort to accelerate their inheritance and their rediscovery of past experiences. Dorothy, the Princess de Lascabanes, ex-wife of a French nobleman and a Catholic convert, never casts off her resentful jealousy of her mother's beauty and dominance. Basil, now Sir Basil Hunter, an eminent but tired West End actor, has a keener perception of the alienating gulf between acted selves and authentic selves. Mrs Hunter's eventual death reframes the lives of others: Sister de Santis finds in her next 'case' an even more rigorous testing of her powers of selfless love; Sister Manhood abandons nursing for marriage with Col Pardoe, a future she had attempted to avoid; Dorothy returns to the comforts of her religion and European society; Sir Basil leaves with a renewed hope that he will be able to play a great tragic role with authenticity. For two individuals her death has a curtailing effect: Lotte Lippmann cuts her wrists in the bath, and Arnold Wyburd continues a drab existence, lit only by the brilliance of Mrs Hunter's sapphire that he keeps as an object of contemplation.

'Eyre All Alone', a poem in fourteen parts by Francis Webb (q.v.), was first published in its entirety in Webb's volume *Socrates* (1961), although parts of it (3, 10, 14) were published in the *Bulletin* in 1959. In Webb's *Collected Poems* (1969) 'Eyre All Alone' was printed as a separate section. The poem begins with the SA settler's 'dream of a stock-route' to WA. The explorer Edward John Eyre (q.v.), who had failed in an alternative attempt to open up the north of SA, sets out to chart a stock-route to the west by way of the Great Australian Bight. The last stanza of the first part, beginning

> Walk, walk. From dubious footfall one
> At Fowler's Bay, the chosen must push on

which refers to the departure of Eyre, John Baxter, Wylie and two other Aborigines from Fowler's Bay to the distant goal of King George Sound, is repeated several times as a sonorous, almost biblical, refrain throughout the poem. The third part tells of Baxter's murder by the two Aborigines; the fifth part reflects Eyre's uncertainty about Wylie's loyalty; the eighth part dwells on the ever-present menace of the Aborigines who shadow them. In the tenth part, 'Banksia', virtually the climax to the sequence, Wylie sights the banksia tree in flower and their hazardous journey across the desert is almost over. Webb's use in this part of the dramatic technique of question and answer to further the narrative ('Wylie, what can you see?/ I see a flower') is particularly effective. Later at Thistle Cove they are given supplies and companionship by the French whaler *Mississippi*, and the sequence ends with Wylie reunited with his tribesmen and Eyre about to make his dramatic entrance into Albany on King George Sound. In his notes to the poem Webb suggests that this journey, in which the hero's greatest

discovery is not a stock-route but himself, might be symbolically interpreted: 'My insistence upon Eyre's aloneness is not an overlooking of Wylie, but comes from my seeing such a journey of discovery as suggestive of another which is common to us all.' The poem re-emphasises Webb's interest, reflected in the earlier 'A Drum for Ben Boyd' and 'Leichhardt in Theatre', not so much in the heroic events of Australia's past as in the characters of the men who shaped and were shaped by those events.

EYRE, Edward John (1815–1901), born Bedfordshire, England, arrived as an emigrant in Sydney in 1833. After experience on a sheep station and in overlanding cattle to Port Phillip and Adelaide, he embarked in 1840 on an epic journey of exploration into central Australia and overland around the Great Australian Bight to King George Sound in WA. In 1841–44 he was a magistrate and protector of Aborigines at Moorundie on the Murray River. He then left Australia to serve as a colonial administrator in NZ (1846–53), St Vincent (1854–60), Leeward Islands (1860–61) and Jamaica (1861–65); in Jamaica he was responsible, as governor-in-chief, for the vigorous and controversial suppression of a Negro uprising that led to his recall and to a royal commission in London. Eyre's *Journals of Expeditions of Discovery into Central Australia and Overland from Adelaide to King George's Sound, in the Years 1840–1*, a classic of exploration literature, was published in 1845; almost a century later the seeds for *Voss* (1957) were sown when Patrick White read the journals during the London blitz. Other writers attracted to the Eyre story include Henry Kingsley in his story 'Eyre's March', Francis Webb in his poem sequence 'Eyre All Alone' (q.v.) and Graham Sheil in his play *The Dead Heart* (1991). Lake Eyre, Eyre Peninsula, Eyre Creek and other geographical features are named after Eyre, who is the subject of Geoffrey Dutton's biography *The Hero as Murderer* (1967), and Malcolm Uren and Robert Stephens's *Waterless Horizons* (1941). Eyre's *Autobiographical Narrative of Residence and Exploration in Australia 1832–1839* (1984) was edited by Jill Waterhouse. After three chapters on his early life leading to his departure for Australia in 1832, it includes the public record of the years 1832–39; part of the material had already been used in Dutton's *The Hero as Murderer*.

EYRE, Frank (1910–88), born Manchester, England, came to Australia in 1949. While in England he published *The Naiad and Other Poems* (1935), *Poems by Frank Eyre & Peter Lagger* (1936), *Selected Poems* (1941), *Loving in Truth* (1942) and *English Rivers and Canals* (1945), and also edited several anthologies including *The Quiet Spirit* (1946). After the war Eyre joined the editorial staff of OUP, became managing editor of Oxford children's book publishing and in 1952 published *Twentieth Century Children's Books*. As editorial manager of OUP in Australia from 1950 to 1975 he, advised by Grahame Johnston (q.v.), made an important contribution to the study of Australian literature by publishing a new series of *Australian Writers and* *their Work*, and books of Australian literary criticism. He also published important books by Australian writers at a time when other Australian publishers were rejecting them, e.g. *The Generations of Men*, *The Australian Legend*. With George Ferguson and others he helped to establish the Australian Book Publishers Association, of which he was president 1961–63. He was a member of the committee which was responsible for the *Commonwealth Style Manual*, and chairman of the one which produced the Victorian government's *Plain English*, and he was also a member of the final board of the CLF before its dissolution. His later publications include *Ian Clunies Ross* (1961), *British Children's Books in the Twentieth Century* (1971), *Scholarly Publishing 1976* (1977) and *Oxford in Australia* (1978).

F

FABINYI, Andrew (1908–78), born Budapest, Hungary, came to Australia in 1939. He joined the publishing firm of F.W. Cheshire, of which he ultimately became publishing director. President of the Australian Book Publishers Association 1965–66, Fabinyi was made OBE in 1960 and was given the Redmond Barry Award in 1974 for his work with the Library Association of Australia. In about forty years of publishing in Australia, Fabinyi produced over 1000 titles by Australian authors; they include works by Xavier Herbert, Alan Marshall, Brian Fitzpatrick, Cyril Pearl, Judah Waten and Bruce Dawe. In 1983 *A Nation Apart: Essays in Honour of Andrew Fabinyi* was edited by John McLaren; it contains a memoir of Fabinyi by John Hooker and views of Australia in the 1980s by writers such as McLaren, Leonie Sandercock, Gwyneth Dow, Laurie Clancy, Ronald Millar, Sol Encel and Belinda Vaughan.

'Face of the Waters, The', a long poem whose title comes from Genesis, 'And the spirit of God moved upon the face of the waters', was first published by R.D. FitzGerald (q.v.) in the *Bulletin* (1944). FitzGerald explained that the poem, in free verse with occasional use of rhyme, was a 'pantheistic view of the universe modified by the recognition of a dualism somehow integral with it'. The poem is an expansion of the lines occurring in 'The Hidden Bole', 'the Nothing (contracted to some blackened point)/ Where wakes the dream, the brooding ultimate'. The poem attempts an account of Creation. The 'utter nothingness' of pre-existence is so inconceivable that a creator – God or some consciousness – is a necessity. But the creator so envisaged is given a duality that assists, and mockingly frustrates, the attempts of life to burst forth from the nothingness. The poem is also seen as a reworking, using terms and concepts of modern physics and metaphysics, of the myth of Creation, with the Nothing (or Chaos) transformed or even hatched (the 'egg' imagery of the poem) by the 'brooding Ultimate' (the spirit). The most puzzling and complex of FitzGerald's poetry, yet accepted as one of his most impressive works, 'The Face of the Waters' has been described by Judith Wright as 'a meditation on no less a subject than Creation, and on the impossibility of meditating on Creation'.

'Faces in the Street', one of the best-known protest poems of Henry Lawson (q.v.), was first published in 1888 in the *Bulletin;* it was revised during the preparation of *Selected Poems of Henry Lawson* (1918). Written in a stirring rhythm from the perspective of a person whose 'window-sill is level with the faces in

the street', the poem focuses on the flotsam and jetsam of the city who pass by from before dawn until after midnight. It concludes with the vision of a revolution which will do away with poverty and the other 'terrors of the street'.

FACEY, A.B. (Albert Barnett) (1894–1982), born in Maidstone, Victoria, grew up on the Coolgardie goldfields and in outback WA. His autobiography, *A Fortunate Life* (1981), which won the NSW Premier's Award for non-fiction for 1981 and which relates his remarkable survival of a series of severe misfortunes, has been described as a microcosm of the earlier life of Australia. After his father died, before he was 2, and he was deserted by his mother, he, a sister and two brothers were looked after by his impoverished grandmother. He began his working life at the age of 8 and suffered periods of extreme hardship and exploitation; his numerous occupations included general station work, droving, railway 'dogging' and boxing in a travelling troupe. During the First World War he served at Gallipoli before injuries incapacitated him; his brother Joseph, who was also at Gallipoli, was killed. Back in Perth in 1915 he married and joined the Perth tramways for a time, before becoming a farmer in the Soldier Settlement Scheme in 1922. By 1934 the Depression and Facey's war injuries led to his return to the city with his family. Re-employed by Perth tramways, he became active in the Tramways Union. Three of his sons served in the Second World War and one was killed in the fall of Singapore. Facey, who had no formal education, taught himself to read and write and began to compile notes on his life soon after the First World War. Facey's *A Fortunate Life* was dramatised by Clem Gorman in 1984 for a production by the Melbourne Theatre Company, revised in 1987 for another production and published the same year. *The World of Albert Facey* (1992) by J.B. Hirst is a social history of the late nineteenth and early twentieth century using *A Fortunate Life* as a framework and linking equivalent Henry Lawson stories with the incidents of Facey's life.

FACTOR, June (1936–), born Lodz, Poland, came to Australia in infancy. She was educated at the universities of London and Melbourne, has taught at tertiary level and is currently an associate at the Australian Centre, University of Melbourne. She has contributed short fiction and poetry to anthologies and periodicals but is best known for her editing of numerous collections of children's folklore, such as *Far out, Brussel Sprout* (1983) and *All Right, Vegemite* (1985). Her book on children's folklore in Australia, *Captain*

Cook Chased a Chook (1988), won the Opie Prize in 1989, awarded by the American Folklore Society. She is also the co-editor with Gwyn Dow of *Australian Childhood. An Anthology* (1991).

FAHEY, Diane (1945–   ), born and educated in Melbourne, spent some years abroad before returning to SA in 1986. Her poetry has been widely published in journals, anthologies and newspapers and in the collections, *Voices from the Honeycomb* (1986), *Metamorphoses* (1988), *Turning the Hourglass* (1990), and *Mayflies in Amber* (1993). She has won several awards including the Caltex Bendigo Advertiser Manuscript Award for 1986, the Wesley Michel Wright Prize in 1987, the Mattara Poetry Prize in 1985 and the 1988 John Shaw Neilson Poetry Prize. With *Voices from the Honeycomb* Fahey established herself as an accomplished poet with an assured style. The lightly regular stanzas of this collection are perfectly attuned to their sustained lyric tone which often evokes the same sense of aesthetic completion and arrested emotion as still-life painting. Tranquillity is sometimes only at the poem's surface formal level, however, for Fahey gives full play to feelings, admitting emotions of fear, anxiety and grief. In 'Snapshots of a City', for instance, a traffic accident is described as 'someone's happiness/ vandalised by a hair's-breadth chance' and in Victoria Market derelicts sit and 'wait with faces open, wounded/ and wrinkled, like pierced hands'. In other poems natural scenes are the ostensible subject, but they are also invariably metaphors of emotion. The poems of *Metamorphoses* are feminist reworkings of classical myths; taking the Western patriarchal stories of Ovid, Euripides and others as a starting point, Fahey rewrites them from the point of view of women, showing how frequently they are the objects of the narratives' familiar violence. 'How often the myth of rape–/ the carrying off, the invasion–/ has been festooned with flowers,/ a sparkling atmosphere, a picnic lunch', muses the narrator of 'That Other Shore', which is a reimagining of the myth of Europa; Danae in the poem of that title experiences the rape of Zeus as 'Pennies from heaven', a 'celestial dew ... With immaculate conceptions/ there's so little to do –'. Accompanied by reproductions of celebrated paintings of mythical events and by explanatory notes, these poems are elegant, witty reconstructions whose irreverence often produces startling insights. *Turning the Hourglass*, constructed in five parts, charts a journey to freedom and self-discovery. In many of the poems the narrator discovers how to 'inherit [the] body more truly, move close to spirit whose home is body'. The meditative poems of *Mayflies in Amber* focus on creatures of the insect world, although they are often metaphors of human and metaphysical concerns. The easy grace and simple language of Fahey's limpid poems may give an initial impression of facility, but they are in fact intricately worked and well burnished.

FAIRBAIRNS, Zoe, see **Feminism and Australian Literature**

FAIRBRIDGE, Wolfe (1918–50), born Cottesloe, WA, was a research officer with the CSIRO. He died from poliomyelitis at the age of 31; his poetry was posthumously collected as *Poems* (1953). Notable poems include 'Denial and Riposte', which won second prize in the *Sydney Morning Herald* competition in 1947; 'The Man Who Caught the Wind', an Aboriginal tale; and 'Consecration of the House', the poignant expression of the poet's quiet expectation of delight in a future that, tragically, was not to be.

FAIRFAX, James Griffyth (1886–1976), born Sydney into the *Sydney Morning Herald* Fairfax family, grew up in England and was largely an expatriate, visiting Australia only for brief periods. A poet of both lyric grace and intellectual subtlety, Fairfax published numerous volumes of verse including *The Gates of Sleep and Other Poems* (1906), *Poems* (1908), *The Troubled Pool and Other Poems* (1911), *The Horns of Taurus* (1914), *Side Slips: A Collection of Unposted Postscripts, Admissions and Asides* (1914), *The Temple of Janus: A Sonnet Sequence* (1917), *Mesopotamia: Sonnets and Lyrics at Home and Abroad, 1914–1919* (1919), *Carmina Rapta* (1919) and *The Fifth Element* (1937). Fairfax served in the First World War; four of his 'Mesopotamia' poems were included in *Valour and Vision: Poems of the War, 1914–18* (1920), ed. J.T. Trotter.

FAIRFAX, John (1805–77), born Warwickshire, England, was apprenticed to the printing trade in 1817. He worked on the London *Morning Chronicle* and was proprietor of the *Leamington Spa Courier* and the *Leamington Chronicle* before a libel suit forced him to the insolvency court and to a decision to emigrate to Australia, where he arrived with his family in 1838. In 1841, in partnership with Charles Kemp, he bought the daily *Sydney Herald;* in 1842 it became the *Sydney Morning Herald* (q.v.). Fairfax bought out Kemp in 1853 and brought his sons into the management; the *Echo* (1875–93), a penny evening newspaper, and the *Sydney Mail* (q.v.) were added to the *Sydney Morning Herald* stable in his lifetime. After Fairfax's death his descendants carried on John Fairfax & Sons, which was formed in 1856 and remained a family company (limited in 1916, proprietary in 1937) until the public company John Fairfax Ltd was formed in 1956. In December 1990, two months before the Fairfax family proprietorship would have completed 150 years of Australian newspaper publishing (it had acquired the Melbourne *Age* in 1983) John Fairfax Group Pty Ltd went into receivership as a result of a takeover bid by 26-year-old Warwick Fairfax. Conrad Black, owner of Britain's *Daily Telegraph*, with his Tourang Consortium bid successfully for John Fairfax Holdings Ltd (the *SMH*, *Age* and *Australian Financial Review*) in December 1991 with a foreign equity limit of 15 per cent. The first chief executive of the new group was South African Stephen Mulholland, appointed 1992.

Gavin Souter's *Company of Heralds* takes the Fairfax story to 1981. His update, *Heralds and Angels: The House of Fairfax* (1991), continues the Fairfax story to 1990; a further updated edition was published in 1992. Another account of the events leading to the Tourang group's purchase of Fairfax is given in Colleen Ryan and Glenn Burge's *Corporate Cannibals: The Taking of Fairfax* (1992).

'FALCONER, Dora', see **LAWSON, Louisa**

FALKINER, Suzanne (1952–), born Sydney, grew up in central NSW and after a university education spent three years travelling in Asia, Europe and South America. She has worked as a publisher's editor and reader and as a freelance writer. She has published a novel, *Rain in the Distance* (1986); a collection of short stories, *After the Great Novelist and Other Stories* (1989); an account of an Italian woman who lived as a man in Australia for nearly twenty years, *Eugenia. A Man* (1988); a history of her family's property, *Haddon Rig* (1981); and two extensive and well-researched studies of writers' responses to the Australian rural and urban landscapes, both titled *The Writers' Landscape*, one subtitled *Settlement* (1992) and the other, *Wilderness* (1992). She has also written the texts for the illustrated books *Australians Today* (1985) and *Australian Aborigines: Shadows in a Landscape* (1980); and has edited *Room to Move. The Redress Press Anthology of Australian Women's Short Stories* (1985) and a collection of essays, *Leslie Wilkinson. A Practical Idealist* (1982), written in tribute to Sydney's first professor of architecture. Falkiner's two books on the writers' landscape are important collections, illustrating the powerful, various impact made by Australia on the writerly imagination; interpreting landscape widely, including historical, social, ethnic, and cultural aspects of the Australian experience as well as the geographical, Falkiner moves 'from the physical landscape or geography of Australia as it was revealed to Europeans to the landscape of the mind, rather than from the body of Australian literature to the real world'. The short stories of *After the Great Novelist* move between a range of countries as Stork, the narrator and detached observer, travels between places which can only be known from a distance, mirroring the distance between contemporary relationships. *Rain in the Distance*, a semi-autobiographical novel, re-creates the loneliness of a childhood in a wealthy family whose preoccupations exclude the children and the later experiences of rootlessness and alienation during years of travel.

FALLAW, Lance (1876–1958), born Gateshead, England, joined the staff of the Rockhampton *Daily Record* in 1908 after a period as a newspaperman in South Africa. He was later editor of the *Charters Towers Telegraph, Cairns Post, Geelong Advertiser* and associate editor of the *Sydney Morning Herald*. He published a collection of verse, *Silverleaf and Oak* (1906), before he arrived in Queensland; later volumes of poetry were *The Ampler Sky* (1909), *Unending Ways* (1926) and *Hostage and Survival* (1939).

FALLON, Mary (1951–) is the author of *The Sexuality of Illusion* (1981), on the development of women's sexuality, and the novel *Working Hot* (1989),which won the Victorian Premier's Literary Award in 1989. A powerful and ambitious attempt to write *écriture*

feminine, *Working Hot* moves between free-verse narrative, letters, marginal notes, catalogues, and drama, avoiding the dominance of a single voice. Beginning with an exploration of a lesbian love affair, and finding its ultimate referents in the female body, the novel is both a dexterous erotic display and a mordant social satire.

FANE, Margaret (Beatrice Osborn) (1888–1962) was born in Melbourne and educated privately. She began to write in mid-life, contributed stories to the *Sydney Mail* and the *Bulletin*, and, with Hilary Lofting, published the collection *The Happy Vagabond* (1928). From 1912 to 1918 she lived with David McKee Wright (q.v.), who was the father of her four sons.

Fanfrolico Press, a fine publishing company, was first established by Jack Lindsay (q.v.) and John Kirtley, a stock-exchange employee with an interest in printing. Kirtley had earlier (1923) printed and published Lindsay's *Fauns and Ladies*, with three woodcuts by Norman Lindsay. In 1925 the Kirtley-Norman and Jack Lindsay collaboration produced in Sydney *Lysistrata*, the first book to carry the imprint of Fanfrolico Press. The unbound issue of *The Passionate Neatherd* by Jack Lindsay followed in 1926 and in the same year Jack Lindsay and Kirtley went to London to establish and expand their publishing activities and to attempt to export to Europe the philosophy propounded by Norman Lindsay in his *Creative Effort* (1920). Fanfrolico's publications included works by Australian, European and English writers, produced on hand-made paper, painstakingly edited or translated and often sumptuously illustrated. After Kirtley's departure from the Press in 1927 his place was taken first by P.R. Stephensen (q.v.) and then in 1929 by Brian Penton. Philip Lindsay was also involved in its management. In 1930 the assets of the Press were liquidated. P.R. Stephensen's account of his involvement in Fanfrolico Press is in *Kookaburras and Satyrs* (1954). Jack Lindsay wrote *Fanfrolico and After* (1962) and Harry Chaplin, *The Fanfrolico Press* (1976). An excellent account of the press is also in Craig Munro's biography of Stephensen, *A Wild Man of Letters* (1984).

FARJEON, Benjamin (1838–1903), born London, broke away from his family's Jewish faith as a youth and came penniless to Australia in 1854. From 16 to 23 he roamed the Victorian goldfields, sometimes digging, sometimes caught up in attempts to establish a modest type of newspaper. He went to NZ in 1861, settled in Dunedin and worked on the *Otago Daily Times*. In 1865 he published his first book, *Shadows on the Snow: A Christmas Story*, which he dedicated and sent to Charles Dickens, his literary idol. Dickens responded kindly and Farjeon returned to England, hoping to make a reputation as a writer. In 1866 he published *Grif: A Story of Australian Life*. Between *Grif* and his death, about fifty other novels were written, some concerned with the urban poor, others more straightforward stories of mystery and crime. Farjeon's Australian experiences, especially on the goldfields, are reflected in such works as *Joshua Marvel*

(1871), *At the Sign of the Silver Flagon* (1875), *The Sacred Nugget* (1885), *While Golden Sleep Doth Reign* (1887), *Basil and Annette* (1890) and *The Betrayal of John Fordham* (1896).

FARMER, Beverley (1941–), born Melbourne and educated at the University of Melbourne, has had a variety of occupations and spent three years in Greece, where she participated in village life, taught English and helped to run a restaurant. She has written two novels, *Alone* (1980, winner of the 1981 Alan Marshall award), which deals in part with lesbian love and incidentally provides a vivid picture of Melbourne's inner suburb Carlton, and *The Seal Woman* (1992); and two collections of short stories, *Milk* (1983, winner of the NSW Premier's Award for fiction) and *Home Time* (1985); and her writer's journal, *A Body of Water* (1990). *Milk* and *Home Time* are companion volumes; not only do several stories in both collections deal with the breakdown or aftermath of a Greek-Australian marriage, but characters from the first reappear in the second and relationships established in the first pursue their distinctive histories. Farmer is preoccupied with dislocation and change, whether the dislocation is that of Australians in Greece or vice versa, or the dislocation caused by death, or decaying or ruptured relationships, or simply the natural evolution of time. Farmer's tightly organised prose, which is often as resonant with compressed meaning as poetry, and her sensuous response to landscape and physical objects are frequently seen as characteristic traits, but her descriptions are never merely decorative; objects and textures convey ways and histories of perception and have human as well as aesthetic significance. *Milk* and *Home Time* also complement each other in that the first explores nurturing and formative influences and sets them against the effects of ageing and loss, while the second considers the meaning of home as birthplace and as marking the point of departure, growth or return. *A Body of Water*, subtitled *A Writer's Notebook*, opens in February 1987 and consists of thirteen monthly instalments interleaved with poems and five short stories. A meditation on the writer's craft, on her reading and her spiritual experience, the journal mirrors its title in fluidity and depth. Ideas, memories, and quotations from a range of other writers mingle with reflections on daily life in Carlton or Queenscliff as the narrator struggles to come to terms with isolation and sterility. The protagonist of *The Seal Woman* is a Danish widow in mourning for her husband lost at sea; her return to Australia and to the house where she spent her honeymoon is both an outer journey and an inner one, leading to self-discovery.

FARRELL, John (1851–1904), was born Buenos Aires, the son of Irish gold-rush immigrants who came to Australia in 1852 from South America. After a limited education he worked mainly as a brewer until he turned to journalism. A radical, he contributed frequently to the *Boomerang* and the *Worker* and enthusiastically shared William Lane's vision of an Australian Utopia. In the 1880s he contributed verse satires and narratives to numerous newspapers and journals, including the *Bulletin*, writing one of its earliest Australian stories, 'One Christmas Day' (1884); his first major book of verse, *How He Died* (q.v.), was published in 1887. Farrell became involved with Henry George of the Single Tax movement, editing two of that movement's Australian journals, but worked mainly for the *Daily Telegraph*, briefly as editor but mostly as columnist, leader-writer and book-reviewer. Two of his minor verse successes were 'Australia to England' (q.v.), a poem written for Queen Victoria's Jubilee in 1897, widely esteemed and publicly praised by Kipling; and 'Hymn of the Commonwealth', sung by massed choirs at the Sydney Commonwealth celebrations. The main collection of his poetry, *My Sundowner and Other Poems*, published posthumously in 1904, was edited by Bertram Stevens. Although Farrell's was a minor poetic voice in the nationalistic radicalism of the 1890s, in his person and character he represented the best of that movement. Mary Gilmore's tribute that he most influenced her life and work is characteristic of contemporary sentiments about him.

FARWELL, George (1911–76), born Bath, England, came to Australia in 1936. He travelled widely in Australia and New Guinea and worked in a variety of occupations, as gold-miner, wharf labourer, radio broadcaster, actor and freelance journalist. He edited *Australian Book News* 1946–48, and was public relations officer for the Adelaide Festival 1959–64. A prolific author, Farwell wrote short stories, biographies, plays, documentary features for radio and television and travel accounts. His study of the Philippines, *Mask of Asia* (1966), won the Moomba-Rothman Award of 1967, but his best-known books are those which reflect his extensive knowledge of Australia. They include *Land of Mirage* (1950), an account of the Birdsville Track; *Vanishing Australians* (1961); *Riders to an Unknown Sea* (1963), a biography of Charles Sturt for young readers; *Ghost Towns of Australia* (1965); *Ned Kelly* (1970); *Requiem for Woolloomooloo* (1971); and *Squatter's Castle* (1973), a biography of a nineteenth-century pastoralist, Edward Ogilvie. *Farwell Country* (1977) is a selection of his writings 1946–76. He also published a collection of short stories, *Surf Music* (1950); memoirs, *Rejoice in Freedom* (1976); and two plays, *The House that Jack Built* (1970), which focuses on the Rum Rebellion and won an award in the Commonwealth Jubilee State play competition of 1951, and *Portrait of a Gentleman*, an award-winning radio play on the subject of Thomas Griffiths Wainewright, first produced in 1940 and included in *Australian Radio Plays* (1946, ed. Leslie Rees). Another play, 'Sons of the South', is set in outback Queensland and deals with the shearers' strike of 1891.

Fatal Shore, The, see **HUGHES, Robert**; **Convict in Australian Literature**

FATCHEN, Max, see *The Oxford Companion to Australian Children's Literature* (1993), pp. 161–2.

Fatty Finn, the comic-strip creation of Syd Nicholls (q.v.), began life in 1923 in the Sydney *Sunday News* and appeared intermittently in several formats until 1977. The great rival of Ginger Meggs (q.v.), the Fatty Finn strip was better drawn but less humorous and ultimately less successful. The adventures of Fatty formed the subject of the classic Australian film *The Kid Stakes* (1927); a modern version of the film, titled *Fatty Finn* and scripted by Bob Ellis and Chris McGill, was made in 1980.

FAUCHERY, Antoine (1823–61), born Paris, came to Melbourne in 1852 and worked on the Victorian goldfields both as a digger and a storekeeper until he left Australia in 1856. His *Lettres d'un Mineur en Australie* were published first in *Le Moniteur Universel* in fifteen instalments and also separately (1857). The letters were translated from the French by A.R. Chisholm and published with drawings by Ron Edwards as *Letters from a Miner in Australia* (1965). Full of radical sympathies, even for the Chinese diggers, the letters give a vivid impression of the goldfields and early Melbourne life. In a later visit to Australia in 1858–59, Fauchery conducted a photographic studio in Melbourne. His photographic studies, with those of English geologist, Richard Daintree, have been collected with text by Dianne Reilly and Jennifer Carew as *Sun Pictures of Victoria: The Fauchery-Daintree Collection, 1858* (1983). The collection includes photos of Le Comte Lionel de Chabrillan, husband of Celeste de Chabrillan, Sir John O'Shannassy, Sir Henry Barkly, after whom the Barkly Tablelands were named, and Fauchery himself, as well as numerous gold-mining scenes and Aboriginal studies.

FAUST, Beatrice (1939–), born Melbourne, into a family with Irish antecedents, lost her mother at birth. Although ambivalent towards the child whose birth had caused the death of his wife, her father, Frederick Fennessy, made sure she had a good education which culminated in a scholarship to the University of Melbourne, where she graduated MA. A founding member of the Council for Civil Liberties and for a brief period president of the Abortion Law Repeal Association in Victoria, in the 1960s, she pursued postgraduate studies on abortion, publicising her views on the issue and attracting controversy as a result. One of Australia's most prominent feminists, she was a founder of the Women's Electoral Lobby and has written several well-researched books on the condition of women. They include *Women Sex & Pornography* (1980) and *Apprenticeship in Liberty. Sex, Feminism and Sociobiology* (1991). In *Apprenticeship in Liberty* Faust argues in favour of diversity of sexual and other ways of living, which she sees as liberating for men as well as women, and puts forward a controversial thesis locating sexual difference in biological make-up. The same emphasis on biological difference characterises *Women Sex & Pornography* where Faust disputes feminist opposition to pornography given the differences she perceives between male and female psychosexual reactions. She has also written a frank account of her addiction to prescribed drugs, *Benzo Junkie: More Than*

a Case History (1993). Like Germaine Greer, with whom she is often compared, Faust is an unclassifiable, independent feminist who is no stranger to controversy even within the ranks of feminism, and who combines scholarship with wit and irony in her writings. She has contributed a chapter on her career to *The Half-Open Door* (1982) and her achievements are described in *Reformers* (1989) by Michelle Grattan and Margaret Bowman.

FAUST, Clive (1932–), born Melbourne, graduated in philosophy from the University of Melbourne, lived in Japan for seven years and became a lecturer at Bendigo College of Advanced Education. Featured in the American magazine *Origin* (July 1978), he was included as a representative of the new wave of Australian poetry in John Tranter's anthology *The New Australian Poetry* (1979). Faust has published three books of verse, *Metamorphosed from the Adjacent Cold*, *Token and Trace* (both 1980), and *Leavetakings* (1986).

FAVENC, Ernest (1845–1908), born Surrey, England, came to Australia in 1864 and worked for fourteen years on stations in north Queensland. He led the 1877 expedition, financed by the *Queenslander*, for which he sometimes wrote under the pseudonym 'Dramingo', to investigate the feasibility of a railway linking Queensland to Darwin. His reputation as an explorer established, Favenc spent several years working for pastoral interests opening up the country along the south-western coast of the Gulf of Carpentaria and across into WA. He then joined the staff of the Sydney *Evening News* and began to turn his adventurous past as an explorer into a lucrative source of fiction and non-fiction. His pastoral and geographic works include *The Great Austral Plain* (1881), *Western Australia* (1887), *The History of Australian Exploration from 1788 to 1888* (1888), *A Century of Progress, 1788–1888* (1902) and *The Explorers of Australia and Their Lifework* (1908). His short fiction includes *'The Last of Six': Tales of the Austral Tropics* (1893), the title story relating the macabre finale on Australian soil of an escape from a French penal island in the Pacific; *Tales of the Austral Tropics* (1894), which includes the stories of the earlier work and an additional two tales; and *My Only Murder and Other Tales* (1899), stories also set in Oceania and north Queensland. His novels are *The Secret of the Australian Desert* (1895), which concerns the fate of the explorer Ludwig Leichhardt; *Marooned on Australia* (1896), based on the wreck of the *Batavia* in 1629; and *The Moccasins of Silence* (1896), an adventurous romance which takes its title from the footwear used by some Queensland Aborigines in the story. Favenc's only volume of poetry, *Voices of the Desert* (1905), attempts to evoke something of the emptiness and silence of the inland. Cheryl Frost wrote *The Last Explorer: The Life and Work of Ernest Favenc* (1983).

FAWKNER, John Pascoe (1792–1869), born London, accompanied his father and family to Van Diemen's Land in 1803, his father having been sentenced to fourteen years' transportation for receiving stolen goods. As a young man in Van Diemen's Land, Fawkner was in constant trouble with the authorities; for aiding and abetting the escape of seven convicts he was given 500 lashes and three years' hard labour. Ever the speculator, he organised an expedition across Bass Strait to Port Phillip in 1835, gained large landholdings and was an influential figure in that colony's rapid development to statehood. On the introduction of responsible government he became the member for the Central Province of Victoria, holding the seat until his death. Fawkner saw the press as an instrument of reform. In 1828 he commenced the *Launceston Advertiser*, was its editor for two years and used the paper as 'the active and avowed friend of the emancipist class in Van Diemen's Land'. In 1838 in Port Phillip, he began the *Melbourne Advertiser*, which was suppressed because Fawkner had no licence; in 1839, with a licence, he began the *Port Phillip Patriot and Melbourne Advertiser* (1839–48). Strongly opposed to the squatting interests, he published a pamphlet, *Squatting Orders* (1854). Hugh Anderson wrote *Out of the Shadow: The Career of John Pascoe Fawkner* (1962) and C.P. Billot published *The Life and Times of John Pascoe Fawkner* (1985) and an edition of Fawkner's private journal 1835–36 entitled *Melbourne's Missing Chronicle* (1982). Fawkner appears as a minor character in Eric Lambert's novel *The Five Bright Stars* (1954).

FEARN-WANNAN, William, see **WANNAN, Bill**

Federation was the movement which promoted the union of the six Australian colonies, NSW, Victoria, Queensland, SA, Tasmania and WA. The idea of a federal union was proposed in the 1840s and 1850s but did not gather momentum until the 1880s and 1890s. Perhaps the most decisive steps were taken at federal conventions held in 1897–98, when a constitution was drafted which, after amendments, was approved at a referendum held in 1899 in all colonies except WA. While an Australian delegation was discussing the constitution with the British government in London, WA voted to join the federal system and the inauguration of the Commonwealth of Australia took place on 1 January 1901. A number of 'writer politicians' were involved in the Federation movement, notably Alfred Deakin and Sir Henry Parkes (qq.v.); 'Price Warung' was active as publicist throughout the 1890s. Federation also attracted the interest of many Australian poets, including John Farrell, whose 'Hymn to the Commonwealth' was sung by massed choirs at the inauguration in Sydney; George Essex Evans, who wrote the patriotic 'An Ode for Commonwealth Day' (1901); Edward Dyson; Mary Hannay Foott; William Gay; A.B. Paterson; Roderic Quinn; and A.G. and J. Brunton Stephens. Two pantomimes with Federation themes staged at the time of the inauguration ceremonies were an updated version of J.C. Williamson's 'Djin Djin' and 'Australis', set in Sydney in 2001.

Fellowship (1914–22), a monthly Melbourne journal and the organ of the Free Religious Fellowship, a group dedicated to an undogmatic religion, was edited by Frederick Sinclaire. Mainly concerned with socialist and pacifist ideas, the journal included some poetry and comment on Australian literature. Sinclaire was a major contributor but others included Vance and Nettie Palmer, 'Furnley Maurice', Bernard O'Dowd, J. le Gay Brereton and Frederick Macartney.

Fellowship of Australian Writers, known also as the FAW, was formally inaugurated in Sydney on 23 November 1928. Claims have been advanced for both Roderic Quinn and Mary Gilmore as its founder but it seems that Gilmore, prompted by Quinn and assisted by Lucy Cassidy, wife of the poet, R.J. Cassidy, arranged the meeting at which J. le Gay Brereton was elected first president. At first the FAW was a Sydney-based organisation but, as membership spread, branches were set up in the other States, Victoria and WA being the first. Membership has waxed and waned in some areas, but at present there is an autonomous fellowship in each State and the Northern Territory, with numerous regional branches in the larger States. In 1955 a federal council was formed and since then the national presidency has been held on a rotating basis by State presidents. The FAW exists to bring writers together and to promote their interests, and, although this has been characteristically done through regular meetings, lectures, newsletters and anthologies, there have also been activities associated with each of the individual organisations. For example, in NSW, a pilgrimage to Henry Lawson's statue in the Domain was for long an annual event; the WA branch has its headquarters in Tom Collins House, bequeathed to it by Joseph Furphy's (q.v.) son in 1948; in Victoria the FAW administers a large number of literary awards (q.v.). Periodically the FAW has incorporated other writers' organisations, such as the Writers' Club in Sydney (amalgamated with the FAW in 1938) and the Queensland Authors' and Artists' Association, which was founded in 1921 and became the FAW Queensland branch in 1959. As well as providing 'fellowship' among writers, the organisation has many times advanced the interest of writers in specifically practical ways, notably in the proposals it put forward in the late 1930s which widened the charter of the Commonwealth Literary Fund (q.v.). For over a decade Vance Palmer and Flora Eldershaw represented the FAW on the advisory board of the CLF. The FAW was also heavily involved in the formation of the ASA in 1963. Other activities it has supported include the opposition to censorship and the pioneering of Australian Authors' Week and Children's Book Week. Among the many prominent Australian writers and publishers who were associated with the FAW in its early years were (in addition to those already cited) 'Steele Rudd', George Mackaness, Marjorie Barnard, Dymphna Cusack, Miles Franklin, Will Lawson, Bert and Dora Birtles, T. Inglis Moore, Leslie Haylen, Frank Dalby Davison and Walter Stone in NSW; Nettie Palmer and 'Furnley Maurice' in Victoria; Paul Buddee, Gavin Casey, Henrietta Drake-Brockman, J.K. Ewers, Katharine Susannah Prichard and Donald Stuart in WA; Joan Woodberry and E. Morris Miller in Tasmania; Madelaine Brunato in SA; and James Devaney, R.S. Byrnes, Martin Haley and Maureen Freer in Queensland. *Dream at a Graveside* (1988), edited by Len Fox, is a history of the FAW 1928–88.

Female Eunuch, The, a feminist analysis of female sexual stereotypes by Germaine Greer (q.v.), was first published in Britain in 1970 and became outstandingly popular after publication in the USA in 1971. Subsequently translated into eleven languages, the book became almost a sacred text for the international women's liberation movement of the 1970s, notwithstanding sporadic criticisms of aspects of its ideology from some feminists. Designed to question 'the most basic assumptions about female normality in order to reopen the possibilities for development which have been successively locked off by conditioning', the book begins with a study of the female body. Confined by male, historically determined definitions of female sexuality, women's perceptions of themselves have stressed passivity and elements which belong to the castrate, such as plumpness, languor, delicacy and timidity. In a section titled 'Soul', Greer next examines ways in which the female stereotype is processed in our consumer society and presented to succeeding generations, perpetually suppressing energy or diverting it from a public, powerful sphere to a private, powerless one. In the third section, titled 'Love', a range of distorted perceptions are examined from 'Romance' to the 'Middle-Class Myth of Love and Marriage', and the nuclear family in particular is subjected to stringent criticism. The fourth section, titled 'Hate', discusses negative aspects of the inevitable estrangement of the sexes, given their mutually destructive, predominantly sadomasochistic perceptions of each other. In her last section, 'Revolution', Greer tentatively suggests some sexual alternatives which might free both sexes from their imprisoning stereotypes and from 'building symbiotic, economically determined' relationships.

Female Factory was the name given, during the early years of settlement in NSW, to an institution at Parramatta for the detention and employment of female convicts; there were similar institutions in Hobart and Launceston. The expression is used in the *Sydney Gazette*, in Peter Cunningham's *Two Years in New South Wales* (1827) and in John Lang's *The Forger's Wife* (1855). A song, 'Australian Courtship', from the *Sydney Gazette* 14 July 1832, with its lines 'But the lass I adore, the lass for me/ Is a lass in the female factory', indicates that male convicts and other colonial males saw the factory as a marriage market. 'Price Warung's' story 'Parson Ford's Confessional' (1892) climaxes in a scene at the Hobart Female Factory in which the inmates revenge themselves on Ford by confessing to some visiting matrons that he is the father of their children. The Female Factory is also referred to in Frank Clune's *Wild Colonial Boys* (1948) when Sam Clift tells Benjamin Hall, father of the bushranger Ben Hall, to avoid 'the flash molls in Sydney Town'

and select his bride from the Female Factory. J.H.M. Abbott in *Out of the Past* (1944) maintains that Australia owes much to the women from the Female Factory, many of whom 'valiantly pioneered the new wild country with their men, and played their parts nobly'. Anne Summers in her feminist history *Damned Whores and God's Police* (1975) suggests that one of the alternative roles available to Australian women, especially in the nineteenth century, derived in part from the Female Factory. Annette Salt wrote *These Outcast Women* (1984), a history of, and commentary on, the Parramatta Female Factory. Salt's book dispels many myths about the factory, placing it accurately in its social context.

Feminism and Australian Literature. In 1902 Australian women were granted, several years before their European and American sisters, the right to vote in federal elections, an event which seemed to justify J.S. Mill's earlier impression, recorded in his letter to Archibald Michie in 1868, of Australia as an enlightened country. It is an impression that is not supported, however, by feminists and some modern historians and sociologists. Feminist reinterpretations of Australian history, in particular, see women as inevitably reduced to the margins of the national life by the nature of the nation's pioneering and convict beginnings; forced into such opposed but equally crippling stereotypes as Anne Summers describes in her history *Damned Whores and God's Police* (1975, revised 1993), women are seen as having been implicitly excluded from the nineteenth century's shaping of the national consciousness. The exclusive masculinity of the historical self-image has been indirectly described by Russel Ward, for instance, in a well-known passage of his seminal cultural history *The Australian Legend* (1958); according to Ward, the chief elements of the 'typically Australian outlook', an ethos which he sees as deriving from convict, working-class, Irish and native-born Australian sources, are

> a comradely independence based on a group solidarity and relative economic plenty, a rough and ready capacity for 'stringybark and green-hide' improvisation, a lighthearted intolerance of respectable or conventional manners, a reckless improvidence, and a conviction that the working bushman was the 'true Australian' whose privilege it was to despise 'new chums' and city folk.

Whatever the historical validity of this implicitly sexist perception of the national character, feminists argue that it was an inevitable part of the cultural baggage of the Australian writer, male or female, from at least the 1890s until the 1950s. Similarly, the masculine, patriarchal, acquisitive and anti-intellectual nature of Australian society, both in actuality and in myth, has been a commonplace of many cultural and general histories, and a dominant theme of feminist accounts. Norman Mackenzie expressed what he saw as the actualities of the situation in his pioneering sociological study *Women in Australia* (1962, assisted by Enid Campbell): 'Australia is more "a man's country" than other industrial democracies', and Miriam Dixson has energetically attacked the traditional myths in *The Real Matilda: Women and Identity in Australia, 1788–1975* (1976): 'there are . . . no women in the pantheon of Australian gods . . . there is an animal, a horse called Phar Lap. The rest tend to be males under all-male and danger-fraught conditions.'

Women writers of the nineteenth and early twentieth centuries formed a variety of responses to the national ethos. Miles Franklin, hailed in her own lifetime as a proponent of bush values, was in fact highly ambivalent, recording her bitter alienation in *My Brilliant Career* (1901) even as she celebrated the Australian landscape. Ada Cambridge, Rosa Praed and Jessie Couvreur were traditionally thought to have escaped into the world of the genteel romance reserved for women, although recent research has demonstrated their feminist concerns and even radical criticism of institutions. Cambridge's preoccupations with gender, class and the institution of marriage are thoroughly explored in the biographies by Margaret Bradstock and Louise Wakeling (1991) and by Audrey Tate (1991), and in a new edition of her volume of poetry, *Unspoken Thoughts* (1988), edited by Patricia Barton. The publication of a previously unknown novella, *A Woman's Friendship*, edited by Elizabeth Morrison in 1988, has further enlarged understanding of her radicalism. Jessie Couvreur ('Tasma'), meanwhile, has emerged as a sophisticated, cosmopolitan, internationally successful writer in the biography by Patricia Clarke (1994). Catherine Spence was well known as a public figure, but the extent of her feminist concerns was only made apparent with the publication of Susan Magarey's biography *Unbridling the Tongues of Women* (1985). Spence realistically tackled a range of women's issues, including the problem of work and patriarchal, religious doctrines although her most radical novels, *Gathered In* (serialised 1881–82) and *Handfasted*, were not published in book form during her lifetime and she eventually abandoned fiction for more direct means. Another sophisticated South Australian novelist, Catherine Martin, had been almost completely forgotten until her novel *The Incredible Journey* was republished in 1987, followed by *An Australian Girl* in 1988. The painstaking researches by Rosemary Foxton and Margaret Allen, meanwhile, have filled in some of the gaps in her biography, although a full-scale account has yet to be written. Remarkably well read and well versed in European culture, Martin retained the stock ingredients of the romance but included strikingly frank considerations of marriage, the limitations of the typical Australian male and of conventional religious, Anglo-Saxon pieties. Barbara Baynton's short stories have long been recognised as fundamentally subversive of the myths of mateship and romantic bush life, but the well-concealed biographical reasons for her bitterness have only recently been exposed, especially in the account by her great-granddaughter, Penne Hackforth-Jones (1989).

One of the most interesting products of the second-wave feminist movement in Australia which dates from the early 1970s has been a re-examination of central literary texts and previous perceptions of them. A number of provocative essays by such commentators as Jill Roe, Anne Summers, Frances McInherny, Elizabeth Lawson, Susan Sheridan, Coral Lansbury, Dale Spender, Carole Ferrier, Jane Sunderland, Delys Bird, Shirley Walker and Helen Thomson have appeared in both feminist and literary journals. At the same time the lives, problems and attitudes of a range of women writers, some of whom were formerly dismissed as minor, or untypically Australian, have been reassessed from a modern perspective and the political and personal aspirations, cultural, sexual and racial assumptions in the work of such writers as Katharine Susannah Prichard, Nettie Palmer, Miles Franklin, Marjorie Barnard, Christina Stead, Jean Devanny, Elizabeth Harrower, Shirley Hazzard, Kylie Tennant, Eleanor Dark, Dymphna Cusack, Betty Roland, Eve Langley and Mary Gilmore are now being extensively and illuminatingly explored. Similarly, assumptions and attitudes of certain male writers such as Henry Lawson, Joseph Furphy, Christopher Brennan, Patrick White, David Ireland, Martin Boyd and Thomas Keneally have also been subjected to a feminist reassessment, with revealing results. A collection of essays, titled *Who Is She?* (1983, ed. Shirley Walker), explores the image of women implicitly held by both male and female writers, and Drusilla Modjeska in *Exiles at Home* (1981) examines the work and problems of women writers 1925–45. Significant biographies which have altered perceptions of the role of women writers in both colonial and post-Federation Australia include Diane Kirkby's of Alice Henry (1991), Patricia Clarke's of Louisa Atkinson (1990), Nancy Phelan's of Louise Mack (1991), W.H. Wilde's of Mary Gilmore (1988), Brian Matthews's of Louisa Lawson (1987), Joy Thwaite's of Eve Langley (1989), Julie Lewis's of Olga Masters (1991), Adrienne Hawley's of Dorothea Mackellar (1989) and Chris Williams's of Christina Stead (1989). Hazel Rowley's biography of Stead (1993), the result of many years of research, rivals David Marr's of Patrick White in detail and extent. Feminist rereadings of the work of Henry Handel Richardson by such critics as Carol Franklin, Catherine Pratt and Elizabeth Lawson have countered earlier interpretations of her as unimaginative and overly dependent on biographical fact; Dorothy Green revised her earlier study *Ulysses Bound* in 1986 and Axel Clark offered another account of the early Richardson in 1990.

Re-examination of literary texts has been accompanied by a reassessment of the standard texts of Australian historiography, such as those by Russel Ward, Manning Clark, Geoffrey Serle, Alan Shaw and C.E.W. Bean, and analyses of their limitations from a feminist point of view. Ann Curthoys in *Arena* 22 (1970), and Kay Daniels in *New History: Studying Australia Today* (1982, eds G. Osborne and W.F. Mandle), outline the gaps in Australian historiography. The pioneering histories of Dixson and Summers and such documentary histories as Beverley Kingston's *The World Moves Slowly* (1977) and Ruth Teale's *Colonial Eve* (1978) have been followed by the major feminist history *Creating a Nation* (1994) by Patricia Grimshaw, Marilyn Lake, Ann McGrath and Marian Quartly.

Norman Mackenzie's *Women in Australia* (1962), updated by S. Encel and Margaret Tebbutt (1974), is the only interpretation of the contemporary position of women which aims to be comprehensive, although several collections confront a range of women's problems in such areas as education, law, work and family. These include *Created Second?*, ed. Barbara Thiering (1973); *The Other Half*, ed. Jan Mercer (1975); *Women, Class and History*, ed. Elizabeth Windschuttle (1980); *Australian Women: Feminist Perspectives*, ed. Norma Grieve and Pat Grimshaw (1981); *Australian Women: New Feminist Perspectives*, ed. Norma Grieve and Ailsa Burns (1986); *Studies in Gender: Essays in Honour of Norma Grieve*, ed. Patricia Grimshaw, Ruth Fincher and Marion Campbell (1992); *Women in Australian Society*, ed. Rosalie Stephenson (1970); and *In Her Own Right*, ed. Julie Rigg (1969). Others which concentrate more on the problems of work, both now and in the past, include *My Wife, My Daughter and Poor Mary Ann* by Beverley Kingston (1975); *Women at Work*, ed. Ann Curthoys, Susan Eade and Peter Spearritt (1975); *The Unequal Half*, ed. Janice Brownfoot and Dianne Scott (1976); *Gentle Invaders*, ed. Edna Ryan and Anne Conlon (1975); *Worth Her Salt*, ed. Margaret Bevege (1982); *Gender at Work* by Ann Game and Rosemary Pringle (1983); *Uphill All The Way* by Kay Daniels (1980); *Girl Fridays in Revolt* by Joan Clarke and Zoe O'Leary (1969); *Double Time: Women in Victoria 150 Years*, ed. Marilyn Lake and F. Kelly (1985); and *The Politics of Work: Gender and Labour in Victoria 1880–1939* by Raelene Frances (1993). *The Half-Open Door*, ed. Patricia Grimshaw and Lynne Strahan (1982), is a collection of autobiographical essays, including some from such women writers as Joyce Nicholson, Thérèse Radic, Lynne Strahan and Kathleen Fitzpatrick, which discuss the problems faced by women in their professional and personal lives. *Stepping Out of History* (1991) is an informative collection of documents of women at work in Australia edited by Marian Aveling and Joy Damousi. *Women Academics: Why So Few?* (1983), a report based on a survey of the universities of Sydney and NSW, provides a mass of data on the experience of women in the field of tertiary education. Other aspects of education are considered in *Fashioning the Feminine: Girls, Popular Culture and Schooling* (1991) by Pam Gilbert and Sandra Taylor; *Gender and Education* (1986) by Paige Porter; and *Her Natural Destiny: the Education of Women in NSW* (1986) by Noelene Kyle. A study which has cast a fresh light on convict women is Portia Robinson's *The Women of Botany Bay* (1988, revised 1993). Other specialist, regional and general studies include *Spinifex and Hessian: Women's Lives in North-Western Australia 1860–1900*, by Susan Hunt (1986); *So Much Hard Work: Women and Prostitution in Australian History*, ed. Kay Daniels (1984); *In Her Own Name: Women in South Australian History* by Helen Jones (1986); *Families in Colonial Australia*, ed. Patricia Grimshaw et al. (1985); *A Woman's Place: Women and Politics in Australia* by Marian Sawer and Marian Simms (1984, revised 1993); Katrina Afford's economic history of women in Australia 1788–1850 (1984); and Jill Julius Matthews's study of the historical construction of femininity in twentieth-

century Australia, *Good and Mad Women* (1984). A particularly well-researched and substantial study is Kerreen Reiger's of the Australian family 1880–1940, *The Disenchantment of the Home* (1985). Judith Allen's *Sex & Secrets* (1990) studies crimes involving Australian women since 1880; Shirley Fitzgerald's *Rising Damp* (1987) is an investigation of social mobility which has much to say on the status and economic deprivation of women, as has Marilyn Lake's study of the soldier settlement scheme in Victoria 1915–38, *The Limits of Hope* (1987). Important general studies are *Exclusion, Exploitation and Extermination: Race Relations in Colonial Queensland* (1975 by Raymond Evans, Kay Saunders and Kathryn Cronin), which includes a pioneering account of the degradation of Black women under colonialism and has appeared in revised editions in 1988 and 1993; and *Gender Relations in Australia: Domination and Negotiation* (1992), ed. Kay Saunders and Raymond Evans. Several essays on the specific problems faced by Aboriginal women, both now and in the past and in both White and Aboriginal society, have been published as well as a collection edited by Fay Gale, *Woman's Role in Aboriginal Society* (1970). Feminist concerns, especially in the work of Sneja Gunew, have also helped to illuminate the migrant experience in Australia.

Audrey Oldfield in *Woman Suffrage in Australia: A Gift or a Struggle?* (1992) has written a revisionist account of a movement which has traditionally been perceived as achieving easy victories; and the results of research into the work of such women as Louisa Lawson, Rose Scott, Vida Goldstein, Alice Henry, Catherine Helen Spence, Adela Pankhurst Walsh, Jean Devanny, Jessie Street and Bessie Rischbieth have also appeared. Contemporary accounts of the first wave of the feminist movement include Jessie Ackermann's *Australia From a Woman's Point of View* (1913) and Mrs F. Anderson's 'Women in Australia' in *Australia: Economic and Political Studies* (1920, eds M. Atkinson and Alice Henry). Jessie Street in her memoirs, *Truth or Repose* (1966), provides an account of feminism in Australia in the 1940s. General and individual biographies of women abound although some of these, which tend to cultivate the 'God's Police' stereotype or which exclusively foster the worthy, pioneering image, are regarded critically by feminists. General collections of biographies include Eve Pownall's *Mary of Maranoa* (1959), 'Denton Prout' and Fred Feely's *Petticoat Parade* (1965), *The Peaceful Army*, ed. Flora Eldershaw (1938), *A Book of South Australia: Women in the First Hundred Years*, ed. Louise Brown et al. (1936), Helen Heney's *Australia's Founding Mothers* (1978), Barbara Jefferis's *Three of a Kind* (1982), *The Changemakers*, eds Suzanne Fabian and Morag Loh (1983), and *200 Australian Women*, ed. Heather Radi (1988). *Fighters and Singers*, ed. Isobel White, Diane Barwick and Betty Meehan (1985), is an important collection of biographies of Aboriginal women, and Vivienne Rae Ellis considers Truganini in *Trucanini: Queen or Traitor?* (1981). Diane Bell has written an important anthropological revisionist study of Aboriginal women in *Daughters of the Dreaming* (1983, revised 1993). Patricia Clarke describes the achievements of women writers and little-known journalists in nineteenth-century Australia in *Pen Portraits* (1988). A *Who's Who of Australian Women* was published in 1982. Several bibliographies on women's affairs have appeared, of which the most comprehensive and best organised is *Her Story* (1980) by Margaret Bettison and Anne Summers. Others include *Women in Australia: An Annotated Guide to Records* (q.v., 1977), *Women in Australian Society* (1977) by Janet Reed and Kathleen Oakes, *Australian Women 1952–1975* (1975) by M.J. Gepp, as well as a range of bibliographies on special items published in magazines and in some of the collections listed. The most substantial bibliography of women writers is Debra Adelaide's (1991), although Margaret Murphy's bibliography of women's fiction to 1987 (1988) and Lurline Stuart's check-list of work by women members of the Lyceum Club, Melbourne, (1993) are also useful.

Since the early 1970s feminist magazines, newsletters and newspapers have proliferated, their variety and their often brief existence reflecting the increasingly pluralistic nature of the women's movement. Several, such as *Refractory Girl*, *Australian Feminist Studies* and *Hecate* (qq.v.), deal occasionally with women writers. They include *Mejane* (1971–74), *Hussy* (1972–), *Vashti's Voice* (1972–76), *Mabel* (1975–77), *Womanspeak* (1975–), *Scarlet Woman* (1975–), *Working Papers in Sex, Science and Culture* (1976–), *Luna* (1975–89), *Lip* (1976–), *Join Hands* (1972–84), *Women's News Service* (1975–79), *Double X* (1975–), *Rouge* (1979–81) and *Australian Women's Book Review* (1989–). A series of well-publicised and influential Women and Labour Conferences (1978, 1980 and 1982) sponsored by departments of Macquarie University and the Australian Society for the Study of Labour History resulted in the publication of papers, many of which are literary, and in the *Women and Labour Conference Bulletin*. Conversely, the reductive value system of the *Australian Women's Weekly* (q.v.) in the 1940s and 1950s is analysed by Bill Bonney and Helen Wilson in *Australia's Commercial Media* (1983) and by Helen Wilson in *Glamour and Chauvinism* (1982). Meanwhile the increasing awareness of women's problems at a government level, the growth of women's studies at universities and colleges, the establishment of Women's Electoral Lobby in 1972, and the proliferation of organisations, groups and movements concerned with the multitudinous aspects of women's affairs, have resulted in a mass of published material since 1970 from the politically radical to the mildly polemical or the official. Radio series concentrating on women's issues and several television programmes and films have been produced. Publishing, also seen as traditionally a male, White, middle-class hegemony, has seen the advent of several feminist presses, including Everywoman Press (Sydney), Sybylla Press (Melbourne), Redress Press, Spinifex Press and Sisters (Melbourne). Another well-established feminist publishing enterprise is Melbourne's Women's Movement Children's Literature Co-operative Ltd, which produces non-sexist materials.

Links between women's movements and women writers have always existed, but it was not until the advent of the women's liberation movement in the 1970s, roughly coinciding with Germaine Greer's *The Female Eunuch* (q.v.), that a large, specific body of self-conscious, feminist literature emerged. Writers who contributed to or had some links with early women's movements include Mary Gilmore, Jean Devanny, Dymphna Cusack, Mona Brand, Miles Franklin, Mary Fullerton, Katharine Susannah Prichard and Betty Roland. Some writers with implicit feminist perceptions, such as Kylie Tennant, Thea Astley, Marjorie Barnard and Gwen Harwood, and others with spiritedly explicit attitudes, such as Dorothy Hewett, Mona Brand and Dymphna Cusack, continued to write during the relatively stagnant period 1940–1970. Unlike their predecessors, feminist writers from 1970 have been greatly sustained by ideas stemming from the international women's movement. Another distinction between the two periods is that for some second-wave feminists at least, Marxism and other intellectual systems have combined more easily with feminist issues, especially at the level of methodology. For such writers as Prichard, Devanny and Roland, party and feminist aspirations were frequently at odds. Working-class women have also had some role in the second period although the movement is still mainly a middle-class one. Feminist themes have dominated women's writing since the 1970s as women's writing generally has emerged into much greater prominence, if not dominance. Indeed, it may well be that the striking achievements of women writers after the 1970s are partly a result of the political and cultural insights offered by feminism; certainly most women writers of note are sensitive to the social constructions of gender if they are not, as a large majority are, explicitly feminist. Crime writing in particular (see Crime Fiction) has offered women new opportunities of subverting a traditional male genre. Fiction writers of the post-1970 period who have written on feminist or semi-feminist themes include Glenda Adams, Jessica Anderson, Jean Bedford, Carmel Bird, Sara Dowse, Suzanne Falkiner, Helen Garner, Barbara Giles, Kate Grenville, Marion Halligan, Susan Hampton, Barbara Hanrahan, Helen Hodgman, Janette Turner Hospital, Elizabeth Jolley, Suzanne Holly Jones, Kathy Lette, Kate Llewellyn, Joan London, Jan McKemmish, Jennifer Rowe, Christine Townsend and Glen Tomasetti (qq.v.). Zoe Fairbairns, the English feminist who visited Australia in 1971 and 1983, draws on her Australian experiences in her novels *Benefits* (1979) and most extensively in *Stand We At Last* (1983). Lesbian novels include Elizabeth Riley's *All That False Instruction* (1975) and Beverley Farmer's *Alone* (1980). Kathy Lette and Gabrielle Carey in *Puberty Blues* (1979), which was also produced as a film in 1983, have written an important exploration of an adolescent, male-dominated subculture of the 1970s.

A large body of short fiction has emerged, mostly published in feminist and literary journals, and numerous anthologies have appeared: *Stories of Her Life* (1979), ed. Sandra Zurbo; *Frictions* (1982), ed. Anna Gibbs and Alison Tilson; *The True Life Story Of . . .* (1981), ed. Jan Craney and Esther Caldwell; *Hecate's Daughters* (1978), ed. Carole Ferrier; *Telling Ways: Aus-*

tralian *Women's Experimental Writing* (1988), ed. Anna Couani and Sneja Gunew; *Eclipsed: Two Centuries of Australian Women's Fiction* (1988), ed. Connie Burns and Marygai McNamara; *The Babe is Wise* (1987), ed. Lyn Harwood, Bruce Pascoe and Paula White (1987); *Feeling Restless: Australian Women's Short Stories 1940–1969* (1989), ed. Connie Burns and Marygai McNamara; *Goodbye to Romance: Stories by Australian and New Zealand Women 1930s–1980s* (1989), ed. Elizabeth Webby and Lydia Wevers; and *Room to Move: the Redress Press Anthology* (1985), ed. Suzanne Falkiner. Colonial women's writing has been recovered in such collections as *From the Verandah* (1987), ed. Fiona Giles; *Happy Endings* (1987), ed. Lydia Wevers and Elizabeth Webby; *Her Selection* (1988), ed. Lynne Spender; and *Colonial Voices* (1989), ed. Elizabeth Webby. Anthologies of interviews and reminiscences include *Eight Voices of the Eighties* (1989), ed. Gillian Whitlock; *A Writing Life* (1990), ed. Guilia Giuffre; *Rooms of Their Own* (1986), ed. Jennifer Ellison; and *Tall Poppies* (1984) and *The Matriarchs* (1987), ed. Susan Mitchell. Women's correspondence and diaries have also been anthologised in such collections as *The Diaries of Ethel Turner* (1979), compiled by Philippa Poole; *Scribbling Sisters* (1984), by Dale and Lynne Spender; the letters of Olive King 1915–20, *One Woman at War* (1986), ed. Hazel King; *Life Lines: Australian Women's Letters and Diaries 1788 to 1840* (1992), ed. Patricia Clarke and Dale Spender; correspondence between such writers of the 1930s and 1940s as Miles Franklin, Jean Devanny, Marjorie Barnard and Katharine Susannah Prichard, *As Good as a Yarn With You* (1992), ed. Carole Ferrier; *A Face in the Glass: the Journal and Life of Annie Baxter Dawbin* (1992), by Lucy Frost; the correspondence of Miles Franklin, *My Congenials* (1993), ed. Jill Rowe; and *The Governesses: Letters from the Colonies 1862–1882* (1985), by Patricia Clarke. General or thematically focused anthologies include a collection of multicultural women's writing, *Beyond the Echo* (1988), ed. Sneja Gunew and Jan Mahyuddin; reflections on place, *Inner Cities* (1989), ed. Drusilla Modjeska; *Moments of Desire: Sex and Sensuality by Australian Feminist Writers* (1989), ed. Susan Hawthorne and Jenny Pausacker; *The Penguin Anthology of Australian Women's Writing* (1988), and *Heroines* (1991), both ed. Dale Spender; *Angry Women* (1989), ed. Di Brown et al.; *Difference* (1985), ed. Susan Hawthorne; *Mrs Noah and the Minoan Queen* (1983), ed. Judith Rodriguez; and *Women's Erotica* (1988), ed. Lyn Giles.

Several autobiographical accounts of feminist experience have also appeared including Zelda D'Aprano's *Zelda: The Becoming of a Woman* (1977) and the anthologies *Brian's Wife, Jenny's Mum* (1975), ed. Gwen Wesson, and *A Book About Australian Women* (1974), ed. Carol Jerrems and Virginia Fraser. *For Love Or Money* (1983), compiled by Megan McMurchy, Margot Oliver and Jeni Thornley, is a companion work to an influential feature film of the same title, which depends partly on interviews and autobiographical accounts. Meanwhile autobiography has become an increasingly popular genre with women writers; significant narratives to appear in the last two

decades include: Jean Devanny's *Point of Departure* (1986), ed. Carole Ferrier; Oriel Gray's *Exit Left* (1986); Kylie Tennant's *The Missing Heir* (1986); Germaine Greer's *Daddy, We Hardly Knew You* (1989); Jill Ker Conway's *The Road from Coorain* (1989); Joan Colebrook's *A House of Trees* (1987); Dorothy Hewett's *Wild Card* (1990); Sally Morgan's *My Place* (1987); Dymphna Cusack's *A Window in the Dark* (1991), ed. Debra Adelaide; Glenyse Ward's *Wandering Girl* (1987) and *Una You Fullas* (1991); Drusilla Modjeska's *Poppy* (1990); Ruby Langford Ginibi's *Don't Take Your Love to Town* (1988); Ida West's *Pride Against Prejudice* (1984); Nancy Keesing's *Riding the Elephant* (1988); Patricia Thompson's *Accidental Chords* (1988); Elizabeth Wynhausen's *Manly Girls* (1988); Betty Roland's *The Devious Being* (1990), *An Improbable Life* (1989) and *Caviar for Breakfast* (1979); and Audrey Blake's *A Proletarian Life* (1984).

From the first years of White settlement, poetry has consistently attracted women writers. Dorothy Hewett, Rosemary Dobson, Marie Pitt, Lesbia Harford and Gwen Harwood are examples of older writers who have written some memorable feminist poems, but since 1970 the form appears to have been regarded as the most accessible as a means of expression. Kate Jennings in her anthology *Mother I'm Rooted* (1975) brings together some of the more recent poets including Stefanie Bennett, Lee Cataldi, Anne Elder, Helen Garner, Jill Hellyer, Sylvia Kantarizis, Peg Clarke, Antigone Kefala, Jennifer Maiden, Carol Novack, Marjorie Pizer, Jennifer Rankin, Judith Rodriguez and Vicki Viidikas. Stefanie Bennett, one of the most prolific of feminist poets, is editor and publisher of the Cochon poetry series, which includes several of her own volumes, and of joint collections such as *Hags, Rags & Scriptures* (1976). Rosemary Dobson in *Sisters Poets 1* (1979) has brought together the work of Anne Lloyd, Kate Llewellyn, Joyce Lee and Susan Hampton. Other poetry anthologies include *The Penguin Book of Australian Women Poets* (1986), ed. Susan Hampton and Kate Llewellyn; *Words from the Same Heart* (1988), ed. Margaret Bradstock and Louise Wakeling; and *Up From Below: Poems of the 1980s* (1987), ed. Irene Coates, Nancy J. Corbett and Barbara Petrie. Women's homosexual poetry is included in Robert Dessaix's collection *Australian Gay and Lesbian Writing* (1993) and in *Falling for Grace: an Anthology of Australian Lesbian Fiction* (1993), ed. Roberta Snow and Jill Taylor.

Several women writers such as Dymphna Cusack, Mona Brand, Betty Roland and, outstandingly, Dorothy Hewett, have contributed feminist or semi-feminist plays throughout their careers stretching from the 1940s. And several of the plays of the 1950s renaissance of Australian drama, including Ray Lawler's *Summer of the Seventeenth Doll* (qq.v., 1957) and Alan Seymour's *The One Day of the Year* (qq.v., 1962), were critical of traditional male values, if they were not otherwise especially feminist. The 1970s renaissance of Australian drama, however, produced a wide range of feminist plays from both male and female playwrights. The Women's Group of the Pram Factory company and later the Melbourne Women's

Theatre Group (q.v.,the subject of Peta Tait's *Original Women's Theatre*, 1993) created several co-operative productions of which 'Betty Can Jump' (1971) is probably the best known. Playwrights whose work was produced by the Australian Performing Group during the 1970s and who showed a high level of feminist awareness include Jack Hibberd, John Romeril, Alex Buzo and David Williamson. Outstanding in this area are Hibberd's *White with Wire Wheels* (q.v., 1970) and Williamson's *The Coming of Stork* (1974) and *The Removalists* (1972). Other plays from these writers which deal, at least in part, with the situation of women are Hibberd's 'Peggy Sue' (1974) and *A Toast to Melba* (1976), Romeril's 'Mrs. Thally F' (1971), Williamson's *Don's Party* (1973) and *The Perfectionist* (1983), Buzo's *Rooted* (1973) and *Coralie Lansdowne Says No* (1974). Ron Blair in 'Perfect Strangers' (1971) and Robin Thurston in 'Sisters' (1974) contribute diverse perspectives on so-called normal and abnormal feminine experience. Thérèse and Leonard Radic have combined in dramatising a selection of women's writing, *Some of My Best Friends Are Women* (1983). Dorothy Hewett has been a dominant figure whose most influential play has been *The Chapel Perilous* (1972), followed by *Bon-Bons and Roses for Dolly* (1976), *The Tatty Hollow Story* (1976) and 'Joan' (1975). Other contemporary feminist playwrights include Alma de Groen, Doreen Clarke, Jennifer Rankin, Suzanne Spunner, Gilly Fraser, Jennifer Compton, Mary Gage, Jill Shearer, Alison Lyssa, Gillian Jones, Katharine Thomson, Hannie Rayson and Oriel Gray. A feature of the feminist theatre has been the establishment of women's theatre groups such as Fool's Gallery, Footfall Theatre and the Home Cooking Company, which have occasionally staged co-operative group productions. Better known to the general public is the cabaret artist Robyn Archer. *Around the Edge* (1992), ed. Roxxy Bent et al., is an anthology of women's plays. *Don't Shoot Darling!* (1987), ed. Annette Blonski, Barbara Creed and Freda Freiberg, is an account of women's independent film-making.

If Germaine Greer's *The Female Eunuch* was a powerful stimulus to the women's liberation movement of the 1970s, subsequent feminists, including Greer herself, have continued to analyse the forces which make for inequality. The national and international feminist critique of institutions and ideologies has been markedly extended by the work of several outstanding feminist critics including Elizabeth Grosz, Meaghan Morris, Ann Curthoys, Sneja Gunew and Moira Gatens. Significant studies in feminist theory include *Jacques Lacan, A Feminist Introduction* (1990) and *Sexual Subversions* (1989), both by Elizabeth Grosz.; *Feminist Challenges: Social and Political Theory* (1986), ed. Elizabeth Grosz and Carole Pateman; *Futur*fall; Excursions into Post-Modernity* (1986), ed. Elizabeth Grosz et al.; *Feminism and Philosophy* (1991), by Moira Gatens; *Crossing Boundaries* (1988), ed. Barbara Caine, Elizabeth Grosz and Marie de Lepervanche; *For and Against Feminism* (1988), by Ann Curthoys; *Feminist Fiction* (1990) and *Engendered Fiction* (1992), by Anne Cranny-Francis; *Feminine Masculine and Representation* (1990), ed. Terry Threadgold

and Anne Cranny-Francis; *Feminist Knowledge* (1990), ed. Sneja Gunew; *Grafts* (1988), ed. Susan Sheridan; *Feminism and the Politics of Difference* (1993), ed. Sneja Gunew and Anna Yeatman; and *The Pirate's Fiancée* (1988), by Meaghan Morris. Influential collections of essays are *Gender, Politics and Fiction* (1985, revised 1992), ed. Carole Ferrier; *Debutante Nation: Feminism Contests the 1890s* (1993), ed. Susan Magarey, Sue Rowley and Susan Sheridan; and *Poetry and Gender* (1989), ed. David Brooks and Brenda Walker. R.W. Connell's work on the construction of gender, typified by his *Gender and Power* (1987), has, like the work of Morris, Greer and Grosz, found an international readership. Greer's most recent work has focused on the mid-life experience of women in *The Change: Women, Ageing and the Menopause* (1991). Significant general feminist studies of women's literature include *Coming Out from Under* (1988), by Pam Gilbert; *A Bright and Fiery Troop* (1988), ed. Debra Adelaide; *Writing a New World* (1988), by Dale Spender; *The Time to Write* (1993), ed. Kay Ferres; *Christina Stead* (1988), by Susan Sheridan; *Women and the Bush* (1988) by Kay Schaffer; and *Stories of Herself When Young* (1990) by Joy Hooton. Two particularly significant essays, the former altering assumptions about the 1890s and the latter about multicultural writing, are Marilyn Lake's 'The Politics of Respectability', in *Historical Studies* (1986) and Sneja Gunew's 'Who's on Whose Margins' in *Gender, Politics and Fiction* (1985). Meanwhile women's studies, in some form, is offered in almost all tertiary educational institutions, while a large number of university courses address gender relations and feminist theory and their interrelationship with post-modernism, cultural studies and post-colonialism. Interdisciplinary in nature, feminist scholarship has proposed new questions and structures, and critiqued established disciplines and bodies of thought. The importance of the new insights was highlighted by three interdisciplinary conferences held in 1986 under the sponsorship of the Humanities Research Centre of the ANU, titled 'Feminism and the Humanities'; feminism, meanwhile, was an important aspect of the controversial annual conference of the Academy of the Humanities in 1992 titled 'The New Humanities', which celebrated the breakdown of disciplinary boundaries.

FENTON, James (1820–1901), born Dunlavin, Ireland, came to Van Diemen's Land in 1834 and in 1840 began farming on the Forth River in thickly forested country deemed unsuitable for settlement. He was the first to apply the technique of ringbarking to clear forest land. Becoming aware of the need of the growing colony of Victoria for housing, he then turned to exploiting his land for its timber; as the land was cleared some of Tasmania's best farm land emerged. After his retirement from farming in 1879 he wrote *A History of Tasmania* (1884) and a book of memoirs, *Bush Life in Tasmania Fifty Years Ago* (1891).

FERGUSON, G.A. (George Adie) (1910–   ), born Sydney, is the son of the noted bibliographer and collector of Australiana Sir John Alexander Ferguson, and grandson of George Robertson (2). While he was a director of Angus & Robertson 1936–70 and its publishing director 1949–70, he consolidated the reputation that the firm had gained as one of Australia's greatest publishing houses. In 1949 he was instrumental in the founding of the Australian Book Publishers Association; the Association's annual book-design awards were inaugurated during his ten-year period as president; he was director of the Association 1971–75. A member of the ABPA committee, the Australian Book Trade Advisory Committee and the Joint Publishers Committee, Ferguson was also involved in the Spicer Committee on copyright revision. An advisor to the Australian government on matters such as the CLF and the Commonwealth Printing Office, Ferguson was also, from its inception, a member of the Book Printing Bounty Advisory Panel; he was made CBE in 1956. He wrote *Some Early Australian Bookmen* (1978), which discusses such identities as the two George Robertsons, D.M. Angus, Samuel Mullen, F.V. Wymark, Sir William Dixson and David Scott Mitchell.

FERGUSON, Sir John Alexander (1881–1969), born Invercargill, NZ, trained as a lawyer in Sydney, where in 1936–53 he was a judge on the Industrial Commission. Ferguson was involved over many years with the Presbyterian Church, the Royal Australian Historical Society, the Public (later State) Library of NSW and the University of Sydney; a member of its Senate, he supported C.J. Brennan at the time of his dismissal. His marriage in 1906 to the daughter of the Sydney bookseller George Robertson (2) stimulated and facilitated his interest in bibliography and book-collecting. Ferguson submitted an article on Henry Kendall to the *Bulletin* in 1900 which was reprinted in 1963 in *Foreshadowings*, and contributed several bibliographical, biographical and historical essays to the Royal Australian Historical Society's *Journal* 1917–31. His major endeavours, however, went into the monumental *Bibliography of Australia* (q.v.), published in seven volumes 1941–69, a pioneering work of scholarship which remains a basic reference work in Australian studies. Ferguson's other lasting memorials are his collection of Australiana, acquired by the National Library of Australia after his death, and the John Alexander Ferguson Memorial lecture, a public lecture on Australian history, bibliography or literature, held at intervals of not less than two years in Sydney and Canberra. The inaugural lecture by G.D. Richardson, *The Instruction and Good of His Country: Sir John Ferguson, Libraries, and the Historical Record* (1977), includes a survey of Ferguson's career. George Adie Ferguson (q.v.) is his son.

'FERRES, Arthur' (John William Kevin), see *The Oxford Companion to Australian Children's Literature* (1993), p. 166.

FERRIER, Carole, see **Feminism and Australian Literature**

FETHERSTONHAUGH, Cuthbert (1837–1925), born County Westmeath, Ireland, came to Australia in 1853 and for the following twenty years was active as jackeroo, explorer and squatter in the developing north Queensland pastoral areas. He was briefly an Anglican minister (1873–75) before resuming his pastoral career; he helped organise the meat-export industry and mined successfully in the Gulf country. The character, the Rev. Herbert Heatherstone, in 'Rolf Boldrewood's' *A Colonial Reformer* (1890) is based on him, and his supposed encounter with the bushranger Bluecap is recalled in Barcroft Boake's poem 'Fetherstonhaugh', in *Where the Dead Men Lie and Other Poems* (1897). Fetherstonhaugh's lively career is outlined in his autobiographical *After Many Days* (1918).

Fiction Fields of Australia, The, an essay by Frederick Sinnett (q.v.), was published in the *Journal of Australasia* in 1856. It was republished in 1966, ed. Cecil Hadgraft. The first critical essay to deal solely with Australian literature, *The Fiction Fields of Australia* has more than historical significance. It raised questions that are still relevant about an Australian literary voice and the ways of representing 'local manners and customs' in fiction, and concluded with useful comments on works by Catherine Helen Spence, Alexander Harris and Charles Rowcroft.

FIELD, Barron (1786–1846), an unsuccessful legal practitioner in England, came to Sydney in 1817 as a judge of the Supreme Court of NSW. In 1819 George Howe, the government printer, published Field's *First Fruits of Australian Poetry* (q.v.). The Colony's unfamiliar flora and fauna attracted him, but he disliked the uninviting terrain, the reversed seasons and the penal nature of the settlement. He saw it as a 'prose-dull land', a land without associations, and left it gladly in 1824. Back in England he edited *Geographical Memoirs on New South Wales* (1825), then went to Gibralter as chief justice. Although Field's claim to be the first 'Austral Harmonist' is presumptuous, 'Botany Bay Flowers' and 'The Kangaroo', in spite of some ridiculing of the colonial scene, are among the first poems to evoke the Australian environment.

FIELDING, Sydney Glanville (1856–1930), born Parramatta, went to sea as a boy but gave up the seafaring life at the age of 24 to join the Anglican ministry, serving for half a century in various parishes in the Bathurst and Sydney dioceses. He published fiction, *The Southern Light* (1895) and *Down to the Sea in Ships* (1900), both of which deal with the adventurous times at sea and ashore of their young heroes; *The New Vicar of Wakefield* (1902), which is based on the vicissitudes of a minister of religion in western NSW and takes in the Boer War; and the futuristic *Australia A.D. 2000: Or, the Great Referendum* (1917). Fielding also published verse, *The Castaway and Other Poems* (1884), as well as several religious tracts.

Fifty Years Ago: An Australian Tale, a novel by Charles de Boos (q.v.), first published in fourteen booklets (1866–67) and then in a single volume in 1867, was also serialised in the *Australian Journal* (1869–70). It was reprinted as *Settler and Savage* in 1906 by A.C. Rowlandson in the NSW Bookstall series. The novel opens with the massacre of the wife and family of the settler George Maxwell by a group of marauding Aborigines from the Maroo tribe led by chieftains Macomo, Atara and Opara. Maxwell and his son Jamie, who survive the attack, swear vengeance on the Blacks and the novel follows, with numerous sub-plots, the hunt for the guilty tribe and its leaders. The Maroo are exterminated, leaving Macomo alone to be hunted down. Jamie, victim of his own obsession for vengeance, is slain by the Blacks, but George Maxwell, when confronted with the suffering and nobility of Macomo, regrets his hatred and comes to a new understanding of the Aboriginal psyche. The novel has sometimes been linked with J. Fenimore Cooper's writing, with Macomo as the Magua figure and Maxwell as a White Deerslayer. The novel successfully captures both the physical environment and the psychological ambience of colonial times; its somewhat revolutionary conclusion in favour of the Aborigines contrasts greatly, however, with their disparagement in other colonial literature.

Film, see **Cinema and Australian Literature**

FINCH, Peter (1916–77), born England, the legal son of an Australian-born soldier, mountaineer and scientist George Ingle-Finch, was brought up by a variety of relatives and friends in Paris, India and Australia. After leaving school in Sydney he worked as a journalist, artist's model, waiter and straight-man in a vaudeville act before becoming an actor for stage and radio. His first successful part in film was as Bill Ryan in *Dad and Dave Come to Town* (1938). In the Second World War he served as a gunner, interrupting his service for the production of films including *The Rats of Tobruk* (1944). After the success of the British-Australian film *Eureka Stockade* (1949) he moved to England where he established an outstanding reputation as a film actor. Films in which he appeared include *The Miniver Story* (1950), *The Wooden Horse* (1950), *The Heart of the Matter* (1953), *A Town Like Alice* (1956), *Robbery Under Arms* (1957), *The Shiralee* (1957), *Far from the Madding Crowd* (1967), *Sunday Bloody Sunday* (1971), *Network* (1976) and *Raid on Entebbe* (1977). He was particularly noted for his portrayal of vulnerable public figures such as Lord Nelson in *Bequest to the Nation* (1973) and Oscar Wilde in *The Trials of Oscar Wilde* (1960). For his role in *Network* he won an Academy Award and was named best actor in America's Golden Globe Awards and (for the fifth time) by the British Film Academy. Finch appears as the character Archie Calverton in George Johnston's novel *Clean Straw for Nothing* (1969). Two biographies of Finch are *Peter Finch* (1979) by Trader Faulkner and *Finch Bloody Finch* (1980) by Elaine Dundy.

Fine Line, a small, Melbourne-based literary magazine published twice annually 1987–90, edited initially by Carmel Bird and Helen Garlick, later Gar-lick and Bev Roberts, featured new poetry and fiction, interviews, essays and reviews. It published two special poetry issues (No.3, 1988; No.8, 1990). Writers featured included Janette Turner Hospital, Marion Halligan, Janine Burke, Diane Fahey, Jan Owen, Mark O'Connor, Barbara Giles, Alex Skovron, Judith Rodriguez and Jennifer Strauss.

FINEY, George (1895–1987), born Auckland, NZ, sold his first drawings to local newspapers at the age of 14. In the First World War he served in France with the NZ forces both as infantry soldier and war artist, and studied briefly at art school in London before settling in Australia in 1919. His first cartoons were published in the *Bulletin*, but in 1921 he began a decade's association with *Smith's Weekly* and won a reputation as a superb caricaturist. Subsequently he worked as a political cartoonist and strip artist for the *Labour Daily*, *Truth*, the *Sunday Sun*, the *Daily Telegraph* and other journals, although he often ran foul of editors and proprietors. A notable Sydney bohemian, Finey worked in many media including pen and ink, brush drawing, ceramics, enamel paint and collage, and was judged by his contemporary, Stan Cross, to be the finest of the *Smith's Weekly* artists. His simple verse is included in *Poems* (1975) and *Book of Finey* (1976) as well as in his entertaining autobiography *The Mangle Wheel* (1981).

FINLAYSON, H.H., see **Dead Heart**

FINN, Edmund ('Garryowen') (1819–98), born Tipperary, Ireland, settled in the infant city of Melbourne in 1841 and worked on the *Port Phillip Herald* for thirteen years before becoming a public servant in 1858. As 'An Old Colonist', Finn published *The Garryowen Sketches* (1880), which was followed by 'Garryowen's' two-volume *The Chronicles of Early Melbourne 1835 to 1852* (1888); both are significant accounts of colonial Melbourne life based on Finn's wide experience and extensive records. A selection from the *Chronicles* was published as *Garryowen's Melbourne*, ed. Margaret Weidenhofer (1967). Finn's son, also Edmund, wrote pantomimes.

FINNIN, Mary (1906–), born Kildare near Geelong, Victoria, trained as an artist, held successful exhibitions of paintings, and has been an art teacher, critic and businesswoman. Her major literary interest has been poetry; her six volumes of verse include *A Beggar's Opera* (1938), *Look Down, Olympians* (1939), *Royal* (1941), *Alms for Oblivion* (1947), *The Shield of Place* (1957) and a collected volume, *Off Shears* (1958–1978) (1979). *The Shield of Place* (the title refers to her commitment to Victoria) includes the ballad 'The Ride of Richard Illidge', which commemorates an epic horse ride of 160 kilometres in a night to save a condemned prisoner from execution. Other poems with local Victorian flavour are 'Bacchus in the Marsh' and 'Rain in Glenrowan'. Mary Finnin also wrote and illustrated the children's book *The Book of Bauble* (1945).

Fire on the Snow, The, a verse drama by Douglas Stewart (q.v.), was written in 1939, and published in part in the *Bulletin* (13 December 1939). Produced as a radio play by the ABC, 6 June 1941, it was published with *The Golden Lover* in 1944. The play traces Captain Robert Scott's Antarctic expedition from 4 January 1912, when Scott and his four companions, Wilson, Bowers, Oates and Evans, set out on the final dash to the South Pole, to the last entry in Scott's diary on 29 March 1912. As the tragedy unfolds, the omniscient announcer traces the historic journey, whose glory the participants themselves are fated never to know. *The Fire on the Snow* is remarkable for its radio drama technique and for its skilful verse variations, which range from the colloquialism of the blindly struggling mortals to the solemn tones of the announcer reporting the progress of their fate.

First Boke of Fowle Ayres, The, a collection of unattributed scurrilous and bawdy verse by such poets as A.D. Hope, James McAuley, O.M. Somerville and Harold Stewart, was published in a limited edition in 1944. Epigrams from it and some verse by Somerville and Hope are included in *Comic Australian Verse* (1972), ed. Geoffrey Lehmann.

First Fleet is the name given to the ships which carried the first convicts to Australia; it is also applied more generally to the passengers of those ships, both during their time on board and in the early years of settlement. The First Fleet comprised two warships (the *Sirius* and the *Supply*), six chartered transports to carry the convicts, and three supply vessels, none of them as big as, for example, a Sydney harbour ferry of the twentieth century. The Fleet left England on 13 May 1787, sighted Van Diemen's Land on 5 January 1788 and arrived at Botany Bay on 18–20 January; just over 1000 people disembarked to form the first settlement. Among the naval and military officers and other personnel who sailed with the convicts were Arthur Phillip, William Bradley, Watkin Tench, David Collins, John White and John Hunter, all of whom published contemporary accounts of the voyage or the early years of settlement. Later fictional accounts were written by 'Louis' Becke and Walter Jeffery, J.H.M. Abbott and Eleanor Dark (qq.v.). In recent years the term 'First Fleeter' has emerged to describe those Australians who can trace part of their family back to a passenger on the First Fleet. One was Miles Franklin; another, Jonathan King, has written *The First Fleet* (1982), an account of the voyage. Other recent publications include the First Fleet journals of Arthur Bowes Smyth, Philip Gidley King and Ralph Clark, each edited by P.G. Fidlon and R.J. Ryan (1979, 1980, 1981); Victor Crittenden's *The Voyage of the First Fleet* (1981) and *A Bibliography of the First Fleet* (1981); Don Chapman's *1788 – The People of the First Fleet* (1981); and John Cobley's (q.v.) *The Crimes of the First Fleet Convicts* (1970). Jonathan King's *The First Settlement* (1984) draws on the journals of the First Fleeters to recount the first two and a half years of White settlement in Australia. Mollie Gillen's *The Founders of Australia: A Biographical Dictionary of the First Fleet*

(1989), the result of twenty years' research, is perhaps the final word on Australia's original White inhabitants. Much less written about, the Second Fleet, dispatched in a hurry in 1789 by the British government partly to relieve the settlement in NSW and partly to relieve the continuing pressure on the gaols, is the subject of Michael Flynn's *The Second Fleet* (1993). It contains biographies of 1500 convicts, seamen and soldiers who sailed with the Fleet, including D'Arcy Wentworth and John Macarthur.

First Fruits of Australian Poetry (1819), by Barron Field (q.v.), contains two poems, 'Botany Bay Flowers' and 'The Kangaroo'. On the title page, the lines 'I first adventure; follow me who list/ And be Australia's second harmonist' indicate Field's claim to be Australia's first poetic voice, and his book is, in fact, the first book of poems published in Australia. With 'Botany Bay Flowers' Field provides the first poetic description of wildflowers and native shrubs of the Sydney bush. 'The Kangaroo' depicts that animal as an antipodean oddity, an anomaly of the animal world yet typical of the equally strange Australian landscape. In spite of Field's amazement and amusement at colonial oddities of flora and fauna there is, in both poems, a sincere note of interest.

FISHER, Lala (1872–1929), born Rockhampton, Queensland, spent the years 1897–1901 in England where she published poetry, *A Twilight Teaching* (1898), and edited *By Creek and Gully* (1899), a mainly prose anthology of Australian writers then in England. Back in Australia she lived first in Charters Towers and wrote for various journals and newspapers, including *Steele Rudd's Magazine*. In 1909, in Sydney, she bought the *Theatre Magazine*, which she edited until 1918. Her later books of verse were *Grass Flowering* (1915) and *Earth Spiritual* (1918). A remarkably progressive and liberated woman for her time, Lala Fisher expressed in her poetry some of the sentiments that the restricting conventions of the day were prone to stifle.

Fisher Library, at the University of Sydney, was named in honour of Thomas Fisher (1820–84), boot-and shoe-shop proprietor of Pitt Street, Sydney, who left the bulk of his large fortune to the University for establishing and maintaining a library. In 1909 the library building was opened and the Fisher bequest was used to stock it with books. Substantial additions were made to the original library building after the Second World War. H.M. Green (q.v.) was Fisher librarian 1921–46; he is largely responsible for its extensive holdings of Australiana.

Fisher's Ghost is Australia's best-known and most-discussed apparition. Frederick Fisher, a ticket-of-leave convict and farmer of the Campbelltown area, disappeared 16 June 1826 from the house of a neighbour, George Worrall. More than four months later, following a supposed sighting by a John Farley of Fisher's Ghost sitting upon the rail of a fence or bridge and pointing to a nearby creek, the body was found and Worrall was hanged for Fisher's murder, 5 February 1827. The story of Fisher's Ghost is outlined in R. Montgomery Martin's *History of the British Colonies* (1835); in 'Fisher's Ghost: A Legend of Campbelltown' by W. Kerr in *Tegg's Monthly Magazine* (March 1836), reprinted in Geoffrey C. Ingleton's *True Patriots All* (1952); in 'Fisher's Ghost' (probably by John Lang) in Charles Dickens's *Household Words* (1853); and in John Lang's story 'The Ghost upon the Rail', from his book of stories *Botany Bay* (1859). A poetic version of Fisher's Ghost, 'The Sprite of the Creek!', by an unknown author, occurs in an early newspaper, *Hill's Life in New South Wales*, 14 September 1832. Fisher's Ghost has been the subject of many other stories, articles, tall tales, a film by Raymond Longford in 1924, and a play by Douglas Stewart in 1960. The creek near which the body was found now bears the name Fisher's Ghost Creek.

FISON, Lorimer, see **Aborigine in White Australian Literature**

FITCHETT, William Henry ('Vedette') (1841–1928), born Lincolnshire, England, came to Australia in 1854 and worked as a jackeroo in Queensland before entering the Methodist ministry in 1866. He was principal for forty-six years of the Methodist Ladies College, Melbourne, columnist of the Methodist church paper the *Spectator*, and editor of a Sunday family magazine, the *Southern Cross*, and the *Review of Reviews*. Fitchett published, in the Melbourne *Argus*, a series of articles that were collected in 1896 as *Deeds That Won the Empire*, a book that ran to thirty-five printings. Other popular historical narratives by Fitchett, under the pseudonym, 'Vedette', include *Wellington's Men* (1900), *The Tale of the Great Mutiny* (1901), *Nelson and His Captains* (1902), *The New World of the South: Australia in the Making* (1903) and *The Romance of Australian History* (1913). Fitchett also wrote fiction, *The Commander of the Hirondelle* (1904), *Ithuriel's Spear* (1906), *A Pawn in the Game* (1908) and *The Adventures of an Ensign* (1917).

FITTON, Dame Doris (1897–1985), born Manila of an English father and an Australian mother, was brought to Sydney at the age of 5. She worked as a secretary before training as an actor with Gregan McMahon and subsequently acting with the Melbourne and Sydney Repertory Societies and in numerous J.C. Williamson productions. In 1930 she founded the Independent Theatre in Sydney, formed from the Turret Theatre repertory company. An important part of the Australian theatrical scene for almost half a century, the Independent provided both actors and playwrights with stage opportunities, producing plays by such authors as Sumner Locke Elliott, Sydney Tomholt, Catherine Shepherd, Gwen Meredith, Max Afford, Coral Lansbury, Douglas Stewart, Peter Kenna, Jack Hibberd, Richard Beynon, Alan Seymour and Betty Roland. The staging of Sumner Locke Elliott's *Rusty Bugles* (q.v.) in 1948 was the Independent's most controversial production, resulting in the play's temporary banning by the NSW government. The Independent also produced a range of international plays and fostered the careers of numerous Australian actors, including Ruth Cracknell, John Meillon, Leonard Teale and Helen Morse. In 1977 lack of funds caused the Theatre's closure. Director of the Independent during its lifetime, Fitton also frequently produced plays or acted in its productions; she was made DBE in 1981. Her autobiography, *Not Without Dust & Heat* (1981), is also a history of the Independent.

FITZGERALD, John Daniel (1862–1922), born Shellharbour, NSW, was an apprentice printer in Bathurst, NSW, before joining the Sydney *Evening News* and later (1890–91) travelling to England and Europe as secretary of the Trades and Labour Council, seeking strike funds. He was editor of *Freeman's Journal* (1899–1904), was called to the Bar in 1900 and, as an alderman of the Sydney City Council (1900–4), was particularly concerned with town planning, housing and municipal reform. His close but stormy relationship with the Labor Party ended in 1916 with his expulsion over the conscription issue. His parliamentary career, which began in 1891, continued until 1920. In addition to publications such as *Greater Sydney and Greater Newcastle* (1906) and *The Rise of the Australian Labor Party* (1915), FitzGerald wrote fiction, *The Ring Valley* (1922), set in rural NSW in the 1860s and 1870s, and *Children of the Sunlight: Stories of Australian Circus Life* (1923). He also wrote *Studies in Australian Crime* (1924), a reference work on Australian crime fiction.

FITZGERALD, R.D. (Robert David) (1902–87), nephew of John le Gay Brereton (q.v.), was born at Hunters Hill, Sydney, where he lived for much of his life. He attended the University of Sydney in 1920–21 but abandoned a science course for surveying. Like many young writers of the early 1920s, FitzGerald came under the influence of Norman Lindsay, and participated, with Hugh McCrae, Kenneth Slessor and Jack Lindsay in the production of the journal *Vision*, in which several of his early poems were published. In 1931–36 he was mostly in Fiji, surveying the vague traditional boundaries of the tribal lands for the Native Lands Commission. In 1936–40 he was a private surveyor in Sydney, then municipal surveyor to the suburban councils of Manly and Ryde. Late in 1940 he joined the Commonwealth Department of the Interior, surveying sites for wartime aerodromes. He remained with the Department of the Interior after the war, ultimately becoming supervising surveyor of the NSW branch of the department before his retirement in 1965. In 1951 he was made OBE; in 1965 he shared the Britannica Australia Award; in 1974 he won the Robert Frost Medallion; in 1982 he was made AM and a life member of ASAL. In 1985 he was awarded an honorary D.Litt. from the University of Melbourne. He gave public lectures in Australian literature at the universities of Melbourne and Queensland in 1959 and 1961 respectively, published in 1963 as *The Elements of Poetry*, and in 1963 spent a semester as a visiting lecturer in poetry at the University of Texas. Best known as a poet, FitzGerald was also a prolific reviewer of, and influential commentator on, modern Australian writing.

His first collection of verse, *The Greater Apollo: Seven Metaphysical Songs* (1927), consists of short meditative poems that reveal the predicament of man torn between the opposing attractions of the transcendent reality ('the Greater Apollo') and the material world. Although he recognises its transience, FitzGerald chooses the visible world with its obvious delights – 'It is enough that trees are trees/ That earth is earth and stone is stone.' His comment in the fourth part of 'The Greater Apollo', 'I look no more for gods among the lace-like ferns and twisted boughs', while further emphasising his decision in favour of the actual, might also be taken to indicate the end of his relationship with the exotic fantasies of the *Vision* group. *To Meet the Sun* (1929), a collection of thirty-three poems including 'The Greater Apollo' series, won recognition in England where it was awarded, before it was published in Australia, the Bronze Medal of the Festival of Arts and Letters sponsored by the Panton Arts club. *Moonlight Acre* (1938), which contains two groups of short poems, 'Moonlight Acre' (the phrase occurring in the poem 'Invasion') and 'Copernicus', and two long poems, 'The Hidden Bole' and 'Essay on Memory' (qq.v.), won the Australian Literature Society's Gold Medal in 1938. It established FitzGerald, in the eyes of many, as the major Australian poet of the 1930s. 'The Hidden Bole', an intricately constructed elegy which contains a central aesthetic truth that transience is an inseparable part of beauty and uses as examples the banyan tree and the famous ballerina Pavlova, represents some of FitzGerald's most sensuous and lyrical writing. 'Essay on Memory', which won the Australia's 150th Anniversary Celebrations Council's sesquicentenary prize for poetry in 1938, insists, in the complex and knotty manner of FitzGerald's long speculative verse, on the vital influence of the past upon the present.

Heemskerck Shoals (1949) incorporates some shorter poems with the long dramatic monologue of that title, one of several works by FitzGerald with a Fijian background. The poem consists of the angry meditations of the Dutch seaman and explorer Abel Tasman, after the near disaster of his expedition on the reef which he named Heemskerck Shoals, near Nanuku Island, Fiji, in 1643. *Between Two Tides* (1952), drawn from *An Account of the Natives of the Tongan Islands* by J.M. Martin (1817), is a very long poem on which FitzGerald worked intermittently over many years. It was awarded the Grace Leven Prize for poetry in 1952. In five parts, the poem relates and discusses the life and exploits of Will Mariner, a young sailor on the privateer *Port au Prince*, which was attacked and burned by Tongan natives in 1806. Mariner survived the massacre of the crew and was adopted by the Tongan chief, Finau. The poem focuses on both Mariner and Finau, guiding the reader to an assessment of the two men and their achievements. Well constructed and impressively written, the poem urges 'the necessity for advance in action', for it is only by 'acts of resolution' that any man can fashion himself a recognisable ident-

ity. At the same time it recognises the fragility of individual human existence, which lasts only 'between two tides', the new, incoming tide washing away all traces of the individual's efforts and achievements. *This Night's Orbit* (1953) reprinted two of FitzGerald's most important poems, 'The Face of the Waters' (q.v.), which meditates on the Creation, and 'Fifth Day', an incident from the trial of Warren Hastings. 'The Wind at Your Door' (q.v.), a poem based on a convict-flogging incident which involved FitzGerald's ancestor Martin Mason, was published in the *Bulletin* (1958) and published separately in 1959. *South-most Twelve* (1962), incorporating the poems written after *This Night's Orbit*, includes the series 'Eleven Compositions: Roadside', and the well-known 'Bog and Candle', published in *Meanjin* (1960). 'The Wind at Your Door' and *South-most Twelve* won the Grace Leven Prize for poetry in 1959 and 1962 respectively. FitzGerald's Australian Poets selection and his American volume *Of Some Country*, published by the University of Texas, both appeared in 1963 and were followed in 1965 by *Forty Years' Poems*. It contains most of his later work and an opening section, 'Salvage', which reprints, with revisions, all the poems that FitzGerald wished to retain from the earliest period of his writing, 1922–30. The salvaged poems deal mainly with the alienation of the artist, e.g. 'Passed By', and romantic love, e.g. 'The Wall' and 'Black Woods'. After a considerable break he published *Product: Later Verses by Robert D. FitzGerald* (1977), its appearance a further proof of his lifetime principle of 'advance in action', of his Carlylean belief that 'Were it but the pitifullest infinitesimal fraction of a Product, produce it, in God's name!' Some of the poems express his protest at Australia's participation in the Vietnam War, others re-create early colonial times in Australia. In 'Just Once', his judgement of the present ('This age of shoddy') seems out of keeping with his normally optimistic view of life and humanity. *Of Places and Poetry*, a collection of FitzGerald's prose, appeared in 1976. He edited a volume of Mary Gilmore's verse in 1963 and the letters of Hugh McCrae in 1970.

FitzGerald was never a popular or fashionable poet. His use of poetry for the carriage of complex, philosophical ideas and for the examination of abstract, intellectual concepts made him less accessible than other contemporary poets. Meanwhile expert literary opinions of his work have varied widely and the prestige he enjoyed from the late 1930s to the 1960s has lately diminished. Some fellow poets and critics have judged his work, in spite of its integrity and painstaking conscientiousness, as ungainly, lacking in lyricism, grace and spontaneity. Opinions to the contrary are also widely held. He continues to be praised as a true and even great poet and has been judged, with Kenneth Slessor, as the major influence that compelled modern Australian poetry to address itself, in a professional manner, to a range of intellectual, philosophical and metaphysical themes that it had rarely attempted before. *R.D. FitzGerald* in the Portable Australian Authors series was published in 1987, edited by Julian Croft.

FITZGERALD, Ross (1944–), born Melbourne, educated at Melbourne High School, Monash University and the University of NSW (Ph.D. in political science), is a well-known historian (Griffith University, Queensland), political commentator, novelist and poet. Two of his novels, *Pushed from the Wings* (1986) and *Busy in the Fog* (1990), and a book of short stories, *All About Anthrax* (1987), record the misadventures of Grafton Everest, an academic at the fictional Bowen University of Queensland. Overweight, underenergetic except in pursuit of food and sex (whether 'oral, anal or solitary' is all the same to him), Everest is applauded or cordially hated by roughly equal proportions of readers and critics – 'brilliantly revolting' (Thomas Shapcott), 'a wonderful creation . . . in the ranks of . . . Portnoy and . . . Lucky Jim' (Barry Humphries) and, by contrast, both he and the stories about him are 'much nearer Grafton than Everest' (John McGregor). *Pushed from the Wings* recounts several weeks in Everest's life while desperately hanging on for tenure in the Arts Department of a new Queensland University. *All About Anthrax* is a series of stories recounting Everest's Melbourne childhood and adolescence, and his academic years both in Australia and overseas. Most had appeared in magazines such as *Quadrant*, *Westerly*, *Overland* and the *Cane Toad Times*. In *Busy in the Fog* Everest has become dean of studies at Bowen University and presides over a situation rapidly slipping beyond repair. The Everest stories, written apparently as intellectual relaxation while Fitzgerald was researching his two-volume *A History of Queensland* (vol. 1 *From the Dreamtime to 1915* in 1982; vol. 2 *From 1915 to the 1980s* in 1984), are brilliantly, savagely satirical of the halls of academe. Fitzgerald's more serious works include, in addition to the history of Queensland, *What It Means to be Human* (1978, essays in philosophical anthropology), *The Sources of Hope* (1979, philosophical perspectives edited by Fitzgerald), *Comparing Political Thinkers* (1980), *Bligh, Macarthur and the Rum Rebellion* (1988, with Mark Hearn), *Labor in Queensland: From the 1880s to 1985* (1989, with Harold Thornton), and *The Eleven Deadly Sins* (1993), a collection of essays on human frailties edited by Fitzgerald, which includes contributions from such writers as Robert Dessaix, Rosemary Sorensen, Graham Little, Gerard Henderson and Blanche D'Alpuget. He has also published a book of poems, *The Eyes of Angels* (1973, in The Saturday Centre Poets Series) and edited (with Ken Spillman) *The Greatest Game* (1988), an anthology of verse, short stories and humorous anecdotes about Australian rules football.

FITZGERALD, Tom (Thomas Michael) (1918–93), born Sydney, into a family of Irish Catholic extraction, joined the Commonwealth Public Service in 1936 after working with his father and brothers in the family's milk-vending business. He studied economics at the University of Sydney, served in the RAAF in the Second World War and in 1946 joined the *Bulletin* as financial journalist. In 1950 he moved to the *Sydney Morning Herald* as commercial editor. The demise of the independent journal *Voice* in 1956 prompted him to found and edit a new journal, *Nation*, modelled on the American weekly the *New Republic* and one of the most influential periodicals on public and cultural affairs during its life 1958–72. One of his closest associates in the enterprise was George Munster (q.v.). Fitzgerald was subsequently editorial director for News Ltd 1970–72 and economic adviser to the NSW Premier 1976–83. Fitzgerald's career is described by K.S.Inglis in *Nation: The Life of an Independent Journal of Opinion 1958–1972* (1989).

FITZ HENRY, Bill (William Ernest) (1903–57) joined the staff of the *Bulletin* as an office boy in 1917 after a brief period with the *Lone Hand*. During his time with the *Bulletin* he was secretary to three editors, S.H. Prior, J.E. Webb and David Adams; wrote the Service Page for many years; wrote paragraphs on writers and artists as 'Fitz', 'W.E.F.' and 'Morehead', and occasional long articles. In his capacity as payer of freelance contributors he was acquainted with many artists and writers and was well known in Sydney bohemian circles; he was an unofficial collector of *Bulletin* history and folklore and at the time of his death (at his desk, in 1957) was completing a history of the *Bulletin*, which remains unpublished. Fitz Henry was at various times secretary of the *Bulletin* Novel Competition (1928–29), the S.H. Prior Memorial Prize, and the Fellowship of Australian Writers. With Cecil Ringstad he edited the *Australian Authors and Artists' Handbook* (1928), and he wrote an introduction to *The Books of the Bulletin* (1955).

FITZPATRICK, Brian (1905–65), born Cudgee near Koroit, Victoria, embraced radical socialism when he became a philosophy student at the University of Melbourne in 1921. He began a career of journalism in 1927 but resigned from the Melbourne *Herald* in 1935. During the Second World War he worked for the Labor government and was subsequently a writer and freelance journalist. A regular columnist for *Smith's Weekly* during the 1940s, he began in 1947 to publish the journal *Australian Democrat*, which was replaced by *Australian News Review* in 1951; from 1958 until his death he edited *Labor Newsletter*. He became general secretary in 1937 for the Australian Council for Civil Liberties and his name has become synonymous with that organisation and its aims. Fitzpatrick published *British Imperialism and Australia* (1939), a work which set Australia's beginnings in the context of social and economic changes then occurring in England, and which won the Harbison-Higinbotham scholarship of the University of Melbourne. Its sequel was *The British Empire in Australia: An Economic History 1834–1939* (1941). His other works were *A Short History of the Australian Labor Movement* (1940), *The Australian People* (1946), *The Australian Commonwealth* (1956) and, with E.L. Wheelwright, *The Highest Bidder* (1965). Fitzpatrick's writings reflect his ideology: his economic works are radical reinterpretations of Australian economic history while his idiosyncratic social histories are based upon his socialist ideals. Don Watson published the biography *Brian Fitzpatrick: A Radical Life* (1979).

FITZPATRICK, J.C.L. (John Charles Lucas) (1862–1932), born Moama, NSW, served a printing apprenticeship then worked on the *Melbourne Punch* (1880) before becoming a journalist on country newspapers in Goulburn, Gunnedah, Narrabri and Parramatta. In 1888 he established the *Windsor and Richmond Gazette*, controlling it until 1899; subsequently he owned the *Molong Argus*, 1904–7. A long-time member of the NSW Legislative Assembly (1895–1930), Fitzpatrick was also the author of several local histories and travel books including *The Good Old Days of the Hawkesbury* (1900), *Eastward Ho* (1905), *Jaunt to Java* (1908) and *Good Old Days of Molong* (1913).

FITZPATRICK, Kathleen Elizabeth (1905–90), born Omeo, Victoria, became associate professor in the department of history, University of Melbourne, where she taught 1930–62. She wrote the biography *Sir John Franklin in Tasmania, 1837–1843* (1949) and edited *Australian Explorers* (1958), one of the first anthologies of the writings of such explorers as Gregory Blaxland, John Oxley, Hamilton Hume, William Hovell, Alan Cunningham, Charles Sturt, T.L. Mitchell, Edward John Eyre, Ludwig Leichhardt, John McDouall Stuart, Robert O'Hara Burke, William John Wills and Ernest Giles. Her monograph *Martin Boyd* (1963) provoked a response, 'Dubious Cartography', by Boyd in *Meanjin Quarterly* (1964). She also published a history of Presbyterian Ladies College, Melbourne, in 1975 and *Solid Bluestone Foundations* (1983), which encompasses the years 1908–28 and recalls her childhood in Melbourne and her student years in Australia and at Oxford. She was made AO in 1989.

'Five Bells', the title poem of Kenneth Slessor's (q.v.) volume of poetry published in 1939 and acknowledged as his major work, is a meditation, compressed into memory's own time-scale as a ship's bell rings five bells in Sydney Harbour, on Slessor's drowned friend Joe Lynch. Able to recapture only disconnected, trivial scraps of the dead man's past existence and unsuccessful in his attempt to understand the significance of Joe Lynch's life, or to decide what purpose gave him life at all, the poet is forced to an admission of the futility of human existence. Although the emphasis is on the impermanence of all human relationships and thus the triumph of time (moved by 'little fidget wheels') over life, the affection expressed for the scruffy, unruly, unimportant Irishman gives the poem a tender and human character. Peter Fitzpatrick discusses the life and death of Joe Lynch in *Australian Literary Studies* (1988) and *The Sea Coast of Bohemia* (1992).

'Five Visions of Captain Cook', first published in *Trio* (1931) by Kenneth Slessor (q.v.), builds the character of Captain James Cook (q.v.) from the reactions of those who sailed with him on his three major voyages. Based on Cook's journals and other contemporary writings, the poem is an important contribution to the voyager theme (q.v.) in Australian literature. The first section, focusing on the first *Endeavour* voyage of 1768–71, recounts Cook's historic decision to sail 'westabout' to Australia. The final section, the most attractive part of the poem, reviews the golden days with Cook through the nostalgic memories of retired sea captain Alexander Home. Full of memorable lines that attest to Slessor's delight in language, the poem is distinguished by its characterisation of Cook and Captain Home and demonstrates that men who change the face of the world inevitably change the lives of those who associate with them.

'FLACK, James', see **LINDSAY, Norman**

FLANAGAN, Roderick (1828–62), born County Roscommon, Ireland, came to Australia in 1840 and worked with the *People's Advocate* and the Melbourne *Daily News* before founding the brief-lived weekly, *Chronicle*, in Sydney in 1851. He joined the *Empire* in 1852 and published in it a series of articles in 1853 on the Aborigines, later published as *The Aborigines of Australia* (1888). In 1854 he joined the *Sydney Morning Herald;* in 1862 his *History of New South Wales with an Account of Van Diemen's Land, New Zealand, Port Phillip, Moreton Bay and Other Australasian Settlements* was published. A collection of his verse, *Australian and Other Poems*, published in 1887, was reprinted in *Roderick Flanagan* (1988) by Arthur Hoyle with a biographical introduction.

'Flash Jack from Gundagai' is an Australian folksong in which a shearer, the self-proclaimed Flash Jack from Gundagai, sings of the shearing sheds and the practices he has experienced. Several times in the song Flash Jack pays tribute to 'Old Tom Patterson on the One Tree Plain'. Patterson was a pastoralist who took up Ulong station in the Riverina in 1871 and added to his holding until it measured more than 120 000 hectares and took in the whole of the One Tree Plain.

Flaws in the Glass, by Patrick White (q.v.), was published in 1981. A collage of his memories of himself from an early age, significant emotional experiences, artistic and religious growth and relationships with family, friends and enemies, *Flaws in the Glass* is a remarkably frank study which has numerous links with his fiction. White's early memories of parents, relatives, servants and nannies are dominated by a sense of difference; born to extrovert, unimaginative parents who are leisured, wealthy and philistine, he is aware of emotions, gifts and interests which are alien to their experience and expectations. Sent at 14 to an English boarding school, which he hates, he nourishes his creative gifts and memories of the Australian landscape: 'Till well into my life, houses, places, landscape meant more to me than people ... It was landscape which made me long to return to Australia while at school in England.' During the grazier son's compulsory spell as a jackeroo, in the Monaro and at Walgett, NSW, he writes three 'immature' novels. After taking his degree in modern languages at Cambridge, he decides to try a writing career in London, supported by an allowance from his father. In London he mingles in bohemian and artistic circles and meets the painter Roy de Maistre, who influences his attitudes to art, music, writing and sex. He is in the USA negotiating the publishing of *Happy Valley* when the Second World War breaks out, but he returns to London and later joins the RAF as an intelligence officer. Posted to the Middle East he experiences the tedium, futility and occasional danger of war in the desert and in 1941 meets Manoly Lascaris, his future life-companion. A year in Palestine provides him with a highly varied human experience and an insight into the Jewish consciousness. A year in Greece is such a fundamentally important experience that he contemplates remaining there, although he fears becoming 'the beachcomber all foreigners become when they settle in Greece – tolerated, but never much more than a joke'. He is demobbed in London, begins to write *The Aunt's Story* and returns to Australia to prepare for Manoly's arrival. Reunited with his mother, Ruth, and his old nurse, Lizzie, he re-experiences feelings of ambivalence towards the first and of empathy with the second. After Manoly's arrival in Australia, they settle on a small holding at Castle Hill on the outskirts of Sydney, where White writes his novels *The Tree of Man* and *The Solid Mandala.* In 1963 they move to more congenial surroundings near Centennial Park, Sydney. The last two sections of *Flaws in the Glass* are titled 'Journeys' and 'Episodes and Epitaphs'; 'Journeys' describes White and Lascaris's travels in Greece, interspersed with White's individual journeys into the recesses of the unknown self: 'The masks I put on in my fictions are very different from those which strangers try to force on me, or to use another metaphor, the characters of whom I am composed cannot include those not yet revealed to me. At the age of sixty-nine I am still embarking on voyages of exploration which I hope may lead to discovery.' 'Episodes and Epitaphs' deals with some significant incidents in White's life, including his late involvement in political issues and his relationships with other writers and artists.

FLEMING, W.M. (William Montgomerie) (1874–1961), born Avon Plains in the Wimmera district of Victoria, spent much of his life as a State and federal parliamentarian. His literary achievements lie mainly in the field of children's literature, e.g. *Bunyip Says So* (1922) and *The Hunted Piccaninnies* (1927), highly imaginative short stories based on the Aboriginal understanding of animals and nature. A regular contributor of verse and prose to the *Sydney Morning Herald* and the *Bulletin*, Fleming also wrote a novel, *Broad Acres* (1939), which was made into a radio serial for the ABC in 1940.

Flesh in Armour (1932), the first novel by Leonard Mann (q.v.), is a fictional account, based to some degree on Mann's own experiences, of the AIF in action on the Western Front in France in the First World War. Unable to find a publisher for the novel in England or Australia, Mann published it himself. The novel's central character is the ex-schoolteacher, now corporal, Frank Jeffreys, a nervous, introverted and sensitive soldier who spends his time at the front in an agony of fear. On leave in London he meets Mary Hatton, who has already had a brief wartime intimacy with Jeffreys's fellow Australian, a rather callow youth, Charley Bentley. Frank and Mary write to each other, fall in love and plan to marry. Frank, however, learns of her affair with Bentley and kills himself with a grenade. Although the Mary–Frank romance runs throughout the novel, most of the book is set in France where the Australian division acquits itself superbly, in the opinion of the author, in the battles of the Somme, Ancre, Villers Brettoneux, Ypres and Mont St Quentin. Jim Blount is the novel's archetypal Australian digger, irreverent of authority, competent and coldly effective in hand-to-hand combat with the enemy but warm-hearted and generous with his Australian mates. He dies charging the enemy trenches single-handed. The battle scenes and characterisation lose little by comparison with Frederic Manning's *Her Privates We* (1930), but the novel has attracted some criticism because of Mann's excessive praise of the Australian fighting soldier.

FLETCHER, Charles Brunsdon (1859–1946), born Somerset, England, came to Sydney as a boy of 13 with his parents, who had earlier emigrated to NZ. Trained as a surveyor, Fletcher turned to journalism in 1893, joined the *Brisbane Courier* as a leader-writer and became its editor in 1898. In 1903 he returned to Sydney as associate editor of the *Sydney Morning Herald* and was its editor 1918–37. One of Fletcher's prime concerns, on which he wrote three books, was the security of the Pacific and the need for Australian interest in its development. His book *The Black Knight of the Pacific* (1944) was a biography of the Pacific Methodist missionary Dr George Brown. Among his Australian works was *Water Magic: Australia and the Future* (1945) on water conservation. His autobiography *The Great Wheel: An Editor's Adventures* (1940) is an illuminating account of the newspaper world.

FLETCHER, Henry (1856–1932), born London, came to Australia in 1872, and lived an itinerant life in Australia, NZ, France and England. He published six works of fiction, including four which chronicled the fortunes of the Wayback (q.v.) family: *The Waybacks in Town and at Home* (1902), *Dads Wayback: His Work* (1904), *Dads and Dan: Between Smokes* (1908) and *The Waybacks Again: Or, Love at Dingo Flat* (1909). An unsophisticated rural family, the Waybacks, who were also the subject of a 1918 film, were modelled on the Rudd family (q.v.) of 'Steele Rudd'.

'Flight of Wild Geese, A', a highly regarded poem by Harold Stewart (q.v.), published in his first volume of verse, *Phoenix Wings* (1948), depicts an imaginary incident concerning Wu Tao–tzu, the great Chinese artist who was commissioned by the Emperor Ming Huang of the T'ang Dynasty to paint a landscape roll. The poem's opening gloss indicates that Wu so enters into the spirit of the scene that he can walk about in the picture at will. One day he wanders over a distant mountain in the roll and is never seen again. During his wanderings Wu meets Chang Chih–ho, 'the Old Fisherman of the Waters and the Mists'. Their ensuing conversation is conducted with traditional Oriental decorum. Wu believes the old man to be evading life by his self-imposed exile; Chang responds that he 'fled not from the world but into it'. The conversation, charged with subtleties and innuendos that range deep into Oriental religious philosophies, is interrupted and illuminated by the sudden arrival and abrupt departure of a flight of geese.

FLINDERS, Matthew (1774–1814), born Lincolnshire, England, entered the Royal Navy at the age of 15, sailed as a midshipman with Vice–Admiral William Bligh to Tahiti in 1791, and was at the naval battle the 'Glorious First of June'. He went to Port Jackson in 1795 in HMS *Reliance* in which George Bass was ship's surgeon, explored the coast around Sydney with Bass in the *Tom Thumb*, circumnavigated Van Diemen's Land with Bass in 1798–99 and returned to England where he published *Observations on the Coasts of Van Diemen's Land, on Bass's Strait and Its Islands, and on Part of the Coasts of New South Wales* (1801). From January to May 1802 Flinders, in command of HMS *Investigator*, mapped the coastline from Fowler's Bay on the Great Australian Bight to Port Jackson, then charted north along the Queensland coast, through Torres Strait and the Gulf of Carpentaria, and completed the circumnavigation of the continent, returning to Port Jackson in June 1803. That momentous voyage proved that Australia *was* 'Terra Australis', the Great South Land. On his way back to England later that year, Flinders put into Port Louis, Mauritius, seeking water and provisions. He was arrested and held on the island by the French governor, de Caen, until 1810, when he was allowed to return to England. From 1810 until his death Flinders worked on the memorable account of his experiences and explorations, *A Voyage to Terra Australis*, which he wished to title *A Voyage to Australia* but was dissuaded by Sir Joseph Banks. After the publication of *A Voyage to Terra Australis* (1814), in which Flinders writes 'Had I permitted myself any innovation upon the original term, it would have been to convert it into 'Australia', as being more agreeable to the ear, and an assimilation of the names of the other great parts of the earth', the name 'Australia' began to be generally used. Flinders has been widely recognised in Australia; his name has been given to streets in towns and cities, to bays, islands, national parks, rivers, reefs and mountain ranges, to Australia's main naval base and to a university in Adelaide. His statues are in several Australian cities but the Mitchell Library in Sydney holds his manuscript collection, donated by his grandson, Sir William Matthew Flinders Petrie, because Sydney was the first city to erect a statue in his memory. Biographical works on Flinders include Ernest Scott's *The Life of Captain Matthew Flinders, R.N.* (1914), James D. Mack's *Matthew Flinders 1774–1814* (1966) and Ernestine Hill's fictional *My Love Must Wait* (q.v. 1941). In addition to his own *A Voyage to Terra Australis*, his explorations are described and assessed in K.A. Austin's *The Voyage of the Investigator 1801–1803*

(1964) and Max Colwell's *The Voyages of Matthew Flinders* (1970). The poems 'Flinders' Map' by John Blight and 'Cape Catastrophe' by J.M. Couper re-create incidents from Flinders's career. When *Matthew Flinders' Private Journal 1803–1814* was published in the Genesis Publications *Voyages of Exploration and Discovery* series in 1986 it was accompanied by a de luxe illustrated biography by Geoffrey C. Ingleton, *Matthew Flinders: Navigator and Chartmaker*. Huguette Ly Tio-Fane Pineo wrote *In the Grips of the Eagle* (1988), a study of the circumstances of Flinders's imprisonment on Mauritius, 1803–10.

Floating World, The, a play by John Romeril (q.v.), was first performed by the Australian Performing Group in 1974 and published in 1975. Les Harding, a member of the AIF during the Second World War and a survivor of the Burma–Thailand railway, has embarked on an *Australian Women's Weekly* 'Cherry Blossom' cruise to Japan with his wife, Irene. Les displays what Romeril regards as the worst characteristics of his generation – philistinism, xenophobia, racism and an aggressive masculinity that manifests itself in crude sexual jokes and gargantuan feats of beer consumption. Irene's natural habitat is lower-middle-class suburbia, with its mindless materialism, processed entertainment and false gentility. Unknown to Les the journey to Japan is about to bring him face to face with his inner, more sensitive self, which has been unable to forget the war, the deaths and sufferings of his mates, his hatred of the Japanese and his guilt that he survived. The blandness of current Australian–Japanese relations, meanwhile, is typified by the useless Dippy-Birds, mechanical drinking storks which are set in motion by the steward according to quaintly phrased Japanese instructions. Against the impressionistically presented background of a pleasure cruise with its third-rate entertainment, pseudo-romance and familiar rituals, Romeril imposes Les's anguished hallucinations; a passenger, Williams, becomes McLeod, an old digger mate; the Malay steward, a Japanese soldier; and Robinson, an ex-RN officer, a spy from the RSL. As he retreats into the unreality of madness Les discovers his true reality, his floating world, where his paranoid identity is at least given coherent meaning by real enemies.

FLOOD, Tom (1955–), born Sydney, the son of Dorothy Hewett (q.v.), grew up in WA, and had a variety of short-term occupations, e.g. wheat sampler, geologist's assistant, bus conductor, until he began writing fiction in 1985. *Oceana Fine* (1989), his first novel, won the 1988 *Australian*/Vogel Award and the Miles Franklin Award, 1990. The title refers to a particularly fast-growing strain of wheat that is capable of turning the vast wheat lands of Western Australia into a veritable ocean of wheat, and wheat and wheat men play a major part in the complicated and tortuous plot. At the book's core is the patriarchal Rex Cleaver, described aptly by John Carroll as 'a Bible-quoting messianic obsessive'. Much of the Cleaver family history is revealed by and to Rex's youngest son Jamie, accompanied by brutal violent events played out against the vast, almost mythic landscape.

FLOWER, Cedric (1920–   ), born Sydney and best known as a painter, has written several studies of Australia's cultural life, including *Duck & Cabbage Tree: A Pictorial History of Clothes in Australia 1788–1914* (1968, rev. edn 1988 *Clothes in Australia*), *The Antipodes Observed: Prints and Printmakers of Australia 1788–1850* (1975), and *Illustrated History of New South Wales* (1981). He also collaborated with his wife Pat Flower in writing for television, including a play, 'Love Returns to Umbrizi', and an award-winning film script, *From the Tropics to the Snow* (1963).

FLOWER, Charles Augustus (?1856–1948), born Port Fairy, Victoria, worked as a jackeroo in Victoria before settling in Queensland, where he overlanded sheep and was employed as an accountant for a firm of railway contractors; he was later a pastoralist for many years in the Roma district of central Queensland. He is credited by some folklorists with the authorship of the overlanding song 'A Thousand Miles Away' (q.v.), which mentions the Roma railway, and 'The Brokendown Squatter', the lament of a pastoralist who has been forced by drought and high rents to give up his run. Similarly, Horace Alfred Flower, the elder brother of Charles (uncle in some less reliable accounts), is claimed as the author of another well-known Australian folk-song, 'The Dying Stockman' (q.v.).

FLOWER, Pat (1914–77), born Kent, England, came to Australia at the age of 14. A prolific writer of radio and television plays, she also wrote satirical sketches for Sydney's New Theatre and numerous crime novels, most of which were published in the Collins Crime Club series and translated into French, German and Italian. One of her television plays, 'The Tape-Recorder', the first play to be produced in colour by BBC 2, was also produced in Australia, Canada and the USA and was published in *The Best Short Plays 1969* (1970); another, 'Fiends of the Family', is included in *Take One* (1972), ed. Richard Lane. In 1967 she won the Mary Gilmore Award for a one-hour television play, 'Tilley Landed on Our Shores'. With her husband Cedric Flower she wrote the award-winning film script *From the Tropics to the Snow* (1963). Her novels include *A Wreath of Water-Lilies* (1960), *One Rose Less* (1961), *Cat's Cradle* (1973) and *Crisscross* (1976).

Flying Doctor, see **FLYNN, John**

Flying Fox and Drifting Sand (1938), by Francis Ratcliffe, is an account of inland Australia following two surveys Ratcliffe undertook for the CSIRO: in 1929–31 when he investigated the flying foxes of Queensland, and in 1935 when he studied soil erosion from SA to Queensland. Ratcliffe's lively description of the wildlife of mangrove swamps and deserts and his anecdotes of outback personalities and incidents have made the book perennially popular.

FLYNN, Errol (1909–59), the swashbuckling Hollywood film hero, was born in Hobart; his father Theodore (1883–1968) was a prominent zoologist and his mother a descendant of a *Bounty* mutineer. After a rebellious childhood, mainly in Australia, Flynn spent several years adventuring in New Guinea before going into films. His heyday was 1935–42, when he played such roles as Captain Blood and Robin Hood. Flynn was a notorious playboy, thrice married and addicted in his later years to drugs, alcohol and young girls; his amorous adventures are said by some to have inspired the current colloquial Australianism, 'in like Flynn' (or 'in like Errol'), meaning to take advantage of a situation, particularly a sexual opportunity. Flynn wrote New Guinea columns for the *Bulletin;* a travel book, *Beam Ends* (1937); a novel, *Showdown* (1946); and the autobiographical *My Wicked, Wicked Ways* (1960). He is the subject of a number of biographical studies, including J.H. Moore's *The Young Errol* (1975) and Charles Higham's *Errol Flynn* (1980); Peter Valenti has written a bio-bibliography (1984) and his abilities as an actor are analysed in *The Films of Errol Flynn* (1969) by T. Thomas, R. Behlmer and C. McCarty; he is celebrated in Rob George's play 'Errol Flynn's Big Adventure Book for Boys' (1977) and in Australian Crawl's popular song 'Oh Errol'. Grahame Bond starred in the Flynn musical 'Captain Bloody' in 1984. Roger McDonald published the novel *Flynn* (1992), based on the feature film released in that year.

FLYNN, John (1880–1951), born Moliagul, Victoria, joined the Home Mission staff of the Presbyterian Church of Victoria in 1902 and was ordained in 1911. In 1912 he was appointed superintendent of the Northern Territory mission area, a position he held for almost forty years. In 1928 he founded the Australian Inland Mission Aerial Service at Cloncurry, Queensland, later known as the Royal Flying Doctor Service. Made OBE in 1933, he was moderator-general of the Presbyterian Church of Australia 1939–42. Flynn published *The Bushman's Companion* (1910) and was editor of the *Outback Battler*, a quarterly magazine (1911–13), and of *Inlander*, another bush magazine (1913–29). He is the subject of Ion L. Idriess's *Flynn of the Inland* (1932) and W.S. McPheat's *John Flynn, Apostle to the Inland* (1963). He is also featured in Ernestine Hill's *Flying Doctor Calling* (1947) and H. Hudson's *Flynn's Flying Doctors* (1956).

Folk-Song and Ballad. In Australia the terms 'folk-song' and 'ballad' describe a body of songs, often but by no means always of anonymous authorship, which tell stories of or depict Australian life and which have had currency among ordinary Australian people as a result of oral performance, particularly between the early days of European settlement and the advent of recordings and the radio. The terms are generally used with others indicating the subject, period, type or audience of the songs, e.g. 'sung ballads', 'traditional songs', '(traditional) bush ballads', '(old) bush songs', 'popular ballads' and 'colonial ballads'. There are different views concerning the most important influences on Australian folk-songs, the main ways in which they were created, and the significance of oral transmission, dismissed by one folklorist as the 'Trench Mouth School of Folklore'. Commentators place little emphasis on the collective composition of the 'folk' (a process satirised as 'composition in committee' and 'immaculate conception'), but most accept that Australian folk-songs are part of popular culture; that they therefore articulate communal values, establishing the Australianness of the singer and the audience; and that the effects of oral transmission can be detected in the textual refinements over time of many songs, in the variants that exist for others (e.g. 'The Wild Colonial Boy', q.v.) and in the transfer of tunes between songs (e.g. 'A Thousand Miles Away', q.v.). No formal census of Australian folk-songs has been undertaken, and estimates vary from 70 to 1500 as to the number which have survived. Most folklorists, however, agree with a central canon of 250–400; among modern collections and indexes, Douglas Stewart and Nancy Keesing's *Old Bush Songs* (1957) has the words of 216 songs, Hugh Anderson's (q.v.) *Australian Song Index 1828–1956* (1957) lists 375 titles and Ron Edwards's (q.v.) *The Big Book of Australian Folk Song* (1976) has the words and music of 308 songs as well as an index of 1800 published songs and recitations; another compilation by Ron Edwards, *200 Years of Australian Folk Song* (1988) indexes over 2000 songs. Some of the folk-songs included in these tallies have as much right to be regarded as part of the folk culture of other countries; this is particularly true of transportation songs such as 'The Black Velvet Band' (q.v.) and 'Van Diemen's Land', which are set for a significant part of their narratives in the convicts' country of origin. These songs clearly originated overseas and were brought to Australia; recent research suggests that there were many similar songs (and many more than has been realised) which have an Australian content but have never had an Australian currency.

The three nineteenth-century experiences of European Australians which contributed most to the creation of Australian folk-song were transportation, the discovery of gold, and pastoral expansion in the period 1860–90. Transportation was the first, although very few of the earliest Australian songs and ballads dealing with the subject have survived; indeed the transportation song best known to modern Australians, 'Botany Bay' (q.v.), was not performed until the 1880s, well after the last convicts had arrived in eastern Australia. In that the popular version of 'Botany Bay' was originally a London parody 'transported' to Australia, it illustrates a common genesis of Australian folk-songs: by the parody, imitation, adaptation and other forms of borrowing from existing English, Irish and, later, American songs; sometimes the words, as in 'Sam Holt' (q.v.); sometimes the tunes, as in the widespread use of 'The Wearing of the Green'; and sometimes both, as in 'The Dying Stockman' (q.v.), which is the Australian remake of an English popular song sometimes set to an American melody, and a song which has itself been subsequently parodied. In that 'Botany Bay' is a music-hall parody of an 1820s broadside, it also illustrates two important influences on

Australian folk-songs: the nineteenth-century popular theatre, and the street ballad which until about 1850 was as popular among certain classes as the modern tabloid newspaper and was thus a major source of news for the urban poor who comprised the bulk of the convicts. The traditional rural folk-ballad of the British Isles was less influential on Australian folk-song than either of these influences.

Most transportation songs are cautionary tales of poachers (e.g. 'Van Diemen's Land') or petty criminals tricked into crime (e.g. 'The Black Velvet Band'), usually told in the first person by the offenders themselves, by their victims (e.g. 'Maggie May') and occasionally by the loved ones they have left behind (e.g. 'A Thousand Miles Away'). The narrative element dominates most in the songs which seem to have emerged, like 'Botany Bay', after the cessation of transportation and are normally sung to jaunty, lilting or rollicking tunes. The most rollicking are 'Ten Thousand Miles Away' and 'Maggie May', partly because they are songs of seamen as well as of convicts. In contrast, the folk-songs which can be more firmly dated to the time of transportation (e.g. 'Van Diemen's Land', 'The Convict Maid', 'The Exile of Erin', 'Jim Jones at Botany Bay', q.v.) and the compositions associated with Francis MacNamara (q.v., 'Frank the Poet'), notably 'Labouring with the Hoe' and 'Moreton Bay' (q.v.), are descriptive rather than narrative, focusing on the dismal experiences of the convicts once they have arrived in Australia. In general, the protagonists in these songs lament their lives as felons but are relatively compliant towards the social systems which led to their transportation. This is not the case, however, with 'Moreton Bay' and 'Jim Jones at Botany Bay', among the most haunting of all Australian songs, which both strike a defiant note at the end. The exhilaration of the convict in 'Moreton Bay' at the death of the tyrannical commandant Patrick Logan, and the vow of Jim Jones to join the bushranger 'Bold Jack Donahoo' (see Donohoe, John) in order to 'shoot the floggers down', provide the kind of evidence supporting speculations that the reason more of the songs sung by the convicts have not survived is that as treason songs they were banned by the penal authorities. Certainly, in later decades it could be dangerous to sing 'The *Catalpa*' (q.v.) in front of the authorities in Fremantle and the Ned Kelly (q.v.) songs to bush policemen in Victoria; certainly also, 'Moreton Bay' and 'Jim Jones at Botany Bay' are among the first Australian protest songs, helping to inaugurate a tradition of anti-authoritarian sentiment, often thought to be a national virtue, which accommodates the best-known Australian song of any description, 'Waltzing Matilda' (q.v.). In tone, the tradition ranges from the lightly mocking irreverence of 'The *Catalpa*' to the revolutionary calls of some shearers' ballads of the 1890s. In time, it ranges from convict songs like 'Moreton Bay' through the convict-bushranger songs centred on Bold Jack Donahoe, who is linked with his legendary descendant 'The Wild Colonial Boy', because both 'scorn to live in slavery/ bound down by iron chains'; then through the bushrangers, themselves part of a wider highwayman-

Robin Hood tradition, of the 1860s and 1870s, notably Ben Hall (q.v.) and Ned Kelly, who sang 'The Wild Colonial Boy' at Glenrowan and quoted 'Moreton Bay' in the Jerilderie Letter; next through the songs of the pastoral workers, which have been called 'democratic in the extreme'; and reaching finally into modern times in such songs as Frank Hardy's 'Sydney Town' and in the work of Eric Bogle and the band Redgum, among contemporary 'folk' commentators. The strong Irish connection in the convict and bushranger songs gives an anti-English dimension to the protest tradition.

By the time transportation to eastern Australia ceased in 1853, the first official discoveries of gold had been made, stimulating the immigration of 'new chum' diggers who, like Billy Barlow and Paddy Malone (qq.v.) of earlier days and the new chum jackeroos of the subsequent pastoral expansion, were the targets for the 'old hands'. Collectively the experiences of the new chums make up one of the categories into which collections of Australian folksongs are normally arranged; that apart, the goldfields are significant in Australian folk-song less for the intrinsic quality of the surviving songs than for the fact that the kaleidoscopic nature of goldfields society meant the introduction of new musical influences and instruments. With the exception of a song like 'The Old Palmer Song', which grew out of and is almost a variant of 'Ten Thousand Miles Away', the songs of the goldfields were seldom anonymous and were usually clearly identifiable folk-songs. This is mainly because the gold rushes attracted to Australia a wide range of professional entertainers, including the notorious Lola Montez, Shakespearean actors such as G.V. Brooke, and troubadours who entertained their audiences by adopting the ditties they had learnt and played in the music-halls of England to the new conditions of Ballarat and elsewhere. The best was the inimitable Charles Thatcher (q.v.), the 'Bard of Bendigo', whose compositions smack of the concert hall but gained currency beyond it because they were published in one of his series of songsters. When, in time, as with songs like 'Look Out Below', they gained through oral transmission a currency beyond both the composer and his songster, they became part of Australian folk-song. In a similar way, other folk-songs which began life as literary compositions have passed from print into oral circulation and thus into the mainstream of Australian folk-song: the songs which derive from the literary balladists of the 1880s and 1890s came into this category, as also do such well-known songs as 'The Eumerella Shore' and 'Ladies of Brisbane'.

Thatcher, it is said, earned far more from singing than he ever did puddling or panning. His lack of success paralleled that of the diggers at large, many of whom became itinerants like the miner turned pastoral worker in 'With My Swag All on My Shoulder':

> With my swag all on my shoulder
> Black billy in my hand
> I've travelled the bush of Australia
> Like a true-born native man.

The half-century or so after the gold rushes, roughly from 1860 to the outbreak of the First World War, are years covering the decades of major pastoral expansion. They are also the years in which the bush became the dominant subject of Australian folk-song; hence, given also that the bulk of Australian folk-songs dates from this period, the generalised use of terms like 'bush songs' and 'bush ballads'. Songs such as 'The Cocky Farmer' and 'The New England Cocky' chronicle the experiences of the small-scale 'cockatoo' farmer who tried to grub a living from the land after the passing of the Selection Acts in the 1860s. His erstwhile enemy on the pastoral frontier was the squatter, whose own struggle is recorded in 'The Broken-down Squatter' and 'The Eumerella Shore'. Allied with the squatter was the 'cadet' jackeroo, whose songs alternated between wonderment at the novelty of bush life and despair at its harshness (e.g. 'The Dying Stockman'). The greatest proportion of Australian folk-songs from this period, however, focus on the men who serviced, albeit grudgingly, e.g. 'Cockies of Bungaree', 'Goorianawa', both selector and squatter: the bush workers, the drovers (although some of the drovers were intending selectors or failed squatters), bullockies, swagmen, shearers and other pastoral nomads of Russel Ward's *The Australian Legend* (q.v., 1958). Mostly isolated on the one hand from the homestead culture of those settled on the land, and on the other from the centres of popular entertainment in the towns and cities, these itinerant bucolics, particularly the shearers, constituted a ballad community which made its own entertainment, often in ways that expressed their collectivist ethic. Their heroes were the bushrangers and others who snubbed their noses at authority. They enjoyed their freedom, had an ambivalent attitude towards 'flashness', admired daring and despised cockies and new chum jackeroos, whose verses they took over and refined in a hard-bitten way, as is shown by a comparison between 'The Wooyeo Ball' and 'The Euabalong Ball' (q.v.). The songs of the bush workers reflect this ethos. Although there are inevitable differences, e.g. the songs of the drovers are action songs and tend to be longer, possibly because they were sung in the saddle, the differences are not as significant as the similarities. Most bush songs are celebrations rather than narratives; they describe aspects of pioneering life in the first person while preserving communal values, and name individual places and people while retaining the essential impersonality of the music of the 'folk'. Many of them come into the category of work or occupational songs (e.g. 'The Overlander', 'The Sandy Maranoa', 'Click Go the Shears', 'The Lime-juice Tub', 'Flash Jack From Gundagai', 'The Old Bullock Dray'), in some cases asserting (e.g. 'The Ryebuck Shearer') or implying (e.g. 'The Overlander') the superiority of the singer to others in his occupation or the superiority of the occupation itself. The dominant mood of the work songs is an acceptance of the occupation bordering on swaggering cheerfulness, although there are some songs (e.g. 'The Backblocks Shearer', q.v.) in which these attitudes are satirised and others still which are rueful (e.g. the shanty songs

'Lazy Harry's' q.v., 'All for Me Grog' and 'The Wild Rover'); sentimental (e.g. 'The Banks of the Condamine', q.v.) or lugubrious (e.g. 'The Dying Stockman' and other jackeroo songs, and most swagmen's songs). Despite the sentimental and the lugubrious, humour which is self-mocking and sardonic, as in most pioneering communities, is an important ingredient.

The Australian bush song seldom reflects, either in theme or melody, the earlier rural folk-ballads of England and Scotland. For example, very few of the bush songs are love songs, and those which are (e.g. 'The Bush Girl', 'The Banks of the Condamine', 'Ladies of Brisbane') characteristically depict the desertion of the female by the male worker using peripatetic necessity as an excuse; equally, very few of the bush songs have the wild, haunting melodies of the traditional rural ballads. Nevertheless, there remained, as in earlier periods, a strong influence from overseas which can be seen in the genre parallels with America (bushranger/outlaw, swagman/hobo, stockman/cowboy); in the links between individual songs and their parent songs in England, Ireland and America; in the imported dances; and in the accompanying instrumentation, although some singing was done unaccompanied and it was common to learn both words and tune from the acknowledged singer of a district.

The influence in the area of instrumentation is conveniently recorded in 'The Drovers's Dream', in which a stockman on watch at night falls asleep and dreams that the fauna put on a concert for him. Early on in the entertainment,

Three frogs from out the swamp where the atmosphere
    was damp,
Came out and gently sat upon a stone.
They unrolled their little swags, took from out their
    dilly bags,
The violin, the banjo and the bones.

The last line forms the title of John Manifold's (q.v.) brief study of bush music (1957); and what is significant about the instruments named is that the popularity of the violin as a folk instrument derived from the popularity of tavern and street fiddlers in eighteenth-century England and Ireland, and that the introduction of the banjo and the bones reflects the spread of the Christy and Negro minstrel culture beyond America. Among other instruments used, particularly for dancing, were the concertina and the accordion, a German instrument which provides the music at 'Kate's Wedding' by 'Steele Rudd'; the Jew's harp and the tin whistle; and a variety of 'indigenous' instruments, such as the gum leaf, bullock bells, the bush bass (traditionally constructed of a tea chest body, a neck of hide or sapling wood, and a rawhide bow), and the lagerphone (beer bottle tops nailed to an upright). The popularity of the indigenous instruments, however, like that of the guitar and the mouth organ which are common instruments in modern bush bands, is a comparatively recent phenomenon; the emergence of the lagerphone, for example, can be linked specifically with the success of the 1950s bush musical *Reedy River* (q.v.). The instruments that were used in the nineteenth century have been seen as influential in the process of melodic erosion of many Australian folk-song tunes. Roger Covell refers in *Australia's Music* (1967) to the 'slack-jawed gumminess' of much Australian folk-song, in part because of the unfortunate musical influence of the popular theatre but in part also because most of the songs were collected in a terminal form, after the Industrial Revolution and at 'the fag end of a tradition'.

Beyond an acknowledgement of their 'vigour', 'vitality', 'immediacy' and 'authenticity', terms often used in tandem with others like 'rough', 'robust' and 'raw', very few claims have been made for the bush songs as poetry despite the occasional literary flourishes (e.g. the internal rhymes of 'The Drover's Dream') which are apparent also in the folk-songs of earlier times: e.g. in 'Frank the Poet's' ballad 'The Seizure of the *Cyprus Brig* in Recherche Bay' and 'Moreton Bay', which was originally a recitation piece rather than a song. More substantial claims have been made, though the genre is still regarded more as 'popular verse' or 'folk literature' than as 'literary poetry', for what is generally called the 'literary ballad': a set of rhyming verses written in a ballad metre, usually with an eye to publication (and thus more often of known authorship than the majority of folk-songs, and less often subject to refinement or erosion through oral transmission). From the beginning, the bush was a dominant subject of the literary ballad, although the form subsequently accommodated nautical and military subjects as well as occupying an urban landscape. Henry Kendall's 'Jim the Splitter' (1880), a satirical portrait of a bush woodcutter, is regarded by some commentators as an early Australian literary ballad. Ten years earlier Adam Lindsay Gordon, himself a dashing horseman and generally accepted as the first literary balladist, wrote 'The Sick Stockrider', 'From the Wreck', 'Wolf and Hound' and the other ballads that went into his *Bush Ballads and Galloping Rhymes* (1870). 'Jim the Splitter' is unlike much of Kendall's other verse, and Gordon was a derivative writer who modelled himself on Tennyson, Swinburne and Browning. Yet descended from Gordon are the literary balladists clustered around the *Bulletin* (q.v.), who in the decades either side of 1900 promoted, as much by the quantity as by the quality of their work, a distinctive, nationalist bush ethos. A.B. Paterson (q.v.) is by common consent the best of the balladists; among others who established a reputation in the *Bulletin* and elsewhere were his fellow 'equestrians' Barcroft Boake, Will Ogilvie and 'Breaker' Morant (qq.v.); the mining balladists, notably Edward Dyson (q.v.); bush humorists such as W.T. Goodge and Thomas E. Spencer (qq.v.); those who focused on farming communities, such as Charles Henry Souter and 'John O'Brien' (qq.v.); others whose range was eclectic, including Henry Lawson, G.H. Gibson ('Ironbark') and E.G. Murphy ('Dryblower') (qq.v.); and others still who went beyond the bush, notably E.J. Brady and later C.J. Dennis (qq.v.).

Although Gordon 'showed the way', in the words of one commentator, there were other influences operating on the literary balladists. That they were read so avidly is in part an effect of the spread of literacy in the latter part of the nineteenth century. At the same time they were part of a widespread movement towards ballad poetry, particularly among frontier communities. The popularity of Paterson, for example, paralleled the popularity of John Hay and Bret Harte in America, Robert Service in Canada, and Rudyard Kipling throughout the British Empire. Third, and perhaps most important, the literary ballads were influenced by the existing folk-songs, despite differences between the two: principally, in the literary ballads, a greater emphasis on third-person action narratives (e.g. 'The Man from Snowy River', 'How M'Dougall Topped the Score', qq.v.); a more wide-ranging sympathy towards the inhabitants of the bush (thus the literary ballads less single-mindedly articulate the prejudices of the pastoral nomads); a greater empathy with and idealisation of the land itself as well as of its inhabitants (e.g. 'Clancy of the Overflow', q.v.); and a greater attention to the rudiments of verse technique. Yet the differences are differences of degree rather than kind, and against them must be set the similarities in subject matter, in the importance of humour, in attitude (e.g. the admiration of the daring, albeit in different circumstances, of the Wild Colonial Boy and the Man from Snowy River), and in the unselfconscious use of the vernacular, which is symptomatic both of a shared, positive response to 'Australianness' and of a common folk origin of the literary ballads and the bush songs. There is clear evidence also of cross-pollination. On the one hand, Paterson acknowledged that he had heard songs such as 'The Wild Colonial Boy' and 'The Old Bark Hut' in his youth (both are recalled also in Lawson's story 'The Songs They Used to Sing'), and specific parallels exist between a song like 'The Dying Stockman' and a poem like 'The Sick Stockrider'. On the other, many of the literary ballads became recitation pieces which formed part of the repertoire of bush singers and entertainers such as Jack Moses (q.v.), and were printed side by side with folk-songs in the popular outback songsters; some of them (e.g. 'Andy's Gone with Cattle', 'The Bush Girl', 'Reedy River', 'The Shearer's Dream', 'The Streets of Forbes', 'Travelling down the Castlereagh') became folk-songs because they had tunes put to them and passed into oral circulation – a process which has continued, to judge by the popularity in 1980 of a musical version of 'Clancy of the Overflow'.

Perhaps the most significant link between the folk-songs and the literary ballads was forged in 1898, when Paterson began assembling the first collection of Australian folk-songs. Published in 1905 as *The Old Bush Songs* (q.v.), the collection sold widely and went through several editions between 1905 and 1932, in which songs additional to the original fifty-five were included; it introduced the bush song to many Australians, including important modern folklorists (e.g. John Meredith, q.v.). In the 1930s, the recitation booklets of 'Bill Bowyang' (see Vennard, Alexander Vindex), which continued a publishing tradition established on the goldfields and consolidated by the *Bulletin Reciter*, kept some of the Paterson texts in circulation.

Neither Paterson nor 'Bill Bowyang' included musical scores in their collections; the first collectors to focus firmly on this aspect of Australian folk-song were musicologists such as Percy Jones (q.v.) and folklorists such as A.L. Lloyd (q.v.), although some of Lloyd's reconstructions have been criticised by some Australian folklorists. In 1951 Vance Palmer's selection of *Old Australian Bush Ballads* was published, the first to include the music of the songs, restored by Margaret Sutherland. It appeared in the same year as the first of Ron Edwards's and John Manifold's *Bandicoot Ballads* (1951–55), a series of broadsheets which made available some of the convict songs; the convict songs had been largely ignored by Paterson, although the text of 'Moreton Bay' had been included in Will Lawson's *Australian Bush Songs and Ballads* (1944). In 1953 Dick Diamond's *Reedy River*, which incorporated several traditional songs and introduced urban audiences to the music and instruments of the bush, was successfully staged; it came at the beginning of a decade of intense activity, in collection and research as well as in performance, which confirmed the revival of interest in Australian folk-song. The revival subsequently accommodated folklorists such as Ron Edwards, Bill and Alan Scott, Hugh Anderson, Wendy Lowenstein and John Meredith; scholars with university connections, including Russel Ward (q.v.) and Edgar Waters; and established writers such as John Manifold (q.v.), Douglas Stewart and Nancy Keesing. Working sometimes in isolation and sometimes in partnership, they substantially enlarged the corpus of Australian folk-song by fieldwork among the surviving traditional singers (e.g. Simon McDonald, Duke Tritton, q.v.; Sally Sloane, Joseph Cashmere and 'Hoop-Iron' Jack Lee) and by research in the libraries which unearthed important sources such as the early newspapers and songsters, and the reminiscences of Jack Bradshaw and Charles MacAlister (qq.v.).

In time, these research workers published collections or studies which reflected their individual emphases; often the collections were cumulative in that they incorporated or consolidated material previously published in broadsheets, chapbooks, pamphlets and journals, or were subsequently revised and expanded. Hugh Anderson's *The Story of Australian Folksong* (1970), an expansion of his earlier *Colonial Ballads* (1955, 1962), and Ron Edwards's *The Big Book of Australian Folk Song* (1976), which incorporates material from successive editions of his *The Overlander Song Book* (first published in 1956) as well as from his *Black Bull Chapbooks* (1954–57), *Bandicoot Ballads* and other compilations, are examples of cumulative collections. Among other anthologies the most important are Stewart and Keesing's *Old Bush Songs* (1957), which takes the Paterson text as its basis, and *Australian Bush Ballads* (1955), both reprinted under their original and other titles; John Manifold's *The Penguin Australian Song Book* (1964); Bill Scott's *The Second Penguin Australian Song Book* (1976); and Russel Ward's *The Penguin Book of Australian Ballads* (1964). These anthologies usually have important introductions or notes on the groupings, origins, significance or transmission of Australian folk-songs. These subjects are also addressed in specialist studies (e.g. Anderson's study of Thatcher, *The Colonial Minstrel*, 1960); in Manifold's imaginative, speculative left-wing interpretation *Who Wrote the Ballads? Notes on Australian Folk Song* (1964), Anderson's *Farewell to Old England* (1964) and Thérèse Radic's *Songs of Australian Working Life* (1989); in more broadly based works, e.g. Ward's *The Australian Legend*, H.M. Green's *A History of Australian Literature* (1961) *The Oxford Companion to Australian Folklore* (1993), edited by Gwenda Beed Davey and Graham Seal, and several folklore compilations; in anthology-commentary combinations (e.g. Anderson's and Meredith's *Folk Songs of Australia and the Men and Women Who Sang Them*, 1967 reprinted in 1979 and a second volume in 1987 with assistance from Roger Covell and Patricia Brown); and in journals ranging from the literary-cultural (e.g. *Meanjin*) to the specialist folklore magazines (e.g. *Singabout, Gumsucker's Gazette, Australian Tradition*, q.v.; *National Folk*) which were issued by the Sydney Bush Music Club, the Australian Folklore Society, the Folk Lore Society of Victoria and other emerging bush music and folklore societies.

As the dates of some of these works indicate, the revival of interest in Australian folk-song continued into the 1960s, attracting the interest of coffee-shop proprietors and corporation recording companies whose executives probably noted the success of some of the Wattle Records (1954–62). The coffee shops no longer employed folk-singers by the end of the 1960s, but in the 1970s and 1980s interest had periodically been renewed: Anderson, Meredith, Manifold, Edwards and others have continued research and publication, folklore festivals have continued to be held, and in Sydney a successful business in recording and publishing has been established by Warren Fahey. Given the major contribution of the bush to Australian folk-song, it is ironic that the modern folk-song movement is essentially an urban phenomenon, centred in the universities and in the trade unions; hence the attraction of the old protest songs and their influence on contemporary songwriters like John Dengate and Eric Bogle. In general, Australian country-dwellers have long forsaken traditional music in favour of travelling country-western shows featuring such singers as Buddy Williams, Reg Lindsay, Slim Dusty and Chad Morgan. Although in some of their songs they draw on an indigenous tradition (Morgan's 'The Fatal Wedding' has parallels with 'The Dying Stockman', and Rolf Harris's 'Tie Me Kangaroo Down Sport' is even more firmly linked), their models are overwhelmingly American: the rural city of Tamworth, NSW, promoted as the home of Australian country music, copies Nashville, Tennessee. Country-western singers such as Lindsay and Morgan are often dismissed as derivative 'hillbillies' by Australian folklorists, yet it was an Australian, John Edwards, who provided the impetus for the scholarly study of country-western music. After the death of Edwards in 1960, his collections formed the basis of the John Edwards Memorial Foundation, established in 1962 at the University of California at Los Angeles, where there is a folklore centre. In March 1987

Australian Folklore, a yearly journal of Australian folklore studies, was commenced from the Centre for Australian Studies at Curtin University, WA, under the editorship of Graham Seal and David Huets.

FOOTT, Mary Hannay (1846–1918), born Glasgow, Scotland, came to Australia in 1853. Educated at a private school in Melbourne, she trained as a teacher and taught 1862–68 before spending five years at the National Gallery School, where she studied under von Guérard and Buvelot. During these years she supported herself by contributing articles and poems to the Melbourne and Sydney *Punch*, the *Australasian*, the *Town and Country Journal* and the *Australasian Sketcher*. In 1874 she married Thomas Wade Foott and three years later accompanied him to south-west Queensland to take up land. After her husband's death in 1884 she went to Brisbane, where she opened a private school and contributed to the *Queenslander* and *Brisbane Courier*; she joined the staff of the *Queenslander* in 1887 and was editor of its women's page for about a decade, writing verse and stories, sometimes under the pseudonym 'La Quenouille'. She published two books of verse, *Where the Pelican Builds and Other Poems* (1885), expanded as *Morna Lee and Other Poems* (1890). Her best-known poem, frequently anthologised, is 'Where the Pelican Builds'; it records, from the viewpoint of the waiting women, the tragedy that so frequently struck the pioneer families – the loss of loved ones who were drawn by the lure of the land further out. Mary Hannay Foott was also a playwright; her comedy 'More Than Kin' was produced at Government House, Brisbane, in 1891 and another play, 'Sweep', was a popular three-act comedy for children. Her mother-in-law, Henrietta Foott, was the author of *Sketches of Life in the Bush* (1872).

'For gorsake stop laughing – this is serious!' was the title of a famous cartoon by Stan Cross (q.v.), first published in *Smith's Weekly* in 1933. The cartoon depicts a workman hanging precariously from a girder on top of a building as he remonstrates in the words of the punch line with a second workman; the second workman has fallen and in seizing the other's trousers has yanked them down over the ankles and is now convulsed with laughter. The cartoon was reprinted and distributed widely, becoming a standard adornment of barbers' shops and hotel bars. It has been seen as an assault on dignity, archetypal of humour in general and of Australian humour in particular.

For Love Alone, a novel by Christina Stead (q.v.), was published in 1944. Set in Sydney and London in the 1930s, it is the story of Teresa Hawkins, an intelligent, ardent young woman, and her search for the ideal passion of love. She attempts to engage the feelings of the unworthy Jonathan Crow, an intellectual young man and advocate of free love, and follows him to London after four years of severe self-sacrifice. In London the mediocrity, corruption and egoistic shallowness of Crow gradually become obvious. With the help of James Quick, however, a devoted older man who takes Teresa to live with him, she is able to abandon her idealised vision. After a brief interlude with Quick's friend, Harry Girton, Teresa advances to new, more detached appreciation of passion and renews her commitment to Quick in full awareness of the compromises that love imposes. *For Love Alone* was produced as a film in 1985.

For the Term of His Natural Life, see **His Natural Life**

FORBES, 'Alexander' (William Anderson) (1839–79), born Banffshire, Scotland, was sent down from King's College, Aberdeen, for a youthful misdemeanour ('either snowballing or lampooning a professor') and came to Australia in 1862, wandering outback Queensland in a variety of menial jobs. His early Australian poems express resentment at his exile and disgust with the colonial environment. Gradually inured to the hardships of colonial life by alcohol, tobacco and the adoption of a rueful, ironic pose, Forbes, known widely as 'Alick the Poet', recovered from his nostalgia for Scotland and began to sing the praises of bush life. He published, as 'Alexander' Forbes, *Voices from the Bush* (1869); one of the earliest bush balladists, he expressed the humour and tragedy of the bush experience.

FORBES, Archibald (1838–1900), elder brother of 'Alexander' Forbes (q.v.) and one of the best-known British war correspondents of the Victorian period, made an extensive and lucrative tour of Australia in 1883, lecturing to capacity audiences on the various campaigns he had witnessed. His book *Souvenirs of Some Continents* (1885) contains an observant account of 'Social Australia' and a moving essay on his 'poor gifted shipwrecked brother' ('A Poet Waif').

FORBES, John (1950–   ), born Melbourne, lived much of his early life in New Guinea, Malaya and Sydney. He graduated from the University of Sydney and has been a teacher of creative writing. He won the Poetry Society of Australia Award in 1972; the H.M. Butterley-F. Earle-Hooper *Southerly* Award for a young writer in 1976 for the poem 'Breakfast'; and was granted a travelling fellowship in 1975. He has co-edited the journal *Leatherjacket;* edits the magazine *Surfers Paradise;* and has published the volumes of poetry *Tropical Skiing* (1976), *On the Beach* (1977), *Stalin's Holidays* (1981), *The Stunned Mullet* (1988) and *New and Selected Poems* (1992), the last including many from the earlier selections and a section of sixteen new poems. Long regarded as a 'cerebral' poet with an outstanding passion for poetry, who conceals his meaning behind deceptive symbolism and subtle post-modernist devices, Forbes catches the essence of the contemporary world with wry accuracy. Although his canvas is small, his compressed lyrics have been compared to Helen Garner's fiction in terms of moral and artistic breadth; in Alan Wearne's words, 'Both the Forbes and Garner visions are generous, both have produced what may amount to guides on living in urban Australia, both chart how love both survives and helps you survive.' In *Ecstasy and Economics: American Essays for*

John Forbes (1992), Meaghan Morris takes Forbes's poem 'Watching the Treasurer' as a starting-point for examining the cult of the economy and the effects of the mass media.

Forefathers (1983) by Nancy Cato (q.v.), described by one reviewer as Australia's *Roots*, is an epic of Australian life covering the period 1824–1969. Tracing the fluctuating fortunes of three families, the Forbes, the Kings and the Browns, over seven generations, as their lives cross and recross, it links them with almost every important event in Australia in that period. The first book (1824–94) introduces a Tasmanian squatting family, the Forbes, and Canadian patriot-convict, Jamie Brown and his family, and ends on a sheep station in Victoria. The second book (1870–1930) follows members of the Brown family through the shearing sheds of NSW and Queensland, through the beginnings of unionism with the shearers, and into the cane-cutting area of Queensland, where the Kanaka people enter the story. The second book ends with Chukka, grandson of Jamie, too old for cane-cutting, becoming 'a swagman, 'Waltzing Matilda' over the dusty roads and camping beside the dry watercourses of inland Australia'. The third book (1853–1933) introduces the King family and its search for gold in SA, WA, South Africa and even in the Klondike of the new territories of Canada. It includes a world trip for the family when the fortunes are high and a side-track to India for engineering and medical missionary work and for William King to meet Elaine Hamilton Forbes. The fourth book (1933–49) follows playboy amateur racing-driver Vincent King through his early life and his marriage to Maggie Pinjarra, who is the great-great-granddaughter of Jamie Brown. Vincent meets an early death in a motor-racing accident. The fifth book (1949–69) tells almost exclusively of the life of Joseph Forbes King, son of Maggie Pinjarra and Vincent King. Born in Queensland and mistakenly believing he is part-Aboriginal, Joseph Forbes King grows up in Adelaide. Visits north awaken his feelings for the coloured people and attending university in Canberra in the 1960s he becomes involved in demonstrations. In Brisbane he physically attacks the Minister for Aboriginal Affairs; the experience of seven days in gaol, when conscripted for Vietnam, means that he cannot face either the army or further prison. He goes to the Blue Mountains intending to take his life at Govett's Leap. Unable to jump, he heads for Sydney and the Harbour Bridge and dies on the train involved in the Granville railway disaster.

TRISH MIDDLETON

Forger's Wife, The, alternatively titled *Emily Orford*, a short novel by John George Lang (q.v.), was published first in the English journal, *Fraser's Magazine*, while Lang was in England in 1853, and appeared in book form in 1855. It later appeared under various titles, two of which, *Assigned to His Wife* and *The Convict's Wife*, reflect something of its plot. The Forger's Wife is Emily Orford, a naive young beauty from an established English family, who succumbs to the practised wiles of an opportunist, Charles Roberts, masquerading as Captain Reginald Harcourt. Not long after their elopement and marriage at Gretna Green, Roberts is arrested for forgery and transported for life to NSW. Emily follows him and succeeds with the help of George Flower, a renowned Sydney 'thief-taker', probably a fictional version of the Sydney identity Israel Chapman, in having Roberts assigned to her as a servant. While Flower is away at Bathurst apprehending some bushrangers, police magistrate Brade, probably a fictional version of the well-known and unscrupulous magistrate Ernest Augustus Slade, attempts, with the connivance of Roberts, who has returned to his old villainous ways, to 'have his way' with Emily. Flower returns in time to save Emily and later kills Roberts, who has turned bushranger. Emily and Flower return to England, where it is revealed that they are half-brother and sister. Emily succeeds to the family estate, marries a faithful suitor of old, and Flower returns to Australia where his particular qualities are more appreciated. From there he apparently attempts to denude the colony of its fauna, for he 'frequently' sends to Emily and her father 'Australian Curiosities such as kangaroos, emus, flying squirrels, parrots and cockatoos'. Although marred by sentimentality, by a 'fate worse than death' morality and by a dependence on coincidence, *The Forger's Wife* has literary potential which its author seems not to have perceived. Its strengths lie in its picture of convict Sydney in which Lang grew up; its casual depiction of violence and death in an era and locale in which the value of individual human life seemed almost negligible; its portrayal of capricious and callous authoritarianism; and its author's skill in conveying the speech rhythms of the various levels of colonial society.

'FORREST, David' (David Denholm) (1924–), born Maryborough, Queensland, saw service as a militiaman in New Guinea in the Second World War. After the war he worked as a bank officer until 1964, when he undertook full-time academic study; he then taught at the Riverina College of Advanced Education, Wagga Wagga. His first novel, *The Last Blue Sea* (1959), one of the best fictional accounts by an Australian of the jungle campaigns of New Guinea, records the attempt by the 83rd Battalion, a battalion of conscript soldiers (chocolate soldiers or 'chockos' as opposed to the volunteer soldiers of the AIF) to advance along the Missim trail towards Salamaua in New Guinea to assist in the ultimate capture of that port. An authentic account of the horrors of jungle fighting and an excellent portrayal of the young Australian soldier, *The Last Blue Sea* won the inaugural Dame Mary Gilmore Award in 1959. 'Forrest's' second novel, *The Hollow Woodheap* (1962), combines light social satire with restrained humour. It uses the institution of banking and its conventions as a metaphor of middle-class respectability; the 'hollow woodheap' is the bank, a shaky edifice even though it prides itself upon solid values. Of 'Forrest's' short stories, which deal mainly with life in small-town and outback Queensland, the best known are 'That Barambah

Mob' and 'The Keeper of the Night'. The former, a humorous cricket classic, turns on the feats of the Aboriginal fast bowler Eddie Gilbert; the latter reveals 'Forrest's' gift for evoking both the understated compassion of the Australian 'battler' and his laconic wit. Connected with the Realist Writers group, 'Forrest' holds forthright views on the role of the writer and has expressed these in an essay, 'The Split-Level Culture' in *Literary Australia*, eds Clement Semmler and Derek Whitelock (1966), and in the 1962 CLF lecture on Patrick White. Under his own name, David Denholm, he has also written an individual interpretation of aspects of nineteenth-century life in Australia, *The Colonial Australians* (1979). It won the ANA Literature Award for 1979.

FORREST, Sir John (Baron Forrest of Bunbury) (1847–1918), born Bunbury, WA, led an expedition to search for Ludwig Leichhardt's party in 1869. In 1870 he explored the south-coast route from WA to Adelaide, and was awarded 5000 acres of land in WA and the gold medal of the Royal Geographical Society. A further expedition to SA by way of the Murchison River and the overland telegraph line in 1874 was also successful. His chief work, an account of his journeys, *Explorations in Australia*, was published in 1875. His later career as surveyor-general, then politician (he was WA's first premier), coincided with the boom in WA development. He entered the first federal parliament, becoming treasurer and, briefly, acting prime minister. Two of his chief successes were the supplying of the WA goldfields with water and the building of the transcontinental railway. F.K. Crowley published in 1971 the first part of a projected two-volume biography of Forrest. Forrest's younger brother Alexander (1849–1901), also an explorer and politician, discovered and explored the Kimberley area of north-west Australia, helping to open that area for pastoral expansion; he wrote *Journal of Expedition from De Grey to Port Darwin* (1880). G.C. Bolton wrote *Alexander Forrest: His Life and Times* (1958).

FORREST, Mabel (1872–1935), born near Yandilla, Queensland, was a versatile writer of short fiction, novels and verse. Her first book was the volume *Poems* (1893); *The Rose of Forgiveness and Other Stories* was published in 1904; another volume of verse, *Alpha Centauri*, followed in 1909 and a novel, *A Bachelor's Wife*, in 1914. Her other publications include a prose and verse collection, *The Green Harper* (1915); a book of verse, *Streets and Gardens* (1922); and a series of novels, *The Wild Moth* (1924), *Gaming Gods* (1926), *Hibiscus Heart* (1927), *Reaping Roses* (1928) and *White Witches* (1929). A collection of her poems submitted to journals in various countries was published as *Poems* in 1927. A freelance writer for more than thirty years, she was immensely popular in the 1920s.

FORSHAW, Thelma (1923–), born Glebe Point, Sydney, served with the WAAAF in the Second World War. She has since been a secretary, advertising writer, freelance writer and book reviewer for such journals and newspapers as the *Bulletin, Nation,* the *Sydney Morning Herald*, the *Age* and the *Australian*. Her short stories, published in many Australian journals, were collected as *An Affair of Clowns* (1967); of these the best regarded is the section 'Some Customs of My Clan', a series of unsentimental, autobiographical sketches of the Hallorans, her mother's Irish-Australian family. She describes this rumbustious family environment with irony and verve.

FORSTER, William (1818–82), grandson of the explorer Gregory Blaxland, was born Madras, India, and in 1829 came to Australia. In 1840–67 he acquired land throughout northern NSW and Queensland, becoming one of the most successful squatters in the pastoral boom of the mid-nineteenth century. Elected to the NSW parliament when it was first constituted in 1856, Forster served almost continuously until his death and held many important offices, including that of premier briefly, 1859–60. A prolific writer of satirical, political and social essays and a sound literary critic with a wide awareness of the developing colonial literary scene, Forster contributed frequently to Robert Lowe's *Atlas* and Daniel Deniehy's *Southern Cross*. Two of his significant verse satires appeared in the *Atlas*, 'The Devil and the Governor', directed against Governor Sir George Gipps, and 'The Genius and the Ghost', an attack on the proposals for the renewal of transportation. His perceptive, if somewhat trenchant, literary criticism is evident in his attack on Francis Fowler, then the darling of Sydney literary society, in the *Empire*, 25 May 1857. Forster published other poetry and verse plays: *The Weirwolf* (1876), which included, in addition to the title work, sonnets on the Crimean War and other poems; *The Brothers* (1877); and *Midas* (1884).

Fortunate Life, A, see **FACEY, A.B.**; **War Literature**

FORTUNE, Mary ('Waif Wander') (?1833–?), born Mary Helena Wilson in Belfast, Ireland, was taken to Canada while still a child by her father. In 1851 she married Joseph Fortune and bore a son before following her father to the Victorian goldfields in 1855 unaccompanied by her husband, whose subsequent destiny is not known. Her keen-eyed observations of the goldfields, 'Twenty-Six Years Ago', were published in the English journal the *Ladies' Companion* 1882–83 and reprinted in the collection *The Fortunes of Mary Fortune* (1989), edited by Lucy Sussex, whose researches recovered some of the history of her life and writing. Mary Fortune's personal life underwent several crises, including the birth of an illegitimate son, the death of her first child and a short-lived marriage to a mounted constable who deserted her for 'marriage' with another woman. A regular contributor under her pseudonym 'Waif Wander' of poetry, short stories and articles to the *Australian Journal*, she supported herself by her writing, eventually restricting herself to crime stories (from the 1870s to 1909). Only one of her novels was published separately, *The Detective's Album* (1871). Selections of her writing are also included in *From the Verandah* (1987), edited by

Fiona Giles and *Happy Endings* (1987), edited by Elizabeth Webby and Lydia Wevers.

Fortunes of Richard Mahony, The, a novel trilogy by Henry Handel Richardson (q.v.), was first published as a sequence. *Australia Felix*, the first volume, which covers twelve years of Richard Mahony's life from the early 1850s, was published in 1917; *The Way Home*, which deals with his subsequent eight years, appeared in 1925; and *Ultima Thule*, the final volume covering his last four years, in 1929. The novel was first published as a trilogy in 1930.

Australia Felix, which is divided into four parts, opens with a 'Proem' describing the death of a miner on the Ballarat gold diggings and the despair of Long Jim, an English lamplighter turned miner, at his own living burial in an alien, harsh and ugly land. The first part begins the story of Richard Mahony, a 28-year-old medical graduate of Edinburgh University and now the keeper of a general store in Ballarat. Against a dense picture of life in Ballarat, Melbourne and Geelong, Richardson gives several individuals prominence; these include Henry Ocock, a shrewd, unscrupulous lawyer emotionally involved with the wife of a squatter, Agnes Glendinning; the volatile and impressionable Purdy Smith, Mahony's childhood friend from Dublin; John Turnham, Mahony's brother-in-law, a political opportunist and typical Victorian family man; John's younger brother, the irresponsible pursuer of gold Ned Turnham; the chemist Tangye, who, like Mahony, is alienated from Australia; the Beamish girls (especially Tilly Beamish), English lower-class migrants in search of husbands; and the ineffective, pretentious old maid Sarah (later Sara and then Zara) Turnham. Although Mahony does not make friends easily, his marriage to 16-year-old Polly (later Mary) Turnham draws him into the life of others. The first part follows Mahony's career until his marriage; the second part deals with the Eureka Stockade, the growth of the varied society of Ballarat and a legal hearing in Melbourne of a claim by Mahony in which Ocock's dubious practices prevail. It concludes with Mahony's decision to start a practice in Ballarat instead of returning to England, a decision which indicates Polly's growing influence. In the third and fourth parts Richardson extends her panoramic picture of a dynamic colonial society in which individuals are subject to great reversals or advances of fortune. Although the Mahonys eventually prosper, financial and family worries beset them. Others, like John Turnham or like Old Devine, who rises from gardener to parliamentary candidate, succeed in their ambitions; or, like Tilly Beamish who enters into a marriage of convenience with Henry Ocock's father, make compromises; or, like Ned Turnham, Tangye and the Beamish parents, suffer degrees of failure. Some, like Glendinning who dies of alcoholic poisoning, are destroyed by Australian conditions. At the same time relationships undergo change; Mahony quarrels with Purdy after he believes his friend has compromised Mary, and Henry Ocock becomes alienated after Mahony is frank about the alcoholism of Agnes, now his wife. The most profound change of all, however, is in the relationship between the Mahonys themselves, in which Mary plays more and more of a maternal role towards her husband. The fourth part concludes with their return to England, Mahony having become thoroughly dissatisfied with life in Australia.

The Way Home begins with his arrival in England and concludes with his final, second return to Australia, a ruined man. In the intervening years he grows disillusioned with English society, returns to Australia to find his investments have made him suddenly rich, attempts to settle into the wealthy community of Melbourne and becomes the father of three children. Eventually afflicted with his old restlessness, he takes his family on a grand tour of Europe that is abruptly terminated when he learns that his investments have failed. During his years as a general practitioner in England, Mahony first attempts to practise at Leicester but finds that the dominance of industry makes life as limited as on the Ballarat gold-diggings. In his next practice at the pretty seaside resort of Buddlecombe, he finds the English social hierarchy offensive and cramping. Nor does he find himself at home in his old 'homes'; in Dublin he discovers that his relatives 'had made giant strides along the road to decay', lavishing the last remnants of vitality on their religious passions; in Edinburgh, on the other hand, Mahony himself feels like a ghost 'returning for a glimpse of the scenes of his youth', displaced by a new generation of hopeful, active students. His experience as a member of Melbourne's plutocracy also proves less than satisfying, notwithstanding his purchase of a well-appointed home, Ultima Thule; the unexpected arrival of children, a son, Cuffy, and twin daughters, Lallie and Lucie; and his growing interest in spiritualism. His sense of loneliness is deepened by his sense of a gulf in temperament between himself and Mary: 'had they, between them, a single idea in common? . . . Did they share an interest, a liking, a point of view? – with the one exception of an innate sobriety and honesty of purpose', he asks himself. Meanwhile his sense of transience is heightened by the suffering and death of John Turnham. Some months later Mahony decides to sell Ultima Thule and take his family to Europe; circumstances and Richard's haste to depart result in his choice of an unscrupulous agent to handle his affairs and, in Italy after an extremely busy period of travelling, the family learns suddenly of his ruin. Two days later Richard leaves alone by the Overland Mail for Egypt, bound thence for Australia.

Ultima Thule takes up his story on his return to Australia, his attempts to establish himself as a medical practitioner, first in Melbourne and then at Barambogie, a small town in northern Victoria. The family's life in Melbourne proves tolerable, although financial worries dominate; these are compounded by a visit from Agnes Ocock, now a pathetic alcoholic, on her way to South Africa, where her husband believes she will be less a subject of scandal. At her death, soon afterwards, only Mary of all her family and friends seems to feel any sorrow. At Barambogie, a place of heat, dust and isolation, the Mahonys' troubles reach crisis-point. The practice fails to prosper, Lallie dies of dysentery, and Richard begins to show clear signs of physical and mental deterioration. After Lallie's death Mary takes the children to the cooler climate of the coast and the practice dwindles to nothing as Richard's increasing strangeness alarms the townsfolk. Although on her return Mary attempts with some success to re-establish good relations at Barambogie, Richard's rapidly deteriorating condition defeats her; when he fails to set a patient's leg properly, he is threatened with a horse-whipping and a lawsuit. He contemplates suicide but resists the temptation and experiences a brief but intense vision of unity of suffering with his fellow men. The family leaves Barambogie and settles briefly at Shortlands' Bluff on the coast, where Richard gets the post of acting health officer. Here his condition rapidly worsens and culminates in total insanity; the crossing of the Rubicon is signalled by his burning of his deeds, mortgages and share scrip. With Henry Ocock's help Mary secures a position as postmistress at Gymgurra, a small settlement in western Victoria, and Richard is placed first in a private nursing home and then, when money has run out, in the government asylum. When Mary visits him there she is appalled at his treatment and engages in a heroic fight to have him released. In this crisis, only Henry Ocock's help is of any avail. Following his release Richard lives contentedly at Gymgurra, devotedly cared for by Mary, until paralysis incapacitates his body. After his death he is buried in the local cemetery, within sound of the sea.

Forty-Two Faces (1962) by John Hetherington (q.v.) is a collection of biographical studies of Australian writers including Katharine Susannah Prichard, Frank Dalby Davison, Xavier Herbert, Alan Marshall, John Morrison, Gavin Casey, Judah Waten, Kylie Tennant, Patrick White, David Martin, Morris West, Hal Porter, Frank Hardy, 'David Forrest', Elizabeth Harrower and Randolph Stow.

FOSTER, David (1944–), born Sydney, to parents who were radio comedians, graduated from the University of Sydney and the ANU, and was a research scientist who worked in the USA and Sydney before resigning in 1972 to become a full-time writer. He has worked as a labourer, swimming-pool manager and attendant, drummer, postman and deckhand on a prawn trawler. His travels are reflected in his fiction: the Outer Hebrides in *Moonlite*, Venice in *Testostero* and the Northern Territory in *Mates of Mars*. His first major publication was a collection of three novellas, *North South West* (1973). Since then he has published a book of verse, *The Fleeing Atalanta* (1975); a second collection of short fiction, *Escape to Reality* (1977); and nine novels: *The Pure Land* (1974, which shared the *Age* Book of the Year Award), *The Empathy Experiment* (1977, science fiction with D.K. Lyall), *Moonlite* (1981, which won a National Book Council Award), *Plumbum* (1983), *Dog Rock: A Postal Pastoral* (1985), *The Adventures of Christian Rosy Cross* (1986), *Testostero* (1987), *The Pale Blue Crochet Coathanger Cover* (1988), *Mates of Mars* (1991); and two novellas published together, titled *Hitting the Wall* (1989). Foster also edited *Self Portraits* (1991), a collection of the transcripts of fifteen interviews with Australian writers, conducted by Hazel de Berg and part of her extensive collection of tapes housed in the National Library. In 1978 he won the Marten Bequest for Prose and the Barbara Ramsden Award in 1974.

One of Australia's most inventive, irreverent and unpredictable novelists, Foster deals largely in black humour, in creating an atmosphere of anomie and dissolution. Described by one reviewer as 'a grim, joyless farceur', he both celebrates and satirises the Australian awfulness, leading his sullen, inarticulate questers on circular journeys or experiences of accelerating disintegration. His concerns are predominantly masculine, a preference which he frankly espouses, as he rejects contemporary social and political orthodoxies, commenting in one interview, 'There are worse motivations than tribal obligations, loyalty to a mate, fear of not being a real man, idle intellectual curiosity.' Tough-minded and cynical, he preserves an ironic distance from his comic creations, whose activities are frequently a fantastic satire on contemporary Australia, which, Foster maintains, provides endless material for farce. Aware of the linguistic links between 'satire' and 'saturate', Foster emulates Gilbert Highet's definition of satire as: 'A continuous piece of verse, or prose and verse, of considerable size, with great variety of style and subject, but generally characterised by the free use of conversational language, the frequent intrusion of the author's personality, a predilection for wit, humour and irony, great vividness and concreteness of description, shocking obscenity in theme and language, an improvisatory tone [and] topical subjects.' At the same time, his work is rich in literary, scientific and mythic allusion, often reworking foreign or historic legends and works of art in a laconic, colloquial idiom. *Plumbum* is a version of the Faust myth, the quest for ultimate power by a motley collection of rock musicians. *The Adventures of Christian Rosy Cross* reinterprets the life of a legendary figure of Rosicrucian texts of the seventeenth century, relocating him in contemporary Australia and investing him with a personality that is distinctly 'Ocker'. *Dog Rock* has echoes of Virgil's *Georgics*, and both *Moonlite* and *The Adventures of Christian Rosy Cross* are reminiscent of Voltaire's *Candide*, played with Beckett-like effects. *Testostero* inevitably suggests Goldoni's *The Venetian Twins*.

The Pure Land traces in three parts the experiences of Albert Manwaring, a Katoomba photographer who departs from Australia for America seeking a fuller life; second, those of his daughter in England; and third, his grandson, who at the end of the novel returns to Katoomba to try and piece together his past. *Moonlite*, rich in historical and literary allusions, parody and comedy, has been variously described as a satire, myth and allegory about imperialism and colonialism. It begins in the Hebridean isle of Mugg, ruled by MacIshmael, who dispossesses his people and forces them to emigrate to the even more remote and pagan island of Hiphoray, where Finbar MacDuffie, an albino later to be called Moonlite, is born. When Christianity comes to Hiphoray, disrupting its patterns and rhythms, Finbar emerges as the minister's

protégé and zealot. Sent to another island to further his education, he eventually finds his way first to Newbridge (Cambridge) and then to the North West Highlands (Australia), a colony in the grip of material obsessions where bottles form the currency and where Finbar is about to become premier before his death at the end of the novel. *Plumbum* traces the fortunes of the five unalluring members of what is eventually the world's most successful heavy-metal band, from the drab, planned dullness of Canberra to the humid unpleasantness of Sydney to the violent nightmare of Calcutta, a city which effectively disperses the group's aspirations to mystic fulfilment. *Dog Rock* and *The Pale Blue Crochet Coathanger* have the same hero, D'Arcy Oliveres, postman, beekeeper and connoisseur of parrots, who knows everything that goes on in his small town. An eccentric murder mystery, pursued by the loquacious D'Arcy, *Dog Rock* is also a brilliant comic portrayal of small-town life. Written throughout in the second person and addressed, as it belatedly turns out, to a dog, *The Pale Blue Crochet Coathanger* includes the same range of fantastic characters, with additions, and is similarly a murder mystery. *Testostero*, subtitled 'A Comic Novel', and set partly in Venice, exploits the comic possibilities of twinhood; Noel and Leon, the putative twin sons of Sir Cyril Surtout-Spoton, are granted different upbringings, Leon given every cultural advantage and Noel consigned to a-cultural Marrickville, NSW. If the novel's diverse settings provide much stuff for comedy, its plot allows for every conceivable and some inconceivable incidents and coincidences. The title of *Mates of Mars* relates to a diverse group of martial arts fanatics, which includes the ex-bouncer Steve Overton, paralysed from the waist down and eventually literally legless; a Jewish professor, Bruce Nonnemacher; a Chinese doctor, Lim; a feminist self-defence teacher, Jade; a male model, Sven; and a Black footballer, Cyril. When this oddly assorted group travel to Cyril's home, Never-fuckinlose in the Northern Territory, they discover the ineffectiveness both of their 'chi' and of their various cultural identities in the face of the uncompromising Aboriginality of the land itself; as in Foster's other novels, entropy is the characteristic experience. The two novellas of *Hitting the Wall* deal with different male protagonists, one an obsessive runner and the other an ex-convict. Both men are linked, however, in their experience of existential loneliness, described by one as 'the ache of being a man in the world . . . an immense loneliness far too vast to have been acquired in the course of one lifetime'. Regarded extremely highly by some critics, Foster is seen by others as an overly eccentric writer who exploits his appetite for fantastic invention at the expense of 'the responsibilities of serious literature'.

FOSTER, Lynn (1913–), born Rose Bay, Sydney, was active in the 1930s and 1940s, adapting plays for radio and writing her own plays; she was in England 1948–58, where she wrote for radio and television. The best known of her plays is *There Is No Armour* (1945), which uses the living-room of the homestead on Minnabooka station to trace the domination of the land over its people over eighty years. Her 1946 play, 'And the Moon Will Shine', which shared the Playwrights Advisory Board Prize, deals with the problems of the generation between the two world wars. She also wrote the novels *The Exiles* (1960) and *Blow the Wind Southerly* (1969).

FOULCHER, John (1952–), born Sydney, graduated with honours from the University of Sydney and has been a teacher in NSW and the ACT. Poetry editor in 1993 of the National Library's *Voices* (q.v.), he has published several volumes of poetry, *Light Pressure* (1983), *Pictures from the War* (1987), *Paperweight* (1991) and *New and Selected Poems* (1993) and shared the National Library Poetry Award in 1988 with the poem 'Kosciusko in Summer', which is also included in *Paperweight* and *New and Selected Poems*. Simple, direct and convincing, Foulcher's poetry reflects common human experiences – joy in the present, regret for the errors and omissions of the past and faith, mixed with a dash of apprehension, for the future. Many of his poems deal with his family – a father who died when he was only a boy and whose death he did not (because of his age) know how to mourn; a mother whose long, slow dying came when he was a grown man and over whom he grieved fully; a wife and children in whom he delights but who arouse his anxiety as they face the daily struggles of life. *Pictures from the War* is about the war of life, its casualties weighed up against its rewards. Foulcher's range is wide. Biblically based poems such as 'Elegy for Lot's Wife', 'Moses at the Jordan' rub shoulders with historically based 'Botany Bay', 'First Fleet', 'Bora Ground', with the richness of the rural scene of 'Kosciusko in Summer', with the dramatic monologue of a woman blind from birth, who regains her sight ('First Sight'), and with the long 'Travel Sequence', and the partly tongue-in-cheek elegy for Don Bradman's final 'duck' which robbed him of a Test batting average of 100. A sensitive observer of both personal relationships and the wider human scene, Foulcher is building a strong reputation as a poet. His work has been set for several years for study in secondary schools.

Foundation for Australian Literary Studies, which is funded by membership subscriptions and by donations, was established in 1966 within the Department of English, University College of Townsville (later James Cook University of North Queensland). As part of its aim to foster the study of Australian literature within the University and the wider community, it has sponsored since 1966 an annual series of lectures, now titled the Colin Roderick Lectures, by a distinguished author (e.g. James McAuley in 1966, Thea Astley in 1978, Les A. Murray in 1982) or scholar (e.g. G.A. Wilkes in 1967, L.T. Hergenhan in 1973, H.P. Heseltine in 1975, Dorothy Green in 1986, W.H. Wilde in 1991). Several of the lectures have been included in the Foundation's monograph series (e.g. G.A. Wilkes's lectures on 'Novelists of Australia' were revised and published as *Australian Literature: A Conspectus* in 1969). The Foundation has also supported occasional seminars, has made since 1967 an annual

award which carries a cash prize, and from 1980 the award of the H.T. Priestley Memorial Medal for the best book published in Australia on any aspect of Australian life. The journalist and historian Gavin Souter has won the award three times (1968, 1976, 1981); among creative writers who have been successful are Douglas Stewart, the inaugural winner Francis Webb (1969), David Malouf (1974), Alan Marshall (1977), Thea Astley (1979), Peter Carey (1989), Joan Dugdale (1991) and Ruth Park (1992).

Foundations of Culture in Australia, The was written by P.R. Stephensen (q.v.) and published in 1936; the first and most important of its three parts had been published the previous year (July 1935) as an editorial essay in the one and only edition of the *Australian Mercury* (q.v.). Subtitled *An Essay towards National Self-Respect*, *The Foundations of Culture in Australia* posits that *'Art and Literature are at first nationally created, but become internationally appreciated'* (Stephensen's italics) and argues that while the English basis of European Australian culture should be recognised, English elements should not be allowed to dominate Australian culture; the contribution of culture to nationalism is the part it plays in a nation's self-definition. Among many targets in the essay were the emphasis on convicts and bushranging in Australian writing, which Stephensen thought confirmed English notions of a colonial Australia; the *Bulletin*, which was attacked for producing a larrikin literature that overstated the national life; the Anglocentrism of curricula in Australian schools and of literature professors in Australia, such as G. H. Cowling; the 'brain drain' of Australian artists and scholars to Europe; and the failure to develop independent economic, business, political and cultural policies in Australia. Chauvinist and iconoclastic, Stephensen's essay most directly influenced the Jindyworobak writers, although it shares, ironically, some of the views and assumptions about literature and humanities espoused by the *Bulletin* in the 1890s, and some of the issues it canvassed about Eurocentricism in university teaching of literature were still being discussed in the 1970s by John Docker and other writers. *The Foundations of Culture in Australia* also expresses many of the political views (e.g. isolationism) which Stephensen took into the Australia First (q.v.) movement. Craig Munro, who wrote the Stephensen biography *Wild Man of Letters* (1984), also wrote a new introduction to the 1987 reprint of *The Foundations of Culture in Australia*.

Four Stories High (1877), by Marcus Clarke (q.v.), comprises in fact five stories: four are told on a Melbourne verandah by the host and by each of his three friends, and the last is told by the host to his son after his friends have left. All five stories originally appeared as unrelated contributions to the *Australasian* in 1870–73; the most significant is 'La Béguine', which has autobiographical relevance.

Fourteen Men (1954), Dame Mary Gilmore's (q.v.) final volume of poems, was published when she was approaching her ninetieth year. The title poem recalls the massacre of the Chinese at Lambing Flat. The volume also contains the well-known poems 'Nationality' (q.v.) and 'The Pear Tree'.

Fourteen Years: Extracts from a Private Journal 1925–1939, by Nettie Palmer (q.v.), was published in 1948. Although the journal extracts are structured according to the author's movements (Caloundra 1925–29, Melbourne 1929–32, Green Island 1932, Kalorama 1932–35, Paris 1935, London 1935–36, Barcelona 1936, Melbourne 1936–39), the unity of the whole is immediately striking. Moving easily among diverse places, cultural milieux, and individuals, the prose passes from humorous personal reflection to incisive social comment, to observation of the natural scene and to meditation on current and past writing. Like the letters of Madame de Sévigné, with which it has been compared, the journal has the same historical value as the reflection of a generation and the same clear perceptions of personalities, places and things. Some of the well-known individuals captured by the journal are John Masefield, F.R. Leavis, Ruth Pitter, Rebecca West, André Gide; and the writers Henry Handel Richardson, Havelock Ellis, Stewart Macky, Will Dyson, Leonard Mann, Louis Esson, Paul Wenz, Frank Dalby Davison, A.G. Stephens, Flora Eldershaw and Marjorie Barnard. *Fourteen Years* was republished in *Nettie Palmer* (1988), ed. Vivian Smith.

FOWLER, Frank (1833–63), born London, came to Australia for health reasons in 1855. He made a living, in his own words, 'as a journalist and bookseller's hack', writing initially for the *Empire* and the *Sydney Morning Herald*. Under the pseudonym 'Cosmopolitan' he wrote a series, 'Sketches in Parliament', in the *Empire* in 1856; as 'A Literary Vagabond' he contributed the series 'Home Senators' to the *Sydney Morning Herald* in 1857; and as editor of the *Month*, which began publication in July 1857, he contributed significantly to literary, political and social discussion of the contemporary colonial scene. He wrote a play, 'Eva', which was performed in Sydney in 1856. By March or April 1858 he was on his way back to England, having stood unsuccessfully in January 1858 as a candidate in the Legislative Assembly elections. It was on the return voyage that he wrote his chief work, *Southern Lights and Shadows*, published in London in 1859, a work in which he gave his observations and impressions of life in the colony. Fowler also published a book of his sketches contributed to the *Weekly Mail* (London), titled *Dottings of a Lounger* (1859), and *Texts for Talkers* (1860). A posthumous collection of his writings, *Last Gleanings* (1864), which indicates his talent in *belles-lettres*, was compiled by his Australian friend Richard Rowe.

FOX, Sir Frank ('Frank Renar') (1874–1960), born Adelaide, was educated in Hobart and edited the *Australian Workman* in 1893 and the Bathurst *National Advocate* in 1895, before becoming chief of the *Age* reporting staff. In 1901 he joined the *Bulletin* and was first editor of the *Lone Hand* 1907–9. In 1909 Fox went to England to pursue the career in conservative journalism for which he was knighted in 1926. He wrote several books based on his activities as a war correspondent and soldier, but his most significant Australian works were the study of Harry Harbord Morant titled *Bushman and Buccaneer* (1902); the political essays *From the Old Dog* (1908); the descriptive work *Australia* (1910); and the novel *Beneath an Ardent Sun* (1923).

FOX, Len (1905–   ), born Melbourne, was a teacher at Scotch College, Melbourne, 1928–32. In 1935 he became Victorian State secretary of the Movement against War and Fascism; in 1939 he went to Sydney where he worked on the Labor Party newspaper *Progress* (1940–45), and on the communist newspaper *Tribune* (1946–55). Fox and his wife, Mona Brand (q.v.), lived in Hanoi 1956–57; on their return journey to Sydney in 1958 he joined the Miners' Federation paper *Common Cause* and was its editor 1965–70. A prolific writer of socio-political pamphlets, Fox has also published verse, short fiction and dramatic works. His verse, which includes *Chung of Vietnam* (1957, children's verse), *Gum Leaves and Bamboo* (1959), *Vietnam Neighbours* (1966), *Gum Leaves and People* (1967) and *Gum Leaves and Dreaming* (1978), clearly reflects his interest in the people of Vietnam and the Australian Aborigines. He also wrote *The Aboriginals* (1978), and edited *Depression Down Under* (1977), recollections of the 1930s in Australia. He was co-editor with Faith Bandler of *The Time Was Ripe* (1983), the history of the Aboriginal-Australian Fellowship, and collaborated with her in a children's novel, *Marani in Australia* (1980), based partly on her father's life. His recent writing includes a biography of his artist uncle, *E. Phillips Fox and his Family* (1985), and an edited history of the Fellowship of Australian Writers, *Dream at a Graveside* (1988).

'Fragment of Autobiography, A' is a long, autobiographical essay by Henry Lawson (q.v.) covering the years up to his father's death on New Year's Eve 1888. It was written between 1903 and 1908 but not published in full until its appearance in modern collections of Lawson's prose. Some of the same incidents are mentioned in two shorter pieces by Lawson: 'From Mudgee Hills to London Town', which has information on his early poems; and '"Pursuing Literature" in Australia', which focuses more directly on his literary career up to the end of the 1890s and contains his famous advice to any young Australian writer: 'go steerage, stow away, swim, and seek London, Yankeeland or Timbuctoo – rather than stay in Australia until [your] genius [turns] to gall, or beer.' '"Succeeding"', a sequel to '"Pursuing Literature" in Australia' and focusing on Lawson's experiences when he went to England, is among recently discovered Lawson material included in Brian Kiernan's selection *The Essential Henry Lawson* (1982).

'FRANC, Maud Jeanne', see **EVANS, Matilda Jane**

'Frank the Poet', see **MACNAMARA, Francis**

FRANKLIN, Sir John (1786–1847), the naval officer and Arctic explorer who died while searching for the North-West Passage, was a nephew of Matthew Flinders (q.v.) and served under him on the *Investigator* in 1801–4. In 1837–43 he was lieutenant-governor of Van Diemen's Land (Tasmania) in succession to Sir George Arthur (q.v.); it was a period of great difficulty because of the faction fighting within Tasmanian politics, which had carried over from Arthur's regime, the economic climate and the uncertainty over Tasmania's future as a gaol or as a free colony. Franklin's disputes with the colonial secretary, John Montagu, an Arthur protégé, erupted in 1842 when Montagu was suspended from office; the Colonial Office disapproved of this action and both censured and recalled Franklin. Franklin's *Narrative of Some Passages in the History of Van Diemen's Land, during the Last Three Years of Sir John Franklin's Administration of Its Government* (1845) is a vindication of his government in which he was supported by his wife, Lady Jane Franklin (1791–1875), who was active in the development of Tasmania's intellectual life. The Franklins made several explorations and excursions during their term of office; David Burn (q.v.) reported one in *Narrative of the Overland Journey of Sir John and Lady Franklin and Party from Hobart Town to Macquarie Harbour*, which was first published serially in *Colburn's United Services Journal* in London in 1843. Franklin's career in the Arctic and Tasmania is chronicled in Nancy Cato's novel, *North-West by South* (1965) and his relationship with his wife is portrayed in Catherine Shepherd's play, 'Jane, My Love' (1951) and described in Penny Russell's *For Richer, For Poorer* (1994); he also appears as a character in William Gosse Hay's *The Escape of the Notorious Sir William Heans* (1919), in which the Franklin–Montagu dispute is mentioned. George Mackaness published *Some Private Correspondence of Sir John and Lady Jane Franklin (Tasmania, 1837–1845)* (1947) and Kathleen Fitzpatrick the biographical study *Sir John Franklin in Tasmania, 1837–1843* (1949). Owen Beattie and John Geiger wrote *Frozen in Time: The Fate of the Franklin Expedition* (1987).

FRANKLIN, Miles ('Brent of Bin Bin') (1879–1954), known to her family as Stella, was born at Talbingo, the grazing property then held by her maternal grandmother, Sarah Lampe, near Tumut, NSW. On that side of the family, Miles Franklin was a fifth-generation Australian, her great-great-grandfather, Edward Miles, having been a convict in the First Fleet. Her Franklin grandparents, of whom there is a fictionalised account in *All That Swagger* (q.v.), arrived as Irish immigrants in 1839. Both sides of the family 'squatted' in the 1840s in the isolated and sparsely settled Monaro region of NSW; the Franklin home station, Brindabella, and the neighbouring run, Bin Bin, have now become familiar names in Australian literature through Franklin's novels. The eldest of seven children, Miles Franklin spent her first ten years at Brindabella. In 1889 the family moved to a smaller, poorer property – Possum Gully of her autobiographical novel *My Brilliant Career* (q.v., 1901) – at Bangalore near Goulburn, NSW. After some years of arduous and monotonous dairy farming, which Franklin loathed, the family moved in 1903 to a smallholding near Penrith and finally in 1914 to the outer Sydney suburb of Carlton. Between the publication of *My Brilliant Career* in 1901 and her departure for the USA in 1906, she made a brief attempt at a nursing career; spent almost two years in a 'Mary-Anne' housemaid role in Sydney and in Melbourne, where she met Joseph Furphy and began a lifetime infatuation with *Such is Life* (1903); developed literary contacts with A.G. Stephens, Norman Lindsay and Henry Lawson, who wrote the preface to *My Brilliant Career;* worked as a freelance journalist for the *Daily Telegraph* and *Sydney Morning Herald* under the pseudonyms 'An Old Bachelor' and 'Vernacular'; and became involved in the Australian feminist movement through friendship with Rose Scott and Vida Goldstein. In the USA she was associated with Alice Henry, another prominent Australian feminist, in the National Women's Trade Union League, for whom she did secretarial and editorial work 1908–15. In England in 1915, in spite of a lifelong detestation of war (the 'lunacy' of the male), she was impelled by deep ties of sentiment and lineage to help in the war effort, serving with the Scottish Women's Hospital at Ostrovo in the Serbian campaigns of 1917–18. In 1919–25 she was assistant secretary with the National Housing and Town Planning Council in London. She visited Australia for three months in 1923–24, an episode which linked her new awareness of County Clare, Ireland, the birthplace of her grandfather Joseph Franklin, with her old memories of the Monaro uplands. The visit formulated that sense of historical perspective that inspired the chronicle novels of 'Brent of Bin Bin' (q.v.) and the family saga, *All That Swagger.* She returned to Australia 1927–31; in that time the 'Brent of Bin Bin' series, beginning with *Up the Country* (1928), began to be published and the identity of their pseudonymous author became the subject of prolonged speculation. After spending 1931 and most of 1932 in England she returned permanently to Sydney to an increasingly eventful literary life. She was awarded the S.H. Prior Memorial Prize for *All That Swagger* (1936), winning it again in 1939 for her collaboration with Kate Baker in an unpublished Furphy biography. *All That Swagger* and novels of the Bin Bin series were broadcast serially over national radio stations and she herself broadcast to schools on 'My Life and My Books'; she was involved in the nationalism of the 1930s; played a leading role in the promotion of Mary Fullerton's (q.v.) poetry; and delivered the CLF lectures in Perth in 1950, afterwards publishing them as *Laughter, Not for a Cage* (1956). By 1948 the sole survivor of her family, she bequeathed her estate to establish annual literary awards, now known as the Miles Franklin Awards (q.v.).

The chief novels published by Miles Franklin in her own name were *My Brilliant Career* (1901); *Some Everyday Folk and Dawn* (1909), an inferior work reflecting the drabness of life in an Australian town (Penrith) and carrying overtones of female suffrage; *Old Blastus of Bandicoot* (q.v., 1931); *Bring the Monkey* (1933, a parody on English detective fiction of the 1920s); *All That Swagger* (1936); and *My Career Goes Bung* (1946), written shortly after the turn of the century as a sequel to *My Brilliant Career* but rejected as early as 1910 by publishers because it was too audacious. Under the pseudonym 'Brent of Bin Bin' she published six novels, *Up the Country* (1928), *Ten Creeks Run* (1930), *Back to Bool Bool* (1931), *Prelude to Waking* (1950), *Cockatoos* (1954) and *Gentlemen at Gyang Gyang* (1956), the last two appearing after her death. In collaboration with Dymphna Cusack she wrote the satirical *Pioneers on Parade* (1939), a tilt at the pretentiousness and snobbery of established Australian society. Following the 1939 collaboration with Kate Baker she wrote *Joseph Furphy: The Legend of a Man and His Book* (1944), much more her own individual work although acknowledging her debt to the original collaborator. In 1963 the autobiographical *Childhood at Brindabella* was published. *On Dearborn Street*, similar in attitude to *My Brilliant Career* but set in Chicago in 1914, was first published in 1981, edited by Roy Duncan. There are about twenty unpublished Miles Franklin novels and plays.

Miles Franklin was one of a small group of Australian women who, born into a colonial society in the ultra-conservative Victorian era, attempted to fulfil themselves according to their own lights and in defiance of the accepted conventions of the day. She exhibited attitudes regarded as psychological aberrations at the time: sexual ambivalence, with attraction and repulsion both present; hostility to the traditional role of women in marriage and childbearing, the latter being seen as the 'most cruelly agonizing of human duties'; and rejection of the idea of a male-dominated society. She had a fetish for privacy and sought refuge from painful confrontations by absenting herself for twenty years from family, friends and country and by adopting literary disguises such as 'Brent of Bin Bin'. She became famous, even notorious, for *My Brilliant Career*, but the long literary silence between it and the advent of the Bin Bin series and *All That Swagger*, combined with her long absence from Australia, meant that the later novels when published in the 1930s were virtually out of date and seen to be part of the old-fashioned nostalgic nationalism that was then passing into Australian literary history. They were out of phase with the bulk of contemporary Australian literary opinion which, rejecting the vociferous outburst of Jindyworobak nationalism, was rapidly becoming international in outlook. But the Bin Bin novels and *All That Swagger*, although never a popular success and often validly criticised as clumsily written, ill-constructed, trivial in incident and vague in characterisation, form part of the chronicle of Australian pioneer life. More recently her work has attracted attention in the feminist revaluation of Australian literature.

Marjorie Barnard wrote the biographical study *Miles Franklin* (1967, an updated edition in 1988 with introduction by Jill Roe); Verna Coleman filled in the biographical gaps with *Miles Franklin in America* (1981); Colin Roderick also published a biography in 1982, *Miles Franklin: Her Brilliant Career*. Carole Ferrier edited *As Good as a Yarn With You* (1992), a selection of letters from Miles Franklin to several other women writers, including Jean Devanny,

Marjorie Barnard and Katharine Susannah Prichard, but the most extensive collection is the two-volume *My Congenials: Miles Franklin and Friends in Letters* (1993), edited by Jill Roe.

FRASER, Eliza (?1798–1858) was the wife of James Fraser, captain of the *Stirling Castle*, a ship that was wrecked on Swain Reef near Rockhampton, Queensland, in May 1836. The survivors of the wreck, including Eliza and her husband, landed on the then Great Sandy Island and were captured by Aborigines; several, including James Fraser, were later murdered. After six weeks of captivity, Eliza and the remaining survivors were rescued by a detachment of the 14th Regiment sent from Moreton Bay. Great Sandy Island was later renamed Fraser Island in memory of Captain James Fraser. In 1837 a *Narrative of the Capture, Sufferings, and Miraculous Escape of Mrs Eliza Fraser* was published anonymously in New York although it purports to include Mrs Fraser's own account. An account of the shipwreck and rescue is given in John Curtis, *Shipwreck of the Stirling Castle* (1838). Eliza Fraser's experiences are recounted in Robert Gibbings's *John Graham, Convict* (1937), in Charles Barrett's *White Blackfellows* (1948) and in Michael Alexander's *Mrs. Fraser on the Fatal Shore* (1971). Patrick White's novel *A Fringe of Leaves* (1976) is substantially based on her adventures; the dust-jacket of the original edition featured one of Sidney Nolan's Eliza Fraser paintings, which also inspired the South African André Brink's novel *An Instant in the Wind* (1976). *Eliza Fraser*, an Australian film scripted by David Williamson, was made in 1976. The history of Fraser Island itself is contained in Fred Williams's illustrated *Written in Sand* (1982).

FRASER, Gilly, see **Feminism and Australian Literature**

FRAZER, Michael (1948–) served as a national serviceman in the Australian Army during the Vietnam War 1969–71 and during that time spent 253 days in Vietnam. In 1984 he published a novel based on his experiences, *Nasho*. Set in Australia and Vietnam between 1965 and 1972, the novel is a searing indictment of Australia's participation in that war and of war in general. The protagonist, Peter Turner, a journalist attached to the Army Information Corps, is an incisive psychological case study revealing the brutalising effects of the ocker ethos when endowed with military authority and placed within an alien, threatening environment. Volunteering for the infantry as a test of his manhood, Turner finds instead that he is consigned to the half-world of propaganda and censorship, tested by grotesque male-proving rites and ultimately dependent on sex and alcohol to forestall his rapid drift into madness.

Frearson's Weekly Illustrated: A Journal for the People, published in Adelaide 1878–84, was incorporated in 1884 into *Frearson's Monthly Illustrated Adelaide News* and continued 1885–95 as the *Pictorial*

Australian. It contained original sketches, poetry and fiction.

FREE, Colin (1925–), a prolific writer for television, has also written dramas and features for radio, stage plays, short stories and novels. His published plays include the stage play *Cannonade of Bells* (1968), a television episode from the serial *Contrabandits; Cage a Tame Tiger* in *Take One* (1972, ed. Richard Lane); and two radio plays, *Nightmares of the Old Obscenity Master* and *A Walk among the Wheeneys* in *Five Plays for Radio* (1975, ed. Arlene Sykes). Several of his stage plays have been produced, including *Cannonade of Bells*, 'Where Did Vortex Go?', *A Walk among the Wheeneys* and a duo of two-act plays titled 'Unspeakable Acts'. His novels include *Carbon Copy* (1972), *The Soft Kill* (1973), *Ironbark* (1976) based on the life of the bushranger Frank Gardiner (q.v.), *Vinegar Hill* (1978) and *Bay of Shadows* (1980). Free has written both serials and single episodes for television and radio, has contributed to such popular television serials as *Rush, Ben Hall* and *Over There*, and has won several awards, including an Awgie and Logie, for his work. He has also written three thrillers under the pseudonym 'Colin Lewis'.

'Freedom on the Wallaby', a poem by Henry Lawson (q.v.), exists in two versions. The first, which has also become a well-known folk-song, is the poem as originally published in the Brisbane *Worker*, May 1891, when it contained a much-quoted reference to Eureka (q.v.) in the last verse:

> So we must fly a rebel flag
> As others did before us,
> And we must sing a rebel song
> And join in rebel chorus;
> We'll make the tyrants feel the sting
> O' those that they would throttle;
> They needn't say the fault is ours
> If blood should stain the wattle.

There were minor changes (e.g. 'bankers' replaced 'tyrants') when the poem was published in the Sydney *Worker* in 1894, and a major revision (including the deletion of the Eureka reference) for publication in *For Australia* (1913), which provides the text of the poem printed in most Lawson collections. Lawson's original poem was inspired by the 1891 shearing strikes in western Queensland; both the title and the last line have become familiar in the rhetoric of social protest, e.g. in Leslie Haylen's Eureka novel *Blood on the Wattle* (1948). The publication of the poem led to its being quoted in the Queensland parliament during a motion voting thanks to the strikebreakers, to which Lawson derisively replied in two further contributions to the Brisbane *Worker*, 'The Vote of Thanks Debate' and 'The Labour Agitator'.

Freeman's Journal, one of the most substantial of the nineteenth-century Australian journals, catered mainly for the Irish Catholic population but appealed to a wide reading public with its literary articles. Published twice weekly 1850–65, thereafter weekly, it retained its title until 1932 when it became the *Catholic Freeman's Journal* and in 1942 was incorporated into the *Catholic Weekly*. Notable literary figures such as W.B. Dalley, Daniel Deniehy, William Forster, Frank Fowler, J. Sheridan Moore and Victor Daley were associated with it. A frequent contributor was Henry Kendall, who conducted a regular feature on Irish writers, 'The Harp of Erin' (1871), and wrote a series of articles titled 'Men and Books' (1871). His controversial poem 'The Gagging Bill' appeared in the *Freeman's Journal* (1879), as did his well-known 'Jim the Splitter' (1880).

Fremantle Arts Centre began in 1972 in the restored Fremantle Lunatic Asylum which had been built in the 1860s as an asylum for deranged convicts. Its founding director was Ian Templeman, now assistant director-general of cultural and educational services at the National Library of Australia, Canberra. Soon after its opening the Centre established seasonal programmes in art and craft classes and in 1976 it established Arts Access which provided workshops for country people and incorporated a book-hire scheme for country and metropolitan book clubs. Creative writing figured prominently in the Centre's activities, supervised by Templeman, himself a poet, and employing recognised tutors, e.g. Elizabeth Jolley. Weekend writing seminars and conferences were held frequently. In 1975 the Centrepress was established; it ultimately became the Fremantle Arts Centre Press with both the Arts Centre and the Arts Centre Press under (until 1989) the direction of Ian Templeman. Since 1990 they have been separate organisations, housed and managed separately, June Moorhouse being the general manager of the Arts Centre and Clive Newman general manager of the press. The Arts Centre publishes *FAR*, a bi-monthly magazine which, among its other contents, includes new creative writing, poetry and fiction, and book reviews and awards two annual prizes for poetry and short fiction, named the John Birch Awards to honour Birch's distinguished service as Fremantle City Librarian. The Centre conducts an annual winter season of local writers reading from their works and co-presents the Writers' Festival with the Festival of Perth every second year.

Fremantle Arts Centre Press has published, since 1976, more than 200 titles with a focus on high-quality literary works of prose and poetry, art, social history, autobiography, biography and children's literature. Among its most successful writers (usually West Australians) are Elizabeth Jolley, Nicholas Hasluck and Philip Salom, although virtually every West Australian author of merit has been published by the press. Its greatest successes have been *A Fortunate Life* by A.B. Facey and *My Place* by Sally Morgan. Strong on WA anthologies, it published in its first year, 1976, *Soundings* (poetry) and *New Country* (short stories) and for many years published a poetry magazine, *Patterns*, four times a year which grew out of the creative writing classes conducted by Ian Templeman and Elizabeth Jolley.

Fremantle Herald, founded in February 1867 by ex-convict James Pearce, who had been transported in the 1850s while still in his twenties, ran weekly until July 1886 when it was amalgamated with the *Inquiry*. Pearce was joined by two other ex-convicts, James Beresford, sentenced to life imprisonment at 56 for forging an endorsement on a bill of exchange (Beresford may have been a former Anglican Dean of Cork) and James Roe, also a former clergyman and sentenced to ten years for a similar offence. Written specifically for the working man and making no distinction between bond and free, the *Herald* opposed the convict system, championed democracy and campaigned for land, education and social reform. It published verse, short fiction and serials, but its major literary feature was a weekly column by Beresford, 'Chips by a Sandalwood Cutter'. Through the musings of the unsophisticated sandalwood-cutter Beresford exposed pomposity and privilege and extolled the simple working-man morality. In 1913 the *Fremantle Herald* was reopened under its own banner but closed again in 1915. A new era began 30 November 1989 when the *Fremantle Herald* was launched for a third existence. Owned, produced and published in Fremantle (and on the same site as the original), its present aim is to carry on the work and reputation of those earlier forebears. The new publisher is Andrew Smith, editor Sian Martin. A regular contributor is academic and literary critic Veronica Brady.

FREMD, Angelika (1944–), born Seelaw, Germany, arrived in Australia in 1956. She taught at high schools in Queensland and Papua New Guinea 1966–86 and has more recently worked as multicultural and community literature officer in Queensland. Co-founder of Phoenix Publications, she was also co-founder and co-editor of *Outrider*. She has published short fiction and poetry in anthologies and periodicals and two novels, *Heartland* (1989) and *The Glass Inferno* (1992). Both novels focus on the experiences of Inge Heinrich, whose family escapes from Germany in the 1950s when she is a child. Presenting an outsider's perspective on Australia of the 1960s, *The Glass Inferno* is a striking feminist psychodrama which focuses on the narrator's search for identity and freedom from the prejudices of gender and ethnicity.

Frere, Maurice, see *His Natural Life*; **PRICE, John**

FRIEDERICH, Werner Paul, see *Australia in Western Imaginative Prose Writings*

FRIEND, Donald (1915–89), born Moree, NSW, lived and painted in England, France and West Africa before the Second World War, in which he served in the artillery and as an official war artist 1945–46, visiting New Guinea and Borneo. After the war he lived in Sydney, Hill End, Europe and Sri Lanka, before ill health forced his return to Australia in 1980. Friend kept a lavishly illustrated diary from the age of 16 until the year before his death. This unique record of his work, life and times, now held in the National Library

of Australia, formed the basis of his first books, *Gunner's Diary* (1943) and *Painter's Journal* (1946). His official work as war artist is collected in Gavin and Colleen Fry's *Donald Friend: Australian War Artist 1945* (1982). Friend's other publications include a historical miscellany, *A Collection of Hillendiana* (1956); *Donald Friend in Bali* (1972); a loosely autobiographical novel, *Save Me from the Shark* (1973); limited art editions, *The Cosmic Turtle* (1976), *Birds from the Magic Mountain* (1977, Balinese folk stories), *An Alphabet of Owls Et Cetera* (1981) and *Songs of the Vagabond Scholars* (1982); an illustrated satire on bushranging and other pioneering traditions, *Coogan's Gully* (1979); *Bumbooziana* (1979), a limited-edition portfolio of pictures and text which ranges beyond its immediate satirical target – scientific and anthropological expeditions and nineteenth-century books of reminiscences – to embrace sexuality and art styles and *Art in a Classless Society and Vice Versa* (1985) in which he lampoons the Australian arts community. Friend also illustrated a nineteenth-century story, *The Surprising Adventures of Blue-Eyed Patty* (1979) and a licentious play by Rochester, *The Farce of Sodom* (1980). A feature-length film on Friend, *The Prodigal Australian* by Don Bennetts, was released in 1991. Barry Pearce assembled the publication, *Donald Friend 1915–1989* (1990), to accompany a major retrospective exhibition of Friend's work in 1990.

Friendly Street, a regular series of public poetry readings, began in Adelaide in November 1975, largely as a result of efforts by Ian Reid, Andrew Taylor and Richard Tipping. Although there is no such place in Adelaide, Friendly Street was the name chosen for the meetings because it indicated the friendly, welcoming atmosphere generated at the monthly (the first Tuesday night) gatherings at the Box Factory, Regent Street, Adelaide. Each year a *Friendly Street Poetry Reader*, selected from the work read at the monthly meetings, is published. There have been seventeen to 1993, the first edited by Richard Tipping in 1976. Other well-known editors have been Ian Reid, Andrew Taylor, Peter Goldsworthy, John Bray, Robert Clark, Graham Rowlands and Jeff Guess. In addition to the annual *Readers* many individual books of verse by Friendly Street regulars have been published, at first and for many years by the small collaborative press Friendly Street Poets, but more recently by Wakefield Press. Twenty-three individual collections have been published. The 1992 anthology, *Tuesday Night Live*, edited by Jerri Kroll and Barry Westburg, is a retrospective collection of about 160 poems by 80 poets, an indication of the variety of the Friendly Street performers. *Tuesday Night Live* also carries a valuable introduction detailing the history of Friendly Street.

Fringe Dwellers, The (1961), a novel by Nene Gare (q.v.), highlights the problems of part-Aborigines who live on the fringes of White society. Noonah and Trilby Comeaway leave the Murchison Mission, where they have been educated, to rejoin their parents in the squalid environment of 'Nigger Hill' on the outskirts of Geraldton, WA. Under pressure from the two girls, the Comeaways move into a housing development which is an experiment in assimilation by the Department of Native Welfare. But the family is unable to live there successfully. The new house is invaded by relatives, Trilby becomes pregnant and the baby is killed by its mother in a more or less deliberate accident, Mr Comeaway goes 'walkabout', the rent is unpaid, the family is evicted and returns to a one-roomed house on a 'native' reservation. Trilby, the rebel against the old life, is finally resigned to the squalid card-playing, wine-drinking emptiness that the novel characterises as the existence of the fringe-dweller. A feature film of *The Fringe Dwellers*, directed by Bruce Beresford, was released in 1986.

Fringe of Leaves, A, a novel by Patrick White (q.v.) based on the adventures of Mrs Eliza Fraser, was published in 1976. In the autumn of 1836 Ellen Roxburgh, previously Ellen Gluyas, and her husband Austin, set out from Sydney on the *Bristol Maid* on their return voyage to England after visiting Austin's reprobate brother Garnet in Van Diemen's Land. In describing the early days of the voyage, White also establishes the inhibited relationship of the Roxburghs, Ellen's past life as a simple farm girl in Cornwall, her marriage to the invalid gentleman Austin, the early years of their marriage and her education in gentility, and the more recent past in Australia. Among Ellen's uneasy memories is her surrender on one occasion to Garnet, a man she thoroughly dislikes. The voyage is disrupted when the ship founders on a reef and the subsequent lengthy ordeal in unseaworthy longboats arouses the unexpected in both crew and passengers. The captain turns rapidly into an ineffective old man whereas others, such as the mate, Pilcher, and even Austin, discover strong instincts of survival. The cabin boy, Oswald Dignam, who is devoted to Ellen, and Spurgeon, the steward, who becomes Austin's friend, both die and Ellen is delivered of a stillborn child. When they finally make land they are attacked by Aborigines and most of them killed, Austin dying from a spear in his neck. Ellen is captured by the tribe, stripped of her clothes apart from a girdle of convolvulus in which she hides her wedding ring, and treated as a slave. Her privations and indignities arouse her sympathy for the Aborigines and grant her an insight into the unity of being and her inevitable implication in the eternal duality of good and evil. Later, when she is rescued by an escaped convict, Jack Chance, she experiences rare moments of passionate or tender communion although both their pasts strain the relationship. When they finally reach civilisation, Chance flees back into the wilderness, wary of colonial justice. Ellen, stripped even of her fringe of leaves and her wedding ring, is discovered by the Oakes family outside their farm and cared for by them until her journey to the prison settlement at Moreton Bay. Her renewed confrontation with society, especially with its authority figures, is imbued with her singular spiritual experience. Peace of mind comes when she visits the rude chapel at Moreton Bay built by Pilcher, the only other survivor of the wreck, and rediscovers what her experiences have taught her, the painful complexity of the religious phrase above its altar, 'God is Love'.

Front Room Boys, The, a play by Alexander Buzo (q.v.), was first performed in 1969 and published in 1970. The Front Room Boys are clerks who work for a large corporation headed by the executives, the Back Room Boys, unseen except for the silent Hendo, who emerges from time to time to exert authority. Two women, Sundra, a typist in search of extramarital diversion, and Pammy, the nubile junior and office mascot, complete the group. Set in twelve scenes to accord with the months of the year, the play explores motives for subservience to established, unjust powers; the acceptance of stereotyped roles and meaningless functions; and the willing complicity of the oppressed in their oppression. In its conformity to rituals and ceremonies, its submission to strong, unseen powers and its need to propitiate those powers with sacrificial scapegoats, this modern urban group follows timeless, primitive tribal practices. Only Jacko, who finally sees the absurdity of their situation, challenges the system and is consequently attacked and ejected by his mates.

FROST, John (1784–1877) was a Chartist who in 1839 led an abortive attack on his birthplace of Newport, Wales; he was sentenced to be hanged, drawn and quartered for this treasonous offence, but the sentence was commuted to transportation for life. Frost arrived in Tasmania in 1840, served part of his sentence at Port Arthur and after securing a conditional pardon in 1854 went to America. He returned to England from exile in 1856 after hearing news of a free pardon, and gave lectures on his experiences which were published as *The Horrors of Convict Life* (1856) and *A Letter to the People of Great Britain and Ireland on Transportation* (1857). Several contemporary accounts of Frost's trial were published. David Williams's *John Frost: A Study in Chartism*, and James Davies's *The Chartist Movement in Monmouthshire* both appeared in 1939, the centenary year of the Newport attack.

FROUDE, James Anthony (1818–94), the English historian and biographer of Thomas Carlyle, visited South Africa, Australia and NZ in 1885 to obtain material for a book, *Oceana, or England and Her Colonies*, published in 1886. As he spent only a few weeks in Australia, his impressions of actual conditions were superficial and even incorrect, but his political vision for the nation as member of a Commonwealth of Oceana was, at least for a period, closer to the mark. Geoffrey Blainey edited an abridged version of *Oceana* in 1985.

Fryer Memorial Library, part of the University of Queensland library, is named after J.D. Fryer, an ex-serviceman who died in 1924 from injuries sustained in the First World War; its establishment in 1927 owed much to F.W. Robinson of the University. The Fryer Library is a significant repository of Australian literature material, including papers of many writers with strong Queensland affiliations, e.g. Thea Astley, John

Blight, James Devaney, George Essex Evans, Mary Hannay Foott, Xavier Herbert, Ernestine Hill, David Malouf and Thomas Shapcott. It also has papers of many other writers, e.g. A.G. Stephens, E.G. Moll, Martin Boyd, Mary Gilmore, and houses a strong drama collection centred on the Eunice Hanger (q.v.) collection of unpublished play scripts but also including Brisbane theatre records and papers of G.L. Dann and Nat Phillips, the straightman for Roy Rene. The Fryer Library published on microfiche the check-list of Australian plays prepared at the University of Queensland, and maintains the index which is the basis of the annual bibliography of Australian literature included in *Australian Literary Studies*.

FULLERTON, Mary Eliza ('E') (1868–1946), born in a bark hut in Glenmaggie, Victoria, became a devotee of literature and a strong campaigner on feminist issues. As 'Alpenstock', she wrote poetry and short fiction for newspapers and journals. She published poetry, *Moods and Melodies* (1908), *The Breaking Furrow* (1921) and *Bark House Days* (1921, published with additional material in 1931), her childhood reminiscences. She also wrote fiction, e.g. *The People of the Timber Belt* (1925) and *A Juno of the Bush* (1930) as well as a descriptive work, *The Australian Bush* (1928). Her friendship with Miles Franklin (q.v.), continued by correspondence after Fullerton left Australia permanently for England in 1922, led to the eventual publication of her poetry in the 1940s under the pseudonym 'E'. The identity of 'E', the author of *Moles Do So Little With Their Privacy* (1942) and *The Wonder and the Apple* (1946), was one of the major literary talking-points of the time; adopted as a mark of reverence for her favourite authors, Emily Bronte and Emily Dickinson, and for her mother, it was revealed after her death. Fullerton was also the author of two novels published under pseudonyms, *Rufus Sterne* by 'Robert Gray' (1932) and *The Murders at Crabapple Café* by 'Gordon Manners' (1933). Another novel, *Clare*, won a prize as one of the best short books of self-revelation submitted to the London publisher Philpot; it was published anonymously in *Two Women* (1923).

'Furphy', a word still used in Australia for a rumour or false report, seems to have originated during the First World War from the gossip around the water-carts (also known as 'furphies') made by the Furphy foundry at Shepparton in Victoria. Ironically, the phrase 'Tom Collins', the pen-name of Joseph Furphy who wrote *Such is Life* (1903) while employed at the foundry from 1883 to 1905, carried the meaning that furphy has now.

FURPHY, Joseph (1843–1912) was born at Yering in the upper Yarra valley in Victoria, the son of Protestant Irish bounty emigrants who arrived in Australia in 1841 and from whom he inherited a capacity for hard work and a love of literature. His elder brother John, who inherited their dourness and religious zeal, was the inventor of the Furphy water-cart and thus directly responsible for the introduction of 'furphy'

into Australian English. Furphy completed his schooling at Kyneton, where he first worked on his father's farm before brief stints on the goldfields and as a threshing-machine operator in the Daylesford district; in 1867 he married a young French girl, Leonie Germaine, and took over her mother's farm and vineyard. The following year he selected land in the Lake Cooper district but was driven off after five years and forced to work as a labourer and to return to the gold-diggings. Around the end of 1877 he moved with his family to the Riverina in NSW to set himself up with a bullock team; based in Hay, he carted wool and other goods on both sides of the Murray River and to stations further north. The life was particularly hard on Furphy and his family, and after his team was virtually wiped out in the 1883 drought, he moved to Shepparton in Victoria to work at his brother's foundry. The move lost Furphy his independence but provided his family with security and gave him the opportunity to read at the local mechanics' institute and to write. In 1889 he began contributing short items and sketches to the *Bulletin*, first as 'Warrigal Jack' and from 1893 as 'Tom Collins'. By 1897 he had finished a 'full-sized novel, title, 'Such is Life'; scene, Riverina and northern Vic.; temper, democratic; bias, offensively Australian', which he tentatively sent to the *Bulletin*'s editor, J.F. Archibald, for an opinion. Archibald passed the manuscript of 1125 pages over to his literary editor, A.G. Stephens (q.v.), who recognised its originality but suggested revisions which Furphy doggedly worked on before *Such is Life: Being Certain Extracts from the Diary of Tom Collins* (q.v.) was eventually published in 1903. His euphoria at seeing the novel in print stimulated Furphy into making two books, *The Buln-Buln and the Brolga* and *Rigby's Romance* (qq.v.), out of the excised portions of the original manuscript, but because of the slow sale and lukewarm reception of *Such is Life* neither was published in book form during his lifetime. In 1905 he moved to WA to join his sons, who had established an iron foundry; he died there seven years later. The house that Furphy built at Swanbourne, a Perth suburb, is now the house of the WA branch of the FAW and is described in Justina Williams's *Tom Collins & His House* (1973). Jean Lang (Jean Lang Crowe), custodian of the Furphy material in Tom Collins House since 1949, has written about Furphy's time in WA, *At the Toss of a Coin: Joseph Furphy: The Western Link* (1986).

Although Furphy's death in 1912 attracted little attention, the eventual recognition of his stature is an important episode in Australian literary history. At Shepparton he had met a young schoolteacher, Kate Baker (q.v.), who along with Furphy's Melbourne friend William Cathels, provided encouragement and assistance during the writing and revision of *Such is Life*. Furphy's death coincided with Kate Baker's retirement from teaching. For the next four decades she devoted herself to promoting Furphy by collecting Furphiana and by arranging for the publication of his works including *The Poems of Joseph Furphy* (1916), a reissue in 1917 of *Such is Life* and a severely edited version in 1921 of *Rigby's Romance*. The efforts of Baker and other admirers of Furphy such as Vance Palmer and A.G. Stephens were rewarded during the 1940s, when his reputation was secured; towards the end of the decade Douglas Stewart was writing that 'An amiable, an estimable madness is abroad in the land. Namely, the deification of Joseph Furphy, *alias* Tom Collins', and protesting with tongue in cheek that 'at a conservative estimate, fifteen thousand articles' on him had been contributed to *Southerly* alone. Furphy texts became available again with the republication of *Such is Life* (1944) and the first full publication of *Rigby's Romance* (1946) and *The Buln-Buln and the Brolga* (1948); together with the release of Baker's material in Miles Franklin's (q.v.) *Joseph Furphy: The Legend of a Man and His Book* (1944), they stimulated the increased interest in Furphy already apparent in the 'Letters to Tom Collins' (q.v.) series in *Meanjin* and confirmed by the Furphy special numbers in both *Meanjin* and *Southerly* (1943, 1945). Considerable attention then was devoted to Furphy's social and political ideas, which made him a central figure in the legend of the Nineties (q.v.). The democratic temper, egalitarianism, nationalism and Christian socialism of his work were explicated by J.K. Ewers among others in *Tell the People!* (1943) and a decade later Furphy's 1897 description of his novel was adopted as the motto for the radical *Overland*. The second major thrust of Furphy commentary in the 1940s was directed towards unravelling the mysteries of *Such is Life*, which had confused most earlier commentators despite the clues offered by Furphy himself in an anonymous review of the novel published in the *Bulletin* in 1903. Most importantly, commentators demonstrated that *Such is Life* is not as structurally formless as its narrator, Tom Collins, would have readers believe; that the relationship between Furphy and his narrator is an ambivalent and ironic one in which, for example, Collins reveals things to the reader which are hidden from himself; that it is an experimental work which in form and design explores the relationship between fiction and reality; and that these complexities of structure and theme provide evidence that *Such is Life* is judged wrongly if judged simply as a rich portrait of bush life in the 1880s. The structure, form and themes of *Such is Life* have continued to detain literary critics and historians since the 1940s. There has been further exploration of the unities of its plot and of the role and morality of its narrator, which has involved discussions of *Rigby's Romance* and *The Buln-Buln and the Brolga*. Attention has also been focused on the philosophy of the novel, e.g. whether life as a mixture of predestination and free will is its central theme; on its balance of comedy and moral seriousness; its ironic modes; its romance and picaresque elements; and Furphy's language and style. John Barnes has written a critical monograph (revised edn, 1979) and edited a Furphy volume in the Portable Australian Authors series (1981). His *The Order of Things: A Life of Joseph Furphy* (1990) is the major biography of Furphy. Julian Croft's *The Life and Opinions of Tom Collins: A Study of the Works of Joseph Furphy* (1991) presents an alternative interpretation of *Such is Life*, that is as a double text – 'Tom Collins's Annals' and 'Joseph Furphy's novel'. In 1991 Frances Devlin-Glass, Robin Eaden, Lois Hoffmann and G.W. Turner produced *The Annotated Such is Life*, an entertaining and informative explanation and unravelling of the difficulties facing the modern reader in Furphy's esoteric and complex masterpiece.

Furphy once described himself as 'half bushman and half bookworm'. Just as his wide experience of bush life gave him the knowledge which informed his writing and made *Such is Life* an important and realistic portrayal of rural Australia, so his wide reading helped fashion the form of the novel and make it an important and original exploration of the relationship between literature and life. The isolation in which Furphy worked is the probable reason for the residual self-consciousness of his literary style, notwithstanding the cleverness and appropriateness of his literary allusions to Shakespeare, the Bible, Sterne and other authors; the effect, when the ponderousness and pomposity natural to the character of Tom Collins are added, is to make *Such is Life* difficult to read, if increasingly enjoyable to reread. The irony, then, is that an Australian classic by an author of strong nationalistic sentiments (despite recent suggestions that parts of *Such is Life* attest to hierarchies of class in rural Australia) is inaccessible to ordinary Australians. Nonetheless, *Such is Life* is significant for the part it played in turning Australian fiction away from the colonial romance, and Furphy remains one of the most significant writers of Australian fiction before the First World War.

G

Gabbett, the convict cannibal in Marcus Clarke's novel *His Natural Life* (q.v., 1874), is based on the Tasmanian convict Alexander Pearce or Pierce (c.1790–1824), who twice escaped with other convicts from Macquarie Harbour, was the sole survivor on each occasion, and was hanged for cannibalism. Clarke read about Pearce in the Molesworth Report on transportation (1837–38); so did 'Price Warung', who used the source for two gruesome stories about convict cannibalism, 'In Shoes of Death: The Tanning of the Hide' and 'The Wearing of the "Shoes of Death"' (1892). Pearce, whose skull is now at the University of Pennsylvania, is the subject of Dan Sprod's *Alexander Pearce of Macquarie Harbour* (1977), which includes information on the other writers, e.g. David Burn, T.G. Ford, Patsy Adam-Smith, who have written up the Pearce story.

Gadfly, a provocative Adelaide weekly founded by C.J. Dennis (q.v.), was published 1906–9. It aimed to encourage Australian literature and art, support nationalistic attitudes such as protection and restricted immigration, and lampoon pomposity and hypocrisy. Its contributors included the writers Dennis, Edward Dyson, 'Grant Hervey', and artists Hal Gye, Will and Ambrose Dyson and Ruby Lindsay.

GAGE, Mary (1940–), born England, where she worked as a freelance journalist and for the London *Times*, settled in WA in 1972. She has written short stories, some of which have been published in *Argosy* and broadcast by the BBC; an unusual book about life in a chicken run, *Praise the Egg* (1981), which won the 1981 Angus & Robertson Writers' Fellowship; and several plays. These include 'C.Y.' (1981), 'The Catalyst' (1973), 'Supermarket' (1975), 'Skin Hunger' (1976), 'Everyone's a General' (1976), *The New Life* (1977), 'Gas' (1977), 'The Same Square of Dust' (1979), based on the life of Charles Kingsford-Smith, 'The Price of Pearls' (1980, co-winner of WA's 150th anniversary play competition) and *My Name is Pablo Picasso* (1984). Her best-known play, *The New Life*, a one-act study of the experience of a British immigrant family, was first produced in 1974.

'Galah', a word of Aboriginal origin, is the name applied to the rose-breasted, grey-backed species of cockatoo found in considerable numbers in inland Australia. Like most types of cockatoo, the galah is a pest to farmers because of its attacks on crops. Its noisy and clowning behaviour has led to the word being used colloquially to denote noisy, foolish people who lack common sense. Popular expressions are 'as mad as a galah' or 'as mad as a gumtree full of galahs'. This derogatory use of galah is widespread in Australian writing, e.g. in Sumner Locke Elliott's *Rusty Bugles* (1948), D'Arcy Niland's *Call Me When the Cross Turns Over* (1957) and David Ireland's *The Unknown Industrial Prisoner* (1971). A 'galah session' is the phrase used to denote a gossip session on the Flying Doctor radio network.

Galahad Jones, a novel by Arthur Henry Adams (q.v.), was published in 1910. The hero, a middle-aged bank clerk with a chivalric spirit, intervenes in the life of a young girl dying of consumption in an effort to bring her happiness. The novel, which successfully combines realism, romance, humour and melodrama, was subsequently reworked by Adams as a play and published in 1914.

GALLAGHER, Katherine (1935–), born Maldon, Victoria, worked as a laboratory assistant and secretary before graduating from the University of Melbourne in 1963. She taught in Melbourne high schools 1964–68 and in 1969 moved to Europe, living first in London and then in Paris (1971–79). Since 1979 she has lived in England. She has contributed widely to poetry anthologies and journals both in Australia and overseas and has published several volumes of verse, *The Eye's Circle* (1974, a second edition 1978), *Tributaries of the Love-Song* (1978), *Passengers to the City* (1985), *Fish-Rings on Water* (1989) and *Finding the Prince* (1993). *Passengers to the City* was short-listed for the National Poetry Award of 1986. Although resident overseas for more than twenty years, her connections with Australia remain strong. *Fish-Rings on Water* was launched at the Poetry Society in London and Gallagher read from it and her other works at the Australian Studies Centre there. Many of her poems are delicate cameos of events and experiences significant to her. Sensitive, imaginative and at ease in either a colloquial or more formal style, Gallagher is especially impressive when she writes of those close to her or of the general human condition where loss, grief or sorrow are conveyed with eloquence and compassion. She also writes short stories and shared the first prize with Finola Moorhead in the 1975 Sun Festival of Stories, Melbourne. She won the Warana Poetry Prize in 1981.

Gallipoli, a word of legendary significance to Australians, is a town (spelt 'Gelibolu' on some modern international maps) in Turkey, which is at the neck of and gives its name to a peninsula bounded on one side by the Gulf of Saros and the Aegean Sea, and on the other by the Dardanelles Straits connecting the Aegean Sea and the Sea of Marmora, which in turn is connected to the Black Sea by the Bosporus. The peninsula was the scene of a campaign, known as the Gallipoli or Dardanelles campaign, in the First World War. Early in 1915, after Russia had asked Britain to help relieve Russian troops fighting the Turks by mounting their own attack on the Turkish forces, it was decided that an attempt should be made to force the Dardanelles, thus opening the way for an attack on Constantinople (Istanbul). After naval bombardments in the Straits, the Allies attempted an amphibious landing on the Aegean side of the Gallipoli peninsula with the objective of crossing overland to capture the Turkish gun emplacements protecting the Dardanelles. Australian and NZ troops formed part of the Allied forces and from 25 April 1915 the Anzacs (q.v.) were put ashore at what came to be known as Anzac Cove. They established a toehold on the ridges above the beach but were unable to make much progress towards winning the summit which commanded the Straits; a stalemate developed in which the impact of troops was reduced by indecision and sometimes incompetent planning, by the threat of disease, and by the unfavourable terrain. The campaign itself foundered and in December 1915 it was decided to evacuate the peninsula. By one estimate almost half a million Allied troops were landed on the Gallipoli peninsula; of those up to a quarter of a million were casualties in one form or another, Australasian casualties numbering 27 594.

The commemoration of Anzac Day, as the anniversary of the first landing at Anzac Cove came to be known, began in 1916 and in time the Gallipoli experience came to be seen as an event of national significance: in broad terms, as the occasion when Australia underwent its baptism of fire and came of age through the heroic sacrifice of its young men, who demonstrated the ideals of Australian manhood. That the sacrifice was made in an imperial rather than national cause illustrates the paradoxes of Gallipoli in particular and Australian nationalism in general. The mythic significance of Gallipoli was firmly established in the writings of the war historian C.E.W. Bean (q.v.), particularly in his *The Story of Anzac*. C.J. Dennis, known as the 'Anzac Laureate', in *The Moods of Ginger Mick* (1916) and *Digger Smith* (1918), and Henry Lawson in 'Song of the Dardanelles' also paid contemporary tribute to the distinctive qualities of the Australian soldier. David McKee Wright's poem 'Gallipoli' celebrates the Australian achievement there; Mary Gilmore's 'Gallipoli' grieves for those who died there. Although in its generalised aspects the myth has been much scrutinised, e.g. by Alan Seymour in *The One Day of the Year* (q.v., 1962), Australian writers have continued to be detained by Gallipoli. A number of them, e.g. Leon Gellert, Ion L. Idriess, Frank Clune, Harley Matthews, were at Gallipoli and recorded their experiences. More recently, Peter Weir's film *Gallipoli* (1981; screenplay by David Williamson, novelisation by Jack Bennett) was a major success in Australia and overseas; Roger McDonald's *1915* (q.v., 1979) won several major literary awards before its adaptation into

a successful television series in 1982; and Albert Facey's memoirs, *A Fortunate Life* (1981), cover the First World War. Although the events of Gallipoli form only part of Weir's film, McDonald's novel and Facey's autobiography, the success of all three illustrates how firm a hold the Gallipoli experience retains on the imagination of Anglo-Saxon Australians. Sidney Nolan painted a notable Gallipoli series; among recent books on Gallipoli are Bill Gammage's *The Broken Years* (1974) based on diaries and personal accounts, Kevin Fewster's *Gallipoli Correspondent: The Frontline Diary of C.E.W. Bean* (1983) and Kit Denton's *Gallipoli, One Long Grave* (1985). Gammage also published, with Peter Weir and David Williamson, *The Story of Gallipoli* (1981). The other side of the Gallipoli story is told in *A Turkish View of Gallipoli Çanakkale* (Kevin Fewster, Vecihi Basarin and H.H. Basarin, 1985). Recent plays about Gallipoli include Clem Gorman's *A Manual of Trench Warfare* (1979), Leonard Radic's *Sideshow* (1987) and Richard Beynon's *Simpson, J. 202* (1991). The Anzac/Gallipoli myth comes under scrutiny in Robin Gerster's *Big-noting. The Heroic Theme in Australian War Writing* (1987), which examines literary formulae used to mythologise the Australian warrior, and in E.M. Andrews's *The Anzac Illusion* (1993), which challenges many aspects of the screen representations of the Anzacs, e.g. in *Gallipoli* and *1915*. Pam Cupper and Phil Taylor compiled *Gallipoli: A Battlefield Guide* (1989).

Galmahra, a University of Queensland magazine, was published three times a year 1921–65. Two of its notable editors were P.R. Stephensen and Cecil Hadgraft. It published, in addition to university news, literary articles, reviews, short fiction and verse.

GAMAS, Citizen, was author of an early play about the French Revolution. Set in 'Austral lands', which were often viewed in eighteenth-century France as 'utopian', *Les Emigrés aux Terres Australes, ou Le Dernier Chapitre d'une Grande Révolution* (1794) was performed in Paris in 1792. An edited, translated version was published by Patricia Clancy in 1984. Other early plays were performed on the English stage including 'Botany Bay' (1787), before the First Fleet reached Australia.

GAMMAGE, W.L., see **Gallipoli**

GARDINER, Frank (Francis Christie) (?1830–1903), born near Goulburn, NSW, was the son of a Scottish free settler named Christie and an Irish-Aboriginal servant girl; he took the name Frank Gardiner around 1860. From 1861 until his capture in 1864 he took part in several daring robberies in central western NSW, often teamed with Ben Hall and Johnny Gilbert (qq.v.). One of the few bushrangers to escape death during capture or execution after it, he was eventually released in 1874 subject to his exile, a controversial decision which brought down the government of Sir Henry Parkes. The bushranger Lardner in 'Rolf Boldrewood's' *Robbery Under Arms* (1888) and *The Miner's Right* (1890) is modelled on Gardiner, who is also the subject of an extensive ballad literature, e.g. 'Frank Gardiner He Is Caught at Last' and 'The Fierce and Bloody Battle of the Weddin Mountains'. Colin Free wrote *Ironbark* (1976), a novel about Gardiner and his exploits, and Edgar Penzig has published a biography, *Frank Gardiner the Bushranger* (1987).

GARDNER, Silvana (1942–), born Zadar, Dalmatia, subsequently Yugoslavia, has had numerous occupations – artist, domestic, nurse, interpreter – and has conducted and co-ordinated creative writing and art workshops. She graduated in fine arts and literature from the University of Queensland and her art work is represented in Australian and overseas galleries. She has published several books of poetry: *When Sunday Comes* (1982), *Hacedor* (1982), *With Open Eyes* (1983), *Children of the Dragon* (1985), *The Devil in Nature* (1987), *Ha Ha Hacedor* (1991) and *Cochineal Red* (1992, Pamphlet Poets series). Her best poems are the brief, enigmatic verses of the early volumes that recall her migrant childhood, including the ambience of the boarding house; her grandmother of the aristocratic profile and the black burial dress lovingly preserved 'for one last modesty'; searching in the sea for ambergris with her father; the name of their new street, 'Hope'; and the barely concealed contempt of her classmates for one of a different ethnic group. *With Open Eyes* describes and characterises a number of individuals: the lost soul, Marjorie; a fisherman and his son; the telegraph linesman; the 85-year-old 'Miss Regina'. It also contains poems written during a visit to America. *Children of the Dragon* was largely inspired by the children she met while conducting art, craft and literary workshops in schools, youth shelters and other places. The second part, 'of the Dragon', deals with the underprivileged youth at the Windsor Youth Emergency Shelter in Brisbane, where she was artist-in-residence for part of 1982. *The Devil in Nature* is more feminist in outlook, with a number of poems wryly and provocatively assessing male–female relationships.

GARE, Nene (1919–94), born Adelaide, was educated at the Adelaide Art School and Perth Technical School. Her publications include the significant novel *The Fringe Dwellers* (q.v., 1961, a film in 1988), which concerns the plight of part-Aborigines who fail in their effort to integrate with White society; *Green Gold* (1963), a novel loosely based on the author's banana-growing experiences at Carnarvon, with a backdrop of the natural hazards of that area of Australia; *Bend to the Wind* (1978), short stories about her friends the Aborigines of WA; and *A House With Verandahs* (1980), an autobiographical account of her family life as a girl in Adelaide, together with a sequel, *An Island Away* (1981), dealing with her experiences when her husband was a patrol officer in Salamaua, Papua New Guinea.

Gargoyle Poets, see *Makar*

GARNER, Helen (1942–), born Geelong, graduated from the University of Melbourne in 1965 and has worked as a secondary school teacher, journalist, freelance reviewer and feature writer and translator. She has written for various media, including film and television, but is best known for her novels and short stories. Her first novel, *Monkey Grip* (1977), which was widely acclaimed and won a National Book Council Award, was released as a film in 1982. Her subsequent publications include two novellas published together, *Honour and Other People's Children* (1980), a collection of short stories, *Postcards from Surfers* (1985), which won a 1986 NSW Premier's Literary Award, and two novels, *The Children's Bach* (1984), winner of a SA Premier's Literary Award in 1986, and *Cosmo Cosmolino* (1992). Garner has also written for television and film, including the screenplay *The Last Days of Chez Nous* (1992). In 1993 she won a Walkley Award for feature journalism for her story in *Time* magazine about the Daniel Valiero case.

Dramatic action and plot are largely absent in Garner's fiction, which is more concerned with the undramatic, daily encounters of modern life, the nuances and shifts in relationships between women and their lovers, friends and children. *Monkey Grip*, *Honour and Other People's Children* and some of the stories in *Postcards from Surfers* deal with a sad world where people attempt, and often fail, to build alternatives to the traditional family. Garner's scrupulous prose, sensitive to language's rhythms, inflexions and shades of meaning, characteristically evokes the loneliness of late twentieth-century life. An austere writer in the sense that she works on a small canvas, she is also morally austere, underlining the imperatives of compassion, understanding and tenderness. Set against a background of 1970s inner-city life in Melbourne, *Monkey Grip* focuses on the fluctuating relationship between Javo, a heroin addict, and the narrator, Nora. A semi-autobiographical novel, it has been widely praised for its re-creation of the familiar, but Garner's realism is always secondary to her stringent morality, for the novel deals with several forms of drug addiction including addictive, destructive relationships. In *Postcards from Surfers* Garner manipulates a variety of different styles and personae from the drunken male monologue of 'All Those Bloody Young Catholics' to the child's diminutive but sharp perspective on ugliness in 'Little Helen's Sunday Afternoon'. Like postcards in their intensity and brevity, these stories affirm experience even as they record its inevitable pain. The two novellas of *Honour and Other People's Children* are linked in their preoccupation with the question of power in relationships and the difficult struggle to maintain an honourable openness and generosity however shifting the emotional circumstances. In *The Children's Bach*, often seen as Garner's most subtly structured novel, the affinity between her moral themes and music is most clearly visible; intertwining the lives of eight people in a complex, polyphonic pattern, and developing the theme of music as an ordering principle, the novel recalls the compressed effects of Bach. *Cosmo Cosmolino*, set in the Nineties decade, and once again concerned with communal living, nevertheless represents a marked change in Garner's work from realism to a mix of realism and surrealism; drawing on a more highly coloured language to develop its theme of salvation and regeneration from physical and moral ugliness, the novel is a bold transition to a more visible spiritual dimension while revealing Garner as a comic writer with a wide-ranging repertoire of dramatic effects.

GARRAN, Andrew (1825–1901), born and educated in London, came to Australia in 1851 because of ill health. He was co-editor of the *Register* 1853–55 then became assistant editor of the *Sydney Morning Herald* in 1856 and editor 1873–85. He edited the *Picturesque Atlas of Australasia* (1886–88) and was a member of the NSW Legislative Council 1887–92. His son was Sir Robert Garran (q.v.).

GARRAN, Sir Robert (1867–1957), son of Andrew Garran (q.v.), was born in Sydney and was called to the Bar in 1890. Private secretary to Edmund Barton in the Federation movement, he published *The Coming Commonwealth* (1897) and collaborated with John Quick in the *Annotated Constitution of the Australian Commonwealth* (1897). A foundation member of the Commonwealth public service, Garran became solicitor-general in 1916 and played a leading role in many undertakings including the establishment of the ANU. He was made GCMG in 1937 and received numerous other honours. Garran's memoirs, *Prosper the Commonwealth*, were published in 1958. *The Gifted Knight* (1983), by Noel Francis, collects Garran's poetry, and includes biography, correspondence and radio broadcasts.

'Garryowen', see **FINN, Edmund**

GARTNER, Jack, see **Hawthorn Press**

GASK, Arthur Cecil (1872–1951), born London, practised as a dental surgeon for more than forty years in England and Australia and wrote more than thirty crime and mystery novels, some of which involve the detective Larose and are set in SA, where Gask lived. The scope and nature of Gask's fiction are indicated by their titles, e.g. *The Red Paste Murders* (1923), *The Shadow of Larose* (1930), *Gentlemen of Crime* (1932) and *The Hangman's Knot* (1936). *The Secret of the Garden* was reprinted in the Wakefield Crime Classics series in 1993.

GASKIN, Catherine (1929–), born County Louth, Ireland, came to Australia as a child. At 16 she startled the Australian reading public by having a successful novel, *This Other Eden*, published. After her second novel, *With Every Year* (1947), she went to England and has since lived in the USA, Ireland and the Isle of Man. Her most successful novel, *Sara Dane* (1954), the story of a convict girl who goes on to make a successful life in Australia, is based partly on the life of Mary Reibey. It sold over two million copies and was made into a television series in Australia in 1982. She produced a stream of other best-sellers, including *Blake's Reach* (1958), *Corporation Wife* (1960), *The Tilsit Inheritance* (1963), *The File on Devlin* (1965), *Edge of Glass* (1967), *Fiona* (1970), *A Falcon for a Queen* (1972),

The Property of a Gentleman (1974), *The Summer of the Spanish Woman* (1977), *Family Affairs* (1980), *Promises* (1982) and *The Ambassador's Women* (1985). Although she has not attracted the interest of literary critics, she is one of the most successful contemporary exponents of the popular romance. Her plots, carefully crafted and woven into a solidly researched background, are the strength of her fiction; her characters, predictable figures who vary little from book to book, are less effective.

Gateway, The (1953), the third volume of poetry by Judith Wright (q.v.), shows the poet moving away from the familiar world of the senses which characterises the earlier volumes, *The Moving Image* (1946) and *Woman to Man* (1949), to begin a quest for self-knowledge. The title poem speaks of 'the traveller' (the poet herself) passing through 'the gateway' to new perceptions. In addition to poems about other searchers for knowledge, e.g. 'The Journey' and 'The Cicadas', the volume contains poems such as 'Old House', 'Train Journey' and 'Eroded Hills', which reflect Wright's long-established interest in her ancestry and the New England environment.

Gathered In, a novel by Catherine Helen Spence (q.v.), was published as a serial in the Adelaide *Observer* 1881–82 and in book form in 1977. Although broadly typical of the nineteenth-century romantic novel, *Gathered In* presents an unusual view of illegitimacy and the moral and philosophical problems that confront those involved. Spence shows that illegitimacy can sometimes involve the father as an unwilling victim and a sufferer, and that an illegitimate child can be anxious not for revenge for himself and his betrayed mother but for his father's good reputation and for the welfare of his half-brothers and sisters. Kenneth Oswald, illegitimate son of Scottish gentleman, Norman McDiarmid, loses his mother when he is 10 years old and unknowingly makes the acquaintance of his father, who wishes to provide for his future without upsetting the present McDiarmid family relationship, which full recognition of the boy would entail. Kenneth later joins another benefactor, his uncle, George Oswald, on his large Australian property Tingalpa, an occasion which allows the author to enlarge on the low-born Australian immigrant who has grown to a graceless colonial prosperity on the sheep's back and by ruthlessly grasping enormous tracts of land. Most of the remainder of the novel is set in the colony in the 1860s, where, by a series of remarkable coincidences, Kenneth meets and rescues his half-sister Sybil from a villainous husband; meets, loves and finally marries Edith Gray, daughter of a nearby English gentleman squatter; becomes so firmly entrenched in the favour of his rough-and-ready but essentially good-hearted Uncle George that the latter makes him heir to his colonial wealth; and is wrongfully arrested for the murder of Uncle George's wastrel son Jim, a 'currency lad', but is acquitted when Sybil's husband, the murderer, flees to America. The last scenes occur in England and Scotland, where Edith agrees to marry Kenneth on condition he first restore his mother's reputation and claim justice from his father. Kenneth reverses the usual course of the illegitimacy novel by refusing, but Edith withdraws her condition when Norman McDiarmid is able to show that his own anguish about the situation has, over many years, made abundant recompense for his early lack of judgement. Thus Kenneth is left illegitimate, but, in view of his being finally 'gathered in' to the bosom of his real family, his marriage to Edith, and his inheritance from his uncle, scarcely lamenting.

In spite of its elaborate, circuitous and melodramatic plot, *Gathered In* is not altogether a failure. Some of the Australian station scenes, e.g. the men's hut at Gray's property, are effectively described although there is the usual implication that to be colonial is to be uncouth and crude, whereas to be English is to be instinctively fine and elegant. Spence's own religious doubts, evident in *An Agnostic's Progress* (1884), are solved in the novel. Religion, especially as exemplified in the itinerant bush missionary David Henderson, is shown to be no grim Calvinistic scheme of rewards and punishments but a process where love of God is expressed through a religion of humanity.

GAUNT, Mary (1861–1942), born Chiltern, Victoria, into the distinguished family of Judge William Henry Gaunt, was one of the first two women admitted to the University of Melbourne, although she failed to complete her degree. From the late 1880s she contributed short stories and articles to such journals as the *Argus, Sydney Mail* and the *Australasian*, earning enough to pay her passage for her first visit to Europe in 1890–91. In 1894 she married a widower, Dr Hubert Miller, and settled happily at Warrnambool. Miller's death in 1900 left her penniless, and determined to maintain her independence she left for London in 1901 to seek her fortune as a writer. She was never to return, becoming an inveterate traveller in Europe, Africa, China and Jamaica, settling finally in Italy. She wrote numerous travel books but her forte was fiction; of over twenty published works, six novels and a book of stories concern Australia. In both her fiction and travel books Gaunt attacked the economic and social inequality of women and conventional ideas of marriage. *Dave's Sweetheart* (1894), her first novel and a treatment of the fallen woman theme, follows the familiar Victorian formula, unlike *The Uncounted Cost* (1910), which was so radical in approach that it was excluded by Mudies and the Times Book Club. Gaunt's second and most significant novel, *Kirkham's Find* (1897), has an Australian setting and is the first to deal with the feminist themes that recur throughout her work. The story of a girl's struggle for independence, *Kirkham's Find* celebrates the advantages of the unmarried state for women and criticises their poor educational and work opportunities. *Deadman's* (1898), set on the 1860s goldfields, is a subversive treatment of the conventional Victorian heroine. Several of Gaunt's later novels are set in Africa, as are the three she wrote in collaboration with John Ridgewell Essex 1904–9; her experiences in China, which reinforced her conviction that revolutionary social change was necessary, are reflected in the novel *A*

Wind from the Wilderness (1919), and the travel book *A Woman in China* (1914). Gaunt's remaining novels with Australian settings are *As the Whirlwind Passeth* (1923) and *Joan of the Pilchard* (1930). *The Moving Finger* (1895) is a book of Australian short stories and *The Ends of the Earth* (1915) also contains Australian tales as well as her 'Scrap of Autobiography'. Ian F. McLaren has published the extensive bibliography *Mary Gaunt. A Cosmopolitan Australian* (1986).

'Gavah the Blacksmith', see **O'DOWD, Bernard**; *Tocsin*

GAY, William (1865–97), born Bridge of Weir, Scotland, emigrated to NZ in 1885 and then to Victoria in 1888 in a vain attempt to ward off tuberculosis. He taught briefly at Scotch College, Melbourne, and was a tutor on a Riverina station and later in Melbourne. He spent the last four years of his life in a Bendigo hospital but maintained his keen interest in writing poetry and helped foster literature in the Bendigo area. He published *Sonnets and Other Verses* (1894), *Sonnets* (1896) and *Christ on Olympus and Other Poems* (1896). A miniature edition of his poems was published posthumously in 1910; *The Complete Poetical Works of William Gay*, edited with a memoir by J. Glen Oliphant, appeared in 1911. His best-known individual poems are those which appeal for the establishment of the Australian Commonwealth, i.e. 'Australia 1894', 'Australian Federation' and 'Australia Infelix'. 'Christ on Olympus', a long poem in blank verse, shows the Olympian deities relinquishing their power to the greater God.

GEASON, Susan, see **Crime Fiction**

GEBHARDT, Peter has contributed poetry to several periodicals and has published two collections, *Killing the Old Fool* (1988) and *Secretary to Praise* (1992). Whether grounded in minute natural events as in 'Horizons' and 'The Rock' or in familiar historical ones, as in 'William John Wills Writes his Ending', Gebhardt's compressed lyrics explore life's paradoxes with irony and compassion.

GELLERT, Leon (1892–1977), born Walkerville, SA, was a schoolteacher before he was wounded at Gallipoli. In 1917 he published *Songs of a Campaign* (see War Literature), which won the University of Adelaide's Bundey prize for poetry and established Gellert as the soldier-poet of the day. In eloquent poems such as 'Through a Porthole', 'Patience', 'The Burial', 'The Diggers' and 'Attack at Dawn', Gellert recorded the dignity and courage of the soldier caught haplessly in the futility of war. In 1919 he published *The Isle of San*, a long allegorical poem divided into six dreams with a prologue and an epilogue and numerous songs and sonnets that are used as interludes between the dreams. In 1928 he included the connecting pieces of *The Isle of San* in a booklet, *Desperate Measures*, which is largely concerned with the vicissitudes of domesticity, Gellert having married in 1918. He taught in Sydney after the war before his friendship with Norman Lindsay,

Sydney Ure Smith and Bert Stevens led him into journalism, initially with *Art in Australia*, then with *Home* and later as literary editor, columnist and book reviewer with the *Sydney Morning Herald* and the *Daily Telegraph*. His later publications included the satirical *These Beastly Australians* (1944), *Week after Week* (1953) and *Year after Year* (1956).

Generations of Men, The (1959) an imaginative blend of history and fiction by Judith Wright (q.v.), tells the story of her grandparents, Albert and May Wright, and May Wright's parents and grandparents, early pioneers of the Hunter Valley district of NSW. The book is based largely on diaries of Albert Wright and on letters and personal reminiscences.

GEOGHEGAN, Edward (?1813–?), born Dublin, arrived in Sydney in 1840. A medical student convicted of obtaining goods on false pretences, he was transported for seven years. He became associated with Francis Nesbitt and within a few years produced ten plays, some of which were adaptations. They include 'Ravenswood' (1843), 'The Last Days of Pompeii' (1844), 'A Christmas Carol' (1844), *The Currency Lass* (q.v., 1844), 'The Hibernian Father' (q.v., 1844), 'Captain Kyd' (1845), 'Lafitte the Pirate' (1845) and 'The Royal Masquer' (1845). As a convict subject to prohibitions in the theatre, Geoghegan was inhibited from publicly claiming authorship of his plays and, in addition, was accused of plagiarism in 'The Hibernian Father'. Geoghegan obtained his freedom in 1846 and later moved to Melbourne where possibly his last play, 'A Trip to Geelong', was produced in 1861.

GEORGE, Rob (1950–), born Mannum, SA, was educated at Adelaide University, where he became interested in writing for the stage. In 1973 he helped to form the Circle Theatre Company for which he wrote, acted and directed until it disbanded in 1977. Closely asociated with the Fringe of the Adelaide Festival, he was also a founder of Adelaide's Stage Company and has written extensively for film, radio and television. His plays and revues include 'Prompt' (1973), 'Les' (1974), 'Snookered' (1974), 'Full Bored' (1975), 'Stairway to the Stars' (1976), 'Lofty' (1977), 'Errol Flynn's Great Big Adventure Book for Boys' (1977), 'Let's Twist Again' (1978), 'Grabbing It' (1979), *Sandy Lee Live at Nui Dat* (performed 1981, published 1983), 'Percy and Rose' (1982), 'Follies' (1982), 'Follies Vulgare' (1982), *The Dynamic Duo* (1985), and 'The Humble Doctor' (1986). His television script 'The First Ninety Days' won an Awgie in 1981 and at the 1979 Edinburgh Festival 'Errol Flynn' won an award for the Best Fringe production. Of his plays for the stage the best known are 'Percy and Rose', based on the relationship between the composer Percy Grainger and his mother, and *Sandy Lee Live at Nui Dat*, an exploration of the impact of the Vietnam War on Australia. George has also written the children's novels *Captain Johnno* (1988), based on his series for television, and *You & Me & Uncle Bob* (1993).

Geraldton Express, a weekly newspaper, began publication in WA in 1878 as the *Victorian Express*; in 1894 it became the *Geraldton Express and Murchison Goldfields News*, in 1897 the *Geraldton Express and Murchison and Yalgoo Goldfields Chronicler*, in 1929 the *Geraldton Guardian and Express* and in 1948 *The Geraldton Guardian*. Usually referred to as the *Geraldton Express*, or the *Express*, it became in the 1890s one of the most important goldfields newspapers, identifying with the working man and aggressively championing the cause of the miners. Its solid core of literary content was largely due to its energetic and progressive editors and journalists, among whom were Alfred Carson, John Drew, C. Andrée Hayward and F.C.B Vosper. In 1880 the *Express* introduced a regular literary supplement which reprinted literary material from the newspapers of the eastern States and overseas. In an editorial in January 1896 Hayward assessed Australian literature, especially the work of the *Bulletin* writers; he also held regular literary competitions for local writers, the material from which was printed in the *Express's* Christmas numbers.

GERARD, Edwin Field ('Gerardy', 'Trooper Gerardy') (1891–1965), born Yunta, SA, worked on the WA goldfields and later served with the AIF at Gallipoli and in the campaigns in the desert. Under the pseudonyms 'Gerardy' and 'Trooper Gerardy' (see War Literature), he contributed poems about the war to journals such as the *Bulletin* and published two volumes of poetry, *The Road to Palestine and Other Verses* (1918) and *Australian Light Horse Ballads and Rhymes* (1919). Sometimes dubbed 'the laureate of the Light Horsemen', Gerard produced in poems such as 'The Horse That Died for Me', 'El Maghara', 'South of Gaza' and 'Riding Song' his most vigorous and effective verse. After the war he was a journalist, then a farmer, and wrote prolifically for the *Bulletin* in verses that reflected nostalgically on the vanished rural life of his youth.

GERSTAECKER, Friedrich (1816–72), born Hamburg, Germany, came to Australia in 1851 by way of the Californian goldfields and various South Sea islands with an established reputation as a novelist and writer of travel books. His stay of less than a year in Australia was hectic; it included an unsuccessful attempt to travel down the Murray River in a homemade canoe, a tramp of 700 miles across country to Adelaide, and a visit to the Bathurst goldfields in NSW. His writings on Australia include a handbook for German immigrants, *Nord-und-Sud Australien: Ein Handbuch fur Auswanderer* (1849); *Narrative of a Journey round the World* (1853), a vivid description of his activities here; *The Two Convicts* (1857), the romantic story of a bushranger which was serialised in the *Examiner and Melbourne Weekly News* (1859–60); and *Im Busch* (1864), a story of the goldfields. An Australian background is also used in several of his other novels. He translated into German Charles Rowcroft's *Tales of the Colonies* (1843).

Getting of Wisdom, The, a novel by 'Henry Handel Richardson' (q.v.), was first published in 1910 and was produced as a film in 1977. Based on 'Richardson's' personal experience as a boarder at the Presbyterian Ladies' College, Melbourne, 1883–87, the novel consists of a series of graphically realised scenes which present the various stages of Laura Rambotham's growth in self and worldly knowledge. At the same time she is unconsciously developing a theory of fiction that she will later use as a writer. At home with her hard-working widowed mother, her sister Pin, and her two little brothers, Laura is used to being dominant, but at school she is immediately subjected to ridicule and hostility both because of her name and her unusual clothes. Although the chilly reception of Mrs Gurley, the awesome lady superintendent, and of the teachers adds to the load of misery she feels in the first six weeks, Laura begins to value life at school for its indirect lessons in experience. One of the first she learns, after an unseemly display of her musical virtuosity, is that 'the unpardonable sin is to vary from the common mould'. Her sense of inner difference is accentuated by her reaction to the public expulsion of Annie Johns, a classmate, for stealing; Laura, who understands Annie's motive better than 'nice-minded girls', is less shocked by the crime than by its punishment and her own thrilled response to its drama. Sex appears to be another area in which she differs from her schoolmates, Laura having no talent for and little real interest in attracting masculine admirers. Anxious to enhance her prestige, however, she invents a romance with the curate, Mr Shepherd. Invited to spend a weekend at his home, she discovers the pedestrian facts about Mr Shepherd, that he is bad-tempered and unattractive, but is unable to resist further opportunities to embellish her passionate tale. Eventually exposed when another girl also visits the Shepherds' home, Laura is completely ostracised and endures a period of intense misery. A seaside holiday is a healing experience, but back at school Laura disciplines herself in socially acceptable behaviour, now bitterly aware that 'the majority is always in the right'. Entry to the prestigious literary society develops her awareness of the differences between literal truth and the truth of fiction, and a deep friendship with an older girl, Evelyn Soutter, who soon leaves school, convinces Laura of the eternal 'fleetingness of things'. Her final lesson is about God; unprepared for her final examinations she fervently seeks His help and is rewarded by being given an opportunity to cheat, which she takes. Deep resentment of God as a pitiless Being succeeds this experience. Laura leaves school for the last time with the 'uncomfortable sense of being a square peg which fitted into none of the round holes of her world', although the narrator hints that she will ultimately find the right one. Her immediate response, however, is to celebrate her freedom by running with complete abandon down the avenue of a public park until she is lost to sight.

GIBBS, May, see *The Oxford Companion to Australian Children's Literature* (1993), pp. 180–1.

GIBSON, G.H. (George Herbert) ('Ironbark') (1846–1921), born Plymouth, England, was a solicitor when he migrated to NZ in 1869 and thence in 1874 to Sydney, where in 1876 he joined the Department of Lands. His work as an inspector in that department took him to many outback stations, where he gained the knowledge of the bush that informs the light-hearted and lively ballads he published under the pseudonym 'Ironbark'. His books of verse are *Southerly Busters* (1878), *Ironbark Chips and Stockwhip Cracks* (1893) and *Ironbark Splinters from the Australian Bush* (1912), the last containing some of the poems from the earlier volumes. He is also the author of *Old Friends under New Aspects* (1883), an unusual depiction of characters from the Old Testament.

GIBSON, Ross (1956–), a graduate of the universities of Queensland and London, has written an analysis of changing literary perceptions of Australia, *The Diminishing Paradise* (1984). Concentrating on the earliest period of European history in Australia, on European imaginings of the great south land prior to settlement and on the inland explorations of the 1830s and 1840s, Gibson explores the concept of a diminishing paradise, the contradictions between actual experiences of Australia by settlers, convicts and explorers and the perennial dream of Utopia which has shaped anticipations of the country. He finds a purgatorial myth embedded in Australian culture, a theme of necessary suffering, which infuses the journals of such explorers as Sturt, Mitchell and Eyre and runs through some of the novels of Patrick White. He has also written *South of the West. Postcolonialism and the Narrative Construction of Australia* (1992), a collection of essays on diverse representations of Australia in literature, art and film which begins with the proposition that 'Australia is presently an unsettled load ballasted with a clutter of cargo – the mythologies of nationalism and colonialism, rural romanticism, hedonist modernism and wildstyle postmodernism'.

GILBERT, John (?1842–65) was a bushranger who took part in about forty armed hold-ups and robberies in NSW 1862–65, often working with Frank Gardiner and Ben Hall (qq.v.). Gilbert was the model for Hulbert in 'Rolf Boldrewood's' *Robbery Under Arms* (1888); his career is the subject of the anonymous satire, 'The Diverting History of John Gilbert', and his death is romanticised in A.B. Paterson's ballad 'How Gilbert Died'. Edgar F. Penzig published *A Real Flash Cove: The Story of the Bushranger John Gilbert* (1983), revised as *Happy Jack* in 1990.

GILBERT, Kevin (1933–93), born Condobolin, NSW, to an Irish father and part-Aboriginal mother, who both died when he was 7, was brought up in welfare homes and by relatives. After a limited education he worked through his teens as an itinerant labourer in towns of western NSW. Married at an early age, and with two children, Gilbert was found guilty in 1957 of the murder of his wife after a domestic argument and was sentenced to life imprisonment. In prison Gilbert, until then almost illiterate, became interested in art and literature. He soon showed a considerable talent for both lino cuts and painting, and his work from prison was exhibited in 1970 by the Australian Council for the Arts. In 1971, after fourteen years in prison, Gilbert was paroled. His play *The Cherry Pickers* (q.v., 1988), a story of Aboriginal seasonal workers, written while he was in prison and staged in Sydney in 1971, earned Gilbert the distinction of being the first Aboriginal playwright to have a play performed in Australia. In 1972 he became associated with the Purfleet Aboriginal Reserve near Taree, NSW, where he instituted community aid projects and worked as a community developer. He also established the Kalari Aboriginal Art Gallery, an experiment in the training of young Aboriginal artists. Gilbert rapidly became active in the wider Aboriginal cause, editing periodicals such as *Alchuringa* and *Black Australian News*, canvassing the federal government for a national inquiry into Aboriginal education, and working for the Centre for Continuing Research into Aboriginal Affairs at Monash University, Melbourne. In addition to *The Cherry Pickers* he published several volumes of poetry, *End of Dreamtime* (1971), *People Are Legends* (1978) and *The Blackside* (1990). His poetry is protest verse, displaying his anger against White society in 'End of Dreamtime', 'People Are Legends' 'Chained'; the indifferent treatment of the Aboriginal people in 'Trying to Save Joan Ella'; the degradation brought into their lives by the hopelessness of their common future in 'Goomee Jack'; the need for violence in order to gain basic land rights in 'Land Claims'; his own personal situation in 'Epitaph: Upon Expiration of the Aspirations of an Aborigine' and the tragedy of the part-Aborigine in 'Inhabitants of the Third World'. His contentious poem 'To My Cousin, Evonne Cawley' in the *Bulletin* (30 September 1980) attacked what he saw as her lack of involvement in Aboriginal problems. Gilbert's main political tract is the prose work *Because a White Man'll Never Do It* (1973), the chief purpose of which was to procure land rights for the Aborigines so that dignity and self-esteem could be restored and a total Aboriginal community re-established. *Living Black* (1978), a collection of interviews conducted by Gilbert with Aborigines from all parts of Australia, won a National Book Council Award in 1978. In *Living Black*, which attempted to give an authentic view of what it meant to be Black, Gilbert incorporated his conversations with Aborigines of all types, urban, reserve, tribal and fringe-dwellers. He proposed a programme of physical and spiritual compensation for 200 years of deprivation, a programme based on the granting of land rights and a regeneration of Aboriginal culture. In 1988 he published the anthology *Inside Black Australia*, which he described as 'the first collection of contemporary Aboriginal oral history from an Aboriginal viewpoint'. His introduction examined the nature of Black poetry and culture and recounted White mismanagement of the Aboriginal situation. *The Blackside* is a composite of *People Are Legends* and his work in the decade following that publication in 1978, with a section of photographs illustrating Aboriginal political activities. In 1992 he published *Child's Dreaming*, a

view of the bush through a Black child's eyes, illustrated by the photographs of Eleanor Williams. Awarded the Human Rights Award for literature in 1988, Gilbert returned it saying he could not accept it until Aborigines were granted human rights. In 1992 he was awarded one of the four-year fellowships to artists of high distinction granted by the federal government.

GILES, Barbara (1912–), born Manchester, England, came to Australia in 1923. She had to postpone her education for some years because of family circumstances but later spent some years teaching in Victoria. She was also involved in migrant education as a teacher and has written about migrants and their experiences in her poetry. She was co-ordinating editor of the magazine *Luna* for eight years and a founding member of Pariah Press Co-operative. A tutor of creative writing and a long-time reviewer for the ABC, Giles has published five books of poetry, all since her mid-sixties, *Eve Rejects Apple* (1978), *Earth and Solitude* (1985), *The Hag in the Mirror* (1989), *A Savage Coast* (1993) and, with Roy Fuller and Adrian Rumble, *Upright Downfall* (1983). *Earth and Solitude*, with its characteristic Giles eye for detail, is about the difficulty of the farming life. *The Hag in the Mirror* has many poems dealing with the mixed emotions of age, the passing of time and the approach of death but Giles, while willing to explore all the attitudes available to those confronting the later stages of life and even death, is positive and forceful in her reactions. Her intimate, simple, lyrical, witty, laconic and occasionally angry poetry carries much appeal. She won the FAW John Shaw Neilson Poetry Award in 1972. Giles has edited and co-edited several anthologies of verse for children and is well known for her children's novels, most of which have a strong element of fantasy. Her children's books include *Bicycles Don't Fly* (1982), *Jack in the Bush* (1983), *Alex is My Friend* (1984), about a lonely child who finds a secret room and a secret diary which helps unravel mysteries of long-ago events, *Flying Backwards* (1985), *Bill* (1988) and *Gone Wild* (1990).

GILES, Ernest (1835–97), born Bristol, England, came to Australia in 1850 and was on the Victorian goldfields in 1852. In the early 1860s he explored the pastoral potential of the western areas of NSW beyond the Darling River, but his chief ambition was to make an overland crossing to WA. In spite of several failures in the early 1870s to find a route from Central Australia to the coast of WA, Giles ultimately crossed from SA to WA in 1875. His expeditions added greatly to the knowledge of the western half of the continent and his journals and published works are among the most perceptive and literary of the writings of the explorers. He published *Geographic Travels in Central Australia from 1872 to 1874* (1875), *The Journal of a Forgotten Expedition* (1880), and *Australia Twice Traversed* (1889). Geoffrey Dutton wrote *Australia's Last Explorer: Ernest Giles* (1970) and extracts from Giles's journals are included in Kathleen Fitzpatrick's selection *Australian Explorers* (1958). Ray Ericksen's

Ernest Giles: Explorer and Traveller 1835–1897 (1978) won a National Book Council Award.

GILES, Zeny (1937–   ), born Sydney, of a Cypriot father and a Kastellorizian mother, was educated at the universities of Sydney and Newcastle and has worked as a teacher at secondary and tertiary level. She has published a novel, *Between Two Worlds* (1981), a collection of short stories, *Miracle of the Waters* (1989), and edited, with Norman Talbot, a collection of stories from the Hunter Valley, *Contrast and Relief* (1981). She has also written three plays, 'The Bargain', 'Dance for the Prodigal' and 'Zorica', and poetry, which has been published in periodicals and anthologies. *Between Two Worlds*, based on her mother's experiences as a Greek migrant child in Australia of the 1920s, is a sensitive representation of the difficulties faced by immigrants from a different culture and of the particular difficulties of their children, claimed by markedly contrasting traditions. The stories of *Miracle of the Waters* are linked by their setting, the Moree hot baths in inland NSW, by the common experiences of cultural difference of those who frequent them, and who look back to earlier existences in Greece, Hungary, Yugoslavia or Poland and by the recurrence of certain characters. Running through the collection is the theme of change, whether curative or destructive. Giles won the Ann Dankwerts Memorial Prize in 1980 and the *Age* Tabloid Short Story Competition Prize in 1981.

GILL, S.T. (Samuel Thomas) (1818–80), born Somerset, England, came to SA in 1839 and established a portrait studio in Adelaide. In 1846 he accompanied J.A. Horrocks's expedition to Spencer Gulf; his diary of that journey was published in the *South Australian Gazette and Colonial Register* (1846), and many of his drawings from the expedition remain in the National Gallery of SA. Gill is represented in George French Angas's *South Australia Illustrated* (1847) by a scene in Hindley Street, Adelaide, and by a scene of the departure of Charles Sturt on his 1844 expedition. In 1852 Gill visited the Victorian goldfields: twenty-four lithographed sketches by him comprise *Victoria Gold Diggings and Diggers As They Are* (1853); many were included as illustrations in John Sherer's *The Gold-Finder of Australia* (1853). Gill's *Scenery in and around Sydney* was published in 1856; he also published *The Australian Sketchbook* (1865), a popular book of lithographed views depicting aspects of Australian rural life (see Overlander). In 1869 he was commissioned by the Melbourne Public Library to do forty sketches of the Victorian goldfields of 1852–53 (see Gold). Selections of his work include Geoffrey Dutton's *The Paintings of S.T. Gill* (1962) and J.E.B. Curry's *The Goldfields Illustrated: The Sketches of S.T. Gill* (1972). K.M. Bowden published the biographical *Samuel Thomas Gill, Artist* (1971) and Michael Cannon edited *The Victorian Goldfields 1852–53: An Original Album* (1982, reprinted 1992) which is Gill's original collection.

GILLEN, Francis James, see **SPENCER, Sir Walter**

GILLESPIE, Bruce, see **Science Fiction**

GILLMORE, Terry (1945–   ) lives in rural Victoria and has contributed poetry to numerous periodicals and has published two collections, *Further, Poems 1966–1976* (1977) and *Surviving the Shadow* (1990).

GILMORE, Dame Mary (1864–1962) was born Mary Jean Cameron at Cotta Walla near Goulburn, NSW. After a bush childhood with sporadic formal schooling she completed her education by assisting in small schools in the Cootamundra, Wagga and Albury districts of NSW. In 1888–89 she taught in the mining town of Silverton, near Broken Hill, where close contact with the militant, working-class community aroused her lifelong interest in the labour movement. In 1890–95 she taught at Neutral Bay and Stanmore in Sydney and became involved in the developing radicalism of the day by supporting the maritime and shearers' strikes of the early 1890s. In those years her friendship with Henry Lawson began and she was influenced by three men, William Lane, John Farrell and A.G. Stephens, who, she said, 'shaped my mind and my life'. In 1896 she joined Lane's New Australia venture in Paraguay and in May 1897, at the Cosme settlement, married a Victorian shearer, William Alexander Gilmore. They returned to Australia in 1902 and settled to an isolated farming existence in the Casterton district of western Victoria. In October 1903 her poetry was featured by A.G. Stephens in the Red Page of the *Bulletin*, and in 1908 she began to edit the Women's Page of the Sydney *Worker*, a task which occupied her until 1931. In 1910 her first volume of poetry, *Marri'd and Other Verses*, was published, and in 1912, when her husband joined his brother on the land in north Queensland, she and her son went back to Sydney. Her campaigns for the welfare of the young and old, sick and helpless, depressed and under-privileged, and her irate and constantly expressed disgust with privilege and corruption in high places filled the pages of the *Worker* and other newspapers for many years. In the two decades 1920–40, she published six volumes of poetry and three of prose. In 1937, in recognition of her literary achievement and her community and social activities, and as a tribute to her growing national status, she was made DBE, an honour which she cherished. During the tense months of 1942 after Singapore fell and the Japanese island-hopped towards Australia, her defiant and well-publicised poem 'No Foe Shall Gather Our Harvest' (q.v.), was a timely booster to public morale. In her remaining years, perched in her tiny flat in the heart of Sydney's bohemian Kings Cross, she continued her writing and encouragement of other writers, her social crusading, and gathering of the diminishing store of pioneer lore and legend. William Dobell's controversial portrait of her was unveiled for her ninety-second birthday in 1957. Her last years passed amid growing public acclaim; her death was mourned by a ceremonial state funeral through the streets of Sydney.

Mary Gilmore's earliest poems, *Marri'd and Other Verses*, are mainly spontaneous reactions, in a colloquial style, to the joys and sorrows of life's daily round; the short, lively lyrics are interspersed with occasional outbursts against injustice and inhumanity. *The Passionate Heart* (q.v., 1918), with its emphasis on the desolation of war, is more mature verse. In *The Tilted Cart* (1925), *The Wild Swan* (q.v., 1930) and *Under the Wilgas* (1932), and in her prose anecdotes and reminiscences, *Old Days: Old Ways* (q.v., 1934) and *More Recollections* (1935), her interest in re-creating pioneer times and her concern with the despoiling of the land and destruction of the Aboriginal tribes are paramount. *Battlefields* (1939) contains her most strongly radical verse. 'The Baying Hounds' depicts the customary Gilmore stance, 'There was no hunted one/With whom I did not run', while 'Contest I Ask' affirms her lifelong belief, 'Better to wounded lie/Than undeclared to die.' In the inscription to her final volume, *Fourteen Men* (q.v., 1954), published when she was almost 90, she faces life's final encounter with the calm judgement that death is 'the last thing left to defeat'. Mary Gilmore's best poetry insists on love, courage and selflessness, and enshrines those values in some fine lyrics. Dymphna Cusack, T. Inglis Moore, Barrie Ovenden and Walter Stone compiled *Mary Gilmore: A Tribute* (1965); W.H. Wilde and T. Inglis Moore edited *Letters of Mary Gilmore* (1980) and Wilde wrote the biography *Courage a Grace: A Biography of Dame Mary Gilmore* (1988).

One-woman dramatic interpretations of the life and work of Mary Gilmore include Theatre ACT's production 'When Butter Was Sixpence a Pound' (Joan Murray, 1983), Melbourne Theatre Company's 'To Botany Bay on a Bondi Tram' (Beverley Dunn, 1984), and the Queensland Art Council's touring season of the same production in 1994. Mary Gilmore is one of the two Australian writers (A.B. Paterson is the other) featured on the 1993 ten-dollar note.

Ginger Meggs, Australia's most famous 'boy' from the 1920s to the 1960s, was the comic strip creation of J.C. Bancks (q.v.). A small red-headed boy in a black waistcoat, he began life in November 1921 as a googly bowler in the first episode of the strip 'Us Fellers'; by the time he became Ginger Meggs in April 1922 he was the central character; had acquired a girl friend, Minnie Peters, and a rival for her affections, Eddie Coogan; and had gathered about him a gang of mates including Benny and Ocker Stevens. For the next thirty years, weekly in the Sydney Sunday *Sun* and other newspapers and annually in *The Sunbeams Book, Adventures of Ginger Meggs* (1924–59), he experienced under Bancks both joy and tribulation. The joys included cricket, football, fishing, fighting, billy cart derbies, 'wagging' school and toughening up curly-headed 'sooks' named Clarence, Cuthbert and Gerald. The tribulations included having to run messages (and the gauntlet of Tiger Kelly), brushes with the law over broken windows, with schoolteachers named Flogger and Canehard over his absence from school, and with his parents, John and Sarah Meggs, over almost any issue. Although the basic ingredients were established in its first year, the success of the strip was consolidated by its visual improvement over the years. Throughout all his adventures Ginger remained sturdily optimistic, self-confident, cunning and quick-thinking, a combination of larrikin, battler, philosopher and humorist. 'Us Fellers' changed its name to 'Ginger Meggs' in 1939, by which time the strip had become the first Australian one to be syndicated overseas. After Bancks's death in 1952 it was drawn by Ron Vivian (1953–74), after Vivian by Lloyd Piper (1974–84), and James Kemsley (1984–). Ginger has been the subject of several children's books, a pantomime written by Ray Lawler in the 1950s, the play, 'Ginge's Last Stand', by Ken Horler (1975) and an Australian film (1982). A selection from the Bancks years was published as *The Golden Years of Ginger Meggs 1921–1952* (1978).

GIPPS, Sir George (1791–1847), after whom the region of Gippsland in Victoria is named, was born in Kent, England, entered the British Army in 1809, and was appointed the ninth governor of NSW in 1837. During his eight years in office, 1838–46, he presided over great changes in the Colony: the cessation of transportation to NSW in 1840 and Alexander Maconochie's penal experiments at Norfolk Island; an increase in migration which almost doubled the population and made more urgent the need to establish a satisfactory education system; demands for separation by the colonists at Port Phillip; the beginnings of self-government through the establishment of a partly elected Legislative Council, which increased tensions between Gipps and the colonists; and turmoil over relationships between the colonists and the Aborigines, most dramatically illustrated by the Myall Creek massacre of 1838. A governor whose contemporary unpopularity during difficult times influenced subsequent judgements of him, Gipps had most trouble with the squatters, who sought security of tenure for their runs and objected to Gipps's attempts to recover land rents in order to provide funds to assist immigration. In 1844, after the announcement of proposals which would implement Gipps's policies, the *Atlas* (q.v.) began publication in Sydney in the squatting interest; as part of the campaign the *Atlas* published the verse satires of Robert Lowe, notably 'Songs of the Squatter', and William Forster. Forster's 'The Devil and the Governor', published in the *Atlas* on 17 May 1845 (republished in *The Unsparing Scourge*, ed. Vincent O'Sullivan, 1988), depicts a visit by the Devil to his friend Gipps and their discussion of contemporary problems. Samuel Prout Hill published *Monody on the Death of Sir George Gipps* (1847). The correspondence between Gipps as governor of NSW and Charles La Trobe, newly appointed as superintendent of the Port Phillip district, was edited by A.G.L. Shaw in 1989.

GLASKIN, Gerald Marcus (1923–), born Perth, WA, served in the Second World War with both the RAN and the RAAF. He began writing short fiction while in hospital during the war; after the war he combined motor merchandising and stockbroking with writing, but became a full-time writer from 1959, spending considerable periods travelling and living outside Australia. Glaskin's first novel, *A World of Our Own* (1955), examines the attempts by a number of ex-servicemen to cope with the post-war world; praised in England and a best-seller in Europe, it won the Commonwealth Literary Award for 1957. His other novels include *A Minor Portrait* (1957); *A Change of Mind* (1959); *A Lion in the Sun* (1960), which he considers his first important novel; *The Beach of Passionate Love* (1961), set in Malaysia; *A Waltz through the Hills* (1961, produced for television in 1967); *Flight to Landfall* (1963); *O Love, O Loneliness* (1964); *No End to the Way* (1965), under the pseudonym 'Neville Jackson'; and *The Man Who Didn't Count* (1965). He has also published short stories, *A Small Selection* (1962) and *The Road to Nowhere* (1967); non-fiction (parapsychology), *Windows of the Mind: The Christos Experience* (1974), *Worlds Within: Probing the Christos Experience* (1976) and *A Door to Eternity: Proving the Christos Experience* (1979); and autobiographical works, *A Bird in My Hands* (1967), *Two Women*, comprising *Turn on the Heat* and *The Eaves of Night* (1975), and *One Way to Wonderland: Letters to a Pen-Friend* (1984). He has written screenplays of several of his novels, a travel book, *The Land That Sleeps* (1961), on Australia's empty North, and numerous prize-winning short stories.

Glass Canoe, The, a novel by David Ireland (q.v.), was first published in 1976 and won the Miles Franklin Award for that year. Narrated by a young golf-course greenkeeper, nicknamed Meat Man because he is sexually well endowed, *The Glass Canoe* describes the customs of an urban tribe of drinkers, who regularly congregate at their watering hole, the Southern Cross pub in an outer area of Sydney, referred to as The Mead. The characters, whose stories or random experiences form much of the kaleidoscopic structure of the novel, include Ernie, who first suffers excessive grief when his mother dies and then horribly murders a girl who appears to be threatening his job; the Great Lover, who combines a prodigious, indiscriminate sexual appetite and submissive domesticity; Aussie Bob, the ex-Englishman who ultimately loses all his four children in car accidents; Serge, the Russian pub fighter of unerring aim and unpredictable anger, who has been barred from the pub although no one has been brave enough to tell him; Eh, a Queenslander who never got over it and has had a wandering but complicated life; and Alky Jack, Meat Man's surrogate father, whose bitterly wise pronouncements on modern life find a willing but uncomprehending audience at the Southern Cross. Alternating with their individual experience is the communal life of the pub, a solid shelter against the so-called life outside of jobs, weddings, dismissals, babies, hunger and defeat. The pub offers 'A sort of past solidified in masonry. The traffic tried to run by all the faster to stay in the present or the past might grab them. But to us, our tomb was where life was: outside was a world fit only to die in.'

Meat Man perceives his tribe as the exploited, hunted victims of an urban world, whose only escape is the glass canoe, the schooner of beer: 'wage and small enterprise sheep and cattle amongst the unattainable riches of civilisation; among tall, unfamiliar buildings, unimaginable processes, incomprehensible aims, scratching a living on the edge of the educated world.' Contrasting with his perspective is that of Sibley, his old schoolfriend, who earnestly documents the anti-social attitudes of the drinkers for his Ph.D. thesis in social psychology. As the narrative progresses, it is clear that much of life at the Southern Cross and outside is mysterious to the stoically acquiescent and perhaps wilfully blind Meat Man. Sibley suddenly disappears, the link between his continued absence and a malodorous beer keg apparently unperceived by Meat Man; a stranger, Vivian, hangs himself in an outer shed for love; Liz the Large is declared dead by her doctor but survives long enough to have the child she did not know she was carrying; Meat Man's girl-friend, whom he calls My Darling, appears to have another life from which he is divided; the brain-damaged victim of a savage mugging leaps on the roof of the Southern Cross and tries to drive the pub like a car; women unexpectedly demand feats of sexual prowess or casually offer themselves in payment for trivial favours; a pub widow hurls her husband's ashes into the bar. Alky Jack's pronouncements on the 'modern cult of animalism and violence' and the hopelessness of attempting to cast off 'the monster on our backs ... absurd, gross, degrading' appear more and more justified by the pattern of events, which culminate in an extended, epic brawl with all the attributes of a ritualistic, tribal blood-letting.

GLASSOP, Lawson (1913–66), born Lawson in the Blue Mountains, NSW, began a career in journalism with the *Newcastle Morning Herald*. In 1940 he joined the AIF serving in the Middle East, where he worked on an army newspaper. After the war he joined the *Sydney Morning Herald* and was a war correspondent in Korea 1950–51. From 1951 to 1960 he was with the Sydney *Daily Mirror*, Sydney *Truth* and Adelaide *Truth* and from 1960 was a columnist and feature writer for the Adelaide *Advertiser*. Glassop's chief literary work was the novel *We Were the Rats* (1944, see War Literature); he also published a children's book, *Susan and the Bogeywomp* (1947), *Lucky Palmer* (1949), a novel about a gambler, and *The Rats in New Guinea* (1963), a sequel to the earlier novel. *We Were the Rats* was banned as obscene by the NSW government in 1946; a modified version of the book was published in 1961. The hero of the novel, a cricketer and furniture salesman, enlists in the Australian Army and after initial training in Australia goes to the Middle East, where he participates in the siege of Tobruk. Later he has a period in Cairo, returns to Australia, marries, and resumes his soldiering in the island campaigns of the Pacific War. A factual account of army life in wartime and an accurate reflection of army language and attitudes, *We Were the Rats* is reportage rather than a creative novel. The crude language, the repellent details of army life, and the blatant sexuality of the book led the appeals judge to describe much of it as 'just plain filthy', an assessment hotly contested by its numerous defenders, including the American writer John Dos Passos. The novel's realistic characterisation and treatment of the extraordinary experiences common to many

Australian volunteer soldiers make *We Were the Rats* a significant addition to Australian war literature.

GLEESON, James (1915–), born Sydney, is one of Australia's best-known painters and art critics, frequently described as Australia's first surrealist. Art critic of the Sydney *Sun* newspaper 1949–76, he became director of the Sir William Dobell Art Foundation in 1971. He has been awarded the OAM and made AO and received an honorary D.Litt. from Macquarie University. Prominent in the debates on surrealism in the 1930s and 1940s, Gleeson contributed verse to such journals as *Angry Penguins, A Comment* and *Stream* and articles to *Art in Australia.* He also produced two groups of poem-drawings in 1938 and 1976, all using poetry written 1938–43 and creating dual written and visual images. His *Selected Poems*, drawn from the same group of poems, was published in 1993. His other publications include *William Dobell* (1964), *Masterpieces of Australian Painting* (1969), *Colonial Painters 1788–1880* (1971), *Impressionist Painters 1881–1930* (1971), and *Robert Klippel* (1983). His work featured prominently in the 1993 exhibition 'Surrealism: Revolution by Night', which appeared in Canberra, Brisbane and Sydney. In the same year the establishment of the James Gleeson Foundation, to which the artist is bequeathing nearly all his art works and possessions, was announced. Gleeson's achievement as an artist is described in Renée Free's *James Gleeson* (1993).

'Glen of the Whiteman's Grave, The', a narrative poem, was first published by Henry Kendall (q.v.) in an undated booklet (?1865); it was later published in *Leaves from Australian Forests* (1869) as 'The Glen of Arrawatta' and republished with minor variations as 'Orara' in 1881. The tale of a lone settler murdered by natives, Kendall's poem is similar in theme to the earlier Charles Harpur narrative 'The Creek of the Four Graves' (q.v.).

GODDARD, Francis, see **MACNAMARA, Francis**

Going Down Swinging, an annual literary magazine begun in 1980 with Myron Lysenko as founding editor (now edited by Kevin Brophy and Lysenko) is an anthology of contemporary writing aimed especially at publishing the work of new, young or innovative writers.

Golconda trilogy is a series of novels by Vance Palmer (q.v.) which centres on the history of Macy Donovan, who has affinities with the politician E.G. Theodore (q.v.) and his rise from small union organiser to premier of Queensland. The series comprises *Golconda* (1948), *Seedtime* (1957) and *The Big Fellow* (1959). *Golconda*, set in a new mining settlement in the Queensland outback just after the First World War, traces the beginnings of Donovan's career. Brought up in the Maranoa district, Donovan has come to Golconda as a water-carter, but a chance meeting with Frank Mahony, a union organiser, changes the direction of his life. In his new role of local union official, Donovan soon becomes dominant on the mining field but is less fortunate in his private life, especially in his inability to establish a relationship with the girl who most strongly attracts him, Neda Varnek. Neda, a sculptor with unconventional attitudes stemming partly from her childhood association with Aborigines, is more powerfully drawn by the primitive landscape, especially by the huge mountain, Golconda, than by its inhabitants. Donovan passes through a period of depression when he discovers that Mahony has been dismissed from his union office for embezzling funds, and when his brief liaison with Carita Keighley, the wife of one of the company managers, comes to an end. Neda's mother, May Varnek, dies and Neda leaves for the interior with Farelli, an Italian bird-catcher, but soon returns disillusioned. Mahony also returns to Golconda, where he falls desperately ill with pneumonia and is nursed back to health by a schoolteacher, Dora Venn, whom he subsequently marries. Donovan wins preselection as the Labor Party candidate in the forthcoming State election and gains the seat. On the plane that takes him to Brisbane is Neda Varnek, bound for Sydney to pursue a career in art. The novel is distinguished by Palmer's evocation of the brooding, dominating mountain, and by the well-realised panorama of diverse individuals who live round its foot. One of the most striking of these is Christy Baughan, an old gouger who has been with William Lane in the New Australia venture.

Seedtime picks up Donovan's history after a gap of two years. He appears to be a failure in Brisbane, given to wild drinking sprees, and has been stabbed in a brawl with an Italian he took to be Farelli. He is admitted to a hospital where he meets Dr Hugh McCoy and his sister-in-law, Nurse Judy Hegarty. Judy's fast-developing love for Donovan fails to move him, although her influence, together with his involvement with the McCoy and Hegarty families, has the effect of widening his aspirations. Meanwhile his political career reaches a crisis when he challenges his party chief and premier, Lambert, over a strike in the sugar industry and is soundly defeated. He returns to Golconda to ensure preselection for the next election; is warmly welcomed by the mining community, especially by Frank and Dora Mahony who now have a son, Peter; wins the seat with an increased majority; is reconciled with Lambert; and becomes engaged to Kitty, Judy's elder sister. Judy leaves to join the Flying Doctor Service and Frank Mahony dies of pneumonia.

The Big Fellow opens twenty years later just after the Second World War. Donovan is now at the height of his power, premier of his State and temporary leader of his party, but he is under threat both in his private and his public life. Neda Varnek comes back from a successful stay abroad and asks Donovan to help Leo, her son by Farelli, who is in a reformatory. His revived feeling for Neda makes Donovan more aware of the flaws in his family life. His sense of disappointment is deepened by the decision of Peter Mahony, whom he has virtually adopted and who has been working as his secretary, to study medicine. At the same time his political career is threatened by a scandal about the sale of government mines. Although a royal commission later clears him, he loses preselection for the Golconda seat. A peaceful interlude with Neda is disrupted by the return of Leo and their relationship is later shattered by Leo's violent confrontation with Donovan and subsequent death in a car smash. Neda leaves Queensland. Donovan's tired marriage is patched up and he leaves Golconda for a new career in federal politics.

Gold was officially discovered in NSW in April 1851, in Victoria in July of the same year and in Queensland in 1867. The rush to the Kimberley district of WA began in 1886, and in 1892–93 the rich Coolgardie and Kalgoorlie fields of that State were discovered. The mass movements to the various goldfields were known as the gold rushes, the alluvial goldfields were known as 'the diggings', and the gold-seekers as 'diggers', a word which has carried into this century as a colloquialism for Australian soldiers of two world wars. Gold mania fundamentally affected the nature of Australian society: the traditional dominance of the pastoralist was thrown off; an enhanced sense of egalitarianism ('Jack's as good as his master') disturbed the existing class strata; the colony's traditional ethnic balance was upset by the polyglot population that swarmed on to the goldfields; an upsurge of republican nationalism sprang from the new population mix and from the possibility of national independence offered by the country's new-found wealth; respect for the traditional values of education, industry and integrity wavered before the onslaught of greed, materialism and sharp practices; and public morality, law and order were threatened by the corruption and licentiousness that thrived on the diggings. The ultimate decline of gold fever produced further change, leading to a renewed interest in pastoral pursuits, a consequent demand to 'unlock the land' and the most significant pastoral reform, the Selection Acts. Gold brought into Australian life a new personality, the bearded, flannel-shirted, cabbage-tree hatted, Chinese-hating digger; a new language, the slangy jargon of alluvial mining; and a new set of legends, Ophir, the Turon, Bendigo Mac, the Welcome Stranger, the 'inimitable' Thatcher, Eureka and the Southern Cross, the Palmer, Paddy Hannan and the Golden Mile, Harold Lasseter and his lost reef. It brought to a land that had known only convictism and the arduous tedium of pioneering a stimulating wave of excitement, glamour and optimism.

Although the profound social and economic changes that gold brought aroused sustained and serious literary comment in the second half of the nineteenth century, contemporary writers sought mainly to capture the spectacular nature of the gold rushes and the dramatic character of life on the diggings. Oral composition (balladry, song and the tall tale) was first in the field. Charles Robert Thatcher (q.v.), balladist and songwriter, was typical of the many itinerant entertainers, whose songs such as 'Who Wouldn't Be a Digger?', 'Where's Your Licence?', 'The Song of the Trap' and 'The Rising

Generation' capture much of the colour and controversy of the goldfields life. Thatcher's compositions, which are included in his various songsters, celebrate contemporary goldfields events and personages and were enormously popular with the digger audiences. Commentaries such as James Bonwick's *Notes of a Gold Digger, and Gold Diggers' Guide* (1852), Samuel Mossman's *The Gold Regions of Australia* (1852), John Capper's *The Emigrant's Guide to Australia* (1853), and John and Samuel Sidney's *The Three Colonies of Australia* (1852), are a pot-pourri of history, geography, description and advice in the guidebook genre. Mrs Charles Clacy's *A Lady's Visit to the Gold Diggings of Australia, in 1852–53* (1853) is a lively personal account of the Victorian goldfields. Similarly spontaneous and informative are David Mackenzie's *The Gold Digger* (1853), which gives an account of a visit to the goldfields in February 1852; C. Rudston Read's *What I Heard, Saw and Did at the Australian Goldfields* (1853), a colourful and humorous account by a goldfields administrator; and *The Gold-Finder of Australia* (1853), ed. John Sherer, an entertaining but fictitious account of a tour of the goldfields, supplemented by stories and articles. Edward Hammond Hargraves (q.v.), popularly but inaccurately accepted as the discoverer of gold in Australia, wrote *Australia and Its Gold Fields* (1855). William Howitt's *Land, Labour and Gold* (1855) forecast that from the melting pot of the goldfields would emerge 'a go-ahead, self-confident, Yankee sort of people'. The discovery and development of the Victorian goldfields is recorded in George Wathen's *The Golden Colony* (1855) and William Kelly's *Life in Victoria* (1859). Somewhat later reflections include James Armour's *The Diggings, the Bush, and Melbourne* (1864); W.J. Barry's *Up and Down* (1879); Charles D. Ferguson's *The Experiences of a Forty-Niner during Thirty-Four Years' Residence in California and Australia* (1888), which includes a discussion of the Eureka uprising; and G.O. Preshaw's *Banking Under Difficulties* (1888), an account of a journey on foot from Melbourne to the Ballarat diggings by a lad of 13, who makes his 'pile' and then turns to the more secure occupation of banking.

Fictional representation of the goldfields is similarly abundant. 'Rolf Boldrewood', himself a Gulgong gold commissioner, wrote several novels with goldfields themes, including *The Miner's Right* (q.v., 1890), which is set in the NSW diggings and contains such ingredients as a successful gold strike, claim-jumping, an attack by bushrangers on a gold escort, anti-Chinese riots, and the hero's return to England to a comfortable existence on the proceeds of Australian gold. Henry Lawson, son of an inveterate optimist whose life was ruled (and ruined) by the golden lure, grew up around the primitive alluvial goldfields of Gulgong and Pipeclay (Eurunderee) in western NSW. He records the colour and squalor, hope and despair, of the diggings in his 'A Fragment of Autobiography', in stories such as 'The Golden Graveyard', 'Payable Gold' and 'An Old Mate of Your Father's', and in poems such as 'The Roaring Days' and 'Eureka'. Edward Dyson (q.v.), the son of a mining engineer, tells graphically of the deep mines in *Below and On Top*

(1898) and *Rhymes from the Mines and Other Lines* (1896), while his classic story 'A Profitable Pub' (1887), better known as 'A Golden Shanty' (q.v.), has echoes of the goldfields with its golden bricks and anti-Chinese sentiments. 'Henry Handel Richardson's' *The Fortunes of Richard Mahony* (1930) opens with descriptions of goldfields life; Katharine Susannah Prichard (q.v.) wrote a trilogy, *The Roaring Nineties* (1946), *Golden Miles* (1948) and *Winged Seeds* (1950), set in the WA goldfields. The WA goldfields also provided the setting for John Arthur Barry's *The Luck of the Native Born* (1898), Hume Nisbet's *The Swampers: A Romance of the Westralian Goldfields* (1897), Hubert Stewart's *Ungodly Man* (1904), a moral tale about the ignobility of striving for material riches, Nat Gould's *The Miner's Cup: A Coolgardie Romance* (1896), Helen Helga Wilson's several anecdotal accounts of the era, e.g. *Gateways to Gold* (1969), *The Golden Miles* (1977) and Denis O'Callaghan's *Memories and Reflections of a Pioneer: Australia 1875–1939* (1988). Australian melodrama of the late nineteenth century was obsessed with the theatrical possibilities offered by the gold era. George Darrell's *The Sunny South* (1883), with its theme of fortune won, lost and regained, was one of Australia's most popular and successful plays. Drury Lane Theatre in London had a long-running success in 1896, *The Duchess of Coolgardie*, by two English writers, Euston Leigh and Cyril Clare, while the rush to Kalgoorlie and Coolgardie is also depicted in 'To the West' (1896) by Alfred Dampier and Kenneth McKay. In 1921 the Pioneer Players staged Louis Esson's 'The Battler', which deals with the chanciness of the prospecting life. Later writers have continued to describe, record, explain and analyse every aspect of the golden revolution. Among such works are Malcolm Uren's *Glint of Gold* (1948); Geoffrey Serle's *The Golden Age* (1963); Nancy Keesing's *Gold Fever: The Australian Goldfields 1851 to the 1890s* (1967). They, and others like them, illustrate the truth of the title of Geoffrey Blainey's comprehensive account of mining in Australia, *The Rush That Never Ended* (1963).

Equally as authentically as in literature, the atmosphere of the gold-rush era was captured and preserved in sketches and on canvas. S.T. Gill (q.v.) joined the gold rush to Victoria in 1852 and spent several years sketching scenes of goldfields life. In 1869 he was commissioned by the Melbourne Public Library to prepare watercolour paintings based on those sketches. Four of his most famous paintings of the goldfields, featured on Australian stamps in 1981, were *Puddling*, *Quality of Washing Stuff*, *Licence Inspected* and *On Route to Deposit Gold*. His original album, *The Victorian Goldfields 1852–53*, was edited in 1982 (reprinted 1992) by Michael Cannon. The diary and drawings of another noted artist of the period, Eugene von Guérard (q.v.), were published as *The Artist on the Goldfields* (1982) with an introduction and annotations by Marjorie Tipping. A television series, 'Peach's Gold' by Bill Peach, was screened by the ABC in 1983 and the book of the series, *Gold*, was published simultaneously.

GOLDBERG, S.L., see **Criticism**

'**Golden Builders**', which takes its title from William Blake's 'Jerusalem', is a 27-poem sequence by Vincent Buckley (q.v.) forming the second half of *Golden Builders and Other Poems* (1976). The sequence emphasises the oppressive impact on the individual human consciousness of an urban environment, in this case the inner Melbourne suburbs where the University sits cheek by jowl with slums, high-rise flats, factories, hospitals and a cemetery. The oppression of noise 'piped up like muzak' from the eternal jack-hammers and ceaseless traffic is the constant accompaniment to the ugliness and sordidness of the city, the 'crouched brick houses', the garbage and rats, the graffiti, a woman seeking an abortion, a self-immolation, and doomed dogs howling in the cages of medical laboratories. Although the overwhelming impression of the poem is of an environment deeply depressing to the human spirit, the underlying theme, as indicated by the introductory reference to Blake and by the 'Practising Not Dying' sequences and other areas of the poem, is that the human spirit can find within itself the strength and resilience to survive.

Golden Miles (1948), a novel in Katharine Susannah Prichard's (q.v.) goldfields trilogy, continues the story of Sally Gough, her friend Dinny Quin, and her descendants, while depicting the period of the mining industry 1914–27. It moves on from *The Roaring Nineties* (q.v., 1946), which juxtaposes man against the natural elements, to a concentration on the dehumanising world of machines, whose oppressive and evil energy dominates not only the slave-like lives of the mining community but also the Aborigines who come in contact with its corruption. A more didactic work, *Golden Miles* traces the democratic impulses which lead to trade unionism, the miners' strikes and the opposition to war with anti-conscription campaigns. Sally, now a mother of four sons, although hesitant at becoming involved in politics, finds that she is more responsive as both the war and the mines deprive her of her sons. The capitalist villain of the piece, Sir Paddy Cavan, who has evolved from the impish but ambitious young rogue in the previous novel, frames her son Tom, a political activist, and her husband on charges of gold-stealing; is implicated in the murder of her Aboriginal friend Maritana; and elopes with her eldest son's wife Amy. Sally's romantic attraction to Frisco, the charming blackguard, reaches its climax in this novel after the death of her husband and as a consequence of Frisco's debilitating blindness. See *Roaring Nineties, The* and *Winged Seeds*.

'**Golden Shanty, A**', one of Australia's most famous goldfields short stories, written by Edward Dyson (q.v.), was published originally as 'A Profitable Pub' in the *Bulletin*'s Christmas issue, 1887. J.F. Archibald used Dyson's story as the title of the *Bulletin*'s first anthology (1890). On an old abandoned goldfield near Ballarat stands the Shamrock Hotel, owned by the Irish-Australian Michael Doyle. Doyle's only neighbours are Chinese fossickers who appear intent on dismantling his hotel brick by brick. Doyle's running battle with the Chinese culminates in their offering him £50 for the building. The elated Doyle family are celebrating this handsome offer when, sharpening his carving knife on one of the hotel's bricks, Doyle discovers the reason for the Chinese enthusiasm for his pub – the bricks are made of gold-bearing clay. Chasing off the 'thavin' hathins', Doyle takes the pub apart himself, collects nearly £2000 in gold, goes off to Melbourne and becomes a Justice of the Peace, where it is his greatest delight to sentence any Chinaman who comes under his jurisdiction to 'foive pound or a month'. Despite its humour, 'A Golden Shanty' reflects the hostility that existed between White men and the Chinese on the goldfields.

Golden West, an annual journal emanating from WA, was founded by R.C. Spear, former editor of the weekly newspaper the *Spectator*, and was published 1906–46, edited by Spear for the whole of its existence. Begun largely as a survey of the State, and characterised by its strong pro-WA attitudes, it was soon expanded to carry short stories, sketches and verse, much of which was nostalgic in tone. Well-known WA literary figures who regularly contributed to the *Golden West* were 'Dryblower' (E.G. Murphy), John Drayton, 'Crosscut' (T.H. Wilson), Julian Stuart, Billy Clare and Spear himself.

GOLDHAR, Pinchas (1901–47), born Lodz, Poland, migrated to Australia in 1928. His book, *Short Stories of Australia* (1939), written in Yiddish, paints a pessimistic picture of the weakening of traditional Jewish family and religious ties in the Australian environment. 'Drummond Street' and 'Newcomers' were published as *Two Short Stories* in 1968. Among his other notable stories are 'The Pioneer', published in the *First Jewish Almanac* (1937), 'The Circumcision' and 'The Last Minyan', published in *Short Stories of Australia*, and 'The Funeral', published in *Coast to Coast* (1944). H. Brezniak published *Pinchas Goldhar: The First Yiddish Writer in Australia: An Assessment* (1968), which includes two short stories.

GOLDSMITH, Andrea (1950–), born Melbourne, has worked as a speech pathologist and as a teacher of creative writing. She has published uncollected short stories and two novels, *Gracious Living* (1990) and *Modern Interiors* (1991). Sharp satires of contemporary mores, both novels are concerned with the experience of women, from the happily divorced central protagonist of *Gracious Living* to the 61-year-old widow of *Modern Interiors*, whose struggle for independence from her status-obsessed family following the death of her husband provides the novel's storyline.

GOLDSTEIN, Vida (1869–1949), born Portland, Victoria, was educated at first privately and then at the Presbyterian Ladies' College. Her mother was a zealous worker for social reform and the women's suffrage movement and her father, a friend of Dr Charles Strong, was prominent on various charitable committees. One of her sisters, Elsie, married the British socialist H.H. Champion. From 1892 to 1898 Vida

conducted a co-educational school in St Kilda with her sisters and from the early 1890s began to take an interest in numerous welfare activities, working closely with Annette Bear-Crawford. By 1899 she had become the recognised leader of the women's movement in Victoria, which was at that time mainly concerned with the suffrage. After Australian women were granted the federal vote in 1902, Goldstein stood as an independent candidate for the Senate in 1903, becoming the first woman parliamentary candidate in the British Empire and polling well notwithstanding ridicule of her candidacy and her failure to win election. Her campaign was assisted by the Women's Federal Political Association, which she headed as president, reforming the association after her defeat into the Women's Political Association. She stood again for the Senate in 1910 and 1917 and for the House of Representatives in 1913 and 1914. In 1899 she founded a feminist newspaper, *Woman's Sphere*, which she continued to edit until its demise in 1905, and in 1909 she launched another, the *Woman Voter*. She also contributed to journals in Australia and overseas. During the First World War Goldstein, a staunch pacifist, became chairperson of the Peace Alliance and formed the Women's Peace Army in 1915. In 1919 she left for Europe to represent Australian women at a Women's Peace Conference and stayed away for three years, thereafter turning her attention to more international issues and withdrawing from public prominence in Australian politics. In her last years she became increasingly involved in Christian Science. Although she acquired an international reputation as a feminist and achieved numerous specific political and legislative reforms in Australia, her death passed almost unnoticed. Janette Bomford has written her biography, *That Dangerous and Persuasive Woman* (1993).

GOLDSWORTHY, Kerryn (1953–), born SA and educated at the University of Adelaide, teaches English at the University of Melbourne. Editor of the *Australian Book Review* 1986–87, she has contributed short stories to numerous literary periodicals and has published one collection, *North of the Moonlight Sonata* (1989). She is also the editor of *Australian Short Stories* (1983) and *Coast to Coast* (1986).

GOLDSWORTHY, Peter (1951–), born Minlaton, SA, grew up in various SA towns and in Darwin. He graduated in medicine from the University of Adelaide in 1974 and has combined the practice of medicine with a busy writing career. He has published four books of short fiction, *Archipelagoes* (1982), *Zooing* (1986), *Bleak Rooms* (1988) and *Little Deaths* (1993); four books of poetry, *Readings from Ecclesiastes* (1982), *This Goes with This* (1988), *This Goes with That: Selected Poems 1970–1990* (1991) and *After the Ball* (1992); two novels, *Maestro* (1989, which has been filmed) and *Honk If You Are Jesus* (1992) as well as *Magpie* (1992), a somewhat madcap pastiche of a novel in collaboration with Brian Matthews. Successful in all three genres Goldsworthy won the 1982 Commonwealth Poetry Prize, the Anne Elder Award for Poetry and the SA Biennial Literary Award, all for *Readings from*

Ecclesiastes; a 1979 WA sesquicentenary literary competition for the story 'Memoirs of a small 'm' marxist'; the 1980 Premio Bancarella literary Award from the Italian Festival of Victoria for the story 'Before the Day Goes'; and the Bicentennial Grace Perry Award for Poetry for *This Goes with This*.

Goldsworthy's poetry, with its laconic Australian idiom, is an attractively intelligent, rueful, sardonic assessment of contemporary life. His observation of people and situations is acute, the acerbity underlying much of what he has to say controlled and alleviated by wry wit and humour. His short fiction is similarly clinical, describing and probing personal relationships and social situations to expose an underlying triviality. Compassionate towards those who are short on social and economic advantages, he is severe towards those of his own affluent set, urging them, as in 'The Affirmative Action Dinner Party' to self-criticism. Many stories reflect his experiences as a G.P. in suburban Adelaide, while others, e.g. 'The Car Keys', 'The Death of Daffy Duck' and 'Pointing the Bone', also have something of a medical basis in that they feature cardiac arrest, near death from asphyxiation and psychosomatic illness. The long story 'Jesus Wants Me for a Sunbeam', from *Little Deaths*, is Goldsworthy at his warm and human best. In the more personal, implicitly autobiographical stories, e.g. 'Requiescat in Pace', 'Frock, Wireless, Gorgeous, Slacks', the narrating self emerges as a good-natured individual, alive to his own foibles. Technically competent and driven effortlessly by spontaneous and effective dialogue, Goldworthy's stories move at a lively, entertaining pace.

His first novel, *Maestro*, is about Paul Crabbe (15 at the beginning of the story), who lives in Darwin with his parents (both amateur musicians and Gilbert and Sullivan addicts) and takes piano lessons from an old Austrian, Eduard Keller, the dominating character of the novel. Keller arrived in Australia after the Second World War, walking away from a past that contained the death of his Jewish wife and son in the Holocaust. As part of his own rejection of a world that had countenanced such brutalities he also walked away from his previous musical passions and ambitions. Despite initial difficulties when the boy's enthusiasm meets the impenetrable wall of the maestro's aphoristic summations of life and music, a strong rapport ultimately develops between them. Years pass; Paul becomes a musician; marries his first real love, Rosie; has children; seeks self-knowledge. During those years the maestro's influence is always present. An absorbing novel, tender, emotional, whimsical, *Maestro* confirmed Goldsworthy's considerable story-telling talent. His second novel, *Honk If You Are Jesus*, is a mixture of science fiction, medical research and romance. The central character is Dr Mara Fox, a gynaecologist with a line of IVF research that takes her to the Schulz Bible College on the Gold Coast where her work on sex cells is funded by the TV evangelist Hollis Schulz, mainly to cure his own infertility problems. Mara, whose own hitherto rather empty life is enriched by her experiences there, achieves self-realisation by ultimately destroying her genetic

engineering experiment. Andrew Riemer wrote *The Ironic Eye: Peter Goldsworthy's Fiction* (1993).

GOODE, Arthur Russell ('Arthur Russell') (1889–1971), born Wedderburn, Victoria, worked as a telegraphist for eighteen years before taking up journalism and ultimately becoming technical editor of *Listener In*, a Melbourne radio journal. A prolific writer of books for boys, usually under the pseudonym 'Arthur Russell', Goode published such successful novels as *Ginger for Pluck* (1926), *Storm Child* (1932), *Snowy for Luck* (1934), *The Sky Pirates* (1946) and *Mason's Circus* (1947). He also published *Twenty-Six Radio Stories* (1931), *Twenty-Six Australian Stories* (1934), *Twenty-Six South Sea Stories* (1936), and, with Bernard Cronin, *Bushranging Silhouettes* (1932).

GOODFELLOW, Geoff (1949–   ), born Adelaide, grew up in a working-class environment, leaving school at 15 to begin almost twenty years of physical labour in a variety of jobs – on building sites, oil rigs, in trucks, and as a self-employed carpenter. Struck down by a severe back injury in 1982, he discovered poetry – in the form of A.B. Paterson – and from that time has followed a successful career as a performance poet and creative-writing teacher. He has taken poetry on to the streets, into clubs and pubs, prisons, schools, colleges and universities. He was a member (with fellow performance poets, Eric Beach and Jenny Boult) in 1984–85 of the SA 'New Mobile Poetry Workshop' and has conducted writing workshops in SA prisons and correctional institutions. He was made poet-in-residence in 1985 at Pembroke School, Yatala Labour Prison and SA rehabilitation and training centres. During 1988 he travelled through Canada, USA, Europe, Great Britain and China giving poetry readings and conducting writing workshops and seminars. He was awarded the Carclew Fellowship of SA in 1988 and in 1989 was appointed to the SA Youth Arts Board. In 1990 he was appointed by the Australia Council as poet-in-residence with CMEU, the Construction, Mining and Energy Union of SA, his role being to paint a poet's-eye view of the workings of a large trade union organisation. The somewhat grizzled and weatherbeaten portraits of Goodfellow on several of his books reflect their contents – tough, direct, no-nonsense but eloquent statements of personal experience. He has published three slim books of verse, *No Collars No Cuffs* (1986), *Bow Tie and Tails* (1989), *No Ticket No Start* (1990) and *Triggers: Turning Experiences into Poetry* (1992), a poetry workshop text for young readers which uses individual poems to demonstrate how poems are 'triggered' and finally written. *Triggers* also provides an insight into Goodfellow's own experiences.

No Collars No Cuffs deals first ('Locked In') with his childhood including an early education at the hands of the nuns, a hazardous experience given his rebellious spirit. Pubs and prisons provide the contexts of the next two sections ('Bending at the Bars', 'Bending Bars') and the book concludes with 'Locked Out', dealing with those (e.g. Aborigines, squatters, battered wives) whom life has treated badly. The most memorable poems in *Bow Tie and Tails* speak also for the distraught, disadvantaged and derelict: 'Poem for Annie' (his battered sister whose three husbands have 'all turned out mongrels'); 'Another City View' (street kids); 'An Old Bloke' (a schizophrenic); 'Epitaph for Robbie' (a young, and dead, drug addict); 'Stretched Out' (a victim of parental molestation now turned prostitute); 'Governor's Pleasure' (young men raped in prison). *No Ticket No Start* contains the poetic fruits of Goodfellow's residency with the CMEU. Mostly poetry of praise for the workers, the collection urges the need to keep fighting the bosses ('it's just another fight/ another bloody year'), the need to keep alive in all good working-class hearts the vision of the 'Light on the Hill'.

GOODGE, W.T. (William Thomas) (1862–1909), born London, went to sea as a steward but left his ship in Sydney in 1882 to go 'on the wallaby' for twelve years in outback NSW. In later life Goodge was a journalist, becoming editor of the Orange *Leader* and for the last nine years of his life contributing a weekly account to the Sydney *Truth* about an imaginary club of boozers, the Gimcrack Club. Goodge's comic journalism is part of the long line of notable Australian writing in that genre which includes the work of Lennie Lower, Alex Macdonald, Ross Campbell and Ron Saw. A popular *Bulletin* poet and assessed by Norman Lindsay as one of Australia's best writers of light verse, Goodge published *Hits! Skits! and Jingles!* (1899). His poems are filled with bush identities such as Temora Mat, Slippery Bill, Brandy Jack and the Melodious Bullocky, and with tall tales of the bush such as the story of Jock McPherson who rode the Oozlum Bird from the Centre to Sydney and back, and of Pat Ahearne who exhibited lobsters at outback shows as 'monster Sydney fleas'. Goodge's best-known poem is 'The Great Australian Adjective' (q.v.), which is also the title of a volume of his verse (1965).

GOODING, Tim (1950–), born Melbourne, has written widely for film, stage and television, especially for the popular series *The Aunty Jack Show*, and for the stage and screen. His stage plays include 'The Great Australian Play' winner of the Elizabethan Theatre Trust Prize for best Australian play in 1978, 'A Bent Repose' (1974), 'A Tent Show Pagliacci' (1978), 'Drums along the Diamantina', 'The Astounding Optimissimos' (1977), 'Paradise Depression Style', 'Rockola', a surrealistic celebration of the death of the rock and roll era produced in Sydney, Melbourne and Adelaide in 1978, and its companion piece, *King of Country* (1992), dealing with rural mythology through country music, first produced in Canberra in 1985 and Sydney in 1986.

GOONERATNE, Yasmine (1935–), born Sri Lanka, into the Dias Bandaranaike family, and educated at the universities of Ceylon and Cambridge, UK, came to Australia in 1972 and holds a personal chair in English at Macquarie University. Foundation director of the University's post-colonial literatures and language centre, she was made AO in 1990 and received the University's first earned D.Litt. in 1981. As well as numerous works of literary criticism and edited anthologies of Asian poetry and prose, Gooneratne has published a novel, *A Change of Skies* (1991); several volumes of poetry including *Celebrations and Departures: Selected Poems 1951–1991* (1991); and *Relative Merits* (1986) an account of her father's family. *A Change of Skies* is a subtle, frequently comic study of cultural misunderstandings which makes fun of both Sri Lankan and Australian attitudes and interweaves journal extracts, dramatic monologues, letters and anecdotes.

GORDON, Adam Lindsay (1833–70) was born at Fayal in the Azores where his mother's father had a plantation. On his father's retirement from a commission with the Bengal cavalry he completed his education in England. After numerous youthful escapades Gordon was, in 1853, banished by his parents to SA, where he enlisted in the mounted police. Resigning from the constabulary after two years' service he drifted about SA dealing in horses and riding in steeplechases. With a sizable legacy from his parents' estate he purchased several properties, married, and lived in Dingley Dell, a small stone cottage still lovingly preserved near the seaside settlement of Port MacDonnell, not far from Mount Gambier. From those years come many stories of Gordon's daring feats of horsemanship, most notably the Blue Lake Leap. He had a brief and unspectacular parliamentary career in 1864–66, an abortive grazing venture in WA in 1866–67, and then conducted a livery stable in Ballarat in 1867–68. After a severe head injury in a riding accident, bankruptcy caused by a fire in the livery stable, and the death of his infant daughter, he left Ballarat for Melbourne. There he lived an unhappy and aimless existence, working spasmodically at his writing and suffering from depression, insomnia and pain from his numerous riding injuries. When an attempt failed to claim heirship to the ancestral Gordon lands in Scotland, he faced financial disaster. On 24 June 1870, the day following the publication of his poems, *Bush Ballads and Galloping Rhymes* (q.v.), he committed suicide on Brighton Beach, Melbourne.

Gordon's published works began with *The Feud* (1864), a ballad inspired by Noel Paton's engravings of scenes from the ballad 'The Dowie Dens o' Yarrow'. *Ashtaroth* (1867), his second publication, a long dramatic poem indebted to the Faust theme, has failed to arouse any critical enthusiasm. The two main volumes on which his poetic reputation rests are *Sea Spray and Smoke Drift* (q.v., 1867) and *Bush Ballads and Galloping Rhymes*. In 1934 a bust of Gordon was unveiled in the Poets' Corner of Westminster Abbey, making him the only Australian poet to have been thus honoured. That mark of recognition reflects the adulation he attracted after his death and through the first decades of the twentieth century. His popularity sprang partly from the romantic aura of his life, his aristocratic background, his exile in the colony, his reckless riding exploits, and the pathos of his death. It sprang, too, from the gratitude of Australian nationalists for his poetry's acclaim of the outback way of life. His verses were loved and recited around camp-fires and in the homesteads and shearing sheds of the backblocks. Yet very little of Gordon's poetry reflects the fragrance of the wattle blossom, the blue of Australian skies, or the camaraderie of Australian mateship. Such Australian flavour is present only in 'The Sick Stockrider', 'A Dedication' (qq.v.) and some parts of 'Ye Wearie Wayfarer'. Most of his poetry is modelled upon the conventional verse derived from his English education and background. Apart from the occasional narrative, notably 'The Rhyme of Joyous Garde', that poetry has little significance. The small Australian segment does, however, have undoubted historical importance, and 'The Sick Stockrider', in particular, is recognised as the poem which sketched in broad outline the territory which later balladists filled with profuse and picturesque detail; it thus pointed literature in a new definably 'Australian' direction. Poems to Gordon and his memory include Henry Kendall's 'The Late Mr A.L. Gordon: In Memoriam' and Will Ogilvie's 'Adam Lindsay Gordon'. Edith Humpris wrote *The Life of Adam Lindsay Gordon* (1934), C.F. MacRae, *Adam Lindsay Gordon* (1968), W.H. Wilde, the monograph *Adam Lindsay Gordon* (1972) and Geoffrey Hutton, *Adam Lindsay Gordon: The Man and the Myth* (1978). Ian F. McLaren compiled *Adam Lindsay Gordon: A Comprehensive Bibliography* (1986).

Gordon & Gotch was established in 1854 in Melbourne as a partnership between Alexander Gordon and John Speechley Gotch to act as news and advertising agents and to distribute newspapers and periodicals from Britain. In 1859 Gordon sold his interest in the business to Gotch and returned to Scotland. Gotch was joined by his brother William in 1860 and brother-in-law Alfred Jones in 1861. Branches were opened in Sydney (1861), London (1867), Brisbane (1875), Perth (1894), Wellington (NZ) (1899) and Launceston (1903). In 1885 Gordon & Gotch became a public company. Chiefly a distributor of periodicals to newsagents and booksellers, Gordon & Gotch is also well known for its publication *Australian Handbook*, a comprehensive volume of facts and information about Australia, published 1870–1906. *Years to Remember: The Story of Gordon and Gotch* was published in 1953.

GORDON, J.W. (James William) ('Jim Grahame') (1874–1949), born Creswick, Victoria, was a mate of Henry Lawson and a possible model for Jack Mitchell (q.v.), one of Lawson's most important fictional characters. The two met in 1892 at Bourke during Lawson's celebrated outback trek, worked together for several months and then parted, to meet again when Lawson went to Leeton in 1916. They remained friends from then until Lawson's death. Gordon wrote under the pseudonym 'Jim Grahame', a name reputedly given to him by Lawson. After 1903 he was a regular contributor of bush verse to the *Bulletin* and other journals, and published three volumes of verse: *Call of the Bush* (1940), *Home Leave and Departing* (1944) and *Under Wide Skies: Collected Verses* (1947). Gordon's recollections of Lawson form part of *Henry Lawson – by His Mates* (1931); Lawson's recollections of Gordon form part of his articles on Yanco contributed to the *Bulletin* in 1916–17.

GORE, Stuart (1905–), born Portsmouth, England, came to Australia in 1910. A jack of all trades, he finally settled on cinematography for a living, touring Australia making films and bringing them to the public in a show titled 'See Australia First'. After war service in the RAAF Gore made industrial and public-relations films in England and subsequently divided his time between writing and lecturing, much of the latter on behalf of the Commonwealth Institute in London. Gore's travel books include *Overlanding with Annabel* (1956), which relates his and his wife's experiences as they travelled in an old Chrysler car through outback Australia. Gore's other publications include the humorous *Holy Smoke* (1968), Saltbush Bill's (q.v.) version of the scriptures, and a novel, *Down the Golden Mile* (1962), set in the goldfields and outback of WA.

GORMAN, Clem (1942–), born Perth, WA, was educated at the University of Sydney, was a freelance stage manager and administrator in Sydney 1967–68, founded the Australian Free Theatre Group and co-founded the theatre magazine *Masque*. From 1970 to 1979 he worked in England as a freelance writer and as an arts administrator before returning to Australia to work in the same field. He has written extensively for television, film and radio, has published books on rock music, experimental theatre and alternative living, has edited a collection of essays by twenty writers on the subject of famous and infamous larrikins, *The Larrikin Streak* (1990), and has written several plays. His first play, 'Let Me In, I'm a Friend of the Band', had a season at the Kings Head, London, in 1978, and his third play, 'The Making of the Documentary d'Arcy Conran', won a special prize in the WA 150th anniversary play competition in 1979. His published plays include *A Manual of Trench Warfare* (1979, performed 1978); *A Night in the Arms of Raeleen* (1983, performed 1981); *The Harding Women* (1983, performed 1981); *The Motivators* (1983, performed 1983); and *The Last Nightclub* (1985). He also adapted A.B. Facey's *A Fortunate Life* for the stage; produced first in 1984 by the Melbourne Theatre Company, the play was revised for another production in 1987 and published the same year.

GOUGER, Robert (1802–46), born London, visited Edward Gibbon Wakefield in Newgate prison to discuss their mutual interest in the colonising of Australia. His *Sketch of a Proposal for Colonizing Australia* was published in 1829, the year he edited Wakefield's *A Letter from Sydney*. Gouger's efforts were largely responsible for the formation in 1830 of the National Colonization Society, whose object was to assist pauper emigration to the colonies, especially SA. At first unsuccessful, Gouger finally prevailed when the SA Colonization Commission was gazetted in 1835 with himself as colonial secretary. He arrived in SA in 1836 but was involved in faction fighting which negated much of his usefulness to the new colony which he had so long championed. In ill health he returned to England in 1845. He published *South Australia in 1837* (1838). His journals were used by Edwin Hodder in the compilation of *The Founding of South Australia* (1898).

GOULD, Alan (1949–), born London, his father a British Army officer and his mother, Valdergur, of Icelandic origin, came to Australia in 1966 after a childhood dominated by the frequent changes characteristic of a serviceman's family. As a student Gould was involved in the anti-Vietnam War protests and demonstrations; he graduated from the ANU with an arts degree and after a few brief casual occupations has settled to a life as a poet and novelist interspersed with occasional periods of teaching. He has lived mostly in Canberra and nearby Queanbeyan, was the founding editor of *Canberra Poetry* and the Open Door Press in Canberra, has been poetry reviewer for *Nation Review*, *Poetry Australia*, and other journals and newspapers, and is editor of the anthology, *Arteries in Stone* (1976). He has published numerous books of poetry, *Icelandic Solitaries* (1978); *Astral Sea* (1981, winner of NSW Premier's Poetry Award); *The Pausing of the Hours* (1984); *The Twofold Place* (1986); *Years Found in Likeness* (1988); *Formerlight* (1992, a *Selected* volume of the previous five books); and *Momentum* (1992).

Much of Gould's early poetry derives from his interest in Norse mythology and early ocean exploration. *Astral Sea* includes the sections, 'The Vinlanders', which owes much to Farley Mowat's reconstruction of Norse voyages in his book *Westocking* (1965), and 'The Songs of Ymir' which tells of the birth of the first man and woman and the first Frost giants. Ymir is killed and from his parts Heaven and Earth are made. *Astral Sea* also contains a series 'Marine Photographs', episodes of shipwrecks and near disasters at sea, mostly from the days of sail. The mesmerising focus of the sea is present also in *The Twofold Place* with its series 'A History of Shipping', which celebrates the feats of endurance and courage of the early seafarers – 'The Phoenician Helmsman', 'An Arab Merchant', 'The Norse Ship', 'Portuguese Carracks' and 'A Dutch Jacht'. *The Twofold Place* takes its title, however, from the imagination, that faculty that allows us to be wherever we wish, in the here and now or the there and then, and to see beyond the object to its deeper significance. Some autobiographical poems, 'Learning to Think', deal with Gould's boyhood of boarding schools, when he encountered two of his chief influences: the Ipswich River which ran alongside the school inspired thoughts of the vast oceans, and the school subject history, 'a constant B grade cinema', provided similarly expanded mental horizons. *Years Found in Likeness* brings another sea sequence, the extended voyager series 'The Great Circle', dealing with the life and explorations of Captain James Cook. Part of the poem was the libretto for a choral symphony commissioned for the 1988 Bicentenary. *Years Found in Likeness* also contains one of Gould's loveliest poems, 'Austral Bluebells in Molonglo Gorge'.

Momentum sees Gould in more experimental mode, using a striking array of poetic and verbal devices to explore emotional states. Intrigued by the archetypal Australian workman, Gould writes observantly and amusedly of the casual dexterity, laconic humour and good-natured contempt for those with more intellectual skills (including poets) characteristic of electricians, roof-tilers, tree-loppers, mechanics and the like. *Formerlight*, the *Selected* volume, which begins, appropriately, with a 'Homage' (from *Icelandic Solitaries*) to another lover of the sea, Joseph Conrad, gathers together an attractive, wide-ranging group of his best poems, establishing his claim to be one of Australia's finest contemporary poets.

Gould has also, however, achieved similar distinction as a fiction-writer. His first novel, *The Man Who Stayed Below* (1984), about a young apprentice's first experiences on a sailing ship under a demonic alcoholic captain, won the James Cook University's Foundation for Australian Literary Studies Award in 1985. *The Enduring Disguises* (1988) contains three linked novellas, autobiographically based. 'The Clayfield' is the story of a young boy growing up in the 1950s at an army base in the English countryside; 'Decay and Honour' is based on the anti-Vietnam War demonstrations in the early 1970s; 'A Paperknife and a Broken Oar' is the story of a friendship between two young men. Gould's fictional *tour de force* is the novel *To the Burning City* (1991), which won the NBC Banjo Award for fiction. It concerns two half-brothers, Len Hengelow and Jeb Corballis. Len's father, Crispin Hengelow, is a bomb-aimer in the RAF in the Second World War; his mother, Elizabeth, an Australian girl who joins the WRAF; Len, aged 4, is sent to a boarding school. Those war years, with the aura of his father as hero-airman and his loving mother, are the only happy times Len is to know. After the war his father leaves them to go on a lifelong crusade of restitution for the damage he had done to individuals in the 'area bombing' of German cities. Len's mother remarries and has another son, Jeb, but Len, bitterly missing and resenting his father, feels an outsider in the new family, and grows more difficult, becoming estranged from all except his father's sister, Aunty Eva. In her house he constructs with enormous care the front end of a Lancaster bomber, in which he plays out his boyhood fantasies of the war years. Len's major purpose, however, is eventually to confront his father with the guilt of his desertion of family. Jeb returns with his mother to Australia to live but goes off, eventually, to search for Crispin Hengelow, now a cult figure in Germany and loved by all whose lives he has helped to reconstruct. Jeb arranges the ultimate confrontation (in the Lancaster cockpit) between Crispin and his son Len, when Crispin is brought to realise the destruction he has caused in the lives of the boy and his mother. Much later Jeb realises the extent of his mother's suffering from Crispin's self-satisfying gestures of restitution to the rest of the world.

GOULD, John (1804–81), born Dorset, England, had published two significant ornithological works, *A Century of Birds from the Himalaya Mountains* (1831–32) and *The Birds of Europe* (1837), before coming to Australia in 1838. He remained in the colonies until 1840 working in Van Diemen's Land, SA and NSW. *The Birds of Australia*, in thirty-six parts and bound in seven volumes, was published 1840–48; a supplementary volume was completed in 1869. The total work includes 681 coloured plates. In addition to many other works he also published *The Mammals of Australia* (1845–63) and *Handbook to the Birds of Australia* (1865); he was at work upon *The Birds of New Guinea and the Adjacent Papuan Islands* at the time of his death, the work being completed by R.B. Sharpe. His name has been honoured in Australia by the establishment of the Gould League of Bird Lovers (1938). Gordon C. Sauer published *John Gould the Bird Man* (1982), a comprehensive chronology and bibliography, and Isabella Tree wrote *The Ruling Passion of John Gould* (1991), a full biography. C.L. Barrett wrote the biographical *The Bird Man* (1938). Elizabeth (1804–41), John Gould's wife and a talented artist, supplied many of the drawings for the colour plates of her husband's books. Her letters from Australia admirably reflect the contemporary colonial scene; A.H. Chisholm wrote her biography, *The Story of Elizabeth Gould* (1944).

GOULD, Nat (1857–1919), who wrote sometimes under the pseudonym 'Verax', was born in Manchester, England, served as a reporter on the *Newark Advertiser*, and arrived in Australia in 1884. He worked on newspapers in Brisbane, Bathurst and Sydney, where 'With the Tide' was serialised in the *Referee*. Published as a novel, *The Double Event* (1891), it was staged in 1893 and established Gould's reputation. Subsequently he wrote over a hundred readable, exciting and popular novels, mostly about the turf and other sports; in many of these, published under such titles as *Jockey Jack* (1892), *The Doctor's Double* (1896), *The Miner's Cup* (1896), *King of the Ranges* (1902), *Bred in the Bush* (1903), *A Sporting Squatter* (1906) and *A Chestnut Champion* (1920), he continued to draw on his Australian experiences even though he returned to England in 1895. Gould's success derived from his clever blending of the mystery story with a sporting subject. Although seldom regarded as a significant Australian novelist, he inaugurated the Australian sporting novel and is still beloved by aficionados of sporting fiction. His volumes of reminiscences, *On and Off the Turf in Australia* (1895), *Town and Bush: Stray Notes on Australia* (1896) and *The Magic of Sport Mainly Autobiographical* (1909), are useful for their information about Australian journalism and theatre as well as about the turf (q.v.) and other sports.

GOVERNOR, Jimmy (1875–1901), a part-Aborigine born at Talbragar River, NSW, achieved notoriety in 1900 when with his brother Joe he committed several murders and eluded capture in northern NSW. He was captured and hanged early in 1901. Frank Clune's *Jimmy Governor* (1959) introduced Thomas Keneally (q.v.) to the story of the Governors, which forms the historical basis of *The Chant of Jimmie Blacksmith* (q.v., 1972), Keneally's novel about Aboriginal dispossession and White racism. Sympathy

for Governor is also displayed in Les Murray's poem 'The Ballad of Jimmy Governor'. Brian Davies wrote *The Life of Jimmy Governor* (1979).

GOW, Michael (1955–), born Sydney and educated at the University of Sydney, joined the Sydney University Dramatic Society in 1975. He has had numerous major acting roles in film, television and stage and written plays for television, radio and stage. His first play, *The Kid* (1983), was workshopped at the Australian National Playwrights' Conference in 1982 and subsequently widely performed. It was followed by 'The Astronaut's Wife' (1984), *Away* (1986), *Europe* and *On Top of the World*, published together in 1987, *1841* (1988), *All Stops Out* (1991) and 'Furious' (1991). Gow has won numerous awards including the 1986 NSW Premier's Award, the Sydney Theatre Critics' Circle Award and two Awgies for *Away*, as well as Green Room, AFI and Penguin awards. Gow's best-known play, *Away*, takes a familiar Australian ritual, the annual Christmas holiday at the beach, and transforms it into the tragi-comic story of a Shakespearean sea-change in the lives of its three contrasting families. With *Europe* and *1841*, which was commissioned for the 1988 Adelaide Festival, Gow broadened his approach to include Australia's colonial history and its relationship with Europe. *The Kid* and *All Stops Out* focus on the contemporary world of the Australian teenager and the experience of alienation, defeat and separation from the older generation; semi-autobiographical, they are linked to *Away* and *On Top of the World* in their continuing preoccupation with the family.

Grace Leven Prize for Poetry, an annual award in memory of Grace Leven, who died in 1922, was established by her friend and admirer 'William Baylebridge' (q.v.); she was his mother's half-sister. The award, first made in 1947 to Nan McDonald's *Pacific Sea*, is for the best volume of poetry published in the preceding twelve months by a writer either Australian-born and writing as an Australian, or naturalised in Australia and resident in Australia for not less than ten years. In 1948 the second award was made to Francis Webb's *A Drum for Ben Boyd*. The prize winners list reads like a roll-call of the greats of Australian poetry, e.g. Judith Wright, R.D. FitzGerald, A.D. Hope, James McAuley, Geoffrey Dutton, William Hart-Smith, Thomas Shapcott, Douglas Stewart, David Campbell, Rodney Hall, Gwen Harwood, John Blight, Vivian Smith, Peter Porter, Rosemary Dobson, Robert Gray, Chris Wallace-Crabbe, Rhyll McMaster, Elizabeth Riddell, John Tranter, Dorothy Hewett, Les Murray, Robert Adamson, Kevin Hart.

GRAHAM, Gordon (1949–), born South Africa, was brought to Australia at the age of 3. His first professional production, *Innocent Bystanders*, published 1985 in *Popular Short Plays for the Australian Stage* vol. II, was presented at the Royal Court Theatre (London) in 1975. His first full-length play, 'Freaks', was produced by Hoopla in 1978. His other plays include 'Rallying Point' (1977), *Demolition Job* (1984), which won an Awgie in 1982 for best stage play, and 'Hanging Together' (1983).

GRAHAM, John (1822–79), born County Tyrone, Ireland, and minister of the Pitt Street Congregational Church, Sydney, in the 1860s and 1870s, published a book of poetry, *Poems: Sacred, Didactic and Descriptive* (1861) and the semi-fictional narrative *Laurence Struilby: Or, Observations and Experiences during Twenty-Five Years of Bush Life in Australia* (1863); the latter gives an account of early life in the colony, some of it in narrative form, other parts including extracts from journals and letters. Most of the story is set in the Bathurst district with a period in the 1830s in Van Diemen's Land. His brother, Charles Graham, published *Memoir of the Rev. John Graham* in 1880.

'GRAHAME, Jim', see **GORDON, J.W.**

GRAINGER, Percy (1882–1961), the Australian composer and pianist, is the subject of two plays, 'Percy and Rose' (1982) by Rob George (q.v.) and *A Whip Round for Percy Grainger* (1982) by Thérèse Radic (q.v.). Elaine Dorum has written a biography, *Percy Grainger: The Man Behind the Music* (1986) and a selection of his correspondence, titled *The Farthest North of Humanness* (1985), was edited by Kay Dreyfus.

GRANO, Paul (1894–1975), born Ararat, Victoria, graduated in law from the University of Melbourne but practised only briefly, working as an insurance salesman, advertising writer, commercial traveller and journalist. He went to Queensland in 1932 and worked in the Main Roads Commission until his retirement. Grano founded the Catholic Poetry Society in Brisbane in 1934 and the Catholic Readers' and Writers' Society in 1943. In 1946 he edited *Witness to the Stars*, an anthology of Catholic poetry of Australia and NZ. A Keatsian dedication to the ideals of truth and beauty, a wistful tone and skilful imagery are the hallmarks of his best verse. His volumes of poetry are *The Roads and Other Poems* (1934), *Quest* (1940), *Poet's Holiday* (1941), *Poems, New & Old* (1945) and *Selected Verse*, published posthumously in 1976.

GRANT, Bruce (1925–), born Perth, WA, has had a long, distinguished career as diplomat, foreign correspondent, international affairs expert and author. He was a foreign correspondent in Europe 1954–64, Nieman fellow at Harvard University in 1959, fellow in political science at Melbourne University 1965–68, Scott fellow at Ormond College 1976–77, writer-in-residence at Monash University in 1982 and visiting fellow at the ANU 1983. Columnist ('Public Affairs') for the *Age* 1968–72, he was Australian high commissioner in India, 1973–76. Consultant to the minister for Foreign Affairs and Trade since 1988, he has been chairman of the Australia Indonesia Institute since 1989. Among his many significant publications are *Indonesia* (1964), which won the Melbourne Moomba Prize for Literature in that year; *The Crisis of Loyalty* (1972), a study of Australian foreign policy; *The Boat People* (1979), an investigatory study commissioned by the *Age* into the events behind that refugee crisis; *Gods and Politicians* (1982), a work on India and Australia; *The Australian Dilemma* (1983); and *What Kind of Country? Australia and the Twenty-first Century* (1988). His short fiction has been published in Australian and overseas journals, including *Meanjin* and the *New Yorker*, and he has written a novel, *Cherry Bloom* (1980).

GRANT, Jamie (James Beresford) (1949–), born Melbourne, graduated from La Trobe University. A brief career in advertising was followed by a decade as sales manager with Cambridge University Press. He managed a Sydney bookshop for a year and is presently editor of Heinemann Australia's Poetry series. He has also been columnist and critic for the *Age Monthly Review* and a freelance journalist and editor. Well known as a critic of poetry, regarded by some as 'accurate and fearless' and by others as negative and destructive, Grant has, over the years, provoked considerable discussion – for example, after his comments on the poets Gary Catalano and Dimitris Tsaloumas, *Australian Book Review*, April 1988. His own published works include *Turn Left at Any Time With Care* (a shared booklet with Graeme Kinross Smith in the Paperback Poets series, 1975), *The Refinery* (1985), *Skywriting* (1989) and *Mysteries* (1993). His love of cricket led to *The Longest Game* (1990, with Alec Buzo).

Demanding from the poets he reviews the highest standards of craftsmanship, Grant strives for similar excellence in his own work. Such excellence is hard won. Many of his poems become protracted chessboard battles with words, each phrase honed, shaped and positioned then followed by others even more worked upon in the search for the ultimate in description or analogy. Landscapes are especially important and his poems are frequently triggered by places and the impressions they leave or the reflections they arouse. Atmosphere and description are his forte, whether of natural scenes as in 'Snowfall over Water', 'Cold Weather', 'River Valley, House for Sale', 'Western District, Discovering Atlantis', or of people combined with places, 'Snow Holiday with Aunt', 'Grandfather's Clock', 'Sunlight at Montacute (Tasmania)', 'The Farmer's Widow, Home Again'. The intrusion of personalities into the poetry (an aunt with cancer, an autistic cousin in an asylum, the death of grandparents, echoes of marital disharmony) usually results in a gloomy reticence – 'ingrown pessimism', to modify slightly one of Grant's own phrases. 'Christopher Codrington' (one of several poems about Grant's unfortunate cousin) won the Northern Territory Government's Red Earth Poetry Award in 1988.

GRATTAN, C. (Clinton) Hartley (1902–80), born Massachusetts, USA, was a journalist and freelance writer in New York 1926–64 and professor of history 1964–74 at the University of Texas, where the Grattan collection of Australian and Pacific material is housed. Grattan made the first of several visits to Australia in 1927, becoming friendly with Percival Serle and 'Furnley Maurice'. That visit resulted in the booklet

Australian Literature (1929), with a foreword by Nettie Palmer. In 1936 the Carnegie Corporation of New York commissioned him to produce a political, economic and cultural synthesis of Australia. The result was the 1942 publication *Introducing Australia*, a work which he described as a non-academic investigation of Australian society but which helped publicise Australia in America. In 1947 he edited *Australia*, a symposium of specialist articles on Australian society. Introduced to Joseph Furphy's writings by 'Furnley Maurice', Grattan published an American edition of *Such Is Life* in 1948. Grattan's interest extended during the Second World War to NZ and the South Pacific. His subsequent publications include a massive work in two volumes, *The Southwest Pacific to 1900*, and *The Southwest Pacific Since 1900* (both 1963).

GRAY, Oriel (1920–), born Sydney, has written numerous plays for stage, radio and television. A member of the Communist Party of Australia until 1950, she was originally closely associated as actor and writer with Sydney's New Theatre. Her political interests are reflected in her stage plays, nearly all of which deal with oppression, exploitation and discrimination, especially racial discrimination. She was married first to the actor John Gray and then to the journalist John Hepworth (q.v.).

Gray's first full-length stage play, *Lawson*, a dramatisation of some of the short stories of Henry Lawson, produced in 1943, included in extract in *Australian One-Act Plays, Book II*, ed. Greg Branson (1962) and published separately and in a full revised version in 1989, was followed by 'Western Limit', 'Had We but World Enough', 'Sky Without Birds', 'Royal Tour', 'Belle and the Bushranger', 'The King Who Wouldn't', 'Let's be Offensive', 'Marx of Time', 'Milestones', 'Antarctic Four', *The Torrents*, which shared first prize with *Summer of the Seventeenth Doll* in the Playwrights Advisory Board competition of 1955, 'My Life is My Affair', *Drive a Hard Bargain* (1958), 'Burst of Summer', which was produced in 1960 and won the play-writing competition of the Little Theatre Guild of Melbourne in 1959, *The Golden Touch* (1965) and *The Ghost of Dog Leg Creek* (1967). *The Torrents* was not published until 1988 in *The Penguin Anthology of Australian Women's Writing*, ed. Dale Spender. Gray also contributed to the popular television serial of the 1970s, *Bellbird*, and wrote the television plays 'Antarctic Four' and 'The Brass Guitar'. In 1985 Gray published an account of her life to 1949, when she decided to leave the Communist Party, *Exit Left: Memoirs of a Scarlet Woman*. A social document of Australia in the 1930s and 1940s, the autobiography is also informative on Communist Party politics and the activities of the New Theatre and incidentally revealing of such individuals as Cedric Flower, James McAuley and John Hepworth. Gray has also written a novel, *The Animal Shop* (1990), a study of several women in the working-class suburb of West Heidelberg, Melbourne, who encounter hardship in various forms but who also discover a sense of community.

GRAY, Robert (1945–), born on the NSW north coast, grew up and was educated at Coffs Harbour, NSW. He left school to become a cadet journalist on a country newspaper but went to Sydney where he wrote for a magazine, was an advertising copywriter, a mail sorter and a bookshop assistant. With a growing literary reputation he became a reviewer of poetry with the *Sydney Morning Herald* and the ABC. He won the Marten Bequest Travelling Scholarship to the USA in 1981 and was a writer-in-residence in Japan. He supports himself almost wholly from his writing, complemented by part-time work when necessary. His first volume of poetry, *Introspect, Retrospect* (1970), was followed by *Creekwater Journal* (1974), *Grass Script* (1979), *The Skylight* (1984), *Selected Poems 1963–1983* (1985), which won the NSW Premier's Award, the Adelaide Festival of the Arts Award and the Grace Leven Poetry Prize, all in 1986, *Piano* (1988), which was added to the original *Selected* to form an expanded *Selected* edition in 1990, and *Certain Things* (1993). In 1990 he was the recipient of the Patrick White Award. He collaborated with Geoffrey Lehmann to produce the anthologies *Younger Australian Poets* (1983) and *Australian Poetry in the Twentieth Century* (1991), and, with Vivian Smith, *Sydney's Poems* (1992).

Applauded by fellow poets – 'the best eye in Australian poetry' (Les Murray) and 'as an imagist he is without a rival in the English-speaking world' (Kevin Hart) – Gray continues to receive increasing recognition. His constant poetic endeavour is to transform all that he sees and experiences in the freshest, most imaginative, yet realistic, verbal equivalents. Such poems as 'A Port of Europe', 'Very Early', 'The Swallows', 'Smoke', 'Under the Summer Leaves', 'Memories of the Coast', 'Journey: The North Coast' and 'A Country Town', are imagistic creations of rare quality. Yet the things described, as he confesses in 'Very Early' from *Piano*, have no need of poetic interpretation.

> 'If no-one saw all this, its existence would go on just
> as well.
> And what is really here no words can tell'.

The north coast, where he grew up, is part of Gray's 'heart's blood' in much the same way as New England is Judith Wright's, Bunyah is Les Murray's. Many of the poems describing the area, 'Journey: The North Coast', 'Within the Traveller's Eye', 'North Coast Town', 'Memories of the Coast', 'Mr Nelson', capture the seedy, defeated, slothful inadequacy of people oppressed by the overpowering heat and humidity in contrast with the prolific, near tropical luxuriance of nature. Some of Gray's poems recall personal events – his boyhood visits to his grandmother, his recollections of his T.P.I. father's alcoholism and his mother's inadequacy in the face of that situation – but they lack any real sense of intimacy. It is almost as if the boy is emotionally dissociated from the personal strife around him. Gray's adult narrators convey something of the same impression. His eye for 'character', however, in 'Under the Summer Leaves' is unerring.

Adept at many verse forms and in both short and long poems, Gray is especially successful in the prose-poem genre. Remarkably accessible to the reader, his poetry denies the tenet of deconstruction that it is impossible to communicate what one means to others. 'Claritas', as Jamie Grant has said of him, is truly the essence of his work.

Great Australian Adjective ('Bloody') was observed to be flourishing in the colony as early as 1859, Frank Fowler noting, in *Southern Lights and Shadows*, that the cornstalk (q.v.) was prone 'to interlard his diction with the crimsonest of adjectives'. In 1894 the *Bulletin* explained the Australian appropriation of 'bloody' thus – 'we call it the *Australian* adjective simply because it is more used and used more exclusively by Australians than by any other allegedly civilized nation.' Three of the best-known literary examples of the crimson adjective's use are C.J. Dennis's 'The Australaise' (q.v.); Joseph Furphy's *Such Is Life* (q.v., 1903); and W.T. Goodge's poem, 'The Great Australian Adjective', about 'the sunburnt – stockman' (for – mostly read 'bloody') whose attempted crossing of a flooded creek on horseback ended thus:

> He plunged into the – creek
> The – horse was – weak
> The stockman's face was a – study
> And though the – horse was drowned
> The – rider reached the ground
> Ejaculating '–!'
> '–!'

In his anthology *Verse in Australia* (1959) Ian Mudie included 'The Man from Tumbarumba' by J. Wolfe. That worthy's pastime was 'shootin' kanga-bloody-roos/ At Tumba-bloody-rumba'. In *They're a Weird Mob* (1957) Nino Culotta, as a new arrival to Australia, tries to make his way to 'Kings-bloody-Cross'.

Great World, The, a novel by David Malouf, was published in 1990 and won the Miles Franklin Award in 1991, the Adelaide Festival Award and two international awards, the 1991 Commonwealth Prize for fiction and the Prix Femina Étranger in France for the best foreign novel. *The Great World* compares and intertwines the destinies of two men, Digger Keen and Vic Curran. Digger, whose name was acquired virtually at birth without any foresight of his destiny as a soldier, is an outwardly unremarkable man with a remarkable memory and a strong sense of allegiance to his home on the Hawkesbury River, the ferry crossing known as Keen's Crossing. Taciturn and unambitious, Digger puts a high value on mateship and represents many of the values traditionally associated with Australian men. Trained by his mother, who had been denied a family context and who had lost several of her children in infancy, to value the past, and to care for his mentally retarded sister Jenny, Digger enjoys a token rebellion as a fighter with a circus before enlisting in the army. Vic Curran, the son of an alcoholic father whom he thoroughly despised and a mother whose death he witnessed and eased at the age of 10, is convinced early that his life in a run-down shack on the edge of sand dunes is a mistake; 'He ought to have

been without hope. But his body was hopeful and he trusted it. Everything he did he looked forward to with an eager impatience'. His hopefulness seems justified after his father's death when he is adopted by the executor of his father's will, Captain Warrender of Strathfield, Sydney, and accepted into the Warrender family as a son. Comfortably off due to a soap factory inherited from Mrs Warrender's father, the family includes two daughters, Lucille and Ellie, an eccentric aunt and a much-loved servant, Meggsie. Soon aware that Mr Warrender has no head for business and alert to Mrs Warrender's anxieties about their financial stability, Vic determines to 'save' the family by cultivating his natural talents for making money. With one of its numerous timeshifts the novel shifts to the POW camp at Changi where Vic and Digger become acquainted. Suspicious of Vic, Digger becomes even more hostile after he inadvertently causes the death of his best friend Mac, a man who had introduced him to music and whose integrity he trusted; Mac's letters from home later become Digger's lifeline during the intense hardships imposed by working on the Burma railway. Although several of their mates succumb to dysentery and other sicknesses while working on the railway, Vic and Digger survive; undeterred by Digger's hostility, Vic nurses him during illness and saves his gangrenous leg by forcing him into a river for the cleansing actions of fish. Digger meanwhile is sustained by his remarkable memory: 'What Digger remembered, and after a certain time in an official capacity, was the name and number of every man in the unit; including those who had been killed or gone missing and been replaced, then the replacements; and where each man was sent after the surrender.' After the war the lives of the two men diverge, although they continue to maintain contact; Vic marries Ellie and becomes an extremely successful if overly daring businessman, whereas Digger returns to the old life at Keen's Crossing, interspersed only with regular visits to Mac's sister-in-law Iris, who becomes his lover. Mr Warrender pursues his literary interests, becoming the well-known poet Hugh Warrender, and Mrs Warrender becomes Vic's partner in enterprising schemes. The next three decades see the deaths of Meggsie, Hugh Warrender and Iris, the loss of Vic's son to the drug world and a maturing friendship between Ellie and Digger; happiness meanwhile largely eludes Vic, who continues to need the stability of his relationship with Digger. When the boom years of the 1980s promise greater scope to Vic's gambling instinct he uses Digger's name as a cover for some of his activities and is on the edge of even greater profits when he suffers a heart attack on the way to Keen's Crossing. His death is followed by the crash of his ventures.

GREEN, Bill (1940–), born Swan Hill, Victoria, has worked as a journalist in North America, Mexico, South East Asia and China as well as Australia. He was a speech-writer and press secretary in Canberra 1972–74 before becoming a breeder and trainer of thoroughbred racehorses and a writer of fiction. He now lives in Melbourne, where he works as a freelance screenwriter. One of the founding editors of *Sunday Review*, he has published the novels *Small Town Rising* (1981), *Born Before the Wind* (1984), *Freud and the Nazis Go Surfing* (1986), *Compulsively Murdering Mao* (1989) and *Cleaning Up* (1993). Combining the ingredients of fast-paced action, well-defined characters and contemporary issues, Green's novels have found a ready market; *Small Town Rising* focuses on racial prejudice in a small Victorian town and *Born Before the Wind* on a get-rich scheme in the horse-racing world. *Compulsorily Murdering Mao*, set in the period of the Vietnam War, is an unrelieved satire of Australian and big-power politics, while *Cleaning Up* satirises an Australia of the near future, when the country has become another state of the USA, controlled by the White House and subject to the megalomania of the American president, thanks to the apathy of Canberra's bureaucracy. *Freud and the Nazis Go Surfing*, Green's most enthusiastically received novel to date, explores a teenager's sexual and other *rites de passage* in a small Victorian town of the 1950s and his encounter with violence and sadism.

GREEN, Cliff(ord) (1934–), born Melbourne, was in the printing trade before becoming a primary school teacher in Victoria. He resigned in 1969 to become a staff writer with Crawford Productions, contributing to such television series as *Homicide*, *Rush*, *Power Without Glory* and *Against the Wind*. Green's major contribution to television writing, however, has been *Marion* (1974), which won an Awgie and the Television Society Award; *End of Summer* which also won an Awgie, and *Summerfield*, both of which were published in *Four Scripts* (1978). Green also wrote the screenplay for the film *Picnic at Hanging Rock* (1975), and two original screenplays, 'Break of Day' and *Burn the Butterflies* (1979). His first stage play, *Cop Out!* (1983), was performed by the Melbourne Theatre Company in 1977. His other publications include a novel, *Break of Day* (1976), based on the screenplay; a collection of short stories, *The Sun Is Up* (1978); the Riverboat Bill books for children (1975, 1981); *Boy Soldiers* (1990), based on his screenplay for children's television; and *Evergreen. The Story of a Family* (1984), a history of his family from 1800. Among his adaptations for television are the series *Lawson's Mates* (1978), *Lucinda Brayford* (1980) and *I Can Jump Puddles* (1981). Green has received numerous Awgies and Penguin awards and was nominated Best Writer in the 1978 awards in Hollywood for his screenplay *Picnic at Hanging Rock*.

GREEN, Dorothy (Dorothy Auchterlonie) (1915–91), born County Durham, England, was educated there and at the University of Sydney. She worked as a broadcaster, journalist and news editor with the news service of the ABC 1942–49 and was co-principal of a well-known girls' school in Warwick, Queensland, 1955–60. She subsequently lectured in English at Monash University, at the ANU, at the Royal Military College, Duntroon, and at the Australian Defence Force Academy. In 1944 she married H.M. Green. Well known as an essayist and reviewer, she was a regular contributor to Australian literary magazines and published significant essays on Martin Boyd, E.L. Grant Watson, 'Henry Handel Richardson', Patrick White, C.J. Brennan, Christina Stead and Kylie Tennant. Her published works include a revised edition of her husband's *History* (1985); an extensively researched biography and critical study of 'Henry Handel Richardson', *Ulysses Bound* (1973), which won the James Cook University's Foundation for Australian Literary Studies Award and the Barbara Ramsden Award and appeared in a revised edition in 1986 titled *Henry Handel Richardson and her Fiction*; a collection of literary essays, *The Music of Love* (1984); three lectures delivered for the Foundation for Australian Literary Studies titled *The Writer, the Reader and the Critic in a Monoculture* (1986), which were reproduced in an expanded collection in 1991 titled *Writer Reader Critic*; and an edition of the writings of E.L. Grant Watson, *Descent of Spirit* (1990). With David Headon she edited *Imagining the Real: Australian Writing in the Nuclear Age* (1987). Her poetry, under the name Dorothy Auchterlonie, appeared regularly in literary magazines and in three collections, *Kaleidoscope* (1940), *The Dolphin* (1967) and *Something to Someone* (1983). She was awarded the OAM in 1984 and made AO in 1988; in 1987 she received an honorary doctorate from the University of New South Wales. Passionately concerned with the larger issues of culture, Dorothy Green approached literature from an interdisciplinary, nonconformist perspective. In her later years her uncompromising convictions on international and local political issues and on the moral responsibility of writers, readers and critics made her one of the most influential cultural figures. *Ulysses Bound* is her most substantial literary achievement, but her distinctive qualities as a critic, reflecting her wide-ranging interests and lightly worn but extensive scholarship, are most visible in her various essays and lectures.

GREEN, Evan (1930–), born Fairfield, NSW, has had a colourful career in radio, television, the motoring industry and, in recent years, as an author of adventure thrillers, most of them set against the vast outback, over which Green travelled in his days as a motoring journalist, covering and participating in some of the car races around Australia. With adventure novels such as *Alice to Nowhere* (1984), *Adam's Empire* (1986), *Kalinda* (1991) and *Bet Your Life* (1992), Green has hit upon a satisfactory formula of the blockbusting family saga, crime and derring-do, romance and suspense. His novels have sold well in Australia and overseas and have been purchased for film and television. *Alice to Nowhere* revolves around a pair of thieves who kill an old lady while stealing opals from a safe in an Alice Springs hotel. The chase takes place along the famous Birdsville Track, the novel highlighting the harshness and heat of the inland. *Adam's Empire*, with sales of a quarter of a million copies, and *Kalinda*, its sequel, are set on an outback sheep station, Kalinda, founded by Adam Ross. Decades of drama and adventure, Black–White relationships, the Second World War and personal, family and economic crises, combine to produce a final happy ending. *Bet*

Your Life is based on a bet accepted by documentary film-maker, Kelly Hunnicutt, that he can elude the police in the outback for seven days. Unknown to Hunnicutt, he has been set up by his estranged wife and his business partner on a theft-and-murder charge. An exciting path is cut through Broken Hill, Tibooburra, Innamincka, Boulia and on to a finale at Alice Springs. Green has also written *Journeys with Gelignite Jack* (1966, echoes of the old Redex trials), *A Bootful of Right Arms* (1975), *Dust and Glory* (1990) and for television, *The Last Explorer* (1978), *Around Australia Days* (1980) and *On the Road* (1984).

GREEN, H.M. (Henry Mackenzie) (1881–1962), born Sydney, was educated in arts and law at the University of Sydney. After travelling in Europe for a year he returned to Sydney in 1907 and spent two years on the staff of the *Sydney Morning Herald*, followed by eleven years with the *Daily Telegraph*. He was librarian at the Fisher Library, University of Sydney, 1921–46. Green was an active member of the Casuals Club and had close personal associations with most of Sydney's leading writers, artists, academics and publishers. Green was married twice, on the second occasion to Dorothy Auchterlonie. Well known as a lecturer, he participated regularly in the arts courses at the University. He also lectured to the WEA and other groups, gave the first lectures in Sydney sponsored by the CLF, and was a familiar broadcaster on Australian literature for the ABC. Evidence of his considerable influence on writers and students of Australian literature survives in his publications and in the Fisher Library's extensive holdings of Australiana.

Apart from numerous essays and reviews, including annual surveys of Australian literature in *Southerly* 1939–51, Green's published writings are *The Story of Printing* (1929) and, with J.A. Ferguson and Mrs A.G. Foster, *The Howes and Their Press* (1936); five lectures, *Australian Literature: A Summary* (1928), *The Poetry of W.B. Yeats* (1931), *A Midsummer Night's Dream* (1933), *Kendall* (1933) and *Wentworth as Orator* (1935); a significant study of Brennan which he originally delivered as two lectures for the English Association, *Christopher Brennan* (1939); *An Outline of Australian Literature* (1930), which, although preceded by Nettie Palmer's *Modern Australian Literature* (1924), was the first comprehensive critical survey to 1928; a further more cursory survey, *Australian Literature 1900–1950* (1951); and *Fourteen Minutes* (1944), a series of radio talks on Australian poetry, revised by Dorothy Green in 1950. Green also published two books of poetry, *The Happy Valley* (1925) and *The Book of Beauty* (1929), and edited *Australian Poetry 1943* (1944) and the influential collection *Modern Australian Poetry* (1946). A writer of short fiction, and the author of an unpublished novel, he is represented in *Australian Short Stories* (1928), ed. George Mackaness. But Green's most important work is his two-volume *A History of Australian Literature* (q.v., 1961). A work of wide scope, thoroughness and painstaking scholarship, it is a mine of information, culled partly from Green's own unique knowledge of Australian writing, and is still

the most significant literary history. The *History* was revised by his widow, Dorothy Green, in 1985.

GREEN, James (1864–1948), born Newcastle-on-Tyne, England, was ordained a Methodist minister in 1893 and served as a chaplain with the Australian Bushmen's contingents in the Boer War and later with the Australian forces in the First World War. His publications include poetry, *The Story of the Australian Bushmen* (1903), *News from No Man's Land* (1917), *The Angels of Mons* (1921) and a collection of religious meditations, *From My Hospital Window* (1935). His fiction includes *The Selector* (1907) and *The Lost Echo* (1910).

GREEN, Judith, see **RODRIGUEZ, Judith**

GREENWAY, Francis (1777–1837), born near Bristol, England, was an architect when transported to NSW in 1814 for forgery. Appointed a government architect in 1816, he was emancipated on the completion of his first assignment, the lighthouse known as Macquarie Tower on South Head, Sydney Harbour. Greenway's many architectural achievements include St James's Church and the Supreme Court in King Street, Sydney; St Luke's Church, Liverpool; St Matthew's Church, Windsor; and the Court House, Windsor. Greenway's reminiscences in the *Australian Almanack* of 1835 provide considerable information about colonial life of the time. M.H. Ellis wrote the biography *Francis Greenway* (1949). A fictionalised account of Greenway's life is given in Andrew Mallon's *Builder of Dreams* (1984).

GREENWOOD, Kerry, see **Crime Fiction**

GREER, Germaine (1939–), born Melbourne, was educated at the Star of the Sea Convent, Gardenvale, and the universities of Melbourne, Cambridge and Sydney. She lectured in English at the University of Warwick 1967–72, was co-founder of the controversial magazine *Suck*, a columnist for the *Sunday Times* 1971–73 and contributor to such periodicals as *Listener*, *Spectator*, *Oz*, *Rolling Stone* and *Esquire*. She also appeared in a British television series and had contacts with rock musicians and other members of the pop culture but did not become a well-known media personality until the American publication of her influential feminist work *The Female Eunuch* (q.v.) in 1971. Attacked by some hard-line feminists, the book was nevertheless hailed generally as a landmark in the women's liberation movement, achieved enormous sales and was subsequently translated into several languages. In 1971 Greer toured the USA to promote the book, appearing on numerous television and radio shows and debating feminist issues with various well-known figures, including Norman Mailer. In Australia reviews were mixed and Greer has continued to have an ambivalent relationship with her homeland, visiting it only fleetingly and spending most of her time in Southern Tuscany and in Essex, England. She had the position of professor at the University of Tulsa 1979–83, was founder-director of the Tulsa Center for the Study of Women's Literature and has been director of Stump Cross Books since 1988. She has also written a historical account of obstacles to female achievement in the field of painting, *The Obstacle Race* (1979); an account of the politics of human fertility, *Sex and Destiny* (1984); a critical study of Shakespeare (1986); under the pseudonym 'Rose Blight' a parodic work, *The Revolting Garden* (1979); an autobiography, *Daddy, We Hardly Knew You* (1989); and an account of the historical, cultural, medical and psychological aspects of women's menopause, *The Change* (1991). Some of her essays and articles were collected in *The Madwoman's Underclothes* (1986); and she has edited *The Uncollected Verse of Aphra Behn* (1989) and, with others, an anthology of seventeenth-century women's verse, *Kissing the Rod* (1988). With books like *The Female Eunuch, The Obstacle Race* and *Sex and Destiny* Greer has appealed to an international market, but her autobiography has more direct relevance for Australia; a quest for her dead father's past, which has unpleasant consequences revealing Reg Greer to have been as fraudulent as his self-adopted surname, it is also a quest for the historical and present meaning of White Australia.

GREGORY, Sir Augustus Charles (1819–1905), born Nottinghamshire, England, arrived in the Swan River colony in 1829 and became a surveyor. In 1855 he led a major exploration and scientific expedition across northern Australia from the Victoria River to Brisbane; his last major expedition was to search for Ludwig Leichhardt in 1858. Thereafter he was Queensland's surveyor-general and its first commissioner for Crown Lands. In addition to numerous pamphlets and reports on various aspects of his administration, his collected papers and records, together with those of his brother and fellow surveyor-explorer, Francis Thomas Gregory (1821–88), were published in 1884 as *Journals of Australian Explorations.* Wendy Birman published *Gregory of Rainworth* (1979); J.H.L. Cumpston wrote *Augustus Gregory and the Inland Sea* (1972).

'GREIG, Maysie' (Jennifer Ames) (?1901–71), born Jennifer Greig Smith, Sydney, won a literary competition at 15, worked as a journalist with the Sydney *Sun* 1919–20, and then went to England where she published *Peggy of Beacon Hill* (1920), which was serialised and later filmed. Permanently resident in England, except for a brief period in Australia in the 1950s, 'Maysie Greig' went on to write about 200 popular romantic novels, few of which have any connection with Australia.

GRENVILLE, Kate (Catherine Elizabeth) (1950–), born Sydney, was educated at the University of Sydney before working at Film Australia as an editor. At the age of 26 she left Australia and spent seven years in Europe and the USA, where she completed a master's degree at the University of Colorado. She has published a collection of short stories, *Bearded Ladies* (1984); three novels, *Lilian's Story* (1985, which won the 1984 *Australian*/Vogel National Literary Award),

Dreamhouse (1986) and *Joan Makes History* (1988); a practical workbook for other writers, *The Writing Book* (1990); and edited, with Sue Wolfe, *Making Stories: How Ten Australian Novels Were Written* (1993), a study of the development of selected novels based on manuscript versions. A powerful writer, Grenville merges comic and gothic modes with innovative effects. Written with astringent wit and in uncluttered prose, the short stories of *Bearded Ladies* recount the experiences of a range of women, whose somewhat wayward progress through relationships, travel or childhood experiences frequently culminates in unpleasant or bizarre discoveries. *Lilian's Story*, loosely based on the eccentric personality of Bea Miles, is a study of a superbly self-confident woman who has the courage to create her own different destiny. Fat and ungainly, Lil makes a virtue of her socially embarrassing difference, growing into an imaginative independence and uninhibited zest for experience, which even a prolonged spell in an institution for the insane cannot quench. Reduced to existing as a derelict in old age, she still decides that her life has been worthwhile, having given a very different twist to her father's early caution that, considering her other handicaps, her future lay in her own hands. *Dreamhouse* focuses on an English couple, Louise Dufrey, the narrator of the novel, and her husband Reynold, who is engaged in completing his doctoral dissertation on Malthus's Theory of Necessary Catastrophe, and their two children, Hugo and Viola. Provided with a decrepit villa in Tuscany by Reynold's supervisor Daniel, the couple are confronted with their several limitations and with the decay of their marriage, in which Reynold's latent homosexuality is more a symptom than a cause. A reworking of an earlier short story, 'Country Pleasures', *Dreamhouse* belongs to an earlier period of Grenville's writing and extends its Gothic suggestiveness into concrete but more mundane realities. *Joan Makes History* is a rewriting of history from the multiple alternative viewpoints of a series of Joans, a composite Australian everywoman, who is also tethered in contemporary life. Thin, plain, flat-chested, Joan is determined to make up for her natural limitations by becoming a woman of destiny but ultimately comes to realise in childbirth that women have always made history, if it is not the traditional male-defined history of public events. Grenville's feminist convictions, most sharply expressed in *Bearded Ladies*, expand in *Dreamhouse* and *Lilian's Story* to criticism of the social confinements suffered by people of both genders.

'Gretel', a short story by Hal Porter (q.v.), was first published in the American periodical *Literary Review* (1963–64) and is included in his collection *The Cats of Venice* (1965). A 45-year-old man, smugly conscious that he is *dégagé* and safe from life, is recalled to his mother's funeral in the provincial Victorian town where he was born and relives an important emotional incident of his youth. At the age of 12 he had flouted his mother's prohibitions to encounter a beautiful young girl, Gretel, who was briefly staying in a secluded part of the house. The most exquisite creature he had ever seen, or was ever to see, she had 'the hair of Rapunzel, of all immolated princesses, of all the children lost in the snow or woods of ballads'. Entranced, he gave her a white china necklace. Now, thirty-three years later, he is appalled to learn that Gretel is still in the town, incarcerated in the asylum for the insane where she has always had to live; now aged beyond her years and hideous, she grimly clings to the china necklace.

GREY, Sir George (1812–98), born Lisbon, Portugal, was an army officer before being attracted to the Australian colonies by the publicity associated with the explorations of Charles Sturt. In 1837–39 he led two abortive expeditions to establish a settlement in north-western Australia. Grey's inaccurate report on the WA country inland of Champion Bay was later followed (1864) by an ill-fated Camden Harbour settlement attempt. An account of that expedition is given in Christopher Richards's *There Were Three Ships: The Story of the Camden Harbour Expedition* (1990). In 1839 Grey was resident magistrate at King George Sound; and in 1840–45 he was governor of SA. In 1845 he went to NZ as governor. His published works in Australia include his compilation of *A Vocabulary of the Dialects of South Western Australia* (1840) and the account of his explorations, *Journals of Two Expeditions of Discovery in North-West and Western Australia during the Years 1837, 38, and 39* (1841). John Rutherford and G.C. Henderson published biographies of Grey in 1961 and 1967; he was the subject of a television series, *The Governor*, in 1979. Grey appears as a character in Graham Sheil's play *The Dead Heart* (1991).

'GREY, Harold', see **ARGLES, Theodore Emile**

GRIFFITHS, Bryn (1933–), born Swansea, Wales, was a seaman in the British merchant navy (1951–58) and a full-time writer (1962–76), before becoming cultural adviser and arts co-ordinator for industry with the Trades and Labour Council of WA; in 1989 he published *Wharfies: A Celebration of 100 years on the Fremantle Waterfront 1889–1989*. His interests lie in community arts, theatre, modern poetry and Celtic history; his books of poetry include *The Mask of Pity* (1966), *The Stones Remember* (1967), *Scars* (1969), *At the Airport* (1971), *The Survivors* (1971), *Beasthoods* (1972), *Starboard Green* (1973), *The Dark Convoys* (1974), *Love Poems* (1980), *The Shadow Beasts* (1981), and *Sea Poems* (1988). His radio plays, 'The Sailor' (1967) and 'The Dream of Arthur' (1968), were broadcast by the BBC.

GRIMSHAW, Beatrice (1870–1953), born County Antrim, Ireland, was educated in France and at the University of London and Queen's College, Belfast. She worked as a journalist in Dublin from 1891 before working for various shipping companies in the Canary Islands, the USA and England. In 1903 she left for the Pacific to report on the region for the *Daily Graphic* and accepted government and other commissions to write tourist publicity for various Pacific islands and NZ. She moved to Papua after being commissioned by the London *Times* and the *Sydney Morning Herald* as a travel writer and stayed there for the next twenty-seven years, becoming a close friend of Sir Hubert Murray (q.v.). Her experiences yielded such books as a novel, *Vaiti of the Islands* (1907), and the travel books *From Fiji to the Cannibal Islands* (1907), *In the Strange South Seas* (1907) and *The New New Guinea* (1910). She also wrote a further thirty-seven books of fiction including a semi-autobiography, *Isles of Adventure* (1930). Best known of these is *When the Red Gods Call* (1911), which was frequently reprinted and serialised and translated into several languages; others include *Guinea Gold* (1912), *The Sorcerer's Stone* (1914), *Kris Girl* (1917) and *The Coral Queen* (1919). *Conn of the Coral Seas* (1922) was filmed by Hollywood as *Adorable Outcast*. Grimshaw managed a plantation near Samarai 1917–22, accompanied exploring sorties up the Sepik and Fly rivers in 1923 and 1926 and joined her brother Ramsay in tobacco-growing in 1934. In 1936 she retired to Kelso, NSW, where she died. Nigel Krauth's novel *J.F. Was Here* (1990) is partly based on Grimshaw's unconventional life. A best-selling writer in the 1920s and sometimes favourably compared with Joseph Conrad, Bret Harte and Robert Louis Stevenson, Grimshaw is now virtually unknown, while all her books are out of print. Susan Gardner, who has carried out extensive research into Grimshaw's life and achievements (described in *Hecate* 13, 1987–88), concludes that she was made up of contradictions, the most extraordinary being that between her explicit anti-feminism and her feminist career.

GRIMSTONE, Mary Leman (c.1800–?), born Hamburg, Germany, was the daughter of Leman Thomas Rede, an English expatriate known in literary circles. In 1826 she went to the colony of Van Diemen's Land for her health and during her three years there wrote most of *Woman's Love* (q.v., 1832), which although set in England was probably the first novel written in Australia. There are passing references to the penal system in *Woman's Love* and in Grimstone's other novels, *Louisa Egerton* (1830) and *Cleone* (1834). She also wrote several short stories based on her Tasmanian experiences, and a letter about the colony which attracted replies in Hobart after it was published in London in 1827.

GRIN, Henri Louis (1844–1921) was the Swiss-born hoaxer 'Louis de Rougemont', whose sensational account of his adventures during thirty-odd years as a castaway among the Aborigines of north-west and central Australia was published in London in the *Wide World Magazine*, 1898–99. 'De Rougemont' was supported by his publishers and by the explorer John Moresby, and lectured to the British Association for the Advancement of Science, but his claims were disputed by 'Louis' Becke and David Wynford Carnegie. He was exposed by the London *Daily Chronicle*, which provided in *Grien ou Rougemont: Or, The Story of a Modern Robinson Crusoe* (1898) the information on Grin's life and Australian experiences from which subsequent accounts derive. 'De Rougemont' was satirised by E.J. Brady in 'Rougemont Outdone' (*Arrow*, 1898–99) and was the subject of a play by Geoffrey Maslen included in *Five Plays for Radio*, ed. Alrene Sykes (1975).

GROSZ, Elizabeth, see **Feminism and Australian Literature**

'GROVER, Marshall' (L.F. Meares) (1921–), born Merrylands, NSW, has published a handful of crime and romance stories under the pseudonyms 'Lesley Malloy', 'Frank Everton' and 'Val Sterling' but has gained a reputation as Australia's most prolific writer of western stories, having published more than 400 titles under the pseudonym 'Marshall Grover' in a career extending over forty years.

GROVER, Monty (1870–1943), born Melbourne, had an extensive career in journalism. He was the foundation editor of the Sydney *Sun* (1910–16), editor of the *Sunday Sun* (1917) and its representative in London (1918–21), and foundation editor of *Sun-News Pictorial* (1922) and the *Evening Sun* (1923). He was magazine editor of the Melbourne *Herald* (1929–30) and first editor of the Sydney labour daily, the *World* (1931–32). His writings include the dramas *The Sleeping Beauty and the Beast* (1903), *The Minus Quantity and Other Short Plays* (1914), *Judah and the Giant* (1915) and *The Time is Now Ripe* (1937), a socialist work. Verses by Grover are included in *The 'Bulletin' Book of Humorous Verses and Recitations* (1920) under the title 'The Man Who Writes *The Bulletin*', and in W.T. Pyke's *The Australian Favourite Reciter* (1907). Grover's memoirs, *Hold Page One*, were published in 1993.

GUESS, Jeff (1948–), born and educated in SA, is a high-school teacher, having graduated from Flinders University. Active in the Friendly Street writing community (he co-edited with Donna McSkimming the No. 12 *Friendly Street Reader*), he has published several small volumes of poetry: *Leaving Maps* (1984); *Four in the Afternoon* (1987); *Painting the Town – the Gawler Poems* (1988); *Replacing Fuses in the House of Cards* (1988), a *Poetry Australia* publication; *Rites of Arrival: Poems from the Museums of the History Trust of South Australia* (1990); *Out of Bounds* (1990); *Selected Sonnets* (1991) and *Early in the Cafe Boulevarde: The Adelaide Poems* (1991). With Anne Brewster he compiled *Inner Courtyard* (1990), an anthology of SA love poetry.

Guess's interest in history is evident in the poems inspired by the SA History Trust museums and by others such as 'The Map Maker' (Flinders and Kangaroo Island), 'Lambing Flat Massacre, 1861', 'Miners Cottages – Paxton Square'. His more personal poems such as 'Making Easter Cakes', 'Collecting Dickens' and 'Spring and Fall' are eloquent and attractive. 'Under Siege Now' won the Canning Literary Award in 1982 and 'The Bee Farm' won the Melbourne Poetry Society Award in 1986.

GULLETT, Henry (1837–1914), born Devonshire, England, came to Australia in 1853 and worked on the

Victorian goldfields. Although he returned to England in 1861, he came back to Melbourne to join the staff of the *Argus*. He later edited the *Australasian* (1872–85), was associate editor of the Sydney *Daily Telegraph* and editor of the weekly *Tribune*. He was acting editor of the Sydney *Morning Herald* in the federal referendum period (1898), federalism being a cause he supported wholeheartedly. After a period as editor of the *Daily Telegraph* (1901–3) he retired from active journalism; from 1908 until his death he was a member of the NSW Legislative Council. Gullett made the *Australasian* the outstanding colonial literary journal of the day; his editorship of three of the major daily newspapers of the time attests also to his status as an Australian newspaperman. A scholarly man, Gullett was president of the Shakespeare Society of NSW 1904–11. He was uncle of Sir Henry Somer Gullett (q.v.) and his mother, Isabella, was a cousin of the poet John Keats.

GULLETT, Sir Henry Somer (1878–1940), born Toolamba West, Victoria, was a member of the literary staff of the *Sydney Morning Herald*, of which his uncle, Henry Gullett (q.v.), had been editor. He later became a war correspondent in the First World War. Director of Immigration (1920–22), an area in which he had long been interested, and then a member of the House of Representatives (1928–40), Gullett was killed in the Canberra air crash 13 August 1940. Gullett was related to fiction-writer Barbara Baynton, through marriage to her daughter; his son, Henry Baynton Somer ('Jo') Gullett, wrote a biographical memoir to the 1965 edition of Baynton's *Bush Studies* and an autobiography, *Good Company* (1992). Sir Henry Gullett's own writings include the immigration booklets *The Opportunity in Australia* (1914), *Unguarded Australia* (1919) and a volume of the official history of Australia in the First World War, titled *The Australian Imperial Force in Sinai and Palestine, 1914–1918* (1923).

'Gumsucker' was a colloquialism, now largely obsolete, for a resident of Victoria. The term is used in William Howitt's *Land, Labour and Gold* (1855), Frank Fowler's *Southern Light and Shadows* (1859) and Nathan Spielvogel's books of reminiscences, *A Gumsucker on the Tramp* (1905) and *The Gumsucker at Home* (1913). Joseph Furphy uses the abbreviation 'sucker' in *Such is Life* (1903). The folklore journal *Gumsuckers' Gazette* (later *Australian Tradition*) is an example of the partial revival of the term.

Gumsuckers' Gazette, see ***Australian Tradition***

Gundagai, a town on the Murrumbidgee River in southern NSW and on the main inland highway between Sydney and Melbourne, has long been a natural meeting-place for travellers. Before the advent of the automobile it was a gathering-spot for teamsters, drovers, shearers and all varieties of bush travellers. It is best known as the spot where the bullocky's dog fouled the tuckerbox, an act commemorated in the teamster song 'Nine (Five) Miles from Gundagai'; in later poems (e.g. by Jack Moses, q.v.), in which the dog guards the tucker box; and in recent times by a bronze statue of a dog on a tuckerbox by the Italian sculptor Rosconi, whose 'Marble Masterpiece' is one of Gundagai's tourist attractions. 'The Road to Gundagai', with its well-known chorus beginning 'There's a track, winding back to an old-fashioned shack', was composed by Jack O'Hagan and included in the repertoire of Australian baritone Peter Dawson. The traditional shearers' song 'Lazy Harry's' (q.v.) celebrates the legendary 'lambing down' pub on the road to Gundagai. A.B. Paterson and R.J. Cassidy ('Gilroony') both wrote poems titled 'The Road to Gundagai'.

GUNEW, Sneja (1946–), born West Germany of a German mother and Bulgarian father, arrived in Australia in 1952. Educated at the universities of Melbourne, Toronto and Newcastle, she has taught in literature and women's studies at tertiary level since 1972, and now teaches in Canada. She has contributed short stories to anthologies and has written extensively on multicultural writing in Australia and the migrant experience. With Loló Houbein, Alexandra Karakostas-Seda and Jan Mahyuddin she compiled the extensive *A Bibliography of Australian Multicultural Writers* (1992); she is also the editor of *Displacements: Migrant Storytellers* (1982), *Displacements II* (1987) and *Feminist Knowledge: Critique and Construct* (1990), with Jan Mahyuddin, *Beyond the Echo: Multicultural Women's Writing* (1988), with Anna Couani, *Telling Ways: Australian Women's Experimental Writing* (1988), with Kateryna O. Longley, *Striking Chords: Multicultural Literary Interpretations* (1991) and with Anna Yeatman, *Feminism and the Politics of Difference* (1993). She has also written *Framing Marginality: Multicultural Literary Studies* (1994).

GUNN, Jeannie (1870–1961) was born Jeannie Taylor in Melbourne, daughter of a journalist. She established a private school with her sister at Hawthorn, a Melbourne suburb, then in 1901 married Aeneas Gunn and went with him to Elsey station on the Roper River in the Northern Territory. She returned to Melbourne after his death in 1903. She published two books, *The Little Black Princess* (1905) and *We of the Never-Never* (q.v., 1908) (see Aborigine in White Australian Literature). The latter, which has sold over half a million copies, is an extended anecdote of the vicissitudes of life in the Territory and has given Australian literature such characters as the Maluka (the boss), Cheon (the Chinese cook) and the Fizzer (the mailman), as well as the Little Missus, Jeannie Gunn herself. An Australian film of *We of the Never-Never* was screened in 1982.

GURNEY, Alex (1902–55), born Portsmouth, England, studied art at Hobart Technical School. In 1926 he published a book of caricatures of leading Tasmanian citizens, *Tasmanians Today*. A cartoonist with numerous newspapers, Gurney was the creator of the comic strip 'Bluey and Curley', which appeared in 1940 and rapidly became one of Australia's most popular strips. It depicted the vicissitudes of army life as seen through the eyes of Bluey, the hard-bitten veteran of the First World War, and his mate Curley, the ingenuous young recruit. Bluey and Curley are important figures in the development of the comic 'ocker' image of the Australian male. Other cartoonists to draw the strip after Gurney's death were Norm Rice and Les Dixon; the latter carried it through until his retirement in 1975, when 'Bluey and Curley' was also retired from the Melbourne *Sun-News Pictorial* where it had first appeared. John Gurney and Keith Dunstan published *Gurney & Bluey & Curley: Alex Gurney and His Greatest Cartoons* (1986).

GURR, Michael (1961–), born Melbourne, studied at the National Theatre Drama School and has written for screen and stage. Playwright-in-residence with the Melbourne Theatre Company in 1982, he has also worked as a director. His published plays include *Magnetic North* (first performed 1982) & *Imitation Real* (first performed 1981 and published with *Magnetic North* in 1983), *A Pair of Claws* (first performed 1983, published the same year and produced as a feature film titled *Departure* in 1986), *What You Wanted* (first performed 1983 and published with *This and That* in 1988), *Dead to the World* (first performed 1986 and published the same year), and *Sex Diary of an Infidel* (first performed 1992 and published the same year). His other plays include 'Indoors', 'The First Church in Hell', 'Three Short Plays', 'On the Horn', 'Man and Beast', 'Emmett Stone', which was also adapted for film, 'The Seamstress and the Publisher', 'The Hundred Year Ambush', 'These Days', 'World's Apart' 'Victoria Bitter' (with Laurence Housman), and 'Dry Storm'. He has also written the screenplay, *Ninety Miles an Hour Down a Dead End Street*. Writing in a style he terms 'heightened naturalism' and generally avoiding 'answers' to the problems he poses, Gurr deals with contemporary issues, such as the ruthlessness of property developers, Australian sex tourists, the fragility of present-day relationships and political repression and torture.

GURR, Robin (1934–), born Sydney, has published six small books of restrained, private poetry which is notable for intricate word-patterns and subtlety of language. They are *Song is a Mirror* (1963), *Music in the Grass* (1971), *A House of Cards* (1975), *Harvest of Birds* (1981), *Masques* (1986) and *The Tiger in the Head* (1987). She has also written books for children, *Red Pepper* (1954), *Bush Outlaw* (1954) and *The Kid and the King* (1980).

GWYNNE, Agnes M. published several romantic novels with Australian settings, e.g. *The Mistress of Windfells* (1921), a station romance of the Victorian Western District; *The Mystery of Lakeside House* (1925), set in a Victorian north-west country town in the period after the First World War; *An Emergency Husband* (?1926), which related the vicissitudes of a young woman compelled to marry to satisfy the terms of an inheritance; and *High Dawn* (1935), a sentimental account of the convict period with a hero badly used by fate. Agnes Gwynne also published two plays, *A Social Experiment* (1908), which won an exhibition of women's work in Melbourne, and *The Capitalist* (1931).

GYE, Hal ('James Hackston', 'Hacko') (1888–1967), born Ryde, Sydney, worked as a law clerk before pursuing three separate careers in Australian art and letters: as Hal Gye, illustrator of the original 1915 edition of C.J. Dennis's *The Songs of a Sentimental Bloke* with the now-famous winged cherubs and illustrator for Angus & Robertson and for the *Bulletin*, the *Melbourne Punch*, the Sydney *Daily Telegraph* and other papers; as short story writer 'James Hackston', who

from 1936 wrote the 'Father' series of stories for the *Bulletin* and published two collections of short fiction, *Father Clears Out* (1966) and *The Hole in the Bedroom Floor* (1969); and as the *Bulletin* poet 'Hacko', whose pithy and often amusing verses appeared through the 1940s and 1950s on the 'Aboriginalities' page of the *Bulletin*. A competent short fiction writer, somewhat in the 'Steele Rudd' and the later Eric Schlunke manner, Gye combines the comedy and the tragedy of rural life in amusing and frequently moving stories. Elizabeth Lane's *Hal Gye: The Man and his Work* (1986) gives Gye's own account of his early years, further biographical data and selections from his art and writings.

H

HACKETT, Patricia (1908–63), daughter of Sir Winthrop Hackett, benefactor of the University of WA, graduated in law in London and practised in Adelaide. Her interest in drama led to her acquiring her own little theatre, the Torch, in Adelaide in 1934 where, in the 1930s and later in the 1950s, she produced, designed the sets for and acted in many plays. In 1938 she published *These Little Things*, a volume of forty-one poems set in Adelaide and in the Solomon Islands where she lived on the island M'bangai, which she owned just before the outbreak of the Pacific War in 1941. The Patricia Hackett Prize was endowed in her memory in 1965 for the best original creative contribution published in *Westerly* (q.v.) each year.

'HACKSTON, James', see **GYE, Hal**

HADDON, F.W. (Frederick William) (1839–1906), born Surrey, England, came to Australia in 1863 to work for the Melbourne *Argus*. He was co-editor of the *Australasian* when it began publication in 1864 as the weekend journal of the *Argus*, and in 1865 became its editor. In 1867 he became editor of the *Argus*; his thirty-one years in that position were not without criticism, especially from the opponents of free trade, which Haddon espoused, but they were the heyday of the *Argus*. Haddon, a friend of Marcus Clarke's, was instrumental in the founding of the Yorick Club in 1868.

HADGRAFT, C.H. (Cecil Huddlestone) (1904–87), born Melbourne, studied at the universities of Queensland and Manchester and in 1956–57 studied and lectured at the University of Omaha and Louisiana State University. In Australia he taught at the University of Queensland, ultimately becoming a reader in its Department of English. He introduced Australian Literature courses into the department in 1964. He was also a major force in the development of the Fryer Library at the University. Hadgraft's critical and scholarly writings include *Queensland and Its Writers* (1959–60), *Australian Literature: A Critical Account to 1955* (1960), a biography of James Brunton Stephens (1969), and, with Ray Beilby, a brief study of Ada Cambridge, Jessie Couvreur and Rosa Praed (1979). He edited new editions in 1962 and 1984 of Henry Savery's early works, *The Hermit in Van Diemen's Land* and *Quintus Servinton*; a new edition in 1969 with Ray Beilby of Jessie Couvreur's novel *Uncle Piper of Piper's Hill* (first published 1889); *Coast to Coast* (1961); with Richard Wilson, *A Century of Australian Short Stories* (1963); in 1966 Frederick Sinnett's *The Fiction Fields of Australia* (first published 1856); and in

1986 *The Australian Short Story before Lawson*. See Criticism.

HADOW, Lyndall (1903–76), born Kalgoorlie, was the sister of the novelist Donald Stuart, and daughter of Julian Stuart, 1891 shearers' strike prisoner, and Florence Collings, one of WA's first women journalists. Long-time editor of the magazine *Our Women*, she was a prolific writer of short stories, reviews and critical articles. Her collection of short fiction, *Full Cycle and Other Stories* (1969), deals with the State's wheat belt, its far north-west and the assimilation of non-British migrants into the more settled south-west. She edited a book of her father's writings, *Part of the Glory* (1967). The WA branch of the FAW created the Lyndall Hadow Annual Award for short stories in 1977; it also published *She Too Is 'Part of the Glory': Lyndall Hadow 1903–1976* (1976).

HAENKE, Helen (1916–78) published two volumes of poetry, *The Good Company* (1977) and *Prophets and Honour* (1979), both characterised by wit, compassion, perceptive awareness of people and fine control of language. She also published a play, *The Bottom of a Birdcage* (performed 1976, published 1978) and *Firebug* in *3 Queensland One-act Plays for Festivals*, vol. 2 (1978). Her unpublished plays include 'Golden Sword' (1961), 'The Passage' (1978), 'Black Out' (1967) and 'Truth to Tell', which won an award in the Ipswich drama competition for 1960.

HAILES, Nathaniel (1802–79), born London, claimed to have enjoyed the acquaintance of such prominent English literary figures as Sir Walter Scott and Thomas de Quincey. He published *The Emigrant and Other Poems* (1833) in England before his departure for SA in 1839. In 1856 he published *The Soul's Journey: A Metrical Fantasy;* as 'Timothy Short' he edited the brief-lived literary magazine *The Wanderer* (1853), in which several of his own poems on Australian subjects were published. His autobiographical 'Personal Recollections of a Septuagenarian' were published serially in the *Observer Miscellany* in 1877.

HALES, A.A.G. (Alfred Arthur Greenwood) (1860–1936), nicknamed 'Smiler', was born Kent Town, SA, and wandered the outback working at a variety of jobs and contributing to country newspapers stories of his experiences, many of which were published in *The Wanderings of a Simple Child* (1890). He was a war correspondent in the Boer War, in which he was taken prisoner, a participant in the rebellion against the Turks in Macedonia in 1903, and a war correspondent in the Russo-Japanese war and the First World War. He then lived in England, where he continued to write a long line of adventure novels, which had begun with *Driscoll, King of Scouts* (1901), a story of the Boer War. His best-known creation is McGlusky, an Australian of Scots descent, who is the hero in 1902 of *McGlusky: Being a Compilation from the Diary of Trooper McWiddy of Remington's Scouts* and who appears in a further eighteen novels. He also wrote a series of sporting novels, and often set his fiction in countries other than Australia. In his Australian period his interest in newspapers is reflected in his founding of the *Coolgardie Mining Review* and the *Boulder Evening Star*. He published a volume of poetry in the bush ballad tradition, *Poems and Ballads* (1909). His autobiographical works are *My Life of Adventure* (1918) and *Broken Trails* (1931).

HALEY, Martin (1905–80), born Brisbane, was a teacher in Queensland. He was, with Paul Grano, a foundation member of the Queensland Catholic Poetry Society and was president of the Catholic Readers' and Writers' Society. Haley published numerous books of verse and translations including *Poems and a Preface* (1936), *More Poems and Another Preface* (1938), *Translations (Mostly)* (1941), *Good Measure: A Century of Epigrams* (1950), *Middle Kingdom* (1952), *Asphodel and Wistaria* (1955, poems from Chinese and Greek), *Preciosa* (1962, poems from Spanish), *Beatrice, Being the Sonnets of Louis Labé 1525–66* (1963), *Lucretia and the Banks of the Anio* (1965), *The Central Splendour (Chung Hua): An Anthology from the Chinese* (1969), and *Trophies: Taken Mostly from the French of José Maria de Heredia* (1972).

HALL, Ben (1837–65), born Breeza, near Tamworth, NSW, was a bushranger who operated in central western NSW in the early 1860s, often in partnership with Frank Gardiner, Johnny Gilbert and others. The exploits of the Hall-Gardiner-Gilbert gang are the subject of Ambrose Pratt's *The Outlaws of Weddin Range* (1911) and Launcelot Booth's *The Devil's Nightcap* (1912), and figure prominently in 'Rolf Boldrewood's' *Robbery Under Arms* (1888), where Hall becomes Wall, Gardiner, Lardner and Gilbert, Hulbert. Two famous bushranging incidents involving the gang, the Eugowra gold escort robbery in 1862 and the raid on Henry Keightley's homestead at Dunn's Plains a year later, are re-created in *Robbery Under Arms*, although 'Boldrewood' transposed the events to the 1850s and made the evil Dan Moran/Dan Morgan (with whom Hall, Gardiner and Gilbert had no contact) leader of the gang. Wall, Lardner and the Eugowra robbery reappear in 'Boldrewood's' *The Miner's Right* (1890). Hall also appears as a character in the novel by Hilda Bridges, *The Squatter's Daughter* (1922), which is based on the successful play (1907) and film (1910) by Edmund Duggan and Bert Bailey. He is the subject of several ballads, including the anonymous 'Brave Ben Hall', 'Ballad of Ben Hall' and 'Ballad of Ben Hall's Gang', John McGuire's bitter 'The Streets of Forbes' and W.H. Ogilvie's 'The Death of Ben Hall'. A television series based on Ben Hall's career was produced

by the ABC in 1975; D.J. Shiel published *Ben Hall* (1983), a detailed reconstruction of Hall's life which sees the outlaw as hero rather than villain. Edgar F. Penzig published *The Sandy Creek Bushranger: a Definitive History of Ben Hall, His Gang and Associates* (1985).

HALL, Edward Smith (1786–1860), born London, came to Australia in 1811 intending to be a gentleman farmer. Unsuccessful on the land, he became active in the commercial life of Sydney, becoming in 1817 the first cashier and secretary of the newly formed Bank of NSW. In 1826 he established with Arthur Hill the *Monitor*, a newspaper which took up the settlers' causes and attacked administrative abuses and incompetence, especially in the rule of Governor Darling. Hall was imprisoned for libel but continued to conduct his campaigns through the *Monitor*, eventually having the pleasure of seeing Darling recalled. From 1838, when he sold the *Monitor*, until 1848 he edited the *Australian*, then worked on Henry Parkes's *Empire*, and finally became a public servant. Hall's struggles for such democratic freedoms as representative government, trial by jury, and freedom of the press and his support of the rights of the native-born led to him being dubbed the 'Colonial Cobbett'. The disputes between the press and Governor Darling are treated in C.H. Currey's *Sir Francis Forbes* (1968). An editorial by Hall figures prominently in 'Price Warung's' story 'Mr Slyde's Auction'.

HALL, James Norman (1887–1951), American novelist and short-story writer, was born in Iowa, served in France in the Lafayette Flying Corps during the First World War and spent some time as a POW in Germany. In 1920 he moved to Tahiti with Charles Nordhoff (q.v.), with whom he collaborated in a series of popular novels, mostly about the South Seas. As well as the novels he published with Nordhoff, the most famous of which are the three dealing with the mutiny against William Bligh, *Mutiny on the Bounty* (1932), *Men against the Sea* (1934) and *Pitcairn's Island* (1934), Hall published verse, novels for adults and children, and an autobiography, *My Island Home* (1952). He also contributed verse, short stories and essays to such periodicals as *Atlantic Monthly*, *Harper's Magazine* and *Saturday Evening Post*. The Bounty trilogy was published in one volume in 1936, *Mutiny on the Bounty*, and was a major source for the film treatments. Another novel with Australian content, *Botany Bay* (1941), was also produced as a film in 1953.

HALL, Ken G. (1901–94), born Sydney, was one of Australia's most successful film producers of the 1930s and 1940s. He made a total of eighteen feature films after founding Cinesound Productions Ltd, a subsidiary of the Greater Union Theatre Group in 1931. Among his most popular productions were four comedies starring Bert Bailey, the first of which was *On Our Selection* (1932). His other films included *The Silence of Dean Maitland* (1934), *Tall Timbers* (1937) and *Smithy* (1946, about Sir Charles Kingsford-Smith). His autobiography, *Directed by Ken G. Hall*, appeared in

1977 updated in 1980 as *Australian Film: The Inside Story*.

HALL, Rodney (1935–), born Birmingham, England, came to Australia after the Second World War. He graduated from the University of Queensland in 1971 and has worked as a freelance script-writer for television and radio, as an actor, as film critic for the ABC, as a youth officer for the Australian Council for the Arts, and as a tutor and lecturer in music and creative writing. Poetry editor of the *Australian* 1967–78, he was poetry adviser to the publishers Angus & Robertson, 1972–75. He has travelled extensively in Europe, Asia and the USA, and for a long period has been actively involved in Aboriginal affairs. He was chairperson of the Australia Council 1990–93, and was made OAM.

A prolific writer, Hall contributed to *Four Poets* (1962) and has published the volumes of poetry *Penniless till Doomsday* (1962), *Forty Beads on a Hangman's Rope* (1963), *Eyewitness* (1967), *The Autobiography of a Gorgon* (1968), *The Law of Karma* (1968), *Heaven, In a Way* (1970), *Romulus and Remus* (1970), *A Soapbox Omnibus* (1973, winner of the Grace Leven Poetry Prize), *Selected Poems* (1975), *Black Bagatelles* (1978) and *The Most Beautiful World* (1981); the novels *The Ship on the Coin* (1972), *A Place Among People* (1975, a prizewinner in the Cook Bicentennial Celebrations Competition), *Just Relations* (1982, winner of the Miles Franklin Award); *Kisses of the Enemy* (1987), *Captivity Captive* (1988, winner of the Victorian Premier's Literary Award), *The Second Bridegroom* (1991) and *The Grisly Wife* (1993); and studies of the artist Andrew Sibley in 1968, and of the writer who has influenced him most, John Manifold, in 1978. He has also edited several significant collections of Australian verse: *New Impulses in Australian Poetry* (q.v., 1968, with Thomas Shapcott), *Australian Poetry 1970* (1970), *Poems from Prison* (1973), and *The Collins Book of Australian Poetry* (1981); a collection of Australian poems and paintings, *Australians Aware* (1975); and three collections of Michael Dransfield's poetry, *Voyage into Solitude* (1978), *The Second Month of Spring* (1980) and *Michael Dransfield. Collected Poems* (1987). He has also written the text of the photographic collection, *Australia – Image of a Nation 1850–1950* (1983) and a meditative travelogue, *Journey Through Australia* (1988). Other awards won by Hall include the Barbara Ramsden Award (1982) and the Poetry Society Prize (1975).

Hall's poetry, ironically detached and frequently witty, is characterised by economy of form and diction, a wide range of tone and a familiarity with myth and legend. His concern with technical virtuosity, especially his use of free, flexible verse-forms and associated patterns of imagery, was evident from the first. Particularly striking is his development of the form he has termed a 'Progression', which consists of a series of short poems, sometimes as many as sixty, each of which is capable of standing alone, but which together form a tightly related unity resembling a single long poem.

Hall's novels emphasise the range of his interests, each one developing a different idea of the novel. *The Ship on the Coin* is a satiric allegory that attacks the apathy, crudity and blindness of bourgeois society; *A Place Among People* is a more conventional 'imagist' novel, that is deliberately open-ended and suggestive. In *Just Relations* he has created a White mythology around an Australian country landscape that is almost as pervasive and substantial as Aboriginal mythology. Set in Whitey's Fall, a small decaying town with a gold-mining past and peopled by a remarkable group of elderly eccentrics, the novel gradually develops a dense web of relations that persuasively knits past, present and future into a pattern of meaning. *The Second Bridegroom* and *Captivity Captive* are the first and last books of a trilogy in which Hall explores the culturally produced meanings of Australia by its Eurocentric invaders. Set in the 1830s, *The Second Bridegroom* is a convict's first-person account of his escape into the NSW bush after being transported for forgery. Protected by a tribe of Aborigines, with whom he lives for some years, he finds himself inexplicably involved in their ceremonies and forced to contend with conflicting ways of knowing the world. Some of the opposed categories which the novel explores by means of the narrator's extended meditations are notions of the primitive and the civilised, order and chaos and colonised and coloniser. *Captivity Captive* uses a historical incident, the mysterious murder of three members of a family on a NSW farm in 1898, as a springboard for exploration of the general theme of captivity, from the cultural imprisonment which perennially sanctions the slaughter of war to the primitive tyranny of family relationships. *The Grisly Wife* completes the trilogy. Set in 1868 (the other two books are set in 1838 and 1898 respectively), *The Grisly Wife* is narrated in free-flowing style by Catherine Byrne, daughter of an Anglican clergyman and wife of Muley Moloch, a preacher, prophet and ex-bootmaker. The revolting odour associated with Moloch's trade, most vividly presented in a scene in which he takes Catherine into a tannery, resembles the unpleasant otherness of the imposed British culture in Australia; as Catherine observes, the bush 'didn't like the smell of us'. Moloch leads a group of women disciples, known collectively as the Houshold of Hidden Stars, to the south coast of NSW, where they found a religious commune. Replicating the familiar biblical story of virgin birth, but ironically undercutting it, *The Grisly Wife* is also a feminist novel in that the women eventually cast out the patriarch. Hall has emphasised that throughout the trilogy he has been concerned to show the shifts in perception of Britain as 'home'; perceived as close by in *The Second Bridgroom*, it is remembered selectively in *The Grisly Wife* and 'only gesturally' in *Captivity Captive Kisses of the Enemy*, set in Australia's near republican future, opposes the careless squanderings of the country's political and business leaders to the subversive perceptions and actions of a few unblinkered individuals. Particularly well received in the USA, Hall's work has been translated into German, Swedish, Danish, French and Chinese.

HALLIGAN, Marion (1940–), born Newcastle, has worked as a teacher and a freelance journalist. In

1992 she was appointed chairperson of the Literature Board of the Australia Council and has served three consecutive two-year terms as chairperson of the Australian National Word Festival. She has contributed short stories to literary periodicals in Australia and overseas and to the collection *Canberra Tales* (1988), and has published three independent collections, *The Living Hothouse* (1988, winner of the 1989 Steele Rudd Award and the Braille Book of the Year Award), *The Hanged Man in the Garden* (1989), and *The Worry Box* (1993); she has also published three novels, *Self-Possession* (1987), *Spidercup* (1990) and *Lovers' Knots* (1992, winner of the 1992 *Age* Book of the Year Award); and *Eat My Words* (1990), a book about food which explores the historical, cultural and mythological aspects of food as well as the aesthetic and physical pleasures of cooking and eating and which won the Prize for Gastronomic Writing in 1991. She has won several short-story awards and in 1990 she won the Geraldine Pascall Prize for book-reviewing and criticism.

Finely controlled irony, assured, elliptical but precise language and a keen sensitivity to place characterise Halligan's short stories. In *The Living Hothouse* the stories range geographically between Australia, NZ and France, and also emotionally as explorations of different moods. As studies of inward experience and the interplay between mood and the outward drama of engagement with others, they are uniformly balanced and controlled, filtered through a fine mesh of irony and sustained by clarity of tone. The stories of *The Hanged Man in the Garden*, set in Canberra, capture specific aspects of life in the national capital, such as the privileged pleasures of a middle-class, largely academic culture and the natural features of a semi-rural, high tableland environment, and juxtapose these certainties with more universal griefs and disappointments; death, betrayal, destructive or fragile relationships and the breakdown of marriage affect some of these characters notwithstanding their immunity from more material anxieties. As in all Halligan's work, descriptions are both aesthetically precise and sensual, sensitive to the idiosyncrasies and fleeting character of landscape, moods, expressions, gestures, foods, rooms or conversations. *Self-Possession*, set within Canberra's academic culture, and partly a comedy of manners, centres on the coming of age of Angela Mayhew, an *ingénue* who is 'educated' by a series of more worldly characters. *Spider Cup* begins with the breakdown of an 18-year-old marriage and the flight of Elinor Spenser, displaced by her husband's mistress, to France. There, while living in a friend's house in a medieval village, she attempts to redefine herself, finding analogies and temporary vengeful consolation between her own situation and a more violent seventeenth-century betrayal. Elinor's work in language as a part-time researcher on a dictionary, has made her aware of the links between language and reality, and she struggles with the notion that her meaning, that is as wife to Ivan her husband, has been destroyed: 'Does a wife only exist when her husband is contemplating her?' Elinor asks herself. 'A wife is called into being only by a husband; therefore does she cease to exist when he stops observing her,

stops regarding her?' She tries out various other possible self-meanings as she contemplates the different lives of other women and is partly comforted, partly discomfited by a temporary physical liaison with her friend, Christophe; finally she discovers that she can choose her meaning of self and that words can be a refuge as they were earlier a threat, finding affirmation in a comment by Sartre: 'Life is nothing until it is lived, but it is yours to make sense of, and the value of it is nothing else but the sense that you choose.' Subtitled *A Hundred-Year Novel*, *Lovers' Knots* traces the fortunes of a Newcastle family from 1911 until the beginning of the twenty-first century. Although a traditional novel in that it spans a chronological period and focuses on one family, *Lovers' Knots* differs from the conventional family saga; constructed around a series of 'snapshots' of the characters taken at different times, rather than as a sequential narrative, it resembles a series of linked stories which perpetually evoke intergenerational ironies, resemblances, echoes and changes. Concerned with unexceptional people, whose lives are not dramatically changed by external circumstances, the novel is almost without a plot, selectively narrating certain experiences of the characters as if they were stopped in time like the family photographs they resemble. At the close of her novel Halligan emphasises that life is not an ordered tapestry but rather ' in a human eye view . . . a matted tangle like water hyacinth in a river, beautiful possibly and charmingly named, but what a pest'. Picking up threads from the past and the future, Halligan unravels both the lovers' knots and the less pleasant tangles, comparing her characters' experience of life to a piece of knitting, 'with its neat patterns thwarted by dropped stitches'. Meanwhile, characters from earlier stories and novels, such as Elinor and Ivan from *Spidercup* and Mikelis from *Canberra Tales*, reappear among the interlinked lives.

HALLORAN, Henry (1811–93), born Cape Town, South Africa, son of L.H. Halloran (q.v.), came to Sydney in 1822, had a successful career in the public service, becoming chief clerk in the Survey Department, under-secretary of the Colonial Secretary's Department and a justice of the peace. He was made CMG after his retirement in 1878. A well-known member of the Sydney literary society of the day and a frequent contributor to the *Month*, *Sydney Morning Herald* and *Sydney Gazette*, he also assisted young writers, e.g., Henry Kendall, for whom he obtained civil service employment. A minor poet himself, he published *Poems, Odes, Songs* (1887) and *A Few Love Rhymes of a Married Life* (1890); made translations from the Greek poems of Anacreon; and wrote numerous commemorative poems for the 1888 centenary.

HALLORAN, L.H. (Laurence Hynes) (1765–1831), born County Meath, Ireland, father of Henry Halloran (q.v.), ruined a career as a chaplain and schoolmaster by indulgence in libellous verse and other acts. Indicted on a minor forging charge in 1818, he was transported for seven years. In 1819 he was given a ticket of leave by Governor Lachlan

Macquarie, opened a private school in 1820, and in 1825 became principal of the Sydney Free Public Grammar School. His unpredictable behaviour, which led to constant litigation, finally deprived him of his schoolmastering career and he then published a journal, the *Gleaner* (1827), a voice for the emancipist cause. Governor Darling, in a kindly gesture, appointed him the Sydney coroner in 1828 but his last years were spent drawing up memorials for people with grievances – his own situation for much of his later life. His numerous publications prior to his transportation were minor poetry and drama. They included, under the pseudonym 'Philo-nauticus', *Odes, Poems and Translations* (1790) and *Newgate: Or, Desultory Sketches in a Prison* (?1819).

HALLS, Geraldine ('Charlotte Jay') (1919–) spent her early years in Adelaide and subsequently travelled widely in Europe and Asia. She has written several thrillers under the pseudonyms 'Charlotte Jay' and 'G.M. Jay'. Published mainly in London, they include *The Knife is Feminine* (1951), *Beat Not the Bones* (1952, winner of the American Edgar Allan Poe Award), *The Fugitive Eye* (1953), *The Yellow Turban* (1955), *The Feast of the Dead* (1956), *The Man Who Walked Away* (1958), *Arms for Adonis* (1960) and *A Hank of Hair* (1964). Her novels as Geraldine Halls include *The Silk Project* (1964), which reflects her knowledge of Thailand and forms a trilogy with two subsequent novels set in India, *The Cats of Benares* (1967) and *The Cobra Kite* (1971); *The Voice of the Crab* (1974), a tense drama set on an island off the coast of Papua New Guinea which intermingles European and indigenous destinies; *The Last Summer of the Men Shortage* (1976), a witty and nostalgic novel which returns to Adelaide in 1945 and explores happy and unhappy love stories which run their course in a 'golden time of sunshine and sentimental songs', notwithstanding the tragedy and death of war; *The Felling of Thawle* (1979), which serio-comically traces the decline of an English country house; and *Talking to Strangers* (1982), a study of an Australian woman, divided by fierce family claims and the need for independence and freedom.

Halstead Press, Angus & Robertson's (q.v.) one-time book-printing department, grew from Eagle Press, established in 1923. Known originally as Halstead Printing Company, its first manager was W. Kirwan; he was succeeded by W.G. Cousins, who was chief of Angus & Robertson's publishing department throughout the 1930s. The press was named Halstead in honour of the town in Essex where George Robertson (2) was born in 1860.

Ham Funeral, The, a play by Patrick White (q.v.), written in 1947, was published in *Four Plays* (1965). Rejected in 1961 by the governors of the Adelaide Festival as too abstract for the general public, a decision that aroused some acrimony, it was produced that year by the Adelaide University Theatre Guild and in 1962 by the Australian Elizabethan Theatre Trust in Sydney. It is an expressionistic play, in which the characters, the two-storey set and the language combine to suggest the conflict in a young artist's emerging consciousness. For the introspective Young Man, life is a struggle between ideality, represented by the Girl, his anima in the upstairs room, and hearty but repellent and frightening reality. The latter is represented by his Landlord, Will Lusty, and his wife, the part-seductive, part-motherly Alma, who inhabit the basement. After a series of incidents ranging from the horrific to the macabre and the comic, the Young Man is able to reconcile ideality and lusty reality and moves out into the world.

HAMILTON, George (c.1812–83), whose diverse experience included a period as a police commissioner, was one of the first to overland cattle between Port Phillip and Adelaide. He wrote a lively account of his adventures, *Experiences of a Colonist Forty Years Ago* (1879), and two entertaining, brief discussions of the role of the horse in Australia, *The Horse: Its Treatment in Australia* (1864) and *An Appeal for the Horse* (1866). A man of many talents, Hamilton also illustrated his own work and some of Sir George Grey's publications.

HAMMIAL, Philip (1937–), born Detroit, Michigan, USA, grew up in America and served with the US Navy. After a period travelling through Europe, Asia and Africa he settled in Sydney in 1972. He has published several small books of verse, *Footfalls & Notes* (1976), *Chemical Cart* (1977), *Mastication Poems* (1977), *Hear Me Eating* (1977), *More Bath, Less Water* (1978), *Swarm* (1979), *Squeeze* (1985), *Pell Mell* (1988), *Travel* (1989, published with Ania Walwicz's *Writing*) and *With One Skin Less* (1994).

HAMPTON, Susan (1949–), born Inverell, NSW, was formerly a teacher in English and creative writing and now lives on a farm in Majorca (Victoria). A poet, prose-writer and anthologist, she won the Dame Mary Gilmore Poetry Award in 1979 and has published two collections of poetry, *Costumes* (1981) and *White Dog Sonnets* (1987). The twenty-three sonnets of the *White Dog Sonnets* (there is also an accomplished longer poem, 'Stranded in Paradise') tell the story of a failing relationship and have been likened to a modern feminist version of the Astrophel and Stella series of Sir Philip Sidney. *Surly Girls* (1989), which won the 1990 Steele Rudd Award and comprises prose poems but includes stories, monologues and performance pieces, is an unusual collection which looks at contemporary women's experience. In all her writing there is warmth, sensitivity and wit. Hampton edited, with Kate Llewellyn, the significant collection *The Penguin Book of Australian Women Poets* (1985). She also co-scripted Ruby Langford Gibini's autobiography *Don't Take Your Love to Town* (1988) and published (with Sue Woolfe, 1984) *About Literature*. Her work is included in *Sisters Poets, 1* (1979), edited by Rosemary Dobson). Hampton was writing fellow in 1993 at the ANU, Australian Defence Force Academy and University of Canberra. See also Feminism and Australian Literature.

HANCOCK, Sir Keith (1898–1988), born Melbourne, was educated at the universities of Melbourne and Oxford. He was professor of history at the universities of Adelaide, 1924–33, and Birmingham, 1934–41. In 1941 he was appointed to the British War Cabinet as supervisor of civil histories. He became professor of economic history at Oxford in 1944 and was director of the Institute of Commonwealth Studies at London University 1949–57. In 1957 he was appointed director and professor of history at the Research School of Social Sciences at the ANU, which he had helped to found. Generally recognised as one of Australia's most distinguished historians, he received many awards and honorary degrees, including the Britannica-Australia Award in 1969. He was knighted in 1953 and made KBE in 1965. Hancock's most influential cultural study is *Australia* (q.v., 1930), although that account is by no means as substantial as some of his later works. His other most significant writings are *Ricasoli and the Risorgimento in Tuscany* (1926); the three-volume *Survey of British Commonwealth Affairs* (1937–42); *Argument of Empire* (1943); *Politics in Pitcairn* (1947); (with M.M. Gowing) *British War Economy* (1949); *Four Studies of War and Peace in This Century* (1961); a two-volume biography of Jan Smuts (1962, 1968); *Discovering Monaro* (1972); and *Today, Yesterday and Tomorrow* (1973). He also co-edited the Smuts papers in 1966 and wrote two volumes of autobiography, *Country and Calling* (1954) and *Professing History* (1976).

HANDFORD, Nourma (1911–), born Queensland, edited the *Australian Women's Digest* for three years, wrote five novels for adults, *High River* (1947), *Murder for Tea* (1949), *Coward's Kiss* (1954), *Blood on the Leaves* (1953) and *Fools of Time* (1958), and several books for adolescent girls. She has also written, as Nourma Abbotsmith, *White Girl, Brown Skin* (1969) and as Norma Abbott-Smith, a biography of Ian Fairweather (1978).

Handful of Friends, A, a play by David Williamson (q.v.), was first performed in 1976 and published the same year. It is an obliquely developed study of betrayal, in marriage, in friendship and in love. The relationships between the five friends involved range over thirty years, although the action of the play, divided into eight scenes, spans only a week. A libellous film script by one of the group is the action's catalyst, but the play's interest centres on the intricately convoluted relations that gradually develop and establish a composite picture of egoism and isolation.

HANGER, Eunice (1911–72), born Rockhampton, Queensland, was educated at the University of Queensland, where she taught from 1955. An enthusiastic proponent of Australian drama, she was active as writer, director and producer in theatre in Brisbane and began the Hanger Collection of unpublished play scripts, which is now held by the University's Fryer Library. Her own published plays are *Upstage* (1952), *An Actor Prepares* in *Never Kill a Dolphin* (1959), and *2D and Other Plays* (includes *The Frogs* and *Flood*) ed. Al-

rene Sykes (1978). Her unpublished plays include 'Tragedy' (1948), 'The Dolls' (1952), 'Well, Well!' (1954), 'For Love or Money', 'Foundations' (1961), 'Short Street' (1962), 'The Lawn Mower', 'Ring the Changelings', 'A Sandwich for the Teacher' (1976), and an adaptation of 'M. Barnard Eldershaw's' *A House Is Built* (1954). She also edited *Australian One-Act Plays Book I* (1962), *Khaki, Bush and Bigotry* (1968), *Six One-Act Plays* (1970) and *Drama for High Schools* (1971).

HANRAHAN, Barbara (1939–91) was born in Adelaide. After her father's early death her mother worked as a commercial artist and she grew up in a household of women, made up of her mother, grandmother and great-aunt. She spent three years at the SA School of Art, taught briefly and then left for London in 1963 to continue her art studies. She thereafter spent extensive periods in England before finally settling in Adelaide. A painter and printmaker with an international reputation, she lectured at the SA School of Art and at art colleges in England, and had numerous exhibitions in Australian cities and in London. Her initiation into authorship was relatively late, stimulated by the death of her grandmother, which released powerful childhood memories of Adelaide. Her published works include two autobiographical novels based on her childhood, *The Scent of Eucalyptus* (1973) and *Kewpie Doll* (1984); an autobiography of her years in England, *Michael and Me and the Sun* (1992); and ten novels, *Sea Green* (1974), *The Albatross Muff* (1977), *Where the Queens All Strayed* (1978), *The Peach Groves* (q.v., 1979), *The Frangipani Gardens* (1980), *Dove* (1982), *Annie Magdalene* (1985), *A Chelsea Girl* (1988), *Flawless Jade* (1989) and *Good Night, Mr Moon* (1992). She also published two collections of stories, *Dream People* (1987) and *Iris in her Garden* (1992) and selected and illustrated the poems of John Shaw Neilson (1985). Alison Carroll has written an account of her career as an artist, *Barbara Hanrahan. Printmaker* (1986).

A writer with a plain but suggestive prose style, Hanrahan was a brilliant creator of atmosphere. Adelaide, which she described as a 'terribly sinister place', represented for her a fascinating contrast between the prim respectability of society, especially Victorian society, and its seamy or horrific underside. She saw her novels as 'concerned with contrasts, contradictions: beauty and horror, love and death, frivolity and menace; the precisely-detailed world of substance, the darker world of instinct; the queerness of mind split from body, the absurd fantasy of the 'ordinary''. These contrasts are already present in *The Scent of Eucalyptus*, a vivid evocation of childhood experience, and in *Sea Green*, the story of a young Adelaide artist who goes to London. In *The Albatross Muff*, however, Hanrahan's gift for Gothic romance and her capacity to re-create an era in full visual detail are given full scope. Set mainly in the middle years of nineteenth-century London, it mingles fairy-tale fantasy and baroque horror. In *Where the Queens All Strayed* Hanrahan turned her attention to Edwardian Adelaide and in *The Peach Groves* to NZ and Adelaide in the 1880s. Both are suggestive, delicately woven blends of frivolity and menace, pretension and primitivism, quaint old-world charm and coarse, unnatural passion. *The Frangipani Gardens*, set in Adelaide of the 1920s, is a compelling exploration of the horror and mystery that lie below the brittle surface of respectable high society. *Dove*, which ranges over three SA generations from the late nineteenth century to the 1930s, focuses mainly on the diverse experiences of a mother and daughter. Hanrahan's last novels are varied first-person life stories, in which she reveals a fine sensitivity to idiosyncratic language, especially the character-revealing rhythms of inward dialogue. *Annie Magdalene* is the story of a working-class Adelaide woman born in 1908; narrated in a matter-of-fact sparse style, Annie's 'autobiography' reveals her to be a wise innocent whose acceptance of hardship and disappointment is both uncomplicated and quietly spirited. *A Chelsea Girl* purports to be the autobiography of Sarah Hodge, who was born in London's Chelsea in the 1890s and whose story reads as if it were oral history. Working most of her life as a cook in restaurants and cafes, Sarah knows a populous, noisy, poverty-stricken Chelsea and stoically survives a series of 'ordinary' tragedies. *Flawless Jade* is the study of a Chinese girl's growth to adulthood against the background of war and revolution. Unfolding chronologically in a series of 114 episodes and narrated by the child Wing-yee, the novel conveys both the hardships and injustices of life in a traditional Chinese family and the understated heroism of its women members. *Good Night, Mr Moon*, narrated by Alexandra May Rodda, born in 1901, is a part-ironic, part-sympathetic re-creation of her ordinary life which is also a contemporaneous social history of suburban Adelaide. The stories of *Dream People*, set mainly in Adelaide from the Depression years to the late 1940s, chronicle the experiences of a quintessential older generation; like Hanrahan's first-person novels, they reveal her distinctive empathy with lives that are 'infinitely obscure', especially the lives of women. *Iris in her Garden*, which is a collection of eight stories centred on her grandmother, aunt and mother and explores the same childhood world as *The Scent of Eucalyptus*, emphasises Hanrahan's continuing debt to her early experience and her ability to work and rework this rich vein. The Barbara Hanrahan Fellowship (a writing fellowship) has been created by the Arts Division of the SA Department of the Arts and Cultural Heritage.

Hansard, the official record of parliamentary debates, is named after T.C. Hansard, who began to print reports from the British parliament in 1803. There is now a *Hansard* for all the Australian parliaments, but the dates of commencement vary, as do the frequency of publication (daily, weekly, by session) and the dates from which the parliamentary debates were formally titled *Hansard*. The first Australian *Hansard* was established in Victoria in 1856 by the *Argus*; it received financial support from the Victorian parliament in 1861 and became independent of the newspaper in 1866. In SA *Hansard* was contracted to the *Register* or the *Advertiser* from its inception in the 1857–58 session of parliament until 1914, when it came formally under the control of the government. Elsewhere, *Hansard* commenced in 1864 in Queensland, 1879 in NSW, 1876 in WA, 1901 for the Commonwealth parliament, 1948 in the Northern Territory and 1979 in Tasmania. Among *Hansard* reporters, J.F. Archibald worked on the NSW staff in 1879 immediately before establishing the *Bulletin*; Ernest Scott on the Victorian *Hansard* 1895–1901 and the Commonwealth 1901–13; and Fred Johns worked in SA from 1914. Before *Hansard*, parliamentary debates and topics were extensively reported in major colonial newspapers; the novelist, Charles de Boos (q.v.), was parliamentary reporter for the *Sydney Morning Herald* in the 1860s and his weekly column, 'The Collective Wisdom of New South Wales' (1867–73), remains a useful source for historians.

HANSCOMBE, Gillian (1945–), born Melbourne and now resident in Britain, has worked as a freelance journalist, teacher, lecturer, saleswoman and academic. Well known for her contribution to lesbian and feminist debates, she has published the collections, *Hecate's Charms* (1975), a verse and prose collection, which was later scored for string quartet and voices and performed in London, *Flesh and Paper* (1986), a verse sequence with Suniti Namjoshi, and *Sybil. The Glide of her Tongue* (1992), a verse sequence with explanatory sections by Suniti Namjoshi. She has also written several books of feminist literary criticism and polemic and the fictional *Between Friends* (1982).

Happy Land, The, a theatrical satire by Marcus Clarke (q.v.), was performed in Melbourne in 1880. Adapted from an 1873 London burlesque of the same title which had lampooned Gladstone and been banned by the Lord Chamberlain, *The Happy Land* satirised the government of Graham Berry, which took steps to ban the piece; it had two performances in Melbourne and was played also in Sydney and Wellington, NZ. Berry's actions aroused controversy in the Victorian press and parliament, where he was attacked by the rebellious politician David Gaunson who, in 1880, defended Ned Kelly.

Harbinger of Light, a monthly journal published in Melbourne, began in 1870 and ran until 1956, after which it was known as *Psychic Science News Magazine*. In addition to articles on psychic and literary topics, it featured fiction serials and poetry. Contributors included Charles Bright and James Smith.

HARCOURT, J.M. (John Mewton) (1902–71), born Melbourne, worked for a time in the pearling industry at Broome, and as a journalist 1926–47, on newspapers in Perth and Melbourne and for the Australian government. He wrote three novels, *The Pearlers* (1933), *Upsurge* (1934) and *It Never Fails* (1937). *The Pearlers* is a lively story with the pearling industry as background; *Upsurge*, an account of Perth during the Depression of the early 1930s in which Perth is seen as a city of middle-class capitalist greed and exploitation, created such a furore that it was branded an indecent publication and became the first Australian novel to be banned by the Commonwealth Book Censorship Board. Officially, the ban was said to be because of its explicit use of sexual detail, but it is more likely that the ban was due to the book's support for a radical political programme and its Marxist analysis of the Depression. Harcourt was shortly afterwards elected president of the Book Censorship Abolition League formed in Melbourne in 1935 and president of a group of left-wing writers formed to welcome the Czech communist and writer Egon Kisch. In the event, Kisch was refused entry to Australia, leaped from his ship and was subsequently deported. A facsimile edition of *Upsurge* with an introduction by Richard Nile was published in 1986. *It Never Fails*, an improbable account of the adventures of a young English immigrant, is a satire on Australian social attitudes.

HARDIE, J.J. (John Jackson) (1894–1951), born Scotland, migrated to Australia in 1911, served in the First World War and spent much of his later life on sheep and cattle stations in northern NSW. He wrote three station romances, *Cattle Camp* (1932, winner of the *Bulletin* prize), *Lantana* (1933) and *The Bridle Track* (1936). Another novel, *Pastoral Symphony* (1939), is an account of the breeding of cattle and sheep by two escaped convicts and their descendants in northern NSW.

HARDING, Lee (1937–   ), born Colac, Victoria, a full-time writer since 1978, is both a science fiction and children's author; the two interests often merge, as in his remarkably successful novel *Displaced Person* (1979, see Science Fiction), a first-person narrative by an alienated adolescent, which won both the Children's Book of the Year Award for 1980 and the FAW Alan Marshall Award for a manuscript novel in 1977. His other works include *The Fallen Spaceman* (1973), *The Frozen Sky* (1976), *The Children of Atlantis* (1976), *Return to Tomorrow* (1976), *The Weeping Sky* (1977, see Science Fiction), *Journey into Time* (1978), *The Legend of New Earth* (1979), *The Web of Time* (1980) and *Waiting for the End of the World* (1983). Dramatisations of *The Frozen Sky*, *Journey into Time* and *The Legend of New Earth* were broadcast on ABC radio in 1978–79. Harding has also edited several significant anthologies of modern science fiction, including *Beyond Tomorrow* (1975); *The Altered I: An Encounter with Science Fiction* (1976, with Ursula Le Guin and others); and *Rooms of Paradise* (1978). Several of his novels have been translated into German, Danish and Swedish.

HARDY, Frank (1917–94), born into a large Roman Catholic family, was brought up at Bacchus Marsh, Victoria, the 'Benson's Valley' of several of his short stories. He left school at 13 and worked as a fruit-picker, road-construction worker, seaman, grocer and cartoonist. Deeply impressed by the sufferings of the 1930s Depression, he joined the Communist Party of Australia in 1939 and later became a member of the Realist Writers' group. He joined the army in 1942, was posted to Mataranka, Northern Territory, and there established a camp newspaper, the *Troppo Trib-*

une, providing the illustrations and most of the written work himself. In 1944 he joined the staff of the army magazine *Salt*. After leaving the army in 1946, he worked part-time as a journalist in Melbourne, meanwhile assiduously gathering information for his novel *Power Without Glory* (q.v., 1950), a semi-fictional account of the millionaire John Wren (q.v.). Because of the book's controversial nature, Hardy published and distributed the first issues himself. In September 1950 he was charged with libel of Mrs Ellen Wren, allegedly the Nellie West of the novel who has a child as a result of an extramarital love affair. After a criminal trial that lasted nine months and aroused keen national interest, he was acquitted; in *The Hard Way* (1961) he gives an account of the writing of the novel and the subsequent trial. *Power Without Glory* has since been translated into several languages, frequently reprinted, and produced as a successful television serial in 1976. His other novels are *The Four-Legged Lottery* (1958), a study of the tragedy caused by gambling; *The Outcasts of Foolgarah* (1971), a slapstick comedy about garbage collectors; *But the Dead Are Many* (q.v., 1975), his most ambitious work and a reconstruction of the personal and political predicaments of a Marxist intellectual after his suicide; *Who Shot George Kirkland?* (1980, co-winner of the ANA Literature Award and an extension of one of the incidents in *Power Without Glory*); and *The Obsession of Oscar Oswald* (1983), an attack on the role of lawyers, financial companies and debt-collectors in modern society, which is accompanied by a booklet ostensibly written by Oscar Oswald, *Warrant of Distress* (1983). Clement Semmler edited *A Frank Hardy Swag* (1982), a collage of Hardy's works. Hardy was well known as a television personality, playwright, songwriter, journalist, lecturer, and writer for radio and television. Well known for his support of the Aboriginal people and in particular of the land claims of the Gurindji of the Northern Territory, he published an account of their 1966 protest at Wave Hill cattle station, *The Unlucky Australians* (1968).

Apart from *Power Without Glory* which, notwithstanding its formal defects, is a coherent and convincing study of a corrupt and corrupting individual, Hardy's most significant achievement lies in the short story. His main short-story collections are *The Man from Clinkapella* (1951), *Legends from Benson's Valley* (1963), republished with one addition in *It's Moments Like These* (1972), *The Yarns of Billy Borker* (1965) (see Borker, Billy) and *Billy Borker Yarns Again* (1967), republished with some additions in *The Great Australian Lover* (1972) and *The Loser Now Will Be Later to Win* (1985). His most carefully structured stories, the studies of the Depression years in rural Victoria in *Legends from Benson's Valley* (e.g. 'The Cockie in Bungaree' and 'The Load of Wood'), illustrate his sympathy with the battler's sufferings, stoicism and humour, and his ear for the laconic Australian idiom. The Billy Borker stories are lighter pieces, tall stories casually narrated by Borker, the ever-thirsty, ubiquitous bar-dweller and folksy humorist. In *The Loser Now Will Be Later to Win* he mingles fact and fiction in stories which celebrate losers and their capacity to surmount material and other forms of loss. Hardy collaborated with his fictional alter ego, Truthful Jones, in three collections of sketches, yarns and stories, in *Hardy's People* (1986), *Great Australian Legends* (1988) and *Retreat Australia Fair* (1990). The archetypal Australian sceptic, suspicious of authority and contemptuous of privilege, Truthful Jones is an appropriate filter for Hardy's brand of demotic yarning.

Hardy was also a playwright. His plays include 'Nail on the Wall', 'Leap Seven Times in the Air', 'The Outcasts of Foolgarah', 'The Ringbolter', which won the 1964 Mary Gilmore Award and *Mary Lives!* (1992), a celebration of the acting career of his sister, Mary Hardy. Two of his plays explore his fascination with Henry Lawson, 'Who Was Henry Larsen?', first produced in 1984, and *Faces in the Street* (1988), a Brechtian interpretation of the writer's life. In several of his plays Hardy himself appears as Ross Franklyn, the name of the central character of *Who Shot George Kirkland?* and Hardy's pseudonym in the early stages of his career.

HARFORD, Lesbia (1891–1927) was born Lesbia Keogh in Melbourne. From an early age she was subject to ill health but possessed a charismatic, eccentric and outspoken personality. After graduating in law and philosophy from the University of Melbourne in 1916, she worked as an art teacher, a confidential clerk in a business office and a freelance social researcher. This last role led her to work for some time in a clothing factory in order to understand women's working conditions. She was a prolific writer of lyrical poetry, some of which was collected after her death by Nettie Palmer and published as *The Poems of Lesbia Harford* (1941); apparently artless and even casual, her slender, remarkably frank lyrics focus on a variety of subjects from love to factory life. Her long-lost novel *The Invaluable Mystery*, probably written 1921–24, was published in 1987 with an introduction by Richard Nile and Robert Darby. The novel, with its background of the internment of German nationals in Australia during the First World War, focuses on Sally Putnam, whose brother and father were interned. The book is a powerful picture of the repression suffered by women in that period. A new edition of her poetry was published in 1985, introduced by Drusilla Modjeska. Darryl Emmerson's play *Earthly Paradise*, based on Lesbia Harford's life, was first performed by the Playbox Theatre Company in Melbourne in 1991 and published by Currency Press the same year.

HARGRAVES, Edward Hammond (1816–91), born Gosport, England, came to Australia in 1834, worked on the Californian goldfields in 1849–50, and returned to Australia in 1851; he began prospecting for gold in the Bathurst–Orange region of NSW, largely because the topography there resembled that of the gold-bearing areas of California. His discovery of gold at Summer Hill Creek and Ophir was said to have begun the Australian gold rushes. In 1855 he published *Australia and Its Goldfields*. His exploits are recorded in Frank Clune's *Golden Goliath* (1946), Jay Monaghan's *Australians and the Gold Rush* (1966) and in most of the historical works associated with the Australian gold-

fields era, e.g. Geoffrey Serle's *The Golden Age* (1963) and Nancy Keesing's *Gold Fever* (1967).

HARNEY, Bill (1895–1962), born Charters Towers, Queensland, was a drover, bushman, soldier in the First World War, lugger captain, patrol officer in the Native Affairs Branch of the Northern Territory, member of several UN expeditions into Arnhem Land, curator of Ayers Rock reservation, and an ardent supporter of the cause of the Aborigines, to whom he was known as 'Bilarni'. His numerous popular books about the Northern Territory, the Aborigines and his own life include *Taboo* (1943), *North of 23°* (1946), *Brimming Billabongs* (1947), *Life Among the Aborigines* (1957), *Content to Lie in the Sun* (1958), *Grief, Gaiety and Aborigines* (1961) and *The Shady Tree* (1963), completed after his death by Douglas Lockwood. With A.P. Elkin he wrote *Tales from the Aborigines* (1959). A skilful raconteur, Harney coloured his writings with a wealth of bush lore and bush humour. *Bill Harney's War* (1983), introduced by Manning Clark, is adapted from a radio programme, 'Harney's War', by John Thompson in the 1950s. A collection of Harney's autobiographical writings, edited by Douglas and Ruth Lockwood, was published in 1990 as *A Bushman's Life*. *West of Alice: A Collection of Poems by Bill Harney*, was compiled by Ruth Lockwood in 1993.

Harp in the South, The, a novel by Ruth Park (q.v.), won first prize in the 1946 *Sydney Morning Herald* novel competition and was published in 1948. Dramatised by Park and Leslie Rees, it was staged in 1949. The novel was also presented as a television miniseries in 1985. Set in the slums of Surry Hills, Sydney, it deals with the fortunes of an Irish-Australian family, the Darcys. Hughie Darcy, the feckless, boisterous father, dominates the household which includes his wife, Mumma, and his two daughters, 19-year-old Roie and Dolour, who is still a schoolgirl. The Darcys' son, Thady, has mysteriously disappeared at the age of 6. Their dilapidated house is shared by three tenants, Patrick Diamond, a solitary Irishman whose Orange fervour reaches boiling-point every St Patrick's Day, and Miss Sheily, a lady who has come down in the world and is forced to live with the illegitimate handicapped son, Johnny, whom she detests. Later Johnny is killed by a truck and Miss Sheily remorsefully and secretly punishes herself. Life for the Darcys grows more exciting after their Irish-born, maliciously humorous grandmother comes to live with them. Meanwhile their lives are affected both by the general teeming life of Surry Hills and by several of their neighbours, such as the Siciliano family and Lick Jimmy, the Chinese greengrocer. Roie's dull life as a factory hand is temporarily lightened by her love affair with Tommy Mendel, an inarticulate Jewish boy, but after the romance fades she finds that she is pregnant. She is unable to face up to an abortion but loses her baby when she is beaten up in a drunken mêlée. After the accident she is severely ill for several months and meanwhile Grandmother, now 86, weakens and dies. Hughie believes for one halcyon day that he has won a lottery prize but is disappointed, Miss Sheily leaves after her marriage to a barrel-organ grinder, Mr Gunnarson, and Roie finds a new lover, Charlie Rothe, marries and has a daughter. The fortunes of the Darcys are continued in Park's next novel, *Poor Man's Orange* (1949) and retrospectively presented in a prequel which she published in 1985, *Missus*.

HARPER, Graeme (1959–), born England, has been a script-writer, teacher of creative writing and co-ordinator of writers' workshops. His novel *Black Cat, Green Field* (1988) won the NBC Qantas New Writers Award. Set in NSW in the latter part of the First World War and after, the novel's central character is 'black cat' Sidney Nelson, recently wounded in Gallipoli and a supporter of the radical Industrial Workers of the World. A former art student, he yearns for the inspiration of Paris but goes to the north coast of NSW to live. The rest of the novel concentrates on family entanglements at Greenfield but ends with Nelson leaving Australia for Paris. Well written, the novel captures the sense of location and period extremely well. Harper has also published a play, *All in Favour* (1985).

HARPUR, Charles (1813–68), born Windsor of emancipist parents, was raised in the Hawkesbury River (q.v.) district; his later use of the pseudonym 'A Hawkesbury Lad' indicates his affection for that area. In young manhood his abrasive and radical personality led to erratic and unsatisfactory employment. His long courtship of Mary Doyle ('Rosa' of his love sonnets) culminated in their marriage in 1850. After a period as an unwilling sheep farmer in the Hunter Valley, Harpur in 1859 was appointed assistant gold commissioner at Araluen. In 1866 the goldfields position was retrenched; in 1867 his farm at Nerrigundah near Eurobodalla was ruined by floods, and his son Charles was killed in a shooting accident. These personal setbacks, combined with the lack of recognition of his literary efforts, made his final years bitter and frustrated.

Harpur's published works include *Thoughts: A Series of Sonnets* (1845), *The Bushrangers, A Play in Five Acts, and Other Poems* (q.v., 1853), *The Tower of the Dream* (q.v., 1865), and several smaller works: a broadsheet, *Songs of Australia, First Series* (1850); a pamphlet containing two poems, titled *A Poet's Home* (1862); and a four-page booklet, *A Rhyme* (1864). The first Harpur collected edition was the posthumous *Poems*, edited by H.M. Martin in 1883. Relied on for some years as the definitive edition of Harpur, it has now been largely discredited because of Martin's arbitrary handling of the text, excising whatever he felt was controversial or radical in Harpur and leaving him as little more than a descriptive nature poet. In 1948 *'Rosa': Love Sonnets to Mary Doyle* was published, edited by C.W. Salier; K.H. Gifford and D.F. Hall edited *Selected Poems of Charles Harpur* (1944), Elizabeth Perkins *The Poetical Works of Charles Harpur* (1984) and Michael Ackland *Charles Harpur, Selected Poetry and Prose* (1986). Elizabeth Perkins has also edited *Stalwart the Bushranger* and *Tragedy of Donohoe* (1987), the first and final versions of Harpur's 1853 play *The Bushrangers*.

In the early years of settlement, when colonial poetry was largely ignored or derided, Harpur's ambition was to be Australia's first authentic poetic voice. He believed that Australian poetry should be modelled upon traditional English verse before seeking its own individuality. Thus his own poetry relies heavily on traditional poetic techniques such as ornamental diction, wide use of personification and metaphor, solemnity of tone and ponderous movement, while attempting on some occasions at least to describe and interpret the colonial Australian scene. Such attempts include his nature poems, 'A Mid-Summer Noon in the Australian Forest' (q.v.), 'Dawn and Sunrise in the Snowy Mountains', 'The Bush Fire' and 'A Storm in the Mountains', which describe some of the typical though more dramatic components of the Australian landscape, and convey a sense of vast distance and wide horizons.

Ignored or badly mutilated in the 1883 collection were several substantial philosophical poems, *The Tower of the Dream*, 'The Witch of Hebron', 'Genius Lost', 'The World and the Soul' and 'The Temple of Infamy'. The long blank-verse dissertation 'The World and the Soul' combines the Darwinian theory of evolution with a highly unorthodox religious view of the universe and its purpose. The subject itself is so complicated and Harpur's treatment of it so unconventional that his editor, Martin, probably at a loss how to handle it, omitted it altogether. Only a few lyrics and choruses of the 2300 lines of 'Genius Lost', a series of poems on the death of Thomas Chatterton, appeared in the 1883 edition. 'Genius Lost', one of the most ambitious of colonial poetic efforts, demonstrates Harpur's grasp of technique and his intellectual capacity. 'The Witch of Hebron' was printed in the 1883 collection with about 400 lines, vital to the understanding of the poem, excised. The best-known Harpur narrative poem, 'The Creek of the Four Graves' (q.v.), the story of settlers murdered by Aborigines, was altered by Martin to highlight the descriptive rather than the narrative areas. The deficiencies of the 1883 collection resulted, for many years, in an undervaluing of Harpur's poetic achievements. Research and scholarship in recent times, however, have increased his reputation, and modern critical opinion sees him as the most substantial of the colonial poets.

In spite of his own unfulfilled dream to be acknowledged as 'the Muse of Australia', Harpur was an influential figure in the mid-century colony. Journals and newspapers such as the *Weekly Register*, the *People's Advocate*, the *Empire* and the *Sydney Morning Herald* carried his wide-ranging political, social and literary commentary, including outbursts against injustice and inequality, satirical tilts at squattocracy and snobbery, defence of the Aborigines, and literary articles and essays. With other currency lads such as Daniel Deniehy, Harpur attempted to direct the colony along the path of egalitarianism and democracy. J. Normington-Rawling published the biography *Charles Harpur, An Australian* (1962) and Judith Wright, a strong advocate of Harpur's talent, the monograph *Charles Harpur* (1963). Elizabeth Perkins's edition, the most complete to date, is accompanied by critical and bibliographical apparatus; Michael Ackland's brings together some of his best-known poetry and prose with correspondence and little-known material. Ackland and Perkins are collaborating in the proposed Academy Editions (q.v.) two-volume *Complete Poems* of Harpur.

HARRINGTON, Edward Phillip (1896–1966), born Colbinabbin near Shepparton, Victoria, served in the First World War in Palestine with the Australian Light Horse. Those experiences are recorded in his first book of verse, *Songs of War and Peace* (1920). He later wandered through the Victorian outback as rouseabout, drover and farmer, saturating himself in the atmosphere of the bush ('Oh the careless, droving, roving life is the finest life of all'). The last of the bush balladists, Harrington enshrines in his poetry such attitudes as mateship, egalitarianism and love of the bush. He lived for a time at Swan Hill in Victoria and later in Melbourne, where he was instrumental in founding the Bread and Cheese Club. His bush balladry is represented in his volumes *Boundary Bend and Other Ballads* (1936), *My Old Black Billy and Other Songs of the Australian Outback* (1940), *The Kerrigan Boys* (1944) and *The Swagless Swaggie and Other Ballads* (1957), which includes some verse from earlier books.

HARRIS, Alexander ('An Emigrant Mechanic') (1805–74), born London, spent his childhood mainly at Windsor in Berkshire, and then returned at the age of 18 to London, where he enlisted in the Guards. Dissolute living led to his desertion and flight to Australia in 1825. Until his return to England in 1840, he worked at numerous occupations including cedar-getting, and established himself on the land. During this period he was converted and after returning to England married his old sweetheart, Elizabeth Atkinson, who had previously refused him on the grounds of irreligion. Elizabeth, who was in the last stages of tuberculosis, died five weeks after their marriage. Harris's second marriage to Ursula Carr in 1842 was incompatible, although there were several children, and the couple eventually separated. After Elizabeth's death Harris became involved in city missionary work in London and wrote widely on life in the colonies. In 1851 he went to America, where he made a living from teaching and writing. He ultimately became an American citizen and died in Canada.

Harris's first book, *Settlers and Convicts: Or, Recollections of Sixteen Years' Labour in the Australian Backwoods* (q.v., 1847), was published under the pseudonym 'An Emigrant Mechanic'. His fictional work *The Emigrant Family: Or, the Story of an Australian Settler* (q.v., 1849) and ascribed to 'the author of *Settlers and Convicts*', a mixture of romantic novel and social history, belongs, as does his first book, to the emigrant literature genre so popular at the time, when interest in the colonies was stimulated by difficult economic conditions in the home countries. Between these two Australian works Harris published, also anonymously, an autobio-

graphical account of his religious conversion, *Testimony to the Truth: Or, the Autobiography of an Atheist* (1848), which again dwells on his Australian experiences, although emphasising their religious effects. In its fourth edition Harris was named as the author and *Settlers and Convicts* was also credited to him. An emigrant handbook, *A Guide to Port Stephens in New South Wales, the Colony of the Australian Agricultural Company* (1849), also linked his name to *The Emigrant Family*. Harris's original anonymity confused modern literary researchers, who were not convinced of his authorship, but the controversy was largely settled by Harris's grandson, Grant Carr Harris, producing corroborative biographical information and an autobiographical work, 'Religio Christi', which was originally published by Harris in serial form in the *Saturday Evening Post* in 1858. An updated account of Harris's life and career and the text of 'Religio Christi' is included in A.H. Chisholm's *The Secrets of Alexander Harris* (1961), but there still remain some unauthenticated biographical details, especially about his time in Australia, and some inconsistencies in Harris's autobiographical writings.

With *Settlers and Convicts* and *The Emigrant Family*, Harris provides the most realistic and comprehensive accounts of early colonial life in Australia. They have been a valuable reference source for social historians, who have found in them informed and accurate comment on such features of the colonial scene as the convict system, the Aborigines, land reform, modes of transport, bushrangers, urban and outback life-styles. Nor are they negligible as literature. *The Emigrant Family*, in spite of its length and its conventional, romantic sub-plots, is one of the major works of fiction of the period.

HARRIS, Max (1921–), born Adelaide, grew up in Mount Gambier. He went from school in Adelaide to journalism to the University of Adelaide, where he obtained a degree in commerce. During the Second World War he worked as a government economist and published two volumes of verse and a novel. He also founded, owned and co-edited the literary and artistic journal *Angry Penguins* (q.v.), which gave expression to the noisy revolutionary modernism in literature and the arts of a group of avant-garde young intellectuals known as the Angry Penguins. The failure of Harris and his co-editors to detect the deliberately concocted nonsense of the Ern Malley hoax (q.v.) and the publication of 'The Darkening Ecliptic' in the Autumn 1944 issue of *Angry Penguins* resulted in ridicule and prosecution for publishing indecent material. Harris's own career in literature, however, suffered little more than a minor setback from the Ern Malley affair. After the war he was involved in many successful literary projects, including the establishment of the Mary Martin bookshop chain (later sold to Macmillan), the creation and editing of *Ern Malley's Journal* (1952–55); the publication of *Ern Malley's Poems* (1961); the founding and editing, with Geoffrey Dutton, of *Australian Letters* (q.v., 1957–68) and *Australian Book Review* (q.v., 1961–74); the publication with Dutton of *The Vital Decade* (1968); the compilation, with Alison

Forbes, of a pictorial history of Australia titled *The Land That Waited* (1967), based on his 1962 film script which won the AFI gold medal; a criticism of present-day Australian values, *Ockers: Essays on the Bad Old New Australia* (1974); a 1988 edition (subtitled the *Complete Poems*) with Joanna Murray-Smith of *The Poems of Ern Malley*.

As drama, art and literary critic, belletrist and, in his own description, 'socio-cultural diagnostician', Harris has been for the past forty years one of Australia's most controversial figures. Some of the fruits of those years of acting as irritant of the political, social, literary and artistic establishment are preserved in *The Angry Eye* (1973), the aptly named collection of Harris's writing from the *Australian* and *Nation* (he has been a columnist on the *Australian* since 1964, a record-breaking period). He also published *The Unknown Great Australian and Other Psycho-biographical Portraits* (1983), a collection of pen pictures of various Australian outsiders and eccentrics; *The Best of Max Harris: 21 Years of Browsing* (1987) which contains thirty-six of his contributions to the *Australian*; and a collection of articles on Australian English, *The Australian Way With Words* (1989). With Geoffrey Dutton he edited a collection of regional comments on a range of Australian politicians, *Sir Henry, Bjelke, Don Baby and Friends* (1971). He was made AO for his services to Australian literature.

Harris's creative writing began with *The Gift of Blood* (1940) and *Dramas from the Sky* (1942), two slight volumes of verse. The poems are love lyrics, responses to the local scene, and reflections on the Spanish Civil War. *The Coorong and Other Poems* (1955) is more noteworthy. Poems such as 'Incident at the Alice', 'Martin Buber in the Pub', 'Apollo Bay to Kingston', 'Allegory of Dante and the Apes' and 'On Throwing a Copy of the *New Statesman* into the Coorong' led readers and critics to hope that Harris would publish more frequently. But the next volume, *A Window at Night*, selected by Robert Clark, who wrote a valuable introduction discussing Harris as a poet, did not appear until 1967 and more than half the poems it contains had been published earlier. Harris had insisted in 'The Faded Years' in *Direction* (May 1952) that there was no room for 'posturing' in poetry and that poetry should establish a real relationship between the poet and the reader. The new poems attract the reader, often in quite different ways e.g. 'A Window at Night' with its intricate intimacy and 'The Death of Bert Sassenowsky' with its ironic narrative of Bert and his oxen disappearing into a volcanic hole in the Mount Gambier district. After another twelve years came the tiny volume *Poetic Gems* (1979), sarcastically titled and puzzlingly ambivalent. Many of the brief poems exhibit both an arrogant contempt for life and a strong fear of death, Harris treating life to the scornful 'Sir-rah' which he claims to prefer that life directs at him, but the *enfant terrible* of the *Angry Penguin* days is still seen in such poems as 'I'm Shagging in the Wagon'. There are some 'gems' nevertheless, e.g. 'Love Poems for the Thompson Children'. Harris's early experimental novel *The Vegetative Eye* (1943) was not a success; he later published a section of another novel,

provisionally titled 'Biography of a No-Hoper' in a 1960 anthology, *Southern Festival*.

HARRIS, Phillip Lawrence, see ***Aussie: The Australian Soldiers' Magazine***

HARRIS, Robert (1951–93), born Melbourne, was involved in the Vietnam War controversy, as were so many of his generation. He had a variety of occupations including labouring work and the teaching of creative writing. In the 1980s he was converted to Christianity and maintained passionate religious convictions until his death, surpassing but not replacing his passion for poetry which was for a long period, his dominant interest. His first book of poems, *Localities*, was published in 1973 and was awarded the Harri Jones Memorial Prize for poetry in 1975. He also published *Translations from the Albatross* (1976), *The Abandoned* (1979), *The Cloud Passes Over* (1986) and *JANE, Interlinear & Other Poems* (1992), which won the C.J. Dennis Prize for poetry. A member of the editorial executive of *Overland* (q.v.), Harris was also the journal's poetry editor for a period.

Harris's early poetry is idiosyncratic and difficult, saturated with abstraction and complex personal attitudes. Evidence of a religious conversion exists in the later books, many of the poems, e.g. 'Ray', 'The Call', 'The Eagle', 'The Prayer of the Blade', celebrating and confirming the significance of God in his life. Throughout his work there is compassion for the underprivileged, especially those 'untouchables' (the mentally and physically defective) who, under the guise of compassion, are 'battered' in playgrounds, offices, workshops and even in their own homes. The later poems, although still prone at times to esoteric thought and density of language, are more accessible to the general reader. *JANE, Interlinear & Other Poems* opens with a sequence, 'Seven Songs for Sydney', exploring the loss of HMAS *Sydney* to the German raider *Kormoran* in 1941. The unusual title of the book points to a sequence of thirty poems dealing with Lady Jane Grey, who lost her head on the block in 1554. In notes to the *JANE* poems Harris indicates that the structure used for most of them is mimetic of the interlinear Bible where the Hebrew text is presented with the English translation printed phrase for phrase directly below. The remaining three sections of the book are 'After the Process', 'Silver Buckle' and 'Recorder Music'. Throughout this last book, as in all of his poetry, there is abundant evidence of 'a profound intelligence at ease with its quest, sure-footed in its isolation', in the words of Fay Zwicky.

HARRISON, Keith (1932–), born Melbourne, taught in Victoria and England before taking up an academic career in the USA. Represented in numerous Australian, English and American anthologies, Harrison has achieved a considerable international reputation as poet, editor, academic and critic. His poetry publications include *Points in a Journey* (1966); *Songs from the Drifting House* (1972), which won a British Arts Council award; *The Basho Poems* (1975), built around a central figure, Basho, whom Harrison describes as 'a kind of trickster figure . . . the kind of figure you see occurring in Red Indian mythology, who essentially upsets the expected order of things', and through whom Harrison deflates the ridiculous, stupid and pompous; *A Town and Country Suite* (1980); *The Sense of Falling* (1980) and *A Burning of Applewood* (1988), a combination of new and selected poems.

HARROP, Les (1948–), born Blackburn, England, and educated in England and Canada, taught in the USA before coming to Australia in 1977; he was poetry editor of *Overland* and later founding editor of *Helix*. Awarded the Greenwood Prize of the Poetry Society of Great Britain in 1976, the Stroud Festival Poetry Prize in 1977 and the Anne Elder Award in 1980, he has published, in Australia, *The Hum of the Old Suit* (1979), a volume of about eighty short poems, many of them in strong colloquial style about people and events from his past.

HARROWER, Elizabeth (1928–), born Sydney, spent her first eleven years in the industrial town of Newcastle, the model for Ballowra in her novel *The Long Prospect* (q.v.). After leaving school she worked as a clerk and studied psychology before discovering her bent as a writer. She lived in London 1951–59; returning to Sydney she worked for the ABC, as a reviewer for the *Sydney Morning Herald*, and for a publishing firm. Harrower has written four novels, *Down in the City* (1957), *The Long Prospect* (1958), *The Catherine Wheel* (1960) and *The Watch Tower* (q.v., 1966), and short stories.

At the centre of all Harrower's novels is an intense psychological drama, a struggle between the strong (as far as position is concerned) and the weak, although the nature and the terms of the struggle vary widely. She has a keen understanding of the motivating forces of selfishness, envy, ignorance, malice, pride, pity and fear and of the way these forces can work within a small familiar group to produce misery for the innocent or defenceless. At a deeper level, her fiction tentatively and searchingly explores the ambivalent problems of responsibility and freedom, guilt and innocence, naivety and experience. *Down in the City* traces the disillusionment of an upper-class woman, Esther Prescott, with the working-class businessman, Stan Peterson, whom she marries after an acquaintanceship of two weeks. Apparently easygoing and fun-loving, Stan turns out to be a racketeer and a paranoid bully. A weak man, unable to abandon either old habits or his old mistress, he finds in Esther a new object on which to vent his grudge against the System. *The Long Prospect* is a more complex exploration of the banality of evil. Here the adult world, seen partly through the consciousness of a child, Emily, reveals itself as both seedy and dangerous, vulgar and destructive. In her progression to a finer moral awareness and a new condition of isolation, Emily is typical of Harrower's heroines. *The Catherine Wheel*, a subtle study of an exceptional and complicated relationship, is her least popular novel. Set in London, it traces the struggle between a young Australian girl, Clemency James, and a penniless, handsome, enigmatic young

man, Christian Roland. Christian's self-indulgence, unpredictable moods, manufactured charm and exhibitionism are convincingly presented, but the struggle between Clem's passive integrity and his uncompromising selfishness becomes somewhat unequal. *The Watch Tower* is a darker exploration of anarchic evil, made more compelling by the novel's ordinary suburban setting. Felix Shaw, a domestic tyrant who lives only to gratify his need for power, is chillingly presented, as is the gradual collusion of his chief victim, his wife Laura. For Clare, Laura's sister, however, suffering is morally rewarding, an illuminating experience both of the enfeebling force of pity and the indomitable power of the self to resist appropriation.

HARRY, J.S. (1939–), born Adelaide, has had a variety of occupations, publishing at infrequent intervals three small books of intense, sensitive and skilled verse. *The Deer Under the Skin* appeared in the UQP Paperback Poets series in 1971, *Hold, for a Little While, and Turn Gently* in 1979 and *A Dandelion for Van Gogh* in 1985. The last-named was short-listed for both the National Book Council awards and the Adelaide Festival Poetry Awards. Increasingly highly regarded for the originality, integrity and technical skill of her work, she was awarded the PEN International Lynne Phillips Poetry Prize in 1987. Meticulous in her fine-tuning (she admits to up to a hundred drafts of some poems), Harry is not interested in evolving a consistent line of technique, each poem being allowed to develop its own voice and method. Her poetry's obsession with language's multiple levels of meaning challenges the reader with its complexity.

HART, Alfred, see **Shakespeare and Australia**

HART, Gertrude, born Melbourne, published a number of novels, including *The Dream Girl* (1912), an unusually told love story, *The Laughter Lady* (1914), an interpretation of the Christmas message, and *Chubby* (1937). In co-operation with Bernard Cronin, Gertrude Hart founded the Derelicts, a club that later became the Melbourne Society of Australian Authors. She contributed poems to *The Little Track and Other Verses* (1922).

HART, Kevin (1954–), born London, came to live in Brisbane at the age of 10. Keenly religious from his youth, his allegiance swung from Baptist to Anglican and in his twenties to Roman Catholicism. He graduated with honours in philosophy from the ANU and won a writing fellowship to Stanford University, California, 1977–78. He gained his Ph.D. from the University of Melbourne in 1986 and has been lecturer in philosophy and English there, senior lecturer in English at Deakin Univeristy and associate professor of English (critical theory) at Monash University. He has written extensively on literary theory and poetry, publishing *The Trespass of the Sign: Deconstruction, Theology and Philosophy* (1989), a radical rethinking of Derrida's writings. He has translated from the Italian the poetry of Giuseppe Ungaretti, *The Buried*

Harbour (1990), and has written a full critical account of the poetry of A.D. Hope (1992) in the Australian Writers Series. His own books of verse are *The Departure* (1978), *The Lines of the Hand* (1981), *Your Shadow* (1984) and *Peniel* (1990), all of his poetry achieving critical recognition; among his awards are the FAW John Shaw Neilson Award 1976, the Mattara Poetry Award 1982, the Harri Jones Award 1983, the Wesley Michel Wright Award in 1984, the Victorian Premier's and NSW State Literary Awards in 1985 (for *Your Shadow*) and the Grace Leven Prize for Poetry in 1992 for *Peniel*. Religious feeling is evident in all his poetry, as is his preoccupation with ageing and death, symbolised by the frequent presence of clocks and references to time:

> Mirrors tell us that we must die
> but clocks announce they know just when

The first section of *The Departure* is entitled 'The Convert'. It recalls his boyhood habit of going to church while 'the family would lounge in bed till ten or so', he meanwhile stepping 'into a day of Grace'. 'The Old' (also from *The Departure*) is an exceptional poem on old age, but its emphasis finally is on the poet's own old age, a spectre that haunts him even in his prime of life.

> Someone old will be inside your flesh
> not long from now –
> I know the one who wants me,
> Sometimes I think I know his thoughts.
> He will know me very well.

There are similar sentiments, and presentiments, in 'The Lines of the Hand', title poem of Hart's second volume, 'Full Moon' and 'My Death', while 'To Christ Our Lord', 'The Yellow Christ' and 'To Our Lady' emphasise the fervour of this verse. *Peniel* marks a departure in technique from earlier volumes where Hart used variable stanza forms and a flexible line scheme, alternating from fluent iambics to equally fluent free verse. *Peniel* is structured into poems each of nine stanzas, each stanza of three pentameter lines. Each of the three sections of the book contains nine poems. Hart's skill with imagery recalls the 'conceit' of the metaphysical poets, while his intellectual subtlety and powerful imagination combine to produce poetry of the highest quality.

HART-SMITH, William (1911–90), born Tunbridge Wells, England, went to NZ as a boy and came to Australia in 1936. He worked in radio in Sydney before enlisting in the Australian Army in 1940. After the war he returned to NZ, where he was involved in adult education and advertising. He was back in Sydney in 1962 as an advertising manager, then radio technician, but went to Perth in 1970 and returned to NZ to live in 1978. He was president of the Poetry Society of Australia 1963–64 and taught creative writing at the WA University of Technology, now Curtin University. His poetry includes *Columbus Goes West* (1943), *Harvest* (1945), *The Unceasing Ground* (1946), *Christopher Columbus* (q.v., 1948), *On the Level: Mostly Canterbury* (NZ) *Poems* (1950), *Poems of Dis-*covery (1959, which includes *Columbus Goes West* and *Christopher Columbus* and which won the Australian Literature Society Gold Medal), *The Talking Clothes* (1966, which shared the Grace Leven Prize for poetry), *Minipoems* (1974), brief verses based on Maori legends and proverbs, and evocations of the WA landscape, *Let Me Learn the Steps* (1977, with Mary Morris), subtitled 'Poems from a Psychiatric Ward' and the result of a briefly disturbed period in 1976. Soon after his arrival in Australia, Hart-Smith became involved with the growing Jindyworobak movement, largely because of his delight in the Australian spirit of place and his fascination with what he saw as the primitive animism of the Aborigines and the romantic mysticism of their legends. From 1940 his poems were regularly featured in the Jindyworobak anthologies and he edited the 1944 volume. Traces of Jindyworobak subjects and sentiment persist in his later poetry. Notable among his numerous Jindyworobak verses were 'The Pleiades', a poem based on Aboriginal legend; 'Moondeen', a character-study of 'the oldest man of the river tribe'; and 'Nullarbor', his account of a brief meeting with a young Aborigine in the desert and his consequent conviction of his own white grotesqueness. Hart-Smith's poetic talents were too considerable, however, to be limited to an expression of Jindyworobak philosophy. His major poetic work is *Christopher Columbus*. With the incisive, delicately constructed, sometimes sombre, sometimes ironic, poems of personal observation, it assured him a small but enthusiastic following among discerning readers, impressed by the clarity, exactness and sensitivity of his observations and by his capacity for communicating those observations in distinctive and often startling imagery. Hart-Smith's *Selected Poems* were chosen and edited by Brian Dibble in 1985; *Hand to Hand, A Garnering*, collected by Barbara Petrie in 1991 after Hart-Smith's death, contains another 250 poems which the poet himself had chosen.

HARTIGAN, Patrick Joseph, see **'O'BRIEN, John'**

HARWOOD, Gwen ('Francis Geyer', 'Walter Lehmann', 'Miriam Stone', 'T. F. Kline') (1920–) was born at Taringa, Queensland. Brought up and educated in Brisbane, she developed strong interests in literature and philosophy as well as music, later becoming organist at All Saints' Church in Brisbane. Her marriage in 1945 to academic linguist William Harwood brought at the same time a reluctant move to Tasmania and the discovery of her lifelong passion for the work of philosopher Ludwig Wittgenstein, which informs her entire opus. Apart from an early isolated poem in *Meanjin* in 1944, her poems, stories, critical essays and reviews have appeared regularly in a wide range of Australian journals and elsewhere since the early 1960s. She has written libretti for composers Larry Sitsky, James Penberthy, Don Kay and Ian Cugley and other occasional words for music. In volume form, Harwood's poetry has appeared in *Poems* (1963), *Poems: Volume Two* (1968), *Selected Poems* (1975), *In Plato's Cave* (Broadsheet, 1977), *The Lion's Bride* (1981),

Journeys: Poems by Judith Wright, Rosemary Dobson, Gwen Harwood, Dorothy Hewett (1982), *Bone Scan* (1988) and *Selected Poems* (1990). *Blessed City: Letters to Thomas Riddell 1943*, finely edited by Alison Hoddinott, appeared in 1990. In one of her many interviews, Gwen Harwood has claimed a 'deep inner necessity . . . to realise in words the moments that gave my life its meaning'. Her work tells the story of her imaginative and intellectual life and its continuing engagement with literature, music, philosophy, painting, with the beauties and cruel laws of the natural world and, as a binding dedicatory thread across its voice through time, her conversation with many friends and, later, the ghosts of many friends.

Many of the poems of her first volume tell of pain, direct physical pain as in 'The Wound', 'In Hospital' and 'Ad Orientem', and the oblique pain of life's passing which seems to bring no sense of fulfilment, either physically ('The Wine is Drunk') or spiritually ('The Old Wife's Tale'). The self-scrutiny of the early poetry seems at its most perturbed in 'Triste, Triste' and most confident in 'O Could One Write As One Makes Love', a poem which suggests this poet's continuing delight in her own flair for word-craft. Her early work creates two ironic figures, Professor Eisenbart (q.v.), whose eight poems constitute the second part of *Poems*, and Professor Kröte (q.v.), soft-hearted anti-hero whose drunken irritability is compensated by his keen eye for the charms of life and keen ear for music, and who, unlike the scarifying Eisenbart, continues to appear in Harwood's latest work.

The use of elaborate personae like Eisenbart and Kröte together with parody, varied masks and pseudonyms, may suggest in this poet a considerable political animus as much as playfulness. The Sydney *Bulletin*'s belated petulant response to its well-deserved hoaxing by the publication in 1961 of two acrostic sonnets by 'Walter Lehmann' wholly vindicated Harwood's double point about editors' prejudice against women poets and farcical incompetence as poetry readers. The poems of the two tragi-comic figures Eisenbart and Kröte, the first an ageing nuclear physicist, the second a frustrated, alcoholic European musician set down in the unrelenting banality of mid-century Australian suburbia, form a running social satire laced with bonedry truths about a bone-dry milieu. Their acid light moves across parlours, patios and beaches, mocking and deft. These poems show a sometimes intricate stanzaic development and tartly rhyme-clipped narrative pace which, in the case of Kröte, can yet indulge a self-ironising, lovable character. Kröte struggles hopelessly with a petty social world impervious to his sensitivities and ill-founded ambitions and can only cry 'Alas!' While Eisenbart's comic satire is bitterly explosive, Kröte's laughter in the suburbs is mellow, wry and attractive. By contrast, other later comic-satiric verse exploits a versatile, parodic balladry and a gift for black humour and the absurd which finally offers a brave, elegant stay against time and the 'sharpness of death' ('Night and Dreams').

Poetry is 'not a perfect game', and if it were we could 'not play' ('Thought is Surrounded by A Halo'). The point goes back to a universal sense of life itself,

and to Eden, so the language 'game' of Harwood's poetry, exhilarating, playful, full of the warmth of good wine and fellowship, can play a deadly earnest. Her work pursues the imperfect game of poetry as part of a love and unquenchable desire for the knowable within a finally unknowable world. From the beginning, she writes of universal problems of existence: growth, ageing, death, and especially the limits of sense and expression. Within traditional metrical forms and subtle musical divisions, her verse achieves a fluid narrative and the sure colloquial tones of contemporaneity. It ranges from ironically structured comedy (the Kröte poems) to free-wheeling virtuoso pieces, abrasive, witty and satirical ('Meditations on Wyatt', 'Night Thoughts: Baby & Demon'), to brief philosophical lyrics, to measured movements of the tragic and deeply moving ('The Violets', 'Father and Child', 'Night Flight', 'Mother Who Gave Me Life'). And across this range there occurs an unusual capacity to blend opposing feelings: the painful with the funny, exhilaration with rue, black jokiness with the death's head, warmth and fun with nostalgia. As 'Mappings of the Plane' so complexly proposes, life as seen here is both exquisitely rhapsodic and sharp with the pain of memory and loss. Both the natural world and the phenomenal world present brilliant images of stability and renewal which turn again and again to violence, brutality or the great abiding swing of returning dark. This, most of all, is a poetry of memory and music and all that these compose; memory is joy and consolation but it is also change and loss.

Harwood's poetry is also a poetry of place, of the cool lights of Tasmania, of its estuarine landscapes, its birds, grasses, frosts, wide cool skies, of Tasmania's tragic history explored tentatively but pungently through a series of poems for the Aborigines which meet a necessary, expressive stop of bewilderment and awe: 'I ask them in no language to forgive/my dreadful freedom in the light of morning' ('After a Dream'). Also, in *The Lion's Bride*, of a part of this island's domestic life, its geese, sheep and cats who summon an eloquent goosegirl and, unabashed, can instruct her (and Wittgenstein) in essential philosophy.

So Kröte's rueful peregrinations record the comic side of Harwood's serious poetic habitation of a world that offers rich beauties in an order perennially treading the edge of chaos. The intolerable is funny, but it is also intolerable and asks eternal questions which have, in Harwood's lexicon, no answer. At the same time, wit, music and the epigrams of philosophy are joys in this verse as much as consolations, and the poetry throughout celebrates the richness of love, friendship, morning light, while it refuses to abandon the fun and mischief of the game of language. Beginning from her 'deep inner necessity . . . to realise in words the moments that gave my life its meaning', Harwood came to believe conversely and with Wittgenstein in the 'power of poetry to infuse experience with value'. The distinctive and impressive poetry which has emerged from these beliefs has led to an increasing critical and widespread popular attention. She was awarded the *Meanjin* Poetry Prize in 1958 and 1959, the Grace Leven Poetry Prize in 1975, the Robert Frost

Award in 1977 and the Patrick White Literary Award in 1978. She received an honorary D.Litt. from the University of Tasmania in 1988 and two further honorary doctorates in 1994 from the University of Queensland and Latrobe University. Her late volume *Bone Scan* won the 1989 Victorian Premier's Literary Award and the J.J. Bray Award in 1990. Her book of letters, *Blessed City* (1990), won the *Age* Book of the Year Award in 1990.

Many critical essays have appeared on Harwood's poetry. Books include Elizabeth Lawson, *The Poetry of Gwen Harwood* (1991); Alison Hoddinott, *Gwen Harwood: The Real and the Imagined World* (1991); Jennifer Strauss, *Boundary Conditions: The Poetry of Gwen Harwood* (1992); and Stephanie Trigg, *Gwen Harwood* (1994, in Oxford's Australian Writers Series).

ELIZABETH LAWSON

HASKELL, Dennis (1948–), born Sydney, gained a Ph.D. from the University of Sydney, and is presently senior lecturer in English at the University of WA, where he also co-edits *Westerly* (q.v.). Both poet and critic, Haskell has published two books of poetry, *Listening at Night* (1984) and *Abracadabra* (1993) and shared a small booklet, *A Touch of Ginger* (1992), with Fay Zwicky. He co-edited, with Hilary Fraser, the anthology of WA poetry of the 1980s, *Wordhord* (1989); with Bruce Bennett, *Myths, Heroes and Anti-Heroes* (1992), twenty-two essays on the literature and culture of countries of the Asia-Pacific region, including Australia; and with Delys Bird a study of Sally Morgan's autobiographical *My Place* (*Whose Place?*) (1992). He compiled *The Sea Poems of Kenneth Slessor*, published in 1990 by Alec Bolton's (then) Officina Brindabella and edited the UQP Australian Authors volume on Slessor in 1991. His other critical work covers Keats and Yeats.

An observant, fluent and accessible poet, Haskell comments perceptively and with occasional humour and disquiet on such everyday realities as relationships with parents, partners and friends and the ups and downs of domesticity. Alert also to the impact of new environments and milieux he has found much poetic material in the years he has spent in the West. Deeply inherent in his poetry, which is often self-searching, is an urge to 'value the ordinary', because in the seemingly commonplace lies perhaps the individual's best hope of personal satisfaction and fulfilment.

HASLUCK, Dame Alexandra (1908–93) was born in Perth with the name Darker, into a family which had been established in WA for four generations. After graduating from the University of WA, she was a teacher before her marriage in 1932 to Sir Paul Hasluck (q.v.). Although the latter's subsequent role as a federal politician, prominent minister and governor-general involved her in a busy public life, she wrote numerous substantial historical and biographical studies. They include *Portrait with Background* (1955, new edition 1989), the biography of Georgiana Molloy, a pioneer botanist of WA; *Unwilling Emigrants* (1959, new edition 1991), a social study of the convict period in WA based upon the letters of a wife in England to her convict husband in Australia; *Evelyn Hill* (1963), a memoir of her mother; *Thomas Peel of Swan River* (1965); and *Royal Engineer: A Life of Sir Edmund Du-Cane* (1973). She also edited the Australian letters (1899–1903) of Lady Audrey Tennyson (1978) titled *Audrey Tennyson's Vice-Regal Days* and, with the title *Remembered With Affection* (1963), some of the letters of Lady Broome (1831–1911); and wrote short stories, *Of Ladies Dead* (1970), and an autobiography, *Portrait in a Mirror* (1981). In 1970 she was awarded an honorary D.Litt. by the University of WA and in 1978 was made a Dame of the Order of Australia.

HASLUCK, Nicholas (1942–), born Canberra, son of Sir Paul and Dame Alexandra Hasluck, graduated in law from the University of WA in 1963 and Oxford in 1966. Following a brief period in Fleet Street as an editorial assistant he returned to Australia in 1967 and since 1968 has been a barrister in WA. He was deputy chairman of the Australia Council 1978–82 and was made AM.

An energetic, almost prolific writer, he has published more than a dozen books since 1976; three volumes of poetry, *Anchor* (1976), *On the Edge* (1981) and *Chinese Journey* (1985, with Christopher Koch); a book of short stories, *The Hat on the Letter 'O' and Other Stories* (1978); *Collage: Recollections and Images of the University of Western Australia* (1987, essays); and seven novels, *Quarantine* (1978), *The Blue Guitar* (1980, republished in 1989 and broadcast on radio 1991), *The Hand That Feeds You* (1982), *The Bellarmine Jug* (1984, winner of the *Age* Book of the Year Award), *Truant State* (1987), *The Country Without Music* (1990, joint winner of the WA Premier's Award for fiction) and *The Blosseville File* (1992). *Quarantine* is a suspense story of the detention of a ship in a quarantine station in the Suez Canal, the events recalled by an ageing lawyer many years later. *The Blue Guitar* enters the middle range of entrepreneurship and commercial corruption as Dyson Garrick attempts to produce and sell a transistorised guitar, the invention of the erratic Herman Strickland. Garrick, a small-time huckster ambitious to enter the world of high finance, is a tawdry character, pursued by Hollins of the Fraud Squad for past shady deals. A slick story in racy language, it belongs more to the crime fiction genre than the proper world of fiction. With *The Bellarmine Jug*, however, Hasluck's skill as a novelist is properly revealed. A complicated story which has its origin in the *Batavia* wreck and massacre off the Abrolhos Islands off WA in 1629 (seen in the novel to be part of a Rosicrucian plot to take over the newly discovered lands of the South Seas), it moves on to the Grotius Institute in Holland in 1948 where an Australian student, Aveline, discovers a long-lost appendix to Pelsaert's account of the *Batavia* events, implicating in the Rosicrucian plot the son of the Great Dutch jurist Grotius, whose pronouncements had morally validated the voyages of the Dutch explorers into the once-forbidden south seas. The novel explores, in considerable detail, the political intrigue and machinations that follow Aveling's discovery, a trail that leads to the Petrov affair in Australia and the decline of Dutch rule in the East Indies.

The tentacles of the plot reach out to involve Leon Davies, (a graduate of Cambridge and present at the Grotius Institute in those times) in a Secret Service grilling many years later as to his communist sympathies. *The Hand That Feeds You* is a satire on contemporary Australian society with its preoccupations of tax evasion, defrauding the welfare system and watching cricket. Satire is also present in much of Hasluck's later fiction. *Truant State*, whose title refers to WA and its 1933 referendum decision to secede from the Commonwealth, is set in the 1920s but exposes much the same kind of doubtful liaison between government and big business that occurred more spectacularly half a century later. It is the story of the successes and failures of the Traverne family, immigrants from England, whose affairs become entangled with the political and financial intrigues of their neighbour, newspaperman Romney Guy, which brings about their ruin. Many colourful incidents from WA's history enliven the novel – the *Catalpa* escape of the Fenian convicts, the gold rushes, the Fremantle quarantine riots, the land booms and busts. The western coast of the continent is the setting for *The Country Without Music* and *The Blosseville File*, the past history, real and imagined of the area, and its present social and cultural milieu proving fruitful for Hasluck's often sardonic probings. In *The Country Without Music* (i.e. one without 'un chant national') the former (1789) French convict settlements on the islands of Gournay and Dupuis (named after heroes of the Revolution) in the Baie de Baudin just off the coast of Grande Terre (Australia) provide the setting for much of the present-day action. The chief characters (and first-person narrators) are Jacqueline Villiers, niece or daughter of Gournay's administrator, Charles Villiers; Gilbert Forel, young radical and Jacqueline's lover, who plans with others to upset Charles Villiers's plan to integrate the islands and their convict descendants (Ilois or Islanders) with Grande Terre; Don Ryan, an Australian investment man who rapes Jacqueline on a business trip to Gournay; and Charles Villiers himself. The fourth section, narrated by Villiers, offers elucidation to the reader who will have struggled in the complex and rapidly moving early stages of the novel to grasp all that is implied or actually occurring. An ambitious novel ('a meditative fantasy' in the words of one critic) which shared the WA Premier's Award for fiction and was short-listed for the Miles Franklin Award with *The Bellarmine Jug*, *The Country Without Music* establishes Hasluck as one of Australia's leading contemporary fiction-writers.

The Blosseville File (Blosseville was the Australian city on Grande Terre opposite the two islands in *The Country Without Music*) is a series of discontinuous narratives – snippets of stories, speeches, interviews, commentaries – gathered together by middle-aged freelance journalist and crime reporter Lucien Chabot, in a file which is to be published in an Eastern state magazine. An ironic exposé of Hasluck's home city – its small-town mentality, the hypocrisy and corruption rampant in its intellectual, literary and commercial circles, the obsession with gathering and flaunting wealth, the influence of its geography upon its present

history – *The Blosseville File* is a polished and eloquent narrative. Another aspect of Hasluck's considerable writing talent is revealed in *Offcuts From a Legal Literary Life* (1993), a volume of sophisticated essays on law, politics, travel and writing.

HASLUCK, Sir Paul (1905–93) was born in Fremantle into a Salvation Army family. He graduated from the University of WA, where he taught history (1939–40, 1947–48). He served on the staff of the *West Australian* 1922–38, and in 1932 married Alexandra Darker (see Hasluck, Alexandra). In 1941 he joined the Department of External Affairs and served on numerous missions to the UN. He was elected to the Australian parliament in 1949, serving as minister for Territories (1951–63), for Defence (1963–64) and for External Affairs (1964–69).

He was governor-general of Australia 1969–74. As well as receiving numerous awards he was made GCMG in 1969, GCVO in 1970, and KG in 1979. Hasluck published numerous papers on historical and political subjects and public administration as well as several collections of verse, *Into the Desert* (1939), *Collected Verse* (1969), *Dark Cottage* (1984), *Crude Impieties* (1991) and a 'discursive essay', *The Poet in Australia* (1975); two volumes of autobiography, *Mucking About* (1977) and *Diplomatic Witness* (1980); accounts of government policy towards Aborigines, *Our Southern Half-Caste Natives* (1938), the influential *Black Australians* (1942, republished 1970); *Native Welfare in Australia* (1953); and *Shades of Darkness* (1988); an account of the Australian administration in Papua and New Guinea 1951–63, *A Time for Building* (1976); a collection of speeches, *An Open Go* (1971); an account of the work of the UN Security Council, *Workshop of Security* (1948); and two volumes in the official history of Australia in the Second World War, *The Government and the People 1939–41* (1952) and *1942–45* (1970). Robert Porter has written a political biography of Hasluck (1993).

HATFIELD, William (1892–1969), born Nottingham, England, son of Joseph Chapman, used his mother's maiden name for his writing, adopting it by deed poll in 1938. He abandoned law studies to come to Australia in 1911, intent on experiencing and writing about outback life. After ten years of bush experience on sheep and cattle stations in the north of SA, in Queensland and in the Northern Territory, he began to write of his adventures. He first published a semi-autobiographical novel, *Sheepmates* (1931), about a young English immigrant, Atherton, who becomes a boundary-rider on a remote sheep property, Borella, in Central Australia. *Desert Saga* (1933) is the story of an Aboriginal boy of the Arunta people, which draws on Hatfield's study of Aboriginal culture in a desert environment. His other fiction, mostly popular romances and boys' books, includes *Ginger Murdoch* (1932) and *Buffalo Jim* (1938), while his descriptive and documentary works include *Australia through the Windscreen* (1936), *I Find Australia* (1937), *Into the Great Unfenced* (1940), *This Land of Ours* (1941), *Australia*

Reclaimed (1944), *Barrier Reef Days* (1948) and *Wild Dog Frontier* (1951).

'Hatter' was a word formerly applied to the lonely eccentrics of the bush, e.g. the solitary shepherd, the gold-fossicker and the boundary-rider. The isolated bush existence often led to the development of strange behaviour patterns, colourfully described as 'kangaroos in the top paddock', in those compelled to endure its monotony, hence the term may have derived from the earlier expression, 'mad as a hatter'. Another theory sees it as a corruption of 'hutter', a term describing the solitary shepherd who lived in a makeshift hut. The term 'hatter' is widely met in literature, e.g. in 'Rolf Boldrewood's' *A Romance of Canvas Town* (1898); George Darrell's play *The Sunny South*, performed in 1883; several of Henry Lawson's stories, e.g. '"Rats"' and 'The Bush Undertaker'; C.E.W. Bean's *On the Wool Track* (1910) and *The Dreadnought of the Darling* (1911); Vance Palmer's *The Man Hamilton* (1928); and Katharine Susannah Prichard's *The Roaring Nineties* (1946).

HAWDON, Joseph (1813–71), born County Durham, England, was one of Australia's first overlanders (q.v.). He drove cattle from the Murrumbidgee area of NSW to the Port Phillip district in 1836, and in 1838 with Charles Bonney made the first overland journey from Howlong, near Albury on the Murray River, to Adelaide. After Hawdon's journey, the overland trail to Adelaide was followed by hundreds of settlers in the following decade. That overlanding epic is recorded in Hawdon's *The Journal of a Journey from New South Wales to Adelaide*, first published in book form in 1952.

Hawk, published weekly in Melbourne, began in 1892 and from 1895 until its demise in 1931 had the title *Hawklet: Sport and Stage*. It contained serial fiction and cartoons by Norman Lindsay.

Hawkesbury River, one of NSW's most scenic waterways, flows into Broken Bay to the north of Sydney. Important from the earliest days of settlement, when farms were established on its fertile flats, the Hawkesbury was discovered by Governor Arthur Phillip in June 1789 while he was examining Broken Bay; he named it after the then Earl of Liverpool, Baron Hawkesbury. The Hawkesbury area was the home of many early colonial identities, e.g. Samuel Marsden, James Ruse, Charles Tompson and Charles Harpur, the last sometimes signing his writings 'A Hawkesbury Lad'. Descriptions of the Hawkesbury landscape, with its background of the Blue Mountains, are frequent in the early colonial writing, e.g. W.C. Wentworth's *Australasia*, Charles Harpur's 'A Storm in the Mountains' and Alexander Harris's *The Emigrant Family*. Charles de Boos's *The Congewoi Correspondence* (q.v., 1874) supposedly emanates from the Hawkesbury region; the area is also important in the poetry of Robert Adamson (q.v.). Histories of the area include Charles Swancott's *Hawkesbury River Saga* (1967) and D.G. Bowd's *Macquarie Country* (1969).

The township of Windsor, established 1794, was one of the earliest settlements on the Hawkesbury; it was one of Governor Macquarie's Five Towns (Richmond, Wilberforce, Castlereagh and Pitt Town were the others) that were planned to be built above the Hawkesbury flood level.

'HAWTHORN, J.R.H.', see **HOULDING, John Richard**

Hawthorn Press, begun by Jack Gartner in the 1930s, became a general publishing and printing house in 1945 and by the late 1960s was publishing exclusive commercial books and some private press books. In 1970 it commenced the series Hawthorn Poets; it played a pioneering role in publishing the works of Australian immigrant poets and in producing local histories and other aspects of Australiana. It closed down in the 1970s, after a disastrous fire.

HAY, Agnes Grant ('Anglo-Australian') (1838–1910), born London, was the mother of novelist William Gosse Hay (q.v.), and related to Edmund Gosse. She published several books of memoirs and fiction, e.g. *After-Glow Memories* (1905), *Malcolm Canmore's Pearl* (1907), *Archibald Menzies* (1908) and *Footprints: A Memoir of the Late Alexander Hay* (1899). Her autobiography, *After-Glow Memories*, which is informative on the social life of early Adelaide, is discussed in Joy Hooton's *Stories of Herself When Young* (1990). The Gosse and Hay families are discussed in Fayette Gosse's *The Gosses: An Anglo-Australian Family* (1981).

'Hay and Hell and Booligal', a poem by A.B. Paterson (q.v.), was published in *Rio Grande's Last Race and Other Verses* (1902). Hay and Booligal, two towns in the remote parts of south-western NSW, with their snakes and mosquitoes, heat and drought, 'sand, and dust, and stacks of flies', are rated in Paterson's poems on a par with Hell. The phrase, abbreviated to 'Hay, Hell and Booligal', denoting the unattractive nature of the isolated towns of the outback, has become a part of Australian idiom.

HAY, Robert Gordon (1933–), born Blair Athol, lectured in mathematics and computer science at the University College of Rockhampton before retirement. His poetry has been widely published in periodicals and anthologies and in a collection titled *Love and the Outer World* (1984). With Anne Lloyd and Stefanie Bennett he is a contributor to the collection *Three North Queensland Poets* (1990). Ranging from the elegiac to the wryly humorous, Hay mostly writes elegantly shaped lyrics which record significant moments of being or relationships with people and landscapes, although he occasionally turns to satiric dramatic monologues.

HAY, William Gosse (1875–1945) was born into a successful Adelaide family with literary connections; his self-made father was an early SA colonist and his novelist mother, Agnes Grant Hay, was related to

Edmund Gosse. Hay was educated at the University of Cambridge, where he decided to become a writer. In 1901 his first novel, *Stifled Laughter*, was published; it was set in Manalia, a fictional name for Australia, as were his next two novels, *Herridge of Reality Swamp* (q.v., 1907) and *Captain Quadring* (q.v., 1912). On his return to Australia in 1901 he settled near Adelaide and was able, because of independent means, to concentrate on his literary work. In 1909 the family home burnt down, an incident which was possibly recalled during the writing of *Strabane of the Mulberry Hills* (q.v.) and which prompted Hay's mother and sister to embark on a visit to Europe; their ship vanished off the African coast. Their deaths disturbed Hay greatly, and while recuperating in Tasmania he became more deeply interested in that State's history. The interest is reflected in *Captain Quadring*, which has some Tasmanian scenes, and in his subsequent novels, *The Escape of the Notorious Sir William Heans* (q.v., 1919), *Strabane of the Mulberry Hills* (1929) and *The Mystery of Alfred Doubt* (1937), which are all focused on Tasmania. A painstaking writer, Hay completed only one other book, *An Australian Rip Van Winkle* (q.v., 1921).

In a statement about his work Hay recalled that 'When I began writing, just before the beginning of this century, Australian novels had relapsed entirely into fifth-rate tales of the 'paddock and stockyard variety', in spurious imitation of 'Rolf Boldrewood's' distinguished work [*Robbery Under Arms*, 1888]. I felt it was necessary to try and raise Australian literature out of that desolate bog, and turned to her tragic and ballad-like history and its proper costumes'. The particular period he chose, and researched carefully, was the decade from the early 1830s, a decade in which his six novels and some of the stories in *An Australian Rip Van Winkle* are set. It was a period of flux in Australia, especially in Tasmania, where the mix of convicts, ex-convicts and free settlers made the future of the colony uncertain. It also had a heroic, romantic quality which attracted Hay, a devotee of Walter Scott, and provided a suitable setting for him to explore such themes as the conflict between good and evil within individuals, the discovery of moral identity, the education towards spiritual freedom through trial and suffering, and the balance between suffering and sin. Such themes are central to Hay's novels, which are characterised by the tribulations faced by the hero or heroine, who are pursued by malicious forces, sometimes associated with a system such as the convict system, and who are tested in hazardous circumstances, often at the climax to the novel; good is detected in courage, endurance and constancy, evil emerges in hatred and jealousy.

The gothic and romance elements in Hay's fiction are demonstrated in his predilection for exotic names (Sligo Quibb, Homely O'Crone, Abelia Oughtryn, Haylin Talmash); in the extreme incidents (fights, fires, escapes); and in the mystery surrounding many of his characters, which partly arises because Hay's narrators seldom know more than his readers at a particular point in the novels and the truth is often presented piecemeal. Balancing these qualities are the careful way Hay builds up a sense of period by his elaborate attention to detail and costume, and his use of the techniques of the historical novelist to establish verisimilitude: for example, the footnotes which admit invention or discuss sources, or the clear indication that his novels are based on the evidence of witnesses, as in the authorial reminders that *The Escape of the Notorious Sir William Heans* is informed by Heans's own letters after his escape. The last technique is employed also in *Herridge of Reality Swamp, Captain Quadring*, and *Strabane of the Mulberry Hills.* There is strong division among commentators on Hay's work. Although his novels have been dismissed as obtuse, overwritten, poorly resolved, stagey, and melodramatic, *The Escape of the Notorious Sir William Heans*, which in some ways recalls Henry Savery's *Quintus Servinton* (1831) and in others anticipates Hal Porter's *The Tower* (1963) and *The Tilted Cross* (1961), is both a successful historical novel and a significant contribution to convict literature. Fayette Gosse published the monograph *William Gosse Hay* (1965) and discusses Hay in her *The Gosses: An Anglo-Australian Family* (1981).

HAYBALL, Doris (1909–48), a Melbourne writer, wrote several plays as well as recollections of mainly British personages whom she met during her travels, *Strawberries in the Jam* (1940), and an account of a visit to the Soviet Union, *Sidelights on the Soviet* (1939). Her published plays are *Blue Willow Pattern* (1944), *Opening Movement: Two Comedies from Australia's Beginnings* (1944), *The Grotesque* in *Eight Plays by Australians* (1934) and *Out of a Clear Sky* in *The Playbill* (1935). Her other plays are 'The Mirror' and 'Old Mr Wintersapple'.

HAYDON, G.H. (George Henry) (1822–91), born Devon, England, emigrated to Australia in 1840 in search of fortune. He became one of Melbourne's earliest commercial sketchers, his work appearing in both Sydney and Melbourne newspapers. Haydon, who studied the Aboriginal way of life and defended the Blacks against the charge of racial inferiority, was especially friendly with Benbo, a well-known Aborigine of the Werribee people. After his return to England he published *Five Years' Experience in Australia Felix* (1846), which brought him recognition as an authority on Australian life. A later novel, *The Australian Emigrant* (1854), with illustrations based on his sketches, gives a short account of the settlement of the Port Phillip District, stressing the egalitarian nature of Australian pioneering life.

HAYES, 'Bully' (William Henry) (?1829–77), born America, was a notorious and legendary South Seas adventurer and blackbirder. His colourful career has been documented by several Australian writers, most notably 'Louis' Becke, who sailed with him and supplied most of the material that 'Rolf Boldrewood' used in *A Modern Buccaneer* (q.v., 1894). *Tom Wallis* (1900), *The Strange Adventure of James Shervinton* (1902), *The Adventures of Louis Blake* (1909) and *Bully Hayes, Buccaneer* (1913) are other Becke books in which Hayes appears or is discussed. Hayes is also the main character in Albert Dorrington's *A South Sea Buccaneer* and *Our Lady of the Leopards* (both 1911) and he appears in Beatrice Grimshaw's *Victorian Family Robinson* (1934), and Will Lawson's *The Laughing Buccaneer* (1935).

HAYGARTH, H.W., see **Bush, The**

HAYLEN, Leslie Clement (1899–1977) was born near Canberra into a large Catholic farming family. After serving in the First World War he worked as a journalist in Sydney and Wagga; later he joined the staff of the *Australian Women's Weekly* in Sydney. He was the Labor member for the federal seat of Parkes 1943–64 and gained a reputation as a witty debater and an eloquent proponent of Australian literature; his maiden speech was a plea for the establishment of a national theatre. As well as numerous articles, pamphlets, occasional verse and short stories, Haylen wrote plays and novels. His published plays are *Two Minutes' Silence* (1933), a well-received anti-war drama first produced in 1930 and also produced as a film in 1933, and *Blood on the Wattle* (1948), a stirring treatment of the Eureka rebellion which requires a cast of over fifty. His other plays are 'Change of Policy' (1934), 'Freedom has a Beard' (1937), and 'The Stormy Blast' (1966). His first three novels, *The Game Darrells* (1933), *The Brierley Rose* (1935) and *Brown Boy Singing* (1940), were serialised in the *Australian Women's Weekly* and later produced as radio serials. They were followed by *New Guinea Newsreel (1945)*, *A for Artemis* (1960, under the pseudonym 'Sutton Woodfield'), and *Big Red* (1965). Most of his novels, especially *Big Red* and *The Game Darrells*, draw on his experience of country life and of the labour movement. Haylen also wrote an account of his second visit to China in 1957, *Chinese Journey* (1959), memoirs of his years in parliament, *Twenty Years' Hard Labor* (1969), and edited the third and fourth short-story collections in the series titled *The Tracks We Travel* (1965 and 1976).

HAYNES, John (1850–1917), born Singleton, NSW, began a career in journalism in Morpeth. He moved to Sydney in 1873 and worked on the *Empire*, the *Australian Town and Country Journal* and the *Evening News;* while sub-editor on the *Evening News* he met J.F. Archibald, with whom he founded the *Bulletin* in 1880. Haynes made a significant contribution to the establishment and early success of the *Bulletin*, but his free-trade economic beliefs clashed with the protectionism of W.H. Traill and by 1885 he had severed his connection with the journal. Haynes was a controversial member of the NSW parliament 1887–1904 and 1915–17. He ran *Haynes Weekly* 1885–87, the *Weekly News* 1890–91, and the *Elector*, later the *Newsletter*, 1895–1917. His version of the early *Bulletin* days was serialised in the *Newsletter* in 1905.

HAYTER, Henry Heylyn (1821–95), born Eden Vale, England, came to Victoria in 1852 and became government statist of Victoria in 1874; his statistical methods were adopted for the whole of Australia. An eager travel author, he published *Notes of a Tour in New Zealand* (1874), *Notes on the Colony of Victoria* (1875),

and *A Handbook to the Colony of Victoria* (1884). He also wrote poetry, *Carboona, A Chapter from the Early History of Victoria* (1885) and *My Christmas Adventure, Carboona and Other Poems* (1887). Hayter's chief creation, however, was the *Victorian Year Book*, published in twenty volumes from 1874; in his yearbooks, commended throughout the world, Hayter made statistics interesting and understandable for the ordinary reader.

HAYWARD, Charles W. Andrée (1866–1950), born Herefordshire, England, was a lawyer in England and South Africa before his arrival in WA in 1894. He joined the *Geraldton Express*, expanding that newspaper's literary interests by examining in January 1896 the achievements of the flourishing *Bulletin* school of writers. His own contributions to the *Geraldton Express* include satire, sonnets, ballads and lyric verse; some of his poems, usually written under the pseudonym 'Viator', were published in 1897 as *Along the Road to Cue and Other Verses*. He left the *Geraldton Express* in 1898 to edit the *Murchison Advocate* at Cue; thereafter he worked on the Kalgoorlie *Sun*, the Perth *Sunday Times* and again the *Geraldton Express*. From 1922 until his death Hayward worked on the staff of the *Bulletin*, contributing copious light and topical verse under various pseudonyms, e.g. 'Thomas the Rhymer'.

HAZZARD, Shirley (1931–   ) was born and educated in Sydney. From 1947 she has lived overseas, in Hong Kong, NZ, Europe and the USA. She is now an American citizen, married to American littérateur Francis Steegmuller, and divides her time between New York and Capri. In 1966 she was awarded a grant by the United States National Institute of Arts and Letters, and in 1980 won the National Book Critics Circle Award. She revisited Australia in 1976 and wrote a lengthy, influential account of her impressions for the *New Yorker* (January 1977). She worked as a clerical employee of the UN 1952–62, and became a passionate opponent of that institution. One of her two extended non-fiction works, *Defeat of an Ideal* (1973), is a well-documented analysis of its weaknesses; the other, *Countenance of Truth* (1990), deals with the case of Kurt Waldheim. In 1982 she was elected to the American Academy and Institute of Arts and Letters. In 1984 she delivered the ABC's Boyer lectures which were published in 1985 as *Coming of Age in Australia.*

Hazzard has written numerous short stories, mainly for the *New Yorker*. Some are collected in *Cliffs of Fall* (1963), and she has also written four novels: *The Evening of the Holiday* (1966), *People in Glass Houses* (1967), *The Bay of Noon* (q.v., 1970) and *The Transit of Venus* (q.v., 1980). An admirer of Flaubert and Turgenev, Hazzard writes with poise and restraint. Her novels and short stories are centrally concerned with the poignant experience of love, its discovery, loss and recollection. She is sensitive to the nuances and minutiae of feelings and to the distinctive flavours of different places and relationships, writing lucid prose that can be evocative, reflective or ironic, but is always compressed in its effects. Apart from one short story,

'Woollahra Road', *New Yorker* (1961), Hazzard has not drawn heavily on her experience of Australia, although the heroines of *The Transit of Venus* are expatriate Australians. The short stories in *Cliffs of Fall* are set in Italy, Switzerland and America; Siena is the setting for *The Evening of the Holiday* and Naples for *The Bay of Noon;* the sterile atmosphere of the UN building in New York is the background of *People in Glass Houses;* and *The Transit of Venus* moves between Sydney, London, New York and Stockholm. A sense of geographical, national and social dislocation is common to Hazzard's very different heroines, and their quest for love is also a quest for a sense of belonging and knowledge of the self. At the beginning of her career the short story provided the perfect form for her concern with love as a general experience and for her gifts of psychological insight, suggestive symbolism and creation of atmosphere. Several, such as 'A Place in the Country' and 'The Picnic' in *Cliffs of Fall*, and 'A Long Short Story' and 'A Crush on Doctor Dance', *New Yorker* (1976 and 1977), are interconnected narratives. *People in Glass Houses* is also a series of portraits connected by the participants' common experience of working for the UN. Both *The Evening of the Holiday* and *The Bay of Noon* are close to the novella in their measured approach, and both are nostalgic treatments of the fragility of unaccountable love. Italy, colourful and passionate but also unpredictable and insecure, provides the suggestive background. *People in Glass Houses*, a witty, satirical work, pillories the suffocating stupidity of organisation life. Underlying the acute sketches of people and incongruous situations is an awareness of the dehumanising effect of a large organisation that exists only for itself, using jargon as its servant of destruction. *The Transit of Venus*, more elaborate, ambitious and extended than her previous work, has established Hazzard as a major novelist. The novel's mannered quality has led to comparisons with Jane Austen and Henry James, but in atmosphere it is thoroughly modern. Although the theme once again is love, the chronological and geographical range is wide, extending from the First World War to the time of Richard Nixon. A self-conscious work of art, its complex ambiguity is heightened by an equivocal narrative technique, discreet but resonant symbolism and an elaborately sculpted structure. Wit and verbal play, psychological insight and a wide-ranging literary allusiveness are other striking aspects.

HEAD, Walter William (1861–1939), born Oakleigh, Victoria, came to prominence as founder and editor, with Arthur Rae, of the labour movement newspaper the *Hummer*, 1891–92. After the newspaper became the *Worker*, Head moved with it to Sydney, where he continued his involvement in the New Australia movement as secretary, later treasurer and trustee, of the New Australia Co-operative Settlement Association and editor of its monthly journal, *New Australia*, 1892–94; Mary Cameron, later Dame Mary Gilmore, helped with the latter. Head resigned as editor of the *Worker* in November 1893 preparatory to leaving for Paraguay, but the death of his son, who became lost in the bush in Victoria, prevented his

departure. Henry Lawson, who was disappointed in his hopes of succeeding Head as editor of the *Worker*, wrote a poem and a story, both titled 'The Babies in the Bush', based on the tragedy. The major Australian point of contact for the New Australia settlers, Head became embroiled in its internecine disputes in 1894; although probably not guilty of financial impropriety, he was personally liable for its debts and disappeared from view to avoid imprisonment. He surfaced again in Tasmania in 1895, probably via NZ, and as Walter Alan Woods, William Ashe Woods and other combinations of the Christian names, he made a new start in the labour movement. Editor of the *Tasmanian Democrat* (1895–96), owner (1898–99) and editor (?1900–9) of the *Clipper*, and involved in the *Clipper*'s successors, the *Daily Post* and the *World*, Woods was a member of the Tasmanian parliament 1906–17 and 1925–31 and Speaker of the House of Assembly, 1925–31. The author of several ballads under the pseudonym, 'John Drayman', he retained contact with Lawson and Mary Gilmore after his departure from Sydney.

Heads of the People, subtitled *An Illustrated Journal of Literature, Whims and Oddities*, was published weekly in Sydney 1847–48; it contained serials, poetry and short fiction. *Heads of the People* serialised Charles Dickens's *Dombey and Son* in 1847 before its publication in book form and carried illustrations by J. Skinner Prout. A notable contributor was D.H. Deniehy.

Heart of Spring (1919), containing fifty-seven poems, was the first published collection of John Shaw Neilson (q.v.). It met a mixed critical reception: A.G. Stephens in the book's preface called Neilson 'first of Australian poets'; Hubert Church described the poems as 'marvellous songs'; David McKee Wright in the *Bulletin* believed the poet to be 'a whispering person, not likely to be heard of again'.

HEATON, Sir John Henniker (1848–1914), born Rochester, England, came to NSW in 1864, working first as a jackeroo, then as a journalist on the *Cumberland Mercury, Goulburn Evening Penny Post, Cumberland Times* and *Australian Town and Country Journal*. He married Rose Bennett, daughter of Samuel Bennett of the *Empire* and often presumed to be the 'Rose Lorraine' of Henry Kendall's love poetry. In 1879 Heaton published the pioneer reference work *Australian Dictionary of Dates and Men of the Time*. From 1883 he lived in England, where he represented Australian interests, especially in the campaign for cheaper postal, telegraphic and freight charges between England and the Australian colonies. A keen collector of Australiana, he once owned the *Endeavour* journals of Sir Joseph Banks. R. Porter wrote *The Life and Letters of Sir John Henniker Heaton* (1916).

HEBBLETHWAITE, James (1857–1921), born Preston, England, was a teacher in England before migrating to Tasmania in 1890 for health reasons and gaining a teaching position at the Friends' School,

Hobart. He was later a minister of religion, initially with the Congregational Church, then the Church of England. A scholar and a graceful if limited lyric poet, Hebblethwaite published five books of poetry: *Verse* (1896); *A Rose of Regret* (1900); *Meadow and Bush* (1911); a collected edition, *The Poems of James Hebblethwaite* (1920); and *New Poems of James Hebblethwaite* (1921). His only novel, *Castlehill* (1895), is a romance associated with the convict period.

Hecate, named after 'the goddess invoked by women who desired freedom from male tyranny' and edited by Carole Ferrier, is published from the University of Queensland. First published in 1975, it gives expression to the creative and critical writing of women and covers many feminist issues.

HEDLEY, Wilma (1927–), born Brisbane, has worked at numerous occupations including acting, secretarial work, gardening and journalism. She has published two volumes of poetry, *Identity* (1968) and *Identity II* (1971). Although small in output, Hedley's compressed, spare poetry which communicates a wide range of feeling from intense anger to bitterness to compassion, has attracted strongly favourable reviews.

Heidelberg School, the first distinctive school of Australian painting, originated in the period 1885–90 after the artist Tom Roberts (q.v.) returned to Australia from Europe, where he had become acquainted with the work of the French Impressionists. Roberts and Frederick McCubbin (q.v.) established an artists' camp in 1885 at Box Hill, Melbourne, and used it as a centre for a modified form of *plein air* and impressionist painting. Emphasising brightness, light and colour, Roberts and McCubbin sought, in Bernard Smith's words, 'to produce a naturalistic interpretation of the Australian sunlit landscape'. In 1888 Roberts was joined by Arthur Streeton and Charles Conder (qq.v.); they moved to a house at Eaglemont, Heidelberg, and established another artists' camp; in 1889 they opened the now-famous '9 x 5' exhibition of Australian Impressionism comprising some 180 oil sketches on cigar-box lids. A second Heidelberg camp, with which Norman Lindsay (q.v.) was connected, was established in 1890 at a house, Charterisville, near Eaglemont, and in the period up to the end of the century the new painting philosophy spread rapidly.

Like the writers of the 1890s, the Heidelberg artists became increasingly nationalistic, seeking out subjects of national interest and significance. Although they were not concerned exclusively with the bush (Roberts and Conder, for example, also produced some remarkable urban paintings), the Australian Impressionists forged their closest links with literature when they emphasised the bush and incidents from bush life. McCubbin's *The Lost Child* (1886), for example, illustrates an incident that had already found literary expression in Henry Kingsley's novel *The Recollections of Geoffry Hamlyn* (1859) and Marcus Clarke's story 'Pretty Dick'. His canvas, *Down on his Luck* (1889), illustrates the type of unfortunate swagman portrayed in Henry Lawson's stories and poems, and in

the verse of A.B. Paterson and Barcroft Boake; his *Bush Burial* (1890) reflects to some extent a scene in Henry Kendall's poem 'A Death in the Bush', and has been used on the dust-jacket of *Leaves from Australian Forests: Poetical Works of Henry Kendall* (1970) in the Australian Classics series. Roberts's paintings associated with outback life, e.g. *Bailed Up* (1888), *Shearing the Rams* (1889), *The Breakaway* (1891), and *The Golden Fleece* (1894), reflect a host of similar incidents from the writings of 'Rolf Boldrewood', Lawson, Paterson, 'Breaker' Morant, Will Ogilvie and others, while the idealisation of the landscape evident in some of the Heidelberg school paintings echoes the attitudes taken by writers such as Bernard O'Dowd, Roderic Quinn and John le Gay Brereton. The relationship between the work of the Heidelberg school and literature linking them to the social and cultural background of the day is discussed in Bernard Smith's *Australian Painting: 1788–1970* (1961). A full account of the Heidelberg artists is given in David Leigh Astbury's *City Bushmen: The Heidelberg School and the Rural Mythology*. Its publication in 1985 coincided with 'Golden Summers', the first national touring exhibition of the School. Astbury also wrote *Sunlight and Shadow: Australian Impressionist Painters 1880–1900* (1989). Two works which question some of the mythology surrounding the School are Eleanor Finlay and Marjorie Morgan's *Prelude to Heidelberg* (1991) and Helen Topliss's *The Artists' Camp: 'Plein Air' Painting in Australia* (1992). The work of women artists of the Heidelberg era, rarely if ever acknowledged, was highlighted by the 1992 exhibition, curated by Juliet Peers and Victoria Hammond, 'Completing the Picture, Women Artists and the Heidelberg Era'.

Helix, a literary journal founded in Canberra by Les Harrop in 1978, later transferred with him to Victoria. Dedicated to publishing Australian and overseas writing in the same journal, *Helix* produced an Ezra Pound special issue in 1982. A book review supplement to *Helix* (9, 10) was published as a separate issue, *Fresh Flounder* (1981). *Helix* ceased regular publication in 1986; its editor, David Brooks, then began to work with *The Phoenix Review*, which took over something of the role of *Helix*, although its future in 1993 also appears uncertain. *The Phoenix Review* is published twice a year.

HELLYER, Jill (1925–), born North Sydney, has been a consistent contributor of poetry to literary magazines such as *Westerly*, *Southerly*, *Meanjin* and *Overland* over many years. Instrumental in founding the Australian Society of Authors, she was its first executive secretary 1963–71 and was made a life member for her services. She has published verse, *The Exile* (1969) and *Song of the Humpback Whales* (1981); a novel, *Not Enough Savages* (1975); and edited a biographical work, *Fifty Years in Psychiatry: D. W. H. Arnott* (1980).

HEMENSLEY, Kris (1946–), writer, critic, editor, publisher, bookshop director, teacher, and passionate about all things literary, was born on the

Isle of Wight, came to Australia in 1966 and quickly settled into the Melbourne literary scene, originally with the Melbourne New Theatre, then at La Mama, where in 1968–70 he helped to produce the poetry workshops that played a significant role in the rise of what has been termed the 'New Australian Poetry' (q.v.). To publish that poetry Hemensley created the mini-magazine *Our Glass*. While in England in 1969–72 Hemensley edited the magazine *Earth Ship* (1970–72), and after his return to Australia continued his literary interests through poetry, prose and editorial activities. He edited a second series of *Earth Ship*, titled *The Ear in a Wheatfield* (q.v., 1972–76), a third series, *The Merri Creek or Nero* (1981–84); in 1985 the selection *The Best of the Ear*, and other associated journals; became an advisory editor to *New Poetry* 1973–74; and was poetry editor of *Meanjin* 1976–78. His own publications of poetry, prose, drama and children's books have been prolific; they include *Two Poets* (1968, with Ken Taylor), *The Going* (1969), *Dreams* (1971), *No Word – No Worry* (1971), *The Soft Poems* (1971), *Mimi* (1973), *Rocky Mountains & Tired Indians* (1973), *Domestications* (1974), *Love's Voyages* (1974), *Here We Are* (1975), *The Rooms and Other Prose Pieces* (1975), *The Poem of the Clear Eye* (1975), *Sulking in the Seventies* (1975), *The Moths* (1978, prose/poetry), *Beginning Again* (1978, prose/poetry), *Down Under* (1978, a comic novel), *Games: An Exhibition 1970–72* (1978, prose), *The Miro Poems* (1979), *A Mile from Poetry* (1979), *Trace* (1984), *Christopher* (1987), and *The Site* (1987). One of Hemensley's many plays, 'Stephany', which was produced, as were several others, at La Mama, was made into a short film in 1972.

Hemensley's literary range is considerable: brief, enigmatic and personal poems such as those in *Domestications;* a long, complex examination of contemporary poetic attitudes in *The Poem of the Clear Eye*; the poetry-prose compositions, such as those in *Here We Are*, where fantasy and realism meet in a startling mix; his many works for radio and screen. An indefatigable Utopian and campaigner for world peace, an active and dedicated literary internationalist, and a regular commentator on Australian writing, Hemensley has long been a colourful and important figure in the Australian literary scene.

Hemisphere: An Asian-Australian Magazine, began publication as a monthly in 1957 and was then issued by the federal government six times a year 1979–84. Edited from 1969 by Ken Henderson, it was intended initially as an extension of the Colombo Plan programme but broadened to reflect a deeper interest in the Asian region. In addition to its variety of historical, sociological and cultural articles, *Hemisphere* had a wide-ranging survey of Australian and Asian writing and a selection of the poetry and short fiction of contemporary writers in both areas. *Hemisphere* produced four annuals and three anthologies, one on Indonesia (1976), two on the Australian Aborigines (1978, 1981).

HENDERSON, W.G. (Walter Gordon [George]) (1870–1957), born Roslyn, near Goulburn,

NSW, became a lawyer and lived at Albury but always maintained a keen interest in the bush and bush life. His first volume of fiction, *Midnight's Daughter and Other Stories* (1907), comprises bush tales, including bushranging stories of the 1840s to 1860s. His other fiction includes the novels *Norah Conough* (1908), which deals with the conflict between large and small landowners of the 1890s; *The Bathers* (1911), which shows the impact of wholesome attitudes of country life on urban and religious conservatism; *Bush Bred* (1922), a romantic tale which is complicated by the impact of Chinese immigrants on the lives of the protagonists; and *Nelligang* (1945), a tale of family problems and life in the bush.

HENEY, Helen (1907–   ), born Sydney, the daughter of Thomas William Heney, was educated at the University of Sydney and lived mainly in Poland 1929–35, working as a translator and a teacher of English. During the war she worked with the Red Cross and was a social worker with UNRRA in various European countries 1945–47. She has published five novels, *The Chinese Camellia* (1950), *The Proud Lady* (1951), *Dark Moon* (1953), *This Quiet Dust* (1956) and *The Leaping Blaze* (1962); a substantial biography of the explorer Sir Paul Strzelecki, *In a Dark Glass* (1961); a well-researched study of Australian women between 1788 and 1822, *Australia's Founding Mothers* (1978); and *Dear Fanny: Women's Letters to and from New South Wales, 1788–1857* (ed., 1985). Apart from *The Proud Lady*, which traces the destiny of a woman set against the dramatic background of Polish history between 1885 and 1939, all Heney's novels have Australian settings. Although some have intricate plots and well-realised historical backgrounds, they are less memorable for their action than for their psychological studies. *Dark Moon*, which deals with the case of a White woman, presumed dead, who is discovered to be living with an Aboriginal tribe and the effects of the discovery on those involved, and *The Chinese Camellia*, which focuses on the impact of a Chinese concubine on an Australian settlement, express most effectively her insight into the relationship between outsider and social group. *This Quiet Dust* and *The Leaping Blaze* both contain striking portraits of egoistic, dominating women.

HENEY, Thomas William (1862–1928), born Sydney, father of Helen Heney, spent a lifetime in journalism. He was editor of the *Sydney Morning Herald* (1903–18), the *Brisbane Telegraph* (1920–23), and the Sydney *Daily Telegraph* (1924–25). He published two novels with outback settings, *The Girl at Birrell's* (1896) and *A Station Courtship* (1899), and two collections of verse, *Fortunate Days* (1886), and *In Middle Harbour and Other Verse, Chiefly Australian* (1890).

HENNESSEY, John David (1847–1935), born London, came to Australia in 1875, lived in Queensland, NSW and Victoria, and combined service as a Methodist and Congregational minister with religious journalism and general editing and publishing. He founded and edited the *Australian Christian World*

1886–91 and in 1894 the *Australian Field*, a weekly agricultural paper. He also tried pineapple farming in the 1890s and became active in political affairs, working for Edmund Barton and the *Federalist*. As well as short stories in magazines in Australia and England, he published several novels including *The Dis-Honourable* (1895), *An Australian Bush Track* (1896), *Wynnum* (1896), *A Lost Identity* (1897), *The Outlaw* (1913), *A Tail of Gold* (1914), *The Caves of Shend* (1915) and *The Cords of Vanity* (1920). He also wrote a book of advice for farmers, *The New Chum Farmer* (1897). Hennessey's novels are characterised by graphic descriptions of the Australian scene, both contemporary and past; sensational, melodramatic plots; and romantically happy conclusions. Particularly striking are *The Dis-Honourable*, which draws on conditions and events in Brisbane of the 1890s, especially on the catastrophic flood of 1893, and *The Outlaw*, which deals with the adventures of an assigned convict forced to turn bushranger by the injustice of his master.

HENNING, Rachel (1826–1914), born Bristol, England, joined her brother Biddulph in Australia in 1854 but returned to England in 1856, homesick and disillusioned by the colony. She came back to Australia in 1861 and, although settling much better on the second occasion and increasingly sensitive to the beauty of the land, never completely overcame her antipathy to what she saw as the crudeness of the colonial environment. In 1862 she and her sister Annie joined Biddulph on his run, inland from Port Denison (now Bowen) in Queensland. In 1866 she married Deighton Taylor, one of her brother's overseers, and settled in NSW, ultimately on a farming property near Wollongong. The popular collection *The Letters of Rachel Henning* (1952, a new edition 1986), edited by David Adams and illustrated by pen drawings by Norman Lindsay, ranges in time from 1853, when Biddulph left England, to 1882; the letters were were mainly written to her sisters Etta and Amy, the former in England and the latter in Australia. A sensitive account of the delights, difficulties and drawbacks involved in the process of migration to, and acclimatisation in, an alien environment, the Rachel Henning letters reveal as much about the personality of the writer as they do about the colony of Australia in the nineteenth century. Of particular interest is the information offered about squatting life in Queensland.

HENRY, Alice (1857–1943), born Richmond, Victoria, was a journalist with the Melbourne *Argus* and the *Australasian* in the 1890s. In 1905 she visited England and the USA to lecture on women's suffrage, later becoming secretary of the Chicago branch of the National Women's Trade Union League and editor, with the assistance of her close friend Miles Franklin from 1910 to 1915 of the League's journal, *Life and Labor*. She returned to Australia in 1933. She published *The Trade Union Woman* (1915) and *Women and the Labor Movement* (1923). Her memoirs, edited by Nettie Palmer, were published in 1944; Diane Kirkby has written her biography, *Alice Henry: The Power of Pen and Voice* (1991).

HENRY, Kristin (1947–), born Chattanooga, Tennessee, USA, came to Australia with her parents when she was 17. During the 1980s she was active in the community movement and has been prominent in the performance poetry sphere. She has two published books of verse, *Slices of Wry* (1985) and *One Day She Catches Fire* (1992, in the Australian Poets series). Her poetry often deals with topical events, childhood experiences ('On Learning That Mothers Die') and feminist concerns such as the way that women's lives are all too frequently submerged by the demands of family and friends. She edited, with Joan Winter, *Valley Voices* (1985), an anthology of Diamond Valley (Victoria) writers.

Henry Lawson by His Mates, edited by J. le Gay Brereton and Lawson's daughter Bertha, was published in 1931. A collection of verse tributes, reminiscences, anecdotes and assessments, most of them first published as journal contributions, it offers an affectionate and somewhat sentimental portrait of Lawson. The contributors include Arthur Adams, H.E. Boote, E.J. Brady, F.J. Broomfield, R.J. Cassidy, Ernest O'Ferrall, W.E. FitzHenry, 'Jim Grahame', Mary Gilmore, T.D. Mutch, Roderic Quinn and Lawson's wife Bertha.

Henry Lawson Literary and Memorial Society, which incorporated the Australian Poetry Lovers' Society in 1973, grew out of the annual commemorative meetings held since 1923 at Footscray Park, Melbourne, where there is now a memorial bust of Lawson, a Lawson tree, and a plaque; Joseph Jones has recorded his impressions of one of the annual gatherings in the pamphlet *The Union Honours Its Dead: Henry Lawson Commemorative Gathering Number Thirty Nine* (1966). The society meets in Melbourne once a month to discuss Australian literature in general as well as Lawson in particular, and since 1960 has published a newsletter, the *Lawsonian*. In Sydney, the Henry Lawson Literary Society was organised in 1928 but is now in abeyance.

HENSHAW, Mark (1951–), born Canberra, has studied medicine and music and has lived in Germany and France. His first novel, *Out of the Line of Fire* (1988), won the 1988 Barbara Ramsden Award and the NBC Qantas New Writers Award of 1989. Henshaw has also published a sequence of meditations, translated into French by Pierre Alien, *Last Thoughts of a Dead Man* (1990). A novel which emphasises and plays with the post-structuralist position that reality is a fictional construct, *Out of the Line of Fire* places itself self-consciously in the tradition of Robbe-Grillet, Pynchon, Calvino, Abish and Handke and aroused a debate on publication between adherents and opponents of post-modernism; described as a *tour de force* by the former, it was denounced as pretentious and anti-humanist by the latter. Elena, one of the novel's characters, describes the nub of its philosophical position: 'there is essentially no difference between a fictional world and the real world . . . each world is particular to the mind that simultaneously perceives and creates it.' Central to this accomplished novel is an interest in language and its paradoxical combination of power with powerlessness, and the bearing this has on issues of narrative, the reliability and unreliability of memory and the problematic nature of identity. The novel takes the form of a dialogue between the Australian narrator, who is tentatively the author of the story, and Wolfi Schonbrun, a young philosophy student from Austria whom he encounters in Heidelberg; Wolfi is a character in the Australian's creation of story, as the Australian becomes a reader of Wolfi's, and as the latter switches in his turn to the role of author and observer of an indeterminate other in his relationship with the drug addict Karl. Described by some critics as a novel about reading, *Out of the Line of Fire* constantly challenges the reader, tantalising and half-fulfilling the normal expectations of unity and finality and engaging the reader's energies directly in the making of story. The novel is constructed in three sections; in the first, the narrator describes his encounter with Wolfi. In this section of the novel the reader is presented with a great deal of material which appears to be disjunct but which also appears to represent segments in a jigsaw, clues to possible final explanations of 'reality'; led on to piece items of knowledge together and to interpret wholes from partially perceived realities, the reader demonstrates the practical implications of Wolfi's abstractly titled thesis 'The Metonymic Perception of Reality'. The more conventionally narrated middle section, relying on a large box of material from the now vanished Wolfi, is narrated by Wolfi himself as he describes among other matters crucial events in his emotional history, including a family holiday in Yugoslavia when he fell in love with his sister Elena, and she with a Greek youth called Alexis; his initiation into sex, orchestrated by his grandmother and administered by a prostitute who resembled his sister; his relationship with a chameleon drug addict called Karl; and his ultimate disclosure that he is the father of his sister's daughter Anya. The third section returns to the original narrator and to a more contemporary, continuous mode of narration, describing the Australian's pursuit of the 'final' truth about Wolfi during a stay in Germany. Discovering that Wolfi has shot himself, that his father is now insane and his mother dead, the Australian visits Elena and is presented with yet another version of the past which accords even more closely to the Oedipal romance but which at the same time undermines the possibility of ever achieving certainty about Wolfi or about any series of events posing as absolute reality. On the one hand an enthralling thriller which focuses on the contrast between middle-class respectability and sadistic or incestuous relationships, on the other the novel both demystifies and exploits the thriller, relying on its psychology of concealment to pose larger questions about the human condition. Henshaw was awarded the ACT Literary Award ($15 000) in 1994.

Henslowe's Annual, published in Sydney 1900–4, was both an artistic and literary annual, written by Australian authors and illustrated by Australian artists.

Its publisher, Leonard Henslowe, was also connected with the brief-lived theatrical weekly the *Dramatic Critic* (1903).

HENTY Family. The Henty family was a pioneering family headed by Thomas Henty (1775–1839), whose wife, seven sons and a daughter all came to Australia. In 1828 Thomas, a Sussex farmer and banker dissatisfied with prospects in England, decided to emigrate to the colonies. The first party, headed by the eldest son, James (1800–82), went to the new settlement of WA in 1829 and to Van Diemen's Land, which became their base, in 1831; Thomas joined them with the rest of the family a year later. Dissatisfied with their failure to secure land in Van Diemen's Land, the Hentys turned their attention across Bass Strait to the unoccupied and virgin territory of the Port Phillip District. Starting initially as whalers at Portland Bay on the south-western coast of what became the colony of Victoria, they moved inland to establish themselves as squatters in the 'Australia Felix' territory explored by Thomas Mitchell. The pioneers of the pastoral industry in Victoria, the Hentys only secured title to their land after protracted wrangling with the NSW governors and the British Colonial Office. Edward (1810–78) and Stephen (1811–72) Henty were central to the Port Phillip operations; of the other sons, Francis (1815–89) succeeded on the station in WA, earlier mismanaged by his brother John (1813–68), the black sheep of the family; Charles (1807–64) and William (1808–81) settled in Tasmania and, like Edward, Stephen and James, became active in politics; and James became a successful merchant in Melbourne after earlier setbacks in Launceston. The early days at Portland Bay are recorded in *Australiana; Or, My Early Life* (1886) by Richmond Henty, son of Stephen; Marnie Bassett's *The Hentys* (1954) is the standard account of the family, which is commemorated by the naming of towns in NSW and Victoria and by a highway linking Horsham and Warracknabeal in the Wimmera district of Victoria. Charles Gee composed the folk-song 'The Henty Song' while *en route* with the first party to WA.

HEPBURN, Edith, see **'WICKHAM, Anna'**

HEPWORTH, John (1921–   ), born Pinjarra, WA, has worked mainly as a journalist and with the ABC. Well known for his column 'Outsight' in *Nation Review*, which he helped establish and of which he was editor for several years, Hepworth is an outstanding if controversial essayist and raconteur. *John Hepworth . . . His Book* (1978), edited by Morris Lurie and illustrated by Michael Leunig, is a collection of his 'Outsight' writings. His other numerous works include several performed plays, 'The Last of the Rainbow' (1963), which won the Lady Manifold competition in 1961, 'A Beast in View' (1959) and 'My Aunt the Unicorn'. He has also written a racy Australian fantasy, *The Multitude of Tigers* (1990), the saga of an attempt to save the last pure-bred Australian blowflies by Foulmouthed Freda and Brave Blowfly Benjamin. Their quest, which is really for the meaning of life, takes them all over Australia and introduces them to a wide range of animal characters. With Bob Ellis he wrote the children's books *Top Kid* (1985) and *The Paper Boy* (1985), based on television plays by Ellis, and with Steve Spears, *The Big Wish* (1990), based on Spears's television play for children. He also collaborated with John Hindle in the pub-crawl guide *Boozing Out in Melbourne Town* (1980), and *Around the Bend* (1983), an account of a 49-day raft trip down the Murray River by 'three middle-aged eccentrics' (Hepworth, Hindle and ABC producer Patrick Amer); it is said to have been 'an excursion kept afloat by rum, Scotch whisky, egotism and the presence of an ABC camera crew'. Once married to Oriel Gray (q.v.), Hepworth figures large in her autobiography, *Exit Left* (1985).

Herald, one of the oldest Australian daily newspapers, began publication in Melbourne as the *Port Phillip Herald* (1840–48); in 1849–55 it was known as the *Melbourne Morning Herald* and from 1855 by the present title. The *Herald* was originally a morning newspaper but was converted into an evening publication in 1869 by David Syme, who took it over briefly in 1858. On 8 October 1990 the *Herald* combined with the *Sun* to become the *Herald-Sun*, an 'all day' newspaper with four issues a day. Under Sir Keith Murdoch it had a reputation between the First and Second World Wars as one of the leading evening newspapers of the British Commonwealth. Edmund Finn worked for the *Herald* 1845–58; later contributors included Marcus Clarke, A.T.Strong, C.J. Dennis and Will Dyson.

HERBERT, Bob (1923–), born Yea, Victoria, has worked in pantomime, vaudeville, radio, television and little theatre as actor, stage hand, stage manager and director, and has written numerous plays. After serving in the AIF and RAAF in the Second World War, he spent four years as a member of the New Theatre, Melbourne, before becoming theatres manager at the University of New England. His plays include 'Campari Rocks', 'Sex and Violets', *Mr Jones* (1973), 'New England Honeymoon', *A Man of Respect* (published in *Biala* 1977), 'An Isolated Case of Heterochromia', which won second prize in the drama section of the 1970 Captain Cook literary competition, *No Names . . . No Pack Drill* (1980), 'The Girl with the Odd-Coloured Eyes' (1981), 'By the Billabong' (1981), and *The Last Wake at She-Oak Creek* (1988). *No Names . . . No Pack Drill*, which deals with a relationship between a young widow and an American deserter, shared first prize in the WA sesquicentenary play-writing competition, has been extensively staged in Australia and was produced as a film with the title *Rebel*.

HERBERT, Xavier (1901–84), born Geraldton, WA, was registered Alfred Jackson, the son of Amy Victoria Jackson and John Jackson, auctioneer. Whether John Jackson or Ben Herbert, Amy's subsequent husband, was Xavier's father is unclear, although various hypotheses are suggested by Frances De Groen, who discovered the previously missing birth certificate and published her findings in *Xavier Herbert's Birth: the Documentary Record* (1988). Herbert's first name, Xavier, was adopted in his twenties. As De Groen emphasises, the obscurity surrounding his paternity and subsequent difficult relationship with his mother and putative father may be psychologically linked, while they undoubtedly provided Herbert with powerful fuel for imaginative reconstruction throughout his literary career. At the age of 12 Herbert moved to Fremantle with his family. Two years later he began work in a chemist shop but continued schooling in order to qualify as a pharmacist. He remained in Fremantle during the First World War, but after training as a pharmacist moved to Melbourne, where he studied medicine for a year and worked as a dispenser in a hospital. He probably wrote for the *Melbourne Truth* in that period. In 1926 his first story was published in the *Australian Journal* under the pseudonym 'Herbert Astor'. By this time he had left Melbourne and gone to Sydney, staying there for a year and apparently writing for *Smith's Weekly* before his wandering took him northwards. In 1927 he reached Darwin, worked as a railway fettler in the Rum Jungle area, and visited the South Pacific. The experiences Herbert gathered in the late 1920s helped to inform his first and last novels, *Capricornia* (q.v., 1938) and *Poor Fellow My Country* (q.v., 1975).

In 1930 Herbert left Darwin for England; during his two years there the Anglophobia apparent in *Poor Fellow My Country* was confirmed but he managed before his return to Australia at the end of 1932 to complete, with the support of Sadie Norden, later his wife, the first draft of *Capricornia*, a long novel about the Northern Territory. In 1933 he wrote stories for the *Australian Journal* and the Sydney *Sun* to help bring Sadie to Australia; then, with the encouragement and advice of P.R. Stephensen (q.v.), also recently returned from England, he settled to the task of revising and reducing *Capricornia*. In 1934 the novel was set in type, but the collapse of Stephensen's publishing company meant that publication did not resume until in 1937 Stephensen accepted it for a new press with which he had become associated. *Capricornia* was officially published in 1938 (the A & R Imprint Classics edition of 1990 has an introduction by Mudrooroo), and in March of that year won the sesquicentenary novel competition. It soon became a best-seller and remains one of the best-known novels of its type and period.

In 1940 Herbert was awarded the first of several CLF fellowships to work on 'The King and the Kurrawaddi'; like several other works given titles and mentioned in Herbert's letters, it was never published. He served in the Second World War, mainly in the Northern Territory and the Pacific; following his discharge in 1946 he left Sydney and finally settled with his wife at Redlynch, near Cairns, in northern Queensland. Alternating writing with a variety of casual occupations and with validating the concluding words of *Disturbing Element*, 'the main thing in life is Living!', he wrote prolifically but published little until the end of the 1950s. The appearance in 1959 of *Seven Emus*, a novella significant mainly for an eccentric system of punctuation which was subsequently abandoned, was the start of a period in which Herbert had four books published in as many years. The others were *Soldiers' Women* (1961), a novel about wartime Sydney originally punctuated in the same form as *Seven Emus* but rewritten after the critical disapproval of that work; *Larger than Life* (1963), a collection of short stories; and *Disturbing Element* (1963, reprinted in 1991), an unsparing autobiography of his first twenty-four years, which some commentators see with *Capricornia* as containing his best work. Then, in 1975 after a decade of preparation and amid much publicity, Herbert's *Poor Fellow My Country* was published. A massive work of about 850 000 words, a third longer than *War and Peace* and the longest novel ever published in Australia, it is Herbert's final statement about Australia in general and the Northern Territory in particular. It won the Miles Franklin Award in 1975, an award which was soon followed by honorary doctorates from the universities of Queensland and Newcastle and by other tributes. Two collections of Herbert's writing have been published since his death, *Xavier Herbert* (1992) edited by Frances De Groen and Peter Pierce, which combines extracts from novels with other fiction, non-fiction and correspondence, and the substantial *South of Capricornia* (1990), edited by Russell McDougall, which reprints stories written before 1934 and often published under pseudonyms.

One of the legendary figures of Australian literary culture in the twentieth century, included in Keith Dunstan's affectionate gallery *Ratbags* (1979), Herbert was a man about whom anecdotes abound and who periodically emerged from the isolation of Redlynch to promote the publication of his books as well as to deliver strongly held opinions about life in Australia. Perhaps influenced by the chronological span of *Disturbing Element*, commentators have discovered in his early experiences some of the crucial influences on the subject matter and thematic concerns of his fiction. The title and substance of the autobiography attested to the difficult relationship Herbert had with his family: terrorised by his father and rejected by his mother, he felt himself the 'disturbing element' in their lives. There are many travellers among the hundreds of characters who inhabit Herbert's fictional work, and most of these are embarked on a search for security, for familial, social or national identity; in particular, the figure of the part-Aborigine, caught between White and Black society, is a dominant one in *Capricornia, Seven Emus, Larger than Life* and *Poor Fellow My Country*. A second and connected influence to emerge from Herbert's early years was his contact at Geraldton with Aborigines and with pioneering European Australians like his engine-driver father. These contacts, together with a strong feeling of both his own and Aboriginal attachment to the land, were consolidated by his wanderings after he left Melbourne, and shaped the outback settings and discussion of man's relationship to the environment that figure prominently in his fiction with the exception of *Soldiers' Women*. The matriarchal world of that novel, however, was no doubt partly shaped by Herbert's experience of his mother's dominance of his childhood

household and by his father's absence on active service in the First World War.

Herbert's literary career was marked by a succession of false starts, multiple drafts, and much revision, and also by the influence the success of his first novel, *Capricornia*, had on his subsequent work. A saga which encompasses the 1880s to the 1930s, *Capricornia* won renown, when first published, as a savage indictment of the treatment of Aboriginal Australians by European Australians. Without minimising the significance of the indictment, subsequent commentators have directed attention to other aspects of Herbert's achievement: the narrative momentum retained throughout the work; the tight control exerted over what appears to be a sprawling canvas of incident and character; the richness with which Herbert establishes his isolated, frontier, fictional territory of Capricornia; the exploration in the novel of human culpability and man's response to the land; the range of its characterisation; and its mixture of comedy, satire and tragedy. The fictional works which have been published since *Capricornia* have been unfavourably compared with it. *Seven Emus*, the plot of which has been summarised by Harry Heseltine as a 'tall story of two confidence tricksters who succeed in the end in outsmarting themselves', is not only flawed by the failed experiment in punctuation but also by the hectoring tone of its sneers at familiar Herbert targets, and by the ponderous prose style. *Larger than Life* is a collection of traditionally plotted stories from the 1930s, 1940s and 1950s. It encompasses familiar territory (northern Australia) and themes (the mistreatment and alienation of ethnic minorities), although several stories attest to the development of Herbert's interest in flying. *Soldiers' Women*, the most uncharacteristic of Herbert's work in its urban setting, which has been equated with Sydney during the Second World War, is a representation of women in wartime, which explores through symbol and narrative the themes of destiny in human lives and the nature of sexuality. Some critics, however, have suggested that Herbert's idiosyncratic views on female sexuality have intruded too much into the novel, in which all sexual relationships outside heterosexual monogamy are condemned. Finally, there is *Poor Fellow My Country*, which has been praised as Herbert's *magnum opus* and condemned by Laurie Clancy as a kind of literary brontosaurus, *Poor Bugger My Book*. In the novel Herbert carries the story of life in northern Australia forward from 1936, the time at which *Capricornia* ends, to 1942. One of its two central characters is Prindy, the part-Aborigine who, unlike Norman Shillingsworth, acquires his Aboriginal identity in the opening chapter and retains it, in the face of White oppression, until his death at the end, a death which represents the wholesale destruction of Aboriginal society. The second major figure is Jeremy Delacy, a hard-bitten pioneer who articulates where Australia has gone wrong, e.g. in letting its citizens become involved in the imperialist wars of 1914–18 and 1939–45; his experience embodies the national tragedy which culminates in the 'Day of Shame', the title of the last section, when Australians flee Darwin in fear of Japanese bombs. Although Prindy's tragedy is realised and Herbert has characteristically exerted some control over his material, *Poor Fellow My Country* clearly suffers from authorial intrusions thinly disguised as Jeremy's lectures to a series of listeners; from the failure of Jeremy to emerge as a moral model and his emergence instead as a self-righteous, quirky, intolerant, paternalistic, sexist bore; from the chauvinist attitudes expressed to all non-Australians; and from the prolixity of the writing. Harry Heseltine and Laurie Clancy have published studies of Herbert (1973, 1981), the former in the OUP Australian Writers and Their Work series, the latter in the Twayne's World Authors series; John McLaren has published a study of *Capricornia* and *Poor Fellow My Country* in the 'Essays in Australian Literature' series in 1981.

'Here Comes the Nigger!', a play by Gerald Bostock, was performed in the Black Theatre, Sydney, in 1976. It concerns a blind Aboriginal poet, Sam Matthews, and a White woman, Odette O'Brien, who is tutoring him for his Higher School Certificate. A loving relationship develops between them but is strongly opposed by racist relatives on both sides. Billy, Sam's brother, warns him that White women 'can screw you up'; Neil, Odette's brother, accuses her of being 'partial to the taste of licorice sticks'. The play, with its distinctive contemporary urban idiom, is a powerful and violent statement on 1970s racism.

Here's Luck, a comic novel by Lennie Lower (q.v.), was first published in 1930. It chronicles the misadventures of Jack Gudgeon, a 48-year-old Sydneysider, after the departure of his wife, Agatha, gives him new freedoms. In company with his sleazy son, Stanley, and later his brother-in-law, George, Gudgeon embarks on a series of drunken escapades which give full rein to Lower's talent for slapstick and his satiric observations of domestic strife and city lowlife. At the climax to the novel, a riotous party is held at the family home, which is burnt down. The party is the occasion also of the reconciliation between Jack and Agatha, although the last page of *Here's Luck* suggests that Jack's decision to settle down may be only a temporary one.

HERGENHAN, L.T. (Laurence Thomas) (1931–), born Bega, NSW, was educated at the universities of Sydney and London, and has taught at the universities of Tasmania and Queensland, where he was director of the Australian Studies Centre 1979–82. Foundation editor of *Australian Literary Studies* (q.v.) in 1963, he has also edited the Portable Australian Authors series (now UQP Australian Authors series) since 1976 and written widely on Australian and English literature; his editorship of *Australian Literary Studies* over more than two decades has significantly advanced Australian literary scholarship. Hergenhan's major Australian publications include an edition of the journalism of Marcus Clarke, *A Colonial City* (1972), a Clarke bibliography (1975), a critical study of fiction about the convicts, *Unnatural Lives* (1983), and an anthology, *The Australian Short Story: From the 1890s to

the 1980s* (1986). He was also general editor of *The Penguin New Literary History of Australia* (1988) and in 1992 received the A.A. Phillips Award for his contribution to the study of Australian literature.

Hermes began in 1886 as an undergraduates' magazine sponsored by the Students' Representative Council of the University of Sydney. Published monthly it ran until 1894; in 1895 a new series began, published twice a term, which continued until 1969 although the magazine failed to appear in 1953, 1955, 1964, 1967 and 1968. In addition to university news, *Hermes* published original verse and literary articles. A special Jubilee number was issued in 1902 to commemorate the fiftieth year of the university; it included a history of the university and an article by Christopher Brennan, 'The University and Australian Literature'. Numerous other subsequently well-known writers either edited or contributed to *Hermes*, including J. le Gay Brereton and A.D. Hope. In recent years *Hermes* has become a national and more populist magazine receiving contributions Australia-wide. A companion *Hermes Papers* accommodates more theoretical and critical interests.

Hermit in Van Diemen's Land, The is a series of thirty prose sketches which first appeared under the pseudonym 'Simon Stukeley' in weekly parts in Andrew Bent's *Colonial Times* June–December 1829. The sketches were then collected in book form by Bent, and the resulting volume, released in 1830 although 1829 appears on the title page, constitutes the first book of essays published in Australia. The acknowledged model for *The Hermit in Van Diemen's Land* was *The Hermit in London*, a series of didactic, anecdotal and descriptive sketches of London life which forms part of a larger series of *Hermit* books, e.g. *The Hermit in the Country, The Hermit Abroad, The Hermit in Edinburgh*, generally attributed to Felix McDonough or Macdonogh. The technique, however, of employing as narrator a wide-eyed visitor (Simon announces himself a native of Yorkshire coming to 'look over' the colony and inhabitants of Van Diemen's Land) not only owes something to a long-established prose genre which accommodates some of the essays of Montesquieu and Goldsmith but also establishes Simon, at least for part of *The Hermit in Van Diemen's Land*, as an early specimen of the 'new chum' type. Characteristically the sketches combine authorial contemplation, satiric description, and narration. They follow Simon from his arrival in Van Diemen's Land, through his meetings with prominent citizens and his peripatetic visits to courts, parties, weddings, schools, farms, and so on in Hobart and the surrounding countryside. Some characters appear in several sketches; two recurring themes are the confusion over Simon's identity, and the rapacity and incompetence of lawyers. Although individual colonists are not named, the precise descriptions of dress, speech and mannerism made identification easy for contemporary audiences, and led to Bent's prosecution for libel by one disgruntled target, the advocate Gamaliel Butler. The case delayed release of the book.

The Hermit in Van Diemen's Land is generally agreed to have been written by Henry Savery (q.v.), the author of the first Australian novel, *Quintus Servinton* (1831); the two works are complementary in their attitude towards the legal system, although *The Hermit* is more openly antagonistic. If Savery was the author he wrote it while in gaol for debt in 1829; the use of a pseudonym is understandable, not least because the convicts were banned by a government order of 1828 from writing for the press. The identification of Savery was first firmly made by Henry Melville in a copy of *The Hermit in Van Diemen's Land* now in the British Library, London; Melville stated that Savery was wholly responsible for the work and that Thomas Wells (q.v.), a fellow debtor in prison, acted as an amanuensis, preparing the copy for the printer. Other contemporaries, however, identified Wells as the author, as also did later writers such as James Bonwick. The only modern text, edited by Cecil Hadgraft (1964), accepts Melville's view and assigns the work to Savery. Also included in this edition are notes on the Hobart citizens, e.g. Sir George Arthur, William Bedford, Andrew Bent, whose identities are confirmed by a contemporary key now held in the Mitchell Library, Sydney.

Hero of Too, The, a novel by David Martin (q.v.), was first published in 1965. It is both a sustained, hilarious comedy and a mild satire on the bushranging (q.v.) tradition and small-town life and politics. Tooramit, a tiny Victorian town faced with the problem of how best to celebrate its founding day, gradually discovers a series of embarrassing truths about its most famous son, the bushranger Dick Grogan. Although many of the Tooramites are aware that Grogan's heroic image is paper-thin and have private reasons for not perpetuating his memory, others have equally good reasons for raising his ghost. Neighbouring Boobyalla, with which Tooramit is locked in traditional rivalry, also yearns to celebrate the Grogan legend. The arrival of a Grogan devotee from Melbourne, a young schoolteacher, Steve Turner, acts as a catalyst to the involved political situation, setting a chain of events in inevitable motion. Not only is Grogan revealed as a feeble and unwilling hero, but unsuspected intricacies of relationships also come to light that link the family of Jack Bollman, shire president and supposedly grandson of the man who shot Grogan in the buttocks in the 'Affair at Tooramit Bridge' in 1874, and that of Klep Quinn, the local nightcart man and an amiable kleptomaniac. The past events, brought fully into light by two of the oldest inhabitants, Pongo Quinn and Lam the Chinese herbalist, prove benign for the younger generation, rearranging George Bollman and Lacy Quinn, and Steve Turner and Clare Lovelett, in more appropriate relationships. They also have a liberating impact on the lives of the middle-aged, such as Jack Bollman, his sister Alison, and his low-pulsed wife Norma.

Herridge of Reality Swamp (1907), William Gosse Hay's (q.v.) second novel, is focused on the experiences of a minister, John Sydenham, who comes to Manalia (Australia) to escape from a romantic scandal in which he is the innocent party. He changes his name to Herridge, goes to work among the convicts, and rescues a would-be suicide who turns out to be the woman who ruined his reputation; in time she marries Sir Ralph Eardley and manages to reduce him to alcoholism, to drive his heiress daughter Ellen towards madness, and to have Herridge imprisoned. Herridge is sent to the isolated penal settlement of Reality Swamp, where Sir Ralph is in charge and Herridge and Ellen fall in love. When the settlement runs short of food, the dominant Lady Eardley plans to remove herself and the officers, leaving the prisoners to starve. Hay himself planned to have Lady Eardley's boat attacked by Aborigines and the only survivor, Ellen, return it to the starving settlement; but at the insistence of Hay's publishers, Herridge leads the party back to civilisation, is pardoned, and settles down with Ellen as his wife in a country vicarage.

HERRON, Margaret (?–1968), born Olive Herron, married C.J. Dennis (q.v.) in 1917. As Margaret Herron she published two novels, *My Dear* (1928) and *Seed and Stubble* (1936), and a biography of Dennis which includes some information about her own life, *Down the Years* (1953). She also selected a collection of Dennis's verse, *Random Verse* (1952).

'HERVEY, Grant' (George Henry Cochrane) (1880–1933), born Casterton, Victoria, was a blacksmith before becoming a journalist, working on newspapers in both eastern and western Australia. He contributed ballads and other verse to the *Bulletin*, and published *Australians Yet, and Other Verses* in 1913. Acquitted in 1905 of attempted murder, 'Hervey' was arrested in 1914 after he offered to provide John Norton with divorce evidence against his wife. Convicted of forgery, he was sentenced to four years' imprisonment; his open letter about prison conditions to the NSW Premier, W.A. Holman, was printed in Vance Marshall's *The World of the Living Dead* (1919). In 1919, posing as an American, 'Madison Harvey', 'Hervey' appeared in Mildura to drum up financial support for a new state; he was exposed by C.J. de Garis and after seeking his revenge through the editorship of the *Mildura and Merbein Sun* was tarred and feathered by de Garis's supporters in 1921. After another gaol sentence for forgery he was, in 1929, briefly editor of the salacious Sydney weekly *Beckett's Budget;* in 1931 he was convicted on a third charge of forgery. At Bathurst gaol he wrote *An Eden of the Good* (1934), a bizarre historical novel set in Tasmania and Sydney in the 1830s. Peopled by historical characters such as Charles Darwin, John Dunmore Lang and William Charles Wentworth as well as by the exotically named governor Sir Dratsum Sneek (the well-known 'Keens Mustard' spelt backwards), the madame Venus Colossal, and the newspaper editor Ebenezer Weaselfidjetts, *An Eden of the Good* focuses on the rise to prosperity of the poet Randolph Cochrane and his brother Walter. At the end of the novel both have married well and depart the 'poisonous convict-minded village of Sydney', Randolph to a new settlement to be named after his wife, Mildura, and Walter to Moreton Bay. Although his central characters share his real name, 'Hervey' begins the novel with the convict experiences of his 'grandfather', George Hervey; another convict in *An Eden of the Good*, the Irish baronet Sir Terence Hayes, bears some resemblance to the title character of William Gosse Hay's *The Escape of the Notorious Sir William Heans* (1919).

HESELTINE, H.P. (Harry Payne) (1931–), born Fremantle, WA, was educated at the University of WA and at Louisiana State University. He returned to Australia in 1956 and taught at the universities of New England and NSW (1959–77) before becoming professor of English at James Cook University of North Queensland; in 1982 he became professor of English in the faculty of Military Studies, Royal Military College, Duntroon, in 1986 professor of English at the Australian Defence Force Academy, becoming rector in 1991. The essays Heseltine has contributed to literary journals such as *Meanjin* since the early 1960s have included important assessments of Henry Lawson, A.B. Paterson, Francis Webb and other Australian writers as well as studies of the Australian literary tradition. He edited *Australian Idiom* (1963) and, with Stanley Tick, *The Writer in the Modern World* (1962); his other publications include monographs on J. le Gay Brereton (1965) and Xavier Herbert (1973); a critical edition of Nathaniel Swan's (q.v.) *Luke Mivers' Harvest* (1991); a biographical and critical study of Vance Palmer (1970) and *Intimate Portraits and Other Pieces* (1969), a selection of Palmer's prose; editions of *The Penguin Book of Australian Verse* (1972), *The Penguin Book of Australian Short Stories* (1976), and *The Penguin Book of Modern Australian Verse* (1981); *Acquainted with the Night: Studies in Classic Australian Fiction* (1979) and *The Uncertain Self* (1986), a collection of his essays on Australian literature. He also wrote the entry on literary criticism (Criticism) in this *Companion*. With Joy Hooton he compiled the second edition of *Annals of Australian Literature* (1992). He was made AO in 1990 for his services to Australian literature.

HESLING, Bernard (1905–87), born Yorkshire, England, came to Australia in 1928. A well-known painter and cartoonist whose work was a familiar feature of the Sydney *Daily Telegraph*, he wrote and drew for a variety of newspapers and magazines, including *Meanjin*, the *Bulletin*, the *Sydney Morning Herald*, *Smith's Weekly*, *Quadrant*, *Nation*, the *New Yorker* and the *Listener*. Art critic for the Sydney *Observer* 1950–55, he lived in Sydney for thirty years before moving to Adelaide. He published a collection of his drawings, *Cartoons* (1945); an illustrated account of Sydney, *Sydney Observed* (1953); and several humorous illustrated autobiographies, *Little and Orphan* (1954), *The Dinkumization and Depommification of an Artful English Immigrant* (1963, later published with the title *The Dinkum Pommie*), *Stir Up This Stew* (1966), *I Left My Tears in the Fridge* (1972), *Around the World on an Old Age Pension* (1974, which includes 'My Picture Book') and *Art Ruined My Career in Crime* (1977). One of his plays, 'My Life with an Interval for Aspirin', was performed

in 1972. He was awarded the OAM for his services to art.

HETHERINGTON, John (1907–74), born Sandringham, near Melbourne, worked for several Melbourne newspapers until the Second World War, during which he served in Greece as war correspondent for the London *Times*, the *Manchester Guardian* and the Melbourne *Herald* group of newspapers. He was editor of the Adelaide *News* 1945–49, deputy editor of the *Argus* 1952–54, and a feature-writer for the *Age* 1954–67. His publications based on his war experience included *Airborne Invasion* (1943), an account of the battle of Crete; *The Australian Soldier* (1943); and *The Winds Are Still* (1947), winner of the *Sydney Morning Herald* war-novel competition. He also wrote several biographies of famous Australians, including two of Sir Thomas Blamey, *Blamey* (1954), and the more substantial *Blamey: Controversial Soldier* (1973); *Melba* (1967); and a monograph on Norman Lindsay (1961) and the authorised account, *Norman Lindsay: The Embattled Olympian* (1973), winner of the Matthew Flinders Award. He published several collective biographical studies, *Australians: Nine Profiles* (1960), *Forty-Two Faces* (q.v. 1962), *Australian Painters* (1963) and *Uncommon Men* (1965). Interested in Victorian architecture and social history, he wrote a history of some Victorian buildings, *Witness to Things Past* (1964), and a history of churches and churchmen in early Victoria, *Pillars of the Faith* (1966). In addition to some uncollected short stories and verse he wrote an account of his childhood at Sandringham, *The Morning Was Shining* (1971). A painstaking, balanced and self-effacing biographer, with a lucid style, Hetherington had unusual ability to appreciate and realise the diverse personalities and interests of his subjects.

HETHERINGTON, Paul (1958–), born Adelaide, has spent much of his life in WA but is now programme development officer of the National Library of Australia in Canberra. While in WA he was editor of the *Fremantle Arts Review* and now edits the monthly *National Library of Australia News* and the quarterly Library journal, *Voices*. He has published the collections *Mapping Wildwood Road* (1990) in the ANL Pamphlet Poets series *Acts Themselves Trivial* (1991), and *The Dancing Scorpion* (1993). His delight in language and his meticulous craftsmanship create lyrical poetry, pleasantly ornamented with metaphor and imagery. His themes spring from the personal but often move out to embrace the more general and universal.

HEWETT Dorothy (1923–) was born and brought up in WA on her father's isolated wheat farm. Until the age of 12 she was educated by correspondence. At 19 her first poetry appeared in *Meanjin*, and by 22 she had won a drama competition and a national poetry competition. Her personal life at this time was turbulent: she failed her university course and attempted suicide. At 19 she joined the Communist Party. Marriage in 1944 to the lawyer and communist writer Lloyd Davies (q.v.), and the birth of a son, provided a brief stability, but the marriage failed and Hewett left for Sydney in 1948. There she lived in the poorer areas and worked in a variety of factory jobs. For nine years she lived with Les Flood, boiler-maker and communist, by whom she had three sons. She became deeply involved in Party activities during the turbulent anti-communist period of the 1950s, but wrote little. In 1959 her novel *Bobbin Up* (q.v.), based on her factory experiences, appeared and won immediate popularity. Her relationship with Flood having come to an end, she resumed her university studies in Perth in 1960 and married Merv Lilley (q.v.), merchant seaman and communist, in the same year. In 1968, disillusioned by Soviet treatment of dissidents, she left the Communist Party. After some years of tutoring at the University of WA, she moved again to Sydney. *Wild Card* (1990), Hewett's acclaimed first volume of autobiography, describes her experiences to 1958. In 1975 Lloyd Davies began a series of libel actions against Hewett and other parties following the publication of a poem in *Rapunzel in Suburbia*; the actions, which stimulated much public debate, are justified by Davies in *In Defence of My Family* (1986).

Her poetry, a continued preoccupation, has appeared in the collections *What about the People!* (1961, with Merv Lilley), *Windmill Country* (1968), *Late Night Bulletin* (1969), *Rapunzel in Suburbia* (1975), *Greenhouse* (1979), *Journeys* (1982), *Alice in Wormland* (1987), *A Tremendous World in her Head* (1989) and *Selected Poems* (1991). But she is also well known as a playwright. Her published plays are *This Old Man Comes Rolling Home* (q.v., 1966, published 1976), *The Chapel Perilous* (q.v., 1971, published 1972), *Bon-Bons and Roses for Dolly* (1972, published 1976), *The Tatty Hollow Story* (1975, published 1976), *The Golden Oldies* (in *Hecate* 1976, and with a radio play, *Susannah's Dreaming*, in 1981), *The Beautiful Mrs. Portland* (*Theatre Australia* 1976), *The Man from Mukinupin* (1979, published 1979), *Golden Valley* (1981, published 1985), *Song of the Seals* (1983, published 1985) and *Joan* (1975, published 1984). Her unpublished plays and musicals include 'Time Flits Away, Lady' (1941), 'Mrs. Porter and the Angel' (1970), 'Catspaw' (1974), 'Miss Hewett's Shenanigans' (1975), 'Pandora's Cross' (1978), 'The Fields of Heaven' (1983), 'Zimmer' (1983), 'Zoo' (1984) and 'The Rising of Pete Marsh' (1988). She has also written radio plays, numerous short stories and a novel, *The Toucher* (1993), and edited a collection of WA literature, *Sandgropers* (1973). The first volume of her *Collected Plays* was published in 1992.

A romantic quest for the intrinsic but elusive self lies at the heart of Hewett's poetry and drama. It determines the emotional range and impact of her work, its vigour and frankness. Critics of her work also claim that her romantic commitment leads to structural weakness, thematic confusion and self-indulgence. After the naturalism of her first professionally produced play, *This Old Man Comes Rolling Home*, Hewett turned to a more expressionistic, free-wheeling theatre, that mixes diverse styles and moods and uses a wide range of effects, visual, verbal and musical. Like Patrick White (q.v.), she uses poetry, music and sym-

bol to portray life's paradoxes and her characters' mingling of perception and delusion. The mixture of black comedy and absurdist allegory in 'Mrs. Porter and the Angel' prefigures the later plays, although the theme of division between dream and reality is dealt with more purposefully in her next most produced play, *The Chapel Perilous*. Reactions to the formidable heroine have ranged from delight to disgust, but the play's vigorous momentum and abrasive variety have made it memorable theatre. The bitch-goddess figure also features in the next three plays: *Bon-Bons and Roses for Dolly* is a part-nostalgic, part-satirical look at the dream-world created by the cinema of the 1930s, in which the heroine, Dolly Garden, is both victim and creator of the dream; *The Tatty Hollow Story* is a more controlled study of the resistance between authentic self and perceived and conditioned selves; *The Golden Oldies* explores the tedium and frustrations of petit-bourgeois, 'respectable' femininity. The musicals 'Catspaw' and 'Joan' are more schematic elaborations of the previous themes via knock-about vaudeville, but *The Beautiful Mrs. Portland* is a return to a more naturalistic, Ibsenesque theatre. Another change is registered in her most unified and objective play so far, *The Man from Mukinupin*. Many of Hewett's dramatic themes, incidents and images are present in her poetry. Apart from some proletarian ballads, her verse is confessional and romantic in theme, wryly humorous, frankly bawdy, varied in tone and rich in imagery. Sexuality is her main subject, seen as both liberation and imprisonment, although increasingly she writes of the fear and attraction of death.

Hewett has won numerous awards for her work including the ABC Poetry Prize (1945 and 1965), the Mary Gilmore short story Award (1960), the *Australian* Poetry Prize (1986), the Angus & Robertson Poetry Prize (1986), the Grace Leven Poetry Prize (1989), the Mattara Poetry Award (1991), the Victorian Premier's Award for non-fiction (1991) and two Awgies (1972 and 1982). She has received several Literature Board writers' grants, is an emeritus fellow of the Literature Board of the Australia Council and has been made AO. Margaret Williams has written a study of her work, *Dorothy Hewett. The Feminine as Subversion* (1992).

HEWETT, Robert (1949–), born Melbourne, graduated in drama from Flinders University and has had extensive experience as an actor in live theatre, film and television. His first play, 'Just . . . One Last Dance', was produced in 1980 by the Melbourne Theatre Company and was followed by *Gulls*, first produced in 1983, winner of the Green Room Award for best new play that year and published in 1984, and *The Adman* (produced and published in 1991). His other plays include 'The Lemming Harvest', 'Rites' and 'Babyface'. *Gulls*, a study of the relationship and mutual frustrations of brain-damaged Bill Clements and his sister Frances, who cares for him in their beachside cottage, deals sensitively and unsentimentally with the theme of physical impairment; *The Adman* focuses on the advertising world, satirically exposing its politics, dubious ethics and obsession with image-making and whatever is current.

HIBBERD, Jack (1940–), born Warracknabeal, Victoria, studied medicine at the University of Melbourne, graduated in 1964 and practised as a doctor until 1973 when he began to work for the theatre full-time. At the beginning of his career he was closely associated, both as writer and director, with the Australian Performing Group, which performed ten of his early plays. In 1976 he left the group although, unlike Barry Oakley and David Williamson, he has remained in Melbourne. Active in public discussion of the arts, he has served a term on the Theatre Board. His first full-length published play, *White with Wire Wheels* (q.v. published in *Plays*, ed. Graeme Blundell, 1970), was followed by *Three Old Friends* (1967) and in 1968 by a sequence of short plays which include 'Brainrot', *Just Before the Honeymoon* (published in *Komos*, 1969), *O, One of Nature's Gentlemen* (1976), *Who?* (also published in Blundell's edition of *Plays*), *This Great Gap of Time, No Time Like the Present*, and a musical drama, 'Jack Juan'. *Commitment* also appeared in 1968 and the following year he was commissioned by the University of NSW Drama Foundation to write 'The Last Days of Epic J. Remorse'. *Dimboola* (q.v., 1974), his best-known play, was first produced by the Australian Performing Group in 1969, but only became successful after David Williamson directed it in 1973. In 1970 the musical extravaganza he wrote with John Romeril, *Marvellous Melbourne* (*Theatre-Australia*, 1977), was produced by the Group, followed by 'Klag' and 'Customs and Excise' (later 'Proud Flesh'); 'Aorta' was produced in 1971 and 'Women!' and *Captain Midnight V.C.* in 1972 (published 1984). *A Stretch of the Imagination* (1973), regarded by some critics as his most important play to date, was also first produced in 1972. His remaining plays include 'Long Time No See' (1968), 'Why an Alternative Theatre?' (1972), 'The Architect and the Emperor of Assyria' (1973–74), 'Sports Show' (1974), *The Les Darcy Show* (performed 1974, published 1976), *Peggy Sue* (performed 1974, published 1982), *A Toast to Melba* (performed 1975, published 1976), *Goodbye Ted* (1975, with John Timlin, published 1983), 'Memoirs of a Carlton Bohemian' (1977), *The Overcoat* (in *Theatre-Australia*, 1977), *Sin* (in *Meanjin* 1978 and with *The Overcoat*, 1981), an opera libretto performed by the Victorian State Opera in 1978, 'A Man of Many Parts' (1980), *Mothballs* (in *Meanjin*, 1980), *Breakfast at the Windsor* (in *Meanjin*, 1981), *A Modest Proposal* (in *The Review*, 1981), *Glycerine Tears* (in *Meanjin*, 1982), *Lavender Bags* (in *Aspect*, 1982), *Liquid Amber* (1982, published 1984), 'Malarky Barks' (1982), *Death Warmed Up* (in *Scripsi*, 1984), and *Odyssey of a Prostitute* (in *Outrider*, 1985). *Squibs: A Collection of Short Plays* (1984) includes several of the above pieces as well as the previously unpublished skits and micro-plays, *A Knotty Problem*, *A League of Nations*, *Asian Oranges*, *The Three Sisters*, *Death of a Traveller*, *See You Tomorrow at Maxim's*, *The Common Touch* and *Below the Belt*. *A Country Quinella* (1984) includes *Dimboola* and *Liquid Amber*, and *Duets* (1989) *The Old School Tie*

and *Glycerine Tears*. The collection *Three Popular Plays* (1976) includes *One of Nature's Gentlemen, A Toast to Melba* and *The Les Darcy Show*. Critical studies of his drama include *Hibberd*, edited by John Hainsworth (1987) and Paul McGillick's *Jack Hibberd* (1988). Abandoning the theatre in 1986, Hibberd returned to medicine and began writing fiction. He has written three novels, *Memoirs of an Old Bastard* (1989), *The Life of Riley* (1991) and *Perdita* (1992). Hibberd has also published translations of poems by Baudelaire, *Le Vin des Amants* (1977), and, with Garrie Hutchinson, *The Barracker's Bible: A Dictionary of Sporting Slang* (1983).

Hibberd's early plays favour a rough, aggressive, cabaret style that is abrasive and disconcerting in impact. He was the first of the new dramatists to explore the contemporary 'ocker' stereotype and the limitations of prevalent Australian male attitudes and rituals from the point of view of both sexes. *White with Wire Wheels* concentrates on male conformity, *One of Nature's Gentlemen* on the exploitative relationships between 'mates', *Peggy Sue* on varieties of female experience of male domination.

Some of his plays, like those of David Williamson, which crystallise and satirise familiar attitudes or myths, engage the audience in the shock of recognition. *Dimboola*, a send-up of the Australian country wedding that is more comic and affectionate than satiric, has become part of the national folklore, and is the most performed of any Australian play; *A Toast to Melba*, *The Les Darcy Show* and *Captain Midnight V.C.* are part comic parody, part affirmative celebration of legendary national figures. But Hibberd is more interested in the possibilities of popular theatre than in sociology. Influenced by Pinter, Beckett and Brecht, Elizabethan and Jacobean theatre, the expressionists from Büchner to Wedekind and nineteenth-century Australian theatre, he draws on a wide range of theatrical modes for his own experimental effects. A loose, episodic structure, broadly drawn characters, scatological humour, songs and other musical effects, and a general, absurdist tenor are recurrent characteristics of his diverse theatre. In his introduction to *Three Popular Plays*, Hibberd develops his concept of a popular, accessible theatre that intermingles 'celebration with satire, fun with gravity, fiction with information, ignorance with politics, slang with poetry'; such a theatre offers no political messages or psychological explanations, but is nevertheless able to 'jolt and agitate within a context of sheer local enjoyment, a whirl of community, and an awareness of a shared heritage and its absurdities'. Especially fascinated by language, he uses the Australian idiom not as a sociological reflector but in an attempt to reanimate and recolour the English language. This reinvigorating effect is particularly obvious in his adaptation of Gogol's story *The Overcoat*, a part-comic, part-sombre evocation of a crazy, absurdist world, and in his monodrama *A Stretch of the Imagination*. In this play, a re-creation over one day of his life by an old man, Monk O'Neill, as he faces death (both literally and in imagination), Hibberd draws heavily on the variety of the vernacular, especially on its ironic capacities. Monk O'Neill is simultaneously a complex individual, an archetypal

Australian and an Everyman figure. Once a man-about-town, scholar, and world traveller, Monk as pioneer, fossicker, explorer, sporting hero and womaniser also embodies ideal aspects of the Australian legend as well as some of its exploitative and destructive aspects. Although death and alienation are the play's starting-points, the underlying mood is strongly positive and life-affirming. Pathetic and dignified, comic and tragic, callous and humane, self-centred and selfless, Monk emerges as a figure of elastic dimensions, a fusion of myth, type and caricature.

Hibberd's fiction draws on some of the same elements which fuelled his plays, such as his interest in language, ambivalent relationship with Melbourne and preoccupation with Australian masculinity. *Memoirs of an Old Bastard* is a Rabelaisian, picaresque tale of an elderly, eccentric millionaire who comes to Melbourne after sixteen years in the Great Dividing Range in search of his lost daughter and rapidly gathers a troupe of grotesquely comic characters with such functional names as Rick O'Shea, the ballistics expert, and Skidmore Rowe, the aristocratic derelict. The novel's plot, which is described by a Frank Moorhouse (q.v.) surrogate (F. Rank-Morgue-house) as a 'dis-ongoing narrative', proceeds at a furious pace, sustained by a cast of hundreds and by Hibberd's fertile linguistic powers. *The Life of Riley*, which has the same picaresque structure and comic ingredients, takes its central character over larger areas of Australia and even overseas. A companion to *Memoirs of an Old Bastard, Perdita* traces the vicissitudes of a girl, abandoned in childhood, and her quest for her father.

'Hibernian Father, The', a popular melodrama by Edward Geoghegan (q.v.), was presented anonymously in Sydney in 1844; it is set in fifteenth-century Ireland. The author was accused of plagiarism by some spectators, who claimed the play borrowed heavily from *The Warden of Galway* by a Rev. Groves, performed in Dublin and published in 1832. Geoghegan refuted the charge and the controversy subsided since the earlier play could not be produced for comparison. Opinion is still divided about the validity of the charge although free adaptations were then common practice.

'Hidden Bole, The', a complex philosophical poem by R.D. FitzGerald (q.v.), was written in 1935 in Sydney while FitzGerald was convalescing from a severe operation. It was published in *Moonlight Acre* (1938). Highly valued by FitzGerald ('my chief claim to be a poet at all'), the poem reflects on the death of the ballerina Pavlova in 1931, moving from that event to a contemplation of the nature and essence of beauty and the relationship between beauty and time. The banyan tree, which puts out aerial roots to reinforce the original sapling, thus producing a maze of trunks, is taken as a natural example of continuous survival, that survival stemming from the original core, the 'hidden bole' itself. The individual blossoms of the tree, coming in profusion from the many trunks, have only a momentary existence and glory, but that glory (beauty) continues with the new blossoms that quickly replace the old. Beauty thus persists because, paradoxically, it is transient. Although the beauty of Pavlova's actual dance seems to die with her, it survives in the memory of those who witness it.

HIDES, Jack (1906–38), born Port Moresby, Papua, was a patrol officer and later assistant resident magistrate and gold prospector. His books *Through Wildest Papua* (1935), *Papuan Wonderland* (1936), *Savages in Serge* (1938) and *Beyond the Kubea* (1939) are a combination of adventure fiction, description and ethnographical studies. J.P. Sinclair wrote *The Outside Man: Jack Hides of Papua* (1969).

HIGGINS, Bertram (1901–74), born Malvern, Melbourne, went to Oxford in 1919 and remained in England until 1930 as a literary journalist, as assistant editor of the *Calendar of Modern Letters* and a reviewer for the *Times Literary Supplement*, the *Spectator*, the *New Statesman*, and the *Sunday Times*. After a brief period in Australia (1930–33), part of which time he worked on Cyril Pearl's short-lived magazine *Stream*, he returned to England, where he served in the RAF in the Second World War. In 1946 he returned to Australia. Higgins published *Mordecaius Overture* (1933), a complex work that saw him recognised by a small coterie as the intellectual and poetic equal of T.S. Eliot, but which remained only dimly understood. Mordecaius, a witness to both the crucifixion of Christ and the destruction of Pompeii, attempts to fit both events into a frame of reference which has some relevance to the confusion of his own life. Higgins's lack of other published works, deplored by his devotees, has been somewhat compensated for by the posthumous edition *The Haunted Rendezvous: Selected Poems* (1980), a selection made by Higgins, in collaboration with Robert King, in the year before his death. In addition to Higgins's best poems, *The Haunted Rendezvous* contains a selection of the sparse critical commentary available on Higgins, most of it written about the time *Mordecaius Overture* was published.

HIGGINS, Henry Bournes (1851–1929), born Ireland, came to Australia in 1870 and graduated from the University of Melbourne with degrees in arts and law in 1875. In 1901 he entered the first Commonwealth parliament and although not a member of the Labor Party became attorney-general in 1904 in J.C. Watson's Labor ministry. As a federal parliamentarian he was influential in the establishment of the CLF. He was made a justice of the High Court in 1906 and president of the Federal Court of Conciliation and Arbitration, in which capacity he was largely responsible for the establishment of the principle of a basic wage for workers. His niece Nettie Palmer wrote an early biography, *Henry Bournes Higgins*, in 1931. John Rickard's *H.B. Higgins: The Rebel as Judge* (1984) won the *Age* Book of the Year Award. An account of his career and influence is included in Stuart Macintyre's *A Colonial Liberalism: The Lost World of Three Victorian Visionaries* (1991). His publications include *Essays and Addresses on the Australian Commonwealth Bill* (1900) and *A New Province for Law and Order* (1922).

HIGHAM, Charles (1931–), born London, became a book-reviewer for the *Sydney Morning Herald* in 1956 and was literary editor of the *Bulletin* 1964–67 before moving to the USA. His first two volumes of poetry, *A Distant Star* (1951) and *Spring and Death* (1953), were published in England. His Australian publications are *The Earthbound and Other Poems* (1959), *Noonday Country* (1966), subtitled *Poems 1954–1965*, and *The Voyage to Brindisi, and Other Poems* (1970). He edited *Australian Writing Today* (1968), *They Came to Australia* (1961, with Alan Brissenden) and *Australians Abroad* (1967, with Michael Wilding). He published a controversial biography of Errol Flynn in 1980, as well as several biographies of American stars.

HIGINBOTHAM, George (1826–92), born Dublin, came to Australia in 1854 after being called to the Bar in England. He combined journalism and law in Australia, writing initially for the Melbourne *Herald*; in 1856–59 he was editor of the *Argus*. Following an interrupted political career during which he campaigned assiduously for extreme secularism in state education, he was appointed to the Supreme Court in 1880, becoming chief justice in 1886. Throughout his political and judicial career Higinbotham was concerned with the conditions of the working man and the rights of women. E.E. Morris wrote *A Memoir of George Higinbotham* (1895), Gwyneth M. Dow *George Higinbotham: Church and State* (1964) and Vance Palmer included a biographical sketch of him in *National Portraits* (1940). He is one of the subjects of Stuart Macintyre's study *A Colonial Liberalism: The Lost World of Three Victorian Visionaries* (1991).

HILL, Barry (1943–), born Melbourne, graduated from the University of Melbourne and has worked as a teacher, psychologist and journalist in Victoria and London. In 1972 he returned to Melbourne as founding editor of the education page of the *Age* but has been a full-time fiction writer since 1975. His documentary of contemporary Australian educational practice, *The Schools* (1977), won a National Book Council Award. Hill has published two books of short fiction, *A Rim of Blue* (1978) and *Headlocks & Other Stories* (1983) and two novellas, *Near the Refinery* (1980), and *The Best Picture* (1988); a collection of poetry, *Raft* (1990), winner of the Anne Elder Poetry Award and *Ghosting William Buckley* (1993), a meditation in verse on the adventures and experiences of escaped convict, William Buckley (q.v.); and *Sitting In* (1991), an account of the industrial dispute at the Altona petrochemical complex 1979–80, which combines autobiography, political analysis and documentary reportage, and won a NSW Premier's Award in 1991. His complex and disturbing short stories written in a polished, spare prose, interpret a range of individual psyches, probing the raw areas of experience and frequently culminating in a Joycean epiphany or moment of insight. 'A Bold Headline' from *A Rim of Blue*, the story of watchmaker-turned-teacher, Charles Bristol, is painfully poignant; 'Headlocks', in which a visitor is battered to death and his body burned by his

erstwhile friends, is casually macabre. *Near the Refinery* deals with the relationship between a dying man and his middle-aged son; it subtly explores sexual taboos and the discrepancy between reality and what passes for observable facts. His most ambitious novel, *The Best Picture*, seeks to interpret and synthesise aspects of Eastern and Western thought through a range of characters, concrete incidents and philosophical reflection. Set mainly in a Buddhist centre in a Queensland rainforest and virtually a plotless novel, it presents a diverse group of individuals at various stages of spiritual journeying. Sensory perception of the world is allied with analysis and conceptualisation, illustrating the book's epigraph from Wittgenstein: 'The human body is the best picture of the human soul.' *Ghosting William Buckley* has a remarkable range of poetic styles and rhythms, adapting well to the varied environments in which Buckley found himself – in the bush with the Aborigines, in Hobart and back in English society. Conceived in the myth cycle of hero banished into the wilderness and his ultimate return, *Ghosting William Buckley* is a complex work, brilliantly executed.

HILL, Ernestine (1899–72), born Rockhampton, Queensland, worked briefly as a public servant before her marriage. A wanderer by nature, she began to indulge her love of travel as early as 1930 and after the death of her husband in 1933 embarked on a life of almost continuous travel and writing. Apart from an adolescent book of verse, *Peter Pan Land* (1916), her first publication was *The Great Australian Loneliness* (1937, republished 1991 in the A & R Imprint Travel Series), an account of five years' travel over outback Australia from Adelaide to Darwin via the Birdsville Track, the Red Centre and Arnhem Land. *Water into Gold*, a history of the Murray River irrigation areas, was published in the same year. Her only novel, *My Love Must Wait* (q.v., 1941), based on the life of Matthew Flinders (q.v.) and published also in England and the USA, sold more than 10 000 copies in Australia, a remarkable achievement in the austerity of wartime. In 1947, in *Flying Doctor Calling*, she gives an absorbing account, spiced with extraordinary anecdotes, of the foundation of the Australian Inland Mission, of the dedication and courage of John Flynn and others, and of the ultimate spread of airborne medical care over two million square miles of inland Australia. By the time she had published the best known of her works, *The Territory* (q.v., 1951), she had been, in her own words, 'twice round Australia by land, clockwise and anti-clockwise . . . three times across it from south to north, many times east and west, and once on the diagonal'. *The Territory* is a book that J.K. Ewers believed 'ought to be in the swag of every Australian'. An anecdotal history of the Northern Territory, it is a stimulating work, coloured by both her purple prose and her affection for the Territory and its inhabitants. In addition to her numerous contributions to newspapers and journals about her experiences, especially to *Walkabout*, Hill wrote 'a personal memoir' of Daisy Bates, *Kabbarli* (1973), in which she claims that she was largely responsible for the writing of Bates's *The*

Passing of the Aborigines (1938). Hill was a commissioner of the ABC, 1942–44.

HILL, Fidelia S.T. (?1790–1854), born Pontefract, Yorkshire, published *Poems and Recollections of the Past* (1840), suggested as the first book of verse written by a woman to be published in Australia.

Hill of Content is the name given to three Melbourne literary ventures: a bookshop, an archive series and a publishing company. The Hill of Content antique and rare-book bookshop was established by A.H. Spencer in Bourke Street, Melbourne, in 1922 and was owned by him until, after a brief period of ownership by Angus & Robertson in 1951, it was bought by Collins Book Depot. Spencer's autobiographical work *The Hill of Content* (1959) highlights the Sydney and Melbourne literary worlds from the turn of the century to the end of the Second World War. The Hill of Content Archive series was launched in 1966 to gather historical documents for educational purposes on various topics, e.g. Hugh Anderson's *Australia in the Depression* (1972) and Margaret Jennings's *Australian Explorers* (1969) and *Australia in the Great War* (1970). The Hill of Content publishing company, formed by a group of employees of the Collins Book Depot in Melbourne in 1965, presents the Archive series and has also published a wide range of Australian writing, e.g. Marjorie Barnard's *Miles Franklin* (1967) and Hugh Anderson's *The Poet Militant: Bernard O'Dowd* (1969).

HILL, Samuel Prout (1812–61), born Devonshire, England, came to Australia in 1841. He alternated residence between NSW and Tasmania in various clerical occupations but made more of a reputation as a man of letters than of business. He published *Tarquin the Proud and Other Poems* (1843) and *Monody on the Death of Sir George Gipps* (1847). Hill was also a respected political writer with the Hobart *Mercury* in the late 1850s.

Hillyars and the Burtons, The, Henry Kingsley's (q.v.) fourth novel, was serialised in *Macmillan's Magazine* 1863–65 and revised for publication in book form in 1865. The novel is subtitled *A Story of Two Families;* these are the Hillyars, English gentry whose story is told contemporaneously with the events depicted by the author-narrator; and the Burtons, a family of Chelsea blacksmiths whose history is chronicled in part by the author but mainly by the retrospective narration of one of the Burton children, James. The narratives, which concentrate on events in England and Australia in the middle and late 1850s, alternate in the early part of the novel but increasingly overlap as the affairs of the several Hillyars become entangled with those of the Burtons. The prehistory of the novel accommodates one such Hillyar–Burton relationship, that between George Hillyar, son of the baronet, and his former servant, Samuel Burton, James's uncle. A reckless youth, George has eventually been despatched as a 'remittance man' to Australia, where Samuel is transported after robbing the Hillyar family home. George's reputation follows him to the colon-

ies but he joins the police and becomes a hero by quelling an attack by bushrangers, thus overcoming the objections to his marriage to Gertie Neville, sister-in-law of the colonial secretary of the colony of Cooksland. The Hillyars return to England, where George hopes to regain the respect of his father and to supplant his favoured and protected younger half-brother, Erne. Erne, meanwhile, has become friendly with the Burton family, particularly the children, James, Joe and Emma and their cousin, Reuben, Samuel's putative son but the child of George Hillyar's secret early marriage, as is eventually revealed. Sir George Hillyar is on the point of changing his will to make it more equitable to his elder son when he suddenly dies; but as the will cannot be found George is able to take over the family seat and to turn out Erne Hillyar, who seeks refuge with the Burtons. *The Hillyars and the Burtons* continues to chronicle the decline of the Hillyars: George's discovery that the will is held by a vengeful Samuel; his desertion of Gertie; Gertie's departure for Australia; her overland walk back to her sister's place; her descent into quiescent madness; the eventual death of the dissipated George; and Reuben's succession to the baronetcy. It also focuses increasingly on the Burtons. After the collapse of the blacksmith's business in London, they emigrate to Cooksland accompanied by Erne, and achieve prosperity: Burton senior becomes part-owner of a coppermine while James and Joseph enter politics. The family's success is tempered at the end of the novel, however, by the death of the saintly Emma just after she has been released from her vow of service to her crippled brother Joe and is free to marry her devoted suitor, Erne. This ironic but sensational climax to *The Hillyars and the Burtons* is characteristic of a novel spoilt also by its contrived plot and by its melodramatic set pieces. Yet the Chelsea scenes of Kingsley's own youth are evoked by James Burton, and the depiction of Cooksland is notable for the way Kingsley captures the complexities of colonial politics. Parallels can be seen between some Cooksland politicians and newspapers, e.g. Dempsey, the *Palmerston Sentinel* and the *Mohawk*, and their Victorian equivalents in the 1850s, e.g. respectively Charles Gavan Duffy, the *Argus* and the *Age*. The success story of the Burtons, who remain in Australia, and the critical view Kingsley seems to take of English gentlemen contrasts with the exploitation of Australia and the celebration of the virtues of the Buckleys and Brentwoods in *The Recollections of Geoffry Hamlyn* (1859), which so offended Joseph Furphy.

'His Father's Mate', Henry Lawson's first story, was published in the *Bulletin*'s Christmas issue in 1888 and later revised for inclusion in *While the Billy Boils* (1896); the original in particular shows the influence of Bret Harte, with whom Lawson was often compared. 'His Father's Mate' is the name given to Isley Mason, who is working an abandoned goldfield with his father Tom and is killed when the soil collapses around a mineshaft. Isley's death is the final tragedy in Tom's life, for his wife had died of a broken heart after Isley's elder brother had been convicted of bushranging. In the melodramatic climax to the story, the elder son, presumably released from prison, comes to the goldfield to become, like Isley, his father's 'mate' only to discover that his father has died.

His Natural Life, a novel by Marcus Clarke (q.v.), was first published in the *Australian Journal* 1870–72 and revised for first publication in book form in 1874; the alternative title, *For the Term of His Natural Life*, was first used in an 1882 edition of the revised version. The revised version has been regularly reprinted, usually under the long title and often from an 1885 reprint of the 1882 edition; the original serial version, which the *Australian Journal* ran again in 1881–83, 1886–88 and 1913–15, was published in 1970, edited by Stephen Murray-Smith. *His Natural Life* has been translated into German, Dutch, Swedish and Russian; several dramatisations were made in 1886–90, film versions were screened in 1907, 1917 and 1926, and a television series in 1983.

Influenced by Charles Reade's *It Is Never Too Late to Mend* (1856), Victor Hugo's *Les Misérables* (1862) and by other fictional treatments of convict life, *His Natural Life* was also informed by Clarke's researches into transportation at the Public Library in Melbourne and by his visit to the Tasmanian penal settlements in 1870. Its protagonist is Richard Devine, alias Rufus Dawes; in the prologue to the revised version he is exposed as the bastard son of Lady Devine and her cousin, Lord Bellasis, and is ordered from home by Sir Richard Devine, who threatens to make his nephew Maurice Frere his heir. That night Richard discovers the body of Lord Bellasis on Hampstead Heath; supposing his putative father to have been the murderer, he takes the name Rufus Dawes when apprehended and is transported for the robbery of Lord Bellasis. One of his guards on the voyage to Australia is Frere, whose hopes for the inheritance have been thwarted by Sir Richard's death. Typhus breaks out and a mutiny is planned by the convicts Gabbett, Vetch and John Rex, assisted by Sarah Purfoy, Rex's lover and nurse to Sylvia Vickers, the daughter of a military officer. Dawes thwarts the mutiny but is one of those tried for it and is sent on arrival to the penal settlement of Macquarie Harbour.

The subsequent sections of *His Natural Life* comprise the bulk of the novel and focus on Dawes's suffering under Frere at Macquarie Harbour and two other famous secondary punishment centres, Port Arthur and Norfolk Island (qq.v.). The Macquarie Harbour scenes open with Dawes in solitary confinement on Grummet Island; after failing to escape overland, he returns to Macquarie Harbour to find another mutiny has been engineered by Rex and that Frere, Sylvia and her mother are among those marooned there. Dawes asserts his natural role to become leader of the group's escape back to Hobart, but on the journey Mrs Vickers dies, Sylvia loses her memory and Frere takes the credit for their survival and Sylvia's hand in marriage. In despair at Sylvia's failure to recognise his contribution at Macquarie Harbour, Dawes is sent to Port Arthur for the original escape; in the Port Arthur chapters the most dismal aspects of transportation life

are presented, including the homosexual rape and flogging to death of the young convict Kirkland, the human tramway and the cannibalism practised by Gabbett, Vetch and others after they escape from Port Arthur. Another escapee is John Rex, who has recognised Dawes's identity and returns to England to impersonate Richard Devine, supposedly lost at sea; the impersonation owes something to the contemporary Tichborne (q.v.) case. The action of the last book of *His Natural Life* is centred on Norfolk Island, where the final stages of Dawes's decline are presented through extracts from the diary of the Reverend James North, an alcoholic chaplain whose kindnesses Dawes had experienced at Port Arthur. The determination of North to save Dawes is paralleled by Sylvia's pity for him and by her resolve to leave her husband because of his continued brutality. Dawes discovers from North that Sir Richard Devine had not murdered Lord Bellasis, and that North had committed the robbery for which Dawes was transported; the real murderer turns out to be Rex, who is pursued to England by Sarah and when exposed by Lady Devine reveals unwittingly that he has killed his own father and is therefore Dawes's half-brother. Rex has a stroke and spends the rest of his life in a kind of living death similar to the one that Dawes has experienced; but the final irony is that when Dawes and Sylvia escape from Norfolk Island, the ship is hit by a cyclone and they are drowned at the moment when Sylvia's memory returns and she and Dawes have been reunited. In the serial version of the novel, which is almost twice as long, the ending is different: Sylvia (called Dora) is drowned, but Dawes and Dora's daughter, Dorcas, survive to prosper on the mainland and return to England. Some of the dramatic film and television adaptations preserve the lives of Dawes and Sylvia. The other major, but not the only, revision is the prologue, reduced from 40 000 to just over 2000 words; in the serial version Dawes is transported for the murder of a business associate, Hans Blinzler, in which neither North nor Rex is involved.

His Natural Life is the most significant and most famous nineteenth-century Australian novel, the major contribution of colonial fiction to the English novel. Profoundly pessimistic, it has been criticised for its melodramatic scenes and unrealistic coincidences, e.g. Sylvia's loss of memory, but its power continues to move modern readers. Although it moves beyond a documentary treatment of the convict system to explore fundamental questions concerning man's capacity for evil, its treatment of transportation played a significant part, along with the works of Caroline Leakey, 'Price Warung' (qq.v.) and others, in consolidating the legend that the convicts were more 'sinn'd against than sinning'.

Historical Journal of the Transactions at Port Jackson and Norfolk Island, An, by John Hunter (q.v.), was published in 1793 in London, where a year later Hunter was selected as successor to Governor Arthur Phillip. One of the first examples of Australian exploration literature, it chronicles the voyage of the First Fleet to Australia, the early days of the colony of

NSW, and Hunter's subsequent voyages, including visits to the Cape of Good Hope for provisions (during which his ship, the *Sirius*, circumnavigated the globe) and to Norfolk Island, where the *Sirius* was wrecked. *An Historical Journal of the Transactions at Port Jackson and Norfolk Island* incorporates material from the journals of Phillip and Philip Gidley King.

Historical Records of Australia (*HRA*), a series of volumes of documents covering several areas of the history of the Australian colonies before 1850, was published in thirty-three volumes 1914–25. When the publication programme for the *Historical Records of New South Wales* (q.v.) terminated in 1902, the Commonwealth government in 1907 took over the task of completing the collection and publication of the early documentary record of Australia. Material already collected, notably the official documents transcribed by James Bonwick (q.v.) and assistants in London, was arranged and indexed 1907–11 and in 1912 Frederick Watson was appointed editor of the *Historical Records of Australia*. As originally envisaged, the project was to take the documentary record from 1811, the year at which the coverage of the *Historical Records of New South Wales* ended, to 1837, later revised to 1856. This plan was found to be impractical, partly because some important pre-1811 documents had not been published in the *Historical Records of New South Wales*, a series which had also excluded documents relating to the other colonies. Watson then suggested that the *Historical Records of Australia* should comprise seven series of volumes: the dispatches between the governors of NSW and the Colonial Office; administrative papers; papers relating to early settlement (including in areas then part of NSW, later of other colonies); legal papers; exploration papers; scientific papers; and ecclesiastical, naval and military papers. Of the thirty-three volumes published, twenty-six belong to the first series (taking the historical record up to 1848), six to the third series (to 1830), and one to the fourth series (to 1827). The *Historical Records of New South Wales* and the *Historical Records of Australia* (known to historians as *HRA)* have documents in common; the main difference between the series, apart from the different chronological coverage, is that the latter is more strictly an official record, excluding the newspaper extracts and other material included in the former. Both series, however, are valuable compilations of the early prose written in Australia; in addition, the *Historical Records of Australia*, which, unlike its predecessor, includes the names of convicts, yields references to early convicts who became significant in Australian literature, e.g. Henry Savery. The cessation of the *HRA* project accelerated the creation of the Australian Archives.

Historical Records of New South Wales, a documentary record of the discovery and early years of British settlement in NSW, was published in seven volumes, the first in two parts, making eight books in all, 1892–1901. Their publication grew out of the collecting of documents for a multi-volume history of NSW, which began under G.B. Barton as a contri-

bution to the 1888 centenary but was abandoned in 1894 with only two volumes published. Volume one, part one, of the *Historical Records of New South Wales* comprises mainly extracts from the logs of Captain James Cook and his subordinates relating to the discovery and exploration of the eastern coast of Australia in 1770. Succeeding volumes comprise governors' dispatches, many of them transcribed by James Bonwick (q.v.), other official and personal documents, and extracts from newspapers and other sources, arranged chronologically 1783–1811 and covering plans for the establishment of the colony of NSW and the first decades of settlement. The *Historical Records of New South Wales*, like the later *Historical Records of Australia*, have been important sources for Australian historians of the twentieth century and are significant in Australian literature as records of early prose written in Australia and as historical sources used by later creative writers. The *Records* were annotated by their editors, Alexander Britton (for the volumes on Phillip published in 1892) and F.M. Bladen (for the succeeding volumes).

Historical Records of Victoria, of which the foundation series has been commissioned by the Victorian government, has Michael Cannon (q.v.) as editor-in-chief. The foundation series covering 1835–39 comprises a projected seven volumes; vol. 1, *The Beginnings of Permanent Government*; vols 2A and 2B, *The Aborigines of Port Phillip*; vol. 3, *The Early Development of Melbourne*; vol. 4, *Communications, Trade and Transport*; vol. 5, *Surveyors' Problems and Achievements 1836–1839*; vol. 6, *The Crown, the Land and the Squatter 1835–1840* have been published 1981–91.

Historical Societies. In each Australian State there now exists a historical society which focuses attention on the history, including literary history, of that State. The oldest is the Royal Australian Historical Society, founded in 1901 as the Australian Historical Society; it received its royal charter in 1918 and has published a journal since 1906 (now quarterly, from 1965 the *Journal of the Royal Australian Historical Society*, known also as *JRAHS*). In the other States, the Historical Society of Victoria was founded in 1909, became the Royal Historical Society of Victoria when it received a royal charter in 1952 and has published the quarterly *Victorian Historical Journal* from 1911 (from 1983 as the *Royal Historical Society of Victoria Journal); the Queensland Historical Society was founded in 1913, became the Royal Historical Society of Queensland when it received a royal charter in 1963 and has published a journal, mainly quarterly, since 1920; the Royal Western Australian Historical Society, founded in 1926, received its royal charter in 1962 and publishes an annual, *Early Days;* the Tasmanian Historical Research Association, founded in 1951, publishes quarterly papers and proceedings; and the Historical Society of South Australia, founded in 1974, publishes an annual journal. With the exception of Tasmania, each of these historical societies is an umbrella organisation to which the local and special interest historical societies within the State are affiliated with varying degrees of formality, e.g. by 1992 270 historical societies within NSW were affiliated with the Royal Australian Historical Society; by 1992 about 200 similar societies within Victoria were affiliated with the Royal Victorian Historical Society. These societies publish newsletters and other material; similarly, the umbrella organisations publish regular bulletins as well as journals and in some cases other publications of historical interest, e.g. the Royal Australian Historical Society has published the early journals of David Collins, John Hunter and Watkin Tench. Apart from the State historical societies, there are history teachers' associations in most States and an academic organisation, the Australian Historical Association, which was formed in 1973.

Although State and professional historical associations were not established until the twentieth century, their *de facto* predecessors were a number of nineteenth-century cultural and scientific bodies with historical interests, e.g. the activity of the SA branch of the Royal Geographical Society of Australasia partly explains the late formation of the Historical Society of South Australia. Many figures significant in Australian history have been associated with the State historical societies; among figures significant in Australian literature and literary history are David Scott Mitchell, Sir John Ferguson, Malcolm Ellis, Colin Roderick and George Mackaness in NSW, Alfred Deakin and Geoffrey Blainey in Victoria, Thomas Welsby in Queensland, Sir Paul Hasluck in WA and E. Morris Miller in Tasmania.

History of Australian Drama, A, by Leslie Rees (q.v.), published in three volumes, is an expansion of his earlier work, *Towards an Australian Drama* (1953). The *History* comprises *The Making of Australian Drama: A Historical and Critical Survey from the 1830s to the 1970s* (1973, revised 1978) and *Australian Drama in the 1970s: A Historical and Critical Survey* (1978, which was revised and expanded in 1987 with the title *Australian Drama 1970–1985*). The volumes cover stage, radio and television drama, commercial and little theatres, repertory groups, theatrical societies, and the role of the universities, government subsidisation and censorship, as well as critical appraisals of the work of individual playwrights.

History of Australian Literature, A, by H.M. Green (q.v.), was published in two volumes in 1961. Apart from a few anomalies and a final chapter which summarises 'The Last Ten Years', the history covers work from 1789 to 1950. Divided into four periods ending roughly in 1850, 1890, 1923 and 1950, the work is further divided within each period into 'pure literature' and 'applied literature'. In the first category Green discusses verse, fiction, drama, essays, criticism, scholarship, oratory and magazines; in the second he discusses, less intensively, histories, descriptive and biographical works, works on law, science, economics, politics, anthropology, psychology, philosophy, geography, education and religion and finally newspapers. In his preface Green stresses that 'a double standard has been definitely and deliberately maintained', works that are of 'value ... to Australian literature' having been included that a history of world literature would have ignored. The two volumes appeared in revised editions (by Dorothy Green) 1984, 1985.

History of Australian Literature, A, by Ken Goodwin in the Macmillan History of Literature series, was published in 1986. Its contents include The Nature of Australian Literature; The First Hundred Years of Colonization; The 'Bulletin' School; National Self Definition; New Reputations of the 1920s and 1930s; Major New Voices of the 1930s and 1940s; The Last Decades of the 'old Bulletin'; Symbolic and SocialRealist Fiction; Mid-Century Directions; The Generation of the 1960s; The Uniqueness of Recent Writing.

HOARE, Benjamin (1842–1932), born Buckinghamshire, England, arrived in Australia in 1856. After founding and editing the *Evening Times* and *Evening Star* in Geelong (1871, 1879) he joined the editorial staff of the Melbourne *Daily Telegraph* in 1886; he was leader-writer for the *Age* 1890–1914. Active in Catholic affairs, he helped found the *Catholic Magazine* in 1888. He published poetry including *The Maori* (1869) and *Figures of Fancy* (1869); essays on political and economic subjects, e.g. *Preferential Trade* (1904) and the pro-British *War Things That Matter* (1918); literary essays and reminiscences, e.g. *Looking Back Gaily* (1927); and a political drama, *Polling Day: Or, Wooed and Won* (1883). His work reflects sincere if naive ideas and strong religious convictions.

Hobart Town Courier was a newspaper founded by James Ross (q.v.) in 1827; it supported the lieutenant-governor of Van Diemen's Land, George Arthur (q.v.), and was thus in opposition to the anti-Arthur journals, notably the *Colonial Times* (q.v.). The *Hobart Town Courier*, which began publication after the pro-Arthur *Hobart Town Gazette* (q.v.) ceased to function as a newspaper, was edited by Ross until 1837, when it was taken over by William Gore Elliston. In 1859 the *Hobart Town Courier* was incorporated in the *Mercury*.

Hobart Town Gazette was founded by Andrew Bent (q.v.) in 1816 and for some years was the official newspaper of the colony of Van Diemen's Land. In 1824 and 1825 it carried criticisms of Lieutenant-Governor George Arthur by R.L. Murray and Evan Thomas, which led to Bent's prosecution for libel. Arthur pirated the title of Bent's newspaper for his own government organ, which was run conjointly by James Ross and George Terry Howe (q.v.), so from June to August 1825 two *Hobart Town Gazettes* were published with the same volume and serial numbers. Bent changed his *Gazette* to the *Colonial Times and Tasmanian Advertiser* (q.v.) 19 August 1825; Arthur's *Gazette* ceased to function in newspaper form in October 1827, when it became the Tasmanian government gazette.

Hobart Town Magazine was the first Tasmanian literary journal and ran for eighteen monthly issues, the first titled the *Hobart Town Monthly Magazine*, in 1833–34. It was edited by Henry Melville assisted by Thomas Richards, who were also its most prolific and important contributors. Richards's fiction sketches, contributed to the *Hobart Town Magazine*, were among the first short stories published in Australia.

Hobart Town Punch, see **Melbourne Punch**

HODGINS, Philip (1959–) grew up on a dairy farm near Shepparton, was educated at Geelong and later moved to Melbourne where he has worked in publishing. He was diagnosed as suffering from chronic myeloid leukaemia in 1983, a personal calamity which has affected both the content and volume of his poetry. He has published widely in anthologies and periodicals and has produced the collections *Blood and Bone* (1986), *Down the Lake with Half a Chook* (1988), *Animal Warmth* (1990), *Up On All Fours* (1993) and *Dispossessed* (1994). *Up On All Fours* was praised by Peter Porter, who welcomed its extension of the Australian pastoral genre, with its 'tradition of yarning, balladry, legend and truculent attitudinising'. Divided into four parts, the work is notable for its heightened formal definition as for its renewed lyric impulse and characteristic lack of sentimentality. Much of the imagery is cool and memorable: 'the little kitchen spreading buttered light'; a farmer dipping his sheep like a gondolier; a dead snake becoming 'a line of common memory lying in the dust'. Poems such as 'Tail Paddock' and 'Driving through the Mallee' explore territory largely unfamiliar to his contemporaries, as in this stanza from 'The Rock Paddocks':

They happen over centuries and stop
when all they have to push against is air.
So slow the paddocks are taken by surprise.
And though it's time to strip this useless crop
the man who owns the paddocks doesn't care.
He knows there's more already on the rise.

Up On All Fours was quickly followed by *Dispossessed*, a novel in blank verse which investigates the tribulations of farming life and the psychology of eight survivors.

In 1986 he won the Wesley Michel Wright Prize, in 1987 the NSW Premier's Award, and in 1988 the Grace Perry Prize and the Prairie Schooner Readers Choice USA Award. The poems of *Blood and Bone* are a frank confrontation with his own and others' mortality, moving from the metaphysical irony of 'The Passenger', which represents his leukaemia as a parasite draining nourishment from 'everything I eat. It gets the vitamins/ from every sorry beer I drink', and whose 'birth will bring me to a corpse', to the rural analogies of the crows of 'From County Down', which bring to mind life's grim, perennial realities and random cruelties. The poems of *Animal Warmth* and *Down the Lake with Half a Chook*, which draw on his childhood experience, mine with individual effects the same rich vein of Australian pastoral experience as

Les Murray and David Campbell. Resurrecting the past is for Hodgins 'a detailed obsession', stimulated by childhood memories of the different tastes of milk straight from the cow, the shapes of gums, the antics of possums, the bar-room tricks of a mate, a paddock 'gridlocked' with hay bales or a confrontation with a goanna. Combining laconic language with striking visual imagery and assured control of phrase, rhythm and syntax, his best poems achieve a Horatian clarity and balance. *Down the Lake with Half a Chook* is divided into three sections, 'Hospital', which returns to his struggle with cancer, 'Boarding School', which focuses on specific childhood memories, and 'Country', which returns with the same Proustian nostalgia as *Animal Warmth* to the rural world. According to 'Sludge' re-creating the dairy-farming past is to be 'exhilarated by the mundane', an experience Hodgins transmits to the reader with tact, candour and freshness. As in his poems on the experience of incurable illness, toughness and humour are striking characteristics, achieved as much by confident control of the poetry's various metrical forms from free verse to more regular structures, as by controlled emotion.

HODGMAN, Helen (1945–), born Scotland, grew up in Essex and Tasmania. She left school at 15, has worked at a variety of occupations and has lived in London and Vancouver. She has written three novels, *Blue Skies* (1976), *Jack and Jill* (1978) and *Broken Words* (1988), all of which have been praised as incisively expressive reflections of contemporary female experience of Australia. *Jack and Jill* won the 1979 Somerset Maugham Prize and *Broken Words* the 1989 Christina Stead Prize in the NSW State Literary Awards. She has also written plays for stage and television. Comic, bleak and savage, Hodgman's novels deal unsentimentally and acutely with modern experience.

HODGSON, C.P. (Christopher Pemberton) (1821–65), born Hertfordshire, England, was in Australia 1839–45 when he engaged in squatting and pastoral activities in southern Queensland and was briefly involved with Ludwig Leichhardt's 1844–45 expedition to Port Essington. On his return to England he published *Reminiscences of Australia with Hints on the Squatter's Life* (1846) and in 1849 a book of verse, *The Wanderer*, and a travel book, *El Ydaiour*, in both of which there are references to Australia.

HOFFMANN, Catherine (1948–), born Hungary, arrived in Australia in 1956. Educated at Monash University, she has worked as a teacher, library assistant and trainee botanist. She has written several short stories and two novels, *Crystal: a Tale of Desire and Flight* (1987) and *Forms of Bliss* (1988). She has also published *Perilous Journey* (1981), which comprises eight interviews with the incurably ill.

HOGAN, J.F. (James Francis) (1855–1924), born County Tipperary, Ireland, came to Australia in 1856. He became a teacher then turned to journalism, being sub-editor of the *Victorian Review* before joining the *Argus*. In 1887 he went to England, became a member of the House of Commons, and returned to Australia for only a brief visit in 1901. Hogan's publications include *An Australian Christmas Collection* (1886), a selection of his own stories; *The Irish in Australia* (1887), his assessment of the Irish contribution to the development of Australia; *The Australian in London and America* (1889); *The Lost Explorer* (1890, on Ludwig Leichhardt); *The Convict King* (1891, on Jorgen Jorgenson); *Robert Lowe, Viscount Sherbrooke* (1893); *The Sister Dominions* (1896); and *The Gladstone Colony* (1898).

HOGUE, Oliver ('Trooper Bluegum') (1880–1919), born Sydney, was a journalist with the *Sydney Morning Herald* before enlisting as a trooper in the Sixth Light Horse regiment. He soon gained a commission and served at Gallipoli and in the desert campaigns; he survived the war only to die in the influenza epidemic in England in 1919. As 'Trooper Bluegum' he wrote articles for the *Sydney Morning Herald* which were collected in two books, both published in 1916, *Love Letters of an Anzac* and *Trooper Bluegum at the Dardanelles*. He also wrote *The Home-Sick Anzac and Other Verses* (1918) and a work of fiction, *The Cameliers* (1919).

HOLBURN, Muir (1920–60), born Sydney, was a journalist with the NSW public service 1947–59; he was president of the NSW branch of the FAW in 1948–50. Although well known as a poet, he did not publish a volume of poetry; with his wife, Marjorie Pizer, he edited *Creeve Roe* (q.v., 1947).

HOLDSWORTH, Philip (1851–1902), born Sydney, was a public servant and member of the literary coterie of Sydney in the second half of the nineteenth century. He was editor of the *Illustrated Sydney News* in the 1880s, a contributor to the *Bulletin*, *Freeman's Journal* and *Athenaeum*, and a founding member of the Athenaeum Club. His only published work was *Station Hunting on the Warrego* (1885), the first poem a long account of a search by two pioneers for pastures for their flocks. He wrote a biographical note to *Poems of Henry Kendall* (1886), edited by Alexander Sutherland.

HOLMAN, Ada (1869–1949), born Ballarat, Victoria, as Ada Kidgell, entered journalism in the 1890s, contributing, as 'Myee', a regular Sydney letter to *Melbourne Punch;* she also wrote for the *Sydney Mail* and *Sydney Morning Herald* under her own name and as 'Marcus Malcolm' and 'Nardoo'. In 1901 she married the politician W.A. Holman (q.v.) but continued to write, sometimes ghosting for her husband. Her publications include travel articles for the *Daily Telegraph* later published as *My Wander Year* (1912); the political novel *Sport of the Gods* (1921): children's fiction, *Little Miss Anzac* (1917), *The Adventures of Woodeny* (1923) and *Elka Reva-Ree* (1928); several plays, including 'Annabel Goes to a Party', 'Mrs Milligan Seeks Her Ideal', 'The Premier's Wife' (1936), 'The Six Queens' and 'The Three Little Dears' (1932); and an autobiography, *Memoirs of a Premier's Wife* (1947). Her strong feminist beliefs are visible in 'The Premier's Wife'.

HOLMAN, W.A. (William Arthur) (1871–1934), born London, came to Australia in 1888. He soon interested himself in the organisation of the NSW Labor Party, and was elected to parliament in 1898 as the member for Grenfell. In a State political career that lasted to 1920, he was premier for nearly seven years, 1913–16 as leader of the Labor Party and 1916–20 as leader of the Nationalist Party. A lawyer, Holman delivered the Macrossan lectures at the University of Queensland, published as *Three Lectures on the Australian Constitution: Its Interpretation and Amendment* (1928). His biography, *Australian Labour Leader* by H.V. Evatt, was published in 1940.

HOLT, Bland (1851–1942), born Norwich, England, as Joseph Thomas Holt, was the son of Clarence Holt, a theatre-manager and actor who had successful seasons in Australia in the 1850s and 1860s. Bland Holt became a professional actor at the age of 14 and returned to Sydney in 1876, after travelling extensively in England and the USA with various companies, to become one of Australia's foremost actor-managers, leasing the Lyceum Theatre in Sydney and the Theatre Royal in Melbourne. Known as the 'King of Melodrama', he presented mainly English melodramas, rewritten for Australia with sensational effects such as live animals on stage and stunts such as balloon ascents and diving scenes. The most famous melodrama staged by Holt, written for him by Arthur Shirley, was 'The Breaking of the Drought' (1902), which included a realistic bushfire and a drought scene in which crows picked at the bones of dead cattle. One of the first plays to have a contemporary setting, 'The Breaking of the Drought' is also remarkable as an early treatment of the theme of bush versus city life. Other melodramas staged by Holt, many of which he enhanced with his own versatile skills as an actor, included 'Riding to Win' (1901), 'A Desperate Game' (1903), 'The War of Wealth' (1903), 'Besieged at Port Arthur' (1905) and 'The Great Rescue' (1907).

HOLT, Edgar (1904–88), born England, had a wide-ranging career as a journalist in Brisbane, Sydney and Melbourne before becoming editor of *Smith's Weekly* 1947–50. He published poetry, *Lilacs out of the Dead Land* (1932) and a book of memoirs, *Politics is People* (1969).

'HOLT, Gavin', see **RODDA, Percival Charles**

HOLT, Joseph (1756–1826) was an Irish Protestant farmer who became embroiled in the rebellion of the United Irishmen in 1798. As a 'general' of the rebels, he led a successful guerilla campaign and only surrendered on condition that he be exiled without trial to NSW. He arrived in Sydney in 1800 and although rearrested in 1800 and 1804 at a time of unrest among the Irish prisoners, eventually secured a pardon in 1809 and returned to Ireland in 1812. His self-vindicating *Memoirs* (1838), which are a contribution to

Australian convict literature (q.v.), include an account of his voyage to Australia on board the *Minerva* and his presence at a celebrated and brutal flogging of two convicts at Toongabbie near Sydney in 1800. The former incident is used by Thomas Keneally in *Passenger* (1979), the latter is re-created by R.D. FitzGerald in his poem 'The Wind at Your Door' (q.v.). A new edition of Holt's memoirs, *A Rum Story* (1988), edited by Peter O'Shaughnessy, indicates a high degree of interference by the 1838 editor, Thomas Croker.

'**Home**' is a term, now largely obsolescent, used by Australians of British descent to refer to Great Britain in general and England in particular; it was most prevalent between the discovery of gold and the First World War and reflected, like the term 'Mother Country', which also referred to Great Britain or England and has had a greater longevity, the then colonial mentality of many Australians. 'Rolf Boldrewood's' account of his visit to Britain, *My Run Home* (1897), is one of many examples of its usage.

Home was published as a quarterly, 1920–42. Its art editor was Sydney Ure Smith, its literary editor Bertram Stevens. Literary contributions included interviews, critical articles, poetry and short fiction.

'**Homecoming**', a poem by Bruce Dawe (q.v.), published in *Beyond the Subdivisions* (1969), tells of the return to their homelands (both Australia and the USA are suggested) of the bodies of soldiers who died in the Vietnam War. With its deliberate air of casual inhumanity ('they're zipping them up in green plastic bags ... they're rolling them out of the deep-freeze lockers'), the poem evokes the dehumanising effect and wastefulness of war. Its final line, 'they're bringing them home, now, too late, too early', hints at the bitterness and controversy that the Vietnam War engendered.

Honi Soit, the students' journal of the University of Sydney, began publication in 1929. It carries university news, political, social and literary articles. It has had several significant periods when its influence in the university has been considerable; its editorial staff and contributors include many names that have been significant in Australian literary, political and sporting life. James McAuley wrote for it 1937–38; Donald Horne was its editor 1941; Neville Wran contributed a column, 'Flotsam and Jetsam', in 1946 and was dubbed 'Beachcomber' for his pains; Craig McGregor wrote film and book reviews in 1954; Robert Hughes contributed illustrations in 1956; Clive James wrote prolifically in 1958, including a long (and unfinished) serial, 'The Hand beneath the Table'; Geoffrey Havers wrote an anti-Anzac Day article in 1958 which is said to have inspired Alan Seymour's *The One Day of the Year* (1962). Others associated with *Honi Soit* include A.D. Hope, Bob Ellis, Ken Horler, Mungo MacCallum, Bruce Beresford, Ron Blair, Richard Walsh, Patrick Cook, Nick Enright, Les Murray, Geoffrey Lehmann, Geraldine Pascall and Sally McInerney.

HOOKER, John (1932–), born NZ and educated at the University of Auckland, has lived in Australia since 1963. He worked for many years in publishing before turning to full-time writing in 1985. His novels include *Jacob's Season* (1971), *The Bush Soldiers* (1984), *Standing Orders* (1986) and *Rubicon* (1990). He has also written an account of the Korean war, *Korea: The Forgotten War* (1989). Hooker's most popular novels, *The Bush Soldiers* and *Standing Orders* focus on modern wars, bringing into play his significant gifts for dramatic action, landscape description and psychological insight. *Rubicon*, set in the Depression years of the 1930s, is a tense drama including murder, racism, violence, corruption and passionate love. He has also written a fictionalised account of the life of Captain James Cook (1987), based on a screenplay by Peter Yeldham.

HOOKER, Patricia was at one time employed in the ABC programme department; she left Australia in the late 1960s to write in London. Her plays include 'A Season in Hell' (1965), which re-creates the personal relationship between the poets Rimbaud and Verlaine; 'Socrates', where the force of truth is ranged against that of malevolence; 'Concord of Sweet Sounds', a study of an ageing concert pianist; 'Twilight of a Hero', about the biblical father-son pair, David and Absalom; and 'The Lotus Eaters' (1968).

HOOTON, Harry (1908–61), born Hampstead, London, migrated to Australia in 1924. Unable to get employment, he wandered widely in Australia, finally settling in Sydney, where he worked for a time as a journalist and became connected with the libertarian group dominated by the philosopher John Anderson (q.v.). An iconoclast who developed a philosophy, he called Anarcho-Technocracy, Power Over Things or the Dictatorship of Art, Hooton appears to have had more influence as a witty raconteur than as philosopher or poet, although he had become a minor cult figure in Sydney by the time of his death. He published three collections of poetry, *These Poets* (1941), *Things You See When You Haven't Got a Gun* (1943), which includes some prose, and *It Is Great To Be Alive* (1961); and with A.D. Hope, Garry Lyle and O.M. Somerville contributed to the booklets of verse, *No. 1, Number Two* and *Number Three* (1943–48). A film on Hooton's life was made by Arthur and Corinne Cantrill in 1972 and he appears as the poet Mulcahy in Hugh Atkinson's novel *Low Company* (1961). His *Collected Poems*, edited by Sasha Soldatow and including an account of his poetic theory and philosophy, was published in 1990.

HOPE, A.D. (Alec Derwent) (1907–), born Cooma, NSW, the son of a Presbyterian minister, spent most of his childhood in rural NSW and Tasmania. He graduated in 1928 from the University of Sydney, and took up a scholarship at Oxford the same year. Returning to a depressed Australia in 1931, he tried various occupations before becoming lecturer in education at Sydney Teachers' College in 1937, lecturer in English there 1938–44, moved to the University of Melbourne in 1945 and in 1951 was appointed to the chair of English at Canberra University College, later part of the ANU. He retired in 1968 to devote himself to poetry, but has continued to lecture and retains a close association with the University as emeritus professor.

Although Hope recognised his poetic vocation early, his work appeared only fugitively until 1955 when his first collection, *The Wandering Islands*, was published. His subsequent collections include *Poems* (1960), *A.D. Hope* (1963), *Collected Poems 1930–1965* (1966, republished in an expanded form 1972), *Selected Poems* (1973), *A Late Picking* (1975), *A Book of Answers* (1978), *The Drifting Continent* (1979), *Antechinus* (1981), *The Tragical History of Dr Faustus* (1982), *The Age of Reason* (1985), *Selected Poems*, selected by Ruth Morse (1986), *Orpheus* (1991), a volume in the Poets on Record series (1972), a lengthy mock-heroic poem, *Dunciad Minor* (q.v., 1970), a play, *Ladies from the Sea* (1987), *Selected Poems*, selected by David Brooks (1992), and a collection of reminiscences, *Chance Encounters* (1992). A selection of his verse has been translated into Italian by G. Distefano, titled *Tre Volti Dell'Amore* (1983). A major figure in Australian critical work since the late 1940s, he has published several collections of essays: *The Cave and the Spring* (1965), *Native Companions* (1974), *The Pack of Autolycus* (1978) and *The New Cratylus* (1979); a study of Judith Wright (1975); a brief survey of Australian literature 1950–62 (1963); a scholarly, imaginative study of a sixteenth-century poem by William Dunbar, *A Midsummer Eve's Dream* (1970); and a variety of smaller monographs on aspects of literature. The international recognition that Hope's poetry has won is reflected in the diversity of his awards which include, among others, the Britannica-Australia Award (1965), the Arts Council Award for poetry (1965), the *Age* Book of the Year Award (1976), the Myer Award (1967), the Levinson Prize for poetry (Chicago, 1968), the Ingram Merrill Award, New York (1969), the Robert Frost Award (1976) and a special NSW State Literary Award (1989). He was made OBE in 1972 and AC in 1981. He has received an honorary D.Litt. from the ANU and the universities of Melbourne and New England as well as Monash University.

The distinctive note of Hope's poetry, authoritative, measured, rich in literary, biblical and mythological allusion and adhering to traditional rhythms and forms, led to his being classed at first as 'classic', 'academic' or 'intellectual'. The lack of any identifiable Australian experience, the satirical dismissal of much of modern life, the diversity of his interests and the emphasis on sexual experience bewildered most early readers. Many saw him as principally a satirist, opposed to the cowardice of technocratic man in preferring tame, vicarious, standardised experience. Certainly, rejection of conforming rituals which stifle life's resources of heroism and energy was, and is, a characteristic theme of Hope's verse. Poems such as 'Private Dick', 'The Brides', 'The House of God' and 'Conquistador' are hilarious treatments of the subject; others such as 'A Commination', 'Easter Hymn' and 'Toast for a Golden Age' are more bitter. But, as *The*

Wandering Islands and the later collections reveal, satire is secondary in Hope's work and springs from his persistent concern with the nature of poetry and the serious, even sacred role that he accords it. As his fine poem 'William Butler Yeats' illustrates, he shares Yeats's romantic, heroic conception of the artist. In 'Invocation' he unequivocally describes the poet as one who 'alone' defends 'That darkness out of which our light is won' and celebrates the working of 'the spirit elect' in his own poetry; and in several other poems he has dealt explicitly with the elect role of the poet. Poetry's complementary communal role emerges in his perception of it as 'Celebration', meaning not just 'admiration and delight' but 'an intellectual assent to the causes that make the natural world an order and a system, and an imaginative grasp of the necessity of its processes'. In essays and poems he has described the poet as one with the gift of night-time vision in a world where others see only by day, and as 'a man continually obsessed with a passion for a synoptic view', concerned always to present his subject, man in all aspects, 'under the aspect of eternity'. The poem 'Conversation with Calliope' and the essay 'The Three Faces of Love' define his conception of the poet's distinctive 'creative way of life', bringing 'new objects of desire into being'.

Hope also sees mythology as playing an indispensable part in this creative reinterpretation; myths embody 'the great commonplaces' that define man's place in the universal order. Yet, as 'An Epistle from Holofernes' affirms, 'myths will not fit us ready made' and 'It is the meaning of the poet's trade/ To recreate the fables and revive/ In men the energies by which they live'. Frequently he refashions myth for his own purposes: 'Imperial Adam' (q.v.) and 'Paradise Saved' deal playfully with the Edenic myth; 'The End of a Journey' casts a new, bleak light on Ulysses' homecoming; 'The Return of Persephone' elicits sympathy for Dis; and in 'Coup de Grâce' even the story of Red Riding Hood is given an unexpected twist.

If Hope confidently sees the poet's task as sacred, he also presents it as hazardous, painful and even terrifying. In much of his verse regularity of form contrasts with strong emotional content, sensuality with intellectual detachment, but within some poems there is a struggle between opposites that is left unreconciled. Poems such as 'Flower Poem' and 'The Watcher', expressive of the terrors and pain of poetic vision, are balanced by others such as 'Pseudodoxia Epidemica' and 'As Well as They Can', which establish an emotional poise between suffering and achieved insight. Similarly, poems such as 'X-Ray Photograph', 'The Dinner' and 'Rawhead and Bloody Bones', testifying to the horrors of the mind's imaginings, are balanced by others such as 'Argolis', 'The Trophy' and 'On an Engraving by Casserius', which express a more harmonious acceptance of life's dualities. In his essays Hope has expressed his conviction of the poet's negative capability, and some of his finest poems are also his most impersonal: 'The Death of the Bird', 'Man Friday', 'Meditation on a Bone', 'Moschus Moschiferus' and 'On an Engraving by Casserius'. Other striking achievements include 'The Double Looking

Glass', a complex, ornate, richly sensual poem, and the simpler 'Ode on the Death of Pius the Twelfth', which celebrates his mature, joyful intuition of a harmonious natural order.

The characteristic duality of his perceptions, both in terms of harmony and ambivalence, is particularly evident in his love poetry. Love is central to his work, and he has not only frequently drawn analogies between the transcending, creative experience of love and that of poetry but also expressed their interdependence. 'Chorale', 'The Gateway' and 'The Lamp and the Jar' are his most explicit celebrations of this dependence. Others such as 'Pygmalion', 'The Coasts of Cerigo', 'Fafnir', 'The Damnation of Byron' and 'The Dinner' are more ambivalent expressions of the conflicting pull of delight and revulsion, surrender and freedom.

Most of Hope's discursive critical work reflects his preoccupations as a poet. Witty, original and incisive, his essays in *The Cave and The Spring, The New Cratylus* and *The Pack of Autolycus* develop his ideas on the nature and forms of poetry, including an energetic defence of rhyme and poetic modes that have fallen into disuse. Regarding poetry as a damaged 'ecology' of forms, he particularly laments the passing of that 'middle form of poetry' successfully resurrected in much of his own verse. As a trenchant, individual, witty reviewer and unrelenting enemy of the second-rate, he has had a strong influence on Australian critical standards and has often been notoriously and valuably unsettling. *Native Companions* reprints some of his essays and reviews written over four decades. *Chance Encounters* recalls incidents from his youth in Tasmania to his years of retirement from academic life. Hope's poetry is the subject of numerous critical essays and of monographs by Leonie Kramer (1979) and Kevin Hart (1992). A bibliography, compiled by Joy Hooton, was published in 1979.

HOPEGOOD, Peter (1891–1967), born Essex, England, came to Australia in 1924 after serving in the First World War. He worked as a hand on a pearling lugger in Broome and a jackeroo on north-west cattle stations; he then became a journalist and freelance writer. A man-of-action turned mystic, Hopegood became obsessed with myth, attempting to indicate in his verse and in several essays that there are correspondences between the myths of diverse races. In the title poem of his first book of verse, *Austral Pan and Other Verses* (1932), the subject is the eternal, ubiquitous spirit of Pan, known to 'Ovid's ancient rustic clan' in rural Italy 2000 years ago and equally present in the Australian bush today – 'his steps outback with glee are bent/ He sniffs the saltbush with content.' Hopegood's echo of the vitalism of the time, and his link with the contemporary vision of poets such as Hugh McCrae, Kenneth Slessor and the Lindsays are evident. His second book of verse, *Thirteen from Oahu* (1940), sees him chiefly in the role of myth-interpreter. Oahu is the Hawaiian Place of the Setting Forth for Hawaiki, the Isles of the Blessed. Regeneration is the central theme and the poems are accompanied by copious explanatory notes, which are often more effective and interesting than the poems

they illustrate. His chief poetic work, *Circus at World's End* (1947), is prefaced by an essay which sets out his poetic/philosophic theory; at the heart of all the myths of the diverse races of the world and of all literature and psychoanalytic theory there is a single underlying concept of earth consciousness, the union of earth and man. Hopegood said that his poems in *Circus at World's End* were 'written in emulation of the skill of the myth-makers' and especially the makers of the traditional ballads. That Hopegood can write effectively in the medieval ballad style is illustrated in 'Swastika Stepmother', which echoes the Scottish 'Lord Randal' but is translated from the German traditional ballad 'Die Stiefmutter'. By adding the word 'swastika' to the title, Hopegood allows the poem to become a reflection on the contemporary German people. *Snake's-eye View of a Serial Story* (1964), Hopegood's first collection for seventeen years, sees him still using myth, from Australian ballad to Maori legend and Scots pibroch. The simplest and least pretentious of his verse, however, is the most effective. Acknowledged by his contemporaries as a significant poet, Hopegood has been roundly attacked for the obscurity of his major poetry; friend and fellow poet R.D. FitzGerald believed that he sacrificed his artistic integrity to his mystical preoccupations. Hopegood published the autobiographical *Peter Lecky by Himself* in 1935, 'Lecky' being the pseudonym he adopted in an earlier literary competition.

HOPGOOD, Alan (1934–), born Launceston, is a well-known stage and television actor, and has written several plays: 'Marcus' (1955); *And the Big Men Fly* (1969), a popular comedy about Australian rules football, first produced in 1963; *The Golden Legion of Cleaning Women* (1979), first produced in 1964; 'Private Yuk Objects', a play about the impact of the Vietnam War on Australian society, first produced in 1966; 'Terribly, Terribly' (1968), a black comedy first produced in Los Angeles in 1967 and in Australia in 1979; and *And Here Comes Bucknuckle* (1980), a sequel to *And the Big Men Fly* and a television serial. Hopgood, best known for his scripts for the *Alvin Purple* films, has also written other film scripts and plays for television, and has won several Awgies.

HOPKINS, F.R.C. (Francis Rawdon Chesney) (1849–1916), born Bombay and educated in England, came in 1865 to Victoria, where he managed various stations, eventually purchasing his own. His plays, all adapted from European works, were very successful, largely due to their production by Alfred Dampier. They include 'Good for Evil' (first performed 1877, published 1875 with the title *Clay and Porcelain*), 'All for Gold' (first performed 1877), 'Only a Fool' (first performed 1880), '£ S D' (first performed 1882) and 'Michael Strogoff' (first performed 1882). He also edited the *Australian Ladies Annual* (1878); published a book of essays, *Confessions of a Cynic* (1882); a book of verse, *Gum Leaves Old and Gum Leaves New* (1902); and two collections of short stories with Australian settings (1908, 1909). His later play, *Reaping the Whirlwind*, published anonymously in 1909, was intended to alert Australians to what he saw as the Asiatic menace.

HOPKINS, Livingston York ('Hop') (1846–1927), born Ohio, USA, was best known as the cartoonist, 'Hop', for the *Bulletin* (q.v.). He served in the American Civil War, and worked mainly in New York as a freelance designer and cartoonist until 1882, when his services were secured for the *Bulletin* by W.H. Traill. He arrived in Australia soon after and was joined by Phil May with whom he contributed greatly to the spread of the *Bulletin*'s popularity and prosperity. Hopkins remained with the *Bulletin* and eventually became a director; his prodigious output has been estimated at 19,000 drawings. His best-known cartoons include those on the Sudan War and Federation and the caricatures of Sir Henry Parkes, Sir George Reid and other public figures. His interpretation of the politicians and the regular appearance of his symbolic figures such as the Little Boy from Manly and a host of allegorical animals did much to project the economic, political, racial and cultural policies of the *Bulletin*, particularly before Federation. In 1880 he prepared *A Comic History of the United States* and in 1904 published *On the Hop*, a selection of his Australian work. In 1929 his daughter Dorothy published the biographical tribute *Hop of the 'Bulletin'*.

HOPKINSON, Simon (1947–), born London, migrated to Australia in 1970 and joined the Melbourne Theatre Company as production manager the same year. In 1971 he founded the Melbourne Theatre Company Youth Theatre and has since held a number of positions on theatre boards and companies as well as directing numerous plays. His first play, performed in 1964, was awarded the Dobell Drama Prize and since coming to Australia he has continued a prolific writing career. His Australian plays include *The Crazy World of Advertising* (1975), 'Jailed!', 'If This Account is not Paid . . .', 'The Stinking, Filthy, Dirty, All-In Pollution Show', 'Prejudice and Outcasts', 'The Blue Jean'd and Stardust Scene', 'A Pile of Secrets' (1972), 'Stopwork!' (1973), 'Thumbscrew Circus' (1974), 'Occupied' (1975), 'Blind Choice' (1976), 'Moving On, Moving On' (1981), 'Whoops!' (1982), 'Greenants – White cans' (1983), *Buffaloes Can't Fly* (1984), 'Sail' (1984), 'Yesterday's Mangoes' (1985) and 'Just a Bloke from Murwillumbah' (1986).

HORNE, Donald (1921–), born Muswellbrook, NSW, was educated at the University of Sydney (he did not gain a degree), where he was strongly influenced by John Anderson (q.v.), became friendly with A.D. Hope, Harold Stewart, Oliver Somerville and James McAuley, and edited *Honi Soit* for a brief period. He served in the AIF 1941–44, was a cadet in the diplomatic service 1944–45 and a reporter for the Sydney *Daily Telegraph* 1945–49. After working in Britain 1950–54, he returned to become involved in a variety of editorial work. He edited *Weekend* (1954–61), the *Observer* (1958–61), *Everybody's* (1961–62), and the *Bulletin* (1961–62 and 1967–72). He was also co-editor of *Quadrant* (1963–66) and contributing editor to *Newsweek International* (1973–76). In 1973 he began an academic career at the University of NSW, which awarded him an honorary doctorate in 1986 and made him emeritus professor on retirement in 1987. Chairperson of the Australia Council 1985–90, he was appointed chancellor of the University of Canberra in 1991 and made AO in 1982.

In the 1960s Horne was in the forefront of the politically conservative polemicists and was a member of the executive of the Australian Association for Cultural Freedom 1962–66. In the late 1960s he moved to support for the Labor opposition, however, and has been one of the most outspoken critics of the dismissal of the Whitlam government in 1975. As well as innumerable essays, reviews and articles he has written several works of social and political comment: *The Lucky Country* (q.v., 1964, 2nd revised edn 1968); *God Is an Englishman* (1969), a study of British society; *Money Made Us* (1976), an analysis of materialist propensities in Australian society; *The Next Australia* (1970), an examination of changes in social and cultural attitudes, in the economy, the political system and foreign policy; *Death of the Lucky Country* (1976), an account of the 1975 political crisis from a Labor perspective; *Time of Hope* (1980), a study of changes in Australian society 1966–72; *Winner Take All?* (1981), an examination of the issues facing Australia after the 1980 election; *The Lucky Country Revisited* (1987), which attempts to redress superficial responses to *The Lucky Country*; *The Great Museum* (1984), a study of cultural monuments and their role as reflectors of changes in socio-political meanings; *The Public Culture* (1986), an analysis of our construction of 'reality', the culturally learned hypotheses about existence and the repertoires of collective habits of thinking and acting which create a sense of national identity; and *Ideas for a Nation* (1989), which explores, in the wake of the Bicentenary, Australia's public culture, the limiting effects of certain myths and stereotypes, especially the national cult of pragmatism and the possibilities of imaginatively reshaping the future. He has also written a social history, *The Australian People* (1972); a portrait of W.M. Hughes, *In Search of Billy Hughes* (1979) which won the Con Weickhardt Award for 1979; three novels, *The Permit* (1965), *But What If There Are No Pelicans?* (1971) and *His Excellency's Pleasure* (1977); an account of his travels in Australia, *Right Way, Don't Go Back* (1978); and an autobiographical trilogy, *The Education of Young Donald* (q.v., 1967), *Confessions of a New Boy* (1985) and *Portrait of an Optimist* (1988). He also provided the text for *Southern Exposure* (1967), a collection of unusual Australian photographs by David Beal, and edited the collections *The Trouble with Economic Rationalism* (1992) and *The Coming Republic* (1992).

Already familiar to readers of the *Bulletin* and the *Observer* as a writer of witty, provocative articles, Horne sprang into general prominence with the publication of *The Lucky Country*. One of the first of a series of critiques of Australian society in the 1960s, it aroused so much interest that its title has become familiar usage, frequently adopted by politicians and others without regard to Horne's intended ironies.

Central to the book and a continuing preoccupation in Horne's work is the thesis that Australia is a derivative and provincial society, obsessed with material pursuits at the expense of excellence in any field except sport. In his later books, and especially in *The Next Australia*, Horne has extended and changed some of the opinions and conclusions of *The Lucky Country*. His novels reveal a versatile talent; *The Permit*, a slapstick comedy, deals with the absurdities of officialdom, the political sphere and the press; *His Excellency's Pleasure* satirises the institution of the governor-general in Australia; *But What If There Are No Pelicans?*, part-allegory, part-fantasy, explores human nature and the possibilities of faith in humanity. Horne's autobiographies, however, are his most striking literary achievement. *The Education of Young Donald* is both a dispassionately honest study of the artist as a child and young man, and a documentary representation of Australian lower-middle-class society in the 1930s; *Confessions of a New Boy* takes up his life story in 1941 when he was conscripted into the army; *Portrait of an Optimist* continues the story to 1958 and his editorship of the *Observer*. The last two volumes of this trilogy are even more self-conscious and self-reflexive than the first; comically deploying a vast array of younger selves, Horne is persistently conscious of a more contemplative self which observes his role-playing from a concealed vantage point: 'In my mind I was a nineteenth century novelist inventing characters in a society.' *Portrait of an Optimist* concludes with the 39-year-old author struggling to find a style that would unite his natural optimism as a child and the pessimism acquired through education.

HORNE, R.H. (Richard Henry) (1802–84), who in 1867 substituted 'Hengist' for his second name, was born Edmonton, near London, and became ambitious for a poetic career after reading Shelley's *Queen Mab*. He became a literary celebrity through his successful editorship of the *Monthly Repository*, and the triumph of his epic poem *Orion* (1843), which ran to six printings in its first year, causing him to be later dubbed 'Orion' Horne. In 1852 he came to Australia, partly to escape a dramatic decline in his personal situation, partly to restore his fortunes on the Australian goldfields. He held and lost minor administrative positions on the Victorian diggings, failed to win election to the Victorian parliament, was briefly and unsuccessfully a commissioner for Melbourne's sewerage and water supply, and drifted, often unemployed, until 1863, when he was made warden of the Blue Mountain goldfield near Trentham in Victoria. There he returned to serious writing. In 1864 *Prometheus the Fire-Bringer*, a lyrical drama, was published and in 1866 he wrote, for the Intercolonial Exhibition of Australasia, *The South Sea Sisters, A Lyric Masque*, which contains his poetic version of an Aboriginal corroboree. Restored to literary prestige and influence, he was an important member of the Melbourne literary circle, centred on the Yorick Club. He returned to England in 1869, continuing to write profusely but unprofitably. Horne's Australian writings, except for his prose work *Australian Facts and Prospects* (1859), were of little

significance in themselves, but the presence in the colony of such an established literary figure did much to bolster the respectability of the literary profession in the hitherto sceptical colonial mind and acted as a stimulus to such rising literary talents as Henry Kendall, Adam Lindsay Gordon and Marcus Clarke. Biographical works include Cyril Pearl's *Always Morning: The Life of Richard Henry 'Orion' Horne* (1960) and Anne Blainey's *The Farthing Poet* (1968). Barry Oakley's play *The Ship's Whistle* (1979) focuses on Horne.

HORNUNG, E.W. (Ernest William) (1866–1921), born Middlesbrough, England, was in Australia 1884–86. He spent most of his life in England and France, where he became a well-known literary figure, a prolific writer of popular romance, crime and mystery fiction. His brief Australian experience is reflected in a number of his novels: *A Bride from the Bush* (1890), said to have been started while he was a tutor at Mossgiel station in the Riverina, reflects the contrast between the cold formality of upper-class English life and the warm open-heartedness of outback Australian life; *Tiny Luttrell* (1893) is similarly in favour of the colonial environment; *Denis Dent* (1903) is partly set on the diggings at Ballarat; and *The Boss of Taroomba* (1894) contains incidents of station life and bushranging. Other bushranging figures are in *Irralie's Bushranger* (1896) and *The Belle of Toorak* (1900); *The Rogue's March* (1896) is set in the convict period. Hornung is also well known as the creator of Raffles, the polished gentleman burglar whose exploits begin in Australia and fill many of his tales, and were carried on by Barry Perowne after Hornung's death. Of particular interest to Australian readers is Hornung's love of cricket, evident especially in his short stories, major collections of which are *Under Two Skies* (1892), *Some Persons Unknown* (1898) and *Old Offenders and a Few Old Scores* (1923).

Horse-racing, see **Turf**

HOSPITAL, Janette Turner (1942–), born Janette Turner in Melbourne, moved with her family to Brisbane in 1950. In Queensland at primary school she suffered harassment from other children and even teachers on account of her 'difference'; the fundamentalist Pentecostal religion of her immediate family imposed visible external differences, which were perceived as particularly dangerous after a diphtheria epidemic exposed the sect's refusal to accept the immunisation programmes of modern medicine. At home, where she never voiced these difficulties, the family provided security, fun and emotional warmth, but the daily crossing from the security of this familiar dimension to the unpredictable hostility of the public one was much later to have significant influence on her writing. The experience of prejudice and group hostility and of the fine line between affluence and poverty, power and powerlessness, home and homelessness, infuses much of her fiction; characteristically preoccupied from the first with the crossing of borders, both her novels and short stories are increasingly concerned with the stark incongruence of cultures and groups, even though physically contiguous. Moving to Mitchelton State High School, where she was able to abandon this early unhappy history, was a substantial liberation and initiated a period of growing self-confidence. She subsequently became a student at Queensland University and at Kelvin Grove Teachers College, completing her BA in 1965. In 1963–66 she taught at Mossman in North Queensland (where her then religious attitudes were strongly challenged) and in Brisbane. Her short story 'You Gave Me Hyacinths' is partly based on the experience at Mossman. In 1965 she married Clifford Hospital, then a Methodist minister, and two years later left for Boston, USA, where her husband completed his Ph.D. at Harvard University in the field of comparative religion and where she worked at the University library and cared for their two children. The family moved to Kingston, Ontario, Canada, in 1971 and Hospital spent the next five years completing an MA in medieval literature and teaching as a casual teacher at high schools, Queen's University, St Lawrence College and maximum- and medium-security penitentiaries for men. A period in India in 1977 during her husband's study leave later provided the background for *The Ivory Swing*. Her first short story, 'Waiting', was published in 1978 in *The Atlantic Monthly*, and received an 'Atlantic First' citation, which led to the publication in 1982 of her first novel, *The Ivory Swing*, winner of the prestigious Canadian Seal Award. In the same year she was awarded first prize for magazine fiction from the Foundation for the Advancement of Canadian Letters. Her subsequent novels are *The Tiger in the Tiger Pit* (1983), *Borderline* (1985), *Charades* (1988) and *The Last Magician* (1992). She has also published two collections of short stories, *Dislocations* (1986, published in Australia with additional stories in 1987) and *Isobars* (1990). As 'Alex Juniper' she published the crime fiction *A Very Proper Death* (1990). Writer-in-residence at the Massachusetts Institute of Technology in Boston for several periods, she has held similar positions at the University of Sydney and La Trobe University. Although her work won recognition almost immediately in Canada and the USA, her reputation has grown more gradually in Australia, largely due to her extended periods of residence overseas and the copyright limitations affecting her first novel, which was not published in Australia until 1991. Her short stories have been published in numerous journals and anthologies including *Latitudes* (1986), *The Australian Bedside Book* (1987), *More Stories by Canadian Women* (1987), *Expressway* (1989), and *Airmail from Down Under* (1991). Other awards she has won include second prize in the Canadian Broadcasting Commission's short-story competition in 1987, and in 1988 the FAW Fiction Award and the Torgi Award of the Canadian Association for the Blind.

Although Hospital spends some part of each year in Canada and the USA, she makes extended visits to Australia, describing Queensland in particular as 'absolutely in my bloodstream' and as 'a permanent mood that I carry around inside my head'. Her work is not narrowly autobiographical, but several characteristic features and concerns have autobiographical roots; these include her interest in dislocations of multiple varieties, reflecting her own experience of mobility between different countries and disparate social, cultural and religious environments; her concern with women's survival within their received social frameworks and especially with the unhappy fates of highly intelligent women unable to surmount external pressures; and her interest in the theme of redemption or grace. No longer a dogmatic Christian, Hospital nevertheless maintains a belief in the possibility of redemption, sometimes opposing the unexpected kindness of a deeply flawed individual to the equally unexpected cruelty of one generally perceived as benevolent. The experience of moving between cultures has also contributed to the post-modernist aspects of her work, reinforcing her impression of memory as subjectively and quirkily selective and her conviction that history and the past are its artefacts, as it has heightened the sensitivity to language which she has described as a lifelong passion. The narrator of one of her most autobiographical short stories, 'After Long Absence', expresses a similar sensitivity: 'I know a lot about words, about their sensuous surfaces, the way the tongue licks at them. And about the depth charges they carry.'

The Ivory Swing describes the experiences of a Canadian couple and their two children in a region of southern India which is singularly isolated from Western culture and where the husband, an academic, has elected to spend his study leave. Juliet, his wife, frustrated by the small-town life in Ontario she is obliged to lead as 'a faculty wife', and half inclined to abandon her marriage for the independence of her own apartment in Montreal and possible reconnection with her old lover Jeremy, welcomes the change as a chance of freedom. The theme of crossed borders is inevitably sounded at the novel's beginning as Juliet attempts to adjust to the unexpected differences, rigidities and utterly opposite values of another culture, and to the impact of these on her own convictions and received attitudes. Obliged to accept a houseboy to conform to Indian expectations, she tries to include him in the family, only to discover that the 'freedom' she confers is more destructive than the caste-determined rules which are a condition of his acceptance as he has been conditioned to accept them. But the line between freedom and responsibility is etched far more clearly by the fate of Yashoda, a young Indian widow whose social constrictions elicit both Juliet's and her husband's sympathy and who finally fatally oversteps the limits of her culturally codified position. As in Hospital's later fiction, although with less emphasis on discontinuity, the lines of cause and effect are tangled and ambiguous; the 'borderline' between accident and preventable tragedy, between the need for rules and the need to break them, is blurred and left open-ended, both for the reader and the characters. The ivory swing, represented by a carving of the Indian gods Radha and Krishna, caught in an embrace on a swing frozen in mid-air, may reflect Juliet's own perception of her inability to choose between marriage and the challenging freedoms which her sister, for instance, has accepted, or the precariousness of human destinies in general, or the difficult moral poise which the shocks of cross-cultural exchange evoke most acutely. *The Tiger in the Tiger Pit* focuses on the family and its paradoxical function as the primary source of comfort and security and the primary source of harm. Set in a small town of Massachusetts and covering a brief period in physical time, the few days leading up to and including a family reunion for the fiftieth wedding anniversary of Edward and Elizabeth Carpenter, the novel backtracks in psychological time as the various family members reflect on crucial events, treacheries and guilts which have separated them from each other and especially from their father, an irascible retired school principal. If the imminent anniversary stimulates an excess of border-crossing between past and present in the minds of the Carpenter family, it is itself an important emotional event, creating a new rift in time and bringing to completion a new phase in the family's individual and collective self-definition. *Borderline*, a far more sophisticated novel, extends Hospital's aims into the realm of metafiction. The novel has many ingredients of a conventional thriller, but whereas the thriller resolves its questions, *Borderline* deliberately leaves them open, emphasising the modern experience of reality as uncertain. The novel's title refers most obviously to the border between the USA and Canada, where three of the main characters meet for the first time and are caught up in the discovery of illegal Salvadoran immigrants hidden among the carcases of a butcher's van. Felicity, the main character, is known throughout indirectly, from the perspective of Jean-Marc, her friend, whose narration of Felicity's story and implicit unreliability as a narrator raise numerous questions about the selectivity of memory, observation and opinion and the consoling, duplicitous nature of all narrative. Aware that it is a simple matter to rearrange the past and that 'yesterday was an hypothesis existing purely by the grace of today', Felicity is as self-conscious a crosser of borders as her narrator, who constantly rearranges her relationships with places and people in his effort to distil her essence to his satisfaction: 'I temper, I stretch, I embroider.' Meanwhile various other realities are juxtaposed and questioned, especially the reality of experience to the reality of news purveyed by the modern media; Hospital has emphasised this aspect of the novel in an interview, describing *Borderline* as concerned with the nature of narrative and the unreality of evil in North America. Felicity anticipates Charade of the next novel; a wanderer, she is sensitive, resilient, independent and self-confident, aware of her own intelligence and talents which she exploits in order to survive. La Magdalena, the illegal emigrant whom Felicity attempts to help and who is first discovered lying in a carcase like a fetus in a womb, is a representation of the damaged woman who continues to intrigue Hospital; trapped by hostile, impersonal but invincible forces, she repeats the experience of Yashoda and anticipates that of Verity Ashkenazy. Felicity's survival skills are also finally inadequate in this world of big-power politics which she challenges, notwithstanding Jean-

Marc's attempts to convince himself that she will return.

In *Charades* Hospital probes the theme of uncertainty even more extensively, invoking the familiar Arabian fairy-tale by placing the story's narration in a lengthy sequence of sexual/story-telling encounters between Charade, a modern-day Scheherazade, and Koenig, an eminent American physicist engaged in work on Heisenberg's uncertainty principle and her kingly opponent/collaborator. Undercut and impeded by frequent timeshifts, and in some instances left ambiguous, the plot represents the contemporary perception of time, bolstered by the insights of theoretical physics. Intrigued by Koenig's demonstrations that modern science is not only unable to provide empirical evidence of certainty but is able to entertain paradoxes which make certainty permanently unobtainable, Charade enlists him as an imaginative equal in her quest for a father. As she sifts the past of her Queensland childhood and the events which preceded her birth, her quest becomes one for a mother and more implicitly and generally one for other more uncertain human goods, including happiness in love and freedom from guilt. If some secrets are discovered, others remain hidden, a condition which Charade ultimately accepts as she accepts the '*necessity* of uncertainty'.

The Last Magician owes its inception to a photograph of the Serra Pelada gold-mine in Brazil published in the *New York Times Magazine*. The analogies between the quarry and the rocky ravine enclosing Newtown railway station with its abandoned buildings and subterranean labyrinth of tunnels are at the heart of Hospital's exploration of the links between Sydney's underworld of depravity and deprivation and the outwardly more salubrious world of the powerful. The principal characters are Charlie Chang, an Australian-Chinese photographer and brothel manager; the brilliant but remote Catherine Reed, an SBS television journalist; the powerful, malevolent Judge Robinson Gray and his vastly different son Gabriel; Cat, a rebellious eccentric, 'feral and sinuous'; and the narrator Lucy Barclay. Tracing the destinies of this group of people born in Queensland and their determining childhood experiences, the novel is partly a detective story and partly a philosophical/psychological study of a society which sacrifices the powerless to the powerful. For Lucy Barclay the distance between the surface world of affluence and security and the underworld is made dramatically vivid when she encounters a madwoman on Brisbane station: 'she saw suddenly that there were parallel worlds, that you could cross a line, that you could fall through a hairline crack and cartwheel giddily down and round and down in slow motion, like moondust in space and how did you know that wasn't your real world, the one you came from and to which you properly belonged?' The last magician of the title is Charlie Chang, whose arresting photographs which both reveal and conceal, enlighten and deceive, are shuffled and reshuffled into patterns creating versions of the past, just as the narrative itself shuffles and reshuffles time. Rich in literary allusions, the novel frequently makes comparisons with Dante's *Inferno*, suggesting that descent into the underworld is necessary for enlightenment. Less explicitly concerned with theoretical physics than *Charades*, *The Last Magician* nevertheless invokes chaos theory, suggesting that in the human world as in the physical, random and trivial events may trigger distant calamities. Hospital's short stories, ranging between Canada, Boston, India, Australia's rainforests and cities, share the fascination with indeterminacy, curving time and the borderlines of things which distinguishes her novels. Many reflect on incorrigible human predatoriness which frequently selects women as its victims, although, like Jolley's, her characters often show a resilient or stoic strength which redeems the otherwise bleak vision.

HOUBEIN, Loló (1934–), born Johanna (Jopie) in Hilversum, Holland, lived as a child through the Nazi occupation of her country and the hardship of the immediate post-war period. She adopted the name Loló at the age of 12 and made the change legal in 1975. In 1958 she emigrated with her second husband and children to Australia, living near Adelaide, in whose public library she read widely in English, which she could not speak on her arrival. She later trained to be a teacher, graduated in arts from the University of Adelaide and undertook postgraduate work in literature at the University of Papua New Guinea. She has taught in Darwin and Adelaide, visited Indonesia, India and Tibet, fulfilling a lifelong dream by meeting the Dalai Lama. Settled in Adelaide, she now pursues her chief interests (her vegetable garden, writing, concern for the Aborigines, feminism, Buddhism) with undiminished passion. Her published works include *Everything is Real* (1984), a group of short stories which she later republished (1992) as *The Sixth Sense*; *Walk a Barefoot Road* (1988); and *Wrong Face in the Mirror: An Autobiography of Race and Identity* (1990). *Wrong Face in the Mirror*, published first in Dutch in 1988, won the Dirk Hartog Literary Award for literary exploration of migration experiences, while *Walk a Barefoot Road* won the ABC Bicentennial Fiction Award. Houbein has won several other short-story awards, including the 'Rolf Boldrewood' Award in 1978 and 1983.

Wrong Face in the Mirror is a disarmingly frank autobiography weaving together the twin stories of her physical and spiritual journeying, from her childhood in wartime Holland to her eventual achievement of the individual and cultural independence that she had long sought. *Walk a Barefoot Road* is the story of Riena Lahman, who as a child is separated from her family in war-torn Holland. Her struggle to survive those years, her wanderings throughout the world and her eventual refuge in the SA countryside form a story of indomitable will, courage and resourcefulness. *The Sixth Sense* contains twenty stories, beginning with 'Everything is Real', one of the 'Boldrewood' Award winners ('No Stranger' is the other). Its message, in the story of the two sisters, Maudy and Mim, is clearly the message of Houbein and her life – 'recognize each moment for what it's worth'. The stories as a whole can be taken, as one critic has said, 'as a guide for wise,

contented and serviceable living'. Houbein also compiled *Ethnic Writings in English from Australia: A Bibliography* (1976).

HOULDING, J.R. (John Richard) (1822–1918), born Essex, England, worked in a lawyer's office both in London, where he was supposed to have met Charles Dickens, and in Sydney, where he arrived in 1839. A country storekeeper for most of the 1840s, he sold out in 1852 and visited England in 1854. The loss of his modest fortune on his return to Sydney in 1855 led to a nervous collapse and to the commencement, while convalescing, of a writing career which lasted until his retirement in the 1890s. Houlding's first novel, *Australian Capers* (q.v., 1867), published under the pseudonym 'Old Boomerang', chronicles the colonial experiences of a 'new chum' (q.v.), Christopher Cockle. Informed by Houlding's own experiences of sharp Sydney businessmen, *Australian Capers* also reflects his Methodist and temperance beliefs, and benefited in the preparation from the advice of the Sydney literary patron N.D. Stenhouse. As 'Old Boomerang' or as 'J.R.H. Hawthorn', the most popular of his several pseudonyms, Houlding published six further novels, *Rural and City Life* (1870), *Investing Uncle Ben's Legacy* (1876), *The Pioneer of a Family* (1881), *Launching Away* (1882), *In the Depths of the Sea* (1885), *A Flood That Led on to Fortune* (1886), and *Australian Tales, and Sketches from Real Life* (1868), a selection of his contributions to the *Sydney Mail*. Strongly moralist in tone, his instructional tales became popular as Sunday school prizes, but *Australian Capers* in particular is interesting as an example of the guidebook genre of fiction; for the vividness of some of its scenes based on Houlding's perceptive observation of Australian life; and for its humour, in which exaggerated metaphor, the use of dialect and puns, and the presentation of immigrant and colonial types are important ingredients.

House Is Built, A, a novel by 'M. Barnard Eldershaw' (q.v.), shared first prize in the *Bulletin's* novel competition of 1928. After serialisation in the *Bulletin* as 'The Quartermaster', it was published in London in 1929, was produced as a play in 1954 after dramatisation by Eunice Hanger and has continued to be popular in England, the USA and Australia. Set in Sydney from the 1830s to the 1880s, it deals with the fortunes of the family of James Hyde. A quartermaster in the Royal Navy, Hyde decides at the age of 50 to set up in the supply business on Sydney's waterfront. He is joined by his two daughters, Fanny, practical, energetic and serious-minded, and Maud, vivacious, beautiful and gregarious, and by his son William, conventional, reserved and priggish. Thanks to the indomitable and innovative energies of the quartermaster and the growing business sense of William, the family's fortunes thrive. Fanny is disappointed in her love for a whaling captain, Hildebrand, but Maud elopes with the son of one of Sydney's wealthiest families, the Gillams, and is soon happily absorbed in her role of wife and mother. William is eventually joined by his English fiancée of five years, Adela Gage, and becomes the father of two temperamentally different sons, James, an apparent replica of his grandfather, and Lionel, less robust and artistic. Adela, who has been keenly disappointed in her romantic expectations of William, has more affinity with Lionel than with James. When the gold rushes of the 1850s provide even greater opportunities for the supply business, the quartermaster sets out for the diggings himself and Fanny finds her true vocation in administration of the waterfront store. Later, only Adela's near death from scarlet fever takes Fanny away from her work, and William's conventional notions prevent her from returning. Embittered, she finds a partial refuge in genteel charity work. Established as one of Sydney's prominent families, the Hydes move to a mansion at Hunter's Hill and James prepares for his role as head of the business. At 20 he falls in love with the volatile Laurel Franklin, the daughter of a business rival. Trapped by Laurel into betraying a business secret and unable to confess his crime to Adela, he takes to his small boat and is drowned in a storm. His death, following closely on private news of his disloyalty, causes the collapse of the quartermaster and he dies after two years of mute paralysis. Although Adela is able to keep the fact of James's betrayal from William, the loss of his son contributes to his early death. Lionel loyally but unenthusiastically takes up the business and after the death of Adela marries the quiet, undemanding Mary Bardon.

HOVELL, W.H. (William Hilton) (1786–1875), born Yarmouth, England, was captain of a vessel trading to South America before settling on the land in Australia after 1813. His explorations in 1824 with Hamilton Hume (q.v.) from the Goulburn district of NSW to Corio Bay in Port Phillip led to the discovery of the Murray River and the pastoral expansion of the Colony. In an ensuing public controversy between the two explorers, Hovell's point of view is given in *Reply to 'A Brief Statement of Facts'* (1855). A character, Captain Travers, in Edward Maitland's novel *The Pilgrim and the Shrine* (1867), is based on Hovell.

'How He Died', the title poem of John Farrell's (q.v., 1887) volume of bush ballads, is a sentimental tale of the station boozer, Nabbage, who gives his life to save his 'little mate', the squatter's boy, Freddie. It was published first in the *Bulletin*, 1883.

'How M'Dougall Topped the Score', the title poem of T.E. Spencer's (q.v.) 1906 collection of verse, is the story of the historic cricket match between Piper's Flat and Molongo. When challenged by Molongo to a single-innings match, the loser to pay for a slap-up lunch at McGinnis's pub, Piper's Flat can only muster ten players. They reluctantly recruit the old Scotsman, M'Dougall, from nearby Cooper's Creek, to make up the number. Molongo are dismissed for 66 and when Piper's Flat in reply are 9 wickets down for 17, M'Dougall marches to the crease. He hits the first ball gently back towards the bowler and in response to his command, 'Fetch It', his aptly named old sheepdog, Pincher, seizes the ball and makes off, with the whole Molongo team in wrathful but vain pursuit ('brain the mongrel with a bat'). M'Dougall, meanwhile, begins his initially swift but eventually ponderous and painful but successful pursuit of the 50 runs needed for victory:

> Then Pincher dropped the ball, and, as instinctively
>   he knew
> Discretion was the wiser plan, he disappeared from view
> And as Molongo's beaten men exhausted lay around
> We raised M'Dougall shoulder high, and bore him from
>   the ground.

Both sides then repair to McGinnis's to celebrate with 'whisky-punch' the historic occasion when 'M'Dougall topped the score'. Spencer's poem celebrates the bushman's talents for devising ingenious but essentially harmless methods of besting a rival; it takes its place alongside A.B. Paterson's accounts of the stratagems of drovers to outwit squatters and of racehorse owners and jockeys to outwit bookmakers.

HOWARD, Campbell, see **Campbell Howard Collection of Australian Plays in Manuscript**

HOWARD, Frederick (1904–84), born London, came to Australia in 1920, entered journalism and was a member of the Melbourne *Herald* staff before and after the First World War. He edited *Stead's Review* 1929–31; his published novels include *The Emigrant* (1928) and *Return Ticket* (1929), which have a romantic theme and an Australian setting.

HOWARTH, R.G. (Robert Guy) (1906–74), born Tenterfield, NSW, graduated from the universities of Sydney and Oxford before being appointed to the English Department at the University of Sydney in 1933. In 1955–71 he was professor of English literature at the University of Cape Town, South Africa. Widely acknowledged by contemporaries as one of Australia's finest literary scholars and regarded as an inspiring and encouraging teacher by a generation of literature students at Sydney, Howarth early in his academic career produced several important works on English literature, e.g. *The Letters of George Gordon, Sixth Lord Byron* (1933). He was an active member of the English Association (q.v.) in Sydney and was foundation editor (1939–56) of *Southerly* (q.v.). He served on the advisory board of the CLF 1950–55, was a foundation member of the Australian Humanities Research Council, and in 1952 was elected a fellow of the Royal Society of Literature. An enthusiastic advocate of Australian literature, he edited Hugh McCrae's *Forests of Pan* (1944) and *The Best Poems of Hugh McCrae* (1961), and collaborated with John Thompson and Kenneth Slessor in *The Penguin Book of Australian Verse* (1958). His editing of the letters of Norman Lindsay was completed after his death by A.W. Barker, who published them in 1979. Howarth's poetry, which has not received sufficient recognition, appeared in the collections *Spright and Geist* (1944), a series of epigrammatic love poems, *Involuntaries* (1948) and *Nardoo and Pituri* (1959); many of his essays on literature are included in his *Literary Particles* (1946).

HOWE, George (1769–1821), the first important government printer in Australia, was born in the West Indies and apprenticed there to the printing trade. He went to London in 1790s, worked on The *Times* and other newspapers, and was transported for shoplifting in 1799. He became government printer soon after his arrival in Sydney in 1800 and in 1802 issued the first book printed in Australia, *New South Wales General Standing Orders.* In 1803 he began publication of the *Sydney Gazette* (q.v.); other publishing initiatives in which he was involved were the natural history and art book *Birds of New South Wales* (1813), Barron Field's *First Fruits of Australian Poetry* (1819) and a series of early almanacs (q.v.). Conditionally pardoned in 1803 and fully emancipated in 1806, Howe was successful in commerce. Two of his sons, Robert and George Terry Howe (qq.v.), followed him into printing and publishing.

HOWE, George Terry (1806–63), born Sydney, a son of the pioneer Sydney pressman George Howe, came to Van Diemen's Land in 1821 and in 1825 founded the first newspaper in Launceston, the *Tasmanian and Port Dalrymple Advertiser.* Later that year he moved his press to Hobart to join James Ross in producing the *Hobart Town Gazette* (q.v.). After the partnership was dissolved in 1827, Howe re-established the *Tasmanian* in Hobart before returning to Sydney.

HOWE, Jack (?1861–1920), born Killarney near Warwick in Queensland, began work as a shearer in the 1870s. In 1892 he established a world-record tally when he shore 321 sheep in eight hours with blade shears; he was equally expert with machine shears when they gained a wider usage. He retired from shearing to become a publican in 1900, and was active also in the union movement. A man with huge hands whose shearing feats were legendary, Howe is mentioned in several shearers' songs (e.g. 'Goorianawa') as well as in poems such as Ian Mudie's 'They'll Tell You About Me'. Howe's fame also explains why a 'Jacky (Jackie) Howe' became established as an Australian colloquialism for a sleeveless flannel shirt of the type worn by shearers and other bush workers.

HOWE, Michael (1787–1818) was a notorious early Tasmanian bushranger (q.v.) who was convicted of highway robbery in York, England in 1811 and transported for seven years. In 1813 he absconded and took to the bush at the head of a gang of desperadoes which terrorised the pioneer settlers of Van Diemen's Land. An amnesty in 1814 led most of the gang to report to the authorities, but by early 1815 Howe had again gathered about him a new well-armed band; martial law was declared and Howe styled himself 'Lieutenant-Governor of the Woods'. In 1817 negotiations between Howe and the *de jure* lieutenant-governor, William Sorell, broke down and he again took to the bush; a year later he was betrayed and clubbed to death near his hut at Shannon River. Cunning, callous, vicious and probably deranged, Howe was the subject of the first non-official book or pamphlet published in

Tasmania, Thomas Wells's *Michael Howe, the Last and Worst of the Bush Rangers of Van Diemen's Land*, published in the year of his death. Other early responses to his sensational exploits are a play by J. Amherst advertised in London in 1821 (no copy has survived), and *Van Diemen's Land* (q.v., 1830), 'W.T. Moncrieff's' extravaganza in which the gang is captured at the end of the play and Howe led away to execution. James Bonwick wrote the biographical *Mike Howe, the Bushranger of Van Diemen's Land* (1873), while Hume Nisbet's *The Savage Queen* (1891), Nat Gould's *King of the Ranges* (1902), and Roy Bridges's *On His Majesty's Service* (1914) are works of popular fiction in which Howe appears.

HOWE, Robert (1795–1829), born England, was the eldest son of George Howe (q.v.), whom he accompanied to Australia in 1800. From boyhood he assisted in his father's printing office and carried on the business after George Howe's death in 1821. He continued to produce the *Sydney Gazette* and the *New South Wales Pocket Almanack*, renamed the *Austral(as)ian Almanack*, as well as publishing the *Australian Magazine*, the first Australian periodical, and Charles Tompson's *Wild Notes, from the Lyre of a Native Minstrel* (1826), the first book of poems by a native-born poet of European descent. After Robert's death the production of the *Gazette* and the *Almanack* was carried on by his widow, Ann.

HOWITT, Alfred William (1830–1908), the son of William Howitt (q.v.), was born in Nottingham, England, and went with his father to the Victorian goldfields in 1852. In 1859 he explored the Lake Eyre region, and in 1861 he was sent by the Royal Society of Victoria to search for Burke and Wills; he arrived only in time to save King, and returned to Cooper's Creek to bring the bodies of Burke and Wills back to Melbourne for burial. One of the few explorers not to publish his journal, he later wrote prolifically in the fields of natural science and anthropology, e.g. *The Native Tribes of South-East Australia* (1904). His biography, *Come Wind, Come Weather* (1971), was written by his granddaughter Mary Howitt Walker.

HOWITT, William (1792–1879), born Derbyshire, England, was in Australia 1852–54, accompanied by his sons Alfred and Charlton, exploring the colony and seeking a fortune on the goldfields. The literary results of those experiences were *A Boy's Adventures in the Wilds of Australia* (1854), *Land, Labour and Gold: Or, Two Years in Victoria* (1855), *Tallangetta, the Squatter's Home* (1857), and *The History of Discovery in Australia, Tasmania, and New Zealand* (1865). *Land, Labour and Gold* is one of the most accurate and comprehensive in the popular contemporary travel-book genre. Based on Howitt's diaries and a series of forty letters written by him at various places in his two-year stay, the book possesses the colour and immediacy of fiction. Howitt was not content, however, with highlighting only the more dramatic aspects of colonial life – cities and towns deserted because of gold fever, raging inflation, the eccentricities of colonial flora, fauna and climate, and the excitement and interest of the Bendigo and Ballarat diggings. He saw it as his duty, at a time when the English parliament was attempting to frame constitutions for NSW and Victoria, to give also a candid and honest exposition of the social and political state of the colonies. After his return to England in 1854 (he ultimately made his home in Rome), Howitt continued an active literary life, he and his wife, Mary Botham, being credited with about 180 published works; a biography of them, *Laurels & Rosemary* (1955), was written by Howitt's great-niece Amice Lee. Of less significance in Australian literature was William's younger brother Richard (1799–1870), who came to Australia in 1840 with a still younger brother, Godfrey, who remained in Australia until his death in 1873, by which time he had become a noted physician, botanist and entomologist. Richard returned to England in 1844 and published, in prose and verse, an account of the colony and his experiences, *Impressions of Australia Felix during Four Years' Residence in That Colony* (1845).

HUBER, Thérèse (1764–1829), born Göttingen, Germany, married Georg Forster who at 18 had accompanied his father, the naturalist Johann Reinhold Forster (1729–98), on Captain James Cook's second voyage around the world (1772–75). She later separated from Forster, who died in 1794, and married Ludwig Ferdinand Huber (1764–1804). Between 1795 and 1829 she wrote about sixty stories and novels, two of which, *Adventures on a Journey to New Holland* (1801) and its sequel *The Lonely Deathbed* (1810), have Australian content. *Adventures on a Journey to New Holland*, was probably completed in 1793; if so it is perhaps the first novel in world literature that has the Australian penal settlement as its background, and draws on German translations of the journals of Arthur Phillip (1789), John White (1790) and John Hunter (1793) by Huber's first father-in-law, Johann Reinhold Forster, and Ludwig Huber's 'New Holland and the British Colony in Botany Bay' (Berlin's *Historical Almanack for the Year 1787*), as sources. Basically a story about people caught up in the aftermath of the French Revolution (with a Welsh rebel miner, Henry Belton, giving a British touch to the penal settlement), *Adventures on a Journey to New Holland* gives only a vague picture of the Australian Colony. The characteristic features of Australian fauna and flora, staples in early English novels about the Colony, are seldom mentioned; the Colony itself appears to have been chosen solely because it provided a contrast between the natural virgin setting and its depraved convict inhabitants and was a suitable site for the confrontation between the protagonists, Rudolph, the French ex-revolutionary, and Belton, the Welsh ex-revolutionary, over the whole question of revolution itself.

In her later years Thérèse Huber attained considerable status in German literary life and was recognised as one of the first professional women writers in German literature. She published numerous short stories and novels, and was editor of the widely read German newspaper the *Morgenblatt für gebildete Stände* in Stuttgart. *Adventures on a Journey to New Holland* and *The*

Lonely Deathbed, translated by Rodney Livingstone and edited by Leslie Bodi, were republished in one volume in 1966.

HUDSON, Flexmore (1913–88), born Charters Towers, Queensland, graduated from the University of Adelaide and was a teacher, freelance writer and seaman in the Australian coastal trade. His published poetry includes *Ashes and Sparkle* (1937), *In the Wind's Teeth* (1940), *With the First Soft Rain* (1943), *Indelible Voices* (1943), *As Iron Hills* (1944), and *Pools of the Cinnabar Range* (1959). He edited *Poetry*, a quarterly, 1941–47, and the 1943 *Jindyworobak Anthology;* contributed numerous short stories to various periodicals and anthologies; and wrote a book of aesthetics, *The Child Discovers Poetry* (1941). His stories were collected by Adam Dutkiewicz, who edited them as *Tales from Corytella* (1987).

Involved in the Jindyworobak movement almost from its beginning, Hudson was strongly committed to the unique Australian spirit of place. Unlike Rex Ingamells, the Jindyworobak founder, however, Hudson wished to interpret the Australian environment, first in his own individual way, then in more universal terms. He was not willing to visualise the Australian landscape specifically through a pattern of Aboriginal legend ('a good many of us find the Alcheringa myth unpalatable and unprofitable'). His love for the Australian countryside, embracing everything from the harshness of the Mallee environment, which produced his much-anthologised 'Drought', to the softer beauty of a Murray River sunrise, gives his landscape lyrics warmth and sincerity. Less effective are his Jindyworobakish radical and political homilies, which are prominent in *Indelible Voices* and which mar the effect of individual poems such as 'To a Boy on His Eleventh Birthday'.

HUGHES, Billy (William Morris) (1862–1952), born London of Welsh parents, migrated to Australia in 1884. Following the maritime strike of 1890 he became secretary of the Wharf Labourers' Union, then established, and became president of, the Waterside Workers' Federation. Elected to the first federal parliament, Hughes later became attorney-general and, in 1915, prime minister. His advocacy of conscription, rejected in national referenda in 1916–17, led to his break with the Labor Party, but he saw the war through as leader of several coalition governments and, from May 1917, as leader of the National Party and prime minister. He forcefully represented Australian interests at the Versailles Peace Conference of 1919, and although his parliamentary fortunes gradually declined thereafter he remained involved in politics until his death. Nicknamed 'The Little Digger' and known widely as 'Billy', Hughes was both idolised and detested in the Australian community. In the heat of the conscription controversies he was the target of derisive songs ('No use for Billy' and 'Billy Hughes's Army'). He was more literally the target for the famous 'Warwick Egg', a putrid missile aimed at him in 1917 in a conscription meeting at Warwick in Queensland. Angered by the local constabulary's refusal to arrest the culprit, Hughes established the Commonwealth police force. With his diminutive stature and aquiline features, Hughes was also the constant target of cartoonists, notably David Low (q.v.). He is the subject of biographies by W. Farmer Whyte (1957), L.F. Fitzhardinge (1964, 1979, two volumes), Donald Horne (1979 and 1983) and Peter Spartalis, *The Diplomatic Battles of Billy Hughes* (1984). Hughes published the autobiographical *Crusts and Crusades* (1947) and *Policies and Potentates* (1950). He appears as a character in the play by Michael Boddy and Bob Ellis, *The Legend of King O'Malley* (1974). Douglas Sladen edited *From Boundary Rider to Prime Minister* (1916), a book of Hughes's speeches.

HUGHES, E.F. (Edward Francis) (1814–79), born Kidderminster, England, and who sometimes wrote under the pseudonym 'Frederick Gundase Shaw', published (in Australia) drama, *Bernard: A Drama of the Year 1848* (1859) and poetry, *Portland Bay: A Poem* (1864), *Efforts to be Heard* (1872), *The Millennium: An Epic Poem* (1873), a ten-book work which encompasses the whole scope of biblical history, and *Lays for Thoughtful Workers* (1875). Hughes had earlier (1846) published in London *The Benighted Traveller: A Tale and Other Poems*. He established the Portland *Chronicle*, which he edited from its inception in 1855.

HUGHES, Lyn (1952–), born South Wales, went to South Africa at the age of 12 and arrived in Australia in 1982. Her two novels are set in South Africa. *The Factory* (1990) is a canning factory staffed by mostly Black women. Deirdre is street-wise, resourceful and resilient; Anthea is naively immersed in an unfortunate love affair. Imprisoned physically and mentally by apartheid, the women's lives are a repetitive round of hardship, violence, violation and deprivation. *One-Way Mirror* (1993) is the story of White woman Rosemary Williston, who falls in love with her art teacher, Louise, destroying her marriage in the process. Louise, a constant seeker of new passions, eventually leaves Rosemary for Nandile, a Black woman who is part of a terrorist group. Louise, and ultimately Rosemary, are caught in the net of suspicion surrounding the group. Although the racial tensions of modern South Africa feature in the novel, it is essentially a personal story – of Rosemary's passion for Louise and her attempt to come to terms with Louise's rejection of her.

HUGHES, Robert (1938–), born Sydney, was educated at St Ignatius College and at the University of Sydney where he graduated in architecture before turning to art criticism when commissioned to write a history of Australian art, a task completed when he published *The Art of Australia* at the age of 28. He left Australia to pursue a career in England and Europe as freelance journalist, specialising in art criticism, an area in which he had worked for the Sydney *Observer* (1958–59) and the *Nation* (1960–64). He contributed regularly to English publications, the *Observer*, the *Spectator*, the *Sunday Times* and the *Daily Telegraph*, then joined *Time* magazine in 1970 as art critic, a position he still holds. As art critic he has written *Donald*

Friend (1965), *Heaven and Hell in Western Art* (1969), *The Shock of the New* (1980), *Lucien Freud Paintings* (1988), *Frank Auerbach* (1990) and has also published monographs on Caravaggio, Brueghel and the Van Eyck brothers. In 1991 he published an historical and cultural work, *Barcelona*, just before the Olympic Games were held in that city, and in 1993 a polemical defence of liberal values, *Culture of Complaint: The Fraying of America*. *The Shock of the New* was filmed for television as an eight-part series; several of his art documentaries were also televised. He twice won (1982, 1985) the F.J. Mather Award of the College Art Association of America for art criticism and in 1988 received the American Academy of Achievement's Gold Plate Award. Such tributes acknowledge Hughes as one of the most successful contemporary art critics. His strength is his capacity to popularise art, to inform and instruct his audience on the fundamentals of art appreciation rather than to confuse them with the professional 'artspeak' common to many critics. In 1990 nearly a hundred pieces of his art criticism from the 1980s, most of them from *Time*, were collected in *Nothing If Not Critical*. Hughes's most significant contribution to Australian literature and culture was his massive 688-page account of Australia's colonisation by convicts, *The Fatal Shore: A History of the Transportation of Convicts to Australia 1787–1868* (1987). Rejecting the theory that Britain established the Australian colony primarily to circumvent French expansion in the Pacific, Hughes saw the penal settlement as an eighteenth-century version of what became all too familiar in the twentieth century as the concentration camp – the 'Gulag' – to which those who threatened British property and wealth, good order and discipline, and the preservation of a British society based on class and privilege could be transported, then largely abandoned. Hughes explores at great length the historical background (both in Britain and the Pacific) to the decision to establish such a 'Gulag'; tells the story of the First Settlement itself; of the continuation of transportation in NSW, Norfolk Island and Van Diemen's Land; of the controversy that grew over the 'System' and its continuance; of its gradual decline and ultimate abolition. He combines the meticulous research of the historian with the imaginative flair of the dramatist and the fictional licence of the novelist to produce a monumental account of Australia's origins. Although not without critics, who question particularly the dramatic and fictional elements, *The Fatal Shore* has won many honours – the W.H. Smith Literary Award (in England) for the most significant contribution to literature in 1987; the Duff Cooper Award (again in England) for the most literary historical work of 1987; the *Age* Book of the Year Award (in Australia) for 1987. For his services to Australian culture Hughes was made AO.

Human Pattern, A, see **WRIGHT, Judith**

Human Toll, a novel by Barbara Baynton (q.v.) published in 1907, depicts the struggles of a bush girl, Ursula Ewart, after she is orphaned and then taken away from the care of Boshy, her father's station hand.

She is raised in town by an unloving Mrs Irvine whose nephew, Andrew Cameron, for a time befriends and protects her; after the death of Mrs Irvine, who has married the rapacious minister, Mr Civil, Boshy returns and is nursed by Ursula through his final illness. Afterwards Ursula returns to her bush home with Mina, a German neighbour who has tricked Andrew into marriage and who has a child by Andrew's partner; appalled by Mina's treatment of the baby, Ursula flees with it into the bush. The child dies, and Ursula becomes both lost and delirious; although in the last ambiguous paragraphs of the novel she seems to be rescued by Andrew; another possibility is that she experiences her final hallucination.

Humbug, a satirical illustrated weekly, was published in Melbourne 1869-70; it was edited by Marcus Clarke (q.v.), whose co-proprietor was Garnet Walch. Other contributors included Charles Bright and James Edward Neild.

HUME, Fergus (1859-1932), born England, trained as a lawyer in NZ and came to Melbourne in 1885. His ambitions to become a dramatist led him to write a novel to attract the attention of theatre managers. The result was the detective story *The Mystery of a Hansom Cab* (q.v., 1886), which was an instant success in Australia and a continuing one in England. Hume, however, sold his rights to *The Mystery of a Hansom Cab* soon after publication of the first edition and did not reap any benefit from the many printings of the novel associated with the Hansom Cab Publishing Company in England. In 1888 Hume settled in England, where he published more than 130 additional novels; of these, only *Madame Midas* (1888), its sequel *Miss Mephistopheles* (1890), *Whom God Hath Joined* (1891) and *High Water Mark* (1911) can be classified as Australian in setting, although several others have Australian associations.

HUME, Hamilton (1797-1873), born Toongabbie near Parramatta, NSW, made several significant journeys of exploration in early colonial times: in 1824 with W.H. Hovell (q.v.) from the Goulburn area of NSW to Corio Bay in Port Phillip, during which they discovered the Murray River, naming it the Hume; and in 1828 with Charles Sturt to the interior of NSW, during which they discovered the Darling River. A controversy between Hume and Hovell over their respective roles in the 1824 expedition led to Hume publishing *A Brief Statement of Facts in Connection with an Overland Expedition from Lake George to Port Phillip in 1824* (1855). William Bland compiled *Journey of Discovery to Port Phillip, New South Wales: By Messrs. W.H. Hovell and Hamilton Hume: in 1824 and 1825* (1831). Jean Prest wrote *Hamilton Hume and William Hovell* (1963) and Alan E.J. Andrews edited *Hume and Hovell 1824* (1981), much of which is devoted to the acrimonious public argument between the two men over their exploits. In 1860 Hume was elected FRGS and spent the latter part of his life as a grazier and magistrate in the Yass district. Joyce Nicholson wrote a fictional account, mainly for children, of Hamilton

Hume's explorations, *Our First Overlander* (1956). Hume is commemorated by the Hume Highway linking Sydney and Melbourne. Frank O'Grady's novel *No Boundary Fence* (1960) is based on the life of Hume.

Hummer, see ***Australian Worker***

HUMPHRIES, Barry (1934-), born Melbourne, was educated at the University of Melbourne, where he appeared in revues. After leaving university he toured Victoria in *Twelfth Night* with Ray Lawler and others, entertaining the company with a party turn in which he impersonated a suburban housewife. Lawler suggested that Humphries incorporate the act into the Melbourne Union Theatre's Christmas revue, and thus in December 1955 Edna Everage (q.v.) made her stage debut in Melbourne. Humphries moved to Sydney, where he established himself as a revue artist with the Phillip Street Theatre. In 1959 he went to England, but before leaving released *Wild Life in Suburbia*, two records of the monologues of Edna and Sandy Stone, the latter a 'decent humdrum little old man' whose character Humphries first created on stage in 1958. Through Edna and Sandy, he satirised the philistinism, emptiness, materialism and pretensions of the Australian suburban middle class.

In England Humphries worked as a theatre and television actor, and in 1962 toured Australia in 'A Nice Night's Entertainment', the first of the one-man shows for which he has become famous. In this and later shows and in several gramophone records of the 1960s, Sandy and Edna remained central to Humphries's presentation of national life, but the introduction of other characters widened the satirical coverage of Australian types: for example, Debbie Thwaite, who spends her entire working holiday in England meeting other Australians; Neil Singleton, whose monologues reveal him as a trendy and manipulative academic; Martin Agrippa, a film-maker who has won the coveted Bronze Scrotum at the Helsinki International Experimental Film Biennale; and Buster Thompson, an ex-public school slob who is pub-crawling his way around Europe. Although their social backgrounds are different, Buster is the prototype of Barry (Bazza) McKenzie (q.v.), a character in a comic strip written by Humphries and drawn by Nicholas Garland which was published for over a decade in the English satirical magazine *Private Eye*. The strip, which focuses on the innocent Bazza's search for sexual satisfaction and his gargantuan capacity for alcohol, cleverly exploits mutual English-Australian prejudices, with the Poms characteristically portrayed as unwashed and avaricious and the Ockers, like Bazza, as unsophisticated vulgarians. Selections from the strip were published in 1968, 1971 and 1979 as well as *The Adventures of Barry McKenzie* (1973) and *Barry McKenzie Holds His Own* (1974), in which are published the scripts written by Humphries and Bruce Beresford for two McKenzie films (1972, 1974). *The Complete Barry McKenzie* appeared appropriately in the bicentennial year 1988.

By the end of the 1960s Humphries's reputation was firmly established in Australia and abroad; in the next decade that reputation was consolidated, particularly in England, with a further series of one-man shows. In 1971 Sandy 'died' while his wife, Beryl, was overseas, although he reappeared in Limbo in 1974 and in 1978, reporting on the response to his death. Characters which Humphries created later include Lance Boyle, a wheeler-dealing union official, Colin Cartwright, self-made businessman and self-pitying father, Morrie O'Connor, a used-picture salesman and Sir Les Patterson (q.v.), Australia's cultural ambassador at the Court of St James whose view of the 'Yartz', a common Humphries target, is presented in *Les Patterson's Australia* (1978) and his *The Traveller's Tool* (1985). Sandy Stone's monologues are preserved in *Shades of Sandy Stone* (1989) and *The Life and Death of Sandy Stone* (1990), and the monologues of a range of characters in John Allen's compilation *The Humour of Barry Humphries* (1984). Despite these later creations, Humphries has been increasingly identified with Edna Everage, who has evolved from the pretentious, self-opinionated suburban housewife of 1955 into an outrageous international superstar. A 'gladdimaniac', made DBE by Gough Whitlam in the second McKenzie film in 1974, eight years before Humphries's own award of AO, she assails her television and stage audiences in two hemispheres, dispenses advice in the *Australian Women's Weekly* and is the 'author' of *Dame Edna's Coffee Table Book* (1976) and *Dame Edna's Bedside Companion* (1982) as well as an autobiography, *My Gorgeous Life* (1989). Under his own name, Humphries has compiled a controversial anthology, *Bizarre* (1965); *The Barry Humphries Book of Innocent Austral Verse* (1968), a collection of 'bad' verse which includes poems of Barcroft Boake, E.J. Brady and Louise Mack as well as more thoroughly primitive poets; *Barry Humphries' Treasury of Australian Kitsch* (1980); the important retrospective *A Nice Night's Entertainment: Sketches and Monologues 1956–1981* (1981); and *Neglected Poems and Other Creatures* (1991), which includes his own and his characters' verse.

Much admired by other writers who have drawn on suburban idioms, Humphries has been identified as 'Australia's only true Augustan' and his material described as 'Joyce Grenfell rewritten by Jonathan Swift'. On stage he has been part-satirist, part-caricaturist, and part-music-hall entertainer, sometimes in league with, sometimes antagonistic to, his audience. His creations are defined and exposed by their names, their dress, their possessions and obsessions, and by their argot. As well as finding the precise identifying phrase (e.g. Sandy having a 'bit of strife parking the vehicle', Sir Les nudging his audience 'Ya with me?'), Humphries brings a creative imagination to bear on Australian idiom, and probably influenced later playwrights such as Alexander Buzo and David Williamson. In particular, some of his phrases, notably the alliterative euphemisms for urination which characterise the speech of Barry McKenzie, have become part of the Australian lexicon. For much of his career Humphries has attacked, with an ambivalent mixture of cruelty and affection, the pretension, self-centredness, prejudices and vulgarity of his imaginary Australian characters, 'accurately based on real people who

have never lived'. The most affectionate portrait has been that of Sandy Stone, in whose making Humphries was influenced by Gertrude Stein's *Three Lives* and Samuel Beckett's *Watt*; Sandy's popularity has been attributed to the depth and sympathy of Humphries's characterisation, which has helped him tap a rich vein of nostalgia in his audiences. The cruellest portraits have led to criticisms that Humphries is misanthropic and reactionary, presenting his overseas audiences with an Australia that is dated and even distorted, an issue raised in Jack Hibberd's *Breakfast at Windsor* (*Meanjin*, 1981). John Lahr's study of Humphries's personality and comic style, *Dame Edna and the Rise of Western Civilization* (1991) and Peter Coleman's *The Real Barry Humphries* (1990) give valuable insights into the sources of his dramatic creativity, but the most revealing study of the roots of his iconoclasm has been provided by Humphries himself in his autobiography, *More Please* (1992). A self-conscious portrait of his elusive self, *More Please* intensively recalls the oppressive dullness of his Melbourne childhood and the even more oppressive years at Melbourne Grammar School where he preserved his individuality by conducting guerilla-type subversion of the School Spirit.

HUNGERFORD, T.A.G. (Thomas Arthur Guy) (1915–), born Perth, WA, grew up in that city during the 1930s Depression and served in the commandos in the Second World War in New Guinea, New Britain and Bougainville. After the war he went with the occupation forces to Japan where his novel, *Sowers of the Wind*, is set. Back in Australia he edited the Australian War Memorial's *Stand Easy* series, writing six of the stories himself. He then freelanced, writing for the *Bulletin*, and in 1954 joined the Australian News and Information Bureau, accompanying the Australian Antarctic expedition in 1954–55. He spent a period as press officer in the New York office of the Australian Consul-General. After his resignation from the bureau in 1967 he travelled in Asia, then returned to WA, where he compiled a book on that State titled *A Million Square: Western Australia* (1969). Subsequently he was a public relations officer for the WA government.

His first book published (third written) is the war novel *The Ridge and the River* (1952) (see War Literature). Based on the Australian commandos' campaign in Bougainville in the Solomon Islands, the novel captures the horror, not only of man fighting against man, which it does with stark bestiality, but also of man attempting to survive the intolerable jungle. *Sowers of the Wind* (1954) grew out of his concern for the mistreatment of the Japanese by the Australian occupying forces after the war. He believed that they were 'sowing a wind of hatred for the future'. Their exploitations of the conquered Japanese, economically and sexually, reveal such a distasteful side to the character of the young Australian troops that Hungerford's publishers, Angus & Robertson, kept *Sowers of the Wind*, written in the late 1940s, back until 1954. Hungerford's three other novels are *Riverslake* (1953), set in a Canberra post-war immigration camp and concerned with the deplorable conditions experienced by

European migrants; *Shake the Golden Bough* (1963), in which the central character, Charlie Dangerfield, a handsome drifter loosely modelled on Australian boxer Tony Madigan, plays on his physical charms to win a niche for himself in the brittle Manhattan society; and *Code Word Macao* (1991), which draws on a year spent in Macao in the 1960s. Hungerford has also written collections of short stories, *Wong Chu and the Queen's Letterbox* (1977), *Stories from Suburban Road* (1984), autobiographical fiction based on affectionate memories of his childhood and adolesence in South Perth, 1920–38; and *Hungerford* (1989), edited by Peter Cowan; and two collections of reminiscences, *A Knockabout with a Slouch Hat* (1985), which deals with his experiences in wartime New Guinea and post-war Japan and Canberra, 1942–51, and *Red Rover All Over* (1986), which ranges from the 1950s to the 1980s. He has also written several radio plays, e.g. 'Help Me Cut Up a Cat' (1972) and 'Looking After Bert' (1976); a stage play, 'The Day It All Ended' (1989); and a book for children, *Swagbelly Birdswatcher and the Prince of Siam* (1989). The inaugural T.A.G. Hungerford Prize in 1990 was won by Brenda Walker's (q.v.) novel *Crush*. He is a member of the Order of Australia.

HUNT, Hugh (1911–), born Surrey, England, was educated at Oxford and the Sorbonne. Director of the Abbey theatre in Dublin 1935–38, of the Bristol Old Vic 1938–48, and the London Old Vic 1950–53, he came to Australia in 1955 as the first executive director of the Australian Elizabethan Theatre Trust, a position he held until 1960. From 1961 to 1977 he was professor of drama at the University of Manchester and was made emeritus professor and CBE in 1977. Instrumental in the founding of NIDA, he also did much to encourage professional theatre companies and the staging of Australian plays. Some of his ideas on drama are expressed in the second series of Kathleen Robinson lectures on drama and the theatre at the University of Sydney, published in 1960 and titled *The Making of Australian Theatre*.

HUNTER, John (1737–1821), born Leith, Scotland, the son of a shipmaster, went to sea in 1754. After extensive experience with the Royal Navy in North America and the West Indies, he was appointed second-in-command of the First Fleet and was in command of the main convoy for part of the journey to Botany Bay. Following the establishment of the settlement at Port Jackson, Hunter was engaged on surveying and magisterial duties, and undertook journeys for Governor Arthur Phillip to the Cape of Good Hope and Norfolk Island, where he was stranded for almost twelve months in 1790 after his ship was wrecked. He returned to England in 1792, published *An Historical Journal of the Transactions at Port Jackson and Norfolk Island* (q.v.) in 1793 and a year later was appointed as Phillip's replacement. He assumed office in September 1795. During his five years as governor he struggled to retain control of the Colony against the power of the NSW Corps and John Macarthur. Recalled in 1799, he handed over to his successor, Philip Gidley King, in 1800 and returned to England, where he vindicated his conduct in *Governor Hunter's Remarks on the Causes of the Colonial Expense of the Establishment of New South Wales* (1802). Hunter is commemorated by the Hunter River; he appears as a character in Eleanor Dark's *The Timeless Land* (1941) and *Storm of Time* (1948), in Mary Gaunt's *As the Whirlwind Passeth* (1923) and in Catherine Gaskin's *Sara Dane* (1954). B.R. Blaze wrote the biography of Hunter, *Great Scot* (1982). The National Library of Australia published *The Hunter Sketchbook: Birds & Flowers of New South Wales drawn on the Spot in 1788, 89 & 90 By Captain John Hunter RN of the First Fleet* in 1989.

Hunter River, discovered in 1797 by Lieutenant John Shortland and named after the then governor of NSW, John Hunter, rises in the Mount Royal Range and after flowing south-west, then south-east, for 470 kilometres, enters the Pacific Ocean at Newcastle. Associated with sheep- and cattle-raising, thoroughbred horse breeding, coal-mining and wine-making, the Hunter also has many literary associations. Judith Wright's original ancestor in Australia, George Wyndham, established the homestead Dalwood there, as she describes in her book *The Generations of Men* (1962) and in her poem 'Old House', both of which describe the Hunter environment in pioneer times. Charles Harpur was associated with the Hunter, living at Patrick's Plains (now Singleton) and the village of Jerry's Plains. Much of the early history of the Hunter is in the papers (University of New England) of Henry and Grace Dangar, who established the estate of Neotsfield at Patrick's Plains and were the district's chief pioneering family. See also Hunter Valley Poets. The standard history is W. Allan Wood's *Dawn in the Valley: the Story of Settlement in the Hunter River Valley to 1833* (1972).

Hunter Valley Poets first emerged as an identifiable literary group with the publishing by Norman Talbot of *XI Hunter Valley Poets + VII* (1966) and the anthology *Hunter Valley Poets* (1973), which presents not only the work of established and lesser-known writers of the region but also a sampling of poetry from schoolchildren. *IV Hunter Valley Poets* (1975) was a first collection from each of four poets of the region, T.H. Naisby, Maureen Bonomini, Denis King and Ross Bennett. T.H. Naisby, more than a poet of a particular place, has also published *The Fabulous Dross* (1979), a second and more expanded collection of verse. Ross Bennett, in addition to publishing another work, *River* (1980), a long poem set mainly in the Upper Allyn, a rainforest area near the Barrington Tops, edited *This Place: Poetry of the Hunter Valley* (1980), an anthology of the prose and poetry of thirty-three writers. Bennett's anthology was accompanied by *The Companion to This Place: Studies in Hunter Valley Poetry and Glossary of Poetic Terms* (1980), which was intended for the valley's secondary school students. *V Hunter Valley Poets* (1978) presents another five first collections, those of Jean Talbot, Christopher Pollnitz, David McQualter, Jess Dyce and Tim McGee. Jean Talbot has also edited *Huntress: Women Poets of the*

Hunter Valley (1981) and Norman Talbot and Zeny Giles have edited *Contrast and Relief: Short Stories of the Hunter Valley* (1981). *Riverrun*, a little magazine produced by Keith Russell and Brian Musgrove, published some of the more experimental of the Hunter Valley poets. Ken Stone published *Hunter* (1980), a collection of poems which expresses his affection for the landscape and people of the region.

HURLEY, Frank (1885–1962), born Sydney, was official photographer to the first Australasian Antarctic Expedition led by Douglas Mawson 1911–13, and in 1914–16 was photographer to the Imperial Trans-Antarctic Expedition. He accompanied the AIF in France in the First World War as an official war photographer with the rank of captain, a title he retained. He was with Ross and Keith Smith on the Australian section of their England–Australia flight; in 1920 he produced the film of this journey, *The Ross Smith Flight*. Between the wars he filmed in New Guinea and was chief cameraman for Cinesound Productions Limited 1932–36, filming such productions as *The Squatter's Daughter* (1933). In the Second World War he was an official photographer for the AIF. A collection of his photographs of both world wars, accompanied by excerpts from his diaries, *Hurley at War*, was published in 1986. His photographic books on Australia include *Sydney* (1948), *The Blue Mountains and Jenolan Caves* (1952), *Sydney from the Sky* (1952), *Tasmania* (1953), *Western Australia* (1953) and *Australia* (1955). Frank Legg and Toni Hurley wrote the biographical *Once More on My Adventure* (1966).

Hussy, see **Feminism and Australian Literature**

HUTCHINSON, Garrie (1949–), born Melbourne, was involved with the La Mama writers' workshops and is a freelance journalist and writer who was speechwriter for the former Australian prime minister, R.J. Hawke. His published poetry includes *Dart Objects: Poured Concrete, 1967–71* (1971), *Nothing Unsayable Said Right: 50 Poems, 1968–72* (1974) and *Terror Australis: Poems* (1975). He has also written numerous works on sport, including *The Barracker's Bible* (1983, with Jack Hibberd), and *Great Australian Football Stories* (1989, formerly *Great Australian Book of Football Stories*). Co-founder of Hoopla Theatre (later Playbox) in 1976 and the Melbourne Writers' Theatre in 1981, he has written for stage, television and film.

His plays include *Fifteen Rounds with Gorgeous George* (1985, published 1987), 'Angela Gets It On', and 'The Dinner Party' (1986). A member of the Theatre Board of the Australia Council 1973–74, he was arts editor of the *National Times* 1986–87.

HUTCHINSON, George (1930–), born Sydney, is a graduate of Sydney University and has worked as a clerk and a teacher. His first full-length play, 'My Shadow and Me', was produced in 1974 and was followed by 'Island on the Rocks' (1977) and a trilogy on turn-of-the-century Australian idealists. *No Room for Dreamers* (1981), which was widely performed in Australia and at the 1980 Edinburgh and Dublin theatre festivals before touring Great Britain and is the first play of the trilogy, is a study of the life of William Chidley. The second, 'The Ballad of Billy Lane' (1982), explores William Lane's utopian endeavours, and the third, *Henry & Peter, Henry & Me* (1985), with music by Terence Clarke, focuses on Louisa Lawson and her relationship with the men in her life, Henry Albury, her father, Peter Larsen, her husband and Henry Lawson, her son. Hutchinson's other plays include 'Good Times Coming', 'Fair and Tender Ladies', and 'Natural Mystic'.

HUTTON, Geoffrey (1909–85), born Southampton, England, came to Australia at the age of 14 and was educated at the University of Melbourne, where his work as editor and writer for *MUM (Melbourne University Magazine)* brought him to the attention of the editor of the *Argus* newspaper. He worked for the *Argus* until 1954 when he joined the *Age*. In the Second World War he was a correspondent in New Guinea and Europe. London correspondent for the *Age* 1957–59, he was a senior leader-writer, theatre critic, book-reviewer and columnist until his retirement in 1974. He continued to contribute book reviews to the *Age* and theatre reviews to the *Australian* in retirement. His publications include a biography of Adam Lindsay Gordon (1978), a history of the first twenty years of the Melbourne Theatre Company, *It Won't Last a Week!* (1975), and short biographies of Nellie Melba (1962) and C.J. Dennis (1976). He also edited a book on Australia's environmentally precious areas, *Australia's Natural Heritage* (1981) and, with Les Tanner, a selection of articles, cartoons, and advertisements from the *Age* to celebrate its 125th anniversary, *125 Years of Age* (1979).

I

I Can Jump Puddles, a childhood autobiography by Alan Marshall (q.v.), was first published in 1955. Outstandingly popular both in Australia and overseas, the book has been translated into several languages and was produced as an award-winning film in Czechoslovakia in 1970 and as a television series in Australia in 1981. The story of a young boy's adjustment to paralysis of the legs after contracting polio at the age of 6, it is also a vivid picture of Victorian country life between the wars. Particularly memorable are Marshall's portraits of a range of individuals, from the men whom the boy encounters in hospital to the swagmen who pass through the little settlement of Turalla; to Mrs Carruthers, who is rich enough to own an Abbot buggy; to the schoolchildren who are both a challenge and a help in his adjustment. These include the stalwart Maggie Mulligan, who on one occasion carries him home in a fireman's lift; Joe Carmichael, with whom Alan hunts for rabbits, and his inconvenient smaller brother Andy (both also figure in Marshall's short stories); and Freddie Hawk, who is a champion at marbles. Determined that his crutches will not be a hindrance, Alan proves himself at fighting, hunting, climbing and swimming, and even teaches himself to ride a horse. Entranced by his father's tales of the bush, he goes on a week-long trip with a teamster, Peter McLeod, and is impressed by the examples of bush mateship that he witnesses. Most striking of all is Marshall's portrait of his father, a horse-breaker, who represents to the boy all that is self-reliant, forthright and compassionate about the Australian rural tradition. The narrative closes as the family prepares to move to Melbourne, cars having begun to replace horses and Alan having won an accountancy scholarship.

Identity, also titled *Aboriginal and Islander Identity* and *Aboriginal and Thursday Islander Identity*, was established in 1971. Its original editor was Barrie Ovenden; later editors included Jack Davis, Michael Anderson, John Newfong and Les Malezer. From a strongly aggressive stance, it reported widely on significant political and social issues affecting Aborigines. It also did much to foster Aboriginal talent in the creative arts, consistently publishing poetry, short stories, and myths, publicising Aboriginal artists and reviewing Aboriginal literature. Its funding was withdrawn in 1982 as a result of what was considered its over-political bias; it then ceased publication.

IDRIESS, Ion (1889–1979) was born at Waverley, Sydney, but educated in several NSW country towns. He attended the Broken Hill School of Mines, started work in an assay office, and at about the age of 16 began a nomadic existence which lasted for a quarter of a century and provided him with the experience which informs his writing. Following a spell as a seaman on coastal ships around Newcastle he worked as a rabbit-exterminator, boundary-rider, rouseabout and drover in western NSW, then mined for opals at Lightning Ridge; while there he began contributing paragraphs to the *Bulletin*'s 'Aboriginalities' column and other journals under such pseudonyms as 'Gouger', 'Up North' and 'Emucrest'. After further experience as gold-fossicker, pearler and station hand in northern Queensland, the Northern Territory, the Torres Strait Islands, Papua and the Great Barrier Reef, he served in the First World War with the Australian Light Horse. Idriess claimed to have 'encircled' Australia in the 1920s, travelling from Central Australia through south-west Queensland to the Gulf country and then across to the Northern Territory and WA; among other occupations he was explorer, surveyor, and hunter of buffalos and crocodiles. In 1927, while on a trip to Sydney, he was encouraged by Alec Chisholm to write up a diary he had kept while marooned on an island off the Queensland coast. The resulting work, *Madman's Island* (1927), was a failure, principally because of the love story which George Robertson (2) had insisted Idriess incorporate in the plot and which was excised from the second successful edition (1938).

After the publication of *Madman's Island* Idriess returned to the outback, but about 1930 settled in Sydney and was a freelance contributor to the *Sunday Pictorial* and other Sydney journals when his mining manual, *Prospecting for Gold*, was published in 1931. In the same year came his first great success, *Lasseter's Last Ride*, an account of the expedition which searched for the rich gold lead which Harold Lasseter (q.v.) claimed to have found some years before. Over the next four decades, writing mainly in the Angus & Robertson office, Idriess became a household name, with more than forty books published; many of them went through several reprints. The best known are

Flynn of the Inland (1932), *The Desert Column* (1932), *Gold-Dust and Ashes* (1933), *Drums of Mer* (1933), *The Cattle King* (1936), *Forty Fathoms Deep* (1937), *Head-hunters of the Coral Sea* (1940), *Nemarluk: King of the Wilds* (1941), a series of six military handbooks in the *Australian Guerrilla* series (1942), *Horrie the Wog-Dog* (1945), *Outlaws of the Leopolds* (1952) and *The Red Chief* (1953). With the exception of 1943 he published at least a book a year from 1931 to 1964, and was made OBE in 1968. Although he kept writing until the end of the 1960s, his heyday was the period from the 1930s Depression until the end of the Second World War.

Several of Idriess's books are novels, e.g. *Drums of Mer*, *Forty Fathoms Deep*, but in the main he wrote basically factual stories, imaginatively re-created, with the invented conversations that are a feature also of the works of Frank Clune. The main territory of his writing is outback and coastal Australia, the Torres Strait Islands and Papua. His subjects include mining, pearling, outback pioneers such as John Flynn and Sidney Kidman, Aboriginal freedom fighters such as Pidgin and Nemarluk, and the war experiences of Australians; *The Desert Column*, based on Idriess's Gallipoli diary, is the first view of the First World War from the point of view of the ordinary soldier. Idriess wrote best when informed by his own experience, combining this with romantic portrayals of heroic individuals from Australia's adventurous past, with a snappy prose style which effectively employs Australian idiom, and with an optimism about the future of the country; several of his works argue for the development of the resources of inland Australia, and several Onward Australia Leagues were established after his *Onward Australia* was published in 1944. His portraits of Aboriginal Australians reflect the prejudices of the time, although he admires their courage and acumen, notes the cohesion of Aboriginal culture, and documents the effects of the Aboriginal–European culture clash. As well as informing an Australian audience about little-known parts of the continent and its near neighbours, he carried on the *Bulletin's* bush ethos and played a significant part in fashioning the legends surrounding the Australian Light Horse and such individuals as Flynn, Kidman and Lasseter.

IGGULDEN, John (1917–   ), born Brighton, Victoria, entered the family's Melbourne engineering business as a youth but has been able to give substantial periods to writing. His published works include *Breakthrough* (1960), a futuristic novel which is partly thriller and partly science fiction; *The Storms of Summer* (1960), a novel set on the Australian east-coast fishing grounds and concerned with the struggle between migrant and Australian fishermen; *The Clouded Sky* (1965), a complex novel in which he examines the proposition that a man needs relationships with various women – passionate, romantic and domestic – and in which the sport of gliding provides a background drawn from Iggulden's personal experience (he was Australian national gliding champion 1959–60); and *Dark Stranger* (1965), a race-relations novel demon-strating the need for the White race to accept the Black on its own merits and for the Black to take pride in Black culture. Iggulden has also published two volumes in his series *The Promised Land Papers* (1986, 1988), which projects his economic vision for Australia.

Illustrated Australian Magazine (Ham's Illustrated Australian Magazine), the first Australian illustrated journal, was published monthly in Melbourne 1850–52; it included creative writing and reviews, and its contributors included William à Beckett, William Westgarth and editor, Thomas Ham (1821–70), a lithographer and engraver. The *Illustrated Australian Magazine* followed eight years after the establishment of the *Illustrated London News*, of which there was an Australian edition in 1888–91 published by W.J. Akhurst 1888–90, and was itself succeeded by several other journals of similar title in the second half of the nineteenth century. They include the *Illustrated Australian Mail* (1861–62), which had Eugene von Guérard and William Strutt as artists; the *Illustrated Australian News*, a Melbourne monthly 1862–96, which incorporated the *Illustrated Melbourne Post* (1862–68); the *Illustrated Adelaide Post* (1867–74); the *Illustrated Adelaide News*, a monthly which was published 1875–80, became *Frearson's Monthly Illustrated Adelaide News* 1880–84 and the *Pictorial Australian* 1885–95; and the *Illustrated Sydney News*, published in two series, 1853–55 (weekly), 1864–94 (monthly 1864–?88, fortnightly ?1888–93, weekly 1893–94), edited in the 1880s by P.J. Holdsworth. These journals generally carried literary contributions.

Imago, a literature magazine originally published twice annually by the School of Communications, the Queensland University of Technology, supported by the Queensland Arts Council, began in 1989. It emphasises Queensland writing and culture but also publishes other Australian writing and writing in translation. From 1992 it has been published by the UQP in association with the above and with assistance from the Australia Council. Its editor from No. 2 has been Philip Neilsen. Bruce Dawe is consulting editor.

Immigrant Experience in Australian Literature. Is the immigrant experience ultimately an invigorating or a mutilating one? This question, applied personally or nationally, has been a recurring theme in Australian literature, but it took almost 200 years before the relationship of minority groups to our perceived national culture came to be regarded as a central issue. Pain, poignancy and bitterness, and courage, vitality and hope – these are the polar tugs and pulls that register the immigrant experience: on the one hand, physical displacement can result in the anguish of rejection, alienation and fragmentation; on the other, it can offer release from (social or political) oppression, a sense of critical distance and a fresh start with a new identity. Migrant writing in Australia traces the process of learning to live with these contradictions.

While it is often said that all non-Aboriginal Australians come from an immigrant tradition, there are important distinctions to be made. Without denying the authenticity of the sense of strangeness expressed by the first British settlers in Australia, it is important to remember that they brought with them their cultural values, and their language. They did not experience the sense of dislocation and disjunction so often captured in the writing of later immigrants – refugees from central Europe or Indochina, for instance, whose minority and outsider status was unquestioningly assumed by the aggressively Anglophone ethos of the dominant Australian culture. It is not surprising to find, then, that early accounts of immigrant life, such as Charles Rowcroft's *Tale of the Colonies; or, The Adventures of an Emigrant* (1843), are untroubled by the rifts and disjunctions of real exile. And Catherine Helen Spence's novel *Clara Morison* (1854), while it focuses on Clara's experience of isolation and separateness, suggests that much of her sense of homelessness arises from the male-dominated society she found in Australia. On the whole, early immigrant literature emphasised the positive, even romantic, aspect of life in Australia: see Charles Harpur's poem 'The Emigrant's Vision', for example. Memoirs, diaries and letters often provide a better sense of the range of early immigrant experience than traditional literature. There is a tendency among some literary scholars to consider memoirs and letters of sociological or historical interest only, assigning them to a lower position on the cultural ladder. Lucy Frost's collection *No Place For A Nervous Lady* (1984) is enough to challenge the assumption that diaries and letters simply document unmediated experience, as is Joseph Jenkins' *Diary of a Welsh Swagman 1869–1894* (1975). Annie Maria Baxter's *Memories of the Past, by a Lady in Australia* (1873) is far from mere recording, being distilled from thirty-five volumes of diaries in which she documented her extensive experience in Hobart and New South Wales.

Within the monoculture that was colonial Australia, the margins were occupied by the Irish. In an attempt to redress what he sees as the subsequently distorted account of the Irish in Australia, T.J. Kiernan allows their letters and memoirs to speak for themselves in *The Irish Exiles in Australia* (1954). More recently, Patrick O'Farrell's *Letters from Irish Australia 1825–1929* (1984) builds on Kiernan's work. John O'Brien and Pauric Travers (eds.), *The Irish Emigrant Experience in Australia* (1991) sheds new light on our cultural history. See also O'Farrell's argument in *The Irish in Australia* (1986), that the Irish settlers' refusal to accept a monolithic culture laid the foundations for the pluralistic society Australia has become. While many Irish settlers were illiterate or semi-literate, their letters home must have emphasised the positive side of the immigrant experience: by the late 1830s Dublin Castle was alarmed by reports that people were committing crimes in order to be transported. *A True History of Bernard Reilly* (1839), the Castle's attempt at deterrence, emphasising the horror and misery of convict life, was widely read and enjoyed in Ireland. Similarly, in poems by Francis Macnamara ('Frank the

Poet'), such as 'A Convict's Tour to Hell' and the better known 'Convict's Lament' (or 'Moreton Bay'), the elegiac Irish sense of exile is tempered by an adventurous urge to cross social and political as well as geographical frontiers.

Australian fiction remained more concerned with reaffirming a romantic view of life than with recognising the immigrants' dilemma. 'Henry Handel Richardson' broke new ground in this regard with her novel trilogy *The Fortunes of Richard Mahony* (1917–1929), which confronts the disabling and overpowering effects of Australian life on some of its new settlers. 'Richardson' was not writing as an immigrant herself but, like many of our writers, as a child of immigrant parents. She had also, through her travels, discovered first-hand the richness of European cultural life. In her trilogy a number of figures, from different backgrounds, suffer a sense of loss and alienation (Long Jim, Tangye), but the focus of the novel is on Richard Mahony, an Irishman in Australia at a time when the term 'immigrant' was unknown. Like 'Richardson's' father, Mahony considered himself an 'emigrant': the centre was deemed to be Britain, and Australia's marginal status was unquestioned. Mahony's restless moving from place to place brings him no nearer to the sense of belonging that eludes him. 'Richardson' deals with one of the imperatives of exile: the emigrant's belief or hope that returning 'home' will heal the split, and the discovery that 'home', in its original sense, is forever lost. After his death, Mahony is fittingly buried within earshot of the ever-changing tides.

A steady flow of Anglo-Celtic immigrants arrived in the early decades of this century, the result of both imperial sentiment and poor social conditions in Britain, and through land settlement schemes many urban dwellers found themselves struggling to readjust to life in a rugged and often hostile rural environment. Interestingly, any bewilderment or sense of dislocation they experienced is not registered in the literature of the time, which is notably insular, conservative and unquestioning. It was not until the arrival of Jewish and European refugees in the 1930s that the complexity of the immigrant experience began to be explored in our literature. Even then, the settled Anglo-Celtic population was too preoccupied with attempts to define themselves as Australians to be receptive to alien newcomers who muddied rather than clarified the picture.

Of the non-Anglo-Celtic traditions in Australia, one of the strongest is the Jewish – and within that minority are a number of minorities: Russian, Polish, Hungarian, German, Austrian and of course British Jews. Approximately 80 000 people in Australia are of Jewish descent (and over half of them live in Melbourne). In the nineteenth century most Jewish immigrants were British. Hilary Rubinstein's history *The Jews in Victoria* (1986) records how these Anglo-Jews did their best to prevent the immigration of European Jews, because they feared that the presence of such distinctively foreign Jews in Australia might encourage the growth of anti-Semitism. For a different perspective on the Anglo-Jewish immigrant experience see Barbara Falk, *No Other Home: an Anglo-Jewish Story*

1833–1987 (1988). A comprehensive history of 200 years of Jewish settlement in Australia is offered by Suzanne D. Rutland in *Edge of the Diaspora* (1988). Amirah Inglis, whose award-winning *Amirah: an un-Australian Childhood* (1983) begins 'I am an Australian perforce and by chance', records how her childhood as a non-religious Jew in Australia was influenced by the arrival of the 'reffos' – Austrian and German refugees from Nazi anti-Semitism. She was embarrassed by their difference, yet forced to confront the fact that she was one of them, 'From 1936 to 1939', she writes, 'Hitler kept us all Jews'. Another interesting account of growing up Jewish in Australia is Elisabeth Wynhausen's *Manly Girls* (1989). In the history of Jewish-Australian writing, Judah Waten's *Alien Son* (1952) occupies a key place; it has long been accepted as part of our mainstream literature, even featuring in Geoffrey Dutton's *The Australian Collection: Australia's Greatest Books* (1985). Waten came to Australia as a child, and the stories that make up *Alien Son* describe the experiences of a Russian/Jewish immigrant family in the early years of this century. Unlike some immigrant writing, these stories are not direct and unmediated autobiography (though they are often read that way). They are a more distanced and literary attempt to capture the way immigrants necessarily establish a new imaginative relationship with the world. The title points to the ambivalence the book explores: the alien (not native) son is part of a community trying to preserve its Russian and Yiddish traditions, yet he considers himself a 'son' of this soil, too. Waten's parallel between the defencelessness of the immigrant and the helplessness of the child, with adolescence and growth to manhood serving as a metaphor for adjustment to a new way of seeing and being in the world, is a trope since used by many immigrant writers. The 'alien son' is also very much a biological son, and Waten subtly captures the way in which 'Mother' and 'Father's' cultural loss carries with it the son's cultural gain. Written in English, *Alien Son* is both an exploration of the immigrant experience of estrangement and a testament to Waten's assimilation. The stories of another Jewish-Australian author, Serge Liberman, trace the changes in perspective as three generations of Australian Jews, pre- and post-war immigrants, try to adjust to a new life without abandoning old traditions in *On Firmer Shores* (1981), *A Universe of Clowns* (1983) and *The Life That I Have Led* (1986).

Assimilation – the merging of diverse cultural elements until all become 'similar' – was official policy during the peak years of immigration that followed the Second World War. Thirty thousand immigrants arrived in 1947, many of them from Central Europe, and there is no doubt about the extreme Anglophone bias exhibited towards these 'new Australians', as Arthur Calwell dubbed them. In November 1946 Calwell publicly expressed his hope that 'for every foreign migrant there will be ten people from the United Kingdom'. Some of the most thought-provoking literature of the immigrant experience deals with the culture shock suffered by refugees from war-torn Europe when they found themselves in a provincial and narrow-minded country which seemed to

them devoid of cultural activity, insensitive to racial difference and aggressively monolinguistic. This experience has been gradually written into our literature, by the refugees themselves and particularly their children. Representative of these accounts is Andrew Riemer's *Inside Outside: Life Between Two Worlds* (1992), which describes how the initial relief of the authors' parents at being safe, and their bright hope for the future in a new land, quickly dissolved in the reality of life in Sydney at the end of the 1940s. With wry humour Riemer describes his early schooling here, the Hungarian-Jewish family's struggles with a new language, and the defensive re-creation of the old culture within the new as immigrants grouped together in racial 'islands' or 'ghettoes'. To the Riemers, what had at first appeared to be a haven soon came to be seen as 'a land of sleepwalkers'. Yet *Inside Outside* is not sentimental; Riemer sees too clearly the dangers of living in the past, harbouring a romantic yearning for the lost home. Implicitly, his book asks 'who were the real sleepwalkers?' An 'alien son' himself, Riemer mastered the language, returned to Europe to find that he felt at least partly Australian, and ended up making Australia his home (and teaching English literature!). Maria Lewitt's autobiographical novel *No Snow in December* (1985), which won a NSW Premier's Award, tells the tale of a Polish-Jewish family who migrated to Australia in 1949. Along with the problems associated with language, housing and employment, the family also had to cope with exploitative fellow Poles. Sometimes it is hard to tell whether the discrimination they experience is real or imagined but this story of the gradual process of becoming Australian is told with ironic verve. A more humorous but lighter tale of Polish immigration is Janka Abrami's *Zat izz Apples, Sir* (1986), an autobiographical account of life in a Melbourne milk bar. Anna Kosloff came to Australia as a refugee from Russia in 1945. Aided by her Australian-born daughter, Anna Bilbrough, she tells her story in *Stateless* (1983; reissued 1989). From Yugoslavia, Magda Bozic migrated to Australia after the war. Her story, *Gather Your Dreams* (1984), is not a horrific tale of hardship and overt discrimination but an account of day-to-day incidents which suggests very powerfully the slow and painful process of settling into a new life. Dutch-Australian Loló Houbein's *Walk a Barefoot Road* (1988) is a moving and readable novel of a representative immigrant experience.

Italian immigrants have been contributing to Australian culture since the 1850s, when adventurers, missionaries, political exiles and educated professionals settled here. John O'Grady (as Nino Culotta) falsely stereotyped Italian immigrants as rather slow-witted labourers in his novel *They're a Weird Mob* (1957). Fortunately, popular perceptions of cultural difference are fluid and changeable – a point made by both Gianfranco Cresciani in *Migrants or Mates* (1988) and Robert Pascoe in *Buongiorno Australia* (1987). Pascoe points out that poetry has been the medium for some of the sharpest expression of the immigrant experience by Italo-Australian writers. M. Coreno's *Yellow Sun* (1980) and S. Bacsi's *Would I Say Hello* (1982) are pertinent in this context, as are works by Lino

Conchas, Paul Depasquale, Franco Paiso and Luigi Strano. Like many Central Europeans, some Italo-Australian writers find the amplitude of prose more suitable to their needs. V. Ercole's novel *No Escape* (1932), set at the turn of the century, describes in a rather leisurely way the settlement and assimilation of an Italian doctor. A very different novel is Rosa Cappiello's *Oh Lucky Country* (1984). Cappiello's immigrant is female, working-class and single, and she rebels against the resultant inferior status imposed on her by the dominant culture in Australia. Her rebellion is linguistic: in a passionate, mood-swinging and at times scatological monologue she pours invective on the attitudes and values she finds oppressive and offensive, and in the process of asserting her own values – and celebrating her difference – she risks the charge of being offensive herself. The vigour, aggression, irony and humour in this novel do not hide the pain of the immigrant experience. Rather, the pain is expressed instead of repressed, and the concept of assimilation is thoroughly and energetically interrogated. Pino Bosi is quite a well-known figure in Australian cultural life. His novel *Australia Cane* (1971), about the experiences of an Italian immigrant's first years in Australia in the 1950s, is unsurprising; it ought to be read alongside the author's *Farewell Australia* (published the following year) in which, leaving after twenty years here, he criticises the attitudes and values of Australia in the 1960s. In *Who is Afraid of the Ethnic Wolf?* (1986) Bosi examines Australian society's attitude to multiculturalism and ethnic broadcasting in the 1980s. Memoirs by Italo-Australians abound. Some examples are O. Bonutto's *A Migrant's Story* (1963), M. Triaca's tale of her grandmother, *Amelia: a Long Journey* (1985), R.A. Baggio's humorous *The Shoe in My Cheese* (1989) and E. Ciccotosto's *Emma; a Translated Life* (1990). Especially recommended is Alfredo Strano's *Luck Without Joy* (1986), a fascinating insight into the struggles of Italian immigrants to make a success in an alien land.

'It cannot be denied that most Greek-Australian writers deal implicitly and explicitly with the issues of writing from the margins; being perceived by the mainstream as marginal; and depicting characters who, almost without exception, perceive themselves and are perceived by others as marginal'. So writes Helen Nickas in the introduction to her study of Greek-Australian women writers, *Migrant Daughters* (1992). The literary contribution of Greek immigrants has been neglected as a topic for study until recently. Many Greek writers chose – and still choose – to write in Greek, with the result that much of their work is not accessible to the majority of Australians, including minority groups from other cultures. Among those whose literary language is English are Vasso Kalamaras, Antigone Kefala and ΠΟ. All have written about the conflict they feel between the land of their heritage and that of their adoption. Kalamaras spent her young womanhood as an immigrant working on a farm near a country town where no interest was shown in literary or artistic activities. Her book *Other Earth* (1977) contains four stories about the sorrows of immigrant life, and six more stories delineating the loneliness of immigrant women in the bush make up *Bitterness* (1983). Yet Kalamaras insists that she does not think of herself as a 'marginalised', or 'ethnic', or even 'multicultural' writer; she is simply a writer, and her subject is the human condition. She has written a play, *The Bread Trap* (1986), about the clash of values experienced by migrants, and has published her poetry bilingually, although her latest collection of poems, *The Same Light* (1989), is all in English. Antigone Kefala is one of the best-known Greek-Australian writers, which is not to say that she is very widely read. Born in Romania, she has French as a second language, Greek as a third and English as a fourth. She writes only in English, but it is an English stylistically influenced by the three languages, with their cultural attitudes, which she absorbed first. She is conscious of this: she tells Helen Nickas, 'the texture of my language is not an English texture. This has made it difficult for me to find an audience. My language is foreign to Australian 'mainstream' audiences.' In her three volumes of poetry, *The Alien* (1973), *Thirsty Weather* (1978) and *European Notebook* (1988), this un-English texture is more evident (and more problematic for Australian English speakers) than in her three volumes of prose. Throughout all her works she is concerned with questions of identity and belonging, with the time it takes to adjust to new perspectives, and with the gaps or vacuums in human experience. In her novella *The First Journey* (1975) the narrator returns 'home', to face the disconcerting experience of 'trying to fit again into the silence of the house and the rooms that did not contain me any longer'. Another novel, *Alexia* (1984), is subtitled *A Tale of Two Cultures*. *The Island* (1984) also deals with homelessness, cultural differences and the problems of identity. Though not a readily accessible writer, Kefala is profoundly interesting. In stark contrast to Kefala is the work of ΠΟ, who was born in Greece and grew up in Australia. ΠΟ revels in not being part of 'mainstream' Australian literature. He is a performance and concrete poet who communicates the immigrant's struggles with the restrictions of an unfamiliar language directly: in his distorted English, with its repetitions and fragmentation, we hear not simply the immigrants' patois but also their frustration, isolation, and determination to communicate. Unafraid to confront issues of race, class or gender, ΠΟ at his best can leave his Anglophone Australian audience feeling uncomfortably caught between amusement, horror and embarrassment. He has compiled an anthology of performance poetry, mostly written by immigrants, entitled *Off the Record* (1985). His latest book is *The Fitzroy Poems* (1989). As a further contrast, and to illustrate the folly of oversimplified generalisation about 'Greek-Australian writing', the work of Dimitris Tsaloumas is worth considering. Unlike ΠΟ, Tsaloumas has been embraced by the literary establishment ever since his first Australian publication, *The Observatory* (1983), a bilingual poetry text with English translations by Philip Grundy which won a National Book Council Award. Tsaloumas writes out of a Greek literary tradition; the influence on his work of Cavafy and Seferis has been noted. Yet he has found a distinct voice for himself, and as his poetry attempts to transcend daily reality he does not write directly of the immigrant experience. Nevertheless, a sense of exile, of isolation, haunts his work. Until recently his poems have all appeared in translation, but those in *Falcon Drinking* (1988) were composed in English. Other acclaimed Greek-Australian writers of the immigrant experience are George Papaellinas, Tony Maniaty and Dimitris Tsoumakas. Beverley Farmer, married to a Greek immigrant, writes fiction about immigrants in Australia from a different perspective; see her stories in *Milk* (1983) and *Home Time* (1985). Angelo Loukakis writes from the point of view of young people growing up in Australia, growing away from the immigrant culture of their parents. His stories have been well received, but compared to other Greek-Australian writers his work is of limited interest and accomplishment. Gillian Bouras, in *A Foreign Wife* (1986), explores the immigrant experience in reverse. Her book tells the story of a marriage between an Australian woman and a Greek-Australian man, and studies the contrast between their cultures. In order to give their sons a tougher and more basic upbringing than that offered in easygoing Australia, the family moves to rural Greece. Bouras describes the struggles and rewards of living in a foreign 'folk' culture. One of these rewards is the release from obsession with the self; faced with an unbridgeable gap between herself and her Greek mother-in-law, the wife voluntarily withdraws her own viewpoints, and discovers this to be an act of growth rather than defeat. Further reading can be found in Con Castan's *Conflicts of Love* (1986), especially the chapter on 'Greek Literature in Australia'. For background, see Andreas Papageorgopoulos, *The Greeks in Australia: A Home Away from Home* (1981).

Writers of Asian background are not widely represented in Australian literature. Mena Abdullah's stories of a child growing up in an Indian family in New England were first published in the *Bulletin*, and have been justly praised. Abdullah is a first-generation Australian, and while her work is informed by her Indian background, it is not 'foreign'; it reflects her education and assimilation into our 'mainstream' culture. Her stories are available in the collection *The Time of the Peacock* (1965, reprinted 1989). More recently, in *A Change of Skies* (1991), Yasmine Gooneratne (born in Sri Lanka) had written movingly and intelligently about the gradual process of adaptation, and particularly about the difficulties the immigrant writer faces in her efforts to find a voice. She explores other aspects of transience and difference in her selected poems, *Celebrations and Departures* (1991). The most numerous group of immigrants from Asia are the Indochinese. In the late 1970s, over a million refugees fled from Indochina. In 1981 there were 50 000 Indochinese in Australia, and at the time of writing there are over 100 000. As yet their writing is not well known, particularly as many do not write in English. The difficulty of articulating (in any language) the severity of their suffering in their home country and during their escape is the theme of Tim Winton's story 'The Oppressed' in R.F. Holt's *Neighbours* (1991). Winton's story is an attempt to give voice to the silent,

and is a good starting point for debate about authenticity in writings about the immigrant experience: is it purely the property of immigrants themselves? Do mainstream Australian writers such as Winton simply appropriate experiences they cannot fathom? Can, and should, the habit of mind which categorises Australian writers into 'mainstream' and 'other' be challenged? These questions are of interest to writers (and readers) from all cultural backgrounds. Canberra writer Uyen Loewald's stories show a curiosity about cultural identity in many of the permutations she observes in Australia. Her *Child of Vietnam* (1987) describes her youth and also brings to life Vietnam's history and cultural distinctiveness. Shu Li has published poetry and prose based on his experience in Cambodia and his escape to Australia, and is currently working on a novel set in Australia. Nancy Viviani's *The Long Journey: Vietnamese Migration and Settlement in Australia* (1984) considers Australia as a country of asylum as well as resettlement, and examines the long-term implications of Vietnamese immigration. Other Australian writers from Asian backgrounds include novelist Don'o Kim, from Korea: *My Name is Tian* (1968) and *The Chinaman* (1984); and poet Ee Tiang Hong, a political exile from Malaysia, whose poems of the immigrant experience are refreshingly free of cliché. See for example 'Coming To' and 'Becoming' in Dennis Haskell and Hilary Fraser (eds.), *Wordhord: a Critical Selection of Contemporary Western Australian Poetry* (1989).

The extent of the Middle Eastern contribution to Australian culture is not reflected in the small volume of writing available in English, though there is a significant literature appearing in Arabic and Greek. Drama, not always the immigrant's chosen medium, appeals to a number of 'Middle Eastern' writers as a vehicle for exploring social issues and questions of tradition, and there has been a notable increase in the public performance of works by immigrant 'middle eastern' authors in Australia since 1988. Names to follow with interest include Samar Attar from Syria, who considers herself both a 'writer in exile' and a 'citizen of the world', and playwrights Charbee Baini and Simon Zaiter, both from Lebanon.

The change in official policy from assimilation to multiculturalism was disconcerting for many post-war immigrants (this is one of the strands of Riemer's *Inside Outside*), and it certainly influenced the course of Australian literature. From the late 1970s foreign literary sensibilities began to assert themselves, preparing the way for the diversity of literary voices that are now widely accepted as Australian, and by the mid-1980s perceptions about Australian literature were changing. As Geoffrey Dutton put it in *Snow on the Saltbush* (1984),

> the Anglo-Saxon snow that kept falling on the Australian saltbush has long since melted. For early immigrant writers exile had provided its own subject matter; with the emergence of second generation writers, at home in two cultures and practised at translating one reality into another, the immigrant experience could be a condition – not simply a visible cause – of their imaginative response to life.

It would be a mistake, however, to think that the transition to multiculturalism was either quick or unproblematic. It was in the 1970s that Billy Snedden, Leader of the Liberal Party, declared: 'We must have a single culture. I am determined we should have a monoculture, with everyone living in the same way, understanding each other, and sharing the same aspirations. We don't want pluralism.' (Quoted in Lois Foster and David Stockley, *Multiculturalism the Changing Australian Paradigm* (1984), pp. 52–3.) Implied in the words 'understanding each other' is the uncompromising expectation that migrants communicate in English; and it is only very recently that writing in languages other than English is beginning to be considered part of 'Australian literature'. Yet a writer's identity is very much bound up in language. Lidija Simkus-Pocius, resisting the pressure to conform, writes poetry in her native Latvian because, she explains, 'to have conformed would have obliterated my essential identity'.

From an Anglo-Australian perspective, multiculturalism may be seen as a policy means of authenticating the pluralistic nature of Australian society, and of institutionalising the rights of different cultures to co-exist on what is in principle an equal footing with Anglo-Australian culture. From the point of view of many immigrants, however, multiculturalism has been interpreted differently. For some it is virtually meaningless, since its effects are so dispersed and hard to qualify. Others see a difficulty in the way it legitimates any minority language and culture vis-à-vis Anglo-Australian culture, but without any reference to the rights and needs of other ethnic communities. In other words it subtly reinforces the self/other oppositions it ostensibly dismantles. Many contemporary writers of the immigrant experience are working towards a dissolution of the binary oppositions inherent in so much that has been thought and written about the immigrant experience: success/failure; assimilation/resistance; centre/margin; remembering/forgetting; inferior/superior. They also want to avoid the paralysis and consequent silence that can come from being caught between two worlds.

The common assumption that there is only one acceptable literary language in Australia is being challenged. Like ΠΟ, Ania Walwicz and Anna Couani deliberately introduce elements from other languages into conventional English, and try to break down the barriers between spoken and written English. The purpose of this experimental and transgressive approach is constructive, not destructive: they are not simply reflecting the fragmentation of the immigrant experience; they are challenging accounts of Australian literature which present it as the product of a unified, unfragmented culture. They want terms such as 'Australian' and 'Literature' not to deny difference, but to reflect fully the diversity of style, genre and language found in the creative writing in this country. There are different emphases in the ways writers choose to describe themselves ('Greek-Australian' or 'Australian Greek', for example), but many prefer not to attach any nationality to their writing. An example is Inez Baranay, who was born in Naples and has lived

in Australia since 1950, whose first language is Hungarian but who has written and published in English. Baranay describes herself as 'without nationality'. This way of transcending the limitations of nationality has its dangers, however. As Jurgensen puts it in *Eagle and Emu*, 'with the prospect of an emerging global monoculture . . . a literature's strains of origin are a precious commodity'. The challenge to Australian literature is to value those 'strains of origin', without simply enshrining 'difference'. We need to recognise that it is possible to have a plural identity, and that different strains or streams can feed into each other to produce something new. After all, the immigrant experience is not so discontinuous with our Anglo-Celtic traditions: starting with the convicts, the double strands of bondage and release have run continuously through Australian history. Peter Carey's novels, for example, may seem to some readers remote from the immigrant experience; but the themes in *Illywhacker* (1985) – of security and belonging, of the death of old fathers and the search for new ones – are far from alien to the immigrant. In that novel Badgery loses an English father (or did he simply pretend to be English?) and finds in the Chinese magician Goon Tse Ying a new father, who teaches Badgery to disappear. And *The Tax Inspector* (1991) celebrates the fertile, female, 'New' Australian, Maria, as the salvation of the degenerate Anglo-Celtic Australian. The immigrant experience makes it possible for us to reread and rewrite Australian culture, through unprecedented unions between what we were and what we have become.

Given the range, volume and diversity of recently emerging non-Anglo-Celtic writing in Australia, anthologies provide an invaluable point of entry. Sneja Gunew (ed.), *Displacements: Migrant Storytellers* (1982) and *Displacements II: Multicultural Storytellers* (1987) are good general collections, as is Peter Skrzynecki's *Joseph's Coat* (1985). R.F. Holt's two anthologies, *The Strength of Tradition* (1983) and *Neighbours* (1991), contain stories by first- and second-generation immigrants from both English-speaking and non-English-speaking backgrounds. Manfred Jurgensen's edited anthologies *Ethnic Australia* (1981) and (with Robert Adamson) *Australian Writing Now*, (1988) contain poetry as well as short fiction. The changing attitude to immigrant writing is caught in Jurgensen's description of the 1988 volume as an 'anthology of contemporary Australian literature which does not accept the distinctions of 'mainstream', 'ethnic' or 'marginal''. A compilation based on similar principles is Jim Kable (ed.), *An Arc of Australian Voices* (1990). Anthologies of Jewish-Australian literature include Nancy Keesing's *Shalom* (1978, reissued 1988); R. and R. Kalechofsky (eds), *Jewish Writing from Down Under* (1984) and Gael Hammer's *Pomegranates* (1988). *Greek Voices in Australia* (1987), ed. George Kanarakis, includes poetry and drama as well as short fiction, and has biographical and critical notes on each author; *Reflections: Selected Works from Greek-Australian Literature* (1988), ed. Thanasis Spilias and Stavros Messinis, represents the work of nineteen authors, some in English, some in Greek. It also contains a thought-provoking introduction by

Con Castan. *Italians in Australia: the Literary Experience* (1991), ed. M. Arrighi, is a collection of Italo-Australian prose with some valuable essays. Other anthologies include Gaetano Rando's bilingual text *Italo-Australian Prose in the 80s* (1988), Vincenzo Cincotta (ed.), *Italo-Australian Poetry in the 80s* (1986) and *Italo-Australian poetry in the 80s II* (1989), and L. Fazzolari (ed.), *Visione di Donne: an anthology of Italo-Australian Women* (1985). See also R.H. Morrison (ed.), *Australia's Italian Poets* (1976), with English translations by the editor. Some other specialised anthologies are R.H. Morrison's *Australia's Russian Poets* (1971); Dmytro Chub (ed.), *On the Fence: an Anthology of Ukrainian Prose in Australia* (1985), featuring the work of twenty-five authors in English; and I. Skof et al. (eds), *Our Paths: Multilingual Collection of Poems, Prose and Drama* (1986), produced by the Association of Yugoslav Writers in Australia and NZ. There are also a number of collections of women's writing which illuminate the immigrant experience, particularly B. Cugliari and D. Bradshaw (eds), *The World is Round* (1985) and S. Gunew and J. Mahyuddin (eds), *Beyond the Echo* (1988). Anglo-Celtic as well as more minority cultural backgrounds are represented in Anna Couani and Sneja Gunew (eds), *Telling Ways: Australian Women's Experimental Writing* (1988) and Drusilla Modjeska (ed.), *Inner Cities: Australian Women's Memory of Place* (1989).

Bibliographies and journals provide more detailed and up-to-date information. The most important bibliography on this subject has been compiled by S. Gunew, L. Houbein, A. Karakostas-Seda and J. Mahyuddin: their *Bibliography of Australian Multicultural Writers* (1992) builds on earlier works, particularly Loló Houbein's pioneering *Ethnic Writing in English from Australia* (1976–84). More selective are Serge Liberman's *Bibliography of Australian Judaica* (1987); and Con Castan's 'Selected Bibliography of Greek-Australian Literature' and Gaetano Rando's 'Selected Bibliography of Italo-Australian Literature', both in S. Gunew and K. Longley (eds), *Striking Chords* (1992). Though outdated, Peter Lumb and Anne Hazel's bibliography, *Diversity and Diversion* (1983), remains valuable for its annotations. There are currently a number of journals which publish new Australian writing, including *Antipodes*, *Aspect*, *Directions*, *Dislocations*, *Migrant 7* and *Rainbow Rising*. By far the most influential journal in the field, however, is *Outrider*, (ed. Manfred Jurgensen), which was established in 1984 by the Literature Board of the Australia Council in response to the interest sustained by conferences on multiculturalism in Sydney and Melbourne. *Outrider* not only features new Australian literature from a range of cultural backgrounds and positions; it also provides a forum for debate on issues relating to the constitution of Australian literature.

For more general or historical studies of Australian immigration, Geoffrey Sherington, *Australia's Immigrants 1788–1978* (1980) and James Jupp's *Immigration* (1991) are recommended; both contain useful bibliographies. Jean Martin in *The Migrant Presence* (1978) challenges the myth of easy assimilation, and points out the importance of self-publishing by migrants in a society where people of Anglo-Celtic background had a monopoly on the construction and validation of knowledge. Other perspectives on the complex reception of migrants include Michael Dugan and Josef Szwarc, *There Goes the Neighbourhood* (1984), Jock Collins, *Migrant Hands in a Distant Land* (1988) and Harry Martin, *Angels and Arrogant Gods* (1989) – a book of anecdotes about the officials and employees in the Department of Immigration and Ethnic Affairs. For more detailed studies of government policy as it affected immigrants, see Alison Ketley, *Assimilation of Migrants in Australia* (1965) and Katharine Betts, *Ideology and Immigration: Australia 1976 to 1987* (1988). The Australian Ethnic Heritage Series offers readable and informative accounts of the contribution to Australian life made by immigrant groups as disparate as the Afghans, the Cornish and the Maltese. Out of a proposed thirty-one titles, sixteen are currently available, for example Edward Duyker, *The Dutch in Australia* (1987), Al Grassby, *The Spanish in Australia* (1983) and W.D. Rubinstein, *The Jews in Australia* (1986).

FRANCES DIXON

'Imperial Adam', a poem by A.D. Hope (q.v.), was first published in 1951. A fresh, sensuous look at the Edenic myth, the poem describes Adam's discovery of Eve, 'Man's counterpart/ In tender parody', their joyous love-making and Eve's subsequent travail in childbirth, aided by the 'first gentle midwives of mankind', the 'gravid elephant', the 'calving hind', the 'she-ape big with young' and the 'teeming lioness'. The poem's final comment on the birth of 'the first murderer' and other possible ambivalences are the subject of influential essays by James McAuley, Vincent Buckley and S.L. Goldberg, to which Hope has replied in his essay 'The Practical Critic', in *The Cave and the Spring* (1965).

In Bad Company and Other Stories (1901), a collection of tales and essays by 'Rolf Boldrewood' (q.v.), includes some of his pieces written in the 1860s, the informative 'How I Began to Write' and the title story, a fictionalised account of the conflicts between the shearers and the squatters in the 1890s, in which 'Boldrewood's' conservative political views are revealed.

In the Days When the World Was Wide, Henry Lawson's (q.v.) first major book of verse, was published in 1896; dedicated to J.F. Archibald, it carried on the title page a sketch by Frank Mahony of Lawson 'humping his bluey'. *In the Days When the World Was Wide* contains many of the best Lawson poems, including famous bush verses such as 'The Roaring Days', 'The Free-Selector's Daughter', 'Andy's Gone with Cattle' and 'Middleton's Rouseabout'; several important poems of political and social protest, including 'Faces in the Street', 'The *Cambaroora Star*' and 'The Star of Australasia'; and the best of Lawson's contributions to the *Bulletin* debate (q.v.). *In the Days When the World Was Wide* went into a revised edition in 1900, when new poems such as 'Past Carin'' were added.

Independent Theatre, see **FITTON, Doris**

Index to Australian Book Reviews, published quarterly with an annual cumulation in the fourth number each year, began in 1965 through the auspices of the Libraries Board of SA. In subsequent years the entries were supplied by the University of Queensland library staff. The *Index* included reviews of books by Australians originating in Australia or of Australian interest. It was suspended in 1980 but one *Index* was issued in 1981.

INGAMELLS, Rex (1913–55), poet and founder of the Jindyworobak movement (q.v.), was born at Orooo, a small town in outback SA. Educated at the University of Adelaide, he was a high-school teacher, freelance journalist, then a representative of a Melbourne publishing firm. His first book of verse, *Gumtops* (1935), carried a foreword by L.F. Giblin stressing the need for Australian poets to give 'their firsthand, direct reaction to nature and man as they find them in Australia'. This directive, P.R. Stephensen's *The Foundations of Culture in Australia* (1936) and Ingamells's irritation with G.H. Cowling's article on Australian literature in the *Age*, 16 February 1935, led to his own prose manifesto, *Conditional Culture* (1938), and the formation of the Jindyworobak movement in 1938. In 1941 Ingamells joined the Australia First movement, whose political aims were to some extent complementary to the literary ambitions of the Jindyworobaks. Ingamells's own political attitudes and his thwarted hopes for a massive takeover of the literary scene by the Jindyworobaks (see the controversy in the *Southerly* editorials of 1941–42) are summed up in his poem 'The Gangrened People', published in *At a Boundary* (1941). In 1951 he was appointed a judge of the Commonwealth Jubilee literary competition and he lectured in Australian literature at the Melbourne Technical College.

Ingamells's publications of poetry include *Gumtops* (1935), *Forgotten People* (1936), *Sun-Freedom* (1938), *Memory of Hills* (1940), *At a Boundary* (1941), *Content Are the Quiet Ranges* (1943), and *The Great South Land* (1945), which won the Grace Leven Prize for poetry. He wrote a novel, *Of Us Now Living* (1952), and a children's story, *Aranda Boy* (1952). He was general editor of the *Jindyworobak Anthologies*, published annually 1938–53, compiled *The Jindyworobak Review 1938–1948* (1948) and edited an anthology for schools, *New Song in an Old Land: Australian Verse* (1943). Although Ingamells's own poetic talent was inadequate for the task of carrying the Jindyworobaks to the eminence he desired for them, he was a competent craftsman with a capacity for graceful imagery and picturesque description. These qualities are particularly evident in poems such as 'Forlorn Beauty', 'Sun-Freedom' and 'Memory of Hills', which are filled also with sensitivity to the spirit of place, and in 'The Forgotten People' and 'Uluru', where his emotional affinity with the Aboriginal people lifts the verse above the ordinary.

INGLIS, Amirah (1926–), born Brussels, Belgium, of Jewish parents from Poland, came to Australia in 1929. Her father, who spent the First World War as a hostage in Russia, and who found the anti-Semitism of his own country intolerable, had emigrated to Melbourne a year earlier. Well educated and politically active, her parents had abandoned the Jewish religion and were members of the Communist Party. Amirah Inglis graduated from the University of Melbourne and later from the ANU and has worked as a teacher, librarian and research assistant. She edited the communist weekly, *The Guardian*, 1948–50 and was married to Ian Turner for a period. Now married to the historian Ken Inglis, she spent 1972–75 in Papua New Guinea, which resulted in the biography *Karo* (1982) and a historical study of race relations, *'Not A White Woman Safe': Sexual Anxiety and Politics in Port Moresby 1920–1934* (1974). She has also written a well-researched account of the Australian response to the Spanish Civil War, which includes information on the attitudes of some writers, *Australians in the Spanish Civil War* (1987), and has edited the letters of Lloyd Edmonds, one of the Australian participants, *Letters from Spain* (1985). Her best-known book is the autobiography *Amirah: an Un-Australian Childhood* (1983), winner of the Royal Blind Society's Talking Book of the Year Award. A frank account of the strangely divided experience of growing up in 1930s and 1940s Melbourne and responding to the polarised demands of the culture of her Australian schools and her family's culture, *Amirah* is valuable both as a personal record and as social history.

INGLIS, Kenneth Stanley (1929–), a graduate of Oxford University and the University of Melbourne and professor of history at the ANU since 1977, was vice-chancellor of the University of Papua New Guinea 1972–75 and previously taught at the University of Adelaide. His publications include *Hospital and Community: A History of the Royal Melbourne Hospital* (1958), *The Stuart Case* (1961), *The Australian Colonists: An Exploration of Social History 1788–1870* (1974), *This is the ABC: the Australian Broadcasting Commission 1932–1983* (1983), and *The Rehearsal: Australians at War in the Sudan, 1885* (1985). He has also edited *Nation: The Life of an Independent Journal 1958–72* (1989) and, with Alan Gilbert, the twelve-volume bicentennial history *Australians: A Historical Library* (1987–88). He is married to Amirah Inglis.

INGLIS, Rob (1933–) has worked as actor, writer, journalist, critic and producer in Australia and England. His plays include 'Voyage of the Endeavour' (1965), which is based on the journal of Captain James Cook; 'Canterbury Tales' (1968), dramatised readings from Chaucer; 'Erf' (1971), a one-actor play about the twenty-first century, presented in Australia and in the USA; 'A Rum Do' (1970), a musical based on the governorship of Lachlan Macquarie; and 'Men Who Shaped Australia, for Better or for Worse' (1968), a one-actor play dealing with significant historical figures.

'INNES, Michael' (John Innes Mackintosh Stewart) (1906–), born Edinburgh, Scotland, was professor of English at the University of Adelaide 1935–45. A distinguished literary scholar and well-known novelist, Stewart used the pseudonym 'Michael Innes' mainly for his detective fiction; novels written or published during his period in Australia, some of which have Australian references, include *Death at the President's Lodging* (1936), *Hamlet, Revenge!* (1937), *Lament for a Maker* (1938), *The Spider Strikes Back* (1939), *The Secret Vanguard* (1940), *A Comedy of Errors* (1940), *Appleby on Ararat* (1941), *The Daffodil Affair* (1942), *The Weight of the Evidence* (1943) and *Appleby's End* (1945).

inprint, a short-story magazine, was published quarterly 1977–83 from the Mitchell College of Advanced Education. Its policy was to encourage new writers; some of those originally published in *inprint* have gone on to establish literary reputations, e.g. James McQueen and Peter Goldsworthy, as has one of its editors, Nigel Krauth. Back in print in 1985 with Bill Turner as editor, it was published thrice yearly but after ten years and twenty-six issues it published its last regular issue in 1987. Thereafter its plan was to publish single-author collections and anthologies, e.g. *Bite a Short Story* (1986) and *W.A. Short Story* (1986).

Inquirer, a weekly WA journal of politics and literature, was established in 1840 under the editorship of Edmund Lochée. More lively in outlook and more alert to literature than its rival the *Perth Gazette*, the *Inquirer* advocated in 1841 the establishment of a literary society in WA, encouraged local writers and presented a regular series of book reviews. Its enlightened racial attitudes are reflected by the series of articles by William Nairne Clark in 1842 defending the Aborigines against charges of racial and intellectual inferiority. In 1851–55 the *Inquirer* published a Saturday supplement, which began with a literary flourish but quickly faded. After 1857 the *Inquirer* (which had incorporated the *Commercial News* in 1855) was also an agent for the purchase of books, a common practice in those times. It ceased publication in 1901.

Inventing Australia: Images and Identity 1688–1980, by Richard White, was published in 1981. An influential study of efforts to explain what it means to be Australian, *Inventing Australia* is founded on the premise that a national identity is an invention and that there 'is no 'real' Australia waiting to be uncovered ... There is no point asking whether one version of this essential Australia is truer than another because they are all intellectual constructs, neat, tidy, comprehensible – and necessarily false.' Analysing the varying cultural constructions of Australia from the images popularised by Dampier and Cook to the plural versions of the 1970s, White focuses on three main influences on identity: European ideas and cultural assumptions, the perceptions of the intelligentsia and those groups in society who are economically powerful.

IRELAND, David (1927–), born Lakemba, NSW, has had a variety of occupations, including greenkeeping, factory work and a lengthy period in an oil refinery. Since 1973 he has been a full-time writer. He first came to notice in 1958 when his play *Image in the Clay* (1964) shared third prize in a competition. He has written some poetry and another play, 'The Virgin of Treadmill Street' (1959), but is best known for his novels, *The Chantic Bird* (q.v., 1968), *The Unknown Industrial Prisoner* (q.v., 1971), *The Flesheaters* (1972), *Burn* (an adaptation of *Image in the Clay*) (1974), *The Glass Canoe* (q.v., 1976), *A Woman of the Future* (q.v., 1979), *City of Women* (1981), *Archimedes and the Seagle* (1984) and *Bloodfather* (1987, 1988 in UK and USA). He won the Miles Franklin Award in 1971, 1976 and 1980, the *Age* Book of the Year Award in 1980 and the Gold Medal of the Australian Literature Society in 1985. He was made AO in 1981.

Ireland uses the novel form in diverse, innovatory and non-representational ways to embody his explorations of the contemporary human condition. His use of fragmented scenes rather than formally constructed chapters and his often opaque narrators are reminiscent of Laurence Sterne, a debt he acknowledges. Like the Brazilian writer Machado de Assis, who has also influenced him, he is concerned with the indifference of the human environment to the individual and with self-betrayal. Pessimistic but not nihilistic, his indictment of the futility of contemporary industrialised existence is satirical and compassionate, humorous and bitter, detached and committed. Underlying his representations of meaningless activity is a philosophical questioning of humankind's true function and purpose, as distinct from its arbitrary functions and stop-gap purposes. Concerned with ways of perceiving the world, his novels evoke the conflict between the urge to order experience and the unruly disorder of reality and its refusal to submit to the categorising impulses of the human mind. *The Chantic Bird*, narrated by an anonymous, underground youth, committed to equalising things by acts of violence, is set in a dehumanising, materialistic and predatory world. The narrator yearns for some transforming magic that will invest life with inherent meaning, but is left with the bleak conviction that it is 'a tale told by nobody'. Ireland's next, more ambitious novel, *The Unknown Industrial Prisoner*, concentrates on the collective experience of workers in an oil refinery owned by a multinational company, Puroil. In this huge industrial complex, man is but another resource, a prisoner of institutionalised incompetence and avarice and of his own weaknesses. This comprehensively worked picture of an inane economic structure, a vast 'termitary', in which everyone, consciously or unconsciously, is subservient, transcends political solutions. *The Flesheaters*, a more absurdist novel which combines social reality and surrealist fantasy, deals once again with an anarchic, predatory world. A tight unity is provided by the growth in self-awareness of the narrator, Lee Mallory, who writes from within Merry Lands, a home for outcasts and incurables. *Burn*, a more modest novel in a realistic mode, describes one day of crisis in the life of a part-Aboriginal family;

concerned less with the conflict between society and outsiders, it probes the grounds of the outcast's inner inertia that partly determines his defeat. *The Glass Canoe*, Ireland's most comic novel, evokes the lost tribal community of the public bar, the last outpost of such traditional male values as mateship, sexual prowess, sport, anti-authoritarianism and support of the underdog. The glass canoe (a schooner of beer) supports the tribe in its escape from the suffocating demands of their otherwise unnatural industrialised life. *A Woman of the Future* is a complete contrast: partly surrealist allegory, it embodies Ireland's hopes and fears for Australia, presenting the future as offering both Arcadian potential and the possibility of further social degradation. In this novel Ireland's subversive juxtaposing of the facetious and the serious, the prophetic and the obscene constantly undermine the reader's expectations and challenge received impressions of what it is to be Australian. *City of Women*, a novel without a male character, traces the inner journey of Billie Shockley, a retired water engineer and lesbian separatist. *Archimedes and the Seagle*, narrated by a red setter dog blessed with certain human powers and a benevolent philosophy, is an optimistic, humorous novel with an underlying conviction that 'at the heart of all things, there is life and strength and joy'. The semi-autobiographical *Bloodfather* traces the growth of the hero's artistic and spiritual consciousness from birth to the age of 16. After working intensively as a visual artist from an early age, David Blood discovers his real vocation is writing; at the same time his awareness of God as immanent creativity deepens and arms him with confidence. Helen Daniel has published a critical account of Ireland's work, *Double Agent* (1982).

IRISH, Lola, born Sydney, worked as a commercial artist and had some success as a playwright for stage and radio before marrying. She has written several popular novels mostly published in London, including *The Touch of Jade* (1962), *Shadow Mountain* (1964), *Time of the Dolphins* (1972), *And the Wild Birds Sing* (1983), winner of an award from the Society of Women Writers), *The Place of the Swan* (1986), *The House of O'Shea* (1990) and *Streets of Dust* (1993). Her plays include 'Where There's a Will' (1937) and 'Three Corners' (1937). *And the Wild Birds Sing, The Place of the Swan* and *The House of O'Shea* form a historical trilogy, set in Australia's colonial era; *Time of the Dolphins* is the story of a middle-aged woman's rebellion against the dullness of a suburban marriage and her choice of a difficult freedom. *Streets of Dust* is a well-researched historical novel, based on the life of Caroline Chisholm (q.v.).

'Ironbark', see **GIBSON, G.H.**

IRONSIDE, Adelaide (1831–67), born Sydney, was well known in the city's cultural circles and familiar with such figures as John Dunmore Lang, Sir Charles Nicholson and Daniel Deniehy. She studied literature and art as well as languages and contributed articles and verse on republican topics to such journals as the

People's Advocate and *New South Wales Vindicator*, before leaving for London in 1855. Attracted to Deniehy, she is said to have refused many brilliant offers of marriage and continued to correspond with him until his death. In January 1856 she and her mother, who appears to have acted as entrepreneur of her daughter's talents, settled in Rome, where she became known as a painter and in spiritualist circles as a medium. Many of her paintings were on religious subjects or represented her visions as a medium; the most famous included 'The Pilgrim of Art' and 'The Marriage in Cana', which expresses her republicanism by modelling the heads of Christ and the bridegroom on Garibaldi. While in Rome she was granted an audience with the Pope and became a member of the exclusive Society of Artists with access to the Pope's private gallery. In 1865 she lived in London, where she became friendly with John Ruskin, who advised her on her drawing. She appears to have won some success as an artist, receiving visits from the Prince of Wales and W. Wentworth, who bought paintings, and winning respect from other artists such as Joseph Severn, Seymour Kirkup and John Gibson. Her death in Rome inspired several eulogies including a poem by Brunton Stephens, although her painting failed to attract continuing attention. Jill Poulton has written a biography of Adelaide Ironside (1987).

IRVIN, Eric (1908–   ), born Newtown, Sydney, left school at 15, becoming, in his words, 'one of the dropouts of the 1920s'. After a succession of occasional jobs he became a journalist, served with the AIF in the Second World War and was on the editorial staff of the *Sydney Morning Herald* 1962–73, when he retired. Irvin published two volumes of poetry, *A Soldier's Miscellany* (1945) and *A Suit for Everyman* (1968). An expert on the Australian theatre in the nineteenth century, he has published numerous articles in scholarly journals in Australia, England and the USA, and the following books: *Theatre Comes to Australia* (1971); *Sydney As It Might Have Been* (1974); *Gentleman George* (1980), a biography of the actor-dramatist George Darrell; *Australian Melodrama* (1981); and a *Dictionary of the Australian Theatre 1788–1914* (1984). He also edited Walter Cooper's play *Colonial Experience*, with a valuable historical introduction, in 1979. He received an honorary D.Litt. from the University of Queensland for his writings on the theatre.

IRVING, John, see *Bystander*

Island, a quarterly journal of literature, the arts and allied disciplines, is produced in Tasmania partly to promote the work of Tasmanian artists and writers. It began as the *Tasmanian Review* in 1979, was *Island Magazine* 1981–90 and is now *Island*. It is supported by the Literature Board, the University of Tasmania and the Tasmanian Arts Advisory Board. The first issue was edited by Michael Denholm, Andrew Sant and Tim Thorne; then until No. 40, 1989, it was edited jointly by Denholm and Sant; since that issue it has been edited by Cassandra Pybus. Denholm and Sant edited *First Rights: A Decade of Island Magazine* (1989). A $10 000 Essay competition for Australian writers was inaugurated by *Island* in 1994.

'It's Harder for Girls', a short story by Gavin Casey, is the title story of Casey's first book of short fiction, which was published in 1942 and won the S.H. Prior Memorial Prize. It is the story of the impoverished Dawson family who live in one of the tumbledown houses that dot the old mining leases on the edge of Kalgoorlie. The father is a loafer and boozer, the mother frail and long-suffering. The older boy, Monk, has a spell in a reformatory, returns without 'any sting left' and settles to the grind of life in the mines, a wife and kids. Johnny, the youngest, narrowly escapes the reform school, takes a job in a local store and attempts to break out of his social class by courting the daughter of one of the staff men at the mines. His efforts come to nothing when the girl is frightened off by the loose reputation of his sister Molly. A fiery, beautiful girl, Molly has basically good instincts but indulges in spells of wildness, usually as a gesture of revolt against the feeling that her future is restricted by her family background. A bank clerk, Sid Polson, visits Kalgoorlie briefly and falls in love with Molly. Before he has time to know much about her he returns to Perth, and when she goes there to work they marry and are extremely happy. Ironically, and tragically, the bank later transfers Sid to Kalgoorlie, where his friends soon enlighten him about Molly's past. Broken-hearted, he leaves Molly and equally devastated, she bitterly resumes the life she had known earlier. Casey's presentation of life in the lower social order as circumscribed and frustrated is characteristic of his fiction: 'it was tough being any sort of a Dawson [but] it was harder for girls.'

J

Jacaranda Press, which took its name from Queensland's famous flowering jacaranda tree, was founded in 1952 by Brian Clouston to produce material by Australian writers, initially for Queensland schools but later for the whole Australian educational network. Jacaranda has produced a wide range of Australian poetry, fiction, natural history, politics and conservation titles; its authors have included Judith Wright, Douglas Stewart, Nancy Cato, Kath Walker, Bill Scott, Russel Ward, Sylvana Gardner, June Epstein and Colin Simpson. Control and ownership of Jacaranda has changed frequently (eight owners in twenty-five years); since 1977 it has been known as Jacaranda Wiley but retains the Jacaranda Press imprint for school and general books. It is presently (1993) owned by John Wiley & Sons (USA).

'Jackeroo' (also 'Jackaroo') was a term originally used to describe a young man, usually with good family connections and often directly from England, working as a station hand, sometimes paying for the privilege, in order to gain experience before taking over his own station. A similar term was 'colonial experiencer' (q.v.) and, although it chiefly emphasised the young man's inexperience, 'new chum' (q.v.). Suggestions of the origin of 'jackeroo' include the Aboriginal word *tchaceroo*, a chattering, garrulous bird; a corruption of 'Jack Carew', said to be the name of one actual young gentleman engaged as a station hand; and a corruption of the term 'Johnny Raw', meaning 'new chum', to 'Jacky Raw' then euphonically to 'Jackeroo'. Widely used in literature, the term is found for example in 'Rolf Boldrewood', Henry Lawson, A.B. Paterson and G.H. Gibson. In his *Old Bush Songs* Paterson includes an anonymous song, 'Jim Sago, Jackeroo', and explains that a jackeroo 'occupies a position much like an apprentice . . . has to work with the men though supposed to be above them in social status'. The song carries the traditional contempt of the experienced bushman for the aristocratic and useless new chum. Still a widely used term to denote a young man gaining experience of the cattle and sheep industry by working on outback properties, 'jackeroo' is now complemented by 'jilleroo' ('jillaroo') the female of the species, the latter dating from the Second World War when female station hands were used in times of manpower shortage. Many Australian writers have worked as jackeroos; a notable example was Patrick White, who drew extensively on his experiences in *The Twyborn Affair* (1979).

JACKMAN, William (1821–?), born near Dartmouth, England, lived with the Aborigines for almost two years in 1837–39 after his ship the *Carib* was wrecked off Nuyts Archipelago. He published a somewhat fanciful account of his experiences in *The Australian Captive: Or, An Authentic Narrative of Fifteen Years in the Life of William Jackman* (1853). The book tells also of Jackman's further adventures in whalers, slavers and merchantmen around the world and contains an appendix with information on Van Diemen's Land and the Australian goldfields.

JACOBSON, Howard (1942–), born Manchester, England, and educated at Cambridge University, spent three years in Australia from 1965, when he lectured in English at the University of Sydney, and a further period in the 1970s when he claims to have worked as labourer to an Italian plasterer and as a publisher's representative in Victoria. Married to an Australian, he now lives in London but has continued to visit Australia. Jacobson has written several successful novels including *Coming from Behind* (1983), a satire on life in an English tertiary institution which opens in Australia, *Peeping Tom* (1984) and *Redback* (1986), which is set in Australia. *Redback* is a comic anatomy of Australia, narrated by Karl Leon Forelock, a graduate with a double first in moral decencies from Cambridge, who has been recruited by the CIA to combat the influence of left-wing intellectuals in Australia. Satirising familiar targets in Australian culture, *Redback* skims the surface of English and Australian prejudices to produce some witty one-liners but little sustained humour. Jacobson has also written a comic account of his travels in Australia in the 1980s, *In the Land of Oz* (1987).

JAFFA, Herbert C., see *Modern Australian Poetry, 1920–70*

'JAMES, Brian' (John Tierney) (1892–1972) was born at Eurunderee, NSW, the son of a schoolteacher, who taught Henry Lawson and whom Lawson commemorated in his poem 'Eurunderee'. 'Brian James' also became a pupil teacher on leaving school, and taught mainly English for thirty-seven years in state high schools in many parts of NSW and in Sydney. He later combined teaching and farming, both of which occupations colour his fiction, before retiring from teaching in 1951. He did not publish any of his writing until 1942, when he sent his first short story to the *Bulletin* and received strong encouragement from the editor of its Red Page, Douglas Stewart, and from Norman Lindsay.

Under his pseudonym he published four collections of short stories, *First Furrow* (1944), *Cookabundy Bridge*

(1946), which won the S.H. Prior memorial Prize, *The Bunyip of Barney's Elbow* (1956) and *The Big Burn* (1965); two novels, *The Advancement of Spencer Button* (q.v., 1950) and *Hopeton High* (1963). He also edited two collections of short stories, *Selected Australian Stories* (1959) and *Australian Short Stories – Second Series* (1963). Norman Lindsay, who regarded 'James' as one of the two best short-story writers Australia has produced, edited, with introductions, *The Bunyip of Barney's Elbow* and *The Big Burn*.

Strongly influenced by Lawson and owing an allegiance to the Lawson country, 'Brian James' writes in the same *Bulletin* tradition that fostered such writers as 'Steele Rudd', Frank Dalby Davison and E.O. Schlunke. Similarly a regionalist, re-creating the life of the hinterland of NSW, 'James' shares with these writers a wry, sardonic sense of humour and a capacity for sharp satire, understated realism and stylistic economy. Distinctive features of his short stories are his eloquent evocations of rich rural landscapes and the joys and hardships of farming, as in 'Bungally' and 'First-Furrow'; his acute insight into the workings of the collective rural or small-town mind, as in 'Shots in the Orchard' (q.v.) and 'Cookabundy Bridge'; and his varied range of bush and town characters. An unsentimental writer, with a sure, satiric eye for the significant social or psychological detail, 'James' creates a wide range of effects, from light family comedy, as in 'Grandfather Celebrates', to macabre farce, as in 'Dolf', which relates a botched attempt to kill a pig, to terse pathos, as in 'Brosie', which deals with the death of a child. Particularly striking are his philosophical, fatalistic sense of humour which accepts defeat and even death as part of life's comic inevitability; his combination of detachment and acute observation; and his relish for the absurd rituals of social life from school speech days to political meetings. Although 'James' is probably best known for such comically extended tales as 'The Bunyip of Barney's Elbow' (q.v.) and 'Hawkins' Pigs', some of his most distinctive stories, such as 'Jacob's Escape' and 'Doolan's Devotions', are subtle explorations of inner, reflective experience.

In his novels 'James' draws on his wide experience of teaching in the NSW system. *Hopeton High*, narrower in scope than *The Advancement of Spencer Button*, is a comic extension of one episode in the life of a typical Australian high school – the acquisition of a 'Warwick Peerless' sound system with loudspeakers in every room, funded by the Parents' and Citizens' Association. He deftly exploits the human comedy of the incident, creating a wide range of characters from the inadequate but aspiring headmaster, Mr Mullett ('Dead Fish'), to the cynical strategies of the more astute teachers, to the political manoeuvrings of ambitious parents. Meanwhile, irreverent but acute observations on the part of both teachers and students on the inane activities inspired by the advent of the sound system provide a constant ironic background. *The Advancement of Spencer Button*, 'James's' most significant achievement and the biography of a NSW high-school teacher, is also a broad picture of life in the State from the 1890s to the 1940s, and an ironical presentation of the working of its educational system. As Spencer Button, the efficient but unexciting hero of the novel, advances from rural Wombat Creek, his birthplace, to the pinnacle of teaching achievement, headmastership of one of Sydney's big high schools, successfully avoiding the hazards posed by malevolent inspectors, aggressive parents, eccentric colleagues and manic headmasters, a richly detailed human comedy unfolds.

JAMES, Clive (1939–), born and educated in Sydney, was literary editor of *Honi Soit* and wrote for university magazines such as *Arna*. He worked briefly for the *Sydney Morning Herald* before settling in England in 1962. After completing a second degree at the University of Cambridge, he became a freelance literary journalist and critic and has written for the *New Statesman*, *Encounter*, the *Listener*, the *Times Literary Supplement* and other publications in England and the USA; in 1972–82 he was the highly respected television critic for the *Observer*, and has an international reputation as a television broadcaster, interviewer and performer, appearing regularly on BBC television. He was made AM in 1992. James's eclectic interests range from high culture to mass entertainment and embrace literature, television, films and popular music. Apart from several mock-heroic epics, e.g. *Peregrine Prykke's Pilgrimage through the London Literary World* (1976) and rock lyrics, he has published books of reviews and literary criticism, such as *The Metropolitan Critic* (1974), *At the Pillars of Hercules* (1979), *From the Land of Shadows* (1982), *Snakecharmers in Texas* (1988) and *The Dreaming Swimmer* (1992); several selections of his television journalism such as *Visions Before Midnight* (1977), *The Crystal Bucket* (1981), and *Glued to the Box* (1983); selections of his verse including *Fan-mail: Seven Verse Letters* (1977), *Other Passports* (1986) and *Poem of the Year* (1983); a book of travel pieces, *Flying Visits* (1984); the autobiographies, *Unreliable Memoirs* (1980), a hilarious account of his experiences growing up in and leaving Australia; *Falling Towards England* (1985), the story of his experiences in London in the 1960s and *May Week Was in June* (1990), which closes in 1968 as his career at Cambridge comes to an end; and three novels, *Brilliant Creatures* (1983), the experiences of a publishing executive who conquers literary London; *The Remake* (1987), which charts the falling fortunes of a Cambridge academic and television performer; and *Brrm! Brrm!* (1991) the story of a Japanese bookshop assistant on a riotous journey to fame and fortune in London. James describes himself as preoccupied with the obvious: 'my field is the self-evident.' Nevertheless he takes pride in casting a fresh light on the prosaic, including himself with self-deprecating wit in that category. 'Born without a sense of proportion, I had it imposed on me by the weight of evidence', he declares in *May Week Was in June* and much of his comedy derives from his re-creation of this negative education. Verbal dexterity, a pungent wit and extraordinary metaphoric inventiveness are surface characteristics of his exuberant writing but behind the facade of frivolity he is often both erudite and serious. Notwithstanding his reputation as an expatriate metropolitan critic, his style and humour have been recognised as quintessentially Australian and have led him to be described, not necessarily unkindly, as 'the highbrow coming on as Chips Rafferty'.

JAMES, Florence (1904–93), born Gisborne, NZ, graduated from the University of Sydney, where she met Dymphna Cusack (q.v.). In the 1930s she worked as a journalist in London, sharing a room for a period with Christina Stead, and returned to Sydney in 1938 after marrying. In the last year of the war she and Cusack, accompanied by three children, shared a cottage in the Blue Mountains and collaborated in writing the children's book *Four Winds and a Family* (1946) and *Come In Spinner* (q.v.,1951), winner of the 1948 *Daily Telegraph* competition. James returned to London and to a career in publishing in 1947, leaving Cusack to make the massive cuts demanded by the *Daily Telegraph*. In the late 1980s the original manuscript of the novel was recovered and James, once again living in Sydney, reassembled the original text for publication in 1988.

JAMES, John Stanley ('The Vagabond', 'Julian Thomas') (1843–96) led a vagabond's life that began in Walsall, England, where he was born, educated and began work in his father's legal office. From there he moved to London, where he got his start as a freelance journalist, and then worked in Wales as a railway clerk and station master before returning to journalism. Around 1872 he went to America, changed his name to 'Julian Thomas', and married, so he later claimed, the widow of a Virginian planter; in 1875 he arrived in Australia. In April 1876 the *Argus* published, under the pseudonym 'A Vagabond', the first of a long series of articles on high and low life and their institutions. The series was extremely popular, partly because of the mystery surrounding its author, and was republished in four parts as *The Vagabond Papers* (1877). A fifth part, with the same main title, was published in 1878 and sketched life in Sydney and Queensland, where James travelled in 1877–78. Thereafter James was mainly occupied in visiting the Pacific, the Orient and Europe writing for the *Argus*. He returned periodically to Victoria, where, at his death in Melbourne, he was remembered for his humanitarianism; his true identity was not publicly known until 1912. Apart from *The Vagabond Papers*, he compiled *The 'Vagabond' Annual* (1877); published eight other descriptive works, including *South Sea Massacres* (1881), *Occident and Orient* (1882) and *Cannibals and Convicts* (1886); wrote two plays, 'No Mercy' (first performed 1882) and, with Alfred Dampier, 'The Nihilists' (first performed 1880 and revised as 'England and Russia', 1885); and was portrayed in Francis Hopkins's play, 'Michael Strogoff' (1882). Michael Cannon has edited two selections of James's journalism, *The Vagabond Papers* (1969) and *Vagabond Country* (1981). James, who worked in Pentridge Gaol, Melbourne, to gather material for articles on penology, is discussed in Denton Prout and Fred Feely's *50 Years Hard* (1967).

JAMES, Winifred (1876–1941), born Prahran, Melbourne, was a journalist in Melbourne before going in 1905 to England, where she became a successful novelist, essayist and writer of travel books. She returned to Australia to live in 1939. Her most successful work was *Letters to My Son* (1910) which, in less than a decade went through eighteen reprintings, and was followed by *More Letters to My Son* (1911). Her other novels include *Bachelor Betty* (1907), *Patricia Baring* (1908), *Saturday's Children* (1910) and *The Gods Arrive* (1941). Her travel books include *The Mulberry Tree* (1913), *A Woman in the Wilderness* (1915), *Out of the Shadows* (1924) and *Gangways and Corridors* (1936).

JANAVICIUS, Jurgis (1926–   ), born Lithuania, arrived in Australia in 1948. His poetry has appeared in anthologies and periodicals and in two collections, *Journey to the Moon* (1971) and *Umph* (1972). The poems of *Journey to the Moon* are spare, witty lyrics, dealing for the most part with the experience of immigration; the comic verse of *Umph*, accompanied by drawings, records the experiences of a lump of live jelly of undefined size which 'observes the outside world through its slightly protruding aperture'. Janavicius is also a cartoonist whose work has been published in *Aspect* and *Outrider*.

Jane Street Theatre, founded by the Old Tote Theatre Company in a small church building in Jane Street in the Sydney suburb of Randwick in 1966, was the venue for numerous productions by NIDA. At a time when Australian drama was generally neglected by theatres, Jane Street produced numerous contemporary plays, providing a Sydney impetus to the 1970s renaissance. Plays staged include Edward Geoghegan's *The Currency Lass*, James Searle's *The Lucky Streak*, Rodney Milgate's *A Refined Look at Existence*, Thomas Keneally's *Halloran's Little Boat* and 'An Awful Rose' and William Marshall's 'King Edward'. Particularly popular and influential was the theatre's 1970 production of *The Legend of King O'Malley*. In 1980 the theatre closed, having proved too small for many productions.

JARDINE Family, including John Jardine (1807–74) and his two elder sons, Francis Lascelles Jardine (1841–1919) and Alexander William Jardine (1843–1920), was an important pioneering family in northern Queensland. John Jardine was appointed superintendent of the settlement to be established at Cape York in 1863; his sons, in a ten-month trek of about 2000 kilometres, overlanded the stock that was to form the nucleus of the settlement. F.J. Byerley edited *Narrative of the Overland Expedition of the Messrs. Jardine from Rockhampton to Cape York, Queensland* (1867) and A.J. Richardson published the *Private Journal of the Surveyor . . . Jardine's Overland Expedition to Cape York* (1867).

JEFFERIS, Barbara (1917–   ), born Adelaide, has been a journalist and has written dramas and documentaries for the ABC. She has also written fiction, characterised by gripping plots and subtle psychological insights, which has been published outside Australia; her novels include *Contango Day* (1954), *Beloved Lady* (1956), *Half Angel* (1959), *Solo for Several Players* (1961), *The Wild Grapes* (1963), *One Black Summer* (1967), *Time of the Unicorn* (1974), and *The Tall One* (1977). She has also published *Three of a Kind* (1982), a biographical work on the Victorian goldfields' actors Susan Woolridge and her daughter Harriet, and on Harriet's daughter Mary Card, who became a renowned needlework designer 1910–40. President of the ASA 1973–76, Barbara Jefferis played a part in the establishment of the Public Lending Right scheme and has published for the society, *Australian Book Contracts* (1983) and *The Good, the Bad and the Greedy: How Australian Publishers are Rated by Their Authors* (1989). She was made AM in 1986.

JEFFERY, Walter James (1861–1922), born into a naval family at Portsmouth, England, went to sea at 15. He served in the Royal Navy and the merchant navy before settling in Australia in 1886. In 1887 he joined the staff of the *Evening News*, moved from there in 1891 to become sub-editor and later editor of the *Australian Town and Country Journal*, and returned to the *Evening News* in 1906 as managing editor. Highly respected in the newspaper world, Jeffery was also an enthusiastic student of maritime history. He published *A Century of Our Sea Story* (1900) and a novel, *The King's Yard* (1903), but of more significance are the fruits of his harmonious collaboration with 'Louis' Becke: three novels, *A First Fleet Family* (1896), *The Mystery of the Laughlin Islands* (1896), and an admired Bounty story, *The Mutineer* (1898), which was the first novel published by Angus & Robertson; a history, *The Naval Pioneers of Australia* (1899); a biography, *Admiral Phillip* (1899); and a miscellany, *The Tapu of Banderah* (1901). In general, Jeffery did the research and rough drafts of these works; Becke did the polishing and negotiated with publishers.

Jemmy Green in Australia, a play by James Tucker (q.v.), was probably written in 1845, although not published until 1955; it was staged at the Adelaide Festival in 1966. A slight three-act comedy, each act consisting of five short scenes, *Jemmy Green in Australia* records the experiences in Australia of the 'new chum' (q.v.) Londoner Jemmy Green, who soon after his arrival is duped into the purchase of a squatting run in the back country stocked by diseased sheep and wild cattle. During his journey there he is robbed by bushrangers and mistaken for an escaped convict; after his arrival his huts are burned by Aborigines, he learns that his sheep have catarrh, and he is served with writs from his employees, his neighbours and Sydney businessmen. He takes advice, declares himself bankrupt, and is released under a new government act in time to save his London sweetheart, Priscilla Peasblossom, from marriage into a rapacious merchant family. Priscilla has inherited a sizable fortune, followed Jemmy to Sydney, and been told that he is dead. The most likely direct source for Tucker when he wrote *Jemmy Green in Australia* was 'Billy Barlow in Australia', a Billy Barlow song first performed in 1843 in Maitland, where Tucker was working. The character

of Jemmy Green, however, was by then already well established on the stage. In 1821 'W.T. Moncrieff' (q.v.) had introduced Jemmy into his popular *Tom and Jerry: Or, Life in London*, which spawned many adaptations, imitations and sequels, including 'Life in Sydney: Or, The Ran Dan Club' (1843); in both plays, as in *Jemmy Green in Australia*, Jemmy's rawness ('greenness') leads to his unwise bidding at an auction.

JENKINS, John (1949–), born Melbourne, writer and journalist, was associated with the rise of the 'New Australian Poetry' and the small magazines which accompanied it. He edited the brief-lived *A and Aardvark* in 1970, and was co-editor, with Walter Billeter, of *etymspheres: The Journal of the Paper Castle* in 1974–75 and, with Rudi Krausmann, of *Aspect* in 1976–77. He has also been involved with Billeter in Paper Castle Publications, publishing with him *Dreamrobe Embroideries & Asparagus for Dinner* (1974); with Robert Kenny in Rigmarole Publications; and with Michael Dugan in *The Outback Reader* (1975). Associate editor of *Helix* (1981–82), he was also editor of the small Brunswick Hills Press 1984–88. His own poetry includes *Zone of the White Wolf and Other Landscapes* (1974), *Blindspot* (1977), *The Inland Sea* (1985), *Chromatic Cargoes* (1986), *The Wild White Sea* (1991) and *Days Like Air* (1992). With Ken Bolton he published *Airborne Dogs* (1988), *The Ferrara Poems* (1989) and *The Gutman Variations* (1992), and edited with Antonia Bruns *Soft Lounges* (1984). He has also written for screen and radio. His first non-fiction book, *22 Contemporary Australian Composers*, appeared in 1988.

JENKINS, Wendy (1952–), born Perth, has published poetry in periodicals and in one collection, *Out of Water into Light* (1979). She also edited with B.R. Coffey a collection of WA writing, *Portrait* (1986) and, with Amanda Curtin, Alfredo Strano's *Luck Without Joy: A Portrayal of a Migrant* (1986).

JENNINGS, Kate (1948–), born near Temora, NSW, was raised near Griffith. At Sydney University in the late 1960s and early 1970s she was active in leftwing politics and feminism and edited the well-known collection of contemporary women's verse *Mother I'm Rooted* (1975). Her own verse has appeared in two widely separated collections, *Come to Me My Melancholy Baby* (1975) and *Cats, Dogs & Pitchforks* (1993). The 1975 collection confronts the difficulties of surviving the pain, disappointments and loneliness of life as a feminist poet enclosed in an a 1970s environment of brittle relationships and ephemeral experience; the verse of the 1993 collection is equally passionate and direct but is both more finely honed and more generous in range and tone, achieving what Jennings has described as the 'fast disappearing' art of 'Saying simple things well or complicated things simply'. In 1979 Jennings left for New York, where she works as a writer and editor. Her subsequent publications, selections of essays, *Save Me, Joe Louis* (1988) and *Bad Manners* (1993) and a collection of short stories, *Women Falling Down in the Street* (1990), reveal a marked shift from her earlier radicalism. 'Save me

Joe Louis' were the last words uttered by a young Negro before he died in an American gas chamber, and Jennings uses them as a starting-point for her frank, self-probing reflections on living in New York, her Riverina childhood, relationship with Australia, her travels, love affairs and years as a militant feminist. The essays of *Bad Manners* range over many subjects including an American election, marriage, ageing, political correctness, feminism and the Australian literary scene. Several of the short stories of *Women Falling Down in the Street* are similarly semi-autobiographical; focusing on obsessions, delusions and eccentricities, they probe the absurdity that underlies everyday reality and question the validity of so-called rational ways of living.

JENNINGS, Paul, see *The Oxford Companion to Australian Children's Literature* (1993), pp. 238–9.

JEPHCOTT, Sydney (1864–1951), born Nariong, Upper Murray, Victoria, lived most of his life in the Mount Kosciusko area, whose beauty and grandeur he claimed influenced his literary imagination. He published two books of poetry, *The Secrets of the South* (1892) and *Penetralia* (1912), which contained some verses from the earlier volume. The short, meditative lyrics are frequently solemn and stately in tone; 'Thredbo River', for example, conveys well the atmosphere of the snow country.

JERROLD, Douglas, see *Black-Ey'd Susan*.

'Jim Jones at Botany Bay', one of the best early Australian folk-songs (q.v.), is the bitter lament of an English convict who has been transported for poaching and who at the end of the song vows defiantly that he will join Jack Donohoe's bushranging gang and take revenge on the 'tyrants' who have ill-treated him at Botany Bay. The reference to Donohoe suggests that the ballad was written around 1830, although it was not collected until 1907, when it was published as a 'typical song of the convict days' in Charles MacAlister's *Old Pioneering Days in the Sunny South* (1907). Usually sung to the tune, 'Irish Mollie, Oh!', 'Jim Jones at Botany Bay' has features which link it with the English street ballad tradition; it is one of the few treason songs, reputedly banned by the authorities, to have survived from the penal days.

Jindyworobak Movement, the most extreme expression of the revival of nationalism in Australia in the 1930s, arose partly as a reaction against contemporary colonialist attitudes and partly as a counter to the international influences that had made steady inroads into Australia's isolation throughout the 1920s. It came into being in 1938 when Rex Ingamells (q.v.) founded the Jindyworobak club in Adelaide, published *Conditional Culture*, a prose manifesto explaining the aims and methods of the movement, and produced the first *Jindyworobak Anthology* of poetry. The anthologies were continued annually until 1953, and in 1948 a historical account of the movement, *Jindyworobak Review* (1938–48), was compiled by Inga-

mells. *The Jindyworobaks* (1979), edited by Brian Elliott in the Portable Australian Authors series, is a comprehensive historical and critical account of the movement. Many writers were associated, with varying degrees of commitment, with the Jindyworobaks. In addition to Ingamells those most closely involved, although briefly in some cases, included Ian Tilbrook, Flexmore Hudson, Max Harris, Ian Mudie, Colin Thiele, David Rowbotham, John Blight, William Hart-Smith, Victor Kennedy, Paul Grano, Roland Robinson, Gina Ballantyne, Nancy Cato, Judith Wright, Gwen Harwood and Geoffrey Dutton. Considerable as the early Jindyworobak body of literary talent was, it contained no outstanding Australian poet. By the mid-1950s the movement had lost much of its impetus but has not even now disappeared entirely: Elliott sees evidence of a Jindyworobak continuation in the work of Xavier Herbert, Les Murray and Peter Porter.

The word 'Jindyworobak' was adapted by Ingamells from 'Jindy-worabak', a term used in the glossary of James Devaney's *The Vanished Tribes* (1929) with the meaning 'to annex, to join'. Ingamells chose the word as the name for the movement because it was 'aboriginal', 'outlandish', i.e. likely to arrest attention, and 'symbolic', i.e. directing Australian writers to what should be their distinctive material. Major stimuli to the creation of the movement were P.R. Stephensen's *The Foundations of Culture in Australia* (1936), an aggressively nationalistic demand for a distinctive Australian culture based largely on the spirit of place, and D.H. Lawrence's sensitive reaction to the bush in his novel *Kangaroo* (1923). Ingamells's first exposition of Jindyworobak philosophy came with *On Environmental Values*, an address delivered in 1937, later expanded into *Conditional Culture*. He applied the term 'Jindyworobak' to 'those individuals who are endeavouring to free Australian art from whatever alien influences trammel it, that is, to bring it into proper contact with its material'. Ingamells insisted that the national culture depended on a clear recognition of 'environment values' and an understanding of Australian history and traditions, primaeval, colonial and modern. Australian writers were urged to express their distinctive environment, not in conventional terms suited to other countries but in language indicating its own primal essence. Ingamells concluded *Conditional Culture* with the celebrated and much-ridiculed linking of the Jindyworobak philosophy with Aboriginal culture. He believed that 'the laws, the customs, and the art of the Australian Aboriginals went to make a culture which was closely bound in every way with their environment'. The inference was that the Jindyworobak culture could best develop by assimilating the spirit of Aboriginal culture and by identifying with it. From Aboriginal art and song modern Australian culture could learn the necessary techniques and from Aboriginal legend ('sublimated through our thought') would come the required 'pristine outlook on life'. The Jindyworobaks, or some of them, came to see a fitting symbol in the Aboriginal 'Dreamtime' (more properly 'Alchera' or 'Alcheringa') the myth of the 'first time', the time of creation itself, the root of all Aboriginal lore. They felt that the order and spiritual wholeness implanted in Aboriginal life through the concept of Alcheringa could be taken as a symbol or image which might provide a key for a larger Australian 'Dreamtime'. Contrary to popular opinion, they had no intention of peddling Aboriginal culture for its own sake. It seemed to them to offer a suitable example of environmental values in action. Misconception of their emphasis on Aboriginal culture, exacerbated by the infrequent but much-publicised Jindyworobak habit of using Aboriginal words in poetry, led to misrepresentation, even ridicule of the movement as a whole. R.H. Morrison's coining of the term 'Jindyworobakwardness' reflected the reaction of many people to the idea of basing modern literary culture on an Aboriginal one. In that the movement was symptomatic of a deeply felt need to perceive and express a sense of national identity, it met with some encouragement and support. In that it attempted to force Australia's literary development into narrow nationalistic channels it failed, both because it was too idiosyncratic and backward-looking and because it was parochial and isolationist. In the final outcome it was simply swept aside by the inevitable movement of Australia after the Second World War into the wider international arena, where the simplicity, perhaps naivety, of the Jindyworobak dream appeared to have no real relevance.

Joe Wilson and His Mates, Henry Lawson's (q.v.) fifth prose collection, was first published in 1901 while Lawson was in England. It contains two sections, sometimes published separately: *Joe Wilson*, which comprises the four major parts of the Joe Wilson (q.v.) sequence; and *Joe Wilson's Mates*, fourteen stories which include the famous 'The Loaded Dog'. The popularity of the *Joe Wilson's Mates* title is confirmed by 'Joe Wilson's Mate', a poem by David Campbell, and *Joe Wilson's Mates*, the title both of modern Lawson selections and of a 1957 film of Lawson's story, 'The Union Buries its Dead', in which Joe Wilson is named as the drowned unionist whose funeral is attended.

Johnno, a novel by David Malouf, was published in 1975 and traces the childhood and early adult life of the narrator, who has returned to Brisbane at the age of 30 on the death of his father. During the Second World War the placid life of the Brisbane seaside suburb of Scarborough, where the child's family is settled, is only mildly disturbed and little happens to alter his perception of Australia as 'familiar and boring' or his acceptance of the rituals of his conventional upbringing. At the age of 13, however, when his friendship with the school rebel Johnno suddenly ripens, his world widens. Johnno, whose father has been posted as missing, is a wiry, reckless, tearaway of precocious sexuality, wide-ranging vituperative powers and impressive mendacity. He exerts a strong influence on a small group of would-be disciples but appears, at times, to place most value on his relationship with the narrator, whom he nicknames 'Dante'. At university,

after a period of separation, Dante and Johnno take to roaming around the town, frequenting fights and brothels, where Johnno delights in disturbing the domestic calm. Dante's relationship with Johnno is as ambivalent as his relationship with Australia; cut off from Johnno because of his inability to be romantic enough and his unwillingness to share fully in his fantasies, he is also cut off from Brisbane, 'a place where poetry could never occur'. Johnno eventually leaves for the Congo to work in a copper-mine; Dante stubbornly hangs on in Brisbane in a routine occupation, surprised at his own lack of ambition but determined 'to make life reveal whatever it had to reveal *here* on home ground, where I could recognize the terms'. Later he visits Johnno in Paris, where he witnesses his bizarre underworld lifestyle before leaving for England, where he settles in the North as a teacher. After three years he is treated by fellow Australians as an expatriate, although he reflects: 'I had once found it odd, gratuitous even, that I should be an Australian. I found it even odder, more accidental, that I should be anything else.' Meanwhile Johnno has moved to Athens, where Dante eventually visits him, discovering that some of his life-force has now been sapped and that his style of life is more mysterious than ever. Back in Brisbane some time later, he runs into Johnno again; now massive and dishevelled, Johnno is working on an oil survey on the Condamine. His sudden, mysterious death by drowning forces Dante to re-examine their relationship, including Johnno's expectations of himself and of Australia. Johnno, he realises, had aimed at 'some dimension in which the hundred possibilities a situation contains may be more significant than the occurrence of any one of them, and a metaphor truer in the long run than mere fact'.

JOHNS, Brian (1936–), born Gordonvale, Queensland, is well known in the fields of journalism and publishing. He worked as a feature-writer for the Australian News and Information Bureau 1956–64, was chief political correspondent for the *Australian* in 1964, special writer for the *Bulletin* in 1965 and leader-writer, chief of staff and chief political correspondent in Canberra for the *Sydney Morning Herald* 1966–74. Publishing director for Penguin Books Australia 1979–87, and then a chief executive for the Special Broadcasting Service, he is now chairman of the ABC.

JOHNS, Fred (1868–1932), born Michigan, USA, of Cornish descent, came in 1884 to SA where he found employment on the *Register*; in 1914 he left to become a Hansard reporter in the SA parliament, and in 1920–25 he was editor of the *South Australian Freemason*. Johns wrote a small volume of patriotic verse, *In Remembrance* (1920), as well as *A Journalist's Jottings* (1922), but is best remembered for his pioneering, meticulous biographical research. *Johns's Notable Australians* (1906), a volume of biographies of living Australians, was revised and updated in 1908 under the original title; in 1912–14 as *Fred Johns's Annual*; in 1922 as *Who's Who in the Commonwealth of Australia*; and in 1927 as *Who's Who in Australia* (q.v.), a title which continued after his death. Johns was also the author of *An Australian Biographical Dictionary* (1934); he endowed the University of Adelaide scholarship for biography which bears his name.

JOHNSON, Colin, see **MUDROOROO**

JOHNSON, Eva (1946–) belongs to the Malak Malak people of the Northern Territory. A feminist, political activist, travelling performer and speaker, she has written several plays including 'Faded Gems' (1981), 'Tjinderella' (1984), which she also directed, and *Murras* (workshopped at the first National Black Playwrights Conference in 1987, produced 1988 and published 1989). In 1984 she was named Aboriginal Artist of the Year. Concentrating specifically on Aboriginal women, *Murras* is an angry play which exposes the historical White neglect of and brutality towards Black Australians.

JOHNSON, Frank C. was an employee of Dymock's, the Sydney booksellers, when he joined with Norman Lindsay and Kenneth Slessor to found *Vision* (q.v.) magazine. He subsequently published Slessor's *Darlinghurst Nights* (1933) and, particularly in the 1940s, a wide range of popular material, e.g. magazines, children's books, comic books and popular fiction.

JOHNSON, J.C.F. (Joseph Colin Francis) (1848–1904), born Adelaide, and widely known as 'Alphabetical' Johnson, became experienced and knowledgeable in mining operations, on which he wrote the successful handbooks *Practical Mining* (1889) and *Getting Gold* (1897). A journalist with the SA *Register*, subsequently proprietor and editor of *Adelaide Punch*, and Minister for Education in SA and the NT 1887–89, he contributed bush verse to the *Savage Club Annual* and the *Observer Miscellany*, and published several collections of fiction and verse that caught, with considerable affection, the atmosphere of bush and mining life and mirrored typical characters from those environments. His published works were *On the Wallaby: Or, Tales from the Men's Hut* (1872), *Christmas on Carringa* (1873), *Over the Island* (1873) and *An Austral Christmas* (1888).

JOHNSON, Patricia (1945–), born Sydney, worked overseas as a journalist until 1976 when she returned to Australia. She has had many television and film scripts produced, has contributed short stories to anthologies and magazines and has published two plays, *Gladbags* (1984) and *And the Bestman Makes Three* in *Shorts at the Wharf* Vol.I (1985). Her unpublished plays include 'The Cocky on the Lawn' and 'Kindred Spirits' (1984).

JOHNSON, Richard (1753–1827), born Yorkshire, England, came to Australia with the First Fleet as Australia's first clergyman. He conducted the first religious service in the colony on 3 February 1788. Johnson's chief interest apart from religion was farming; Watkin Tench judged him 'the best farmer in the colony'. He returned to England in 1800. Johnson wrote *An Address to the Inhabitants of the Colonies Established in New South Wales and Norfolk Island* (1794), the first book published with the intention of being distributed throughout the Colony. George Mackaness edited *Some Letters of Rev. Richard Johnson* (1954); biographical studies include James Bonwick's *Australia's First Preacher* (1898), W.H. Rainey's *The Real Richard Johnson* (1947), and Neil K. Macintosh's *Richard Johnson* (1978); the last-named is the most comprehensive. Johnson appears as a character in Thomas Keneally's novel *The Playmaker* (1987) and in the play which it inspired, *Our Country's Good* (1988), by Timberlake Wertenbaker.

JOHNSON, Stephanie (1961–), born NZ, is a freelance writer who has spent several years in Australia and has contributed to Australian periodicals and anthologies. She has published a collection of poetry, *The Bleeding Ballerina* (1987), a collection of short stories, *The Glass Whittler* (1989) and a novel, *Crimes of Neglect* (1992). She has also written plays for stage, radio and screen and in 1986 won the Bruce Mason Playwright's Award (NZ). Johnson's stories, which have been praised for their technical competence, deal with loneliness, ageing, death and failed or failing relationships. *Crimes of Neglect* explores the inward and outward journey of Bea, a 44-year-old alcoholic whose purposeless moves between NZ and Australia mirror her sense of the meaningless nature of life.

JOHNSON, Susan (1956–), born Brisbane, grew up in Sydney and worked as a journalist with the *Courier-Mail*, the *Australian Women's Weekly*, the *Sun-Herald*, the *Sydney Morning Herald* and the *National Times*. Since 1984 she has been writing full-time and now resides in Hong Kong. She has written three novels. *Messages from Chaos* (1987) explores the difficulties of contemporary relationships when liberation frequently shades into exploitation, as the protagonist, 29-year-old Anna Lawrence, discovers in her long-continued affair with a married man. *Flying Lessons* (1990) is the story of two women of different generations, Emma James and her granddaughter Ria Lubrano, whose situations and sense of unfulfilled potential are both alike and different. *A Big Life* (1993) traces the career of Billy Hayes, born in the Sydney slums of Glebe into a family of six children which loses its relative peace and harmony when the father, Jack, returns several years after the end of the Great War. Billy finds a niche for himself with a Chinese tumbling family of Reggie and Lily Tsang. Eventually his acrobatic talent is sold off by his avaricious father to a travelling troupe with whom he goes overseas. As he grows older Billy's life becomes totally centred on his talent, his artistry as a tumbler. In time he marries the incompatible Bubbles Drake and has a child but remains permanently arrested in his childhood dream of the 'big life' of success and perfection as 'a working artist whose material was air'. As the years pass he demonstrates little or no capacity to participate in the real world. In the final pages Johnson allows him 'some sort of glimmer of understanding' that 'life is about balance' but the reader remains unconvinced that 'balance' for Billy has any wider meaning than that which has so far dominated his life.

Susan Johnson has co-edited *Latitudes: New Writing from the North* (1986, short fiction) and has contributed her own short stories to several anthologies, *Millennium* (1991), *Country Childhood* (1991) and *Storia* (1991).

JOHNSTON, Dorothy (1948–), born Geelong, was educated at the University of Melbourne, trained as a teacher and has taught English and worked as a researcher in the field of education. In 1979 she moved to Canberra and is a member of the group of seven women writers who published a joint collection, *Canberra Tales* (1988). Johnston's stories have appeared in periodicals and in such anthologies as *Frictions* (1982) and *The State of the Art* (1983). She has also published three novels, *Tunnel Vision* (1984), *Ruth* (1986), and *Maralinga, My Love* (1988, highly commended in the ABC Bicentennial Awards). In 1991 she won the inaugural ACT Literary Award. *Tunnel Vision*, set in a massage parlour, the normal euphemism for a brothel, is an ironic, subtle and even lyrical exploration of the experiences of three women who work there, Lil, the narrator and novitiate in prostitution, Freda, the cynic whose life is a 'continuous open-ended complaint', and Maria, whose capacity to dream buoys them all up, at least for a while. Run by Harry Cod, an entrepreneur who sees himself as in the entertainment business, the parlour is a run-down shed in Port Melbourne, an emblem of the gentle corruption which pervades the story. It is characteristic of the unexpected atmosphere of this novel, which evades sociology and ideology as firmly as pornography, that relations between the women themselves and some of their clients are surprisingly tender. *Ruth*, set in the mid-1970s against the political ferment of the period and partly located in a Melbourne women's refuge, traces the search for self of Ruth Cassidy, housewife and mother. Markedly passive and, as it turns out much later, haunted by the loss of an earlier child, Ruth leaves her husband for a women's refuge but fails to find a satisfying alternative way of life, and finally disappears from the novel in its last section, titled 'Waiting for the Dismissal!'. The allusion to the dismissal of the Whitlam government underlines Johnston's attempt to link public and private; Ruth's disappearance and the consequences for her family emphasise the significance of Auden's poem 'Musée des Beaux Arts', which is the novel's epigraph, on the everyday nature of suffering and the indifference of both human and natural worlds to the extreme experiences of others. *Maralinga, My Love* (the novel's title is an echo of the 1959 screenplay by Marguerite Duras, *Hiroshima, Mon Amour*), focuses on the atomic tests of 1956–57 undertaken by the British government at Maralinga, SA and grew from Johnston's visit to the area in 1986 shortly after the royal commission into the tests had begun. Written from the perspective of a young Australian soldier, Graham Falconer, who participates in the tests and who slowly uncovers their physical, cultural and psychological consequences, the novel uses a disconnected narrative and bare, understated prose style to evoke the passivity and confusion which characterised post-colonial Australian society in the 1950s and led to uncritical acquiescence in a decade of testing. Graham's search for the truth begins when he and his friend and mentor, the scientist Charlie Hamilton, find traces of cobalt radiation. Later Graham becomes a technician in the nuclear industry, gains a degree in physics and a position as defence scientist. While his determination to pursue the facts strengthens, Charlie Hamilton fears the issue is potentially too personally damaging and defects. Emphasising the carnival atmosphere of the preparations for the tests and the strange male bonding that the explosion elicits, the narrative is sewn with subtle ironies evoking the bizarre aspects of the Australians' complicity in the degradation of their land and the gendered assumptions and needs which are in part the psychological grounds of this collusion in self-betrayal. Graham's quest also affects his marriage, and just as his growth to responsibility and recognition of unnatural dependence mirrors the nation's growth from the passive simplicities of the Menzies years to the challenging complexities of the Vietnam period, Deborah, his wife, abandons the dependent attitudes of a 1950s wife. But the main character of the novel is Maralinga itself, a desert landscape of haunting power, which grips the imagination of the central protagonist with increasing tenacity, confronting him with a series of difficult loyalties, to himself, to the land, and to history; as he comments towards the end of the novel: 'It's a funny thing loyalty. It comes at you in such devious ways.'

JOHNSTON, George Henry (1912–70) was born in Malvern, Melbourne, the son of a tramway sheds foreman. After education at state schools he became an apprentice lithographer in a commercial art studio, meanwhile studying art at the National Gallery School. A series of imaginative articles about sailing ships gained him a start as a journalist on the staff of the *Argus* and during the Second World War his syndicated dispatches from battle zones in New Guinea, China, Burma, India, Italy and the north Atlantic appeared regularly in national and overseas newspapers. He also wrote two accounts of the war at sea, *Grey Gladiator* (1941) and *Battle of the Seaways* (1941); a graphic description of his experience in New Guinea, *New Guinea Diary* (1943); a contemporary and historical account of the Australian army, *Australia at War* (1942); and a description of the Australian war effort for American readers, *Pacific Partner* (1944). His *War Diary 1942* was published in 1984. Brought up on the myth of Anzac, he turned finally towards pacifism as a result of his experiences of war and disillusionment with Western policies in China in 1945. After the failure of his first marriage he married Charmian Clift (q.v.) in 1947 and joined the staff of the Sydney *Sun*, which sent him to London in 1951 as its European editor. He resigned from the position in 1954, having decided to rely solely on his writing for support, and with his wife and three children spent the next ten years on the Greek islands of Kalymnos and Hydra.

The difficulties and joys of their years there are described in his novel *Clean Straw for Nothing* (q.v., 1969) and in Charmian Clift's *Mermaid Singing* (1956) and *Peel Me a Lotus* (1959). In 1964, when his novel *My Brother Jack* (q.v., 1964) won the Miles Franklin Award, he returned to Australia and lived in Sydney until his death from tuberculosis, a disease that had threatened his life for several years.

A prolific writer, Johnston produced a range of novels, short stories and plays for radio and television. Although many of his books are 'potboilers', such as the series of thrillers published under the pseudonym 'Shane Martin', several of his novels achieve distinction. Among the most notable are *Moon at Perigee* (1948), published in London with the title *Monsoon* (1951), *The Cyprian Woman* (1955), *The Darkness Outside* (1959), *Closer to the Sun* (1960), *The Far Road* (1962) and *The Far Face of the Moon* (1965). But his outstanding achievement is his semi-autobiographical trilogy *My Brother Jack*, *Clean Straw for Nothing* and *A Cartload of Clay* (1971). His other writings include *Journey Through Tomorrow* (1947), a description of his travels in India, China, Tibet, Burma and Japan; *Skyscrapers in the Mist* (1946), an account of a wartime visit to New York; three novels with Charmian Clift, *High Valley* (1949), which won first prize in the 1948 literary competition of the *Sydney Morning Herald*, *The Big Chariot* (1953) and *The Sponge Divers* (1956), published in the USA with the title *The Sea and the Stone* (1955); and a popular collection of essays, *The Australians* (1966), lavishly illustrated with photographs by Robert B. Goodman. A collection of his and Charmian Clift's short stories, *Strong Man from Piraeus*, selected by Garry Kinnane, appeared in 1983. Johnston also edited two collections of essays by Charmian Clift. Other awards that he won include the Miles Franklin Award for *Clean Straw for Nothing* and the Literary Guild Award of the USA for *Closer to the Sun*. There are two well-known portraits of Johnston, by Russell Drysdale and Ray Crooke and an award-winning biography by Garry Kinnane was published in 1986. One of his sons was the poet Martin Johnston (q.v.).

A victim of his natural fluency and the necessity of writing to make a living, Johnston did not achieve a work of major importance until *My Brother Jack*. An absorbing, frank study of early experience, the novel is also a remarkable social document, a densely textured re-creation of life in Melbourne between the wars. The semi-autobiographical narrator, David Meredith, appears in both *Closer to the Sun* and in *The Far Road*, although neither develops his Odysseus qualities. *My Brother Jack*, which deals with David's youth and early manhood, begins the story of his journeyings in quest of meaning. Doomed to be an expatriate, David never inwardly conforms to accepted patterns but constantly seeks to find and assert his own. Rejecting first his family, then his own false values, his marriage and finally his country, he seems to find at the end of the novel authentic freedom in his union with Cressida Morley. *Clean Straw for Nothing* has a kaleidoscopic structure, criss-crossing time from 1945 to 1968 and covering Meredith's experiences in Melbourne, Sydney, London and Greece. The mood of the novel,

heavy with creative, emotional and material failure, is darkened even further by Meredith's inability to grasp the promised freedom. His voyaging has resulted in a baffled awareness of unfulfilled dreams and the near collapse of his marriage. In the unfinished novel *A Cartload of Clay*, Meredith, now deprived of a future, ceaselessly probes the past to discover a meaning. Left with 'only the brittle present, fragmenting at a touch, and the long accumulated mucked-up obscurity of the past, with all its unlearned lessons', he concludes that the only pattern to life is the search itself.

JOHNSTON, Grahame (1929–76), born Wellington, NZ, was educated at Victoria University, Wellington, and at the University of Oxford. He came to Australia in 1954 and taught at the University of Queensland and the ANU, and was professor of English at the University of Melbourne (1963–65) and at the Royal Military College, Duntroon (1968–76). Originally a medievalist, Johnston later worked in American literature and particularly in Australian language and literature, where he won a reputation as critic, editor, bibliographer and lexicographer. His *Australian Literary Criticism* (1962) was an early critical anthology devoted to Australian literature and the beginning of a successful relationship with the Australian branch of OUP. Adviser on Australian literature to the press from the early 1960s, he became an active general editor of its Australian Writers and Their Work and Australian Bibliographies series, compiled the *Annals of Australian Literature* (q.v., 1970), and edited the *Australian Pocket Oxford Dictionary* (1976), a major contribution to the study of Australian English (q.v.).

JOHNSTON, Martin, (1947–90), born Sydney, the son of George Johnston and Charmian Clift (qq.v.), worked as a cadet reporter, a freelance book reviewer, and as a subtitler and sub-editor for SBS television. Brought up partly in Greece, he returned there to live for some years and also travelled widely in Europe. He published the collections of poetry *Shadowmass* (1971), *The Sea-Cucumber* (1978), and *The Typewriter Considered as a Bee-trap* (1984); a novel, *Cicada Gambit* (1984); and a series of translations of modern Greek poetry, *Ithaka* (1973). He also wrote an introduction to a reprint of Charmian Clift's essays, *The World of Charmian Clift* (1983). His novel, which concerns a young Greek chess player who earns a precarious living in bohemian Sydney, is experimental in form, notable for its central character and its city setting. A selection of his poetry and prose, edited by John Tranter, was published in 1993 and includes some poems not published in book form before, essays, book reviews, excerpts from interviews and family photographs. The selection allows for a more complete view of Johnston than was previously available, underlining his wide-ranging interests, scholarly background and political commitment. Tranter's introduction also throws light on his early death from alcoholism, suggesting that the cultural shifts he experienced in childhood and the consequent sense of rootlessness, coupled with his parents' style of living and subsequent family tragedies were major contributions. Cerebral, occasionally inaccessible and responsive to literary traditions different from those recognised by other Australian poets of his generation, Johnston found it difficult to reach a wide audience. Martin Duwell has suggested that reading his poetry sometimes draws on skills similar to those required for reading chess, a game which was one of Johnston's obsessions; Christopher Pollnitz, who ranks the title poem of *The Sea-Cucumber* as 'one of the handful of major Australian poems this decade', sees particular creative strengths in his tangential position. Tranter's poem 'Cicada Gambit' describes Johnston as 'Exiled by circumstance and inclination/ from the land and language of his childhood' and as declining to Darlinghurst, where he exchanged 'the dialect/ of Callimachus and Cavafy for the meat-pie-eaters'/ drab vernacular'. 'Without Preamble: Martin Johnston 1947–1990' in Kate Jennings's collection of verse *Cats, Dogs & Pitchforks* (1993) reflects on his achievements and early death.

JOLLEY, Elizabeth (1923–   ), born Birmingham, England, of an English father and a Viennese mother, grew up in the 'black country' of Britain's industrial Midlands. The tensions caused by her mother's sense of exile and her father's pacifist beliefs, both exacerbated by the circumstance of war, have provided rich material for her fiction. With her younger sister, she was educated privately until the age of 11, when she was sent to a Quaker boarding school. At 17 she began her nursing training in London, and was soon exposed to the physical and psychological horrors suffered by wounded servicemen as well as gaining further insights into institutional life. In 1959 she migrated to WA with her husband, who was a university librarian, and her three children. In Australia she has worked as a nurse, a domestic cleaner, a door-to-door salesperson and, very briefly, in real estate. She was a part-time tutor in creative writing and literature at Fremantle Arts Centre 1974–85 and has taught at Curtin University and several other tertiary institutions. She began writing early but was late to win publication or recognition. In the 1960s some of her stories were accepted by the BBC World Service and by Australian journals, but her first book was not published until 1976. She then won immediate recognition in Australia and from 1983, with the publication of *Mr Scobie's Riddle* and *Miss Peabody's Inheritance*, internationally, especially in the USA. Jolley's publications since 1976 give the impression of a steady rate of production, but their chronology of publication does not represent their history of composition; *My Father's Moon* and *Cabin Fever* were the first novels she wrote, followed by *Palomino* and *Milk and Honey*; and some have gone through periods of revision or temporary abandonment or have coincided with the writing of others reflecting her non-linear creative process. Her published works include the short-story collections *Five Acre Virgin* (1976), *The Travelling Entertainer* (1979) and *Woman in a Lampshade* (1983); the novels *Palomino* (1980, co-winner of the Con Weickhardt Prize), *The Newspaper of Claremont Street* (1981), *Miss*

Peabody's Inheritance (1983), *Mr Scobie's Riddle* (q.v., 1983, winner of the Western Australia Week Award for fiction and the *Age* Book of the Year Award), *Milk and Honey* (1984, winner of the NSW Premier's Prize for fiction), *Foxybaby* (1985), *The Well* (1986, winner of the Miles Franklin Award), *The Sugar Mother* (1988), *My Father's Moon* (1989, winner of the *Age* Book of the Year Award), *Cabin Fever* (1990) and *The George's Wife* (1993, winner of the *Age* Book of the Year Award); and the collection of autobiographical pieces, speeches and articles, *Central Mischief*, edited by Caroline Lurie (1992). A diary she kept before she published any of her novels and which records her experience after buying a small hobby farm was published as *Diary of a Weekend Farmer* in 1993. She has also written numerous radio plays, broadcast by the ABC, 'Night Report' (1975) which won a special award in the Sound-Stage competition of 1975–76, 'The Performance' (1976), 'The Shepherd on the Roof' (1977), 'The Well-Bred Thief' (1977), 'Woman in a Lampshade' (1979), 'Two Men Running' (1981), which was awarded an Awgie in 1982, 'Paper Children' (1988) and 'Little Lewis Has Had a Lovely Sleep' (1988); her poetry and stories have also appeared in numerous journals and anthologies. Her awards also include the State of Victoria Short Story Award in 1966, 1981 and 1982 and the Canada/Australia Literary Award in 1989; in 1987 she was awarded an honorary doctorate by the WA Institute of Technology. She is an Officer of the Order of Australia (AO).

The characters of Jolley's stories and novels are in varying degrees society's misfits; whether they are old, foreign, lonely, eccentric, poor, or simply regarded as deviant, they are outsiders, dispossessed and diminished. The sadness of their lives is frequently moderated by the imaginative inventiveness of their strategies for survival, described with a mix of wry affection, dark humour, compassion and satirical realism. Inhabiting various forms of prison, such as the old people's home of *Mr Scobie's Riddle*, the educational establishments of *Miss Peabody's Inheritance* and *Foxybaby*, the Gothic boarding house of *Milk and Honey*, the maternity home of *Cabin Fever*, and the isolated farm of *Palomino*, they often survive because of an understated but gritty conviction of significance and an openness to the bizarre, cross-grained aspects of living, however painful. Jolley has said that she is interested in the individual's particular form of loneliness or fear which imposes life on the fringe, 'I suppose I'm interested to explore the inside of people's survival'. In an extended essay, 'Who Talks of Victory?', she has commented that 'Bitter knowledge, grief and unwanted realisation, often in greater proportion, go side by side with acceptance, love and hope . . . . No one comes out on top in my fiction [but many of my characters] would endorse the apostles' injunction 'and having done all to stand'.' Cruelty, emotional manipulation, territorial aggression and financial exploitation are also natural to some of her characters, however, and although Jolley emphasises the importance of empathy and compassion, her underlying view of the human condition and human nature is necessarily bleak. The world of her fiction has a realistic surface, which is subject to unpredictable surprises, shocks, bizarre twists and flights of fantasy; a dissonant wit and resilient comic impulse combined with open-ended plots or startling resolutions unsettle the reader's expectations and erode assumptions about what is 'normal'. The self-consciousness of Jolley's art, which includes an intricate treatment of interlocking narrative frames, overt fictionality and playful manipulation of the reader's curiosity about the relationship between author and characters enhances the formal pleasures of her work, although it is not radically experimental. Her subtle studies of embattled individuals are also richly suggestive of the power of psychic processes, the workings of deferred desire and displaced repression. Her fiction has also been interpreted in terms of musical structure, practising variation and counterpoint, and interplaying independent themes or melodic fragments. This musicality extends between texts as well as within them so that characters and situations recur through the novels and short stories, developing from a germinal point in an earlier collection or concluding or explaining themselves in a later one. The cleaning woman who is the main character of *The Newspaper of Claremont Street* appears earlier in stories centring on the family of Mrs Morgan and her family recurs in *Mr Scobie's Riddle*; a postscript to *Palomino*, 'The Libation', is included in *Woman in a Lampshade*. In her short stories characters are often interwoven, repeating themselves in modified forms, reflecting each other, increasing the effect of human complexity. Some stories, focusing on a central character, have the loose unity of a cycle. Certain themes, incidents, landscapes, types, and situations recur, although variety rather than sameness is the keynote of her fiction. She is particularly preoccupied with the experience of displacement, whether it is the alienation suffered by those incarcerated in an old people's home or the bewilderment of the European migrant confronted with the strange Australian landscape or the reverse experience of the Australian traveller in a Europe which does not fit received expectations.

Palomino, a sombre novel suggestively set in a harsh inland landscape, and frequently criss-crossing between past and present, explores the lesbian relationship between a deregistered obstetrician, the 60-year-old Laura, and a much younger woman, Andrea. Tormented by her sexual relationship with her brother, which has concluded in pregnancy, Andrea is the more passive of the two. Both women and their ultimate self-sacrificing decision are interpreted with sympathy, while the flowering of their relationship and its exposure to external threats are counterpointed with the emotional and physical poverty of a family of squatters on Laura's isolated property. *The Newspaper of Claremont Street* deals with a familar theme in Jolley's fiction, 'over-devotion', or the destructive, unwilling dependence that can bind people together. This novel is one of her most comic, however, a rich cultivation of Jolley's talent for the eccentric and macabre. The book's protagonist, called Newspaper or Weekly because of her habit of spreading news between the homes she cleans, saves her money to fulfil her secret dream of buying a house in the country; almost prevented from achieving her goal by a widowed former employer, Nastasya 'Nasty' Torben, Weekly ultimately resolves her predicament in a blackly comic way. The central theme of *Mr Scobie's Riddle*, which is set in a nursing home, is the moral one of sensitivity to the needs of others. Jolley's poignant, unsentimental presentation of the vulnerable aged inmates is a tragi-comic exploration of greed, egotism and the fear of death. In this place of dislocation and diminishment, two individuals achieve a kind of redemption; Mr Scobie, one of the elderly inmates prevented from returning home by younger relatives and pursued in predatory fashion by the home's matron, and Heather Hailey, whose imaginative energy and openness to life lead her to important insights about human meaning and value notwithstanding her inhuman, value-drained environment.

Miss Peabody's Inheritance is one of Jolley's most artful, self-reflexive novels, exploring the processes of both writing and reading: as she comments, 'So much depends in the writing of a novel on the impact of the imagination on someone else. A great deal depends too on the fiction which is mounted on truth ... the writer creates the imagined land from fragments of the real thing.' Miss Peabody is another dispossessed individual, trapped in a drab existence as a London office worker and dutiful daughter, subservient to the demands of a bedridden mother. Another novelist, the Australian Diana Hopewell, author of a lesbian romance, *Angels on Horseback*, is supposedly responsible for half the text and for offering Miss Peabody her ultimate inheritance. After initiating a correspondence with Diana Hopewell, Miss Peabody becomes her ideal reader, privileged to receive the text of a new novel in successive letters. Reading becomes an education in writing as she shares in the creative process, meanwhile creating her own imaginative version of the admired novelist and the Australian bush. The links, dualities and echoes between the novel in process and life in process suggest the power of the imagination and the ambiguous relationships between fiction and reality, mind and art, and subjectivity and life.

Milk and Honey, Jolley's most poetic and expressionistic fiction, is a haunting blend of naturalism, fantasy, allegory, fairy tale and Gothic romance. Rich in literary, biblical, and mythical allusions, the novel is concerned with metaphysical issues, especially the nature of love in various aspects, sexual, familial and even love of country and its paradoxical dual potential for harm or help. Placing William Blake's poem on Love from *Songs of Experience* as the first of the novel's epigraphs, and juxtaposing it with the well-known passage from *Exodus* referring to the Israelites' promised land as a 'land flowing with milk and honey', Jolley describes the journey of Jacob, the novel's protagonist and narrator, to self-knowledge and a kind of redemption. The novel begins almost at the end of Jacob's story, when he appears to be living a shrunken existence as an ineffective door-to-door salesman; alienated from his wife and daughter and almost wholly friendless, tormented by the loss of his love, Madge, filled with a nameless remorse, oppressed by 'the chill discomfort of poverty' and living in a cold little house on the edge of an industrial wasteland, he has lost the power he once had as a musician since one of his hands is now no more than a claw. His passage to this grievous situation is a complicated one, involving a series of choices between alternative ways of seeing, living and loving, which Jacob appears to have made or has been led to make, almost unconsciously. At the age of 13 he was introduced as a student of music and resident guest into a family of refugees from Vienna, headed by Leopold Heimbach, and comprising his unmarried sisters Tante Rosa and Tante Heloise, his daughter, the maidenly Louise and his handicapped, physically grotesque son, Waldemar. The Heimbachs continue to live as if they are in Europe, shutting out the actualities of Australia with collective determination and confirming their resistant cultural identity with numerous old-world rituals. Jacob, who inherits a fortune, is their guarantee of security, in Jolley's terms, the fragment of an Austrian cone on which this fully formed one settles, drawing sustenance from it 'in order to preserve themselves and remain unchanged for as long as possible'. *Milk and Honey* is concerned throughout with numerous dualities or opposed qualities, but the opposition of Europe and Australia, the new world and the old, is the most immediate. The claustrophobic but compelling charms of living in this imported European environment, where he is explicitly treated like a prince, subvert Jacob's will to escape to the open air of outside Australia, represented most vividly by Madge; wife to the boring but good-natured Norman, a plump, brashly everyday woman who makes no pretence to artistic vocation and plays a violin for money, Madge becomes Jacob's lover. Almost involuntarily, however, he becomes betrothed to Louise, just as earlier he had involuntarily acquiesced in the fiction that he had accidentally killed Waldemar who apparently suffered from a weak heart and died as a result of one of Jacob's playful blows: 'I looked upon myself as a murderer and considered my imprisonment quite in order. I had no wish to be free.' But Waldemar's presence continues to brood over the action and the reader is not surprised to discover that the family has secretly maintained him in an upstairs room. It is possible that the physically gross, incestuous and violent Waldemar is the Hyde to Jacob's Dr Jekyll, a projection of his morally deteriorating inner self and that the childish game of choosing which of the two closed hands contains a gift which initiates their relationship ('"Which hend you hev?"' Waldemar demands of Jacob, holding 'his porky face . . . suddenly close'), and which results in Jacob receiving a cockroach, predicts his choice of Blake's self-centred Love which 'builds a Hell in Heaven's despite'. The novel's close, nevertheless, suggests the possibility of redemption following growth into mature self-knowledge, that 'Perhaps the rubbish in a person's life could be pushed somewhere beneath a smooth skin. Perhaps a shining and elastic skin could grow and, in place of a decrepit human being, there could be something radiant and glowing'.

In *Foxybaby* Jolley returns with a larger cast of characters and a farcical outer plot to the same stratagem of framing a work-in-progress with a story about its writer and another about its audience as she used in *Miss Peabody's Inheritance*. When the novelist Alma Porch agrees to tutor a creative drama course for a group of middle-aged women who are enrolled in a 'Better Body Through the Arts' weight-loss course at a campus in a place called Cheatham East, she provides the ingredients for striking contrasts between the riotous sexual and other caperings of students and staff and the sombre story they begin to mime; eventually the fictions fuse, art and life become indistinguishable from each other and the sexual theme is extended into a statement about the erotic adventure of authorship. Characteristically unsettling in the mix of modes and shifts of mood, *Foxybaby* is also characteristic in its unsettling transformation of figures of caricature to figures who are fully human. Gothic atmosphere and finely modulated horror characterise *The Well* which is a study of love become distorted and destructive. Hester Harper, the lame only daughter of a WA landowner, and the orphan she 'adopts', Katherine, enjoy or appear to enjoy a relationship in which Hester provides for the girl out of the fortune which she has previously carefully hoarded. All is changed after their car hits a man and they throw the body down the well; the fragility of their bond is thereafter dramatically exposed at the level of plot while at the novel's deeper psychological levels the well takes on the role of symbol, focusing the concerns with memory and the unconscious which weave through the narrative.

The subject of Jolley's eighth novel, *The Sugar Mother*, her most extended study of a marriage, is partly fictionality. Left to fend for himself for a year while his wife Cecilia goes abroad for a medical fellowship, the childless 54-year-old Edwin Page is drawn into a relationship with a young woman, stage-managed by her mother and complicated by other friends, which appears as if it will issue in surrogate motherhood. If the juxtapositions and shocks are less extreme than in Jolley's other fiction, the novel has cumulative destabilising effects.

My Father's Moon, *Cabin Fever* and *The George's Wife* represent a radically new direction in Jolley's writing, suggested earlier in a few short stories, but not fully developed until these three complementary novels. Semi-autobiographical, subtle and gently elegiac, they return to the English scenes of her youth. A poignant retrospective search for the lost father and the study of a young life damaged by careless people, *My Father's Moon* records the sadness aroused by unattainable ways of being, the irreversible drift from early securities and intimacies and the power of unconscious drives and repressions. *Cabin Fever* fills in some of the gaps in *My Father's Moon* and takes the narrator, Vera, a few years further in her destiny. *The George's Wife* brings her to Australia and to her final destiny as wife and nurse to a wheelchair-bound husband. Reminiscent of Chekhov in their revelation of 'life's depths at the very moment when [they seem] to reflect its shimmering surface', these novels probe the past and the mind's act of remembering with tact and sometimes painful honesty.

The selected writings of *Central Mischief*, indispensable for an understanding of Jolley, include autobiographical information and numerous statements on her preoccupations and creative life.

JOLLIFFE, Eric (1907–), born Portsmouth, England, came to Australia in 1914 and spent his late teens as a bush worker. He studied art in Sydney and in the late 1930s became a regular contributor of cartoons to the *Bulletin*. He worked briefly for *Smith's Weekly* after the Second World War but established his reputation with his cartoon series 'Saltbush Bill' and 'Witchetty's Tribe' in *Pix*, and 'Sandy Blight' in the *Sun-Herald*; in 1973 he established his own magazine, *Jolliffe's Outback*. Saltbush Bill and Sandy Blight are farmers whose experiences form part of the Dad and Dave (q.v.) tradition of rural humour. 'Witchetty's Tribe', a series dominated by busty Aboriginal women in tribal 'suburbia', has been criticised for its patronising Eurocentricism, although Jolliffe has often protested his deep love and respect for the Aborigines whom he has visited regularly in outback Australia. More than a hundred books of Jolliffe's cartoons have been published; he also illustrated *Corroboree* (1946), which includes poems and stories by other authors.

Jonah, a novel by Louis Stone (q.v.), was first published in 1911. Set in Sydney's working-class districts in the early years of the twentieth century, it is the story of a larrikin, Joe Jones or Jonah, leader of a street 'push'. A hunchbacked outsider rejected as a child by his family, Jonah leads a fierce existence that acknowledges only the solidarity of the gang. His discovery of his love for his son, offspring of his liaison with the unattractive Ada Yabsley, revolutionises his life, turning him into a successful capitalist, owner of a large shoe shop. Ada's mother, Mrs Yabsley, a washerwoman of generous proportions and instincts, helps his early rise. Happiness eludes the ruthless Jonah, however; Ada lapses into alcoholism and is killed in a fall that has been partly caused by the intervention of Clara Grimes, a refined music teacher to whom Jonah is attracted. He ends by forming a marriage of convenience with his saleswoman, Miss Giltinan. The destiny of his old friend Chook, another larrikin, contrasts with that of Jonah. Chook marries the courageous Pinkey and finds emotional rather than material happiness. *Jonah* was made into a television series by the ABC in 1982 and has been adapted for the stage in two versions, by John O'Donoghue in 1979 and by John Romeril and Alan John in 1986. The novel was also the basis for the musical, *Jonah Jones*, performed by the Sydney Theatre Company in 1985.

JONES, Doris Egerton (1889–1973), born Adelaide, was educated in WA, SA and Victoria and travelled extensively within Australia and overseas. She turned to fiction-writing after her plans for a career in law were abandoned because of ill health. Her novels are *Peter Piper* (1913), *Time O'Day* (1915), *Green Eyes* (1915), *The Coconut Planter* (1916) and *The Year Between* (1918). *Peter Piper* was well received at the time; A.G. Steph-

ens in the *Bookfellow* saw it as 'the most Australian story since Stella Franklin's *My Brilliant Career*', and in some respects, especially in the heroine's early boy-like status, it resembles Franklin's novel. It lacks Franklin's grim realism, however, and before long resorts to the facile solutions of women's romance novels. Jones's later novels attracted only minor critical interest. She also wrote the play *Governor Bligh* (1930), which was performed in Sydney and Melbourne and collaborated with Emelie Polini in the play 'The Flaw', produced in Sydney in 1923.

JONES, Evan (1931–), born Preston, Victoria, was educated at the University of Melbourne and Stanford University in the USA. Jones has taught history and English at the University of Melbourne and the ANU. He has published four volumes of poetry, *Inside the Whale* (1960), *Understandings* (1967), *Recognitions* (1978) and *Left at the Post* (1984). He edited, with Geoffrey Little, *The Poems of Kenneth Mackenzie* (1972) and wrote the monograph *Kenneth Mackenzie* (1969). In the 1950s Jones was one of a group of writers at the University of Melbourne which included Vincent Buckley and Chris Wallace-Crabbe. His early poetry is seen as being in a 'rigidly imitation Classical manner'; his later poetry, although more modern in both technique and language, retains its emphasis on traditional values. Strongly personal in tone, Jones's poetry subjects life, himself and human relationships to a close and mildly sardonic scrutiny.

JONES, John Joseph (1930–), born London, migrated to Australia in 1948 and has been a teacher of English in WA. Singer, musician, poet, theatre director and playwright, Jones is a well-known WA identity. As a folk-singer he compered and sang at the first Winthrop folk festival for the ABC. From his 1964 recitals at the Adelaide Festival of Arts sprang his five records of ballads, *Five Australian Ballads*, *Songs and Ballads of Australia*, *Songs of John Shaw Neilson*, *Australian Songs and Ballads* and *Ballads of Durack and Sorensen*. His performed plays include 'Wildflowers' (1957), 'Tea Towels and Earrings' (1958), 'New Found Country' (1963), 'Harvest' (1964), *The Undivided* (1965), *Sturt* (1972), 'Loving Lady' (1974, on Caroline Chisholm), 'Bitter Grapes' (1975) and 'The Hamburger Man' (1985). He has also published an opera, *My New-Found Country* (1963), *Love* (1983, sonnets and paintings) and *A Day at Hiroshima, Parkerville and Other Poems* (1983).

JONES, Joseph Jay (1908–) taught at the University of Texas for over forty years until his retirement in 1975, when he was made emeritus professor. An enthusiastic promoter of Australian and Commonwealth literature studies in the USA and the author of numerous books on world literature, he first visited Australia in 1953. He is the author of *Radical Cousins* (1976), a comparative study of nineteenth-century Australian and American writers, and he edited the Australian section of the Twayne's World Authors series and the special Australian number of the *Texas Quarterly* reprinted as *Image of Australia* (1962). With his wife

Johanna Jones he has co-authored pamphlets on Henry Lawson, *Authors and Areas of Australia* (1970), and a history of the Australian novel, *Australian Fiction* (1983).

JONES, Margaret (1923–), a well-known journalist and previously foreign and literary editor for the *Sydney Morning Herald*, spent periods in Washington, London and South East Asia and was one of the first three Australian journalists to be accredited to the People's Republic of China in 1973. She has written two novels, *The Confucius Enigma* (1979) and *The Smiling Buddha* (1985). *The Confucius Enigma*, set in the 1970s, is a political thriller, which draws on Jones's experiences in China and imaginatively extends historical-political events such as the disappearance in 1971 of Lin Piao. The plot of *The Smiling Buddha*, set in an imaginary country in South East Asia, Khamla, unites the stories of Gillian Herbert, wife of an English academic, Peter Casement, an Irish-American journalist, and the political affairs of Khamla itself. Jones has also written an account of her impressions of England in the 1980s, *Thatcher's Kingdom* (1984).

JONES, Percy (1914–92), born Geelong, was educated at the University of Melbourne and overseas and was vice-director of the Melbourne University Conservatorium of Music 1950–72. A member of the Catholic clergy, he was interested mainly in church music, although he was an early modern collector of Australian folk-songs (q.v.) and ballads. Donald Cave has recorded his memoirs in *Percy Jones, Priest, Musician, Teacher* (1988).

JONES, Rae Desmond (1941–), born Broken Hill, graduated in 1976 from the University of Sydney. He has worked at various occupations and as a teacher. Jones has published four books of verse, *Orpheus with a Tuba* (1973), *The Mad Vibe* (1975), *Shakti* (1977), and *The Palace of Art* (1981). He also published a novel, *The Lemon Tree* (1990), the short-story collection *Walking the Line* (1979), and one side of the poetry record *Two Voluminous Gentlemen* (1977). He was the founding editor of the modern poetry journal *Your Friendly Fascist*. Jones's early poetry, personal in tone, modernistic in language and theme, and violent in attitude, reflected his own individual 'mad vibe', a term that he adopted to indicate the anti-social, self-destructive characteristic present in most people but dominant in some. His later poetry focuses more on the external world.

JONES, Rod (1953–) graduated from the University of Melbourne in 1976 and has worked as a teacher although he now writes full-time. He has written two novels, *Julia Paradise* (1986) and *Prince of the Lilies* (1991), and contributed short stories to magazines; in 1987 he won the *Canberra Times* National Short Story Award.

Julia Paradise attracted immediate attention, winning the SA Festival Award in 1988 and has since been translated into several languages. A powerful, many-layered novel, it explores psychic experience, crossing and recrossing the boundaries between dream and reality. Julia Paradise, a morphine addict with an interest in taking photographs of human degradation and brutality, is the wife of William Paradise, a Methodist missionary and director of a mission for girls in Shanghai in the 1920s. She begins a sexual relationship with her psychiatrist, Kenneth Ayres, intriguing him with her stories of the incestuous advances of her father, which appear to offer the ingredients of an even more interesting 'case' than any encountered by Freud. Eventually she binds him even closer with her knowledge of his killing of a child prostitute in an act of sodomy. Shifting between tropical northern Australia and China, where the characters are ultimately caught up in political upheavals as the Nationalist Party gains power, the novel combines sensuous descriptions of physical and psychical worlds with intriguing intensity as the reader is drawn into the narrative's mysterious, brilliant-coloured jigsaw of meanings. *Prince of the Lilies*, which opens in the 1970s, concerns the relationships between Charles Saracen, an archaeologist, his German wife Magda, their son Dylan, and Nicholas and Tasma Amelis, an American couple living in Crete. The island, with its burden of Western myth and the romance of ancient Greek culture established by such archaeologists as Sir Arthur Evans, represents the cultural meanings which prevent individuals such as the Saracens from attaining self-understanding. Fact or fiction, stories of the Minoan civilisation are powerful beasts in the labyrinth of the mind, and Jones interweaves archaeology and psychoanalysis in this study of subjective interpretations of reality. In a paper delivered at a 1987 writers' conference, Jones has described his conception of the imagination as associated with both darkness and light, with 'the unconscious, subterranean mines, magnetic poles, archaeology, the camera obscura, sleepwalking' and with 'light, vision, the key, ignition, fission, explosion – in a word, connection'. The power of fiction comes from 'the wild places of the unconscious mind' and 'If dreams are 'the royal road to the unconscious', then the imagination is the royal bridge between the unconscious and the world'.

JONES, Suzanne Holly (1945–) has written two novels, *Harry's Child* (1964), a study of a relationship between a teenage girl and her middle-aged guardian, and *Crying in the Garden* (1974), narrated by a patient in a psychiatric clinic. Distinguished by a striking, impressionistic style, both novels explore elusive elements in human relationships.

JONES, T. Harri (1921–65), born Llanafan, Wales, served in the Royal Navy during the Second World War and graduated from the University of Wales in 1947. In 1951–59 he taught English at the naval dockyard in Portsmouth before his appointment as lecturer in English at Newcastle University College. He published three books of poems: *The Enemy in the Heart* (1957), *Songs of a Mad Prince* (1960) and *The Beast at the Door* (1963). An active and popular member of the Newcastle community who did much to foster poetry in the Hunter River district, Harri Jones died by drowning 29 January 1965. A posthumous volume, *The Colour of Cockcrowing*, was published in 1966, and *The Collected Poems of T. Harri Jones*, bringing together all four volumes and some uncollected poems, was edited by Julian Croft and Don Dale-Jones in 1977.

In Jones's unpublished poem 'Thinking to Write an Ode' are the lines 'Thinking to write an ode, I thought of my country' and 'Thinking to write an ode, I thought of love!'. Wales and love are the constant subjects of his mostly elegiac poetry. The poems written in Australia about his sense of exile from his country are mainly collected in the second section, 'Hiraeth', of *The Beast at the Door*; typical of them is 'The Welshman in Exile Speaks'. The progress of love is recorded almost chronologically in his published verse; the early sensuous enjoyment and the 'impatient debonair' love of 'The Bridegroom' give way to a bewilderment about the loss of personal identity in love, to a state of disillusionment and hostility, and finally, in the 'Eros' poems of *The Beast at the Door*, to a resigned acceptance of disappointment and futility. A deeply personal poet, Jones had scarcely time to achieve the potential that his verse seemed to promise. His long poem, 'Cotton Mather Remembers the Trial of Elizabeth How: Salem, Massachusetts, 30th June 1692', reconstructs the thoughts of the Calvinist preacher and judge as he writes of the Salem witch trials; it is notable for its evocation of character and its subtly ambivalent exploration of the nature of good and evil. Julian Croft's study, *T.H. Jones* (1976), has a brief biography and a sensitive and detailed commentary on the poet's work; Croft had been a student of Jones. The poet is commemorated in the Harri Jones Memorial Prize for poetry.

JORGENSON, Jorgen (1780–1841) was an adventurer born Jorgen Jorgensen in Copenhagen; he changed his surname in 1817. At 15 he went to sea, and was in Australian waters in 1801–5, first at Port Jackson, later at Port Phillip and Van Diemen's Land. In 1809 he was involved in proclaiming Iceland independent of Denmark, and subsequently styled himself 'ex-King of Iceland'. In 1826, after years of adventure, debauchery and some ill fortune, he returned to Australia under sentence of transportation for life. He spent most of his time in Tasmania, where he was a minor explorer and where he eked out a living in the 1830s as an exterminator of Aborigines, as a convict constable, and as a contributor to the press. Jorgenson's 'A Shred of Autobiography' was published in the *Hobart Town Almanack* in 1835 and 1838 and republished in monograph form in 1981. His stormy career was detailed by J.F. Hogan in *The Convict King* (1891); by Marcus Clarke in *Old Tales of a Young Country* (1871); and by Frank Clune and P.R. Stephensen in *The Viking of Van Diemen's Land* (1954). Jorgenson appears as a character in several historical novels about Tasmania, e.g. Roy Bridges's *The Cards of Fortune* (1922) and William Hay's *The Escape of the Notorious Sir William Heans* (1919). N.J.B. Plomley discovered in the Mitchell Library Jorgenson's uncompleted account of the customs of the Aborigines and his part in Governor Arthur's plans to round them up; it was

published in 1991 in unconstructed form with a comprehensive commentary, titled *Jorgen Jorgenson and the Aborigines of Van Diemen's Land*.

JOSE, A.W. (Arthur Wilberforce) (1863–1934), who has been described as 'one of the best Australians ever born and educated in England', was born in Gloucestershire, England, and at 19 emigrated to Australia for his health. In 1885–99, after experience in the bush, he worked mainly as a teacher and university extension lecturer; after a five-year interlude spent in South Africa, India and England, he returned to Australia as correspondent for the London *Times* (1904–15). Jose's first publication was *Sun and Cloud on River and Sea* (1888), an early Angus & Robertson collection of verse written under the pseudonym 'Ishmael Dare'; later he made substantial contributions to Australian writing as a historian, editor, essayist. His *A Short History of Australasia* (1899), expanded as *History of Australasia*, went through fifteen editions by 1929. Among other works, he wrote the naval volume in the *Official History of Australia in the War of 1914–1918* (1928), two volumes of essays, *Two Awheel and Some Others Afoot in Australia* (1903) and *Builders and Pioneers of Australia* (1928), and was editor-in-chief of the first edition of the *Australian Encyclopaedia* (1925–26). Jose's most significant work, however, was *The Romantic Nineties* (q.v., 1933), which played an influential part in the development of the legend of the Nineties (q.v.). A publisher's reader for many years, he edited major collections of Henry Lawson and A.B. Paterson.

JOSE, Nicholas (1952–), born London, grew up in Traralgon, Perth and Adelaide. He was educated at Oxford University and the ANU and has since lived in Canberra, England, Italy and China. In 1986–87 he spent eighteen months teaching and writing in China, at the Beijing Foreign Studies University and the East China Teachers' University in Shanghai. He was cultural counsellor at the Australian embassy in Beijing 1987–90 and was there when the demonstrations erupted in Tiananmen Square in 1987. His interest in China grew from his study of the language, but his family has traditionally had links with the country; his grandfather was born in China and his great-grandfather worked there as a missionary in the 1890s. Jose drew on the latter's diaries and letters to research his novel about China, *Avenue of Eternal Peace* (1989). His other novels are *Rowena's Field* (1984) and *Paper Nautilus* (1987), and he has also published two collections of short stories, *The Possession of Amber* (1980) and *Feathers or Lead* (1986). Jose's short stories are varied in range, characters and settings, reflecting his travels and experience of other cultures; loneliness, unreciprocated love, homesickness and the tenacity of past pain are some of the emotions he explores and if he has a realistic rather than an optimistic perception of the human condition, he sometimes allows hope and even restored happiness to resolve some of his stories. He is pre-eminently a subtle, evocative writer, however, who relies on imagery rather than plot to express a narrative's essence. Structured in three sections spanning a decade, *Rowena's Field* opens in Adelaide in 1970 and traces the experiences of Rowena Sunner, her flight from the stultifying values of her family and her search for love. In contrast to the polished cameos of Jose's stories, it is a generously built novel, reminiscent of Victorian fiction in its broad scope and traditional structure. The first section, 'Adelaide', set in the period of Vietnam War, which impinges on Rowena's destiny, deals with her loss of Hal, her lover, who is killed in grotesque circumstances; in the second section, 'Therapy', she travels in Europe and finds some consolation by teaching at a school for intellectually disadvantaged children, and in the third she comes full circle, returns to SA, marries unhappily, becomes a mother and is reconciled with her own mother. The men in her life are shadowy, ineffective figures, but the women, especially her aunt Flo, who brings her back to Australia by leaving her an inheritance, have a powerful impact. In her search for equilibrium as she journeys from Australia to Europe and back again, Rowena mirrors the experiences of some of Jose's other characters who can only come completely to terms with Australia by travelling abroad and rediscovering the country from a distance. The central character of *Paper Nautilus*, Jack Tregenza, is an outwardly unremarkable man whose inarticulate stoicism and capacity for self-sacrifice find a natural centre in the young life of his niece Penny; beginning with Penny's wedding in 1965, the novel backtracks in a series of digressions from that date to trace Jack's relationship with his more charismatic brother, Peter, and their war experiences. The delicate nautilus shell, acquired with difficulty and rarely as whole, is an emblem of Jack's tenacity and sensitivity as a surrogate father. In *Avenue of Eternal Peace* Jose presents the Chinese and China through the eyes of a visitor trying to come to terms with the country as well as his own life. Wally Frith, an expert on cancer, whose wife has died of the disease, goes to China to recover from his loss, to trace a family tradition and make contact with another doctor in his field. The theme of personal relationships expands to become a story of freedom and oppression, issues which are emphasised in the afterword Jose attached to the novel after actual political events reinforced his fictional conclusions. Emphasising the impossibility of writing a book about China, Jose prefers to see China as the element in which the novel is plunged and presents contemporary Beijing through the eyes of the individuals Frith encounters in his quest, including expatriate eccentric Westerners, Chinese academics, students, artists, officials and businessmen. The sub-plots multiply and become intertwined, establishing an intriguing collage of the culture as Frith belatedly explores his family's ties with China and falls in love with a woman who finally chooses independence and China rather than marriage to a Westerner.

Journal of Australasia (1856–58), also known as the *Illustrated Journal of Australasia* for part of 1857–58, was a Melbourne monthly which contained serial and short fiction, poetry and literary articles. Thomas McCombie and Henry Gyles Turner contributed to the journal, which is best known as the original place of publication for *The Fiction Fields of Australia* (q.v, 1856) by Frederick Sinnett, editor in 1857.

Journal of Australian Literature, which commenced in June 1990, is edited by Subhas Chandra Saha and emanates from the Department of English, Manipur University, Imphal, India. Many of the contributors are Indian academics and writers.

Journal of Commonwealth Literature, see **Association for Commonwealth Language and Literature Studies**

JOYCE, Alfred (1821–1901), born London, England, came to Australia in 1843. He and his older brother George, who had arrived in 1840, paid £50 for a run of 10 000 acres in the Loddon River district of Victoria, which they named Plaistow after the family home in Essex. After his marriage in 1853 Alfred took over Norwood, a 37 000-acre property nearby, but after a period of prosperity he was driven into the hands of the banks and by 1887 had lost the property. In 1896–98 he set down his reminiscences, but they remained unpublished until 1942 when G.F. James (a significant figure in Australian publishing) edited *A Homestead History*, which comprises two sections: 'The Reminiscences, 1843–51', which relate the establishment of Plaistow and experiences in the Port Phillip District up to the Joyce brothers' purchase of Norwood in 1851; and 'The Letters, 1851–64', most of which were written at Norwood and recount the development of the station during the gold-rush period and up to the building of the permanent homestead in 1864.

JURGENSEN, Manfred (1940–), born Flensburg, then in Denmark now in West Germany, came to Australia in 1961 after living in Germany, Switzerland and the USA. He was educated at the universities of Melbourne and Zurich and now holds a personal chair in German literature at the University of Queensland, which awarded him the degree of D.Litt. in 1991. Interested in the study of comparative literature and bilingualism in poetry, Jurgensen has written more than thirty books, including studies of Goethe, Grass, Frisch, Bachmann and Bernhard. His poetry collections in English are *Signs & Voices* (1973), *A Kind of Dying* (1977), *A Winter's Journey* (1979), which records details of a return visit to Flensburg, *South Africa Transit* (1979), *The Skin Trade* (1983), *Waiting for Cancer* (1985), *Selected Poems 1972–1986*, edited by Dimitris Tsaloumas (1987), *My Operas Can't Swim* (1989), *Continental Flicks and Other Passions* (1989) and *The Partiality of Harbours* (1989). In 1979 his novel, *Wehrersatz* (1978), about a Flensburg man trying to escape national service, was made into a film for television in Germany. Jurgensen has written two novellas in English, *A Difficult Love* and *Break-Out*, published together in 1987, and a collection of short stories, *Intruders* (1992). *Break-Out*, a revision of a 1977 novella, satirises middle-class reactions to the 1975 dismissal of the Whitlam government; *A Difficult Love* is both an intense study of Australian materialism from an immigrant viewpoint and an exploration of complex male–

female relationships. Founding editor of the multicultural magazine *Outrider* (q.v.), he has also edited the magazine's separate collections titled *Australian Writing Now* (with Robert Adamson, 1988), *Outrider 90* (1990), *Earth Wings* (1991) and *Queensland Words and All* (1993), and a celebration of *Outrider*'s first decade, *Queensland: Words and All* (1993). He is also the editor of a significant anthology of writing by authors whose first language is not English, *Ethnic Australia* (1981), winner of the 1984 NSW Premier's Ethnic Award, and editor of *Queensland Studies in German* and *German-Australian Studies*. With Alan Corkhill he edited a collection of essays titled *The German Presence in Queensland* (1988) and has written a substantial history of German-Australian writing 1930–90, *Eagle and Emu* (1992). Jurgensen has written plays, *Rückkehr ins Exil* [*Return to Exile*] (published 1963, performed 1964) and *The Unit* (published 1984, performed 1988); his script, *Das Gift der Heimat/Native Poison*, was made into a film in 1989. Jurgensen's other writing in German includes the novel, *Versuchsperson* (1986), the literary diary, *Deutsche Reise* (1990) and the poetry collections, *Stationen* (1968), *aufenthalte* (1969), *innere sicherheit* (1979) and *Erste Gegenwart* (1988).

JURY, C.R. (Charles Rischbieth) (1893–1958), born Glenelg, SA, was educated at Oxford, served with the British Army in the First World War and became a lecturer in English at the University of Adelaide in 1933. In 1946–49 he was professor of English at the University; the chair was later named in his honour. A considerable contemporary influence on the SA literary scene, he held strictly classical and traditional concepts of poetry. Represented in *Lamps and Vine Leaves* (1919) with Vernon Knowles and E.J. Morgan, he also published *Spring is Coming and Other Poems* (1906), *Perseus and Erythia and Other Poems* (1912), *Love and the Virgins* (1929, expanded in 1958), *Galahad, Selenemia, and Poems* (1939), *Icarius* (1955, a Greek drama), *The Sun in Servitude and Other Plays* (1961) and *Well Measur'd Song* (1968); the last is an essay on prosody, in particular on his own use of quantitative and quasi-quantitative verse, edited by Barbara Wall and D.C. Muecke.

K

Kabbarli', see **BATES, Daisy**

KAHAN, Louis (1905–), born Vienna, Austria, was a clothes designer and illustrator in Paris before enlisting in the French Foreign Legion and serving for a time as a war artist with the Allied armies in North Africa. In 1947 he came to Australia and worked as a stage designer and full-time artist; his work is represented in all the major galleries. In 1960 he began a series of portrait sketches of important literary figures in *Meanjin*; many of these are included in Kahan's *Australian Writers: The Face of Literature* (1981). In 1962 he won the Archibald Prize with a portrait of novelist Patrick White. A collection of his paintings and drawings, edited by Lou Klepac and titled *Louis Kahan* (1990), includes a substantial biographical introduction and bibliography.

KALAMARAS, Vasso (1932–), born Athens, Greece, of Roumelian and Cretan descent, was educated in Athens in a cultural milieu dominated by music, ballet, theatre and literature. In her late teens she married Leonidas Kalamaras, whose father had migrated to WA in 1924. In 1951 she and Leonidas joined his father in tobacco farming at Manjimup, WA. She returned with the family for a year to Greece in 1960–61, publishing there a collection of poems, *Stalagmaties (Droplets)* (1959) and *Other Earth. Greek-Australian Stories* (1961). While in Greece she also wrote a play, *The Bread Trap*, which was performed in Perth in 1983. An account of the year back in her original homeland, *Impressions of a Journey* (1977), was also published in Greece where it encountered some criticism, although the book won the Tsakalos Literature Prize (Athens) for prose in 1978. *Impressions of a Journey* reveals her continuing emotional attachment to her origins. After the collapse of the tobacco market led the family to seek employment in Perth, Kalamaras began teaching Greek classes to adult Australians at the Claremont College of the Arts and from 1973 has taught modern Greek at the Perth Technical College. Her impressions of the immigrant experience and its hardships inform all her writing. Although bilingual, Vasso Kalamaras writes mainly in Greek and uses translators (Reg Durack, June Kingdon, Con Castan, David Hutchison) to assist her in presenting her work in English. Those English translations include *Other Earth* (1977), *Twenty Two Poems* (1977), *Landscape and Soul. Greek Australian Poems* (1980), *Bitterness* (1983, five stories), *The Bread Trap* (1986) and *The Same Light* (poetry and short fiction 1989). Her other plays include 'Holidays in Greece' (1983), 'Phrynê (1984), 'Karagiozis Strikes It Rich' (1987),

'Karagiozis the Interpreter' and 'Karagiozis the Milk-bar Owner'. The winner of several literary prizes in Greece and Australia, Kalamaras is widely represented in Australian anthologies, e.g. *Decade* (1982), ed. B.R. Coffey, *The Strength of Tradition. Stories of the Immigrant Presence in Australia 1976–1981* (1983), ed. R.F. Holt, and *Joseph's Coat: An Anthology of Multicultural Writing* (1985), ed. Peter Skrzynecki. An account of her life and work is given in Con Castan's *Conflicts of Love* (1986).

KALESKI, Robert (1877–1961), born Burwood, Sydney, was a dog owner from the age of 6 and became during his life an expert on Australian dogs, including the dingo. In 1893 he began improving the blue heeler strain of cattle dog; he also established breeding standards for the kelpie and barb varieties of sheepdog. Under various pseudonyms, including 'Falder', he wrote articles on dogs, other animals and rural topics for the *Sydney Mail*, *Sydney Morning Herald*, *Bulletin* and *Bookfellow*. Some of his articles and stories appeared in book form as *Australian Barkers and Biters* (1914). He also compiled *The Australian Settler's Complete Guide* (1909).

KAN, Diana (1934–), born and educated in Melbourne, studied at the Art Institute of RMIT and began publishing poetry in the 1970s. A series of poems, 'The Hill of the Cross', was included as a special feature in *On the Move*, published by the joint Board of Religious Education of Australia and NZ. Her own published books are *Happy Families and Other Poems* (1973) and *The Bird-man* (1984). She was joint winner of the Patricia Hackett Prize for Poetry in 1983.

Kangaroo is an animal of the Macropodidae ('great-footed') family; other members of the family of over sixty species include wallaroos, wallabies, rat and tree kangaroos. The name was first met with by Captain James Cook when he encountered Aborigines near the site of present Cooktown in northern Queensland. Readily adopted by the early colonists, the name occurs frequently in colonial writing: Watkin Tench, Charles Harpur, Henry Kendall and Alexander Harris, for example, all record their surprise at the unfamiliar animal. Barron Field (q.v.) in his poem 'The Kangaroo' sees the bounding marsupial as an almost malicious afterthought of the Creator, made in defiance of all zoological propriety. The identification of the kangaroo with Australia (Field called it 'thou spirit of Australia') is seen in its presence on the Australian coat of arms; as the symbol 'The Flying

Kangaroo' of Australia's international airline Qantas; as the nickname, 'the Kangaroos', of Australia's representative rugby league football team; and as the symbol Matilda at the Commonwealth Games, 1982.

Writers of children's fiction have used the kangaroo family to considerable effect; the most successful literary kangaroo, however, is undoubtedly Victor Barnes's *Skippy the Bush Kangaroo* (1968), which was filmed as an Australian television series. By the end of 1969 eighty countries had bought the *Skippy* series. A new series was produced in 1992 and sold internationally. A feature film was screened in 1969. The English novelist D.H. Lawrence used *Kangaroo* as the title of his Australian novel, published in 1923.

Kangaroo (1923), a novel by D.H. Lawrence (q.v.) based on his experiences in Australia May–August 1922, is set in the same period. The writer and poet Richard Lovat Somers (Lawrence's self-portrait) and his wife Harriet (a picture of Frieda Lawrence) arrive in Sydney, where they rent a small suburban bungalow, Torestin. Convinced that in Europe 'everything was done for, played out, finished', Somers has come to the 'newest country' to 'start a new life and flutter with a new hope'. In Sydney the Somers become friendly with their neighbour, a returned digger, Jack Callcott, his wife Victoria, and his brother-in-law William James ('Jaz') Trewhella. Jack Callcott attempts to draw Somers into connection with a secret right-wing political movement, made up mainly of returned soldiers and committed to the aim of eventually seizing power. Although Somers does not really care about politics, which he sees as no more than a 'country's housekeeping', he is intrigued by his meetings with Kangaroo, the charismatic Jewish leader of the movement and in public life Benjamin Cooley, an eminent lawyer. Nevertheless he remains uncommitted, dedicated to his instinctive need to keep his individuality isolated. After a few weeks in Sydney, the Somers rent a cottage, Cooee, at Mullumbimby (Thirroul), a coastal mining town south of Sydney. There Somers continues his unsuccessful struggle to direct his marriage into the 'Pacific Ocean . . . [of] lord-and-masterdom', while Harriet attempts to reach 'the Atlantic of pure companionship'. Meanwhile at Canberra Hall in Sydney, Somers also meets Willie Struthers, the labour movement leader, although he is as unattracted by the 'generalized love' of socialism as he is by Kangaroo's 'great general emotion'. His ultimate rejection of Kangaroo, which is accompanied by feelings of terror and revulsion, recalls Lawrence's wartime experiences in England when he was persecuted for his refusal to subscribe to the 'wave of criminal lust' that possessed the nation from 1916 to 1919. Before leaving Australia for the USA, Somers has a last terrifying contact with the digger movement when it disrupts a labour meeting in Sydney, causing extensive casualties; Jack Callcott derives a passionate satisfaction from the violence, but Kangaroo is shot and later dies of his wounds. *Kangaroo* was produced as a film in 1985.

KANTARIZIS, Sylvia, see **Feminism and Australian Literature**

KATA, Elizabeth, born Sydney, married a Japanese concert pianist in 1937 and lived in Japan for a decade which included the Second World War. Her first novel, *Be Ready with Bells and Drums* (1961), the story of a blind girl and her friendship with a Black American in New York, achieved international success after it was published in New York titled *A Patch of Blue* and was produced as a film, winning the Award of the Writers' Guild of America for the best-written 'American' drama of 1965. Kata subsequently spent two years working as a screenwriter in Hollywood and has also written for television. Her other publications include the novels *Someone Will Conquer Them* (1962), *Child of the Holocaust* (1979), *Tilda* (1979), *The Death of Ruth* (1981) and *Kagami* (1989), and the collection of short stories *With Kisses on Both Cheeks* (1981).

KAUFMANN, Walter (1924–), born Berlin, of Jewish descent, was adopted at the age of 2 and arrived in Australia in 1942 after his adoptive parents were arrested by the Nazis. He joined the Australian Army and later worked on the Melbourne waterfront, in abattoirs and as a sailor. In 1955 he returned to Berlin, where he has continued to live. A member of the Realist Writers' Group in Melbourne, he published a novel in Australia which draws on his experiences of Nazi Germany, *Voices in the Storm* (1953). Two of his subsequent novels, published in Berlin, are set in Australia, *Crossroads* (1961, translated into German in 1966) and *Wohin der Mensch Gehort* (*Where A Man Belongs*) (1963) and a collection of short fiction, *The Curse of Maralinga and Other Stories* (1959) includes some Australian material. Kaufmann has also written other novels with European settings, a further collection of short stories and two autobiographies, *American Encounter* (1966) and *Kindheit* (1970, translated into English in 1972, titled *Beyond the Green World of Childhood*). Kaufmann has won the Mary Gilmore Award and in Germany the Heinrich Mann Prize and the Theodor Fontane Prize for Art and Literature.

KAVANAGH, Paul (1941–), born Sydney, graduated from the University of Sydney and gained his Ph.D. at the University of Newcastle, where he presently teaches English. He has published two volumes of poetry, *Wild Honey* (1974) and *The Summerhouse* (1978). Closely involved with the Mattara Spring Poetry Festivals, he has edited several of their anthologies, *The Members of the Orchestra* (1981), *Instructions for Honey Ants* (1983), *Poem of Thanksgiving* (1985), *Properties of the Poet* (1987), *Hunter Kids' Book* (1988), *Pictures from an Exhibition* (1989) and *The Sea's White Edge* (1991). In 1988 he collaborated with Allan Chawner in two exhibitions of poetry and photographs, *Soundings* (1988). He edited (with Peter Kuch) *Conversations: Interviews with Australian Writers* (1991), the writers being Vincent Buckley, Bruce Dawe, Rosemary Dobson, Marion Halligan, Shirley Hazzard, Dorothy Hewett, Alec Hope, Elizabeth Jolley,

David Malouf, Les Murray, Peter Porter, Randolph Stow and David Williamson.

'KAYE, Louis' (Noel Wilson Norman) (1901–81), born Claremont, Tasmania, spent considerable time as a young man on outback stations in WA, where he assimilated the atmosphere that characterises his novels. A successful contributor of short fiction to overseas magazines, 'Kaye' is best known in Australia as a writer of popular fiction. His first novel, *Tybal Men* (1931), is the story of a WA sheep station founded by the pioneer Maclean family and the difficulties of maintaining the heritage; an additional virtue of the book is its authentic presentation of the Aborigines. He wrote twelve more novels including *Trail of Plunder* (1931), *Desert Herbage* (1932), *The End of the Trail* (1933), *The Desert Boss* (1934), *Tightened Belts* (1934), *Pathways of Free Men* (1935), *The Dark Gods* (1935), *The Lonely Land* (1935), *Black Wilderness* (1936), *Darkened Camps* (1936), *Vanished Legion* (1937) and *Tracks of Levask* (1938). *Trail of Plunder* is a reflective work on the passing of the bushranging days; *The End of the Trail* takes the author to the 'real Australia', the desert lands where pastoralists attempt to survive in a battle against the elemental forces of nature; *The Desert Boss* emphasises the brutalising effect of the arid-land environment on certain types of men; *Tightened Belts* (1934) describes an old prospector's discovery of a rich opal field; *Pathways of Free Men* (1935) underlines the allure of far horizons to the stockman; and *Tracks of Levask* (1938) has, as do several of 'Kaye's' later novels, the basic ingredients of the American western.

KEAN, Charles (1811–68) and **Ellen** (1806–80) were actors who toured Australia under contract to George Coppin 1863–64. Charles Kean was the son of Edmund Kean, the celebrated tragedian. Although their career in England had been successful, crowned by Charles Kean's appointment as director of Queen Victoria's private theatricals in 1848, it had not been lucrative and the colonial tour was designed to finance their anticipated retirement. Their stay was plagued by a series of illnesses and managerial problems but was not unsuccessful and helped to foster Australian interest in serious theatre. J.M.D. Hardwick edited *Emigrant in Motley: The Journey of Charles and Ellen Kean in Quest of a Theatrical Fortune in Australia and America, as Told in Their Hitherto Unpublished Letters* (1954).

KEENE, Daniel (1955–), born Melbourne, has written for both stage and television. His first plays, 'Four Quarters', 'Bitch Heart' and 'Car Crash at the O.K. Corral', were produced at the La Mama theatre. Of his subsequent plays for stage, seven have played in New York and others have been staged in most of Australia's capital cities. They include 'Echoes of Ruby Dark' (1983), 'La Place Tango', 'The Hour Before My Brother Dies', 'Isle of Swans', 'The Snake Pit', 'The Fighter', 'Angel's Tomorrow' (1986), *Cho Cho San* (produced 1984, published 1987), and the trilogy 'Silent Partner' (1992), 'Low' and 'Tom'.

Keep Him My Country (1955), a novel by Mary Durack (q.v.), is set in the 1950s on a cattle station in the Kimberleys of WA, where the author's parents and grandparents settled in the late nineteenth century. The manager of Trafalgar station, and central character in the novel, is Stan Rolt, grandson of the original pioneer. Stan takes over the running of the station on a temporary basis, expecting to stay only two years then to return to his university studies. He has a brief, idyllic love affair with the Aboriginal girl Dalgerie, but she is reclaimed by tribal law and returns to her own people. Depression and the war compel Stan Rolt to stay on at Trafalgar, and when after fifteen years the opportunity to depart finally comes, he finds himself unable to go. Through his love for Dalgerie, his understanding of her affinity with the land and his own long and close association with it, a bond has been forged which he is unable to break. Mary Durack gives an account in the novel of the varied and demanding activities of an outback cattle station, and also presents the dilemma of the Aborigines, faced with conflicting attachments to old tribal and new White environments. Her main concern, however, is to convince the White people of the outback that they must grow into the same spiritual harmony with the land that the Aborigines have achieved by generations of patient and loving understanding of it.

KEESING, Nancy (1923–93), born Sydney, graduated from the University of Sydney and was a social worker at the Royal Alexandra Hospital for Children 1947–51. She was also a freelance writer and active in numerous literary organisations, e.g. the English Association (committee member 1940–73); ASA, whose journal, the *Australian Author*, she edited 1971–74; the Literature Board (member, 1973–74 and chairperson 1974–77); and the National Book Council. She published a critical study of Douglas Stewart (1965) and a selection of the poetry of Elsie Carew with critical commentary, *Elsie Carew* (1965); she also edited *Australian Postwar Novelists* (1975) and, with Douglas Stewart, the important anthologies *Australian Bush Ballads* (1955), *Old Bush Songs* (1957) and *The Pacific Book of Bush Ballads* (1967); and compiled *Gold Fever* (1967), *Transition* (1970, an ASA anthology), *The Kelly Gang* (1975), *The White Chrysanthemum* (1977), *Henry Lawson: Favourite Verse* (1978), *Shalom* (1978, Australian Jewish short stories, reprinted 1988 with five additional stories), *Lily on the Dustbin: Slang of Australian Women and Families* (1982) and *Just Look Out the Window* (1985). She also wrote children's novels, *By Gravel and Gum* (1963) and *The Golden Dream* (1974); two books of memoirs, *Garden Island People* (1975) and *Riding the Elephant* (1988); a biographical work, *John Lang and 'The Forger's Wife'* (1979); and collections of poetry, *Imminent Summer* (1951), *Three Men and Sydney* (1955), *Showground Sketchbook* (1968) and *Hails and Farewells* (1977). She was made AM for her services to literature.

KEFALÁ, Antigone (1935–), born Braila, Romania, of Greek parents, has lived in Romania,

Greece, NZ and Australia. She graduated from Victoria University, Wellington, in 1960, has worked as a librarian, as an arts administrator and as a teacher of English as a second language, and is a prominent commentator on Australian multicultural writing. She has published four books of poetry, *The Alien* (1973), *Thirsty Weather* (1978), *European Notebook* (1988) and *Absence: New and Selected Poems* (1992); and three short novels, *The First Journey* and *The Boarding House*, under the title *The First Journey* (1975), and *The Island* (1984). In *Alexia: A Tale of Two Cultures* (1984) she has retold her experiences as a migrant in the form of a novel for children. She has also translated the poetic manifesto of I.P. Koutsocheras, *Men, for the Rights of Man, Rise!* (1974). Migration is an important theme in Kefalá's work but it is largely a starting-point for exploring larger themes of estrangement, from others, from self and from 'reality'. Her novels, which concentrate more on inward development than external action, are clearly the work of a poet, sensitive to the aura of words and images. In all three, the central narrator (Alexi, a young Bucharest student, in *The First Journey* and Melina, a young Greek migrant, in *The Boarding House* and *The Island*) are engaged in a search for stability and meaning in which language figures as a seductive but unreliable agent. The same mood of unbelonging characterises her poems; austere and unrelenting in their confrontation of loneliness and death, they combine strength with delicacy, flexibility with precision.

KELEN, Christopher (1958–), born Sydney, the son of Stephen Kelen and the brother of S.K. Kelen (qq.v.), is resident in Japan, where he teaches English. He has published verse in numerous anthologies and periodicals and in the collection *The Naming of the Harbour & the Trees* (1992). He has also published a novel, *Punk's Travels* (1980). In 1988 Kelen won first prize in the Australian Bicentennial/ABC poetry competition. *The Naming of the Harbour & the Trees* contains travel poems, political pieces, drug poems and numerous other inventives, all couched in the typically innovative and intellectually sharp Kelen fashion.

KELEN, Stephen (1912–), born Budapest, Hungary, and educated at the University of Budapest and at Karlovo University at Prague, arrived in Australia in 1939. He published in leading Hungarian newspapers from the age of 17. In 1939 he volunteered for the Australian Army and served in New Guinea and North Borneo and in Japan as a member of the British Occupation Forces. During the 1940s and 1950s he worked as an author and journalist with ABC radio, writing documentaries and features and dramatising short stories and plays. As well as numerous short stories, feature articles and radio plays published in Australia and overseas, Kelen has published the novels *Heed McGlarity* (1945), *Freedom is a Rainbow* (serialised in the *Bulletin* in 1957), and *Goshu* (1965); the novellas *Gold in Laos* (serialised in *Wireless Weekly* in 1941) and *Camp Busters* (serialised in the *Australian Journal* in 1957); the collection of short stories, *Camp Happy and*

Other Stories (1944); the autobiographies *I Was There* (1941), *Jackals in the Jungle* (1942) and *I Remember Hiroshima* (1983); the biography *Uphill All the Way: Murdoch Stanley McLeod's Story* (1974); and the stage plays 'The Sun Shines Black in the Valley' (1963), 'Shadow of the Crabbe' (1965), 'Some Years Later' (1965, with Sylvia Kelen), 'Fission in the Ointment' (1965, with Sylvia Kelen), 'The Intruders' (1965) and 'Illicit Petting' (1988, with Sylvia Kelen). Kelen has won several awards for his work, including a prize in the 1948 *Sun-News Pictorial* short-story competition for his short story 'The Olympic Runner' and second prize in a 1958 United Nations competition for *Freedom is a Rainbow*. In 1986 he was awarded an OAM for services to literature.

KELEN, Stephen K. (1956–), born Sydney, the son of Stephen Kelen and brother of Chistopher Kelen (qq.v.), studied philosophy and literature at Sydney University and has worked as a Commonwealth government public servant and as a teacher of creative writing. His poetry has appeared in numerous periodicals, in several anthologies and in the collections *The Gods Ash Their Cigarettes* (1978), *To the Heart of the World's Electricity* (1980), *Zen Maniacs* (1980), *Atomic Ballet* (1990), and *Dingo Sky* (1993). He has also edited the collection *(The) Final Taxi Review* (1981). In 1973 Kelen won the *Poetry Australia* prize for writers under 18. Contemporary issues and concerns mingle with the small incidents of daily life in Kelen's witty, often lightly ironic verse; reflecting his various travels and wide reading and frequently sharply suggestive, it also reflects a relish of what is paradoxical and quirky and a detached, almost anthropological interest in contemporary idioms and icons. Described as 'rarely self-conscious', Kelen in fact occasionally satirises the pretensions of poetry while expressing his delight in it, suggesting in 'The Boy With the Sun in his Pocket', for instance, that it may be necessary to 'accept the sky has its own significance/ & is not waiting for your interpretation/ or metaphor' if one is to find 'the perfect cliche'.

KELLAWAY, Frank (1922–), born London of Australian parents, graduated from the University of Melbourne in 1948 and worked as a librarian and as a lecturer at the Preston Institute of Technology in Melbourne. His volumes of poetry are *Beanstalk* (1973) and *Mare's Nest* (1978). He has also written fiction, *A Straight Furrow* (1960), *The Quest for Golden Dan* (1962) and *Golden Dan* (1976), and verse libretti for the music of George Dreyfus in operas performed in Australia and abroad. He won first prize in the inaugural National Poetry Competition in 1986.

KELLEHER, Victor (1939–), born London, completed his university education in South Africa and has been an academic at universities in South Africa, NZ and Australia. A successful writer of novels for children, he has won three Children's Book Council Awards (1983, 1987 and 1991), an Australian Science Fiction Achievement Award (1984), a Peace Prize for Children's Literature (1969) and a WA Young

Readers Book Award (1982). His books for young readers include *Forbidden Paths of Thual* (1979), *The Hunting of Shadroth* (1981), *Master of the Grove* (1982), *Papio* (1984), *The Green Piper* (1984), *Taronga* (1986), *The Makers* (1987), *Baily's Bones* (1988), *The Red King* (1989), *Brother Night* (1990), *Del-Del* (1991) and *To the Dark Tower* (1992). Many of these novels are potentially directed at adults as well as older children. Kelleher has also written adult fiction, including a volume of short stories, *Africa and After* (1983, republished 1987 as *The Traveller*) and five novels, *Voices from the River* (1979), *The Beast of Heaven* (1984), *Em's Story* (1988), *Wintering* (1990) and *Micky Darlin'* (1992). *Voices from the River*, set in Central Africa in the 1950s and structured as a mosaic of narratives, focuses on the complex relationship between a missionary and two younger men, his 'adoptive' sons, and its violent ending. *The Beast of Heaven*, a science fiction set in an environment ruined by nuclear war, is similarly preoccupied with aggression and the urge to oppress and subdue others perceived as inferiors. *Em's Story* is the story of a horrific journey through the Kalahari desert at the turn of the century by Emma Wilhelm; recorded sixty years later by her granddaughter Eva, the story is gradually integrated into Eva's present as Emma's history becomes hers. *Wintering* focuses on the corrupted idealism of some members of the anti-Vietnam War movement of the 1960s as a means of exploring the relationship between public and personal histories, past and present, Black and White cultures in Australia and different ways of interpreting the past. *Micky Darlin'*, made up of nineteen linked stories, describes the experiences of a boy of Irish extraction growing up in wartime and post-war London in an extended and rumbustious family; cared for by his grandparents, since his parents fail to do so, Micky is initiated early into the seamy side of adult life.

KELLOW, H.A. (Henry Arthur) (1881–1935), born Fifeshire, Scotland, was educated at the University of Glasgow and was a schoolmaster in Airdrie and Glasgow before accepting the headmastership of Rockhampton Grammar School in 1912. He remained there until his death; the critic, Cecil Hadgraft, was a pupil and returned to teach at the school. Before leaving Scotland, Kellow had written a study of Robert Burns, compiled an anthology of Scottish verse and had published *A Practical Training in English* (1911). In Rockhampton he wrote *Queensland Poets* (1930), a pioneering critical study. He is the subject of a monograph by Lorna McDonald (1981).

KELLY, Gwen (1922–), born Gwen Smith at Thornleigh, an outer Sydney suburb, is a graduate of the University of Sydney who has combined a career in secondary and tertiary teaching with the writing of several novels, *There Is No Refuge* (1961), *The Red Boat* (1968), *The Middle-Aged Maidens* (1976), *Always Afternoon* (1981) and *Arrows of Rain* (1988). In 1980 she published, with Anthony J. Bennett, a volume of selected poems, *Fossils and Stray Cats*. A successful short-story writer with wide representation in Australian journals and periodicals and one collection, *The*

Happy People and Others (1988, introduced by Anthony J. Bennett), she has won four Henry Lawson prose Awards. In 1981 she was presented by the Society of Women Writers with the first Hilarie Lindsay Award for achievement by a woman writer and won the award again in 1989. *There is No Refuge*, Kelly's most autobiographical novel, deals with the experiences of a young girl student at Sydney University in the 1930s and her response to the religious and moral challenges she meets there. *The Red Boat*, set in Canada, explores the long-lasting emotional damage caused by intense childhood relationships and the struggle of the heroine, Joan Paterson, to escape the past. *The Middle-Aged Maidens* is a satirical study of life in a private girls' school. *Arrows of Rain* covers forty years in the life of the Drayton family (1932–72); beginning with the opening of Sydney's Harbour Bridge, and closing with the advent of the Whitlam government, the novel is a family saga linking relationships and external events. *Always Afternoon*, set 1915–18, studies the impact on the local residents of an internment camp for Germans at Trial Bay, NSW, and a love affair between a young Australian woman and one of the prisoners; it was produced as a mini-series for Australian television in 1988 and subsequently in Germany, where it was titled *Prisoners in Paradise*.

KELLY, Kate (1862–98), Ned Kelly's sister, was a supporter of the Kelly gang although she neither played as active a role as is attributed to her in Australian folklore nor became a disgrace to the family after Ned's death by trading on the notoriety of the Kelly name. Present at the siege of Glenrowan, she pleaded Ned's case with the governor of Victoria and with Melbourne theatre audiences on the night of his execution. Following the release of her mother from prison in 1881, she worked in Adelaide, toured as an equestrienne, worked on a central western station in NSW, and moved in 1886 to Forbes, where she married in 1888 and was drowned a decade later; she is buried near Ben Hall in Forbes cemetery. Frank Hatherley's play 'Ned Kelly's Sister's Travelling Circus', later titled 'Kate Kelly's Roadshow', was first performed in 1980; Jean Bedford's novel *Sister Kate* was published in 1982.

KELLY, Ned (1855–80) was the eldest son of an Irish ex-convict, John 'Red' Kelly (1820–66), who was transported to Van Diemen's Land in 1842, went to the mainland when his sentence expired, and married Ellen Quinn in 1850; he appears as a character in Eric Lambert's Eureka novel *The Five Bright Stars* (1954). After his death Ellen moved with the children to a small selection between Greta and Glenrowan in north-eastern Victoria, the 'Kelly country' as it has become known. Along with the Lloyds and the Quinns, relatives with whom they sometimes feuded, the Kellys formed part of the rural poor, suspected of duffing cattle and other crimes but also persecuted by the police. In 1870, after a previous acquittal for robbery under arms, Ned was sentenced to six months' hard labour for assault and offensive behaviour, and in 1871 to three years' gaol for receiving a stolen horse.

Following his release he stayed out of trouble for several years but eventually became involved again in the theft of stock, partly because he was provoked, like others of the clan, by the actions of the local squatters in impounding the cattle of the selectors. In April 1878 a trooper named Fitzpatrick went to the Kelly shanty to arrest Dan Kelly (1861–80), Ned's brother, for stealing horses. What happened there has never been completely established but Fitzpatrick, later dismissed from the police force, claimed he had been shot by Ned, who was almost certainly not present. Dan went into hiding in the Wombat Ranges, where he was joined by Ned. In October Ellen Kelly received three years' hard labour for her part in the attempted murder of Fitzpatrick; later that month the Kellys, together with Joe Byrne, Steve Hart and a fifth man, Tom Lloyd Jnr, who was never identified as a member of the Kelly gang, surprised a police camp at Stringybark Creek, where, according to one account, Constable Lonigan was reading a copy of *The Vagabond Papers*. In the ensuing affray Lonigan, his fellow constable, Scanlon, and Sergeant Kennedy were killed, but the fourth policeman, McIntyre, escaped to give evidence at Ned Kelly's trial.

Within a week the gang had been outlawed, but avoided capture for nearly two years, not least because of the 'bush telegraph' operated by sympathisers. In December 1878 the bushrangers 'stuck up' a bank at Euroa, and in February 1879 made a similar raid at Jerilderie in NSW. On both occasions they cleared more than £2000 and lavishly entertained their victims; at Jerilderie, Ned produced a written vindication of his conduct which has become known as the Jerilderie Letter. The climax to the gang's adventures came at the end of June 1880, when the Kellys, Hart and Byrne ensconced themselves in a hotel at Glenrowan, planning to derail a special police train sent up from Melbourne; it is probable that they hoped to spark off a wider rebellion in the area. (A Bertram Chandler fantasy novel, *Kelly Country* (1983), shows what might have happened if the Kellys had won at Glenrowan). The plan was foiled when the local schoolmaster, Curnow, receiving permission to leave the hotel to go home, warned the train crew. In the battle between police and the gang, Byrne, Hart and Dan Kelly died in the hotel and Ned, clad in metal armour, was wounded and captured. Tried in October 1880 for one of the Stringybark Creek murders, he was convicted, sentenced to death and executed on 11 November; by one account his last words were 'Such is Life'. The anniversary of his death falls on the same day as two other events of significance to Australians: the Armistice ending the First World War, and the dismissal of the Whitlam government in 1975.

The Kelly gang was the last of the famous bushranging gangs and for many colonists in 1880 the capture of Ned meant safety from a cold-blooded killer. Such was the view of most of his pursuers, among whom John Sadleir, in *Recollections of a Victorian Police Officer* (1913), left a well-known account from the law-and-order side; George Farwell, in *Ned Kelly, What a Life!* (1970), takes the same view. Yet 32 000 people petitioned for Ned's reprieve, and since his execution the Kelly legend in Australian folklore has grown and been celebrated in song and dance, verse and prose, paint and film. The legend's sympathy for the Kellys has its origin in the several factors which made them underdogs: they were of the selector class, disadvantaged by the inequitable distribution of land by urban legislators in favour of the squatters; they were of Irish and convict origins; and they were subject to a legal system which showed its severity in Sir Redmond Barry's sentencing of Ellen and Ned Kelly and which was administered by a force of police whose incompetence was satirised during the long pursuit of the gang and whose shortcomings were exposed in a subsequent royal commission (1881–83). Added to this, Ned was brave (to be as 'game as Ned Kelly' is to show the same kind of pluck that made him fight on despite multiple wounds at Glenrowan), a superb bushman, loyal to his mates and, although something of a 'larrikin', possessed of the kind of daring and gallantry both at Euroa and Jerilderie that place him within a wider outlaw/highwayman folk tradition. Most of the Kelly folk-songs and ballads, including the anonymous 'The Kelly Gang', 'The Kellys, Byrne and Hart', 'Kelly was Their Captain' and 'Farewell to My Home in Greta', express this view of Ned and his circle. Several works in the same tradition are J.J. Kenneally's influential *The Complete Inner History of the Kelly Gang and Their Pursuers* (1929), which carries a testimonial by Ned's brother, Jim and was a major source for Frank Clune's best-selling *The Kelly Hunters* (1954); Max Brown's fine biography, *Australian Son* (1948), which first published some of the Kelly songs and the Jerilderie Letter; Eric Lambert's novel *Kelly* (1964), which presents Ned as an 'underground saint'; and noted novelist Robert Drewe's *Our Sunshine* (1991), told mainly in the first person and with fictional licence, which sees Ned as the victim of his background and times and which is an imaginative re-creation of the inner life of the man, Kelly.

A second view of the Kellys has emerged through what Graham Seal (*Ned Kelly in Popular Tradition*, 1980) has called the 'media tradition', which has exploited the sensational aspects of the story. From the start, the exploits of the Kelly gang were media events, as evidenced by the contemporary booklet *The Kelly Gang: Or, The Outlaws of the Wombat Ranges* (1879); the popularity of Thomas Carrington's sketches for the Melbourne press; the photographs taken at Glenrowan and sold later as postcards; and the several Kelly plays performed before Ned's capture, during his trial, and immediately following his execution. Within the same tradition can be placed J.J.G. Bradley's serialised story *Ned Kelly: The Ironclad Australian Bushranger* (1881), Nat Gould's novel *Stuck Up* (1894), Ambrose Pratt's *Dan Kelly* (1911), which exploits the rumours of Dan's escape from Glenrowan (the rumour-mongering is satirised in Nettie Palmer's ballad 'The Mystery Man'), Roy Bridges's romance, *The Fenceless Ranges* (1920), the Kelly stage melodramas of Dan Barry and Arnold Denham (1898–99), and the six Kelly films made 1906–70. Some of these works, influenced by the oral tradition, offer unashamedly sympathetic portrayals of the Kellys, but a more characteristic note is one of ambivalence towards Ned and his fellow hero-criminals. Something of the same ambivalence is to be found in Douglas Stewart's play *Ned Kelly* (q.v., 1943), in the two series (1946–55) of Kelly paintings by Sidney Nolan and in Robert Drewe's novel *Our Sunshine* (1991); both Stewart and Nolan explore Ned's symbolic significance and their work, together with David Campbell's Kelly poems in *Devil's Rock and Other Poems 1970–72* (1974) and the Kelly comics and modern songs, has done much to keep the legend alive.

Third, Ned Kelly has loomed large in Australian historical writing, including the general histories of Australia such as Manning Clark's *A History of Australia*; studies in the Australian tradition such as Russel Ward's *The Australian Legend* (1958); the early bushranging histories of James Bonwick, Charles White, George Boxall and Jack Bradshaw; and a number of specific studies. The centenary of Ned's capture and execution saw moves for a retrospective pardon; the screening of the television series *The Last Outlaw*; and the publication or reprinting of numerous Kelly books, including studies of the Kelly legend by Graham Seal (*Ned Kelly in Popular Tradition*) and Keith Dunstan (*Saint Ned*), the biographical interpretation by John Molony (*I Am Ned Kelly*), *Ned Kelly, after a Century of Acrimony*, by the folklorists John Meredith and Bill Scott, and Gary Langford's black comedy *The Adventures of Dreaded Ned*. Of the many other works published earlier, the most important are perhaps David Martin's satiric novel debunking the bushranging legend, *The Hero of Too* (1965), the collection of papers edited by Colin Cave as *Ned Kelly: Man and Myth* (1968), Charles Osborne's *Ned Kelly* (1970), Brian Carroll's *Ned Kelly, Bushranger* (1976), and especially John McQuilton's *The Kelly Outbreak 1879–1880* (1979), which places the exploits of the Kelly gang within the phenomenon of agrarian protest and social banditry. John H. Phillips, a criminal lawyer and a supreme court judge, reconstructs Kelly's trial in *The Trial of Ned Kelly* (1987) and Ian Jones in *The Friendship that Destroyed Ned Kelly, Joe Byrne and Aaron Sherritt* (1992) takes a fresh look at the role of Aaron Sherritt in the events leading up to Glenrowan. Despite its central character and the brief appearance of policemen named Kennedy and Scanlon, Thomas Keneally's children's fantasy, *Ned Kelly and the City of the Bees* (1978), is of little significance to the Kelly story beyond demonstrating that Ned's name still sells books. Jean Bedford's *Sister Kate* (1982) loosely reconstructs the life of Ned's sister Kate Kelly.

KEMP, Edward (1822–?), born near Hobart, was the author of the early political satire *A Voice from Tasmania* (q.v., 1846). He was the son of the pioneer settler Anthony Fenn Kemp (1773–1868), who was involved in the Rum Rebellion and who makes a brief appearance in 'Price Warung's' story 'The Evolution of Convict Hendy', and in Henry Savery's *The Hermit in Van Diemen's Land* (1830).

KENDALL, Henry (1839–82), born near Milton on the NSW south coast, spent his impressionable boyhood in the coastal districts of Illawarra in the south and the Clarence River in the north. Their cool moist rainforests, deep-shadowed gullies and lush pastures became the centrepieces of Kendall's best-known poetry, the landscape lyrics such as 'Bell Birds', 'September in Australia', 'Araluen' (qq.v.) and 'Narrara Creek'. After a difficult childhood with loving but impractical parents, and a stint of two years at sea in a whaler, Kendall settled into the literary coterie of Sydney, making his mark with poems in Sydney journals and newspapers from 1859 onwards. His first volume, *Poems and Songs* (q.v.), was published in 1862 with the assistance of J. Sheridan Moore. Although generously received by local and some English critics, the volume failed to sell its first edition of 500 copies. Beset by debts and personal problems, including a growing dependence on both literary patronage and alcohol, Kendall sought a new life in Melbourne after his marriage in 1868; his second volume, *Leaves from Australian Forests* (q.v.), was published there in 1869. The failure of the Melbourne venture, which led to increasing poverty, alcoholism and the death of his daughter Araluen, brought his return to Sydney in 1870, where the rapid disintegration of his personal and literary life continued. This painful period, described by him as 'The Shadow of 1872', brought alienation from his wife and periods of treatment for addiction in the Gladesville asylum. He was restored to health and sanity, and cured of alcoholism, by the extraordinary kindness of the Fagan family, timber merchants of Gosford and Sydney, who for two years, 1873–75, supervised his rehabilitation in their home near Gosford. In 1876 Kendall was reunited with his wife and family when he began a new life at the Fagan timber mill at Camden Haven on the north coast of NSW. His return to writing was signalled by his winning the *Sydney Morning Herald's* International Exhibition poetry competition in 1879 and by the publication of his final volume, *Songs from the Mountains* (q.v.), in 1880. In 1881 he was appointed inspector of forests by Sir Henry Parkes, the long-time patron whom Kendall offended many times but never more deeply than with his satire 'The Gagging Bill' in 1879. Kendall's health deteriorated under the strain of the travelling and work associated with his new position; he died in Sydney of phthisis when only 43.

Kendall's literary reputation, extraordinarily high in his own lifetime and immediately after his death but never at the same peak in this century, still rests chiefly on his lyric poetry. 'Bell Birds', 'September in Australia' and 'The Song of the Cattle Hunters', with their elaborate word pictures, extravagant melody and haunting melancholy, endeared themselves to succeeding generations of Australian readers and established Kendall as a favourite schoolroom poet. Some modern critical opinion, while not denying the importance of these popular lyrics, has drawn attention to the many-sided nature of Kendall's poetic talent, ignored when the nationalistic fervour of the 1890s and the early decades of this century dismissed his work as derivative. Kendall's neglected narrative poems, whether with an Australian setting such as 'The Glen of Arrawatta' or 'A Death in the Bush', or with biblical backgrounds such as 'King Saul at Gilboa' and 'Manasseh', or based on the Homeric legends of Ulysses such as 'The Voyage of Telegonus', now attract attention because of their significant themes and their controlled narrative skill. Kendall's affectionate though tart commentaries on the colonial outback types, e.g. 'Bill the Bullock Driver' (q.v.) and 'Jim the Splitter' are now seen to have anticipated Henry Lawson and A.B. Paterson's portraits of similar bush characters. In the role of literary hatchetman, as in the satires 'The Gagging Bill' and 'The Song of Ninian Melville' and to a lesser extent 'The Bronze Trumpet', he reveals a vindictiveness that does not surprise those who know the correspondence of his early manhood. His love poetry, especially 'Rose Lorraine' and 'At Nightfall', which tell of his lost love for Rose Bennett, and the poignant 'Araluen' and 'On a Street', which reflect his guilt over the broken years 1869–72, are powerful statements of the problems of his troubled life. His patriotic verse, such as 'The Far Future', which attempts to create new loyalties and new hopes; his public poems, written for important occasions such as the 1879 International Exhibition in Sydney; his memorial verses for Charles Harpur, James Lionel Michael and Adam Lindsay Gordon; and his attempt in the fragmentary 'The Australian Shepherd' to begin the first Australian rural epic, all support the claim that Kendall was the most substantial poet of the colonial period. T.T. Reed compiled the definitive edition of Kendall, *The Poetical Works of Henry Kendall* (1966) and wrote *Henry Kendall: A Critical Appreciation* (1960). W.H. Wilde published the biographical and critical account *Henry Kendall* (1976). Ian F. McLaren compiled *Henry Kendall: A Comprehensive Bibliography* (1987) and Russell McDougall edited *Henry Kendall: The Muse of Australia* (1992), which includes excerpts from Kendall's work and essays about his life and work by various authors.

KENEALLY, Thomas (1935–) was born in Sydney, where he completed his schooling after some years at Kempsey, Wauchope and Taree on the NSW north coast. At 17 he commenced study for the Catholic priesthood, a vocation he abandoned in 1960 before ordination; the experience informed his early fiction, e.g. *Three Cheers for the Paraclete*, which focuses on a young priest's conflict with his superiors. He worked as a schoolteacher and clerk before the publication of his first novel, *The Place at Whitton*, in 1964. Since then he has been mainly a full-time writer, although in 1968–69 he lectured in drama at the University of New England; he has travelled widely in Australia and overseas, and has lived abroad for extended periods, in 1975–76 mainly in the USA and in 1970–71 in England. In 1987 he visited Eritrea, where he encountered war at first hand and lived with the Eritrean People's Liberation Front. *The Place at Whitton* and Keneally's second novel, *The Fear* (1965), which he has republished in condensed form titled *By the Line* (1989), won some praise among reviewers, but his first major success was *Bring Larks and Heroes* (q.v., 1967), which won the Miles Franklin Award. His subsequent novels are *Three Cheers for the Paraclete* (1968),

which also won the Miles Franklin Award; *The Survivor* (1969), which shared the Cook Bicentenary Award in 1970 and was filmed for television in 1971; *A Dutiful Daughter* (1971); *The Chant of Jimmie Blacksmith* (q.v., 1972), which won awards from the *Sydney Morning Herald* and the Royal Society of Literature and was filmed in 1978; *Blood Red, Sister Rose* (1974); *Gossip from the Forest* (1975), which was filmed for television (1978); *Season in Purgatory* (1976); *A Victim of the Aurora* (1977); *Passenger* (1979); *Confederates* (1979); *The Cut-Rate Kingdom* (1980), a magazine novel with modern advertisements and photography contemporary with its setting, Australia and New Guinea during the Second World War; and *Schindler's Ark* (q.v., 1982) which won the *Los Angeles Times* Prize for fiction and the prestigious Booker McConnell Prize in the UK (for which Keneally had previously been short-listed with *The Chant of Jimmie Blacksmith, Gossip from the Forest* and *Confederates*); *A Family Madness* (1985); *The Playmaker* (1987); *Towards Asmara* (1988); *Flying Hero Class* (1991); *Woman of the Inner Sea* (1992); and *Jacko* (1993). Apart from involvement in the television and film adaptations of his fiction, Keneally has written stage adaptations of *Bring Larks and Heroes* (*Halloran's Little Boat*, first performed 1966, published 1975), and *Gossip from the Forest* (performed and published 1983); three other plays, *Childermas* (1968), 'An Awful Rose' (1972) and *Bullie's House* (1981); scripts for television (e.g. the Bligh episode in *Behind the Legend* series, 1974) and film (e.g. *Libido*, 1973); a children's fantasy, *Ned Kelly and the City of the Bees* (1978); and *Moses the Lawgiver* (1975), a book written to complement an English television series. He has written several accounts of his travels, the lavishly illustrated *Outback* (1983); the similarly well-illustrated *Now and In Time To Be: Ireland and the Irish* (1991), a description of his journey around Ireland which is a self-conscious return to the home of his forebears and a quest for the country's place in Australia's immigrant experience; and *The Place Where Souls Are Born* (1992), which charts his travels in the American south-west and his search for the vanished Indian tribes. Keneally's interest in the past is also illustrated by his contribution with Patsy Adam-Smith and Robyn Davidson to *Australia: Beyond the Dreamtime* (1987). He has written two novels under the pseudonym 'William Coyle', *Act of Grace* (1988) and *Chief of Staff* (1991); and an account of his views on republicanism, *Our Republic* (1993). A fellow of the Royal Society of Literature, chairperson of the Australian Society of Authors 1987–90, a member of the Literature Board of the Australia Council 1985–88, and president of the National Book Council 1985–89, Keneally was made AO in 1983. Apart from numerous critical articles on Keneally's fiction, there is one book-length study, Peter Quartermaine's *Thomas Keneally* (1991). His novel *The Playmaker* inspired a play by Timberlake Wertenbaker, *Our Country's Good* (1988), which has been produced in several countries and in Australia.

A fluent writer who has on several occasions stated that he writes for a middlebrow not an academic audience, Keneally is a novelist who is both popular – overseas as well as in Australia – and serious. The range of his fiction is apparent in his prose, which moves from the idiomatic and vernacular to the symbolic and rhetorical; in his choice of subject matter, which is mainly Australian up to *The Chant of Jimmie Blacksmith* and has since included France, England, America, Antarctica, Yugoslavia, Poland, Eritrea and Byelorussia; and in his diverse use of fable (e.g. *A Dutiful Daughter*), fantasy (e.g. *Passenger*), parable (e.g. *Bring Larks and Heroes*) suspense (e.g. *The Survivor, A Victim of the Aurora, Flying Hero Class*) and other modes. Many of his novels have either an autobiographical starting-point (e.g. the importance of Catholicism in *The Place of Whitton, The Fear* and *Three Cheers for the Paraclete*; or his adventures in the Eritrean war in *Towards Asmara*); or reflect his interest in history. *Bring Larks and Heroes*, set in early NSW, is informed by Watkin Tench's writings and by Keneally's knowledge of the Vinegar Hill (q.v.) uprising by Irish convicts in 1804. *The Playmaker* returns to 1789 and the first dramatic production in Australia; *The Chant of Jimmie Blacksmith* is a fictional re-creation of the Jimmy Governor (q.v.) episode in the history of European–Aboriginal relations in Australia. The subject of *Blood Red, Sister Rose* is Joan of Arc, a figure who recurs in other Keneally novels, notably *A Place at Whitton* and *A Dutiful Daughter*. The setting of *Gossip from the Forest* is the Armistice negotiations at the end of the First World War. *Season in Purgatory*, in which Tito makes an appearance, focuses on the Yugoslav partisans during the Second World War and *Confederates* on the 1862 campaigns of Stonewall Jackson in the American Civil War. *Schindler's Ark* uses 'the texture and devices of a novel to tell a true story', that of the German industrialist Oskar Schindler, who saved more than a thousand Jews from the gas chambers during the Holocaust. In 1993 *Schindler's Ark* was made into an award-winning film, *Schindler's List*, directed by Steven Spielberg. On more than one occasion the links between history and Keneally's fiction have caused controversy, e.g. in the parallels drawn between *Season in Purgatory* and an earlier work on the same subject, Bill Strutton's *Island of Terrible Friends* (1961) and in the objections raised when *Schindler's Ark* was awarded the Booker Prize that the novel was less fiction than 'faction'.

Yet despite Keneally's ability to capture convincingly the texture of history, notably in *Gossip from the Forest, Schindler's Ark* and *Confederates*, his novels are not simply historical reconstructions, nor is his imagination enslaved by the past. Several of his works, e.g. *Three Cheers for the Paraclete, A Dutiful Daughter, Passenger, 'An Awful Rose', Flying Hero Class*, are contemporary in setting or in the issues they address, e.g. religious belief, abortion, familial relationships, terrorism and the plight of displaced peoples. Those works that are 'historical' remain also, as Keneally suggested of *Bring Larks and Heroes*, 'essentially contemporary', forging links between the past and the present. *Bring Larks and Heroes*, described by him as 'a parable for the present', was written during the Australian experience of Vietnam, an experience influential in 'Childermas', an anti-war play commissioned by the Australian Committee of Responsibility for Children in Vietnam. The historical framework so overtly established in *The Chant of Jimmie Blacksmith* offers an implicit explanation for the current state of Black–White relationships in Australia. *Blood Red, Sister Rose*, to take a third example, is in part a novel about how myths are established. In two of his latest novels he intermingles contemporary and past experience with diverse but pronounced refracting effects; in *Woman of the Inner Sea*, set in 1980s NSW, the central character returns to a older, simpler Australia after her life has been overturned by a terrible tragedy; *A Family Madness* interweaves the surface ordinariness of contemporary Sydney and the labyrinthine nightmare of Byelorussia of the Second World War in a complex pattern of divided loyalties and responsibilities. But in all his novels, the past serves to evoke moral connectedness and our general implication in the brute tragedy of history.

Subsidiary to this general theme is the recurring one of the predicament of the ordinary individual, vulnerable in the midst of a hostile world. This preoccupation is reflected in the extreme situations that his characters find themselves in, e.g. in times of war (eight of the novels); the sense of fragility and absurdity of the body and of life itself; and the prevalence of violence, e.g. the murders, hangings, sacrifices, butchery, blood and witchcraft that commentators have noticed as staples in his fiction. The attempts of Keneally's protagonists to act with integrity, decency or honour are characteristically at odds with the demands of the systems of authority that mankind constructs: religious systems (as in *Three Cheers for the Paraclete*); political systems of various forms (e.g. communism in *The Fear*, Naziism in *Schindler's Ark*, regionalism in *A Family Madness*); systems of kinship (e.g. the family in 'An Awful Rose' and *A Dutiful Daughter*, race in *The Chant of Jimmie Blacksmith*). In some Keneally novels the individual is oppressed by the combinations of authority (e.g. Halloran by both Church and State in *Bring Larks and Heroes*), in others by their conflict (e.g. *Confederates* and the other war novels). The irony is that humanity constructs and codifies authority, and that individuals (e.g. Halloran, Erzberger in *Gossip from the Forest*) are drawn to seek moral protection or justification for their conduct within the systems. Thus humanity is collectively responsible for what has been made of the world, although some critics have argued persuasively that it is Keneally's women (e.g. Ettie Bumphass in *Confederates*, Barbara Glover in *A Dutiful Daughter*) who are made to bear the moral burden. That issue apart, the recognition of collective complicity and guilt, and Keneally's mixing of comedy and tragedy, offer what little hope there is in his fictional worlds.

KENNA, Francis (1865–1932), born Maryborough, Queensland, worked in a post office, was a teacher, member of the Queensland parliament and a newspaperman. He was editor of the Queensland *Worker*, the *Clarion*, the Brisbane *Sun* and the Charters Towers *Telegraph*, and owned and edited the Bangalow *Herald* and the *Logan and Albert Bulletin*, now the *Gold Coast Bulletin*. A regular *Bulletin* poet, Kenna often used the pseudonym 'K'; he contributed to the *Bulletin* debate in the 1890s, siding with Henry Lawson and satirising A.B. Paterson with his parody 'Banjo of the Overflow'. Kenna published two volumes of verse, *Songs of a Season* (1895) and *Phases* (1915), which range from the easy vernacular of the bush ballad to elegiac poetry of considerable intensity. A devoted Labor Party man, Kenna shared the sentiments of poets such as Lawson and Barcroft Boake, fulminating against the 'Lords of the Money' and their oppression of the working class.

KENNA, Peter (1930–87) was born in Sydney into a large Irish Catholic family and at the age of 10 began to work with a concert party entertaining troops. After leaving school at 14, he worked in a variety of jobs, meanwhile performing with amateur theatre groups. By the 1950s he was an established radio actor and joined the Australian Elizabethan Theatre Trust on its formation in 1954. In 1959 his play *The Slaughter of St. Teresa's Day* won the General Motors-Holden national playwrights' competition, was subsequently widely performed in Australia and was produced on radio and television in Australia and Britain. Between 1960 and 1971 Kenna lived mainly in London, where his play *Talk to the Moon* (1977) was first produced in 1963, although he visited Australia briefly to direct his farce 'Muriel's Virtues' at the Independent Theatre in 1966. In 1971 he returned to live permanently in Sydney, where he re-established his name with a number of productions. His published plays are *The Slaughter of St. Teresa's Day* (1972), *A Hard God* (1974), *Three Plays* (*Talk to the Moon*, *Listen Closely* and *Trespassers Will Be Prosecuted*) (1977), *Mates in Drag Show* (1977), and *Furtive Love* (1980).

The Slaughter of St. Teresa's Day, set in Sydney's inner suburb Paddington in the 1950s, deals with the criminal underworld of the city and one of its prominent female individuals. It effectively combines naturalism, sensational events, comedy and sentiment, and touches on one of Kenna's characteristic themes, the difficulty of establishing and maintaining intimate human relationships. This theme is more obvious in his working-class family drama *Talk to the Moon*, and in his play for two actors, *Trespassers Will Be Prosecuted*; set in a culvert beneath a railway line, the latter is a territorial battle between an aging alcoholic tramp and an adolescent boy, in which the corruption and innocence, aggressions and needs of both, are laid bare. *Listen Closely*, a farce which turns on a country father's attempt to impose a ritual of initiation on his son and the reactions of the various women involved, is also an effective satire of Australian middle-class mores. Kenna's best-known play, *A Hard God*, which draws heavily on his Irish Catholic boyhood and has aroused memories of familiar experiences in many of his audiences, is concerned with the difficulties and comforts of the Catholic religion, the effects of time and the experience of loss. The play's structure, and its division between the experience of the older members of the Cassidy family and Joe Cassidy's adolescent relationship with another boy, reflect Kenna's interest in combining an expressionistic, thematically developed

form with representational realism. Kenna conceived *A Hard God* originally as part of a trilogy and later completed it with the further two plays, *Furtive Love* and 'An Eager Hope' to form 'The Cassidy Album'. The trilogy was first performed at the Adelaide Festival in 1978. *Furtive Love*, which takes up the story of Joe Cassidy, now an actor and author, a decade later, centres on the conflict between his homosexuality and his religion; 'An Eager Hope' returns to the home of the Cassidy family, where Joe, now in his thirties, unsuccessfully fights kidney disease, whereas his brother Francis evades suffering by means of his facile charm. Kenna's short play *Mates*, a confrontation between Sylvia, a transvestite homosexual and a nightclub performer, and Perce, an old shearer who is firmly heterosexual, is a further exploration of the theme of the absence of intimacy in modern life and the inadequacy of relationships, including sexual ones.

KENNEDY, Victor (1895–1952), born Eaglehawk, Victoria, spent a lifetime in journalism and freelance writing in WA, Queensland and Victoria. A Jindyworobak in outlook, he wrote *Flaunted Banners* (1941), an essay in defence of the Jindyworobak movement, and edited the Jindyworobak anthology of verse for 1942. His poetry includes *The Unknown Anzac and Other Poems* (1917), *Farthest North and Other Verses* (1928), *Light of Earth* (1938) and *Cyclone: Selected Poems* (1949). With Nettie Palmer he wrote the biographical and critical work *Bernard O'Dowd* (1954).

KENNY, Robert (1950–), born Melbourne, was co-founder and co-editor until 1974 of *Contempa* magazine and publications. In 1974 he founded the Rigmarole of the Hours (q.v.) series of publications. He co-edited with Colin Talbot the verse anthology *Applestealers* (1974) and with Kris Hemensley and Walter Billeter, *3 Blind Mice* (1977). Writer, editor and graphic designer, he has published several books of verse, *Dead Oceans Poems* (1975), *'Poem'* (1975), *Dark Lyrics* (1987) and *Fear* (1991). His prose includes fiction, *A Book of Detection* (1978), *Etcetera* (1978) and *The Last Adventures of Christian Doom* (1982).

KENT, Jean (1951–), born Chinchilla, near Brisbane, spent her early formative years (as her poetry shows) in subtropical Queensland. She completed an arts degree in psychology in 1971 and has worked mainly as a counsellor with TAFE in NSW. She has contributed poetry and short fiction to literary journals and anthologies and has won numerous prizes, e.g. the 1988 and 1989 Henry Kendall competitions, the Patricia Hackett Award in 1982 and 1990, the National Library Award 1988, the Mary Gilmore Award and the Anne Elder Award, both in 1990, for her first collection, *Verandahs* (1990) and the FAW John Shaw Neilson Award in 1992 for her second collection, *Practising Breathing* (1991).

Jean Kent returns many times in her poetry to the innocent days of childhood, *Verandahs*, for example, opening with nostalgic memories of her parents' and grandparents' homes in southern Queensland, of the country school 'hardly bigger than a kitchen' which she attended, of hours spent high in the branches of a Moreton Bay fig tree trying to see over the range to the city and ocean, of her invalid father (to whom the book is dedicated) 'communing with nature' on his beloved verandah every afternoon, of their country neighbours given to few words and long silences, and of Christmases with 'cousins cousins cousins aunts and uncles, mothers fathers'. Poems of more mature experiences, focusing on her work as a counsellor, subsequent homes and different places, are less animated, finding harmony only in flowers, gardens, poetry and thoughts of childhood. Although 'After Reading Poetry in My Lunchbreak' appears to question whether poetry has any relevance for ordinary life, in other poems the implied answer is affirmative, while the minutiae of day-to-day living (e.g. her small gem 'To the Ironing Board') provide the impetus for much of their whimsical creativity. *Practising Breathing* is more ambitious than *Verandahs*, including longer, more sombre poems, e.g. the long sequence of the title poem about a young man's suicide and the 'Poems after the Death of a Young Child'.

KENTISH, N.L. (Nathaniel Lipscomb) (1797–1867), born Hampshire, England, arrived in NSW in 1830 to take up a government surveying appointment. He lost his job in 1833 and in 1834–38 ran the *Sydney Times*, a pro-emancipist newspaper with a strong verse content which was published irregularly but sold strongly in competition with the *Sydney Herald*, later *Sydney Morning Herald*. Briefly an emigration agent, Kentish returned to surveying and spent most of the 1840s in Van Diemen's Land; in 1849 he went to Port Phillip, where he was gaoled for horsewhipping a newspaper editor, then returned to Sydney, where his last years were spent. A self-promoting controversialist, Kentish became embroiled with officialdom wherever he went and published several pamphlets in which he justified his conduct. Besides these, he wrote two descriptive works, *The Present State of New South Wales* (1835) and *The Political Economy of New South Wales* (1838), and several verse essays and miscellanies including *Essay on Capital Punishment* (1842); *The Bush in South Australia* (1836); the bibliographical curiosity *Work in the Bush, Thoughts in the Bush, and Life in the Bush, of Van Diemen's Land* (1846); and *The Question of Questions* (1855), which reprints the broadsheet verse anthems with which Kentish, self-styled 'Amateur Poet Laureate' of Victoria, celebrated the separation in 1851 of that colony from NSW.

KER WILSON, Barbara (1929–   ), born Sunderland, England, has lived in Australia since 1964. She has had long experience in the publishing industry with OUP, Bodley Head and Collins in England, and with A&R, Hodder & Stoughton and UQP in Australia. A freelance editor and consultant editor for young adult fiction with UQP, she has written many books for children over a period of nearly forty years, most of them with a strong element of folklore and social history; among them are stories about such Australian identities as the koala, kangaroo, dingo and magpie. She collected Aboriginal legends told to Daisy Bates in *Tales Told to Kabbarli* (1972). Her adult fiction comprises *Jane Austen in Australia* (1984), a meticulously researched historical novel written in a sub-Austen style, and *The Quade Inheritance* (1988), which begins with the establishment in Somerset of Selbury Quade estate by the ruthless Dame Margery Quade in the sixteenth century. Her nineteenth-century descendant, Imogen Quade, equally obsessed with the estate, comes to grief over her obsession. The story spans Victorian England and the newly established colony in Australia. She has also compiled several books of Australian stories for children and young adults.

KERBY, Corinne, a radio broadcaster, television compère and civil rights activist, published two collections of poetry, *Mainly Affirmative* (1968) and *The Living Thing* (1971). Celebrations of marital and family love, the lyrics of *Mainly Affirmative* are more accessible than those of *The Living Thing*, although their certainties are already ringed round with a sense of transience and mortality. Even more sparing of language and crafted with delicacy, the poems of Kerby's second collection share the metrical assurance, clear images and condensed thought of *Mainly Affirmative*; in this collection, however, the surface control contrasts with a turbulent, almost despairing struggle for existential meaning.

KERR, Colin (1912–82), born Adelaide and educated at the University of Adelaide, joined the staff of the *Advertiser* in 1935. He served with the 2nd AIF in the Middle East and the Pacific during the Second World War and in 1966 was appointed to the staff of the SA Archives where his interest in the early history of the State resulted in several books. His publications include a biography of Sir Archibald Grenfell Price, *Archie* (1983); an annotated collection of excerpts from letters and diaries of ordinary settlers in South Australia, *A Exelent Coliney: The Practical Idealists of 1836–46* (1978); a military history, *Tanks in the East* (1945); and with his wife, Margaret Kerr, a series of books in Rigby's Pageant of Australia series, *The River Men* (1975), *The Gold-Seekers* (1975), *The Overlanders* (1975), *Twelve Makers of Australia* (1975), *Australian Pioneers* (1976), *Australian Explorers* (1978), *Australian Bushrangers* (1978), *Port Phillip Bay* (1979), *Australia's Early Whalemen* (1980), *Port Jackson, Today and Yesterday* (1980) and a history of the Royal Adelaide show, *Royal Show* (1983).

KERR, D.B. (Donald Bevis) (1920–42), killed in air operations in New Guinea in the Second World War, was a poet whose talent was recognised by critics such as Max Harris and Geoffrey Dutton. A founder of the *Angry Penguins* journal and a leading figure in the avant-garde poetry movement of the early 1940s, Kerr is represented by the small posthumous collection, *Death Be Not Proud* (1943).

KERR, Sir John (1914–91), born Balmain, into a working-class family, was educated at Fort Street

High School and the University of Sydney and was admitted to the Sydney Bar in 1938. He was principal of the Australian School of Pacific Administration for three years, returned to the Bar in 1949, and was later president of the NSW Bar Association and the Law Council of Australia. He played a prominent part in the Industrial Relations Society and the Council on New Guinea Affairs, was appointed to the federal Bench in 1966 and in 1972 became chief justice and lieutenant governor of NSW. Governor-general of Australia 1974–77, he exercised controversial reserve powers of the Crown to dismiss the Whitlam government in November 1975 after the Senate denied Supply in October. Australia's greatest constitutional crisis since Federation, the event aroused and continues to arouse fierce debate. Kerr's autobiography, *Matters for Judgement* (1978), presents his side of the affair as well as describing his earlier career and including reminiscences of Sir Thomas Blamey, Alfred Conlon, James McAuley, H.V.Evatt, Sir Robert Menzies and numerous politicians and legal figures.

KERSHAW, Alister (1921–   ), born Melbourne, was a member of the city's artistic counter-culture of the 1930s and 1940s, contributing to such magazines as *Comment* and *Angry Penguins*. He left Australia in 1947 and was secretary for some years to the British writer Richard Aldington, but has lived in France for much of his life. During the 1960s he was the ABC's Paris correspondent and has published some of his talks in *A Word from Paris* (1991). His other publications include five books of poetry, *The Lonely Verge* (1943), *Excellent Stranger* (1944), *Defeat by Time Past* (1947), *Accent & Hazard* (1951) and *Collected Poems* (1992); *A History of the Guillotine* (1958), which is to some extent also a study of the French character, and *Murder in France* (1955), an account of seven of France's most notable murderers; reminiscences of friends, *Adrian Lawlor: A Memoir* (1981) and *The Pleasure of Their Company* (1986), which recalls numerous 'nonconformists' he has encountered including Lawlor and P.R. Stephensen; *Hey Days* (1991), a personal record of Melbourne in the 1930s and 1940s; and *Village to Village: Misadventures in France* (1993), an account of his time in France just after the Second World War. Written partly as a response to Richard Haese's study *Rebels and Precursors, Hey Days* is a lively, frankly opinionated account of the period's cultural battles including the Ern Malley hoax and of such artists, writers and other cultural figures as David Strachan, Albert Tucker, Olga Cohn, James Gleeson, Sidney Nolan, Bernard Smith, Geoffrey Dutton, Max Harris, John and Sunday Reed, Adrian Lawlor and Denison Deasey.

KIDDLE, Margaret (1914–58), born South Yarra, Melbourne, graduated from the University of Melbourne (BA, MA), where she later taught history. She wrote two children's books, *Moonbeam Stairs* (1945) and *West of Sunset* (1949), and a biography, *Caroline Chisholm* (1950), but her chief work was *Men of Yesterday: A Social History of the Western District of Victoria 1834–1890* (1961). Based largely on the family records of the early pioneers, *Men of Yesterday* begins with a prologue that describes Australia Felix and its Aboriginal inhabitants prior to White settlement and examines the conditions in Scotland and Ireland that led to large-scale emigration in the 1830s and 1840s. The first part depicts the pioneering ventures in Australia Felix from Van Diemen's land and overland from NSW. The second part has a chapter on the Victorian goldfields and outlines the problems associated with the land Acts. The third part sees the squatter dynasties firmly entrenched on magnificent merino studs with elaborate but practical rural homesteads and alternative mansions in Melbourne.

KIERNAN, Brian, see **Criticism**

Kiley's Run, from the poem 'On Kiley's Run' by A.B. Paterson (q.v.) published in *The Man from Snowy River and Other Verses* (1895), is usually identified with the station Narambla, where Paterson was born and spent many happy boyhood times. In its opening verses the poem presents an attractive glimpse, in the usual Paterson manner, of the carefree existence and camaraderie of bush life. But with droughts and unpaid overdrafts, Kiley's Run is eventually lost and passes through the bank to an absentee landlord in England. As Chandos Park Estate, it becomes merely an investment. Paterson had in 1888 written a pamphlet, 'Australia for Australians', urging land reform; 'On Kiley's Run' is a further attack on the evils of the land grant system, made more personal by its echoes of a situation that had occurred in the poet's own family years earlier.

KIM, D'Ono (1938–   ), born North Korea, arrived in Australia in 1961, after travelling in China, Russia, Vietnam and Japan. He has studied linguistics and English literature at the universities of NSW and Sydney, has taught in schools and colleges and worked as a librarian. He is the author of three novels, *My Name is Tian* (1968), *Password* (1974) and *The Chinaman* (1984); and several libretti with the composer Anne Boyd, 'Death of Captain Cook', 'Coal River', 'My Name is Tian' and 'The Cycle of Love'. A play, 'The Bell', written for stage and published in *Outrider 90* (1990), was later performed on radio and afterwards adapted as a libretto. *My Name is Tian*, set during the Vietnam War, traces the story of a peasant boy, Tian, born into a traditional Vietnamese family but confronted with conflicting ideologies which create division and alienation; *Password*, set in an ostensibly fictional country, 'Tartaria', focuses on the moral dilemma of a Chinese intellectual who becomes a member of the Japanese military élite after the fall of Nanking; *The Chinaman*, which can be read as adventure novel or allegory and has a contemporary Australian setting, explores intercultural relationships and like *Password* combines inner and outer experiences. Addressed to a meditative reader, Kim's slender but sophisticated novels reflect on the dilemmas posed for the individual conscience by the blind forces of history.

Kimberleys, or more properly the Kimberley, a vast, sparsely settled area of tropical north-western Australia, was named after the Earl of Kimberley, a former colonial secretary. Settlement of the Kimberleys followed Alexander Forrest's (q.v.) explorations in 1879; sheep were introduced into the western part of the region by Julius Brockman in 1879; the southern area began to be settled in 1881; by 1885 cattlemen from western Queensland – the Duracks, Nat Buchanan and others – had overlanded stock to the eastern area. Gold, discovered at Hall's Creek, led to an influx of settlement and the establishment of the port of Wyndham. The history and physical geography of the Kimberleys are recounted in such works as Alexander Forrest's *Journal of Expedition from De Grey to Port Darwin* (1880), Gordon Buchanan's *Packhorse and Waterhole: With The First Overlanders to the Kimberleys* (1933), Ion L. Idriess's *Over the Range* (1937), *One Wet Season* (1949) and *Outlaws of the Leopolds* (1952), J.K. Ewers's *With the Sun on My Back* (1953), Leslie and Coralie Rees's *Spinifex Walkabout* (1953) and Mary Durack's *Kings in Grass Castles* (q.v., 1959) and *Sons in the Saddle* (1983). The Kimberley region is now a major contributor to Australia's export of beef and iron ore.

KING, Jonathan (1942–), born Geelong, a descendant of Philip Gidley King, was educated at Geelong Grammar and spent three years as a jackeroo before becoming a journalist. He later studied at the universities of Melbourne and London, worked as a current affairs reporter for ABC television and as a lecturer in political science at the University of Melbourne from 1977 to 1982. He was the major force in arranging a re-enactment of the voyage of the First Fleet in 1987–88, a project which took ten years to realise and which is the subject of one of his books, *The Battle for the Bicentenary* (1989). His other publications include *The Other Side of the Coin: A Cartoon History of Australia* (1976), *Stop Laughing, This is Serious: A Social History of Australia in Cartoons* (1978), *Waltzing Materialism* (1978), *The First Fleet* (1982), *Philip Gidley King* (1981, with John King), *The First Settlement: the convict village that founded Australia 1788–90* (1984), and '*In the Beginning. . .*' (1985), a collection of the documents that gave rise to the establishment of a European nation in Australia.

KING, Philip Gidley (1758–1808), born Cornwall, England, was second lieutenant of the *Sirius* in the First Fleet and superintendent of the Norfolk Island settlement established in March 1788; he was its lieutenant-governor 1789–96. King succeeded Governor John Hunter at Port Jackson in 1800. An energetic administrator, he tried to eliminate the rum trade and other malpractices, developed agriculture and coal-mining, extended exploration by land and sea, expanded the Colony's public works programme and improved the lot of convicts and emancipists. The journal of his experiences was published as an appendix to Hunter's *An Historical Journal of the Transactions at Port Jackson and Norfolk Island* (1793) and separately in 1980. King was the subject of some of the 'pipes' (q.v.) circulating in the Colony at the time; during his governorship the *Sydney Gazette* began publication. He is featured in H.V. Evatt's *Rum Rebellion* (1938); his

wife, the first governor's wife to live in Australia, is the subject of Marnie Bassett's *The Governor's Lady* (1940); and a biography by his descendants, Jonathan King and John King, was published in 1981. He is the subject of Victor Crittenden's *King of Norfolk Island* (1993).

KING, Phillip Parker (1791–1856), son of Governor Philip Gidley King, was born at Norfolk Island, where his father was lieutenant-governor. Trained as a surveyor, King was given command of the cutter *Mermaid* in 1817 to explore the north-western coast of Australia, the first of four such voyages he made between then and 1821. In 1826 he published *Narrative of a Survey of the Intertropical and Western Coasts of Australia*, partly illustrated by his own sketches. His connection with Australia was resumed in 1832 when he returned to the colony as a substantial landowner; in 1834 he became resident commissioner of the Australian Agricultural Company, which he had joined as a shareholder in 1824. King's exploits are discussed in G.C. Ingleton's *Charting a Continent* (1944) and G.S. Ritchie's *The Admiralty Chart: British Naval Hydrography in the Nineteenth Century* (1967). Dorothy Walsh edited *The Admiral's Wife: Mrs. Phillip Parker King* (1967).

Kings Cross, known colloquially as 'the Cross', and a byword throughout Australia for bohemianism, is a small area of the inner Sydney suburbs of Darlinghurst and Potts Point. With a long-established reputation for its colourful citizenry, its cosmopolitan life-style and its exciting night life, Kings Cross has always been regarded as the 'sin centre' of Sydney, a constant allure in days gone by to those escaping from the tedium of the bush on their annual jaunt to the city or to those city-dwellers who want to escape, usually on a Saturday night, from the respectable monotony of the suburbs. It was beloved of writers such as the bohemian Marien Dreyer (q.v.), the impeccably respectable Dame Mary Gilmore, who lived for over thirty years at 99 Darlinghurst Road in a comfortable – and at times delighted – propinquity with strip joints, brothels and nightclubs, and *bon vivant* Kenneth Slessor (q.v.), a *habitué* of the area for even longer. The Cross has often been prominent in the literature of Sydney. Slessor's poems about Kings Cross, best known of which is 'William Street' (q.v.), have been published separately as *Darlinghurst Nights* (1981) with the original *Smith's Weekly* illustrations by Virgil Reilly. Slessor and Robert Walker published *Life at the Cross* (1965); other personal reminiscences include Robin Eakin's *Aunts up the Cross* (1965); Rennie Ellis's *Kings Cross Sydney: A Personal Look at the Cross* (1971); and Ricki Francis's *96 Kings Cross* (1972) and *Kings Cross Hooker* (1974). Historical accounts of the Cross include Freda MacDonnell's *Before Kings Cross* (1967) and the nostalgic recall of the war years by the Kings Cross Community Aid and Information Service, *Kings Cross 1936–1946* (1981). The phrase 'Kings-bloody-Cross' in 'Nino Culotta''s *They're a Weird Mob* (1957) aptly illustrates the combined impact of that unique part of the Sydney environment and the colloquial Australian language on the migrant consciousness.

Kings in Grass Castles (1959), an account of the Durack family's part in the saga of the pastoral expansion in Australia in the period 1853–98, was written by Mary Durack (q.v.). Patrick (Patsy) Durack, the author's grandfather, born in County Galway, Ireland, in 1834, arrives in Australia with his family in 1853. Three months later, after the death of his father in an accident, he is left at the age of 19 as the provider for his mother and seven other children. He takes a cartload of merchandise (on credit) to the Ovens diggings in Victoria, sells it profitably and digs for gold until he has accumulated £1000. In 1867 he settles the family on a small property at Dixon's Creek near Goulburn. In 1862 he marries Mary Costello from a neighbouring Irish family and with her brother, John, 100 horses and 400 cattle, heads north of Bourke, believing that 'out there between the Warrego and the Paroo are kingdoms waiting to be claimed'. In the drought-stricken outback Durack and Costello lose their stock and are themselves saved from death only by the intervention of Aborigines, who escort them to safety. In 1867 both families leave their Goulburn properties and set off north. In 1868 they reach the Cooper's Creek (q.v.) area where they settle at the now famous stations Thylungra (Durack) and Kyabra (Costello). By 1873 the registered holdings of the two families in the vast plain watered by the Cooper, the Diamantina and the Georgina Rivers total eleven million acres. In the good years that follow (1874–77) they see the Channel country and the Cooper's Creek district opened up to closer settlement and cattle-grazing over the spot where Burke and Wills had died only fifteen years earlier. The urge to 'poke along up North', which continues to grip both Patsy Durack and John Costello, then quite wealthy men, is probably a symptom of the consuming land hunger that stems from their deprived Irish background. Costello sells Kyabra for £60 000 and later moves off into the Gulf Country. In 1882 Stumpy Michael, Patsy's brother, sails from Brisbane to Darwin, thence to the mouth of the Ord River in the Kimberleys (q.v.) and explores the country with a view to the Duracks moving there. Following his favourable report the decision is made to leave Thylungra and in June 1883 in probably the greatest droving epic in Australian pastoral history, 7250 cattle leave Cooper's Creek on the 3000-mile trek to the Ord. The journey takes two years and three months; less than half the stock survive and the total cost is £70 000. The Duracks' arrival coincides with the Kimberley gold rushes, but the development of the properties – Argyle, Rosewood, Ivanhoe – goes on largely under the control of M.P. (Michael) Durack, Patsy's eldest son and the father of the author. The economic collapse of 1890–91 brings financial ruin to Patsy Durack, bearing out the truth of the statement he made back in the 1878 heyday, 'We are kings in grass castles that may be blown away upon a puff of wind'. In 1893 Mary Durack, Patsy's wife, dies and in 1896 he visits Ireland. He dies in Fremantle in 1898, melancholy and dispirited at the collapse, as he

sees it, of his life's work. In the book's epilogue Mary Durack briefly traces later events in the family history, including her brother Kim's role in the Ord River irrigation project and the disposal by her father of the Kimberley empire in 1950.

Kings in Grass Castles is not simply the story of a family. It is a wide-ranging social history in which the family's exploits are seen in the wider context of pastoral expansion in the second half of the nineteenth century. As well as analysing the colonial problem of land rights, it describes the lifestyle of outback communities; examines the role of the Irish immigrant in the pioneering days; assesses, without rancour or prejudice, religious divisions in colonial Australia; portrays, with fairness to both sides, the conflict between the frontier settlers and the Aborigines; and describes, with considerable flair and expertise, the constantly changing natural wonders of the country from southern NSW to the Kimberleys. The sequel, *Sons in the Saddle* (1983), continues the Durack story during the lifetime of Mary Durack's father, M.P. (Michael) Durack.

KINGSFORD-SMITH, Sir Charles (1897–1935), born Hamilton, Queensland, served in the Royal Flying Corps in the First World War, and then pioneered a mail route between Geraldton and Derby for the WA Airways; he later formed a transport company with fellow aviator Keith Anderson. In 1927 Kingsford-Smith, known nationally as 'Smithy' in later years, and Charles Ulm made a record flight around Australia and in 1928 in their Fokker aircraft *Southern Cross* they became the first men to fly across the Pacific Ocean from America to Australia. Numerous other significant flights followed: to England in record time; the first east-to-west crossing of the Atlantic Ocean; the first aerial circumnavigation of the globe. Smithy and Ulm established the first Australian National Airways in 1930 and made abortive attempts to establish air-mail services between Australia and England. In 1935 Smithy and T. Pethybridge were lost off the coast of Burma. A national hero after whom the Sydney airport at Mascot has been named, he has been the subject of numerous biographies, including Beau Sheil's *Caesar of the Skies* (1937), Ward McNally's *Smithy: The Kingsford-Smith Story* (1966), Pedr Davis's *Charles Kingsford-Smith: The World's Greatest Aviator* (1977) and John Pickering's *The Routes of the Valkyries* (1977, which also deals with Charles Ulm). His autobiography, *My Flying Life* (1937), was ghosted by Geoffrey Rawson. Two plays about Kingsford-Smith are Mary Gage's 'The Same Square of Dust', co-winner of the WA 150th anniversary play competition in 1979 and Richard Lane's 'Boy on an Old Bus'. A popular film of his career, *Smithy*, produced by Columbia Pictures, directed by Ken Hall, was released in 1946 and his life was the subject of a television series in the 1970s. His career has some parallels with that of Roy Hilman in Roger McDonald's novel *Slipstream* (1982).

KINGSLEY, Henry (1830–76), the younger brother of the English novelist Charles Kingsley (1819–75), was born in Northhamptonshire, England. His early life was spent in Devon, where parts of *The Recollections of Geoffry Hamlyn* (q.v.) and *Ravenshoe* are set, and in Chelsea, which is recalled in *The Hillyars and the Burtons* (q.v.). In 1850 he matriculated to Oxford where he was more interested in sport than in his studies; although he did not row in the boat race against Cambridge, he won an event at the 1852 Henley regatta. In 1853 he left without a degree and migrated to Australia. He spent 1854 on the Victorian goldfields, e.g. Bendigo and Beechworth, visited NSW in 1855 and returned to Victoria in 1856 by way of the Monaro; he also spent some time at Langi Willi station near Skipton, where a start was made on *The Recollections of Geoffry Hamlyn*. The novel was completed on his return to England, published in 1859 and met with some success. His next novel, *Ravenshoe* (1862), was also well received and encouraged Kingsley to make writing his career, but thereafter he struggled to support himself and his wife and in 1869 accepted the editorship of the Edinburgh *Daily Review*. He covered the Franco-Prussian War as correspondent for the *Review* in 1870, and then settled in London in 1871. Three years later he moved to Cuckfield, Sussex, where he died.

In all Kingsley published twenty works, most of them novels. There is Australian material in *Tales of Old Travel Re-Narrated* (1869), a bushranging story, 'The Two Cadets', in *Hetty and Other Stories* (1871), essays on the explorers Charles Sturt and Edward John Eyre in *Hornby Mills and Other Stories* (1872), and some Australian scenes in *The Boy in Grey* (1871) and *Reginald Hetherege* (1874), but Kingsley's two major contributions to Australian literature are his family chronicles, *The Recollections of Geoffry Hamlyn* and *The Hillyars and the Burtons* (1865, a facsimile edition with introduction by Leonie Kramer 1973). They are both emigrant success stories in the line initiated by Charles Rowcroft, Alexander Harris and others, but whereas, ironically, *The Hillyars and the Burtons* is the more Australian in allegiance, *The Recollections of Geoffry Hamlyn* was more significant for the development of Australian literature. A celebration of pastoral Australia 'before the Gold', it inaugurated the colonial romance continued by 'Rolf Boldrewood' and others. In describing it as 'that immortal work, the best Australian novel', 'Boldrewood' echoed Marcus Clarke's judgement, 'the best Australian novel that has been, or probably will be written'. In contrast, Joseph Furphy (q.v.) objected to its unrealistic picture of bush life in nineteenth-century Australia and dismissed it as 'exceedingly trashy and misleading' in *Such is Life* (1903), in which he purports to tell the real story of the Buckleys (q.v.) of Baroona. The twentieth-century decline in popularity of *The Recollections of Geoffry Hamlyn* paralleled Kingsley's status in English literature, which led S.M. Ellis to write *Henry Kingsley 1830–1876: Towards a Vindication* (1931). Recent studies include W.H. Scheuerle's *The Neglected Brother: A Study of Henry Kingsley* (1971), John Barnes's *Henry Kingsley and Colonial Fiction* (1971), and J.S.D. Mellick's comprehensive biography, *The Passing Guest: A Life of Henry Kingsley* (1983). Mellick also edited the

Kingsley volume in the Portable Australian Authors series (1982). 'Rolf Boldrewood' wrote of Kingsley in his *Old Melbourne Memories* (1884) and portrayed him in his pastoral romance *Babes in the Bush* (1900).

KINGSTON, Beverley (1941–), born Sydney, was educated at the University of Queensland and Monash University. Associate professor of history at the University of NSW since 1980, she has published the pioneering feminist history *My Wife, My Daughter, and Poor Mary Ann: Woman and Work in Australia* (1975) and vol. 3 of the *Oxford History of Australia, Glad Confident Morning* (1988). She has also edited *The World Moves Slowly: A Documentary History of Australian Women* (1977).

KINSELLA, John (1963–), born Perth, has studied at the University of WA and travelled extensively in Europe, the Middle East and Asia. Editor of the poetry magazine *Salt*, he has published his own poetry in numerous periodicals and anthologies and in the collections *Night Parrots* (1989), *The Book of Two Faces* (1989), *Eschatologies* (1991) and *Full Fathom Five* (1993); *SYZYGY*, an experimental poem, was published separately in 1993. Kinsella also contributed, with Anthony Lawrence, to the volume *Ultramarine* (1991) and edited an anthology of verse from the magazine *Salt*, *The Bird Catcher's Song* (1992). Often responsive to paintings or to the WA landscape, whose light, heat and dryness are prominent features, Kinsella's poetry is both intense and freshly lyrical. Myth-making is also a characteristic, *Night Parrots* including sequences on Lasseter and Nebuchadnezzar and *Eschatologies* an extended version of the Lilith myth.

KIPLING, Rudyard (1865–1936) visited Australia for two weeks in November 1891. In his autobiographical fragment *Something of Myself* (1937) he describes how he was welcomed in Melbourne and asked by a 'leading newspaper' to write a report on the Melbourne Cup, an offer he declined. If the brevity of his visit meant that Kipling the man was not well known in Australia, his work was a different matter. Immensely popular in Australia, it was regarded as a model of narrative realism, while his attitudes contributed markedly to the developing sense of a distinctive national identity in the 1890s. Qualities of his writing admired by contemporary Australian critics were its freshness, vigour, graphic power, humour, local colour and lively language, all qualities emulated by the *Bulletin* writers, notwithstanding the anti-imperialism of that paper. His sympathy with the downtrodden and interest in social reform foreshadowed Henry Lawson's creed as expressed in 'The Uncultured Rhymer to His Cultured Critics', while his plain-speaking interest in the darker aspects of life found a ready audience in those writers for the *Bulletin* who wrote of the hardships of bush life. Although Lawson resented any comparison with Kipling, his short stories were sometimes seen by reviewers as following in the Englishman's footsteps in terms of language, narrative technique and structure. The two authors addressed similar audiences and published in similar cheap editions, designed to meet as wide a public as possible. Some of the values they espoused were interchangeable, particularly those connected with national identity or the distinctive attributes of the national type. As Richard White has emphasised in *Inventing Australia* (1981), the cluster of values surrounding the democratic idea of 'The Coming Man', which were current at the turn of the century and which stressed manliness, practicality and the outdoor life, could be shared by political philosophies ranging from Kipling's imperialism to the *Bulletin*'s republicanism: 'Their values were generally democratic, although not necessarily radical, emphasising the worth of the 'Common Man', often at the expense of his political and military leaders'. Similarly, Lawson's preference for the bush worker as opposed to the squatter was paralleled in Kipling's idealisation of the 'common man' over the cultivated English gentleman. Meanwhile as a ballad-writer of 'strength and substance', Kipling was seen as particularly attuned to the outpost consciousness which Australians shared with other regions of the Empire; as one reviewer expressed it in terms that Paterson would have approved, Kipling 'is the first writer who has brought home to the insular Englishman the grandeur of his empire across the seas and the great qualities of the men who have won and are still upholding it'.

KIRBY, Reginald (1901–50), born Buckinghamshire, England, became a minister in the Baptist Church and arrived in Australia in 1936, serving as a padre in the RAAF in the Second World War. A prolific writer of adventure and romance fiction, Kirby published such books as *Basing House* (1943), *Beaufighter* (1943, on the war in New Guinea), *Pearl Harbour Pilot* (1944, about American pilots in the New Guinea campaign), *So Lovers Dream* (1945), *Girl of the Sierras* (1946) and *Wind of the Morning* (1950).

KIRKPATRICK, John Simpson (Private **Jack Simpson**) (1892–1915), known affectionately as 'The Man with the Donkey', was born South Shields, Tyneside, England, jumped ship in Australia in 1910, carried his swag to northern Queensland and then worked on coastal shipping before enlisting in the AIF. Politically radical and distrustful of the English ruling class, he enlisted more as a means of returning to England than for the patriotic reasons established by the myth surrounding his name. On 25 April 1915, the day of the landing on Gallipoli, he obtained a donkey, the first of several, and from then on worked day and night carrying the wounded from the front lines to the beach. Three weeks later, he and his last donkey were killed by shrapnel. Although no award for valour was made to Simpson, such awards then being given only for single acts of valour, his name became legendary for qualities of self-sacrifice and bravery. There is a statue of The Man with the Donkey at the Melbourne Shrine of Remembrance, a bronze by W. Leslie Bowles at the Australian War Memorial, Canberra, and a statue in South Shields erected in 1988 to mark Australia's bicentenary. T. Walsh wrote *The Man and the Donkey* (1948) and Sir Irving Benson, *The Man with*

the Donkey (1965). Richard Beynon has written the play *Simpson J. 202* (1991), which uses military records and letters Simpson wrote to his mother. Peter Cochrane's *Simpson and the Donkey: The Making of a Legend* (1992) examines the historical construction of the Simpson legend. Vietnam veteran Tom Curran also published a Kirkpatrick biography in 1992.

KIRWAN, Sir John (1869–1949), born Liverpool, England, came to Australia in 1889 and worked as a journalist in Brisbane, Melbourne and Adelaide before becoming editor-in-chief of the *Kalgoorlie Miner* and the *Western Argus*, where he remained until 1926. A long-time member of parliament and a member of the Senate of the University of WA 1912–24, he was knighted in 1930. In addition to numerous articles on the history of WA he published *An Empty Land: Pioneers and Pioneering in Australia* (1934) and the autobiographical *My Life's Adventure* (1936).

KISCH, Egon, see **HARCOURT, J.M.**

KLEIN, Colleen (1921–), born Blacktown, Sydney, began writing poetry under the tutelage of A.D. Hope but later turned to short fiction and the novel. Her fiction includes *The Heart in the Casket* (1977), *The Pomegranate Tree* (1977), *Deirdre Kincaid* (1978), *Women of a Certain Age* (1979) and *A Space for Delight* (1988). Much of her fiction concerns women and the various situations – as lovers, wives, mothers – that life finds them in. *Women of a Certain Age*, for example, depicts the boredom, bitterness and sense of futility that some women experience in middle age. *The Heart in the Casket* tells of the paradox of parenthood – its joys and sorrows, highs and lows. *A Space for Delight* is an account of three generations of women, their lives seemingly different but basically similar. In her fiction the hallmarks of her poetry – symbolism, concern with language and conciseness – are evident. She has also published two plays in a volume titled *From Blacktown to St Ives* (1978).

KNOPWOOD, Robert (1763–1838), born Norfolk, England, went to Port Phillip with the expedition of David Collins in 1803 as chaplain. When the projected settlement at Port Phillip was abandoned he went on to Hobart, where he was clergyman and magistrate. Knopwood kept a diary of his thirty or more years in Tasmania; an extraordinary document with eccentric spelling, it gives an enlightening account of the early days of the Tasmanian colony. Parts of it were published in *Historical Records of Port Phillip* (1879) and *Proceedings of the Royal Society of Tasmania* (1946–47), and also provided valuable information for Marjorie Tipping's *Convicts Unbound* (1988), an account of the first settlement in Tasmania. Mabel Hookey edited *Bobby Knopwood and His Times* (1929) and wrote the biographical *The Chaplain* (1970). Mary Nicholls edited *The Diary of the Reverend Robert Knopwood 1803–1838* (1977). He appears as a benevolent figure in 'Price Warung's' story 'The Procession of the Buttercup'.

KNORR, Hilde (1920–), born in the Warragul–Moe district of Victoria, studied music in Melbourne before marrying the Bavarian-born sculptor Hans Knorr. She began writing in 1958, contributing articles and short stories to newspapers and magazines, and has published three novels, *Shoemaker's Children* (1975), *The Mystic Lake* (1976), *Group with Lady* (1978); two collections of short stories, *Fire Won't Burn Stick* (1972), and *A Private Viewing* (1982); a volume of poetry, *From an Australian Homestead* (1980); and an account of her and Hans Knorr's earlier lives and their experiences after marriage, *Journey With a Stranger* (1986). She has also written the non-fiction books *Merriang: An Early Victorian Homestead* (1981) and with Hans Knorr, *Religious Art in Australia* (1967). Concerned with the subtleties of human relationships and the equally subtle, unpredictable workings of destiny, Knorr deals with a range of characters and experience in her short fiction. Reconciliation, either with others or with wounding events of the past, is one of her major themes. Both *Shoemaker's Children* and *The Mystic Lake* are set in rural Victoria; in the first the eldest girl of a large family is selected by her strong-willed aunt to help her farm a barely tamed, drought-stricken tract of land; the second recounts the experiences of the Delany family who open a hotel in a small Victorian township during the Great Depression, linking their experiences over several generations and the history of the hotel to those of their community. *Group with Lady*, set in 1940s Melbourne and narrated in the first person, focuses on the difficulties and unexpected crises connected with running a boarding house.

KNOWLES, Conrad (1810–44), born England, the son of a Wesleyan minister, was well educated and came as a colonist to WA at the age of 18; finding poor prospects there, he moved to Hobart, where he became a tutor in 1830. A scandal seems to have cut short his appointment and he moved to Sydney, where he soon became one of the leading actors at Barnett Levey's Theatre Royal when it opened in 1832. He was a versatile, popular but heavily overworked actor, often playing several parts at one performance, presenting many Shakespearean roles including Australia's first Hamlet and Lear, and becoming involved in management at the Theatre Royal and later at the Victoria Theatre and others. The strain of overwork, however, frequently showed in his acting. In 1837 he left for England with the actress Mrs Harriet Jones, but by 1838 they were back in Sydney. In his absence, other actors had replaced him in popularity, a situation that worsened with the arrival of Francis Nesbitt in 1842, and although he tried a series of acting-managing positions at theatres in Sydney and Melbourne, none was successful and he died of overwork. He is the author of *Salathiel: Or, the Jewish Chieftain*, performed and published in 1842, a pseudo-historical 'literary' drama with a turgid plot.

KNOWLES, Lee (Lee Jean Johnson) (1941–), born WA, is a dance teacher who performs Middle Eastern dances and was previously a writer with the WA Education Department. Living on an ocean-going yacht in Fremantle Boat Harbour she writes poetry which features the Fremantle, Swan River, Indian Ocean milieux. Her three books of poetry are *Cool Summer* (1977), *Dial Marina* (1986) and *Sirocco Days* (1993). She has won several awards, including the Tom Collins Poetry Prize (1980), Mazzucchelli's Love Poem Competition (1986) and the WA Week Award in 1987 for *Dial Marina*.

KNOWLES, Marion Miller (1865–1949), born Wood's Point, Victoria, was a teacher in Victorian schools in the 1880s and 1890s; between 1899 and 1927 she conducted a women's column and children's page in the Melbourne *Advocate*. She was a prolific writer of simple poetry and fiction dealing with experiences of Australian bush life, often filtered through devout Roman Catholic attitudes. Her poetry includes *Songs from the Hills* (1898), *Fronds from the Blacks' Spur* (1911), *Roses on the Window Sill* (1913), *Songs from the Land of the Wattle* (1916), *Love, Luck and Lavender* (1919) and *Ferns and Fancies* (1923). Her *Selected Poems* was published in 1935. Her fiction includes *Country Tales and Sketches* (1896), *Barbara Halliday* (1896, partly autobiographical), *Shamrock and Wattle Bloom* (1900), *The Little Doctor* (1919), *Meg of Minadong* (1926) and *Pretty Nan Hartigan* (1928). She is featured in J.R. Stevens's *Adam Lindsay Gordon and Other Australian Writers* (1937).

KNOWLES, Vernon (1899–1968), born Adelaide, worked on the Adelaide *Register* then went to England to continue a journalistic and writing career; he remained an expatriate but the influence of his Australian boyhood frequently surfaces in his work. His partly autobiographical novel *Eternity in an Hour* (1932) contains memories of childhood events in Adelaide and descriptions of the bush setting of creeks and gullies. His other works of fiction include *Bypaths* (1921, which combines prose and verse), *The Street of Queer Houses and Other Tales* (1925), *Here and Otherwhere* (1926), *Beads of Coloured Days* (1926), *The Ladder* (1929), *Pitiful Dust* (1931) and *Two and Two Make Five* (1935). His poetry includes *Songs and Preludes* (1917), *Poems* (1925), *The Ripening Years* (1927) and *Love is My Enemy* (1947). He also wrote a verse play, *Prince Jonathan* (1935) and a critical work, *The Experience of Poetry* (1935). He is represented, with C.R. Jury and E.J.R. Morgan, in *Lamps and Vine Leaves* (1919). Paul Depasquale has published an appreciation, *The Life and Work of Vernon Knowles* (1979).

KNOX, James (?1810–65) arrived in Hobart from England about 1832. An indefatigable contributor to journals and newspapers, he published *Poetic Trifles* (1838), a small book of simple immigrant lyrics which he claimed as the first book of poetry published in Tasmania.

KOCAN, Peter (1947–), born Newcastle, NSW, spent much of his boyhood in Melbourne, later returning to NSW where, at 19, he was sentenced to life imprisonment for the attempted murder of the then leader of the Australian Labor Party, Arthur Calwell.

He spent the next ten years either in gaol or in Morissett Mental Hospital. In that period he became engrossed in poetry, publishing a small booklet, *The Other Side of the Fence* (1975), dealing largely with the experience of being in an institution. In 1980 he published a second book of poems, *Armistice*, followed by two semi-fictional works, *The Treatment* (1980) and *The Cure* (1983, published in one volume in the USA in 1985), based on his incarceration. The protagonist of the fiction is Len Tarbutt who, like Kocan, progressed from gaol to the maximum-security section of an institution for the criminally insane, thence to open-ward custody and finally freedom. Since his release, with considerable assistance from the Literature Board of the Australia Council, Kocan has maintained himself as a full-time writer. By 1985 he had published a third book of poetry, *Freedom to Breathe*, the title poem adapted from Solzhenitsyn's prose poem indicating that Kocan now felt his 'lost faith' finally returning. Many poems of *Freedom to Breathe*, however, ('Retards Out Walking', 'Post Mortem' and 'Morissett Winter') imply the persistence of past traumas. Other poems show him attempting to breathe that freedom by visiting legendary literary places abroad – Culloden, Cambridge, Glastonbury – although even these create a sense of the 'loner' seeking the spiritual fulfilment that continues to prove elusive. A later work of fiction, *Flies of a Summer* (1988), is a fantasy of a future Dark Age, the modern world as we know it having been destroyed when 'the whole sky caught fire'. The new but primitive world is ruled by a vicious tribe, the Margai, who keep the remnants of the human race in subjection as a source of slave labour. Finally, a young human, Rowan, by exercising the virtues of courage, loyalty, determination and resourcefulness, leads his people to a new destiny. In *Standing With Friends* (1992) Kocan appears finally to have achieved his freedom. The times, as he sees them, are sadly out of order, but compassion, faith and affection may yet set things right. The simple, modest, finely crafted poems are themselves filled with compassion for the sufferers in a world characterised by, at best, insensitivity and, at worst, brutality and viciousness. The victims are many and varied – the savagely murdered Anita Cobby, the suburban family suffering from the Recession, the three unmourned, innocent policemen murdered by the Kelly gang at Stringybark Creek, a puppy chained up and growled at by its inhumane owner, a little girl killed and her unrepentant, uncomprehending killer. Keenly interested in amateur theatricals as writer, actor and producer, Kocan has written several plays, including 'The Card Players' (1979), 'Who Do You Think You Are?' (1982), 'The Walking Stick of the Desert' (1983), 'Home Fires Burning' and 'The Plot Sickens' (1986), some of which have been performed. He won the 1982 Mattara Poetry Prize for 'From the Private Poems of Governor Caulfield' and the 1983 NSW Premier's Literary Award for *The Cure*.

KOCH, C.J. (Christopher John) (1932–), born Hobart, has lived for extensive periods in Europe and America and has travelled in Asia. He worked for more than ten years as a producer for the ABC, becoming head of radio for schools, but resigned in 1973 to write full-time. Apart from some striking uncollected poetry, some of it anthologised, he has written four novels: *The Boys in the Island* (q.v., 1958, extensively revised in 1974), *Across the Sea Wall* (1965, a heavily revised version in 1982), *The Year of Living Dangerously* (q.v., 1978) and *The Doubleman* (1985). *The Year of Living Dangerously* won the 1978 *Age* Book of the Year Award and a National Book Council Award in 1979; it was made into a film of the same title by Peter Weir in 1982, the screenplay being written by Weir, David Williamson and Koch. *The Doubleman* won the 1985 Miles Franklin Award. Koch has also published a collection of essays, *Crossing the Gap* (1987), and has collaborated with Nicholas Hasluck in *Chinese Journey* (1985), which is a joint response to their visit to China in 1981 at the invitation of the Chinese Writers' Association.

The Boys in the Island, an unsentimental account of a boy's childhood and adolescence in Tasmania and Melbourne, received wide acclaim. Although the boy's experiences are captured with immediacy, it is his fresh openness to experience as he restlessly pursues his dream of a paradisal, illimitable state that is memorable. Striking aspects of the book are the youth's disillusioning love affair, described with lucid honesty, and his excited response to the magical lure of the big city. *Across the Sea Wall*, written entirely in the present tense, spans six years and is set partly in India, partly in Australia. It deals with the strange, obsessive relationship between a young Australian and a Latvian showgirl and traces a similar pattern of dream and disillusionment. Koch's concentration on visionaries had led earlier to his being classed with Patrick White and Randolph Stow, but the reception of this novel was very mixed. *The Year of Living Dangerously* revived Koch's reputation. Set in Indonesia in 1965 just before the fall of Sukarno, it is an engrossing, densely packed narrative which is both diverse and unified, convincingly meshing public and private worlds and setting the unpredictable political events against a spiritual and cultural background. *The Doubleman* and *Crossing the Gap* have further established Koch's reputation and clarified his consistent preoccupations. *The Doubleman*, set in Hobart of Koch's childhood and in 1960s Sydney, is narrated by Richard Miller, a victim of the post-war polio epidemic and, by the 1960s, a Sydney television producer. Miller's fascination as an isolated child with an imaginary fairy world is extended into adulthood both for himself and for others with ultimately destructive effects. In this story, the yearning for an otherness which will complete and transform the self takes the form of contemporary off-beat cults, but it has links with the obsessive quests, the vaguely but deeply felt absences and doomed attempts to control and dominate which characterise the central figures in his preceding novels. Koch's protagonists, in trying to reconcile the elusive power of dream and everyday actualities are all, spiritually speaking, suffering a postcolonial malaise. As a Tasmanian, Koch feels he has a special advantage in understanding Australia's post-colonial experience, which in *Crossing the Gap* he has described as a tension 'produced by the consciousness of another lost landscape and society'. If in Tasmania it was less difficult for previous generations to 'put together the lost totality of England', its inhabitants can no more escape the characteristic Australian experience, which he describes as 'a pathos of absence: the essential experience emerges as one where a European consciousness, with European ancestral memories, is confronted by the mask of a strange land, and by a society still not certain of its style'. The essays of *Crossing the Gap*, which chart his development as an artist and combine literary criticism, evocation of place and analysis of the changing map of Australian culture, have the unifying theme of the necessary and inevitable shift from Empire to a new Asia-Pacific consciousness. Describing Australia as living in 'interesting times', Koch concludes that his compatriots face the challenge of finally and thoroughly absorbing the new hemisphere in which they live while retaining their European heritage.

'Kodak', see **O'FERRALL, Ernest Francis**

KOMNINOS (Komninos Constantine Zervos) (1950–), born Richmond, Melbourne, of Greek parents, has an honours degree in science but since 1985 has devoted much of his life and energy to furthering performance poetry in Australia. His published works include *The Komninos Manifesto* (1985), *The Second Komninos Manifesto* (1986), *The Last Komninos Manifesto* (1987), *Wordsports* (1989), *High Street Kew East* (1990), *Komninos: The Poet and His Poetry* (1991), *On the Way to the Fridge for a Snack* (1991), *The Baby Rap* (1992) and *The Venus of Marrickville* (1993); and the plays *Sophisticated Souvlaki* (1986) and *Amnesty Project* (1990). His performances have taken place in schools, libraries, prisons, factories, pubs, clubs, on street corners and in writers' trains.

Komninos's poems tell of life as it is lived in everyday places – the work place, the pub, suburban homes, city streets – and reflect the situations people face in the family, with friends, enemies and fellows. The poems are usually humorous or sad, often satirical and dramatic, mostly boisterous and lively. His instructions to a rock and roll audience on how to appreciate poetry reveal the attitude of the performance poet to audience participation.

> If you feel like sleeping, sleep
> or chatting at the back of the crowd
> if you feel like snoring, snore
> but please don't snore too loud
> – if you feel like laughing, laugh
> if you feel like shouting, shout
> if you feel like clapping, clap
> that's what poetry's all about.

Reactions to such performance have been mixed. Komninos's own comments indicate the difficulties facing the performance poet: 'most think you're a poof – they all think you're a bludger.' To offset audience scepticism the performance poet has to work harder than his more traditional counterpart, the published poet:

> you have to make your words electric
> to sizzle with energy and still be euphoric
> to dabble and dribble in dialectic metaphoric
> without too much boring didactic rhetoric
> to spell out the truth and still have aesthetic
> to bend words and change words 'til they're brightly
> neonic
> to capture the sounds at speeds supersonic

The performance poet's goal, finally, is

> to free the words from their traditional prisons
> of books and libraries and academic institutions,
> to undress them, expose them to the whole
> population . . .
> to take the words off the page, give them wings,
> and let them fly to new destinations.

Komninos's most effective poems include 'childhood in richmond' which gives glimpses of the sadness of a young boy growing up in a household where economic and social pressures were intense; 'bustalk', which catches the speech cadences and rhythms of women gossiping on a bus; 'it's great to be mates with a koori', which is riotously rollicking and full of easy rhythm; 'i hate cars', which effectively displays the verbal power of performance poetry.

The traditional poet's attitude to performance poetry like Komninos's is ambivalent. Geoff Page, for example, sees value in the attempts of performance poets to win back some of poetry's earlier entertainment function which has been largely surrendered to television, but he warns that in the process they risk underestimating the true depth of their art as poets. The rapid growth of performance poetry has led, however, to increased sales of books of poetry and to greater public awareness of poetry as entertainment. In 1993 Komninos won the $20 000 Ros Bower Memorial Award for outstanding achievement in Community Arts. Ros Bower was the first director of the Australia Council's Community Arts Board.

Komos, published quarterly 1967–73 from the Monash University English Department, contained articles and discussions on drama and theatre. Some playscripts were issued as supplements. An index was published in 1973.

Kookaburra, sometimes referred to as the Laughing Jackass, is an Australian member of the kingfisher family of birds. It makes a loud, harsh noise resembling raucous human laughter, that was often regarded as fiendish and mocking by the early pioneers. Specimens of the kookaburra were taken to England by Sir Joseph Banks from Captain James Cook's first visit to Australia in 1770. In Captain Arthur Phillip's *The Voyage of Governor Phillip to Botany Bay* (1789) and in Surgeon-General John White's *Journal of a Voyage to New South Wales* (1790) there are engravings of a kookaburra, labelled the Great Brown Kingfisher, although Phillip notes the Aboriginal name, 'kookaburra'. The term 'laughing jackass' is recorded as early as 1797 in the notes of the ex-convict Thomas

Watling. Later writers, such as Henry Kendall, used the term 'gooburra', a version of which ('goburra') is found in Mary Anne FitzGerald's *Australian Fur and Feathers* (1889). Forty-five variations of the name are listed by A.H. Chisholm in *Bird Wonders of Australia* (1934). Like its compatriots the kangaroo and the emu, the kookaburra has often been used as an Australian symbol, e.g. as trademarks for Australian products, on badges of Australian military units, as a laughing motif on the Australian version of Movietone news in cinemas during the 1930s–1950s, and as striking dust-jacket illustrations on specifically Australian books. The bird is widely and variably featured in Australian children's literature, e.g. May Gibbs portrays the kookaburras as 'goodies' in the struggle against Mrs Snake and the evil Banksia men in *Snugglepot and Cuddlepie*, while Norman Lindsay's kookaburra in *The Magic Pudding* (1918) is the complete larrikin. Other writers such as Leslie Rees and Ida Rentoul Outhwaite have created well-known fictional kookaburras, e.g. Kurri Kurri and Johnny Kookaburra. Well adapted to illustration because of its striking features, the kookaburra has been immortalised in the paintings of Neville Cayley (senior) and in the illustrations of Hal Gye. The kookaburra's habit of making its first loud outburst at dawn has given it the name 'the settler's clock' or 'the bushman's clock'. Two significant works on the kookaburra are the ornithological investigation *Kookaburras* (1970) by Veronica Parry and the profusely illustrated, anecdotal *The Laughing Australian* (1982) by Toby and Juliana Hooper.

KOTZE, Stefan von (1869–1909), born Oschersleben, Germany, worked for some years in Australia as a journalist, contributed verse to the *Bulletin* in the late 1890s, and published his impressions of the country in local newspapers. In 1903 he published a German version, *Australische Skizzen*, which was subsequently translated back into English by L.L. Politzer, titled *Australian Sketches* (1945). Von Kotze also published travel books about Australia in German and edited an anthology of the short stories of Edward Dyson and C.A. Jeffries, translated into German, *Geschichten aus Australien* [*Tales from Australia*] (1909); some of the stories were subsequently reprinted in his collection *Im Australischen Busch* [*In the Australian Bush*] (1911).

KRAMER, Dame Leonie (1924–), born Melbourne, was educated at the universities of Melbourne and Oxford. She was professor of Australian literature at the University of Sydney 1968–89 and is now emeritus professor and chancellor. She has been a member of numerous community and educational boards and committees and chairperson of the ABC 1981–83. Editor of *The Oxford History of Australian Literature* (1981), she has written studies of 'Henry Handel Richardson', including *Henry Handel Richardson and Some of Her Sources* (1954), *A Companion to Australia Felix* (1962) and *Myself When Laura* (1966). She has edited or selected several collections including the 1961 volume of *Australian Poetry* and the 1963–64 volume of *Coast to Coast*; a selection of Hal Porter's writing (1971), and, with A.D. Hope, of Henry Ken-

dall's (1973); a selection of poetry, essays and personal commentary by James McAuley (1988); the collected poems of David Campbell (1989); and the general selections *My Country* (1985) and, with Adrian Mitchell, *The Oxford Anthology of Australian Literature* (1985). She has also written a critical study of A.D. Hope's poetry (1979) and, with R.D. Eagleson, *Language and Literature: A Synthesis* (1976) and *A Guide to Language and Literature* (1978). She was made OBE in 1976 and DBE in 1983; in 1986 she received the annual Award from the *Encyclopaedia Britannica*. She was awarded an honorary D.Litt. by the University of Tasmania and made honorary LL D by the ANU and the University of Melbourne.

KRAUSMANN, Rudi (1933–), born Mauerkirchen, Austria, came to Australia in 1958 but returned to Europe for three extended periods before settling in Sydney in 1966. He has worked as a journalist in Salzburg, as a language teacher in Sydney and Melbourne, and is now a freelance writer and editor. In 1975 he founded *Aspect: Art and Literature*, a magazine which attempted to bring the visual and literary arts together and ran until 1989. He also edited the collection *Recent German Poetry* (1977) and with Michael Wilding a collection of Australian short stories in German, *Air Mail From Down Under* (1990). His own published works include the prose collection *From Another Shore* (1975), and three volumes of poetry, *The Water Lily and Other Poems* (1977), *Paradox* (1980, illustrated by Brett Whitely) and *Flowers of Emptiness* (1982). Krausmann is also a playwright; his published plays include *Everyman: A Sentence Situation* (1978), republished in his collection *Three Plays* (1989), which also includes *The Perfection* and *The Word*. His other plays are 'The Leader' (1980), based on the diaries of the German architect Albert Speer, and 'Life Is Nothing New' (1982), based on the work of the Russian revolutionary poet Mayakowsky.

KRAUTH, Nigel (1949–), born North Sydney, was educated at the universities of Queensland and Newcastle and the ANU and has taught English at the universities of Papua New Guinea and Queensland, the Mitchell College of Advanced Education at Bathurst, where he helped to found *inprint*, and Griffith University. Krauth's novel 'The Jolly Swagman Affair' was co-winner of the *Australian/Vogel* Award for 1982; published in 1983 as *Matilda My Darling*, it is a fictional investigation of events surrounding the composition of 'Waltzing Matilda' (q.v.) in 1895. Krauth has written two further novels, *The Bathing Machine Called the Twentieth Century* (1988) and *J.F. Was Here* (1990). Set in the little coastal town of Booloominbah, *The Bathing Machine Called the Twentieth Century* is a deftly written allegory commenting on Australian materialism, secularism and history of oppression; *J.F. Was Here* focuses on two individuals whose histories as victims of society resemble each other, John Freeman, dying of AIDS at the age of 40, and Ina, his grandmother, who suffered for her defiance of colonial rule in Papua New Guinea. A composite character, Ina is partly based on Beatrice Grimshaw (q.v.). Krauth has also written short stories, radio plays and one stage play, *Muse of Fire* (1985), which is set in 1910 and concerns the beginnings of the Australian Film Industry and its impact on live theatre. Like his novels, the play, which includes Louis Esson as a character, reflects Krauth's interest in literary history and his concerns about contemporary Australia. Krauth has also edited *New Guinea Images in Australian Literature* (1982) and, with Elton Brash, *Modern Poetry from Papua New Guinea* (1972) and *Traditional Poems, Chants and Songs of Papua New Guinea* (1973). With Caron Krauth he has written several books for young readers, *Sin Can Can* (1987), *Rack Off Rachmaninoff* (1989) and *I Thought You Kissed With Your Lips* (1990).

KROLL, Jeri (1946–), born New York, USA, where she gained a Ph.D. from Columbia University, came to Australia in 1978 and has taught at Adelaide and Flinders universities. She has published four collections of poetry, *Death as Mr Right* (1982), winner of second prize in the Anne Elder Award of 1982, *Indian Movies* (1984), *Monster Love* (1990) and *House Arrest* (1993), and a collection of short stories, *The Electrolux Man* (1987). With Robert Clark she edited the eighth number of *Friendly Street Poetry Reader* and, with Barry Westburg, *Tuesday Night Live: Fifteen Years of Friendly Street* (1993). Her poetry and short stories have appeared in numerous periodicals and anthologies. Economy of expression and striking metaphors are characteristic of both Kroll's poetry and short fiction. The poems of her first two collections move between Australia, New York and India, exploring the personalities of places and the difficulties, ambivalences, pleasures and pains of relationships. Sharply observant and coolly witty in their response to the variety and pressures of contemporary existence, they explode female and male stereotypes. Motherhood is the subject of *Monster Love*, but an ambivalent, unsentimental motherhood which represents frankly the frustrating, exhausting experience of caring for a small child and rereads the personal and cultural past from the new/old perspective of maternity. Set partly in America and partly in Australia and projected via a series of narrative perspectives, the stories of *The Electrolux Man* range from the bizarre to the mundane, detailing the tensions, contradictions, griefs and absurdities of contemporary experience. In 1981 Kroll won the *Artlook* National Poetry contest.

Kröte, Professor, a creation of the poet Gwen Harwood (q.v.), is a European musician who finds himself alienated in a materialistic Australian environment, where he must keep body and soul together by teaching music and giving performances. Most of the Kröte poems were published in Gwen Harwood's second collection *Poems: Volume Two* (1968), but her continued interest in him is indicated by his reappearance in several of the 'New Poems' of her *Selected Poems* (1975) and in 'A Music Lesson', 'A Scattering of Ashes' and 'The Silver Swan' of *The Lion's Bride* (1981). Sympathetically portrayed by her ('I should think I like Kröte'), the professor of music, with his vagaries of behaviour and unfulfilled dreams and expectations, is in constant conflict with, but never defeated by, the unsympathetic and stuffily conventional society which surrounds him.

Kunapipi, a journal of Commonwealth literature, including Australian, began in 1979 as a continuation of the *Commonwealth Newsletter*. Published twice yearly from the Department of English, University of Aarhus, Denmark, *Kunapipi*, with its emblematic serpent of creativity from Australian Aboriginal culture, is edited by Anna Rutherford.

KYNASTON, Edward (1924–), born Aberystwyth, Wales, came to Australia in 1957 and taught in high schools before becoming education columnist and correspondent for the Perth *Independent* (1969–71) and literary editor of *Nation Review* (1972–75). His published works include *The Penguin Book of the Bush* (1977) which, in the guidebook mode, tells of such bush activities as 'Practical Camping' and 'Orienteering' and of such bush hazards as 'Getting Lost and Other Emergencies' and 'Bush Beasts', and *A Man on Edge* (1981), a biography of Baron Sir Ferdinand von Mueller which won the Con Weickhardt Award for 1982. He edited *Australian Voices* (1974), a collection of verse and pictures and, with Richard Bates, *Thinking Aloud: Interviews with Australian Educators* (1983).

L

LABILLIÈRE, Francis Peter (1840–95), born Melbourne, went to England in 1859 and was called to the Bar in 1863. An advocate of imperial federation, he was made secretary of the Imperial Federation League in 1884. In 1878 he published the two-volume *Early History of the Colony of Victoria*, which includes personal reminiscences and makes detailed uses of documentary material. In 1894 he published *Federal Britain: Or, Unity and Federation of the Empire*.

LACK, Clem (1901–72), a well-known Queensland journalist and historian, began his career on the *Gympie Times* in 1918. He was subsequently on the staff of the *Courier-Mail* (1920–40), the *Telegraph* (1940–44) and the Melbourne *Age* (1944–48), and in 1948 returned to Brisbane to work for the State's Public Relations Bureau. He retired in 1966 but continued as a freelance writer. Fellow and later vice-president of the Royal Historical Society of Queensland, he edited the Society's journal, wrote numerous articles on Queensland's history, edited the Queensland centenary book, *Queensland, Daughter of the Sun* (1959), co-authored other books on Queensland's history with Sir Raphael Cilento and Harry Stafford, and wrote an independent history, *Three Decades of Queensland Political History 1929–1960* (1962). He also published a volume of verse, *The Fields of Amaranth and Other Poems* (1936), and a collection of essays on Celtic legends and sagas, *A Bookman's Essays* (1969).

LADDS, Dulcie Dunlop (1906–72), born Brisbane, lived for some years on a banana plantation in southern Queensland after directing a studio of dancing and dramatic art in Brisbane. Two selections of the numerous short stories which she contributed to such periodicals as *Everylady's Journal*, the *Australian Journal* and Queensland's *Sunday Mail* were published, *Marriage is Monotonous* (1944) and *The Lighted Window* (1944). She also wrote several plays, one of which, *We Have Our Dreams* (1957), won the 1942 C.J. Dennis prize, was widely performed in Australia and translated into German for performance by the Stadt Theatre of Baden-Baden. L. Tarnawski has written her biography, *Such Stuff as Dreams* (1987).

LAKE, David (1929–), born India, spent his childhood in Calcutta. A graduate of the University of Cambridge, he taught in English schools until 1959 and at tertiary level in Vietnam, Thailand and India 1959–67; in 1967 he joined the University of Queensland. He has contributed verse to such periodicals as *Westerly*, *Southerly* and *Makar* and has published one collection, *Hornpipes & Funerals* (1973), and a satiric poem, *The Portnoyad*, first published in 1970. He has also written academic studies of renaissance literature, and several science-fiction (q.v.) novels including *The Changelings of Chaan* (1985) and a series culminating in *The Fourth Hemisphere* (1980), as well as a continuation of *The Time Machine* by H.G. Wells, *The Man Who Loved Morlocks* (1981). He won the Ditmar Award for the best long fiction/fantasy in 1982.

LAKE, Joshua (1848–1908), born Sussex, England, a graduate of Oxford University and a schoolmaster, was friendly with Alexander Leeper, whom he assisted in the founding of the *Melburnian*. He contributed to *Cassell's Picturesque Australasia* (1887–89) and to the Australasian supplement to *Webster's International Dictionary* (1898). Editor of the anthology *Childhood in Bud and Blossom* (1900), which includes contributions from A.B. Paterson, Ada Cambridge, John Sands and E.E. Morris, he also wrote a libretto, *Vercingetorix: Or, Love and Passion* (1881), and contributed sonnets to the anthology *Town Halle, Melbourne* (1881).

LALOR, Peter (1827–89), Irish-born leader of the Eureka Stockade (q.v.), migrated to Victoria in gold rushes of 1852. Elected commander-in-chief of the diggers on Bakery Hill, Lalor was wounded in the attack on the Stockade. From 1855 until his death he was an elected member of the Legislative Council, then a member of the Victorian parliament. Lalor's account of Eureka is in his 'Statement on the Ballarat Rebellion', *Age* and *Argus* 10 April 1855, and in further statements in the *Ballarat Star* 12 January 1857 and the *Geelong Advertiser* 21 September 1864 and 3 March 1874. Raffaello Carboni's (q.v.) account of Lalor's activities at Eureka is in *The Eureka Stockade* (1855). All the significant historical accounts of Eureka emphasise Lalor's role; those which particularise him include Clive Turnbull's *Eureka: The Story of Peter Lalor* (1946) and C.H. Currey's *The Irish at Eureka* (1954). Lalor been celebrated in such fictional accounts of Eureka as Edward Dyson's *In The Roaring Fifties* (1906) and Jack Lindsay's *Rebels of the Goldfields* (1936); in poems such as Henry Lawson's 'Eureka (A Fragment)', written as a eulogy after Lalor's death, and 'The Fight at Eureka Stockade'; and in the several plays relating to the incident but particularly in Leslie Rees's 'Lalor of Eureka' (1939).

La Mama, one of the most important influences in the 1970s 'new wave' of Australian theatre, originated in 1967 as a 'coffee-house' or 'café' theatre through the enthusiasm of Betty Burstall. In an abandoned underwear factory behind a vacant lot in Faraday Street,

Carlton, an inner Melbourne suburb popular with students, academics, artists and writers, Betty Burstall established the intimate, non-commercial type of theatre she had experienced in New York in 1965; in 1976 management of the theatre was taken over by Ann Eckersley and Liz Jones. Such writer-oriented theatres worked with few of the trappings of traditional theatre – props, make-up, large casts, elaborate stages and plush auditoriums. Writers such as Jack Hibberd, David Williamson, Barry Oakley and John Romeril all had plays performed at La Mama in its first years. An actors' workshop was established there; from it developed the Australian Performing Group (q.v.) which based itself at the nearby Pram Factory in Carlton. Poetry workshops inspired by Kris Hemensley, Michael Dugan and others have also, over the years, used La Mama for their meetings; the early 'workshops' provided a considerable impetus to the 'New Australian Poetry' (q.v.) movement of the late 1960s and early 1970s. *La Mama. The Story of a Theatre* (1988) consists of interviews with Betty Burstall and Liz Jones conducted by Helen Garner, comments by writers, artists, poets, producers and actors who contributed to the life of La Mama and a chronology of plays performed.

La Mama Poetica is the name given to a series of regular poetry readings which began at La Mama in February 1985, presented by Mal Morgan and John Irving. The poets presented at the first meeting were Carmel Bird, Rosemary Nissen, Komninos, Frank Kellaway, Shelton Lea and Mal Morgan. In 1989 Morgan edited an anthology collected from the readings at La Mama Poetica in the four years since it had been established. A combination of new and unknown poets, it includes work from Myron Lysenko, Ken Taylor, Kevin Brophy, Geoff Goodfellow, Komninos, Michael Sharkey, Morgan, Carmel Bird, ΠΟ, Eric Beach, Barbara Giles, Alex Skovron, Jenny Boult, John Irving, Alan Wearne, Robert Harris and Jas H. Duke.

LAMBERT, Elisabeth (1918–), born England, went to Jamaica as a teenager before coming to Australia. She worked as a journalist and feature-writer in Sydney as well as a court reporter and theatre critic. She contributed verse in the 1940s to such periodicals as *Meanjin*, *Southerly* and *Angry Penguins*, and edited with Harry Roskolenko the September 1944 issue of the American magazine, *Voices*, which was devoted to Australian poetry. She also published three collections of verse, *Insurgence* (1939), *The Map* (1940) and *Poems* (1943), and a novel, *The Sleeping House Party* (1951). She went to New York to live in 1951.

LAMBERT, Eric (1918–66), born Stamford, England, and educated in Sydney, served in the Second World War in the Middle East, New Guinea and Singapore. He began writing stories in the late 1940s and in 1951 published *The Twenty Thousand Thieves* (q.v.), a novel based on his war experiences. Lambert became a member of the Communist Party in 1947 and was active in left-wing literary circles for almost a

decade after the war; he joined the Realist Writers and was a member of the first editorial board of *Overland*. In 1955 he was an Australian delegate to the Helsinki peace conference; he stayed on in England after the conference, alienating the Australian literary left with his 'on-the-spot' dispatches, the first of them possibly written in London, which reported the Hungarian uprising of 1956 and, more significantly, were published in the conservative Sydney newspaper the *Daily Telegraph*. In all, Lambert wrote seventeen novels under his own name and a number of novelisations of films under the pseudonym 'D. Brennan'. His most successful work was *The Twenty Thousand Thieves* which has had numerous editions and reprintings and has become a paperback classic of war literature. Informed both by Lambert's abhorrence of war and his admiration of the ordinary Australian soldier, the novel exhibits its contempt for the officer class and was attacked in the 1950s by some ex-officers for its unflattering portrait of the Australian Army. Lambert's other war novels include *The Veterans* (1954), *Glory Thrown In* (1959) and *MacDougal's Farm* (1965), the last based on a visit to the notorious Changi POW camp at the end of the war. He also wrote a biography of Oscar Wilde's parents, *Mad with Much Heart* (1967); and two Eureka novels, *The Five Bright Stars* (1954) and *Ballarat* (1962), which, like his Ned Kelly novel *Kelly* (1964), are strongly anti-authoritarian and introduce as characters historical personages such as Raffaello Carboni, John Pascoe Fawkner, Charles Thatcher and Lola Montez. Zoe O'Leary's biography of Lambert, *The Desolate Market* (1974), focuses on his literary and political activities both before and after his break with the Australian Left.

LAMBERT, George Washington (1873–1930), born St Petersburg, Russia, of American-English parentage, was educated in England and arrived in Australia in 1883. A station hand, clerk and shop assistant before establishing himself as an artist, Lambert was a cartoonist and illustrator of poems for the *Bulletin* from 1895. In 1900 he was awarded a travelling scholarship and went to England, where he lived mainly as a portrait-painter. In 1917–20 he was an AIF war artist, visiting Palestine, France and Gallipoli; he returned in 1921 to Australia, where he was active in the Society of Arts and the Contemporary Group, which he formed with Thea Proctor. Lambert's earliest extant portrait is of his brother-in-law, A.W. Jose, whose work he illustrated and with whom he was involved in the *Australian Magazine*. Apart from his war paintings, he is best known for *Across the Black Soil Plains* (Art Gallery of NSW), a tribute to the Australian pioneering spirit; it won the 1899 Wynne Prize but was subsequently criticised by Joseph Furphy for inaccuracy of detail. Lambert sculpted the Sydney memorial to Henry Lawson, using Lawson's children as models. Featured in *Art in Australia* in 1924 and 1930, Lambert is the subject of J.S. MacDonald's *The Art and Life of George W. Lambert* (1920) and Amy Lambert's *Thirty Years of an Artist's Life* (1938). Andrew Motion has written *The Lamberts: George, Constant & Kit* (1986), Constant being George's son and an important English composer, Kit being Constant's son, a rock band manager ('The Who') and record company owner.

LAMOND, Hector (1865–1947), born Broughton Creek on the NSW south coast, entered journalism after a printing apprenticeship. In 1890–95 he was editor of the *Chronicle* in Carcoar before moving to Sydney, where for over two decades he was associated as manager and editor with the *Worker*, later *Australian Worker*. He resigned in 1916 over the conscription issue, which split the Labor Party, and was a Nationalist member of the federal parliament 1917–22; in later life he was a country newspaper proprietor. A son-in-law of the pioneer unionist W.G. Spence, he helped Spence in the writing of *Australia's Awakening* (1909) and other work. It was Lamond who persuaded Mary Gilmore to write the Women's Page in the *Worker*.

LAMOND, Henry George (1885–1969), born Carlo Creek in northern Queensland, was educated in Brisbane and worked on stations in Queensland. He used this experience in sketches and stories contributed to journals in Australia and overseas; his speciality was the animal tale. The best-known of his books was *Big Red* (1953, published in the USA as *Kangaroo*). His other publications include *Tooth and Talon* (1934), *An Aviary on the Plains* (1934), *Amathea* (1937, published in the USA as *Kilgour's Mare* 1943), *Brindle Royalist* (1946), *Dingo* (1945, published in Australia as *White Ears the Outlaw*, 1949), *The Manx Star* (1954), *Towser, Sheep Dog* (1955), *The Red Ruin Mare* (1958) and *Sheep Station* (1959).

LA NAUZE, J.A., see **DEAKIN, Alfred**; **MURDOCH, Sir Walter**

'LANCASTER, G.B.' (**Edith Joan Lyttleton**) (1874–1945), born Epping Forest, Tasmania, into a pioneering family, spent part of her childhood in NZ. She subsequently travelled widely but lived for some time in Australia. As 'G.B. Lancaster' she contributed stories to the *Bulletin* and the *Lone Hand* and published thirteen works of fiction: *Sons O' Men* (1904), *A Spur to Smite* (1905), *The Tracks We Tread* (1907), *The Altar Stairs* (1908), *Jim of the Ranges* (1910), *The Honourable Peggy* (1911), *The Law-Bringers* (1913), *Fool Divine* (1917), *The Savignys* (1918), *Pageant* (1933), *The World Is Yours* (1934), *Promenade* (1938) and *Grand Parade* (1943). Of these only *A Spur to Smite*, *Jim of the Ranges* and *Pageant* have Australian settings. *Pageant*, 'Lancaster''s best Australian novel and winner of the Australian Literature Society's Gold Medal, draws on the records of 'Lancaster''s own family in its presentation of the fortunes of a Tasmanian family from 1826 to the twentieth century. The novel's attempts to present Tasmanian history as a colourful pageant result in woodenness and contrived effects, although some of the characters have vitality.

LANDOLT, Esther (1893–1943), born Switzerland, was the author of two novels of Swiss life written in German, *Das Opfer* (1937) and *Delfine* (1939), which

was awarded the Schiller Prize. In 1937 she accompanied her husband, Dr Moritz Meyer, to Australia and wrote a further two novels in German but with Australian settings, *Ewige Herde (Eternal Flock)* (1942), and *Namenlos (Nameless)* (1946). *Ewige Herde* gives a finely detailed, unsentimental picture of life on a Victorian sheep station; drought, bushfire, rats, rain and frost prove to be implacable enemies to all human endeavour, although the novel also celebrates human resilience and courage. *Namenlos*, the story of a Swiss who settles in Melbourne, is distinguished more by its psychological insight into the dual consciousness of the migrant than by its presentation of Australian life.

LANDOR, Edward Willson (1811–78), a WA poet and essayist, wrote a satirical account of early WA life, *The Bushman: Or, Life in a New Country* (1847).

LANDSBOROUGH, William (1825–86) was the Scots-born son of a clergyman who emigrated to NSW in 1841 and became an expert bushman. In 1861–62 he led a search party for Burke and Wills; although unsuccessful in the search, he completed the first north–south crossing of the continent, discovering good grazing land in the process. His *Journal of Landsborough's Expedition from Carpentaria, in Search of Burke and Wills* and *Landsborough's Exploration of Australia from Carpentaria to Melbourne*, ed. J.S. Laurie, were published in 1862 and 1866 respectively. They stirred pastoral interest in the Gulf country, as Mary Durack's *Kings in Grass Castles* (1959) demonstrates. His pioneering role is recalled in *Bowen Downs, 1863–1963* (1963), ed. D.S. Macmillan, and is commemorated by townships in Queensland and Victoria.

Landtakers, a novel by Brian Penton (q.v.), published in 1934 as the first of a projected trilogy, was followed only by *Inheritors* (1936). The chief 'landtaker' of the novel, Derek Cabell, is an informant of its unnamed narrator, who is piecing together from letters, gossip and memoirs an account of Queensland's pioneering days in order to understand the roots of the national psyche. Arriving in Australia in 1842 intending to make his fortune and return quickly to his native Dorset, Cabell takes a job as an overseer on Murrumburra station, 40 miles from the penal settlement of Moreton Bay. The convict experience is important in *Landtakers* because its legacy of conflict and hatred characterises Cabell's experience of pioneering life and most of his personal relationships. At Murrumburra Cabell is bullied by the brutal lessee Bob McGovern, but during a flood manages to engineer his escape and that of the convict Joe Gurney. Together they overland a mob of cattle and sheep into the hinterland of Queensland where, threatened by Aborigines whom Cabell massacres and by a succession of natural and man-made hazards, e.g. fire, flood, drought, loneliness and threats to his security by later settlers, he struggles over the next seventeen years to establish himself as a squatter. Recovering from a nightmarish journey in which he gets lost while taking his wool clip down to Brisbane, Cabell encounters Emma Surface, an ex-convict, whose degraded past he does not discover until after their marriage. Their relationship becomes a paradoxical one: Cabell is repelled by his knowledge of Emma's history but released from his selfishness by his passion for her; Emma loathes Cabell's brutality towards her but sees in the marriage, and in her children, the focus of *Inheritors*, her chance to achieve respectability. At the climax to *Landtakers* Gurney, who has been ordered by Cabell to leave the station when it emerges that he knows of Emma's past, is allowed to return. During his absence he has met McGovern, who arrives in the district to take up an overseer's position on an adjoining property; McGovern is seemingly much changed in character but later returns to his bullying ways. Gurney, long fearing McGovern's power to return him to imprisonment for his original escape from Murrumburra, hopes Cabell will kill McGovern. It is Emma, however, who kills him while he is fighting with Cabell. The novel concludes with Cabell's renunciation of his long-held plans to return to England. *Inheritors*, the sequel to *Landtakers*, brings the story of the Cabell family forward to the end of the century, and explores the destructive relationship between Cabell and his children.

Like other novels of the 1930s, *Landtakers* offers an iconoclastic revaluation of Australia's past. Influenced by 'Henry Handel Richardson's' *The Fortunes of Richard Mahony* (1930), it powerfully portrays the revenge of the environment on those who try to 'take' from the land. The world of the novel, characterised by violence and cruelty, peopled by characters who, if not broken, are brutalised by their experience and only survive because of their vitality, doggedness and courage (qualities admired in Penton the journalist), is a sobering contrast to more romantic accounts of pioneering life.

'LANE, Elizabeth' (Eileen Elizabeth Farmers) (1918–), born on a farm in the Wimmera region of Victoria into a family of limited means and twelve children, has contributed short stories and articles to periodicals and written two autobiographical novels, *Mad as Rabbits* (1962) and *Our Uncle Charlie* (1964). Dealing with such incidents as snakes in the lavatory, squabbles between siblings, an alcoholic, gambling uncle's brief conversion to the Salvation Army, the strategies of travelling salesmen and the overly enthusiastic sermonising of the local preacher, Lane's narratives extract a nostalgic but gritty humour from family crises and everyday rural life. In the 1940s she became friendly with the illustrator and fiction-writer Hal Gye, and contributed an affectionate memoir and informative biography, *Hal Gye: The Man and his Work* (1986), to a reprint of his *The Hole in the Bedroom Floor* and some of his stories.

LANE, Richard, born Sydney, began writing plays for radio in the 1930s and is one of the most prolific of writers for television and radio. He spent eight years with Macquarie Broadcasting as writer and producer, and later worked as a freelance writer for commercial radio in Sydney and for the ABC. Author of Aus-

tralia's first television serial, *Autumn Affair*, for ATN 7, he also worked on the television serial *Motel*. His *The Remittance Man* is included in *Australian Radio Plays*, ed. Leslie Rees (1946), and his adaptation for television of Jon Cleary's novel *You Can't See Round Corners* is included in the collection he edited, *Take One: A Selection of Award-Winning Australian Radio and Television Scripts* (1972). His other plays for radio and television include 'Pointless Design', 'Eureka Stockade', 'Boy on an Old Bus' (about Charles Kingsford-Smith), 'Gods in Wedlock', 'The Purple Jacaranda' and 'What About Next Year?'.

LANE, William ('John Miller', 'Tohunga') (1861–1917), born Bristol, England, of Irish-English parentage, worked his passage to America at the age of 16. After a series of casual jobs he turned to the printing trade as a compositor, then journalist, on a Detroit newspaper. His American experience developed his radical interests; his socialist thinking was moulded by the Americans Henry George and Edward Bellamy, and later by his reading of Karl Marx. His strong racist attitudes, especially his implacable hostility towards the Chinese, also date from his American period. Lane returned to England briefly in 1885 with a wife and daughter but in the same year came to Australia to join other members of the family already in Queensland. He became a journalist in Brisbane, where in 1887 he founded a branch of the Bellamy Society and established, with Alfred Walker, the weekly newspaper the *Boomerang*. He became deeply involved with the 'New Unionism' and with the planning of the Queensland Australian Labour Federation, a federal organisation of unions. In 1890 he became editor of the Brisbane *Worker* in which he advocated full-scale socialism, supported the maritime strike of 1890 and the shearers' strike of 1891, campaigned for the rights of women in letters under the pseudonym 'Lucinda Sharpe', and persistently mooted the idea of a 'Co-operative Commune' either in Australia or abroad. Disappointed in the prospects for socialism/communism in Australia after the failure of the strikes in 1890–91, he established in 1891, and became chairman of, the New Australia Settlement Association with the object of organising a communist colony in South America which would be the vanguard of world communism. Lane led the New Australia (q.v.) expedition to Paraguay in the *Royal Tar* in 1893, but when the original settlement broke up in discord he and his followers formed another settlement, Colonia Cosme. He visited England in 1896 on an unsuccessful recruiting trip for the Cosme settlement, returned to Cosme in February 1898 and left permanently in August 1899. After three months as editor of the Sydney *Worker* he became in 1900 the leader-writer of the *New Zealand Herald* in Auckland (1900) and its editor in 1913. As 'Tohunga' (Maori for 'prophet') he wrote voluminously on social and political topics, but his stance grew increasingly conservative. After his death he was praised in the NZ press as a great editor and imperialist, but the radical Australian press, apart from some sporadic recriminations about his change to conservatism, contented itself with remembering the intense idealism of his younger years. Lane's first novel, *White or Yellow? A Story of the Race War of A.D. 1908,* was serialised in the *Boomerang* in twelve episodes in 1888 under the pseudonym 'Sketcher', but his chief literary work was the novel *The Workingman's Paradise* (q.v., 1892), written under the pseudonym 'John Miller' to raise funds to help the unionists gaoled for conspiracy in the shearers' strike of 1891. His writings for the *New Zealand Herald* were published as *Selections from the Writing of 'Tohunga'* in Auckland in 1917. Lane is the subject of Lloyd Ross's *William Lane and the Australian Labor Movement* (1937), and he and his philosophies are analysed in Michael Wilding's introduction to the 1980 facsimile of *The Workingman's Paradise.* He features in Vance Palmer's play about the shearers' strike of 1891, *Hail Tomorrow* (1947), in Graham Shiel's play 'New Australians Rehearse the Working Man's Paradise' (1983) and in George Hutchinson's 'The Ballad of Billy Lane' (1982); his work for New Australia is comprehensively examined in Gavin Souter's *A Peculiar People: The Australians in Paraguay* (1968). Hume Nisbet's *A Dream of Freedom* (1902) deals unfavourably with New Australia.

LANG, John Dunmore (1799–1878), born Greenock, Scotland, arrived in Sydney in 1823 as the city's first Presbyterian minister. For the next fifty years he was an energetic and controversial figure in the colony's religious and political scene. He established the Scots Church and the Australian College in Sydney; was a member of the Legislative Council; was dismissed from his ministry by the Australian synod but retained his own congregation based on the Scots Church; and campaigned assiduously for the abolition of transportation, Protestant immigration, the separation of Victoria and Queensland from NSW, a system of national education, republicanism and federation. On the statue erected to his memory in Wynyard Park (close by the Scots Church) are the words 'Patriot and Statesman'. Lang wrote numerous historical, political and religious books and pamphlets, lectured widely, addressed countless meetings, and wrote public letters on every possible topic of colonial interest. James Bonwick, indefatigable researcher, dubbed him 'The Father of Australian Literature'. His main published works are *An Historical and Statistical Account of New South Wales both as a Penal Settlement and As a British Colony* (1834), referred to by the *Westminster Review* as 'The History of Doctor Lang, to which is added the History of New South Wales'; *Transportation and Colonization* (1837); *The Coming Event: Or, the United Provinces of Australia* (1850); and *Freedom and Independence for the Golden Lands of Australia* (1852). His several volumes of poetry are consolidated in *Poems: Sacred and Secular* (1872), which is chiefly religious in tone but contains some satire, humour, and translations from Greek and German. Lang was also closely associated with the newspapers the *Colonist* (1835–40), the *Colonial Observer* (1841–44) and the *Press* (1851). A valuable picture of Lang is given in *John Dunmore Lang – Chiefly Autobiographical, 1799 to 1878* (1951), ed. Archibald Gilchrist, but the most substantial biography is Don Baker's *Days of Wrath: A Life of John*

Dunmore Lang (1985). Baker had previously (1972) edited Lang's autobiographical account of his life up to 1843, *Reminiscences of My Life and Times*. A complementary volume to the Baker biography is the bibliography compiled by Ian F. McLaren, *John Dunmore Lang: Turbulent Australian Scot* (1985). Lang is the 'Scotch parson' the title character meets in Henry Savery's novel *Quintus Servinton* (1831); he also appears briefly in James Tucker's *Ralph Rashleigh* (1952) and other historical fiction as well as in contemporary polemical verse.

LANG, John George (1816–64), born Parramatta, was the second son of sea captain and landowner Walter Lang and Elizabeth Harris, the daughter of convict parents. Lang was educated at William Cape's school in King Street, Sydney, and at Sydney College, from which he received the first gold medal awarded 'in approbation of his talents, acquirements and general good conduct'. In 1837 he went to England to study law at Cambridge but was sent down for unspecified indiscretions ('Botany Bay tricks, not gentlemanly tricks') and completed his legal training at the Middle Temple, proceeding to the Bar in May 1841. Lang returned to Australia with a wife and child in 1841 but early in 1842 left for India where his wife's brother was a successful barrister. His brief stay in Australia and his sudden departure have been attributed to his Jewish and emancipist backgrounds, a combination not well accepted in the exclusive Sydney society of the day, and to some injudicious public statements about representative government and colonial law which made him unpopular with, and ridiculed by, the colony's political and legal circles. In 1843–45 he practised law in Calcutta then moved, for his health's sake, to the hill city of Meerut. He became editor and ultimately owner of the *Mofussilite* ('up-country man'), an English-language newspaper, publishing much of his own work in its columns. Financial success from his legal and newspaper pursuits enabled Lang to spend most of 1853–59 in England and Europe, where he was a well-known and popular literary figure, contributing to many leading journals and newspapers, especially *Fraser's Magazine* and Charles Dickens's *Household Words*. He returned to India in 1859, remarried in 1861 and died, according to the *Madras Times*, 'a melancholy example of wasted talents and degraded abilities'. The enigma surrounding the life and personality of John Lang has not, even a century later and in spite of considerable literary research, been completely solved. Lang published nine novels, a volume of short stories and a travel book, *Wanderings in India* (1859), first published serially in *Household Words*. It appears probable that he was also the author of *Legends of Australia*, an anonymous work of fiction published in four parts, of a projected twelve, in 1842. A romance about an aristocratic transportee who is followed to the colony by his beautiful wife and ultimately finds happiness, it bears some resemblance to *The Forger's Wife* (q.v., 1855), one of Lang's later novels with an Australian setting. Authorship of *Legends of Australia* would entitle Lang to the distinction of being the first Australian-born novelist. *Legends* of *Australia* has been republished (1989) by Victor Crittenden's Mulini Press. Crittenden has also published in the Australian Books on Demand series the novel *Lucy Cooper* (1992), which he ascribes to Lang (it was first published as a serial in *Sharpe's London Magazine* in 1846 and had not since been published in book form). Lang's most significant Australian work was *Botany Bay: Or, True Tales of Early Australia* (1859), a fictional but factually based series of stories about early Sydney, some parts of which were published initially in *Household Words*. The best known of the tales is 'The Ghost upon the Rail', the story of Fisher's Ghost (q.v.). Lang's Indian novels are also significant in their field for they aptly convey, in gentle satire, English social life in India in the period before the Mutiny. *John Lang & 'The Forger's Wife'* (1979), edited by Nancy Keesing, contains a facsimile of the novel and a biographical outline.

LANG, John Thomas (1876–1975), born Sydney, was Labor premier of NSW 1925–27 and 1930–32 and became a legendary figure in Australian history during the 1930s Depression. The controversy surrounding him was at its most acute after February 1931, when he instituted the 'Lang Plan', a scheme devised to withhold interest payments on British loans and reduce the interest on private ones. The plan caused a deep split between the NSW and federal branches of the Labor Party. Dismissed by the State governor in May 1932, Lang was soundly defeated at the election held shortly afterwards. A populist and an effective orator, who was both passionately loved and hated, Lang was known as the 'Big Fella' by his supporters and often received popular endorsement for his course at political meetings in the familiarly chanted phrase 'Lang is right!'. He continued to have a strong hold over the State party machine until 1939 and attracted a large following for even longer. Expelled from the Party in 1943, he served as an independent member in the federal parliament 1946–49. In 1971 he was readmitted to the Party through the efforts of younger members. Editor of the weekly newspaper the *Century* until his death, Lang wrote three autobiographical accounts, *I Remember* (1956), *The Great Bust* (1962) and *The Turbulent Years* (1970). His political career has been the subject of numerous studies, including Bethia Foott's *Dismissal of a Premier* (1968), Robert Cooksey's *Lang and Socialism* (1971) and *Jack Lang* (1977), a collection of essays edited by Heather Radi and Peter Spearritt. Miriam Dixson wrote *Greater than Lenin: Lang and Labor 1916–1932* (1977) and Bede Nairn *The 'Big Fella'. Jack Lang and the Australian Labor Party 1891–1949* (1986). Lang was a brother-in-law of Henry Lawson.

LANG, Mary (1914–), born Sydney, grew up in the Monaro district and in Sydney, completing her education in London where her first book of poems, *The Strange Battalion*, was published in 1933. In 1936 she published a second collection, *Tom Groggin*, which was well received, but she is now best known for *Home Was Here* (1987), a history of her Irish ancestors, Edward Redmond (c.1767–1840), transported in 1799 after taking part in the rebellion of 1798 and his wife

Winefred Dowling and their descendants. Meticulously researched, the family history is mingled with the general history of NSW, providing a graphic picture of everyday life in the early days of White settlement as well as remarkable portraits of dominant individuals, such as Sir Henry Browne Hayes and John Macarthur.

LANG, W.H. (William Henry) (1859–1923), born Selkirk, Scotland, a medical practitioner and brother of the Scottish scholar and poet Andrew Lang, was editor of the *Pastoralists' Review* for a time. He published a descriptive account, *Australia* (1908), with drawings by G.W. Lambert; and a novel, *The Thunder of the Hoofs* (1909), which is set partly in Scotland and partly in the Riverina and deals extensively with such sports as cricket, racing and hunting. He also edited *Racehorses in Australia* (1922) with K. Austin and S. McKay.

LANGFORD, Gary (1947–), born NZ, moved to Sydney in 1974. A versatile writer, he has contributed to numerous NZ and Australian anthologies and periodicals, and has written for television, stage, radio and film. He has published seven volumes of poetry, *The Family* (1973), *Four Ships* (1982), *The Pest Exterminator's Shakespeare* (1984), *Bushido* (1987), *Strange City* (1988), *Love at the Traffic Lights* (1990) and *Jesus the Galilee Hitch-Hiker* (1991); two collections of short stories, *The Death of James Dean* (1978), of which one, 'The Dying Man', shared the Patricia Hackett Prize in 1975, and *A Library is a Place of Love and Other Stories* (1989); five novels, *Death of the Early Morning Hero* (1976), which won second prize in an Angus & Robertson literary award, *Players in the Ballgame* (1979), *The Adventures of Dreaded Ned* (1980), a black comedy on the Ned Kelly legend, *Vanities* (1984, winner of the Alan Marshall Award in 1983), which is the story of a famous Sydney actress and her daughter and focuses on alcoholism, and *Pillbox* (1985), which deals with the abuse of prescribed drugs; two collections of plays and dramatic sketches, *Getting On* (1986) and *Lovers and Others* (1986); and a book for children, *A Classical Pianist in a Rock 'N' Roll Band* (1989). He also won the Vera Bladen Poetry Award in 1970.

LANGFORD (GINIBI), Ruby (1934–), born Coraki, NSW, at Box Ridge Mission, was brought up there and at Bonalbo where she lived with relatives after her mother deserted the family and her father, a log-cutter and carter, was forced to find work where he could. Whereas life at the mission was humiliating and packed with imposed hardships, her years at Bonalbo were amongst her happiest. She went to high school at Casino and at the age of 15 moved to Sydney where she trained as a clothing machinist. The mother of nine children, whom she raised mostly on her own after their fathers left, Langford lived for eleven years near Coonabarabran, living in tents or tin shacks and working at fencing, burning off, lopping, ring-barking and pegging kangaroo skins; subsequently she lived in other areas of Australia but invariably gravitated to Redfern, Sydney, and to work in clothing factories. Her autobiography, *Don't Take Your Love to Town* (1988), written with the help of Susan Hampton and winner of a Human Rights Literary Award in 1988 and the Pandora Women's Writing Award of 1989, describes her survival of numerous disappointments and tragedies, such as the deaths of children and the desertions of lovers, and her determined battle with economic hardship and homelessness. Humorous and poignant, *Don't Take Your Love to Town* is a strikingly frank picture of life between the White and Black cultures. Although her experience of wandering resembled the life of her tribal ancestors, most of the supportive aspects of that life had disappeared: 'I felt like I was living tribal, but with no tribe around me, no close-knit family. The food-gathering, the laws and songs were broken up, and my generation at this time wandered around as if we were tribal but in fact living worse than the poorest of poor whites, and in the case of women, living hard because it seemed like the men loved you for a while and then more kids came along and the men drank and gambled and disappeared'. Langford has also contributed short stories and articles to anthologies and periodicals and has published a collection of autobiographical stories and poems, *Real Deadly* (1992).

LANGLEY, Eve (1908–74), born Forbes, NSW, went to NZ in 1932, made a disastrous marriage with artist and art teacher, Hilary Clark, had three children and later returned to Australia, where at first she played an active role in the Sydney literary scene but spent the latter part of her life as a recluse in her shack, Iona-Lympus, in the bush near Katoomba in the Blue Mountains. Few other details of Eve Langley's later life were publicly known before Joy Thwaites's biography *The Importance of Being Eve Langley* (1990) was published, but her eccentricities certainly were; she dressed in mannish clothes, wore a white topi, carried a sheath knife in her belt, was obsessed with guns, had Oscar Wilde as an alter ego, and lived as an isolate. Her twin novels, *The Pea Pickers* (q.v., 1942) and *White Topee* (1954), contain numerous clues to the enigma of her life. *The Pea Pickers* was acclaimed by Douglas Stewart as 'the most delightful novel' to have been written by an Australian; by Norman Lindsay as 'a sport of genius'; and by Hal Porter as 'a superb and haunting work'. Much of that early enthusiasm has faded, but the novel is still the subject of debate; some modern critics see it as an extreme example of the nationalist tradition, while others are critical of the elaborate prose style that often obliterates the narrative itself. *White Topee* is an extension of *The Pea Pickers*, both novels being centred on the narrator, Steve, who attempts to reconcile the twin demands of her nature: the intellectual, with a need for expression in thought, poetry and art, and the emotional, which seeks fulfilment in personal love. The conflict in the novels is often expressed sardonically; Steve alternates between poet and clown, ecstatic and sublime at one moment, wryly self-deprecatory the next. *The Pea Pickers* concludes with Steve not fully in command of her turbulent nature; *White Topee* brings a greater measure of self-understanding: 'I really didn't want to be loved

. . . What I really wanted was to be a man, and free for ever to write and think and dream'. In the fictional tug-of-war Steve's psyche is stretched to breaking-point but survives; it would seem that in the real world Eve Langley's did not. *The Importance of Being Eve Langley* combines biography and literary analysis.

LANSBURY, Coral (1929–91), born Melbourne, was professor of English and dean of graduate studies at Rutgers University, USA. The daughter of actors and the cousin of Angela Lansbury, she performed as a child in J.C. Williamson productions and had her first radio script accepted at the age of 13. She studied for her first degree at the University of Sydney, where she frequently contributed to *Hermes*, and continued to write plays for radio in the 1940s and 1950s; one of her plays, *Krubi of the Illawarra*, won the Henry Lawson prize for poetry and was published in *Hermes* (1949). After gaining her doctorate at Auckland University, she moved permanently to the USA in 1969. Her other plays for radio and television include 'The Bronze Plain', 'Mockery Bend', 'The Bombora', 'The Gate of the Sea', 'The Living Rock', 'Court of Angels' and 'Account Rendered at Ringarra'. She also wrote some verse and several works on nineteenth-century English fiction as well as the polemical *Arcady in Australia* (1970), a study of perceptions of Australia in nineteenth-century English literature. Developing the thesis that the Australian bush ethos was a literary importation rather than of native, folk origin, *Arcady in Australia* draws illustrations from such writers as Charles Dickens, Bulwer-Lytton and Charles Reade and explores the influence of such emigration publicists as Samuel Sidney. In the latter years of her career Lansbury concentrated on fiction, publishing four novels, *Ringarra* (1985), *Sweet Alice* (1986), *Felicity* (1987) and *The Grotto* (1989). Lansbury was the mother of the prominent lawyer Malcolm Turnbull.

LANSDOWN, Andrew (1954–), born Pingelly, WA, and a graduate of Murdoch University, has worked as an education officer in various WA prisons. He has published six books of poetry, *Homecoming* (1979), *Counterpoise* (1982), *Windfalls* (1984), *Waking & Always* (1987), *The Grasshopper Heart* (1991) and *Between Glances* (1993); two books for children, *A Ball of Gold* (1981) and *With My Knife* (1992); a collection of short stories which originated in his experience as Writer in the Community in the Shire of Kalamunda 1984–85, *The Bowgada Birds* (1986); and an analysis of homosexual activism, *Blatant and Proud* (1984). An imagist in the tradition of Wallace Stevens, Lansdown's short poems have been praised for their precise observation and keen insights; inventive both metrically and in terms of imagery, his poems are also frequently characterised by a religious, celebratory sense of a Maker immanent in natural and human worlds. *Between Glances* won the 1994 SA Festival Award for Poetry.

LA PÉROUSE, Jean-Francois de Galaup, Comte de (1741–88), born Albi, France, joined the navy at 15, developed interests in navigation and oceanography and was made a captain in 1780. In 1785 he was selected by Louis XVI to lead an exploratory expedition into the north and south Pacific, to complete the unfinished work of Captain James Cook. The expedition, made up of two ships, *La Boussole* and *L'Astrolabe*, sailed to South America, rounded Cape Horn, and sailed to the Sandwich Islands and Alaska, turning south to explore the coast as far as California. La Pérouse then sailed across the Pacific and surveyed the coasts north of Korea; in September 1787 he put in to Kamchatka and sent an account of his voyage thus far back to Paris. Published in 1797 in four volumes, titled *Voyage de La Pérouse autour du Monde*, the account includes much valuable cartographic and scientific information. From Kamchatka La Pérouse's expedition set course south for New Holland and in December at Samoa encountered a major setback when natives attacked some of the crew of the *L'Astrolabe*, killing the commander and eleven men. La Pérouse left without taking reprisals and reached Botany Bay 24 January 1788, six days after the arrival of the First Fleet, although bad weather prevented his landing for some days. Governor Phillip, who had left for Port Jackson, did not meet La Pérouse, but cordial relations were established with the remaining British officers and the French established a camp on the north shore of Botany Bay. Six weeks later La Pérouse sailed from Botany Bay and was never heard from again. Not until 1828 was it discovered that the expedition had been wrecked at Vanikoro, Santa Cruz, north of the New Hebrides. Apart from La Pérouse's own account, the only remaining record of the expedition is an anonymous pamphlet, *Fragmens du dernier voyage de la Pérouse* (1797), which may have been written by Père Receveur, a scientist on the expedition who died at Botany Bay. Biographies of La Pérouse include Sir Ernest Scott's *Laperouse* (1911) and John Dunmore's *Pacific Explorer* (1985). Russell Shelton's *From Hudson Bay to Botany Bay* (1987) is a popular history of the La Pérouse expedition. Shane McCauley gives an account (by La Pérouse to his wife) of his last voyage in the poem 'La Pérouse to Eleanor' in *The Butterfly Man* (1991). A museum in honour of La Pérouse was opened at Botany Bay in 1988.

Larrikin in Australian Literature. Although the term 'larrikin' did not emerge in Australia until the 1860s, and was widely used only in the period 1870–1910, the symptoms of larrikinism were evident in the behaviour of 'currency' lads who, as early as 1819, were accused of rowdy behaviour such as drinking, brawling, profanity and gambling. The *Sydney Gazette* reported critically on the activities of 'larky boys' in 1825. The cabbage-tree mobs, young native-born men whose name came from their wearing of the broad-brimmed hats woven from cabbage tree palms, were also forerunners of the larrikin pushes, in that they roamed the Sydney streets of the 1830s and 1840s abusing and assaulting the citizenry. Their activities are criticised in G.C. Mundy's *Our Antipodes* (1852) and Charles MacAlister's *Old Pioneering Days in the Sunny South* (1907). Larrikinism, in the shape of hooliganism and loutish behaviour, appears to have originated in

the Colony in the Sydney Rocks area, but it soon came to be a common phenomenon in the inner city and poorer, crowded areas of both Sydney and Melbourne. Suggestions for the origin of the term 'larrikin' include a rolling Irish pronunciation of 'larking' (i.e. fooling about, playing about) by a police sergeant (both a Jack Staunton and a Sergeant Dalton have been named) in the courts of the day; a diminution ('Larry') of the Irish name Lawrence, together with 'kin'; an existing Cornish word which meant 'larker'; a corruption of the two words 'leary kinchen', meaning a knowing or cunning fellow; and a Worcestershire and Warwickshire dialect word meaning mischievous fellow. As described by Sidney J. Baker, the larrikin's distinguishing features were that he was young, between the ages of 15 and 25, was a city-dweller, dressed with exaggerated precision, extracted comfort from being a member of a gang, looked upon refinement in social conduct as a form of weakness, spoke in a weird jargon which it seemed only his kind could understand, and was given to periodical violence. Larrikin dress ran to a surprising neatness, described in *Jonah* (q.v.) as 'tight-fitting suits of dark cloth, soft black felt hats, and soft white shirts with new black mufflers round their neck in place of collars'. Their ornamented, pointed and heavy boots, known as 'Romeos', were lethal weapons in street brawls. The larrikin's violent behaviour is described in Marcus Clarke's *A Colonial City* (edited by L. Hergenhan 1973), T.E. Argles's *Pilgrim* (1877), R.E.N. Twopeny's *Town Life in Australia* (1883), J.A. Froude's *Oceana* (1886) and with some gusto in a poem, 'Kicking Their Livers Out', in the seamy Sydney weekly the *Dead Bird*. The linguistic innovations of the larrikin have been, in the main, a passing phenomenon, as a modern reading of W.T. Goodge's contemporary slang poem 'The Great Australian Slanguage' (1897) and of the works of Louis Stone, Edward Dyson and C.J. Dennis verifies. Certain larrikin expressions, however, e.g. 'king hit', 'blue' and 'stoush' from street fighting; 'tart', 'sheila' and 'good sort' from the larrikin's assessment of the female; 'bludger', 'queen' and 'poof' from his abhorrence of effeminacy, have made a definite impact on the vernacular language. That the larrikin's push (mob) was a recognisable feature of city life at the turn of the century is reflected in the notoriety of such street gangs as Sydney's the Livers Push of Glebe, the Waterloo Push, the Blues Point Mob and Melbourne's Bouverie Street Push, the Fitzroy Murderers and the Richmond Dirty Dozen. In literature the push is prominent in the fiction of Louis Stone and Edward Dyson, and in Henry Lawson's poem 'The Captain of the Push' (q.v.). Two minor novels by Ambrose Pratt, *King of the Rocks* (1900) and *The Great 'Push' Experiment* (1902), give an authentic picture of Sydney larrikinism, but the classic larrikin works, in a relatively small literary field, are Louis Stone's *Jonah* (1911), Edward Dyson's *Fact'ry 'Ands* (1906), *Benno and Some of the Push* (1911) and *Spats' Fact'ry* (1914); and C.J. Dennis's chief works, *The Songs of a Sentimental Bloke* (q.v., 1915) and *The Moods of Ginger Mick* (1916). In those works the larrikin's viciousness, his lovesick sentimentality and his twisted sense of mateship (an inverted *noblesse oblige* which compels him to join in kicking a common enemy into insensibility) are all demonstrated. His less reprehensible qualities are also demonstrated, e.g. jauntiness of spirit even in adversity, cheery optimism, amused contempt for pompous and incompetent authority, and a strong streak of vulgarity. These latter characteristics, which are important in modern usages of 'larrikin' and 'larrikinism', have led to the larrikin being regarded with affectionate tolerance rather than with animosity. James Murray's *Larrikins: 19th Century Outrage* (1973) is a comprehensive account of the larrikin phenomenon in Australia and contains both an extensive bibliography of larrikin literature and a glossary of larrikin terms; Clem Gorman edited *The Larrikin Streak: Australian Writers Look at the Legend* (1990), which examines larrikinism as a facet of the Australian character, from the Sydney Push to contemporary times.

LASERON, Charles Francis (1887–1959), collector at Sydney's Technological Museum 1909–29 and a fellow of the Royal Zoological Society of NSW, was born Wisconsin, USA, and brought to Australia as a child. He served at Gallipoli during the First World War and published a small volume of reminiscences and extracts from his diary, *From Australia to the Dardanelles* (1916). Assistant biologist to Sir Douglas Mawson on the first Australasian Antarctic expedition 1911–14, he wrote an account of his experiences, *South with Mawson* (1947), which graphically relates the nature of the hazards encountered by the group and the personalities and qualities of the individual men. He also wrote two popular geological accounts of Australia, *The Face of Australia* (1953) and *Ancient Australia* (1954).

LASSETER, 'Harold Bell' (Lewis Hubbard) (1880–1931), born Bamganie near Meredith, Victoria, left behind, following his death in the Petermann Range in 1931, one of Australia's greatest enigmas – the existence or not of a gold reef of extraordinary size and richness ('Lasseter's Lost Reef'). The true facts of Lasseter and his reef appear to have been finally settled by the research of Gerald Walsh for the *ADB* (1983). Lasseter was in America from 1901 to 1908, then returned to Australia where he took up a small farm at Tabulam on the Clarence River, NSW. He saw some service in the AIF in the First World War in Australia but the military authorities kept him only briefly, discharging him twice as unfit for service. In 1925–30 Lasseter worked as a carpenter in Canberra and on the Sydney Harbour Bridge, of which he claimed, unsuccessfully, to be the original designer. In 1929 he claimed that he had, in about 1911, discovered 'a vast gold-bearing reef in Central Australia'. Government authorities, having interviewed Lasseter, lost interest in his claim. In 1930 Lasseter repeated his story to a John Bailey, president of the AWU central branch in Sydney (dating the find this time about 1897) and a well-equipped expedition led by Fred Blakeley and guided by Lasseter, left Alice Springs on 21 July 1930 to search for the reef. In September the expedition abandoned the search but Lasseter carried on, at first with

Paul Johns, an Englishman, but later alone. A search party led by Bob Buck claimed to have found Lasseter's body and buried it at Shaw Creek in the Petermann Range in March 1931. Walsh argues that Lasseter had never before been in central Australia and had not discovered any reef. The existence of such a reef had been suggested in earlier literature, e.g. Simpson Newland's *Blood Tracks of the Bush* (1900), J.D. Hennessey's *The Bush Track* (1896) and Conrad Sayce's *Golden Buckles* (1920), while the American Harold Bell Wright, whose Christian names were used by Lasseter, wrote *The Mine with the Iron Door* (1923), a work on the same theme. Versions of Lasseter's story have been told in Ion Idriess's popular *Lasseter's Last Ride* (1931, seventeen printings in four years), in Errol Coote's *Hell's Airport* (1934, republished in 1981 as *Hell's Airport and Lasseter's Lost Legacy*), in Edward Harrington's poem 'Lasseter's Last Ride', in Fred Blakeley's *Dream Millions* (1972) and in A. Stapleton's *Lasseter Did Not Lie!* (1981). Ivan and Jocelyn Smith published *The Die-Hard* (1979), an illustrated poem about Lasseter and he features in a section of John Kinsella's book of poems, *Night Parrots* (1989). The work that claims to be the definitive history of Lasseter is Billy Marshall-Stoneking's *Lasseter – The Making of a Legend* (1985), but Murray Hubbard has published a later work (1993), *The Search for Harold Lasseter*. A facsimile of the diary kept by Lasseter on his last expedition was published in 1986.

'Last of His Tribe, The', a widely anthologised poem by Henry Kendall (q.v.), was first published in the *Sydney Morning Herald*, 1864. In it Kendall captures the attractive nature of Aboriginal life and sentimentally mourns its passing.

LA TROBE, Charles Joseph (1801–75), born London and educated in Switzerland, was tutor to the family of the Swiss Count de Pourtales (1824–27) and accompanied him on a tour of America (1832–34). Washington Irving, who accompanied them on a tour of the prairies, published an account of the journey and La Trobe also published *The Rambler in North America: 1832–1833* (1835) and *The Rambler in Mexico 1834* (1836). Appointed superintendent of the Port Phillip District in 1839, he was on excellent terms with his senior, Governor Gipps, but had constant problems with the Melbourne colonists, who frequently resented economic and political aspects of the link with NSW; he won some popularity, however, in 1849 when he took a bold stand on transportation. In 1851–54 La Trobe was lieutenant-governor of Victoria after the colony gained representative government. After gold was discovered at Ballarat in 1851, La Trobe faced a chaotic period of government, made worse by his decision to wrest a revenue from the goldfields in the form of monthly licence fees. A cultured and religious gentleman, La Trobe gave his support to the establishment of numerous cultural, educational and charitable institutions. He left Australia in 1854. An extensive collection of his letters and papers is held by the State Library of Victoria, which has named its Australiana collections after him. Victoria's third university is also named in his honour. His career is described in a biography by A. Gross (1956) and in Geoffrey Serle's *The Golden Age* (1963); his letters, edited by F.J. Blake, were published in 1975 and the correspondence between him and Governor George Gipps was edited by A.G.L. Shaw in 1989. La Trobe's brother, John Antes La Trobe, an English clergyman, published a collection of sacred lyrics (1850) and other books on church music as well as a collection of verse, *The Solace of Song* (1837), which has been wrongly attributed to Charles La Trobe.

La Trobe Library, the section of the State Library of Victoria which holds the Library's special collections of Australiana, has several important manuscript collections relating to such authors as Mary Grant Bruce, Rex Ingamells, Victor Kennedy, Louis Lavater, Percival Serle, Henry Gyles Turner and R.H. Croll. It also holds the substantial J.K. Moir collection, as well as papers relating to Melbourne's literary associations and journals. Information about the collections is contained in the *Catalogue of the Manuscripts, Letters, Documents, etc. in the Private Collection of the State Library of Victoria* (1961). The twice-yearly *La Trobe Library Journal*, which has been published since 1968, lists recent acquisitions as well as including bibliographical and other articles of relevance to Australian literature.

'LAUDER, Afferbeck', see **MORRISON, A.A.**

LAVATER, Louis (1867–1953), born Melbourne of a Swiss father who came to Victoria during the 1851 gold rush, was educated at Wesley College and began a medical course at the University of Melbourne which he soon abandoned for music. Subsequently prominent in Melbourne's musical circles, he was at various times president of the Association of Music Teachers of Victoria, music critic for several Melbourne newspapers, frequent adjudicator of musical competitions and founder of the Guild of Australian Composers. Also a well-known literary figure, he contributed verse and short stories to numerous anthologies and to such journals as the *Lone Hand* and the *Bulletin*, and edited the little magazine *Verse* (1929–33). He also published three collections of verse, *Blue Days and Grey Days* (1915), *A Lover's Ephemeris* (1917) and *This Green Mortality* (1922), and edited a popular anthology, *The Sonnet in Australasia* (1926), revised in a second edition edited by Frederick Macartney (1956). Among his musical compositions were *Swagman's Treasure: Five Camp-fire Ditties* (1937).

LAWLER, Ray (1921–), born Footscray, Melbourne, left school at 13 to work in a foundry. Ten years later a growing interest in amateur dramatics and play-writing led to his leaving the foundry to act in variety shows in Brisbane. He subsequently worked as actor and producer with the National Theatre company, Melbourne, and as director of the Melbourne Union Theatre repertory company. One of his plays, 'Cradle of Thunder', was produced in Melbourne in 1949 and won the National Theatre Movement's Jubilee play competition. In 1955 his outstandingly successful play *Summer of the Seventeenth Doll* (q.v.) shared first prize with Oriel Gray's *The Torrents* in a competition organised by the Playwrights Advisory Board. *The Doll*, as it is familiarly called, was first staged by the Union Theatre of Melbourne University with Lawler in the role of Barney in 1955, and in 1956 in Sydney by the Australian Elizabethan Theatre Trust. John Sumner produced both productions, as well as a subsequent revival in 1977 by the Melbourne Theatre Company. After extensive touring in Australia, *The Doll* was produced in 1957 in London at the New Theatre, where it enjoyed a highly successful long run. A production in New York in 1958 failed to attract audiences, but it was produced as a film in 1960 starring Ernest Borgnine and Anne Baxter and was included in *Ten Best Plays of the American Season 1957–58*, edited by Louis Kronenberger. *The Doll*, which has been produced in numerous European countries and frequently restaged in Australia, was first published in 1957 and is now studied in schools as a classic of the national theatre. With Richard Beynon's *The Shifting Heart* (1958) and Alan Seymour's *The One Day of the Year* (1962), *The Doll* seemed to herald a flowering of Australian theatre that in fact failed to sustain itself, unlike the renaissance of the 1970s. After the success of *The Doll* Lawler lived in Denmark, England and (most extensively) in Ireland. He visited Australia in 1971 for a production of his play 'The Man Who Shot the Albatross' and returned in 1975 to work as deputy artistic director, literary adviser and subsequently actor with the Melbourne Theatre Company. Apart from some adaptations of works by other authors, produced by the BBC, other plays by Lawler which have been staged include *The Piccadilly Bushman* (first produced 1959, published 1961), 'The Unshaven Cheek' (1963), 'A Breach in the Wall' (1967) and two framing plays to *The Doll*, *Kid Stakes* (first produced 1975) and *Other Times* (first produced 1976). All three plays were produced together in two day-long performances in 1977 by the Melbourne Theatre Company, published as *The Doll Trilogy* in 1978 and in a revised form in 1985, and revived in 1985 by the Sydney Theatre Company to celebrate the thirtieth anniversary of *The Doll*. In 1958 Lawler won the London *Evening Standard* Award. Lawler's play 'Godsend' (1982) is a reworking of 'A Breach in the Wall'. He was made OBE in 1980 and is an emeritus fellow of the Australia Council.

Although the contemporary popularity of *The Doll* coincides with a national nostalgia for the recent past, the play had a more revolutionary impact in 1955. Concerned with the terminal stage of an unconventional relationship between two cane-cutters and their Melbourne girlfriends, a relationship that depends on conventional national assumptions, it was the first successful play to examine critically Australian myths and attitudes. Some of the underlying themes of the play, such as the limitations of mateship and of received Australian stereotypes of masculinity and the outback, have become familiar in contemporary drama. All three of Lawler's affectionately realised characters are attracted to vitalist, ennobling and supposedly free aspects of the Australian legend, but the legend's inadequacies, which they experience rather than acknowledge, finally impose tragic, life-denying consequences. *Kid Stakes* and *Other Times*, the first dealing with the beginning of the relationship and the second with a critical later stage, complement *The Doll* but add nothing to its dramatic urgency. *The Piccadilly Bushman*, which deals with the ambivalences of Australian/English loyalties, especially those experienced by the artist, is much less universal in its effects and has been less sympathetically received. With 'The Man Who Shot the Albatross', his remaining Australian play, Lawler turned his attention to history and the fate of Governor William Bligh. Impressionistic in structure and setting, the play is a powerful exploration of an enigmatic figure, combining imaginative psychological penetration with authentic historical fact.

LAWLOR, Adrian (1890–1969), painter and art critic, was born London and arrived in Australia in 1910. He served with the AIF in the First World War, studied art for a short period at the National Gallery School in Melbourne, but did not begin painting seriously until 1930. His provocative, modernist works made an immediate impact, although by 1940 he had given up painting for art criticism for the *Sun* newspaper and literary magazines, and for radio broadcasting. Lawlor also wrote some verse, some of which appeared in *Vision* and in *Poetry in Australia 1923* (1923), ed. Jack Lindsay and Kenneth Slessor, and a novel, *Horned Capon* (1949). A witty polemicist and one of the boldest proponents of modernism, Lawlor deals with the controversial issues of the Australian art world of the time in his *Arquebus* (1937). Alister Kershaw, friend and admirer of Lawlor, has written a memoir of him (1981) as well as further reminscences in *The Pleasure of Their Company* (1986) and *Hey Days* (1991).

LAWRENCE, Anthony (1957–), born Tamworth, NSW, left school at 16 and became a jackeroo in the Riverina. He later travelled overseas for three years. The next seven years he spent in Wagga Wagga, NSW, trying to become a teacher. While there he and David Gilbey organised a successful association for Wagga Wagga writers. He taught for a time, then went to the north coast of WA, where he wrote and worked as a fisherman. A literary fellowship enabled him to remain at Geraldton, indulging his two passions, writing and fishing. His travel experiences are reflected in such poems as 'Sandstorm', 'Negere Desert', 'Bethlehem', 'Island Meditation', 'Heraklion' and 'Incident at Heraklion'. 'The Flight Sonnets', from his first book, *Dreaming in Stone* (1989), describe the swifts and barn owls of Northumbria. From his time on the land came 'The Art of Killing', 'Shooters' and 'Cro-Kill'. They highlight the casual savagery that is a part of the daily life on the land. The killing process in Lawrence's poems lacks the saving grace of a natural and essential rural order that characterises similar actions in, for example, Les Murray's poem 'Blood'. 'Blood Oath', the major sequence of Lawrence's second book *Three Days Out of Tidal Town* (1991), describes a real-life incident in which two

young jackeroos meet their deaths fleeing from their vicious, crazed boss in the desert. 'Blood Oath' was runner-up in the Grace Perry Memorial Award in 1988. Numerous other poems from the WA period deal with fishing, but Lawrence's chief obsession is poetry: 'wherever I turn, poetry astounds me with its quiet visitations . . . my poetry my love'. His third book of poetry, *The Darkwood Aquarium* (1993), deals in part with his own childhood and adolescence while focusing also on other young passionate and stormy characters. One of the book's four sections, 'Howling in Tandem', pays homage to, but at the same time shows Lawrence freeing himself from, the influence of those who played a part in his becoming a poet. In the coastal section he believes he has achieved the type of poetry he is most comfortable with – narrative with a strong lyrical vein. He has also written *A Book of Dying Sayings* (1991).

LAWRENCE, D.H. (David Herbert) (1885–1930), the English novelist, came to Australia from Ceylon in 1922, arriving with his wife Frieda at Fremantle on 4 May. In Perth, where he stayed for two weeks, he met some of the local literati and the Quaker nurse Mollie Skinner (q.v.), with whom he collaborated in a novel, *The Boy in the Bush* (q.v., 1924). Katharine Susannah Prichard, who missed meeting him, later corresponded with him and attempted to interest him in Australian literature. After leaving Perth, the Lawrences arrived in Sydney on 27 May. They spent a brief time in the city and then rented a house, Wyewurk, at Thirroul, a mining village on the NSW coast, where they remained until their departure for San Francisco on 11 August. In eastern Australia Lawrence appears to have led a deliberately isolated life, mainly devoted to the writing of his novel, *Kangaroo* (q.v., 1923). The extent of his involvement in and knowledge of Australian political life is uncertain; although Lawrence's letters, Frieda Lawrence's autobiography *Not I, But the Wind* (1935), and his numerous biographers suggest that his involvement was minimal, recent researches have tentatively suggested that he may have had personal knowledge of a secret political organisation. Of these, the most substantial is Robert Darroch's *D.H. Lawrence in Australia* (1981).

In his letters Lawrence describes Australia as 'a weird country – fascinating – but humanly non-existent' and in both *The Boy in the Bush* and *Kangaroo* he vividly expresses his response to the 'subtle, remote, *formless* beauty' of the bush, its indifference to humanity, its 'fern-world' aura and separation from history. Almost equally evocative are his descriptions of Australian suburbia and the ramshackle impermanence of small coastal settlements. In *Kangaroo* the inability of the land's White inhabitants to relate to each other or to Australia is a dominant theme; in *The Boy in the Bush* the bush becomes a shaping force, a source of mysterious vitality and freedom. Lawrence's perceptive descriptions of the Australian landscape have been frequently praised, but his interpretation of the national character has aroused some fierce dissent. Describing Australia in *Kangaroo* as a land where 'nobody felt *better* than anybody else, or higher; only better off', where 'Demos was ... his own master, undisputed, and therefore quite calm about it' and as a 'vast continent ... really void of speech', Lawrence was critical of what he saw as intellectual and spiritual lethargy, a lack of individuality and a general exaltation of the average. In Jack Callcott, his prototypical Australian, drawn from the Australians he met on board ship and from the pages of the *Bulletin*, which he read avidly, he develops his idea that the Australian indifference is not stoic but is based on recklessness and an unpredictable propensity for violence.

Written in six weeks, although he later revised the manuscript in Mexico, *Kangaroo* is strongly autobiographical, reflecting the almost daily flow of Lawrence's thoughts and impressions while in Australia. Richard Somers, the restless hero, is a barely disguised picture of Lawrence, as Harriet, his wife, is of Frieda, and many of the domestic incidents are drawn directly from their Australian experience. Described by Lawrence as a 'thought-adventure', the novel's apparent formlessness expresses the flow of Somers's inner life; his attraction to and withdrawal from politics; his European memories; his concern with the fundamental question of authority in marriage, society and politics and with the attractions and dangers of democracy, fascism and socialism. For Somers/Lawrence the practical aims of political parties are far less important than their potential for the spiritual regeneration that his wartime experiences, described at length in *Kangaroo*, had convinced him was humanity's only hope: 'What Richard wanted was some sort of new show: a new recognition of the life-mystery, a departure from the dreariness of money-making, money-having and money-spending'. In *Kangaroo* Lawrence appears to be searching for the same religious answer, 'The Great God who stands dark on the threshold of the phallic me', that was to concern him in *The Plumed Serpent* (1926) and *Lady Chatterley's Lover* (1928). It is probable that in Somers's ambivalent relationship to the figure of Kangaroo, alias Benjamin Cooley, a charismatic lawyer and leader of a secret right-wing group, Lawrence develops his response to Whitman's idea of generalised love, an issue he also deals with in his 'Essay on Democracy' which he was revising in 1922. Some readers have assumed, however, that Lawrence was transferring his observations of incipient Italian fascism to Australia, and others have suggested a range of 'originals' of Kangaroo, including Lawrence's friend S. Koteliansky and Sir John Monash. Lawrence's description of NSW politics and the digger movement, once regarded as pure fabrication but which surprisingly foreshadows the formation of the New Guard of Colonel Eric Campbell in Sydney in 1931–32, has been defended as close to fact, based on local observation and reading of the *Bulletin*, even if not, as Darroch suggests, on personal encounters with officials of the King and Empire Alliance. Darroch's thesis has been supported by further research by Andrew Moore (*Overland*, 1988, 1990, 1991) and is extensively debated by Bruce Steele in *Meridian* (1991) and Joseph Davis in *D.H. Lawrence at Thirroul* (1989); an exhaustive study

of the Lawrences' stay at Thirroul, Davis's book blends personal reminiscence, geography, local and public history, 'political sleuthing' and literary criticism.

Lawrence's concern with the dark gods and the growth of an inner life also shapes the WA adventure story *The Boy in the Bush*, affecting particularly the novel's conclusion which is totally different from the original written by Mollie Skinner. Largely neglected by Lawrence critics as a collaboration, the novel is, however, distinctly Lawrentian in atmosphere and preoccupations. The critical edition of the novel, edited by Paul Eggert (1990) in the Cambridge Edition of Lawrence's Letters and Works, has an extensive discussion of the collaboration.

Other Australians whom Lawrence knew in Europe included Jack Lindsay and P.R. Stephensen; the latter's Mandrake Press was responsible for the publication of reproductions of some of Lawrence's controversial paintings in 1929 and for his essay *A Propos of Lady Chatterley's Lover* (1930). Lawrence's Australian experience has been made the subject of a play by David Allen, *Upside Down at the Bottom of the World* (1981), and the circumstances of the genesis of *Kangaroo* form part of the background of Margaret Barbalet's novel *Steel Beach* (1988).

LAWSON, Bertha (1876–1957), born Bertha Bredt in Bairnsdale, Victoria, was working as a nurse when she met Henry Lawson (q.v.) in 1895. She married him the following year; they had two children and lived in WA, NZ, Sydney and England until Bertha won a judicial separation in 1903. Lawson claimed that the portrait of Mary in the Joe Wilson stories was informed by his marriage to Bertha, who is also the subject of 'To Bertha', the dedicatory poem of *Children of the Bush* (1901); the bitterness between them after the separation, when Lawson spent time in gaol for arrears of maintenance, emerges in several poems, e.g. 'The Separated Woman', included in *For Australia and Other Poems* (1913). Bertha's account of the 1896–1902 period is included in *Henry Lawson by His Mates* (1931) and *My Henry Lawson* (1943), which was ghosted by Will Lawson.

LAWSON, Henry (1867–1922) was born on the goldfields at Grenfell, NSW, the eldest son of Niels Hertzberg Larsen (Peter Lawson, 1832–88), a Norwegian ex-sailor, and his wife, Louisa (see Lawson, Louisa); his surname was registered as Lawson, which became the family one. Peter and Louisa had been living near Mudgee at New Pipeclay, later called Eurunderee (q.v.), and returned there soon after Lawson's birth. They moved to the Gulgong goldfields in 1871, but settled back at New Pipeclay on a selection in 1873. In 1883 they separated, Louisa moving to Sydney to become active in publishing and the women's movement.

Henry's early life was difficult: the family was poor, the tensions between his parents have some parallels in the short stories, particularly in 'A Child in the Dark, and a Foreign Father' (q.v.), and from the age of 9 he was afflicted by deafness. He attended several schools at Eurunderee and Mudgee – John Tierney, one of his teachers, was the father of the comic novelist and short-story writer 'Brian James' – and then worked with his father on building contracts until 1883, when he joined Louisa. Over the next few years he was based in Sydney, worked mainly as a coach-painter and, influenced by his mother's radical friends, became interested in the republican movement. In 1887 his first published prose piece appeared in the *Republican*, of which he became nominal publisher, and his first poem, 'A Song of the Republic' (q.v.), in the *Bulletin*. The *Bulletin* also published his first short story, 'His Father's Mate' (q.v.), several days before his father's death on New Year's Eve 1888. In 1890 he left Sydney to find work in Albany, WA, where he wrote for the *Albany Observer*. He returned in September 1890 before accepting early in 1891 an offer of employment on the radical Brisbane newspaper the *Boomerang*, to write a digest of news from the provincial press. After six months he was retrenched and returned to Sydney, then in the grip of the depression of the Nineties (q.v.). To this point Lawson had established himself primarily as a writer of verse: some of his enduring poems of bush life, e.g. 'The Teams', 'Andy's Gone With Cattle', 'The Roaring Days' (qq.v.), date from before 1892; so do the major poems of social and political protest, e.g. 'The Watch on the Kerb', 'Faces in the Street', 'Freedom on the Wallaby', 'The Army of the Rear', which made him the obvious model for Arty, the People's Poet, in William Lane's *The Workingman's Paradise* (1892). But from the time of his return to Sydney after working with the *Boomerang*, his talent as a writer of short stories began to emerge as he drew more and more on his own observation to supplement his past experiences and the experiences of his family. In 1892, despite the diversion of the *Bulletin* debate (q.v.), which he conducted with A.B. Paterson about the right way to represent bush life, he wrote the Arvie Aspinall (q.v.) series, his first major fiction sequence, and a series of bush stories including 'A Day on a Selection', 'The Drover's Wife' (q.v.) and 'The Bush Undertaker'. Later that year, unable to find regular work, he was funded by J.F. Archibald and went on a celebrated trip to Bourke, where he worked as a house-painter for some months before tramping with his swag to Hungerford and back in the midst of a fierce drought. The experience, his first of the real outback, was crucial for Lawson in several ways: it confirmed the horrors of bush life; it not only provided him with the immediate copy for such stories as 'Hungerford' and 'The Union Buries Its Dead' (q.v.), but also by its intensity enslaved his imagination to the point where his fiction subsequently became repetitive; and it gave him in J.W. Gordon (q.v.) one of the models for Jack Mitchell (q.v.), his most important fictional character, as well as the models for the bush workers whose mateship (q.v.) he celebrates in 'Send Round the Hat' and other stories.

In 1893 Lawson wrote up his outback trip in stories and sketches contributed to the *Bulletin*, the Sydney *Worker* and *Truth*; the influence of journalism on his fiction is an important one, particularly in the links between his brief sketches and the paragraphs of

journals like the *Bulletin*. With the depression at its worst, he went to NZ for seven months, travelling part of the time with the original of another of his fictional characters – the 'sharper', Steelman (q.v.). He returned on the expectation of a position with the *Worker*, which had become a daily; when this venture failed and the *Worker* reverted to a weekly he continued with it, first as provincial editor and then as a prolific salaried contributor. At the end of 1894 his first collection, *Short Stories in Prose and Verse*, was published. It was a poor production, but nevertheless confirmed his growing reputation, which was consolidated by the appearance in 1896 of the first two volumes in a long publishing partnership between Lawson and Angus & Robertson: *While the Billy Boils* (q.v.), generally considered as his best prose collection, and *In the Days When the World Was Wide* (q.v.), a collection of verse. By now he had met Bertha Bredt (see Lawson, Bertha), the stepdaughter of W.H. McNamara, a radical Sydney bookseller; her sister married the politician J.T. Lang. Soon after their marriage in 1896 the Lawsons went to WA then continued their itinerant life by travelling in 1897 to NZ, where they taught at a Maori school at Mangamaunu, near Kaikoura. Although he eventually became frustrated by the isolation of Mangamaunu, Lawson wrote steadily and was relatively free of his dependence on alcohol, which had become apparent a decade before. His drinking problem surfaced again on their return to Sydney in 1898, especially during his membership of the bohemian Dawn and Dusk Club, but he managed to complete contracts with Angus & Robertson, which resulted in the publication in 1900 of two more collections of prose, *On the Track* and *Over the Sliprails*, and a collection of verse, *Verses Popular and Humorous* (q.v.). Like many of his books they consisted largely of material first published in Australian periodicals and subsequently revised. An essay, '"Pursuing Literature" in Australia', published in the *Bulletin* in 1899, shows his dissatisfaction at this time with Australia and his wish for wider recognition for his work. In 1900 Lawson left with his wife and two children for England, assisted in the endeavour by the governor of NSW, Earl Beauchamp, the bibliophile David Scott Mitchell, and the publisher George Robertson. In England he wrote some of his finest stories and published *The Country I Come From* (1901), a selection of his previous work; *Joe Wilson and His Mates* (q.v., 1901), which is dominated by the Joe Wilson (q.v.) sequence; and *Children of the Bush* (q.v.,1902), which contains the material subsequently published as *Send Round the Hat* (1907) and *The Romance of the Swag* (1907). By 1902 the climate, poverty, illness and perhaps other unexplained reasons caused the Lawsons to leave England, the marriage failing. Thereafter, with the exception of a few weeks immediately following their return to Sydney, Lawson lived apart from Bertha and the children, with increasing bitterness on both sides.

Lawson's best work was now behind him, and the remaining twenty years of his life were years of spasmodic literary output in which he produced more verse than prose, and of steady personal disintegration. He was in and out of prison, particularly 1905–10, for drunkenness and arrears of maintenance, spent some time in mental and 'convalescent' hospitals and became a familiar sight on the streets of Sydney, a dishevelled, cadging drunk. That he survived so long was the result of the devotion of friends, old literary colleagues such as J. le Gay Brereton and E.J. Brady but in particular George Robertson, who assisted him financially, and Mrs Isabel Byers, a woman twenty years his senior who regularly provided care and lodging for him after 1904. There were political friends as well, including T.D. Mutch (q.v.) and W.A. Holman, which led to his being granted a sinecure in 1916 to live in Leeton, a prohibition area, in order to write material advertising the Murrumbidgee Irrigation Area; during his year or so there he met J.W. Gordon from the Bourke days. The interest of parliamentarians in him was also in evidence in 1920–22, when he was awarded a CLF pension and negotiations were conducted between the federal and NSW governments over a supplement to the pension.

The ostensible reason for Lawson's deterioration was his collapse into alcoholism and mental illness, although several commentators, viewing his dependence on alcohol more as a symptom than as a cause, have suggested other sources for his decline: the failure of his marriage; the death of his close friend Hannah Thornburn (q.v.) just before his return from London; and, perhaps more significantly for his reputation as a prose-writer, an artistic crisis in the same period deriving from a failure of creativity, which led to his eventual increasing reliance on melodrama, contrivance and romance, features of some of his very first stories. Brian Matthews's *The Receding Wave* (1972) is the most important study of Lawson's achievement and decline; signs of the decline can be detected in the prose collections, the Joe Wilson sequence apart, immediately following *While the Billy Boils*; they are more in evidence in the two new collections published after his return from England, *The Rising of the Court* (1910) and *Triangles of Life* (1913). That Lawson had little new to say explains the return to the past which is characteristic of his later prose. In 1912–20 he essayed a new and flabby city series, 'Elder Man's Lane', published in the *Bulletin*; but more typical of his work were the autobiographical pieces, in particular the long 'A Fragment of Autobiography' (q.v.), begun in 1903 and recalling his life up to 1888, and the stories such as 'Grandfather's Courtship' which went back even further. To some extent this nostalgia was stimulated by visits with Mutch to Eurunderee in 1914 and by the memories evoked after the reunion with Gordon in Leeton, as the 1916 *Bulletin* sketch, 'By the Banks of the Murrumbidgee', reveals.

Lawson's decline after 1902 did not mean, however, that he lost his appeal for the Australian public. In part this was because his verse, in such volumes as *When I Was King* (1905), *The Skyline Riders* (1910), *For Australia* (1913), *My Army, O, My Army* (q.v., 1915) and *Song of the Dardanelles* (1916), continued to strike a popular chord. Some of his best-known poems, e.g. 'One-Hundred-and-Three' and 'Black Bonnet' (q.v.), date from this period; he was particularly prolific during the First World War, when his poetic affirmation of the imperial link was such as to see him later accused of jingoism and apostasy of his socialism and republicanism of the 1880s. A second reason for his continuing appeal was the publishing programme of George Robertson (2), who republished Lawson's earlier prose and verse, often in series bearing such titles as *While the Billy Boils*, as well as arranging for the first collection of poetry, *Selected Poems of Henry Lawson* (1918). Also involved in the preparation of *Selected Poems* was David McKee Wright (q.v.), who edited Lawson extensively while working on the much-criticised *Poetical Works of Henry Lawson* (1925). Notwithstanding the scholarly edition of Colin Roderick, *Poetical Works of Henry Lawson* has been the most popular collection of Lawson's verse and has remained in print under various titles.

In 1921 Lawson suffered a cerebral haemorrhage, from which he recovered sufficiently to be still writing reminiscences of his visit to London when he died at Abbotsford on 2 September 1922. The extent of the Lawson legend in his lifetime can be measured by the fact that he was the first Australian writer granted a state funeral. Since his death he has remained Australian literature's most famous son, commemorated by a statue in the Sydney Domain, sculpted by George Lambert using Lawson's children as models, and by memorials elsewhere, as well as by his appearance on the Australian ten-dollar note when decimal currency was introduced in 1965. He has been the subject of one-man shows by Leonard Teale and Robin Ramsay, and of numerous plays, films, stories, readings and television series. In Melbourne there is a Henry Lawson Literary and Memorial Society (q.v.), which publishes the *Lawsonian* and conducts an annual gathering at the 'Lawson Tree' at Footscray. In Sydney, apart from the Domain statue, there is a Henry Lawson Bookshop and a Henry Lawson Literary Society, and the FAW conducted for some years annual pilgrimages to his grave at Waverley cemetery and to the Domain statue. In Grenfell, the local high school and a festival are named after him; in Mudgee and Eurunderee there are memorial shelters and the Eurunderee School which he attended was restored in 1989 by local Lawson enthusiasts. Sydney University undergraduates compete annually for the Henry Lawson Prize for Poetry. The Lawson publishing industry has not remained confined to reprints deriving from the earlier Angus & Robertson collections. The same publishers issued *The Stories of Henry Lawson*, edited by Cecil Mann (q.v.) in 1964, which was trenchantly criticised. Not until the appearance in 1972 of *Henry Lawson: Short Stories and Sketches 1888–1922* and *Henry Lawson: Autobiographical and Other Writings 1887–1922*, the first two of Colin Roderick's three-volume edition of Lawson's prose, was a reliable text established. Roderick had earlier edited several Lawson selections: in 1967–69 he edited the three-volume *Henry Lawson: Collected Verse*, which provided an authoritative text of the poetry, and subsequently *Henry Lawson: Letters 1890–1922* (1970), the anthology *Henry Lawson Criticism 1894–1971* (1972) and *Henry Lawson: the Master Story Teller: Prose Writings* (1984–85). An important edition which organises Lawson's work in order of its composition is Leonard Cronin's (introduced by Brian Kiernan) two-volume *A Camp-Fire Yarn – Complete Works 1885–1900* and *A Fantasy of Man – Complete Works 1901–1922* (1984). Kiernan also wrote *The Essential Henry Lawson* (1982), which includes recently discovered material. Important biographical studies, some of them anecdotal, include his daughter Bertha Lawson and J. le Gay Brereton's collection of tributes, *Henry Lawson by His Mates* (q.v., 1931); his wife Bertha's *My Henry Lawson* (1943); Denton Prout's *Henry Lawson: The Grey Dreamer* (1963); W.H. Pearson's *Henry Lawson Among Maoris* (1968); the controversial *In Search of Henry Lawson* (1978) by Manning Clark; Colin Roderick's *The Real Henry Lawson* (1982) and Xavier Pons's *Out of Eden: Henry Lawson's Life and Works* (1984), a psychoanalytical study of Lawson's life and works which attempts to explain Lawson's failures rather than his successes. The most substantial biography is Colin Roderick's *Henry Lawson: A Life* (1991), the culmination of a lifetime of research and writing. Some of the most interesting commentary on Lawson's life has appeared in significant critical studies, among them A.A. Phillips's *The Australian Tradition* (1958) and *Henry Lawson* (1970), Stephen Murray-Smith's monograph, *Henry Lawson* (1975), and Brian Matthews's *The Receding Wave* (1972). These works represent only a fraction of the published material on Lawson, much of which remains in periodicals or is to be found in collections of essays and critical anthologies. In 1989 Chris Kempster published *The Songs of Henry Lawson*; Lawson's poems set to music in the 1980s and 1990s have featured in the ABC National radio programme 'On the Wallaby', in Frank Hardy's play 'Faces in the Street' and the Dick Diamond revival *Reedy River*.

In general there have been two schools of Lawson criticism: a popular one which has seen many of Lawson's short stories as artless yarns and regards him as the poet of the people, a folk-writer whose galloping rhythms and facility for rhyme articulate the voice and attitudes of Australians; and a professional one, which sees mainly historical interest now in the poetry and finds enduring virtues in the prose. Despite the continuing appeal of the stirring calls for social change in 'Faces in the Street' or 'Freedom on the Wallaby', the lyricism of 'Andy's Gone With Cattle' or 'Black Bonnet', the sardonic sharpness of 'The Uncultured Rhymer to his Cultured Critics' or 'The Captain of the Push' (q.v.), and the robust balladry of 'The Roaring Days', only Roderick among recent critical writers has argued for more than a handful of Lawson's poems. Far more attention, particularly among literary critics, has been focused on the quality of the prose. Lawson's well-plotted, humorous magazine stories, notably 'The Loaded Dog' and 'Bill the Ventriloquial Rooster' (qq.v.), continue to be admired and anthologised, but more and more the apparent artlessness of Lawson's stories has been recognised as the work of a conscious craftsman seeking the effect of naturalness. The peak of Lawson's achievement is now usually seen to be in *While the Billy Boils* and *Joe Wilson and His Mates*. These fifty or sixty stories and sketches include the best of Mitchell and Steelman, e.g. 'Enter Mitchell', 'Shooting the Moon' and 'The Geological Spieler'; sketches such as 'The Drover's Wife', 'An Old Mate of Your Father's', '"Rats"', 'In a Wet Season', 'The Union Buries Its Dead' and 'Going Blind', in which he drew most effectively on his early life, the Bourke trip and his experiences in the city; and the emerging alienation and isolation of Joe and Mary Wilson in '"Water Them Geraniums"' and 'Brighten's Sister-in-law' (q.v.). In stories like these Lawson's fundamentally pessimistic fictional bush world is memorably and dramatically realised. Central to the presentation are the sharpness and selection of detail, Lawson's documentary quality; the use of an involved narrator, sometimes a character like Mitchell or Wilson, sometimes ostensibly Lawson himself, to establish a natural colloquial voice and an ironic tone, an important ingredient in Lawson's humour; immense sympathy for the victims or survivors of the bush in his characterisations; and a deceptively lucid, understated prose style. Together, these qualities mean that Lawson did more than write the Australia of the 1890s: at his best he has few superiors anywhere in the field of the short story.

LAWSON, Louisa (1848–1920), the mother of Henry Lawson (q.v.) but an important figure in her own right in the history of Australian radicalism, feminism and publishing, was born near Mudgee, NSW, the daughter of Henry Albury and his wife Harriet Wynn; a version of Henry's wooing of Harriet is presented in Lawson's 'Grandfather's Courtship'. In 1866 Louisa married Niels Hertzberg (Peter) Larsen, a Norwegian ex-sailor some years her senior; they moved soon after to the Grenfell goldfields – where Henry, the first of their five children, was born – before returning to New Pipeclay, near Mudgee, where they were based until 1883, apart from a stint at Gulgong. The marriage had its periods of tension, with Larsen usually characterised as gentle with his children but somewhat stolid, and Louisa as strong-willed, temperamental and increasingly frustrated with the poverty of selection life. Henry Lawson's 'A Child in the Dark, and a Foreign Father' (q.v.), in presenting substantially this view of the parents, is somewhat unfair to Louisa, who had married Peter under pressure and whose hard-working, poverty-stricken and isolated life during the seventeen years of her marriage no doubt provided the model for the bushwomen who appear in his other stories. Her radicalism and sensitivity could find no outlet at New Pipeclay and in 1883 she moved to Sydney, where she was quickly in contact with leading figures in the spiritualist, republican and women's movements. By 1885 her house was a meeting-place for reformists, and in 1887 she took over the radical monthly the *Republican* (q.v.). The following year she founded the *Dawn* (q.v.), the first Australian feminist journal, and the Dawn Club; active also in the women's suffrage movement, she established the Association of Women in 1889, merging her activities with those of Rose Scott and the Womanhood Suffrage League in 1891. In 1894 Louisa brought out Henry's first collection, *Short Stories in Prose and Verse*; it was poorly produced and contributed to the estrangement between mother and son. Louisa's own published work includes a novel, *Dert and Do* (189?), and a book of poems, *The Lonely Crossing* (1905). She invented a new buckle for post-office mailbags but the piracy of the invention and the subsequent litigation contributed to her failing health and the closure of the *Dawn* in 1905. The subject of Lorna Ollif's *Louisa Lawson: Henry Lawson's Crusading Mother* (1978) and of George Hutchinson's play *Henry & Peter, Henry & Me* (1985), Louisa was featured on an Australian ten-cent postage stamp during International Women's Year (1975). Brian Matthews wrote the controversial award-winning biography *Louisa* (1987), and Olive Lawson, Louisa's great-granddaughter, has edited excerpts from the *Dawn* 1888–95, titled *The First Voice of Australian Feminism* (1990). Patricia Clarke's *Pen Portraits* (1988) offers an account of Louisa Lawson and her publication of the *Dawn*. See also 'Drover's Wife, The'.

LAWSON, Sylvia (1932–), born Sydney, is a great-granddaughter of Louisa Lawson. She writes in the genres of history, journalism and fiction and in all three is concerned with the political dimensions of reading, writing, filming and viewing. She has written substantial essays on cultural history, media policy and the concept of 'national' cinema and has contributed articles to such journals as *Nation*, the *London Review of Books* and *Australian Society*. Her short stories have appeared in several anthologies. Her most extensive work is *The Archibald Paradox* (1983). Both a biography of J.F. Archibald (q.v.) and an exploration of the paradoxical institutions and discourses that shaped his life and his journal, *The Archibald Paradox* is also concerned with the cultural phenomenon that was the *Bulletin* and with its post-colonial history and interpretation. It won the NSW Premier's Award for non-fiction in 1984.

LAWSON, Will (1876–1957), born Durham, England, was brought to Australia as a child and educated in Brisbane. In the 1890s his family moved to Wellington, NZ, where Lawson worked as a clerk for an insurance company. In 1912, after contributing some verse to the *Bulletin*, he came to Sydney where he joined the staff of the *Evening News* and later worked as a freelance writer for newspapers and magazines, including the *Bulletin* and *Smith's Weekly*. A familiar figure in Sydney's bohemian circles, he was friendly with such writers and artists as Roderic Quinn, Edward and Will Dyson, Percy Lindsay, Randolph Bedford and Livingston Hopkins. Enthusiastic about Australia's sailing and coaching past, especially the coaching days, Lawson wrote numerous ballads, publishing six collections, *The Red West Road* (1903), *Between the Lights* (1906), *Stokin' and Other Verses* (1908), *The Three Kings* (1914), *Bush Verses* (1943) and *Bill the Whaler* (1944). He also drew on the same sort of material for several novels, including *The Laughing Buccaneer* (1935), *When Cobb and Co. Was King* (1936), *Old Man Murray* (1937), *In Ben Boyd's Day* (1939), *Red Morgan Rides* (1940), *Bound for Callao* (1942), *Black Diamonds* (1945), *The Lady of the Heather* (1945), *Forbidden*

Gold (1945), *Paddle-Wheels Away* (1947) and, with Tom Hickey, *Galloping Wheels* (1947) and *Moira of Green Hills* (1950). He also edited an anthology, *Australian Bush Songs and Ballads* (1944); and wrote several descriptive and historical works about Australia and NZ, of which the best known are *Harpoons Ahoy* (1938) and *Blue Gum Clippers and Whale Ships of Tasmania* (1949). Although not related to Henry Lawson he was a friend of Bertha Lawson and collaborated in her reminiscences of her husband, *My Henry Lawson* (1943).

LAZAR, John (1801–79), the first entrepreneur of serious theatre in Adelaide, was born in Edinburgh and arrived in Sydney in 1837. Adopting the name Lazarus, he claimed to have appeared in well-known London theatres and began his Australian dramatic career by playing Shylock at Sydney's Theatre Royal. Manager of the Theatre Royal from December 1837 to March 1838, and actor and stage manager at the Victoria Theatre until late 1840, he appears to have had more talent as an administrator than an actor. In 1841 Lazar leased the newly established Queen's Theatre in Adelaide and with the help of his daughter Rachel, who appeared as both actress and dancer, he presented Adelaide audiences with Shakespearean plays, burlettas, farces and operas. A depressed economy contributed to the lack of interest in his entertainments and he was forced to abandon his lease in November 1842 and return to Sydney, where he again managed the Victoria Theatre (1842–44 and 1846). In 1848 he returned to Adelaide as an associate of George Selth Coppin and on this occasion enjoyed some popularity as a comedian and manager. In the 1850s he abandoned the theatre for a jeweller's and silversmith's business in Adelaide, became an alderman of the city council in 1853 and was mayor of Adelaide 1855–58. In 1859 he retired from the council, and in 1863 settled in NZ where he worked in local government as an administrator.

'Lazy Harry's' is perhaps the best-known Australian folk-song to chronicle the notorious 'lambing down' of shearers by shanty-keepers. In the song two shearers travel through the Riverina towards Sydney but go on a spree at Lazy Harry's shanty on the road to Gundagai and are relieved of their shearing cheques. The rueful tone of 'Lazy Harry's' is repeated in other Australian folk-songs about bush workers in shanties, e.g. 'The Wild Rover' and 'Across the Western Plains' (also known as 'The Jolly Jolly Grog'). Both songs are included in A.B. Paterson's *Old Bush Songs* (1905). In each the protagonist has spent his money on drink and is about to depart, the former to return like the prodigal son to his parents, the latter to resume as an itinerant bush worker on the Riverina's western plains.

LEA, Shelton (1946–), born Melbourne, left school at the age of 12 and spent periods in gaol as a young man, including eighteen months in Goulburn Gaol at the age of 18. While there he wrote love poems for detainees, payment being in tobacco. Part-performance poet (he declares he will read poems wherever he can find an audience), part-critic of contemporary Australian life and attitudes, he is 'by birth and nature urban', with inner-city areas his natural habitat. His comfortable milieu is the city pubs – 'great brewing palaces of beer' – and city life, with its violence, crime, drugs, alcoholism, gutter and park derelicts ('in defence of drunks', 'coming down – delirium tremens'). Shelton Lea also writes of love in his more tranquil verse ('having watched you', 'love poem', 'i dream of the soft slide of light'). His complaint about the sterility of modern Australian life and politics is evident in 'i'm here today for a whinge' and 'occupied' – where he accuses, in Jindyworobakish accents:

we are occupied by our own greed . . .
we are making of this place a desert,
a land of rutted soil
of ruined earth, leached of its true wealth,
its dreamtime,
rather than living in harmony, as once the koories did,
treating this land as a kindred soul

Many of Lea's poems are slanted towards performance, carrying within such verses as 'The Dip's Dilemma' and 'Picnic Day at the Drouin Races', echoes both of C.J. Dennis and an early Bruce Dawe. Commenting on the modern proliferation of easygoing, slang-type verse (including much of his own) Lea says that the times themselves prohibit traditional-type verse, ('well-ordered thoughts well shaped and moulded into a perfectly metrical form'). There are too many distractions in modern society – television, the media and 'the accostation of cars and trucks/ the imperterbable [sic] rumble of suburbs and/cities'. Lea has published several books of verse, *Corners in Cans* (1969), *Chrysalis* (1972), *The Paradise Poems* (1973), *Chockablock with Dawn* (1975), *Palantine Madonna* (1978), *Poems from a Peach Melba Hat* (1985), *I am Nebuchadnezzar* (1991) and a *Poets on Record* (1976, tape recording with text).

Leader, the weekly companion of the *Age* (q.v.), began publication in 1856 as the *Melbourne Leader* and changed its title to the *Leader* in 1862; it ceased publication in 1957. It contained a literary section which included serials, short stories, and news and information on books and writers. James Smith and Marcus Clarke were prominent early contributors to the *Leader*; at the turn of the century Mary Grant Bruce began her literary career when she took over the *Leader's* children's page.

LEAKEY, Caroline Woolmer ('Oliné Keese') (1827–81), born and educated in Exeter, England, returned there after spending five years (1848–53) in Tasmania with her sister. Her life was dominated by ill health and a strong Christian faith. The former limited her schooling, made her an invalid for most of her time in Australia, caused her return to England and severely restricted her activities after 1871; the latter led her, when able, to become involved in a variety of charitable works and to write for the Religious Tract Society and the *Girls' Own Paper*. Religion and the

problems of sickness and death are major themes in her collection of poems *Lyra Australis*, published under her own name in 1854, and important ingredients also of *The Broad Arrow* (q.v.), a novel about the convict system which was informed by her Tasmanian experiences and published under her pseudonym in 1859. Immensely popular in its time but subsequently out of print and neglected, *The Broad Arrow* is the only convict novel, apart from *Lucy Cooper* (see Lang, John) to have a female convict as its hero and is one of the first to be based on first-hand experience of a convict settlement. Recent rereadings emphasise the novel's implicit feminism and opposition to the colonial penal system, themes which transcend its surface evangelicalism. A memoir of Leakey by her sister Emily, *Clear Shining Light*, was published in 1882.

LEASON, Percy (1889–1959), born Kaniva, Victoria, served an apprenticeship as a lithographer in Melbourne, and then moved in 1917 to Sydney, where he established himself as a cartoonist on the *Bulletin*. Lured back to Melbourne in 1924 to work on the *Melbourne Punch* and its successor, *Table Talk*, he eventually renewed his association with the *Bulletin* before settling in America in 1938. A precise draughtsman with a fine sense of detail, Leason won a reputation not only for his cartoons, especially the series on the country town, Wiregrass, but also for his illustrations of the works of Australian authors, notably for the drawings included in the *Selected Poems of Henry Lawson* (1918). Those drawings and much of Leason's work emphasise the legendary Australian bush humour. He published a series of articles on his boyhood in the magazine *Pandemonium* in 1934. His comic art is well illustrated in *Wiregrass, a Mythical Australian Town: the Drawings of Percy Leason* (1986), edited by Garrie Hutchinson.

Leaves from Australian Forests, the second volume of verse published by Henry Kendall (q.v.) in 1869, contains the well-known lyrics 'Bell Birds' and 'September in Australia'; the important narratives 'The Glen of Arrawatta' and 'King Saul at Gilboa'; the love poem 'Rose Lorraine'; and memorial poems to Charles Harpur, James Lionel Michael and Adam Lindsay Gordon.

LEE, Gerard (1951–   ), born Melbourne, grew up in Melbourne and Brisbane, and graduated from the University of Queensland in 1974. He has worked as a teacher, clerk, journalist and house-painter and has contributed verse and short stories to a range of periodicals including *Ear in a Wheatfield, Meanjin, Riverrun, Magic Sam, Semper Floreat* and *Makar*. Lee has published a collection of prose poems, *Manual for a Garden Mechanic* (1976); a collection of short stories, *Pieces for a Glass Piano* (1978); two novels, *True Love and How to Get It* (1981), *Troppo Man* (1990); and *Eating Dog* (1993), a selection of his experiences from two decades of wandering. He has written several screenplays including *Sweetie*, co-authored with Jane Campion and winner of the 1989 AFI Award for best screenplay. A witty writer with a deceptively naive narrative style,

Lee frequently satirises contemporary Queensland lifestyles, from numerous varieties of the alternative to the mainstream. *True Love and How to Get It*, set in Coolangatta and suburban Brisbane, has been praised as an authentic representation of contemporary southern Queensland; the episodic story of the sexual and other adventures of a picaresque hero, narrated by an omniscient author in a wryly comic style that is reminiscent of Fielding, the novel presents a range of social scenes from the bizarre to the bourgeois. *Troppo Man*, set in Bali, opposes Australian naivety to Asian complexity with black comic effects.

LEE, Ida (1865–1943), born Kelso, NSW, into one of the earliest pioneering families, married Charles Marriott and is occasionally referred to as Ida Marriott. She wrote several historical accounts, some of which contain extracts from previously unpublished journals, including *The Coming of the British to Australia, 1788–1829* (1906), *Commodore Sir John Hayes* (1912), *The Logbooks of the 'Lady Nelson'* (1915), *Captain Bligh's Second Voyage to the South Sea* (1920), *Early Explorers in Australia* (1925); and edited *The Voyage of the 'Caroline' from England to Van Diemen's Land and Batavia in 1827–28* by R. Hare (1927). She also published a collection of verse, *The Bush Fire and Other Verses* (1897).

LEE, Joyce (1913–), born Murtoa, Victoria, has been a pharmacist with the Richmond Community Health Centre, a lecturer in poetry writing at Victoria College, Toorak, and has been involved with Pariah Press. She has published verse, 'Poems from the Wimmera' in *Sisters Poets 1* (1979), *Abruptly from the Flatlands* (1984) and *Plain Dreaming* (1991). Her reminiscences about her childhood in the Wimmera in the 1920s, featured in her books, are the best of Joyce Lee's writing. They indicate, as has traditionally been the case, that the landscape and environment are among the strongest inspirers of poetry. Joyce Lee won the Grenfell Henry Lawson Festival of the Arts Award in 1978 and the MacGregor Prize for Poetry, 1982.

Leeuwin, an occasional journal published in WA in five issues 1910–11, was edited by Alfred Chandler ('Spinifex') and A.G. Plate. Its most noteworthy literary articles were four contributions by A.G. Stephens on 'The Manly Poetry of Western Australia'.

Legend of King O'Malley, The (1974), a two-act musical and burlesque comedy by Bob Ellis and Michael Boddy (qq.v.), is based on the life, both factual and apocryphal, of King O'Malley (1854–1953), an eccentric hero of the Australian Labor movement. First produced in 1970 by NIDA at Sydney's Jane Street Theatre and frequently revived, it is often compared to Ray Lawler's *Summer of the Seventeenth Doll* (1957) for its stimulating effect on Australian drama. In 1970 it won the James Cook bicentennial play competition, two Awgie Awards in 1971 for the best script in any medium and the best play and the Australian Producers' and Directors' Guild Award for the best script in any medium in 1971. The play opens in the form of a meeting of the revivalist Waterlily Rock-bound Church, which according to his own account O'Malley founded in Texas, and follows his career until his arrival in Queensland. Hounded by his alter ego, Angel, who appears in various disguises, e.g. as a devil wearing army boots and bloomers, a swagman, Long John Silver and a fortune-telling beggar, O'Malley eventually makes his way to the first federal parliament, which transpires to be a troupe of tired vaudeville artists led by W.M. (Billy) Hughes. Later, O'Malley is alienated from Hughes over the conscription issue (1916–17) and loses his seat. But he outlasts them all and when he dies is taken off to the next world accompanied by a rousing hymn from the chorus. A fast-moving series of comic, music-hall sketches linked by song, dance and mime, the play also makes some serious statements about Australian political life.

Legend of the Nineties, The, an influential work of cultural criticism by Vance Palmer (q.v.), was published in 1954. It attempts to take dispassionate stock of the Nineties (q.v.), a decade that became invested with mythic significance for many Australians by the end of the Second World War. After opening with a generalised description of the period, 'which turned the eyes of Australians inward and impelled them to discover themselves and their country', Palmer moves on to chapters on the composition of the population, on the period's oral literature and its myth-making, on Utopian aspirations and ventures, the role of the *Bulletin*, the literature of Henry Lawson, A.B. Paterson, Bernard O'Dowd, Joseph Furphy and others, and on the political ferment of the time and its resolution. In his last chapter, 'A Lost Tradition', he speculates on the continuing significance of the decade for the national consciousness of Australia.

LEGG, Frank (1906–66), born England, came to Australia in 1927. After working as a freelance journalist in Sydney, Melbourne and Adelaide, he joined the staff of the Adelaide *News* in 1937. He also began to establish a reputation as a broadcaster on ABC radio. In 1940 he joined the AIF and served in the Middle East, sending back a series of articles, 'Tales of Tobruk', to the *ABC Weekly*. In January 1944 he went to New Guinea as an ABC war correspondent and covered the retreat of the Japanese to the ultimate surrender in Tokyo Bay. After the war he became one of the best-known commentators on ABC radio and television. He published the biographies *The Eyes of Damien Parer* (1963), *The Gordon Bennett Story* (1965), *Once More on My Adventure* (1966, with Tom Hurley and on Frank Hurley); an account of his and others' war experiences based on diaries, recorded talks and official reports to the ABC, *War Correspondent* (1964); and a collection of reminiscences of his cats, *Cats on Velvet* (1966).

LEHMANN, Geoffrey (1940–), born Sydney, graduated with degrees in arts and law from the University of Sydney, where he also studied German literature and was associated with fellow poet Les Murray co-editing the magazines *Arna* and *Hermes*. Lehmann practised as a solicitor and lectured in law at the University of NSW. He is now a partner in a major international accounting firm in Sydney. His published verse consists of *The Ilex Tree* (1965, a shared volume with Les Murray), *A Voyage of Lions and Other Poems* (1968), *Conversation with a Rider* (1972), *From an Australian Country Sequence* (1973), *Extracts from Ross' Poems* (1976), *Ross' Poems* (q.v., 1978), *Nero's Poems* (1982), *Children's Games* (1990), and *Spring Forest* (1992). His *Selected Poems* was published in 1976. Lehmann has also written a novel, *A Spring Day in Autumn* (1974); edited the anthologies *Comic Australian Verse* (1972, retitled *The Flight of the Emu, Contemporary Light Verse*, 1990), *The Younger Australian Poets* (1983, with Robert Gray), and *Australian Poetry in the Twentieth Century* (1991, also with Gray); published a book of art criticism, *Australian Primitive Painters* (1977), which is a selection of the work of painters Irvine Homer, Charles Callins, James Fardoulys, Sam Byrne and Harry Bastin.

In *The Ilex Tree* Lehmann's predilection for family poetry is shown in the four 'Pieces for My Father' and the long seven-part poem 'For William Rainer, My Grandfather'. *A Voyage of Lions and Other Poems* is dominated by the much-admired historical series 'Monologues for Marcus Furius Camillus, Governor of Africa', and other shorter poems with an ancient Roman setting. As a background to the observations and meditations of the ageing Camillus there is a passing parade of Roman decadence – victory marches, lavish banquets, slave girls, gladiators, ornate villas, lush vineyards and olive groves. The monologues, which are also included as the opening section of Lehmann's later *Selected Poems*, convey well the fatal combination of opulence and ennui that marks a civilisation near collapse. The highlights of the series are the dolphin and lion poems. The capture and transhipping of the African lions to the Colosseum ('A Voyage of Lions') are taken up by the following poem, 'Colosseum', and in a later volume, 'Colosseum at a Distance'. The lion sequence pinpoints the ultimate barbarity of Roman civilisation, the charnel-house of the Colosseum where the burial pits were 'So foul that workmen digging two thousand years later/ Sickened by the smell will lay down their spades'. *Conversation with a Rider* combines poems on historical personages such as Pope Alexander VI and Cellini with those on family and friends. The sequence of eleven poems, which recalls experiences from the life of Lehmann's father, lovingly and good-humouredly charts the close relationship between the two. The 'Roses' sequence, with its patterning of natural beauty and grace against man's destructiveness, is more complex, both technically and thematically, than Lehmann's usual lucid, undemonstrative compositions.

Ross' Poems, Lehmann's most popular and impressive work, is a long poem segmented into seventy-five separate pieces. Taking as persona Lehmann's then father-in-law, Ross McInerney, the poem describes his experiences as a farmer in central-western NSW. Partly memoirs, partly anecdotes and partly reflections, the poems build up a composite of close-knit family life in a typically Australian rural community. *Ross' Poems* form part of the Australian 'vernacular

republic' of Lehmann's fellow poet Les Murray, and are an important illustration of the modern resurgence of interest in the bush and its people. In *Nero's Poems* Lehmann returns to the ancient world which had intrigued him in *A Voyage of Lions*. He resumes the successful dramatic monologue of the Camillus poems to explore the enigma of Nero and to examine and even account for that ruler's bizarre character and conduct. The poems are accompanied by Lehmann's introductory comments on Nero. *Spring Forest* incorporates much of the original *Ross' Poems*, revised and expanded with thirty new poems added. Essentially a single poem and accompanied by photographs, *Spring Forest* is based on the life and stories of Ross and Olive McInerney as was *Ross' Poems*. *Children's Games*, a quiet, restrained, meditative collection deals initially with the problems associated with a marriage breakdown, its impact on the participants and the children. The latter part of the book includes an unusual series of cryptic sonnets.

LEICHHARDT, Ludwig (1813–?48), born Trebatsch, Prussia, studied philosophy, languages, natural science and medicine in Germany, England and France before coming to Australia in 1842 to study natural science in a hitherto unexplored environment. In 1844–45 he led an overland expedition from Brisbane to Port Essington, a journey of almost 5000 kilometres. After an abortive attempt in 1846–47 to cross the continent east–west from the Darling Downs to the coast of WA, Leichhardt tried again in March 1848, setting out from the Condamine River near the present township of Roma, but the expedition disappeared virtually without trace. In spite of nine major searches over a period of almost a century the disappearance of Leichhardt's expedition still remains one of the great mysteries of the Australian bush.

Leichhardt's own records of his explorations are contained in diaries, notebooks, sketch-books and letters, many of which are in the Mitchell Library. He published *Journal of an Overland Expedition in Australia from Moreton Bay to Port Essington* (1847). His *Letters*, collected and translated by Marcel Aurousseau, were published in 1968. The Leichhardt saga and the controversial character of the man himself have inspired a large body of writing, chief of which are the descriptive and biographical works of A.H. Chisholm, *Strange New World: The Adventures of John Gilbert and Ludwig Leichhardt* (1941, republished 1973 as *Strange Journey*); E.M. Webster, *Whirlwinds in the Plain* (1980) and *An Explorer at Rest* (1986); Gordon Connell, *The Mystery of Ludwig Leichhardt* (1980); Colin Roderick, *Leichhardt: The Dauntless Explorer* (1988); and Dan Sprod, *Proud Intrepid Heart* (1989), which reproduces Leichhardt's journal of his expedition of 1846–47. Leichhardt and his fate have also inspired poets such as Henry Kendall, who wrote the long poem 'Leichhardt' and whose first published verses were four stanzas ('Oh, Tell Me Ye Breezes') pondering the explorer's disappearance. A.B. Paterson wrote 'The Lost Leichhardt', Francis Webb examines the enigma of Leichhardt's character in 'Leichhardt in Theatre' and he appears in the play by Janis Balodis, *Too Young for Ghosts (1985). The most celebrated fictional representation of him is in Patrick White's novel *Voss* (1957). An interesting offshoot of the fatal Leichhardt expedition concerns one of his team, Clarsen, who was allegedly seen in the 1860s, while living with the Aborigines, by one Andrew Hume, who later went on two unsuccessful expeditions to find him. Les Perrin gives an account of those expeditions in *The Mystery of the Leichhardt Survivor* (1990).

'Leichhardt in Theatre', a poem by Francis Webb (q.v.), was published as 'Leichhardt Pantomime' in the *Bulletin*, 1947. In 1952 it was published with other poems in a revised form with a new title, 'Leichhardt in Theatre', in a volume of that name. The opening section of the original poem, 'Introduction in a Waxworks', was replaced by a segment titled 'Advertisement', and the 'Epilogue' of the original poem was omitted. The poem's central figure is the explorer Ludwig Leichhardt (q.v.). The poem opens with a vision of the earlier explorer Charles Sturt who, thwarted in his several attempts to establish the existence of an inland sea, left an 'Impasse at the Centre'. The solving of that 'Impasse' provided much of the lure for Leichhardt. Webb's portrait of Leichhardt begins by emphasising the visionary side of his nature ('This is a land where man becomes a myth'), then, by introducing a clown and by the use of a type of music-hall doggerel, he pictures Leichhardt as a buffoon who does not know 'north from south' but who is clever at 'playing with windmills in the Never Never'. Glimpses of Leichhardt's expeditions follow: the first triumphant journey of fifteen months and 5000 kilometres to the Gulf of Carpentaria, marred only by the death of botanist John Gilbert; and the second journey, a farcical failure led by the equally farcical figure of Leichhardt. In the interval between the second and third expeditions Leichhardt is forced to confront the painful realisation of the conflicting duality of his nature. The third expedition, although only briefly exposed in the poem, sees purpose and significance restored. The outcome is seen as uncertain, but that is unimportant – the venture is everything ('Where they will go, how perish – this is nothing'). In its use of psychological analysis and self-analysis for characterisation rather than the simple observer technique employed in 'A Drum for Ben Boyd', 'Leichhardt in Theatre' is more skilful and subtle than the earlier Webb poem. It builds up a fascinating and deeply unified vision of the enigmatic and contradictory character of the Prussian explorer. Douglas Stewart included 'Leichhardt in Theatre' in his anthology *Voyager Poems*, in 1960.

LETT, Lewis (1878–1967), born Waddingham, England, came to Australia in 1910. Shortly afterwards, he settled in Papua as superintendent engineer of a large development company. In 1911 he and his partner, G.H. Thomas, found petroleum in the Gulf of Papua and prospected an extensive area of jungle for further indications, Thomas dying in the attempt. Lett travelled extensively in Papua before settling in Port Moresby, where he acted as Reuters' correspondent, contributing to the London *Times*, the *Manchester Guardian* and other overseas and Australian newspapers. He published a biography of Sir Hubert Murray (1949); several accounts of Papua including *Knights Errant of Papua* (1935), *The Papuan Achievement* (1942), *Papuan Gold* (1943) and *Papua: Its People and Its Promise* (1944); and a collection of short stories of Papuan life, *Savage Tales* (1946).

LETTE, Kathy (1958–   ), born Sydney, has worked for radio and television as an interviewer and writer. At the age of 15 she and Gabrielle Carey created a cabaret act, the 'Salami Sisters', and subsequently collaborated in the popular novel, later produced as a film, which is a satirical study of a 1970s surfie culture, *Puberty Blues* (q.v., 1979). In 1988 she spent some time in Hollywood writing for a television comedy series before moving to London in 1990 as a television interviewer in the BBC talk show 'Behind the Headlines'. Lette's other publications include *Hit & Ms* (1984), a flippant guide to surviving the eighties; *Girls' Night Out* (1987), a collection of stories which focus on a group of women in their early twenties and which mimic the attitude of one of the characters who 'revelled in being scandalous. She didn't just lampoon sacred cows, she milked them dry, then barbecued them'; a novel, *The Llama Parlour* (1991), which satirises American west-coast culture from the perspective of an Australian innocent, a 'Crocodile Dundette'; and *Foetal Attraction* (1993), a hilarious novel about Maddy Wolfe's experiences in love, in London and ultimately in childbirth, which is also a satire on England and the English. As Maddy reflects shortly after her arrival, 'Being in England was like living amongst some remote and foreign tribe. Maddy felt as bamboozled by the unwritten etiquette and exotic rituals as Captain Cook must have been when witnessing aboriginal tribesmen attaching coconuts to their penises'. Lette has also written three plays, *Grommitts* (produced in 1987 and published 1988), which centres on the subgroups within the teenage culture of an Australian high school; *Perfect Mismatch* (produced in 1985 and published the same year in *Shorts at the Wharf, Vol. 1*); and 'Wet Dreams', produced in 1985.

LETTERS, F.J.H. (Francis Joseph Henry) (1897–1964), born Queensland, graduated from the University of Sydney in 1918 and practised as a barrister 1927–37 before joining the foundation staff of the New England University College in 1938 to lecture in classics and English. He published several works of academic criticism on classical and European literature; a collection of general essays, *In a Shaft of Sunlight* (1948); and three volumes of poetry, *Darkness and Light* (1934), *The Great Attainder* (1943) and *Aurora Australis* (1963). A collection of essays on classic literature, *For Service to Classical Studies*, was published in 1966 in his honour. He was awarded an honorary D.Litt. by the National University of Ireland in 1956.

Letters to Live Poets (1969), the major work of Bruce Beaver (q.v.), comprises thirty-four confessional-type poems in a *livre composé*. It was influenced by the NZ poet James K. Baxter's *Pig Island Letters, Life Studies* by Robert Lowell and *Letters from Darkness* by Lawrence Durrell; in its turn *Letters to Live Poets* influenced the style and direction of much Australian poetry of the 1970s. Written with obsessional purpose and speed (forty-nine poems in as many days in 1966) because Beaver believed he was losing his rationality, the *Letters* are directed to the 'not-impossible creative reader, a live poet in his or her own sense'. They begin with a letter to the American poet Frank O'Hara, recently killed in a bizarre fashion when crushed by a beach buggy while sunbathing. The opening letters despairingly catch certain appalling aspects of contemporary life: the Vietnam War ('infants blistered and skinned alive by napalm'); international complicity in corruption ('your country's president ... among us like a formidable virus'); the rank commercialism of modern society ('keyed to obsolescence'); the vegetable existence and mindless passivity of today's people who demand only the material trivia of life, none of its beauty and fullness. Other letters recall painful episodes of Beaver's early life ('damn my childhood') and the ever-present threat of mental illness ('so it's one day at a time spent checking the menagerie of self'). From Letter XIX, whose self-revelations are taken up more fully in Beaver's later work *As It Was*, the tone changes. Its comfortable opening, 'I welcome the anonymity of the middle years', reflects a growing note of self-confidence born out of an ironic acceptance of himself and of the achievement of a limited kind of working arrangement with his environment. Although the early despair subsides, the sense of futility does not completely disappear and the *Letters*, 'never to be posted', close with the recognition of at least one supreme saving gift – that of the 'living word'.

'Letter[s] to Tom Collins' is a series of letters supposedly addressed to Joseph Furphy through 'Tom Collins' (q.v.), which discuss either Furphy's works and their reception, or Australian literature and society in the 1940s in the light of Furphy's critical and social attitudes. The series was published in *Meanjin*, commencing with 'Brian Vrepont's' 'Letter to Tom Collins: "New" Verse – and *Meanjin* Trends' in 1941 and concluding with Sidney Baker's 'Letter to Tom Collins: Demise of the *Bulletin*' in 1946; other contributors include James Devaney, Kylie Tennant, Nettie Palmer, Miles Franklin, Manning Clark and A.A. Phillips. The device of addressing Collins or the deceased Furphy himself as a way of commenting, usually critically, on contemporary Australian society has been periodically revived, e.g. in *Overland* in 1957.

LEUNIG, Michael (1945–   ), born Melbourne into a working-class family, is one of Australia's best-known cartoonists. He was conscripted into the army during the Vietnam War, but was rejected on physical grounds and spent two years at Swinburne Film and Television School. He worked at first for the short-lived *Newsday*, but came into prominence after he moved to *Nation Review*, where his cartoon of a ferret

became the newspaper's symbol ('lean and nosy like a ferret'). After the demise of *Nation Review*, he moved to the *Age*. His whimsical cartoons create a sad, absurd, often original world, inhabited by playful ducks, genderless humanoids and eternal innocents such as Mr Curly and Vasco Pyjama. He has also attained cult status in England, where four of his books have been published and in the USA, where a café has been named after him. Vasco Pyjama became the hero of a play scripted by Ingle Knight, 'The Voyage of Vasco Pyjama', staged in 1991, and in 1993 another play based on his work 'State of Bewilderment' was produced in Britain and Australia. Leunig's compassionate if quirky representation of mundane affairs is often hopeful about the human predicament, an attitude which colours the prayers he has published in the *Age*, which address everyday experiences from love to the common cold. His cartoons have even been linked to the religious thought of the German theologian Karl Rahner in *Michael Leunig and Karl Rahner: A Common Philosophy* (1992) by John Honner. Leunig has published several collections of cartoons, including *The Penguin Leunig* (1974), *The Second Leunig* (1979), *The Bedtime Leunig* (1981), *A Bag of Roosters* (1983), *Ramming the Shears* (1985), *The Travelling Leunig* (1990), *Introspective* (1991) and *Everyday Devils and Angels* (1992); two books of his prayers, *A Common Prayer* (1990) and *The Prayer Tree* (1991); and a collection of his verse, *A Book of Poesy* (1992).

LEVEY, Barnett (1798–1837), born London, arrived in Sydney in 1821 to join his brother Solomon, who had been transported in 1815 but had become a prosperous merchant. Barnett Levey worked for his brother for about four years, before going into business as merchant and auctioneer with an interest in banking. He achieved some financial success but was temperamentally unsuited to commercial life. A man of impulse and unrealistic ambitions, he opened his own retail and wholesale warehouse, established one of the first lending libraries, and built a flour-mill, wheat store and windmill on the site of his warehouse between Colchester and George Streets. A great lover of the theatre, he nourished grandiose, entrepreneurial projections, took a prominent part in Sydney's cultural events, performing as a singer at concerts, and from 1826 was actively engaged in establishing the first permanent theatre in Australia. In November 1827 he founded a company to finance the theatre, which was to be included in his Colchester Street property. Hindered by acrimonious disputes with Governor Darling and the colonial secretary over his mill, by financial worries, by his own mercurial, irascible nature, and by the unwillingness of others to finance the theatre, Levey mortgaged his property to do so. Meanwhile he faced great opposition from the government and clergy in his repeated bids to gain a theatrical licence. To acquire more money he converted the front of his building into the Royal Hotel and in July 1829 obtained a licence to present balls and suppers and, later, concerts in his hotel. In August he held a vocal and instrumental concert ostensibly in the Royal Hotel, referred to as the Assembly Rooms, but which was in fact held in his Theatre Royal, designed by Francis Greenway to accommodate 700 people. The first concert was succeeded by others, at all of which Levey himself performed. In November he performed in a one-man show titled 'At Home', which proved highly popular with the audience but incurred the wrath of the colonial secretary. By December 1830 Levey, still unable to obtain a theatrical licence, was forced to sell his hotel, store, granary and mill and to turn to working as an auctioneer, watchmaker and estate agent. Governor Darling's replacement by Governor Bourke, however, resulted in a more relaxed attitude to theatrical performances and in April 1832 Levey was granted a licence. Levey's original Theatre Royal, now owned by Cooper and Levey, was redesigned and enlarged by John Verge. While the theatre was being adapted, Levey and his company presented entertainments and plays on a temporary stage in the converted saloon of the Royal Hotel. The company opened their first season on 26 December 1832 with Douglas Jerrold's *Black-Ey'd Susan*. Enormously popular, Levey's company presented performances of a variety of plays from melodrama to farce to Shakespearean drama three nights a week in its first season, which ran to July 1833. The expanded Theatre Royal, capable of seating at least 1200, was opened in October 1833. To the end of its turbulent life the Theatre Royal company experienced more lows than peaks, owing to perennial disputes between Levey and his players, unruly audiences, some careless performances and some poor houses. Charles Harpur, who was briefly an actor, took Levey to court to recover money from him, and legal actions between Levey and other players were a constant phenomenon. Actors of some note who performed with the company included Conrad Knowles, John Meredith, George Buckingham, Joseph Simmons, Eliza Winstanley and John Lazar. John Simmons joined Levey as partner in 1834. In 1835, worn out by the difficulties of running the company, Levey lost control of the theatre to other lessees although in 1836 he briefly resumed management. In April 1837 he staged his last great entertainment, the spectacle *Napoleon Buonaparte*. He died in October, leaving his widow and four children in poverty. Mrs Levey, assisted by others including Joseph Simmons, continued to run the theatre until March 1838, when the opening of the Royal Victoria under the directorship of Joseph Wyatt ensured the demise of the company. In October 1838 Wyatt bought the Royal Hotel and the Theatre Royal to house his own company. Barnett Levey's life and achievements are described by Eric Irvin in *Theatre Comes to Australia* (1971), and in Ian Bevan's *The Story of the Theatre Royal* (1993). He appears as the character 'Barney Little' in Eliza Winstanley's novel *Margaret Falconer* (1860).

LEVI, John (1934–), born Melbourne, is a graduate of the University of Melbourne and Monash University and spent five years of rabbinic studies in America and Israel before becoming rabbi of Temple Beth Israel, Australia's largest Jewish congregation. With G.F.J. Bergman he co-authored *Australian Genesis: Jewish Convicts and Settlers 1788–1850* (1974); he also compiled *The Forefathers: A Dictionary of Biography of the Jews in Australia 1788–1830* (1976).

LEVY, Julia Ethel, who frequently used the pseudonym 'Juliet', published several lightweight and conventional one-act plays, novels and volumes of poetry in the 1920s. Her plays include *The Way Out* (1925), *The Snob* (1925), *The Proposal* (1926), *Woman Disposes* (1927) and the three-act piece *The Choice* (1928). Her novels include *A Soul of Sincerity* (1923), *God's Good Woman* (1926), *Devotion* (1927) and *The Snob and the Lady* (1929); her collections of verse are *Songs of Solace* (1922) and *Signposts on Life's Highway* (1926).

LEWIN, J.W. (John William) (1770–1819), born England, arrived in Sydney in 1800. His *Birds of New Holland with Their Natural History* was published in London in 1808; the 1813 edition issued in Sydney with the title *Birds of New South Wales* was the first illustrated book published in Australia and was printed by George Howe.

LEWIS, Brian (1906–91), born Lottah, Tasmania, was the youngest in a family of eight. A distinguished architect and dean of the Faculty of Architecture and Building at the University of Melbourne 1947–71, he was educated at Wesley College, Melbourne and the universities of Melbourne, Liverpool and London. He served in the AIF 1940–43. He wrote two autobiographical accounts of his childhood in Melbourne, *Sunday at Kooyong Road* (1976) and *Our War: Australia during World War I* (1980). Focusing on the suburban ritual of Sunday from 1909 to the early 1920s and following his younger self from the age of 3 to 15, Lewis provides in *Sunday at Kooyong Road* a part-nostalgic, part-ironic picture of his district's social codes and practices and its bitter sectarian rivalries and disputes. *Our War*, which builds on the same memories, is a more intensely researched general study of attitudes on the Australian home front to the First World War. Anglophile Presbyterians, staunchly loyal to the ends of empire, Lewis's family adjusted slowly to the realities of the war which was to 'blow [the family] apart'; interweaving the naive perceptions of his child self with mature knowledge of the blunders and wastage, *Our War* is both social history and autobiography. It includes reminiscences of Sir John Monash, Nellie Melba and the young Robert Menzies.

LEWIS, Julie (1925–), born Perth and educated at the University of WA, has worked as a teacher in schools and in adult education and community groups. She began writing in 1964, mainly for radio. Her short stories have been published in periodicals and anthologies and in two collections, *Double Exposure* (1981) and *The Walls of Jericho* (1987); she has also written the biographies *Jimmy Woods: Flying Pioneer* (1989) and *Olga Masters: A Lot of Living* (1991), and with P.A.E. Hutchings, *Kathleen O'Connor: Artist in Exile* (1987); an account of the radio work of Catherine King, *On Air* (1979); and has edited a selection of radio scripts, *Unlimited Scope* (1983), and, with Shane McCauley, the anthology *Breakaway* (1980). Concentrating mainly on domestic life and the experience of women and written in compressed, spare prose, the stories of *Double Exposure* and *The Walls of Jericho* explore silences and barriers in relationships, the insidious tokens of change or resistance to change, the recognition of turning-points, or the experience of coming to terms with separation, difference and loneliness.

LEWITT, Maria (1924–), born Lodz, Poland, arrived in Australia in 1949. In Australia she has worked as an outdoor machinist, shop assistant and secretary. Her publications in English include the autobiographical novels *Come Spring* (1980), winner of the Alan Marshall Award in 1978, and *No Snow in December* (1985), winner of the NSW Premier's Award for Ethnic Writing. Her short stories which have appeared in numerous anthologies and periodicals, were awarded first prize in the 1972 CAE Adult Association Writers' Short Story Competition. She has also written a novel for secondary school children, *Just Call Me Bob* (1976). *Come Spring*, based on Lewitt's experiences in Poland as a member of a part-Jewish family during the Nazi occupation, is a fast-paced, compelling account of living daily on the edge of catastrophe; at 15 Irena, Lewitt's narrator, was conscious of being at the threshold of life, entranced by 'the idyllic beauty of the European summer of 1939', but the succeeding years of horror and occasional despair were introduced suddenly by the murder of her father, beaten to death by the Gestapo. Death thereafter became a regular companion, in company with brutality, betrayal, starvation and fear; presenting this grim story in spare prose and through the eyes of an adolescent girl, who manages to find love in the midst of general destruction and who undergoes the normal conflicts of youth, Lewitt achieves a strong impression of authenticity and a fine balance between horror and lyricism. *No Snow in December* continues the narrator's experiences as a migrant in Australia, recording the misconceptions and problems of the non-English-speaking newcomer and the difficulties of coming to terms with the residual horrors of war.

'LEYS, Simon' (Pierre Ryckmans) (1935–), born in the district of Uccle in Belgium, was a law student at the University of Louvain when, in 1955, he visited China as part of a youth delegation. After completing his law degree, he spent several years studying Chinese language and literature in Taiwan. After completing his doctorate he went to Hong Kong to carry out research and by 1970 had published four scholarly books, including two translations of Chinese memoirs. He came to Australia to work at the ANU and in 1971 his book *The Chairman's New Clothes*, which deals with the horrors of Chairman Mao's Cultural Revolution, was published. It was followed in 1977 by *Chinese Shadows*, a Book of the Month Club selection in the USA. In 1988 he became professor of Chinese studies at the University of Sydney and in 1990 was elected to the Belgian Academy of French Language and Literature to fill the chair left vacant by the death of novelist Georges Simenon. Ryckman's novel *The Death of Napoleon*, written originally in

French, was published in 1991 and won the NSW Christina Stead Literary Award for fiction in 1992. Setting history aside, he has Napoleon escape from St Helena on a Portuguese seal-hunting lugger. In an amusing account of Napoleon's attempt to re-establish himself as emperor, he has him meet a variety of farcical obstacles, since no one believes his story. He is arrested for not paying a hotel bill and is given a guided tour of the battlefield of Waterloo. He finally arrives in Paris but becomes involved in the fruit trade, ultimately failing in his attempt to resume his career. In Ryckmans's words, the book 'has nothing to do with history, politics, or even with Napoleon himself'.

LHOTSKY, John (1795–?), born Galicia (now part of Poland) of Czechoslovakian parents, was a trained naturalist and doctor who arrived in Sydney in 1832. In 1834 he explored the Argyle and Monaro districts of NSW, publishing on his return *A Journey from Sydney to the Australian Alps*; this lively, somewhat eccentric, and incomplete work was first issued in sixteen-page parts to subscribers (1834–36) and then bound in book form (dated 1835). After failing to secure a scientific post in NSW, Lhotsky went in 1836 to Van Diemen's Land, where he worked as a scientist, lecturer and journalist before leaving for England in 1838; the last reference to him overseas is in 1865. A controversial colonist during his six years in Australia, Lhotsky was an important early natural historian, explorer and geologist; his *A Song of the Women of the Menero Tribe* (1835) is the first arrangement of Aboriginal music. He contributed widely to scientific journals overseas as well as writing political and scientific articles for the *Sydney Gazette*, the *Sydney Monitor* and the *Sydney Herald* in Sydney and the *Hobart Town Courier*, *Colonial Times* and *Tasmanian and Austral-Asiatic Review* in Hobart. In Sydney Lhotsky also helped edit the *New South Wales Magazine* (1833), edited the *Reformer* (1836) and wrote all of the *New South Wales Literary, Political and Commercial Advertiser*, a short-lived periodical (1835–36), some of the issues published with part of *Illustrations of the Present State and Future Prospects of the Colony of New South Wales* (1835); the *Illustrations* parts were published anonymously but were written by Lhotsky and were bound together (1836), like the earlier *A Journey to the Australian Alps*. In Hobart he wrote the three weekly numbers of *Information for the People* (1837), which included a description of Tasman's Peninsula. Lech Paszkowski edited *Dr. John Lhotsky: The Turbulent Australian Writer Naturalist and Explorer* (1977), which includes biographical information on Lhotsky's birth (previously reckoned as 1800), and a year later appeared Alan E.J. Andrews's edition of Lhotsky's *Journey* which includes material recently discovered at the British Library.

LIBERMAN, Serge (1942–), born Fergana, Russia, the son of Polish Jewish refugees who fled to Russia when Germany invaded Poland, spent much of his early childhood in Displaced Persons Camps before arriving in 1951 to settle in Melbourne. He graduated in medicine in 1974 and now combines writing and editorial activities with work as a medical practitioner. Treasurer and member of the Editorial Board of the Australian Jewish Historical Society, he edited the *Melbourne Chronicle* 1977–84, was associate editor of *Outrider* 1984–85, and previously literary editor of the *Australian Jewish News*, the *Australian Times* and *Menorah*. He also compiled a *Bibliography of Australian Judaica* (1987), edited by Joy Young. He spent some time in Israel after completing his medical course. He describes himself as 'doctor, migrant, citizen, human being, Jew'.

Liberman's books of short fiction are *On Firmer Shores* (1981, winner in manuscript of the Alan Marshall Award for 1979); *A Universe of Clowns* (1983, winner in manuscript of the Alan Marshall Award for 1980 and of the Ethnic Affairs Commission Award in the 1984 NSW Premier's Literary Awards); *The Life That I Have Led* (1986, winner in manuscript of the Alan Marshall Award for 1984) and *The Battered and the Redeemed* (1990).

Many of the sixteen stories in *A Universe of Clowns* tell of the Jewish subculture that flourished in Melbourne after the Second World War. Like other Jewish writers of the post-Holocaust generation Liberman is strongly aware of the impact of that tragedy on the lives not only of those who had been directly involved but of the generation that followed. His stories stress the combined effect on Liberman's own generation of an inherited Jewish culture, the Holocaust and contemporary life. The opening story 'Seeds' from *The Life That I Have Led* is the archetypal Jewish story, evoking the commitment, voluntary or otherwise, of the Jewish boy to his ancestry, his Jewishness. The soul of his dead grandfather flows into the boy's soul – 'his soul enters into me and with his soul he brings still more, whole hosts of souls, generations of souls, the ever-surviving souls of my people that through me they may continue.' But the contemporary world pulls in a different direction. In 'Discovery in Venice' the Jewish boy, Reuben, has become an *apikoros* – a heretic – having married a Catholic girl, Marguerite. On the honeymoon trip to Europe Reuben visits a synagogue in what was once a Jewish ghetto in Venice and Marguerite prays at the Madonna's statue in the Church of Frari. There is brought home to both of them a perturbing uncertainty about their future together. The Holocaust is never far away in Liberman's stories; the young Jew's awareness in 'Survivors' of the tragic past of his parents and others of their vintage becomes the medium through which he can forgive them for their present petty traits.

'The Storyteller', from *The Battered and the Redeemed*, is rich in Jewish lore, much of it passed on by the story-telling mother to her son. The obsession of the growing boy to write of this inheritance is tempered, however, by the advice of his teacher, Jacob Kuznitz, who, in a Yiddish parable, urges the values of contemporaneity and relevance. Contemporaneity brings with it, of course, stories of the Holocaust – 'stories that like some repetitive driven ritual filled our lounge room and our kitchen of a mid-week evening or a Sunday afternoon' – and that bring with them the names Auschwitz, Bergen-Belsen, Treblinka, Maydanek, Buchenwald, names of reverence but also of terror and nightmare. Impaled on his dilemma of either writing of his Jewish heritage or of the continuing tribulations faced by modern Jewry, he comes to realise that they are inseparable.

The Holocaust has echoes, too, in 'Music' where the boy meets three old men, Glick, Freilich and Hoffnung, whose music during the war (pleasing to their German masters) kept them from the gas chambers. Even now, in old age, the memory of the terror of those times drives them into the same hysteria of playing that once saved their lives. 'Requiem' brings to two other young people, Jewish boy Asher and Catholic girl Genevieve, the full awareness that 'Discovery in Venice' had hinted was lying in wait for the honeymooners Reuben and Marguerite, i.e. the recognition that 'East is East and West is West', that 'Moses will ever remain Moses, and Jesus, Jesus', or as Asher's father had more pithily put it – 'one bed can sleep two people, but never will it accommodate two peoples.'

Liberman's other stories reflect on the sadness of unfulfilled lives wherever they are; it is not only the survivors of the Holocaust or Jews of the present generation who comprise the battered and the redeemed. They are everywhere. Liberman brings to the short story a depth and intensity that is more characteristic of the European than the Australian tradition.

Life, a popular monthly magazine published in Melbourne 1904–38, was edited by J.S. and W.H. Fitchett and was concerned with local and international affairs. W.H. Fitchett wrote much of the material until his death in 1927. The magazine published some articles and verse by Australian writers and reprinted poetry and prose from overseas sources. In 1938 it was superseded by *Life Digest*, which ran until 1961, becoming increasingly journalistic and less literary.

'Life-Cycle', one of Bruce Dawe's (q.v.) best-known poems, was published in his volume *An Eye for a Tooth* (1968). Both a satire on, and a celebration of, the Victorian obsession with Australian rules football, the poem presents the ingredients of the Saturday afternoon football ritual – the wearing of the club colours and the shouting of club nicknames ('Tigers', 'Demons', 'Saints'); the barracking chant ('Carn ... carn'); the abuse of umpires ('ooohh you bludger'); and the football spectator's fare ('hot pies and potato-crisps'). Like some mass opiate, Aussie rules adds meaning to otherwise meaningless lives. Old-timers by boundary fences 'dream of resurgent lions and centaur-figures from the past' and visualise present salvation 'in the six-foot recruit from Eaglehawk'. With his parody of the threnody 'For the Fallen', Dawe catches, in serio-comic fashion, the analogy between the football game and life itself.

> They will not grow old as those from more
> northern States grow old,
> for them it will always be three-quarter time
> with the scores level and the wind advantage
> in the final term.

'Life in Sydney: Or, the Ran Dan Club', an anonymous adaptation of *Tom and Jerry: Or, Life in London* (1821) by 'W.T. Moncrieff' (q.v.), was written in 1843 but refused a performance licence by the colonial secretary on the grounds that it was libellous. The adaptation uses the same names for its principal characters as well as the Jemmy Green who is also the subject of James Tucker's *Jemmy Green in Australia* (q.v., 1845). The script of the play is by various authors, including H.C. O'Flaherty, who also seems to have been prominent in its promotion.

LIGHT, William (1786–1839), born Malaya, served in the British Army and travelled widely in Europe before his appointment in 1836 as surveyor-general of the new colony of SA. In 1836–37 he selected the site, surveyed and laid out the plan of Adelaide and is generally recognised as the founder of that city. He also explored the SA coast and surveyed part of the hinterland of the colony before conflicts with his superiors caused his resignation. Light wrote *A Brief Journal of the Proceedings of William Light* (1839), a vindication of his activities in SA; an accomplished artist, he also published *Sicilian Scenery* (1823) and *Views of Pompeii* (1828). The Lighthouse Theatre Company of SA is named after him; there are several biographical studies of Light including G. Finkel's *William Light* (1972), David Elder's *The Art of William Light* (1987) and Geoffrey Dutton's *Founder of a City* (1960, expanded in 1992 with Dutton and Elder in collaboration. Elder also wrote the introduction to the 1984 Wakefield Press's edition of Light's *Brief Journal and Australian Diaries*). Max Afford's play *Awake My Love*, first titled 'William Light the Founder', won the SA centenary competition in 1936 and was published in 1960; it centres on the conflicts between Light and the SA governor John Hindmarsh. Early settlers who wrote commemorative poems on Light include Caroline Carleton in *South Australian Lyrics* (?1860) and Fidelia Hill in *Poems and Recollections of the Past* (1840).

LILLEY, Merv (1919–), born Rockhampton, left school early, served in the army 1941–44, and has worked as drover, cane-cutter, seaman and wharf labourer. He has contributed verse and songs to numerous periodicals and is represented in several well-known anthologies. He collaborated with Dorothy Hewett, whom he married in 1960, in a volume of verse with a socialist theme, *What About the People?* (1962), has published an independent collection, *Cautious Birds* (1973), and a collection of stories, reminiscences, poems and bush cookery ideas titled *Git Away Back! A Knockabout Life* (1983).

Lilley's Magazine was founded and edited by Norman Lilley (1876–1941), who was familiar with many of Sydney's writers and for some years conducted the literary page of the Sydney *Worker*. The magazine appeared monthly June–October 1911 and provided a much-needed outlet for several artists and writers, including Hugh McCrae, C.J. Brennan, Mary Gilmore and Lionel Lindsay.

'LINDALL, Edward' (Edward Ernest Smith) (1915–), born Adelaide, worked as a journalist for many years and during the Second World War served in the Middle East and New Guinea. He started writing in 1948 during an extended stay in England, sold his first fiction, a short story, in 1949, and subsequently contributed several stories to the *Saturday Evening Post*. He has since become a popular author in the USA, Australia and Britain, having written numerous adventure novels mostly set in outback, northern Australia. They include *Stranger Among Friends* (1956), *No Place to Hide* (1959, republished in 1961 titled *The Paper Ghost*), *Untamed Land* (1961), *The Killers of Karawala* (1961), *A Kind of Justice* (1964), *Northward the Coast* (1966), *A Time Too Soon* (1967), *The Fires of Kiwai* (1968), *Roar of the Lion* (1969), *A Gathering of Eagles* (1970), *The Last Refuge* (1972) and *Season of Discovery* (1978).

LINDESAY, Vane (1920–), the cartoonist 'Vane', was born in Sydney, became senior artist on *Salt* during the Second World War and subsequently worked for the Melbourne *Herald*, the *Argus* and the *Australasian Post* where he illustrated the Australiana feature 'Come in Spinner' by Bill Wannan. A book-illustrator and theatrical designer as well as a cartoonist, Lindesay has conducted extensive research into the history of Australian comic art. He has written *The Inked-In Image* (1970), a social and historical survey of Australian comic art, *The Way We Were*, on Australian popular magazines (1983), and has contributed numerous articles to *The World Encyclopedia of Cartoons* (1980). He also wrote the introduction to and designed the book *Caricatures* (1985), about fellow artist Noel Counihan. Vane Lindesay was given an Award of Honour in 1991 by the Australian Book Publishers Association in recognition of his contribution to Australian book design and production.

LINDSAY, Sir Daryl (1889–1976), born Creswick, Victoria, was the brother of Percy, Lionel, Norman and Ruby Lindsay. After some experience on sheep and cattle stations he enlisted in the AIF in 1915 and served in France. After his return to Australia in 1919 he became known for his landscapes and equestrian studies, but is most widely known as a gallery director and art adviser. He was director of the National Gallery of Victoria 1942–55; helped to establish the National Trust of Australia; from 1953 was a member of the Commonwealth Art Advisory Board and its chairman 1960–69; and was chairman of the interim council for the Australian National Gallery 1968–71. He was knighted in 1956. In 1922 he married Joan à Beckett Weigall (Joan Lindsay). His only work of literary interest is *The Leafy Tree* (1965), an autobiography and account of the Lindsay family.

LINDSAY, Harold Arthur (1900–69), born Adelaide, travelled extensively in Australia before starting work as a commercial bee-keeper in 1928 and as a farmer in 1933. In 1940 he joined the army as a special instructor in bushcraft, teaching survival techniques to Australian and American servicemen in Australia,

New Guinea and New Britain. His *The Bushman's Handbook* (1948), one of his most popular books, was published in three editions. After the war he became a full-time writer and broadcaster, contributing a weekly 'Naturalist's Diary' column to the *Age* for several years, as well as numerous articles to geographical and naturalist magazines. He published five novels for adults, *The Red Bull* (1959), *Sweeps the Wide Earth* (1960), *Janie McLachlan* (1961), *Faraway Hill* (1963) and *And Gifts Misspent* (1964); *The Red Bull*, drawing on his knowledge of forestry and bushfire, has been the most acclaimed. He wrote the juvenile novel *The Arnhem Treasure* (1952) and, with Norman Tindale, three books for children: *The First Walkabout* (1954, winner of the 1955 Children's Book of the Year Award), *Rangatira* (1959) and *Aboriginal Australians* (1963).

LINDSAY, Jack (1900–90), son of Norman Lindsay (q.v.), was born Melbourne and brought up in Brisbane. He graduated from the University of Queensland in 1921. Although hardly aware of his father during his childhood after his parents separated, he came strongly under Norman's influence from 1919 and in 1921–26 was a part of the lively cultural life of Sydney that he described in *The Roaring Twenties* (q.v., 1960). Profoundly impressed by his father's ideas, especially as expressed in *Creative Effort* (1920), he was the major force behind the establishment of the journal *Vision* (q.v.). He also edited with Kenneth Slessor and Frank Johnson the anthology *Poetry in Australia 1923* (1923). His first book of verse, *Fauns and Ladies* (1923), was illustrated by Norman Lindsay's woodcuts. In 1926 he left for England with the object of establishing himself as a poet and disseminating the Lindsay aesthetic via the Fanfrolico Press (q.v.), which he founded and ran with Jack Kirtley and P.R. Stephensen. The same motives prompted his establishment of the journal the *London Aphrodite* (q.v., 1928–29). By 1930 Lindsay's contact with a wider culture and international political issues had counteracted the influence of his father's ideas and by 1936 he had moved from Nietzscheanism to Marxism, a commitment that persisted. His importance to the Soviet cause was recognised in 1968 when he was awarded the Soviet Badge of Honour, but he remained a philosophical adherent rather than a political activist. During the war he worked as a private in the signals corps and then in the War Office as script-writer for army drama groups. He subsequently supported himself by his prodigious writing. Poet, dramatist, editor, historian, translator, classical scholar, biographer, novelist and critic, he had a formidable international reputation, especially in the last five fields. Author of over 150 books, he also contributed to many of the better-known journals in Australia and England. Although he never returned to Australia, he retained a lively interest in its culture and frequently contributed to Australian literary debates. His autobiographical trilogy, *Life Rarely Tells* (1958), *The Roaring Twenties* (1960) and *Fanfrolico and After* (1962), is particularly valuable as socio-cultural history. The collection *Decay and Renewal* (1976) brings together some of his essays on Australian and international literature, and in 1985 his novel about the 1917 conscription referendum, written in 1937, was published, titled *The Blood Vote*. Paul Gillen has edited a compendium of his writing, *Jack Lindsay. Faithful to the Earth* (1993). In 1968 his services to Australian literature were recognised by a D.Litt. from the University of Queensland. In 1980 he was elected a life member of the Association for the Study of Australian Literature; in 1981 he was made AM. *Culture and History: Essays Presented to Jack Lindsay*, edited by Bernard Smith, was published in 1984. Lindsay was the model for the character Willie Weaver in Aldous Huxley's novel *Point Counter Point*.

LINDSAY, Jane (1920–) is the daughter of Norman and Rose Lindsay (qq.v.). She has written a novel, *Kurrajong* (1945), a humorous, realistic story of rural folk, and *Portrait of Pa* (1973), an autobiography which includes reminiscences of her father, particularly of his latter years at Springwood.

LINDSAY, Lady Joan (1896–1984), born Joan à Beckett Weigall, was related to the Boyd family and became a member of the Lindsay family when she married Sir Daryl Lindsay (q.v.) in 1922. She was born in Melbourne and educated at the Clyde Girls Grammar School, the basis for the Appleyard College of *Picnic at Hanging Rock* (q.v., 1967). Although she studied art at the National Gallery School in Melbourne, writing became her main interest. Her first book, written under the pseudonym 'Serena Livingstone-Stanley' and titled *Through Darkest Pondelayo* (1936), parodies, among other things, feminine literature of the genteel variety, British colonialism and accounts of exploration; complete with photographs and 'Appendicites' the book purports to be edited by 'Barnaby Whitecorn D.D.'. Its humour has been compared to that of the Marx brothers. Her next two books, *Time Without Clocks* (1962) and *Facts Soft and Hard* (1964), are autobiographical. The former is a series of reminiscences of her married life before the outbreak of the Second World War; the latter describes her impressions of a visit to the USA. Her best-known book, *Picnic at Hanging Rock*, was made into an internationally successful film in 1975. A carefully crafted, suggestive and intriguing work with mythic overtones, it is shaped by her characteristically penetrating insights into human behaviour. Also prominent in the novel is her preoccupation with the ambiguities of time, especially the disparities between man-made time, natural time and time of the mind. In 1987 the novel's eighteenth and final chapter titled *The Secret of Hanging Rock* was published, although it barely alters the story's mystery. Joan Lindsay also wrote a children's book, *Syd Sixpence* (1982).

LINDSAY, Sir Lionel (1874–1961), born Creswick, Victoria, etcher, watercolour painter, wood-engraver, black-and-white artist, book-illustrator and art critic, was the brother of Percy, Norman, Daryl and Ruby Lindsay. After a period of work as a pupil-assistant at the Melbourne Observatory and some training in drawing at the National Gallery School in Melbourne, he worked as a freelance artist and journalist for weeklies in Melbourne and Sydney including the *Hawk* (later the *Hawklet*), and the *Free Lance*. He taught himself the techniques of etching and engraving, in which he became a master, and pioneered local interest in them. After a visit to Spain 1901–2 he settled in Sydney, working as a cartoonist on the *Evening News* and meanwhile establishing his reputation as an artist in Australia and overseas. In 1903 he married Jane Dyson, the sister of Will Dyson. He travelled extensively, visiting Spain, France, Italy, North Africa and India 1926–35, and continued to work and exhibit after his return to Australia in 1935. His work is held extensively by Australian and overseas galleries. He was knighted in 1941 for his services to art and was a trustee of the Art Gallery of NSW 1919–29 and 1934–49.

In addition to several collections of his art work, Lindsay produced numerous works of art criticism including an entry on Arthur Streeton's Australian paintings, 'The Art of Arthur Streeton', in a special edition of *Art in Australia* (1919), *The Art of Ernest Moffitt* (1899), *Conrad Martens* (1920), *The Art of Hans Heysen* (1920) and *Charles Keene* (1934). An outspoken and articulate critic of modernism in art, he expressed his views most provocatively in *Addled Art* (1942). His autobiography, *Comedy of Life* (1967), includes reminiscences of other members of the Lindsay family and of the artists, writers, musicians and well-known figures with whom he was familiar. Although he worked closely with his brother Norman in his early years their ideas eventually diverged and the relationship was severed in 1922. Joanna Mendelssohn has written his biography, *Lionel Lindsay* (1988).

LINDSAY, Norman (1879–1969) was born Creswick, Victoria, the fourth son of Jane and Robert Lindsay, who was an Irish-born doctor; of the Lindsays' family of ten children, five were to become prominent artists. Norman Lindsay's work spans various fields: painter, etcher, illustrator, cartoonist, sculptor and model-maker. He also wrote numerous works of fiction, philosophical, polemical and autobiographical essays, literary criticism, art appreciations, reviews and reminiscences. Although he classed himself primarily as an artist, he was more significant in the literary sphere, where his positive aesthetic credo and charismatic personality had a profound influence. Educated at Creswick Grammar School after a delicate childhood, Lindsay left home at 16 to join his brother Lionel in Melbourne and earn his living as an artist. His first novel, *A Curate in Bohemia* (1913), describes his lively, precarious student life in Melbourne, supported mainly by the topical drawings for a local weekly, the *Hawklet*, that he 'ghosted' for Lionel. In 1901 he attracted the attention of J.F. Archibald and moved to Sydney, where he joined the staff of the *Bulletin* as a black-and-white artist. His association with the *Bulletin*, later expanded to reviewer, essayist and fiction-writer, lasted until two years before his death. From the first his work attracted controversy: his characteristic bacchanalian paintings were often

condemned as immoral or irreligious; during the First World War his war cartoons aroused protests; and two of his novels, *Redheap* (q.v.) and *The Cautious Amorist*, were banned for a period within Australia. In 1931, after a police prosecution was launched against an issue of *Art in Australia* devoted to his work, he left for America, but soon returned. Apart from another earlier stay in Europe 1909–10, he remained firm in his conviction that an artist worked best within his own country. Lindsay was married twice. By his first marriage to Kate Parkinson he had three sons, Jack, Raymond and Philip; by his second wife, Rose Soady (Rose Lindsay) he had two daughters, Jane and Helen. He bequeathed a large part of his work to the University of Melbourne and the remainder to the National Trust of Australia on condition that it was preserved in the house at Springwood, NSW, where he lived for more than fifty years.

Lindsay's novels are *A Curate in Bohemia* (1913), *Redheap* (1930, banned in Australia until 1958 but published in the USA as *Every Mother's Son*), *Miracles by Arrangement* (1932, published in the USA as *Mr. Gresham and Olympus*), *The Cautious Amorist* (1932, banned in Australia 1934–58), *Saturdee* (q.v., 1933), *Pan in the Parlour* (1933), *Age of Consent* (1938), *The Cousin from Fiji* (q.v., 1945), *Halfway to Anywhere* (1947), *Dust or Polish?* (1950) and *Rooms and Houses* (1968). His children's novels are *The Magic Pudding* (q.v., 1918) and *The Flyaway Highway* (1936). Three works develop his aesthetic ideas: *Creative Effort* (1920), *Hyperborea* (1928) and *Madam Life's Lovers* (1929). *My Mask* (1970) is an autobiographical work, *The Scribblings of an Idle Mind* (1966) is a collection of philosophical essays, and *Bohemians of the Bulletin* (1965) describes some of the well-known personalities with whom Lindsay worked. Two anthologies, *Norman Lindsay's Book, No. I* (1912) and *Norman Lindsay's Book, No. II* (1915), contain some of his sketches and stories. Numerous selections of his art work have been published and Lindsay also illustrated many of his own books and those of other Australian authors, including Hugh McCrae, Leon Gellert, A.B. Paterson, Jack Lindsay, Kenneth Slessor, Dulcie Deamer, Kenneth Mackenzie and Douglas Stewart. There is as yet no comprehensive collection of Lindsay's prolific writings for the *Bulletin*, *Art in Australia*, the *Lone Hand* and other journals, although Keith Wingrove has edited a selection of his fiction-writing and art and literary criticism in *Norman Lindsay on Art, Life and Literature* (1990). His involvement with various publishing ventures, such as the Fanfrolico Press and the Endeavour Press, however, is well documented.

Writers who were directly influenced by Lindsay's aesthetic credo included R.D. FitzGerald, Hugh McCrae, Kenneth Slessor, Kenneth Mackenzie, Douglas Stewart and, of course, Jack Lindsay, although his indirect influence, coinciding with a traditional, vitalist strain in Australian literature, is inestimable. His ideas probably achieved their most concentrated effect in the 1920s, especially during the existence of the journal *Vision*, established by Jack Lindsay and himself. An ardent admirer of Nietzsche, Rabelais and Plato, Lindsay saw aesthetic values as the only values in a disordered world and 'creative effort' as the 'one enduring element in man's life'. By perpetual self-discovery and self-expression the great creative artist was seen as gifted with the power to penetrate contingent reality to life's eternal, natural essence. Key values in his credo were beauty, passion, youth, vitality, sexuality and courage. The artist's mission, inevitably separating him from the passionless, materialistic majority, naturally involved a continual resistance to all outwardly imposed restrictions. For the wowser and all kinds of humbug and pretension, Lindsay had an invincible contempt. His admiration for the ancients and the Italian Renaissance, and his conviction that true art was life-affirming and a quest for joy, were deepened by his hatred of 'modernism'. The First World War confirmed his intuition that modern civilisation was anti-life. Although social, political and religious issues failed to interest him, the implications of his attitudes were élitist, reactionary and anti-religious.

Lindsay's ideas are prominent in his novels, especially his conviction of the importance of sexual self-expression. *A Curate in Bohemia* is a vivid picture of Melbourne bohemian life in the 1890s, enlivened by Lindsay's liking for Dickensian oddities. But his talent for keen social observation and comedy is at its height in the trilogy on small-town life based on his memories of Creswick, *Saturdee*, *Redheap* and *Halfway to Anywhere*. Lindsay brilliantly captures both the pretentious adult life of a sleepy country town at the turn of the century and the spontaneous, if undercover, sexual energy of his youthful heroes and heroines. *Pan in the Parlour*, also set in a fictional country town, is a more schematised presentation of his ideas on the connection between sexuality and creativity; although lively and witty, it is less substantial than *Redheap* and *The Cousin from Fiji*. Both *Age of Consent* and *The Cautious Amorist* are popular comic novels but limited by Lindsay's preference for adolescent sexuality. *Miracles by Arrangement*, set in Sydney between the wars and concerned with the marital dilemma of a middle-aged couple, is his most successful and balanced attempt to deal with the world of his adult life. *Dust or Polish?* and *Rooms and Houses* are slacker works: the former, an attempt at a conventional novel, lacks Lindsay's distinctive satirical energy and the latter, ostensibly set in Melbourne in 1899, is an assortment of his diverse reminiscences and attitudes. Both Lindsay's novels for children are remarkable achievements: *The Magic Pudding*, a versatile blend of fantasy, droll humour, satire and comic verse, is probably Australia's favourite children's book; *The Flyaway Highway*, though less popular, has the same elements and both are enhanced by Lindsay's distinctive illustrations.

The centenary of Lindsay's birth was marked by the publication of his fantasy *Micomicana* (1979), ed. Jane Lindsay; by a collection of his letters (1979), ed. R.G. Howarth and A.W. Barker; and by *The World of Norman Lindsay* (1979), ed. Lin Bloomfield. A collection of his war cartoons 1914–18 was published in 1983, ed. Peter Fullerton. Accounts of Lindsay's life and work include Douglas Stewart's personal memoir (1975), John Hetherington's authorised biography *Norman*

Lindsay: The Embattled Olympian (1973), and Jane Lindsay's *Portrait of Pa* (1973).

LINDSAY, Percy (1870–1952), born Creswick, Victoria, was the eldest son of Robert Lindsay and brother of Norman, Lionel, Daryl and Ruby Lindsay. He studied art at Ballarat and Melbourne and later became a well-known landscape painter, particularly noted for his use of light and for tranquil paintings of trees. He was also a proficient black-and-white artist. From 1918 he lived in Sydney, but during the 1890s he was prominent in Melbourne's intellectual bohemian circles which included his brothers, Norman and Lionel, and such figures as Max Meldrum, Ernest Moffitt and Will Dyson. Renowned for his ebullient, gregarious and genial personality, Percy Lindsay remained a bohemian all his life. His son Peter also became a painter.

LINDSAY, Philip (1906–58), born Sydney, son of Norman Lindsay and brother of Jack Lindsay, was a prolific writer of historical fiction. He tried journalism in Australia before leaving in 1929 for England, where he remained. His first printed book was a collection of verse in a limited edition, *An Affair of Philip Lindsay's* (1925). A writer for film and an acknowledged specialist on medieval England, he wrote over forty historical novels and numerous works of non-fiction, mainly historical biographies. His autobiography, *I'd Live the Same Life Over* (1941), includes reminiscences of other members of the Lindsay family and of several Australian writers such as R.D. Fitzgerald, Kenneth Slessor and P.R. Stephensen. Cressida Lindsay, Philip Lindsay's daughter by his first marriage, is also a novelist.

LINDSAY, Raymond (1903–60), born Melbourne, was the second son of Norman and Kate Lindsay and the brother of Jack and Philip Lindsay. He grew up in Brisbane after the break-up of his parents' marriage and worked for the Brisbane *Courier* before following Jack to Sydney in 1921. In Sydney he studied at Julian Ashton's art school and renewed contact with his father, although unlike Jack he failed to become a disciple and was not involved in the *Vision* school; his bohemian activities during this period are described in Philip Lindsay's *I'd Live the Same Life Over* (1941). He achieved some success as an artist, married the potter Loma Latour, and by the 1930s had acquired respectability; the only one of the three Lindsay brothers to remain in Australia, he made a living from freelance illustration work, reading for publishers, as art critic for the *Daily Telegraph*, and from occasional sales of paintings. His second wife was Joan Skinner. In 1959 Jack Lindsay wrote to his brother seeking background material for his autobiography *The Roaring Twenties* (1962); Raymond Lindsay's extended reply, a graphic account of bohemian life in Sydney between the wars, was published in 1983, titled *A Letter from Sydney*.

LINDSAY, Rose (1885–1978), born Sydney as Rose Soady, was the second wife of Norman Lindsay. After a childhood of some hardship, she began work as an artist's model at the age of 18 and later modelled for many of Lindsay's paintings. They had two children, Jane and Helen. Rose Lindsay wrote two books: *Ma and Pa* (1963), which recounts her childhood experiences as one of a large family, is also a lively picture of Sydney in the 1890s; and *Model Wife* (1967), a collection of reminiscences which includes descriptions of many of the well-known personalities who gathered at the Lindsays' home at Springwood.

LINDSAY, Ruby (1885–1919), born Creswick, Victoria, painter and illustrator, also known as 'Ruby Lind', was the sister of Percy, Lionel, Norman and Daryl Lindsay. For several years before her marriage to Will Dyson in 1909, she studied art in Melbourne, meanwhile contributing drawings and cartoons to the *Hawklet*, the *Lone Hand* and other journals. She left for England with her husband and brother Norman in 1909, and continued to work as a pen-and-ink artist until her death in the influenza epidemic. Her daughter Betty also became a talented artist. Will Dyson's *Poems in Memory of a Wife* (1919) commemorates her personality, as does an introduction to a collection of her drawings published in 1920.

LiNQ (Literature in North Queensland), a quarterly literary journal emanating from James Cook University in Townsville, Queensland, was first published in 1971.

LINTERMANS, Tony (1948–   ), born on a farm in Victoria, has worked as a teacher, speechwriter and editor. He has written for radio and television and has published poetry and short stories in numerous periodicals and anthologies. In 1986 he won the Northern Territory Red Earth Poetry Award, in 1987 the John Shaw Neilsen Poetry Award, the Grenfell Henry Lawson Award, the Harold Kesteven Poetry Prize, the Poetry Day Prize and the *Age* Short Story competition, in 1988 the *Asiaweek* Short Story Prize and in 1991 the Springvale Short Story Competition and the FAW State of Victoria Short Story Award. He has published two collections of poetry, *Inside the Circle* (1979) and *The Shed Manifesto* (1989), and a book for children, *Town Tales* (1981). Lintermans's spare, arresting poems frequently centre on aspects of rural landscapes as starting-points for striking metaphoric insights illuminating and transforming the mundane. His landscapes, sometimes explicitly dependent on the perceiving eye, are vigorously and idiosyncratically alive: in poems which celebrate the mysterious energy of nature ('Nothing moves except mystery, the splendour/ of not knowing what makes this place ache/ beauty'), a creek 'meanders towards oblivion', 'Brown grass dithers on the ridge', or from the top of Mount Hotham 'valleys peel off like pages in a prayer book/ viciously crumpled'. Other poems express the poignant pain of loneliness or lost love, or wittily evoke the wry experience of achieving middle age. One of his best known, 'The Shed Manifesto', reminiscent of Murray's 'Wearing Shorts', and dwelling with loving detail on sheds and their place in male culture, is characteristic in combining imaginative breadth and

concentration on the concrete: 'whatever his car, career, position, a man's shed/ is coagulation, unburdened essence of himself. It is also the shed itself.' Lintermans's short stories, often focusing on urban life, resemble his poems in range, wit and assurance.

Lip, see **Feminism and Australian Literature**

'LISLE, Mary' (1897–1973), born in the Riverina, NSW, lived and farmed at Coonamble after her marriage to D.M. Cornish in 1925. She contributed verse to such periodicals as *Country Life*, the *Bulletin*, *Poetry*, *Southerly*, *Prism* and *Vision*; and published two collections, *The Secret Fire* (1947) and *The Inlander* (1968).

LITCHFIELD, Jessie (1883–1956), born Sydney as Jessie Phillips, was a pupil of Mary Gilmore. In 1908 she married a tin-miner, Valentine Litchfield, and travelled with him in many parts of the Northern Territory until 1917, meanwhile raising seven children. Her reminiscences of ten years of wandering, *Far-North Memories*, were published in 1930. She also contributed poems and short stories to the *Bulletin*, *Age* and *Woman's Mirror*, and was editor of the *Northern Territory Times* in Darwin 1930–42 until the family was evacuated after enemy bombing. She returned to Darwin in 1946 to work as a librarian and in 1951 unsuccessfully contested the Territory's federal seat in parliament as an independent candidate. The Jessie Litchfield Award, established in her will and administered by the Melbourne Bread and Cheese Club, is presented annually to a new and unknown writer. Her biography, which also includes several of her poems, *Jessie Litchfield – Grand Old Lady of the Territory* (1982), was written by her granddaughter, Janet Dickinson.

Literary Awards. The rewarding of Australian writers began soon after the establishment of the first colony when in 1818 Lachlan Macquarie, governor of NSW, awarded Michael Massey Robinson two cows from the government herd for his services as an antipodean 'poet laureate'. Macquarie's decision inaugurated government patronage of Australian literature, and throughout the nineteenth century and even later there are similar instances of support for writers, notably through the creation of employment opportunities in government departments: Henry Kendall, for example, was appointed a government inspector of forests in NSW in 1881, his widow was appointed superintendent of cleaners in a government office in 1884, and Henry Lawson was one of several *Bulletin* authors who found employment in the office of the NSW government statistician, which became known as the *'Bulletin* Bards' Refuge'. But such public or semi-public assistance was at best intermittent and depended upon the personal sympathies of individual politicians or public servants; it was not until the twentieth century that Australian writers began to receive prizes and awards on a regular basis.

There are now more than fifty literary prizes, or types of prizes, awarded regularly (usually annually) in Australia, each falling into one of two main categories. The first and smaller category comprises the awards which *sustain* creative activity, in the sense of supporting a writer during the creation of a work. These awards include some which are available in several fields including literature and journalism, e.g. the Churchill Fellowships awarded by the Winston Churchill Memorial Trust, or the Anzac Fellowships awarded by the NZ government, and others which are restricted to literature. Notable among the latter are the fellowships and other writing grants awarded annually by the Literature Board (q.v.) of the Australia Council. Like its predecessor, the Commonwealth Literary Fund (q.v.), the Literature Board spends a significant amount of its budget on direct assistance to writers, including the provision of pensions and emeritus fellowships and the support of writers-in-residence programmes; it has also funded such prizes as the Children's Book of the Year Award and the National Book Council (qq.v.) awards which began in 1973 and since 1988 have been known as the NBC Banjo Awards, after A.B. Paterson.

The second award category comprises those prizes and awards which *reward* the writer (publisher, illustrator, etc.) for a completed, and usually published, literary work, and includes awards funded or sponsored by governments, e.g. the SA government's Biennial Literature Prizes awarded in conjunction with the Adelaide Festival; by business corporations, e.g. the Shell Book of the Year Award; by newspapers, e.g. the *Age* Book of the Year Awards (q.v.); by publishers, e.g. Angus & Robertson and the Australian Book Publishers' Association Book Design Awards; by writers' groups, e.g. the FAW which administers and/or funds more than a dozen awards; by educational institutions, e.g. the Foundation for Australian Literary Studies; by miscellaneous organisations, e.g. the ANA's Award, the Winton Tourist Promotion Association's Bronze Swagman Award; and by individuals, e.g. the Grace Leven Poetry Prize (q.v.) awarded under the will of 'William Baylebridge'. A third category comprises the awards or prizes received by Australian writers from overseas sources, including the Booker McConnell Prize awarded to Thomas Keneally in 1982 for *Schindler's Ark*, the Canada-Australia Literary Award and in 1992 the NZ-Australia literary award which includes reciprocal visits and a cash prize. The Commonwealth Writers' Prize was established by the Commonwealth Foundation in 1987 in association with the Book Trust and the Overseas League. It was first won by an Australian in 1990 – Robert Drewe for the *The Bay of Contented Men*. The most important is the Nobel Prize awarded to Patrick White for *The Eye of the Storm* in 1973. White used the Nobel Prize money to establish a trust which administers the Patrick White Award, usually given to an older writer of distinction whose work is deemed to have been given insufficient recognition. Other writers to have funded awards are Miles Franklin and 'Baylebridge'. Among writers to have awards named after them are 'Rolf Boldrewood', Alan Marshall, Anne Elder, Mary Gilmore, A.B. Paterson, C.J. Dennis, Christopher Brennan, 'Steele Rudd', and John Shaw Neilson (qq.v.). There are also a number of defunct awards, e.g. the S.H. Prior (q.v.)

Memorial Prize and the Encyclopaedia Britannica Awards, and others which have been awarded intermittently, e.g. by the *Sydney Morning Herald*.

Although the direct assistance provided by the Literature Board covers all forms of creative literature, most Australian awards and prizes carry more specific restrictions, which range from those which demand an Australian subject or theme, e.g. *Age* Book of the Year; to those which are restricted within genre, e.g. the Miles Franklin Award (q.v.) for a published novel, the Bronze Swagman Award for bush verse; to those which carry age, occupational, ethnic or other restrictions, e.g. the Patrick White Award, the Blackbooks Award for Aboriginal writers, illustrators and publishers. Similarly, there is a wide range in value of the prizes regularly awarded for individual works. Among the richest are the *Australian*/Vogel National Literary Award; the most prestigious include the *Age* Book of the Year, the Children's Book of the Year, the Miles Franklin Award, the National Book Council Awards, the NSW Premier's Literary Awards retitled the NSW State Literary Awards from 1988, and thereafter to be named in honour of Christina Stead, Douglas Stewart and Kenneth Slessor, the SA government's Biennial Literature Prizes, the Victorian Premier's Literary Awards begun by John Cain in 1985, the fiction and non-fiction awards celebrating Vance and Nettie Palmer, the WA Premier's Awards, first presented in 1991, and the Gold Medal of the Australian Literature Society now awarded by ASAL. The ACT Literary Award was upgraded in 1993 to $20 000, allowing for publication of a biennial anthology of writers from the ACT, and $5000 for the ACT Book of the Year Award for a book published by a Canberra author. Some of the most important literary awards are described elsewhere in this volume, usually under their titles, e.g. the Miles Franklin Award. Information on new awards and the winners of existing ones is provided regularly in such journals as *Australian Author*, *Notes & Furphies* and *Southerly*. Nicole Strang edited *Australian Literary Awards & Fellowships* (1991).

Literary Criterion, a prominent Indian quarterly journal of English studies edited by C.D. Narasimhaiah, has on two occasions been devoted exclusively to Australian literature (1964, 1980). On both occasions the issues were reprinted as *An Introduction to Australian Literature* (1965, 1982) edited by Narasimhaiah.

Literary Guide to Australia, see **Oxford Literary Guide to Australia**

Literary News (1) was an early Sydney weekly journal which was published for six months 1837–38 and included sketches and poetry. Its proprietor, James Tegg, edited the journal in conjunction with William à Beckett.

Literary News (2) was a Melbourne weekly journal which ran for just over a year 1882–83. Avoiding politics, it focused on literature, theatre, art and science, and included reviews of books and theatrical productions, poetry, short stories, serials and literary news from Australia and overseas. Two notable contributors were 'Australie' (Emily Manning) and 'Australienne' (Frances Holden), the latter a contributor to other literary journals and active in social reform and women's rights.

Literature and Aesthetics, the annual journal of the Sydney Society of Literature and Aesthetics, commenced publication in 1991, its policy to include 'not only papers in philosophical aesthetics on any or all of the arts', but also papers on literature and literary theory. It also includes poems, short fiction, essays and black-and-white art.

Literature Board, one of the three art-form boards which form part of, and are responsible to, the Australia Council (q.v.), was established in 1973; it comprises eight members including a chairman (the first was Geoffrey Blainey), who normally serve for four years and include representatives from different regions within Australia and of a variety of literary interests. It also has a Grants Committee, a Community Access Assessment Committee, a Literary Magazines Assessment Committee and a Writing for Performance Assessment Committee. The Literature Board dispenses federal government support to literature and took over the functions of the Commonwealth Literary Fund (q.v.) but with a greatly increased budget: the first full allocation of the Literature Board was four times that of the final budget ($300 000) of the CLF. With increased funding, the Literature Board has been able, particularly in its early years, to broaden the support to Australian literature provided by the CLF, although assistance is offered in the same four areas: direct assistance to writers through the provision of pensions, now replaced by emeritus fellowships, and several types of fellowships and grants to established and developing writers; assistance to publishers through a per-page subsidy for approved titles; assistance to literary journals; and assistance in a wide variety of promotional activities including grants to festivals, associations and educational institutions. The Board is committed to the pursuit of excellence and to the fostering of creative literature, although it also supports non-fiction. The greatest proportion of its allocation goes in direct assistance to writers, and its innovations in this area include emeritus fellowships (pensions); longer-term fellowships (Category A of up to four years for writers of substantial achievement and shorter, Category B, fellowships for developing writers); writers' projects grants and grants to educational institutions for writer-in-residence programmes, and specific type projects such as Asian/Pacific writing fellowships and Art and Working Life fellowships. Other notable aspects of its activities have been the promotion of Australian literature overseas and the development of the Public Lending Right scheme. Martin Johnston's novel *Cicada Gambit*, published in 1984, was the thousandth title to be published with the assistance of the Board. By 1987 1000 writers had been assisted with grants and more than $20 million disbursed. Thomas

Shapcott (q.v.), who served as the Board's director 1983–90, published *The Literature Board: A Brief History* (1988).

Literature in New South Wales (1866), by George Burnett Barton (q.v.), is one of the first substantial assessments of the development of literature in the colony. Although Barton states that Australia is too young to possess a national literature, he attempts a detailed account and critical assessment of the whole body of indigenous writing. He finds that in every field of letters the colony has produced something of value and in many instances there is evidence of 'undoubted genius'. In some areas, especially poetry, fiction and exploration narrative, he sees the 'rough groundwork' of a national literature laid. The remarkably wide-ranging and perceptive survey covers newspapers, periodicals, poetry, fiction, oratory, history, biography, travel writings, philology, physical science, geography, law and theology. Both *Literature in New South Wales* and its companion volume, *The Poets and Prose Writers of New South Wales* (q.v., 1866), were commissioned for the Paris Exhibition of 1867.

Literature of Australia, The, an influential collection of critical essays edited by Geoffrey Dutton, was published by Penguin Books in 1964 and in a second edition in 1976. The collections include general essays on such topics as the social setting, poetry, fiction and drama; essays on selected individual writers; and detailed bibliographies. The collections were succeeded by *The Penguin New Literary History of Australia* (q.v., 1988), edited by Laurie Hergenhan.

Literature of Western Australia, The (1979), edited by Bruce Bennett, is a volume in the Western Australian Sesquicentenary Celebrations series. It contains descriptive rather than definitive discussions of diaries, letters, journals, fiction, poetry, drama, children's books, newspapers and literary journalism. Its contributors include Peter Cowan, Veronica Brady, Nicholas Hasluck, Fay Zwicky, Bill Dunstone, Barbara Buick, Maxine Walker, Bill Bunbury and Don Grant.

Little Company, The, a novel by Eleanor Dark (q.v.), was published in 1945. Set in wartime Sydney, it deals mainly with the experience of Gilbert Massey, a middle-aged bookseller and author of leftist political inclination. After an unhappy childhood dominated by his father William Massey, a sanctimonious religious hypocrite, Gilbert has drifted into marriage with their housekeeper's daughter Phyllis Miller, a similarly sanctimonious self-martyr. Gilbert's now hearty dislike of Phyllis is shared by Marty, his vehemently feminist sister who is also an author, and by Nick his younger brother, a voluble Marxist. Of the Masseys' two daughters, Virginia and Prue, Gilbert is closer to Prue, the flippant Virginia having slipped into a life of promiscuity. An important relationship in both Gilbert's and Marty's youth has been that with the now dead Scott Laughlin, an unsuccessful Labor candidate. Deserted by his wife Denny for Jerrold

Kay, a celebrated cartoonist, Laughlin had died early, as had his daughter Janet, Marty's close friend. The union of Denny and Jerrold produced a daughter, Elsa Kay, who becomes involved in an unsatisfactory love affair with Gilbert; Elsa had been brought up by her mother to regard the Laughlin family as a destructive influence. Against the background of national insecurity, Gilbert and Marty, both afflicted with a 'creative paralysis', struggle with their individual insecurities. Although the affair with Elsa soon comes to an end, Gilbert finds it releases his creative block and he begins a novel about Scott Laughlin. His relationship with Phyllis, which deteriorates still further after the death of Virginia from a complicated pregnancy, reaches its nadir when Phyllis unsuccessfully attempts suicide. At the close of the novel she is temporarily confined to a nursing home, and life for the Masseys resumes what normality it can in abnormal times.

LITTLE, William (1839–1916), born Cumberland, England, arrived in the Colony in 1851. He was mayor of Ballarat in the 1890s; he used the pseudonym 'Lambda' for two works of fiction, *The Trinity of Man* (1896) and *Visit to Topos* (1897), and numerous booklets of verse including *Reveries* (1896), *A Dream of Paradise* (1904) and *Sonnets by Lambda* (1908).

LITTLEJOHN, Agnes, a regular contributor of short stories and verse to the *Sydney Mail* and the *Sydney Morning Herald* from before the First World War until the 1930s, published several works of fiction and collections of verse 1907–39. Described in reviews of the time as graceful, charming, spontaneous and fluent, her work has now more historical than literary value, reflecting in its willed floweriness very conventional, imported notions of beauty. Her fiction includes *The Daughter of a Soldier* (1907), *A Lapse of Memory* (1909), *Mirage of the Desert* (1910), *The Breath of India* (1914), *The Silver Road* (1915), *Star Dust and Sea Spray* (1918), *Rainbow Dreams* (1919), *The Sleeping Sea-Nymph* (1921), *The Lost Emerald* (1924) and *The Pipes o' Pan* (1939). Her verse was published under the following titles: *Verses* (1914), *Poems* (1915), *Patriotic Poems* (1915), *War Poems* (1916), *Lyrics and Lyrical Prose* (1927), *Lyrics and Mystic Sketches* (1928), *The Lady of the Doves* (1929), *The Guardian of the Gate* (1933), *The Unforgotten Watch* (1935), *Drowsy Hours* (1936) and *Lighthouse Keepers* (1938).

LIVERANI, Mary Rose (1939–), born Glasgow, the daughter of a ship's rigger, came to Australia at the age of 13 when her family migrated to Wollongong, NSW. In *The Winter Sparrows: Growing Up in Scotland and Australia* (1975), she vividly re-creates her early years in the Glasgow slums and her experiences in Australia until the time she left school. The book has been acclaimed as a landmark in Australia's migrant literature.

LIVERMORE, Reg (1938–), born Parramatta, is a well-known actor, singer, dancer and female impersonator. He began his career at the Phillip Street Revue Theatre in Sydney and after a period at the

Ensemble, of which he was a foundation member, worked with the State Theatre companies in Victoria, SA and NSW. After collaborating in the writing of such musical shows as 'The Good Ship Walter Raleigh' (1962), 'West of the Black Stump' (1965), 'Gone Potty' (1969) and 'Lasseter' (1971), and independently writing the rock musical 'Ned Kelly' (1978), Livermore devised a series of one-man shows which have given scope to his individual, abrasive, energetic style. They include 'Betty Blokkbuster Follies', 'Wonder Woman', 'Sacred Cow', 'Son of Betty' and 'Firing Squad'. Occasionally compared to Barry Humphries in the range of personae that he presents and his interpretation of female identities, Livermore is a less specifically Australian satirist.

LLEWELLYN, Kate (1940–), born Tumby Bay, SA, has worked as a registered nurse and joint owner/director of an art gallery and now lives at Leura in the Blue Mountains region of NSW, where she writes full-time. The mother of three children, she became a writer after first undertaking university study in 1970. She has contributed verse and prose to numerous periodicals and anthologies, including *Sisters Poets 1* (1979), and has published five books of poetry, *Trader Kate and the Elephants* (1982, joint winner of the Anne Elder Award for poetry), *Luxury* (1985), *Honey* (1988), *Figs* (1990) and *Selected Poems* (1992); and the prose works *The Waterlily* (1987), *Dear You* (1988), *The Mountain* (1989) and *Angels & Dark Madonnas* (1991). With Susan Hampton she edited the anthology, *The Penguin Book of Australian Women Poets* (1986). Llewellyn's verse has a distinctive direct voice that is rueful, sensual and witty, whether interpreting familiar classical myths from a contemporary, feminist perspective or reflecting on the minutiae of everyday existence. Unafraid of the physical aspects of life and often frankly earthy about female sexuality, her verse celebrates the arrival and departure of love, childbirth and childhood, the familiarity become strangeness of parent–child relationships, foreign cities, gardening and simple natural phenonema which suggest the complexities of human experience. A journal of one year of her life at Leura (1985–86), *The Waterlily* describes a range of experiences from the trivial to the traumatic, both of which are made richly significant. *Dear You*, partly a sequel to *The Waterlily* and partly an erotic novel, is written in the form of letters to a lover abroad. Writing about 'the immense trivialities that make up the profound truths of our lives', the protagonist of *Dear You* is a middle-aged feminist who is passionate about every aspect of her life – her work, her garden, her love – and who is brutally honest about her feelings and disappointments. Llewellyn has remarked that her life 'is simply the paddock I plough when I write. I do it, not because it is unique or from a sense of my own importance, but rather because it is held in common with the lives of other women in this place and this time. It is its commonality that I value'. Loss and a sense of vulnerability are undoubtedly elements of that commonality as the third volume in her autobiographical trilogy, *The Mountain*, written in the form of letters to her daughter Caro, demonstrates.

Angels & Dark Madonnas is the journal of her travels in India and Italy, recorded with the same direction and freshness of perception.

LLOYD, A.L. (Albert Lancaster) (1908–), born London, was the son of folk-singers who had died by the time he came to Australia in the middle 1920s. Over the next eight or nine years Lloyd worked mainly in the bush in NSW, learning a number of folk-songs and ballads in the years before the revival of interest in Australian folk-music after the Second World War. From 1950 Lloyd worked as a freelance folklorist and ethnomusicologist, paying a return visit to Australia in 1970 to lecture and perform. His major interest and writing was in British and European music, but he made a number of albums of Australian folk-songs, including *The Banks of the Condamine* (1957) and *Across the Western Plains* (1958), and helped establish songs like 'Flash Jack from Gundagai', 'The Euabalong Ball' and 'The Lime-Juice Tub' within the canon of Australian folk-song and ballad.

LLOYD, Anne, see **Feminism and Australian Literature**

LLOYD, Jessie (1843–85), born Jessie Bell, near Launceston, lived on stations near Gunnedah and Coonamble after her marriage to George A. Lloyd, later a NSW politician. Jessie Lloyd, using the pseudonym 'Silverleaf', began writing short stories, essays and poems in 1878 for such periodicals as the *Echo*, the *Illustrated Sydney News* and the *Sydney Mail*. She also published three novels, *The Wheel of Life* (1880); 'All Aboard', which was serialised in the *Echo* in 1879; and 'Retribution', serialised in the *Illustrated Sydney News* 1884–85. In 1881–82 she contributed a regular series on various aspects of bush and station life, titled the 'Silverleaf Papers', to the *Illustrated Sydney News*. The mother of four children, two of whom received a boarding-school education on the proceeds of her writing, Jessie Lloyd wrote in an easy, graceful way on the aspects of outback life which were likely to have a general appeal. Joan McKenzie has written her biography, *Silverleaf, the story of Jessie Lloyd* (1986). Patricia Clarke includes an account of her life and work in *Pen Portraits* (1988).

'Loaded Dog, The', by Henry Lawson (q.v.), is probably the best-known short story in Australian literature, a standard children's favourite and anthology piece. One of the Dave Regan sequence, it chronicles the misadventures of Dave and his mates, Andy Page and Jim Bently, after they make a cartridge in order to blast fish from a waterhole. Their dog, Tommy, retrieves the cartridge, accidentally sets the fuse alight at their camp-fire, and then follows them in turn as they desperately try to escape his attentions. Eventually Tommy pursues Dave to a nearby shanty and drops the cartridge when molested by the resident cattledog, a vicious creature, which is blown to pieces. The story was written in 1900 and published in *Joe Wilson and His Mates* (1901).

LOCH, Frederick (1889–1954), who worked as a farmer in Gippsland in his early years, served at Gallipoli in the First World War and wrote, under the pseudonym 'Sydney de Loghe', a novel about his experiences, *The Straits Impregnable* (1916). After marrying Joice Nankivell (q.v.) he spent eighteen months in Ireland 1920–21 as a freelance journalist before volunteering to serve with Quaker relief units in Poland. The Lochs settled in Greece 1923–39, combining work for refugees with writing, worked for Polish refugees in Bulgaria and Romania 1939–44, and returned to Greece after the war. Loch wrote two further novels under his pseudonym, *Pelican Pool* (1917) and *One Crowded Hour* (1918), and another under his real name, *Three Predatory Women* (1925). With his wife he wrote two descriptive books, *Ireland in Travail* (1922) and *The River of a Hundred Ways* (1924). Some of his experiences are described in Joice Nankivell's autobiography, *A Fringe of Blue* (1968).

LOCK, Arnold Charles Cooper (1897/8–1965), an Adelaide author and an officer of the PMG who subsequently transferred to Queensland, wrote seven novels under the pseudonym 'Charles Cooper'. They include *The Turkish Spy* (1932) and *Reflected Glory* (1934), both of which are war novels, the first dealing with Australians in the Middle East and the second set in France; *Satan's Mercy* (1934), *The Soul of Tak-Ming* (1935), *By Command of Yee-Shing* (1937), *Hong Kong Mystery* (1938) and *West in the East* (1941). Under his real name, Lock wrote several books which reflect his extensive travels in Australia including *Tropics and Topics* (1949), *People We Met* (1950), *Travels Across Australia* (1952), *Destination Barrier Reef* (1955) and *Tropical Tapestry; From Capricorn to Cape York* (1956).

LOCKE, Sumner (Helena Sumner Locke Elliott) (1881–1917), born Sandgate, Brisbane, who died the day after the birth of her son, the playwright and novelist Sumner Locke Elliott (q.v.), was herself a playwright and novelist. In 1908 her play, 'The Vicissitudes of Vivienne', was produced in Melbourne, but her reputation was more firmly established with the popular Mum Dawson books sketching selection life: *Mum Dawson, Boss* (1911), staged by Bert Bailey in 1917, and *The Dawsons' Uncle George* (1912). In both, Mum is a female version of 'Steele Rudd's' Dad Rudd (see Rudd Family) and presides as matriarch over a family of yokels whose misadventures are humorously portrayed. The success of the Dawson books prompted another selection volume, *Skeeter Farm Takes a Spell* (1915), although Locke's last novel, *Samaritan Mary* (1916), is set in the USA where she lived during part of the First World War. *In Memoriam Sumner Locke* (1921) contains poems by Sumner Locke and verse tributes which attest to her popularity. As Sinden Marriott, 'Dear One', she is an important presence in her son's novel *Careful, He Might Hear You* (q.v., 1963) and as Sidney in his *Waiting for Childhood* (1987), which also draws on the history of her family.

LOCKWOOD, Douglas (1918–80), born Natimuk, Victoria, joined the Melbourne *Herald* in 1940. Sent to Darwin in 1942, he witnessed the bombing of the city before serving with the AIF in New Guinea and the Solomons and as a war correspondent in the South Pacific. In 1946 he returned to Darwin, where he remained until 1968 apart from a two-year stay in London. Managing editor of the *Herald*-owned *South Pacific Post* in Port Moresby 1968–71, he was editorial manager and then manager of the *Herald* in Melbourne 1971–73 and managing editor of the *Bendigo Advertiser* from 1975. He wrote numerous books on Darwin and the people and way of life of the Northern Territory, including *Crocodiles and Other People* (1959); *Fair Dinkum* (1960); *Life on the Daly River* (1961, with Nancy Polishuk); *I, the Aboriginal* (1962), a biography of a Northern Territory Aborigine, which won the *Advertiser* Prize; *We, the Aborigines* (1963); *The Shady Tree* (1963, with Bill Harney); *Up the Track* (1964); *The Lizard Eaters* (1964); *Australia's Pearl Harbour: Darwin 1942* (1966); *Northern Territory Sketchbook* (1968, with Ainslie Roberts); *The Front Door* (1968), a history of Darwin 1869–1969; and *My Old Mates and I* (1979). Lockwood also won the London *Evening News* Award in 1957 and the Walkley Award in 1958.

LOEWALD, Uyen (1940–), born Vietnam, experienced life under the Japanese, the Chinese, the Viet Minh and the French and was imprisoned for six months without trial during the Diem regime. In 1964 she married an American diplomat and accompanied him in 1965 to the USA, where she helped in the compilation of the army handbook for Vietnam and taught Vietnamese at the CIA language school in Washington. In 1970 she and her husband migrated to Australia where she has worked as a caterer and chef and has been a member of the Multicultural Arts Advisory Committee of the Australia Council. She has written short fiction and poetry for periodicals and anthologies and an autobiography, *Child of Vietnam* (1987). The latter describes the vicissitudes of her life in Vietnam during the country's succeeding political upheavals and her struggle to survive hunger, hardship of various forms and humiliation.

LOGAN, Patrick (1791–1830) was a Scots-born soldier and explorer who came to NSW in 1825 and was appointed later that year as commandant of the penal station at Moreton Bay; he was harsh in his treatment of the convicts, and is presented as a tyrant in the folk-song 'Moreton Bay' (q.v.). Killed by Aborigines, possibly encouraged by the Moreton Bay convicts, Logan is the subject of Charles Bateson's biography *Patrick Logan* (1966), Jessica Anderson's novel *The Commandant* (1975) and Thomas Shapcott's poem 'Portrait of Captain Logan'.

LOHREY, Amanda (1947–), born Hobart, grew up in Battery Point near the waterfront; her father, grandfather and great uncle were waterside workers with strong union loyalties. Lohrey was educated at the University of Tasmania before accepting a scholarship to Cambridge University, although she did not complete her course there. She has worked as a research officer and a visiting lecturer at the University of Technology, Sydney, and is married to a Tasmanian politician, Andrew Lohrey. She has published two novels, *The Morality of Gentlemen* (1984) and *The Reading Group* (1988). Publication of *The Reading Group* led to a libel action by Senator Terry Aulich in 1989, subsequently settled out of court, and the pulping of 1,000 unsold copies, events which aroused debate and some strong protests from the literary community; the novel was reissued several months afterwards. An unusual fictionalised study of a waterfront industrial dispute of the 1950s, the Hursey case, *The Morality of Gentlemen* uses Brechtian strategies to present different perspectives; well paced and planned, the novel uncovers the personal roots of much outwardly disinterested political activity and the discrepancy between actual events and issues and public perceptions of them. Set in an unnamed Australian city suffering a fierce heatwave, which has contributed to the ring of bushfires in the surrounding hills, *The Reading Group* presents a bleak vision of Australia's future as a country starkly divided between the 'haves' and the 'have nots', but distracted by a political circus from confronting the unpleasant realities; the divisions are most starkly imaged in the contrast between the pretentious but unfinished plaza in the city's centre and the human jungle which is 'off-Plaza'. Although the nation's political structure embraces such sinister institutions as the Committee of Public Safety and the New Emergency Powers, the political realities are left vague, reflecting the apathy and ignorance of the main characters. The plot is structured around what was once a left-wing reading group which is still loosely united by social, professional and family ties, but the idealism which had earlier fired its eight members is now dissipated, replaced by confusion, apathy and self-distracting pursuits; *The Reading Group* differs from Orwell's and Huxley's political novels in that it projects social and political evil into the present rather than the future and exposes its frivolous, mundane roots, although like them it evokes the involuntary way in which ordinary people are drawn to accede to repugnant policies.

London Aphrodite, a periodical edited by Jack Lindsay and P.R. Stephensen and published in London by the Fanfrolico Press, ran for a planned six issues 1928–29. Named as a rebuttal of the conservatism of J.C. Squire's *London Mercury*, it was committed to the same aesthetic attitudes as *Vision*. Some prominent English authors, including Aldous Huxley, contributed, although the majority were Australian. Jack Lindsay, the dominant force, used the pseudonym 'Peter Meadows' for several articles. Other Australian contributors were Norman Lindsay, Hugh McCrae, Kenneth Slessor, Philip Lindsay, Brian Penton, P.R. Stephensen, Les Robinson, W.J. Turner, Bertram Higgins, E.J. Rupert Atkinson and Edith Hepburn ('Anna Wickham').

LONDON, Joan (1948–), born Perth, graduated from the University of WA, lives in Fremantle, has taught English as a second language and is a bookseller. Her first book of short stories, *Sister Ships* (1986), won that year's *Age* Book of the Year Award. Another collection, *Letter to Constantine*, was published in 1993. *Sister Ships* contains eight stories, the title story relating the experiences of three recently matriculated schoolgirls on a voyage to England, and with 'First Night' focuses on the turbulence that adolescence brings. 'Lilies' and 'The Girls Love Each Other', with its background of gossip from a hairdressing salon, concern relationships between mothers and daughters. *Letter to Constantine*, quietly controlled and understated, probes relationships and analyses mental states with a subtle irony that hints at more than it reveals. 'Maisie Goes to India', for example, links the personal and cultural in an absorbing mix.

Lone Hand, an illustrated monthly modelled on the London *Strand* magazine, was published in two series in unbroken sequence 1907–21. A journal which remained under the control of the *Bulletin* for most of its life, the *Lone Hand* was planned by J.F. Archibald who gave it the name he had originally wished to confer on the *Bulletin*. After Archibald's mental collapse in 1906 delayed publication of the first issue, Frank Fox took over as editor 1907–9; he was followed by A.H. Adams (1909–11), Bertram Stevens (1912–19) and Walter Jago (1919–21). Major contributors included Randolph Bedford, Will and Edward Dyson, Mabel Forrest, Norman Lindsay, Ernest O'Ferrall, Rod Quinn and Adams himself. The *Lone Hand* was a success in its early years (its first issue of 50 000 sold out in three days, and its second in one) and was responsible for such innovations in journalism as the beauty contest and columns by famous people. Its decline was attributed to increasing competition after the First World War, evidenced by the departure of Jago to edit the rival, *Aussie*. Cyril Hannaford compiled an index to the *Lone Hand* for the period 1907–13 in 1967, and Kit Taylor *A History with Indexes of the Lone Hand, the Australian Monthly* (1977).

LONG, Gavin (1901–68), born Foster, Victoria, was the son of George Long, Bishop of Bathurst and later Newcastle, and the founder of the Australian Army's education service. Educated at the University of Sydney, Gavin Long worked first as a teacher and then as a journalist for the Sydney *Daily Guardian*, the *Argus* and the *Sydney Morning Herald*. Attached to the British expeditionary force in France as correspondent for Australian morning newspapers, he also covered the war in Libya and Greece as officially accredited correspondent for the AIF. He was recalled to Australia in 1941 and made two visits to New Guinea. In 1943 he was appointed general editor of the official history *Australia in the War of 1939–45* (q.v.). Of the 22-volume history, Long wrote three himself, *To Benghazi* (1952), *Greece, Crete and Syria* (1953) and *The Final Campaigns* (1963), and his wartime diaries and notes were widely used in the writing of the Service volumes of the history. In 1963 Long resigned as general editor to become a research fellow at the ANU. He also wrote a one-volume history of Australian par-

ticipation in the Second World War, *The Six Years War* (1973), and a study of General Douglas Macarthur as military commander (1969). An unpretentious but painstaking historian, Long presented a systematic, balanced account of events in a factual, fluent style.

Long Odds, Marcus Clarke's (q.v.) first novel, was serialised in the *Colonial Monthly* 1868–69 and revised for publication in book form (1869); the serial version, which was issued as *Heavy Odds* in 1896, includes two instalments written by G.A. Walstab. Set almost entirely in England, *Long Odds* recounts the tragedy of Cyril Chatteris, who makes an unfortunate marriage with Carry Manton while in disfavour with his father, Saville Chatteris. After the death of his elder brother, Cyril becomes the family heir, conceals the marriage and becomes engaged to his cousin, Kate Ffrench, but the truth is discovered by Rupert Dacre. Cyril plots to rid himself of Carry by compromising her with Dacre, but their planned elopement enrages him and he murders Dacre after Dacre's victory in a House of Commons election for which they are both candidates. With the truth revealed to Kate and Saville, Kate marries Bob Calverley, a member of the squattocracy who is visiting England, loses money gambling and is duped by Dacre into buying a poorly performing racehorse against which Dacre and his cronies bet heavily. Bob hears of the plot and foils it, wins a race at 'long odds' which recovers his fortune, and takes Kate back to Australia to his new station, where Cyril turns up in the last chapter as a dying swagman.

Long Prospect, The, a novel by Elizabeth Harrower (q.v.), was published in 1958. Emily Lawrence, on the edge of adolescence, has lived with her twice-widowed grandmother, Lilian, at Ballowra since she was 4. Her parents, both colourless, unimaginative individuals, have drifted apart, Harry to manage in the outback, Paula to run a hat shop in Sydney. An eventual reconciliation is likely, however, as they share a Hollywood concept of marriage. Lilian, a vulgar, insensitive, domineering woman, is more interested in her own complicated love life than in her granddaughter and Emily is conscious that her life is as bleak and featureless as the industrial town of Ballowra. The one previous bright period in her experience, stemming from her relationship with one of Lilian's boarders, a young woman, Thea, had ended with Thea's departure. Emily, aware of being inwardly alienated from her parents, her grandmother and her grandmother's friends, particularly dislikes Mr Rosen, her grandmother's sycophantic suitor. Neither her school friends nor Dotty, the kindly 'daily help', can provide the stimulating companionship she seeks. When Lilian takes in another boarder, Max, a scientist who also happens to be Thea's old lover, Emily's life changes dramatically. Max treats her as an individual, introduces her to books and music and provides her with someone to love. Although Max grows increasingly and uneasily aware that he cannot stay in Ballowra, their relationship is terminated unpleasantly and abruptly. Disaster ensues when Rosen and another of Lilian's friends, Billie Duncan, both of whom have suffered recent humiliations, find gratification in implying that there is a sexual relationship between Max and Emily. Lilian is privately unconvinced but their innuendoes coincide with her desire to exert her supremacy. She calls in Paula and Harry as reinforcements, and Max leaves after an unpleasant scene. The experience ironically unites the parents and three months later Emily, still mourning her loss of Max, moves to live with them in their sterile new flat in Sydney. Later, however, she realises that the experience has been valuable: 'she was responsible for her actions. What had been amorphous and unreliable in her seemed, now, to be solid'.

LONG, Richard (1873–1948), born England, was brought to Australia at the age of 5 and settled at Sandringham, Melbourne. A ship's carpenter and joiner, he was a member of the Socialist Party of Victoria, the Free Religious Fellowship and the Australian Peace Alliance and was familiar with such prominent individuals as John Cain, Adela Pankhurst, Marie Pitt, Bernard O'Dowd and Frederick Sinclaire. From 1911 he began contributing verse and articles to the *Socialist* and later verse to *Fellowship* and *Birth*, some of which was reprinted in his one collection, *Verses* (1917), with a foreword by Sinclaire.

LONGBOTTOM, Audrey, born Coramba, a small north-coast town near Coffs Harbour, NSW, began to write poetry and prose after attending the University of Wollongong as a mature-age student. She has published three groups of poems, *Relatives and Reliques* (1979), *Replay* (in *Trillium*, 1983) and *The Solitary Islands* (1986), which contains most of the poems from *Replay*. *Relatives and Reliques* has five sections, 'Under Mount Keira', '10 Mins from Shops', 'Traveller's Tales', 'Conditioned Response' and 'Relatives and Reliques'. It contains, as does *The Solitary Islands*, poems of personal experience, reflections on and reminiscences about life and people. There is a nostalgic, occasionally acerbic and regretful tone in poems such as 'Reflections', 'You Can See how the Town's Come On', 'After Taste' and 'Character Piece'. In general, however, her treatment of people, the past and the contemporary scene, is benign, such criticism being tempered by gentle humour and quiet understanding. She won the Grenfell Henry Lawson Award for verse in 1981.

LONGFORD, Raymond Hollis (1878–1959), born Melbourne as John Walter Longford, later adopted the name Raymond Hollis. He went to sea before becoming an actor with various companies in Australia and NZ. After acting in three films produced by Charles Cozens Spencer in 1911, he directed several films for Spencer, beginning with *The Fatal Wedding* (1911), and became one of the most innovative of Australian film directors. Although he found it difficult to get continuity of work, he directed more than thirty silent films, including *The Romantic Story of Margaret Catchpole* (1911), *Sweet Nell of Old Drury* (1911), *The Midnight Wedding* (1912), *Australia Calls* (1913), *The Silence of Dean Maitland* (1914), *The Mutiny of the Bounty*

(1916), *The Sentimental Bloke* (1919), *On Our Selection* (1920), *The Blue Mountains Mystery* (1921) and *The Dinkum Bloke* (1923), of which only *The Sentimental Bloke* and *On Our Selection* have survived as complete copies. After reaching his peak in the 1920s, Longford was employed only in minor productions as associate director or actor by the 1930s and finally broke with the film industry, spending his last years as a night watchman. During his most creative years he was closely associated with Lottie Lyell (1890–1925), who worked variously as actress, writer, co-director and co-producer. The Australian film industry now presents an annual award in Longford's name for outstanding work in cinema.

LONGSTAFF, Sir John (1861–1941), born Clunes, Victoria, studied art in Paris from 1887, returning to Australia in 1895 where he became a leading portrait-artist. He won the Archibald Prize in 1925, 1928, 1929, 1931 and 1935, the last for a portrait of A.B. Paterson. Well known among his paintings are the portrait of Henry Lawson in the NSW Art Gallery, *Burke and Wills* in the National Gallery of Victoria and *Breaking the News* in the WA Art Gallery. The April 1931 number of *Art in Australia* was given over to his work; Nina Murdoch published *Portrait in Youth of Sir John Longstaff* (1948).

LORD, Gabrielle (1946–   ), born Sydney, was educated at the universities of Sydney and New England, gaining an honours degree in arts. She worked as a Commonwealth employment officer for nine years, but a Literature Board grant in 1978 allowed her to write *Fortress* (1980), the first of a group of thriller-mystery novels which have established her reputation in that genre. With the sale of the film rights of *Salt* (1990) she has been able to write full-time, turning her attention to scripts for screen and television as well as novels. Her fiction includes *Short Stories of Marcel Ayme* (1980), *Fortress* (1980), *Tooth and Claw* (1983), *Jumbo* (1986), *Salt* (1990) and *Whipping Boy* (1992). She has also written six episodes (1987–88) for the television series *Last Resort* and co-authored an account of her convent education, *Growing up Catholic* (1986).

Lord's first novel, *Fortress*, tells of a two-day ordeal by country schoolteacher Sally Jones and her twelve Sunny Flat pupils when they are abducted and held for ransom by four city hoodlums and petty criminals. The story has its basis in a similar real-life incident involving teacher Mary Gibb and her pupils in Victoria some years earlier. Terrified at first, the teacher and her pupils gradually weld into a resourceful team determined to thwart the villains. They escape twice and are recaptured but when the kidnappers dwindle to two, teacher and children hide in a cave which they turn into a 'fortress' and dispatch the last two villains in a bloodthirsty finale. *Tooth and Claw* is a suspense thriller where an innocent woman, Beth, and her dog Sam, living on a lonely farm, are pitted against a vengeful former employer who is looking for heroin hidden on the farm by the woman's dead husband. *Jumbo* links the fortunes of discontented teacher Verity Unicombe with her former student, teenager Lisa

Brand, who is driven to despair and ultimately suicide by her inability to find work and by her pessimism about the future for herself and others like the three small Hennessy children whom she babysits part-time. *Salt*, a futuristic thriller, is set in Australia in 2075. Lovers Sando and Hedda, looking for Sando's former mentor, venture out of the walled city of Sydney into the environmental and social wasteland that the rest of the country has become – a wasteland devastated by salt pollution, soil erosion, radiation, illicit experiments with bacteriological weapons, genetic engineering, organ banks and political corruption. *Whipping Boy*, a violent, fast-paced thriller, has lawyer Cass Meredith involved in investigating a paedophile ring in Sydney, a task that leads her and her 8-year-old son into jeopardy. As with all her fiction, *Whipping Boy* blends realistic characterisation with a complex, ingenious plot, a combination that has brought Gabrielle Lord an enthusiastic readership.

LORIMER, Philip Durham (1843–97), born Madras, India, was a Scotsman who migrated to Sydney in 1861, worked mainly as an overlander in Queensland in the 1860s, and in the 1870s became a swagman poet known to many as 'Old Phil the Poet'. He spent much of his time wandering in outback NSW and Victoria, repaying the hospitality of diggers, bush workers, station owners and newspaper editors with extempore verse. His *Songs and Verses* (1901), mainly descriptive and lyrical verse, contains an appreciation by E.A. Petherick and incorporates material published in two earlier selections.

Lot's Wife, a weekly student newspaper published at Monash University, began fortnightly publication in 1961 titled *Chaos*, changing its name in June 1964. Concerned mainly with politics, student news, educational issues and the cultural life of the university, the newspaper has occasionally published original contributions from well-known writers, as well as substantial interviews.

LOUKAKIS, Angelo (1951–), born Sydney, of Greek parentage, graduated from the University of NSW and has worked as a teacher of English as a second language, as a multicultural education project officer, as a welfare worker and freelance journalist. In 1993 he was appointed literature publisher at Angus & Robertson. He has written screenplays and short stories, some of which have been published in anthologies and periodicals, and in two collections, *For the Patriarch* (1981, winner of a NSW Premier's Literary Award) and *Vernacular Dreams* (1986). He has also written a novel, *Messenger* (1992). His stories deal with the diverse experience of first- and second-generation Greeks and Italians in Australia, as well as with the Australian rediscovery of European roots. *Messenger*, more a sequence of linked stories than a novel, concentrates on the growth of a boy of Greek parentage in Sydney of the 1950s and 1960s. Mediator and interpreter for his parents in a foreign culture, Manny Kanellis is the messenger of the title; for Dimitri, his father, Australia remains not just unknowable but

cruelly indifferent to his hopes, while Sophia, his mother, finally abandons the marriage and returns to her 'homeland'. Loukakis's screenplay *Dancing* (1980) was awarded a prize for production at the Melbourne Film Festival.

LOVE, Harold (1937–), a reader in English at Monash University, has written several books relevant to Australian culture. They include *The Golden Age of Australian Opera: W.S. Lyster and his Companies 1861–1880* (1981) and a biography of the influential theatre critic and journalist James Edward Neild (1989), which is also a significant study of nineteenth-century Melbourne culture. Love has also edited *The Australian Stage: A Documentary History* (1984).

Love Me Sailor (1945), by Robert Close (q.v.), is the story of a voyage of the windjammer *Annabella* with a cargo of Chilean nitrate from Mejillones to San Francisco. The voyage is complicated by the presence on the ship of a lone female passenger, Ella Miller, whose past history and present conduct show her to be a nymphomaniac on the verge of insanity. Her effect on the crew is catastrophic; their lust for her produces sexual rivalries and jealousies that lead to arguments, fights, knifings, accidents, insanity and death. Although the captain appropriates her for his own sexual use, some of the crew, especially the second mate, Bill Hawkins, Christenson, Spider Lukes and the steward, Catspaw, vainly attempt to satisfy their own passion for her. The young apprentice Ernie sees her in an idealistic, romantic light and constantly defends her against his shipmates' foul-mouthed talk. After the captain is hurt in an accident, Bill Hawkins takes over the ship and is about to satisfy his desire for Ella when they are caught in a hurricane and he is forced to employ all his seamanship skill to save the ship. When the danger has almost passed Ella is swept overboard by a huge wave and Ernie sets out to rescue her in a rowing boat. He gets the naked girl into the boat but she believes him to be the devil and pushes him overboard to his death. Soon after, she is taken back aboard the *Annabella* but the crew, regarding her now with contempt, put her aboard a passing steamer.

'LOVEGOOD, John', see **WATSON, Grant**

LOVELESS, George (1797–1874), born Tolpuddle near Dorchester, England, became the best-known of the famous Tolpuddle Martyrs, the six agricultural workers also called the Dorchester Labourers, who were dealt with as criminals when they attempted in 1833 to protect their livelihood against the rapacious local landowners by forming a rural trade union, the Friendly Society of Agricultural Labourers. Convicted in 1834 of administering unlawful oaths, the Martyrs were sentenced to seven years' transportation; Loveless was separated from his colleagues and sent to Van Diemen's Land where he impressed the lieutenant-governor, George Arthur, with his integrity and character. Early in 1837, after pardons had been issued in London to the prisoners, Loveless left Australia and later migrated from England to Canada. His book *The*

Victims of Whiggery (1837) is an account of his arrest and trial and his experiences in Australia. In 1982 'Tolpuddle', a radio play by Alan Plater and Vince Hill, highly sympathetic to Loveless, was broadcast in London; H.V. Evatt wrote *Injustice within the Law* (1937) about the Tolpuddle Martyrs.

'Love's Coming', a brief lyric poem by John Shaw Neilson (q.v.), was published in the Sydney *Sun* in 1911. It was later set to music by Dr W.G. Whitaker of the London College of Music. Acknowledged as one of Neilson's most attractive lyrics, there is a perfect harmony between the poem's simple but artistic form and its delicate imagery.

LOW, Sir David (1891–1963), the creator of Colonel Blimp and as 'Low' one of the most significant cartoonists of the twentieth century, was born NZ and came to Australia at the age of 20 to become a staff artist on the *Bulletin*. With an early style which showed the influence of his *Bulletin* predecessor Phil May, Low made his reputation with *The Billy Book* (1918), in which he caricatured the Australian prime minister W.M. 'Billy' Hughes. In 1919 he moved to England, where he became famous as a political cartoonist with the *Star*, the *Evening Standard*, the *Daily Herald* and the *Manchester Guardian*. Apart from *The Billy Book*, he published *Low's Annual* (1908) and *Caricatures* (1915) before his departure for England; his caricatures include a celebrated portrayal of Henry Lawson. Among his later publications was *Low's Autobiography* (1956), which includes reminiscences of his work with the *Bulletin*. An appreciation of Low's life and work by Colin Seymour-Ure and Jim Schoff was published in 1985.

LOWE, Eric (1889–1963), born Birriwa, NSW, into a well-known pioneering family, was a pastoralist before the First World War in which he served in the Australian Light Horse. He subsequently worked at numerous rural occupations, travelled for a time, spending some years in Denmark, and trained as an engineer and accountant. He wrote a trilogy dealing with station life, *Salute to Freedom* (1938), *Beyond the Nineteen Counties* (1948) and *O Willing Hearts* (1951). *Beyond the Nineteen Counties*, chronologically the first volume of the series, recounts the early history of the pioneering Stewart family; adapted for radio by Colin Roderick, it was serialised in 1949. Lowe's major achievement, however, is his study of a single complex individual, Robin Stewart, in *Salute to Freedom*, which covers the period 1902–36. *Framed in Hardwood* (1940), Lowe's remaining novel, also draws on his rural experience.

LOWE, Robert (1811–92), from 1880 Viscount Sherbrooke, was born in Nottinghamshire, England, and was a successful scholar at Oxford, where in the late 1830s he was a private tutor whose pupils included Charles Reade. An albino, he came to NSW to seek his fortune in 1842 after being warned of impending blindness, and in his eight years in the colony won renown but not always popularity as a politician, ora-

tor, journalist and satirist. In 1843 Lowe was appointed to the Legislative Council by Governor Gipps, although he soon fell out with Gipps over his proposed squatting regulations. Lowe was a leading contributor of satiric poems, e.g. 'Songs of the Squatters', poems attacking the Gladstone Colony and pungent articles to the *Atlas* (q.v.), but by 1847 he had broken with the squatting interest, whose land monopoly he opposed. Active also in the development of educational policies and in the opposition to the resumption of transportation, Lowe left Australia in 1850; subsequently he was a leader-writer for the London *Times* and a long time Liberal member of the British parliament, serving as Gladstone's chancellor of the exchequer (1869–73) and home secretary (1873–74). Lowe's Australian poems are included in his *Poems of a Life* (1885); several of his Australian speeches were published in Sydney during the 1840s. Lowe has been the subject of biographies by A.P. Martin, *Life and Letters of the Right Honourable Robert Lowe, Viscount Sherbrooke* (1893), J.F. Hogan, *Robert Lowe, Viscount Sherbrooke* (1893), and Ruth Knight, *Illiberal Liberal: Robert Lowe in New South Wales 1842–50* (1966).

'Lower Bohemia' was a series of six sketches by Marcus Clarke (q.v.), published in the *Australasian* in 1869. With the earlier 'Night Scenes in Melbourne' in the *Argus* (1868) and 'A Melbourne Alsatia' in *Colonial Monthly* (1869), the 'Lower Bohemia' sketches show Clarke to be an important predecessor of 'The Vagabond' (John Stanley James) in depicting Melbourne lowlife.

LOWER, Lennie (1903–47), born Dubbo, NSW, was educated in Sydney. After leaving school, he served briefly in the army and navy and carried his swag in Queensland and NSW before settling into journalism. At 23 his first piece was published in *Beckett's Budget*, a Sydney scandal sheet; soon after, he joined the *Labor Daily* as a humorous columnist, and moved from there to the *Daily Guardian* and *Smith's Weekly*. In 1930 his widely acclaimed comic novel *Here's Luck* (q.v.) was published; a sardonic record of the tribulations of Jack Gudgeon, suburban battler, it established Lower's reputation beyond Sydney. From *Smith's Weekly* Lower moved to the *Daily Telegraph*, the *Sunday Telegraph* and the *Australian Women's Weekly*, but after being dismissed by Sir Frank Packer, allegedly for insulting Noel Coward, returned to *Smith's Weekly* in 1940. The books following *Here's Luck* comprise sketches mostly selected from his regular newspaper contributions; they include *Here's Another* (1932), *Life and Things* (1936), *The Bachelor's Guide to the Care of the Young and Other Stories* (1941), *Loweritis* (1940) and *Lennie Lower's Annual* (1941). A well-known character in Sydney journalistic circles, whose periods of depression were punctuated by absurdist escapades that are a feature also of his writing, Lower was widely mourned after his early death. Two of his Sydney friends, Cyril Pearl and the artist 'Wep' (W.E. Pidgeon), prepared the selection of his work *The Best of Lennie Lower* (1963); Tom Thompson introduced the 1983 selection *Here's Lower* and the 1988 *The*

Legends of Lennie Lower, both illustrated by cartoonist Patrick Cook. Barry Dickins's play 'The Sadness of Lennie Lower' (1981) was published as *Lennie Lower* (1982). Bill Hornadge has written a biography and appreciation of Lower, *Lennie Lower: He Made a Nation Laugh* (1993).

Lower's humour, primarily verbal, has the flavour of the 1930s and 1940s, reflected in such idioms as 'whacko', 'mug', 'galoot' and 'lair' and in its preoccupation with six o'clock hotel closing and meals of steak and eggs in 'greasy spoon' cafes. Both in the titles of his pieces, e.g. an article on chess titled 'By Rook or by Crook', and within the body of the text, e.g. in the report of a Lower character who dies of a cold as a result of shoeing draught-horses, he had habitual recourse to punning; the danger of tiring his readers by repetition was minimised by his piecemeal method of publishing his work and by a self-mocking authorial voice. The Lower scripts characteristically focus on domestic life or place a subject, usually male, in chauvinist, outrageous fantasy situations which allow full play to Lower's talent for the one-line gag, cynicism and sense of the slapstick dimension to life. Among regular satirical targets are the conformism of suburban life, nagging wives, wowsers of any kind, and those who make life difficult for the ordinary people with whom he sympathised.

LOYAU, George Étienne (1835–98), born London, arrived in Sydney in 1853 and spent seven years travelling extensively in Australia and working at a range of occupations from gold-digger to private tutor. From the 1860s to the 1880s he had extensive experience in journalism and as a newspaper editor in Queensland, NSW, Victoria and SA, editing the *Maryborough Chronicle* (1861–62), the Gawler *Bunyip* (1878–79) and the *Illustrated Adelaide News* (1880–81). He also published three volumes of verse, *The Australian Seasons* (1871), *Australian Wild Flowers* (1871) and *Colonial Lyrics* (1872); an autobiographical account titled *The Personal Adventures of George E. Loyau* (1883); and two collections of biographical studies, *The Representative Men of South Australia* (1883) and *Notable South Australians* (1885). Founder and editor of the short-lived Adelaide magazine, the *Australian Family Herald* (1877), he also edited *The South Australian Annual: Australian Tales by Well Known Writers* (1877). Hugh Anderson wrote the biography, *George Loyau: the Man Who Wrote Bush Ballads* (1991). It incorporates two rare songbooks, *The Queenslanders' New Colonial Camp Fire Song Book* (c.1865) and *The Sydney Songster* (c.1869), with lyrics and musical scores, both songbooks written by Loyau.

LUBBOCK, Adelaide (1906–81), born London, the daughter of Sir Arthur Stanley, governor of Victoria during the First World War, and a descendant of Sarah Siddons and Owen Stanley, became a leading singer at Sadlers Wells. She grew up partly in Australia and wrote an account of her childhood, *People in Glass Houses: Growing Up at Government House* (1977). Based partly on her mother's letters back to England, her autobiography records the Stanleys' difficulties in dealing both with the Australian natives and the more rebellious natives who were their children. Reflecting the aristocratic prejudices of her parents, and the internecine disputes between the State governors and the governor-general of the period, the book is also informative on the imperial relationship between Australia and Britain and on personalities of the period, such as Nellie Melba and Squizzy Taylor. Lubbock also wrote an account of a later visit to Australia, *Australian Roundabout* (1963), and a biography of Owen Stanley (1968).

Lucinda Brayford, a novel by Martin Boyd (q.v.), was published in 1946. The novel comprises four parts, the early section dealing in a leisurely way with Lucinda's antecedents and her Australian childhood at the turn of the century. Descended from two very different English grandfathers, her nature reconciles the daredevil energies of the one with the aesthetic, religious sense of the other. After a period of struggle, her parents become wealthy and her expected brilliant future seems to be assured when she marries a well-connected Englishman, Hugo Brayford, aide-de-camp to the governor of Victoria. Their return to Hugo's English home, Crittenden House, begins both the outward decline of Lucinda's fortunes and her spiritual growth. After the birth of a son, Stephen, she discovers her husband's infidelity, although his severe wounding in the war prevents her from seeking a divorce. An affair with one of her husband's friends, Pat Lanfranc, proves equally disillusioning. Meanwhile the ideals of her brother-in-law, Paul Brayford, who pursues his concept of a civilised existence at his villa in Provence, strengthen her instinctive belief in the goodness of the natural world. This belief is put to the test of sorrow when her son becomes a martyr to the pacifist cause during the Second World War.

Lucky Country, The, by Donald Horne, a critique of Australian society in the 1960s, was published in 1964 and won unprecedented popularity. Frequently reprinted, and published in a second revised edition in 1968, its title has become a common idiom for Australia, although not always with the sense that Horne intended. Horne defines Australia as 'a lucky country run mainly by second-rate people who share its luck'. Provincial and derivative, content with the second-rate but fortuitously prosperous, 'it lives on other people's ideas, and, although its ordinary people are adaptable, most of its leaders (in all fields) . . . lack curiosity about the events that surround them'. Taking for his image of Australia 'a man in an open-necked shirt, solemnly enjoying an ice-cream' at the beach, his 'kiddy . . . beside him', Horne defines the Australian dream and what it is to be an Australian. He analyses what he sees as the country's social, cultural, political and religious attitudes, as well as attitudes to work and leisure, the place of women, migrants, Aborigines and intellectuals, the relationship with Britain, America, Asia and Oceania, the political and educational systems, industry and the unions, the bureaucracy and the press. In his last chapter he examines the possibilities of the nation's continuing to live on its luck. Underlying his criticisms is an enthusiasm for the ordinariness and for what he defines as the 'innocent happiness' of Australian life.

LUFFMANN, Laura Bogue (1846–1929), born Lauretta Lane in England, was educated in France and married a Melbourne horticulturist, Carl Bogue Luffmann. As Laura M. Lane and before her arrival in Australia, she wrote several books for children as well as a biography of Alexander Vinet (1890) and an adult novel, *Gentleman Verschoyle* (1875). In Australia she was prominent in women's movements, wrote numerous articles for the Australian, South African and American press, edited the *Woman's Voice* and as 'Una' contributed to the Sydney *Daily Telegraph*. She also wrote an Australian novel for children, *Will Aylmer* (1909), and an adult novel, *A Question of Latitude* (1912). The Laura Bogue Luffmann literary competition was established in her memory.

LUKIN, Gresley (1840–1916), born Launceston, Tasmania, was an actor before becoming a public servant in Queensland, where he drafted Selection Acts for the Lands Department. In 1873 he became editor of the *Brisbane Courier* and the *Queenslander* and was associated on both journals with Ernest Favenc and W.H. Traill. His other major connection with Australian journalism was with the *Boomerang*, which he bought from William Lane in 1890; soon after its collapse in 1892 he left Australia for NZ. During his long career (1896–1916) as editor of the Wellington *Evening Post*, he employed Arthur Adams as a reporter.

Luna, a general literary magazine, was published 1975–89 with the support of The Friends of Women's Arts in Victoria and the FAW. Although *Luna* emphasised women's issues and the work of women, its editorial criteria were based on the quality of the work to be published; thus the work of men as well as women was represented in its pages. Its editorial collective was led by Barbara Giles.

LUNN, Hugh (1941–), born Brisbane, began his career as a journalist on the *Courier-Mail* before leaving for London where he worked on the London *Daily Mirror* and then joined Reuters. He was sent to Vietnam in 1967 as a correspondent and later worked for Reuters in Singapore and Indonesia before joining the *Australian* in 1971. He was for several years assistant editor of the *Australian* and also its Queensland editor. Well known as a feature-writer, he has won five national awards including three Walkley Awards as well as the *Age* Book of the Year Award in 1985 for *Vietnam: A Reporter's War* (1985). Lunn's books include an unauthorised biography of the Queensland premier who became identified with his State as a symbol of its conservatism, *The Life and Political Adventures of Johannes Bjelke-Petersen* (1978), which has appeared in several subsequent editions; the collections of feature articles, *Behind the Banana Curtain* (1980) and *Queenslanders* (1984); and the humorous bestselling memoirs of growing up in Queensland, *Over the Top with Jim* (1989), adapted for a second edition in 1992 titled *Jim & Me*; *Head Over Heels* (1992); and *Fred & Olive's Blessed Lino* (1993). *Vietnam: A Reporter's War* is a gripping account of his thirteen months in the country when he witnessed numerous horrors, experienced battle at first hand, was educated in the power of propaganda and lost four of his closest friends. Lunn's memoirs of his Brisbane childhood and early years on the *Courier-Mail* are vivid re-creations of Queensland of the 1950s and 1960s.

LUNN, Richard (1950–), born Sydney, has worked as a teacher in Australia and England and lectured in creative writing at the Macarthur Institute of Higher Education. His publications include *Pompeii Deep Fry* (1980), which won the Anne Elder Award for poetry, and two books of short stories, *The Divine Right of Dogs* (1982) and *The Taxidermist's Dance* (1990). His story 'Tennis with My Father', published in the *Age* and included in *The Taxidermist's Dance*, won the 1987 *Age* short-story competition. Affection and resentment colour the adolescent's recollections of his father's sporting skill, but there is finally a moment when that skill is stripped away to reveal an ordinary mortal, and a whole boyhood of envy is dissipated. Many of Lunn's stories are set in boyhood; by contrast others, e.g. from 'The True Mask' section of *The Taxidermist's Dance*, have more bizarre settings and characters. There is 'Marco the Molasses Man', whose flesh stretches like elastic; 'Mr Videlius', who, with his weird friends Retcini, Fargoblad and Chrome, seems to have stepped straight from a Toulouse-Lautrec tableau; and 'Giselle's Admirer', who is nothing less than a vampire.

LURIE, Morris (1938–), born Melbourne of Jewish parents from Poland, studied architecture and worked for a time in advertising before becoming a full-time writer. He lived overseas, in Greece, Denmark, Morocco and England with frequent visits to New York, 1965–73. His stories have been widely published in Australia and in such overseas magazines and newspapers as the London *Daily Telegraph*, *Esquire*, the *Transatlantic Review*, *Argosy*, the *New Yorker*, *Punch*, the London *Times, Antaeus* and *Penthouse*. He has published six novels, *Rappaport* (1966), *The London Jungle Adventures of Charlie Hope* (1968), *Rappaport's Revenge* (1973), *Flying Home* (1978), *Seven Books for Grossman* (1983) and *Madness* (1991); six collections of short stories, *Happy Times* (1969), *Inside the Wardrobe* (1975), *Running Nicely* (1979), *Dirty Friends* (1981), *Outrageous Behaviour* (1984), and *The Night We Ate the Sparrow* (1985); five collections of prose pieces which he refers to as 'reportage', *The English in Heat* (1972), *Hackwork* (1977), *Public Secrets* (1981), *Snow Jobs* (1985) and *My Life as a Movie* (1988); three plays in the collection *Waterman* (1979), which includes *Jangle, Jangle* and *A Visit to the Uncle* as well as the title play; a collection of stories and a screenplay, *Two Brothers Running* (1990); an autobiography, *Whole Life* (1987); and several children's books including *The Twenty-Seventh Annual African Hippopotamus Race* (1969), *Arlo the Dandy Lion* (1971), *Toby's Millions* (1982), *The Story of Imelda Who Was Small* (1984) and *Heroes* (1987). His stories are also represented in several anthologies and in the collection *The Most Beautiful Lies*, ed. Brian Kiernan (1977).

Lurie's Jewish qualities, especially his humour, are often described as reminiscent of such American writers as Isaac Singer, Saul Bellow and Phillip Roth, although other characteristics such as his preoccupation with loneliness in an empty land and the cult of taciturnity mark him as distinctively Australian. Describing himself as having grown up 'in a strange bubble of isolation' as a result of his parents' double alienation, from contemporary Poland and from Australia, Lurie is interested in all types of cultural displacement. The comic protagonists of his novels and stories are all solitary, homeless figures, misfits, romantic dreamers, hapless shlemiels, perpetual tourists or bewildered expatriates. Rappaport, the hero of his first novel, of *Rappaport's Revenge* and of several short stories, is a self-centred, overweight, aspiring antique dealer with a less than keen nose for a bargain, cursed with a suffocating Jewish mother, a surly father and an innate incapacity to lead a normal existence. In London in *Rappaport's Revenge* he stands out as even more of an oddity, becoming a part-comic, part-painful test of friendship for Friedlander, the more conventional narrator. Leo Axelrod of *Flying Home*, Lurie's most complex novel, leaves Australia, his birthplace, for Israel, the emotional 'home' of his parents and grandfather, and gradually discovers that a relationship has more human substance than a place. Charlie Hope of *The London Jungle Adventures of Charlie Hope* is another outrageously comic figure, even more larger-than-life than Rappaport, who operates in the surreal world of advertising, fascinating the rather immature narrator with his capacity for grandiose near successes and massive failures. *Seven Books for Grossman* has a professor of literature writing pornography for Jewish editor Grossman in order to pay off his gambling debts. The seven books are parodies of celebrated authors such as Faulkner, Hemingway and others.

Lurie's inventive talents are particularly well suited to the short story. In several he explores the mysteries, frustrations, comedy and pathos of family relationships, concentrating especially on outwardly prickly but inwardly anguished father–son relations. Observant of nuances in human relationships, Lurie often combines delight in a farcical, outrageous situation with an understanding of its poignant relevance to universal experience. In the same way his gift for comic dialogue, for the devastating quip or the brilliant aphorism, is joined by a Pinteresque awareness of the way language both masks and reveals meaning. Generally in his stories a wry, self-deprecating humour forestalls sentimentality or self-indulgence, the verbal and situational comedy effectively distancing pain and nostalgia. Nevertheless, the general aura of loneliness, rootlessness and emptiness persists; as Lurie has commented, 'It's funny on the surface, but what I'm talking about is not really funny'.

Whole Life is Lurie's most acute and intimate exploration of loneliness and rootlessness. Maintaining that the business of his autobiography is 'to investigate why I am how I am', he probes with brutal honesty and compassion his continuing love-hate relationship with a smothering mother and a sardonic father and the impact of their extreme cultural isolation on his conviction of homelessness. Essentially Jewish, *Whole Life* nevertheless reflects familiar experience. As Ron Elisha has commented, it 'cries out for the sorrow of all children. For the daily damage done to them. For the essential, inescapable grievous injury they suffer simply by their continued existence within the crushing confines of the family'.

LYCETT, Joseph (c.1775–1828), born Staffordshire, England, was a professional portrait and miniature-painter who was convicted of forgery in 1811 and sentenced to transportation for fourteen years. After arriving in Sydney in 1814, he worked as a clerk in the police office but was convicted of forgery again in 1815 and sent to Newcastle. His work on the plans of a Newcastle church led to a conditional pardon and in 1819–20 he travelled extensively in NSW and Van Diemen's Land, completing a series of drawings of Australian life. Three of his drawings sent by Governor Macquarie to Lord Bathurst are believed to have won him an absolute pardon in 1821. Lycett returned to England in 1822 and in 1824–25 published his *Views in Australia: Or, New South Wales, and Van Diemen's Land Delineated* in thirteen parts, reissued in a single volume in 1825. Little is known of the rest of Lycett's life, although a pencilled note in a copy of his *Views* held by the Mitchell Library states that he committed suicide after being charged again with forgery. A delicate and perceptive artist at his best, Lycett was not averse in his *Views* to presenting a Europeanised version of the Australian landscape to suit London tastes. The National Library of Australia has published *The Lycett Album* (1990), which reproduces twenty watercolour paintings, believed to have been completed in the 1820s, depicting aspects of Aboriginal life in NSW. The paintings are accompanied by a commentary by Jeanette Hoorn.

Lyceum Miniature, a monthly paper published in Melbourne 1878–79, circulated among members of the Melbourne and Sydney Progressive Lyceums. The paper published news of the society and original contributions from members consisting of articles on general topics, short stories and verse. Alfred Deakin was editor from January 1878 to January 1879.

LYLE, Garry, a Melbourne poet, founder and publisher of the untitled booklets of verse *Number One*, *Number Two* and *Number Three* (1943–48), contributed verse to such periodicals as *Bohemia* and *Venture*, and published one collection, *Eighteen Poems* (1940). His verse is also represented in the anthology *Dawnfire* (1941), ed. John Cremin.

LYNCH, Arthur Alfred (1861–1934), born near Ballarat of an Irish father who had taken part in the Eureka rebellion and of a Scottish mother, graduated from the University of Melbourne in 1886, and also trained as a civil engineer. He later studied science, physiology, psychology and electrical engineering in

Europe, qualified as a doctor in London, worked for a time as a journalist and in 1892 tried unsuccessfully to enter the House of Commons as a Parnellite candidate. He served with the Boers during the Boer War. In 1901 he was elected to the House of Commons as Nationalist candidate for Galway but was imprisoned and tried for treason in 1902. Convicted in 1903, he was sentenced to life imprisonment but was released on licence a year later after Theodore Roosevelt interceded with Edward VII, and subsequently won a free pardon. A prominent Irish member of parliament until 1918, he was active in British interests during the First World War. The author of nearly thirty books on a range of subjects including science, psychology, ethics and the Irish problem, Lynch also published an autobiography, *My Life Story* (1924); five volumes of verse, some of which shows a satirical wit, *A Koran of Love* (1894), *Our Poets!* (1894), *Religio Athletae* (1895), *Prince Azreel* (1911) and *Sonnets of the Banner and the Star* (1914); and two works of fiction, *Poppy Meadows* (1915) and *O'Rourke the Great* (1921). A man of wide-ranging interests and talents, Lynch in his combination of affection for Australia and fierce love of Ireland is an extreme representative of a common political phenomenon in Australia before 1918.

LYNCH, Joe, see **'Five Bells'**

LYNG, Jens Sorensen (1868–1941), born Hasle, Denmark, came to Australia in 1891, was for a time secretary to the botanist Baron von Mueller and served with the Australian forces in New Guinea 1914–18. He edited the *New Guinea Government Gazette* and later founded the *Rabaul Record.* On his return to Australia he worked for the Commonwealth Bureau of Census and Statistics until his retirement in 1933. Editor of the Melbourne Scandinavian journal *Norden* for ten years, he wrote several fiction works in Danish and a novel in English, *Teddy Wilkins' Trials* (1910), the story of a Danish printer in Melbourne. He also wrote several general books in English including *Non-Britishers in Australia* (1927, winner of the Harbison-Higinbotham Prize), *The Road to Canberra* (1931) and *The Scandinavians in Australia, New Zealand and the Western Pacific* (1939). Lyng also founded the *Australian National Review.*

LYONS, Dame Enid (1897–1981), born Smithton, Tasmania, married the future prime minister J.A. Lyons in 1915 and became the mother of twelve children. After her husband's death she became the first woman member of the federal parliament in 1943, and later the first woman to hold ministerial office. She retired from politics in 1951 but was a commissioner of the ABC 1951–62. She wrote an account of her early life and marriage, *So We Take Comfort* (1965); a volume of political reminiscences, *Among the Carrion Crows* (1972); and a series of short essays and sketches on aspects of daily life, *The Old Haggis* (1969). Kate White has written *A Political Love Story: Joe and Enid Lyons* (1987).

LYSSIOTIS, Tes, born in the Wimmera district, Victoria, of Greek parents, taught drama and media studies for eight years at high school after completing a course at Rusden State College. She began writing and directing plays from 1978; an ensemble piece for women, 'Girls Talk', was performed at the Why Not Theatre in 1980 and was followed by 'I'll Go To Australia and Wear a Hat' (1982), a bilingual play in Greek and English based on the experiences of her mother, who was a proxy bride. In 1984 she founded the Filiki Players and in the following year presented 'The Journey', an innovative, multilingual play which is a compendium of four earlier plays and which subsequently toured in NSW, the ACT and Queensland. Only one of her plays has been published so far, *The Forty Lounge Cafe* (1990); based again on her mother's experiences in Australia and Greece, the play explores her exploitation as a child and young woman and her struggle to transmit the Greek culture to her Anglocentric daughter. Lyssiotis's other plays are 'Come to Australia They Said' (1982–83), 'Hotel Bonegilla' (1984), 'On the Line' (1984), 'The Uncle from Australia' (1985) and 'The White Sports Coat' (1989).

LYSTER, William Saurin (1828–80), operatic entrepreneur, was born in Dublin. He first came to Australia in 1842, and after various overseas military adventures formed an opera troupe in San Francisco with his brother Frederick. In 1861 the troupe travelled to Australia and, after beginning a successful season in Melbourne, which was to become Lyster's base, continued to tour Australasia for the next six years. After an unsuccessful season in San Francisco in 1868, followed by dispersal of the troupe, Lyster formed another company which he brought to Australia in 1870 and continued to present both English and Italian operas successfully in Australia until his death. His career is described by Harold Love in *The Golden Age of Australian Opera* (1981).

M

MACALISTER, Charles (1830–1908), born Scotland, came to Australia in 1833 and spent much of his life in the Goulburn district of NSW. His book of reminiscences, *Old Pioneering Days in the Sunny South* (1907), vividly recalls aspects of colonial life, e.g. the effects of transportation, overlanding experiences, the gold discoveries, the selection experiment and the bushranging phenomenon, and presents MacAlister's recollections of Daniel Deniehy, Robert Lowe and other nineteenth-century notables. A significant source book for Australian folklorists, *Old Pioneering Days in the Sunny South* includes a number of early folk-songs.

MACARTHUR, Elizabeth (1767–1850), born Elizabeth Veale, married John Macarthur (q.v.) in 1788 and accompanied him to England with the Second Fleet in 1789–90. She was to become the mother of nine children, and to encounter extraordinary difficulties and challenges as manager of the Macarthur property at Parramatta during her husband's long absences from the colony 1801–5 and 1809–17. Her letters and journal, since published in part in several collections and more comprehensively in *The Journal and Letters of Elizabeth Macarthur 1789–1798* (1984), edited by Joy Hughes, reveal her keen interest in world affairs, the Aborigines, colonial politics, Australian fauna and flora, and pastoral management in which she was a pioneer, making a significant contribution to the development of the wool industry. After John Macarthur died in 1834, having been declared insane in 1832, Elizabeth continued to live at Elizabeth Farm for the next sixteen years, communicating by letter with some members of her family, such as her sons Edward and John, who returned to England. Her achievements are recorded in Averil Mackenzie-Grieve's *The Great Accomplishment* (1953), Hazel King's *Elizabeth Macarthur and her World* (1980) and Lennard Bickel's *Australia's First Lady* (1991).

MACARTHUR, Emmeline (Emmeline Falbe) (1828–1911), born at Vineyard Cottage on the Parramatta River, NSW, was the daughter of Hannibal Macarthur, nephew of John Macarthur; her mother, Anna Maria, was the daughter of Philip Gidley King. In 1847 she married George Leslie, the younger brother of Patrick Leslie, and moved to a property at Canning Downs, where she suffered numerous hardships culminating in Leslie's death from tuberculosis

in 1860. Emmeline's second marriage in 1865 to Captain Vigant Falbe, a distinguished sailor, was also short, although it produced two boys before Falbe's death in 1871. An observant witness to Australia's early history, Emmeline Macarthur kept letters, newsclippings and notebooks, which she drew on in old age for her memoirs, which were circulated within the family for some years; unpublished until they were discovered by subsequent descendants, they were published in the *Bulletin* (1954) and in 1988 in a volume titled *My Dear Miss Macarthur. The Recollections of Emmeline Maria Macarthur (1828–1911)*, arranged and edited by Jane de Falbe.

MACARTHUR, John (1767–1834) **and Family** exercised a considerable influence on the growth of the merino wool industry and on the political affairs of NSW during the Colony's first fifty years. John Macarthur, a lieutenant in the NSW Corps, and his wife Elizabeth (q.v.) came to Australia in June 1890. By 1794 they had established Elizabeth Farm House on a grant of 40 hectares in the Parramatta district. Macarthur's appointment in 1793 as inspector of public works and his position as paymaster of the NSW Corps placed him in such advantageous circumstances that he rapidly became one of the most powerful men in the Colony. After quarrels with successive governors, John Hunter and Philip Gidley King, and a duel with his commanding officer William Paterson, Macarthur was sent to England for court martial. He returned in 1805 with a grant of 2000 hectares of land of his own choosing and with plans to promote the fine wool industry in the Colony; he took up his grant in the Cowpastures area, establishing the historic property Camden Park. In 1808 he played a leading role in deposing Governor William Bligh and returned to England in 1809, again to answer for his actions. Although threatened with arrest if he returned to the colonies, in 1817 he was back in Australia where he exercised considerable influence on the inquiry of Commissioner J.T. Bigge in 1819, quarrelled with Governor Lachlan Macquarie, continued on bad terms with Macquarie's successor Sir Ralph Darling, helped to found the Australian Agricultural Company, the Australian Bank and the Australian and Sydney Colleges, and energetically promoted his pastoral interests. Macarthur was survived by his wife Elizabeth and by his sons Edward (1789–1872) and James (1798–1867); the latter published *New South Wales: Its Present State and Future Prospects* (1837), ghosted by Edward Edwards. James, a leading figure in NSW politics before self-government, was the father of Elizabeth, who in 1867 married Captain

A.A.W. Onslow, thus originating the Macarthur-Onslow family. Macarthur is the subject of M.H. Ellis's biography *John Macarthur* (1955) and is included in Vance Palmer's *National Portraits* (1940). Sibella Macarthur-Onslow edited *Some Early Records of the Macarthurs of Camden* (1914). Differing versions of some of the events of the Macarthur period are given in Ellis's biography and in H.V. Evatt's *Rum Rebellion* (1938). Ross Fitzgerald and Mark Hearn have written *Bligh, Macarthur and the Rum Rebellion* (1988) and J.M. Ward *James Macarthur: Colonial Conservative 1798–1867* (1981).

MACARTNEY, F.T. (Frederick Thomas) (1887–1980), born and educated in Melbourne, left school at 12 and followed a variety of occupations including stints as a clerk, a bookkeeper on a Riverina station, a shorthand reporter, a freelance journalist and a Victorian government employee, until his appointment in 1921 to the Northern Territory public service. Macartney returned to Melbourne in 1933 and, apart from 1942–47 when he was employed as a public servant and 1948–54 when most of his energies were devoted to the revision of E. Morris Miller's bibliography *Australian Literature* (q.v., 1940), he worked as a freelance broadcaster, reviewer (in 1935–38 for *All About Books*) and university extension and CLF lecturer.

Active in Melbourne literary circles from his early twenties, Macartney helped to found the Melbourne Literary Club in 1916 and was editor of its journal, *Birth*, in 1920; he was prominent in the Australian Literature Society, PEN and the FAW. Although he contributed short stories to periodicals and anthologies and illustrated some of his books with linocuts, his main creative activity was as a writer of cool and crafted verse which ranges from the densely philosophical to the lightly satiric. His major volumes were *Preferences* (1941) and *Selected Poems* (1961), which both include material from earlier volumes, e.g. *Dewed Petals* (1912), *Earthen Vessels* (1913), *Commercium* (1917), *In War-Time* (1918), *Poems* (1920), *Something for Tokens* (1922), *A Sweep of Lute-Strings* (1929), *Hard Light* (1933), *Ode of Our Times* (1944), *Gaily the Troubadour* (1946) and *Tripod for Homeward Incense* (1947). He is better known, however, for the abridgement and re-arrangement of the Miller bibliography, published in 1956 under their joint names as *Australian Literature: A Bibliography to 1938 . . . Extended to 1950*. 'Miller and Macartney', as *Australian Literature* has become known, remains an indispensable tool for students of Australian literature, although contemporary criticism of the work led Macartney to publish *An Odious Comparison Considered in Its Relation to Australian Literature* (1956). His other work includes *A Historical Outline of Australian Literature* (1957) which comprises the historical introduction to 'Miller and Macartney'; *Australian Literary Essays* (1957); an autobiography, *Proof Against Failure* (1967); a biography, *Furnley Maurice (Frank Wilmot)* (1955); a revision of Louis Lavater's 1926 anthology, *The Sonnet in Australasia* (1956); and the 1947 number of *Australian Poetry* (1948).

McAULEY, James (1917–76), born Lakemba, NSW, was educated at the University of Sydney where he gained his MA in 1940 with the thesis 'Symbolism: An Essay in Poetics', a topic which foreshadows the classical stance he later adopted in his poetry. Although he was regarded by some as an arch-conservative in later life, McAuley's university days were filled with the usual dalliances with atheism, anarchism, radicalism and idealism. Drafted for military service in 1942, he was appointed to the Australian Army Directorate of Research and Civil Affairs under A.A. Conlon, where he helped to train the personnel of the Australian New Guinea Administration Unit (ANGAU), whose postwar task was to re-establish civil administration in the island. Thereafter New Guinea was a major factor in McAuley's life. In 1946–60 he was a member of the instructional staff of the Australian School of Pacific Administration in Sydney. He visited New Guinea frequently, becoming deeply interested in the problems facing its primitive society and fascinated by its exotic landscape. His writings on New Guinea, published throughout the 1940s and 1950s in the journal *South Pacific*, won him an international reputation among scholars of Oceania. In 1956 he became editor of the literary and current affairs journal *Quadrant* (q.v.); in 1961 he was appointed reader in poetry at the University of Tasmania, Hobart, then professor of English, occupying the chair until his death. McAuley was instrumental in establishing *Australian Literary Studies*, and was president of the Australian Association for the Teaching of English 1970–75. In 1972 he won the Britannica-Australia Award; in 1975 he was made AM.

McAuley's first collection of verse was *Under Aldebaran* (q.v., 1946). In 1947–49 he wrote 'Prometheus', 'The Death of Chiron', 'The Ascent of Heracles' and 'The Tomb of Heracles', the four poems which make up his important work 'The Hero and the Hydra', first published together in his second volume, *A Vision of Ceremony* (q.v., 1956). Using the Greek tales based on the Prometheus legend, McAuley comments adversely on modern civilisation and affirms traditional moral and spiritual values. His *Selected Poems* appeared in 1963. The epic narrative *Captain Quiros* (q.v.) was published in 1964. *Surprises of the Sun* (1969), a series of mainly autobiographical lyrics, disappointed critics who felt that after *Captain Quiros* McAuley would continue to write public poetry with substantial themes. Two of the poems, 'In the Huon Valley' and 'St. John's Park, New Town', reflect McAuley's reaction to his new Tasmanian environment, a reaction more fully explored in the posthumous collection *A World of Its Own* (1977), where his handwritten poems in praise of the Tasmanian east-coast area near Coles Bay are combined with paintings and drawings by Patricia Giles. *Collected Poems 1936–1970* appeared in 1971, and in the year he died *Music Late at Night: Poems 1970–1973* and *Time Given: Poems 1970–1974* were published; both titles reflect his awareness of approaching death. McAuley's chief prose works are *The End of Modernity* (1959), essays on modern literature, art and culture in general, written mainly from a traditional religious viewpoint; *The Personal Element in*

Australian Poetry (1970), the texts of his 1968 lectures for the Foundation for Australian Literary Studies; and *The Grammar of the Real* (1975), essays and literary criticism. *A Map of Australian Verse: The Twentieth Century* (1975) combines samples of the work of Australian poets with critical commentary, biographical and bibliographical information.

One of the so-called 'University' poets of the 1950s, McAuley was considered a classicist because of his belief, expressed in 'The Magian Heresy' (*Quadrant*, September 1957), that in the 'high world of Virgil and Chaucer and Dante and Shakespeare . . . the true proportions of things are recognized' and because of his stance, taken in 'An Art of Poetry' *(A Vision of Ceremony)*, that 'only the simplest forms can hold/ A vast complexity'. McAuley eschewed 'individual, arbitrary/ And self-expressive art', demanding (and providing in his own writing) traditional control and order, grace and precision. Such attitudes explain his impatience with what he saw as the self-indulgent, 'immense deviation' of the avant-garde verse of the 1940s and the resultant Ern Malley hoax (q.v.). Those opposed to his viewpoint saw his stance as arch-conservative and his attitudes as reactionary. To some of his admirers the graceful autobiographical lyrics of his later volumes represent his most pleasant poetry, but they do little to enhance the reputation and prestige he gained from the more substantial earlier works, *Under Aldebaran*, *A Vision of Ceremony* and *Captain Quiros*. His final years, however, brought an increasing recognition of his stature as critic and intellectual, although his reputation as a poet, has, since his death, suffered a decline. Peter Coleman wrote *The Heart of James McAuley: Life and Work of the Australian Poet* (1980); Leonie Kramer edited *James McAuley* (1988), which includes a personal commentary and a selection of McAuley's poetry and essays; and Lyn McCredden wrote *James McAuley* (1992) in Oxford's Australian Writers series. The James McAuley Lecture is delivered annually at the University of Tasmania in his honour. An account of McAuley's involvement in the Ern Malley hoax is contained in Michael Heyward's *The Ern Malley Affair* (1993).

MACCALLUM, Mungo Ballardie (1913–), grandson of Sir Mungo William MacCallum (q.v.) and son of Mungo Lorenz MacCallum, was born in Sydney, educated at the University of Sydney and began work as a journalist and as writer and producer for ABC radio. During the Second World War he edited the army education journal *Salt*. After studying television in Britain and Europe, he was involved as producer, announcer and interviewer in ABC television for several years, producing its opening night of television in 1956. He has since worked as a freelance radio and television broadcaster, film and arts critic, and playwright. In 1966 his radio play 'Five Days' was entered for the Italia Prize; another radio play, 'Stone-bloody-henge', won an Awgie in 1972 and he has written documentary film scripts, poetry and two novels, *A Voyage in Love* (1956) and *Son of Mars* (1963). Formerly television and book critic for *Nation*, he is also a well-known contributor to journals and newspapers.

In 1968 he edited a collection of essays, *Ten Years of Television*. His autobiography, *Plankton's Luck*, was published in 1986.

MACCALLUM, Sir Mungo William (1854–1942), born Scotland, was educated at the universities of Glasgow, Leipzig and Berlin before his appointment in 1879 as professor of English, University College of Wales at Bangor. In 1887 he was selected by a committee that included Matthew Arnold, Leslie Stephen and Max Muller to a new chair of modern literature at the University of Sydney; after his retirement in 1920 he was successively acting warden and warden (1923–24), vice-chancellor (1925–27, during the time Christopher Brennan was dismissed from the university), deputy chancellor (1928–34) and chancellor (1935–36). He was knighted for his services to education in 1926 and honoured by doctorates from the universities of Glasgow and Oxford.

MacCallum's first major publication was in the field of German philology, but his international reputation in English studies was established with the expository *Tennyson's Idylls of the King* (1894), and particularly with *Shakespeare's Roman Plays and Their Background* (1910), which remains a significant study. A man of massive learning who found his colonial appointment some hindrance to his scholarly endeavors, he was enormously influential, not only in the University of Sydney, where he developed the tradition of Elizabethan scholarship in its English department, but also in the intellectual and cultural life of NSW. He was chairman of trustees of the Public Library of NSW 1906–12, during which time the Mitchell Library opened, helped to found the CLF, was NSW representative on its central committee 1917–29, and was instrumental in the formation of the Shakespeare Society and the Australian English Association; foundation and life president of the latter 1923–42; he gave several lectures on English literary topics which were published as pamphlets, and was the subject of a special number of *Southerly* in 1944. His other publications include a biblical verse drama, *Queen Jezebel* (1930), a biography of the Sydney headmaster A.B. Weigall (1913), and *The Dramatic Monologue in the Victorian Period* (1925). His son, Mungo Lorenz MacCallum (1883–1933), was a lecturer in law at the University of Sydney, edited several plays of Shakespeare, and was leader-writer for the *Sydney Morning Herald* 1919–32; his grandson, Mungo Ballardie MacCallum (q.v.), is a journalist and writer; and his great-grandson, Mungo Wentworth MacCallum (1941–), a journalist and satirist, is the author of *Mungo's Canberra* (1977), *Mungo on The Zoo Plane* (1979) and *The Oxford Book of Australian Political Anecdotes* (1994).

McCAULEY, Shane (1954–), born Surrey, England, has lived mostly in WA, although he completed his postgraduate education in Sydney before working for the WA Department of TAFE. His poetry and short stories have appeared frequently in anthologies and periodicals and he has published three collections of poetry, *The Chinese Feast* (1984), *Deep-Sea Diver* (1987) and *The Butterfly Man* (1991). He has also written a play, 'The All-Nite Cafe', performed in Perth in 1978. With Julie Lewis he edited the anthology *Breakaway* (1980). In 1976 he won the Tom Collins Short Story Prize and in 1988 the UTA/*Poetry Australia* Bicentennial Poetry Prize; in 1983 he was co-winner of the Tom Collins Poetry Prize. McCauley's poetry, ranging from philosophical contemplation to dramatic monologue to love lyric, reflects his wide interests and reading. Particularly striking is his interest in history, which includes Australia's history. The latter has inspired some poems on military themes such as 'The Landing', which captures the impotence of men locked into a situation they cannot escape in 'the scrub' of war and the absurdity of their transient emotional reactions to the crisis, and 'Dardanelles Spring', which compares the ancient peace of the Gallipoli Peninsula where no men had walked for a thousand years with the dead men now littering the landscape, 'hands raised/ In the supplication rigor brings,/ Ignored but for insect interrogation'. Other poems spring from the cultures of ancient Greece, China and Japan, such as 'An Old Samurai Arranges Flowers' which opens his third collection and which contrasts the aesthetic delicacy and control of Japanese culture with its historical violence. For the old man the ascetic way of life in painful old age is a matter of pride, a challenge to a purer stoicism: 'My chest is as thin as these immaculate/ Paper walls, but in my small way/ a harmony can be re-instated', while the inoffensive carnations he is arranging, 'easier to preserve than human lives', suggest the grim reality of war: 'Swift as the shock of the sword/ Releasing exploding chrysanthemums/ Hidden in the neck, the sprawl/ Of depleted bodies, war's spattered banners'. Similarly, the characteristically elegant, humorous title poem of his third collection garners Eastern wisdom in a quest for balance and the sort of maturity which recognises the need to 'be a little gnarled' to 'Love what is imperfect' in the self. But some of his most attractive poems spring from personal inward experience, such as 'Visitor', a brief poignant lyric on lost love. Technically assured and sustained by coherent imagery and subtle internal rhymes, McCauley's poetry is formally sophisticated and well matured if in some poems the emotional intensity strikes the reader only at second or third reading.

McCOMBIE, Thomas (1819–69), born Aberdeenshire, Scotland, arrived in Melbourne in 1841, where he briefly tried squatting before becoming editor and part-proprietor of the *Port Phillip Gazette* 1844–51. He was a member of the Port Phillip Legislative Council 1856–59, then returned to England where he gave authoritative opinions on such colonial matters as the Aborigines, gold and the convict system, and reflected publicly on various methods of colonisation. He returned to Australia in 1866 but, discovering he was terminally ill, went back to England to die. His two main novels are *Arabin: Or, The Adventures of a Colonist in New South Wales* (q.v., 1845) and *Frank Henly: Or, Honest Industry Will Conquer* (1867), unexceptional works of literature but worthwhile because of their enthusiasm for, and realistic account of, life in Aus-

tralia. He also published historical and descriptive prose which includes *Australian Sketches* (1847, second series, 1861), *Essays on Colonization* (1850) and *The History of the Colony Of Victoria from Its Settlement to the Death of Sir Charles Hotham* (1858).

McCONNEL, Ursula, see **Aboriginal Song and Narrative in Translation**

McCRAE, George Gordon (1833–1927), born Leith, Scotland, son of Andrew Murison McCrae and Georgiana Huntly McCrae (q.v.) and father of the poet Hugh McCrae (q.v.), came to Australia in 1841. The family settled in 1843 at Arthur's Seat on the Mornington Peninsula, an area described in his mother's journal and in his *Recollections of Melbourne & Port Phillip Bay in the Early Forties* (1987, originally published in the *Victorian Historical Magazine* 1911–12). McCrae entered the civil service in Melbourne in 1854, ultimately rising to the post of deputy registrar-general. Artistic in temperament, he became an important member of the Melbourne cultural and literary scene, being one of the founders of the Yorick Club and an associate of such literary figures as Marcus Clarke, Henry Kendall, Adam Lindsay Gordon and R.H. Horne. Two of McCrae's poems, *Mamba ('The Bright-Eyed'): An Aboriginal Reminiscence* and *The Story of Balladeadro* (both 1867), are among the earliest Australian poems on Aboriginal themes. They found favour with contemporaries such as Henry Kendall, who judged McCrae 'the highest poet in Australia' whose voice was for 'scholars and thinkers only', but they soon came to be considered too romanticised and unrealistic in their treatment of the Aborigine. *The Man in the Iron Mask* (1873), a long poem in blank verse, was enlivened, like all McCrae's work, by some graceful passages, but its story of the imprisonment of a mysterious royal Frenchman held little attraction for Australian readers. A further collection, *The Fleet and Convoy and Other Verses*, was published in 1915, and his only novel, *John Rous*, in 1918.

McCRAE, Georgiana Huntly (1804–90), the mother of George Gordon McCrae and grandmother of Hugh McCrae (qq.v.) was the natural daughter of George, Marquis of Huntly, later fifth Duke of Gordon. Educated in London at a convent school run by aristocratic refugees from the French Revolution, she became an accomplished linguist and talented musician. Her forte, however, was painting, especially portraiture, a talent that was nourished by several distinguished teachers. After leaving school she lived for seven years at Gordon Castle, followed by a period in Edinburgh where she attempted to earn her living from portrait-painting. In 1830 she married a lawyer, Andrew McCrae, who migrated to Australia in 1839. Georgiana followed in 1841 and the family lived in various areas of Victoria, including Arthur's Seat near Frankston, Melbourne, where Andrew farmed. She painted some portraits and miniatures in Australia, but was better known during her lifetime as a cultured, witty and resourceful woman, the friend of most of the colony's political and cultural figures. Some of her journals covering the period 1838–65, supplemented by George Gordon McCrae's diary 1846–47, were edited by Hugh McCrae and were first published in 1934 titled *Georgiana's Journal*. One of the most valuable records of Melbourne life in the 1840s, the journal is also remarkable as the reflection of a distinctive, lively personality. Extracts from some of Georgiana McCrae's English notebooks (1804–29) were also published in *Southerly* (1946, 1947), and some of her letters and drawings are listed in H.F. Chaplin's bibliography *A McCrae Miscellany* (1967).

McCRAE, Hugh (1876–1958), born Melbourne, son of George Gordon McCrae and grandson of Georgiana Huntly McCrae (qq.v.), was initially articled to a Melbourne architect but, influenced by the Norman Lindsay set that included Randolph Bedford, Lionel Lindsay, Edward and Will Dyson, sought a living by freelance writing and illustration. In 1904 he moved to Sydney where he became involved with J.F. Archibald, A.G. Stephens and Frank Fox. In 1914 he went to the USA, where he attempted to earn a living as an artist and actor, but suffered extreme financial hardship. Back in Australia, he played Adam Lindsay Gordon in an Australian film released in 1916, performed in Shakespearean productions and was employed as a decoder in the wartime Censor's Office in Melbourne. In 1922 he returned to Sydney and continued to live there apart from a few years at Camden. Co-editor of the *New Triad* (1927–28), he also wrote poetry, prose, drama and letters, gave radio talks and public lectures, wrote for newspapers and compiled and edited personal and family memoirs. In 1953 he was made OBE.

McCrae's first collection of poetry is *Satyrs and Sunlight* (q.v., 1909), illustrated by Norman Lindsay; the title was also given to a 1928 collection of his poetry. McCrae's other volumes of poetry include *Colombine* (1920); *Idyllia* (1922) which contains a short extract from the work McCrae hoped would be his masterpiece, the verse drama 'Joan of Arc', a further extract being included in the 1928 *Satyrs and Sunlight*; *The Mimshi Maiden* (1938); *Poems* (1939), a selected volume; *Forests of Pan* (1944), containing a number of earlier poems which were not reprinted in *Poems* (1939); and *Voice of the Forest* (1945). R.G. Howarth, who edited *Forests of Pan* and arranged and introduced *Voice of the Forest*, also edited *The Best Poems of Hugh McCrae* (1961), which includes the whole of the incomplete 'Joan of Arc'. A selection of his poems made by Douglas Stewart was published in the Australian Poets series in 1966. McCrae wrote a musical fantasy, *The Ship of Heaven* (1951), which was produced in 1933; a prose work, *The Du Poissey Anecdotes* (1922); and a prose collection, *Story-Book Only* (1948), which includes the *Du Poissey* pieces and his reminiscences of his father and his times, *My Father and My Father's Friends*, first published in 1935. He edited *Georgiana's Journal* (1934), the diaries of his grandmother. McCrae also wrote an endless stream of letters to friends and acquaintants, each beautifully handwritten letter illustrated with figures and scenes and often accompanied by a verse composed for the occasion. A selection of his letters was edited by R.D. FitzGerald in 1970. A Hugh McCrae number of *Southerly* appeared in 1956.

McCrae's poetry has consistently attracted a small band of devotees: fellow Rabelaisian Kenneth Slessor, who believed that *Satyrs and Sunlight* (1909) ushered modern Australian poetry into being; Mary Gilmore, who was delighted by McCrae's verbal artistry and regarded him as Australia's finest poet; literary historian H.M. Green, who saw him as 'a prince of lyrists' with 'as near an approach to pure beauty as can be made by means of the purely physical'; and Judith Wright, who found in him 'a poet to love and admire and be proud of'. With the gradual disappearance of the generation who knew McCrae personally, much of that ardour has evaporated. Recent judgements tend, in the main, to reject the whimsy, the exotica and the seductive carnival of colour and sound that characterise his verse, finding instead incoherence of thought and lack of control over imagery and syntax; in effect, little more than imaginative chaos. He remains, however, of importance in Australian literary history, both because he anticipated the *Vision* school and because he offered, with other lyrists, an alternative to the balladry that had dominated Australian poetry in the preceding generation.

McCUAIG, Ronald (1908–93), born Newcastle, NSW, began writing for radio in 1927 and was employed by *Wireless Weekly* 1928–38. During the Second World War he worked for the ABC and for *Smith's Weekly*. He was a special writer and occasional literary critic for the *Sydney Morning Herald* 1945–46, and *Smith's Weekly* 1947. In 1949 he joined the editorial staff of the *Bulletin* where as 'Swilliam', he wrote much topical verse and numerous literary and theatre reviews. He also became fiction editor of the *Bulletin*. McCuaig's poetry publications include *Vaudeville* (1938), *The Wanton Goldfish* (1941) and the cumulative collections, *Quod Ronald McCuaig* (1946) and *The Ballad of Bloodthirsty Bessie and Other Poems* (1961, which was a 'collected' based on the earlier three). He also wrote *Tales out of Bed* (1944, essays and short stories) and *Australia and the Arts* (1972). He edited the 1954 edition of *Australian Poetry* and published the children's books *Gangles* (1972) and *Tobolino and the Amazing Football Boots* (1974). With his shrewd, and sometimes crude, satirical observations of life, his talent for dry and witty cynicism, and his delicately humorous love lyrics, McCuaig seemed likely to occupy an important place in the post-war poetry scene; however, the success of 'The Ballad of Bloodthirsty Bessie' (q.v.), a rollicking fantasy which combines greed, lust, religious mania and superbly portrayed indifference to human life, was followed by virtual poetic silence. The best of McCuaig's serious work is in *Vaudeville*. Among his best-known poems are 'The Commercial Traveller's Wife', 'Au Tombeau de mon Père', 'Music in the Air', 'The Passionate Clerk to his Love' and 'Bessie'. His *Selected Poems*, published in 1992 with an introduction by Peter Kirkpatrick, confirms that McCuaig was a highly original avant-garde poet, who was both satirical comedian and serious artist. In 1992, not long before his death, McCuaig was presented with a NSW State Special Award for his outstanding contribution to Australian literature.

McCUBBIN, Frederick (1855–1917), born West Melbourne, studied at the National Gallery of Victoria School, later becoming a master there. A prime mover in the development of the nationalistic Heidelberg School (q.v.), McCubbin began his interpretation of the local scene with *The Lost Child* (1886), a typical colonial tragedy that had already found literary expression in Henry Kingsley's novel *The Recollections of Geoffry Hamlyn* (1859) and Marcus Clarke's story 'Pretty Dick'. Other McCubbin paintings to illustrate the hardship and melancholy of pioneer life so consistently emphasised in colonial writing are *Down on His Luck* (1889), *Bush Burial* (1890), *On the Wallaby Track* (1896) and *The Pioneer* (1904). McCubbin is the art teacher of heroine Delie Gordon in Nancy Cato's novel *All the Rivers Run* (1958). The opening chapters of Katharine Susannah Prichard's novel *The Pioneers* (1915) are an imaginative interpretation of McCubbin's painting of similar title; the same painting is discussed in Mary Marlowe's novel *The Ghost Girl* (1921). J.S. MacDonald edited *The Art of Frederick McCubbin* (1916); Okko Boer compiled *Frederick McCubbin: The Man and His Art* (1980), a folio of reproductions of McCubbin's paintings with commentary; Ann Galbally wrote the biographical *Frederick McCubbin* (1981). Andrew MacKenzie's *Frederick McCubbin 1855–1917: 'The Proff' and his Art* (1990) includes extensive commentary on the portraits, correspondence and biographical information. Kathleen Mangan, McCubbin's daughter, recalls him in her autobiographies *Daisy Chains, War, then Jazz* (1984) and *Autumn Memories* (1988).

McCULLOUGH, Colleen (1937–), born Wellington, NSW, of Irish Catholic stock, was educated at the University of Sydney. After brief periods as schoolteacher, library assistant and journalist, she worked as a neurophysiologist in Sydney and England and at the Yale University's School of International Medicine 1967–76. Her first novel, *Tim*, published in the USA in 1974, depicts the relationship between Tim Melville, an unskilled labourer with the mind of a child and the body of an Adonis, and Mary Horton, a plain spinster in her forties. Although *Tim* met with some commercial success and was made into a film, its critical reception has been unenthusiastic. Her second novel, *The Thorn Birds* (q.v., 1977), a colourful and sometimes bizarre story that chronicles the fortunes of several generations of the Cleary family on Drogheda station in northern NSW, was selected from a proof copy by the United States Literary Guild. As a result it became a best-seller in both hardback and paperback; a television series was screened in 1983. Her next novel, *An Indecent Obsession* (1981), is set in the psychiatric ward of a small military hospital in the South Pacific soon after the end of the Second World War. A novel about duty (the 'indecent obsession'), it has the prescribed mix of best-selling ingredients – romance, sex, violence and paranoia. *A Creed for the Third Millennium*

(1985) is set in the twenty-first century with the Earth and Mankind under threat from a new Ice Age. The bureaucracy of the day, in the shape of the Department of the Environment, attempts to conjure up a new 'messiah' (Dr Joshua Christian, i.e. Jesus Christ) to inspire the depressed population. Following the somewhat controversial novella *The Ladies of Missalonghi* (1987), McCullough turned to the historical epic on a blockbusting scale. The three novels so far (1993) published in her saga of Ancient Rome, in a planned series of six, have been *The First Man in Rome* (1990), which begins in 110 BC, *The Grass Crown* (1991) and *Fortune's Favourites* (1993). Massive novels with huge casts (forty-eight main characters are specified, for example, in *The Grass Crown*) and prodigious plot structures, the Masters of Rome series represents an extraordinary research and writing effort, one calculated perhaps to rival that other mammoth, also in six volumes, Edward Gibbon's *The Decline and Fall of the Roman Empire* (1776–88). Perhaps Australia's most affluent writer, Colleen McCullough now lives on Norfolk Island.

MACDONALD, Alexander (1) (1878–1939), born Scotland, spent some time in WA and Queensland and served with the Australian contingent in the Boer War. A keen traveller and prospector, he wrote several accounts of his adventures, including *In Search of El Dorado* (1905), *In the Land of Pearl and Gold* (1907) and *Through the Heart of Tibet* (1910), the first two of which deal partly with Australia. He also wrote adventure stories, mostly addressed to the young male reader and extolling the active life and traditional public-school virtues; several of them draw upon his Australian experience. They include *The Lost Explorers* (1906), *The Pearl Seekers* (1907), *The Quest of the Black Opals* (1908), *The Island Traders* (1908), *The White Trail* (1908), *The Hidden Nugget* (1909) and *The Invisible Island* (1910).

MACDONALD, Alexander (2) (1915–73), a well-known Sydney journalist, was born Sydney but spent most of his boyhood in a Catholic seminary in Scotland. At 16 he was reunited with his father, who was mining for gold in north Queensland, before joining the ABC in Sydney as a continuity writer. He later became a gag-writer for such comedians as Jack Davey and Roy Rene, moved to commercial radio and wrote a weekly column of radio reviews for *Smith's Weekly*. He also contributed feature articles and humorous columns, radio and television reviews to a range of newspapers including the *Daily Telegraph*, *Sydney Morning Herald*, *Sun*, *Daily Mirror* and the *Sunday Telegraph*. Some of his pieces for the *Daily Telegraph* and *Sunday Telegraph* are reprinted in his collection *Don't Frighten the Horses* (1961). He also wrote a humorous autobiography, *The Ukelele Player under the Red Lamp* (1972), which includes vivid pictures of bohemian life in Sydney in the 1930s and 1940s, as well as reminiscences of Peter Finch, Roy Rene and Kenneth Slessor.

McDONALD, Andrew (1942–), born England, came to Australia in 1971 and has worked as a lecturer in English and in television. He has published poetry in anthologies, periodicals and newspapers and in two collections, *Absence in Strange Countries* (1976) and *The One True History* (1984). In 1979 he won the Ian Mudie Award. Rich in literary allusion and sometimes addressing jokes or puns to an implied academic reader, McDonald's first collection is in the tradition of Hardy, Gunn and Larkin, although his second is more decidedly Australian; varied in range from the macabre to the elegiac, and reflecting among other matters his travels, his responses to the country of his birth and to Australia, the difficulties of creative work, the challenge of language, and family relationships, his verse is equally varied in metrical structure.

MACDONALD, Donald Alaster (1859–1932), born Melbourne, worked on the staff of the *Argus* from 1881 until his death. Its correspondent during the Boer War, he wrote a well-received account of the siege of Ladysmith, *How We Kept the Flag Flying* (1900). Also well known as a naturalist, contributing essays and the column 'Nature Notes' to the *Argus* and other articles to the *Australasian* under the pseudonym 'Gnuyang', he published two collections of reprinted essays which represent his fluid style, enthusiastic response to nature and feeling for childhood experience, *Gum Boughs and Wattle Bloom Gathered on Australian Hills and Plains* (1887) and *Sweet-Scented Flowers and Fragrant Leaves* (1897). Another collection of his essays on a range of subjects was published after his death, titled *The Brooks of Morning* (1933). His cricket and football commentaries established a new trend in sports writing and were a popular, regular feature of the *Argus*. He also wrote two books for children, *The Bush Boy's Book* (1911), based on his column 'Notes for Boys', in the *Argus*, and *At the End of the Moonpath* (1922); and, with J.F. Edgar, a novel, *The Warrigals' Well* (1901).

McDONALD, Nan (1921–74), born Eastwood, Sydney, was educated at the University of Sydney. As publishing editor for Angus & Robertson she made a considerable contribution to the publication of Australian literature in the decades following the Second World War. She edited the annual anthology *Australian Poetry* in 1953. Her own volumes of poetry are *Pacific Sea* (1947), which won the inaugural Grace Leven Prize for poetry, *The Lonely Fire* (1954) and *The Lighthouse and Other Poems* (1959). Her *Selected Poems* was published in 1969. *Pacific Sea* captures in smooth, attractive verse the beauty of the Sydney bushlands, the grandeur of the Hawkesbury district and the pleasant seascapes of the NSW south coast. In philosophic poems such as 'The Ship' and 'The Tollgate Islands' she probes the future, wondering 'what dark fee, what cruel payment' life may exact from her. *The Lonely Fire*, more powerful and at times quite sombre, uses a series of masks, like the old tramp in the title poem, to lay bare the human condition. 'The Lighthouse' is a long dramatic study of a lighthouse-keeper who spends three days of terror fighting to regain his self-control after discovering the dead body of his companion.

MACDONALD, Robert Maclauchlan (1874–?) wrote a series of boys' adventure stories set in New Guinea, the South Pacific and Australia, which are now mainly remarkable for their improbable plots, shallow characters and frank expressions of racist prejudice and imperial pride. They include *The Great White Chief* (1907), *The Rival Treasure Hunters* (1909), *Chillagoe Charlie* (1909), *The Secret of the Sargasso* (1909), *The Gold Seekers* (1910), *The Moon God's Secret* (1910), *Danger Mountain* (1911), *The Opal Hunters* (1912) and *The Pearl Lagoons* (1911). Macdonald also wrote an account of his travels as a prospector, *Opals & Gold* (1928).

McDONALD, Roger (1941–), the son of local historian Lorna McDonald, was born at Young, NSW, educated at Temora and Bourke before attending Scots College, Sydney and the University of Sydney. He was a high-school teacher and a radio and television producer with the Education Department of the ABC in Brisbane and Hobart before becoming, in 1969, a professional editor with UQP, which published his two volumes of poetry, *Citizens of Mist* (1968) and *Airship* (1975). In his seven years with the press McDonald was involved with the Paperback Poets series which both reflected and stimulated the 'New Australian Poetry' (q.v.); his selection from the first series was published in 1974 as *The First Paperback Poets Anthology*. In 1976 he moved to Canberra to work on *1915* (q.v.), a novel about the Gallipoli experience. Published in 1979, *1915* proved an outstanding success, winning the *Age* Book of the Year Award and the SA government's Biennial Literature Award; Peter Yeldham adapted it into a seven-part television series which was shown in 1982. In 1981 he was awarded the Canada-Australia Literary Prize. His subsequent work includes the novels *Slipstream* (1982), *Rough Wallaby* (1989) and *Water Man* (1993); the semi-autobiographical *Shearers' Motel* (1992), winner of the Banjo Award for non-fiction in 1993; the fictionalised biography *Melba* (1988), and the script of the television miniseries of the same name (1988); the television script *John Simpson* (1988); a novel, *Flynn* (1992), based on the 1992 screenplay of the life of Errol Flynn by Frank Howson and Alister Webb; the text of *Michael Willesee's Australians* (1988), based on dramatised television portrayals of thirteen Australians; and *Reflecting Labor: Images of Myth and Origin over 100 Years* (1991). He also edited *Gone Bush* (1990), a collection of essays by Australian writers about bush places of significance to them.

In the intensely political world of Australian poetry since the 1960s McDonald has been much admired for his editorial activities, which helped significantly to establish or consolidate the reputation of a number of (mainly younger) Australian poets. His own poetry occupies a corner of Les Murray's 'Vernacular Republic' and is distinguished by a selection of detail and by metaphoric observations which give freshness and resonance to his metaphysical exploration of experience. His fiction also reflects his intention to 'write out of the Australian character and in the Australian accent': in practice this has often meant the exploration of the

Australian character within a historical framework, as in *Citizens of Mist* which includes poems on Adam Lindsay Gordon and other historical subjects; in *1915*, which, although explicitly described by McDonald as 'a work of the imagination', embodies also considerable research; and in *Slipstream*, a novel about a pioneer aviator of the 1920s and 1930s whose career loosely resembles that of Charles Kingsford-Smith. The interpretation offered of Gallipoli has preoccupied reviewers of *1915*, often to the distortion of the novel, in which the domestic scenes set in Australia are as important as the war scenes in establishing its major theme, the search of the four central characters for a coherent shape to their existence. A second point of discussion concerning *1915* has been the evaluation of McDonald's transformation from poet into novelist, which perhaps influenced him to jettison some of the lyricism in *1915* in the preparation of *Slipstream*, written in plainer, understated, allusive prose in keeping with the elusiveness of its central character, Roy Hilman. In *Rough Wallaby* McDonald allows satire to slip the leash for the first time. Chief among his targets is that well-worn Australian myth – mateship – but several other attitudes and groups are also deflated in the novel's farcical situations.

McDonald is clearly, in some part of his psyche, a writer by default, one who would rather be a 'doer' than a 'scribe', who would rather experience it first and then, if so inclined, comment on it. Time spent writing makes him chafe for the taste of real life – as he admits. The impulse comes, he says, 'to drop everything and head west'. So he learned to cook, drove out one morning from his then Braidwood property, waved the family goodbye and went off to join a team of Maori shearers as 'Cookie'. The experiences of the next few months yielded *Shearers' Motel*, an amalgam of observation, description, narration and characterisation, presenting McDonald at his most relaxed.

Considerably more complex than *Shearers' Motel*, *Water Man* is a story based on two attempts, half a century apart, to find artesian water for the D'Inglis property Croppdale and the nearby township of Logan's Reef. The first attempt is in 1939 when Gunner Fitch and his wife Rosan arrive to fulfil Fitch's contract with William D'Inglis. It ends in violence and drama. The search for water is taken up fifty years later with a new set of characters, many of whom, e.g. Gunner's son Mal and William's grandson Stuart, have links with the earlier characters and events. Water is found and numerous resolutions ensue. A complex study of psychological and environmental forces at work upon characters and events, *Water Man* is an ambitious work.

MACDONNELL, J.E. (James Edmond) ('Macnell') (1917–), born Mackay, Queensland, joined the RAN as an ordinary seaman at the age of 17. He spent fourteen years in the navy, saw action in the Second World War and finished his career as a commissioned gunner. A contributor of stories and articles to the *Bulletin* under the pseudonym 'Macnell', he joined the *Bulletin* in 1948 to write the weekly 'Personal Items' page. He also contributed articles on naval actions in the war which were subsequently published as a book, *Valiant Occasions* (1952), and supplemented his previous non-fictional naval account, *Fleet Destroyer* (1945). His first novel, *Gimme the Boats*, was published in 1953. MacDonnell left the *Bulletin* in 1956 to write full-time for Horwitz publications, for whom he has subsequently written an average of twelve wide-selling paperback novels a year. Almost all set against a naval background, several are a series focusing on the exploits of individual sea warriors, the most popular of whom is Jim Brady. Horwitz has also published a series of reprints under the general title *The J.E. MacDonnell Classic Library*. MacDonnell has also written several books for boys under the pseudonym 'James Macnell'.

McFADYEN, Ella May, see *The Oxford Companion to Australian Children's Literature* (1993), p. 273.

McFARLANE, Brian (1934–), associate professor of English at Monash University, is the author of the first Australian book to examine the relationship between literature and film, *Words and Images* (1983); his subsequent studies include *Australian Cinema 1970–1985* (1987), and *New Australian Cinema: Sources and Parallels in American and British Film* (1992). He has also published a critique of Martin Boyd's Langton novels (1980), and with John Barnes edited a selection of verse, *Cross-Country* (1984, 2nd edn 1988).

McFARLANE, Ian (1937–), born England, came to Australia in 1954. He worked in the Defence Department and in the Australian Diplomatic Service, which took him to Tel Aviv and Hong Kong. He has published the popular thrillers *The Jerusalem Conspiracy* (1984), *The Siberian Sparrows* (1990) and *Shadows* (1992).

McGARVIE, William (1810–41), born Glasgow, had some journalistic experience on the *Glasgow Herald* before coming to Sydney in 1828 where, through his involvement in the Australian Stationery Warehouse and its attached circulating library run by Robert Howe, he became one of Australia's earliest booksellers. McGarvie's *Catalogue of Books* (1829) of the library was the first catalogue of books issued in Australia. With Alfred Ward Stephens and Frederick Michael Stokes as partners, McGarvie imported a printing press and began publication of the *Sydney Herald* (later the *Sydney Morning Herald*, q.v.), in 1831. McGarvie sold out to the other two after only a month, and later returned to bookselling.

MACGILLIVRAY, John (1822–67), born Aberdeen, Scotland, studied medicine and zoology before accepting, in 1842, an appointment as assistant naturalist in HMS *Fly* on a surveying voyage to Australia and New Guinea. He spent three years with the *Fly*, assiduously collecting specimens whenever the ship anchored off the coast. He joined as naturalist, assisted by T.H. Huxley and James Fowler Wilson, another surveying voyage to Australia in HMS *Rattlesnake* 1847–50. His work in the natural history and exploration of Australia is recorded in his *Narrative of the Voyage of H.M.S. Rattlesnake* (1852). In 1853 he again visited Australia and the Pacific as naturalist on HMS *Herald* and subsequently spent some years in Sydney before in 1864 settling at Grafton, where he continued his work in natural science.

McGRATH, Raymond Herbert (1903–77), born Sydney, studied arts and architecture at the University of Sydney, where he was art director of *Hermes*. He also studied painting under Julian Ashton and won a reputation as a woodcut artist. Well known in literary circles, he contributed short stories to *Art in Australia* and other journals and anthologies, and published a collection of verse, illustrated, bound and printed by himself on J.T. Kirtley's private press, *The Seven Songs of Meadow Lane* (1924). At the age of 23 he won the Wentworth Travelling Scholarship to London, and later settled in Dublin; he became one of the leading architects of the modern movement. He is one of the poets recalled by J. le Gay Brereton in his reminiscences of Sydney's literary life in *Knocking Round* (1930).

McGREGOR, Craig (1933–), born Jamberoo, NSW, left school at 16 to join the *Sydney Morning Herald*. He studied part-time at the University of Sydney in the 1950s, meanwhile establishing a reputation as a journalist. In the 1960s he spent four years in England, working partly as a freelance journalist, and then lived for several years in the USA on a Harkness Fellowship. He has written an analysis of Australia's culture, history, social mores and political attitudes, *Profile of Australia* (1966), revised and published in 1980 titled *The Australian People*; two novels, *Don't Talk to Me About Love* (1971), winner of the Xavier Society Prize, and *The See-Through Revolver* (1977); numerous short stories, which have appeared in Australian and overseas magazines and newspapers and in the collection *Real Lies* (1987); the texts of several photographic studies of Australia, *The High Country* (1967), *To Sydney with Love* (1968), *Life in Australia* (1968) and *The Great Barrier Reef* (1974); and an account of the 1983 Australian federal election, *Time of Testing: The Bob Hawke Victory* (1983). His interest in popular culture and music is reflected in the essays he has written for such newspapers as the *New York Times*, *Observer*, *Spectator* and *New Statesman*; in his anthology of essays on Bob Dylan (1972); and in his collections of essays on Australian society in the 1960s, *People, Politics and Pop* (1968); on American society, *Up Against the Wall, America* (1973); and on Western society in general and Australian society in particular, *Soundtrack for the 'Eighties* (1983). He has also written scripts for films and for a rock-opera, *Hero*, and has edited a collection of interviews with Australian writers and artists, *In the Making* (1969) and another with Australians who are prominent in various fields, *Headliners* (1990). He has twice won the Walkley Award for journalism. McGregor has written a self-portrait, 'The Public Mode', in *Australian Book Review* (February 1984).

McGUIRE, Frances (1900–), born Glenelg, SA, as Frances Cheadle, was educated at the University of Adelaide and later worked as a biochemist on insulin research and was one of the founding editors of the Adelaide literary periodical *Orion*, which ran 1919–21. In 1927 she married Paul McGuire (q.v.) and subsequently lived in Europe, Asia and the USA. Well known as a freelance journalist, she has published two novels, *September Comes In* (1961) and *Time in the End* (1963); a history of the RAN (1948); an account, with Paul McGuire, of the war service of HMAS *Parramatta*, *The Price of Admiralty* (1944); a novel for children, *Three and Ma Kelpie* (1964); a series of part-satirical, part-pious fairy-tales, *Twelve Tales of the Life and Adventures of Saint Imaginus* (1946); a history of the Australian theatre (1948) with Paul McGuire and Betty Arnott; and an account of her childhood in SA, which is also a social history, *Bright Morning: The Story of an Australian Family before 1914* (1975). She has also translated the autobiography of John Gerard, *The Flight of the Falcon* (1954). Co-founder of the Dante Alighieri Society of SA, she has won cultural awards from the Italian government.

McGUIRE, Paul (1903–78), born Peterborough, SA, was educated at the University of Adelaide and in 1927 married Frances Cheadle (see McGuire, Frances) with whom he collaborated in two books. He was special overseas correspondent for various newspapers before serving in the RAN Volunteer Reserve during the Second World War. European correspondent for the *Argus* from 1945, he was appointed Australian delegate to the General Assembly of the United Nations in 1953 and was Australia's first ambassador to Italy 1953–59. He was decorated by both the Italian and the Australian governments and was made CBE in 1950. A well-known lecturer on international politics, McGuire published four influential books on current affairs, *Australia: Her Heritage, Her Future* (1939), subsequently revised and reprinted several times with the title *Australian Journey*; *Westward the Course* (1942), a survey of Asian and Pacific countries, which went to press the month Pearl Harbour was bombed and became a best-seller; *The Three Corners of the World* (1948); and *There's Freedom for the Brave* (1949). He also published a booklet of poems, *The Two Men and Other Poems* (1932), and a series of popular crime novels which were subsequently translated into several languages. These include *Murder in Bostall* (1931), *Three Dead Men* (1931), *The Tower Mystery* (1932), *Murder by the Law* (1932), *There Sits Death* (1933), *Death Fugue* (1933), *Murder in Haste* (1934), *Daylight Murder* (1934), *7.30 Victoria* (1935), *Born to be Hanged* (1935), *Prologue to the Gallows* (1936), *Threepence to Marble Arch* (1936), *Cry Aloud for Murder* (1937), *W.I.* (1938), *Burial Service* (1938) and *The Spanish Steps* (1940). A selection of his poems, edited by Paul Depasquale, was published in 1980.

MACILWAINE, Herbert C., born England, spent some years in Australia before returning to London, where he worked as a publisher's reader. He published two books of short tales which draw upon his

Australian experience, *The Twilight Reef* (1897) and *The Undersong* (1903), and some novels which describe Australian bush life from the point of view of an English migrant, including *Dinkinbar* (1898), *Fate the Fiddler* (1900), *The White Stone* (1900) and *Anthony Britten* (1906).

MACINNES, Colin (1914–76), son of the novelist Angela Thirkell (q.v.) and her first husband, James Campbell McInnes, and brother of the writer Graham McInnes (q.v.), was brought to Australia in 1920 after his mother married George Thirkell (q.v.). After an education in Melbourne he returned to England in 1930. During the Second World War he served in an intelligence unit and based his first book, *To the Victors the Spoils* (1950), on his experiences. He wrote nine novels, of which two, *June in Her Spring* (1952) and *All Day Saturday* (1966), are set in Australia. Some of his essays, contributed to such British periodicals as *Encounter*, *New Left Review* and *Twentieth Century*, are reprinted in the collection *England, Half English* (1961). He also wrote a monograph on the painter Sidney Nolan (1961), and a pictorial account, *Australia and New Zealand* (1964). A biography of MacInnes by Tony Gould, *Inside Outsider*, was published in 1983.

McINNES, Graham (1912–70) was the son of the novelist Angela Thirkell (q.v.) and her first husband, James Campbell McInnes, and the brother of the novelist Colin MacInnes (q.v.). Brought to Australia in 1920 after his mother married George Thirkell (q.v.), he was educated in Melbourne; in 1934 he left for Canada, which subsequently became his permanent home. He worked as a university lecturer, art editor of a Toronto newspaper and producer for the Canadian Film Board before joining the Canadian diplomatic service in 1948. As well as numerous film scripts and articles on art, he wrote two books on Canadian art (1939 and 1950), but is best known in Australia for his autobiographical sequence *The Road to Gundagai* (q.v., 1965), *Humping My Bluey* (1966), *Finding a Father* (1967) and *Goodbye, Melbourne Town* (1968).

The Road to Gundagai, which deals mainly with his schooldays and culminates with his mother's permanent departure for England in 1930, is both a sociological study of Melbourne in the 1920s and a vivid re-creation of the joys and fears, humiliations and enthusiasms of childhood. Particularly striking are his portraits of his mother and stepfather, and the intimate, detailed picture of the family's daily life in suburban Malvern. *Humping My Bluey*, less integrated than the earlier volume but still an effective re-creation of youthful life in Melbourne of the 1930s, retraces the events of his last year at school and his years at the University of Melbourne; it ends with his departure for Canada in search of his father. *Finding a Father* deals with his experiences in Canada and London and closes with his marriage and return to Canada in 1938. In *Goodbye, Melbourne Town*, which he described as a coda to his autobiographical sequence, McInnes explores further youthful memories of Melbourne.

MACINTYRE, Elisabeth, see *The Oxford Companion to Australian Children's Literature* (1993), pp. 274–6.

MACK, Amy (1876–1939), the sister of Louise Mack (q.v.), was born in Port Adelaide. She edited the women's page of the *Sydney Morning Herald* 1907–14 and served in the ministry of munitions, London, 1916–17. Between 1909 and 1928 she published fourteen collections of bushland stories for children. Her major collections are *A Bush Calendar* (1909), *Bushland Stories* (1910), *Birdland Stories* (1910), *Waterside Stories* (1910), *Bush Days* (1911), *Scribbling Sue and Other Stories* (1913), *Tom-tit's Nest and Other Stories* (1914) and *The Wilderness* (1922). Anthropomorphic animals and plants feature in her stories, although Mack implicitly includes much natural science and history. Her gifts for drama and realism, her sensitive recording of the natural world and avoidance, on the whole, of an overly didactic tone, make her stories still accessible. Nancy Phelan's biography *The Romantic Lives of Louise Mack* (1991) is also informative about Amy Mack.

MACK, Louise (1870–1935), born Hobart, was the daughter of a Wesleyan minister whose career took the family later to Adelaide and then to Sydney. She was educated at Sydney High School, which she drew on for her popular books for girls *Teens* (1897), *Girls Together* (1898) and *Teens Triumphant* (1933), and where she edited the *High School Magazine*. From 1898 until 1901, when she left for London, she was the author of the *Bulletin*'s 'A Woman's Letter'. From 1901 she lived for some years in England and Italy, edited a newspaper for the English residents of Florence for a period, and was in Belgium at the outbreak of war in 1914. She recorded her intrepid adventures in Antwerp and Brussels in *A Woman's Experiences in the Great War* (1915). Married twice, to J.P. Creed and Allen I. Leyland, Mack published several novels for adults, most of which are light romances and draw on her impressions of Europe and Australia: *The World is Round* (1896), *Children of the Sun* (1904), *The Red Rose of a Summer* (1909), *In a White Palace* (1910), *Theodora's Husband* (1909), *The Romance of a Woman of Thirty* (1911), *Wife to Peter* (1911), *The Marriage of Edward* (1913), *Attraction* (1913), *The Music Makers* (1914), *The House of Daffodils* (1915) and *The Maiden's Prayer* (1934). *An Australian Girl in London* (1902) records her impressions of Britain. She also published a volume of poetry, *Dreams in Flower* (1901, reprinted in *A Southern Garland*, 1904), and several short stories, some of which were reprinted in *The Bulletin Story Book* (1901). Mack's breathless style, described as 'ecstatic' by a contemporary reviewer, and her concentration on a conventional version of love, have tended to date her novels although her perceptions are often fresh and her vitality undeniable. She is at her best and her least conventional in her writing for girls, especially in the school trilogy *Teens*, *Girls Together* and *Teens Triumphant*, which is lively, realistic and unpretentious. She was the sister of Amy Mack (q.v.). Nancy Phelan's biography of Louise Mack, who was her aunt, *The Romantic Lives of Louise Mack* (1991), is a vivid portrait of an impetuous but courageous woman which is also informative about literary Sydney in the 1890s and Mack's friendships with Ethel Turner, Christopher Brennan, George Lambert, Henry Lawson, J.F. Archibald and A.G. Stephens.

MACKANESS, George (1882–1968), born Sydney, graduated from the University of Sydney in 1907 and was head of the department of English at Sydney Teachers' College 1924–46. In a long and distinguished career as educationist, historian, author, bibliographer and bibliophile, Mackaness received honorary degrees from the universities of Sydney and Melbourne, was president and fellow of the Royal Australian Historical Society, president of the FAW, a member of the CLF advisory board, and a trustee of the Public Library of NSW; he was made OBE in 1938.

Mackaness excelled in editorial and anthologist roles. Between 1935 and 1962 he edited, and sometimes translated from their original languages, forty-six small volumes dealing with such diverse subjects as Robert Louis Stevenson's association with Australia, the goldfields, the correspondence of Samuel Marsden, Richard Johnson and John Cotton, early Tasmanian history, and the discovery and exploration of the Moreton Bay District. The series, reduced to forty-four volumes titled *Australian Historical Monographs*, was reprinted in 1981. Mackaness's most significant works are the biographies *The Life of Vice-Admiral William Bligh, R.N., F.R.S.* (1931), *Sir Joseph Banks: His Relations with Australia* (1936) and *Admiral Arthur Phillip* (1937). His poetry anthologies began in 1913 with *Selections from the Australian Poets* and *The Children's Treasury of Australian Verse*, both in collaboration with Bertram Stevens (q.v.). In 1934 he edited the familiar anthology *The Wide Brown Land* in collaboration with his daughter Joan. His other anthologies include *Australian Short Stories* (1928), *Essays, Imaginative and Critical, Chosen From Australian Writers* (1933, with J.D. Holmes) and *Poets of Australia* (1946). Other Mackaness publications of interest are *The Art of Book-Collecting in Australia* (1956), in which he records his experiences as a bibliophile; *The Books of the Bulletin: An Annotated Bibliography* (1955, in collaboration with Walter Stone), a record of the *Bulletin* books 1888–1952; and *Bibliomania: An Australian Book Collector's Essays* (1965).

MACKAY, Angus (1824–86), born Aberdeen, Scotland, was educated in Sydney and began a varied career as a journalist when he succeeded James Martin as editor of the *Atlas* in 1847. Subsequently he worked on the *People's Advocate* in Sydney, was a goldfields correspondent for the *Empire* and the *Argus*, edited the *Bendigo Advertiser*, was proprietor of the *Riverine Herald*, foundation editor of the *Queenslander* and helped to found the Sydney *Daily Telegraph*. In 1868–77 and 1883–86 he was a member of the Victorian parliament, serving several terms as a minister. He was the author of *The Great Gold Field* (1853) and *A Visit to Sydney and the Cudgegong Diamond Mines* (1870).

McKAY, Claude (1878–1972) was born at Kilmore, Victoria, where he began his journalistic career on the *Kilmore Advertiser*. In the next decade he was a journalist in Seymour, Melbourne, Warrnambool, Bendigo, Brisbane and Sydney before he became a publicist for a circus and, in 1908, a press agent, talent scout and house author for the theatrical entrepreneur J.C. Williamson. In 1918, while seconded as a government war-loan publicist, he met Sir James Joynton Smith. With Smith and R.C. Packer, McKay founded *Smith's Weekly* (q.v.) and was its editor or editor-in-chief 1919–27 and 1939–50; he was also involved in the management of the *Daily Guardian*, which ran the first Miss Australia contest in 1926–27, and was managing director of *Smith's Weekly* briefly in the 1930s. With Harry Julius, McKay published *Theatrical Caricatures* (1912); he also wrote a book of memoirs, *This is the Life* (1961) and ghosted Joynton Smith's autobiography, *My Life Story* (1927).

McKAY, Hugh (1877–?), born Melbourne, studied medicine in a desultory way at Melbourne University in the 1890s while leading a bohemian existence and becoming familiar with such literary figures as E.J. Brady, Louis Esson and Spencer Brodney (qq.v.). He eventually became a registered chemist after a period spent as a freelance writer. A member of the T.M.J. (the Too Much Jesus Society), McKay developed an interest in the speculative possibilities of science and a personal aesthetic based partly on Nietzschean ideas, publishing a series of articles and short stories in the *Lone Hand* 1908–10, similar to the genre which H.G. Wells popularised. Regarded as a genius by some of his contemporaries and noted for his satirical wit, he published light verse in the *Bulletin*, which consistently rejected his serious poetry. From 1915 to 1921 he ran a pharmacy in North Perth but then returned to Sydney, where he reverted to bohemianism in the company of the sons of Norman Lindsay and the *Vision* group of writers. Some of his poetry was included in the *Vision* anthology *Poetry in Australia: 1923*, but his only individual collection is *In the Changing Crystal* (1909). He later became the science writer for *Smith's Weekly* and a journalist on the staff of the *Daily Telegraph*, abandoning serious literature and becoming more reclusive. Memorable more for his distinctive personality, recalled by several of his friends in their autobiographies, than for his achievements, McKay has been described as a significant figure in the pre-1914 cultural scene.

MACKAY, James Alexander Kenneth (1859–1935), born Wallendbeen, NSW, was a member of the NSW Legislative Council and vice-president of the Executive Council 1899–1900, and a distinguished military officer, rising to the rank of major-general. In 1897 he raised the 1st Australian Horse, a volunteer cavalry regiment recruited from NSW country districts and commanded the NSW Imperial Bushmen's Contingent in South Africa 1900–1. Chairman of a royal commission on the administration of Papua 1906–7, his personal account, *Across Papua*, was published in 1909. He was director-general of the Australian Army reserve during the First World War. He frequently contributed articles and verse to Australian newspapers and, as Kenneth Mackay, published two novels, *Out Back* (1893) and *The Yellow Wave: A Romance of the Asiatic Invasion of Australia* (1895), and three collections of verse, *Stirrup Jingles from the Bush and the Turf* (1887), *A Bush Idyl* (1888) and *Songs of a Sunlit Land* (1908).

MACKELLAR, Dorothea (1885–1968) was born in Sydney into a well-established and wealthy family, and was educated privately and at the University of Sydney, acquiring a facility for languages which proved useful during her wide-ranging travel in Australia and overseas. At 19 she wrote a poem (the second verse of which is probably the best-known stanza in Australian poetry) which was published in 1908 in the London *Spectator* as 'Core of My Heart'. When revised and published in her first book, *The Closed Door* (1911), it carried the title 'My Country' (q.v.), and has become familiar to generations of Australian schoolchildren. Mackellar published three further volumes of poetry, *The Witch-Maid* (1914), *Dreamharbour* (1923) and *Fancy Dress* (1926), which confirm her delight in nature as well as her facility at verse translations, but for many Australians she remains the author of one famous poem. With a sculpture of her on horseback in the centre of the town, Gunnedah in NSW claims Dorothea Mackellar for its own. Her family owned a substantial property in the district, which she often visited. Its typical Australian scenery is said by some to have provided the inspiration for 'My Country'. Before prolonged ill health forced her largely to abandon writing in the middle 1920s she also wrote three novels, *The Little Blue Devil* (1912), *Outlaws Luck* (1913), and *Two's Company* (1914), the first and last in collaboration with Ruth Bedford. Made OBE in 1968, she was for some years active in and patron of the English Association. A collection of her poetry was published in 1971 as *The Poems of Dorothea Mackellar* and *My Country and other Poems* in 1982. *I Love a Sunburnt Country: The Diaries of Dorothea Mackellar* was edited by Jyoti Brunsdon in 1990 and Adrienne Howley, who nursed her for the last decades of her life, has written a biography, *My Heart, My Country: The Story of Dorothea Mackellar* (1989).

McKELLAR, John (1881–1966), born Greenock, Scotland, settled in Melbourne, where he worked as a journalist and developed connections with the Jindyworobak poets. He contributed to *Merringek*, and published a series of pamphlets 1946–54 to express his strong views on a range of subjects including conscription, evolution, Christianity and politics. He also published two novels, *Sheep without a Shepherd* (1937) and *Tree by the Creek* (1961), an imaginative account of the Burke and Wills expedition of 1860–61 narrated by John King, the sole survivor, and originally an award-winning radio script. In 1951 some of McKellar's essays were collected as *Digging at Roots*.

McKELLAR, J.A.R. (John Alexander Ross) (1904–32), born Dulwich Hill, Sydney, left school at

15 to work in a bank. At a time when he was regarded as a poet of some potential, encouraged by such writers as Kenneth Slessor, Hugh McCrae and H.M. Green, and was also establishing a reputation as an athlete, McKellar died suddenly of pneumonia. He contributed poetry to the *New Triad* and published one collection in his lifetime, *Twenty-Six* (1931), selected by Kenneth Slessor. Some of his poems have appeared in anthologies but it was not until 1946 that his *Collected Poems* was published, edited by J.W. Gibbes; *Southerly* published a commemorative issue in 1944. A keen classical student, McKellar expressed his admiration for Greek literature in his choice of subject and style.

McKEMMISH, Jan (1950–), born Tongala, Victoria, has written two novels, *A Gap in the Records* (1985) and *Only Lawyers Dancing* (1992). A feminist thriller which subverts the ideology of the genre by rejecting the tone of male, heroic confidence in unravelling a tangle of events as if it were a hazardous crossword puzzle, *A Gap in the Records* is a more lifelike tangle of false leads, lies, imperfect information and scraps of truth; its plot is based 'entirely on the notion that the world is a big place and truth stranger than fiction'. The male hero is replaced by a group of four women, a 'hen's party', composed of 'Some of the best brains in the country', although they are ordinary-looking women, who disarm suspicion; the story which emerges piecemeal from the plot's collage is of a global empire of finance, espionage and political manipulation. Constructed on the notion that 'We live in a world of no truth', the novel is also a postmodernist challenge to the reader, twisting away from the 'profundity' of an ending, and admitting instead the fictiveness of the reader's as well as the author's purposes: 'There are gaps in every record. They can be filled'. The hero of *Only Lawyers Dancing* is also a woman, a psychologist turned lawyer who defends a crime boss charged with murder, eventually discovering the truth and resolving her relationship with her father at the same time.

McKenzie, Barry, a film and comic-strip character created by Barry Humphries (q.v.) and the artist Nicholas Garland, embarked on a series of adventures in the English satirical magazine *Private Eye* in 1963. An Australian innocent abroad, Barry, or 'Bazza' to his mates, was the stereotyped, uncultivated Australian in London, perpetually failing in his quest for 'sheilas' who would 'come across', but finding recompense in alcohol. Selections from the *Private Eye* strip, which ran until 1974, were published in 1968, 1971 and 1979, as were the scripts (1973) of two McKenzie films, *The Adventures of Barry McKenzie* (1972) and *Barry McKenzie Holds His Own* (1974), written by Humphries and the film director Bruce Beresford; both comic strip and film satirise the English as much as the Australians. The popularity of Barry McKenzie, which can be measured by the number of his phrases which have become part of Australian English (q.v.), helped focus attention on and promote discussion of the 'ocker' (q.v.) stereotype during the 1970s, when 'Bazza' was a generic term for such stereotypes. 'Bazzaland' also had a brief currency as a synonym for Australia. *The Complete Barry McKenzie* appeared in 1988.

MACKENZIE, David, a clergyman who visited Australia 1835–45 and 1848–52, published an account of his experiences, *Ten Years in Australia* (1851), which was an expansion of his *The Emigrant's Guide: Or, Ten Years Practical Experience in Australia* (1845) and which proved popular with English readers, especially after the discovery of gold. Mackenzie deals with a range of aspects of colonial life including the 'Literature of Botany Bay'. He also wrote *The Gold Digger: A Visit to the Gold Fields of Australia in February 1852*, which was first published with the third edition of *Ten Years in Australia* in 1852.

MACKENZIE, Kenneth ('Seaforth') (1913–55), born Perth, was educated at Guildford Grammar School, Muresk Agricultural College and the University of WA. His periods of education were all incomplete: at 16 he ran away from school and never returned, his stay at Muresk lasted a year, and he left university without taking a degree. After moving to Sydney in 1934 at the suggestion of Norman Lindsay, he tried journalism, but his dislike of routine, combined with an increasing dependence on alcohol, made him an unreliable employee. He married Kathleen Bartlett, an art teacher, in 1934 and they had two children. In 1942 he was drafted into the army and served as a corporal attached to a compound of Italian prisoners at the POW camp at Cowra. A mass breakout of Japanese prisoners there in 1944 was used by Mackenzie as the subject of his novel *Dead Men Rising* (q.v.). After some time in an army hospital in 1945, he attempted to rejoin the civilian work-force but his handicaps persisted and the family was eventually forced to separate. During his last few years Mackenzie lived on a very small property at Kurrajong owned by his wife, while she supported their children in Sydney by teaching sculpture. In 1955, during a visit to a friend at Goulburn, he drowned in a creek.

His novels, all first published under the pseudonym 'Seaforth' Mackenzie, include *The Young Desire It* (q.v., 1937), which won the Australian Literature Society's Gold Medal, *Chosen People* (1938), *Dead Men Rising* (1951) and *The Refuge* (1954). Two collections of poetry under the name Kenneth Mackenzie were published in his lifetime and two posthumously. They include *Our Earth* (1937, illustrated by Norman Lindsay), *The Moonlit Doorway* (1944), *Selected Poems* (1961, ed. Douglas Stewart) and *The Poems of Kenneth Mackenzie* (1972, ed. Evan Jones and Geoffrey Little). Several uncollected short stories were also published and he left manuscripts of others as well as radio plays and an uncompleted novel.

Preoccupations that persist in Mackenzie's distinctive fiction include alienation, discontinuity and obsessive parent–child relationships, although the success of his treatment of them varies. *The Young Desire It*, based on his experiences at school, attempts themes previously unexplored in Australian fiction. An intensely introspective account of a boy's experience of love, both homosexual and heterosexual, it

shows a poet's sensitivity to experience and language. *Chosen People*, which includes two of the characters of the earlier novel though with a different narrative focus, is sophisticated and technically assured but lacks depth. Although *Dead Men Rising* is a well-realised and varied work, it is uneven in tone and unequal to its potentially interesting subject. In *The Refuge*, narrator and protagonist are combined in the figure of the crime reporter Lloyd Fitzherbert, who relives his relationship with his secret wife Irma and his eventual murder of her. Carefully crafted, the novel has a well-controlled narrative although there are some absurdities of plot and character.

Mackenzie's early poetry, with its penchant for romantic melodrama and vitalist themes, shows the influence of Norman Lindsay and Hugh McCrae. His second collection is marked by an unusually frank exploration of sexual relationships. Later he began to write a more austere poetry which turns on the themes of pain, isolation, time, family relationships and death and which achieves, at its best, a controlled tranquillity and compassion. Among his finest pieces are those he wrote about his experiences in hospital, published for the first time in full in the 1972 collection. Evan Jones wrote the critical study *Kenneth Mackenzie* (1969).

McKIE, Ronald (1909–91), born Toowoomba, Queensland, was educated at the University of Queensland and worked as a journalist on various newspapers in Australia (e.g. Melbourne *Herald*, *SMH* and *Daily Telegraph*), Singapore and China. He served with the AIF for a time in the Second World War before becoming a war correspondent in Burma and Italy; he later reported the Potsdam Conference in Berlin and the Quisling trial in Norway. After the war he returned to the *Daily Telegraph*. As a journalist-writer he published prolifically, e.g. documentary works such as *This Was Singapore* (1942, written after the Japanese capture of the city), *Malaysia in Focus* (1963), *The Company of Animals* (1965), *Bali* (1969) and *Singapore* (1972). His war writings include *Proud Echo* (1953), the story of the exploits of HMAS *Perth*; *The Heroes* (1960), the story of the little-known Rimau party, a group of twenty Australian and British servicemen who were beheaded by the Japanese for their raid on Japanese shipping in Singapore harbour; and *Echoes from Forgotten Wars* (1980). His novels include *The Mango Tree* (1974, an account of his boyhood in Bundaberg, Queensland, which won both the Miles Franklin and the Barbara Ramsden Awards), *The Crushing* (1977) and *Bitter Bread* (1978, which recalled the Depression days in Melbourne). *We Have No Dreaming* (1988) is McKie's own story of his life which includes some of his experiences as a war correspondent.

McKINLAY, John (1819–72), born Scotland, migrated to NSW in 1836. He soon became well versed in bushcraft and made money by trading in squatting leases, taking up a number of stations west of the Darling 1850–60. In August 1861 he was chosen to lead the SA Burke Relief Expedition, after the explorers Burke and Wills failed to return. His subsequent journey of exploration towards the Gulf of Carpentaria, the second to cross the continent from south to north, was recorded in his *McKinlay's Journal of Exploration in the Interior of Australia* (1862). In 1865 he made further explorations in the Northern Territory before settling down as a pastoralist near Gawler.

McKINNEY, Jack (1891–1966), born Melbourne, spent a large part of his life working as a freelance journalist and on the land as farmer, drover, shearer and jackeroo. He wrote short stories for the *Australian Journal* and other periodicals; a novel, *Crucible* (1935), which drew on his experiences of the First World War and won first prize for a work of fiction by a member of the armed forces; and several plays. Of these, *The Well*, published in *Khaki, Bush and Bigotry* (1968, ed. Eunice Hanger), was first produced in 1960 and won a minor play-writing prize; *Next Door*, included in *Australian One-Act Plays, Book I* (1962, ed. Eunice Hanger), is an adaptation of Act I of *The Well*. An experimental playwright, McKinney attempts to enliven the naturalistic, rural Australian play with expressionistic elements and an innovative approach to language. Interested also in philosophy, he published a brief exposition of his thinking, *The Challenge of Reason* (1950), which was superseded by his longer work *The Structure of Modern Thought* (1971). He was the husband of Judith Wright.

MACKLIN, Robert (1941–), born Brisbane, left school at 16 to work as a jackeroo before joining the *Courier-Mail* as a cadet journalist. In 1964 he joined the *Age*, and in 1967 became press secretary to the deputy prime minister, John McEwen. His next position as an information officer in Manila led to his directing, editing and narrating several documentary films on Asian countries. He is currently a columnist and arts editor for the *Canberra Times*. He has published four popular novels, *The Queenslander* (1975), *The Paper Castle* (1977), *Newsfront* (1978, based on a screenplay by Bob Ellis), and *The Journalist* (1979, adapted from a screenplay by Edna Wilson and Michael Thornhill); and has collaborated with Frank Galbally, a prominent lawyer, in a murder mystery, *Juryman* (1982). He has also written the controversial book *The Secret Life of Jesus* (1990). *The Queenslander* traces the history of a young man as he progresses from youth in suburban Brisbane to life as a jackeroo in the Queensland outback and subsequently as a journalist and writer in Brisbane; *The Paper Castle*, set partly in Canberra, Queensland and Asia, deals with the world of politics and international affairs.

McKNIGHT, Roger (1925–), born Jamestown, SA, served in the AIF in the Second World War and has subsequently worked as a dairy farmer and woodworker. He has published poetry in anthologies and periodicals and in two volumes, *You Can Hear Grass Grow* (1970) and *The Grass-Trees* (1988). Relying mainly on the rural landscape, he draws analogies between natural features and phenomena and human emotions and experiences, often in a mood of whimsy or fantasy.

MACKY, Stewart, brought up in NZ, graduated in medicine from the University of Melbourne and subsequently practised his profession in SA and Melbourne. A keen amateur actor, producer and playwright, he was a friend of Vance Palmer and Louis Esson and an active member of the Pioneer Players, although his disillusionment with audience reactions and the demands of his profession made his contribution short-lived. His plays, 'John Blake' and *The Trap*, were produced in Melbourne in 1922 by the Players. Both draw upon Australia's convict past, *The Trap*, which is included in *Best Australian One-Act Plays* (1937) ed. William Moore and Tom Inglis Moore, being a dramatised version of a short story by 'Price Warung'. In the 1930s Macky spent some time in London. A cousin of W.J. Turner, he was friendly with Aldous Huxley, James Stephens and S.L. Koteliansky. His work with the Pioneer Players is described by Vance Palmer in his *Louis Esson and the Australian Theatre* (1948).

McLAREN, Jack (1884–1954), born Melbourne, the son of a puritanical Presbyterian clergyman, ran away from home at 16. After a year's wandering in the bush he became a cabin boy on a sailing vessel bound for South Africa. These early, severe experiences are graphically described in *Blood on the Deck* (1933), revised in 1947 with the title *My First Voyage*. He was subsequently mate on a timber schooner trading along the Queensland coast and tried a variety of occupations in the Pacific, northern Australia and New Guinea, before in 1911 settling on the west coast of the Cape York Peninsula where he established a coconut plantation. His account of his eight years on Cape York, *My Crowded Solitude* (1926), distinguished by his detailed observations of the area's natural life and including succinct descriptions of his hardships and achievements and more extended accounts of Aboriginal life, was popular both in England and overseas. During these years McLaren also began to contribute prose sketches to the *Bulletin*, often using the pseudonym 'Jack McNorth'. He moved to Sydney in 1919 to work as a freelance writer, and subsequently lived in Melbourne before settling in 1925 in London, where he eventually established a reputation. A familiar radio broadcaster in England, McLaren contributed articles and short stories to English, American and Australian magazines. He published three other autobiographical travel books, *My Odyssey* (1923), which describes his experiences in Papua, Thursday Island and the Solomons, *My South Seas Adventures* (1936), and *My Civilized Adventure* (1952). He also wrote numerous short stories and novels, which are competent if undistinguished adventure stories or romances based on his experiences in northern Australia, the Pacific Islands and New Guinea. Generally sympathetic, if occasionally paternalistic, towards the indigenous peoples of these areas, McLaren interprets their way of life in his travel writings with sensitivity and even deference. His novels and short-story collections include *Red*

Mountain (1919), *The White Witch* (1919), *The Skipper of the 'Roaring Meg'* (1919), *The Savagery of Margaret Nestor* (1920), *The Oil Seekers* (1921), *Feathers of Heaven* (1921), *Fagaloa's Daughter* (1923), *Spear-Eye* (1925), *The Hidden Lagoon* (1926), *Isle of Escape* (1926), *The Sun Man* (1928), *A Diver Went Down* (1929), *The Money Stones* (1933), *The Devil of the Depths* (1935), *The Crystal Skull* (1936), *Their Isle of Desire* (1941), *The Marriage of Sandra* (1946), *Stories of Fear* (1946), *Stories of the South Seas* (1946) and *New Love for Old* (1948). Of these, one of the most distinctive is *The Sun Man*, a romance set on Thursday Island, which includes some graphically described diving scenes. McLaren's knowledge of diving also animates one of his best short stories, 'A Diver Went Down'. In addition he published a volume of verse, *Songs of a Fuzzy-top* (1926), the love story of a South Sea Islander; and *Gentlemen of the Empire* (1940), an account of the work of district commissioners, patrol officers and other officials in some of 'the British Empire's tropical outposts'.

McLAREN, Philip (1943–), born Redfern, Sydney, a descendant of the Kamilaroi people of NSW, is a freelance producer of television and film documentaries. During the late 1960s and 1970s he lived overseas, working in television and advertising. His novel *Sweet Water – Stolen Land* (1993) which interweaves the destinies of his families, one Black and the other White, is a powerful re-creation of the historical dispossession of the Aboriginal people. *Sweet Water – Stolen Land* won the David Unaipon Award for Black writing in 1992.

MACLEAN, Donald Findlay (1874–1937), born Hotspur, Victoria, left school at 12 and became a bush missionary at 20, later entering the Baptist ministry. After serving as a padre in the First World War he travelled extensively, meanwhile contributing frequently to Australian magazines and newspapers. In 1927 he returned to Melbourne, where he worked in radio. Maclean published three novels, *The Man from Curdie's River* (1907), which deals with the career of a bush missionary in western Victoria; *John Scarlett, Ganger* (1912), an account of the adventures of a welfare worker among railway labourers; and *The Luck of the 'Gold Moidore'* (1920), an adventure story concerning quests for gold in the sixteenth century, which was originally published as a serial in England with the title 'The Mahogany Ship'.

McLEAN, Donald James (1905–75), born Broken Hill, trained at Sydney Teachers' College and became one of Australia's foremost educationists. Headmaster of several government schools, he published three influential books on education, *The Education of the Personality* (1952), *Nature's Second Sun* (1954) and *Children in Need* (1956), and edited a collection of essays on Australian educational policies, *It's People That Matter* (1969). Editor of all the publications of the NSW Department of Education in the 1960s, he was also educational correspondent for the *Sydney Morning Herald*, and one of the initiators of the ASA. McLean also wrote three novels which draw upon his own and his

family's experiences at Broken Hill and in outback NSW, *No Man Is An Island* (1955), *The Roaring Days* (1960), and *The World Turned Upside Down* (1962).

McLEOD, Alan Lindsay (1928–), born Sydney, was educated at the University of Sydney, where he edited the magazines *Vesperis* and *Descant*, and has taught for many years in the USA. The author of numerous articles on Australian literature and of three collections of poetry, *The Change of Light* (1953), *Beyond the Cresting Surf* (1959) and *Chautauqua Canticles* (1962), he has also edited, with Richard Preston, *The Lincoln Anthology 1951* (1951), a selection of writing by young Australians including Lex Banning, Sylvia Lawson and Reba Ginsburg, and the essay collections *The Commonwealth Pen* (1961) and *The Pattern of Australian Culture* (1963). McLeod has also edited *Australia Speaks* (1969), a selection of speeches, and an account of Walt Whitman's reputation in Australia and NZ (1964).

McLEOD, Marjorie (1893–) was born in Dimboola, Victoria. Founder of the Swan Hill National Theatre, of which she was director and producer for many years, she worked as a teacher of speech and as an actor and writer for ABC radio before moving to Swan Hill in 1946. Two of her plays were published in anthologies, *Travail* in *Eight Plays by Australians* (1934) and *Moonshine* in *Five Plays by Australians* (1936), and she also published *Within These Walls* (1948), a four-act historical play first produced in Melbourne in 1936, and *Four Period Plays* (1958). The last-named collection comprises *Within These Walls*; *Mine a Sad One*, which is based on an imaginary incident in the life of the explorer Robert O'Hara Burke and was first produced in 1956; *A Shillingsworth*, a study of a Melbourne family in the Depression, which was first produced in 1931 and won first prize in the Australian Literature Society competition; and *Horizons*, a study of the experience of New Australians in the Murray River district, which was first produced in 1952. She has also published a poetry collection, *Verses from Swan Hill* (1946), which includes a verse drama, 'The Enchanted Tryst'; and an account of her experience with the Swan Hill National Theatre, *All the World's a Stage* (1980).

MACLEOD, William (1850–1929), born London of Scots descent, arrived in Australia in 1855. Like his stepfather, James Anderson, he became an artist, and established a reputation as a portrait-painter, designer of stained glass, and illustrator for such journals as the *Sydney Mail* and the *Illustrated Sydney News*. He was a regular contributor to the *Bulletin* (q.v.) from its inception in 1880. Following the departure of W.H. Traill from the management of the journal in 1886, Macleod withdrew from his involvement with the *Picturesque Atlas of Australasia* and became managing director in 1887; he remained in that position until his retirement in 1927, retaining financial control of the *Bulletin* throughout the second editorship of J.F. Archibald and that of his successors. The Archibald–Macleod partnership (1886–1903) presided over the most successful years of the *Bulletin*, and clearly Archibald benefited from Macleod's sound business sense. 'Without Archibald after Traill left there would have been no *Bulletin*', suggested A.G. Stephens, 'without Macleod, or some similar manager, there would have been no *Bulletin* long'. Macleod's career both as artist and *Bulletin* proprietor was enthusiastically sketched by his widow, Agnes Conor Macleod, in *Macleod of 'the Bulletin'* (1931).

McMAHON, Gregan (1874–1941), actor and theatrical producer, was born in Sydney and in 1896 graduated from the University of Sydney. A member of the Sydney University Dramatic Society, McMahon also performed in amateur theatre, and in 1900 decided to leave the firm of solicitors for which he was working to join Robert Brough's comedy company. In 1911 he established the Melbourne Repertory Theatre Company, formed mainly of well-trained amateurs. Notwithstanding its lack of a permanent theatre, the Company produced a range of avant-garde international plays, as well as plays by Australian writers such as Louis Esson, William Moore, Blamire Young, Arthur Adams, Helen Simpson and Alfred Buchanan. In 1918, when the effects of the war were clearly restricting the activities of the Company, McMahon accepted a professional engagement in Sydney with the Tait brothers, who had taken over the J.C. Williamson firm. Still committed to the idea of an alternative theatre, McMahon was able to use his position with J.C. Williamson's to establish, with the backing of the Tait brothers, the Sydney Repertory Theatre Society. Australian playwrights were inactive during this period and McMahon, though sympathetic to Australian drama, produced only four Australian plays between 1920 and 1927 and these were by obscure playwrights. In 1926, after the Taits purchased the Comedy Theatre in Melbourne, it was agreed that McMahon should produce three months of repertory theatre there each year with the Melbourne Society. Financial losses in 1928, however, led the Taits to impose economic restrictions on the societies, which both failed to accept. McMahon continued to produce plays for the Taits as director of a semi-professional society in both Sydney and Melbourne and in 1929 formed the group known as the Gregan McMahon Players. Backed by a series of theatrical entrepreneurs, the group included some able actors, the most brilliant being Coral Browne, and continued to stage at least eight productions a year until McMahon's death. Producing plays by such writers as Shaw, Chekhov, Ibsen, Galsworthy and Pirandello, McMahon provided an alternative, serious theatre for thirty years at a time when Australia was culturally isolated and its entertainment industry was dominated by foreign stars and commercially successful, internationally popular productions. He was made CBE in 1938. His personality and work have been recorded by two of his ex-students, Doris Fitton in her autobiography *Not Without Dust & Heat* (1981) and Hal Porter in *The Watcher on the Cast-Iron Balcony* (1963).

McMASTER, Rhyll (1947–), born Brisbane, has published three books of poetry, *The Brineshrimp* (1972), for which she was awarded the Harri Jones Memorial Prize; *Washing the Money* (1986), which shared the Victorian Premier's Literary Award (the C.J. Dennis Award) for Poetry in 1985 and won the Grace Leven Poetry Prize for 1986; and *On My Empty Feet* (1993). In all her books she recalls scenes and events from childhood – 'freeze frames' as she aptly describes them. Poems such as 'Crab Meat', 'Underneath the House', 'Profiles of My Father', 'Washing the Money' and 'Eeling' describe specific moments of a seemingly placid and secure childhood in clear and unpretentious language. More sophisticated imagery enhances poems on other subjects and themes. 'Vertebrae' and 'Light' are more complex poetic constructions, combining close observation of external details with a compelling sense of strangeness and mystery. The central poem of *On My Empty Feet*, 'My mother and I become victims of a stroke', a powerful study of a stifled life, unites with others evoking alienation, fragmentation and displacement. Rhyll McMaster has also written short fiction and been a reviewer of fiction for the *Sydney Morning Herald* and in 1994 became poetry editor for the *Canberra Times*.

McMILLAN, Robert (1848–1929), born Edinburgh, came to Australia in 1893 and worked as a freelance journalist before editing the *Stock and Station Journal* until 1917, when he was appointed editor of the *Grazier* (Queensland), before returning to the *Stock and Station Journal* in 1921. It became *Country Life* in 1924. One of the foundation members of the New South Wales Institute of Journalists, he was its first secretary. His column 'Science Gossip', under the pseudonym 'Gossip', was very popular with country readers and was partly republished in his *Science Gossip for Young and Old* (1907). He also wrote a series of popular books on such subjects as philosophy, religion and science, including *Origin of the World* (1913), *The Story of a Microscope* (1914), *No Breakfast* (1905) and *Why We Do It* (1919); an account of his travels, *There and Back* (1903); a novel for young people, *The Voyage of the 'Monsoon'* (1900); and three collections of prose pieces, *Australian Gossip and Story* by 'Globetrotter' (1895), *Unsuccessful Competitors* (1897) and *Cities of the War* (1917).

McMULLEN, Sean (1948–), born Melbourne, gained his MA at the University of Melbourne and a Diploma in Computer Science at La Trobe University. He is a systems analyst with the Bureau of Meteorology and has made a considerable reputation as a writer of science fiction. He won the 43rd World Science Fiction Convention Competition Prize in 1986 and the 1992 Ditmar Science Fiction Award for his short story 'Alone in his Chariot'. His debut collection of stories, *Call to the Edge* (1992), is wide-ranging in time and place. Memorable stories of the collection are 'The Colours of the Masters', 'The Eyes of the Green Lancer', 'Alone in His Chariot', 'The Deciad' and 'Destroyer of Illusions'. 'The Colours of the Masters', published in the prestigious *Fantasy and*

Science Fiction, is about an early invention that turned sound into colours and a modern computer technique converting those colours back to sound. 'The Deciad', his 1986 prize-winning story, is the memoir of an ancient Roman stonemason. All the stories in *Call to the Edge* reflect on the near possible rather than the impossible, the hallmark of good Science Fiction writing.

McNALLY, Ward (1917–91), born NZ as Clifford Douglas Keane, had an exceptionally deprived childhood. After running away from home at 13, he had some success as a boxer before he was convicted of housebreaking and sentenced to imprisonment. In 1950 he came to Australia, where he travelled widely, working mainly as a journalist. Editor of the *Centralian Advocate* in Alice Springs and some Queensland newspapers in the late 1960s, he also spent some time in Fiji, where he edited the *Fiji Times* and the *Herald*. A passionate advocate of the Aboriginal people, McNally wrote two books about their treatment by White society, *Goodbye Dreamtime* (1973) and *The Angry Australians* (1974). He also wrote two descriptive accounts of Australia, *Australia, the Challenging Land* (1965) and *Australia, the Waking Giant* (1969); two biographies of Sir Charles Kingsford-Smith, *Smithy* (1966) and *The Man on the Twenty-dollar Note* (1976); an account of mining in Broken Hill, *To Broken Hill and Back* (1975); two frank autobiographies which have aroused the interest of sociologists and social historians, *Cry of a Man Running* (1968) and *Man from Zero* (1973); a pseudo-autobiographical novel for the late teenager about a boy's depressed childhood in Sydney, *Supper at Happy Harry's* (1982); and a biography of T.G. Strehlow, *Aborigines, Artefacts and Anguish* (1981).

MACNAMARA, Francis (1811–?), a convict who was probably the writer best known as 'Frank the Poet' and also as Francis Goddard, was born in Ireland and transported to NSW in 1832. His original offence was stealing but he may, in addition, have been a political agitator. Certainly he was a recalcitrant during his first decade in Australia: he absconded several times, suffered numerous floggings and other punishments, and served extended terms as a member of a chain gang. In 1839, while employed as a shepherd with the Australian Agricultural Company, he composed 'A Convict's Tour to Hell' (q.v.), an anti-authoritarian satire which passed into oral tradition. In 1842 MacNamara was sent to Port Arthur, where his conduct improved to the point that he was given a ticket of leave in 1847 and his freedom in 1849. Known as a composer of cheeky, extempore verse, he reputedly farewelled the audience which had come to see him off at Launceston with the verse, which exists in several versions:

> Land of Lags and Kangaroo,
> Of 'possum and the scarce Emu,
> The farmer's pride but the prisoner's Hell
> Land of Buggers [Bums] Fare-thee-well!

MacNamara's movements after leaving Tasmania are largely unknown, although John Meredith and Rex

Whalan in *Frank the Poet: The Life and Works of Francis MacNamara* (1979), who first linked 'Frank the Poet' with the Francis MacNamara transported in 1832, suggest he may have been 'the Poet', a balladeer living in a Melbourne doss-house whom Marcus Clarke wrote about in 1868. Among the other poems associated with 'Frank the Poet', who appears as a character in Michael Boddy's play 'Cash' (1972), are a ballad about Bold Jack Donohoe (which may have been the source of the later 'Wild Colonial Boy' song about Jack Doolan), and the convict laments 'Labouring with the Hoe', which shows the influence of Robert Burns, and 'The Convict's Arrival', known also as 'Moreton Bay' (q.v.).

McNEIL, Eugénie (1886–1983) was born into a French/English family, proprietors of a once prosperous jewellers' business in Sydney. Her father, Leopold Delarue, died when she was 6 and she and her sister Lydia were brought up by their mother in the countryside south of Sydney near what is now Lidcombe. Eugénie McNeil's recollections of her childhood and adolescence were collected and related by her daughter, Eugénie Crawford, in two publications, *A Bunyip Close Behind Me* (1972) and *Ladies Didn't* (1984). These lightly humorous accounts give a detailed picture of life of the period and especially the conventions which confined girls and women. *A Bunyip Close Behind Me* takes the sisters up to 1902 when their mother suddenly decided to continue their education in France. *Ladies Didn't*, which closes with Eugénie McNeil's marriage in 1910, follows their fortunes in France and back in Australia where their economic difficulties caused by the decline of the family business made little difference to their zest for contemporary fashions and such innovations as the motor car. Related with delicate irony, these reminiscences have found a wide audience both for their humour and their period charm.

McNEIL, Jim (1935–82), born Melbourne, began to write plays while in Parramatta gaol where, since 1967, he had been serving a lengthy sentence for armed robbery and wounding a policeman. A member of the Resurgents Discussion and Debating Society at Parramatta, McNeil took part in weekly drama workshops. One of his first plays, *The Chocolate Frog* (1973), written to communicate the realities of prison life to outsiders, was first publicly performed in 1971 and has been frequently staged since. Another, originally titled 'The Last Cuppa', was reworked by McNeil, was first given a professional performance in 1972 with the title *The Old Familiar Juice* and was published in 1973 with *The Chocolate Frog*. In 1974, while still imprisoned, McNeil won a grant from the Australian Council for the Arts. He was released in 1975, married for the second time (to the actor Robyn Nevin), but was unable to cope with the pressures of outside life and died of alcoholism. His third play, *How Does Your Garden Grow* (1974), is his most complex and won the Awgie Award for the best script of 1975; 'Jack' (1977), his last, is a less coherently developed piece. His *Collected Plays* were published in 1987.

McNeil's plays, especially 'Jack', deal realistically with the violent, sordid aspects of prison life, but a quiet form of comedy, both verbal and situational, is their most memorable quality. Particularly striking is his ability to give his claustrophobic, unnatural world a universal, natural dimension and to re-create the monotonous triviality of prison existence while investing it with significance, humour and even tenderness.

McNICOLL, David (1914–), born Geelong, Victoria, and one of Australia's best-known journalists, began his career as a cadet on the staff of the *Sydney Morning Herald*. A war correspondent during the Second World War, he covered the campaigns in the Middle East and the invasion of Normandy. He was special correspondent 1945–54 for the Sydney *Daily Telegraph* to which he contributed the front-page column 'Town Talk', and was editor-in-chief of Sir Frank Packer's newspaper empire 1953–72. He has published two volumes of verse, *Air Mail Palestine* (1943, see War Literature) and *The Round Dozen* (1947); and a volume of memoirs, *Luck's a Fortune* (1979), in which he draws on his familiarity with prominent politicians and his memories of Packer.

MACONOCHIE, Alexander (1787–1860), born Edinburgh, Scotland, had a career in the Royal Navy and was the first professor of geography at the University of London before going to Hobart Town in 1836 as private secretary to the lieutenant-governor, Sir John Franklin. In 1838 he wrote a condemnation of the convict system, *Report on the State of Prison Discipline in Van Diemen's Land*, as a result of which he was dismissed from his position, but he was later appointed superintendent of the Norfolk Island penal settlement in 1840. In his four-year period of office he implemented enlightened penal theories which are expounded in *Crime and Punishment* (1846), which led to his recall by Governor Gipps; subsequently he was governor of Birmingham prison and is presented sympathetically in this role as O'Connor in Charles Reade's novel *It Is Never Too Late to Mend* (1856). Alexander Harris's novel *The Emigrant Family*, published in 1849 just after Maconochie's period on Norfolk Island, was dedicated to him 'in testimony of the soundness of the principles he has endeavoured to introduce into penal discipline'. He is the subject of J.V. Barry's *Alexander Maconochie of Norfolk Island* (1958) and appears in several 'Price Warung' stories, notably 'Captain Maconochie's "Bounty for Crime"' and 'Secret Society of the Ring'.

McPHERSON, Alpin (James) (1841–95), better known as the bushranger, 'The Wild Scotchman', was born in Inverness-shire, Scotland, and emigrated with his family to Moreton Bay in 1855. The only Queensland bushranger of note, he was active in 1865–66 before his imprisonment on St Helena Island, Moreton Bay. After his release in 1874 he worked as a stockman and station overseer and came into contact with Sylvester Browne, who is alleged to have passed on McPherson's story, which he was fond of telling, to his brother 'Rolf Boldrewood' (q.v.) for use in the celebrated bushranging novel *Robbery Under Arms* (1888); the bushranging incidents in the novel, however, are drawn from the careers of several other bushrangers. An ineffective lawbreaker, one of the few bushrangers to have been actually wounded by the notoriously incompetent policeman, Sir Frederick Pottinger, and first captured while reading quietly by the Lachlan River, McPherson is the subject of P.W. McNally's *The Life and Adventures of the Wild Scotchman* (1899) and P.H. McCarthy's *The Wild Scotsman* (1975).

MACQUARIE, Elizabeth (1778–1835), the daughter of John Campbell of Airds, Scotland, was the second wife of Governor Lachlan Macquarie (q.v.), and accompanied him to the colony of NSW in 1809. The journey is recorded in her lively journal 'Diary of Journey from England to New South Wales 1809'. A loyal supporter of her husband in the various faction fights into which he was drawn, she also took an interest in the welfare of women convicts and the Aborigines. Her knowledge of architecture was also of use to her husband's architect, Francis Greenway. After leaving Australia in 1822, she and her husband settled in England on the Macquarie estate at Jarvisfield, although Macquarie had not long to live. His last days in 1824 are recorded in Elizabeth's letters to her friends in NSW (1825). Her life is described in Marjorie Barnard's *Macquarie's World* (1941), Malcolm Ellis's *Lachlan Macquarie* (1947), Lysbeth Cohen's *Elizabeth Macquarie* (1979) and John Ritchie's *Lachlan Macquarie* (1956). She also appears as a character in Eleanor Dark's historical novel *No Barrier* (1953). Her name has been applied to various natural and man-made features of Sydney, one of which is Mrs Macquarie's Chair overlooking Sydney Harbour.

MACQUARIE, Lachlan (1761–1824), born Ulva in the Scottish Hebrides, had, before his appointment as governor of the colony of NSW, seen army service in Canada, America, India and Egypt. One of the Colony's longest-serving (1809–21) and most successful governors, Macquarie largely healed the rift caused by the John Macarthur–Governor William Bligh disputes, expanded the settlement by systematic exploration, instituted an energetic public works programme, promoted cultural and civil amenities, developed education, treated the Aborigines humanely and introduced a policy of enlightened treatment of the emancipists. The last policy produced friction with the 'exclusives' ('pure merinos') of the Colony and was a significant cause of the Bigge (q.v.) inquiry. True to his own prediction that 'my name will not be readily forgotten', Macquarie has been commemorated in Australia by streets, towns, ports, harbours, islands, rivers, lakes and a university named in his honour. M.H. Ellis wrote the biography *Lachlan Macquarie: His Life, Adventures and Times* (1947). Marjorie Barnard wrote *Macquarie's World* (1941), Anthony Hewison edited *The Macquarie Decade* (1972), and he is the subject of a substantial biography by John Ritchie (1986). Macquarie's *Journals of His Tours in New South Wales and Van Diemen's Land 1810–1822* was published in 1956. *The Age of Macquarie* (1992), edited by James Broadbent and Joy Hughes, is a broad biographical and historical study. He is the major character in Alexander Buzo's play *Macquarie* (1971) and also appears as a character in the novels *A Rebel of the Bush* (1914) by John Sandes, *Sally: The Tale of a Currency Lass* (1918) by J.H.M. Abbott, and *No Barrier* (1953) by Eleanor Dark.

McQUEEN, Humphrey (1942–), born and educated in Queensland, has taught history at secondary and tertiary level. A member of the Labor Party early in his career, he became disillusioned with parliamentary socialism and in 1968 was appointed chairman of the Revolutionary Socialists in Melbourne. His *A New Britannia: An Argument Concerning the Social Origins of Australian Radicalism and Nationalism* (1970) is a New Left history, an analysis of the effects of the Protestant-capitalist ethos on Australian society. Particularly critical of the myths of egalitarianism and mateship, the history drew a series of strong reviews including responses from other interpreters of Australia's cultural history, such as Arthur Phillips and Russel Ward. McQueen has also published an account of racism in Australian society, *Aborigines, Race and Racism* (1974); a provocative assessment of the media, *Australia's Media Monopolies* (1977); an alternative social history from the 1890s, which includes accounts of the treatment of the Aborigines, migrants, the unemployed and women, *Social Sketches of Australia 1888–1975* (1978); an account of the emergence of modernist painting in Australia, which also deals with the Ern Malley hoax and the links between modernist art and literature, *The Black Swan of Trespass* (1979); a study of Australia's economic past and its implications for the future, *Gone Tomorrow: Australia in the 80s* (1982); a collection of provocative essays on a range of topics, *Gallipoli to Petrov* (1984); an analysis of the evolution of recent Australian art which focuses on the work of Keith Looby, *Suburbs of the Sacred* (1988); a record of his two years as visiting professor at Tokyo University, *Tokyo World* (1991); and a historical analysis of relations between Japan, Australia and the USA which posits a radically different Australian defence policy, *Japan to the Rescue* (1991). With Kay Daniels and Bruce Bennett he edited *Windows onto Worlds. Studying Australia at Tertiary Level* (1987).

McQUEEN, James (1934–), born Tasmania, has worked at a variety of occupations including ship's cook, fruit-picker, weatherman on Macquarie Island and window-dresser. He studied at the National Art School, Sydney, and completed a four-year course in accountancy, but at the age of 40 returned to Tasmania to grow orchids. Although he did not begin writing until 1975, he has won several awards and short-story competitions including the State of Victoria Award in 1978 and 1979, the Air New Zealand PEN Award in 1978 and 1979 and the Henry Lawson Prose Award in 1979 and 1982. He was co-winner of the *Age/Tabloid Story* Award in 1981. Involved in the 1980s movement to protect the Franklin River, he turned down writers' grants in protest against the treatment of protesters

and wrote a book on the issue, *The Franklin – Not Just a River* (1983). He has published five novels, *A Just Equinox* (1980), the story of an artist divided by the demands of art and alcohol; *Hook's Mountain* (1982), a study of a man's destruction by conflicting passions, by the need to preserve the mountain wilderness which is his home and by homicidal impulses deriving from his military past; *The Floor of Heaven* (1986), the story of a man's search for identity after a shocking discovery about the identity of his father; *White Light* (1990) and its sequel *The Heavy Knife* (1991). *White Light*, set mainly in Thailand, concerns the confrontation between two migrant Australians, one a building contractor, Tony Caramia, who spent part of his youth in Auschwitz and the other, a nurseryman, Erich Ritter, who was once a guard at the concentration camp. The confrontation has surprising and semi-healing consequences for them both. Alternating the Buddhism of Thai village life with sharply realised scenes from Auschwitz, McQueen develops a complex moral pattern which emphasises the ambiguities latent in notions of responsibility, conscience, justice and forgiveness. *The Heavy Knife* explores some of the same territory as Ritter's son, detective sergeant Karl Ritter, comes to terms with his father's past and his own aggressive tendencies. McQueen has also published six collections of short fiction which vary widely in subject and tone, *The Electric Beach* (1978), *The Escape Machine* (1981), *Uphill Runner* (1984), *Death of a Ladies' Man* (1989), *Lower Latitudes* (1990) and *Travels With Michael and Me* (1992).

MADIGAN, C.T. (Cecil Thomas) (1889–1947), geologist and explorer, was born at Renmark, SA, and educated at the University of Adelaide where he won distinction. After accompanying Douglas Mawson on the Australasian Antarctic Expedition 1911–14, Madigan served in the Royal Engineers in the First World War, pursued further study in natural science at Oxford as a Rhodes scholar and served in the Sudan civil service 1920–22. In 1922 he was appointed lecturer in geology at the University of Adelaide. He began geological investigations of Central Australia in 1927, making various expeditions into the area in the 1930s, and in 1939 led the first scientific expedition across the Simpson Desert. His account of the expedition, *Crossing the Dead Heart* (1946), understated, deliberately unsensational but nevertheless vivid and enlivened by his knowledge of human nature, has maintained its popularity. An earlier book, *Central Australia* (1936), includes accounts of his journeys up to 1932. President of the Royal Society of South Australia in 1936 and of the geographical section of ANZAAS in 1937, Madigan received the Murchison Grant of the Royal Geographical Society in 1941. He served in the Second World War 1940–43.

Magic Pudding, The, an outstandingly popular novel for children by Norman Lindsay (q.v.), was first published in 1918 and is frequently compared in its appeal to Lewis Carroll's *Alice in Wonderland*. The plot relates to misadventures of three friends, Bunyip Bluegum, Bill Barnacle and Sam Sawnoff, in their efforts to save their magic pudding from two professional Puddin' thieves, Watkin Wombat and Possum. The pudding, which plays a vocal but passive part in the story, has a variety of flavours and an endless life. After a series of comic encounters, the friends elude their enemies by coming to the end of the story and settle down at the home of Benjamin Brandysnap, an elderly dog and market-gardener. The narrative is enlivened by Lindsay's distinctive illustrations and comic verse; the verse was separately published as *Puddin' Poems* (1977).

MAGOFFIN, Richard (1937–), known as 'The Boredrain Balladist', is a writer of bush verse, songs and yarns and is well known in outback Queensland for his recitations. He is the author of the often-reprinted *We Bushies* (1968), *Chops and Gravy* (1972), *Fair Dinkum Matilda* (1973), which is an important contribution to Waltzing Matilda (q.v.) literature, *Down Another Track* (1982) and *Waltzing Matilda: Song of Australia* (1983). *'How Would You Be?'* (1984) is a selection of verse from earlier publications.

Magpie, one of Australia's best-known and most prolific birds, belongs to the crowshrike family. It is especially notable for its melodious carolling, particularly at dawn and dusk, and for its aggression, dive-bombing or swooping on unsuspecting humans in the nesting season. Its name has been adopted by football teams that wear the bird's black-and-white colours, e.g. Collingwood in Melbourne. The bird's sturdy personality is well expressed in James McAuley's poem 'Magpie', and Judith Wright's 'Magpies'. As part of the typical Australian scene it is mentioned in Judith Wright's poem 'Old House', and James Lister Cuthbertson's 'The Australian Sunrise'. *Magpie* is the title of the short-lived weekly periodical published in Melbourne 1865–66.

MAHONY, Frank (1862–1916), born Melbourne, went with his parents to Sydney at the age of 10. He worked in an architect's office after leaving school, but in the 1890s became established as a black-and-white illustrator and watercolour artist for the *Bulletin*, the *Sydney Mail*, the *Antipodean* and other journals. He gained a reputation for his bush subjects, notably horses and swagmen; his portrait of Henry Lawson 'on the wallaby' became the frontispiece of Lawson's *In the Days When the World Was Wide* (1896). Mahony also illustrated Lawson's *While the Billy Boils* (1896), some of the works of A.B. Paterson and Ethel Pedley's *Dot and the Kangaroo* (1899); he was one of the Heptarchs of the Dawn and Dusk Club, his job being to predict, through paint, the winner of the Melbourne Cup. He was an instructor for the Art Society of NSW before his departure for England in 1901; in later years he was a contributor to the *Lone Hand*.

MAIDEN, Jennifer (1949–), born Penrith, NSW, left school at 13 and spent several years working at casual jobs before returning to study, graduating BA from Macquarie University at the age of 24. Since then she has been a professional writer, has tutored in creative writing, conducted writing workshops and seminars in the western suburbs of Sydney and been poet-in-residence at the ANU and the University of Western Sydney. She has published numerous books of poetry: *Tactics* (1974), *The Problem of Evil* (1975), *The Occupying Forces* (1975), *Mortal Details* (1977, poems and two short stories), *Birthstones* (1978), *The Border Loss* (1979), *For the Left Hand* (1981), *The Trust* (1988), *Selected Poems* (1990), *Bastille Day* (1990), *The Winter Baby* (1990) and *Acoustic Shadow* (1993). She has won several poetry prizes, including the English Association Prize, the Harri Jones Memorial Prize, the Grenfell Henry Lawson Festival of Arts Award, the NSW Premier's Prize (the Kenneth Slessor Award) and the Victorian Premier's Award (the C.J. Dennis Award), the last two for *The Winter Baby*. She has also written two novels, *The Terms* (1982) and *Play with Knives* (1990).

Jennifer Maiden's first volume, *Tactics*, brought a new and distinctive poetic voice – complex, intense, private, and urgent in its effort to distil thoughts and emotions into language that seemed barely expansive enough to contain them. It proved to be the first glimpse of what one critic (Martin Duwell) called 'Maidenland', a terrain that demanded skill and patience if the reader was to negotiate a way successfully but one that offered considerable rewards if the effort were made. Her second volume, *The Problem of Evil*, is set totally in 'Maidenland'. The long title section appears to be based on a military encounter in which two female partisans are captured by a male invading force. One is killed, the other tortured but ultimately rescued as the withdrawing invaders poison the land they are leaving. The rescued partisan is unable to warn her fellows about the land – 'I harsh on wordless phlegm to warn/ those keepers from their soil.' The reader is kept well enough in touch with what is happening if agile enough to make the leap from one informative rock to another across the stream of the narrative. The other sections of the book are 'Mobiles', 'The Sponge', and 'A Solstice Miscellany', all concerning shadowy incidents occurring in 'Maidenland'. The challenging complexity of the whole volume stems from subtleties of thought and theme cleverly couched in even more subtly manipulated language. *The Occupying Forces* is a series of poems integrated by the usual experiences and preoccupations of life, while *Birthstones* is structurally based on introductory poems related to each month's precious or semi-precious stones. *The Border Loss* and *For the Left Hand*, the latter a special issue of *Poetry Australia*, present the usual problems for the reader of unravelling sufficient clues to trace the patterns of thought developed by means of a highly original structure of language and image. *The Trust*, however, is more accessible. *Bastille Day*, a brief volume in the NLA Pamphlet Poet Series, takes its title from the poet's wedding day, 14 July 1984.

The *Selected Poems*, which carries a tribute from A.D. Hope on its cover ('great originality of line and image'), contains selections from all the earlier volumes and a group of new poems, 'Fin de Siécle' (1988–89), highlighted by the poignant 'Tiananmen Square'.

The Winter Baby explores an entirely new landscape, peopled now with recognisable figures. The shadowy, anonymous personae of 'Maidenland' have given way to real flesh and blood – 'the winter baby' herself, Katharine Margot Toohey; the poets Doug Stewart and Bob FitzGerald, who like to sit with backs against a wall; Donna, who has done the Assertiveness Course at the Tech.; and an MP caught off-guard in a morning interview. 'Maidenland', valid and justifiable as it undoubtedly once seemed to its creator, has faded and the poet is content to accept the change:

> Poems about poems don't seem
> as abstract as once they did.

In *Acoustic Shadow*, a collection in the Australian Poetry Series by Penguin, the tone is assured, the commentary confident, the effect crisp, lucid, controlled. An acute observer of the contemporary scene, Maiden links local politicians (Joan Kirner, Janet Powell, Cleary of Wills) with those larger on the world stage (Nelson Mandela, George Bush, Saddam Hussein), blends local radical feminists with overseas terrorists (the Locherbie disaster) and allows bulls at the Sydney Show to share the spotlight with the travelling Guggenheim Exhibition. There are many family oriented poems. Perhaps the most entertaining poem is the long 'Guarding the Cenotaph'; a high-school cadet stands guard in the black hours before dawn against the possible incursions of the 'Rape-in-War' protestors. He ultimately confronts a lone protestor, a young university girl who wants to spray four lines of Elizabeth Riddell's 'The Soldier in the Park' on the Memorial. He convinces her to settle for a single phrase from Kenneth Slessor and they depart to the beach to celebrate their own encounter.

Play with Knives is an impressive psycho-thriller. Its story revolves around the young woman Clare, who, as a 9-year-old, killed three smaller children. When the novel begins she is 16 and undergoing psychological assessment by the narrator to determine if she is suitable for release on probation. Tension mounts as the lives of Clare and her psychologist become emotionally and intellectually interwoven.

MAITLAND, Edward (1824–97), born Ipswich, England, was educated at Cambridge and destined for the church, but suffered a crisis of faith and left England for Mexico, California and Australia in 1849. Appointed commissioner of Crown Lands and police magistrate at Wellington, NSW, in 1854, he married a year later the granddaughter of the explorer W.H. Hovell. President of the Goulburn School of Arts, which he helped to found, Maitland propounded the casting off of colonial ties and attitudes in his lectures. In 1858 he left for England after delivering a lecture published as *The Meaning of the Age* (1858). In England he wrote several novels which draw partly on his Australian experience. *The Pilgrim and the Shrine* (1868) gives vent to his political and spiritual ideas as well as providing pictures of life on the Australian goldfields. One of the novel's characters, Captain Travers, is based on Hovell, and another, Mary, on Mary Woolley, the wife of John Woolley; John Woolley is also

mentioned by name. Mary Woolley is also the basis of the heroine of his next novel, *Higher Law* (1870). His subsequent fiction was more mystical and psychological, anticipating in some respects the views of C.G. Jung. *By and By* (1873) is particularly speculative, expressive of Maitland's radical ideas on a range of social institutions. Although Maitland acquired a reputation as a writer, mainly for the *Spectator* and the *Examiner*, his friendship with the feminist and spiritualist Dr Anna Kingsford, and his own spiritualist ideas aroused suspicion, hostility and ridicule. His reputation was irretrievably damaged by his book *England and Islam* (1877), a passionate attempt to expose the dangers of materialism in politics and science. In 1896 he published a two-volume work, *Anna Kingsford*, which was to have an important influence on C.J. Brennan. Other works which were influential among those sympathetic to his views were *The Keys of the Creeds* (1875), *The Soul and How It Found Me* (1877) and, with Anna Kingsford, *The Perfect Way* (1882). Maitland's exploration of spiritualism and psychic phenomena stimulated or coincided with similar explorations in Australia, reflected particularly in the linked interests of such figures as C.J. Brennan, Alfred Deakin, John le Gay Brereton, Dowell O'Reilly and John Woolley.

Makar, a magazine of new writing published by Makar Press, ran 1960–80, edited successively by Graham Rowlands, Martin Duwell and Rodney Wissler. It began as the quarterly magazine of the English Society of the University of Queensland, its title using the Middle Scots form of the word 'maker', meaning poet. In 1972 one of the quarterly editions was replaced by three small books of verse which inaugurated the Gargoyle Poets series, the name deriving from the University of Queensland's gargoyles, four of which had been depicted on *Makar*'s covers. With Martin Duwell as general editor, the Gargoyle Poets series included works by Graham Rowlands, Alan Wearne, Richard Packer, Peter Annand, Antigone Kefala, Rae Desmond Jones, Kris Hemensley, Graeme Curtis, John Griffin, Stephanie Bennett, Eric Beach, Carol Novack, John Tranter, Shelton Lea, Philip Neilsen and Jennifer Maiden. *Makar* also conducted a series of interviews with significant contemporary writers; some of those interviews (and others unpublished in the journal) were incorporated into *A Possible Contemporary Poetry* (1982) edited by Duwell. Duwell also co-edited *The Honey-Ant Men's Love Song* and the thirty years' accumulation of bibliographies in *Australian Literary Studies*, *The ALS Guide to Australian Writers: A Bibliography 1963–1990* (1992).

'**Mallee**', an Aboriginal word, is applied to scrub and certain low-growing, multi-stemmed eucalypts which are found in low-rainfall areas of southern Australia, especially in north-western Victoria; by extension it refers to areas where mallee eucalypts predominate. The word, which seems to have come into use in the late 1840s, was given official sanction in 1883 in the *Mallee Pastoral Leases Act of Victoria*. Certain animals and birds natural to this sort of environment have also acquired the name, e.g. mallee fowl, mallee hen and mallee kangaroo. The term 'mallee' is used colloquially to denote an area far from civilisation, as in the expression 'take to the mallee', i.e. go out into the remote areas of the bush; 'fit as a mallee bull' is a common expression denoting good health and virility, usually through hard physical work and tough conditions. The best-known part of the mallee scrub is its large underground root system, renowned for its burning qualities in an open fireplace; C.H. Souter's poem 'The Mallee Fire' praises these qualities.

The mallee country is the setting of several novels, including Patricia Stonehouse's *The Years of Forgetting* (1914), John Truran's *Green Mallee* (1932), Benjamin Cozens's *The Princess of the Mallee* (1903), Roy Bridges's *Merchandise* (1918) and Catherine Martin's *An Australian Girl* (1890), but the life of the area is best commemorated in the ballads of C.H. Souter, one of whose collections is titled *The Mallee Fire* (1923). The poet John Shaw Neilson spent his early manhood in the Mallee; in his autobiography he tells of an existence of poverty and misery accentuated by the severe climate, dust storms, rabbit plagues, droughts and the long desperate wait for a cash crop.

MALOUF, David (1934–   ), born Brisbane of Lebanese and English parents, was educated at the University of Queensland. He lived in Europe 1959–68, and worked for a time as a relief teacher in London before taking up a permanent teaching position at Birkenhead. He taught English at the University of Sydney 1968–77, but now devotes himself to full-time writing, living partly in Australia and partly in southern Tuscany. Well known as a poet, Malouf has published the volumes of verse *Bicycle and Other Poems* (1970), published in New York with the title *The Year of the Foxes and Other Poems* (1979), *Neighbours in a Thicket* (1974), *Poems 1975–76* (1976), *Wild Lemons* (1980), *First Things Last* (1980), *Selected Poems* (1981), *Selected Poems* (1991) and *David Malouf: Poems 1959–89* (1992). He has also written the novels *Johnno* (q.v., 1975), *An Imaginary Life* (1978), *Harland's Half-Acre* (1984), *The Great World* (q.v., 1990) and *Remembering Babylon* (1993); four novellas, *Child's Play*, which was first published in 1981 with *Fly Away Peter* (titled here *The Bread of Time to Come*) and republished in 1982 with two other novellas, *The Prowler* and *Eustace* (the retitled *Fly Away Peter* was also published separately in 1982); a group of autobiographical essays, *12 Edmonstone Street* (1985); a play, *Blood Relations* (1988); and a collection of short stories, *Antipodes* (1985). Malouf also contributed verse to the collection *Four Poets* (1962) and has edited an anthology of Australian verse, *Gesture of a Hand* (1975) and, with others, *We Took Their Orders and Are Dead* (1975). He contributed to the collection *New Currents in Australian Writing* (1978) and is the author of the libretto of Richard Meale's opera *Voss*, which is based on Patrick White's novel, and of *Baa Baa Black Sheep: A Jungle Tale* (1993), the libretto for an opera with music by Michael Berkeley. *David Malouf* (1990), edited by James Tulip in the UQP Australian Authors series includes *Johnno*, short stories, poems, essays and an interview.

An exceptionally diverse writer, Malouf is concerned with certain fundamental, consistent and unifying themes: the relationships between past and present, continuity and change, animal and human, and the role of language as a mediator of experience. Drawn by the force of his own early experience, and regional in his preoccupations in that much of his poetry and fiction re-creates his childhood in Brisbane, Malouf is nevertheless thoroughly European in his interests and attitudes. *Johnno*, his most outwardly autobiographical novel, which has been much praised as a realistic presentation of wartime Brisbane, has been followed by the ostensibly different *An Imaginary Life*. A meditative book close to a prose poem and dealing with the last years of Ovid, the Roman poet, in exile on the shores of the Black Sea and his strangely maturing relationship with a wolfchild, *An Imaginary Life* narrates an inner history, whereas *Johnno* is more concerned with outer change. In *An Imaginary Life* Roman sophistication is confronted with primitive animality and for Ovid the confrontation results in a subtle dying into life. *Child's Play*, an apparently factual and even documentary account of the experience of an Italian terrorist bent on perfecting his assassin's task, has again an inward, poetically suggestive direction. As the assassin meticulously studies his victim, a great writer, he gradually comes to see himself as mysteriously linked to his victim, an organic part of the great man's work and the inevitable agent of his life's conclusion. Personal time is overtaken by an objective, impersonally shaping time, which finally rushes both assassin and victim towards their predestined 'event'. *The Prowler* is a comically orchestrated foray into the sexual repressions and fantasies of the suburbs; *Eustace* is a more chilling account of innocence confronted with a dangerous stranger. *Fly Away Peter*, set in Queensland before the First World War, is the compressed but subtly worked story of crucial events in the life of Jim Saddler, a dedicated bird-watcher, who becomes drawn into the war. In Queensland, Saddler's life enriches those of Ashley Crowther, his employer, and Imogen Harcourt, an eccentric English photographer. The idyllic, life-affirming landscape of a Queensland swampland contrasts with the nightmarish, destructive horror of the trenches, and both experiences are present in Imogen's final transcendent vision of all life, anonymous or notable, as having integrity, dignity and a unique presence. The central figure of *Harland's Half Acre*, Frank Harland, is another study of the artist-figure which continues to intrigue Malouf. Partly structured like *Johnno* and *An Imaginary Life* around two opposite individuals, and in this case their families (the artist Harland, 'mother' to his all-male household of Irish descent, and Phil Vernon, member of a wealthy 'English' family and Harland's friend and legal adviser), the novel returns to the lush, exotic world of Queensland to re-create one of the numberless rich cultures which Malouf perceives as making up the mysterious country called Australia. A chronological narrative covering several decades, it is superficially a more conventional novel, although it is less concerned with material events than with the distances between events and human interpretations of

them. Harland, aware of the costs of his father's soft-
ness and self-indulgence, chooses to stand side-on to
life, and to submerge his own natural needs for community and fellowship in an austere sense of singular
duty, leading his life in 'ambiguous' places, neither
inside nor out, from a condemned picture palace at the
end of a Southport pier to a tent on Bribie Island in
Moreton Bay. From his youth Harland is obsessed
with the need to reclaim the family's lost inheritance,
the pastoral land with the nostalgic name Killarney.
The dream turns sour when tragedy intervenes but
Harland grows to understand that he has created
another unexpected but more real legacy in his art:
'When all was done and the fragments garnered and
laid side by side, he would have laid bare say half an
acre. It wasn't much, no more than a glimpse. But as
much as one man might catch sight of'. The linked
essays of *12 Edmonstone Street* form one of Malouf's
most revealing and subtle studies of the relation between place and self. Analytical rather than nostalgic,
the collection explores ways of seeing and knowing
and the roles played by architecture, landscape, region
and cultural grouping. In the section of the book
named after his childhood home, Malouf's retrospective exploration of the intricate personality of the old
Queensland weatherboard house and the impress of its
features on the growing child's consciousness is also an
extended meditation on the complex power of memory. Mapping this early reality is another venture into
the pattern of mythologising places which he sees as a
necessary part of finding a home in culture. The last
section of the collection deals with crossing boundaries and with the countering perennial experience of
exile; accompanying his father on a train journey
between Queensland and NSW, the young David
is disappointed to find the experience of boundary-
crossing negligible, only to be profoundly shocked by
the sight of three Japanese prisoners in the dark of a
goods van. Suddenly confronted by a 'vast gap of darkness', the child is aware of being on 'a different train',
bringing him at last 'to a different unnameable destination'. In *The Great World* Malouf enters familiar
Australian territory with a story of war experience and
mateship. The narrative contrasts the personalities of
two men and their experiences in the Second World
War, Digger Keen, the archetypal, taciturn Australian, gifted with a photographic memory, and Vic
Curran, whose ambition and drive take him from poverty to the top of the business world. On the one hand
an epic history, *The Great World* is, on the other, a
more intimate history, recording the unrecorded, and
mapping the inner topographies of self and the effects
of time, change and memory. Malouf has described
himself as attempting to reconcile the individual to all
the lines that bind past and present, natural, social,
cultural, linguistic and familial, and in this novel, concerned partly with the emergence of a more complicated post-war Australia, he has re-created the past in
all its immediacy, confusion and muddle. Working at
close quarters, Malouf's prose invests what seems
small with transcendent significance so that the greatness of the world is transposed from the 'major' realm
of public events to the 'minor' detailed one of ordinary

lives and 'insignificant' events. *Remembering Babylon*,
set mainly in a mid-nineteenth-century settlement in
Queensland, is a compressed epic, centring on the
theme of exile and the strange challenge posed by one
who, like William Buckley, had lived with the Aborigines, becoming 'a white black man'. The thirteen
stories of *Antipodes* range widely in moods, settings
and subject matter but are united in their concentration on antipodean states and experiences, dark and
light, youth and age, tenderness and violence, loss and
gain, boredom and hope, inheritance and dispposses-
sion. As in his other fiction, Malouf's spare, rumina-
tive prose concentrates on the 'grainy reality' of his
characters' experience, lit by occasional, externally unremarkable epiphanies. The title of this collection is
appropriate to all his work, for his fictional worlds are
typically constructed in terms of correspondences,
analogies and opposites and are concerned with gaps
and discontinuities, the geographical and cultural distance between Europe and Australia, generational,
class, gender and social differences, and different ways
of perceiving. In all his novels he constructs dual-
faceted perspectives based on such oppositions as
centre and periphery, wild and civilised, self and other.
Above all he is interested in the gulf between the Australian landscape and the inherited language of naming, with its consequent sense of loss, which he
describes as a fall from innocence peculiar to Australia;
the artist offers a chance to 'get past that actual fall to
some kind of personal reconciliation between
language and what is made'. As one of the characters
of his short stories puts it, 'the world as we know it is
in the last resort the words with which we imagine
and name it'.

Malouf's verse, distinguished by arresting images
and an urbane, dispassionate tone, shows the same
delight in concrete detail and the same interest in the
immediacy and tenacity of the past as his prose fiction.
Language is once again celebrated as bridging past and
present, change and permanence, the perceiving 'eye'
and the material object, the individual life and the
totality of things. Describing the poet in 'A Poet
Among Others' as one 'holding/to the is-ness of
things', Malouf has sometimes been compared to
Wallace Stevens although his work resists categories.
If European and American roots are revealed as powerful creative forces, childhood experience and the distinctive cultural and historical inheritances that make
up his exotic Australia are equally powerful. Malouf's
one play, *Blood Relations*, uses dream sequences and
inner dialogue to dramatise the characters' inner
journeyings; drawing to some extent on Shakespeare's
The Tempest, the play recasts the theme of forgiveness
and atonement in an Australian context.

Malouf has won numerous awards, including the
1974 Grace Leven Prize, the 1974 Foundation for Australian Literary Studies Award, and the Australian
Literature Society's Gold Medal in 1974 for *Neighbours
in a Thicket*; the NSW Premier's Literary Award in
1979 for *An Imaginary Life*; the *Age* Book of the Year
Award for 1982 for *Fly Away Peter*; and the Australian
Literature Society's (now ASAL's) Gold Medal in 1983
for *Child's Play* and *Fly Away Peter*. *The Great World*

won the 1991 Miles Franklin Award, the Adelaide Festival Award and two international awards, the 1991 Commonwealth Prize for fiction and the Prix Femina Étranger in France for the best foreign novel. *Antipodes* won the Vance Palmer Prize for fiction in the Victorian Premier's 1985 Literary Awards. *Remembering Babylon* won the NSW Premier's Prize for fiction in 1993. In 1988 Malouf was awarded the inaugural Pascall Prize (the richest literary prize in Australia) for excellence in creative writing. Malouf was made AO in 1987. His work is the subject of studies by Philip Neilsen (1990), Karin Hansson (1991) and Ivor Indyk (1993).

Man, a monthly magazine which was published in Sydney but circulated widely in Australia, began publication in 1936; modelled on *Esquire*, its arrival reflected the increasing Americanisation of Australian society. In its early years it had a strong literary component: as 'Gilbert Anstruther', Russel Clarke was its literary editor, Ion Idriess edited its 'Australiana' section, and its contributors included J.H.M. Abbott, Frank Clune, Vance Palmer, Ruth Park, P.R. Stephensen, Dal Stivens and E.V. Timms. After the Second World War and particularly from the 1950s, it became primarily a 'girlie' magazine but failed to withstand the competition from more explicit magazines such as *Playboy* and *Penthouse* and ceased publication in 1974.

'Man from Ironbark, The', one of A.B. Paterson's most humorous ballads, was published in the *Bulletin* (December 1892). A city barber, who pretends to cut the throat of the man from Ironbark, gets more than he bargains for when the bushman, holding his throat to 'save his vital spark', wrecks the barber's shop. In Ironbark the oft-told story reinforces traditional bush suspicion of the city and leads to a pronounced fashion in beards.

'Man from Snowy River, The', first published in the *Bulletin* (April 1890), is the title poem of A.B. Paterson's (q.v.) first collection *The Man from Snowy River and Other Verses* (1895), the most successful volume of poetry ever published in Australia. Other well-known Paterson poems in the collection include 'Clancy of the Overflow', 'The Man from Ironbark', 'A Bush Christening' and 'The Travelling Post Office'. Paterson's story of the Snowy River poem's origin is that it was not based on a specific event but was written to describe the cleaning up of wild horses in his district. Wanting to create a character who could ride better than anybody else he 'naturally' chose a man from the Snowy mounted on a typical horse of the district, a half-thoroughbred mountain pony. Various names have been suggested in an attempt to identify the original Man from Snowy River; they include Jim Troy, Jack Riley, whose grave in the Corryong cemetery has a tablet naming him as Paterson's character, Owen Cummins, Jim Spencer, Jack Clarke and Lachie Cochrane. Probably Australia's most famous poem, 'The Man from Snowy River' tells of a hectic chase after the valuable colt

from 'Old Regret' who had broken out of his station yard and joined the wild bush horses. A select band of horsemen gather at the homestead to take part in the chase; among them is 'a stripling on a small and weedy beast' who is at first excluded but is finally allowed to join the hunt because Clancy of the Overflow indicates that he and his horse come from the Snowy River country, a sure sign of courage and skill. The wild horses flee to the shelter of the mountains and when the pursuing riders fail to turn them before they reach the summit of the first mountain, the colt's owner angrily stops the chase, declaring 'We may bid the mob good day/ No man can hold them down the other side'. The Man from Snowy River has other ideas. At breakneck speed he gallops his horse down the steep mountain side, runs the mob relentlessly until 'cowed and beaten' they are brought back single-handedly by him to the station. Around the hills of Kosciusko the ride becomes a legend; with its combination of courage, daredevilry and horsemanship, qualities much prized in rural Australia from pioneer times, the ride has also become part of Australian legend. A highly successful Australian film was shown in 1982. A series of paintings inspired by the film, which illustrate the poem line by line, was done by Robert Lovett in 1984.

Man-shy, a novel by Frank Dalby Davison (q.v.), first serialised in *Australia* 1923–25 and published in a cheap home-bound edition by his father, Frederick Davison, in 1931, won the Australian Literature Society's Gold Medal and has been frequently republished. Written from the perspective of a wild red heifer, the novel describes her life and that of outback 'scrubber' cattle in general. Although the heifer successfully and courageously resists several attempts to take or kill her, the fast approach of civilisation spells doom for her kind and at the end freedom for her also means death. The simple story, told with restrained lyricism, reflects Davison's belief in the power of the spirit to surmount physical defeat.

Man Who Loved Children, The, a novel by Christina Stead (q.v.), was published in 1940. Set in Baltimore and Annapolis in the USA of the 1930s, the novel nevertheless draws on the author's childhood memories of Sydney. The title ironically refers to Sam Pollit, a compelling portrait of a complacent, egocentric, infantile adult, whose optimistic humanitarianism and cheerful *bonhomie* mask his tyrannical, self-righteous, self-deceptive motives. Opposed to him are his second wife, Henrietta or Henny, and, increasingly as the novel develops, his daughter by his first marriage, Louisa. The other members of the Pollit family include six younger children and, in the background, a diverse group of relatives. As Henny and Sam (temperamental opposites in that she lives in the real as much as he in the ideal) foster their mutual hatred, the children tenaciously survive as uneasy subjects and shifting allies in the struggle. The development of Louisa's understanding of the situation and her final rejection of Sam provides the story's main movement, although the family's external fortunes also progressively decline. Sam, who has depended on his father-in-law's support in the Conservation Bureau where he works, is beset with enemies when he dies. In addition the family is forced to leave their spacious home Tahoga House, which Henny fails to inherit, and they move to a run-down part of Annapolis. There Sam, suspended from work, devotes his manic energies to his family's activities at the same time as he neglects to provide for their material welfare, and Henny sinks deeper and deeper into despair. Her threats of suicide inspire Louisa with the idea of winning freedom for the children by killing both parents, but her attempt results in Henny's actual suicide through cyanide poisoning. Louisa's confession is disbelieved by her wilfully sanguine father, and the novel closes as she leaves home to find her own destiny.

Mandrake Press was formed in London by P.R. Stephensen and bookseller Edward Goldston, in 1929. It developed out of the Fanfrolico Press (q.v.) and produced some Fanfrolico-type publications as well as a volume of reproductions of D.H. Lawrence's paintings and his essay *A Propos of Lady Chatterley's Lover*, and works by Liam O'Flaherty and Aleister Crowley. By late 1930, economic circumstances and meddling by the controversial Crowley contributed to the demise of the press. An excellent account of the press is in Craig Munro's biography of Stephensen, *A Wild Man of Letters* (1984).

MANIATY, Tony (1949–), born Brisbane of a Greek father and an Anglo-Australian mother, spent more than twenty years as a journalist in radio and television, working with the ABC, SBS, Radio Australia and the BBC, and is now mainly a reviewer and writer of fiction. He has published two novels, *The Children Must Dance* (1984) and *Smyrna* (1989), and an autobiography of his boyhood, *All Over the Shop* (1993). *The Children Must Dance* is set in a former Portuguese colony to the north of Australia. Nicholas Ranse, nephew of Sam Goddard, who had reputedly shot himself three weeks earlier, arrives at the island of Inhumas, to collect his naturalist uncle's books. He sets out to solve the mystery of Goddard's death (which proves to have been murder) but becomes involved in the struggle between Fragas, the revolutionary forces on the island, and the Livres, the occupiers. *The Children Must Dance* arose out of Maniaty's coverage of the Timor fighting in 1975. It gained him a NSW Premier's Fellowship and the Marten Bequest. In 1985 he won the *Canberra Times* National Short Story competition with a story that he used as the basis of his novel *Smyrna* (1989). Autobiographical in that its chief character, Harry Tekarios, a radio journalist, is Maniaty himself, *Smyrna* has Tekarios visiting Greece and Turkey in 1984 to trace the past of his father who left Greece for Australia as a refugee in 1922. The novel brings Harry into a number of brief relationships but its strength is its creation of an atmosphere of 'Greekness', both in the people and the land. Maniaty also edited *The Power of Speech: 25 Years of the National Press Club* (1989).

MANIFOLD, J.S. (John Streeter) (1915–85) was born in Melbourne into one of the oldest and richest rural families of western Victoria. After an education at the University of Cambridge, where he was a friend of the poet David Campbell (q.v.), he joined the Communist Party and was later employed as editor-translator by a German publishing firm in the Rhineland. During the Second World War he was in the British army intelligence corps. By 1949, when he returned with his English wife to Australia, he was recognised in England and the USA as a rising literary star. His Communist Party allegiance caused family difficulties, so Manifold left Victoria to live in Brisbane. He became occupied with freelance writing, the composition and teaching of music, the collection and recording of bush songs and ballads and the establishment of the Realist Writers (q.v.) group. Manifold's early books of poetry are *Verses 1930–1933* (1933), *The Death of Ned Kelly and Other Ballads* (1941), *Trident* (1944, with David Martin and Hubert Nicholson) and *Selected Verse* (1946). After his return to Australia he produced *Nightmares and Sunhorses* (1961) and *Op. 8: Poems 1961–69* (1971). His *Collected Verse* was published simultaneously in 1978 with Rodney Hall's *J.S. Manifold: An Introduction to the Man and His Work*; his volume *On My Selection* (1983) includes his old favourites and a number of new poems. His interest in bush ballads and songs led to *Bandicoot Ballads* (1953), broadside forms of Australian folk-songs which were set to music and sung at the weekly music nights at Manifold's house in Wynnum, Brisbane; *The Violin, the Banjo & the Bones: An Essay on the Instruments of Bush Music* (1957); *The Queensland Centenary Pocket Songbook* (1959), of which he was chief editor; and the popular, much-reprinted *The Penguin Australian Song Book* (1964), which includes musical scores and notes on provenance. In 1964 he published *Who Wrote the Ballads? Notes on Australian Folksong*, an important book on the origins of Australian folk-song and balladry. Two of his works on music which reflect Manifold's early academic background, *The Music in English Drama (from Shakespeare to Purcell)* (1956) and *Music of the Elizabethan Stage* (1964), although highly acclaimed overseas, have been largely ignored in Australia. Manifold was an important but neglected poet. His preference was for the lyric, especially in the style of the seventeenth century; for satire, often aggressive and violent; for lively, swaggering verse set, with touches of a Byronic romanticism, in an Australian Arcadia; and for war poetry. His elegy 'The Tomb of Lt. John Learmonth A.I.F.' (q.v.) is perhaps his best and best-known poem.

MANN, Cecil (1896–1967), born Cudgen, NSW, served with the AIF at Gallipoli and in France in the First World War and was on active service also in the Second World War. In 1923–25 he was a journalist with the *Sydney Morning Herald*, then spent the rest of his working life with the *Bulletin*, as editor of the Red Page and later associate editor of the journal. His publications of well-crafted fiction include the volumes of short stories *The River and Other Stories* (1945) and *Three Stories* (1963), as well as a novel, *Light in the*

Valley (1947). He edited the first series of *Coast to Coast* (1941), *The Stories of Henry Lawson* (1964), *Henry Lawson's Best Stories* (1966) and *Henry Lawson's Humorous Stories* (1967).

MANN, David Dickenson (?1775–?), born England, was convicted of forgery in 1798 and sentenced to transportation, arriving in Sydney in 1799; he prospered in the Colony and was granted an absolute pardon in 1802. Involved in the Rum Rebellion, he accompanied George Johnston to England in 1809 and gave evidence at his court martial. In 1811 he published *The Present Picture of New South Wales*, an important early descriptive work about the Colony and specially significant as it includes a statistical survey.

MANN, Dame Ida (1893–1983), born London, an international authority on eye diseases, the first professor of ophthalmology in Britain and the first woman to hold a chair at Oxford University, left school early and spent three years working as a clerk before she discovered her vocation. Studying at night, she matriculated in 1914 and began her life as a student at the London School of Medicine for Women. She held a number of positions as an ophthalmic surgeon and researcher, including senior surgeon at Moorfields Eye Hospital and in the Second World War was head of a research team for the Ministry of Supply. Appointed professor of ophthalmology at Oxford University in 1945, she became an honorary fellow in 1947. In 1944 she married W.E. Gye, director of the Imperial Cancer Research Fund, and accompanied him to Perth, WA, on his retirement in 1949. She continued to live in WA after his death in 1952, although she travelled extensively. In Australia she continued her research and extended it to include the epidemiology of WA. In a series of surveys in the 1950s she uncovered the high incidence of trachoma among Aborigines and subsequently isolated and cultivated the organism and extended her research to New Guinea, the Trobriand Islands, Taiwan and South America. The recipient of numerous honours, she was made CBE in 1950 and in 1980 appointed DBE for services to Aboriginal welfare. As well as textbooks on her subject and travel books, Ida Mann wrote an autobiography, *The Chase* (1986), edited by Ros Golding. A frank and inward story, the autobiography reveals her energy and appetite for life, disregard for social convention and streak of mysticism which recognised 'a veiled and mysterious It (or Id) . . . that all-knowing, timeless universal subconscious within me which opens up the inevitable future with alluring flashes, so that I do not know whether it chases me or I pursue it'.

MANN, Leonard (1895–1981), born Toorak, Melbourne, worked as a clerk in the public service before serving in France in the First World War. After the war he graduated in law from the University of Melbourne and in the 1930s was secretary of the Victorian Employers' Federation. In that period he published *Flesh in Armour* (q.v., 1932) and two other works of fiction, *Human Drift* (1935) and *A Murder in Sydney*

(1937), as well as his first book of verse, *The Plumed Voice* (1938). In the 1940s and 1950s he was a senior public servant; after his retirement he farmed at Macclesfield in the Dandenong Ranges. In 1960 he moved to Olinda, also in the Dandenongs, and later to Inverloch in South Gippsland, locales which allowed him the privacy to write. His later novels are *Mountain Flat* (1939), *The Go-Getter* (1942), *Andrea Caslin* (1959) and *Venus Half-Caste* (1963); his other volumes of poetry are *Poems from the Mask* (1941), *The Delectable Mountains* (1944) and *Elegiac and Other Poems* (1957). Less regarded as a poet than a novelist, Mann exhibits much the same attitudes in all his writing: criticism of a world order which sanctions the barbarity of war and the social and economic strictures that depress the lives of ordinary people, yet a sense of optimism about the innate worth of life itself. Rugged, prosy and careless as it sometimes is, his poetry is often strikingly effective. His novel *Flesh in Armour* is particularly effective in battle narrative, character portrayal and dialogue, but tends to overemphasise the 'remarkable' qualities of the Australian 'digger'. *Human Drift* is a story of the Victorian goldfields in their halcyon days and climaxes in the Eureka Stockade. *A Murder in Sydney*, set in contemporary urban life, has a complicated psychological family framework in which a daughter murders her father's fiancée, partly to vindicate her dead mother's memory, partly as an act of self-indulgence. *Mountain Flat*, set in a small community struggling to survive, combines the fierce lust of land-ownership with a somewhat tangled romantic interest. *The Go-Getter* tells how ex-soldier Chris Gibbons is tempted, in the Depression, towards a corrupt business deal but resists finally, partly because of his own basically decent nature, partly through the influence of a 'good woman' in his life. Andrea Caslin of the novel of that title uses her intelligence and her sexuality to advance her material interests and is one of the earliest female characters in Australian fiction to do just that. *Venus Half-Caste*, an important novel in the saga of the part-Aborigine attempting to find a meaningful role in a White-dominated society, is about the beautiful and intelligent Beatrice Ledden's fight to be accepted in that society and the impact on her life of three men, two of whom are White and one part-Aborigine. The young White lawyer Phillip Roke takes possession of Beatrice in order to satisfy his own bizarre lust and then murders the elderly White surgeon Mr Panner, who, he believes, has stolen her from him. Beatrice ultimately finds happiness with Vic Pegram, himself the son of a White station-owner and an Aboriginal girl with whom he had a casual liaison.

MANN, Phillip Grenville, born Sydney, was educated at the University of Sydney and served in the Second World War. He drew on his war experiences for his first radio play, 'The Seas Between', which won the Lux Radio Theatre competition of 1946. After some years of freelance writing for radio, he spent seven years in London, where he wrote for radio, television and stage, becoming well known after the success of his television series *Pentecost Road*. Mann returned to Sydney in the 1960s to work as a television drama editor for the ABC. In 1961 his television play 'The Attorney General' won the Sydney Journalists' Club drama competition, was subsequently produced overseas, and as a stage production by the Melbourne Theatre Company with the title 'Day of Glory'. Another play produced on radio and television in Australia and overseas, 'The Sergeant from Burralee', was also produced by the Melbourne Theatre Company in 1970. Mann's other stage plays include 'Sky High', *Eight Days a Week* (1972) and *How Sleep the Brave* (1982). He has also published two novels, *The Keys of Heaven* (1966), based on his historical series for television, *The Patriots*, and *Candles in the Sun* (1978).

MANNERS-SUTTON, Dorothy (1895–1972), born Sydney as Doris Dinham, wrote for Melbourne newspapers and magazines before leaving for South Africa and Europe in the 1920s. Fluent in five languages, she was Paris correspondent for the London *Daily Telegraph* and travelled extensively in Africa. In 1932, in Libya, she married Salvatore Gentile, an engineer of Fascist sympathies in the Italian Army and a member of a noble Sicilian family. Over the next years she moved between Italy and England and in 1936 visited North America to promote her writing. Her marriage was unsuccessful, and after the entry of Italy into the war, Doris Gentile fled north to Genoa with her two children. In 1943 she failed in her attempt to cross the border into Switzerland, and was trapped for the remainder of the war without means of support on the Italian side of the border, living in great hardship in the village of Civiglio just above Como. She became involved with the partisans and in helping Allied airmen to escape out of Italy. The full extent of her involvement in the resistance movement and her role in the crucial events of the last days of the Republic of Salo have still to be unravelled and reconstructed. After the war she was repatriated to Britain and then migrated to Canada, where she worked as a reader and editor for Longmans Green in Toronto. The Canadian experiment did not work out and she returned to London. Eventually in 1970 she followed her children to Australia, where she died in 1972. As Doris Manners-Sutton she published three novels. The first, *A Marked Soul* (1923), is a love story in which the action moves from Tasmania in the early nineteenth century to the trenches of France in the First World War as damned souls transmigrate. She herself was later very critical of this first novel. The later two, *Black God: A Story of the Congo* (1934) and *The Last Secret* (1939), are set in the Congo with Africans as the main protagonists. While unknown in Australia, both were widely and favourably reviewed in Britain and North America, and the former was selected as Book of the Month by the Book of the Month Club in the USA. She appears to have published nothing after the war, but her papers include the manuscripts of a number of unpublished novels and short stories, including two which claim to be autobiographical and relate to her experiences in Italy, 1943–45.

ROSLYN PESMAN COOPER

MANNING, Emily (1845–90), the daughter of Sir William Manning, a prominent lawyer and politician, was born and educated in Sydney. After a period in England, when she began her career in journalism by contributing to such periodicals as C.F. Yonge's *Monthly Packet of Evening Readings*, she returned to Sydney in the early 1870s to become one of the first women to contribute regularly to Australian newspapers and journals. Marriage to Henry Heron and the subsequent birth of six children made no interruption to her prolific writing. Either anonymously or as 'Australie', she contributed to the *Sydney Morning Herald* and the *Australian Town and Country Journal* and was briefly on the staff of the *Illustrated Sydney News* and the *Sydney Mail*. She wrote on art and literature as well as on the public questions of the day but was best known as a poet; her book *The Balance of Pain and Other Poems* was published in 1877. A well-known member of Sydney society, she is featured in Ruth Bedford's *Think of Stephen* (1954) and was linked romantically with David Scott Mitchell.

MANNING, Frederic (1882–1935), born Sydney, son of Sir William Manning, four times lord mayor of that city, had a limited formal education, being taught mainly by private tutors because he suffered from bronchial asthma. He went to England for eighteen months at the age of 16, with Arthur Galton, former private secretary to Sir Robert Duff, governor of NSW. He returned to Australia with his parents but after three years was back in England and lived with Galton in Lincolnshire near the town of Bourne, whose name he gave to the protagonist, Private Bourne, of *The Middle Parts of Fortune* (q.v.). Through Galton, who acted as mentor, educator and friend, Manning became devoted to a scholastic, recluse-like existence, steeping himself in literature and the classics. Before the First World War Manning published *The Vigil of Brunhild* (1907, poetry), *Scenes and Portraits* (1909, prose) and *Poems* (1910), and was a reviewer for the *Spectator*. At the outset of the war Manning took the unexpected step of joining the King's Shropshire Light Infantry Regiment as a private. He served, as did Private Bourne of his novel, on the Somme front in August 1916 and on the Ancre front in November, being back in England by the end of the year. During 1917 he was a subaltern in Ireland, where the British Army had been sent to quell disturbances. Personality clashes with his fellow officers, a dislike of the pretensions of the officer class and continuing poor health led to his resigning his commission in 1918. Manning's post-war life was uneventful. He returned to an isolated existence, with study and writing his twin pursuits. He published *Eidola* (poetry) in 1917 and wrote the *Life of Sir William White* (1923), White being the designer of the first dreadnought; he also edited Walter Charleton's *Epicurus's Morals* (1926). In 1929 *The Middle Parts of Fortune: Somme & Ancre 1916* was published anonymously, an expurgated edition appearing in 1930 as *Her Privates We* by 'Private 19022' by which name and form it was known until the original was published in 1977. Manning died of pneumonia in 1935, virtually unknown in Australia and largely neglected by critics in England after the initial surge of excitement about his novel. *The Middle Parts of Fortune*, whose autobiographical basis has been traced by L.T. Hergenhan, is now internationally acknowledged as one of the most comprehensive and authentic documents of the First World War. *Scenes and Portraits*, which discusses historical personages such as Machiavelli and Francis of Assisi, is a series of dialogues and discussions rather than stories, dealing with the problems of transience, the anguish of human existence and the reconciliation of the burdens of mankind with a belief in a merciful, benevolent deity. Jonathan Marwil wrote the biography *Frederic Manning: An Unfinished Life* (1988) and Verna Coleman *The Last Exquisite: A Portrait of Frederic Manning* (1990).

MANNIX, Daniel (1864–1963), Roman Catholic archbishop of Melbourne, was the son of a tenant farmer in County Cork, Ireland. Educated at Maynooth College, he became its president in 1903. In 1913 he joined Archbishop T.J. Carr of Melbourne as coadjutor and became archbishop in 1917. An extremely influential and forceful figure, he was prominent in several controversies which affected Irish and Catholic Australians. Strongly opposed to the suppression of the 1916 Irish rebellion, he campaigned against conscription during the 1916 and 1917 referenda and was an equally dominant protagonist in the recurrent debate about state aid to non-government schools. Energetic in the field of education, he helped to found numerous Catholic schools, and in 1923 established the Corpus Christi seminary at Werribee. His opposition to both capitalism and communism sharpened and often polarised political and religious debate in Victoria and led to the formation in 1937 of the National Secretariat of Catholic Action by the Catholic bishops in Australia and the emergence of the Catholic Social Movement, presided over by B.A. Santamaria. Typical of the attitudes of many Australian Catholics contemporary with Mannix were those of poet Vincent Buckley (q.v.) in *Cutting Green Hay* (1983): 'the feelings he commanded were unique, not only in their intensity but in their kind . . . what many felt for Mannix . . . was an amalgam of reverence, love and fierce approval'. That there was also, and still are, contradictory appraisals of Mannix and his achievements can be gauged from the controversy in *Quadrant* (Jan/Feb 1991) between James Griffin and Timothy O'Leary on the entry on Mannix in *ADB*, vol. 10. Several biographies have been written of Mannix, including those by Cyril Bryan (1918), Frank Murphy (1948), Niall Brennan (1964), Michael Gilchrist (1982) and B.A. Santamaria (1984). Colin Kiernan in *Daniel Mannix and Ireland* (1980) traces the influence of Irish nationalism on Mannix. He appears as the character Archbishop Malone in Frank Hardy's novel *Power Without Glory* (1950) and in Barry Oakley's (q.v.) play *The Feet of Daniel Mannix* (1975).

MANSELL, Chris (1953–) graduated with an economics degree from the University of Sydney. She founded *Compass*, a poetry and prose magazine, and

was its editor 1978–87. A participant in the NSW Poets in Schools programme 1983–84, a writer-in-residence at WAIT in 1985 and lecturer in writing at the universities of Wollongong and Western Sydney, she has published several brief books of poetry, *Delta* (1978), *Heart, Head & Stone* (1982), *Redshift/Blueshift* (1988) and *Shining Like a Jinx* (1991, winner of the 1988 USA Amelia Chapbook Award). A passionate believer in the complexity of language, Mansell looks upon ambiguity and experimentation with structure as essential poetic activities. Deeply interested in the techniques of poetry, she rejects the conservatism and conformity of the past but acknowledges the vital criteria of reader accessibility – that all writing must ultimately communicate.

MANSFIELD, Katherine (1888–1928), the NZ writer of Australian descent, published her first professional writing in Australia. Encouraged by a NZ journalist, Tom L. Mills, she contributed four prose pieces to the *Native Companion* (1907), edited by E.J. Brady, Brady's acceptance strengthening her resolve to pursue a writing career. They are 'Vignettes', 'Silhouettes', 'In a Cafe' and 'In the Botanical Gardens' (signed 'Julian Mark'). Mansfield also made one contribution to the *Triad* in 1908 and one to the *Lone Hand* in 1909. In 1977 her contributions to the *Native Companion* were republished in Jean E. Stone's bibliographical study *Katherine Mansfield: Publications in Australia 1907–09*. Mansfield's last year of life is the subject of Alma De Groen's play *The Rivers of China* (1988).

MANSFIELD, Ralph (1799–1880), Methodist missionary and newspaper editor, was born Liverpool, England. He arrived in Sydney in 1820 and soon became prominent in the activities of the colony's Methodists, as well as editing the *Australian Magazine*. After difficulties had developed in his relationship with the British Committee, he resigned as a missionary in 1828 and in 1829 became joint editor with Robert Howe of the *Sydney Gazette*, and sole editor after Howe's death, a position he held until 1832. Subsequently he was a businessman and bookseller and in 1840–54 he was leader-writer and unofficial editor of the *Sydney Morning Herald*. An early demographer, Mansfield published *Analytical View of the Census of New South Wales for the Year 1841* (1841) and a similar work for 1846.

MANT, Gilbert (1902–), born Sydney, was a journalist with the *Daily Telegraph* 1925–30 and subsequently worked for Reuters in Australia, Britain and Canada. He joined the AIF in 1940 and went to Malaya with the first contingent of Australian troops in 1941. After serving for fourteen months he rejoined Reuters as its Australian news editor and returned to Malaya as a war correspondent after the outbreak of war with Japan, eventually escaping from Singapore in a British destroyer. His account of the Malayan campaign, *Grim Glory* (1942), was followed by a more personal account of his experiences as a soldier and war correspondent, *You'll Be Sorry* (1944), both republished as *The Singapore Surrender* in 1992. Mant has published two novels, *Glamour Brat* (1941), the story of a male Shirley Temple who comes to Australia and is kidnapped in the Blue Mountains, and *Gone Tomorrow* (1948); a collection of verse and stories, most of which were previously contributed to the *Australasian* and the *Bulletin*, *Holy Terror and Other Stories and Verse* (1923); a book for children, *Buttercup* (1969); an account of his experiences as a member of the press corps covering the 1932–33 bodyline cricket tour of Australia, *A Cuckoo in the Bodyline Nest* (1992); and a history of the Agricultural Council of NSW, *Show People* (1985). He also edited *Soldier Boy: the Letters of Gunner W.J.Duffell 1915–18* (1992), correspondence from an Australian soldier on active service in France.

Manuscripts: A Miscellany of Art and Letters, a Victorian magazine, ran, mainly quarterly, 1931–35. A vehicle for moderately advanced literary and art criticism, *Manuscripts* also became, especially in its later years, the publisher of avant-garde poetry. A contemporary section on European literature was included in its final two issues. Contributors included Hugh McCrae, Nettie Palmer, K.S. Prichard, Blamire Young and Clive Turnbull; it was edited by Harry Tatlock Miller and others.

MAQUARIE, Arthur (1874–1955), born Dubbo, NSW, as Arthur Frank Macquarie Mullens, later changed his name by deed poll. After graduating from the University of Sydney in 1895 he worked in England as a freelance writer, in Italy as a teacher of English, and also lived in France and Spain; he was active in the Royal Society of Literature and organised the British committee which promoted intellectual harmony among the Allies in the First World War. He wrote several plays on medieval subjects and several volumes of lyrical verse, but is most significant for the assistance he provided to Henry Lawson in London in 1900–1; as well as writing articles about Lawson which helped introduce him to literary London, Maquarie arranged meetings with editors, publishers and literary agents, and lived with Lawson while part of the Joe Wilson sequence was being written. Lawson's poignant portrait of Maquarie's struggle as a hack writer in London forms part of recently discovered material and is included in Brian Kiernan's *The Essential Henry Lawson* (1982).

Margin, which stands for Monash Australiana Research Group Informal Notes, is a literary/critical/historical magazine which began in 1977 at Monash University under the editorship of Dennis Davison. Published annually to begin with, it now usually appears twice annually.

MARIN LA MESLÉE, Edmond Marie (1852–93), born France, settled in Australia in 1876 and was private secretary to the French consul-general before becoming a public servant. Instrumental in the foundation of the Geographical Society of Australasia, he travelled extensively in eastern Australia and wrote an account of his impressions which was published in France in 1883 as *L'Australie Nouvelle*; an English edition, edited and translated by Russel Ward, appeared in 1973. A committed Austrophile, Marin la Meslée was a propagandist for Australia in France. He was interested in Federation and did research for Sir Henry Parkes.

MARKS, Harry (1923–77), born Melbourne, worked for a Melbourne advertising agency, was president of the Victorian FAW, and was one of the first Australian novelists to write about the experience of migrants. The main protagonists of both his novels are Jews, *The Heart Is Where the Hurt Is* (1966) dealing with a German-Jewish girl who comes to live with her Melbourne relatives a few years before the Second World War, and *Unicorn among the Wattles* (1979) describing the experience of a young Jewish man at Gallipoli and in Australia. Marks also edited, with Oscar Mendelsohn, an anthology of contemporary prose, *Australian New Writing* (1973) and wrote a biography of Alan Marshall, *I Can Jump Oceans: The World of Alan Marshall* (1976).

MARLOWE, Mary (1884–1962), born Marguerite Mary Shanahan at St Kilda, Melbourne, was a granddaughter of Sir John O'Shanassy, premier of Victoria. She began her career as an actor although she came from a middle-class Catholic family which regarded the profession as disreputable. After acquiring some minor roles in Australia, she went to London in 1910, and eventually achieved moderate success in Britain, the USA and Canada. Returning to England she published two novels, *Kangaroos in King's Land* (1917), which draws on her early experience of London, and *The Women Who Wait* (1918), a war novel intended to impress British women with the need to produce children. In 1920 she returned to Australia and joined the staff of the Sydney *Sun*, eventually writing a weekly theatre column for the newspaper, signed 'Puck'. She retired from journalism in 1946 but continued as a part-time writer of Dorothy Dix letters 1953–57. During the 1930s Depression she began to supplement her income by radio broadcasting and by 1935 had become an established interviewer of stage and film celebrities, and a regular commentator on a range of topics from household hints to world events. Her subsequent novels, all of them written to the romantic, escapist formula popular with such magazines as the *Australian Woman's Mirror*, which serialised several of them, include *The Toll Gate of Mars* (1917), *The Ghost Girl* (1921), *Gypsy Royal* (1923), *A Child by Proxy* (1925), *An Unofficial Rose* (1927), *Said the Spider* (1929), *Psalmist of the Dawn* (1934) and *Island Calm* (1940). Her autobiography, *That Fragile Hour*, was published in 1990.

MARRINGTON, Pauline (1921–   ), born Canada, was partly educated in England. In Australia she studied art and has taught at a Sydney girls' school. She has written two novels, *The October Horse* (1975) and *A House Full of Men* (1979); and an account of life on Norfolk Island based on the reminiscences of an Islander and recording some of the spoken language specific to Norfolk, *In the Sweet Bye and Bye: Reminis-*

cences of a Norfolk Islander (1981). Her two novels are traditional historical narratives dealing with the convict period.

MARSDEN, Samuel (1765–1838), born Yorkshire, England, was a blacksmith and a lay preacher when he attracted the attention of an Evangelical society within the Church of England, which sent him in his twenties to the University of Cambridge. In 1794 he arrived in NSW to take up a chaplaincy to which he had been recommended by William Wilberforce. Although he revisited England in 1807–9 and made several missionary voyages to NZ, he was based mainly at Parramatta, where he engaged in farming and was a magistrate as well as a minister. A controversial colonist, Marsden argued with Lachlan Macquarie, W.C. Wentworth and John Dunmore Lang among others, and published several vindications of his conduct; he retained a correspondence with Barron Field after Field's return to England in 1824. Known as the 'Flogging Parson', he was much criticised for his severity to the convicts, and appears in this light in 'Price Warung's' story 'Mr Slyde's Auction'; he also figures in several historical novels and plays. A.T. Yarwood wrote the biography, *Samuel Marsden: The Great Survivor* (1977).

MARSHALL, Alan (1902–84) was born Noorat in western Victoria. At the age of 6 he contracted infantile paralysis, which left his legs permanently crippled. After his family moved to Melbourne when he was 16, he attended business college and later worked as an accountant for a struggling shoe company. His main interest, however, was writing and he won several short-story competitions, although publication eluded him. In 1935, when the shoe company closed down, he turned to freelance writing. He contributed numerous topical, whimsical sketches to newspapers in Melbourne, Brisbane and Adelaide, and for many years contributed a 'lonely hearts' column to the women's magazine *Woman*. Another similar column, titled 'Alan Marshall's Casebook', was a regular feature of the *Argus* until that newspaper's demise in 1957; he also collaborated in a regular cartoon strip for the *Argus*, titled 'Speewa Jack'. Several of his short stories, meanwhile, were published in such periodicals as *Smith's Weekly*, the *Bulletin*, *ABC Weekly*, *Bohemia* and *Meanjin*. During the war Marshall travelled Australia by horse-drawn and motorised caravan, gathering messages from servicemen's families to be published in *A.I.F. News*; he also lectured for the army education service. Enthusiastic about the outback, he continued to travel widely in Australia after the war and spent some time in Hong Kong and China.

Although Marshall's reputation as a writer was slow to gain ground, it increased dramatically after the publication of his childhood autobiography, *I Can Jump Puddles* (q.v., 1955). The book has sold over three million copies, has been translated and published in numerous overseas countries, proving particularly popular in the former Soviet Union and eastern Europe, and was produced as an award-winning film in Czechoslovakia in 1970, and as a television series in Australia in 1981. Marshall himself also became a fam-

iliar national figure, particularly well known to schoolchildren. He was made OBE in 1972, AM in 1981 and received the Soviet Order of Friendship in 1977.

Marshall published five collections of short stories, *Tell Us About the Turkey, Jo* (1946), *How's Andy Going?* (1956), *Short Stories* (1973), later published as *Four Sunday Suits* (1975), *Hammers over the Anvil* (1975) and *The Complete Stories of Alan Marshall* (1977); an autobiographical trilogy, *I Can Jump Puddles* (1955), *This Is the Grass* (1962) and *In Mine Own Heart* (1963); an account of a visit to Arnhem Land, *Ourselves Writ Strange* (1948), later published with the title *These Were My Tribesmen* (1965); a description of his travels in Australia, *These Are My People* (1944); two collections of his newspaper sketches, *Pull Down the Blind* (1949) and *Bumping into Friends* (1950); a novel, *How Beautiful Are Thy Feet* (1949); an interpretation of Aboriginal myths, *People of the Dreamtime* (1952); two books for children, *Whispering in the Wind* (1969) and *Fight for Life* (1972); and a series of sketches of Australian country life originally contributed to *Permewan's Review* and *Australasian Post*, *Alan Marshall's Australia* (1981). He also wrote an account of the Melbourne businessman Sidney Myer and his emporium, *The Gay Provider* (1961) and, with Sreten Bozic, a play, *A Stone in My Pocket* (1974). *Alan Marshall Talking* (1978) records his yarns and Harry Marks has written an account of his life, *I Can Jump Oceans* (1976). John White has written an account of his association with the Victorian Writers' League (1987).

Underlying all Marshall's writing is a simple code, grounded in an optimistic faith in humanity, that values social solidarity, tenacity, work and physical courage. Distinctive features of his work include an open response to both the natural world and the world of children, an ability to describe graphically scene, character and incident, and to reproduce the Australian idiom. His most-loved stories are those which centre on the instinctive life of animals, such as 'The Grey Kangaroo', 'My Bird', 'The Three-Legged Bitch' and 'The Gentleman'; or which re-create the world of early childhood, such as 'Tell Us about the Turkey, Jo' (q.v.), 'Little Girl', 'Crossing the Road' and 'How's Andy Going?'; or which recall personalities and minor incidents from his early life in rural Victoria as in the *Hammers over the Anvil* collection; or which rely on the broadly humorous effects of the outback tall story, such as 'They Were Tough Men on the Speewah'. Rapidly sketched characters, a simple story-line culminating in a moment of revelation, a boy observer who is often crippled, and the impression of a speaking-voice narrating events, are recurrent characteristics of his short fiction. 'Trees Can Speak', perhaps his most technically accomplished story, is archetypal in its use of these ingredients to achieve a simple but striking effect. His autobiographies, like his novel, consist of loosely connected anecdotes or reminiscences which combine to form a vivid social history of rural Victoria in the early years of this century and of Melbourne in the 1920s and 1930s. The Alan Marshall Award for literature which contains a strong narrative element and whose purpose is to entertain the reading public is awarded annually through the Victorian branch of the FAW. His name is now given to the award for children's literature in the Victorian Premier's Literary Awards. The Shire of Eltham, Victoria, where Marshall once lived, gives an annual Alan Marshall Award for short fiction.

MARSHALL, Alan John (1911–67), zoologist and explorer known familiarly as 'Jock' Marshall, grew up in Penshurst, NSW. He lost an arm in a shooting accident at the age of 16 but was nevertheless a keen sportsman. Educated at the universities of Oxford and Sydney, where he supported himself by part-time journalism, he took part in explorations of the New Hebrides, New Guinea and the Arctic and led the Oxford University expedition to Jan Mayen in 1937. He taught anatomy and zoology at the universities of Oxford, Yale, California, and London, before his appointment in 1960 as professor of zoology and comparative physiology at Monash University. During the Second World War he served in army intelligence leading a special force ('Jock Force') behind Japanese lines in New Guinea. He published numerous scientific papers, and books on natural history, zoology and the conservation of wildlife, e.g. *The Men and Birds of Paradise* (1938), for which he was an active campaigner; *The Black Musketeers* (1937), an account of his experiences in the New Hebrides; an account of the work of Charles Darwin and T.H. Huxley in Australia (1970); and, with Russell Drysdale, a lively and popular description of a journey in north-western Australia in 1958, *Journey Among Men* (1962). His *Australia Limited*, first published in 1942, went to six printings by 1945; a deeply critical account of the Australian character, it echoed the sentiments of many at the time. Marshall is given a chapter in John Hetherington's *Uncommon Men* (1965).

MARSHALL, James Vance (1887–1964), born Casino, NSW, was an inveterate traveller, working at a range of occupations from bank clerk to railway ganger to purser on a banana ship. A prominent member of the Labor Party and union organiser, he was active also in British labour politics. An ardent campaigner against conscription in the First World War, he was imprisoned under the government of W.M. Hughes. He wrote two pamphlets relating to his prison experiences, *Jail from Within* (1918), a series of autobiographical sketches, and *The World of the Living Dead* (1919), a collection of poems and sketches of similar context, which includes a preface by Henry Lawson, with whom Marshall was friendly. He also wrote *Timely Tips for New Australians* (1926) under the pseudonym 'Jice Doone'. A subsequent tale, *The Children* (1959), republished in 1961 with the title *Walkabout*, which describes the experiences of two White children, sole survivors of a plane crash in the outback, and an Aboriginal boy, was apparently written by an English author who collaborated with Marshall in that he used, with his consent, his notes on outback life deriving from his period as a sandalwood-cutter in the Northern Territory. Some subsequent books, similarly reliant on his notes, have been published

under his name, including *A River Ran Out of Eden* (1962), *My Boy John That Went to Sea* (1966) and *A Walk to the Hills of the Dreamtime* (1970). *The Children* proved popular at the time of its publication and was also produced as a film, but it has subsequently been described as 'a good record of white Australian folklore about Aborigines'.

MARSHALL, Rocky (1924–), born Adelaide, left school at 14 and worked as a rural and industrial labourer, serving in the RAAF in the Second World War. It was not until his late fifties that he began writing. He travels the outback gathering tales of bush characters for his stories and his narrative poetry. At folk gatherings he is well known for his recitations and his playing of the harmonica. He has had numerous writer-in-residence stints at SA schools. His books for children include *This Was My Valley* (1983), the story of his childhood, first by the seaside and later on a soldier settlement block between the wars. *Hidden Valley* (1983) has the same bush setting but is written as a fantasy. His verse includes *Front Bar Politicians* (1984) and *Down the Track* (1985). He has won the Kapunda Bush Verse Award, 1984, 1986, the SA Folk Federation Song Writing Award, 1984 and the Laura Literary Award, 1989. His book *King of Kimberley* (1988) is the story of 'Pigeon' (Tjandamara) who was declared an outlaw when he tried to drive White settlers from his people's land during the settlement of the Kimberley region in the 1890s.

MARSHALL, William Leonard (1944–), born Sydney, has worked as a proofreader, mortuary attendant, schoolteacher, postman, chemical worker and storeman. He lived in Hong Kong, Switzerland, Wales and Ireland before returning to Australia in 1983. His first novel, *The Fire Circle*, a concentrated tale of guilt and violence set in a construction camp in the WA desert, was published in 1969. His other novels include *The Age of Death* (1970) and *The Middle Kingdom* (1971), as well as numerous detective mysteries in a series titled 'The Yellowthread Street Mysteries'. He has also written plays, including 'King Edward', based on the abdication of Edward VIII, which was produced in Sydney in 1971, and *The Twinkling Ornaments of the Night*, published in *Five Plays for Radio* (1975), ed. Alrene Sykes.

MARSHALL-HALL, G.W.L. (George William Louis) (1862–1915) was born in London, where he studied at the Royal College of Music. In 1888 he was appointed conductor of the choral and orchestral societies of the London Organ School, and in 1891 Ormond professor of music at the University of Melbourne. A charismatic but impetuous and volatile personality, he was frequently involved in acrimonious debates with music critics in Melbourne's newspapers. He also became well known as a conductor and in 1892 founded the Marshall-Hall Orchestra, recognised by visiting musicians as equal to European first-rank orchestras. In 1895 he established, with W.A. Laver, the University's Conservatorium of Music. In 1897 he published two booklets of verse, *Hymn to Sydney* and *A*

Book of Canticles, neither of which attained a circulation of fifty copies, but which succeeded in offending large numbers of citizens by their alleged eroticism. His next collection, *Hymns, Ancient and Modern* (1898), aroused ill-founded claims of irreverence and lasciviousness, and prompted the University council to dismiss him, an action which sparked an intense controversy. He subsequently established a private conservatorium in East Melbourne, the Marshall-Hall Conservatorium. In 1914 he was again appointed to the Ormond Chair but died shortly afterwards. He also published two historical tragedies, *Aristodemus* (1900) and *Bianca Capello* (1906); another collection of verse, *To Irene* (1896); and wrote both music and libretti for three operas. At his death, Sir Herbert Brookes published a part-prose, part-verse elegy in his memory, *At the Graveside*. Thérèse Radic published *G.W.L. Marshall-Hall: Portrait of a Lost Crusader* (1982), an introduction to the Marshall-Hall collection of the Grainger Museum, which includes a brief biography of Marshall-Hall.

MARSHALL-STONEKING, Billy (1947–), born and raised in the USA, came to Australia in the early 1970s to teach, first at Lake Koorat High School. He spent some time at Yandamincka in the NT, then moved to Papunya in Central Australia. He had a long association with the Pintupi people of Central Australia making several significant documentary films (he also went to film school in Sydney) including *Desert Stories* (1984) and *Nosepeg's Movie* (1988). Poet, playwright, screenwriter, he wrote *Lasseter: The Making of a Legend* (1985), a substantial work on Harold Bell Lasseter of the Lost Reef fame, and was co-writer of the ABC TV series *Stringer* (1988). Active in performance poetry, he won the Bill Harney, 1988 Poetry Prize for his poem, 'Seasons of Fire'. His book *Singing the Snake*, consisting of poems from the Western Desert 1979–1988, was published in 1990 and a play, *Sixteen Words for Water*, dealing with Ezra Pound, in 1991. His 'auto-fictography' *Taking America out of the Boy* was published in 1993.

MARTENS, Conrad (1801–78), prominent colonial artist, was born London and joined HMS *Beagle* in 1833 on its scientific cruise to Patagonia and Tierra del Fuego, becoming a close friend of Charles Darwin. In 1835 Martens came to Sydney; he sketched and painted the Port Jackson, Illawarra and Blue Mountains areas and later the New England and Darling Downs districts. Accounts of Martens and his work include Lionel Lindsay's *Conrad Martens: The Man and His Art* (1920) and J.G. Steele's *Conrad Martens in Queensland* (1978).

MARTIN, A.E. (Archibald Edward) (1885–1955) worked for a time with C.J. Dennis on the *Gadfly* and as publishing agent for the J.C. Williamson firm. He wrote radio serials, four books on place names in Australia and six novels, several of which were serialised in the *Australian Women's Weekly*. They include *Common People* (1944), which won the *Weekly's* novel prize in 1942, *Sinners Never Die* (1944), *The Misplaced Corpse*

(1944), *Death in the Limelight* (1946) and *The Chinese Bed Mysteries* (1955). His last novel, *The Hive of Glass* (1962), a study of small-town life in NSW, was completed after his death by his son, J.T. Martin. *The Misplaced Corpse* was reprinted in Wakefield Press's Australian Crime Classics series in 1992, *Sinners Never Die* in 1993.

MARTIN, A.P. (Arthur Patchett) (1851–1902), born Kent, England, was brought to Australia in 1852. A member of the Victorian public service, he took an active role in Melbourne's literary life and was editor of the *Melbourne Review* from its inception in 1876 until he left for London in 1882 to work as a journalist. Martin edited three anthologies which included contributions from prominent Australian writers, *An Easter Omelette* (1879), *Oak-bough and Wattle-blossom* (1888) and *Over the Sea* (1891); wrote one of the earliest surveys of Australian literature, *The Beginnings of an Australian Literature* (1898); the historical accounts *Australia and the Empire* (1889) and *True Stories from Australasian History* (1893), and a biography of Robert Lowe (1893). A composer of conventional, romantic verse, he contributed to various anthologies such as *Hash* (1877), *The 'Vagabond' Annual* (1877) and *Under the Gum Tree* (1890); and published three collections, *Lays of Today* (1878), *Fernshawe* (1882) and *The Withered Jester* (1895). *Fernshawe*, which includes some prose sketches, reprints material from the *Melbourne Review* and other journals, e.g. 'Two Australian Poets' (on Adam Lindsay Gordon and J.B. Stephens). He also wrote a book of verse and fiction, *Sweet Girl Graduate* (1876). His wife was Harriette Anne Martin.

MARTIN, C.E.M. (Catherine Edith Macauley) (1847–1937), born on the Isle of Skye, was the daughter of Samuel Nicholson Mackay, a crofter, and Janet Mackay. In 1855 the family arrived in Adelaide and moved to Naracoorte, presumably to help work pastoral properties belonging to other Highland families. The death of Samuel in about 1856 was a major blow. Little is known of Catherine Martin's education, but she appears to have gained a knowledge of French and German. By the early 1870s she was living in Mount Gambier, where she ran a school with her sister Mary. From at least 1868 she published poetry and verse translations in the Mount Gambier and Adelaide newspapers and in 1874, under the initials M.C., her first book, *The Explorers and Other Poems*. After moving shortly afterwards to Adelaide, where she became friendly with Catherine Spence (q.v.), she published what appears to be her first novel, *The Moated Grange*, serialised in the *South Australian Chronicle and Weekly Mail* in 1877. In the same year she took a position as a clerk in the Education Department but lost it in 1885, possibly as a result of discrimination. She married Frederick Martin in 1882 and lived for a time at the Alma gold-mine near Waukaringa where Frederick was the accountant. This experience provided her with material for her novel, *The Silent Sea* (1892). Her best known novel, *An Australian Girl* (q.v.), had been published anonymously in 1890. Between 1890–1904 and 1904–7 the Martins travelled extensively in

Europe, Catherine contributing a series, 'Vignettes of Travel', to the *Age*, as well as stories to the *Leader* and a serial novel, *At a Crisis*, to the *Adelaide Observer* in 1900. Her travel experiences also informed the anonymous novel *The Old Roof-Tree: Letters of Ishbel to Her Half-brother, Mark Latimer* (1906). After Frederick Martin died in 1909 Catherine made several more trips abroad and continued to take a lively interest in literature, social issues and international relations. Her last novel, *The Incredible Journey* (1923), was published under her own name. Martin's other publications which have been traced so far include articles, reviews and short stories contributed to the *Victorian Review*, the *Melbourne Review*, the *Age*, the *Leader*, the *South Australian Chronicle and Weekly Mail* and the *Observer Miscellany*. Extremely reticent, Martin left little in the way of biographical or bibliographical records. Her work, popular with her contemporaries, was subsequently neglected, although two of her novels, *An Australian Girl* and *The Incredible Journey*, were republished in 1987.

An advanced writer for her time, and unusual in that she has no interest in the bush ethos, Martin is concerned with social issues, religion and philosophy, anticipating several of the themes of such writers as Martin Boyd, 'Henry Handel Richardson' and, in her few realistic images of bush life, Barbara Baynton. *An Australian Girl* presents a perceptive, intellectually alive and idealistic heroine, whose sceptical view of marriage proves tragically well founded. Out of print for many years and often described as a conventional nineteenth-century genteel romance with the standard preoccupation with love and courtship, *An Australian Girl* is more the account of one woman's spiritual pilgrimage in which personal loss is finally transcended by the discovery of a religious humanism that is reminiscent of George Eliot's. Martin's originality emerges in her realistic but sympathetic treatment of her well-rounded characters and her imaginative penetration of their inner life; in her transcendence of an ostensibly conventional plot; and in her treatment of such large themes as religion, the realities of marriage, the pursuit of happiness and the nature of civilisation. Particularly striking are her finely detailed descriptions of the Mallee country, which is the background of the early part of the novel. The final scenes, set partly in Berlin and dominated by intense anguish, doomed love, and music, anticipate some of the atmosphere of 'Henry Handel Richardson's' *Maurice Guest* (1908). *The Incredible Journey* is a sympathetic and knowledgeable story of the journey of two Aboriginal women, Iliapo and Polde, over hundreds of miles of desert country to retrieve a little boy who had been kidnapped by a White man. *The Old Roof-Tree*, supposedly made up of letters written from England, Holland, Germany and Italy, ranges over a large span of subjects from religion and philosophy to painting and visions of an ideal social future, and reflects Martin's horror of the poverty and inequalities of English life as well as her witty, colonial perception of English manners at the turn of the century. Her verse collection includes a long narrative poem, 'The Explorers', on the Burke and Wills story,

which includes an idyllic vision of the Australian future, as well as some ballads and lyrics and translations from Herder, Goethe, Schiller and other European poets.

MARTIN, David (1915–) was born Ludwig Detsinyi into a Jewish family in Hungary and subsequently changed his name by deed poll. He was brought up in Germany, a country for which he has ambivalent feelings and which he left at 17. After some time in Holland, where he worked on the reclamation of the Zuider Zee, and a year in Palestine, where he lived on a kibbutz, he served as a first-aid orderly in the International Brigade in Spain 1937–38. In 1938 he settled in London, where he worked for the *Daily Express* and later for the European service of the BBC. He married Richenda Powell, a schoolteacher and writer, in 1941. He was literary editor of *Reynolds News* 1945–47, and foreign correspondent in India for the *Daily Express* 1948–49. In 1949 he visited Australia, was impressed by the peaceful, extrovert life, and decided to stay. For many years a member of the Communist Party, Martin left it in 1956 but retains his left-wing sympathies.

Although German is his native language, Martin began writing verse in English in the 1940s and had established a reputation as a poet, short-story writer, novelist and playwright before his arrival in Australia. He has published eight collections of verse, *Battlefields and Girls* (1942), *Trident* (1944, with Hubert Nicholson and John Manifold), *From Life* (1953), *Rob the Robber* (1954, under the pseudonym 'Spinifex'), *Poems of David Martin 1938–1958* (1958), *Spiegel the Cat* (1961), *The Gift* (1966) and *The Idealist* (1968). His verse has also appeared in numerous anthologies including *Eight by Eight* (1963) and *Modern Australian Writing* (1966). He has written six novels, *Tiger Bay* (1946), *The Stones of Bombay* (1949), *The Young Wife* (q.v., 1962), *The Hero of Too* (q.v., 1965, published in New York as *The Hero of the Town*), *The King Between* (1966, published in New York as *The Littlest Neutral*) and *Where a Man Belongs* (1969); two collections of short stories, *The Shoes Men Walk In* (1946) and *Foreigners* (1981); two autobiographical narratives, *Fox On My Door* (1987), which blends short story, essay and autobiography, and *My Strange Friend* (1991), a more substantial account of his life which is also informative about other writers; numerous books for children, including *Hughie* (1971), *Frank & Francesca* (1972), *Gary* (1972), *The Chinese Boy* (1973), *The Cabby's Daughter* (1974), *Katie* (1974, with Richenda Martin), *Mister P and His Remarkable Flight* (1975), *The Devilish Mystery of the Flying Mum* (1977), *The Man in the Red Turban* (1978), *The Mermaid Attack* (1978), *The Girl Who Didn't Know Kelly* (1985) and *Clowning Sim* (1988); and a collection of verse for children, *I Rhyme My Time* (1980). In *Armed Neutrality for Australia* (1984) he has projected a radically different Australian defence policy. Two of his plays, 'The Young Wife' and *The Shepherd and The Hunter*, have been produced, and the latter published in 1946; *Tiger Bay* has been produced as a film and *Frank & Francesca* as a serial on ABC television. As well as numerous essays and reviews, he has edited two collections of verse, *Rhyme and Reason* (1944) and *New World, New Song* (1955); written a travel book, *On the Road to Sydney* (1970); and provided the text for a collection of photographs on migrant life in Australia, *I'll Take Australia* (1978). He was made AO in 1988 and in 1991 won the Patrick White Award.

Martin's novels have diverse settings and themes, ranging from the Cardiff dockside area of *Tiger Bay* or the tiny Indo-Chinese kingdom of Lhaodia of *The King Between* to the small Australian country town of Tooramit of *The Hero of Too*. Variety of tone is also a marked feature of his work. *The Young Wife*, a powerful and sombre domestic drama played by Greek migrants in contemporary Melbourne, sensitively explores an archetypal theme; the Rabelaisian *The Hero of Too* wittily but affectionately explodes a number of Australian myths; *Where a Man Belongs*, Martin's most autobiographical and ambitious novel, is both complex and searching; *The King Between*, a comic fantasy on the theme of neutrality, is a virtuoso display of his satirical skills.

Martin's writing for children, directed mainly at teenagers, shows the same verve and, for the most part, the same uncompromising realism. Several of his novels concentrate on the struggle of the outsider: *Frank and Francesca* deals with migrants, *Hughie* with an Aboriginal boy, *The Chinese Boy* with Chinese experience on the Australian goldfields of the 1860s. Particularly notable are *The Cabby's Daughter*, the story of the experience of a motherless girl in 1903 as she confronts adult realities for the first time, and *Mister P and His Remarkable Flight*, an account of a lonely boy and his racing pigeon, written from the perspectives of both the boy and his bird.

Martin's verse has moved from simple and stirring revolutionary themes that address 'all who love life and peace above war and death' *(From Life)* to the more personal, lyrical and complex. His predilection for humorous satire emerges in some shorter poems and in *The Idealist*, a narrative about a Reverend Eric Green who chooses to live literally as a Christian. His comic versatility is seen at its best in *Spiegel the Cat*, a narrative poem based on a tale by the nineteenth-century Swiss writer Gottfried Keller.

MARTIN, Sir James (1820–86), born County Cork, Ireland, was brought to Sydney as an infant by his parents and was educated at W.T. Cape's academy. In 1838 his *The Australian Sketch Book*, a collection of fifteen essays imitative of Washington Irving, was published; with the possible exception of Henry Savery's *The Hermit of Van Diemen's Land* (1830) it was the first book of essays published in Australia and included 'The Pseudo-Poets', which criticised Charles Harpur, Charles Tompson and others. Martin contributed to the *Australian* after leaving school and was its acting editor in 1839; in 1845–47 he was editor and manager of the *Atlas*. He qualified as a solicitor in 1845 and in 1848 began a long career in conservative politics which culminated in the premiership of NSW (1863–64, 1866–68, 1870–72). Knighted in 1869, Martin was a distinguished chief justice of the colony in 1873–86. He gave his name to Martin Place in the central busi-

ness district of Sydney and is the subject of Elena Grainger's *Martin of Martin Place* (1970). Anthony Trollope regarded him as the best Australian speaker he heard in his time in Australia.

MARTIN, Philip (1931–   ), born Richmond, Melbourne, graduated from the University of Melbourne in 1958 and has taught at Monash University, Melbourne. Critic, translator and script-writer for radio and television, Martin is probably best known as a poet. His volumes of poetry include *Voice Unaccompanied* (1970), *A Bone Flute* (1974), *From Sweden: Translations and Poems* (1979), *A Flag for the Wind* (1982) and *New and Selected Poems* (1988). Martin was an important influence on Bruce Dawe (q.v.) in the 1950s.

Marvellous Melbourne, a phrase commonly applied to Melbourne in the nineteenth century to describe its growth in prosperity from the 1850s to the late 1880s, derived from an account of the city written by the English journalist George Augustus Sala, following a visit in 1885, and published in the *Argus*, the *Australasian*, the *Sydney Morning Herald* and the London *Daily Telegraph*. The phrase immediately stuck in the popular imagination and summed up for Melburnians their long-established confidence in their city's material progress, its thriving commercial, social and cultural life, and its dominance over Sydney. This pride was reflected in the popular press, in the statements of political, business and church leaders, and in the work of the city's chroniclers such as Alexander Sutherland's *Victoria and Its Metropolis* (1888) and H. Perkins's *Melbourne Illustrated and Victoria Described* (1880). Alfred Dampier used the phrase as the title for one of his popular melodramas (staged 1889), written in collaboration with J.H. Wrangham and possibly others; but the myth received its most ornate literary treatment in the public poems produced by Victorian poets on appropriate occasions, from R.H. Horne's 'Lyric Masque', commissioned for Melbourne's Intercolonial Exhibition of 1866, to Reverend William Allen's *The Centennial Cantata* (1888), written for Melbourne's Centennial International Exhibition. The phrase was also frequently adjusted to express less attractive aspects of the city; the deficiencies of its sanitation led to the title 'Murderous Melbourne', celebrated in the Sydney *Bulletin* in 1889 in the following terms:

> Sing hey! for the City that's Queen
> Of the continent known as Australia
> Where the gutters are slimy and green
> And all sorts of terrors assail yer . . .

Four years later, the city's financial scandals gave the *Bulletin's* cartoonists plenty of material for their theme of 'Marvellous Smellboom'. Another familiar theme was the contrast between Melbourne's prosperity and its seamier underside; John Stanley James's *The Vagabond Papers* (1876–77) presents authentic descriptions of the city's slums; John Freeman's *Lights and Shadows of Melbourne Life* (1888) exploits the sensational aspects of the same topic; and Fergus Hume's novel *The Mystery of a Hansom Cab* (1886) paints a dramatic contrast between the two sides of Melbourne's life. After the severe depression of the 1890s, Melbourne began to attract the adjective 'Miserable' in the popular press and the theme was a common one with contemporary historians and literary figures. Both Alfred Deakin and Charles H. Pearson wrote of the disadvantages and social evils of the city; George Essex Evans's poem 'In Collins Street' (1898) reflects a familiar feeling of unease and disillusionment; and the theme of the evil city is treated with particularly incisive bitterness by Bernard O'Dowd in his poem 'The City' (1901). The myth of 'Marvellous Melbourne' has been thoroughly explored by Graeme Davison in *The Rise and Fall of Marvellous Melbourne* (1978). It has also given rise to a popular extravaganza by John Romeril and Jack Hibberd, *Marvellous Melbourne* (1970), which presents a dense, lively picture of nineteenth-century Melbourne with Alfred Dampier at the centre of the action, and explores political and social analogies with modern Victoria. Jim Davidson's *The Sydney-Melbourne Book* (1986) looks at the social, cultural and political differences between the two rival cities, known as 'Tinsel Town' and 'St. Petersburg' to many in the literary fraternity.

Mary Poppins, see **TRAVERS, Pamela**

MAS, Joan (1926–74), born Sydney as Joan Morgan, was a freelance writer for the ABC and was for a time editor of *Poetry Magazine*. She contributed verse to numerous Australian anthologies and periodicals as well as to overseas journals, and published two collections *Isis in Search* (1966) and *The Fear and the Flowering* (1975).

Masque, a review of the performing arts, was published six times a year in Sydney 1967–71. Edited by John Allen, it included contributions from playwrights, producers and drama critics such as Roger Covell, Robert Helpmann, Alan Seymour and John Tasker.

MASS, Nuri (1918–), born Melbourne, spent some years in Argentina as a child, returning to Australia at the age of 12. After graduating from the University of Sydney she was an editor with Angus & Robertson, Consolidated Press and the Sydney *Sun*, and established her own private press, the Writers Press. She subsequently practised as a chiropractor. Her books for children include *Australian Wild Flower Fairies* (1937), *The Little Grammar People* (1942), *Magic Australia* (1942), *The Wizard of Jenolan* (1946), *The Wonderland of Nature* (1964), *Many Paths – One Heaven* (1965), *China – The Waking Giant* (1966), and *Australian Wild-flower Magic* (1967). She has also written five novels for adults, *Randy Blair* (1955), *The Gift* (1969), *Donna Roon* (1970), *As Much Right to Live* (1971) and *Don't Kill It – It's Me* (1972); a collection of verse, *Just Give Us Time* (1984); and an account of Argentina, largely drawn from her mother's records, *Where the Incas Trod* (1956).

MASSINA, A.H. (Alfred Henry) (1834–1917), born London, arrived in Melbourne in 1855. After an unsuccessful stint on the Victorian goldfields he returned to his former trade of printing, and in 1859 he helped form Clarson, Shallard & Co, which became Clarson, Massina & Co in 1868 and A.H. Massina & Co, the present name, in 1876. Among the firm's publications were the *Colonial Monthly* and the *Australian Journal; His Natural Life* was serialised in the latter 1870–72, Massina allegedly locking Clarke in an office so that instalments could be completed. Massina also published Adam Lindsay Gordon's *Bush Ballads and Galloping Rhymes* (1870), presenting Gordon with the account the day before Gordon's suicide. He was chairman of the Melbourne *Herald* board 1902–9. Ronald G. Campbell wrote *The First Ninety Years, the Printing House of Massina, Melbourne, 1859–1949* (1949).

MASTERS, Olga (1919–86), born Pambula, NSW, worked as a journalist for the *Cobargo Chronicle* before leaving for Sydney in 1937. She married Charles Masters, a schoolteacher, in 1940 and for the next twenty years lived in a series of small and large NSW country towns. By 1961 she was the mother of seven children, several of whom were to win prominence in various fields. In 1955 she resumed her career as a journalist, working casually as a district correspondent for the Lismore *Northern Star*, and later writing for other newspapers, including the *Manly Daily*, the *Land* and the *Sydney Morning Herald*. Everyday rituals and activities were the staple of Masters's journalism, which she frequently described as the long apprenticeship behind her sudden success as a fiction-writer. Beginning her writing career belatedly in 1975, she soon began to win awards for her short stories. Her first collection, *The Home Girls* (1982), won a National Book Council Award, and was followed by *A Long Time Dying* (1985), a series of linked stories, and two novels, *Loving Daughters* (1984) and *Amy's Children* (1987). A further short-story collection, *The Rose Fancier* (1988), a stage play, *A Working Man's Castle* (1988) and a collection of her journalism, selected by Deirdre Coleman, *Reporting Home* (1990), were published posthumously. In 1991 Julie Lewis's biography, *Olga Masters – A Lot of Living*, was published.

The stories in *The Home Girls*, set in the rural landscape of Masters's childhood, deal with the quotidian experience of economically depressed communities. Working on a small canvas, Masters develops unillusioned but compassionate studies of family and small-town relationships. Bleak and threadbare as are the lives of most of her characters, the dullness of their world is made dramatic and complex by Masters's keen eye for vivid detail, and her discovery of the significant in the trivial, the comic in the tragic. The linked stories of *A Long Time Dying*, set in Cobargo of 1935, 'a terribly dull place', pursue the theme of confinement, especially women's economic, social and psychological confinement. Sensuality in this gossip-ruled environment may be a doubtful gift, and although the home is a central theme it is experienced as part-haven, part-prison. In Masters's first novel,

Loving Daughters, two talented sisters are rivals for the love of an English minister, newly arrived in their 1920s town. Their struggle, which is really a quest for some autonomy, is doomed to disappointment from the first, given the uncongenial nature of their social circumstances. *Amy's Children* charts the life-course of a woman who initially breaks through economic and social boundaries, only to return to an oppressive situation. In her last collection, *The Rose Fancier*, Masters extends her studies of economic and emotional impoverishment from the 1880s to the 1980s.

Materfamilias, a novel by Ada Cambridge (q.v.), was published in 1898. The retrospective narration of incidents in the life of a Melbourne matron, Polly Braye, the novel opens with her leaving home, almost immediately to marry, after her father takes a second wife. Although Polly's marriage is unsuccessful, she voyages to Melbourne when she hears her husband is ill there; *en route* she falls in love with the captain of the ship, Tom Braye, whom she marries when it is discovered that her first husband has died. The bulk of *Materfamilias* chronicles significant events in the marriage of Polly and Tom: the birth of their four children, although Polly's favourite son, Bobby, is later killed in a shooting accident; the struggle to establish themselves, which is alleviated by a legacy from Polly's aunt; Tom's retirement from the sea to take up pig-farming outside Melbourne; the education and courtship of their eldest children, Harry and Phyllis; the silver wedding anniversary of Polly and Tom; and at the end of the novel, the birth of the first grandchild and the marriage of Harry to Emily Blount, whom Polly has long resisted. The most fully drawn of Cambridge's characters, Polly, despite her vitality and exuberance, reveals herself as wilful, possessive, self-deceiving, inconsistent and increasingly jealous, attitudes which Cambridge's implied feminism sheets home to her powerlessness.

'Mateship', a much-discussed term in Australian literary, historical and cultural commentary, emerged in the second half of the nineteenth century; it derives from the word 'mate', used in Australian English as a synonym for 'cobber', which denotes a habitual companion, associate, friend or partner. 'Mate' has also been used as a mode of address, which is often friendly and implies equality, as in the famous "ow yer goin' mate, orright?' in *They're a Weird Mob*, (1957); sometimes neutral, as in the common reply 'Sorry, mate, haven't got a clue' to a request for information; and sometimes hostile, as in the threatening 'Watch it, *mate*'. The comradeship and mutual support which form part of 'mateship', and the fact that it is an exclusively male phenomenon, an 'informal male-bonding institution involving powerful, sublimated homosexuality' in the words of polemicist Miriam Dixson, were noticed by Alexander Harris in the 1840s. In *The Emigrant Family* (1849) Harris noted that 'The Australians . . . are growing up a race by themselves; fellowship of country has already begun to distinguish them and bind them together'; in *Settlers and Convicts* (1847) he expressed surprise at the extent of the 'exertions bushmen of new countries, especially mates, will make for one another, beyond people of the old countries'. Mateship has also been discovered in the following decade among the Eureka rebels, but as a term it gained a wider currency in the 1890s. In part this was an indirect consequence of the late nineteenth-century interest in the 'Coming Man', a question addressed by such writers as Marcus Clarke, Francis Adams and 'Rolf Boldrewood', but more important were the propagandists for the emerging union movement (the group loyalties and brotherhood of 'mates' were contrasted by W.G. Spence with the treachery of 'scabs') and the numerous, if varied, references to mateship in the writings of Henry Lawson. Mateship also figures in the work of C.E.W. Bean and others writing about Australian soldiers in the First World War. Its importance in the Anzac tradition, celebrated in Leonard Mann's novel *Flesh in Armour* (q.v., 1932) and scrutinised in Alan Seymour's play *The One Day of the Year* (1962), is reinforced by a 1983 survey which showed that mateship is regarded by the participants as the main reason for the higher survival rate of Australians in Japanese POW camps in 1942–45. The several social, political and military contexts in which mateship has been used in the 1890s and later has contributed to the semantic extension of the term beyond a collection of qualities such as comradeship and mutual support among males towards its status almost as a creed, certainly a term around which have clustered a number of associations, values, practices or ideals: associations such as the link with the bush and with Australianness, noticed by Harris, consolidated by Lawson and present in other writers, e.g. 'Duke' Tritton, Alan Marshall and even Mary Grant Bruce; male values and practices such as manliness and drinking beer; ideals such as egalitarianism, democratic political and social reform, and Utopianism. In the hands of some writers mateship has become a synonym for these associations, practices, values or ideals. For example, in H.G. Oxley's *Mateship in Local Organization* (1974) the term is largely dispensed with after the title in favour of the egalitarianism which is the focus of the book. Similarly, mateship in the narrow sense is only one of the ingredients which make up the stereotypical Australian in Russel Ward's *The Australian Legend* (q.v., 1958), a stereotype which Ward sees as a national self-image, also partly a myth, which originated with the convicts, developed through the character and experience of the itinerant bush workers in the second half of the nineteenth century and was publicised by such journals as the *Bulletin* (q.v.). Yet because Ward's typical Australians exhibit not only mateship but also the characteristics associated with it, phrases like 'the Australian ideal of mateship' and 'one huge myth of mateship' have become the shorthand of commentators on, and critics of, Ward's Australian legend (e.g. Humphrey McQueen, q.v.) and the other myths, e.g. the Anzac tradition, about national character with which it has been linked. To take a third example, mateship and other manifestations of 'maleness' such as 'ockerism', 'larrikinism' and male chauvinism have been used interchangeably in critiques, particularly those by feminists and journalists, of Australian society and historiography.

It is largely because of the flexibility with which the term has been used that discussions of, and attacks on, mateship have paralleled the discussions of the Australian legends into which it so centrally fits. Broadly, commentators have focused on four issues: the extent to which mateship is uniquely or even distinctively Australian (although it is doubtful whether in any other country an all-male club like the Melbourne Bread and Cheese Club (q.v.) would specify that its journal, *Bohemia*, was published in the interest of Mateship, Art and Letters; or a journal like *Realist Writer*, in its first issue, use the word 'mateship' as a code word for the radical tradition it was asserting); the extent to which it is a true description of Australian (male) behaviour; whether, even if not a true description, it forms part of the Australian self-image of (male) Australians, at least at one stage in Australian history, or whether instead it is a myth created by historians and others; and finally, its value as an ideal or a mode of behaviour. In most of these discussions Australian literature has been one of the main sources of evidence to which commentators have turned. As well as citing some of the numerous examples which can be found within Australian folk-song and ballad attesting to the ideal or practice of comradeship and mutual support among Australian males, e.g. 'How Gilbert Died', 'The Dying Stockman', 'Sam Holt', 'The Sick Stockrider', Ward adduces evidence from Harris, Lawson and the writings of Marcus Clarke, 'Price Warung', Anthony Trollope, Friedrich Gerstaecker and Joseph Furphy. Although the evidence of these authors is seen as positive about the existence and value of mateship, some of it at least is open to different interpretation, even in the case of 'Warung', who had strong egalitarian beliefs and whose story 'Secret Society of the Ring' climaxes in the self-sacrifice and mateship of the convict Felix. The famous Convict Oath (q.v.) in 'Warung's' story 'The Liberation of the First Three' is cited by Ward and several other writers as evidence of the freemasonry of the convicts, an early form of mateship. The story, however, recounts how three convicts kill three other convicts with whom they are chained and have sworn the oath, and in the sequel ('The Liberation of the Other Three') two survivors murder the third and then kill each other, making an ironic mockery of the oath. Similarly, the work of other Australian writers has been cited as evidence of the darker side of mateship. To take a few examples among many: the theme of men as predators in Barbara Baynton's (q.v.) fiction finds bitter expression in the ironically titled 'Squeaker's Mate', a story which chronicles the desertion of the morally stronger female by her male partner after she has her back broken in an accident; the exclusiveness, hostility and even violence towards outsiders such as women, class traitors and different racial or ethnic groups finds expression in Gavin Casey's (q.v.) *It's Harder for Girls* (1942), in some of John Morrison's stories, e.g. 'Bo Abbott', in the crucifixion of Himmelfarb in Patrick White's *Riders in the Chariot* (1961), in the brutality of the larrikins (q.v.) in Louis Stone's *Jonah* (1911) and in

the murder of Sibley in David Ireland's *The Glass Canoe* (1976). Among dramatists, Ray Lawler's *Summer of the Seventeenth Doll* (1957) shows the fragility even of a long-term mateship and Jack Hibberd, one of a number of Australian playwrights to scrutinise national myths, exposes the ethic as insular and imprisoning in *White with Wire Wheels* (q.v., 1970).

Something of the darker side of mateship is also seen in the work of the writer most closely identified with its celebration, Henry Lawson. According to J. le Gay Brereton in *Henry Lawon by His Mates* (1931), 'More than any other writer who ever dipped a pen, [Lawson] has made clear to all men an ideal that has always been cherished in the bush, and in our growing towns, and has helped to fix it as a national inspiration. In his life and in his writings he exalted the idea of "mateship" – an ideal of personal devotion, trust and generosity, irrespective of class or creed.' The ideal to which Brereton refers, implied in the numerous titles of stories (the first, 'His Father's Mate', as well as 'An Old Mate of Your Father's', 'His Mother's Mate', 'Macquarie's Mate', 'Meeting Old Mates', 'A Sketch of Mateship', 'Mateship', 'The Stranger's Friend', and 'Their Mate's Honour') finds perhaps its fullest expression in poems like 'The Glass on the Bar' in *Children of the Bush* (1902), which is prefaced by the moving verse tribute to 'The Shearers',

> No church-bell rings them from the Track,
> No pulpit lights their blindness –
> 'Tis hardship, drought and homelessness
> That teach those bushmen kindness:
> The mateship born of barren lands,
> Of toil and thirst and danger –
> The camp-fare for the stranger set,
> The first place to the stranger

It also includes stories such as 'That Pretty Girl in the Army', '"Lord Douglas"', 'A Sketch of Mateship', 'His Brother's Keeper' and the much-anthologised 'Send Round the Hat' (q.v.), which chronicles the fellowship and practical support which 'The Giraffe', Bob Brothers, offers to all those in need. Yet several qualifications need to be made to the impression Brereton leaves of Lawson as a celebrant of mateship. First, *Children of the Bush* is seen as the start of Lawson's decline as a writer, his succumbing to the sentimentality and contrivance that marked his first work; his sentimentalising of mateship in the volume is both a symptom of this and a contrast to the more critical appraisal found in his other writings. For example, in 'The Cant and Dirt of Labour Literature' published in the *Worker* in 1894, Lawson suggests that mateship 'is an egotistic word' implying a state of things 'too angelic to exist among mortals'; the mortals we encounter in Lawson's stories include Steelman and Smith, who are given to sharp practices in their conduct with other human beings, and other groups of men whose mateship is seen by H.P. Heseltine, in an ironically titled article, 'Saint Henry – Our Apostle of Mateship' (*Quadrant*, 1961), to be a combination of 'cruel practical joking, irresponsible behaviour, and, occasionally, even dishonesty'. Second, as even 'The Shearers' makes clear in ''Tis hardness, drought, and homelessness/ That teach those bushmen kindness', mateship is commonly presented by Lawson as a defensive tactic rather than as an ideal, a code of conduct which is one of the protections against poverty, as in the Arvie Aspinall stories, notably 'A Visit of Condolence' where mateship unites the urban poor against rapacious capitalists; illness, as in '"Going Blind"'; or the terrible conditions of bush existence, as in 'Hungerford' or the best of the Mitchell stories, where mateship is implicit and not always confined to the itinerant workers rather than bosses like Baldy Thompson. Even then, what remains finally memorable about Lawson's fiction is not the partnerships which in sum attest to the triumph of mateship, but the gallery of loners, hatters and battlers, who at best survive (the Drover's Wife, Mitchell, the bushman in '"Going Blind"') and at worst are defeated (Mrs Spicer). The relentless realism which is a major source of Lawson's fictional achievement finds no better expression than in 'The Union Buries Its Dead', in which the emptiness of the ritual in which a group of bushmen bury an unknown unionist (therefore 'mate') is confirmed by a consistently ironic nihilism. After noting the hard, dry Darling River clods rebounding on the coffin, the narrator explains:

I have left out the wattle – because it wasn't there. I have also neglected to mention the heart-broken old mate, with his grizzled head bowed and great pearly drops streaming down his rugged cheeks. He was absent – He was probably 'Out Back'. For similar reasons I have omitted reference to the suspicious moisture in the eyes of a bearded bush ruffian named Bill. Bill failed to turn up – and the only moisture was that induced by the heat.

Terry Colling, a family therapist, has written a critical study of mateship, which he sees as an obstacle to men's emotional growth, *Beyond Mateship: Understanding Australian Men* (1992).

MATHERS, Peter (1931–), born Fulham, England, was brought to Australia in infancy. He left school at 16 to undertake an agricultural course and has had numerous occupations which have taken him all over Australia and which include farming, labouring, wool-classing, work in a brewery and in the Victorian public service. He lived in Britain and Europe, mainly in London 1964–67, where he combined research for stockbrokers and literary scholars with writing. The literary research led to a year in the USA attached to the University of Pittsburgh as adviser to students studying theatre; he has comically described this experience in his article 'Pittsburgh Identity: 0000000621' in *Overland* (1968). He has published two novels, *Trap* (1966), which won the Miles Franklin Award, and *The Wort Papers* (1972); and a collection of short stories, *A Change for the Better* (1984); and has written several plays, including 'The Catch', 'Possums', 'The Station Master', 'A Small Drop', 'A Shirt Tale' (1985), 'The Mountain King' (1985), 'Pelaco Hill' (1985), 'Bats' (1986), 'Grigori

Two' (1987), 'Caught' (1987), 'Urbiculture' (1987), 'Travelling' (1988), 'More Urbiculture' (1988) and 'The Real McCoy' (1988).

An ebulliently comic, innovative and inventive writer, Mathers is exceptional in his variety and range. He sees the writer's role as one of preaching and practising subversion, holding up 'authoritative' claims to ridicule and analysis, reflecting the reality of disorder rather than the myth of order; as he has commented in an interview: 'Pattern and order can be pleasant. But . . . If we feel that disorder is necessary, it's to be disorder'. His novels are deliberately negligent of novelistic rules, shaped not in orderly chronological form, but fluid, digressive and web-like. Both *Trap* and *The Wort Papers* are dislocated but connected jumbles of episodes, yarns, individual histories and reflective meanderings that fuse fact and fiction, past and present, cultural myth and private reality, the order of external history and the chaos of inner experience. Both novels offer a varied number of perspectives on contemporary and past Australian society, mediated by numerous narrative voices, tones and styles. While vivid comic incident and incisive social satire dominate the foreground, time sequences are constantly dislocated, localities abruptly change, narrators overtake each other and even blur. Gradually a pattern emerges that presents actual history as a complex dynamic movement, simultaneously chaotic and integrated, chronological, continuous and circular.

Trap is to some extent the diary of a young conformist social worker, David David, who is hired by a group of people belonging to the Establishment, to interrogate, analyse and subdue Trap, a part-Aboriginal iconoclast. The entries in David's diary, covering one year, but extending as far back as the early nineteenth century and to places as dissimilar as Tierra del Fuego and Hobart, are mainly in flashback and record the insidious growth of his doubt under Trap's subversive influence. As the tale approaches its climax – David's almost total lapse into an outlaw-consciousness – the digressions are less extensive and the voices of Trap and David merge. Trap's casual but devastating power stems, as his name suggests, from his stubborn singularity, his resistance to categories, his genius for unpredictable independence in a materialistic, secular society that prizes categorised order at the expense of imagination and poetry. Trap denies validity to established mores in various ways: by simply existing as a charismatic embodiment of anarchy; by violating accepted standards in the most comically outrageous way possible as when, gaoled for infringing a township's embargo on Aborigines in swimming pools, he kills (police-) man's best friend, his dog; or by exaggerated over-commitment to the System, such as his ingenious 'improvement' to the hangman's trap during his period of working for Vulcan and Trap Scaffoldwrights. Eventually, the full threat of Trapism, the blurring of Black and White uncovered by David's investigations, emerges: Trap is revealed as sharing ancestry with prominent capitalists and aristocrats, the Australian historical myth is reversed and the subservient, fringe figure of the Aborigine is presented as a central, disturbing power.

The Wort Papers, also written in semi-diary form and covering an even wider social and historical spectrum, purports to be the jumbled manuscript of the Wort family history, compiled by the iconoclastic, anarchic Percy Wort and threatening the security of his bourgeois brother Thomas. Although in both novels rebellion and political action are presented as comically ineffective, the anarchic characters in *The Wort Papers* are more passive and accidentally anti-social in their effects than in *Trap*; in both novels, however, they retain such an invincible, inalienable freedom that the outward severity of their various persecutions and hardships becomes more of a comic fantasy. The pattern, meanwhile, of their impacts on society, reinforced and mirrored by Mathers's flexible form, creates an impression of Australian history as an intricate maze of contingent but involuntarily significant destinies. In both novels Mathers's energetic, resourceful use of language, his powers of verbal slapstick, comic exaggeration, witty parody and incisive satire contribute markedly to the overall destructive effect. Mathers is an emeritus fellow of the Literature Board of the Australia Council.

MATHEW, Ray (1929–), born Sydney, was a NSW schoolteacher (1949–51), a freelance journalist (1951–52), a member of the CSIRO (1952–54) and a tutor and lecturer with the University of Sydney (1955–60). In 1961 he left Australia, has subsequently lived in London, Italy and New York and now lives permanently in the USA where he is a freelance writer and art critic. One of Australia's most enterprising playwrights of the 1950s, Mathew wrote a series of experimental dramas which anticipate a number of themes and modes used by writers of the late 1960s renaissance. His published plays include *We Find the Bunyip* in *Khaki, Bush and Bigotry* (1968, ed. Eunice Hanger), a satirical rural comedy first produced in 1955; *The Bones of My Toe* in *Australian One-Act Plays, Book One* (1962, ed. Eunice Hanger); and *A Spring Song* (1961), the story of a young male schoolteacher and his involvement in the crises and relationships of a country family, first produced in 1958. His unpublished plays include 'The Boomerang and the Bantam' (1952); 'Church Sunday' (1950) and 'Lonely Without You' (1957), the last two of which are one-act plays set in the bush; 'Sing for St. Ned' (1960), a comic musical satire on the Ned Kelly myth, which anticipates the rough style of *The Legend of King O'Malley*; and 'The Life of the Party' (1961), a sophisticated comedy set against the bohemian background of Kings Cross, which was produced in London in 1961 and was a finalist in the London *Observer*'s international play competition in 1957 but has been neglected by Australian theatres. He has also written two radio plays, 'The Love of Gotama' (1952), and an adaptation of Euripides's *Medea* (1954). Mathew's attempts to achieve a new, suggestive realism by means of unusual verbal techniques and indeterminate, even circular plots which deliberately avoid the expected climaxes of the 'well-made play' were not fully appreciated by Australian audiences of the 1950s. It was his misfortune to be writing ahead of his time and he is now often classed with Peter Kenna and Jack McKinney as one of the 'lonely playwrights'. Mathew also published three volumes of verse which demonstrate his unusual verbal techniques and ability to create a well-defined regional identity, *With Cypress Pine* (1951), *Song and Dance* (1956) and *South of the Equator* (1961); and a collection of short stories, most of which draw on his experiences of rural NSW and Sydney and were previously published in the *Bulletin* and *Southerly*, *A Bohemian Affair* (1961). He also contributed stories to another collection with Mena Abdullah, *The Time of the Peacock* (1965), and is represented in numerous anthologies. His other publications include a novel, *The Joys of Possession* (1967), which is partly autobiographical and draws on his talent as social comedian, and studies of Miles Franklin (1955) and Charles Blackman (1965).

'Matilda', the colloquial term for a swag (q.v.) or bedroll, probably derives from the German word *mathilde*, meaning a female travelling-companion, probably imported into the vernacular during the gold rushes from the speech of SA German immigrants visiting the goldfields. The phrase, 'to waltz matilda', meaning to carry one's swag or live as a swagman, has received its most famous usage in 'Waltzing Matilda' (q.v.). In Henry Lawson's short story '"Rats"' the matilda reverts to its human origins in the crazed antics of an old bushman.

Mattara Spring Festival Poetry Prize, sponsored by the Hunter District Water Board and the University of Newcastle and under the administration of the Department of English of the University, has been awarded annually since 1981 and has come to be recognised as one of the more important annual verse prizes. In 1981 the prize was shared by Les Murray and Kevin Hart; in 1982 it was won by Peter Kocan for 'From the Private Poems of Governor Caulfield'; in 1983 by Craig Powell for 'Five Pieces for a Homecoming'; in 1984 by John A. Scott for 'St Clair'; in 1985 by Diane Fahey for 'Poem of Thanksgiving'; in 1986 by Lily Brett for 'Poland'. Later winners have included Kristophe Saknussenm, John Bennett and Gabrielle Davieu. Selected entries for the prize have been incorporated into anthologies: *The Members of the Orchestra and Other Poems* (1981), edited by Paul Kavanagh; *Lines from the Horizon and Other Poems* (1982), edited by Christopher Pollnitz; *Instructions for Honey Ants and Other Poems* (1983), edited by Paul Kavanagh; *Neither Nuked nor Crucified and other Poems* (1984), edited by Pollnitz; *Poem of Thanksgiving and other Poems* (1985), edited by Kavanagh; *An Inflection of Silence* (1986), edited by Pollnitz; *Properties of the Poet* (1987); *Pictures from an Exhibition* (1989); and *The Sea's White Edge* (1991), the last three edited by Kavanagh. In 1991 a new sponsor, Butterfly Books, the publishing house established by Ross Blackwood, lent its support to Mattara. Awards in that year totalled $10 000, with a youth prize of $4000.

MATTHEWS, Brian (1936–), born St Kilda, Melbourne, graduated from the University of Melbourne and worked as a teacher before joining the staff of Flinders University in 1969. He was chairperson of the Literature Board of the Australia Council 1990–92, and was appointed director of the Australian Studies Centre, London in 1992. He has written a study of Henry Lawson, *The Receding Wave* (1972), and an unusual biography of Louisa Lawson, *Louisa* (1987), which won in 1988 the Victorian Premier's Award, the NSW Premier's Award, the Gold Medal of the Australian Literature Society and a half share in the John Hetherington Bicentennial Biography Prize. Matthews is also a creative writer and has published two collections of short stories and essays, *Quickening and Other Stories* (1989) and *Oval Dreams: Larrikin Essays on Sport and Low Culture* (1991); and is co-author with Peter Goldsworthy of the novel *Magpie* (1992). His lectures for the Foundation for Australian Literary Studies were published in 1987 titled *Romantics and Mavericks: The Australian Short Story*, and he has also edited selected stories by Henry Lawson (1971). Many of the spare, polished stories of *Quickening* concentrate on experiences of separation in relationship or on the discrepancy between outer image and inner reality; others touch on the weird, although Matthews always grounds his fiction in the tangible. Matthews's comic gift, present in his first collection, comes to the fore in the essays of *Oval Dreams*, which concentrate hilariously on cricket and football, although several are autobiographical, looking back nostalgically to his working-class boyhood in St Kilda or reflecting on unfortunate experiences as an academic. *Louisa*, an explicitly self-conscious biography which admits the elusiveness of the biographical subject and the unnatural nature of biography, attempts to circumvent the difficulty by creating an alternative persona, 'Owen Stevens', whose voice mixes with that of the 'biographer'.

MATTHEWS, Harley (1889–1968), born Harry Matthews, at St Leonards, Sydney, served in the First World War at Gallipoli and in Egypt and France. Although he was qualified as a solicitor and had experience as a journalist, he became a vigneron at Moorebank near Sydney in 1922; his vineyard was a popular gathering-place for writers in the 1930s. Suspected of being a member of the Australia First movement, Matthews was imprisoned for six months in 1942; cleared by the royal commission into the movement in 1945, he was awarded £700 compensation. He spent the remainder of his life on a small farm at Ingleburn on the outskirts of Sydney.

Matthews published several books of verse, the first two of which (1912, 1916) had the same title, *Under the Open Sky*, but contained mostly different poems. To *Trio* (1931), which he shared with Kenneth Slessor and Colin Simpson, he contributed the Gallipoli narrative poem 'Two Brothers'. One of his best early poems, *The Breaking of the Drought*, was published as a separate pamphlet in 1940. *Vintage* (1938), a group of four war poems and four lyrics, also contained 'Two Brothers'. His best book of mostly lyrical verse, *Patriot's Progress* (1965), reflects Matthews's independent spirit, love of the rural scene and scorn for convention and materi-

alism. His two books of short stories are *Saints and Soldiers* (1918), which captures much of the character of the Australian soldier, and *Wet Canteen* (1939), which contains a mixture of previously published and new tales. He also wrote a three-act play, *We Are the People* (1940), and edited an anthology of short stories, *Pillar to Post* (1944).

MATTHEWS, Jill Julius (1949–), convener of the women's studies programme at the ANU, has contributed articles to numerous anthologies and periodicals and has written a study of the historical construction of femininity in twentieth-century Australia, *Good and Mad Women* (1984).

'MAURICE, Furnley' (Frank Wilmot) (1881–1942), born Collingwood, Melbourne, published most of his work under the pseudonym 'Furnley Maurice', a combination of the names of two of his favourite Melbourne haunts, Ferntree Gully and Beaumaris. Inclined to nationalism and radicalism by his background, 'Furnley Maurice' published his first verses in Bernard O'Dowd's radical journal *Tocsin*. He worked for thirty-five years, from errand boy to manager, in Cole's Book Arcade in Melbourne, was active in the Melbourne Literary Club which sponsored the magazine *Birth*, printed on his own treadle press, was a member of Louis Esson's Pioneer Players, became the successful manager of Melbourne University Press, helped to establish the Victorian branch of the FAW, was on the advisory board of the CLF and presented the fund's inaugural lectures on Australian literature at the University of Melbourne. 'Maurice's' early poetry, *Some Verses* (1903) and *Some More Verses* (1904), are home-made booklets produced on an old hand printing press which also produced his small and short-lived monthly magazine the *Microbe*. After *Unconditioned Songs* (1913) came some of 'Maurice's' most significant work, the poetry which contains his reaction to the First World War. In the poem 'To God: From the Warring Nations' (q.v.) and in the volume *Eyes of Vigilance* (1920) he expresses his disgust at the glamorising of war, at the pressures on young men to enlist and at the criminality of war itself. His radical-nationalist views are evident in his condemnation of Australia for departing from the nationalist dream of moulding her separate destiny to follow the European pattern of ancient hatreds between nations. During the war he also wrote, for his two small sons, some excellent children's verse, *The Bay and Padie Book* (1917). *Arrows of Longing* (1921) with its preface by Bernard O'Dowd, also reflects 'Maurice's' deep concern, with the memory of war still fresh, for the future of Australia and of the human race in general. 'Maurice' was fundamentally a townsman but he loved the bushland of the Dandenong Ranges, as his poem 'The Gully' (1925), which has been equated with Bernard O'Dowd's 'The Bush', indicates. 'Maurice's' most significant literary achievement is *Melbourne Odes* (q.v., 1934). In the preface to the odes 'Maurice' expounds the principles of modern European and American poetry and stresses the need for new methods, techniques and objectives for Australian poetry. In the

Odes 'Maurice' seeks to employ the best features of the modern movement in verse; the work is thus experimental and educational and its impact on the development of modern Australian verse, though long and perhaps still underestimated, is undoubted. Vance Palmer wrote *Frank Wilmot (Furnley Maurice)* (1942); Hugh Anderson, *Frank Wilmot (Furnley Maurice): A Bibliography and a Criticism* (1955); and F.T. Macartney, *Furnley Maurice (Frank Wilmot)* (1955). The impact of his life is also discussed in David Walker's *Dream and Disillusion* (1976), and he is one of *The Three Radicals* in W.H. Wilde's monograph of that title (1969).

Maurice Guest, a novel by 'Henry Handel Richardson' (q.v.), was first published in 1908. Set in Leipzig at the turn of the century, it deals with the fatal passion of an idealistic young English student of music, Maurice Guest, for an Australian woman, Louise Dufrayer. Louise, several years older than Maurice but disturbingly attractive, is deeply involved in an unequal relationship with a Polish musician of genius, Schilsky. Maurice, who has grown up in a cheerless, middle-class home, totally bereft 'of the great gladness, the ideal beauty of life', romanticises both his passion for music and his passion for Louise. In his sentimental idealism he differs from his friends Madeleine Ware, a purposeful, realistic, sympathetic girl who repeatedly attempts to rescue Maurice from his self-destructive path, and Dove, a shallow egoist who is easily able to adapt to his disappointments in love and whose busy concern for others satisfies his mild lust for power. The enigmatic, unpredictable Heinz Krafft, another talented student, who also seems to have been sexually involved with both Schilsky and Louise, appears to be inspired with a more malevolent urge to manipulate others. Ephie Cayhill, on the other hand, a childlike American, is completely vulnerable in this milieu, especially after she falls in love with Schilsky. The latter, who casually encourages her passion while attempting to disentangle himself from Louise, is making plans to leave Leipzig and further his career with the financial help of yet another admirer. Maurice quarrels violently with Schilsky after he discovers these facts at a drunken party. Although Louise has barely noticed Maurice up to this point, he shows his devotion to her in the crisis following Schilsky's sudden departure by taking Ephie to her apartment. The American girl, in despair at her enlightenment about Schilsky and Louise, is removed from Leipzig by her family. Two months later, Maurice, who has attempted to subdue his passion for Louise, discovers that she is living in a state of apathetic withdrawal, and takes over the management of her practical affairs. After their relationship becomes one of close companionship, Maurice proposes marriage and is rejected, Louise realising that 'there is something irreconcileable in their two natures'. Shortly after, however, she suddenly consents to accept him as a lover, hoping perhaps to escape from her ennui in this way. In July they spend an idyllic two weeks in the country. Back in Leipzig, Maurice throws himself into his work, which he has previously

neglected, but becomes increasingly uneasy about Louise's uninterest in everything except sensual passion. By October Louise is aware that for her 'the whole affair had been no more than an episode' and Maurice is made to realise that 'to him the gradual unfolding of their love had been a wonderful revelation; to her, a repetition, and a paler and fainter one, of a tale she already knew by heart'. Their relationship rapidly degenerates: Maurice, maddened by her inconstancy and his discovery of her relationship with Krafft, beats her in despair. Krafft suddenly disappears from Leipzig, although he continues to write to Maurice denigrating Louise. His departure is also followed by the suicide of his inscrutable but devoted mistress Avery Hill. Maurice, now aware that Louise is indifferent to him and will return to Schilsky but powerless to surmount his feelings, which he now recognises have passed beyond 'tenderness, faithfulness, respect' to become simply 'the morbid possession by a woman's face', commits suicide. The novel concludes with a glimpse of Schilsky and Louise, now married, two years later; Schilsky, now *Konzertmeister* in a large south German town, is firmly set in his career and Louise, of whom it is said that 'an English chap shot himself on her account', is still exerting her power over other men. In 1954 the novel was produced as a film titled *Rhapsody* and starring Elizabeth Taylor.

MAWSON, Sir Douglas (1882–1958), born Shipley, Yorkshire, was brought to Australia as a child. He graduated in engineering and science at the University of Sydney and in 1907 accompanied Shackleton's expedition to Antarctica; he was knighted for his exploits on both that and the 1911–14 Australasian Antarctic expedition and was awarded many honours, including the King's Polar Medal, the Founder's Medal of the Royal Geographical Society and the first David Livingstone Centenary Medal of the American Geographical Society. Professor of geology at the University of Adelaide from 1920, Mawson was also responsible for setting up the first Australian National Antarctic research expedition in 1947 and for establishing an Antarctic division of the Department of External Affairs in 1948. One of the Australian Antarctic bases is named after him, as is the Mawson Institute in Adelaide, established in 1961 to further Antarctic research. Mawson published *The Home of the Blizzard* in 1915, acknowledged as one of the finest books on the polar areas; it was published in a popular edition in 1930. His solitary journey back to base during the 1912 expedition after the disappearance of his two companions down a crevasse is told in Lennard Bickel's *This Accursed Land* (1977), and Bickel has also reconstructed the explorer's experiences in *Mawson's Will* (1977). His *Antarctic Diaries*, edited by Fred and Eleanor Jacka, were published in 1988 and C.F. Laseron, assistant biologist on the 1911–14 expedition, contributed another perspective with *South with Mawson* (1947). Paquita Mawson, the explorer's wife, published the biography *Mawson of the Antarctic* (1964). Literary responses to Mawson's heroism include a sonnet by Geoffrey Dutton, 'On the Death of Sir Douglas Mawson'. In 1982 the ABC produced a television documentary, 'Douglas Mawson – The Survivor' (which reconstructs the ill-fated 1912 expedition), to mark the centenary of his birth.

MAY, Phil (1864–1903), born and educated in Leeds, England, was becoming known as a cartoonist in London when he was lured to Australia by W.H. Traill in 1885 to work for the *Bulletin*. He remained with the *Bulletin* for three years, produced about 800 drawings, and helped Livingston Hopkins to establish the journal's reputation in the field of black-and-white art. In Australia May developed his characteristic economy of line, although it is doubtful whether, as is commonly thought, the *Bulletin*'s inadequate printing facilities were the cause. On his return to England he became famous on *Punch* and other journals; his best-known Australian drawings were the caricatures of politicians such as Sir Henry Parkes and Sir John Robertson and the series 'Things We See When We Go Out Without Our Gun'. A.G. Stephens edited *Phil May in Australia* (1904), a collection of May's *Bulletin* cartoons.

MAZA, Bob has worked extensively as an actor, director, playwright and as a consultant in theatre, radio, film and television. One of the original members of the Black Theatre in the early 1970s with the production 'Basically Black', he has appeared in numerous television series, including 'Women of the Sun', 'White Man's Legend' and 'Rainbow Serpent'. His plays include 'Tiddalik', 'Rain for Christmas', 'Mereki' and *The Keepers*, first performed in 1988 and published in *Plays from Black Australia* (1989).

MEAD, Philip (1953–), born Brisbane, and educated in Australia, England and the USA, has contributed poetry to numerous anthologies and periodicals, published the collections, *Songs from Another Country* (1975), *Be Faithful Go* (1980), *The Spring-Mire* (1982) and *This River is in the South* (1984). Poetry editor for *Meanjin* until 1994, he has taught creative writing at the University of Melbourne as Lockie fellow, and has been associated with poetry-publishing since 1972. With John Tranter he edited *The Penguin Book of Modern Australian Poetry* (1991), and with Gerald Murnane and Jenny Lee, *The Temperament of Generations: Fifty Years of Writing in Meanjin* (1990). With Alan Gould, David Brooks and Mark O'Connor, Mead was one of the founders of the journal *Canberra Poetry*. The natural landscape is often the grounding for Mead's meditative poetry, although he is concerned mostly with inward experience, the consciousness of mutability, the curious paradoxes of memory, the contradictory power and impotence of words, or the promise of meaning offered by the natural scene and doubts about its validity, as in 'Looking Towards the Major Mitchell Plateau'. In this poem the landscape offers new access to the 'inner city of the heart, overlaid by now/ with crumbled brick and dust and written words/ but still chequered with the weathers/ of the four-fold year'; but turning away from it, 'the rain at our backs/ like a coat', it is more difficult 'to know how we will live . . . What is the order of our lives? What continues

to sing/ in its blessing?' Other poems take paintings, memories of a Queensland childhood, or Australian myths and historical figures as lyrical starting-points.

Meanjin, a journal known as *Meanjin Papers* (1940–47), *Meanjin* (1947–60, 1977–) and *Meanjin Quarterly* (1961–76), began in Brisbane in December 1940 with an eight-page edition of eight poems, two each by the editor, C.B. Christesen (q.v.), James Picot, Brian Vrepont and Paul Grano. Bi-monthly in 1940–42, *Meanjin* has been quarterly since 1943. It takes its name from the Aboriginal words *migan* (spike) and *chagun* (earth, place, land), the composite word 'meanjin' (*mianjin*), referring to the site where Brisbane was first established. In 1945 *Meanjin* moved with Christesen to Melbourne, where the University of Melbourne gave it the home it has occupied to the present time. The constant battle for financial viability has seen *Meanjin* partly supported from Christesen's own resources then assisted by grants-in-aid from the Lockie Bequest, University of Melbourne (since 1949), from the CLF and the Literature Board, and the Ministry for the Arts, Victoria. *Meanjin* certainly owed its survival to its long-standing (1940–74) editor Clem Christesen. He was succeeded by Jim Davidson (1974–82), who changed the appearance of the magazine, introduced new features such as the regular interviews with contemporary writers, but retained much of the traditional *Meanjin* political stance and interests. In 1982 Judith Brett became editor. Perceiving *Meanjin*'s role as offering 'a broad review of ideas with a strong contemporary focus', she encouraged articles on general cultural matters as well as literary. In 1987 Jenny Lee became *Meanjin*'s fourth editor and continued the journal's traditional role as an organ of socio-political and literary comment as well as creative writing. Christina Thompson became editor in 1994. Opinions of *Meanjin*'s political leanings have ranged from a 'fellow-travelling publication' (the description of James McAuley, editor of *Meanjin*'s right-wing rival *Quadrant*) to Christesen's own phrase, 'democratic left of centre', which more accurately describes its liberal humanist stance. *Meanjin*'s task, according to Christesen in his 1951 commentary 'The Wound as the Bow' on the magazine's first decade of existence, was to offer 'disinterested criticism that is interested in all pertinent ideas', to be 'flexible because of its inflexible sincerity' and 'as a matter of principle' to be 'unattached to any one principle'. Other judgements have obviously differed. Financial support was withheld in 1948–49, and during the 1950s political and intellectual opposition to the *Meanjin* stance became widespread. The number and intensity of its polemical articles increased in the late 1960s with the Vietnam War, and Christesen, on his retirement in 1973, is reputed to have indicated (in a letter to Jim Cairns) his satisfaction that he did 'not allow *Meanjin* to become a right-wing *Quadrant* type of magazine'. Although *Meanjin* has regularly published or focused on overseas writing, its major literary importance has been in its publication of Australian poetry and short fiction and its establishment of a body of seminal criticism on a wide range of Australian writers. A review of arts and letters for much of its life, it has also paid attention to music, cinema and the other arts, and has periodically investigated contemporary Australian society, as in its 'Austerica' and 'Godzone' series in the 1960s and its 'State of the Nation' articles in the 1970s. Important new work by established writers such as A.D. Hope, James McAuley, Douglas Stewart, Judith Wright, Patrick White, Randolph Stow, and by younger writers such as Frank Moorhouse, Les Murray and others has been published in *Meanjin*. Special numbers of *Meanjin* have been devoted to writers, e.g. Joseph Furphy (3, 1943) and Vance Palmer (2, 1959); genres, e.g. Australian theatre and drama (3, 1964); Aboriginal writing (4, 1977); and traditions, e.g. the 'St Petersburg or Tinsel Town' issue on cultural traditions in Sydney and in Melbourne (1, 1981). *On Native Grounds* (1968), edited by Christesen, and *Sideways from the Page* (1983), a selection of Davidson's interviews with writers, are both volumes which reprint material first published in *Meanjin*. The Meanjin Press, also associated with the journal, published several volumes in the 1940s, e.g. Judith Wright's *The Moving Image* (1948) and Nettie Palmer's *Fourteen Years* (1948). Lynne Strahan's *Just City and the Mirrors: Meanjin Quarterly and the Intellectual Front, 1940–65,* a history of *Meanjin* and the literary life of that first quarter-century of the journal's existence, was published in 1984. In 1990 *Meanjin's* fiftieth anniversary was celebrated with the publication of *The Temperament of Generations: Fifty Years of Meanjin*, an anthology of essays, poetry, fiction and correspondence from the journal's archives, edited by Jenny Lee, Phillip Mead and Gerald Murnane. Clement Semmler's review of that anthology, *Quadrant* (July 1991), provides another significant account of *Meanjin*, its role and history.

MEARS, Gillian (1964–) grew up in Grafton, NSW, and was awarded a communications degree from the University of Technology, Sydney, in 1985. She has published two collections of short stories, *Ride a Cock Horse* (1988, winner of a Commonwealth Writer's Prize in 1989) and *Fineflour* (1990), and a novel, *The Mint Lawn* (1991). Mears continues to live in the northern rivers district, which provides the setting for much of her fiction; the Fineflour River which weaves in and out of the interconnecting stories in the collection of that name also flows through the decaying semi-tropical town which is the setting for *The Mint Lawn*. The novel centres around Clementine, whose emotional development was arrested at 17 when her mother was killed in a car accident, and who now, in her twenties, lacks the initiative to escape the stultifying atmosphere of the town and her miserable marriage to Hugh, her former music teacher. Alternating Clementine's first-person narrative in the present with a third-person account of her childhood up to the time of her mother's death, Mears reconstructs and interprets Clementine's life with layer upon layer of minutely observed emotional and physical detail. At the end of the book, with the help of a lover, and having at last come to some understanding of her father, Clementine is able to leave the town, the river,

her husband, and the 'remembered sadness' of her mother's early death and her own failure to fulfil her childhood promise. *The Mint Lawn* won the *Australian*/Vogel literary Award for 1990.

KAY WALSH

MEEHAN, Maurilia (1951–), teacher of English as a second language, won the FAW State of Victoria Short Story Award in 1988. She has published *Performances* (1990, short fiction) and *Fury* (1992, a novel). *Performances*, parts of which were earlier published in magazines such as Deakin University's *Mattoid*, is a series of vignettes about the occupants of the Domain Street flats. The caretaker's flat is occupied by Edna, the housekeeper, who attracts men to her by feeding them and gets rid of them, when she needs to, by cutting off the food supply. Other occupants include Neil the novelist, who is involved with a girl in his creative writing class; Bob and Alice, who have been married eight years and have no children; Djuna, who is involved with her employer Hermie; and several Vietnamese squatters. Meehan carries another odd group of characters into *Fury*, a novel in two time-zones and places, Northcote (Melbourne) in 1993 and revolutionary Paris in 1789–93. The Northcote Community Theatre Group is staging a play by Bette the tattooist about the exploits of Frenchwoman Olympe de Gouges (known as 'Fury') during the revolutionary years in France. Alice, a French-Canadian by birth, and married to Gerry, who is obsessed with samurai sword drill, is a look-alike of Olympe and is to play the main role. Bruce, the play's director, who regards lesbians as 'the last frontier' to be conquered, Carla, a none-too committed inhabitant of that 'frontier', and Bette's old love Sean, who sleeps in a gum tree on the Yarra bank, are other characters in the contemporary scene. By walking in one door of a theatrical costume supplier's shop and out another, Alice passes from the Melbourne scene to Paris in 1789. The second part of the book concerns Olympe de Gouges and Gouverneur Morris, the United States Ambassador to France. Again the characters are more like caricatures: Olympe, married at 15, widowed at 16 and producing, in her widowhood, numerous children for the Republic; Morris, tall and with a wooden leg, which proves somewhat difficult in the many affairs in which he engages. Olympe carries on a vociferous campaign for the rights of women and is about to be guillotined when she changes places with Alice, going to a new life in twentieth-century Melbourne. Whimsical, often tongue-in-cheek but with a serious feminist undertone, *Fury* is well crafted, entertaining and attractively written.

Mejane, see **Feminism and Australian Literature**

MELBA, Dame Nellie (Helen Porter Armstrong) (1861–1931) was born Helen Mitchell in Melbourne and studied music with Pietro Cecchi, an Italian tenor. In 1882 she accompanied her father, a building contractor, to northern Queensland, where she married Charles Armstrong, manager of a sugar plantation, the same year. Although a son was born in 1883, the marriage soon failed and Melba returned to Melbourne to begin her singing career. In 1886 she sailed for London with ambitions of making a name in opera, but was at first unsuccessful and moved to Paris, where the well-known teacher Madame Marchesi undertook to make 'something extraordinary' of her. She appeared for the first time as Madame Melba, the title deriving from her native city, late in 1886 and made a triumphant debut in *Rigoletto* in Brussels in 1887. Her career thereafter progressed with few setbacks and for many years she sang at Covent Garden, was equally successful in Europe and the USA and regarded as unrivalled in many of her twenty-five operas. She toured Australia 1902-3 and from 1909 lived partly in Europe and partly in Australia. Actively associated with the Melbourne University Conservatorium of Music and a highly successful fund-raiser for the Australian Red Cross during the First World War, she was made DBE in 1918 and GBE in 1927. She made her final appearance at Covent Garden in June 1926 and her last Australian appearance at Geelong in November 1928. In May 1927 she sang the national anthem at the opening of Parliament House, Canberra. Her reminiscences, *Melodies and Memories*, appeared in 1925 and she also contributed to a substantial anthology of Australian writing, *Melba's Gift Book of Australian Art and Literature* (1915), and to the *Australian Soldiers' Gift Book* (1918), edited by Ethel Turner and Bertram Stevens. The numerous biographies of Melba include Agnes G. Murphy's *Melba* (1909), Percy Colson's *Melba: An Unconventional Biography* (1932), Joseph Wechsberg's *Red Plush and Black Velvet* (1961), Geoffrey W. Hutton's *Melba* (1962), John Hetherington's *Melba* (1967), and Thérèse Radic's *Melba. The Voice of Australia* (1986). William R. Moran compiled *Nellie Melba: a Contemporary Review* (1985), a collection of contemporary opinions and reminiscences of Melba, which also includes a discography. Maie Casey offered a reassessment in *Melba Revisited* (1975) and her life has been the subject of three plays, *Melba* (1976) by Paul Sherman, *A Toast to Melba* (1976) by Jack Hibberd and *Peach Melba* (1990) by Thérèse Radic and a novel by Roger McDonald, *Melba* (1988). The phrase 'to do a Melba' derives from her many 'retirements'.

Melbourne, the capital of Victoria (q.v.), is situated in the southern part of the State, along the lower reaches of the Yarra River; at the mouth of the Yarra is Port Phillip Bay, beyond which is Bass Strait, separating Victoria from Tasmania. Intending pastoralists were the first to settle in the Melbourne area. In 1835 John Batman, acting for the Port Phillip Association from Van Diemen's Land, explored parts of the area and claimed to have purchased land from the Aborigines; later that year John Pascoe Fawkner camped along the Yarra. After any purchases from the Aborigines were declared null and void by the colonial government in New South Wales, settlement began in earnest in Melbourne and other parts of the Port Phillip District (q.v.), as Victoria was called until separated from New South Wales in 1851. Incorporated as a town in 1842 and proclaimed a city in 1847, Melbourne underwent a boom following the discovery of gold; an impression of the boom city is given in 'Henry Handel Richardson's' *The Fortunes of Richard Mahony* (1930). Named after the prime minister of England, Melbourne was designated 'Marvellous Melbourne' in the 1880s; its character then is analysed in Graeme Davison's *The Rise and Fall of Marvellous Melbourne* (1978). John Arnold edited *The Imagined City: Melbourne in the Minds of Its Writers* (1983), which includes extracts from more than two dozen writers. Dame Nellie Melba took her stage name from Melbourne. Michael Cannon's *Old Melbourne Town* (1991) gives a guided tour of Melbourne in the period 1836-51, the years before the gold rushes, as does Paul de Serville's *Port Phillip Gentlemen*, whose emphasis is on early Melbourne society. His *Pounds and Pedigrees* (1991) is a 'Who's Who' of the city in the post-gold rush era. Alister Kershaw looks at the artistic avant-garde of Melbourne of the 1940s in *Hey Days: Memories and Glimpses of Melbourne's Bohemia 1937-1947* (1991). Two novels with contemporary Melbourne settings are Steven Carroll's *Remember Me, Jimmy James* (1992) and Tom Petsini's *Raising the Shadow* (1992). *Margin*, a publication from Monash University, begun in 1977, has a particular interest in nineteenth-century Melbourne.

Melbourne Advertiser, published at Port Phillip by John Pascoe Fawkner from 1 January to 23 April 1838, began as a handwritten sheet carrying classified advertisements, shipping and travel notices and a 'Poet's Corner'. From 5 March to 23 April the sheet appeared in printed form, thus becoming the first printed publication in Melbourne. Suppressed because of failure to comply with the Newspaper Act, it was re-established as the *Port Phillip Patriot and Melbourne Advertiser* (1839-48).

Melbourne Bulletin, a weekly paper, was published 1880-86 and was owned and produced by Edmund Finn, Alex McKinley, John Booth and others. Subsequently absorbed into *Melbourne Punch*, the paper contained general articles on socio-political, religious and business matters, as well as theatrical notices and some fiction and light verse.

Melbourne Chronicle, subtitled *Independent Cultural-Social Periodical*, began publication in 1975, published by the Jewish National Library and Cultural Centre, 'Kadimah'. It includes Jewish-Australian creative and critical writing.

Melbourne Cup is a handicap horse-race run over 3200 metres (formerly 2 miles) on the first Tuesday in November at Flemington racecourse in Melbourne. First run in 1861, it soon became an event of national significance and was commented on by visitors such as 'Mark Twain' and prominent journalists such as 'Garryowen' and 'The Vagabond'. Numerous nineteenth-century plays have Melbourne Cup scenes, e.g. *Marvellous Melbourne* (1889); in Alfred Dampier's adaptation of Nat Gould's *The Double Event* (staged 1893) and William Anderson and Temple Harrison's 'Winning Ticket' (1900) the Cup race was staged with live horses. Other writers to have used 'the Cup' and its rituals in their work include Adam Lindsay Gordon, Ada Cambridge, Marcus Clarke, Victor Daley, Jessie Couvreur, Douglas Sladen, Arthur Wright, Nat Gould, Ambrose Pratt, A.B. Paterson, C.J. Dennis, Rosa Praed and Alexander Buzo. Among Australian artists, Charles Nuttall published a series of humorous sketches, *Peter Wayback Visits the Melbourne Cup* (1902), and Frank Mahony's Dawn and Dusk Club colleagues required him to predict, through paint, the Melbourne Cup winner.

Melbourne Journal: Australian Serial Tales, Short Stories and the Literature of the Day, an illustrated fortnightly newspaper, appeared 1894–1927. Advertising 'Thrilling Tales of Romance and Adventure: Interesting, Instructive, and Amusing Home Reading', the newspaper included serials and original and reprinted short stories, as well as articles on local and overseas news.

Melbourne Morning Herald, see **Herald**

Melbourne Odes (1934) are among the most important poems of 'Furnley Maurice' (q.v.). The opening ode, 'Melbourne and Memory', won the Melbourne centenary poetry competition. Other odes in the volume deal with places and events familiar in the life of the city: the Victoria Markets, the annual agricultural show and orchestral concerts in the Melbourne Town Hall. Together they represent the first attempt by an Australian poet to depict life in the modern city. 'Upon a Row of Old Boots and Shoes in a Pawnbroker's Window', with its grim account of the plight of the unemployed of the 1930s Depression and its macabre description of the ghostly march of the boot-pawners, is a powerful radical commentary on the economic misery and injustice of the time.

Melbourne Punch, the best, most famous and longest-running of the colonial imitations of London *Punch*, was founded in 1855 by Edgar Ray and Frederick Sinnett. An illustrated humorous weekly which included articles on society and politics, satirical verse and prose and cartoons, it merged with *Table Talk* (1885–1939) in 1929. Sinnett was succeeded as editor by James Smith (1857–63) and Charles Bright (1863–66). Prominent early contributors included Butler Cole Aspinall, Charles Gavan Duffy, R.H. Horne, and the cartoonists Thomas Carrington and Nicholas Chevalier. *Melbourne Punch* was a significant colonial literary magazine but was even more important for the part it played in the development of an Australian tradition of political caricature. Of the other Australian imitations of *Punch*, three separate magazines carried the title *Sydney Punch* (1856, 1857, 1864–88), the third of them founded also by Ray and numbering Daniel Deniehy, Garnet Walch and later William Macleod among its contributors; *Adelaide Punch*, like its Melbourne counterpart, carried cartoons by Carrington and ran intermittently 1868–84, when it was incorporated into the *Lantern*; *Tasmanian Punch* ran 1866–68 (1867–68 as *Hobart Town Punch*) and was revived in

1870; *Queensland Punch* (1868–85) published work by Ernest Favenc, Henry Halloran, and J. Brunton Stephens before it was incorporated into *Queensland Figaro*; and there were even two versions of *Ballarat Punch* (1857, 1867–70). The best study of *Melbourne Punch* and other colonial equivalents of London *Punch*, which include humorous weeklies such as *Humbug* and *Touchstone*, is Marguerite Mahood's *The Loaded Line* (1973).

Melbourne Review, a quarterly magazine which ran 1876–85, was modelled on the English magazines *Contemporary Review* and *Fortnightly Review*. Edited by H.G. Turner, later assisted by A.P. Martin and Alexander Sutherland, the magazine attracted contributions from such writers as G.B. Barton, Marcus Clarke, Sir Henry Parkes, Catherine Spence, David Syme, Ethel Turner and Jessie Couvreur.

Melbourne Theatre Company, titled the Union Theatre Repertory Company until 1968, was established in 1953 under the auspices of the University of Melbourne, administered by John Sumner and located in the Union Theatre on the campus. Wal Cherry directed the Company for three years and Ray Lawler for one, but Sumner had been the director for thirty-one years when he retired in 1987. He was succeeded by Roger Hodgman. In 1959 the Australian Elizabethan Theatre Trust came into association with the Company, although it was not until 1966 that the MTC left the Union Theatre and established a permanent theatre in the city at Russell Street. In 1973 the MTC took over St Martin's theatre and four years later the much larger Athenaeum. In 1979 it established Athenaeum 2, a small theatre appropriate for more intimate plays as its third venue. In 1984 the Company left the Athenaeum and moved to the Playhouse at the Victorian Arts Centre. The largest and most prestigious repertory company in Australia, the MTC has dominated Melbourne theatre for the last four decades. As well as producing a wide range of international plays, the Company has frequently produced Australian plays, often supporting a playwright-in-residence. Outstanding plays staged for the first time by the MTC include Ray Lawler's *Summer of the Seventeenth Doll*, Vance Palmer's *Prisoner's Country*, Patrick White's *A Cheery Soul*, Alan Hopgood's *And the Big Men Fly*, Alexander Buzo's *Macquarie*, and David Williamson's *Jugglers Three*. Geoffrey Hutton has written an account of the Company's first twenty years in *It Won't Last a Week* (1975).

Melbourne University Magazine, a student magazine known familiarly as *MUM* and published annually 1907–79, started as a review of the university year with contributions in prose and verse, photographs, and notes on the activities of colleges, societies and sporting clubs. Eventually expanded into more of a literary publication, with a strong interest in political, philosophical and social issues, the magazine often included original contributions from Australian writers as well as significant interviews. Contributors included Vincent Buckley, Tim Burstall, Max Harris, A.D. Hope, Bruce Dawe and R.G. Menzies.

Melbourne University Press, see **University Presses**

Melbourne Women's Theatre Group was formed in 1974, largely by women who were dissatisfied with their perceived role in the collective of the Australian Performing Group (q.v.). It was the first and largest group to advance women's theatre in Australia, providing support for women directors, designers and playwrights, many of whom subsequently pursued successful careers. The constitution of the Group defined its objectives as 'performance, encouragement and promotion of drama, music, art, literature, film production and exhibition and other cultural activities within a feminist framework'. Between 1974 and 1977, when it disbanded, the Group generated at least twenty-five drama productions and art programmes, organised the community arts festivals, 'Out of the Frying Pan' (1974), 'Sister's Delight Festival' (1975) and 'The Summer Solstice Celebration' and developed some of the first multicultural theatre. Early Group-created revues such as 'Women's Weekly Vol One' (1974) and 'The Love Show' (1974) confronted conventional gender constructions; subsequent productions which explored the institutions of marriage and motherhood, mother–daughter relations, women's sexuality and women and madness included 'Documentary Theatre' (1974), 'Women and Children First' (1974), 'Add a Grated Laugh or Two' (1975), 'Women Times Three' (1975), 'Wonder Women's Revenge' (1976), 'The Power Show' (1977) and 'Edges' (1977). Street theatre and travelling shows developed by the Group included 'A Woman's Place' (1975), 'The Travelling Medicine Show' (1976) and 'She'll Be Right Mate' (1976). The Group is described by Peta Tait in *Original Women's Theatre* (1993).

MELLER, Leslie (1892–1962), born Adelaide, a land-valuer in the SA civil service before his enlistment in the first AIF, wrote two novels, *Quartette* (1932) and *A Leaf of Laurel* (1933); the latter has continued to attract some attention as a novel of the First World War and includes some graphic descriptions of life at Gallipoli. Anthony Hyde, the hero, comes from a wealthy SA pastoralist family, and is an aspiring writer with a 'passion for beauty', who finds little in common with his fellows after enlisting in the first SA infantry battalion to leave Australia, although he manages to simulate a show of mateship. Involved in the landing at Gallipoli, he is wounded twice and spends an extended period in Cairo, grateful that he can play the part of the 'willing non-participant' since he had at least put rifle to shoulder whereas others had been struck down in the first hours. Both at Gallipoli and in Cairo, a ring, bought from an Egyptian prostitute, plays a dominant part in his life, as if it were a mascot. In Cairo he abstains from full intimacy with Arab women, for fear of 'fearful decay', but enjoys their company in 'rooms where commerce of the body was handled like any other daily trade of the bazaars',

meanwhile finding gratification in the sense that his memory was filling with precious 'stuffs' which could one day be 'catalogued in fine words for others to read'. Repatriated, he is restless at home and attempts to cure his mood by embarking on a walking trip in the Adelaide hills; his adventures include a strange sexual encounter with the young wife of an alcoholic old man and another with the daughter of the landlord of an isolated hotel; dominated by a prurient interest in anything to do with illicit sex, the landlord becomes determined to obtain the prostitute's ring, an endeavour which results in the death of his daughter, killed by a blow intended for Anthony, and his own descent into insanity.

'MELVILLE, Captain', see **Bushranger in Australian Literature**

MELVILLE, Henry Saxelby Melville Wintle (1799–1873), born England, always used the name, Henry Melville, and probably arrived in Hobart late in 1827. In 1830 he bought the *Colonial Times* from Andrew Bent and published Henry Savery's *Quintus Servinton* (1831), the first Australian novel: three years later he founded the first literary monthly in Tasmania, the *Hobart Town Magazine* (q.v.). During the 1930s he was involved in the running not only of the *Colonial Times*, which passed out of his hands in 1839, but also of the *Tasmanian*, its offshoot the *Tasmanian and Austral-Asiatic Review*, and the *Trumpeter*, an advertising paper. In the Tasmanian ventures he combined forces with Robert Lathropp Murray (q.v.) and was critical of Governor Arthur's administration. While in prison for contempt of court in 1835 he wrote 'A Few Words on Prison Discipline', which formed part of the pioneering *The History of the Island of Van Diemen's Land, from the Year 1824 to 1835* Inclusive (1835); like his anti-government pamphlet, *Two Letters Written in Van Diemen's Land* (1834), it was published anonymously. In the 1840s Melville engaged primarily in agricultural pursuits and in the study of the occult and freemasonry, on which he published several later works. After leaving Tasmania in 1849, he settled in England, where he published in 1851 the work known in different editions as *Australasia and Prison Discipline* and *The Present State of Australia*. His activities as a journalist, editor and publisher are discussed in E. Morris Miller's *Pressmen and Governors* (1952).

MENDELSOHN, Oscar (1896–1978), born Queensland, was an industrial chemist, a public analyst and examiner of questioned documents, a composer and conductor of music and a wine and food expert. He was at various times federal president, State president, immediate past president and vice-president of the Fellowship of Australian Writers, and was the driving force behind the establishment of FAW awards, activities which won him the OBE. He also edited the magazine *Focus* in the 1940s. His varied interests led to several books including *A Waltz with Matilda* (1966), a study of the origins of the famous ballad which claims that Harry Nathan of Queensland composed the music and that A.B. Paterson plagiarised the words from an anonymous bush song collected during the preparation of his anthology of bush ballads. Mendelsohn also edited with Harry Marks a selection of Australian short stories, *Australian New Writing* (1973).

MENNELL, Philip (1851–1905), born Newcastle, England, qualified as a solicitor before coming to Australia in the middle 1870s. He founded and edited the *Bairnsdale Advertiser* 1877–82, and wrote for the *Age* in Melbourne 1882–83 before returning to London as the *Age*'s representative 1883–91, and later as editor of the *British Australasian* 1892–1905. Active within the London Anglo-Australian community (called the 'AAs' by Marcus Clarke), Mennell edited *In Australian Wilds* (1889), which carried contributions by B.L. Farjeon, C. Haddon Chambers, 'Tasma' and others; contributed to similar anthologies, e.g. A.P. Martin's *Oak-bough and Wattle-blossom* (1888), and wrote a descriptive travel work and emigrants' guide on WA, *The Coming Colony* (1892), which derived from a return visit to Australia in 1891. He paid later visits in 1895 and 1900 as correspondent for the London *Times* and *Morning Post* respectively. His most important work, however, was *The Dictionary of Australasian Biography (1855–1892)* (1892), which includes historical material as well as biographies of colonial worthies.

MENZIES, Sir Robert (1894–1978), prime minister of Australia 1939–41 and 1949–66, was born at Jeparit, Victoria, and worked as a lawyer before entering federal politics in 1934. His published works include *Rule of Law during War* (1917), *Studies in the Australian Constitution* (1933), *Speech Is of Time* (1958), *Central Power in the Australian Commonwealth* (1962), and two volumes of reminiscences, *Afternoon Light* (1967) and *The Measure of the Years* (1970). Appointed a Knight of the Thistle in 1963, he was also made Lord Warden of the Cinque Ports on his retirement in 1966. Numerous biographies of Menzies have been published, including Kevin Perkins, *Menzies: Last of the Queen's Men* (1968), Cameron Hazlehurst, *Menzies Observed* (1979) and Sir Percy Joske, *Menzies 1894–1978* (1978); a collection of his witticisms, compiled by Ray Robinson, was published in 1966. Known familiarly as 'Ming the Merciless' and 'Pig-iron Bob', Menzies was frequently the butt of satirists and cartoonists. He is the subject of a long satirical poem, *Rob the Robber* (1954), by 'Spinifex' (David Martin), appears in an extensive role in Barry Oakley's play *Beware of Imitations* (1985), is a character in Amanda Lohrey's novel *The Morality of Gentlemen* (1984), and as a young man, suitor to the author's sister, in Brian Lewis's autobiography *Our War* (1980). More recent studies include Sir John Bunting's *Menzies: A Portrait* (1988), Judith Brett's *Robert Menzies' Forgotten People* (1992), which won both the 1993 NSW Literary Award for non-fiction (shared) and the 1993 A.A. Phillips Prize in the Victorian Premier's Literary Awards, and A.W. Martin's substantial biography, *Robert Menzies: A Life. Volume 1. 1894–1943* (1993). Menzies's 1941 diary, edited by A.W. Martin and Patsy Hardy, *Dark and Hurrying Days*, was also published in 1993.

'MERANDA, Wolla', see **POYITT, Gertrude**

MERCER, Harold (1882–?), born Brisbane, served in the First World War, studied law before becoming an actor, and was also an active unionist. A contributor of verse and short stories or prose sketches to the *Bulletin* and other journals, often under the pseudonym 'Hamer', he published four collections of short stories, *The Search for the Bonzer Tart* (1920), *The Lady Who Was French* (1929), *The Adventures of Mrs. Parsley* (1942) and *Romances in Real Life* (1944); a romance of the Pacific, *Amazon Island* (1933); and a collection of verse, *The Frequent Lover* (1928).

MERCIER, Emile (1901–81), born Noumea, New Caledonia, of French parentage, came to Australia as a young man (1919 and 1923 have both been suggested) and was a clerk and translator while studying art under Julian Ashton. He had his first cartoons and joke drawings published in the early 1920s but was forced to work at many part-time jobs, including those of 'spruiker' and music-hall actor, while making freelance contributions to the *Bulletin, Melbourne Punch, Smith's Weekly*, and other journals. From 1940 he obtained more regular work as the illustrator of Lennie Lower's *Smith's Weekly* column; as political cartoonist for *Truth*, for which he also created two comic strips, and the *Daily Mirror*, and as writer-illustrator of comics for Frank Johnson; in 1949–68 he was a full-time cartoonist with the Sydney *Sun*. Mercier published more than twenty comic books and books of cartoons; many of his comic-book protagonists, e.g. Mudrake the Magician, Tripalong Hoppity, Speed Umplestroop, were the satirical equivalents of the heroes of cinema serials and other strips, e.g. Mandrake, Hopalong Cassidy, Speed Gordon. His *Sun* cartoons, now affectionately remembered, were irreverently topical, contemptuous of pretension, and characterised by oddball characters, e.g. an old gent with a long white beard who often appeared on stilts, numerous stray animals such as yaks and cats with immodestly raised tails; by zany details, e.g. the springs on which the cartoon often sat; and by absurd alliterations and repetitions, e.g. phrases like 'Post no Gravy' and words like 'shrdlu', which confirm the verbal-visual mix of his work. Mercier's humour, although intensely Australian in content and target, has its parallel overseas in the humour of the Goons and the Goodies.

Mercury, the major Tasmanian newspaper, was founded in 1854 by John Davies and George Aubey Jones, who incorporated the *Hobarton Guardian*, which they had taken over in 1852, into their new newspaper, which was named the *Hobarton Mercury* 1854–58, and the *Hobart Town Daily Mercury* 1858–60. A morning daily from 1858, the *Mercury* incorporated a number of other Hobart newspapers, including the *Colonial Times* in 1857, the *Tasmanian Daily News* in 1858, the *Hobart Town Courier* in 1859, and the *Illustrated Tasmanian Mail* in 1935. The Davies family retained control of the *Mercury* until 1895, when a public company was formed, in which the Herald and

Weekly Times company of Melbourne has a significant interest.

MEREDITH, Gwen (1907–), born Orange, NSW, was educated at the University of Sydney. In 1939 she contributed to a long-running radio serial, *Fred and Maggie*. *Blue Hills*, her outstandingly popular radio serial, which was broadcast four days a week 1949–76, was preceded by another serial with a farming background, *The Lawsons*, which ran 1943–49. Both drew on the Australian nostalgia for the bush and were sustained by Meredith's gift for developing a drama of slowly unfolding human relationships and for creating ordinary characters faced with problems such as romantic love, business difficulties, or the onset of old age. Sensitive to some extent to changing social mores and frequently topical in its public concerns, *Blue Hills* never succumbed to permissive sexual standards. The series provided regular employment for a range of well-known actors including John Meillon, John McCallum, Queenie Ashton, Nellie Lamport, June Salter, Rod Taylor, Madge Ryan and Ray Barrett. Meredith also wrote other plays for radio and stage, including a three-act comedy, *Wives Have Their Uses* (1944); *Great Inheritance* in *Australian Radio Plays* (1946, ed. Leslie Rees) and *Modern Short Plays* (1951); and 'Cornerstone', a stage-play produced in 1955; several novels based on the radio serials, *The Lawsons* (1948), *Blue Hills* (1950), *Beyond Blue Hills* (1953), and *Into the Sun* (1961); and, with her husband, Ainsworth Harrison, a travel book, *Inns and Outs* (1955). In 1967 she was made MBE and in 1977 OBE.

MEREDITH, John (1920–), born and educated at Holbrook, NSW, worked in the pharmaceutical industry before becoming a full-time writer in 1978. At 14 he bought a copy of A.B. Paterson's *Old Bush Songs* (q.v.), which inspired his long-term interest in Australian folk-song (q.v.) and folklore. A founding member of the Sydney Bush Music Club, he was first editor of its journal, *Singabout*. With Hugh Anderson, Meredith compiled *Folk Songs of Australia and the Men and Women Who Sang Them* (1967); a second volume from his tape-recorder trip through the bush was published in 1987, with assistance from Roger Covell and Patricia Brown. He also compiled other song-books, e.g. *Reedy River Song Book* (1953), *Songs from the Kelly Country* (1955), and several *Bushwacker Broadsides* (1955–60). His other publications include important studies of Bold Jack Donahue, *The Wild Colonial Boy* (1960, rev. edn 1982); Francis MacNamara, *Frank the Poet* (1979, with Rex Whalan); Ned Kelly, *Ned Kelly, After a Century of Acrimony* (1980, with Bill Scott); 'Duke' Tritton, *Duke of the Outback* (1983); and *The Coo-ee March* (1981). With Joan Clarke, Meredith wrote a ballad opera, 'The Wild Colonial Boy', first produced in 1955; a second ballad opera, 'How Many Miles from Gundagai', has also been produced.

MEREDITH, Louisa Anne (1812–95), born Louisa Anne Twamley at Birmingham, England, married her cousin Charles Meredith in 1839 and went with him to NSW, where he had pastoral interests. In 1840 they moved to Tasmania, where Charles was a successful member of parliament 1860–79. An energetic, talented and strongly independent woman, Louisa wrote and illustrated several autobiographical books which are vividly descriptive of colonial life and society and native flora and fauna, including *Notes and Sketches of New South Wales* (1844), *My Home in Tasmania* (1852) and *Over the Straits; A Visit to Victoria* (1861). She also published numerous illustrated books of poetry, e.g. *Some of My Bush Friends in Tasmania* (1860), *Our Island Home* (1879) and *Bush Friends in Tasmania, Native Flowers, Fruits and Insects* (1891); poetry for children, e.g. *Waratah Rhymes for Young Australia* (1891); and several novels including *Phoebe's Mother* (1869), *Tasmanian Friends and Foes, Feathered, Furred, and Finned: A Family Chronicle of Country Life* (1880), which is of most relevance to Australia and includes coloured plates from her own drawings, and *Nellie* (1882). It has been said of her that she was 'a poet in feeling, an artist by instinct, a naturalist by force of circumstances, a keen botanist, and an ardent lover of landscape scenery'. She won numerous medals and prizes for her paintings at exhibitions in England, Australia and India and after the death of Charles Meredith was awarded a small pension by the Tasmanian government. She may well have been the first person granted a government pension in Australia for services to science, literature and the arts. Vivienne Rae Ellis's biography *Louisa Anne Meredith: A Tigress in Exile* (1979) gives a vivid impression of this resourceful and talented woman.

MERRITT, R.J. (Robert James) (1945–), born Cowra, NSW, one of nine children of an Aboriginal labourer, was brought up on Erambie Mission. He attended Cowra primary and high schools, where he was an outstanding student, but was later unable to find any work other than seasonal manual labour. He has since spent long periods in prison. His play *The Cake Man* (q.v., 1978, rev. edn 1983), the first play by an Aboriginal playwright to be performed in Australia and first performed in 1975, recalls his childhood experiences of Erambie Mission. He has also written the screenplays *Running Man* (1982) and *Short Change* (1983), and produced several video recordings with Aboriginal themes.

Merry-Go-Round in the Sea, The, a novel by Randolph Stow (q.v.), was published in 1965. Set in Geraldton, WA, 1941–49, the novel is a semi-autobiographical, nostalgic re-creation of an Australian childhood. The story concentrates on the growth of a boy, Rob Coram, who is 6 when the novel opens, and less extensively on the experience of his much-loved older cousin, Rick Maplestead. During the years covered by the first section of the novel, when Rick is away at war, Rob's experiences within his extensive family reinforce his yearning vision of life as familiar and circular, as safe in its movement as the merry-go-round he rode as a child. The second section of the novel, which deals with the years after Rick's return, ends with the destruction of this comfortable vision of circularity and the realisation of life as linear, transient and lonely.

MICHAEL, James Lionel (1824–68), born London, was educated in languages and the arts and entered the legal profession in England. He came to Australia in the gold-rush period but preferred the more comfortable existence of the Sydney legal world to a stint on the goldfields. He became a member of the Sydney literary coterie of the day, contributing verse, essays and literary criticism to the *Month*, edited by James Sheridan Moore, and the *Southern Cross*, edited by D.H. Deniehy. He extended patronage to the fledgeling poet Henry Kendall, allowing him access to his ample library and employing him as a clerk. Near bankruptcy, Michael went to Grafton in 1861 to open a legal practice but died there by drowning. He published a collection of lyric poems, *Songs Without Music* (1857) and a semi-autobiographical narrative poem, *John Cumberland* (1860). His poetry is pleasantly smooth and graceful but devoid of originality or significant theme. Kendall wrote two poems in tribute to Michael after his death, 'James Lionel Michael' and 'Lines to J.L. Michael'. Sheridan Moore published *The Life and Genius of James Lionel Michael* (1868). Geoff Page wrote a series of short poems reflecting on Michael's life and character and pondering on the puzzle of his death; titled 'From the Life and Death of James Lionel Michael', the poems were published in *Instructions for Honey Ants*, the 1983 Mattara Spring Festival anthology. Ian McLaren has published *James Lionel Michael: a Comprehensive Bibliography* (1989).

MICHELL, Keith (1928–), born Adelaide, taught art before leaving Australia in 1948 to work with the Old Vic Theatre school. He made his first West End appearance in 1951 and has since become a well known actor, particularly renowned for his role in the BBC series *The Six Wives of Henry VIII*. Formerly artistic director of the Chichester Festival Theatre, he also established a reputation as a painter, an illustrator of children's books, and a singer whose novelty song 'Captain Beaky and his Band' rose to the top of the pop charts in 1980. He has toured Australia on several occasions, and in 1981 appeared in his own play produced by the Melbourne Theatre Company, 'Pete McGynty and the Dreamtime', an Australian version of Ibsen's *Peer Gynt*.

MICKLE, Alan (1883–1969), born Melbourne, lived mostly as a full-time writer, although he developed an interest in painting late in life. His publications include eight collections of philosophical essays 1910–47; several volumes of reminiscences, including *Of Many Things* (1941), *Many a Mickle* (1953) and *My Lady Life* (1960); a book for children, *The Trio from Rio* (1942); two novels, *The Pilgrimage of Peer* (1938) and *The Execution of Newcome Bowles* (1948); a book of sporting reminiscences, *After the Ball* (1959); and six collections of poetry, of which only the juvenile verse has continued to receive attention, *The Poor Poet and the Beautiful Lady* (1931), *Pemmican Pete and Other Verses* (1934), *The Great City* (1935), *The Loony Cove* (1940),

Mine Own Land (1944) and *The Ballad of Flatfoot Fred* (1944).

Middle Parts of Fortune: Somme and Ancre 1916, The, a novel by Frederic Manning (q.v.), was published anonymously in 1929 and was not published again in its original form until 1977. An expurgated edition was published in 1930 under the title *Her Privates We*, with the author's identity partly revealed by the pseudonym 'Private 19022' (Manning's army number). It was not until the 1943 reprint of *Her Privates We* that the author was clearly revealed as Manning, an Australian-born writer, who had served with the British Army in France in the First World War. The novel covers parts of the Somme and Ancre fighting in the latter part of 1916 and revolves around a small group of British soldiers, chief of whom is Private Bourne, a shadowy, enigmatic character who is so obviously superior in background and potential to his fellow soldiers in the ranks that he is vainly badgered by his commanding officers to seek a commission. Bourne's two closest comrades are Shem and Martlow. Martlow and Bourne both die in action and Shem is wounded. Other characters pass in and out of the narrative, including the fine officer Captain Malet, the deserter Miller, and the soldier 'Weeper' Smart, whose behaviour patterns and nickname reveal his precarious hold on sanity. The novel seldom describes the actual fighting, concerning itself more with the repetitive trivia of the soldiering life behind the lines: moving in and out of billets, drilling, scrounging, gossiping, quarrelling, getting mail from home, searching perfunctorily in one despondent French village after another for the elusive 'bon time!'. The few battle scenes are, however, intensely dramatic and Bourne's death at the end of the novel deeply moving. In spite of the novel's recreation of the horror of war and the spiritual ennui that swamps men's souls in such protracted, hopeless situations, it emphasises such positives as the men's pride in themselves as soldiers ('we're a fuckin' fine mob'), their deep involvement in the comradeship of the trenches, and their almost perverse determination to endure the unendurable. Although it records, with undoubted authenticity, monotonous blasphemous soldier talk, the novel fails to capture the ironic, earthy wit emphasised by other Australian war writers.

Midnite: The Story of a Wild Colonial Boy, an outstandingly popular children's novel by Randolph Stow (q.v.), was published in 1967 and later translated into several languages. Midnite is a good-natured, almost handsome, not very clever boy of 17 who, on the advice of his shrewd Siamese cat, Khat, becomes a famous bushranger. His gang consists of his animals, Red Ned, a noble horse; Gyp, a sheepdog; Dora, a silly cow; and Major, an irascible cockatoo. Midnite's adventures land him in gaol several times, incite the anger of Queen Victoria, and engage him in contests with the charming but disreputable Trooper O'Grady. Midnite eventually makes good as the law-abiding gold-discoverer Mr Daybrake. For the older reader *Midnite* is also delightful satire which has fun with familiar aspects of the Australian romantic tradition from bushrangers to explorers.

'Midsummer Noon in the Australian Forest, A', published in the *Empire*, 1858, is Charles Harpur's (q.v.) best-known and most-anthologised descriptive poem. Although often praised for its creation of the hushed somnolent atmosphere of the summer noonday in the Australian bush, the poem lacks Australian definition.

Miles Franklin Award is made annually from the estate of Miles Franklin (q.v.) for a published novel portraying some aspects of Australian life. Its value stood at $20 000 in 1991. If the judges consider that there is no novel of sufficient merit, a radio or television play may be considered for the award. The list of awards is as follows: 1957, *Voss* by Patrick White; 1958, *To The Islands* by Randolph Stow; 1959, *The Big Fellow* by Vance Palmer; 1960, *The Irishman* by 'Elizabeth O'Conner'; 1961, *Riders in the Chariot* by Patrick White; 1962, *The Well-Dressed Explorer* by Thea Astley and *The Cupboard under the Stairs* by George Turner; 1963, *Careful, He Might Hear You* by Sumner Locke Elliot; 1964, *My Brother Jack* by George Johnston; 1965, *The Slow Natives* by Thea Astley; 1966, *Trap* by Peter Mathers; 1967, *Bring Larks and Heroes* by Thomas Keneally; 1968, *Three Cheers for the Paraclete* by Thomas Keneally; 1969, *Clean Straw for Nothing* by George Johnston; 1970, *A Horse of Air* by Dal Stivens; 1971, *The Unknown Industrial Prisoner* by David Ireland; 1972, *The Acolyte* by Thea Astley; 1973, no award; 1974, *The Mango Tree* by Ronald McKie; 1975, *Poor Fellow My Country* by Xavier Herbert; 1976, *The Glass Canoe* by David Ireland; 1977, *Swords and Crowns and Rings* by Ruth Park; 1978, *Tirra Lirra by the River* by Jessica Anderson; 1979, *A Woman of the Future* by David Ireland; 1980, *The Impersonators* by Jessica Anderson; 1981, *Bliss* by Peter Carey; 1982, *Just Relations* by Rodney Hall; 1983, no award; 1984, *Shallows* by Tim Winton; 1985, *The Doubleman* by C.J. Koch; 1986, *The Well* by Elizabeth Jolley; 1987, *Dancing on Coral* by Glenda Adams; 1988 - date of award changed from year of publication to year of award; 1989, *Oscar and Lucinda* by Peter Carey; 1990, *Oceana Fine* by Tom Flood; 1991, *The Great World* by David Malouf; 1992, *Cloudstreet* by Tim Winton; 1993, *The Ancestor Game* by Alex Miller; 1994, *The Grisly Wife* by Rodney Hall.

MILES, William John (1871–1942) was a Sydney businessman who met P.R. Stephensen (q.v.) in 1935 and employed him as his assistant to conduct the *Publicist*, a monthly dominated by Miles's rationalist, isolationist political views. Miles published Stephensen's *The Foundations of Culture in Australia* and financed the publication of Xavier Herbert's *Capricornia* (1938). Influenced in his last years by the biological theories of Morley Roberts, Miles was the father of the famous Sydney eccentric Bea Miles (1901–73), who was well known for her evasion of taxi and bus fares and for her recitations of Shakespeare and other writers.

MILGATE, Rodney (1934–), born Kyogle, NSW, is a well-known painter as well as a playwright and poet and has worked as an art teacher and as an actor in stage productions and on radio and television. He has had numerous exhibitions of his paintings, both in Australia and overseas, and has won several prizes including the prestigious Blake Prize on three occasions. He has published some poetry, including *Fourteen Stations of the Cross ... A Sequence of Poems Accompanying Fourteen Paintings* (1991), and one play, *A Refined Look at Existence* (1968), which was staged during the first Jane Street theatre season in 1966. Fast-moving, freewheeling, impressionistic and satirical, the play is a mock-heroic portrayal of the impact of a pop singer on contemporary society; the most popular of the 1966 season, it heralded the arrival of a new kind of 'total' or 'rough' theatre in Australia. Milgate's other plays include 'At Least You Get Something Out of That' (1968), 'Grass Up to Your Ears' (1977), 'Buckets With Holes in Them' (1977), 'A Golden Pathway To Europe' (1980) and 'Destiny's Mill' (1981).

MILLER, Alex (1936–), born London, emigrated to Australia at the age of 17. He worked on the land in Queensland and travelled the whole of Australia before attending the University of Melbourne where he graduated in English and history in 1965. He began writing in 1972 and teaches writing courses in Melbourne. He was co-founder of the Anthill Theatre and a founding member of the Melbourne Writers' Theatre. He has written three novels, *Watching the Climbers on the Mountain* (1988), *The Tivington Nott* (1989) and *The Ancestor Game* (1992), which won the Miles Franklin Award for 1993 and the 1993 Commonwealth Writers Prize; and the plays 'Kitty Howard' (1978) and *Exiles* (1981).

Watching the Climbers on the Mountain is set in the Central Highlands of Queensland and is a story of passion and violence involving station-owner Ward Rankin, his frustrated wife Ida, and the accommodating and available young English stockman Robert Crofts. *The Tivington Nott* is also set in country that Alex Miller knew after working for two years as a young farm labourer in the West of England. The story takes place in Somerset on the borders of Exmoor. The young farmworker is given the magnificent stallion Kabara to groom. Without status or power in this closed social system where the hunt is the symbol and sport of the aristocracy, the lad comes to know a secret that those above him would love to share – the whereabouts of the legendary Tivington nott, the nott stag which has eluded the local hunters for years. Given the task of riding Kabara on a hunt, the boy proves himself the equal of his masters and is finally accorded their respect. The moor country and its animals are the true protagonists of the novel; the humans are far less heroic. The prolonged description of the even more prolonged hunt sequence gives the novel the air of an English 'Man from Snowy River' sequence. Miller's talent for creating atmosphere is obvious; nowhere is it better displayed than in the opening sequence where the maddened bull is briefly let loose upon a waiting cow.

The Ancestor Game (q.v.), an impressive novel in rich, evocative prose, links the stories of the Chinese Australian Lang Tzu and Gertrude Spiess, of German and Asian descent, with Steven Muir of English background. Lang Tzu, great-grandson of Feng who arrived in Australia in 1848 four generations earlier and made a fortune on the goldfields, is the central character, although ancestry itself is more pivotal than the personae. Equally a chain that binds and a link that secures, mixed ancestry proves to be an ambivalent inheritance.

MILLER, E. (Edmund) Morris (1881–1964), born Natal, South Africa, was brought to Melbourne in infancy. Educated at the University of Melbourne, he worked for the Public Library of Victoria 1900–13. In Melbourne he was active in both library and public affairs and became friendly with Alfred Deakin; secretary of the Imperial Federation League, he published two pamphlets (1911, 1912) in support of its aims. He also published a pioneering book on librarianship in Australia, *Libraries and Education* (1912). In 1913 Morris Miller was appointed lecturer in mental and moral science at the University of Tasmania, where he subsequently held the positions of professor of philosophy and psychology (1922–51) and vice-chancellor (1933–46). In Hobart his activities were remarkably diverse; as well as running the Department of Philosophy and Psychology without an assistant until 1950, he became prominent in the field of mental health; in 1920 he drafted a Mental Deficiency Act which became a blueprint for other States. One outcome of his activities in this area was his psychological study *Brain Capacity and Intelligence* (1926). He was also active in the general educational field, helping to found the WEA in Tasmania. He held the post of honorary librarian of the University of Tasmania 1919–45 and was responsible for extensively building up the holdings of the library, which is now named after him; he also helped to form the Australian Library Association in 1928 and was chairman of the board of trustees of the Public Library of Tasmania 1922–43. For the last three decades of his life Morris Miller devoted himself to the bibliography of Australian literature and in 1932 began the eight years' research leading to his monumental work *Australian Literature from Its Beginnings to 1935 . . . with Subsidiary Entries to 1938* (q.v., 1940). Created emeritus professor on his retirement and made CBE in 1963, he received numerous other awards, including the Gold Medal of the Australian Literature Society. Apart from the works already mentioned and numerous essays, reviews and pamphlets, Morris Miller published four studies of Kant's philosophy, (1911, 1913, 1924, 1928); a brief study of Henry Savery and Mary L. Grimstone, *Australia's First Two Novels* (1958); and an exhaustive account of early journalism in Tasmania, *Pressmen and Governors* (1952). Morris Miller is now probably best known for his two-volume descriptive and bibliographical survey of Australian literature. A fundamental reference work, it is full of detailed information

that is unavailable elsewhere and is particularly useful for the period from 1850, when J.A. Ferguson's *Bibliography of Australia* (1941–69) ceases to cover literature, until 1937 when the National Library's *Annual Catalogue of Australian Publications* began publication. Although a second edition of *Australian Literature* appeared in 1956 revised and updated by Frederick T. Macartney, it by no means replaced the 1940 publication. John Reynolds and Margaret Giordano have written a biography of Miller, *Countries of the Mind* (1985), and Linda Rodda has compiled a listing of his published works and manuscripts, *E.M.M.* (1970).

'MILLER, John', see **LANE, William**

MILLETT, John (1921–) served as a RAAF air gunner in Britain during the Second World War, and subsequently practised as a lawyer in Sydney and on the Gold Coast. He has contributed poetry to numerous Australian and international periodicals and has published several collections, *Calendar Adam* (1971), *The Silences* (1973), *Love Tree of the Coomera* (1975), *West of the Cunderang* (1977), *Tail Arse Charlie* in *Poetry Australia* (1982) and as a chapbook in the USA in 1983, *Come Down Cunderang* (1985) and *The Nine Lives of Big Meg O'Shannessy* (1990). He has also written a play with Grace Perry, *Last Bride at Longsleep* (1981), and an eight-part verse novella, *Blue Dynamite* (1987), also published as a chapbook in the USA in 1987 and adapted for stage in 1988. Another publication, *Voyeur from Australia*, was published in the USA in 1988. An elusive and strikingly individual poet, Millett has a strong sense of place and a fascination with language, which he uses with zest and dexterity. His gift for sharp imagery and his pronounced, self-conscious use of a persona add power and colour to such spiritually autobiographical sequences as *Calendar Adam* and *Love Tree of the Coomera*. *Tail Arse Charlie*, his simplest work, which was broadcast on radio in a dramatised version in 1981–82, is a powerful anti-war sequence, bolstered by photographs and records from the Australian War Memorial. Partly based on his memories of the air war, it is also evocative of the experience of all the 'old-young men' involved in the Battle of Britain. Millett was for a long period associated with *Poetry Australia* (q.v.).

MILLISS, Roger (1934–), born Katoomba, NSW, graduated from the University of Sydney in 1956 and worked as a teacher before spending some years as a journalist in Moscow, where he was employed as a translator on the *Moscow News*, and in Nairobi and London. A committed communist, he worked on *Tribune* 1966–70 and was an actor and director with Sydney's New Theatre for many years. Milliss's publications include an autobiography, *Serpent's Tooth* (1984); a history of Tamworth, *City on the Peel* (1980); and an account of Aboriginal relations with White settlers in northern NSW 1818–40, titled *Waterloo Creek: the Australia Day Massacre of 1838, George Gipps and the British Conquest of New South Wales* (1992). He is the editor of *The Wallabadah Manuscript: Recollections of the Early Days by William Telfer Jr* (1980), and co-author, with Barry Dwyer and Bruce Thomson, of *Mastering the Media: a Guide to the Discriminating Use of the Mass Media* (1971). Milliss has also written for television and radio. The central subject of *Waterloo Creek* is the 1838 massacre which took place about 60 kilometres south-west of Moree near Snodgrass Lagoon, when up to 300 Aborigines of the Weraerai tribe were killed by a force led by Major J.W. Nunn, but the book is also a meticulously researched, encyclopaedic treatment of related topics; these include the governorship of Governor Gipps, anthropological evidence concerning the Kamilaroi and neighbouring peoples in NSW, the political influence and manipulations of White settlers of the period and the career of George Augustus Robinson. *The Wallabadah Manuscript*, the reminiscences of William Telfer (1841–1925), draws partly on the stories of Telfer's father who migrated to Australia in 1825 and worked for the Australian Agricultural Company. An authoritative account of the settlement of northern NSW 1840–60, it is also informative on the history of relations between the White settlers and Aborigines from the 1830s. *Serpent's Tooth*, one of Australia's most striking autobiographies, is the story of Milliss's political and emotional development and his relationship with his father, Bruce Milliss; a successful Katoomba businessman, Bruce Milliss left the Catholic Church for the Communist Party of Australia, transferring his religious zeal to the Party and bringing up his son in the same faith. He was also active in the Labor Party, becoming Chifley's campaign director, and building up trade opportunities with communist China and the Soviet Union. Beginning and ending with Bruce Milliss's death in 1970, *Serpent's Tooth* is partly an elegiac study of a passionate father–son relationship, and the explosive influence of diverging political beliefs; it is also a valuable social history, densely informative on the CPA and its history from the 1930s.

'MILLS, Martin', see **BOYD, Martin**

Miner's Right, The, a novel by 'Rolf Boldrewood' (q.v.), was serialised in the *Australian Town and Country Journal* in 1880, published in book form in 1890, and adapted for the stage in 1891. The hero of the novel is Hereward Pole, an Englishman of good breeding who emigrates to Australia to seek on the Turon goldfields of NSW the fortune that will allow him to marry Ruth Allerton, a squire's daughter. After four years he and his three partners are successful, but their claim is jumped; they win the case before the goldfields commissioner William Blake, but a court appeal is lodged and Pole goes to the Oxley goldfields while awaiting the decision. There he again strikes a rich lead, which he leaves to visit Sydney with the gold escort to help an old friend, Jane Morsley, escape her villainous husband Ned. The escort is attacked *en route* by bushrangers and the wounded Pole nursed back to health by Jane; he returns to Oxley, where an anti-Chinese riot is quelled. With the appeal dismissed and both claims flourishing, Pole looks forward to selling up and returning to England, but he receives a letter from Ruth's father breaking off the

relationship because of a libellous report that Jane has become Pole's mistress. Jane herself is murdered, and Hereward accused of the crime. Acquitted following Ned's arrest, he is honoured by a dinner on his departure from the goldfields and goes to Sydney to be reunited with Ruth, who has travelled with her family to Australia for her health. After a final tour of the goldfields Hereward returns with his bride to England to establish his own estate.

A typical 'Boldrewood' success story of an English gentleman, *The Miner's Right* has weaknesses of plot, style and characterisation that led Joseph Furphy to parody it in *The Buln-Buln and the Brolga* (1948); a comparison between Hereward Pole and Dick Marston, the narrator of *Robbery Under Arms* (1888), explains why *Robbery Under Arms* is the more successful novel. That *The Miner's Right* has endured at all derives from the strength of the minor characters, together with the fact that 'Boldrewood' drew extensively on his Gulgong experiences of the 1870s and transferred them to a story, set in the 1850s and 1860s, in which he was able to re-create other historical incidents such as the Lambing Flat riots.

Mirage, The (1955), a novel by F. Bert Vickers (q.v.), has also been published in Russia and in East Germany, resulting in considerable correspondence between Vickers and European students about the Aboriginal situation in Australia. The novel's principal characters are two Aborigines, Freddie Adams and the girl Nona. Freddie Adams, growing up as part-Aboriginal, is alien to both the tribal life of the Aborigines and to White society, and the discrimination he suffers ultimately brings about his destruction. A well-planned novel with warm and realistic characters, *The Mirage* convincingly argues for greater racial tolerance by White Australians.

MITCHEL, John (1815–75), born Derry, Ireland, was an Irish lawyer and nationalist who became actively involved in the Young Ireland movement in 1845. Assistant editor of the *Nation* under Charles Gavan Duffy, later premier of Victoria, he launched the *United Irishman* in 1848 and was soon arrested for sedition. He was sentenced to transportation, and arrived in Hobart in 1850; in 1853 he escaped to America, where he became a controversial journalist. Mitchel's *Jail Journal* (1854) includes an account of his Australian experiences, which were also written up by Marcus Clarke in *Old Tales of a Young Country* (1871), and published in a version edited by Peter O'Shaughnessy titled *The Gardens of Hell* (1988). Several of his Young Ireland colleagues were also transported to Australia, where they briefly ran the journal the *Irish Exile* (1850–51). Biographies of Mitchel include P.S. O'Hegarty's *John Mitchel* (1917) and Seamus MacCall's *Irish Mitchel* (1938), and he is one of the Irish nationalists featured in Patsy Adam-Smith's *Heart of Exile* (1986).

MITCHELL, David Scott (1836–1907), book-collector, was born in Sydney, the son of Dr James Mitchell (1792–1869), a prominent colonial surgeon and businessman from whom he inherited estates. Educated at the University of Sydney, Mitchell was admitted to the Bar in 1858 but never practised; after a broken romance with Emily Manning in 1864 and the death of his parents in 1869 and 1871, he lived in increasing seclusion to pursue his interest in books. For twenty years from the 1860s he collected mainly English literary works, but from about 1886 devoted himself to the aim of collecting every document relating to Australia, the Pacific, the East Indies, and Antarctica. He bequeathed to the trustees of the Public, now State, Library of NSW his collection and an endowment of £70 000; the collection of about 60 000 volumes and other material formed the basis of the collection of the Mitchell Library (q.v.), which was opened in 1910.

MITCHELL, Elyne (1913–   ), born Melbourne, the daughter of the military commander Sir Harry Chauvel, married Thomas Mitchell in 1935 and has subsequently lived on a station on the upper Murray in the foothills of the Victorian Alps. She has drawn on this alpine landscape and its wild horses for many of her popular children's books, which have been translated into several languages and published in Britain and the USA. They include the popular Silver Brumby series, beginning with *The Silver Brumby* (1958) which was made into a successful film in 1993. She has also written two novels for adults, *Flow River, Blow Wind* (1953) and *Black Cockatoos Mean Snow* (1956); a part-historical, part-autobiographical account of discoverers of the Snowy Mountains region (1985) and a collection of descriptive essays that deal with aspects of the same region, *Images in Water* (1947); an illustrated collection of prose, poetry and photographs chronicling her love of the mountains, *A Vision of the Snowy Mountains* (1988); reminiscences of skiing and climbing experiences, which reflect her prowess as a champion skier and her sensitive response to the alpine landscape, *Australia's Alps* (1942); a detailed, often lyrically expressed chronicle of her work on the family station during the Second World War, *Speak to the Earth* (1945); a history of the Australian Light Horse (1978); an account of her parents and her early life, *Chauvel Country* (1983) and another of her experiences in the Snowy Mountains from the time of her marriage, *Towong Hill* (1989). She was made AO in 1988.

Mitchell, Jack is a major character in the fiction of Henry Lawson (q.v.), appearing in about forty sketches and stories; he is an important figure in *While the Billy Boils* (1896), although there are Mitchell stories in later Lawson volumes, including *On the Track* (1900), *Over the Sliprails* (1900) and *Children of the Bush* (1902). Described in 'Enter Mitchell' as 'short, and stout, and bow-legged, and freckled, and sandy', Mitchell, as he is usually called, reveals at the end of that story that he was once a cab-driver for five years in Sydney; more characteristically he appears as a bushman who has been on the track for several years carrying his swag. Mitchell is an evolving, complex character in his own right but is most significant as a narrator, particularly in *While the Billy Boils*, where his understated, laconic yarns help establish the authen-

ticity of Lawson's fictional world. A number of bushmen whom Lawson met have been suggested as models for Mitchell, including Arthur Parker, with whom he worked in the Blue Mountains in 1887; Bill Louisson, a foreman in NZ; and J.W. Gordon (q.v.), also known as 'Jim Grahame', with whom Lawson travelled during his outback trek in 1892–93. In 'By the Banks of the Murrumbidgee' Lawson states that in 1892–93 he travelled as Joe Swallow (one of his literary pseudonyms) and Gordon as Jack Mitchell; but it is also clear that Mitchell is a composite character, independent of any model, and that in the Mitchell stories Lawson drew on a wide range of experiences, including those of his family, rather than simply on his experiences with Gordon.

Mitchell Library, which is housed in the State Library of NSW in Sydney, was opened in 1910 as a result of the bequest of the bibliophile David Scott Mitchell (q.v.). The Mitchell collection, one of the world's significant national collections, includes not only the most extensive and important collection of Australiana but also material relating to NZ, the Pacific and other regions near Australia. The Mitchell Library's *Dictionary Catalog of Printed Books* was published in 1968, with a first supplement appearing in 1970; part of its manuscript catalogue has been published (1967, 1969), as well as an index to periodicals covering 1944–63 (1950–67). Phyllis Mander-Jones, long-time member of the Mitchell Library staff, published *Sources of Australian Literature in the Mitchell Library Sydney* (1962) and contributed a chapter on the library to Charles Barrett's anthology *Across the Years* (1948), and another long-time staff member, Anne Robertson, prepared *Treasures of the State Library of New South Wales* (1988), which describes the Australiana collection of the State Library, including the Mitchell and Dixson collections. The library's early history is described by G.D. Richardson in *The Colony's Quest for a National Library* (1960).

MITCHELL, Mary (1893–1973), born Melbourne, was educated in Australia and Europe. In 1923 she returned to Australia, and until 1932 worked with the Victorian Junior Red Cross. She published about twenty popular novels, many of them with romantic, even fantastic plots. They include *A Warning to Wantons* (1934), *Pendulum Swing* (1935), *Viper's Progress* (1939), *Dark Tapestry* (1942), *Prelude to Jesting* (1950) and *Birth of a Legend* (1956). Her best-known novel, *A Warning to Wantons*, was translated into several languages and produced as a film in 1948. Afflicted with blindness in her later years, Mitchell also wrote a well-received account of the experience of the blind, designed to improve relations between them and the sighted, *Uncharted Country* (1963).

MITCHELL, Sir Thomas (1792–1855), born Craigend, Scotland, went to NSW in 1827 as assistant surveyor-general, succeeding to the main position in 1828 on the death of John Oxley. In 1831–36 Mitchell made three exploratory expeditions: to northern NSW in the Namoi, Gwydir and Barwon River areas;

to the Darling River from the point where Charles Sturt had explored in 1828 down to its junction with the Murray River; and finally along the Lachlan, Murrumbidgee and Murray Rivers and up the Darling River towards Menindee, then back to the Murray and into what is now Victoria, which he called Australia Felix, thence south and west until he came across the Henty brothers near Portland. Rapid settlement of Victoria followed the third expedition. Mitchell's account of his explorations is contained in *Three Expeditions into the Interior of Eastern Australia* (1838). Following further explorations in 1845–46 to find an overland route to Port Essington and/or a great north-flowing river, he published *Journal of an Expedition into the Interior of Tropical Australia* (1848). The experiences of his final years, including a prolonged visit to England (1852–54) during which he sought to interest the Admiralty in a propeller for steamships modelled on the Aboriginal boomerang, are contained in J.H.L. Cumpston's biography (1955). The best literary stylist of the Australian explorers, Mitchell published a translation of the *Luciad* of Camoens (1854). He is featured in William Hay's book of sketches, *An Australian Rip Van Winkle* (1921) and is the subject of a biography by William C. Foster, *Sir Thomas Livingston Mitchell and his World 1792–1855* (1985). *Major Mitchell's Map 1834: The Saga of the Survey of the Nineteen Counties* (1992), by Alan E.J. Andrews, examines Mitchell's attempt to map the NSW colony between 1827 and 1834.

'Mo', see **RENE, Roy**

Modern Australian Literature (1900–1923), a brief but comprehensive account by Nettie Palmer (q.v.), was published in 1924 and won the Lothian Prize for an essay in Australian literature since 1900. Although preceded by *An Introduction to the Study of Australian Literature* (1922) by Zora Cross, it is the first systematically critical survey to be published in book form. Written in an agreeable, readable style, enlivened by frequently striking epithets and analogies, the book makes many judgements which are still fresh. The conclusion presents a bleak picture of the Australian writer's isolation in the 1920s and the absence of 'facilities for ordinary publishing'. The monograph incidentally led to Nettie Palmer's discovery of 'Henry Handel Richardson': Mrs Mary Kernot, an acquaintance of both Nettie Palmer and the novelist, surprised to find no mention of 'Richardson', lent Nettie Palmer her books and thus initiated the intense interest that led to her *Henry Handel Richardson* (1950), the first full-length study of that writer.

Modern Australian Poetry, 1920–70: A Guide to Information Sources (1979), by Herbert C. Jaffa, is a bibliographical guide covering Australian poetry from Kenneth Slessor to the new Australian poets of the late 1960s and early 1970s. Sections annotating bibliographies, bibliographic guides, background reference material, critical studies and anthologies precede author check-lists which cover the author's work and an annotated selection of bibliographical and critical material. The author sections are organised within the categories of major poets (Slessor, R.D. FitzGerald, A.D. Hope, Douglas Stewart, Judith Wright, James McAuley), important and established poets (e.g. David Campbell, Francis Webb, Les Murray), Jindyworobak poets, Angry Penguins poets, expatriate poets, other poets of the 1940s–1960s, and younger poets. The companion volumes to *Modern Australian Poetry* are *Modern Australian Prose* by A. Grove Day and *Australian Literature to 1900* by Barry Andrews and William H. Wilde (qq.v.).

Modern Australian Prose, 1901–75: A Guide to Information Sources (1980), by A. Grove Day, is mainly a reference guide to twentieth-century Australian prose, although the last of its four sections lists critical material on modern Australian drama. The first part is an annotated listing of bibliographies and bibliographical guides, background reference works, literary history and criticism, materials on Australian English, periodicals and anthologies. The second part provides a bibliographical and critical guide to fifty-four authors; the third annotates selected non-fiction titles, including material on Aborigines. The companion volumes to *Modern Australian Prose* are Herbert Jaffa's *Modern Australian Poetry* and Barry Andrews and William H. Wilde's *Australian Literature to 1900* (qq.v.).

Modern Buccaneer, A (1894), a fictionalised account of the career of 'Bully' Hayes, was published by 'Rolf Boldrewood', but roughly two-thirds was the work of 'Louis' Becke (q.v.). As a fledgeling author, Becke sent a narrative about Hayes to 'Boldrewood' in 1893 and was paid, expecting that it would form only the framework for a work. When Becke protested about the use of the material, 'Boldrewood' publicly acknowledged his indebtedness.

Modern Times: The National Affairs Monthly, the successor to *Australian Society* (1982–92), is concerned with a wide range of social, economic and political issues and includes articles and reviews on literary and cultural affairs.

MODJESKA, Drusilla (1946–   ), born England, has lived in Australia since 1971. Educated at the ANU and the University of NSW, she has taught at the University of Technology, Sydney, and has worked in publishing. She has written an influential study of a group of women writers between the wars, which includes Miles Franklin, Katharine Susannah Prichard, Marjorie Barnard, Dymphna Cusack, Flora Eldershaw, Eleanor Dark, Nettie Palmer and Jean Devanny, *Exiles at Home: Australian Women Writers 1925–45* (1981); informative on the general cultural milieu and the effects of the Great Depression, *Exiles at Home* also concentrates on the relationships between the women, their political affinities and the issues that concerned them, and the difficulties they faced in balancing feminism, nationalism and socialist ideals. She has also written *Poppy* (1990), a biography of her mother which is as much an autobiography. It has won the 1990 Herb Thomas Literary Award, the

NBC Banjo Award for non-fiction, the 1991 Talking Book of the Year Award and the Douglas Stewart Prize for non-fiction in the 1991 NSW State Library Awards. A 'mixture of fact and fiction, biography and novel', *Poppy* depends on diaries, letters, conversations, family papers and stories, memory and imagination. Modjeska has also edited *Inner Cities: Australian Women's Memory of Place* (1989), a selection of extracts which attempts to explore the interrelationship between place and the inner life; and *Sisters* (1993), an anthology of reflections on the experience of being a sister by such writers as Elizabeth Jolley, Helen Garner, Gillian Mears, Dorothy Hewett, Beth Yahp and Modjeska herself. With Marjorie Pizer she edited *The Poems of Lesbia Harford* (1986); and with Susan Dermody and John Docker, *Nellie Melba, Ginger Meggs and Friends: Essays in Australian Cultural History* (1982).

MOFFITT, Ian (1929–), born Sydney, has worked for several Australian newspapers, including the Sydney *Mirror*, the *Australian*, the *Sydney Morning Herald* and the *Bulletin*, after beginning his career in Hong Kong on the staff of the *South China Morning Post*. He spent some years in New York as head of the News Ltd bureau, but gave up journalism in 1978 to write full-time. He has written a critique of Australian attitudes to conservation, the arts, the press, sport, foreign policy, migrants and racism, *The U-Jack Society* (1972); the text of an illustrated work, *The Australian Outback* (1976); several novels which have been well received, *The Retreat of Radiance* (1982), *The Colour Man* (1983, published in the USA as *Presence of Evil*, 1985), *Blue Angels* (1987), *Death Adder Dreaming* (1988) and *Gilt Edge* (1991); a collection of short stories, *The Electric Jungle* (1993); and a collection of journalism and short stories, *Deadlines* (1985). *The Retreat of Radiance*, which draws on his experiences in China during the civil war, deals with a 19-year-old Australian journalist, Quinn, who witnesses a Nationalist massacre and returns to the Far East thirty years later to seek vengeance. Frequently compared in style, pace and tone to the work of 'John le Carré', the novel has been praised for its depth of characterisation and authentic background. For four months after publication it remained on the best-seller list. Moffitt's subsequent novels are well-crafted, fast-paced, unpretentious thrillers, which have led one reviewer to describe him as 'George Johnston without the pain, Neville Shute without the sentimentality'. The nine short stories of *The Electric Jungle* (1993) explore fantasy worlds and characters, beginning with 'Street Angel, House Devil', a suspenseful story of a serial rapist/murderer outwitted by his next potential victim. Moffitt goes on in other stories such as 'The Emperor of Waterford' to outrageous but harmless flights of fancy. The novella 'The Electric Jungle', however, enters the eerie world of mental imbalance where obsessive behaviour brings fear and terror to all concerned.

MOIR, J.K. (John Kinmont) (1893–1958), born Normanton, Queensland, was brought up in Queensland, but spent his adult life in Melbourne. A business-

man, he was, in his spare time, an avid collector of Australiana, his home in Richmond becoming well known to students of Australian literature, authors and bibliophiles. In 1957 his large collection of books, photographs, prints and other memorabilia was donated to the La Trobe Library. An ardent devotee of Australian literature, particularly interested in Adam Lindsay Gordon, he was co-founder and Knight Grand Cheese (president) of the Bread and Cheese Club and editor of its monthly bulletin *Bohemia*; patron of the Gordon Lovers' society; life member of the Australian Literature Society and of the Henry Lawson society; and member of the Poetry Lovers' Society and of the C.J. Dennis Memorial Committee. His only published work was a history of Australia's first electric tram (1940), but he also wrote biographies of Gordon and of Edward Devine, coach-driver for Cobb & Co. He was made OBE in 1952.

MOLL, E.G. (Ernest George) (1900–), born Murtoa, Victoria, was educated at schools in NSW. In 1920 he left for the USA and studied at Lawrence College, Wisconsin, and Harvard University. From 1928 to 1966 he was professor of English at the University of Oregon. Moll's verse, which is represented in numerous Australian anthologies, has appeared in several collections, including *Sedge Fire* (1927), *Native Moments* (1931), *Campus Sonnets* (1934), *Blue Interval* (1935), *Cut from Mulga* (1940), *Brief Waters* (1945), *Beware the Cuckoo* (1947), *The Waterhole* (1948), *The Lifted Spear* (1953), *Poems 1940–1955* (1957), *The Rainbow Serpent* (1962), *Briseis* (1965), *The Road to Cactus-land* (1971) and *The View From a Ninetieth Birthday* (1992). He has also written a critical study, *The Appreciation of Poetry* (1933); and *Below These Hills: The Story of a Riverina Farm* (1957), an account of his family's farm, established in 1910. Strongly indebted to his rural Australian experience, Moll has often been classed as a regionalist, although his work is by no means restricted to Australian subjects.

MOLONEY, Patrick (1843–1904), born Melbourne, graduated in medicine from the University of Melbourne in 1867. One of the editors of the *Australian Medical Journal* and a contributor to the *Melbourne Punch*, he wrote verse for the *Australasian* as well as a series of papers headed 'Under the Greenwood Tree'. He was a member of the Yorick Club and is recalled in Hugh McCrae's *My Father and My Father's Friends* (1935) and in *Yorick Club Reminiscences* (1911). His verse also appeared in several contemporary anthologies and his sonnet sequence, *Sonnets: Ad Innuptam*, originally published in the *Australasian* under his pseudonym 'Australis', in *An Easter Omelette* (1879), edited by A. Patchett Martin.

Monaro is the name of the geographical district that now extends from south of the Australian Capital Territory to the Victorian border and eastward from the alpine area of the Great Dividing Range to the escarpment that abuts on to the far-south coastal plain of NSW. Discovered in 1823 by Captain M.J. Currie, it has been known by a variety of names, Monaroo,

Manaroo, Moneiro, Monera, all of which are said to derive from the Aboriginal word *manaroo* meaning woman's breast, the name denoting the rounded nature of the hills of the original district. The 1840 Moneroo Squattage District, much larger than the present Monaro, extended from north of the present NSW city of Goulburn well down into the modern State of Victoria; Henry Kingsley's *The Recollections of Geoffry Hamlyn* (1859) is partly set in this extended area. The Monaro soon figured in Australian writing. John Lhotsky records his travels through it in *A Journey from Sydney to the Australian Alps* (1835); Paul de Strzelecki explored it, giving a Polish name, Kosciusko, to Australia's loftiest peak; Henry W. Haygarth records details of squatting life in the area in his *Recollections of Bush Life in Australia during a Residence of Eight Years in the Interior* (1848); W.A. Brodribb does the same in retrospect in *Recollections of an Australian Squatter* (1883); and Charles Cozens records his experiences as a convict constable in the Monaro *in Adventures of a Guardsman* (1848). Mentioned in fiction as early as 1849 in the novel *The Emigrant Family*, the Monaro is assessed by Alexander Harris as 'the best grazing grounds for horned cattle within the Australian colonies'. Harris describes it as 'far above the sea, and utterly bare of forest over its main expanse; its winter is piercing and desolate. Its extent is such that in some parts a rider may tire a good horse two days in succession in passing across from bush to bush'. In more recent Australian literature it has featured as the home of A.B. Paterson's legendary Man from Snowy River (Tim Hall has written *'Banjo' Paterson's High Country*, 1989); as the birthplace of Miles Franklin and the setting of many of her novels; and as the well-loved country of poet David Campbell, sometimes referred to as 'The Man from the Monaro'. The chief study of the district is W.K. Hancock's *Discovering Monaro* (1972).

MONASH, Sir John (1865–1931), born Melbourne of Prussian-Jewish extraction, graduated in arts, law and engineering from the University of Melbourne. Before the First World War he practised successfully as an engineer, pioneering construction in reinforced concrete. A citizen soldier, he was commissioned in 1908, became colonel of an infantry brigade in 1913, and commanded the 4th Infantry Brigade at Gallipoli. He quickly established his reputation as a commander in France 1917–18 and succeeded General Birdwood in command of the Australian Corps in March 1918. At the close of the war his reputation exceeded that of any other Australian general; he was described by Sir Basil Liddell Hart as having 'probably the greatest capacity for command in modern war among all those who held command'. Monash subsequently gave an account of the main action in which he was involved in *The Australian Victories in France in 1918* (1920). His *War Letters*, edited by F.M. Cutlack, were published in 1934 and both publications reveal his wide-ranging intellect and interests, his humanity, administrative capability, and shrewd psychological insight. After the war he was prominent in the development of electrical power in Victoria. He was vice-chancellor of the University of Melbourne and received numerous other honours; in 1958 Victoria's second university was named after him. Monash's military achievement is described in C.E.W. Bean's official history of the First World War and several biographies have been published, although the most substantial is Geoffrey Serle's award-winning *John Monash* (1982). P.A. Pedersen has published a densely researched study of his achievements as a military commander (1985).

MONCKTON, Charles Arthur Whitmore (1873–1936), born Invercargill, NZ, was a magistrate in New Guinea from 1897 and became well known for his punitive expeditions against rebellious tribes. A controversial figure, who resigned from the service after he was reprimanded for exceeding his instructions in an exploratory expedition, he later served in the First World War. He published three books on his experiences in New Guinea, *Some Experiences of a New Guinea Resident Magistrate* (1921), *Last Days in New Guinea* (1922) and *New Guinea Recollections* (1934). An unabashed imperialist with firm ideas on the treatment of 'savages' and the virtues and vices of his White colleagues, Monckton wrote a dramatic prose which made his books popular with British readers. Inaccuracies in *New Guinea Recollections*, however, damaged his reputation.

'MONCRIEFF, William Thomas' (William George Thomas) (1794–1857) was theatre manager, critic, editor of play texts and dramatist and wrote well over a hundred plays for the English stage in the 1820s and 1830s; two of them, the burletta *Tom and Jerry: Or, Life in London* (produced 1821, performed Sydney 1834), and the extravaganza *Van Diemen's Land: Or, Tasmania in 1818* (q.v.) (produced 1830, published 1831), are significant in Australian literature. In adapting for the stage Pierce Egan's (1772–1849) enormously popular series of sketches of London life, 'Moncrieff' introduced into *Tom and Jerry* the character of Jemmy Green, a raw ('green') East-Ender. His popularity was such that he survived in the similar figure of the 'new chum' (q.v.) in the plays *Jemmy Green in Australia* (q.v.) by James Tucker and 'Life in Sydney: Or, the Ran Dan Club' (q.v.), an adaptation of *Life in London* possibly by H.C. O'Flaherty. *Van Diemen's Land* was one of the earliest plays about Australia produced in England and owed its writing to the desire of 'Moncrieff''s' colleague, the actor and theatre manager Robert Elliston (1774–1831), to celebrate the arrival of his two sons, William and Henry, in Van Diemen's Land. 'Moncrieff''s' propensity to respond to the theatrical fashion of the day and adapt the novels of writers like Sir Walter Scott and Charles Dickens led the latter to present him satirically in *Nicholas Nickleby*.

MONTEZ, Lola (Maria Dolores Eliza Rosanna Gilbert) (1818–61), born Limerick, Ireland, eloped with a young army officer, Thomas James, in 1837 but was deserted by him in India. She returned to England in 1842, trained as a dancer in Spain and as Donna Lola Montez made her London theatre debut in 1843.

Hissed off the stage when her identity became known (her hypocritical husband had earlier won a separation because of her adultery aboard ship returning from India), she reappeared in Europe, where she became the mistress of Franz Liszt, Alexandre Dumas, and King Ludwig I of Bavaria, among others. Created Countess Marie von Landsfeld by Ludwig, she exercised political influence until the riots which broke out against her in 1848 caused the King to abdicate. By 1849 Lola was back in London, where she bigamously married a second young army officer; after his death in 1850 she returned to the stage and toured Europe and America, where in gold-rush California she first performed her provocative Spider Dance. Another bigamous and broken marriage later she toured Australia for almost a year (1855–56), opening on most occasions in the farrago 'Lola Montez in Bavaria'. In Sydney she avoided arrest for debt by undressing and daring a sheriff to arrest her, in Melbourne the Spider Dance appalled some respectable citizens and was parodied by George Coppin, notably in his role of Scrumptious Katunka, Egyptian Professor of the Spider Dance in 'Coppin in Cairo' (1858); Montez, however, had successful if scandalous seasons in Adelaide and on the goldfields. After leaving Australia she returned to America, where, in San Francisco, William Robertson satirised her in the play 'A Trip to Australia, or Lola Montez on the Fanny Major'. In later years her physical decline was paralleled by her moral reformation, and she became known on the lecture platform.

A number of historical and fictional accounts of goldfields life mention Lola Montez, including Eric Lambert's novel *Ballarat* (1962); in 1958 the musical 'Lola Montez', by Alan Burke, Peter Benjamin and Peter Stannard was performed in Sydney. Among recent accounts of her life are Doris Foley's *The Divine Eccentric: Lola Montez and the Newspapers* (1969), which includes her autobiography and American reports of her Australian experiences, Ishbel Ross's *The Uncrowned Queen* (1972), Amanda Darling's *Lola Montez* (1972) and the anonymous *Lola Montez: The Tragic Story of a 'Liberated Woman'* (1973). Raymond A. Bradfield has written an account of her career on the Australian goldfields, *Lola Montez and Castlemaine* (1980).

MONTGOMERY, Alexander (1847–1922) was born in Londonderry, Ireland. In 1870, in the course of extensive travels, he visited Melbourne, where he worked for a time as a journalist. After further travel in the Malay Archipelago, he arrived in Sydney, where he worked for the *Evening News* and the *Echo*, and contributed to the *Bulletin*, directing the 'Aboriginalities' page. He wrote several serials for the *Australasian* and other newspapers, using such pseudonyms as 'Montalex', 'Sardonyx' and 'Heretic', as well as a historical novel with a European setting, *The Sword of a Sin* (1898) and a collection of short stories, *Five Skull Island and Other Tales of the Malay Archipelago* (1897).

Month, a monthly literary and critical journal established in Sydney by Frank Fowler, was edited by him July 1857 to April 1858 and then by J. Sheridan Moore until its demise in December 1858. Its contributors included R H. Horne, Richard Rowe and J.L. Michael. Fowler's stated aims for the *Month* included a denunciation of Australian philistinism and the creation of a national literature based on the highest standards of European excellence. Among his own contributions to the *Month* was a series of nine travel essays titled 'Sydney and Its Suburbs'. Much of the magazine's material was not particularly Australian in character, although it did offer reviews of Australian books and occasional serials on bush life; its highlight was the series 'The World of Books'. Under Moore's editorship, the *Month* became less substantial as a literary journal and perished through financial difficulties. An account of the journal's foundation and fortunes is included in Ann-Mari Jordens's *The Stenhouse Circle* (1979).

MOODIE HEDDLE, Enid (1904–), born Elsternwick, Victoria, was educated at the University of Melbourne and taught in Australia and England 1927–34. In 1935–46 she was educational adviser in Australia to Longmans Green and to William Collins and in 1947–60 educational manager for Longmans in Australia. The author or editor of more than thirty books, Enid Moodie Heddle wrote two books of verse, *Solitude* (1937) and *Sagitta Says* (1943); and *Boy on a Horse* (1957, with H.J. Samuel), the story of Adam Lindsay Gordon. She published *Australian Literature Now* (1949) and *How Australian Literature Grew* (1962) but is best known as editor of the Boomerang Books series, which includes *The Boomerang Book of Australian Poetry* (1956) and *The Boomerang Book of Legendary Tales* (1957), both of which won Children's Book Council Awards. Moodie Heddle edited the Australian editions of *The Poet's Way* (1942, 1943, 1944), *Discovering Poetry* (1956, 1957) and *A Galaxy of Poems Old and New* (1962).

Moondyne, a novel by John Boyle O'Reilly (q.v.), was published in America in 1879 and in Australia a year later; originally a serial in the Boston *Pilot*, which O'Reilly edited after his escape from WA in 1869, it began publication in November 1878 as 'Moondyne Joe', the title of one of the three or more American editions published in 1879, but the title was changed to 'Moondyne' the following February. Although only the first and last of its five sections are set in WA, it is generally accepted as the State's first novel. It was filmed in 1913. The first part of *Moondyne* focuses on the title character, a convict of heroic stature who has effected several escapes in the Colony, originally from the cruel ex-convict Isaac Bowman, to whom he has been assigned. He takes to the bush and joins an Aboriginal tribe, which christens him Moondyne and leads him to the gold-mine of which there have long been rumours in the Colony. Recaptured by Bowman, now an officer in the penal service, Moondyne offers to lead him to the gold-mine in return for his freedom. Bowman predictably reneges on the bargain, escapes with the gold to return to civilisation, but is pursued by Moondyne and eventually dies in the desert; Moondyne himself escapes, to reappear later in the novel as the compelling penal reformer Mr Wyville. The focus now shifts to Will Sheridan, a Lancashire seaman whose love for Alice Walmsley is thwarted by the evil Sam Draper and who deserts his ship in Singapore and becomes successful in the sandalwood trade in WA. After nine years he returns to England to find that Alice is in prison for murdering the child she bore in an unwittingly bigamous marriage to Draper. While in London he meets Wyville, who has interested himself in Alice's case, believes her innocent, saves her from despair, and is eventually to discover the real murderer, Draper's original wife. Having persuaded the English authorities of the efficacy of his penal theories which, like those of Alexander Maconochie, are based on the reformation rather than the punishment of the offenders, Wyville returns to Australia as comptroller-general of convicts; also on the ship the *Hougoumont* (on which O'Reilly was transported to Australia) are Sheridan, Sister Cecilia, who has befriended Alice in prison, Draper and his wife Harriet, who confesses her crime. In Australia Wyville successfully puts his theories into practice, Will and Alice are reunited and take over Wyville's estate, and Wyville dies heroically (he drowns in a bushfire!) trying to save Sam and Harriet Draper.

Moondyne is a poorly constructed novel, perhaps because of its weekly publication in the *Pilot*, with more than its share of cliché-ridden melodramatic set pieces. It has more than historical interest, however, for the way O'Reilly integrates the legendary experiences of the convict bushranger 'Moondyne Joe' (q.v.), with his own experiences and ideas, e.g. the scenes on board the convict ship, and the ideas articulated by the idealised Wyville and his sympathisers on the noble savages, freedom, politics and religion. In addition, *Moondyne* is remarkably prescient in its prediction about the importance of gold in WA's history and its presentation of WA as a cinderella State anticipates some later thinking in that State.

'MOONDYNE JOE' (Joseph Bolitho Jones) (?1827–1900) was a WA convict bushranger (q.v.), who was born in Wales, sentenced to transportation in 1848 and arrived at Fremantle in 1853. He established his reputation in the period 1860–73, when he made several daring escapes from gaol, remaining at large for long periods; on one occasion the authorities were forced to confine him to a specially reinforced cell, from which he escaped when allowed out for medical treatment. John Boyle O'Reilly's novel *Moondyne* (1879), titled *Moondyne Joe* in some editions, traded on the reputation of Jones and probably helped perpetuate his reputation for gallantry. More recently, Ian Elliot's *Moondyne Joe* (1978) has separated the man and the myth, and Roger Montgomery's folk musical, 'Moondyne Joe', was presented at the Perth Festival in 1982.

MOONEY, Ray (1945–), born Melbourne, has studied at the Victorian College of the Arts and the Australian Film and Television School and has worked as a barman, physical education teacher, builder and theatre director. He began his career as a writer while serving a term in prison, where his first play, *A Blue Freckle* (published 1984), was performed. His other plays include 'The Dominator' (1982), *Everynight, Everynight* (1985, a condemnation of the prison system), 'Angel of the Graveyard' (1979), 'The Final Siren' (1980), 'Lost Victoria' (1984), 'A Cat from Across the Road' (1985), 'Hard Labour Mate' (1981, with Peter Oyston), 'Autobiography of an Extra' (1982, with Judy Ferrier) and *Black Rabbit* (1988), which centres on the impact of White culture on Aboriginal society in the early nineteenth century. He has also written a novel based on his experience of criminality, *A Green Light* (1988).

MOORE, George Fletcher (1798–1886), born County Tyrone, Ireland, practised as a lawyer in that country before emigrating to the Swan River settlement in 1830. His accounts of the vicissitudes of life in the colony were published in *Extracts from the Letters and Journals of George Fletcher Moore* (1834) edited by Martin Doyle, and *Diary of Ten Years' Eventful Life of an Early Settler in Western Australia* (1884), Moore's own expanded version. Sympathetic to the Aboriginal people, he also published an Aboriginal vocabulary in 1842.

MOORE, Joseph Sheridan (1828–91), born Dublin, migrated in 1847 to Sydney and became a Benedictine monk and headmaster of Lyndhurst College, Glebe. After many disagreements with his superiors, including Archbishop Polding, he left Lyndhurst in 1856 and only rejoined the church in 1872, although he edited the Catholic magazine *Freeman's Journal* 1856–57. Well known, if not universally popular, in Sydney's literary milieu, Moore was familiar with such men as N.D. Stenhouse, Richard Rowe, James Lionel Michael, Daniel Deniehy, W.B. Dalley, Henry Kendall, John Woolley and Frank Fowler, and edited the *Month* (q.v.). An energetic teacher, he claimed proficiency in a range of subjects, including classics, languages, geography and science, meanwhile bolstering his precarious financial fortunes by literary journalism and lecturing. His publications include a collection of poetry, *Spring Life Lyrics* (1864); a collection of essays which also includes some verse and professes to initiate Irish-Australians into Irish history and customs, *The Ethics of the Irish under the Pentarchy* (1872); and a biography of Michael (1868). Aspects of his career are discussed in *The Stenhouse Circle* (1979), by Ann-Mari Jordens.

MOORE, Maggie (1851–1926), born Margaret Sullivan in San Francisco, came to Australia with her husband J.C. Williamson (q.v.) in 1874. She starred with him in the long-running, commercially successful play *Struck Oil* (q.v.) before touring in England, Ireland and the USA. In 1879 the Williamsons returned to Australia, where Moore became a versatile and outstandingly popular actress and singer, playing numerous roles in light opera, including Josephine in the first authorised performance of *HMS Pinafore* by Gilbert and Sullivan. After relations between Moore and Williamson became strained, she formed her own company and in 1894 defeated an injunction by Williamson designed to prevent her production of *Struck Oil*. She divorced Williamson in 1899 and in 1901 married H.R. Roberts, continuing to appear as an actor until 1924, when the fiftieth anniversary of her arrival in Australia was marked by large concerts. She died in San Francisco.

MOORE, Tom Inglis (1901–79), born Camden, NSW, was educated at the universities of Sydney and Oxford and taught in the USA and at the University of the Philippines (1928–31). In 1934–40 he was on the staff of the *Sydney Morning Herald* as reviewer and leader-writer. After service in the Second World War he joined the Canberra University College, later the ANU, where he remained until his retirement in 1966. He was a long-serving member of the CLF advisory board and active in the FAW, the ASA and the English Association. His creative writing includes a novel, *The Half Way Sun: A Tale of the Philippine Islands* (1935); a radio play in verse, *We're Going Through* (1945), broadcast by the ABC; and three books of verse, *Adagio in Blue* (1938), *Emu Parade: Poems from Camp* (1941) and *Bayonet and Grass* (1957). As an editor he published *Best Australian One-Act Plays* (1937, with William Moore); *Australia Writes: An Anthology* (1953); *Henry Kendall* (1957), the introduction to which contained a major scholarly reappraisal of Kendall's work; *Poetry in Australia* (1964, in collaboration with Douglas Stewart); and *Letters of Mary Gilmore* (1980, in collaboration with W.H. Wilde). His critical writing includes *Modern American Poetry* (1935), *Six Australian Poets* (1942), *The Misfortunes of Henry Handel Richardson* (1957), *Mary Gilmore: A Tribute* (1965, with others), and *Social Patterns in Australian Literature* (1971).

Moore's poetry, largely of love and war, appeals because of its attractive imagery, its spontaneity of feeling, whether of joy in loving or anger at the plight of a war-torn world, and its sprinkling of Australian symbols to explain and illustrate universal attitudes. His valuable contribution as a pioneer teacher of Australian literature and as one of its earliest scholarly critics was recognised when he was made OBE in 1958.

MOORE, William (1868–1937), born Bendigo, Victoria, was art and drama critic for the Melbourne *Herald* and later for the Sydney *Daily Telegraph*. His interest in the theatre led to the presentation of four 'Australian drama nights' which ran in Melbourne 1909–12. During these informal drama sessions Moore staged several one-acters of his own as well as plays by Louis Esson, Katharine Susannah Prichard and others. He combined with the Melbourne Repertory Theatre for the third drama night in 1911 and this group continued the staging of Australian plays after Moore's drama nights ceased. One of Moore's one-act plays, *The Tea-Room Girl*, was published in 1910 and he also edited, with T. Inglis Moore, *Best Australian One-Act*

Plays (1937). His major achievement was *The Story of Australian Art* (1934); he also published two semi-fictional works, *City Sketches* (1905) and *Studio Sketches* (1906). He was married to Dora Wilcox.

MOOREHEAD, Alan (1910–83), born Melbourne, was educated at the University of Melbourne, where he edited the *Melbourne University Magazine*. He subsequently worked for five years for the Melbourne *Herald*, before leaving Australia for Europe in 1936. In London he joined the *Daily Express*, was sent to Gibraltar in 1937 and in 1940 to the Middle East, where he soon established himself as the outstanding correspondent of the North African war. His three books about the war in Africa, *Mediterranean Front* (1941), *A Year of Battle* (1943) and *The End in Africa* (1943), republished together titled *African Trilogy* in 1944, proved highly popular; the trilogy was also published in an abridged version, *The Desert War* (1965). His other significant war book is *Eclipse* (1945). In 1946 Moorehead retired from active journalism to write full-time and lived mainly in Italy. His other books include biographies of Winston Churchill (1955 and 1960) and General Montgomery (1946); historical narratives, *The Traitors* (1952), *Gallipoli* (1956), *The Russian Revolution* (1958), *The White Nile* (1960), *The Blue Nile* (1962), *Cooper's Creek: The Real Story of Burke and Wills* (1963), *The Fatal Impact: An Account of the Invasion of the South Pacific 1767–1840* (1966) and *Darwin and the Beagle* (1969); travel documentaries, *Rum Jungle* (1953), *The Villa Diana* (1951) and *No Room in the Ark* (1959); two novels, *The Rage of the Vulture* (1948), which was produced as an American film titled *Thunder in the East*, and *A Summer Night* (1954); and an autobiography, *A Late Education* (1970). Awards won by Moorehead include the 1956 *Sunday Times* Book Prize, the Duff Cooper Memorial Award (for *Gallipoli*) and the Royal Society of Literature Award (for *Cooper's Creek*). He was made CBE in 1968 and AO in 1978. A biography by Tom Pocock, *Alan Moorehead*, was published in 1990.

MOORHEAD, Finola (1947–) grew up in Mornington, Victoria, and was educated at the University of Tasmania, before working as a teacher for four years. She became a full-time writer in 1973. She has contributed short stories to periodicals and to such anthologies as *Room to Move* (1985), *The Best of the Ear* (1985), *Difference* (1985), *Frictions* (1982) and *The True Story . . .* (1981); has published a collection of prose, *Quilt* (1985) and a manifesto, *A Handwritten Modern Classic* (1987); and two novels, *Remember the Tarantella* (1987) and *Still Murder* (1991), which won the 1991 Victorian Premier's Award for fiction. Moorhead has also directed and written plays including 'Stud' (1973), 'Edges' (1977), and 'It Might as Well be Loneliness'. A selection of short stories, poems, autobiographical fragments and reflections on the writing process and the special challenges facing the woman writer, *Quilt* is a feminist collage which celebrates the capacities of contemporary women writers and the 'richness of the female heritage in terms of strength, endurance and various forms of oppression'. A complex novel, begun in response to a challenge from Christina Stead to write an interesting novel 'with no men in it at all', *Remember the Tarantella* interweaves strands of plot and theme in a non-linear form; as Moorhead's epigraph warns, the reader must be willing to go 'astray', entering 'the mosaic of chipped experiences, employing the wings of dream'. In quest of an 'everywoman' figure contrary to the 'sorry women' in much feminist writing 'who were not in control of their own downfall', Moorhead opted for a large group of women protagonists: 'the singular does not compute when one investigates the nature of the feminine'. Temporarily united in a range of social and political groupings and more permanently within the novel's formal patterns in that they represent every letter of the alphabet, the female characters are presented as responding as dancers to their shifting destinies in a fluid pattern which moves in time from 1980 to 1981 and in place from Europe to South and North America, to Afghanistan and back to Australia. At the centre of the web, in so far as it has a centre, is the author's alter ego, the taxi-driver/writer Iona, who observes rather than orchestrates some of the patterns; she is accompanied by further vowel characters, Arachne, Etama, Oona and Ursula, who contribute to the spiral structure and interact with the other consonant characters in the novel's comprehensive A–Z inclusiveness; a novel of ideas, which recalls literary precedents such as Joyce's *Ulysses* as boldly as it utilises astrology, numerology, geometry, tarot and myth, *Remember the Tarantella* also highlights the process of writing, frequently shifting point of view, tone and style and drawing on multiple genres. An intricately worked psychological murder mystery, which subverts the genre while using its strategies, *Still Murder* makes the initial crime symbol and symptom of a society that is intrinsically and incorrigibly violent. A crime, which seems to begin with the discovery of a body in a suburban park, and is the subject of an investigation by an ambitious young detective gradually emerges as part of a chain of violence initiated by the rape of a young Asian girl in Vietnam. Examining the murder from the partial, fragmentary points of view of a number of people involved, Moorhead allows Detective Constable Margot Gorman a major role; after she is detailed with minimal information to guard a female inmate of a psychiatric ward, she is progressively enabled to piece the jigsaw together, although she is less privy to the whole story than the reader. Meanwhile she moves from a confident professional stance to one which includes greater understanding of both herself and her society. Subverting the consolatory ending of the 'whodunnit' which 'solves' the crime by a process of rational deduction and formal investigation, *Still Murder* indicts the violent act as part of a entrenched system of oppression founded in traditional male patterns of behaviour, in which the police themselves are deeply implicated.

MOORHOUSE, Frank (1938–   ), born Nowra on the south coast of NSW, was a cadet journalist on the Sydney *Daily Telegraph* and then worked on country newspapers before returning to Sydney to edit the *Australian Worker* in 1963 and to become an organiser for the WEA. Subsequently he edited *City Voices*, an inner-city newspaper modelled on New York's *Village Voice*, and was a union organiser for the AJA; his active interest in the welfare of writers in Australia has also included a stint as president of the ASA and involvement in a test case aimed at winning income for authors whose work had been photocopied in educational institutions. In 1957 Moorhouse's first story was published in *Southerly*, but in the 1960s he found it difficult, partly because of the explicitness of his fiction, to have work accepted by the established literary quarterlies. He found his outlets instead in smaller publications, often on the radical fringe, and in men's magazines; a publisher of the latter brought out his first collection of stories, *Futility and Other Animals* (1969). The appearance in 1972 of *The Americans, Baby* (q.v.) established Moorhouse's reputation as a leading exponent of short fiction in Australia, a reputation that has been confirmed by his later collections, *The Electrical Experience* (q.v., 1974), *Conference-ville* (q.v., 1976), *Tales of Mystery and Romance* (1977), *The Everlasting Secret Family and Other Secrets* (q.v., 1980), *Room Service* (1985), *Forty-Seventeen* (1988) and *Lateshows* (1990). A *Selected Stories* was published in 1982, republished in 1985 as *The Coca Cola Kid*. In 1993 Moorhouse took a fresh direction with the publication of his historical novel *Grand Days*, a study of the League of Nations and the work of the idealistic Edith Campbell Berry; written in a realist genre, reminiscent of Stendhal and Zola, the novel explores the ways in which a large, complex bureaucracy was used to further initiatives for world peace. It won the 1994 SA Festival Award for fiction. Co-founder in 1972 of the alternative fiction magazine *Tabloid Story* (q.v.), Moorhouse edited the last issue of *Coast to Coast* (1973), the anthologies of contemporary short fiction, *The State of the Art* (1983) and *Fictions* (1988), and a selected edition of 'Steele Rudd's' stories in 1987. His other work includes screenplays, for the film *Between Wars* (1974) and for short films of two stories from *The Americans, Baby*, 'The Girl from the Family of Man' (1969) and 'The Machine Gun' (1971) as well as 'The Girl Who Met Simone de Beauvoir in Paris' (1980), and *The Everlasting Secret Family* (1988); and columns and contributions written for the *Bulletin*. Some of the *Bulletin* material is included in *Days of Wine and Rage* (1980), a 1970s retrospective edited and dominated by Moorhouse. The influence of journalism in his fiction can be seen not only in the catchy titles and clipped prose style of the stories but also in the use of some of the techniques of American 'new journalism', notably a scene-by-scene method of construction and an extensive use of realistic dialogue. Another influence which emerges in his fiction is the Andersonianism (see Anderson, John) of the Libertarian Society circles in which Moorhouse moved in Sydney, which includes a belief in enquiry, a rejection of absolutes, and suspicion of political and other enclosing systems.

Moorhouse has been widely identified as a Balmain (q.v.) writer; the label derives from the congregation of intellectually oriented, politically radical, sexually experimental writers, artists and academics who gathered there from the late 1960s. The link with Balmain is strongest in *The Americans, Baby* and *Tales of Mystery and Romance* and evocatively recalled in *Days of Wine and Rage*, but is not as important as his innovative narrative method: the 'discontinuous narrative', a phrase which forms the subtitle of *Futility and Other Animals, The Americans, Baby* and *The Electrical Experience* and remains an important element in the later collections. As Moorhouse has described it, once he got beyond the apprentice stage

> and was starting to write stories which (looking back on it) were departures from the essentially social realist type story of the time, I found . . . that the stories were clustering. I wasn't writing a novel, but one story suggested the next. I was writing about one locality or one group of people, and even though the connections were often oblique, tangential, and at first not altogether perceived by me, they were real and growing.

The tension between connection and fragmentation, implied in the paradoxical word 'discontinuous', is a distinctive feature of the narrative form, which has its parallels, although Moorhouse was not specifically influenced by these writers, in the stories of Henry Lawson, Judah Waten and J.D. Salinger. Although individual Moorhouse volumes focus on particular localities and groups, e.g. the 'urban tribe' of *Futility and Other Animals*, T. George McDowell's country town world in *The Electrical Experience*, and the 'academic rodeo' of *Conference-ville*, there are enriching connections within and between the collections, e.g. incidents alluded to in one story become the focus of another, or characters appear and reappear. Thus Cindy Braughtin ages from a university student in *Futility and Other Animals* to a history lecturer in *The Everlasting Secret Family*, and is a character in *The Americans, Baby* and *Conference-ville*. Yet the links between Moorhouse's narratives have been recognised as molecular rather than linear and the sense of elusiveness and fragmentation is reinforced by the piecemeal way a reader is forced, as a result of the organisation of the stories and the variation in point of view, to put together the history of individual characters who flit in and out of focus. It is also reinforced by the astringent prose style, with its emphasis on discrete paragraphs; by the inclusion of fragments as well as stories in some collections; and even by the physical make-up of the books.

The effect of discontinuity is to sharpen the reader's awareness of uncertainty and ambiguity, an ambiguity which encompasses not only the formal characteristics of the stories but also the extent to which they are autobiographical and historical, and the links between Moorhouse himself and his various and increasingly self-conscious authorial voices. Moorhouse's *raison d'être* for his choice of form is that it corresponds to experience. Much of his fiction, focused on subcultural, submerged groups, emphasises change and the resulting social and personal tensions. Thus the 'central dilemma' of the members of the urban tribe in *Futility and Other Animals* is 'of giving birth, of creating new life': they leave home, move to the city,

experience sexual liberation, try to overcome the sense of futility that accompanies their loss of equilibrium. *The Americans, Baby*, which like *Futility and Other Animals* is rapidly acquiring the status of a historical chronicle of the late 1960s and early 1970s, explores the ineffectiveness of political activism and the way sex can act as a destabilising force, fragmenting personality. The title of *The Americans, Baby* is a reference to the Americanisation of Australian society that many commentators have noticed. The American influence is important also in *The Electrical Experience*, which focuses on the generation gap between T. George McDowell, a south-coast soft drinks manufacturer who, influenced by his visit to a Rotary convention in America, has tried to create order and shape to his existence, and his neurotic daughter Terri, who emerges in *The Americans, Baby* as 'unstable as jazz'. The ironic family motif recurs in *Tales of Mystery and Romance*, which contrasts the narrator's past conventional, coherent world with his present unattained hopes centred on Milton, the academic friend who has rejected him; and in *The Everlasting Secret Family*, in which the four sections are linked by the secrets, most of them relating to sexuality, which are shared with the reader in each.

The process of living can be seen to produce uncertainty, ambiguity, even chaos in the lives of Moorhouse's characters; freedom, it seems to be increasingly implied, comes from spontaneity and impulse, from accepting the fragmentations and discontinuities of a changing world. Not to do so is to risk becoming as lifeless as Hugo and the unnamed history lecturer in *The Americans, Baby*. Both pride themselves on the order and shape to their existence yet Hugo's relentless self-sufficiency (he even makes his own soap) becomes terrifyingly claustrophobic for anyone he comes in contact with; similarly, the history lecturer, who tries to arrive at a formula for living in the story, 'Will power + natural sex-drive + intelligence + personal organisation + aggression = sexual success' (*Futility and Other Animals*) is reduced in 'Letters to Twiggy' (*The Americans, Baby*) to pouring out obscenities when his obsession with forming a relationship with the pop star Twiggy is thwarted by the response of a series of identical form letters. The emphasis on a flexible attitude towards life's ambiguities has led some commentators to see Moorhouse's fictional world as profoundly pessimistic and fundamentally pointless. Something of that pointlessness is obvious in the François Blase stories of the 1985 collection *Room Service*, which is subtitled *Comic Writings of Frank Moorhouse*. Blase, Moorhouse's alter ego, is an incessant traveller of the world (courtesy of an extraordinarily generous editor) sending back accounts of his endeavours. This is the world of international hotels, expensive restaurants, hired Mercedes and 'cultural delegates' like Blase for whom this environment becomes their cocoon. Blase (Moorhouse) is seen by one critic (Tom Thompson) as 'Les Patterson gone semiological'. There are other stories in *Room Service* that have appeared previously and been revised for this book. The section 'Oral History of A Childhood' begins with 'Mechanical Aptitude', wherein a frustrated father becomes impatient with his mechanically incompetent son and goes on to recount the ritual torments and pleasures of schooldays.

Forty-Seventeen brings the narrator Ian to the verge of middle age and the hazards posed by that to sexuality and other hedonistic pursuits. Most of these previously unpublished stories are linked by memory, by conversation, by recurring characters and by family history into a less 'discontinuous narrative' than usual. Ian, the archetypal bush-bred, masculine-oriented Australian is at the crossroads and, growing intensely neurotic, is attempting to establish some meaningful philosophy that may assuage the doubts that will inevitably become certainties. The 'Seventeen' applies to his ex-wife Robyn (17 when he married her) dying of cancer and his present girl-friend, also 17. As usual with Moorhouse Australian life and culture are both affectionately and ruthlessly exposed.

Lateshows, a collection of short prose pieces, has three sections, The Club: 'Contemporary Protocol', full of whimsical, deft, comic anecdotes; The Movie, 'Working with Makavejev', an account of the project of turning his stories into the long-delayed film *The Coca Cola Kid*; and The Cabaret, 'The Cabaret Voltaire', much of which is a sequence of increasingly frenetic monologues by last year's disastrous panel chairman at the Arts Festival trying to gain himself a place at the next one. In depicting as he does some of the absurdities of intellectual and cultural life in Australia, Moorhouse joins that long line of Australian humorists typified by Ross Campbell, Barry Humphries, Clive James and Max Gillies. Among the many awards he has won for his fiction are the NBC Banjo Award in 1975, Awgie Award 1984, *Age* Book of the Year Award 1988, UK *Blitz* Magazine Book of the Year for 1988 and the ALS Gold Medal 1989 (the last three for *Forty-Seventeen*). He was made AM in 1985.

MORAN, Herbert Michael (1885–1945), a distinguished cancer specialist and outstanding rugby union player, was born in Sydney, educated at the universities of Sydney and Edinburgh and served in the First World War. He subsequently worked in Italy, Abyssinia and England, occasionally returning to Australia. He published three mainly autobiographical books, *Viewless Winds* (1939), *Beyond the Hill Lies China* (1945) and *In My Fashion* (1946). The first and last of them demonstrate his keen but sardonic wit and his strong, trenchant opinions, especially on such topics as the medical, academic and religious professions. *Beyond the Hill Lies China*, the most fictionalised of his books, includes a portrait of C.J. Brennan as Charles Maginn.

MORAN, Patrick Francis (1830–1911), born Ireland and educated at the Irish College in Rome, was ordained in 1853, established a distinguished reputation as academic and ecclesiastic and became archbishop of Sydney in 1884; he was created cardinal in 1885. In Australia he established several orphanages, hospitals, schools and churches, as well as two seminaries and was particularly active in the field of education. In secular affairs he proved to be a strong supporter of the Labor Party and a powerful advocate of Federation. He published a *History of the Catholic Church in Australasia* (1895), a work of extensive research. Vance Palmer includes an account of Moran in his *National Portraits* (1940) and his career is also described in J.G. Murtagh's *Australia, the Catholic Chapter* (1946), Patrick Ford's *Cardinal Moran and the A.L.P.* (1966) and Patrick O'Farrell's *The Catholic Church and Community in Australia* (1977), and *The Irish in Australia* (1986).

MORANT, Harry Harbord (?Edwin Henry Murrant) (?1864–1902), whose death by firing-squad at Pretoria, South Africa, 27 February 1902 provoked one of the most prolonged controversies in Australian military history, was a minor balladist of the 1890s. His origins are somewhat uncertain. By his own account he was born at Bideford, Devon, in 1865, son of Admiral Sir Digby Morant. Subsequent research (*In Search of Breaker Morant, Balladist, and Bushveldt Carbineer* by Margaret Carnegie and Frank Shields, 1979) strongly suggests that he was Edwin Henry Murrant, born at Bridgwater, Somerset, 9 December 1864, son of Edwin Murrant and his wife Catherine, née Riely; that he sailed for Australia from Plymouth 1 April 1883; that he landed in Townsville in northern Queensland in June 1883; that he took a job with a travelling rodeo and ended up in Charters Towers where, on 13 March 1884 he married a Daisy May O'Dwyer who was later to become the well-known Australian identity Daisy Bates. The marriage supposedly lasted a few brief weeks, Morant, by which name he was known in April 1884 according to Charters Towers court records, taking off on a nomadic life of droving and horse-breaking. His skill and daring as a horse-breaker and rider led to his nickname 'The Breaker'. He developed a widespread reputation for riotous and unpredictable behaviour, but his horsemanship, swagger, poetry, and cheerful nature generally won him more friends than enemies. He enlisted in the SA Mounted Rifles to get to the Boer War and ultimately joined the Bushveldt Carbineers, dubbed 'the Buccaneers', a cavalry regiment especially formed to combat the Boer commandos. After the death and mutilation of his close friend Captain Hunt at the hands of the Boers, Morant was court-martialled with several others for the murder of some Boer prisoners and a German missionary, and executed with another Australian, P.J. Handcock. Morant and his associates, although almost certainly guilty of the charges against them, came to be regarded by many as pawns in the game of war and politics sacrificed by Kitchener to appease the German government or expended in an effort to secure a cease-fire in the war.

Although Morant's literary talent was meagre, the bizarre circumstances of his life and death have added piquancy to the public image of him as a poet. His first verses, 'A Night Thought', signed by 'The Breaker', were published in the *Bulletin* in 1891. During the next ten years he wrote about sixty poems for the *Bulletin* with occasional contributions to the Sydney *World News* and the *Windsor and Richmond Gazette*. Best known of his verses are 'Since the Country Carried Sheep', 'West by North Again', 'Who's Riding Old Harlequin Now?', 'Stewed' and 'Beyond His Jurisdiction'; 'Butchered to Make a Dutchman's Holiday', written in Pretoria Gaol on the eve of his execution, was featured on the *Bulletin* Red Page 19 April 1902. *The Poetry of 'Breaker' Morant: from the Bulletin 1891–1903* was published in 1980 with a foreword by David McNicoll. Although Morant did not publish a volume of verse, selections of his work are included in some of the books that have been written about him. He was one of the multitude of 'back-block bards' of the 1890s; his verse is lively, breezy, and entertaining, and conveys in an ebullient, rough-and-ready fashion both the flavour of outback life and the laconically humorous, devil-may-care attitude of the Australian bushman of legend. A notable Australian film, *Breaker Morant*, focusing on the events in South Africa, was released in 1980. Paintings by Pro Hart illustrated a Breaker Morant series which was compiled by Dawn Ross and published in 1981. Kit Denton, who wrote *The Breaker* (1973), a fictionalised account of Morant's exploits, has reversed his attitude to his subject in *Closed File* (1983), where Morant is assessed as a vicious, amoral type. Other works on Morant include F.M. Cutlack's *Breaker Morant* (1962), Frank Fox's *Bushman and Buccaneer, Harry Morant* (1902) and George R. Witton's *Scapegoats of the Empire* (1907), Witton being one of the Bushveldt Carbineers who was imprisoned with Morant and later released from an English prison.

'MORDAUNT, Elinor/Elenor' (Evelyn Mary Clowes) (1872–1942), born Nottinghamshire, England, came to Australia in 1902 and remained for nine years. Some of her contributions to the *Bulletin* and *Lone Hand* were published as *Rosemary, That's for Remembrance* (1909); her first fictional work, *The Garden of Contentment*, was published in 1901. Her impressions of Victoria are recorded in *On the Wallaby through Victoria* (1911). In later years she wrote prolifically: over thirty novels and books of short fiction, several accounts of her extensive travels in many out-of-the-way places, and an autobiographical work, *Sinabada* (1937). Of her novels, *A Ship of Solace* (1911), which describes her voyage to Melbourne in 1902, *Lu of the Ranges* (1913), *The Pendulum* (1918), *The Dark Fire* (1927) and *The Real Sally* (1925) have some Australian background.

MORELL, Musette (Moyra Martin) (1898–1950) wrote various plays for radio, including *Webs of Our Weaving, The Better Road* and *Even the Birds of the Air*, published in 1948 under the title *Three Radio Plays.* Her other plays include 'His Gentle Art of Making Enemies' (a study of James Whistler), 'The World His Oyster' (about Alexandre Dumas), 'Brolgah the Beautiful', and *The Quick and the Dead* (in *Australian Writers' Annual*, 1936). Two popular animal serials for children, broadcast on ABC radio, were published as books, *The Antics of Algy* (1946) and *Bush Cobbers* (1948); she also published two collections of plays for children, *Australian Youth Plays* (1948) and *Ten Puppet Plays* (1950).

MORGAN, Daniel (1830–65), born Campbelltown, NSW, a bushranger who took the name of the pirate Morgan, was the son of Sydney prostitute Kate Owen and cabbage-seller 'Gypsy' Fuller. Notoriously cruel and probably insane, Morgan was the model for the evil, snake-eyed Moran in 'Rolf Boldrewood's' *Robbery Under Arms* (1888) and is the subject of Edward Harrington's ballad 'Morgan', Francis Webb's poem 'Morgan's Country', and the Australian film *Mad Dog Morgan* (1976). Morgan is the subject of a novel by Will Lawson, *Red Morgan Rides* (1940), and of two biographies, Margaret Carnegie's *Morgan: the Bold Bushranger* (1974) and Edgar F. Penzig's *Morgan the Murderer* (1989).

MORGAN, Gail (1953–), born Sydney, graduated MA in English from the University of Sydney and has combined a career as a writer with teaching English as a foreign language. She has lived and worked in Central Australia and New Guinea (and has used them as the setting for two of her novels) as well as England and France. She has written poetry and plays; published three novels, *Promise of Rain* (1985), *Walk to Kulentufu* (1988), and *Patent Lies* (1993); and a fantasy, *The Day My Publisher Turned into a Dog* (1989). *Promise of Rain* takes Lucy Stapleton from her primary schooldays with the nuns at Five Dock, an inner Sydney suburb, to Alice Springs, where she teaches an adult literature class and falls in love with Titus Hayes, a part-Aborigine. The racist White Alice Springs community exacts its vengeance on them, attempting to lynch Titus for a rape he did not commit and bringing home to Lucy the virtual impossibility of a life together for them. Deftly drawn characters are the old Irish nun from the early part of the novel, Mother de Bosco, and the full-blood Aboriginal woman Esther (the mother of Titus), from the latter part. *Walk to Kulentufu* begins in Bondi and later moves to the Sepik country of New Guinea. The Polish immigrant Wojtek becomes involved with Anne Shanahan who deals in native artefacts. In the village of Kulentufu, where Anne hopes to start a trout hatchery, the difficult, irascible Pole insults a native leader by touching his wife. The ritual killing that follows claims Anne, who offers herself in place of Wojtek. *The Day My Publisher Turned into a Dog* is a highly entertaining satirical tilt at publishers, written from the viewpoint of the struggling writer, one Jane Hardacre, who wishes to make the transition from saga to serious writer. Sometimes gentle, sometimes steel-toed, the satire is amusing and well-directed. *Patent Lies* interleaves contemporary interpretations of a 'lost' journal of Captain James Cook (q.v.) on the part of five diverse individuals with extracts from the journal itself.

MORGAN, John (?1792–1866), born near Portsmouth, England, served with the royal marines before coming to the Swan River settlement in 1828. At Perth he served as magistrate, justice of the peace and barracks master and in 1834 took up a police magistracy in Van Diemen's Land. Three years later he tried farming and then journalism. Foundation editor of the *Hobart Town Advertiser* (1839), he also established the *Tasmanian Weekly Dispatch* (1839–41) and edited the *Morning Advertiser* (1841) and the *Britannia and Trades' Advocate* (1846–51). Before coming to Australia, Morgan published in 1824 *The Emigrant's Note Book and Guide*; he also collaborated with William Buckley in *The Life and Adventures of William Buckley* (1852).

MORGAN, Mal (1936–), of Polish-Jewish extraction, was born in England and came to Australia at the age of 12. Now a pharmacist at Melbourne Royal Children's Hospital, he was one of the 'underground' poets of the late 1960s 'New Poetry' revolution in Australia, attending poetry readings at La Mama run by Kris Hemensley and Michael Dugan in 1969 and involved with the small poetry magazine explosion – *Crosscurrents*, *Our Glass*, *Great Auk*, *Flagstones*, *Free Poetry*, *Parachute*, *Mindscape* – of those years. Seldom included in the early 'New Australian Poetry' anthologies, Morgan has in recent years become a well-known 'performance' poet; he convened La Mama Poetica poetry readings 1985–91 and edited the anthology *La Mama Poetica* (1989), has directed the Montsalvat National Poetry Festivals, and organises regular readings, frequently performing his own work. His publications include *Poemstones* (1976), *Statues Don't Bleed* (1984), *A Handshake with the Moon* (1987) and *Once Father and God* (1992). His poetry communicates a concern for humanity, anger at such evils as racism and delight in satirising pretentiousness and hypocrisy. For Morgan, love is the greatest worker for good. Most of his poems are brief, pointed and questioning, self-consciously Jewish in their irony and wry wisdom.

MORGAN, Sally (1951–), born Perth, WA, grew up there as Sally Milroy. Her mother Gladys was part-Aboriginal, her father a White returned soldier who had been a POW and who committed suicide when Sally was 9. She and her four brothers and sisters were raised by Gladys and Nan (Daisy), their grandmother who was also part-Aboriginal. Morgan graduated BA from the University of WA and WAIT, majoring in psychology. Her publications include the celebrated autobiography *My Place* (1987); the biography *Wanamurraganya* (1989); *The Flying Emu and Other Australian Stories* (1991, a collection of Aboriginal tales and legends); and *Sistergirl* (1992, a play that has been widely performed). She is also an accomplished artist, whose paintings are included in several important collections including the Australian National Gallery in Canberra, and have been particularly successful in the USA. In 1993 her print *Outback* appeared on a UN stamp, one of thirty paintings and sculptures chosen by an international panel of art historians to illustrate each article of the Universal Declaration of Human Rights. She won the FAW Patricia Weickhardt Award in 1988, the Order of Australia Association Book Prize in 1988, and the Human Rights and Equal Opportunities Award of 1987, all three for *My Place*.

She again won the Human Rights Award for 1989 for *Wanamurraganya*.

My Place begins as a warm, conventional account of Sally's early childhood years in a household dominated by the alcoholism and unpredictable behaviour of her father. Her mother Glad and grandmother Nan (Daisy) combine to rear the children, attempting to disguise their Aboriginality by claiming they are of Indian origin. After Glad's admission of their Aboriginal background the nature of the book changes, the emphasis turning from Sally herself to the histories of her mother and grandmother. More information is disclosed when Sally's great-uncle Arthur (Daisy's brother) appears. Arthur and Daisy were born on Corunna Downs Station near Marble Bar, owned by the Drake-Brockman family in the 1890s, the offspring of a full-blood Aboriginal woman and a White man. As all children of Aboriginal women and White men were taken away from the mother to be raised, Daisy later went to Perth as a servant in the Drake-Brockman household and her daughter Gladys to the Parkerville Children's Home. Uncompromising in her efforts to get at the truth of her background and to fully trace her family history, Sally and her mother travelled to the Corunna Downs area. Both Gladys and then Nan felt compelled by that journey and its emotional impact to elaborate the painful history of all that had happened in their lives. From it all Sally Morgan finally came to understand her 'place'. The true importance of *My Place* is that it contains a story, the essence of which was repeated countless thousands of times in the early part of this century. Much more effectively and poignantly than a myriad historical studies and documentary accounts, the simple but anguished stories of Daisy, Arthur and Gladys Corunna have exposed the reality of White racism in Australia. An extraordinarily successful book, which is humorous, sad, painful and deeply poignant, *My Place* has sold more than half a million copies.

Sally Morgan combined with Jack McPhee, a contemporary of her grandmother, and her own tribal grandfather, to write an account of McPhee's life, *Wanamurraganya*. Her play *Sistergirl* links two old women, the alcoholic Aboriginal Rosy and her White counterpart, Irishwoman Miss Murphy, who are in hospital together, both 'drying out' from their recurrent bouts of drinking. Delys Bird and Dennis Haskell edited (1992) a collection of critical essays titled *Whose Place?: A Study of Sally Morgan's My Place*.

MORPHETT, Tony (1938–), born Sydney, worked for the ABC as an interviewer and reporter, before he became a freelance writer for radio and television. One of the best-known writers for ABC television, and the author of the popular series *Dynasty*, he originated the series *Certain Women* and contributed to *The Sullivans*, *Ben Hall*, *Against the Wind* and *Seven Ages*. He has won numerous television awards including two Awgies for best script of the year (in 1973 and 1979). He has also written stage plays, one of which, *I've Come about the Assassination*, is included in Eunice Hanger's anthology *Six One-Act Plays* (1970); and four novels, *Mayor's Nest* (1964), a lively satire in which the mayor of Parramatta becomes dictator of Australia; *Fitzgerald* (1965); *Dynasty* (1967), a family boardroom drama which became the basis of his television series; and *Thorskald* (1969), a multifaceted study of an Australian artist. He has also written *A Hole in My Ceiling* (1985), a collection of addresses on his Christian faith, and two books for young readers, *Quest Beyond Time* (1985), based on his television script of the same title, and *The Distant Home* (1993).

MORRIS, E.E. (Edward Ellis) (1843–1902), born Madras, India, was educated at Rugby and Oxford, and in 1875 came to Australia to take up the position of headmaster of the Melbourne Church of England Grammar School. In 1883 he was appointed professor of English, French and German languages and literature at the University of Melbourne, a position he held until his death. He published an important, pioneering work on Australian English (q.v.), *Austral English* (1898), and a biography of his father-in-law George Higinbotham, chief justice of Victoria (1895). He also edited *Cassell's Picturesque Australasia* (1887–89).

'MORRIS, Julian', see **WEST, Morris**

MORRIS, Meaghan (1950–   ) was educated at the University of Sydney and in Paris. A full-time writer who has worked as a professional critic and lectured in art and media studies, she is one of the most influential feminists, especially in interpreting French feminist post-structuralist theory and in promoting interdisciplinary post-modernist studies both within the academy and between it and other cultural groups. She has published *The Pirate's Fiancée: Feminism, Reading, Post-modernism* (1988), a collection of essays ranging from photography to Paul Hogan to deconstruction, and from cinema to Mary Daly, Susan Sontag and Jean Baudrillard; and *Ecstasy and Economics: American Essays for John Forbes* (1992), essays which take two poems by John Forbes as starting-points for reading both the beach and the politician Paul Keating as cultural sites reflecting a new diversity. Morris has also edited two collections of essays, with Paul Foss, *Language, Sexuality & Subversion* (1978), and with John Frow, *Australian Cultural Studies* (1993).

MORRIS, Myra (1893–1966), born Boort, Victoria, was brought up in the Mallee district. A freelance writer, she published verse, short stories and articles in newspapers and magazines. Her collections of verse include *England and Other Verses* (1918) and *White Magic* (1929). She also published a collection of short stories, *The Township* (1947); two novels, *The Wind on the Water* (1938) and *Dark Tumult* (1939); a novel for children, *Us Five* (1922); and edited the selected poems of 'Capel Boake' (1949). Morris's simple, rhythmic, ballad-style verses, which exuberantly reflect her love of the outdoor life, found a ready acceptance in the 1920s and 1930s. As a novelist she competently handles narrative and character, revealing a keen insight into the difficulties faced by women in inadequate marital relationships. But her talents for domestic realism and naturalistic description, especially of rural environments, are best suited to the short story.

MORRISON, A.A. (Alistair Ardoch) (1911–   ), born Melbourne, the brother of R.H. Morrison (q.v.), worked as an artist and graphic designer, mainly in Sydney, before becoming a full-time painter. As Professor 'Afferbeck Lauder', Professor of Strine (q.v.) studies at the University of Sinny, he published several 'papers' on strine in the *Sydney Morning Herald* in 1965. Some of these were subsequently republished in his books *Let Stalk Strine* (1965) and *Nose Tone Unturned* (1966), both illustrated by 'Al Terego'. He has also published compilations of Knightsbridge English for the uninitiated, *Fraffly Well Spoken* (1968) and *Fraffly Suite* (1969); a compendium, *Fraffly Strine Everything* (1969); and, under the name Alistair Morrison, a comic miscellany, *The Scrambled Egghead* (1971).

MORRISON, G.E. (George Ernest) (1862–1920), journalist, doctor and expert on Chinese affairs, often referred to as 'Chinese Morrison', was born at Geelong College, where his father was principal. He began a medical course at the University of Melbourne but failed his exams and travelled for a period in the South Seas, contributing influential articles to the *Age* on the evils of the Kanaka trade. Sent to New Guinea as correspondent for the *Age* in 1883, he succeeded in penetrating well into the hinterland but was seriously wounded by natives. He went to Edinburgh for treatment and continued his medical studies there, graduating in 1887. After some further travel, he left for China in 1893. In *An Australian in China* (1895) he describes his hundred-day journey from Shanghai to Rangoon in 1894, made with very little money and little knowledge of Chinese. Appointed special correspondent for the London *Times* in the Far East in 1895, he travelled widely in China, Thailand and Manchuria, providing the *Times* with accurate and often anticipatory reports of the country's troubled affairs and relations with Russia and Japan; in 1897 he became the first permanent correspondent of the *Times* in Peking. He resigned from that position in 1912 to become political adviser to the new Chinese government. Several biographies have been written, including Frank Clune's *Chinese Morrison* (1941), W.A. Morrison's *Ernest Morrison* (1962) and Cyril Pearl's *Morrison of Peking* (1967); A.B. Paterson included an account of his life in *Happy Dispatches* (1934). A two-volume edition of his correspondence, edited by Lo Hui-Min, was published 1976–78.

MORRISON, John (1904–   ), born Sunderland, England, migrated to Australia in 1923. A member of the Realist Writers Group, Morrison first published his short stories in trade union magazines. His published works include novels, *The Creeping City* (1949) and *Port of Call* (1950); collections of short stories, *Sailors Belong Ships* (1947), *Black Cargo* (1955), *Twenty-Three* (1962), and *John Morrison, Selected Stories* (1972), selected by Ian Reid). Penguin later reprinted most of his stories in three volumes, *North Wind* (1982), *Stories of the Waterfront* (1984, illuminating his experiences on the Melbourne waterfront in the 1930s and 1940s) and *This Freedom* (1985). A further selected volume, *The Best Stories of John Morrison*, was published in 1988. Morrison also published a collection of memoirs and reflective essays, *Australian By Choice* (1973) and the partly autobiographical *The Happy Warrior* (1987) which also contains his assessment of writers such as Alan Marshall, Judah Waten, Vance Palmer and himself. Translations of his stories, either singly or in collections, have been published in numerous countries, including China, Japan, Poland and the former Soviet Union. He was awarded the Gold Medal of the Australian Literature Society for *Twenty-Three* and in 1986 received the Patrick White Award. He is a Member of the Order of Australia.

Although Morrison's socialist convictions are reflected in his choice of subjects and his naturalistic mode, he is an undogmatic, sensitive observer. Restricted to a narrow span of action and unexceptional individuals, his short stories characteristically record a particular, frequently undramatic, human situation, such as a family argument, a chance meeting in the bush, an interchange between passengers in a halted railway carriage, a conflict between a worker and his employer. Recurrent themes include isolation, whether imposed by psychological or physical conditions, and the destructive power of possessions or possessive attitudes. 'The Man on the 'Bidgee', 'Pioneers' and 'Goyai' are particularly striking studies of the former, 'It Opens Your Eyes', 'This Freedom' and 'Morning Glory' of the latter. Of his more extended narratives, 'The Battle of Flowers' describes an absurd but implacable and destructive struggle between two sisters to worst each other at their hobby of gardening; 'To Margaret' is a delicate study of young love opposed to middle-aged possessiveness; 'Black Night in Collingwood', a particularly popular story, deals with the impact of football on a typical Melbourne family. Morrison's range is wide but his attitude is consistent and is revealed implicitly in his novels and short stories as a belief in the simple virtues of work, loyalty and self-discipline. Although he avoids the experimental, usually preferring an uncomplicated linear progression and first-person narration by a reliable narrator, he achieves in his best narratives, such as 'Pioneers' and 'Goyai', a powerful, cumulative suggestiveness. His revealing stories of waterfront workers, mostly more documentary than fictional, are frankly partisan in their sympathies, although 'The Drunk' explores the ambivalences of the creed of mateship in a working situation. His novels, episodic in form, concentrate on a small number of characters set against a restricted environment.

MORRISON, R.H. (Robert Hay) (1915–), born South Yarra, Melbourne, the brother of Alistair Ardoch Morrison (q.v.), studied modern languages at the University of Melbourne and was employed by the army as an Italian translator during the Second World War. He worked for the ABC, mostly as a radio and television State news editor, before resigning in 1968 to pursue his interests as a poet, verse translator and literary reviewer. He has published the volumes of poetry *Lyric Images* (1954), *Opus 4* (1971), *Leaf-fall* (1974), *In the Ear of Dusk* (1977), *The Secret Greenness and Other Poems* (1978), *For the Weeks of the Year* (1981), *Poems for an Exhibition* (1985) and *Poems From My Eight Lives* (1989). His other publications include translations of Mandelstam's poetry (1990) and of Pushkin's (1951) and the more general translations *Australia's Russian Poets* (1971), *Australia's Ukrainian Poets* (1973), *Australia's Italian Poets* (1976), *One Hundred Russian Poems* (1979), *Ancient Chinese Odes* (1979) and *Sonnets from the Spanish* (1980). He has also compiled a collection of verse by South Australian poets, *A Book of South Australian Verse* (1957).

MORRISON, Sally (1946–), born Sydney, was educated in Canberra and is a scientist at the University of Melbourne. She has written a novel, *Who's Taking You to the Dance?* (1979); a collection of short stories, *I Am a Boat* (1989); and a play, 'Hag', performed at the 1976 National Playwrights Conference. Morrison's short stories reflect the difficulties of maintaining emotional relationships in post-1960s Australia and of adjusting to change. *Who's Taking You to the Dance?*, set in the last three days of a country high school in 1962, and told by a cross-section of narrators, is the story of several final-year students, their friends, parents and teachers.

MORTLOCK, J.F. (John Frederick) (1809–82), born Cambridge, England, was convicted in 1843 of attempting to murder his uncle, who he believed had defrauded him of his inheritance. He was transported for twenty-one years, arrived in Australia in 1844, and served the first part of his sentence on Norfolk Island, where he was tutor to the family of ex-Tasmanian journalist, Gilbert Robertson. In 1857 he returned to England but was arrested and transported again in 1858 to complete his sentence; he settled finally in England in 1864. Mortlock wrote more than a dozen pamphlets in which he vigorously pursued the claims to his inheritance, but his major work is the memoir, *Experiences of a Convict*, which reflects Mortlock's wide knowledge of the Australian penal settlements. It was published in five parts in 1864–65 and republished in 1965, edited by G.A. Wilkes and A.G. Mitchell. A.E. Clark-Kennedy has written a biography of Mortlock, *Cambridge to Botany Bay* (1983).

MORTON, Frank (1869–1923), born England, came to Australia at the age of 16. He spent some years in Singapore and India, where he worked as a journalist, and returned to Australia in 1894. He contributed to the *Bulletin*, the *Brisbane Courier* and the Hobart *Mercury*, before moving to NZ, where he worked for the *Otago Daily Times* and, as editor, for the monthly magazine the *Triad*. While in NZ he published a collection of verse, *Laughter and Tears: Verses of a Journalist* (1908) and two novels, *The Angel of the Earthquake* (1909) and *The Yacht of Dreams* (1911). Back in Sydney by 1914, he contributed to the *Bulletin*, the *Lone Hand*, *Native Companion*, *Bookfellow* and other journals, and became the main contributor to the Australian edition of the *Triad* 1915–23. Gregarious and broad-minded, he was a familiar host to Sydney's bohemia in the 1920s. He also published the subsequent poetry collections *Verses for Marjorie* (1916), *The Secret Spring* (1919) and *Man and the Devil: A Book of Shame and Pity* (1922).

MORTON, William Lockhart (1820–98), born Cambusnethan, Scotland, studied engineering before migrating to Australia in 1841. A hard-working and innovative pastoralist who invented the sheep dip and the swing gate for drafting sheep, Morton was handicapped by adverse circumstances and personal tragedy, as well as by his inflexible, hypersensitive and censorious personality. He was also a keen and effective explorer, who meticulously recorded his observations on his trips in northern Queensland and the Mallee and Gippsland districts of Victoria, publishing *Notes of a Recent Personal Visit to the Unoccupied Portions of Northern Queensland* (1860) and *Suggestions for the Formation of a New Settlement in Australia* (1861). Morton published a series of accounts of his experiences in *Once A Month*, 1884–86, including his encounter with the bushranger Frank Gardiner. In 1978 the accounts were published as *Adventures of a Pioneer*, edited by J.O. Randell.

MOSES, Jack (1860–1945), born Sydney, spent most of his working life as a commercial traveller in wine, and became known on the agricultural show circuit of NSW and other States both as a salesman and as a reciter of Australian ballads; *The Bulletin Book of Humorous Verses and Recitations* (1920) was dedicated to him as a 'good Australian' who was 'for many years a *Bulletin* reciter in the bush'. One of his favourite authors was Henry Lawson, who in the poem *Joseph's Dreams* (1923) refers to Moses in stating 'my best friend was a Yid'; Moses recalled their friendship in *Henry Lawson by His Mates* (1931). A long-time contributor to the *Bulletin*, the *Sydney Mail*, *Smith's Weekly* and other journals, Moses wrote *Beyond the City Gates* (1923), a volume of sketches and poems in which he celebrates bush life as the 'matrix of our Australian nation', and *Nine Miles from Gundagai* (1938), a volume of verse; the title piece is the well-known poem about the dog on the tucker box at Gundagai (q.v.). After his retirement Moses settled again in Sydney, where he was an affectionately regarded street character who distributed postcards of his poems.

Mother and Son, a three-act play by Louis Esson (q.v.), was first produced in 1923 by the Pioneer Players and was published in 1946. Set in Gippsland, it deals mainly with the relationship between a young man, Harry Lind, and his possessive mother. Harry rejects the girl his mother prefers, brings home a barmaid of dubious reputation, is rejected in turn for a rival squatter, and finally killed in a riding accident.

Mother's Offering to Her Children, A, written anonymously by 'A Lady Long Resident in New South Wales' and published in 1841, was an early Australian book written especially for children. In the form of a dialogue it contains naive and trivialised anecdotes of the Aborigines and their customs as well as stories of shipwrecks on the Australian coasts. Marcie Muir in *Charlotte Barton: Australia's First Children's Author* (1980) indicates that its author was Charlotte Barton (1797–1862) mother of the first Australian-born woman novelist, Louisa Atkinson. Charlotte Barton's second husband (her first was James Atkinson) was George Barton. The book was previously attributed to Lady Gordon Bremer. A copy of the book was sold at auction in 1991 for $17 600, a record price for a rare Australian book.

MOTHERWELL, Phil (1946–), actor and playwright, was associated with the La Mama theatre and the Pram Factory Group which produced several of his plays. His published works include the plays *The Surgeon's Arms* in *Seven One-Act Plays*, ed. Rodney Fisher (1983), *Dreamers of the Absolute* (1985) and *Steal Away Home* (1988). He has also written two novellas published together, *Sideshow* and *Mr Bastard* (1977) and two film scripts, *Fat Tuesday* and *Hat Trick*. Motherwell's unpublished plays, some of which have been produced by the Troupe Theatre, Nimrod and overseas theatres, include 'The Yellow Girl', 'The Laughing Bantam', 'Island', 'The Beatnik and the Dead Dog', 'The Native Rose', 'The Weight' (1973), 'The Year Lacertis' (1974), 'Pecking Orders' (1976), 'The Fitzroy Yank' (1980), 'Held in Camera' (1980) and 'The Bodgie Tree' (1988). Many of Motherwell's plays concern the power games played out in the underworld of petty criminality and drug-taking, although *Dreamers of the Absolute*, set during the Russian revolution of 1917, extends this theme to political terrorism.

MOUBRAY, (MOWBRAY), Philip (?–1903), who died at Narrandera, was well known in the 1890s as a *Bulletin* writer under the pseudonym 'Scotty the Wrinkler'; he adopted the name for his contributions after meeting in the Riverina a Scottish shepherd who claimed to be an expert on wrinkles. Of Scots descent himself, Moubray seems to have been a British Army officer who served in India and Abyssinia before travelling to America and then Australia where, among other occupations, he was miner, drover, tutor, cook, and whaler. His gently cynical, often humorous *Bulletin* contributions consist mainly of paragraphs published in such columns as 'Aboriginalities'; he celebrates the freedoms of bush life and attacks cant and humbug. His death prompted Henry Lawson's poem 'The Passing of Scotty', published in the *Bulletin* 12 November 1903. A collection of his writings was published as *The Swag* around 1900.

MOUNTFORD, C.P. (Charles Pearcy) (1890–1977), one of Australia's best-known ethnologists, was born in the SA outback settlement of Hallett. A post-office mechanic in the 1920s, he was sent to the Northern Territory where his contacts with the Aboriginal people of the area stimulated his lifelong interest in their culture and resulted in a series of books on Aboriginal art, myths, rituals and music, many of them illustrated with his own photographs. The best known are *Brown Men and Red Sand* (1948), *The Art, Myth and Symbolism of Arnhem Land* (1956), *The Tiwi, Their Art, Myth and Ceremony* (1958), *Winbaraku and the Myth of Jarapiri* (1968), and *Ayers Rock* (1965). Three of his most popular interpretations of Aboriginal music, *The Dreamtime* (1965), *The Dawn of Time* (1969) and *The First Sunrise* (1971), illustrated by Ainslie Roberts, were published together in 1973 titled *The Dreamtime Book*. Although he was removed from the conventional areas of teaching and research, Mountford established a significant reputation as an ethnologist and led two National Geographic expeditions, one to Arnhem Land and the other to Melville Island, as well as eight expeditions into inland Australia for the University of Adelaide. He received numerous awards for his skills as anthropologist and photographer. His biography, *Monty*, by Max Lamshed, was published in 1972.

Moving Image, The (1946), the first volume of poetry by Judith Wright (q.v.), takes its title from Plato's 'Time is a moving image of eternity'. The title poem is a philosophical meditation on the metaphysical role of the poet as interpreter of the processes of change wrought by time. The volume includes poems celebrating her affection for New England, e.g. 'South of My Days' and others which present figures and themes from Australia's past, e.g. 'Bullocky', 'Bora Ring' and 'Remittance Man'.

'Mr. Butterfry', the title story of Hal Porter's (q.v.) collection *Mr. Butterfry and Other Tales of New Japan* (1970), was first published in the *Bulletin* in 1968. In a Tokyo bar frequented by expatriate Australians, the narrator encounters Blue, a man with whom he had been friendly eighteen years earlier during the postwar occupation of Japan. When he had first known him, Blue had been a cheeky, self-confident if boring individual in love with his major's housegirl. Now a commercial traveller, he seems strangely embittered and his cheekiness has degenerated into foul-mouthed brashness. He is known to the Japanese bar hostesses in the many bars he visits as 'Mr. Butterfry', the loathsome, uncouth barbarian. For the narrator the source of his bitterness is not clear, although it transpires he has lost the fortune he made on the black market, until he is invited to visit his home. There he meets his now-detested, ex-housegirl wife; she has contracted her husband's brand of verbal abuse and forcefully returns his hatred, notwithstanding the presence of a stranger. It becomes clear that she has used her husband's fortune to buy modelling careers for their daughters Lana and Shirley. Aware that there is no way back for 'Mr. Butterfry' and that his abuse of the bar hostesses is a kind of blind revenge, the narrator leaves this 'ageing terrier of a spiv snarling and sniffing in the daily darker corners of [his] prison'.

Mr Scobie's Riddle, a novel by Elizabeth Jolley (q.v.), was published in 1983 and won the WA Week Award for fiction and the *Age* Book of the Year Award. Set in St Christopher and St Jude's Hospital for the Aged, it opens with hilarious brief excerpts from Night Sister Shady's reports and the responses from Matron Hyacinth Price, which sketch in the activities of a group of nocturnal poker players and convey the impersonality, verging on cruelty, of the nursing staff. For Mr Scobie, a retired music teacher who longs to return to his home, and for the two other elderly men who share his room, Mr Privett and Mr Hughes, the hospital is a place which systematically, if casually, destroys their independence, health and finances. The deathliness of the institution, emphasised by the frequent actual deaths of the old people which are as casually erased as they are treated and by the farcical incidents which often involve the patients' natural functions, is relieved only by the manic energies of two young nursing aides, Frankie and Robyn. Manipulated in different ways by his niece for his remaining money and by his more sympathetic if shady nephew Hartley in various nefarious schemes, Mr Scobie is appalled by the spiritual wilderness that is the hospital but finds a kindred spirit in Miss Hailey, a fellow music-lover and would-be novelist. One of the victims of Matron Price, who is herself a victim in a 'strangling complication' of lives which includes bigamy, fraud and blackmail, Miss Hailey is more eccentric than insane; she also preserves such moral qualities as charity and generosity even though she 'had not been at the place she had once called home for many years'. Mr Scobie's riddle, which poses the question/certainty of death: 'What is it that we all know is going to happen but we don't know when or how?' is also, as his last days demonstrate, concerned with life and what makes for goodness. On his deathbed he supplies the answer by quoting Blake: 'Where Mercy Love and Pity dwell, There God is dwelling too', an answer which receives a more extended hopefulness in the commune which Hartley, Frankie, Robyn and others establish on the site of Mr Scobie's old home. Miss Hailey, who is invited to join them there but who refuses the invitation, perceives the commune as a sort of promise of tenderness in contrast to her own life, which has 'offered [her] much but it has been mainly suffering'.

Mrs. Pretty and the Premier, a play by A.H. Adams (q.v.), was first produced in Sydney in 1914, published the same year and produced in London two years later. A light comedy, the play ironically mixes up the male world of politics and the female one of marriage, to the detriment of the former. The central character, William Power, a Labor State premier with little social finesse, finds himself in a political and personal dilemma when a reporter from an opposition paper sees him with a veiled lady, Mrs Pretty, in compromising circumstances. The situation is complicated by Mrs Pretty's engagement to the leader of the opposition and her position as one of the landholders threatened by Power's new bill to reclaim large estates. To extricate himself, Power claims that the lady is his secret wife and the action turns upon Mrs Pretty's reactions to the situation.

MUDIE, Ian (1911–76), born Hawthorn, SA, was a freelance writer who also worked as a publisher's editor and lecturer in creative writing. Active in literary affairs, he was federal president of the FAW, regularly conducted the Writers' School held in conjunction with the Adelaide Festival and frequently addressed school and adult groups on Australian literature. In 1978 the SA FAW instituted the annual Ian Mudie Award for poetry with an Australian theme.

A prolific poet, Mudie published numerous volumes of verse, including *Corroboree to the Sun* (1940), *This Is Australia* (1941), *The Australian Dream* (1943), *Their Seven Stars Unseen* (1943), *Poems* (1945), *Poems 1924–1944* (1945), *The Blue Crane* (1959), *The North-Bound Rider* (1963), winner of the Grace Leven Prize for poetry, *Look, The Kingfisher* (1970) and *Selected Poems 1934–1974* (1976), which contains about forty uncollected poems written while he was in his early sixties. He also edited numerous works and anthologies, including *Poets at War: An Anthology of Verse by Australian Servicemen* (1944) and the *Jindyworobak Anthology* (1946); and wrote several histories, chief of which are *Riverboats* (1961), an account of the paddle-steamers that plied the Darling–Murray waterways, and *The Heroic Journey of John McDouall Stuart* (1968).

A member of the Australia First movement and attracted to Rex Ingamells's Jindyworobak movement through his patriotism, affinity with the landscape, and concern and respect for the Aborigines and their lore, Mudie was a strident champion of the 'good old days' of pioneer Australia. Aggressively conservationist, much of his early poetry tells of a once lovely land 'turned to barrenness, made dead by the lust of men', and of once proud tribesmen, dispossessed so that their lands, 'cut up and divided by Torrens title', could be given to the White man for his 'five-roomed coffins'. 'This Land' and 'This is Australia' are representative of Mudie, the ardent nationalist, the Jindyworobak proselytiser. Sensitive also to the paradox of 'a harsh land . . . that scorches its flowers of spring', Mudie sought to employ a poetic language that captured the spirit and character of the land and the people who survived there. He settled in the main for spare, laconic and often colloquial style. At its best that style produced poetic flashes, at its worst it was prosaic and slangy. His most popular successes were the colloquial 'They'll Tell You About Me' (q.v.), 'Hey Blue, It's Raining', and 'I Wouldn't Be Lord Mayor'. Mudie's poetry is, however, not confined to Jindyworobak and nationalist preoccupations. *The North Bound Rider*, the prize-winning collection of 1963, has numerous reflections on city and suburban life. Personal lyrics are plentiful in *The Blue Crane* (1959), *Look, The Kingfisher* (1970) and *Selected Poems 1934–1974* (1976). Popular for his camaraderie, yarns and good nature, Mudie embodied much of the best and most characteristic features of the traditional bush ethos.

MUDIE, James, see **Convict in Australian Literature**

MUDROOROO (Colin Johnson) (1939–), born Narogin, WA, was raised in a Roman Catholic orphanage and had minor brushes with the law as a young man before leaving for Melbourne, where he worked for a period in the Victorian public service. Active in Aboriginal cultural affairs, he is a member of the Aboriginal Arts Unit committee of the Australia Council and was a co-founder with Jack Davis of the Aboriginal Writers, Oral Literature and Dramatists Association. He has also helped to initiate courses in Aboriginal literature at several Australian universities. After travelling widely in Australia and spending seven years in India where he lived for some time as a Buddhist monk, he settled in Bungawalbyn in northern NSW, to write full-time. A prolific writer of poetry and prose, his publications include the novels *Wild Cat Falling* (1965), the first novel to be published by an Aboriginal writer, *Long Live Sandawara* (1979), *Doctor Wooreddy's Prescription for Enduring the Ending of the World* (1983), *Master of the Ghost Dreaming* (1991), *Wildcat Screaming* (1992) and *The Kwinkan* (1993); the verse collections *The Song Circle of Jacky* (1986), *Dalwurra* (1988) and *The Garden of Gethsemane* (1991); a study of modern Aboriginal literature, *Writing from the Fringe* (1990); and an autobiographical narrative, *Doin Wildcat* (1988). Mudrooroo is also one of the editors of the first comprehensive anthology of Aboriginal writing, *Paperbark* (1988), and has written several plays including 'Big Sunday' (1987) and 'Mutjinggaba' (1989). *The Mudrooroo/Muller Project: A Theatrical Casebook* (1993), edited by Gerhard Fischer in collaboration with others, intermingles a play by Mudrooroo with a German play by Heiner Muller about the impact of the French revolution in Jamaica. *Wild Cat Falling* was released as a film in 1975. Mudrooroo has won several awards including the Jessie Litchfield Award in 1965, the Patricia Weickhardt Award in 1980 and the WA Literary Award for poetry in 1989.

Wild Cat Falling outlines the search of a young part-Aborigine for a meaningful existence in a White world which excludes him, because of his colour and background, from its rewards and privileges. As an outcast on the fringes of White society, his instinctive reaction is to attack that society, fruitlessly, as the novel indicates. Near the end of the novel, as he awaits capture on an attempted murder charge, he is given a new sense of identity and purpose when he meets and talks with old Noongar, a tribal elder turned rabbiter. *Long Live Sandawara* is the story of a part-Aboriginal youth, Alan, who, inspired by the heroic flight of Sandawara (based on the legendary Pidgin) against his people's oppressors, attempts to establish his own modern Aboriginal resistance group in the slums of Perth. Although the result is inevitable failure, mainly because of the ironies and contradictions of human nature and the human situation, the heroic archetype of Sandawara set up in the novel remains undiminished. Ion Idriess had also dealt with Sandawara's rebellion in the Kimberley district in *Outlaws of the Leopolds* in 1952 but Idriess's point of view is that of a White supremacist; twenty-seven years later Mudrooroo uses the historical incident to stimulate pride in Black opposition to the European culture. In both *Doctor Wooreddy* and *Master of the Ghost Dreaming* G.A. Robinson (q.v.) is a major figure. *Master of the Ghost Dreaming*, an allegory of Robinson's dealings with the

Tasmanian Aborigines, is also concerned with contemporary race relations. Countering the efforts of Robinson to 'civilise' the natives are those of Jangamuttuk, an Aboriginal elder who struggles to instil traditional beliefs in the young men of his tribe in the face of change. Whereas *Dr Wooreddy* presents the grim physical reality of George Augustus Robinson's mission, *Master of the Ghost Dreaming* draws on 'magic realism' to suggest that the Aborigines are the final winners in a spiritual sense. Both novels, however, infuse Australian history with symbolism and mythology drawn from Aboriginal and Eastern cultures and attempt to develop a philosophical vision of the historical events which will have meaning for contemporary Aborigines. *Wildcat Screaming*, set mainly in Fremantle prison, continues the misfortunes of the hero of *Wildcat Falling; The Kwinkan*, ostensibly the transcripts of thirteen recording sessions made in 1992 and dealing with the career of Dr Watson Holmes Jackamara, satirises the political hypocrisy and greed of contemporary Australia. Mudrooroo's poetry, often markedly satirical of White society, combines innovative treatment of the poetic traditions of his culture with a wide range of other poetic traditions, both Eastern and Western.

MUELLER, Baron Sir Ferdinand von (1825–96), botanist and explorer, was born in Germany and arrived in Australia in 1847. In 1853 he was appointed foundation government botanist of Victoria and carried out extensive explorations of the Victorian hinterland, greatly extending the knowledge of Australian plant species. He also later accompanied or conducted expeditions in the Northern Territory, Queensland, WA and Tasmania. Appointed director of the Melbourne Botanic Gardens in 1857, he established what is now the National Herbarium but was deprived of his directorship in 1873 because of a demand that more attention be paid to the gardens' aesthetic appeal. One of the founders of the Royal Society of Victoria and the University of Melbourne, von Mueller received numerous awards and honours, including election as FRS (1861) and as president of the Australasian Association for the Advancement of Science (1890). His numerous publications on Australian plants include the twelve-volume *Fragmenta Phytographiae Australiae* (1858–82); with George J. Bentham, the seven-volume *Flora Australiensis* (1863–78); and the two-part study *Systematic Census of Australian Plants* (1882, 1889). His work is described in biographies by Margaret Willis, *By Their Fruits* (1949) and Edward Kynaston, *A Man on Edge* (1981).

MUIR, Marcie (1919–   ), born Perth, has worked for many years on Australian children's literature. She has published volume I (1774–1972) of *Australian Children's Books: A Bibliography* (1992), an expanded and updated version of her earlier two-volume work, 1970 and 1976; Kerry White compiled volume II (1973–88) of the *Bibliography*. Muir has also edited a collection of tales for children, *Strike-a-Light the Bushranger* (1972) and an anthology of poetry and prose for children, *Under the Pepper Trees* (1987); written an account of

Charlotte Barton, Australia's first children's author (1980); and a *History of Australian Children's Book Illustration* (1982), which supersedes her earlier *Australian Children's Book Illustrators* (1977), and which records the image of Australia presented to children from the early romanticised misconceptions of overseas publishers to the realism of such contemporary artists as Dick Roughsey. She has also published an edition of C. Langloh Parker's *My Bush Book* (1982), which includes a discussion of Mrs Parker's life and her literary contribution; and *Anthony Trollope in Australia* (1949); with Robert Holden she has written an illustrated account of the life and work of Ida Rentoul Outhwaite (1985). In 1984 Muir won the inaugural Nan Chauncy Award and in 1988 the Redmond Barry Award and in 1978 shared with her husband, Harry Muir, an Adelaide bookshop proprietor and founder of the Wakefield Press, the National Book Council's Bookman of the Year Award.

MUIR, Thomas, see **Scottish Martyrs**

MUIRDEN, Bruce, see **Australia First**; *Austro-vert*

Mulga Bill, the central figure in A.B. Paterson's (q.v.) poem 'Mulga Bill's Bicycle' published in *Rio Grande's Last Race and Other Verses* (1902), is one of Paterson's well-known comic folk-characters. Concerned to keep abreast of progress, Bill turned away 'the good old horse that served him many days' and 'caught the cycling craze'. After a brief but spectacular encounter with the 'two-wheeled outlaw', Bill ended up, with the cycle, in Dead Man's Creek. There he left it, the lesson learned: 'a horse's back is good enough, henceforth for Mulga Bill.' Mulga Bill takes his name from his habitat, the mulga, which in colloquial speech denotes the remote bush or outback. Will Ogilvie's poem 'The Mulga Mail', demonstrates how news travels through the outback via the bush telegraph (see Bush).

Mulini Press, see *Australian Books on Demand*

MULLEN, Samuel (1828–90), born Dublin, was apprenticed to bookseller William Curry, in whose shop he met fellow apprentice George Robertson (1) (q.v.), and emigrated with him to Australia in 1852. After five months working as a station hand at Mount Bute, he joined Robertson as an assistant in the latter's bookshop in Melbourne. He travelled to London to take up the position of manager of Robertson's London branch in 1857, but when Robertson appointed his brother William Robertson in his stead the two men fell out and never spoke to each other again. Mullen returned to Melbourne in 1859 and opened up his own bookshop and a successful library, based on Mudie's of London and the first of its kind in Australia. He retired in 1889 and William, a bookseller and stationer of Ballarat, joined with A.G. Melville and Leonard Slade to acquire Samuel's business. They traded as Melville, Mullen & Slade, in 1900 became Melville and Mullen, and in 1921 merged with George Robertson & Co to become Robertson & Mullens, the well-known Melbourne bookshop and publishing firm.

MUM, see *Melbourne University Magazine*

MUNDY, Godfrey Charles (1804–60), an officer in the British Army, came to Australia in 1846 as deputy adjutant-general of the military forces in Australia. He left in 1851 after accompanying Governor FitzRoy in several journeys into outback NSW and visiting Victoria, Van Diemen's Land and NZ. In 1852 he published *Our Antipodes: or, Residence and Rambles in the Australasian Colonies. With a Glimpse at the Goldfields*. Illustrated with his own sketches and deftly and wittily written, *Our Antipodes* went through four editions and is still a useful source of historical information. The section which narrates Mundy's visit to Van Diemen's Land in the summer of 1850–51 has been published separately titled *A Record of Observations in Van Diemen's Land* (1986).

MUNSTER, George (1925–84), born Vienna, left Austria with his family in 1938, arriving in Australia the following year. A brilliant student, he studied English and philosophy at the University of Sydney, where he was taught by John Anderson, and co-edited *Hermes*. In 1949 he returned to Europe, worked for a period as a supply teacher in London and in Iraq tutored for the British Council. Back in Australia in the 1950s he became friendly with Tom Fitzgerald and collaborated with him in the production of the independent fortnightly *Nation*, which ran 1958–72. Munster became the periodical's business manager, but also took on the role of associate editor on occasion and was one of its main contributors both under his own name and under pseudonyms. From 1972 to 1978 he was the Sydney editor of *Nation Review*, worked in the publishing division of Angus & Robertson 1978–81 and as a freelance writer 1981–84. In 1980 Munster and Richard Walsh tried to publish *Documents on Australian Defence and Foreign Policy 1968–1975*, hitherto unpublished official memoranda, briefings and cables, but the book was ordered to be withdrawn by the High Court. Munster subsequently published *Secrets of State. A Detailed Assessment of the Book They Banned* (1982). His study *Rupert Murdoch: A Paper Prince* (1985), winner of a NSW State Premier's Award that year, was published posthumously. The George Munster Award for Freelance Journalism was established to honour his achievement.

MURDOCH, Anna (1944–   ), born Scotland, came to Australia in 1954 and was a journalist in Sydney on the *Daily Mirror* and the *Australian* before marrying newspaper proprietor Rupert Murdoch. She has published three novels: *In Her Own Image* (1985), a tempestuous tale centred on a family Christmas reunion on an Australian sheep farm; *Family Business* (1988) and *Coming to Terms* (1991), a story of the absurdities and eccentricities of country town life.

MURDOCH Family is significant in the history of the twentieth-century Australian, and latterly British

and American, newspaper industry. Sir Keith Murdoch (1885–1952), the nephew of Sir Walter Murdoch (q.v.), was born in Melbourne, began his career in journalism in 1903 as a district correspondent for the *Age*, had a brief and unsuccessful sojourn in England 1908–9 before returning to the *Age* as a reporter. He was a Melbourne correspondent of the *Sun* from 1912 to 1915, when he was narrowly defeated by C.E.W. Bean in an AJA ballot to be Australian war correspondent. The same year he left for England to become manager of a cable service; *en route* he visited Gallipoli, and his subsequent report of conditions there to the Australian and British governments was significant in the recall of Sir Ian Hamilton and the evacuation of Gallipoli. Murdoch remained in England until his appointment as editor of the Melbourne *Herald* in 1921. Fighting off Sir Hugh Denison's attempt to enter Melbourne journalism, Murdoch, as managing director and chairman of the Herald and Weekly Times company, proceeded to build the company into a position of prominence in Australian journalism, with interests in the *Advertiser* and *News* in Adelaide, the *West Australian* in Perth, and the *Courier-Mail* in Brisbane. He was also a significant figure in the establishment of the Australian newsprint industry and the development of cable services, and during the Second World War was director-general of information. He is the subject of Desmond Zwar's *In Search of Keith Murdoch* (1980).

Murdoch's sudden death in 1952, three years after his retirement from the Herald and Weekly Times, left his family with a controlling interest only in News Limited, which ran the *News* and the *Sunday Mail* in Adelaide. Rupert Murdoch (1931–   ), born Melbourne and educated at Oxford University, worked briefly in London on the *Daily Express* before returning to Australia to join News Limited. He was based in Adelaide for the rest of the 1950s; in 1960 he expanded into NSW with the purchase by News Limited of the *Daily* and *Sunday Mirror* and a chain of Sydney suburban newspapers. In 1964 Murdoch founded the *Australian* and launched his assault on Fleet Street in 1969 with the purchase of *News of the World* and the *Sun*. In the 1970s and 1980s News Limited and its associated companies continued expansion – in Australia with the purchase of the Sydney *Daily* and *Sunday Telegraph* (1972) but also into NZ, the USA and elsewhere in the UK. Apart from interests in television, records, magazines and numerous other areas, Murdoch's companies founded the *National Star*, later the *Star*, in 1974 in New York; purchased the *San Antonio Express* (1973), the New York *Post* (1976) and *Village Voice* (1977), the *Boston Herald* (1982) and *Chicago Sun-Times* (1983) in the USA; and the *Times* and *Sunday Times* (1980) in the UK; by 1984 he controlled over eighty significant newspapers and magazines. When he became a US citizen he bought Twentieth Century Fox and Metromedia. His involvement in Sky Television brought the Murdoch Empire to the brink of disaster, but the late 1980s saw his fortunes rise again dramatically.

A controversial figure who has been admired for his business acumen and criticised for lowering newspaper standards, he is the subject of a stream of biographical works including Simon Regan's *Rupert Murdoch: A Business Biography* (1976), Michael Leapman's *Barefaced Cheek: The Apotheosis of Rupert Murdoch* (1983), George Munster's *Rupert Murdoch: A Paper Prince* (1985), Richard Belfield's et al. *Murdoch: The Decline of an Empire* (1991) and William Shawcross's *Rupert Murdoch* (1992, a shorter US edition titled *Murdoch*). Rupert Murdoch's wife Anna (q.v.) is a novelist.

MURDOCH, Nina (1890–1976), born Melbourne, worked first as a schoolteacher. A contributor of verse to the *Bulletin*, she won a prize for a sonnet on Canberra and subsequently published two collections, *Songs of the Open Air* (1915) and *More Songs of the Open Air* (1922). In 1914 she joined the staff of the Sydney *Sun* and transferred to the Melbourne *Sun* in 1922. Retrenched from the *Herald* in 1930, she began working in radio broadcasting, managing Children's Corner on 3LO from the inception of the ABC, and founding the children's programme 'The Argonauts', which she ran until 1934, when she moved to Adelaide. She also published three novelettes, which have been popular with both adults and children, *Miss Emily in Black Lace* (1930), *Portrait of Miss Emily* (1931) and *Exit Miss Emily* (1937); a biographical account of Sir John Longstaff, *Portrait in Youth* (1948); and four books which reflected her keen interest in travel.

MURDOCH, Sir Walter (1874–1970), born Aberdeenshire, Scotland, came to Melbourne in 1884. Educated at the University of Melbourne, Murdoch worked as a private tutor and as a country schoolmaster before starting a school in Camberwell in 1897. He ran another school in Warrnambool 1901–3, but in 1904 was appointed to a lecturing position in English at the University of Melbourne. A familiar figure in literary and academic circles in Melbourne, a member of various literary societies and founder and editor of *Trident*, Murdoch was friendly with many prominent individuals; one of his students and a lifelong friend was Nettie Palmer. Murdoch was widely known for his contributions to the *Argus*. His weekly column, titled 'Books and Men' and signed 'Elzevir', ran 1905–13, and in a second series, 1919–38. One of his first ventures as a critic, an essay on Australian poets of the 1890s, published in the *Argus* in 1899, drew trenchant reactions from such writers as Edward Dyson, 'Rolf Boldrewood' and A.G. Stephens. During his years in Melbourne Murdoch also contributed leaders and anonymous book reviews to the *Argus*, and contributed to many other newspapers and periodicals under such pseudonyms as 'Aden', 'Nick O'Teen', 'W.L. Forbes' and 'Diogenes T. Moxhaye'.

When in 1911 he was not appointed to the chair of English, which had been left vacant since the death of E.E. Morris in 1902, Murdoch took a full-time position on the literary staff of the *Argus*. In 1912, however, he was appointed to the chair of English at the newly founded University of WA and moved to Perth. During his years in WA his reputation as a public figure grew, both because of his regular contributions to the *Argus* and the *West Australian* and because of his regular radio talks, which were particu-

larly influential in the 1930s and 1940s and continued until the 1960s. The publication in 1930 of *Speaking Personally*, a collection of some of his pieces for the *Argus*, followed by other collections, made his name familiar throughout Australia. In 1939 he retired from the teaching staff of the university but was re-elected to the Senate 1941–43, and served as chancellor 1943–48. His writing career meanwhile continued unabated. After his association with the *Argus* ceased in 1938, he began a regular syndicated column for the Melbourne *Herald*. In 1945 his journalism took a new turn when he began a weekly series of much briefer essays titled 'Answers', which took the form of responses to readers' questions; this series, which appeared for varying periods in all States of Australia and in NZ, ceased in 1964. His last journalistic venture was a series titled 'Afterthoughts', which appeared in the *Australian* 1965–68. Murdoch was made CBE in 1939 and knighted in 1964; in 1970 WA's second university was named after him. His daughter Catherine, also a well-known broadcaster, married the poet and critic Alec King; the newspaper proprietor Sir Keith Murdoch was his nephew and Rupert Murdoch is his grand-nephew.

Although Murdoch wrote some verse and short stories, his natural medium was the essay. He published several collections of essays which had previously only appeared in newspapers, *Loose Leaves* (1910), *Speaking Personally* (1930), *Saturday Mornings* (1931), *Moreover* (1932), *The Wild Planet* (1934) and *Lucid Intervals* (1936); the last five of these are brought together in his *Collected Essays* (1938); another subsequent collection, *The Spur of the Moment* (1939), is included in the second edition of *Collected Essays* (1940); *Steadfast* (1941) is his last collection of new essays. Other selections, which are all reprinted from the above collections, include *The Two Laughters* (1934), *Selections from Walter Murdoch* (1941), *72 Essays* (1947), *Selected Essays* (1956) and *The Best of Walter Murdoch* (1964). *Answers* (1953), largely reprinted in *My 100 Answers* (1960), is selected from the *Herald* series of essays in miniature. He also wrote a biography of Alfred Deakin (1923) and edited two well-known anthologies, *The Oxford Book of Australasian Verse* (1918), titled in later editions *A Book of Australian and New Zealand Verse*, and *A Book of Australasian Verse* and, with Henrietta Drake-Brockman, *Australian Short Stories* (1951). Of his many school editions and textbooks *The Struggle for Freedom* (1903) and *The Australian Citizen* (1912) are interesting both as records of social and political attitudes of the time and as reflections of Murdoch's personal philosophy. J.A. La Nauze published an account of Murdoch's life (1977) and edited, with Elizabeth Nurser, *Walter Murdoch and Alfred Deakin on Books and Men: Letters and Comments 1900–1918* (1974).

As Murdoch himself commented, he only wrote one 'real' book, that is, his biography of Deakin, but probably no other Australian writer has enjoyed so wide and sympathetic an audience, especially from the 1930s to the late 1950s. His essays and his radio talks shared the same characteristics: whimsical, often shrewd, humour, an easy, conversational but economical style and a disarming, persuasive, personal flavour. Writing or talking urbanely on a wide range of subjects, from tripe and onions and tin-openers to the nature of man and the meaning of life, he frequently dealt, in a light and original way, with familiar, ordinary ideas. *Loose Leaves* consists entirely of literary essays, but Murdoch turned more and more to the general, topical essay, although his wide reading and enthusiasm for literature were always manifest. A liberal humanist, he professed a traditional morality which derived from his Presbyterian background and his years in the distinctive cultural milieu that was Melbourne's from the 1890s to 1914. A courageous and often effective critic of pretension, and an enemy of the 'suburban spirit', he deliberately encouraged his readers in what he saw as the healthy habit of scepticism and his faith in 'the sacred duty of growling'. Occasionally, and particularly in the 1930s, his independent attitudes involved him in economic, educational, political, and even religious controversy. He was also, on occasion, the centre of literary controversy; his survey of Australian literature for a special supplement of the London *Times*, published in 1938, aroused the anger of several Australian writers for its excessive concentration on the nineteenth century. A protest from the FAW resulted in a letter of apology from the *Times*. Equally acrimonious was the response in *Southerly* and elsewhere to the 1945 edition of the *Book of Australasian Verse* which, it was claimed, was totally unrepresentative and out of date. Although Murdoch showed some interest in Australian writing during his career, his real literary affinities were with nineteenth-century English literature.

As an essayist, however, Murdoch eluded criticism for the most part by keeping to general, uncontroversial topics. Some of his essays are purely fanciful; others touch on his travels; others on his literary interests; and others deal with his detestation of pretension and jargon. A great number use an apparently trivial topic to introduce consideration of some universal subject, such as patriotism, tolerance, true democracy, civilisation or education. In his later series, 'Answers', the topics became even more general, covering such questions as 'Can One Be a Snob and a Christian?', 'What Is a Perfect Day?', or 'Does It Ever Rain Cats and Dogs?'.

MURNANE, Gerald (1939–   ), born Melbourne where he now lives, spent part of his childhood in rural Victoria. He has worked as a primary school teacher, publications officer and editor for the Victorian Department of Education and as a freelance editor, and is now a lecturer at Victoria College. He has written four novels, *Tamarisk Row* (1974), *A Lifetime on Clouds* (1976), *The Plains* (1982) and *Inland* (1988); and two collections of short stories, *Landscape with Landscape* (1987) and *Velvet Waters* (1990, winner of the 1991 Barbara Ramsden Award). With Jenny Lee and Philip Mead he edited *The Temperament of Generations: Fifty Years of Writing in Meanjin* (1990). Murnane's first novel, *Tamarisk Row*, a study of an Australian Catholic childhood in 1940s rural Victoria, contains the seeds of all his later fiction, not in the sense that it presents a unifying thesis or central idea, but in the sense that it is the first exploration of a philosophical, social and emotional territory that is essentially Murnane's and is both tiny and vast. Fascinated by the mystery of the everyday and by the phenomenon that nothing is as it seems to be, Murnane is also intrigued by the interpretive/misinterpretive powers of language and is in agreement with Musil's contention that 'thoughts are the graveyard of the mind', inevitably buried by the heavy power of words. He has also described a phrase from Herbert Read, comparing thought to a contour of mind which the artist is bound to follow as being 'a magical phrase . . . It has helped me in time of trouble in the way that phrases from the Bible or from Karl Marx probably help other people'; the comment emphasises his interest in the geography of mind and the interdependence between mind and place, between the observed and the observer. Clement Killeaton, the boy protagonist of *Tamarisk Row*, plays an elaborate game with marbles which he uses partly to represent racehorses and to dream of winning; dreaming of winning is related to dreaming of knowing, in that both are quests into the unknown. Clement associates knowing with sexual knowledge and other specific mysteries, but the notion of a hidden territory within the external visible one is returned to again and again in *Tamarisk Row* and in Murnane's other fictions. Like the marbles which fascinate Clement, Murnane's 'reality' is iridescent, prismatic and mysterious, both solid and insubstantial, fixed and changing, and coloured by the whorls of imagining. *A Lifetime on Clouds* focuses on another, slighter older dreaming child, and his frequently comic attempts to surmount the dislocations between the repressive strictures of the Catholic Church and his experience of a burgeoning sexuality. *The Plains* describes the failed attempts of a would-be film-maker to make a film about a certain enigmatic anonymous territory which has some affinity with the Western District of Victoria and the American prairie. The more the film-maker learns of life on the Plains, the more elusive and even impossible as a filmic topic does it become; the narrator's journey meanwhile becomes a journey into the self's inward zone. *Landscape with Landscape*, a series of six stories, might also be described as a novel since the stories are really one man's alternative biographies, which give free rein to Murnane's obsession with secret places concealed within obvious ones and with the self as multiple. *Inland*, which concentrates on a writer writing about writing, is preoccupied with ideas of authorship and readership and their insidious collaborations; combining widely separated geographical areas, such as the plains of south-west Hungary, the Yorkshire moors and the familiar Murnane territory of south-west Victoria, *Inland* is also narrowly focused on one man's inward meditations on language and its relation to possible realities. The stories of *Velvet Waters*, written in a spare, emotionally concentrated prose, circle the question of fiction-making and the writer's creative processes. Murnane's work is the subject of a monograph edited by John Hanrahan in the 'Footprint New Writers' series (1987), a study in Oxford's Australian

Writers series (1993) by Imre Salusinszky, who has also published an annotated bibliography of Murnane (1993), and is included in Helen Daniel's study of eight contemporary writers, *Liars* (1988).

MURPHY, Edwin Greenslade (1866–1939) was born in Victoria but joined in the great gold rush to Coolgardie in WA in 1893. From prospecting he turned to journalism and the writing of topical verses, becoming, as 'Dryblower', one of the best-known and most colourful identities of the West. For forty years he wrote a column of jingles, 'Verse and Worse', for the Perth *Sunday Times*. Two collections of his verses were published, *Jarrahland Jingles* (1908) and *Dryblower's Verses 1894–1926* (1926). He also published a novel, *Sweet Boronia: A Story of Coolgardie* (1904). Unpretentious in style, his poems are humorous and full of affection for the ordinary toilers of the world; his pseudonym 'Dryblower' was the name given to the rudimentary apparatus used by miners in the waterless West to separate the gold from dirt and gravel. Murphy's personality and career are described in Arthur L. Bennett's *Dryblower Murphy. His Life and Times* (1982).

MURPHY, Peter (1945–), born Melbourne, works as a teacher and has published four collections of verse, *Escape Victim and Other Poems* (1974), *Seen & Unseen* (1975), *Glass Doors and Other Poems* (1977) and *Lies* (1983); and two collections of short stories, *Black Light* (1979) and *The Moving Shadow Problem* (1986); and plays for radio and stage including 'Glitter' (1977) and 'Illuminations' (1986).

MURRAY, Anna Maria (1808–89), born Balliston, Ireland, came to Sydney in 1827 and married Captain George Bunn, a shipowner, whaler and sealer. Widowed early, she wrote a melodramatic novel under the pseudonym 'An Australian' and titled *The Guardian* (1838), the first novel to be printed and published on the mainland of Australia, Henry Savery's *Quintus Servinton* (1831) having been published in Hobart Town. An account of her life is included in Gwendoline Wilson's *Murray of Yarralumla* (1968).

MURRAY, David Christie (1847–1907), born Staffordshire, had established a solid reputation as a war correspondent and popular novelist before he arrived in Australia in 1889 to give a series of lectures in Melbourne, Sydney and Brisbane. During a subsequent tour of NZ he fell in with Harry St Maur's theatrical company and thence returned to Australia in 1890 to assist in the production of a number of plays (including *Jim the Penman*, in which he himself acted for the first time, and his own comedy *Chums*). His three articles on 'The Antipodeans' appeared in *The Contemporary Review* in 1891 and were widely criticised for their inaccurate use of statistics and their stress on the increasing prevalence of anti-British sentiment in Australian culture.

MURRAY, Elizabeth Alicia (1820–77), born Elizabeth Poitier in Portland, Jamaica, moved to Ireland in 1844 and married Captain Virginius Murray, who was a goldfields' commissioner in Australia 1852–59. A colourful character, he is mentioned in William Howitt's *Land, Labour and Gold* (1855). Elizabeth Murray followed her husband in 1855 with their five sons and stayed in St Kilda while he travelled around the goldfields. She disliked the colony and returned to England in late 1859, leaving her oldest son behind with his father. Virginius Murray died in 1861. On her return to England Elizabeth Murray wrote a novel based on her experience, *Ella Norman; or, a Woman's Perils* (1864); the author of several previous novels she no doubt wrote *Ella Norman* to improve her finances although it is also likely that the book is an attempt to convince the British government and the benevolent societies of the real difficulties confronting the numerous young women who were persuaded to emigrate in the hope of securing a husband. The story of a governess's tribulations, and a damning account of contemporary Australia, *Ella Norman* castigates the crudity of social life and the corruption of those in power. A feminist novel in that it explicitly attacks the exploitation of women and presents a positive picture of the capabilities and independence of colonial women, it was republished in 1985.

MURRAY, George Gilbert Aime (1866–1957), born Sydney, the son of the pastoralist and politician Sir Terence Aubrey Murray and his second wife Agnes Edwards, and the brother of Sir Hubert Murray (q.v.), was educated in Australia at Moss Vale and Mittagong before leaving for England in 1877. After achieving brilliant results at Oxford, he was appointed professor of Greek at Glasgow at the age of 23. In 1889 he married Lady Mary Howard. An influential critic and Hellenist, whose translations made Greek literature available to English readers, he was appointed Regius professor of Greek at Oxford in 1908. He was foundation chairman of the League of Nations Union 1923–38 and president of its successor, the United Nations Association, and was awarded the Order of Merit in 1941. He returned to Australia briefly in 1892. In his *Unfinished Autobiography* (1960) Murray describes his schooldays, when he was often intensely miserable due to bullying, and his love of the bush. As Francis West comments in *Gilbert Murray. A Life* (1984), Murray's 'Australian childhood shaped his emotions, fired his indignation about life, [and] remained an affectionate memory and a yardstick for his achievement'.

MURRAY, James (1927–), born Ireland, grew up in Melbourne and was educated at the University of Melbourne; after a period as a teacher he entered the Anglican priesthood. Well known as a feature-writer for newspapers and as a broadcaster and columnist and religious affairs correspondent for the *Australian*, he has also been an editor for *Reader's Digest*. He has published an account of his travels in Indonesia, *The Mask of Time* (1970), a study of the larrikin 'pushes' of Sydney and Melbourne, *Larrikins: 19th Century Outrage* (1973), an account of criminal behaviour of various forms and degrees and its causes, *Sprung: A Study in*

Victims (1974), and an autobiography of his childhood, *The Paradise Tree: An Eccentric Childhood Remembered* (1988). He has also edited *New South Illustrated: The Sketches of F.C. Terry* (1973, first published as *The Australian Keepsake*, 1855), and provided the text for *Sydney: An Illustrated History* (1974).

MURRAY, Sir John Hubert (1861–1940), born Sydney, the son of the pastoralist and politician Sir Terence Aubrey Murray, and his second wife Agnes Edwards, and the brother of Gilbert Murray (q.v.), was educated in Melbourne and Sydney before leaving for England in 1878. After winning first-class honours at Oxford, he trained for the Bar. In 1886 he returned to Australia, wher e he worked as a lawyer, before sailing for Cape Town as a special service officer in command of a troop ship in 1900. In his ten months in South Africa he saw action near Pretoria and supervised the burning of Boer farms, a duty which he hated. In 1904 he was appointed chief judicial officer of British New Guinea, a position he held for the next thirty-five years. More liberal and forward-looking than most of his contemporaries, he imposed the death penalty only twice and opposed the amalgamation of German New Guinea and Papua, fearing that the combined territories would be governed less humanely. He was appointed CMG in 1914 and KCMG in 1925. He published two books on Papua, *Papua or British New Guinea* (1912) and *Papua of Today* (1925). There are two substantial biographies of Murray by Lewis Lett (1949) and Francis West (1968); West also edited his selected letters (1970).

MURRAY, Les (Leslie Allan) (1938–   ), born Nabiac in the Manning River district of the lower north coast of NSW, spent his childhood and adolescence on his grandfather's dairy farm in the nearby Bunyah district. His Murray forebears had arrived on the Manning in the 1840s and he has always been proud of both his Gaelic and pioneer Australian ancestry. A placid but solitary rural childhood ended when he was 12 with the death of his mother, an event recalled in his 'Three Poems in Memory of My Mother, Miriam Murray née Arnall'. In 1957 he began an arts degree at the University of Sydney. After four years of pursuing his own interests – usually in the Fisher Library or in the company of kindred literary spirits such as Geoffrey Lehmann and Bob Ellis – he left without a degree but with something of a reputation as a wit and an intellectual and with an attraction to Roman Catholicism, which faith he later officially embraced. In 1962 he married Budapest-born Valerie Morelli. During 1963–67 he was a translator of foreign scholarly and technical material at the ANU. In 1965, after the collaborative volume *The Ilex Tree* (with Lehmann) won the Grace Leven Prize for poetry, Murray attended the British Commonwealth Arts Festival Poetry Conference at Cardiff. In 1967 he resigned his ANU position and lived with his wife and two children for more than a year in England and Europe. He was briefly (1970) a public servant in Canberra but returned to Sydney (Chatswood) determined to make a career as a full-time writer. Aided, over the years, by numerous Literature Board grants, several editorial positions, income from book reviews, articles and essays in newspapers and journals, and royalties and prizes from about twenty books of poetry and prose, he could be said to have adequately achieved that aim. From 1973 to 1979 he was editor of Grace Perry's *Poetry Australia*, holding the fort as long as he could against the inroads of the so-called New Poetry, of 'literary modernism', that surfaced in Australia in those years. One of his complaints about post-modernism was that it removed poetry from widespread, popular readership, leaving it the domain of a small intellectual clique. From 1976 to 1991 he was poetry editor of Angus & Robertson and in 1990 became literary editor of *Quadrant*. By 1978 his literary stature was such that he became writer-in-residence at the University of New England (the first of several such literary tenancies to be held by him) and he began to be invited to represent Australia (and poetry) at overseas literary festivals and conferences. By the 1980s he was widely recognised as one of Australia's leading contemporary poets and literary personalities. His poetry has won numerous awards, among them the Grace Leven Prize on three occasions – *The Ilex Tree* in 1965, *The Boys Who Stole the Funeral* in 1980 and *Dog Fox Field* in 1991; the Captain Cook Bicentenary Literary Competition Prize for 'Seven Points for an Imperilled Star' included in *Poems Against Economics* (1972); the C.J. Dennis Memorial Prize for *The Vernacular Republic* (1976); the National Book Council Award for *Lunch and Counterlunch* (1975); the Canada-Australia Literary Award, the FAW Christopher Brennan Award, the NSW Premier's Award for Poetry and the Australian Literature Society's Gold Medal, all in 1984 and all for *The People's Otherworld*; the 1993 C.J. Dennis Award in the Victorian Premier's Literary Awards, the NBC Banjo Award for poetry in 1993, and the 1993 NSW Premier's Literary Award, all for *Translations from the Natural World* (q.v.). Two of his volumes, *The Daylight Moon* (1987) and *Dog Fox Field* (1990) became the annual choices of the UK Poetry Society. In 1989 he was awarded an Australian Creative Arts Fellowship; in 1991 he was the subject of an ABC television programme in the True Stories series; he has been made AO and has received an honorary D.Litt. from the University of New England.

Notwithstanding his success in the literary world both in Australia and overseas and his high public profile, Murray never wavered in his resolve to return to the privacy of Bunyah to live. In 1975 he was able to buy back part of the lost family farm and returned there for brief recuperative periods whenever possible. In late 1985, after an exhausting lecture and reading tour of Canada, North America and Europe, he returned with his family permanently to Bunyah – 'I had been twenty-nine years away', he lamented in 'The Idyll Wheel'. Long labelled by the tabloids 'The Bard of Bunyah', he had finally taken up his favourite poet-in-residence position. The return did not, however, indicate an indolent, bucolic retirement. Two anthologies of verse compiled and edited, four further volumes of poetry written and two books of essays published since his return attest to his continuing contribution to Australian writing.

Murray's volumes of poetry are *The Ilex Tree* (1965, with Lehmann), *The Weatherboard Cathedral* (1969), *Poems Against Economics* (1972), *Lunch & Counterlunch* (1974), *The Vernacular Republic* (1976, a Selected Poems volume which has been regularly updated, e.g. 1983, 1984, 1986, 1988), *Ethnic Radio* (1977), *The Boys Who Stole the Funeral* (1980), *The People's Otherworld* (1983), *The Daylight Moon* (1987), *Dog Fox Field* (1990) and *Translations from the Natural World* (1992). In 1991 a *Collected Poems* in the A & R Modern Poets series was published; a selection from his previous volumes (except *Dog Fox Field*) rather than a full *Collected* edition, it won the 1992 FAW Barbara Ramsden Award. He has collected the best of his book reviews, articles and essays in four prose volumes, *The Peasant Mandarin* (1978), *Persistence in Folly* (1984), *Blocks and Tackles* (1990) and *The Paperbark Tree* (1992). He edited *The Australian Year* (photographs by Peter Solness) in 1985; subtitled *The Chronicle of Our Seasons and Celebrations*, it is a well-informed, lyrical and loving evocation of Australia. Murray's two anthologies are *The New Oxford Book of Australian Verse* (1986) and the *Anthology of Australian Religious Poetry* (1986). *The New Oxford Book of Australian Verse* (critically well received) is a somewhat eccentric collection with no more than three poems from any one writer, no accompanying notes about poets or poems, no long-standing favourite A.B. Paterson characters, a sprinkling of religious poems and numerous (thirty-one) translations of Aboriginal songs and song-cycles. It is also a typical Murray selection in that more than half the book illustrates the Murray reverence for the land and the landscape and the Murray belief in the Bush and Bush values. The bulk of the poems in the religious anthology come from the post-Second World War period. Unorthodox, in that the term 'religious' in the title is sometimes loosely interpreted, the anthology has proved popular with readers, necessitating a second edition within five years of publication. It incorporates the work of many of Australia's best poets – James McAuley, A.D. Hope, Judith Wright, Rosemary Dobson, Bruce Dawe, Francis Webb, Roland Robinson, Kevin Hart and Murray himself – twenty-three of his own pieces. Murray's account of the compiling of the anthology was given in the 1986 Aquinas Lecture, later reproduced in *Blocks and Tackles*.

There is a richness and diversity in Les Murray's poetry which quickly disposes of the simplistic labelling of 'disguised autobiography' that some critics have occasionally sought to apply to it. Murray himself does not accept that his 'various books constitute chapters of the one work' but there is, nevertheless, an obvious unity and wholeness in much of his writing. At the core of that unity is his consistent commitment to the ideals and values of what he sees as the real Australia, that is, the Australia centred – as the nationalistic 1890s version has it – on its rural heartland, the Bush. For Murray that rural-centred Australia (his 'vernacular republic'), although superficially modified by modern times and technologies, exists today essentially the same as it was in earlier times.

The continuing themes of much of his poetry are those inherent in that traditional nationalistic identity – respect, even reverence, for the pioneers; the importance of the land and its shaping influence on the Australian character; admiration for that special Australian character, down-to-earth, laconic ('we are a colloquial nation') and based on such Bush-bred qualities as egalitarianism, practicality, straightforwardness and independence; special respect for that Australian character in action in wartime ('the country soldiers'); and a brook-no-argument preference for the rural life over the sterile and corrupting urban environment. Such themes appear early in his published poems, e.g. in 'Noonday Axeman' from *The Ilex Tree* and 'Evening Alone at Bunyah' from *The Weatherboard Cathedral*. 'Noonday Axeman' reveres the toil and endurance of the pioneer Murrays:

A hundred years of clearing, splitting, sawing,
a hundred years of timbermen, ringbarkers, fencers
and women in kitchens, stoking loud iron stoves
year in, year out, and singing old songs to their children.

From those pioneers, and others like them, have come, for Australia, 'the rough foundation of legends'. Wielding his own noonday axe where his 'great-great-grandfather . . . with his first sons' had done the same, he acknowledges the claim that the land and the past have on him. Distracted as he would certainly be down the years by 'the talk and dazzle of cities' he knew that 'the city will never quite hold me. I will be always coming back here . . .' In 'Evening Alone at Bunyah' the finality of 'This country is my mind. I lift my face and count my hills' indicates the only course open to Murray when those distractions have ultimately been put aside. The final return to Bunyah took longer than he would have anticipated and the poems themselves trace the continuing saga of loss and recovery – 'The Away-bound Train', where he dreams of his 'left-behind hills' on one of his half-reluctant journeys back 'to the twentieth century'; 'Blood', where his 'smart city life' has made him momentarily squeamish about the slaughter of the pig, until his cousin's mild reproof reminds him of the natural rural order that requires such acts; 'SMLE', where, on another brief visit to Bunyah, he goes out shooting, a country action that when done 'rightly according to its nature' is one of the rare valid uses to which a rifle is put; 'The Bulahdelah-Taree Holiday Song Cycle' (q.v.), where he and his family, and other city families like them, crowd back briefly to the country for the Christmas holidays to recover their origins, 'walking out, looking all around, relearning that country'; 'Cowyard Gates', where the old house he lived in as a boy has finally been pulled down, an event which he partly blames on his own repeated desertions of it; 'Laconics: The Forty Acres', where having at last bought back 'our beautiful deep land', he can plan in detail for the ultimate return. And when the recovery has been effected there are poems to tell of that – 'Extract from a Verse Letter to Dennis Haskell', where what has been regained ('the milk and honey I came home for') are 'Trees, space, waterbirds – things of that ilk/ plus people of my own kind'. The distractions of 'this metropolitan century' are at last rejected with the ultimatum that the years away finally brought: 'get out of Yuppie City or go mad'.

'Aspects of Language and War on the Gloucester Road' has him safely returned, nostalgically recalling events from his own and Bunyah's past. In 'The Idyll Wheel' he describes, in a baker's dozen poems (there are two Aprils), the month-by-month cycle of the first year back. A labour of love, 'The Idyll Wheel', which appeared in a limited edition in 1989, in parts in *Dog Fox Field* and *in toto* in the 1991 *Collected*, is rich in verbal imagery. Heart, mind and eye banquet on Keatsian colours – 'purple, foam-white, skims of leek and sherry, tawny, bronze and citrine, rosy-blue' – and on the beauty of Spring:

Burning days ... die out over west mountains/ erased with azure

Emerald kingparrots, crimson-breasted, whirr/ and plane out of open feed sheds

Poddy calves wobbling in their newborn mushroom colours

Bees and pollen drift/ through greening orchards.

The preference for rural life and values exhibited in the above poems is private and personal. That same preference was aired in a more universal, public and hence more controversial, manner in Murray's essay 'On Sitting Back and Thinking about Porter's Boeotia', published in 1978 in Elkin's *Australian Poems in Perspective* and later included in *The Peasant Mandarin*. Porter's judgement of Australia, in 'On First Looking into Chapman's Hesiod', was that it was Boeotian in character and attitude and likely to remain so, Boeotian equating to primitive, unpolished, uncultured and over-traditional. 'Australians', he said, 'are Boeotians', and he described the Boeotian poet Hesiod in terms clearly applicable to Murray:

Like a Taree small-holder splitting logs
And philosophising on his dangling billies

Chris Wallace-Crabbe later saw Murray somewhat similarly – 'Oscar Wilde in moleskins' – though Murray, indeed, has a marked preference for shorts and 'Wellies'. In his thoughts on Porter's poem Murray dated the fundamental tension that has long existed between the two models of civilisation – the rural and the urban – from the rivalry that sprang up between the newly established Athens of the sixth century BC and the older, rural Boeotia. Urban-minded Athens grew scornful of traditional, pastoral Boeotia, whose people and ways it held to be boorish and old-fashioned and whose art and culture it saw as unsophisticated and unexciting. Porter envisaged 'a new land' of the future where the individual would be valued for his intellect and culture but Australia was unlikely to become that new land, being too limited by its Boeotian past and present. Murray, however, saw merit in Australia's Boeotian-ness – it was the only true distinctiveness that Australia possessed ('our distinctiveness is still firmly anchored in the bush').

Australia, he felt, could become Porter's 'new land', but only if it retained the Boeotian quality that came with its beginnings, only if it refused to allow that rural character to be swamped by an imported, imposed Athenian culture. Among the distinctive Boeotian figures are the Aborigines – 'their culture is a Boeotian source of immeasurable value to us all'. There is 'wisdom in Australia's Boeotian-ness' and the idea of our 'deliberately remaining Boeotia is full of exciting possibilities'

It would be something indeed, to break with Western culture by not taking, even now, the characteristic second step into alienation, into élitism and the relegation of all places except one or two urban centres to the sterile status of provincial no-man's-land largely deprived of any art or any creative self-confidence. This is what is at stake.

In each of his volumes Murray has produced memorable poems. *Poems Against Economics* (1972) is a composite of three sequences, 'Seven Points for an Imperilled Star', which won the Captain Cook Bicentenary literary competition in 1970, 'Juggernaut's Little Scrapbook' and 'Walking to the Cattle Place' (q.v.). The 'Imperilled Star' sequence includes 'Toward the Imminent Days', an epithalamium for his friends Geoff Lehmann and Sally McInerney. 'Walking to the Cattle Place', a complex meditation sequence of sixteen 'cow' poems (few poets have found poetry in dairy cows) is given some framework but little explanation by Murray's comment, 'I set out to follow a cow and I found a whole world, a spacious, town-despising grassland where Celt and Zulu and Verdic Aryan were one in their concerns.' The most substantial poem in *Ethnic Radio* is 'The Bulahdelah-Taree Holiday Song Cycle' (q.v.), a group of thirteen poems (songs) in the style and metre of R.M. Berndt's translation of 'The Moon-bone Song' from the Wonguri linguistic group of the Aboriginal Mandjigai (Manjikai) tribe of north-eastern Arnhem Land. A remarkable fusing of ancient Aboriginal and modern White Australian urban and rural cultures (for example, the Pacific Highway in holiday time is described in terms of the all-giving Rainbow Snake), the 'Holiday Song Cycle' is an imaginative poetic statement of the Jindyworobak dream that White Australians should have the same affinity with the environment as the Aborigines had, and is also another emphatic illustration of the loss suffered when children grow up and desert their rural origins for urban life.

The Boys Who Stole the Funeral (q.v.), a sequence of 140 sonnets, is a novel-in-verse. Two young men, Kevin Forbutt and Cameron Reeby, steal the body of a First World War veteran, Clarrie Dunn (Kevin's great-uncle), from a Sydney funeral parlour and carry it by car to the old man's native place, an isolated spot named Dark's Plain on the NSW north coast. In carrying out the old man's wish to be buried at Dark's Plain, Kevin manages also to escape from the unrewarding urban environment into a more satisfying rural existence.

The People's Otherworld (the title a joking reference once made by him to Australia), in which Murray allowed an exuberance of language that matched his customary rich visual imagination, so dazzled the critics and literary judges that it won virtually every poetry prize in 1984. Several poems both admire and question the impact of modern technology, especially where it is dramatically changing the once familiar face of the urban landscape. Commenting on the book he remarked, 'The old idea that Murray only writes about rural stuff is an exaggeration'. In spite of that protest about a critical view that has really never been widely held, 'the governing pastoral vision with all its ambivalence toward technology', in the words of Lawrence Bourke, remains firmly in place in these poems. 'The Sydney Highrise Variations' (first published in the *Bulletin*, 1980) contains five poems. The first, 'Fuel Stoppage on Gladesville road bridge in the year 1980', sets the scene. Compelled by a car breakdown to wait 'atop a great building of the double century' (the bridge), Murray has the opportunity to take in the 'View of Sydney, Australia, from Gladesville road bridge'.

In 'The Flight from Manhattan' he attributes the modern Sydney city skyline to the New York skyscraper influence. The remaining pieces, 'The C19-20' and 'The Recession of the Jones', link the technology that produces such vast urban structures to the cargo cult of consumerism that consumes the lives of so many in contemporary times. 'Variations' certainly reflects Murray's awestruck wonder at the miracles of modern technology, but the ultimate message of the poems is regret that, in the onward march of technological genius, the old, familiar, accessible and fondly remembered Sydney that he knew has been all but obliterated. 'Machine Portraits with Pendant Spaceman', which shared the 1981 Mattara Poetry Festival Prize, is a spectacular set of ten Spenserian stanzas divided by a single sonnet (the 'Pendant Spaceman'). This is a free-wheeling, exuberant set of verses, crammed with poetic devices and sparkling with witty verbal flourishes. The machines portrayed – e.g. a bulldozer, combine seeder, satellite dish, space shuttle, crane, geophone and river ferry – demonstrate the mechanical ingenuity that Murray clearly admires but carry with them a somewhat intimidating mystique that raises the question whether they indeed are the slaves or the masters. The poems of *The Daylight Moon*, wide-ranging as ever, include a number of narratives (tall tales of the bush) based on local oral history – e.g. 'The Megaethon: 1850, 1906–29', the story of the steam engine ordained by its owner to be walked from Sydney to the Hunter Valley; 'Physiognomy on the Savage Manning River', starring the tempestuous Isabella Mary Kelly; and 'Federation Style on the Northern Rivers' in which the astute storekeeper, J. Cornwell, to save his impecunious rural customers, outwits the city auditor. Prominent in *The Daylight Moon* also are poems dealing with the return to Bunyah, e.g., 'Extract from a Verse Letter to Dennis Haskell' and 'Aspects of Language and War on the Gloucester Road'. Murray's stated aims for *Dog Fox Field* – to recover, or learn, the art of brevity and to use

rhyme freely – were born of his long-held desire to make poetry accessible to a wider reading public. Poems such as 'The Up-to-date Scarecrow', 'Midnight Lake', 'The Ballad of the Barbed Wire Ocean', 'Spotted Native Cat', 'The Tin Wash Dish' and 'Low Down Sandcastle Blues', while admittedly brief and mostly rhyming, are, at best, semi-doggerel. Defending this marked change in technique Murray indicated (in *Blocks and Tackles*) his admiration for similar nineteenth-century verse – 'newspaper' verse and the populist poetry of the *Bulletin* school – which was, he said, 'a colloquial middle-voice poetry' that caught 'a great deal of ordinary human experience' and shared it 'in an unfussed way with a broad range of people'. Until *Dog Fox Field* Murray, a truly modern bushman, had made no attempt to actually locate himself or his poetry in the Boeotian world of the Bush, no matter how strongly he and his poetry had urged the worth of that world. Some critics have seen little merit in his attempt to restore and revalue the colloquial poetry that was characteristic of it. *Dog Fox Field*, in spite of some exceptional poems – 'The Transposition of Clermont', 'The Emerald Dove', 'Hastings River Cruise' and 'Spring' – sometimes gives the impression of a poet momentarily out of sorts with himself, his muse and even the world about him. *Translations from the Natural World* indicates, having been published by Heinemann in the Australian Poetry series, that Murray's break with Angus & Robertson is complete. A multi-award winner, it also sees him return to his full capacity for brilliantly conceived and executed poetry. The book takes its title from the second section (of three) subtitled 'Presence'. Each of the forty poems in 'Presence' takes a particular natural object and attempts to 'translate' the essential presence of that object into poetry, and to link such individual presences to the one all-encompassing presence of the natural (which includes the human) world.

The Peasant Mandarin gathers together a first selection of Murray's prose, the book reviews, articles and essays that he had written from 1972 to 1977. Two articles on the plight of the impecunious artist/writer and the need for both governmental and private support, 'Patronage in Australia' (1972) and 'Patronage Revisited' (1977), helped to bring that subject more fully into public debate to the benefit of writers. 'The Australian Republic' (originally in *Quadrant* April 1976), while deploring the lack of a true political republic, takes comfort in our possession of the one that is 'inherent in our vernacular tradition', our Vernacular Republic. Complementing the 'Republic' is 'The Flag Rave' in which he rejects the 'three quarters of a national flag' that Australia has and commends (while submitting four of his own designs) the Eureka Flag. *Persistence in Folly* (1984), a further prose collection, includes the major essay 'The Human Hair Thread', in which he pays tribute to the Aborigines and to the Jindyworobak movement, acknowledging aspects of both as the sources of his own view of the Australian psyche. *Blocks and Tackles* brought together his articles and essays from 1982 to 1990. 'Poems and Poesies' and 'Poemes and the Mystery of Embodiment', complex examinations of the inner workings of poetry and an essay on the timber-working history of the lower north coast, are notable pieces. *The Paperbark Tree*, published in England, contains thirty-eight prose pieces, all of which have appeared in other publications.

Lawrence Bourke's *A Vivid Steady State* (1992) is the first of an undoubted stream of major critical works on Murray destined to appear in the future.

Murray River, more than 2500 kilometres long, rises in the Australian Alps just south of Mt Kosciusko, flows for much of its distance as the border between NSW and Victoria, then enters SA and reaches the ocean through the waters of Lake Alexandrina. The Murray was discovered in 1824 by Hamilton Hume and William Hovell who named it the Hume, and was charted by Charles Sturt who renamed it after Sir George Murray, then secretary of state for the colonies. Sturt travelled by boat in 1830 from Gundagai, on the Murrumbidgee River to Lake Alexandrina and back again. Following the tracks of these early explorers, and others such as Sir Thomas Mitchell, overlanders and pastoralists soon occupied the river and its environs. The Murray exploration literature includes Hume and Hovell's *Journey of Discovery to Port Phillip* (1831) compiled by William Bland, Charles Sturt's *Two Expeditions into the Interior of Southern Australia* (1833), and T.L. Mitchell's *Three Expeditions into the Interior of Eastern Australia* (1838). Settlement literature of the Murray region includes travellers' and pastoralists' memoirs and reminiscences such as T.F. Bride's *Letters from Victorian Pioneers* (1898); R.V. Billis and A.S. Kenyon's *Pastures New* (1930) and *Pastoral Pioneers of Port Phillip* (1932); and Joseph Hawdon's *The Journal of a Journey from New South Wales to Adelaide* (first published 1952). Allan Morris's *Rich River* (1953) is a historical account of the Murray riverboat trade, based on the McCulloch Carrying Company papers; Ian Mudie's *Riverboats* (1961) also highlights the colour and excitement of the river trade; Charles Shaw's poem 'Murray Memory' is a nostalgic re-creation of the riverboat days. G.W. Broughton wrote *Men of the Murray* (1966), Joe Anderson, *Murray Riverman: The Life of George Freeman* (who worked on the Murray for some thirty years) (1986) and John Larkins and Steve Parish published *Australia's Greatest River* (1982). The major fictional work in which the Murray and its riverboats are the central characters is Nancy Cato's trilogy *All the Rivers Run* (1958), *Time, Flow Softly* (1959) and *But Still the Stream* (1962). A rewritten combination of the three volumes was published as a single volume, *All the Rivers Run* (1979), and a television series was screened in 1983. Max Fatchen published two books about the river for children, *The River Kings* (1966, a TV series in 1991) and *Conquest of the River* (1970). Tom Collins in *Such is Life* (1903) loses his trousers trying to cross the Murray, which also figures prominently in *Rigby's Romance* (1948).

MURRAY, Robert William Felton Lathrop(p) (1777–1850), born Shropshire, England, was baptised Robert Felton Lathropp but took the additional surname of Murray, claiming connection with a

baronetcy, after coming of age; there have also been suggestions, usually discarded, that he was a natural son of George III. Commissioned in the army in 1797, Murray served in the Peninsular Wars, and may have met Napoleon in exile at Elba; the meeting, although never confirmed, has been taken by some as evidence either that Murray was acting as emissary for the royal family and was indeed of royal parentage, or that he was engaged in undercover work for the government. As a consequence, his conviction for bigamy in 1815 has been interpreted as a trumped-up charge designed to remove an embarrassing witness from England. Murray fought vigorously in petitions, e.g. *An Appeal to the British Nation* (1815), and broadsides, e.g. *The Case of Captain Murray* (1842), to overturn the conviction, but was transported to Australia. He served his sentence in Sydney before moving to the developing colony of Van Diemen's Land, where for over two decades he was a prominent polemicist and newspaper editor. Under the pseudonym 'A Colonist', Murray wrote a series of letters in the *Hobart Town Gazette* in 1824–25 attacking the administration of Lieutenant-Governor George Arthur. Briefly editor of the *Hobart Town Gazette* (1825) and its successor the *Colonial Times* (1825–26), Murray founded *Murray's Austral-Asiatic Review* in 1828. Founded as a monthly magazine rather than as a newspaper in order to circumvent Arthur's licensing provisions, the *Austral-Asiatic Review* ran until 1845; it underwent several changes of name and was intermittently amalgamated with the *Tasmanian*. After 1828 Murray was more kindly disposed towards Arthur but remained a firm defender of press freedom and wrote vigorously from a humanitarian stance on transportation and press freedom.

MURRAY-SMITH, Stephen (1922–88), born Melbourne, was educated at Geelong Grammar, which inspired in him both a dislike of authority and an ideal of community, and at the University of Melbourne. After serving with the AIF as a commando in New Guinea during the Second World War, he lived in London and Prague 1948–51. A member of the Communist Party of Australia for thirteen years, he became organising secretary of the Australian Peace Council, and a prominent member of the Melbourne Realist Writers Group. Editor of the *Realist Writer* 1952–54, in 1954 he founded the magazine *Overland* (q.v.), which he edited until his death. A reader in education at the University of Melbourne, and editor of the series *Melbourne Studies in Education* to 1982, he was also chairman of the National Book Council for two years from 1981. One of the greatest passions of his later years and the stimulus for several books was the social dynamics of island communities, especially those of Bass Strait; for the last twenty-five years of his life he returned annually with other writers and friends to Erith Island for a communal holiday. Murray-Smith edited a range of books including two collections of short stories, *The Tracks We Travel* (1953) and, with Judah Waten, *Classic Australian Short Stories* (1974); a collection of writing from *Overland*, *An Overland Muster* (1965); an edition of Marcus Clarke's *For the Term of His Natural Life* (1970); with Leonie Sandercock, a selection of Ian

Turner's writing, *Room for Manoeuvre* (1982); and the journals of the missionary voyages of Canon Marcus Brownrigg 1872–85, *Mission to the Islands* (1979). With Edgar Waters he compiled the collection *Rebel Songs* (1947) and, with John Thompson, *Bass Strait Bibliography* (1981). He wrote a short study of Henry Lawson (1962, 2nd edn 1975); an autobiography based on a series of lectures delivered at James Cook University in 1979, *Indirections* (1981); an account of a visit to Antarctica 1985–86, *Sitting on Penguins* (1988); and compiled an extensive *Dictionary of Australian Quotations* (1984) and a guide to English usage in Australia, *Right Words* (1987). Under the pseudonym 'Simon Ffuckes', he compiled with Ken Gott ('Sebastian Hogbotel') a collection of bawdy songs, *Snatches & Lays* (1973), which includes verse from such writers as A.D. Hope, James McAuley and Robert Brissenden. In 1981 he was made AM.

MUSGROVE, George (1854–1916), born Surbiton, England, into a theatrical family, came to Victoria at the age of 12, and later worked for W.S. Lyster. In 1880 he had his first entrepreneurial success with Offenbach's *Tambour Major* at the Melbourne Opera House; in 1882 he entered into partnership with George Garner and J.C. Williamson, and with one interruption continued to work as Williamson's partner until 1899. Musgrove energetically and imaginatively produced shows until 1914, with varying degrees of commercial success, and fostered the careers of several successful stars, including Nellie Stewart, with whom he formed an alliance, and Dame Nellie Melba.

MUSKETT, Alice Jane ('Jane Laker') (1869–1936), born Melbourne, studied painting with Julian Ashton, who made three portraits of her, and at the Académie Colarossi in Paris. She exhibited annually from 1890 with the Art Society of NSW and with the Society of Artists, Sydney, from 1895. In 1928 she endowed the Phillip Muskett prize at Ashton's Sydney Art School in memory of her brother. She also published verse and short stories and, as 'Jane Laker', a novel, *Among the Reeds* (1933). Partly autobiographical, the novel expresses feminist attitudes, exploring the dilemma of women forced to choose between family and career.

MUSPRATT, Eric (1899–1949), born England, led an extremely colourful life as a traveller or professional tramp, and a womaniser. His travels, which took him around the world four times and included several visits to Australia, were interspersed by brief periods in prison in South Africa and England. He served in the AIF in both world wars and subsequently settled in Victoria. He published five autobiographical accounts, *My South Sea Island* (1931), his most popular book, which sold particularly well in America, *Wild Oats* (1932), *The Journey Home* (1933), *Greek Seas* (1933) and *Fire of Youth* (1948); and three novels which draw heavily on his unusual experiences, *Ambition* (1934), *Going Native* (1936) and *Time is a Cheat* (1946).

MUTCH, T.D. (Thomas Davies) (1885–1958), born London and educated in Sydney, became a rural worker before joining the staff of the labour newspaper the *Worker*. In 1902 he met Henry Lawson (q.v.), to whom he offered friendship and practical assistance during the long years of Lawson's decline. Active in local government and newspaper unionism, he held office in the AJA and entered politics in 1917, distributing a broadsheet testimonial from Lawson to his Botany electors during his first campaign. He served in the NSW parliament 1917–30 and 1938–41, and as minister for education was the subject of Lawson's satiric poem 'The Parsin for Edgerkashun', published in the *Lone Hand* in February 1921; later that year Lawson retracted this 'cowardly attack on an old friend and mate' in a poem titled 'A Song of Mutch and Little', which was reprinted as *Henry Lawson's Message to the Electors of Botany* in Mutch's 1925 election campaign. For over forty years a trustee of the Public Library of NSW, Mutch was active also in the Royal Australian Historical Society and the Society of Australian Genealogists, which named an annual lecture after him; he conducted extensive research into early Australian history and genealogy and his indexes to historical material are now in the Mitchell Library. His writings include important biographical articles and reminiscences about Lawson, an edition of the journals of Lachlan Macquarie (1956), and historical material used in radio scripts.

My Army, O, My Army! and Other Songs, the book of poems which briefly re-established Henry Lawson (q.v.) as a leading verse commentator on public events, was published in 1915; the following year the contents of the volume were reassembled and published as *Song of the Dardanelles*. The poems in *My Army, O, My Army!*, which were mostly written in 1914–15 and first published in the *Bulletin*, reflect Lawson's reaction to the outbreak of the First World War. His early enthusiasm for the war as good for national character is apparent in *My Army, O, My Army!*; so also is the imperial fervour which stands in contrast to his socialist republicanism of the 1880s. The title poem, however, in which the army referred to is the same army of the poor as in 'The Army of the Rear', is remarkably prophetic of the Russian Revolution.

My Brilliant Career (1901), the first of the novels published by Miles Franklin (q.v.) in her own name, was written and revised in the period September 1898 to November 1899, when the author was 19. Henry Lawson wrote the preface for it, offered the opinion that it 'beats *Jane Eyre* or the *African Farm*' and helped to have it published in England by Blackwoods. The novel's heroine, Sybylla Melvyn, a girl of 16, rebels against the stagnant life on her parents' dairy farm at Possum Gully and against the inevitable fate of teaching or marriage that awaits her; both forms of 'slavery' are distasteful to her, but she sees marriage as particularly degrading. Rescued temporarily by a period with her affluent grandmother at the congenial station homestead, Caddagat, she faces interwoven problems – her sexual ambivalence which is characterised by strong physical attraction to eligible young squatter Harold Beecham, and an equally strong physical revulsion which causes her to slash his face with a whip when he attempts to kiss her; and her fierce insistence on retaining her independence. The ultimate disqualification of Harold Beecham is that 'he offered me everything – but control'. The novel's setting in the picturesque Monaro district, its close description of station and farming life, its poignant assessment of the barren existence in the bush for a sensitive girl or woman, and its love of the Australian landscape led Lawson to declare it 'true to Australia – the truest I ever read'. With its strong autobiographical links, the novel brought both fame and distress to its author. She later claimed that friends and relatives were hurt by the book's personal disclosures and that she was embarrassed by the publicity and by their reaction. Sale of the book was stopped by her in 1910 and she refused permission on many occasions for its reprinting. An Australian film of the book was made in 1979.

My Brother Jack (1964), a novel by George Johnston and the first of his semi-autobiographical trilogy, was succeeded by *Clean Straw for Nothing* (q.v., 1969) and *A Cartload of Clay* (1971). It won the Miles Franklin Award and was adapted for television by Charmian Clift. Set in lower-class Melbourne, mainly between the wars, it deals with the different histories of the narrator, David Meredith, and his brother Jack. Beginning in 1919, when both Meredith parents return from the First World War to resume the care of their four children, the story describes first the effect on the Meredith family of the war's aftermath, brought home most forcibly to the two boys by the disabled soldiers their mother brings home to nurse, then the gradual reduction to humdrum normality and later the social upheaval of the 1930s Depression. Jack, straightforward, frankly virile, the epitome of the mythical Australian, engages in an uninhibited pursuit of adventure, whereas David, introverted and escapist, becomes absorbed in a private world of writing. As Jack attempts to wrest a living from the bush, undergoes severe suffering during the Depression and takes on family responsibilities, David, while ostensibly committed to his apprenticeship to a printing firm, establishes himself as a correspondent for the *Morning Post* under the benevolent patronage of its editor, Mr Brewster. Released by the Depression from this ambiguous situation, and his career as a reporter on the ascendant, he becomes involved with, and subsequently marries, Helen Midgely. But he soon recognises that his marriage is a mistake, largely because of his friendship with a colleague, Gavin Turley, and he quickly escapes from it with the outbreak of war. As David becomes increasingly aware of his growing, but unmerited reputation as the courageous war correspondent, Jack's genuine heroic potential is frustrated by an accident and he never sees action. The novel ends as the war comes to a close and David embarks on a serious relationship with Cressida Morley, a girl who represents the freedom and vitality he has always sought.

'My Country', a poem by Dorothea Mackellar (q.v.), was first published as 'Core of My Heart' in the London *Spectator* 5 September 1908, but was published in the *Sydney Mail* 21 October 1908 as 'My Country', the title which has acquired fame in Australian literature. A recitation and anthology favourite, 'My Country' is a poem of six eight-line stanzas which contrasts a love of the English landscape,

> The love of field and coppice,
> Of green and shaded lanes,

with the poet's love of Australia represented, for example, in its famous second stanza:

> I love a sunburnt country
> A land of sweeping plains,
> Of ragged mountain ranges,
> Of droughts and flooding rains.
> I love her far horizons,
> I love her jewel-sea
> Her beauty and her terror
> The wide brown land for me!

Most versions of the poem print 'rugged' in the third line, although Mackellar is recorded as having intended 'ragged'. Similarly, there are several versions of the poem's origins: by one account it was written in response to the 'anti-Australianism . . . of many Australians we knew', by another it was inspired by the breaking of the drought on the Mackellar property of Torryburn, near Maitland in NSW. The popularity of 'My Country' is evidenced in the way some of its phrases have been appropriated: *The Wide Brown Land* is the title of anthologies of Australian verse edited by Joan S. and George Mackaness (1934), one of the best-known anthologies, and by Douglas Stewart (1971), and several publications have adopted or adapted the phrase 'a sunburnt country'. Despite the preference for 'a sunburnt country' in her most famous poem, Mackellar was attracted in other moods to other landscapes. For example, in 'Merry England' *(Dreamharbour*, 1923) she writes that

> England wrapped me in her cloak
> Silvery-grey, silvery-gold,
> Silvery-grey and gold and green,
> Whose touch can heal the sorest stroke –
> Mother and Priestess, Nurse and Queen.

My Love Must Wait (1941), a novel by Ernestine Hill (q.v.), is based on the life of Matthew Flinders. Carefully researched from Flinders's manuscripts and given additional atmosphere and colour by her own retracing of his circumnavigation of the continent, sometimes using a copy of the charts that he had made more than a hundred years earlier, Ernestine Hill's novel is an imaginative and highly sympathetic portrait of the celebrated navigator. In addition to her detailed accounts of his voyages culminating in his proof, by circumnavigation in 1802–3, that Australia was indeed 'Terra Australis', Ernestine Hill provides many interesting biographical details of Flinders: his daydreams of Robinson Crusoe islands during his boyhood in the Lincolnshire village of Donington; his youthful friendship with George Bass, the apothecary's apprentice in the nearby town of Boston; his opinion of Bligh of the *Bounty* with whom he sailed to the Pacific as a midshipman; his adventures with Bass in *Tom Thumb*; his marriage to Ann Chappell in 1801; his long imprisonment 1803–10 on Mauritius because of the vindictiveness of the French governor, General de Caen; his reunion with his wife in 1810 after nine years' separation; his arduous work of preparing the monumental text of his explorations, *A Voyage to Terra Australis* (1814), and his claim to be recognised as the first user of the name 'Australia'. In an unusual concluding chapter to the novel, Ernestine Hill abandons the fictional mode to reveal the remarkable emotional affinity that developed between her and Flinders: 'Matthew Flinders, long dead, became to me as a friend'. The final chapter, a résumé of the achievements of Flinders, also adds some later family history and outlines the various ways in which the navigator's exploits have since been recognised in Australia.

My Note Book, a weekly literary journal published in Melbourne 1856–59, edited by Thomas Lockyer Bright, Charles Bright and J.E. Neild, included verse, theatrical notices, prose sketches, serials and book reviews as well as articles on current affairs. Contributors included David Blair, R.H. Horne, George Gordon McCrae and James Smith.

Myall Creek Massacre, 9 June 1838, was a highly publicised atrocity in which twenty-eight Aborigines were shot and their bodies burned by twelve White men, eleven of them convicts, on the Myall Creek run of squatter Henry Dangar in the northern tablelands of NSW, north-west of the present township of Guyra. Governor George Gipps, in spite of the widely held view in the Colony that it was absurd to punish White men for the extermination of the Aborigines, and in the face of outraged editorial comment of such newspapers as the *Sydney Morning Herald*, proceeded to charge eleven of the White men with murder. Although they were acquitted on the first charge of murdering two Aboriginal adult males, seven were found guilty of a subsequent charge of murdering an Aboriginal child and were executed 18 December 1838. The massacre and trial were prominently featured in many later accounts of the Aboriginal problem in the Colony, e.g. in Alexander Harris's *Settlers and Convicts* (1847), R. Therry's *Reminiscences of Thirty Years' Residence in New South Wales and Victoria* (1863) and T.F. Bride's *Letters from Victorian Pioneers* (1898). 'Myall' (*myal*) an Aboriginal word meaning 'wild' or 'savage', came to be used generally to denote the hostile native of the less settled areas. There is a sympathetic poem by Mary Gilmore titled 'The Myall in Prison' and Charles Harpur, who witnessed the Myall Creek executions, wrote a poem, 'An Aboriginal Mother's Lament', based on the massacre. The massacre is also described in *The Wallabadah Manuscript* (1981), and features in Philip McLaren's novel *Sweet Water – Stolen Land* (1993).

MYERS, David (1942–   ), professor of comparative literature at the University of Central Queensland, has lectured at the universities of Adelaide, Toronto and Cologne. He has published a collection of poems, *The Oversexed Canary* (1981); an interpretation of Patrick White's short stories, *The Peacocks and the Bourgeoisie* (1978); a study of Australia's national legends, *Bleeding Battlers From Ironbark: Australian Myths in Fiction & Film 1890s–1980s* (1987); a collection of short stories, *Mudmaps to Paradise* (1987); and a humorous, loosely connected group of stories in which Queensland or its facsimile is the main character but which are also dominated by Myron Byron, 'a successful schizophrenic and an authentic postmodernist', *Cornucopia County* (1991). He has also edited a collection of essays titled *The Great Literacy Debate: English in Contemporary Australia* (1992).

Mystery of a Hansom Cab, The, a novel by Fergus Hume (q.v.), was first published in Melbourne in 1886. A significant early example of detective fiction, it was a huge success both there and in England, where the Hansom Cab Publishing Company, in which Hume had no financial interest, was formed. A stage adaptation of the novel, first staged in Australia by George Darrell in 1888, later had a long run in London; Barry Pree wrote a later adaptation (1961). Written in the style of Emile Gaboriau (1832–73), the father of the detective novel in France, *The Mystery of a Hansom Cab* opens with the *Argus* report of the murder of an unknown man in a Melbourne cab. Detective Gorby, assigned to the case, pieces together the identity of the man, Oliver Whyte, a rake recently arrived from England who has been paying court to a Melbourne beauty, Madge Frettlby. Gorby's suspicions fall on Madge's fiancé Brian Fitzgerald, who is tried for the murder but acquitted when a missing witness, Sal Rawlins, turns up at the last moment to testify that Fitzgerald had been visiting a dying woman in a Melbourne slum at the time of the murder. The second part of the novel unravels the mystery of both the murder and Fitzgerald's hostility since his arrest towards his prospective father-in-law, Mark Frettlby. The dying woman, a former actress named Rosanna Moore, has revealed to Brian that she is Mark Frettlby's wife, long thought dead, that Sal is their daughter and that Madge is therefore illegitimate. As Rosanna and Whyte have been blackmailing Mark Frettlby, Brian is convinced that Frettlby is the murderer; however, Frettlby's confession to the marriage, discovered after his death from a heart attack, states that the murderer is Whyte's companion Roger Moreland, who hopes also to blackmail Frettlby. Moreland's suicide after his arrest allows the secret of Madge's illegitimacy to be preserved and she and Brian leave Australia after their marriage for a new life overseas. A parody of *The Mystery of a Hansom Cab*, titled *The Mystery of a Wheelbarrow, or Gaboriam Gaborooed* (by 'W. Humer Ferguson'), was published in 1888.

N

NAGEL, Charles, see **Shakespeare and Australia**

NAISH, John (1923–63), born Wales, served in the British Army during the Second World War and came to Australia in 1950. He worked as a cane-cutter, labourer, miner, barman, clerk and fruit-picker, spent some time in Fiji and returned to Australia in 1958. He published two novels, *The Cruel Field* (1962), which deals with life on the canefields; *That Men Should Fear* (1963), a study of an affluent Australian farming family and its struggle with an incurable inherited disease; and an autobiography, *The Clean Breast* (1961). His plays include *The Claw* in *Australian One-Act Plays Book II*, ed. Greg Branson (1962), *Deuteronomy* in the Derwent Series of *Australian One-Act Plays*, 2nd series (1961), 'The First Mrs Peters', 'The Maoris', 'The Paul Davis Affair' and 'The Strange Black Creatures'.

NAMATJIRA, Albert (1902–59), the Aboriginal artist, was born at Hermannsburg Lutheran Mission near Alice Springs, where he received some education; a member of the Arrernte (Aranda) people, he was also initiated into tribal life. He became acquainted with Rex Battarbee, an Australian artist, who taught and encouraged him in the 1930s, held several exhibitions of his landscape paintings from the late 1930s to the 1950s and described his work in *Modern Australian Aboriginal Art* (1951). While he was celebrated in the south for his work, Namatjira was refused the benefits of White civilisation in the Northern Territory. His application for a grazing lease was rejected in 1948 and he was unable to build a house in Alice Springs. In 1957 he was granted full citizenship, which enabled him to purchase alcohol legally, but which also put him under pressure to share this, as all other things, with his people. He was sentenced to six months' imprisonment for supplying alcohol to an Aborigine in 1958 and died in 1959 soon after his release from confinement. As he painted in watercolour, Namatjira was regarded by many critics during his lifetime as working outside the Aboriginal tradition. A major retrospective exhibition at the opening of the Araluen Arts Centre in Alice Springs in 1984 was followed by a reassessment of his work, which recognised that his painting expressed an Aboriginal spirituality and identity with the landscape. Accounts of his life and work include C.P. Mountford's *The Art of Albert Namatjira* (1944), Victor Hall's *Namatjira of the Aranda* (1962) and Joyce D. Batty's *Namatjira: Wanderer Between Two Worlds* (1963). *The Heritage of Namatjira: The Watercolourists of Central Australia* (1992) ed. Jane Hardy, J.V.S. Megaw and M. Ruth Megaw and published in association with a touring exhibition of the same name, and Nadine Amadio's *Albert Namatjira: the Life and Work of an Australian Painter* (1986), place his work within the history and stylistic development of Aranda art and discuss his influence on later Hermannsburg watercolourists, including his sons, Enos, Ewald, Oscar and Kevin, and a number of grandchildren.

NANDAN, Satendra (1939–), born Fiji of Indian descent, is a graduate of the universities of Delhi, Leeds and the ANU. He taught at the University of the South Pacific 1969–87, was elected to the Fijian Parliament in 1982, as Fiji's first Labour MP, and again in 1987, when he became Minister for Health, Social Welfare and Women's Studies in the short-lived Bavadra coalition government, ousted by the military coup of 1987. He now lives in Canberra, where he teaches at the University of Canberra. He has written a novel, *The Wounded Sea* (1991), based mainly on his childhood, although it includes an account of the events of 1987. Before coming to Australia Nandan published two volumes of verse, *Faces in a Village* (1979) and *Voices in the River* (1985). He is the editor of *Language and Literature in Multicultural Contexts* (1983).

NANKIVELL, Joice (?–1988), born Queensland and brought up partly in Gippsland, published a collection of prose and verse for children, *The Cobweb Ladder* (1916); a collection of sketches of bush and city life, *The Solitary Pedestrian* (1918); and an account of life in Moscow from 1923 to the death of Lenin, *The Fourteen Thumbs of St Peter* (1926). Her *Collected Poems* appeared in 1980. With her husband, Frederick Loch (q.v.), she also published an account of a visit to Ireland 1920–21, *Ireland in Travail* (1922); and of life in Eastern Poland after the First World War, *The River of a Hundred Ways* (1924). The Lochs settled in Greece 1923–29, combining work for refugees with writing, worked for Polish refugees in Bulgaria and Romania 1939–44, and returned to Greece after the war. Their experiences are described in Joice Nankivell's autobiography *A Fringe of Blue* (1968), which she published under her married name.

NANNUP, Alice (1911–), born on a Pilbara station of an Aboriginal mother and a European father, was removed from her community at the age of 12 and sent south to be trained as a domestic servant. After her marriage in 1932 she raised ten children. Her account of her struggle with hardship and poverty and her encounters with White ignorance and prejudice, told frankly and without rancour to Lauren Marsh and Stephen Kinnane, was published in 1992, titled *When the Pelican Laughed.*

NAPIER, Sydney Elliott (1870–1940), born Sydney, trained as a solicitor. He served with the AIF during the First World War and returned in 1919 to Australia, where he worked as a legal officer and freelance journalist; in 1925 he joined the *Sydney Morning Herald*. Subsequently assistant editor of the *Sydney Mail* and leader-writer of the *Sydney Morning Herald*, he compiled, with P.S. Allen, *A Century of Journalism: The Sydney Morning Herald and Its Record of Australian Life 1831–1931* (1931). He contributed prose and verse to numerous English and Australian journals and newspapers, and published a collection of essays, *The Magic Carpet* (1932); a collection of biographical sketches, *Great Lovers* (1934); and two collections of verse, *Potted Biographies* (1930) and *Underneath the Bough* (1937). He also wrote a history of the Sydney Repertory Theatre Society (1923); a series of travel accounts, *On The Barrier Reef* (1928), *Walks Abroad* (1929), *Men and Cities* (1938) and *This Roundabout* (1938); and edited *The Book of the Anzac Memorial* (1934).

NATHAN, Isaac (1790–1864), musician and musical librarian to George IV, was born in Kent of Polish-Jewish parents. A friend of Lord Byron, he persuaded him in 1814 to write a series of poems on Hebrew subjects, which he set to adaptations of ancient Jewish chants and titled *Hebrew Melodies* (1815). Deprived of patronage by Byron's flight from England in 1816 and the death of his pupil, Princess Charlotte, Nathan composed musical comedies and operatic pieces such as *Sweethearts and Wives* (1823) and *The Alcaid* (1824). His *An Essay on the History and Theory of Music* (1823) acquired a European reputation and in 1829 he edited *Fugitive Pieces and Reminiscences of Lord Byron*. By 1837 Nathan's financial state was precarious and, unable to obtain payment for secret services he had rendered William IV before his death, he left for Australia. In Sydney he rapidly acquired the status of leading musician and composed several odes to mark public events, including 'Australia the Wide and Free' (1842), 'Currency Lasses' (1846) and 'Leichhardt's Grave' (1846). In May 1847 his romantic opera *Don John of Austria*, the first opera to be composed and produced in Australia, was performed in the Victoria Theatre. Another Australian achievement of note is his miscellany *The Southern Euphrosyne and Australian Miscellany* (1849), which includes sections on Aboriginal music. Studies of Nathan include those by C.H. Bertie (1922) and O.S. Phillips (1940) and Catherine Mackerras's *The Hebrew Melodist* (1963).

Nation: An Independent Journal of Opinion, a fortnightly periodical, was founded and edited by Tom Fitzgerald and published in Sydney 1958–72. George Munster, business manager, occasional associate editor and prolific author of articles both under his own name and under pseudonyms, was a major contributor to the journal's continuance. Caslon Press, run by Francis James, produced the journal. Representing mainly the views of the liberal left, *Nation* attracted a range of contributors including Cyril Pearl, H.G. Kippax, W. McMahon Ball, Max Harris, Sylvia Lawson, Ken Inglis, Brian Johns, Manning Clark, Robert Hughes, Hugh Stretton, Judah Waten and Bob Ellis. Many writers, employed by other newspapers, used pseudonyms. *Nation* covered a full range of topics including economics, urban planning, literature and the visual and performing arts, cultural events and issues, and foreign policy. At the time of its inception, the Labor Party was still handicapped by ideological differences and the Liberal Party was imprisoned within outdated post-colonial attitudes; *Nation*, it was hoped, would appeal to those small 'l' liberals who were virtually disenfranchised. With the *Observer* the journal had a marked impact on the level of Australian journalism, raising the standard of debate in a period of radical change. *Nation: The Life of an Independent Journal of Opinion 1958–1972* (1989), edited by Ken Inglis, reprints some of the articles published in the journal and provides information both on *Nation* and its contributors and cultural context. *Nation* merged with the *Review* to form *Nation Review* in 1972.

Nation Review, a weekly newspaper published in Melbourne, ran 1972–81 and was formed by the merger of the Sydney *Nation* (q.v.) and the Melbourne *Review* (q.v.). Radical and provocative, in accordance with its self-adopted nickname 'The Ferret', *Nation Review* frequently published controversial articles on Australian writers, pugnacious literary debates and outspoken book reviews and theatrical notices. Michael Leunig (q.v.) frequently contributed cartoons expressive of the spirit of the newspaper. Richard Walsh (q.v.) compiled a selection, *Ferretobilia: Life and Times of Nation Review* (1993).

National Anthem. Until 1974 'God Save the King' or 'God Save the Queen' was the Australian national anthem, before 1901 because the Australian colonies 'belonged' to Great Britain and after 1901 because it became the national anthem of the Commonwealth of Australia. There has, however, been a long history of dissatisfaction in some quarters with 'God Save the King/Queen' and many Australian writers or composers have attempted to compose an alternative anthem. Among them were the republican John Dunmore Lang, who included an 'Australian Anthem' and an 'Australian Hymn' in his *Aurora Australis* (1826); Nathaniel Kentish, who was one of several writers who composed national songs in the 1850s, around the time of the separation of Victoria from NSW; James Brunton Stephens, who wrote a new national anthem in 1902 to the music of 'God Save the King'; A.H. Adams, whose 'Fling Out the Flag' won first prize in an anthem competition sponsored by the Musical Association of NSW in 1913; and Marie Pitt, who won an ABC competition in 1945 with 'Ave Australia'. Neither these compositions nor the many others submitted at the several competitions organised since Federation, e.g. one run by the Australian Council for the Arts in 1973 which attracted 2500 verse entries, won any popular support to replace 'God Save the Queen/King', but three songs have had their champions: 'Advance Australia Fair', composed about 1878 by Peter Dodds McCormick; 'Song of Australia', composed by Carl Linger in 1860; and 'Waltzing Matilda' (q.v.), Australia's most famous song and the one most closely identified with the country by non-Australians. In 1974, after a sample poll of these three songs at which 'Advance Australia Fair' received just over half the vote, the then prime minister, E.G. Whitlam, announced that 'Advance Australia Fair' would supersede 'God Save the Queen' as the national tune (i.e. its words were not then officially recognised), except during the presence of the Queen or when it was necessary to acknowledge Australian links with the royal family, when both would be played; in 1975–76 the governor-general's salute combined the first six bars of 'God Save the Queen' and the last few bars of 'Advance Australia Fair'. This decision was modified in 1976 by the then prime minister, Malcolm Fraser, whose government reinstated 'God Save the Queen' for royal, vice-regal and defence occasions and for others left optional the choice between 'God Save the Queen' and 'Advance Australia Fair'. Thus at the 1980 Olympic Games 'God Save the Queen' was played when Australian swimmers won gold medals, but for the equivalent ceremonies at the 1982 Commonwealth Games the choice was 'Advance Australia Fair'. These guidelines, laid down formally in 1978 after a national poll at which the figures were approximately 43 per cent for 'Advance Australia Fair', 28 per cent for 'Waltzing Matilda', 18 per cent for 'God Save the Queen' and 10 per cent for 'Song of Australia', remained in force until April 1984, when the federal government announced that 'Advance Australia Fair' (with some words modernised or made non-sexist) would become the national anthem except during the presence of the Queen, when 'God Save the Queen' would be played.

National Book Council was created in 1973 to promote books and book use and to bring together a variety of organisations and individuals who had an interest in, or concern for, books. Foundation members of the Council, which has rapidly expanded since its inception, included the ASA, the Australian Book Publishers' Association, the Library Association of Australia, the FAW, the Australian Booksellers' Association, the Australian Library Promotion Council, the Book Trade Group, the Children's Book Council and the National Library. Managed by a governing council (assisted by the Literature Board of the Australia Council and Arts Victoria) which draws representatives from professional and trade organisations, the National Book Council has instituted a system of annual literary awards, sponsored book fairs and Australian Book Week, and publishes material relevant to the book trade, as well as the revived monthly *Australian Book Review* (1978–   ). The National Book Council administers, among others, the Qantas New Writers Award, the Lysbeth Cohen Memorial Prize and the Turnbull Fox Phillips Poetry Award. The

NBC's newsletter, *Thumbnail*, is published bi-monthly.

Since 1988 the NBC's annual literary awards, for books published in Australia, have been known as the NBC Banjo Awards. Since 1991 they have been sponsored by Carlton and United Breweries, having been chiefly funded by the Literature Board of the Australia Council 1973–86. The first NBC Award for Australian literature was to Roland Robinson for his autobiography *The Drift of Things* (1973). NBC Awards are for fiction and non-fiction. Winners for fiction have included Murray Bail (*Homesickness*, 1980), David Foster (*Moonlite* 1981), Peter Carey (*Bliss*, 1982), Olga Masters (*The Home Girls*, 1983), Peter Carey (*Illywhacker*, 1985), Morris Lurie (*Whole Life*, 1988), Peter Carey (*Oscar and Lucinda*, 1989), Thea Welsh (*The Story of the Year 1912 in the Village of Elza Darzins*, 1990), Tim Winton (*Cloudstreet*) and Glenda Adams (*Longleg*) both 1991, Alan Gould (*To the Burning City*, 1992), and Liam Davison (*Soundings*, 1993). Some poets have been awarded prizes, e.g. Dimitris Tsaloumas, Les Murray, Alan Wearne. Biographers Elsie Webster, Geoffrey Serle, Brenda Niall, David Marr and Drusilla Modjeska and autobiographers Albert Facey and Bernard Smith have also been prize-winners.

National Institute of Dramatic Art (NIDA) was founded in 1958 under the auspices of the University of NSW, the Australian Elizabethan Theatre Trust and in association with the ABC 'to encourage the knowledge and appreciation of drama, opera, music and all the arts of the theatre, and in particular to provide training for young people who wish to enter the profession of theatre as actors, directors, designers and stage-managers'. Located on the campus of the University, which originally provided financial assistance as well as makeshift accommodation, NIDA moved into purpose-built buildings incorporating a theatre in 1988. NIDA offers courses in acting, technical production, design, directing, theatre crafts, production management and voice and movement studies to a small group of stringently selected students. Professor Robert Quentin, head of the University's department of drama and a member of the University of NSW Drama Foundation (q.v.), was founder and first director of NIDA (1958–63); Tom Brown (1963–68) and John Clark (1968–   ) were subsequent directors. It has been financially supported by the Commonwealth government through the Australian Elizabethan Theatre Trust, the Australia Council, the Tertiary Education Commission and the then Department of the Arts, Sport, the Environment, Tourism and Territories. NIDA has founded theatre companies characterised by a commitment to Australian drama, including the Old Tote Theatre Company (q.v.), which was established in 1963 and became independent in 1969, and Jane Street (q.v.), which functioned between 1966 and 1980. Well-known NIDA graduates include Kate Fitzpatrick, Garry McDonald, Helen Morse, Judy Davis, Mel Gibson, Robyn Nevin, Aubrey Mellor, Jim Sharman, Colin Friels, Hugo Weaving, Sandy Gore and Peter Kingston.

National Library of Australia was known as the Commonwealth National Library from 1923 to 1960, developed from 1901 from the parliamentary library, and was finally established as an autonomous corporate body by the National Library Act of 1960. The Petherick Collection Act of 1911 secured for the library the extensive collection related to Australasia and the Pacific assembled by E.A. Petherick (q.v.) and the inclusion of legal deposit provision in the Copyright Act of 1912 enabled the library to claim one copy of Australian publications free of charge. Other important collections acquired by the library were those of Sir John Ferguson and Rex de C. Nan Kivell. Dispersed in various buildings in Canberra from its early years, the several collections were brought together in one building in 1968. C.A. Burmester has compiled *National Library of Australia: Guide to the Collections* (1974, 1977, 1980 and 1982). The bibliographical services of the library are reflected in a range of regular publications including *Australian National Bibliography, Australian Government Publications, Australian Books, APAIS: Australian Public Affairs Information Service* and *ABC (Acquisition, Bibliography, Cataloguing) News*. In 1981 the library launched a national on-line shared cataloguing network, the Australian Bibliographical Network (ABN), which, by June 1991, was being used by more than 1100 client libraries, including virtually every Australian library of significant size. As retrospective files were added to the database, ABN rapidly began to supplant the function of the National Library's *National Union Catalogue of Monographs (NUCOM)*, which has now closed, although it may still need to be consulted for pre-1970 foreign titles. ABN claims a comprehensive coverage of Australiana, current and retrospective. A subset of the ABN database is the *National Union Catalogue of Serials (NUCOS)*.

In the 1940s the library began to develop major archival collections, leading to its establishment as the Commonwealth Archival Authority; the archives division was reconstituted separately in 1961, becoming the Commonwealth Archives Office (now Australian Archives), taking responsibility for federal government archives from the library, which continued to develop its collection of non-public records and manuscripts. These include numerous significant collections of literary manuscripts, and large collections relating to exploration and the early years of settlement and to the political history of the Commonwealth of Australia. Many of these are listed in *Principal Manuscript Collections in the National Library of Australia* (1973, 3rd edn 1992), *Guide to Collections of Manuscripts Relating to Australia* (on microfiche, 1990, Suppl. 1992–), and in *The People's Treasures: Collections in the National Library of Australia* (1993), ed. John Thompson. There are descriptive guides to the collections of the Poetry Society of Australia, Kate Baker, Mary Gilmore, Henry Kendall, Vance and Nettie Palmer, 'Henry Handel Richardson', Kenneth Slessor, Judah Waten, and others. The library also maintains a publishing department which has published numerous Australian literary texts, bibliographies and studies of Australian writers, traditionally based on its own collections. Its Oral History Collection numbers more than 30 000 recordings and interviews. In recent years the library's aim to develop its role as the 'cultural memory of society' has seen a more outward-looking publishing programme, resulting in the Pamphlet Poets series (q.v.) and the journal *Voices*, edited by Paul Hetherington, which presents information relating to the collections and services of the library as well as poetry, short fiction, articles and reviews. The library has also sought to strengthen its links with the contemporary literary and publishing community through exhibitions, lectures, poetry readings and the NLA poetry prize, awarded in 1986 and 1988. It also publishes *National Library of Australia News*, a monthly journal of news from the library. In 1991 a special issue of *Australian Academic and Research Libraries*, devoted to the National Library and edited by Peter Biskup and Margaret Henty, was published as *Library for the Nation*. The library sponsors the 'Australian Voices' Essay series in *Australian Book Review* and administers its annual TDK Australian Audio Book Award.

National Portraits, a collection of twenty-five brief biographical studies of significant figures in Australian history by Vance Palmer (q.v.), was first published in 1940. Palmer chose his figures either 'because of their representative character' or 'because they seemed ... true pioneers, originating ideas and tapping springs that were later to enrich the national life'. Most of the figures are drawn from the 1850s or, more substantially, from the 1890s. Each portrait includes an outline of the individual's career and character and an assessment of his contribution to Australian life, especially to what Palmer sees as its distinctive democratic substance. As history, the collection is oversimplified, but as a cultural document it has value in the light it sheds on the general myth of the 1890s and on Palmer's particular credo.

National Times, a weekly newspaper published in Sydney from February 1971 to 1986, generally addressed itself to an educated, affluent, middle-class reader and dealt with current political, social and economic issues. The newspaper also included substantial critical and biographical articles on Australian literature, interviews with writers, short stories, book reviews and theatrical notices from all the major cities. An anthology of *National Times* writings on being Australian was published in 1986, titled *The Way We Are: A National Portrait by the National Times*.

'Nationality' is a brief poem published in *Fourteen Men* (1954) in which Mary Gilmore (q.v.), while conceding the need for internationalism, acknowledges the pre-eminent claims of race and blood:

> All men at God's round table sit
> And all men must be fed;
> But this loaf in my hand,
> This loaf is my son's bread.

'Native' was a term used from the 1830s, like 'currency' (q.v.), to indicate a White person born in the

Australian colonies. The expression was commonly used in fictional and factual literature of the middle nineteenth century, e.g. Alexander Harris's *The Emigrant Family* (1849). Compound words were formed to indicate indigenous flora and fauna as contrasted with the English species, e.g. 'native dog', 'native pear'.

Native Companion, a monthly magazine published in Melbourne, appeared from January to June and August to November 1907. Edited by Bertram Stevens for its first six issues, the magazine included verse, short stories, literary notes and articles, and book reviews. E.J. Brady took over the editorship from August 1907 and the magazine's contents became more substantial, varied and representative of Australian literature. Contributors included Mary Gilmore, Hugh McCrae, Sumner Locke, Randolph Bedford, Louis Esson, 'Furnley Maurice' and Roderic Quinn. Katherine Mansfield contributed prose sketches to the last two issues.

Naught to Thirty-Three, published posthumously in 1944, is Randolph Bedford's (q.v.) racy and nostalgic autobiography covering the years between his birth in 1868 and his departure overseas in 1901. Like the volumes of reminiscences by G.A. Taylor, A.W. Jose and Norman Lindsay, *Naught to Thirty-three* paid tribute to the *Bulletin's* encouragement of Australian writers and helped to foster the legend of the Nineties (q.v.) as a golden decade.

NAYMAN, Michele (1956–), born London and educated in Johannesburg and Melbourne, has had a varied career. She holds a degree in town planning from Melbourne and a master's degree in journalism from Columbia University, New York. She has worked as a journalist and a marketing executive in Australia, Asia and Europe. Now a freelance writer, she has published a book of poetry, *What You Love You Are* (1977) and two books of fiction, *Faces You Can't Find Again* (1980) and *Somewhere Else* (1989). The sketches in *Somewhere Else* recount the somewhat erratic adventures of Laura Michaels in Melbourne, Hong Kong, Jerusalem, Denver and Venice in the 1970s and early 1980s. The fiction is structured in a staccato, fragmentary fashion to suit the situations it depicts. The overall assessment of the worth of human relationships is pessimistic in the extreme, but the occasional character, the much-put-upon actress Sallyanne O'Connor, for example, has a sad resilience which shines through her rather dismal existence.

Ned Kelly, a play by Douglas Stewart (q.v.), partly in verse, was written during 1940 for stage production, won an ABC prize for drama in 1942, when it was produced as a radio play, and was published in 1943. The play has been staged many times and was chosen for a special performance during the Olympic Games in Melbourne in 1956. The four-act, three-hour drama begins with the four members of the bushranger gang, Ned Kelly (q.v.), Joe Byrne, Dan Kelly and Steve Hart, holding up the bank at Jerilderie, NSW. Later, in a long, drawn-out scene in the Jerilderie Hotel, the outlaws proclaim, often in verse, their justification of past depredations and their romantic, cavalier view of themselves. Opposed to their braggadocio is the stubborn insistence of the Reverend Gribble on their ultimate downfall. Act Two, sixteen months later, is set in the gang's hide-out in the ranges. The tension of men living on their nerves pervades the scene. Isolated from the outside world by the vastness of the bush and apprehensive of every noise, they are driven to desperate measures: the killing of the informer, Aaron Sherritt, and the decision to carry the war to the police by setting a trap at Glenrowan. After Sherritt's death, they take over the hotel and township of Glenrowan and await the wrecking of the train carrying the pursuing police. Following Curnow's treachery and Joe Byrne's assessment that the Kelly legend is 'a bitch legend – wrong from the start', the play ends with the death of three members of the gang and Ned's dramatic but vain onslaught on the police in his legendary armour.

The play's strengths are its characterisation, its background and its functional use of poetry. The imaginative, intelligent Joe Byrne exemplifies the futility of the outlaws' crusade against law and order. Ned, the central figure in spite of the importance of Byrne, conveys a chilling sense of neurotic instability that inevitably brings about the gang's undoing. The historical explanation of the bushranging ethos in Australia and the attraction it has always held for the Australian temperament and nature are convincingly explored. The play's poetry is used to convey the epic quality that Stewart sees in the bushranger story. Successful though the poetry is in a literary sense, it has sometimes provided an obstacle to the play's stage presentation, for it has proved difficult to create the suspension of disbelief that allows an audience to accept the startling change in the bushrangers' language from the casually colloquial to the elevated and solemn.

NEIDJIE, Bill (1925?–), born Alawanydjawany, NT, spent most of his childhood in his father's country, Bunitj Clan land on the western side of the East Alligator River. When he was about 12 he followed his mother to Cape Don, where he lived for five or six years. Before the Second World War Neidjie had a variety of occupations for which he was paid in kind, working for eight years at timber-mill camps and spending some time at Darwin. He subsequently worked for many years as a deck-hand on a lugger on the north coast, but returned intermittently to his clan's land, and permanently in 1979. In the same year he was a claimant in the Alligator Rivers Stage II land claim, and as a result of this claim the Bunitj people of the Gagudju language group were awarded title to their land. Neidjie's talks with Keith Taylor were recorded in 1982 and published in 1989, edited by Taylor and titled *Story About Feeling*. Arranged according to themes and illustrated by the work of Aboriginal artists, *Story About Feeling* is an imaginative response to landscape and people, which helps to initiate White readers into the contradictory Aboriginal ways of conceiving the world. Some of Neidjie's stories are also included in his *Kakadu Man* (1986), which he produced with Stephen Davis and Allan Fox.

NEILD, J.E. (James Edward) (1824–1906), born Doncaster, Yorkshire, was interested in art, music and the theatre from an early age, but trained as a medical practitioner. Politically radical, he was a personal friend of John Bright and was active in the movement for repeal of the Corn Laws. He came to Australia in 1853, spent some time at the Castlemaine diggings and later worked as a chemist in Melbourne. In 1855 he joined the staff of the *Age*, meanwhile trading in the pharmaceutical business. Between 1856 and 1861 he was theatrical critic of *My Note Book*, the *Examiner* (writing under the name 'Christopher Sly') and the *Argus*; from 1865 to 1890 he was theatre critic for the *Australasian*, writing as 'Jacques' or 'Tahite'. A prominent member of Melbourne's cultural life, who knew R.H. Horne, Charles Bright, Patrick Maloney, Annie Maria Dawbin, John Dunn, E.E. Morris and George Coppin, Neild wrote and acted in productions for the Garrick Club and was a foundation member of both the Yorick Club and the Melbourne Shakespeare Society. His outspoken reviews antagonised a number of actors, theatrical managers and journalists, including James Smith and Marcus Clarke (qq.v.), with whom he conducted public feuds in the theatrical press. He began medical practice in Melbourne in 1861, soon became an influential member and office-bearer of the Medical Society of Victoria and edited the *Australian Medical Journal* 1862–79. He was lecturer in forensic medicine at the University of Melbourne, 1865–1904, was acting coroner and city medical officer of health for a time, and was prominent in a wide range of professional societies and institutions connected with public health. He contributed numerous articles to the *Herald*, the *Melbourne Punch*, the *Weekly Review* and the *Victorian*, published a critical essay, *On Literature and the Fine Arts in Victoria* (1889) and a theatrical novel under the pseudonym 'Cleofas', *A Bird in a Golden Cage* (1867). Harold Love has published a biography, *James Edward Neild: Victorian Virtuoso* (1989).

NEILSEN, Philip (1949–), born Brisbane, was educated at the University of Queensland, where he gained a Ph.D. He has taught at several Queensland universities, specialising in literature and cultural studies. He has published some short stories, but his main interest has been verse, which he has contributed to various periodicals, newspapers and anthologies, including *Poet's Choice*. He has published three collections of verse, *Faces of a Sitting Man* (1975), *The Art of Lying* (1979) and *Life Movies* (1981). Flexible and accessible, Neilsen's verse frequently mingles an easy wit and a sinister surrealism with unpredictable effects. Several, such as 'Veronica Lake', 'The Poet Imagines Himself an SS Officer', 'Superman in Our Town', 'Son of Dracula' and 'The Bushranger Comes Home', take a fresh, humorously disturbing look at familiar myths and cultural heroes. With Barry O'Donohue he published *We'll All Go Together* (1984) and he edited *The Penguin Book of Australian Satirical Verse* (1986), which was republished in a revised version in 1993 as *The Sting in the Wattle: Australian Satirical Verse*. He has also written *Imagined Lives: A Study of David Malouf* (1990). Neilsen has edited the literary magazine *Imago*, and is chairman of Warana Writers' Week, the Brisbane literary festival.

'NEILSEN, Ted' (James Rowntree) (1936–), born Hobart, graduated BA from the University of Tasmania and began acting with the Theatre Royal Company in 1955. He spent ten years working in England before, in 1971, settling in Melbourne, where he has worked as a tutor of improvisational drama and script-writing. By 1971 he had also become a professional writer and playwright and won a FAW playwriting competition in 1974. He has since written for screen and seen his plays produced by numerous theatres. They include 'The Solo Flight of Rose Bates' (1972), 'Ordinary Decent' (1974), 'Time Will Tell', 'Breakout', 'The Bell Jar' (1976), *Oh* (first produced 1978, published 1984), *Let Me In* (first performed 1978 and included in *Seven One-Act Plays* (1983), ed. Rodney Fisher), *Quadraphenia* (first performed 1980, published 1984), 'Last Paradise', 'Save the Wombat', *The Family Room* (first performed 1985, published 1987 and winner of the Best New Play Prize in the National Playwrights Awards in 1984), 'Juice', 'The St Kilda Soirees of Bonnie Smith' (1985), 'Every Prospect of Success' (1987), *Country Heat* (1990, an actor-inspired play) and 'Mates' (1991).

NEILSON, John (1844–1922), the father of John Shaw Neilson (q.v.), was born in Scotland and came to Australia at the age of 9. Proficient at a variety of bush trades, he worked at shearing, sheep-herding and road-making, married in 1871 and settled at Penola. In 1881 he took up land at Minimay in the south-west of Victoria, but was severely handicapped by lack of capital and in 1889 moved to Nhill, where he was forced to rely on road-making for a living. Another move in 1895 to Sea Lake in the central Mallee proved disastrous and again he had to turn to manual work. At the turn of the century he took up land at Eureka, where he lived by wheat-growing. The father of nine children, he was married twice. Although he was entirely self-educated, he acquired a reputation as a bush poet, contributing verse from his early thirties to the Mt Gambier newspapers and the *Adelaide Punch*, and later to the *Australasian* and other journals, and winning two prizes (in 1893 and 1897). Much of his verse has been lost but three volumes have been published, *Poem for Recitation: Love's Summer in the Snow* (1893), *The Men of the Fifties* (1938) and *The Song of the Shearer* (1960). His life is described in James Devaney's *Shaw Neilson* (1944); in *John Shaw Neilson* (1972) by Hugh Anderson and L.J. Blake; and in *The Autobiography of John Shaw Neilson* (1978).

NEILSON, John Shaw (1872–1942), born Penola, SA, was the eldest son of Scottish-born parents, John Neilson (q.v.) and Margaret McKinnon. Beset by debts the Neilson family moved in 1881 to a selection at Minimay in the Wimmera region of western

Victoria. Poor as the country was, it proved rich in associations and experiences for the young poet. He revelled in the limitless space of the inland and was fascinated by the bird and animal life. Recollections of life at Minimay are seen in his poem 'The Poor, Poor Country', where his own attitude is made clear – 'in that poor country no pauper was I.' Neilson's formal education lasted only two and a half years, including a final year at Minimay when he was 13. In 1889 the family moved north to Dow Well, near the new township of Nhill. By 1895 they had taken up blocks in the Mallee country, where life continued to be difficult and unproductive. The clearing of the scrub, the severe climate, the terrible dust storms, the rabbit plagues, the drought years 1895–1903, and the long despairing wait for a cash crop all made for an existence of poverty and misery. In 1896 Neilson's poem 'Polly and Dad and the Spring Cart' was published in the *Bulletin*, thus beginning a relationship with A.G. Stephens, his literary adviser, editor and financial mentor, that spanned almost forty years. Stephens's influence on Neilson's literary career was not wholly beneficial and his editorial liberties with the poetry were excessive, but without his guidance and promotion the inexperienced bush poet would have made little or no impact. Neilson's eye trouble began in 1905 and his resultant inability over the years to read anything but large print was a great hindrance to his writing. Until 1928 Neilson was an itinerant labourer, clearing land, navvying in quarries, on roads and railways, fencing, potato-digging, fruit-picking – work that seemed incompatible with the delicate poetry he produced. In 1901, J.F. Archibald of the *Bulletin* published 'Sheedy was Dying' (q.v.) and asked for more. In 1905 Stephens bought three poems (for £1), including 'The Land Where I Was Born'. The *Bookfellow* (1907) published 'Old Granny Sullivan' (q.v.) with a full-page illustration by Dagmar Ross. In 1909 twenty-eight of Neilson's poems were published in Randolph Bedford's *Clarion*. 'Love's Coming' (q.v.) was published in the Sydney *Sun* in 1911, and in October 1912, Stephens used it and 'You and Yellow Air' to illustrate an article on him. The first proposed volume of his poetry, *Green Days and Cherries*, remained unpublished except for three proof copies. His first published volume, *Heart of Spring* (q.v., 1919), was followed in 1923 by *Ballad and Lyrical Poems* and by *New Poems* in 1927. In 1928 a position was secured for him as messenger with the Country Roads Board in Melbourne. This supposedly congenial position with a guaranteed weekly wage was expected to lead to increased writing, but the city environment lowered his poetic impulse. His *Collected Poems*, edited by R.H. Croll, was published in 1934 and *Beauty Imposes* in 1938. In 1941, his health failing, he went to Queensland to visit James Devaney (q.v.), who had replaced Stephens as his friend and adviser, and he died soon after in Melbourne of heart trouble. After his death Devaney edited *Unpublished Poems* (1947); in 1970 *Witnesses of Spring: Unpublished Poems* was edited by Judith Wright, Val Vallis and Ruth Harrison; in 1981 *Green Days and Cherries* finally appeared, edited by Hugh Anderson and L.J. Blake.

Most of the Australian poetry written in the 1890s and the first two decades of this century is now less regarded than when it was written, but the best work of Neilson, who felt that 'five shillings seems a good deal for people to pay for my verses', has so grown in esteem that he is now claimed by some to be pre-eminent among Australian lyrists. The incongruity between the grace, delicacy and subtlety of his poetry and his hard life and rough background have also made him Australia's chief literary enigma, but those who knew him well have never subscribed to the popular theory that he was merely a literary fluke. Victor Kennedy found him remarkably well informed and intellectually aware, 'steeped in the current philosophies – rationalism, evolution, the labour movement and Australian poets and poetry'. The immediate impression his poetry gives, with its spareness, brevity and uncomplicated structure, is that of simplicity, even naivety. Some of it *is* naive, even trivial and banal. But in his finest work the combination of disturbing mysticism and haunting language, well exemplified in the enigmatic 'The Orange Tree' (q.v.), shows him to be a sensitive and unusually gifted poet. The John Shaw Neilson Society was formed in 1987 in Footscray and the Victorian branch of the FAW annually honours his memory with the John Shaw Neilson Award for poetry. *The Autobiography of John Shaw Neilson* was published in 1978 with an introduction by Nancy Keesing. Hugh Anderson compiled *Shaw Neilson: An Annotated Bibliography and Checklist, 1893–1964* (rev. edn 1964). Cliff Hanna wrote *The Folly of Spring: A Study of John Shaw Neilson's Poetry* (1990) and edited *John Shaw Neilson* (1991), a collection of poems, letters, memoirs and autobiographical fragments. Darryl Emmerson has written a play based on his life, 'The Pathfinder', first performed at the Spoleto Festival, Melbourne, in 1986.

NELSON, Jeremy Lockhart (1933–), born Sydney, grew up in the Hunter Valley and was educated at the University of Sydney. Now retired from Sydney Grammar School, he has lived in India, Greece and England. He has published two books of verse, *City of Man* (1983) and *Diagrams of Paradise* (1989).

NELSON, Penelope (1943–), born Sydney, was educated at the University of Sydney and Macquarie University. She has been a TAFE teacher, and has worked in community relations and as a member of the ABC National Advisory Council. She is presently a freelance writer, a reviewer for the *Weekend Australian* and lives near Narrabri, NSW. She has written two novels, *Medium Flyers* (1990) and *Prophesying Backwards* (1991). *Medium Flyers* might well be subtitled 'Women in Commerce' or 'Career Women', the narrative paralleling the fortunes of several women, two of whom are 'high flyers' in their chosen occupation, the travel industry (Roxane Rowe, and Olwyn Tierney). The other two are 'medium flyers' (Prue Lambert, an investigator in the Commission for Business Ethics and Olwyn's daughter, Margot, an academic at the Yagoona Institute of Further Education). The women's lives run along predictable courses of love affairs, marriages, family and business crises, jealousies and struggles to survive and advance. *Prophesying Backwards* also has parallel plots, relating the experiences of Sigrid Larsen, schoolteacher, at the turn of the century and her granddaughter Denise, liberated university student in the 1960s. Racism, unwanted pregnancies, the temperance movement and thwarted lives characterise the Victorian era plot; the modern plot brings the illusion of freedom but not the substance.

Neos, later *Neos Young Writers*, originated in Glebe, Sydney, in 1981 as a magazine for young writers. Dedicated to the new and experimental, it was an important outlet for students and ran (supported by the Literature Board and the NSW English Teachers Association, among others) from 1981 to 1985. Its final volume was published in book form as *House of Words: the very last Neos*.

NESBITT, Francis (?1810–53), born England as Francis Nesbitt McCron, came to Sydney in 1842 and soon established himself at the Victoria Theatre as a highly popular tragedian, even described by some critics as 'the best actor in the Southern hemisphere'. In 1843–44 he was instrumental in staging the plays of the convict-writer Edward Geoghegan, including 'Ravenswood' (1843), which he presented as his own. His career underwent several vicissitudes in Sydney and in Hobart and Launceston where he played for some time, partly because of his occasional drunkenness and partly because of the fading popularity of his declamatory style.

'Never Never' describes the vast, remote, inland area of northern Australia, in particular north-west Queensland and the Northern Territory. Frederic de Brébant Cooper in *Wild Adventures in Australia* (1857) suggests that the term's origin lies in the Aboriginal expression *nievah vahs*, meaning unoccupied land. Many writers, e.g. 'Rolf Boldrewood' in *A Colonial Reformer* (1890) and A.J. Boyd in *Old Colonials* (1882), use the term without indicating its source. Jeannie Gunn, whose popular work *We of the Never-Never* (q.v., 1908) gave the expression widespread currency, romantically asserted that the farthest outback was called the Never Never 'because they who have lived in it and loved it *never never* voluntarily leave it'. By contrast, many believe that it is so called because those who succeed in getting out of it swear that they will 'never never' return to it. The best description of the Never Never and of the lifestyle that goes with it is in Henry Lawson's poem 'The Never-Never Land'. Lawson sees it as a land of 'wide wastes of scrub and plain', of blazing and hopeless deserts, where man has named its few distinctive features Mount Desolation, Mount Dreadful and Mount Despair, but a land where mateship flourishes. Laura Palmer-Archer wrote the fictional *Racing in the Never Never* (1899) and 'Gurney Slade' a travel book, *Through the Never Never* (1935).

Nevermore (1892), a novel by 'Rolf Boldrewood' (q.v.), was first published as a serial in the *Centennial Magazine* 1889–90. One of the few 'Boldrewood' novels in which an English-born hero meets tragedy, *Nevermore* recounts the adventures of Lance Trevanion, who leaves his Cornwall home to seek fortune on the Australian goldfields. He succeeds at Ballarat but is seduced into crime by the Lawless family and is gaoled, then sent to the Williamstown hulks. He escapes and moves to the Omeo goldfields, but again falls into crime and is murdered by his evil partner, Caleb Coke, and Lawrence Trevenna, Lance's double, with whom he has quarrelled on the voyage to Australia. Trevenna impersonates Lance to his fiancée, Estelle, when she visits Australia but both the impersonation and the murder are exposed at the altar; after her return to England, Estelle discovers that Trevenna is Lance's natural half-brother, a device which owes something to *His Natural Life* (1874). The Lawless family, modelled on the family of Ned Kelly, recurs in two later 'Boldrewood' novels, *The Last Chance* (1905) and *The Ghost Camp* (1902). *Nevermore* is a melodramatic work but there are some effective goldfields scenes in which 'Boldrewood' draws on experiences that are also put to good use in *The Miner's Right* (1890).

NEVILLE, Jill (1932–), born Sydney, the sister of Richard Neville, went to Britain in 1951 and has lived in London and Paris. She has worked as a teacher, copywriter, social worker, journalist and critic, has published literary criticism and poetry in such periodicals as the *Times Literary Supplement*, the *Observer* and *London Magazine* and has contributed a column to the *Sunday Times*. She has written six novels, *Fall-Girl* (1966), *The Girl Who Played Gooseberry* (1968), *The Love Germ* (1969), *The Living Daylights* (1974) *Last Ferry to Manly* (1984), and *Swimming the Channel* (1993). Her first novel is partly autobiographical and includes a fictionalised portrait of the poet Peter Porter, whom she met on board ship *en route* to England, and their tumultuous love affair. A witty, ironic study of a distinctly Australian experience, the 1950s *rite de passage* of the extended stay in Britain, *Fall-Girl* is also a feminist tale which brings its heroine to a point of self-confidence if not happiness. Neville's other novel with Australian content is *Last Ferry to Manly*, which focuses on a vulnerable woman who has left behind damaging experiences in France and London and gone to ground in a seedy flat at Manly; erotic love continues to elude her, although love in the sense of *caritas* accompanies her at the close. An intricately worked novel with a sharply observed sense of place and numerous shifts between times and places, *Last Ferry to Manly* dramatises in spare, sometimes lyrical prose the complex fate of the individual who is torn between Europe and Australia; it includes a fictionalised portrait of Edmund Campion.

'NEVILLE, Margot' (Margot Goyder) (1903–) and **Anne Neville Goyder Joske** (1893–) were sisters who combined under the pseudonym 'Margot Neville' to write twenty-four murder mysteries between 1922 and 1966 beginning with *Mariette is Stolen* (1922) and ending with *Head on the Sill* (1966); they also published a play, *Horses Don't Care* (1936). Transferring the basic ingredients of the British police mystery to Australia, the Neville novels are well-articulated, competent essays in suspense which are often resolved by an ostensibly unimportant clue, patiently uncovered by the heroes, Inspector Grogan and Detective Sergeant Manning. Although set in Australia, the novels have little local colour.

NEVILLE, Richard (1941–   ), editor of the student magazines *Tharunka* and *Noise*, was joint founder with Richard Walsh and Martin Sharp, a graphic artist, of the controversial Sydney magazine *Oz* in 1963. Given a six-months' prison sentence (which was later quashed) on the grounds of obscenity, Neville went to London in 1966 and re-established *Oz* with Felix Dennis and Jim Anderson as co-editors. In 1971 the editors were subjected to a sensational trial on a charge of issuing a publication likely 'to corrupt public morals', were sentenced to fifteen months' imprisonment, but were freed on appeal. Neville also defeated a deportation order which was issued after the trial. In 1973 *Oz*, grown familiar if not respectable, expired. Neville has since travelled extensively, worked as a journalist and broadcaster in Sydney, London and New York, and returned in 1979 to Australia, where he has worked in television. He has published *Play Power* (1970), an analysis of the Youth Movement and the antagonistic alliance between the New Left and the 'Underground of hippies, beats, mystics, madmen, freaks, yippies, crazies, crackpots, communards etc,'; a novel, *Playing Around* (1991); and, with Julie Clarke, an account of the mass murderer Charles Sobhraj (1979). In 1991 a television series titled 'Trials of Oz' was screened. Neville's wife, Julie Clarke, has published a collection of essays, *Floating in the Fast Lane* (1991).

New Australia was the name of the co-operative socialist settlement established originally by William Lane (q.v.) in Paraguay in 1893. The abortive shearers' and maritime strikes of 1891, the severe drought of 1892, and the economic depression of 1892–93 confirmed for many working-class people their belief that a true socialist existence was not possible in Australia. In 1891 William Lane established the New Australia Co-operative Settlement Association and sent Alfred Walker to negotiate a land grant for such a settlement from the government of Argentina, but Paraguay was eventually chosen. The New Australia Office was opened at Elizabeth Street, Sydney, and a monthly journal, *New Australia*, commenced publication in November 1892 under the editorship of Walter Head. The Association purchased a 598-ton sailing ship, the *Royal Tar*, which, carrying 220 colonists and their children, left Sydney 16 July 1893, arriving off Montevideo 11 September 1893. By small boat and train the settlers were transhipped to Las Ovegas, the site for the New Australia settlement. Within a few months the settlement had broken into irreconcilable factions. By July 1894 Cosme, a breakaway settlement of Lane's staunchest followers, had been established. The original New Australia gradually disintegrated, its assets being sold and divided in 1897, but vestiges of it survive even today in the district known as Nueva Aus-

tralia. Cosme prospered until 1898 but after Lane's return to live in NZ in 1899 it, too, gradually broke up and by 1909 had ceased to exist as a separate society, being absorbed into the Paraguayan community. The journals *New Australia, Cosme Monthly* and *Cosme Evening Notes*, the last two edited by Mary Gilmore (q.v.), then Mary Cameron, contain much of the history of the New Australia movement, and a bibliography of material held in the Mitchell and National libraries was published as *New Australia and Cosme* (1965). A full account of New Australia is in Gavin Souter's (q.v.) *A Peculiar People: The Australians in Paraguay* (1968), republished in 1991 with a postscript chapter.

Vance Palmer's play *Hail Tomorrow* (1947) concerns Lane's Utopian dream, while numerous songs and verses sing the settlement's praises, e.g. 'The Men of the New Australia' by Mary Gilmore, 'Over There in Paraguay' by 'A Bushman', 'It's Nice to Live in Paraguay' by 'The Doctor' and 'The Man from Bogantungan' by Hilda Lane, William Lane's niece, who was born at Cosme in 1899. Hume Nisbet wrote an unfavourable account of New Australia, *A Dream of Freedom* (1902).

'New Australian', a term for immigrant, gained currency during the period of accelerated immigration after the Second World War to promote assimilation and to replace less desirable terms such as 'reffo', 'Balt', 'boong', 'wop' and 'pommy'. It has largely been confined to non-English-speaking immigrants.

New Australian Poetry was the vague and somewhat grandiloquent title bestowed by its proponents on the wave of poetry, mainly from young poets of the so-called 'Generation of '68', which found expression in poetry readings and in the small and often briefly lived magazines which sprang into existence in the late 1960s and 1970s. Although the practitioners of the new poetry held various, and sometimes opposing, views on its character, attitude, and limits, they felt a common antagonism to the mainstream of Australian poetry as represented by the work, for example, of A.D. Hope, R.D. FitzGerald, Judith Wright and James McAuley, who had dominated Australian poetry for the previous quarter of a century. The new poets judged the established poetry to be, in its form and content, traditional and conservative to the point of atrophy. The new poetry movement took much of its inspiration from contemporary American poetry as represented in, for example, Donald Allen's *The New American Poetry* (1960) and Donald Hall's *Contemporary American Poetry* (1962), both of which were having an impact in Australia in the mid-1960s. The movement sought to have contemporary Australian poetry reflect a similar modernity of attitude and technique. The genesis of the movement is difficult to be exact about but the obvious originating forces were, in Melbourne, the poetry readings held at Monash University 1967–69, and the poetry workshops 1968–69 at the La Mama (q.v.) Theatre and other venues; and, in Sydney, the 1964 birth of Grace Perry's *Poetry Australia* (q.v.), the annual Balmain poetry and prose competitions, the poetry readings run by Robert Adamson (q.v.), and the 1971 rise of the journal *New Poetry* from the ashes of *Poetry Magazine* (q.v). The movement's growth was spurred by the rise of a myriad of little magazines that carried the poetry and the message. Magazines such as *Our Glass, Mok, Crosscurrents, The Great Auk* and *Free Poetry* flourished briefly and disappeared but were replaced by others almost immediately, some, such as *Parachute Poems* and *Flagstones*, being equally short-lived, others, such as *The Saturday Club Book of Poetry* and *Contempa*, proving more durable. Such magazines, and the rapid development of printing technology, allowed the new poets easy access to the publication both of their individual poems and small inexpensive volumes of their work, access which had previously been available only to poets with an established reputation. These publication opportunities were augmented in the 1970s by the emergence of such printing houses as South Head Press, Outback Press, Wild and Woolley and Rigmarole of the Hours; by the increased activity of UQP, which catered for the new poetry in its Paperback Poets series and anthologies; and by the traditional publisher, Angus & Robertson, which introduced an innovatory Poets of the Month series. In addition to the dissatisfaction with existing poetry and the impact of contemporary international writing, other causes of the rise of the new poetry are said to have been the influence of the 1950s decade in which the new poets grew up; the ready availability of tertiary education to their generation; the influence of the new rock music; the impact of drugs; the sense of outrage that accompanied the Vietnam War and Australia's participation in it; conscription; the belief in poetry as part of the weaponry in the struggle for wider freedom; and the impact of such poets as Francis Webb and Bruce Beaver (qq.v.). Although many poets who published during the period were involved in the movement to some degree, the more important figures were Beaver, Thomas Shapcott, Rodney Hall, Robert Adamson, John Tranter, Kris Hemensley, Michael Dugan, Bruce Dawe, Les Murray, Michael Dransfield, Charles Buckmaster, Ken Taylor, Robert Kenny, Garrie Hutchinson, Walter Billeter, Vicki Viidikas, Mal Morgan, Paul Smith, Alan Wearne and John A. Scott. Many of these worked independently of the literary cliques that developed and many were not in agreement with each other or even with the theory of a 'New Australian Poetry'. The new poetry is represented in the anthologies *Australian Poetry Now* (1970) and *Contemporary American & Australian Poetry* (q.v. 1976), both edited by Shapcott; *Applestealers* (1974), edited by Kenny and Colin Talbot; *The New Australian Poetry* (1979), edited by Tranter; and *The Younger Australian Poets* (1983), edited by Robert Gray and Geoffrey Lehmann. *New Impulses in Australian Poetry* (q.v., 1968), edited by Hall and Shapcott, is not properly descriptive or illustrative of the movement, although it indicates the changes that were then emerging.

That the 'New Australian Poetry' would inevitably be supplanted by a similar movement, and that the 'Generation of '68' had become the anti-establishment establishment, to be replaced by a further anti-establishment force, was foreshadowed by the October 1977 special issue of *Australian Literary Studies*, titled 'New Writing in Australia'. The new poetry was subjected to considerable criticism in Richard Packer's 'Against the Epigones', *Quadrant* (1975) and Mark O'Connor's 'The Graying of the Underground', *Overland* (1979). The explosion of poetry in the decade 1970–80, and the resultant confusion over standards, is well exemplified in Thomas Shapcott's article 'Australian Poetry 1970–1980: Some Statistical Observations', *Australian Literary Studies* (1983). The extent to which the then contemporary American poets had an influence on the New Australian Poetry is investigated in *The American Model: Influence and Independence in Australian Poetry* (1983), edited by Joan Kirkby. Many of the standard-bearers of the New Australian Poetry movement of the 1960s and 1970s have become recognised leaders in the poetic scene of the 1990s, e.g. Tranter, Scott, Adamson, Dawe and Wearne, to name but a few.

'New Chum' was a phrase, derived from prison slang, which was originally used in Australia to describe a newly arrived convict, a usage which occurs in James Tucker's novel *Ralph Rashleigh*. From about 1840 it had come to mean any new arrival but particularly one, e.g. a well-connected young Englishman sent out to gain 'colonial experience' (see 'Colonial Experiencer'), who betrayed his ignorance and inexperience in the colonies. A number of anonymous Australian folk-songs record the experiences of the new chum, including 'I've Been to Australia-Oh' and 'The Settler's Lament', which both tell of new chums being 'taken down'; 'A New Chum in the Country', in which the reverse happens; and 'The New Chum's Farewell to Queensland', a long, inventive curse which concludes

> To stay in thee, O land of Mutton!
> I would not give a single button,
> But bid thee now a long farewell,
> Thou scorching sunburnt land of Hell!

Another folk-song new chum is Billy Barlow who, as a stage character in his own right and as a source for James Tucker's 1840s play *Jemmy Green in Australia* (q.v.), helped to inaugurate the long tradition of the new chum on the nineteenth-century Australian stage; a famous later example of this stock character is Charles Harold Vane Cholmondeley Vane Somers Golightly in Alfred Dampier and J.H. Wrangham's *Marvellous Melbourne* (first performed 1889), a role played by Dampier himself. The term 'new chum' was most often used in a derogatory way, with 'old hand' its antonym. Henry Lawson, however, provides a spirited defence of the type in his poem 'The New Chum Jackaroos', and some new chums themselves, e.g. Percy Clarke in his reminiscences, *The New Chum in Australia* (1886), and Paul Wenz in his *Diary of a New Chum* (1908), exploited the currency of the phrase without discomfort. Among prominent fictional new chums are Christopher Cockle in J.R. Houlding's *Australian Capers: Or, Christopher Cockle's Colonial Ex-*

perience (q.v., 1867) and Ernest Neuchamp, the hero of 'Rolf Boldrewood's' *A Colonial Reformer* (1890).

New England. The New England district of NSW, of which Armidale is the main city, is a high plateau covering about 27 000 square kilometres of fine grazing land. The European history of New England dates from 1818, when John Oxley crossed its southern areas; its occupation began in 1832 when H.C. Sempill moved north from the Hunter Valley to occupy a station which he named Wolka (now Walcha). The name 'New England' came into use about 1836. Armidale took its name from G.J. MacDonald, commissioner of Crown Lands, who established a station in the area in 1839 and named it after his father's estate in Scotland. New England has many historical and literary associations. The Myall Creek massacre (q.v.) of Aborigines took place there in 1838; a similar but later massacre is recalled in Judith Wright's 'Nigger's Leap, New England'. Judith Wright, who grew up in New England, has celebrated its history and landscape in her poems 'South of My Days' and 'For New England' and in her historical works *The Generations of Men* (q.v., 1959) and *The Cry for the Dead* (1981). The bushranger Thunderbolt was active in the New England area in the 1860s and was killed near Uralla in May 1870. 'Rolf Boldrewood' was a goldfields commissioner stationed at Armidale 1884–85. The privations of the poor selector, especially in New England's severe winters, are recalled in the anonymous ballad 'The New England Cocky'. The colour and excitement of the district's history are captured in Robin B. Walker's *Old New England* (1966) and in E.C. Sommerlad's *The Land of 'the Beardies'* (1922), published to mark the jubilee of the town of Glen Innes. *The Wallabadah Manuscript* (1980), edited by Roger Milliss, also contributes to the historical coverage of the district. The Armidale and District Historical Society has done much to record the district's pioneer past.

New Holland, the name given by Dutch explorers in the seventeenth century to that part of the Australian continent west of the meridian passing through Torres Strait, was occasionally subsequently applied to the continent as a whole. By the 1820s the name Australia had established itself. W.J. Gordon in 1888 published *The Captain General: Being the Story of the Attempt of the Dutch to Colonize New Holland*, one of a number of works which investigated, fictionally and otherwise, the attempts by the Dutch to anticipate British colonisation of the continent. Two popular modern historical novels about the establishment of settlement in WA, the scene of the early Dutch discoveries, are Rix Weaver's *Behold, New Holland* (1940) and *New Holland Heritage* (1941).

New Impulses in Australian Poetry (1968), an anthology of Australian poetry of the 1960s, was edited, with an introduction, by Rodney Hall and Thomas W. Shapcott (qq.v.). The keynote of these 'new impulses' was 'a suspicion of idealism, and an inbred awareness of the consequences of totalitarian beliefs'.

Authoritarianism in religion and politics was eschewed, as was the concept of national and international aggression. Major established poets such as Kenneth Slessor, Judith Wright and A.D. Hope are not represented because the editors felt that their poetry of the decade added little to their already defined stances. Their contemporaries, however, Gwen Harwood and Francis Webb, are given considerable space because they are important influences on younger poets.

New Literature Review began publication in 1975 as the successor to *Arna* (q.v.). Its first issue contained poetry, e.g. by Vivian Smith and Chris Wallace-Crabbe, short fiction, e.g. by Frank Moorhouse and Michael Wilding, critical articles, and a *Tabloid Story* supplement. Since the second issue in 1977 it has been published twice yearly and has been a solely critical journal which has focused on new literatures in English, including Australian literature, and literary theory. Since 1988 it has been jointly supported by the New Literatures Research Centre of the University of Wollongong and the English Department of the University of NSW and is now titled *New Literatures Review*.

New Poetry was the magazine of the Poetry Society of Australia (q.v.). It replaced *Poetry Magazine* in 1971, which had replaced *Prism* (q.v.) in 1961, as a result of a dispute among the Society's members over the amount of non-Australian writing that the magazine should contain. Edited initially by Robert Adamson and Carl Harrison-Ford and later mostly by Adamson alone, *New Poetry* was published bi-monthly, quarterly and sometimes irregularly until 1982. One of Australia's major poetry magazines, *New Poetry* played an important role in the rise of the 'New Australian Poetry' (q.v.) during the 1970s and, by publishing contemporary American poetry in particular, kept Australian poets and readers abreast of modern developments in poetic form and content. It published an extensive range of contemporary poetry from well-known Australian and overseas poets, as well as lesser-known writers and previously unpublished writers. It also contained critical articles, reviews, notes and comments.

New South Wales Bookstall Company, see **ROWLANDSON, A.C.**

New South Wales General Standing Orders, a selection of governors' orders, was, when published in 1802, the first book printed in Australia.

New South Wales Magazine, owned and edited by Ralph Mansfield, was published monthly in Sydney, August 1833 to March 1834. The magazine included general news items, religious material, serials, short stories, poetry and literary reviews. Henry Halloran and John Lhotsky were contributors. A second monthly *New South Wales Magazine* was published in Sydney in 1843.

New Theatre (Australia), a federal organisation which has affinities with the American New Theatre movement and sponsors a 'committed', broadly socialist theatre, was formed in the early 1950s to link various New Theatres or workers' theatre groups which had formed in Sydney, Melbourne, Brisbane, Perth, and later Newcastle. The Sydney and Melbourne groups, formed in 1932 and 1936 respectively, were the first to establish themselves as serious theatres, adopting the name New Theatre League in 1936, shortened to New Theatre in 1945. Some of the other State groups enjoyed periods of intense activity, but only the Melbourne and Sydney New Theatres are now operational. Although New Theatre has been seen as a predominantly left-wing organisation, subject at times to mild attempts at censorship on the part of State governments, the theatres have staged a range of international and classical plays and have presented the work of numerous Australian playwrights, including Louis Esson, Leslie Rees, Betty Roland, Katharine Susannah Prichard, Oriel Gray, Dymphna Cusack, Barry Oakley, John Romeril, Sumner Locke Elliott and Mona Brand. *Reedy River*, first performed in 1953, was New Theatre's most popular and widely staged production. Oriel Gray's *Exit Left* (1985) includes an account of her long involvement in New Theatre and Angela Hillel has written a history of Melbourne New Theatre 1936–86, *Against the Stream* (1986), which lists the plays produced in that period.

New Triad, edited by Hugh McCrae and Ernest Watt and published in Sydney, appeared monthly April 1927 to July 1928. The magazine included short stories, articles, verse and theatrical notices and attracted such contributors as Louis Esson, R.D. FitzGerald, H.M. Green, Vance Palmer, Dora Wilcox, David McKee Wright and Les Robinson.

NEWLAND, Simpson (1835–1925), born Staffordshire, England, came to Australia as a small child, settling with his parents in the Encounter Bay area of SA. As a young man he travelled the outback, ultimately becoming a squatter along the Darling River. He returned to Adelaide in 1876 and in 1881 was elected to the SA House of Assembly, where he began a lifelong advocacy of the development of the Northern Territory through the building of a transcontinental railway and development of the SA river system, on which subjects he wrote numerous pamphlets. His chief literary work was the novel *Paving the Way* (1893), the title a tribute to the pioneers who had 'paved the way' for the development of the country. The novel's long, loose and rather melodramatic narrative incorporates many features of pioneering life including squatting, the Aborigines, and women of the outback. A less effective novel, *Blood Tracks of the Bush*, was published in 1900. Newland's *Memoirs* (1926), written when he was nearly 90, gives a vivid account of the early days of SA settlement and considerable details of Aboriginal life and customs.

Newsfront, a film directed by Phil Noyce and dealing with the Australian newspaper world of the 1940s, was released in 1978. Bob Ellis wrote the screenplay and Robert Macklin published a book based on the film in 1978. One of the most popular and influential productions of the 1970s renaissance in Australian film, *Newsfront* is also one of the more intelligent re-creations of the 1940s decade, which found favour with Australian audiences in the late 1970s.

Newspapers in Australian Libraries: A Union List (1959–60, 4th edn 1984–85), published by the National Library of Australia, is published in two parts, the first listing overseas newspapers and the second listing Australian newspapers. The standard guide to the location of newspapers in Australia, it is arranged by place of publication, with an index of titles.

NIBBI, Gino (1896–1969), born Fermo, Italy, lived intermittently and for lengthy periods in Australia. After first settling in Melbourne in 1928, he opened a bookshop, the Leonardo, which became a meeting-place for artists and writers in the 1930s. A trenchant critic of the local art scene and promoter of the avant-garde, he travelled widely in Australia, gathering material for articles for the Italian press. Although he was naturalised in 1940, he remained emotionally attached to his original homeland and returned to Italy to live in 1947. He made three subsequent visits to Australia but returned finally to Rome in 1963. Apart from his journalism, two of his publications relate to Australia, the collections *Il Volto degli Emigranti (The Face of the Emigrants)* (1937) and *Cocktails d'Australia* (1963), sketches and stories of migrant life in Australia.

NICHOLLS, Charles Frederick (1826–?) and **Henry Richard** (1830–1912), born London, were brothers who became Chartists in 1848 and emigrated to Australia in the early 1850s. They were both involved in the movement leading to the Eureka Stockade, but left before the attack and were afterwards active in the campaign to secure release of the rebels. In later years Charles was a mining investor, prospector, explorer and promoter, owned and edited the Melbourne *Evening Star* (1867–69) and wrote *Democracy and Representation* (1871). Henry pursued mainly a career in journalism, as writer for the *Ballarat Times*, editor and proprietor (1875–83) of the *Ballarat Star*, editor of the *Mercury* in Hobart (1883–1912), and contributor under the pseudonym 'Henricus' to the *Argus* and *Australasian*. He also wrote a brief satirical pamphlet, *An Essay on Politics in Verse* (1867). In the 1980s members of the 'new right' in Australian politics and business took Henry Nicholls as their figurehead when forming the H.R. Nicholls Society.

NICHOLLS, Syd (1896–1977), born Tasmania, studied art at the Royal Art Society in Sydney and was a prominent cartoonist for the *Bulletin* and the left-wing journal *Direct Action* during the First World War. During the 1930s he pioneered the Australian adventure comic strip with the pirate strip 'Middy Malone', but his best-loved creation was Fatty Finn (q.v.); *Fatty Finn's Weekly* (1934–35) was the first Australian comic book.

NICHOLSON, John Henry (1838–1923), born England, was a close friend of Ludwig Leichhardt and came to Australia in 1854. He tried various occupations, including prospector, theatre manager, bird-collector and schoolteacher, finally settling in Queensland. In his later years he suffered periodic bouts of mental illness. He wrote verse, plays and prose sketches, acquired a temporary and local reputation for his patriotic song 'Rouse Australians!' in the late 1880s, but is now best known for his moral and religious allegory *The Adventures of Halek* (1882) and its sequel *Almoni* (1904). The autobiography of a pilgrim from the sensual level of existence to the intellectual to the spiritual, *Halek* is greatly inferior but obviously indebted to such books as *The Pilgrim's Progress, Erewhon* and *Gulliver's Travels*. Nicholson also published two volumes of humorous prose sketches, *The Mysterious Cooks* (1867) and *My Little Book* (1873); a volume of prose and verse, *The Opal Fever* (1878); two collections of verse, *Hubert and Other Poems* (1879) and *A Book of Verses* (1916); the dramas *Moike: Or, Melbourne in a Muddle* (1886), *The Spanish Coachman* (1888) and *Hubert* in the 1879 verse collection; and *Recreations of a Registrar* (1904).

NICHOLSON, Joyce (1919–), born Melbourne, daughter of D.W. Thorpe, publisher, was herself managing director and proprietor of the family publishing firm. She was also co-founder and director of Sisters Publishing. She has edited *Australian Bookseller and Publisher* and *Australian Books in Print* and has written over thirty books, many for children and many based on actual events and people. They include *Our First Overlander* (1956), *Man Against Mutiny* (1961), *A Goldseeker* (1970), *Freedom for Priscilla* (1974, first published in 1963 as *A Mortarboard for Priscilla*) and *The Convict's Daughter* (1976). A feminist, she has written a study of sex-role conditioning, *What Society Does to Girls* (1975); has been an active participant in the Women's Electoral Lobby, for whom she edited the *WEL Broadsheet* for three years; and has published *The Heartache of Motherhood* (1983). She was made AM in 1983.

Night the Prowler, The, a novella by Patrick White (q.v.), is included in his collection *The Cockatoos* (1974). It was also adapted for film in 1976 and was published in its dramatised form in 1978.

'Night We Watched for Wallabies, The', one of the best-known stories by 'Steele Rudd' (q.v.), appears in *On Our Selection* (1899). The story sketches the annoyance of the sons of Dad Rudd when they are forced to spend a cold and windy night helping their father prevent the wallabies from ravaging the wheat crop. The next morning they learn the real reason for their outdoors vigil – their mother has given birth again.

NILAND, D'Arcy (1919–67) was born at Glen Innes, NSW, into a large Irish Catholic family. After leaving school at 14 he worked in a woolshed, then at 16 went to Sydney, where he was a copy-boy for the Sydney *Sun* but soon lost his job because of the Depression. He then 'went bush' for several years, working at a variety of occupations: opal-gouger, blacksmith's striker, shearer, circus hand, fencer, fruit-picker, rouseabout and member of a travelling boxing troupe. In 1942 he married the writer Ruth Park (q.v.), and after a period of travelling in country areas they settled in Surry Hills, Sydney. Their joint autobiography, *The Drums Go Bang!* (1956), describes the early years of their marriage and their various attempts to wrest a living from writing. Niland, already well known for his short stories in *Smith's Weekly* and other magazines, won international fame after the publication of his best-selling novel *The Shiralee* (1955). Later filmed with Peter Finch in the main role, it was selected by many book clubs and as book of the month by newspapers in Australia and overseas. As well as articles, plays for radio and television, ballads and hundreds of uncollected short stories, Niland wrote six novels, *The Shiralee* (1955), *Call Me When the Cross Turns Over* (1957), *Gold in the Streets* (1959), *The Big Smoke* (1959), *The Apprentices* (1965) and *Dead Men Running* (1969). He also published four collections of short stories, *The Ballad of the Fat Bushranger* (1961), *Logan's Girl* (1961), *Dadda Jumped Over Two Elephants* (1961) and *Pairs and Loners* (1966); with Leslie Raphael, a collection of ballads, *Travelling Songs of Old Australia* (1966); and a book on the writer's craft, *Make Your Stories Sell* (1955). He worked for many years on a biography of Les Darcy the boxer, after whom he was christened, but died before it was completed. *The Penguin Best Stories of D'Arcy Niland*, selected by Ruth Park, was published in 1987. Many of his short stories and several of his novels have been translated into other languages and have appeared in international anthologies. Niland won several minor literary prizes for his work including second prize in the 1948 *Sydney Morning Herald*'s short-story competition and third prize in the novel section with *Gold in the Streets*. In 1961 he won, with Ruth Park, a British award for their television play 'No Decision'; and *Dead Men Running* also proved popular when it was produced as an ABC television serial. Of the Nilands' five children, their twin daughters Kilmeny and Deborah are well known as illustrators.

Niland's Irish Catholic childhood and his experiences as a bush worker in the 1930s Depression were seminal. Strongly influenced by the realist writers of the 1890s, his own work is a rich source of social history, capturing the life of both rural and urban Australia from the 1930s to the 1950s. A versatile and lively writer, he has a gift for graphically evoking atmosphere, incident and memorable characters, as well as an ability to create suspense. Uninhibited in his use of language, he is particularly adept at producing the rhythm and flavour of colloquial idiom. As far as characterisation and plot development are concerned, his approach tends to the picaresque and is more suited to the short story than the novel. His occasional tendency to sentimentality, especially in his creation of female characters, is avoided for the most part in *Dead Men Running*, which is held together by a well-controlled, retrospective design and by the predominance of its complex main character. Ruth Park's second volume of autobiography, *Fishing in the Styx* (1993), includes a well-rounded study of Niland.

Nimrod Street Theatre Company was founded in 1970 by John Bell and Ken Horler and was an attempt to offer an alternative, younger, more radical and generally appealing theatre than was then available to Sydney audiences. First located in a former stable and gymnasium in Nimrod Street, Kings Cross, the Company moved in 1974 to a more capacious building, an old tomato-sauce factory in Surry Hills. In this new venue, where an intimate atmosphere between cast and audience was maintained and extended to a downstairs theatre, the Nimrod continued to foster Australian drama, producing the work of such playwrights as Ron Blair, Jack Hibberd, Alex Buzo, Jim McNeil, Peter Kenna, Bill Reed, David Allen, Stephen Sewell, Michael Gow, Dorothy Hewett, David Williamson, Alma de Groen, Steve Spears and Louis Nowra as well as international playwrights. Following a further move to the larger York theatre in the Seymour Centre in 1984, the company faced financial difficulties and largely shed its commitment to Australian drama and devoted itself to the classics. When funding subsidies from the NSW government and the Australia Council were not renewed for 1988, the Company went into liquidation.

1915, a novel by Roger McDonald (q.v.), was first published in 1979, and won the *Age* Book of the Year and the SA biennial literature awards; in 1982 a seven-part adaptation by Peter Yeldham was shown on Australian television. The narrative of *1915* is told primarily from three alternating perspectives, those of Walter Gilchrist, Billy McKenzie and Frances Reilly. Walter, sensitive, uncertain, from a relatively well-off farming family, and Billy, confident, knowing, something of a larrikin, are two boys from the bush in NSW, whose ambivalent relationship, a mixture of friendship and rivalry, is established in the opening pages of the novel. As they grow up in the period immediately preceding the First World War, their rivalry is focused on their desultory pursuit of the unsettled and flirtatious Frances, whom Billy meets on a visit to Forbes and introduces to Walter. As 1913 turns into 1914 the shadows of war settle over the country town of Parkes, disrupting the texture of life there. When war is declared, Billy and Walter soon join up, Billy making the more comfortable transition into service life. The war affects their relationship with Frances: just before their departure for the Front, Walter establishes an intimate relationship with Frances, and Billy one with Diana Benedetto, Frances's best friend.

The second half of the novel is concerned primarily with the experiences of Walter and Billy as Anzacs at Gallipoli, but there are both temporal and geographical shifts in the narrative. For example, while at Gallipoli, Walter recollects his last days in Sydney before embarkation and his experiences while training in Egypt, and there are chapters which chronicle Frances's betrayal of Walter by her pursuit of the rich landowner Robert Gillen, and the death of Diana, who is drowned while carrying Billy's child. At the Front, as in the early days of recruitment, Billy settles more comfortably into the experiences of war, winning repute as a sniper. Wally, on the other hand, experiences most of the awfulness of war: its carnage, the appalling confrontations with and randomness of death, the omnipresent and drugging fear of extinction which makes comrades out of soldiers because of a lust for remembrance. At the end of the novel, however, Wally is captured and presumably preserved, but Billy is destroyed. Wounded while on sniping patrol in an attempt to save Walter, whom he sights under threat in a trench, Billy is invalided back to Australia and placed in an asylum after he visits and physically attacks Frances, whom he blames for Diana's death.

1915 has elements of the war novel and the historical novel, but its main focus is the evolution of its central characters and their search for a meaning and shape to their existence. The view the novel offers of Gallipoli has attracted the attention of reviewers, yet the war scenes are integrated with and paralleled by the Australian and Egyptian scenes. Walter, Billy and Frances are seeking throughout the novel to create a mosaic out of the fragments of experience but what war does for Frances and Diana, no less than for Walter and Billy, is make them aware of the forces for disintegration.

'Nineties' is a word used to describe the 1890s, a significant and even legendary decade in Australian history and literature. Historically, it was a period in which the labour movement gained representation in parliament (the first Labor government in the world was formed briefly in Queensland in 1899); progressive social-welfare legislation and political reforms were implemented; and a national self-awareness found expression in the Federation movement, climaxed by the proclamation of the Commonwealth of Australia on 1 January 1901. But countering these achievements were an economic depression, the worst experienced in the colonial period, which began in 1889 and peaked in 1892; a severe financial crisis the following year, characterised by the collapse of a number of banks; the end of the land boom; a decline in the pastoral industry, exacerbated by the long drought from 1895 to 1903; industrial conflict, notably in the shearing and maritime industries, in which the unions lost more disputes than they won; and massive unemployment of up to 30 per cent. As well, the beginning of a new technological age was signalled by the arrival of the motor car, electric street lighting and cinema, and by improvements in transport and communication which made Australia less isolated from Europe.

These momentous and contradictory events have produced fluctuating responses among commentators. Several volumes of reminiscences published from the end of the First World War, e.g. G.A. Taylor's *Those*

Were the Days (1918), A.W. Jose's *The Romantic Nineties* (1933), Randolph Bedford's *Naught to Thirty-Three* (1944), Norman Lindsay's *Bohemians of the Bulletin* (1965), looked back nostalgically and helped foster the legend of the Nineties as a 'golden' decade in the development of Australia: a decade when, specifically, Australian writers and artists looked inwards and found an authentic identity distinct from the cultural models of Great Britain. As articulated by the memoirists and in the writings of later radical nationalist commentators such as Vance Palmer in *The Legend of the Nineties* (1954), A.A. Phillips, Russel Ward and H.M. Green, Australian literature was finally born in the 1890s. The midwife was the *Bulletin* (q.v.), which, under J.F. Archibald and A.G. Stephens, encouraged writers and illustrators to discover a 'real' Australia in which the importance of the bush was stressed, and to affirm, in short sketches and ballads written in a natural idiom, certain distinctive values: national pride, egalitarianism, republicanism, collectivism, Utopianism, scepticism. A major symbol in this version of the Nineties is the pastoral worker; the major creative publicists are Henry Lawson, 'Banjo' Paterson and Joseph Furphy. Furphy's famous, though tongue-in-cheek, description of his novel *Such is Life* (1903), 'temper, democratic; bias, offensively Australian', has been taken as a motto for the spirit of the age.

Since the Second World War, and more particularly from the 1960s, the Nineties has undergone revaluation. Literary historians and critics, noting the darker side to the history, have made several corrections to the legend: for example, in suggesting that the *Bulletin* was xenophobic, racist, provincial, sexist and bourgeois as well as (or perhaps rather than) radical, nationalist and youthfully zestful; that the bush ethos it promoted was in some senses a romantic escape from the disillusionment with and despair of the realities of urban life; that the accepted model of the *Bulletin* writer does not accommodate some of its notable contributors, e.g. the Celtic Twilight lyricists, or more significantly a writer such as Christopher Brennan, whose concerns were moral and metaphysical and whose literary heritage was European; and that literary nationalism and the promotion of an Australian identity were not *Bulletin* inventions, but had been a concern of many colonial writers in the century before 1890. The extent to which the glow surrounding the Nineties has been dissipated is measured by the 'sense of alienation and loss' which Leon Cantrell, the editor of *The 1890s* (1977), an anthology devoted to the period, sees as its 'principal literary hallmark'. John Docker, long interested in the Nineties, while also challenging the traditional interpretation of the decade, asserts, in *The Nervous Nineties: Australian Cultural Life in the 1890s* (1991), the impact of American culture on the Australia of the time. He analyses significant American texts and their influence and places the basic 1890s Utopian and anti-Utopian influences, e.g. the *Bulletin*, the *Dawn*, Lawson's stories, William Lane's *The Workingman's Paradise*, again under scrutiny. Some commentators have warned of the danger of replacing an old orthodoxy, the golden Nineties, with a new one, the gloomy Nineties, but the revaluation of the Nineties has at least contributed to an acceptance of the complexities and contradictions that emerged in the literature of the period. Just as, for example, nationalism itself was an amalgam of allegiances to an emerging Australia, an individual colony like NSW, and even Britain itself, so Australian literature was both inward-looking *and* influenced by international movements such as Utopianism, feminism and the growth of literary journalism. Similarly, there has been an increasing acceptance of an ambivalence towards the bush and city in many Nineties writers, and of the inadequacy of a simplistic response to writers like Lawson and Furphy. The vitality and variety of Nineties writing, including critical writing, have survived; less so the uniqueness of the decade, particularly as more attention is directed to earlier Australian literature. Stephen Alomes and Catherine Jones edited *Australian Nationalism: A Documentary History* (1991) and Noel McLachlan wrote *Waiting for the Revolution: A History of Australian Nationalism* (1989).

NISBET, Hume (1849–1923), a Scottish artist who was an associate of John Ruskin, taught art at Edinburgh and exhibited at the Royal Scottish Academy, visited Australia 1865–72, 1886 and 1895. On his first visit he travelled extensively in eastern Australia and tried acting in Melbourne. He published more than forty books of fiction (many of which draw on his Australian experience), plays, verse, works on art and painting and accounts of his travels. Novels and short-story collections which are set in or refer to Australia include *The Land of the Hibiscus Blossom* (1888); *Doctor Bernard St Vincent* (1889); *Bail Up!* (1890); *The Savage Queen* (1891), which includes Truganini, Michael Howe and G.A. Robinson as characters; *The Black Drop* (1891); *The Bushranger's Sweetheart* (1892); *The Divers* (1892); *A Bush Girl's Romance* (1894); *A Sweet Sinner* (1897); *The Swampers* (1897), which was banned because of scurrilous references to public figures in NSW; *In Sheep's Clothing* (1900); *Children of Hermes* (1901); *A Losing Game* (1901); *Mistletoe Manor* (1902); *Wasted Fires* (1902); and *A Dream of Freedom* (1902), which deals unfavourably with William Lane's founding of New Australia in Paraguay. Several of his novels and short stories focus on one of his most individual characters, an Australian-born Chinese detective, Wung-Ti, based on an individual whom Nisbet met in Melbourne. Nisbet's travel writings which have reference to Australia are *My Illustrated Diary of a Voyage from London to Australia* (1890) and *A Colonial Tramp* (1891). His verse, some of which is Australian in context, was published in several collections, *Memories of the Months* (1889), *The Matador and Other Recitative Pieces* (1893), and *Hathor and Other Poems* (1905). Hackneyed as far as plots and characters are concerned and crammed with the stock ingredients of bushrangers, convicts, squatters and Aborigines, Nisbet's novels have more historical than literary interest, although his anachronistic and outspoken comments and prefaces on such topics as racial prejudice in Australia and especially the treatment of the Aborigines, enliven his turgid narratives.

NISSEN, Rosemary (1939–), previously the proprietor-manager of Abalone Press, has taught creative writing, been a librarian and is an alternative health practitioner. She has published two books of verse, *Universe Cat* (1985) and *Small Poems of April* (1991), as well as co-editing several publications, e.g. *Directory of Australian Poets 1980* (1980), *The Great White Hunter Meets Darkest Africa* (1986), *Surprise Witness* (1988) and *Yarra Valley Writers* (1990).

'No Foe Shall Gather Our Harvest', a stirring poem written by Mary Gilmore (q.v.) in 1940, proved a remarkable morale booster in the tense days of the Japanese threat to Australia in 1942. The poem, with its refrain 'No foe shall gather our harvest/ Or sit on our stockyard rail' was at the time considered as a possible battle hymn, even national anthem.

NOLAN, Cynthia (?1913–76) was born in Tasmania into a wealthy pastoral family. A sister of John Reed (q.v.), she had connections with the Angry Penguins (q.v.) group of writers and artists in the 1940s. Several Australian writers, including George Johnston and Patrick White, have recorded their impressions of her personality. As Cynthia Reed, she published two novels, *Lucky Alphonse* (1944) and *Daddy Sowed a Wind!* (1947), although after her marriage to Sidney Nolan (q.v.) in 1948 she published under her married name. She wrote another novel, *A Bride for St Thomas* (1970), which draws heavily on her experiences as a student nurse, and several travel books, *Outback* (1962), *One Traveller's Africa* (1965), *Open Negative* (1967), *A Sight of China* (1969) and *Paradise, and Yet* (1971). *Open Negative*, her most sympathetically received book, describes a visit to the USA and her experiences in a New York hospital while undergoing treatment for tuberculosis.

NOLAN, Sir Sidney (1917–92), born Melbourne into a working-class family, left school at 15 and two years later enrolled in the Art School of the National Gallery of Victoria. In 1940 he held his first exhibition of abstract paintings, which aroused some controversy and even a destructive attack by one enraged viewer armed with a can of green paint. He served in the army 1942–45 and was stationed in the Wimmera, which gave him his first taste of the Australian open landscape and determined the form of his interest in the Ned Kelly legend. A visit to Central Australia in 1949 resulted in a series of paintings on the explorations of Burke and Wills, which won him the Dunlop Art Prize in 1950. In the 1940s he was encouraged by John Reed, president of the Contemporary Art Society and brother of Cynthia Reed (see Cynthia Nolan), whom Nolan married in 1948. A member for a time of the publishing firm Reed & Harris, Nolan also became friendly with Max Harris and was one of the editors of *Angry Penguins Broadsheet*. In 1952 he met George Johnston, spent an extended period with him on the island of Hydra in 1955 and was subsequently portrayed by Johnston as Tom Kiernan in his novel *Clean Straw for Nothing* (1969). From 1950 Nolan lived abroad, and gained an outstanding international repu-

tation; he returned to Australia at regular intervals. His two Ned Kelly series are perhaps his most famous paintings; inspired partly by the stories of his grandfather, a trooper in the Kelly era, they illustrate his Irish-Australian temperament, his literary streak and his strong feel for the strange individuality of the Australian landscape. Nolan also drew on other Australian myths for series of paintings on the story of Eliza Fraser and on Gallipoli (qq.v.). His Gallipoli series, consisting of 252 paintings, produced over thirty years, was donated to the nation in 1977. Another series, 'Ern Malley', comments on the Ern Malley poems and includes portraits of members of the Angry Penguins group. He illustrated the work of Randolph Stow, Patrick White, Alan Moorehead, Colin MacInnes, George Johnston, Robert Lowell and Charles Osborne and designed the dust-covers of C.P. Snow's novels, many of which allude to his work. A selection of Nolan's own verse, *Paradise Garden*, illustrated by his paintings, was published in 1971. In 1972 he produced a film, *Kelly Country*, and co-operated in several films and television programmes on his life and work, including *The Dreaming, Spinning Thing* (1967), *Nolan at Sixty* (1977), *Sidney Nolan: An Australian Dream* (1982) and *It is of Eden I was Dreaming* (1983). He was awarded the Britannica-Australia Award in 1969, made CBE in 1963, knighted in 1983 and was made AM in 1983 and AC in 1988. In 1983 he also received the Order of Merit. Several biographical and critical accounts of Nolan have been published, including *Sidney Nolan* (1961), by Kenneth Clark, Colin MacInnes and Bryan Robertson, *Sidney Nolan: Myth and Imagery* (1967), by Elwyn Lynn, *Sidney Nolan: Such is Life* (1987), by Brian Adams and *Sidney Nolan* (1987), by Jane Clark.

NOONUCCAL, Oodgeroo (1920–93), of the Noonuccal tribe of Stradbroke Island off the Queensland coast near Brisbane, was the first of the modern Aboriginal protest writers. Known for most of her life as Kath Walker, she returned to her tribal name in 1988 in opposition to the Bicentenary celebrations. She was educated only to primary school level, then at 13 worked in domestic service in Brisbane. At 16 she wanted to be a nurse but was rejected because she was an Aborigine. By 1961, when she was State secretary of the Federal Council for the Advancement of Aboriginals and Torres Strait Islanders, she was deeply involved in the Aboriginal activist movement. She campaigned strenuously and successfully for the 1967 abolition of Section 52 of the Australian Constitution which discriminated against Aborigines. In the 1970s she served as chairperson of the National Tribal Council, the Aboriginal Arts Board, the Aboriginal Housing Committee and the Queensland Aboriginal Advancement League. In her life and through her writings she constantly sought to generate cultural self-pride by emphasising the value of her people's way of life. This crusade often led her to criticise White Australian attitudes and to demand basic Aboriginal rights. She was made MBE but returned the honour in 1988 in protest at the federal government's failure to legislate nationally for Aboriginal land rights. She was awarded honorary doctorates by Macquarie University and Griffith University. Her first volume of poetry, *We Are Going* (1964), is not, as its title might imply, an indication of her resignation to the loss of Aboriginal identity. She meant it, in her own words, 'as a warning to the white people: we can go out of existence, or with proper help we could also go on and live in this world in peace and harmony . . . the Aboriginal will not go out of existence; the whites will'. Her second volume, *The Dawn Is at Hand* (1966), won the 1967 Jessie Litchfield Award. *My People: A Kath Walker Collection* (1970) reprinted the poems of the two earlier collections, together with some new poems, short stories, essays and speeches. *Stradbroke Dreamtime* (1972) is a collection of thirteen whimsical stories of her childhood and fourteen traditional stories from Aboriginal folklore or new ones in traditional form. She also published children's books, *Father Sky and Mother Earth* (1981), illustrated with her own art work, and *Little Fella* (1986), and, with her son, Kabul Oodgeroo Noonuccal, *The Rainbow Serpent* (1988). As Oodgeroo Noonuccal she provided stories and verse for the illustrated volumes *Australian Legends and Landscapes* (1990) and *Australia's Unwritten History* (1992).

Her best-known poems, 'We Are Going', 'Gooboora, the Silent Pool' and 'Last of His Tribe' express nostalgia for the lost Aboriginal past, while anger at White intolerance and cruelty is expressed in poems such as 'Dark Unmarried Mothers', 'Acacia Ridge' and 'God's One Mistake'; a sense of fairness, nevertheless, compels her to admit, in 'Civilization' and 'Integration – Yes!', that some benefits have flowed to the Aboriginal people from contact with White culture. 'Aboriginal Charter of Rights' is a straightforward declaration of the basic rights of her people, while 'Tribal Justice' and 'The Food Gatherers' idealise the Aboriginal existence of primitive times. 'I Am Proud' is an angry assertion of pride in her Black identity, conforming with her description of her poetry as 'sloganistic, civil rightish, plain and simple'. Oodgeroo also won the FAW Patricia Weickhardt Award in 1977 and the Mary Gilmore Award. In 1977 she won the Black Makers Award in San Francisco for her performance in the film *Shadow Sister*. Ulli Beier has written *Quandamooka. The Art of Kath Walker* (1985), which includes biographical information and some of Oodgeroo's art work.

NORDHOFF, Charles (1887–1947), an American citizen, was born in London but lived in the USA from the age of 3. Educated at Harvard University, he served in the First World War in France, where he met his future collaborator, James Norman Hall (q.v.). In 1920 they visited Tahiti, where Nordhoff remained until 1941. He published several South Seas novels independently 1919–29. With Hall he published some non-fiction works and the following novels, many using glamorous incidents of South Seas history: *Falcons of France* (1929), *Mutiny on the Bounty* (1932), *Men against the Sea* (1934), *Pitcairn's Island* (1934), *The Hurricane* (1936), *The Dark River* (1938), *No More Gas* (1940), *Botany Bay* (1941), *Men Without Country* (1942)

and *The High Barbaree* (1945). Their best-known books, the trilogy (1932–34) dealing with the Bligh (q.v.) mutiny and the subsequent settlement on Pitcairn Island, were published together in 1936, titled *The Bounty Trilogy;* several of Nordhoff and Hall's books met Hollywood's formula for romantic adventure films. The Nordhoff-Hall collaboration has been described by Paul L. Briand in *In Search of Paradise* (1966).

Norfolk Island, situated about 1500 kilometres east-north-east of Sydney, was discovered by James Cook on 10 October 1774 and was used as a prison settlement 1788–1814 and 1825–56. In 1856 the penal settlement was finally abolished and descendants of the *Bounty* mutineers were transferred from Pitcairn Island. Settlers from Australia and NZ, known locally as 'mainlanders', have since joined the 'islanders', and in 1914 the island became an external territory under the administration of the Australian government.

First settled by Philip Gidley King with a small group of convicts and some free men on the orders of Governor Phillip, the island's first period as convict settlement 1788–1814, was relatively unremarkable. Some disturbances between troops and convicts arose, especially under the administration of Major Robert Ross, and there were some abortive convict rebellions and periods of near-famine. When the penal settlement was re-established in 1824, however, following the report of Commissioner J.T. Bigge, the object was to segregate there the worst type of convict, Norfolk becoming, in the words of Governor Ralph Darling, 'the place of extremest punishment short of death'. For the next twenty-five years the island, which held an average of 1500 to 2000 desperate convicts, had a reputation as a natural paradise turned into hell, and was administered with great severity; the only relative respite occurred under the administration of Alexander Maconochie (q.v.) (1840–44). Mutinies and insurrections were frequent, especially under the infamously repressive administration of Joseph Childs (1844–46), the model for 'Price Warung's' (q.v.) Commandant Scragge, and John Price (1846–50), the model for Marcus Clarke's (q.v.) Maurice Frere. Norfolk's years as a convict settlement have been freqently commemorated in Australian fiction, most notably in Clarke's *His Natural Life* (1874), 'Price Warung's' short stories including *Tales of the Isle of Death (Norfolk Island)* (1898), but also in Eliza Winstanley's *Twenty Straws* (1864), Mark Jeffrey's *A Burglar's Life* (1893), Roy Bridges's *The Fires of Hate* (1915) and Thomas Gillard Ford's short stories, *Inhumanity* (1935). Margaret Hazzard's *Punishment Short of Death: A History of the Penal Settlement at Norfolk Island* (1984) describes the two periods of convict settlement, the first as an extension of the colony at Port Jackson, the second as a place of punishment. Victor Crittenden wrote about Philip Gidley King's time on the Island in *King of Norfolk Island* (1993).

Norm and Ahmed, a one-act play by Alexander Buzo (q.v.), was first produced in 1968 and first published in 1969. The play's action, which consists simply of a midnight conversation between Norm Gallagher, a middle-aged, average Australian, and Ahmed, a young Pakistani student, probes the inadequacy of the 'Aussie' self-image. Norm, the typical beer-drinking, rough-and-ready good mate and family man, supporter of the 'fair go', the RSL, the Leagues Club, sport and law and order, the unthinking cog in the industrial system, unwittingly reveals his inner anxiety and unconscious insufficiency as he talks to the politely formal student. The suspense aroused by his ambivalent behaviour, varying from the threatening to the friendly, culminates in his physical attack on the student and the succinct phrase 'Fucking boong'. The final line of the play led to prosecutions for obscenity when it was performed in Melbourne and Brisbane, although in the latter case the prosecution was quashed.

NORMAN, Lilith, see *The Oxford Companion to Australian Children's Literature* (1993), p. 318.

Northern Perspective, published originally by the Darwin Institute of Technology (now the Northern Territory University) began in 1977 under editor Barry Bannister (1977–91) and later Lyn Riddett. Published twice yearly (Dry Season, Wet Season) it includes work by new and established writers who have 'a northern perspective'. It also publishes winning and highly commended entries in the annual NT literary awards.

Northern Territory is the middle section of the northern half of Australia; originally part of NSW, then SA, it became the Northern Territory of Australia in 1911 and was administered by the federal government until self-government in 1978. Its history, geography, character and legendry have been dealt with in such works as A. Grenfell Price's *The History and Problems of the Northern Territory, Australia* (1930), W.E. ('Bill') Harney's *North of 23°* (1946), *Australia's Frontier Province* (1950) by C.L. Abbott, for nine years the administrator of the Northern Territory, Ernestine Hill's *The Territory* (q.v., 1951), Douglas Lockwood's *Up the Track* (1964), J.H. Kelly's *Struggle for the North* (1966), Glenville Pike's *Frontier Territory* (1972) and Alan Powell's *Far Country: A Short History of the Northern Territory* (1982). The Northern Territory is depicted as Capricornia in Xavier Herbert's novel *Capricornia* (1938) and figures largely in his *Poor Fellow My Country* (1975). David Headon edited *North of the Ten Commandments: A Collection of Northern Territory Literature* (1991).

NORTON, Ezra, see **NORTON, John**; *Truth*

NORTON, John (1858–1916), a colourful Sydney newspaper editor at the turn of the century, was born in Brighton, England, and endured an unhappy childhood in which he was maltreated by his stepfather. He was a private secretary to an architect before entering journalism. In 1884 he arrived in Australia and soon established himself as a reporter on the *Evening News* and as a publicist for the labour movement; among the works he wrote at that time were *The Australian Labour Market* (1886) and the Australian material in *The History of Capital and Labour* (1886). In 1890, after a stint as editor of the *Newcastle Morning Herald*, he joined the recently established radical weekly, *Truth* (q.v.), which he edited 1891–92 and 1896–1905; he bought into the journal in 1896 and owned it outright from 1899 until his death. Under Norton *Truth* was notorious for its focus on political, sexual and domestic scandal (e.g. during the Dean case), some of it relating to Norton's own violent private life. After his death *Truth* came under the control of his son Ezra (1897–1967), who subsequently established the tabloid *Daily Mirror*. In 1958, when Cyril Pearl's sensational exposé of John Norton and his milieu, *Wild Men of Sydney*, was in the process of publication, Ezra threatened legal action for libel and is often credited with influencing the passing of stricter defamation laws in that year. A later study of Norton, Michael Cannon's *That Damned Democrat* (1981), reprints a selection of Norton's alliterative editorials and has information on his political activities, which saw him several times elected to parliament (where he was several times ejected for disorderly conduct), as well as on his crusades in *Truth* on behalf of the underprivileged.

Nosey Alf is the disfigured boundary-rider in Joseph Furphy's *Such is Life* (1903) who turns out to be a woman, Molly Cooper, in disguise. Furphy's idea for the characterisation came from his awareness of the double life led by Johanna Jorgensen (1843–93), who had also been kicked in the face by a horse as a young woman.

Notes & Furphies, published by the Association for the Study of Australian Literature (q.v.) since 1978, includes short articles, reports of Australian and overseas conferences, information about work-in-progress, awards and competitions, biographical notes on Australian writers, lists of theses on Australian literature since 1976 and miscellaneous news. Edited for its first eleven years by Julian Croft and Ken Stewart (twenty-one issues), it was taken over in 1989 by David English and Jim Sillitoe.

NOVACK, Carol, see **Feminism and Australian Literature**

NOWRA, Louis (1950–) was born in Melbourne and studied English at La Trobe University without taking a degree. Best known as a playwright, he has published *Albert Names Edward* in *Five Plays for Radio* (1975), ed. Alrene Sykes, *Inner Voices* (1977), *Visions* (1979), two plays published together, *Inside the Island* and *The Precious Woman* (1981), *Sunrise* (1983), *The Song Room* in *Seven One-Act Plays* (1983) ed. Rodney Fisher, *The Golden Age* (1985) *Capricornia* (1988), from the novel by Xavier Herbert, *Così* (1992) and *The Temple* (1993). His other plays include 'Kiss the One-Eyed Priest' (1973), 'Sleezee' (1977), 'The Death of Joe Orton' (1980), 'Spellbound' (1982), 'Prince of Homburg' (1982), 'Royal Show' (1982), 'Byzantine Flowers' (1990), 'Summer of the Aliens', and

'Radiance'. He has also translated and adapted European plays, such as *La Dame aux Camellias* and *Cyrano de Bergerac*, and written operas, film scripts, and plays for radio and television. His television play 'Displaced Persons' (1985) had a wide impact and was followed by 'Hunger' (1986) and 'The Lizard King' (1987). Nowra is also attracted by fiction and has published two novels, *The Misery of Beauty* (1976), which won the fourth Angus & Robertson fellowship, and *Palu* (1987). *The Cheated* (1979), a collection of newspaper reports of personal catastrophes or tragedies, reflects his interest in extreme situations. *Louis Nowra*, ed. Veronica Kelly (1987) includes interviews with Nowra and critical articles on his work. Nowra won the Canada/Australia Literary Award in 1994.

Sometimes classed with Stephen Sewell as representing a second wave of Australian drama, Nowra is like Sewell in his interest in black comedy, gothic passions and an epic style of theatre which studies individuals in broad historical and political contexts. Nowra is concerned more with exploring timeless questions about human motivation, aspirations and interdependence than with re-creating a specific Australian environment, although most of his dramatic situations are analogical reflections of Australia history. Fascinated by post-colonial contexts in particular and their resonances for Australia, he frequently implies the repressed presence of the Aboriginal experience within the Australian cultural consciousness. *Inside the Island, Sunrise, The Golden Age* and *Capricornia* have recognisable Australian settings; *Inner Voices* takes place in Russia of 1794, *Visions* in Paraguay of the 1860s, *The Precious Woman* in China of the 1920s, *Così* in a Melbourne mental institution and a suburban backyard. In all his plays, however, the external setting is less important than the inner one, 'the landscape of the mind'. The structure of his stage plays, usually composed of succinct, visually striking emblematic scenes, partly determines his characteristic Brechtian effect of simultaneous engagement and detachment. Both *Albert Names Edward* and *Inner Voices* deal with the experiences of abnormally isolated and unformed young men: Edward, who suffers from total amnesia, presents himself as a *tabula rasa* to an older man, Albert, and becomes, finally, Albert's mental replica; the central protagonist of *Inner Voices* is Ivan, the 24-year-old claimant to the Russian throne, whom Catherine II has kept imprisoned since infancy and who, at the beginning of the play, knows only his own name. In both plays Nowra is preoccupied with the power of language as an instrument of domination and as a means of interpreting and defining the world. For Ivan, the search for subjective and objective knowledge is fatally conditioned by the warped structure of his 'education' at the hands of his tyrannical instructor and 'liberator', Mirovich. The close of the play sees him in almost the same situation that he was in at the beginning; trapped in his palace/prison, he is surrounded by the indecipherable voices of his followers, whose tongues he has had removed. *Visions*, where the scope of the action is social and national, dealing with the fates of President Lopez of Paraguay and his wife Eliza Lynch, a one-time Paris courtesan, concentrates more on the inner lives of the dominators than of the victims. Both, however, emerge as fatally corruptible by half-truths masquerading as absolutes. *The Golden Age*, often described as his most accomplished achievement, concerns the discovery of a White tribe living in total isolation in the Tasmanian wilderness. The remnants of a group of convicts and prospectors, the tribe had evolved an individual culture and language which appears superficially alien to the two young professional men who discover them in 1939 while bushwalking. Returning the tribe to 'civilisation' at the brink of the Second World War and narrating both their rapid demise and the horrors of war, allows Nowra to contrast barren modernity and a more organic, 'natural' way of living. The opposition is not a simplistic one, however, but a complex exploration of issues Nowra had considered in his earlier work, the challenge of the irrational and uncultivated to perceptions of what is 'real' and valuable, the shallowness of Australia's transplanted culture and the destructiveness of imperial patterns of oppression. The play's close with a promise of unity between the one survivor of the tribe, Betsheb, and Francis, one of their discoverers, is a tentative gesture of hope, undercut by warnings implicit in the Greek theatrical fragments which act as a frame for the main play.

Nowra's novels are concerned with the same unsettling issues as his plays. *The Misery of Beauty*, narrated by a physical grotesque christened Frogman, and assistant to a magician, Earl, who is both dominating and dependent, deals with the unique experience of the excluded, isolated individual. *Palu*, set mainly in Papua New Guinea, is narrated by the wife of the crazed president of the country as she awaits execution. In her division between a primal, exotic culture and an acquired, Western one, *Palu* challenges both ways of knowing the world.

NUCOS: National Union Catalogue of Serials, see **Serials in Australian Libraries**

NUTTALL, Charles (1872–1934), born Melbourne, began his education in art at that city's National Gallery School and contributed drawings to the *Bulletin*. In 1902 he painted *Opening of the First Commonwealth Parliament* and published *Representative Australians*, a series of portrait sketches, as well as *Peter Wayback Visits the Melbourne Cup* (1902), a series of humorous sketches. He became a cartoonist with *Table Talk* in 1904; in 1905 he joined the *New York Herald*. Back in Australia in 1910 he had regular exhibitions of drawings and sketches, illustrated *Pals*, a boys' weekly, wrote stories and articles, and in 1933 published *Melbourne Town* with reproductions of Melbourne drawings.

NYOONGAH, Mudrooroo Narogin, see **MUDROOROO**

O

OAKES, Russell (1910–52) was an officer in the Australian Army and served in New Guinea during the Second World War. He wrote verse, short stories (one of which, 'No-one Spoke', won an award) and plays for radio and stage. His published plays include the one-act *Judgment* (?1951) which is set in wartime Papua, and *Enduring as the Camphor Tree* (1967), which is based on a Chinese love story and was first produced in Melbourne in 1946. His other plays include 'Invisible Circus', 'The Alchemist', 'The Arrival of Arthur', 'Carry On, Sergeant', 'The Egg', 'The Embarrassing Proviso', 'In Puris Naturalibus', 'The Substantial Phantom', 'These Little Pigs', 'The Voice of Jerome Keddle', 'Drowned Valley', 'Publicity Unlimited', 'The Tree that Chose Itself', 'Water Goes East', and 'Wool Gathering'.

OAKLEY, Barry (1931–) was born in Melbourne and educated at the Christian Brothers College, St Kilda, and at the University of Melbourne. He taught at secondary schools in central and northern Victoria and in Melbourne 1955–62, meanwhile writing copiously, although publication eluded him. In 1963 he lectured in humanities at the Royal Melbourne Institute of Technology, worked as an advertising copywriter 1964–65 and as a copywriter for the federal Department of Trade and Industry 1966–73. During these years he lived mainly in the inner suburbs of Melbourne, with his wife and six children. He now lives in Sydney and is literary editor of the *Australian*. Oakley has published four novels, *A Wild Ass of a Man* (1967), *A Salute to the Great McCarthy* (1970), which was produced as a film, *The Great McCarthy*, in 1976, *Let's Hear It for Prendergast* (1970) and *The Craziplane* (1989); a collection of short stories, *Walking Through Tigerland* (1977), which reprints only some of his stories that have appeared in magazines and newspapers since 1955; a collection of reminiscences and reviews, *Scribbling in the Dark* (1985); and numerous plays, *Witzenhausen, Where Are You?* in *Meanjin* (1967) and *Six One-Act Plays* (1970), ed. Eunice Hanger; *A Lesson in English*, which first appeared in *English in Australia* (1968) and was published with Ron Blair's *The Christian Brothers* (1976); *The Feet of Daniel Mannix* (1975); *Bedfellows* (1975); *Buck Privates* in *Nation Review* (1977); *Scanlan* in *Meanjin* (1978); *The Ship's Whistle* (1979); *The Great God Mogadon and Other Plays* (1980), which includes *Witzenhausen. Where Are You?*, *The Hollow Tombola*, *Buck Privates*, *Eugene Flockhart's Desk* and *Scanlan*; *Marsupials and Politics: Two Comedies* (1981), *Beware of Imitations* (first performed 1973, published 1985) and 'It's a Chocolate World' (1968). He has also written two books for children, *How They*

Caught Kevin Farrelly (1972) and *A Letter from Hospital* (1975). In 1970 Oakley shared the Captain Cook Bicentenary Award with Thomas Keneally, in 1982 he won the Canada/Australia Literary Award and in 1988 an Awgie for *The Feet of Daniel Mannix*.

Oakley's novels are picaresque comedies in which the hero/victim pits his manic energies against an absurd but conformist world. Oakley, who sees himself as refracting rather than recording reality, is interested in the riddle of 'Middle Australia', the enigma of 'Glen Waverley Man, *homo suburbiensis*, forever patrolling and mowing his front lawn'. Satiric and iconoclastic, but also sympathetic and affirmative, his fiction attacks many targets in a free-wheeling, amiable way including religion, sport, suburbia, academia, publishers, avant-garde artists, public servants, schoolteachers and advertising executives. Two of his most potent topics are Catholicism, especially Catholic education, and the norms of life in Melbourne, which he presents with penetrating irony. *A Wild Ass of a Man*, his most exuberant and inventive novel, traces the progress of a luckless, innocent young man called Muldoon, who perpetually strives but always fails to make an imprint on his society and who ends by suffering a revolving crucifixion on a ferris wheel at Luna Park. *A Salute to the Great McCarthy*, which restricts itself to Australian rules football and the doomed rise of a young star player from the country, has almost the same satirical impact and frenetic pace, if not the same episodic variety, as *A Wild Ass of a Man*. In *Let's Hear It for Prendergast*, Prendergast, the tallest poet in the world, with a mission to destroy all Melbourne's sacred cows, is granted an unwilling 'normal' interpreter, Morley; as Prendergast chaotically progresses to his fate of self-immolation in fires that consume Melbourne's Exhibition building, he exposes indirectly the equally chaotic absurdity of the city's pretensions and social conventions. *The Craziplane*, once again set in Melbourne, centres on the tangled relationship between the middle-aged Frank Minogue, once Australia's greatest living playwright, and a young Sydney journalist commissioned to interview him. A witty exploration of the city's pub and theatre life of the 1980s, the novel exploits the traditional Melbourne–Sydney rivalry. Oakley's gifts for satire and for evoking the absurd are seen at their best in his short stories. Frequently using the epistolary form, he interprets various experiences of failure and isolation – discarded husbands, restive priests, failed writers, jaded public servants, tired academics, bored housewives; immediate, ironic, witty and often hilariously comic, they have an underlying seriousness that seems to regard failure as the universal price of being human.

Oakley is probably best known for his drama, however, and for his associations with other dramatists such as John Romeril, David Williamson, Jack Hibberd and Alexander Buzo. His earliest plays were performed at the La Mama theatre, although his non-partisan stance and ironic subtleties are often at odds with the approach of doctrinaire 'rough' theatre. His first play to be produced was *From the Desk of Eugene Flockhart* (its original title) at the Emerald Hill Theatre in Melbourne in 1967; set in a Canberra public service office, it is an uproarious attack on the deadening absurdities of office life which has similarities with Buzo's more intricate play *The Front Room Boys* (1969). The subject of *Witzenhausen, Where Are You?*, one of the first plays to be produced at La Mama (in 1968), is a mystic messenger in a large car company who causes a disruption by locking himself in the lavatory, passing subversive messages on toilet paper under the door to the dismayed staff and finally disappearing in a flash of light. 'It's a Chocolate World' is a comic but compassionate treatment of the problems of an unhappily married research officer in a large international firm, Candy Bar Inc. A later play which deals similarly with the effects of power on people and with the incongruities between public façades and private realities, and which has affinities with Oakley's short story 'Malvolio', is the radio play *The Great God Mogadon*. Two plays which were highly successful at the Pram Factory and are more in keeping with its 'rough' theatre are *The Feet of Daniel Mannix* and *Beware of Imitations*; the former, a vaudevillean-style production, draws on the life of the Roman Catholic Archbishop Daniel Mannix, and moves from his descent on Melbourne from heaven, clutching a wrench and a tube of Tarzan's Grip, to his western-style shoot-out with W.M. Hughes over conscription, to his association with John Wren and 'Greensleeves' (B.A. Santamaria) and his conflict with 'Dr Bert Effort' (H.V. Evatt). *Beware of Imitations* centres on the life of ex-prime minister 'Sir Wilfred McLuckie' (R.G. Menzies), Warden of the Ports and Brandies, the Garters and the Privy Seal, who is spending his last days in a private nursing home, tended by Roy, his valet, a former digger and staunch member of the RSL, now sustained by whisky and visits to the TAB. In dreams and re-enactments the pair play out the highs and lows, the aspirations and the disappointments of the prime minister's career. Two later plays, the farce, *Politics*, which has a more general theme, and *The Ship's Whistle*, which focuses on the life of the nineteenth-century poet R.H. Horne, show the same flair for comic exaggeration, verbal display and serious buffoonery.

Three plays which reflect Oakley's literary interests are *The Hollow Tombola*, a sharp satire on Patrick White's novel *The Solid Mandala* (1966), *Scanlan*, a part-comic, part-pathetic parody of a conference paper delivered by a middle-aged, paranoid, nervously debilitated academic on the poet Henry Kendall, and *A Lesson in English*. The last, performed at La Mama in 1969, deals comically at first with a teacher's unlucky efforts to interpret Marvell's poem 'To His Coy Mistress' to rowdy schoolboys, and ends in a moment of

rare communication between teacher and boys on the real nature of sexuality. Oakley's other more naturalistic plays include *Buck Privates*, a subtle exploration of the private yearnings of Lovelock, a Dried Fruits publicity officer, and his old school rival Daley, now a middle-aged priest; *Marsupials*, a study of the complexities and paradoxes of one man's relationship with his wife, her ex-lover, his work, his role as a father and, with the greatest paradox of all, Australia; and *Bedfellows*. The last named is Oakley's most extended treatment of relationships, a funny/sad look at a tired marriage between a university lecturer, editor of a literary magazine and Carlton resident, Paul Cummins, and his wife Carol, part-time student and mother of two. Shaken out of their usual boredom by a mutual disclosure of extra-marital affairs, especially Carol's with Bill Butler, rising writer and Paul's best friend, the couple re-examine their feelings in a way that mixes the mundane, the farcical and the anguished.

O'BRIEN, Eris (1895–1974), Archbishop of Canberra and Goulburn 1953–67, was born at Condobolin, NSW, and entered the priesthood in 1918. He studied overseas 1934–38, gaining a doctorate from the University of Louvain, Belgium, for his work *The Foundation of Australia (1786–1800)* (1937). O'Brien also published the *Life and Letters of Archpriest John Joseph Therry* (1922), *The Dawn of Catholicism in Australia* (1928) and *The Establishment of the Hierarchy in Australia* (1942). He is the author of a three-act play, *The Hostage* (1928), dealing with the life of Father Jeremiah O'Flynn, an Irish priest who was expelled by Governor Macquarie; Michael Massey Robinson appears as a character. O'Brien was made CMG in 1957.

'O'BRIEN, John' (Patrick Joseph Hartigan) (1878–1952), born Yass, was ordained as a Roman Catholic priest in 1903. In 1910, after a curacy of seven years at Albury, he was appointed inspector of Catholic schools in the Goulburn diocese. He administered the last rites (prematurely) in 1911 to Jack Riley of Brigenbrong, who had some claims to having been A.B. Paterson's 'The Man from Snowy River'. He was priest-in-charge at Berrigan in 1916 and parish priest at Narrandera 1917–44. He published two volumes of verse under the pseudonym 'John O'Brien', *Around the Boree Log and Other Verses* (1921) and *The Parish of St Mel's* (1954), the latter a tribute to his Narrandera parish. A selection of his poems, illustrated by the paintings of Patrick Carroll, was published in 1978 as *Around the Boree Log*. He also wrote *On Darlinghurst Hill* (1952), the centenary volume of the Sacred Heart parish, Darlinghurst, and a series of articles, 'In Diebus Illis', recording the achievement of the pioneer clergy in Australia, published originally in the *Australasian Catholic Record* and later in book form, *The Men of '38 and other Pioneer Priests* (1975). The 'John O'Brien' poetry is simple, homely balladry centred on the Irish-Australian, Catholic, rural communities. Its great successes are 'Said Hanrahan' (q.v.), 'The Old Bush School', 'At Casey's, After Mass' and 'Tangmalangaloo'. The *Around the Boree Log* poems were made popular by the recitations of John Byrne ('The Joker'); they were made into a film in 1925; twenty of them were set to music by Dom. S. Moreno of New Norcia, WA, in 1933. 'O'Brien's' nephew Frank Mecham published the biography 'John O'Brien' and the Boree Log in 1981.

Observer (1) was an Adelaide weekly associated with the *South Australian Register*. Absorbing the *Adelaide Examiner* (1841–43), it began publication in 1843 as the *Adelaide Observer*, its title until 1905, and ran until 1931, when it was itself incorporated into the *Chronicle*. Catherine Helen Spence's novels *The Author's Daughter* and *Gathered In* were first published as serials in the *Observer* in 1867 (as 'Hugh Lindsay's Guest') and in 1881–82 respectively. Her work was also included in the *Observer Miscellany* (1875–79), an annual literary selection from the *Observer*.

Observer (2), a fortnightly newspaper published in Sydney and edited by Donald Horne, ran 1958–61, when it merged with the *Bulletin*. A liberal-conservative polemical newspaper concerned with local political and international affairs, the *Observer* also published substantial literary articles, book reviews, short stories, verse and theatrical notices. Many of Australia's leading writers either contributed to or were reviewed by the newspaper. Regular contributors included Chris Wallace-Crabbe and Desmond O'Grady. Peter Coleman was on the editorial staff.

'Ocker' is a word in current usage denoting someone uncouth, boorish or uncultivated, usually an Australian male. The origin of the word is uncertain, although it existed innocently from at least the 1920s until the end of the 1960s, best known as a nickname for people with the Christian name of Horace or Oscar, as in 'Ocker' Stevens, a character in the comic strip 'Ginger Meggs', or with the surnames O'Connor and O'Connell. In its present sense it seems to have superseded 'Alf' during the 1970s, possibly as a result of the television portrayal by the actor Ron Frazer of the beer-swilling philistine Ocker in the television series *The Mavis Bramston Show*; other famous stage Ockers include Barry Humphries's 'Bazza' McKenzie and Les Patterson, and Paul Hogan. For some social commentators the Ocker is an Australian national type, as in Max Harris's *Ockers* (1974); the stereotype is explored in such plays as Alexander Buzo's *Norm and Ahmed* (1969) and John Romeril's *The Floating World* (1975). Recent neologisms include 'Ockerina' for the female of the species, 'Ockerdom' and 'Ockerism', although there is some evidence that 'Ocker' is now under threat from 'Norm'.

'O'CONNER, Elizabeth' (**Barbara McNamara**) (1913–), the daughter of Eric Lowe, was born at Dunedoo, NSW, and studied art at Adelaide and Sydney before teaching at a Brisbane girls' boarding school. After marrying a cattle-station manager, she spent many years in outback areas of northern Australia and now lives in Cairns. She has written two autobiographical accounts of life on large cattle

stations, which have proved perennially popular, *Steak for Breakfast* (1958) and *A Second Helping* (1969), and three novels, all of which are set in northern Queensland, *The Irishman* (1960), *Find a Woman* (1963) and *Spirit Man* (1980). Of these, *The Irishman*, which deals with the experiences of an Irish teamster, Paddy Doolan, and his two sons against a colourful panorama of Gulf country life, has received most attention. Produced as a film in 1978, the novel also won the Miles Franklin Award in 1960. *Find a Woman* is a family comedy which describes the revolutionary impact of a new wife on the masculine idyll of two middle-aged brothers; *Spirit Man*, set in the mid-1930s, is a tense racial drama. 'O'Conner' has also written a book for children, *The Chinese Bird* (1966).

O'CONNOR, Mark (1945–), born Melbourne, the son of a judge, graduated in English and classics (after abandoning engineering) from the University of Melbourne, then taught briefly but has spent most of the time since as a full-time writer, especially of poetry. While resident in Canberra in the early 1970s, he was editor of *Canberra Poetry* 1973–75, and won the *Poetry Australia* Biennial International Prize with his first published poetry in 1973, winning the same award in 1975.

A travelling scholarship, the Marten Bequest Travelling Scholarship, allowed him to spend several years in Europe, chiefly in Italy. He returned to Australia in 1980 and was attached to James Cook University in Townsville in 1982, which was also a return to the Barrier Reef, the inspiration of his first book of poetry, *Reef Poems* (1976). His experiences in North Queensland, and his poetry, were the subject of a 1985 documentary in the ABC TV series 'A Big Country'. In 1984 he was writer-in-residence for the NSW National Parks; a knowledgeable amateur biologist, he has had a lifelong concern for the Australian environment and its protection. A series of Literature Board Fellowships and numerous prizes for his work have enabled him to continue his writing. In 1987–88 he was the Thomas Ramsay Science and Humanities Scholar at the Museum of Victoria, and he has been writer-in-residence in several academic institutions, notably at East China University; in 1993 he won the substantial ACT Literary Award, after which he took up a residency at the University of Oregon. Among the numerous minor poetry and short fiction awards that O'Connor has won are the Shell *Artlook* Prize (1979), the Commonwealth Short Story Prize (1979), the London *Times* Kenneth Allsop Memorial Prize (1980), the FAW John Shaw Neilson Poetry Award (1981), the Tom Collins Poetry Prize (1983), the Charles Thatcher Prize (1985) and the Grace Perry Prize (1988). His chief publications have been poetry: *Reef Poems* (1976); *The Eating Tree* (1980, a collection of poems based on his European experiences); *The Fiesta of Men* (1983); *Poetry in Pictures: The Great Barrier Reef* (1986, a republication of *Reef Poems* in conjunction with photographer Neville Coleman); *Selected Poems* (1986); *Poetry of the Mountains* (1988, the subject being the Blue Mountains of NSW, photographs by Ian Brown); *The Ship Trans-Time* (1989, inspired by the

Museum of Victoria's collections); *The Great Forest* (1989) and *Fire-Stick Farming: Selected Poems 1972–90* (1990). O'Connor has also edited the anthology *Two Centuries of Australian Poetry* (1988); published three lectures on poetry, *Modern Australian Styles* (1982); written a book of prose, *Words on Paper: An Introduction to Alphabetic Theory* (1983); contributed seven episodes to the radio Science Show, 1984–85, and written several plays.

Section One, 'Coelenterate Islands', from *Reef Poems* highlights the teeming life of that North Queensland paradise, the birds (herons, gannets, sea-eagles, terns and cormorants) holding pride of place. The threat of man's pollution ('On a rusted drum of poison') spoils an otherwise perfect scenario. *The Fiesta of Men* captures incidents and atmospheres of O'Connor's wanderings through Greece, Italy, Yugoslavia, Norway, England's Lake District ('Wordsworth's House at Rydal') and North Queensland where, in 'Planting the Dunk Botanic Gardens', he tells of his own almost frenzied attempt to establish a huge tropical garden on E.J. Banfield's paradise island. 'Riding a Hired Lambretta', from *The Fiesta of Men*, won the 1981 John Shaw Neilson Poetry Award. O'Connor's first *Selected Poems* adopts the unusual practice of segmenting the poems by years rather than by the books in which they were published. The years range from 1972 to 1984, with only 1981 missing. *Poetry of the Mountains* is saturated with the natural beauty of the Blue Mountains of NSW, the verbal brilliance of the poems complemented by some striking photographs. 'Fire-Stick Farming' from the Blue Mountains poetry provides the title for O'Connor's second *Selected* volume. The book is again segmented by periods, rather than by published volumes. A remarkably fine collection, *Fire-Stick Farming* reinforces the impression that O'Connor's poetry draws strongly on the external natural scene, and the diversity of flora, fauna and landscapes. Interwoven with those externals, however, are frequent, sensitive insights into the nature of existence itself. A poet who has won a popular following, O'Connor has also won a reputation as one of Australia's major contemporary nature poets.

O'DOHERTY, Eva (1830–1910), born Ireland as Mary Eva Kelly, was an early contributor of nationalistic ballads and poems to Charles Gavan Duffy's magazine *Nation*, earning for herself the name 'Eva of the *Nation*'. She became engaged to Kevin Izod O'Doherty, a medical practitioner and political activist, who was sentenced to transportation in 1848. After O'Doherty was set free in 1854, the two married, lived for a time in Paris and Dublin and finally settled in Brisbane, where O'Doherty practised medicine and had some success as a politician. In 1886 they returned to Ireland, where O'Doherty joined the Irish National Party and was briefly a member of the House of Commons, before returning to Queensland. Eva O'Doherty published two collections of verse, *Poems* (1877) and *Poems* (1880). Popular as O'Doherty's verse was in her lifetime both in Ireland and Queensland, her predictable themes, images and rhymes are now only of historical interest. Ross and Heather Patrick

have written *Exiles Undaunted: the Irish Rebels Kevin and Eva O'Doherty* (1989).

O'DONOGHUE, John (1929–), born Newcastle, has worked as a teacher, lecturer and director of community programmes for Newcastle College of Advanced Education. Of his several plays for stage three have been published, *A Happy and Holy Occasion* (1976), a study of a 1940s working-class Catholic family of Irish origin; *Abbie & Lou, Norman & Rose* (1993), which focuses on the relationship between Louis Stone (q.v.) and his wife Abigail, and between Norman and Rose Lindsay (qq.v.); and *Essington Lewis: I am Work* (1987), an interpretation of the steel magnate who built up BHP and his impact on Australian industrial history. Both his first two published plays, embedded in Newcastle's past, are markedly regional. O'Donoghue's other plays include 'Jonah' (1979, an adaptation of the novel by Louis Stone) and 'In the Field Where They Buried Peter Pan' (1982).

O'DONOHUE, Barry (1947–), born Innisfail, Queensland, was conscripted into the Australian Army in 1967 and spent a year on active service in Vietnam. He now lives in Brisbane and is writing, in prose and poetry, of his Vietnam experiences. He has been involved in several magazines in an editorial capacity, e.g. *Image*, *The Border Issue*, *Arts National* and *LiNQ* and has also edited *Queensland Youth Festival Young Writers 1979* (1980) and a collection of contemporary Queensland poetry, *Place and Perspective* (1984). He has published short stories, articles, literary reviews and poetry widely in Australia. His poetry has also appeared in France, Canada and the USA. His verse has been published in several collections, *From the Edge of the World* (1979), *Addiction to False Landscapes* (1981), *Latitudes South* (1983), *View from a First Floor Window* (1983) and, with Philip Neilsen, *We'll All Go Together* (1984).

O'DOWD, Bernard (1866–1953), born Beaufort, Victoria, the son of Ulster immigrants, grew up in Ballarat, strongly compelled by his Irish background and the events of the recent Eureka Stockade to radical socialism. He had both arts and law degrees before he was 30, a considerable achievement for those times. After periods of teaching, O'Dowd moved to Melbourne, entered the State public service by way of the crown solicitor's office, and ultimately became chief parliamentary draftsman in 1931. He married Eva Fryer in 1889 but later left her for the socialist poet Marie Pitt, with whom he lived from 1919. O'Dowd's strong radical tendencies found full expression in Melbourne at the turn of the century. He was a member of the Progressive Lyceum, edited its manual, the *Lyceum Tutor*, until his views became too vehement even for that coterie of radicals, and attended Charles Strong's Australian Church, which was renowned for its radical sermons and debates and its emphasis on intellectual freedom. His first writings of note appeared in the *Bulletin* and in the *Tocsin* (q.v.), a journal which he produced and edited. His *Tocsin* column 'The Forge', under the pseudonym 'Gavah the Blacksmith', consistently attacked the Establishment and the injustices of the contemporary social system. His belief, which he shared with Walt Whitman, that the poet's true socialist role was to further the best interests of mankind was contained in his 1909 address *Poetry Militant* (q.v.). His first volume of poetry, *Dawnward?* (q.v., 1903), indicated by its question mark O'Dowd's uncertainty about Australia's future direction. The sonnet 'Australia' (q.v.) is the volume's best-known poem. *The Silent Land* (1906) speculates about a mystic world which exists beyond the physical world, influencing and being influenced by it. *Dominions of the Boundary* (1907) examines the nature and purpose of the deities such as Hermes, Vulcan and Bacchus and attempts to bestow contemporary significance on them. *The Seven Deadly Sins* (1909), a series of sonnets on those sins, contains some unusually fine imagery. *The Bush* (q.v.), O'Dowd's most substantial and worthwhile poem, envisages a future in which Australia occupies a place of glory similar to that occupied by Greece and Rome in antiquity. O'Dowd's last major composition was *Alma Venus* (1921), a remarkable but largely ignored poetic exploration of the mystery of sex. From 1921 until his death in 1953 O'Dowd maintained an almost complete poetic silence. Apart from radical verse like *Dawnward?* and *The Bush*, in which he assumed the role of standard-bearer of the nationalist radical movement, O'Dowd's poetry made little impact. His concern with 'Poetry Militant' made his verse too obviously didactic for general taste and his predilection for classical allusions made it largely incomprehensible to the ordinary reader. But he attempted to make a meaningful examination of Australian life and not simply describe, as the balladists had done, its more picturesque aspects. He also wrote a book of essays, *Fantasies* (1942). Victor Kennedy and Nettie Palmer wrote *Bernard O'Dowd* (1954) and Hugh Anderson, *Bernard O'Dowd* (1968).

O'FARRELL, Henry James (1833–68), born Arran Quay, Dublin, arrived in Melbourne in 1841. An epileptic, alcoholic, paranoid with Fenian sympathies, O'Farrell shot and wounded the visiting Duke of Edinburgh at Clontarf, 12 March 1868. He was hanged 21 April 1868. The incident accentuated sectarianism in a colony that was already strongly divided on Protestant and Roman Catholic lines. Henry Kendall wrote two poems about the incident, 'In Hyde Park' and 'Australia Vindex', both published in the *Sydney Morning Herald*, 26 March 1868; they echo Australian shame at the assassination attempt and anger at O'Farrell, whose name, Kendall believed, was sure to become 'a byword for hisses and hate'. The events are recorded in Brian McKinlay's *The First Royal Tour 1867–1868* (1970).

O'FARRELL, Patrick James (1933–), born NZ, and Australian only by adoption, is professor of history at the University of NSW. His chief interests are the history of the Irish in Australia and the role of the Catholic Church in Australian history. He has published *Harry Holland: Militant Socialist* (1964), *The Catholic Church in Australia: A Short History 1788–1967*

(1968), revised as *The Catholic Church and Community in Australia: A History* (1977, updated 1985, 1992), *Documents in Australian Catholic History 1788–1968* (2 vols, with Deirdre O'Farrell, 1969), *Letters from Irish Australia 1825–1929* (1984), *The Irish in Australia* (1986, updated 1993) and *Vanished Kingdoms: Irish in Australia and New Zealand* (1990). He won the NSW Premier's Literary Award for non-fiction in 1987 and the Ernest Scott Historical Prize in 1990 for *The Irish in Australia*. All O'Farrell's work is characterised by an eloquent style and a highly imaginative and original interpretation of events. *Vanished Kingdoms*, subtitled *A Personal Excursion*, draws on the experiences and history of his own parents to bring to vivid life the day-to-day experiences of a typical Irish-Australian family.

O'FERRALL, Ernest Francis (1881–1925), born Melbourne, joined the staff of the *Bulletin* in 1907. A popular writer of short stories and sketches for the *Bulletin* and the *Lone Hand*, often under the pseudonym 'Kodak', O'Ferrall is represented in numerous anthologies. He published two collections of stories, *Bodger and the Boarders* (1921) and *Stories by 'Kodak'* (1933), and a collection of verse, *Odd Jobs* (1928). O'Ferrall's stories have mainly urban settings. Lightly satiric, they rely heavily on situational comedy, especially on bizarre but credible incidents arising from boarding-house life, on the predictable but originally handled collisions between shrewish, unattractive landladies and drunken male boarders. His most famous story, 'The Lobster and the Lioness', which has affinities with Henry Lawson's 'The Loaded Dog', recounts an encounter between a drunken boarding-house inmate and an escaped lioness which he mistakes for a dog.

Official History of Australia in the War of 1914–1918, The, begun in 1919 when C.E.W. Bean (q.v.) was appointed official historian, was completed in 1942. *The Official History of the Australian Army Medical Services in the War of 1914–1918* (three vols, 1930, 1940, 1943) by A.G. Butler was also under Bean's general editorship. Bean wrote the first six volumes of the general history *The Story of Anzac* (1921, 1924) and *The Australian Imperial Force in France* (1929, 1933, 1937, 1942). Volume 7, *The Australian Imperial Force in Sinai and Palestine 1914–1918* (1923), was written by Sir Henry Gullett; 8, *The Australian Flying Corps in the Western and Eastern Theatres of War, 1914–1918* (1923), by F.M. Cutlack; 9, *The Royal Australian Navy, 1914–1918* (1928), by A.W. Jose; 10, *The Australians at Rabaul* (1927), by S.S. Mackenzie; 11, *Australia during the War* (1936), by Ernest Scott; 12, *Photographic Record of the War* (1939), annotated by C.E.W. Bean and H.S. Gullett. Bean's single-volume abridgement, *Anzac to Amiens*, was published in 1946. One of Australia's most impressive and massive historical works, the *Official History* has elicited great praise from military historians all over the world. It is an absorbing amalgam of military, social and political history, offering a lively analysis, frequently by anecdote and inference, of the Australian character, especially of Australia's fighting men; it is a sustained illustration of Bean's view of the democratic basis of the national life and society. *The Official History* has been republished by UQP, beginning in 1981.

O'FLAHERTY, H.C. (Henry Charles) (?–?1854) was theatre musician, actor and playwright. Little is known of his life apart from his marriage to the actress Eliza Winstanley, in 1841. He was probably the author of the burletta 'Life in Sydney: Or, The Ran Dan Club' (1843), and he also wrote a play as a vehicle for his wife, 'Isabel of Valois: Or, The Tyrant Queen', produced in 1842. Between 1841 and 1846 when they left for England, the O'Flahertys played at all three of Sydney's theatres, with visits to Tasmania and Melbourne. After they left Australia Eliza's career eclipsed his and he sank into oblivion, Eliza reverting to her maiden name in 1847.

OGILVIE, Will (William Henry) (1869–1963), born near Kelso, Scotland, arrived in Australia at the age of 20, drawn to the colony by his love of horses and adventure, and by his admiration for the poet Adam Lindsay Gordon, whose tragic story had captured his imagination. He spent twelve years in a nomadic existence on far-flung stations like Belalie on the Warrego and Maroupe in SA, droving, mustering, breaking in horses and capturing, in hastily scribbled, buoyant, romantic verses, the many experiences of outback life. A prolific contributor to the *Bulletin* and popular also with readers of the *Australasian* and the Mount Gambier *Border Watch*, he published his popular and best-known volume of verse, *Fair Girls and Gray Horses* (1898), before his return to Scotland in 1901. The poems, a mixture of ballads and lyrics, celebrated 'all Fair Girls' and 'all Gray Horses', for Ogilvie believed that 'Golden and Gray are the loves to hold'. The classic droving poem 'From the Gulf', with its nostalgic refrain 'Store Cattle from Nelanjie', the sentimental, horsebreaker poem 'The Riding of the Rebel', and the poem that celebrated the courage and endurance of the teamsters, 'How the Fire Queen crossed the Swamp', are examples of Australian balladry at its best. But it is in lyrics such as 'A Telltale Tryst' and 'The Bush, My Lover', where the loveliness of fair girls blends with the shimmering Australian moonlight, that Ogilvie's singular contribution to the verse of the period lies. In the mostly pragmatic and masculine world of bush verse, his was virtually the only, and certainly the best, romantic voice. His later volumes of Australian content, *Hearts of Gold* (1903), *The Australian* (1916) and *Saddle for a Throne* (1952), compiled by Thelma E. Williams and published by R.M. Williams, were all published in Australia, although Ogilvie did not return to this country. In Scotland Ogilvie continued to write verse and was acclaimed for his Border poetry by such luminaries as Hugh MacDiarmid, but died in relative obscurity. He wrote an account of his Australian adventures in *My Life in the Open* (1908).

O'GRADY, Desmond (1929–   ), born Melbourne, has worked as literary editor of the *Bulletin* and since 1962 has lived as a freelance journalist in Rome. His short stories have been collected in *A Long Way from Home* (1966) and *Valid for All Countries* (1979). He has also published a novel, *Deschooling Kevin Carew* (1974), and has written a number of plays including 'Heart of the Wise' (1958), *Other Side of the Ocean* (1985), *Let's Hear it for Carboni* (1987), 'Marriage Gamblers' (1991), and the radio script 'Randall's Choice'. A skilful raconteur, with a plain but expressive style and a keen eye for the odd and the eccentric, O'Grady gives his stories diverse settings, ranging from Europe to Asia to Australia. Frequently his central character is an outsider, a misfit, an exile or a returned expatriate; an Australian in Rome or a Hungarian in Melbourne, the O'Grady hero is afflicted with a divided consciousness and a vague sense of displacement and dispossession, although his predicament is interpreted as comic or even farcical. As the hero reluctantly absorbs his unpredictable experience and the perverse irony of his circumstances, he 'progresses' from a state of fragile certainty to one of total bewilderment. O'Grady's Australian Catholic childhood has provided him with much of his absurd material. Several of his short stories, including the trio 'Memoirs of Catholic Boyhoods' in *Valid for All Countries*, draw on the comic, discomfiting collisions between the simple rigidities of an Australian Catholic education and the complex actualities of modern adult life. *Deschooling Kevin Carew*, which draws heavily on this material, relates Carew's excessive but uncertain efforts to come to terms with his religious conditioning. In 1985 he published *Raffaello! Raffaello!*, a biography of Raffaello Carboni. O'Grady has also written histories of early Christianity, published overseas.

O'GRADY, Frank (1910–87) was working as an employee of the Sydney City Council when he wrote his first novel, *The Golden Valley* (1955). The story of a pioneering family in NSW in the 1830s, it was followed by five similar historical novels: *Goonoo Goonoo* (1956), *Hanging Rock* (1957), *No Boundary Fence* (1960), which is based on the life of Hamilton Hume, *Wild Honey* (1961) which includes the bushranger Fred Ward as a character, and *The Sun Breaks Through* (1964). O'Grady also wrote a biography of Francis James McGarry, *Francis of Central Australia* (1977).

O'GRADY, John Patrick (1907–81), born Sydney, the eldest of eight children, spent most of his childhood on a remote New England farm and had no formal education until the age of 12. He qualified as a chemist but never found the profession satisfying and in 1936 began work as a commercial traveller selling medical goods, meanwhile writing short stories, plays and poems, some of which were published in the *Bulletin*. During the Second World War he served in New Guinea and Borneo, left the army in 1950 and worked successively as a pharmacist, a builder's labourer, a teacher of pharmacy for the NZ government in Samoa, and a fisherman. In 1957 his novel *They're a Weird Mob*, supposedly written by an Italian migrant journalist turned Sydney builder's labourer, Nino Culotta, was an instant and continuing success. Nino Culotta's bewildered but sympathetic perceptions of

Australian habits and language and his progress from outsider to insider provided a perspective on national attitudes that many Australians found fresh and congenial. The book was produced as a film in 1966. O'Grady subsequently wrote two more Nino Culotta books, *Cop This Lot* (1960) and *Gone Fishin'* (1962), and sixteen books under his own name, none of which proved as popular. They include *No Kava for Johnny* (1961), a novel based on his Samoan experience; *Aussie English* (1965); *Gone Troppo* (1968); *O'Grady Sez* (1969), a collection of short stories and verse; *Are You Irish or Normal?* (1970); *Aussie Etiket* (1971); *Gone Gougin'* (1975); and *There Was a Kid* (1977), an account of his New England childhood. O'Grady, occasionally described as the Rolf Harris of Australian literature, had a keen ear for the Australian idiom, especially of the 1950s, but he overworked his material.

O'HARA, J.B. (John Bernard) (1862–1927), born Bendigo, was educated at the University of Melbourne, where he achieved distinction, and became a lecturer in mathematics and physics at Ormond College in 1886. In 1889 he established a girls' school, South Melbourne College, of which he was headmaster until 1917. Katharine Susannah Prichard and Elsie Cole were two of his pupils and protégées. A respected poet in his lifetime, he won a prize in a competition connected with the Melbourne Exhibition of 1880, although his bland, meditative verse, reminiscent of the late Victorians, has now dated. He published nine collections of verse, mostly short lyrics, although his second volume, *Songs of the South Second Series: The Wild White Man and Other Poems* (1895), includes a narrative poem relating the adventures of William Buckley. His other volumes are *Songs of the South* (1891), *Lyrics of Nature* (1899), *A Book of Sonnets* (1902), *Odes and Lyrics* (1906), *Calypso and Other Poems* (1912), *The Poems of John Bernard O'Hara* (1918), *At Eventide* (1922) and *Sonnets and Rondels* (1925).

'O'HARRIS, Pixie' (Rhona Olive Pratt) (1903–91), born Cardiff, Wales, migrated to WA in 1920 but later moved to Sydney. Wife of Bruce Pratt, aunt of Rolf Harris and close friend of Miles Franklin, she wrote and illustrated about twenty books for children, and acquired a considerable reputation as an illustrator by the mid-1920s. Some of her most popular books are the fairy-tales *Pearl Pinkie and Sea Greenie* (1935), *The 'Pixie O'Harris Fairy Book'* (1925), *Marmaduke the Possum* (1943) and *Marmaduke and Margaret* (1953), in which her conventionally pretty artwork complements the fantasy. She also wrote a series of romantic stories for girls, beginning with *The Fortunes of Poppy Treloar* (1941). After a decline in popularity of fairy-stories in the 1950s, she ceased writing and illustrating children's books for a time and concentrated on a career as a landscape and portrait artist. A revival of interest in her work has seen a number of her books reprinted in recent years and also the publication of a number of new titles such as *The Pixie O'Harris Cavalcade of Cats* (1981) and *The Little Grey Mouse* (1982). As well as illustrating the work of other children's authors, she illustrated work by C.J. Dennis, Frank

Dalby Davison and Ruth Bedford. Her autobiography *Was It Yesterday?*, illustrated by herself, was published in 1983, followed by *Our Small Safe World: Recollections of a Welsh Childhood* in 1986. She was made MBE in 1976.

'Old Bark Hut, The' is an anonymous Australian folk-song which exists in several versions; the best-known one introduces the singer as Bob the Swagman, who chronicles the misfortunes he experiences while living on rations in an old bark hut, poorly furnished and open to the elements. The song was one of the most popular of Australian folk-songs in the nineteenth century. Its jaunty melody, simple four-line stanza, and chorus which repeats the last line of each verse, permit the kind of extension which gave rise to the legend that a party of shearers once started singing the song as their train pulled out of Bourke, and finished it as the train arrived at Central Station in Sydney.

Old Blastus of Bandicoot, a novel by Miles Franklin (q.v.), was originally published in 1931 in England, but many copies of that edition were destroyed in a fire. Set in the Murrumbidgee ranges, the novel traces the course of a feud between the rival pioneer families the Lindseys and the Barrys. William Barry, nicknamed 'Old Blastus' because of his fondness for that mild expletive, has two daughters: Mabel, seduced by a Lindsey boy, with a resultant illegitimate son; and the younger Dora who, ignorant of the family 'shame', is compelled to a cloistered existence by her over-protective father. The original Lindsey-Barry romance is in time repeated with Dora and Ross Lindsey, although not with the same result. All comes to a happy conclusion when Old Blastus heroically saves the Lindsey estate from a bushfire, thus clearing up the old feud. Mabel marries and leaves the district taking her 'shame' with her and Dora marries young Ross Lindsey. The novel's routine plot and outdated moral attitudes are its weaknesses; its strength lies in the character of Old Blastus, at times a figure of fun and the butt of Miles Franklin's feminism, at other times something of a hero in spite of himself,

'OLD BOOMERANG', see **HOULDING, J.R.**

Old Bush Songs Composed and Sung in the Bushranging, Digging and Overlanding Days, The was compiled and edited by A.B. Paterson (q.v.) in 1905. The first major collection of Australian folk-songs, it rescued from oblivion many old ballads and songs which had existed precariously as songs or recitations around the camp-fires and in the shearing sheds of the outback. The first edition contained about fifty songs; by 1926 the fifth edition contained more than seventy, some with choruses, many with footnotes and identification of the tunes to which they were sung. Among the well-known inclusions were 'The Wild Colonial Boy', 'The Eumerella Shore', 'The Stringy Bark Cockatoo', 'The Dying Stockman', 'The Old Bark Hut' and the Paddy Malone songs.

Old Days: Old Ways (1934) are reminiscences and anecdotes of the pioneering days by Mary Gilmore (q.v.). A companion volume, *More Recollections*, was published in 1935. In vivid and lyrical prose she tells of the struggle to survive the hazards and discomfort of bush life, the epic feats of the teamsters in servicing the outback, the Aborigines and their lore, and the beauty of the land before its ravage by the onward march of civilisation.

'Old Granny Sullivan', a sentimental poem by John Shaw Neilson (q.v.), was published in the *Bookfellow* in 1907; A.G. Stephens published it again in 1916 as a leaflet and it was also used in school publications. Based, according to Neilson, on an old lady who lived in Penola when he was a boy, the poem recounts the typically sad story of a woman in early colonial times.

Old Tales of a Young Country, a series of fifteen historical tales by Marcus Clarke (q.v.), was published in 1871; all but one of the series had appeared in 'Old Stories Retold' in the *Australasian* 1870–71. A by-product of the research for *His Natural Life* (1874), *Old Tales of a Young Country* reveals a similar opposition to the effect of authority on individual freedom and focuses on romantic incidents and individuals of Australian history; subjects include George Barrington, William Buckley, Jorgen Jorgenson, John Mitchel, the Rum Rebellion and Macquarie Harbour.

Old Times in the Bush of Australia (1895) is James Kirby's account of the trials and experiences of bush life in Victoria during the 1840s. Kirby came to Australia from Northamphire in 1839 and went to the Swan Hill area of Victoria in 1846. One of Victoria's earliest pioneers, he was encouraged in 1894 by the then Governor of Victoria, Lord Hopetoun, to compile his memoirs. *Old Times* has much information about the Aborigines, the bushrangers and life on the goldfields in the 1840s–1860s.

Old Tote Theatre Company, founded in 1963 by the University of NSW in association with the Australian Elizabethan Theatre Trust, derived its name from its first home, an old racecourse totalisator in the grounds of the University. Robert Quentin, one of the founders of the Company and head of the University's Drama Department, was co-director with Tom Brown 1963–65; he was succeeded by Robin Lovejoy, who became director in 1969 after Brown's resignation. In 1978 Sir Robert Helpmann was appointed artistic director. Originally closely associated with NIDA, the Old Tote became an independent company in 1969 and moved to a larger building on the University campus, the Parade Theatre. A professional company of high standing, the Old Tote staged mainly international, lavishly produced plays which catered for an affluent, middle-aged audience. In 1968, however, the company produced with scant success a series of Australian plays: Thomas Keneally's 'Childermas', Rodney Milgate's *A Refined Look at Existence* and *At Least You Get Something Out of That*,

Dorothy Hewett's *This Old Man Comes Rolling Home*, Alexander Buzo's *Norm and Ahmed*, and Douglas Stewart's *The Fire on the Snow*. Funding for the company transferred to the Australian Council for the Arts in 1968, but in 1978 the Theatre Board decided to discontinue the Old Tote's subsidy and the company consequently dissolved. Its history is given in Josephine South's *Ten on the Tote* (1973).

O'LEARY, P.I. (Patrick Ignatius) (1888–1944), born Adelaide, was an organiser for the SA labour movement in his early years. He later worked as a journalist for newspapers in Broken Hill, Adelaide and Melbourne. Editor of *Design*, he was also editor in Melbourne of the *Advocate* 1920–44, dominating the literary page and contributing poetry, political comment and leading articles. Connected with the Pioneer Players, he was also a member of the Bread and Cheese club. Pseudonyms he used included 'M', 'Historicus', 'Francis Davitt' and 'P.I.O.L.'. Some of his essays, which include several studies of Australian writers, were published in 1954, edited by Joseph O'Dwyer and titled *Bard in Bondage*. Although O'Leary tends to be prolix and even declamatory when his Irish nationalism is aroused, as in 'The Heroes of Easter Week', his judgements are often sound. He also edited an anthology, which includes verse by Roderic Quinn, E.J. Brady, John Shaw Neilson, Edward Harrington and others, *The Bread and Cheese Book* (1939), and published a volume of his own verse, *Romance and Other Verses* (1921).

OLIVER, Murray (1951–), born Broken Hill, NSW, has worked as writer, actor and producer, particularly in theatre-in-education and community theatre. He was a founder in NSW of the children's circus Pipi Storm, and in 1981 formed Bent Pin Productions in WA. His plays include 'True Luv' (1979), 'The Elastic Band' (1979), 'The Fake Cafe' (1982, with Mandy Browne and Ken Kelso), *Couples* (1982, with Mandy Browne), 'The All Night Oasis' (1983), *The Buck Stops Here* (1984, a study of a businessman on retirement facing the personal costs of his career), *Confessions from the Male* (1984, an examination of a range of male roles and stereotypes), and 'Space Invaders' (1985).

'On First Looking Into Chapman's Hesiod', by Peter Porter (q.v.), published in his verse collection, *Living in a Calm Country* (1975) is central to the understanding of Porter's relationship with Australia. The vehicle of the poem is the purchase at a village fête of a copy of Chapman's *Hesiod* and Porter's recognition of the similarity of the attitudes of Boeotian poetry to Australian life; both are robust and innocent, essentially physical and direct in their emotions. Porter identifies his own preference as the European 'Athenian' culture of 'precept and the Pleiades'. The evocation of Australia is sharp in visual and aural detail but the irony is tender and amused rather than scabrous, as in his earlier satires on human folly; his admiration for Australian modes is also made clear. In view of Porter's self-avowed lack of simple and direct response, the poem's tone even suggests partial envy of such Australian modes. His exile from Australia is explained as a feeling of homelessness, a seeking for the 'permanently upright city' which is not London but the 'new land', the world of ideas which dominates his poetry, especially the later volumes *The Cost of Seriousness* (1978) and *English Subtitles* (1981). In an interview with Bruce Bennett (*Westerly*, 1982) Porter spoke of the 'new land' as the republic of the imagination 'where everyone is as gifted as the great men of the past and where you are made welcome as a confrère'. His preference is personal, imposing no clear-cut advocacy of the exiled over the native, more a resignation to the difference between his attitude and the Australian. See also Murray, Les.

JEFF DOYLE

On Our Selection, 'Steele Rudd's' (q.v.) first book, is a series of sketches of selection life on the Queensland Darling Downs; it was first published in 1899 and contained twenty-six stories. In 1909, when 'Rudd' sold the rights of *On Our Selection* and its immediate sequel, *Our New Selection*, to A.C. Rowlandson of the NSW Bookstall Company, the last ten chapters, deleted from subsequent editions, were included in *Stocking Our Selection*.

As originally contributed to the *Bulletin* the *On Our Selection* sketches were about different families, but, on the suggestion of A.G. Stephens, 'Rudd' reworked them for the book so that they focused on the experiences of the Rudd family (q.v.), although Steele himself does not emerge as a character until *From Selection to City* (1909). 'Starting the Selection', the first story, depicts the family's arrival at Shingle Hut from Stanthorpe and Dad's first attempt at sowing a crop; subsequent sketches, of which 'The Night We Watched for Wallabies', 'Cranky Jack' (qq.v.) and 'Kate's Wedding', the best known and most anthologised, chronicle the struggle of the family to survive a harsh and fickle climate, the poorness of the soil, and the exploitation of cockatoo farmers like Dad Rudd by storekeeper and squatter alike. There are moments of comedy and indeed high farce in *On Our Selection*, but the book emphasises the harshness of pioneering life; it was not until *Our New Selection* and subsequent volumes that the family became relatively comfortable. *On Our Selection* was a major publishing success; one estimate put its sales to 1940 at 250 000. The sale of the rights to Rowlandson meant, however, that 'Rudd' did not reap the benefits of its popularity, except in higher fees for the rights to his other books. Similarly, the agreement he reached with Bert Bailey and Julius Grant for the stage adaptation of *On Our Selection* worked to the entrepreneurs' rather than to 'Rudd's' advantage. 'Rudd' had no involvement in the dramatisation of *On Our Selection*, which was also highly popular for many years after its first production in 1912; a sound film of the play was screened in 1932 and led to three further films starring Bailey as Dad. Both the play and the film were influential in the transformation of Dad and his second son, Dave, into stereotypes of the rural hayseed, although 'Rudd' himself, in resorting primarily to farce in his later work,

was also partly responsible. Raymond Longford's classic silent film version (1920) of *On Our Selection*, with a print of which 'Rudd' toured Australia in 1922, is closer in spirit to the 1899 book.

Once a Month: A Magazine for Australasia, a monthly magazine published in Melbourne 1884–86, included articles on literary topics, short stories and verse, much of which was reprinted.

Once a Week, see **Saturday Night**

One Day of the Year, The, a play by Alan Seymour (q.v.), was first produced in 1960 and published in 1962. The 'One Day' is Anzac Day, the servicemen's day of commemoration, commemorated by Alf Cook, a Sydney working-class man who served in the Second World War, as the most sacred day of the year. Anzac Day for Alf is bound up with his strong but otherwise undefined faith in mateship, his masculinity, his pride in Australia and his contempt for other races, nations and classes. In other years his participation in the Dawn Service had been reverently witnessed by his son Hughie, now a university student, but for Hughie Anzac Day has become a symbol of bigoted and ignorant working-class attitudes from which he seeks to free himself. His disaffection has been encouraged by his friendship with another student, Jan Castle, a girl from Sydney's upper-class North Shore; they determine to produce an article and pictures for the university newspaper, exposing the national day of mourning as a national day of 'boozing'. Hughie, who soon realises that for him the issue is far from clear-cut, is torn by conflicting feelings of loyalty and love, anger, disgust and pity as his embattled father strives to redefine what the day means for him; that for one day he is not just an insignificant lift-driver but a man of status: 'They make a fuss of y' for once. The speeches and the march . . . and y're all mates. Y're mates an' everythin' seems all right.' The conflict between father and son is watched helplessly but sympathetically by Hughie's mum Dot and by Wacka Dawson, an old friend of the family and an original Anzac, whose own response to the 'Day' is far more muted than Alf's. By Act III, which takes place some days after Anzac Day, Hughie's friendship with Jan is at an end despite her realisation that her father's class, by sustaining 'patriotic' institutions and through media propaganda, is instrumental in perpetuating the legend. At the close of the play Hughie has decided to remain at home for the time being, having reached an uncomfortable truce with his father.

O'NEIL, Lloyd (1928–92), one of the pioneers of modern Australian publishing, joined Angus & Robertson when he was 16. In 1955 he went to Jacaranda Press in Queensland, one of the earliest Australian educational publishing houses. In 1960 he moved to Melbourne to establish Lansdowne Press, whose first book was *How to Play Aussie Rules*. The touring guide *Explore Australia* sold more than half a million copies. He later sold Lansdowne Press to create the Lloyd O'Neil Publishing Group, producing more than 3000 titles. In 1987 he sold his interests to Penguin Books and became part of the Viking O'Neil imprint. He was made AM in 1990 for his services to Australian publishing. He is commemorated by the Lloyd O'Neil Award, awarded for services to the book industry.

Opinion, a monthly magazine published in Sydney, which included verse, literary essays, notes on literary societies and appreciations of past and contemporary Australian writers, appeared from May to October 1935. Its first issue included a highly sympathetic review of Patrick White's volume of verse *The Ploughman* (1935).

'O'RANE, Patricia', see **DARK, Eleanor**

'Orange Tree, The', one of John Shaw Neilson's (q.v.) best-known poems, was inspired by the beauty of the orange groves at Merbein near Mildura in the Murray River irrigation area, where Neilson was fruit-picking in 1917. The poem was completed in 1919 and published in his *Ballad and Lyrical Poems* (1923). Neilson's comments, 'I was struck with the very beautiful light there is in May . . . the dark green of the orange trees and beautiful sunlight give them enchantment hard to describe', explain the genesis of the poem. He partly attributes the mysticism of the poem to his reaction to a print of Botticelli's *Spring*. In the poem the young girl's instinctive response to the beautiful light that glows within the orange tree has sometimes been interpreted as youth's innate understanding of the natural beauty of life, an understanding that requires none of the hapless and complex explanations offered by the experience of age.

O'REILLY, Bernard (1903–75), born Hartley, NSW, was a member of a pioneering family which opened up the McPherson Ranges on the border of NSW and Queensland. He became a national hero in 1937 when he single-handedly searched for and discovered a crashed plane on the Lamington Plateau and rescued the two survivors. He served in New Guinea and Borneo during the war, and subsequently ran a well-known tourist lodge in the Lamington National Park. He published a popular account of the exploits of his family and a record of the 1937 rescue, *Green Mountains* (1940), which was later produced as a film, *Sons of Matthew*; two collections of memories, *Cullenbenbong* (1944), and *Over the Hills* (1963); a collection of verse, *Songs from the Hills* (1971); and a book for children, *Wild River* (1949). A television documentary of his life was made in 1975.

O'REILLY, Dowell (1865–1923), born Sydney, was elected to the NSW parliament in 1894. He later taught at his old school, Sydney Grammar, and then became a public servant in Sydney. In 1914 his first wife died and in 1917 he married his cousin, Marie Miles. The correspondence of their courtship, *Dowell O'Reilly From His Letters* (1927), edited by his wife, reveals much of his personality and character. The contemporary and friend of Henry Lawson, John le Gay Brereton, and Mary Gilmore, O'Reilly was active

in the Sydney literary scene. Because he was such a rigorous critic of his own writing, O'Reilly's output was small but impressive. His verse includes *Australian Poems* (1884) and *A Pedlar's Pack* (1888), both published under the pseudonym 'D'. His fiction includes the novel *Tears and Triumph* (1913) and *Five Corners* (1920), short stories of excellent quality. *The Prose and Verse of Dowell O'Reilly* (1924) is a composite selection of his work. Eleanor Dark the novelist was his daughter.

O'REILLY, John Boyle (1844–90), born Drogheda, Ireland, was a printer and reporter in Ireland and England before becoming a Fenian. In 1863 he enlisted as a trooper in the British Army for the express purpose of winning his fellow soldiers to the cause but was arrested in 1866. After stints in prisons at Millbank, Portsmouth and Dartmoor – there are Millbank scenes in his novel *Moondyne* (q.v., 1879) and the Dartmoor experiences are presented fictionally in *The King's Men* (1884) – O'Reilly was transported to WA in 1868 on the *Hougoumont*, the last convict ship to be sent to the Australian colonies; he helped edit the *Wild Goose*, a journal produced on board the ship. In 1869 he staged an extraordinary escape to America, where he became prominent in Boston as editor of the *Pilot* and as a publicist and lecturer on Irish affairs. In 1875 he was part of the daring plan organised by the Clan na Gael to rescue six Irish prisoners from Fremantle gaol. The plan was successfully carried out in 1876 and is celebrated in the Australian folk-song 'The Catalpa'. O'Reilly's sudden death in 1890, from an accidental overdose of chloral, stunned the Irish community in Boston, where a memorial to him was erected as well as in his native Drogheda. The heroic dimension of his life is captured in J.J. Roche's hagiographic *Life of John Boyle O'Reilly* (1891), a work which incorporates his poems and speeches; in W.G. Schofield's anecdotal *Seek for a Hero: The Story of John Boyle O'Reilly* (1956) and in Paul Buddee's children's book *The Escape of John O'Reilly* (1973). He was the model for Morres Blake in Rosa Praed's novel *Outlaw and Lawmaker* (1893). Like other transported political prisoners, including George Loveless, Thomas Muir and John Mitchel (q.v.), O'Reilly had a relatively brief sojourn in Australia and has a larger reputation overseas. In Ireland he is remembered as a folk-hero, his poetry is included in standard anthologies of Irish political verse, and he himself edited an anthology, *The Poetry and Song of Ireland* (1887); in the USA he is remembered additionally as a fine sportsman who composed the important sporting treatise *Ethics of Boxing and Manly Sport* (1888). He wrote several volumes of verse, including *Songs from the Southern Seas* (1873), *Songs, Legends and Ballads* (1878), *The Statues in the Block* (1881), and *In Bohemia* (1886); in each there are poems relating to Australia, notably several verse narratives. His major contribution to Australian literature, however, was *Moondyne*, generally recognised as the first WA novel and significant in convict literature. Although clumsily constructed and melodramatic, *Moondyne*, the story of a convict who escapes with the help of Aborigines and eventually returns in disguise to WA as a penal reformer, is of interest for the way O'Reilly meshes his own experiences with those of the convict bushranger 'Moondyne Joe' (q.v.), and for the views it offers on transportation from the point of view of an idealistic ex-convict.

'ORION', see **HORNE, R.H.**

OSBORNE, Charles (1927–), born Brisbane, studied music in Brisbane and Melbourne and worked in literary and musical journalism and as an actor before leaving Australia in 1953. He earned a living in England by freelance writing and occasional acting before becoming assistant editor of *London Magazine* 1958–66; he joined the Arts Council of Great Britain in 1966 and was its literature director 1971–86. He has published several books on literature and music, including a substantial biography in 1980 of W.H. Auden, with whom he was friendly from the 1960s. His books which have relevance to Australia include a biography of Ned Kelly (1970), and another of the Australian actor Max Oldaker (1989), a collection of poems, illustrated by Sidney Nolan, *Swansong* (1968), and an autobiography, *Giving It Away: Memoirs of an Uncivil Servant* (1986), which includes a chapter on his Australian years. He also edited the handbook *Australia, New Zealand and the South Pacific* (1970) and the collection of short stories *Australian Stories of Today* (1961).

O'SHAUGHNESSY, Edward (1801–40), born Ireland, was transported for false pretences in 1824. In Sydney he worked out his sentence as a reporter on the pro-convict *Sydney Gazette*, which he edited 1833–35; subsequently he wrote for its rival, the *Sydney Herald*. During his time with the *Gazette* he wrote lyrical and satiric verse as well as some of the first Australian theatre reviews.

O'SHAUGHNESSY, Peter (1923–), actor and producer, has produced numerous Australian plays, including John Courtney's 'Off to the Diggings' and James Tucker's *Jemmy Green in Australia* at the Adelaide Festival in 1966. He has played the major Shakespearean tragic roles both in Australia and overseas and is well known for his one-act show 'Diary of a Madman', an adaptation of Gogol's short story. In 1968 he collaborated with Graeme Inson and Russel Ward in *The Restless Years*; a lavishly illustrated anthology of documents, ballads, poems, letters, extracts from journals, newspaper reports and advertisements, *The Restless Years* ranges from 1770 to 1901 and is based on an award-winning television programme, produced by O'Shaughnessy. In the 1950s he also wrote and produced with Jeff Underhill a popular children's play, 'The Bunyip and the Satellite'. He edited the memoirs of Joseph Holt, published under the title *A Rum Story* (1988), and the journal of John Mitchel, titled *The Gardens of Hell: John Mitchel in Van Diemen's Land, 1850–1853* (1988).

O'SULLIVAN, Edward William (1846–1910), journalist, trade unionist and politician, was born at Launceston and was apprenticed to the printing trade with the Hobart *Mercury* at an early age. He subsequently became a reporter, moved to Sydney in 1869, and returned to Hobart in 1871 to found the *Tasmanian Tribune*. In 1874 he sold out to work as a journalist on the mainland. Editor of the *Evening Tribune-City News* (1874), *St Arnaud Mercury* (1875–78), *Democrat* (1884) and *Freeman's Journal* (1896–99), he also worked for the *Argus*, Sydney *Daily Telegraph* and *Australian Star*. He was a member of the NSW parliament 1885–1910. One of the creators of the Protectionist Party of the 1880s, O'Sullivan was minister for Public Works 1899–1904 and was responsible for significant development of the railways and tramway systems. The author of a number of melodramas including 'The Eureka Rebellion' (1907) and 'Cooee' (1906), both of which drew on his earlier play 'Eureka Stockade' (1898), 'A Quiet Little Dinner' (1908), and 'Keane of Kalgoorlie' (1908), which he co-authored with Arthur Wright, O'Sullivan also published a novel in the 1890s, *Esperanza: A Tale of Three Colonies*, and a collection of sketches, stories and speeches, *Under the Southern Cross* (1906). Bruce Mansfield has written his biography, *Australian Democrat* (1965).

OTTLEY, Reginald Leslie, see *The Oxford Companion to Australian Children's Literature* (1993), p. 328.

Our Glass, a Melbourne magazine associated with the rise of the 'New Australian Poetry', was edited by Kris Hemensley (q.v.). It contains a selection of the poetry from the La Mama poetry workshops and was published 1968–69.

'Outback' denotes the remote and sparsely settled inland districts of Australia but does not indicate such extreme remoteness as is implied in a similar expression, the 'Never Never' (q.v.). The noun 'Outback' and the adverb or adjective 'outback' occur frequently in Australian writing in the latter part of the nineteenth century, e.g. in 'Rolf Boldrewood's' novel *Ups and Downs* (1878) and in Henry Lawson's celebrated poem 'Out Back', but are much more common in this century; the original, semi-colloquial expression is now an orthodox term. Although the outback has been widely romanticised in Australian writing, especially by such bush balladists as A.B. Paterson and Will Ogilvie, the other side of the picture is forcibly given by Lawson, who concludes his 'Some Popular Australian Mistakes' with the wish 'that Australian writers would leave off trying to make a paradise out of the Outback Hell'. Thomas Keneally's *Outback* (1983) records his impressions of the Northern Territory, its people and legends, the volume capturing in splendid illustrations the quality of the landscape.

Outback Press was formed in Melbourne in 1973 by Colin Talbot, Morris Schwarz, Mark Gillespie and Alfred Milgrom. Intent on publishing books of interest to young thinking people, it has produced such volumes as *Applestealers, Mother I'm Rooted, The*

Collapsible Man and *The Outback Reader: A Collection of Australian Contemporary and Experimental Short Fiction*. An associate company is Dingo Books.

Outbreak of Love, a novel by Martin Boyd (q.v.), was published in 1957. The third in a tetralogy dealing with the Langton family, the narrative is mainly concerned with Diana von Flugel, aunt to Guy Langton, the novel's occasional narrator, and daughter to Alice of *The Cardboard Crown* (1952). Diana's 23-year marriage to a feckless musical genius, Wolfgang ('Wolfie') von Flugel, is at a point of crisis, first because she has discovered that her husband has a vulgar mistress, and second because she is attracted to Russell Lockwood, an agreeable, cultivated dilettante. Diana's plans to leave for Europe with Russell are frustrated by Wolfie's continuing dependence on her, by her unwillingness to embarrass her recently married daughter, Josie, and by the declaration of war in 1914.

OUTHWAITE, Ida Rentoul, see *The Oxford Companion to Australian Children's Literature* (1993), pp. 328–9.

Outlook, a bi-monthly socialist journal edited by Helen Palmer (q.v.), ran 1957–70. Although the magazine's main concerns were political, it included some theatrical notices and reviews of cultural studies as well as attracting such writers as Russel Ward, Merv Lilley, Jack Lindsay, Len Fox and Ian Turner. Some of Helen Palmer's writing for the journal was reprinted in *Helen Palmer's Outlook* (1982), edited by Doreen Bridges.

Outrider: A Journal of Multicultural Literature in Australia, published in Brisbane under the general editorship of Manfred Jurgensen, began publication in 1984. The journal, which aims to add another dimension to Australian culture by promoting the creative work of immigrant writers and artists and has frequently debated multicultural issues, includes poetry, short stories, essays and addresses, plays, criticism, bibliographies, reviews and art work. As well as drawing attention to the contribution 'immigrant writers' make to Australian literature, the journal seeks to emphasise the place of Australian literature within the context of world literature. Of the 400 authors published over the first eight years, approximately half were born outside Australia. *Outrider* was published twice a year until 1989 and became an annual magazine in 1990. See also Jurgensen, Manfred.

Over the Sliprails, a collection of seventeen stories by Henry Lawson (q.v.), was published in 1900; in the same year it was combined with *On the Track*. Lawson's fourth collection of stories and sketches, *Over the Sliprails* includes material written in the early 1890s as well as at the end of the decade. Its range encompasses an Arvie Aspinall story; 'The Hero of Redclay', one of Lawson's longest stories, which grew out of his attempt to write a play for Bland Holt; stories which focus on the experiences of well-known Lawson characters, e.g. Mitchell, Steelman, Stiffner; and

stories which reflect his travels to Bourke, NZ and WA.

Overland, one of Australia's major contemporary literary magazines, began publication in Melbourne in 1954. It originally incorporated the *Realist Writer*, a left-wing journal which had begun publication under editor Bill Wannan in 1952 but severed its connection with the Realist Writers groups (q.v.) after the Hungarian uprisings of 1956. The original role of *Overland* was, in Ian Turner's words, 'to develop a radical tradition, including within that the Marxist tradition; to encourage a working-class audience and working-class writers ... and to take part in polemics against the Right'. *Overland's* successful struggle to survive the factional difficulties and lack of government patronage in its early years was largely due to the energy and devotion of its original and long-standing editor, Stephen Murray-Smith (q.v.), and Ian Turner. Others involved in its continued existence have been John McLaren, Barrett Reid, Nancy Keesing, Leonie Sandercock, Ken Gott, Gwen Harwood and Martin Duwell. *Overland* gives expression to a diversity of literary and social attitudes and opinions but its overall tone and spirit reflect its motto, 'Temper democratic, bias Australian', derived from Joseph Furphy's description of *Such is Life* (1903). *An Overland Muster* (1965), an anthology of writing from the pages of *Overland* between 1954 and 1964, was edited by Murray-Smith. Barrett Reid took over as editor with no. 112, October 1988, following Murray-Smith's death in that year. The same issue contained tributes to Murray-Smith.

'Overlander', a parallel term to 'drover' (q.v.), derives from 'overland', an English word meaning simply 'over the land', and is a term peculiar to Australia. An 'overlander' is defined in H.W. Haygarth's *Recollections of Bush Life in Australia* (1848) as 'one who makes long expeditions from one colony to another with stock, either for the purpose of finding new pasture land on which to establish himself, or to take advantage of a favourable market'. The earliest overlanders, notably Charles Bonney, Joseph Hawdon and Alexander Mollison, who followed in the tracks of the explorers had, by the early 1830s, reached the Murray and Monaro regions and, by the late 1830s, the Port Phillip and Adelaide districts. In the second half of the nineteenth century the real sagas of the overlanders occurred with the stocking of the vast runs in the Cooper's Creek area, northern Queensland, the Gulf country and the Kimberley region of north-west WA. Among these élite and intrepid stockmen were D'Arcy Uhr, Sydney and Alfred Prout (commemorated in Mary Hannay Foott's ballad 'Where the Pelican Builds Her Nest'), Nat Buchanan (q.v.), Sam Croaker, John Costello and the Duracks. In addition to Haygarth's book the overlander is discussed in such memoirs and historical writings as Sir George Grey's *Journals of Two Expeditions of Discovery* (1841), Frederic de Brébant Cooper's *Wild Adventures in Australia* (1857), C. Wade Browne's *Overlanding in Australia* (1868), Gordon Buchanan's *Packhorse and Waterhole*

(1933), Ernestine Hill's *The Territory* (1951), Joseph Hawdon's *The Journal of a Journey from New South Wales to Adelaide* (first published 1952), Mary Durack's *Kings in Grass Castles* (q.v., 1959), Garry Hogg's *The Overlanders* (1961), H.M. Barker's *Droving Days* (1966), Eleanor Smith's *The Beckoning West: The Story of K.S. Trotman and the Canning Stock Route* (1966), Margaret Ford's *Beyond the Furtherest Fences* (1966), Jeff Carter's *In the Tracks of the Cattle* (1968), and Alexander Fullerton Mollison's *An Overlanding Diary* (first published 1980, from the original manuscript presented to the State Library of Victoria in 1886). The overlander is represented in many works of fiction including Alexander Harris's *The Emigrant Family* (1849), Marcus Clarke's *Old Tales of a Young Country* (1871), Vance Palmer's *The World of Men* (1915), and Donald Stuart's *The Driven* (1961). He is also depicted in Australian short stories and poetry, including A.B. Paterson's 'With the Cattle', Will Ogilvie's 'From the Gulf' and Roland Robinson's 'The Drovers'. Traditional overlanding ballads and folk-songs include 'A Thousand Miles Away' and 'The Overlander'; the latter celebrates the overlander's free life and probably dates from the 1840s. Ron Edwards published *The Overlander Song Book* (1971), not all the songs of which are concerned with the overlanders. An Australian film, *The Overlanders* (1946), featured the driving of 85 000 head of cattle from the north of WA to the Queensland coast in 1942 as part of the wartime scorched-earth policy. One of S.T. Gill's famous watercolours, *Overlanders* (1865), depicts two men on horseback moving across a great flat stretch of semi-arid country with their dogs and packhorses behind them. 'The Overland' is a term that has come to be applied generally to the vast outback districts through which the stock routes ran, and to the stock routes themselves, e.g. the Canning, the Great North Road and the Georgina. *Overland* is one of Australia's distinguished literary journals.

OWEN, David (1956–), born Zimbabwe of a Welsh father and Canadian mother, grew up in Malawi and Swaziland and was educated in South Africa, where he lived for ten years. After working for some years in London, he migrated to Melbourne in 1986 and now lives in Tasmania. He has published the novels *Eden* and *Venter & Son* (published together, 1988), which draw on his experience of South Africa; *Coping With Pleasure* (1990), a satire on 'yuppie' attitudes of 1960s Australia; and *Bitters End* (1993), a darker, part-surreal exploration of grief, loss and love, set in a parched Australian landscape.

OWEN, Jan (1940–), born Adelaide, has worked as a librarian and as a teacher of creative writing. She has published poetry in numerous periodicals and anthologies and in three collections, *Boy With a Telescope* (1986), *Fingerprints on Light* (1990) and *Blackberry Season* (1993). In 1981 she won the Ian Mudie Award, in 1984 the Jessie Litchfield Prize, and in 1985 the Grenfell Henry Lawson Award; her first collection also won the Mary Gilmore Prize and the Anne Elder Award. A poet with a keen eye for detail, who is also

sensitive to nuance, Owen concentrates on significant moments of experience, or significant natural scenes which express a human meaning. 'Pear Tree', for instance, begins with a moonlit vision of the tree and radiates outwards into an intense, highly compressed reflection on time, loss and change; 'Poppies' and 'Red Carnations' are even more subtle expressions of the insidious, delicate quality of natural transience which implicitly includes human experience; 'Orthodera ministralis' is an elegantly witty statement on the praying mantis and the human associations of the contradiction expressed in his predatory/pious behaviour. Other poems reflect on family relationships, celebrate joyful memories or express the poignancy of loss and the resilience of grief. The poems of *Fingerprints on Light* are particularly wide-ranging, garnering topics from diverse cultures, periods and places, although they show the same sensitivity to minutiae and the links between physical and human nature.

Oxford Companion to Australian Children's Literature, The, by Stella Lees and Pam MacIntyre, was published in 1993. Accompanied by original illustrations, the *Companion* includes entries on individual authors and general entries on such topics as the Children's Book Council and Criticism of Children's Literature.

Oxford History of Australian Literature, The, edited by Leonie Kramer, was published in 1981. The history comprises an introduction by Kramer, surveys of fiction (by Adrian Mitchell), drama (by Terry Sturm) and poetry (by Vivian Smith) and includes a descriptive bibliography (by Joy Hooton).

Oxford Literary Guide to Australia, The, published in 1987 under the general editorship of Peter Pierce and researched by many contributors throughout Australia, was sponsored by Mobil Australia and OUP in collaboration with ASAL. The Literary Guide provides an extensive coverage of the links and associations of many places with Australian writers and books. Grouped according to State or Territory, and in alphabetical order, the entries give writers' places of birth, domicile and death and the association between actual places and their counterparts in Australian literature. An index of authors provides biographical details and links authors with places named in the text. A second edition was published in 1993.

OXLEY, John (?1783–1828), born Yorkshire, England, entered the Royal Navy as a midshipman and travelled to Australia in HMS *Buffalo* in 1802. He was appointed surveyor-general of NSW in 1812 and undertook in 1817–18 a series of exploratory journeys in the Lachlan, Macquarie, Castlereagh, Peel and Hastings Rivers regions of NSW. Unable to trace fully the Macquarie and Lachlan Rivers, Oxley subscribed to the theory of a vast inland sea, a theory later disproved by the journeys of Charles Sturt. Oxley's *Journals of Two Expeditions into the Interior of New South Wales* (1820), with its detailed description of the colony's interior, was the forerunner of the large body of later exploration literature. His further expeditions led to the discovery of the Tweed and Brisbane Rivers and the establishment of a penal settlement at Moreton Bay. His name is commemorated in the township Oxley, near the junction of the Lachlan and Murrumbidgee rivers and in the Oxley Highway, which runs from Nevertire to Port Macquarie. A contemporary account of Oxley's exploration achievements is included in Barron Field's *Geographical Memoirs on New South Wales* (1825).

Oz, see **NEVILLE, Richard**

P

PACKER, Sir Frank (1906–74), born Sydney, a well-known and influential media proprietor, was the son of Robert Clyde Packer (1879–1934), managing director of *Smith's Weekly*, 1919–33, and general manager of Associated Newspapers, 1931–33. Frank Packer began his career as a cadet reporter on his father's newspaper the *Daily Guardian* in 1923. He had become general advertising manager by 1927 and in 1933, with E.G. Theodore, founded Australia's best-known women's magazine, the *Australian Women's Weekly*. Packer was managing director of Consolidated Press from 1936 and chairman from 1957. The group, now Australian Consolidated Press, publishes a range of popular magazines such as the *Bulletin, Cleo,* the *Australian Home Journal* and the *Australian Women's Weekly*, as well as a number of suburban and country newspapers, and holds large interests in radio stations in Victoria and WA. The group also owned the Sydney *Daily Telegraph* (q.v.), and the *Sunday Telegraph*, although these were sold to Rupert Murdoch's News Ltd in 1972. Chairman of television corporations in Melbourne and Sydney and credited with great right-wing political influence, Packer was also well known in racing and yachting circles. An authorised biography by Richard Whitington was published in 1971. Sir Frank Packer's two sons, Clyde Packer (1935–) and Kerry Packer (1937–), have also become well-known figures. Clyde Packer was a member of the NSW Legislative Council, 1964–76, and from 1959 was involved as administrator and part-owner of his father's publishing empire. From 1970 he was joint manager of the television corporations but resigned from all his positions in the Packer industries 1972–73. He now lives in Los Angeles, where he owns an entertainment agency and a magazine, *New Times*. Owner and founder of the Sydney magazine *Forum*, he has also been a major supporter of *Quadrant*. Kerry Packer has succeeded to his father's publishing and television empire, and has extended the group's interests into mining, real estate, film production and leisure industries. In 1977 he became a controversial figure in his own right when he launched World Series cricket. He was made AC in 1983. Journalist Paul Berry published *The Rise and Rise of Kerry Packer* (1993), which also deals extensively with the Packer dynasty.

PACKER, Richard (1935–) was born NZ, where he worked mostly as a journalist. Since his arrival in Australia in 1966 he has worked in advertising. He has published two collections of poetry, *Prince of the Plague Country* (1964) and *Being out of Order* (1972), which includes his verse play for radio, 'The Uncommercial Traveller'. He has also written two other plays, *The Powerhouse* (1972) and 'The Applicant'.

Paddy Malone is a 'new chum' Irishman, who, in several Australian folk-songs and ballads (q.v.), chronicles his misfortunes after emigrating to Australia; like Billy Barlow and Jemmy Green, he probably originated as a stage character. Two of the Paddy Malone songs, 'Paddy Malone in Australia' and 'Paddy's Letter, 1857', were included in A.B. Paterson's *Old Bush Songs* (1905) and date from the second half of the nineteenth century.

PAGE, Geoff (1940–), born Grafton, attended The Armidale School before going on to the University of New England. His family's connection with the Clarence River district dates back to the middle of the nineteenth century; the river's influence on him and his family is summed up in the admission,

> The Clarence that I know has flowed
> through every second of my life.

It has flowed, too, through much of his poetry, giving it the same essential spirit of place that Bunyah gave to Les Murray, New England to Judith Wright and Gippsland to Eve Langley. Page went to Canberra to teach in 1964 and has remained there. He was, for some years, in charge of the English Department of Narrabundah College and has been writer-in-residence at several educational institutions e.g., Wollongong University, the Australian Defence Force Academy, Curtin University (WA), as well as a member of academic groups visiting and lecturing in Europe, America and China.

Page's beginning as a writer was modest; he shared a volume of UQP's Paperback Poets series in 1971 with Phillip Roberts. In the following seven years he published two more books of poetry, *Smalltown Memorials* (1975) and *Collecting the Weather* (1978). The years 1980–92 were extraordinarily prolific, however. In that time he published seven books of his own poetry, *Cassandra Paddocks* (1980), *Clairvoyant in Autumn* (1983), *Collected Lives* (1986), *Smiling in English, Smoking in French* (1987), *Footwork* (1988), *Selected Poems* (1991) and *Gravel Corners* (1992). He also edited *Shadows from Wire: Poems and Photographs of Australians in the Great War* (1983), *Century of Clouds: Selected Poems of Guillaume Apollinaire* (translations – with Wendy Coutts, 1985) and *On the Move: Australian Poets in Europe* (1992). He has also written two novels, *Benton's Conviction* (1985), the story of David Benton, vicar of a small New England country town during the First World War, who faced a conflict between the nationalistic fervour of his parishioners and his own questioning of the relevance of the war to Australia and indeed to those same parishioners who were so willingly sacrificing their sons; and *Winter Vision* (1989), the story of 55-year-old Canberra history teacher Roy Porter, who in the mid-1990s shares pacifist sentiments (and his bed on occasions) with his colleague Libby Sexton, as the world comes again to the brink of nuclear war between Russia and the United States.

Page also published *Invisible Histories* (1989), a selection of his well-crafted, lucid and unpretentious prose with poems from earlier books. His *Invisible Histories* are imagined events that usually have a basis in fact or imagined fact, e.g. the explorer Sturt journeying to the interior; an invented squatter, Edward Coledale, who believed that land taken from the Aborigines should be returned to them; the dreams of Edward Hargraves, who believed (erroneously) that his discovery of gold would lead to a baronetcy.

Page's poetry was influenced from the beginning by American writers such as William Carlos Williams, especially Williams's plain use of language, evocation of strong physical and spiritual realities and expression of a distinctive personality. Much the same virtues are present in Page's own poetry. The physical reality is his ancestry and its relationship with the Clarence River country, and his immediate family – father and mother, son – and then his extended family of grandparents, cousins and other relatives. The spiritual reality is the inevitability of old age and death and the ultimate nothingness. The physical reality of his family and farming background gives a remarkable warmth to his poetry and runs through all his books, e.g. grandmother and grandson together in 'Detail', and memories of his father in 'Departure and Return', both from *Cassandra Paddocks*, as well as the striking hymn of praise ('Grit') for his mother and other pioneer women. *Collected Lives* is the story of the whole family; each of the six sections recounts the life of one member of the Page family, the poet's own life being represented in it ('1940– '). When that life is complete, it is his wish, expressed in 'Codicil' from *Gravel Corners*, that his ashes be consigned in 'a long descending curve' to the waters of the Clarence. *Gravel Corners*, which ends with two poems about his father (to whom the book is dedicated), 'The Proverb' and 'My Father in His Silver Frame', brings Page's celebration of his family to a fitting conclusion. The spiritual reality in Page's poetry, his concern with transience and death, is perhaps responsible for the melancholy note which has frequently been said to mark his work. Page is not, however, a sombre poet; he has a remarkably ironic eye but makes only the gentlest of mischief with it. War, with its cost of so many innocent lives and the brutal massacre of Aborigines in the early stages of settlement are also topics that he returns to frequently in his writing. While age and death greatly occupy him there is solace in the comfort that the aged – husband and wife – can bring to each other in their final years. From 'Love at the End' comes the thought,

Fingers linked, we float towards that last
stopped moment when one will hand the other through

alone
to disbelief . . . and silence.

The proof of Page's considerable appeal as a poet is his presence in so many contemporary anthologies. Among his most popular poems are 'Grit', 'Bondi Afternoon 1915', 'Inscription at Villers-Bretonneux', 'Cassandra Paddocks', 'Detail', 'Roots and Branches' and 'Country Nun'. His sequence 'Five Australian Maps' (published later in *Gravel Corners*) won the Queensland Premier's Poetry Prize in 1990.

PAGE, Tony (1952–), born Melbourne, travelled in Europe and Asia after graduation and has worked as a teacher and as a film and theatre critic. He has contributed verse to numerous periodicals and to the anthology *La Mama Poetica* (1989). He has published two collections, *They're Knocking at My Door* (1986) and *Satellite Link* (1992).

Palmer, The, one of Australia's most notable goldfields, was opened up after the discovery of gold in 1873 by prospector James Venture Mulligan on the banks of the Palmer River in the hinterland of Cooktown in northern Queensland. The wildest of all Australian diggings, the Palmer was especially notable for the large number of Chinese who gathered there and their maltreatment by the White diggers. The history of the Palmer is recorded in Hector Holthouse's *River of Gold* (1967), but much of its atmosphere is caught in such traditional songs as 'The Old Palmer Song', 'The Golden Gullies of the Palmer' and 'The Palmer Days'.

PALMER, Aileen (1915–88), daughter of Vance and Nettie Palmer and sister of Helen Palmer (qq.v.), was born in London and educated at the University of Melbourne. She served with the British medical unit and medical service of the International Brigade in Spain 1936–38 and with the London Auxiliary Ambulance Service, 1939–43. She contributed verse to such journals as *Overland, Meanjin, Southerly, Vietnam Advances* and *Realist Writer* and published two collections, *World Without Strangers?* (1964) and *Dear Life* (1957), under the pseudonym 'Caliban'. Judith Keene has written a poignant account of her life and ultimate mental breakdown in *Crossing Boundaries: Feminisms and the Critique of Knowledges* (1988), ed. Barbara Caine et al.

PALMER, Helen (1917–79), daughter of Vance and Nettie Palmer and sister of Aileen Palmer (qq.v.), graduated from the University of Melbourne and was a high-school teacher and writer. During the Second World War she was in charge of education services by WAAAF personnel throughout Australia. Her published writings are *Australian Teacher in China* (1953), which records a visit to China in 1952; *Beneath the Southern Cross* (1954), a story about Eureka that was later serialised on ABC radio's children's session; and, with Jessie MacLeod, a series of Australian historical texts directed mainly at schools (1954, 1956, 1961, 1964). Other school texts that she wrote independently are *Our Sugar* (1949), *Fencing Australia* (1961) and *'Banjo' Paterson* (1966). Her poem 'Ballad of 1891' became a highlight of the musical *Reedy River* (1953). She also founded and edited the journal *Outlook: An Australian Socialist Review;* some of her writing for the journal is collected in *Helen Palmer's Outlook* (1982), ed. Doreen Bridges. She was a member of the Communist Party of Australia until expelled in 1957.

PALMER, Nettie (1885–1964) was born Janet Gertrude Higgins at Bendigo, Victoria. She graduated from the University of Melbourne in 1909 and in 1910 left for Europe to study languages, first in London, then in Marburg and Paris. She returned to Australia in 1911, completed her MA degree at the University of Melbourne in 1912 and left again for London in 1914 to marry Vance Palmer (q.v.). Their marriage was to be a remarkable literary partnership, of great importance to Australia's cultural life. Although Nettie Palmer's life centred mainly on her husband and her two daughters, Aileen and Helen, she made an independent contribution and there were important distinctions between her work and her husband's. At a personal level she seems to have been at least as influential as Vance Palmer and in particular her relationship with 'Henry Handel Richardson' was important. Her prolific literary journalism, especially during the 1920s and 1930s, when Vance Palmer was concentrating on creative work and when Australian publishing and literary debate were at a low ebb, was of inestimable significance. She moved easily in international literary circles and in 1935 she attended the Writers' Congress in Paris. There she made contact with the Australian writer Christina Stead (q.v.) and with many international writers, including André Gide, Paul Elvard, André Malraux and E.M. Forster. Only a few of her penetrating impressions there are recorded in her published journal extracts *Fourteen Years* (q.v., 1948), although others survive in manuscript form. Nettie Palmer was also in the forefront of the Palmers' practical work for refugees and immigrants, especially during the Spanish Civil War; two pamphlets express her urgent concern, *Spanish Struggle* (1936) and *Australians in Spain* (1938). In addition, she frequently worked closely with Vance Palmer in research for his novels and in particular on the 1937 abridgement of Joseph Furphy's *Such is Life*. Like her husband, she was a familiar broadcaster on ABC radio in the 1940s and 1950s and on several occasions lectured in Australian literature for the CLF. After her husband's death in 1959 she continued to write, concentrating on her projected autobiography, but rapid deterioration of her health prevented its completion.

Her published work consists of two volumes of poetry, *The South Wind* (1914) and *Shadowy Paths* (1915); a critical appreciation, *Modern Australian Literature 1900–1923* (q.v., 1924); a collection of essays, *Talking It Over* (1932); a memoir of her uncle, Henry Bournes Higgins (1931); *Fourteen Years: Extracts from a Private Journal, 1925–1939* (1948); a study of 'Henry Handel Richardson' (1950) and, with Victor Kennedy, one of

Bernard O'Dowd (1954); and *The Dandenongs* (1952), an unusual account of the Dandenong country near Melbourne which mingles personal reminiscence and history. Another account, of Green Island, Queensland, that she worked on in 1932 and that has been described as 'a minor Australian *Walden*', was never published. She also edited two collections of short stories, *An Australian Story Book* (1928) and *Coast to Coast* (1950) and, with Frances Fraser, a collection of women's writings, *Centenary Gift Book* (1934). In addition, she edited or introduced several other works by Australian writers. In 1953 letters she received from 'Henry Handel Richardson' were published, and she was also for a short time editor of the periodical *Birth*. In 1977 Vivian Smith edited a selection of her and Vance Palmer's letters, 1915–63, and in 1988 an edition of *Fourteen Years* with selected poetry, articles, reviews and essays. In 1959 when *Meanjin* published an issue in tribute to the Palmers, some attempts were made to assess her contribution, but Drusilla Modjeska, who has written extensively on her difficulties and achievements in *Exiles at Home* (1981), and Vivian Smith in his study *Vance and Nettie Palmer* (1975) and in other essays and introductions have done the most to establish her reputation.

Nettie Palmer's creativity found its fullest scope in her prose work; her poems, mainly simple lyrics, are now interesting mainly as period pieces. Until 1988 and Vivian Smith's collection titled *Nettie Palmer*, little of her criticism had appeared in book form apart from *Talking It Over* and the pioneer study *Modern Australian Literature 1900–1923*. Papers that she contributed articles to in the 1920s included the *Brisbane Courier*, *Argus*, Brisbane *Telegraph*, *Bulletin*, *Woman's Mirror* and Brisbane *Sunday Mail*. Her personal column, titled 'A Reader's Notebook', appeared in *All About Books*, 1928–38, but many of her most extended pieces were published in the *Illustrated Tasmanian Mail*, 1927–33. Written with ease, humour and perception on contemporary as on classical literature, on international and on Australian writers, her notices display a fine sense of proportion, independence and integrity. A keen student of comparative literature, she knew French, German and Greek, and later studied Spanish to have access to South American literature. A vigorous proponent of Australian writing, she contributed five articles on 'Henry Handel Richardson'; other writers who received substantial appreciations, some for the first time, include Miles Franklin, Katharine Susannah Prichard, Paul Wenz, Joseph Furphy, 'Price Warung', Barbara Baynton, Shaw Neilson, Bernard O'Dowd, Henry Tate, 'M. Barnard Eldershaw', Martin Boyd, Frank Dalby Davison, R.D. FitzGerald and Dowell O'Reilly. Her collection *An Australian Story Book* brings together work by well-known and lesser-known writers and reflects her desire to foster interest in disparate Australian writing. The commissioned study of Henry Bournes Higgins reflects her personal piety for his memory and her sense of shared values. Her *Henry Handel Richardson* (1950), which was the first full-length study of the novelist, written after an association of twenty-five years, is revealing as biography and deals with issues that are still central. The account of Bernard O'Dowd's life and work, a reshaping of the incomplete manuscript left by Victor Kennedy, is an invaluable one, especially of his origins and influences. Perhaps her most enduring work is *Fourteen Years*, a unique document in Australian literature that moves easily from personal reminiscence to accounts of literary and personal meetings in Australia and overseas. Striking features of the work are the easy, conversational tone and graphic individual portraits, the revealing presentation of varying cultural milieux and the impression throughout of a distinctive, illuminating mind. Restricted in its original edition to 500 copies, *Fourteen Years* did not for many years reach the widespread audience it deserves. The Victorian Premier's Awards includes a Nettie Palmer Award for non-fiction.

PALMER, Vance (1885–1959) was born at Bundaberg, Queensland, the youngest in a family of eight. His father was a schoolmaster with diverse literary interests and his childhood was spent in a succession of Queensland country towns. He rejected the idea of a university education, spent some time as a private secretary, and in 1905 left for London, where he stayed for two years earning his living as a 'Grub Street hack'. He returned to Australia by way of Finland, Russia and Japan, tried salesmanship and schoolteaching, and spent some time as tutor, bookkeeper and drover in north-west Queensland. Five of his early novels and many of his short stories reflect these experiences. In 1910 he revisited London, this time making contact with several British writers, most importantly with A.R. Orage, the editor of the *New Age*, who encouraged his writing and influenced his social philosophy. He returned briefly to Australia in 1912, travelling through USA and Mexico, which was at that time in revolution. In 1914 he married Janet Higgins (see Palmer, Nettie) in London. Before their return to Australia in September 1915, Palmer had begun his literary career with collections of poetry, *The Forerunners* (1915), and short stories, *The World of Men* (1915), and with numerous articles for the *New Age*, the *Manchester Guardian Fortnightly*, and the *British Review*. His return to Australia at the height of imperialist fervour generated by the war quickened his commitment to his own culture and his concern for the development and preservation of its distinctive identity. A vigorous opponent of conscription, he nevertheless enlisted in the AIF in 1918 and was sent overseas, but was too late to see action. For the next decade, spent at Emerald, Palmer was actively engaged in the cause of Australian literary nationalism as an essayist and reviewer and as a leading member of the Pioneer Players (q.v.). This period also saw the publication of another collection of poetry, *The Camp* (1920), a collection of plays, *The Black Horse and Other Plays* (1924), and five novels: *The Shantykeeper's Daughter* (1920), *The Boss of Killara* (1922), *The Enchanted Island* (1923), *The Outpost* (1924) and *Cronulla* (1924). Both *The Enchanted Island* and *The Outpost* were published under the pseudonym 'Rann Daly', and *The Outpost* was rewritten and republished as *Hurricane* in 1935. Palmer later dropped his first four novels from his list of publications. In 1925 the

Palmers left for Caloundra, a small fishing port in Queensland. Freelance literary journalism, largely undertaken by Nettie Palmer, provided a living, while Vance Palmer worked on a group of novels: *The Man Hamilton* (1928), *Men are Human* (1930), *The Passage* (q.v., 1930), *Daybreak* (q.v., 1932) and *The Swayne Family* (1934). In order to educate their daughters, Aileen and Helen, the family returned to Melbourne, 1929–32, spent some time at Green Island, Queensland, in 1932 and then at Kalorama, Victoria, 1932–35, before revisiting Europe in 1935–36, where they witnessed the beginning of the Spanish Civil War. Apart from another visit to Europe in 1955 and winter holidays in Queensland, Palmer lived in Melbourne for the rest of his life. By the 1940s his reputation as Australia's pre-eminent cultural figure was well established, reinforced by his regular talks and reviews for the ABC. He served on the CLF, 1942–53. His other publications are the novels *Legend for Sanderson* (1937), *Cyclone* (1947) and the trilogy *Golconda* (1948), *Seedtime* (1957) and *The Big Fellow* (1959) (see *Golconda* trilogy); the collections of short stories *Separate Lives* (1931), *Sea and Spinifex* (1934), *Let the Birds Fly* (1955) and the reprinted selection *The Rainbow-Bird and Other Stories* (1957); the plays *Ancestors*, in *Best Australian One-Act Plays* (1937), and *Hail Tomorrow* (1947); and the essays and studies *National Portraits* (q.v., 1940), *A.G. Stephens: His Life and Work* (1941), *Frank Wilmot (Furnley Maurice)* (1942), *Louis Esson and the Australian Theatre* (1948) and *The Legend of the Nineties* (q.v., 1954). He also edited a collection of short stories, *Coast to Coast* (1945); was instrumental in both the reissue of Joseph Furphy's *Such is Life* in 1917 and the abridged edition (1937); and compiled a collection of bush ballads, *Old Australian Bush Ballads* (1951). *Intimate Portraits* (1969), ed. H.P. Heseltine, is a selection of his essays and talks, and a selection of his and Nettie Palmer's letters, edited by Vivian Smith, was published in 1977. Apart from Heseltine's small selection, no attempt has been made to collect or select from his vast number of essays for such journals as *Fellowship*, the *Bulletin*, the *ABC Weekly*, *Birth*, the *New Triad* and *Meanjin*, or from his talks and reviews broadcast for the ABC, 1941–59. In 1959, when *Meanjin* published a special issue in tribute to Vance and Nettie Palmer, many of the writers for whom Palmer had been an important influence expressed their appreciation. His preoccupations and achievements are explored in Harry Heseltine's *Vance Palmer* (1970), Vivian Smith's *Vance Palmer* (1971) and *Vance and Nettie Palmer* (1975) and David Walker's *Dream and Disillusion* (1976).

The pervading theme of all Palmer's work is his firm belief in an 'Australia of the spirit' and in literature as its influential and lasting expression. For Palmer, Australian literature was, or should be, an integral part of the fabric of national life, an expression of its inner spirit and values, its distinctive 'undertones'. As he asserted in an early essay, writers 'must be at one with the purposes and aspirations of the people and their hearts must beat in unison with them'. A profound admirer of Henry Lawson, Barbara Baynton, Bernard O'Dowd and Joseph Furphy, he saw the 1890s as the period in which their national identity was first revealed to Australians, primarily through the work of the *Bulletin* writers. He perceived this revealed national consciousness as robust, masculine, close to nature and physical work, democratic, taciturn, sardonic, frugal, unsentimental and communal; he rapidly saw the communal concept as a threatened ideal, subject to erosion by the materialism of the expanding cities. These values inform his own work. Five of his first novels, *The Shanty Keeper's Daughter, The Boss of Killara, Cronulla, The Man Hamilton* and *Men Are Human*, are station novels, set in the Queensland outback, although only the last two seriously engage with his subject. These begin to develop the elements of Palmer's best work: controlled narrative technique, unpretentious prose style, lyrical evocation of place, and preference for psychological rather than physical action, all of which combine to form an understated realism. *The Passage*, set in a small Queensland fishing port similar to Caloundra, brings these elements to full realisation; his best-known novel, it is distinguished by the gradual lyrical development of the numinous relationship between the central figure, Lew Calloway, and his natural surroundings. *Daybreak* has the dramatic unity and achieved insights of the best of Palmer's short stories. The complexities of family relationships which figure in *The Passage* are also the subject of *The Swayne Family*, Palmer's one novel with an urban setting, although explored here more thoroughly and subtly. *Legend for Sanderson* and *Cyclone* are less assured works, but in the *Golconda* trilogy Palmer attacks his socio-cultural themes from a panoramic conspectus and with renewed, shaping purpose. Palmer's talent is most at home in his short stories. 'The Foal', 'The Rainbow-Bird', 'The Red Truck', 'Mathieson's Wife', 'The Birthday' and 'Greta' provide ideal scope for his characteristic style of ironic detachment and controlled tone. They achieve a muted realism and deceptively artless effect which is similar to Henry Lawson's. Several of his most effective stories concentrate on a crucial childhood initiation into the complex adult world. His verse, characterised by simple forms and generalised emotions, clearly fails as a means of giving rein to his keenest concerns, although 'The Farmer Remembers the Somme' is one of Australia's most effective war poems. His plays, mostly set in the outback, are marred by obviously manipulated plots and stilted dialogue; his most ambitious, *Hail Tomorrow*, is an attempt to express the meaning of William Lane's career and the 1890s. Palmer's wide-ranging literary journalism displays tact, discrimination and practical, intuitive evaluations rather than critical theories or strikingly original perceptions. His series of books on key national figures written between 1940 and 1954, and especially his seminal *The Legend of the Nineties*, reflect his preoccupation with the inner life of Australia and his concern to preserve its distinctive democratic quality. The Victorian Premier's Awards include a Vance Palmer Award for fiction.

PALMER-ARCHER, Laura (1864–1929), who also used the pseudonym 'Bushwoman', was the sister of E.F. O'Ferrall and the wife of a station-owner. She contributed short stories to the *Australasian* and the *Australian Town and Country Journal* and published two works of fiction, *A Bush Honeymoon and Other Stories* (1904) and *Racing in the Never Never* (1899). Lively, humorous and written in a direct, unpretentious style, her stories vividly convey the dramas and hazards, tedium and deprivations, personalities, idioms and social convention of bush life in the 1890s.

Pamphlet Poets is a set of beautifully produced pamphlets in individual paper wallets emanating from the National Library of Australia, each containing eight poems by a single writer. The series began in 1990, the first series comprising John Bray's *Tobacco: A Valedictory and Other Poems*, Sarah Day's *Sarah Day*, Rosemary Dobson's *Seeing is Believing*, Paul Hetherington's *Mapping Wildwood Road*, Jennifer Maiden's *Bastille Day* and Tom Shapcott's *In the Beginning*. Series 2 in 1992 comprised Silvana Gardner's *Cochineal Red*, Peter Goldsworthy's *After the Ball*, Gwen Harwood's *Night Thoughts*, Judith Rodriguez's *The Cold*, Philip Salom's *Tremors* and John Tranter's *Days in the Capital*.

Pandemonium, a monthly magazine published in Melbourne and edited anonymously by Mervyn Skipper (q.v.), ran 1934–35. A response to the unstable world situation of the time, *Pandemonium* satirised a wide range of contemporary topics from capitalism and imperialism to Australian censorship and communist peace movements. Striking features of the journal are Skipper's bold cartoons and the prominence given to the views of such controversial figures as the psychologist G.W.R. Southern and the economist Major Douglas. *Pandemonium* also included book reviews, theatrical notices, articles on Australian literature and short stories by Skipper, Percy Leason and Vance and Nettie Palmer.

PANKHURST, Adela (1888–1961), the daughter of Emmeline Pankhurst, was born in England and became prominent in the suffragette movement and in socialist agitation before leaving for Australia in 1914. One of the most formidable leaders of the feminist movement in Australia and a prominent socialist, Pankhurst threw her energies into the organisation of the Women's Political Association, renamed the Women's Peace Army, and the fight against conscription. In 1917 she joined the Victorian Socialist Party, wrote frequently for the *Socialist* and edited *Dawn*, a socialist newspaper for children. In the same year she married Tom Walsh, a militant trade-unionist. The founding of the Communist Party of Australia engaged the energies of Pankhurst and Walsh for a time, but they were soon alienated by the Party's ideological disputes and subsequently became staunchly anti-communist. Pankhurst's ideas found their widest scope during her association with the Australian Women's Guild of Empire, a middle-class organisation whose newspaper, the *Empire Gazette*, she edited. She visited Japan in 1939–40 with her husband, joined with him in urging closer ties between Australia and Japan, stood unsuccessfully as an independent candidate for the Senate in 1940, was briefly attracted to the

Australia First movement founded by W.J. Miles and P.R. Stephensen (qq.v.), and was interned during the Second World War. No stranger to imprisonment, having spent time in Strangeways and Pentridge, she was released in October 1942 when she went on a hunger strike. Pankhurst withdrew from political life following the death of Tom Walsh in 1943; she died in poverty after having been received into the Catholic Church in 1960. She published a play, *Betrayed* (1917), which is a propagandist, anti-conscription piece, and four political pamphlets, *Put up the Sword* (1915), *After the War, What?* (1917), *Conditions in Japan* (1940) and *What We Should Know about the Orient* (1940). Her life and achievements are described by David Mitchell in *The Fighting Pankhursts* (1967).

PAPAELLINAS, George (1954–), born Sydney of Cypriot Greek parents, was educated at the University of Sydney and the NSW Institute of Technology. He has worked in a variety of occupations including taxi-driving, lecturing in professional writing at the University of Technology and in creative writing at Deakin University and Tranby Aboriginal College in Glebe, Sydney. In 1985 he founded the Writers in the Park readings at Sydney's Harold Park Hotel and has organised Carnivale's writers' week for several years. He has contributed short stories to anthologies and has published one collection, *Ikons* (1986); he is also the editor of two collections sponsored by Carnivale, *Homeland* (1991), short stories, essays and poems by twenty-six Australian writers which concentrate on the meaning of Australia as home, and *Harbour* (1993), prose pieces by seventeen authors on the theme of the harbour. *Ikons* contains eight linked stories of three generations of a Greek family living in Australia; each story presents a different viewpoint on the experience of cultural uprooting and of the central character, Peter, the Australian-born son, culminating with his disastrous visit to his parents' 'homeland'.

Paperback Poets, a series initiated by UQP in 1970, presented a wide range of contemporary Australian poetry. The first series of eighteen books, mostly edited by Roger McDonald, was published 1970–73, and comprised David Malouf's *Bicycle and Other Poems* (1970), Michael Dransfield's *Streets of the Long Voyage* (1970), Rodney Hall's *Heaven, in a Way* (1970), Andrew Taylor's *The Cool Change* (1970), Geoff Page and Philip Roberts's *Two Poets: The Question and Single Eye* (1971), J.S. Harry's *The Deer under the Skin* (1971), R.A. Simpson's *Diver* (1972), Dransfield's *The Inspector of Tides* (1972), Rhyll McMaster's *The Brineshrimp* (1972), Richard Tipping's *Soft Riots* (1972), Thomas Shapcott's *Begin with Walking* (1972), Leon Slade's *Slade's Anatomy of the Horse* (1972), David Lake's *Hornpipes & Funerals* (1973), Judith Rodriguez's *Nu-Plastik Fanfare Red and Other Poems* (1973), Andrew Taylor's *Ice Fishing* (1973), Rodney Hall's *A Soapbox Omnibus* (1973), Manfred Jurgensen's *Signs and Voices* (1973), and Vicki Viidikas's *Condition Red* (1973). *The First Paperback Poets Anthology*, edited by McDonald, was published in 1974.

The second series of nineteen books was published 1974–81 and comprised Jennifer Maiden's *Tactics* (1974), Paul Kavanagh's *Wild Honey* (1974), Robert Gray's *Creekwater Journal* (1974), McDonald's *Airship* (1975), Page's *Smalltown Memorials* (1975), Graeme Kinross Smith and Jamie Grant's *Turn Left at Any Time with Care* (1975), Robin Thurston's *Believed Dangerous* (1975), Peter Skrzynecki's *Immigrant Chronicle* (1975), Tipping's *Domestic Hardcore* (1975), Roberts's *Will's Dream* (1975), Peter Kocan's *The Other Side of the Fence* (1975), Simpson's *Poems from Murrumbeena* (1976), Andrew McDonald's *Absence in Strange Countries* (1976), Alan Wearne's *New Devil, New Parish* (1976), Martin Johnston's *The Sea-Cucumber* (1978), Alan Gould's *Icelandic Solitaries* (1978), Kevin Hart's *The Departure* (1978), Gary Catalano's *Remembering the Rural Life* (1978), and Susan Whiting's *Between Breaths* (1981). *Consolidation: The Second Paperback Poets Anthology* comprising selected poems from the second series, edited by Thomas Shapcott, was published in 1981.

PARADISSIS, Aristides (George) (1923–), born China of Greek parents, arrived in Australia in 1949. After gaining a Licence en Droit from the Universite l'Aurore, Shanghai, he completed further studies at the universities of London and Melbourne and at La Trobe University. He has taught at secondary and tertiary level in China, Egypt and Australia and was lecturer and senior lecturer in French, Spanish and European literature at La Trobe University 1967–85. He has contributed poems in English to anthologies and periodicals and has published three collections, *A Tree at the Gate* (1971), *The City of the Tree* (1981) and *The Bing Book of Verse. Poems in Memory of Bing Crosby* (1983).

Paraguay, see **New Australia**; **NOWRA, Louis**

PARER, Damien (1912–44), born Malvern, Victoria, was the youngest of a large family of Spanish-Irish heritage, and spent his early years on King Island in Bass Strait. In 1933 he was employed by Charles Chauvel on the camera crew making the film *Heritage*, and he worked on further films with Chauvel 1935–36, including *Forty Thousand Horsemen*. He joined a Commonwealth film unit in 1939 and in 1940 accompanied the AIF to the Middle East. Documentaries he produced of Australian troops in action in Greece and Syria and at Tobruk include *The Fall of Bardia* (1941), *The Relief of Tobruk* (1941) and *The RAAF in the Western Desert* (1942). In 1942 he joined the Australian forces in New Guinea and produced numerous documentaries, several of which were to become internationally well known; one, *Jungle Warfare on the Kokoda Front*, was awarded an Oscar in 1943. Late in 1943 Parer joined the American forces to cover the invasion of the Pacific and was killed at the landing on Peleliu. Probably Australia's best-known photographer, Parer also became legendary for his courage, unswerving dedication to the camera and unpretentious, if eccentric, personality. His career is described by Frank Legg in *The Eyes of Damien Parer*

(1963) and by John Hetherington in *Australians: Nine Profiles* (1960).

PARK, Ruth (1922–   ) was born in Auckland, NZ. She spent her early childhood in isolated areas of NZ and in several of her books has drawn on her memories of the NZ bush and the Maori culture. After experience as a journalist and editor of children's books, she came to Australia in 1942 and married the writer D'Arcy Niland (q.v.). Her autobiography, *A Fence Around the Cuckoo* (1992 which won the Foundation for Australian Literary Studies Award), describes both the hardships and the joys of her childhood in depressed NZ and the difficulties she encountered in her struggle to become a writer. Wartime conditions resulted in the newly married Nilands leading a wandering life in the outback for a time, but they eventually settled in the slum area of Surry Hills, Sydney, and turned to full-time writing. They wrote at first a variety of material, radio plays and documentaries, short stories, articles and song lyrics, and even gag scripts for a local comedian. Two of Park's novels, *The Harp in the South* (q.v.) and *Poor Man's Orange*, are based on their experience in Surry Hills, and the Nilands' joint autobiography *The Drums Go Bang!* (1956) also refers to this period although Park's acclaimed second volume of autobiography, *Fishing in the Styx* (1993), gives the most comprehensive account. By the mid-1950s the Nilands had become known as a successful writing couple, who managed to combine full-time careers and parenthood. After D'Arcy Niland died in 1967, Park visited London, where she worked for a film company. From 1973 to 1985 she lived on Norfolk Island. Park has written nine novels for adults, *The Harp in the South* (1948), which won the 1946 *Sydney Morning Herald* novel competition, was produced as a television series in 1985 and has been translated into numerous languages, *Poor Man's Orange* (1949), published in the USA as *12 1/2 Plymouth Street* (1951), *The Witch's Thorn* (1951), *A Power of Roses* (1953), *Pink Flannel* (1955), *One-a-Pecker, Two-a-Pecker* (1957), published in USA as *The Frost and the Fire* (1958), *The Good Looking Women* (1961), published in 1962 as *Serpent's Delight*, and *Swords and Crowns and Rings* (q.v., 1977), which won that year's Miles Franklin Award. In 1987 she selected *The Penguin Best Stories of D'Arcy Niland*. Collaborating with the illustrator, Cedric Emanuel, she has also written a guide to Sydney (1983) and another to Tasmania (1987); a factual book about Australia for German readers, *Der Goldene Bumerang (The Golden Boomerang)* (1955); and numerous plays for radio and television, including, with D'Arcy Niland, a television play, 'No Decision', which won a British award in 1961. Many of her books, but especially *The Harp in the South, The Witch's Thorn* and *Swords and Crowns and Rings*, have been best-sellers in Australia and overseas and have been frequently selected by book clubs. In 1985 she published *Missus*, a prequel to *The Harp in the South* and the chronological first in the trilogy which is completed by *Poor Man's Orange*. Park has won distinction as a prolific writer of children's fiction and is well known to younger children as the creator of the Muddle-Headed Wombat series. The series, which originated as a radio drama sequence on the ABC children's session, has resulted in fourteen books, published 1962–81, all illustrated by Noela Young's lively drawings. Of her numerous other children's books, the most notable are *The Hole in the Hill* (1961), *The Road under the Sea* (1962), *Uncle Matt's Mountain* (1962), *The Ship's Cat* (1961), *The Sixpenny Island* (1968), *Callie's Castle* (1974), *Come Danger, Come Darkness* (1978), *Playing Beatie Bow* (1980), which won the Children's Book of the Year Award for 1981 as well as several awards in the USA and was released as a film in 1985, and *When the Wind Changed* (1980), which won the 1981 NSW Premier's Award. She has also written short stories and plays for young readers, including *The Uninvited Guest*, published in 1978 in the Australian Youth Plays series. In 1993 Park won the Lloyd O'Neil Award for services to the book industry.

Park's gifts for dramatic action and credible, graphically drawn characters are apparent in her first two novels, dealing with the hardships of a poverty-stricken Irish-Australian family and their Surry Hills neighbours. The sordid actuality, pathos and ebullient humour of slum life are sympathetically realised in both. In *The Witch's Thorn* and *Pink Flannel*, both of which draw on her memories of NZ, she brings to life a wide range of eccentric characters, as well as the peculiar world of childhood. *A Power of Roses* and *Good-Looking Women* are family dramas, set once again in the inner suburbs of Sydney, but in *Swords and Crowns and Rings* Park breaks new ground. The novel is a sensitive re-creation of social change in Australia 1907–30 and a fable-like odyssey whose hero is a dwarf. The same vigorous characteristics enliven Park's fiction for children. In the Muddle-Headed Wombat series her enjoyment of zany dialogue, comic nonsense and absurdly human animal characters finds full scope. Her books for teenage children, such as *Callie's Castle, Come Danger, Come Darkness* and *Playing Beatie Bow*, show a perceptive understanding of adolescence, which, in the last two, combines with gripping re-creations of nineteenth-century Australia. She was made AM in 1987.

PARKER, Catherine Langloh (1856–1940), born Catherine Field at Encounter Bay, SA, spent much of her childhood on her father's station, Marra, on the Darling River, where Aboriginal children were her companions. In 1879 she went with her husband, Langloh Parker, to pastoral properties in northern NSW and Queensland where she collected native legends and stories. After Langloh Parker's death she married Percival Stow and returned to SA. Her *Australian Legendary Tales* (1896), under the name Mrs K. Langloh Parker, was the first substantial collection of Aboriginal legends and tales. Although not regarded as a scholarly treatise on, or penetration of, the complex mysteries of Aboriginal custom and tradition, Catherine Parker's tales capture such features of Aboriginal lore as the belief in Baiame, the All-Father; the wanderings of Wurrunna, the culture-hero, and the significance attached to Mullee Mullees, Doowis, Yowis and Mingga, or spirit trees. Her other Aboriginal legend publications are *More Australian Legendary Tales* (1898), *The Walkabouts of Wurrunnah* (1918) and *Woggheeguy* (1930). She also wrote the factual *The Euahlayi Tribe: A Study of Aboriginal Life in Australia* (1905). A selection from her earlier volumes of tales, titled *Australian Legendary Tales*, selected and edited with an introduction by Henrietta Drake-Brockman and illustrated by Elizabeth Durack, was published in 1953 and won the Children's Book of the Year Award for 1954. Six of the *Tales* were adapted for use in Vashti Farrer's *Tales of the Dreamtime* (1975). In 1982 her narrative of her years on Bangate Station, 1870–1901, was published, together with a background and biography by Marcie Muir, as *My Bush Book: K. Langloh Parker's 1890s Story of Outback Station Life*.

PARKER, David (1943–   ), born Adelaide and educated at the universities of Adelaide, Flinders and Oxford, teaches English at the ANU. He has contributed short stories to *Southerly*, the *Australian*, *Quadrant* and the *Adelaide Review* and has published one collection, *The Mighty World of Eye: Stories/Anti-Stories* (1990) and a novel, *Building on Sand* (1988), which was short-listed for the Miles Franklin Award.

PARKES, Sir Henry (1815–96), born Warwickshire, England, grew up in Birmingham, where he received only a meagre education. Unsuccessful business ventures as a young man led to his departure from England in 1839, a situation which he deplored in some verses, 'A Poet's Farewell'. In Australia he tried a variety of jobs – agricultural labourer, clerk, ivory- and bone-turner – before turning to politics, supporting the causes of liberalism and anti-transportation. He was assisted financially, in 1850, to become an editor of the newspaper the *Empire* (q.v.), an important voice in the developing democracy of the day. He was elected to the Legislative Council in 1854 and the first Legislative Assembly in 1856. Years of political and commercial crises followed, his fortunes in both arenas fluctuating wildly, but Parkes, a natural survivor, became premier in 1872, a position he was to hold on five subsequent occasions. His major administrative achievement was the Public Instruction Act of 1880 which ensured 'free, secular and compulsory' education in NSW. Often called the 'Father of Federation', Parkes played a key role in the Federation conventions of 1890–91. The *Bulletin*'s famous cartoon after his death, which shows 'The Little Boy from Manly' closing a huge volume, titled simply 'Parkes', indicates the scope of his achievements and the impact of his personality throughout half a century of public life. He is portrayed in George Darrell's play 'The Lucky Lot' (1890). An important figure also in the colonial literary milieu, he was a friend of Charles Harpur and the long-suffering patron of Henry Kendall. His own publications include the volumes of verse *Stolen Moments* (1842), *Murmurs of the Stream* (1857), *Studies in Rhyme* (1870), *The Beauteous Terrorist and Other Poems* (1885), *Fragmentary Thoughts* (1889) and *Sonnets and Other Verse* (1895). His chief prose work is the autobiographical *Fifty Years in the Making of Australian History* (1892). He wrote *Australian Views*

of England (1869) as well as numerous political pamphlets. A collection of letters to his family, *An Emigrant's Home Letters*, was edited in 1896 by his daughter Annie. Biographies of Parkes include C.E. Lyne, *Life of Sir Henry Parkes* (1896), Sir Thomas Bavin, *Sir Henry Parkes* (1941) and Robert Travers, *The Grand Old Man of Australian Politics* (1992), but the outstanding account of his life and work is A.W. Martin's *Henry Parkes* (1980), which won the Barbara Ramsden Award. Martin also edited *Letters from Menie: Sir Henry Parkes and His Daughter* (1983).

PARKIN, Ray (1910–   ), born Melbourne, served with the RAN, 1928–46, and has written three accounts of his experiences in the Second World War. *Out of the Smoke* (1960) narrates the sinking of the cruiser HMAS *Perth* in the Sunda Strait; *Into the Smother* (1963) records the experiences of Australian servicemen on the Burma–Thailand railway; *The Sword and the Blossom* (1968) continues the author's experiences in Japan until the end of the war. Quietly narrated, reflective and balanced, Parkin's accounts, which he has illustrated with his own drawings, have been internationally acclaimed.

PARKINSON, Sydney (?1745–71), born Edinburgh, Scotland, went as botanical draughtsman with Sir Joseph Banks in the *Endeavour* in 1768. During the voyage he made over 1000 drawings and sketches and compiled vocabularies of the natives of Tahiti and New Holland. He died of dysentery on the voyage. His drawings were later used, with scant acknowledgement, in John Hawkesworth's *An Account of the Voyages Undertaken by the Order of His Present Majesty for Making Discoveries in the Southern Hemisphere* (1773); Stanfield Parkinson compiled his brother's book, *A Journal of a Voyage to the South Seas, in His Majesty's Ship, the Endeavour*, in the same year. D.J. Carr edited *Sydney Parkinson: Artist of Cook's Endeavour Voyage* (1983).

Parramatta, after Sydney the oldest settlement in Australia, is located 24 kilometres west of Sydney at the head of the Parramatta River and is a city within the metropolitan area of Sydney. The site, discovered by Governor Phillip 23 April 1788, was settled in November that year. Until 1792 Parramatta was the major settlement, Sydney being reserved as a depot for stores, and it retained social importance as the seat of the governor, even after Sydney became the commercial centre. The first land grant issued in Australia was made at Parramatta to James Ruse (1760–1837), who was the Colony's first successful farmer; many other notable pioneers settled in the area, including John Macarthur, whose home, Elizabeth House, is still standing. The area has figured frequently in Australian historical fiction and is the background to Mary Gaunt's novel *As the Whirlwind Passeth* (1923), Ethel Turner's novel *Seven Little Australians* (1894), Ethel Anderson's short stories *At Parramatta* (1956), David Ireland's novel *The Glass Canoe* (1976), and part of Donald Horne's autobiography, *The Education of Young Donald* (1967). James Jervis wrote *The Cradle*

City of Australia: A History of Parramatta 1788–1961 (1961).

PARRY, Anne Spencer (1931–85) graduated BA from the University of NSW and was a psychotherapist in private practice in Sydney. She wrote *The Land Behind the World* series, a group of fantasy stories written mainly for children, although appreciated also by adult readers. The series began with *The Land Behind the World* (1976) and continued with *The Lost Souls of the Twilight* (1977), *The Crown of Darkness* (1979) and *The Crown of Light* (1980). In the four books listed, one of the chief characters, Zaddik, was the guide and mentor of Bara in the land of Shemara. Parry returned to Zaddik's childhood in *Zaddik and the Seafarers* (1983) and *Beyond the Outlandish Mountains* (1984). Parry collaborated with Marjorie Pizer in *Below the Surface: Reflections on Life and Living* (1982).

PARSONS, Philip, see **Currency Press**

PARTRIDGE, Eric Honeywood (1894–1979), born NZ, was brought to Australia in 1907 and after service in the AIF, 1915–19, completed a degree at the University of Queensland. In 1921 he went to Oxford and after graduation taught at the universities of Manchester and London. In 1927 he founded the Scholartis Press, which he directed for the next four years, publishing a wide range of books with a bias towards younger writers. *Glimpses* (1927), Partridge's volume of short stories under the pseudonym 'Corrie Denison', was published by the press as was his first slang lexicography, *Songs and Slang of the British Soldier 1914–1918* (1930), compiled with John Brophy. After the Scholartis Press foundered in 1935, Partridge began a career as a lexicographer of unconventional English, which continued until his death. His major dictionaries, which include Australian slang, are *A Dictionary of Slang and Unconventional English* (1937), *A Dictionary of the Underworld* (1949) and *Origins: A Short Etymological Dictionary of Modern English* (1958). All have been repeatedly revised and enlarged. Partridge's other outstanding achievements include *Usage and Abusage* (1942), *Shakespeare's Bawdy* (1947) and *English: A Course for Human Beings* (1949). An indefatigable researcher and compiler, Partridge also produced dictionaries of abbreviations, etymological dictionaries, guides to punctuation, collections of quotations and several anthologies of essays on language and literature. Of these the best known are *A Dictionary of Clichés* (1940), *A Dictionary of Catch Phrases* (1977) and *A Charm of Words* (1960). He also edited numerous collections of prose and verse, and early in his career published several studies of European literature. An unpretentious scholar, whose main object was to be readable, Partridge was also not averse to publishing potboilers such as *The 'Shaggy Dog' Story* (1953) and *Comic Alphabets* (1961). His autobiographical writing includes *The First Three Years* (1930), an account of the Scholartis Press; *A Covey of Partridge* (1937) and *The Gentle Art of Lexicography* (1963). His reminiscences of the First World War include 'Frank Honywood, Private' in *Three Personal Records of the War* (1929) and 'A

Mere Private' in *Glimpses*; *Frank Honywood, Private* was republished in 1987, edited and introduced by Geoffrey Serle. The best introduction to his work is David Crystal's anthology *Eric Partridge in His Own Words* (1980). Partridge received two academic honours, both Australian: an honorary D.Litt. from the University of Queensland and an honorary fellowship of the Australian Academy of the Humanities.

'PARTRIGE, Sydney' (Kate Margaret Stone) (1871–1953) was the wife of Hal Stone (1872–1956), whose private Wayside Press produced numerous publications by Australian writers and who edited the magazines the *Red Ant, Ye Kangaroo* and *Ye Wayside Goose*. She published two collections of verse, *The Lie and Other Lines* (1913) and *The One Life and Other Verses* (1936); two novels, *Rocky Section* (1907) and *The Mystery of Wall's Hill* (1921, with Cecil Raworth); and a collection of short stories reprinted from the *Bulletin*, the *Australasian* and other magazines, *Life's Wallaby* (1908).

PASCOE, Bruce (1947–   ), born Richmond, Melbourne, is managing director of Pascoe Publishing. A Churchill fellow in 1985, he has had numerous occupations – teaching, farming, the hotel trade, journalism, education consultancy. Pascoe has written several books of fiction including *Night Animals* (1986, short stories) and *Fox* (1988, a novel) as well as a play, 'Dearly Beloved' (1982).

His short stories are said to reflect two famous bush archetypes – the pathos and tragedy of bush life as revealed in McCubbin's painting *Bush Burial* and the simple, undemanding, laconic nature of bush people as reflected in the writings of Henry Lawson. Many of the stories of *Night Animals* are, in fact, about bush people and events; in their simple, direct style they come close to another bush archetype – the yarn. Pascoe is also interested in Aboriginal culture and several stories reflect badly on White brutality towards Blacks. His novel, *Fox*, has a part-Aborigine as its protagonist. Jim Fox leaves his family farm on the Murray after fighting with his cruel father, who finally dies of his injuries. The novel traces Jim's life on the run until he reaches Arnhem Land and gradually comes to recognise and accept his Aboriginality. With Lyn Harwood and Paula White, Pascoe edited a book of stories by contemporary Australian women writers, *The Babe is Wise* (1987), and collaborated with Professor Zhu Twngqiang of Hangzhou University in a book of translations of the work of contemporary Australian authors, *A Selection of Contemporary Australian Fiction* (1992). Pascoe's most valuable contribution to Australian writing, however, has been his editing and publishing (since 1982) of a quarterly journal of short fiction, *Australian Short Stories*, thus providing a valuable forum for the appearance of the work of writers who might otherwise have remained unpublished. *Australian Short Stories* includes experimental as well as traditional short fiction.

Passage, The, a novel by Vance Palmer (q.v.), was published in 1930 and won first prize in the *Bulletin's*

1929 novel competition and the Gold Medal of the Australian Literature Society. Set in a small Queensland fishing port (possibly Caloundra), it deals mainly with the life of a fisherman, Lew Calloway, the eldest son and breadwinner of the Calloway family of five children, and incidentally with that of their neighbours. Lew has an attachment to the slow rhythms of life at The Passage which is deep, instinctive, inarticulate and tenacious, unlike his brother Hughie and sister Marnie, who yearn for the bustling activity of the city. Anna Calloway, their mother, anxious that her children should have wider opportunities than those of their relations, Tony and Rachel Calloway, only belatedly understands the meaning of Lew's organic bond to The Passage. Although the novel's action moves quietly and undramatically, the Calloways undergo various vicissitudes in its course: Hughie, whose charm and quick energy seemed to augur success, eventually fails in the city and returns to The Passage to take up his old job of managing the local store; Lew allows his first chance of a relationship with Clem McNair to pass him by, makes a disastrous marriage with Lena Christensen, suffers the death of his son Peter, loses Lena to her previous lover Craig, and is finally reunited with Clem. The ebb and flow in individual lives is also mirrored in the difference between the changing fortunes of Lavinia, a neighbouring tourist resort, and the stability of life at The Passage.

Passionate Heart, The (1918), a volume of poems by Mary Gilmore (q.v.), was dedicated to 'The Fellowing Men', the soldiers of the First World War. Poems such as 'The Measure', 'The Satin of the Bee', 'Corn' and 'Gallipoli' tell of the loss and heartache of war as seen through a woman's eyes and reflect the general disenchantment with war that followed the Allied victory in 1918. Other poems, such as 'Life-Song', 'Life at Autumn' and the title poem, carry the typical Mary Gilmore affirmation of life.

'Past Carin'', a poem by Henry Lawson (q.v.) which records the lament of a bush woman whom hardship and tragedy have made 'past carin'', was published in 1899. It subsequently became the title of the second part of '"Water them Geraniums"', a story in the Joe Wilson (q.v.) sequence, which chronicles the spiritual disintegration and death of the bush woman Mrs Spicer.

PATCHETT, Mary, see *The Oxford Companion to Australian Children's Literature* (1993), pp. 335–6.

PATERSON, A.B. (Andrew Barton) (1864–1941), widely known as 'Banjo' Paterson from the pseudonym 'The Banjo', which he adopted for his early contributions to the *Bulletin*, was born at Narambla Station, near Orange, NSW. Growing up in the bush on Illalong Station near Yass, NSW, he had an early acquaintance with identities such as drovers, teamsters and even bushrangers, with occasions such as picnic race meetings, and with relationships such as the animosity between squatters and drovers. Those early

experiences provided him with a fund of incidents, characters and scenes, which his later writings turned into legend. After early schooling in the small town of Binalong he completed his education in Sydney, then entered a lawyer's office as clerk, and was ultimately admitted as a solicitor. A literary celebrity after the rapturous reception of *The Man from Snowy River and Other Verses* in 1895, the handsome, well-bred, athletic Paterson rapidly became the toast of the country; he is portrayed as such in Nigel Krauth's novel *Matilda, My Darling* (1983). His later life was full of glamour and adventure. He went crocodile-hunting and buffalo-shooting in the Northern Territory, dived for pearls with the Japanese at Broome, was a war correspondent in the Boer War, and travelled to China to cover the Boxer Rebellion. Back in Australia he was successively editor of the Sydney *Evening News* and the *Australian Town and Country Journal*. In the First World War he was initially a war correspondent but, dissatisfied with his inability to get to the front in France, returned to Australia and enlisted in the Remount Service which provided horses for the Australian cavalry in the Middle East. After the war he returned to journalism, edited the *Sydney Sportsman*, continued to indulge his love for all sports, especially the turf (q.v.), and wrote further verse and fiction as well as scripts for radio. He had lived periodically in the country on the property Coodravale on the upper Murrumbidgee, fulfilling the dream he had expressed years earlier in 'A Mountain Station', but from 1919 he lived in Sydney.

Paterson's books of verse are *The Man from Snowy River and Other Verses* (1895), *Rio Grande's Last Race and Other Verses* (1902), *Saltbush Bill J.P. and Other Verses* (1917), and the children's book *The Animals Noah Forgot* (1933). A *Collected Verse* was published in 1923. His fiction comprised two novels, *An Outback Marriage* (1906) and *The Shearer's Colt* (1936); and short stories, *Three Elephant Power and Other Stories* (1917). Reminiscences of his travels and adventures were brought together in the semi-autobiographical *Happy Dispatches* (1934). He also compiled the seminal anthology *Old Bush Songs* (q.v., 1905). Paterson left several unpublished works, including 'Racehorses and Racing' and 'Illalong Children', both of which were published in 1983 in a two-volume edition, collected and introduced by his granddaughters, Rosamund Campbell and Phillipa Harvie, *Singer of the Bush* (writings 1885–1900) and *Song of the Pen* (writings 1901–41). Published by Lansdowne Press as *The Complete Works of Banjo Paterson*, it remains a best-seller. A recent selection by Richard Hall reprints some of Paterson's journalism, *Banjo Paterson. His Poetry and Prose* (1993).

Paterson is the chief folk-poet of Australia. 'Waltzing Matilda' (q.v.), Australia's national song, and 'The Man from Snowy River' (q.v.), Australia's national narrative poem, substantiate that claim. Add such folk-figures as 'Clancy of the Overflow', 'Saltbush Bill', 'The Man from Ironbark' and 'Mulga Bill' (qq.v.), set them 'On Kiley's Run', at 'Conroy's Gap', along 'The Road to Gundagai' or 'By the Grey Gulf Water', have them sing 'A Bushman's Song', dream 'A Dream of the Melbourne Cup', swap old yarns of 'Father Riley's

Horse' and 'The Geebung Polo Club', or ruefully recount 'How the Favourite Beat Us', and the outlines of the map of Australian folklore are broadly drawn. That mythical map's outlines coincide with actual geographical boundaries. It begins in the western plains of NSW, takes in the Murrumbidgee and the Monaro, heads north to the Queensland Downs and the Northern Territory, encompassing the whole limitless outback. It is 'the land of lots o' time', signposted with fabled names, the Overflow, the Castlereagh, the Snowy, Dandaloo, Gundaroo, Come-by-Chance, Hogan's Gap, Hay and Hell and Booligal. It is Australian Arcadia, created by all the bush balladists and in his more optimistic moods even contributed to by Henry Lawson himself, but it is indisputably Paterson country. Whether Australian Arcadia ever existed in the way Paterson pictured it is problematical, but the general Australian populace has long been beguiled by his vision. The first edition of *The Man from Snowy River* sold out in the week of publication; it went through four editions in six months and still outsells any other volume of Australian poetry ever published. The Arcadian view was strongly challenged in the *Bulletin* debate (q.v.) with Lawson in 1892–93, but Paterson did not, in his own opinion, ignore those aspects of the outback which coloured Lawson's attitude – the minor irritants like dust, heat and flies, or the darker calamities like droughts, floods, despair and tragedy. His Arcadians simply accepted their lot, good or bad, with cheerful, laconic patience.

Paterson is the supreme balladist of the horse. In bushman fashion he viewed the horse as an animal trained for and useful in specific tasks and he admired it for its excellence in those tasks, one of which is racing. Racing involves feats of speed, courage and endurance and there is plenty of human drama associated with it. 'Rio Grande's Last Race', 'Father Riley's Horse', 'The Old Timer's Steeplechase', 'Mulligan's Mare' and 'In the Droving Days' are notable Paterson stories of the horse, but 'The Man from Snowy River' is the undisputed classic of that genre. Paterson belongs also to the stream of nationalist-radical writers that the 1890s nurtured. In 'A Bushman's Song' he is the radical, putting the case for the ordinary drover and shearer against the squatter and the absentee landlord, while 'Song of Federation', 'Song of the Future' and 'Old Australian Ways' express nationalist sentiments.

Paterson is commemorated in the Banjo Paterson Award made biennially by the Orange Festival of Arts Committee for one-act plays and poetry and the National Book Council's annual awards which, since 1988, have been known as the Banjo Awards. The major biographical and critical study for many years was Clement Semmler's popular *The Banjo of the Bush: The Work, Life and Times of A.B. Paterson* (1966). Semmler has also edited, with an introduction, *The World of 'Banjo' Paterson* (1967) and the beautifully illustrated *The Collected Verse of A.B. Paterson* (1992) and has written *A.B. Paterson* (1967) in the Great Australian series, *A.B. Paterson* (1965) in OUP's Australian Writers and Their Work series and *A.B. 'Banjo' Paterson* (1992) in UQP's Australian Authors series.

Colin Roderick in the recent (1992) biography *Banjo Paterson: Poet by Accident* combines his own lengthy experience of the bush poet genre with wider-ranging research into much primary Paterson material.

Patrick White Literary Award is an annual award established by Patrick White (q.v.) in 1973 with the proceeds of the Nobel Prize for Literature which he won that year. It is awarded to an older Australian writer whose work, in the opinion of the administrators of the fund, has not received the critical acclaim or the financial rewards it deserves. The following writers have won the award: Christina Stead (1974), David Campbell (1975), John Blight (1976), Sumner Locke Elliott (1977), Gwen Harwood (1978), Randolph Stow (1979), Bruce Dawe (1980), Dal Stivens (1981), Bruce Beaver (1982), Marjorie Barnard (1983), Rosemary Dobson (1984), Judah Waten (1985), John Morrison (1986), William Hart-Smith (1987), Roland Robinson (1988), Thea Astley (1989), Robert Gray (1990), David Martin (1991), Peter Cowan (1992), and Amy Witting (1993).

PATTERSON, Henry (1867– ?), born Scotland, came to Australia in 1878 and acquired ownership of several country newspapers in Victoria. A prolific, conventional and flowery poet who specialised in elevated, patriotic themes, Patterson published nine volumes of verse. They are *The Litany of Liberty* (1918), *Song of the Anzacs* (1918), *Sunrise Hymns and The Litany of Liberty* (1919), *Morning Songs* (1922), *More Morning Songs* (1924), *Joan of Domremy* (1925), *The King's Chamberlain* (1939), *Armageddon* (1940) and *Kingdom Come* (1944). Both *The King's Chamberlain* and *Armageddon* were published under the pseudonym 'Bartimaeus'.

Patterson, Sir Les, a character created by Barry Humphries (q.v.) in 1974, was originally presented as the entertainments officer of a well-known Sydney licensed club, the St George Leagues Club, but developed into an Australian cultural attaché abroad; from 1978 the recently knighted Australian cultural attaché at the court of St James. A chauvinistic, obscene, vulgar ex-politician, who has survived the fall of E.G. Whitlam's government, Sir Les is part larrikin and part ocker (q.v.), the means whereby Humphries can attack both Australian philistinism and government support for the arts. The views of Sir Les on Australian cultural life are presented in *Les Patterson's Australia* (1978).

PAULL, Raymond (1906–72) began his career as a journalist for the *Argus* and transferred to the ABC news service in 1939. He enlisted in the AIF in the Second World War and was later war correspondent for the ABC in the South Pacific. He wrote a well-researched account of the Kokoda campaign, *Retreat from Kokoda* (1958), which was reissued several times and became regarded as a classic military history; focusing on the experience of both the ordinary Australian and the ordinary Japanese soldier, the history also exposes the bungling and petty jealousies at senior levels, implicating General Blamey as a major culprit. Paull also wrote a history of the gold town Walhalla, *Old Walhalla* (1963).

Pea Pickers, The (1942), a novel by Eve Langley (q.v.) with a strong autobiographical basis, is a story of two sisters, aged 18 and 19, who leave their Dandenong home to taste the free and wandering life. Dressed as boys, a half-hearted disguise that only partly conceals their sex, and answering to the names Blue and Steve, they journey to Gippsland, their soul-country, where their ancestors had first gone by bullock dray. They work as apple-packers and Steve, whose feverish preoccupations are an obsession to be loved and a counter-conviction that her beloved land 'loved me for my virginity and would be with me while I kept it', meets her first love, Kelly Wilson, 'bow-legged, booted and spurred'; he demonstrates his gallantry in Gippsland male fashion by taking her rabbit-shooting. Kelly, who feels 'like a bottle of yeast that must soon explode', ultimately loses interest as Steve clings to 'the cold but happy ideal of the virgin'. Steve and Blue become mates with another Gippslander, Jim. Estimable in most respects, Jim is an embarrassment to them on social occasions such as Sunday tea at the boss's house because of his rapid and continuing plunder of the tea table. After apple-packing and trips to the vineyards at Rutherglen on the Murray and the maize fields at Tumut in NSW, they rejoin Jim for the pea-picking at Metung on the Gippsland lakes. The grand passion of Steve's life now appears in the person of Macca Mackinnon, 'a short fair bloke with a slow voice', and she becomes, again, tortured by conflicting desires. She reads the *Aeneid* to Macca in the moonlight and they lie, afterwards, decorously on (not in) her bed. While Steve agonises the night away, the puzzled but equable Macca finally falls asleep. A pragmatic Gippslander, Macca ultimately sidesteps the complexities of Steve; proclaiming to her his satisfaction with 'the uncloying cleanliness' of her passion he indulges, on the side, in less complicated frolics with the local girls. At Metung the itinerant Italian workers enter the narrative: Peppino, who always wears green socks ('Dese me mudder makes') and avows distraught, unintelligible love for Blue by letter; Domenic Gatto ('Tomcatto'), who is prone to drawing the Australian coat of arms and hollowly crying 'Viva l'Owstralia'; and the amorous Puglisi ('Rudolph Valentino … he not dead while I alive'). Later, while hop-picking in the Australian Alps, they encounter more such characters: another Italian, 'The Little Black Flea', whose continual wail of despair at Steve's indifference to him, 'no luna ancora' (no moon yet), becomes her own cry for Macca; and another Australian mate, the lisping Charlie Wallaby and his mare 'Blothum' (Blossom). After a winter of near starvation in the Alps, relieved only by their adroitness in stealing food from the Italians and pumpkins from nearby fields, they return in the spring with renewed optimism to another pea-picking season at Metung. Her idyll over, Blue finally returns to normality by going home to Dandenong to marry her patient suitor, but Steve, still virginal, still obsessed by love, vows to stay on in Gippsland in 'pure and poetic solitude', a reminder to the errant Macca, now comfortably 'sweet on a cattleman's daughter', of 'flawless love' and 'ideal faithfulness'. *The Pea Pickers* was republished in 1991 in Angus & Robertson's Imprint series with an introduction by Lucy Frost.

Peach Groves, The, a novel by Barbara Hanrahan (q.v.), was published in 1979. Although Adelaide of 1884 is the opening setting, the scene soon shifts to North Island, NZ. Blanche Dean, bored with her genteel existence and her respectable husband George, decides to visit her brother Harry in NZ. She is accompanied by her two small daughters, Ida and Maud. For the perceptive Ida and later for the more superficial Maud, NZ reveals itself as a place of mystery, danger and corruption. Not only does Uncle Harry have an illicit relationship with his wife's half-Maori sister Tempe, but Tempe also proves to have witch-like powers. The dangers surrounding the Deans multiply when they visit the Peach Groves, the property of Mr Maufe, Harry's apparently kindly friend. Mr Maufe's strange family includes his wife Zillah, who takes refuge in obsessive sketching, and his shy son Oc, who is afflicted with an outsize head. But it is Mr Maufe who turns out to be the most frightening, a pederast with murderous designs on Maud. Blanche, unaware of these undercurrents, succumbs to her own form of corruption in a recurrence of her incestuous relationship with Harry, an incident that the children witness. The family returns to Harry's residence, Harry repents his sin of incest, the revengeful Tempe, after attempting to poison Blanche and corrupt Maud, is drowned, and Mr Maufe suffers a stroke when his attempt to strangle Maud is intercepted by Oc. Chastened, and looking forward to the dull respectability of Adelaide and George, Blanche sails for Australia. Maud has emerged from the experience unchanged but Ida has grown up and away from the influence of her mother.

PEARCE, Harry Hastings (1897–1984), born Creswick, Victoria, worked as a gold-miner and farm labourer and lived in NZ for fourteen years before settling in Melbourne. A professed atheist and rationalist, he published several pamphlets in support of his views. A member of the Melbourne Bread and Cheese Club, treasurer and secretary of the Australian Poetry Lovers' Society from 1948 until its demise in 1973, and editor of its little magazine, the *Poetry Lover*, 1955–73, he was also active in the Henry Lawson Memorial and Literary Society and in the Folklore Society of Victoria. He published two collections of poetry, *The Song of Nature* (1948) and *Dreams and Arrows* (1969); a narrative poem, *Thomas Kennedy's March from Creswick's Creek* (1954), written to commemorate the centenary of Eureka; and a detailed argument concerning the origins of 'Waltzing Matilda' (q.v., 1971).

PEARL, Cyril (1906–87), born Fitzroy, Melbourne, graduated from the University of Melbourne where he was editor of *Stream*, and subsequently became a well-known Sydney journalist; he edited the *Sunday*

Telegraph 1939–49, *A.M.* 1949–54 and the *Sunday Mirror* 1960–61. A prolific social historian and biographer, he wrote an influential account of some of Sydney's controversial figures such as John Norton, *Wild Men of Sydney* (1958); biographies of R.H. Horne, *Always Morning* (1960), George Ernest Morrison, *Morrison of Peking* (1967), Dan Deniehy, *Brilliant Dan Deniehy* (1972) and Charles Gavan Duffy, *The Three Lives of Gavan Duffy* (1979); studies of nineteenth-century sexual mores, *The Girl with the Swansdown Seat* (1955) and *Victorian Patchwork* (1972); accounts of curious incidents in Australian history, *Rebel Down Under* (1970), *Five Men Vanished* (1978) and *The Dunera Scandal* (1983), the story of Jewish refugees who spent part of the Second World War in an Australian prison camp, which was also produced for television; satirical studies of Australian attitudes, *So, You Want to Be an Australian* (1959) and *So, You Want to Buy a House and Live in It!* (1961); a novel, *Pantaloons and Antics* (1964); a history of beer in Australia, *Beer, Glorious Beer* (1969); an account of Hardy Wilson's work (1970), of James Joyce's Dublin (1969) and of Robert Burns (1958); and edited a selection of the work of Lennie Lower, *The Best of Lennie Lower* (1963). Pearl was also a well-known television personality.

PEARSON, C.H. (Charles Henry) (1830–94), born London, studied history at Oxford and was professor of modern history at King's College, 1855–64, and lecturer in modern history at Trinity College, Cambridge, 1869–71. Editor of the *National Review* in 1862, he also contributed to the *Saturday Review* and the *Spectator*. In 1871 Pearson migrated to SA where he had bought a farm, but in 1874 accepted a post at the University of Melbourne. In Melbourne he became friendly with such prominent individuals as Alfred Deakin and George Higinbotham. A strong advocate of education for women, he was headmaster of the Presbyterian Ladies College 1875–77, and presented an influential report on public education in Victoria in 1878. Leader-writer for the *Age* 1874–85 and the *Leader* 1880–84, Pearson entered Victorian politics in 1878 and held various ministerial positions, 1886–90. In 1892 he left for England, where he was made permanent secretary to the Victorian agent-general's office, but was retired two years later. Pearson published *History of England during the Early and Middle Ages* (1868) and other historical works, but his main achievement was *National Life and Character* (1893). The most influential contentions of the book included predictions of the growth of the power of the state, and the rise of the working classes and of undeveloped nations such as China. This last influenced Australia's subsequent immigration policies. Some of his reviews and critical essays were collected in 1896, edited by H.A. Strong; John Tregenza has written an account of his life, *Professor of Democracy* (1968). Pearson's autobiography, with others' reminiscences of him was published in 1900, edited by William Stebbing. He is one of the subjects of Stuart Macintyre's *A Colonial Liberalism: The Lost World of Three Victorian Visionaries* (1991).

PEDLEY, Ethel C., see *The Oxford Companion to Australian Children's Literature* (1993), p. 339.

PELL, Olive (1903–), born Kalgoorlie, has worked as a secretary and librarian. She has written numerous radio features, short stories, plays for radio and television, and has published three collections of poetry, *Gold to Win* (1964), *I'd Rather Be a Fig!* (1976) and *Patient Reaction* (1991).

Penguin New Literary History of Australia, The, a project developed by ASAL in collaboration with *Australian Literary Studies* (*ALS*) under the general editorship of Laurie Hergenhan, was published in 1988. In five parts, the Penguin *History* deals mainly with issues rather than individual writers; it is a collection of thirty-four essays by different contributors with an introduction by Hergenhan. It comprised the October 1988 issue of *ALS*.

PENN-SMITH, Frank (1863–1935), born Lancashire, England, came to Tasmania in 1880 and worked as a farmer and prospector. He lived on the mainland 1900–5, when he left for overseas, revisited Tasmania briefly in 1922 and finally settled in England. His autobiography, *The Unexpected* (1933), was well received at the time of publication. He also published *Hang!* (1925), a collection of short stories and animal fables, and a collection of verse, *Austral Lyrics and Fugitive Pieces* (189?).

Penola, a town near the south-eastern border of SA and Victoria, has literary connections with poets Adam Lindsay Gordon and John Shaw Neilson (qq.v.). Gordon was stationed there for two years (1853–54) while a trooper in the SA Mounted Police, rode in steeplechase races there and bought a small property in the district. Julian Tenison-Woods began his friendship with Adam Lindsay Gordon while Woods was a priest at Penola in 1857. In 1872 John Shaw Neilson was born at Penola, where his father (and poet) John Neilson had a property. John Shaw Neilson's 'Old Granny Sullivan' is based on an old lady who lived at Penola.

PENTON, Brian (1904–51), born and educated in Brisbane, began a long career in journalism with a brief spell on the *Brisbane Courier;* at 19 he went to England to freelance for eighteen months before returning to Australia to join the *Sydney Morning Herald*. As its 'Special Correspondent', Penton contributed a daily column, 'From the Gallery', reporting on the events and personalities of the new federal parliament in Canberra. Its irreverent tone led to complaints from politicians, to Penton's recall to Sydney at the end of 1927, and his resignation from the *Herald* soon after. He spent most of the Depression years in England, where in 1929–30 he was P.R. Stephensen's successor as business manager of the Fanfrolico Press, which published Jack Lindsay's translation *The Mimiambs of Herondas* (1929), with an introduction by Penton, and in 1930–32 was a reporter on the *Daily Express*. While in England Penton also contributed to the *London*

Aphrodite and helped to place Norman Lindsay's *Red-heap* with publishers. In 1933 he began a long associ-ation with the Sydney *Daily Telegraph*, first as the author of the 'Sydney Spy' column, which ran daily 1934–35 and became a forum for his wide-ranging interests, and then as editor of the newspaper from 1941 until his death. Aggressively anti-Labor, Penton campaigned vigorously during the Second World War years to limit the amount of government censor-ship imposed on Australian newspapers. The dispute, the subject of Penton's *Censored!* (1947), flared most seriously in 1944, when issues of the *Telegraph* and the *Sydney Morning Herald* were suppressed.

Penton was a flamboyant and fearless journalist who has been ranked alongside J.F. Archibald as an outstanding editor, although some of his staff, e.g. Don Whitington in *Strive To Be Fair* (1977), have re-corded their resentment at his aggression and authori-tarianism. The crusading spirit which informed countless editorials and columns is evident also in two polemical works, *Advance Australia – Where?* (1943) and *Think – Or Be Damned* (1941), iconoclastic dis-cussions of contemporary society, which have their parallel in works like Donald Horne's *The Lucky Country* (1964) and Ronald Conway's *The Great Aus-tralian Stupor* (1971) a generation later. *Think – Or Be Damned*, in particular, offers sardonic comments on some of the myths about Australia's historical devel-opment; on a larger scale, Penton's two novels *Land-takers* (q.v. 1934) and *Inheritors* (1936), parts of a projected trilogy that was never completed, explore the same territory. Generally described as a 'saga' novel, a term which perhaps does less than justice to the inner life of the characters, *Landtakers* chronicles pioneering life in rural Queensland in the period 1842–64. Its focus is Derek Cabell, an innocent immi-grant who arrives in Australia intending only to make his fortune and return to England, but who stays and is changed dramatically by the rigours he is forced to endure. *Inheritors*, the sequel to *Landtakers*, takes the story of the Cabells forward to the 1880s and 1890s, and explores the destructive relationship between the successful but brutalised Cabell and his four children. Although the plots of Penton's novels are sometimes clumsy in construction and melodramatic, *Landtakers*, in particular, offers a powerful vision of the colonial experience and its legacies.

PEPWORTH, Barbara (1955–), born Sydney, was educated at Macquarie University. She has pub-lished two novels, *Early Marks* (1980) and *The Light Fantastic* (1990); and has written scripts for radio, po-etry and short stories and the plays 'Happy Families' (1979) and 'Performing Seals' (1984). In 1975 she won the FAW Short Story Award and the Ford Award for young playwrights. Narrated in the present tense, *Early Marks* is the frank, sometimes hilarious story of a young girl's formative years, ranging from sexual experiences to the difficulties of relationships with parental figures and friends. *The Light Fantastic*, concentrating on a group of shallow, chronically dissatisfied people, exploits the multiple meanings of

words and their punning potential to create a sharp, sustained attack on contemporary society.

'Peripatetic Philosopher, The' was a weekly column written by Marcus Clarke (q.v.) under the pseudonym 'Q' for the *Australasian*, 1867–70; a selec-tion from the series was published as *The Peripatetic Philosopher* in 1869 and was Clarke's first book. 'The Peripatetic Philosopher' was also a Clarke pseudo-nym, most notably for his 'Lower Bohemia' sketches in the *Australasian* and *Argus* in 1869.

PERRY, Fiona (1958–), born Brisbane, now lives in Townsville where she conducts a drama studio and is the artistic director of a youth theatre company. She has published *Pharaohs Returning* (1991), in the Pen-guin Australian Poetry series (a short volume with Alison Croggon's *This is the Stone*). The title poem is in a group of 'Five Sonnets for Egypt', based upon Lord Carnarvon's discovery of the tomb of Tutank-hamen. The 'Pharaoh Returning' would find, says Perry, 'desecration after desecration . . . nothing to worship'. Egypt and the past are strong elements in Perry's work, which also includes poems about Maria Theresa, Empress of Austria, Marie Tagliani, the first ballerina to dance on the tips of her toes, and the more contemporary subject of Sylvia Plath's suicide. The personal is also present in her poetry e.g., 'Nursery Song', 'Mango Season', 'Acknowledgment' and 'Committed'.

PERRY, Grace (1927–87), born Melbourne, was educated in Queensland and Sydney, then graduated in medicine from the University of Sydney in 1951. She combined family life with a career as a paediatri-cian and an extremely energetic involvement in con-temporary literary affairs as poet, editor, publisher, founder member of the ASA and convenor/organiser of numerous Sydney poetry workshops and writing schools. At Berrima, where she lived in her last years, she ran a 2000-acre property and maintained an interest in stud breeding. She was editor of *Poetry Magazine*, 1961–64; in 1964 she inaugurated *Poetry Australia* (q.v.), which she edited until her death. She founded South Head Press in 1964. Her own pub-lished poetry began with teenage volumes, *Staring at the Stars* (1942) and *I Live a Life of Dreams* (1943). Her first mature volume, *Red Scarf* (1963), is in two sec-tions: 'Where the Wind Moves', love poems in which natural scenery, usually seascapes, is used to reflect personal emotions; and 'Red Scarf', striking poems born out of her experiences as a doctor, which express the horror and fascination of disease and death. *Frozen Section* (1967), notable also for its considerable medical sequence, reflects the problem that is nearly always present in Grace Perry's writing, the accommodation of the clinical detachment of the physician with the sensitive involvement of the poet. *Two Houses* (1969) contains the sequence 'Notes on a Journey', small intense landscape images of the picturesque Warrum-bungles and western NSW, and poems of contempor-ary events such as President Lyndon B. Johnson's Australian visit. *Black Swans at Berrima* (1972), an ambitious sequence of more than a hundred individual lyric pieces, begins with the building of the historic magistrate's house at Berrima, describes a journey from Sydney to Berrima, and explores the passing of time and the approach of age and death. Following *Berrima Winter* (1974), Perry published *Journal of a Surgeon's Wife and Other Poems* (1976), the title poem a long verse diary of the experiences of an immigrant doctor's wife in early colonial Australia. The poem captures the sense of exile that so oppressed the early settlers. Another book of poetry, *Snow in Summer* (1980), was followed in 1981 by a play, with John Millett, *Last Bride at Longsleep. Poetry Australia* No. 119 (1989) consists of poetry by Perry with German translations by Margaret Diesendorf. In 1985 Perry won the NSW Premier's Special Award for services to literature, and in 1986 was made AM.

Perth, the capital of Western Australia (q.v.), is situated in the south-west corner of the State on the banks of the Swan River; the centre of the city is about 16 kilometres from the mouth of the Swan, where the port of Fremantle is located. The site for Perth was chosen in 1829 and the city, named after Perth in Scotland, was founded in that year by Captain James Stirling with the establishment of the Swan River Colony (q.v.). Very much a convict settlement in its early years, Perth was proclaimed a city in 1856 and incorporated in 1871. It underwent great changes during the gold-rush era of the 1890s. George Seddon and David Ravine compiled *A City and Its Setting*, the story in words and pictures of Perth from colonial outpost to modern city.

Perth Gazette, see ***West Australian***

PETERSON, Ralph (1921–), born Adelaide, served in the army during the Second World War and became a radio actor and script-writer for such comedians as Roy Rene, Dick Bentley and Jack Davey. He also wrote radio serials for the ABC and two verse plays for radio, one of which, 'The Problem of Jonny Flourcake', led to his departure for England in 1949 to work for the BBC. In London he scripted work for Tony Hancock and Benny Hill and had two stage plays produced, 'The Square Ring' (1951) and 'The Night of the Ding Dong' (1954). 'The Square Ring', which deals with a boxer's comeback, was also produced in Melbourne the same year and in the USA. Ealing Studios produced it as a film starring Jack Warner, Kay Kendall and Sid James, and Peterson rewrote it in the form of a novel, published in 1954. 'The Night of the Ding Dong', a historical drama set in Adelaide of 1870, was produced in Britain and the USA in 1954 and toured Australia in 1966. Peterson returned in 1954 to Australia where he has remained, apart from a period overseas 1959–64, becoming well known as a writer for film, radio and television. Award-winning television serials he has written include *My Name's McGooley, What's Yours?* (1966–69), *Rita and Wally*, (1968, winner of two Logie Awards and the Grenfell Henry Lawson Award) and *Dad and Dave* (1972, winner of an Awgie Award). Other stage plays by Peterson that have been produced are 'The Mating of Ulick Dooley' (1965), 'The Big Boat' (1965), winner of the *Australian*'s play-writing competition, and *The Third Secretary* (1972). A naturalistic political play, *The Third Secretary* deals with the defection of a Russian diplomat and has been linked with the celebrated defection of Vladimir Petrov in 1954, although the link is extremely tenuous. Peterson has also written another novel, *Greater the Truth* (1956), a study of a journalist's crisis of conscience. Peterson has won several other Logie Awards.

PETHERICK, E.A. (Edward Augustus) (1847–1917), born Somerset, England, arrived in Melbourne at the age of 6 and joined the bookselling and publishing firm of George Robertson (1) (q.v.) in 1862. In 1870 Robertson chose him to reorganise the London branch of the firm, which he managed from 1873 until Robertson's retirement in 1887, when he set up his own business, Colonial Booksellers' Agency. Bankrupted in 1894, Petherick lost most of his book stocks to E.W. Cole of Melbourne, but his magnificent collection of Australiana, begun in 1865, was saved. After unsuccessful efforts to present the collection to the nation, he brought it to Australia in 1908 and in 1909 it was acquired by the library committee of federal parliament, Petherick obtaining an annuity of £500 a year in consideration. The Petherick Collection Act was passed in 1911. Appointed government archivist in 1911, Petherick worked at the task of collecting titles for an all-embracing bibliography of Australasia and Polynesia. Although the Victorian section was published in the *Victorian Historical Magazine* in 1911 and 1912 and the NSW section in the *Torch* 1888–90, it remains in manuscript in the National Library of Australia, where the Petherick Collection is housed. Petherick won renown as a bibliographer in 1882 with his *Catalogue of the York Gate Geographical and Colonial Library* (1882) and *Catalogue of Books Relating to Australasia* (1899). As a publisher he issued the *Colonial Book Circular and Bibliographical Record* (1888), later the *Torch*, and *Collection of Favourite and Approved Authors* (1889).

PETSINIS, Tom (1953–), born Macedonia, Greece, came to Australia in 1959, grew up in Fitzroy, Melbourne, and studied mathematics at the University of Melbourne. He teaches at the Victoria University of Technology. Two of his plays, 'The Drought' and 'The Thief', were performed at the Anthill Theatre, Melbourne. He has also published a novel, *Raising the Shadow* (1992) and a book of poetry, *The Blossom Vendor* (1992). *Raising the Shadow* is a novel within a novel. Alex Senka, a young generous-hearted Greek, is sacked for defending a fellow workmate by fighting his antagonist. Unable to find another job he gradually drifts into despair and depression. Dave Weston, a writer who lives in a room in the same lodging house as Senka, begins a novel based on Senka's experiences. Senka reads the novel as it progresses and gradually comes to believe that the character portraying him in the novel is actually himself and that the events in the novel, which are running ahead of the events in real life, will actually occur. Tragedy ensues when he sets out to follow the fictional events. Cleverly contrived, the novel depicts life imitating art rather than the customary reverse. *The Blossom Vendor* re-creates scenes, events and characters from Petsinis's original homeland and other European countries. The poems are set in such places as Thassos, Salonika, Florence, Rome, Alexandria and are peopled by an assortment of literary, mythical, historical and colourful characters. Among the last-named are the 'The Blossom Vendor', 'The Book Vendor' and 'The Lottery Vendor' – all three from Salonika. Direct and economical, the poems convey with imaginative precision the essence of place and character. Petsinis won the Greek Australian Cultural League's Literary Competition 1989 and 1990.

Phar Lap, Australia's most famous racehorse, was actually foaled in NZ in 1926. He created a sensation on the Australian turf, 1929–31, when he won thirty-six races, including the major classics in NSW and Victoria and the Melbourne Cup in 1930. His death in mysterious circumstances in California in 1932 added to his legend and occasioned many sentimental verse tributes; since then he has been the subject of Peter Porter's poem 'Phar Lap in the Melbourne Museum', Isabel Carter's chronicle *Phar Lap* (1964), Stephen Mastare's play 'Phar Lap, It's Cingalese for Lightning, Y'Know', produced in Melbourne in 1977, and Michael Wilkinson's *The Phar Lap Story* (1980). An Australian film, *Phar Lap: Hero to a Nation*, was screened in 1983; Helen Townsend wrote a novel, *Phar Lap* (1983), based on the film.

PHELAN, Nancy (1913–), born and educated in Sydney, lived in England for several years and has travelled widely in the Pacific Islands, Europe, Asia and the Middle East. She has written three novels, *The Voice beyond the Trees*, winner of third prize in the *Sydney Morning Herald*'s 1950 novel competition and published in 1985, *The River and the Brook* (1962) and *Serpents in Paradise* (1967); two volumes of autobiography, an account of her childhood in Sydney, *A Kingdom by the Sea* (1969) and *The Swift Foot of Time* (1983), which deals with her experiences in England in the 1930s and 1940s; several travel books, including *Welcome the Wayfarer* (1965), *Pillow of Grass* (1969), *Some Came Early, Some Came Late* (1970), *The Chilean Way* (1973) and *Morocco is a Lion* (1982); two short novels published together, *Home is the Sailor* and *The Best of Intentions* (1987, which won the 1988 Townsville Foundation for Australian Literary Studies Award); and a biography of the musician Charles Mackerras (1987). Phelan is a niece of Amy and Louise Mack (qq.v.), and has written a lively and imaginative biography of the latter, *The Romantic Lives of Louise Mack* (1991), which interweaves family lore, personal knowledge, intensive research and sympathetic projections of Mack's inner life, based partly on her prolific writing.

'Phil the Poet', see **LORIMER, Philip Durham**

PHILLIP, Arthur (1738–1814), born London, joined the Royal Navy as midshipman in 1755; by 1781 he had gained the rank of captain. In 1786 he was appointed captain-general of the proposed expedition to NSW and governor of the projected convict settlement. On 13 May 1787 the First Fleet sailed from Portsmouth and Phillip, in HMS *Supply*, reached Botany Bay 18 January 1788. Disappointed in Botany Bay as a place for the settlement, he explored the Port Jackson district, finally selecting a suitable cove that he named Sydney Cove. On 26 January 1788, now celebrated as Australia Day, a party was landed at Sydney Cove and a ceremony marked the founding of the British settlement. A humane, decisive, energetic and determined governor, Phillip was sustained by a positive vision of the Colony's future, as many of his memoranda and letters preserved in the *Historical Records of New South Wales* reveal. The official account of the expedition to NSW and the founding of the settlement, titled *The Voyage of Governor Phillip to Botany Bay* and first published in 1789, is a compilation from the official dispatches of Phillip and from accounts by several of his officers; it contains detailed appendices and is illustrated with maps, plans and drawings of native flora and fauna. Frequently reprinted, the most accessible edition is that edited by J.J. Auchmuty (1970); also important are the accounts by Watkin Tench, John White, John Hunter and David Collins. Of the accounts of Phillip's life those by G.D. Milford (1935), George Mackaness (1937), 'M. Barnard Eldershaw' (1938) and Alan Frost (1987) are the most substantial. He appears in J.H.M. Abbott's novel *Sydney Cove* (1923), but the most extensive fictional interpretations of his governorship are in Eleanor Dark's *The Timeless Land* (1941) and Michael Talbot's *To the Ends of the Earth* (1987).

PHILLIPS, A.A. (Arthur Angell) (1900–85) was born in Melbourne of Jewish ancestors who had arrived in Australia from England in the 1820s, and of parents who were strongly nationalistic in sentiment; his father was president of the ANA. Phillips studied at the universities of Melbourne and Oxford before becoming a schoolmaster at Wesley College, 1925–71. While on the committee of the English Association, his interest in Australian literature was aroused by a request from England for a list of Australian poets for inclusion in a British Empire anthology. His own publications began with an anthology of Australian and English poetry, *In Fealty to Apollo* (1932, with Ian Maxwell) and a prose anthology, *An Australian Muster* (1946). Phillips's first major impact on the Australian literary scene came with his article 'The Cultural Cringe' (q.v.) in *Meanjin* (1950), in which he expresses his dissatisfaction with the prevailing Australian attitude of cultural servility. He published *Thinkers At Work*, a book on logical writing (1946, with A. Boyce Gibson); edited *Five Radio Plays* (1949), which includes Douglas Stewart's *The Fire on the Snow; Ten Tales: A Collection of Short Stories* (1951); *Presenting Ideas* (1952, with Mary Phillips); and *Australian Poetry* (1956). A selection of his critical articles from *Meanjin* and *Overland* was published as *The Australian Tradition* (q.v.,

1958), a work which emphasises the importance of the democratic theme in the development of a distinctive Australian literary tradition. *The Australian Tradition* established him as one of Australia's leading critics and the book itself has become an integral part of the literary heritage it posits. Phillips edited, with valuable introductions, *Bernard O'Dowd* (1963) and Barbara Baynton's *Bush Studies* (1965), and compiled *Coast to Coast* (1968), which emphasises rural and country town stories and reflects Phillips's belief in the importance of the Henry Lawson–Joseph Furphy tradition. His chief critical work, *Henry Lawson* (1970), although directed towards an American reading public, adds to the contribution he made to Lawson studies with his earlier articles, 'Henry Lawson as Craftsman' and 'Henry Lawson Revisited', included in the 1966 edition of *The Australian Tradition*. *Responses* (1979), edited by Brian Kiernan, is a selection of Phillips's literary journalism in his characteristic lucid, fresh and pugnacious style. A.A. Phillips, long associated with the FAW and with *Meanjin*, was awarded an honorary D.Litt. from the University of Melbourne in 1975 and was made foundation patron of ASAL in 1978. The A.A. Phillips Award from ASAL, introduced in 1986 and presented on an occasional basis for excellence in Australian literary scholarship, was presented for the inaugural occasion to W.H. Wilde, Joy Hooton and Barry Andrews for *The Oxford Companion to Australian Literature* (1985). The Victorian Premier's annual awards includes the A.A. Phillips Award.

PHILLIPS, Charles Walter ('Denton Prout') (1910–), born Broadford, Victoria, spent most of his working life as a public servant, ending his career as chief electoral officer of Victoria. He has written an important biography of Henry Lawson, *Henry Lawson: The Grey Dreamer* (1963) and two books with Fred Feely, *Petticoat Parade* (1965), a collection of biographies of colonial women, and *50 Years Hard: The Story of Pentridge Gaol from 1850 to 1900* (1967).

PHILP, J.A. (James Alexander) (1861–1935), born Stirling, Scotland, was a journalist in Queensland and sub-editor of the *Bulletin*, to which he also contributed short stories. He published two collections of verse, *Jingles That Jangle* (1918) and *Songs of the Australian Fascisti* (1923). His short stories, several of which are set in NZ, where he was educated, were collected in 1916, titled *Some Bulletin Stories*.

PHIPSON, Joan, see *The Oxford Companion to Australian Children's Literature* (1993), pp. 342–4.

Phoenix, the literary annual of the University of Adelaide Union, was published irregularly 1935–50 and included verse, short stories and book reviews. Contributors included Rex Ingamells, Clement Semmler, C.R. Jury, Max Harris, Ian Mudie, Flexmore Hudson, Hal Porter and Brian Elliott.

Phoenix, Review, The, see *Helix*

'ΠΟ' (1951–), born Greece, has been resident in Australia since infancy. A draftsperson in the Victorian public service, he is well known out of working hours as an anarchist and a reader and writer of concrete verse. Regarded initially as a bizarre figure by some, ΠΟ has proved extremely durable, writing and promoting poetry for more than two decades, especially that concerned with and emanating from Melbourne's large immigrant population. A member of a number of collective presses, he has edited such underground poetry magazines as *Fitzrot, Born to Concrete, Free, Free Too, Free Read, i's and e's* and *9.2.5*, and is a familiar contributor to such magazines as *Ploughman, Contempa, Magic Sam, Luna* and *Your Friendly Fascist*. An enthusiastic supporter of poetry readings in schools, prisons, universities, at political demonstrations and on radio, ΠΟ has played a leading role in the upsurge of performance poetry. He has contributed verse to several anthologies and published numerous collections including *Fitzroy Brothel* (1974), *Poems by Pi O* (1974), *Shade* (1974, with Stephanie Bennett), *Emotions in Concrete* (1975), *Street Singe* (1976), *Pi O Revisited* (1976), *Humble Pi* (1977), *Panash* (1978), *The Fuck Poems* (1982) and *Re: The National Neurosis: Ockers* (1983). *The Fitzroy Poems* (1989) is a selection of his poetry, much of it in a Greek-Australian dialect. He edited *Off the Record*, a collection of works by about fifty Australian poets working in pubs, cafés, clubs and on the streets, and *Missing Form: Concrete, Visual and Experimental Poems* (1981).

Picnic at Hanging Rock, a novel by Joan Lindsay (q.v.), was first published in 1967 and made into an internationally successful film in 1975. On St Valentine's Day 1900, a party of nineteen schoolgirls and two mistresses from the fashionable Appleyard College picnic at Hanging Rock, a volcanic mass in the Mt Macedon area of Victoria. A tragedy strangely disfigures the idyllic outing: three girls, Miranda, Irma Leopold and Marion Quade, and their teacher, Greta McCraw, mysteriously disappear from the face of the rock. The incident has profound, progressive effects on numerous lives, most notably on a young Englishman, Michael Fitzhubert, who is drawn by his single vision of the beautiful Miranda and later succeeds in finding one of the girls, Irma Leopold. Four other deaths eventually flow from the initial tragedy, including that of the headmistress of the College, the evil Mrs Appleyard. In 1980 Yvonne Rousseau developed five possible explanations for the girls' disappearance in *The Murders at Hanging Rock* and has included further commentary in *The Secret of Hanging Rock* (1987), the novel's previously unpublished final chapter, which concludes with Miranda and Marion crawling into a hole in the rock while Irma waits outside.

PICOT, James (1906–44), born England, came to Australia in 1923 and graduated from the University of Queensland. In 1941 he enlisted in the AIF and died as a POW on the Burma–Thailand railway. He was one of the four contributors of verse to the first issue of *Meanjin*, which published a selection of letters, personal recollections and critical appreciations of his work in 1954. His extant poems were collected after his death, titled *With a Hawk's Quill* (1953). Influenced by such poets as Robert Browning, T.S. Eliot and Gerard Manley Hopkins, Picot was a brilliant linguist, who had a promising career in prospect as poet and critic.

Picturesque Atlas of Australasia, a lavishly illustrated descriptive work which also covers the history, geography and development of the Australian colonies, NZ, and parts of the Pacific (e.g. New Guinea, Fiji), was a publishing enterprise initiated by American book salesman Silas Lyon Moffett and J.W. Lyon, who had worked on the successful *Picturesque Canada* (1882–85). They interested a number of Australian journalists and artists in an equivalent Australian project, and the Picturesque Atlas Publishing Company was formed with William Macleod as chairman. The *Picturesque Atlas* was published in parts (?1883–86) and as a three volume set in 1886; it was several times reprinted and updated, e.g. in 1892 as *Australasia Unlimited*, but the publishing venture was unsuccessful and the methods used to promote the work led to changes to the law to protect consumers. Andrew Garran was nominal editor with F.J. Broomfield and F.J. Donohue as assistant editors. Literary contributors included Broomfield, Donohue, G.B. Barton, James Smith, W.H. Traill, Baron von Mueller and Ada Cambridge (writing as Ada Cross). Artists whose work was featured in the *Atlas*, which was significant not only for the quality of its wood-engravings but also because the project brought artists and engravers to Australia who had experience with recently developed techniques, were F.B. Schell, Macleod, Frank Mahony, A.H. Fullwood, Tom Roberts, and Julian Rossi Ashton.

PIDDINGTON, W.R. (William Richman) (1815–87), born London, was brought up in the book trade. He migrated to NSW in 1838 and in 1848 formed a partnership with a Sydney bookseller, W.A. Colman. When the partnership foundered fourteen months later, Piddington went into business on his own and published Charles Harpur's collection *The Bushrangers* (1853). A prominent figure in public affairs, Piddington opposed transportation and campaigned for constitutional reform. Elected to the NSW parliament in 1856, he served in several governments and was treasurer in two ministries headed by Henry Parkes, with whom he was friendly. Appointed to the Legislative Council in 1879, on Parkes's recommendation, he was chairman of committees 1885–87.

PIDGEON, William Edwin (1909–81), the cartoonist 'Wep', was born in Paddington, Sydney, and began an art cadetship with the *Evening News* in 1925; the following year he had his first comic strip published in the *Sunday News*. For more than two decades with the Sydney press he worked, in a style which shows the influence of Phil May, for the *Daily Guardian*, the *Sun*, the *Daily Telegraph*, and, most import-

antly, the *Australian Women's Weekly*, where he formed a partnership with Lennie Lower and drew 'In and Out of Society', a domestic strip which gently focuses on marital discord. Although best known for his comic strips and cartoons, Pidgeon illustrated many books, e.g. John O'Grady's *They're a Weird Mob* (1957), and won the Archibald Prize for portraiture in 1958, 1961 and 1968, after he gave up newspaper work in 1949.

PIKE, Douglas Henry (1908–74), born China, the son of a missionary, came to Australia in 1924 and was manager of a pastoral property and a minister of religion before becoming a lecturer in history at the University of Adelaide. He was appointed professor of history at the University of Tasmania in 1961 and general editor of the ADB (q.v.) in 1964. He published two influential histories, *Paradise of Dissent: South Australia 1829–1857* (1957), an encyclopaedic account of the settlement of SA and the role of dissenting religious attitudes, and *Australia: The Quiet Continent* (1962), a general history of Australia. As general editor of the first five volumes of the ADB, he won the Encyclopaedia Britannica Award in 1971. He was also advisory editor of the Great Australians Series (1955–75) in which OUP, with Pike's assistance, published about sixty small monographs, the majority of which at that time had to be written from primary sources. Many of the scholarly authors recommended by Pike have since published major biographies of the subjects of their Great Australians monographs.

'PILGRIM, A (The)', see **ARGLES, Theodore Emile**

'PINDAR JUVENAL', see ***Van Diemen's Land Warriors, The***

PINNEY, Peter (1922–92), born Sydney, and grandson of the colonial administrator Sir Hubert Murray, was educated in Sydney and served in New Guinea during the Second World War. He worked as an opal-digger, wharf labourer and seaman, but his main interest was travel. An eccentric traveller, who often moved round the world without money or passport, he ultimately settled in Brisbane as a freelance writer for television and film. He wrote several vivid accounts of his travels: *Dust on My Shoes* (1951), a description of a journey on foot in the Middle East and Asia; *Who Wanders Alone* (1954); *Anywhere But Here* (1956); *The Lawless and the Lotus* (1963); and *Restless Men* (1966), dealing with his travels in northern Australia. John Borthwick edited *The Road to Anywhere* (1993), a selection of the best of Pinney's travel writings. He also wrote two novels, *Road in the Wilderness* (1952) and *Ride the Volcano* (1960), the first of which draws on his war experiences; an account of a crocodile-shooting expedition, *To Catch a Crocodile* (1976); with Estelle Runcie, *Too Many Spears* (1978), the biography of Frank Jardine, government resident and police magistrate in the Cape York Peninsula in the 1860s; and a trilogy based on the diaries he kept while serving as a commando in the New Guinea-Bougainville campaigns, *The Barbarians* (1988), *The Glass Cannon* (1990) and *The Devil's Garden* (1992). Johnno, the narrator of the diaries, fights the war on two fronts, against the Japanese and against his superiors and eloquently expresses the hazards, frustrations and grim daily realities faced by the infantrymen.

Pioneer Players was a company formed in 1921–22 in Melbourne by Louis Esson, Vance Palmer and Stewart Macky (qq.v.). Although financially limited and composed of amateur players, apart from the actor George Dawe, the company aimed at producing simple plays expressive of the life of ordinary Australians and as nationally inspiring as those staged by the Abbey Theatre in Ireland. The first season in 1922 saw the production of Esson's 'The Battler' and *The Woman Tamer*, Stewart Macky's 'John Blake' and *The Trap*, and plays by Gerald Byrne and Vance Palmer. The following year the company produced *Mother and Son* and *The Drovers* by Louis Esson, *Travellers* and *The Black Horse* by Vance Palmer, and plays by Katharine Susannah Prichard, Alan Mulgan, Frank Wilmot and Ernest O'Ferrall. To Esson's deep disappointment, the plays failed to attract popular following and although he managed to organise a single night's performance of his play *The Bride of Gospel Place* in 1926, the death of George Dawe and the departure of the Palmers saw the end of the project.

Pipes were anonymous, scurrilous verses, which were occasionally circulated in NSW during the early years of settlement and which lampooned those in authority from the governor down. The name may derive from the verb 'to pipe', meaning to observe and victimise an individual, or from the habit of folding the lampoon in the shape of a pipe. The first pipes, directed against Governor King, were written in 1803 and others to suffer from the lampoons were Samuel Marsden and Lieutenant-Colonel George Molle. W.C. Wentworth is known to be author of some pipes and other alleged authors are Michael Massey Robinson and some officers of the NSW Corps.

PITT, Marie (1869–1948) was born at Doherty's Corner, a small mining town in Gippsland as Marie McKeown and received little schooling owing to her family's extreme poverty. After she married William Pitt, a Tasmanian farmer, later a gold-miner, in 1893, she lived in mining and farming areas of Tasmania, moving to Bairnsdale in 1905 and subsequently to Melbourne after her husband contracted miners' phthisis. Pitt died in 1912 and Marie supported her three children by writing for newspapers and clerical work. A familiar figure in feminist and socialist circles, a member of the Victorian Socialist Party, and, with Frederick Sinclaire, editor for a time of the *Socialist*, she wrote several ballads which have an underlying note of social protest. Friendly with such writers as Vance and Nettie Palmer, Mary Gilmore and Louis Esson, she was particularly influenced by Bernard O'Dowd, with whom she lived from 1920. Her verse, which first began to appear in the *Bulletin* in 1900, and subsequently appeared in the *Clarion*, *Birth* and the

Socialist, was published in four collections, *The Horses of the Hills* (1911), *Bairnsdale and Other Poems* (1922), *The Poems of Marie E. J. Pitt* (1925) and *Selected Poems* (1944). Pitt's best-known work is contained in her studies of landscape, her most radical verse being omitted from the 1944 selection. In 1944 she won the ABC's national song lyric competition with 'Ave Australia'. Colleen Burke has written a biography of Pitt, *Doherty's Corner* (1985), which includes a selection of her poetry and prose.

PIZER, Marjorie (1920–), born Melbourne and educated at the University of Melbourne, lives in Sydney where she works as a psychotherapist. She has published several collections of poetry, *Thou and I* (1967), *To Life* (1969), *Tides Flow* (1972), *Seasons of Love* (1975), *Full Summer* (1977), *Gifts and Remembrances* (1979), *To You, the Living* (1981), *The Sixtieth Spring* (1982), *Selected Poems 1963–1983* (1984), *Equinox: Poems* (1987), *Fire in the Heart* (1990) and *Journeys* (1992), and with Anne Spencer Parry, *Below the Surface* (1982). She has also edited an anthology of poetry, *Freedom on the Wallaby* (1953); a selection of stories and poems by Henry Lawson, *The Men Who Made Australia* (1957); and with her husband, Muir Holburn, a collection of verse by Victor Daley, *Creeve Roe* (1947). Pizer and Holburn were founders of the Pinchgut Press in 1947, which published *Creeve Roe* and *Freedom on the Wallaby* and which was revived in 1975 to publish Pizer's poetry and Anne Spencer Parry's series of fantasy novels. With Drusilla Modjeska she edited *The Poems of Lesbia Harford* (1985). Pizer's poems celebrate the simple things and everyday compensations of life in the face of death, war and transience.

PLACE, Fiona (1958–), born Sydney, graduated from the University of Sydney and studied in the Writing Program of the NSW University of Technology. She has been writer-in-residence at Westmead Hospital and at the Prince Henry Hospital. She has also lectured in creative writing at the University of Western Sydney. Her first novel, *Cardboard* (1989), won the NBC Banjo Qantas New Writers Award in 1990. *Cardboard*, an impressive novel both in its literary qualities and its treatment of the theme of anorexia, is narrated by Lucinda, who guides the reader through the extraordinary horrors she endures in finally making her way out of the labyrinth. *When Eating is Everything* (1991) is a book Place co-authored on eating problems.

Playwrights Advisory Board was founded in 1938 by Leslie Rees, Rex Rienits and Doris Fitton, with the object of fostering Australian theatre. Although the Board had no production capacity, it negotiated productions with both professional and amateur theatres, acted as an intermediary in the nomination and collection of royalties, and advised both theatres and playwrights on scripts. Rees was chairman of the Board during its existence; Fitton and Rienits soon withdrew, but numerous others worked for the Board for varying periods, including Dymphna Cusack, Sumner Locke Elliot, May Hollinworth, Sydney

Tomholt, Gwen Harrison, Alrene Sykes, George Farwell, Alan Ashbolt and Richard Lane. The Board was instrumental in securing publication of Australian plays, and was active in opposing censorship and in the running and judging of play competitions. One of the most important competitions, held in 1955, yielded two first-prize winners, *Summer of the Seventeenth Doll* by Ray Lawler, and *The Torrents* by Oriel Gray; the Board was later active in securing professional production of Lawler's internationally successful play. Other significant competitions in which the Board was involved were those of 1956, when first prize was awarded to Richard Beynon's *The Shifting Heart*, and 1961, when first prize was shared by Hal Porter's *The Tower* and Robert Amos's *When the Gravediggers Come*. After 1963 the Board ceased operations, its functions having been taken over by various commercial agencies and by the Australian Elizabethan Theatre Trust.

Pluralist, a magazine which described itself as 'of the non-popularist left' and adopted the subtitle *A Journal of Social and Literary Criticism* from its third issue, was published irregularly in Sydney 1962–69. Edited by Richard Appleton, W. Maidment and others, it included articles of general literary or philosophical interest and some verse and short stories. Contributors included Bruce Beaver, Norman Talbot, Frank Moorhouse, John Tranter and Clive James.

Poems and Songs, Henry Kendall's (q.v.) first volume of verse, was published in 1862. Many of these early Kendall poems attempt, however imperfectly, to reflect the spirit and character of Australian life and to picture the beauty of the Australian coastal landscape. Kendall the sentimental young romantic is also evident in them. Well-known poems include 'The Muse of Australia', 'Wild Kangaroo', 'The Curlew Song' and 'Morning in the Bush'.

Poetry: A Quarterly of Australian and New Zealand Verse, founded and edited by Flexmore Hudson, was published in Adelaide, 1941–47. Uncommitted to any particular ideology, the magazine published a mixture of notable and negligible talents; it changed its subtitle in 1946 to the *Australian International Quarterly of Verse* to reflect the subsequent inclusion of British, Irish and American poets. Contributors included Judith Wright, 'Brian Vrepont', Gina Ballantyne, Rex Ingamells and A.D. Hope.

Poetry Australia, a quarterly poetry magazine founded, managed and edited by Grace Perry (q.v.), was first published in 1964 when Perry led a movement away from the Poetry Society of Australia (q.v.) and its journal *Poetry Magazine*, later *New Poetry* (q.v.). Both *Poetry Australia* and the publishing house South Head Press were the result of Perry's resolve to produce a fine poetry magazine devoid of factions, fostering Australian talent but also one which was truly international. *Poetry Australia*, aided by editorial advice and assistance from poets such as Bruce Beaver and Les Murray (joint editor Nos 66–73), and from critics and academics such as Ronald Dunlop, James Tulip, Clement Semmler and Leonie Kramer, has published both new and established Australian writers, as well as modern overseas poetry. It has also published special issues of NZ, Canadian, Italian, Japanese, Dutch and Flemish, American, Gaelic, French, Austrian, Swedish and Papua New Guinean poetry; commemorative issues on Francis Webb and David Campbell; Young Poets issues; regional poetry of the various Australian States and special issues devoted to individual poets, e.g. John Millett, Heather Cam, Peter Goldsworthy, Meredith Wattison. Based in Sydney, *Poetry Australia* has also played a leading part in poetry readings and workshops, in literary seminars, and in visits by overseas writers of distinction. An account of the *raison d'être* of *Poetry Australia* and its history is given by Les Murray in 'Inside *Poetry Australia*', *Quadrant* (1983). *Poetry Australia – Twenty One Years* (1985), a collection of about thirty-five poems mostly by well-established Australian poets, celebrates twenty-one years of publication. The prize awarded in connection with that twenty-first milestone went to Keith Russell's 'The Trains South'. In its later years Grace Perry and John Millett were responsible for publication with assistance from guest editors for the special issues. It has been edited since 1988 by John Millett. Its achievements were recognised in 1985 by the NSW Premier's Special Literary Award.

Poetry Magazine, see **Poetry Society of Australia**

Poetry Militant is the name given to the poetic credo expressed by Bernard O'Dowd (q.v.) in a presidential address to the Australian Literature Society in 1909. The poet is to be 'the ferment who alters for the better, the ordered, natural, inert sequence of things'; his role is to accelerate the process of intellectual and moral evolution. Poetry Militant stresses the need for the poet to concern himself with worthy themes, e.g. politics, religion, sex, science, social reform, and with simple forms. It eschews 'Poetry Triumphant', the poetry of beauty and ornamentation, until the proper social order has been achieved.

Poetry Monash, emanating from the English Department of Monash University began in July 1977 under the editorship of Dennis Davison. Initially published twice yearly and later thrice yearly, it contained poems from writers and students associated with Monash. In 1987 Davison, having edited it about twenty times, became its business manager and Lynette Wilson succeeded him as editor.

Poetry Society of Australia was founded in Sydney in 1954 to encourage the study of poetry and to establish an active fellowship with a love of poetry as a common bond. In addition to performances by members of the Society (Shelley's *The Cenci* was produced in its first year), lectures and poetry competitions, the Society commenced publication in July 1954 of a journal, *Prism*. *Prism* was superseded in 1961 by *Poetry Magazine*, a bi-monthly publication edited, until 1964, by Grace Perry, assisted by Roland Robinson and others. *Poetry Magazine* ran until 1970 when a dispute over the question of how much space should be devoted to American and English writers saw its disappearance and replacement by *New Poetry* (q.v.) in February 1971.

Poets and Prose Writers of New South Wales, The (1866), edited by George Burnett Barton (q.v.), is a supplementary volume to *Literature in New South Wales* (q.v.), published earlier the same year. Whereas the earlier volume is a comprehensive account of the literature of the colony, the supplement concentrates on important writers. The writers discussed are W.C. Wentworth, John Dunmore Lang, Charles Harpur, William Forster, James Martin, Henry Parkes, D.H. Deniehy, Robert Sealy, W.B. Dalley, Henry Kendall, Henry Halloran, T.L. Mitchell, J.L. Michael and G.R. Morton. Both volumes were compiled for the Paris Exhibition of 1867.

Poet's Choice, see **ROBERTS, Philip**

Poets of the Month was a series of slim booklets of verse published monthly by Angus & Robertson, each booklet featuring the work of a single poet. The booklets were consolidated in several series, 1976–80.

Poets on Record, a series of recordings of well-known Australian poets reading from their own works, was published by UQP and edited by Thomas Shapcott. The series ran 1970–75.

POIGNANT, Axel (1906–86), born England of Anglo-Swedish parentage, was educated partly in Sweden. He arrived in Australia in 1926 and began to pursue an interest in photography when he moved to Perth in 1930. By the mid-1930s he had extended the range of his work to include press photographs, and began to experiment with the photo-story. Fascinated by the Australian landscape, wildlife and outback personalities, Poignant also photographed several Australian writers and artists. He developed a strong affinity with the Aborigines, which is reflected in his highly popular book for children, *Piccaninny Walkabout* (1957), redesigned and retitled *Bush Walkabout* in 1972. He spent two months with the Aboriginal people of Arnhem Land in 1952, producing an invaluable record of their traditional way of life. In 1956 Poignant left Australia and settled in London, where he worked as a freelance photo-journalist for such newspapers as the *Observer* and the London *Times*. His other books on Australia are *Bush Animals of Australia* (1949) and *The Improbable Kangaroo and Other Australian Animals* (1965). A selection of his photographs was published in 1982, titled *Axel Poignant: Photographs 1922–1980*.

Policy and Passion, a novel by Rosa Praed (q.v.), was published in 1881, adapted for the stage by Edward Reeve (q.v.) in 1884, and republished in 1887 as *Longleat of Kooralbyn;* like other Praed novels, it is set in Leichardt's (*sic*) Land (Queensland) and informed by Praed's experience of her family's property Maroon (Kooralbyn in the novel), and of political activities in Brisbane (Leichardt's Town). *Policy and Passion* centres on the passions of Thomas Longleat, self-made premier of Leichardt's Land, his daughter Honoria, and the people with whom they become emotionally involved: Thomas with Constance Vallancy, the wife of a politician opposed to Longleat, Honoria with Hardress Barrington, the dissolute second son of an English baronet who has been sent to the colonies by a disappointed mother and who turns Honoria away from her long-term and faithful suitor, Dyson Maddox. Meeting Constance early in the novel, Longleat travels back to Leichardt's Town with her, and as their relationship develops is persuaded to appoint her husband to a police magistracy in the country. This action, together with a controversy about railway extension, contributes to the fall of his government, although he is successful at the polls. Barrington, meanwhile, pays a series of visits to Kooralbyn while staying with friends nearby, and attracts the interest not only of the strong-willed Honoria, whose need for excitement has caused her to reject the stolid Dyson's appeal, but also of Angela Ferris, the delicate artistic daughter of Anthony Ferris, storekeeper at Kooralbyn, who is jealous of Longleat's success. Barrington, motivated partly by Honoria's wealth, declares his love; when Honoria, fearing his growing mastery, escapes to Leichardt's Town, he follows and is eventually successful in his proposal, although the match is violently opposed by Longleat, who wishes her husband to be an Australian such as Maddox. Longleat's opposition leads to his estrangement from his daughter and to her meeting Barrington in secret.

The third volume of the novel opens with the death of Angela from a fever; her father, blaming Barrington and Honoria for her decline, revenges himself on the Longleats by informing Vallancy of the affair between Constance and the premier. Vallancy's return to Leichardt's Town, confirmation of the liaison, and subsequent scene with Constance results in her decision to leave the colony, and Longleat's problems are compounded by the fact that Barrington has compromised Honoria when their secret night-time meeting becomes public, although Dyson Maddox saves her reputation by pretending that he and Honoria are engaged. The reconciliation of Honoria and her father is, however, short-lived; on information originating from Ferris, the leader of the parliamentary opposition exposes Longleat's ex-convict past. He commits suicide, although at the end of the novel Dyson, whose engagement has become reality, has married Honoria and succeeded in politics.

POLITZER, Ludwig, editor of the *Centenary Journal 1934–35* (1935) and the author of two volumes of verse, *Autumn Leaves* (1934) and *In Introspective Mood* (1944), compiled several useful bibliographies of French, German and Dutch writing on the subject of Australia (1952, 1953). He also compiled a bibliography of Leichhardt literature (1953), translated some of Leichhardt's letters (1944) and Stefan Kotze's *Australian Sketches* (1945).

POLLARD, James ('Mopoke') (1900–71), born Yorkshire, England, migrated to WA at the age of 14. After the First World War, in which he served with the AIF and was severely wounded, Pollard took up land under the soldier settlement scheme but soon abandoned farming for writing. A well-known writer on natural history, a frequent contributor to *Walkabout* and, as 'Mopoke', the author of a column on natural history in the *West Australian*, Pollard also contributed short stories to such newspapers as the *Australasian* and the *Western Mail*. Some of these were collected in 1948, titled *Twenty-Eight Tales*. He wrote two novels for children and three for adults; his adult novels, *The Bushland Man* (1926), *Rose of the Bushlands* (1927) and *Bushland Vagabonds* (1928), are distinguished more by their incidental naturalist descriptions than by any literary features.

POLLARD, Rhys (1948–) grew up in Melbourne and spent eight months in Vietnam in 1968 as a national serviceman before training as an engine-driver with Victorian railways. He is the author of a novel about his war experience, *The Cream Machine* (1972). Written from the point of view of the infantryman, the novel is not concerned with the politics of Australia's commitment to the Vietnam War but concentrates rather on the day-to-day experiences of the ordinary soldier preoccupied with surviving.

'Pom', 'Pommy' are Australian words denoting an English immigrant or national, and are often used derogatively, as in 'pommy bastard'. The origin of 'pommy' is uncertain: derivations from the acronym POME (Prisoner of Mother England), from 'pomegranate', and from rhyming slang (from 'immigrant' via 'pommygrant') have been suggested. H.J. Rumsey uses the expression in his novel *The Pommies* (1920).

Poor Fellow My Country, a novel by Xavier Herbert (q.v.), was published in 1975 and won the Miles Franklin Award for that year; about 850 000 words, it is the longest Australian novel ever published. Set mainly in and around the Northern Territory, like Herbert's earlier novel *Capricornia* (q.v., 1938), *Poor Fellow My Country* shares many of *Capricornia*'s themes, techniques and concerns, e.g. the majesty of the land, the motif of the journey, the destruction of Aboriginal society. Chronologically it follows *Capricornia* in depicting the tragic effects of White settlement in Australia, although its time-span is much more concentrated, covering the years 1936–42. Among the several dozen characters whose histories are narrated, the most important are Jeremy Delacy, a hard-bitten, idealised pioneer, at odds with many of his fellow Whites, whose talents, prejudices and passions find some parallels in Herbert himself; the women whom Jeremy influences, notably his part-Aboriginal second wife Nanango, the aristocratic Lydia Lyndbrooke-Esk, the idealistic Alfie Candlemass, and the Jewish refugee Rifkah; Jeremy's grandson

Prindy, who is of Irish, English and Aboriginal descent, responds to Jewish and Indian as well as Aboriginal culture in the novel and whose death signals the end of hopes of an integration of culture and belief in Australia; Bobwirridirridi, 'Cock-Eye Bob' to the Whites, and perhaps the finest piece of characterisation in the novel, an Aboriginal wise man who meets Prindy and adopts him as tribal protégé in the opening scene; representatives of the institution of White society, e.g. the police sergeant, Dinny Cahoon, who believes Prindy to be his son, anthropologist, Fabian Cootes, protector of Aborigines, Eddie McCuskey, and British military commander of the Australian Army Sir Mark Esk, Lydia's father; and numerous railway workers, pioneering families and outback types.

'Terra Australis', the first of *Poor Fellow My Country*'s three books, covers 1936–37 and is summarised by Herbert as 'Blackman's Idyll Despoiled by White Bullies, Thieves and Hypocrites'. That summary is elaborated, for the first but not the last time, early in 'Terra Australis' by Jeremy to a stock inspector visiting his property Lily Lagoons, a sanctuary where Jeremy tries to live in harmony with the environment and its original inhabitants. In contrast, the disruption and attempted control of Aboriginal practices twice results in violence in 'Terra Australis': first, the pursuit of Prindy after he leaves Lily Lagoons with Bobwirridirridi to undergo the first stage of his initiation culminates in the death of Willy Ah Loy, his adoptive father; later, the deaths of Nelyerri, Prindy's mother, and Njorjinga, his tribal uncle, have their origins in the attempted separation of Prindy and Nelyerri by the authorities at Port Palmerston (Darwin), where they are brought after Willy's murder. The other major focus of 'Terra Australis' is Jeremy's relationships with Lydia Lyndbrooke-Esk and Alfie Candlemass. He meets Lydia, the fiancée of the land baron Lord Vaisey, at the Beatrice River races, an annual Territory occasion and a recurring event in *Poor Fellow My Country;* she falls in love with him but is rejected, along with her fascist philosophy, during a tour of Lily Lagoons and surrounding areas, in which she is shown the realities of outback life. Similarly, Alfie Candlemass, who has come to the Territory imbued with idealism and been disillusioned by the corruption and insensitivity of government, falls in love with Jeremy when they meet at the Beatrice River races the following year; although Jeremy rejects her advances also, he rekindles her desire to effect social and political change. She returns south to write and become involved in Australia Free, a nationalist movement modelled on Australia First (q.v.).

The second book of *Poor Fellow My Country*, sardonically titled 'Australia Felix – Whiteman's Ideal Sold Out by Rogues and Fools', covers the period 1937–39, when the Beatrice River races are postponed because of the onset of the Second World War. Against a background of the worsening international situation, much of the action of 'Australia Felix' is centred on Lily Lagoons, where Prindy finds temporary refuge from representatives of authority such as Cahoon and McCuskey, into whose hands he has fallen after witnessing the deaths of his mother and uncle following their escape from Port Palmerston. Two new visitors to Lily Lagoons are Sir Mark Esk, who is sufficiently impressed by Jeremy's beliefs and integrity to eventually ask him to take over military command of the northern region, and Rifkah, a Jewish refugee who finds in Lily Lagoons and in her experience with Prindy of Aboriginal culture an inner harmony that radiates to others around her; her understanding of the land and its inhabitants is in contrast to the lack of perception of the government anthropologist Fabian Cootes. The outside world, however, threatens Rifkah when she is arrested and faces deportation on the grounds that she is a communist, although she finds refuge, after barely escaping death while on the run from the security police, at Leopold Catholic mission off the coast, which she has already visited with a party from Lily Lagoons. Prindy joins her there under the guardianship of the church after himself escaping from Dinny Cahoon, whose death he engineers in the process. Jeremy, meanwhile, has become involved in Australia Free and journeys to Sydney and Melbourne to help Alfie inaugurate it as a political party, cleanse it of its fascist and anti-Semitic elements, and direct it towards fulfilling its responsibilities to the Aborigines. He fails in the attempt, and returns to Lily Lagoons at the end of 'Australia Felix' to live on his old individualistic terms.

The title of the final book, 'Day of Shame – A Rabble Fled the Test of Nationhood', refers to the mass exodus from Darwin in 1942 in the face of the Japanese attack. The progress of the war again forms part of the background, and again Jeremy journeys south, this time at the request of Mark Esk that he join his staff and report on conditions in Malaya. A meeting with the officer who led his brother to death at Gallipoli convinces Jeremy that the sacrifice of the Australian Army to imperial rather than nationalist ends is being repeated; he resigns his commission but before leaving Sydney is badly beaten up with Alfie during a political meeting in the Domain. She loses the child Jeremy has fathered during the Australia Free interlude, and becomes disillusioned with Jeremy when in her eyes he fails to act with spirit when they are unfairly detained for security reasons after the fracas. Soon after his return to the Territory, Jeremy discovers that Lily Lagoons is to be commandeered by the army; with his sanctuary there invaded, he creates another one further away from civilisation, where he is joined briefly by Prindy and Rifkah before they return to the Leopold mission, where they have spent much of the time during Jeremy's absence. At the mission Rifkah, who has been pursued by several men since her arrival in Australia, finds fulfilment in her relationship with a priest; Prindy, too, has become attached to Savitra, the daughter of an Indian hawker who has several times sheltered him. The idyll of Rifkah, Prindy and their lovers is interrupted by their enforced evacuation for military reasons, but their arrival in Port Palmerston coincides with the Japanese bombing, and they escape back to Jeremy's camp in company with Bobwirridirridi, who has retained his Aboriginal claim on Prindy despite Prindy's ability to accommodate other cultures. It is in the region of Jeremy's camp that the final tragedies of *Poor Fellow My Country* occur: when Prindy's initiation is interrupted by Savitra's search for him, she is brutally murdered for her intrusion; Jeremy's pursuit of her results only in Prindy's death, in that Prindy's attention, distracted by Jeremy's cry during the trial by ordeal Savitra's intrusion has forced upon him, means that he is speared; and Jeremy too, having caused Prindy's death, is speared by Bobwirridirridi. The final chapter of the novel is an epilogue set some years after the war, in which the profound pessimism of the novel is confirmed by the description of how post-war development of the Northern Territory has completed the destruction of Aboriginal society; for example, the Rainbow Pool and the Painted Caves, central to the novel's presentation of Aboriginal belief, have been despoiled by mining and tourism. A.J. Hassall edited *The Making of Xavier Herbert's Poor Fellow My Country* (1988). The novel has also inspired paintings by Robert White, published in 1978.

Port Arthur, about 160 kilometres from Hobart on the south-eastern coast of Tasmania, was a notorious penal settlement 1830–77. A natural penitentiary because of its situation on Tasman Peninsula and of the narrowness of Eaglehawk Neck, a narrow isthmus joining Tasman and Forestier peninsulas, Port Arthur is descibed in detail in Marcus Clarke's novel *His Natural Life* (1874) and figures prominently in much other convict literature. Among many works on Port Arthur is Margaret Weidenhofer's *Port Arthur: A Place of Misery* (1981).

Port Phillip District, which became the State of Victoria (q.v.), has its origin in Governor Phillip King's naming of the large inlet on the central Victorian coast on which the major cities of Melbourne and Geelong now stand, Port Phillip Bay. The earliest attempt to establish a settlement at Port Phillip was by David Collins; J.H. Tuckey's account of that expedition, *An Account of a Voyage to Establish a Colony at Port Phillip in Bass's Strait*, was published in 1805. The Port Phillip Association was formed in Hobart early in 1835 to attempt again to establish a settlement at Port Phillip where, soon after, John Batman (q.v.) established himself. The first successful overland expedition from NSW into the Port Phillip District was that of W.H. Hovell and Hamilton Hume in 1824–25. The titles of most early Melbourne newspapers, e.g. the *Port Phillip Herald*, *Port Phillip Gazette*, *Port Phillip Patriot*, confirm the currency of the term in the 1830s and 1840s. An important foundation document in the history of White settlement in the Port Phillip District is the journal kept by William Todd at Indented Head on the Bellarine Peninsula in 1835. Todd's *Journal* was published in 1990, edited by Philip L. Brown. Descriptive and historical writings on the Port Phillip District include J.B. Clutterbuck's *Port Phillip in 1849* (1850), E.M. Curr's *Recollections of Squatting in Victoria, Then Called the Port Phillip District* (1883) and T.F. Bride (ed.) *Letters from Victorian Pioneers* (1898). Early settlers of the Port Phillip District include the

McCraes, the Furphys and the family of 'Rolf Boldrewood'. Early Port Phillip society is described in Paul de Serville's *Port Phillip Gentlemen* (1980) and in the contemporary reminiscences *Georgiana's Journal* (1934).

Port Phillip Gazette, one of Victoria's earliest newspapers, was published in Melbourne, sometimes daily and sometimes weekly, 1838–51; in 1844–51 it was edited by Thomas McCombie (q.v.). A modern *Port Phillip Gazette* was published in Melbourne, 1952–56, edited by Desmond Fennessy.

Port Phillip Herald, see **Herald**

Port Phillip Patriot and Melbourne Advertiser, see **FAWKNER, John Pascoe**

PORTEOUS, R.S. (Richard Sydney) (1897–1963), born Melbourne, served in the Australian Light Horse in the First World War and subsequently worked on a cattle station in central Queensland and on Australian coastal vessels. During the Second World War he served in the navy, before working as mate on cargo ships on the Queensland and New Guinea coasts. His experiences led to a series of sea stories contributed to the *Bulletin*, often under the pseudonym 'Standby'. As 'Standby' he published a novel, *Sailing Orders* (1949), and two collections of short stories, *Little Known of These Waters* (1945) and *Close to the Wind* (1955). As R.S. Porteous, he published another collection of short stories, *Salvage* (1963); two novels of cattle-station life, *Brigalow* (1957) and *Cattleman* (1960), which won the *Courier-Mail*'s centenary novel competition; and three novels for young readers, *Tambai Island* (1955), *The Tambai Treasure* (1958) and *The Silent Isles* (1963).

PORTER, Dorothy Featherstone (1954–), born Sydney, was educated at the University of Sydney and has taught creative writing at the University of Technology, Sydney. Her poetry has appeared in numerous periodicals and anthologies and in five collections, *Little Hoodlum* (1975), *Bison* (1979), *The Night Parrot* (1984), *Driving Too Fast* (1989) and *Akhenaten* (1992). She has also written a novel for young adults, *Rookwood* (1991). Sensuous and sharply witty, Porter's finely honed lyrics are charged with an immediate rhythmic energy and strikingly original imagery. The *Bison* collection draws on Porter's interest in music, painting, sculpture, and the figures of myth and legend. The poems of *The Night Parrot* circle around the description of the rare bird in the *Reader's Digest Complete Book of Australian Birds* ('Some naturalists believe it to be extinct, but there is evidence to suggest that a few individuals may survive in the spinifex country of the interior') to create an original companion or occasional adversary and spokescreature of the libido. *Driving Too Fast* moves from objective presentations of Carmen and Don Jose, Truganini, the Antarctic explorers Oates and Wilson, and British twins who chose to speak to no one but each other and

are now incarcerated separately in a psychiatric hospital, to personal erotic poems of electric intensity: 'Our love stabs so deep/ I'm amazed the cuts/ can't fountain a power/ to fight death/ to the death.' Akhenaten, king of Egypt from 1378 BC to 1362 BC, is the subject of the collection of that title, which imagines the extraordinary/ordinary experiences of a man who attempted to eradicate all the old gods and replace them with one, Aten, the sun. The volume includes his perception of Nefertiti, his cousin and wife, who loves, despairs and hates. *Rookwood* is a suspenseful, bizarre story of a young girl's probing of the past and her discovery of family secrets.

PORTER, Hal (1911–84), the eldest of six children, was born in Melbourne, and educated mainly at Bairnsdale in Gippsland, where his family moved when he was 6. He began writing early and had a number of short stories and poems published in school magazines. After leaving school he worked briefly as a cub reporter on the *Bairnsdale Advertiser* but then turned to schoolteaching, living in Williamstown 1927–37. In 1929 the death of his mother, who is lovingly recalled in the first volume of his autobiography, *The Watcher on the Cast-Iron Balcony* (q.v. 1963), was a severe blow. Although he was writing steadily in the 1930s and 1940s, he published little. He married in 1939 and in the same year suffered a severe traffic accident which kept him in hospital for twelve months and prevented him, to his regret, from taking part in the Second World War. Divorced in 1943, he never remarried. He spent the rest of the war in Adelaide, where he taught at private schools, and resumed his writing. In 1942 fourteen of his stories were published in a limited edition, titled *Short Stories*. After the war Porter had numerous occupations, including cook, actor, hotel manager, hospital orderly, theatrical producer, schoolteacher and librarian. He was attached as a teacher to the Occupation Forces in Japan 1949–50, an experience which proved seminal; his last appointment was as a librarian at Bairnsdale and Shepparton, 1953–61, after which he became a full-time writer. By that time he had published two novels and a collection of poetry, as well as numerous uncollected short stories, but his reputation was not firmly established until the mid-1960s. He won most major literary awards in Australia, some of them more than once. In 1967 he received, with Randolph Stow, the Britannica-Australia Award; in 1982 he was made AM. An intimately revealing biography by Mary Lord was published in 1993.

A prolific and versatile writer, Porter published three novels, *A Handful of Pennies* (1958), *The Tilted Cross* (q.v., 1961) and *The Right Thing* (1971); three collections of poetry, *The Hexagon* (1956), *Elijah's Ravens* (1968) and *In an Australian Country Graveyard* (1974), which includes his own drawings; seven collections of short fiction, *Short Stories* (1942), *A Bachelor's Children* (1962), *The Cats of Venice* (1965), *Mr. Butterfry and Other Tales of New Japan* (1970), *Selected Stories* (1971), *Fredo Fuss Love Life* (1974) and *The Clairvoyant Goat* (1981); three autobiographical works, *The Watcher on the Cast-Iron Balcony* (1963), *The Paper Chase* (1966) and *The Extra* (1975); and three plays, *The Tower* in *Three Australian Plays* (1963), *The Professor* (1966) and *Eden House* (1969). Another play, 'Parker', was produced 1972. He also wrote an account of modern Japanese life and culture, *The Actors* (1968), and a history of his home town, *Bairnsdale: Portrait of an Australian Country Town* (1977), both of which are illustrated by his own drawings, the latter extensively; and a book of theatrical biography, *Stars of Australian Stage and Screen* (1965). In addition, he wrote numerous magazine articles and some uncollected short stories and poems, and edited two collections of short stories, *Coast to Coast* (1962) and *It Could Be You* (1972), and one of poetry, *Australian Poetry* (1957). *Hal Porter* (1980), edited by Mary Lord, is an extensive selection of his writing; updated in 1989 in UQP's Australian Authors series, it makes available a revised edition of *A Handful of Pennies* and additional commentary on Porter. Another collection of his stories, *Selected Stories* (1991), is introduced by Fay Zwicky. Giovanna Capone has written a study of his fiction, *Incandescent Verities* (1990).

The most immediately striking aspect of Porter's short fiction is his style, which is markedly different from that of earlier Australian short-story writers. A self-conscious stylist, he adopted an intricate, densely woven prose that is studiedly extravagant, crammed with spectacular and often idiosyncratic images. Exuberantly witty but controlled and precise in its effects, his style is not just concerned with verbal display but is a conscious attempt to capture the complex texture of experience. Porter once said that his main aim was 'to write with many-planed clarity, to achieve an incandescence', and described himself as constantly 'burnishing' and 'pruning' his prose. Although he was occasionally accused of excessive decoration and inappropriate 'baroque' effects, and an obsessive interest in the grotesque, the violent and the melodramatic, he steadily won more sympathetic appreciations. His short stories have a variety of settings ranging from Earl's Court, London, to a typical Australian country town, to Venice and to Japan, but they are essentially those of a regional writer, interested in the actuality of Australian life, past and present. This interest is apparent in the thirty stories of *A Bachelor's Children*, where Porter's remarkable ability to evoke atmosphere and to re-create time and place in full solidity of detail has wide scope. Many of his stories are nostalgic in that they deal with the loss of innocence, the death of illusion or past happiness, and the destruction of love. Stories such as 'At Aunt Sophia's', 'Miss Rodda' and 'The Cuckoo' deal with varieties of violent initiation from the safe familiarity of childhood into the unpredictable realities of the adult world; others such as 'Fiend and Friend', 'Uncle Foss and Big Bogga' and 'Country Town' explore the changed quality of the past from the perspective of the present. Violent events, suicides, deaths, disfigurements and monstrosities are common to many, although their plots are less memorable than the authentic evocation of character, situation and place. Porter's gift for pungent satire is more noticeable in *The Cats of Venice* collection, in such stories as 'Vulgar's the Word' and 'Party

Forty-Two and Mrs. Brewer'; in others, such as 'Great Aunt Fanny's Picnic', 'Say to Me Ronald!' (q.v.) and 'The Cats of Venice', satire fades imperceptibly into social commentary. Others, such as 'Francis Silver' or 'Gretel' (q.v.), return to the familiar themes of lost innocence and the changed past. The seven stories in *Mr. Butterfry and Other Tales of New Japan* are extended character studies, centring on aspects of cultural opposition and based, like *The Actors*, on Porter's disillusionment with Japan after a return visit in 1967. The title story, 'Mr. Butterfry' (q.v.), is archetypal in its finely modulated effects and cumulative impact. The nine stories of the *Fredo Fuss Love Life* collection are similarly extended accounts of past incidents and diverse personalities; deceptively artless, they are virtuoso displays of his wide range of effects. Throughout Porter's short fiction the pressure of personally remembered experience can be felt, reinforced by his frequent use of an older, semi-autobiographical narrator, and by numerous similarities between characters and incidents in the short stories and his autobiographies.

Porter's novels have had a less sympathetic reception. *A Handful of Pennies*, which is set in post-war Japan and deals, often satirically, with tragi-comic aspects of East–West opposition, is an episodic work with a heavily encrusted style. *The Tilted Cross*, however, is more successfully integrated; set in colonial Hobart Town, it is a concentrated and compelling re-creation of a society that is fundamentally anti-Christian. *The Right Thing*, located in contemporary Australia, explores the power of a calcified social code; schematic and didactic, it has brilliant moments and some well-realised characters, but is finally more memorable for its parts than as a whole.

But Porter is best known for his three autobiographies, especially *The Watcher on the Cast-Iron Balcony*. A work of sustained imaginative power, it is a remarkably vivid re-creation of childhood and youthful experience that fully extends Porter's ability to present the past as an immediate, almost tangible, present. Particularly striking are his acute awareness of the effects of time and the unique phenomenon of memory, and his frank, retrospective self-analysis; the latter is made more compelling by the constant impression of an older narrator who, from his experienced perspective, watches the child who is also a watcher, an analyst both of the inner self and of the external changes in his widening world. *The Watcher* takes Porter to the age of 18 and the death of his mother; *The Paper Chase* covers the period between 1929 and 1949. More lighthearted in mood, less nostalgic and structurally coherent, and less of an immediate social record, its main theme concerns the narrator's growing awareness of schism between the needs of the creative artist and of the man. *The Extra*, which takes Porter to the 1970s, takes its title from one of his poems and emphasises his stance as observer rather than as participant. Concerned more with events and people than with the self, this volume contains numerous portraits of Australian writers.

Porter regarded his plays less seriously than his other work, and both *The Tower* and *Eden House* are frank entertainments; the former is a satirical melodrama set in colonial Hobart Town and the latter, set in contemporary Melbourne, is a satirical family comedy. Although both have two-dimensional characters and a stylised action, they are sustained by Porter's practical knowledge of stagecraft. *The Tower* was first produced in 1964, *Eden House* in 1969, on television in 1970, and as a stage play in London with the title *Home on the Pig's Back* in 1972. *The Professor*, which turns once again to the gulf between occidental and oriental culture, is a far more serious work; subtle and perceptive, it is a compelling study of love and lust and the degrees between them. It was first produced, with the title *Toda-San*, in Adelaide in 1965 and in London in 1966.

Porter's verse is both less abundant and less original than his prose work. Framed in traditional forms, his poems dwell in a brief way on many of the same general themes as his fiction: the passage of time, the fact of death, the anguish of disillusionment and the paradoxes of personality.

PORTER, Peter (1929–), born Brisbane, educated as a boarder at Church of England Grammar School and then Toowoomba Grammar school, worked in 1947–48 as a cadet journalist for the *Courier-Mail*. After a short time in business in 1951, and always disquieted about Australia, he left for England where, apart from a brief period in 1954, he remained until 1974, when he returned at the invitation of the Adelaide Festival for a longer stay. In England he developed connections with many other young poets, notably with the writers known as The Group. Since 1974 he has visited Australia much more frequently, but he still makes his home in central London. He has worked as a bookseller, journalist, clerk and advertising copywriter. Since 1968 he has lived as a full-time freelance writer, apart from producing poetry, providing contributions and reviews for journals such as *New Statesman*, *London Magazine*, the *Observer*, *Times Literary Supplement*, *Encounter*, and the *New Review*, and from the late 1980s *Scripsi*, *Overland* and *Westerly*. He has broadcast regularly for the BBC, has been a judge for numerous literary prizes, and has had appointments as writer-in-residence in universities and academies in the UK and Australia. Porter is the author of thirteen major volumes of verse, as well as a collected and a selected volume, a number of smaller volumes of verse and libretti, four volumes of illustrations and poems made in collaboration with Arthur Boyd, and a number of unpublished radio scripts broadcast by the BBC. He is now widely considered as one of the finest poets writing in English of the late twentieth century; he has been awarded a number of honorary D.Litts, the Duff Cooper Memorial Prize (1983), The Whitbread Prize for Poetry (1988), and the Gold Medal of the Australian Literature Society (1990).

His early poetry, *Once Bitten, Twice Bitten* (1961), *Poems Ancient and Modern* (1964) and A. Alvarez's selection for *Penguin Modern Poets 2* (1962) displays an ironic wit tinged with melancholy, formal structural control, wide variety of subject matter, skilful use of aphorisms, and the strong influence of several earlier writers, chiefly Auden. Such poems as 'Story from a Time of Disturbance' and 'An Anthropologist's Confession' with their acute verbal play and lurid, even scabrous, details, highlight a variety of social follies with an Auden-like control and pleasure in detailed satire. 'Your Attention Please', 'Soliloquy at Potsdam' and 'The Frankenstein Report' among other early works reveal the influence of Browning's monologues. In this early verse too is the first fruit of his experiences of being an outsider in the English scene. In 'Beast and Beauty' and 'Made in Heaven' the persona of the self-deprecating outsider scathingly attacking English folly comes close at times to self-pity and envy. This edgy tonality marks much of Porter's early and middle works and may have contributed to the difficulty of empathy which some early and partly critical reviews express. It may also have contributed to the paradoxical situation that for some critics, in particular Australians, Porter's verse was too English, while for others it was not English enough. As such his early work was mostly neglected in his homeland, and treated with respectful if somewhat 'outsider' interest in the UK. Already notable in the early volumes, all of Porter's verse is full of dense cultural allusions, a focus which only widens as his knowledge of Europe is enhanced by time and modified by an increasing though often diffidently amused awareness of modern popular culture, mostly from the USA.

In some early work the affirmation of human capacity afforded by art, its ability to balance modern life's artlessness, in poems such as 'John Marston Advises Anger' or 'Homage to Gaetano Donizetti', is countered by nagging doubts about the fictional deferral of real experience (a theme of great centrality in later volumes) in 'What a Lying Lot the Writers Are'. At one level the sheer enjoyment of ideas, irony and paradox pervades Porter's early poetry, buoying it and demonstrating art's ability to make palatable the essential difficulty and hopelessness of life; at another it is the very art itself, the language which distances the poet from the experience. None of this is handled in straightforward language. Porter's intellect is reflected in his verse, difficult, dense but highly rewarding.

In this early verse the ambivalent adoption of European civilisation counters an uneasy, often mistrustful, attitude to Australia. Porter had expressed (*Times Literary Supplement*, 1971) his self-exile in part as his own version of the cringe, as an aversion to Australian bluntness and physicality, and to its lack of sophistication in response to complexity in life and art; this attitude is reflected in such poems as 'Sydney Cove, 1788' from *Poems Ancient and Modern* and 'The Recipe' from his third volume, *A Porter Folio* (1969). Other poems, which recall a bitter-sweet boyhood in Brisbane and Queensland, 'A Christmas Recalled' and 'Two Merits of Sunshine', are melancholy rather than antagonistic. Others take up family history, presenting it as a means of discussing traditions of Australian culture. Notable here is 'Forefathers' View of Failure' from *Once Bitten*, which delves into a tradition of country town poems taken up with greater scope by Les Murray and Geoff Page.

Two small volumes, *Words without Music* (1968) and *Solemn Adultery at Breakfast Creek: An Australian Ballad* (1968), the latter a collaboration with musician Michael Jessett, were followed by *A Porter Folio* (1969) and *The Last of England* (1970), which consolidated his reputation as a difficult but valuable poet. These volumes continue his use of witty personae ('The Return of Inspector Christopher Smart', 'A Consumer's Report'), widen the range of formal experiments ('The Sanitized Sonnets', 'The Widow's Story') and develop a more personal voice which, though still involved with complex analysis of art confronting experience, often laments the poet's inability to feel except through the mediation of art.

Two volumes of translations, *Epigrams by Martial* (1971), and *After Martial* (1972), cover a wide range of topics together with an increasing confidence and maturity; both are evident in one of his finest volumes, *Preaching to the Converted* (1972). 'La Déploration sur la Mort D'Igor Stravinsky', 'Fossil Gathering', 'May 1945', and several other poems continue the exploration of aesthetic immortality opposing physical death, each poem twisting the focus of enquiry as Porter's discrimination of all gradations of meaning becomes a moral pursuit, a way of living in and through the world of ideas.

A small collection, *A Share of the Market* (1973), and two collaborations with Arthur Boyd, *Jonah* (1973) and *The Lady and the Unicorn* (1975), precede his seventh major volume, *Living in a Calm Country* (1975); all confirm the growing trend of urbane complexity in his work. Not regarded as one of his finest books, *Living in a Calm Country* contains, nonetheless, a number of significant poems, two of which have become central to understanding Porter's evolution. The theme of increasing age, as it is linked to both an increased understanding of life and art, and as it points to mortality and loss, has always featured in Porter's verse. In 'The Story of My Conversion' he laments the condition of the poet/intellectual, having been converted by inclination and age to the seriousness and difficulty of the life of ideas. Moving into the realm of the over-forties, which he dubs 'the new land of disappointment', Porter looked forward even in his own forties towards death as the only certainty, and to the failure of a life of the mind to learn, to accept, simplicity. Another poem of major importance, 'On First Looking into Chapman's *Hesiod*' (q.v.), refracts that situation through Porter's differences with Australia, at once the lost land of simplicity, and a satirised Boeotian land of inadequacy.

Another small volume, *Les Très Riches Heures* (1978), preceded the next and, of the middle work, the best single volume of his verse, *The Cost of Seriousness* (1978). This volume was universally praised by critics for its display of a new maturity, especially in its approach to the darker and tragic sides of love, an area which Porter's perceived detachment and earlier (claimed) lack of experience had denied him. That ironic lack of experience was just one of the profoundly handled subjects in the volume, the central poems of which find a tragic expression for the untimely death of the poet's first wife in 1974. In *The Cost of Seriousness* the sufficiency of art's, of language's, consolation in the face of deeply felt grief is subjected to rigorous inspection; it is often found to be unable to 'alter human circumstances or alleviate human distress'. In two of the finest poems in an outstanding volume, 'An Exequy' (q.v.) and 'The Delegate', refuge in art is found wanting as the poet seems the more isolated by its making. Paradoxically, this stance seemed to provide a moving consolation for many of the reviewers. It is probably still his best-known volume. From this volume on the relation of Porter's biography to his art was almost totally fused, and from it the readership detected even greater depths of emotion allied to the perception of a melancholic intellect; Porter's verbal skills, meanwhile, were rapidly gaining him recognition as one of the finest poets in the language.

With the next volume, *English Subtitles* (1981), Porter took up the theme of loss and artistic inadequacy, with 'Alcestis and the Poet' and 'Good Ghost, Gaunt Ghost', while the theme of ageing reappeared in a number of outstanding pieces: 'The Werther Level', 'What I Have Written I Have Written', 'The Unfortunate Isles', and 'At Lake Massaciuccoli'. In this volume seriousness as a mode of living is re-examined and found to provide at least the most effective means of sustaining life in the face of a world of superficial values. Against the specious life of late twentieth-century culture Porter poses the value of serious art and the moral value of a satirical eye and ear of the poet always ready to point at folly, as he does in the significant final poem of the volume, 'Landscape with Orpheus'.

In 1983 his *Collected Poems* was awarded the Duff Cooper Memorial Prize and he returned to Australia as writer-in-residence for the University of Melbourne. The *Collected* revived interest in the early satirical and formally innovative Porter and reinforced the general perception of him as more than a mere skilled aphorist. The next volume, *Fast Forward* (1984), whose title indicates Porter's increasing focus on the ironies of modern popular culture, demonstrates a refreshing new series of Porter voices, reflecting the effects of new influences, including Ashbery, Stevens and a few other trans-Atlantic poets as well as Gray and Murray among many Australians. Another of the Porter-Boyd collaborative volumes, *Narcissus* (1984) also came out in 1984.

Nineteen eighty-seven saw another residency, this time at the University of WA, and the volume *The Automatic Oracle*, which was awarded the Whitbread Prize for Poetry in 1988 and received highly favourable reviews. Porter was now widely known in Australia, and in parallel his verse contained a larger proportion of material rehabilitating his childhood in newer and often nostalgic lights. But the linguistic agility and philosophic eye were as vigorous as ever. His satirical eye was more definitely turning to popular culture and the political state of Thatcherite Britain and its parallels in Reagan's USA. In this volume these matters are controlled by the metaphor of the title. The title poem 'The Automatic Oracle' sees the oracle as both the language of the poet and his task as a priestly messenger warning of the ills of political expediency. As always Porter's emphasis in this volume falls on his need to preserve the values and responsibilities inherent in words.

These themes are evident also in the next two volumes, *Possible Worlds* (1989) and *The Chair of Babel* (1992). In 1988 he produced *Mars*, another collaboration with Boyd, and in between the solo volumes published *A Porter Selected* (1989). Nineteen eighty-nine was Porter's sixtieth year and his interest in age and ageing provided a series of occasions to muse on the value of verse in the face of mortality, history and memory, in poems such as 'The Child at Sixty' from *Babel* and 'Night Watch' and 'They Come Back More' from *Possible Worlds*. Many of the poems in the first volume present a harder-edged dystopian view of England than earlier views. 'An Ingrate's England' and the last poem of the volume, 'The New Mandeville', are typical if significant examples and present almost Swiftian images of the old world. In this and his last volume, *The Chair of Babel*, Porter reassesses the differences between the real and the mental geographies of his perceptions of the old world and of Australia as two among many 'possible worlds'. The melancholic certainty lodged in the earlier verse in the old world seems less secure in these later volumes, while the assertion that art is the best weapon available is strongly held and argued, as it has been from the middle work of the late 1970s and early 1980s. To that end Porter is fascinated by, but resistant to, the linguistic jargon of academic, or political power which he aphorises as 'cultspeak' in 'The Chair of Babel'. Against this the poet may be reduced to the seemingly lowly task of explication, as in 'The Village Explainer' or 'His Body to Blaise Pascal'; or of becoming the 'Cassandra of the market-place', as Porter styles one of his 'babbling' voices, although these become the callings of essential salvation, the means of surviving the specious life of the next century.

Nineteen ninety also saw the award of the Gold Medal of the Australian Literature Society and a number of other markers of recognition of his high status within his own country. By the end of the 1980s many articles and chapters had begun to pay him the attention he deserved. *Peter Porter: A Bibliography 1954–1986* (1990), compiled by John R. Kaiser, was followed by the critical biography by Bruce Bennett, *Spirit in Exile: Peter Porter and His Poetry* (1991) and the shorter critical analysis by Peter Steele, *Peter Porter* (1992) in the Australian Writers Series.

JEFF DOYLE

POTTINGER, Sir Frederick (1831–65), born India, was an Eton-educated guards officer who succeeded to a baronetcy in 1856 but dissipated his inheritance and was forced to emigrate to Australia. He was a mounted trooper in NSW until the discovery of his title led to rapid promotion. During 1862–65 he was an inspector of police in central-western NSW, a persistent, unlucky and sometimes incompetent hunter of such bushrangers as Ben Hall, Frank Gardiner and John Gilbert; like most of them he died young, when he accidentally shot himself jumping on board a coach. An earlier incident, in which his pistol failed to discharge and Gardiner escaped, was recorded in the anonymous ballad 'The Bloody Field of Wheogo', and may have given rise to the phrase 'even blind Freddie couldn't miss it'. As Sir Ferdinand Morringer, Pottinger is sympathetically portrayed in 'Rolf Boldrewood's' *Robbery Under Arms* (1888).

POUSSARD, Wendy (1943–), born Melbourne, has worked in many Third World countries. Director of the International Women's Development Agency, a community-based organisation which works with international women's groups, and previously a staff member of the Asian Bureau of Australia and editor of the *Asian Bureau Newsletter*, she has published several books dealing with life in the Third World and the experiences of Asian refugees, including *Today is a Real Day* (1981). Her verse, which reflects her commitment to the peace movement and familiarity with Asian poetry and politics, has appeared in numerous periodicals and anthologies and in two collections, *Outbreak of Peace. Poems and Notes from Pine Gap* (1984) and *Ground Truth* (1987).

POWELL, Craig (1940–), born Wollongong, graduated in medicine from the University of Sydney in 1964, later specialising in psychiatry. In 1972 he left Australia to spend ten years in Canada, where he trained in psychoanalysis. Returning to Australia permanently in 1982, he won the 1983 Mattara Spring Festival Poetry Prize for 'Five Pieces for a Homecoming'. In private practice in Sydney as a psychoanalyst, he also teaches at the NSW Institute of Psychiatry. A contributing editor of *Phoenix Review*, he edited *New Canadian Poetry* as no. 105 of *Poetry Australia*, 1986.

Widely represented in anthologies, journals and newspapers, Powell has published seven books of poetry, *A Different Kind of Breathing* (1966), *I Learn by Going* (1968), *A Country without Exiles* (1972), *Selected Poems* (1978), *Rehearsal for Dancers* (1978, published in Canada), *A Face in Your Hands* (1984, *Poetry Australia* no. 97), *The Ocean Remembers It Is Visible: Poems 1966–1989* (1989, in the *Quarterly Review of Literature*, Princeton, New Jersey) and *Minga Street: New and Selected Poems* (1993). Powell's prize-winning 'Five Pieces for a Homecoming' is included in *A Face in Your Hands*, and three of the 'Pieces' are also in *Minga Street*. The latter includes poems from most of the earlier volumes, with a group of new poems.

'Bringing the Hay in on Mike's Farm' (the third of 'Five Pieces') captures the essential quality of Powell, especially his combination of realism and mysticism. The bales of hay are like poetry itself, 'dark at the very centre'. The precise but imaginative observer is evident in his description of the Australian male, 'the men you work with bandy scabrous insults/ they are embarrassed by liking each other'. 'The Milk Run' (the fourth of 'Five Pieces') captures the madcap joy of youthful exploits such as riding on the milkman's and baker's cart, while reflecting ruefully on time's capacity to mar that young innocence with later tragedies. Many of Powell's poems reflect on events of his life ('The Horse Gang', 'Boomerang', 'The Snapshot Never Taken', 'Obituary', 'The International') and the people closest to him ('Death Poems for My Father', 'Katie at Twenty-One'). His association with fellow poets is manifest in his dedications – *A Face in Your Hands* to David Brooks, 'Spring Thaw' to Francis Webb ('I Loved Your Friendship'), 'The Child Explains' to Brooks and a poem titled 'For Bruce Beaver in Sydney'. Powell structures his poetry tightly and forcefully, preferring the broken-line schema, which often leads to staccato and emphatic effect. An early poem, 'Tree and River Bank', which concerns two of his family, the dead grandfather of 81 and the dead son of three weeks, won the Henry Lawson Festival Award in 1969. He also won the *Poetry Magazine* Award in 1964. He is a leading figure in the literature and psychiatry seminars held for a decade in Canberra at the Australian Defence Force Academy and latterly in Sydney.

POWELL, S.W. (Sydney Walter) (1878–1952), born England and educated partly in South Africa, served in the Boer War before coming to Australia in 1904. He joined the army and was drafted to Thursday Island, where he began writing for the *Bulletin* under the pseudonym 'Wyben'. He left Australia in 1908, spent some time in NZ and Tahiti but returned in time to enlist in the AIF. A participant in the landing at Gallipoli, he was wounded and invalided back to Sydney in 1916. His war poem 'Gallipoli' was awarded first prize in the John Masefield competition, 1932, and included in his collection, *One-Way Street and Other Poems* (1934). Powell subsequently traded in the Paumotu Archipelago before joining the Commonwealth public service; in 1925 he returned to England. Powell wrote seventeen romances and novels, 1920–37. Those which have Australian characters or associations include *The Maker of Pearls* (1920), *The Great Jade Seal* (1922), *The Game* (1925) and *Noah's Ark* (1935). He also published a volume of short stories, *Tales from Tahiti* (1928), and an account of his travels, *Adventures of a Wanderer* (1928).

POWER, Helen (1870–1957) was born at Campbell Town, Tasmania, the granddaughter of a surveyor-general of Tasmania. A distinguished member of Hobart's literary community, she contributed verse to the *Bulletin*, the *Australasian* and numerous poetry magazines, especially during the years 1912–32. Her work, which is represented in several anthologies, appeared in two collections, *Poems* (1934) and *A Lute with Three Strings* (1964), introduced by Clive Sansom. Conventional and simple, Power's lyrics dwell on such themes as death, love, growing old, the loss of friends and the persistence of the past in the present.

Power Without Glory, a novel by Frank Hardy (q.v.), was first published in Melbourne in 1950 and led to his trial for criminal libel. After proceedings that lasted nine months and aroused keen public interest, Hardy was acquitted. He described the writing of the book and subsequent trial in *The Hard Way* (1961).

Power Without Glory has since been translated into several languages and was produced as a successful television serial by the ABC in 1976. Divided into three sections which span the years 1890–1950, the novel narrates the fortunes of its anti-hero, John West (q.v.).

Born into one of the poorest working-class families of Carringbush, Melbourne's inner suburb of Collingwood, West takes his first step on the road to wealth and power when he rigs a pigeon race, and quickly progresses to running an illegal and crooked totalisator disguised as a tea-shop. Accomplices in his rapid rise include his brother Joe and his cronies Sugar Renfrey, Barney Robinson, Piggy, Flash Alec, Cauliflower Dick and Mick O'Connell; some of these have been identified as contemporary Melbourne figures, as have other characters in the novel. West's older brother Arthur, who becomes a member of the West machine on his release from a long prison term for rape, is more of a liability that West doggedly endures for the sake of their mother. Apart from Sugar Renfrey, few of his early cronies survive to share his later life of respectability, and some, such as Barney Robinson, die violent deaths. Meanwhile West's relationship with David Garside, a brilliant lawyer, furthers his early career most effectively. By the time of the First World War, West has a reputation as a wealthy philanthropist, an important friend of the Roman Catholic Archbishop Daniel Malone (see Mannix, Daniel), and of others in high places, but his secret career is studded with infamous incidents. He is involved in three murders and in the attempted murder of a detective; he bribes police, magistrates and police witnesses; he attempts to bribe the judiciary; he strives, with only limited success, to manipulate politicians, in particular the idealistic Labor member Frank Ashton (Frank Anstey); and in all his gambling enterprises consistently cheats his customers. Inadequate in his personal relationships, West finds that his private life deteriorates as surely as his public one flourishes. His wife Nellie has a child in mid-life after a one-sided affair with a young labourer and subsequently lives a disabled, reclusive existence; his talented elder daughter Marjorie, alienated from him by her choice of a foreign husband, subsequently dies in a German concentration camp; his son John becomes an alcoholic and eventually commits suicide; his younger daughter Mary defiantly leads her own life as a member of the Communist Party, then leaves Australia and dies before West's longed-for reconciliation can take place. Public affairs also soon pass beyond West's influence and he comes to be valued only as a convenient source of funds for the projects of others. At the end of the novel West faces death, an embittered, lonely and frustrated old man, an unconscious victim of the cash nexus. The novel is overcrowded and untidy, but is a compelling study of one man's single-minded pursuit of powerful forces which he fails to understand and which finally overtake him, as well as a vivid representation of Melbourne life, especially before the First World War.

POWERS, John (1935–   ), born Melbourne, spent his early years as a jackeroo and labourer, travelling around Australia, and has since worked as a freelance journalist, teacher and public servant. His one-act play 'The Hot Centre of the World' (1971), subsequently produced as a film by Tim Burstall, won two film awards, and he has written two further full-length plays, *The Last of the Knucklemen* (1974) and 'Shindig' (1975). *The Last of the Knucklemen*, Powers's most popular play, focuses on the tense relationship between nine miners in a mining camp of north-western Australia and effectively displays his gifts for rumbustious action and an earthy vernacular. It was produced as a film in 1978. 'Shindig', set in the opal-mining town of Lightning Ridge, complicates a similar situation with the presence of numerous women. Powers has also written *The Coach* (1978), a study of the famous Melbourne footballer Ron Barassi, and *Australian Sports Heroes* (1982) and has edited, with Alan Mahar, *Prose Writing for Australians: an Anthology of Feature Articles and Short Stories* (1985).

POWNALL, Eve, see *The Oxford Companion to Australian Children's Literature* (1993), pp. 351–2.

POYITT, Gertrude ('Wolla Meranda') (1867–1950), born Sunny Corner, Victoria, trained as a teacher, which remained her profession before and after marrying George Nicol Williams in 1891; their son died soon after birth and Williams was killed in a mining accident in New Caledonia in 1904. A subsequent marriage to a Mr Yates ended after six months. Encouraged by Julien de Sanary, a Frenchman from New Caledonia who lived with her at Sunny Corner from 1920 until his death in 1929, and using the pseudonym 'Wolla Meranda', she published her first novel, *Poppies of the Night*, in a French translation in 1922 (*Pavots de la Nuit*); the English version was not published until 1930. Poyitt published at least two further novels, *Vila of the Isles* (1930) and *The Red River of Life* (1931). There is evidence that she wrote several more which she published at her own expense although records have now been lost; they include *The Summer Seas*, *In Mulga Town*, *Big Jack of Mittewa Creek*, *The Perfidy of Jane Forster*, and *Gold Dust of Mittewa Creek*. A feminist who was critical of contemporary conventions governing marriage and the education of girls and a staunch conservationist and pacifist, Poyitt acquired the reputation of a witch in Sunny Corner, exacerbated by her articles on the occult published in the *Bookfellow* in 1920–21. This interest also informed the book *Light and Outer Darkness* (1935) and two further lost books, *The World Tongue* and *What is Truth*. Poyitt, who was herself a poet, also edited a volume of the poetry of de Sanary in 1931.

PRAED, Rosa (1851–1935), born in Bromelton, near Beaudesert, Queensland, was the daughter of Thomas Murray-Prior, a pastoralist and later a public servant and politician. Brought up on stations in the Burnett River district, which Murray-Prior left in 1858 after the Hornet Bank massacre, and at Maroon, near Bromelton, she also experienced political and social life in Brisbane before her marriage in 1872 to Arthur Campbell Praed. They lived at Praed's station at Port Curtis, near Gladstone, for three years; the isolation and appalling conditions are recalled in Rosa's first novel, *An Australian Heroine* (1880), in *Sister Sorrow* (1916), and particularly in the ironically titled *The Romance of a Station* (1889). In 1875 they sold up and settled in England where, as Mrs Campbell Praed, Rosa established herself as a popular novelist and dramatist; she revisited Australia 1894–95 and although she continued to live in England, maintained contact with relations and friends and frequently drew on her Australian experiences in her fiction. Her play *Ariane*, adapted from the novel *The Bond of Wedlock* (1887), was a controversial production in 1888 in its portrayal of the limitations of marriage, but was a commercial success. Among her acquaintances were Oscar Wilde, who is portrayed in *Affinities* (1885); the politician Justin McCarthy, with whom she collaborated on three novels and whose letters she edited and amplified as *Our Book of Memories* (1912); and J.B. O'Reilly, whom she met on a visit to America and who was the model for the politician bushranger Morres Blake in *Outlaw and Lawmaker* (1893). Other Australian figures to appear in her work are James Tyson in *Mrs Tregaskiss* (1895) and Sir George Bowen in *Nùlma* (1897). Of Praed's forty-odd works of fiction, almost half have Australian settings or associations; as well as *An Australian Heroine, The Romance of a Station* and *Outlaw and Lawmaker*, they include *Policy and Passion* (q.v., 1881), *The Head Station* (1885), *Miss Jacobsen's Chance* (1886), *Mrs. Tregaskiss* (1895), *Nùlma* (1897), *Dwellers by the River* (1902), *Fugitive Anne* (1903), *The Ghost* (1903), *The Maid of the River* (1905), *The Lost Earl of Ellan* (1906), *The Luck of the Leura* (1907), *A Summer Wreath* (1909), *Opal Fire* (1910), *Lady Bridget in the Never-Never Land* (1915) and *Sister Sorrow* (1916). Her other works include contributions to the Anglo-Australian anthologies by Arthur Patchett Martin and others; reminiscences of her Australian experiences, *My Australian Girlhood* (1902), in which J. Brunton Stephens is portrayed, and *Australian Life: Black and White* (1885); and a number of novels, particularly from *As a Watch in the Night* (1900) onwards, which reflect her interest in spiritualism and the occult. Among other beliefs she embraced astral bodies, telepathic communication and reincarnation; after separating from her husband she lived with Nancy Harward, 1899–1927, and believed Nancy to be the reincarnation of a Roman slave girl. Praed's story of this, *Nyria*, caused something of a sensation when published in 1904, and was succeeded by *Soul of Nyria* (1931) after Nancy's death. Praed also believed that her family tragedies were a consequence of her own past as a priestess in classical times. Her daughter, born deaf, died in a mental asylum, and of her three sons, one died in a car accident, one was gored to death by a rhinoceros, and the third committed suicide. Praed's philosophical interests and her relationship with Nancy Harward are discussed in Colin Roderick's *In Mortal Bondage: The Strange Life of Rosa Praed* (1948). Three of her novels, *The Bond of Wedlock, Outlaw and Lawmaker* and *Lady Bridget in the Never-Never Land*, were republished in 1987, 1988 and 1987 respectively, and Chris Tiffin has published a bibliography of her writing (1989).

Praed has often been bracketed with Ada Cambridge and Jessie Couvreur (qq.v.), e.g. in Raymond Beilby and Cecil Hadgraft's monograph on the three writers (1979), and has been categorised as a writer of women's formula romance fiction who succumbed to the cultural cringe (q.v.) both in writing of colonial life for a 'Home' market and in her admiration of English breeding. Yet, despite the exotic set pieces in some of her novels, the melodramatic resolutions of some of her plots, and her observation of the crudities of colonial society, she was responsive to her Australian experience, even to the mystery and power of the bush, notwithstanding its harshness. Several of her novels apart from *An Australian Heroine* and *The Romance of a Station* are informed by her knowledge, and that of her family, of pastoral and political life in Queensland, designated in her fiction as Leichardt's (*sic*) Land: her memories of Naraigin station in the Burnett district are drawn on in *Mrs. Tregaskiss*, and of Maroon in *Policy and Passion, The Head Station* and *Outlaw and Lawmaker; Policy and Passion, Nùlma* and *Miss Jacobsen's Chance* reflect her acute awareness of colonial politics in the years after Queensland's separation from NSW; and *The Lost Earl of Ellan* and *Lady Bridget of the Never-Never Land* use the experiences of her brother and sister elsewhere in Queensland. Although many of Praed's heroines are victims of 'Anglomania', and seem to prefer the English gentleman to the Australian suitor who characteristically completes the love triangle, that preference often ends in the kind of disillusionment that Honoria Longleat experiences in her relationship with Hardress Barrington in *Policy and Passion*, generally believed to be her best work. Australian men, despite their subjugation of colonial women, are admired for their bluff honesty, endurance and steadfastness. The limitations of marriage and the idealisations of love can be set against the failure of her own marriage and are prominent themes throughout her work.

Pram Factory, see **Australian Performing Group**

PRATT, Ambrose (1874–1944), born Forbes, NSW, was for some time a solicitor, but turned to journalism and was on the staff of the *Age* from 1905 and the *Industrial Australian and Mining Standard* 1918–27. His thirty novels, which deal with such facets of Australian life as the convict and bushranger eras and the mining and larrikin periods, include *The Great 'Push' Experiment* (1902), a story of the larrikin gangs; *Three Years with Thunderbolt* (1905), the narrative of William Monckton, who accompanied Thunderbolt; *The Remittance Man* (1907); *The Outlaws of Weddin Range* (1911), on the Ben Hall gang; *The Big Five* (1911); *Her Assigned Husband* (1916); and *Lift up Your Eyes* (1935). Pratt was a sinophile, who opposed the White Australia policy and attempted in his play 'Point in Time', performed by the Gregan McMahon Players in 1941, to educate Australian audiences in Chinese thought. Of his many other publications, several with

Australian interest include *David Syme: The Father of Protection in Australia* (1908) and *The Handbook of Australia's Industries* (1934). His commissioned biography of Sidney Myer was eventually published in 1978.

PREE, Barry, see *Mystery of a Hansom Cab, The*

PRICE, Evadne ('Helen Zenna Smith') (1901–85), born at sea off the NSW coast to English parents, was educated in NSW and England. She worked briefly as an actor in London but turned to journalism, writing a column, 'As A Woman Sees It', for the *Sunday Chronicle*. She later worked for the *Sunday Graphic* and for the *Daily Sketch*, where she met her second husband, Kenneth Attiwill (q.v.). Her first husband was C.A. Fletcher. During the late 1920s Price established a reputation as a writer for children; her 'Jane Turpin' stories were serialised monthly in *Novel Magazine* and also apeared in book form 1928–47. The author of numerous books of popular fiction for adults, she also wrote radio and television scripts, as well as plays for the London stage, two of which were published, *The Phantom Light* (1949), which ran for two years, and *Once a Crook* (1943, co-authored with Kenneth Attiwill). A war correspondent for *People* in the 1940s, she claimed to have been the first woman journalist to enter Belsen, where she encountered the war criminal Irma Groetz; she subsequently interviewed Goering and covered the Nuremberg trials.

Her pseudonym, 'Helen Zenna Smith', was adopted for her best-selling novel *Not So Quiet . . . Stepdaughters of War* (1930). The novel's genesis was complex. Approached by A.E. Marriott to write a spoof of E.M. Remarque's *All Quiet on the Western Front* (1929) ('All Quaint on the Western Front' by 'Erica Remarks'), Price offered instead to write a realistic account of a woman's experience of war. She made contact with Winifred Young, an ambulance driver at the French front in the First World War, and made use of her diary for first-hand descriptions of destruction and atrocities. An immediate best-seller, although many were too shocked by its contents to accept their truth, the novel was serialised in *People* and in *Collier's Weekly* (USA). In France *Not So Quiet* was awarded the Prix Severigne as 'the novel most calculated to promote international peace'. Four other 'Helen Zenna Smith' novels followed, *Women of the Aftermath* (1931), *Shadow Women* (1932), *Luxury Ladies* (1933) and *They Lived With Me* (1934). *Not So Quiet* was republished by Virago in 1988 with an introduction by Barbara Hardy. Price also achieved celebrity as an astrologer for *She* magazine and for television, and, in Australia, for *Vogue*, compiling astrological pieces for her last book, *She Stargazes* (1965). After living in Sussex for some years, she returned to Australia in 1976 and died in Sydney.

PRICE, George Frederick, see **DARRELL, George**

PRICE, John (1808–57), born Cornwall, England, was a notorious commandant of the Norfolk Island penal settlement in the 1840s and the model for Maurice Frere in Marcus Clarke's *His Natural Life* (1874). The links between Frere and Price are discussed in Sir John Vincent Barry's *The Life and Death of John Price* (1964). Price also appears in 'Price Warung's' story 'John Price's Bar of Steel'.

PRICHARD, Katharine Susannah (1883–1969), born Levuka, Fiji, was the daughter of Tom Prichard, editor of the *Fiji Times*. Her childhood, re-created in her children's book *The Wild Oats of Han* (1928), was spent initially in Tasmania, and then in Melbourne. On matriculating from South Melbourne College, where she came under the influence of poet and teacher J.B. O'Hara, she spent two years as a governess at Yarram in South Gippsland and then at Turella sheep station in the far west of NSW. Returning to Melbourne to teach, she attended night lectures in English literature under the auspices of Walter Murdoch.

In 1908 Prichard made her first trip to London as a freelance journalist for the Melbourne *Herald* and on her return accepted a position with the newspaper as social editor of the women's page for two years. In 1912 she again left for England to pursue her career as a writer. Her first novel, *The Pioneers* (1915), won the colonial section of the Hodder & Stoughton novel competition and was made into an Australian film in 1916 (and remade in 1926). Drawn from her memories of Gippsland, the novel was a romantic period tale of escaped convicts, cattle-duffing and people in the act of creating a new and better life. Although seen as a germinal work containing both stylistic and thematic aspects later to be developed by the author, *The Pioneers* has much in common, in terms of contrived plot and characterisation, with its successor, *Windlestraws* (1916), a melodramatic romance involving an impoverished Russian prince, a female dancer and the London theatrical scene; the latter was written before *The Pioneers*, but published after it.

In 1916 Prichard returned to Australia. She married Hugo Throssell (VC recipient) in 1919, went to live in WA and immersed herself in both politics and writing; the first, some critics say, to the detriment of the second. In 1920 she became a founding member of the Communist Party of Australia and served for a period on its central committee. She wrote some simple political pamphlets such as *The New Order* (1919), and later a book, *The Real Russia* (1934), which reported on her experiences and observations as a traveller in the Soviet Union the previous year. She founded, with Cecilia Shelley, the Unemployed Women and Girls' Association in Perth and, after the Labor Party's decision to exclude women from the movement against war and fascism, she established the Modern Women's Club in 1938. She was elected, in 1935, federal president of the Australian Writers' League (an organisation she had helped to establish the previous year) and three years later became a founding member of the WA branch of the FAW which later nominated her for a Nobel Prize.

Her initial attempt to embody political concepts in her novels came with the publication in 1921 of *Black Opal*, a study of the opal-mining community of Fallen Star Ridge which seeks to maintain the ethos of independent ownership of mines and to stave off the threat to its way of life from capitalism. Although her next novel, *Working Bullocks* (1926, republished 1991 in Angus & Robertson's Imprint Classics with an introduction by Ivor Indyk), stressed the political nature of work in the Karri timber industry of WA and the alienation of man's labour implicit in its title, its primary focus was far more aesthetic. Regarded as rich in literary merit, it sought to explore the elemental attraction existing between man and his environment through the central characters of Red Burke, as powerful as the bullock teams he drives, and Deb Colburn, the primitive child of nature. The more polished *Coonardoo* (q.v.), which shared the 1928 *Bulletin* novel prize and was praised as the first realistic and detailed portrayal of an Aborigine, and *Working Bullocks* are regarded as the basis for Katharine Susannah Prichard's literary reputation.

Her other novels include *Haxby's Circus* (1930), which traces the struggles of Gina Haxby, who is deformed as a result of a circus accident, and her counterpart, the hunchback clown Roca. Together Gina and Roca attempt to maintain both the circus and their self-respect. *Intimate Strangers* (1937) is a psychological study of the marital breakdown of Greg and Elodie Blackwood, with a not very credible reconciliation through their joint work for a new social order. The poorly constructed *Moon of Desire* (1941) is a flimsy and unbelievable adventure story transporting its protagonists from Broome to Singapore in search of a fabulous pearl. Her most contentious work is the WA goldfields trilogy, which was published separately as *The Roaring Nineties* (q.v., 1946), *Golden Miles* (q.v., 1948) and *Winged Seeds* (q.v., 1950). This trilogy, with its mass of historical detail, is a dynamic 'story of an industry' seen through the lives of the central heroine, Sally Gough, and the archetypal prospector, Dinny Quin. In *The Roaring Nineties*, Prichard traces the period of early pioneering and prospecting and the growth of companies; in *Golden Miles*, the impact of the First World War and conscription, and the industrial strife of the 1920s. In *Winged Seeds*, its name taken from the novel's last image of a Kalgoorluh nut breaking over the grave of an Aboriginal woman and symbolising the renewal of life and hope, she completes the trilogy through the Great Depression to 1946. On the one hand the trilogy has been criticised for its didacticism, its subordination of character to propaganda and its overwhelming historical documentation; on the other it has been praised for its political concerns by such people as Jack Lindsay in *Meanjin Quarterly* (1961) and Jack Beasley in *The Rage for Life* (1964). Her last novel, *Subtle Flame* (1967), was a manifestation of her increasing desire for world peace and centred on a middle-aged newspaper editor who suffers a personal and political crisis during the era of the Korean War which causes him to leave both family and job to crusade for peace and nuclear disarmament.

Numerous short stories of uneven quality have been collected and published in *Kiss on the Lips* (1932), *Potch and Colour* (1944), *N'Goola* (1959), *On Strenuous Wings* (edited by Joan Williams, 1965) and *Happiness* (1967). One story, 'The Grey Horse', which cleverly juxtaposes the virility of a stallion with the frustration of a farmer, won the 1924 *Art in Australia* Award and, with symbolic sketches like 'The Cow' and 'The Cooboo', has been a popular choice for anthologies. Prichard published two volumes of poetry, *Clovelly Verses* (1913) and *The Earth Lover* (1932). Her several plays include *Brumby Innes* (1940, which won the 1927 *Triad* Award for the best Australian three-act play) and *Bid Me to Love* (published posthumously in 1974).

Two critical books on her writing are Jack Beasley's *The Rage for Life: The Work of Katharine Susannah Prichard* (1964), reworked and extended as *A Gallop of Fire* (1993), and Henrietta Drake-Brockman's monograph *Katharine Susannah Prichard* (1967), while information on her life is to be found in her autobiography *Child of the Hurricane* (1963) and a biography by her son Ric Throssell (q.v.), *Wild Weeds and Wind Flowers* (1975). Throssell has also collected many of her articles and polemics in one volume, *Straight Left* (1982) and a selection of her stories in *Tribute* (1988). Her books have been translated into many languages and in 1983 *The Roaring Nineties*, previously out of print, was re-issued to commemorate the centenary of her birth. Some of her correspondence with Miles Franklin and other women writers is included in Carole Ferrier (ed.) *As Good as a Yarn with You* (1992). Richard Nile wrote *The Making of a Really Modern Witch: Katharine Susannah Prichard 1919–1969* (1990) and John Hay and Brenda Walker edited *Katharine Susannah Prichard Centenary Essays* (1984). The inaugural Katharine Susannah Prichard Annual Lecture was given by Veronica Brady in Perth in 1988.

SANDRA BURCHILL

PRINGLE, J.M.D. (John Martin Douglas) (1912–), born Scotland, was educated at Oxford and was on the editorial staff of the *Manchester Guardian* 1934–39, assistant editor 1944–48, special writer for the London *Times* 1948–52, and deputy editor of the *Observer* 1957–62. In 1952 he came to Australia, where he was editor of the *Sydney Morning Herald*, 1952–57, 1965–70, and managing editor of the *Canberra Times*, 1964–65. *Australian Accent* (1958), a frank discussion of Australian attitudes, politics, culture and social mores, is Pringle's best-known and most influential book. He has also written a collection of essays on aspects of Australian life, some of them literary, *On Second Thoughts* (1971); an account of Australian art, *Australian Painting Today* (1963); and reminiscences of his career in journalism, *Have Pen: Will Travel* (1973). He has made a selection of Ethel Anderson's stories, *The Best of Ethel Anderson* (1973), and written *The Last Shenachie* (1976), a biography of Angus John Macdonald (1900–75), oral historian of Scotland who lived in Australia for forty-seven years.

PRIOR, S.H. (Samuel Henry) (1869–1933), born Brighton, SA, was educated at Glenelg and Bendigo,

and at 21 became editor of the *Barrier Miner* in Broken Hill. He moved to the *Bulletin* in 1903, becoming associate editor in 1912 and editor 1915–33; his family held a controlling interest in the *Bulletin* 1927–60. Under Prior the *Bulletin* became less oriented towards the bush and more conservative, but continued to encourage Australian writers; novel-writing contests which he initiated in 1928 and 1929 drew a large response, including such entries as *A House Is Built* (1929), *Coonardoo* (1929) and *The Passage* (1930). The S.H. Prior Memorial Prize of £100 was instituted by the *Bulletin* after Prior's death, and was awarded 1935–46; winning entries later published include *Tiburon* (1935), *All That Swagger* (1936), *Joseph Furphy: The Legend of a Man and His Book* (1944) and *The Battlers* (1941).

Prism, the journal of the Poetry Society of Australia (q.v.), appeared in July 1954, edited by Peter Daventry, and was thereafter published, usually monthly, until it was succeeded in 1961 by *Poetry Magazine*. *The Poetry Society of Australia: First Anthology* (1956), edited by Wesley Milgate and Imogen Whyse in 1957, was a selection of verse from the pages of *Prism*.

PRITCHARD, Selwyn (Selwyn Pritchard Hughes) (1933–), born England and educated at Oxford University, lives in Tasmania, where he is a secondary school teacher. He has contributed verse to numerous periodicals in Australia, NZ, North America and UK and has published the collections *Homage to Colonel Rainborough* (1984), *Being Determined* (1990), *Stirring Stuff* (1991) and *Quack Quack Floreat* (1991).

Prizes, see **Literary Awards**

Prometheus, intended as the annual student magazine of the Canberra University College and subsequently of the ANU, has appeared irregularly since 1933. The magazine has attracted verse and literary articles from a range of contributors associated with the University, including T. Inglis Moore, L.H. Allen, A.D. Hope, R.F. Brissenden, Manning Clark, Alan Gould, Nick Jose, Mark O'Connor and David Campbell.

Prospect, a journal published by a group of Catholic laymen from the University of Melbourne, appeared quarterly 1958–64. The journal, which published literary articles, verse and book reviews, attracted a range of contributors including Vincent Buckley, A.D. Hope, Evan Jones, James McAuley, Francis Webb and Chris Wallace-Crabbe.

'PROUT, Denton', see **PHILLIPS, Charles Walter**

PROUT, J.S. (John Skinner) (1805–76), born Plymouth, England, came to Australia in 1840 and lectured on art in Sydney. An artist and lithographer, he organised in Hobart the first art exhibition held in Australia, and followed it with other successful exhibitions. He returned to England in 1848 but may have paid a subsequent visit to Australia. During his stay he published *Sydney Illustrated* (1842–44), with letterpress by John Rae, *Tasmania Illustrated* (1844–46) and *Views of Melbourne and Geelong* (1847). He also provided illustrations for the journal *Heads of the People*. After his return he published two popular works, *An Illustrated Handbook of the Voyage to Australia* (1852) and *A Magical Trip to the Gold Regions* (1853). His drawings were also used to illustrate E.C. Booth's *Australia* in 1876. A catalogue of the 1987 exhibition of Prout's work, *Skinner Prout in Australia* (1986), contains a biographical outline by Tony Brown and Hendrik Kolenberg.

Puberty Blues (1979) by Kathy Lette and Gabrielle Carey (qq.v.) is a mainly comic representation of 1970s surfie culture, as experienced by two 13-year-old 'surfie-chicks'. Set in Cronulla, Sydney, the novel reaches hilarious levels in the contrasts between the blindly materialist preoccupations of parents and other authority figures and the innovative strategies pursued by their offspring, bent on being 'cool'; 'cool' behaviour included sex, alcohol, going to the drive-in and the beach, and drug-taking. At the beach, the young male surfies are a dominant tribe, governed by a strict hierarchy and subject to complicated codes and taboos, a pattern of behaviour which includes the possessions they prize only second to their surfboards, their girlfriends; to graduate into the surfie gang a girl had to wear certain clothes, display a mild form of rebellion against authority and know all about sex: 'You had to be not too slack, but not too tight. Friendly but not forward. You had to wear just enough make-up but never overdo it. You had to be interested in surfing, but not interested enough to surf.' Sue and Debbie, the narrators of *Puberty Blues*, eventually tire of being on the margins of life and take to the surf themselves, an action which declares their rejection of a culture which stifles real relationships and induces such boredom that only drugs can relieve it. The book's epilogue, recounting the destinies of others in the group and the occasional glimpses of a sordid underworld which claims some less lucky girls, reveals the darker side of this adolescent subculture. *Puberty Blues* was produced as a film in 1983.

Public Lending Right, a federal government scheme which compensates authors and publishers for the multiple use of books in public lending libraries, was instituted in July 1975; the Literature Board and writers' organisations such as the ASA were instrumental in its implementation. Under the provisions of Public Lending Right, authors in 1984 were paid 66 cents ($1.07 in 1994) and publishers 16.5 cents (26.8 cents in 1994) for each estimated copy of a book held in public lending libraries in Australia, the amount of payment being calculated after annual surveys of library bookstocks. The scheme was administered by the Australia Council 1976–80, when it passed back to the federal government.

Publicist was a monthly founded and edited by William John Miles (q.v.) and conducted with the assistance of P.R. Stephensen (q.v.) from July 6 until

Stephensen was interned in March 1942. Miles died in January 1942, and Stephensen edited the last few issues of the journal. Apart from Miles and Stephensen, contributors to the *Publicist* included George Farwell, Xavier Herbert, Rex Ingamells, Alister Kershaw, John Manifold, Harley Matthews, Ian Mudie and C.W. Salier, although not all these writers were sympathetic to the chauvinist, isolationist, anti-Semitic, pro-Japanese political views increasingly espoused by the journal. The Publicist Publishing Company was also responsible for the publication of the first edition of Xavier Herbert's *Capricornia* (1938).

PULVERS, Roger (1944–   ), born New York into a Jewish-American family, studied political science, Polish and Russian at the universities of California, Harvard and Warsaw. He taught at Kyoto Sangyo University in Japan 1967–71, before moving in 1972 to Australia to teach Japanese at the ANU. In 1979–82 Pulvers was director and writer-in-residence at the Playbox Theatre Company and now lives in Japan. Some of his plays were performed by the Australian Theatre Workshop in Canberra, La Mama and the Playbox Theatre Company. They include 'Bones' (1973), 'The Fat Lady' (1973), 'The Senator from California' (1974), 'Ice' (1974), 'The Covenant of the Rainbow' (1974), 'Fair Go', later titled 'Joe' (1975), 'Drop Drill' (1976), *Yamashita* (1977, published in Japanese in 1970 and in English in 1981), 'Cedoona' (1978), 'Witold Gombrowicz in Buenos Aires' (1978), *Bertolt Brecht Leaves Los Angeles* (1979, published 1982), 'Australia Majestic' (1980), a radio play, 'Coma Berenices' (1980), *Dreamtime* (1985) and *News Unlimited!* (1986). He has also translated plays by European authors, some of which have been staged; has published two other plays, *The Perfect Crime of Mrs Garigari* (1970), and *General MacArthur in Australia* (1978); a book of short stories, *On the Edge of Kyoto* (1969); and a novel, *The Death of Urashima Taro* (1981). Pulvers's theatre, which is expressionistic, experimental and highly unconventional, notwithstanding traces of Japanese traditional drama, has occasionally been described as inaccessible to the general audience. His themes are shaped by his opposition to American policies and social mores and his admiration for Japanese culture; few of his plays deal with Australian subjects, although 'Australia Majestic' concerns Americans in Australia during the Second World War and his novel, a self-conscious anti-thriller, centres on the outbreak of Japanese POWs from a camp at Cowra in 1944.

Punch, see **Melbourne Punch**

PURNELL, Kathryn, born Vancouver, Canada, was educated there and later at the University of Melbourne. She married an Australian and has lived in various parts of the world. She has been a creative writing tutor and an active member of literary organisations such as the Society of Women Writers, and an editor in the *Luna* collective. Her published works include poetry, *Pandora* (1979), *Safari* (1979), *Trillium* (1983, with Audrey Longbottom and Susan McGowan),

Otway Country (1984) and *Magic Perhaps* (1987). She has edited several anthologies, including *A Spin of Pink Heath* (1980), *A Spin of Gold Wattle* (1982) for the Society of Woman Writers, and *Herb Spin* (1984). She has also edited the fiction anthologies *Remember* (1984), and *Journeys* (1986). Her strongly compassionate and sensitive poetry has won numerous awards, e.g. the Victorian Premier's Literary Award 1966, the Society of Women Writers' Award 1972, the International Poetry Society's UK Prize 1979 and the Charles Meeking Poetry Prize for Women 1979.

PUSELEY, Daniel ('Frank Foster') (1814–82), born Devon, England, was a commercial traveller and a hosier and silk merchant. He acquired a distinguished reputation as a public speaker on literary and political subjects. In 1854 he visited Australia, and after his return published a general description titled *The Rise and Progress of Australia, Tasmania, and New Zealand* (1857) under the pseudonym 'An Englishman'. He revisited Australia in 1857 before settling in England, where he devoted himself to literature and philanthropic works. Puseley published several novels under the pseudonym 'Frank Foster' 1872–76; he also published drama, poetry and essays on contemporary issues.

Push, The, see **Larrikin in Australian Literature**

PYBUS, Cassandra, born Snug, Tasmania, and educated at the University of Sydney, is a sixth-generation Tasmanian. Editor of the quarterly magazine *Island* (q.v.), she has also edited *The Rest of the World is Watching* (1990), a collection of essays on the environmental movement in Tasmania. She is the author of *Community of Thieves* (1991), a personal study of Aboriginal dispossession in Tasmania, which provides fresh insights into the personality and motives of George Augustus Robinson (q.v.), and *Gross Moral Turpitude* (1993), a revisionist account of a university scandal of the 1950s, the Orr case, which produced long-lasting bitter divisions.

PYKE, Lillian, see *The Oxford Companion to Australian Children's Literature* (1993), pp. 353–4.

Q

'Q', see **CLARKE, Marcus**

Quadrant, the magazine of the Australian Association for Cultural Freedom, an offshoot of the International Congress for Cultural Freedom set up in 1950 to counter what was seen as the threat of Communism to intellectual and cultural freedom throughout the world, commenced publication as a composite political, social and literary journal in 1956. Its foundation editor was James McAuley and while he was its sole editor (1956–63) it bore the McAuley stamp of conservatism and traditionalism in culture and literature. It changed from a quarterly to a bi-monthly in 1964 and was co-edited by McAuley and Donald Horne 1964–67, by McAuley and Peter Coleman (q.v.) 1967–75, and since 1975, when it became a monthly, by various editors, including Coleman, Elwyn Lynn, H.W. Arndt, Roger Sandall and Robert Manne. Partly through McAuley's influence and partly through the influence of its long-standing literary editor Vivian Smith, *Quadrant* has been especially notable for the high quality of its poetry and for some significant criticism. *Quadrant: Twenty Five Years*, edited by Peter Coleman, Lee Shrubb and Vivian Smith, an anthology from the journal's first quarter-century, was published in 1982.

Queensland Authors' and Artists' Association, see **Fellowship of Australian Writers**

Queenslander, a weekly newspaper published in Brisbane, was the companion of the *Brisbane Courier* and appeared 1866–1939. Edited first by Angus Mackay and in the 1870s by W.H. Traill, the newspaper numbered Alexander Boyd and Ernest Favenc among its contributors, serialising Boyd's *Old Colonials* 1875–76 and financing a Favenc expedition in 1878–79. As well as news summaries and items of topical interest, the *Queenslander* included short stories and verse. Mary Hannay Foott was its literary editor in the 1890s.

Quentin Massys is a didactic verse play about a fifteenth-century Dutch painter by Alfred Deakin (q.v.). It was written in his teens and published in 1875 though never produced. Although Deakin later burned all but a few copies, the play has survived and shows energy, vitality and mature perception.

QUICK, Sir John (1852–1932), born Cornwall, was brought to Australia in infancy and left school at 10 to work in an iron foundry. Later he worked as a journalist and in 1874 gained a scholarship to the University of Melbourne, where he studied law. He gained his doctorate in 1882. He was a member of the Victorian parliament 1880–89 and became a prominent figure in the Federation movement. He was a member for Bendigo for twelve years in the federal parliament, was chairman of the first Tariff Commission 1905–7 and postmaster-general 1909–10. He was knighted in 1901 for his outstanding contribution to Federation. After electoral defeat in 1913 he returned for a time to legal practice. He was deputy president of the Federal Arbitration Court 1922–30. Quick wrote several legal works and combined with Sir Robert Garran in *The Annotated Constitution of the Australian Commonwealth* (1901), which includes a valuable historical account of the Federation movement. He spent his last years working on a series of bibliographies of Australian writing, in co-operation with F.J. Broomfield, Firmin McKinnon, Bernard Cronin, E. Morris Miller and others. After his death Miller continued his work, which resulted in *Australian Literature from Its Beginnings to 1935* (q.v., 1940). L.E. Fredman edited *Sir John Quick's Notebook* (1965).

QUIN, Tarella (1877–1945), born Tarella station, near Wilcannia, NSW, also wrote under her married name, Daskein, and was one of Australia's most successful writers of fairy-stories for children. Humour, irony, a fluent, dramatic style and fantasy reminiscent of Lewis Carroll enliven her stories, several of which were illustrated by Ida Outhwaite. They include *Gum Tree Brownie* (1907, later enlarged with changed title), *Freckles* (1910), *Before the Lamps are Lit* (1911), *The Other Side of Nowhere* (1934) and *Chimney Town* (1934). She also wrote the novels for adults, *A Desert Rose* (1912), *Kerno* (1914) and *Paying Guests* (1917). Paul Depasquale has written a brief appreciation of her life and work (1981).

QUINLAN, Lucille Mary, see **War Literature**

QUINN, Patrick (1862–1926), born Sydney, was the brother of Roderic Quinn and father of Marjorie Quinn (1889–1972), who wrote poems and short stories. He was a member of the NSW parliament 1898–1904, was deputy commissioner of trade for NSW in San Francisco for six years, returned to Australia in 1917 and subsequently worked on the staff of the Sydney *Daily Telegraph*. He published verse and fiction in the *Bulletin*; a musical drama, *Captain Cook* (1891); a detective novel, *The Jewelled Belt* (1896); and a collection of short stories, *The Australian Storyteller for an Idle Afternoon* (n.d.). After his death some of his poems were collected and edited by Marjorie Quinn, titled *Selected Poems* (1970).

QUINN, Roderic (1867–1949) was born in Sydney of Irish parents who had come to Australia about 1853. He was educated in Sydney with his lifelong friends E.J. Brady and C.J. Brennan, studied law briefly, was a country schoolteacher, then returned to Sydney as a freelance journalist. His chief publications are the romantic novel *Mostyn Stayne* (1897) and three books of verse, *The Hidden Tide* (1899), *The Circling Hearths* (1901) and *Poems* (1920), his major volume. He also wrote short stories for the *Bulletin*. From the mid-1890s to the mid-1920s Quinn made a modest living from his poetry, which was greatly admired by his contemporaries. Although linked with Victor Daley (q.v.) as poets of the so-called Celtic Twilight, Quinn lacked Daley's easy, lyric artistry. He often attempted more, however, for in addition to capturing the spirit and atmosphere of the Australian outdoors he sought a hidden meaning beneath the externals of life and nature.

Quintus Servinton, a novel by Henry Savery (q.v.), was written in 1829 or 1830 in Hobart, where early in 1831, despite the 1830 date on the title page, it was published by Henry Melville. It is generally regarded as the first Australian novel by reason of its place and date of publication and its author's residence, although several earlier works of fiction contain Australian scenes and *Quintus Servinton* itself was printed expressly for sale in England, where the first and second of its three volumes are set, giving it status also as a regional English novel of manners. It may not, however, have been the first novel written in Australia, for Mary Leman Grimstone wrote most of *Woman's Love* (1832) while resident in Hobart in 1826–29. *Quintus Servinton* was published anonymously, but the identification of Savery as author is readily made possible by the close parallels between Savery's experiences and those of his protagonist and by the extensive use of the name Servinton, within the Savery family. The main difference between the experiences of Savery and those of Quintus Servinton is the devotion to Quintus of the idealised Emily, whose spiritual superiority to her husband has been seen by some critics as inaugurating a significant theme in Australian literature.

A moral tale with elements of the picaresque and the allegory, *Quintus Servinton* demonstrates the virtues of moderation, discipline, prudence and humility, the dangers of selfishness, ambition and wilfulness, and the need to recognise the ways of Providence as inscrutable but wise. The novel purports to be a fictionalised biography written by an unnamed author who meets the 60-year-old subject, Quintus, in the first chapter, when he is laid up at the Servinton home in Devonshire with an ankle dislocated in a walking accident. In the course of his convalescence he is given a manuscript which details the experiences of Quintus during the first forty years of his life. He secures permission to use the manuscript as the basis of a fictionalised biography, subsequently published in Hobart rather than in London because of the author's posting to Australia; the story of Quintus occupies all but the last few pages of the rest of the book. It begins in 1772 just before Quintus's birth, with a gypsy's prophecy made to his father that in the fourth decade of his life his fifth son would thrice be in danger of his life, would undergo great reverses of fortune, but would thereafter live happily and peacefully. Determined to strengthen his son's character in case the prophecy should come true, Servinton sends Quintus away to boarding school. He remains there for over five years, becoming captain of the school but exhibiting also some of the petulance and overweening self-confidence that are to bring about his downfall. Leaving school for a clerkship in London, Quintus has early success both in business and society, and has several flirtations before falling in love with the beautiful Emily Clifton, whom he courts and marries. Emily is a model of moral balance, virtue and loyalty against which the immature, erratic but basically decent Quintus is measured. After experiencing both the peaks and troughs of business life, the former the reward of his intelligence and acumen, the latter resulting sometimes from providential bad luck but more often from his dangerous self-confidence, Quintus arrives at his thirty-first year in partnership in business in the west of England. His downfall commences when, having extended the credit of his firm beyond its resources, he starts signing fictitious bills of exchange. Discovering that this activity constitutes forgery punishable by death, Quintus panics and decides to flee to America; his boat is delayed by unfavourable winds and when he sees his partner arriving on board with a constable he throws himself into the sea but is rescued and brought back to face trial. His second brush with death comes when he takes legal advice to plead guilty. Condemned to death, he is reprieved at the last moment and transported to Australia, where the last quarter of the novel is set.

Resolving to be a model prisoner, Quintus is treated well in the prison hulks and on the voyage out, during which he finds congenial company in a Scottish minister modelled on John Dunmore Lang. On arrival he is at first given a comfortable government billet in Sydney and the freedom to dabble in business, but this leniency is resented and the secretary of state in England is persuaded to order that his privileges be denied. The decline in his fortunes affects his relationship with Emily when, after several years, she follows Quintus to Australia with their son Olivant. Persuaded by Alverney Malmers to whom she had been entrusted for protection by her family, Emily temporarily leaves Quintus, who attempts suicide. He is saved by one of his remaining friends and reconciled with Emily, who returns to England and eventually secures his pardon. Meanwhile Quintus has learnt moderation; he waits patiently for his release, which comes as the gypsy foretold in his forty-first year. With Emily and Olivant he voyages back to England to a congenial retirement in Devonshire. *Quintus Servinton* was reprinted by the University of NSW Press in 1984 as *The Bitter Bread of Banishment*, a quote from Shakespeare's *Richard II* which appears as an epigraph to one of Savery's chapters.

Quiz, a satirical social and sporting journal published in Adelaide, appeared weekly 1889–1930. Edited by Alfred C. Chandler and H. Congreve Evans, among others, the journal included short stories, verse and theatrical notices.

R

RADIC, Leonard (1935–   ), born Melbourne, studied English at the University of Melbourne, where he also edited the student magazine *Farrago*; he has been a theatre critic for the *Age* since 1974. He has written several plays which include *The General* (1974, produced in 1965), 'Ordeal by Fire' (1972), *The Particular* (1974, produced in 1965), *Cody versus Cody* (1980, produced in 1975), *A Clean Sweep* [and] *Ground Rules* (1984, both produced in 1979), 'Now and Then' (1983), 'The Brotherhood' (1986) and *Side-Show* (1987, produced 1971). With his wife Thérèse Radic he has written *Some of My Best Friends Are Women* (1983, produced in 1976), a compilation of songs and readings on the theme of Australian women. Radic is caricatured as Leonardo Radish in Jack Hibberd's play *Dimboola* (1974). He has also edited the two-volume collection, *Short Plays for the Australian Stage* (1987) and written a critical account of Australian theatre, *The State of Play. The Revolution in the Australian Theatre since the 1960s* (1991).

RADIC, Thérèse (1935–   ), born Footscray, Melbourne, has a Ph.D. in music history from the University of Melbourne. She has contributed to numerous journals and encyclopaedias on her subject and has written the biographies *G.W.L. Marshall-Hall: Portrait of a Lost Crusader* (1982), *Bernard Heinze* (1984) and *Melba. The Voice of Australia* (1986). She is also a playwright. Her plays include 'Sisters-in-Law', 'Forty Watt', *Some of My Best Friends Are Women* (1983, co-authored with her husband, Leonard Radic, and first produced in 1976), *A Whip Round for Percy Grainger* (1984, first performed in 1982), 'Cinders' (1985), *Madame Mao* (1986), an epic study of the life of Jiang Qing and the fate of female ambition in Chinese and by implication any culture, *Peach Melba* (1990, first performed 1989), an exploration of the public and private lives of Nellie Melba, which uses music from her repertoire as counterpoint, and *The Emperor Regrets* (1992). She has also compiled *A Treasury of Favourite Australian Songs* (1983) and *Songs of Australian Working Life* (1989).

RADLEY, Paul (1962–   ), born Waratah NSW, left school at 16 to work as a storeman. He has published three novels, *Jack Rivers and Me* (1981), winner of the 1980 *Australian*/Vogel Award, *My Blue-Checker Corker and Me* (1982) and *Good Mates!* (1985). Radley, who explores the territory of boyhood and family life, has set his novels in a fictional country town of the 1950s, Boomeroo. *Jack Rivers and Me*, narrated by a perceptive 5-year-old, James Oxford 'Peanut' Delarue, recounts the history of the boy's relationship with his invisible but charismatic friend Jack Rivers. *My Blue-Checker Corker and Me* deals with the progress to maturity of a 12-year-old boy after the death of his beloved racing pigeon, the prized blue-checker that he named Corker. Both novels are sensitive to the ebb and flow of family experience and to the colourful texture of country existence. Particularly striking is Radley's verbal energy and his ear for the idiosyncrasies of the regional idiom of the Boomeroosters as well as for the more individual private language of siblings, friends, parents and grandparents. *Good Mates!*, set in Boomeroo in the late 1930s and 1940s, recounts the story of Monte's dead father, Chid Howard, and his mate Nick.

RAFFERTY, Chips (1909–71), the film and television actor whose lanky build and weathered features made him the popular conception of the archetypal Australian, was born John Goffage, the son of a Broken Hill miner. He tried a range of occupations including station hand, cane-cutter, shearer, drover, pearl-diver and miner before he was selected by Cinesound Productions for two small parts in the local films *Come Up Smiling* (*Ants in His Pants*, 1938), and *Dad Rudd, M.P.* (1940). His first major part was in *Forty Thousand Horsemen* (1940), produced by Charles Chauvel. Although he had no formal training, he became a well-known international actor, particularly in demand for character parts. He starred in such films as *Mutiny on the Bounty, Eureka Stockade, The Overlanders, Bitter Springs, The Rats of Tobruk, The Sundowners* and *Kangaroo*. He also starred in popular television serials in Britain, the USA and Australia, including *Gunsmoke, Big Valley* and *Dead Men Running*. During the Second World War he served in the RAAF, apart from a brief period when he was released to make *Rats of Tobruk* with Peter Finch and Grant Taylor. During the 1950s he also founded a film company which produced several successful films such as *The Phantom Stockman* and *King of the Coral Sea;* the business collapsed after the advent of television. Bob Larkins wrote *Chips: The Life and Times of Chips Rafferty* (1986).

Ralph Rashleigh, a novel generally assigned to the convict James Tucker (q.v.), was probably written in 1844–45, although the later date of 1850 has been suggested. It was first published in severely edited form in 1929 as a convict memoir by an unknown author. In 1952 the original text was published (reprinted 1992 in the A & R Imprint Classics series), edited by Colin Roderick, whose research uncovered the links between Tucker and the novel. Subtitled *The Life of an Exile, Ralph Rashleigh* purports to be a squatter's record of the reminiscences of a convict, who is given the name of Rashleigh (because he acts rashly); this narrative frame, established in the preface, is of no significance to the rest of the novel, although it parallels the device used in another early convict novel, *Quintus Servinton* (1831).

In structure *Ralph Rashleigh* is a picaresque novel with elements of the cautionary tale, the prisoner's memoir, the Robinson Crusoe cast-away novel and the guidebook genre made popular by Tucker's contemporaries Alexander Harris and Charles Rowcroft. It records the adventures and experiences of Ralph from his descent into crime before 1820 until his death at the hands of Aborigines in 1844, although the last three-quarters of the novel concentrates on the eight or nine years following his arrival in the Colony of NSW in the mid-1820s. The first part is set in England, where Ralph, the son of a London shopkeeper, is apprenticed to a conveyancer. After two years he is allowed to occupy lodgings and begins his life of crime by passing counterfeit coins. Eventually arrested and imprisoned for twelve months, he leaves gaol wise in criminal ways and successfully carries out several daring burglaries. To his dismay he loses the proceeds of a bank robbery in a disastrous fire, and soon after is arrested for a burglary he did not commit. Ralph's sentence of death is commuted to transportation.

On arrival in Australia he is sent to Emu Plains, where the rigours of work in a government gang are relieved only by opportunities to take part in theatrical entertainments or to work for free settlers during harvest. Ralph spends two years at Emu Plains and then travels to the Campbelltown district to be assigned to an emancipist farmer; on the journey there he enjoys the revels of an Irish family and the hospitality offered by Bob Marshall, a model yeoman farmer. Ill-treated at his place of assignment, he complains to the local constable and is held in custody pending the resolution of his case; the gaol is attacked by bushrangers and Ralph taken prisoner by the murderous Foxley and his companions. The gang, of which Ralph becomes an unwilling member, commits several atrocities, including the capture of an overseer, who is pegged out on an anthill and eaten alive by soldier ants, and an attack on the home of a settler, whose daughters are raped. Eventually the gang is caught, and Ralph and the remaining survivor are convicted and condemned. Reprieved for the second time, on this occasion on the gallows, Ralph is sent to Newcastle, where he is forced to endure several floggings and the privations of work in a gang. In company with seven other convicts, he escapes northwards, where the party is racked by internal feuding and attacked by Aborigines. The sole survivor of a flash flood while he is building a canoe to escape Australian waters, Ralph becomes a member of an Aboriginal tribe, whose ceremonies and lifestyle are briefly described. He spends a peaceful four years in its company, but hostility towards him increases following the death of his protector; in the company of two Aboriginal women, he reaches the northern tip of Australia, where he rescues two women from a shipwreck. He accompanies them to Sydney and after a period of assignment to the father of one of the women, he becomes a free settler in the New England district.

Partly because of the circumstances of its composition and discovery, *Ralph Rashleigh* has attracted the attention of commentators on Australian fiction. If Tucker's authorship is assumed, it is one of the few, and undeniably the best, fictional treatment of transportation written by a convict and provides a link between the memoirs of Tucker's fellow prisoners and the novels about the System written in the second half of the nineteenth century. It also, as Roderick suggests, adheres to the paradigm of the well-established English criminal novel, with the dimensions of punishment and redemption extended to a colonial setting. Although the brutality of the penal officials is not ignored in *Ralph Rashleigh*, notably in the Emu Plains and Newcastle scenes, neither is the brutality of the convicts and ex-convicts themselves, which has led to suggestions that the protest against the System in the novel is undercut by Tucker's desire to come to terms with his experience by embracing it. Other approaches to the novel have focused on its contribution to the depiction of the bushranger and the Aborigine in Australian literature, the comparative brutalities of civilised and savage society, and the search for freedom implicit in Ralph's journeys in the novel.

RAMSAY-LAYE, Elizabeth ('Isabel Massary') was the author of two early Australian novels of manners, *Social Life in Sydney* (1866, revised edition issued as *Memories of Social Life in Australia Thirty Years Ago*, 1914) and *Our Cousins in Australia* (1867). A collection of short stories, *A Two Year's Folly, and Other Stories* (1916) also has some Australian content. Both novels deal with urban middle-class families attempting to overcome the stigma of convict antecedents; in *Social Life in Sydney* the brother and sister Margaret and Gerald Bright make their way in Sydney society through many reversals of fortune. Margaret marries Edmund Milner and leads a life of comfortable seclusion which is disrupted by the return of her convict father; Gerald prospers in business but is led into questionable speculation by Phryn, Milner's discredited clerk. The saintly Margaret dies in a bushfire while fulfilling her duty to her father, but Gerald repairs the family's fortune and wins happiness and respect. In *Our Cousins in Australia* the Philipson family leads cousins Mark and Christina Dare into immoral behaviour and, eventually, financial ruin. In this case the Philipsons, whose parents are both former convicts, are irrevocably degenerate and carry the additional burden of Jewishness. An anonymously published autobiographical work, *Social Life and Manners in Australia: Being Notes of Eight Years Experience by a Resident* (1861), is frequently attributed to Elizabeth Ramsay-Laye, but as the author of this work spent eight years in Victoria in the 1850s, including two years on the goldfields at Forest Creek, and does not appear to have visited NSW, the attribution (based on a guess by a British bookseller) may not be correct. This work presents a lively, optimistic picture of life on the diggings and in Melbourne which is explicitly addressed to women readers.

KAY WALSH

RAMSON, W.S., see **Australian English**

RANKEN, George (1827–95), born Ayrshire, Scotland, trained as a surveyor and emigrated to Australia in 1851. He pursued various occupations in Queensland and became commissioner for Crown Lands in 1868. Following a violent incident with his expartner, William Rea, Ranken was charged with attempted murder in 1869, but was acquitted and moved to Sydney, where he became an estate agent, alderman and, in 1886, mayor. He wrote for the *Sydney Morning Herald* on land questions under the pseudonym 'Capricornus', and in 1879 was a member of a royal commission into the Lands Department, whose report subsequently provided the basis for important legislation. Ranken also published two novels, *The Invasion* (1877), under the pseudonym 'W.H. Walker'; and *Windabyne* (1895), previously serialised in the *Australian Magazine* (1878–79); *Bush Essays* (1872); and *The Federal Geography of British Australasia* (1891). A digressive, discursive narrative of station life in NSW, *Windabyne* is his most significant literary achievement.

RANKIN, Jennifer (1941–79), born Sydney as Jennifer Haynes, graduated from the University of Sydney and worked both in England and Australia in the social sciences and education. Married first to John Roberts, and then to the painter David Rankin, she also lived for a period with Frank Moorhouse, who dedicated *Futility and Other Animals* to her. Her poetry, which was published widely in magazines in Australia, England and the USA, appeared in four collections, *Ritual Shift* (1976), *Earth Hold* (1978), illustrated by John Olsen, *The Mud Hut* (1979, published in Canada) and the posthumous *Collected Poems* (1990), edited by Judith Rodriguez. She also wrote plays for stage and radio including *Razorback Mountain Journey* (included in *Collected Poems*), 'Night Spaces', 'Surfaces', 'I Heard the Door Close', 'A Steady Face', 'Catwalk', 'The Darling's Been Done' and *Bees* published in *Theatre Australia* (1976). Rankin's intense, compressed poetry often deals with repressed childhood experiences and relationships, the loss of a father, mental and physical illness, adult love and experiences of vulnerability.

RATCLIFFE, Francis, see *Flying Fox and Drifting Sand*

RAYMENT, Tarlton (1882–1964), born Reading, England, came to Australia in 1902 and worked as a professional beekeeper and commercial artist. A fellow of the Entomological and Zoological societies of London, he published several books and numerous articles as a result of his research into Australian native bees, and was a regular contributor to *Walkabout* 1939–50, writing under his own name and under the pseudonyms 'Ralph Darling', 'Kavai', 'Johan Moorst' and 'Moroka'. As well as numerous radio scripts and short stories, he wrote *The Prince of the Totem* (1933), a collection of Aboriginal legends and fairy-tales pre-viously broadcast on radio; *The Valley of the Sky* (1937), winner of an award in a 1935 world novel competition, and based on Angus McMillan's discovery of Gippsland, which was subsequently translated into several European languages; and *Eagles and Earthlings* (1945), a collection of verse commemorating the Allied air crews of the Second World War. He also contributed short stories to several leading newspapers. His biography, *The Melody Lingers On*, by Lynette Young, was published in 1967.

RAYMOND, Vicki (Vicki Kathleen Irwin) (1949–), born Daylesford, Victoria, lived as a child in Adelaide, later settling in Tasmania, where she gained a BA; in 1981 she moved to London. Her first book of poems, *Holiday Girls and Other Poems* (1985) won the British Airways Commonwealth Poetry Prize for a best first volume. She was one of four poets to represent Australia at Struga Poetry Evenings in Yugoslavia. Her second volume of poems, *Small Arm Practice*, was published in 1989. Witty, ironic but sensitive to those who deserve sensitivity, she has a discerning eye for foibles and vanities. The title poem, 'Holiday Girls' (in both volumes) is a perceptive view of the British holiday mania as well as a poignant account of the tragedy of those unlucky girls. Her *Selected Poems* was published in 1993.

RAYSON, Hannie (1957–), born Melbourne, is a graduate of Melbourne University and the Victorian College of the Arts and is a freelance journalist, editor, playwright and script-writer. Her plays for stage include 'Please Return to Sender' (1980), 'Leave it Till Monday' (1984), *Mary* (1985), 'Yack' (1985), *Room to Move* (1985), which won an Awgie, and *Hotel Sorrento* (1990). Interested in the question of cultural identity and changing social roles, Rayson presents characters who grapple intellectually and emotionally with shifting contemporary attitudes, often with serio-comic effects. *Mary*, first produced in 1982, focuses on the relationship between a Greek, immigrant mother and her 16-year-old daughter. *Room to Move*, an extremely popular comedy, explores the problems of post-feminist men, the limitations of mateship and the difficulties of women, especially older women, in adjusting to new opportunities for independence. *Hotel Sorrento*, the study of a particular family of sisters who have variously stayed in or left Australia, is also concerned with larger questions of cultural belonging, loyalty and betrayal.

READE, Charles (1814–84), the nineteenth-century English novelist and dramatist popular in his own time and remembered chiefly for the medieval romance *The Cloister and the Hearth* (1861), had several literary connections with Australia although he never visited the colonies. After education at Oxford University, where he studied privately for a time with Robert Lowe, Reade was called to the Bar but pursued instead a career as a dramatist. In 1853 his sixth play, *Gold*, was performed successfully in London; a five-act melodrama, the third and fourth acts set in Australia, the play exploited the current interest aroused by the discovery of gold. It focuses on the experiences of a poor English farmer, George Sandford, who emigrates to Australia and earns the £1000 which allows him to marry his sweetheart, Susan Merton, thus thwarting the plans of another suitor. Over the next three years Reade, his experience of Australia enlarged by the descriptive writing of Peter Cunningham, William Howitt and others, reworked the *Gold* material into a novel, published in 1856 as *It Is Never Too Late to Mend*. Reade developed his celebrated documentary method in writing *It is Never Too Late to Mend*. He retained the success story of George Sandford, changing his name to George Fielding, but the novel became famous for its other major plot, the story of a thief, Thomas Robinson, a minor character in *Gold*, who goes to Australia with Sandford. Influenced by *Uncle Tom's Cabin* and by his visit to Birmingham and Reading gaols and other institutions, Reade made his story of Robinson's experiences before his transportation a savage indictment of the English prison system. The novel impressed Marcus Clarke, who adapted Reade's novel *Foul Play* for the stage and referred to Reade in the preface of *His Natural Life* (1874). Dramatisations of *It Is Never Too Late to Mend* were popular on the Australian stage and formed part of the repertoire of Alfred Dampier.

READE, Harry (1927–   ), born Murtoa, Victoria, had only four years of schooling and at 13 began work as a labourer in a foundry. He subsequently 'did just about everything' from working as a stand-up comedian to cartoonist to wharfie; he has been a journalist in Moscow, a seaman in the Danish merchant navy and was with Fidel Castro's force at the Bay of Pigs. At 53 he wrote his first play and has since published three dramas, *The Naked Gun* (1982), *Bucks' Night at Susy's Place* (1982) and *You'll Die Laughing* (1988). He has also written a collection of humorous reminiscences, *An Elephant Charging My Chookhouse* (1987). A free-wheeling Brechtian play, *The Naked Gun* exposes the links between the gun culture, war, the media and masculine drives; *Bucks' Night at Susy's Place* explores violence in domestic relationships; *You'll Die Laughing*, set on Cape York Peninsula and played between several outback characters of varied ethnic origin, an unconventional undertaker and two American tourists, makes comic capital out of the subject of death.

Realist Writers Groups, collectives of active communist and left-wing writers, were established throughout much of Australia in the period 1944–64. The first group was set up in Melbourne in 1944, spreading to Brisbane 1950, Sydney 1952, Perth 1960 and Newcastle 1963. In 1960 a National Council of the Groups was also set up and became linked internationally to similar groups in NZ, Canada and America and in countries under communist rule. Defined by their constitution as 'literary organizations of the working class movement', the Groups' intentions were 'to carry forward the revolutionary and democratic traditions of Australian literature'. By 1970 or a little later the Groups had fallen into decline. The first journal (from the Melbourne group), the *Realist Writer*, appeared quarterly in roneoed form March 1952 to April 1954 when it was incorporated in *Overland* (q.v.). Bill Wannan edited the first two issues and Stephen Murray-Smith the subsequent seven. Contributors included David Martin, Frank Hardy, Laurence Collinson, John Manifold, John Morrison, Eric Lambert and Katharine Susannah Prichard. A second *Realist Writer*, from the Sydney branch, again in roneoed form, appeared in 1958 edited by Frank Hardy, and from 1960 appeared at least three times a year until its demise in 1970. When the National Council of the Groups was formed in 1960 the *Realist Writer* came under its aegis. In 1964 the journal's name was changed to *The Realist*. For much of the period 1962–70 it was edited by Ray Williams. Its contributors included, in addition to those already named, Len Fox, Wilma Hedley and Ron Tullipan. Many of the writers named were members of the Groups.

Recollections of Geoffry Hamlyn, The, a novel by Henry Kingsley (q.v.), was first published in 1859. A chronicle of three families, the Buckleys (q.v.), the Thorntons and the Brentwoods, it covers the period from the 1780s to 1858, focusing on the period after 1820. The novel is narrated by the bumbling bachelor Geoffry Hamlyn; ostensibly the story is read aloud to Major and Agnes Buckley and Captain Brentwood at Baroona station in 1857, where the first chapter is set, but in the last pages of the novel it is revealed that Hamlyn has revised and enlarged the oral version. The first part of *Geoffry Hamlyn* is set mainly at Drumston in Devon, England, where Major Buckley has settled with his wife after being forced to sell the family seat of Clere; other inhabitants of the village include the Rev. John Thornton, his daughter Mary, his sister and his nephew, Thomas Troubridge, Mary's suitors James Stockbridge and George Hawker, the German Dr Mulhaus, and Hamlyn himself. Rejected by Mary, Stockbridge emigrates to Australia with Hamlyn; Mary elopes with the wild and ignoble George, which causes her father to have a stroke and the couple to be pursued by Major Buckley to London, where they are married. George falls into bad company and eventually into crime. After he is arrested for forgery, Mary struggles home with her baby to be reunited with her father on his deathbed. The second part of the novel is set in Australia, where the Buckleys and Thorntons emigrate to join Stockbridge and Hamlyn as pastoralists in the Monaro region; they are followed out by Dr Mulhaus. Mary settles on Toonarbin in partnership with Thomas Troubridge, the Buckleys on Baroona near the station of Captain Brentwood and Mrs Mayford; despite such hazards as bushfires and attacks by Aborigines, which result in the death of Stockbridge, their breeding makes success inevitable. Much of the focus of the Australian scenes, however, is on the affairs of the next generation: Sam Buckley, Alice and Jim Brentwood, Charles Hawker, Cecil Mayford. The conflict between Cecil and Sam over their love for Alice is resolved by her acceptance of Sam, whose heroic qualities are tested when bushrangers enter the district and he rescues Alice just before her house is besieged. During the attacks both Cecil and Charles are killed, Charles by the notorious bushranger Captain Touan, who turns out to be his father, George Hawker. George is hanged for the murder, which allows Mary to find happiness at the end of the novel by her marriage to Thomas Troubridge. They remain in Australia; Sam and Alice, however, return to England rich enough to reclaim Clere, where they are eventually joined by their parents and Hamlyn himself. They are visited by the successful soldier Jim Brentwood and by Dr Mulhaus, who has been revealed to be a baron wounded at the battle of Jena.

An emigrant success story which presented Australia largely as a pastoral Eden, *The Recollections of Geoffry Hamlyn* influenced the direction of Australian fiction by providing a romance model for later successful writers such as 'Rolf Boldrewood'. The Anglocentric attitudes revealed in the novel and its lack of realism led to its dismissal by Joseph Furphy in *Such is Life* (q.v., 1903), and for much of the twentieth century its historical importance was alone emphasised. Recent commentators, however, have stressed its mythic qualities as well as Kingsley's ability to depict landscape.

Recruiting Officer, The, a play by George Farquhar and staged by a group of convicts in honour of the King's birthday, was the first play performed in the colony of NSW (4 June 1789). The historical event is the basis of Thomas Keneally's novel *The Playmaker* (1987), and of the play which it inspired, *Our Country's Good* (1988) by Timberlake Wertenbaker.

Red Page, the major literary section of the *Bulletin* (q.v.) 1896–1961, was so named because it appeared on the inside of the journal's distinctive red cover. The Red Page was the innovation of A.G. Stephens (q.v.), who developed it from 'Books of the Day' and 'The Bulletin Book Exchange', the lists of new literature with occasional editorial comment that replaced advertisements in the *Bulletin* 1894–96. Stephens, satirised as the Red Page Rhadamanthus in Victor Daley's poem 'Narcissus and Some Tadpoles' (1899), was editor of the Red Page until 1906 and was succeeded by A.H. Adams, Bertram Stevens, David McKee Wright, Cecil Mann and most importantly Douglas Stewart (1940–61). A selection of Stephens's Red Page criticism was published as *The Red Pagan* (1902); some of Stewart's criticism is included in *The Flesh and the Spirit* (1948) and *The Broad Stream* (1975).

Red Sky at Morning, a play in three acts by Dymphna Cusack (q.v.), was first produced in 1935 and published in 1942. Set in 1812, the action takes place at an inn at Parramatta. Alicia, a well-born lady who has been trapped into an illicit relationship with a sadistic officer of the NSW Corps and who is now fleeing from him, renews her acquaintance with Michael, an Irish convict, at the inn, where she has taken refuge from a fierce storm. Three years earlier Michael had suffered a flogging after Alicia had been seen speaking to him. Michael and Alicia agree to

escape together by ship but the officer, in pursuit of Alicia, arrives at the inn and, recognising Michael and intent on subjecting him to further humiliation, buys him as a servant from the landlord. Meanwhile he disregards the pleas of Emma, the landlord's daughter, who is engaged to Michael. While the officer sleeps, heavily sedated by the alcohol Michael has given him, Michael makes plans for their escape. Next day the collapse of a bridge under flood water appears to have frustrated his hope of escape with Alicia. Convinced that they love each other, however, and that their only hope is to go forward, they decide to brave the swollen river and are drowned.

Redheap, a novel by Norman Lindsay (q.v.), was published in the USA in 1930 with the title *Every Mother's Son;* banned in Australia until 1958, it was published in 1959. Part of Lindsay's trilogy on small-town life in the 1890s that includes *Saturdee* (q.v., 1933) and *Halfway to Anywhere* (1947), it relates the amatory adventures of Robert Piper, aged 19, and his sister Ethel, aged 20. Robert's reckless love affair with Millie Kneebone, the daughter of a local parson and an alcoholic mother, almost terminates in parenthood and matrimony. Ethel, however, adroitly manages her indiscretions, eventually depriving her sister Hetty of the eligible Dr Niven. Against the background of Redheap's torpor and repressive pretensions is ranged an array of memorable characters, from the senile but libidinous Grandpa Piper to the grandiloquent, irreverent tutor, Mr Bandparts, dogged by his partiality for beer.

Redoubt, begun in 1988 under the editorship of David Reiter, is generally published three times a year to highlight the work of promising young writers and to act as a practical vehicle for Professional Writing Students of the University of Canberra to improve their editing, design, production and distribution skills. It includes fiction, poetry, features, reviews, essays on literary, cultural, social, philosophical issues and trends. Edited by Patricia Munro (1990–93) *Redoubt*'s literary advisors have been Michael Wilding and, before her death in 1993, Margaret Diesendorf.

REED, A.W. (Alexander Wyclif) (1908–79), formerly chairman of the NZ publishing firm A.H. & A.W. Reed, and a nephew of Sir Alfred Hamish Reed, who established the firm in Dunedin in 1911, wrote numerous accounts of Aboriginal legends, several of them for young readers. They include *Aboriginal Fables* (1965), *Myths and Legends of Australia* (1965) and *The Mischievous Crow* (1969). He wrote on Australian place-names, *Aboriginal Place Names and Their Meanings* (1967), and *Place Names of Australia* (1973); compiled *An Illustrated Encyclopedia of Aboriginal Life* (1969); edited extracts from Captain James Cook's journals, *Captain Cook in Australia* (1969); and wrote recollections of Sir A.H. Reed, *Young Kauri 1875–1975* (1975). He also wrote several Australian educational books and books for children. The publishing house of A.H. & A.W. Reed, which extended to Sydney in 1963, has published numerous works of Australian literature and history. The history of the publishing firm is described in A.W. Reed's autobiography *Books Are My Business* (1966) and in *The House of Reed* (1957), by A.H. and A.W. Reed.

REED, Bill (1939–), born Perth but educated in Adelaide, has worked as a book editor and journalist since the early 1960s in Canada, England and Australia and as publishing director for A.H. & A.W. Reed. Best known as a playwright, he has published several plays, *Burke's Company* (1969), *Mr Siggie Morrison with His Comb and Paper* (1972), *Cass Butcher Bunting* (1977), which won first prize in Monash University's first play-writing contest in 1977, and *Truganinni* (1977, a series of three plays, *White Exercises, Pantagruel In-Between* and *King Billy's Bones*). His other plays include 'The Pecking Order' (1972), 'The Old Pig Rat', 'Jack Charles Is Up and Fighting' (1972), 'Just Out of Your Ground' (1975), 'You Want It, Don't You Billy?' (1976), 'Paddlesteamer' (1975, under the pseudonym 'Barvar Adele'), 'Bullsh' (1977), 'More Bullsh' (1978), *I Don't Know What to Do with You* (1980), 'Hit and Run' and 'English Expression'. He has also published six novels, *Dogod* (1977), *The Pipwink Papers* (1978), *Me, the Old Man* (1979), *Stigmata* (1980, winner of the ANA Literature Award), *IHE* (1982) and *Crooks* (1984). *Burke's Company*, focusing on the last days of the Burke and Wills expedition, interweaves experiences of Burke, Wills and King on the trek, of William Brahe as he waits at Cooper's Creek, and the proceedings of the subsequent court of inquiry, to form an intense but necessarily inconclusive study of respective guilt. Both *Cass Butcher Bunting*, which explores the feelings of three trapped miners just before the final cave-in, and *Mr Siggie Morrison with His Comb and Paper*, a goon-like, vaudevillean production, have dying as a central theme. The three plays based on the life of Truganini are studies of fear, violence and racism, ranging from mime to farce-melodrama to tragedy. Nearly all Reed's plays are distinguished by his innovative treatment of language to create a disturbing atmosphere verging on the surreal.

REED, John (1901–81), born Tasmania into a wealthy pastoral family, trained as a lawyer, although he later abandoned law for art. President of the Contemporary Art Society, Melbourne, 1940–43 and 1953–58, he was founder and director of the Museum of Modern Art and Design of Australia in Melbourne 1958–65, and with his wife Sunday was one of the most influential proponents of modernism in Australian art. Artists whose work was fostered by the Reeds include Sidney Nolan, John Perceval, Arthur Boyd, Albert Tucker, Joy Hester, Danila Vassilieff and Charles Blackman. Part-owner with Max Harris of the publishing firm Reed & Harris, which published work by numerous Australian authors including Peter Cowan, Dal Stivens, Alister Kershaw, Geoffrey Dutton and Max Harris, Reed was a prominent member of the Angry Penguins group and joint editor and publisher of *Angry Penguins*. A brother of Cynthia Nolan and an energetic patron of Sidney Nolan, Reed was instrumental in gaining international recognition of Nolan's Ned Kelly series of paintings. The work of John and Sunday Reed is commemorated in the Heide Park and Art Gallery, Heidelberg, Melbourne, and described by Richard Haese in his *Rebels and Precursors* (1981). Alister Kershaw gives a more negative picture of John Reed in his reminiscences, *Hey Days* (1991).

REED, Sunday, see **REED, John**

Reedy River, a musical play based on Australian folk-songs gathered by the actor John Gray, with a script by Dick Diamond (q.v.), was first produced by the Melbourne New Theatre in 1953, when it attracted large audiences; published in 1970, the play has since been regularly revived. The rather sketchy plot concerns a group of shearers who in spite of the failure of the strikes of the 1890s continue to oppose the use of scab labour. The play's real attractiveness lies in its combination of folk-songs and ballads (q.v.) sung to the accompaniment of a bush band. The title song comes from Henry Lawson's poem 'Reedy River'; other well-known pieces include 'Click Go the Shears', 'The Eumerella Shore', 'Flash Jack from Gundagai' and 'The Old Black Billy', most of which carry nostalgic echoes of the nationalist and radical sentiments of the 1890s and continue to appeal to urban audiences.

REES, Arthur J. (1877–1942), born Melbourne, was for a time on the staff of the *Age*, then joined the *New Zealand Herald* and, while still in his twenties, left for England. He lived for some time as a freelance journalist but soon acquired a reputation as a prolific writer of detective stories, none of which reflect his Australian experience. Several of his novels were translated into other languages.

REES, Coralie Clarke, see **CLARKE, Coralie**

REES, Leslie (1905–) was born in Perth and educated at the University of WA, where he edited the student magazine the *Black Swan*. He spent some time on the staff of the *West Australian*, before winning a scholarship to study in London in 1929. In London in 1931 he married Coralie Clarke (q.v.). He was the senior drama critic on the London weekly *Era* 1931–35, and met many prominent British and European writers. He returned in 1936 to Sydney, where he reviewed plays and films for the *Sydney Morning Herald* before being appointed federal drama editor for the ABC, a position from which he retired in 1966. Well known as a drama critic with international interests, Rees has had a strong influence on Australian drama through his work with the ABC and his twenty-five years chairmanship of the Playwrights Advisory Board. His wide-ranging experience is recorded in his autobiography *Hold Fast to Dreams* (1982). In 1981 he was made AM.

Rees has written two histories of Australian drama, *Towards an Australian Drama* (1953) and the more ambitious *A History of Australian Drama* (q.v., 1973, 1978, 1987) which won the 1978 Townsville Foundation for

Australian Literary Studies Award; and has edited four collections of plays, *Australian Radio Plays* (1946), *Australian Youth Plays* (1948), *Modern Short Plays* (1951) and *Mask and Microphone* (1963). Of his own plays, *Sub-Editors Room*, the first Australian play to be televised, is included in *Best Australian One-Act Plays* (1937), edited by William Moore and T. Inglis Moore, and *Mother's Day* in *Six Australian One-Act Plays* (1944). He also collaborated with Ruth Park in a dramatisation of her novel *The Harp in the South*, produced in 1949 and published in 1987. His other plays include 'Lalor of Eureka' (1937), which won a Melbourne New Theatre competition.

As well as numerous articles, memoirs and critical essays, Rees has written four travel books in collaboration with his wife: *Spinifex Walkabout* (1953), *Westward from Cocos* (1956), *Coasts of Cape York* (1960) and *People of the Big Sky Country* (1970). He is also one of Australia's best-known and most prolific children's writers. He has written four adventure stories, *Quokka Island* (1951), *Danger Patrol* (1955), *Boy Lost on Tropic Coast* (1968) and *Panic in the Cattle Country* (1974); an animal fantasy, *Mates of the Kurlalong* (1948); a series of popular stories centring on a local Tom Thumb called Digit Dick (1942–82); and an extensive and informative series of nature stories dealing with Australian fauna. Of these the most popular are *The Story of Shy the Platypus* (1944), *Two-Thumbs: The Story of a Koala* (1953), *The Story of Sarli the Barrier Reef Turtle* (1947), *The Story of Aroora the Red Kangaroo* (1952) and *The Story of Karrawingi the Emu* (1946), which won the 1946 Children's Book of the Year Award. Several of the tales have been reprinted in two collections (1958, 1974) and others have also been translated and published in the former Soviet Union and other countries. Rees broke new ground in *Here's to Shane* (1977), a story of a deaf boy's battle with his handicap.

REES, Lloyd (1895–1988), born Brisbane, the seventh of eight children, received an education in European culture from his French-Mauritian mother. After studying art at Brisbane Technical College, he worked for a brief period for the Queensland Government Printing Office. His pen drawings of Brisbane, a city he transformed into a Parisian ideal of 'boulevards, riverside quays, graceful bridges, trees, squares and fountains', came to the attention of Sydney Ure Smith, and led to his employment in 1917 by the commercial art firm of Smith & Julius in Sydney. He became friendly with other artists such as Roland Wakelin, Percy Leason and Grace Cossington Smith, was exhibited by the Society of Artists and received favourable attention from Lionel Lindsay. After visiting Europe in 1923, he supported himself by drawing illustrations part-time for Farmers' department store. His marriage in 1926 to Dulcie Metcalf ended tragically when she died a year later, a loss which seriously affected his painting. In 1931 he married Marjory Pollard, his wife for fifty-three years, and began to attract recognition as a painter. His son Alan was born in 1934 and the family moved to Northwood, NSW, to a house designed by Rees as an Italian villa. From the 1940s Rees won numerous prizes and awards, held frequent exhibitions and was honoured with a retrospective exhibition at the Art Gallery of NSW in 1942. In 1946 he started to teach painting and drawing to architectural students at the University of Sydney and attracted great affection from his students. He was made CMG in 1978 and AC in 1985 and received an honorary D.Litt. from the University of Sydney in 1970. Rees's lyrical, light-filled paintings ranged widely in subject matter, reflecting his love of landscape; regions and cities which stimulated his art included Paris and Chartres, Tuscany, the south coast of NSW, Sydney Harbour, the Bathurst region, central Australia, Tasmania and early Canberra. His youthful passion for Brisbane's St John's Cathedral persisted in later life, resulting in a series of paintings of cathedrals. He made frequent visits to Europe, which had a strong influence on his painting of Australian subjects, to the exent that Europe and Australia co-existed in his work. In his later years, when he continued to paint free-flowing works in rich, luminous colours, he became well known as an activist to preserve the environment and an anti-nuclear energy protester. Rees wrote two volumes of autobiography, which are also informative on the history of Australia's visual arts culture, *The Small Treasures of a Lifetime* (1969) and *Peaks and Valleys* (1985). In 1990 a dramatic tribute, 'Swimming in Light', was performed in Melbourne. Renée Free has written widely on Rees, e.g. *Lloyd Rees Retrospective* (1968), *Lloyd Rees* (1972), *Lloyd Rees: The Later Work* (1983, updated in 1990 as *Lloyd Rees: The Last Twenty Years*).

REEVE, Edward (1822–89), born England, arrived in Sydney in 1840, and after some years as a teacher and then clerk, joined the staff of the *Sydney Morning Herald* in 1857. He contributed articles on various subjects to contemporary journals, was associated with the literary group which included Frank Fowler, Joseph Sheridan Moore and Nicol Drysdale Stenhouse, and with their founding of the *Month*. He became the first curator of the Nicholson Museum at the University of Sydney in 1860 and, in 1871, a founder and honorary secretary of the NSW Academy of Art. His blank verse tragedy *Raymond, Lord of Milan* (1851), first produced for a four-night run in Sydney in 1863, was revived in 1950. The play has some good verse and incidental scenes but lacks unity and direction. In 1882 in the *Sydney Mail* he also published a long, well-written and tightly constructed romance, 'Friends and Foes; Or, The Bride of Bernbeck'; and in 1884 'Passion', his adaptation of Rosa Praed's novel *Policy and Passion* (q.v., 1881), was staged in Sydney.

Referee, a Sydney weekly newspaper, was launched in 1886 to compete with the Melbourne *Sportsman* and later the *Arrow* and *Sydney Sportsman* for the attention of a burgeoning sporting public. During its fifty-odd years' existence it was dominated by W.F. Corbert and his son Claude but in earlier days Nat Gould and 'Smiler' Hailes were prominent contributors. Its demise in 1939 resulted less from the competition of rival sporting journals than from the increasing popularity of evening newspapers such as the *Sun*.

Register, the first SA newspaper and for most of its life the great rival of the *Advertiser*, began publication in 1836; its first issue was produced by George Stevenson (q.v.) and was published in England, as were other publications relating to early SA, but it resumed in Adelaide in 1837. Titled the *South Australian Gazette and Colonial Register* (1836–39), the *South Australian Register* (1839–1900) and the *Register News-Pictorial* (1929–31), the *Register* became a daily in 1850 and was absorbed by the *Advertiser* in 1931. Catherine Helen Spence was a major contributor both to the *Register* and its weekly companion the *Adelaide Observer*.

REIBEY, Mary (1777–1855), born Mary Haydock, Lancashire, England, was convicted of horse-stealing in 1790 while masquerading as a young lad and was transported to NSW in 1792. In 1794 she married Thomas Reibey (1769–1811), a young Irishman who became one of the Colony's most successful traders and merchants. When Reibey died, Mary, then the mother of seven children, took over his business interests and became one of the leading members of the new emancipist society favoured by Governor Lachlan Macquarie. An enterprising and successful businesswoman, she eventually owned several ships, substantial properties in the heart of Sydney and in Tasmania and established the Reibey dynasty, which included her grandson Thomas, a member of the Tasmanian State parliament for twenty-five years and, briefly, premier of that State. Her biography, *Mary Reibey – Molly Incognita* (1982) by Nance Irvine, was launched at Mary Reibey's Coffee Palace in the Rocks, Sydney, at a 1982 reunion of the Reibey family. Irvine has also edited a collection of Reibey family letters 1792–1901 (1992).

REID, Sir George Houstoun (1845–1918), premier of NSW (1894–99) and prime minister of Australia (1904–5), was born in Scotland and came to Australia in 1852. He began his working life in 1858 as clerk to a Sydney merchant, but subsequently gained a position in the colonial treasury and studied law, which he began to practise in 1879. Elected to the NSW parliament in 1880, he proved to be an active, skilful politician and a colourful debater with a gift for witty repartee. His vacillation over Federation led to his becoming known as 'Yes-No' Reid in a series of cartoons by Livingston Hopkins. He retired from politics in 1908, was Australian high commissioner in London 1910–16, and held the seat of Hanover Square in the House of Commons 1916–18 as an independent imperialist. Reid's publications include a collection of five essays on free trade (1875), which won him honorary membership of the Cobden Club; an account of his own colony, *An Essay on New South Wales, the Mother Colony of the Australias* (1876); a volume of autobiography, *My Reminiscences* (1917); and a poem, *Lines Addressed to New South Wales on the Opening of the First Australian International Exhibition* (1879). He also wrote the foreword to Barbara Baynton's *Cobbers* (1917). Extracts from his London notebooks and letters, illustrative of Australia's role in the planning and execution of the Gallipoli campaign, and selected by his granddaughter, Anne Fairbairn, were published in the *Australian* (1981). Some of the most trenchant criticisms of Reid are contained in Alfred Deakin's *The Federal Story* (1944). A biography by W.G. McMinn, *George Reid*, was published in 1989.

REITER, David P. (1947–), editor of the literary magazine *Redoubt* (q.v.) 1988–90, has published poetry in many Australian, North American and European periodicals and in two collections, *The Snow In Us* (1989), which largely reflects his experience of Canada, and *Changing House* (1991), winner of the 1989 Queensland Premier's Poetry Award.

Remittance Man, A was usually the black sheep of the family, sent out to the colonies from England so that he would no longer be an embarrassment at home. He was usually sustained by regular remittances of money from the family in England. Often an inebriate or isolate, the remittance man was recognised by his faded aristocratic air and his inability to cope with the rough-and-ready colonial life. Well-known portraits of the type are in Henry Lawson's 'The Story of 'Gentleman-Once'' in *Children of the Bush* (1902), Ambrose Pratt's *The Remittance Man* (1907) and Judith Wright's poem 'Remittance Man' in *The Moving Image* (1946). References to remittance men, usually in derogatory terms, are widespread in writing of the late nineteenth century, e.g. in Nat Gould's *On and Off the Turf in Australia* (1895) and 'Mark Twain's' *Following the Equator* (1897).

Removalists, The, a play by David Williamson (q.v.) first performed in 1971 at the La Mama Theatre, has been widely performed in Australia and in London and New York. It was published in 1972, was co-winner of the 1971 British George Devine Award and also won two Awgies. Set partly in a small police station and partly in a suburban home, the cast includes the authoritarian, pontificating Sergeant Simmonds; Ross, his impressionable junior; Fiona Carter, a young housewife who reluctantly makes a complaint about her physically abusive husband Kenny; her socially pretentious sister Kate; and a removalist. After Fiona's complaint, orchestrated by her domineering sister and exploited for its sexual possibilities by Simmonds, the two policemen offer to help Fiona move out. The sexually frustrated Simmonds aspires, fruitlessly, to a liaison with Kate. In Act Two Kenny arrives home early and immediately engages aggressively with Simmonds. Both men are committed to a tough self-image which stresses sexual and fighting ability. First Simmonds methodically bashes Kenny and then Ross, who has been ceaselessly humiliated all day, explodes into violence at Kenny's taunts. Kenny appears to die, recovers, matily discusses a call-girl racket with Simmonds, and then collapses with a cerebral haemorrhage. After some panic-stricken recriminations, Simmonds and Ross fall to blows in an attempt to claim that Kenny died while resisting arrest.

'RENAR, Frank', see **FOX, Sir Frank**

RENE, Roy (1891–1954), born Adelaide as Henry Van der Sluys, was also known as Harry Sluice but took the stage name of Roy Rene. Initially a boy soprano, Roy Boy, Rene in 1916 formed with Nat Phillips a comedy partnership, Stiffy and Mo, which delighted Australian vaudeville audiences until the end of the 1920s. Phillips was Stiffy, the straight man who fed lines to Mo, characteristically made up with chalk-white face and black beard as he leered and lisped catch-phrases like 'Strike me lucky'. A city-oriented clown who remained enormously popular on the Australian stage after the breaking of the Stiffy and Mo partnership, Rene had success also on radio in the late 1940s; as Mo McCackie he presided over *McCackie Mansions*, an establishment also inhabited by Mo's stupid son Young Harry, his layabout relative 'Orrible 'Erbie, next-door neighbour Lasho, and the sweetly spoken visitor Spencer the Garbage Man. *Mo's Memoirs*, ghosted by Max Harris and Elisabeth Lambert, was published in 1945; John Thompson included Rene in his *Time to Remember* (1962) and his scriptwriter, Fred Parsons, wrote the biographical tribute, *A Man Called Mo* (1973). Rene has also been the subject of a musical tribute, 'Mo', by George Dreyfus (performed 1972), and of Steve J. Spears's play *Young Mo* (first performed 1976, published 1977).

RENTOUL, Annie Rattray, see *The Oxford Companion to Australian Children's Literature* (1993), pp. 361–2.

Republican, a Sydney radical journal, ran for ten issues 1887–88; for part of the time, when it was under the management of Louisa Lawson, her son Henry was nominal publisher and had his first prose articles published there. The *Republican* is the subject of Lawson's poem 'The Cambaroora Star'.

Review, a weekly newspaper published in Melbourne 1970–72, was titled *Sunday Review* until July 1971 and in March 1971 incorporated the *Sunday Observer*. In July 1972 the newspaper merged with the Sydney *Nation* to form *Nation Review*.

Review of Reviews for Australasia was published monthly in Melbourne 1892–1914, when its title changed to *Stead's Review of Reviews*. From 1931 to 1934, when it ceased publication, the magazine was titled *Today*. *Review of Reviews* included some material from the parent British edition, reprinted extracts and cartoons from Australian periodicals to give a general survey of affairs, and included reviews of Australian books and articles on Australian artists and writers. One of the most useful surveys of contemporary Australian newspapers appeared as a series from July 1892 to September 1893.

REYNOLDS, Henry, see **Aborigine in White Australian Literature**

RICHARDS, Max (1942–), born Timaru, NZ, moved to Australia in 1973 to become playwright-in-residence at La Mama theatre. He has written numerous plays for radio, television screenplays and several plays for stage. These include 'Queue' (1973), *Sadie & Neco* (1978), 'Night Flowers', 'Mirrors', 'Sand/Tombstone/Tree' (1975), 'Cripple Play' (1976), *Love Play* (1988) and 'Murderer's Barbecue' (1988). He has also published a collection of poetry, *Under Mount Egmont and Other Poems* (1983).

RICHARDS, Thomas (1800–77), born Wales, trained as a doctor in London and moved in literary and journalistic circles before he came to Australia in 1832 as surgeon on an emigrant ship. He settled in Van Diemen's Land where, in 1833, he edited the *Tasmanian* and collaborated with Henry Melville in the production of the *Hobart Town Magazine*; after it ceased publication in 1834 he ran a correspondence agency to assist the poor and illiterate to communicate with the government. In 1837 he was assistant editor of the *Hobart Town Courier* and for about a decade from 1837 was associated with the *Colonial Times*; in the 1850s he returned full-time to medicine but in his later years was active on the *Mercury*. Richards was a talented journalist whose varied output included polemical and descriptive essays and dramatic criticism; his fictional sketches contributed to the *Hobart Town Magazine* make him one of the pioneers of the short story in Australia.

'RICHARDSON, Henry Handel' (Ethel Florence Lindesay Robertson) (1870–1946) was born in Melbourne, the elder daughter of a physician, Walter Lindesay Richardson, who had emigrated to Australia in 1852. Strikingly dependent on autobiographical and family experience for her creative writing, 'Richardson' drew heavily on her father's life for the central character of her novel trilogy *The Fortunes of Richard Mahony* (q.v.), although she made several significant changes. Like Mahony, Walter Richardson was born in Dublin, trained at the University of Edinburgh, came to Australia during the gold rushes of the 1850s in an attempt to recoup his family's fortunes, worked first as a storekeeper and then as a general practitioner and in 1855 married a much younger girl, also recently arrived from England, Mary Bailey. By the time of Ethel's birth fifteen years later, Walter Richardson was a prosperous, prominent figure in Melbourne society and had retired from general practice in 1869 when his investments in stocks returned him a small fortune. Four years later he took his wife and two daughters on a grand tour of Europe but his visit was cut short by the sudden failure of his investments and his abrupt return to Australia to rebuild his practice. The next four years were dominated by the family's frequent changes of home in Victoria as Walter Richardson vainly attempted to re-establish himself, meanwhile contending with rapidly increasing symptoms of what was brain disease leading to dementia. In 1878 he was admitted to a private asylum in Melbourne and later spent some time in the government asylum. He died in 1879 after some months in the care of his family at Koroit, a remote village in western Victoria where Mary Richardson had been appointed postmistress. Ethel Richardson's memories of Koroit were distasteful, although she was happier at Maldon after the family moved there in 1880. From the ages of 13 to 17 she was a boarder at the Presbyterian Ladies College, Melbourne, an experience she drew on for her novel *The Getting of Wisdom* (q.v.), although, unlike its heroine, Laura Rambotham, she won distinction there, especially as a musician. In other respects, however, her experience was close to Laura's, especially in her strong attachment to another, older girl. In 1888 her mother resigned from the postal service and took her two daughters to Europe so that Ethel could continue her musical studies at Leipzig Conservatorium. 'Richardson's' childhood in Australia left her with strong memories of the Australian landscape, a precocious but lasting awareness of the dark side of human experience and a conviction of her own distinctive apartness.

Life in Germany proved to be liberating and intellectually stimulating; she discovered European literature, in which she read widely, and began to concentrate on her own creative talent, ultimately abandoning music for writing. She also met her future husband, J.G. Robertson, a Scotsman and a doctoral student in German literature, who had a profound influence on the direction of her cultural interests. A year after her marriage in 1895 'Richardson' published translations from the German J.P. Jacobsen's Danish novel *Niels Lyhne*, which she titled *Siren Voices* and afterwards described as having 'stirred [her] as few books have ever done either before or since', and B. Björnson's *The Fisher Lass*. She began her own first novel, *Maurice Guest* (q.v.), in 1897 in Strasbourg, where her husband had been appointed as lecturer at the university. The death of her mother that year, which was a severe blow, gave rise to a short story, 'Death', published in 1911, later titled 'Mary Christina' and included in *Two Studies* (1931). As at Leipzig, 'Richardson' led an active social life at Strasbourg. After 1903, however, when she moved to London with her husband, who had been appointed to a chair of German at the University of London, 'Richardson's' life quickly set into the solitary pattern that was to continue until her death. Common to nearly all the reminiscences of 'Richardson' is the picture of a deliberately isolated figure, hard at work in an upper-storey, sound-proof study, devotedly attended by first her husband and then her companion-secretary, Olga Roncoroni.

Maurice Guest, published by Heinemann in 1908 under the semi-pseudonym that she later described as deriving from the Irish side of her family, received varying reviews although it was praised by several prominent writers of the time, including Hugh Walpole and Somerset Maugham. *The Getting of Wisdom*, written as a light relief from *Maurice Guest*, appeared in 1910 but failed to attract immediate attention. In London 'Richardson' began the painstaking research for *Australia Felix*, the first volume of the trilogy *The Fortunes of Richard Mahony*, which was to occupy her for twenty years. In 1912 she visited Australia for two months to check details for the trilogy, but then remained in England for the rest of her life. *Australia Felix*, completed in 1915, was published in 1917 and sold reasonably well although it was neglected in Australia. *The Way Home*, the middle volume of the trilogy and 'Richardson's' favourite, was published in 1925 but sold so poorly that Heinemann refused in 1928 to publish the last volume, *Ultima Thule*. Published in 1929 at J.G. Robertson's expense, it was an immediate success and was quickly reprinted by Heinemann and by Norton in the USA. The trilogy, published as one volume for the first time in 1930, has been frequently reprinted and translated into Swedish and Danish. Well known in England, Europe, the USA and Australia by the mid-1930s, 'Richardson' was awarded the Australian Literature Society's Gold Medal (1929) for *Ultima Thule*. As well as two collections of short stories, *Two Studies* (1931) and *The End of a Childhood* (1934), some other short stories collected in *The Adventures of Cuffy Mahony* (1979), several uncollected articles and a volume of unfinished autobiography, *Myself When Young* (1948), 'Richardson' produced one other major piece of fiction, *The Young Cosima* (1939). Some of her letters to Nettie Palmer were published in the latter's study of 'Richardson' (1950) and in a separate edition in 1953. The death of 'Richardson's' husband in 1933 was an irreparable loss, after which she moved to Sussex, and the Second World War proved to be even more of a personal ordeal than the First. As one of her critics has commented, all three countries in which she lived, Australia, Germany and England, offered 'Richardson' distinctive experiences and gifts, but 'it is open to question whether any . . . gave her a home'.

At Leipzig 'Richardson' became interested in German romanticism and in French, Russian and Scandinavian writers of the nineteenth century. She read both Dostoevsky and Freud some years before English translations of their work were available and was also particularly influenced by Swedenborg, Goethe, Ibsen, and Flaubert as well as Jacobsen. Swedenborg's work probably reinforced the interest in spiritualism that she shared with her father (she was a lifelong member of the Society for Psychical Research); and she found much in the German world-view of the time to confirm her own pessimistic perception of the human condition as inevitably limited and subject to constant change. Although 'Richardson' owes much to the European tradition of scientific realism, especially so far as a concern for accurate documentation, psychological veracity and narrative impartiality is concerned, she is also preoccupied with romantic themes such as love and spiritual and artistic fulfilment. In *Maurice Guest* realism and romanticism combine in the study of an aspiring artist who lacks the talent to achieve his ambition and who becomes the victim of an obsessive love, leading finally to his suicide. Against the well-realised background of Leipzig's musical world, 'Richardson' carefully and objectively traces the successive stages of Maurice's corrosive passion, his failure in everything except acceptance of his fate. Some readers have uncovered a debt to Nietzsche in its theme, especially in 'Richardson's' treatment of Maurice's opposite, the genius and free spirit, Schilsky; others, however, have stressed the novel's ironic undercurrents that imply an objective attitude to the concept of the artist-hero. *The Getting of Wisdom*, described by 'Richardson' as a 'merry little book', is comically ironic in tone, but has a serious subject, the story of an artist's painful inner growth during her impressionable adolescent years. The freshness, clarity and honesty of 'Richardson's' presentation of youthful experience have often been praised, although at the time some regarded the book as a satire on education, and 'Richardson' subsequently claimed, probably falsely, that she was denied admittance to the Presbyterian Ladies College in 1912 as a result of her fictional treatment of the school. In her picture of Laura, her 'odd and unaccountable' heroine, she undoubtedly drew heavily on her own experience, but Laura differs from herself in certain respects, most importantly in her outward failure. The wisdom that Laura acquires takes various forms, none of which derives from her formal education, but all of which concern the nature of truth and honesty, the force and forms of passion, and the ambivalent need to be individual and conform. Like Mahony, Laura learns that nothing is permanent and that life inevitably involves loneliness, disillusionment and loss.

If *The Getting of Wisdom* has acquired the status of a classic in the genre of childhood autobiography, it is *The Fortunes of Richard Mahony* that is generally judged to be 'Richardson's' major achievement and one of the showpieces of Australian literature. The trilogy has been variously defined as an emigrant novel, a chronicle of colonialism in Australia, a study of failure or of an ill-matched marriage, an analysis of the 'complex fate' of dual nationality, or, simply, as 'a book about money'. The central subject, however, is Mahony himself, in accordance with 'Richardson's' view of the importance of character: 'I never cease to believe that character-drawing is [the novel's] main end and object, the conflict of personalities its drama.' In *Australia Felix*, which presents a varied, densely packed picture of Victorian colonial life, Mahony gradually emerges as a man suffering from cultural alienation; *The Way Home* records, from a narrower perspective, his successive failures to find 'home' in any sense; *Ultima Thule* places him firmly in the foreground and traces the final stages of his self-destruction. Lack of unity, an excessive and cramping attention to detail and stylistic clumsiness have been some of the charges levelled at the trilogy, although some critics have found that 'Richardson' shapes and illuminates her material in minutely detailed ways. Some of these include her use of recurrent images, especially of confinement and burial, age and youth, of recurrent incidents, scenes and objects and of contrasting or parallel characters, so that the work is held together by a pattern of interlocking ironies and reveals several layers of meaning. Although *Ultima Thule* is generally regarded as the most assured and moving volume of the trilogy, the whole has been described as similar to a symphony, of which the 'Proem' to *Australia Felix* is the overture. In her portrait of Mahony, 'Richardson' undoubtedly invested the facts of her father's life with her own personality traits and emotional experience. Afflicted with a romantic dilemma, an awareness that there is no permanence, coupled with an ineradicable yearning for an ideal point of rest, Mahony pursues his fate as relentlessly as Maurice Guest. His relationship with his wife, the practical, common-sense Mary, defines both the absurdity and the magnificence of his search, as 'Richardson's' use of a third observer in *Ultima Thule*, the child, Cuffy, emphasises its poignance and suffering. Ultimately Mahony emerges as an Everyman figure, as the epigraph to *Australia Felix* suggests, an illustration of the universal human vulnerability to pain and loss.

With the trilogy and the four stories dealing with Cuffy Mahony in *The End of a Childhood*, 'Richardson' exhausted her family experience and attempted in *The Young Cosima* a different sort of historical novel, a study of the relationships between Wagner, Liszt, Hans von Bülow and Cosima von Bülow. Within the framework of this familiar story of genius and passion 'Richardson' attempts to re-examine some of the problems of art and life that had preoccupied her in *Maurice Guest*. In this last novel, however, her prose lacks energy and she fails to achieve that impression of felt life which is, for the most part, a marked feature of her work. Studies of 'Richardson' include Leonie Kramer's *Henry Handel Richardson and Some of Her Sources* (1954) and *Myself When Laura* (1966); Vincent Buckley's monograph *Henry Handel Richardson* (1961); Dorothy Green's extensive biographical and critical analysis *Ulysses Bound* (1973, revised in 1986); Karen McLeod's *Henry Handel Richardson* (1985); and Axel Clark's *Henry Handel Richardson: Fiction in the Making* (1990). In 1992 Carol Franklin edited *The End of a Childhood: The Complete Stories of Henry Handel Richardson*.

RICKARD, John (1935–), reader in history at Monash University, is the author of a significant study, *Australia. A Cultural History* (1988), which sets the contribution of writers in a wide socio-political context. He has also written *Class and Politics: New South Wales, Victoria and the Early Commonwealth 1890–1910* (1976), winner of the Ernest Scott Prize, and *H.B. Higgins: The Rebel as Judge* (1984), which won the *Age* non-fiction Book of the Year Award.

RICKARDS, Harry (1847–1911), born Henry Benjamin Leete in London, took the stage name of Harry Rickards and established a reputation as a singer of music-hall comic songs. On his first visit to Australia beginning in 1871, Marcus Clarke wrote vaudeville sketches for him; Rickards made subsequent tours in 1885–87, and from 1892 made Australia his home; in 1893 he took a lease on the Garrick Theatre in Sydney, renaming it the Tivoli and establishing himself as a successful vaudeville entrepreneur, with theatres in Melbourne, Adelaide, Perth, Kalgoorlie, Brisbane and NZ, becoming reputedly the largest single-handed music-hall manager and proprietor in the world. Frequently visiting England, Rickards was responsible in the decades either side of 1900 for the Australian engagement of many overseas variety entertainers. One of his few failures was a lecture tour by the hoaxer 'Louis de Rougemont' in 1904.

RIDDELL, Alan (1927–77), born Townsville, Queensland, was educated in Scotland and lived in Greece, Spain and France, as well as Australia, where he worked as a journalist for the *Age, Daily Telegraph* and *Sydney Morning Herald.* Founder of the Scottish poetry review *Lines*, which he edited 1952–55 and 1962–67, he contributed verse to Australian and overseas journals and anthologies and published four collections, *Beneath the Summer* (1952), *Majorcan Interlude* (1960), *The Stopped Landscape* (1968) and *Eclipse* (1972). Editor of the Scottish section of *Young Commonwealth Poets '65* (1965), he also edited the anthology *Typewriter Art* (1975). In 1956 Riddell won the Heinemann Lyric Prize and a Scottish Arts Council Prize in 1968. Originally a traditional poet, he became interested in concrete and visual poetry in the 1960s.

RIDDELL, Elizabeth (1910–), born Napier, NZ, settled in Australia in 1928, when she was hired by Ezra Norton to work on the Sydney *Truth*. In due course she established a reputation as one of Australia's most distinguished journalists, winning a Walkley Award for a series of articles on the brewing industry. From 1935 to 1939 she lived mainly in England, where she worked briefly for the *Daily Express*. Sent to New York at the outbreak of war to open the bureau of the *Daily Mirror*, she was transferred to London and Europe, where she saw some action behind the lines and witnessed the German defeat and withdrawal. She later worked for *Smith's Weekly* and the *Daily Telegraph*, and was a special writer with the *Australian* and News Limited Group, before becoming a freelance book-reviewer and feature-writer. In 1935 she married another journalist, 'Blue' Greatorex, who died in 1964. She has published six collections of poetry, *The Untrammelled* (1940), *Poems* (1948), *Forbears* (1961), *Occasions of Birds* (1987), *From the Midnight Courtyard* (1989) and *Selected Poems* (1992). She has won the Grace Leven Prize, the Christopher Brennan Award in 1991 and the NSW State inaugural Book of the Year Award for *Selected Poems* in 1992, and was awarded the Gold Medal of the Australian Literature Society in 1993.

Riddell's poetry, controlled, spare, frequently witty and lightly lyrical, concrete and sensuous, has been compared to that of Judith Wright and Kenneth Slessor, although the sparsity of her writing and the period of silence from 1961 to 1987 resulted in a relative critical neglect. Death has been a recurring theme in her verse from *The Untrammelled*, but the overall effect is nevertheless of gaiety and colour. Surety of expression characterises all her collections, but her later poetry is more sardonic and analytical; as Riddell herself has commented in an interview in *Tall Poppies* (1984): 'I've nothing to lose. I'm trying to write totally what I mean. When I was younger I was very addicted to the beautiful phrase. Now I'm ruthless with it.'

Ride On Stranger, a novel by Kylie Tennant (q.v.), was published in 1943. Shannon Hicks, an intelligent, independent girl in search of a role that will add meaning to her life, restlessly tries and discards a series of occupations and relationships. Although she works desperately hard in each succeeding missionary venture, whether it is in radio or in the United Council for the Defence of Labour, her keen awareness of the egoism that underlies human motive inevitably undermines her commitment. Her ultimate marriage to John Terrill, a young unambitious farmer, seems an achievement of happiness, but even this is disrupted by the war and Terrill's unexpected enlistment and death. By the end Shannon has found through suffering that her only home is her own stoic independence and acceptance of the claims of others.

Riders in the Chariot, a novel by Patrick White (q.v.), was published in 1961 and won the Miles Franklin Award. Set mainly in the Sydney suburbs of Sarsaparilla and Barranugli (qq.v.), it deals with the lives and final spiritual meeting of four 'illuminates': Mary Hare, an elderly spinster; Mordecai Himmelfarb, a Jewish refugee from Germany; Ruth Godbold, a housewife; and Alf Dubbo, a tubercular part-Aborigine. Miss Hare, the small, unattractive and unloved daughter of incompatible parents, lives on in the crumbling mansion Xanadu built by her half-mad father, Norbert Hare. Tortured by her memories of her father's violent death, which she had witnessed, and uneasy in most human relationships, she has a natural affinity with birds and animals and an instinct for spiritual truth. The latter quickly alienates her from her newly engaged housekeeper Mrs Jolley, whose vulgar materialism and capacity for evil is only surpassed by her more sinister friend Mrs Flack. Both ladies have annihilated their husbands with their versions of 'married love'. The most important event in Miss Hare's later life is her friendship with Mordecai Himmelfarb. The brilliant son of a devoutly orthodox mother and a shallow, worldly father, Himmelfarb discovers his faith belatedly, although he is early recognised as a *zaddik* by others. After studying at Oxford and service in the First World War, he becomes a professor of English in Germany and marries the devout Reha Liebmann. The growing force of anti-Semitism eventually disturbs the quiet of their devoted marriage. Himmelfarb loses his post and Reha is seized by police one night when he is absent. After a period of hiding, protected by his friends the Stauffers, Himmelfarb gives himself up, is transported to a concentration camp in Poland and escapes during an uprising. He briefly visits Israel but decides to settle in Australia, where he finds employment in Harry Rosetree's Brighta Bicycle Lamps factory. Harry Rosetree, formerly Haim Rosenbaum, now assimilated and living with his wife Shirl and 'the kids' in their texture-brick house in Paradise East, finds Himmelfarb's orthodoxy disturbing. Others who are impressed by his spirituality are Miss Hare, Ruth Godbold and Alf Dubbo. After a childhood in rural England, Ruth Godbold had settled in Australia where she had gone into service. Her spiritual superiority, amounting to saintliness, had reluctantly impressed one of her employers, the frivolous Mrs Chalmers-Robinson. Now the mother of a large family, married to a violent, alcoholic husband, Ruth lives in a temporary shed and takes in washing. Her genius for love touches Miss

Hare, Himmelfarb and, briefly, Alf Dubbo, and on one occasion even extends to retrieving her husband from the local brothel. Alf Dubbo, the fourth 'illuminate', lives on the margins of their lives. Born on a reserve to an Aboriginal mother and an indeterminate father, he had been adopted by the Reverend Timothy Calderon, Anglican rector of Numburra, and his widowed sister Mrs Pask. Before he is forced to flee by the Reverend's homosexual advances, Alf discovers the joy of painting. He lives for a while with the degenerate Mrs Spicer, mistress of a humpy set on a rubbish dump, and later with Hannah, a city prostitute, and her homosexual friend Norm Fussell. He contracts syphilis, of which he is cured, and tuberculosis, which rapidly worsens. Picking up work when he needs it to support his obsession of painting, Dubbo encounters Himmelfarb at Rosetree's factory, where he works as a sweeper. The forces of good and evil clash when Himmelfarb, long the object of Mrs Flack's venom, is half-lynched or crucified by her secret son Blue and his mates at the factory. Later the same day Himmelfarb's house is burned, although he has been previously rescued by Mrs Godbold. Nursed by Mrs Godbold and Miss Hare and watched over by Alf Dubbo, he dies on Good Friday. Harry Rosetree, unhinged by the incident, commits suicide; Alf Dubbo finds expression in paint for the elusive vision of the chariot of fire that all four 'illuminates' have in common but dies once it is completed. Miss Hare disappears and Xanadu is destroyed to make way for fibro homes. Mrs Jolley and Mrs Flack remain locked in a mutually destructive relationship. Only Mrs Godbold, now widowed and a grandmother, remains to testify to the divine mystery realised by the visionaries.

RIDLEY, William, see **Aborigine in White Australian Literature**

RIEMER, Andrew (1936–), born Budapest, Hungary, came to Australia with his parents when he was 10. Educated at the universities of Sydney and London, he was a distinguished member of the English Department of the University of Sydney until 1994. Like other younger members of the post-war influx of migrants from Europe to Australia, Riemer came under the influence of two cultures, the one inherited from family, the other imposed by the new environment. Again like many other young migrants, he felt the inherited culture less than older family members who, as 'The Living Dead', always remained spiritually, emotionally and intellectually within it. Riemer returned to Europe, at first briefly and later on a more extended visit, to probe the connection established by the first decade of his life and the influence of his family and ethnic background. To some extent Europe (Hungary and Austria), had always existed for him as 'a country of the mind' which had been fashioned by the fantasies and inner longings created by both personal memories and family reminiscences. The story of those two visits is contained in *Inside Outside* (1992) and *The Habsburg Café* (1993). *Inside Outside* deals largely with growing up in Australia, where contemporary experiences tended to conflict

with the emotional ties attaching him to 'the mythic motherland'. That first visit to Europe brought both the acceptance and evaluation of those ties. *The Habsburg Café*, a mixture of reminiscence, autobiography, travelogue and family history, assesses both the realities of contemporary Europe and the presence and influence of the past, and indicates his rootedness in Australia, although he can never claim to belong fully. Both books are important and impressive accounts of the immigrant experience. Riemer is also the author of several books of Shakespearean criticism and is a regular book-reviewer for the *Sydney Morning Herald*, the *Age* and *Australian Book Review*.

Rigby's Romance, a novel by Joseph Furphy (q.v.), was in its original form the fifth chapter of Furphy's major work *Such is Life* (1903), but was excised from that novel during revision. Serialised in the Broken Hill newspaper the *Barrier Truth* in 1905–6, *Rigby's Romance* was published in truncated form in 1921 and in full in 1946.

As in *Such is Life* and *The Buln-Buln and the Brolga* (1948), the latter also created out of material deleted from the former, the narrator of *Rigby's Romance* is Tom Collins (q.v.), who at the opening of the novel (April 1884), soon after the events of *Such is Life*) is on his leisurely way to fulfil a contract to clear a Riverina run of cattle. Between Echuca and Yooringa, where he expects to cross the path of an old friend, the American Jefferson Rigby, he meets two women also in search of Rigby; one of them, Kate Vanderdecken, is Rigby's former sweetheart. After reaching Yooringa and helping to facilitate the reunion between Rigby and Kate, Collins repairs to the banks of the nearby Murray River to fish for a 30-pound cod known to be in the area. He is joined by the bullock-drivers Robert Dixon and Steve Thompson, both of whom appear in *Such is Life*; Rigby himself; the kangaroo-hunter Smith; a trapper named Furlong; the farmer Binney and his brother-in-law, the Methodist minister Harold Lushington. The bulk of the novel comprises the yarns swapped among these men and their discussions and arguments about politics, religion and ethics, and the law, until Furlong eventually catches the fish and the party breaks up. Thompson, Dixon, Rigby, Furlong and Smith all tell stories of love affairs that end in unhappiness or failure, an important theme in *Such is Life*, although as the night wears on the socialist Rigby, despite the efforts of Tom and Steve to deflect him, increasingly dominates the conversation as he expounds his political ideas. In doing so, he forgets the appointment he has made with Kate and returns to her hotel next morning to discover that she has left Yooringa.

At one stage in his career Furphy preferred *Rigby's Romance* to all his other writing, although most commentators see it as slighter than and much inferior to *Such is Life*. *Rigby's Romance* is the less complex and less subtle work, although Rigby articulates many of Furphy's views on state socialism. The novel also contains similar surprises of plot to *Such is Life*, e.g. the revelation that Thompson is the man in Furlong's story who provided assistance when the trapper needed desperately to go to his dying wife. It enlarges our understanding of some of the characters of *Such is Life*, e.g. in the extra information which confirms Thompson's pessimistic view of life, and explores some of the same themes. Just as, in the long work, Tom's obsession with theory contrasts with his inability to interpret experience, so Rigby's idealistic concern that one should be responsible for one's fellows contrasts with his inability to keep his appointments in life. The ironic contrasts between theory and practice and between belief and experience are emphasised throughout *Rigby's Romance* and provide some of the novel's best moments, notably in Dixon's account of a courtship that fails because he is influenced by his reading of *Jane Eyre* into 'bullyragging' his girl. Dixon's earthy narrative of the story of Moses, the 'knowledge ill-inhabited' which causes him to mistranslate the Latin phrases he has acquired, and the elaborate code by which his profanities are recorded and satirised, are among the other comic highlights of the novel.

Rigmarole of the Hours, based in Melbourne, was a small press which operated 1974–79, publishing seventeen titles of new writings in Australia. Initially it was a magazine, *Rigmarole of the Hours*, which intended to publish books as special issues; after the first number in August 1974, edited by Robert Kenny, the magazine disappeared and the press began publishing books by writers such as Katherine Gallagher, Walter Billeter, Kris Hemensley, Robert Kenny, Laurie Duggan and Jennifer Maiden. Rigmarole of the Hours stopped publishing in 1980 but resumed in 1982 as Rigmarole Books when John Jenkins joined Kenny. It then published works by Anna Couani, Philip Jenkins, Ken Bolton, Anna Walwicz and Gerard Lee, but closed again at the end of 1986.

RIGNOLD, George, see **Shakespeare and Australia**

'RILEY, Elizabeth', see **Feminism and Australian Literature**

'Ringer', a term used to denote a stockman or a champion shearer, as in the famous ballad 'Click Go the Shears, Boys', or more recently any individual of exceptional ability, occurs frequently in Australian literature. See also Shearer in Australian Literature.

'Rio Grande's Last Race', one of A.B. Paterson's (q.v.) favourite ballads, is the title poem of his second collection of verse, *Rio Grande's Last Race and Other Verses* (1902). The poem's theme, a jockey's premonition of death, is unusual in Paterson, who prefers to applaud the deeds of racehorses and riders or to depict the humour and irony associated with the turf. Jack Macpherson's dream of his last fatal ride on Rio Grande is a traditional rather than a bush ballad. The language, which matches the sombre theme, is lifted above the usual colloquial style of the bush poem and the narrative moves with impressive urgency towards its fatal climax.

Riverina is a district in south-western NSW. Its borders have never been formally established but are generally taken to be the Lachlan and Murrumbidgee Rivers in the north and west, although sometimes the country beyond the Lachlan-Murrumbidgee towards the Darling River is counted; the Murray River in the south; and in the east an imaginary line from Albury northwards through the city of Wagga Wagga to the town of Condobolin. The Riverina, which is divided roughly in two (north and south) by the Murrumbidgee after it separates from the Lachlan, is a predominantly rural district, wheat-producing to the east and more suitable for wool further west; there are many arid parts, notably the Old Man Plain and the country between Hay and Booligal celebrated in A.B. Paterson's poem 'Hay and Hell and Booligal'. The Murrumbidgee Irrigation Area, in the centre of the Riverina, produces citrus, cereals and wine, although it was an area of prohibition when Henry Lawson was sent there to 'dry out' in 1913. Within the borders of the Riverina are, as well as the cities of Albury, Wagga Wagga and Griffith, smaller towns such as Jerilderie, where Ned Kelly staged a daring raid in 1879 and is said to have composed the Jerilderie Letter, and Deniliquin, near where 'Rolf Boldrewood' was living in 1865, when he wrote one of his first sketches, *Shearing in Riverina*.

The Riverina rivers were explored by John Oxley, Thomas Livingstone Mitchell and Charles Sturt, who all left journals of their expeditions. Pastoral settlement began in the 1830s, and other principal towns grew up around points on the various rivers across which stock was ferried southwards in the 1840s and 1850s; selectors first took up land in the 1860s. There are Riverina scenes or characters in a number of station romances and other works of fiction, including Randolph Bedford's *True Eyes and the Whirlwind* (1903), Carlton Dawe's *Love, the Conqueror* (1925), Mary Gaunt's *The Moving Finger* (1895), Nat Gould's *Racing Rituals* (1922), Thomas Heney's *The Girl at Birrell's* (1896), E.W. Hornung's *Irralie's Bushranger* (1896), Jessie Couvreur's *In Her Earliest Youth* (1890), F.J. Thwaites's *The Broken Melody* (q.v., 1930), Lilian Turner's *April Girls* (1911), Arthur Wright's *A Rogue's Luck* (1909), *Gambler's Gold* (1911) and *The Outlaw's Daughter* (1919) and E.O. Schlunke's *Stories of the Riverina* (1965). Among visitors to the area who recorded their impressions was Morley Roberts in *Land-travel and Sea-faring* (1891).

The two Australian writers most closely associated with the Riverina, however, are Joseph Furphy, who worked as a bullocky in the Riverina for ten years and whose *Such is Life* (1903) depicts life there in the early 1880s; and Miles Franklin, who as 'Brent of Bin Bin' published three volumes of a station saga set in the Murrumbidgee area: *Up the Country* (1928), *Ten Creeks Run* (1930) and *Back to Bool Bool* (1951).

A derivation from, and possible early alternative to, 'Riverina' is 'Riverine', as in the folk-song 'Banks of the Riverine', and in 'Price Warung's' *Tales of the Riverine* (1898), where it refers to the Murray River, its reaches and foreshores.

RIVETT, Rohan (1917–77), born Melbourne, a grandson of Alfred Deakin and son of the eminent scientist Sir David Rivett, was educated at the universities of Melbourne and Oxford. He joined the *Argus* in 1939, was a war correspondent in Malaya and was taken prisoner by the Japanese. *Behind Bamboo* (1946), his best-known book, is a detailed account of his experiences in prison camps and on the Burma–Thailand railway. In 1951 Rivett became editor-in-chief of Adelaide *News* and later a director of News Ltd, and was director of the International Press Institute at Zurich 1961–64. He returned to Melbourne in 1964 and worked as a freelance journalist and as a radio and television commentator on international affairs. As well as contributing to numerous books about Australia, he wrote a biography of Herbert Brookes, *Australian Citizen* (1965); a short history, *Australia* (1968); a series of lectures delivered for the Foundation for Australian Studies, *Writing about Australia* (1969); and a biography of his father, *David Rivett* (1972).

Road to Gundagai, The, a childhood autobiography by Graham McInnes (q.v.), the son of Angela Thirkell (q.v.), was published in 1965. The narrative opens in 1920 at Fremantle, where the Thirkell family, comprising Angela, her new husband George Thirkell ('Thirk'), her sons Graham and Colin, aged 8 and 6, and her 'lady-help' Mabel Baden, land on their way to Melbourne after a difficult seven-weeks' voyage aboard the troop-ship SS *Friedrichsruh*. After a six-months' visit to Tasmania, where they stay with Thirk's parents, they settle in the Melbourne suburb of Malvern. McInnes vividly describes both the general life of Melbourne in the 1920s, the city's sights, sounds and seasons, rituals, celebrations and social attitudes, and his individual experiences. The last include his education at Scotch College, holiday visits to country properties owned by their friends, Basil and Nell Hall, his brief career in the scouts, relationships with a varied sequence of 'lady-helps', with Thirk's relatives, and his maternal grandparents, and his brief associations with eminent friends of his mother such as the classical scholar Alexander Leeper, the artists Thea Proctor and Arthur Streeton, General Sir John Monash and the Papuan administrator Sir Hubert Murray. Most compelling of all is his picture of life at 4 Grace Street, Malvern, dominated by his literary mother, who remains doggedly committed to her Oxbridge values despite her imprisonment in a country which she considers fit only 'for Warrant Officers'.

The contrast between the parents' worlds ('With mother everything was sharp and tight and on schedule. Bells rang, cannons boomed, gongs clanged, flags were run up and the form was more important than the substance. With Dad it was a world of laissez-faire, sudden impulses, timeless cheerful whistling, odd tasks begun and never finished') gradually widens into an unbridgeable gulf; as Angela devotes herself to writing and broadcasting, Thirk retreats into his passions of stamp-collecting and standard roses, his small engineering firm TAMECO and the Naval and Military Club, where the Anzac dream is ever fresh. After Thirk is eased off the board of TAMECO fol-lowing the crash of 1929 and Graham wins a scholarship to the University of Melbourne, Angela leaves permanently for England with Colin and her youngest son, Lance. *The Road to Gundagai* was followed by three further autobiographies, *Humping My Bluey* (1966), *Finding a Father* (1967) and *Goodbye, Melbourne Town* (1968).

'Roaring Days, The' is a phrase referring nostalgically to the gold rushes. Its best-known literary use is in Henry Lawson's poem 'The Roaring Days', written from Lawson's boyhood memories of Gulgong and Pipeclay. The poem was first published in the *Bulletin* in 1889.

Roaring Nineties, The (1946), a novel by Katharine Susannah Prichard (q.v.), is the first part of a socialist-realist trilogy intended to document the history of the WA goldfields and tell the story of the development of the State's gold industry. *The Roaring Nineties* explores the early prospecting days, the wild rushes to the new fields of the Cross, Coolgardie and Kalgoorlie, the diggers' struggle for alluvial rights, and exploitation by wealthy foreign companies. Against this broad historical tableau are set the life and experiences of Sally Gough, the protagonist. The daughter of an Australian pioneer, Sally is married to an English gentleman who, caught in the madness of gold-fever, chases the 'yellow siren'. The novel follows Sally's attempts at financial independence as she cooks and runs boarding houses for the miners, offending the aristocratic prejudices of her husband Morris, who feels she is abrogating her dignity and breeding indifference to his wishes. Yet she is a dutiful wife and devoted mother, who believes implicitly in marriage as a contract and so she repels the emotional attraction which draws her to Frisco, a prospecting partner of Morris. Attuned to the fundamental principles of life on the goldfields, Sally encompasses the loyalty and egalitarian impulses of the workers and is responsive to the hardships and injustices suffered by the ordinary people and her Aboriginal friends. See *Golden Miles* and *Winged Seeds*.

SANDRA BURCHILL

Roaring Twenties, The (1960), the middle volume of Jack Lindsay's autobiographical trilogy, describes his life in Sydney 1921–26. A vivid picture of Sydney's cultural life at that time, it includes reminiscences of members of the Lindsay family, especially of Jack Lindsay's father Norman, and his brothers Raymond and Philip. As well as profiles of important literary figures such as Chris Brennan, Hugh McCrae, Kenneth Slessor and R.D. FitzGerald, Lindsay gives an account of the establishment of the journal *Vision* and of the Fanfrolico Press.

Robbery Under Arms, a novel by 'Rolf Boldrewood' (q.v.), was first published as a serial in the *Sydney Mail* 1882–83. With minor revisions, it was published in book form in 1888 and again in a one-volume edition, with further deletions which reduced the 269 000 words of the original to 231 000 in 1889.

The 1889 edition proved very popular and was reprinted over thirty times in the next fifty years. An adaptation by Alfred Dampier and Garnet Walch was first staged in 1890 and became part of Dampier's repertoire. *Robbery Under Arms* has been filmed three times (1907, 1920, 1957) and serialised on radio both in England and Australia.

The narrator, Dick Marston, awaiting execution at the start of the novel, decides to tell the cautionary tale of his life as a bushranger. Led into crime by their father, Ben Marston, Dick and his brother Jim join Ben and the aristocrat Captain Starlight (q.v.) in driving a mob of stolen cattle overland from NSW to SA. With the proceeds Dick and Jim holiday in Melbourne, where they take up with the sisters Kate and Jeannie Morrison and then work their way back to the family selection at Rocky Flat, where Dick is captured and sentenced, along with Starlight, to Berrima Gaol. After an escape is effected by Jim and Starlight's part-Aboriginal assistant, Warrigal, the gang turns from cattle-stealing to bushranging; they elude capture through the assistance of the Barnes family and because they have a secret hide-out, Terrible Hollow, which is probably based on Horse-stealer's Gully in the Gwydir district near Inverell, NSW. The news of the discovery of gold eventually draws Dick, Jim and Starlight to the Turon fields, where they have some success as miners, and Jim brings Jeannie from Melbourne to marry her. Kate, however, has married unhappily and runs a hotel on the goldfields; when she discovers Dick's love for Grace Storefield, who lives on the next farm at Rocky Flat, she betrays the brothers and Starlight. Jim is captured but rescued by Dick, and Starlight also eludes capture; back at Terrible Hollow, they embark on a second series of bushranging adventures, the gang now enlarged by the inclusion of Moran, Wall, Hulbert, Lardner and others. Moran, Wall, Hulbert and Lardner are based on the bushrangers Daniel Morgan, Ben Hall, John Gilbert and Frank Gardiner. Similarly, some of the subsequent exploits of the gang, including the robbing of the gold escort, Starlight's appearance at the Turon races while the police under Sir Ferdinand Morringer are looking for him elsewhere, and the raid on a squatter's homestead, are based on the exploits in the 1860s of the Hall-Gardiner-Gilbert gang. Starlight, Dick and Jim plan to go to America and escape, but *en route* to Queensland they are again betrayed by Kate and also by Warrigal; in the ensuing battle with police, Starlight and Jim are killed. At the end of the novel, Dick's death sentence is commuted through the intervention of George Storefield, the former neighbour of the Marstons, whose respectability and progress to wealth and position are contrasted throughout the novel with Dick's wildness and decline. When he leaves gaol twelve years later he marries Grace and settles in Queensland.

ROBERTS, Barney (1920–), born Flowerdale, Tasmania, where he lives on a farm, was a POW in the Second World War. He has published two books of verse, *The Phantom Boy* (1976) and *Stones in the Cephissus* (1979); a novel, *The Penalty of Adam* (1980); an

autobiography of childhood, *Where's Morning Gone?* (1987), which won a Tasmanian Bicentennial Literary Award; an account of his years in Europe as a prisoner of war, *A Kind of Cattle* (1985); and a collection of short stories, *Tales I Carry with Me* (1988). *Where's Morning Gone?* revisits the lost world of Tasmania's 1930s with the same outward simplicity and nostalgic, homely detail as T.A.G. Hungerford's re-creation of the west in *Stories from Suburban Road*. *A Kind of Cattle*, which avoids both the bravura and self-pity of some war writing, won a special award for the international year of peace in the NSW Premier's literary awards. Roberts also won the 'Rolf Boldrewood' Short Story Award in 1974.

ROBERTS, Bev (Beverley Dale) (1939–) has made an important contribution to the Australian literary scene in her various roles as assistant editor of *Meanjin*, as Victorian literature field officer and as co-ordinator of the Victorian Writers' Centre. Her own books of poetry are *The Transvestite Next Door* (1986), *Here Come the Pumpkins* (1991) and *The Exorcism Trip* (1991). A subtly humorous and modest poet, Bev Roberts writes with sensitivity and quiet charm about both the good and bad of life. Where there has been pain or injustice there is little rancour in their recollection, while the myriad irritations and irritators of daily life are quenched with wit and imagination. People, places, the past, mortality and the pleasure of poetry itself are the regular themes of her writing.

ROBERTS, Morley (1857–1942), the English writer who published over eighty books including stories of the sea, travel and other adventures, historical romances and novels and studies dealing with psychological, medical and literary topics, came to Australia early in 1877. He worked in Melbourne and on stations in the Riverina, returned to England at the end of 1879 and subsequently revisited the country in the course of other travels, recording his experiences in *Land-travel and Sea-faring* (1891) and *A Tramp's Note-book* (1904). Several of his short stories have Australian settings, the best-known being 'King Billy' of *King Billy of Ballarat and Other Stories* (1892), the story of a Ballarat Aborigine with a taste for fine clothes. Other Australian sketches are in *The Reputation of George Saxon and Other Stories* (1892), *Bianca's Caprice* (1904), *The Grinder's Wheel* (1907) and *The Madonna of the Beech Wood* (1918). He also wrote several Australian romances and included some Australian material in others. Novels which are wholly or partly set in Australia are *The Adventures of a Ship's Doctor* (1895), *The Adventures of the Broad Arrow* (1897), a romance about the discovery of a lost tribe descended from escaped convicts which anticipates the tale of 'Louis de Rougemont', *The Flying Cloud* (1907), *Hearts of Women* (1919) and *Women and Ships* (1932). In *The Private Life of Henry Maitland* (1912), based on the life of his friend George Gissing, Roberts includes thinly veiled references to his own travels in Australia.

ROBERTS, Nigel (1941–), born Wellington, NZ, has lived in Australia since 1965 and teaches art.

One of the significant identities of the poetry revolution in Australia in the late 1960s–1970s, Roberts was a leading member of the Balmain Poetry Group 1970–76 and was associated with the magazines *Free Poetry*, *Package Deal* and *Living Daylights*. Roberts has published only two volumes of poetry, *In Casablanca for the Waters* (1977) and *Steps for Astaire* (1983), but is a prominent figure in the Australian poetry scene. He is represented in such 'New Poetry' anthologies as John Tranter's *The New Australian Poetry* (1979) and Gray and Lehmann's *The Younger Australian Poets* (1983). A witty and ironic poet, Roberts writes with lively, biting relevance about the modern scene and is innovative with verse forms and techniques. Informal in language, experimental with the shape of the poem on the page, and iconoclastic in his ribald derision of sacred cows, either in life or poetry, Roberts is one of the more strikingly individualistic of contemporary writers.

ROBERTS, Philip (1938–), born Canada, studied at the universities of Acadia (Canada), Oxford and Sydney, and has worked as a sub-editor for Reuters news agency in London, and as a public relations consultant. In 1967–79 he taught English at the University of Sydney and since 1980 he has been a writer, now resident in Canada. Founding editor of Island Press, Sydney, 1970–79, he was poetry editor of the *Sydney Morning Herald* 1970–74, and editor of the annual anthologies, *Poet's Choice*. He began writing poetry at Oxford, where he was encouraged by Robert Graves, and has published six collections, *Just Passing Through* (1969), *Single Eye in Two Poets* (1971, with Geoff Page), *Crux* (1973), *Will's Dream* (1975), *Selected Poems* (1978) and *Letters Home* (1990). Cosmopolitan, sophisticated, condensed and polished, Roberts's poetry has a musical finesse that reflects his talents as a pianist. *Will's Dream*, his most ambitious and extended work, is a sequence of poems which deftly builds up an original interior world and which features four characters, one of whom is Will, the dreamer of the sequence. The poems of *Selected Poems* and the earlier collections are taut, witty, deceptively laconic comments on a multiplicity of subjects, some of them literary. Island Press, in addition to publishing *Poet's Choice*, has produced works by Kevin Gilbert, Martin Johnston, Robert Adamson, Phillip Hammial, Andrew Taylor, Ken Bolton, J.S. Harry and many others. Roberts has also written *How Poetry Works* (1986) and *Plain English: A User's Guide* (1987).

ROBERTS, Ted (1931–), born Sydney, spent twelve years in advertising and sales promotion and has worked as a freelance writer, mainly for television and cinema. He has written episodes for such television series as *Homicide*, *Division Four*, *Rush*, *Certain Women*, *Patrol Boat* and *A Country Practice*; plays for television, such as *Lindsay's Boy*, included in *Five Plays for Stage, Radio and Television* (1977, ed. Alrene Sykes), 'Three Men of the City', 'Wilde's Domain', 'The Amorous Dentist', 'Straight Enough' and 'The Kiss and Ride Ferry'; and feature films for cinema, *Bush Christmas* and *The Settlement*.

ROBERTS, Tom (1856–1931), born Dorchester, England, arrived in Australia in 1869. He trained as an artist in Melbourne and London. One of the famous Heidelberg School (q.v.) of painters, who practised a modified form of impressionism and attempted to capture the essence of Australian light and colour, Roberts is sometimes referred to as 'the father of Australian painting'. He was one of the first to paint outback subjects; among such works are his *Shearing the Rams*, *The Breakaway*, *The Golden Fleece* and *Bailed Up!* He painted *Opening of the First Federal Parliament of the Commonwealth of Australia*, a remarkable work which hangs in the High Court of Australia in Canberra. His close friend R.H. Croll published *Tom Roberts: Father of Australian Landscape Painting* (1935), and edited *Smike to Bulldog* (1946), the letters of Arthur Streeton (q.v.) to Roberts. Peter Batey's entertainment 'From Smike to Bulldog' is also based on the letters. Virginia Spate published the monograph *Tom Roberts* (1972), listing 481 of his paintings. Helen Topliss extended the number to 770 paintings and drawings in her two-volume work *Tom Roberts 1856–1931. A Catalogue Raisonné* (1985).

ROBERTSON & MULLEN, see **ROBERTSON, George** (1); **MULLEN, Samuel**

ROBERTSON, George (1) (1825–98), born Glasgow, was a fellow apprentice with Samuel Mullen (q.v.) in the Dublin firm of William Curry, booksellers. In 1852 the two friends emigrated to Australia (coincidentally arriving on the same day as E.W. Cole), Mullen to follow a life on the land and Robertson, after selling a case of second-hand books on the Melbourne wharf, to open a bookshop in Russell Street. By 1855 Robertson was thriving as a retail and wholesale bookseller, publisher and stationer and Mullen joined him as his assistant. In 1857 Robertson opened a London office and Mullen was sent to England to manage it only to find, on his arrival, that the job had been given to William Robertson, George's brother. From that time Robertson and Mullen were completely estranged and it was not until 1922, long after both men were dead, that the two companies, George Robertson & Co and Melville & Mullen came together as the now famous firm of Robertson & Mullen. In 1860 Robertson bought the derelict property at 69 Elizabeth Street, Melbourne, and built a magnificent new bookshop. The Elizabeth Street premises (now numbered 107) were occupied for many years by the firm of Robertson & Mullen and later by the Melbourne branch of the Sydney firm Angus & Robertson. Robertson opened a Sydney branch in 1860 under the charge of William Maddock, a notable early Sydney bookseller to whom he sold the Sydney business in 1862. By 1875 Robertson was back in Sydney at 125 Pitt Street and later also at 361 George Street. He opened branches also in Adelaide and Brisbane. Through the Robertson bookshops passed names destined to become legendary in Australian bookselling and publishing: William Dymock, David Angus, George Robertson (2), George Philip, E.J. Dwyer and T.V. Carroll. E.A. Petherick (q.v.)

was, at one time, manager of Robertson's London branch. The publisher of more than 600 titles, George Robertson produced many of the works of Adam Lindsay Gordon, Henry Kendall, Marcus Clarke, 'Rolf Boldrewood', G.G. McCrae and James Bonwick. In 1861–89 he published *George Robertson's Monthly Book Circular*, a list of new books and periodicals, sometimes with notes and short literary reviews, and the Melbourne journals *Melbourne Review* and *Tatler*, 1879–85 and 1897–98. Robertson retired from active bookselling and publishing in 1890. John Holroyd, veteran bookseller and formerly head of the rare books departments of Robertson & Mullen in Melbourne and then of Angus & Robertson in Sydney, published the biography *George Robertson of Melbourne* (1968).

ROBERTSON, George (2) (1860–1933), born Halstead, Essex, England, was apprenticed to James Maclehose, publisher and bookseller to the University of Glasgow. In 1879 he migrated to NZ and came to Sydney in 1882. By coincidence he found employment in the Sydney branch of George Robertson (1) (q.v.), bookseller and publisher of Melbourne, where a fellow employee was David Mackenzie Angus (q.v.), with whom in 1886 he formed the Australian publishing and bookselling firm of Angus & Robertson (q.v.). After Angus's death in 1901 Robertson continued in partnership with Frederick Victor Wymark, a longtime employee, and Richard Thomson, who had bought Angus's share of the business; in 1907 the partnership was converted into a public company.

The firm's interest in Australiana sprang largely from George Robertson and Wymark. They collected and sold countless books, pamphlets, manuscripts, prints and maps from all over the world relating to Australia and influenced such major collectors as David Scott Mitchell and Sir William Dixson. George Robertson's evidence to a parliamentary committee in 1905 on the value of the Mitchell and Dixson collections was instrumental in the establishment of the Mitchell Library. In the 1920s he bought a controlling interest in a Sydney printery, the Eagle Press, which he retitled Halstead Press. A dominant figure among Australian publishers of his time, George Robertson was always highly esteemed and affectionately regarded by the writers whom he assisted. Henry Lawson referred to him as 'The Chief', while Mary Gilmore commented in a 1932 letter, 'I never think of you that I do not see Australia. You and she are inseparable.' A selection of George Robertson's correspondence, titled *Dear Robertson: Letters to an Australian Publisher*, was published in 1982 and in a revised edition in 1993, edited by A.W. (Tony) Barker, a former A & R editor. Much of the early history of Angus & Robertson is contained in George Ferguson's (Robertson's grandson) *Some Early Australian Bookmen* (1978).

ROBERTSON, Gilbert (1794–1851) was a West Indian farmer who migrated to Van Diemen's Land in 1822. He entered journalism in the 1830s, edited the *Colonist* in 1832 and was proprietor of the *True Colonist* (1834–44), which was a daily, the first in Australia, in 1835, and the *Horn Boy* (1834–38). Known as the 'Tasmanian Cobbett', Robertson was not only an uncompromising opponent of the lieutenant-governor, George Arthur, in the fight for press freedom in Tasmania, but was also involved in controversies with fellow pressmen R.L. Murray, James Ross and William Gore Elliston. He later settled on Norfolk Island where the memoirist John Mortlock worked for him.

ROBERTSON, John George (1867–1933), born Glasgow, Scotland, graduated in science from the University of Glasgow in 1889. In the same year he left for Leipzig, where he studied European languages and literature, gaining his doctorate in 1892, and where he met the future novelist 'Henry Handel Richardson' (q.v.) whom he married in 1895. After a period as lecturer at Strasbourg University, he was offered a chair in German at the University of London in 1903. A distinguished and productive scholar, Robertson was prominent in making London a centre of German studies, published numerous works on German writers and in 1905 founded the *Modern Language Review*, which he edited for four years. Robertson, who undoubtedly influenced the literary interests of his wife, directing her towards Scandinavian literature, took immense pains to leave her free for writing by protecting her from domestic and other cares. One of her most perceptive critics, he wrote an essay titled 'The Art of Henry Handel Richardson' (1928–29), first published with *Myself When Young* (1948).

ROBERTSON, Marjorie contributed short stories to periodicals and anthologies and published one collection, *In One Town* (1946), and a novel, *To Ripen or to Kill* (1953). With Mary Cecil Woods she also published the legal guide *Leaves from a Woman Lawyer's Casebook* (1947) under the pseudonym 'Marjorie Woodson'.

ROBERTSON, Tim (1944–), born Braintree, England, migrated to Australia in 1953. A member of the Australian Performing Group 1972–77, he collaborated with John Romeril in 'A Night in Rio and Other Bummerz' (1972) and has since acted in and written for theatre, film and television as well as directing numerous productions. His plays and musicals include *Waltzing Matilda. A National Pantomime with Tomato Sauce* (1984, with John Romeril), *Mary Shelley and the Monsters* (1983), 'Tristram Shandy, Gent' (1985), 'Charles the Last' (1976), and, with Don Watson and others, 'Manning Clark's History of Australia' (1988). He has also written the novel *Dimboola* (1978), adapted from Jack Hibberd's play.

ROBINSON, George Augustus (1788–1866), born London, emigrated in 1824 to Hobart, where he established himself as a builder and manifested philanthropic concerns. In 1829 he was given the task of conciliating the Aborigines on Bruny Island and from

1830 to 1834 contacted tribes in all parts of Tasmania with a view to persuading them to join the new settlement at Flinders Island. Although the settlement was under Robinson's general superintendence, it was managed by commandants who saw themselves as gaolers. Mortality among the Aborigines was high, the population having shrunk from 4000 to 150 by 1835. In October 1835 Robinson took control of the settlement and attempted, unsuccessfully, to inculcate the remaining Aborigines with the Protestant ethic and nineteenth-century European village values. His failure did nothing to erode the confidence of the White settlers in their plans to 'civilise' the native tribes, and in 1838 Robinson was appointed chief protector of Aborigines at Port Phillip, where he remained for the next eleven years. His protectorship was undistinguished and his assistants condemned by Governor Gipps for inefficiency, although he made several journeys to SA, NSW and the Murray Valley, which yielded valuable information about the tribes. His Port Phillip journals, edited by Ian D. Clark, were published in 1988, and George Mackaness edited his report of his 1844 journey into South Eastern Australia (1941). After the protectorate was abolished in 1849, Robinson returned to England in 1852 and settled at Bath. Truganini (q.v.) assisted Robinson in contacting the tribes of Tasmania and accompanied him to Port Phillip. Robinson's Tasmanian journals and papers 1829–34 were published in 1966, titled *Friendly Mission* and edited by N.J.B. Plomley, and his career has been described by Lyndall Ryan in *The Aboriginal Tasmanians* (1981). Plomley's *Weep in Silence* (1987), an extensive history of the Flinders Island settlement, discusses Robinson's role, which he interprets as more benign than that of his successors; Vivienne Rae-Ellis, however, in a study based on Robinson's private journals and correspondence as well as the official material, *Black Robinson* (1988), challenges the view that he was a 'friend' to the Aborigines. Cassandra Pybus in *Community of Thieves* (1991) presents Robinson as a man of contradictory motives and meditates on his legacy to present-day Tasmanians. Robinson appears as a character in Bill Reed's plays about Truganini (1977), in Hume Nisbet's novel *The Savage Queen* (1891) and in Robert Drewe's novel *The Savage Crows* (1976); C.S. Ross's novel *Dick Arnold* (1893) includes references to his work.

ROBINSON Les(lie) (1886–1968), born Sydney, contributed verse, short stories and articles to numerous periodicals and several anthologies and published one collection of stories, *The Giraffe's Uncle* (1933). Temperamentally unstable and unable to maintain long-term employment, he was a familiar member of Sydney's bohemia for many years, supporting himself by writing freelance for the *Melbourne Punch*, *Art in Australia*, *Smith's Weekly* and the *Worker*. In later life he led a hermit existence in caves on Middle Harbour. His life and personality are described in Peter Kirkpatrick's *The Sea Coast of Bohemia* (1992).

ROBINSON, Michael Massey (1744–1826), lawyer turned blackmailer, arrived in NSW as a convict in 1798. His legal experience gained him appointment as secretary to the deputy judge-advocate of the Colony. Corrupt use of his office and the charge of 'promoting discords', probably by the writing of lampooning verses known as pipes (q.v.), saw him in 1805 at Norfolk Island. Pardoned in 1811, he advanced to principal clerk in the police office before he died. Under Governor Lachlan Macquarie, Robinson composed odes to celebrate the birthdays of George III and Queen Charlotte 1810–21. With one exception they were published in the *Sydney Gazette* and read by Robinson at the annual birthday ceremonies at Government House. In 1818 and 1819 he was repaid 'for his services as Poet Laureate' by a grant of two cows from the government herd, probably the first royalties to a poet in Australia. The odes, in the stilted flowery language of the public-poem genre, lavished praise not only on the royal couple but also on their subjects, who were energetically evangelising the new southern land to the British way of life. The odes blatantly flattered Macquarie also, for the governor, accepting Oliver Goldsmith's opinion that a bold peasantry was its country's pride, favoured the development of peasant farming and a cottage economy, and Robinson depicted the settlement in the romanticised manner of Macquarie's hopes for it. On Macquarie's resignation Robinson lost his poetic 'office' but vented some of his spleen on Governor Sir Thomas Brisbane by celebrating in several ballads the virtues of Macquarie over his successor. Twenty-seven of Robinson's poems, including twenty royal birthday odes, were published by George Mackaness in his monograph *Odes of Michael Massey Robinson* (1946). He appears as a character in Eris O'Brien's play *The Hostage* (1928). Robinson's role in Macquarie's vision of a neo-classical culture in NSW is examined by Robert Dixon in *The Course of Empire* (1986).

ROBINSON, Roland (1912–92), born County Clare, Ireland, was brought to Australia when 9 years old. After a brief schooling he began work as a rouseabout on a sheep station near Coonamble, NSW, and subsequently worked as a boundary-rider, railway fettler, fencer, dam-builder, factory-worker, ballet-dancer, gardener and golf-course groundsman. He was a book reviewer and ballet and literary critic for the *Sydney Morning Herald*, editor of *Poetry Magazine* 1965–69, and president of the Poetry Association of Australia. During the Second World War he worked in the Northern Territory, an experience which provided contact with tribal Aboriginal life to add to his existing familiarity with detribalised Aborigines from his youthful wanderings in the bush and his later experiences in the 1950s when, with the assistance of CLF grants, he gathered stories from the Aborigines of NSW. Strongly attracted to the Australian landscape and spirit of place long before the Jindyworobak movement and before he met its founder, Rex Ingamells, in 1944, Robinson came to be accepted as the best and most dedicated of the Jindyworobak poets, but he is not as stereotyped as the Jindyworobak label would imply. His published verse began with *Beyond the Grass-tree Spears* (1944), twenty-one brief poems, the first of which indicates, in its opening lines, Robinson's poetic stance:

> I made my verses of places where I made
>   my fires;
> of the dark trees standing against the blue-
>   green night
> with the first stars coming; of the bare plains
>   where a
> bird broke into running song, and of the
>   wind-cold scrub
> where the bent trees sing to themselves, and
>   of the night
> black about me, the fire dying out, and the
>   ashes left.

Later volumes include *Language of the Sand* (1949), *Tumult of the Swans* (1953), and *Deep Well* (1962), which incorporated selections from the earlier volumes and added new poems exploring his pantheistic vision of the land and its primal inhabitants, the Aborigines, and in other verses examining the 'deep well' of his own self. *Grendel* (1967) has, in addition to its Aboriginal legends, a section on the impact of White settlement that tends, especially in a poem such as 'The Pioneers', to suggest the ultimate meaninglessness of all human endeavour. *Altjeringa and Other Aboriginal Poems* (1970) is a collection of Robinson's earlier, but revised, Aboriginal poems. The first part of the volume contains translations of poems that he had gathered from the Aborigines themselves; the second part has his own poetry on Aboriginal themes. *Selected Poems* (1971), a surprisingly small collection, is made up of poems mostly in accord with the Jindyworobak movement. His eighth volume of poetry, *The Hooded Lamp*, was published in 1976; a second *Selected Poems* (1983) was edited by A.J. Bennett and Michael Sharkey and a third in 1989, edited by Robert Gray. Robinson's prose collections, which include his own and Aboriginal work, indicate, by their titles, his deep interest in Aboriginal lore and narrative. They include *Legend & Dreaming* (1952), *The Feathered Serpent* (1956), *Black-feller, White-feller* (1958), *The Man Who Sold His Dreaming* (1965), *Aboriginal Myths and Legends* (1966), *The Australian Aboriginal in Colour* (1968) and *The Nearest the White Man Gets* (1989). The last is a book of Aboriginal narratives and poems from NSW with an introductory essay by Norman Talbot. He published three autobiographical volumes, *The Drift of Things* (1973, NBC Award winner), *The Shift of Sands* (1976), and *A Letter to Joan* (1978). Robinson was awarded the OAM, received the Patrick White Award in 1988, the FAW Christopher Brennan Award in 1989 and in 1991 a D.Litt. from the University of Newcastle. He was also an emeritus fellow of the Australia Council.

Rocks, The, a name applied to a small harbourside area of Sydney west of Sydney Cove, is distinguished by configurations of sandstone. The area was settled early and had acquired its name by 1803. By the mid-nineteenth century, frequented by sailors and the crews of whaling vessels, it had also acquired a notorious reputation. The Rocks 'Push' of the 1890s also added to the area's colourful image and is featured in the novels *King of the Rocks* (1900) by Ambrose Pratt and *An Outback Marriage* (1906) by A.B. Paterson, and Henry Lawson's poem 'The Captain of the Push'. Well-known Australians who lived in the area include George Howe, Henry Kendall, Sir Edmund Barton, Sir George Reid and Conrad Martens. The area was also visited by Joseph Conrad and Jack London, both of whom stayed at the Ship and Mermaid Hotel, which London also used as the setting for one of his short stories. The area is described in Isadore Brodsky's *Heart of the Rocks of Old Sydney* (1965) and Alan Sutherland's *The Rocks* (1965). The 1980s redevelopment of the Rocks area attempted to recapture something of the atmosphere of Old Sydney.

RODD, Lewis Charles (1906–79), born Sydney, was the husband of Kylie Tennant. The son of a sea captain, he describes his early years in *A Gentle Shipwreck* (1975), which is also a revealing account of life in poverty-stricken Surry Hills, Sydney, before the First World War. He subsequently became a primary school headmaster and produced a number of literary studies for use in schools as well as editing two anthologies of Australian essays: *Venturing the Unknown Ways* (1965, with Donald McLean), and *The Australian Essay* (1968). His biography of John Hope, rector of Christ Church, St Laurence (1972), is also a social history.

'RODDA, Emily', see **ROWE, Jennifer**

RODDA, Percival Charles ('Gavin Holt') (1891–?), born Port Augusta, SA, was a journalist on the *Age* before going in 1919 to the USA, where he became a music critic for *Musical America*. In 1926 Rodda went to London and lived from then on in England and France, where he established a world-wide reputation as a writer of crime and mystery fiction under the pseudonym, 'Gavin Holt'. His best-known creation was the criminologist Professor Bastion, who first appeared in the novel *Six Minutes Past Twelve* (1928), and was the chief character in a long series of books. Rodda's first novel, *The Fortunes of Geoffrey Mayne* (1919), appeared in A.C. Rowlandson's Bookstall series. Both it and *The Scarlet Mask* (1926) are stories of the Australian bushranging days. There are only incidental associations with Australia in his other novels.

RODERICK, Colin (1911–) was born Mt Morgan, Queensland. He was foundation professor of English at James Cook University 1965–76, editor for Angus & Robertson 1945–65, and director 1961–65, and has written extensively on Australian literature. Some of his most significant achievements are his editions of Henry Lawson's work, *Collected Verse* (1967–69) and *Collected Prose* (1972). He has also edited other Lawson anthologies; Lawson's letters (1970); a selection of critical writing on Lawson (1972); a collection of his writings which chart the development of his creative life, *Henry Lawson. Master Storyteller* (1985); and has written several biographical and critical accounts, including *Henry Lawson: Poet and Short Story*

Writer (1966), The Real Henry Lawson (1982) and Henry Lawson. A Life (1991). His other writings on Australian literature include three studies of fiction, the first two combining selections and commentary, The Australian Novel (1945), 20 Australian Novelists (1947) and An Introduction to Australian Fiction (1950); a translation of Miska Hauser's Letters from Australia 1854–1858 (1988), edited with Hugh Anderson; a companion to Walter Murdoch's essays (1945); a lecture on the nature of Australian literature, Suckled by a Wolf (1968); a biographical account of Rosa Praed, In Mortal Bondage (1948); and the biographies Miles Franklin: Her Brilliant Career (1982), Leichhardt, the Dauntless Explorer (1988) and Banjo Paterson: Poet by Accident (1993). He also edited James Tucker's Ralph Rashleigh (1952) and Jemmy Green in Australia (1955); compiled a collection of travel writings, Wanderers in Australia (1949) and a collection of short stories, Australian Round-up (1953); and has written an account of the murderer John Knatchbull (1963), which includes Knatchbull's autobiographical narrative, and a historical novel, The Lady and The Lawyer (1955). Made emeritus professor soon after his retirement, Roderick was also awarded an honorary D.Litt. by the University of Caen (France) and James Cook University (1977, 1991). He is also a Commander of the British Empire (CBE). In 1966 he established the Foundation for Australian Literary Studies in Townsville; its annual lectures on Australian literature are named in his honour.

RODRIGUEZ, Judith (1936–   ), born Perth as Judith Green and brought up in Brisbane, was educated at the universities of Queensland and Cambridge. She has taught literature and/or conducted professional writing courses in many parts of the world – England, the West Indies, America, several Australian universities and institutes of higher education – and has been active also as poet, anthologist, editor, reviewer and writer-in-residence. She taught at La Trobe University, Melbourne, 1969–85, later at the Macarthur Insitute, Sydney, and since 1989 has been lecturing in professional writing at the Victoria College, Melbourne. She has had writing residencies at Ormond College, the University of Melbourne, Royal Melbourne Institute of Technology and Rollins College, Florida. From 1979 to 1982 she was poetry editor of Meanjin and has edited the Penguin Australian Poetry Series since 1989. She has also edited Mrs Noah and The Minoan Queen (1983, Australian women poets); Swedish Poets in Translation (1985, with Thomas Shapcott); a selection of poems from twenty years of the Australian (1985, with Andrew Taylor); and a collection of Australian poems (1946–88) in Italian (1988). She has collected the poems of Jennifer Rankin (1990), written (with Vicki Pauli) the art text, Noela Hjorth (1984), compiled a poetry-writing course (1976), and edited the Foundations of Professional Writing Series 1988–89. Her own poetry includes Nu-Plastik Fanfare Red (1973), Water Life (1976), Shadow on Glass (1978), Mudcrab at Gambaro's (1980), Witch Heart (1982), Floridian Poems (1986), New and Selected Poems: The House by Water (1988) and The Cold (1992). In 1962 she shared (with A Question of Ignorance) the volume Four Poets;

the other poets were David Malouf, Rodney Hall and Donald Maynard.

Judith Rodriguez's early poems (Nu Plastik Red, Water Life, Shadow in Glass) often deal with personal, family and domestic experiences, but they also range out to cover women's experience more broadly. With Mudcrab at Gambaro's a new emotional experience provides an exultation that is palpable, the word 'mudcrab' itself coming to stand for excitement, joy, fulfilment, the ingredients of a new situation. Witch Heart (1982) brings the obverse side, the aftermath of divorce and the sense of dislocation that follows such a personal upheaval ('Leaving', 'Leaving the Trees', 'Travelling'). Always vigorously responsive to experience, she specifies 'clarity' and 'energy' as desirable qualities in any writing. Such qualities are abundantly evident in her own poetry, as is a reliance on the expressiveness of direct and forthright language, enhanced frequently by intricate verbal sound-patterning and effective imagery. In 1974 she began making linocuts and woodcuts for book decorations, some of which are included in Water Life, Shadow on Glass and New and Selected Poems. She won the inaugural SA Biennial Prize for Literature in 1978 for Water Life, the International PEN/Peter Stuyvesant Prize for Poetry and the Shell/Artlook Prize for Mudcrab at Gambaro's.

ROE, Paddy (1912?–   ), born on Roebuck Plains station near Broome, WA, has worked as a drover and windmill-repairer throughout the Kimberley region. An unofficial ombudsman who negotiates between government agencies and the Aboriginal communities of the Kimberley region, he is regarded as outstandingly knowledgeable about traditional tribal life. He has published a collection of stories, edited by Stephen Muecke, gularabulu (1983), and with Stephen Muecke and Krim Benterrak contributed to Reading the Country (1984). The latter is an attempt to convey different meanings and interpretations of a place, Roebuck Plains, as experienced by all three individuals who are in one sense or another 'foreigners'. If Roe is a 'foreigner' to painting and the European artefact of the book, Adelaide-born Muecke is a foreigner to Roebuck Plains and to painting, and the Morrocco-born painter Benterrak is a foreigner to the Plains and to the communications theory which underlies Muecke's work.

'ROHAN, Criena' (Deirdre Cash) (1924–63), born Melbourne, was the daughter of Leo Cash, poet and Marxist, and Valerie Cash, a talented singer. After her parents separated, she was brought up by her grandmother in SA, by aunts in Melbourne, and then boarded at the Convent of Mercy in Mornington, Victoria. She studied singing at the Albert Street Conservatorium before working as a singer in nightclubs and as a teacher of ballroom dancing, meanwhile enjoying the freedoms of post-war Australia. Her first marriage, which issued in a son, failed, and she subsequently married a coastal seaman, Otto Olsen, and had a daughter. She published two novels, The Delinquents (1962) and Down by the Dockside (1963), both of which deal with the experiences and love affairs of working-class, urban youngsters. Although they fit within the social-realist genre, they are not propagandist and are enlivened by Rohan's versatile style, which ranges from the colloquial to the lyrical, and by her lively sense of humour. *The Delinquents* was produced as a film in 1989. In the same year it was listed in a group which the Festival of Light considered should be removed from the NSW high school curriculum because of a 'hidden agenda of sex education'. Rohan died of cancer before her last book was published. Republished in 1984 and 1986, with introductions by Barrett Reid, the two novels found an appreciative 1980s audience.

ROLAND, Betty (1903–), born in the Victorian Mallee town of Kaniva as Elizabeth Maclean, later adopted her father's christian name. After leaving school at 16 she worked as a journalist for *Table Talk* and *Sun News-Pictorial*; married in 1923; and in 1928, at a time when Australian drama was generally neglected by theatres, saw her first play, *The Touch of Silk* (q.v., 1942) produced by the Melbourne Repertory Theatre. Her marriage failed in 1933 and she eloped with a prominent Australian communist, Guido Baracchi, to Russia, where she stayed for fifteen months working as a journalist. After returning to Australia in 1935 and joining the Communist Party, she wrote a series of political plays and sketches that were frequently performed as street theatre. Of these, 'Are You Ready, Comrade?', which won a competition in 1938 and was widely performed in theatres, is the only full-length piece. By 1939, after she had become disillusioned with communism, she abandoned political plays and, after the breakdown of her nine-year relationship with Baracchi, became a prolific writer for radio. She had been introduced to the artist Justus Jorgensen, and his followers by Mervyn Skipper (q.v.) in the 1920s and became an intermittent member of the artists' colony he established at Montsalvat near Eltham, Melbourne, living there in 1941 and from 1947 to 1950. From 1952 to 1961 she lived in London, where she established a successful career as a freelance writer. In 1972 she was invited back to Montsalvat to work on Mervyn Skipper's extensive archive on the community, a task which absorbed her until 1979 and resulted in *The Eye of the Beholder* (1984). Partly autobiography and partly an interpretation of Jorgensen and his followers, it is densely informative on aspects of Australia's cultural life from the 1920s to the 1940s. Artists, writers and academics who are discussed include Max Meldrum, Percy Leason, Jim Minogue, Colin Colahan, George Chalmers, Clarice Beckett, Mervyn and Lena Skipper, Dolia Ribush, Vance and Nettie Palmer, Max Teichmann and William Macmahon Ball. Roland has also written three other autobiographies: *Caviar for Breakfast* (1979), an account of her experiences in the Soviet Union which includes some discussion of her relationship with Katharine Susannah Prichard; *An Improbable Life* (1989), which deals with her childhood, marriage to Ellis Davies, the loss of her son, and the beginnings of her career as a writer; and *The Devious Being* (1990), which describes the breakdown of her relationship

with Baracchi and her struggle to survive as a writer in the post-war years. All four autobiographies are remarkably frank about her intimate experiences, her relationships with well-known individuals and her knowledge of the Australian political and cultural scene over four decades. Roland's other published plays are *Morning*, which was included in a 1937 anthology and *Granite Peak*, a three-act play about Central Australia which was televised in Britain and published in 1988 with a revised version of *The Touch of Silk*. One of her early serials, *A Woman Scorned*, became the basis of a popular television serial of 1983, titled *Return to Eden*. She also scripted the first full-length talking feature film made in Australia, *The Spur of the Moment*, produced in 1931. Her other writings include several children's books, travel accounts, and three novels: *The Other Side of Sunset* (1972), *No Ordinary Man* (1974) and *Beyond Capricorn* (1976).

ROLFE, Patricia, see *Bulletin*

ROLLS, Eric C. (1923–), born Grenfell, NSW, has farmed near Narrabri. His poems have appeared in four collections, *Sheaf Tosser* (1967), *The Green Mosaic* (1977), *Miss Strawberry Verses* (1978) and *Selected Poems* (1990). A versatile, exuberant poet with a gift for satire, wry irony and the macabre as well as for the simple nature lyric, Rolls focuses mainly on his farming and family experiences in *Sheaf Tosser* and on his memories of New Guinea in *The Green Mosaic*. Both collections demonstrate his keen interest in animals and the processes of nature. *Miss Strawberry Verses* is a collection of humorous poems for children. Rolls has also written an account of the importation into Australia and subsequent proliferation of the rabbit and other pests, *They All Ran Wild* (1969), which won the Cook Bicentenary Award for a work of non-fiction. Revised for children and titled *Running Wild* (1973), it also won the John Franklin Award. Rolls's other writings are *The River* (1974), an autobiographical essay reflecting his farming experiences in the Namoi River district; *Doorways: A Year of the Cumberdeen Diaries* (1989), accompanied by photographs by John Peel, which partly recounts his research into the history of the Chinese in Australia and partly describes the way of life on his farm at Cumberdeen; *Sojourners: the Epic Story of China's Centuries-Old Relationship with Australia* (1992); *A Million Wild Acres* (1981), a natural and social history of the Pilliga forest in central NSW which won the 1981 C.J. Dennis Award and the *Age* Book of the Year Award; *Celebration of the Senses* (1984), a partly autobiographical work which explores the joy to be gained from the five senses; and *From Forest to Sea: Australia's Changing Environment* (1993), a series of reflections (some of which have been published before) on such topics as trees, conservation, land use and development and his own forays into and across the Australian countryside. He has also edited *An Anthology of Australian Fishing* (1991). In 1992 Rolls was made AM.

Romantic Nineties, The, an influential volume of reminiscences and essays by A.W. Jose, was published in 1933. The most important of its four sections is the title one, in which there are brief chapters on authors, artists, editors, journals and club life of the 1890s. Jose's exuberant picture of the decade as the 'birth-years of Australian literature' helped to foster the romantic legend of the Nineties (q.v.).

ROMERIL, John (1945–   ), born Melbourne, was educated at Monash University, graduating in 1970. In 1968 he joined the theatre ensemble which was to become the Australian Performing Group and remained strongly committed to its aims and style of theatre. Most of his plays have been performed by the Group, first at La Mama and later at the Pram Factory. His published plays include *Chicago, Chicago* in *Plays* (1970), edited by Graeme Blundell, *The Kitchen Table* and *Brudder Humphrey* in *Komos* (1973), *I Don't Know Who to Feel Sorry For* (1973), *The Floating World* (q.v., 1975), *Marvellous Melbourne* in *Theatre-Australia* (with Jack Hibberd, 1977), *Bastardy* (1982), *Mrs Thally F* in *Seven One-Act Plays* edited by Rodney Fisher (1983), *The Kelly Dance* (1986), *Legends* (with Jennifer Hill and Chris Anastassiades, 1986), *The Accidental Poke* in *Popular Short Plays for the Australian Stage*, vol. 1, edited by Ron Blair (1985) and *Definitely Not the Last* (1989). Selections from *Mickey's Moomba*, produced in 1979, have also been published in *Meanjin* (1978). His unpublished plays include 'A Nameless Concern' (1968), 'The American Independence Hour' (1969), 'Mr Big the Big Big Pig' (1969), 'In a Place Somewhere Else' (1969), 'Dr Karl's Kure' (1970), 'Whatever Happened to Realism' (1969), 'Rearguard Action' (1971), 'Christie in Love' (1971), 'And the Beast' (1972), 'He Can Swagger Sitting Down' (1972), 'A Night in Rio and Other Bummerz' (1973), 'The Earth, Air, Fire and Water Show' (1973), 'The Golden Holden Show' (1975), 'The Dudders' (1976, with John Timlin and reworked in 1980 by Romeril and titled 'The Dud War'), 'The Radio-Active Horror Show' (1977), 'Carboni' (1980), 'The 700,000' (1980), 'Samizdat' (1981), 'The Centenary Dance' (1984), 'Jonah Jones' (1985, with music by Alan John), 'Top End' (1986), 'The Imposter' (1987), 'Lost Weekend' (1989), 'Black Cargo' (1991), 'Working Out' (1991), 'Reading Boy' (1991) and 'Bring Down the House' (1992). Romeril was also one of the authors of the Pram Factory's collaborative productions, *Waltzing Matilda* (1974, published 1984) and 'The Hills Family Show' (1975). His work for film includes *The Great McCarthy* (1975), an adaptation of Barry Oakley's novel *Salute to the Great McCarthy;* of his work for television, *Six of the Best*, a series for young people written for the ABC's Education Unit and published in 1984 is the most substantial. In 1976 he won the first Canada-Australia Literary Award.

Romeril, who has described himself as a 'community pen', is concerned to rouse Australians from what he sees as their political apathy. Confining himself mainly to 'agit-prop' (agitational-propaganda) theatre, he has written several street plays and plays for demonstrations, e.g. 'Mr Big the Big Big Pig', 'Whatever Happened to Realism', for factory tours, restaurants, children and women's liberation groups. Several of his more finished productions, such as *Chicago, Chicago* and *Marvellous Melbourne*, have been rewritten to fit the needs and demands of the acting group. Influenced strongly by Brecht, he prefers a rough, bold, abrasive, improvisational, free-wheeling, musical theatre that is collaborative in its growth, obviously political in its message and broadly humorous in its effects. *Chicago, Chicago* and 'He Can Swagger Sitting Down' focus on alienation and violence in American society, *Mickey's Moomba* deals with American cultural imperialism; 'The Golden Holden Show' with multinationals, Liberal politics and the Holden car industry; *Mrs Thally F* with extremes of suburban isolation; 'The Dudders' with American–Australian relations during the Second World War; 'The Radio-Active Horror Show' with the uranium industry; 'Samizdat' with repressive activities of the Queensland police force. 'Carboni' is an adaptation of Raffaello Carboni's account of the Eureka Stockade. Plays in which Romeril's interest in a particular human scene merges with his political aims are *I Don't Know Who to Feel Sorry For*, 'Top End' and *The Floating World*. The first, a part-naturalist, part-absurdist play, explores some fundamental human needs and attitudes; *The Floating World* concentrates on the depths that underlie an Australian male stereotype, a middle-aged 'ocker'; and 'Top End', set in Darwin on the eve of the defeat of the Whitlam government in 1975 interweaves personal and political disillusionments and betrayals. Romeril's political interests are also prominent in his bold reworking of Louis Stone's novel *Jonah* in 'Jonah Jones' into an attack on Western capitalism; presenting Jonah as a victim of the system, Romeril portrays his degeneration into exploiter and war-monger as politically inevitable. All Romeril's plays are flexible pieces, which have often evolved after extensive workshopping and which invite reworking by the actors and active participation from the audience. This flexibility is most obvious in *The Kelly Dance*, which interweaves the Ned Kelly story and participatory bush dancing, and *Legends*, which was intensively workshopped over a six-month period by writers, students from two Victorian High Schools, eight actors and students and staff from the Victorian College of the Arts. Romeril's interest in stimulating works of the 'collective imagination' is well expressed in his introduction to *The Kelly Dance* where he states that from 'the number of "found" sources used throughout (folk songs, folk music, poems, newspaper reports, official documents etc) it should be apparent that not just the living had a hand in shaping the play so did the dead, Ned Kelly amongst them'. Gareth Griffiths has edited a collection of critical essays, *John Romeril*, in the Australian Playwrights Series (1993).

RONAN, Tom (1907–76), born Perth, the son of Jim Ronan, stockman and cattle-station manager, spent his childhood in the inland areas of north-west Australia. At the age of 14 he joined his father as an apprentice stockman and subsequently worked as a rouseabout and drover and as a ship's clerk and shell-opener on pearling boats at Broome. During the Second World War he served with the AIF and in

1950–70 lived with his wife and eight children on an old property, Springvale, near Katherine. Ronan published five novels, *Strangers on the Ophir* (1945), *Vision Splendid* (1954), *Moleskin Midas* (1956), *The Pearling Master* (1958) and *Only a Short Walk* (1961); a biography of his father, *Deep of the Sky* (1962); and two volumes of autobiography, *Packhorse and Pearling Boat* (1964) and *Once There Was a Bagman* (1966). His last collection, *The Mighty Men on Horseback* (1977), includes sketches, yarns, short stories and previously unpublished sections of *Vision Splendid* which won the 1951 Commonwealth Jubilee literary competition. Ronan, described by his publishers as having boiled 'either a stockman's billy can or a drover's quart pot of tea by the side of almost every watercourse between Wyndham and Camooweal, and between Darwin and Oodnadatta', describes the landscape and social life of outback northern Australia from the early nineteenth century to the 1950s with an engaging impression of authenticity. His short stories, novels and autobiographies, written in a plain but vigorous prose and enlivened by his understated humour, are rich in portraits of eccentric outback types.

RONCORONI, Olga (1893–1982), born England of Italian extraction, was a close friend of 'Henry Handel Richardson' and her executrix and lived with her from 1920 to 1946 as companion and secretary. As a young girl she acted, sang, played and composed music for the family's theatrical performances at Broadstairs, where they were known as the Popular Purple Pierrots and which they staged in order to mend their failing fortunes. Later she played the piano in cinemas managed by her father at Broadstairs, Rochester and Lyme Regis, where she became friendly with 'Richardson' and her husband John Robertson. She suffered from agoraphobia and first stayed with the Robertsons in order to receive treatment in London. Subsequently gaining the Licentiate Diploma of the Royal Academy of Music, she taught Dalcroze eurythmics at a girls' school until Robertson's death in 1933. She thereafter devoted herself to 'Richardson's' welfare. The strain of the Second World War, when their house was vulnerable to bombing raids, and of caring for 'Richardson' in her last illness contributed to Roncoroni's own ill health from 1946 and she subsequently spent long periods in psychiatric hospitals. Using Robertson's notes and diaries, Roncoroni completed 'Richardson's' autobiography, *Myself When Young* (1948), from the time of her marriage to her departure for London. She also edited, with Edna Purdie, reminiscences of 'Richardson' in 1957.

Rooted, a three-act play by Alexander Buzo (q.v.) was first performed in Australia in 1969 and published in 1973; it has also been staged in USA and England. Bentley, a Sydney civil servant in his mid-twenties, is successively stripped of his home, wife, possessions, livelihood and mates by the never-seen, all-powerful Simmo. Although the situations are often farcical and the characters two-dimensional, the picture of a hollow, image-obsessed culture that emerges is serious and credible. Both Bentley, the born loser who ineffectually apes the required attitudes, owns the required technological possessions and mouths the required clichés, and the super-successful Simmo whose amazing feats on the sportsfield, in bed, in the pub or in the business world are constantly recounted, express the sterility of this generation's aspirations. Simmo, appropriately unseen, represents the generalised public ideal of the 1970s young middle class of both genders, just as Bentley embodies its private fears.

ROSA, S.A. (Samuel Albert) (1866–1940), born Sydney, was educated in London, became a journalist in America and then returned to Australia, where he worked for the Sydney *Truth* (1901–23, 1934–40) and the *Labor Daily* (1925–34). An advocate of revolutionary socialism, he was expelled from the NSW Labor Party and formed a short-lived socialist party. His published fiction, *The Coming Terror: Or, the Australian Revolution* (1894), was published in 1895 as *Oliver Spence*. He was also the author of the political analyses *Federation* (1898), *The Federal Bill Analysed* (1899) and *The Invasion of Australia* (1920) and of the autobiographical *The Troubles of An Editor* (1936).

ROSE, Peter (1955–), spent his boyhood in Wangaratta, and graduated from Monash University. He worked as a medical bookseller before joining OUP, Australia, where he is publisher of general and reference works, among which is this Second Edition of the *Oxford Companion to Australian Literature*. Rose has published two books of poetry, *The House of Vitriol* (1990) and *The Catullan Rag* (1993). His poem 'Vantage' was awarded the St Kilda Centenary Poetry Prize in 1990; 'The Catullan Rag' won the Queensland Premier's Poetry Prize in 1991 and 'Dog Days' won the same prize in 1992. Rose won the Harri Jones Award in 1991.

A late first book (Rose was thirty-five when it was published), *The House of Vitriol* reflects Rose's major cultural interests – literature, music and the classics. It is marked by a somewhat sardonic, self-deprecatory tone that appears resigned to the limits life is likely to impose. 'Pathology', 'These Questions I would Ask', 'Imagining the Inappropriate', 'Darlinghurst Poem' and 'Three Fingers of Gin' are quietly pessimistic evaluations of personal and social situations. Self-revelation is not, however, Rose's aim; the reader is mostly kept at arm's length by a persistent ironic mask, complex language and obscure references and allusions. His frequent use of rare and archaic words and inventive analogies has led to accusations of poetry that is mostly 'gesture and flourish' (John Foulcher). Some of that 'flourish' (e.g. 'the sadness of ancients/ craning for trams', 'rousing and ringing/ as a coital cry') is, however, spectacular and effective. Links with T.S. Eliot have been suggested; the title poem, 'The House of Vitriol', has echoes of 'The Wasteland' and 'Ash Wednesday', and there are Prufrockian touches in other poems.

The Catullan Rag has two sections, the first of St Kilda scenes, concerts, the crowded loneliness of city life, and personal frustrations. In many of them, 'Confetti', 'Miseracordia', 'Sacrifice', 'Notionalism', associations are in Rose's own words 'becoming quite wild and uncontrolled'. Occasionally the mask slips, as in 'Dog Days', perhaps Rose's most effective poem. It tells of a walk through the park with his affable old dog, who takes frequent 'aromatic detours'. The walk eases the tensions built up by a literary festival he has just left. Frustrated with his present way of life, he thinks back to a more carefree past in 'some convivial harbour' where there is 'wine and fish and company'. That past is, however, neither available nor, if it were, would it now be satisfying. In spite of himself he seeks more order, certainty and even discipline.

> I long in my own way
> for the faint impress of the collar,
> the slow bruise of the familiar,
> the sharp tug on the gnostic leash.

The prize-winning 'Vantage' voices a moment of accord with life around him springing from a loving and satisfying relationship.

'The Catullan Rag', fourteen pieces imitating the Roman poet Catullus, but in contemporary tone and mode, make up the second section of the book. Brilliantly targeted are Lesbia, a NASAL (read ASAL) conference, and the poet Suffenus (read any number of ASAL literary 'personalities'). Inaccessible to some, Rose is, nevertheless, making a significant impact on the contemporary literary scene, representing in Peter Porter's judgement, 'an enterprising new voice [in] Australian poetry'.

ROSKOLENKO, Harry (1907–80), born New York, was self-educated and worked at numerous occupations including sailor, law clerk, factory-hand and patent-researcher before joining the US Army in 1942. Posted to the Pacific area, he made numerous visits to Australia in the 1940s, became friendly with poets of the *Angry Penguins* group, and contributed to Australian magazines. Two volumes of his poetry were published in Australia, *A Second Summary* (1944) and *Notes from a Journey* (1947), illustrated by Sidney Nolan. When he returned to America in 1945 he acted as the *Angry Penguins* representative, acquiring contributions from such writers as Kenneth Rexroth and Harold Rosenberg and contributing a 'Letter from America'. With Max Harris he also edited the tenth issue of *Angry Penguins Broadsheet* and, with Elisabeth Lambert, edited an Australian issue of the American poetry magazine *Voices* (1944). Roskolenko subsequently travelled widely and was a familiar contributor to such magazines as *New York Times Book Review*, *New Republic* and *Partisan Review*. He published novels, travel books, autobiographies and several collections of poetry, some of which reflect his experience in Australia. In 1969 he visited Australia again and in 1970 published another collection of poetry in Melbourne, *American Civilization*, illustrated by several well-known Australian artists.

ROSMAN, Alice Grant (1882–1961), born Kapunda, SA, contributed numerous sketches, stories and poems to Australian anthologies, newspapers and magazines, including the *Bulletin*, the *Australasian*, *Sydney Mail*, *Steele Rudd's Magazine*, the *Native Companion* and the *Lone Hand*. She had her own page on C.J. Dennis's *Gadfly* 1906–9, was Adelaide correspondent for the *Bulletin* 1908–11, using the pseudonym 'Rosna', and worked also for the *Evening Post* and the *Daily Herald*. In 1911 she left for London, where she was on the literary staff of the *British Australasian* 1915–20 and the editorial staff of the *Grand Magazine* 1920–27. She gave up journalism for full-time writing in 1927 and established an international reputation as a popular novelist, one of her novels, *The Window* (1928), becoming a best-seller. Novels which include Australian characters are *Miss Bryde of England* (1915), *The Tower Wall* (1916), *The Back Seat Driver* (1928) and *The Sixth Journey* (1931). Rosman's mother, Alice Mary Bowyer Rosman, published a verse collection, *An Enchanted Garden* (1916).

ROSS, James (1786–1838) was born and educated in Scotland and was a successful schoolmaster in England before emigrating to Van Diemen's Land in 1822. He farmed near Hobart until 1825, when he was appointed joint government printer with George Terry Howe and editor of the *Hobart Town Gazette*. In 1827 the partnership was dissolved, with Ross remaining government printer and the *Gazette* changing from a newspaper to a government information organ. Soon after, Ross founded the *Hobart Town Courier* (q.v.), which he ran until 1837. Both in the *Gazette* and the *Courier* he supported the controversial lieutenant-governor of Van Diemen's Land, George Arthur, and was thus inevitably attacked by his fellow pioneering pressmen, including Andrew Bent, Henry Melville, Gilbert Robertson, and R.L. Murray. Among other publishing activities, Ross wrote *An Essay on Prison Discipline* (1833), ran the short-lived *Hobart Town Chronicle* (1833) and the early literary periodical the *Van Diemen's Land Monthly Magazine* (1835), and issued eight almanacs 1829–36, usually with the *Hobart Town Almanack* as part of the title. The 1835 volume contained the first part of Jorgen Jorgenson's autobiography, and was a source for Marcus Clarke's *Old Tales of a Young Country* (1871). Ross's narrative of his early years in Van Diemen's Land, first published in the *Hobart Town Almanack* in 1836, was published as *The Settler in Van Diemen's Land* in 1975.

ROSS, Lloyd (1901–87), born Melbourne, the son of the revolutionary socialist R.S. Ross (1875–1931), founder of the Victorian Railways Union, editor of the *Socialist* and author of *Eureka – Freedom's Fight of '54* (1914), was a graduate of the University of Melbourne. He earned his living as an adult education teacher, mainly for the WEA, and as a freelance journalist. Secretary of the NSW branch of the Australian Railways Union 1938–43 and 1952–69, and public relations officer of the post-war reconstruction programme, he was a member of the Communist Party of Australia in his youth, but left the party before the Second World War and subsequently became vehemently anti-communist. From 1961–68 he was president of the Australian Association for Cultural Freedom, an anti-communist body. His keen interest in the labour movement and politics is reflected in the numerous articles he wrote for Australian and international trade union and political journals. He wrote *William Lane and the Australian Labor Movement* (1937), a classic labour history which was reprinted in 1980; and a biography of John Curtin (1977), whom he had known since childhood. Ross also wrote several plays, two of which have been published, *On the Edge of the Future* in *Eight Plays by Australians* (1934), and *The Rustling of Voices* in *Best Australian One-Act Plays* (1937), ed. T. Inglis Moore and William Moore. He was made OBE in 1972.

Ross' Poems (1978), a collection of seventy-five poems by Geoffrey Lehmann (q.v.), is illustrated by old photographs of some of the personalities and places mentioned and by etchings of rural scenes done by Sally McInerney, 'Sally' of the poems. *Ross' Poems* traces the establishment by Ross and Olive McInerney, Lehmann's then parents-in-law, of the property Spring Forest near Cowra in the Lachlan Valley of central-western NSW in the period just after the Second World War. Interspersed with incidents and events in the development of Spring Forest are Ross's memories of his own rural childhood. The poems present an analytical ('my laboratory is the dust where I stand') account of country life and a catalogue of country characters, including the bagman Mr Long, who, walking all day on the western plains, sustains himself 'with a line of trees on the horizon'; Ross's father who at 87 still rides a horse; his Auntie Bridge who at 80 still plants trees; and the parsimonious neighbour who sends his horses to the knackery when their working lives are over. The poems also carry Ross's country-wise reflections on such features of modern life as 'lurid newspaper headlines' that contain 'all the trash of our world'; the constant exposure to violence, the built-in obsolescence of modern machines, and the insidious attraction that the city ('the son and daughter stealer') holds for young people. The undemonstrative Lehmann style adapts easily to the flat, laconic tones of the countryman narrator, but a judicious use of reverie frequently elevates the poems from an ordinary to a highly imaginative plane. Some of the poems were published in 1976 in the Poets of the Month series, as *Extracts from Ross' Poems*. Lehmann's *Spring Forest* (1992) is an expanded and revised edition of *Ross' Poems*.

ROSSER, Bill (1927–), born Brisbane, left school at the age of 11 unable to read or write, but subsequently educated himself and served with the RAAF during the Second World War. He is the author of *This Is Palm Island* (1978), an account of the Palm Island Aboriginal Reserve which Rosser first visited in 1974 and which was then run with extreme repression and destructive results. The story of the Palm Islanders' struggle to throw off this oppressive system sanctioned by the Queensland Aborigines Act, *This is Palm Island*, is based on Rosser's interviews with numerous people living on the reserve. Rosser's subsequent books are *Dreamtime Nightmares* (1985), the personal stories of eight Aborigines which illustrate

the historical exploitation of Aboriginal people on the vast pastoral holdings of far west Queensland and the Northern Territory; *Up Rode the Troopers* (1990), an account of White manipulation of the mounted Aboriginal Native Police in Queensland in the 1890s, based on Rosser's talks with Cyclone Jack, a surviving member of the Telemon tribe; and *Return to Palm Island* (1994). *Dreamtime Nightmares* shared the inaugural W.E.H. Stanner Award of the Australian Institute of Aboriginal Studies and the Ethnic Award in the 1987 NSW Premier's Literary Awards; *Up Rode the Troopers* won the Ruth Adeney Koori Award.

Rouge, see **Feminism and Australian Literature**

ROUGHSEY, Dick (1924–85), born Langunarnji, an island near Mornington Island in the Gulf of Carpentaria, had a tribal name, Goobalathaldin, meaning 'water standing on end', which has been anglicised to Roughsey (Rough Sea). His childhood was spent with the tribe in the bush before he was taken to a Presbyterian mission to be educated. After primary school education he returned to tribal life, but in the Second World War worked on Queensland cattle stations and as a deckhand on a coastal supply ship. Later, at Kurumba Lodge at the mouth of the Norman River, he met an Ansett pilot, Percy Trezise, who encouraged him to paint. He became proficient in both the traditional Aboriginal method of bark painting and the Western method of painting in oils, and held successful exhibitions of his work in many Australian cities. Roughsey's *Moon and Rainbow: The Autobiography of an Aboriginal* (1971) is the story of his early life and the legends and customs of his people, the Lardil tribe. The book, which is profusely illustrated, presents in considerable detail Aboriginal beliefs about conception, birth, death and the life hereafter. He also published *The Giant Devil Dingo* (1973), the legend of Eelgin the grasshopper woman, who taught Gaiya the giant dingo to hunt and kill men for food. When the giant dingo is killed, the medicine man makes from his bones two small dingoes to be man's friends and helpers. The book, illustrated in magnificent colour, was named the Children's Picture Book of the Year for 1973 by the Children's Book Council. The award was repeated for a similar book, *The Rainbow Serpent* (1975), which deals with a legend forming the basis of much Aboriginal tradition. Roughsey joined with Percy Trezise to produce *The Quinkins* (1978), *Banana Bird and the Snake Men* (1980), *Turramulli the Giant Quinkin* (1982), *The Magic Firesticks* (1983), *Gidga* (1984) and *The Flying Fox Warriors* (1985). In 1973 Roughsey was appointed chairman of the newly established Aboriginal Arts Board; in 1976 he was awarded the Patricia Weickhardt Award for an Aboriginal writer.

ROUGHSEY, Elsie (Labumore) (1923–85), born at Goonana (Mornington Island) in the Gulf of Carpentaria, was partly brought up in a mission and later worked as a nursing assistant and teacher's aide. Married to Dick Roughsey (q.v.), she is the mother of six children. She grew up in two cultures, that of her people, the Lardils, and the White culture of the mission; after initiation at the age of 8 into the strangely rule-governed world dominated by the missionaries, she spent a period in the bush with her own people during the Second World War when the island was evacuated. In her autobiography, *An Aboriginal Mother Tells of the Old and the New* (1984), Elsie Roughsey compares the two ways of life; whereas in the mission 'All the laughs and fun were ended among the people. Then sad, quiet, frightness, shyness came and made everything change rather different', in the bush 'you are really walking the proud land, back again with mums and dads and able to move around wherever you want to go . . . no one was too sad about anything, but lived that peaceful life amongst our old tribal people'. Edited by Paul Memmott and Robyn Horsman, *An Aboriginal Mother Tells of the Old and the New* has retained the unusual syntax of the manuscript which reflects the author's use of a blend of standard English, Aboriginal English and tribal language. Optimistic and even-handed, the narrative meditates on the Aboriginal identity of past and future while providing a vivid picture of the author's unusual life through a period of radical change. Elsie Roughsey also collaborated with Virginia Huffer in her study of the experiences of tribal women on Mornington Island, *The Sweetness of the Fig: Aboriginal Women in Transition* (1980).

'Rouseabout', derived from 'rouse', meaning to stir from a state of apathy, sleep or inaction, was the name given to the ordinary station hand. A common figure in Australian literature, the rouseabout is given his best-known literary embodiment in Henry Lawson's poems 'Middleton's Rouseabout', which records the progress of the laconic, unquestioning, practical Andy, 'type of a coming nation', from station hand to station-owner, and 'Ballad of the Rouseabout'. Two traditional songs entitled 'Rouseabout' give a complete picture of the 'Generally Useful . . . poor bloody rouseabout'; one is by an anonymous author, the other by Jim Lawson. The author of the novel *Jackeroo* (1891), otherwise known only by his initials P.G.A., used 'Rouseabout' as his pseudonym.

ROWBOTHAM, David (1924–), born Toowoomba, Queensland, served in the RAAF in the Pacific in the Second World War and subsequently studied at the universities of Queensland and Sydney, where he won prizes for his poetry. He has worked as a journalist, broadcaster and academic; from 1969–79 he was literary and theatre critic for the *Courier-Mail* and from 1980–87 its literary editor. A prominent Australian poet since the 1940s and a regular contributor to the *Bulletin* when Douglas Stewart was editor of the Red Page, Rowbotham has published eight collections of poetry, *Ploughman and Poet* (1954), *Inland* (1958), *All the Room* (1964), *Bungalow and Hurricane* (1967), *The Makers of the Ark* (1970), *The Pen of Feathers* (1971), *Selected Poems* (1975) and *Maydays* (1980); a novel, *The Man in the Jungle* (1964); and a selection of short stories, *Town and City* (1956). He has also edited an anthology of verse and prose, *Queensland Writing* (1957). Among

other awards Rowbotham won the Grace Leven Prize for Poetry in 1964 and second prize in the Cook Bicentenary literary competition. He was made AM, and, in 1988, emeritus fellow of Australian Literature by the Australia Council.

Originally perceived as primarily a poet of the Queensland landscape, preoccupied with transience and the pattern of life in rural Australia, Rowbotham has moved in his later work towards a more idiosyncratic vision that resists categorisation. Writing in a bare, physically precise and metrically conservative style, he often explores fundamental philosophical problems through reflection on homely objects and ostensibly ordinary themes. Included by critics and fellow writers, e.g. David Malouf, as among those who have been involved in a radical redefinition of Australian poetry, Rowbotham has also gained international attention. His *Selected Poems* and *Maydays* have been particularly praised, e.g. in the USA, for their skilful conjunction of personal, national and universal themes. J. Strugnell has written the monograph *Focus on David Rowbotham* (1969).

ROWCROFT, Charles (1798–1856), born London, was the son of Thomas Rowcroft, East Indian merchant and London alderman who became British consul in Peru, where he died in Simon Bolivar's uprising. After an Eton education, Rowcroft went in 1821 to Hobart Town and took up a grant of 2000 acres. He remained only four years in the colony, returning in 1826 to England by way of Brazil. In 1843 he published his first novel, *Tales of the Colonies* (q.v.), a work which was partly a description of life in the colony, partly a guide for intending settlers and partly a sensational tale of the hazards of Van Diemen's Land in its pioneer times. His second Australian novel, *The Bushranger of Van Diemen's Land* (1846), recounts the violent exploits of both White and Black bushrangers in the south-east of the island. Of his other novels, only *An Emigrant in Search of a Colony* (1851) is connected with Australia. In England, Rowcroft edited *Hood's Magazine and Comic Miscellany*. See Aborigine in White Australian Literature; Bushranger in Australian Literature.

ROWE, Jennifer (1948–), born Sydney, was educated at the University of Sydney and has worked in publishing and as editor of the *Australian Women's Weekly*. As 'Emily Rodda' she has written several children's books, including *Something Special* (1984), *Pigs Might Fly* (1986), *The Best-Kept Secret* (1988), *Finders Keepers* (1990) and *Crumbs!* (1990). She won the CBC Book of the Year for Younger Readers in 1985, 1987 and 1991. She has also written books for adults, including *Grim Pickings* (1987), *Murder by the Book* (1989), *Death in Store* (1991), *The Makeover Murders* (1992) and *Stranglehold* (1993). *Grim Pickings* was produced as a television screenplay in 1989. In the tradition of Agatha Christie and Dorothy Sayers in terms of plot, Rowe's crime fiction is well crafted and fast paced; like other women writers of mystery novels, she creates a female detective figure, the outwardly unprepossessing Verity Birdwood, and includes acute portraits of both male and female characters. *Murder by the Book*, set in a publishing firm, draws on her experience as editor at Angus & Robertson. See also Crime Fiction.

ROWE, John (1936–), a graduate of the Royal Military College, Duntroon, has seen active service in Malaya, Kashmir, Borneo and Vietnam. He has written six novels, most of which deal with sensational political events. His first novel, *Count Your Dead* (1968), written while he was serving with the Defence Intelligence Agency in Washington, is critical of the American role in the Vietnam War and was followed by his resignation from the army. His second, *McCabe P.M.* (1972), deals with a political crisis following the assassination of an Australian prime minister by an Aboriginal extremist. His other novels are *The Chocolate Crucifix* (1972), *The Warlords* (1978), *The Jewish Solution* (1980), and *Long Live the King* (1984). He has also written an account of the Australian experience in Vietnam in the Time-Life series (1987).

ROWE, Penelope (1946–), born Sydney, the sister of Gerard Windsor (q.v.), graduated in arts from the University of Sydney. Formerly a teacher and a journalist with the *Sydney Morning Herald* and *Daily Telegraph*, she is presently a writer and editor with SBS TV. She published her first novel, *Dance for the Ducks*, in 1976. The story of Erica's student years, marriage to fellow student Ambrose, and the strains brought into the marriage by the birth of children and her mental illness, is semi-autobiographical. A later novel, *Tiger Country* (1990), turns back to the childhood of the heroine, Margaret-Anne Milton ('Matti'). As she waits by the bedside of her dying father, 'Matti' relives his years of sadistic treatment of her ('It was for your own good. I wanted you to grow up independent, principled, upright. That's all I wanted'). Some years before his death Matti is reconciled with her father but she is never forgiven by her mother for refusing to follow her own self-sacrificing example. *Unacceptable Behaviour* (1992), a book of short fiction, also contains stories ('Albatross', 'Kubla Khan in Autumn' and 'Melba Manchester') which appear to have a personal connection. Others ('Love Story', 'Francis Drake Goes to Sea', 'Motherlove', 'Running Mates' and 'Raymond Belvedere's Bit of Fun') are tender, sombre, pathos-filled, waspish and bizarre in turn, their characters reflecting Rowe's view of humanity – 'we are all so flawed'. A powerful writer, Rowe creates situations and characters that make for intense reading.

ROWE, Richard ('Peter Possum') (1828–79), born Doncaster, England, came to Australia in 1853 and worked first as a tutor before being befriended by literary patron N.D. Stenhouse (q.v.) and becoming part of the Sydney 1850s literary *coterie* that included Frank Fowler, J. Sheridan Moore, Henry Kendall, Henry Halloran and Daniel Deniehy. A regular contributor to the *Month*, the Sydney *Punch*, *Freeman's Journal* and the *Sydney Morning Herald*, Rowe published a collection of his essays and verse as *Peter Possum's Portfolio* (1858), one of the first such colonial collections; he returned to England in 1858. He published numerous

books for boys, including several, such as *The Boy in the Bush* (1869), *Roughing It in Van Diemen's Land* (1880) by 'Edward Howe' and *Fred Leicester: Or, the Southern Cross and Charles's Wain* (1889), which have Australian settings. Among his best works are *Episodes in an Obscure Life* (1871) and *Friends and Acquaintances* (1871), part of his writings about the London poor. Rowe is described in Ann-Mari Jordens's *The Stenhouse Circle* (1979).

ROWLAND, John Russell (1925–), born Armidale, NSW, joined the Department of Foreign Affairs in 1944 and served in London, Washington, Saigon, Malaysia, Paris, Moscow and other East European countries. He was ambassador in Moscow 1965–68, and in Paris 1979–82, and is an Officer of the Order of Australia (AO). He has published five collections of poetry, *The Feast of Ancestors* (1965), *Snow and Other Poems* (1971), *Times and Places* (1975), *The Clock Inside* (1979) and *Sixty* (1989). Rowland writes an elegant, controlled poetry, which often deals with the Australian landscape, re-creates the atmosphere of other countries or celebrates the daily realities of family life. One of his best-known poems, 'Canberra in April', evokes the social and physical landscape of the national capital of the 1950s and 1960s. He has also edited translations of poems by Andrei Voznesensky, *The Sculptor of Candles* (1985).

ROWLANDS, Graham (1947–), born Brisbane, was educated at the University of Queensland and Flinders University, SA, where he gained a Ph.D. He has been an academic, freelance journalist, educational editor and reviewer and presently lectures in Australian politics and crime prevention planning at Adelaide College of TAFE. He was one of the chief organisers of the Friendly Street (q.v.) poetry group in Adelaide and, for many years, poetry editor of *Overland*. He also edited *Dots over Lines* (1980), an anthology of then recent SA poetry and, with Pauline Wardleworth, *No 9 Friendly Street Poetry Reader* (1985). His own books of poetry include *Stares and Statues* (1972, the first of the Gargoyle Poets series), *Replacing Mirrors* (1975), *Poems Political* (1976), *Adam Scolds* (1976, with Grahame Pitt and Lyndon Walker), *Dial-a-Poem* (1982), *On the Menu* (1988) and *Selected Poems* (1992).

ROWLANDS, Lesley (1925–), born Carcoar, NSW, was educated at the University of Sydney, before travelling in Europe. She has written short stories and two popular humorous books on her travels, *Why Can't the English?* (1959, illustrated with line drawings by Cedric Flower) and *On Top of the World* (1961). She has also written a novel, *A Bird in the Hand* (1965), which focuses with comic effect on the efforts of the protagonist, Clem Bird, to escape the bonds of respectability, a job, matrimony and the social ambitions of his North Shore mother.

ROWLANDSON, A.C. (Alfred Cecil) (1865–1922), born Daylesford, Victoria, joined the NSW Bookstall Company, then owned by Henry Lloyd, as a tram ticket seller in 1883 and became owner of the company in 1897. He turned it into one of Australia's most successful book-publishing and selling ventures, publishing in paperback about 200 titles by Australasian authors and selling four to five million copies, mainly through the Bookstall's eight shops and many railway bookstalls. The books, in coloured wrappers, mostly novels of adventure or romance, with an occasional book of short stories, sold for one shilling per copy, rising to one shilling and threepence per copy during the First World War, when paper was scarce and expensive, but reverting to the popular 'bob' after the war. The Bookstall series (or 'Bookstalls') include novels by Arthur H. Adams, J.A. Barry, 'Louis' Becke, Randolph Bedford, E.J. Brady, Edward Dyson, Beatrice Grimshaw, Norman Lindsay, Sumner Locke, Vance Palmer, 'Steele Rudd', Thomas E. Spencer and A.G. Stephens. The brightly coloured covers were designed and illustrated on occasions by the then largely unknown Norman and Lionel Lindsay and George Lambert. The remarkable sales of these Australian books confirmed Rowlandson's intuition that the Australian reading public was keen for local reading matter, and the impact of his company on the development of Australian writing was considerable. A biographical work, *The Late Alfred Cecil Rowlandson: Pioneer Publisher of Australian Novels* (1922), has a foreword by R. Wynn and appreciative articles by A.G. Stephens and Bertram Stevens. A novel, *The Rival Physicians* (1909) by 'Paul Cupid', has been attributed to Rowlandson. Harry F. Chaplin has written two descriptive and bibliographical articles about the Bookstall series in *Biblionews* (1961). Carol Mills published *The New South Wales Bookstall Company as a Publisher* (1991), with notes on its authors and artists and a list of its publications.

RUBINSTEIN, Gillian (1942–), see *The Oxford Companion to Australian Children's Literature* (1993), pp. 372–3.

Rudd Family. The Rudd family's fortunes are chronicled in a series of books about selection life written by Arthur Hoey Davis under the pseudonym 'Steele Rudd' (q.v.), the narrator of the series, who appears as a character in the seventh volume. The series began with *On Our Selection* (q.v., 1899) in which Murtagh Joseph Rudd, known primarily as Dad (see Dad and Dave), brings his family from Stanthorpe to his selection at Emu Creek on the Darling Downs. Accompanying Dad are his wife Ellen (Mother), his sons Dan, Dave and Joe, his daughters Kate and Sarah (sometimes called Sal), and the as yet unnamed narrator, Steele. In the course of *On Our Selection*, which focuses on the struggle of Dad and the family to establish themselves on the selection, three further children are born: the twin boys, Bill and Tom, and another son, unnamed in the story in which he is born, 'The Night We Watched for Wallabies' (q.v.), but eventually christened Bartholomew. After the first few sketches, the eldest son, Dan, is seldom at Shingle Hut, the family home, although he reappears periodically in the Rudd family volumes along with

the eldest daughter, Norah, a schoolteacher elsewhere in Queensland. Dan is the black sheep of the family and his farming experiences are the subject of *The Book of Dan* (1911).

On Our Selection is the best and most famous of the Rudd volumes. There are nine others, through which, and according in general to the sequence of publication, the subsequent fortunes of the family are traced. In *Our New Selection* (1903), the Rudds begin to prosper: Shingle Hut is sold and Dad takes up the better holding of Saddletop, which he leaves temporarily after his election to parliament. *Dad in Politics and Other Stories* (q.v., published 1908, written 1904) records his experiences as a vociferous backbencher and the disillusionment with governments which causes him to resign his seat and return to Saddletop in *Back at Our Selection* (1906), in which there is mention of another daughter, Amelia. Meanwhile, Kate has married the neighbour, Sandy Taylor, in 'Kate's Wedding', an *On Our Selection* sketch; the struggle of Kate and Sandy to establish their selection at Sleepy Creek, which parallels the initial hardships of Dad and Mother at Shingle Hut, is the subject of *Sandy's Selection* (1904), in which Dad becomes parsimonious in his prosperity. His meanness is confirmed when Dave gets married in *Back at Our Selection* and in the later *Grandpa's Selection* (1916), by which time Dad has become Grandpa, a widower living with Joe.

The other Rudd volumes are *Stocking Our Selection* (1909), which includes the last part of *On Our Selection* (where Uncle Peter, an important character in *Sandy's Selection*, was introduced), together with a further seven stories featuring Dad in the city with Norah; *From Selection to City* (1909), which introduces Steele as a character, the next son in line to Joe, and traces his movement from bush work into the public service; *The Book of Dan* (1911); and *The Rudd Family* (1926), by which time the Emu Creek area is known as Ruddville, Sarah and Joe have married, Bill, Frank, Eileen and Peggy are the children at home, and Uncle Sam Rudd pays a visit. In the stage adaptation of *The Rudd Family* (1928) the Rudds become the Dicksons, using material from an earlier play. The final appearance of the Rudds in fiction occurs in the last novel, *The Green Grey Homestead* (1934), in which Dave and Joe visit the selector Dick Gall around the time in which *On Our Selection* or *Back at Our Selection* are set, and have to be hauled home by Dad.

The success of *On Our Selection* owed much to 'Rudd's' ability to write from his experience. The commercial popularity of the later books owed something to his willingness to let his characters evolve, e.g. the emergence of Dad's meanness and the development of Joe's stutter, and to vary the focus on different members of the family in succeeding volumes. Nevertheless Dad and Dave were the most important characters in the family and in exploiting their popularity 'Rudd' made them increasingly farcical after *On Our Selection*. He was influenced by his illustrators and perhaps also by the stage and screen adaptations of his work, in which he had little part: *Grandad Rudd* (1918), adapted from *Grandpa's Selection*, and the stage version of *The Rudd Family* were his work but he made little direct contribution to the stage adaptation of *On Our Selection* (1912), starring Bert Bailey (q.v.), the sound film (1932) based on it, and the three later Rudd spin-off films. Bailey became identified with Dad, and in time Dad and Dave moved beyond the Rudd family to become comic stereotypes, notably in the Dad and Dave radio serial produced by George Edwards. In addition, there have been several versions of the Rudds, including 'Rudd's' other fictional families, the Dashwoods, the Davidsons, the Duffs (in *On Emu Creek* (1923) in which Mrs Duff is identified as Joe's daughter), the Pettigrews and the Kaytons. Among other writers to be influenced by 'Rudd' are Henry Fletcher, in his novels about the Wayback family in which the patriarch is Dads Wayback and Dan Wayback is the equivalent of Dave Rudd; and Sumner Locke, in her novels about the Dawson family in which Mum Dawson is the counterpart of Dad. Although the first film in the series preceded the silent version of *On Our Selection* (1920), the several films (1918–37) about the Hayseed family clearly also benefited from the popularity of the Rudds.

'RUDD, Steele' (Arthur Hoey Davis) (1868–1935), born Drayton on the Darling Downs in Queensland, was the son of a blacksmith, Thomas Davis, who in 1870 selected land at Emu Creek, where the family moved in 1875. Maurice French has suggested that Thomas Davis was originally Thomas Davies, transported for burglary in 1849 (*Australian Literary Studies*, 1989). Arthur Davis left school in 1880 and worked on local properties and shearing sheds until 1885, when he moved to Brisbane to become a clerk in the public service. In 1889 he transferred to the sheriff's office in the Justice Department and was promoted to under-sheriff in 1902; he was retrenched from this position in 1904. Around 1890 he began contributing rowing skits to the Brisbane *Chronicle* under the pseudonym 'Steele Rudder' (the Christian name derives from his admiration for the English essayist, the surname from boating); 'Rudder' had been contracted to 'Rudd' by the time his first sketch about selection life, 'Starting the Selection', appeared in the *Bulletin* in April 1895. The popularity of 'Rudd's' contributions encouraged the *Bulletin* management to publish in 1899 an illustrated collection, *On Our Selection* (q.v.), and its success was repeated four years later with the sequel *Our New Selection*.

Davis believed that his identification in 1897 with his pseudonym had been influential in his retrenchment. As Richard Fotheringham has suggested, Davis's pseudonymous self took on a socially constructed life of its own, which was very different from his historical self. Davis was an articulate, cultured man of the world, a city-dweller for much of his life, and a conscious literary artist; 'Rudd' was a shy bushman, out of place in the city and a naive presenter of outback 'realities'. In 1897, refusing offers on re-appointment at a lower level in the public service, Davis opted to trade on his popularity and founded *Steele Rudd's Magazine* (q.v.), an illustrated monthly to which he was a major contributor. In 1909 he bought a

farm not far from Emu Creek, where he continued to write and became prominent in local affairs. In 1912 the stage adaptation of *On Our Selection* by Bert Bailey and Edmund Duggan was a huge success, but 'Rudd', as he will now be termed, benefited little from the royalty payments. Similarly, the arrangement he made with A.C. Rowlandson of the NSW Bookstall company for later editions of *On Our Selection* and *Our New Selection* worked to his disadvantage, except in higher payments for the rights to his other books. In 1917 he moved to Brisbane and revived his magazine as *Steele Rudd's Annual* (1917–23), later *Steele Rudd's* (1924–25), and *Steele Rudd's and the Shop Assistant's Magazine* (1926–27). But although Raymond Longford's (q.v.) silent film version of *On Our Selection* (1920) and its sequel *Rudd's New Selection* (1921) kept his name before the public, his personal and financial affairs continued to decline in the 1920s and 1930s. Major setbacks were the failure of the film version of his first novel, *The Romance of Runnibede* (1928), and the bankruptcy of the producer of the stage adaptation (1928) of *The Rudd Family*. 'Rudd's' son, Eric Drayton Davis, has written *The Life and Times of Steele Rudd* (1976) and Harry Reade the play 'The Execution of Steele Rudd' (1982).

A prolific contributor to his own and other journals, 'Rudd' published about two dozen works of fiction, wrote several plays based on his books (though not the script for the Bailey-Duggan *On Our Selection*), and in addition to the three silent films based on his work there were four sound features starring Bailey as Dad: *On Our Selection* (1932), *Grandad Rudd* (1935), *Dad and Dave Come to Town* (1938) and *Dad Rudd M.P.* (1940). One of 'Rudd's' best plays, *The Old Selection*, was never performed and was believed lost but was discovered in 1986 and published in 1987, edited by Richard Fotheringham. His most important work went into the ten volumes in which he chronicles the fortunes of the Rudd family: *On Our Selection* (1899), *Our New Selection* (1903), *Sandy's Selection* (1904), *Back at Our Selection* (1906), *Dad in Politics and Other Stories* (q.v., 1908), *Stocking Our Selection* (1909), *From Selection to City* (1909), *The Book of Dan* (1911) *Grandpa's Selection* (1916), and *The Rudd Family* (1926). The success of the Rudd volumes, particularly the first half of the sequence, clearly influenced 'Rudd's' direction as a writer. With the exception of three novels, *In Australia* (1908), which shows the influence of Nat Gould, *The Romance of Runnibede* (1927) and *The Green Grey Homestead* (1934), and the autobiographical *The Miserable Clerk* (1926), his other books are almost a copy of the Rudd books formula, a series of sketches about families and characters working selections on the Darling Downs or visiting Brisbane. Of these, the best is *The Poor Parson* (1907), in which the central character is Duncan McClure, the subject also of a play by 'Rudd'. Of the others, *On An Australian Farm* (1910) and its sequel *The Dashwoods* (1911), *We Kaytons* (1921), and *Me an' th' Son* (1924) all chronicle the experience of countrymen and their families in the city; *The Old Homestead* (1917) centres on Abe Pettigrew, a Dad Rudd figure toiling with his family at Ironbark; *Memoirs of Corporal Keeley* (1918) traces the shearing life of a young bush worker before his enlistment and service in Gallipoli and France; and *On Emu Creek* (1923) studies the problems of an urban innocent, who moves to a selection after his retrenchment from the public service.

'Rudd' was at his best when writing out of his early experiences. In one sense that generalisation applies to most of his books, but it is particularly true of *On Our Selection*, in which the struggles of the Rudd family parallel those of his own family in the later 1870s and early 1880s. Dad, however, was not based directly on his father, and of the characters in *On Our Selection* only the rouseabout Cranky Jack (q.v.) is drawn directly from real life. *On Our Selection* and its immediate sequels succeeded also because of 'Rudd's' pictorial gifts and because the presentation of the members of the Rudd family, particularly Dad, Dave, Joe, Mother and Kate, was both rounded and unsentimental. But particularly from *Dad in Politics* onwards the dominant tone was farce, present in the earlier volumes but there both a comment on and a relief from the struggles of pioneering life; together with the effects of 'Rudd's' illustrators and the presentation of Dad and Dave on stage, screen and radio, the later Rudd volumes helped transform Dad and Dave into stereotypes of rural yokels. The later Rudd volumes and the other sketches of Darling Downs life came finally to rely less and less on 'Rudd's' experiences than on his use of a previously successful formula. Of his later work, only *The Miserable Clerk* and *The Green Grey Homestead* have much of the strength of *On Our Selection*. Although 'Steele Rudd's' stories have not, in the last generation or two, weathered as well as the writings of A.B. Paterson or Henry Lawson, they remain representative of pioneering life on the land. Frank Moorhouse's edition of *A Steele Rudd Selection* (1987), which selects and groups stories from 'Rudd's' twenty-four books into a novel-like combination, does much to re-establish 'Rudd' as relevant to modern readers. It also, by virtue of the introduction, 'Frank Moorhouse Reflects on Steele Rudd', reaffirms the Bush – fact or fancy – as an integral part of the Australian legend. 'Rudd's' name is commemorated by the Steele Rudd Award in Brisbane's annual Warona Writers Week. The richest short-story award in Australia ($10 000 in early 1990s), it is given to a collection of short stories by an Australian author. It has been won by such notable writers as Thea Astley, Marion Halligan, Susan Hampton and Kate Jennings.

RUHEN, Olaf (1911–89), born NZ, pursued numerous occupations including deep-sea fishing before serving in the RNZAF during the Second World War. In 1947 he moved to Sydney, where he worked for the *Sun* and the *Sydney Morning Herald;* he resigned in 1956 to work as a freelance writer after several of his short stories had been accepted by the *Saturday Evening Post*. His extensive travels in Australia, the South Pacific and New Guinea are reflected in both his documentary and fictional writing. He published five novels; *Naked Under Capricorn* (1958), *White Man's Shoes* (1960), *The Flockmaster* (1963), *The Broken Wing* (1965) and *Scan the Dark Coast* (1969); two collections

of short stories, *Land of Dahori* (1957) and *Lively Ghosts* (1964); documentary accounts of New Guinea, *Mountains in the Clouds* (1963), of the South Pacific, *Tangaroa's Godchild* (1962), of the whale-hunters of Tonga, *Harpoon in My Hand* (1966) and of the bullock-drivers of Australia, *Bullock Teams* (1980); an account of a Japanese shipwreck in the South Pacific, *Minerva Reef* (1963); a biography of Lawrence Hargrave (1977); a novel for children, *Corcoran's the Name* (1967); an account of an aspect of Australia's prehistory for children, *The Day of the Diprotodon* (1976); and a manual for writers, *Writing: The Craft of Creative Fiction* (1964). He also edited an anthology of short stories, *South Pacific Adventure* (1966).

RULE, Edgar John, see **War Literature**

Rum Rebellion was the name given to the deposing of Governor William Bligh (q.v.) by the officers of the NSW Corps, 26 January 1808. The NSW Corps was known as the 'Rum Corps' because it had attempted, more or less successfully, to obtain the monopoly on the sale of rum in the Colony. Leaders of the rebellion were Lieutenant Colonel George Johnston, commanding officer of the Corps, and John Macarthur (q.v.). The events are recounted in H.V. Evatt's *Rum Rebellion* (1938), George Mackaness's *The Life of Vice-Admiral William Bligh* (2nd edn, 1951), M.H. Ellis's *John Macarthur* (1955) and Ross Fitzgerald and Mark Hearn's *Bligh, Macarthur and the Rum Rebellion* (1988). The Rum Rebellion features in many fictional and dramatic re-creations of events from Bligh's life, e.g. J.H.M. Abbott's semi-historical novel *The Governor's Man* (1919), Doris Egerton Jones's play *Governor Bligh* (1930), Eleanor Dark's novels *Storm of Time* (1948) and *No Barrier* (1953), George Farwell's play *The House That Jack Built* (1950), Brian Medlin's play 'Governor Bligh' (1955), and Ray Lawler's 'The Man Who Shot the Albatross' (1971). Rob Inglis wrote a musical, 'A Rum Do' (1970), in which the rum trade is highlighted.

'Run' is a term found in Australia as early as 1804. In its earliest use it referred to a large, open and reasonably well-grassed area for grazing sheep or cattle. Originally an English dialect word, it became widely used to denote specific characteristics of the Australian pastoral scene, e.g. 'sheep-run', 'cattle run'. It is found in many fictional and factual accounts of life in the colony, e.g. in Alexander Harris's *The Emigrant Family* (1849), and has been frequently used in the titles of fiction and poetry, e.g. Miles Franklin's *Ten Creeks Run* (1930) and A.B. Paterson's 'On Kiley's Run'.

RUSDEN, George ('Yittadairn') (1819–1903), born Surrey, England, accompanied his Anglican minister father to Maitland, NSW, in 1834. He worked as property manager in south-western NSW before two years of adventure in China 1847–49. Back in Australia, he became associated with education, publishing *National Education* (1853), an early proposal for State-directed education; he was also active in local politics and cultural affairs. An enthusiastic writer on political, religious and literary topics, Rusden published a poem, *Moyarra: An Australian Legend in Two Cantos* (1851), an account of two Aboriginal lovers who die because they transgress tribal law, and several documentary works, including *The Discovery, Survey and Settlement of Port Phillip* (1871), *Curiosities of Colonization* (1874), and the important *History of Australia* (1883). Rusden's educational policies are the subject of A.G. Austin's *George William Rusden and National Education in Australia 1849–1862* (1958).

Rusty Bugles, a play by Sumner Locke Elliot (q.v.), was first performed at the Independent Theatre, Sydney, in October 1948. Although the audience was enthusiastic, the play's 'blasphemous' language was brought to the attention of the chief secretary of NSW who temporarily banned further production. After much public debate, the play was performed again by the end of the month, although some deletions were made. It was subsequently produced with great success in the other capital cities of Australia, except Brisbane, and toured NZ, with less success, in 1952. In 1964 Doris Fitton revived the play at the Independent, and the New Theatre staged it successfully in 1979; it has been broadcast several times on ABC radio and was produced on television in 1965. Included in Eunice Hanger's collection *Khaki, Bush and Bigotry* (1968), *Rusty Bugles* was also published separately in 1980.

Comprising ten scenes that convey the experiences of the protagonists over six months in 1944, it is set in a remote army camp in the Northern Territory. The action opens with the arrival of Private Rod Carson and his initiation into the monotony, discomfort and ugliness of camp life, alleviated only by the nightly game of 'swy' (two-up), the arrival of the mail, bickering, the occasional unsatisfactory and public call home, the hope of leave or of replacements. His campmates include Des Noland (The 'Gig Ape'), the good-natured butt of rough-house jokes; Mac, the unpopular shirker who finally gets leave when his wife deserts him only to be held back by the dermatitis that he has been encouraging; the taciturn Ken Falcon, who eventually 'goes troppo'; the cheerful, resourceful Ot, who is granted longed-for leave only to discover that his girlfriend has married another; Chris and Ollie, the versatile youngsters who take on the role of camp clowns; the eternally depressed Keghead Stephens; and the universally detested petty official, Sergeant Brooks. The play's absence of plot and its circular movement, which at the close brings back the men who had vowed they would never return, emphasises the meaningless, desultory progress of the soldiers' experience.

RYAN, Gig (Elizabeth) (1956–), born England, worked on the feminist journal *Luna* 1975–78, and has had various casual occupations. A songwriter and singer, she has also performed with 'Disband', whose album *Six Goodbyes* (the title also of one of her own group of poems) was released in 1988. She has published four books of poems: *The Division of Anger* (1980), which shared the Anne Elder Poetry Award, *Manners of an Astronaut* (1984), *The Last Interior* (1986)

and *Excavation* (1990). An extremely original and distinctive voice, Ryan melds her poems from disparate, cryptic fragments and fractured syntax, forming striking images from the unlikely, ugly clutter of contemporary urban life. Her difficult, intense and pain-filled poetry, which unsentimentally and often poignantly reflects a hostile world, combines the personal and the political, implicitly illustrating their complicity. Intimate relationships, sexual desire, the flight of love, the pursuit of power, events on the world stage and the perverse human tendency to inflict hurt on self and others intermingle in poems which speak directly and with uncompromising urgency. As one reviewer has commented, 'this is a poetry where really fundamental problems about content, life, words and styles are being dragged to the light and investigated.' Spare, technically taut, sharply witty, her poems often probe the experiences common to those who have chosen the ghetto life of the inner city. *Excavation* is subtitled 'arguments and monologues', a fitting description of many of her poems which are interior monologues, characterised by hard-edged feelings which range from anger to a fatalistic acceptance of loss to a wry humour. But Ryan is also a lyrist with an outstanding linguistic ability to create aesthetically exciting moments from what is emotionally painful. In her simply titled 'Poem', for instance, what might in other hands have become a long drawn out lament for lost love is turned into an intensely compressed and moving expression of the perennial contrast between the uncaring serenity of the external world and inner anguish:

> The day is beautiful
> He doesn't love me
> Pieces of me fly in formation
> Across the sky's blue lung

If Ryan's vision is a dark one, her expression of it is intrinsically stimulating, especially to other creative writers.

RYAN, Les, see **Shearer in Australian Literature**

RYAN, Lyndall, see **Aborigine in White Australian Literature**; **ROBINSON, George Augustus**

RYAN, Peter (1923–), born Melbourne, served in New Guinea in the Second World War and subsequently worked in public relations. He was director of Melbourne University Press 1962–88. He has published a segment of autobiography, *Fear Drive My Feet* (1959), describing his experiences in New Guinea 1942–43. As one of a small group of Australian commandos who linked up with the New Guinea Volunteer Rifles under the joint title Kanga force and who stayed on in New Guinea after the fall of Lae and Salamaua to maintain contact with the indigenous people and observe and harass Japanese movements, Ryan underwent extraordinary dangers and hardships. He has also written an account of the gold rush at Mount Kare, New Guinea, in the 1990s, *Black Bonanza* (1991), edited the *Encyclopaedia of Papua and New Guinea* (1972) and written a short biography of Judge Redmond Barry (1972).

S

SACCHI, Filippo (1887–?), born Vincenza, Italy, graduated from the University of Padua and joined the staff of the *Corriere della sera*, one of Italy's major newspapers, in 1914, subsequently travelling extensively as a special correspondent in Europe and Australasia. He arrived in North Queensland in 1925 but was back in Italy by 1926, and was excluded from journalism by the emerging Fascist regime. In 1932 his novel about Italian immigrants to Queensland, *La Casa in Oceania*, the first novel written by an Italian about Australia, was published. The novel's central character, Giorgio Breglia, a young man from Piedmont, sets up a business in Brisbane importing American agricultural machinery, which fails owing to his association with a dishonest compatriot. Moving to Ingham in an attempt to mend his fortunes, he becomes friendly with an Englishman, John Cobley, who persuades him to go part-share in establishing a cane farm, an enterprise which comes to an end when Cobley suddenly tires of it. Giorgio then joins an Italian cane-cutting gang, and persists through the season although the effort almost breaks him, finally saving enough to buy a farm at Lilypond. The stories of Cobley and Giorgio intersect romantically with those of two women, Mary Bartlett and Romana Canzi, and although Cobley departs to wander in other parts of Australia, Giorgio and Romana find happiness and settle down on their farm. Historically accurate and including some incidental characters, buildings and places drawn from real life, *La Casa in Oceania* describes Queensland life and the work of cane-cutters in vivid detail.

'Said Hanrahan', one of the most popular and frequently anthologised of the poems of 'John O'Brien' (q.v.), was published in *Around the Boree Log and Other Verses* (1921). The poem catches to perfection the legendary pessimism of the farmer, who sees prospects of ruin in every variation of weather. The lugubrious lament of the poem, 'We'll all be rooned', has passed into Australian folklore.

SALA, George Augustus (1828–95), born London, was a scene-painter and engraver before establishing himself as a journalist with *Household Words, Temple Bar* (which he edited) and, most notably, the London *Daily Telegraph*. In his heyday he was the best-known figure of the London newspaper scene. Widely travelled, he lectured and toured Australia in 1885; while in Melbourne (where his wife died and is buried) he coined the phrase 'Marvellous Melbourne' (q.v.), which soon became a popular description of the city. During his Australian tour Sala wrote a series of thirty-two articles for the *Daily Telegraph* entitled 'The Land

of the Golden Fleece'; these were reprinted in the *Argus*, (to which he also addressed a few letters), *Australasian* and *Sydney Morning Herald*. After his return to England he published *The Life and Adventures of George Augustus Sala* (1895), which contains a few pages of Australian impressions, but he never completed his projected book on the colonies. Sala also wrote stories, 'The Australian Night's Entertainments', purporting to be 'related by convicts at the Antipodes while lying in their hammocks after sunset'; they were published in the short-lived journal *Chat* in 1848. Marcus Clarke is said to have been influenced by Sala's journalistic attitude and style. Judy McKenzie has written of Sala in 'G.A.S. in Australia: Hot Air Down Under?', *Australian Literary Studies* (1992).

SALOM, Philip (1950–), born in the Brunswick Junction farming district of WA, trained to be a scientist but later completed a degree in English and turned to writing as a career. From 1983 to 1989 he wrote poetry while tutoring in creative writing at Curtin University, WA, and held several writer-in-residences – in 1985 at Perth City Council, in 1988 at the WA College of Advanced Education, in 1989 at Singapore National University. Particularly active in the WA literary scene, he has been a judge of numerous WA literary awards and a member of several literary committees, e.g. the 1987 Bicentennial Publications Grants Panel, and in 1989 a committee member of the Katharine Susannah Prichard Foundation. In 1987 he was an Australian representative and guest writer at the Struga International Poetry Readings in Yugoslavia. He has also organised DISK READINGS, Perth's major venue for regular literary readings.

Salom has published (to 1993) six books of poetry – *The Silent Piano* (1980), which won the 1981 Commonwealth Poetry Prize; *The Projectionist* (1983), winner of the 1984 WA Literary Award for Poetry; *Sky Poems* (1987), which repeated his success in the Commonwealth Poetry competition (the only writer to have won the award twice) and which also won the 1988 WA Literary Award for Poetry; *Tremors* (1992) in the NLA Pamphlet Poets Series; *Barbecue of the Primitives* (1989), another WA Literary Award winner and *Feeding the Ghost* (1993). *Sky Poems*, in particular, reflects the influence on Salom of the hill country (the Darling Range) near Perth, where he has lived for some time. The sky itself is prominent in some of that poetry. Salom is much more than a landscape poet, however; his work traverses a broad range of subjects, many of which stem from mundane experience but are then transformed by his fine craftsmanship and intellectual agility into rich and provocative poetry. A poet already formed, as the success of his first book which dealt mainly with his family and historical figures indicates, Salom has expanded energetically into more conceptually sophisticated and stimulating writing with each successive volume. He forges, in the words of the critic, 'the best aspects of the Symbolist and Surrealist traditions' into a highly distinctive and distinguished body of poetry, much of which illustrates his own assertions that 'the mind is the biggest city of all' and that the poet's true role is 'to know the times, to question the times into intensity'. Among his notable poems are 'Poets and Allegories', 'Properties of the Poet', the clever and amusing 'The Sex of Autostrada Driving', 'Barbecue of the Primitives' and the three pieces on the Swedish tenor Jussi Borling.

Salom published his first novel, *Playback*, in 1991. It emulated the success of his poetry, winning the WA Premier's Award for Fiction in 1992. The story of folklorist Jack Biner's attempt to gather on his tape recorder the oral history of the small country town of Windrup, not far from Perth, *Playback* has mystery, murder, intrigue, and abundant and enthusiastic sex. Biner soon stumbles on the town's guilty secret, the death of a young man in a shooting during a bushfire some years earlier. A Polish migrant, Tadek Bukowski, was blamed (he is also now dead) but there is an undercurrent of suspicion and rumour that a local businessman, Payne, was the killer. Biner stumbles equally quickly on to local artist Laura Ridout, whose husband runs the district's agricultural research station where he is experimenting, unsuccessfully, with bull semen for artificial insemination. Laura and Jack spend much of the book engaged in their own practical, and very successful, version of insemination. Ultimately, Payne is unmasked and Jack and Laura appear headed for a more permanent, if uneasy, alliance. A well-plotted novel, with intriguing if not wholly believable characters, and with Salom's talent with language strongly evident, *Playback* is well-realised fiction.

Salt (1), an army journal, published weekly, later fortnightly, in Melbourne 1941–46, included short stories, poems, articles and drawings by personnel to whom it was distributed. A book-review section, 'Dustjackets Off', was a regular feature of *Salt* and it also had a 'Great Authors' series, including prominent Australian writers, e.g. Jon Cleary, Xavier Herbert, Alan Marshall, Vance Palmer and Kylie Tennant. Staff members included Mungo MacCallum, Frank Hardy, Ambrose Dyson and Vane Lindsay. Frank Hardy's autobiographical *The Hard Way* (1961) recounts some of the exploits of *Salt*'s writers.

Salt (2), a literary journal, edited by poet John Kinsella, was launched by John Forbes early in 1992 at the Harold Park Hotel, Sydney, a meeting-place for writers. Devoted primarily to poetry, it prefers to feature poets in depth, usually a sequence of poems, e.g. Robert Harris's (q.v.) *Jane, Interlinear* and poems and excerpts from Robert Adamson's (q.v.) memoirs, *Wards of the State*. Issues 3 and 4 comprised an anthology of contemporary poetry, *The Bird-Catcher's Song*.

Saltbush Bill, one of A.B. Paterson's (q.v.) best-known characters, appeared in five poems, 'Saltbush Bill' (in *The Man from Snowy River and Other Verses*, 1895), 'Saltbush Bill's Second Fight' and 'Saltbush Bill's Gamecock' (both in *Rio Grande's Last Race and Other Verses*, 1902), and 'Saltbush Bill, J.P.' and 'Saltbush Bill on the Patriarchs' (both in *Saltbush Bill, J.P. and Other Verses*, 1917). As a drover in charge of travelling sheep, Saltbush Bill sparks fear and anger in the hearts of squatters like Stingy Smith, on to whose best runs his sheep always manage to stray. When his natural cunning occasionally fails him, his determination usually wins the day. Grown old and grey, respectability comes to Bill, for 'Edward Rex' appoints him a justice of the peace. Bill discovers in the fine print of his high office that he can charge £1 for an inquest on a fire. Over the course of a week, while Bill's sheep feed freely on a nearby run, twenty-five 'residences' in the local Aboriginal camp are destroyed by fire. With his £25 from fees Bill is able to spend Christmas with his sister in the South. There, as loving uncle to his sister's 'little rouseabouts', he recounts, in a superb outback analogy, the drover's version of the patriarchs. Isaac is the squatter; Jacob, his son, takes to the droving track, 'for any boy that's worth his salt will roll his swag and roam'. On his uncle Laban's run Jacob works, not for 'the speckled and spotted' animals of Genesis but, in Bill's words, for 'the roan and strawberry calves'. In the character of Saltbush Bill, Paterson incorporates many of the qualities he considered essential for survival in the rough and tumble of outback life: determination, ingenuity, a wry sense of humour and a talent for sharp practices.

SALTER, Elizabeth (1918–81), born Adelaide, studied arts at the University of Adelaide and music at the Elder Conservatorium. She left Australia in 1952 to work with Dame Edith Sitwell, whose life she recorded in her biographies *The Last Years of a Rebel* (1967) and *Edith Sitwell* (1978). She also wrote biographies of John Peter Russell (1976), Daisy Bates (1971) and Robert Helpmann (1978); and a series of detective novels, *Death in a Mist* (1957), *Will to Survive* (1958), *There Was a Witness* (1960), *The Voice of the Peacock* (1962), *Once Upon a Tombstone* (1965) and *Tails She Dies* (1977).

'Sam Holt', an Australian folk-song in which a bushman sardonically recalls the seamy past of a former mate, Sam Holt, who has finally succeeded as a digger and returned to a gentleman's life in England, was originally a poem, 'A Ballad of Queensland', written by G.H. Gibson (q.v.) and published in the *Bulletin* 26 March 1881. A parody on the English popular song of the 1840s, 'Ben Bolt', 'Sam Holt' passed into oral currency and was included as an anonymous composition in A.B. Paterson's *Old Bush Songs* (1905). The opening lines of 'Sam Holt',

Oh! don't you remember Black Alice, Sam Holt –
Black Alice, so dusky and dark,
The Warrego gin, with the straw through
    her nose,
And teeth like a Moreton Bay shark

are quoted with minor variations in Xavier Herbert's *Capricornia* (q.v., 1938) and illustrate the racist attitudes of much of Australian folk-song and ballad. Earlier parodies of 'Ben Bolt' were written by the goldfields entertainer Charles Thatcher.

SANDES, John (1863–1938), born Cork, Ireland, and educated at Oxford, migrated to Australia in 1885 and for fifteen years from 1887 worked for the *Argus* as music and drama critic. One of the first contributors to the 'Oriel' column of the newspaper, he also used the pseudonym independently. In 1903 Sandes joined the Sydney *Daily Telegraph* and attended the London peace conference in 1919 as that newspaper's representative. From 1925 to 1938 he edited *Harbour*, a monthly shipping magazine. Sandes's topical, patriotic poetry found a ready audience, especially his 'With Death's Prophetic Ear', a poem on the Boer War which was published in numerous contemporary anthologies. He published five collections of verse, *Rhymes of the Times* (1898), *Ballads of Battle* (1900), *The House of Empire* (1909), *Landing in the Dawn* (1916) and *The Escort* (1925); three adventure novels, *Love and the Aeroplane* (1910), *Designing Fate* (1912) and *The Call of the Southern Cross* (1915); and, under the pseudonym 'Don Delaney', a group of novels mainly with bushranging themes, *Gentleman Jack, Bushranger* (1911), *For Turon Gold* (1913), *The Captain of the Gang* (1913), *A Rebel of the Bush* (1914) and *The White Champion* (1917).

SANDS, John (1818–73) was a famous early Australian printer and stationer who was born in Sandhurst, England; a fifth-generation engraver and printer, he came to Australia for health reasons in 1837 and set up business in Sydney. In 1852, in partnership with his brother-in-law Thomas Kenny, he expanded into Melbourne; when Kenny retired in 1861, the firm, which had been joined by Dugald MacDougall in 1860, became Sands & MacDougall. After Sands's death, his widow divided the business so that John Sands Ltd, run by the Sands family, operated in Sydney and Sands & MacDougall, run by the MacDougall family, operated from Melbourne. Under various titles, Sands was one of the largest booksellers and stationers in Australia, and published an important series of almanacs (q.v.), directories and gazetteers covering Melbourne, Sydney, Adelaide and country areas in NSW and Victoria. In 1881 the John Sands company became the first Australian firm to issue Christmas and New Year cards. A centenary history of Sands & MacDougall was compiled by H.P. Down and published in 1956.

'Sandy Maranoa, The' is a rollicking Australian folk-song which celebrates the life of the overlanders moving cattle to and from the Maranoa pastoral district in central-southern Queensland, through which runs the Maranoa River, named by Sir Thomas Mitchell in 1846. 'The Sandy Maranoa' was included in A.B. Paterson's *Old Bush Songs* (1905) as an anonymous composition, 'The Maranoa Drovers', but claims have been made that it was composed at the end of the nineteenth century by a young Queensland stockman, A.W. Davis.

Sandy's Selection, see **Rudd Family**

SANSOM, Clive (1910–81) lived in London until 1950, when he migrated to Tasmania. A speech educationalist, he was the author of several collections of verse or verse plays on religious and historical themes, *In the Midst of Death* (1940), *The Unfailing Spring* (1943), *The World Turned Upside Down* (1948), *The Witnesses and Other Poems* (1956), *The Cathedral* (1958), *Dorset Village* (1962), *Return to Magic* (1969), *Francis of Assisi* (1981); and a novel, *Passion Play* (1951). His *Selected Poems*, chosen by Ruth Sansom, were published in 1990 and four of his verse plays, titled *Four Verse Dramas*, in 1991. His poem 'The Witnesses', one of the prize-winning entries of the Festival of Britain competition, was also published in *Poems 1951* (1951) and separately in 1971. In addition, Sansom compiled anthologies of poetry for adults, including *The English Heart* (1945) and *The World of Poetry* (1959), as well as numerous anthologies of verse and plays for children. *Clive Sansom by Forty Friends*, edited by Ruth Sansom, was published in 1990.

SANT, Andrew (1950–) was born and lived on the outskirts of London until he came to Australia with his family in 1962. He graduated in arts from La Trobe University and has revisited England and travelled in Europe. He lives in Tasmania and has been a part-time teacher, editor and writer. He was joint editor of *Island Magazine* 1979–89, co-editing with Michael Denholm the anthology *First Rights: A Decade of Island Magazine* (1989). He has produced for radio, *First Hearing: New Verse by Australian Poets* (1982, 1990) and *Antarctica: The Imagined Continent* (1986); has been a member of the Literature Board of the Australia Council; and has edited *Toads: Australian Writers: Other Work, Other Lives* (1992), in which twelve Australian authors (e.g. Robert Drewe, Kate Jennings, Marion Halligan, James McQueen, Peter Goldsworthy, Elizabeth Jolley, David Foster, John Forbes) describe the problems of being a writer. Sant's four books of verse (to 1993) are *Lives* (1980), a small book of twenty-one poems, *The Caught Sky* (1982), *The Flower Industry* (1985) and *Brushing the Dark* (1989).

Sant's strength as a poet lies in his capacity for keen and sensitive observation and in his ability to capture nuances of character and scene. The title poem of *Lives*, for example, catches to perfection the emigrant Dutch farmer Henk Ramek, who 'drinks regularly to celebrate the good life' here in Australia, and his wife, who, stoically milking the cows, greets his stumbling return home from the pub with 'you olt buggar'. Two other poems involving these two are 'A Small Holding' and 'Milking Three Cows at Nightfall'. Other notable Sant poems are the three-poem series 'Rural

Episodes', 'Literacy Lessons' (the vicissitudes of teaching English to unemployed youths), 'A Mount Wellington Sequence', 'Old Woman in Apple Country', 'The Beekeeper's Directory', 'Kelp Harvesters (King Island)' and the popular 'Homage to the Canal People', where those who ply the canals, 'cloth caps pulled down against complacency', view with mildly contemptuous indifference the passing parade of towns and villages.

SANTAMARIA, B.A. (Bartholomew Augustine) (1915–   ), born West Brunswick, Melbourne, graduated in arts and law from the University of Melbourne. Catholic activist and, from 1957, president of the National Civic Council, he has published numerous political books including *The Price of Freedom* (1964), *Point of View* (1969), *The Defence of Australia* (1970) and *The Australian Labor Movement: The Issue of Control (1966–71)* (1971). He has also written an autobiography, *Against the Tide* (1981), which includes a chapter on James McAuley (q.v.), a biography of Daniel Mannix (1984), and *Australia at the Crossroads: Reflections of an Outsider* (1987). He is caricatured as Greensleeves in Barry Oakley's play *The Feet of Daniel Mannix* (1975).

Sara Dane, see **GASKIN, Catherine**

SARIBAN, Michael (1939–   ), born Berlin, of Russian parents, arrived in Australia in 1948. He began a career in librarianship at the National Library but moved to Brisbane in 1966. He has published two collections of verse, *At the Institute for Total Recall* (1984) and *A Formula for Glass* (1987).

Sarsaparilla, one of Patrick White's (q.v.) fictional outer Sydney suburbs, represents the materialism, ugliness and 'exaltation of the average' that he deplores. It features in his novels *Riders in the Chariot* (1961) and *The Solid Mandala* (1966); in his plays *A Cheery Soul* (1965) and *The Season at Sarsaparilla* (1965); and in several of the short stories collected in *The Burnt Ones* (1964). In *Flaws in the Glass* (1981), White indicates the connections between Sarsaparilla and Castle Hill, where he lived 1948–63.

Saturday Club Book of Poetry, The, a Sydney magazine, was edited by Patricia Laird. First published in 1972 as an issue dedicated to Kenneth Slessor, it was replaced in 1977 by *Scopp*, a magazine that included prose as well as poetry, also edited by Laird. *Scopp* ceased publication in 1980.

Saturday Night, a weekly magazine published in Melbourne, ran 1879–94, changing its title to *Once a Week* in 1881; in 1894 it was incorporated into the *Weekly Budget*. It included some serials and short stories.

Saturdee, a novel by Norman Lindsay (q.v.), was published in 1933, illustrated by the author. A revised version of a series of short stories published 1908–19, it forms part of his trilogy on small-town life in the 1890s that includes *Redheap* (q.v., 1930) and *Halfway to Anywhere* (1947). The novel centres on the escapades of 12-year-old Peter Gimble and his friends Conkey Menders, Bullyo Peddlar, Bufflehead and others as they unremittingly pursue fun, freedom and the mysteries of the female in the face of Redheap's sleepy but repressive narrowness. Distinctive aspects include Lindsay's humorous insight into the amoral world of the schoolboy and the pretensions of the adult, his versatile characterisation and zestful narrative.

Satyrs and Sunlight: Silvarum Libri, the first volume of poems by Hugh McCrae (q.v.), was published in Sydney in 1909. The first part of the title, *Satyrs and Sunlight*, was also used for McCrae's 1928 collected verse. The seventy-nine poems, mainly short lyrics, were highly regarded by the bohemian literary set of the day, of which Norman Lindsay was the centre. Poems such as 'I Blow My Pipes', 'The Satyr's Lass', 'Bacchanalia', 'Fantasy' and 'Muse-Haunted', filled with fauns and nymphs, dryads, centaurs, Bacchanals and the god Pan, all whirling and cavorting in an exultant, sensuous vitality, were a startling contrast to the homespun balladry of the previous two decades.

SAVAGE, Georgia, born Launceston, Tasmania, has lived most of her adult life in Victoria, whence she returned in 1984 after several years in Queensland. Now a full-time writer, she has published four successful novels and won the 1992 Canada-Australia Literary Award. Her first book was *The Tournament* (1983). The hero, Finney Kitto, a young man who falls under the spell of Marigold, a woman twice his age, is being questioned about her sudden death. He escapes from custody and finds his way to where Marigold's son Simon is engaged in a chess tournament. There he finally comes to terms with himself and his relationship with Marigold. By comparison with the later novels *The Tournament* lacks tension and realism. Her second book, *Slate and Me and Blanche McBride* (1983), recalls the circumstances of the Patricia Hearst kidnapping in America some years ago and the involvement of Hearst in the kidnap gang's activities. Savage's book has the brothers Slate and Wyn Jackson robbing a bank, killing a policeman and abducting a hostage, schoolgirl witness Blanche McBride. The novel describes the later events and their effect on Blanche. *The Estuary* (1987), whose incidents may have some autobiographical basis, sees Vinny Beaumont leave Victoria after the death of her husband and go to Queensland to live in her mother's old home, The Estuary. The novel recalls the earlier events of Vinny's life – her childhood, early marriage, birth of her daughter Clare, her young husband's death in an accident at work, her prolonged grief and the estrangement it brings from Clare. In Queensland she becomes involved with the family who run a private hotel, nicknamed 'The Bananas', with a Yugoslav, Jan Tadic, to whom she is attracted and with a lesbian, Marcia. Eventually she is reconciled with Clare. The novel is intended, in Savage's words, 'to show how one woman coped with problems which I believe are more or less universal to women'. *The House Tibet*

(1989) is more substantial, ambitious and complex. Victoria Ferguson, 13, leaves her Melbourne home after being violated by her architect father. She and her half-mute younger brother James make their way by train and bus to the Gold Coast where they take on new identities, Morgan le Fay Christie and J-Max, and become involved with a group of other youthful runaways, several of whom become their loyal friends and supporters. After numerous adventures, including working in the laundry of a brothel, Morgan and J-Max come to stay at the derelict old house named Tibet, and become involved with the 80-year-old ex-Cambridge scholar, lawyer and farmer, Xam, whom they help during an asthma attack. From Xam, Morgan gains a sense of being loved and begins to come to terms with the trauma of incest. J-Max begins to learn to speak. Eventually Morgan is also reconciled to her mother and father, who have put their own lives into better order as a result of those tragic events. *The House Tibet* has strength, conviction and some fine characterisation. The relationship between Morgan, J-Max and Xam is explored with great sensitivity and understanding.

SAVERY, Henry (1791–1842), the first Australian novelist and essayist, was born in Somerset, England, the son of a prominent Bristol banker; his movements thereafter until his marriage in 1815 are not known with certainty, although the evidence of his strongly autobiographical novel, *Quintus Servinton* (q.v., 1831), suggests that he was educated at a grammar school and that he spent his early manhood in London. After his marriage he moved to near Bristol, where he was engaged in business as a sugar-refiner until bankrupted in 1819; in 1819–22 he was editor of the *Bristol Observer* and an insurance broker. In 1822 he returned to sugar-refining and soon became the dominant partner in the business, but overreached himself financially and forged fictitious bills to meet his debts. Panicking at the prospect of detection, he fled, planning to escape to America, but was captured in dramatic circumstances at Cowes in the Isle of Wight within half an hour of his ship's sailing. Brought back to Bristol, he was advised to plead guilty but was condemned to death. Reprieved almost at the last moment, he was transported to Van Diemen's Land and arrived in Hobart in 1825.

Savery was soon involved in controversy: he was appointed to clerkships in the colonial administration and gained permission to bring his wife and child to join him, which led to accusations that he had received favoured treatment from the lieutenant-governor of the colony, George Arthur, who had to defend his actions to the Colonial Office in London. In 1827 Savery was assigned to the superintendent of the Van Diemen's Land Establishment, a development company which did not prosper; in the ensuing investigation he was exonerated of any financial malpractice. In 1828 Eliza Savery, encouraged by her husband's misleading reports of his prospects, arrived in Hobart to find him in debt; within a week he had attempted suicide, his despair possibly increased by rumours of a shipboard liaison between his wife and

Algernon Montagu. When Eliza left Hobart early in 1829 Savery's debts had landed him in prison; during his fifteen months' incarceration he probably wrote the sketches of Hobart life and people which were published under the pseudonym 'Simon Stukeley' in the *Colonial Times* 1829, as *The Hermit in Van Diemen's Land* (q.v.), which, when issued in book form in 1830, was the first book of Australian essays. Some uncertainty remains concerning Savery's authorship of *The Hermit in Van Diemen's Land;* there is no doubt, however, about his authorship of *Quintus Servinton*, the first Australian novel. Subtitled *A Tale Founded upon Incidents of Real Occurrence*, it records in fictional form the main incidents in Savery's life until 1829, except that Quintus's wife remains faithful to her husband and eventually secures his release. After his own release from prison, Savery underwent periods of assignment until securing his ticket-of-leave in 1832; it was temporarily withdrawn in 1833 following complaints that he had run the *Tasmanian* during the absence of Henry Melville (q.v.), who published *Quintus Servinton* and included Savery material in the *Van Diemen's Land Almanack* for 1831. For several years from 1833 Savery was mainly engaged in pastoral pursuits securing his conditional pardon in 1838, but he again overreached himself financially, again resorted to forgery, and was sent to Port Arthur after a trial presided over, ironically, by Algernon Montagu. He died there early in 1842, his decline graphically described by David Burn in *An Excursion to Port Arthur in 1842* (1842).

In some respects Savery's tragic life is of more interest than his writing, but *The Hermit in Van Diemen's Land* offers a valuable picture of colonial Tasmania, and *Quintus Servinton*, in addition to its autobiographical and historical significance, is of some interest in the way, as a cautionary tale, it links convict fiction with the convict memoirs (see Convict in Australian Literature). Again, although there is no evidence that Henry Kingsley read the novel, *Quintus Servinton* looks forward to *The Recollections of Geoffry Hamlyn* (1859) in its admiration of prudence and moderation, and disapproval of wilfulness and self-centredness, to which Quintus no less than Mary Hawker is victim. There have been suggestions also that William Hay was influenced by *Quintus Servinton* in writing *The Escape of the Notorious Sir William Heans* (1919), in which Savery appears as a minor character.

'Say to Me Ronald!', a short story by Hal Porter (q.v.), was first published in the *Bulletin* in 1961. An amusing study of well-intentioned individuals afflicted with language difficulties and notions of good form inherited from their respective, very different cultures, it is one of Porter's most popular stories. Perrot, an Adelaide schoolteacher, has been tutoring Ronald Wee San Wat, the 17-year-old son of a Singapore millionaire exiled in Australia during the Second World War. Aghast when Wee gratefully presents him with a massive golfbag, Perrot is finally persuaded in lieu to attend afternoon tea with Wee and his sisters. At their hot, over-furnished flat, Wee's well-plied whisky and the cement-like 'melting-moments' of the Misses Wee help to frustrate the determined efforts of both sides to achieve a social success and the party rapidly degenerates into a farcical fiasco.

SAYCE, C.H. (Conrad Harvey) (1888–1935), born Hereford, England, and educated in England, was a well-known architect who was resident for some time in Australia and designed some of the buildings of the University of WA. He also wrote a series of adventure novels, which have conventional plots and wooden characters but which reflect an intimate knowledge of outback localities and conditions. They are *The Valley of a Thousand Deaths* (?1920), *Golden Buckles* (1920), *In the Musgrave Ranges* (1922), *The Golden Valley* (1924), *The Splendid Savage* (?1928) and *Comboman* (1934). Sayce also used the pseudonym 'Jim Bushman'.

SAYERS, C.E. (Charles Edward) (1901–80) worked on the staff of the *Age* for many years, and published four novels, *The Jumping Double* (1923), *Boss of Toolangi* (1924), *Green Streaked Ring* (1930) and *Desperate Chances* (1930); a biography of David Syme (1965); and numerous local histories. He also edited several historical and literary texts including James Bonwick's *Western Victoria* (1970) and *John Batman* (1973), 'Rolf Boldrewood's' *Old Melbourne Memories* (1969), John Morgan's *The Life and Adventures of William Buckley* (1967) and the 1969 edition of *Letters From Victorian Pioneers*.

SAYER, Mandy (1963–), born Sydney, has a degree in creative writing from Indiana University, USA. She won the 1989 Myrtle Armstrong Fiction Award, the 1989 Keisler Poetry Award and the 1989 NSAL Literature Merit Award for short fiction. Her memoir, 'Dreamtime Alice', was a finalist in the 1988 *Australian*/Vogel Award; in 1989 she won that Award with her first novel, *Mood Indigo* (1990). Both it and its sequel, *Blind Luck* (1993), trace the misfortunes of the Partridge family – husband and father, the drug-addicted musician Len; wife and mother Nancy, who begins well enough but disintegrates under the stress of Len's committal to a psychiatric institution and the pressure of keeping the children and becomes an alcoholic housekeeper and 'live-in' companion to anyone willing to employ her; the children, Ned, Wanda and Rose. Rose is the central character, 4 years old at the beginning of *Mood Indigo* and an adolescent in *Blind Luck*. Sayer has also written a play, *Blind Faith* (1991).

SCANLON, Herbert (1899–?) served in the First World War and published numerous collections of short stories, nearly all dealing with the experience of war. They include *Recollections of a Soldier's Life* (1919), *Into Turkish Harems* (?1922), *Gay Mademoiselles, Sly Digs and Wedding Bells* (192?), *In a Nutshell* (1921), *Humoresque* (1922), *Bon Jour Digger* (1922), *Triolette* (1923), *The Vengeance of Etna* (1924), *Forgotten Men* (1927), *The Deathless Army* (1927), *Veterans of War* (1928) and *Great Short Stories* (?1932). Many of Scanlon's books on war were one-shilling paperbacks, sold by door-to-door salesmen to help unemployed servicemen.

Scarlet Woman, see **Feminism and Australian Literature**

Scarp, published initially by the Department of English at the University of Wollongong, began life as *First Draught* in September 1980, three issues of that title being edited by a collective which included James Wieland. The title *Scarp* began with Autumn 1982; *Scarp* is published twice yearly and is now under the aegis of the School of Creative Arts, with a strong graphic art as well as literary content. In conjunction with Five Islands Press, *Scarp* publishes the work of new poets.

Schindler's Ark (1982) by Thomas Keneally (q.v.), won the 1982 Booker McConnell Prize. Based entirely on facts ascertained from official documents, interviews, testimonies, correspondence and private papers, the book uses, in Keneally's words, 'the texture and devices of a novel' to tell the authentic story of the protection of thousands of Jewish lives in the Second World War by the German industrialist Oskar Schindler (1908–74). Born in the Czechoslovakian industrial city Zwittau, Schindler follows the German invasion into Poland, where in Cracow he establishes an enamelware factory. Within a few months he is employing 150 Jewish workers and his Emalia factory begins to develop among Jews the reputation of a haven. Arrested on several occasions for 'racial improprieties', Schindler has a charmed life, buying and blackmailing himself out of trouble. As the Holocaust develops the Jews are gathered into vast labour camps; one such camp is at Plaszow, near Cracow. Knowing the intolerable conditions experienced by his Jewish employees in Plaszow, Schindler gains permission to build, at his own expense, a camp for them in the grounds of his Emalia factory. It becomes a relative paradise, Schindler devoting vast sums of money and practising all kinds of stratagems and subterfuges to build up its population. In 1944 Emalia is ordered disbanded and the workers scheduled for 'relocation' at the extermination camps of Gross-Rosen and Auschwitz. Schindler succeeds in having the factory, now committed to armaments, re-established at Brinnlitz in Moravia. He compiles a list of several thousand 'essential' workers; at a time when the crematoria of Auschwitz alone are consuming 9000 victims a day it becomes a 'list of life'. In a supreme irony that pleases Schindler immensely, his new armament factory does not produce a single shell in the course of its existence. At the end of the war a bodyguard of Jewish ex-prisoners saw Schindler to safety in Switzerland. An international Jewish relief organisation helped him settle on a farm in Argentina in 1949, but he returned to Germany in 1958. In 1961 he was welcomed ecstatically in Israel and declared a Righteous Person, a peculiarly Jewish honour extended to Gentiles. He was awarded the Cross of Merit by the West German government in 1966; by his own wish he was buried in Jerusalem.

Keneally's claim that the techniques of the novel are suited to the portrayal of a character of such ambiguity and events of such magnitude is validated in the work, which is a valuable contribution to the literature of the Holocaust. In 1993 *Schindler's Ark* was made into an award-winning film, *Schindler's List*.

SCHLUNKE, E.O. (Eric Otto) (1906–60), born Reefton, near Temora, NSW, lived most of his life on the family sheep and wheat property Rosenthal, near Reefton. Schlunke's ancestors were among the group of German Lutheran settlers who came to Australia under the sponsorship of George Fife Angas and who settled mainly in the Barossa Valley of SA. An efficient and enterprising farmer, Schlunke was also a skilled writer of fiction. He published two collections of short stories, *The Man in the Silo* (1955) and *The Village Hampden* (1958) and Clement Semmler edited a selection, *Stories of the Riverina* (1965, reprinted 1984); the last, except for seven stories, is selected from the earlier collections. Schlunke wrote three novels, *Rosenthal* and *Foray on Freeling*, both published serially in the *Sydney Morning Herald* in 1939, and *Feather Your Nest*, published serially in the *Bulletin* in 1954. A regionalist, Schlunke captured in his fiction the essence of the Riverina and central-western NSW – its sunbleached expanses of wheat paddocks and sheep runs, red-brown soil, dusty townships and drily taciturn inhabitants, especially those of the old German extraction. Sardonically humorous and slyly debunking in the 'Steele Rudd' manner, Schlunke was also, in his later works, a social satirist. His notable humorous stories include 'The Cowboy from Town', 'Once a Sheep Stealer', 'The Man in the Silo' and 'The Enthusiastic Prisoner', the last one of several stories he wrote about Italian POWs who worked as agricultural labourers in the Riverina in the Second World War. Schlunke liked to depict, as in 'Riding the Boom', 'Into My Parlour' and 'Sale of a Car Owner', the machinations of such archetypal city slickers as car salesmen, real estate agents and stockbrokers, who cheated the naive and seemingly slow-witted country folk. Beneath the ironic humour of his stories, a trace of seriousness is sometimes present, 'The Man Farther Out', for example, hinting in science fiction style at the future problems inherent in the greedy mismanagement of the land. Schlunke's biographical novel *Rosenthal* has been highly commended. It tells of three generations of German-Australian farmers: Adolph Weismann, the pioneer ancestor who established Rosenthal, his son Karl and grandson Otto (Schlunke himself). It recounts their pioneer experiences, the traumas of the First World War which was an agonising period for Germans in Australia, and their struggles to survive the boom-bust syndrome of the 1930s Depression years. An authentic documentary of the effect of the rigorous creed of Lutheranism on the lives of those enmeshed in its rules and customs, *Rosenthal* is also an absorbing study of childhood and schooling in the Australian outback. It glows, as does all Schlunke's writing, with affection for the landscape and the rural life. Schlunke's wife Olga, lover of art, music and literature, published poems in the *Bulletin*.

Science Fiction (Speculative Fiction) (SF). Van Ikin concludes his introductory survey in *Australian Science Fiction* (1982) with the assessment that 'the Great Australian SF Novel is yet to be written'. For many readers and critics more basic questions are whether the terms 'Great Novel' and 'Science Fiction' or 'Speculative Fiction' are, in fact, compatible; whether SF has any place in the mainstream of literature; and, if it has, how is it to be defined, and what are its limits and extent. The 'inclusive' view, towards which majority opinion tends, accepts SF as a legitimate literary form, anticipates the ultimate birth of 'the Great Australian SF Novel', and is inclined to locate SF itself within the genre of fantasy literature.

One of the earliest Australian fantasy stories is the anonymously authored 'Oo-a-deen', which appeared in the *Corio Chronicle and Western Districts Advertiser* (October 1847). Sated with the delights and vices of the old world, a young man comes to Australia, where he finds 'Ooadeen, the country of Mahanacumans . . . a country fair as the 'land of promise' seen by the Hebrew Lawgiver from the top of Mount Pisgah'. His illicit romance with the beautiful Ooadeen maiden, Yarranee, leads to his banishment and he passes the rest of his life 'wedded in thought and memory to Ooadeen' but fails in all his efforts to find it again. 'Oo-a-deen' represents one of the earliest appearances in Australian literature of the 'lost civilisation' motif; confronted with this mysterious and unknown continent, writers fell to conjecturing about the possible existence in Australia's unexplored vastness of older civilisations and lost kingdoms. Speculation became more pronounced in the final two decades of the nineteenth century, when the Lemurian legend gripped the imagination of writers the world over. 'Lemuria' had been used in the 1850s by C.L. Sclater to refer to a lost continent of prehistoric times extending from the coast of Africa to Malaysia and including Australia. Australian fantasies that embrace aspects of the Lemurian theme (White explorers, strange peoples, unknown regions and fabulous treasures) include J.F. Hogan's *The Lost Explorer* (1890), Ernest Favenc's '*The Last of Six': Tales of the Austral Tropics* (1893) and *The Secret of the Australian Desert* (1896), W.H. Willshire's *A Thrilling Tale of Real Life in the Wilds of Australia* (1895), J.D. Hennessey's *An Australian Bush Track* (1896), G. Firth Scott's *The Last Lemurian* (1898), and Henry Grin's *The Adventures of Louis de Rougemont* (1899). Favenc, an explorer-writer, was particularly intrigued by the dimly known, mysterious, tropical regions of Australia and viewed them with typical Lemurian romanticism. Firth Scott's novel discovers the lost civilisation of Lemuria in the Australian desert; the two heroes, Dick Halwood and the lapsed English aristocrat 'Yellow Hatter', trick Tor Ymmothe, queen of Lemuria, into allowing them to take a fortune in gold out of the kingdom, but the 'Hatter' falls in love with the queen and seeks to return. Such stories, remote though they are from modern science/speculative fiction, carry occasional suggestions of advanced technical achievements, e.g. *The Last Lemurian* has a water-powered artificial doorway guarding the entrance to the legendary kingdom.

A frequent component of the Lemurian legend is Utopianism. Fantasy literature itself is often oriented to Utopia; sometimes it depicts a Shangri-La existence in a newly discovered paradise (as in 'Oo-a-deen'); sometimes the Utopia is the ordinary world turned into paradise by a sudden change in material fortunes, e.g. hidden treasure discovered. One of the first major works of Utopian SF actually set in Australia is Joseph Fraser's *Melbourne and Mars: My Mysterious Life on Two Planets* (1889). *Melbourne and Mars* is the story of Adam Jacobs, who comes to Australia in 1828 with his mother and convict father, has a successful business career, experiences the depression of the 1840s, and seeks to restore his fortune on the goldfields. In middle age he has persistent dreams of a second infancy and it is gradually revealed that he is living again in childhood in the Utopian civilisation of the planet Mars, with its vastly superior social system. The Martian lifestyle is also presented in considerable technical detail, e.g. people travel by a contraption resembling a flying fish which rises spirally and then progresses forward by giant sweeping strokes of its fins. Other Utopia-oriented works include S.A. Rosa's *The Coming Terror: A Romance of the Twentieth Century* (1894), in which a rebellious country overthrows its established authorities by the use of a poisonous gas ('Panmort') and enters into a period of Utopian prosperity; G. Read Murphy's *Beyond the Ice: Being a Story of the Newly Discovered Region round the North Pole* (1894), in which Dr Frank Farleigh, sole survivor of an Arctic expedition, is saved by members of a highly advanced civilisation in the 'Fregida' (North Pole) area and becomes indoctrinated in their ways; and W.H. Galier's *A Visit to Blestland* (1896) where a boatload of people is transported on a mysterious cloud to the planet Blestland, where sectarian hatred and personal rivalry are nonexistent.

Widely regarded as the first classic of Australian SF, Erle Cox's *Out of the Silence* (1925) is a work in which science and fantasy are in equal proportions. Alan Dundas discovers beneath his land the remnants of a highly advanced civilisation, and the body, in suspended animation, of a beautiful woman, Earani. Restored to life, Earani reveals to Dundas the philosophy of her civilisation and explains to him something of its ingenious gadgetry, e.g. death rays, light without heat, tablet meals, sophisticated and powerful eavesdropping devices. Although attracted to her, Dundas is appalled by the plans she unfolds to develop the world along the lines of controlled genetics. Ironically, she is killed and civilisation as we know it is saved by a primitive weapon (a knife) wielded by the most primitive of all passions (the jealousy of Dundas's jilted lover, Marian Seymour).

Although interplanetary travel is occasionally mentioned in earlier fiction, e.g. *A Woman of Mars* (1901) by 'Mary-Ann Moore-Bentley' and *The Germ Growers* (1892) by Robert Potter, it is not until *Vandals of the Void* (1931) by J.M. Walsh ('H. Haverstock Hill') that Australian SF enters the era of spaceships, interplanetary alliances, battles in space and extra-terrestrial beings with weird physical characteristics and remarkable intellectual powers. In *Vandals of the Void*, legit-imate space traffic is harassed by unknown enemies and the Interplanetary Guard is assigned to sort out the trouble. The Guards' own ships are attacked and some of the planets (Earth, Mars and Venus) are saved in an epic clash in the now famous *Star Wars* fashion. Significant features of *Vandals of the Void* are the realistic scientific explanations of events and devices, e.g. robots and ray tubes, and the provision of a Buck Rogers-type hero, Space Captain Sanders of the Interplanetary Guard. 'M. Barnard Eldershaw's' *Tomorrow and Tomorrow* (1947), set in Australia in the twenty-fourth century, illustrates the fact that literary craftsmanship rather than theme is the real prerequisite for literary acceptance. The book's chief character, Knarf, a writer of the twenty-fourth century, divides his attention between his own contemporary life and that of the early twentieth century, when the 'Australians', who had taken over from the first White 'Pioneers', had inherited the land from its original dwellers, the 'First People' (Aborigines). In Knarf's time the errant Murrumbidgee of 400 years earlier sits 'quiet and full between canal-like banks, tame and sure' and that fruitful land, once named 'Riverina', has been renamed the Tenth Commune. The interesting traditional aspect of the novel is its sophisticated twenty-fourth century perspective on present Australian history; its SF interest lies in the author's attempt to convey a picture of Australian society of that century. By the mid-twentieth century SF was a recognisable literary commodity in Australia, with Ivan Southall's Simon Black series catering for a new generation of young SF fans and the Commonwealth Satellite Space Station stories of Frank Bryning accommodating older readers. Bryning's stories, given continuity by the presence of the female scientist Dr Vivien Gale, and set in the twenty-first century, combine intriguing plots with highly realistic scientific content.

In the decades 1940–60 American SF had only a limited impact in Australia although the Melbourne Science Fiction Club, founded in the early 1950s, prospered. During the Second World War and through the 1950s (the Golden Age of American SF) there was, because of the dollar imbalance, an embargo on the importation of American publications into Australia which was not lifted until after 1960, by which time Australia had virtually missed out on the influence of that remarkable period of growth in the USA. It is from as late as 1975 that the current and continuing boom in Australian SF dates. In that year the 33rd Annual World SF Convention (Aussie Con One) was held in Melbourne with American writer Ursula Le Guin as the central conference figure. The success of Aussie Con One created a new climate for Australian SF; new publishing houses for SF sprang up, e.g. Norstrilia Press, Void Publications, while established presses such as the UQP and Wild & Woolley showed increased interest; new SF magazines came into being, e.g. *Science Fiction: A Review of Speculative Literature*; writers' workshops were conducted which led to the emergence of new writers and anthologies of SF writing; and the Literature Board, which had helped fund Aussie Con One, continued to give generous assistance to the publication of SF writing. Aussie Con Two was held in Melbourne in 1985; *Contrary Modes* is a collection of papers from that conference.

Important Australian SF writers include George Turner, A. Bertram Chandler (qq.v.), Frank Bryning, Lee Harding (q.v.), Victor Kelleher (q.v.), Wynne Whiteford, John Baxter, Jack Wodhams, Freda McLennan, Damien Broderick (q.v.), Yvonne Rousseau, David J. Lake (q.v.), Terry Dowling, Greg Egan, Cherry Wilder, Philippa Maddern, Lucy Sussex, Bruce Gillespie, Van Ikin, Francis Byrne, Petrina Smith, David Grigg, Paul Voermans, Russell Blackford and John Alderson. Occasional venturers into SF, usually with conspicuous success, include mainstream writers Michael Wilding, Dal Stivens and Peter Carey. Film producer Peter Weir, with his provocative films *The Cars That Ate Paris* (1974), *Picnic at Hanging Rock* (1975) and *The Last Wave* (1977), has also made a significant contribution, in a different medium, to Australian fantasy.

With William Noonan, George Turner is Australia's longest-established reviewer, critic and proponent of SF writing. He is also the creator of the SF trilogy *Beloved Son* (1978), *Vaneglory* (1981) and *Yesterday's Men* (1983), novels that are set in the twenty-first century after the nuclear holocaust. Turner eschews the 'apocalyptic' SF novel, 'with everybody slapped back to the caves and three-headed mutants springing up everywhere'. He uses instead the power of biological science and such forms of bio-warfare as crop toxicity, defoliants, soil poisons and self-limiting insect plagues. Meticulously based on the most accurate, if speculative, science knowledge that research can produce, Turner's SF writing is also concerned to investigate the sociological implications of a science-dominated future and to probe the individual's situation in that future. Above all, he is concerned with literary standards; the SF novel should be 'a work of art, or at least of craftsmanship, in its own right'. A. Bertram Chandler, a writer of SF stories from the 1940s until his death in 1984, was Australia's most prolific and successful writer in the traditional SF mould. Crammed with adventures on the outer rim of the galaxy, Chandler's books are escapist excitement of high quality. His publications include *Rendezvous on a Lost World* (1961), *Beyond the Galactic Rim* (1963), *Into the Alternate Universe* (1964), *Space Mercenaries* (1965), *The Road to the Rim* (1967), *The Rim Gods* (1968), *Alternate Orbits* (1971), *The Broken Cycle* (1975) and *The Wild Ones* (1984), which retains Chandler's celebrated Space Captain Grimes. One of his more unusual is the 'alternative history' fantasy of Australia, *Kelly Country* (1983), which considers what might have happened if Ned Kelly had won the siege of Glenrowan. Chandler is commemorated by the A. Bertram Chandler Award, instituted in 1992. Lee Harding, whose SF anthologies have stimulated interest in Australian SF, has written numerous novels including *A World of Shadows* (1975), *Future Sanctuary* (1976), *The Weeping Sky* (1977), *Displaced Person* (1979) and *The Web of Time* (1980). *Displaced Person*, which Harding describes as 'a schizophrenic fantasy' is a poignant story about adolescence. Teenager Graeme Drury gradually loses contact with the ordinary world around him and drifts away from family and friends into a dim, grey world, peopled only by others like himself. Its fine characterisation and subtle fantasy won it the Alan Marshall Award for 1978. *The Weeping Sky*, a remarkably imaginative work, describes with brilliant visual detail the impact on a rather primitive society of the terrifying sight of the sky rent by a gaping, weeping wound. Damien Broderick (q.v.) wrote the fantasy *The Dreaming Dragons* (1980, runner-up that year in the John W. Campbell Award for the best SF novel in the world), which posits a new prehistory of the human race; David J. Lake has published *Walkers on the Sky* (1976), *The Gods of Xuma* (1978), *The Fourth Hemisphere* (1980), *The Man Who Loved Morlocks* (1981), Lake's sequel to H.G. Wells's *The Time Machine*, *The Ring of Truth* (1982), *The Changelings of Chaan* (1985) and *West of the Moon* (1988). Jack Wodhams's *Future War* (1982) contains four unusual stories on the theme of the title; he is particularly acclaimed for the story 'One Clay Foot'. Wynne Whiteford has written several successful SF novels, *Breathing Space Only* (1980), *Thor's Hammer* (1983), *The Hyades Contact* (1987) and *Lake of the Sun* (1989), the last-named winning the 1990 Ditmar Award, the annual Australian SF award. Victor Kelleher's *The Beast of Heaven* (1984) won the Australian SF Achievement Award for that year. Terry Dowling, among the major SF writers of the 1990s, has published collections of short stories and a novel, *Wormwood* (1991), which won the Ditmar Award for 1992. The same year saw the publication of Sean McMullen's debut collection of stories *Call to the Edge* (1992), which was popularly received. Of the more mainstream writers, David Ireland's *A Woman of the Future* (1979) is largely fantasy, while Stivens, Wilding and Carey have all dabbled, quite impressively, in fantasy, e.g. Carey's 'Report on the Shadow Industry', Wilding's 'The Man of Slow Feeling' and Stivens's 'The Gentle Basilisk'.

Anthologies have probably done more to advance the cause of Australian SF than any individual writer or individual novel. The earliest significant anthologies were John Baxter's *The Pacific Book of Australian SF* (1968) and *The Second Pacific Book of Science Fiction* (1971). The Baxter anthologies contain stories by Harding, Bryning, Chandler, Wodhams and Broderick and by mainstream fiction-writers Wilding, Olaf Ruhen, Douglas Stewart and George Johnston. Damien Broderick's *The Zeitgeist Machine* (1977) also includes fantasy fiction as distinct from pure SF in works by Wilding, Carey, Stivens, G.M. Glaskin and John Romeril. Paul Collins maintained the impetus from the 1975 Aussie Con One with his Void Publications' four anthologies, *Other Worlds* (1978), *Envisaged Worlds* (1978), *Alien Worlds* (1979) and *Distant Worlds* (1981). Lee Harding combines stories from Australian and overseas writers in *Beyond Tomorrow* (1976) and *Rooms of Paradise* (1978); his best-known anthology, *The Altered I* (1976), contains the fruits of Ursula Le Guin's writers' workshop that followed Aussie Con One. George Turner's anthology *The View from the Edge* (1977) gathers together the stories and Turner's critical notes from a Monash University writers' workshop conducted by Turner, the American Vonda McIntyre, and the English writer Christopher Priest. In 1979 Rob Gerrand edited the anthology *Transmutations*. At Aussie Con Two in 1985 the anthologies *Strange Attractors: Original Australian Speculative Fiction*, edited by Damien Broderick (who also edited the 1988 anthology *Matilda at the Speed of Light*), and *Urban Fantasies*, edited by David King and Russell Blackford, were launched. Blackford had earlier written *The Tempting of the Witch King* (1983), a work belonging to the heroic fantasy subgenre. In 1990 Van Ikin edited *Glass Reptile Breakout and Other Australian Speculative Stories*, in 1992 Bill Congreve, *Intimate Armageddons*, and in 1994 Van Ikin and Terry Dowling, *Mortal Fire. Best Australian SF*.

Australian SF magazines began in the 1950s with *Scientific Thriller* (1948–52), *Thrills Incorporated* (1950–52), *Future Science Fiction* (1953–55), *Popular Science Fiction* (1953–55) and *Science Fiction News* (1953–59). More substantial magazines of SF criticism and commentary began with John Bangsund's *Australian Science Fiction Review* (first series 1966–69), which was nominated in 1967 to receive an award at the International Science Fiction Convention for the best amateur SF magazine of that year. Bangsund's magazine was incorporated into *Scythrop* 1969–71 but reappeared as a second series of *Australian Science Fiction Review* in 1986, edited and produced by the Science Fiction Collective and continued until 1991. *SF Commentary*, which began in January 1969, was collated by Harding, printed by Bangsund and edited by Bruce Gillespie. *Science Fiction: A Review of Speculative Literature*, edited by Van Ikin, began in 1977, as did *The Cygnus Chronicler* edited by N.J. Angove. *Eidolon: The Journal of Australian Science Fiction and Fantasy*, a quarterly journal devoted to the development of speculative fiction in Australia, began in 1990, as did *Aurealis, the Australian Magazine of Fantasy and Science Fiction*. Emanating from WA, *Eidolon*'s April 1992 issue was a special Harlan Ellison number.

The most complete account of Australian SF writing, with illustrative extracts, is *Australian Science Fiction*, edited and introduced by Van Ikin (of the University of WA) in UQP's Portable Australian Authors series. Van Ikin gives a chronological survey of Australian SF and includes a bibliography. His article 'Adding New Co-ordinates to the Chart: The Place of Australian SF in the Literary Mainstream' in *Contrary Modes* (Aussie Con Two) updates the argument about the status of science fiction. To acknowledge his achievement in the SF field, Van Ikin was awarded the inaugural A. Bertram Chandler medal in 1992. Other significant SF bibliographical works include S.L. Larnach, *Materials towards a Checklist of Australian Fantasy to 1937* (1950) and Graham Stone's *Australian Science Fiction Index 1925–1967* (1968), with a supplement to 1975.

Scopp, see **Saturday Club Book of Poetry, The**

SCOTT, Sir Ernest (1867–1939), born and educated in England (although he did not attend a university), worked as a journalist in London and in 1892 migrated to Australia, where he joined the staff of the Melbourne *Herald*. He was on the staff of the Victorian *Hansard* 1895–1901 and the Commonwealth *Hansard* 1901–13. In 1912, after the publication of his impressive histories, *Terre Napoléon* (1910) and *Lapérouse* (1912), was appointed professor of history at the University of Melbourne, a position he held until 1936 when he retired as emeritus professor. His other publications include *The Life of Captain Matthew Flinders, R.N.* (1914), an important early history, *A Short History of Australia* (1916), *Men and Thought in Modern History* (1920), *History and Historical Problems* (1925) and *Australian Discovery* (1929). Scott also wrote *Australia during the War*, vol. 11 of *The Official History of Australia in the War of 1914–1918* (1936). The Ernest Scott Prize, a biennial award, is granted to a scholar of Australian or NZ history; it was awarded for 1991–92 to Anne Salmond for *Two Worlds: First Meetings between Maori and European, 1642–1772* (1991).

SCOTT, John A. (1948–   ), born Sussex, England, graduated from Monash University, Melbourne and spent some years writing for television and radio (e.g. the Aunty Jack Show and the Gary McDonald Show) before lecturing in media studies and professional writing at the Canberra College of Advanced Education (later University of Canberra). He then joined the Creative Arts Department of the University of Wollongong.

Although Scott was a leading figure in the lively poetry scene at Monash in the 1960s, winning the University's Writing Awards in 1966–67, and contributed to the burgeoning poetic revolution of the period, winning the Poetry Society of Australia Award in 1970, it was with the long narrative poem, 'St Clair', that he established himself as a leading contemporary poet. 'St Clair' won the 1984 Mattara Poetry Prize, appearing in the 1984 Mattara anthology *Neither Nuked nor Crucified*, and was published in 1986 with two other lengthy works by Scott, titled *St Clair: Three Narratives*. The other two were 'Preface', which won the 1985 Wesley Michel Wright Award from the University of Melbourne, and 'Run in the Stocking'. A revised edition of the 'Three Narratives' was published in 1990 with an introduction by Christopher Pollnitz who had published 'St Clair' initially in the Mattara anthology. Pollnitz demonstrates that much of the 'Three Narratives' has been present in Scott's work for a number of years; that 'St Clair', for example, is St Clair Convalescent in *The Barbarous Sideshow* of 1976; that Carl Brouwer, the chief figure of 'Preface', is contained to some extent in the character Gus, in *From the Flooded City* of 1981, and that Brouwer, Finchley Watson and Julia feature in *The Quarrel with Ourselves* and *Confession* of 1984, while other poems from those books have echoes of the self-investigations of Dover Anderson/Terry Rutherford in 'Run in the Stocking'. The degree of interconnectedness between Scott's poems, both in the repetition of poems from one volume to another and in the extension and expansion of parts of poems from one volume to another, has been readily admitted by the poet, who sees such repetitions, expansions and reworkings as a writer's natural attempt to attain the ultimate goal of a 'finished' work.

The first of the 'Three Narratives', 'Preface', a series of prose poems, has the narrator, Finchley Watson, committed to examining a series of letters written by Carl Brouwer to his former lover, Julia. The letters cover more than eighteen months, from March 1982, during which Carl leaves Sydney to begin an obsessive search (leading to his death) for A––, the original, quintessential female. Full of sexual obsessions, the letters show Carl drifting towards ultimate mental disintegration. The second narrative, 'St Clair', whose nineteen sections are all in verse, is set in an English psychiatric institution run by the government to 'condition' (by either rehabilitation or destruction) its political dissidents. Both those treated (e.g. the academic, Sheehan) and those administering the treatment (e.g. the psychologist, Warren) are shown to be victims of the barbarity that masquerades as modern (especially politically motivated) psychiatry. The third narrative, 'Run in the Stocking', is a psychological mystery-thriller, set in a totalitarian Australia of the twenty-first century. Whether academic Terry Rutherford, who had become an outspoken opponent of the government, did murder his lover Anne Morris and then commit suicide, or whether Dover Andersson, refashioned in a contrived hospital operation, is actually Rutherford, now removed from society by deleting his old identity and being given a new, less harmful one, is the central question. All three narratives – a combination of varied techniques that require considerable mental agility in the reader – extend the boundaries of contemporary Australian poetry. Not all critics are enthused by such techniques; 'tricky formlessness' that leads to the 'removal of narrative coherence' and a slavish adherence 'to post-structuralist insistence on the writer's automatism' is how the narratives are seen by fellow poet Fay Zwicky. Scott's shorter poems are well exemplified in *Singles*, where the reader attunes with ease to the sensitivity and dexterity of such stylish works as 'My Favourite Things', 'The Chicago Blues Style', 'The Park', 'The Passing, at Boho' and 'Breath'. Notable poems from other volumes include 'The Celebration' (*From the Flooded City*), 'The Apology' (*Translations*) and the translations of the French poet Emmanuel Holquard (*Translations*).

Scott's first novel, *Blair* (1988), has as its hero transplanted English academic Eric Blair, and as its setting the Centre of Human Achievement, in an Australian university. Scott lampoons the academic world, as numerous others have before him, peopling it with inept, bumbling, ridiculous figures. Deftly drawn characters combine with amusing dialogue to produce a better than usual piece of slapstick fiction.

What I have Written (1993), a novella, has three sections each with a different narrator, the first by the writer Christopher Houghton, the second by his wife Sorel Atherton, and the third by Houghton's friend and publisher Jeremy Fayrfax. Houghton's section, which comprises his 'novella' within the overall novella, tells of his encounter (he is Avery in the 'novella') in Paris with Frances Bourin (Catherine in the 'novella') and the sexual obsession that follows. Houghton (Avery) has to leave Paris and return to Melbourne before the relationship between them has time to develop. That relationship is continued (both in the 'novella' and the novella) through a passionate, uninhibited correspondence, but Houghton finally breaks free to return to his wife Sorel (Gillian in the 'novella'). He then has a stroke and dies. Sorel's section is one of consuming jealousy over her husband's supposed 'affair', a jealousy not assuaged at all by the very real doubt whether the affair existed on any level other than the fictional (i.e. in the 'novella'). The third section is that narrated by Jeremy Fayrfax, who has long been in love with Sorel and who aids and abets Houghton in the 'affair' hoping that it might lead to his winning Sorel. The 'novella', especially in the letters written by Catherine (Frances Bourin), is filled with sexual fantasies and obsessions. On the literary level the book explores the subtle differences between fiction and reality.

John A. Scott's published poetry includes *The Barbarous Sideshow* (1975), *From the Flooded City* (1981), *Smoking* (1983), *The Quarrel with Ourselves*, and *Confession* (1984, two volumes in one), *St Clair: Three Narratives* (1986, revised version 1990), *Singles: Shorter Works 1981–1986* (1989) and *Translations* (1990). *St Clair: Three Narratives* shared the 1986 Victorian Premier's Literary Award.

SCOTT, Margaret (1934–), born Bristol, England, graduated MA from Cambridge and Ph.D. from the University of Tasmania. She came to Australia in 1959 and taught at the University of Tasmania from 1966 to 1989, her chief academic interests being seventeenth-century drama and modern Australian poetry. She has written several books of poetry, *Tricks of Memory* (1980), *Visited* (1983) and *The Black Swans* (1988). Her first novel was *The Baby-Farmer* (1990). With Vivian Smith (q.v.) she edited the anthology *Effects of Light: The Poetry of Tasmania* (1985). She won the Borestone Mountain Poetry Award in 1974 and 1976. *The Baby-Farmer*, a novel set in nineteenth-century England, is a factual, fast-paced, macabre story of a woman who bought babies from their unwed or uncaring mothers and killed them.

SCOTT, Maria J. (d.1899), born Maria Barney, wrote five semi-religious, sentimental and romantic novels which rely on such plot devices as substituted infants and mistaken identities and are rich in villains, usually lawyers, and saintly deaths, usually of children. They are *Annine* (1871), *Pearl and Willie* (1873), *A Many Coloured Bubble* (1874), *Not So Ugly* (1874) and *A Brother or Lover? A Sister or Bride? and the Lights and Shadows of Hazleglen* (1872). For her second, third and fifth novels Scott used the pseudonyms 'Mist' or 'M.I.S.T.'.

SCOTT, Natalie (1928–) has written both as Natalie Scott and Louise Kent (children's fiction). A teacher of creative writing (the University of NSW and Macquarie University), she has also been a journalist and has lived in England and Europe as well as Australia. Her children's books include *Firebrand* (1968), *Hullabaloo* (1969), *Please Sit Still* (1969), *Wings on Wednesday* (1969) and *The Wizard of the Umbrella People* (1971). Her adult fiction comprises two novels, *Wherever We Step the Land is Mined* (1980) and *The Glasshouse* (1985), the latter a somewhat unusual novel in that it focuses on a woman who enjoys independence and its benefits in the form of beauty, love and security. Alexandra Pawley, the narrator, is an architect who marries a rich husband. Abandoned by him, she retains the comfortable pattern of her former married existence and satisfies her lifelong appetite for the beauty of material things, an appetite which is explained in the novel by a flashback to childhood.

SCOTT, Patricia Ethel, see **STONEHOUSE, Ethel**

SCOTT, Rose (1847–1925), born Glendon, NSW, into a well-known Australian family, was the cousin of the book-collector David Scott Mitchell. She became involved in the women's suffrage movement in 1891 when she was appointed secretary of the Womanhood Suffrage League, and subsequently took a prominent part in the achievement of a number of reforms affecting women and children. President of the Women's Political Educational League 1902–10, Scott was also president of a local branch of the London Peace Society and international secretary of the National Council of Women of NSW, but her main influence derived from her wide circle of acquaintances, which included several leading politicians. She was also well known to numerous Australian writers, including J.F. Archibald, Victor Daley, Henry Lawson, Louisa Lawson, Miles Franklin, A.B. Paterson, Bernard O'Dowd, Barbara Baynton, E.J. Brady and Mary Gilmore. Scott wrote some verse and short stories, but had little time for literary creativity, although some of her illustrated limericks were published in the *Bulletin*. Miles Franklin contributed an account of her achievement in *The Peaceful Army* (1938), ed. Flora Eldershaw, and Judith Allen has written the substantial biography *Rose Scott: Vision and Revision in Feminism* (1994).

SCOTT, Rosie (Judy Rosemary) (1948–), born Wellington, NZ, studied English and drama, has worked in social work and counselling and was involved in publishing and film-scripting. She now writes full-time. Her first book was a collection of poems, *Flesh and Blood* (1985), followed by a play, *Say Thank You to the Lady* (1985), which won the Bruce Mason *Sunday Times* Award and was the basis for the film *Redheads*. She has also published a collecton of short stories, *Queen of Love* (1989), but her major works have been the novels *Glory Days* (1988, short-listed for the NZ National Book Awards), *Nights with Grace* (1990), *Feral City* (1992, short-listed for the NBC Banjo Award for Fiction) and *Lives on Fire* (1993).

Rosie Scott is a significant voice in contemporary women's fiction. In all her novels the experience of one central female character dominates the narrative; such a character is the narrator, for example, in both *Feral City* and *Lives on Fire. Nights with Grace*, set in the idyllic Pacific Island of Rarotonga, tells of 17-year-old Grace finding first passionate love with a handsome New Zealander who is surveying the Pacific Islands for the harmful effects of pesticides and agriculture sprays. Tangential to this tenderly told love affair, which ends without damage to Grace's psyche, are the exploits and affairs of two other powerful women characters, Mara, Grace's mother, a willing victim all her life to a self-confessed 'unruly sex drive', and Porora, the Rarotongan, who is the one outspoken voice against the destruction of her island's culture and heritage by the tourist industry.

The 'feral city' of the novel of that title is Auckland, NZ, of the not too distant future. It is a city whose centre is a wasteland, inhabited by the human dregs (drug addicts, alcoholics, AIDS sufferers, dispossessed old people, street kids, gangs of malevolent hooligans) that a callous modern society and incompetent, corrupt governments have condemned to permanently degraded existences. Returning to the 'feral city' where she had grown up in the bookshop run by her parents, Faith has behind her, at 38, a dead drug-addict husband, her own cured addiction, a purposeless existence and a strong desire to renew the deep bond that had existed between her and her sister Violet. Together the sisters reopen the dilapidated bookshop and bring a little joy and hope to the city-dwellers. Unknown to Faith, Violet has long led the reform movement to improve the conditions within the city. In a huge rally organised to prick the consciences of political and social leaders, Violet is shot and killed. Faith ultimately finds comfort in her sister's courage and in the memory of their childhood together as well as some precarious hope for her own personal happiness in the devotion of Redfern, leader of one of the city's gangs. The real focus of the novel is the 'feral city' of the future whose ugliness, squalor and horror can only be combated by the compassion and moral integrity of people like Violet.

Lives on Fire focuses on Belle, the 40-year-old wife of Tyler, and mother of Kate and Patrick, two self-centred, grown-up children who have quit the parental home but who continue to plague Belle with their demands. Belle is temporarily in Brisbane where Tyler is fulfilling a building demolition contract. When beautiful young actress/call-girl Sky comes to stay with them, Tyler becomes obsessed with her. Belle is forced to come to terms with the new situation. As a short-term solution she attempts to salvage the lives of some of the Brisbane street kids by forming them into a group of travelling actors. The languid tropical Queensland climate creates a lush, hothouse ambience, with both nature and human nature in a permanent state of sexual and emotional arousal. The novel is thus replete with sensual sights, sounds and smells. Belle's long and anxious analysis of her life as wife and mother, her bitter memories of the harrowing love-hate relationship in the family process, and social issues such as the plight of the urban poor, the non-recognition of the Aborigines and the treatment of those classified as 'juvenile delinquents' are other important features of *Lives on Fire*.

Scottish Martyrs was a name given to five men who, inspired by the French Revolution, became such strong advocates of parliamentary and constitutional reform that an alarmed British government subjected them to sedition trials in 1793–94 and had them transported to the infant colony of NSW. Thomas Muir (1765–99), Maurice Margarot (1745–1815), Thomas Fyshe Palmer (1747–1802) and William Skirving (?–1796) came out in the *Surprize* in 1794, and Joseph Gerrald (1760–96) arrived a year later. Although the Scottish Martyrs were well treated as political prisoners, only Margarot, who during his time in the colony was suspected both of being a government informer and of plotting rebellion, lived long enough to return to Britain. Of the others, Gerrald and Skirving died soon after arrival; Muir escaped in 1796 with the intention of making his way to America, but only reached France and died there of wounds received on the harrowing journey; and Palmer died enfeebled at Guam, on his way home at the expiration of his sentence. The post-trial decline of the Scottish Martyrs meant that they made little contribution to transportation literature, although Palmer wrote an account of his and Skirving's ill-treatment on board the *Surprize* after a trumped-up charge of mutiny, which includes his reaction to NSW and was published in 1797 as *A Narrative of the Sufferings of T.F. Palmer, and W. Skirving, . . . on Board the Surprise Transport*, and Muir wrote an account of his exile which was lost during his last years in Paris. In 1796, however, *The Telegraph: A Consolatory Epistle from Thomas Muir, Esq., of Botany Bay, to the Hon. Henry Erskine*, which was written, not by Muir but probably by a Scottish minister, George Hamilton, was published anonymously in Edinburgh. This poem, a satire relating mainly to Scottish university politics, has been claimed as the first separately published imaginative work set in the colony of NSW. Frank Clune wrote *The Scottish Martyrs* (1969).

'Scotty the Wrinkler', see MOUBRAY, Philip

Scripsi, primarily a literary magazine supported by the Literature Board and by the Victorian Ministry of the Arts, began in 1981, taking its name from Pontius Pilate's assertion 'Quod scripsi, scripsi' ('What I have written, I have written'). *Scripsi* offers a wide variety of contemporary Australian and international fiction, poetry and literary criticism as well as art criticism. Some of its issues have included whole books of poetry, e.g. Laurie Duggan's *The Epigrams of Martial* in 1990, and some have been special issues, e.g. on James Joyce. Among its editors have been Peter Craven, Michael Heyward and Andrew Rutherford. Now published by OUP, *Scripsi* appears three times a year and is one of Australia's major contemporary journals.

Script, Screen & Art, a monthly journal published in Sydney and concerned with film, television, art and the performing arts in Australia, began publication in 1968 and frequently includes interviews with or information on writers for the visual media.

'SCRIVENER, Mark' was a pseudonym of Marcus Clarke derived from 'Marcus Scrivener', the nickname given to Clarke by his schoolmate Gerard Manley Hopkins.

SCUTT, Jocelynne A. (1947–), born Subiaco, WA, is a feminist lawyer, who holds degrees in law from universities in Australia, England and the USA and who has held several prominent posts including commissioner and deputy chairperson of the Law Reform Commission, Victoria, 1984–86. She has written and edited numerous books on the legal status of women and criminology. They include the collections of essays *For Richer, For Poorer: Money, Marriage and Property Rights* (1984, with Di Graham), *Growing Up Feminist: The New Generation of Australian Women* (1985), *Different Lives* (1987), *Lionel Murphy: A Radical Judge* (1987), *The Baby Machine* (1988), *Breaking Through: Women, Work and Careers* (1992), *As à Woman: Writing Women's Lives* (1992) and *Glorious Age: Growing Older Gloriously* (1993). As 'Melissa Chan' she has written crime fiction, e.g. *Too Rich* (1991), *Getting Your Man* (1992) and *One Too Many* (1993).

Sea Spray and Smoke Drift (1867) is the first collection of poems by Adam Lindsay Gordon (q.v.). The main poem of the collection is 'Ye Wearie Wayfarer'. There are several ballads, e.g. 'The Roll of the Kettledrum', and some melancholy personal poems in which Gordon regrets his youthful follies and wasted opportunities. 'Hippodromania', a poem in five parts, is an indication of the importance of horses and horse-racing both to Gordon and to Australia.

SEARLE, James (1938–   ), born Sydney, where he has practised as an architect, is the author of *The Lucky Streak* (1972), one of the plays performed at the first Jane Street Theatre season in 1966. Searle first wrote revue sketches for the Illawarra Theatre Guild and a pantomime, 'Aladdin', performed in the 1960s. His subsequent writing for theatre has included 'The First Theatre of Pollution Play' (1972), 'A Married Man' (1974) and 'The National Hero and the Daily Press'. *The Lucky Streak*, a working-class comedy set in a boarding house and dealing loosely with the subject of gambling, achieves subtle Pinteresque effects with well-worn situations and ostensibly stock characters.

Season at Sarsaparilla, The, a play by Patrick White (q.v.) first produced in 1962, was published in *Four Plays* (1965). The set is formed of the kitchens of three houses in Sarsaparilla (q.v.) belonging to the Knotts, a young couple expecting their first baby; the more affluent Pogsons, who have two daughters, Judy and Joyleen ('Pippy'); and the lower-class Boyles. The hot weather, the imminent birth and a variety of mating rituals, echoed by the constant barking of dogs pursuing a bitch on heat, emphasise that this is the 'season' at Sarsaparilla. In the course of the play Mavis Knott has her baby; Judy Pogson rejects the romanticism of Roy Child, Mavis's brother, and accepts the 'loving-kindness' of Ron Suddards; Nola Boyle has an affair with her husband's mate; Pippy Pogson learns about life's cycle of birth, copulation and death; Roy Child abandons his teaching job for a life of adventure; and Julia Sheen kills herself after discovering she is pregnant to Mr Erbage, a local councillor. Only Girlie Pogson, for whom 'it's a man and a washing-machine that counts', remains untouched by the natural forces.

Second Fleet, The, see **First Fleet, The**; **Transportation**

'Secret Society of the Ring' is one of several stories by 'Price Warung' (q.v.) about the Ring, a convict secret society which was supposed to have flourished on Norfolk Island in the 1840s; Marcus Clarke also wrote about the Ring, making Rufus Dawes one of its leaders in *His Natural Life* (1874). 'Secret Society of the Ring', originally published in the *Bulletin* in 1892, centres on the attempt by Captain Alexander Maconochie (q.v.) to weaken the power of the Ring by showing a kindness uncharacteristic of Norfolk Island commandants towards the convicts. The attempt fails when Reynell, an incorrigible convict and Ring member who has been won over by Maconochie, is condemned to death by the secret society at one of its ceremonies. The warrant to execute Reynell is given to one of his mates, Bill Felix; although Felix provokes a sentry into shooting him, his sacrifice is in vain because Reynell, who has been placed in solitary confinement by Maconochie when he learns of the sentence passed by the Ring, commits suicide before hearing news of Felix's death.

'Selection', or **'Free Selection'**, were terms which after 1860 particularly referred to the choosing of a portion of land for farming purposes; the land so chosen eventually came to be called a 'selection' and the person working it a 'selector' or 'free selector'. Selection was an attempt at land reform: the extent of the squatters' (q.v.) monopoly over land tenure in Australia can be measured by the fact that in 1860 4000 squatters controlled under lease or licence 160 million acres of land from the Darling Downs in Queensland through NSW and western Victoria up to the northern part of SA, paying an average of less than a farthing an acre in rent for their runs. Agitation to 'unlock the lands' to allow greater opportunities for small-scale farming grew in the 1850s, and Selection Acts to achieve these ends were passed in all the Australian colonies 1858–72; the most famous were the two Acts finally shepherded through the NSW parliament by Sir John Robertson in 1861. Essentially, the Selection Acts allowed anyone to select in designated areas a block of crown land for agricultural purposes. The size of the selection permitted varied in different colonies within limits of 40 and 640 acres (16.19 and 259 hectares), as did the provisions regarding price, usually £1 per acre; method of payment; selection before or after land had been surveyed; and requirements for residence and improvements. The Selection Acts led to bitter conflict between the selectors and the squatters, who adopted various practices to strengthen their hold

on the land. Two of the most prevalent were 'dummying', the employment of people to select land and then hand it over after the title was complete, as practised by Barefooted Bob in *Such is Life* (1903); and 'peacocking', the selection of choice pieces of land, for example around water, so that adjoining land was useless. In general, the selection experiment, which owed something to agrarian Utopianism, was a failure. The attempt to establish a yeomanry succeeded best in SA, but squatting interests remained entrenched in Queensland and parts of Victoria, even though in both colonies, as elsewhere, the pastoralists lost political ground. The selectors were hampered by their own ignorance and inexperience and by the vagaries of soil, climate and geography; many of them became 'cockatoo' (q.v.) farmers, barely scratching a living from the land, despised by squatters and itinerant bush workers alike, and exploited by storekeepers and middlemen. An additional effect was the exacerbation of rural class tensions. The bushranging activities of Ned Kelly (q.v.), for example, can be linked with the oppression felt by selectors in north-eastern Victoria in the 1870s.

Selection has been a significant theme in Australian literature. Several Australian writers, notably 'Steele Rudd', Henry Lawson and Mary Fullerton, were from selector families; others, including Joseph Furphy and George Essex Evans, had unsuccessful stints working selections, and Barbara Baynton's first marriage was to a selector. The most extensive treatment of the experiences of the selectors occurs in 'Steele Rudd's' *On Our Selection* (1899) and other volumes in which he drew on his own experiences as he chronicled the fortunes of the Rudd family (q.v.). The selectors' grim struggle for survival, as depicted in the early Rudd books, is also mirrored in some of the stories and poems of Lawson, e.g. '"Water Them Geraniums"' and 'A Day on a Selection', and stories of Baynton, e.g. 'Bush Church' and 'The Chosen Vessel'. The conflict between selector and squatter is the subject of Lawson's story 'The Bush Fire', and is featured in some of Rosa Praed's station romances; in other novels, e.g. Anthony Trollope's *Harry Heathcote of Gangoil* (1874), E.S. Sorenson's *The Squatter's Ward* (1908) and Albert Dorrington's *Children of the Cloven Hoof* (1911); in T.E. Spencer's poem 'Moods of the Bush' and in several folk-songs, e.g. 'The Eumerella Shore' (q.v.). Among other Australian writers on the selection theme are Mary Fullerton, in poems like 'The Selector's Daughter' and in the autobiographical *Bark House Days* (1921); W.H. Traill, who established a reputation as an investigative journalist when he probed dummying on the Darling Downs in 1874 and later wrote digests of Selection Acts for the Queensland government; the balladists Will Ogilvie in 'Abandoned Selections' and A.B. Paterson in the poem 'The Free Selector's Daughter'; M. Broda Reynolds in two novels, *The Selector Girl* (1917) and *Dawn Asper* (1918); Sumner Locke (q.v.), in her sketches of Mum Dawson, and Henry Fletcher in his *Wayback* (q.v.) family series, which both show the influence of 'Rudd'; and Frank Dalby Davison in *Forever Morning* (1931). A fine painting by Arthur Streeton, *The Selector's Hut (Whelan on the Log*) (1890), captures the atmosphere of the selection.

SEMMLER, Clement (1914–), born Eastern Well, SA, attended Murray Bridge High School and graduated MA in English language and literature from the University of Adelaide. He taught in SA high schools (e.g. Unley High) until in 1942 he chose a career with the ABC in preference to a lectureship at the then New England University College. He remained with the ABC for thirty-five years, becoming its deputy general manager (1965–77). Among his achievements at the ABC may be counted his popularisation of jazz music programmes on radio, his role in the establishment of ABC television and the part he played in the development of such programmes as *Four Corners*, *The Critics* and *Six O'Clock Rock*. Active in community affairs after his retirement from the ABC, he was chairman of the Sydney City Art Institute Board (1982–84), deputy president of the Library Council of NSW (1980–83) and chairman of the Alexander Mackie CAE Council (1977–81). His numerous publications include *For the Uncanny Man* (1963), *A.B. (Banjo) Paterson* (1965), *Barcroft Boake: Poet of the Stockwhip* (1965), *Kenneth Slessor* (1966), *The Banjo of the Bush* (1966), *The World of Banjo Paterson* (1967), *The Art of Brian James* (1972), *Douglas Stewart* (1974), *The ABC – Aunt Sally and Sacred Cow* (1981) and *Pictures on the Margin: Memoirs* (1991). He has edited a collection of short fiction by E.O. Schlunke, *Stories of the Riverina* (1965) and a collection of Frank Hardy's writings, *A Frank Hardy Swag* (1982). With Derek Whitelock he edited *Literary Australia* (1966) and on his own account, *Twentieth Century Australian Literary Criticism* (1967), two early, seminal collections of literary and cultural essays. He was also the editor of the 1965–66 short-story collections *Coast to Coast* (q.v.). He continued his writing on Slessor, which began with the 1966 monograph in the British Writers and Their Work series, by editing *The War Diaries of Kenneth Slessor* (1985) and *The War Despatches of Kenneth Slessor* (1987), which added most significantly to previously published biographical and critical works. His work on Paterson also continued with his 1992 editions, *A.B. 'Banjo' Paterson: Bush Ballads, Poems, Stories and Journalism* and *The Collected Verse of Banjo Paterson*. His book of memoirs, *Pictures on the Margin*, is both whimsical and attractive and reveals Semmler's undoubted skill as an essayist. It is enlightening in its exposure of the intrigue behind the hallowed portals of the ABC and BBC and in its account of such distinguished people as the Caseys, Patrick White, Slessor, J.I.M. Stewart ('Michael Innes') and others whom Semmler came to know during his career. Semmler has also been for many years a notable reviewer of Australian books.

He was awarded a D.Litt. in 1969 by the University of New England on the basis of his published works, the first such award by the University. His contribution to Australian literature was recognised in 1972 when he was made OBE and in 1989 when he was made AM.

Semper Floreat, a student magazine/newspaper of the University of Queensland, was published 1932–76 and frequently included original literary contributions and articles on Australian literature. In 1977 it was replaced by a multi-campus weekly newspaper, *Gamut*, but returned in 1980, titled *Semper*.

'Send Round the Hat', a story by Henry Lawson (q.v.) included in *Children of the Bush* (1902), is a celebration of mateship (q.v.). Set in Bourke, where Lawson worked for some months in 1892, it focuses on 'The Giraffe', Bob Brothers, a Victorian shearer whose kindness leads him regularly to send round his hat collecting for those in distress. Among the bush workers who are 'touched' by the Giraffe are Jack Mitchell, Lawson himself, Barcoo Rot, One-Eyed Bogan and Jack Moonlight, who at the end of the story send round the hat among themselves when they learn the Giraffe is leaving Bourke to get married. Other *Children of the Bush* stories in which these characters are grouped in Bourke are 'That Pretty Girl in the Army' and '"Lord Douglas"'.

Sentimental Bloke, see ***Songs of a Sentimental Bloke, The***

'September in Australia', a well-known Henry Kendall (q.v.) lyric poem, was published in *Leaves from Australian Forests* in 1869. The poem celebrates, in a riot of alliterative musical phrases, the coming of the Australian spring.

Serials in Australian Libraries: Social Sciences and Humanities (SALSSAH), published in four volumes by the National Library of Australia (1968–74), listed locations and holdings of periodicals in Australian libraries. From 1984 it was superseded by *NUCOS: National Union Catalogue of Serials*, published on microfiche in March and September of each year.

SERLE, Geoffrey (1922–), born Melbourne, son of Percival Serle, has taught history at the University of Melbourne and Monash University. He has written two influential histories of Victoria, *The Golden Age* (1963), winner of the Ernest Scott prize, and *The Rush to be Rich* (1971), which won the Townsville Foundation for Australian Literary Studies Award; a history of high culture in Australia, *From Deserts the Prophets Come* (1973), which won a National Book Council Award in 1974 and was revised in 1987 titled *The Creative Spirit in Australia*; and *John Monash: A Biography* (1982), which won the *Age* Book of the Year Award, the Con Weickhardt and Wilke Awards and first prize in the National Book Council awards. He has also written memoirs of his father, *Percival Serle* (1988) and of Sir John Medley (1993). General editor for part of the ADB, he has also edited the journals *Historical Studies* and the *La Trobe Library Journal* and co-edited, with Alan Davies, *Policies for Progress* (1954). He is an Officer of the Order of Australia (AO).

SERLE, Percival (1871–1951), born Elsternwick, Victoria, worked for twenty years in a life assurance office before becoming chief clerk and accountant at the University of Melbourne. In 1910 he married the artist Dora Beatrice Hake. Moderately successful with investments, he was able to retire in 1920 to pursue his cultural interests, although he ran a second-hand bookshop in the Eastern Market, Melbourne, in the Depression years 1931–36. He was guide-lecturer at the National Gallery of Victoria 1929–38, curator of the Art Museum of the Gallery 1934–36, and member of the council of the Victorian Artists' Society for about forty years. He was also president of the Australian Literature Society 1944–46. Serle's first publication was an edition, with notes, of *A Song to David and Other Poems* (1923) by Christopher Smart, the eighteenth-century English poet. Serle's meticulous scholarship is evident in *A Bibliography of Australasian Poetry and Verse: Australia and New Zealand* (1925), a much-needed reference work of Australian literature at that time, to which later bibliographies were indebted. To complement his *Bibliography* he published, in collaboration with 'Furnley Maurice' and R.H. Croll, *An Australasian Anthology* (1927), a standard Australian literary work not supplanted until after the Second World War. His most significant work, laboured over for almost twenty years, was his *Dictionary of Australian Biography* (1949). It comprises more than 1000 biographical sketches of prominent Australians or people connected closely with Australia. In 1944 Serle edited the poems of 'Furnley Maurice' and in 1951 published *A Primer of Collecting*. Serle brought to all his literary work a rigorous sense of, and passion for, scholarship. A commemorative number of *Southerly* was published in 1953 and his son, Geoffrey Serle, has written the memoir *Percival Serle* (1988).

Settlers and Convicts: Or, Recollections of Sixteen Years' Labour in the Australian Backwoods, a fictional-factual account of life in the colony of NSW, in the emigrant handbook genre, by Alexander Harris (q.v.), was published in 1847 under the pseudonym 'An Emigrant Mechanic'. The book is a lively and informative account of sixteen years of colonial adventuring. It is filled with stories of brushes with bushrangers, Aborigines, convicts, colonial police, cattle-stealers, greedy squatters, and the denizens of Sydney's Rocks area. The 'mechanic' begins as a carpenter in the Five Island territory (Illa Warra), then becomes a sawyer and cedar-cutter, first around the Hawkesbury River, later as far north as the Manning River. His attempts to join the squatter ranks lead him to the 'Australian prairies' of near-western and south-eastern NSW, where he discovers a good run, 'a fine tract of flats of good grass, open timbered, and stretching a good mile and a half along a creek side'. After marriage, parenthood and years of the routine but never dull life of a far-out station, the 'mechanic' returns to England.

The book seriously examines the main problems of colonial life, commenting on land regulations, the iniquities of the convict system, the moral and religious needs of the population, and the maltreatment of the Aborigines (see Aborigine in White Australian Literature). It includes advice and guidance for potential emigrants, ranging from the best method of becoming a squatter to the provisioning of an up-country station. The striking quality of the landscape is expansively described, and there are graphic accounts of the perennial hazards of colonial life: bushfires, floods, snakes, attacks by Blacks, and getting lost in the vastness of the bush.

Seven Little Australians, a children's novel by Ethel Turner (q.v.), was first published in 1894. The novel centres on the Woolcott family, who live in a large, rambling house on the Parramatta River, nicknamed Misrule. The family comprises Captain Woolcott, his second wife Esther, and seven children who range from babyhood to early adolescence, Meg, Pip, Judy, Nell, Bunty, Baby and Esther's baby, the General. Mischievous and imaginative, the children easily influence their young stepmother and are nearly always a match for their earnest, well-meaning but stern father, whether they are engaged in daring adventures or unwisely attempting to be good. After a particularly embarrassing incident involving Pip and the adventurous, high-spirited Judy, arrangements are made for Judy to go to boarding school. While Judy is away her elder sister Meg indulges her adolescent fantasies, making Herculean efforts to be beautiful and tight-lacing her waist. Influenced by her more sophisticated friend Aldith MacCarfy, she half-encourages the attentions of a neighbouring young man, Andrew Courtney, although she prefers his brother, Alan. She is led unwittingly into a compromising situation, which is complicated by her use of the unreliable 6-year-old Bunty as messenger. Alan substitutes himself for Andrew but realises her innocence and later becomes firmly attached to her. When Bunty lames one of his father's horses with a cricket ball, he hides in a disused shed, where to his amazement he meets Judy, who has escaped from school, walking the 70 miles home. The children conceal her presence, stealing food and furniture from the house, until Bunty, under the stress of a particularly severe whipping from his father, blurts out their secret. Captain Woolcott's anger is disarmed by his discovery that Judy's lungs have been affected, and she is taken home to be carefully nursed. To help her recovery, it is arranged that Esther and the children will visit Esther's parents at their station, Yarrahappini. There they enjoy the excitements of bush life and make the acquaintance of Mr Gillet, an exiled Englishman prone to episodes of alcoholism. Meg's mixed relationship with Mr Gillet contributes to her maturing. When Esther attends a ball the children are taken by bullock-cart to a picnic ground 14 miles away and there Judy saves the baby, the General, from a falling tree but suffers a broken back. While Pip goes to get a doctor 10 miles away and Mr Gillet returns home for help, Meg comforts the suffering, dying Judy. Her death deeply affects her family, although life eventually resumes an outward normality. Frequently reprinted, *Seven Little Austral-*

ians was produced as an ABC television serial in 1975.

Seven Poor Men of Sydney, a novel by Christina Stead (q.v.), was published in 1934. Set in Sydney in the 1920s, it deals with the experiences of a group of people which includes the printers Joseph Baguenault, Tom Withers, Baruch Mendelssohn; their employer Gregory Chamberlain; Michael Baguenault, an emotionally disturbed returned soldier; Tom Winter, a librarian; and Kol Blount, a paralysed youth. The other important characters are Catherine Baguenault, Michael's half-sister, and Fulke and Marion Folliot, bourgeois intellectuals and social reformers. Linked tenuously by work, friendship, interests, love or family, they are mostly alike in their oppression by poverty and their final defeat. Unconventional in structure, with little in the way of plot and few dramatic incidents, the novel is shaped by its concentration on the diverse emotional lives of its protagonists. Although the inner landscape is more important than the outer, both are expressed with poetic intensity and cumulative, impressionistic effect. The most striking individuals are the idealistic, introspective rebels and half-lovers Michael and Catherine, whose emotional struggles end in suicide for Michael and incarceration in a mental home for Catherine. The intellectual Baruch Mendelssohn is the wisest and most balanced of the group, although he is merely one of the refracted responses to experience explored by the author and by no means her representative. At the opposite extreme to Michael and Catherine stands Joseph, their dull, unimaginative but dependable cousin, who finds a limited salvation in domesticity. Others, like Winter and the Folliots, find refuge in simplistic ideologies, or like Withers in business schemes and feuds. Kol Blount, the cripple, expresses both in his person and his moving 'In Memoriam' the frustrations and limitations of their inimical world.

SEWELL, Stephen (1953–), born Liverpool, NSW, grew up in Granville. He studied science at Sydney University 1970–74 and during these years became involved in fringe theatre at the Stanley Palmer Culture Palace, a youth centre at King's Cross. In 1975 two one-act plays by Sewell were staged at the Palace, 'Kangaroo' and 'A New Boarder'. In the same year Sewell moved to Brisbane where he wrote scripts for ABC children's radio and became associated with the La Boîte Theatre Comany which staged *The Father We Loved on a Beach by the Sea* in 1978. In 1980 Sewell moved back to Sydney after spending a period with the Australian Performing Group in Melbourne that year. Sewell's published plays for stage include *The Father We Loved on a Beach by the Sea*, in *Three Political Plays*, ed. Alrene Sykes (1980), *Traitors* (1983) first produced in Melbourne in 1979 and in London in 1980, *Welcome the Bright World* (1983), winner of an Awgie for the best new play of 1982, *The Blind Giant Is Dancing* (1983), which won the NSW Premier's Literary Award, *Dreams in an Empty City* (1986), *Hate* (1988), *Sisters* (1991), and *The Garden of Granddaughters* (1993). His unpublished plays are 'Miranda' (1989) and 'King

Golgrutha' (1991). He has also written film scripts and plays for television. Peter Fitzpatrick's *Stephen Sewell* (1991) is a critical study of his work.

Sewell was committed first to Catholicism and then to Marxism, attitudes which have provided a religious dimension to his work. Preoccupied with guilt and redemption and the problem of evil, he frequently draws on Christian myth, even though his approach to familiar metaphors may be more problematic than conclusive. *The Father We Loved on a Beach by the Sea* contrasts a father who helplessly submits to a coercive system and his two sons who fiercely rebel against it; both alternatives prove to have destructive effects. *Traitors*, set in Leningrad in 1927, concerns the experiences of a group of ordinary people, although its theme is the collapse of the communist ideal in the face of Stalinism. *Welcome the Bright World* concerns conflict within the family group, community and state. *The Blind Giant Is Dancing* traces the moral decay of an erstwhile man of principle through the corrupting influence of power politics. The action of *Welcome the Bright World*, which consists of sixty scenes and requires a large cast, ranges from 1974 to 1981; the mathematician Max Lewin is part of a network of personal and political relationships, with his lonely wife, terrorist daughter, radical physicist colleague and sinister political employers. Deluding himself that his relationship to his work is purely that of a disinterested scientist, he nevertheless provides the state with the means of destroying his daughter and his friend. *Dreams in an Empty City*, set in Sydney, is a study of corporate conspiracy with an explicit Christian frame of reference; conceived on a grand scale with fifty-five scenes and forty-five speaking roles, the play is nevertheless tightly unified by its premise that the 'bit-players' also change and shape the world and that no one is a passive actor in a pre-ordained script. *Hate*, 'Miranda' and *Sisters* are plays on a smaller scale. *Sisters*, a play for two actors, explores a complicated family relationship and charts the characters' reassessment of the transition from childhood to adulthood and their coming to terms with death, regret and guilt. *Hate* has a similar intense concentration of focus but deals with the large moral themes of the earlier plays. As in *Dreams in an Empty City* the Christian theme is prominent, although here Sewell also draws on the resources of the Gothic thriller in the central confrontation of innocence and evil. 'Miranda', Sewell's most stripped-down play and an intensive exploration of raw emotions and the anatomy of despair, comes closest to Sewell's own description of his theatre as a 'a roller-coaster ride on razor-blades'.

A revolutionary playwright in that he deals with large political and moral isues and is attempting to 'define a new aesthetic in the performing arts' which will 'antedate the cultural forms with which we are familiar', Sewell is sometimes classed with Nowra and White as belonging to an internationalist stream in Australian theatre. He has defined the broad theme of his work as an attempt 'to appropriate the world dramatically', to show the interpendence of personal and political, individual and national, national and international. Rejecting the term 'political' playwright, he is interested in combining a broad representation of powerful historical forces with a focus on the apparently powerless individual, exposing their intricate interactions. Although the characters of *Traitors, Welcome the Bright World* and *The Blind Giant is Dancing* are not historical figures and have a sense of insignificance and powerlessness, they are revealed as makers of history as well as victims. Sewell's elaborately developed epic style of theatre, Brechtian in terms of dialectical structure and alienating techniques, and his mixing of naturalistic and expressionistic modes, have challenged both actors and audiences.

SEYMOUR, Alan (1927–   ) was born in Perth, and was brought up by his eldest sister after the death of his parents. Educated at state schools in Perth, he spent some time as a freelance film and theatre critic in Sydney, worked for the ABC in the late 1940s and 1950s and directed operas for the Sydney Opera Group 1953–57. Since 1961 he has lived overseas, mostly in London, where he was theatre critic for *London Magazine* 1962–65. More recently he has lived in Turkey, which has led to a play dealing with modern Turkish politics and an adaptation for the stage of *The Wind from the Plain* by the Turkish novelist Yashar Kemal. A cosmopolitan and experimental playwright in the main, he has written 'Swamp Creatures' (1957), *The One Day of the Year* (q.v., 1960, published 1962), 'The Gaiety of Nations' (1965), 'A Break in the Music' (1966), 'The Pope and the Pill' (1968), 'The Shattering' (1973) and 'The Float' (1980). He has also written a novel, *The Coming Self-Destruction of the United States of America* (1969), and a novel-adaptation of his play *The One Day of the Year* (1967); two radio plays, 'A Winter Passion' (1960) and 'Donny Johnson' (1965); and from the 1960s to the 1980s numerous television plays of which 'The Runner' (1960) is the most significant.

'Swamp Creatures' has a macabre, compelling atmosphere, reminiscent of Tennessee Williams; ostensibly about two middle-aged sisters, one of whom is engaged in unnatural monster-producing experiments, the play expresses common fears of a future nuclear disaster. The play for which Seymour is best known in Australia, *The One Day of the Year*, is the least typical of his work because of its simple naturalism; rejected by the Adelaide Festival's board of governors in 1959 on the grounds that its treatment of Anzac Day, the servicemen's national day of commemoration, might give offence to such groups as the RSL, it was first staged by an amateur organisation, the Adelaide Theatre Group, in 1960. In 1961 it was given a professional production in Sydney, supported by the Australian Elizabethan Theatre Trust. Performed in London the same year and subsequently widely staged in Australia, the play has become almost as well known as Ray Lawler's *Summer of the Seventeenth Doll* (1957) and is popular as a school and university text. The subject of the play is not so much Anzac Day as the familiar antagonisms between generations, exacerbated in this instance by rapid social change and disparity in education. Seymour explores the opposing points of view of digger-father and university-educated son with sensitivity and insight, developing especially the pathos of the father's situation and breaking new ground in his energetic exploitation of the Australian vernacular and the inadequacies of the ocker/digger stereotype.

Of Seymour's other plays, 'Swamp Creatures', 'Donny Johnson' and 'A Break in the Music' are ostensibly set in Australia, although the first two could be set anywhere. 'Donny Johnson', winner of the 1960 Sydney Journalists' Club competition, is a modern Australian rock version of the Don Juan legend; 'A Break in the Music' draws on Seymour's family memories of Australian life in the 1930s and 1940s. Much of his work has a political dimension: 'The Gaiety of Nations' has the Vietnam War as its subject, and *The Coming Self-Destruction of the United States of America* deals with American race relations. His other stage and television plays range over a wide number of countries and situations.

Shabbytown Calendar (1975), by Thomas Shapcott (q.v.), with cover design and illustrations based on the paintings of Charles Blackman, is a series of twelve sequences of poems, one for each month of the year. 'Shabbytown' is Ipswich, the Queensland city where Shapcott spent much of his early life. The poems reflect, with gentle irony for the most part but sometimes with acerbity, the barrenness of provincial life. Symbols of that barrenness range from events such as church socials, engagement parties and service club activities, to local identities such as retired schoolmasters, salesmen and shopkeepers. Victims of it include Tommy Jennings who commits suicide and the anonymous housewife who every day buys groceries, lingerie, books and magazines – 'something that might alter the world'. Shapcott also reflects on Shabbytown's influence on his own personality and character and sees the dramatic tropical climate as a factor in the eccentricity of the inhabitants' behaviour. The series contains brief memorial poems to Francis Webb and Michael Dransfield.

Shakespeare and Australia. Although there are no references to Terra Australis in Shakespeare's plays – though there are to the Antipodes (q.v.) – the playwright has been enormously significant in the cultural history of Australia; indeed Shakespeare was one of the names considered for the new national capital after the creation of the Commonwealth of Australia. The first recorded performance of a Shakespearean play (*Henry IV*) took place in Sydney in 1800, and as a professional theatre developed in NSW and the other colonies from the 1830s, Shakespeare's plays were intermittently performed at benefits or other special performances in the theatres, like Barnett Levey's Theatre Royal in Sydney, that catered mainly for the melodramas, comedies and farces imported from London. Auctioneers' and booksellers' catalogues from the 1820s onwards attest to the popularity of editions of Shakespeare, and in the same decade Edward Smith

Hall, like many subsequent Australian newspaper proprietors, adopted Othello's 'Nothing extenuate,/ Nor set down aught in malice', as a motto for his *Sydney Monitor*.

Most early significant Shakespearean performers, such as Conrad Knowles, Australia's first Hamlet, and Eliza Winstanley, a notable early Lady Macbeth who went on to successes in England and America, were immigrant amateurs without prior theatrical training. One of Knowles's contemporaries, however, Joseph Simmons, claimed prior English experience and in the 1840s a steady stream of English provincial actors and actresses started to flow into the colonies, including Francis Nesbitt in 1842 and George Selth Coppin (q.v.) the following year. Coppin's main stage reputation was as a comic actor, but as an entrepreneur and manager he was prominent in arranging, particularly in the decades following the discovery of gold, the theatrical tours by American, English and other overseas performers which remained a distinctive feature of Australian theatrical history well into the twentieth century. The repertoires of these performers were by no means always focused on or even included Shakespeare, but among the established Shakespearean performers Coppin was instrumental in bringing out were G.V. Brooke in 1855, Charles and Ellen Kean (q.v.) in 1863, and Alfred Dampier (q.v.) in 1873. Other notable touring actors and actresses who presented Shakespearean programmes were Edwin Thomas Booth and Laura Keene in 1854, Barry Sullivan (q.v., arrived 1862), Charles John Mathews (1870) and George Rignold (1876). Arrivals in the twentieth century have included Oscar Asche (1909); the Old Vic with Laurence Olivier and Vivien Leigh in *Richard III* (1948) and with Robert Helpmann and Katharine Hepburn in *The Taming of The Shrew* (1955); the Shakespeare Memorial Theatre in 1950 and 1953, headed by Anthony Quayle; and its successor, the Royal Shakespeare Company, with Peter Brook's *A Midsummer Night's Dream* in 1973. Helpmann and Asche, who carried a pocket edition of Shakespeare in his swag while roaming southern NSW for some months in the 1880s, were Australian-born performers who had won a reputation overseas. Similarly, Keith Michell and Leo McKern, who both toured with Quayle, established Shakespearean reputations in England, while other actors such as Ron Haddrick and John Bell had seasons at Stratford before returning to Australia. In recent years actor Mel Gibson has distinguished himself in a film version of *Hamlet*.

Many of the Shakespearean performers who visited Australia left reminiscences of their travels, e.g. Daniel Edward Bandmann's *An Actor's Tour: Or, Seventy Thousand Miles with Shakespeare* (1885) and several remained to play a significant part in Australian theatrical history, including influencing acting styles. Brooke (1855–61) and Sullivan (1862–66) had long tours encompassing several seasons and some experience in management. Brooke's leading lady, Fanny Cathcart (q.v.), settled and matured as an actress in Australia, encouraged her brother, James Cathcart, to visit, and married George Darrell, who thought his melodrama, *The Sunny South*, inferior only to *Hamlet*.

Alfred Dampier retained, like James Cathcart, a reputation as a Shakespearean actor even though some of his energies were directed towards adapting, producing and performing Australian material. Perhaps most significant of all was George Rignold (George Richard Rignall, 1839–1912), whose presentation of *Henry V* in 1876 (twenty-four performances) was the first long run of a Shakespearean play in Australia. After later tours of Australasia and America he was based from 1887 in Sydney, where he was a partner in Her Majesty's Theatre in 1887–95, alternated Shakespeare with melodrama and flew Henry V's standard whenever in residence at his Middle Harbour home.

Touring performers, however, have not been restricted to capital cities, nor have Shakespearean companies only come from overseas. Numerous reminiscences of Australians attest to Shakespearean performances in small country towns: William Walker, for example, records in his *Reminiscences* (1890) a performance of *Othello* at Windsor around 1850 when an actor named Kemble (possibly the same Henry Kemble who had vegetables and other food thrown at him by enraged audiences in Hobart in 1859) painted one side of his face black and alternated his profile to play both Othello and Iago. Towards the end of the century Dan Barry (q.v.) was a legendary outback manager who 'murdered' Shakespeare most touring Saturday nights, and W.J. Holloway ran an Australian Shakespeare company, which starred the colonial-born actress Essie Jenyns (1865–1920). Later still, Alan Wilkie (1878–1970), who had previously toured widely in Great Britain, Asia and South Africa, came to Australia in 1916 and in 1920 formed a Shakespearean company. In the following eight years Wilkie staged about 14 000 performances of Shakespeare's plays, a tribute both to appreciative Australian audiences and the energetic actor-manager and his leading lady wife, Frediswyde Hunter-Watts. Wilkie was made CBE in 1926. In 1951 John Alden (1908–62), born Taree, NSW, began a decade's regular touring with a Shakespearean company. In 1958 the Young Elizabethan Players, attached to the Australian Elizabethan Theatre Trust in Sydney, and later to the Melbourne Theatre Company, began bringing Shakespeare to thousands of city and country children. These schools' companies had a home base in organisations which have also included Shakespeare in their repertoires. Similarly, in contemporary times, Shakespearean plays form part of the repertoires of regional professional companies and a variety of amateur dramatic organisations. Some of the professional companies, e.g. Nimrod in Sydney, have developed a strong tradition in Shakespeare.

From early colonial days, performances of Shakespeare attracted the newspaper reviews and journal articles that are an important primary source for Australian theatre historians. A notable example of a controversial performance was Walter Montgomery's interpretation of Hamlet in 1867, which led to a spirited correspondence in the Melbourne press. *The Hamlet Controversy: Was Hamlet Mad?* (1867) reprinted the comments of David Blair, Charles Bright, R.H.

Horne, Sir Archibald Michie, J.E. Neild and James Smith. All contributed to the intellectual life of Melbourne in the second half of the nineteenth century, but Neild and Smith in particular had long careers as dramatic critics and wrote some of the best Australian theatre reviews. With Blair and others they also helped in 1884 to found the Melbourne Shakespeare Society, which claimed at one time to be the largest in the world, fostered the reading and study of Shakespeare, and sponsored prizes such as an annual essay prize which Mary Grant Bruce won three times. In Sydney the Shakespeare Society of NSW was in existence 1900–?36, and published a *Shakespeare Quarterly* in 1922–24. A second Shakespearean journal was the *University Shakespeare Journal*, which was associated with the University of Adelaide's Shakespeare Society and published briefly in 1886–87; the same society also published its annual *Proceedings* for at least a decade either side of 1900. A Shakespeare Society was formed in Brisbane in 1919 and in Tasmania in the 1930s, while even a country town such as Wagga Wagga could boast in 1895 of a Shakespeare Society and in 1922 of a Shakespeare Club. If the reviews of Shakespearean productions form part of the extensive history of Shakespearean performance in Australia, they also form part of an extensive body of Australian writing about the playwright and his work. The list of books includes editions of the plays, biographical, textual and critical studies, and bibliographies; it extends from William à Beckett's *Lectures on the Poets and Poetry of Great Britain* (1839), which had a Shakespearean component, to contemporary works published both in Australia and overseas. Among editions of the plays, the most significant are perhaps Rignold's acting arrangements of several of the plays published between 1876 and 1879; the Australasian Shakespeare, a series of seven plays published 1916–20, each edited by a different academic or educationist, including J. le Gay Brereton, A.T. Strong, T.G. Tucker and Walter Murdoch; other school series such as OUP's Australian Students' Shakespeare (general editor J.J. Stable) and the Australasian Students' Shakespeare (1936–37, edited by Murdoch and Albert Booth Taylor); the Challis Shakespeare, a series under the general editorship of G.A. Wilkes and A.P. Riemer, which began publication in 1980; and the contributions by Australians to notable series of the plays published elsewhere, such as the editions for the Arden Shakespeare (*Timon of Athens*, 1959, *The Merry Wives of Windsor*, 1971) and the New Penguin Shakespeare (*As You Like It*, 1968) by H.J. Oliver (1916–82). Among textual studies, the most important is *Stolne and Surreptitious Copies* (1942) by Alfred Hart (1870–1950), an American-born scientist and educationist who arrived in Melbourne in 1879 and was active in the Melbourne Shakespeare Society. *Stolne and Surreptitious Copies*, written in isolation from libraries and scholars overseas, although it won recognition there, is a study of the provenance of the 'bad' quartos, the pirated editions of single Shakespeare plays published before the famous First Folio of 1623. Two hundred and thirty-odd copies of the First Folio survive, one of them in the State Library of NSW's Shakespeare Tercentenary Memorial Library of

Shakespeare material. The library was opened in 1923 to commemorate the tercentenary of Shakespeare's death; the quatercentenary of his birth in 1964 occasioned displays and exhibitions in libraries throughout Australia. An early bibliography, Percy Joseph Marks's *Australasian Shakespeareana* (1915), lists Australian and NZ books, journals, articles, pamphlets on and references to Shakespeare up to 1913.

There have been many biographical, critical and other studies, apart from the contributions to Australian and overseas academic journals and the addresses and lectures to Shakespeare and other literary societies. In the nineteenth and early twentieth centuries most of the Australian books on Shakespeare were by amateur scholars: doctors, clergymen, public servants, journalists, educationists, businessmen. Several focused on the authorship question, including Hugh Junor Browne, who, in *The Grand Reality* (1888), presented Shakespeare's experiences in spirit life as received by a Melbourne medium and in *The Baconian Authorship of Shakespeare's Plays Refuted* (1898) gave an account of an interview with Shakespeare in which the playwright told how he had written the plays while under spirit control. The comic balladist, W.T. Goodge, in *Hits! Skits! and Jingles!* (1899), reached the same conclusion more succinctly ('Who Wrote the Shakespere Plays'):

> Shakespere's the author, I'll vow,
> And nothing my faith can be shakin',
> For it would be ridiculous, now
> If we talked about 'Lamb's Tales of Bacon'.

Other studies published in this period included the politician Sir Josiah Henry Symon's *Shakespeare Quotation* (1901) and *Shakespeare at Home* (1905), both included in his *Shakespeare the Englishman* (1929); the drama critic Austin Brereton's *Romeo and Juliet on the Stage* (1662–1890) (1890); the historian and public servant G.W. Rusden's *William Shakespeare: His Life, His Works and His Teaching* (1903); the politician Henry Gullett's *The Making of Shakespeare and Other Papers* (1905); *Shakespeare's Plays* (?1908–9) by the journalist E.H.C. Oliphant (1862–1936), who later taught Elizabethan literature in the USA; and *The True Text of Shakespeare and His Fellow Playwrights* (1923) by the businessman and philanthropist Thomas Donovan (1843–1929), who also edited Shakespeare and presented his extensive Elizabethan library to the University of Sydney. Increasingly, however, and notwithstanding Hart's *Stolne and Surreptitious Copies*, his earlier *Shakespeare and the Homilies* (1934) and the contributions to Shakespearean studies of Eric Partridge, the major studies have come from Australian universities, many of them by academics who settled in Australia or studied overseas. A notable early example was *Shakespeare's Roman Plays and Their Background* (1910) by Sir Mungo MacCallum (q.v.) who developed the University of Sydney's tradition in Shakespearean and Elizabethan studies. Subsequent works include E.H. Sugden's *A Topographical Dictionary to the Works of Shakespeare and His Fellow Dramatists* (1925); Cowling's *A Preface to Shakespeare* (1925); A.J.A. Waldock's *Hamlet: A Study in Critical Method*

(1931); J. le Gay Brereton's *Writings on Elizabethan Drama* (1948); D.R.C. Marsh's *The Recurring Miracle* (1962), *Shakespeare's 'Hamlet'* (1970) and *Passion Lends Them Power* (1976); A.P. Riemer's *A Reading of Shakespeare's 'Antony and Cleopatra'* (1968) and *Antic Fables: Patterns of Evasion in Shakespeare's Comedies* (1980); Dennis Bartholomeusz's *Macbeth and the Players* (1969); Philip Martin's *Shakespeare's Sonnets* (1972); E.A.M. Colman's *The Dramatic Use of Bawdy in Shakespeare* (1974); S.L. Goldberg's *An Essay on King Lear* (1974); Alan Brissenden's *Shakespeare and the Dance* (1981) and his edited collection of essays, *Shakespeare and Some Others* (1976); and Jane Adamson's *Othello as Tragedy* (1980).

The number of editions of the plays and studies of Shakespeare and his work lends credence to E. Morris Miller's 1940 claim that Shakespeare had dominated the Australian study of literature. The significance of the playwright extends, however, beyond the performance of his plays and the various publications about him. The statues to Shakespeare, the reports of fancy-dress balls held on his birthday in which the guests dressed in appropriate costume, the performance of operas derived from Shakespearean themes, the names of public houses (e.g. the Shakespeare Tavern in the basement of the first theatre in Hobart), theatres (e.g. the Twelfth Night Theatre in Brisbane) and racehorses (e.g. Malvolio won the 1891 Melbourne Cup), all attest to Shakespeare's contribution to an enduring English influence on the cultural history of Australia. Finally, the response of and influence on Australian writers should be noted. An early example is Charles Nagel's burlesque *Shakespericonglommorofunnidogammoniae* (1843) in which Macbeth suggests to Othello that he should prevent Ophelia's desertion to Richard III because of her valuable property in NSW; Shakespeare also appears in several nineteenth-century pantomimes. Charles Harpur's play *The Bushrangers* employs Shakespearean verse and has Falstaffian characters; Harpur also wrote a poem on Shakespeare, as did James Hebblethwaite, J.B. O'Hara, David Campbell and numerous other writers. Around the turn of the century Joseph Furphy in *Such is Life* (1903) and other works consistently alludes to Shakespeare, often for comic effect; Henry Lawson in 'Mateship in Shakespeare's Rome' gives his version of *Julius Caesar* and also refers to *Timon of Athens;* and C.J. Dennis in *The Songs of a Sentimental Bloke* (1915) includes an account of a visit by the Bloke and Doreen to a performance of *Romeo and Juliet*, which is as famous in Australian literature and as funny as the Duke's rendition of Shakespeare in *Huckleberry Finn* in American literature.

Among more recent writers, Kenneth Mackenzie wrote a radio play, 'The Young Shakespeare'; 'M. Barnard Eldershaw's' novel *Tomorrow and Tomorrow and Tomorrow* (1983) takes its title from *Macbeth;* Eunice Hanger's play *Upstage* (1952) gathers together several Shakespearean heroines to compete for the title of Miss Shakespeare; the Nimrod pantomime 'Hamlet on Ice' (1971) featured Grahame Bond, the author and star, as the ageing schoolboy Terry Shakespeare, of the hilarious *Boy's Own McBeth* (1980), set in Dunsinane

Boys' School; and David Williamson wrote a much-criticised Australian-idiom adaptation of *King Lear*, which was performed in 1978.

SHAPCOTT, Thomas (1935–   ), born and educated at Ipswich, Queensland, left school at 15 and worked as a clerk in his father's accountancy business. He completed an accountancy degree in 1961 and was a public accountant until 1978. He graduated in arts from the University of Queensland in 1967. In 1973–76 he was a member of the Literature Board and its director 1983–90, and is currently (1993) executive director of the National Book Council. As critic, editor and anthologist, Shapcott was an influential supporter of the 'New Australian Poetry' (q.v.) that sprang up in the late 1960s. In addition to being one of the most interesting of present-day poets he continues to be a major reviewer of and authority on contemporary Australian poetry.

Shapcott's publications include the poetry collections *Time on Fire* (1961), which was awarded the Grace Leven Prize; *Sonnets 1960–1963* (1964); *The Mankind Thing* (1964); *A Taste of Salt Water* (1967), which won both the Sir Thomas White Memorial Prize and the Myer Award for poetry; *Inwards to the Sun* (1969), which also won the Myer Award for poetry; *Fingers at Air* (1969); a group of poems for opera, *The Seven Deadly Sins* (1970); *Begin with Walking* (1972); *Shabbytown Calendar* (q.v., 1975); *Selected Poems* (1978, rev. edn 1989); *Turning Full Circle* (1979), *Welcome* (1983), *Travel Dice* (1987) and *In the Beginning* (1990). He has also published novels, *Flood Children* (1981), *The Birthday Gift* (1982), a book of 'prose inventions', *Stump & Grape & Bopple-Nut* (1981), *White Stag of Exile* (1984), *Hotel Bellevue* (1986), *The Search for Galina* (1989) and *Mona's Gift* (1993); a collection of essays, articles, speeches, reviews and autobiographical reflections titled *Biting the Bullet: A Literary Memoir* (1990); two collections of short stories, *Limestone and Lemon Wine* (1988) and *What You Own* (1991); several books for young readers; and a history of the Literature Board (1988). He has also written two studies of the artist Charles Blackman, *Focus on Charles Blackman* (1967) and *The Art of Charles Blackman* (1990). He edited the anthologies *New Impulses in Australian Poetry* (q.v., 1968, with Rodney Hall), *Australian Poetry Now* (1970), *Contemporary American and Australian Poetry* (1976) and *Consolidation: The Second Paperback Poets Anthology* (1982). Other distinctions Shapcott has won include the Canada-Australia Literary Award (1978) and the Struga Golden Wreath International Poetry Award (1989). In 1989 he was awarded an honorary D.Litt. by Macquarie University and made AO the same year.

Shapcott's verse reflects his interest in experimental poetic techniques, although his early poetry, as seen in *Time on Fire* and *The Mankind Thing*, is conventional in both form and theme. It is also largely autobiographical, reflecting the country boy's distaste for the garish city environment; the wakening of young love; courtship, marriage, parenthood; and a preoccupation with transience. The fourteen-part 'Two and a Half Acres', the story of the poet, his wife and child settling on their small property, is typical of this intimate, lyrical early verse. With *A Taste of Salt Water* and *Inwards to the Sun*, self-understanding ('Self's the unique toy that I grapple with') and the ultimate understanding of human nature, especially in the light of transience, become his abiding concerns and are illuminated by a wide use of mythology, history, religious and social commentary. In these volumes Shapcott's interest in innovatory techniques is illustrated, e.g. in the blank opening page of *Inwards to the Sun* ('This Blank Page . . . is where I begin to exist'), and in the experimental settings of 'Night Songs' and 'Ceremony for Cedar'. That interest is given free rein in his book of experimental verse, *Fingers at Air*. Substantial Shapcott poems of this period are 'The City of Acknowledgement', a fourteen-part ironic treatment of the life of Christ; the sonnet sequences 'Suite of Sonnets' and 'Minotaur'; and the historically based 'Portrait of Captain Logan'. Shapcott's best-known and most widely acclaimed work is *Shabbytown Calendar*; 'Shabbytown' is the poet's home town of Ipswich, its 'calendar' ranging over a year from the 'mango weather' of January to the thunderstorms and Christmas bells of the following December. The course of life in the provincial town is conveyed with precision and irony. Shapcott's volume of *Selected Poems* is structured in four chronological sections from 1956 to 1976; his volume *Turning Full Circle* comprises eight sections of prose poems; *Welcome* contains a selection of his most important work since the *Selected Poems* and indicates a new poetic direction consolidated in his subsequent collections and the revised *Selected Poems*.

Shapcott's fictional writing is also striking and original, although it has attracted a less appreciative audience. *Hotel Bellevue* links the fate of an old Brisbane hotel, demolished by the Queensland government, with a general theme of violation and fragmentation. Both the protagonist of the novel, Boyd Kennedy, an academic who is representative of a general middle-class, middle-age anomie, and the place, tropically seedy and fecund Brisbane, are recurrent motifs in Australian fiction, although Shapcott melds them in original ways. *White Stag of Exile* is a complex biographical portrait of Karoly Pulszky, founding director of the Hungarian National Gallery, compelled to flee to Australia after he was accused of incompetence and embezzlement. Shapcott draws on contemporary documents, family reminiscences and secondary sources but refrains from direct authorial interpretation of the mosaic of data, preferring to imply the problematic nature of all biography. Pulszky, nevertheless, emerges as a man who is less understanding of himself and his cultural dilemma than his biographer in this ambitious, stimulating study. The protagonist of *The Search for Galina*, David Cumberland, shares some of the frustrations of his predecessor, Boyd Kennedy, but the novel is more than a part-ironic, part-sympathetic story of mid-life frustration. Like *White Stag of Exile* it opposes European complexity to Australian ordinariness and naivety, investing the opposition with mythic resonances. An epistolary novel, *Mona's Gift* is set in Sydney of the 1940s and employs some of the same biographical strategies as *White Stag*

of Exile, although in the former Shapcott has highlighted the speculative nature of biography. The reconstruction of a passionate woman's life and her wartime love affair, *Mona's Gift* is also an effective period novel. The stories of *Limestone and Lemon Wine*, set mainly in fictional Limestone, which has affinities with Ipswich, are assured explorations of place, alienation and transience; sensitive to the complex fate of provincialism, they revolve around money, power, betrayal and disillusionment. In *What You Own* Shapcott ranges widely in time and space in stories which explore the implications of possession, whether of memory, cultural baggage, inheritance or goods and objects.

SHARKEY, Michael (1946–   ), born Canterbury, NSW, has had a varied and colourful career, graduating BA from the University of Sydney and Ph.D. from the University of Auckland. An academic at Bond and New England universities, he has also been writer-in-the-community at the Blue Mountains City Library, for whom he edited *Out of the Blue: Blue Mountains Writing* (1991). A volatile and voluble poet who is keen on performance poetry (he was a member of La Mama Poetica), Sharkey writes with colloquial directness and élan. Deeply sympathetic towards the 'battler' and 'toiler', he is antagonistic and even contemptuous towards those, such as run-of-the-mill politicians, who display a lack of humanity. While fully aware of formal literary tradition, his own verse is often experimental to the point of formal anarchy. His many publications include *Woodcuts* (1978), *Loose Federation* (with Julian Croft, 1979), *Barbarians* (1981), *Robert Solay's Dreaming* (1983), *The Way It Is: Selected Poems* (1984) and *Alive in Difficult Times: Poems 1985–1991* (1991). He has also edited the *Illustrated Treasury of Australian Humour* (1988) and is writing a biography of David McKee Wright. With A.J. Bennett he edited *Selected Poems (1944–1982)* (1983) of Roland Robinson, and with A.J. Bennett and Winifred Belmont, the verse anthology *No Standing* (1980).

SHARP, William ('Fiona Macleod') (1855–1905), the English poet, essayist and biographer of Rossetti, Shelley, Heine and Browning, visited Australia in 1876 and travelled in NSW and Victoria. His *The Human Inheritance* (1882) contains poetry written in response to his Australian experience. Flavia Alaya wrote the biography *William Sharp – 'Fiona Macleod'* (1990).

'SHARPE, Lucinda', see **LANE, William**

SHAVE, Lionel (1888–1954), born Hawthorn, Melbourne, was a Melbourne advertising agent. He wrote numerous competent but lightweight plays for stage and radio, some of which were broadcast overseas. He also published the collection *Five Proven One-Act Plays* (1948), which comprises *A Sirius Cove, Red and Gold, That's Murder, The Resignation of Mr Bagsworth* and *Twelve Moons Cold*.

SHAW, Bruce, see **Aboriginal Song and Narrative in Translation; Aboriginal Writing/Testimony in English**

SHAW, Charles (1900–55), born Melbourne and orphaned early, worked at a variety of occupations in rural areas of Victoria and on country newspapers, before joining the literary staff of the *Bulletin* in 1939. Some of his short stories were published in two collections, *Outback Occupations* (1943) and *A Sheaf of Shorts* (1944); a popular collection of his ballads, *The Warrumbungle Mare*, appeared in 1943. Shaw also wrote the best-selling international novel *Heaven Knows, Mr Allison* (1952), which was subsequently produced as an American film; a mystery story, *Who Could Hate Purcey?* (1944), as well as four mystery stories under the pseudonym 'Bant Singer', *You're Wrong, Delaney* (1953), *Don't Slip, Delaney* (1954), *Have Patience, Delaney!* (1954) and *Your Move, Delaney* (1958); and two novels for children, *The Green Token* (1943) and *The Treasure of the Hills* (1944).

SHAW, Janet (1959–), born Melbourne, is a teacher of creative writing. She has written stories for children (*My Hiding Place*, 1984) and a book of short fiction, *In This House* (1990). She has won several awards for short stories including the Judah Waten Story Writing Competition in 1987 for 'All the Columns'. Her fictional world is based largely on the seemingly innocent domestic scene but there is often an undercurrent of the sinister and bizarre in her work. *My Hiding Place* won the 1983 A & R Writers for the Young Fellowship.

SHAW, Winifred (1905–), born Maitland, NSW, married R.M. Taplin and was interned in Singapore's Changi prison camp during the Second World War. She subsequently lived in England. While still in her teens she published three collections of lyrical ballads which show a striking technical control, *The Aspen Tree* (1920), *The Yellow Cloak* (1922) and *Babylon* (1924).

Shearer in Australian Literature. The wool industry in Australia began with the introduction of merino sheep into the colony of NSW in 1797 and the export of merino wool from John Macarthur's (q.v.) flock to England in 1808. With the opening of new pastoral areas, central and western NSW, the Hunter Valley, the Darling Downs in Queensland, the Australia Felix districts of Victoria, thirty million hectares of grazing land became available for sheep farming. The shearing industry that sprang from this pastoral expansion developed in three phases. Before 1850, when flocks were relatively few in number, shearing was done either by the owner, his family and a few permanent employees, or by a small group of itinerant shearers. The simple open-air shearing process of that early period, adapted to whatever facilities of water and grass were available, is described in books of reminiscences such as *A Homestead History* (1942, ed. G.F. James), the memoirs of early squatter Alfred Joyce in the Port Phillip District, and *Recollections of Squatting in Victoria (1841–1859)* (1883) by E.M. Curr. Peter Freeman, in *The Woolshed: A Riverina Anthology* (1980), describes an etching from an 1852 London journal, the *Leisure Hour*, which depicts an Arcadian scene with father and son kneeling on the grass taking off the fleece with knives. The few professional shearers, either 'Derwenters' from Van Diemen's Land or 'Sydneys' from NSW, were paid ten shillings per hundred sheep (thirty shillings per hundred in the labour shortages of the gold rushes, $125 per hundred in 1994). With the spread of fencing wire over the outback in the late 1850s and 1860s, flock numbers increased rapidly, the wool clip improved dramatically and the second phase, with large numbers of professional shearers using blade shears, began. From that period sprang many of the characteristics of the shearing legend: the ragtag, itinerant army of workers, the idiosyncratic vocabulary, the colourful personalities, the strictly observed customs and codes of conduct and behaviour, and the host of ballads and songs. Significant among contemporary accounts of the blade-shearing days is 'Rolf Boldrewood's' *Shearing in Riverina, New South Wales* (1983, first published 1871). 'Duke' Tritton in *Time Means Tucker* (1964) tells of the last blade shearing at Conimbia Station on the Castlereagh, describes the blade-shearing process and pays tribute to the blade shearers for the dramatic improvement in shearing conditions in that period. With the introduction of machines, the third phase of shearing began. The first patent for a shearing machine was granted in 1868; the first complete shearing of a flock by machines occurred at Dunlop Station, Louth, on the Darling in 1888. To accommodate machine shearing and the changed shearing process, the modern shearing shed, with its board, stands, pens and long string of workers behind the shearer, e.g. the 'pony', 'picker', 'broomie', 'skirter', 'dagboy', 'tarboy', 'woolroller', 'classer' and 'presser', came into being. The character of the shearer and of shearing life in both the blade and early machine period is preserved in the pages of the *Bulletin* in the closing years of the nineteenth century; there is, for example, a collection of shearing terms in the *Bulletin* (1898). C.E.W. Bean's documentary *On the Wool Track* (1910) and Tritton's autobiography *Time Means Tucker* are two of the major chronicles of the shearing life and lore of that time. Other works which include the shearer are Nat Gould's *On and Off the Turf in Australia* (1895), which describes the shearing at Winbar Station and a shearing strike there in 1894; and two retrospective accounts, William Hatfield's *Sheepmates* (1931), and H.M. Eastman's *Memoirs of a Sheepman* (1953), which gives the squatter's viewpoint on union shearing. Eastman's chapter 'A Shearers' Race Meeting' displays something of the lighter side of shearing life, as does *Time Means Tucker* with its post-shearing activities such as picnic race meetings, sprees and lively country dances.

In the creative literature of the late nineteenth and early twentieth century the shearer is a ubiquitous but never dominating presence. Shearers pass casually through much of Henry Lawson's writing, but his story 'A Rough Shed' presents the harsh reality of the shearing environment, while 'The Shearer's Dream' (q.v.), with the ecstatic lines

> Oh, I dreamt I shore in a shearers' shed,
>   and it was a dream of joy,
> For every one of the rouseabouts
>   was a girl dressed up as a boy,

expresses, as does another Lawson poem, 'The Shearing Shed', and Frank Moorhouse's satiric story 'The Drover's 'Wife'', the sexual deprivation of the shearer's world. Other Lawson shearing poems include the rouseabout verses 'The Ballad of the Rouseabout', 'The Greenhand Rouseabout' and 'The Boss's Boots'; the bitter 'Out Back', which pours scorn upon the myth of the carefree, idyllic life of tramping from one 'jolly' shearing shed to another; 'Shearers', which emphasises the mateship and camaraderie of those in the profession; and 'The Boss-Over-the-Boards', which describes something of the worker versus management syndrome. Other shearing poetry includes 'John Drayman's' nostalgic ballad 'I Don't Go Shearing Now', whose wistful lines

> Every year I get a longing,
>   as the shearing time draws nigh,
> To saddle up and slither, and
>   to have another try
> At the game I loved so dearly

indicate the appeal of the shearing life to the Australian male. Will Ogilvie's 'Northward to the Sheds' expresses the excitement and anticipation as the time for the annual migration to the sheds approaches, and A.B. Paterson's 'Shearing at Castlereagh' gives shearing something of the quality of a good-natured and boisterous game where the characters combine to dispatch 'another bale of golden fleece ... branded "Castlereagh"'.

The shearer has flourished most, however, in folksong and ballad. The best-known shearing song is 'Click Go the Shears' (q.v.), which probably dates from the 1890s or early 1900s. The song which best reflects the male world of the shearer and the mysterious appeal of mateship is 'The Banks of the Condamine' (q.v.). The shearer's incorrigible habit of boasting is reflected in such songs as 'The Ryebuck Shearer' and 'Flash Jack from Gundagai', while the supreme example of the shearer tall story is the ballad 'Bill Brinks'. Bill, who shears 200 sheep a day and drinks with the same gusto, is given sulphuric acid by a barman who hates him. Several days later Bill reappears at the pub, demanding more of the 'new' brew and complaining (only mildly) that every time he coughs his whiskers catch fire. Incompetent shearers are pilloried in 'I'm Tomahawking Fred, the Ladies' Man', 'tomahawking' being a term to indicate that the wool appears to have been hacked off with an axe. The shearer's close analysis of the other sex is usually expressed in sheep terminology, as in the song 'The Euabalong Ball' (q.v.). Some of the toughest shearing sheds are mentioned in the song 'Goorianawa'. The legendary shearers' spree after the shed cuts out is illustrated in 'The Keg of Rum', while the practice of 'lambing down', i.e. cheating the drunken shearer on

the spree by corrupt innkeepers, is seen in 'Lazy Harry's' (q.v.). In 'The Big-Gun Shearer', one who has been lambed-down by the faraway Sydney experts offers the advice:

> Head for the nearest wayside shack
> It's not so far when you've got to walk back.

Famous shearing personalities include blade shearer Jack Howe (q.v.), who shore 321 sheep in a day in 1892; Jimmy Gibbs, whose strength and stamina were unaffected even when he was in the grip of the 'Barcoo spews'; and Don Munday who amazed a British audience by shearing a sheep in eighty seconds. Known as 'The Champion Western Australian Sheep Shearer', Munday wrote an account of his shearing life, *Tin Dog, Damper & Dust* (1991). The terminology of the shearing industry, including such picturesque expressions as 'dreadnought' (a clumsy, blundering shearer) and 'Cunnamulla Gun' (a 'flash' shearer whose big tallies only occur in a burst of wind-baggery in the Cunnamulla pub), has been discussed in the *Bulletin* article of 1898, in *The Australian Language* (1945) by Sidney J. Baker and particularly in *The Terminology of the Shearing Industry* (1965) by J.S. Gunn.

The greatest single crisis in the shearing industry was the shearers' strike of 1891, which resulted in the imprisonment of a number of shearers on conspiracy charges, produced a dramatic outburst of radicalism and republicanism, with the Eureka flag flown at the camps of the striking shearers and Henry Lawson's 'Freedom on the Wallaby' (q.v.) expressing the rage of the unionists. Accounts and analyses of the strike are given in W.G. Spence's *Australia's Awakening* (1909), Julian Stuart's (q.v.) *Part of the Glory: Reminiscences of the Shearers' Strike Queensland 1891* (1967) and in an anonymous manuscript in the Mitchell Library, 'The Shearers' Strike, January to June 1891'. The gaoling of the shearers on the conspiracy charge was the spur to William Lane's novel *The Workingman's Paradise* (1892), where the strike is part of the background. The strike is also the subject of E.S. 'Milky White' Emerson's narrative poem 'Jock McPhail (A Tale of the 1891 Shearers' Strike)' and George Farwell's play 'Sons of the South', and is significant also in Vance Palmer's play *Hail Tomorrow* (1947) and Nigel Krauth's novel *Matilda, My Darling* (1983). The title story of 'Rolf Boldrewood's' *In Bad Company* (1901) is hostile to the strikers. In the Australian film *Sunday Too Far Away* (1975), the itinerant nature of the shearing life, its radicalism and the problems inherent in its closed male society are portrayed. The popular and frequently staged musical play *Reedy River* (1970), with its echoes of the shearers' strike, highlights such shearing songs as 'Click Go the Shears' and 'Flash Jack from Gundagai'. The shearer has been immortalised also in Tom Roberts's painting *Shearing the Rams*. Patsy Adam-Smith published a comprehensive historical and anecdotal account of the shearers and shearing, *The Shearers* (1982); Les Ryan, author of several authoritative textbooks on shearing, has also published a novel, *The Shearers* (1975), which re-creates the tough life of the shearing sheds. Written in the 1950s, it was rejected at the time by publishers because of its ribald but authentic language. Ryan's book also includes a valuable glossary of the shearers' idiom. Roger McDonald's *Shearers' Motel* (1992), which won the NBC Banjo Award in 1993, portrays the shearing sheds in modern times with the comfort of air-conditioned caravans, microwaves, mobile phones and refrigeration.

SHEARER, Jill (1936–) has lived mainly in Queensland and has written some poetry and short stories for children and adults, but is best known as a playwright. She has won numerous awards and competitions and written several full-length and one-act plays; they include 'But I Won't Wear White' (1972), 'Ships That Pass' (1973), 'The Trouble With Gillian' (1974), 'Who the Hell Needs Whipbirds' (1974), 'The Job' (1974), 'Release Lavinia Stannard' (1975), *Catherine* (1976, published 1977), *The Foreman* (1973, published 1977), *The Boat* (1975, published 1977), 'The Expatriate' (1976), *Echoes* (1978), 'Computer Man' (1980), *The Kite* (1976, published 1980), *Stephen* (1980), *Nocturne* (1980), 'A Woman Like That' (1986), 'Comrade' (1987) and *Shimada* (1987, published 1989, and produced on Broadway in 1992). *The Boat* is included in the collection *Can't You Hear Me Talking To You?* ed. Alrene Sykes (1978); Shearer's independent collection, *Echoes and Other Plays* (1980), includes *Stephen*, *Nocturne* and *The Kite*. A writer with an acute ear for the subtleties of dialogue, Shearer tends to favour the one-act play with an ordinary setting, into which an element of the bizarre intrudes. Her most complex play is *Catherine*, a play within a play, which moves from contemporary time to 1790 and the voyage of Catherine Crowley, mother of William Charles Wentworth (q.v.), to Australia with the Second Fleet.

'Shearer's Dream, The', one of the poems of Henry Lawson (q.v.) which was subsequently set to music and became an Australian folk-song, was written in 1901. It tells the story of a shearer who, until he wakes up and finds that he has been dreaming, imagines himself in a shed with electric fans and mahogany pens, shearing sheep that have been washed before they are shorn, and served drinks every hour by female rouseabouts who also attend to the other 'needs' of the shearers. The poem first appeared in print in a story, also titled 'The Shearer's Dream', which was included in *Children of the Bush* (1902). Mitchell and Lawson, camped for the night, listen to the song coming from an adjoining camp, although the singer is silenced before he reveals that he 'woke with my head in the blazin' sun to find ''twas a shearer's dream'; this ending, however, was revealed when the poem was published in *When I Was King* (1905). A similar Australian folk-song is 'The Drover's Dream', in which the drover dreams that the bush fauna put on a concert for him until he is rudely awakened by his boss, demanding to know where the sheep have gone.

SHEARSTON, Trevor (1946–), born Sydney, graduated from the University of Sydney in 1967 and spent the following seven years (until 1976) teaching in Papua New Guinea, an experience that has been the main influence on his life and his writing. His first book of fiction was *Something in the Blood* (1979, reprinted 1983, 1984), a collection of fifteen stories. The overall theme of the collection, reflected in the title, is that the power to rule is intrinsically a polarising force, producing the opposed groups of rulers and ruled. The Australian colonial authorities in Papua New Guinea before independence often exercised their power without sensitive regard for the people over whom they ruled – exercised it brutally as in the story 'Boi', and with an amalgam of sentimental paternalism and contemptuous racism as in 'Leaving Molly', where retiring plantation-owner Farrell leaves a generous sum for his house servant Gabriel but burns his house down, saying 'No coon lives in the house I built for Molly. Ever.' The novels that have followed, *Sticks That Kill* (1983), *White Lies* (1986) and *Concertinas* (1988), are all similarly set in Papua New Guinea. *Sticks That Kill* is an absorbing account of some of the events leading up to Australia taking over control of Papua from the British, as seen through the eyes of newcomer John Rhys. *White Lies*, with descriptions matching the mystery and menace of the settings, is a story of the conflict between two stubborn men, White missionary Richard Wakely and Black medicine man Sebo. The conflict, in which the supposedly enlightened White man proves as primitive as his Black counterpart, ends in tragedy – Sebo and his son Yaru slain by the Gewa tribesmen who seize an opportunity to unleash old tribal passions, the new church burnt to the ground, and the collapse of Wakely's obsessive attempt to mould the Black man in the White's image. *Concertinas* further emphasises the spell cast by Papua New Guinea; the novel's protagonist Chris Davage had taught there for some years, but is married with two children and teaching in Canberra, when he meets again the native girl Timii, whom he had once taught. He goes back to Papua New Guinea and becomes involved not only with Timii but also with her radical activities to free West Papua from Indonesian domination. Timii is killed, Davage expelled from Papua New Guinea, but, with his marriage at stake, his children alienated and his teaching job lost, he remains unable to break free from the obsession that has dominated his life. A skilful writer, Shearston has won a high place in the contemporary popular fiction scene.

'Sheedy Was Dying', a poem by John Shaw Neilson (q.v.), published in the *Bulletin* 1901 Christmas number, records the lonely death that usually comes to drifters in the outback.

SHEIL, Graham (1938–), born Melbourne, has combined the management of a wholesale optical company with a career as an author. He has published short stories in numerous periodicals and anthologies and in two collections, *War's End* (1981) and *Islands* (1986). He has also written a novel, *Christmas Trees in the Sky* (1991), and several plays including 'Mad Like Lasseter' (1977), 'Work-A-Day World' (1981), 'New Australians Rehearse the Working Man's Paradise', based on William Lane's efforts to create a Utopian society in Paraguay (1983), 'This is the Way the World Ends' (1987), 'Christmas Trees in the Sky' (1989), *River of Fire* (1991), *Bali: Adat* (1991) and *The Dead Heart*, a study of the explorer Edward John Eyre (1991). He has won several awards for his short fiction including the *Sun-News Pictorial* Award, the 'Rolf Boldrewood' Award, the Syme Newspapers Australia Day Award, and the Bicentennial State of Victoria Award. The linked stories of *War's End*, set mainly in rural Victoria in the years immediately after the Second World War, are based on autobiographical experience and relate the development of a boy into adulthood, his quest for a heroic model, pursuit of his writing vocation and coming to terms with the failed figure of his father. The subjects of the more varied stories of *Islands* range from the fire-bombing of Dresden to Bali to the familiar territory of *War's End*; firmly directed and punctuated with well-rendered dramatic or comic scenes, Sheil's stories have as an underlying theme the perennial isolation of human kind. *Christmas Trees in the Sky* returns to the fire-bombing of Dresden, interweaving the experiences of several witnesses of the atrocity, an Australian POW, his German supervisor and the latter's wife.

SHEINER, Robin (1940–), born Perth, is a fifth-generation Australian who has gained first-hand knowledge of migrant experience by marrying into an immigrant family. She has written short stories and two novels, *Smile, the War is Over* (1983) and *Beyond the Pale* (1989). Set in Perth of the 1940s, *Smile, the War is Over* follows the fortunes of a group of young women and the impact on their lives of the huge influx of American servicemen, incidentally conveying the social texture of life in the wartime city; *Beyond the Pale* focuses on post-war European immigrants in 1950s outer suburban Perth and their attempt to adjust to an alien landscape.

Shepherd, later replaced by the stockman, drover and jackeroo, was a familiar figure in the colonies before the introduction of fencing wire on pastoral holdings in the 1850s. The shepherd prevented the sheep from wandering, escorted them to water and fresh pastures, and protected them from depredations by Blacks and dingoes. The solitary shepherd was sometimes himself the victim of marauding Aborigines, who killed him and made off with his flock. He was usually dressed in a rough serge suit tied at the waist with a leather belt; mostly bearded and long-haired, he wore a cabbage-tree hat or a less durable one made of plaited kangaroo grass. The itinerant shepherd made a rough shelter each night from branches and leaves; in more settled areas he lived in a rough slab hut with a dirt floor, occasionally with a wife and family for company but more often with a hutkeeper who kept watch over the sheep at night. Detached for long periods from the company of fellow humans, the shepherd often grew erratic in behaviour, such a misfit when restored to society that he could only return to the solitude that had become natural to him. Henry Kendall, himself a shepherd when a young man, planned a major poetic work, 'The Australian Shepherd', using the sheep-

herder as the central figure around which to weave the epic story of life in the bush. Only fragments of this work were completed, e.g. 'A Death in the Bush'. Prominent in most histories of the pastoral age, the shepherd is discussed in James Bonwick's *Romance of the Wool Trade* (1887) and is the central subject of W.R. Glasson's *Our Shepherds* (1942); the latter also contains a selection of shepherd vocabulary and slang. Artist S.T. Gill painted the well-known work *Sleeping Shepherd*.

SHEPHERD, Catherine (1902–76), born Rhodesia (Zimbabwe) and educated in Wales, came to Australia in the 1920s. In the 1930s and 1940s she wrote plays and dramatic adaptations of classic novels for radio which included 'Lethe Wharf', 'Seapiece', 'Exit Socrates', 'The Flying Swan', 'I Saw the New Moon', 'Three Mile Cross', 'Sabotage', 'A Citizen of the World', 'The Valiant Tinker', 'The Heroic Journey', 'Balzac', 'The Golden Cockerel', 'Arthur of Van Diemen's Land', 'The Hayfield' and 'The Judas Sheep'. She also wrote several stage plays, *Daybreak* (1942) and 'Jane, My Love' (1951), and a children's novel, *Tasmanian Adventure* (1964).

SHERER, John (1810–?), born Edinburgh, trained as a printer and published, 1844–81, sixteen miscellaneous works which include histories, travel books, pamphlets and general reference works. He also edited the popular narrative *The Gold-Finder of Australia: How He Went, How He Fared, And How He Made His Fortune* (1853), which was once regarded as an authentic account of Sherer's own entertaining adventures on the Australian goldfields. It has since been established that Sherer never visited Australia but derived most of his ideas for *The Gold-Finder* from S.T. Gill's *Sketches of the Victorian Goldfields* (1852) and other oral and printed accounts, and published the book to tap the lucrative English market for informative literature on the gold discoveries.

SHERMAN, Paul (1933–), born Brisbane, has worked as journalist, high school teacher and actor. He has written short stories and poems, and the plays *Melba*, produced 1974, published 1976, and *The Mangrove Man*, produced 1977–78 and published in *Australian Theatre Workshop One Act Plays, Series 1* (1978). *Melba*, an interpretation of Dame Nellie Melba, has a more documentary and external approach than Jack Hibberd's contemporary *A Toast to Melba* (1976). Sherman has also written the libretto of a musical, *Captain Starlight*, produced in 1964 and published in 1988 and the plays 'The Hero of Too' (an adaptation of David Martin's novel), 'Jungles' and *The Murder of Gonzago* (1988).

Shifting Heart, The (1960), a play by Richard Beynon (q.v.), was first produced in Sydney in 1957 after winning first prize in the 1956 Playwrights' Advisory Board competition. Set in Collingwood, a working-class Melbourne suburb, on Christmas Eve, the play deals with the fortunes of an Italian immigrant family, the Bianchis: Poppa, Momma, a son, Gino and a daughter, Maria, who is married to an Australian, Clarry Fowler, and is anxiously waiting for the birth of her child, having previously suffered two miscarriages. Gino appears to be drawn to the local dance hall, where he attracts the violent attentions of the local, racist youths, a fact which receives scant sympathetic attention from Clarry, despite Maria's anxiety. The Bianchis have a friendly, if noisy, relationship with one set of neighbours, the Pratts; with their other neighbours they are in a state of warfare, Momma resorting to blocking their drains and depositing garbage over their fence. Act Two ends with Gino's death following a fight in which it is unclear whether he was aggressor or victim, although chauvinist Australian attitudes have clearly played a part. The birth of Maria's baby is precipitated by the news and by her angry conflict with Clarry, whom she blames for the tragedy. Act Three takes place on Christmas Day. The baby is safely born and Clarry and Maria reconciled, Clarry maintaining with an inarticulate show of sentiment that his son's name will be Gino.

SHILLINGLAW, J.J. (John Joseph) (1831–1905), born London, came to Australia in 1852 during the gold rush and held various public service appointments in Victoria. A member of the Yorick Club and of the literary society the Cave of Adullam, he acquired a reputation as a historian, contributed to various Victorian periodicals and in 1869 took over the *Colonial Monthly*. He published six books but his most important achievement was the discovery and editing of a number of documents relating to the early history of the Port Phillip settlement, published in 1879 as *Historical Records of Port Phillip*. His personality is described in Hugh McCrae's *Story-book Only* (1948).

'Ship of Ice, The', a long, dramatic poem by Rosemary Dobson (q.v.), won the *Sydney Morning Herald* prize for poetry in 1946 and was published in three parts in that newspaper in 1947. The ship of ice is the English schooner *Jenny*, which lay locked in the Antarctic ice from 1823 to 1860 until discovered by a whaling vessel. 'Snap-frozen' as it were in an instant of time, the bodies of the crew had been perfectly preserved, caught for thirty-seven years in their frozen postures until released by discovery into conventional death. The poem's seven individual voices (the captain, his wife, and five of the crew) comment on the event in the light of their own personalities and philosophies.

'Shiralee', according to D'Arcy Niland (q.v.), who wrote the novel *The Shiralee* (1955), was a particular type of swag (q.v.), one shaped like a leg of mutton, carried over the shoulder by a strap or rope, which usually balanced some other load, probably a tucker bag on the chest. The origin of the word is unknown. A film of Niland's novel, with Peter Finch (q.v.) as the swagman Macauley, was screened in 1957.

'Short Shift Saturday', one of Gavin Casey's best-known short stories, published in *It's Harder for Girls*

(1942), focuses on the gulf that grows between partners in marriage and, on the broader level, of the even greater gulf that exists between the sexes in male-dominated Australian society. Set in Kalgoorlie, the story is based on the different reactions of man and wife to the sight of a drunken miner being thrown out of a hotel. In the woman's eyes a drunken beast, the miner Don Bell, is viewed more sympathetically by the husband, who knows Bell has silicosis and is soon to die. That night, in bed, the husband ponders the gulf that has grown between them over the years: 'I wanted to touch her, to make some sort of contact with her.' That gulf is seen to be due both to the Australian male habit of turning to his mates and beer 'because bars are the most cheerful places I know' and to the Australian woman's inability to cope with the ethos of masculinity and mateship that is so destructive to harmonious marital and family relationships. See also *Casey's Wife* in Casey, Gavin.

SHOTLANDER, Sandra (1941–), born Melbourne, has worked as a teacher, actor and director in England, the USA and Australia. She set up 'Mime and Mumbles', a theatre of the deaf, and directed their first production at the Pram Factory in 1974. She has written poetry and short stories, and has written for television, radio and stage. Her plays include *Framework* (1984), first produced in 1983 and co-winner of an international play-writing competition, *Blind Salome* (1985), *Angels of Power* in an anthology of that title edited by Susan Hawthorne and Renate Klein (1991) and 'Is That You Nancy?' (1991).

'Shots in the Orchard', a short story by 'Brian James' (q.v.), was first published in the *Bulletin* (1944). Typical of 'James's' ability to interpret the collective small-town mind, it concerns a domestic tragedy in the otherwise crime-free town of Templeton and the townsfolk's subsequent enjoyment and assimilation of the incident. When Enoch Rath, a despised 'shrimp' of a man, shoots both his wife and her lover Tommy Ramsbottom, he arouses surprise and sympathy in many of his neighbours on the grounds of his courage and marksmanship. Eventually, however, Enoch's refusal to talk about the shooting and the town's long-standing preference for Tommy lose him so much support that the court's failure to hang him is regarded as a mistake. Mrs Ramsbottom, a 'poor colourless little woman' with four children, is held much to blame and leaves the district.

SHRUBB, Peter (1928–) graduated from the University of Sydney and Stanford University and has lectured in English at the University of Sydney. A late starter as a fiction-writer, Shrubb has published three books, *A List of All People and Other Stories* (1982), *Family Matters* (1988) and *Living Alone* (1989). *Family Matters* has four separate stories, 'A Love Affair', 'Wedding', 'At Work' and 'The Freutzer Sonata', while *Living Alone* traces the experiences of Helen Richman, both in the five years of her marriage to Harry Richman and after she moves out from her comfortable Woollahra home to a seedy flat (and some seedy neighbours) at Bondi.

'SHUTE, Nevil' (Nevil Shute Norway) (1899–1960), born Middlesex, England, trained at first as a Royal Flying Corps gunnery officer, although he failed his final medical examination. After a brief period in the British infantry in 1918, he studied at Oxford University and in 1923 joined the de Havilland Aircraft Company as an engineer. His first published novel, *Marazan*, appeared under the pseudonym 'Nevil Shute', in 1926; two earlier attempts, 'Stephen Morris' and 'Pilotage', were published after 'Shute's' death as one volume under the title *Stephen Morris* (1961). In 1924 'Shute' left de Havilland to work on the R100 airship project, which was halted in 1930 following the disastrous crash of the rival F101 airship. 'Shute' then helped to found a new aircraft-manufacturing company, Airspeed Ltd, for which he worked as managing director until 1938, when the success of his novels *So Disdained* (1928) and *Lonely Road* (1932) prompted him to turn to full-time writing. On the outbreak of the Second World War, however, he joined the Royal Navy Volunteer Reserve, and was set to work on weapons developments; in 1944 he was sent to Normandy with the invasion fleet as correspondent for the Ministry of Information. Novels that draw on his war experiences are the outstandingly popular *Pied Piper* (1942), which established 'Nevil Shute' as a household name in the English-speaking world, *Most Secret* (?1945) and *Pastoral* (1944). In 1945 'Shute' resigned from the navy and visited Burma, again as a ministry correspondent, an experience he incorporated in his novel *The Chequer Board* (1947). *No Highway* (1948), his next novel, returned to his experience in the aviation industry and dealt prophetically with the problem of structural fatigue in aircraft. In 1948–49 'Shute' flew his own plane to Australia in search of novelistic material, an experience which resulted in two of his best-known novels, *A Town Like Alice* (q.v., 1950) and *Round the Bend* (1951). In 1950, disappointed with the current British political scene, he decided to live permanently in Australia. Subsequent novels dealing mainly or partly with Australia are *The Far Country* (1952), *In the Wet* (1953), *Beyond the Black Stump* (1956), *On the Beach* (1957), *Requiem for a Wren* (1955) and *The Rainbow and the Rose* (1958).

'Shute' wrote more than twenty novels in all and an autobiography up to the year 1938, *Slide Rule* (1954). His books draw heavily on his experiences, his travels and his professional expertise, especially his knowledge of aircraft and weaponry; most of them are concerned with contemporary issues or problems and several, such as *What Happened to the Corbetts* (1939), which deals prophetically with the civilian destruction caused by bombing raids, and *On the Beach*, which focuses on the actuality of a nuclear holocaust, have appealed to the common anxieties of readers. Perennially popular, his novels are characterised by naturalistic, fast-moving plots; diverse settings; credible if unexceptional characters; an easy style; serious, if old-fashioned, moral purpose and happy or optimistic endings. Several have been produced as films including *Scotland Yard Commands*, a version of *The Lonely Road* (1937), *No Highway in the Sky* (*No Highway*) (1951), *On the Beach* (1959 made in Australia), and *A Town Like Alice* (1958), which was also produced as a television serial in 1981. Julian Smith has written the biographical critical study *Nevil Shute* (*Nevil Shute Norway*) (1976). Cathy Giffuni compiled the bibliography *Nevil Shute* (1988).

Sibyl (1978–83), a feminist magazine, produced four times a year at the University of WA by a small women's collective, included, among articles on feminist issues, interviews with Australian women writers and book reviews.

'Sick Stockrider, The', a popular and well-known poem of Adam Lindsay Gordon (q.v.), was written in 1869 and published in *Bush Ballads and Galloping Rhymes* (1870). The ballad of the dying stockman, with its creed of mateship, its laconic acceptance in true bush style of whatever life and death may offer, led Marcus Clarke to assert that in Gordon's work lay the beginnings of a national school of Australian poetry. 'The Sick Stockrider' is accepted as the progenitor of the Australian literary ballad but differs markedly in tone and language from the later bush ballads of the *Bulletin* school. See Folk-Song and Ballad.

SIDNEY, John, see **SIDNEY, Samuel**

'SIDNEY, Neilma' (Neilma Gantner) (1922–), born San Francisco, a daughter of the prominent businessman Sidney Myer, grew up in Melbourne and Sorrento. She lived in California for some time, worked for many years for International Social Service and is now settled in Bermagui, NSW. She has published three novels, the autobiographical *Beyond the Bay* (1966), *The Return* (1976) and *The Sweet Cool South Wind* (1993); three collections of short stories, *Saturday Afternoon* (1959), *The Eye of the Needle* (1970) and *Sunday Evening* (1988); and a travel book, *Journey to Mourilyan* (1986).

SIDNEY, Samuel ('A Bushman') (1813–83), born Birmingham, England, was baptised Samuel Solomon but throughout his career as a journalist was known as Samuel Sidney. His long-term interest was in English agriculture, but for several years either side of 1850 he was an acknowledged expert on Australian emigration. In 1847 'A Bushman's' *A Voice from the Far Interior of Australia* was published, written by Sidney from material supplied by his younger brother John, who had spent six years in NSW. *A Voice from the Far Interior of Australia* became the initial section of the wide-selling *Sidney's Australian Hand-book: How to Settle and Succeed in Australia* (1848) by 'A Bushman', also written by Sidney, possibly in collaboration with his brother. Its success led the Sidneys to establish *Sidney's Emigrant's Journal* (1848–50), which ran as a weekly until John returned to Australia in 1849, and then as a monthly. Samuel subsequently wrote the popular pot-pourri *The Three Colonies of Australia*

(1852) and a homiletic novel, *Gallops and Gossips in the Bush of Australia* (1854). Influenced by Caroline Chisholm, Alexander Harris and Robert Lowe, he was an opponent of the theories of Edward Gibbon Wakefield, who, like him, never went to Australia, and argued that the Australian colonies were an ideal location for working-class settlement. He contributed articles on Australia to Charles Dickens's *Household Words;* his influence on Dickens, Edward Bulwer-Lytton and Charles Reade, and on the creation of an Arcadian myth about Australia, are discussed in Coral Lansbury's *Arcady in Australia* (1970).

'Silkworms, The', a poem by Douglas Stewart (q.v.), was published in *Quadrant* (1957). Generally regarded as one of Stewart's finest lyric poems, 'The Silkworms' belongs, according to its author, to 'a sequence of suburban satires' inspired by his residence in a Sydney northern suburb, St Ives. The poem's opening phrase, 'All their lives in a box!', represents not only the silkworms but also their human counterparts, the suburb-dwellers. The human situation in which freedom of action and choice is limited by environment-conditioned attitudes is linked to the inertness of the silkworm's existence consequent upon generations of confinement and restriction. The poem's deliberate but restrained gravity, its measured but unemphatic tone and quiet, relaxed movement accentuate the tragic frustration of the situation it represents.

'Silverleaf', see **LLOYD, Jessie**

SIMMONS, Joseph (1810–93), born England, arrived in NSW in 1830 and in 1834 joined Barnett Levey in ownership and management of the Theatre Royal, where he also performed as an actor and was the Colony's first Macbeth. After much discord, Simmons terminated his partnership with Levey, but was once again manager, after Levey lost control of the theatre, 1835–36, and 1837–38, after Levey's death; in between he performed in Van Diemen's Land. Simmons also managed the Royal Victoria Theatre 1838–39 and 1842. In 1843 he opened the small City Theatre in Sydney with his own company, but was forced to close after only a few weeks. Best known as a comedian, Simmons played the role of Lanty O'Liffey in Edward Geoghegan's *The Currency Lass* in 1844; he also wrote several dramatic pieces, including 'New Engagements' (1842) and 'The Duellist' (1844). He seems to have retired from the stage in 1845, although he reappeared at his benefit in 1879.

SIMMONS, Samuel Rowe (1871–1952) was a Melbourne printer who established two small private presses, the Argonaut Press and the Simmons Press, which published his own verse and criticism and other works, e.g. the poems of the English writer Christopher Smart. Of Simmons's six books, the most important were *Sonnets and Other Verses* (1925), published under the pseudonym 'Oswald Gray', and *A Problem and a Solution* (1946), a textual study of Marcus Clarke's first novel, *Long Odds* (1869). A prominent member of the Bread and Cheese Club, Simmons also

prepared a bibliography of Clarke which was enlarged by L.T. Hergenhan and published in 1975.

SIMON, Ella (1902–81) was born at Purfleet mission on the outskirts of Taree, NSW, to a part-Aboriginal mother and a White father, but was reared by her grandparents. The first Aboriginal woman to be made a justice of the peace (in 1962), she devoted much of her life to the mission and witnessed the changes brought about by the 1930s Depression when the practice of preventing people with Aboriginal blood from leaving the reserve without permission was instituted. At the age of 55, for instance, she was issued with a certificate of exemption from provisions of the Aboriginal Protection Act, a 'dog certificate', which she bitterly resented. Knowledgeable about Aboriginal culture, she was also a devout Christian, although she suffered prejudice within and without the church and felt herself to be divided between the two cultures. Her autobiography, *Through My Eyes* (1978), is a revealing account of the difficulties and indignities faced by Aboriginal people of her generation.

'Simon Stukeley', see **SAVERY, Henry**

Simpson and his donkey, see **KIRKPATRICK, John Simpson**

SIMPSON, Colin (1908–83), born Sydney, worked for several years as a journalist for such Sydney newspapers as the *Daily Telegraph* and the *Sun*, the latter of which published one of his most brilliant coups, the revelation of the facts of the Ern Malley hoax. In 1947 he joined the ABC as a writer of travel documentaries and from 1950 worked as a freelance writer of well-researched and popular travel books. The best known are *Adam in Ochre* (1951), which is partly based on an Australian-American expedition Simpson accompanied to Arnhem Land in 1948, sponsored by the National Geographic Society; *Adam with Arrows* (1953) and *Adam in Plumes* (1954), both of which describe life in New Guinea; *Greece, the Unclouded Eye* (1968); and *The New Australia* (1971). Simpson also wrote a novel, *Come Away, Pearler* (1952); a biography of Charles Kingsford-Smith (1937); and contributed verse, 'Infidelities', to *Trio* (1931) with Harley Matthews and Kenneth Slessor. Vice-president of the ASA, Simpson was prominent in gaining the Public Lending Right legislation for Australian authors. He was made OBE in 1981. He is one of the authors featured in David Foster's *Self Portraits* (1991).

SIMPSON, Helen (1897–1940), granddaughter of a French marquis who had settled at Goulburn in the mid-nineteenth century, was born in Sydney and educated in Australia, although she left for England at the age of 16. She subsequently visited Australia several times, most notably in 1937 when she gave several talks for the ABC. During the First World War she worked in decoding for the British Admiralty, later studied music at Oxford, and in 1927 married Denys John Browne, a nephew of 'Rolf Boldrewood'. In England she quickly acquired a reputation as a novelist, a writer of historical biography, a radio broadcaster and later a politician; in 1938 she stood unsuccessfully as Liberal candidate for the Isle of Wight. Two of her novels have Australian content, *Boomerang* (1932), winner of the James Tait Black Memorial Prize, and *Under Capricorn* (1937); and *The Woman on the Beast* (1933), a trio of fantastic novellas, includes one set in Australia in 1999. Both *Boomerang* and *Under Capricorn* have involved, highly coloured plots, lightly sketched but credible characters, and a lively, humorous and sophisticated narrative style. *Under Capricorn*, produced as a film by a British studio in 1949, directed by Alfred Hitchcock and starring Michael Wilding and Ingrid Bergman, is a tale of passion and misunderstanding set in colonial NSW and deals with the fortunes of an ex-convict and Irish groom, married to an aristocratic Irish lady; *Boomerang*, a more ambitious novel, relates the history of four generations of a family of French origin both in Australia and elsewhere. Simpson's other work includes a volume of poetry, *Philosophies in Little* (1921); the novels *Acquittal* (1925), *The Baseless Fabric* (1925), *Cups, Wands and Swords* (1927), *Mumbudget* (1928), *The Desolate House* (1929), *'Vantage Striker* (1931), *Saraband for Dead Lovers* (1935, which was also produced as a film), *The Female Felon* (1935) and *Maid No More* (1940); three novels written in collaboration with Clemence Dane; the historical biographies *The Spanish Marriage* (1933) and *Henry VIII* (1934); an account of Mary Kingsley, *A Woman Among Wild Men* (1938); and a translation of a selection from Louis-Sebastian Mercier's *Le Tableau de Paris* (1933). She also published several plays, *Pan in Pimlico* in an anthology, *Four One-Act Plays* (1923); *A Man of His Time* (1923), an interpretation of the life of Benvenuto Cellini, produced by Gregan McMahon in 1923; and *The Women's Comedy* (1926). An earlier play, 'Masks', was produced by the Sydney University Dramatic Society in 1921. Ben Hutchison compiled *Bibliography of Helen Simpson* (1988).

SIMPSON, Mary (1884–?), born Stawell, Victoria, contributed numerous humorous sketches and short stories to the *Bulletin*, the *Australian Journal* and *Woman's Mirror* for more than two decades. Some were collected and published under the title *'Tell-Tale' Stories from the Bulletin* (1926), and one, 'Santa Claus', was reprinted in Nettie Palmer's *An Australian Story-Book* (1928) and George Mackaness's *Australian Short Stories* (1928). Simpson, who used the pseudonym 'Weeroona', also wrote comedies and one-act plays, e.g. *Crossing Swords with Fate* (1940), a play based on the life of Adam Lindsay Gordon.

SIMPSON, R.A. (Ronald Albert) (1929–), born Melbourne, studied at the Royal Melbourne Institute of Technology and taught in schools in England and Australia before his appointment in 1968 to the Chisholm Institute of Technology where he is senior lecturer in art. Poetry editor of the *Bulletin* 1963–65, he has been poetry editor of the *Age* since 1969. His poetry has appeared in numerous anthologies, in *Eight by Eight* (1963), in *Twelve Poets 1950–1970* (1971, ed. Alexander Craig) and in numerous collections, *The*

Walk along the Beach (1960), *This Real Pompeii* (1964), *After the Assassination and Other Poems* (1968), *Diver* (1972), *Poems from Murrumbeena* (1976), *The Forbidden City* (1979), *Selected Poems* (1981), *Words for a Journey: Poems 1970–1985* (1986) and *Dancing Table – Poems and Drawings 1986–1991* (1992, in the Penguin Australian Poetry Series). He has also edited *Poems from the Age 1967–79* (1979).

One of a group of Melbourne poets that came to prominence in the late 1950s and included Vincent Buckley, Evan Jones, Chris Wallace-Crabbe, Alexander Craig and Noel Macainsh, Simpson has written, over thirty years, a consistently urbane, understated and cerebral poetry that is more international than Australian in style. His collections include some light satires and verse on political subjects, but his preoccupations are the texture of ordinary life, the difficulties and joys of communication, both in art and with people, and the tensions between the desire for permanence and the reality of change, between aspiration and actuality. Complex but intelligible, spare and rigorous in thought and expression, often ironic and provocative, Simpson's verse has an analytical sensitivity that is sometimes uncompromisingly directed at the self. In his later work he achieves a relaxed, flexible and deceptively artless style. Throughout much of his work there is a faintly elegiac tone, but the sadness is phlegmatic rather than acute. That tone is struck in the words of 'Making', the final poem of *Dancing Table*.

> I dislike
> every poem
> I've ever written
> but I'm stuck with them.
>
> But even now
> I'm fashioning another
> stitching patches together.

Long overdue recognition of his achievement came with the 1992 Victorian FAW Christopher Brennan Award.

SINCLAIR, James Patrick (1928–), district commissioner in the Eastern Highlands of New Guinea until 1975, has written numerous books about New Guinea and northern Australia. They include *Behind the Ranges* (1966); *The Outside Man* (1969), a biography of Jack Hides (q.v.), a New Guinea explorer and writer; *Sepik Pilot* (1971), a biography of the Australian aviator and founder of Sepik Airways, Bobby Gibbes; and *Kiap: Australia's Patrol Officers in Papua New Guinea* (1981).

SINCLAIRE, Frederick (1881–1954), born Auckland, NZ, studied for the Unitarian ministry at Manchester College, Oxford, where he achieved distinction. In 1908 he arrived in Melbourne, where he became prominent in the Victorian Socialist Party, co-edited the *Socialist* 1911–13 with Marie Pitt, and edited the organ of the Free Religious Fellowship, *Fellowship*, 1914–22, to which Vance Palmer, Louis Esson and 'Furnley Maurice' contributed. In 1911 he left the Unitarian ministry to further the aims of the Free Religious Fellowship, founded that year. An outspoken opponent of conscription, he advanced his pacifist and socialist ideas and his search for a 'living theology' in the pages of *Fellowship* and other journals. In the late 1920s he left Melbourne for Perth, where he lectured in English, and was professor of English at the University of Christchurch, NZ, 1932–46. He published three collections of essays, *Annotations* (1920), *Lend Me Your Ears* (1942), and *A Time to Laugh and Other Essays* (1951). David Walker in *Dream and Disillusion* (1976) has given an account of his aspirations and their affinity with those of Louis Esson, Vance Palmer and 'Furnley Maurice' and H. Winston Rhodes has written an informative memoir (1984).

Singabout, the magazine of the Sydney Bush Music Club, founded 1954, was published intermittently 1956–67. Less eclectic in coverage than its Victorian equivalent *Australian Tradition*, it comprised mainly words of songs together with articles, reviews and news items on folk-music and folklore societies. Edited by John Meredith, 1957–62, *Singabout* numbered Merv Lilley and John Manifold among its contributors.

'Singapore', a poem by Mary Gilmore (q.v.), was published in the *Australian Women's Weekly* in March 1942, soon after the fall of Singapore to the Japanese forces in the Second World War. Much weakened because of wartime censorship from its original scathing indictment of corruption and ineptitude, the poem echoed the widespread belief that Australian troops in Malaya, and possibly the ultimate safety of this country, had been needlessly sacrificed to other Allied interests.

SINNETT, Frederick (1830–66), born Hamburg, Germany, emigrated to Australia in 1849 because of tuberculosis, which eventually caused his death. After working as surveyor and explorer in SA he moved to journalism in Melbourne, where he helped to found and edit *Melbourne Punch*, was involved in the management of the Melbourne *Herald* and the Geelong *Daily News*, and was employed as leader-writer by the *Argus* 1857–60. He returned to Adelaide in 1859, where he ran the first ice works and the first evening newspaper, before returning to Melbourne and the *Argus* a year before his death. Sinnett wrote *Account of the Rush to Point Curtis* (1859), based on his visit to the Queensland goldfields as *Argus* correspondent, and prepared *Account of the Colony of South Australia* (1862) for the International Exhibition in London; but his most significant work was *The Fiction Fields of Australia* (q.v. 1856, reprinted 1966, ed. Cecil Hadgraft), the first extended critical essay devoted to Australian literature. His brother, Alfred Percy Sinnett, was a prominent theosophist and writer in England, and his son, Percy (1859–82), who wrote under the pseudonym 'Per Se', produced the anthology *Wattle Blossom* (1881).

Sisters Poets, see **Anthologies**; **Feminism and Australian Literature**

SKINNER, Mollie (Mary Louisa) (1876–1955), born Perth, WA, was educated in England and at the age of 23 returned to WA, where she worked as a nurse and also tried journalism. A Quaker by religion, she later worked in the London slums and, in the First World War, in India. Her wartime experiences stimulated her first book, *Letters of a V.A.D.* (1918), which is set on the Western Front and was published in England under the pseudonym 'R.E. Leake'. Her acquaintance with D.H. Lawrence began in 1922; they collaborated on *The Boy in the Bush* (q.v., 1924), a story about the experiences of a young English immigrant, Jack Grant, in the WA outback of the 1880s; it was shown as a TV series in 1984. Her later books were *Black Swans* (1925), a romance set in WA in the nineteenth century, which received a preface by Lawrence, but which was published separately; *Men Are We* (1927), a collection of Aboriginal stories; *Tucker Sees India* (1937); *WX – Corporal Smith: A Romance of the A.I.F. in Libya* (1941); and *Where Skies Are Blue* (1946). Another unpublished novel, 'Eve in the Land of Nod', was also worked over by Lawrence. Her autobiography, *The Fifth Sparrow*, with a foreword by Mary Durack, was published in 1972. Mollie Skinner's collaboration with Lawrence is discussed in detail in the critical edition of *The Boy in the Bush* edited by Paul Eggert (1990) in the Cambridge Edition of Lawrence's Letters and Works.

SKIPPER, Mervyn (1886–1958), born Adelaide, was associated with the Eastern Extension Cable Co. 1902–24, and spent some time in Borneo and the Malay States. He was subsequently Melbourne representative of the *Bulletin* and contributed frequently to the *Lone Hand* and other journals and newspapers. In 1933 he briefly left the *Bulletin* to establish the monthly magazine *Pandemonium* (q.v.), but was forced to return to the newspaper at a lower salary and reduced status after *Pandemonium* failed to prosper. The *Bulletin*'s editor was also disapproving of his and his family's close association with the painter Jurgus Jorgensen and the artists' colony he had established at Montsalvat in Eltham, Melbourne, which had acquired some notoriety. The Skipper family, including his son and two daughters, were the most permanent members of the community, while Skipper himself was Jorgensen's most devoted disciple. Betty Roland's *The Eye of the Beholder* (1984) traces Jorgensen's powerful ambivalent influence on the family. While in Borneo Skipper collected stories of the jungle, which he wove into fantasies for children and published in two collections, *The Meeting-pool* (1929) and *The White Man's Garden* (1930). Lively and humorous, the tales are told by the animals, birds, insects and plants of the jungle and reflect the natural biases, abilities and predilections of the various creatures involved. More realistic and unpredictable, if less memorable, than Kipling's *Just So Stories*, they have been translated into several European languages.

SKOVRON, Alex (1948–), born Poland, spent a year in Israel before coming to Australia in 1958. Educated at Sydney University (MA), he has worked in

Sydney and Melbourne as an editor. In 1979 he edited *The Concise Encyclopaedia of Australia* and has since published two highly regarded volumes of poetry, *The Rearrangement* (1988), which won both the FAW Anne Elder Award for Poetry and the Mary Gilmore Award, and *Sleeve Notes* (1992). A highly intelligent and sophisticated poet (one critic has referred jocularly, but respectfully, to his work as 'Poems with a Capital P'), Skovron can be intellectual, abstract and formal and at other times pragmatic and plain-speaking. His concern is that poetry should not be a momentary experience for the reader, that it should offer continuing insights and experiences. His range is wide and versatile: in language – from the polished and erudite to the simple, even colloquial; in form – from the complex, intricate and formal to blank and free verse; in theme – from the past, the future, history, philosophy, music, the shape of reality, the complexity of the human situation to the ordinary and mundane. His notable poems include the narratives from *The Rearrangement*, e.g. 'Lines from the Horizon', 'Fugue' (which won the 1983 Wesley Michel Wright prize), and the title poem itself, a sixteen-sonnet sequence recording an old man's obsession with order in his library, a ritual that both sustains and diminishes him. Music is one of the chief themes of *Sleeve Notes*, the title poem in twelve parts being inspired by Mozart's life and music and 'Elgar Revisits Worcestershire, 1984' in which the composer's ghost angrily comments on modern man's inability to truly know 'my music's dark communion'. The personal reminiscences, 'The Waterline Poems' and the reflective 'Life' are also impressive. Making few concessions to attract a wide and popular audience ('I want the reader to make a journey with each poem'), Skovron has met with considerable acclaim from fellow poets.

SKRZYNECKI, Peter (1945–   ), born Germany of Polish-Ukrainian descent, came to Australia in 1949 and grew up mainly in Sydney. He has worked as a teacher. His poetry has appeared in several collections, *There, Behind the Lids* (1970), *Head-waters* (1972), *Immigrant Chronicle* (1975), *The Aviary: Poems 1975–1977* (1978), *The Polish Immigrant* (1982), *Night Swim* (1989) and *Easter Sunday* (1993). He has also written a novel, *The Beloved Mountain* (1988) and two collections of short stories, *The Wild Dogs* (1987) and *Rock 'n' Roll Heroes* (1992), and edited an anthology of writing from Australians of non-English-speaking backgrounds, *Joseph's Coat* (1985). He won a prize in the Cook Bicentenary competitions of 1970, the Grace Leven Prize in 1972 and the Henry Lawson Short Story Award in 1985.

Immigrant experience in a new land is the dominant theme of Skrzynecki's gently lyrical and accessible poetry. In the earlier collections the dominant experience of loss is most closely associated with the father's irretrievable loss of home and the son's equally irretrievable separation from experience of that particular home. In the later collections a more personal, contemporary sense of loss, associated with separation

from wife and children and with the emotional impact of a serious heart attack, makes itself felt. Technically assured and controlled, Skrzynecki's poetry is also remarkable for delicacy of observation and sensitivity to landscape, expressed in direct, precise and unaffected language. The same sense or premonition of loss and cherishing of memory expressed in his poetry colour his short stories. Although Skrzynecki focuses largely on the experience of growing up as a child of migrant parents, he also deals with experiences that are more general, such as youthful encounters with death, sexuality and grief. Set in the mid-1960s, *The Beloved Mountain* covers the last few weeks of Dominic Zagubic, the only son of European immigrants. Unable to find stability in religion, relationships or in allegiance to his parents' homeland, he is finally killed in full view of Mount Warning, his beloved mountain, which had once seemed to offer hope and meaning.

SKUTHORP(E), Lance (1870–1958), born Kurrajong, NSW, a legendary buckjump rider and showman, formed Australia's first professional rodeo or 'wild west' show in the 1890s and toured country towns for almost forty years. He showed his horsemanship by repeating Adam Lindsay Gordon's famous Blue Lake leap. Skuthorpe's best-known and much-anthologised short story is 'The Champion Bullock Driver'; the bullocky demonstrates his talents of whip work and persuasive language by getting several panels of fencing to move of their own accord. Jack Pollard published the biography *The Roughrider* (1962), later titled *The Horse Tamer*.

SLADE, Ernest Augustus (1805–78) was an English army officer who formerly served in Australia before returning in 1832 to Sydney, where in 1833–34 he was superintendent of the convict barracks and a police magistrate. Forced to resign because of scandals surrounding his domestic arrangements with his female convict servants, he returned in 1836 to England, where he boasted to a parliamentary committee on transportation that his improved cat-o-nine tails, if properly administered, had never failed to break the skin in four lashes. Slade is presented as the corrupt and vicious Slyde in several 'Price Warung' stories, notably 'Mr Slyde's Auction', and was the model for the seducer, Brade, in John Lang's novel *The Forger's Wife* (q.v., 1855).

'SLADE, Gurney' (**Stephen Bartlett**) was a prolific writer of both children's and adult fiction. His early books were tales of adventure set in the South Seas and Australia, e.g. *Pleasure Island* (1924), *The Pearlers of Lorne: A Story for Boys* (1925), *The Fifteen Men* (1925) and *The Black Pyramid* (1926). *The Pearlers of Lorne, Lovers and Luggers* (1928) and *Captain Quid* (1937) have the pearling industry of north-west Australia as their backdrop. *Ships That Pass in the Night Clubs* (1926) is about a shipboard romance and its aftermath. He also wrote a travel book, *Through the Never Never* (1935).

SLADE, Leon (1931–), born Melbourne, has published three collections of verse, *Wilderness* (1970), *Slade's Anatomy of the Horse* (1972), and *Bloodstock Breeding* (1979). Often humorous or satirical, Slade uses colloquial diction and imagery to express his urban, contemporary themes.

SLADEN, Douglas (1856–1946), born London, took an arts degree at Oxford before coming in 1879 to Victoria, where his uncle, Sir Charles Sladen, had been premier and where he graduated in law from the University of Melbourne. He was appointed as the first lecturer in modern history at the University of Sydney in 1883, but returned to England the following year. In spite of his brief Australian experience he was considered in England something of an Australian literary expert, but his editorial judgements were not so well esteemed in Australia, for example by A.G. Stephens. Sladen's publications began with the rather ordinary verses, *Australian Lyrics* (1883) and *A Poetry of Exiles* (1883). His anthology *Australian Ballads and Rhymes* (1888) was the basis for two similar works, *A Century of Australian Song* (1888) and *Australian Poets 1788–1888* (1888). Although unimaginative and conventional in their selection of poems, the anthologies aroused interest in England in Australian poetry (see Anthologies). His keen interest in the Australian poet, Adam Lindsay Gordon (q.v.) led to his editing Gordon's *Poems* (1912) and, with Edith Humphris, the biographical *Adam Lindsay Gordon and His Friends in England and Australia* (1912). He was secretary of the Adam Lindsay Gordon Memorial Committee, which was responsible for Gordon's bust being placed in the Poets' Corner of Westminster Abbey in 1934, and to mark that occasion he edited *Adam Lindsay Gordon: The Life and Best Poems of the Poet of Australia* (1934). Sladen also wrote several minor novels; edited a volume of W.M. Hughes's speeches, *From Boundary-Rider to Prime Minister* (1916); was editor of the original English *Who's Who;* and published two autobiographical works, *Twenty Years of My Life* (1915) and *My Long Life* (1939).

SLESSOR, Kenneth (1901–71) was born in Orange, NSW, of German-Scottish ancestry. His father, Robert Schloesser, was a mining engineer, but came from a distinguished family of musicians, and was something of a polymath himself. Margaret, his wife, presumably shared some of her husband's intellectual interests as she was a schoolmistress at the time that they met. Both her parents came from the Hebrides. Her father ran a store in Orange and became mayor of that municipality. Perhaps the most influential aspects of this diverse inheritance for Kenneth were his father's intensely serious philosophical musings and his mother's strong Presbyterianism. That the family name was anglicised in 1914 to avoid unpleasantness consequent upon their Germanic connections may also have left a mark on the young Slessor. Certainly his first poems published in the *Bulletin* (q.v.) while he was still at school are anxious to convey an appropriate patriotism; they celebrate the 'derring-do' of the

Anzacs, and Slessor remained devoted to the myth of the Australian soldier for the rest of his life.

Despite his early effusions in a popularist mode, the young Slessor soon developed his serious work in a different, more aristocratic direction, while maintaining an involvement with popular writing through his burgeoning career as a journalist. Slessor worked for the Sydney *Sun* from 1920 to 1925, and then briefly for the *Melbourne Punch* and Melbourne *Herald*. In 1927 he returned to Sydney and joined *Smith's Weekly*, with which he stayed until 1939 and the outbreak of the Second World War. The 1920s and 1930s were the years of his productivity as a poet. He published his first volume, *Thief of the Moon*, in 1924 and this was followed by *Earth-Visitors* (1926), *Trio*, with Harley Matthews and Colin Simpson (1931), *Cuckooz Contrey* (1932), *Darlinghurst Nights and Morning Glories* (1932) and *Five Bells* (1939). A selection of his work, published under the title *One Hundred Poems* in 1944, was reprinted with an additional two poems in 1957. Since then this selection of Slessor's poems has been reprinted over and over again. Another volume of light verse (*Darlinghurst Nights* was the first) edited by Julian Croft entitled *Backless Betty from Bondi* was published in 1983. A selection of Slessor's literary essays and other prose writings, *Bread and Wine*, appeared in 1970.

The poems in Slessor's first two volumes pursue the great themes of the Romantic-Symbolist tradition, turning obsessively upon the conflicts between art and nature, beauty and time. A fear of death, that most difficult of subjects for the Romantic imagination to confront, lurks behind many of the utterances. Here too is manifest the powerful influence of Norman Lindsay (q.v.). Slessor met the Lindsays in the early 1920s and collaborated with Norman and Jack in the production of a short-lived periodical, *Vision* (q.v.), which gained a certain notoriety for what many considered to be its salacious content. The magazine was a proponent of Norman Lindsay's aesthetic – a hotchpotch of ideas deriving from Plato, Nietzsche and other thinkers in the European symbolist tradition. According to Lindsay, art was transcendental and gave access to Life which was distinct from the humdrum, quotidian concerns of mere existence. In the highly decorative, even ornate, surfaces of Slessor's early poems one feels the strain of the poet's desire to escape into these magical realms of art and Lindsayan Life. But often the reader is struck by artifice rather than art – an exercise of skill rather than an expression of deep thought or feeling. In a few poems, however, 'The Night Ride', 'A City Nightfall', 'Winter Dawn' Slessor prefigures the direction of his later work. In these poems we have a sense of the world of lived experience, and also a sense of how this world is, for Slessor, threatened by death and meaninglessness.

The poems included in *Cuckooz Contrey* and *Five Bells* demonstrate a more refined diction than in the earlier work and a willingness to experiment with rhythm and rhyme, although it must be said that such experiment was conducted within well-defined parameters. Slessor never went as far as T.S. Eliot, say, in the disruption of conventional syntax and metre.

There is some broadening of overt subject matter in the poems of the later 1920s and 1930s, but Slessor's obsessions remain recognisably constant. There is a penchant for evoking a romantic and decorative past that sits uneasily against the increasing bitterness with which Slessor regards the modern world. His famous poems, *Captain Dobbin* and *Five Visions of Captain Cook*, are essays in poetic portraiture which are concerned with the role of memory and imagination in the construction of myth. It is significant that both poems, despite their manifest charm, have elements in them which celebrate the past at the expense of the present, and more darkly intimate the defeat of all experience (including imagination and memory) by time. This latter theme finds its greatest expression in Slessor's most important poem, 'Five Bells'. This constitutes an elegy for Joe Lynch, drowned in Sydney Harbour, and explores yet again the equivocal relationship between art, time and death. Although through the operations of memory and imagination the poet can retrieve and express aspects of the dead man so that he becomes 'part of an idea', the poet also expresses his (and the poem's) failure to resurrect or even hear Joe's voice. It is no wonder that this poem was the herald of a poetic silence that was to last from 1944 to the poet's death in 1971, broken only by two further lyric poems which arose out of his experience during the war.

In 1939 Slessor was appointed as an official war correspondent and between 1940 and 1944 spent time with Australian troops in England, Greece, the Middle-East and New Guinea. His *War Diaries* and *War Despatches*, edited by Clement Semmler, were published in 1985 and 1987 respectively. 'Beach Burial', an elegy for dead sailors, plays on the obvious irony that death makes no distinction between the Allied and the Axis dead. More poignantly the poem intimates the vulnerability of memorials and the distance between the living and the dead. 'An Inscription for Dog River', Slessor's other war poem, is altogether slighter than 'Beach Burial' but nevertheless effectively satirises the vainglory of the Australian General Blamey.

This perhaps was the most political poem Slessor wrote in his adult career. It is a striking feature of his work that despite living through the 1930s, a decade of political turmoil in Australia and overseas, politics and social themes are never allowed to intrude into his poetry. Slessor shared Norman Lindsay's very conservative belief that art including poetry was 'above' politics. And even in Slessor's very accomplished light verse, where we sometimes glimpse some of the seedier aspects of Sydney, these are dealt with in tones which are devised to maximise fun and minimise critique. Like many of his 'serious' poems, the light verse also provides evidence of Slessor's highly ambivalent attitude towards women.

On resigning his position as a war correspondent, Slessor returned to the Sydney *Sun*, where he remained as leader-writer and literary editor until 1957. Thereafter he worked for the *Daily Telegraph* and *Sunday Telegraph* as a leader-writer and book-reviewer. Although he wrote no further poetry, he maintained his literary interests through various jobs as editor and adviser. He compiled the 1945 anthology *Australian Poetry* and co-edited *The Penguin Book of Australian Verse* (1958). In 1953 he became a member of the advisory board of the CLF and in 1968 a member of the National Literature Board of Review. Between 1956 and 1961 he edited the literary magazine *Southerly*, typically insisting that it remain a purely *literary* periodical that did not dabble in politics. A *bon vivant*, Slessor relished his period as president of the Sydney Journalists Club 1956–65, a position which gave him considerable influence over the city's literary and journalistic scene.

Ironically in the years of his poetic silence his reputation steadily increased, and today this shows little sign of diminution. In 1991 Geoffrey Dutton (q.v.) published a biography of the poet, and John Tranter (q.v.) and Philip Mead chose to begin their *Penguin Anthology of Modern Australian Poetry* with selections from Slessor's work. In the same year Dennis Haskell provided a new selection of Slessor's writings including letters, journalism, light verse as well as some of the better-known poems. Notwithstanding Slessor's limited output and the mixed quality of some of his early work, he remains undoubtedly one of Australia's most important poets.

ADRIAN CAESAR

SLIGO, John (1944–), born NZ, graduated from Cambridge University before working for FAO, United Nations, in Rome and later as a film and television journalist. Now living in Sydney, he works as a freelance writer. He has published three novels, *The Cave* (1978, winner of the NZ PEN Award), *The Concert Masters* (1983) and *The Faces of Sappho* (1990); and three novellas published together, *Final Things* (1987, winnner of a NSW State Premier's Award in 1988). The novellas of *Final Things*, set in NZ, cover the period from the Second World War to 1967, and deal with separate groups of characters, although they are interwoven into a trilogy 'in intention but not by plot'; common themes are the experiences of outsiders in small, closed communities and confrontations with death, the 'final thing'. Confronting death also provides each of the main characters with a transcendent understanding of life and initiation into its deeper spiritual meanings. An ambitious novel with an unusual structure and huge time-span, *The Faces of Sappho* is a far-reaching critique of Western civilisation and its growth from masculine values. Returning to the androgynous Sappho as a metaphor for the possibilities of human development which were lost before the birth of Christ, the novel focuses on the experiences of a New Zealander, David Beauford, and his passion for the philosophy of the lesbian poet; although David ultimately suicides, his tragic experience, explored after his death by family members and friends, bears fruit in their greater understanding of truths concealed by the 'twisted ... lines of history'. Both this novel and *Final Things* reflect Sligo's dislike of the provincial attitudes and brutalised notions of masculinity which he maintains he encountered in his childhood in Australia and NZ.

Slow Natives, The, a novel by Thea Astley (q.v.), first published in 1965, won the Miles Franklin and Moomba Awards. Set mainly in suburban Brisbane, the novel explores a series of sterile relationships, both emotional and spiritual. The Leverson family, which comprises the sensitive but bored Bernard, his equally bored but dull wife Iris, and their precocious son Keith, is the focus. Others, whose lives are also empty and whose malaise touches on theirs, include the spiritually alienated Sister Matthew and Father Lingard; Gerald Geoghegan, Iris's lover; the sexually frustrated Miss Trumper and her severely deprived garden-boy, Chookie. When Keith attempts to punish his parents for their apparent indifference by running away, he meets Chookie, who is also in flight from an encounter with Miss Trumper which he interprets as rape. Their escapade ends in a car crash in which Chookie is killed and Keith loses a leg.

'SLY, Christopher', see **NEILD, J.E.**

SMITH, Bernard (1916–   ), born Sydney, art critic and professor of contemporary art and director of the Power Institute of Fine Arts at the University of Sydney 1967–77, has written several influential histories of art in Australia, which are also important as histories of ideas and cultural movements. They include *Place, Taste and Tradition* (1945), *European Vision and the South Pacific 1768–1850* (1960, 2nd edn 1985) and *Australian Painting 1788–1960* (1962, extended to 1990 with additional chapters by Terry Smith, 1991). He has published several collections of essays and lectures, including *The Antipodean Manifesto* (1975), *The Spectre of Truganini* (1980), *The Death of the Artist as Hero* (1988) and *The Critic as Advocate* (1989). *Imagining the Pacific: In the Wake of the Cook Voyages* (1992) brings together several connected essays on European imagined constructions of the Pacific region. With Rudiger Joppien he prepared the three-volume edition *The Art of Captain Cook's Voyages* (1985–88) and has collaborated in editing *Baudin in Australian Waters* (1988, with Jacqueline Bonnemains and Elliott Forsyth) and *The Art of the First Fleet* (1988, with Alwyne Wheeler). He has also edited *Concerning Contemporary Art* (1975), *Documents on Art and Taste in Australia* (1975) and *Culture and History* (1984), essays presented to Jack Lindsay. A collection of essays edited by Anthony Bradley and Terry Smith, *Australian Art and Architecture*, was published in his honour in 1980. Nancy Underhill's *Making Australian Art 1916–49: Sydney Ure Smith, Patron and Publisher* (1991) is informative on his key relationship with Ure Smith. Bernard Smith has also written an autobiography, *The Boy Adeodatus* (1984), which is both an absorbing social and cultural history and a significant literary achievement, re-creating the lives and social context of his two mothers, his natural mother and his foster mother. Subtitled *The Portrait of a Lucky Bastard*, it is written in the third person and concludes in his twenty-fourth year, his year of decision, when he gave up painting in favour of art history and criticism. Emeritus professor of the University of Sydney, Smith has received numerous awards and distinctions includ-

ing an honorary D.Litt. from the University of Melbourne, the Ernest Scott Prize in 1962 and both a National Book Council Award and a Victorian Premier's Literary Award for *The Boy Adeodatus*.

SMITH, Graeme Kinross, see **Australia's Writers**

SMITH, James (1820–1910), born Kent, England, had a successful and varied publishing and journalistic career in England before migrating in 1854 to Australia, where he became leader-writer and dramatic critic for the *Age*. He rapidly became one of the colony's most influential newspapermen and public figures. Editor of the *Leader* (1856), *Melbourne Punch* (1859), the *Australasian* (1871) and the *Evening Mail* (1881), he was founding editor of the satirical magazine *Touchstone* in 1869 and was closely associated with both the magazines titled *Victorian Review* (1860–61, 1879–86). Also closely associated with the *Argus*, as leader-writer, dramatic, literary and fine arts critic 1856–96, he was asked to retire in 1896 due to his 'leaning towards spiritualism'. He was Victorian Parliamentary Librarian 1863–69. He helped establish the Garrick Club (1855), the Melbourne Shakespeare Society (1884), the Alliance Française (1890) and the Dante Society (1896); as a trustee of the Public Library, Museums and the National Gallery of Victoria 1880–1910, he exerted considerable influence on the cultural life of Melbourne. His own publications include the important *Cyclopedia of Victoria* (1903–5), *From Melbourne to Melrose* (1888) and *Junius Unveiled* (1909); a play, 'Garibaldi', was performed at the Prince of Wales theatre, Melbourne, in 1860. Smith also published the novels *The Secret of the Sphinx* (1906), the story of Moses as communicated by a spirit medium, and the autobiographical 'Ralph Penfold', serialised in the *Victorian Review* in 1861. His reminiscences, 'Recollections of an Octogenarian', were published in the *Leader* in 1907. Lurline Stuart has published *James Smith. The Making of a Colonial Culture* (1989), which is also an important study of Smith's Victorian milieu.

SMITH, Sir James Joynton, see **Smith's Weekly**

SMITH, Jan (1935–   ), born Queensland, studied economics and has worked as a journalist, secretary and artist's model. She has written two novels, *An Ornament of Grace* (1966) and *The Worshipful Company* (1969). Narrated by Marina Hamilton, a girl in her twenties who is pursuing a career in journalism in Sydney after casting off a conventional relationship, *An Ornament of Grace* is a witty exploration of urban life and the difficulties faced by the so-called liberated woman in a man's world; *The Worshipful Company* deals with the fortunes of three young women in Sydney of the 1960s as they attempt to create alternative destinies to the conventional suburban ones led by their mothers but who find the new social and sexual freedoms incompatible with their deepest needs.

SMITH, Sydney Ure (1887–1949), born London, was brought to Australia in infancy and studied art at the Julian Ashton school in Sydney, where he became friendly with a group of young artists, including Norman Lindsay and Will Dyson. A pioneer of art publishing in Australia, he started the publishing house Art in Australia, in 1916 with Bertram Stevens as co-editor. He also founded and edited the influential periodical *Art in Australia* (q.v.), as well as *Home*, and wrote and edited several books on the work of Australian artists. The Art in Australia company was sold to John Fairfax & Sons in 1934, and in 1939 Ure Smith established the firm of Ure Smith, which produced high-quality publications, mostly on art and related subjects. A well-known etcher and artist, he published several collections of his etchings and drawings and also illustrated numerous works by other authors, including *Glimpses of Old Sydney* (1928) and *Old Colonial By-Ways* (1928) by Charles H. Bertie and *The Sydney Book* (1947) by Marjorie Barnard. His love of Sydney is also reflected in the anthology of literary references to the city that he illustrated and edited, *The Charm of Sydney* (1918). With Gwen Morton-Spencer he edited the magazine *Australia National Journal* (1939–47) and its annual anthologies, *Australia Week-End Book* (1942–46). President of the Society of Artists (1921–48), and trustee and vice-president of the Art Gallery of NSW, Ure Smith also organised numerous overseas exhibitions. Nancy Underhill's *Making Australian Art 1916–49: Sydney Ure Smith, Patron and Publisher* (1991) is an informative account of Ure Smith's achievements and influence and includes chapters on his relationships with Norman Lindsay, George Lambert and Bernard Smith.

SMITH, Vivian (1933–) was born and grew up in Hobart, Tasmania. He graduated with an MA in French from the University of Tasmania, where he taught French for ten years. After moving to Sydney he completed a Ph.D. in English at the University of Sydney, where he is now a reader in English. He has published five volumes of verse, *The Other Meaning* (1956), *An Island South* (1967), *Familiar Places* (1978), *Tide Country* (1982), which won the NSW Premier's Poetry Prize and the Grace Leven Prize, and *Selected Poems* (1985). He edited *Australian Poetry 1986* and *1988*; *Young St. Poets Anthology* (1981), and co-edited, with Margaret Scott (q.v.), *Effects of Light: The Poetry of Tasmania* (1985) and, with Robert Gray, *Sydney's Poems* (1992). His edition *Nettie Palmer: Her Private Journal 'Fourteen Years', Poems, Reviews and Literary Essays* appeared in 1988. He has published monographs on James McAuley (1965) and Vance Palmer (1971) and critical studies, *Vance and Nettie Palmer* (1975) and *The Poetry of Robert Lowell* (1974). He also edited *Letters of Vance and Nettie Palmer 1915–1963* (1977) and wrote the poetry section of *The Oxford History of Australian Literature* (q.v., 1981). Other publications include *Tasmania and Australian Poetry* (1984) and a book for young people in French, *Les Vigés en Australie* (1967).

Smith's first poems were published in the *Bulletin* while he was still at school. His first volume, *The Other Meaning*, reveals Tasmania as the focal point of his work. This early poetry, seen by Kenneth Slessor as

reflecting 'a gaunt, stony, achromatic landscape', is romantic in its symbolist imagery, linguistic musicality and melancholy pensiveness. Influenced by Judith Wright and Kenneth Slessor, it shares their preoccupation with landscape and sea, the latter 'an inescapable element' for a Tasmanian. Poems like 'Bird Sanctuary', 'In Summer Rain', 'Myth', 'Bedlam Hills' and 'Thylacine' are attractive lyrics fusing a personal inner world with a vividly evoked and precisely observed external scene.

An Island South, named for Tasmania, conveys the island's cold, still luminosity and searches 'for a vision in which contradictions are held in balance' and doubt and pain and fragmentation can be withstood. A group of savagely comic satires introduces a new detachment and toughness of tone. Longer lyrics ('Warmth in July', 'Hobart', 'Late April, Hobart') respond sensitively to the scenes and implications of autumn.

Familiar Places celebrates places that have become meaningful to the poet – Sydney ('Twenty Years of Sydney', 'Balmoral Summer') and Tuscany ('Il Convento, Batignano') joining with the first familiar place, Tasmania ('View from the Domain, Hobart' and 'Back in Hobart'); and the memory of three women (two of them Tasmanian artists, the third a Sydney refugee from Vienna), whose highly individual and isolated lives reflect wider human issues.

Tide Country brings together the two poles of Smith's imaginative world, Tasmania and Sydney. Les Murray writes of Smith as 'Slessor's natural successor in evocations of Sydney Harbour and its surrounds which few really match'. A new, less intimately congenial environment brings fresh imaginative alertness and a harder-edged quality to the verse. The book includes a section of translations ranging from the French Renaissance poet Maurice Scève to the German modernist Paul Celan and continues Smith's main preoccupations with related notions of permanence and decreation, loss and endurance, decay and renewal.

Selected Poems contains a large group of new poems and shows Smith increasingly concerned with the scrutiny of modes and codes of behaviour, the odd, the unexpectedly poignant, observed in the animal as well as the human world ('Dung Beetles', 'At the Parrot House, Taronga Park'). The language becomes grittier, the rhythmic texture of the verse more complex. The book contains a series of prose poems of memories of Hobart in the 1940s, as well as many unrhymed free forms. At the same time the lyrical aspect of Smith's poetry continues with new controlled intensity ('Still Life', 'Tasmania').

Smith has commented on his own work:

> Looking back over my poems I find that they are concerned with various attitudes of mind – how to go on living fully and humanly without dogma or theory – on a provisional basis so to speak – but without becoming the victim of unstructured experience.

Smith's Weekly, an uninhibited Sydney newspaper which won an overseas reputation for its raciness and for the quality of its black-and-white art, was published 1919–50. It was named after Sir James Joynton

Smith (1858–1943), an English-born adventurer who became a successful businessman and lord mayor of Sydney, and provided the funds which allowed Claude McKay and R.C. Packer, assisted by an ageing J.F. Archibald, to produce the first issue. Packer remained with the newspaper until 1931, Smith until 1939, and McKay intermittently until 1950; Kenneth Slessor was editor 1935–39 and editor-in-chief in 1939–40. Aggressively nationalist and somewhat racist, *Smith's* championed the cause of the digger, espoused the White Australia Policy, and was aggressively anti-communist; it rivalled the *Bulletin* with its blend of sporting and other news, satire and visual humour in which horse-racing, Dad and Dave and the Anzacs were regular subjects. Among many notable artists who drew for the journal were Cecil Hartt, George Finey, Frank Dunne, Jim Russell and Stan Cross, whose famous cartoon, 'For gorsake stop laughing – this is serious'! (q.v.), was first published in *Smith's* in 1933. Among its best-known writers were the sporting reporter Jim Donald, the satirists Lennie Lower, Ronald McCuaig and Alexander Macdonald, and the political commentator Brian Fitzpatrick. Smith's memoirs, *My Life Story*, were published in 1927, and George Blaikie's *Remember Smith's Weekly?* in 1966. Claude McKay's autobiography, *This is the Life* (1961), also contains much information about the newspaper.

Snowy River, made legendary in Australian folklore by A.B. Paterson's poem 'The Man from Snowy River' (q.v.), rises in the Snowy Mountains near Mt Kosciusko in NSW and flows into Bass Strait, 450 kilometres away, in the Gippsland district of Victoria. First explored in 1840 by Paul Strzelecki (q.v.), who named Mt Kosciusko, the area was named Muniong (or Munyang) by the geologist W.B. Clarke after the Aboriginal word for the region, but the name Snowy Mountains caught public imagination and was later officially adopted. The Snowy Mountains are the source of many rivers; others, in addition to the Snowy, are the Tumut and a major tributary of the Murray, the Swampy Plain. The spring run-off from the heavy winter snows provides the water for the Snowy Mountains hydro-electric scheme which was completed in 1972. The alpine country through which the Snowy initially flows is ruggedly beautiful; its lofty grandeur influenced, and is reflected in, the poetry of Sydney Jephcott (q.v.). Elyne Mitchell (q.v.), who lives in the alpine country, draws on it for the background to her popular children's Silver Brumby series, her book of essays *Images in Water* (1947), her experiences as a skier and climber in the area, *Australia's Alps* (1942), and her work on the family property during the Second World War, *Speak to the Earth* (1945). Douglas Stewart's poem 'The Man from Adaminaby', is about the drowning of the old township by the Snowy hydro-electric scheme. A TV series depicting the human drama associated with the development of the Snowy Scheme was screened in 1993. *Men Who Built the Snowy* (1982) by Ivan Kobal tells of the engineering genius that achieved the scheme.

Social Alternatives (1977–), a quarterly magazine, which provides a forum for debate on social, cultural and economic issues, and focuses on alternative proposals for positive social change, is published in Queensland and includes articles and reviews of literary interest.

Society of Women Writers (Australia) was founded in 1925 with the object of drawing together women writers from a variety of fields and promoting the publication of Australian books. An honorary organisation with affiliations with the Society of Women Writers and Journalists, London, it includes numerous distinguished Australian authors.

Solid Mandala, The, a novel by Patrick White (q.v.), was published in 1966. Set in pre-war and contemporary urban Australia, it is divided into four sections. The first describes the elderly twin brothers Arthur and Waldo Brown, as they are glimpsed by two housewives, Mrs Poulter and Mrs Dun, from the 8.13 bus from Sarsaparilla to Barranugli (qq.v.). Shabbily dressed, they are accompanied by their scruffy dogs and trudge along hand in hand; 'it was difficult to decide which was leading and which was led'. The second and longest section, titled 'Waldo', describes the brothers' present and past, largely as realised by Waldo's repressed, embittered consciousness. Brought to Australia from England in childhood by parents who were always inadequate in terms of their own dreams, Waldo has been dogged by resentful embarrassment at his own inadequacies and, even more, those of his father and his backward brother, Arthur. Although Waldo frequently hates Arthur, they seem doomed to live side by side, sharing the same house, parents, relationships, experiences, habits, aspirations, and even the same bed. Waldo's cultural ambitions are fated to be stillborn; his promising relationship with Dulcie Feinstein, daughter of a middle-class Jewish family, comes to nothing and is surpassed by Arthur's intimacy with her, and even his dog is only technically his own. Waldo's resentment of Arthur's invasion of every area of his life and of his superior gifts of self-expression reaches a crescendo when he discovers his brother in the library, previously his own preserve, reading such spiritually important works as *The Brothers Karamazov*. In his anger he physically ejects Arthur and later, intolerably chafed by the yoke that joins them, plans his brother's death. The third section, titled 'Arthur', presents several of the same facts and events, although this time refracted by Arthur's more relaxed, open and perceptive consciousness. Despite his apparent slowness, Arthur, more spiritually alive than his brother, is in quest of a vision of totality that is most suggestively hinted at in the idea of the mandala as the 'dwelling of the god'. It is embodied for him most persistently in the four glass marbles that he lovingly treasures. Unlike Waldo, Arthur establishes genuine communication with Dulcie Feinstein and her family and with Mrs Poulter. His tentative vision is expressed most notably in his dance of the mandala for Mrs Poulter and in his gifts of the marbles: the golden one to Mrs

Poulter, the knotted one to Waldo and the blue one to Dulcie. The whorled marble, expressive of the cloudy ambiguities of life, he keeps for himself. The novel's final section, 'Mrs Poulter and the Zeitgeist', returns to the consequences of Waldo's murderous feelings for his brother. Waldo's dead body, abandoned by the appalled Arthur and hideously disfigured by the dogs, is discovered by Mrs Poulter. Arthur, unhinged by the corrosive force of Waldo's hate, is led away to an institution.

SOMERVILLE, Oliver M. (?–1947), a Sydney poet who was acquainted with such writers as A.D. Hope, Harry Hooton, James McAuley, Harold Stewart and Garry Lyle, contributed to such periodicals as *Arna* and *Hermes* and to the collection *The First Boke of Fowle Ayres* (q.v.). Politically and personally eccentric, he is remembered for his impact on the cultural life of the University of Sydney, e.g. by Donald Horne in his *The Education of Young Donald* (1967).

'Song of the Republic, A' was Henry Lawson's (q.v.) first published poem; a stirring appeal to the 'Sons of the South' (the original title) to bring about a new social order, it appeared in the *Bulletin* in October 1887. The circumstances of its composition, acceptance and publication are recorded in Lawson's 'A Fragment of Autobiography'.

Songs from the Mountains, Henry Kendall's (q.v.) final volume of verse, has an interesting publishing history. When first published in December 1880 it included a satirical poem, 'The Song of Ninian Melville', which heaped abuse upon the then member for Northumberland in the NSW parliament. Because the publishers feared a libel action by Melville the volume was hurriedly withdrawn, the satire replaced by a poem, 'Christmas Creek', and the volume re-issued in January 1881. Kendall's best collection, *Songs from the Mountains*, contains the autobiographical lyrics 'Mooni' and 'Narrara Creek', and the well-known character pieces 'Bill the Bullock Driver' (q.v.) and 'Jim the Splitter'. The dedicatory poem of the volume, 'To a Mountain', reveals Kendall's understanding and acceptance of the problems that had so embittered his early life and his new sense of self-reconciliation.

Songs of a Sentimental Bloke, The (1915), the colloquial verse narrative that bestowed on C.J. Dennis (q.v.) the title 'Laureate of the Larrikin', tells of the courtship and marriage of Bill, a larrikin of the Melbourne streets, much given to 'gettin' on the shick', and his 'ideal tart', Doreen, whose 'lurk' was 'pastin' labels in a pickle joint'. Other characters in the story, Ginger Mick and Rose of Spadgers, were used by Dennis in later volumes to continue the series. An immediate best-seller, the book went through five printings in three months and has been frequently adapted for the stage, film and television. Although it has never recaptured its first popularity and has sometimes been accused of gross exaggeration in its vernacular style and unrealistic characterisation, it

occupies a unique position in the folk-literature of Australia, immortalising and romanticising the city larrikin who was a feature of Australian urban life in the early part of the twentieth century.

SORENSEN, Jack (1907–49), born Kalgoorlie, WA, of mixed Danish, Irish and English heritage, was a WA boxing champion, shearer, newspaper representative and balladist whose poems appeared regularly in the *Bulletin* and in the newspapers of the WA gold-fields. His publications were *The Gun of Glindawor* (1932), *The Lost Shanty* (1939) and *The Collected Poems of Jack Sorensen, 1907–1949*, published posthumously in 1950. *The Collected Poems*, with such segments as 'Shearing Ballads and Rhymes of the North-West', 'Goldfields Verse' and 'Songs of the Kimberleys', illustrates the themes of Sorensen's verse. A new collected edition, *The Ghosts of Bayley Street*, was published in 1992.

SORENSON, E.S. (Edward Sylvester) (1869–1939), of mixed Norwegian and Australian parentage, was born at Dyraaba near Casino, NSW. His life was spent in a variety of bush occupations: farming, dairying, droving, shearing and prospecting for gold. A member of the FAW, a contributor to the *Bulletin* and an enthusiastic naturalist, Sorenson published numerous volumes of fiction interspersed with verses about the bush. His major publications were *The Squatter's Ward* (1908), *Quinton's Rouseabout and Other Stories* (1908), *Life in the Australian Backblocks* (1911), *Friends and Foes in the Australian Bush* (1914), and *Chips and Splinters* (1919).

Soundings (1993), a novel by Liam Davison (q.v.), won the 1993 NBC Banjo Award for Fiction. Set in the Westernport Bay area of Victoria, the novel begins in the 1820s when the sealers who carried on their brutal trade in the area were visited first by the French ship *L'Astrolabe* and its scientists, then, soon after, by a survey group with convict labourers under explorer William Hovell. In the novel's first time frame the significant figure is the White sealer, Kerrison, who brutalises his Aboriginal wife, finally bludgeoning her to death as if she were no better than a seal. The second time-frame of the novel extends from the late 1890s to the 1920s. Here there are more substantially drawn characters, Jasper Black the channel-drainer and his wife Anna, the uncomely daughter of ruthless land developer Theodore Drost. Jasper and Anna, in spite of her family's protests, settle to a life in the swamps in a drab hut of corrugated iron and hessian. Jasper attempts, obsessively, to clear about 15 acres of marsh-land to create a farmlet. A brief period of relative happiness for them ends when their child, Edgar, drowns. They then grow apart, Anna regretting her lost comfortable life in her father's house and both she and Jasper unable to offer each other comfort in their grief. The murky waters of the drainage channels and the bay itself ultimately claim them both. The third time-frame is the present. Its sole occupant of any substance is Jack Cameron, who has resigned from his job as photographer with the Ministry of Lands, and is living in a rented house on the bay. Intent on making a living from portraits, he becomes, instead, obsessed with the area itself, spending most of his time photographing it rather than people. He sets up an old photo-finish machine he has bought from a greyhound track disposal and focuses his camera on the machine's narrow slit, recording the single scene visible through the slit, a scene that varies with the passing minutes and hours. To his amazement Cameron captures on film, as he moves his machine to various vantage points in the swamps and around the waterline, images of objects and events that he himself has not been able to see. There are several boats, including a pleasure cruiser floundering just off shore, a party of men up to their waists in water searching one of the channels, a little child running towards the water, a man bludgeoning what appears to be a seal but may well be a woman, a man strapped to a triangular frame, his back bloodied. These are all events from the past, certainly not witnessed by the photographer but somehow captured by his camera as if they were occurring in the present. Thus the theme of the novel – that the past, the present and the future are all part of 'one perpetual moment ... an everlasting now!' Gradually the introverted, lonely Jack Cameron of the present becomes dominated by the Anna Black of the past. He seeks her constantly, delving ever deeper into the swamps trying to capture her face on his film. At the final moment of the novel he appears to meet her, joining her in the murky depths.

With its notion of the eternal 'now', the co-existence of all time-frames, past, present and future, *Soundings* departs from the traditional chronological narrative structure. The three time-frames merge, ebbing and flowing through and across each other in the three parts of the book. Difficult at first for the reader, that fluidity ultimately becomes effective, even unobtrusive. Dialogue is sparse; the mesmerising flow of description and narration is often unbroken for pages on end. Sombre, claustrophobic and compelling, *Soundings* is a remarkable novel.

SOUTER, C.H. (Charles Henry) (1864–1944), born Scotland, came to Australia in 1879 and spent three years in the bush before returning to Scotland to train as a doctor. After a journey to China as a ship's surgeon and some years in NSW he settled in a practice in SA. He began to contribute ballads to the *Bulletin* in 1896, sometimes using the pseudonyms 'Nil' and 'Dr Nil', and published four collections of verse, *Irish Lords and Other Verses* (1912), *To Many Ladies and Others* (1917), *The Mallee Fire and Other Verses* (1923) and *The Lonely Rose and Other Verses* (1935). Souter wrote bush ballads and sea shanties as well as lyrical verse. His bush ballads, which reflect the daily life of the small farms of SA, are sensitive to the experience and idiom of a wide range of personalities, both male and female. Some of his most memorable are 'Irish Lords', 'Pump'kin Time', 'When the Missus Is Away' and 'Harvestin'. His rhythmic, suitably salty, sea shanties, such as 'What the Red-Haired Bo'sun Said' and 'Blue Peter', are less individual and distinctive but found a ready audience. D.H. Souter

(1862–1935), sometimes mistakenly believed to be related to C.H. Souter, was a long-term *Bulletin* cartoonist and illustrator. His book *The Ticket in Tatts*, edited by Stephan Williams, was published in 1988.

SOUTER, D.H., see **SOUTER, C.H.**

SOUTER, Gavin (1929–), born Sydney, joined the staff of the *Sydney Morning Herald* after graduating from the University of Sydney in 1948. As a representative of the newspaper he spent 1950–51 in New York and 1968–70 in London. He has written a history of the European relationship with New Guinea, *New Guinea – The Last Unknown* (1963); a profile of Sydney, *Sydney* (1965), titled in subsequent reprints *Sydney Observed*, illustrated by George Molnar; an account of the settlements of New Australia and Cosme in Paraguay under the leadership of William Lane, *A Peculiar People* (1968, republished in 1991 with an important postcript by Souter); an autobiography of his childhood in Sydney, NSW and Queensland 1939–45, *The Idle Hill of Summer* (1972); a history of the British–Australian relationship from Federation to 1919, which won the award of the Foundation for Australian Literary Studies, *Lion and Kangaroo* (1976); *Company of Heralds* (1981); *Acts of Parliament* (1988); and the sequel to *Company of Heralds*, *Heralds and Angels: The House of Fairfax 1841–1990* (1991, updated 1992). Written to mark the 150th anniversary of the *Sydney Morning Herald*, *Company of Heralds* is also a socio-historical document, especially significant as an account of the role of the press in Australian political life; it won the 1981 award of the Foundation for Australian Literary Studies. The writing of *Heralds and Angels* coincided with the demise of the Fairfax Company. *Acts of Parliament* traces the history of the federal Parliament's legislature from 1901 to 1988. Souter has won the H.T. Priestley Memorial Medal three times (1968, 1976, 1981).

South-Asian Register, published quarterly in Sydney 1827–28, carried poetry, literary reviews and articles on literary subjects.

South Australian Advertiser, see **Advertiser**

South Australian Chronicle, South Australian Weekly Chronicle, see **Chronicle**

South Australian Gazette and Colonial Register, see **Register**; STEVENSON, George

South Australian Magazine, the first SA literary periodical, was published as a monthly 1841–43. Founded by James Allen, a pioneering SA journalist who was associated with several early Adelaide newspapers and periodicals, it included literary articles, serial fiction and poetry.

South Australian Register, see **Register**

'South of My Days', published in *The Moving Image* (1946), is the poem that chiefly characterises Judith

Wright (q.v.) as the poet of the New England countryside. The poem echoes her affectionate memories of the 'clean, lean hungry country' in which she was born and grew up. It contains, too, fragments of stories from that countryside's pioneer past – drovers and bushrangers, desperate droughts and starving cattle, and the legendary coaches of Cobb & Co.

South Pacific Association for Commonwealth Language and Literature Studies, see **Association for Commonwealth Language and Literature Studies**

SOUTHALL, Ivan (1921–), born Melbourne, left school at the age of 14 to work for the Melbourne *Herald* before joining the RAAF in 1942. In the same year he published at his own expense a collection of short stories for adults, *Out of the Dawn*. Posted to England, he served in Coastal Command, was awarded the DFC, and at the end of 1944 was transferred to RAAF headquarters in London as a writer in the historical section. In 1946 he returned to Melbourne and resumed work as a photo-engraver, but in 1947 gave up his job in favour of casual work that would leave more time for writing. For many years one of Australia's best-known writer of serious children's fiction, whose books have been published in numerous countries and translated into several languages, he has frequently travelled and lectured overseas. Southall's first nine books for children, which form a series published in 1950–61, centre on an incredibly courageous, resourceful and stoical airman Simon Black (*Meet Simon Black, Simon Black in Peril, . . . in Space, . . . in Coastal Command, . . . in China, . . . and the Spaceman, . . . in the Antarctic, . . . Takes Over, . . . at Sea*). *Hills End* (1962), his next children's book, is a complete departure from his previous work and reflects a strong interest in the real-life problems, emotions and experiences of young people. The many novels that follow *Hills End* have continued to explore this vein of realism; they include *Ash Road* (1965), *The Fox Hole* (1967), *To the Wild Sky* (1967), *Sly Old Wardrobe* (1968), *Let the Balloon Go* (1968), *Finn's Folly* (1969), *Chinaman's Reef is Ours* (1970), *Bread and Honey* (1970, also published with the title *Walk a Mile and Get Nowhere*), *Josh* (1971), *Over the Top* (1972), also published as *Benson Boy* (1973), *Head in the Clouds* (1972), *Seventeen Seconds* (1973), *Matt and Jo* (1973), *Fly West* (1974), *What about Tomorrow* (1977), *King of the Sticks* (1979), *The Golden Goose* (1981), *The Long Night Watch* (1983), *A City Out of Sight* (1984, a sequel to *To the Wild Sky*), *Christmas in the Tree* (1985), *Rachel* (1986), *Blackbird* (1988) and *The Mysterious World of Marcus Leadbeater* (1990). Southall has also published several non-fiction books for young people. Much of Southall's fictional and non-fictional writing for children has links with the books he has written for adults, especially those that derive from his wartime experiences, *They Shall Not Pass Unseen* (1956), a popular history of 461 Squadron, RAAF; *Bluey Truscott* (1958), a memoir of one of Australia's most famous air aces; and *Softly Tread the Brave* (1960), an account of the work of mine-disposal officers. Southall also drew on these experiences for six adventure stories for adults published in his War in the Air series 1958–60. His other writing for adults includes a biography of Godfrey Hirst, *The Weaver from Meltham* (1950) and an account of missionary work in the outback, *Parson on the Track* (1962). Some of his lectures on writing for children were collected in 1975, titled *A Journey of Discovery*. Southall has received numerous awards in Australia, the USA and Europe; they include the Children's Book of the Year Award in 1966, 1968, 1971 and 1976, and the Picture Book of the Year Award in 1969; in 1971 he was awarded the British Library Association Carnegie Medal, in 1972 the Zilver Griffell of Holland, in 1974 the Australian Writers' Award and in 1988 the USA Child Study Committee Book of the Year (for *Rachel*). In 1981 he was made AM.

Southall combines an outstanding ability to identify with and to realise the thoughts, feelings and agonies of childhood and adolescence with a gift for evoking suspense in scenes of gripping action. A realist who deals frankly with contemporary and universal problems ranging from physical disability to psychological instability and emotional inadequacy, he makes few concessions to his youthful audience. His first three serious books for children, *Hills End, Ash Road* and *To the Wild Sky*, form a group in that they are all about groups of children who face disaster without adult help and with varying degrees of success; in all of them the central theme is the growth to maturity. *Finn's Folly* is an even more harrowing and probing story of disaster in which three adults are killed in a road accident, a foggy hillside is made treacherous with overturned drums of deadly cyanide and a mentally retarded boy wanders without protection. *Chinaman's Reef Is Ours* explores love-hate relationships in a dying mining town. *The Fox Hole* concentrates on a tense drama between a frightened child and his greed-crazed uncle. *Let the Balloon Go*, which was produced as a film in 1975 and is a compelling story of a handicapped boy's bid for independence, is the first of a series of studies of individual growth towards adulthood, which include *Bread and Honey, Josh, What About Tomorrow, King of the Sticks* and *The Mysterious World of Marcus Leadbeater*. With *Josh, Head in the Clouds, Matt and Jo* and *Over the Top* Southall explores a new vein of humour. See also *The Oxford Companion to Australian Children's Literature* (1993), pp. 395-7.

Southerly, the quarterly journal of the Sydney branch of the English Association (q.v.), was founded in 1939 under the editorship of R.G. Howarth and A.G. Mitchell; Howarth was sole editor 1945–55 and subsequent editors have been Kenneth Slessor (1956–61), Walter Stone (1962), G.A. Wilkes (1963–87) and Elizabeth Webby (1988–). In its early years it gave coverage to English and American literature but from 1944, when Angus & Robertson (publishers 1944–71) became involved in its production, it gave increasing attention to Australian writing; from Slessor's editorship it has been subtitled *A Review of Australian Literature*. *Southerly* publishes creative work, chiefly short stories and poetry, as well as criticism and reviews. Apart from 1960, when no issues appeared, *Southerly* has continued to play a significant part in the study of Australian literature, particularly through its contribution to the establishment of a body of criticism on significant Australian writers such as C.J. Brennan, 'Henry Handel Richardson' and Patrick White. It sponsors the H.M. Butterly F. Earle-Hooper Award, named after two active members of the English Association, for the best *Southerly* contribution in creative writing or literary criticism by a writer who is not yet established. Its fiftieth anniversary issue (1989) includes many articles that illustrate its importance to Australian literature over half a century, including S.E. Lee's history of *Southerly* 1942–89. The issue No. 3, 1991, edited by Webby and Ivor Indyk, titled *Memory*, took a retrospective look at Australian literature over the course of *Southerly*'s existence.

Southern Australian, an early SA newspaper, was published weekly and semi-weekly 1838–51. Founded soon after the establishment of the colony of SA in response to the anti-gubernatorial views expressed by George Stevenson (q.v.) in the *South Australian Gazette*, it changed its title to the *South Australian* in 1844.

Southern Cross (1), a notable constellation in the southern heavens, whose four chief stars are in the shape of a cross, was first described as a 'cross' shape by Andrea Corsali in 1517 and first officially segregated and named *Crux* by the astronomer Royer in 1679. Five of the stars of the constellation are represented on the flag of the Commonwealth of Australia. The Southern Cross has been frequently evoked or used as a nationalistic title.

Southern Cross (2) is the name of the flag hoisted by the rebellious diggers of the Eureka stockade (q.v.). Raffaello Carboni in his *The Eureka Stockade* (1855) describes the flag as 'silk, blue ground, with a large silver cross, similar to the one in our southern firmament; no device of arms, but all exceedingly chaste and natural'. Len Fox (q.v.) gives an account of the flag's history in *The Strange Story of the Eureka Flag* (1963); Louis Esson called his Eureka play *The Southern Cross* (1946).

Southern Cross: A Magazine for the People, a monthly journal published in Sydney and edited in succession by Maxwell Keely and Charles Turner, ran 1898–1900. It included some general literary articles and original poetry and short stories.

Southern Cross: A Weekly Journal of Politics, Literature and Social Progress, founded and edited by Daniel Deniehy (q.v.) as a vehicle for his political and literary ideas, was published in Sydney and ran 1859–60. Apart from Deniehy (whose well-known prose satire, *How I Became Attorney-General of New Barataria*, was first published in the *Southern Cross* in 1860), other well-known contributors included Charles Harpur, R.H. Horne and William Forster.

Southern Lights and Shadows: Brief Notes of Three Years' Experience of Social, Literary, and Political Life in Australia was written by Frank Fowler (q.v.) while returning to England from Australia in 1858 and was published in 1859. Fowler records his experiences of life in Sydney; compares Sydney and Melbourne, to the latter city's advantage; gives a series of brief comments on the colonial press of the day; vividly describes such characters as bullock-drivers, city larrikins and modish young colonial belles; trenchantly criticises the new parliamentary system of self-government; and provides anecdotes from his country travels. Written in haste, *Southern Lights and Shadows* was undoubtedly a 'pot-boiler', pandering to the eager market in England for descriptive works on the colony. Although it was a rather mild document overall and one of the more interesting of the contemporary accounts of Australian life, its errors and exaggerations provoked some criticism and hostility in the colony. Its shortcomings are discussed in the preface to R.H. Horne's *Australian Facts and Prospects* (1859).

SOUTHEY, Robert, see **Convict in Australian Literature**

Span, see **Association for Commonwealth Language and Literature Studies**

SPEARS, Steve J. (1951–), born Adelaide, studied law at the University of Adelaide before deciding to follow a career in theatre. He has published eight plays, *Africa – A Savage Musical* (produced 1974), *Mad Jean* (produced 1978) and *People Keep Giving Me Things* (published with the preceding two plays in *Early Works*, 1978); *The Elocution of Benjamin Franklin* (q.v.) in *Drag Show* (1977); *The Resuscitation of the Little Prince Who Couldn't Laugh as Performed by Young Mo at the Height of the Great Depression of 1929* (or *Young Mo*) in *Theatre-Australia* (1977); *King Richard* in *Three Political Plays* (1980), ed. Alrene Sykes; *Glory* (1988); and *Froggie* (1988). His other plays, some of which have been performed in the USA, include 'Stud' (1973), 'Eliza Q' (1975), 'There Were Giants in Those Days' (1978), 'The Death of George Reeves' (1979), 'Friends of the Family' (1980) and 'When They Send Me Three-and-Fourpence' (1982). Spears has also written for radio and television and worked as an actor; founding member of the Balmain Boys cabaret troupe, he has appeared in the production *Balmain Boys Don't Cry* and in the films *Mad Max II* and *The Empty Beach*. He has won several literary prizes including three Awgies and one Off-Broadway Award.

An innovative and lively playwright, Spears is at home in a wide range of theatrical modes from vaudeville to naturalism. The protagonists of 'The Death of George Reeves' and 'There Were Giants in Those Days' are the larger-than-life cartoon-strip characters Batman, Superman and Wonderwoman, whom Spears reveals as privately human and limited; *Young Mo* (produced in 1976), re-creates the life and personality of the famous Australian comic, Roy Rene; *King Richard* (produced in 1978), part-thriller, part-farce, part-political satire, focuses on a confrontation between a convicted murderer and a State premier, which reveals their basic similarity. But Spears is best known for his one-actor play *The Elocution of Benjamin Franklin* (first produced in 1976), a complex study of a middle-aged transvestite, which has been widely staged in Australia as well as in London, New York and San Francisco, and which won the National Critics' Award of Cleveland, Ohio. *Glory*, a play for two female actors, centres on the death of 75-year-old Gloria, suffering from Alzheimer's disease. *Froggie*, a black comedy and a version of a familiar fairy-tale, concerns an armless man who grows arms for the woman he loves. Spears has also published a series of autobiographical essays, *In Search of the Bodgie* (1989); and collaborated in writing books for young readers based on his screen plays *The Big Wish* (1990, with John Hepworth) and *Mr Edmund* (1990, with Tom Shapcott).

Spectator was the title of four Australian journals. Richard Thompson's *Spectator*, with original verse and reviews, was published weekly in 1846; the *Spectator: Journal of Literature and Art*, published fortnightly 1858–59, was edited by Cora Anna Weekes; the *Spectator*, edited by Edward Langton, contained articles on political and literary topics as well as original prose and verse and ran monthly 1865–67. In 1900–5, the *Spectator*, a WA weekly, was published and edited by R.C. Spear, carried short fiction, verse, book reviews and literary comment, and was illustrated with satirical cartoons by Ben Strange.

Speewah (Speewaa, Speewa), the home of great men and tall tales, was a mythical station in Australian folklore from about 1870 to the 1950s. Ernestine Hill places it near Swan Hill on the Murray River, but it has also been located by other writers in Queensland and the Kimberleys. Its chief character is Crooked Mick of the Speewah who, though no giant by Speewah standards, often uses Ayers Rock to 'stone the crows'. Other celebrities of the Speewah are Big Bill and Slabface Joe. Crooked Mick features in Alan Marshall's story, 'They were Tough Men on the Speewah', in *How's Andy Going* (1956), in Julian Stuart's anecdotes in the *Australian Worker* in the 1920s, and in Bill Wannan's *Crooked Mick of the Speewah* (1956). David Campbell included a poem, 'The Speewah Picnics', in *The Miracle of Mullion Hill* (1956). The comic strip *Speewa Jack*, written by Alan Marshall and drawn by Doug Tainsh, ran in the *Argus* 1954–57, and later briefly in the *Age*. Its central character, Speewa Jack, was noted for his tall stories, many of which related to the goldfields and bushranging days.

SPENCE, Catherine Helen (1825–1910), born near Melrose, Scotland, where she was educated, migrated to SA with her family in 1839. She became a governess at 17, largely because she felt that experience as a teacher would advance her literary ambitions. In 1854 she published anonymously *Clara Morison: A Tale of South Australia during the Gold Fever* (q.v.), a novel she described as 'more domestic than exciting'. In 1856 she

published, also anonymously, a second novel, *Tender and True: A Colonial Tale*. Her interest in social reform, which first expressed itself in her disaffection with the existing electoral system, began in 1858 after she had read an article by John Stuart Mill on proportional representation. In 1861 she published *A Plea for Pure Democracy*, which advocated the Thomas Hare system of proportional representation. The first novel under her own name, *Mr. Hogarth's Will*, which had been earlier serialised as 'Uphill Work' in the Adelaide *Weekly Mail* in 1863–64, was published in 1865. It was followed in 1868 by *The Author's Daughter*, which had been published serially as 'Hugh Lindsay's Guest' in the Adelaide *Observer* in 1867. Among her continuing social concerns were the removal of destitute children from institutions into normal homes and the provision of increased educational opportunities for the very young and for adolescent girls; such concerns were expressed in the articles published in the *Register* in 1878 as 'Some Social Aspects of South Australian Life'. Her social commentary, *The Laws We Live Under* (1880), became the first civics or social studies textbook to be used in Australian schools. In 1881–82 her novel *Gathered In* (q.v.) was serialised in the *Observer* but was not published in book form until 1977. Another novel, *Handfasted* (1984), was unpublished in her lifetime, its themes and sentiments considered too advanced for the time. In 1884 she published, anonymously, *An Agnostic's Progress from the Known to the Unknown*, an allegorical work which is also part-autobiography, reflecting the shift from Calvinism to Unitarianism, which brought her relief from the religious despondency of her early life. *A Week in the Future*, serialised in the *Centennial Magazine* in 1888–89 and republished in monograph form in 1987, was probably her last fictional work, although indications of other writings exist. Her public participation in social causes then became more pronounced. She made lecture tours of the USA and Britain speaking on the inequalities of the voting system; helped to form the Effective Voting League of SA; became Australia's first female political candidate in the federal convention elections of 1897; was vice-president of the Women's Suffrage League of SA; and helped establish a SA branch of the National Council of Women. A Catherine Spence Prize for the best woman student in economics has been annually awarded at the University of Adelaide, and the SA government awards an annual social sciences scholarship in her name.

More emphasis is usually placed on Spence's role as pioneer feminist and social reformer than on her literary achievements, but with *Clara Morison*, which Frederick Sinnett in 1856 judged 'decidedly the best Australian novel we have met with', and with *Gathered In* she made a considerable contribution to colonial Australian fiction. Her *Autobiography*, which she began and which was completed after her death by her companion, Jeanne F. Young, was published in 1910. Jeanne F. Young also published *Catherine Helen Spence: A Study and an Appreciation* (1937). Helen Thomson has edited *Clara Morison* and other writings by Spence in the then Portable Australian Authors series (1987), Elizabeth Gunton has compiled a bibliography

(1967) and Susan Magarey has written a biography, *Unbridling the Tongues of Women* (1985).

SPENCE, Eleanor (1928–   ), a well-known children's writer, and author of *The October Child* (1976, winner of the CBC Book of the Year Award in 1977 and included in the Honours List of the International Board on books for Young People in 1978), also wrote an autobiography, *Another October Child* (1988). Spence's writing for children is described in *The Oxford Companion to Australian Children's Literature* (1993), pp. 397–8.

SPENCE, W.G. (William Guthrie) (1846–1926), born in the Orkney Islands, Scotland, came to Australia in 1853. A miner on the Victorian goldfields from an early age, he was prominent in labour affairs and became general secretary of the Amalgamated Miners' Association, president of the Amalgamated Shearers' Union and a conspicuous figure in the maritime strike of 1890 and the Queensland shearers' strike of 1891. He became general secretary of the AWU in 1894; in 1898 he was elected to the NSW Legislative Assembly and in 1901 to the Commonwealth parliament. Spence wrote the *History of the A.W.U.* (1911) and *Australia's Awakening: Thirty Years in the Life of an Australian Agitator* (1909), which gives an interesting if biased view of social conditions in Australia at the end of the nineteenth century. Spence also became known in bush society, via a bush ballad by F.J. Murray, as the owner of a mythical station, Spence's Station; it was an attempt by rural landowners to present him to his followers as a man of property.

SPENCER-BROWNE, Reginald (1856–1943), born Appin, NSW, joined the staff of the *Brisbane Courier* in 1882, after a period as sub-editor of the *Townsville Herald* and editor of the *Cooktown Herald*. As associate editor of the *Queenslander*, he encouraged the work of the poet George Essex Evans. Commissioned in the Queensland Mounted Infantry in 1887, he had risen to major before the outbreak of the Boer War, in which he served with distinction. He later devoted much of his time to Queensland's light horse regiments, and in 1915 joined the AIF as colonel and saw action at Gallipoli, before being 'retired' to command of the Australian training depots in Egypt and England. He was formally retired in 1921 as honorary major-general and in his later years became a famous Queensland identity. He published a series of bush and mining yarns, *Romances of the Goldfield and Bush* (1890); two collections of poetry, *Shadow and Shine* (1874) and *The Last Ride* (1875); and reminiscences, *A Journalist's Memories* (1927), previously published in the *Courier* and invaluable as a source for the history of Queensland.

SPENCER, T.E. (Thomas Edward) (1845–1911), born London, visited Australia at 18 and returned in 1875 to settle in Sydney, where he became a building contractor and a prominent figure in industrial arbitration. He is best known for his humorous ballads, several of which, e.g. 'How M'Dougall Topped the Score' (q.v.), 'Why Doherty Died' and 'O'Toole and McSharry', have become familiar recitation pieces. His ballads, frequently contributed to the *Bulletin*, appeared in two collections, *How M'Dougall Topped the Score and Other Verses and Sketches* (1906) and *Budgeree Ballads* (1908), reprinted in 1910 as *Why Doherty Died*. He also published a novel, *Bindawalla* (1912), and short stories, most of which deal with the experiences of another popular character, a loquacious Irish-Australian lady, Mrs Bridget McSweeney, *The Surprising Adventures of Mrs Bridget McSweeney* (1906), *A Spring Cleaning and Other Stories by Mrs Bridget McSweeney* (1908), *The Haunted Shanty* (1910) and *That Droll Lady* (1911).

SPENCER, Sir Walter Baldwin (1860–1929), born Lancashire, England, became the first professor of biology at the University of Melbourne in 1887. He joined the W.A. Horn expedition into Central Australia in 1894 and met his future collaborator, Francis James Gillen (1856–1912), who for twenty years had worked with the Arunta tribes among whom he was accepted as an initiate. Spencer and Gillen subsequently lived with the Arunta and allied tribes for lengthy periods and were permitted to observe their sacred ceremonies, previously unwitnessed by Europeans. The results of their studies were published in 1899, titled *The Native Tribes of Central Australia*. Later they spent a year studying the Warramunga and more northerly tribes, which resulted in *The Northern Tribes of Central Australia* (1904). Spencer made further investigations after Gillen's death, visiting Central Australia in 1923 and 1924, and published a revision and extension of his earlier work with Gillen, *The Arunta* (1927). Spencer also published *Native Tribes of the Northern Territory of Australia* (1914) and two more popular accounts of his work, with Gillen, *Across Australia* (1912) and *Wanderings in Wild Australia* (1928). The journal of Spencer's last expedition to Tierra del Fuego, where he died, was published in 1931, edited by R.R. Marett and T.K. Penniman, *Spencer's Last Journey*. A man of wide interests, Spencer co-edited the *Australasian Critic* in 1890 with the classicist T.G. Tucker and as trustee and vice-president of the National Gallery of Victoria encouraged the work of Australian artists, many of whom, such as the Lindsay brothers, Streeton and Roberts, were his personal friends. D.J. Mulvaney and J.H. Calaby have written his biography, *'So Much that is New': Baldwin Spencer 1860–1929* (1985). A selection from about 1800 photographs taken by Spencer 1894–1926 was published in 1982 as *The Aboriginal Photographs of Baldwin Spencer*.

SPENDER, Dale (1943–   ), born Newcastle, is a prominent feminist, who has published over thirty books and is the founder of numerous women's publishing ventures. She was educated at the universities of Sydney, Wollongong and New England before spending over a decade in Britain, where she gained her doctorate and taught women's studies at the Institute of Education, University of London. Her publications include *The Spitting Image: Reflections on*

Language, Education and Social Class (1976, with Garth Boomer), *Man Made Language* (1980), *Women of Ideas and What Men Have Done to Them* (1982), *Invisible Women: The Schooling Scandal* (1982), *There's Always Been a Women's Movement this Century* (1983), *Scribbling Sisters* (1984, with Lynne Spender), *For The Record: The Making and Meaning of Feminist Knowledge* (1985), *Mothers of the Novel* (1986), *Writing a New World: Two Centuries of Australian Women Writers* (1988), and *The Writing or the Sex?* (1989). She is also the editor of the collections *Learning to Lose* (1980, with Elizabeth Sarah), *Men's Studies Modified* (1981), *Feminist Theorists* (1983), *The Penguin Anthology of Australian Women's Writing* (1988), *Heroines* (1991) and *Living by the Pen* (1992), and co-editor of the collections *The Knowledge Explosion* (1992, with Cheris Kramarae) and *Life-Lines: Australian Women's Letters and Diaries 1788–1840* (1992, with Patricia Clarke). She is a niece of the politician Sir Percy Spender.

SPIELVOGEL, Nathan (1874–1956), born Ballarat, worked as a teacher in rural areas of Victoria and at Ballarat and contributed short stories, sketches and verse to the *Lone Hand*, the *Bulletin* and other newspapers. Many of his short stories dealing with Jewish life in Ballarat appeared regularly in the Jewish press, the *Bulletin*, the *Dimboola Banner* and other newspapers under such pseudonyms as 'Genung', 'Eko', 'Ato' and 'Ahaswar'; some were collected in *Selected Stories of Nathan Spielvogel* (1956). His impressions of Europe during a lengthy visit, titled *A Gumsucker on the Tramp* (1905), ran into four printings and was followed by *The Gumsucker at Home* (1913). Spielvogel also published sketches of school life and farming, set mainly in the Wimmera district, *The Cocky Farmer* (1907); a series of sketches dealing with the experiences of an unorthodox schoolmaster, *Old Eko's Note-Book* (1930); a collection of verse, *Our Gum Trees* (1913); several brief histories of Ballarat's institutions as well as a general history of the city (1935); a popular account of the Eureka rebellion, *The Affair at Eureka* (1928); and a ballad, *The Call of the Wandering Jew* (1940). Some of Spielvogel's articles and talks for radio have been published in two volumes (1974 and 1981), titled the *Spielvogel Papers*.

'Spinifex', the name of a creeping, salt-tolerant grass that is abundant on Australian seashores, is also popularly used to denote the tussock grass that covers much of the inland. Sometimes used as a pseudonym by writers, e.g. Alfred Chandler and David Martin, 'spinifex' was also used in the titles of books, especially about WA, e.g. D.W. Carnegie's *Spinifex and Sand: A Narrative of Five Years' Pioneering and Exploration in Western Australia* (1898).

Spinner (1924–27), a monthly poetry magazine, was published in Melbourne, edited by R.A. Broinowski. Numerous poets of the time, including Dorothea McKellar, Zora Cross, Mary Gilmore, Louis Lavater and 'Furnley Maurice', were contributors to the magazine, which also included brief reviews, biographical notes and photographs. Issues of *The Spinner* were also reprinted as annual volumes 1925–27, titled *Poetry in Australasia*.

Springwood, a residential centre and tourist resort in the Blue Mountains area of NSW, was named by Governor Macquarie. It was the home of Norman Lindsay from 1912 until his death in 1969. The grounds of his property, which was actually owned by his wife, Rose Lindsay, and is set in 10 hectares of bush, were landscaped by Lindsay himself and decorated with many of his sculptures to express his dream of an Australian Arcadia. After Lindsay died the property became part of the National Trust and in 1973 was officially titled the Norman Lindsay Gallery and Museum. The house contains a representative collection of pencil and pen drawings, etchings, watercolours, oil paintings, books, ship models and statuary, bequeathed by Lindsay to the nation.

SPUNNER, Suzanne, see **Feminism and Australian Literature**

'Squatter' is a word which probably derived from the American term 'to squat', meaning to settle on unclaimed land without a title. The term has now gone out of general use, the modern approximation being 'grazier' or 'pastoralist'. When first used around the 1830s, 'squatter' was a derogatory term applied mainly to convicts who settled on unoccupied land on the outskirts of the settlement. By the 1840s it was used to describe all those who grazed stock beyond the borders of the Nineteen Counties proclaimed by Governor Darling as the limits of settlement. By the end of the 1860s the squattocracy was firmly established in spite of the bitter political struggles of the 1850s and 1860s and the passing of various Selection and Land Acts aimed at producing more equable land distribution. Thereafter 'squatter' became, and remained, something of a class term, denoting wealth and power. The squatters did not, however, succeed in fulfilling W.C. Wentworth's 1853 ambition of establishing a colonial peerage based on 'our Shepherd Kings'; that proposal was ridiculed out of existence by Daniel Deniehy's derisive comments about a 'bunyip aristocracy'. Notable among the many squatters' memoirs and reminiscences are W.A. Brodribb's (q.v.) *Recollections of an Australian Squatter* (1883), E.M. Curr's (q.v) *Recollections of Squatting in Victoria* (1883) and James Kirby's *Old Times in the Bush of Australia* (q.v., 1895). Notable fictional squatters include the Bractons in *The Emigrant Family* (1849), the Buckleys in *The Recollections of Geoffry Hamlyn* (1859), the Delacys in *All That Swagger* (1936), the Mazeres and Pooles in the 'Brent of Bin Bin' (q.v.) novels, Stewart of Kooltopa in *Such is Life* (1903) and the Cabells in *Landtakers* (1934) and *Inheritors* (1936).

The squatter is frequently an unpopular figure in literature. One of the earliest expressions of distaste for his greed is Charles Harpur's sonnet 'On the Political and Moral Condition of Australia in 1845'. He is pictured as arrogant, ruthless, avaricious and miserly, the implacable enemy of the small selectors in the many selection stories of 'Steele Rudd' and Henry Lawson;

of swagmen down on their luck in Lawson's stories and in poems such as A.B. Paterson's 'Waltzing Matilda'; or of travelling drovers like Saltbush Bill (q.v.) who wage ceaseless battles with squatters like Stingy Smith. In Henry Kingsley's fiction, in some of the station romances of Rosa Praed (q.v.) and in the novels of Miles Franklin, the representation of the squatter is much more favourable.

A factual account of the squatting era in Queensland and the Kimberleys is given in Mary Durack's *Kings in Grass Castles* (1959) and in Victoria in Margaret Kiddle's *Men of Yesterday* (1961). The early development of squatting is outlined in S.H. Roberts's *The Squatting Age in Australia 1835–1847* (1935). Geoffrey Dutton wrote *The Squatters: An Illustrated History of Australia's Pastoral Pioneers* (1985).

Squatter's Dream, The, a novel by 'Rolf Boldrewood' (q.v.), was first published as a serial in the *Australian Town and Country Journal* in 1875; radically changed, it was published as *Ups and Downs* (1878), 'Boldrewood's' first book, and republished under the original title in 1890. *The Squatter's Dream* is strongly autobiographical: the experiences of its hero, Jack Redgrave, who sells his cattle-run, Marshmead, and suffers a decline in fortune are similar to those of 'Boldrewood', who after selling his Victorian run, Squattlesea Mere, in 1861 failed on two sheep stations and was forced to go droving. In the serial version Jack wakes up to find himself at Marshmead, with the sale advertisement on the table before him unposted; in the novel version he completes the sale, buys a bigger station, fails on it, but eventually recoups his fortunes sufficiently to buy back Marshmead.

STABLE, J.J., see **Anthologies**

'STANDBY', see **PORTEOUS, R.S.**

STANLEY, Owen (1811–50), a Royal Navy officer, commanded HMS *Britomart* in the expedition to effect a settlement at Port Essington in 1838, and HMS *Rattlesnake* in its coastal survey of New Guinea 1846–50. His name is commemorated in the Owen Stanley range of New Guinea. A significant artist, Stanley recorded the Port Essington expedition in valuable sketch-books. The original *Narrative of the Voyage of H.M.S. Rattlesnake* was edited by John MacGillivray in 1852. Marnie Bassett has published *Behind the Picture: H.M.S. Rattlesnake's Australia–New Guinea Cruise 1846 to 1850* (1966); Adelaide Lubbock has written the biography *Owen Stanley R.N.* (1968).

STANNER, W.E.H. (William Edward Hanley) (1905–81), born Sydney and educated at the University of Sydney and the London School of Economics, was professor of anthropology at the ANU 1964–70 and was made emeritus professor in 1971. An influential interpreter of Aboriginal culture and its interaction with Australia's European heritage, he published among other books in his field, *On Aboriginal Religion* (1964), *White Man Got No Dreaming: Essays 1938–73* (1979) and *After the Dreaming*, the Boyer lectures he

delivered in 1968 and first published that year but frequently reprinted.

Starlight, Captain is the Byronic hero of mysterious but aristocratic origins in 'Rolf Boldrewood's' bushranging classic *Robbery Under Arms* (1888), and the leader of the bushranging gang briefly mentioned in Adam Lindsay Gordon's poem 'The Sick Stockrider'. The popularity of 'Boldrewood's' novel and the dramatic adaptation of it by Alfred Dampier (1890) have led to much speculation about the model for Starlight; Dampier recorded that after stage performances of *Robbery Under Arms* he was several times approached by men claiming to be the original. Although Frank Pearson (1837–99) had been active as the bushranger 'Captain Starlight' in the Bourke district in 1868, it is unlikely that he was the model. 'Boldrewood', whose novel incorporates the experiences of several bushrangers and transposes them to a different historical period, himself claimed that Starlight was a composite character based partly on 'Captain Midnight' and Harry Redford (?1842–1901); a major incident in the novel, in which Starlight's gang steals a mob of cattle and 'overlands' it from Queensland to SA, parallels a similar drive in which Redford was involved in 1870. The Starlight legend is assessed in Frank Clune's *Captain Starlight: Reckless Rascal of 'Robbery Under Arms'* (1945) and in the more definitive *Starlight: The Man and the Myth* (1972) by P.H. McCarthy. A musical, *Captain Starlight*, was produced in 1964 with libretto by Paul Sherman, and published in 1988.

'Station' is a term first recorded in 1815 to describe an area inland from the settlement at Port Jackson where government stock were grazed. From the 1820s it began to be accepted as any tract of land on which privately owned sheep or cattle were grazed under the supervision of an overseer. It came into later general use to denote a large pastoral property, and many compounds were formed to give additional detail, e.g. 'head station', 'back station'. The term was widely used in fictional and factual accounts of the colony, e.g. Rosa Praed's novels *The Head Station* (1885) and *The Romance of a Station* (?1889). Samuel Mossman and Thomas Banister's *Australia, Visited & Revisited* (q.v., 1853) has chapters on 'A Sheep Station' and 'A Cattle Station', as has Alexander Forbes's *Voices from the Bush* (1869); A.B. Paterson's poem 'A Mountain Station' describes the difficulties of coping with the problems of the pastoral life. Large and well-known stations include Victoria Downs (written of by Jock Makin in *Big Run*, 1970, frequently reprinted) and Wave Hill in the Northern Territory, Bowen Downs and Barcaldine in Queensland (written of by Margaret Reeves in *A Strange Bird on the Lagoon*, 1985) and Thylungra and Kyabra in the Cooper's Creek area; perhaps the best-known in literature are the Elsey, of Jeannie Gunn's *We of the Never-Never* (q.v., 1908), and Billabong, in the children's novels of Mary Grant Bruce (q.v.).

STAUNTON, Madge (1917–), born Coolangatta, Queensland, taught and practised in the visual arts for many years. She did not begin writing until the early

1970s but has contributed poetry to numerous periodicals and has won the Henry Lawson Festival Award twice and the Silver Jubilee Henry Lawson Festival Award in 1982. She has published two collections, *The Cleaving Edge* (1982) and *Heritage of Air* (1984).

STEAD, Christina (1902–83) was born and educated in Australia, but spent the greater part of her life abroad. Her mother died in 1904; her father, David Stead, an eminent naturalist, Fabian socialist, and humanitarian, married for the second time in 1907 and subsequently raised an extensive family. After graduating from Sydney Teachers' College in 1921, Christina Stead taught for some time but resigned in 1924. For the next few years she worked in an office, practising severe economies in order to save her fare to Europe. She left Australia in 1928 not, as she later emphasised, to escape, but to satisfy a wandering impulse and to follow the man with whom she was in love. In 1928–29 she worked in offices in London, fell seriously ill as a result of her previous privations, and wrote *Seven Poor Men of Sydney* (q.v.) as a determined effort 'to leave something behind'. In London she also met her husband, William Blake, a man of diverse gifts who successfully combined banking and Marxism as well as the writing of fiction and works on political economy. They moved to Paris in 1929 and for the next five years Stead worked as a secretary with a French bank, an experience she later put to good use in her novel *House of All Nations*. Her first published work, *The Salzburg Tales*, appeared in 1934, followed a few months later by *Seven Poor Men of Sydney*. Her third book, *The Beauties and Furies*, a story of student life in Paris, appeared in 1936 and *House of All Nations*, written in Spain just before the outbreak of the Civil War, in 1938. The Blakes lived in the USA 1937–47. Three of her novels directly reflect her American experience: *Letty Fox: Her Luck* (1946), *A Little Tea, A Little Chat* (1948) and *The People with the Dogs* (1952). *The Man Who Loved Children* (q.v., 1940), although ostensibly set in the USA, is based on her childhood, and again in *For Love Alone* (q.v., 1944) she draws heavily on her Australian experience. Returning to Europe in 1947, the Blakes travelled widely before settling in 1953 in England, where they remained until William Blake's death in 1968. *Dark Places of the Heart* (New York, 1966), republished the following year in England as *Cotters' England* (q.v.), is Stead's only novel with an exclusively English setting. Her remaining works include a volume of four novellas, *The Puzzleheaded Girl* (1967), and the novels *The Little Hotel* (1973), a reworking of some earlier short stories, *Miss Herbert (The Suburban Wife)* (1976), and *I'm Dying Laughing* (1986), published posthumously and edited by Stead's literary executor, R.G. Geering. Geering also edited her uncollected short stories, *Ocean of Story* (1986), which created something of a furore when it was judged the winner of the Victorian Premier's Award for Fiction in 1986, then was ruled ineligible by the Awards Committee because the author was dead; the award then went to Peter Carey's *Illywhacker*. Stead also edited two anthologies of short stories and translated three diverse French books into English. In 1969 Stead revisited Australia for the first time since 1928 and in 1974 returned to make it her home. A selection of her correspondence, edited by Geering, was published in two volumes in 1992, *A Web of Friendship (1928–1973)* and *Talking into the Typewriter (1973–1983)*.

Until 1965 none of Stead's novels was published in Australia and her long absence and life of travel militated against her formal recognition here and elsewhere. In 1967 she was rejected for the Britannica-Australia Award on the grounds that she had ceased to be Australian, although she received the Patrick White Award in 1974. The critical appreciation of her work has been fitful: from the first her novels received some discerning reviews both in Australia and overseas, but they did not win a more general following until the late 1960s following Randall Jarrell's enthusiastic introduction to a reprint of *The Man Who Loved Children* (1965). Stead's work, now widely taught in Australia and overseas, has stimulated several critical and biographical studies including those by R.G. Geering (1969), Joan Lidoff (1982), Diana Brydon (1987), Susan Sheridan (1988), Kate Stern (1989) and Chris Williams (1989). Hazel Rowley's biography (1993) is a well-researched study, comparable to David Marr's of White in terms of comprehensiveness. The American critic Judith Kegan Gardiner has written the study *Rhys, Stead, Lessing and the Politics of Empathy* (1989).

From the beginning Stead's distinctive quality, which cannot be defined in terms of place, theory or tradition, has intrigued and challenged readers. In form, style, and subject matter her work is experimental. Immediately striking are her strong imaginative power and range, her verbal brilliance, detachment and acute penetration of character. Her concentrated emotional intensity, interest in extraordinary passion, keen sense of the grotesque and use of fantasy have led to comparisons with D.H. Lawrence, Dostoevsky and Dickens, although her singular talent resists comparisons and categories. Both her dramatic scenes and external, physical descriptions are remarkably immediate and particular, but her approach is always inward and emotionally interpretive rather than outward and naturalistic. The irrational world of subconscious emotion is the focus of her interest, not the rational world of the senses. Firmly denying the idea of a 'necessary atmosphere', she described herself as a psychological writer for whom 'personality is a private passion'. Although she possessed firm political convictions, she remained independent of both political and literary theory, approaching her material as a detached, impartial observer, who explores rather than manipulates characters and events.

Her first published work, *The Salzburg Tales* (1934), immediately established the unusual nature of her writing. A group of diverse tales, similar in structure to *The Canterbury Tales* and *The Decameron*, it is a buoyant work which ranges from the supernatural to the legendary, romantic, macabre, naturalistic and satirical. *Seven Poor Men of Sydney* (1934) appeared an anomaly in Australian fiction of the 1930s. Lacking both a conventional plot and a central protagonist, and written in a lyrically meditative manner, it explores the inner lives of a group of casually connected people, who live under the pressure of poverty. In *The Beauties and Furies* (1936) romantic grotesquerie gets somewhat out of hand, but *House of All Nations* (1938) shows firmer control: epic in scale, encyclopaedic in detail, cinematic in form, it is a scathing account of the world of international finance, although once again the eccentricity of private obsession rather than generalised class interest holds the foreground. Radical in her political convictions and well aware of the facts of economic exploitation, Stead consistently avoids the reductions of ideology in her fiction; instead she presents exploitation and ideology as part of the texture of life, private as well as public, meshed as intricately into family relations as into social ones. Nowhere is this more apparent than in her greatest achievement, the autobiographical *The Man Who Loved Children* (1940), an acknowledged masterpiece of twentieth-century fiction. An intensely realised, unsentimental study of a claustrophobic family, this novel revisits the bitter, frustrated and tragi-comic world of childhood, while remaining keenly sensitive to the needs and susceptibilities of its rulers, the adults. Although the emotional growth of the child Louisa charts the contours of the story, sympathy is not reserved for her but extends to all the participants, even to the monstrous, egoistic father, Sam Pollit. Two other novels approach this one in significance: *For Love Alone* (1944) and *Cotters' England* (1966). Her three American novels are lesser works, although characteristically vigorous and penetrating. *Letty Fox: Her Luck* (1946), a lengthy, picaresque novel with a diverse cast of characters, takes up the theme of freedom which figures also in earlier novels; *A Little Tea, A Little Chat* (1948) is interesting for its portrait of another unpleasant male egoist, Robbie Grant; *The People with the Dogs* (1952) is a quieter work, a re-creation of the mellow, communal life of an American country estate. Her last three novels are very different: *Miss Herbert* (*The Suburban Wife*) is a concentrated study of a commonplace personality, *The Little Hotel* a complex exploration of a cross-section of life casually brought together in a Swiss hotel, *I'm Dying Laughing* a subtle study of an American couple's deteriorating marriage and political idealism from the 1930s to the 1950s.

STEELE, Peter (1939–   ), born Perth, was educated there and in Melbourne. A Jesuit priest, he has been provincial superior of the Society of Jesus in Australia and now holds a personal chair in English at the University of Melbourne, where he has taught since 1966. He has published poetry extensively in periodicals and in two collections, *Word from Lilliput* (1973) and *Marching on Paradise* (1984). He has also written several critical works including *Jonathan Swift: Preacher and Jester* (1978), *Expatriates: Reflections on Modern Poetry* (1985), *The Autobiographical Passion: Studies in the Self on Show* (1989) and a study of Peter Porter in the Australian Writers series (1992). A poet with a strong sense of order and balance, Steele links worship of God with passion for language, and poetry with celebration of the divine.

Steele Rudd's Magazine (1904–7) was the first of several journals exploiting the popularity of the 'Steele Rudd' (q.v.), pseudonym of Arthur Hoey Davis. An illustrated monthly, it contained contributions from George Essex Evans, Victor Daley, G.A. Taylor and others as well as from 'Rudd' himself. The journal was subsequently revived as *Steele Rudd's Annual* (1917–23), *Steele Rudd's* (1924–25) and *Steele Rudd's and the Shop Assistant's Magazine* (1926–27). Although dominated by 'Rudd's' contributions, many of which also went into his books, it continued to publish other well-known Australian writers and artists.

Steelman, a character in several stories by Henry Lawson (q.v.), was reputedly modelled on a '"commercial traveller" out of Wellington' whom Lawson met during his first visit to NZ in 1893–94; Smith, Steelman's dim-witted and naive offsider, was Lawson's conception of 'the weaker side of myself'. A travelling confidence man who survives on the sharpness of his wits, Steelman is usually triumphant, although his success is only partial in the best-known Steelman story, 'The Geological Spieler'. A bush type and the focus for some of Lawson's best yarns and tall stories, he lacks the complexity of other recurring characters in Lawson's fiction such as Jack Mitchell and Dave Regan.

STELLMACH, Barbara (1930–   ), born Queensland, has written numerous plays, which have been frequently produced. She has published *4 Australian Plays* (1973), which comprises *Dark Heritage*, a three-act drama with a theme of racism; *Dust Is the Heart*, a one-act tragedy which evokes the hardship and loneliness of the outback; *Hang Your Clothes on Yonder Bush*, an award-winning comedy; and *Legend of the Losers*, a chronicle drama based on the legends surrounding the bushranger Frederick Ward (Captain Thunderbolt). Her other published plays are *Not Even a Mouse* (1978), a three-act thriller, and *From the Fourteenth Floor You Can See the Harbour Bridge* (1980). Her unpublished plays include 'The Trysting Tree' (1960), 'Love Song for Opal' (1966), 'The Sooner to Sleep' (1967), 'Time in Balance' (1971), 'The Merry-Go-Round' (1971), 'Shadow on a Stable' (1973), 'One to Chase the Birds Away' (1984), 'The Poor Dead Roses' (1985) and 'The Shadow of the Cross' (1985). She has also published a collection of verse, *Between the Leaves* (1991).

STENHOUSE, N.D. (Nicol Drysdale) (1806–73), born Scotland, graduated from the University of Edinburgh and subsequently practised as a solicitor. A protégé of the book-collector and philosopher Sir William Hamilton, Stenhouse became acquainted with several literary men in Edinburgh, including Thomas De Quincey, with whom he corresponded. In 1839 he emigrated to Sydney, where he set up a legal practice and became the centre of a circle which included numerous writers and intellectuals. In particular, he provided financial and moral support to Daniel Deniehy, Charles Harpur and Henry Kendall and was friendly with Frank Fowler and Richard

Rowe, with whom he associated in the establishment of the periodical *Month*. The owner of an extensive library, he also provided his friends with access to European cultural developments. He exercised a wider influence on colonial society of the 1850s and 1860s through his involvement with the Sydney Mechanics' School of Arts (president 1867–73), the Free Public Library of Sydney, Sydney College, and the University of Sydney (member of the Senate 1869–73). The Stenhouse library is now in the Fisher Library of the University of Sydney. Ann-Mari Jordens in *The Stenhouse Circle* (1979) gives an account of Stenhouse's life and his cultural milieu.

STEPHEN, Harold (1841–89), the son of George Milner Stephen, a lawyer, colonial administrator and convert to spiritualism, and a relation of Sir Leslie Stephen, was born in England and educated in Melbourne and Germany. Editor for a time of *Sydney Punch*, he published three volumes of short stories and novelettes, *The Golden Yankee* (1877), *Saved by a Ring* (n.d.) and *Lily's Fortune* (1886), and edited and contributed to the anthologies *Our Exhibition Annual* (1878) and *Fizz, Home-Made for Christmas Use* (1881), which both include contributions from G.G. McCrae, Henry Kendall and Henry Halloran, and *Our Christmas Budget* (1872). He also wrote an account of the colourful life of his father, *George Milner Stephen and His Marvellous Cures* (1880), and *Vagabonds and Their Dupes* (1879), a reply to 'Julian Thomas' (John Stanley James) who had earlier written an 'exposure' of spiritualism, *Mediums and Their Dupes* (1879).

STEPHENS, A.G. (Alfred George) (1865–1933), born and educated at Toowoomba, Queensland, was in 1880 apprenticed to a Sydney printer and in 1886 admitted to membership of the NSW Typographical Association. In 1888 he returned north to take up an appointment as editor of the *Gympie Miner* after it had been taken over by supporters of Thomas McIlwraith and the Queensland Nationalist Party. Stephens became a leading member of the Gympie Literary Circle, reporting its meetings in the *Miner*. Stephens also edited and largely wrote the *Apostle*, the organ of the local secular association. In a *Miner* editorial in May 1890 on the visit of Henry George, he wrote 'Truth is not in extremes', suggesting the even-handed view of political questions characteristic of his later writings.

At the end of 1890 Stephens went to Brisbane and became sub-editor of the radical *Boomerang*, to which he contributed leaders, features, social jottings, *faits divers* and a regular column, 'The Magazine Rifler', which surveyed the latest numbers of the English and American journals. When he left the *Boomerang* in October 1891 it was in the hands of a liquidator and Stephens received the office bible in lieu of wages. He then joined the staff of the Cairns *Argus*, becoming editor by the end of 1891 and part-owner in 1892. He instituted a literary supplement and ran an essay competition as he had done on the *Miner*. Stephens himself won the prize of £25 in a competition run in conjunction with the North Queensland Separation

League for his essay 'Why North Queensland Wants Separation', later published as a pamphlet in 1893. The essay criticised the control over the north wielded by Brisbane and the south, and attacked the general concepts of political and economic centralisation. In 1893 Stephens finished another polemical essay on Queensland politics, *The Griffilwraith, Being an Independent Criticism of the Methods and Manoeuvres of the Queensland Coalition Government, 1890–1893*. The pamphlet attacked the coalition government of the factions led by Sir Samuel Griffith and Sir Thomas McIlwraith which had ended the two-party system in the legislature. Immediately after the pamphlet's publication, Stephens left on a trip overseas, using funds from the sale of his interest in the *Argus* at the end of 1892. He travelled in America, Canada and Europe. *A Queenslander's Travel Notes*, published on his return to Sydney in 1894, was a collection of the articles he had sent back to Australian journals and newspapers during his trip. Stephens criticised the pretensions and decorums of traditionalist Europe, and in the half of the work devoted to America used the high divorce rate, drug abuse, poverty and crime, side by side with American 'progress' and smugness about its achievements, to define what he saw as the peculiar and contrary American character. At the end of 1893 Stephens was working in Fleet Street for the *Daily Chronicle* when J.F. Archibald offered him a sub-editorship on the Sydney *Bulletin* (q.v.), which he took up in 1894. By that time the *Bulletin* was a major intercolonial publication, and with Archibald's return to the editorship in 1886, it entered a period of high literary consciousness. It encouraged local authors, advocated literary nationalism and promoted a distinctive model of the short story. From the time of his arrival Stephens contributed literary notices and comments, and full-scale articles on George Eliot, Conan Doyle, and the Brontes had appeared in July 1895. In August 1896 the first Red Page (q.v.) appeared, a full-page literary section developed from the prototype 'Books of the Day' and 'Book Exchange' columns, also on the inside front cover, which Stephens conducted from September 1894. Stephens continued his cosmopolitan interests, dividing comment among Australian, American, English and European writers. He frequently called for a greater awareness of overseas trends and standards. 'Is there a single Australian', he asked in January 1897, 'who could pass an examination in Huysmans, Maeterlinck, or Verhaeren?' Stephens's broad views on politics and his international literary tastes were consistent with his favourite critical yardstick, the concept of 'universality'. The concept recurs throughout his writings and indicates an absolute standard of critical appraisal beyond mutable and transitory criteria such as a work's national or moral value.

Stephens was, however, a nationalist critic in that he encouraged and welcomed new *Bulletin* writers as signs that Australian literature was growing toward maturity. Joseph Furphy, Shaw Neilson, Hugh McCrae, Mary Gilmore, Miles Franklin and Roderic Quinn all acknowledged his personal encouragement and guidance, and as controller of the *Bulletin's* publishing division from 1897 Stephens saw most of these writers into print in book form for the first time. Under Stephens the *Bulletin*'s publishing activities were greatly expanded, beginning with Barcroft Boake's *Where the Dead Men Lie and Other Poems* in 1897 and producing twenty-five further volumes over the next nine years. Stephens acted as editor, literary agent and book designer. His editorship saw the publication of the classics *On Our Selection* (1899) by 'Steele Rudd' and *Such Is Life* (q.v., 1903) by Furphy; the *Bulletin* anthologies *The Bulletin Reciter* (1901), *The Bulletin Story Book* (1901) and *A Southern Garland* (1904); and the first volumes of verse by Will Ogilvie, Arthur Adams, Louise Mack, E.J. Brady, W.T. Goodge and Bernard O'Dowd. Stephens's role as editor of the *Bulletin*'s book division alone guarantees him a place of permanent importance in the history of Australian literature.

In 1902 Stephens's own volume of poems, *Oblation*, was published privately, with illustrations by Norman Lindsay. In 1904 he saw through the press two lavish folios of the *Bulletin* artists Phil May and Livingston Hopkins, and a selection of his own essays from the *Bulletin* on social and literary topics, *The Red Pagan*, was issued in the same year under the paper's imprint. The volume expresses some of Stephens's characteristic literary attitudes, including the criterion of universality, the emotional impact necessary in great art, the sexual and racial conditioning of artistic creativity, and the correlation of artistic genius with insanity. Stephens believed that the emotive qualities of poetry derived from a 'female' species of creativity. It has been argued that this made Stephens's poetic preferences lachrymose and led to bias in his selections of the work of Daley and Neilson. His views about the psychopathological origins of artistic creativity were derived from the writings of Havelock Ellis and through the latter from Francis Galton's *Hereditary Genius* (1869) and Cesare Lombroso's *L'Uomo di Genio* (1888). These views underpinned Stephens's emphasis on biography in his criticism and sometimes precluded from high praise writers who lacked the correct racial or temperamental qualifications.

In 1906 Stephens left the *Bulletin*. Archibald had stood down as editor in favour of James Edmond in 1902, and Stephens's relations with William Macleod, its former artist and now business manager, were prickly. He had also fallen out with Henry Lawson and Norman Lindsay. Stephens had a bluff, dogmatic side to his personality which sometimes irked acquaintances and which, according to Lindsay in *Bohemians of the Bulletin* (1965), was the reverse side of his emotional temperament. Stephens may also have been dissatisfied with the conditions and limitations of his role at the *Bulletin*. On 1 November 1906 the Red Page announced his departure and the establishment of his business venture, the Bookfellow, a literary bookshop named after the monthly literary magazine he had run for five issues from January 1899. In 1907 Stephens revived the *Bookfellow* (q.v.). Its files contain a high standard of discussion of Australian, English and European contemporary writers and artists. By 1907, however, the magazine and the shop were in trouble, and in June the shop's stock and much of

Stephens's own library were auctioned 'without any reserve'. In 1894 Stephens had married Constance Smith; the couple now had six dependent children, and financial necessity compelled a move to NZ, where Stephens accepted an offer from his old editor, Gresley Lukin, of a job on the Wellington *Evening Post*. Stephens maintained an aloof demeanour at the *Post* and in 1909 returned to Sydney, reviving the *Bookfellow* and working as a freelance journalist. The magazine lasted intermittently until 1925 (partly supported by Mary Gilmore) and fulfilled an important literary role. It provided an outlet for Shaw Neilson, Hugh McCrae and Mary Gilmore, and as he had done at the *Bulletin* Stephens also published books under the paper's imprint. In his last years the stream of Stephens's work hardly abated. He planned future publishing projects, toured NSW and Victoria giving lectures on Australian literature, published another volume of verse, *The Pearl and the Octopus and Other Exercises in Prose and Verse* (?1911) and several pamphlets of his own poems, wrote a novel, *Bill's Idees* (1913), two plays, *The Australian Flower Masque* (1924) and *Capturing the Bushranger* (1924), and edited textbooks and anthologies for Australian schools, as well as producing significant critical studies of Henry Kendall and Christopher Brennan (1928, 1933). Rated by many as Australia's most influential pioneer man of letters, Stephens, especially through his editorial work and his steady stream of authoritative criticism, stimulated the development of Australian writing to a marked degree in the decades spanning the nineteenth and twentieth centuries. Leon Cantrell has edited *A.G. Stephens: Selected Writings* (1978) and Stephens's diary in *Cross Currents* (1981, ed. Bruce Bennett); P.R. Stephensen and Vance Palmer wrote, respectively, the biographical works *The Life and Works of A.G. Stephens* ('The Bookfellow') (1940) and *A.G. Stephens: His Life and Work* (1941). Valerie Lawson's book *Connie Sweetheart: The Story of Connie Robertson* (1990), chiefly about Stephens's daughter Constance Robertson, a well-known Sydney journalist and editor 1917–62, has much interesting personal material on Stephens himself.

DOUG JARVIS

STEPHENS, Alfred Ward (1804–52), born Portsmouth, England, arrived in Sydney in 1829 and joined the *Sydney Gazette*. In 1831 with Frederick Stokes and William McGarvie he established the *Sydney Herald*, later the *Sydney Morning Herald;* by 1836 he was sole editor and proprietor. Under his guidance, and with Edward O'Shaugnessy as leader-writer, the newspaper became an important influence in the struggle for representative government, the cessation of transportation and the more ready accessibility of land for colonists, including security of tenure for squatters. In 1839 Stephens sold the *Herald* back to Stokes and participated, with considerable ill luck, in pastoral activities, dying a virtual pauper.

STEPHENS, Edward James (1846–1931), born London, came to Melbourne in 1853, served an apprenticeship in the printing trade and began a lifelong career in country newspapers by establishing the *Horsham Times* in 1873. Other newspapers which he founded or held an interest in were the *Broken Hill Times*, the *Dimboola Banner*, the *Omeo Telegraph*, the *Warragul News*, the *Yarram Chronicle* and the *Nhill Free Press* and *Nhill Mail*, both of which had published early poems of John Shaw Neilson. By his work in developing the provincial press in the country areas of Victoria, Stephens helped to overcome the isolation of rural communities.

STEPHENS, James Brunton (1835–1902), born Bo'ness near Edinburgh, received a sound Scottish education, including a period at the University of Edinburgh. He was a private tutor and schoolmaster both before and after his migration to Queensland in 1866. Following the publication of several volumes of verse, and to acknowledge his growing literary stature, he was appointed to the civil service, ultimately becoming acting under-secretary to the colonial secretary in Brisbane. After the death of Kendall in 1882 Stephens became the leading literary figure of the period. He contributed both creative works and literary comment to important newspapers and journals, including the *Bulletin;* his poetry appeared in contemporary anthologies such as Douglas Sladen's *A Century of Australian Song* (1888); and he figured prominently in contemporary critical works such as H.G. Turner and Alexander Sutherland's *The Development of Australian Literature* (1898). He attempted fiction, publishing two novels in Scotland as well as *A Hundred Pounds* (1876), an Australian story; he wrote an ineffective drama, *Fayette: Or, Bush Revels* (1892); but his major successes were the poetry *Convict Once* (q.v., 1871), *The Black Gin* (1873), *The Godolphin Arabian* (1873) and *My Chinee Cook* (1902). Despite the contemporary respect for him and the present-day acknowledgement of his undoubted influence on the literary scene during the two decades prior to the end of the nineteenth century, his own poetry now arouses little enthusiasm among readers and critics. He is extensively discussed in H.A. Kellow's *Queensland Poets* (1930); Cecil Hadgraft wrote the biographical study *James Brunton Stephens* (1969). He is the poet featured in Rosa Praed's reminiscences, *My Australian Girlhood* (1902).

STEPHENS, John (1806–50), born Northumberland, England, became a bookseller after leaving school. In 1832 he helped to found the influential antislavery journal the *Christian Advocate*, and after further experience in journalism was engaged by George Fife Angas to write promotional material for the new colony of SA. In 1839 he published *The Land of Promise*, a second edition of the same work titled *The History of the Rise and Progress of the New British Province of South Australia*, and a pamphlet attacking the unfavourable picture of the colony presented by another writer. In 1842 Stephens emigrated to SA, where he founded the *Observer* in 1843, took over the *Register* in 1845 and printed some of the colony's first almanacs as well as his brother Edward's periodical, the *Adelaide Miscellany of Useful and Entertaining Knowledge* (1848–49) which

was succeeded by his own *Stephens's Adelaide Miscellany* (1849).

STEPHENSEN, P.R. (Percy Reginald) (1901–65), a flamboyant and controversial figure known familiarly as 'Inky' Stephensen, was born at Maryborough, Queensland, and spent his early years at Biggenden. He was educated at Maryborough, where he was taught briefly by V. Gordon Childe, and at the University of Queensland, where he was a contemporary of Jack Lindsay and Eric Partridge. Elected Queensland Rhodes Scholar for 1924, Stephensen went to Oxford University where he was a controversial left-wing student, nearly expelled for communist activities. In 1927 he became associated with Lindsay and Jack Kirtley in the publishing activities of the Fanfrolico Press (q.v.) in London. Stephensen's version of his two years as business manager of the press, during which he was also involved in the publication of the *London Aphrodite* (q.v.), is told in *Kookaburras and Satyrs* (1954), although other narratives of the Franfrolico days differ in detail and emphasis. In 1929 he started the Mandrake Press (q.v.), which published D.H. Lawrence; Stephensen had by this time established his reputation as an ebullient conversationalist and after one long meeting with him Lawrence wrote that next morning 'the walls still shook'. Stephensen was also familiar with such well-known figures as Augustus John, Sacheverell Sitwell, Rhys Davies and Aldous Huxley; he is thought to have been the model for Huxley's Cuthbert Arkwright in *Point Counter Point*. The Mandrake Press had collapsed by 1931 and after struggling to support himself in England by freelance literary work, Stephensen returned to Australia late in 1932. He had already collaborated with Walford Hyden in the preparation of the biography *Pavlova* (1931), the first of many works which he co-authored or 'ghosted', and had had published on his own account a translation of Nietzsche (1922), *The Legend of Aleister Crowley* (1930), the life story of Harry Buckland, *Master of Hounds* (1931), the prose or verse texts for three slim, illustrated satires, *The Sink of Solitude* (1928), *Policeman of the Lord* (1928) and *The Well of Sleevelessness* (1929), and a volume of short stories, *The Bushwhackers* (1929). Some of these works reveal a crusading spirit, e.g. *Policeman of the Lord* against censorship and wowserism, while *The Bushwhackers* reflects a nostalgia for Stephensen's bush childhood mixed with social criticism of Australia.

In Australia, Stephensen worked for a year as managing director of the Endeavour Press, a book-publishing outlet of the *Bulletin*, and then established his own company, which published Eleanor Dark, 'Henry Handel Richardson' and other authors before going into liquidation early in 1935. During this period Stephensen met Xavier Herbert, also recently returned from England, whom he helped considerably in the revision of *Capricornia*. Although the exact nature of his assistance to Herbert has been the subject of some dispute, Stephensen clearly deserves much of the credit for finally getting the book into print. An editorial essay on Australian culture published in the *Australian Mercury* (q.v.) in July 1935 brought

Stephensen to the attention of W.J. Miles (q.v.), a successful Sydney businessman who encouraged Stephensen's increasing isolationism, anti-communism and anti-Semitism as well as his already aggressive nationalism and Anglophobia. Miles published *The Foundations of Culture in Australia* (1936, subtitled *An Essay Towards National Self Respect*), an expansion of the *Australian Mercury* editorial which became a significant cultural document of the 1930s, drawing support in particular from Rex Ingamells, Ian Mudie and other Jindyworobak writers. Miles also employed Stephensen to write for the *Publicist* (q.v, 1936–42), an Australia First monthly which espoused the Miles line and published the work of a number of Australian authors. Although the outbreak of war caused the *Publicist* to modify its sympathies towards Germany and Japan, its views were monitored by the government, as were the activities of the Yabber Club and the isolationist Australia First (q.v.) movement, which was formally founded by Stephensen and others later in 1941. In March 1942, Stephensen was one of sixteen Australia First members arrested in Sydney and subsequently interned; he was not released until August 1945. Both Stephensen, portrayed as 'The Bloke', and Australia First, called Australia Free, are caricatured in Herbert's *Poor Fellow My Country*.

After internment, Stephensen lived in Victoria and stayed clear of literary and other controversies for several years, although he continued as a collaborator with Frank Clune (q.v.), with whom he had begun work in the mid-1930s. In 1956 he returned to Sydney to pursue a career mainly as a historical writer and researcher specialising in books on the sea. Apart from his work with Clune, for which he is accorded co-authorship status for *The Viking of Van Diemen's Land* (1954) and *The Pirates of the Brig Cyprus* (1962), he collaborated on several books with the English seamen W.H. Jones and Sir James Bissett, and published on his own account, *Sydney Sails* (1962) and *The History and Description of Sydney Harbour* (1966). His other writings, mainly pamphlets, include *The Life and Works of A.G. Stephens* (1940), with whose career Stephensen identified; *Philip Dimmock: A Memoir of a Poet* (1958); and four volumes of an edition of the poems of 'William Baylebridge' (1961–64). These publications make Stephensen the author, co-author, or acknowledged editor of more than twenty works, and he ghosted many more. Despite his breadth of writing, vigorous style and the historical importance of *The Foundations of Culture in Australia*, he was most influential as a literary and cultural promoter, an iconoclast who did much to put into practice his commitment to Australian writing. His assistance in the publication of *Capricornia* was the best-known example of his commitment. Craig Munro has written a densely researched biography, *Wild Man of Letters: The Story of P.R. Stephensen* (1984), an FAW Award winner which is also a major contribution to the history of publishing in Australia and a significant cultural history; Munro also contributed a new introduction to the 1986 reprint of *The Foundations of Culture in Australia*. Noel Macainsh has included Stephensen in his study of the influence of Nietzsche on Australian writers,

Nietzsche in Australia (1975) and Alister Kershaw has recalled his personality in *The Pleasure of Their Company* (1986).

STEVEN, Alexander Gordon (1865–1923), born London, came to Australia in infancy. He studied medicine at the University of Melbourne, but was prevented by ill health from completing the course. His lyrical, introspective verse appeared in five volumes during his lifetime, *The Witchery of Earth* (1911), *Wind on the Wold* (1914), *Poems* (1918), *Revolt* (1919) and *Lures* (1923), and in a posthumous collected edition, *Collected Poems* (1925), with a foreword by Hugh McCrae.

STEVENS, Bertram (1872–1922), born Inverell, NSW, became a solicitor's clerk in Sydney but abandoned law to become a prolific editor of works on Australian literature and art, in which role he exerted a considerable influence on the development of Australian culture in the first quarter of the twentieth century.

Stevens's first editorial venture was John Farrell's *My Sundowner and Other Poems* in 1904. He then edited George Essex Evans's *The Secret Key and Other Verses* (1906) and *An Anthology of Australian Verse* (1906), which was revised and enlarged in 1909 as *The Golden Treasury of Australian Verse*, one of the first significant Australian anthologies (q.v.). In 1911 he edited, with a memoir, Victor Daley's *Wine and Roses*, and in 1920 an edition of the poems of Henry Kendall. His other editorial works include *The 'Bulletin' Book of Humorous Verses and Recitations* (1920), several anthologies of verse for children, anthologies of verse in collaboration with George Mackaness, and critical and illustrative art works on Norman Lindsay, Arthur Streeton, Conrad Martens, Hans Heysen and others. In 1909–10 Stevens edited the Red Page of the *Bulletin*, in 1907 the first five issues of the *Native Companion*, and in 1912–18 the *Lone Hand*. One of the founders in 1916 of *Art in Australia*, he was involved editorially in it until his death; he was also connected editorially with the journals, *Commerce*, from 1918, and *Home*, from 1920. A founding member of the Dawn and Dusk Club and the Casuals Club, Stevens helped numerous writers in financial and other ways; he attempted with others to rehabilitate Henry Lawson, and assisted the families of John Farrell and Victor Daley after their deaths.

STEVENSON, George (1799–1856), born Berwick-upon-Tweed, England, was an author and editor who produced the first issue of the *South Australian Gazette and Colonial Register* (see *Register*), published in England in 1836. He then went with the first colonists to SA to continue the *Gazette*, which had fallen foul of the government and which became the *South Australian Register* by the time he withdrew from the journal in 1842. In 1845 he founded another *South Australian Gazette and Colonial Register*; from 1847 until it ceased publication in 1852 it was titled the *South Australian Gazette and Mining Register*.

STEVENSON, Robert Louis (1850–94) paid four visits to Australia during the period (1888–94) that he was based in Samoa: February–April and August–September 1890, January–February 1891 and February–April 1893. On each visit his presence was prominently noticed in Australian newspapers; in 1893 he met J.F. Archibald and visited Julian Ashton's artists' camp at Balmoral. There are Sydney Domain scenes in *The Wrecker* (1892), written partly in Australia by Stevenson and his stepson Lloyd Osbourne. Other Stevenson publications associated with Australia are the rare collaborative work *An Object of Pity*, printed in Sydney in 1891, and *Father Damien* (1890), a pamphlet defending the Pacific 'leper Priest' Father Joseph Damien (1841–89) from an attack by a Honolulu missionary; the pamphlet was printed in Sydney after its publication in the *Australian Star* (1890) as 'In Defence of the Dead'. Stevenson, whose associations with Australia are the subject of a pamphlet by George Mackaness (1935), which inaugurated his Australian Historical Monographs series, had real affection for Sydney, although the poor effect it had on his constitution caused him to dub Australia the 'New South Pole'.

STEWART, Douglas (1913–85), born Eltham, Taranaki Province, NZ, came to Australia in 1933, expecting to take up a position as light-verse writer on the *Bulletin* staff. When that position did not eventuate he returned to NZ in 1934, visited England in 1937, then came back to Australia in 1938 to become assistant to Cecil Mann, editor of the Red Page. In 1940 he took over the Red Page and remained its editor until 1961. With the *Bulletin* change of ownership Stewart joined Angus & Robertson as literary editor. He retired from Angus & Robertson in 1971 but actively continued his own literary career, consolidating his reputation as writer and critic.

Stewart's first publications were two volumes of poetry, *Green Lions* (1936) and *The White Cry* (1939). This early poetry is characterised by a delight in the beauty and colour of the NZ landscape and by an exuberance of language. Two small books of wartime verse, *Elegy for an Airman* (1940) and *Sonnets to the Unknown Soldier* (1941), followed. The title poem of the earlier volume commemorates Stewart's boyhood friend Desmond Carter, who was killed in action with the RAF in 1939. Stewart's first 'Australian' book of verse, *The Dosser in Springtime* (1946), contains both lyrics and ballads. The title poem, with its humorous account of an old cave-dweller's arousal by the sight of a girl bathing in a creek, sees Stewart giving expression for the first time to the gently ironic and whimsical strain that became characteristic of his later writing. 'The River' (from *The Dosser*), a poetic meditation on the spiritual and intellectual influences of his NZ boyhood, is one of Stewart's best poems. *Glencoe* (1947) is a sequence of twenty-six ballads based on the infamous slaughter of the Macdonald clan by the Campbells in 1691. *Glencoe* has been praised for its sustained and dramatic balladry, and applauded for its theme, a protest against barbarity, cruelty and violence in any age. *Sun Orchids* (1952), in addition to numerous small nature

pieces, also contains 'Worsley Enchanted', a sequence of seventeen poems based on Shackleton's Antarctic expedition of 1914. This sequence indicates, as does his verse drama *The Fire on the Snow* (q.v.), his attraction to Antarctic exploration and the explorer-figure (see Voyager). 'Terra Australis', also in *Sun Orchids*, describes a chance meeting between, and a comparison of notes by, two explorer/adventurer idealists, Pedro Fernandez de Quiros, a sixteenth-century Portuguese seaman, and William Lane, the founder of the Utopian socialist colony New Australia in Paraguay. That meeting allows Stewart to reflect, ironically but not too destructively, on the way in which human idealism is often thwarted by the weaknesses of human nature. Commissioned in 1954 to produce a script for a projected film, *Back of Beyond*, Stewart travelled along the Birdsville Track (q.v.) and published his reaction to the desolate Australian interior in a poem sequence of that title. The sequence begins at Marree in SA, 'the corrugated-iron town/ In the corrugated-iron air'; describes such identities as 'The Whipmaker', 'The Afghan', 'The Dogger', and an Aboriginal rainmaker; casts sidelong glances at red desert grasshoppers, dingoes, wild mules, and bicycle lizards; and concludes, 300 miles north, at Birdsville, an undistinguished little desert town, whose glory lies in the fact that Leichhardt and Sturt once trod its dusty street. *The Birdsville Track* (1955) also contains Stewart's customary meticulous observations on small birds, animals, flowers and landscapes. The best of these lyrical re-creations of his visual and spiritual experiences in the Australian landscape are 'Brindabella', 'Spider Gums' and 'The Snow-gum'. Stewart's final volume of poetry, *Rutherford* (1962), emphasises, in Leonie Kramer's phrase, 'intellectual voyagers' rather than the physical explorers of earlier volumes. In the title poem the NZ atomic scientist Rutherford is addressed as 'the great sea-farer of science'. The most ambitious of Stewart's poems, 'Rutherford' examines the problem of the human need to extend the spirit and intellect to their fullest, even when the consequences are unforeseeable. The poem decides that there is no choice but to accept the destiny inherent in searching, restless human nature. 'The Silkworms' (q.v.), from *Rutherford*, is widely regarded as Stewart's finest individual poem, both for its sensitive and imaginative insight and for its perfect fusion of technique and theme. Stewart's *Selected Poems* was published in 1963 as *Australian Poets: Douglas Stewart*, other editions appearing in 1966 and 1973, the 1973 edition in A & R Modern Poets (reprinted 1993) differing from the earlier two in the Australian Poets series. *Collected Poems 1936–1967* (1967), which Stewart arranged in reverse chronological order, begins with a section 'The Flowering Place' that includes numerous satirical and explorer poems written since *Rutherford* or unpublished in earlier volumes.

Stewart also wrote six verse dramas, four of which were intended as radio plays. *The Fire on the Snow*, his greatest literary success, deals with Captain Robert Scott's tragic expedition to the South Pole in 1912. It was performed on radio by the ABC in 1941, was published in 1944, has been produced and published in many countries, and has been studied by countless Australian schoolchildren. *Ned Kelly* (q.v.), written as a stage play during 1940, had its first performance in an abbreviated form as a radio play in 1942. It follows the affairs of the Kelly gang of bushrangers from the robbery of the Jerilderie bank to their last stand in the hotel at Glenrowan. *The Golden Lover*, first performed on radio in 1943, was published with *The Fire on the Snow* in 1944. Based on the Maori legend of the Golden Lover, the play traces a Maori eternal triangle: Whana, the 'golden lover', chief of the Maori fairy people ('the people of the mist'); Ruarangi, the cuckolded, unimaginative real-life husband; and between them Ruarangi's beautiful, wilful wife, Tawhai. On the husband's side are the conventional forces of family, tribe and traditional morality; the 'golden lover' can call on romance, passion and the lure of the forbidden fruit. Convention wins, and the play's message is that it mostly does, for 'golden lovers' are myths, no part of the world of reality. A warm and humorous play which catches the Maori character and the NZ background, *The Golden Lover* is one of Stewart's most spontaneous and pleasant works. 'The Earthquake Shakes the Land' (performed in 1946) is set against the background of the Maori Wars of the 1840s; *Shipwreck* (1947) is a play based on the bloody events that followed the wrecking of the Dutch ship *Batavia*; *Fisher's Ghost* (1960) is a lighthearted romp around the well-known legend from colonial times (see Fisher's Ghost).

Stewart's published fiction consists of one collection of short stories, *A Girl with Red Hair* (1944), and a handful of other stories in the *Bulletin* and *Coast to Coast*. The collected stories reflect the leisurely, uncomplicated NZ of Stewart's youth, its unspoiled landscape and poetic Maori names. The title story concerns a beautiful and sensitive young woman who has a capacity for a higher destiny than that offered by her humble background. Although trapped in a loveless marriage, she is spiritually freed by the birth of her daughter ('a girl with red hair'), seeing in the child her own symbolic rebirth. Stewart's book of essays, *The Seven Rivers* (1966), named for the seven coastal streams of his Taranaki province, is a delightful discourse on fishing, informed by his attractive wit and wisdom and memorable for its graceful, fluent prose. A selection from it, *Fishing Around the Monaro*, was published in 1978.

Stewart's greatest contribution to Australian literature, however, came from his twenty years' editorship of the Red Page, his ten years as publishing editor with Angus & Robertson, and his lifetime encouragement of Australian writers. In the Red Page, Stewart adopted encouragement and enthusiasm as his editorial philosophy, largely to counteract the apathy with which local writing was usually met. Although occasionally over-generous, he not only gave continued encouragement to established writers but accurately assessed the potential, and assisted in the development, of such major new writers as Judith Wright, James McAuley, Francis Webb, David Campbell, Rosemary Dobson and John Blight. Stewart's critical judgements on the literature of his

editorial years are included in his two books *The Flesh and the Spirit* (1948) and *The Broad Stream* (1975). His publications as anthologist and editor include *Australian Bush Ballads* (1955), *Old Bush Songs and Rhymes of Colonial Times* (1957) and *The Pacific Book of Bush Ballads* (1967), all in collaboration with Nancy Keesing; *Voyager Poems* (1960); *Kenneth Mackenzie: Selected Poems* (1961); *Modern Australian Verse* (1964), with an introduction that stresses his belief that literature should provide joy; *Hugh McCrae: Selected Poems* (1966); *Short Stories of Australia: The Lawson Tradition* (1967); and *The Wide Brown Land* (1971), Australian verse. His suggestion that there should be annual anthologies of Australian poetry and short stories led to the introduction in the early 1940s of the *Australian Poetry* and *Coast to Coast* series. He also published reflections on some of Australia's famous literary figures, *Norman Lindsay: A Personal Memoir* (1975), *A Man of Sydney* (1977) on Kenneth Slessor, and *Writers of the Bulletin* (1977). In 1955–70 Stewart was a member of the advisory board of the CLF; in 1960 he was made OBE for his services to Australian literature and later AO; in 1967 he received the Sydney Myer Award for the best volume of poetry in that year; and in 1968 he received the Britannica-Australia Award in the humanities. *Springtime in Taranaki* (1983), in the typically sensitive Stewart mode, is his autobiographical account of his first twenty-five years. *Douglas Stewart's Garden of Friends* (1987) consists largely of excerpts from his diaries relevant to his association with Australian writers and literature, complemented by the illustrations of his wife, Margaret Coen, and with an afterword by his daughter, Meg Stewart. Meg also wrote the story of her mother, Margaret Coen, watercolorist, in *Autobiography of My Mother* (1985). Nancy Keesing wrote *Douglas Stewart* (1965) in the Australian Writers and Their Work series and Clement Semmler the 1974 volume on him in the Twaynes World Author series.

STEWART, Harold (1916–   ), born Drummoyne, Sydney, studied briefly at the Conservatorium of Music and the University of Sydney, and was a member of the Australian Army's Directorate of Research and Civil Affairs 1942–46, as also was James McAuley. In 1944 Stewart and McAuley perpetrated the famous Ern Malley hoax (q.v.); Stewart's role in this affair and its subsequent effect on him is examined in Michael Heyward's *The Ern Malley Affair* (1993). After the war Stewart was a journalist, lecturer, bookshop salesman and radio broadcaster for the ABC. His first books of verse were *Phoenix Wings: Poems 1940–46* (1948) and *Orpheus and Other Poems* (1956). The poems of *Phoenix Wings*, many of them drawing on Chinese literature and culture, reveal Stewart's deep interest in the Orient, an interest that took him to visit and, from 1966, to live permanently in, Japan, where he studied under Bando Shojun, a Shin Buddhist priest and scholar at the Shin-shu Buddhist University, and where he ultimately became a member of the Shinshu Buddhist sect. In Kyoto he has eked out a frugal existence by teaching English, and publishing the popular volumes of translations of Japanese haiku, *A Net of*

Fireflies (1960), *A Chime of Windbells* (1969) and *The Exiled Immortal: A Song Cycle* (1980).

Stewart's poetry has attracted a devoted following. *Phoenix Wings* and *Orpheus* have been praised for their observation and understanding of a culture other than Australian, and for the fine descriptive and narrative qualities of poems such as 'A Flight of Wild Geese' (q.v.) and 'The Ascension of Feng'. As an expatriate, his more recent work has not been well known in Australia. The haiku translations, which are accompanied by his essays on the history, philosophy and technique of haiku, have been criticised by experts on the culture and language of Japan as too idiosyncratic in approach. The haiku, however, which allows, in Stewart's view, the achievement of 'perfection in little things', is a suitable vehicle for combining his own predilection for sensuous imagery with epigrammatic succinctness. *By the Old Walls of Kyoto*, subtitled *A Yearly Cycle of Landscape Poems*, Stewart's most recent verse (1981) and his *magnum opus*, is a long poem in twelve parts, which celebrates the beauty and significance of Kyoto and pays personal homage to it. Stewart has declared it 'his spiritual autobiography'. He has been awarded an emeritus fellowship of the Literature Board of the Australia Council.

STEWART, John Innes Mackintosh, see 'INNES, Michael'

STEWART, Nellie (1858–1931) was the stage-name of Eleanor Stewart Towzey, born Sydney, who made her theatrical debut at the age of 5 with Charles Kean in *The Stranger*. Star or principal boy in the 1870s and 1880s of numerous pantomimes and comic operas staged by the J.C. Williamson 'triumvirate', which included Arthur Garner and George Musgrove, she later formed a liaison with Musgrove, an earlier marriage having failed. Some of her most successful roles included Marguerite in Gounod's *Faust* (1888) and Nell Gwynne in *Sweet Nell of Old Drury* (1902), which was produced as a film in 1911. She was also the star in *Paul Jones* (1889), *Blue-Eyed Susan* (1892), *Sweet Kitty Bellairs* (1909) and *What Every Woman Knows* (1910). She sang at the opening of the first federal parliament in 1901; her autobiography, *My Life's Story*, was published in 1923. Marjorie Skill wrote the biographical *Sweet Nell of Old Sydney* (1974).

'Still Life', one of the best-known of Rosemary Dobson's (q.v.) painting poems, was first published in the *Bulletin*, 1946. It describes a painting by an unknown seventeenth-century artist of a table set for a simple, sacramental meal of bread and wine. The never-to-be-consumed meal is one of the many examples in Rosemary Dobson's poetry of the permanence of art. A belated sharer in the meal (as all are who have gazed at the painting down the centuries), the poet involuntarily reaches out to break the loaf and pour the wine that awaited the arrival of an unknown guest 300 years ago.

STIRLING, Sir James, see **Swan River Colony**

STIVENS, Dal (1911–), born Blayney, NSW, has worked as a bank officer, freelance journalist, public servant and court reporter. He served in the Army Education Service, 1943–44, the Department of Information, 1944–49, and was press official at Australia House, London, 1949–50, when he resigned to try freelance writing. During his years in London his short stories appeared in such well-known newspapers and magazines as *Lilliput*, the *Times Literary Supplement, John o' London's* and the *Observer*, and were frequently broadcast by the BBC. In 1963 Stivens became the foundation president of the ASA, with which he has continued to work closely. An amateur naturalist, he has contributed to Australian and international natural history journals and has since made a reputation as a painter; in 1974 he held the first exhibition of his paintings, which have also been reproduced in *Art in Australia*.

Stivens's short stories are represented in numerous anthologies and have appeared in eight collections, *The Tramp and Other Stories* (1936), *The Courtship of Uncle Henry* (1946), *The Gambling Ghost and Other Tales* (1953), *Ironbark Bill* (1955), *The Scholarly Mouse and Other Tales* (1957), *Selected Stories: 1936–1968*, introduced by H.P. Heseltine (1969), *The Unicorn and Other Tales* (1976) and *The Demon Bowler and Other Cricket Stories* (1979). He has also published four novels, *Jimmy Brockett* (1951), *The Wide Arch* (1958), *Three Persons Make a Tiger* (1968) and *A Horse of Air* (1970); a book for children, *The Bushranger* (1978); a work on natural history, *The Incredible Egg* (1974); and edited *Coast to Coast 1957–58* (1958). He won the Miles Franklin Award in 1970 for *A Horse of Air* and the Patrick White Award in 1981.

His first collection of stories, based on his experience of rural life during the 1930s Depression, includes human psychological studies and stark sketches of natural life; in both, Stivens reveals a keen insight into the disillusionments, frustrations and cruelties of ordinary existence. 'The Tramp' describes the unsuccessful but spirited attempt of a tramp to win a small prize of money by surviving a side-show boxing contest; 'Pearl Before Swine' evokes the inarticulate feelings of rough men in a bar at the sight of a fresh, innocent girl; in 'Mr. Bloody Kearns', a train guard, conscious of his own insecurity and of the power of the inspector, finds himself throwing a swagman off the train. In his subsequent collections, Stivens explores a range of genres and displays a distinctive comic gift, most popularly in his tall tales and cricketing stories. 'The Courtship of Uncle Henry', a richly rural tale, recounts the transformation of Uncle Henry from tractable, long-suffering swain to despotic husband; 'The Gambling Ghost' deals lightly with the relationship between Frying-Pan Fred and some ghostly gamblers, ending with Fred's own unconscious crossing of the barrier between life and death; 'The Batting Wizard from the City' describes the superhuman feats of an unknown city cricketer, faced with the menace of a local bowler known as the Demon. His tall tales recount such events as Rawhide Harry's capture of the giant groper that has run away with the farmer's plough and Cabbage-Face Ned's duel with a bushranger. Another distinctive genre that has attracted Stivens is the adult animal fable; stories such as 'The Scholarly Mouse', 'The Blue Wren' and 'The Remarkable Cockerel' are a mingling of fantasy and reality, which also probe human inadequacies, fears and failings. Characteristics of Stivens's short fiction include a comic combination of hyperbole and understatement, a deft economy of treatment and a narrative stance that is both detached and sympathetic. His novels are as diverse and experimental as his stories. *Jimmy Brockett*, set in Sydney 1905–38, is the story of a ruthless, brash, manipulating businessman who makes his fortune in boxing, newspapers and racing, rises to political eminence and ends his life lonely, bitter and malicious; *The Wide Arch* is both a murder story and a psychological drama, reminiscent of *Hamlet*; *Three Persons Make a Tiger*, an allegorical fairy-tale based on an oriental legend, satirises aspects of contemporary life; *A Horse of Air*, Stivens's most ambitious and complex novel, is the story of a mystical search for a rare bird, the night parrot, in Central Australia, seen through the eyes of the leader of the expedition, Harry Craddock, a wealthy, amateur ornithologist, and his wife, Joanna, and qualified by comments from the psychiatrist who treats him and the footnotes of his friend who has edited the manuscript.

STOCK, Ralph (1881–?) contributed short stories and his first novel, *The Recipe for Rubber* (1911), to the *Lone Hand*. He recorded his early travels in Canada, the South Seas and Australia in *The Confessions of a Tenderfoot* (1913), and a subsequent voyage to the South Pacific in a small sailing ship in *The Chequered Cruise* (1916). After war service in France, Stock was invalided to England and later sailed again for the South Seas. This journey is described in his most popular work, *The Cruise of the Dream Ship* (1921), and is also the subject of a book by his sister and sailing companion, Mabel Stock, *The Log of a Woman Wanderer* (1923). Stock also published two other novels, *Marama* (1913), a tale of the South Pacific, and *The Pyjama Man* (1913), a romance of a playwright and an unhappily married Sydney girl; and four volumes of short stories, mostly tales of the Pacific set in Fiji and the surrounding islands and dealing with the experiences of traders, planters and beachcombers, *Tadra of the Lagoon* (1914), *Beach Combings* (1920), *South of the Line* (1922) and *Uncharted Waters* (1924).

Stockman, see **'Drover'**

Stockwhip, a weekly free-thought newspaper established by John Edward Kelly (1840–96) in February 1875, ran until September 1876, when a court case forced Kelly to cease publication. Purchased by H.N. Montague, who changed the title to the *Stockwhip and Satirist*, the newspaper continued fortnightly from October to November 1876, when its title was changed to the *Satirist*. It ceased publication in January 1877. A vehicle for Kelly's outspoken views on politics, religion and the land question, and for his support of Sir Henry Parkes, the *Stockwhip* aimed, unsuccess-

fully, to avoid scurrilous personal abuse in its attacks on 'religious, social, commercial and political charlatans'. G.H. Gibson was a regular contributor of satirical poetry, and Havelock Ellis, who may also have been a contributor, mentions the newspaper in his novel *Kanga Creek* (1922). J.F. Archibald, founder of the *Bulletin*, acknowledged that his conception was influenced by the *Stockwhip*, the 'short-lived audacious Sydney weekly ... which had battled against the smug and respectable'. Margaret Woodhouse has published *An Index to 'The Stockwhip' 1875–1877, with a Life of John Edward Kelly, 1840–1896* (1969).

STONE, Louis (1871–1935), born Leicestershire, England, was brought to Australia in 1884 and lived for some time in Redfern and Waterloo, the poorer suburbs of Sydney that he used as the setting for his novel *Jonah* (q.v.). After combining attendance at the University of Sydney (although he did not take a degree) with training as a primary school teacher, he began his teaching career in 1895. He spent some years in country areas of NSW but returned permanently to Sydney in 1904. In about 1908 he married another teacher, Abigail Allen, who shared his musical interests. At this time he was also working on his novel *Jonah*, painstakingly gathering material for his representations of the city's life. The novel was completed in 1909, published in London in 1911 and republished in Sydney in 1933. By 1912 the effects of a debilitating nervous illness which led to his long periods of absence and early retirement in 1931 were already apparent. His next novel, *Betty Wayside*, appeared first in full as a serial in *Lone Hand* in 1913–14, and in book form in 1915, bowdlerised to accord with the publisher's ideas of suitable family reading. Apart from two short stories, one published in *Norman Lindsay's Book No. II* (1915) and the other in *The Australian Soldiers' Gift Book* (1917), Stone's remaining major work was a three-act play, *The Lap of the Gods* (1923). Drama appealed strongly to him as a medium and in 1920 he took the play to London in a bid to gain production. He was unsuccessful but claimed to have received encouragement from John Galsworthy and others. In 1923 the play won second place in a competition run by the *Daily Telegraph*, which also published it that year, although it was not produced until 1928, when Gregan McMahon undertook its presentation. Reviews were mixed and the production, which seems to have been inadequate, was withdrawn after one week. Another one-act play, *The Watch That Wouldn't Go*, was published in *Triad* in 1926.

Stone is chiefly remembered for his novel *Jonah*, the story of a larrikin (q.v.), Joe Jones, leader of a city 'push'. In dealing with an urban rather than a rural environment Stone broke new ground, although his lead was not immediately followed, nor did *Jonah* receive much initial attention apart from an enthusiastic review by A.G. Stephens. Not the first to use the larrikin as a subject, he was the first to make him popular. Striking naturalistic descriptions of place and incident, authentic dialogue and a well-realised array of diverse characters are the novel's distinctive attributes. Although his characters are credible and interesting,

Stone's imagination is visual and dramatic rather than analytical and novelistic; he is more concerned to render the colourful surface of life than to probe its depths. *Betty Wayside* is set in Sydney's lower-middle-class suburbs, Paddington and Woollahra, and deals with the emotional relationships of a woman pianist of potential genius. It is an uneven work, flawed by some weak writing and Stone's uncertain attitude to his protagonist. *Jonah* is a striking achievement, but Stone, whose natural bent seems to have been dramatic, was unfortunate to be writing at a time when Australian drama lacked an audience. Stone is the subject of John O'Donoghue's play *Abbie and Lou, Norman and Rose* (1993), which portrays his attempts to establish himself as a writer and his relationship with Norman and Rose Lindsay.

STONE, Walter (1910–81) was a well-known Australian book-collector, publisher, printer, editor and bibliographer. He was educated in Orange and Parramatta, and for some years worked on an Auburn newspaper, eventually becoming editor. Some of his newspaper articles on Australian literature brought him to the attention of Christopher Brennan, who befriended him. In 1956 he bought the Wentworth Press, which he managed with his sons. The first work he produced as a private printer, under the imprint Talkarra Press, was an edition in 1953 of one hundred copies of Dulcie Deamer's poem *Blue Centaur*. Later, under the imprint Stone Copying Co., he produced the various bibliographies in the Studies in Australian Bibliography series. He was probably best known as a book-collector, however, especially to other Australian bibliophiles and writers; he was a founder member and office-bearer of the Book Collectors' Society of Australia, editor of its journal *Biblionews*, and the owner of an extensive collection of Australiana which included books, manuscripts, photographs and memorabilia of many of Australia's writers. Federal president of the FAW and later State president, and founder member and patron of the Christopher Brennan Society, he was also an office-holder of the ASA and a member of the English Association. In 1975 the National Book Council named him Bookman of the Year; in 1981 he was awarded the OAM.

Apart from numerous bibliographies in periodicals and books, and reviews, bibliographical and biographical essays in journals, Stone compiled four separate bibliographies, *Henry Lawson: A Chronological Checklist of his Contributions to 'The Bulletin' (1887–1924)* (1954); *Joseph Furphy, an Annotated Bibliography* (1955); *The Books of the Bulletin 1880–1952* (1955, with George Mackaness); and *Christopher John Brennan* (1959, with Hugh Anderson). He took over the editorship of *Southerly* for a year (1962), and edited James Mudie's 1837 account of the colony of NSW, *The Felonry of New South Wales* (1964), as well as several popular selections of Lawson and Paterson and *Treasury of Australian Folklore* (1980). Jean Stone wrote his biography, *The Passionate Bibliophile* (1988), and a catalogue of his collection was published in 1987. The Walter Stone Memorial Award for Literature is named in his honour.

STONEHOUSE, Ethel (1883–1964), born Nhill, Victoria, contributed verse early in life to the *Bulletin* and the *Australian Journal*. She published two volumes of verse, *The Road of Yesterday* (1916) and *The Caravan of Dreams* (1923), and fifteen novels, most of which appeared under the pseudonym 'Lindsay Russell', although she also used the name 'Harlingham Quinn'. In 1914 she married a Harley Street specialist, John McNaught Scott, but appears to have found the relationship oppressive and creatively deadening if her last novel, *Earthware*, is to be seen as autobiographical. After her husband's death she maintained a solitary existence at Mortlake, Victoria, and spent the last years of her life as a patient of Royal Park psychiatric hospital. Her novels are *Smouldering Fires* (1912), *Love Letters of a Priest* (1912), *Kathleen Mavourneen* (1913), *Sands o' the Desert* (1913), *Souls in Pawn* (1913), *The Years of Forgetting* (1914), *The Eternal Triangle* (1915), *The Gates of Silence* (1915), *The Interior* (1916), *The Woman Who Lived Again* (1916), *Sons of Iscariot* (1916), *That Woman from Java* (1916), *The Gates of Kut* (1917), *Land o' the Dawning* (1917) and *Earthware* (1918). Set in Australia, Britain, India and Indonesia, many of Stonehouse's novels are preoccupied with women's frustration with patriarchal systems, whether of class or religion. In particular, the plot of *Smouldering Fires*, which hinges on the seduction and desertion of a young Catholic woman by a priest, was repeated in several of her subsequent novels.

STOW, Randolph (1935–), born Geraldton into a long-established WA family, was educated at the University of WA. His varied career has included periods of lecturing in English literature at the universities of Adelaide, WA and Leeds, eighteen months of intensive travel in the USA, work on an Aboriginal mission and as an anthropologist and cadet patrol officer in New Guinea. Since 1966 he has lived permanently in England. His novels are *A Haunted Land* (1956), *The Bystander* (1957), *To the Islands* (q.v., 1958, rev. edn 1982), *Tourmaline* (q.v., 1963), *The Merry-Go-Round in the Sea* (q.v., 1965), *Visitants* (1979), *The Girl Green as Elderflower* (1980), and *The Suburbs of Hell* (1984). He has also written an outstandingly popular novel for children, *Midnite* (q.v., 1967), and two libretti for operas with music by Peter Maxwell Davies, *Eight Songs for a Mad King* (1969) and *Miss Donnithorne's Maggot* (1974). He has published collections of poetry including *Act One* (1957), *Outrider* (1962), *A Counterfeit Silence* (1969) and *Randolph Stow Reads from His Own Work* (1974) and has edited *Australian Poetry* (1964). Anthony J. Hassall has edited *Randolph Stow* (1990) in the Portable Australian Authors series, which includes *Visitants*, episodes from other novels, poems, stories, interviews and essays. Stow's work, which won recognition early, has received several prizes including the 1958 Miles Franklin Award, the Gold Medal of the Australian Literature Society in 1957 and 1958, the Britannica-Australia Award in 1966, the Grace Leven Poetry Prize in 1969 and the Patrick White Literary Award in 1979. The Randolph Stow Fiction and Poetry Award was established in WA in 1987.

The seriousness of Stow's aims and the distinctive nature of his talent were obvious from the first, although his work has aroused a variety of critical reactions. His use of different narrative techniques and his mingling of realism, symbolism, myth, allegory and romance, make his fiction difficult to classify. Sensational, melodramatic plots, obsessive, even demonic, characters and imagistic prose characterise his first two novels. Although in both the WA landscape is brilliantly rendered, Stow's method is not predominantly naturalistic but dramatic and poetically suggestive. His persistent theme, imperfectly developed in these first two novels, is general and universal: human kind's metaphysical isolation and its implication as oppressor and victim in a cruel system. For Stow the uneasiness of time-conscious European culture in the timeless, haunted Australian environment is a peculiarly apt metaphor of this condition. This mythopoetic concern is more apparent in his next two, more assured, novels. *To the Islands* describes the journey to death of an old missionary, Heriot, which is also a spiritual expiatory journey in which he transcends his White heritage. *Tourmaline*, a powerful exploration of the interplay of power in an isolated but representative community, is also a blend of allegory and realism. Shaped by a quasi-religious theme which draws on Chinese Taoism, it has no social message but probes the essence of the human condition. *The Merry-Go-Round in the Sea*, Stow's most popular novel in Australia, achieves several effects at once. Set in Geraldtown in the 1940s, it is an intimately realised study of a particular boy's growth into adolescence which has also a deeper philosophical significance as an expression of transience and isolation. *Visitants*, set in Papua in 1959, has a concentrated atmosphere of mystery, touching on the other-worldly; using the divergent perspectives of a group of individuals of varying cultural backgrounds, it explores a sequence of strange, violent events. *The Girl Green as Elderflower* is a traditional romance which merges life in Suffolk of the 1960s with medieval myth. Completed before the ending of *Visitants* was written, the more hopeful *Girl Green as Elderflower* complements the bitter theme of its published predecessor. *The Suburbs of Hell*, part naturalistic thriller and part medieval morality, works in metafictional and explicit literary ways to involve the reader in the knowledge that death is unpredictable and ubiquitous; set in Tornwitch, a fictional version of Harwich, Essex, the novel creates as dense a human and physical English landscape as the *Merry-Go-Round in the Sea*'s Australian one. Stow's smaller volume of poetry reflects, like his fiction, his Australian experience, his feeling for landscape, his wide reading and interest in myth and folklore, his sense of dynasty and preoccupation with time, transience and isolation. Technically assured and traditional in form, his verse achieves, at its best, a simple, spare lyricism. Stow's work is the subject of monographs by Ray Willbanks (1978) and Anthony J. Hassall (*Strange Country*, 1986).

Strabane of the Mulberry Hills, a novel by William Gosse Hay (q.v.), was published in 1929. Set in Tasmania in 1841 it recounts the experiences of Newton Caillemont, whose letters to his solicitor friend form the substance of the narrative and who as a boy comes to stay with the owner of Strabane, Haylin Talmash. A widower, Haylin has adopted two nieces, Miss Molly and Miss Flo; their skittish conduct offends him, however, and after he becomes convinced that an attempt has been made to poison him he orders them from the house and substitutes Newton as his heir. The rest of the novel focuses on the attempts by the sisters to repossess Strabane and their inheritance, although Newton faces the additional problem of an attack by the bushranger Martin Cash and his gang. At the end Strabane is burnt but rebuilt and Newton returns to live there.

STRACHAN, Tony (1948–), brought up in Papua New Guinea, trained as a dancer and actor in Sydney and London, was dancer and choreographer with the Australian Dance Theatre 1975–76, and resident actor with the South Australian Theatre Company 1978–80. His first play, 'Food', was produced in 1976 at the Space, Adelaide, and was followed by 'Dole City' (1977), 'The Solution' (1980), 'Slice' (1981, with Kim Carpenter), *Eyes of the Whites* (1983), which deals with New Guinea during Australia's administration, 'The Plot' (1983), 'The Times of George Tudor' (1985), *The Harlequin Shuffle* (1985), winner of the *Advertiser* award for the best new play of 1985, *State of Shock* (1986), a study of violence in Aboriginal society and its causes and 'Learn or Burn!'(1991). He has also written for radio.

STRAHAN, Lynne, see **Feminism and Australian Literature**; *Meanjin*

STRAUSS, Jennifer (1933–), born Heywood, Victoria, was educated at the Universities of Melbourne and Glasgow and Monash University (Ph.D.). She has taught at the universities of New England and Melbourne and since 1964 at Monash where she is currently associate professor in the Department of English. Her poetry has appeared widely in anthologies and she has published several collections, *Children and Other Strangers* (1975), *Winter Driving* (1981) and *Labour Ward* (1988). Especially sensitive to the experience and predicaments of women, she writes with wit, irony and pathos of such subjects as the passage of time, the presence of death, motherhood and love. She often examines the past to reveal how the lives of women have been limited and diminished by the role that history has allotted them. Personal poems based on experience – e.g. 'An End to Innocence', 'Et Ego in Arcadia', 'The Snapshot Album of the Innocent Tourist', 'Pine Cones', 'My Grandmother' and 'Tending the Graves' – are sensitive combinations of emotion, wit and realism. 'Tending the Graves', a particularly effective poem, shows that not even with death do the dead release their hold on the living. She won the *Westerly* Sesquicentenary Prize in 1979. Jennifer Strauss, as critic, has published *Stop Laughing! I'm Being Serious: Three Studies in Seriousness and Wit in Contemporary Australian Poetry*, lectures which she gave on Judith Wright, John Forbes and Chris Wallace-Crabbe in 1989 for the Foundation for Australian Literary Studies in Townsville. She has also published *Boundary Conditions: The Poetry of Gwen Harwood* (1992), edited *The Oxford Book of Australian Love Poetry* (1993), and is preparing the Collected Poems of Mary Gilmore.

Stream (July–September 1931), a monthly magazine published in Melbourne, which described itself as a 'medium of international art expression', had an avant-garde outlook and published articles on overseas literary movements as well as some original poetry and articles on Australian literature. Contributors included Bertram Higgins, Edgar Holt, A.R. Chisholm, Nettie Palmer, Cyril Pearl and Adrian Lawlor.

STREET, Jessie, see **Feminism and Australian Literature**

STREETON, Sir Arthur (1867–1943), born Mount Duneed, Victoria, studied art at the National Gallery School, Melbourne, and became part of the Heidelberg School (q.v.). His best works, Australian landscapes and scenes, include *Still Glides the Stream, Golden Summer, Circular Quay* and *Redfern Station*. R.H. Croll edited *Smike to Bulldog* (1946), the letters of Streeton to fellow artist Tom Roberts (whose nickname was Bulldog); the correspondence was the basis of Peter Batey's entertainment 'From Smike to Bulldog'. A more comprehensive record of this correspondence is *'Letters from Smike'. The Letters of Arthur Streeton 1890–1943* (1989), edited by Ann Galbally and Anne Gray. Anne Kern has published the biographical study *Arthur Streeton: The Man and His Art* (1981) and Christopher Wray, *Arthur Streeton: Painter of Light* (1993).

STREHLOW, T.G.H. (Theodor George Henry) (1908–78) was born at Hermannsburg, central Australia, where his father, Carl Strehlow (1871–1922), was in charge of the Lutheran mission. After graduating from the University of Adelaide, he investigated central Australian Aboriginal languages and ceremonial traditions for the Australian National Research Council 1931–34, and worked in native administration in Central Australia 1936–42 before serving with the army in the Second World War. He subsequently joined the English Department at the University of Adelaide, later becoming reader in Australian linguistics. He spent long periods in central Australia 1953–65, recording Aboriginal myths, songs and sacred ceremonies. His published work includes *Aranda Phonetics and Grammar* (1944), *Aranda Traditions* (1947), *Dark and White Australians* (1957), *Songs of Central Australia* (1971), *Central Australian Religion* (1978), and two art studies, *Rex Battarbee* (1956) and *Nomads in No-man's-Land* (1961, an account of Albert Namatjira). Strehlow also wrote *Journey to Horseshoe Bend* (1969), a record of his father's desperate but unsuccessful journey to seek medical help for his fatal illness, attended by himself, then 14, and his mother. A moving account of a journey of extreme suffering and hardship, *Journey to Horseshoe Bend* also re-creates the world of Carl Strehlow, his aspirations and achievements, which included the translation of the Lutheran catechism into Aranda, his disappointments over twenty-eight years at Hermannsburg, difficulties with the Mission Board and inability to understand the mythology of the Aboriginal people. Ward McNally wrote a biography of T.G.H. Strehlow, *Aborigines, Artefacts and Anguish* (1981). The Strehlow Research Foundation was founded in 1978.

STRETTON, Hugh (1924–), born Melbourne, graduated from Oxford University, where he was a fellow of Balliol College 1948–54, before taking up an appointment as professor of history at the University of Adelaide, where he is now emeritus professor and visiting fellow in economics. He served as deputy chairman of the SA Housing Trust 1973–89. An influential writer, who has focused primarily on the problems of managing suburban land and living as a springboard for considering wider Australian issues, Stretton has been described as a radical conservative who questions the old orthodoxies from a practical, humane point of view. His publications include *The Political Sciences* (1969), *Ideas for Australian Cities* (1970), *Housing and Government* (1974), *Capitalism, Socialism and the Environment* (1976, winner of the *Age* Book of the Year Award in 1976), *Urban Planning in Rich and Poor Countries* (1978) and *Political Essays* (1987, winner of the Victorian Premier's Literary Award in 1987). He has been awarded an honorary D.Litt. from the ANU and an honorary LL D from Monash University. *Markets, Morals and Public Policy* (1989), ed. Lionel Orchard and Robert Dare, is a collection of essays which celebrate his work, written to mark his retirement.

'Strine', a term invented to represent the way Australians pronounce the word 'Australian', is now also used by some commentators as a synonym for Australian English (q.v.), Australian speech and the word 'Australian' itself when used as an adjective. The inventor of Strine is Alistair Morrison (q.v.) who under the pseudonym 'Afferbeck Lauder' (Strine for 'alphabetical order'), wrote *Let Stalk Strine* ('Let's Talk Australian') (1965), a satire on the elisions and transliterations of uneducated speakers of Australian English. A famous example of Strine is 'Emma Chisit', for whom the English writer Monica Dickens once autographed her novel in a Sydney store not realising that the shopper had asked, 'How much is it?'

'Stroke', a seven-poem sequence by Vincent Buckley (q.v.), was first published in *Quadrant* (1965). The poem describes the familiar events associated with the death of a parent: the hospital bedside, where the embarrassed visitors ('voyeurs of decay') engage in stiff, platitudinous conversation; the son's guilt over the lifetime lack of communication between himself and his father; and memories of the father in his prime compared with his present state. In the 'life studies' genre, which Buckley was one of the first Australian poets to employ, 'Stroke' conveys, in spite of its calm, almost detached phrasing, the anguish that the son feels, not simply because of the imminent death of his father, but because of the gulf between them that even at the end seems unbridgeable.

STRONG, Sir Archibald Thomas (1876–1930), born Melbourne, the son of Herbert Augustus Strong (1841–1918), professor of classics at the University of Melbourne, was taken to England in 1883 and was educated at Liverpool, Oxford, and in Germany. In 1901 he returned to Melbourne, where he edited the short-lived *Trident* and was for many years literary critic for the *Herald* and lectured in English at the University of Melbourne. He also served as president of the Melbourne Literature, the Melbourne Shakespeare and Mermaid societies. From 1922 to 1930 he was professor of English at the University of Adelaide and was knighted in 1925. One of the founders and trustees of the Melbourne Repertory Theatre under Gregan McMahon, he was also vice-president of the Adelaide Repertory Theatre. He published three collections of conventional verse, *Sonnets and Songs* (1905), *Sonnets of the Empire* (1915) and *Poems* (1918); three collections of essays, *Peradventure* (1911), *Three Studies* (1921) and *Four Studies* (1932); *A Short History of English Literature* (1921) and a translation of *Beowulf* (1925). He also contributed the chapter on Australian literature to the first edition of the *Australian Encyclopaedia* (1925). He was chief Commonwealth film censor 1919–22.

Struck Oil is an appropriately named play that J.C. Williamson (q.v.) originally purchased in California from Sam Smith, an itinerant Irish woodchopper. It was expanded by Clay Greene and later revised by Williamson himself. Set in the American Civil War period, with a simple, melodramatic plot, the drama offered histrionic scope for Williamson and his wife Maggie Moore; when they brought it to Australia in 1874 it was enormously successful, providing the financial base for Williamson's theatrical empire. The Williamsons toured with the play in India, Europe, Britain and the USA, 1875–78, and frequently revived it in Australia.

STRZELECKI, Sir Paul (1797–1873), born Poland of aristocratic background but no accompanying wealth, arrived in Australia in 1839 after a series of indiscretions and misadventures, acquiring along the way a practical knowledge of mineralogy and geology. In attempting to construct a geological map of the Colony he reached the southern Alps and climbed and named Mount Kosciusko, after the Polish democratic leader Tadeusz Kosciuszko. He later performed important geological and exploration surveys in Tasmania and returned in 1843 to England, where he published *Physical Description of New South Wales and Van Diemen's Land* (1845) for which he received the founder's medal of the Royal Geographical Society. He also published *Gold and Silver* (1856) to support his claim of having been the earliest discoverer of gold in NSW. Biographies of Strzelecki include B. Strzelecki's *Biography of Count Paul Edmund de Strzelecki* (1935), Geoffrey Rawson's *The Count: A Life of Sir Paul Edmund Strzelecki* (1953), Helen Heney's *In a Dark Glass: The Story of Paul Edmund Strzelecki* (1961) and Marian Kaluski's *Sir Paul E. Strzelecki* (1985). H.P.G. Clews wrote *Strzelecki's Ascent of Mount Kosciusko, 1840* (1973). The Strzelecki Ranges of Gippsland, Victoria, are named after him. The title of 'Count', by which he was often known, was self-awarded.

STUART, Donald (1913–83), son of Julian Stuart, an early *Bulletin* writer and radical of the 1890s, and brother of Lyndall Hadow, a noted short-story writer, was born at Cottesloe, WA. After a limited education he took to the bush, working as horse-breaker, drover, stockman, prospector, miner, well-sinker and fencer. He was a POW in the Second World War and in later years a prolific novelist, freelance broadcaster for the ABC in Perth, writer of numerous short stories and the federal president of the FAW. His novels began with *Yandy* (q.v., 1959), a fictional-factual account of the establishment of the Pindan Co-operative in 1946, when about 800 striking stockmen on the pastoral stations inland from Port Hedland, WA, broke the long-established system of working Aboriginal stockmen for little pay and of segregating Aborigines from Whites. *The Driven* (1961), one of the best of his outback novels, is the story of a great cattle trek across the north-west of WA in the late 1930s. *Yaralie* (q.v., 1962) uses the part-Aboriginal girl of the title to examine the problem facing people of mixed race. A succession of other novels followed, including *Ilbarana* (1971), about an Aboriginal boy, its sequel *Malloonkai* (1976), *Walk, Trot, Canter and Die* (1975), *Drought Foal* (1977), and *Wedgetail View* (1978). Stuart also wrote a six-novel autobiographical series, *The Conjuror's Years*, which begins with *Prince of My Country* (1974) and concludes with *I Think I'll Live* (1981). Stuart's *Morning Star, Evening Star: Tales of Outback Australia* (1973) is a collection of short stories, colourful yarns which capture the colloquial idiom and humour of the rough-and-ready outback type. A simple and direct writer, Stuart uses character rather than plot to reinforce his theme of the intrinsic worth of the individual, whatever his colour. The background to most of his fiction is the tough north-west country, the Pilbara, over which he wandered most of his life. He died in Broome in 1983. Jean Lang Crowe wrote *Hear the Stars: A Personal Biography of Donald Stuart* (1988).

STUART, John McDouall (1815–66) was a Scots-born son of an army captain; he emigrated to SA in 1838 and was a member of the inland exploration party of Charles Sturt in 1844–46. During 1858–62 he led four explorations into central and northern Australia: in 1860 he reached the centre of the continent and in 1861 made a valiant attempt, in competition with the Burke and Wills expedition, to cross Australia from south to north. The major record of his journeys is *Explorations in Australia: The Journals of John McDouall Stuart* (1864, ed. William Hardman). Stuart's life and achievements are discussed in Mona Stuart Webster's *John McDouall Stuart* (1958), Douglas Pike's *John McDouall Stuart* (1958), T.G.H. Strehlow's *Comments on the Journals of John McDouall Stuart* (1967) and Ian Mudie's *The Heroic Journey of John McDouall Stuart* (1968). The Stuart Range, west of Lake Eyre, and the Stuart highway from Darwin to Port Augusta commemorate his name. W.P. Auld's recollections of Stuart and his final expedition, of which he was a member, were published in 1984.

STUART, Julian (1866–1929), born Eagleton, NSW, of Scottish ancestry, worked on his parents' farm in the Hunter Valley until 18, then went to Sydney where in 1887 he joined the civil service. In 1888 he went to the upper Dawson Valley in Queensland and became interested in the Shearers' Union, which had been established by W.G. Spence in 1886 at Ballarat, Victoria. In 1890 he was at Barcaldine when the shearers' strike was brewing; in 1891 he was elected chairman of the Central Queensland Labourers' Union at Clermont. Arrested in March 1891, he was convicted of conspiracy under an old law which had already been repealed in England and sentenced to three years' gaol. On his release he went to WA, where he took up journalism, wrote radical poetry and remained active in politics. His verses were already known in the *Bulletin* under the pseudonym 'Curlew'; much of his poetry in the *Geraldton Express* and the *Coolgardie Miner* appeared under the pseudonym 'Saladin'. In 1903–6 he edited the *Westralian Worker* and was a member of the WA parliament. He was later a clerk in the WA public service but retained his interest in the bush, the goldfields and the working class. Stuart was prominent in the halcyon days of bush balladry and radical poetry that flourished in WA newspapers at the turn of the century. His radicalism is succinctly expressed in the lines

> I am deformed by labor
> I am the working man
> Cursing the fate that holds me
> A dull-browed Caliban.

Lyndall Hadow, Stuart's daughter, published *Part of the Glory: Reminiscences of the Shearers' Strike, Queensland 1891 From the Pen of Julian Stuart* (1967). The novelist Donald Stuart (q.v.) was his son.

'STUKELEY, Simon', see **SAVERY, Henry**

STURT, Charles (1795–1869), born India into an East India Company family, joined the army and arrived in Australia in 1827. He achieved fame as an explorer, in particular for his discovery in 1828–30 of the Darling and Murray (q.v.) rivers and for his leadership of an extremely difficult journey from Adelaide into the centre of Australia in 1844–46. One of the most literate of Australian explorers, Sturt wrote *Two Expeditions into the Interior of Southern Australia* (1833) and *Narrative of an Expedition into Central Australia* (1849). Henry Kingsley's essay 'The March of Sturt' focuses on Sturt's river journeys, which are also the subject of the novel by J.K. Ewers, *Who Rides on the River?* (1956). Jane Sarah Doudy wrote *Magic of Dawn: A Story of Sturt's Explorations* (1924); Michael Langley, *Sturt of the Murray* (1969); Daniel Brock, *To the Desert*

with *Sturt* (1975) and Margaret Carnegie and Keith Swan, *In Step with Sturt* (1979). Max Harris wrote the poem 'Sturt at Depot Glen', and Francis Webb, 'Sturt and the Vultures'. A modern appraisal of Sturt, together with a medical commentary by Sir Kenneth Noad, is given in Edgar Beale's *Sturt: The Chipped Idol* (1979). Sturt is commemorated by Sturt's Stony Desert, the Sturt Highway and Sturt's Desert Pea, the last the floral emblem of SA.

'Such is Life' are supposedly the last words spoken by Ned Kelly on the scaffold; the words also form the title of Joseph Furphy's (q.v.) famous novel, although it is not known whether Furphy knew of the connection between Kelly and the expression.

Such is Life, a novel by Joseph Furphy (q.v.), was published by the *Bulletin* in 1903; details of its preparation and reception are provided in the entry on Joseph Furphy. A second 'edition', made up from surplus *Bulletin* sheets with a new title page and a preface by Vance Palmer (q.v.), was published in 1917, and an abridgement in 1937 in which Nettie Palmer had a major hand. The 1944 edition was the first to sell widely and was an important factor in the emergence of Furphy as a major figure in Australian literature.

Furphy objected to the type of colonial romance made popular by 'Rolf Boldrewood' and Henry Kingsley, whose *The Recollections of Geoffry Hamlyn* (1859) is dismissed as 'exceedingly trashy and misleading' in *Such is Life*, where an alternative history of the Buckley family (q.v.) is presented. As a result he made *Such is Life* as little in form like a conventional novel as possible and as much like the 'jumble of incident, dialogue, reflection, etc'. that he described life to be to A.G. Stephens in 1897. In this sense *Such is Life* is an experiment in realism, 'a novel based on a theory of the novel', as A.D. Hope suggested in 1945. *Such is Life* is subtitled *Being Certain Extracts from the Diary of Tom Collins*; Tom Collins (q.v.) is the principal narrator, who takes the opportunity of being 'Unemployed at last!' (the opening line of the novel) to enlarge on certain entries in his collection of diaries and thus provide his readers with a 'fair picture of Life, as that engaging problem has presented itself to me'. He decides to amplify a week's record, choosing at random the entry for 9 September 1883, when as a deputy-assistant-sub-inspector in the NSW public service he camps with a group of bullockies, including Steve Thompson, Cooper and Dixon, on the edge of Runnymede run in the Riverina; among the yarns swapped at the camp is Cooper's tale of his sister's disfigurement when kicked by a horse and her subsequent jilting and suicide. Collins recounts the events of that day and the following morning, during which he exchanges his horse for that of another itinerant arrival at the camp, and helps the bullockies avoid the impounding of their teams for foraging without permission on Runnymede grass; he then realises that the events of the next day are not suitable material for narration. He opts instead to amplify the diary record of the ninth day of each succeeding month, a method which is followed in the next five chapters, the bulk of the novel, covering the events of October 1883 to February 1884. In Chapter II he tells of his visit to the home of Rory O'Halloran; on the journey there he passes a swagman whom he chooses not to disturb in order to let him rest, only to discover next morning that the swagman has died. Chapter III focuses on the hilarious incident in which Tom loses his trousers in attempting to cross the Murray River, gets 'bushed' in attempting to get back to his camp at night, disturbs a number of travellers returning from a church picnic and eventually steals a pair of trousers at a farm after diverting the attention of the household by burning a haystack. In Chapter IV he provides assistance to the reclusive bullock-driver Warrigal Alf Morris, whose team has strayed from the track while he is ill with a fever; Collins twice rescues them from capture by boundary-riders and arranges help for Alf, who during his fever reveals something of his life and tells of four husbands who responded differently to the infidelity of their wives, asking Tom to judge which acted best. In Chapter V Tom again meets Steve Thompson, one of a number of fellow travellers whose animals are impounded for trespassing in a well-grassed paddock on Mondunbarra run; while camped overnight they recount three stories of children lost in the bush, including Thompson's tragic tale of the death of Mary O'Halloran, Rory's daughter, who perishes just before her rescuers reach her. Chapter VI finds Tom at Runnymede, where he has been waiting at the homestead for the arrival of the mail to complete his government business; he is ordered to Nyngan, which allows him to escape the advances of Maud Beaudesart, the housekeeper at Runnymede, and spends that night in the company of the disfigured Runnymede boundary-rider Nosey Alf Jones, whom Collins tells of his assistance to Warrigal Alf. At this point in the novel Collins decides that his final proposed diary entry (9 March 1884) is also unsuitable material for narration; he chooses instead to amplify the entry for 28–29 March, the 'arbitrary departure' of dates allowing him to chronicle Nosey Alf's departure from Runnymede and to end *Such is Life* back at the station homestead, where he discovers that his ruse to undermine Maud's marriage plans by having his character blackened by an employee of Runnymede has failed.

In opting to chronicle the events of one day per month, Collins states that 'no one of these short and simple analyses [chapters in the novel] can have any connection with another'. In fact, there are a number of connections within *Such is Life*, apart from the beginning and ending at Runnymede and the several appearances of such characters as Thompson. For example, the mystery of the saddle, which Tom finds on his newly acquired horse the morning after the swap in the first chapter, is cleared up more than 200 pages later, when Tom realises that it has been stolen previously from one of the Runnymede hands; the tramp, Andrew Glover, whom Tom meets just before he loses his trousers, turns up at Runnymede in the last pages of *Such is Life* and reveals to Tom, though neither recognises the other at first, that he has been gaoled for burning the haystack; and most important of all, it emerges from the clues Tom leaves that

Cooper's sister Molly is Nosey Alf in disguise, and that Warrigal Alf is the now repentant fiancé, who had jilted her. The Molly Cooper–Warrigal Alf–Nosey Alf relationship, which establishes, perhaps ironically, a romantic dimension to *Such is Life*, is not realised by Tom, who fails to make similar connections between incidents elsewhere in the novel and thus lacks the intuition on which he prides himself. He also sees himself as possessing a 'limpid veracity', but reveals himself to be a polysyllabic 'windbag'. That Tom is so obviously lacking in self-knowledge has led to disagreement among commentators about the central philosophy of the novel, whether, through Tom, Furphy is suggesting that life is a series of decisions between alternatives, but that once a decision is made events are beyond the control of the individual until another decision is necessary. The 'unfettered alternative followed by rigorous destiny' is a pattern Tom sees operating tragically in the death of the swagman and comically in the loss of his trousers. The idea of the controlling alternative is not firmly adhered to throughout the novel, however, and Tom's responsibility for the swagman's death and for the loss of his trousers is only part of Furphy's concern to emphasise throughout *Such is Life* the 'ageless enigma' of life as suggested by the title of the novel. The relativity of truth and the difficulty in establishing reality are part of that enigma, the recognition of which makes it necessary to accept life's ironies and ambiguities. Moreover, Furphy's relationship with Collins, like the form and themes of the novel, is itself ambiguous. Tom's inadequacies are exposed, but he has his moments of perception and is also the mouthpiece for some of Furphy's ideas, e.g. the democratic temper of *Such is Life*, as well as the vehicle for much of the humour central to the novel: for example, as self-mocking victim as in the loss of the trousers, or as an ironically unknowing character, when he fails to connect Warrigal Alf and Nosey Alf because his mind is filled with 'Ouida', the contemporary romancer. Even Tom's inflated diction, which stands in contrast to the natural idiom of such as Steve Thompson, enables Furphy not only to display his reading of Shakespeare and other authors but also to satirise the habitual swearing of so many of his bush companions. In 1991 Frances Devlin-Glass, Robin Eaden, Lois Hoffman and G.W. Turner published *The Annotated 'Such is Life' by Joseph Furphy*. Some idea of the complexity of Furphy's book can be gauged from the fact that the 297 pages of the novel have required 266 pages of annotations.

SULLIVAN, Barry (1821–91), born England of Irish parents, trained as a lawyer but became an actor and by 1844 was playing leading Shakespearean roles in Scotland and England. In 1862 he arrived in Melbourne, played in a variety of Shakespearean plays in Melbourne and Sydney, and managed the Theatre Royal in Melbourne 1863–66, acquiring considerable popularity as both actor and manager. He left for London in 1866 and continued his successful career, touring North America several times and appearing frequently in Ireland, until ill health forced him from the stage in

1887. R.P. Whitworth, a Melbourne playwright, based a popular farce, 'Catching a Conspirator' (1867), on an incident from one of Sullivan's visits to Ireland; arrested as an alleged Fenian, Sullivan was forced to prove his identity by declaiming passages from Shakespeare.

Summer of the Seventeenth Doll, an outstandingly popular play by Ray Lawler (q.v.), was first produced in 1955, published in 1957 and produced as an American film in 1960. The action, set in 1953, takes place in the faded living-room of a Victorian house in Carlton, Melbourne. The room's otherwise undistinctive furnishings are enlivened by a collection of sixteen kewpie dolls, some stuffed north Queensland birds, a variety of tinted coral and a collection of tropical butterflies. The dolls are mementos of the years of a relationship between Roo, a cane-cutter, and Olive, a barmaid. Seventeen years earlier they, with their friends Barney and Nancy, began an unconventional arrangement in which the men spent their five-month lay-off season in the city with the girls, working in the cane-fields for the other seven months. Roo (short for Reuben) is the epitome of the bronzed Anzac, rugged and taciturn; Barney, his little mate and an inveterate womaniser, is more gregarious and articulate. For Olive, who regards the men as 'a coupla kings' compared to the 'soft city blokes' and even as 'two eagles flyin' down out of the sun and coming south every year for the mating season', this arrangement is far superior to marriage. Nancy, however, has recently defected, exchanging the romance of the lay-off for more lasting qualities in her marriage to a bookish city man. The changed realities of the situation are more completely grasped by Emma, Olive's wiry, acerbic, unsentimental mother; its past romance and warmth by Bubba Ryan, the 22-year-old girl from next door. Nancy's place in the seventeenth summer has been taken by Pearl, a prim widow, who sees a chance of remarriage in the situation. The arrival of Roo and Barney insinuates further hints that this summer will be different; Roo's leadership of the gang had been successfully challenged by a younger man, Johnnie Dowd, and he had spent most of the winter in Brisbane; Barney had failed to follow him. Roo's acceptance of a city job, the inability of Pearl to join in the jollity, the unresolved tension between Barney and Roo, exacerbated by the arrival of Johnnie Dowd and the failure of the ritualistic celebrations to live up to the past, culminate in a fight between the two men. The following morning reveals that Olive has removed all traces of her mementos; Roo, aware that he is too old for cane-cutting, proposes to settle for marriage and work in the city, but Olive angrily rejects him. He leaves despairingly with Barney, unable to respond to his mate's rallying sentiments that 'there's a whole bloody country out there – wide open before us'.

Lawler later wrote two plays to complement *The Doll, Kid Stakes* (produced 1975), which deals with the beginning of the relationship in 1937, and *Other Times* (produced 1976), which is set in 1945 and traces the impact of the war and of time on the foursome. The three plays were published as *The Doll Trilogy* in 1978, and revised in 1985.

SUMMERS, Anne (1945–), born Deniliquin, NSW, educated at the universities of Adelaide and Sydney, is best known as a writer, editor and feminist; in 1983–86 she was head of the women's unit in the Prime Minister's Department. Mainly resident in the USA from 1986, she was editor and joint owner of the magazines *Ms* and *Sassy*, and subsequently editor at large for Lang Communications. In 1992 she was apointed short-term adviser on women's affairs to Prime Minister Paul Keating. One of the founders of the magazine *Refractory Girl*, she has also been prominent in practical aspects of the women's liberation movement. Political correspondent of the *Australian Financial Review*, she became the first woman president of the national press gallery in 1982 and won the Walkley Award for journalism in 1976 for her report on conditions in prisons in NSW. Her polemical book *Damned Whores and God's Police: The Colonization of Women in Australia* (1975, updated 1993 with a reassessment of the achievements of the women's movement), is an attempt to begin the process of reanalysing Australian society and history and to suggest a new framework 'in the light of the insights and assumptions of the new feminism'. Summers sees Australian women as historically imprisoned within the two stereotypes indicated by her title. Her study of both the contemporary and historical condition of women is well documented and includes some discussion of Australian women writers as well as a fresh perspective on most of the key historical and cultural studies of Australia. Summers has also written an account of the 1983 general election in Australia (1986) and compiled, with Margaret Bettison, a bibliography of writing by Australian women on general topics as well as on literature, *Her Story: Australian Women in Print 1788–1975* (1980). She is an Officer of the Order of Australia (AO).

SUMMONS, John (1952–), born Sydney, graduated from the University of New South Wales and is a teacher of English as a second language. His plays include 'White-Washed', 'Behind a Great Man', 'An Unexpected Guest', 'The Revival', 'The Boss', 'The Rivals', *Lamb of God* (1979), 'The Sower and Reaper' (1980), *The Coroner's Report* in *Popular Short Plays* vol. II (1985, ed. Ron Blair), 'The Savage Heart', 'Adventure at Whaler's Bay', 'The Devil You Know' and *Kamikaze Kate (and the Sword of Captain Kuroda)* (1989).

SUMNER, John, see **Melbourne Theatre Company**

Sun, a Sydney afternoon newspaper and the great rival of the tabloid *Daily Mirror* (1941–90), began publication in 1910, superseding the *Star* as Sir Hugh Denison's (q.v.) first venture into newspaper-ownership. Innovatively edited by Monty Grover (1910–17), it was aggressively marketed, with a motto ('Above All "for Australia"') and a masthead (1910–76, Phoebus

Apollo's seven-horse chariot before a rising sun) which became familiar to generations of Sydney readers. Denison's Sun Newspapers ran the *Sun* until 1929, when it was merged with Samuel Bennett Ltd to form Associated Newspapers; in 1953 the *Sun*, politically conservative for much of its life, came under the control of the Fairfax press. Notable editors were Adam McCay (1917–19), Delamore McCay, Thomas Dunbabin, and B.J. Tier (1959–73); long-term staff included the actor, broadcaster and novelist Mary Marlowe, who was theatre critic and reporter 1921–46. In modern times dominated by advertising, the *Sun* was described as early as 1929 as something printed on the back of retailers' advertisements; a weekday newspaper, it published a Saturday edition until 1974. The *Sun* ceased publication 14 March 1988.

The *Sunday Sun* began publication in 1903 as the Sunday companion of the *Star*. Although for many years after Denison's acquisition of the newspaper it carried the title of the *Sun* and may have appeared to be its Sunday edition, it came in effect to be a separate newspaper with its own editor, e.g. Grover in 1917–20, 1921–22, and later Eric Baume and Colin Simpson; Grover introduced a 'Sunbeams' children's page which was first edited by Ethel Turner and starred Ginger Meggs (q.v.). A notable scoop by the *Sunday Sun* was its exposure of the Ern Malley hoax (q.v.) in 1944. The *Sunday Sun* incorporated the *Sunday Guardian* in 1931 and was merged with the *Sunday Herald* (1949–53) to form the *Sun-Herald* in 1953. Fred Peterson was editor in 1956–76 of the *Sun-Herald*, which ran Leon Gellert's columns 'Something Personal' and 'Speaking Personally', until 1961.

Sun News-Pictorial, a Melbourne morning daily, began publication in 1922 when the proprietor of the Sydney *Sun*, Hugh Denison, attempted to establish a Melbourne outlet for his operations. In 1925 Denison sold the newspaper to the Herald and Weekly Times company; the *Sun News-Pictorial* then became the morning companion of the afternoon *Herald*. On 8 October 1990 it combined with the *Herald* to become the *Herald-Sun*, a 24-hour paper, i.e. four editions per day.

Sunday Times, founded in Perth in 1897 by F.C.B. Vosper, was WA's first Sunday newspaper. It linked up in 1901 with the Kalgoorlie *Sun*, another Sunday newspaper, established by Arthur Reid and James MacCallum. Both papers combined to initiate a period of literary activity in WA, centring on goldfields themes, both contemporary and nostalgic. C.W. Andrée Hayward alternated editorship of the papers in the period 1901–12, and contributors included such well-known literary figures as J.P. Bourke ('Bluebush'), Alfred Chandler ('Spinifex'), Julian Stuart ('Saladin'), E.G. Murphy ('Dryblower'), T.H. Wilson ('Crosscut') and Francis Ophel ('Prospect Good'). The Christmas numbers of each paper were literary-oriented; in addition to numerous poems, sketches and short stories, they often contained literary articles. In 1910 Alfred Chandler published an assessment of Australian poetry in a ten-article series in both papers;

throughout 1901–10 both papers ran 'The Bookfellow', a syndicated literary column by A.G. Stephens.

Sundowner, see '**Swag**'

Sundowners, The, a novel by Jon Cleary (q.v.), was published in 1952, adapted for radio presentation by Max Afford and produced as a highly successful film in 1961 starring Deborah Kerr and Robert Mitchum. Set in Australia of the 1920s, it deals with the experiences of Paddy Carmody, a wandering drover, his wife Ida and their 14-year-old son Sean. Although Paddy is temperamentally committed to their wandering life, Ida yearns for a permanent home and is bitterly disappointed when their chances of buying a share in a farm are destroyed by Paddy's gambling spree. Their love survives the crisis, however. The novel also describes Sean's growth from childhood as he adjusts to changes in his relationship with his father and learns from the lives of other men such as Venneker, Bert McKechnie and Ern Bateman.

Sunny South, The, an outstandingly popular melodrama by George Darrell (q.v.) and his only extant work, first produced in 1883 and first published in 1975, was frequently revived in Australia until the 1890s. Darrell, playing the lead, took the play to London in 1884 where it seemed set for a long run had he not suffered a severe accident on stage. With its ebullient humour, vitality, and acute social observation, the play crystallises the distinctive qualities of Australian melodrama, although its Anglophilia soon became outdated.

SUTHERLAND, Alexander (1852–1902), born Glasgow, came to Australia at the age of 14, graduated from the University of Melbourne, and in 1877 became headmaster of a school, Carlton College. He retired in 1892 but was forced by the depression of 1892–93 into journalistic work and wrote leaders for the *Argus* and the *Australasian*. He tried unsuccessfully in 1897 and 1901 to gain election to the Victorian parliament, became registrar of the University of Melbourne in 1901 and lecturer in English following the death of E.E. Morris. He edited the first posthumous collections of Henry Kendall's poetry (1886 and 1890); wrote the manual *Victoria and Its Metropolis: Past and Present* (1888); with his brother George, *The History of Australia* (1877); and collaborated with H.G. Turner in one of the earliest surveys of Australian literature, *The Development of Australian Literature* (q.v., 1898). He was on the editorial staff of the *Melbourne Review*, for which he wrote several significant critical articles; published *Thirty Short Poems* (1890); and wrote short stories. He also wrote on philosophical and scientific subjects, his most notable work being the pioneer study *The Origin and Growth of the Moral Instinct* (1898). His friend and collaborator H.G. Turner wrote the appreciation *Alexander Sutherland* (1908).

SUTHERLAND, George (1855–1905), born Scotland, the brother of Alexander Sutherland (q.v.), was brought to Australia in 1864, taught for some time after graduating from the University of Melbourne, but then turned to journalism. Regarded as an outstandingly cultivated and versatile journalist, he was on the staff of the *South Australian Register* 1881–1902, when he joined the editorial staff of the *Age*. With his brother Alexander he wrote *The History of Australia* (1877), and published on his own account the historical and descriptive sketches, *Tales of the Goldfields* (1880). He wrote accounts of SA in *Australia: Or, England in the South* (1886) and *The South Australian Company* (1898), as well as geographical studies and practical works on vinegrowing and livestock-handling. An inventor, he patented a successful photographic engraving process and in *Twentieth Century Inventions* (1901) discussed a range of current and possible future inventions. His daughter, Margaret Sutherland the composer, collaborated with Vance Palmer in the collection *Old Australian Bush Ballads* (1951).

SUTTOR, William Henry (1834–1905), born NSW, was a prominent pastoralist and member of both houses of the NSW parliament. He contributed a series of historical sketches dealing with pastoral life, gold-mining, bushrangers and Aborigines to the Sydney *Daily Telegraph*. They were subsequently collected, titled *Australian Stories Retold and Sketches of Country Life* (1887). His grandfather, George Suttor (1774–1859) wrote memoirs of his life as a pioneer settler (published 1948) which are informative of life in Sydney in the early years of the nineteenth century.

'Swag' was originally an English word meaning the general booty or spoils from a robbery or theft and it is still used colloquially in that sense to mean a large quantity of goods. It was applied in 1819, by James Hardy Vaux in his 'flash' vocabulary, only to stolen wearing apparel, linen and piece goods. Later in the nineteenth century the term came to be part of the vocabulary of the Australian outback meaning, according to an 1857 definition, 'portable luggage that can be carried on the person'. That meaning has persisted to the present day, although many other different words, e.g. 'matilda', 'shiralee', 'bluey' and 'drum', have been used to denote the bundle of possessions that itinerant work-seekers (and avoiders) carried from place to place. The swag, a tightly rolled, sausage-shaped bundle, usually contained a blue blanket, hence 'bluey' for the swag itself, a waterproof sheet, spare clothes and personal odds and ends. The swag was slung over the shoulder by a piece of leather or rope and from it hung a sugar bag of food and a billy (q.v.) for making tea. Carrying the swag has been variously described as 'humping the bluey', 'humping the drum' and 'waltzing matilda'. Derivatives of swag include 'swagman' and 'swaggie', while variations of 'swagman' include 'bagman', from the English term for a commercial traveller; 'tramp', applicable to all itinerants, especially in the Depression years of the 1920s and 1930s; 'sundowner', because of the habit of arriving at a homestead or station at sundown, thus avoiding the risk of having to work for food; and 'whaler', itinerants like the *Bulletin*'s 'Scotty the Wrinkler', who travelled the inland rivers such as the Murrum-

bidgee, the Murray and the Darling. The profession of swag-carrying has produced a large vocabulary of associated colloquialisms, e.g. 'on the wallaby' denoting being on the track, and 'roll the swag' meaning to quit one's job. The swag and its carriers have been widely featured in Australian literature from the early colonial works of Alexander Harris, *The Emigrant Family* (1849), through and beyond the 1890s in Henry Lawson's *While the Billy Boils* (1896), *In the Days When the World Was Wide* (1896) and *On the Track* (1900), Barcroft Boake's *Where the Dead Men Lie* (1897), Barbara Baynton's *Bush Studies* (1902), John Farrell's *My Sundowner and Other Poems* (1904), John le Gay Brereton's *Swags Up!* (1928), E.P. Harrington's *The Swagless Swaggie and Other Ballads* (1957) and up to modern times in D'Arcy Niland's *The Shiralee* (1955). Among the best descriptions of the life and hard times of the swagman are Lawson's poems 'Out Back' and 'Knocked Up' and his short story 'Some Day'; John Shaw Neilson's poem 'The Sundowner'; Louis Esson's poem 'Whalin' Up the Lachlan'; 'J.P.B.'s' poems about derelict swaggies, 'His Story' and 'His Last Stage'; and A.J. Boyd's sketch 'The Swagsman' in *Old Colonials* (1882). The swag and the swagman have also been celebrated in folk-songs and ballads, e.g. 'Australia's on the Wallaby', 'Humping Old Bluey', 'Three Little Johnny Cakes', 'The Reedy Lagoon', 'The Old Bark Hut', 'The Ramble-eer', 'With My Swag All on My Shoulder' and 'My Old Black Billy'. The Australian literary journal *Overland* has a page of topical comment, initiated by its late editor, Stephen Murray-Smith, titled 'Swag'. The Bronze Swagman Award (a bronze statuette of a swagman, sculpted by Daphne Mayo, and a Winton opal) is awarded annually by the Winton Tourist Promotion Association for the best bush verse of the year. Edel Wignell edited a collection of prose and poetry about swagmen in 1985, titled *A Bluey of Swaggies* and Allan Nixon wrote *The Swagmen* (1987), subsequently produced for television.

SWAN, Nathaniel Walter (1834–84), born Ireland and educated at the University of Glasgow, came to Victoria during the gold rushes. He became acquainted with Henry Kingsley, who advised him to take up writing, and with Adam Lindsay Gordon, Marcus Clarke and Henry Kendall. A contributor to numerous colonial newspapers, he edited the *Ararat Advertiser* and the *Pleasant Creek News* and was for a time proprietor of the *Stawell News*. Three publications by Swan were issued, *Tales of Australian Life* (1875), which includes a short novel, 'Marie Denton', and short stories dealing mainly with life on the diggings; *A Couple of Cups Ago* (1885), a collection of short stories, again reflecting his experiences of the diggings and of station life; and *Luke Mivers' Harvest* (1899), a novel for which he won the *Sydney Mail* prize in 1878 and which includes some effective descriptions of the Australian landscape, although the plot is unwieldy and the characters indistinct. *Luke Mivers' Harvest*, edited and introduced by Harry Heseltine, was published in UNSW's Colonial Texts series in 1991.

Swan River Colony, the infant colony of WA, took its title from the Swan River, on whose northern banks a settlement was established in 1829. Although Captain James Stirling (1791–1865) was not the first to discover the Swan River (it was found by Willem de Vlamingh, a Dutch seafarer, in 1697) he surveyed it in 1827 and became governor of the first settlement. Literature from the infant Swan River colony comprised mainly diaries, journals, letters and memoirs; representative samples, often published much later than the events they portray, include G.F. Moore's *Diary of Ten Years Eventful Life of an Early Settler in Western Australia* (1884); J.G. Hay's *The Visit of Charles Fraser ... to the Swan River in 1827* (1906); Peter Cowan's compilations, *A Faithful Picture: The Letters of Eliza and Thomas Brown at York in the Swan River Colony 1841–1852* (1977) and *A Colonial Experience: Swan River 1839–1888* (1978); and *The Tanner Letters: A Pioneer Saga of Swan River & Tasmania* (1981, ed. Pamela Statham). *Swan River Saga* (1975), a play by Mary Durack, re-creates the experiences of Eliza Shaw, an important pioneer woman. The well-known Swan River Aborigine, Yagan (q.v.), and the problem of White–Black relationships in pioneer times, are featured in Mary Durack's *The Courteous Savage: Yagan of Swan River* (1964) and in G.F. Moore's *Diary*. Popular modern historical novels about the colony are Rix Weaver's *Behold, New Holland* (1940) and *New Holland Heritage* (1941) and Phyllis Hastings's *The Swan River Story* (1968). In its first decade the Swan River colony boasted about ten newspapers, the most significant of which were the *Perth Gazette* and the *Swan River Guardian*.

Swords and Crowns and Rings, a novel by Ruth Park (q.v.), was published in 1977 and won the Miles Franklin Award. Set mainly in rural Australia 1907–32, it is the story of a dwarf's quest for self-acceptance, love and dignity. Jackie Hanna is fortunate in his mother, Peggy, and his stepfather, Jerry MacNunn. Their determination to discount his disability supports him during his childhood at Kingsland, a small town in NSW. He is also sustained by his close relationship with Cushie Moy, his 'princess', the daughter of a local bank employee and his class-conscious wife. After leaving school the only employment available to Jackie is on a fruit farm in the High Valley country owned by Jerry's German relations, the Linzes. Oafish and brutish in the extreme, the Linz brothers treat Jackie with the same cruelty that they show to all the members of their family. Only Maida, their young sister, who invites herself to Jackie's bed, and Hof, the eldest brother, show any kindness. After a particularly vicious and humiliating attack by the brothers, Jackie flees home and is passionately reunited with Cushie. But he soon decides to return to the Linz orchard as a gesture of self-respect, unaware that Cushie is pregnant. Mrs Moy secretly arranges an abortion in Sydney and Cushie is dispatched to be cared for by her eccentric, promiscuous Aunt Claudie and her lesbian housemate Iris. Cushie's humiliating experiences in Sydney strengthen her determination to break free from her dominating mother and she escapes to live with her wealthy grandmother in Balmain. Meanwhile, for Jackie, returning to the Linz farm has meant a forced marriage to the pregnant Maida. The child is stillborn but the couple find happiness on the shores of the River Dovey where Jackie works for a milk supplier, Lufa Morgan. Five years later when their son Carlie is seven months old, they are visited by Maida's embittered mother Eva. The visit ends tragically: Maida, Carlie and Eva die during a fire, Jackie's part in the catastrophe becomes a matter of notoriety and he discovers incidentally that Maida's first pregnancy has been to one of her brothers. After some time in the outback, Jackie in 1931 learns of his mother's death and returns to Kingsland, which has been affected by the Depression. The now elderly and grief-stricken Jerry MacNunn is forced to abandon the family shop and father and son take to the road, along with thousands of others, in search of work. Their journey, which is a sequence of hardships, terminates several months later in Sydney. There Jerry recovers some happiness and dignity and Jackie learns more of the world, finally coming to terms with his dwarfism. His odyssey is complete when chance reunites him with Cushie Moy.

S.W. Silver & Co'.s Australian Graziers' Guide, see 'BOLDREWOOD, Rolf'; Almanacs

Sydney, the oldest city in Australia and the capital of New South Wales, is situated on the eastern coast of the continent. It developed around Port Jackson (Sydney Harbour) and now extends northwards to the Hawkesbury River, southwards past Botany Bay (the original landing place of the First Fleet) and westwards to the Nepean River. It takes its name from Viscount Sydney, home secretary to whom Arthur Phillip reported, but was never officially named, evolving from Sydney Cove, near the present Opera House, where the first settlement was established. Very much a convict settlement in its early years, Sydney began to be laid out during Governor Macquarie's term of office; its first municipal council was formed in 1842. Overtaken briefly by Melbourne during the latter part of the nineteenth century, Sydney is now the largest city in Australia; 20 per cent of Australians live there. Patricia Holt edited *A City in the Mind: Sydney Imagined by its Writers* (1983). She turns to writers such as Ada Cambridge, Christina Stead, Donald Horne to draw out the character of certain corners of Sydney, and traces the changing moods of the city from mid-nineteenth to late twentieth century. Numerous other books on Sydney include Tom Thompson (ed.), *The View from Tinsel Town* (1985), which contains essays on Sydney and its culture stemming from the 1985 Sydney Festival; Jim Davidson's *The Sydney-Melbourne Book* (1986), which looks at the social, cultural and political differences between the two rival cities, known to the 'literati' as 'Tinsel Town' and 'St. Petersburg'; Louise Johnson's *Gaslight Sydney* (1984), which presents a traveller's view of Sydney of the past; Shirley Fitzgerald's *Sydney 1842–1992* (1992), commissioned by the Council of the City of Sydney to commemorate the sesquicentenary of its incorporation; Peter Kirkpatrick's *The Sea Coast of Bohemia: Literary Life in Sydney's Roaring Twenties* (1992); Jan Morris's *Sydney* (1992) and Margaret Throsby's *Sydney People and Places* (1992). Robert Gray and Vivian Smith edited the sesquicentenary celebratory work *Sydney's Poems* (1992).

Sydney Delivered: Or, The Princely Buccanneer is a short farce by David Burn (q.v.) published in 1845 under the pseudonym 'Tasso Australasiatticus', but never performed. The work, which has more vitality than Burn's serious dramas, is set in Tahiti and deals with an Anglo-French confrontation, thus reflecting Burn's interest in colonial defence and general naval matters. The play was reprinted in facsimile form in 1989 edited by Patricia Clancy.

Sydney Gazette (1803–42), Australia's first newspaper, was first published by George Howe (q.v.); it remained in the control of the Howe family for much of its life. Significant contributors included Charles de Boos, Henry Halloran, Edward O'Shaughnessy, Michael Massey Robinson and Charles Tompson; in addition, the advertisements and notices in the *Gazette* provide valuable evidence of the literary interests and habits of the colonists during the foundation years of settlement. Mainly pro-government, the *Sydney Gazette* eventually succumbed to the competition of the *Sydney Morning Herald* and the effects of the 1840s depression.

Sydney Mail, the weekly companion to the *Sydney Morning Herald*, was published 1860–1938. Like its rival the *Australian Town and Country Journal*, it was popular with both country and city readers, and combined general news with agricultural, pastoral, mining, sporting and literary features and included illustrations. A.B. Paterson was its Boer War correspondent, and 'Rolf Boldrewood' had his *Robbery Under Arms* serialised there in 1882–83. Its editors included W.H. Traill, F.W. Ward (1879–84), Edwin Burton (1885–98), J.P. Dowling (1895–1905) and W.R. Charlton (1905–38).

Sydney Monitor, a prominent early Australian newspaper, began publication in 1826 as the *Monitor*, its title until 1828, and ran mainly as a weekly or semi-weekly until 1841. For much of its time under the control of its founder Edward Smith Hall (q.v.), the 'Australian Cobbett', the *Monitor* was aggressively pro-convict and anti-government in its early years, particularly during the governorship of Sir Ralph Darling. It welcomed Darling's more liberal successor, Sir Richard Bourke, although siding with James Mudie, who was contemptuous of convicts, during Mudie's disputes with Bourke in 1834. In 1835 the *Monitor* published extracts from Charles Harpur's play *The Bushrangers* (1853) under the title 'The Tragedy of Donohoe'.

Sydney Morning Herald, the oldest surviving Australian newspaper, commenced publication as a weekly, the *Sydney Herald*, in 1831; two of its three founders, William McGarvie and Alfred Ward Stephens (qq.v.), alternated ownership during its first decade. In 1840 it became a daily and the following year was bought by John Fairfax (q.v.) and Charles Kemp, and in 1842 took its present title. In the 1840s it became established as Sydney's leading newspaper, a position retained despite competition from the *Empire* under the youthful Henry Parkes (qq.v.) and after 1879 from the *Daily Telegraph* (q.v.). From 1853, when Fairfax bought out Kemp, until 1956, when a public company was formed, the *Sydney Morning Herald* remained under the financial control of the Fairfax family. A conservative organ for most of its life, the *Sydney Morning Herald* – or 'Granny' to many of its readers since about 1850 – is, along with the *Age* (q.v.) (which the Fairfax Group absorbed in 1983), Australia's most famous newspaper and one of the few to achieve a world-wide reputation. Its editors have included several prominent names in Australian journalism, notably John West (1854–73), Andrew Garran (1873–85), William Curnow (1886–1903), Thomas Heney (1903–18), C. Brunsdon Fletcher (1918–37), H.A. McClure Smith (1938–52), and John Douglas Pringle (1952–57, 1965–70) and its staff or contributors a number of prominent Australian writers, including S.J. Baker, C.E.W. Bean, Marcus Clarke, Leon Gellert, Charles Harpur, Montague Grover, A.B. Paterson, and Catherine Helen Spence (qq.v.). The company publication of John Fairfax & Sons, *A Century of Journalism: The Sydney Morning Herald and Its Record of Australian Life 1831–1931* (1931) has extensive information on the first hundred years of the *Sydney Morning Herald* and on other Fairfax publications; its more recent history, and information on the activities of the Fairfax organisation in radio, television and other ventures, is detailed in Gavin Souter's prize-winning *Company of Heralds: A Century and a Half of Australian Publishing by John Fairfax Limited and Its Predecessors 1831–1981* (1981); his later work, *Heralds and Angels* (1991, updated in 1992) gives an account of the *Sydney Morning Herald* falling into receivership after the Warwick Fairfax downfall and the Conrad Black takeover in 1991. See also Fairfax, John; Souter, Gavin.

Sydney Punch, see **Melbourne Punch**

Sydney Quarterly Magazine, published by the Sydney Quarterly Magazine club, ran 1883–92 and included some articles on literary subjects and some original poetry. J. le Gay Brereton was a contributor.

Sydney Studies in English, an annual publication jointly sponsored by the Department of English at the University of Sydney and the Sydney branch of the English Association (q.v.), began publication in 1975. Designed to strengthen the relationship between the university and the study of English at secondary level, it often publishes papers on texts set for study in schools. Co-edited (1992) by G.A. Wilkes and A.P. Riemer, it is now mainly devoted to criticism and scholarship in English literature.

Sydney University Magazine, the first magazine of the University of Sydney, ran for three issues in 1855, sponsored by Dr John Woolley, edited by three students, Alexander Oliver, James Stewart Paterson and William Windeyer, and assisted by Henry Parkes, then editor of the *Empire*. Surprisingly nationalistic in its social, cultural and political aims, the *Magazine* included some original verse, the first episode of a serialised novel, and essays on English literature, all contributed anonymously. Two subsequent journals, published in 1878–79 and 1885, had the same title although the 1878–79 journal edited by Joseph Sheridan Moore was not published under the auspices of the University; its contributors included Henry Kendall, Henry Halloran and Moore.

Sydney University Review, founded and administered by the University Union, ran for five issues 1881–83. According to its first issue the *Review* intended to provide 'a platform' from which Australian writers could 'express their matured thoughts' and to act 'as a nursery for aspirants to literary fame' and aspired to attract contributions from numerous eminent Australians. Some poetry by Henry Kendall, Henry Halloran, Emily Manning and C.E.W. Bean is included in its issues, although articles on education, theology, history and legal matters predominate. Articles of literary interest include W.B. Dalley's obituary essay on Kendall (December 1882) and George Knox's review of the first century of Australian verse (July 1883).

SYKES, Roberta (Bobbi) (1943–), born Queensland, a prominent activist for Aboriginal rights, left school at 14 and has had numerous occupations. She was the first executive secretary of the Aboriginal Embassy erected on the lawns in front of Parliament House, Canberra, in 1972; has written and lectured widely on race relations in Australia, the USA, Great Britain, Jamaica and NZ; has worked voluntarily for the Aboriginal medical and legal services; and was the first person of Aboriginal descent to graduate from Harvard University, where she earned first a master's degree and then a doctorate in education. She is also a member of the Australian Advisory Committee on the Environment. She has written an analysis of twenty-one years of Black Australian experience, *Black Majority* (1989) and an account of the nature and consequences of non-Aboriginal educational systems for the Black community, *Incentive, Achievement and Community* (1986); contributed to a debate with Senator Neville Bonner, *Black Power in Australia* (1975); helped Colleen Shirl Perry, one of the founders of the Aboriginal medical and legal services, to compose her autobiography, *Mum Shirl* (1981); and published a collection of poems, *Love Poems and Other Revolutionary Actions* (1979). She was awarded the 1981 Patricia Weickhardt Award for an Aboriginal writer. See also Aboriginal Writing/Testimony in English.

SYME, David (1827–1908), newspaper proprietor, was born and educated in Scotland and joined the Victorian gold rush in 1852. In 1856 he purchased a half-share in the fledgling *Age* (q.v.) newspaper from his brother Ebenezer (1826–60) and on Ebenezer's death took over the management of the paper. Under Syme for almost half a century, the *Age* supported protection and adopted a liberal radical stance, growing substantially in political influence until in the 1890s it had acquired a virtual power of veto over ministerial appointments. A man of few friends, Syme was nevertheless on terms of intimacy with Alfred Deakin, who became his protégé in journalism and politics. Syme also won minor repute as a political economist with the publication of *Outlines of an Industrial Science* (1876). The subject of biographies by Ambrose Pratt in 1908 and Charles Sayers in 1965, Syme was also the subject of Ranald Macdonald's 1982 Daniel Mannix memorial lecture, *David Syme* (1982). His career and influence are discussed in Stuart Macintyre's *A Colonial Liberalism: The Lost World of Three Victorian Visionaries* (1991).

SZYMANSKI, Leszek (1933–) was born and educated in Warsaw. In 1956 he became editor of an independent literary magazine, the *Contemporary*, which took its title from a literary group he founded. Szymanski left Poland in the 1960s and spent some time in Australia; he now lives in Los Angeles. He has published a collection of short stories, some of which are set in Australia, *Escape to the Tropics* (1964) and the autobiographical *On the Wallaby Track* (1967); an account of some of his experiences in Australia, *Living with the Weird Mob* (1973); *Warsaw Aflame* (1967), a description of the German occupation of Poland; and *Candle for Poland* (1982), an account of the Solidarity movement.

T

Table Talk, an illustrated Melbourne journal established by Maurice Brodzky, who edited it until 1903, ran 1885–1939, merging with *Melbourne Punch* in 1929. Strongly literary in flavour, it carried short fiction, serials, poetry, sketches, literary and theatrical reviews, and biographical sketches.

Tabloid Story, a publishing experiment designed to provide an outlet for new short fiction, was devised in 1972 by Michael Wilding, Frank Moorhouse (qq.v.) and Carmel Kelly, joined later by Brian Kiernan and Colin Talbot; in 1975 control of the magazine passed to a group of Melbourne writers. Dissatisfied with the lack of opportunities available through the established literary magazines for short fiction that did not conform to the Lawson tradition, the founders of *Tabloid Story* developed the concept of preparing a tabloid fiction supplement ready for printing which could be offered free to an established journal; in return, the host journal would print the *Tabloid Story* issue and publish it as a supplement, supplying additional copies to the editors for distribution to subscribers and contributors. Assisted by a CLF grant, *Tabloid Story* first appeared in October 1972 in *National U*, the newspaper of the Australian Union of Students. With continuing government support, it was later hosted by other student newspapers, e.g. *Newswit, Semper Floreat, Honi Soit, Lot's Wife, Tharunka*; by radical or fringe newspapers and little magazines, e.g. *Living Daylights, Nation Review, New Literature Review, Warringah Women's Times*; and by more middle-of-the-road journals, e.g. *Bulletin, Australian Book Review*. The fiction in *Tabloid Story* was characterised by its sexual explicitness, the radical, political and social stance of many of its writers, and its eclecticism of form and techniques, including fabulist, process and confessional stories. Among contributors to *Tabloid Story*, apart from Moorhouse, Wilding, Kelly and Talbot, were Murray Bail, Peter Carey, Laurie Clancy, Kris Hemensley, Elizabeth Jolley, Rudi Krausmann, Peter Mathers, Dal Stivens and Vicki Viidikas. Michael Wilding's selection from the first nineteen issues of *Tabloid Story*, published in 1978 as *The Tabloid Story Pocket Book*, includes an account of the magazine's evolution. It ceased publication in 1980.

TAIT Family was involved in theatrical and concert management in Australia for many years. The family included five sons of John Turnbull Tait (1829–1902), a Scotsman who migrated to Victoria in 1862: Charles Tait (1868–1933), John Henry Tait (1871–1955), James Nevin Tait (1876–1961), Edward Joseph Tait (1878–1947) and Frank Samuel Tait (1883–1965). One of the earliest achievements of Charles, John and James was the production of a popular film, *The Story of the Kelly Gang* (1906). In 1908 John and James, guided by their brother Charles, established a concert bureau, J. & N. Tait, which rapidly expanded into theatrical management. They were later joined by their brothers Edward and Frank. In 1920 the Taits merged with the giant of theatrical management in Australia, J.C. Williamson Ltd, and were responsible for the visits of numerous world artists such as Pavlova, Paderewski, Harry Lauder and Gracie Fields; from 1920 to the 1950s they dominated the production of ballet and opera in Australia. The family's achievements are recorded in Viola Tait's *A Family of Brothers* (1971).

Taking Stock (1953), edited by W.V. Aughterson, one-time professor of education at the University of Melbourne, is a collection of assessments of mid-twentieth-century Australian society. Concerned to preserve and defend the good aspects of Australian life, *Taking Stock* examines the problems facing Australia in the second half of the century. Contributors are Aughterson, W. MacMahon Ball, W. D. Borrie, Robin Boyd, Donald Cochrane, Allan McCulloch, P.H. Partridge, A.A. Phillips, G.V. Portus, Geoffrey Sawer and W.H. Stanner. Phillips contributed the essay 'Australian Literature', and Alan McCulloch 'Australian Art'.

TALBOT, Colin (1948–) has worked as a journalist and in radio and has spent some time in the USA. He has published two novels, *Massive Road Trauma* (1975) and *Sweethearts* (1978); a collection of his journalism, *Colin Talbot's Greatest Hits* (1977); a collection of verse, *Creek Roulette* (1973); and has compiled, with Robert Kenny, an anthology of poetry, *Applestealers* (1974). He has been a director of Outback Press and was involved in *Tabloid Story*.

TALBOT, Norman (1936–), born Suffolk, England, has taught English at the University of Newcastle since 1963 and has published several collections of verse, *Poems for a Female Universe* (1968), *Son of a Female Universe* (1971), *The Fishing Boy* (1973, illustrated by John Montefiore), *Find the Lady* (1977), *Where Two Rivers Meet* (1980), *The Kelly Haiku & Other Widdershin Tracks* (1985) and *Four Zoas of Australia* (1992, introduced by Gwen Harwood). A strong supporter of the arts in the Newcastle area, Talbot was founder and president of Nimrod publications, which has published the work of more than 200 Hunter Valley writers as well as collections of writing by disabled people. A colleague of the Welsh-born poet T. Harri Jones, Talbot published the poem *The Seafolding of Harri Jones* (1965), after Jones's death by drowning. With Zeny Giles he edited *Contrast and Relief* (1981), short stories from the Hunter Valley. He also edited and introduced the verse of T.H. Naisby, *The Pink Tongue* (1990).

Tales of the Colonies: Or, The Adventures of an Emigrant was published in London in 1843 by Charles Rowcroft (q.v.) but was attributed to 'A Late Colonial Magistrate'. The preface reveals the emigrant guidebook nature of the novel: 'this book was written with the view of describing the process of settling in a new country; the precautions to be taken; the foresight to be exercised; the early difficulties to be overcome; and the sure reward, which awaits the prudent and industrious colonist.' It purports to be the journal of William Thornby, who emigrates to Van Diemen's Land, settles on a grant of land, establishes a house and farm and experiences such hazards of pioneer life as sheep-stealers, bushrangers, Aboriginal attackers, floods, snakes, eagles and wild cattle. The novel also provides a prolonged account of the convict system as it operates in Van Diemen's Land. A highly popular work, *Tales of the Colonies* was translated into both French and German. See Aborigine in White Australian Literature.

'Tasma', see **COUVREUR, Jessie**

TASMAN, Abel Janszoon (?1603–59), the Netherlands mariner and explorer, undertook between 1633 and 1649 numerous trading and military voyages for the Dutch East India Company; two of these expeditions, 1642 and 1644, resulted in important discoveries about Australia. Tasman subsequently engaged in private trading and became one of the largest landowners in Batavia. His journal of his 1642 voyage to Van Diemen's Land and NZ was first published in England in 1694. There have been numerous biographies of Tasman, including James Backhouse Walker's (1896), and Andrew Sharp has written an account of his voyages (1968). In addition to Tasmania itself his name has been applied to numerous geographical and other features. Tasman's achievements have been celebrated in poems by Frances Sescadorowna Lewin (1889) and E.J. Brady (1909) and he is the hero of R.D. FitzGerald's well-known poem 'Heemskerck Shoals' (1949). He also appears in Ernest Favenc's novel *Marooned on Australia* (1896). Extracts from the journals, edited by Edward Duyker, were published in 1992.

Tasmanian was an early Tasmanian newspaper which had a complicated publishing history over twenty years, involving several prominent pioneering journalists. A weekly for most of its life, it was founded in 1825 by George Terry Howe in Launceston as the *Tasmanian and Port Dalrymple Advertiser*; later that year Howe moved his press to Hobart to help produce the *Hobart Town Gazette*. In 1827 he re-established the *Tasmanian* but sold it several months later to

J.C. Macdougall, who in 1829 amalgamated the journal with R.L. Murray's *Murray's Austral-Asiatic Review* to form the *Tasmanian and Austral-Asiatic Review*. The two journals amalgamated, usually under the title of the *Tasmanian and Austral-Asiatic Review*, in 1829–33, 1834–37 and 1841–45; in 1834 and 1837–41 they co-existed in Hobart. Murray was involved in the proprietorship either of his own *Austral-Asiatic Review* or of the amalgamated journal throughout this period; Macdougall sold his interests to Henry Melville (q.v.) in 1831 but resumed his involvement in 1838. Other journalists who wrote for or helped to edit the *Tasmanian* in one or other of its forms were Thomas Richards and Henry Savery. In 1845 the journal was incorporated into the *Colonial Times*.

Tasmanian Punch, see **Melbourne Punch**

TATE, Henry (1873–1926), born Prahran, Melbourne, was a successful musician, composer and music critic for the *Age* (1924–26), as well as a poet and short-story writer. His ideas for an individual and distinctive Australian music are contained in *Australian Musical Possibilities* (1924). An active participant in the Australian Institute of Arts and Literature, Tate worked with Louis Esson, William Moore and Bernard O'Dowd. He joined Moore and Dora Wilcox in a musical version of their play 'The Dangerous Moonlight', and composed musical settings for the poems of 'Furnley Maurice', titled *Songs of Reverie*. His verse included *The Rune of the Bunyip (Four Grotesques)* (1910), *Lost Love* (1918) and a collected edition, *The Poems of Henry Tate* (1928). His short stories appeared in the *Bulletin*, the Sydney *Sun*, and in Melbourne newspapers.

TAYLOR, Adolphus George (1857–1900), born Mudgee, NSW, was a teacher and journalist there and in Bathurst before entering politics in the early 1880s. In 1890 he became first editor of *Truth*; replaced by John Norton in 1891, he returned to the position 1893–96. A colourful figure known by such nicknames as 'Giraffe' and 'The Mudgee Camel', Taylor was rumbustious and unstable but had a flair for investigative journalism and for the rough and tumble of colonial politics. His satire *The Marble Man* was published in 1889.

TAYLOR, Andrew (1940–), born Warrnambool, Victoria, studied arts and law at the University of Melbourne, where Vincent Buckley encouraged his interest in poetry. He graduated MA from Melbourne and studied and travelled in Europe and the USA, returning to Australia in 1965. From 1971 he taught in the English Department of the University of Adelaide and is now professor at Edith Cowan University, WA. Active in the Australian literary scene, Taylor has been involved in various writers' organisations and has officiated as chairperson of Writers' Week at the Adelaide Festival of the Arts. He has also been a member of the Literature Board of the Australia Council and was made AM for his services to literature. He took part in the poetry readings at La Mama in 1968 and was active in SA's Friendly Street poetry group, editing, with Ian Reid, the second Friendly Street anthology in 1978. His numerous collections of poetry began with *The Cool Change* (1971). Then followed *Ice Fishing* (1973), *The Invention of Fire* (1976), *The Cat's Chin and Ears* (1976), *Parabolas: Prose Poems* (1976), *The Crystal Absences, The Trout* (1978), *Selected Poems 1960–1980* (1982, updated *1960–1985*, 1988), *Travelling* (1986, regional winner of the British Airways Commonwealth Poetry Prize) and *Folds in the Map* (1991). He has edited a collection of short fiction, *Unsettled Areas* (1986), with Ian Reid the second annual *Friendly Street Poetry Reader (1978), with Judith Rodriguez Poems Selected from the Australian's 20th Anniversary Competition* (1985) and with Russell McDougall *(Un)common Ground: Essays in Literature in English* (1990); translated with Beate Josephi selected poems from four German writers in a collection titled *Miracles of Disbelief* (1985); written a book for children, *Bernie the Midnight Owl* (1984); and the first full-length deconstructive study of the Australian poetic tradition from Lawson to Tranter, *Reading Australian Poetry* (1987). He has also written the libretti for two operas, *Letters of Amalie Dietrich* (1988) and *Barossa* (1988). The two *Selected* volumes offer a good sample of Taylor's poetry; the 1982 edition has sections from *The Cool Change* (poems from 1960 to 1970), *Ice Fishing* (poems from 1970 to 1972), *The Cat's Chin and Ears* (1971 to 1973), *The Invention of Fire* (1973 to 1975) and a group of poems from 1975 to 1980, while the 1988 edition adds a substantial group from *Travelling*. *Parabolas*, short, often anecdotal, prose pieces that Taylor wrote while visiting Berkeley and Yale in 1975, are part of both books. Taylor has omitted *The Crystal Absences, The Trout* because it was conceived as a single poem and would not, he felt, benefit by division. That omission is unfortunate because *The Crystal Absences*, poems written on a regular basis while his wife Beate was visiting her parents in Germany, are sensitive and appealing love poems.

Because of his Melbourne academic background Taylor's early poetry has sometimes been regarded as based upon and influenced by the Melbourne University writers of the 1960s and 1970s, *The Invention of Fire*, for example, being linked to Chris Wallace-Crabbe. Taylor is, however, an innovative, individual and experimental poet. Athough his poetry is wide-ranging in reflecting his extensive travels, it is also narrowly and finely focused, contemplative and inward. Open-ended and unemphatic, his poems are frequently meditations which record the irresolutions and disconnections of living and are receptive to the contradictions and ambiguities of an indefinite self: 'Better to choose what isn't you/ if you is what you want to find.' Both landscape and language figure prominently, often as persistent testimonies to the gulf between human need and actuality. Concerned with the substance, solidity and endurance of landscape, compared with the transience of human experience, Taylor is also preoccupied with landscape's unreliability and the way that its existence defies appropriation by ideas even as it is determined by them: 'Landscape without ideas of it/ hasn't been seen.' Writing a 'difficult' poetry, especially in earlier collections, Taylor

seeks to transcend the imposed difficulties of language: 'there are times/ words have to be trodden on/ and ridden across and scraped over/ before they'll reveal the reticence/ that knows how to speak/ if you know how to listen' ('Yugoslav Triptych').

Travelling has three sections: a sequence of poems 'Parts of the World', where the landscape is seen as, above all, a landscape of the mind, whose true meaning lies not in its physical self but in the meaning and significance that the poet brings to it; a second section of lyrics on various themes; and a long poem of eighteen sections, 'Travelling to Gleis-Binario', based on Taylor's travels through Europe. To the uninitiated 'Gleis-Binario' might appear to be a geographical locality; Taylor explains that it, too, is a locality of the mind, conjured up by combining the German and Italian words for that part of a railway station where one boards the train. *Travelling* is Taylor in his characteristically wry, meditative, polished poetic mode. *Folds in the Map* (1991) has some droll, enigmatic and clever poems, mixing prosaic subjects such as 'Spoons' ('I count them, like my friends'), 'Radio', 'Dish Drainers', 'Wineglass', 'Letterboxes' with pertinent philosophic comments. In the final section the importance of relationships both to places and people, a regular characteristic of his poetry, notably in *The Crystal Absences*, is reaffirmed. 'Walluf am Rheim', a fine poem that integrates intellect and emotion, affirms the sanctity of family.

TAYLOR, Geoff (1920–), born England, grew up in Australia and served in the RAAF during the Second World War. He flew briefly on operations with an RAF squadron of the Bomber Command before he was shot down in October 1943 and spent two years as a POW. After the war he returned to Melbourne, where he has worked in journalism and advertising. His first book, *Piece of Cake* (1956), recounts his experiences as a POW and most of his subsequent novels have drawn on his knowledge of flying and of Germany. They include *The Hollow Square* (1958), *Court of Honour* (1966), *Beware the Wounded Tiger* (1971), *The Nuremburg Massacre* (1979) and *The Hour of the Octopus* (1978). He has also written three other novels, *The Crop Dusters* (1960), which focuses on the exploits of agricultural pilots; *Dreamboat* (1962), a farcical story set in the world of advertising; and *Day of the Republic* (1968), a political fantasy of the future; *Sir* (1963), a tribute to his old headmaster, which is also an autobiography of childhood; a children's fantasy, *Blueberg* (1960); and *Return Ticket* (1972), an account of a return visit to Germany.

TAYLOR, G.A. (George Augustine) (1872–1928), born Sydney, first became known as an artist and cartoonist, a contributor of drawings to the *Bulletin*, the *Worker*, the *Sunday Times*, the *Referee* and the London *Punch*. A member of the Dawn and Dusk Club, and a particular friend of Victor Daley, he wrote his reminiscences of its personalities, *Those Were the Days* (1918), which is also valuable as a record of Sydney in the 1890s. In 1898 he launched a highly original comic paper, *Ha-Ha*, although it survived for only three issues. Subsequent periodicals that he founded and edited fared better and reflected his fervent nationalism and his numerous interests, aviation, engineering, radio technology and town planning. They include *Building*, the *Australasian Engineer*, the *Soldier*, the *Commonwealth Home* and the *Radio Journal of Australia*. He achieved original work in aviation and radio, constructing and successfully flying in 1909 a full-size biplane, the first flight in Australia of a manned heavier-than-air machine; his son, P.G. Taylor, flew with Charles Kingsford Smith. A prolific journalist, Taylor also published several minor works of fiction, *The Christmas Swag* (1902), *The Schemers* (1914), and *There!* (1916), as well as *The Sequel: What the Great War Will Mean to Australia* (1915), his most ambitious attempt to express his political ideas in fiction. He also published two collections of verse, *Songs for Soldiers* (1913) and *Just Jingles* (1922), and a travel book, *The Ways of the World* (1922). J.M. Giles has written *Some Chapters in the Life of George Augustine Taylor* (1957).

TAYLOR, Kay Glasson ('David Hamline') (1893–), born Kywanna, Queensland, published her first book, *Ginger for Pluck*, a children's story of station life, under the pseudonym 'David Hamline' in 1929. Her other children's stories and popular fiction include *Pick and the Duffers* (1930), *Many Years: A Story of Russia during the War and the Revolution* (1931), *Wards of the Outer March* (1932), which won second prize in the *Bulletin* novel competition in 1930, and *Bim* (1947).

TAYLOR, Ken (1930–), born Ballarat, Victoria, trained and worked as a journalist before travelling in Europe 1949–51. He later farmed in Queensland then joined the ABC as a radio drama producer in 1962. Interested in South-East Asia studies, he took up a Harkness Fellowship to study in the USA in 1965 but switched his interest to literature, studying at Cornell University. Back in Australia in late 1967 he became active in the emerging La Mama poetry workshops, and returned again in the 1980s to La Mama Poetica. His first poetry was published in *Two Poets* (1968), shared with Kris Hemensley). During the 1970s he became a well-known documentary film-maker specialising in natural history. His first major book of verse was *At Valentines*, published in 1975 but containing numerous poems written in the 1960s at Cornell and in Australia. 'At Valentine's – part one' was read at La Mama as early as 1969. A long poem with extremely short lines, it is based on Taylor's boyhood memories of holidays spent with his grandparents; a pot-pourri of sights, sounds and atmospheres, it conjures up countless echoes of the past – an Australian bushfire; old gramophone records that sent forth their music 'from a verandah to the bush'; 'bottles by the thousands'; tins by the tonne; card games; rainy days and nights; Miss Howell and her cottage, which smelt 'of sour milk on old stones'; the ever-present desiccating Australian sun; old-style cars with 'side running boards' and many other pieces of flotsam, stored up in countless similar Australian homes and sheds of the period. Somewhat similar in its montage effect is the impressive 'Pictures from the Sea', a kaleidoscope of

colour and action with a long string of vivid images of bird and marine life, and scenes of maiming and killing by man and animal, all associated with the sea and its environs. *A Secret Australia* (1985), Taylor's second major book of verse, contains, in the 'Selected Poems' section, the best of his earlier work as well as a group of new poems and an essay on Taylor and his poetry (the title piece) by Robert Kenny, first published in *3 Blind Mice* in 1977 and expanded and updated for this edition. The 'new poems' include the laconic but precise 'Flying into Meekatharra', 'John Olson at Lake Eyre 1977' and 'The Twelve Apostles' poem as well as the nostalgic 'Old Songs', 'The Modern World' and 'The Alexandria Tea Rooms – Ballarat'. Taylor also wrote 'At Valentine's – part two', which, with its emphasis on modern ugliness, draws the contrast between his 'secret Australia' (comparable to Les Murray's 'vernacular republic') and today's Australia which 'we own . . . the way a cripple owns a street'. A poet of deft and attractive images, Taylor often strikes an elegiac note.

'Teams, The', Henry Lawson's (q.v.) well-known ballad celebrating the bullock wagons that helped to open up the country in pioneering times, was first published in 1889; it is a popular anthology and recitation piece. Renowned for their strength, the bullock teams became the subject of many tall stories, notable among which was the occasion when one team became stuck in the river and was pulled out when another team was hitched on. In the process the bends in the river were straightened. The teams were not always composed of bullocks; those made up of horses, controlled by teamsters, were equally well known. The most famous account of the feats of the horse-drawn wagons is Will Ogilvie's poem 'How the *Fire Queen* Crossed the Swamp'.

TEGG, James (1808–45) and his brother, **Samuel Augustus** (1813–?), sons of Thomas Tegg, publisher and bookseller of Cheapside, London, arrived in Australia in 1834 and opened a bookshop in George Street, Sydney, in January 1835. Samuel returned to England the same year but in 1836 came back to open a bookshop in Hobart. Although primarily a bookseller, James Tegg was also an active and important publisher. He published *Tegg's New South Wales Pocket Almanac and Remembrancer* annually 1836–44, and *Tegg's Monthly Magazine*, edited by himself and devoted to general literature, in 1836. In the latter's first number appeared the celebrated story of Fisher's Ghost (q.v.). Other works published by James Tegg include *Literary News*, a weekly which he edited with William à Beckett, 1837–38, and works by James Martin, Henry Parkes, William Hovell and Hamilton Hume, and J.H. Plunkett. He was also involved in the *Handbook for Emigrants* published by his father in 1839.

Samuel Augustus Tegg added a circulating library to his Hobart bookshop in 1839, opened a further bookshop in Launceston in 1844 and left Tasmania in 1847 for London. He published works by David Burn, James Bonwick and Nathaniel Kentish.

Telegraph, a Brisbane daily afternoon newspaper, began publication in 1872; it was owned by the Telegraph Newspaper Company until 1955, when it came under the control of the Herald and Weekly Times group. A number of figures prominent in journalism in Queensland, e.g. Theophilus Pugh and George Hall, and in NSW, e.g. Thomas Heney and F.W. Ward, edited the *Telegraph*; Nat Gould's first Australian appointment was on the *Telegraph*, 1884–87.

TELFER, William, see **MILLISS, Roger**

'Tell Us About the Turkey, Jo', the title story of Alan Marshall's 1946 collection, describes the narrator's encounter with a small boy, Jimmy, and his elder brother Jo. Jimmy's delight in his brother's accounts of various disasters which have befallen himself in the past and his pride in the minor scars and bruises that resulted are interrupted by the arrival of their sister and the news that they have a new baby sister. Jimmy is unimpressed by the news and urges his brother to recount the story of 'how I got chased by the turkey'.

TEMPLEMAN, Ian, see **Fremantle Arts Centre**

TENCH, Watkin (?1758–1833), born Chester, England, entered the marine corps in 1776 and went with the First Fleet to Botany Bay. An enthusiastic explorer, he participated in expeditions which discovered the Nepean and Hawkesbury rivers and penetrated south as far as the Razorback Range fringing the Camden valley. Tench left the Colony in 1792 and continued his military career until his retirement with the rank of lieutenant-general in 1821. His valuable and lively accounts of the establishment of the Colony are *A Narrative of the Expedition to Botany Bay* (1789) and *A Complete Account of the Settlement at Port Jackson in New South Wales* (1793); they were combined as *Sydney's First Four Years* (1961), edited by L.F. Fitzhardinge.

TENISON-WOODS, Julian Edmund (1832–89), born London, migrated to Australia in 1854. Ordained a Roman Catholic priest in 1857, he was appointed to Penola, SA, where he befriended Adam Lindsay Gordon. Director-general of Catholic schools in SA from 1867, he edited various religious magazines; he published about 150 scientific papers after he relinquished his parochial duties in 1883 and became a wide-ranging scientific observer and investigator of the physical world of Australia, the East Indies and Japan. Two of Tenison-Woods's most significant works are *A History of the Discovery and Exploration of Australia* (1865) and a serialised survey, 'Australian Biography', in the *Australian Monthly Magazine* 1866–67. His biography, *Life of the Reverend Julian Edmund Tenison-Woods*, by G. O'Neill was published in 1929, and Margaret M. Press has written a fresh view of his career in *Julian Tenison Woods* (1979). His letters to William Henry Archer, a leading Catholic layman of Victoria, have been published titled *The Archer Letters* (1983), edited by Anne V. Player.

TENNANT, Kylie (1912–88), born Manly, NSW, had varied experience as journalist, publicity officer for the ABC, barmaid, church sister, reviewer and lecturer. She frequently tried to acquire first-hand experience for her novels, including taking to the roads with the unemployed in the 1930s Depression, living in Sydney's slums and with Aboriginal communities, travelling with itinerant bee-keepers and even spending a week in gaol. In 1932 she married the teacher and social historian Lewis Charles Rodd. She encountered numerous personal difficulties, including illness and the attempted suicides of her husband and son, both of whom predeceased her. Her novels include *Tiburon* (q.v. 1935) which won the S.H. Prior Memorial Prize, *Foveaux* (1939), *The Battlers* (q.v., 1941), which won both the S.H. Prior Memorial Prize and the Australian Literature Society's Gold Medal, *Ride On Stranger* (q.v., 1943), *Time Enough Later* (1943), *Lost Haven* (1946), *The Joyful Condemned* (1953, published in its full form with the title *Tell Morning This* in 1967), *The Honey Flow* (1956) and *Tantavallon* (1983). She also wrote *Speak You So Gently* (1959), an account of life in Aboriginal co-operatives; *Australia: Her Story* (1953), a popular history of Australia; a biography of the former Australian Labor leader H.V. Evatt (1970); *Ma Jones and the Little White Cannibals* (1967), a collection of short stories; a series of plays and books for children, including *All the Proud Tribesmen* (1959), winner of the 1960 Children's Book Award; *Tether a Dragon* (1952), a prize-winning play about Alfred Deakin; *The Man on the Headland* (1971), an account of the Diamond Head area of NSW; and an autobiography, *The Missing Heir* (1986). She also edited three collections of short stories.

A vigorous, versatile, high-spirited and witty writer, her fiction ranges from the satiric to the poetic and expresses a richly comic but sympathetic appreciation of multifarious humanity. The protagonists of her novels are usually the dispossessed and underprivileged slum-dwellers, juvenile delinquents, the unemployed, tramps and nomads of all descriptions. By no means an ideologue, she is more delighted with the spirited waywardness of her disparate outcasts than concerned to offer political or social remedies. Nevertheless, politics, education, the law and the bureaucracy are all subjected to her satirical wit. Characteristically, she affirms the value of life in the face of a clear perception of the tragedy of the human condition, a vision that is implicit in her richly suggestive descriptions of the indifferent Australian landscape, both natural and urban. A descriptive rather than a dramatic writer, she is more interested in groupings of people than in individuals and in general activity than in a single shaping action. Her prose style is flexible and expressive, moving easily from poetic suggestiveness to racy vigour. Margaret Dick has written a study of her fiction (1966). Tennant was made AO in 1980.

Terra Australis, meaning 'the South Land', and its derivatives Terra Australis Incognita (the unknown South Land), Terra Australis Nondum Cognita (the not-yet-known South Land) were Latin phrases printed on maps from the earliest times to represent the concept of a great undiscovered landmass in the southern oceans. The dream of discovering Terra Australis became an obsession that haunted the sea voyages of Spain, Portugal and England from the sixteenth to the eighteenth century. In 1568 Alvaro de Mendana discovered the Solomon Islands; in 1605 Pedro Fernandez de Quiros (see *Captain Quiros*) named the New Hebrides, in error, Austrialia del Espiritu Santo. Numerous Dutch voyagers, e.g Jansz, Hartog, Tasman, touched, often unwittingly, on the shores of Hollandia Nova, and the English explorers William Dampier and James Cook, the latter always sceptical of the existence of a great southern continent other than New Holland, made the first significant landfalls on the Australian coastline. It was not until Matthew Flinders (q.v.) circumnavigated the Australian continent in *Investigator*, 1801–3, and reported his findings in *A Voyage to Terra Australis* (1814), that the ghost of 'a great south land' other than Australia was laid to rest. The particular interest of 'Terra Australis' for Australian writers is evident in such poems as 'Australasia' by W.C. Wentworth, 'The Story of Abel Tasman' by Frances S. Lewin, 'The Dream of Dampier' by G.H. Supple, *Captain Quiros* (q.v.) by James McAuley, 'Five Visions of Captain Cook' (q.v.) by Kenneth Slessor; and in 'Terra Australis' poems by McAuley, Douglas Stewart and Chris Wallace-Crabbe. R.H. Major published *Early Voyages to Terra Australis, Now Called Australia* (1859) and Alan Frost *Terra Australis to Australia* (1988).

Territory, The (1951, republished 1991), an omnium gatherum of Northern Territory history, geography, legend, tall tale and folklore, was written by Ernestine Hill (q.v.) and illustrated by Elizabeth Durack. It is a Who's Who of Territory identities: the explorers John McDouall Stuart and Ludwig Leichhardt; the first overlander, D'Arcy Wentworth Uhr, who drove cattle from Queensland to Darwin in 1872; the legendary bushman Nathaniel ('Far Away') Buchanan, who helped establish several of the early stations; the Buffalo Bill of Australia, Rodney Spencer, who shot 6000 buffalo in three years; the horse-breaker Jack Macleod, who is the Quiet Stockman of *We of the Never Never* (1908); and unsung heroines such as Katie Rogers, Phoebe Farrar and Hazel Gaden, Territorian wives and mothers. Its pages are filled with fabled names: cattle stations such as the Elsey, Wave Hill, Brunette Downs, Victoria River Downs; stock routes such as the Canning, the Great North Road, the Georgina; and rivers such as the Victoria, the Ord, the Daly and the Roper. It describes significant events in the Territory's history: the construction of the overland telegraph line; the gold and diamond rushes at Pine Creek and in the Kimberleys; the early agricultural experiments with sugar, tobacco, coffee and rice; and the growth and development of Darwin, Australia's 'front gate'. It abounds in anecdote: macabre and grim, as in the Aboriginal massacres at the Barrow Creek telegraph station and at Daly River; and humorous, as in the exploits of the poddy-dodgers and brand-forgers. It concludes with an illuminating appendix of Territory phrases, which are frequently a combination of pidgin and bush colloquialisms.

Tharunka, a student newspaper of the University of NSW, began publication in 1953, and has frequently contained reviews and articles on Australian literature as well as some original poetry and short stories. In the early 1970s the newspaper became a significant underground libertarian publication under the editorship of Wendy Bacon, Val Hodgson and Alan Rees. Their publication of uncensored erotica, serialised banned books and obscene cartoons led to numerous prosecutions for obscenity, a week's goal term for Bacon, and the resignation of the editors to produce an independent magazine titled *Thorunka* (later *Thor*). Frank Moorhouse includes a description of this period in his collection *Days of Wine and Rage* (1980).

THATCHER, Charles (1831–78), born Bristol, England, was a flautist in theatre orchestras in London before seeking his fortune on the Victorian goldfields in 1852. Failing as a digger, Thatcher became a favourite goldfields entertainer, composing and singing catchy songs with topical local subjects. After several years in NZ (1861–66) he returned to Victoria, resuming his career as an entertainer, before leaving the Colony in 1869 to live again in England. Thatcher's songs, usually represented in anthologies of Australian folk-songs and ballads, were published as broadsheets in contemporary newspapers, and in such collections as *Thatcher's Victoria Songster* (1855), *Thatcher's Colonial Songster* (1857) and *Thatcher's Colonial Minstrel* (1859). Hugh Anderson (q.v.) compiled a selection of Thatcher's songs, *Goldrush Songster* (1958), and wrote the biography *The Colonial Minstrel* (1960). In Eric Lambert's novel *The Five Bright Stars* (1954) Thatcher engages in a singing contest with another character.

THATCHER, Dick (Richmond) (1842–91), brother of Charles Thatcher, was born Brighton, England. From 1871 he lived in NSW and was a journalist on the *Empire*, the *Evening News* and the *Australian Town and Country Journal*. He founded the *Upper Hunter Courier* at Murrurundi and edited the *Western Independent* at Bathurst. He edited several anthologies of stories, poems and articles, notably *Something to His Advantage* (1875), *Thatcher's Holiday Book* (1881) and, with Grosvenor Bunster, *It Runs in the Blood* (1872). He wrote fiction, including *Mr Newcombe in Search of a Cattle Station* (1868), *A Travelled Actor* (1881) and the biographical *Life and Times of Jem Punch* (1885).

Theatre-Australia, a monthly magazine edited by Bruce Knappett, Robert Page and Lucy Wagner, was published 1976–82. It included reviews of stage productions throughout Australia, playscripts, interviews with playwrights, directors and actors, a section on film, television and radio and general theatrical news.

Theatre Board, one of the original seven arts boards of the Australia Council (q.v.), was established in 1973; it received an annual allocation, the largest given to any of the seven boards, which was distributed to support drama and dance, principally in the form of grants to companies and theatres. It had a similar structure to the Literature Board (q.v.), which also assists theatre in Australia by awarding writing grants to dramatists, by subsidising the publication of Australian plays and by contributing to the cost of the Australian National Playwrights Conference. The Theatre Board has now been replaced by the Performing Arts Board, one of three art-form boards of the Australia Council.

Theatre Buildings in Australia to 1905 (1971), by Ross Thorne, is a detailed description, accompanied by numerous drawings, of the major theatres in Australia from the first settlement until the advent of cinema. The result of much original research, Thorne's study also focuses on historical and sociological changes and the impact of such events as the gold and mining booms on entrepreneurs, audiences and players. Thorne has also published *Picture Palace Architecture in Australia* (1976) and *Cinemas of Australia via U.S.A.* (1981).

Theatre in Australia, see ***Australian Stage, The***

Theatregoer, titled *Australian Theatregoer* in the first four issues, a magazine founded and edited by F.R. Harvey, published in Sydney and concerned with live theatre in Australia, appeared at irregular intervals 1960–63. It included reviews of productions, interviews with playwrights and actors, general articles on drama, and playscripts by Australian and English dramatists. In the December–January 1961–62 issue *Theatregoer* was published with *Australian Theatre Year*.

THEODORE, E.G. (Edward Granville) (1884–1950), born Port Adelaide, began his political career in the mining districts of northern Queensland and was Queensland premier 1919–25 before entering federal politics. He was treasurer and deputy prime minister 1929–30 in the James Scullin Labor ministry, resigned over a mining scandal in 1930, returned to parliament after being exonerated but lost his seat in 1931 and turned to business, helping to establish Australian Consolidated Press. In 1942 Prime Minister John Curtin invited him to accept the honorary wartime post of director-general of Allied Works, which he held until the end of the war. Vance Palmer drew on his career for the central character of his *Golconda* trilogy (q.v.), Macy Donovan, and he also figures as Ted Thurgood in Frank Hardy's novel *Power without Glory* (1950). Irwin Young wrote *Theodore: His Life and Times* (1971).

THERRY, Sir Roger (1800–74), born Cork, Ireland, arrived in Sydney in 1829 after being called to the English and Irish bars. He acted as attorney-general in NSW in the 1840s and served as a judge in Victoria and NSW. He also pursued a political career, although his Catholic religion aroused opposition. Generally well regarded as a judge, Therry acquired some notoriety for his championing of the rights of Catholics and his work as a pamphleteer. He retired from the Bench in 1859, returned to England and published his *Reminiscences of Thirty Years' Residence in New South Wales and Victoria* (1863), which immediately sold out in England. A second edition was recalled after reviews in Sydney had objected to some of Therry's opinions. Valuable as commentary on contemporary personalities and customs, the *Reminiscences* are particularly interesting on transportation.

'They'll Tell You About Me' is the title of Ian Mudie's (q.v.) celebrated pot-pourri of Australian myth, legend, tall tales, folklore and history. In ironic, colloquial language and spiced with the good-natured braggadocio that has come to be recognised as the stock-in-trade of the brash Australian male, the poem is a treasure chest of such Australiana as Eureka, Ned Kelly, the Man from Snowy River, Waltzing Matilda, the Dog on the Tuckerbox, Lasseter's Lost Reef, the Sydney Harbour Bridge, and Gallipoli.

THIELE, Colin (1920–), born Eudunda, SA, graduated from the University of Adelaide in 1941 and served with the RAAF in the Second World War. He taught in SA high schools 1946–56, before joining Wattle Park Teachers College of which he was principal 1965–73 and director 1974–80. A prolific writer of verse, fiction, children's books, radio plays, historical, environmental and educational texts and an editor of verse anthologies, short stories and one-act plays, Thiele has published more than ninety books, many of which have gone into multiple reprints and popular paperback editions. A leading literary figure, especially in SA, he is the author of numerous radio features and documentaries and has been active in numerous bodies associated with literature and education. He was made AC in 1977.

Thiele's strongly nationalistic poetry comprises *Progress to Denial* (1945), an elegy to a soldier killed in the Second World War, which won the W.J. Miles poetry prize; *Splinters and Shards* (1945), also largely war poems; *The Golden Lightning* (1951); *Man in a Landscape* (1960), which won the Grace Leven Prize for poetry; *In Charcoal and Conté* (1966); *Selected Verse* (1970); and *The Best of Colin Thiele* (1980), a combined selection of prose and verse. Although he has written novels and short stories for adults including *Labourers in the Vineyard* (1970) and *The Seed's Inheritance* (1986), Thiele's most successful fiction has been for children. *The Sun on the Stubble* (1961), a story of the German immigrant farmer family the Gunthers, was commended in both the Miles Franklin and Australian Children's Book of the Year Awards for 1962. *Storm Boy* (1963), Thiele's classic children's novel set on the Coorong, was made into a successful film in 1976 and won the Netherlands Award of the Silver Pencil. His other significant children's books include *The Rim of the Morning* (1966); *Blue Fin* (1969), a story of the tuna-fishing industry which was commended in the Hans Andersen Award in 1972 and filmed in 1978; *The Fire in the Stone* (1973), a story of the opal fields which won the Edgar Allan Poe Award in the USA; *Albatross Two*

(1974), a story set on an offshore oil rig; *Magpie Island* (1974); *The Hammerhead Light* (1976); *The Sknuks* (1977), a fable for small children which won the Austrian State Prize in 1979; *The Valley Between* (1981), which won his first Australian Children's Book of the Year Award; *The Shadow on the Hills* (1977); *Pinquo* (1983), which won the Austrian State Prize in 1986; *Coorong Captive* (1985); *Shatterbelt* (1987); and its sequel, *Aftershock* (1992). His environmental, historical and educational works include *Barossa Valley Sketchbook* (1968, illustrated by Jeanette McLeod); *Range without Man* (1974), on the North Flinders Ranges; *The Little Desert* (1975); *The Bight* (1976); and *Grains of Mustard Seed* (1975), a history of the SA Department of Education. Thiele also wrote the biography, *Heysen of Hahndorf* (1968). See also *The Oxford Companion to Australian Children's Literature* (1993), pp. 411–13.

THIRKELL, Angela (1890–1961), the well-known English novelist, spent some years in Australia and wrote one novel with Australian associations. The daughter of the classicist John W. Mackail, professor of poetry at Oxford, she was also the granddaughter of Edward Burne-Jones and was related to Rudyard Kipling and Stanley Baldwin. After a private education, she married James Campbell McInnes, a distinguished singer, in 1911 and had two sons, Graham McInnes and Colin MacInnes (qq.v.), and a daughter who died in infancy. The marriage ended in divorce in 1917 and the following year she married an Australian captain in the AIF, George Thirkell (q.v.). After some time in Sheffield, the Thirkells left for Australia in 1920 aboard a troop-ship, the *Friedrichsruh*; their journey became the subject of Angela Thirkell's novel *Trooper to the Southern Cross* (q.v., 1934), published under the pseudonym 'Leslie Parker'. In Australia they spent some time in Tasmania and then settled in Melbourne, where George Thirkell managed a works that produced motor accessories and Angela Thirkell became well known in cultural and social circles. Her Australian friends included such prominent individuals as Dame Nellie Melba, Sir John Monash, Ernest Scott, Arthur Streeton, Thea Proctor, Sir Hubert Murray and the governor-general, Lord Forster. Prompted partly by literary ambition and partly by lack of money, she began to contribute articles and short stories to English and Australian magazines and to broadcast on radio. She detested the restrictions of her life in Melbourne, however, and although another son, Lance, was born in 1921, her marriage to Thirkell rapidly deteriorated. The situation became critical after her husband's business failed during the Depression and she left permanently for England in 1929 with her sons Colin and Lance. Graham McInnes remained in Melbourne until 1934. In London Angela Thirkell recognised her true milieu and almost immediately began the writing career that resulted in thirty-five novels and made her one of England's best-known middle-brow woman novelists. Her years in Melbourne are memorably recorded in Graham McInnes's autobiographies *The Road to Gundagai* (q.v., 1965) and *Humping My Bluey* (1966) and are also

described in Margot Strickland's biography *Angela Thirkell* (1977).

THIRKELL, George (1891–1959) was born into an English family that had been settled in Tasmania since 1820. After graduating B.Sc. from the University of Tasmania he served at Gallipoli and in Europe. Three diaries that he kept at Gallipoli were referred to by the official war historian C.E.W. Bean. During his leaves in London he became friendly with many members of the upper class, was entertained by the Countess of Strathmore at Glamis Castle, and in 1918 married Angela McInnes, who was to become the well-known novelist Angela Thirkell (q.v.). The Thirkells left for Australia in 1920 and settled in Melbourne. When Angela left permanently for England in 1929 George Thirkell lived on in Melbourne, an increasingly pathetic figure. Lance Thirkell was educated in England and has had a distinguished career with the BBC. George Thirkell's personality has been memorably recorded in Angela Thirkell's novel *Trooper to the Southern Cross* (q.v., 1934), where he appears as the protagonist, Major Bowen, and in Graham McInnes's autobiographies *The Road to Gundagai* (q.v., 1965) and *Humping My Bluey* (1966), where he appears as 'Thirk'.

Thirty Years in Australia, a memoir by Ada Cambridge (q.v.), was published in 1903 and in 1989, edited by Margaret Bradstock and Louise Wakeling; it covers 1870–1900 and encompasses Cambridge's marriage to the clergyman George Cross, their almost immediate departure to Australia, and their life there spent mainly in the country districts of Victoria. Written with wit, compassion, humour and candour, *Thirty Years in Australia* chronicles Cambridge's struggles to make the best of things as the wife of a bush parson, the sense of exile, which remained with her for 'about seven-eighths of that long time in Australia', and the evolution of her literary career; one chapter deals with a memorable visit to Sydney in 1887, which she relished for the opportunity it gave her to meet writers and painters. The companion memoir, *The Retrospect* (1912), records her impressions and recollections of her youth when she was finally able to revisit England in 1908. She delighted in her liberation from exile but recognised the insularity of English society.

This Old Man Comes Rolling Home, a play by Dorothy Hewett (q.v.), was first performed in 1967 and published in 1976. Set in the 1950s in Redfern, one of Sydney's poorer suburbs, it presents a cross-section of working-class folk, bound together by their hardships and resilient humour. Central to the play are the vicissitudes within the large Dockerty family, headed by the feckless and alcoholic Laurie Dockerty, once the belle of Bundaberg, and her perpetually optimistic husband, Tom. Other striking characters are Julie Dockerty, the forceful eldest daughter; Edie, the strong, practical wife of Lan Dockerty; and Don Dockerty, a young spiv.

THOMAS, Evan Henry (?1801–37) was born in Ireland and arrived in Hobart in 1822, the year in which his poems in the *Hobart Town Gazette* were the first to be published in the infant colony of Van Diemen's Land. In 1824 he was appointed editor of the *Gazette* by Andrew Bent, with whom he fought strenuously to preserve the freedom of the press; Thomas wrote the famous editorial referring to George Arthur, later lieutenant-governor of Tasmania, as a 'Gideonite of Tyranny', for which Bent was imprisoned for libel. After his resignation from the *Gazette*, Thomas lived mainly at Launceston, where his play *The Bandit of the Rhine* was published in 1835; although the first Australian play to appear in book form, no copies of *The Bandit of the Rhine* are extant. Thomas also may have had a hand in the early satire *The Van Diemen's Land Warriors* (q.v., 1827).

THOMAS Family, well known in SA newspaper circles, included Robert Thomas (1781–1860), who was born in Wales, migrated to SA and in 1836 established, with George Stevenson, the *South Australian Gazette and Colonial Register*, later the *Register*. His second son, William Kyffin Thomas (1821–78), was connected with the paper, as were his grandsons, Sir Robert Kyffin Thomas (1851–1910) and Evan Kyffin Thomas (1866–1935), the latter also editing *Diary and Letters of Mary Thomas* (1915), a record of his grandmother's life as a pioneer in SA. Evan Kyffin's son, Archer Kyffin Thomas (1906–78), ultimately became editor of the Melbourne *Herald* (1945–56), editor-in-chief of the Herald and Weekly Times (1962–66) and chairman of Australian Associated Press (1966–68).

THOMES, William Henry (1824–95), born Portland, USA, worked on ships on the Californian hide trade before joining the gold rush to San Francisco. In 1851–55, during a visit which also took in Hawaii and China, Thomes worked on the Victorian goldfields as digger and storekeeper before returning to the USA to become a journalist and publisher. He used the Australian experience in two popular novels, *The Gold Hunters' Adventures: Or, Life in Australia* (1864) and its sequel *The Bushrangers* (1865), which together established his reputation. Among his later publications were *On Land and Sea* (1883), an account of his Californian experience and the most highly regarded of his dozen or so books, and another popular novel, *The Belle of Australia* (1883).

THOMPSON, John (1907–68), born Melbourne, was a war correspondent in New Guinea and Java 1945–46, and subsequently made a career as a broadcaster with the ABC. He was well known as an interviewer and published a series of interviews with prominent Australian poets in *Southerly*, as well as two collections of profiles of famous Australians, based on interviews, *On Lips of Living Men* (1962) and *Five to Remember* (1964). He also published four collections of his own poetry, *Three Dawns Ago* (1935), *Sesame and Other Poems* (1944), *Thirty Poems* (1954), winner of the Grace Leven Poetry Prize, and *I Hate and I Love* (1964); edited *Australian Poetry 1965* (1965) and, with Kenneth

Slessor and R.G. Howarth, *The Penguin Book of Australian Verse* (1958); and compiled *Alfred Conlon: A Memorial* (1963). His wife, Patricia Thompson (q.v.), describes his personality and achievements in her autobiography, *Accidental Chords* (1988).

THOMPSON, Patricia (1912–87), born Auckland, NZ, came to Australia in childhood and was educated at Sydney Girls High. In the late 1920s she became involved in Doris Fitton's Independent Theatre and worked with such individuals as Peter Finch, Frank Harvey, John Alden and William Rees. She left for London in the 1930s and was secretary for a period to the Australian painter Colin Colahan, who introduced her to her future husband, the poet John Thompson (q.v.). In 1938 the Thompsons returned to Perth, where John worked for the ABC; then associated with the Communist Party of Australia, they were friendly with Katharine Susannah Prichard and prominent in cultural circles, especially in the Patch Theatre. After moving to Collaroy in the late 1940s they adopted a child, Jack, of the same age as their natural son Peter; both men later achieved prominence, Jack as an actor and Peter as a journalist for the ABC. A subsequent move to Paddington, Sydney, led to the Thompsons' founding of the Paddington Society, forerunner of similar resident action groups in the 1950s. Patricia Thompson's autobiography, *Accidental Chords* (1988), is a frank, inward account of her relationship with her talented but dominant mother and incidentally informative about cultural circles in Sydney and Perth and the workings of the Communist Party in the war years. She also wrote accounts of the Northern Territory, *Our Northern Treasure House* (1956), and of the work of several Australian artists, *Twelve Australian Craftsmen* (1973), as well as the texts of three regional books in the Sketchbook series. She edited an edition of Mrs Clacy's *A Lady's Visit to the Gold Diggings of Australia in 1852–53* (1963) and, with Susan Yorke, *Lives Obscurely Great: Historical Essays on Women of New South Wales* (1980).

THOMPSON, Richard (1810–65), born England, was transported to NSW in 1834 for fourteen years for theft of silver. After a conditional pardon in 1842 he worked as a journalist in the Port Phillip District, then on the *Australian* in Sydney. He was editor of Robert Lowe's *Atlas* 1844–45, of another weekly serving the squatting interests, the *Spectator*, in 1846, and of the *Australian* 1847–48. In 1856 he edited the *Report of the Proceedings . . . to Celebrate the Establishment and Inauguration of Responsible Government in the Colony of New South Wales*. Thompson's other literary interests lay in supplying scripts for Sydney's theatrical activities and acting as a drama critic.

THOMPSON, Tom (1953–), born Parkes, NSW, was educated at Macquarie University and has worked as a bookshop manager and freelance journalist and publisher. Literary publisher until 1993 for Angus & Robertson, he was associate publisher with Collins Australia 1988–89, publisher for the Australian Bicentennial Authority 1984–88, editor of Red Press publications 1978–82 and associate editor at Currency Press 1977–79; he has also edited the magazines *Dodo*, *Leatherjacket* and *Australasian Small Press Review*. He has published two collections of verse, *The Island Hotel Dreams* (1977) and *From Here* (1978), and one of short stories, *Neon Line* (1978). He has edited *The View from Tinsel Town* (1985), the proceedings of the 1985 Sydney Writers' Festival in which fifteen writers discuss some of the cross-currents of Australian literature, and co-edited the prose anthology, *Island in the Sun* (1980); is co-author of two selections from the speeches of contemporary politicians; and selected and introduced two selections from Lennie Lower's writings, *Here's Lower* (1983), and *The Legends of Lennie Lower* (1988). He has also written *Growing Up in the 60s* (1986), an account of his childhood in Wagga Wagga, Broken Hill and Wollongong. With Elizabeth Butel he wrote the local history *Kings Cross Album* (1984).

THOMSON, Katherine, actor and playwright, was a founding member of Wollongong's Theatre South and began her work in the theatre with the Australian Theatre for Young People in 1969. Her plays include 'A Change in the Weather' (1982), 'Tonight We Anchor in Twofold Bay' (1986), 'A Sporting Chance' (1987), 'Darlinghurst Nights' (1988), *Diving for Pearls* (produced 1991, published 1992) and *Barmaids* (produced 1991, published 1992, and winner of an Awgie the same year). 'Darlinghurst Nights', a nostalgic musical, draws on 'Five Bells' and other poems by Kenneth Slessor (q.v.); 'A Change in the Weather', based on the stories of women at work in Wollongong, was subsequently produced as a film; 'A Sporting Chance', commissioned by Magpie at the State Theatre Company of SA, is a play for young people; *Barmaids* explores the humour, pathos and cruelty of public house life; *Diving for Pearls*, set in 'A coastal industrial city in contemporary Australia', focuses on the experiences of two ordinary people overtaken by change.

Thorn Birds, The, a novel by Colleen McCullough (q.v.), was published in the USA in 1977, and became a best-seller. The novel is divided into seven chronological sections, each section covering a set period between 1915 and 1969 and highlighting a particular character from the story. The first section, 1915–17, set in NZ, introduces the Roman Catholic Cleary family who are lifted out of their struggling farming existence by Paddy Cleary's ageing sister Mary Carson, who brings them to Australia to manage Drogheda station in north-western NSW. The remaining six sections plot the affairs of the Cleary family and introduce two other important characters, Mary Carson and the Catholic priest Ralph de Bricassart. The Cleary family is headed by Fiona ('Fee'), the Protestant daughter of an important NZ pioneering family, the Armstrongs. She disgraces them by bearing a child out of wedlock and is married off to Paddy Cleary, the dairy hand on the Armstrong property. Paddy and Fiona come to love each other but Paddy is killed early in the novel in a bushfire. Other male Cleary characters include Frank, Fiona's love-child,

who is imprisoned on a manslaughter charge; Hal, who dies of croup as a small child; Stuart, who is killed in an encounter with a wild pig; and the other sons, Jack, Hughie, Bob, James and Patrick, who are less relevant to the story. Meggie, the only Cleary girl and perhaps the chief character interest in the novel, later becomes involved with the handsome Gillanbone parish priest, Ralph de Bricassart, who has resisted Mary Carson's infatuation with him but who advances to eminence as Cardinal de Bricassart as the result of Mary's giving Drogheda to the church. Meggie has a child by Ralph, Dane, who becomes a priest but dies in a drowning accident. Meggie's other child, Justine, by her husband Luke O'Neill, becomes a talented Shakespearean actress. The backdrop to this complicated plot is the Australian outback, with its dramatic landscapes, vast distances, isolation, bush camaraderie, and natural hazards. The novel was screened as a television series in 1983.

THORNBURN, Hannah (1878–1902) was a bookkeeper and clerk when she met Henry Lawson (q.v.) around 1897. Lawson became infatuated with her, may have planned to leave his wife Bertha for her and was shattered by her death just before he arrived back from England in 1902. The subject of the poems 'To Hannah' and 'Hannah Thomburn' (*sic*), Hannah has also been identified in such other Lawson poems as 'Ruth', 'The Lily of St Leonards', and 'Do They Think That I Do Not Know?'.

THORNE, Tim (1944–   ), born Launceston, Tasmania, was educated at the University of Tasmania. During the 'poetry revolution' of the 1960s he lived briefly in Sydney (1967–68) and was associated with *Poetry Magazine*, later *New Poetry*. He won a writing scholarship to Stanford University in California in 1971–72 and in 1978 the Marten Bequest Travelling Scholarship for poetry. He has worked as a teacher of modern languages, an editor and full-time writer. Keenly involved in the development of literature within the Tasmanian community, he organises Launceston's annual Poetry Festival which awards the 'Poetry Cup' to the poet whose reading of his own work elicits the loudest audience response. He edited *Civil War/North* (1989), a small collection of poetry from northern Tasmania, and *Lozenge* (1992), poems by Kathy Allen and others. His own published works include *Tense Mood and Voice* (1969), *The What of Sane* (1971), *New Foundations* (1976), *A Nickel in My Mouth* (1979), *The Atlas* (1982) and *Red Dirt* (1990). Thorne's poetry is critical of the corruption and inhumanity of an unfeeling world, of the phoney and second-rate in modern society and culture. Wry and ironic rather than explosively angry, Thorne probes with precision and wit. His poems incorporate, at times, events and episodes of his own life and of Tasmanian history as well as occurrences in the wider contemporary world. The personal poems of 'White Diamond Gloom', for example, from *Red Dirt* are courageous and moving; those concerned with places, especially the Tasmanian scene, are sensitive and responsive. Tough, witty, technically innovative and confident, Thorne's is a distinctive poetic voice.

'Thousand Miles Away, A' is an Australian folk-song dating from the last decades of the nineteenth century which celebrates the overlanders travelling westwards in Queensland to muster cattle 'On the far Barcoo, where they eat nardoo, a thousand miles away'; the song was included as an anonymous composition in A.B. Paterson's *Old Bush Songs* (1905), but Charles Augustus Flower (q.v.) has been identified as the author by some writers. 'A Thousand Miles Away' is one of three folk-songs and ballads which share the same rollicking tune. The others are 'Ten Thousand Miles Away', a London music-hall song of the 1840s and later the seamen's song in which the singer is joining his convict lover who has 'taken a trip on a government ship/ Ten thousand miles away'; and 'The Old Palmer Song', in which the singer is *en route* to the Palmer diggings in Queensland, which opened up in 1873. The 'Ten Thousand Miles Away' tune formed the basis for the popular theme-song of the 1970s television series *Rush*.

Three Miss Kings, The, a novel by Ada Cambridge (q.v.), was serialised in the *Australasian* in 1883, and republished in book form in 1891. The first of Cambridge's novels to win her recognition in England as well as Australia, *The Three Miss Kings* is set in Melbourne at the time of the Great Exhibition of 1880 and traces the fortunes of Elizabeth, Patty and Eleanor King after they are orphaned and left with meagre incomes. Assisted by Paul Brion, the son of the family solicitor, the inexperienced sisters settle in Melbourne, where they are discovered by a leader of society, Mrs Duff-Scott, who protects them and tries to arrange suitable marriage partners. Each falls in love, though not always with Mrs Duff-Scott's choice: Elizabeth with the English visitor Kingscote Yelverton, Patty with Paul Brion, Eleanor with Mr Westmoreland. Each, however, finds obstacles in the path towards marriage: Yelverton's religious and philanthropic beliefs are unconventional, Paul and Patty offend each other's pride, Mr Westmoreland seems interested in marrying for money. Towards the end of the novel it is discovered by chance that the three Miss Kings are in reality the daughters of Kingscote Yelverton, the uncle of Elizabeth's suitor, and are thus heirs to the Yelverton fortune, which the younger Kingscote has been holding in trust. Her doubts already resolved, Elizabeth marries Yelverton and lives at the family seat, while Patty and Eleanor return to Australia to be married to their lovers. Although conventionally resolved, *The Three Miss Kings* offers ironic comment on class relationships in 'Marvellous Melbourne' and chronicles the rituals of society life, including the Melbourne Cup; there is also reference to the hanging of Ned Kelly.

THROSSELL, Ric (1922–), the son of the novelist Katharine Susannah Prichard (q.v.) and of Captain Hugo Throssell VC, was born in Perth. In 1943, after war service in New Guinea, he joined the Department of External Affairs and served in the Australian legations in Moscow and Rio de Janeiro, was appointed director of the Commonwealth Foundation in London in 1980 and retired in 1983. He has been closely associated with the Canberra Repertory Society as actor, director and writer. His published plays, several of which have won awards, are *Valley of the Shadows* (1949, first produced 1948), *Devil Wear Black* (1955), *Suburban Requiem* (produced 1955) in *Australian One-Act Plays. Book One* (1962, ed. Eunice Hanger), *The Day Before Tomorrow* (1969, first produced 1956), and *For Valour* (1976, first produced 1960 and winner of the Mary Gilmore Award of 1959). His other plays include 'Sailor's Girl' (1945), 'Epitaph for the Unborn' (1955), 'A Kiss and a Promise' (1956), 'If Thy Heart Offend' (1957), 'Legend' (1958), 'The Contemporary Approximation' (1958), 'Dr Homer Speaks' (1963, produced in 1965 with the title 'The Sweet Sad Story of Elmo and Me'), 'The Death of Damien Burr' (1965), 'The Fourth Course' (1971) and the children's play 'South Sea Gold Bay'. Throssell has also written an informative biography of his mother, *Wild Weeds and Wind Flowers* (1975), and edited a collection of her short stories, *Tribute* (1988), and another of her articles on politics, literature and women's affairs, *Straight Left* (1982). A versatile playwright, Throssell has written satires (*Devil Wear Black* and 'Dr Homer Speaks'), naturalistic plays ('The Death of Damien Burr' and 'Legend'), and plays with a serious, polemical purpose (*The Day Before Tomorrow* deals with nuclear war). Particularly striking is *For Valour*, a representative study of a First World War hero's economic and personal decline after returning to Australia. Throssell has also written two novels, *A Reliable Source* (1990) and *In a Wilderness of Mirrors* (1992); and an autobiography which was runner-up in the 1989 NBC Banjo Awards, *My Father's Son* (1989). Partly a biography of his father Hugo Throssell, and beginning with his father's suicide in 1933, *My Father's Son* also relates the difficulties of his own career as a diplomat under constant surveillance by ASIO from the 1950s, suspected of sharing his mother's political views and even of treachery.

THWAITES, F.J. (Frederick Joseph) (1908–79) was born at Balmain, Sydney, but spent time as a child at his grandfather's station at Narrandera in the Riverina district, a region which figures prominently in his fiction and where he personally sold the first copies of *The Broken Melody* (q.v., 1930). It was followed, 1932–73, by another thirty novels and three travel books; the best known, apart from *The Broken Melody*, are *Broken Wings* (1934), *The Melody Lingers* (1935), *The Mad Doctor* (1935), *Rock End* (1937), *Fever* (1939), *Whispers in Tahiti* (1940) and *Shadows Over Rangoon* (1941). Thwaites published more than a dozen of these titles under his own imprint and others were published under the imprint of the Harcourt Press, named after his wife Jessica Harcourt, an actor who played the role of Sarah Purfoy in the 1926 film version of *His Natural Life*. Virtually all the novels went through several editions or impressions (one estimate calculates fifty-four reprintings of *The Broken*

Melody alone) and at the peak of his popularity, 1930–60, Thwaites was possibly the largest-selling Australian author. In 1938 Ken Hall made a film of *The Broken Melody* with music by Alfred Hill. Thwaites's novels are characteristically sentimental romances in which a range of locales is covered (the Riverina, Sydney, Thursday Island and London in *The Broken Melody*, other parts of Australia as well as the East, Africa and the Pacific in subsequent novels) as his heroes and heroines win through tribulation, sometimes injury or self-inflicted disgrace, to happiness. As well as exotic settings, sensational plots and steamy covers, the successful Thwaites mixture incorporated a shrewd topicality, cumulative effect titles, e.g. *The Broken Melody*, *Broken Wings*, *The Melody Lingers*, a political and social conservatism that allowed identification with the major characters, and a tempestuous prose style.

THWAITES, Michael (1915–), born Brisbane, won a Rhodes Scholarship to Oxford and served with the Royal Naval Volunteer Reserve 1939–45. He lectured in English at the University of Melbourne for three years, served with ASIO 1950–71, and was deputy head of the Parliamentary library 1971–76. Winner of the Newdigate Prize, Oxford, in 1938 and the King's Medal for poetry in 1940, he has contributed verse to numerous anthologies and has published four collections, *Milton Blind* (1938), *The Jervis Bay and Other Poems* (1942), *Poems of War and Peace* (1968) and *The Honey Man* (1989). He has also written *Truth Will Out* (1980), an account of the defection of the Russian diplomat Vladimir Petrov in 1954. Traditional in rhetoric and theme, Thwaites's poetry reflects his commitment to the Moral Rearmament movement and his admiration for such poets as John Masefield.

Tiburon, a novel by Kylie Tennant (q.v.) serialised in the *Bulletin* in 1935 and illustrated by Norman Lindsay, was also published separately in the same year and awarded the S.H. Prior Memorial Prize. Set in a small NSW town in the early 1930s, it deals partly with the experiences of a young teacher, Jessica Daunt, recently posted to the town, and her love affair with Paul White, a member of the town's most despised family. The novel's more general theme turns on the conflict between the outcast unemployed and the 'respectable' citizens, especially as that conflict is illustrated in the obsession of the policeman, Scorby, with the White family. Lively and comic, *Tiburon* presents a vivid picture of the narrowness and complacency of small-town life.

Tichborne Case was a *cause célèbre* in England in the 1860s and 1870s. In 1865 a world-wide advertisement for Roger Tichborne, heir to a baronetcy, produced a Wagga Wagga butcher, Thomas Castro, probably one Arthur Orton, as the claimant. He was believed by the mother but disputed by the family; a civil action in 1871–72 led to Castro's imprisonment for perjury. The case has similarities with John Rex's impersonation of Richard Devine in *His Natural Life* (1874) and Lawrence Trevenna's impersonation of his half-brother, Lance Trevanion, in 'Rolf Boldrewood's' *Nevermore*

(1892). Marcus Clarke traded further on the Tichborne name in his novel *Chidiock Tichborne* (1893), which had nothing to do with the case, and the plot of Ada Cambridge's *The Three Miss Kings* (1883) shows its influence. The melodrama 'Tichborne: Or, Is He Butcher or Baronet' was performed in Sydney in 1877. D. Woodruff published *The Tichborne Claimant* (1957) and Michael Roe *Kenealy and the Tichborne Cause* (1974).

Ticket-of-Leave System, which enabled convicts to work for wages and select their own masters before their sentences were concluded, was first instituted by Governor Phillip in 1790. The system was subject to a certain amount of abuse and dispute under Macquarie, and his successor, Sir Thomas Brisbane, published regulations for the issue of tickets in 1822 which were expanded in 1827 by Governor Darling. Ticket-of-leave holders were not allowed to leave their districts of employment and tickets would be withdrawn for misconduct. In 1832, contrary to the advice of Governor Bourke, more stringent rules, which also deprived convicts of the right to own property, were laid down by imperial Act; Bourke then granted conditional pardons, which had a long history of use during transportation (q.v.), to some prisoners instead of tickets-of-leave. The system was also used in Van Diemen's Land and was given further refinements at Norfolk Island where prisoners under Alexander Maconochie could earn tickets by gaining marks for good conduct. James Tucker's loss of his ticket-of-leave in 1844 meant that he was sent to Port Macquarie, where *Ralph Rashleigh* was probably written; Henry Savery's was withdrawn in 1833 on the grounds that he had dabbled in newspaper management. There are numerous references to tickets-of-leave in Australian convict literature, e.g. in the stories of 'Price Warung'.

TIERNEY, John, see '**JAMES, Brian**'

TIGHE, Harry (1877–1946), born near Newcastle, NSW, lived mainly overseas from the age of 17, although he returned to Australia for lengthy periods. The author of sixteen novels, some of which, such as *Archie Wynward of Glen of Imaal* (1903), *A Man of Sympathy* (1908), and *The Four Candles* (1909), draw on his Australian experience, he also wrote numerous plays for the London stage. One of these, 'Open Spaces' (1927), retitled 'The Bush Fire' (1931), is set in Australia. His published plays include *Jean* (1901) and *The Atonement* (1929). His later impressions of Australia are recorded in his semi-fictional *As I Saw It* (1937).

Tilted Cross, The, a novel by Hal Porter (q.v.), was published in 1961. Set in Hobart 1845–46, it deals partly with the last bitter and despairing months of the life of the transported forger and suspected poisoner, Judas Griffin Vaneleigh. The character is based on Thomas Griffiths Wainewright (q.v.), although Porter slightly alters the historical facts to suggest that Wainewright's wife may have been the guilty party. Vaneleigh's life becomes involved with that of the low-born son of an actor, Queely Sheill, whose inborn Christian feelings are stirred by Vaneleigh's sufferings. Both Sheill and Vaneleigh live in the notorious and insalubrious Campbell Street, but have contact with the other, polite extreme of Hobart society when they visit Cindermead, the property of Sir Sydney Knight, where Vaneleigh is to paint the portrait of his wife, Lady Rose. There Queely's good looks arouse the passions of both Asnetha Sleep, Sir Sydney's crippled sister, and his wife, who is currently between lovers, and the jealousy of Asnetha's Black page, Teapot. Again Queely responds to his feelings of compassion, although Vaneleigh warns him that pity will beget infamy. The forces of lust, hatred, envy, despair and bitterness that secretly govern relations at Cindermead combine to trap Queely: he is unjustly arrested for theft, imprisoned, and attempts to escape with the help of his friends, Polidorio Smith and Pretty Dick. Badly injured in the attempt, he suffers a hideous operation in the criminal hospital and dies of gangrene on Christmas Eve. Life, meanwhile, continues at Cindermead in its apparently civilised manner and Vaneleigh, now seriously ill, enters hospital.

Time is Not Yet Ripe, The, a political comedy by Louis Esson (q.v.), was first performed in Melbourne in 1912 and published in the same year. Reminiscent of the theatre of Bernard Shaw and Oscar Wilde and particularly memorable for its lively heroine, Doris Quiverton, the play is a witty exposé of the unreality of political life.

Timeless Land, The, a novel by Eleanor Dark (q.v.) published in 1941, is the first volume of her historical trilogy. The succeeding volumes are *Storm of Time* (1948) and *No Barrier* (1953). The trilogy was reprinted as one edition in 1963 and presented as a television series by the ABC in 1980. *The Timeless Land* concentrates mainly on the first five years of European settlement at Port Jackson. Even before the arrival of the First Fleet, Bennilong and his father, Wunbula, have watched for the return of the winged boat that Wunbula had seen several years previously, the *Endeavour*, captained by James Cook, that had visited eastern Australia in 1770. Against a background of authentic historical events, Dark then traces the destinies and experiences of the historical (and some fictional) characters. After the arrival of the First Fleet at Botany Bay and their removal to Sydney Cove in 1788, Bennilong and his wife Barangaroo and others of his tribe observe the activities of the White people with amazement and, in Bennilong's case, fascination. One of their number, the gentle Arabanoo, is captured and kept as part-guide, part-prisoner, part-friend by Governor Phillip, but dies later in the smallpox epidemic that afflicts many of the Aborigines. Among the convicts the experiences of Ellen Prentice, her husband Andrew and son Johnny are prominent; among those in authority, the experiences of Phillip, William Dawes, David Collins, Watkin Tench and Richard Johnson. Andrew Prentice escapes in 1789 and survives with the help of the inland tribes, taking an

Aboriginal woman, Cunnembeillee, as wife. Later his discovery of some of the cattle that had wandered from the settlement contributes to his sense of security. After two and a half years of isolation from the home country, the European settlers face starvation but the arrival of the *Lady Juliana* in June, forerunner of the Second Fleet, averts disaster. The *Lady Juliana* also brings the first family of free settlers, Stephen and Harriet Mannion and their 6-year-old son, Patrick. Meanwhile Bennilong has become a willing captive, frequently enlivening Phillip's life with his amorous or quarrelsome exploits. Colbee, who is captured with him towards the end of 1789, escapes. By 1791 Andrew Prentice's hide-out is threatened by exploring parties and by the settlement of an estate by Mannion and his convict labourers. After Harriet's death giving birth to another son, Miles, Mannion takes Ellen Prentice as his housekeeper/mistress. Andrew Prentice makes plans to move further westward but dies saving Cunnembeillee and their son in a flash flood. By a strange series of coincidences, his son Johnny inherits his secret farm. Accompanied by Bennilong and the young Immerawanye, Phillip sails for England. The epilogue describes Bennilong's return three years later with Governor Hunter after a bleak experience in England, the desertion of his second wife Goooorooaroooboolo, his inability to recover his sense of wholeness, and the growing faction fights and difficulties that threaten the new settlement.

Storm of Time, which continues the saga from 1799 to 1808, narrates the fortunes of the Colony under the governors Hunter, King and Bligh, as well as those of the Mannion and Prentice families. *No Barrier* picks up the action in February 1808 and covers the first five years of the governorship of Macquarie as well as the destinies of Patrick Mannion, his brother Miles, his young stepmother Connor and her second husband Mark Harvey, Johnny Prentice and his second mate Emily, and Dilboong, Bennilong's daughter. The narrative ends with the crossing of the Blue Mountains in 1813.

TIMMS, E.V. (Edward Vivian) (1895–1960), born Charters Towers, Queensland, served in both world wars and made a reputation as a writer of historical romances, some of which are set in Australia and others in Europe. They include *The Hills of Hate* (1925), *James! Don't Be a Fool* (1927), *The Cripple in Black* (1930), *Whitehall* (1931), *Conflict* (1934), *Far Caravan* (1935), *Alicia Deane* (?1932), *Ten Wicked Men* (1937), *Maelstrom* (1938), *Dark Interlude* (1939), and *James! How Dare You!* (1940). After the war Timms began a historical saga of nineteenth-century Australia beginning with *Forever to Remain* (1948); the other volumes in the saga are *The Pathway of the Sun* (1949), *The Beckoning Shore* (1950), *The Valleys Beyond* (1951), *The Challenge* (1952), *The Scarlet Frontier* (1953), *The Fury* (1954), *They Came from the Sea* (1955), *Shining Harvest* (1956), and *Robina* (1958). When he died he was still at work on the eleventh volume, *The Big Country* (1962), which was finished by Alma Timms, who also wrote the penultimate book in the sequence, *Time and Chance* (1971). E.V. Timms also wrote many short stories and plays, several novels for young readers, scripts for cinema and radio and a biography, *Lawrence, Prince of Mecca* (1927), under the pseudonym 'David Roseler'. He adapted *The Hills of Hate* for Raymond Longford's 1926 film and later his novel *Forever to Remain* was produced as a musical.

TIPPING, Richard Kelly (1949–), born Adelaide, studied literature, media and philosophy at Flinders University in 1968 and 1970–72. He lived in Balmain in the period of the New Poetry movement, has travelled widely both abroad and in Australia and has worked as a psychiatric nurse and in the film industry. He has also been active in sculpture, graphics and photography. He now lectures in communication and media arts at the University of Newcastle. He is also a performance poet and often accompanies his poetry with his own music, on the banjo-ukulele, jaw harp and didgeridoo. He edited the first *Friendly Street Poetry Reader* in 1977 and co-edited *Mok* (1968–69) and *News and Weather* (1973). His screenprints and sculptures have featured in several exhibitions including *The Everlasting Stone* (Adelaide, 1978), *Word Works* (Sydney and Melbourne, 1980) and *Outside Inside* (Brisbane, 1981), and he has produced large-scale installations for the Adelaide Festival, the Festival of Sydney and the Sydney Biennale, 1982. His sculptures and graphics are in the collections of many public galleries. During five years of travelling around Australia he photographed a variety of interesting sights, which are included in *Signs of Australia* (1982) and are described by him as 'photo-poems'. He has also written for film – *Long Time Journey* (1979) – and the word works and ideographics, *The Sydney Morning* (1989). In 1986 Tipping began production of *Writers Talking*, a series of documentary portraits (films) of Australian writers who have spent considerable parts of their working lives overseas, e.g., Peter Porter, Randolph Stow, David Malouf, Sumner Locke Elliott. He has published three main books of verse, *Soft Riots* (1972), *Domestic Hardcore* (1975) and *Nearer by Far* (1986), but other poems are in manuscript form at the National Library. Listed among his other publications are *Airpoet* (1979), *Living on the Edge* (1984), *Headlines to the Heart* (1985), *The Diverse Voice* (1986), *Five O'Clock Shadows* (1979) and the play *Skinny and the Windowcleaner* (1975).

Soft Riots*, which contains, in Tipping's words, 'rhythms from my own breathings', has two sections, 'Balmain' and 'Stirling'. Many of the poems are of short lines, often single words, giving a fractured visual appearance and conveying, when read, a staccato effect. Often too, they are of strange shapes (e.g., 'the poster said'). The two frequently discussed poems of 'Stirling' are 'Multiple 1' and 'Multiple 2'. The girl who is their subject is of such quality that 'her beauty doesn't need/ the painted flourish of this praise'. Tipping's poetry is a far cry from 'painted flourish', the spareness and cryptic quality of the language carrying no flourish whatsoever. *Domestic Hardcore* also has two sections, 'Stirling and Beyond' and 'Mostly Balmain'. Notable poems include the 'Images' series and the long 'Soursobs'. *Nearer by Far* contains poems selected

from a large body of work accumulated over the ten years after *Domestic Hardcore*. It is Tipping's best collection with some trenchant political and satirical poems allied to fine landscape verse. As always with Tipping the result is witty, inventive and lively writing.

TISHLER, Joseph (1871–1956), born NZ but resident most of his life in Victoria, was a fanatical contributor of atrocious, but distinctive and often unconsciously funny, verse to the *Bulletin* under the pseudonym 'Bellerive'. Most of his naive, unrhythmic outpourings were printed in the answers to correspondents column over a period of forty years. *The Book of Bellerive* (1961) is a selection of his verse, edited by Douglas Stewart, who dubbed him 'Australia's Worst Poet'.

TITTENSOR, John (1941–), born Melbourne, graduated in French from the University of Melbourne and has been a teacher, editor, translator and writer. Since 1983 he has been resident in France. He has written *Year One: A Record* (1984) and *Carmody Comes Home* (1988). In 1982 his two children, Jonathan and Emma, were burnt to death in a house fire. *Year One* is a selection of his own notes and diary entries written in the first thirteen months after his children died. The extracts provide both a tender and a harrowing record of his grief, his celebration of the children's all-too-brief lives and his determination to triumph over the tragedy. An important and impressive book, *Year One* is a remarkable human document. *Carmody Comes Home*, by contrast, is a zany, exuberant account of Kevin ('Kevvie') Carmody returning to Australia (having escaped from a English madhouse) on hearing of the death of his mother. Kathleen Carmody's body has been taken over by a group of nuns (of quite strange habits) who intend to make her a saint because of her supposed curing of her neighbour, Myrtle Garlick, of paralysis.

'To God: From the Warring Nations', a poem by 'Furnley Maurice' (q.v.), first appeared in the *Book Lover* in 1916, with the word 'weary' in the title instead of 'warring'. It was published with the new title in *Eyes of Vigilance* (1920). The poem's theme is humanity's general guilt for war and its horror. In 1916 it met a mixed reception; its pacifist plea angered patriots, who saw it as an attack on the nation's will to fight, but it echoed the mood of the anti-war faction of the time.

To the Islands, a novel by Randolph Stow (q.v.) published in 1958 (rev. edn 1982), won the Miles Franklin Award and the Gold Medal of the Australian Literature Society. Set in the wilderness area of northwestern Australia, the novel deals with the last days of Heriot, an old, disillusioned and weary missionary, director of an Anglican Aboriginal mission for many years. Heriot's bitterness reaches a peak when Rex, the man he detests and blames for the death of his foster daughter, defiantly returns to the mission. After an encounter with Rex in which Heriot attacks him with a stone, presumably killing him, the missionary sets out into the wilderness in search of the islands, which according to Aboriginal myth are the islands of death. Justin, another Aborigine, insists on accompanying and caring for him. Heriot's journey is both physical and spiritual, an attempt to expiate his personal and racial guilt towards the Aboriginal people. Gradually he moves towards the quietism and resignation demonstrated by the Aborigines, thus transcending his Western tradition. Finally Justin consents to leave him alone with his vision before the onset of death, and returns to meet the rescue party and the recovered, forgiving Rex.

Tocsin, subtitled *The People's Penny Paper*, a weekly radical Melbourne journal expressing the main socialist thinking of the day, began publication in 1897, largely under the influence of Bernard O'Dowd (q.v.). The title page carried a sketch of a bell-ringer ('tocsin' means an alarm bell) by Norman Lindsay. The *Tocsin* platform, published in each volume, represented a mixture of the ideas and philosophies of Henry George, Edward Bellamy, the Fabians and the emerging political Labor Party. O'Dowd's regular column in *Tocsin* was 'The Forge' by 'Gavah the Blacksmith'. The journal was known as *Labor Call* 1906–53 and as *Labor* from 1953 until its demise in 1961.

TOLMER, Alexander (1815–90), born England of a French father and a German mother, spent some of his early years at sea and in the British cavalry, and in 1840 migrated to SA, where he joined the police, rising to commissioner in 1852. In 1847 he opened up an improved mail route between SA and NSW and was responsible for a successful gold escort between Mount Alexander, Bendigo, Ballarat and Adelaide. An intemperate man, he was first demoted in 1853 and then dismissed in 1856, although he rejoined the police for a turbulent nine months in 1859. He subsequently began trading in a small cutter near the mouth of the Murray, tried sheep-farming and made an unsuccessful attempt to win the reward for the first south–north crossing of the continent. His *Reminiscences of an Adventurous and Chequered Career at Home and at the Antipodes* (1882), is an entertaining contemporary memoir.

Tolpuddle Martyrs, see **LOVELESS, George**

TOMASETTI, Glen (1929–   ), born Melbourne, has travelled widely in Australia and overseas. She has written poetry, songs, radio and stage plays and works frequently as a contemporary troubadour, playing her own songs on the guitar. She has published a collection of her songs, *Songs from a Seat in the Carriage* (1970), and two novels, *Thoroughly Decent People* (1976) and *Man of Letters* (1981), which won the FAW Australian Natives Association Literary Award. Dissatisfied with the conventional rural, male version of Australian history, Tomasetti presents another less celebrated aspect of the past in *Thoroughly Decent People*; a representation of the daily family life of ordinary Melbourne people of the 1930s, it has been praised for its sociological authenticity. *Man of Letters* is a sardonic study of a certain male type, a cloistered academic whose romantic notions finally confront real experience.

'Tomb of Lt. John Learmonth, A.I.F., The', an elegy by J.S. Manifold (q.v.) in memory of a school friend who had been captured in Crete in the Second World War and later died in a German prison camp, was first published in *New Republic* in 1945. Written while Manifold himself was involved in the German offensive in the Ardennes in 1944, the poem is both a tribute to the unpretentious quality of common human heroism as exemplified in John Learmonth's hopeless stand against the Germans in Crete and a linking of that courage to 'the old heroic virtues' that are part of Australia's past, as exemplified in the 'die hard, die game' attitude of such outback characters as the swagmen and the bushrangers.

TOMHOLT, Sydney (1884–1974), born Melbourne, fought in France in the First World War, travelled widely thereafter in China, Mongolia and the Philippines and returned to Sydney in 1932. In Australia he wrote dramatic pieces and serials for radio and later became film and drama critic for the *Sydney Morning Herald*. A serious dramatist, as Bernard Shaw recognised, with a flair for atmosphere and emotional and dramatic intensity, he ranges from realism to poetic symbolism, anticipating the work of Patrick White. Unlike his fellow playwrights, the physical environment interested him less than the inner, psychological one. Although he wrote at a time when Australian plays lacked a theatre and his work was only occasionally produced, either by repertory companies or on radio, he published a collection of ten one-act plays in 1936, titled *Bleak Dawn and Other Plays*. Of these *Bleak Dawn* and *Anoli the Blind* (qq.v.) are the most striking. Another drama, *Searchlights*, was included in *Best Australian One-Act Plays* (1937).

Tomorrow and Tomorrow and Tomorrow, a novel by the collaborating writers known as 'M. Barnard Eldershaw' (q.v.), was published in 1947. Marjorie Barnard (q.v.), who was the predominant author, described the circumstances of its writing and publication in *Meanjin* (1970). Wartime conditions resulted in an abbreviated title and other excisions by an over-zealous censorship, and it was not until 1983 that the novel was published in full with its complete title. The setting is divided between one day in the twenty-fourth century and several decades of the twentieth, as Knarf, a dedicated writer modelled on Frank Dalby Davison, reads his historically retrospective novel to Ord, his friend and a great archaeologist. Looking back at Australia's past from his materially secure but spiritually torpid Utopia, Knarf describes how the First People, the Aborigines, who had lived in harmony with the land, had been succeeded by the tough-spirited Pioneers. The descendants, the Australians, had allowed themselves 'to be dispossessed by the most fantastic tyranny the world had ever known, money in the hands of a few' and had endured the Third World

War, pestilence, internal subversion, the destruction of Sydney and finally total loss of sovereignty. Australia, tamed by twenty-fourth century technology and governed by a small, enlightened élite, is enjoyed by the Third People. The Riverina has become the Tenth Commune as Australia has become part of a smoothly functioning global order in which war, competition, violence, suffering and struggle are things of the past. Two-thirds of the novel are concerned with the past, especially the 1930s and 1940s, and centre on the sufferings of an Australian Everyman, Harry Munster, a poultry farmer turned Sydney truck-driver. Saddled with a lazy, selfish wife, Ally, Harry endures the privations of rural and city life, the death of a son, the indignity of unemployment during the 1930s Depression, and the gradual souring of a late love affair and is finally killed in the bombing of Sydney. Thereafter the story of the past expands into a more general social panorama, though dominated by various figures from Harry's past. When invasion by foreign powers seems inevitable, an underground group led by the Marxist Sid Warren destroys Sydney by fire. Meanwhile in the novel's present, to which the narrative returns at intervals, Knarf's idealistic son Ren has reached the culminating point of his efforts to revitalise the idea of liberty. A motion to allow public opinion some force is to be put to the people that day. Ren's friend Sfax has perfected a votometer which can record unvoiced thoughts, and Oran, a powerful official from the Technical Bureau, has arrived to observe the experiment. Military forces stand by in case they are needed. But to Ren's dismay apathy turns out to be the real enemy and the votometer records 62 per cent as indifferent to the motion.

TOMPSON, Charles (1807–83), born Sydney, tried farming before beginning a career in the public service, ultimately rising to be clerk of the Legislative Assembly. Tompson's chief work is *Wild Notes, from the Lyre of a Native Minstrel* (q.v., 1826). A 'currency lad', he was the first poet to attempt an appreciation of the beauty of the local landscape. His verse invests it with an arresting, picturesque quality and an aura of romantic sadness. One of the earliest conservationists, Tompson adopts a condemnatory tone towards the destructive effects of progress on both nature and the Aboriginal people. Although occasionally attractive with fresh and original imagery, his polished verses, heavily apostrophic, ponderous in tone and ornate in language, belong largely to the poetic tradition of the eighteenth century; *Wild Notes* was the first volume of poetry, written by a poet born here, to be published in Australia.

Touch of Silk, The, a play by Betty Roland (q.v.) which was first produced in 1928, was originally published in 1942 and has been frequently revived on stage and radio. Tragedy ensues when Jeanne, the charming, homesick French wife of Jim Davidson, a shell-shocked digger, contributes in a moment of thoughtlessness to the desperate financial plight of their drought-stricken farm. Although the plot creaks in places, the unsympathetic physical and emotional environment of the bush, in which Jeanne finds herself, is evoked with oppressive effect, as is her relationship with her malevolent mother-in-law.

Touchstone, subtitled **A Saturday Journal of Criticism, Commentary, and Satire**, was published weekly in Melbourne 1869–70. Henry Kendall, who was in Melbourne, was briefly its editor; it published literary articles and reviews but its tone was largely satirical. A later weekly of the same title, with some literary content, was published briefly in Ballarat at the end of 1883, edited by 'Tom Touchstone' (Thomas Bury), and was a considerable influence on the radical poet Bernard O'Dowd.

Tourmaline, a philosophical novel by Randolph Stow (q.v.), was published in 1963. Based on the opposing ideas of Taoism and Christianity, the key to its theme is contained in Stow's sequence of poems titled 'From "The Testament of Tourmaline": Variations on Themes of the *Tao Teh Ching*', published in 1966. Tourmaline is an isolated, WA mining town, a place of heat and dust, but so cut off from outer society that it is an allegorical rather than a realistic entity. Significant individuals in the town are Kestrel, the arrogant hotel owner, Deborah, his part-Aboriginal mistress, Byrne, his drunken nephew, and Tom Spring, the wise storekeeper. The narrator of the story, who also participates in the drama, describes himself as The Law of Tourmaline. One day a young man, Michael Random, half-dead from exposure in the desert, is dumped in town. Michael, who reveals himself to be a diviner, is soon regarded as the town's spiritual saviour, although both Kestrel and the quietist Tom Spring refuse their allegiance. Michael fails to discover water although he finds a gold reef, and eventually leaves Tourmaline, defeated, his place as leader filled by the bullying Kestrel. Tom Spring dies at his store although his quietist perspective lives on in his spiritual descendant, Dave Speed, the desertdweller.

Tower of the Dream, The, published by Charles Harpur (q.v.) in a pamphlet in 1865, is a long poem in blank verse, interspersed with songs. Highly symbolic, the poem, which delves into the division between conscious knowledge and unconscious forces in the life of man, uses allegorical devices such as a monster, a lake, a tower and a maiden. Apart from fellow poet Henry Kendall's obsession with it ('the greatest of Australian poems') the poem aroused little contemporary interest. More recent critical opinion sees it, and Harpur's other philosophical verse, as evidence of a wider poetic talent than the corrupt 1883 collection of his poetry indicates.

Town and Country Journal, see **Australian Town and Country Journal**

Town Like Alice, A, a novel by 'Nevil Shute' (q.v.), was published in 1950. Narrated by an elderly lawyer, Noel Strachan, it is an account of the experience of an

English girl, Jean Paget, who in 1947 at the age of 27 inherits a small fortune from her uncle. Jean has grown up in Malaya and England and is working in Malaya at the outbreak of the Second World War. Just before the fall of Singapore, Jean goes to Batu Tasik near Kuala Lumpur to say goodbye to her friends the Hollands. Captured by the Japanese, Jean is one of a group of fourteen women and nineteen children held prisoner for forty-five days in such severe conditions that one child dies. The group is dispatched to Singapore on foot, guarded by four soldiers. After they have been on the march for several days, one of the older women dies and they are diverted to Port Swetenham, 30 miles away, where a ship should be waiting for them. The ship does not arrive, and after a wait of eleven days and the death of another child they are ordered to walk to Port Dickson 50 miles away. For the next two months, unwanted by the Japanese Army, they wander over Malaya; others of their party die, including Mrs Holland and her two older children. They meet two Australian soldiers, Ben Leggatt and Joe Harman, who obtain medicines and soap for them. Joe Harman, a ringer from northern Australia, is drawn to Jean, whom he nicknames Mrs Boong, assuming that she is married and that the child which she carries is hers. When Joe steals five chickens for Jean's group from the local Japanese commanding officer, Captain Sugamo, he is discovered and is crucified by Sugamo. Guarded now only by a sergeant, the women are sent on their way again. By August 1942 the party, now reduced to seventeen, has reached a small village called Kuala Telang, where their guard dies and where they are allowed to stay to work in the paddy fields. They remain there for three years, and are repatriated at the end of the war; Jean, discovering that both her mother and brother have died, takes up clerical work in London. When Strachan informs her of her inheritance, she decides to return to Malaya to build a well for the village which had befriended her group. In Malaya she discovers that Joe Harman has survived the crucifixion and decides to fly to Australia to find him. Meanwhile in London, Strachan is visited by Joe who is searching for Jean, having discovered that she is unmarried. Strachan sends Joe off on his return journey, refraining from telling him that Jean is already there. At Alice Springs Jean discovers that Joe is managing a station in the Gulf country, Midhurst, near Willstown. She spends several days at Willstown, where she discovers that Joe is returning from England; amazed at the general deprivation of the town, she makes plans to establish a shoe factory and an icecream parlour. Joe and Jean are reunited at Cairns and decide to marry. Helped in a practical way by Strachan and Joe, Jean is successful in her business ventures in Willstown and achieves fame when she rides over 40 miles to get help for an injured man. After three years Joe is making plans to buy Midhurst station, Jean is the proprietor of several flourishing businesses at Willstown, which she intends to transform into a town like Alice, and they are the parents of two children. *A Town Like Alice* was produced as a film in 1956 and as an Australian television series in 1980.

TOWNEND, Christine (1944–), born Melbourne, now lives in Sydney and has published short stories and poetry in several periodicals and anthologies. She is also the author of two novels, *The Beginning of Everything and the End of Everything Else* (1974) and *Travels With Myself* (1976), and of several books on animal liberation. Townend's novels focus on a young woman's quest for self-fulfilment which takes her to different cultures both within and without Australia.

TRAILL, W.H. (William Henry) (1843–1902), born London, arrived in Australia about 1860. He worked on stations in Queensland, including a period on Maroon, where Rosa Praed was brought up, and as a public servant in Melbourne and Brisbane until the middle 1870s, when he went into journalism. In 1881 he wrote the leader for the *Bulletin* (q.v.) which led to the Clontarf libel case and the imprisonment in 1882 of its founding editors, J.F. Archibald and John Haynes. As editor and proprietor or major shareholder, Traill ran the *Bulletin* 1881–86; his regime was a period of consolidation during which he installed new machinery, developed the *Bulletin*'s political and economic philosophy, established its tradition of black-and-white art, and set it on its way to becoming the legendary 'Bushman's Bible'. Before his *Bulletin* years, Traill was proprietor of the *Darling Downs Gazette*, a reporter for the *Queenslander* and *Brisbane Courier*, and editor of the *Sydney Mail*. After his departure he edited the *Australian Star* (1887–89) and *Truth* (1893), was a member of the NSW parliament 1889–94 and engaged in pastoral and mining speculations. In his last years he worked mainly on journalistic assignments for the Queensland government, preparing, among other commissions, *A Queenly Colony* (1901).

TRAIN, George Francis (1829–1904), American-born entrepreneur, spent three busy and profitable years in Victoria in the gold-rush period 1852–55. He was partly instrumental in Freeman Cobb establishing Cobb & Co. (q.v.) and mooted the idea of a Melbourne-based American style of federal government for Australia. He published his autobiography, *My Life in Many States and in Foreign Lands* (1902). Clive Turnbull wrote *Bonanza: The Story of George Francis Train* (1946); Willis Thornton, *The Nine Lives of Citizen Train* (1948); and E. Daniel and Annette Potts edited *A Yankee Merchant in Goldrush Australia: The Letters of George Francis Train 1853–55* (1970).

TRAINOR, Leon (1945–), born Geraldton, grew up in Perth and was educated at the University of WA. In 1970–72 he lived in Italy and France. He now lives in Canberra, where he works in the public service. He has published two volumes of poetry, *Memory's Apprentice* (1977) and *Benediction* (1979); and a novel, *Livio* (1988). Concerned with place and belonging, *Livio* traces the experiences and inner life of Livio Guglielmini, an Australian of European parents, who finds himself to be a foreigner both in Europe, where he lives for a decade, and in Australia after his return.

Transit of Cassidy, a novel by George Turner (q.v.), was published in 1978. Cassidy Edwards, once an arrogant star of the boxing ring, is the anti-hero. His downward course begins when he loses a challenge fight because his wife and children fail to attend. Thirteen years later, his adolescent son Mike seeks him out, but their reunion turns into a violent confrontation culminating in Cassidy's death. As Mike searches for his father a complex, many-sided picture of Cassidy emerges as we see him through the eyes of all those whom he later alienated: Paddy, his brother; Perce, his dedicated manager; Eleanor, his wife; and Jack Wild, the sports writer. Meanwhile the compassionate attitude of Rod Trelawney, who knows Cassidy best, leads Mike to a more mature understanding of his father.

Transit of Venus, The, a novel by Shirley Hazzard (q.v.), was published in 1980 and won the National Book Critics' Circle Award in the USA. The first part, titled 'The Old World', opens in southern England in the 1950s with the arrival of Ted Tice, a scientist, at the home of Professor Sefton Thrale, with whom he is to work on the siting of a large telescope. Ted, who has been on a walking tour, arrives at the house in the middle of a violent storm. At the Thrales', Caro Bell, the woman he is to love for the rest of his life, crosses his destiny for the first time. Caro and her sister Grace are young Australians brought up in Sydney by their half-sister Dora, a neurotic, self-dramatising martyr, after their parents' early death in a ferry accident. Grace is already engaged to Christian Thrale who, like his father the professor, is conventional and self-centred. Caro is about to enter government service. The sisters, indissolubly bound by their childhood experience, are dissimilar in both appearance and temperament, Caro giving the impression of a dark, strong nature, whereas Grace seems as easygoing as she is fair. Dora's emotional dependence on her sisters appears to be suddenly resolved by her marriage to a Major Ingot and departure for Portugal. Although Caro enjoys friendship with Ted Tice, she falls in love with Paul Ivory, a sophisticated young playwright. Ivory flirts with Caro but becomes engaged to a local heiress, the insipid Tertia Drage. His relationship with Caro deepens but is broken off when Tertia is made aware of the love affair and Caro realises that the discovery will make no difference to the status quo. In distress Caro leaves abruptly for London. In the second part, titled 'The Contacts', Caro is impelled by her love to resume her affair with the now-married Paul. Ted follows her progress from a distance, and at the same time successfully pursues his career despite his public criticism of the work of Professor Thrale. Grace becomes involved in her role of wife and mother. After some years, Tertia Ivory becomes pregnant, Paul breaks off the affair and Caro goes through a period of intense misery. Her suffering is exacerbated when Ingot deserts Dora and the ensuing financial and emotional burden falls exclusively on her shoulders, even though Christian Thrale inherits a large fortune on his father's death. In the third part, titled 'The New World', Caro meets and falls in love with an American writer and peace worker, Adam Vail. She marries him and moves to New York, where she is happy, although Adam's daughter Josie, a victim of the protest culture of the 1970s, makes no secret of her resentment. Ted Tice, now despairing of ever winning Caro, marries an old friend, Margaret. Christian Thrale, meanwhile, makes a brief excursion into danger by having an affair with a young typist, Cordelia Ware. Although Cordelia suffers, Christian's insensitivity shields him from pain. By contrast, Grace, at the age of 43, feels the anguish of a deep, unsatisfied passion when she falls in love with a young doctor, Angus Dance. The final part, 'The Culmination', brings several destinies full circle. Adam Vail dies suddenly. Then Caro discovers from a chance meeting with Paul Ivory that he had many years earlier failed to save the life of a man who was blackmailing him. Ted Tice had been made aware of his crime on the very day that he had arrived at the Thrale house to work with Sefton, but had remained silent. The discovery of Ted's integrity stirs Caro's love for him. Paul, however, grief-stricken because of his son's imminent death from leukemia, sees himself as visited with retribution for a life of evil. Later, when Caro meets Ted by chance in Stockholm, they declare their love and decide to live together.

Translations from the Natural World (1992), a book of poems by Les Murray (q.v.), won the NSW Literary Award, the Victorian Premier's Award and the NBC Turnbull Fox Phillips Award, all in 1993. The first of its three sections contains the long poem 'Kimberley Brief', Murray's verse travelogue of his trip from Broome up to the Kimberley region. The second section, 'Presence', contains the 'translations from the natural world'. The forty mostly brief poems, many of which, by presenting the complex of external characteristics that together illuminate the inner nature of a particular object – a cockspur bush, a mollusc, pigs, stone fruit, sunflowers, cuttlefish – re-create something of the essential 'inscape' of Gerard Manley Hopkins. The 'translation' of these objects into the 'poetic' world is striking in its verbal brilliance. 'The Wedding at Berrico' of the third section is, by contrast, unembellished, characterised by the quiet cadences of 'may you/ always have each other, and want to' and the calm recognition that the marriage vows of a daughter move her 'to the centre of life/ and us gently to the rear'.

Transportation, the banishing from Great Britain of offenders against the law, was regularised by the Transportation Act of 1718; under its provisions the responsibility for carrying out the penalty of transportation fell on the masters of the ships which carried the offenders into exile. Until the War of Independence most transportees went to the American colonies or the West Indies, but in 1784 an Act was passed which authorised the British government to select another place for the reception of convicts. In 1786 the eastern coast of New Holland (Australia), discovered by Lieutenant James Cook in 1770, was chosen; in 1787 the First Fleet left under Captain Arthur Phillip for the Colony which, on arrival, was named New South Wales, and where the government continued to maintain and employ convicts. There were strategic and commercial arguments as well as administrative and penal ones for a British settlement in the South Pacific; the relative importance of trade, defence and the problem of the prisons is the subject of *The Founding of Australia*, ed. Ged Martin (1978), and Alan Frost's *Convicts and Empire* (1980), although most contributors to the 'Botany Bay Debate', as it has come to be called, accept that the penal reason was a significant one. Robert Hughes's *The Fatal Shore* (1987) sees Britain's wish to rid itself of the elements that threatened its privileged class society as the main motivation behind the Botany Bay scheme. Robert King's interpretation and translation of Alexandro Malaspina's report, *The Secret History of the Convict Colony* (1990), investigates the notion that the Australian colony was settled because Britain wanted a position of commercial and political advantage in the struggle for supremacy in Europe.

About 150 000 convicts were transported to the eastern part of Australia 1787–1852, 80 000 to NSW, which ceased receiving convicts after 1840, and virtually all the remainder to Van Diemen's Land, later Tasmania, which received about 37 000 convicts after 1840. The importance of the convict experience in Tasmanian history is reflected in Tasmania's dominance as the setting of so much Australian convict literature. Of the other colonies, NSW incorporated Victoria until 1851 and Queensland until 1859, although Moreton Bay was a remote penal settlement in 1824–39; South Australia was founded as a separate colony in 1836 and never formally received convicts although, like Victoria, it was a place where 'Vandemonians' settled; and Western Australia received just under 10 000 convicts over a long period, 1829–68. The origins of the convicts are analysed in L.L. Robson's *The Convict Settlers of Australia* (1965), which, with A.G.L. Shaw's *Convicts and the Colonies* (1966), George Rude's *Protest and Punishment* (1978) and Hughes's *The Fatal Shore* (1987), are standard studies of the convict experience. The research of Robson, Shaw and others has established a profile of the convicts at odds with the 'convict legend'. The legend, influenced by the literary treatment of transportation, is of some longevity among Australians and postulates that the convicts, 'more sinn'd against than sinning', were the victims of a repressive legal system in England and a brutal penal one in Australia, and were characteristically Irish political prisoners, English poachers, or minor offenders forced to commit crimes to feed starving families, or innocents like Rufus Dawes in *His Natural Life* (1874). All four types of convict were transported to Australia but most were urban offenders convicted at least once before transportation, whose crime was often underestimated in order to prevent trial on a capital charge. Roughly a quarter of those convicted of crimes in England in the period 1788–1840 underwent transportation.

The voyage to Australia on a convict transport, the subject of Charles Bateson's *The Convict Ships 1787–1868* (1959), Jonathan King's *The First Fleet* (1982) and Michael Flynn's *The Second Fleet* (1993), could be hazardous, either because of the conditions or because of weather or war, or, less often, because of rebellion. Despite the rebellions in *Ralph Rashleigh*, *His Natural Life* and other convict novels, there were relatively few such insurgencies either on board ship or after landing: the seizure in 1829 of the brig *Cyprus* (q.v.) is a notable example of the former; the Vinegar Hill (q.v.) uprising is perhaps the most famous of the latter. There is an extensive First Fleet literature (see First Fleet), almost solely from the official side, although later convict memoirs usually incorporated an account of the voyage as part of the transportation experience. Once at the colonial settlements, the earliest convicts were employed on the construction of public works or in tending government farms, but as the number of free settlers, ex-convicts and emancipists (q.v.) increased, so did the practice of assignment, the assigning of a convict to a master or masters who maintained the convict in clothing and rations. An equally common problem, and a major theme in the creative literature about transportation, was the 'lottery of assignment', a phrase used to describe the defenceless position convicts were placed in regarding the conduct of their masters. After serving part or all of their sentence convicts were eligible to receive a ticket-of-leave (q.v.), which permitted them to seek employment in a specified area, or a conditional pardon, the condition being that they remain in the colony.

During Lachlan Macquarie's term as governor the number of convicts greatly increased, partly as a result of the end of the Napoleonic Wars. Macquarie is generally recognised as having had a liberal attitude towards the acceptance of emancipists into society; although vindicated in the 1812 report of a British parliamentary committee investigating transportation, his policy aroused the ire of many settlers. In 1819–21 J.T. Bigge (q.v.) investigated Macquarie's administration on behalf of the British government; his reports were critical of Macquarie and led to a tightening up of the 'System', as it came to be called. That many of the worst excesses of the System occurred after the Bigge investigation, during a period when the great majority of convicts (just over 80 per cent) was sent to Australia, helps to explain why so little convict, as distinct from historical, fiction deals with transportation before 1820; Thomas Keneally's *Bring Larks and Heroes* (1967) and Colin Free's *Vinegar Hill* (1978) are among the exceptions. The practice of assignment continued after 1820, but those remaining in government service were worked arduously in gangs, often engaged on the construction of roads. A variety of punishments, of which the lash was the most prevalent, awaited both assignee and road gang member, and for the more recalcitrant there were the secondary punishment centres, where reconvicted convicts were sent. Port Arthur (q.v.), where the first Australian novelist, Henry Savery, was sent after a colonial forgery conviction in 1840, Macquarie Harbour, Norfolk Island (q.v.) and Port Macquarie were the most notorious of these settlements.

During the decades after 1820 the tightening up of the System coincided with an increase in the controversy about the efficacy of transportation. The widely fluctuating views expressed included arguments that the colonies had made sufficient progress to be allowed to develop free of the convict taint; that convict labour should be retained; that transportation had failed both because crime had not declined and too many emancipists had done well; and that the System was still brutal and in need, if not of abolition, at least of reformation. Not all the combatants had first-hand experience of Australia, e.g. Richard Whately, whose attacks on transportation were sternly contested by George Arthur (q.v.), who believed in the severity of transportation and that his own colony of Van Diemen's Land should be the gaol of the empire. One of the main consequences of the controversy was the British parliamentary select committee of 1837–38, whose report, usually called the Molesworth Report after its chairman, Sir William Molesworth (1810–55), led to the cessation of transportation to NSW and to Van Diemen's Land becoming the focus of the new probation system, which abolished assignment, required a period of compulsory labour for all convicts and established a strictly regulated process by which a convict passed 'through' his sentence. The convict memoirist John Mortlock underwent the probation system. By 1846 the economic depression forced an end to the probation system. A revised system, whereby convicted prisoners would spend the first two stages of their sentence in England before coming to Australia holding a ticket-of-leave or a conditional pardon, led to strongly resisted moves for a revival of transportation to NSW. The last convicts arrived in Tasmania in 1853, although WA, chronically short of labour, continued to receive them for another decade and a half.

The effects of the convict experience on the development of Australia have been the subject of some speculation; the male ethos, anti-authoritarianism and egalitarianism, antagonism towards large pastoral landowners, and development of a harsh penal code are among the suggested legacies. Both the generalisations and their origins in the convict experience are difficult to prove; what is more certain is that most convicts stayed in Australia and thus helped to establish the ambivalent relationship of its citizens with England. Among those who stayed were several who played a pioneering role in Australian publishing and newspapers, and a number of the first creative writers. See also Convict in Australian Literature.

TRANTER, John (1943–   ), born Cooma, NSW, grew up in an isolated farming district of the State's south-east coast. He studied arts at the University of Sydney for two years then left to work casually and travel overseas in 1967. Back in Australia he resumed his course, graduating in 1970. He was Asian editor (in Singapore) for A & R 1971–73, then worked as an editor and producer for the ABC in Brisbane until 1977. He has since been a publisher (Transit Poetry, 1981–83), editor (NSW Department of TAFE, 1983–84), teacher of communication, and writer-in-residence (NSW Institute of Technology, Macquarie University and ANU). He travelled through the USA and

Europe (1985–86), reading his own and other Australian poetry and lecturing on Australian literature. He was arts coordinator for the ABC 1987–88, and was in charge of Radio Helicon, the ABC's weekly Radio National cultural and arts programme. Well known as a literary reviewer, he has also been a member of the Literature Board of the Australia Council, and poetry editor of the *Bulletin*, a position he left in 1993.

Tranter has named his chief recreation as 'work' and his long list of publications substantiates that claim. His books of poetry are *Parallax* (1970), *Red Movie* (1972), *The Blast Area* (1974), *The Alphabet Murders* (1975), *Crying in Early Infancy: 100 Sonnets* (1977), *Dazed in the Ladies Lounge* (1979), *Selected Poems* (1982), *Gloria* (1986), *Under Berlin: New Poems 1988* (1988), *The Floor of Heaven* (1992), *Days in the Capital* (1992) and *At the Florida* (1993). He edited *Poetry Australia's Preface to the 70s* issue (1970); the anthologies *The New Australian Poetry* (1979), *The Tin Wash Dish* (1989), *The Penguin Book of Modern Australian Poetry* (1991, with Philip Mead) and *Martin Johnston: Selected Poems and Prose* (1993).

In the Introduction to *The New Australian Poetry* Tranter trenchantly argued the cause of post-modernism (he used the term 'modernism' at that time) and illustrated in the anthology the work of poets who had been attempting to practise it during the 1960s and 1970s. In rejecting the traditional, humanist-based dicta of poetry's methodology and function, he formulated such tenets for the 'new' poetry as:

'words – the fragments of language the poet places in the special framework of a poem – have a reality more solid and intense than the world of objects and self-perception'; 'self signature – the work validates its own technical innovations'; 'self-reference – the method is reflected consciously in the medium'; 'emphasis on individualist values as against an agreed social value'; 'fragmentation as against synthesis and harmony'; 'an intention to disrupt the canons of the art form and the preconceptions of the consumer'.

Because many 'consumers' have not been prepared to abandon their 'preconceptions' of poetry, post-modernism has not subsequently had the total flowering that Tranter and others had hoped for. The pages of Australia's literary journals during the 1970s and 1980s have seen the arguments for and against aired on many occasions. In much of his own poetry John Tranter has observed the Nietzschean maxim, 'the apparent world is the only true one' and the Wallace Stevens insistence that 'poetry should resist the intelligence/ Almost successfully'. Yet he has also, as Kate Lilley has indicated, 'embedded in his poetry a gesturing towards the reader' that falls somewhat short of post-modernism; he creates, in fact, a pact with the reader which, while it may sometimes result in mutual disappointment, often leads to 'mutual investment'.

Tranter's first collection, *Parallax and Other Poems*, published in 1970 as a special issue of *Poetry Australia*, indicated his remarkable technical ingenuity. *Red Movie* is notable both for its profusion of eccentrics and derelicts ('a landscape/ built with dust and vomit') and its succession of brilliantly effective cameos ('morning hunches, like a gathering of men/ in damp overcoats, waiting for something to happen'). The title section is prefaced by the words:

> that which can be studied is the pattern of processes which characterize the interaction of personalities in particular recurrent situations or fields which 'include' the observer.

The title section contains five pieces, 'The New Field of Knowledge', 'Extract from the Ice Diary', 'The Death Circus', 'The Failure of Sentiment and the Evasion of Love' and 'The Knowledge of Our Buried Life'. Their obscure references, ambiguous syntax, disjointedness, fragmentary discourse and esoteric asides do little, however, to include the reader.

Crying in Early Infancy is a collection of one hundred sonnets, about seventy of which are included in Tranter's *Selected*. The traditional sonnet is among the most formal (in terms of theme and structure) of all poetry but Tranter revels in setting that tradition on its ears. His sonnets are lively, often colloquial, conversation pieces, their easy idiomatic fluency scurrying them along in verse paragraphs that appear to have slipped the authorial leash. They often begin with emphatic yet enigmatic statements:

'Yeats rises in the breathless air/ as simple as a spelling error';
'It's easy to be awfully sick,/ though difficult to do it well';
'Giving up women is worse than animal laxatives';
'They burn the radio and listen to the blues';
'It's bad luck with a coughing baby';
'My daughter's playing with her bloodstained doll again'.

Throughout the series there is a succession of brilliant images which, although often apparently disparate and unconnected, complement the sonnet's tone and atmosphere. Fellow poet Andrew Taylor sees many of these sonnets intelligible in terms of a 'conventional expectation of meaning in poetry'. *Dazed in the Ladies Lounge* contain several poems which have been singled out by critics to indicate the post-modernist penchant for concealing meaning behind a curtain of obscure references, symbols and thematic culs-de-sac. They include (and they are among Tranter's 'chosen') 'Leavis at the London', 'Sartre at Surfers Paradise', 'Foucault at Forest Lodge', 'Roland Barthes at the Poets Ball', 'Enzenberger at "Exiles"'. They conform, with striking stylishness, to the post-modernist belief that the language of the poem has a 'reality more solid and intense than the world of objects and self-perception'. In *Under Berlin: New Poems 1988* (which won the Grace Leven Poetry Prize in 1988) the word 'new' in the title presages a different newness from the same word in the 1979 *The New Australian Poetry*. The early poems of *Under Berlin* are 'new' in that Tranter drops into the traditional role of poet-as-communicator. He does it with such natural ease that, attractive and pleasing though it is, the suspicion arises that he is merely illustrating that writing in this manner is rather like riding a two-wheeled bicycle with trainer wheels – simple enough but unexciting. Yet Tranter's admission (in an interview after *The Floor of Heaven* was published) that 'poetry is meant to be read by

other people' seems to place a new emphasis on the consumer.

Such poems as 'Country Veranda' ('Dry Weather' and 'Rain'), 'North Light', 'Widower' and 'South Coast After Rain, 1960' are graceful, lucid and nostalgic. Equally effective are those where the ugliness of modern life predominates – the 'Letter to America' series, 'Glow-Boys', and 'Those Gods Made Permanent', which indicts the entertainment industry for its worship of crime, violence, war and pornography. Although accepting the inevitable future – 'at the end of the show/ death knocks us down' – the poet opts for pleasing while there is still a little time left to please and be pleased: 'I want to be gentler, teasing the audience so they chuckle not sob.' The later poems of *Under Berlin* ('Sex Chemistry') return to postmodernist style – multi-voiced, multi-personed, multi-puzzled – and couched in the familiar Tranter onrush of colloquial idiom that always suggests, but is never really intent on, explication. *The Floor of Heaven* taps the rich vein of long verse narratives which seem to fascinate contemporary writers. Tranter's four story-poems 'Gloria', 'Stella', 'Breathless' and 'Rain' share some of the same characters and much of the same setting – the scenario of lives blighted by anger, greed, passion, betrayal, mischance and character flaws. Brutalities abound – the son who carves up his father's face so that his eyes are 'chopped up like soft-boiled eggs'; the disfigured Vietnam veteran who tries to blow up his brother with a grenade and becomes himself 'just pieces everywhere'; the Porsche driver who crashes his car through a metal fence and ends up with a metal pole through his neck. Alcohol, drugs and sex – all misused – become ineffectual crutches for their hapless victims. Despite the long catalogue of horrors the narrative tone is only occasionally sensitive and sympathetic (as in the first story, 'Gloria'). In the main it is as chillingly indifferent as the reaction of those to whom the stories are told. Language, as always in Tranter, is expertly manipulated, juxtaposing wonderfully innocent lyricism and flatly brutal colloquialisms. Judged a *tour de force*, *The Floor of Heaven* sets the seal on Tranter's literary achievements to this point, confirming his position as one of Australia's most impressive, and influential, writers.

At the Florida, which won the 1993 *Age* poetry award, has three sections, the last of which is technically interesting. Section 3 contains thirty poems which provide a variation, as Tranter explains, of the 'haibun', a form developed in seventeenth-century Japan, consisting of a mixture of prose and verse, usually a short prose passage followed by a haiku. Tranter reverses the order, a twenty-line stanza of free verse followed by a paragraph of prose. The 'haibun' variations are yet another indication of Tranter's still-questing, still-probing poetic psyche. As many of the poems of *At the Florida* reveal, time has done little to clarify for Tranter the enigmas contained in such *curriculum vitae* entries as childhood, schooldays, family life, love, unfulfilment, ageing and death. No matter how finely life is filtered through the mind and soul, and scrutinised ultimately in the poetry, understanding seems always just beyond reach.

Tranter's considerable poetic achievements over more than a quarter of a century have been recognised by the Australia Council (a Creative Arts Fellowship in 1990) and by fellow poets who acknowledge his role as innovator and experimentalist.

TRAVERS, Pamela Lyndon (1906–), the author of *Mary Poppins* (1934), was born in Queensland and grew up there and in NSW. Her Irish father and a succession of Irish-born nannies encouraged her interest in myth and fantasy. Her father's death when she was 7, which resulted in the family's move to a town south of Sydney, also prevented her from completing her education at the University of Sydney where she had won a scholarship. Before leaving for Europe in 1924 she worked as a journalist and actor. In England she once again worked as a journalist, was befriended by 'AE' (G.W. Russell), who published her poetry in his *Irish Statesman* and was of great influence on her writing, met W.B. Yeats, and established a reputation as a drama critic and travel essayist in the *New English Weekly*. *Mary Poppins* grew from her story-telling to two children while recuperating from a serious illness in Sussex. On the outbreak of war, she moved to the USA, but returned to England in 1945 and has since lived intermittently in both countries. The subsequent Mary Poppins books include *Mary Poppins Comes Back* (1935), *Mary Poppins Opens the Door* (1943), *Mary Poppins in the Park* (1952), *Mary Poppins from A to Z* (1962), *Mary Poppins in the Kitchen* (1975), *Mary Poppins in Cherry Tree Lane* (1982), *Mary Poppins and the House Next Door* (1988). Travers's other publications are *I Go By Sea, I Go By Land* (1941), the fictional diary of an 11-year-old girl evacuated from England to the USA in the Second World War; a travel book, *Moscow Excursion* (1934); four gift books, three of which, *Aunt Sass* (1941), *Ah Wong* (1943) and *Johnny Delaney* (1944), draw on her childhood; an account of the first post-war Christmas carol service at St Paul's, *The Fox at the Manger* (1963); a story based on the monkey-lord Hanuman of Hindu myth, *Friend Monkey* (1971); a retelling of the Sleeping Beauty fairy-tale, *About the Sleeping Beauty* (1975); a reworking of a Middle Eastern story, *Two Pairs of Shoes* (1980); and a collection of essays and stories previously published in *Parabola*, the magazine of myth and tradition for which Travers has been consulting editor since 1976, *What the Bee Knows* (1989). Some of her poetry is also included in *Poetry in Australia 1923* (1923, ed. Jack Lindsay and Kenneth Slessor) and in *The New Countries* (1929, ed. H. Bolitho). She was made OBE in 1977 and in 1978 received an honorary doctorate of humane letters from Chatham College, Pittsburgh. Patricia Demers has written a study of her work, *P.L. Travers* (1991), and Staffan Bergsten has written an account of her use of myth (1978).

Tree of Man, The, a novel by Patrick White (q.v.), was published in 1955 and won the Gold Medal of the Australian Literature Society. Extending from the 1880s to the 1930s, it describes the lives of Stan Parker and his wife Amy, who clear a piece of land in NSW for a mixed farm. During the early years of their marriage the couple achieve an inarticulate but poignant and dignified communion, although their responses to experience soon begin to diverge. External crises such as floods and fire shape their lives and meanwhile other people settle nearby: the inadequate Quigley family, eventually reduced to Doll Quigley and her mentally defective brother, Bub; the loquacious Mrs O'Dowd and her alcoholic husband; Mrs Gage, the postmistress whose 'queer' husband paints pictures and eventually hangs himself; and Armstrong, the butcher, who becomes a man of means. After some childless years, the Parkers have two children, Ray, a naturally vicious boy, and Thelma, delicate and reserved. Amy finds contentment in the becalmed years of child-rearing. Only her novelettish dream about a beautiful socialite, Madeleine, a visitor to the Armstrongs' property Glastonbury, disturbs her peace; this too evaporates when Madeleine, trapped in a fire at Glastonbury which destroys her hair, is rescued by Stan. Stan, however, yearns for some transcendent fulfilment. Especially after the First World War, in which he participates, he becomes withdrawn and longs to 'express the great simplicities in simple, luminous words for people to see. But of course he could not.' Many changes take place in the post-war years. Amy, divided from Stan by his reticence, has a casual affair with a commercial traveller, discovered and grieved over by her husband. Ray, who as a child has found a vent for his aimless cruelty in cutting his name in green trees and stealing birds' eggs, and in his sadistic treatment of the farm hands, Fritz the German and Con the Greek, drifts into his destiny of petty criminal. Before he is shot dead in a club brawl he is married to a Methodist girl, Elsie Tarbutt, who has a son. Both Elsie and the grandson become closer to Amy than her own children. Ray's later liaison with a showgirl, Lola, produces another grandson, although Amy refuses to recognise him. Thelma makes a prudent marriage with her employer, Dudley Forsdyke, and pursues a childless and sterile existence in the city. Doll Quigley finally does away with her infantile brother Bub and ends her life in an institution. Amy's relationship with the O'Dowds stagnates for long periods but quickens at times of crisis such as Ray's death and Mrs O'Dowd's discovery that she has cancer. Towards the end of Stan's life a mixed, ugly, suburban development overtakes their farm and it is eventually subdivided and sold up. The novel closes on the day of Stan's death. Seated in the centre of his circular garden, which is enclosed within other circles, the last circle of all being 'the cold and golden bowl of winter', Stan is accosted by a young man with a fundamentalist religious message. He is pressed into a moment of articulate illumination: 'the old man, who had been cornered long enough, saw, through perversity perhaps, but with his own eyes. He was illuminated.' Pointing with his stick to a gob of spittle, 'That is God', he said. Both his spiritual separation from Amy and the circularity of life is emphasised by her interruption of his vision with a delighted account of her rediscovery of a wedding gift, a silver nutmeg grater. Shortly afterwards he dies, but his vision will persist in his grandson, who dreams of writing 'a poem of life, of all life'.

Triad, a monthly magazine published 1915–27, was founded in NZ, transferred to Sydney and edited successively by C.N. Bayertz, Frank Morton and L.L. Woollacott, although Morton did most to sustain it. Self-consciously cultured and independent in its social attitudes, the *Triad* included reviews of literature, music, art and drama, original poetry, articles and general news of interesting events and people. Better-known contributors included Hugh McCrae, Kenneth Slessor, 'Furnley Maurice', Ethel Anderson, Randolph Bedford, Will Lawson, Mary Gilmore, Louis Esson and Cecil Mann. It was succeeded by the *New Triad*.

Tribune, the weekly newspaper of the Communist Party of Australia, published in Sydney, began publication in December 1920 titled the *Australian Communist*. Titled the *Communist* 1921–23 and the *Worker's Weekly* 1923–39, the newspaper suspended publication from May 1940 to January 1941 and resumed as the *Tribune*. In 1943 it incorporated *Forward* and in 1967 the *Guardian* (Victoria) and the *Queensland Guardian*. *Tribune* has occasionally published articles and reviews of Australian literature, especially of the socialist-realist school. Mary Gilmore wrote its socio-political column, 'Arrows' (1954–61).

Trident was published in Melbourne May 1907 to April 1909 and edited by Walter Murdoch, A.T. Strong, Bernard O'Dowd, B.A. Levinson, H.H. Champion and J.G. Latham. Numerous Melbourne writers, including 'Furnley Maurice' and Vance Palmer, and some of the editors contributed to the magazine.

TRIST, Margaret (1914–86), born Dalby, Queensland, held various jobs in Sydney, with the Farmers and Graziers Co-operative Company, as a secretary of the State Government's Western Lands Commission and with the ABC, where for a time she was a script assistant for John Thompson (q.v.). She wrote three novels, *Now That We're Laughing* (1945), *Daddy* (1947) and *Morning in Queensland* (1958, republished as *Tansy* in 1991), and two collections of short stories, *In the Sun* (1943) and *What Else Is There?* (1946). Written in an understated, often lightly humorous way and dealing with ordinary domestic experience, Trist's novels and stories are particularly attuned to the nuances of small-town life. *Morning in Queensland*, the story of a young girl's growing up in a small Queensland town, is her most finished, extended study of a country community, although several of her short stories are effective and varied re-creations of the same milieu. One of the earliest contributors to *Southerly*, Trist published short stories in a range of Australian periodicals and anthologies, some of which were translated into European languages.

TRITTON, 'Duke' (Harold Percy Croydon) (1886–1965), born Five Dock, Sydney, was well known as a folk-singer and source of Australian folk-songs (q.v.) and stories. Tritton had a scanty education and a series of labouring jobs before going off in 1905 with a mate, 'Dutchy' Holland, to try his luck in the shearing sheds. He spent his last years in Sydney, where he became a popular performer of bush songs. The story of his four years battling round the bush was told much later as a serial in the *Bulletin* (1959) and then published as *Time Means Tucker* (1964). A simply written, leisurely yarn of shearing, droving, fossicking for gold, swagging and odd-jobbing in outback NSW, *Time Means Tucker* is a mine of information about bush life and people in the early years of the twentieth century. John Meredith wrote the biographical *Duke of the Outback* (1983). Tritton's daughter, Linda McLean, has written an account of her childhood which includes reminiscences of her father, *Pumpkin Pie and Faded Sandshoes* (1981).

TROLLOPE, Anthony (1815–82) had been retired from the Post Office for three years when he left England in May 1871 to visit his son Frederic, who was the proprietor of a station near Grenfell, NSW. On the voyage out Trollope wrote a novel, *Lady Anna* (1874), which was serialised in the *Australasian* from May 1873; he arrived in July 1871 and during the next year, before travelling on to NZ, visited each of the Australian colonies, recording his impressions in a series of letters for the London *Daily Telegraph* which form the basis of *Australia and New Zealand* (1873). He made a second, briefer, visit to Australia in 1875; his letters from that journey, published in the *Liverpool Mercury*, were reprinted in *The Tireless Traveller*, edited by Bradford A. Booth (1941). Trollope's reputation as a novelist meant that he was fêted in Australasia; at Gulgong in 1871, for example, he was honoured by a luncheon presided over by Thomas Alexander Browne, 'Rolf Boldrewood'. Apart from *Australia and New Zealand*, which is a perceptive account of the colonies from an imperialist's point of view, Trollope wrote two novels with a significant Australian content, *Harry Heathcote of Gangoil* (1874) and *John Caldigate* (1879). *Harry Heathcote of Gangoil* focuses on the selector–squatter conflicts which characterised pastoral life in NSW after 1861; the squatter-hero is modelled on Trollope's son. In Garnet Walch's 1873 pantomime *Australia Felix* the Demon of Gloom, Kantankeros, is subjected to the Curse:

> May Trollope make you, oh! how low to grovel,
> The hero of his next Australian novel!

In *John Caldigate*, recognised as the better novel, Australia is seen as a frontier environment which is significant in Caldigate's moral development. Trollope's posthumous *Autobiography* (1883) discusses his Australian experiences, which are the subject of Marcie Muir's *Anthony Trollope in Australia* (1949). The Australian section of his *Australia and New Zealand* was republished in 1968, edited by R.B. Joyce and P.D. Edwards, and again in 1988 in Travel Classics; Edwards also edited *Harry Heathcote* in a 1992 World Classics edition; Jim Davidson, later editor of *Meanjin*, edited the parallel volume on Trollope's visit to South

Africa (1973). Frederic Trollope's letters to his parents, edited by P.D. Edwards and titled *Anthony Trollope's Son in Australia* (1982), are informative on the difficulties of colonial life, while his experiences form an interesting contrast with those of Dickens's sons.

Trooper to the Southern Cross, a novel by Angela Thirkell (q.v.), was first published in 1934 under her pseudonym, 'Leslie Parker', and in 1939 as *What Happened on the Boat*. Based on her own memories of a voyage to Australia in 1920, the novel describes the experiences of a group of English and Australian passengers aboard a troop-ship, the *Rudolstadt*, returning to Australia from England after the First World War. The interest of the account owes a great deal to Thirkell's choice of narrator, Major Bowen, an Australian doctor. Cheerful, extrovert, resourceful and simple-hearted, if limited by his class and time, Bowen narrates events in a straightforward, succinct manner that is both consciously and unconsciously humorous. Some of the novel's chapter titles indicate its tone: 'How I Got with the Diggers', 'Larry Gives Us the Dinkum Oil', 'The Digger Isn't a Bad Chap' and 'Good Old Aussie Once More'. Recently married to an English girl, Celia French, whom he frequently describes as a 'bonzer kid' or his 'little missus', Bowen narrates the circumstances of their embarkation on the unseaworthy *Rudolstadt*, once a German troop-ship and now crammed with several hundred restless diggers returning home, as well as some prisoners. At sea, troubles proliferate, compounded by ineffective commanding officers, inadequate supplies and tropical heat. Bowen describes the varying relations, the frictions and love affairs between the passengers, and interprets a range of individuals from 'Mrs Jerry', the indomitable wife of his friend Colonel Fairchild, to Cavanagh, one of the prisoners, to Colonel Bird, the ineffective but 'white' senior doctor. Particularly useful in a crisis are the resourceful Sergeant Higgins and the padre, Father Glennie, whose Christian behaviour tempers Bowen's poor opinion of the Roman Catholic faith. At the same time he paints a vivid picture of the average digger, his sardonic, rough sense of humour, anti-authoritarianism, loyalty to those officers who have won his respect and open contempt for those who have not, his kindness and occasional cruelties. Rioting between the diggers and the local populace breaks out at Colombo, and after leaving that port the situation aboard ship becomes increasingly dangerous; the chance of mutiny is a major anxiety, the soldiers having stolen most of the officers' guns, there is insufficient water, food supplies for the children run short, the ship develops steering problems and Higgins is severely injured in a fight. At Fremantle, after a fierce brawl breaks out between the diggers and the crew, several passengers leave the ship to go home by rail. Eventually, with a guard of armed officers protecting the crew, the *Rudolstadt* limps home to Melbourne.

TRUEBRIDGE, Benjamin Arthur, see **'VREPONT, Brian'**

TRUGANINI (?1812–76), one of the last full-blooded Tasmanian Aborigines to live on the island, assisted George Augustus Robinson (q.v.), who named her 'Lallah Rookh', in his missionary activities and in his attempts to settle the Tasmanian Aborigines on Flinders Island. In 1847 she and a handful of surviving Aborigines were resettled in Oyster Bay in her tribe's traditional territory. By 1869 she and William Lanney, 'King Billy', were the only two full-bloods still alive, Lanney dying in March of that year. The story of Truganini's life is told in Vivienne Rae Ellis's controversial *Trucanini: Queen or Traitor?* (1976) and a film, *Truganini: The Last of Her People*, recalling her last years, was made in 1976. Bill Reed wrote the three-play series *Truganini* (1977). Gwen Harwood recalls an incident from Truganini's life in 'Looking towards Bruny' and makes a general comment on the White treatment of the Tasmanian Aborigines in 'Evening, Oyster Cove', both poems from *The Lion's Bride* (1981). Vivienne Rae Ellis and Nancy Cato collaborated in the novel *Queen Trucanini* (1976) and Truganini appears as a character in Robert Drewe's *The Savage Crows* (1976), Jan Roberts's *Jack of Cape Grim* (1986) and Mudrooroo's *Doctor Wooreddy's Prescription for Enduring the Ending of the World* (1983). The Boyer Lectures for 1980, given by Bernard Smith, were titled *The Spectre of Truganini*. There are busts of Truganini and her husband Wooreddy by Benjamin Law (made in 1836) in the Australian National Gallery and other galleries.

Truth, one of the first Australian Sunday newspapers, was founded in Sydney in 1890 by W.N. Willis; its first editor was A.G. Taylor. In its early days *Truth* gave emphasis to sport, the theatre and mining but changed its direction after the arrival on the staff of John Norton (q.v.). Norton established its reputation in the 1890s when Henry Lawson and 'Price Warung' were prominent contributors, both as a crusader for the disadvantaged and as a muckraker with a gamey nose for sexual, criminal and political scandals. Norton was editor in 1891–92, was replaced in 1893 by W.H. Traill, who tried to make the newspaper more wholesome, and returned in 1896. S.A. Rosa took over as editor in 1906, although Norton remained owner of the newspaper from 1899 until his death in 1916, when it came under the control of his son Ezra. Under Ezra Norton *Truth* continued to be a success by combining sport and scandal; there were editions in all the mainland States, a venture initiated by John Norton at the turn of the century. In 1958 the parent edition changed its title to the *Sunday Mirror*, which passed into the hands of Rupert Murdoch in 1960, and ceased publication in 1979.

TSALOUMAS, Dimitris (1921–), born on the island of Leros, grew up there under the Italian occupation and experienced at first hand a German attack on the island. He came to Australia in 1952, studied at the University of Melbourne and later taught modern languages and English. After moving to Australia he ceased writing poetry until 1974, but has since published several collections in his native language. By

1983 he had established the reputation in Greece as an important poet of the post-war period, and the first selection of his poetry in English, *The Observatory* (1983), mostly translated by Philip Grundy, won the 1983 NBC Award. His second book of English verse, *The Book of Epigrams* (1985), also consists of translations by Grundy in association with Tsaloumas, but since then three collections of poetry written directly in English have appeared, *Falcon Drinking* (1988), *Portrait of a Dog* (1991) and *The Barge* (1993). Tsaloumas has also translated a selection of Australian poetry into Greek in the collection *Contemporary Australian Poetry* (1985) and has edited the selected poems of Manfred Jurgensen (1987). Tsaloumas has disclaimed the description 'ethnic' writer, with its implications of a cultural ghetto, preferring to be described as an Australian Greek writer. Drawing on traditional Greek forms and techniques, his poetry in English is a conscious attempt to wed what is essentially Greek with the idioms and texture of Australian English. Densely metaphoric and technically assured, it draws on a range of styles from epigrammatic simplicity to Byzantine lushness, all modulated by a distinctive, authoritative voice which is by turns humorous, sardonic and deftly witty. Con Castan has written a critical account of his work, *Dimitris Tsaloumas, Poet* (1990).

TUCKER, James (?1808–?88), the probable author of the important early convict novel *Ralph Rashleigh* (q.v.) and other works, was born in Bristol, England, and was said to be 18 when convicted in 1826 of sending a threatening letter to his cousin. Sentenced to transportation for life, he arrived in Sydney early in 1827 and was sent to Emu Plains at the foot of the Blue Mountains, where he may have taken part in theatrical activities. For most of the 1830s he was in Sydney employed in the colonial architect's office; he won a ticket-of-leave in 1835 and although he lost it for drunkenness in 1839 regained it in 1840 when he went to Maitland. In 1844 he again lost his ticket-of-leave and was sent to the penal settlement of Port Macquarie, where he was engaged as a storekeeper. He was in Goulburn in southern NSW in 1849–53, probably left there for Moreton Bay, but thereafter fades from the convict records. It is now thought that he died in Sydney in 1888, although he has been linked with a James Tucker who died at Liverpool Asylum in 1866.

While at Port Macquarie Tucker seems to have initiated theatrical entertainments, and also is said to have written several literary works; manuscripts of two, *Jemmy Green in Australia* (q.v., first published 1955) and 'The Grahames' Revenge' (by 'Otto von Rosenberg'), and a novel, *Ralph Rashleigh* (by 'Giacomo di Rosenberg'), have survived. The existence of these works was first noticed publicly in the *Sydney Morning Herald* in 1892, when their authorship was linked with Francis Greenway. In 1920 the manuscripts were brought to an exhibition organised by the Royal Australian Historical Society, whose president sent *Ralph Rashleigh* to London, where it was published in 1929, in a severely edited form, as a convict memoir. After patient research in 1949–51 Colin Roderick established the connections between Tucker and the manuscripts, and was responsible for the editions of *Ralph Rashleigh* and *Jemmy Green in Australia* which were published in 1952 and 1955 respectively. The case for Tucker's authorship rests on four grounds: the fact that the manuscripts are in his hand; the link between the 'Rosenberg' pseudonym and the same alias used in the letter which caused Tucker's arrest; the 1950s oral testimony of an old Port Macquarie resident; and parallels between the movements of Ralph Rashleigh in the novel and Tucker's documented experiences as a convict. Some commentators, however, notably M.H. Ellis in an exchange with Roderick in the *Bulletin* December 1952 to February 1953, have argued that Tucker was a copyist whose known writing, e.g. the 1826 letter, does not reveal the kind of literacy and education required of the author of *Ralph Rashleigh*. Although Ellis's claims for Greenway as an alternative seem weaker than the claims for Tucker, Tucker's own claims have not been established with complete certainty. Whatever the outcome of the authorship dispute, *Jemmy Green in Australia*, an adaptation of a 'Billy Barlow' song Tucker probably heard in Maitland, is a characteristic example of 'new chum' literature, and *Ralph Rashleigh* is an important contemporary account of the convict system.

TUCKER, Margaret (Lilardia) (1904–), born Margaret Clements, near Deniliquin, NSW, was brought up on the missions Moonahcullah and Cummeragunja, which were both near the Edwards River. She and her three sisters were cared for by an aunt and uncle while their mother worked at nearby stations and homesteads and their father was away shearing and wandering. Margaret Tucker describes this mainly happy childhood in her autobiography *If Everyone Cared* (1977); surrounded by numerous relatives and friends, the children were raised with a strong sense of a rich cultural identity, although the tribal lore and language were being rapidly eroded. When she was 13, however, she suffered a disastrous change when, to the enormous distress of her mother, she was forcibly removed with two of her sisters from the mission school by policemen and taken to a training establishment for Aboriginal girls at Cootamundra. Here she was trained for domestic service and subjected to numerous humiliations and semi-starvation. Assigned to a White family as a servant in 1919, she suffered even worse humiliations, was denied contact with her mother, deprived of food and warm clothing and occasionally physically abused. After she attempted suicide, the Aborigines Protection Board intervened and her conditions improved. Transferred to a more compassionate family, she was nevertheless constantly reminded of her inferior status and eventually ran away. After a short period at large she surrendered to the Board and was sent to a sheep station, 25 miles from Walgett, for three years. She subsequently lived in Melbourne, where she found difficulty in finding employment during the economic depression, married a White man, much to the initial disapproval of his family, and had a daughter. The latter part of *If Everyone Cared* is a more fragmentary if happier story of her discovery of the Moral Rearmament movement, overseas travelling and achievement of a new sense of personal dignity. The first Aboriginal woman to be appointed to the Aborigines Welfare Board, she was later made MBE. Criticised by some reviewers as overly conciliatory, *If Everyone Cared* is nevertheless a graphic account of the harsh treatment suffered by Aborigines of Margaret Tucker's generation.

TULLIPAN, Ron (1917–), born into a well-known Queensland circus family, pursued numerous occupations in the outback before serving with the AIF in the Second World War. He subsequently travelled extensively and studied art in London, before returning to Australia. A socialist-realist writer, he has published numerous short stories, mainly in the *Australian Journal*, some novels which he now describes as 'entertainments', and three more serious novels. These are *Follow the Sun* (1960), which deals with the effects of changes in the sugar industry on the lives of ordinary people; *March into Morning* (1962), which won the Mary Gilmore Award and describes the inner growth of its working-class protagonist against a background of grim experiences from depression and war to flood and personal tragedy; and *Daylight Robbery* (1970), which develops the drama of a bushranging incident.

Turf, The. The first organised race meeting in Australia took place at Hyde Park, Sydney, in 1810 although it was some years later (1825) before the first turf club was formed and some years after that (1842) before the formation of the historically most important club in NSW, the Australian Jockey Club (AJC). The same pattern of development was repeated in the other colonies: for example, in Victoria racing began in 1838 and the Victoria Racing Club (VRC) was formed in 1864. For much of the nineteenth century these, their rival and other clubs, including many in the rural districts, held their own meetings, but gradually the administration of racing became regularised. In 1859 the AJC introduced a weight-for-age (WFA) scale, based on 1 August as the official 'birthday' of horses; in 1878 the *Australian Stud Book* began publication to register thoroughbred horses; and in 1912 thoroughbred horse-racing, with meetings still run by individual clubs, came under the jurisdiction of the Australian Rules of Racing. Meetings of unregistered horses continued for some years on the 'pony' race-courses, but such racing only survives in the picnic race meetings held in some country areas; the picnic race meeting, now usually an annual festive occasion, is a survival from race meetings 'got up' on such places as the goldfields, where sharp practices were often indulged in, e.g. the ringing in of Rainbow at the Turon Races in *Robbery Under Arms* (1888). Most thoroughbred racing is flat racing, although steeplechase and hurdle races were more popular in the nineteenth century when Adam Lindsay Gordon (q.v.) was a champion steeplechase jockey, and the Grand National Hurdle, the Grand National Steeplechase, still run in Melbourne, and the Great Eastern Steeplechase, run in Adelaide, have long traditions. Each, significantly, is a handicap race, for despite the classic races such as the AJC, Victoria and Australian Derbys and other WFA races, there is more popular interest in a number of handicap events on the Australian racing calendar. Of these, the most famous is the Melbourne Cup (q.v.), first run in 1861 and already a national day when 'Mark Twain' wrote about it in *Following the Equator* (1897) and when a Cup scene was included in the 1893 stage version of Nat Gould's novel *The Double Event* (1891). Melbourne Cup day, with its sweepstakes and the cessation of work for the duration of the race broadcast, is the November ritual featured in Alexander Buzo's *The Front Room Boys* (1970); it has produced an extensive literature, some of it about its two most famous winners, Carbine (1890) and Phar Lap (q.v., 1930).

The Australian passion for the turf in particular and for sport and gambling in general are common observations in writings about Australian society, particularly those of visitors like 'Mark Twain', Anthony Trollope and Thomas Wood; *Cobbers* (1934), for example, contains an account of Wood's first night in Australia in the 1930s, which was spent at the 'trots'. Trotting, the racing of specially bred horses in which the driver is pulled in a sulky by a horse using either a pacing or a trotting gait, is also popular in Australia. Some creative writers have deplored these passions, seeing in them evidence of the kind of anti-intellectualism satirised in A.D. Hope's *Dunciad Minor* (1970):

> . . . Now all the Austral Scene,
> Race-track, pub, football-ground, poker machine –
> Pleasing enough to these Yahoos, perhaps,
> To whom all books are made with bets, poor chaps!

Despite the attacks of Hope and others, including Joseph Furphy, Henry Lawson and Patrick White, many Australian writers have had a personal commitment to the turf. A.B. Paterson (q.v.) is perhaps the most notable apart from Gordon, although Vincent Buckley has written several racing poems as well as a perceptive and autobiographical account of the Australian racing tradition.

The racing theme is a significant one in Australian literature, even setting aside the many literary works in which racing plays an incidental part, e.g. the racing scenes in *Robbery Under Arms*, or the news of a Melbourne Cup success which is important in the resolution of the play *Marvellous Melbourne* (1883). The most famous novelist of the turf was Nat Gould, who spent a decade in Australia from 1884, wrote for the *Referee*, one of the many sporting newspapers which have had long lives, and moved from sports reporting to fiction in the early 1890s. He wrote more than 130 sporting novels, most of which were about racing, in which he drew regularly on his Australian experiences; he also wrote reminiscences, including *On and Off the Turf in Australia* (1895), and *The Magic of Sport* (1909). Although his reputation was perhaps larger in England, he virtually inaugurated the Australian sporting novel; his most prominent descendant was Arthur Wright (q.v.), advertised as the 'Australian Nat Gould', whose novels contain the Gould blend of sporting (usually racing) subject with elements of the detective story and the romance. Among other, but less well-known, racing novelists who briefly flourished were Leon Breaker, Robert Adam and Con Drew, while several popular novelists have written fiction either about racing, e.g. Ambrose Pratt, W.N. Willis, 'Smiler' Hales, or in which experiences both on or off the turf figure prominently, e.g. Jessie Couvreur in *In Her Earliest Youth* (1890). Racing scenes or subjects were common in the Australian melodramas of the second half of the nineteenth century and in many early Australian films.

The racing novel tradition of Gould was satirised in 'Done for the Double by Knott Gold', a story included in A.B. Paterson's *Three Elephant Power and Other Stories* (1917). Yet Paterson not only wrote a novel about racing, *The Shearer's Colt* (1936), to the Gould formula, but also is central to a second Australian literary tradition in which racing plays a significant part. Paterson is generally regarded as the leading literary balladist of his generation, and of all the *Bulletin*'s 'equestrian' balladists, who include Barcroft Boake, Will Ogilvie and 'Breaker' Morant, Paterson is the one who wrote most about horse sports, polo, as in 'The Geebung Polo Club', as well as racing. Many of his racing poems, e.g. 'Father Riley's Horse', 'How the Favourite Beat Us', are narratives which recount the plans for ill-gotten gain of dishonest racehorse-owners, bookmakers or jockeys. Comic exaggeration, a rural setting and a sporting subject are common ingredients in these poems, which form part of an Australian tall-story tradition which also accommodates the poems of 'Arthur Ferres' (J.W. Kevin) and Thomas E. Spencer, the cricket fantasies of Dal Stivens, and several Billy Borker racing yarns by Frank Hardy (q.v.). Elsewhere, Hardy is less amused about the social effects of racing. *The Four-legged Lottery* (1958) is an indictment of the effects of gambling on the individual, and *Power Without Glory* (q.v., 1950) focuses on the network of corruption established by John West through his 'tote' and other gambling enterprises; gambling is also featured in Lawson Glassop's novel *Lucky Palmer* (1949). The language of gambling has contributed significantly to Australian English, particularly in the area of informal usage, as also have racing and trotting generally: e.g. the colloquialism 'further behind than Walla Walla', meaning to be delayed or at a serious disadvantage, derives from the champion pacer of the 1930s, Walla Walla, which gave away starts of up to 260 metres behind the scratch mark. Similarly, the prominence of champions like Walla Walla or significant events in the history of the turf has produced a body of occasional verse on the subject of racing. This tradition seems to have its origins in the newspaper forecasts of the early racing tipsters of the 1840s and 1850s, although there is a racing description in Edward Kemp's satire *A Voice from Tasmania* (1846). By the 1860s Adam Lindsay Gordon was predicting the result of the Melbourne Cup in verse narratives included in *Sea Spray and Smoke Drift* (1867). In subsequent years, racing disasters as well as triumphs have provided the occasion for comment. Two notable examples are the death of the champion hurdle jockey of the 1880s, Tommy Corrigan, which produced a tribute from Paterson, and the death of Phar Lap in the USA in 1932, which produced a series of sentimental eulogies.

If racing has made its contribution to Australian literature, the reverse has also happened. At the AJC's annual Expressway Stakes meeting, minor races are named after Australian poets, e.g. Adam Lindsay Gordon, 'Banjo' Paterson, Will Ogilvie, Mary Gilmore, Henry Kendall, Henry Lawson and Dorothea Mackellar.

TURNBULL, Clive (1906–75), born and educated in Tasmania, worked as a journalist on the staff of the *Mercury*, the *Argus* and the Melbourne *Herald*. His publications include two collections of verse, *Outside Looking In* (1933) and *14 Poems* (1944); several books on Australian art; a history of the destruction of the Tasmanian Aborigines, *Black War* (1948); a biography, *Essington Lewis* (1963); a concise history of Australia (1965); and a number of biographical sketches of Australian personalities. These comprise *Bluestone* (James Brunton Stephens, 1945), *Mulberry Leaves* (Charles Whitehead, 1945), *Bonanza* (George F. Train, 1946), *Eureka* (Peter Lalor, 1946), *These Tears of Fire* (Francis Adams, 1948) and *Frontier* (Paddy Hannan, 1949). The sketches were combined as *Australian Lives* (1965).

TURNBULL, Gilbert Munro (1890–1938), born Llandudno, Wales, qualifed as an architect before leaving for the USA, Canada, Mexico, Tahiti and Papua. In Papua, where he lived 1913–34, Turnbull worked as government architect; he retired to Bellingen, NSW. He published numerous anecdotal paragraphs and articles as well as over ninety short stories in Australian magazines, including the *Bulletin*, sometimes using the pseudonym 'Tauwarra'. He also published four novels, *Disenchantment* (1932), *Paradise Plumes* (1934), *Mountains of the Moon* (1935) and *Portrait of a Savage* (1943). Critical of the pretensions and hypocrisy of White society, Turnbull attempted in his novels to subvert imperial attitudes. His anachronistic empathy with the Papuan perspective on colonialism in *Portrait of a Savage* deterred numerous English and Australian publishers from publishing the book for some years and led to its denunciation in Australia as 'unclean'.

TURNER, Alexander Frederick (1907–), born England, came in 1925 to WA, where he worked as a bank officer in rural towns. He served in the AIF 1942–46, and subsequently worked for the ABC as drama and feature producer. Turner, whose career as a playwright for radio extended from the 1930s to the 1960s, won numerous awards for his radio and stage plays, including first prize in the 1939 Perth Drama Festival for his three-act play *Royal Mail*. Several of his plays were published, *Hester Siding* (1937), which includes the stage plays *Centurion*, *Not the Six Hundred*, *The Old Allegiance* and *One Hundred Guineas*, and the radio plays *Hester Siding*, *All Stations*, *Strong Archer* and *Coat-of-Arms*, as well as some verse previously contributed to the *Western Mail* and the *Bulletin*; *Australian Stages*

(1944), a verse play for radio; and *Royal Mail and Other Plays* (1944), which includes the radio plays *Wheat Boat*, *Sea Power*, *In Thy Most Need* and *After Three*, and the stage play *The Golden Journey*. Another of his radio plays, *Conglomerate*, is included in *Australian Radio Plays* (1946, ed. Leslie Rees). Turner's other plays include 'The Neighbours', 'Champion Bay', 'Westward Journey', 'I'm a Dutchman', 'Star at the Irwin', 'Flight from Granite' and 'Buccaneer Bay'. At first Turner wrote historical plays reflecting his English background, but he soon moved to dramas evocative of the WA landscape, such as *Hester Siding*, *Royal Mail* and *Conglomerate*, or of the Australian experience of war, such as *Wheat Boat*, 'The Neighbours', and 'Westward Journey'. Although his stage plays were successful, his understated, quiet, poetically suggestive style was more suited to radio.

TURNER, Ethel (1870–1958) was born in Yorkshire, the second child of G.W. Burwell, who died within two years of her birth. Her mother's second marriage was to Henry Turner, whose name was adopted by Ethel and her sister Lilian (see Turner, Lilian) but who also died young. In 1880 Mrs Turner with her three daughters left for Sydney, where she married Charles Cope, a clerk in the NSW public service. While still in her teens Ethel, with Lilian, edited a schoolgirls' magazine, *Iris*, which was superseded by the *Parthenon* and which stimulated her gift for children's fiction. Later she contributed to the *Bulletin* and, as 'Dame Durden', was responsible for the children's column of the *Illustrated Sydney News*, later incorporated in the *Australian Town and Country Journal*. Her best-known children's novel, *Seven Little Australians* (q.v.), was first published in 1894, followed by its sequel, *The Family at Misrule*, in 1895. *The Story of a Baby*, an adult novel, appeared the same year. By 1895 her reputation was well established in Australia and her short stories were appearing regularly in Australian and English magazines. She continued to write after her marriage to the lawyer H.R. Curlewis, later Judge Curlewis, in 1896 and eventually published twenty-seven full-length novels as well as numerous collections of short stories and anthologies of verse and fiction. Her other publications were *The Little Duchess and Other Short Stories* (1896), *The Little Larrikin* (1896), *Miss Bobbie* (1897), *The Camp at Wandinong* (1898), *Three Little Maids* (1900), *Gum Leaves* (1900), *The Wonder-Child* (1901), *Little Mother Meg* (1902), *Betty & Co.* (1903), *Mother's Little Girl* (1904), *A White Roof-Tree* (1905), *In the Mist of the Mountains* (1906), *The Stolen Voyage* (1907), *Happy Hearts* (1908), *That Girl* (1908), *Ethel Turner Birthday Book* (1909), *Fugitives from Fortune* (1909), *Fair Ines* (1910), *The Raft in the Bush* (1910), *The Tiny House* (1911), *Fifteen and Fair* (1911), *The Apple of Happiness* (1911), *An Ogre Up-to-date* (1911), *Ports and Happy Havens* (1912), *The Secret of the Sea* (1913), *Oh, Boys in Brown!* (1914), *Flower o' the Pine* (1914), *The Cub* (1915), *John of Daunt* (1916), *Captain Cub* (1917), *St Tom and the Dragon* (1918), *Brigid and the Cub* (1919), *Laughing Water* (1920), *King Anne* (1921), *Jennifer J.* (1922), *Nicola Silver* (1924), *The Undergardeners* (1925), *Funny* (1926) and *Judy and Punch* (1928). She

also edited, with Bertram Stevens, *The Australian Soldiers' Gift Book* (1918), and compiled, with her daughter Jean Curlewis (q.v.), *The Sunshine Family: A Book of Nonsense for Girls and Boys* (1923). Selections from Ethel Turner's diaries 1889–1930, compiled by her granddaughter Philippa Poole, were published in 1979.

Although Ethel Turner wrote mainly children's books, some of which, such as *Seven Little Australians*, *The Family at Misrule*, *Miss Bobbie* and *Flower o' the Pine*, are still read by children, she has also always attracted adult readers. Drawing on the tradition of domestic fiction established by such writers as Louisa M. Alcott and Charlotte Yonge, she invested her children's stories with specifically Australian, middle-class characteristics and values. The two most successful of the group of novels dealing with the Woolcott family, *Seven Little Australians* and *The Family at Misrule*, are deliberately anti-heroic in tone, concerned with the activities of real children who have an engaging capacity for mischief and rebellion. The children of these novels, three sons and four daughters of an army officer who range from babyhood to young adulthood, undergo a multitude of experiences from punishments to bush picnics, love affairs to sicknesses; and both their daily, confused experience of the complicated process of growing and its overall, long-term nature are realistically expressed. All Ethel Turner's best novels show an understanding of children's interests, needs and anxieties, as well as an insight into the irritations, tensions and joys of family relationships. Dealing mostly with large families and interested more in city life than in the outback, her novels frequently present parents as inadequate, negligent, tyrannical or simply absent, removed by death or separation; if trustworthy authority figures are lacking, however, the sustaining solidarity of the family emerges as a thoroughly adequate substitute. Two novels which deal in a particularly realistic and humorous way with the unheroic world of children are *The Little Larrikin* and *Miss Bobbie*; the former also reveals Ethel Turner's awareness of the hardships and evils of city life as well as her attitude to social injustice. Although she never equates money with gentility, she values good taste, education and cultivated attitudes, regarding a middle state of genteel comfort as the ideal environment, as *Fugitives from Fortune* most explicitly suggests. With the outbreak of the First World War her democratic and socialist inclinations became more pronounced; her three war novels, *The Cub*, *Captain Cub* and *Brigid and the Cub*, stress the disciplining effects of patriotic sacrifice on both men and women. Ethel Turner's range is limited and she has a tendency to lapse into sentimentality or melodrama, especially in her studies of older adolescents, but she has created some perennially convincing children, such as Judy, Meg, Pip and Bunty of *Seven Little Australians* and the madcap heroine of *Miss Bobbie*. Other qualities that are likely to make her best work durable are her humour, empathy with children and representative pictures of Australian middle-class life of the early twentieth century. Brenda Niall compares the fictional worlds of Ethel Turner and Mary Grant

Bruce (q.v.) in *Seven Little Billabongs* (1979). Her relationship with Louise Mack (q.v.) is described in Nancy Phelan's *The Romantic Lives of Louise Mack* (1991). See also *The Oxford Companion to Australian Children's Literature* (1993), pp. 421–5.

TURNER, George (1916–   ), born and educated in Melbourne, has become acknowledged not only as an important mainstream novelist but as Australia's best-known science fiction (q.v.) critic and a leading SF writer. In the Second World War he served in the Middle East, Africa and New Guinea. His first novel, *Young Man of Talent* (q.v., 1959), which was published the same year in New York with the title *Scobie*, was virtually unnoticed. His second, *A Stranger and Afraid* (1961), the first of a tetralogy set in a fictional small Victorian town called Treelake, also aroused little interest, although its successor, *The Cupboard under the Stairs* (1962), was widely acclaimed and shared the Miles Franklin Award for 1962. The remaining novels of the Treelake series are *A Waste of Shame* (1965) and *The Lame Dog Man* (1967). Turner's other mainstream novel is *Transit of Cassidy* (q.v., 1978), which deals with the moral deterioration of a boxing champion. Turner is now recognised as a major figure in science fiction writing and criticism and has published several novels in this genre, *Beloved Son* (1978), *Vaneglory* (1981), *Yesterday's Men* (1981), *The Sea and Summer* (1987, published in the USA as *Drowning Towers*, and winner of the Commonwealth Writers S.E. Asia Pacific Award and the Arthur C. Clark Award), *Brain Child* (1991) and *The Destiny Makers* (1993); and a collection of science fiction stories, *A Pursuit of Miracles* (1990); he has also edited another collection, *The View from the Edge* (1977). He has described science fiction as 'the literature of preparation for change' rather than the 'spinning of fairy-floss' and in *The Sea and Summer*, a realist novel set in Melbourne of 2044–2051 he projects a vision of the future when environmental and economic chaos cause vast changes in the lives of a typical family. His first three science fiction novels form a trilogy in which he also contemplates Australia's future, not just in the light of possible technological change, but as a result of contemporary policies. Turner's own science fiction writing so far fits his definition of the genre's two major claims to originality, the 'presentation of new metaphors for the human condition' and the delineation of the normal 'with the 'one small change' that results in a new perspective'. In the autobiographical *In the Heart or in the Head* (1984) he meditates revealingly on the reasons for his shift in allegiance from mainstream to science fiction at the age of 62.

Turner's Treelake series reveals him as a competent, conventional novelist with a flair for tailored plots, convincing characters and credible incidents. His main interest in the tetralogy is the interaction between the individual and his social environment and the effects the latter has on the psychiatric adjustment of the former. Jimmy Carlyon, the central character of *A Stranger and Afraid*, faces a moral struggle when, as district employment officer, he discovers some chicanery which also implicates his mother and other members of his family. Jimmy is also a minor character in *The Cupboard under the Stairs*, which turns mainly on the rehabilitation of Harry White after six years in a mental hospital. *A Waste of Shame* describes the self-destruction of another inhabitant of Treelake, the alcoholic carpenter Joe Bryen. *The Lame Dog Man* returns to the fortunes of Jimmy Carlyon and Harry White with the addition of the strange destiny of an ex-convict, Teddy Johnson. In all the novels the town of Treelake exists more to provide links between the various identities than as a specifically realised entity. Turner's first novel, *Young Man of Talent*, a complex, dramatic study of a private struggle between antipathetic personalities against the background of war, is his most powerful and suggestive work. *Transit of Cassidy* shows a fine insight into adolescent experience and returns to the study of the corrosive effects of uncontrolled egoism.

TURNER, George William, see **Australian English**

TURNER, Henry Gyles (1831–1920), born London, emigrated to Victoria in 1854 and was for many years general manager of the Commercial Bank of Australasia. Well known in Melbourne's literary circle, in 1875 he helped to found the *Melbourne Review*, which he subsequently edited with Alexander Sutherland. His publications include two histories, *A History of the Colony of Victoria* (1904) and *The First Decade of the Australian Commonwealth* (1911); an account of Eureka, *Our Own Little Rebellion* (1912); and, with Alexander Sutherland, *The Development of Australian Literature* (q.v., 1898). Turner also wrote an appreciation of his friend and collaborator, *Alexander Sutherland* (1908).

TURNER, Ian (1922–78), born East Melbourne, had a variety of occupations including secretary of the Australasian Book Society and a turbulent political career before becoming an academic in 1964. At his death he was associate professor of history at Monash University. Active in the Australian labour movement, he wrote several books on its history; compiled *The Australian Dream* (1968), a historical collection of anticipations about Australia from the time of James Cook; and edited *Cinderella Dressed in Yella* (1969), a collection of lighthearted, irreverent children's rhymes. A fanatical follower of Australian rules football, he was famous for his annual Ron Barassi Memorial lecture, instituted in 1967, and, with co-author Leonie Sandercock, wrote a history of the game, *Up Where, Cazaly?* (1981). After his death friends made a selection of his essays and articles, *Room for Manoeuvre* (1982); a special number of *Overland* (October 1979) contains numerous tributes from writers and historians.

TURNER, Lilian (1867–1956), born Yorkshire, England, came to Australia in 1881. With her better-known sister, Ethel Turner (q.v.), she edited the schoolgirl magazines *Iris* and *Parthenon*, and similarly wrote extensively for children. Her first book, *The Lights of Sydney* (1896), won first prize in Cassell's novel competition in 1894, and she published a further twenty novels for children 1902–31 as well as a book of short stories, *Written Down* (1912). Her novels, written for the older teenager, reflect Australian middle-class life and concentrate on the experience of girls, particularly girls with a creative bent who have to struggle for recognition. Aware of hardship and injustice, she frequently portrays motherless families, as in *Betty the Scribe* (1906), *Three New Chum Girls* (1910) and *Anne Chooses Glory* (1928), and is adept at representing the tensions and changing relationships of family life. Overshadowed by her more successful sister and handicapped by financial hardship and ill health, Lilian Turner had to keep writing to support her family, although when she died all her books were out of print.

TURNER, Walter James (1884–1946) was born and educated in Melbourne. He left Australia in 1907 to study in Europe, and served in the First World War, during which he published his first volume of poetry, *The Hunter and Other Poems* (1916). In London he was music critic for the *New Statesman* (1915–40), *Truth* (c.1920–37), and the *Modern Mystic* (1937); drama critic for the *London Mercury* (1919–23) and the *New Statesman* (1928–29); literary editor of the *Owl* (1919), the *Daily Herald* (1920–23) and the *Spectator* (1941–46). His range of interests, lively intellect and unconventional personality made him a significant member of the cultural groups of Bloomsbury and Garsington. He was acquainted with W.B. Yeats, who greatly admired his poetry and later collaborated with him in BBC poetry programmes, Arnold Bennett, Robert Graves, T.S. Eliot, Virginia Woolf, Aldous Huxley and Artur Schnabel. His uninhibited speech and writing nevertheless made him many enemies and Lady Ottoline Morrell, in particular, never forgave him for his representation of her in *The Aesthetes* (1927). Turner's poetry first won admiration as belonging to the Georgian school, but he later rejected the Georgians and experimented with more symbolist forms. He published sixteen volumes of poetry, two plays, including the successful comedy *The Man Who Ate the Popomack* (1922), and several critical works on music, painting and literature. He also published several comic, semi-autobiographical works of fiction, of which one, *Blow for Balloons* (1935), includes references to his Australian experience. Turner is the author of the familiar lines 'Chimboroso, Cotopaxi, They have stolen my heart away' often quoted in English verse anthologies. Wayne McKenna has written an account of his life and work, *W.J. Turner* (1990), and edited his *Selected Poetry* (1989).

'TWAIN, Mark' (Samuel Langhorne Clemens) (1835–1910) visited Australia in 1895 as part of a world lecture tour to recoup losses his publishing company had suffered; his route took him from Sydney to Melbourne, Adelaide, Ballarat, Bendigo and Tasmania. His *Following the Equator: A Journey Around the World* (1897), published also as *More Tramps Abroad* (1897), includes the material republished in 1973 as *Mark Twain in Australia and New Zealand*; notable comments are the references to 'Ballarat English', which satirises the elisions of Australian English, and the observation of the Melbourne Cup (q.v.) as a national ritual. Brian Kiernan's edition of contemporary short fiction, *The Most Beautiful Lies* (1977), also takes its title from Twain's *Following the Equator*. Miriam Shillingsburg has written an account of his visit to Australia and NZ based on his notebooks, letters and newspaper reports, *At Home Abroad: Mark Twain in Australasia* (1988).

24 Hours, a journal published by the ABC since 1976, was begun primarily as a monthly programme guide to ABC-FM radio. Between 1976 and 1980 it incorporated *The Critic*, a journal of book reviews and book news; from July to December 1988 it was published as *Australian Listener*. While still providing a guide to ABC-FM and Radio National, and focusing on the discussion of 'fine music', from October 1990, under editor Suzy Baldwin, the magazine has developed as an important Australian arts forum, containing book and drama reviews, interviews with writers, and articles of broad cultural interest. Regular contributors include Robert Dessaix, Robyn Williams, Michele Field and Humphrey McQueen.

Twenty Thousand Thieves, The, Eric Lambert's (q.v.) first novel, was published in 1951; Lambert arranged its publication himself, following the example of his friend Frank Hardy with *Power Without Glory* (1950). A popular success, informed by Lambert's experiences during the Second World War, *The Twenty Thousand Thieves* chronicles the experiences of an infantry battalion in the Middle East, notably their part in the defence of Tobruk and in the battle of El Alamein. The main character of the novel, its title deriving from a label given to the Allied forces by the broadcaster Lord Haw Haw, is Dick Brett, one of the few survivors of the platoon on which *The Twenty Thousand Thieves* is focused; Brett's experiences parallel those of the author himself. While not ignoring the larrikin and racist sides of the ordinary Australian troops, the novel pays tribute to their courage and endurance in the face of the carnage and futility of war and incompetent officers like the drunken colonel Fitzroy Orme.

Two Fires, The (1955), a volume of poetry by Judith Wright (q.v.) written at the time of the Korean War, sees, in the title poem, mankind threatened by a nuclear holocaust. The poem reflects the uncertainty that worried people as they witnessed the brinkmanship of statesmen prepared to run unimaginable risks to achieve their objectives. Poems such as 'For Precision', 'The Man beneath the Tree' and 'Gum Trees Stripping' also show humankind baffled in the painstaking search for things that should come effortlessly, e.g. love and truth, and indicate that in the natural world there are modes of existence whose simplicity and completeness deflate the human ego.

Two Worlds of Jimmie Barker, The (1977) is the life story of part-Aborigine Jimmie Barker (1900–72).

Born Cunnamulla, Queensland, he was the son of a German boundary-rider, originally called Bocher, and an Aboriginal mother. His grandmother was a full-blood member of the Murawari tribe. Deserted by his father, the family lived first at Mundiwa, on an Aboriginal reserve, where Barker learned of Murawari customs and language, and then at Milroy, where his mother worked for station managers. Apart from economic hardship, these years were happy ones for Jimmie and his brother Billy, but in 1912 they were compelled to move to a mission at Brewarrina. There he encountered racist attitudes, harsh treatment and extremely poor living conditions. After the age of 12 his schooling became 'part-time' and at 15 he was persuaded to leave his family to take up an 'engineering apprenticeship', but found himself working as an unpaid station hand at Tottenham with a chaff shed as his bedroom. In 1917 he was sent some distance from the station to live on his own as cattle-herd for eight months; the unfriendliness he encountered at the station was relieved only by the kind attentions of the wife of one of the station managers. After he showed building skills when helping to construct a house for his employer, he was treated more kindly and enjoyed a brief period of happiness when he discovered that his love for a White girl was reciprocated; she died in the influenza epidemic of 1919, however, and he returned to his people at Brewarrina. He discovered the mission to be in the last stages of decay, 'a paradise for gamblers and drunks' in which the manager took part. His four and a half years' 'apprenticeship' at Tottenham had resulted in £30, paid to the Aborigines Protection Board. Banned temporarily from the mission after a disagreement with the manager, he worked at several jobs at Brewarrina, and carried his swag for a period. After his mother's death in 1922 he decided to remain at the mission as handyman, given the prejudice he encountered outside, and made a happy marriage two years later to Evelyn Wighton, eventually becoming the father of six children. A new manager in 1930 made great improvements in the mission but four years later was succeeded by others who were in varying degrees dishonest, incompetent or harsh. In 1941 Evelyn died after the birth of their sixth child and the succeeding years were a struggle to maintain the family. After a disagreement with a new, particularly vindictive, assistant manager, Barker left the mission, abandoning the home and garden he had built up and took various jobs in and around Brewarrina; in 1946 he began work at Brewarrina hospital as a handyman, remaining there for seventeen years. In his last years he moved to Lightning Ridge to mine opals and developed his interests in the Murawari language and culture. It was this which eventually brought him into association with Janet Mathews, who was then carrying out research for the Australian Institute of Aboriginal Studies. She recorded his life story, which was published as *The Two Worlds of Jimmie Barker* (1977); a sensitive account of one man's experience of Australian acculturation policies and his sense of 'living between two worlds', the autobiography is also informative on older forms of Aboriginal culture and life within the missions.

TWOPENY, Richard (1857–1915), born Rutland, England, came to Australia in 1876 and joined the literary staff of the *South Australian Register*. In 1877 he left the *Register* and held a series of appointments connected with various great exhibitions, including those in Paris (1878), Sydney (1879) and Melbourne (1880 and 1888). He also managed private exhibitions in Adelaide and Perth (1881) and Christchurch (1882). He edited the *Telegraph* in Christchurch (1881–82), the *Daily Times* in Otago (1882–90), and in 1891, following the shearers' strike, was invited to found and edit the *Australasian Pastoralists' Review*; he remained a proprietor of the newspaper until 1915. From 1896 he frequently made lengthy visits to Europe and England, where he died. Twopeny is best known for his observations on life in Adelaide, Sydney and Melbourne, *Town Life in Australia* (1883), a record that has been frequently used by later historians. Witty and urbane, Twopeny writes discerningly of regional differences within Australia and of differences between Australian and English society; topics that he discusses include houses, furniture, servants, food, dress, social relations, religion and morals, education, politics, business, amusements, newspapers and the state of Australian culture.

Twyborn Affair, The, a novel by Patrick White (q.v.), was published in 1979. Composed of three sections, it deals with an individual for whom sexuality is problematical. Eddie or E, the child of an eminent circuit judge, Judge Edward Twyborn, and his wife Eadie, a lady with transvestite tendencies, has a male body and a female consciousness. In the first part of the novel E appears in her feminine aspect as Eudoxia Vatatzes, the young mistress of Angelos, an ageing Greek merchant from Smyrna with Byzantine imperial fantasies. The two are staying at a small French town, St Mayeul, and the time is February 1914. An Australian couple, E. Boyd ('Curly') Golson and his wife Joan, friends of the Twyborns, are also staying at St Mayeul. Joan, who has lesbian tendencies, becomes fascinated with Eudoxia and finally the threat of discovery forces the Vatatzes to leave. During their flight Angelos dies in a boarding-house, releasing Eudoxia from a relationship that had become oppressive. In the second phase of the novel E appears as Lieutenant Eddie Twyborn returning to Australia after the war, in which he has been decorated. He is reunited with his parents although they remain bewildered about the reasons for his previous sudden disappearance. Unable to establish frank links with them, he escapes by taking a job as jackeroo on a property, Bogong, owned by Greg Lushington. He makes a strong impression on everyone at Bogong: Greg Lushington feels a fatherly affection for him which he returns; Marcia, Greg's wife, takes him as her lover; Mrs Tyrrell, the manager's housekeeper, finds him as congenial as a daughter; Don Prouse the manager, deserted husband and Marcia's ex-lover, depends on his sympathy and later responds to the latent homosexuality that Eddie's physique arouses in him. The most natural, authentic relationship seems to be the arranged marriage between an illiterate stockman, Denny Allen, and Dot, the unattractive daughter of a rabbiter, Dick Norton, who is also the incestuous father of her baby. Disillusioned by the sexual exploitation he finds in both male and female, Eddie disappears once more. Afterwards his mother learns in a letter from Marcia that her fourth son, who was possibly also Eddie's, had, like her previous three sons, died in infancy. After a gap of more than a decade, E appears as the middle-aged Eadith Trist, madam of a high-class brothel in London, partly financed by an aristocratic patron, Lord Gravenor. For Eadith, morality is a complexity that conventional attitudes cannot begin to comprehend. Gravenor loves Eadith passionately, but their relationship is strained by her unwillingness to reveal the truth. Only after their last meeting when the war has intervened does she realise that he would love her 'in whatever form' she appeared. She receives news that her father is dead, learns that her mother is in London and is affectionately united with her, despite her change in sex. Persuaded by her mother to return home to Australia, she resumes her role as Eddie and hands the brothel over to Eadith's housekeeper/confidant. On the way to his mother Eddie dies in a bombing raid which also destroys the hotel where his mother is staying.

TYRRELL, James (1875–1961), born Sydney, lived as a boy at Balmain, where his father kept refreshment rooms. In 1888 Tyrrell joined the bookselling firm of Angus & Robertson and progressed from errand-boy to manager before he left to found his own shop in 1905. He moved to Adelaide to open another bookselling business in 1910 but in 1914 returned to Sydney, where he joined J.F. Archibald in a publishing venture, Tyrrells Ltd, and founded his famous secondhand bookshop. Frequented by most of Sydney's writers and literary identities, the shop is celebrated in such poems as Henry Lawson's 'The Song of Tyrrell's Bell', Roderic Quinn's 'Tyrrell's Bookshop' and Kenneth Slessor's 'In Tyrrell's Bookshop'. Tyrrell's memoirs, *Old Books, Old Friends, Old Sydney* (1952), which include his boyhood reminiscences of Sydney and his recollections of numerous identities of the book world, are an invaluable record of Sydney's social and cultural scene in the 1880s–1905. Individuals he recalls include the booksellers the George Robertsons of Melbourne and Sydney, David Angus and William Dymock; the writers Henry Lawson, J.F. Archibald, C.J. Dennis, Victor Daley, Norman Lindsay and A.B. Paterson; the public figures Sir Henry Parkes, W.M. Hughes, Sir William Dixson and Cardinal Moran; and the book collector David Scott Mitchell, with whom he had frequent dealings. Tyrrell also published a compilation of Australian Aboriginal place-names (1933), a reminiscence of David Scott Mitchell (1936), and *Postscript: Further Bookselling Reminiscences* (1957), which includes the poems of James Lionel Michael as transcribed by Henry Kendall.

TYSON, James (1819–98), born Narellan, NSW, was a famous pioneer pastoralist who made money as a butcher on the Bendigo goldfields in the 1850s and then bought large properties in the Deniliquin area of south-western NSW. He eventually owned more than two million hectares of land in NSW, Victoria and Queensland. A bachelor whose frugality was a byword in the outback, Tyson was nicknamed 'Hungry' Tyson by the *Bulletin*; he was, however, a major benefactor of the Women's College at the University of Sydney and of the University as a whole. He is the model for Abstinens Levison in 'Rolf Boldrewood's' *A Colonial Reformer* (1890) and is commemorated in A.B. Paterson's poem 'T.Y.S.O.N.'.

U

ULLATHORNE, William Bernard (1806–89), born Yorkshire, England, was ordained in 1831 and came in 1833 to Sydney, where for the next decade he was actively involved in the development of Catholicism in Australia. A fervent opponent of transportation (q.v.), he wrote *The Horrors of Transportation* (1838) and other polemical works, gave evidence before the British parliamentary inquiry into transportation in 1838, and influenced later writers about the convict system. These included 'Price Warung', who presented Ullathorne sympathetically as Nellathorne in several of his early stories. Ullathorne's autobiography, written in 1867 and dealing largely with his work in Australia, was published in 1891 in an expurgated form and in 1941 from the original draft, edited by Shane Leslie and titled *From Cabin-Boy to Archbishop*. A biography by Cuthbert Butler, *The Life & Times of Bishop Ullathorne, 1806–1889*, was published in 1926.

Ulitarra, launched in 1992 at the Harold Park Hotel, is a literary magazine, published twice yearly. It was launched by Michael Wilding and Les Murray and its inaugural issue included an extract from a Les Murray verse novel in progress. *Ulitarra* is published by Kardoorair Press, Armidale. One of its chief aims is to promote Aboriginal writing. Its first poetry competition in 1993 was won by Lola Stewart. Michael Sharkey is its poetry editor.

UNAIPON, David (1872–1967), the first Aboriginal writer to have a book published in Australia, was born at the Point McLeay mission in the Tailem Bend area of the Murray River. He was educated at the mission school and then spent most of his life in Adelaide, where he was encouraged in his writing and work for his people by the Aborigines' Friends' Association; he was awarded the Coronation Medal in 1953. Unaipon's chief work, *Native Legends* (1929), written in an elevated and somewhat archaic style, contains two stories, 'The Release of the Dragon Flies by the Fairy Sun Beam' and 'Youn Goona the Cockatoo', with two short pieces which provide some anthropological and mythological background to the legends, and a longer piece, 'Hungarrda: Jew Lizard'. The Christian virtues and values that are illustrated in Unaipon's legends are shown to be similar to Aboriginal values. A collection of Unaipon's legends was published, without acknowledgement, by W. Ramsay Smith as *Myths and Legends of the Australian Aboriginals* (1930). The David Unaipon Award has been inaugurated as an annual competition restricted to Aborigines and Torres Strait Islanders for an unpublished book-length work of any

nature. It was won in 1992 by Phillip McLaren's *Sweet Water – Stolen Land*.

Uncle Piper of Piper's Hill, a novel by Jessie Couvreur (q.v.) published under her pseudonym 'Tasma', was serialised as 'The Pipers of Piper's Hill' in the *Australasian* 1888, and published in book form a year later. It was republished in 1988 with an introduction by Margaret Harris. Set on board an emigrant ship, in 1860s Melbourne and in up-country Barnesbury, a fictional portrait of Malmsbury, where Couvreur lived after her marriage, the novel opens with the genteel but impoverished Mr Cavendish unwillingly *en route* to Australia with his wife and two daughters, Sara and Margaret, where they are to join Mrs Cavendish's brother, Tom Piper, who has prospered in Australia after beginning as a butcher; also on board to take up a colonial ministry is the Reverend Francis Lidiat, whose widowed mother had emigrated to Australia, become the second Mrs Piper, but died less than a year later in childbirth. In Melbourne awaiting with Piper the arrival of the Cavendish family are George, a son by Piper's first marriage; Laura, his stepdaughter, Lidiat's sister; and Louisa, his daughter by the second marriage. George is in love with Laura but Piper warns him that he will be disinherited if their marriage takes place. On arrival in Melbourne, Lidiat's connection with the Pipers is discovered and he becomes a regular visitor at Piper's Hill, where the Cavendishes take up residence. The novel records the relationship between the two families, including Laura's rivalry with Sara, her equal in beauty, and Cavendish's dislike of the Piper patronage. Long in love with the wilful Sara though beloved by the less good-looking Margaret, Lidiat proposes marriage just before leaving for his Barnesbury parish; Sara rejects this proposal but accepts a second one after Piper tells the profligate George that his debts will only be paid on condition that he gives up gambling and marries one of the Cavendish sisters. Sara rethinks her acceptance when subject to a third proposal, this time from Reginald Hyde, a visiting heir to a baronetcy, and suitable pairings are effected in the aftermath of a crisis at Barnesbury, where Louisa is gravely injured while on a visit to Lidiat and Laura. Margaret's devoted nursing of Louisa opens Lidiat's eyes to her virtues, and Laura and George are reconciled after Piper withdraws his objections as a consequence of Louisa's recovery. Only Sara, her engagement to Hyde now also behind her, remains unmarried at the end of the novel.

Uncle Piper of Piper's Hill won wide praise at the time of publication, and was compared with *His Natural Life* (1874) and *Robbery Under Arms* (1888). It was subsequently criticised for the novelistic resolution of its plot and for its lack of 'Australianness', although the desiccated Cavendish is more 'Tasma's' target than the opinionated and authoritarian Piper. It remains an important early urban novel which is enlivened by the strength of its characterisation, particularly the title character and his sister, and its wryly satirical observation of middle-class life.

Under Aldebaran (1946), the first volume of poetry published by James McAuley (q.v.), is a mixture of introspective and philosophical poems which represent, in Vincent Buckley's words, 'an affirmation of the values which give real life and real stability to society'. One of the chief poems in the volume is 'The Blue Horses', which is inscribed in honour of Franz Marc, one of the founders of the Blue Rider expressionist movement in Germany and creator of the famous painting *The Tower of the Blue Horses*; the poem seeks to find in art a panacea for the 'malice, fraud and guile' of the modern world 'gone bad' as well as an escape for the individual to 'spaces infinite'. 'The Incarnation of Sirius' is a warning that the forces of revolution bring not the desired changes but a 'bloody and aborted' vision, a world of bestiality and chaos; 'Henry the Navigator' praises men of foresight and courage who, like the Portuguese prince who 'saw no distant seas, yet guided ships', are vital to the realisation of mankind's full potential; and 'The Family of Love' reflects McAuley's own incertitude and inner turmoil. Other notable poems of the volume are the epithalamium 'Celebration of Love', and the trio 'Terra Australis', 'Envoi', and 'The True Discovery of Australia'; the last reflects both McAuley's frustration with Australian attitudes ('the faint sterility that disheartens and derides'), and his indissoluble link with the environment ('there you come home').

'Union Buries Its Dead, The', a widely anthologised story by Henry Lawson (q.v.), was written in 1893. The story, which chronicles the funeral procession and burial service for a young unionist who has drowned in the Darling River, has been cited as evidence of mateship (q.v.) among outback workers of the 1890s, but the flatness of the prose and the grim, ironic tone of the narrator establish 'The Union Buries Its Dead' as one of Lawson's most pessimistic, even nihilistic, pictures of bush life.

University of New South Wales Drama Foundation was established in 1965 in association with the Australian Elizabethan Theatre Trust (q.v.). The purpose of the Foundation was to promote the practice and study of the theatre arts in NSW, particularly through the drama organisations at the University, such as the National Institute of Dramatic Art (NIDA) and the Jane Street Theatre (qq.v.), and to administer funds for this purpose.

University Presses. There are two types of university presses in Australia. The first comprises the scholarly presses established by several Australian universities: Melbourne University Press (MUP, established 1922), University of Queensland Press (UQP, 1948), University of Western Australia Press (1954), New South Wales University Press (1961), Sydney University Press (1964, which was taken over by Oxford University Press in 1988), Australian National University Press (1966, which was taken over by Pergamon in the early 1980s) and Deakin University Press (1980). These presses form the membership of the Association of Australian University Presses (established 1965), which publishes annually *Scholarly Books in Australia*; some of them evolved from a publications unit within the university (e.g. the ANU Press from the university's publication section, established in 1964). Within all Australian universities there are departments or organisations which publish material independently of the university presses, e.g. the Department of English, University of Queensland, which has published *Australian Literary Studies* since 1979, the University of Tasmania Library, and the Centre for Research in New Literatures in English (CRNLE) at Flinders University.

The second type of university press comprises the Australian branch of an overseas university press. The main example of this type is the Australian branch of Oxford University Press (OUP). In 1890 E.R. Bartholomew established an Oxford presence in Australia with biennial selling trips as representative of OUP, Hodder & Stoughton and other firms; in 1908 an OUP office was opened in Melbourne, with Bartholomew as manager until 1922, when he was succeeded by his son, E.E. Bartholomew (1922–49). Although Australian books, e.g. F.M. Robb's edition of Adam Lindsay Gordon, were published by OUP in London as early as 1912, and from the 1930s OUP published and printed educational books in Australia, it was not until after the Second World War that the Australian branch changed its orientation from sales to publishing. Frank Eyre, managing editor of the Australian branch of OUP 1950–75, has recorded its history in *Oxford in Australia 1890–1978* (1978).

Although all university presses in Australia publish scholarly, educational and more general books in a range of disciplines, they have each developed particular strengths and traditions, e.g. UQP in contemporary fiction, poetry and criticism, MUP in biography and Australian history, the University of Western Australia Press in regional history, OUP in children's literature, lexicography, Australian history and Pacific studies. Roger McDonald (editor UQP, 1969–76), Frank Wilmot (manager MUP, 1932–42), Peter Ryan (director MUP, 1962–88) and Eyre are examples of university press employees of significance in Australian literary and publishing history. Important Australian literature series emanating from the university presses include UQP's Paperback Poets, Poets on Record, Australian Authors (formerly Portable Australian Authors), and Studies in Australian Literature; Sydney University Press's Australian Literary Reprints; and OUP's Australian Writers and Their Work, Australian Bibliographies and from 1992 a new Australian Writers series. The 70th anniversary of MUP in 1992 was marked by a History of Publishing in Australia seminar. In 1993 Laurie Muller, general manager of UQP, received the NBC medal to honour professional commitment and excellence in the book world.

Unknown Industrial Prisoner, The, a novel by David Ireland (q.v.), was published in 1971, and won the Miles Franklin Award. Reminiscent of the work of Gogol and Solzhenitsyn, it deals with the dehumanising life of a vast oil refinery owned by a multinational company called Puroil. A comprehensive representation of men caught up in a ruthless but inane system, compared to a termitary in its activity, the novel exposes the company's reliance on incompetence, avarice, self-seeking and subservience. By using a fragmented narrative structure and a multiplicity of individual perspectives, Ireland builds up an impression of a collective experience in which work and slavery are equated. Soubriquets for the characters such as the Enforcer, the Python, the Garfish and the Good Shepherd heighten the sense of confinement within work roles. The attitudes and experiences of three more fully developed characters structure the narrative. They include the violent and confused Glass Canoe, who futilely seeks to live within the system and win its rewards; the Great White Father, who offers the workers the reliefs of alcohol and sex in his haven in the mangroves called Home Beautiful; and the Samurai, a complex figure who pursues a pattern of dedication that he finds difficult to define and justify. Although disaffection with the system is widespread, the final explosions that rock Puroil are not the result of a planned rebellion, but a haphazard amalgam of individual resentments.

Unspoken Thoughts, a volume of poems by Ada Cambridge (q.v.), was published anonymously in London in 1887. A.G. Stephens appears to have been the originator of the myth that Cambridge withdrew the collection three days after publication, no doubt because some poems embarrassed her clergyman husband George Cross. Recent research has revealed that Cambridge withdrew the collection five years after publication, probably for professional and artistic reasons. Remarkably outspoken for their time, the poems in *Unspoken Thoughts* question faith, marriage and the social order. *The Hand in the Dark*, Cambridge's later collection, contains revised versions of many of the poems in *Unspoken Thoughts*. Patricia Barton has edited and introduced a recent edition of *Unspoken Thoughts* (1988).

UPFIELD, Arthur (1890–1964), born Gosport, England, arrived in Australia in 1910, largely through the insistence of his draper parents, who were convinced that he had no intention of settling to the conventional white-collar career they had planned for him. He was immediately attracted to the outback, following a variety of itinerant occupations including muleteam driver, boundary-rider, opal-digger, shearer, seasonal fruit-picker, and fencer. After four years in the AIF in the First World War, he resumed his nomadic outback life and began writing. His first novel,

The House of Cain, appeared in 1928. Between then and his death he published thirty-two novels; for the last twenty-five years of his life he was able to support himself and his family solely by his writing, largely because of the popularity of his books in the USA, where he was the first foreign writer admitted as a full member of the Mystery Writers' Guild of America. Many of his novels, such as *The House of Cain*, *The Barrakee Mystery* (1929), *The Sands of Windee* (1931) and *A Royal Abduction* (1932), belong to the 'thriller' category, but he includes more substantial themes in works such as *Gripped by Drought* (1932), which gives an account of the effects of a prolonged drought in western NSW; *The Widows of Broome* (1950), which deals with the death throes of the pearling industry in north-west Australia; *Death of a Lake* (1954), which is set against the effect on the environment of a lake drying up in north-western NSW; and *The Will of the Tribe* (1962), which examines contemporary racial attitudes. The background to his novels – bush lore, Aboriginal customs, the landscape, outback camaraderie – has been acclaimed more than his slow-moving plots and unexceptional prose style. Upfield's chief literary creation, and a major reason for the success of his books, is the part-Aboriginal detective-inspector Napoleon Bonaparte, usually referred to as 'Bony', who first emerges in *The Barrakee Mystery* and is featured in most of the later novels. Bony combines the mystic intuitiveness of his Aboriginal mother with the sophisticated intelligence of his White father. Bony, based according to Jessica Hawke's *Follow My Dust!* (1957) on a well-educated part-Aboriginal Queensland tracker, Leon Wood, has been an extremely popular creation, for some readers rivalling Sherlock Holmes.

UREN, Malcolm (1900–73), born Adelaide, moved to Perth as a boy. He worked for some years on the literary staff of the *West Australian*, served as a war correspondent during the Second World War, and was a newspaper executive with the *West Australian* group 1953–65. He also edited the *Western Mail* (1941–53), the *Broadcaster* (1942–52) and *Milady* (1948–52). He wrote numerous local histories as well as an original account of the *Batavia* wreck, *Sailormen's Ghosts* (1940); with Robert Stephens, a biography of Edward John Eyre, *Waterless Horizons* (1941); an account of Governor James Stirling, *Land Looking West* (1948); and a history of the WA goldfields, *Glint of Gold* (1948).

USHER, Rod (Roderick Macleod) (1946–), born in the USA, has lived for extended periods in Britain and Spain. A journalist for twenty-five years, he is a former literary editor of the *Age* and has also worked for the London *Sunday Times* as chief sub-editor and *Time* magazine as deputy editor of the South Pacific edition. He has written two non-fiction books and two novels, *A Man of Marbles* (1989) and *Florid States* (1990) and has published two collections of poetry, *Above Water* (1985) and *Smiling Treason* (1992). Wide-ranging in subject and style, his poetry includes ballads, love poems and humorous reflections on aspects of natural and man-made worlds. *A Man of Marbles* centres on a Melbourne greengrocer of Greek origin, Stavro ('Stan') Kristopolis, whose natural innocence makes him a misfit in an environment that is normally corrupt. A holy fool, he is bound to fail in the world's terms as he succeeds in his own. As a result of his innate kindness he is accused of murder and undergoes a prison sentence, none of which detracts from his natural serenity: 'It was a serenity that many of the warders . . . noted, and Stan remained this way through the contruction of the jigsaw that would eventually depict the balanced shining scales of justice. He got annoyed, at times, flattened, suffered loneliness and fear, but his reserves were never plumbed.' A novel of subtle nuances, *A Man of Marbles* achieves the difficult feat of celebrating passivity. *Florid States*, set in the isolated Overton valley, is partly a convincing study of the experience of schizophrenia, both from the sufferer's point of view and from that of one who comes to love him. Ned Quinn, a teacher of English, who is subject to intermittent attacks of the illness, becomes romantically attached to Jennifer Duncan, a lonely widow and member of a Queensland counter-culture group, which has settled near the Condamine. Although Ned and Jennifer experience a period of idyllic happiness, bigotry and ignorance eventually conspire to separate them.

UTEMORRAH, Daisy (1922–94), see *The Oxford Companion to Australian Children's Literature* (1993), p. 429.

V

'Vagabond, The', see **JAMES, John Stanley**

VALLIS, Val (1916–), born Gladstone, Queensland, was educated at the University of Queensland (MA) and London University (Ph.D.) and served with the AIF 1941–46, spending some time in New Guinea. He taught at the University of Queensland, becoming reader in English, and has been involved in opera, both as critic for the *Australian* and as a lecturer at the Queensland Conservatorium of Music. His poetry has appeared in the collections *Songs of the East Coast* (1947) and *Dark Wind Blowing* (1961). He also edited, with R.S. Byrnes, *The Queensland Centenary Anthology* (1959), and, with Judith Wright, *Witnesses of Spring* (1970) by Shaw Neilson. Vallis delivered the 1988 Colin Roderick lectures for the Foundation for Australian Literary Studies, *Heart Reasons, These*, on poets Neilson, R.D. FitzGerald, Elizabeth Riddell, Ray Mathew and Eve Langley.

Van Diemen's Land was the name originally given to Tasmania in 1642 by its discoverer, Abel Tasman, in honour of the governor-general of the Dutch East Indies, Anthony Van Diemen. Although the name Tasmania was in use for the colony by the 1840s, it was not until 26 November 1855 that the new designation was officially proclaimed, principally because of the association between 'Van Diemen's Land' and convictism. 'Van Diemen's Land', used in numerous early geographical, historical, descriptive and autobiographical works, e.g. G.W. Evans, *A Geographical, Historical, and Topographical Description of Van Diemen's Land* (1822), was the title of 'W.T. Moncrieff's' 1830 London play, and of a well-known Irish street ballad, also regarded as an Australian folk-song (q.v.), in which a poacher laments the rigours of his life as a convict in Van Diemen's Land. The term is also the source of the word 'Vandemonian', which was applied to Tasmanians for much of the nineteenth century, and was particularly used in reference to ex-convicts from the island.

Van Diemen's Land, one of the earliest plays about Australia, was written by 'William Thomas Moncrieff' (q.v.) and first performed in London in 1830 to celebrate the arrival in Australia of William Gore Elliston and his brother. A four-act extravaganza, the play focuses on the experiences of the new settler John Hardy, and the romantic entanglements of his children, John, who meets again his sweetheart Eliza, wrongly transported for stealing from the family home, and Amelia, who marries the 'new chum' settler James Gooseberry. Eliza's innocence is established during the climax to the play, when Hardy is attacked by bushrangers and assisted by friendly Aborigines. In writing *Van Diemen's Land*, 'Moncrieff' exploited the reputations of Bennelong, Michael Howe, James Hardy Vaux and Ikey Solomon, who all appear as characters, often in situations which bear no resemblance to historical experience. Among other points of interest are the songs, e.g. 'The Lincolnshire Poacher', 'The Ram of Derby', which make up one of the play's several elements, and the favourable pictures presented of the Aborigines, e.g. in the marriage between Bennilong's sister Kangaree, and Gooseberry's servant Darby Ballylaggin.

Van Diemen's Land Gazette and General Advertiser, one of the first Australian newspapers, was published in Hobart Town in 1814. Andrew Bent assisted George Clark in the production of the newspaper.

Van Diemen's Land Warriors: Or, the Heroes of Cornwall, The, the first book of Tasmanian verse, was published in 1827. A satire on the ineffectual attempts to capture the bushranger Matthew Brady, it narrates the misadventures of a group of citizens who, contemptuous of the failure of Governor Arthur and his soldiers to capture Brady, decide to do the job themselves. In the first of the poem's three cantos, each of ten tradesmen displays his bravado in punning couplets applicable to his trade. In the second, the Tailor is elected leader and the party sets out, but has to retrace its steps when it is discovered that the gunpowder has been forgotten; when they start again and stumble across what they think to be the gang, they flee in fright. In the final canto, Snip explains that he has run away to cover the gang's retreat; they return and discharge their firearms, only to discover that the 'gang' is a herd of donkeys. The noise awakens two soldiers, who arrest Snip and his associates on suspicion that they are the bushrangers; released by a magistrate, they eventually meet Brady, who has them all flogged, relieves them of their trousers and forces them to return in shame to their homes. *The Van Diemen's Land Warriors* is a rare work, possibly because it was suppressed. Its author, 'Pindar Juvenal', has been tentatively identified as Robert Wales, an officer of the Tasmanian courts.

Vashti's Voice, see **Feminism and Australian Literature**

VAUX, James Hardy (1782–?), born Surrey, England, was transported for theft and in 1801 arrived in Sydney, where he worked as a clerk. Despite a term of trouble following his forgery of Governor King's initials, he ingratiated himself with the chaplain and magistrate Samuel Marsden and with King, who took him back to England in 1807. Vaux, however, became insubordinate after his sentence expired and deserted once the ship reached Portsmouth. Convicted again of theft in 1809, he was again transported and reached Sydney in 1810. In 1811 he was sentenced to twelve months' hard labour for receiving property stolen from the judge-advocate, Ellis Bent, and sent to the Newcastle penal settlement. In January 1814 he attempted to escape from the Colony, but was recaptured and returned to Newcastle. At Newcastle he wrote a slang dictionary included in his autobiography, *Memoirs of James Hardy Vaux*. The manuscript came into the hands of Barron Field, who arranged for its publication in 1819. Vaux's life continued to be as colourful as his *Memoirs*; he received a conditional pardon in 1820, the terms of which he broke in 1829, when he absconded from his employment. He went to Ireland, where he was convicted in August 1830 under the alias 'James Young' for passing forged bank notes. Transported again to Sydney, he arrived in May 1831, was recognised and sent to Port Macquarie penal settlement. In 1837 he was allowed to return to Sydney and although he was soon in further trouble and was sentenced to two years' imprisonment, he was released in 1841 and disappeared thereafter from public notice. During his career Vaux also married three times, probably bigamously. His *Memoirs*, the first full-length autobiography written in Australia, presents a fascinating, graphic picture of London's underworld; his flash vocabulary, the first dictionary compiled in Australia and a valuable glossary of London slang, has been frequently used by subsequent lexicographers of Australian English (q.v.). Vaux's life has also been the subject of drama: he appears in 'William Thomas Moncrieff's' (q.v.) play *Van Diemen's Land* (1830) and is the subject of Ron Blair's ballad opera *Flash Jim Vaux* (first produced in 1971 and published in 1990).

VENNARD, Alexander Vindex ('Bill Bowyang', 'Frank Reid') (1884–1947), born Winton, Queensland, worked as a journalist in Brisbane, becoming editor of the *Port Denison Times*. He later moved to Sydney where he wrote for the *Sydney Morning Herald*, Sydney *Sun*, *Bulletin* and the London *Daily Mail*. In 1915 as 'Frank Reid' he enlisted in the AIF and served at Gallipoli and in Egypt. With David Barker and Charles Barrett he produced *Kia Ora Coo-ee*, a monthly magazine for Australian and NZ troops which achieved a large circulation. Back in Australia, he moved to the north, adopted the pseudonym 'Bill Bowyang', and contributed a regular column, 'On the Track', to the *North Queensland Register*. As 'Bill Bowyang' he published a series of booklets of bush ballads and recitations 1932–40 with such titles as *Australian Bush Recitations*, *Bill Bowyang's Bush Recitations* and *Old Bush Recitations Collected by Bill Bowyang*. Part Six in the *Bush Recitations* series was republished by Hugh Anderson in 1992. As 'Frank Reid' he also wrote *The Fighting Cameliers* (1934) and *Toilers of the Reef* (1925), a book for children.

Venture: An Australian Literary Quarterly, edited by Rex Ingamells (q.v.), appeared for one issue only (July 1937) and was superseded by *Venture: Jindyworobak Quarterly Pamphlet* (1939–40). Ingamells's 1937 editorial, titled 'Concerning Environmental Values', was published in 1938 as part of his book *Conditional Culture*. *Venture* included poetry, short stories and articles from such contributors as Leonard Mann, Max Harris, Victor Kennedy, Flexmore Hudson and Garry Lyle.

Verandah, a small literary magazine produced annually by the Toorak Association of Students, Victoria College, began in 1986 with the aim of giving a voice to new and innovative writers and artists.

VERNON, Barbara (1916–78) spent her early life at Inverell in northern NSW, apart from a period of service in the WAAAF during the Second World War. In 1959 she moved to Sydney, where she worked for several years as a freelance writer and then joined the ABC drama department, first in radio and then as a television script editor. A prolific author, she wrote radio and television plays, features, revue sketches, stage plays and children's plays. One of her stage plays, *The Multi-Coloured Umbrella*, published in *Theatregoer* (1961), won second prize in the Sydney Journalists' Club competition of 1956 and was subsequently widely produced. Her other published plays are *The Passionate Pianist* (1958), which forms part of a trilogy, *The Growing Year*, and includes 'The Bishop and the Boxer' and 'First Love'; and *King Tide Running*, written with Bruce Beaver and included in *Australian One-Act Plays: Book Three* (1967, ed. Musgrave Horner). Her other plays include 'Enough to Make a Pair of Sailor's Trousers', 'The Questing Heart', 'Naked Possum', 'Dusty Frangipanni' or 'No Picnic Tomorrow', 'Lancelot and the Lady', 'The Loquat Tree' and 'Silver Bells and Cockle Shells', and the children's plays 'The Sleeping Planet', 'Theseus and the Minotaur', 'Hullaballo Belay!' and, with Bec Robinson, 'Swords to the Rescue'. In 1967 Vernon originated and planned the popular television serial of the 1960s and 1970s, *Bellbird*, and subsequently published the novels *Bellbird: The Story of a Country Town* (1970), which is based on the first twenty episodes, and *A Big Day at Bellbird* (1972), part of which was used as the script for the film *Country Town* (1971). She also contributed to another popular television serial of the 1970s, *Certain Women*.

Verse, a bi-monthly poetry magazine published in Melbourne and edited by Louis Lavater (q.v.), succeeded the *Spinner* (q.v.) and appeared 1929–33. Although *Verse* generally published poetry that was conventional and nondescript, the magazine also attracted such contributors as 'Furnley Maurice', Frederick Macartney, Mary Gilmore, Paul Hasluck, R.H. Croll and Hal Porter.

Verses Popular and Humorous, Henry Lawson's (q.v.) second book of verse, was published in 1900, just before his departure for London. The volume included early work such as 'The Captain of the Push', and 'The Grog-an'-Grumble Steeplechase', a parody of A.B. Paterson, but most of the poems, e.g. 'The Lights of Cobb and Co.', 'The New Chum Jackaroo', 'The Uncultured Rhymer to His Cultured Critics' and 'Reedy River', had been written after the publication of Lawson's *In the Days When the World Was Wide* (1896). *Verses Popular and Humorous* was reissued several times in two parts, *Popular Verses* and *Humorous Verses*, although in the volumes published under those two titles in 1924 the selection and arrangements are significantly different.

VICKERS, Bert (1903–85), born Oldbury, England, left school at 12, came to Australia in 1925 and worked in a variety of jobs, cook's rouseabout, shearer's cook, wool-classer and general hand, in the WA wheat-belt. After an accident while he was in the army he occupied his time in hospital by taking a course in journalism conducted by Alan Marshall for the Army Education Service. Encouraged to write fiction by Marshall, Vickers had almost immediate success, a manuscript novel, *First Place to the Stranger*, winning a *Sydney Morning Herald* award in 1946. In spite of its success, the unpretentious but authentic account of the experiences of a young urban immigrant in the Australian bush (based on his own and his parents' experiences) was not published until 1956. Vickers's best novel, *The Mirage* (1955), based on the life and prospects of part-Aborigines, is both convincing social documentary and effective fiction. His other works include *Though Poppies Grow* (1958), an account of the erosion by corruption, privilege and a growing class-consciousness, of the traditional Australian values of mateship and a 'fair go', especially as seen in the vilification of those who supported the Peace Movement in the 1950s; *No Man Is Himself* (1970), a story of the human problems associated with life in the isolated outback as well as a further indictment of White treatment of the Aborigines whose demands for land rights he ardently supported; and *Without Map or Compass* (1974) and *A Stranger No Longer* (1977), two largely autobiographical works. *Without Map or Compass* shared the 1975 NBC award. Vickers also wrote plays and talks for radio. In 1971 he was made a life member of the FAW in WA, having been that branch's president 1965–66.

Victoria, the smallest (just over 227 000 square kilometres) mainland Australian State but second only to NSW in population, comprises the south-eastern corner of the Australian continent and is bordered by NSW in the north and South Australia in the west. Originally part of NSW, it was known as the Port Phillip District (q.v.) until its separation in 1851 from NSW, with which it shares the Murray River as a border. It remained the British colony of Victoria until its incorporation in the Commonwealth of Australia in 1901. Victoria was briefly settled in 1803–4 by a party under David Collins (q.v.), and in 1826–28 the explorers Hamilton Hume and William Hovell reached Port Phillip Bay, on which the present capital, Melbourne, stands. Permanent settlement began in the middle 1830s, when John Batman and John Pascoe Fawkner (qq.v.) independently established themselves at Port Phillip, and the Hentys (q.v.) also crossed from Van Diemen's Land to settle further west at Portland Bay. After Sir Thomas Mitchell (q.v.) reached Portland Bay overland from NSW in 1836, the 'Australia Felix' part of Victoria was quickly settled by squatters, who included the novelist 'Rolf Boldrewood'. Victoria made rapid progress after the discovery of gold, and for a period in the 1880s, the heyday of 'Marvellous Melbourne' (q.v.), was the most populous Australian colony. The progress of Victoria in the decades following the discovery of gold is an important theme in Henry Handel Richardson's trilogy *The Fortunes of Richard Mahony* (1930). A three-volume social history, *The Victorians*, was published in 1984 to celebrate the 150th anniversary of European settlement in Victoria. The volumes were written by Richard Broome, Tony Dingle and Susan Priestley. A similar 1984 celebratory volume was Don Garden's *Victoria: A History*.

Victorian: A Weekly Journal of Politics, Literature, Irish and Catholic Intelligence, Colonial, Foreign and General Information, published in Melbourne 1862–64, was edited by Daniel Deniehy and included poetry and prose, book reviews and theatrical notices. Contributors included Charles Harpur and R.H. Horne.

Victorian Review, a monthly magazine published in Melbourne 1879–86, was edited by H. Mortimer Franklyn. The magazine, which included literary articles, verse and fiction as well as discussions of current affairs, attracted a wide range of notable contributors, including Marcus Clarke, Catherine Helen Spence, E.E. Morris, G.B. Barton, Jessie Couvreur, Victor Daley, David Blair, Francis Adams, Edmund Finn and 'Mark Twain'. An earlier *Victorian Review* was published weekly 1860–61, and included R.H. Horne, James Smith and Charles Whitehead as contributors.

VIDAL, Mary Theresa (1815–73), born Devon, England, came to Australia with her husband in 1840 but returned to England in 1845. Her popular book *Tales for the Bush*, first published in Sydney in 1845, has little to do with Australia. It is a series of brief, morally edifying stories intended to instil a proper sense of Christian duty into servants and other members of the lower social classes. She also wrote *Cabramatta, and Woodleigh Farm* (1850), only the first part of which, the story 'The Cabramatta Store', is concerned with Australia. It is set in the Nepean district of NSW and deals mainly with the minutiae of domestic life of the day, although it features some of the stock ingredients of pioneer life such as bushrangers, droughts, floods and bushfires. Her only other Australian-centred work, the novel *Bengala: Or, Some Time Ago* (1860), is set in a fictitious township, probably Penrith, NSW, where her husband ministered. *Bengala* uses the domestic and community concerns of a small colonial rural society to frame a melodramatic and romantic tale. One of the earliest women fiction-writers in Australia, Mary Theresa Vidal is linked by her grandmother to the famous English portrait artist Joshua Reynolds. Her granddaughter was the novelist Faith Compton Mackenzie, in whose autobiography, *As Much As I Dare* (1935), Vidal briefly figures. *Bengala* was republished in 1990 in UNSW Colonial Texts series, edited by Susan McKernan, now Lever.

VIDLER, E.A. (Edward Alexander) (1863–1942), born London, where he worked in publishing, arrived in Melbourne in 1888. He edited the *Evening News* in Geelong and the *Tatler* and the *Spinner* in Melbourne. In 1908 he became head of George Robertson's publishing department, and began his own publishing venture in 1918 when the department closed. He also wrote several art monographs and books for children and edited *The Adam Lindsay Gordon Memorial Volume* (1926), *Art and Letters: Hassell's Australian Miscellany 1921–22* (1922) and, as 'Paul Vedder', the *Dramatic Year* (1886–87). An enthusiast of Australian drama, he wrote two plays, a verse drama, *The Rose of Ravenna* (1913) and *Pan Calls* (1926) in the series *Australian Repertory Plays*, which he published 1925–28. Vidler was instrumental in the foundation of the Australian Institute of Arts and Literature in 1921 and received a CLF pension in 1939 in recognition of his services to Australian art and literature.

View, see *Vista*

Viewpoint, see **Australian Writers Guild**

VIIDIKAS, Vicki (1948–   ), born Sydney of an Australian mother and Estonian father, left school at 15 and worked in various occasional jobs. At 16 she began writing poetry for reasons she termed 'therapeutic' and 'confessional', and had her first poem, 'At East Balmain', published when she was 19. She has published three books of verse, *Condition Red* (1973), *Knäbel* (1978) and *India Ink* (prose poems, 1984), and a volume of short prose, *Wrappings* (1974). As a result of several prolonged visits to India and the East she became interested in Indian life and the Hindu religion, an interest that is reflected in her poetry. *Indian Ink* captures more successfully perhaps than any Australian writer before her the spirit and ambience of the Asian subcontinent. Viidikas's aim in both poetry and prose has been to write about the realities, as she sees them, of such subcultures as those centred on drugs, crime, alternative sexualities, or general non-conformist attitudes. Such subcultures are illustrated in *Wrappings*, a volume of thirty-one prose pieces. The poems of *Condition Red* and *Knäbel* are written mainly from experiences of love and sexuality. In her search for authenticity Viidikas has insisted that the spontaneity and immediacy of emotion, however chaotic and disturbed, should be reflected in the poetic form.

VILLIERS, Alan (1903–82), a well-known sailor and author of more than thirty books on maritime history and affairs, was born in Melbourne. His father, Leon Joseph Villiers, was a union organiser and writer, whose poems were published in the *Bulletin*. On the staff of the Hobart *Mercury* 1924–29, Villiers combined sailing voyages of all descriptions and journalism until the Second World War, when he served in the Royal Navy; from the 1930s he was mainly resident in England. Villiers's best-known maritime adventures include his voyages in the Danish schoolship *Joseph Conrad* (1934–36), the barque *Parma* (1931) and the *Mayflower* replica (1956). He also commanded square-rigged ships for such films as *Moby Dick* (1955), *Billy Budd* (1961) and *Hawaii* (1965). Villiers published several narratives of personal voyages, such as *Falmouth for Orders* (1928), *By Way of Cape Horn* (1930), *Voyage of the 'Parma'* (1933), *Sons of Sinbad* (1940), *Cruise of the Conrad* (1937) and *The New Mayflower* (1958); general autobiographical accounts, such as *The Set of the Sails* (1949) and *Give Me a Ship to Sail* (1958); maritime histories, such as *Vanished Fleets* (1931), *The Cutty Sark* (1953) and *Captain Cook* (1967); and several books for children, of which the best known is *Whalers of the Midnight Sun* (1934).

Vinegar Hill, which took its name from the Vinegar Hill in Ireland where the United Irishmen suffered defeat in 1798, was the site of the first rebellion in Australia. In March 1804 a rising of 200 Irish convicts from the government farm at Castle Hill was quashed at Vinegar Hill, near the Parramatta–Windsor road 43 kilometres from Sydney; the leader of the government forces was George Johnston, himself later a rebel in the deposing of Governor Bligh. The uprising in Thomas Keneally's *Bring Larks and Heroes* (1967) is loosely based on the Vinegar Hill episode, which is re-created in Colin Free's novel *Vinegar Hill* (1978) and Richard Butler's *Against the Wind* (1978), a novelisation of the television series; R.D. FitzGerald's poem 'The Wind at Your Door' mentions the Castle Hill rebels, although the flogging of convicts in the poem, witnessed by Joseph Holt (who was detained after Vinegar Hill), took place earlier. Vinegar Hill was renamed Rouse Hill by Governor Macquarie; the Sydney suburb Bellevue Hill was also known as Vinegar Hill for some years after 1804. Lynette Ramsay Silver has written a history of the Vinegar Hill uprising, *The Battle of Vinegar Hill* (1989).

Vision (1923–24), a periodical edited by Jack Lindsay, Kenneth Slessor and Frank C. Johnson (qq.v.), was published in Sydney. It lasted only four issues but was of major importance. Jack Lindsay was the main force behind the magazine's production, but its inspiration derived chiefly from Norman Lindsay, who also provided the title and contributed illustrations and essays. The editors, who looked forward to a 'Renaissance' of 'creative passion' beginning in Australia, opposed both European modernism and the nationalist strain in Australian writing. Looking back to the Greeks and such European writers as Shakespeare, Byron, Burns, Villon, Browning, Rabelais and Nietzsche, they espoused a romantic, vitalist credo. The same ideas were continued in two other periodicals, the *London Aphrodite* (1928–29) and the *Australian Outline* (1933–34). Contributors to *Vision* included Kenneth Slessor, Jack Lindsay, Hugh McCrae, Adrian Lawlor, Dorothea Mackellar, R.D. FitzGerald, Dulcie Deamer, Louis Lavater, Philip Lindsay and Blamire Young. An important dispute between Jack Lindsay, Kenneth Slessor and Norman Lindsay on the circumstances of the magazine's publication and its influence later took place in *Southerly* (1952 and 1953).

Vision: A Magazine of the Arts, Science and Australiana (1963–72), published by the Adelphi Students' Library, Sydney, and edited by Bruce Skurray and others, superseded *Friends of the Glenaeon Library* (1961–63). Numerous poets contributed verse to the magazine including Joan Mas, Imogen Whyse, A.D. Hope, Martin Haley, 'Mary Lisle' and Flexmore Hudson.

Vision of Ceremony, A (1956), James McAuley's (q.v.) second collection of poetry, published after his conversion to Roman Catholicism, reflects his personal certainty and joy in his new faith and confidence that its 'vision of ceremony', ritual, order and beauty, can transfigure the material world. The central poem of the volume, 'Celebration of Divine Love' (one of the 'Black Swan' lyrics), affirms that creation, 'grown timeless and distraught', can be renewed by the love of God in whom 'are all things in perfection found'. Other 'Black Swan' lyrics include 'Invocation', 'To the Holy Spirit', 'To a Dead Bird of Paradise' and 'Canticle'. 'New Guinea', subtitled 'In Memory of Archbishop Alain de Boismenu, M.S.C.', expresses both the impact of New Guinea upon McAuley and his wonder at the noble faith of de Boismenu, a faith that makes 'life become authentic'. The mythological tales of the Prometheus legend, 'The Hero and the Hydra', 'A Leaf of Sage', a brief and highly effective rendering of a tale from the *Decameron*, and the long and discursive 'Letter to John Dryden', add variety to the volume which won the Grace Leven Prize for poetry in 1956.

'Vision of Melancholy, A Fragment, The', by 'C.S.', the first poem published in Australia, appeared in the *Sydney Gazette* 4 March 1804.

Vista (April 1946, December 1946 and a third, undated issue), the magazine of the Brisbane Catholic Readers' and Writers' Society, was edited by Martin Haley, Paul Grano and J.P. McGoldrick. Titled *View* in its first issue, the magazine included literary articles and reviews and verse; contributors included 'Brian Vrepont', James Devaney, James Picot, Peter Miles and Mary Finnin.

Vivisector, The, a novel by Patrick White (q.v.), was published in 1970. The life of an eminent artist, Hurtle Duffield, from his childhood at the turn of the century to his death in the late 1960s is the novel's subject.

Born into a large working-class family in Sydney, the son of a rag-and-bone man and a washerwoman, Hurtle is conscious at an early age of his apartness from them. He begins to spell his way through the Bible, draws on the walls and in the dust of the yard. On several occasions he is taken by his mother to her wealthy employers, the Courtneys, and becomes entranced by the splendours of their luxurious mansion, Sunningdale. He also attracts the attention of Sunningdale's mistress, the exquisite Alfreda Courtney who, with the approval of her husband Harry, buys Hurtle from his parents for £500. The purchase satisfies Alfreda's pride in her ability to recognise genius, and Harry's longing for a manly son in compensation for his having only a hunch-backed daughter, Rhoda. As Hurtle's relationships with both Alfreda and Rhoda grow in intensity, other significant experiences shape his life: a visit to Harry's property at Mumbelong, the suicide of his tutor, Mr Shewcroft, which he reproduces on the walls of his bedroom, and a tour of Europe during which he fleetingly sees Rhoda naked at the washstand. Eventually oppressed by Alfreda's near-incestuous love, Hurtle escapes to the First World War. In the succeeding years he casts off his Courtney identity and associations and remains for a time in France washing dishes and studying art before returning to Sydney. A prostitute, Nance Lightfoot, falls passionately in love with him but commits suicide when she perceives the truth – that he is fated to use relationships for his art as dispassionately as a vivisectionist uses animals.

The next stage of Hurtle's life opens when his reputation is established and he is settled in a decaying old mansion in Flint Street, Sydney, his home for the rest of his life. Important relationships in his middle years include those with his mistress, Hero Pavloussi, the wife of a Greek shipping magnate, and with the socialite Olivia Davenport. Olivia has figured earlier in his life as his mysterious patron, Mrs Lopez, and earlier still as Rhoda's upper-class friend Boo Hollingrake, the identity to which she finally reverts. After accompanying the intensely egoistic Hero to Greece in an abortive attempt on her part to achieve redemption, Hurtle returns to Flint Street and his life of wrestling with ultimate reality through art. Of the varied range of others who fugitively but significantly touch his experience, the most important are Maurice Caldicott, his agent who also loves him; Cec Cutbush, a grocer; Mothersole, a widower; Mrs Valkov, the mother of his last mistress; Shuard, the music critic; and Don Lethbridge, his servitor after his first stroke. Towards the end of his life, Hurtle rediscovers Rhoda, now an impecunious old woman given to caring for the local cats, and provides her with the bottom floor of his house. His last, most serious sexual relationship is with a young pianist, Kathy Volkov, his artistic and vivisectionist equal. His final years are marked by the contrast between his eminent but bland public identity and the sordid actualities of his private struggle to express the truth of his experience. Crippled by a stroke, he fights back in a last effort to find the liberating vision of God that has obsessed him, but dies from a second attack.

Voice: The Australian Independent Monthly, published Sydney 1951–56 and titled *A.I.M.* in its first issue, was edited by Harold B. Levien. Supported by the Australian Labor Party, the WEA and socialist groups, *Voice* was mainly concerned with current affairs but also carried reviews and articles on Australian literature. Contributors included Russel Ward, Alan Marshall, Max Harris, John K. Ewers, A.D. Hope and T. Inglis Moore.

Voice from Tasmania, A, a verse satire written by Edward Kemp (q.v.), was published in 1846. The major target of the poem is the governor of Van Diemen's Land, John Eardley-Wilmot, although there are attacks on Kemp's fellow littérateurs, including David Burn, Nathaniel Lipscomb Kentish and R.L. Murray. *A Voice from Tasmania* has some historical interest as the first book by an Australian-born author to be published in Tasmania; the racing description included in the poem is an early specimen of the genre, preceding the better-known work of Adam Lindsay Gordon by almost two decades.

Voices, the quarterly journal of the National Library of Australia, began in 1991, edited by Paul Hetherington (q.v.). It presents information relating to the collections and services of NLA and publishes material based on research by the library's Harold White fellows (e.g. Dennis Haskell on Kenneth Slessor's poetry) as well as poetry, short fiction and book reviews. Its poetry, fiction and reviews editors are appointed annually and have included Peter Rose, Elizabeth Jolley, Nick Jose and Jan Owen. NLA also sponsors the Australian Voices Essay series published in *Australian Book Review*.

VON BRANDENSTEIN, C.G., see **Aboriginal Song and Narrative in Translation**

VON GUÉRARD, Eugene (1811–1901), born Vienna, Austria, came to Australia in 1852, participated in the gold rushes and later, as artist, accompanied expeditions by the explorers A.W. Howitt and G.B. von Neumayer. He became curator of the National Gallery of Victoria and head of its art school before returning to Europe in 1882. He published an album of lithographs, *Australian Landscapes* (1867). Marjorie Tipping edited his diary, *An Artist on the Goldfields* (1982, an expanded edition in 1992), a collection of succinct and perceptive comments accompanied by drawings of the events described. *Eugene von Guérard* (1982), by Candice Bruce, Edward Comstock and Frank McDonald, contains fifty colour plates, von Guérard's journal, a biography and a survey of his works, techniques and exhibitions.

VOSPER, F.C.B. (Frederick Charles Burleigh) (1869–1901), born Cornwall, England, emigrated at 15 to Bolivia, where he took part in two sporadic revolutions. He arrived in Queensland in 1886 and worked as timber-miller, drover, boundary-rider and miner, before working for newspapers at Eidsvold, Maryborough, Bundaberg and Charters Towers. During the 1891 shearers' strike he was tried for sedition on the grounds of an inflammatory editorial, but was ultimately acquitted. A year later, however, his involvement in a mining strike resulted in his receiving a sentence of three months' imprisonment. By 1893 he was alienated from a large segment of the Queensland labour movement and moved to WA. He edited the Murchison *Miner*, the *Miner's Right* and, from 1894 until 1897, when he was elected to the Legislative Assembly, the *Coolgardie Miner*. He also subsequently established and edited the Perth *Sunday Times*. Probably the most brilliant and persuasive orator on the WA goldfields, he became a powerful force in arousing opposition to the government on a wide range of issues. A member of the Australian Institute of Mining Engineers, he was one of the founders of the Geological Society of Australasia and author of *The Prospector's Companion* (1894), which was widely used on the WA goldfields in the 1890s. Few of his political pamphlets, such as his influential *A Social Armistice*, have survived.

Voss, a novel by Patrick White (q.v.), was published in 1957 and won the Miles Franklin and the W.H. Smith awards. The narrative opens in colonial Sydney of 1845, where the German explorer Voss, whose experience has affinities with that of Ludwig Leichhardt (q.v.), is preparing to cross the continent from one end to the other. For Voss the desert exists purely as a worthy challenge for his will, a place where he can rival the Almighty and wrest superhumanity for himself. At the house of one of his patrons, Mr Bonner, a wealthy merchant, Voss meets Laura Trevelyan, Bonner's niece, an intelligent, sensitive girl though outwardly a rather stiff bluestocking. Laura and Voss have only four meetings before he departs, but their relationship develops a fierce intensity. Perceiving the truth about his expedition, she challenges him in a 'wrestling' of minds and although the contest does nothing to alter his purpose Voss is already strongly influenced by her transforming power. Of the other members of his expedition, Palfreyman, an ornithologist, Harry Robarts, a simple, physically powerful boy, Frank Le Mesurier, a young, inwardly anguished poet, and Turner, a soured, cunning individual, only Palfreyman, a man of profound Christian humility, offers Voss any moral challenge at this point. After a sea trip to Newcastle the group stays at the beautiful property, Rhine Towers, belonging to the cultivated Mr Sanderson. Two new members join the expedition: a wealthy young pastoralist, Ralph Angus, and an emancipated convict, Judd. At Rhine Towers, Voss's Nietzschean will to power is slightly undermined by several softening experiences, not least his memory of Laura, and he decides to ask Mr Bonner for her hand. Before setting out into the harshest country the group stays at a squalid outpost, Jildra, where they acquire two inscrutable Aborigines, Dugald and Jackie. Side by side with the vicissitudes of Voss and his group in the wilderness, White develops Voss's intense relationship and eventual 'marriage' with Laura, conducted both by letter and by telepathy, and the events of life at the Bonners' in Sydney. When Rose Portion, the Bonners' maid, is found to be pregnant, Laura participates so intensely in her experience that the birth of the child Mercy, from which Rose dies, is also hers. Meanwhile in the desert misfortunes proliferate: Voss is injured, cattle are lost or stolen, food runs short, Turner and Le Mesurier become ill, and the party is constantly dogged by watchful Aborigines. Palfreyman, speared by the Blacks, dies in a Christ-like way, and Judd, Angus and Turner turn back. The severe sufferings of Voss's last days, Le Mesurier's suicide, Harry Robart's death and Voss's decapitation at the hands of Jackie, are also shared by Laura as she is consumed by a fever in Sydney. The final section of the novel is in two phases; the first, taking place two years later when Laura has become a mistress at an academy for young ladies, describes retrospectively the deaths of Angus, Turner and Jackie and the failure of a further expedition under Colonel Hebden to establish Voss's fate. The second phase, taking place several years later, narrates the contrasting fates of Laura, now headmistress of the academy and mother of Mercy, and her cousin Belle Radclyffe, mother of a large family, and the contrasting interpretations of Voss. Destined to figure in history books, regarded as a saint by the now confused Judd, and as a 'poor, twisted fellow' by Sanderson, he was, as Laura comments, a man like other men, composed of good and evil. *Voss* has been produced as an opera with libretto by David Malouf (q.v.) and music by Richard Meale.

VOWLES, George (1844–1928), born Ipswich, became a schoolteacher in NSW and Queensland and published *Sunbeams in Queensland* (1870), the first book of verse by a Queenslander. H.A. Kellow's *Queensland Poets* (1930) devotes a chapter to Vowles, but his disharmonious, anglicised imitations of Romantic models have been neglected by other critics.

Voyager. The voyager theme in Australian poetry is recognised and illustrated in Douglas Stewart's anthology *Voyager Poems* (1968). The theme embraces all adventurers and discoverers down the centuries, but it concentrates on particular voyagers such as William Dampier, James Cook and Abel Tasman, who discovered the Australian continent, or others like George Bass, Matthew Flinders, Ludwig Leichhardt and Charles Sturt, who explored it. The poetry applauds the results of their efforts – colonisation and settlement – but, more importantly, emphasises their vision, skill and courage in battling against the unknown. The voyager theme is present in early colonial literature, as the titles 'Dampier's Dream' and 'The Story of Abel Tasman' and eulogies on the lost explorers Burke and Wills testify, but its unusually strong appeal in this century for Australian poets is demonstrated in such poems as Kenneth Slessor's 'Five Visions of Captain Cook', R.D. FitzGerald's 'Heemskerck Shoals', William Hart-Smith's 'Christopher Columbus', Francis Webb's 'Leichhardt in Theatre' (qq.v.) and Alan Gould's 'The Great Circle' in *Years Found in Likeness* which deals, as does Slessor's 'Five Visions', with the life and explorations of Cook.

'VREPONT, Brian' (Benjamin Arthur Truebridge) (1882–1955), born Melbourne, where he eventually became a teacher of violin at the Melba Conservatorium, also lived in Queensland and WA and tried a variety of occupations, including that of masseur. He began publishing serious poetry late in life and in 1939 won the C.J. Dennis Memorial Prize for his poem on soil erosion, 'The Miracle'. Apart from some ephemeral writing for children, his publications are *Plays and Flower Verses for Youth* (1934), *The Miracle* (1939) and *Beyond the Claw* (1943). 'Vrepont's' best verse, simple and Wordsworthian in tone, reveals a strong but unsentimental response to nature. Surprisingly experimental for his generation, he uses some unusual, idiosyncratic forms that are clearly influenced by his musical interests.

W

WAINEWRIGHT, Thomas Griffiths (1794–1847) was born near London and as a young man showed both literary and artistic talent. A contributor to the *London Magazine*, he became known to such writers as Charles Lamb, William Hazlitt, Thomas Hood, Thomas de Quincey and Charles Dickens. In 1822 and 1824 he committed forgery to gain access to his capital, which was held in trust. Later he was suspected of having poisoned his uncle, his mother-in-law and his sister-in-law in order to obtain money, although the poisonings were never proved. His forgeries discovered in 1835, he was arrested in 1837 and sentenced to transportation for life. He arrived in Hobart in 1837 and worked at first on the roads and then as a wardsman in Hobart Hospital. His health declined and he was granted some freedom, which he used to take up painting again. Finally granted a ticket-of-leave in 1846, he died of apoplexy the following year. Forty of the paintings he did at Hobart, which are considerable achievements, are in existence. In 1825 he published *'Some Passages' in the Life, Etc of Egomet Bonmot, Esq.*, and his collected *Essays and Criticisms* were edited by W. Carew Hazlitt in 1880. After his death a nefarious legend grew up about his name, perpetuated by such novels as Bulwer-Lytton's *Lucretia* (1853), and Charles Dickens's *Hunted Down* (1860). This popular version of his life also appears in *The Criminal* (1890) by Havelock Ellis and in Oscar Wilde's collection of essays *Intentions* (1891), and is perpetuated by some of his later biographers. Robert Crossland's *Wainewright in Tasmania* (1954), however, is a balanced account. In Australian fiction Wainewright figures briefly in Edward Dyson's *In the Roaring Fifties* (1906), but he is given the most extensive treatment in Hal Porter's *The Tilted Cross* (q.v., 1961), where he appears as Judas Griffin Vaneleigh, and in Porter's radio play 'The Forger', broadcast by the ABC in 1983. George Farwell's radio play, *Portrait of a Gentleman*, included in *Australian Radio Plays* (1946, ed. Leslie Rees), also deals with his life.

WAKEFIELD, Edward Gibbon (1796–1862) was born in London into a Quaker family of modest means, although his own ambitions appear to have been grandiose. After some success in the diplomatic service and an earlier, short-lived marriage, from which he acquired a substantial fortune, he abducted a young heiress from school in 1826 and married her although he was soon induced to return her to her parents; Wakefield was sentenced to three years' imprisonment. His experiences in Newgate transformed his life, leading to his critical study of transportation and colonisation. His observations of prison life led to his publication of various works on criminal justice, chief of which was his *Facts Relating to the Punishment of Death in the Metropolis* (1831). His *A Letter from Sydney* (1829), written in prison, and published with Robert Gouger (q.v.) as editor, which first expounded his ideas on systematic colonisation, caused some controversy in Sydney, where it was accepted as the work of an Australian colonist. Wakefield further developed his colonial theory in his major works *England and America* (1833) and *A View of the Art of Colonization* (1849). His economic, social and political theories, which attracted numerous adherents, played a part in the establishment of an assisted migration scheme to NSW in 1831 and in the formation of the SA colony in 1836. In the latter enterprise his work, *The New British Province of South Australia* (1834), was particularly influential. Wakefield was also connected with the parliamentary investigation of transportation in 1837, which led to its abandonment. Although he never visited Australia, he was active in the theoretical and practical aspects of the colonisation of NZ, to which he migrated in 1853 and where he died. He also visited Canada in 1838 with Lord Durham, the governor-general, and was a valuable adviser to three Canadian governors 1841–44. Of the numerous biographies of Wakefield, the most significant are those by R. Garnett (1898), A.J. Harrop (1928), Irma O'Connor (1928), and P. Bloomfield (1961); Richard C. Mills in *The Colonization of Australia (1829–42)* (1915) examines Wakefield's achievements in colonisation and colonial policy. His *Collected Works*, edited by M.F. Lloyd Prichard, were published in 1968.

WAKELING, Louise Katherine (1950–), born Sydney, was educated at the universities of NSW and Adelaide. She has published poetry and short stories in numerous periodicals and is the author of a novel, *Saturn Return* (1990). With Margaret Bradstock (q.v.) she edited an edition of Ada Cambridge's autobiography *Thirty Years in Australia* (1989) and collaborated with her in a biography of Cambridge, *Rattling the Orthodoxies* (1991). Bradstock and Wakeling also edited with others the collection *Edge City on Two Different Plans* (1983) and co-edited *Words from the Same Heart* (1988). A joint collection of their poetry, *Small Rebellions*, was published in 1984.

WALCH, Charles Edward (1830–1915), the son of an English major and brother of Garnet Walch, was brought to Van Diemen's land in 1842. Walch's father bought the bookselling business of Samuel Tegg and renamed the firm J. Walch & Son, trading with his eldest son James. Charles Walch spent some years at sea and at the Victorian gold-diggings before entering into partnership with his brother James of the bookselling firm. He worked in London as buyer for the firm 1854–58 and 1861. In 1859 he instituted *Walch's Literary Intelligencer and General Advertiser* (q.v.), which became a standard reference work, as did his *Walch's Tasmanian Almanack.* Walch published one semifictional narrative that included some verses, *The Rovers* (1884), and a collection of essays published in two parts, *The Story of the Life of Charles Edward Walch* (1908).

WALCH, Garnet (1843–1913), born Broadmarsh, Tasmania, was mainly educated in England, returning to Australia in 1860 and taking up a career of journalism; his first full-time job was with the Sydney *Punch.* In 1872 he settled in Melbourne, where he became a member of the Athenaeum Club and of the group which included Marcus Clarke and R.P. Whitworth, and where he became a prolific writer of burlesques, extravaganzas, pantomimes and farces, producing about thirty works, many of them hack adaptations but contributing to the Australian stock of folk humour. In Sydney in the late 1860s he had already written for the Sydney stage. His first identifiable work for the stage is 'Love's Silver Dream; or, The King, the Goddess and the Fays of Fairyland, or, Harlequin Pygmalion and the Golden Demon of the Yawning Chasm', produced in Sydney in December 1869 at the Adelphi Theatre. Other Walch productions in Sydney included 'Conrad the Corsair' (1870) and 'Prometheus; or, The Man on the Rock' (1870). Walch's work during this period was done in collaboration with Rosa Cooper and for her company; an English actor, Cooper was active in Victoria in the early 1860s and in Sydney later in the decade. In Sydney Walch attracted the attention of George Darrell (q.v.) and was engaged in 1871 to write a Christmas extravaganza for the Victoria Theatre, 'Trookulentos, the Tempter; or Harlequin Cockatoo, the Demon of Discontent, the Good Fairy of Contentment and Four-Leaved Shamrock of Australia'. The 'Trookulentos' libretto was extensively reworked for Melbourne in 1873 and became Walch's outstanding script, *Australia Felix: or, Harlequin Laughing Jackass and the Magic Bat* (1873), republished in 1988, edited by Veronica Kelly with introduction and notes. A lively celebration of things Australian, the extravaganza also satirises topical personalities and issues. In 1872 Walch began a lengthy collaboration with Harry Rickards (q.v.). After leaving Sydney Walch became the leading dramatist for two decades in Melbourne. His other published plays include *Hey Diddle Diddle* (1878) and *Jack the Giant Killer* (1891). He also frequently collaborated with Alfred Dampier (q.v.) in adaptations and original productions, produced two books of verse, a life of General Gordon, a fantasy-narrative, *On the Cards; or, A Motley Pack* (1875) and edited a range of anthologies and popular annuals including *Hash* (1877).

Walch's Literary Intelligencer and General Advertiser, a monthly newsletter 1859–91, was published in Hobart Town and Launceston by J. Walch & Sons, a firm which has been a significant publisher of Tasmanian material. Edited by Charles Walch (q.v.), it carried lists of new books and periodicals, articles on literary and cultural topics, literary notices and reviews and became a standard reference work.

WALES, Robert, see *Van Diemen's Land Warriors, The*

WALFORD, Frank (1882–?) was educated in Sydney and tried various occupations including crocodile-hunting, buffalo-shooting, droving and fishing in northern Australia before turning to journalism. He published two booklets of verse, *Starlight and Haze* (1919) and *The Eternal Ego* (1921); a collection of short stories, *The Ghost and Albert and Other Stories* (1945); and five novels, several of which proved popular, *Twisted Clay* (1933), *The Silver Girl* (1935), *And the River Rolls On* (1939), *The Indiscretions of Iole* (1940) and *A Fool's Odyssey* (1942). He also edited various small short-lived periodicals, including *Walford's Weekly* (1918).

Walkabout, a monthly magazine published by the Australian National Travel Association, began publication in November 1934. It was founded by Charles Henry Holmes (1891–1981), who edited it until 1957. Consisting mainly of articles about the flora, fauna and geographical regions of Australia and neighbouring countries, *Walkabout* has frequently included informative articles by or about Australian writers. The title derives from 'walkabout', a term of European origin which originally denoted a period of nomadic wandering on the part of Aborigines. The expression 'to go walkabout' has lost much of its original racist or disparaging overtones, and is now applied to anyone who wanders the country in a leisurely manner, or to anything that has been mislaid.

WALKER, Brenda (1957–), born northern NSW, was educated at the University of New England and ANU before moving to Perth in 1984 to teach at the University of WA. She has published numerous articles and reviews, especially on Australian women's writing, contributed short stories and verse to periodicals and anthologies and edited with David Brooks the collection *Poetry and Gender* (1989) and, with Delys Bird, *Elizabeth Jolley: New Critical Essays* (1991). She has also written the novels *Crush* (1991), winner of the 1990 T.A.G. Hungerford Award for a first work of fiction, and *One More River* (1993). Ostensibly a murder mystery, *Crush* is also about writing or the need to narrate and its connection with the need for a father; as the epigraph from Barthes expresses the human situation: 'Isn't story-telling always a way of searching for one's origin, speaking one's conflicts with the law, entering into the dialectic of tenderness and hatred?' *One More River* is chiefly the tale of Faith (and faith), an elderly woman who lives alone on an island. Those previously in her life are all dead – her son Winson, her brother Lance, her brutal father. Across the river to her island comes Winton, an escaped prisoner. She gives him sanctuary and ultimately travels with him to Kings Cross, Sydney. Between them develops a closeness that is more than friendship, less than love, more than an ordinary parent–child affection, less than the intimacy of husband and wife. That bond serves its purpose for both of them, releasing them into a new life with new horizons. Finally, Winton leaves for the airport with his passport and Faith finds new vistas in the unlikely environs of Sydney's sin centre. With its ingenious structure (spatially interesting typography), its subtle allusions that indicate depths beyond the scope of an escape story, its parable-like tone and its implications of rebirth through love and understanding, *One More River* rises well above the level of popular fiction.

WALKER, David, see **Criticism**; *Dream and Disillusion*

WALKER, Kath, see **NOONUCCAL, Oodgeroo**

'WALKER, Lucy' (Dorothy Lucie Sanders) (1907–87), born Kalgoorlie, WA, published novels both under her own name and her pseudonym. Chiefly romance and light fiction, they included several set in Perth, e.g. *Pepper Tree Bay* (1959) and *Monday in Summer* (1961). Other titles among her forty wide-selling novels are *Fairies on the Doorstep* (1948), *Waterfall* (1956), *Love in a Cloud* (1960), *The Man from Outback* (1964), *The River Is Down* (1967) and *The Runaway Girl* (1975).

WALKER, Lyndon (1951–), born Townsville, Queensland, had an itinerant childhood as the family followed his meteorologist father around Australia and to Papua New Guinea. He graduated in psychology from La Trobe University in 1983 and has published his poems in Australian anthologies and overseas. The best of his poetry is in *Singers and Winners* (1984). A keen observer of contemporary life and insistent on the need for 'emotional truth' in his (and all) writing, Walker is a talented poet who excels in the short lyric. 'There is no need to travel to America' indicates that what we fear most in contemporary American society exists also in our own. In 1976 he shared (with twenty poems) a small Cochon publication, *Adam Scolds*, with Graham Rowlands and Grahame Pitt and was featured in *Cosh*, an earlier anthology. *The Green Wheelbarrow*, another small poetry collection, was also published in 1976.

WALKER, Thomas (1) (1804–86), born Leith, Scotland, came to Sydney about 1822. A merchant, banker and land speculator, Walker subsequently made a large fortune in NSW and devoted a substantial proportion to charitable projects. In 1837 he rode overland with three friends to Port Phillip, and published his journal of the trip, *A Month in the Bush of Australia* (1838).

WALKER, Thomas (2) (1858–1932), born Lancashire, England, had a colourful and wandering career in Canada, the USA, England, NZ, NSW and South Africa before finally settling in WA. In 1874 he migrated to Canada, where he set up as a spiritual medium; he was implicated in a felonious killing but escaped indictment and left for England where he worked for the *Preston Herald*. He then worked as a spiritualist and journalist in the USA before coming to Sydney in 1877 under the sponsorship of Australian spiritualists. After a chequered career in NSW and some further wanderings overseas, during which he published a book of verse in South Africa, he abandoned spiritualism and established himself in Sydney as a secularist spokesman and populist campaigner. His second volume of verse, *Bush Pilgrims*, was published in 1885 and in the same year he enjoyed the success of his dramatisation of *His Natural Life* (1874) and the production of his own play, in which he acted, 'Marmondelle the Moor'. In 1887 Walker was elected to the Legislative Assembly, where he had a vociferous career, which suffered a reversal in mid-1892 when he inadvertently shot and wounded a clergyman. Convicted of being drunk and disorderly, he immediately set up as a temperance lecturer and in 1899 arrived in WA in that role. He wrote for and edited the *West Australian Sunday Times*, worked for the Kalgoorlie *Sun* and the *Kalgoorlie Miner* and in 1905 was elected to the Legislative Assembly, where he remained until 1932, successfully combining politics, farming and law. He was attorney-general 1911–16 and speaker 1924–30. Apart from some polemical works, Walker published *Felony of New South Wales, by an Old Identity* (1891).

WALKER, William (1828–1908), born Glasgow, Scotland, came to Australia in 1837. A solicitor and member of the NSW parliament 1860–69, he was appointed to the Legislative Council in 1887 and was also prominent in civic, charitable and educational affairs. He published a collection of lectures and articles, *Miscellanies* (1884), which includes his lecture *Australian Literature* (probably 1864), the first separate work of Australian criticism. His other published works include the poem *The Flood, 1850* (1860), *Poems Written in Youth* (1884), *Recollections of Sir Henry Parkes* (1896) and *Reminiscences* (1890). See Criticism.

WALKER, William Sylvester (1846–?), who also wrote as 'Cooee', was a nephew of 'Rolf Boldrewood' and was born in Heidelberg, Melbourne, and later experienced station life and mining in NSW. He spent some time in NZ, tried diamond-mining in South Africa, and finally retired to Devon, England. He published two collections of short stories, *When the Mopoke Calls* (1898) and *From the Land of the Wombat* (1899), and seven novels, *Native Born* (1900), *Virgin Gold* (1901), *In the Blood* (1901), *Zealandia's Guerdon* (1902), *The Silver Queen* (?1908), *What Lay Beneath* (1909), *Blair's Ken* (1910) and *At Possum Creek* (1915). His work is marked by superficial characterisation and sensational, geographically wide-ranging, complicated plots; for the modern reader his stories have more historical than literary interest, especially in their incidental reflections of bush life.

'Walking to the Cattle-Place: A Meditation', a sixteen-poem sequence by Les Murray (q.v.), was first published in *Poetry Australia* (1972). In the opening poem, 'Sanskrit', the poet, listening to the familiar sounds of cattle nearby in the night, repeats to himself the Sanskrit words for the various stages of a cow's life and vows that for the coming day he 'will follow cattle'. In the following sequence, 'Birds in Their Title Work Freeholds of Straw', the dairy-farm children bring in the cows for the morning milking, a detested chore in 'the child-labour districts' that leads inevitably to the late-morning schoolroom scene of 'children dead beat at their desks'. 'The Names of the Humble' shows the cows at eyeball range and as he watches the regular circling movement of champing jaws the poet joins the ruminants by pondering on the vast ingestion of grass by cows down the ages. If he envies the cow one thing it is her stolid, cud-chewing indifference, 'her ease with this epoch'. 'The Artery' sees the herd disturbed by a passing 'beef mob' being driven to the abattoirs where, ultimately, 'out of cool rooms they crowd into our veins'. 'Death Words' reflects on the cows' habit of stampeding at the death of one of their number. The sequence then becomes extremely complex, breaking into fragments which contain Hindu and Krishna motifs. With 'Boopis' it returns to the cows, the opening lines, 'Coming out of reflections/ I find myself in the earth', indicating the meditative digression of the previous verses. The long concluding poem, 'Goloka', takes its title from the cow heaven of Krishna on Mount Maru.

Labelled by Murray as 'cow' poems, the Cattle-Place verses are among his most controversial and complex. The cattle, often set against historical and allegorical backgrounds, are used to carry deeply symbolic interpretations of the actual world.

WALL, Dorothy (1894–1942), see *The Oxford Companion to Australian Children's Literature* (1993), pp. 436–7.

Wallabadah Manuscript, The, see **Myall Creek Massacre**; **New England**; **MILLISS, Roger**

'Wallaby, The' ('The Wallaby Track'), phrases frequently used in Australian writing, are based on the wallaby, the smaller species of the kangaroo. The phrase 'the wallaby track', indicating the tracks of the outback, became in the late nineteenth century shortened in conversational idiom to 'the wallaby' and the phrase, 'to go on the wallaby', meant to go tramping around the country, somewhat like a swagman. The most famous use of the term is Henry Lawson's radical poem 'Freedom on the Wallaby' (q.v.), which is also the title of Muir Holburn and Marjorie Pizer's anthology *Freedom on the Wallaby* (1953). E.J. Overbury in his *Bush Poems* (1965) has a poem, 'The Wallaby Track', and 'Australia's on the Wallaby' and 'The Wallaby Brigade', are well-known folk-songs. Frederick McCubbin's famous painting *On the Wallaby Track* (1896) portrays man, wife and child boiling the billy by the side of a bush track. Nicholas Enright's play *On the Wallaby* (1982) re-creates the 1930s

Depression, when many homeless men wandered the outback looking for work or food.

WALLACE, John, who also used the pseudonyms 'Aintree', 'Texas Ranger' and 'Gerald Grantham', wrote thirteen crime, mystery, racing and adventure novels 1937–42. His complicated, action-filled plots are rapidly propelled by means of his abbreviated prose style and predictable, lightly observed characters; although several are ostensibly set in Australia, their location is really indeterminate. The titles of his novels give some indication of their subjects and tone, e.g. *Millionaire Gangster* (1937), *The Sedan Murder Mystery* (1938), *Vengeance of —–?* (1939), *Dead 'un Wins* (1940), *Dope Runners* (1940) and *Invasion* (1940).

WALLACE-CRABBE, Chris (1934–), born Richmond, Melbourne, was educated at Melbourne and Yale universities. In 1961–63 he was Lockie fellow in Australian literature and creative writing at the University of Melbourne and in 1965–67 Harkness fellow in the USA. From 1968 he has lectured in English at the University of Melbourne where he holds a personal chair. Since 1989 he has been director of the Australian Centre at that University. In 1987–88 he held the visiting chair of Australian Studies at Harvard. He is general editor of the new OUP Australian Writers Series. Wallace-Crabbe's published volumes of verse are *The Music of Division* (1959), *Eight Metropolitan Poems* (1962), *In Light and Darkness* (1963), *The Rebel General* (1967), *Where the Wind Came* (1971), *Selected Poems* (1973), *The Foundations of Joy* (1976), *The Emotions Are Not Skilled Workers* (1979), *The Amorous Cannibal* (1985), *I'm Deadly Serious* (1988), *For Crying Out Loud* (1990) and *Rungs of Time* (1993). He has edited the poetry anthologies *Six Voices* (1963), *Australian Poetry* (1971), *The Golden Apples of the Sun* (1980), *Clubbing of the Gunfire: 101 Australian War Poems* (1984, with Peter Pierce) and *From the Republic of Conscience* (with Kerry Flattley, 1992). He has compiled two selections of critical essays by various writers, *The Australian Nationalists* (1971) and *Multicultural Australia: The Challenges of Change* (1991, with David Goodman and D.J. O'Hearn) and several selections of his own articles, reviews and lectures, *Melbourne or the Bush* (1974), *Toil & Spin* (1979), *Three Absences in Australian Writing* (1983, the Colin Roderick lectures for the Foundation for Australian Literary Studies, Townsville) and *Falling into Language* (1990). He has also written a novel, *Splinters* (1981), set in Melbourne in the late 1960s, which examines the impact of the growing sense of chaos in contemporary life. His *Poetry and Belief* (1990) is the text of the 1989 James McAuley Memorial lecture.

Wallace-Crabbe's early poetry in *The Music of Division* and *In Light and Darkness* is, by his own admission, 'four square and syllogistic . . . written by a Lockean rationalist'. In the middle of unemphatic glimpses of the limited possibilities of life ('Ancient Historian', 'Fog at Midnight' and 'In Light and Darkness') there is a remarkable poem, 'The Wintry Manifesto', which is an affirmation of the potentialities of the here and now: 'our greatest joy to make an outline truly/ And know the piece of earth on which we stand.' The early volumes also reveal Wallace-Crabbe as a poet of the Melbourne suburbs, whose chief reaction is compassion for the shabby and often bewildered participants of modern city life, tempered by gentle irony. With his third volume, *The Rebel General*, Wallace-Crabbe turned towards more public and political themes, a trend accentuated in later volumes. The title poem, a portrait of failure and futility, is the centre-piece of a group of poems titled 'Brief Lives', mostly sardonic character sketches of figures such as Noah, King David and the young concubine Abishag. Wallace-Crabbe's changing poetic ambitions are reflected in his statement before the publication of *Where the Wind Came*: 'After stoical-formalist beginnings, I seek a poetry of Romantic fullness and humanity. I want to see how far lyrical, Dionysian impulses can be released and expressed without a loss of intelligence.' *Where the Wind Came* opens with the long poem 'Blood Is the Water', which concerns a Latin-American military dictator who has engineered power through a well-planned coup; the poem examines the motives and consequences of such dictatorial seizures of power. Wallace-Crabbe's freer approach to form is evident in the sequence 'Going to Cythera', where a thin line separates poetry from prose. His *Selected Poems*, a severe pruning of the first four volumes, is unusual in its grouping of seven poems from various volumes under the heading 'Meditations'. Wallace-Crabbe saw these meditative poems as a 'recurring series', part of a 'continuous landscape of debate'. The poetry of *The Emotions Are Not Skilled Workers*, is, in spite of a sometimes debonair and breezy tone, philosophically grave, even sombre. In 'The Shapes of Gallipoli' he joins the long line of Australian poets who have written on a subject rooted in Australian history. That Wallace-Crabbe could express greater satisfaction with 'The Shapes of Gallipoli', set though it is in 'mundane local conditions', than with 'Blood Is the Water', which is set in a 'laboriously constructed but finally metaphysical banana-republic', is a measure of his liberation from his 'stoical-formalist beginnings'.

The Amorous Cannibal also has as its centre Wallace-Crabbe's Melbourne, including the university campuses, suburbia with its gardens and houses and works of art. With consummate ease he handles both satirically clever lyrics and longer, more extended discourses, all characterised by an essential humanity and free-ranging wit and manifesting his philosophy: 'I believe it our duty to manage joy. We were put on this earth to be joyous.' In *For Crying Out Loud* that joy is partly tempered by an elegiac note, a sombre consideration of the loss that death has brought. Notable poems include 'The Shining Gift', 'Air Force, Burma 1942', 'The Otways' and 'The Ibis'.

One of a group of so-called Melbourne University poets who emerged in the late 1950s (e.g. Vincent Buckley, Evan Jones, A.R. Simpson), Wallace-Crabbe took a stance somewhere between the mainstream poetry of the late 1940s and 1950s and the 'New Poetry' of the 1960s and 1970s. He has continued to be his own voice – not (in his words) a 'Tranterite' (John Tranter, the standard-bearer of the post-modernists) nor a 'Bushie' nor a 'Squatter'.

His poetry has won numerous awards including the John Masefield Award in 1956, Farmer's Prize for Poetry 1974, the Grace Leven Poetry Prize for 1985 and the Dublin Prize for 1987.

Some of Wallace-Crabbe's views on Australian literature and critical theory are included in *Three Absences* and *Falling into Language*. Australian writing is deficient, he believes, in romantic love, in fully developed metaphysical views and in radically new poetic or prose forms. *Falling into Language* is a collection of essays on language, poetry, autobiography, memory and dreams. Especially interested in autobiography's construction of self, he argues for its centrality in literature.

WALLACE-CRABBE, Robin (1938–), born Melbourne, the brother of Chris Wallace-Crabbe (q.v.), is a well-known artist. He has published three novels, *Feral Palit* (1978), a powerful study of a city-bred man's inability to come to grips with rural living; *Goanna* (1982), a strikingly unusual account of the spiritual odyssey of a contemporary Melbourne businessman, and *Dogs* (1993); a family history which is partly a witty parody of family history and claims to trace the descent of the Wallace-Crabbes from a claimant to the Pictish throne, *Australia, Australia* (1989); and several thrillers under the pseudonym 'Robert Wallace', e.g. *To Catch a Forger* (1988), *Pay Day* (1989) and *Floodrain* (1991).

WALLEY, Richard has worked as a director, designer, actor, musician, dancer and choreographer. Founder of the Middar Aboriginal Dance Company, he has also worked in radio and television in the USA, UK, Canada and Denmark. His play *Coordah*, first performed in 1987, is included in *Plays from Black Australia* (1989).

WALSH, J.M. (James Morgan) (1897–1952), born Geelong and educated in Melbourne, is best known as an extremely prolific writer of crime mysteries, mostly located in England. His first novel, *Tap-Tap Island* (1921), was first serialised in the Melbourne *Leader*, his second, *The Lost Valley* (1921), was a prize-winner in the C.J. De Garis competition; his third was *Overdue* (1925). After experience in auctioneering and book-selling, Walsh visited England in 1925 to negotiate with publishers, returned to Victoria but left for permanent residence in England in 1929. Pseudonyms he used include 'John Carew', 'George M. White' and 'H. Haverstock Hill'; he also wrote in collaboration with E.J. Blythe and Audry Baldwin. His first three novels, which are adventure romances, are set in New Guinea and western Victoria and he also wrote two Australian detective stories, *The Man behind the Curtain* (1927) and *The League of Missing Men* (1927). The five adventure stories that he wrote under the pseudonym 'H. Haverstock Hill', *Anne of Flying Gap* (1926), *Spoil of the Desert* (1927), *The Golden Isle* (1928), *Golden Harvest* (1929) and *The Secret of the Crater* (1930), range between New Guinea, the Northern Territory, Gippsland, WA and the South Seas.

WALSH, Richard, see **Angus & Robertson**; **NEVILLE, Richard**

WALSTAB, George Arthur (1834–1909), born and educated in London, migrated with his parents to Australia in 1852. After service with the Victorian mounted police and with the Indian Army, he turned to journalism in 1860. Editor in 1862 of the Calcutta *Englishman*, he returned to Melbourne in 1865 and in the late 1860s was editor of the *Australian Journal*, the *Australasian Monthly Review*, and the *Colonial Monthly*. Bankrupted in 1869, he was a public servant (1873–80) and subsequently worked on the Melbourne *Herald.* Several Walstab novels were serialised in the *Australian Journal* and the *Colonial Monthly* during 1867–69; an earlier novel, *Looking Back* (1864), won him notice in London. Perhaps more important for Australian literature were his involvement in the founding of the Yorick Club and the two chapters of *Long Odds* (1869) that he wrote in 1868 when it was being serialised in the *Colonial Monthly* and Marcus Clarke was incapacitated.

'Waltzing Matilda' is the title of Australia's most famous song. The phrase 'to waltz Matilda', meaning to carry a swag on one's travels, was in existence by the 1890s and probably derived from two German words: *walzen*, which was applied to apprentices travelling around from master to master; and *Mathilde*, a girl's name which became generic for a female travelling companion and then for a bedroll. The song chronicles the experiences of a swagman waltzing his Matilda who has camped by a billabong or waterhole; as he is boiling his billy, a jumbuck (sheep) comes to drink at the billabong, and is captured by the swagman for food. The swagman is then accosted by the owner of the sheep, a squatter, who is accompanied by three mounted policemen; to escape arrest the swagman jumps into the billabong and is drowned near the coolibah tree shading the billabong. 'Waltzing Matilda' became enormously popular, particularly among Australian troops, has assumed the status of an unofficial national anthem, and remains the song most closely identified with Australia among overseas people. Its anti-authoritarian sentiments probably prevented its selection as the national anthem (q.v.) in a 1977 national poll (28 per cent of the vote compared with 43 per cent for 'Advance Australia Fair'), although its sympathy for the underdog has been seen as characteristically Australian and as a significant reason for its continuing appeal.

The provenance and transmission of 'Waltzing Matilda' have been the subject of some dispute. The most generally accepted version is that the words were written early in 1895 by A.B. Paterson (q.v.) at Dagworth station near Winton. Paterson was on a visit to western Queensland and while staying at Dagworth heard Christina Macpherson, the sister of the owner, Robert Macpherson, play 'Craigielea', a march adapted from the Scottish song 'Thou Bonnie Wood

of Craigielea', which she had first encountered at the Warrnambool races the previous April. In putting the words to the tune Paterson drew on several experiences during his three weeks at Dagworth: the discovery while riding of a dead sheep with a forequarter missing; a picnic at Combo waterhole, near where a suicide had taken place; and the casual after-dinner use of the phrase 'Waltzing Matilda', which took the fancy both of Paterson and Macpherson. The song was performed publicly for the first time in Winton in April 1895 and spread quickly in Queensland. A wider audience was reached after 1903 when Marie Cowan adapted Paterson's words and the 'Craigielea' tune as remembered by Macpherson to produce the version that has become the standard popular one. This audience was enlarged further by its inclusion in Thomas Wood's (q.v.) *Cobbers* (1934). Paterson, whose own 'Waltzing Matilda' was first published in his *Saltbush Bill, J.P.* in 1917, approved the adaptation, which was printed as part of an advertising leaflet wrapped around Billy Tea, and later in music broadsheet form. The Matilda Highway was the name given to a new sealed tourist trail that crosses the land of the pioneers – from Burke and Wills to Banjo Paterson – and passes through such outback towns as Barcaldine, Blackall and Winton.

The Paterson-Macpherson origin for 'Waltzing Matilda' was established by Sydney May in *The Story of Waltzing Matilda* (1944 and 1955). May found support from John Manifold, who in *Who Wrote the Ballads?* (1964) links it with the treason songs of the convicts, but alternative theories have been proposed: by Oscar Mendelsohn, in *A Waltz with Matilda* (1966), who claims that Paterson plagiarised the words from an anonymous bush song collected during the preparation of his anthology *The Old Bush Songs* (1905), and that Harry Nathan, a Toowoomba musician, composed the music; and by Harry Pearce, in *On the Origins of Waltzing Matilda* (1971), who claims that there were originally two 'Waltzing Matildas', one written by Paterson and Macpherson which became a variant now known as the Queensland or Buderim version, and an earlier version (the popular one) in the preparation of which a Winton pianist, Josephine Pene, drew on her knowledge of the English marching song 'The Bold Fusilier'. Richard Magoffin's *Fair Dinkum Matilda* (1973) convincingly refutes the theories of Mendelsohn and Pearce and, while correcting some of May's conclusions with new evidence, substantiates the gist of his argument. Nigel Krauth's novel *Matilda, My Darling* (1983), set in Winton in 1895, has Paterson composing 'Waltzing Matilda' after hearing Robert 'McPhee's' story of his disturbing a swagman at the Combo waterhole, although the verse in which the swagman defies the squatter is written as a tribute to a party of shearers whom Paterson also meets during his stay. The Combo waterhole also figures in the novel as the place where the body of a unionist is discovered by a private detective sent up from Brisbane to investigate his disappearance.

WALWICZ, Ania (1951–), born Swidnica, Poland, arrived in Australia in 1963. A visual artist, she is a graduate of the Victorian College of the Arts, Melbourne, and has had several exhibitions. Her prose and poetry has been published very widely in anthologies and periodicals in Australia and Europe and she has published the collection *Writing* (1982, reprinted in 1989 in *Travel/Writing*) and the novels *Boat* (1989), which won the New Writing Prize in the Victorian Premier's Literary Awards, and *Red Roses* (1992). A performance poet, she has performed in Australia, England, Switzerland and France and has been writer-in-residence at several tertiary institutions. She has also written plays, including 'Girlboytalk' (1986), 'Dissecting Mice' (1989) and 'Elegant' (1990). Incantatory and repetitious, Walwicz's prose poems exploit the subconscious effects of language, often exposing the reader to the linguistic alienation suffered by the non-English-speaking migrant and deconstructing familiar linguistic affirmations of 'normality'. A group of poems (for example, 'So Little', 'Poland', and 'New World') focus on the first encounters with the new culture: in the old country the family was 'big and big time' but 'Here we were so little. We were nothing. We were none and naught and no money. We were no speak.' After travelling in the white snow 'that was nowhere' and 'in the blue ocean that was nowhere', the family gets to 'a place where we were less and had less and were less and less and grew smaller every day'. Others, such as 'wogs', which view the immigrant from the perspective of the settled, explore all the familiar anxieties of racism. In all Walwicz's work, however, feminism intersects with the immigrant experience, concentrating on the struggle to reclaim the self from smallness and even invisibility, which is also a struggle with the claims of the past. Registering and resisting the constructions of gender which increasingly imprison the growing girl-self, Walwicz's novels adopt a repetitious, unconventional language which disowns normal syntax and the artificial rules of grammar to deconstruct the imprisoning social constructions; at the same time, and notwithstanding passages reflecting frustration, intense struggle and even paralysis, a fluid, serial, many-layered identity is claimed which is an exultant realisation of creative strength: 'I am here. This is where I now am. This is my place. On my page. This is here for me. This place is a dot in my space. I choose to place myself where I am.' Self-conscious not just about the writing process but about the processes of thinking and feeling, Walwicz's original writing seeks to break normative and restrictive codes of being and challenge the ideologies of power and authority, whether of gender, nationality, status or language.

WANNAN, Bill (William Fielding Fearn-Wannan) (1915–), born Victoria, has travelled widely in Australia and abroad and served in the Pacific with the AIF in the Second World War. His first published work was a poem, *The Corporal's Story* (1943). Now widely known as a leading collector of, and authority on, Australian folklore and humour, especially of the sort of humour that was the staple of such periodicals as *Smith's Weekly* and the *Bulletin*, Wannan has compiled numerous collections of ballads, yarns, anecdotes

and legends. He is also well known for his column 'Come In, Spinner!' contributed to the *Australasian Post* 1955–80. His published work includes the frequently reprinted collections *The Australian* (1954), *Tales from Back o' Bourke* (1957), *Bullockies, Beauts and Bandicoots* (1960), *Hay, Hell and Booligal* (1961), *A Treasury of Australian Frontier Tales* (1961), *Fair Go, Spinner* (1964), and *My Kind of Country* (1967); accounts of bushrangers, *Tell 'Em I Died Game* (1963), notorious colonial figures, *Very Strange Tales* (1962), and famous Australians, *Legendary Australians* (1974); dictionaries of humour, traditional invective and folk anecdotes, *A Treasury of Australian Humour* (1960), *Australian Folklore* (1970), *Folklore of the Australian Pub* (1972), *With Malice Aforethought* (1973), *Robust, Ribald and Rude Verse in Australia* (1972) and *Dictionary of Australian Humorous Quotations* (1974); anthologies of writing by and about the Irish in Australia, *The Wearing of the Green* (1965), and the Scots, *The Heather in the South* (1966); and a satire on Australian local histories, *Chronicles of Boobyalla* (1979). He has also edited an anthology of urban short stories, *Australian Pavements* (1964), a selection of Marcus Clarke's writing, *A Marcus Clarke Reader* (1963), and in 1952 the Melbourne periodical the *Realist Writer*.

War Literature. Australian war literature covers a wide spectrum of emotional and intellectual responses to war, ranging from the general and relatively uncomplicated support for Britain and 'the Empire' during the Boer War and the two world wars to the controversy and division that accompanied Australia's participation in the Vietnam War, and from patriotic pride in the Anzac legend, especially strong during and after the First World War, to the disillusionment with such patriotic and heroic ideals that began to appear in some of the writings of the Second World War and became widespread in the literature, especially the fiction, of the Vietnam War. Responses also range from compassion to horror, anger, and fear, and from bitterness to a humour which is usually tinged with irony. Although mateship figures prominently, love (for women or family) is less in evidence, although, especially in works published after 1945, hatred appears in various forms – not only against the official enemy (as in some of the POW narratives of the Second World War), but also against such unofficial enemies as the military police, politicians, the civilian population, Allied troops (if perceived to be sexual rivals or unreliable in battle) and certain types of military officers. Most Australian war literature is direct and realistic in style, and, being traditional and unadventurous in form and technique, has been little influenced by modernist and post-modernist literary movements of this century.

Boer War (1899–1902). The Boer War produced little memorable Australian war literature. Volumes containing examples of the imperialistic verse popular at the time are *Ballads of Battle* (1900) by Melbourne journalist John Sandes ('Oriel'), *War Songs, 1899–1900* (1901) by W.H. Dawson and *The Collected Verse* (1928) by George Essex Evans. Two individual poems in similar vein are John B. O'Hara's 'Australia's Call to Arms' and Garnet Walch's 'The Lion's Cubs', which appeared in *The Coo-ee Reciter* (1904), compiled by W.T. Pyke. In its sentimental, pro-British propaganda and old-fashioned rhetoric, Sandes's poem 'A Call from England' is typical of the genre:

There came a cry forth speeding o'er the
   mighty Indian main,
A whisper that was borne upon the breeze,
'Twas the voice of England calling, and
   the words were clear and plain,
'Come and help me, O my children overseas . . . '

Not everything published by Sandes, however, is imperialistic. In 'Death Song of the Boers', there is a note of sympathy for the enemy's threatened way of life. Mixed attitudes are also found in the war poems of A.B. ('Banjo') Paterson included in his *Rio Grande's Last Race* (1902). Paterson, who served as a war correspondent, ends his poem 'Johnny Boer' on the confident note that the Boer will be made to run, but in 'On the Trek' the thoughts of the war-weary Australian soldiers return to peacetime life in rural Australia. Henry Lawson's verses, on the other hand, are consistently hostile to the British cause and to Australian participation in the war, as the ironic 'Our Fighters (From a Worldly Point of View)' (1899) and 'The Blessings of War' (1900) indicate. A similarly hostile view of the war is expressed by Monty Grover in the poem 'I Killed a Man at Graspan', subtitled 'The Tale of a Returned Australian Contingenter Done into Verse', in which the author manages to catch the genuine confessional tone of guilt and regret. Memories of the look in the eyes of a dead enemy soldier lead the speaker to reject the traditional heroic view of war and to assert that 'If the Empire ask for me later on/ It'll ask for me in vain'. The poem, like those by O'Hara and Walch, appeared in *The Coo-ee Reciter* (1904).

Of the personal narratives of the war, *On the Veldt* (1902) is a plain, factual account by R.C. Lewis, the officer commanding the Tasmanian Imperial Bushmen, W.T. Reay's *Australians in War* (1900) and Frank Wilkinson's *Australia at the Front* (1901) are works by Australian war correspondents, while James Green's *The Story of the Australian Bushmen* (1903) is a chaplain's account. The most sensational personal narrative of the war is George R. Witton's *Scapegoats of the Empire* (1907). It deals with the author's army life from the outbreak of the war until his release from prison in England and return to Australia in 1904, and includes an account of the events that culminated in the court-martial and execution by the British Army of Lieutenants P.J. Handcock and Harry Harbord Morant. 'Breaker' Morant, a minor poet, is said to have written the bitter lines 'Butchered to Make a Dutchman's Holiday' a short time before his death. He is the subject, in addition to several biographical works, of the two novels *Where Day Begins* (1911) by Alfred Johnston Buchanan and Kit Denton's *The Breaker* (1973). These are the only Australian novels on the Boer War to warrant mention, apart from A.G. Hales's *McGlusky* (1902), the first of a long series of novels narrating the

varied adventures of that aggressive, eponymous hero. The most outstanding single literary work on the Boer War is J.H.M. Abbott's *Tommy Cornstalk* (1902), a personal narrative which emphasises in a spirit of national pride the initiative, independence and fighting abilities of the bushmen who were the core of the Australian mounted troops in South Africa. Direct, lucid and literate, Abbott's account expresses not only national pride but also the personal impressions and opinions of a soldier who experienced a good deal of active service and held strong opinions about the capabilities of the British Army and the character of the Boer. Abbott returns to the subject of the war in some of the fictional sketches and stories of his *Plain and Veldt* (1903), and occasionally in his volume of journalistic articles, *An Outlander in England* (1905), especially in the chapter in which he criticises the emphasis on pomp and circumstance in Britain's army during peace-time.

First World War (1914–18). Australian poetry of the First World War began with slim volumes of patriotic and imperialistic rhetoric by civilian versifiers such as L.E. Homfray's sixteen-page pamphlet *Australians, Awake!* (1915). Several of Homfray's poems are simply pious utterances about the troops abroad and their families at home – e.g. 'Sons of Australia' heaps scorn on those unwilling 'to fight for [their] country – or fall'. In 'List to the Call' in *The Call to Arms* (1915), Winsome Jennings expresses similar sentiments, urging the 'shirkers' to 'Fight for Australia, the King and the Flag'. Similar volumes include *Hoisting Our Flag on the Anzac Redoubt* (1917) by George Smith ('Patrius'), *At Vancouver's Well* (1917) by Australia's chaplain-general, J.L. Rentoul, and *Troop Trains* (1917) by Alice Gore-Jones. J.D. Burns's 'For England', from *In the Dawning of the Day* (1916), Henry Lawson's 'England Yet', from *Selected Poems* (1918), and Christopher Brennan's 'Irish to England' and 'Kitchener', from his volume *A Chant of Doom* (1918), are more worthwhile examples of this loyalist verse. Many of Brennan's other war poems, however, including 'A Chant of Doom' are little more than anti-German propaganda. Pride in the achievements of the Australian troops mingles with an elegiac strain in such poems as L.H. Allen's 'Gallipoli', first published in 1916 and reprinted in *Patria* (1941), Mary Gilmore's 'These Fellowing Men' from *The Passionate Heart* (1918), 'William Baylebridge's' sonnet sequence *A Wreath* (1915), and John Le Gay Brereton's 'The Dead' and 'Anzac' from *The Burning Marl* (1919). Disillusionment with war is the main mood in Mary Gilmore's 'The Measure' from *The Passionate Heart*, Brereton's 'Transports' and 'The Patriot' from *The Burning Marl*, 'Furnley Maurice's' 'To God: From the Warring Nations' (1916) and Zora Cross's *Elegy on an Australian Schoolboy* (1921).

Of the soldier-poets, many were rhymesters and balladists in the popular tradition. Typical of them was Tom Skeyhill, who published *Soldier Songs from Anzac* (1915) and *A Singing Soldier* (1919). In his poem 'Shrapnel' the colloquial style and simple humour characteristic of much of this unpretentious writing are captured in his description of a shell landing nearby while he is sitting in his dug-out chewing his Queensland bully beef and his 'biscuit 'ard as wood':

> When, boom! I nearly choked meself,
> I spilt me bloomin' tea;
> I saw about a million stars
> An' me dug-out fell on me.

Skeyhill, who was blinded by an exploding shell, became an international figure during the war years through his lecturing and fund-raising and subsequently recovered his sight in 1918 after an operation. Other popular soldier-versifiers are James Andrews (*Garrison Ginger*, 1919), Peter Austen (*Bill-Jim*, 1917), Norman Campbell (*The Dinki-Di Soldier*, 1918), who all wrote in imitation of C.J. Dennis's popular humorous war poem *The Moods of Ginger Mick* (1916), J.P. O'Donnell (*Songs of an Anzac*, 1918), F.S. McDonnell (*The History They Have Made*, 1919), William Michael McDonald (*Soldier Songs from Palestine*, 1918), and Edwin Gerard ('Trooper Gerardy') whose two volumes *The Road to Palestine* (1918) and *Australian Light Horse Ballads and Rhymes* (1919) represent the best in the popular narrative tradition. In ballads such as 'Lofty Lane', 'Riding Song', 'North of Jerusalem' and 'Garden Post', Gerard gives vivid descriptions of desert warfare and the feelings of the Australian troopers involved. The best of the more literary soldier-poets were probably Leon Gellert, Frederic Manning, Harley Matthews and Vance Palmer. Gellert's *Songs of a Campaign* (1917) contains some fine vignettes of the Gallipoli experience and its aftermath of illness and desolation. Manning's *Eidola* (1917) expresses the protracted agony and horror of war on the Western Front in a series of poems that alternate between the realistic and visionary modes of presentation. In Palmer's *The Camp* (1920), the long title poem offers an interesting comment on the dehumanising effect of military training on the human spirit, while the short piece 'The Farmer Remembers the Somme' perfectly encapsulates the trauma of war. Matthews's best war poems are the three narratives about Gallipoli published in *Vintage* (1938) – 'The Day Before', 'Two Brothers' and 'True Patriot'. Other, less significant, volumes of verse are Martin Boyd's *Retrospect* (1920), which contains some poems on post-war psychological problems, Reginald Godfrey's elegiac *Anzac Memorial Poems* (1925), Henry Weston Pryce's *Your Old Battalion* (1926) and Oscar Walters's *Shrapnel Green* (1931), which contains the effective humorous poem 'One Sunday Mornin''.

In 1983 an anthology of more recent poems on the war by poets too young to have been participants but who had grown up under the shadow of the Vietnam conflict was published under the title *Shadows from Wire*. Edited by Geoff Page, the volume juxtaposes poems by nineteen poets, including Page, Les Murray, Hal Porter, Roger McDonald, Chris Wallace-Crabbe, David Malouf, John Tranter, Thomas Shapcott, Dorothy Hewett, Michael Dransfield, David Campbell and Kevin Hart with contemporary photographs held by the Australian War Memorial to suggest some of the ironies and ambiguities now present in the modern Australian response to the First World War.

The early prose writings on the war fall into three main categories – patriotic effusions, humorous fiction and descriptive accounts. The first group includes Oliver Hogue's *Love Letters of an Anzac* (1916), his personal narrative *Trooper Bluegum at the Dardanelles* (1916) and his sketches and poems making up *The Cameliers* (1919); E.F. Hanman's ('Haystack') personal narrative *Twelve Months with the 'Anzacs'* (1916); Roy Bridges's volume of sketches *The Immortal Dawn* (1917); and Mabel Brookes's novels *Broken Idols* (1917), *On the Knees of the Gods* (1918) and *Old Desires* (1922). The humorous fiction encompasses 'Steele Rudd's' novel *Memoirs of Corporal Keeley* (1918), Gladys Hain's volume of short sketches *The Coo-ee Contingent* (1917) and A.G. Hales's *McGlusky's Great Adventure* (1917) and *Ginger and McGlusky* (1917). The best of the many descriptive accounts of the war include J.L. Beeston's *Five Months at Anzac* (1916), David Doull's *With the Anzacs in Egypt* (1916), F.S. Loch's ('Sydney de Loghe') *The Straits Impregnable* (1916), C.E.W. Bean's *Letters from France* (1917), H.W. Dinning's *By-Ways on Service* (1918) and T.A. White's *Diggers Abroad* (1920). C.E.W. Bean also edited *The Anzac Book* (1916), an anthology of contributions from Australian soldiers on Gallipoli, which included some of his own writings and photographs.

The best of the early volumes of short stories on the war are *Saints and Soldiers* (1918) by Harley Matthews, and *An Anzac Muster* (1921) by 'William Baylebridge'. The direct realism and simple unpretentious prose style of *Saints and Soldiers* contrast strongly with the indirectness, artifice and idiosyncrasy of style of *An Anzac Muster*, although both contain some effective humour. The year 1923 saw the first publication of the short story 'Two Masters' by Arthur Wheen, a fable in which Christian virtue is contrasted with military *virtus*, already an important element in Anzac mythology. Of the other prose writings of the period, C.E.W. Bean's official two-volume history of Gallipoli, *The Story of Anzac* (1921, 1924), rapidly became one of the most potent influences on the evolution of the Anzac tradition and retains interest for its fine blending of historical and literary qualities. Most of the more memorable prose writings, however, belong to the years following 1927. The volume of short stories *Glimpses* (1928) by Eric Partridge ('Corrie Denison') contains the story 'A Mere Private', dealing with the experiences of an infantryman who serves in Egypt, Gallipoli and France. In 1929 Partridge published what is virtually a personal narrative, 'Frank Honywood, Private', which appeared in the composite volume *Three Personal Records of the War* (by R.H. Mottram, John Easton, and Eric Partridge). He followed this with 'From Two Angles', a more imaginative war narrative, which appeared in 1931 in the miscellany *A Martial Medley*. Partridge's account of the Battle of Pozières, one of the most terrible battles on the Western Front, which forms part of 'Frank Honywood, Private', is especially memorable. In 1928 A.L. McLean's unfinished personal account, *War Vistas*, and T.W. White's personal account of wartime flying, captivity and escape from the Turks, *Guests of the Unspeakable*, appeared, followed in 1934 by John

Halpin's story of suffering and humiliation as a prisoner of the Turks, *Blood in the Mists*.

The outstanding Australian novel on the First World War first appeared in 1929. This was Frederic Manning's *The Middle Parts of Fortune*, which was reissued the following year in expurgated form with a new title, *Her Privates We*. Manning's novel draws on his experiences as an expatriate Australian, who served with an English county regiment in France, but the nationality of his characters is less important than the universal truths about life and human nature which they embody. The author's Australian origin may be detected behind the portrait of his central character, but Manning's moral vision, integrity and artistry are such that his novel triumphantly transcends the limitations implied by such terms as 'documentary realism' and 'national ethos'. It is thus a very different novel from the other well-known Australian novel on the war, Leonard Mann's *Flesh in Armour* (1932), which is a tribute to the courage, independence and mateship of the ordinary Australian soldier. It is also an elegy to the Australian dead, inspired by Australia's high casualty rate during the war, and a protest against the horrors of modern technological war. Frank Dalby Davison's hybrid narrative *The Wells of Beersheba* (1933) is a reconstruction in literary terms of a number of historical events associated with the Anzac Light Horse Division in Sinai and Palestine, culminating in the famous Light Horse charge on Turkish trenches at Beersheba. Leslie Meller's novel *A Leaf of Laurel* (1933) contains in its first section scenes relating to Gallipoli. J.P. McKinney's *Crucible* (1935) gives a realistic account of war experience in France and becomes increasingly cynical about such concepts as heroism and honour. Martin Boyd's *Lucinda Brayford* (1946) concludes with anti-war scenes; his later novel *When Blackbirds Sing* (1962) is even more strongly pacifist in tone, ending with the returned Australian protagonist tossing his war medals into the dam on his peaceful Australian farm.

Some more recent novels on the war (all by non-participants) are Thomas Keneally's *Gossip from the Forest* (1975), Roger McDonald's *1915* (1979), David Malouf's *Fly Away Peter* (1982), and Geoff Page's *Benton's Conviction* (1985). Keneally's novel, which has also been published as a play, tells of the bizarre events surrounding the signing of the Armistice in a carriage at a railway siding in France and is written mainly in dialogue form. McDonald's *1915* is an ambitious and technically sophisticated novel, in which the events of the Gallipoli expedition acquire significance from links with the Australian social scene of the time and with the author's philosophical ideas on life and art. *Fly Away Peter* is an anti-war novel, in which the horrors of trench warfare and the destructive violence of man are presented against a background of the peaceful Australian countryside and the natural rhythms of renewal. *Benton's Conviction* tells of the crisis of conscience that leads a small-town Anglican vicar to oppose the war and the conscription referendum of 1916 and of the resulting conflict that alienates him from his bishop and the majority of his congregation. The novel offers no final solution to the dilemma: the vicar is assaulted and subjected to indignities by the son of a local landowner, who subsequently meets his death in action in France.

Important personal accounts of the war were written by John Lyons Gray ('Donald Black'), H.R. Williams and Martin Boyd. Gray's *Red Dust* (1931), the story of his experiences as a trooper in Palestine, expresses the author's pride in the AIF and intense disillusionment with war. Similar pride is dominant in Williams's *The Gallant Company* (1933), while disillusionment predominates in the war section of Boyd's autobiography *A Single Flame* (1939), as the author traces his growing sense of isolation from his fellow officers in first the Buffs Regiment and then the Royal Flying Corps. Other interesting personal accounts were written by Ion L. Idriess, Joseph Maxwell, E.J. Rule, May Tilton, G.D. Mitchell, Sir John Monash, and A.B. Facey. Idriess's *The Desert Column* (1932) deals straightforwardly with experiences on Gallipoli as well as in Sinai and Palestine, while VC winner Maxwell's *Hell's Bells and Mademoiselles* (1932) deals with experiences on Gallipoli and in Egypt and France. Rule, the author of *Jacka's Mob* (1933), was an officer in the same battalion as Albert Jacka, the first Australian VC winner in this war, and his book describes events on Gallipoli and in France in a direct, objective fashion. May Tilton's *The Grey Battalion* (1933) tells of her experiences as a nursing sister and contains a vivid account of the carnage resulting from the third battle of Ypres, which culminated in the ferocious battle of Passchendaele. Mitchell's *Backs to the Wall* (1937) earned praise from both C.E.W. Bean and H.M. Green. The description of the great frost in France during the bitter winter of 1916–17 is especially memorable. Monash's *War Letters* (1934, ed. F.M. Cutlack) give some interesting insights into the character of this intelligent and highly educated Australian commander. Published many years later than the preceding personal accounts, A.B. Facey's autobiography *A Fortunate Life* (1981) contains, in its short war section, some vivid, moving and impressively honest memories of the author's Gallipoli experiences. In simple prose Facey re-creates, in the first part of his book, the harsh conditions under which life was lived by many Australians in the years before the war and the fortitude displayed, which helped the author and his companions to withstand the hardships and horrors encountered on Gallipoli.

Second World War (1939–45). Three outstanding Australian poems of the Second World War were written by poets who, although they saw active service, would not normally be thought of as war poets. These are David Campbell's taut ballad of the New Guinea campaign, 'Men in Green' (1943), J.S. Manifold's affectionate epitaph on a courageous soldier, who fought and died in Crete, 'The Tomb of Lieutenant John Learmonth, A.I.F.' (1945), and Kenneth Slessor's elegy to the drowned sailors of all nations, 'Beach Burial' (1944). Other noteworthy occasional poems on the war include Dorothy Auchterlonie's (Dorothy Green's) 'Soldiers Abroad', Rosemary Dobson's 'Windfall Apples', Donovan Clarke's 'Ruin Ridge', Geoffrey Dutton's 'Abandoned Airstrip, Northern

Territory', Mary Gilmore's brief lyric 'The Swallow at Kings Cross', Kenneth Mackenzie's love fantasy, 'The Tree at Post 4', David Malouf's 'The Year of the Foxes', Leonard Mann's 'Anzac Day, 1943', Harley Matthews's 'Resurgence', Elizabeth Riddell's 'The Soldier in the Park', Douglas Stewart's sonnet sequence 'Sonnets to the Unknown Soldier', Francis Webb's 'The Gunner', Judith Wright's elegy 'To A.H., New Year 1943', Russel Harte's 'Landing at Lae' and Peter Middleton's 'War in Papua'.

Typical of the volumes of war verse written by mothers, wives and other relatives of Australian servicemen which appeared during the war or shortly afterwards are Gwen Bessell-Browne's *The Road to Kokoda* (1943), Joan Kinmont's *This, My Son* (1943), Nora Kelly's *1940–1942* (1944), and Coralie Clarke's *Silent His Wings* (1946). Many of the volumes written by servicemen follow the tradition of popular Australian verse. Tip Kelaher's *The Digger Hat* (1942) contains a number of patriotic ballad-like pieces together with a few poems like 'Nostalgia', written in a more formal lyrical manner. Bert Beros, a Canadian who served with the AIF in the Middle East and New Guinea, first achieved fame with the sentimental title poem of his volume *The Fuzzy Wuzzy Angels* (1943), in which he paid tribute to the loyalty, devotion, and gentleness of the native bearers during the New Guinea campaign. Most of the poems in Maurice Clough's *The Fighting 'Ninth'* (1943) and *We of the A.I.F.* (1943) are confident, patriotic and optimistic in mood. 'What War Can Give a Man' emphasises the power of war to cement relationships between men; 'Invasion Landing', which describes an action against the Japanese, is representative of Clough's better work. David McNicoll's *Air Mail Palestine* (1943) is, in the words of a contemporary reviewer, 'a pleasing documentation of the places where the A.I.F. ... fought'; but the volume contains the occasional gem like 'Ski Patrol'. The most successful poems in Paul Buddee's *Stand To* (1943) are the humorous and satirical pieces. Humour is the keynote of J.F. Dettman's *Here Was Glory* (1944), a collection of colloquial pieces in the style of C.J. Dennis.

The most significant volumes of serious war poetry by Australian servicemen came from Tom Inglis Moore, Shawn O'Leary, John Quinn, Maurice Biggs, Eric Irvin, J.A. Henderson, Val Vallis, Kevin E. Collopy, Michael Thwaites, W.S. Kent Hughes and John Millett. In the title poem of Moore's *Emu Parade* (1941) irritation at the trivialities of army life is succeeded by a more positive attitude towards the Allied cause, which in 'Wardens of Wisdom' bursts out in the form of satire against academics and undergraduates who believe they are 'too valuable to go and fight'. O'Leary's *Spikenard and Bayonet* (1941) is a collection of twenty short poems based mainly on the author's experiences in the Middle East and written in a variety of verse forms. Quinn's *Battle Stations* (1944) contains two good descriptive poems, 'Troopship by Day' and 'Troopship at Night', and a number of shorter pieces in which death in war is treated from different angles and with varying degrees of emotional intensity, ranging from the dirge-like effect of 'The Dead' to the

over-wrought incitements to kill in 'Action'. One of his better poems is 'A Foxhole for the Night'. Four of Biggs's poems in *Poems of War and Peace* (1945) were cited by the reviewer in the *Bulletin* as 'the finest group of poems turned out by any Australian in the forces'. Biggs's 'Spring Offensive, 1941', 'What the Bullets Sang' and 'Christmas, 1941' are powerful, individual statements about war. Irvin's poems in *A Soldier's Miscellany* (1945) are sensitive, reflective pieces which describe the jungles of New Guinea and other places and highlight the brief moments of physical contentment in a soldier's life. In Henderson's *The World is Wide* (1946), two of the Mediterranean poems, 'Two Desert Graves' and 'The Middle Sea', stand out because of the author's concern with the deeper issues of time and eternity. Vallis's *Songs of the East Coast* (1947) contains two good poems on death in war, 'Flotsam' and 'The Gannet and the Soldier'. Kevin E. Collopy, like Henderson a member of the RAAF, included in his *The Splendid Hour* (1951) a number of sensitive and skilfully executed sonnets which pay tribute to courage and commemorate, with pity but without bitterness, death in its various forms. His 'Night Flight over Hamburg' is a successful narrative poem. The narrative mode is also employed, but more extensively, in *The Jervis Bay* (1943) by Michael Thwaites and *Slaves of the Samurai* (1946) by W.S. Kent Hughes. The title poem in the former volume, one of the few poems dealing with naval warfare, tells in longish rhyming couplets and in dramatic fashion the story of the unequal fight between the British escort vessel *Jervis Bay* and the German pocket battleship *Admiral Scheer* during the battle of the Atlantic. Kent Hughes's volume, an ambitious poem in thirty-one cantos, 'written at odd times, on odd scraps of paper, in many odd places', is an effective account in heroic couplets of Australian POW experience. In *The Jervis Bay*, and in a subsequent volume, *The Honey Man* (1989), Thwaites also published a number of appealing short personal poems on the war. Written in a more modernist style, John Millett's anti-war sequence of fifty-one poems, *Tail Arse Charlie* (1982), vividly evokes the traumas of modern war, as seen from the perspective of a former RAAF air gunner. Other, less significant, writers of war verse include Robert S. Byrnes (*Endeavour*, 1954), Louis H. Clark (*Romance and Reality*, 1944), Colin Thiele (*Splinters and Shards*, 1945 and *Progress to Denial*, 1945), Eric Locke (*From Shore to Shore*, 1944), Bill Wannan (*The Corporal's Story*, 1943), T.W. White (*Sky Saga*, 1943) and, although not Australian-born, Patrick Hore-Ruthven (*The Happy Warrior*, 1943).

Four early volumes devoted wholly or in part to war fiction, which appeared in 1944, were Peter Cowan's *Drift*, G.H. Fearnside's *Sojourn in Tobruk*, Lawson Glassop's *We Were the Rats* and James Aldridge's *The Sea Eagle*. Probably the best of Cowan's stories relating to the war in *Drift* is 'Saturday Afternoon', which skilfully creates through the use of laconic dialogue the very essence of war's boredom and monotony, as experienced by two servicemen on their day of rest in an Australian city. Fearnside's stories are often little more than anecdotes, sometimes realistic and at other times in the tradition of the Australian 'tall story', such as the humorous ghost story 'A for 'Arris'; but even the realistic sketches are enlivened by the author's sense of life's ironies and oddities. The first part of Glassop's novel *We Were the Rats* deals with the hero's civilian life in Australia before the war, the remainder with army life in Australia, Palestine and North Africa. The book's strength lies in its frank and realistic documentation of 'digger' talk, attitudes and behaviour, aspects of which shocked some of the original readers and led to its being banned in 1946 and republished in revised form in 1961. *We Were the Rats* is not an anti-war novel, despite its revelation of the carnage of war, and the author pays tribute to the bravery and mateship of the Australian soldier. Glassop later wrote a sequel, *The Rats in New Guinea* (1963), more in the tradition of popular war fiction. Aldridge's *The Sea Eagle* is concerned with escape through the German lines by some Australian soldiers left behind on the island of Crete after the Allied withdrawal. The author concentrates on the adventurous elements of his story but does not ignore the political issues dividing the resistance fighters who help the Australians to avoid capture. Aldridge also wrote the war novels, *Signed with their Honour* (1942) and *Of Many Men* (1946), which, like *The Sea Eagle* reflect his knowledge of various European theatres of war gained as a war correspondent. *The Winds Are Still* (1947), by John Hetherington, is the best of the escape novels set in the Mediterranean. Concerned with a group of Australian and British servicemen who are cut off behind the German lines in Greece, sheltered for a while in the home of a Greek family, and subsequently assisted by other Greek patriots, the novel has popular appeal as a story of adventure and love. But it is also a realistic account of war experiences and contains some good studies of both Allied and Greek characters. *The Twenty Thousand Thieves* (1951) by Eric Lambert is a novel which pays tribute to the exploits of the Australian Ninth Division in the Middle East; its merit lies in its vivid descriptive style, seen most obviously in the Tobruk and El Alamein battle sections, its vigorous narrative movement and its lively cast of Australian 'type' characters, as found among the other ranks; its weakness is in its politically motivated distortion of the characters of some of the officers. Despite the gruesome scenes of death and destruction Lambert's emphasis falls less on the horrors of war than on the heroism of the ordinary Australian fighting soldier. Other fictional works set in the Mediterranean area are Richard Beilby's novels *No Medals for Aphrodite* (1970) and *Gunner* (1977) and W.H. Williams's romantic narratives *Bardia Blow-Up* (1959) and *Benghazi Blitz* (1960). *No Medals for Aphrodite* is another escape story set in Greece and follows a similar plot line to that of *The Winds are Still*, although at a somewhat more consistently popular level. *Gunner*, a bitter and disillusioned novel concerned as much with sex as with war, opens in Alexandria where a young AIF soldier is living as a deserter. Through a series of flashbacks the novel effectively describes the disastrous Cretan campaign, in which the central character has taken part as a member of the Sixth Division. Williams's books are little more than adventure yarns,

recounting the exciting exploits of a purely fictitious group of Australian desert raiders.

Three novelists who wrote about the wartime home front were Kenneth Mackenzie, Dymphna Cusack and Xavier Herbert. In *Dead Men Rising* (1951) Mackenzie writes about the demoralising routine of garrison soldiers guarding Italian and Japanese POWs at a camp near 'Shotley' (Cowra) in NSW. The novel's climax is based on an historical incident, an uprising by Japanese prisoners. Cusack's *Come In Spinner* (1951), written in collaboration with Florence James, and Herbert's *Soldiers' Women* (1961) both deal with wartime life in Sydney, and in particular with the lives of a number of women caught up in the frenzied atmosphere of a garrison city. The former tends towards an unsentimental feminist view of woman's lot, the latter displays a predominantly male cynicism and produces effects that fluctuate between the comic, the tragic and the bizarre. Thomas Keneally also wrote a political novel set in Australia during the war called *The Cut-Rate Kingdom* (1980).

Two of the outstanding novels of the war are set in the mountains and rainforests of islands in the Pacific area. These are T.A.G. Hungerford's *The Ridge and the River* (1952) and G.R. Turner's *Young Man of Talent* (1959). The main strength of Hungerford's short novel lies in its tight form and vivid descriptive style, which re-create with immediacy and intensity the physical exhaustion and mental strain of war in the jungle and the atmosphere of the oppressive, damp jungle itself. Also impressive is the author's skilful treatment of the characters' inner conflicts and the personal relationships among them, which are conveyed through lively colloquial dialogue and through brief passages of reverie and flash-back. Hungerford also published in 1985 *A Knockabout with a Slouch Hat*, a collection of reminiscences covering the years 1942–51. Turner, in *Young Man of Talent*, goes a good deal further than Hungerford in character development. With a psychological subtlety rare in Australian war fiction, he creates in Sergeant Peter Scobie a highly individualised and complex character, whose considerable intellectual gifts prove to be tragic flaws in the circumstances of the wartime situation in which he finds himself. The odd relationship that develops between the educated Scobie and the primitive, almost animal-like, private soldier Andy Payne ends in violence and tragedy and the novel explores the degree to which the responsibility can be sheeted home to Scobie's pride, insincerity and overweening confidence.

Other jungle warfare novels were written by Peter Pinney, Eric Lambert, Jon Cleary, V.H. Lloyd, Leonard P. Manning, 'David Forrest' and Ron Tullipan. Pinney's *Road in the Wilderness* (1952) is somewhat deficient in form and characterisation, but includes vivid descriptions of the jungle and a realistic account of war, particularly the hardships, the diseases, the brutality of killing and the fear. Lambert's *The Veterans* (1954), a sequel to *The Twenty Thousand Thieves*, begins with episodes condemning black-marketing during the war and military bungling and bastardry inflicted on seasoned troops by the High Command in Australia and concludes with scenes set in New Guinea, where many of the veterans from the Middle East campaigns meet their deaths in a demoralising war that reduces them to primeval 'creatures of the mud'. The tone is bitterly anti-war, anti-officer, anti-army, anti-civilian and anti-American. In *The Climate of Courage* (1954) Jon Cleary also deals with Australian Middle East veterans returning to their homeland, then departing for the war in New Guinea. Its final section, loosely based on a historical incident, describes the fortunes of a small group of soldiers retreating before the Japanese in New Guinea. The troops' deep disillusionment with jungle warfare is epitomised in the words of one of the characters, 'I keep thinking what a lovely war it was in the Middle East.' Cleary's other war writings include a creditable volume of war sketches and stories, *These Small Glories* (1946), with settings in Greece, Crete and the Middle East and which deal with such varied topics as the brutality of war, the anguish of a lovers' separation and the joyous oddity of characters thrown up by war, such as the glass-eating hero of 'The Magnificent Czech'. Lloyd's *The Hidden Enemy* (1957) is partly realistic war novel and partly romantic tale. Describing the rescue by an Australian infantry company under Captain John Grant of a party of women marooned at a mission station during the early stages of the Japanese invasion of New Guinea, it offers a credible account of military operations within a plot in which emotions run strong and actions and motives are not always fully convincing. A more documentary kind of truth is exuded in Manning's *Assignment New Guinea* (1958), an account in fictional form of the battle against the Japanese in the Markham Valley region of New Guinea. 'Forrest's' *The Last Blue Sea* (1959), the story of a group of militia soldiers pitted against the Japanese in New Guinea, contains some vivid descriptive writing. Only in part a war novel, Tullipan's *March into Morning* (1962) opens with an account of Australia in the years of the Depression before the war and concludes with an account of Australia in the post-war years. L.H. Evers, T.A.G. Hungerford, and Hal Porter wrote novels about the Australian occupation forces in Japan after the war. All three are concerned to emphasise the moral disintegration that overtakes an army of occupation as a result, particularly, of sexual promiscuity and black-marketing. In Evers's *Pattern of Conquest* (1954) and Porter's *A Handful of Pennies* (1958) the moral issues receive fairly superficial treatment. Hungerford, however, in *Sowers of the Wind* (1954), offers not only skilful characterisation and description but also a successful embodiment of a number of significant moral themes, involving such issues as integrity, responsibility for one's own actions, guilt and conscience.

Novels about the war at sea include the purely adventurous fiction of J.E. Macdonnell such as *Gimme the Boats!* (1953), which portrays his popular RAN character Petty Officer Jim Brady, Wal Watkins's toughly written tale of a mutiny on an Australian destroyer against its martinet of a captain, *Wayward Warriors* (1970), and Jack Harvey's documentary novel of the merchant navy, *Salt in Our Wounds* (1954). Harvey's novel, which is based on his own experiences in an open boat in 1944, is the story of the hardships endured by thirty-nine seamen, survivors of a torpedoed oil-tanker who, after enduring machine-gunning by a Japanese submarine, fight for their lives in a small boat adrift on the Indian Ocean for forty-three days. Similarly documentary in style is Norman Bartlett's novel about the war in the air, *Island Victory* (1955), which details incidents befalling members of an RAAF Kittyhawk squadron during a campaign on a Pacific island in the closing stages of the war. As the author observes: 'The events in this book all happened. It is fiction only in so far as events have been rearranged in a coherent pattern.' Part of the book is concerned with the adventures of a pilot who parachutes into the jungle and travels through enemy-held territory to safety. Bartlett also edited for the Australian War Memorial the volume *Australia at Arms* (1955), which contained, *inter alia*, David Campbell's short story 'Recco over Rabaul', a tersely written account of a reconnaissance flight by a RAAF Hudson aircraft over Japanese-held territory. The story was later republished as 'Zero at Rabaul' in Campbell's volume of short stories *Flame and Shadow* (1976). Other documentary novels about aerial warfare mostly concern life in Britain with the RAF, such as Ray Ollis's *101 Nights* (1957), Geoff Taylor's *The Hollow Square* (1958) and Olaf Ruhen's *The Broken Wing* (1965).

Ivan Chapman's *Details Enclosed* (1958) and H.V. Clarke's *The Tub* (1963) are also documentary novels, the former dealing with the experiences of two Australian soldiers in POW camps in Europe and the latter with four Australian POWs in the hands of the Japanese from the time of the fall of Singapore until the end of the war. Clarke also wrote *When the Balloon Went Up* (1990), a volume of serious and humorous short stories based on his experiences and those of other soldiers of the Eighth Division both before and after the fall of Singapore. Three novels by well-known civilians which contain sections illustrating the traumatic effects of POW experience at the hands of the Japanese are 'Nevil Shute's' *A Town like Alice* (1950), Randolph Stow's *The Merry-Go-Round in the Sea* (1965), and David Malouf's *The Great World* (1990).

Vastly different from such works and from each other are three other novels, Geoffrey Dutton's *Andy* (1968), John Vader's *Battle of Sydney* (1971) and Thomas Keneally's *Schindler's Ark* (1982). *Andy* is an irreverent comic novel about airforce life and the amorous adventures of its eponymous hero, and *Battle of Sydney* deals with a conjectured invasion of Australia by the Japanese. *Schindler's Ark*, on the other hand, is set in Germany and is best described as a work of 'faction', in that it employs the fictional techniques of the novel form to tell the true story of a remarkable person, Oskar Schindler, a complex character who under the guise of operating a factory for the Nazi war effort, managed to save the lives of many European Jewish workers destined for death in Auschwitz and other notorious concentration camps.

Much of the non-fictional prose written about the war, e.g. books by war correspondents, belongs to the areas of journalism and contemporary history rather than to literature. It is in those categories that the writings of such outstanding Australian war correspondents as Alan Moorehead, Chester Wilmot and John Hetherington should largely be placed, although occasionally a war correspondent's book such as Osmar White's *Green Armour* (1945) and Geoffrey Reading's *Papuan Story* (1946), through its greater concentration on events the author himself participated in or witnessed and its more personal style, may lay claim to recognition as a personal narrative. The *War Diaries* (1985) and the *War Despatches* (1987) of the poet and official Australian war correspondent Kenneth Slessor are among the more outstanding of such writings, the *Diaries*, in particular, containing a good deal of criticism of those responsible for the conduct of the war and of military censorship. The war correspondent George Johnston is also significant, to some extent, for his *New Guinea Diary* (1943), but more particularly for his success in transmuting the raw material of his life as a war correspondent into the stuff of literature in the final section of his highly acclaimed novel *My Brother Jack* (1964).

One of the earliest personal accounts of army life is Donald Friend's *Gunner's Diary* (1943), a frequently droll account of the author's experiences of military training in Australia, and its sequel *Painter's Journal* (1946), which ends as the author is about to forsake his career as an undistinguished private soldier for that of a distinguished official war artist. Another early account of army life, albeit of a very different kind, is Mary Kent Hughes's *Matilda Waltzes with the Tommies* (1943), an unusual story of military service and travel by an Australian doctor who voyages to England to enlist in the RAMC because the Australian Army will not accept service from women doctors. Bruce Robinson's *Record of Service* (1944) records the author's experiences as a doctor with the AIF during the New Guinea campaign. Two other early personal accounts (both 1944) are P.C. Neasbey's *Blokes I Knew* and Leslie Taylor's *So Passed My Year*, the latter describing the author's experiences as a YMCA welfare officer. Two more significant books published in 1944 were Denis Warner's *Written in Sand*, the story of the desert campaign in North Africa written by a private soldier of the Ninth Division, and the anonymous *Word from John*, a volume of letters edited by John and Richard Ackland. Although restricted by the inevitable censorship of the war years, these letters provide an interesting account of the life of an AIF officer in the Middle East and New Guinea from the time of his sailing from Australia in April 1940. Of the army memoirs published after the war, David Selby's *Hell and High Fever* (1956) effectively recounts the adventures of a group of Australian soldiers who survived the Japanese capture of Rabaul and retreated to the southern coast of New Britain, where they enjoyed a precarious freedom, full of dangers and hardships, for several months until rescued. Selby tells his story simply, vividly, modestly and without sensationalism or bitterness. Equally effective is Peter Ryan's impressive story of danger, hardship and fortitude in New Guinea, *Fear Drive My Feet* (1959), a personal account of the experiences of a young ANGAU officer while patrolling the

isolated and rugged country bordering the Lae-Salamaua region during 1942–43, usually in close proximity to the enemy. The book, a saga of heroic conduct, ends with reflections on the folly and vanity of war. Malcolm Wright gives an account of his coast-watching and guerrilla activities in New Britain in *If I Die* (1965). Other later army memoirs include Ken Clift's *The Saga of a Sig* (1972), subtitled *The Wartime Memories of Six Years Service in the Second A.I.F.*, and *The Soldier Who Never Grew Up* (1976), a collection of anecdotes and stories; G.H. Fearnside's *Half to Remember* (1975); Henry ('Jo') Gullett's *Not as a Duty Only* (1976); H.D. Steward's *Recollections of a Regimental Medical Officer* (1983); Peter Pinney's trilogy *The Barbarians* (1988), *The Glass Cannon* (1990), and *The Devil's Garden* (1992); and Fred Airey's *The Time of the Soldier* (1991). Clift wrote about the war in unvarnished soldier's language and was a man who, in the words of one of the introductions: 'must have been a headache to his seniors at times, but after many demotions in non-commissioned ranks ... finally won his commission through sheer fighting ability.' Fearnside, author of the earlier volume of stories *Sojourn in Tobruk* (1944), gives in *Half to Remember* some well-written reminiscences as an infantry sergeant at Tobruk and as an infantry officer in the Aitape-Wewak campaign. Gullett, grandson of Barbara Baynton, subtitled his book *An Infantryman's War* and writes effectively of his experiences, initially in the ranks in the Middle East, then, after gaining a field commission following the battle for Bardia, in Greece and New Guinea, and subsequently with the British forces on the Second Front in Europe. Steward's account of the hard-fought Syrian and Kokoda campaigns is full of praise for the courage and endurance of the troops of the Seventh Division, and is a clear and vivid piece of historical writing. Peter Pinney's three books constitute a slightly fictionalised personal account of commando activities in New Guinea and Bougainville, based on the author's illegally kept diaries, and reflect several of the recurrent themes in Australian literature of the Second World War – hostility towards Duntroon-trained officers, an endorsement of the more larrikin-like elements in the Anzac tradition and of courage without heroics, and a fiercely racist attitude towards the Japanese foe. Fred Airey was the product of the more rigid military discipline of the British Army, with which he had served during the First World War. After migrating to Australia he joined the Australian Army, subsequently earning a fearsome reputation as a strict disciplinarian in the role of RSM of a machine-gun battalion. His account of his life, which included a lengthy period of imprisonment in Japanese POW camps, is written in a simple, vigorous prose style. Air force memoirs include Gordon Powell's *Two Steps to Tokyo* (1945), John Beede's *They Hosed Them Out* (1965), D.E. Charlwood's *No Moon Tonight* (1956) and Ivan Southall's *Fly West* (1974). Powell relates in an episodic, anecdotal fashion various experiences observed and shared as a chaplain with the RAAF on Pacific islands to the north of New Guinea. Beede and Charlwood served with the RAF's bomber command, the former in the extremely vulnerable position of rear gunner and the latter as a navigator. Charlwood's book is a restrained, moving and convincing account of the high losses of life and the fears, tensions and sense of comradeship among those airmen lucky enough to survive their compulsory quota of flying missions over Europe. Southall, the author of several books about the war, including the biography *Bluey Truscott* (1958), tells the story of his own service with the RAAF 461 Squadron while flying Sunderlands during the Battle of the Atlantic. Patrick White also includes an account of his service with the RAF as an intelligence officer in the Middle East in his 'self-portrait' *Flaws in the Glass* (1981). Two Australian women who describe their wartime lives are Pat Studdy-Clift and Nancy Wake. In *Only Our Gloves On* (1981) the former writer describes her life on an Australian farm, while in *The White Mouse* (1985) Wake includes a lengthy account of her dangerous activities in France as a member of the French Resistance Movement and the Special Operations Executive. The story of the Australian contributions to the success of allied Signals Intelligence during the war is given in two books, whose publication was long delayed by Security considerations. These are Geoffrey Ballard's *On Ultra Active Service* (1991) and Jack Bleakley's *The Eavesdroppers* (1992).

POW and escape stories are conspicuous among the personal narratives of the war. Early volumes which deal with the Mediterranean and European theatres of war include L.J. Lind's *Escape from Crete* (1944), Edwin N. Broomhead's *Barbed Wire in the Sunset* (1944), and John Buckland's *Adriatic Adventure* (1945). These were followed soon after the war by Paul Brickhill's *The Great Escape* (1950) and Geoff Taylor's *Piece of Cake* (1956). Brickhill, a fighter pilot shot down and captured in Tunisia, tells an exciting story of tunnelling to escape from a German POW camp. Taylor, shot down near Hamburg during one of bomber command's night raids, tells of hardship and hunger in a German POW camp until the end of the war. The year 1985 saw the publication of two further accounts of POW experience in Europe, Ian Ramsay's *P.O.W.: A Digger in Hitler's Prison Camps, 1941–1945* and Barney Roberts's remarkably tolerant account of POW life, *A Kind of Cattle*. These were followed in 1991 by Charles Robinson's sensitive description of service with a field ambulance unit in the Middle East, followed by capture and escape, *Journey to Captivity*. The hardships endured by Australian prisoners in the hands of the Germans were generally less severe than those endured by prisoners of the Japanese. The accounts by the latter group of prisoners constitute the most harrowing body of personal narratives in Australian literature. Their suffering was touched on in Graeme McCabe's brief, tersely written *Pacific Sunset* (1946), but the full picture of sadistic brutality and callous neglect on the part of the captors did not emerge until the appearance of such books as Rohan Rivett's *Behind Bamboo* (1946), Roy H. Whitecross's *Slaves of the Son of Heaven* (1951) and Russell Braddon's *The Naked Island* (1952). In *Behind Bamboo* Rivett tells how, after escaping from Singapore where he had been a leading member of the news staff of the Malayan

Broadcasting Service, he was captured by the Japanese in Java and subsequently sent to prison camps in Burma and Thailand. The third part ('Burma Railway'), the grimmest section of the book, shows the experienced journalist at work, combining personal observations and experiences with historical material consulted after his release. Roy H. Whitecross, in *Slaves of the Son of Heaven*, limits himself to describing what he experienced and witnessed in POW camps in Singapore, Burma, Thailand, Indo-China, South Malaya and Japan. It is a remarkably objective account of stoical endurance and chronic suffering occasioned by brutality, dietary deficiencies, tropical diseases, and shortage of medical supplies. In Russell Braddon's *The Naked Island* objectivity is replaced by a highly personal style reflecting the author's bitterness, not only towards the Japanese but also towards the British High Command, the British civilian population of Malaya and the many officers who illustrated the pettiness, inflexibility and folly that he came to associate with the military mind. An indignant and caustic book, *The Naked Island* reflects the emotional state of its author at the time when he wrote it. A change of attitude was to appear in its sequel *End of a Hate* (1958). Betty Jeffrey's *White Coolies* (1954) and Jessie Elizabeth Simons's *While History Passed* (1954), later republished as *In Japanese Hands* (1985), are both personal accounts of the suffering endured by the thirty-two Australian army nursing sisters who, of the sixty-five who escaped from Singapore on the tiny ship *Vyner Brooke*, survived its bombing and sinking and escaped the massacre that overtook twenty-one of their original number after their landing on the coast of Sumatra. The tale of their captivity in Japanese hands is told with great restraint by Betty Jeffrey and with somewhat more emotion by Jessie Simons. Restraint also characterises *The Rising Sunset* (1957), in which Ken Attiwill, an Australian journalist who served with the British Army, tells the story of his captivity in camps in Java and Japan, and Ray Parkin's *Into the Smother* (1963) and *The Sword and the Blossom* (1968), in which the author, a survivor of the sinking of HMAS *Perth* in Sunda Strait in 1942, records his experiences as a prisoner working on the Burma–Thailand railway and in Japan. Norman Carter, an Australian radio scriptwriter who was in Malaya at the time of its fall, tells the story of his imprisonment with members of the Australian 8th Division and how he helped to organise stage productions in camps on the Burma railway in *G-String Jesters* (1966). Significant later accounts of POW life include Kenneth Harrison's *The Brave Japanese* (1966), later republished as *Road to Hiroshima* (1983), *The Albert Coates Story* (1977) by Albert Coates and Newman Rosenthal, Stan Arneil's *One Man's War* (1980), Hugh V. Clarke's *Last Stop Nagasaki* (1984), E.E. Dunlop's *The War Diaries of Weary Dunlop* (1986), and Keith Wilson's *You'll Never Get Off the Island* (1989). Harrison, a sergeant in an Australian anti-tank regiment, was captured in Malaya and endured the hardships of POW life in several places including the Burma railway and Japan. While describing the brutality of his Japanese captors, he takes pains to acknowledge their bravery and explain the reasons for their brutality towards prisoners, but without forfeiting critical judgement of their faults. Harrison writes with vigour and a feeling for style. *The Albert Coates Story* is a hybrid work, part-biography and part-autobiography. In the first and third sections Rosenthal supplies details of Coates's earlier and later years; the middle section is basically Sir Albert Coates's first-person account of his experiences as a doctor tending Australian and other POWs in Japanese hands. Coates, who was senior surgeon to the AIF in Malaya, gives a terse and balanced account of events. *One Man's War*, Arneil's diary record of his captivity in Changi, Thailand and Johore, supplemented by later summary sections and pictorial illustrations, is a moving, restrained, balanced, and comprehensive account of a POW's life. The author, an infantry sergeant, objectively records his sufferings in Thailand, and occasionally expresses criticism of the more brutal Korean guards and Japanese officers, together with his anger at acts of incompetence by British and Australian military authorities; he also describes the times in Changi when his life was less wretched. Hugh V. Clarke's *Last Stop Nagasaki* is a lucid account of his experiences as a POW in Japan, where he laboured for much of the time in a Nagasaki shipyard. Clarke is also the author, or part-author, of several other books of a more historical nature dealing with POW experiences, including *Twilight Liberation* (1985) and the Time-Life volume *Prisoners of War* (1988, written in collaboration with Colin Burgess and Russell Braddon). *The War Diaries of Weary Dunlop* provides a comprehensive record of the life of a senior medical officer in various POW camps and provides a fascinating insight into the mind of a truly remarkable individual. While not concealing the brutality of his captors, the book reflects the author's later belief in the need for reconciliation between all men and recognition of a common humanity. Keith Wilson's experiences as a POW were confined to Singapore island and his account of captivity in *You'll Never Get Off the Island* is accordingly less harrowing than the accounts in a number of other POW narratives. His portrayal of the Japanese and Korean guards records not only their brutality but also their occasional acts of kindness and humanity.

Three dramas about the war require mention: Sumner Locke Elliott's *Rusty Bugles* (performed 1948, published 1968), Alan Seymour's *The One Day of the Year* (performed 1960, published 1962) and John Romeril's *The Floating World* (performed 1974, published 1975). *Rusty Bugles*, originally banned by the chief secretary of NSW on the grounds of its 'blasphemous and indecent' dialogue, is a naturalistic anti-war play, whose mood alternates between earthy comedy and pity as it documents the boredom and frustrations of a group of young soldiers stationed at an ordnance depot in the Northern Territory during 1944. *The One Day of the Year*, also a naturalistic work, is a serious exploration of the significance of Anzac Day in the Australian national consciousness and the generation gap as it exists between a working-class, returned-soldier father and his university-educated son. *The Floating World* is experimental in technique; through a mixture of naturalistic and expressionistic scenes set on a cruise ship bound for Japan in 1974, Romeril at first satirises and later evokes sympathy for his returned-soldier hero, whose memories of sufferings and indignities as a POW in Japanese hands and guilt as a survivor ultimately undermine his sanity.

Korean War (1950–53) and Vietnam War (1962–73). The Korean War generated little Australian war literature. In *Korean Diary* (1955) Frank Clune gives an informal but undistinguished journalistic account of what he saw as a UN war correspondent visiting Japan and Korea; and in such narratives as *Mig-Meat* (1960), a story of Australian jet pilots in action in Korea, William R. Bennett wrote about the war at the 'popular fiction' level. The only significant work to emerge from the Korean War was A.M. Harris's novel *The Tall Man* (1958), which won a prize in the *Sydney Morning Herald* literary competition for 1957 under the title *No Flowering Road*. Harris's novel, the story of a mission behind enemy lines led by an Australian military intelligence agent, is both a good story and a realistic account of the dangers, hardships and brutality inherent in the Korean situation, but its success is limited by the shadowiness of the portrayal of the unnamed Australian hero, the lack of serious themes and a mechanical reliance on authorial omniscience in the sections devoted to the earlier careers of various characters.

The Vietnam War inspired a much larger amount of literature in both verse and prose. The verse published during the course of the conflict was mainly protest poetry written by civilians; representative collections are an anthology containing prose as well as verse, titled *We Took Their Orders and Are Dead* (1971) and a special issue of the journal *Overland* (54, 1973), titled *Vietnam Voices: A Retrospect*. An introductory statement in *We Took Their Orders and Are Dead*, which was edited by Shirley Cass, Ros Cheney, David Malouf and Michael Wilding, points out that all the writers contributed to 'register their opposition to the military involvement of Australia and her American and other allies in the war in Vietnam'. A similar statement in the *Overland* issue, which was compiled by R.H. Morrison, speaks of Australia's 'shame' over her entry into the Vietnam War and describes the poems themselves as 'a record of anguish and of protest'. Poets represented include Dorothy Green, Bruce Beaver, R.F. Brissenden, David Campbell, C.B. Christesen, Dennis Davison, Bruce Dawe, Geoffrey Dutton, R.D. FitzGerald, Len Fox, Rodney Hall, A.D. Hope, Nancy Keesing, Craig Powell, Tim Thorne, John Tranter, Chris Wallace-Crabbe and Judith Wright. Among the small number of noteworthy poems which appeared during the war are A.D. Hope's 'Inscription for Any War' (later republished as 'Inscription for a War'), 'Questions for Kaspar' by Dorothy Auchterlonie (Dorothy Green), Len Fox's 'Vietnam Graves' and Bruce Dawe's 'Homecoming'. Most of the poems published during the post-war years were written by servicemen or their relatives and are more sympathetic to the role and sufferings of those who fought in Vietnam. Thus *Homecoming* (1991), an anthology compiled by Jean R. Williams, contains poems such as Peter Moore's

'Missing in Action' and Elizabeth Megrath's 'Veteran's Wife', which dwell on the nightmares and lingering traumas of the Vietnam experience; while in *Sorrow is Knowledge* (1992), compiled by Audrey Greenway, Colin Price's 'Five Young Men' lays the blame for the deaths of the young soldiers on 'greedy old men' responsible for Australia's participation in the war and Robert S. Kearney's 'Lads?' takes to task the civilian population for its rejection of the returned veterans.

Similarly, the prose literature of the war was written both by people who saw service in Vietnam and by those who did not. One of the few impressive prose extracts about the war in *We Took Their Orders and Are Dead* is a passage describing a Viet Cong ambush in which an American army officer meets a particularly gruesome death at the hands of an old man and a boy. This passage on the death of Major Hatton is taken from Hugh Atkinson's novel *The Most Savage Animal* (1972), a civilian author's novel of protest set partly in Europe and partly in Vietnam. Novels set either entirely or mainly in Vietnam include John Rowe's *Count Your Dead* (1968), Kenneth Cook's *The Wine of God's Anger* (1968), Rhys Pollard's *The Cream Machine* (1972), William Nagle's *The Odd Angry Shot* (1975), *When the Buffalo Fight* (1980) by 'David Alexander' (Lex McAulay), John Carroll's *Token Soldiers* (1983), Michael Frazer's *Nasho* (1984) and D.J. Dennis's *One Day at a Time* (1992). Rowe's novel concentrates on the American contribution to the conduct of the war, with Australian characters playing subsidiary and somewhat inglorious roles. Although Rowe raises a number of pertinent questions about Australia's motives for intervention, he devotes most of his novel to a critical examination of American methods of conducting military and 'civil affairs' operations. He also explores differences in national characteristics with an unflattering candour that exposed him to official disapproval, since at the time of publication he was still a commissioned officer in the Australian Army. The novel reflects the author's respect for humane and civilised values and also for the traditional military virtues such as courage and honour. There is little or no respect for the military virtues valued by professional officers of the Australian Army in the disillusioned, anti-war novels of Cook, Carroll and Frazer. The narrator of *The Wine of God's Anger* is a young Australian soldier whose Catholic upbringing has led him to enlist to 'save the world from Communism' but who at the end, guilt-ridden over his involvement in the war, sits in a Bangkok bar as an army deserter. Much of the effect of the novel derives from the wry, confidential style, which conveys the narrator's initial naivety, his growing mental confusion, and an ultimate sense of nightmare expressed through the black comedy of napalm-produced mayhem during modern warfare. *Token Soldiers* and *Nasho* also stress the folly and futility of Australia's participation and military role in the war and the traumatic effects of the war on its young soldiers. Both novels go even further than *The Wine of God's Anger* in exposing the brutalising effect of army life and war on soldiers, illustrated by the sadism of Carroll's Sergeant Savage and the mental

and moral collapse of Frazer's protagonist, Turner. Like the three preceding novels, *The Odd Angry Shot* focuses on a young Australian soldier, whose story in this instance is told in a style of raw realism, complete with blasphemies, indecencies and crude humour. The death and maiming caused by the war, the frantic quest for pleasure during rest-and-recreation leave, the larrikinism and defiance of petty military authority among Australian soldiers are all brought out, as are their feelings of bitterness against the Australian civilian population who show them insufficient understanding and gratitude. Also expressed is their sense of pride in their professionalism as soldiers. Covering virtually the same range of activities as *The Odd Angry Shot* but with a more cynical attitude towards traditional Anzac mythology, is *The Cream Machine*, which is narrated in a breathless kind of prose style that is not always successful. *One Day at a Time* employs the time-frame of a single day in Vietnam during the 1968 Tet Offensive, tracing the experiences, sometimes humorous but usually serious, of several characters, most of whom belong to a small army aviation unit. Incidental criticism is levelled at the militaristic attitude of a certain type of army officer, the shortage of up-to-date military equipment available to the Australian forces in Vietnam, and the sabotaging of the war effort by militant trade unionists in Australia. More traditional in technique and more conservative in its attitudes to the Vietnam War and the Anzac legend is the documentary novel *When the Buffalo Fight*. Closely based on events that befell members of the Australian First Battalion during their tour of duty in 1965 and 1966, this novel pays tribute to the fighting ability and efficiency of the Australian troops, often at the expense of the troops of South Vietnam and the USA. Like *The Most Savage Animal* and *The Wine of God's Anger*, Dymphna Cusack's *The Half-Burnt Tree* (1969) is the work of a civilian novelist. It is set in Australia and deals with the unhappy life of a returned serviceman, maimed and disfigured by napalm burns. It also contains sections in which the brutality of the fighting in Vietnam is recalled with horror and loathing.

One of the outstanding personal narratives on the war is Hugh Lunn's *Vietnam: A Reporter's War* (1985), a vivid and comprehensive account of Lunn's experiences as a Reuters war correspondent both in the field and in the cities of Vietnam during the years 1967–68. Like John Rowe, Lunn concentrates on the American war effort, giving little space to the largely peripheral activities of the Australian troops, although the guerrilla warfare skills of the Australian soldiers receive due acknowledgement. Lunn is especially critical of the manipulation and distortion of the news which occurred at the daily official briefings given by the US military spokesmen, irreverently termed the 'Five O'clock Follies', and of the inability of the American High Command to perceive the futility of its hopes of winning the war. Two interesting personal accounts of infantry operations by Australian troops are Terry Burstall's *The Soldiers' Story* (1986) and Gary McKay's *In Good Company* (1987). The highlight of Burstall's book is his description of the battle of Long Tan, in which he took part as a member of D Company, 6RAR, an engagement for which the company was awarded a Presidential Citation by Lyndon Johnson. McKay's book is a straightforward account of his tour of duty as a platoon commander during 1971. Burstall and McKay subsequently published additional books on Vietnam. Burstall's *A Soldier Returns* (1990) shows him as more sceptical about Australia's motives for being in Vietnam, the effectiveness of the Australian troops in Vietnam, and their treatment of the local population. McKay's *Vietnam Fragments* (1992) is a lengthy and wide-ranging oral history of Australians in the Vietnam War, based on interviews. Other collections of interviews and of brief personal accounts devoted to the Vietnam War include *Desperate Praise* (1982), edited by John J. Coe, *Memories of Vietnam* (1991), edited by Kenneth Maddock, and *A Decade of Dissent* (1992), edited by Greg Langley.

J.T. LAIRD

Waratah is the Aboriginal and common name for a bright flowering shrub of the genus *Telopea*, which grows in NSW, Victoria and Tasmania. The floral emblem of NSW, the waratah has figured frequently in Australian writing and has been particularly popular for its nationalist cachet in the titles of anthologies, collections, periodicals and school books.

WARD, Frederick ('Captain Thunderbolt') (1835–70), a bushranger who acquired legendary status, was born at Windsor, NSW, and worked as a horse-breaker and station hand in the Muswellbrook and Mudgee districts. In 1856 he was sentenced to ten years' imprisonment at Cockatoo Island for horse-stealing, received a ticket-of-leave four years later but was again found guilty of horse-stealing. In 1863 he escaped from Cockatoo Island with another prisoner, Frederick Brittain, probably assisted by his wife Mary Ann, a part-Aborigine also known as 'Yellow Long'. Ward carried out a series of armed robberies in the New England district 1865–70, at first with associates and later alone or with apprentice bushrangers. His success in eluding arrest was frequently attributed to his riding skills, although the ineptitude of the police undoubtedly contributed. Ward, now known as 'Thunderbolt' or 'Captain Thunderbolt', also achieved, apparently undeservedly, the altruistic reputation of a Robin Hood and of a gallant in his dealings with his women victims. He was finally shot at Uralla, NSW. One of his apprentices, William Monckton, subsequently published *Three Years with Thunderbolt* (1905), edited by Ambrose Pratt (q.v.), and Monckton's account forms part of an alternative version of the legend by Annie Rixon, *The Truth About Thunderbolt* (1940). Jack Bradshaw, however, who claimed to be personally acquainted with Ward, questioned parts of Monckton's account in his *The True History of the Australian Bushrangers* (?1924). The Thunderbolt legend has been celebrated in verse, drama, ballad and fiction; it is alluded to in the anonymous *Reminiscences of Australian Early Life by a Pioneer* (1893), and drawn on by J.M. Macdonald in his novel *Thunderbolt* (1894) and Francis Adams in his *John Webb's End* (1891); it is

celebrated in the anonymous ballads 'A Day's Ride' and 'Those Bould Bushrangers', and appears in Judith Wright's poem 'South of My Days' and Les Murray's 'At Thunderbolt's Grave in Uralla'. Ward's life has also been the subject of two popular films, *Thunderbolt* (1910) and *Captain Thunderbolt* (1953), both of which present him as a folk-hero. Annie Louisa Rixon wrote a fictionalised account of his life, *Thunderbolt* (1945), and two recent biographies are *Thunderbolt* (1987) by Bob Cummins and *A Ghost Called Thunderbolt* (1987) by Stephan Williams.

WARD, Glenyse (1949–), born Perth, was taken from her parents when a year old and placed in an orphanage; two years later she was taken to the Wandering Brook mission run by a German Roman Catholic order, where she received some education before employment in domestic duties. At 16 she was sent out into domestic service, working for a White farming family, named the Bigelows in her autobiography, who lived near Busselton. She describes the extremely insensitive treatment she received during this period and her spirited response in *Wandering Girl* (1987); assigned to the nameless status of a 'dark servant', she is also assigned a tin cup in place of the china used by her employers. Although she makes some sympathetic White friends, her escape is ultimately organised with the help of some Aboriginal friends from the mission. Ward's subsequent autobiography, *Unna You Fullas* (1991), describes her years in the mission; a graphic account of an institution which was as severely disciplined as an army barracks, *Unna You Fullas* is also sensitive to the values of the German nuns, foreign and inappropriate though they were. Ward also describes with some nostalgia the way that the children formed themselves into a tight family, preserving their slender memories and fragments of Aboriginal language, and contriving to make themselves a home in their emotionally barren environment.

WARD, Mrs Humphry, see **ARNOLD, Thomas**

WARD, Russel (1914–), born Adelaide, was professor of history 1967–79 and is now emeritus professor and deputy chancellor of the University of New England. After graduating from Adelaide University, he taught at secondary schools, served with the AIF and held a number of academic positions but failed during the 1950s to gain permanency as an academic because of his controversial political opinions. In 1983 the University of New England awarded him a D.Litt. for his published work and in 1986 he was made AM. He has written several socio-cultural, historical accounts of Australia, of which the most influential has been *The Australian Legend* (q.v., 1958). His other writings include an autobiography, *A Radical Life* (1988); three histories, *Australia* (1965, revised in 1982 as *Australia Since the Coming of Man*), *A Nation for a Continent: The History of Australia 1901–1975* (1977) and *Finding Australia: The History of Australia to 1821* (1987); and two well-illustrated and documented socio-cultural studies, with Peter O'Shaughnessy and Graeme Inson, *The Restless Years, Being Some Impressions of the Origin of* *the Australian* (1968) and, with Graeme Inson, *The Glorious Years of Australia Fair from the Birth of the Bulletin to Versailles* (1971); and, with John Robertson, three compilations of select documents in Australian social history titled *Such Was Life* (1969–86). He has also translated Edmond Marin la Meslée's *L'Australie Nouvelle* (1973) and edited *The Penguin Book of Australian Ballads* (1964).

'Ward Two', a poem sequence in eight parts by Francis Webb (q.v.), was first published in its entirety in Webb's volume *The Ghost of the Cock* (1964), although separate parts had been published in the *Bulletin* and *Meanjin* in 1962. The sequence is probably set in the male ward of the Parramatta Psychiatric Centre, where Webb was a patient in 1962. The stark hospital setting, the poet's own well-known mental illness, and the deep compassion and sensitivity of the poem, have contributed to make it one of Webb's best-known works. Central to the poem is the acknowledgement that only in the real world, even if that world is the seemingly crippled world of Ward Two, can any individual make a meaningful existence. The opening segment, 'Pneumo-Encephalograph' (a device to locate brain tumours), counterpoises the cold, clinically beautiful, scientific apparatus of psychiatry and the human agony that has brought it into being and in the service of which it functions with magnificent precision. Other sections of the poem describe the ward's inmates through the sensitive and understanding eyes of a fellow sufferer: the moronic Harry, writing his letter; the 'Old Timer', the 'small grey mendicant man', whose wistful plea for communication melts the poet into instant compassion; the Homosexual; and the Old Women who visit the ward on Sunday afternoons. In the poem's final segment, 'Wild Honey', where the poet watches a girl combing her golden hair, the apprehension of the beauty of that ordinary everyday action brings the recognition that in 'the tiny, the pitiable, meaningless and rare' lie the stars themselves – in 'sacred dishevelment' perhaps, but the stars nevertheless.

WARDELL, Robert, see *Australian* (1)

WARNECKE, George, see *Australian Women's Weekly*

'WARREGO, Paul', see **WENZ, Paul**

'Warrigal', spelt 'waregal', 'warragle', 'woregal' and 'worragul', was the Aboriginal word for the dingo (q.v.) or wild dog. Colonial poets such as Henry Kendall used the word in their verse rather than the more common but less poetic 'dingo'. Kendall's poem 'The Warrigal' carries a grudging note of admiration for the dog which, although 'fierce and fickle and strange', possesses determination, resourcefulness and cunning. The word was later used to denote anything wild and savage, especially an Aborigine. Examples of its use in this way are 'Rolf Boldrewood's' *Robbery Under Arms* (1888), where Warrigal is Starlight's Aboriginal associate, and *The Squatter's Dream* (1890),

where 'warrigul devils' is used to describe the Blacks. Wild horses are described as 'warrigals' or 'brumbies' in Gilbert Parker's *Round the Compass in Australia* (1892). Joseph Furphy's creation 'Warrigal Alf' Morris is the disguised bullock-driver in *Such is Life* (1903). The town of Warragul in western Gippsland, Victoria, derived its name from the plentiful wild dog population in the area when the settlement was formed about 1865.

'WARUNG, Price' (William Astley) (1855–1911), born Liverpool, England, was brought to Australia in 1859 and educated in Melbourne. He was an itinerant journalist 1875–90, when he settled in Sydney. His career peaked in the early 1890s, when he was the *Bulletin*'s most prolific contributor of short stories and was well known as a radical journalist and political commentator. After he broke with the *Bulletin*, he devoted himself to the labour and Federation movements, being editor of the *Australian Workman* in 1893 and organising secretary of the Bathurst People's Federal Convention in 1896; in 1897 he wrote for *Truth* and thereafter lived virtually as a recluse, his decline exacerbated by ill health and drug addiction.

'Warung's' interest in Australian history was aroused as a youth and he claimed to have spent twenty years researching the background for his stories, mainly of convict life, which were published in six series in the *Bulletin* 1890–94, and *Truth*; about half of these contributions were included in the volumes *Tales of the Convict System* (1892), *Tales of the Early Days* (1894), *Tales of the Old Regime and the Bullet of the Fated Ten* (1897), *Half-Crown Bob and Tales of the Riverine* (1898), based on his experiences at Echuca 1876–78, and *Tales of the Isle of Death (Norfolk Island)* (1898). 'Warung's' best-known work includes the imaginative reconstruction of convict Ring freemasonry in 'The Bullet of the Fated Ten' and 'Secret Society of the Ring'. His indictment of the British administrators of 'the System' paralleled his strong early support of republicanism, added valuable literary fuel to the anti-imperialist fire of J.F. Archibald, and played a significant part in consolidating the legend that the convicts were more sinned against than sinning. Some of his lesser-known comic stories are included in *Tales of the Convict System* (1975), ed. Barry Andrews, who also wrote the biographical and critical study *Price Warung (William Astley)* (1976). See Convict in Australian Literature.

Wasters, The, a play by A.H. Adams (q.v.), was first produced in 1910 and published in 1914. Reminiscent of Ibsen's *A Doll's House*, the drama explores the position of women via the relationship between John Dangar, a man exclusively and wastefully dedicated to his business, and his neglected wife Baby.

Watch Tower, The, a novel by Elizabeth Harrower (q.v.), was published in 1966. After the early death of their father, Laura and Clare Vaizey find that their opportunities narrow. Their unconcerned, chronically lazy mother, Stella, removes them from boarding-school to live with her in a Sydney flat, arranges for Laura to attend business college and enrols the 9-year-old Clare in the local school. Bound by their duties at home and at school or work, the girls have no outside interests or friends and even the outbreak of the Second World War scarcely touches them. Laura becomes increasingly useful to her employer, the businessman Felix Shaw. He is a restless individual, apparently deliberately unpleasant except with the succession of young men whose goodwill he vainly attempts to buy. When Stella abruptly decides to leave for England, Felix casually proposes marriage to Laura although their relationship so far has been a business one. He buys a beautiful house at Neutral Bay, which Laura persuades herself is a guarantee of happiness. Felix's behaviour, enigmatic and unpredictable at best, rapidly deteriorates to the level of manic violence. For Clare he comes close to the Bluebeard figurine given to him by one of his reluctant protégés, Peter Trotter. Laura, working harder than ever, although now she is unpaid, desperately tries to propitiate him, frequently sacrificing Clare's feelings in the process. As she grows older, Clare, who is both participant and detached observer, becomes aware of the 'collusion' in the situation: 'There was nothing not depraved, perverted. There was no feeling of sufficient grace to earn the august name of suffering.' Nevertheless, pity for her sister binds her to their shared life. Felix, meanwhile, delights in all forms of psychological cruelty as well as physical violence and deliberately cultivates an atmosphere of uncertainty, selling both house and businesses as the mood takes him. Finally, years later, the arrival of another unfortunate protégé, a Dutch refugee called Bernard, provides Clare with such a positive experience of usefulness that she finds the spirit to abandon the Shaw household. Although she elects to find her destiny alone, she is grateful to Bernard: 'Because of him that futile, wasted, lacerated thing behind her – her life – was transmitted into an apprenticeship of infinite worth.'

Watcher on the Cast-Iron Balcony, The, the first volume of an autobiographical trilogy by Hal Porter (q.v.), was published in 1963. His early years at Kensington, Melbourne, 1911–17, are dominated by his keen, sensuous, detailed awareness of his material surroundings and by his consciousness of his parents as simple fatherly and motherly essences whom he implicitly trusts. After his family moves to Bairnsdale, Gippsland, however, when he is 6, he becomes far more aware of his mother's distinctive qualities, her creative vitality, humour and courage. He attends first the primary school, State School 754, and then Bairnsdale High School, where he does well, avoids sport, discovers literature, and makes a variety of friends. He suffers mild bereavements, falls in and out of love, enjoys the frequent gatherings of his mother's relations, responds insensibly to the political events of the time and profoundly to the familiar rhythms of small-town life between the wars and the lavishness of the Gippsland landscape. By 1927 he is 16, a cadet reporter on the *Bairnsdale Advertiser* and anxious to escape home, which now houses six children, and experience city life. After getting a job as junior

teacher in a state school at Williamstown, he leaves to spend the next crowded eighteen months teaching schoolchildren, going to the theatre, making another set of friends, studying drawing at Melbourne National Gallery and acting under the tutelage of Gregan McMahon. But an 'avalanche' of suffering begins with an unfortunate love affair with an older teacher, the involvement of two of his pupils in a fatal accident, and culminates in the sudden death of his mother which he is called home to witness.

WATEN, Judah (1911–85) was born in Odessa, Russia, into a Jewish family which settled in 1914 in a small town in WA, where his father earned a living as a hawker. In 1926 the family moved to Melbourne. Waten had a variety of occupations ranging from kitchen hand to schoolteacher but his paramount interests were writing and politics. In 1931–33 he visited Europe and then England, where he became involved in the Unemployed Workers' Movement, and served a three-month term in Wormwood Scrubs prison as a result of his political activities. A dedicated communist, he had a difficult relationship with the Communist Party of Australia and eventually became a member of the pro-Soviet segment. He was also a member of the Realist Writers group and had close connections with overseas writers, especially in the USSR. In 1985 he was posthumously awarded the Patrick White Award. Prominent in the FAW and other literary organisations, he was one of the founding members of the Literature Board 1973–74 and was made AM in 1979.

Waten began writing early but failed at first to find his true direction because of his enthusiasm for such writers as James Joyce, John Dos Passos and Michael Gold. In the 1940s, however, he turned to his childhood for inspiration and began the series of short stories that culminated in the popular collection *Alien Son* (q.v., 1952). Some of his novels have been translated into other languages and several of his stories have appeared in overseas anthologies.

Waten wrote seven novels, *The Unbending* (1954), *Shares in Murder* (1957), *Time of Conflict* (1961), *Distant Land* (1964), *Season of Youth* (1966), *So Far No Further* (1971) and *Scenes of Revolutionary Life* (1982); a collection of impressions of childhood experiences, *Alien Son* (1952), and another of autobiographical essays and short stories, *Love and Rebellion* (1978); an account of a visit to the former Soviet Union, which also contains some autobiography, *From Odessa to Odessa* (1969); and a brief history of the Depression years in Australia, 1929–39, in the *Australia since the Camera* series (1971). He also wrote a book for children, *Bottle-O!* (1973); co-edited two collections of short stories, with V.G. O'Connor, *Twenty Great Australian Stories* (1946) and, with Stephen Murray-Smith, *Classic Australian Short Stories* (1974); and translated a book by the Jewish writer Herz Bergner, *Between Sky and Sea* (1946).

Waten described his *Alien Son* cycle, a series of loosely connected stories dealing with the experiences of a European Jewish migrant family in Australia at the time of the First World War, as 'a kind of novel without architecture'. In these plotless sketches, humour and pathos, detachment and sympathy, psychological insight and social detail blend to evoke the flavour of Jewish life. Australian society, meanwhile, perceived as alien and hostile but necessary by the older Jews, becomes more and more an exciting challenge for the children. *The Unbending*, also a study of a Jewish migrant family of the same period, retains the solidity and resonance of *Alien Son*, although here the family is presented in more detail, and Australian political themes are given more prominence. Waten's representations of the strong-willed, courageous Hannah Kochansky and her romantic, eternally optimistic husband Solomon, are the most compelling of his studies of Jewish parents. Reactions to his treatment of the local political struggle have varied widely, however. *Shares in Murder* is not a detective thriller as its title and subject suggest, but a shrewd, documentary-type exploration of human corruption and police psychology. *Time of Conflict*, the story of a young Australian's inevitable evolution into a communist, achieves a sense of felt life in the descriptions of the hero's early hardships, but some critics have found that concentration on Communist Party politics from the 1930s to the 1950s weakens some of the novel's fabric. *Distant Land* is a return to the Jewish migrant theme, although this time the action extends from before the First World War to the late 1940s. In *Season of Youth* Waten deals with an Australian working-class boy with literary ambitions who attempts to find encouragement in the bohemian circles of Melbourne in the 1930s. *So Far No Further*, a novel with a contemporary setting, deals with the experiences of Jewish and Italian post-war migrants and the inevitable gap between parents and grown children. *Scenes of Revolutionary Life* views the 1930s Depression through the eyes of a communist activist and aspiring writer. The National Library of Australia has published a guide to its holdings of Waten's papers (1976). Following his death in 1985 the annual Judah Waten Story Writing Competition, sponsored partly by the Melbourne PEN club, was inaugurated.

Water under the Bridge, a novel by Sumner Locke Elliot (q.v.), was published in 1977 and produced as a television series in 1980. The celebrations following the opening of the Sydney Harbour Bridge in 1932 dominate the beginning of the story and bring together some of the various individuals whose destinies are intertwined: the wealthy Mazzini family; the unpleasant opportunist Archie Ewers; the youthful Neil Atkins, the novel's central character; the journalist and ex-country girl Maggie McGhee; the English teacher and critic T.C. Shallicott; and two sisters, who seem doomed to spinsterhood in Mosman, Ila and Geraldine Flagg. Neil is drawn into the Mazzinis' orbit by the fact that he goes to school with their son Ben and is assumed to be his friend, and by his fascination with their beautiful, restless daughter Carrie. Unknown to him, his foster mother, Shasta Davies, has earlier had a serious affair with the father, Luigi Mazzini. Others are also drawn to the family: Geraldine Flagg desperately but futilely attempts to break out of suburban stagnation and form a relationship with the disturbed Ben; Shallicott, who becomes the generous Maggie's lover, is bound by a formal commitment to Honor Mazzini and dies in a plane crash on his way to keep his promise; Maggie loses first Shallicott and then Neil to the Mazzinis, although at the close of the novel in 1973 there are suggestions that she will finally win Neil. Archie Ewers, handicapped by his unconscious vulgarity, plays a peripheral role for the most part, but at one point his vengeful interference costs one of Maggie's friends, Don Brandywine, his life. The Mazzinis become a subject of national gossip when the parents are brutally attacked by an unknown assailant, Luigi dying as a result and Mrs Mazzini surviving only to lead a vegetable existence. Later, after Ben's death, it emerges that the tragedy was of their own making and that Ben, tortured by the discovery that Luigi was not his father, had been the assailant. Contrasting with the glamour, melodrama and unreality of the Mazzinis is the earthy reality of Neil's ambivalent relationship with Shasta. Dominated by her pity for the infant Neil after his parents' death, Shasta had been forced to abandon her work and her prospects of a permanent relationship to care for him. Now, in impoverished middle age, she alienates him with her violent oscillations between oppressive care and hysterical recriminations; at the same time she holds him by her jaunty heroism, her suffering, integrity and generosity. After a long period of acrimonious separation following Neil's decision to live with Carrie Mazzini, their original relationship is reversed when she suffers a stroke. Finally, when Neil is offered an acting opportunity in London, he is forced to leave her in a nursing home, although she contrives to have the last word. The novel closes with Neil's return to Australia in 1973 as a famous actor, his last meeting with Carrie and his reunion with Maggie.

WATKINS, Griffith (1930–69), born Christchurch, NZ, came to WA at the age of 6. Educated at the University of WA, he taught art at secondary school and at Claremont Teachers College. He also worked as a gold-miner and stockman in order to gain copy. From the late 1950s he published poetry and short stories in numerous periodicals and won several awards including the *Weekend News* Short Story Competition, the UWA Simpson Prize and the 1966 Henry Lawson Prize for poetry. In 1969 he took his own life by drowning. In 1967 his novel *The Pleasure Bird* was published and in 1990 a selection of his poetry and fiction, *God in the Afternoon*, selected and edited by Peter Jefferey.

WATLING, Thomas (1762–?), born Scotland, received a good education, especially in art. In 1788 he was charged with forgery and in 1791 was transported to NSW, where he was assigned to the surgeon-general and naturalist John White. Letters to his aunt, which Watling had begun at Cape Town and continued in the Colony and which were critical of various aspects of the administration, were published in 1794 as *Letters from an Exile at Botany-Bay*. In 1797 he was given an absolute pardon and lived for a time in Calcutta, where he earned a living as a miniature painter, before returning to Scotland. Some of his work, including landscapes, natural history drawings and studies of Aborigines, has survived in the so-called Watling Collection, held in the British Museum. David Campbell's poem 'The Watling Collection' describes his thoughts as he examines 'these first moving records' of the Colony, which Watling viewed as a place where 'little good' would come from 'the coupling of rogue and whore'.

WATSON, Elliot Lovegood Grant (1885–1970) was born at Staines, Middlesex, the son of a barrister who died young. Brought up mainly by his mother, Watson was influenced by her passion for Darwinism and read biology at the University of Cambridge. Watson visited Australia three times, in 1887 with his mother who was recuperating from the death of his younger brother, in 1910–11 and in 1912. On his second visit he was a member of a scientific expedition led by the anthropologist Alfred Radcliffe-Brown, who intended to study the marriage customs of the Aborigines in north-western Australia. Daisy Bates and a Swedish cook, Louis Olsen, were the only other European members of the party. With Brown, Grant Watson travelled to the Upper Murchison, Bernier Island and the Gascoyne, an experience which profoundly affected his later life and turned him towards the writing of fiction. In his autobiography, *But To What Purpose* (1946), he describes the impact of the desert and the Aboriginal culture on his European consciousness. Already unsettled in his own culture by his reading of Nietzsche, Ibsen, Jacobsen, Conrad and Hardy, and dissatisfied with mechanistic explanations of the world, Grant Watson felt that his European conventions suffered 'an objective devaluation' in Australia: 'It was in a way a unique experience, not so much understood and valued at the time, but valued and partly understood *afterwards*. It had lifted me, or perhaps sunk me, above or below the orthodox horizon of vision.' From this experience sprang his interest in psychology, especially in the work of Jung and Steiner; his fascination with what he called 'the great Shadow', the problem of evil; and his commitment to what he termed 'the philosophy of the fringe', the belief that 'in the centres of civilisation life was withering away' and that 'human life was centripetal, having its sources at the circumference, and that it drove inward towards congestion and death'.

The author of over thirty books, including novels, works on natural history, essays and some poetry, Grant Watson wrote six novels with Australian settings, *Where Bonds Are Loosed* (1914), *The Mainland* (1917), *The Desert Horizon* (1923), *Daimon* (1925), *The Partners* under the pseudonym 'John Lovegood' (1933), and *The Nun and the Bandit* (1935, reprinted 1993). His collection of short stories *Innocent Desires* (1924) includes several with Australian settings, as well as his first piece of fiction, a story titled 'Out There', which deals with European–Aboriginal relations and which he contributed to the *English Review* in 1913. *Journey under the Southern Stars* (1968) and *Departures*

(1948) describe some of the outward events of his visit to Australia which he had dealt with earlier in *But to What Purpose*. Familiar with a number of established writers and editors such as Edward Thomas, Austin Harrison, Muriel Draper, Havelock Ellis and Norman Douglas, Grant Watson also knew Joseph Conrad, who made copious critical comments on the manuscript of *Where Bonds Are Loosed*.

Although Grant Watson was one of the earliest writers of fiction to deal with the Aboriginal culture without ethnocentric prejudice, *Where Bonds Are Loosed* is concerned more with relations between European characters on a remote Australian island, based on his experience on the islands of Bernier and Dorré, than with Aboriginal life. For the central character, Sherwin, however, life takes on some of the primitive freedom experienced by the Aborigines. In *The Mainland*, a sequel to *Where Bonds Are Loosed*, Grant Watson develops the theme of the challenging emptiness, the spiritual purity of the desert, and the entangling complexities of civilisation. *The Desert Horizon* and *Daimon*, its continuation, engage more rigorously with the idea of solitude as either ennobling or degrading. Interwoven through the life of the central character, Martin O'Brien, is the mystical attraction of the desert, which he experienced as a child and continues to feel as an 'inner exaltation' and even as 'the core of his life'. Martin gives up his attraction to the desert for the sake of his wife Maggie, but returns to it as an old man; Maggie, aware now that the desert is not evil but is beyond good and evil and expresses the mysterious, uncomprehended, non-human part of life, follows her husband's solitary search and is reunited with him before they both die. *The Partners* deals more sparingly and ironically with a similar concept of the desert as amoral and non-human; *The Nun and the Bandit*, which has an even simpler plot and a shorter time-span, develops further Grant Watson's ideas on the co-existence and co-determination of good and evil that only the desert lays bare.

Grant Watson's novels are uneven and often overweighted with ideas, although enlivened by his sensitive response to the WA landscape. Historically anomalous, they are interesting in that they foreshadow themes used by later novelists; his feeling for the metaphysical implications of the Australian desert links him to Randolph Stow and Patrick White, his sympathy for the Aboriginal culture to Xavier Herbert, and his sensitivity to the experience of women in a predominantly male environment to contemporary feminist writers. His radical scientific ideas, and in particular his questioning of Darwinist dogma, which were well ahead of his time, have now come to the fore; some of his scientific articles and extracts from *But to What Purpose* and *Departures* are included in the collection edited by Dorothy Green, *Descent of Spirit* (1990); his *The Mystery of Physical Life* (1964, reprinted 1992) is based on his scientific studies and experiences among the Aboriginal people of north-western Australia. Paul Cox has produced two films, loosely based on Grant Watson's novels, *The Nun and the Bandit* and *Exile*.

WATSON, Kathleen (1870–1926) was born in Wales and came to Australia as a young woman. The author of three novels, *The Gaiety of Fatma* (1906), *The House of Broken Dreams* (1908) and *Henriette Says!* (1921), and two collections of prose pieces, *Litanies of Life* (1897) and *Later Litanies* (1913), she wrote on romantic or sentimental themes. Her favourite mood is a stoical nostalgia; her favourite subjects are ill-fated love, death, exile, loneliness, altruism and motherhood. Her *Litanies* record the individual, regretful reflections of a group of lonely women; *The House of Broken Dreams* focuses on the emotional experience of a mother whose only son seems marked for tragedy from the outset; *The Gaiety of Fatma* recounts the experiences and extraordinary charity of a Franco-Arab girl who marries a Scottish baron shortly before his death, and visits London and Scotland before devoting herself to the Algerian poor. Watson is also represented in *Melba's Gift Book* (1915).

Wattle was the popular name given to the *Acacia* genus of plants found in abundance in the Colony by the early settlers. They brought with them from England the 'wattle and daub' method of building shelters, i.e. using long pliant twigs known as 'wattles', plastered over with mud. The acacia provided a ready source of such twigs, hence were named 'wattles'. The presence of the wattle in literature is noted as early as Adam Lindsay Gordon's lines 'In the spring when the wattle gold trembles/ Twixt shadow and shine' and Henry Kendall's phrase 'yellow-haired September'. The popularity of the wattle as an Australian motif is seen in its widespread use in the titles of early Australian books of verse and anthologies, e.g. George Wright's *Wattle Blossom* (1857), *Wattle Blossom. An Australian Annual* (1881), edited by Percy Sinnett, and *Oak-bough and Wattle-Blossom* (1888), edited by A. Patchett Martin. The wattle's acceptance as a national emblem is evident in Henry Lawson's poem 'Waratah and Wattle', and in his dire prediction that if Australian society did not become more egalitarian, 'blood should stain the wattle'. Leslie Haylen wrote the play *Blood on the Wattle* (1948), and one of David Campbell's most memorable brief poems is 'Under Wattles'. The wattle blossom is featured on the Australian coat of arms. A sprig of wattle was laid on the coffin of the Unknown Australian Soldier by the Governor-General at the entombment ceremony at the Australian War Memorial, 11 November 1993.

'Wayback', a synonym for 'outback', refers to the parts of Australia remote from settlement; it has also come to refer to the inhabitants of those areas. Examples of the usage of 'wayback' include *The Wayback* (1926), Sarah Musgrave's account of pioneering life in south-western NSW, and the Waybacks, a family of unsophisticated rural folk in a series of novels by Henry Fletcher. 'Wayback' is also commonly used in Australia as an instruction to dogs working sheep and cattle, as in Merv Lilley's autobiographical *Git Away Back!* (1983).

Ways of Many Waters, The (1899), the first volume of verse by E.J. Brady (q.v.), established him as Australia's balladist of the sea. John Masefield praised the poems as 'the best yet written about the merchant sailor and the man of war's man'. Notable poems include 'Lost and Given Over', 'Tallow and Hides', 'The Great Gray Water' and the title poem, 'The Ways of Many Waters'.

We of the Never-Never (1908) is a factual account of thirteen months spent by the author, Jeannie Gunn (q.v.), and her husband, Aeneas (1862–1903), at the Elsey cattle station on the Roper River about 500 kilometres south of Darwin. The narrative commences in January 1902 with the couple at Darwin about to travel to the Elsey, where Aeneas is to become manager. In spite of spirited attempts by the station workers to prevent an Unknown Woman ('probably a snorter') from intruding into their all-male world, Jeannie Gunn battles on horseback through the hazards of the wet season to the Elsey. 'A nice little place', the Elsey is of undisclosed extent, but its front gate is 70 kilometres from the homestead. The homestead turns out to be 'mostly verandahs and promises' but in the months that follow it is made more habitable through the intermittent exertions of an itinerant bush carpenter, Johnny. Other vexations to the 'little missus' are the Aboriginal girl servants, who quickly 'knock up longa work', and a recalcitrant Chinese cook, Sam. The narrative follows the station activities throughout the year culminating in the celebration of the Gunn's first Christmas there. The episodic plot is primarily a device to illustrate the characters, notable among whom are the Sanguine Scot, a bushman of the old type, 'full of old theories, old faiths and old prejudices', whose one fear is that the onward march of civilisation will not leave 'enough bush to bury a man in'; the Quiet Stockman, 'six foot two of bone and muscle' but sparing of speech; the Dandy, 'only a dandy in his love of sweet clean clothes and orderly surroundings', and with a capacity 'for finding something decent in everybody'; the Fizzer, the outback mailman who makes his hazardous trips to the far-flung stations to give them eight mails a year; Cheon, the new Chinese cook, 'the jolliest old josser' in the territory; and the Maluka (Aeneas Gunn), 'the best boss that a man ever struck'. The idyll ends suddenly and tragically: Gunn dies of malarial dysentery in March 1903 and Jeannie Gunn returns to civilisation. *We of the Never Never* has sold over a million copies and has been read by generations of Australian schoolchildren. A film of the book was screened in 1982. The homestead site at the Elsey is now a national reserve. The recent publication of Aboriginal testimony relating to the Elsey area has necessitated a revisionist assessment of the native of *We of The Never-Never* and acknowledgement of its unconscious racism.

We Took Their Orders and Are Dead: An Anti-War Anthology (1971), edited by Ros Cheney, David Malouf, Michael Wilding and Shirley Cass, includes work by numerous Australian poets and prose-writers and was compiled as a protest at Australia's military involvement in the Vietnam War with the USA. The title is taken from a line of A.D. Hope's poem 'Inscription for Any War'. See also War Literature.

WEARNE, Alan (1948–), born Melbourne, has been part of the Australian poetry scene since the late 1960s when he was involved in the Monash poetry readings which helped formulate new directions for Australian poetry. Although he was included in John Tranter's anthology *The New Australian Poetry* (1979), Wearne has not been as widely anthologised as others in the New Poetry movement. He published two small books of verse, *Public Relations* (1972) in the Gargoyle Poets series and *New Devil New Parish* (1976) in the UQP Paperback Poets series. The latter included a verse novella, *Out Here*, which indicated the literary path that Wearne was soon to follow with conspicuous success. Commissioned in 1978 by Penguin to write a verse novel on the strength of one chapter completed out of a projected ten, Wearne laboured for eight years to produce the epic work *The Nightmarkets* (1986). An instant success, it won both the NBC Banjo Award and the Australian Literature Society's Gold Medal in 1987. Although subtitled 'a novel', *The Nightmarkets* virtually defies plot summation. The 'action' is presented in ten chapters – dramatic monologues by six of the major characters of the book. Ian Metcalfe, in more central focus than most of the other characters, is a pot-smoking, lazy, part-time public servant, student, lover, and so-called 'investigative' journalist, who guides the reader into the Melbourne of the middle 1960s and then through to 1980. In the opening chapter he recounts his brother Robert's conscientious objection to the Vietnam War and his six months on a prison farm; the euphoria of Labor's return under Whitlam in 1972; the sacking of the Whitlam government in 1975; the nation 'post-Gough'; and the relapse of many of the 1960s radicals into apathy, conservatism or overseas wanderings. Metcalfe tells also of his two girl-friends – first Sue Dobson, then 18 and the pair of them 'apprentice lovers', and, later, Allison. Metcalfe narrates two other chapters (2 and 4) and the concluding one; his monologues thus provide the central theme around which the other narrators and their stories ebb and flow. Sue Dobson, now a journalist, gives her account of the same years, first in Chapter 2, 'The Bistro Variations', and then in Chapter 6, 'Climbing up the Ladder of Love', the two longest chapters of the book. Sue's 1960s radicalism and 1970s–80s feminism are the most deeply held attitudes of all the characters but even they manage to get temporarily sidelined while she becomes involved with John McTaggart, one-time federal Liberal MP and now founder of the New Progress Party. McTaggart narrates one chapter, 'After the Tribe', as does his mother, the tough, amiable old Liberal party campaigner Elise McTaggart. Ian's brother Robert, seeking a political career as Labor member for O'Dowd, also has a chapter. The prostitute hostess Terri, from the Crystal Palace Health Spa and Businessman's Club, is also a narrator and central to the action. The most honest, likeable and realistic of all the characters, she exposes the shortcomings of

the others. Deliberate stereotypes of the period, the characters are exuberantly portrayed, especially by means of their speech patterns – 'strine', colloquial Australianisms, drug and dope 'lingo'. Intensely familiar with the personality of Melbourne, *The Nightmarkets* has been likened to Joyce's *Ulysses*, not only because of its stream-of-consciousness technique but also because of its sense of place and its linking of locality, history, language and social mores.

WEBB, Beatrice (1858–1943) and **WEBB, Sidney** (1859–1947), the Fabian writers and social reformers, visited Australia in 1898. Their observations of Australian society proved to be surprisingly inaccurate from a sociological point of view; although they met numerous public men, politicians, educationists and writers, they appear to have been handicapped by their English preconceptions and their total ignorance of Australian issues, circumstances and history. Their Australian diary, edited by A.G. Austin and titled *The Webbs' Australian Diary 1898* (1965), is an important addition to knowledge of the Webbs rather than of Australia.

WEBB, Francis (1925–73) was born Francis Charles Webb-Wagg in Adelaide; after the death of his mother in 1927 he was raised in Sydney by his paternal grandparents (Webb) from whom he gained his interest in books, music, sailing and the seas. He had a reasonably happy and trouble-free childhood and adolescence and served with the RAAF 1943–45. He trained as a wireless air gunner in Canada but did not see action in the war. In 1946 he began an arts course at the University of Sydney but abandoned it in 1947 to return to Canada, where he was employed as a publisher's reader. In 1949 he went from Canada to England, where he suffered his first mental breakdown. He returned to Australia in 1950, spent the years 1953–59 in England, much of the time in hospitals in Birmingham and Norfolk, and came back to Australia in 1960. Throughout the 1960s Webb struggled unavailingly against schizophrenia and spent most of the decade in mental institutions in NSW and Victoria.

Webb's published works are *A Drum for Ben Boyd* (1948), *Leichhardt in Theatre* (1952), *Birthday* (1953), *Socrates and Other Poems* (1961), and *The Ghost of the Cock* (1964). His *Collected Poems* was published in 1969. 'A Drum for Ben Boyd' (q.v.), first published in the *Bulletin* (1946), is a long poem about the Scottish merchant-entrepreneur Benjamin Boyd. Webb also uses a heroic figure in the poem 'Leichhardt in Theatre' (q.v.), which was published in the *Bulletin* (1947), an abridged version appearing in his second volume of poetry in 1952. That volume, *Leichhardt in Theatre*, contains some of Webb's most significant shorter verse, e.g. 'Morgan's Country', 'Melville at Woods Hole', 'Dawn Wind on the Islands', 'On First Hearing a Cuckoo' and 'A View of Montreal'. *Birthday* (1953) takes its title from his radio verse play 'Birthday' about the final days of Adolf Hitler in the bunker in Berlin; it also contains the sequence of poems 'The Canticle' (q.v.), dealing with St Francis of Assisi, and several fine individual pieces, e.g. 'Galston' and 'End of the

Picnic'. Most of the poems of Webb's next volume, *Socrates and Other Poems* (1961), had been written in Norfolk, England, following a long period of illness and recuperation during the late 1950s. Dedicated to Dr F.W. Klinghardt, who had supervised his recovery, and to the Australian poet David Campbell, who had much to do with his subsequent return to Australia, *Socrates* contains the most mature and assured of Webb's poetry, including his new concept of the artist's function (which W.D. Ashcroft has termed 'meditative purposefulness'). *Socrates* contains Webb's chief lyric poems, e.g. 'Bells of St. Peter Mancroft' and 'Five Days Old', and some of his most technically innovative and skilfully crafted verses, e.g. 'The Yellowhammer', 'Light' and 'Mousehold Heath'. *Socrates* also includes the fourteen-verse sequence 'Eyre All Alone' (q.v.), Webb's finest analysis of a heroic figure, in this case the Australian explorer Edward John Eyre. Webb's mental ordeals are revealed in such poems as 'The Brain-washers', 'Hospital Night' and 'A Death at Winson Green'. In the title poem, a dramatic monologue by Socrates just before his death, there is an unusual and impressive air of acceptance of the order of things; it reflects perhaps one of his few brief periods of remission.

> ... I front the grieving
> Song of the long spear that is your lifted voice
> And coolly read the outcome in your eye, my star.

Webb's final volume, *The Ghost of the Cock* (1964), was compiled largely from his unpublished poems written before his admission to Callan Park hospital in the early 1960s. The title piece is a radio verse play in three acts, to be accompanied by the scherzos of Bruckner's ninth and seventh symphonies, in which Michael and Tobias descend to earth intending to 'ferry to eternity' the sole human survivors (a man and a woman) of a nuclear war. Accused by the surviving animal inhabitants of cruelty and selfishness, the humans are forgiven and saved only by the intercession of the cock. The last volume contains two of Webb's finest poetic achievements, 'Ward Two' (q.v.), a powerful and moving sequence set in the Parramatta psychiatric centre, and 'Around Costessy', a sequence centred on the Norfolk village of Costessy and conveying impressions of the Norfolk countryside. In the seventh part of 'Around Costessy', i.e. 'In Memoriam: Anthony Sandys, 1806–1883', Webb again defines the function of the creative artist. Webb's long-standing attraction to music, glimpsed in the earlier 'Tallis to Vaughan Williams' in *Birthday*, is indicated more strongly in this volume in 'Gustave Mahler' and 'Brahms at Bruckner's Funeral'. The *Collected Poems*, with a preface by Sir Herbert Read, adds a section 'Early Poems 1942–1948' to those volumes already mentioned. Important among Webb's uncollected poems is 'Lament for St. Maria Goretti', published in *Poetry Australia* (1973).

Francis Webb has drawn his greatest commendations from fellow poets: he was posthumously given the Christopher Brennan Award by the FAW. The most-publicised estimation of him is Sir Herbert Read's judgement that he is not inferior to Rilke,

Eliot, Pasternak and Robert Lowell. Similar high opinions came from Douglas Stewart, who maintained that in his profoundly original writing Webb created 'a new language ... a new imagery'. David Campbell insisted that Webb 'went higher than any other poet who has ever written in Australia'. Bruce Beaver sees the 'touch of genius' in Webb's capacity to 'take the earth-bound and spiritualise it, turning it into a holy fire of music'. Other reactions to the total body of Webb's poetry have been ambivalent. The earlier poetry, in which historical figures such as Boyd and Leichhardt are represented, has been generally well received, *A Drum for Ben Boyd* winning the 1948 Grace Leven Prize for poetry. In the later extremely complex poetry the obsessively religious nature of his personal response to experience, the brilliance of his language and intensity of imagery have combined to categorise him as an extraordinarily gifted, though esoteric and somewhat inaccessible poet. Something of a cult-figure since his death, Webb exercised considerable influence in the development of some of the new attitudes that spread through Australian poetry in the late 1960s and 1970s. The September 1975 number of *Poetry Australia* is a Francis Webb commemorative issue. Michael Griffith and James McGlade published an annotated collection of Webb's work, *Cap and Bells: The Poetry of Francis Webb* (1991) and Griffith also wrote *God's Fool: The Life and Poetry of Francis Webb* (1991). A collection of seminar papers which contains biographical information, *Francis Webb – Poet and Patient*, was published in 1983.

WEEKES, Cora Anna, born England, left with her husband for the USA in 1857 and started a literary paper in Texas, the *Southern Age*, under the patronage of Governor Pease and the Bishop of Texas. After the paper failed to prosper, she established the *Athenaeum* in San Francisco but was attacked in rival papers as an impostor and plagiarist. She and her husband moved to Sydney, where in July 1858 she initiated and edited an Australian magazine, the *Spectator: Journal of Literature and Art*, personally soliciting subscriptions from business firms in Melbourne and Sydney. The attacks she had suffered in San Francisco were taken up by the press in Sydney and Melbourne and included claims that the Weekes had surreptitiously left the USA after obtaining a large amount of money in subscriptions and leaving behind a number of debts. George W. Weekes refuted the claims and Cora Weekes published a spirited defence of women's right to employment in the fourth issue of the magazine. The magazine failed to appear after January 1859 and its editor's further career is unknown. Although the *Spectator* published some mediocre material, it included some well-reasoned and forcefully expressed articles on contemporary issues, including Cora Weekes's feminist lecture 'Female Heroism', probably the first to be given in Australia by a woman. 'Female Heroism' is reprinted in *Colonial Voices* (1989), edited by Elizabeth Webby, and Cora Weekes's Australian career is described by Patricia Clarke in *Pen Portraits* (1988).

WEIR, Peter, see **Gallipoli; Science Fiction**

Well Dressed Explorer, The, a novel by Thea Ast-ley (q.v.), was published in 1962 and was co-winner of the Miles Franklin Award. It is a close, chronological study of a journalist, George Brewster, a supreme ego-tist with an insatiable appetite for sexual adventure. A practised charmer, with as wide a repertoire of appro-priate roles and emotions as of journalistic clichés, he creates general destruction by instinctively exploiting relationships. He remains, throughout, engagingly oblivious of his shallow self-absorption.

WELLER, Archie (Irving Kirkwood, Kirk Weller) (1957–), who also uses the pseudonym 'R. Chee', born Perth, WA, grew up on an isolated farm and spent eight years in a boarding school. He has worked in a variety of occupations, as a farm and wharf labourer, stablehand, printer, gardener and rouse-about. He spent a period as writer-in-residence at the ANU in 1984. Weller's main work, the novel *The Day of the Dog*, was first published in 1981 and won the WA Fiction Week Award in 1982. It was also made into a film and was republished in 1991 to coincide with that film. Set in the twilight world of alcohol, sex and crime that seems, according to Weller, to be the inevi-table habitat of Aborigines and part-Aborigines, *The Day of the Dog* has as its central character the young part-Aborigine Doug Dooligan, who has recently been released from a stint in Fremantle prison. Although intent on pursuing a normal life, Doug, from his first day of freedom, is drawn back into his old brutalising milieu of violent young petty crimi-nals, alcohol and promiscuous sex, compounded by the lack of opportunities for self-improvement and White prejudice, especially from White police. Doug has a brief but erratic period of work, both in the city and later on his brother-in-law's farm, but is eventu-ally persuaded (when drunk) to join his mates in a robbery that goes wrong, resulting in the murder of a storekeeper's wife. Weller's other significant works of fiction are the stories collected in *Going Home* (1986), which includes nine short stories and a novella, 'Cooley'. The title story tells of young Aboriginal footballer and artist Billy Woodward, returning on his twenty-first birthday to the camp where he grew up and where his family, whom he had shunned for the past few years, still lives. The old environment of al-cohol and crime catches up with him and, although innocent, he is implicated in a robbery in the nearby town. It is in the novella 'Cooley' that much of the blame for Aboriginal problems is sheeted home to the White community which begins its persistent degra-dation of the Black protagonist when he is bullied by White boys in the school yard as a 6-year-old. Cooley, unable to cope with the years of humiliation and prejudice, takes his gun and seeks his own justice, but is ultimately killed himself. As Weller says, if you are 'born a half-caste' you 'die a half-caste . . . that's life boy'. Like much of Weller's fiction the story of Cooley is that of 'a small-town half-caste who tried to raise himself out of the dirt and who was kicked back down again'.

Weller has won several awards for his short stories, e.g. a National Short Story competition in 1977 for 'Dead Dingo' and in 1979 for 'Going Home'; McGregor literary awards in 1980 for 'Sandcastles' and in 1982 for 'Fish and Chips' (the last-named included in *Going Home*); the FAW Lyndall Hadow-Donald Stuart Award in 1984 for 'Storm' and the ABC Award in 1988 for 'Frankie My Man'. He also won the Pa-tricia Weickhardt Award for an Aboriginal writer in 1983. With Colleen Glass he compiled *Us Fellas* (1988), an anthology of Aboriginal writing. His other works include the plays 'Sunset and Shadows' (1989) and 'Nidjera' (1990); the films *Tilt* (with Duan Crozier, 1978) and *The Day of the Dog* (with James Ricketson and others); *Chronicle of the Blue Elves* (1991) and *Journey of the Stone People* (1991).

WELLS, Ernest (1902–), a lawyer and public ser-vant, is the author of two books for children and three novels for adults, *Hemp* (1933), *Brave Music* (1934) and *Dirk Spaanders* (1936). *Hemp*, set partly in the convict era, includes numerous colourful subjects from pirates and whaling to the Victorian gold rush; *Brave Music*, a chronicle novel, has an action-filled plot ranging from the mid-Victorian period in Australia and England to the outbreak of the First World War; *Dirk Spaanders* is a buccaneering romance set in the seventeenth century.

Wells of Beersheba, The, an account by Frank Dalby Davison (q.v.) of the Australian Light Horse in a crucial battle during the Palestine campaign of 1917, was first published in 1933 and revised in 1947. Well researched, historically accurate, and written with spare realism, the story celebrates the heroic endur-ance of man and beast.

WELLS, Thomas (1782–1833), born London, was convicted of embezzlement in 1816 and transported to the colony of Van Diemen's Land. Wells was the author of *Michael Howe: The Last and Worst of the Bush Rangers of Van Diemen's Land* (1818), the first 'general work of literature' (J.A. Ferguson) published in Aus-tralia. During five years' imprisonment for debt in the late 1820s, Wells was involved, probably as amanuen-sis, in the preparation of *The Hermit in Van Diemen's Land* (q.v., 1830), although some contemporary obituarists and later historians, e.g. James Bonwick, credited him with the authorship of the work.

WELSH, Thea (1949–) has, since graduating from university, worked in several administrative and re-search positions in Canberra, Adelaide and Sydney. She is manager of the Australian Screen Directors Association. Her first novel, *The Story of the Year of 1912 in the Village of Elza Darzins* (1990), won the NBC Banjo Award for Fiction and the Commonwealth Writers' Prize for this region. The story concerns Erika Cavanagh, who begins a short-lived career as translator at the State Film Board by translating, from Latvian into English, and subtitling, the Russian-made film named in the title. Unable to understand the film fully until she happens to see it without sound, she finally 'scriptdoctors' it, radically rewriting all the dialogue. Fearing disastrous repercussions when her subterfuge is discovered, she is astonished to find it shown in Cannes with French subtitles, translated directly from her own.

WENTWORTH, William Charles (1790–1872), son of surgeon and magistrate D'Arcy Wentworth and Catherine Crowley, a transportee, was born *en route* from Sydney to Norfolk Island. Educated in England, Wentworth returned to Australia in 1810 and was appointed acting provost-marshal by Governor Lachlan Macquarie in 1811. He crossed the Blue Mountains with Blaxland and Lawson in 1813 and returned to England to study law 1817–20. In 1819 he published *A Statistical, Historical, and Political Description of the Colony of New South Wales* in which he foreshadowed such radical reforms for the Colony as trial by jury and a Legislative Assembly elected on a property franchise with no exclusion of emancipated convicts from that franchise. While at Cambridge in 1823 he wrote the poem *Australasia* (q.v.), which was a distinguished entry in the chancellor's poetry competition for that year. Returning to Australia in 1824, Wentworth began publishing, with Robert Wardell, the *Australian* (q.v.), a newspaper which promoted radical, emanicipist political reforms. Wentworth was instrumental in the creation of the Australian Patriotic Association in 1835, which under his guidance was to draft a proposed constitution for NSW. A substantial landowner, he became increasingly conservative and from 1843 onwards, when he took his place as an elected member of the Legislative Council, advanced the cause of the large pastoralist interests at the expense of small landowners. In 1852, under Wentworth's leadership, the Legislative Council demanded and received approval for self-government for NSW; Wentworth was chairman of the committee formed to draft the constitution. His proposal for a colonial peerage, dubbed by Daniel Deniehy (q.v.) 'a bunyip aristocracy', came to nothing. His active political career finished in 1861 and he returned to England to live in 1862. His biography by A.C.V. Melbourne, *William Charles Wentworth* was published in 1934. Charles Harpur's satiric poem 'The Patriot of Australia – An Heroic Poem in Ten Cantos' takes Wentworth as subject. It was republished in the *Penguin Book of Australian Satirical Verse* (1986).

WENZ, Paul (1869–1939), born Rheims, France, went to school with André Gide, with whom he remained friendly. He came to Australia in 1892 after extensive travels in North Africa, South America and NZ, married an Australian girl and worked as a jackaroo and pastoralist in various parts of Australia. He finally established a station, Nanima, in NSW where he died. Although his books deal mainly with Australia, he remained a French citizen, frequently revisited his native country, and served with the Franco-British hospital service in the First World War.

Wenz published two collections of short stories which deal mainly with his Australian experiences, *A l'autre Bout du Monde* (*At the Other End of the World*) (1905) and *Sous la Croix du Sud* (*Under the Southern Cross*) (1910), titled *Contes Australiens* (*Australian Stories*) from the second edition; an account of his early years in Australia, *Diary of a New Chum* (q.v., 1908, translated into French by Denis Wenz, *Un Australien tout neuf*, 1989), the only work he wrote in English; and four Australian novels, *Le Pays de Leurs Pères* (*The Land of Their Fathers*) (1919), *L'Homme du Soleil Couchant* (*The Sundowner*) (1923), *Le Jardin des Coraux* (*The Coral Garden*) (1929) and *L'Écharde* (*The Thorn*) (1931). His other writings are *Bonnes Gens de la Grande Guerre* (1918), *Choses d'Hier* (1919) and *Il Était une Fois un Gosse* (1930). Wenz used a pseudonym, 'Paul Warrego', for *A l'autre Bout du Monde* and *Diary of a New Chum*. He also translated into French *Love of Life* by Jack London, whom he met on the latter's visit to Sydney.

An acute and compassionate observer of Australian outback life, particularly fascinated by the daily experience of sheep stations, Wenz describes a wide range of bush individuals in his fiction – station hands, new chums, swagmen, boundary-riders, Aborigines, Chinese cooks and, especially, children. As aware of the hardship and potential tragedy of bush life as Barbara Baynton (q.v.), and as unsentimental, he is a more openly sympathetic recorder of its burdens, limitations and griefs. His gifts of keen observation, psychological insight, irony, dramatic compassion and eloquent understatement are seen at their best in his short stories. These range from the lightly humorous, such as 'Cinquante-cinq Minutes de Retard' ('Fifty-five Minutes Late') in which the birth of a child delays a train, to the poignant, such as 'Son Chien' ('His Dog'), an account of the relationship between an old swagman and his dog, to the starkly horrific, such as 'La Hutte des Becs-Cuillers' ('The Spoonbill Hut'), the tragic story of a new chum boundary-rider.

Wenz's *L'Homme du Soleil Couchant*, which deals with an Englishman-turned-swagman who finally makes good as a prosperous settler, is rich in vivid, detailed descriptions of bush life and memorable minor characters. *Le Pays de Leurs Pères* concerns mainly the experiences of backblock Australian soldiers in wartime England. Although Wenz humorously exploits the social gaucheries of the Australians to some extent, he also creates a clear impression of the bushman's integrity and simplicity. *Le Jardin des Coraux*, uncharacteristic of Wenz's fiction in its narrow scope, is set mainly on an island off the coast of Queensland and combines scenes of idyllic beauty with scenes of horror and violence. With *L'Écharde*, his darkest novel, Wenz returned to the Australian bush; a tale of an unusual evil passion, it has a powerful dramatic action. Jean-Paul Delamotte has written an account in French of Wenz's life with selected extracts from his fiction and correspondence, *Paul Wenz: A la Recherche d'un Ecrivain Perdu* (1987) and Maurice Blackman has edited and translated the collection *Diary of a New Chum and Other Lost Stories* (1990), which includes Wenz's correspondence with Gide, Miles Franklin and Christopher Brennan.

West Australian (1879–), successor to the *Perth Gazette* (1833–79) and the *Western Australian Times* (1874–79), became a daily in 1885. Its editors have included Charles Harper, Sir John Winthrop Hackett, Sir Alfred Langler, C.P. Smith, H.J. Lambert, E.C. de Burgh, W.T.G. Richards, M.C. Uren and D.B. Smith. Literary material in the *West Australian* has included regular columns on writers and books; its contributors have included well-known WA literary figures such as J.K. Ewers, Henrietta Drake-Brockman and Walter Murdoch.

West Coast Writing is a paperback series of WA short fiction and poetry published by the Fremantle Arts Centre Press with Judith Rodriguez as consultant editor. The series began in 1976 with Nicholas Hasluck's *Anchor and Other Poems*. Authors whose work is featured include Hasluck, T.A.G. Hungerford, Alan Alexander, Lee Knowles, Alec Choate, Justina Williams, Peter Cowan, Philip Salom, Fay Zwicky, Andrew Lansdown and Caroline Caddy, James Legasse, Joan London, Elizabeth Jolley, Julie Lewis, Philip Collier and Strephyn Mappin.

WEST, John (1809–73), born and educated in England, arrived in Tasmania as a Congregational minister in 1838. An effective and leading advocate for the abolition of transportation, he wrote *The History of Tasmania* (1852) as part of the campaign; despite its polemical zeal it is one of the best nineteenth-century Australian histories. In 1854 West became editor of the *Sydney Morning Herald*, remained with the paper until his death, and helped consolidate its reputation in Australian journalism.

West, John is the central character of Frank Hardy's novel *Power Without Glory* (q.v., 1950). A semi-fictional study of a Melbourne multimillionaire, John Wren, the novel gave rise to a charge of criminal libel against Hardy.

WEST, Morris (1916–), born St Kilda, Melbourne, graduated from the University of Melbourne in 1937 and taught in schools in Tasmania and NSW. For twelve years he was a member of the Christian Brothers order but left the order in 1940 before taking his final vows. During the Second World War he served as a cipher officer at Darwin and was also private secretary to W.M. Hughes for a brief period. His first novel, *Moon in My Pocket*, a semi-autobiographical account of a disillusioned religious, was published in 1945 under the pseudonym 'Julian Morris'. West worked as publicity officer for a Melbourne radio station 1944–45, and was managing director of Australian Radio Productions, a company he founded, 1945–54. West left Australia in 1955 to pursue a career as a writer and published two novels in 1956 to finance his venture, *Gallows on the Sand* (1956) and *Kundu* (1957). His account of the slum urchins of Naples, *Children of the Sun* (1957), brought him wide attention, and with *The Devil's Advocate* (1959) he became an international best-selling novelist. His subsequent novels, which have frequently demonstrated his

knack of predicting world issues and even events, have sustained him in this position. His books have been published in twenty-seven languages and have sold more than sixty million copies. From 1955 West lived in Austria, Italy, England and the USA but returned to Australia in 1980. His other novels are *The Big Story* (1957), *The Second Victory* (1958) which was made into a film in 1986, *McCreary Moves In* (1958, as 'Michael East'), *The Naked Country* (1960, as 'Michael East'), *Daughter of Silence* (1961), *The Shoes of the Fisherman* (1963), *The Ambassador* (1965), *The Tower of Babel* (1968), *Summer of the Red Wolf* (1971), *The Salamander* (1973), *Harlequin* (1974), *The Navigator* (1976), *Proteus* (1979), *The Clowns of God* (1981), *The World Is Made of Glass* (1983), *Cassidy* (1986), *Masterclass* (1988), *Lazarus* (1990), *The Ringmaster* (1991), and *The Lovers* (1993). West has also written plays, some of which are dramatised versions of his novels, 'The Illusionists' (1955), *The Devil's Advocate* (1961), *Daughter of Silence* (1962), *The Heretic* (1969) and 'The World Is Made of Glass' (1982). Some of his novels, such as *The Shoes of the Fisherman*, *The Big Story* and *The Salamander* have also been produced as films. A former chairman of the National Book Council and the National Library Council, West is an AM and has won numerous awards including the Heinemann Award, the Black Memorial Prize, the Dag Hammarskjold Prize, and the Conference of Christians and Jews' Brotherhood Award. West deals with serious, often religious themes, as in *The Devil's Advocate* and *Daughter of Silence*, and internationally significant political events, as in *The Ambassador* and *The Tower of Babel*.

Westerly, a literary magazine but concerned also with historical, social and political issues, commenced publication in 1956 as a student-edited magazine of the arts union of the University of WA under the editorship of R.W. Smith. From 1963, when it was first assisted by a CLF grant, *Westerly* began quarterly publication. By contrast with its fellow journals *Meanjin*, *Overland* and *Quadrant*, *Westerly* began with neither a commitment to a particular ideology nor a well-known editorial identity. It thus became a forum magazine, although some continuity of editorial opinion and character was achieved in the late 1950s through the presence of Peter Cowan and John Barnes, and from 1975 when Cowan and Bruce Bennett became joint editors after publication of the magazine was transferred to the English Department of the University of WA. Dennis Haskell joined the editorial team in 1985, and Delys Bird in 1993, following the departure of Bruce Bennett. Concerned from its beginnings to propagate local, national and international interest in Australian writing and culture, *Westerly* has sought a continuing discussion of the nature and character of Australian literature, and of the need for Australian studies in universities and schools. *Westerly*'s publishing preference has been mainly for fiction, e.g. it published early work by Frank Moorhouse, Murray Bail and Michael Wilding, and the Patricia Hackett Prize, awarded from 1965 onwards for the best annual contributions, usually went to prose writers. The 1950s saw greater emphasis on art and poetry. *Westerly* Indexes, such as those compiled by Linda Goldstiver (1956–77) and Susan Miller (1984–88), are useful bibliographical guides. *Westerly 21: An Anniversary Selection* (1978), edited by Bennett and Cowan, is an anthology from the magazine's first twenty-one years of publication. Recognition of geographic and cultural links with the Asia-Pacific region has resulted in increasing contributions by and about that area, reflected in the anthology *Westerly Looks to Asia* (1993) edited by Bennett, Cowan, Haskell and Susan Miller.

Western Australia, the largest Australian State (more than 2.5 million square kilometres in area, and occupying just less than a third of the Australian continent), was possibly discovered in 1616 by Dirk Hartog. It was not part of the original claim for the eastern part of Australia made by Governor Arthur Phillip in 1788, but in 1826 British interest began with the arrival of a small penal party from New South Wales. In 1829 a permanent settlement, the Swan River colony (q.v.), was established near the present capital of Perth and the territory west of the 129th meridian, the then western limit of New South Wales, was designated the British colony of Western Australia. Although many older West Australians were unenthusiastic about Federation (q.v.), the State became part of the Commonwealth of Australia.

Western Australian Monthly Magazine, an early periodical published in Perth, ran from October 1843 to March 1844 and included some original poetry.

Western Mail, a weekly newspaper of WA, ran 1885–1955 when it was incorporated in the *Countryman*. In 1897 the first Christmas edition of the *Mail* was published; the Christmas editions (or Annuals) became lavish, hundred-page productions with substantial literary content, including the winning entries of the *Mail's* annual short-story competition. Contributors included well-known WA literary figures, e.g. Julian Stuart, J.K. Ewers, Henrietta Drake-Brockman and Mary Durack. Ffion Murphy and Richard Nile compiled *The Gate of Dreams: The Western Mail Annuals 1897–1955* (1990), a selection of poems, stories and illustrations from the Christmas Annuals.

WESTGARTH, William (1815–89), born Edinburgh, Scotland, migrated to Melbourne in 1840. In Melbourne his career as an import merchant prospered and he soon began his prolific publications. In the 1840s he founded the Benevolent Society and was prominent in the Melbourne Mechanics' Institute and the Port Phillip separation movement. By 1849 he had become one of the most respected public men in Victoria, a spokesman for those of broadly liberal sympathies who opposed the conservative Anglican establishment. In 1850 Westgarth represented Melbourne in the NSW Legislative Council and headed the poll for Melbourne in the 1851 election for the new Legislative Council of Victoria. Absent in Britain in 1853–54, he was appointed on his return chairman of the commission of inquiry into the Eureka rebellion. In 1857 he returned to London, where he established a share-broking firm and subsequently played a prominent part in the granting of colonial loans and the general promotion of the Australian colonies. Active in 1862–64 in the campaign against the continuation of transportation to WA, he also helped to found the Colonial Institute in 1869 and was one of the preliminary committee of six which founded the Imperial Federation League. In 1888 he paid a last visit to Australia and on the voyage out wrote his *Personal Recollections of Early Melbourne & Victoria* (1888), among the most outstanding pioneer reminiscences. Westgarth's other major works on Australia include *Australia Felix* (1848), *Victoria, Late Australia Felix* (1853), *Australia: Its Rise, Progress and Present Condition* (1861), *The Colony of Victoria* (1864), and *Half a Century of Australasian Progress* (1889). Described by historians of Victoria as the outstanding sociological thinker of the colony, Westgarth was both an effective, practical man and a perceptive intellectual. His major works on Victoria are primarily informative and unpretentious, but in their questioning of circumstances and events and their discussion of social and political assumptions, they reveal his powers as an original thinker.

Westralian Worker, published in Kalgoorlie 1900–12 and in Perth 1912–51, when it was incorporated in *Australian Worker*, printed considerable radical verse in the editorial periods of Wallace Nelson (1901–3) and Julian Stuart (1903–6).

WESTWOOD, William (1820–46) was transported at 16 to NSW for forgery. In 1840, after brutal treatment at the hands of his overseer, he absconded and became a bushranger in the Goulburn district; he established a reputation for politeness and became known as 'Jacky-Jacky'. In the period 1841–46 Westwood was imprisoned at, but managed to escape from, Cockatoo Island in Sydney and Port Arthur and Glenorchy in Tasmania, where he was also a bushranger. Eventually sent to Norfolk Island, he led, in July 1846, a riot involving most of the prisoners on the island; he was convicted of the brutal murder of a warder and executed later that year. Westwood is often cited as an example of a convict brutalised and then broken by his treatment. He is mentioned in many bushranging and convict histories and volumes of reminiscences, e.g. by Charles MacAlister and by Martin Cash, who was on Norfolk Island but not involved in the 1846 riot. The play by Thomas McCombie and J.M. McLachlan, 'Jackey Jackey, the N.S.W. Bushranger', refused a performance licence in NSW in 1845, was staged in Geelong, Victoria, in 1853. Westwood's autobiography, originally published in the *Australasian* in 1879, was published with biographical notes by Stephan Williams in 1990.

Wet, The, the rainy season in central and northern Australia from December to March, has frequently figured in Australian fiction. Novels in which the Wet plays a dominant role are 'Nevil Shute's' *In the Wet* (1953) and *A Town Like Alice* (1950), Mrs Aeneas

Gunn's *We of the Never-Never* (1908), and Xavier Herbert's *Capricornia* (1938).

'Whaler' or **'waler'** was the name given to that species of swagmen who travelled, not along the outback tracks, but on the inland rivers. These river tramps, usually possessors of a canoe or home-made small boat in which they carried their possessions, paddled along the rivers living off the land as they went, either fish from the river or sheep from its banks. The *Australian National Dictionary* gives the origin of the term as one who fished for 'whales', i.e. Murray cod. Best-known among them were the 'Murray Whalers', 'Darling Whalers' and 'Murrumbidgee Whalers', all taking their names from the main inland rivers. Henry Lawson's sketch 'The Darling River' depicts the whaler as 'mostly a withered little old madman'. Mary Gilmore wrote 'The Song of the Waler' in *The Tilted Cart* (1925); Louis Esson wrote 'Whalin' Up the Lachlan'; and C.H. Winter ('Riverina') wrote 'The Whaler's Odyssey'. George Dunderdale wrote of the whaler in his *The Book of the Bush* (1898). A noted whaler was the *Bulletin* contributor 'Scotty the Wrinkler' (Phil Mowbray). 'Waler' is also a word for an Australian-bred horse, named after the colony of NSW, used extensively in the cavalry in the Boer War and the First World War.

WHATELY, Richard (1787–1863), born London, was an Oxford professor before his appointment as Anglican archbishop of Dublin in 1831. A man whose main hobby was the theory and practice of boomerang-throwing, although he never visited Australia, Whately became an implacable opponent of transportation (q.v.). His *Thoughts on Secondary Punishments in a Letter to Earl Grey* (1832) provoked *Observations upon Secondary Punishment* (1833), George Arthur's (q.v.) defence of secondary punishment (the further incarceration of convicts in colonial places of confinement such as Port Arthur and Norfolk Island). Whately responded with *Remarks on Transportation . . . in a Second Letter to Earl Grey* (1834), to which Arthur replied in *Defence of Transportation* (1835), and later wrote *Substance of a Speech on Transportation, Delivered in the House of Lords* (1840); all three publications are important examples of transportation literature and influenced the anti-transportation movement. Whately's reference to Norfolk Island as an 'Isle of Death' gave 'Price Warung' the title of his last series of convict stories (1898). David Burn, however, wrote *Vindication of Van Diemen's Land* (1840) in response to Whately's criticism of the moral tone of the colony.

WHEATLEY, Nadia (1949–   ), born Sydney, was educated at the University of Sydney and Macquarie University. A well-known reviewer and writer for younger readers, she has published short stories for adults in several periodicals and anthologies. Her publications include *Five Times Dizzy* (1982), *The House That Was Eureka* (1984), *Dancing in the Anzac Deli* (1984), *1 is for One* (1985), *The Blooding* (1987) and *My Place* (1987, with Donna Rawlins). *My Place* was CBC Book of the Year for Younger Readers 1988, and also

that year won the Eve Pownall Award and a YABBA, as well as an IBBY Honorary Diploma in 1990; *Dancing in the Anzac Deli* won an IBBY Honorary Diploma in 1986; *Five Times Dizzy*, which was also produced for television, won a NSW State Literary Award in 1983; *The House That Was Eureka* won a NSW State Literary Award in 1985. Wheatley has also edited two volumes of the writings of Charmian Clift, *Trouble in Lotus Land* (1990) and *Being Alone With Oneself* (1991), and a collection of short stories by Australian writers, *Landmarks* (1991). A writer who challenges younger readers, Wheatley deals with the difficulties faced by Aborigines or by non-English-speaking newcomers to Australia, with environmental issues and the effects of social change; *My Place* is the history of a plot of ground in inner Sydney, seen through the eyes of children who live near it and who are divided decade by decade from 1988 to 1788.

WHEEN, Arthur (1897–1971), born NSW, served with distinction in the First World War, won a Rhodes Scholarship in 1920, and later became librarian at the Victoria and Albert Museum, London. His well-known short story, *Two Masters* (1929), an analysis of the moral problems posed by war, was originally published in *Hermes* (1923). Wheen also translated works of war literature, including Erich Remarque's *All Quiet on the Western Front* (1929).

When Blackbirds Sing, a novel by Martin Boyd (q.v.), was published in 1962. The fourth in a tetralogy dealing with the Langton family, the novel follows the fortunes of Dominic, who is also the subject of *A Difficult Young Man* (1955). In this novel Guy Langton's role as narrator is relinquished. Dominic leaves his wife Helena, with whom he has been happy, to join the English forces in the First World War. In England he becomes an efficient officer and drifts into an affair with Sylvia Tunstall, although later feelings of guilt alienate him from Sylvia and from the war effort. The act of killing a German soldier in hand-to-hand combat turns him into a pacifist. After a period in military hospital, where he is deeply stirred by the fate of a mutilated friend, Dominic returns to Australia, which he sees as the innocent hemisphere. There, however, his wife's incomprehension of his pacifist position deepens his sense of spiritual rootlessness.

'Where the Dead Men Lie', the best-known poem by Barcroft Boake (q.v.) and the title poem of his only volume of verse (1897), was published in the *Bulletin* (1891) under the pseudonym 'Surcingle'. In the poem Boake uses the contemptuous name 'Moneygrub' to denote the typical wealthy absentee landlord who lives in city luxury provided for him by the ordinary men and women of the outback; 'out on the wastes of the Never-Never' they give their lives in the one-sided struggle against poverty, privation and the harshness of the land.

While the Billy Boils, Henry Lawson's (q.v.) first major collection of prose, was published in 1896. The fifty-two stories of *While the Billy Boils*, generally considered Lawson's best book, include the most significant Mitchell and Steelman yarns and several stories, e.g. 'The Union Buries Its Dead' and 'The Drover's Wife', which are central to his creation of a pessimistic bush world. *While the Billy Boils* proved to be a popular title, not merely in terms of sales for the original volume; the publisher George Robertson reprinted a number of Lawson's works under a series title, The Billy Boils, and the Lawson selection which was filmed in 1921 also bore the title *While the Billy Boils*, as do some modern selections of Lawson's prose.

WHITE, Charles (1845–1922), the uncle of Mary Gilmore (q.v.), was born in Bathurst, NSW, and became a reporter on his father's *Bathurst Free Press*, which he edited 1884–1902. As a police roundsman in the 1860s, White reported on the activities of the local bushrangers, including Ben Hall, Frank Gardiner and John Gilbert; he remained interested in the subject and wrote *The Story of the Bushrangers* (1891–92), which later became the popular *History of Australian Bushranging* (1900–3). Equally important as a work of history, though less known, is his *Convict Life in New South Wales and Van Diemen's Land* (1889).

WHITE, Gilbert (1859–1933), born Cape Town, South Africa, was successively bishop of Carpentaria and of Willochra and wrote numerous theological works as well as the descriptive accounts *Round about the Torres Straits* (1917) and *Thirty Years in Tropical Australia* (1918). He also published six volumes of verse, *Melchior and Other Verses* (1893), *Night* (1897), *The World's Tragedy* (1910), *Australia* (1913), *The Poems of Gilbert White* (1919), *The Later Poems of Gilbert White* (1930) and *Selected Poems of Gilbert White* (1932). A biography by J.W.C. Ward, *White of Carpentaria*, was published in 1949.

WHITE, John (1757/58–1832), born Sussex, England, was chief surgeon in the First Fleet. A keen naturalist, he kept a journal in which he made notes of birds in the Colony and which he sent to a London friend, Thomas Wilson, in November 1788. It was published in 1790 as *Journal of a Voyage to New South Wales*, was immediately successful and subsequently widely translated. White also contributed drawings to *The Voyage of Governor Phillip to Botany Bay* (1789). Although his capacities as a surgeon were severely tested in the new settlement, especially after the arrival of the Second Fleet in June 1790, he kept up his naturalist interests and after October 1792 was assisted by the convict and artist Thomas Watling. Before he left the Colony in December 1794, White received grants of land, which he retained until 1822. He died in England after further service in the RN.

WHITE, Myrtle Rose (1888–1961), born Acacia Dam near Broken Hill, NSW, lived in the outback for most of her life and published several popular books about her experiences: *No Roads Go By* (1932), *For Those That Love It* (1933), *Beyond the Western Rivers* (1955) and *From That Day to This* (1961). Of these, *No Roads Go By* has acquired the status of a classic; an account of the seven years she spent in an isolated area at Lake Elder between Lake Frome in SA and the NSW border with her station-manager husband and three children, the book was later described by John Flynn as one of the most potent influences on his determination to establish the Flying Doctor Service. White's books combine starkly realistic representations of the loneliness and hardships of outback life with wry humour, lively descriptions of the mischievous activities of young children and an unpretentious style.

WHITE, Patrick (1912–90) was a member of a family of pastoralists that has been established in Australia for several generations. Born in London, he was brought back to Australia at the age of six months and educated first at private schools in NSW and, from the age of 13, at Cheltenham College, England. *Thirteen Poems*, a collection privately printed in Sydney in about 1930, dates from his years at Cheltenham. In 1929 he returned to Australia, where he spent two years as a jackeroo and one reading history for entrance to King's College, Cambridge. At Cambridge, however, he decided on modern languages, a study which took him on frequent visits to France and Germany. After graduating in 1935 he moved to London where he became friendly with other artists, writers and musicians, both English and Australian. His first published novel, *Happy Valley*, appeared in 1939, but his main ambition at this time was to write for the stage. Two 'inferior comedies', as he has described them, 'Bread and Butter Women' and 'The School for Friends', were produced at Bryant's Playhouse, Sydney, in 1935; in the same year he also wrote sketches and lyrics for intimate revues staged by Herbert Farjeon at the Little and Gate theatres, London. Two short stories, 'Cocotte' and 'The Twitching Colonel', and some poetry, later included in his collection *The Ploughman* (1935), appeared in prominent London journals. In 1939 he went for an extended visit to the USA where he wrote his novel *The Living and the Dead* (1941). He joined the RAF in 1941 and was an intelligence officer in the Middle East. Experience of the desert, coupled with a subsequent year's stay in Greece, stimulated his yearning for 'the scenes of childhood'. Demobilisation left him with the alternatives of turning into what he later described as 'the most sterile of beings, a London intellectual', or of 'returning home, to the stimulus of time remembered'. After a visit to Australia in 1946 he chose the latter and returned permanently in 1948. His play *The Ham Funeral* (q.v.) was written in London in 1947 and another play that has since been lost, 'Return to Abyssinia', was performed at Bolton's Theatre, London, that year. He completed the novel *The Aunt's Story* (q.v., 1948) on the 1948 sea voyage to Australia. He settled at first on a small farm at Castle Hill on the outskirts of Sydney but in 1964 moved to Centennial Park near the centre of the city.

Although White lived a secluded life in Australia, he occasionally made public statements on national issues such as the war in Vietnam, environmental matters and Aboriginal affairs. He was also involved in the 1972 federal election campaign that resulted in a Labor government and in the protests after its dismissal in 1975. In 1976 he withdrew from the Order of Australia in protest against some of the government's policies. He contributed generously to Aboriginal schools, donated a collection of works by Australian painters to the Art Gallery of NSW and, with his 1973 Nobel Prize, established the Patrick White Literary Award (q.v.). White's other writings are the novels *The Tree of Man* (q.v., 1955), *Voss* (q.v., 1957), *Riders in the Chariot* (q.v, 1961), *The Solid Mandala* (q.v., 1966), *The Vivisector* (q.v., 1970), *The Eye of the Storm* (q.v, 1973), *A Fringe of Leaves* (q.v, 1976), *The Twyborn Affair* (q.v., 1979) and *Memoirs of Many in One* (1986); the collections of short stories *The Burnt Ones* (1964) and *The Cockatoos* (1974); the plays *Four Plays by Patrick White (The Ham Funeral, The Season at Sarsaparilla, A Cheery Soul* (qq.v.) and *Night on Bald Mountain)* (1965, reissued as *Collected Plays Volume 1*, 1985), *Big Toys* (q.v. 1978), *The Night the Prowler* (1978), *Netherwood* (1983) and *Signal Driver* (1983); and the autobiography *Flaws in the Glass* (q.v., 1981). The brief prose reflections of *Three Uneasy Pieces* were deliberately published in 1987 to avoid the Bicentennial and in 1989 he published a collection of his public statements on such issues as the environment, nuclear disarmament, uranium-mining, republicanism and the Bicentennial, *Patrick White Speaks*, edited by Christine Flynn and Paul Brennan. His essay 'The Prodigal Son' in *Australian Letters* (1958) is an important statement on his work and reasons for living in Australia. In 1973 White won the Nobel Prize for *The Eye of the Storm* and his other awards include the Gold Medal of the Australian Literature Society for *Happy Valley* and *The Tree of Man*, the Miles Franklin Award for *Voss* and *Riders in the Chariot* and the W.H. Smith Literary Award for *Voss*.

Although White's work received some important early appreciations in Australia it was not until the overseas acclaim of *The Tree of Man* that it began to arouse more general, if still ambivalent, interest. Ambivalence, in turn, was also a dominant feature of White's response to Australia. On the one hand critical of Australia's 'exaltation of the average', of 'the Great Australian emptiness in which the mind is the least of possessions . . . and . . . the march of material ugliness does not raise a quiver from the average nerves', he emphasised the crucial link between the land and his creativity. Only in Australia could he achieve 'the state of simplicity and humility [which] is the only desirable one for artist or man'. Here he 'began to see things for the first time. Even the boredom and frustration presented avenues for endless exploration; even the ugliness, the bags and iron of Australian life, acquired a meaning'. Much of the distinctive energy, dynamism and constructive conflict of his work springs from this source. In his early fiction White's debts to the European tradition, especially to such writers as James Joyce, D.H. Lawrence, Virginia Woolf and T.S. Eliot, are easy to discover, but from *The Aunt's Story* onwards his original talent appropriated and shaped the novel in a strikingly distinctive

way. He described his writing as a 'struggle to create completely fresh forms out of the rocks and sticks of words', a struggle that each work resolves differently. White never repeated himself, each novel creating a fresh perspective even while remaining faithful to his central preoccupations. The most immediately impressive features of his work are a protean, creative energy that releases itself in uninhibited, confident play, mordant wit, sharp clarity of observation, zestful comedy and a sure grasp of a wide variety of idioms, people, places and incidents. Particularly striking is his prophetic tone, that seems to enhance every powerfully seized detail with transcending significance. A novelist of dualisms, White combines Swiftian satire and Blakean vision, an ability to render the everyday in all its palpable and even sordid actuality and at the same time invest it with illuminating intensity. Although he belonged to no specific creed, he frequently described himself as a religious artist whose intention was to 'convey a splendour, a transcendence which is . . . there above human realities'. Concerned above all with consciousness, his work bears witness to the immanence of all worlds in the immediately apparent one, expressed most succinctly in the epigraph to *The Solid Mandala*: 'There is another world, but it is this one.' Rational processes or a commitment to the material can only apprehend a fraction of the totality of being and both the sterile intellectual and the shallow materialist are familiar figures in his fiction. Contrasting with these are the visionary few, those who are courageous enough to explore the non-rational world and accept the inevitable suffering and solitude that the spiritual quest brings: 'True knowledge only comes of death by torture in the country of the mind' (*Voss*). Necessarily set apart, in that their unusual openness to experience frequently appears as outward eccentricity or even madness, the saints of White's world are nevertheless bound to the rest of humanity in their frailty and capacity for evil. Failure, furthermore, is a necessary feature of the spiritual journey: 'The mystery of life is not solved by success, which is an end in itself, but in failure, in perpetual struggle, in becoming' (*Voss*). Nor does spirituality preclude the carnal or the material; the physical existence both of objects and of the self, grasped in an intensely palpable way by White's visionaries, is frequently the means to their experience of heightened, psychic awareness. Thus objects often act as hinges between the worlds of consciousness, such as the butterflies in *Voss*, the cracks in the path or the gob of spittle in *The Tree of Man*, the glass marbles in *The Solid Mandala* and the little red-eyed hawk in *The Aunt's Story*. White is preoccupied with the complex dualisms of existence on the one hand, and with totality and the possibilities of integration on the other. He sees ambivalence as present in everything: good and evil, body and spirit, joy and suffering, love and hate, life and death, male and female, dream and actuality, time and eternity. For White's visionaries, however, in their fugitive experiences of the immanent spiritual world, the eternal co-existence of thesis and antithesis blends into a higher cosmic synthesis. The difficulties of transmitting such a vision are overcome by White's urgent, dynamically suggestive imagery and his expressive eccentricities of language and syntax. Frequently his use of uniting mandalic symbols, such as the heavenly chariot in *Riders in the Chariot*, the glass marbles in *The Solid Mandala* and the storm in *The Eye of the Storm*, shape and complicate his fictional structures with a visionary dimension. Deliberately poetic in its effects, his work depends on the cumulation of detailed effects and is consciously indebted to the arts of music and painting: speaking of *Voss*, for instance, he said: 'Always something of a frustrated painter and a composer *manqué*, I wanted to give my book the textures of music and sensuousness of paint, to convey through the theme and characters ... what Delacroix and Blake might have seen, what Mahler and Liszt might have heard' ('The Prodigal Son').

In White's first novel, *Happy Valley*, a dark study of a small community in NSW, some of his characteristic preoccupations, such as the necessity of suffering, emerge. Although self-conscious literariness and a novelettish quality betray it as an early work, the powers of strikingly original description and interest in human motive are already apparent. *The Living and the Dead*, a conventional novel of manners set entirely in England, is a distinct advance in skill and polish and shows a confident assimilation of literary debts. Impressive for its social comedy and representation of Edwardian and post-First World War England, it lacks the cohering force of White's later positive vision and fails to resolve the problem posed by its title: how to live rather than merely exist.

It is in his third novel, *The Aunt's Story*, that White's powerful originality first firmly declares itself. Theodora Goodman, an outwardly unattractive spinster, is his first extended study of the visionary individual, bent on a solitary quest for the ultimate reality. The first section of the novel, dealing with Theodora's early life in Australia, combines an outer, representational movement with an inner, poetically suggestive one. But after Theodora is freed by the death of her mother to pursue her singular vision, the narrative becomes appropriately surreal and expressionistic, although still organically connected to the earlier section. The last brief phase of the novel takes on a sustained lyricism as Theodora penetrates to a state of total lucidity that is interpreted by witnesses as madness. In *The Tree of Man* White attempts a much broader canvas. Epic and even biblical in tone, it narrates the lives of a pioneering couple, Stan and Amy Parker, from youth to old age. White said that he tried to suggest in this novel 'every possible aspect of life, through the lives of an ordinary man and woman. But at the same time ... to discover the extraordinary behind the ordinary, the mystery and poetry which alone could make bearable the lives of such people'. The novel includes a representation of rural life as a felt actuality, but Stan and Amy's inner lives and especially the increasing conflict between Stan's intuitions of meaning and the outer confusion are the centre of interest. The vision that is granted to him before his death comprehends both the unity of being and the inevitable isolation of the self. *Voss* turns back to the 1840s to the experience of a German explorer

who has affinities with Ludwig Leichhardt. Moving with a deft wit between the complacent materialism of colonial Sydney and the stark agonies of Voss and his followers in the desert, White transforms the explorer myth into a metaphor of modern alienation and arrogant individualism. As Voss pits himself against the desert in an act of self-deification, Laura Trevelyan, his betrothed, commits herself to a struggle for his soul. The spiritual, emotional contest between the two, conducted telepathically and culminating in their 'marriage' and mutual discovery of a higher but immanent reality, is counterpointed with actual events both in the wilderness and in Sydney.

Riders in the Chariot, White's most controversial novel, introduces a more idiosyncratic group of novels which seemed at the time to mark him to his critics as both aloofly patrician and bitterly misanthropic. Although its savage social satire and portentous tone have alienated some readers, White's virtuoso mastery of a wide range of modes and the sustained grandeur of his informing religious conception are impressive. Set in his imaginary Sydney suburbs of Sarsaparilla, Barranugli (qq.v.) and Paradise East, it is structured by a brilliant realisation of the inner and outer lives of four illuminates: Miss Hare, a spinster; Mordecai Himmelfarb, a Jewish refugee; Ruth Godbold, an Australian housewife; and Alf Dubbo, a tubercular Aboriginal artist, whose painting of the heavenly chariot finally expresses the transcending vision that unites the four. Contrasting with these is a range of wittily seized satirical creations such as the plastic ladies of suburbia, Mrs Jolley and Mrs Flack, and the perfectly assimilated Jews, Harry and Shirl Rosetree. *The Solid Mandala* has the same setting as *Riders in the Chariot* but is a more modest, relaxed and unified novel. The outwardly uneventful but inwardly dramatic lives of twin brothers Arthur and Waldo Brown are the centre of interest. The two brothers, yoked by genes, experiences and habit, love and hate, are also divided by their differences: the bright but neurotic Waldo forever shuts himself off from growth by his emotional solipsism, whereas the mentally backward Arthur effectively communicates with others and pursues a transcending mandalic vision. In *The Vivisector* White treats a difficult and complex subject, the act of creation and its costs as realised from within the artist's consciousness. Hurtle Duffield, the artist-protagonist, is the vivisector who cuts up living experiences and relationships for the purposes of his art. But Hurtle also comprehends art as an avenue to a realisation of the Divine Vivisector, God, and both the successive women in his life and his paintings represent stages in his quest for a perception of pure being. The quest culminates in his final attempt, disrupted by his last stroke, to paint God. As a background to Hurtle's experiences, described with uncompromising honesty, is White's most comprehensive and intimately realised picture of the changing Australian social milieu.

The Eye of the Storm moves to a study of a life which is itself conceived as a work of art. Ostensibly a conventionally structured novel, it extends White's basic preoccupations in a completely different direction.

Elizabeth Hunter, once a brilliant socialite and a rich, sensual, materialistic woman, now into her eighties, is dying in her Sydney mansion, perceived as a house-shrine by the nurses and servants who devotedly revolve around her. Mrs Hunter's crucial experience, during the eye of a cyclone, of harmony between her inner, essential self and the outer void has determined the rest of her life, especially the act of dying. Flawed as she is, her strength and intense authenticity of being is communicated in varying degrees to her servants, her lawyer and to her two inauthentic children, the Princess de Lascabanes and Sir Basil Hunter. The comic brilliance of White's conception of Sir Basil, the weary actor for whom life and acting are perpetually fused, is one of the novel's highlights. *A Fringe of Leaves*, an ostensibly artless, modest novel, demonstrates once again the unpredictable nature of his talent. Ellen Gluyas, a simple farm-girl, who marries a gentleman, Austin Roxburgh, undergoes a searing but spiritually illuminating experience after her shipwreck off the Queensland coast in the 1830s. Stripped of social position, possessions and even clothes, and treated as a slave by an Aboriginal tribe, Ellen is reduced to the core of her self. Rescued later by an escaped convict, she experiences real passion for the first time. Her ordeal initiates her into a condition of spiritual harmony that yet recognises the implication of all in 'the brutality of life'. *The Twyborn Affair*, more deliberately fractured and the least metaphysical of his works, deals extensively with the bisexual theme that also appears in earlier work. Apparently composed as three distinct novellas with three distinct protagonists, the novel eventually reveals that all three are in fact the same. The child of Mr Justice and Mrs Eadie Twyborn of Sydney is born with a dual sexual identity and appears at first as Eudoxia Vatatzes, the mistress of an old Greek; then as Eddie Twyborn, war hero and jackeroo; and lastly as Eadith Trist, madam of a high-class London brothel. *Memoirs of Many in One* claims on its title page to be edited by White and to be the narration of an elderly Greek woman, Alex Xenophon Demirjian Gray. A memorable, comic and gallant figure, Alex struggles through the handicaps and difficulties of old age and in the face of her daughter's insensitive mothering to make sense of her history. A playful and even self-parodying book, *Memoirs of Many in One* celebrates the joy of creating for its own sake.

Although his novels have won the most attention, White's shorter fiction also displays his characteristic style and effects, though in a more dramatically compressed way. If he was deprived of the cumulative, complex effects of the novel, he nevertheless found scope in the short-story form for a wide variety of tones, moods and settings. Of his two early, uncollected stories, 'Cocotte' (1940) and 'The Twitching Colonel' (1937), the latter is important for the creation of Colonel Trevellick, the first of White's unorthodox visionaries. *The Burnt Ones* (1964) brings together a group of stories published over several years. The range of the eleven stories, four of which are set in Greece and seven in Australia, extends from farce to pathos, from the surreal to the intensely psychologi-cal, from the satirical to the compassionate. As the collective title indicates, most of the central figures of these stories are alienated individuals suffering from an inward malaise. In all of them, but especially in 'Down at the Dump' and 'Willy Wagtails by Moonlight', White's eye for the significant, illuminating detail, his graphically expressive powers of description and satirically puncturing wit combine to create a virtuoso performance. Of the six novellas and stories collected in *The Cockatoos* (1974), some of which date from the 1960s, four have Australian settings or characters. Darker in tone and less enlivened by imagery than *The Burnt Ones*, they have the same general theme of alienation in the midst of bourgeois life. In all of them, simple and orthodox situations are transformed by White's ability to render both the surface tedium of life and its inner intensity.

White's plays represent a watershed in the history of the Australian theatre, initiating a period of experimental drama. After the controversial staging of his 1947 play, *The Ham Funeral*, in 1961, production of the remaining three of *Four Plays* (written from 1961 to 1962) followed in quick succession. *The Ham Funeral*, given its date, is an extraordinary foray into an expressionistic mode in which the set and the characters become a schematic representation of the central figure's personality. Like *The Aunt's Story*, the play treats of ways of being, although the Young Man resolves his struggle to come to terms with life differently from Theodora. *The Season at Sarsaparilla* presents once again White's version of Australian suburbia, although this time with more affection. This play most effectively embodies White's characteristic movement, noted by R.F. Brissenden, between the 'individual struggling to come to terms with himself and with the universe' and 'the cyclic processes of living, impersonal, inscrutable and inescapable'. *A Cheery Soul*, an adaptation of a short story, is dominated by the striking dramatic creation of Miss Docker, a blindly self-righteous individual who alienates all those around her with her 'sin of goodness'. *Night on Bald Mountain*, the most lyrical but least successful of the plays, has an overly schematic structure that is stated rather than dramatically achieved. *Big Toys*, less expressionistic than his earlier plays and ambitious in its social and political comment, is a compressed work that draws on caricature, melodrama, parody and music to express its subject of compromise and class betrayal. In *Netherwood* and *Signal Driver* he mixes realism, surrealism, symbolism, fantasy and satire in an exploration of the themes of loneliness, alienation and the problematic nature of contemporary Australian society.

Major studies of White's work include Patricia Morley *The Mystery of Unity* (1972), Ingmar Bjorksten *Patrick White* (1973), J.R. Dyce *Patrick White as Playwright* (1974), Peter Beatson *The Eye in the Mandala* (1976), William Walsh *Patrick White's Fiction* (1977), David A. Myers *The Peacocks and the Bourgeoisie* (1978), Brian Kiernan *Patrick White* (1980), John A. Weigel *Patrick White* (1983), Peter Wolfe *Laden Choirs: The Fiction of Patrick White* (1993), Ann M. McCulloch *A Tragic Vision* (1983), Karin Hansson *The Warped*

Universe (1984), John Colmer *Patrick White* (1984), Caroline Bliss *Patrick White's Fiction* (1986), Hilary Heltay *The Articles and the Novelist* (1983), Mari-Ann Berg *Aspects of Time, Ageing and Old Age in the Novels of Patrick White 1939–1979* (1983), May-Brit Akerholt *Patrick White* (1988), David Tacey *Patrick White. Fiction and the Unconscious* (1988), Rodney Edgecombe *Vision and Style in Patrick White* (1989), Laurence Steven *Dissociation and Wholeness in Patrick White's Fiction* (1989), T.M. Stein *Illusions of Solidity* (1990), Mark Williams *Patrick White* (1993), and Gordon Collier *The Rocks and Sticks of Words: Style, Discourse and Narrative Structure in the Fiction of Patrick White* (1992). Two collections of critical essays have been published, *Ten Essays on Patrick White* (1970, ed. G.A. Wilkes) and *Critical Essays on Patrick White* (1990, ed. Peter Wolfe). In 1991 David Marr published a substantial biography of White, which has won numerous awards, and in the same year individuals from various fields combined to produce *Patrick White. A Tribute* (compiled by Clayton Joyce).

White Thorntree, The, a novel by Frank Dalby Davison (q.v.), was published in 1968. Lengthy and complex, set in middle-class Sydney between the wars, it concentrates exclusively on the place of sexuality in modern culture. The story begins with the relationship of the outwardly normal couple Norma and Jeff Mitchell, who stand at the centre of the novel, and ends with the violent deaths of Jeff and his mistress. The first book, 'Babes in the Wood', a retrospective exploration of the Mitchells' experience before marriage, includes brief sketches of the sexual history of a range of relatives and reveals an encyclopaedic knowledge of all types of sexual repression and aberration. The second book, 'The Fringe Dwellers', turns its attention to the sexual life of the so-called 'abnormal' individuals, many of whom have tenuous links with the central couple. The third book, 'The Promised Land', turns on the theme that the marital happiness promised by romantic myth is an illusion. The destructive power of both sexuality and the yearning for romance is illustrated in the lives of three couples, the Mitchells, the Teasdales and the Gillespies, and in the violent ends which litter the latter part of the book. In the fourth book, 'The White Thorntree', fate seems negligently to destroy one last chance of romantic love. Although the novel concentrates narrowly on the search for sexual happiness and its inevitable frustration, it is clear that the characters are also searching for love, fellowship, purpose and meaning. The conflict between the claims of conformism and individual need is a central theme in Davison's fiction, although here his vision is at its bleakest.

White with Wire Wheels, a play by Jack Hibberd (q.v.), was first produced in 1967 and published in *Plays* (1970, ed. Graeme Blundell). Mal, Simon and Rod, young Australian executives who live together, pursue a stereotype of the good bachelor life; beer, their hopes of promotion, cars and girls are the main topics of their scabrous conversation, the last two, assessed frequently in terms of 'performance', emerging

as almost synonymous. A new girl, Helen, enters their lives soon after they have all failed in their individual relationships with girl-friends. Helen, who is played by the same actor as plays the part of the other three women, is adept at male expletives, refuses to be ignored, and, in an expressionistically realised scene, succeeds in penetrating their fragile barriers against self-consciousness. Disturbed by the experience, the three decide to get drunk at their favourite pub in the hills, 'thrash' the Valiant 'to death' and 'really write themselves off!'

WHITECROSS, Roy H., see **War Literature**

WHITEFORD, Wynne, see **Science Fiction**

WHITEHEAD, Charles (1804–62), a neglected minor English poet, novelist and dramatist, was born in London. He earned a precarious living as a man of letters, contributed to periodicals, edited *The Library of Fiction* (1836) for the publishers Chapman & Hall, and compiled biographies of highwaymen, one of which, *Jack Ketch* (1834), aroused some interest. He also received some favourable recognition after the publication of his poem *The Solitary* in 1831, and one of his plays, *The Cavalier*, was performed in 1836; but his most significant literary achievement, *Richard Savage* (1842), a novel based on the life of a figure he found congenial, was virtually unrecognised. A member of the Mulberry Club and familiar with Charles Lamb, Charles Dickens, Douglas Jerrold and William Thackeray, Whitehead appears to have gradually alienated his friends because of his alcoholism. In 1857 he migrated to Melbourne, where he already knew R.H. Horne, and was befriended by James Smith and J.E. Neild. In Melbourne Whitehead wrote for the *Examiner, Melbourne Punch* and *My Note Book*. His novel *Emma Latham* was serialised in *My Note Book* from February 1858 and a verse drama, *Spanish Marriage*, appeared in the *Victorian Monthly Magazine* in July 1859. Whitehead's poverty and alcoholism, which was probably in part due to his excessively shy and nervous disposition, became more extreme in Australia. In early 1862, after having been charged in court with 'lunacy, caused through drink', Whitehead applied for admission to the Yarra Bend Asylum, was refused and was eventually picked up in the streets when close to death. His death in July in Melbourne Hospital went unnoticed by his friends and their subsequent efforts to retrieve his body from its pauper's grave were unsuccessful. Whitehead's life is the subject of the English writer H.T.M. Bell's *A Forgotten Genius* (1884) and of Clive Turnbull's *Mulberry Leaves* (1945).

WHITINGTON, Don (1911–77) grew up in Tasmania and worked in his youth as a jackaroo, woolclasser and freelance journalist. He later worked on the staff of the Sydney *Daily Telegraph*, the *Sunday Mail* and the *Courier-Mail*, and early in the Second World War became head of the *Daily Telegraph's* Canberra bureau. In 1947 he began an independent national weekly newsletter, *Inside Canberra*, and later instituted another newsletter, *Money Matters*, and two newspapers, the *Northern Territory News* and the *Mount Isa Mail*. Well known to Australian federal politicians, Whitington wrote a range of guides to and accounts of federal politics as well as two novels, *Treasure upon the Earth* (1957) and *Mile Pegs* (1963), and an autobiography, *Strive To Be Fair* (1978).

WHITLAM, Edward Gough (1916–   ) graduated in arts and law at the University of Sydney and practised law before becoming a Labor member of the Australian parliament in 1952. In a political career spanning twenty-six years he was prime minister 1972–75, a period known as the 'Whitlam era' which was brought to a close with his dismissal by the then governor-general Sir John Kerr, provoking one of the few major political crises in Australia's history. Following his retirement from politics Gough Whitlam – as he is familiarly known – played important cultural and political roles, e.g. chairman of the Australian National Gallery, chairman of the Australia-China Council, executive of the Board of UNESCO 1985–89. He has been a visiting fellow/professor of various universities, e.g. ANU, Adelaide, Harvard. Appointed QC, he has also been awarded honorary D.Litts from the universities of the Philippines, Sydney and Wollongong. He is a Companion of the Order of Australia. His numerous writings have been mainly concerned with Australian politics, foreign policy, the Constitution, public administration, the law and the 'Whitlam era'. His published works include *The Labor Government and the Constitution* (1976), *On Australia's Constitution* (1977), *Reform during Recession* (1978), *The Truth of the Matter* (1979, republished 1983), *A Pacific Community* (1981), and *The Whitlam Government 1972–1975* (1985).

The Whitlam Government 1972–1975, a detailed account, contains chapters on foreign affairs, the economy, industrial relations, national resources, transport, housing, immigration, the Aborigines, women, arts, the environment, the media and law reform. *The Truth of the Matter* gives Whitlam's view of the Kerr controversy; a different perspective is offered in numerous works including H.O. Browning's *1975 Crisis: An Historical View* (1986). *The Whitlam Phenomenon* (1986) is a collection of speeches given at the Victorian Fabian conference, 1985, in which the influence of his government's policies is discussed by Whitlam and by Gareth Evans, Race Matthews and others. Political biographies of Whitlam include *A Certain Grandeur* (1978) by Graham Freudenberg and *The Leader* (1980) by James Walter. Deane Wells compiled *The Wit of Whitlam* (1976).

WHITMAN, Walt (1819–92), the American poet, had a substantial influence on some Australian writers. He corresponded with Francis Adams but his most enthusiastic admirer was Bernard O'Dowd, who was introduced to his work by Thomas Bury ('Tom Touchstone'), the writer of a regular column for the Ballarat *Courier* in the 1880s. In the early 1890s, O'Dowd, who was at the time the dominant spirit of the Australeum, a small group which met to discuss literary and socio-political affairs, corresponded with Whitman and received some positive, if paternalistic, encouragement; O'Dowd also delivered several public lectures on Whitman's work. Another writer, who arrived in Australia in 1888, William Gay (1865–97), was the author of two monographs on Whitman (1893, 1895). The O'Dowd–Whitman correspondence and a range of Australian commentaries on Whitman's work are collected and edited by A.L. McLeod in *Walt Whitman in Australia and New Zealand* (1964). The influence of Whitman on Australian writers is also discussed in Joseph Jones's *Radical Cousins* (1976).

Who's Who in Australia, a biographical dictionary of prominent Australians, has been published by the Herald and Weekly Times company since 1933. The 1933 publication covered 1933–34; since then *Who's Who in Australia* has appeared triennially 1935–50, in 1955, triennially 1959–91 and annually 1992–93; its editors have been Errol Knox 1933–35, J.A. Alexander 1938–65, J.S. Legge 1968–77, W.J. Draper 1980–87, Keith A. Cadman 1988, Ann C. Howie 1991–92 and Michael Wilkinson 1993. The predecessors of *Who's Who in Australia* were the biographical dictionaries of Fred Johns (q.v.), the last titled *Who's Who in Australia* (1927); Johns sold the rights to the Herald and Weekly Times before his death; it was purchased by *Information Australia* from the Herald and Weekly Times in 1989. A rival *Who's Who in Australia* published by the International Press Association, appeared in 1922, 1927 and 1929.

Who's Who of Australian Writers was published in 1991 by publishers D.W. Thorpe in association with the National Centre for Australian Studies, Monash University. Edited by Raylee Singh, Kirsten Alexander and John Arnold, it lists about 5000 writers and their published works together with other personal and literary details.

'WICKHAM, Anna' (Edith Hepburn) (1884–1947), born London, came to Australia in infancy and was educated in Brisbane but returned to England in 1904 to pursue a literary career. From 1905, when she married Patrick Hepburn, she lived in London and was the friend of numerous writers, including Natalie Barney, Kate O'Brien, Dylan Thomas, Malcolm Lowrey, Ezra Pound, David Garnett and D.H. Lawrence. A compulsive writer of poetry, she was encouraged by Harold Munro and Louis Untermeyer. Her publications include two minor plays for girls, *The Seasons* (1902) and *Wonder Eyes* (1903); the volumes of poetry, *Songs* (1911), by 'John Oland'; *The Contemplative Quarry* (1915), *The Man with a Hammer* (1916) and *The Little Old House* (1921), all under the 'Anna Wickham' pseudonym. A combined volume, *The Contemplative Quarry* and *The Man with a Hammer*, was published in the USA in 1921 and her *Selected Poems* in 1971. In 1984 R.D. Smith edited a collection of her poetry and prose, *The Writings of Anna Wickham*, which includes her 'Fragment of an Autobiography' and extensive biographical information. Much of

Wickham's verse reflects her ambivalence about marriage, social convention and the conflicting claims of family and art.

WIGHTON, Rosemary (1925–94), see *The Oxford Companion to Australian Children's Literature* (1993), p. 447.

WILCOX, Dora (1873–1953), born Christchurch, NZ, worked as a teacher in NSW and with the VAD in England during the First World War. Her second husband was Australian art historian William Moore. Some of her poems appeared in Australian magazines and in 1927 she won a *Sydney Morning Herald* prize for an ode celebrating the opening of the Commonwealth parliament. Two of her plays were published, *Commander Capstan* (1931) and *The Fourposter* in *Best Australian One-Act Plays* (1937), edited by William Moore and T. Inglis Moore. She also published three volumes of poetry, *Verses from Maoriland* (1905), *Rata and Mistletoe* (1911) and *Seven Poems* (1924), although only the last collection contains poems drawn from her Australian experience.

'Wild Colonial Boy, The', one of Australia's best-known folk-songs (q.v.), tells the story of an Irish-born bushranger (q.v.), named Jack Doolan, who terrorises the squatters, holds up the Beechworth mail coach in the 1860s, robs Judge MacEvoy, and is eventually killed when surrounded by three troopers, Kelly, Davis and FitzRoy, to whom he refuses to surrender. Several versions of 'The Wild Colonial Boy', which is often sung to the Irish tune 'The Wearing of the Green', e.g. by Ned Kelly at Glenrowan, have survived: in some of them MacEvoy is called Macaboy, and Jack Doolan is variously Jim or John Dowling/Duggan/Dublin/Dolan/Davis. That the hero of the song always has the initials 'JD' has led many folklorists, e.g. John Meredith in *The Wild Colonial Boy* (1982), to argue that the Wild Colonial Boy was a fictitious character and that the song is an 1860s variant of the 'Bold Jack Donahoe' (see Donohoe, John) cycle of songs and ballads, which, as a result of oral transmission, acquired a new set of characters and events. The argument is strengthened by a chorus beginning 'Come along, my hearties, we'll roam the mountains high,/ Together we will plunder, together we will die', which is common to versions of both ballads, and by the fact that the songs are traditionally linked in Irish folk-music. John Manifold, however, in *Who Wrote the Ballads?* (1964), speculates that there was a bushranger of the 1860s named Jack Doolan and that his experiences were celebrated by taking over the existing Bold Jack Donahoe songs. Further investigation has established a Judge Macaboy and families of Dowlings, Doolans, etc. in the Beechworth district in the 1860s, but as yet no bushranger named Doolan has emerged. Whatever the origins of the song, 'The Wild Colonial Boy' is well known overseas and is sung by John Wayne in the film *The Quiet Man*. In Australia, its popularity is such that 'wild colonial boys' became a phrase describing the bushrangers in general, as in Frank Clune's book *Wild Colonial Boys*,

and, indeed, any Australian sharing their bravado and daring. In contrast, the heroic image of the bushranger is satirised in David Martin's novel *The Hero of Too* (1967), in which Dick Grogan is a 'mild' colonial boy whose adventures are the subject of 'Dauntless Dick Grogan', a ballad imitation of 'The Wild Colonial Boy' which prefaces the novel. In 'Steele Rudd's' stage play *Gran'dad Rudd* (1918) a recalcitrant cow is encouraged to give milk by a rendition of 'The Wild Colonial Boy'.

WILDING, Michael (1942–) was born at Worcester, England, and studied at Oxford University before arriving in Australia to take up a lectureship at the University of Sydney in the early 1960s. In 1967–68 he taught at the University of Birmingham but in 1969 he returned to Sydney, where he is now professor of English at the University of Sydney. Apart from *Australians Abroad* (1967), an anthology co-edited with Charles Higham, and *Cultural Policy in Great Britain* (1970), co-authored with Michael Green and Richard Hoggart, Wilding's first major publications were in the field of English literature: he edited *Three Tales* by Henry James (1967), *Marvell: Modern Judgements* (1969) and *The Tragedy of Julius Caesar and The Tragedy of Marcus Brutus* (1970) by John Sheffield, a patron of Dryden, and wrote a monograph on *Paradise Lost* (1969). Although Wilding has continued throughout his career to work in the fields outside Australian literature – e.g. as editor, with Stephen Knight, of *The Radical Reader* (1977, 1982) and as author of *Political Fictions* (1980), an important study which includes discussion of D.H. Lawrence's *Kangaroo*, and of *Dragons Teeth: Literature in the English Revolution* (1987) – he has become increasingly important in Australian writing, not only as a writer of fiction but as editor, publisher, scholar and critic. In 1971 he co-edited, with Shirley Cass, Ros Cheney and David Malouf, the anti-war anthology *We Took Their Orders and Are Dead*. Since then he has published several collections of short stories, *Aspects of the Dying Process* (1972), *The West Midland Underground* (1975), *Scenic Drive* (1976), *The Phallic Forest* (1978), *Reading the Signs* (1984), *The Man of Slow Feeling* (1985, a selection of the previous four volumes), *Under Saturn* (1988, four long short stories or short novellas) and *Great Climate* (1990); and four novels, *Living Together* (1974), *The Short Story Embassy* (1975), *Pacific Highway* (1982) and *The Paraguayan Experiment* (1985). Some of these works were published by Wild & Woolley, the alternative publishing house Wilding established in 1973 with Pat Woolley. He was also associated in the foundation of the short-fiction magazine supplement *Tabloid Story* (q.v.); in 1978 Wilding edited *The Tabloid Story Pocket Book*, a retrospective anthology which includes an account of the venture. His other publications include a scholarly edition of William Lane's novel *The Workingman's Paradise* (1980) and several significant contributions to Marcus Clarke studies: a Portable Australian Authors edition (1976), a separate edition of Clarke's short stories (1983) and a critical monograph (1977). His *The Radical Tradition* (1993), the 1992 Colin Roderick Lectures for the Foundation for Australian Literary

Studies, is a discussion of the social, historical and intellectual background to the writings of Lawson, Furphy and Christina Stead.

As a writer of fiction, Wilding has often been labelled as one of the Balmain writers who gathered in that Sydney suburb from the late 1960s and documented its radical life-style. Yet despite the links with other inner-city writers such as Frank Moorhouse (q.v.), which extend beyond their involvement in *Tabloid Story* to each writing stories to answer the other's (Moorhouse in *Tales of Mystery and Romance*, Wilding in *Scenic Drive*), Wilding has developed in such a way as to defy categorisation simply as a chronicler of the urban subcultural milieu, as in *Living Together*. The radicalism apparent in his publishing activities and in his revaluation of writers such as Clarke and the subjects of *Political Fictions* finds expression also in his fiction; rejecting the realist mode, he is an experimental writer whose stories and novels, rich in allusions to literature beyond Australia, display his willingness to employ a variety of forms, e.g. fantasy, romance, fable, parable, the comic and the surreal. A major theme in his work, Bruce Clunies Ross has suggested, is the way people 'define themselves through stories, deliberately authored inventions and rumours . . . creating legends about their world'. Thus 'Hector and Freddie', a story from *The West Midland Underground* (which also contains a fictional account of Wilding's publishing activities), focuses on the power of stories to define existence, and in *The Short Story Embassy*, a fiction in which the characters are creating fiction, those characters are aware of the way they can thus structure reality. As Lazlo concludes, 'I am not going to write that I will write no more for fear that might become an irreversible state . . . The novel structures what has happened to us; with the short story we sketch our future actions.'

In *Pacific Highway*, one of Wilding's more optimistic works, the locale moves 'out of the terrace house' to the north coast of NSW, where a small community retreats into nature. Described as an attempt at 'literary ecology', the novel shows the paradoxes of mankind's response to nature by juxtaposing the attitude of the narrator's community and those who threaten its ideals.

The Paraguayan Experiment re-creates in fictional form the William Lane 'New Australia' experiment, drawing on documentary data but taking liberties with the characters. *Reading the Signs*, the most wide-ranging and varied of his short fiction collections, contains autobiographical accounts of Wilding's childhood and youth in England and his later life in Australia and his reactions to and involvement in the literary bohemia of Sydney. It provided the basis for a TV programme in England in 1988. *Under Saturn* has four self-contained but thematically linked long stories, 'Under Saturn', 'Campus Novel', 'Way Out That Summer' and 'Writing a Life', all of them preoccupied with paranoia. *Great Climate* is the first British publication of a group of Wilding's best-known stories, its title deriving from the one saving grace that Australia has for most British people. Included are 'Reading the Signs', 'The West Midland Under-

ground', 'The Man of Slow Feeling' and 'Aspects of the Dying Process', the title stories of his earlier major collections.

Wild Notes, from the Lyre of a Native Minstrel (1826), by Charles Tompson (q.v.), was the first volume of poems by an Australian-born writer to be published in Australia. The volume, containing the long poem 'Retrospect', together with odes, elegies, and miscellaneous verses, gives a picture of the foundation of the Colony and a description of the landscape from the well-disposed 'currency' viewpoint. Contrary to the title, the 'wild notes' are well-polished verses, strikingly ornate in a stereotyped, traditional style.

Wild Swan, The (1930) is the most significant book of verse by Mary Gilmore (q.v.), including her favourite themes – nature, the Aborigines, wholehearted commitment to life, and love. She mourns, in several poems, the passing of the wild swans, a beloved feature of the landscape of her youth.

WILKES, G.A. (Gerald Alfred) (1927–), born Punchbowl, NSW, foundation professor of Australian literature at the University of Sydney, has edited numerous Australian literary texts and written several studies of Australian literature. The latter include the monographs *New Perspectives on Brennan's Poetry* (1953), *Australian Literature: A Conspectus* (1969), *R.D. FitzGerald* (1981) and *The Stockyard and the Croquet Lawn: Literary Evidence for Australian Cultural Development* (1981). He also edited *Australian Poetry* (1963) and *Ten Essays on Patrick White* (1970); from 1963 to 1987 he was editor of *Southerly*. He has also published *A Dictionary of Australian Colloquialisms* (1978, 2nd edn 1985), *Exploring Australian English* (1986), and was special Australian consultant to *The New Collins Dictionary of the English Language* (1979) and companion volumes. *Reconnoitres*, a collection of essays in his honour, edited by Margaret Harris and Elizabeth Webby, was published in 1992.

WILKIE, Alan, see **Shakespeare and Australia**

WILLEY, Keith (1930–84), born Boonah, Queensland, grew up in that State. He worked as a journalist on newspapers throughout Australia, as well as in New Guinea; spent some time as a professional crocodile-shooter; and gained a degree late in life in history at the ANU. He was the senior lecturer in journalism at the Darling Downs Institute of Advanced Education at the time of his death. In 1961–63 he won three Walkley Awards for journalism. He wrote a study of Australian humour in times of hardship, *You Might as Well Laugh, Mate* (1984), and several accounts of his experiences and acquaintances in the Northern Territory and New Guinea, *Eaters of The Lotus* (1964), *Assignment New Guinea* (1965), *Crocodile Hunt* (1966), *Naked Island and Other South Sea Tales* (1970), *Boss Drover* (1971), *Tales of the Big Country* (1972), *Ghosts of the Big Country* (1975), and *The Drovers* (1982); an account of Ludwig Leichhardt, *Strange Seeker* (1966); and a well-researched, detailed history of the destruction of the Aboriginal tribes of the Sydney region, 1788–1850s, *When the Sky Fell Down* (1979). He collaborated with other authors and photographers in books about Queensland and New Guinea, and with Frank Flynn in *Northern Gateway* (1963), *Northern Frontiers* (1968) and *The Living Heart* (1979). Willey also edited *Newsnewsnews* (1982), a selection of about 300 items from newspapers over the past century and collaborated with Bruce Elder and Jacqueline Kent in *Memories: Life in Australia since 1900* (1988). Willey's life and writings were a constant search for the Australian identity. He found his version of it in the bush ethos and tall tales and songs in the manner of Slim Dusty.

'William Street', a brief poem by Kenneth Slessor (q.v.) published in *One Hundred Poems 1919–1939* (1944), describes the main traffic artery that runs from the city up to Kings Cross (Sydney) as it would have appeared in all its garish flamboyance in the 1930s. The poem is part of Slessor's defence of his 'patch' – 'you find it ugly, I find it lovely.'

WILLIAMS, Harold Roy, see **War Literature**

WILLIAMS, Justina (1916–), born Coolgardie, WA, has been a journalist on the *West Australian* and the *Daily News*, and an active supporter of radical and feminist causes over many years. Active also in the FAW, she has published three collections of poetry, *The Dreaming Vine* (1970), *By All the Clocks* (1975) and *People and Peace* (1986); a book of short fiction, *White River and Other Stories* (1979); two socio-political histories, *The First Furrow* (1976) and *Trade Unionism* (1978); and a children's story, *The Bird Girl* (1984). She also edited *Tom Collins and his House* (1973). Her autobiography, *Anger and Love* (1993), chiefly concerns her support for the left-wing movement in WA in the face of concerted opposition.

WILLIAMS, Maslyn (1911–), born England, grew up in NSW on rural properties in the New England and Southern Highlands districts, after the deaths of both his parents. His early interest in writing, music and films led to a career in film-making. He was appointed as writer-producer to the Official War Film and Photographic Unit in 1940 and served in the Middle East and the Pacific. He subsequently made films in Europe, Australia and New Guinea, gaining several awards, including a gold medal at the Venice Biennale. In 1962 he gave up film-making to concentrate on writing and is the author of several books on China, Cambodia, Papua, New Guinea and Indonesia. He has written four novels, *The Far Side of the Sky* (1967), *The Benefactors* (1971, published as *Dubu* in the USA), *Florence Copley of Romney* (1974) and *The Temple* (1982), and an autobiography, *His Mother's Country* (1988). In 1988 Williams won the FAW Christina Stead Award and the Douglas Stewart Prize in the 1989 State literary awards for *His Mother's Country*. Written in the third person, the autobiography describes both his experiences in 1920s New England, the lives and personalities of numerous individuals he

encountered, and the distinctive identity of the landscape which ultimately claimed his loyalty. Williams is an emeritus fellow of the Literature Board of the Australia Council.

WILLIAMS, Max, born Redfern, Sydney, where he spent a very deprived childhood during the 1930s Depression, had his first brush with the law at the age of 5 and at the age of 10 was committed to an institution for wayward boys. He spent most of the next thirty years in prison. He has contributed to *Poems from Prison* (1973) and *Australians Aware* (1975), both edited by Rodney Hall, and to *Poet's Choice*. He has also published three collections, *The Poor Man's Bean* (1975), *Hard Is the Convict Road* (1977) and *Baronda* (1977), and has written an autobiography, *Dingo! My Life on the Run* (1980).

WILLIAMS, Ruth, see *The Oxford Companion to Australian Children's Literature* (1993), p. 450.

WILLIAMS, Victor (1914–), born Perth, was a farm worker and schoolteacher in WA before serving with the Australian Army in the Second World War. He has written four books of verse, *Harvest Time* (1946), *Into Battle With a Song* (1953), *Hammers and Seagulls* (1967) and *Three Golden Giants* (1977), as well as *The Years of Big Jim* (1975), a biography of Jim Healy, waterfront union official.

WILLIAMSON, David (1942–) was born in Melbourne and brought up in Bairnsdale in north-eastern Victoria. After graduating in mechanical engineering, he studied social psychology and lectured in both subjects at the Swinburne Institute of Technology before becoming a success in the commercial theatre. His first full-length play, *The Coming of Stork*, the basis of the 1969 film *Stork*, was first performed at the La Mama theatre in 1970. His next two plays, *Don's Party* (q.v.) and *The Removalists* (q.v.), were also both performed in 1971 by the alternative theatre (*Don's Party* by the Australian Performing Group and *The Removalists* at the La Mama theatre) before moving on to the commercially successful productions at the Playbox Theatre and the Royal Court theatre in London. His published plays include *The Removalists* (1972), *Don's Party* (1973), *Three Plays: The Coming of Stork. Jugglers Three. What If You Died Tomorrow* (1974), *The Department* (q.v., 1975), *A Handful of Friends* (q.v., 1976), *The Club* (q.v., 1978), *Travelling North* (1980), *The Perfectionist* (1983), *Sons of Cain* (1985), *Emerald City* (1987), *Top Silk* (1989), *Siren* (1991), *Money & Friends* (1992), *Brilliant Lies* (1993) and *Sanctuary* (1994). Five of his plays have also been republished in his *Collected Plays. Volume 1* (1986). An unpublished play is 'Celluloid Heroes' (1980). Film versions have been made of several of his plays and he has also written other scripts for film, a medium that he admires, including *The Last Bastion, Peterson, Eliza Frazer, Gallipoli* and *Phar Lap*. He has won several awards, including part of the British George Devine Award for *The Removalists*, Awgies on eleven occasions and four AFI awards. As well as receiving widespread Australian production, several of his plays have been performed in New York and London. Brian Kiernan has written a biography of Williamson's writing career (1990) and his work is the subject of two collections of criticism, *Williamson*, edited by Peter Fitzpatrick (1987) and *David Williamson* edited by Ortrun Zuber-Skerritt (1988). Film Australia made the film *David Williamson: Compulsive Playwright* in 1986. Williamson has been awarded an honorary D.Litt. from both Monash University and the University of Sydney.

Raucous wit, naturalistic plots and settings, fast-moving, scatological dialogue and recognisable social types, brilliantly seized and satirised, are familiar characteristics of Williamson's plays. Writing mainly for, and of, his own affluent, educated, permissive generation, he seeks to represent what he sees as the 'awful uniqueness' of Australian life. More interested in rituals of social interaction than in individuals or issues, he has a keen eye for the power games played by any group, whether an academic department, a football club or a party. Colliding temperaments are the subject of his comedy and the hypocrisies, insecurities, defences, aggressions, betrayals and complicities that they generate. Although his subject range is narrow and his attitude comically detached, his plays have a fluid diversity of emotional tones, from the farcical to the sad. Often this emotional range is dependent on a subtext that subtly undercuts the crudities of the dialogue.

The Coming of Stork, an exuberantly crude romp about the complicated sexual adventures of one girl and a group of graduate technologists, is more concerned with farcical effects than serious comment. *The Removalists*, however, is a profound, tightly structured exploration of the links between violence, sexuality and uniformed authoritarianism. A serious tone also underlies the comic satire of *Don's Party*, a study of middle-class, older graduates, subservient to a materialist culture they profess to despise. *Jugglers Three*, *What If You Died Tomorrow* and *A Handful of Friends*, similar in their upper middle-class settings, have a finer insight into female experience. *Jugglers Three* explores the embittered or indifferent relationships of a married couple and the wife's current and ex-lovers. *What If You Died Tomorrow*, Williamson's most autobiographical play, concentrates on one embattled evening in the life of a successful novelist, under pressure from his agent, publishers, mistress and parents. *A Handful of Friends*, subtle and finely worked, probes the intricacies of failed relationships. With *The Department* and *The Club* Williamson turns to the comic interactions of role-playing within bureaucracies, the first an academic department, the second a football club. *Travelling North* is a quieter, less satirical study of a pair of lovers who, in old age, attempt to discard their expected roles. 'Celluloid Heroes' satirises the mores of the film industry, and *The Perfectionist* comically explores the marital limitations of a certain academic type. In *Sons of Cain*, set in the office of a leading newspaper, Williamson turns his attention to the wider issues of corruption in government, police and big business, reaffirming his commitment to social criticism. *Emerald City*, Williamson's term for sophis-

ticated, go-getting Sydney, satirises the Australian film industry while probing the characters' difficulties in reconciling would-be humanitarian concern and self-interest. *Top Silk* is a narrower study of power relations in family life and their links with wider social tensions, while *Siren*, a situation comedy with elements of farce, exploits the potential for the pursuit of sex and power inherent in the temporary relationships set up by undercover police activities. *Money & Friends*, set in the economically insecure 1990s, is a hard-hitting satire of the aggressive, money-hungry drives of a group of professional people which set firm limits on their capacity for friendship. *Brilliant Lies*, which deals with sexual harassment at home and in the workplace, explores what Williamson terms 'the war between the sexes'.

WILLIAMSON, J.C. (James Cassius) (1845–1913), Australia's most successful theatrical entrepreneur, was born in Pennsylvania, USA. He achieved some success as an actor in the USA, particularly after starring in *Struck Oil* (q.v.), with his wife Maggie Moore (q.v.). In 1874 he came to Australia with *Struck Oil* under contract to George Coppin and, on the crest of the play's success, toured England, Europe and the USA, returning to Australia in 1879 and leasing the Melbourne Theatre Royal, in 1880. Two years later he formed an association with his major competitors, Arthur Garner and George Musgrove, which was popularly known as 'the Triumvirate' and dominated Australian theatrical life. Surviving several changes of membership, the J.C. Williamson 'Firm' continued to thrive and to absorb competitive organisations, controlling theatres in Sydney, Melbourne, Adelaide and Brisbane and becoming a proprietary company, J.C. Williamson Theatres Ltd, in 1907. Although the Williamson 'Firm' generated productions and tours by overseas actors, its opposition to the avant-garde and commitment to long, profitable runs of star-studded shows tended to repress the development of local theatre. Williamson was also co-author with Bert Royle of a popular pantomime, 'Djin Djin Japanese Bogeyman' (1895). A biography of Williamson, *J.C.W.* by Ian C. Dicker, was published in 1974, and Ian Bevan has written of him in *The Story of the Theatre Royal* (1993).

WILLIS, William Nicholas (1858–1922), one of the *Wild Men of Sydney* in Cyril Pearl's (q.v.) book (1958) dealing with Sydney journalism and politics at the turn of the century, was born in Mudgee, NSW, and was a country storekeeper and landowner before entering politics. A member of the NSW parliament 1889–1904, he was one of the founders of the radical *Truth* in 1890, and was involved in its management until 1896. In 1905 he was implicated in a political scandal over the sale and lease of land and was extradited from South Africa to stand trial; discharged, he settled in England, where he wrote several sensational novels under his own name dealing with sport, sex and crime. A further dozen works, dealing with the same subjects and written under the pseudonym 'Bree Narran' have also been attributed to Willis but may have been written by his son, e.g. *One Night* (1919), *Three Nights* (1919), and *Seven Nights* (1919).

WILLOUGHBY, Howard (1839–1908), born Birmingham, England, migrated to Victoria in 1857 and made a reputation as a journalist by reporting on the Maori wars in NZ in 1862–63. His examination of the convict system in WA appeared in the *Argus* and as a pamphlet, *Transportation: The British Convict in Western Australia* (1865). He was editor of the Melbourne *Daily Telegraph* (1869–77) but returned to the *Argus*, becoming its editor in 1898. Among his other publications are *Australian Pictures Drawn with Pen and Pencil* (1886), his observations on Australian life, and *Australian Federation* (1891).

WILLS, William John, see **BURKE and WILLS**

WILLMOT, Eric (1936–), born southern Queensland, moved frequently in childhood, attending primary school at various places in Queensland and the Northern Territory. Instead of attending secondary school he worked as a drover and horse-breaker in remote parts of northern Australia. After serious injury in a rodeo accident, he returned to study and graduated from Newcastle University, spending a decade thereafter as a teacher of mathematics. After completing a master's degree in education planning, he joined the Commonwealth Department of Education, where he was particularly concerned with Aboriginal education. In 1978 he was appointed to the then Canberra College of Advanced Education as lecturer and later moved to the ANU to work on a project on indigenous teacher training. Principal of the Australian Institute of Aboriginal Studies 1981–84, he has subsequently had a prominent career as an academic and public servant, including a period as professor of education at James Cook University (1985–87) and as secretary of the ACT Department of Education and the Arts (1987–92). He has published a novel, *Pemulwuy: The Rainbow Warrior* (1987), which celebrates the life of a heroic leader of the Eora people of the Sydney region who first encountered the shock of White settlement, and a thriller, *Below the Line* (1991). A polymath, Willmot has published in a number of disciplines, including anthropology, and in 1981 won the Inventor of the Year Award and the Medaille d'Or at Geneva for his invention of a Variable Radio Transmission System. In 1987 he was awarded an honorary D.Litt. by Newcastle University. His Boyer lectures, *Australia, the Last Experiment* (1987), which deal with the nature and future prospects of the new mixed societies like Australia, the USA and South Africa, were highly acclaimed. He was made AM in 1987.

WILMOT, Frank, see **'MAURICE, Furnley'**

WILMOT, Chester (1911–54), born Melbourne, a graduate of the University of Melbourne, was a war correspondent for the ABC in Greece, Syria, Tobruk and New Guinea, and subsequently for the BBC in western Europe. He was the BBC's special correspondent at the Nuremberg trials 1945–46, and later became well known as writer and broadcaster for the BBC. He was also military correspondent for the London *Observer*. Wilmot published two books, an account of the 1941 siege of Tobruk, *Tobruk* (1944), which is based on official documents, Wilmot's own observations, and the accounts of men engaged in the fighting; and an authoritative, well-researched and highly praised history of the Second World War, *The Struggle for Europe* (1952).

WILSON, Edward (1813–78), born Hampstead, London, migrated to the Port Phillip District in 1842 and took up farming. In 1848 he and J.S. Johnston purchased the Melbourne *Argus* and incorporated the *Daily News* in 1852. In those newspapers he voiced his conviction that Port Phillip should be separated from NSW and that transportation should cease. He published an account of his travels in Australia and NZ, *Rambles at the Antipodes* (1859), illustrated by S.T. Gill.

WILSON, Edwin (1942–), born Lismore, NSW, was educated at the University of NSW. He has taught science in secondary schools, and worked for a period as a lecturer at Armidale Teachers College and as education officer at the Australian Museum, Sydney. Since 1980 he has worked in Community Programs at the Royal Botanic Gardens, Sydney. He has contributed verse to numerous periodicals and anthologies and has published the collections *Banyan* (1982), *The Dragon Book* (1985), *Songs of the Forest* (1990), *The Rose Garden* (1991) and *The Botanic Verses* (1993). Reflecting his interest in plants, his delicately worked poems often use the vegetable world as a starting point for subtle, wry meditations on the human condition. He has also published the novels *Liberty, Egality, Fraternity!* (1984) and *Wild Tamarind* (1987), as well as pictorial histories and guides to Sydney's major public gardens and parks.

WILSON, Erle (1898–), born Scotland, travelled widely before settling in Australia. He published three novels for adults, *Coorinna* (1953), *Minado, the Devil-Dog* (1955) and *Adams of the Bounty* (1958); the first two reflect his interest in animal life, the last is a treatment of the Bligh mutiny. He also wrote books for children, including *Churinga Tales* (1950), a collection of Aboriginal stories, and *Far-away Tales* (1954), a collection of South Sea legends.

WILSON, William Hardy (1881–1955), born Campbelltown, NSW, was a notable and influential architectural theoretician and watercolour artist. He lived for an extensive period in London and also travelled widely in Europe, the USA and China, before settling finally in Australia in 1930. A qualified architect, he abandoned his profession in 1927 to devote himself to writing and drawing and published several polemical, philosophical and prophetic works. These include two fictional narratives, the semi-autobiographical accounts of the wanderings and meditations of an Australian architect, *The Dawn of a*

New Civilization (1929) and *Eucalyptus* (1941), and *Yin Yang* (1934), a Utopian fantasy. Hardy Wilson's most enduring works are *The Cow Pasture Road* (1920), which focuses on the Camden district of NSW and includes his own illustrations; *Old Colonial Architecture in New South Wales and Tasmania* (1924), a collection of finely executed drawings; and *Grecian and Chinese Architecture* (1937).

WILSON, Helen Helga (1902–91), born Mayne at Zeehan, Tasmania, spent her early years in the WA goldfields area, where her father was a mining engineer. A graduate of the University of WA, she published several anecdotal, historical accounts of the goldfields, including *Gateways to Gold* (1969), *Westward Gold!* (1973), *The Golden Miles* (1977) and *Cyclone Coasts* (1980); the novels, *The Golden Age* (1959), *Quiet, Brat!* (1958), *Where the Wind's Feet Shine* (1960), *If Golde Rust* (1961), *Island of Fire* (1973), *Bring Back the Hour* (1977), *The Mulga Trees* (1980) and *The House at Hardie's Corner* (1984); two collections of short stories, *A Show of Colours* (1970) and *The Skedule and Other Australian Short Stories* (1979); and three of verse, *Songs of Empire* (1941), *Occasional Verse, 1942–1943* (1943), and *The Letters of Huang Hu* (1946). In 1980 she was awarded the OAM.

Wilson, Joe is an important character in ten stories by Henry Lawson (q.v.); most of them have Joe as narrator and were written in 1900–1 while Lawson was in England. The best known and most admired of the stories are the four which comprise the Joe Wilson sequence in *Joe Wilson and His Mates* (q.v., 1901): 'The Courtship of Joe Wilson', 'Brighten's Sister-in-Law' (q.v.), '"Water them Geraniums"' and 'A Double Buggy at Lahey's Creek'. The sequence traces the development of the relationship between Joe and his wife Mary, from the time of their courtship until, six or seven years later, Joe is beginning to prosper.

In 'The Courtship of Joe Wilson', the gawky Joe first encounters Mary Brand when he is working as carpenter with his mate Jack Barnes at the homestead where Mary is in service; their innocent romance is encouraged by Jack but stutters along uncertainly until Mary is insulted by a passing shearer, whom Joe fights. 'Brighten's Sister-in-Law' opens with news of the birth at Gulgong of Jim, the first child, two years after the marriage, although the main incident of the story, developed from a poem Lawson had written in 1899, takes place when Jim is rising 3 and Joe and Mary have just moved to a selection at Lahey's Creek. Jim has been staying with relations at Gulgong and while travelling back to the selection with his father comes down with a fever. Having experienced Jim's convulsions as a baby, Joe panics, but is guided by the vision of a woman he sees in the branches of a tree to a nearby shanty, where Jim is nursed through the fever by the shanty-keeper's sister-in-law. '"Water them Geraniums"' deepens the tragic mood of the series. It begins with the move to Lahey's Creek and details Mary's profound disappointment on arrival, the quarrel in which Joe's drinking problem is raised, and Joe's worry that Mary will become a 'gaunt, haggard Bush-

woman' like Mrs Spicer on the adjoining selection. The second part of the story, 'Past Carin'', also amplified from an earlier poem, covers the first year or so on the selection; a second child is born but the focus of the story is Mrs Spicer, who shows the same kind of courage in adversity as the woman in 'The Drover's Wife', which has some incidents in common with '"Water them Geraniums"', but is eventually broken by poverty and isolation and dies 'past carin''. 'A Double Buggy at Lahey's Creek' returns to something like the mood of 'Joe Wilson's Courtship'. Joe has a good year on the selection and surprises Mary with a new double buggy, which has been provisioned by their friends and by shopkeepers in Gulgong. But just as the sentimentality of 'Joe Wilson's Courtship' is controlled by Joe's retrospective narration, so it is clear, when Joe and Mary talk 'more than we'd done for years' the night the buggy arrives, that hardship has placed strain on the marriage.

The Joe Wilson sequence has been justly admired for its controlled presentation of the process of alienation and disintegration wrought by the experience of bush life. It was Lawson's most extended piece of fiction although the order of composition of the four stories differs significantly from the chronological sequence as arranged in *Joe Wilson and His Mates*. Of the remaining Joe Wilson stories, '"Shall We Gather at the River?"', 'His Brother's Keeper' and 'The Story of "Gentleman-Once"' were published in *Children of the Bush* (1902) and centre on Peter M'Laughlan, the bush missionary, reformed alcoholic and befriender of the down-and-outs. Joe is 17 when he hears M'Laughlan's sermon in '"Shall We Gather at the River?"' and 23 or 24 in the other two stories, in which the central incident is Peter's rescue of Jack Barnes from the drink after a shearing stint, which takes place just before the time of 'Joe Wilson's Courtship'; the links with the Joe and Mary stories are not strong, however, and the choice of Joe as narrator is of little more significance than the appearance of Jack Mitchell (q.v.) on the track in 'The Story of "Gentleman-Once"'. In contrast, 'James and Maggie' and 'Drifting Apart', both published in *Triangles of Light* (1913), are later stories than those in the *Joe Wilson and His Mates* sequence. 'James and Maggie' deals with the courtship of James, Joe's brother-in-law who lives at the Lahey's Creek selection from the time of '"Water them Geraniums"', and Maggie Charlesworth, who lives at the home of the local squatter; and 'Drifting Apart' is almost a sequel to 'The Double Buggy at Lahey's Creek' and chronicles the estrangement and eventual reunion between Joe and Mary during a trip to Sydney and back. In the final story, 'Joe Wilson in England', included in *Rowlandson's Commonwealth Annual*, Lawson himself, rather than Joe, is the narrator, who records the reactions of the Wilsons to England, where Joe is the representative of an English wool firm. An unfinished Joe Wilson story, identified by Brian Kiernan in recently discovered Lawson material, is included as 'Going on the Land' in his selection, *The Essential Henry Lawson* (1982).

That Lawson wrote the intensely personal Joe Wilson stories when his own marriage was under strain clearly influenced his presentation of Joe and Mary; there are further links between the Wilsons and the Lawsons in that Joe is dependent on alcohol, that Mary is 'German in figure and walk' in '"Water them Geraniums"', and that in 1916 Lawson stated that 'Mrs Joe Wilson was . . . a portrait of Mrs Henry Lawson (as I idealized her then)'. It is equally clear, however, that the four major stories were informed by other experiences of Lawson (he also claimed in 1916 that Joe, at various points, was 'my uncle by marriage', 'my father and myself') as well as by a creative imagination that transformed experience into what is regarded, with *While the Billy Boils* (1896), as the peak of his achievement.

'Wind at Your Door, The', a poem by R.D. Fitz-Gerald (q.v.), was first published in the *Bulletin* (1958). It is based on the uprising of Irish rebel convicts at Castle Hill in 1804 although the incident of the flogging depicted in the poem took place at Toongabbie in 1800. The poem has two central characters: the poet's ancestor, Martin Mason, surgeon, magistrate, and seemingly callous overseer of the brutal flogging of a convict; and the poet's namesake, Morris Fitzegarrel, the stoic convict victim. In these two figures and their history, FitzGerald sees the continuing problem, on both the national and the individual level, of the Australian identity. On the general level is the problem of the nation adapting to its development from a 'jail-yard'; on the personal level is the problem of individual Australians (in this case the poet himself) adapting to both sides of their ancestry, authoritarianism and rebellion against authority. The poem indicates that the wind that blows the blood and flesh from the lacerated back of the convict Fitzegarrel into the faces of the bystanders will continue to blow the memory and the impact of that event, and scores of similar events, into the present and future Australian consciousness. FitzGerald's personal compromise is to accept that both the characters in the poem and others like them are equal victims. The convict Fitzegarrel also appears in Thomas Keneally's novel *Passenger* (1979).

WINDSOR, A.L. (Arthur Lloyd) (1833–1913) was born on the way to the West Indies, where his father's family were plantation-owners. Educated in England, where he established a reputation in literary and journalistic circles, he arrived in Australia in 1863 to become editor of the *Argus*. He left that newspaper in 1865, edited the *Mount Alexander Mail* at Castlemaine 1865–69, and became editor of the *Age* in 1872, a position he held until his retirement in 1900. He was president of the Australian Institute of Journalists in 1892; his book of essays, *Ethica: Or, Characteristics of Men, Manners and Books*, was published in 1860.

WINDSOR, Gerard (1944–), born Sydney, the son of well-known doctor Harry Windsor and brother of novelist Penelope Rowe, graduated MA at the ANU, tutored in English at UNSW (1979–80) and worked as an editor in the Subtitling Unit of SBS tele-vision (1982–85). He now writes full-time. Concentrating chiefly on short fiction, he has (to 1993) published two books of stories, *The Harlots Enter First* (1982) and *Memories of the Assassination Attempt* (1985); a short novel, *That Fierce Virgin* (1988); and a collection of biographically based anecdotal reminiscences, *Family Lore* (1990). In much of his writing his Irish Catholic family background, Catholic education and feeling for Ireland, where he lived for a time, is a considerable presence and influence. *The Harlots Enter First*, which contains most of his early attempts at short fiction, is dominated by the Irish-Catholic connection, especially in such stories as 'In Waverley Cemetery, the Faith of our Fathers', 'Pathology Tests', 'The Easy Steps of Father Michael O'Leary' and 'The Irishman Takes to His Boat'. More widely praised and highly regarded, his second book, *Memories of the Assassination Attempt and Other Stories*, confirmed the presence of a remarkably original and highly talented short-story writer. Catholic and Irish situations and influences are still present but less dominant. The title story tells of a French priest, who escaped to America, reflecting on his involvement in an earlier attempt to assassinate Napoleon. Every time he celebrates Mass he sees again, and feels the guilt of, the death of a 14-year-old girl blown apart by the bomb meant to kill the Emperor. Many of Windsor's stories blend the everyday with the bizarre in a highly credible fashion. In 'Can These Bones Live?' a married couple, who are at odds, and their children explore an Irish graveyard, meanwhile parrying the children's questions by speaking ambiguously, and often hostilely, to each other. 'Wedding Presents for Breakfast' focuses on another disquieting marriage, and the strange tale of a married woman who left her wedding presents unopened from her wedding day to her death. 'The Life of a Man's Man' shows that the lot of the subservient partner in a homosexual match is little different from a heterosexual marriage. 'The Archbishop or the Lady' shows the effect on a one-time novice to the priesthood of the death of Archbishop Mannix.

Windsor's autobiographically based book *Family Lore* is his most effective and attractive writing. An extended family of surgeons, veterinarians, pathologists, writers, grandfathers and fathers, grandmothers and mothers, brothers, sisters, aunts and uncles wander in and out of his stories uttering or inspiring five generations of anecdotes and cautionary tales. After the slow, discursive beginning of 'Starting the Family', 'Romance as a Beginning', 'In the Garden' and 'Virgins, Widows and Penitents' are more lively, with a pleasant mixture of drama and humour.

Many of the stories revolve around doctors, hospitals, operations and good, practical medicine (e.g. the 'impacted faeces' segment). The underlying passion of the book, however, is the author/son's desire to truly know the father who dominated the family and who dominates the second half of the book itself, and for the father to know him. The true sage, however, and the most entertaining character, is the grandfather, whose reminiscences, homilies, wit and forthrightness overshadow the rest of the cast in the first half.

That Fierce Virgin, Windsor's only novel, is a bizarre story involving a 36-year-old Irish doctor, Maura Boland, illegitimate daughter of Nell Boland. Maura shares a one-night stand with an unnamed Australian marketing man who is in Ireland to learn the religious accessories trade. It is her annual practice to become pregnant to a casual lover and then to go to England for an abortion – 'I always have one at this time of year.' An eccentric, whose motives seem a mixture of seeking sexual satisfaction and a perverse pleasure in exercising power over the foetus, Maura is an extraordinary piece of characterisation. On this particular occasion her Australian lover attempts in vain to abort the abortion itself.

Winged Seeds (1950), the final novel of Katherine Susannah Prichard's (q.v.) goldfields trilogy, examines the period from the mining depression of 1936 through to the end of the Second World War. The focus increasingly moves to Sally Gough's communist grandson, Bill, his involvement with Paddy Cavan's stepdaughters Pam and Pat, who share his revolutionary sentiments, and his eventual death in a war fought against fascism. The final scene in which a kalgoorluh nut sheds its seeds as Sally and Dinny bury their Aboriginal friend, is a symbolic affirmation of the ideas expressed in the trilogy; 'the life force' which 'strives towards perfection' will ensure that seeds sown in the past for a better system come to fruition. See *Roaring Nineties, The* and *Golden Miles*.

Sandra Burchill

WINSTANLEY, Eliza (1818–82), born England, came to Australia in 1833, making her first stage appearance at Barnett Levey's Theatre Royal the next year. A versatile, hard-working actor, she showed a particular flair for tragic roles, learning a great deal from her mentor, Conrad Knowles. She married H.C. O'Flaherty (q.v.) in 1841 and in 1846 left with him for England, where her career prospered. In 1847 she left for a successful run in the USA, often playing leading Shakespearean roles. She returned to London in time to join the company formed by Charles Kean at the Princess's Theatre in 1850, and shared in Kean's achievements for the next eight years, appearing in several command performances before the Queen at Windsor. She turned to writing as a means of support in the 1850s when she was widowed and was becoming too stout and old for the theatre. *Shifting Scenes in Theatrical Life* (1859) is her first novel in book form. She was previously assumed to be the author of 'Lucy Cooper', a short novel published anonymously in the *Illustrated Sydney News* (1854), although Victor Crittenden in his 1992 edition of *Lucy Cooper* attributes it to John Lang. Her other novels, stories and articles, which often draw on her Australian experiences, were frequently serialised in *Bow Bells*. From 1865 to 1866 she also edited and contributed to *Fiction for Family Reading*, collections of short stories issued in weekly parts. She finally abandoned her acting career in 1864, returned to Australia in 1880 and died in Sydney two years later of diabetes and exhaustion. Her Australian novels include *Margaret Falconer* (1860), *Twenty Straws*

(1864), *Des Moro* (1866), *What Is to Be, Will Be* (1867) and *For Her Natural Life* (1876, republished by Mulini Press in 1992), and three novels serialised in the *Sydney Mail*, *Bitter Sweet* (1860), *Which Wins?* (1861) and *A Lonely Lot* (1863).

WINTER, S.V. (Samuel Vincent) (1843–1904), born in the Goulburn River district of Victoria, founded the Catholic newspaper the *Advocate* in 1868 and managed it for three years before passing it to his brother Joseph (1844–1915), who managed it until his death. In 1871 he purchased the Melbourne *Herald* in partnership with John Halfey and others, took over the editorship of the paper three years later and rapidly built up its circulation. He also founded and edited the *Sportsman* (1881) and was active in the ANA, local government and charitable organisations. Nicknamed 'Stormy' Winter, he was well known for his quick temper, his drive and vituperative powers, as well as his generosity. Fiercely committed to the Irish Home Rule movement in Victoria, Joseph published the *Irish-Australian Almanac and Directory* from 1870.

WINTON, Tim (1960–), born Scarborough, WA, and educated in Perth and Albany and at the WA Institute of Technology, has been a full-time writer since 1982. Winton lived for two years in France, Ireland and Greece before returning to Australia in 1989. His first novel, *An Open Swimmer* (1982), shared the 1981 *Australian*/Vogel National Literary Award; his second, *Shallows* (1984), won the Miles Franklin Award in 1984; his collection of stories *Scission* (1985) won the 1985 WA Council Week Literary Award; and his novel *Cloudstreet* (q.v., 1991) won the NBC Banjo Award and the 1992 Miles Franklin Award. His other publications are the novels *In the Winter Dark* (1988) and *That Eye, the Sky* (1986); the collections of short stories *Minimum of Two* (1987) and *Blood and Water* (1993); the novels for younger readers *Jesse* (1990), *Lockie Leonard, Human Torpedo* (1990), *The Bugalugs Bum Thief* (1991) and *Lockie Leonard, Scumbuster* (1993); and *Land's Edge* (1993), autobiographical meditations about his relationship with place.

Winton has described himself as a novelist with a firm sense of place, specifically the WA coast which figures markedly in his fiction: 'I write about small places; about people in small situations. If I get a grip on the geography, I can get a grip on the people . . . the people I responded to the most when I was discovering literature were the people who had their characters out in landscape.' In several of Winton's novels the central protagonist is a young man in quest of identity and meaning. Jerra Nilsam of *An Open Swimmer* is already burdened by guilt and sad experience when the novel opens; unable to recover from his relationship with his best friend's mother, Aunt Jewel, he is desperately searching for the talisman which will restore his earlier innocent wholeness, just as he also searches for the rare pearl in the turrum fish which he has glimpsed and lost as a child. The spontaneity of his friendship with Sean, the best mate of his childhood, has eroded as their choice of futures has diverged, Sean choosing the security of a commercial career in the city, Jerra having opted to drop out of his university course. Jerra's encounters with an old man who lives a reclusive existence on the edge of the beach appear to offer some hope of enlightenment, but the experience finally reinforces the young man's sense that there is no escape from guilt and that like the protagonist of one of Winton's short stories he has been so 'broken' that only an obscure sort of grace can rescue him. Unlike the 'open swimmers' of fish which receive the pearl, he is doomed to be a cave fish which sees nothing. *Shallows*, set in Angelus, WA, the last land-based whaling station in Australia, focuses on the relationship between Cleve Cookson and his wife Queenie; whereas Queenie, the direct descendant of one of the original settlers and whalers, Nathaniel Coupar, becomes a passionate protester against whaling, a crusade which ends in confusion, violence and defeat, Cleve immerses himself in the journals of Nathaniel Coupar in an attempt to fix his sense of wavering purpose and uncertain identity. Like other older, 'wiser' figures in Winton's fiction, Coupar proves an uncertain mentor and Cleve's quest proves even more fruitless than Queenie's. The novel closes with a more hopeful suggestion of meaning, however, in the resistant life and awesome power of the whales themselves, which appear to touch the spirits of the young couple in ways which words and political activity failed to do. As in *An Open Swimmer*, sea imagery and detailed description of watery life carry much of the emotional meaning of the story, and much of its suggestive power, creating a view of the world which one reader has described as 'ambiguous, opalescent, aqueous; populated with misty shapes now closing in, now drifting out of focus; alive with a bright light that can darken unpredictably to the sinister blue-black of impenetrable depth; and full of beauty and corruption brought into gruesome companionship'. Narrated by a 12-year-old boy, Ort Flack, who is keenly observant of the lives of his friends and relations, *That Eye, the Sky* explores with tragi-comic effect his own and his family's vicissitudes following a car accident which makes his father a paraplegic; an uncompromisingly realistic picture of an idiosyncratic group of people, *That Eye, the Sky* is also concerned with the emotional and spiritual difficulties, consolations, and challenges of loving and believing in God. *In the Winter Dark* is a departure from Winton's earlier novels, exploring with chilling and suspenseful effect the mysterious psychological links between four characters who inhabit an isolated valley called the Sink and who, oppressed by past guilts, are unable to unite to discover the one responsible for a series of mutilations of their animals. *Cloudstreet*, Winton's most substantial novel in terms of length, deals with the connected lives of two families in Perth, the Lambs and the Pickles, from 1943 to 1964; when the feckless gambler Sam Pickles achieves his one windfall, a large, rambling house (number one Cloud Street) in the form of a bequest from his brother-in-law, he rents half of it to the large, bustling Lamb family, whose sense of purpose and different destiny make a sharp contrast; balancing the small-town innocence of Perth during the immediate post-war decades with the gothic idiosyncrasies of both families, *Cloudstreet* celebrates lives which are mixed, both tragic and comic, grotesque and graceful. The short stories of *Scission* and *Minimum of Two* are spare, subtle, multilayered studies of the challenges offered by close relationships and the difficulties of achieving and maintaining a sense of individual wholeness and purpose. Death, self-doubt and loneliness are omnipresent aspects of the life of his protagonists, although Winton frequently leaves their fates open-ended; others such as Jerra Nilsam and Queenie Cookson, familiar figures from his novels, continue their quests to come to terms with the past. A collection of critical essays, *Reading Tim Winton*, edited by Richard Rossiter and Lyn Jacobs, was published in 1993.

'WITTING, Amy' (Joan Levick) (1918–), born Joan Fraser at Annandale, Sydney, attended the University of Sydney, where she was a member of the group of intellectuals and poets which included James McAuley and Harold Stewart. She later taught French and English at secondary level. She has contributed short stories and poems to such magazines as *Quadrant*, *Overland*, *Westerly* and the *New Yorker* and has published three novels, *The Visit* (1977), *I for Isobel* (1989, winner of the FAW Barbara Ramsden Award in 1989) and *A Change in the Lightning* (1994); a short-story collection, *Marriages* (1990); and two collections of poetry, *Travel Diary* (1985) and *Beauty is the Straw* (1991). She has also written textbooks on language. In 1974, under the pseudonym 'Chris Willoughby', Witting submitted to issue eight of *Tabloid Story* a story mirroring and parodying what she perceived as the mindless sexism of some earlier contributors; issue eight was subsequently published as a supplement to *Education*, the journal of the NSW Teachers' Federation, arousing fierce protests from teachers and parents and from politicians when it was tabled in Parliament. Although Witting's first novel was received with strongly favourable reviews, it was soon remaindered and she encountered difficulties in securing publication of *I for Isobel* until it won support from a London publisher. *The Visit* focuses on a group of people in a small country town, Bangoree. Outwardly sleepy and 'normal', Bangoree in fact is the home of fierce passions which include the hopelessness of unreciprocated love, envy, well-nourished hatred and even the longing of a husband for his wife's death. As in Witting's subsequent novel, literature plays a shaping role, re-enacting itself in the lives of the characters and bringing together with dramatic consequences literary detection and detection in its more familiar sense. Meanwhile ordinary lives are made more than ordinary and are subtly intertwined with the public life of the town in a style which has led one reviewer to compare Witting to 'that master of provincial pathos, Chekhov'. *I for Isobel*, the story of a young girl's emergence from the destructive circle of hatred caused by a mother's moral sickness and a father's indifference, presents both the resistant integrity of her sense of self and the corruption of her surroundings with incisive dramatic realism. Structured as a series of five self-contained episodes, distanced from each other by time, the story follows Isobel from her home and Catholic school in a working-class suburb in Sydney to a boarding house after she has undergone the liberation of her mother's death, to encounters with university students which are both expanding and constricting, to a nadir of alienation and destructiveness which is surprisingly and suddenly transcended. Interpreting the familiar world of the family as a place of gothic proportions, subject to emotional enormities, Witting's approach is also basically comic, presenting Isobel as alive to the farcical or absurd quality of the various situations she finds herself in, as she is to their potential for pain, pathos and sometimes even tragedy. Not unlike 'Richardson's' heroine of *The Getting of Wisdom*, Isobel has a keen, observant intelligence which makes her particular getting of wisdom remarkably rapid, a series of fine insights which arrive at the sort of detachment which is in effect the state of grace she had sought to achieve as a child. The short stories of *Marriages* reveal a deep psychological understanding which comprehends the unhappiness driving acts of cruelty as well as the suffering of those who are its victims. The range of tone and subject is remarkable, shifting from the rural settting of 'Survivors' and its exploration of casual gender relationships which is comparable to Baynton's stories in bleakness, to the delicate evocation of happiness touched with mortality of 'A Bottle of Tears', to the humour resilient in the face of disaster of 'Goodbye Ady, Goodbye Joe'. Some are almost as long as a novella, others are highly economical, but all compress their insights into small space. Working with a fine scalpel, Witting anatomises motives, unconscious impulses, the dynamics of relationships, the nuances of language and physical expression. Witting's poetry, diverse in range, tone and voice, is cerebral, sensual, witty and, like her fiction, often deftly ironic. Uniting the diversity as a thematic undercurrent is a tempered response to time, change and the certainty of death, an Auden-like awareness that 'The moment of our desolation/ Will be some other's consolation'. Witting received the Patrick White Award in 1993.

WODHAMS, J., see Science Fiction

Woman of the Future, A, a novel by David Ireland (q.v.), was published in 1979, and won the Miles Franklin, the National Book Council and the *Age* Awards. A mixture of surrealistic, realistic and allegorical modes, it has a discontinuous narrative structure that renders experience in a piecemeal but composite way. Set in an unspecified time in the near future, it is the story of Alethea Hunt from conception to the age of 18 when she disappears and, it is implied, turns into a leopard. Alethea, who does everything superlatively and who is to some extent representative of Australia, has a sense of herself as unique and as having untapped resources; she remains virginal, however much her sexual capacity is exploited. The actuality of the surrounding Australian life is degraded and ugly, however. Alethea lives in a rigid social structure, divided between the privileged serving class and the

so-called Free who are condemned to a life of futility. Surreal physical aberrations match the social distortions: a man grows a coffin out of his side, some people sprout branches and leaves, a girl has a proliferation of vulvas in her armpits. Alethea's final transformation is interpreted in a visionary way that celebrates Australia's magnificent potential.

Woman Tamer, The, a one-act comedy by Louis Esson (q.v.), was first produced in 1909 by William Moore and published in 1911. Set in the Melbourne slums and coloured by a racy, underworld vernacular, the action relates the downfall of the arrogant and lazy Chopsey Ryan, who is supplanted in the heroine's affections by tough guy Bongo Williams, just out of gaol.

Woman to Man (1949), the second volume of poems published by Judith Wright (q.v.), takes its title from the opening poem, a delicate, sensitive, yet forthright statement of the special relationship between man and woman as sharers in the act of conception. The sequential poems 'Woman's Song' and 'Woman to Child' are equally compelling statements of woman as mother. The poet's preoccupation with time is evident in 'Letter to a Friend', 'Spring after War' and 'The Bones Speak', but echoing as they do the optimism of her earlier poem 'The Moving Image', they indicate time's regenerative as well as destructive power.

Woman's Love, Mary Leman Grimstone's (q.v.) didactic and early feminist novel set among the provincial aristocracy in south-west England, was published in 1832. Although not set in Australia, *Woman's Love* was written during Grimstone's sojourn with her sister in Van Diemen's Land 1826–29 and is probably, therefore, the first novel written in Australia.

Womanspeak, see **Feminism and Australian Literature**

Women of the Sun (1983), a series of four self-contained television plays, each dealing with an episode of Aboriginal history as seen through an Aborigine's eyes, was written by Hyllus Maris and Sonia Borg. First screened in 1982, it won the 1982 United Nations Association of Australia Media Prize and an Awgie in 1983. Hyllus Maris, who won the Patricia Weickhardt Award in 1982 for *Women of the Sun*, was an Aboriginal rights worker, sociologist and educator.

'Women of the West, The', see **EVANS, George Essex**

WONGAR, B. (Banumbir, Birimbir) (Sreten Bozic) (1932–   ) is the Aboriginal name of a writer, born Sreten Bozic, from Yugoslavia. He had a difficult and hazardous childhood during the war years and as a young man but in 1958 was finally successful in escaping to France. After two years in Paris he came to Australia and lived for a decade in the NT, where he made a tribal marriage and encountered Aboriginal culture at first hand. After his wife died in the 1970s he moved to Melbourne. Wongar's writing first appeared in 1970 and won immediate recognition and literary awards for its understanding of Aboriginal culture. His short stories, signed B or Birimbir (and later Banumbir) Wongar, appeared in such varied periodicals as *Les Temps Modernes* (Paris), *Atlantic Monthly*, *London Magazine* and *Australian Women's Weekly*. A collection of short stories 'from Vietnam', titled *The Sinners* and with a foreword by Alan Marshall, appeared in 1972, and another, titled *The Track to Bralgu* with a foreword by Alan Paton, in 1978. As Sreten Bozic he also collaborated with Alan Marshall in a non-fiction book, *Aboriginal Myths* (1972). Received enthusiastically overseas, where they won approbation from such figures as Simone de Beauvoir, and were translated into German, Hungarian, Russian and Serbo-Croat, Wongar's books were slow to win publication or attention in Australia. Described in the publisher's note to *The Track to Bralgu* as an Aborigine born in northern Australia in the late 1930s but educated overseas, his European origins were not fully disclosed until 1981 when Robert Drewe summed up in the *Bulletin* the results of a prolonged search for his identity. Critics in Australia have been largely preoccupied with issues of authenticity and legitimacy, although some readers have more recently emphasised Wongar's distinctive ability to negotiate two cultures and present two realities. It has been suggested that he is writing in a new genre, termed 'Aboriginalism', and that his work is a challenging, imaginative hybrid, blending and extending both European and Aboriginal ways of thought. His other books include the novels *The Trackers* (1978), the trilogy *Walg* (1983), *Karan* (1985) and *Gabo Djara* (1987), and *Marngit* (1991); the collections of short stories *Babaru* (1982) and *The Last Pack of Dingoes* (1993); the plays *A Stone in My Pocket* (1973, published as Sreten Bozic) and *Balang an Village* (1973); and a collection of poetry, *Bilma* (1984). He also contributed to *Ethnic Australia* (1981), edited by Manfred Jurgensen. He has won the PEN International Award for his trilogy of novels, the American Library Association Award for *Babaru* and a prize from the *Observer* for his poetry. *The Trackers* deals with an Asian architect in Australia who wakes one morning with a black skin and is compelled to look at White culture from the outside. Wongar's trilogy concentrates on the division between Black responses to the land as an extension of humankind and White preoccupation with material exploitation. Although subtitled a novel, *Marngit* is a loosely linked collection of stories, largely narrated by animals and birds; as in the collection *Babaru*, the distinctions between human and animal, living and dead, dream and waking are blurred and shifting.

WOOD, G.A. (George Arnold) (1865–1928), born and educated in England, was Challis professor of history at the University of Sydney from 1891 until his death. His quality as an influential teacher of great personal magnetism and independent mind has been recorded by one of his students, R.M. Crawford, in his biography '*A Bit of a Rebel*' (1975). Wood's major research work was *The Discovery of Australia* (1922).

WOOD, Thomas (1892–1950), the English composer, visited Australia 1930–32 and published a delightful record of his travels, *Cobbers* (1934), in which he printed the words and music of 'Waltzing Matilda' without realising copyright might be involved but percipiently praised it as being 'Good enough to be the unofficial National Anthem of Australia'. Further impressions of Australia are recorded in his autobiography, *True Thomas* (1936). *Cobbers*, which owes a great deal to Wood's gregarious qualities, includes graphic descriptions of Australian landscapes and ways of life and work, both urban and rural. Enlivened by his personal, easy style, it includes numerous original comments on the national character, language and humour and distinctive summations of regional differences. Victoria is described as having sobered down 'after a riotous youth ... It creases its trousers and goes to Church'; Hobart 'has the air of an English country town which has shed its old houses and wandered down to the sea for a rest'; Sydney is 'an exotic: a lovely and petulant spend-thrift, going its own wilful headstrong vivid way; self-centred, yet open-hearted; absurdly vain, yet very likeable'. Wood's later book, *Cobbers Campaigning* (1940), is a tribute to Australia's part in the First World War.

WOODBERRY, Joan (1921–), born in outback northern NSW, has lived in Tasmania since 1959. Educated at the universities of Sydney, Melbourne and Tasmania, she has been a teacher and librarian and lived for periods in the Middle East, Greece and London. A well-known writer for younger readers, she has written scripts and one-act plays for radio, especially for the BBC; her books for children include a series focusing on the character Raffles, one of which, *Rafferty Rides a Winner* (1961), was co-winner of the 1962 CBC Book of the Year Award. Her other books for children include *Come Back Peter* (1968), *Ash Tuesday* (1968), *The Cider Duck* (1969) and *A Garland of Gannets* (1969); she has also written the texts for several books in the regional Sketch Book series, edited several anthologies of writing by members of the Tasmanian Fellowship of Australian Writers and written a study of the emancipist publisher Andrew Bent and his struggle with Governor Arthur, *Andrew Bent and the Freedom of the Press in Van Diemen's Land* (1972).

WOODHOUSE, Jena (1949–), born Rockhampton, has worked as a teacher of creative writing and of English as a second language and as a freelance editor and writer. Winner of the FAW John Shaw Neilson Award for poetry in 1986, of the Rothmans Foundation Prize in 1988 and of an Australian-Greek Travel Award in 1987, she has published poetry in numerous periodicals and anthologies. She has also published the collection *Eros in Landscape* (1989) and the novella *Metis, the Octopus and the Olive Tree* (1993).

WOODHOUSE, Margaret, see *Stockwhip*

WOODS, Walter Alan, see **HEAD, Walter William**

WOOLDRIGE, Susan (1819–87), born Susan Brown at Westminster, England, had been an actor for twenty-nine years when she arrived in Australia in 1853 with her husband and two daughters. In the 1850s she appeared in numerous theatrical productions on the Victorian goldfields, mainly at Bendigo, as did her daughters Harriet and Nellie. In 1863 she moved to Melbourne, where she was engaged by George Selth Coppin (q.v.) and was increasingly successful, frequently touring in Victoria and SA and appearing in productions in Sydney. Her last appearance was in 1886. Barbara Jefferis in *Three of a Kind* (1982) gives an account of her life and those of her daughter, Harriet Wooldrige, and granddaughter, Mary Card.

WOOLFE, Sue (1950–) grew up in the Blue Mountains, NSW, and graduated from the universities of Sydney and New England. She has taught in NSW secondary schools and at Sydney TAFE. She has written textbooks on language and literature (1975, 1984) and has scripted (*Maestro's Company*, 1984), directed and produced documentary films and edited subtitles for SBS television. Her 1989 novel, *Painted Woman*, was runner-up in the ABC Bicentennial Awards. In three sections, *Painted Woman* is the story of Frances, only child of a well-known artist who, given to violence and egotism, strangles his wife. Frances grows up under the domination of her father's personality, her life having no individual meaning outside his orbit. She almost marries, fleeing in her wedding dress from the church, and thereafter spends her life with him, painting under his directions. Ultimately she comes to know the true nature of her father when she discovers a painting of him done by her mother that reveals 'a mean, dishonest, ignorant face. A face that knows nothing'. She also ultimately comes to recognise and accept her own artistic talent. Woolfe published, with Kate Grenville, *Making Stories: How Ten Australian Novels Were Written* (1993), the novelists including Peter Carey, Thomas Keneally, Helen Garner, Patrick White, Jessica Anderson, David Ireland and Finola Moorhead.

WOOLLEY, John (1816–66), born Hampshire, England, was first principal and professor of classics at the University of Sydney. He arrived in Sydney in 1849 to prepare for the opening of the University in 1852. An influential educationalist, he was particularly prominent in an attempt to expand the Sydney Mechanics' School of Arts. He was also well known in literary circles and was friendly with N.D. Stenhouse, Henry Kendall, J. Sheridan Moore and Daniel Deniehy. Some of his Australian lectures were collected and published in 1862, titled *Lectures Delivered in Australia*.

WOOLLEY, Pat (1947–), born California, USA, worked as a fashion designer and singer 1966–69, and came to Australia in 1970 where she worked as a printer, publisher and bookseller. Presses with which she has been associated include Tomato Press, Wild & Woolley, which she founded with Michael Wilding and of which she is managing director, and Redress Press. She has written on collectives, *The Art of Living Together* (1978), and has edited *The Wild and Woolley Comix Book* (1977) and *All About Grass* (1973). In 1986 she established Australia In Print Inc., which by means of a monthly catalogue of new Australian books kept USA readers and booksellers aware of Australian writing.

WOOLLS, William (1814–93), born Hampshire, England, came to Australia at the age of 17 and subsequently became a schoolmaster and an Anglican clergyman. His personality is described by one of his students, 'Rolf Boldrewood', in *In Bad Company and Other Stories* (1901). Woolls was one of Australia's first essayists, his *Miscellanies in Prose and Verse* appearing in 1838. An authoritative botanist, whose work was useful to Ferdinand von Mueller, he wrote several scientific books as well as articles published in proceedings of the Linnean Society. He also published three booklets of verse, *The Voyage* (1832), *Australia* (1833) and *In Memory of R.D. FitzGerald* (1892), grandfather of the prominent Australian poet of the same name; and a sermon in memory of the novelist Caroline Atkinson (1874).

Worker, a Brisbane labour journal, was established as a monthly but ran mainly as a weekly 1890–1974. A trades union organ, it carried labour news, political articles and reports, fiction and poetry; among prominent contributors in the 1890s were Francis Adams, John Farrell and Henry Lawson. The *Worker* emerged at a time of labour agitation in Queensland and in its early days was more strongly established than its NSW equivalent the Sydney *Worker*, which it incorporated in 1892–93. The best-known editor of the *Worker* was its founding one, William Lane, whose novel *The Workingman's Paradise* was serialised in the journal in 1891. Later editors included the poet and politician Francis Kenna, and the journalist and writer H.E. Boote.

Worker (Sydney), see **Australian Worker**

Working Papers in Sex, Science and Culture, see **Feminism and Australian Literature**

Workingman's Paradise, The, a novel by William Lane under the pseudonym 'John Miller', and subtitled *An Australian Labour Novel* to emphasise its openly propagandist attitudes, was published in 1892. In his preface Lane explains that the novel's purpose is to assist the fund for the unionists imprisoned for conspiracy in the shearers' strike of 1891 and to explain socialism to the world at large. The novel's title, ironically used, is a phrase taken from Henry Kingsley's novel *The Recollections of Geoffry Hamlyn* (1859).

The novel is in two parts, 'The Woman Tempted Him' and 'He Knew Himself Naked'. Its protagonists, Nellie Lawton, a Sydney dressmaker (claimed by Mary Gilmore to be a fictional representation of her) and Ned Hawkins, a Queensland bushman, meet in Sydney in the summer of 1888–89. Nellie, an ardent socialist, introduces the naive, generous-hearted Ned to the squalor and destitution of Sydney's poorer areas: the grimy slums themselves; the sweated labour of the rag trade and restaurants; Paddy's Market, the festering sore of Sydney's poverty; the prostitutes and beggars who live off the streets and sleep in the parks; the circle of radical intelligentsia (e.g. Connie and Harry Stratton, and Geisner), where social solutions are aired in 'a medley of conversation'. Notable incidents include the recitation of F.J. Broomfield's poem 'The Vision of Labour', by the poet Arty, thought to be modelled on Henry Lawson; Nellie's illustration of practical socialism by kissing a sleeping prostitute; and the indoctrination of young Ned by Geisner with the principles of Marxism and new unionism. The second part takes place after an interval of two years. The maritime strike of 1890 has failed, the shearers' strike of 1891 is imminent and Ned is now an active, dedicated unionist. Several stereotyped incidents, e.g. the death of a young child through deprivation and the moral ruin of Nellie's younger sister through poverty, cause Nellie to refuse to marry Ned. She vows never to bring children into the degradation and misery that constitute working-class life. Ned is inspired to confront capitalism even more strongly and returns to Queensland to implement the shearers' strike.

Woroni, a student journal of the Australian National University, began publication in 1947 and has occasionally attracted original work from poets and writers living in the Canberra region.

'Wowser', defined by *The Macquarie Dictionary* (1981) as 'a prudish teetotaller' or 'a killjoy' and by C.J. Dennis as 'an ineffably pious person who mistakes this world for a penitentiary and himself for a warder', is a term of uncertain origin. It is popularly accepted to be an acronym coined by John Norton, owner of the newspaper *Truth*, signifying 'We Only Want Social Evils Remedied (or Righted)'. Alec H. Chisholm, however, has suggested that the word derives from 'rouser', a term for religious fanatics current in Victoria in the 1870s. The wowser, who has been a persistent figure in Australian cultural life but who appears to have had his heyday from the 1880s to the end of the First World War, was frequently depicted in cartoons in the *Bulletin* and other newspapers during those years. He invariably appeared bearded, wearing a small flat hat or a gimlet and carrying the universal symbol of a wowser, an umbrella. Numerous Australian writers have inveighed against wowsers, including Norman Lindsay, C.J. Dennis, Frank Hardy, Hugh McCrae, A.D. Hope, Douglas Stewart, Dal Stivens, Geoffrey Dutton and Dorothy Hewett; others have suffered the effects of wowserism in the form of censorship. Keith Dunstan in *Wowsers* (1968) has written 'an account of the prudery exhibited by certain outstanding men and women in such matters as Drink, Smoking, Prostitution, Censorship and Gambling'.

WREN, John (1871–1953), a Melbourne sports promoter and financier, was born into a poor family at Collingwood, where he ran an illegal, but highly profitable, totalisator 1893–1907. He later acquired interests in racecourses and other sporting enterprises and in 1916 took control of the interstate boxing enterprise Stadiums Ltd. In 1915 he acquired the Brisbane *Daily Mail*. Wren, frequently accused of illegal and even criminal activities and of political manipulation, appears as the central character, John West, in Frank Hardy's novel *Power Without Glory* (q.v., 1950). Hardy, charged with criminal libel (of Mrs Wren only) in 1951, was acquitted after a nine-month trial and gave an account of the writing of the novel and of his trial in *The Hard Way* (1961). Wren also appears as a character in Barry Oakley's play *The Feet of Daniel Mannix* (1975). There are two accounts of his life, Niall Brennan's *John Wren: Gambler* (1971) and Hugh Buggy's *The Real John Wren* (1977), Buggy being one of Wren's lifetime friends and his book a rebuttal of Hardy's *Power Without Glory*.

WRIGHT, Arthur (1870–1932), born near Bathurst, was a writer of fiction, usually with a background of horse-racing, other sports and crime. He published numerous novels and stories including *Keane of Kalgoorlie* (1907), *A Rogue's Luck* (1909), *Gambler's Gold* (1911), *Rung In* (1912), *In the Last Stride* (1914), *Under a Cloud* (1916), *Over the Odds* (1918), which contains three other stories, *The Breed Holds Good* (1918), *When Nuggets Glistened* (1918), *The Outlaw's Daughter* (1919), *A Game of Chance* (1919), *A Rough Passage* (1920), *Fettered by Fate* (1921), *A Colt from the Country* (1922), *The Squatter's Secret* (1927), *A Good Recovery* (1928), *A Crooked Game* (1928) and *Gaming for Gold* (1929). Occasionally classified with Nat Gould, Wright nevertheless lacks Gould's ease, versatility and range. His novels are characterised by simple, 'low-life' characters, straightforward if action-filled plots, rough humour and sketchily realised Australian backgrounds. Four of Wright's novels were produced as films, *Keane of Kalgoorlie* and *Gambler's Gold* in 1911, *In the Last Stride* in 1916, and *A Rough Passage* in 1922, and he also won an award for his screenplay 'The Loyal Rebel' (1915).

WRIGHT, David McKee (1869–1928), born Ireland, was educated in Ireland and London, and in 1887 migrated to NZ. There he worked on sheep stations, studied for the Congregational ministry and from 1890 contributed to many NZ journals. In 1905 he gave up the ministry and in 1907 began work as a journalist on the *New Zealand Mail*. Four of his volumes of verse were published in NZ, *Aorangi and Other Verses* (1896), *Station Ballads* (1897), *Wisps of Tussock* (1900) and *New Zealand Chimes* (1900), and some of his poems appeared in Australian periodicals. In 1909 he moved to Sydney, where he worked as a freelance writer for the *Bulletin* and other newspapers before succeeding Arthur H. Adams as editor of the *Bulletin*'s Red Page. He continued to write prolifically in prose and verse, often using such pseudonyms as 'Curse O' Moses', 'Pat O'Maori', 'George Street' and 'Mary McCommonwealth'. In 1918 he published his most substantial collection of verse, *An Irish Heart*, and in 1920 was awarded a prize for a poem commemorating the visit of the Prince of Wales, as well as the Rupert Brooke Memorial Prize for a long poem titled 'Galli-poli' (published in 1920 in the *Bulletin*). Wright also wrote some plays, although these, with much of his verse and prose writings, are uncollected; a prose play-let is included in the *Australian Soldiers' Gift Book* (1918). Like Victor Daley, Wright was strongly influenced by Irish history and legend, although his verse is generally thinner and less striking. The best-known characteristics of his prolific output are an indistinct but pervasive nostalgia for Ireland, visual, general imagery, firmly handled rhythms and a generally optimistic content. But Wright also published a great deal of work which had nothing to do with Ireland and which included satirical verse on political and social life in Australia and NZ. His longest satire, 'Apollo in George Street', written under the pseudonym 'Gillette', includes shrewd observations on contemporary poets, artists, editors and novelists. Regarded as a minor figure in Australia's Celtic tradition, Wright was in fact a more varied, innovative writer, sensitive to intellectual movements and well versed in different cultures and genres. It has been suggested that his disputes with Hugh McCrae and Norman Lindsay over their interpretation of classical art and literature may have led to his continuing disparagement. An influential, sometimes controversial, editor of the Red Page, Wright also edited *Poetical Works of Henry Lawson* (1925). After his death Zora Cross entered his novel 'Julian the Apostate' in the *Bulletin* story competition, where it was commended. Wright, who had been previously married in NZ, lived 1912–18 with the writer Margaret Fane, who was the mother of four of his sons, and with Zora Cross from 1918 until his death; they had two daughters.

WRIGHT, Judith (1915–) was born at Thalgaroch Station, near Armidale, NSW, into a pastoralist family whose roots go back on her paternal grandmother's side to the original settlement of the Hunter Valley in the 1820s. Her father, Phillip Arundell Wright (1889–1970), prominent New England pastoralist, and benefactor of New England University, wrote the autobiographical *Memories of a Bushwacker* (1971). She grew up on the family property Wollomombi (Wall-amumbi), near Armidale, in the heart of the New England tableland, and her love for that countryside, her 'blood's country', runs through much of her early poetry. Educated at New England Girls School, she read English at the University of Sydney, and visited England and Europe, 1937–38 before settling in Sydney to work and write. She published an occasional modest, thoughtful poem, e.g. 'The Hanging Avalanche of Days' in *Southerly* (1940), but with the entry of Japan into the war she returned to help out at Wollomombi, then badly beset by manpower problems. The homecoming, which brought the rediscovery and reassessment of her attachment to the countryside and the opportunity to think deeply about her art, led to her first intensive creative period. From the old stockman Dan's tales of the early days of the district and later from the diaries of her grandfather, Albert Wright, came material that filled much of her early

writing, stories that in her own words at the time, 'still go walking in my sleep'. Several fine poems about the war, 'The Trains', 'The Company of Lovers', 'To A.H. New Year, 1943', were written at this time. In 1943–47 she worked at the University of Queensland, where she met and married J.P. McKinney (q.v.), philosopher and writer whose influence, some believe, has been emphatic in her poetry. Since Wright's publication of *The Moving Image* (q.v., 1946), she has been a prolific poet, literary critic, anthologist, editor, children's writer, short-story writer, supporter of the Aboriginal land rights cause and active conservationist. She has received honorary D.Litts from seven Australian universities, and many awards for her writing, e.g. the Grace Leven Prize twice, the Britannica-Australia Award, the Christopher Brennan Award of the FAW and the ASAN World Prize for Poetry. In 1970 she was elected a foundation fellow of the Australian Academy of the Humanities; she has been a member of the governing body of the Australia Council and a creative arts fellow of the ANU. In her role as conservationist and activist she was for a number of years president of the Wildlife Preservation Society of Queensland, a member of the Committee of Enquiry into the National Estate, secretary of the Aboriginal Treaty Committee and life member of the Australian Conservative Foundation. In 1992 she received the Queen's Gold Medal for Poetry, the first Australian to receive the award. She was earlier awarded an emeritus fellowship of the Literature Board of the Australia Council.

Her chief volumes of poetry after *The Moving Image* have been *Woman to Man* (q.v., 1949); *The Gateway* (q.v., 1953); *The Two Fires* (q.v., 1955); *Birds* (1962); *Five Senses* (1963), (her first selected volume); *Judith Wright* in the Australian Poets Series (1963); *City Sunrise* (1964); *The Other Half* (1966); *Alive: Poems 1971–1972* (1973), *Fourth Quarter and Other Poems* (1976) and *Phantom Dwelling* (1985). Her *Collected Poems 1942–1970*, *The Double Tree: Selected Poems 1942–1976* and *A Human Pattern: Selected Poems* were published in 1971, 1978 and 1990 respectively. A further more substantial collection, 1942–85, was published in 1994 as well as a bilingual work, *The Flame Tree*, fifteen poems translated into Japanese by Nobuo Sakai and Wright's daughter Meredith McKinney. She has written children's fiction, including *Kings of the Dingoes* (1958), *The Day the Mountains Played* (1960) and *The River and the Road* (1966), and a book of short stories, *The Nature of Love* (1966); edited several anthologies, including *A Book of Australian Verse* (1956), *New Land, New Language* (1957) and *The Poet's Pen* (1965), and two selections of John Shaw Neilson's poetry (1963 and 1970); written monographs on Charles Harpur and Henry Lawson; narrated her family's history in *The Generations of Men* (q.v., 1959) and its sequel, *The Cry for the Dead* (1981); published a selection of her essays and reviews, *Because I Was Invited* (1975); written a seminal book of Australian poetic criticism, *Preoccupations in Australian Poetry* (1965); and, in her role as conservationist, has published *The Coral Battleground* (1977) and a book of essays, *Going on Talking* (1992), the second half of which focuses on her anxiety about the environment. Her struggle for the welfare of the Aborigines is given expression in *The Cry for the Dead*, *We Call for a Treaty* (1985) and *Born of the Conquerors* (1991). In an essay for the Tasmanian Wilderness Calendar (1981) she sums up the basis of her desire to fight the Aborigines' cause:

> Those two strands – the love of the land we have invaded and the guilt of the invasion – have become part of me. It is haunted. We owe it repentance and such amends as we can make ...

The appearance of *The Moving Image* in 1946 brought a sense of excitement and anticipation to the Australian literary world of the time; its impact was summed up in Douglas Stewart's *Bulletin* review: 'These poems promise anything, everything, the world.' The poems were acclaimed for their lyric beauty, brilliant craftsmanship and emotional honesty. The volumes following *Woman to Man*, except for the whimsical *Birds*, were received with less general enthusiasm. Wright herself has often expressed discomfiture by the view that those early poems, which she recently described as having 'dropped off several incarnations back', should be the yardstick of all her work. She has been supported by some critics who see that in her later poetry 'she made the harder choice of seeking, through private struggle, to wring from poetry a new vision of the world' (H.P. Heseltine). In the later volumes she reached beyond the easily perceived world of the senses in a search for an ultimate reality, perception or self-knowledge. In *The Gateway* she refers to 'the Traveller', and many of the poems in that collection and following volumes are a record of her 'travelling', her pilgrimage towards that reality and knowledge. Her initial view of the poet as the creative interpreter of the universe and its eternal processes of change still remains, however, at the centre of her poetry. Her recognition of 'the continuity of experience through time' leads her to accept the world as an interdependent community of all living things (human, animal, plant) and her use of nature as a stepping-stone to a deeper exploratory probing of universal human questions is still a satisfying basis from which the reader can proceed to an understanding and appreciation of her total work. In later volumes, especially in 'Shadow' (1970), the closing section of her *Collected Poems 1942–1970*, she attacks the evils of modern society, especially its abnegation of responsibility for the brutality that daily characterises world affairs. Her next three volumes, *Alive*, *Fourth Quarter* and *Phantom Dwelling*, chart yet another watershed in her poetic and philosophical approach. Shirley Walker has described *Alive* as 'a period of stasis', the poetry seeking through meditation 'the pattern of past experience'. Thus Walker sees the poems emphasising, in an elegiac tone, the significance of continuity, the importance of memory. From *Fourth Quarter* on, however, there is a resurgence of energy, as if the limitations of physicality are now dismissed and creative power, undiminished by increasing age, remains as ample recompense. *Phantom Dwelling* goes a step further, reinforcing, with its freshness, strength and clarity, that sense of limitless poetic power still available to her. Many *Phantom Dwelling* poems are familiar in theme – nature, love, her family and its pastoral links (past and present). The six poems of 'For a Pastoral Family' give a partly nostalgic but judicious assessment of the past viewed from the present, and a present still much aligned in attitude and outlook to the past. The things of nature – flora, fauna, the land itself – are still paramount to her, still retain their own 'thisness' ('The remnant of a mountain has its own meaning'). *Phantom Dwelling* ends with twelve short poems titled 'The Shadow of Fire: Ghazals' (Ghazals being a species of Oriental lyrics), in which the interface between ageless natural phenomena (a rockface, a rockpool, a flowering heath) and impermanent individual human life (our 'phantom dwelling') is again lovingly and carefully explored but with an increased, and seemingly new-won, equanimity. *A Human Pattern*, the Selected Volume of all her poetry to that point (1990), reveals the extraordinary substance, or as one critic called it, the 'nobleness', of Judith Wright's overall poetic achievement.

W.N. Scott wrote the biographical *Focus on Judith Wright* (1967), A.K. Thomson edited *Critical Essays on Judith Wright* (1968), A.D. Hope wrote the monograph *Judith Wright* (1975) and Shirley Walker, *The Poetry of Judith Wright: A Search for Unity* (1980), updated as *Flame and Shadow: A Study of Judith Wright's Poetry* (1991, in the UQP Studies in Australian Literature).

WRIGHTSON, Patricia, see *The Oxford Companion to Australian Children's Literature* (1993), pp. 457–8.

Writers in Action is a selection from recordings made at the 'Writer's Choice' evenings held by the Centre for Continuing Education at the University of Sydney. Each writer speaks about his or her work and engages in a question-and-answer session with the audience. Published by Currency Press (q.v.) and edited by Gerry Turcotte, the first volume of *Writers in Action* (1990) featured Alex Buzo, Peter Carey, Jack Davis, Helen Garner, Janette Turner Hospital, Ruby Langford, Amanda Lohrey, David Malouf, Les Murray and Roberta Sykes.

Writers in the Park: The Book 1985/86 (1986), edited by Carol Christie and Kim O'Brien, is a selection of previously unpublished works performed in the first year of the writers' nights at the Harold Park Hotel. As well as prose and poetry the book contains articles, a montage and a separate photographic text. More than an anthology it is a document of and a commentary on cultural life in Sydney.

Y

Yabber (Yabba) Club was a club which met weekly in the Shalimar café in Sydney during the late 1930s and early 1940s. Originally formed by P.R. Stephensen, W.J. Miles and others to discuss the editorial policy of the *Publicist*, the Australia First journal, its meetings subsequently embraced literary and cultural topics. Eleanor Dark, Frank Dalby Davison, Miles Franklin, Lionel Lindsay and T. Inglis Moore were among writers 'permanently invited', and Franklin, Xavier Herbert, Harley Matthews and Ian Mudie were among writers who attended.

YAGAN (?–1833), a WA Aborigine who acquired a reputation for patriotism, courage and resourcefulness, was sentenced to detention for killing a White man in 1832 but soon escaped. He was proclaimed an outlaw in April 1833 with his father, Midgigoroo, following the massacre of other Whites, and was shot for the reward in July 1833 by a young shepherd, William Keates. Yagan's escapades are described in G.F. Moore's *Diary of Ten Years Eventful Life of an Early Settler in Western Australia* (1884). An extended account of his activities is in W.B. Kimberly, *History of West Australia* (1897). Mary Durack wrote *The Courteous Savage: Yagan of Swan River* (1964).

YAHP, Beth (1964–), born Malaysia of Chinese-Thai parentage, came to Australia in 1984 to study at the University of Technology, Sydney. To support her writing she has worked at whatever casual jobs were available. She co-edited *My Look's Caress* (1990), a collection of Australian short romance fiction, and wrote *The Crocodile Fury* (1992), an intriguing story of the lives of three generations of women in a Malaysian convent – the grandmother, who has been 'a ghost chaser', the mother who works in the convent laundry and the daughter (for the most part the narrator) who gets her somewhat diminished education at the convent in return for her and her mother's labours. *The Crocodile Fury* won the Prize for First Fiction in the 1993 Victorian Premier's Literary Awards.

Yandy (1959), a novel by Donald Stuart (q.v.), gives a fictional account of the establishment of the Aboriginal Pindan Co-operative in WA in 1946. The station Aborigines of north-west WA, led by Winyerin, or Dooley as he is called by the White people, and assisted by the help and advice of a White man, Don McLeod, strike for better conditions and more tolerant racial attitudes. The Aborigines turn to 'yandying' for a livelihood, i.e. shaking minerals from alluvial dirt by the use of a special dish. In spite of confrontations with police and White society, the Aborigines remain steadfast. They discover the profitable mineral wolfram and begin to construct a new life.

Yaralie (1962), a novel by Donald Stuart (q.v.), is the story of a young part-Aboriginal girl, Yaralie. After her mother's death the young girl shares with her father, a stockman-turned-prospector, an itinerant life in outback WA. They are separated when he goes south to recover from a stroke and she endures the cruelty and intolerance customarily extended to the Aborigine. As a girl of 15 she falls in love with young Raymond Mendoza, of Filipino extraction, and they resume the old life of prospecting. At the end of the novel Yaralie has a final meeting with her dying father and tells him of the child she is carrying, a child of mixed descent, Australian, Scottish, Aboriginal and Filipino, 'a child of the country', one who would form part of the future generations that would people the North-West. In Stuart's and the old man's words, 'They'll be the *real* people of Nor'-west, the people who know it and understand it, the way it's got to be known and understood.' The novel's strength is its compelling picture of the harsh but beautiful inland environment and the precarious existence of those who live in fragile affinity with it.

Yarra River flows (Sydneysiders believe that to be a euphemism) from Mount Baw Baw, east of Melbourne, about 250 kilometres to Port Phillip Bay. Discovered by Charles Grimes in 1803, the river was named Yarra Yarra by J.H. Wedge in 1835. On its banks, John Batman (q.v.) decided, was 'the place for a village' – the present city of Melbourne. More often the subject of derisive comments than of panegyrics, the Yarra is nevertheless an essential part of the Melbourne scene. It has given its name to the 'Yarra Banker', originally a specialist in the art of loafing, more recently a soapbox orator who harangues the passing crowds, especially on a Sunday afternoon. When the Murray River became part of the boundary between NSW and Victoria, the term 'Yarrasiders' denoted the Victorians as opposed to 'Sydneysiders', who lived north of the Murray. Some of the picturesque aspects of the river are captured in Bill Beasley and Brian Carroll's *River Yarra Sketchbook* (1973).

YARRINGTON, W.H.H. (William Henry Hazell) (?–1920), a clergyman with numerous literary friends, published several volumes of verse in book and pamphlet form 1880–1919. They include *University Prize Poem and Other Verses* (1880), *Coelestia* (1882), *Turning to the East* (1890), *Australian Verses* (1892), *Sonnets on Ritualism* (1901), *The Man of Principle* (?1904), and *Crossing the Mountain* (1919). He also edited the anthology *Prince Alfred's Wreath* (1868), which includes poetry by Henry Kendall and J. Sheridan Moore. Yarrington is one of the minor targets of Kendall's satiric poem *The Bronze Trumpet*.

YATES, Renate, born Renate Raubitschek in Vienna, Austria, grew up in Sydney, graduating in dentistry from the University of Sydney. She practised her profession in London for a period before returning to Australia and now writes full-time. She has contributed short stories to numerous periodicals and anthologies and has published the novels *Social Death* (1984), *Rural Pursuits* (1988) and *The Narcissus Conspiracy* (1991); and the collection of short stories *Fine Bones* (1985). Entertaining mysteries, Yates's novels are also humorous satires which reveal a sharp eye for human foibles and vanities. Spare, sharply perceptive and well honed, the short stories of *Fine Bones* are subtitled *Chronicles of Death Life and Love*, although they deal mostly with death, both of the body and the spirit; a child grows up and discovers his irrelevance to the lives of his apparently indulgent grandparents, a wife contrives the death of her husband's lover by an act of telekinesis, a mother brings about the divorce of her son from his 'unsuitable' wife, a girl's prophecy that she will die at 40 is fulfilled.

Year of Living Dangerously, The, a novel by Christopher Koch (q.v.), was published in 1978, won the *Age* Book of the Year and the National Book Council Awards, and was made into a film in 1982, scripted by Koch, Peter Weir and David Williamson. It is set in Jakarta in 1965 against the backdrop of the mysterious intrigues that culminated in Sukarno's fall. Public events have strange, revolutionary effects on the lives and relationships of Guy Hamilton, an Australian news correspondent; his remarkable Chinese-Australian cameraman, Billy Kwan; and the woman they both love, Jill Bryant. Oppressive, unpredictable and latently violent, the external situation powerfully complements the suspenseful, personal vicissitudes.

YELDHAM, Peter, born Gladstone, NSW, worked as a script-writer for radio before leaving for England in 1956 and establishing a reputation as a writer for film and television as well as a playwright. His plays include 'Birds on the Wing' (1969), 'She Won't Lie Down' (1971), *Fringe Benefits* (1977), 'Lighting Up Time' (1977) and *Seven Little Australians* (1989). For the screen he has written *Comedy Man* (1964), *The Liquidator* (1966), *The Long Duel* (1968), *Age of Consent* (1969) and *Boundaries of the Heart* (1989). He has written popular novel adaptations and series for TV, e.g. *The Timeless Land, Sporting Chance, The Lancaster Miller Affair, Captain James Cook, Run from the Morning, 1915, Ride on Stranger, All the Rivers Run, The Far Country, Tusitalia, The Alien Years, Heroes, Naked Under Capricorn* and *Heroes: The Return*. His radio scripts include *Stella, East of Christmas, Reunion Day, The Cabbage Tree Hat Boys, A Visit from Anna* and *Thunder on the Snowy*. He won the British Writers Guild Award 1963, Australian Awgies 1980, 1983, 1986, 1989 and the Penguin

Award 1982. He was awarded the OAM for his services to screen and television.

You Can't See Round Corners, a novel by Jon Cleary (q.v.), was published in 1947 and won second prize in the *Sydney Morning Herald*'s novel competition of 1946. It was also produced as a film and as a television series. Set mainly in Sydney during the Second World War, it is the story of 21-year-old Frankie McCoy, who has experienced poverty in childhood, has learnt to depend on his wits and holds an inarticulate grudge against the social system. A basically weak individual who lacks self-knowledge, he drifts inevitably towards his shabby fate. Conscripted into the army, he hates the boredom and regimentation and soon deserts. After Margie, his girlfriend of seven years, rejects him in consequence, he becomes involved with another, more sexually experienced girl, Myra. Entangled in gambling debts, he robs a shop and then inadvertently kills Myra in a fit of frustrated passion. A reconciliation with Margie leads to his apprehension by the military police, his death and the discovery of his crimes.

Yorick Club, which included most of the prominent Victorian writers of the 1860s, was founded by Frederick William Haddon in 1868 and grew from the informal meetings he held during 1867–68 at his rooms in Spring Street, Melbourne. Established 'for the purpose of bringing together literary men and those connected with literature, art or science', it included among its earliest members Adam Lindsay Gordon, Hamilton Mackinnon, J.J. Shillinglaw, Marcus Clarke, James E. Neild and George Arthur Walstab. Clarke was the Club's first secretary, although he left it soon afterwards to form a more bohemian group, the Cave of Adullam. Henry Kendall became a member during his stay in Melbourne and later literary members included George Gordon McCrae and Patrick Moloney. At first a lively and informal gathering of writers, committed to practical jokes and all-night suppers, the Yorick soon dwindled into a respectable institution. By 1871 its entry rule had been altered to include 'professional men' and the financial pressures of the 1890s caused further enlargements. The original Yorick Club was wound up in 1894. *The Yorick Club: Its Origin and Development, May 1868 to December 1910* (1911) by Thomas Carrington is an account of its history and membership, and Hugh McCrae describes some of its activities in *My Father, and My Father's Friends* (1935).

Young Desire It, The, a novel by Kenneth Mackenzie (q.v.), which was first published in 1937 under his pseudonym, 'Seaforth Mackenzie', won the Gold Medal of the Australian Literature Society. An account of a year in the life of a sensitive 15-year-old boy, Charles Fox, it deals with his intellectual, emotional and sexual awakening when he leaves home and his protective mother to enter boarding school. One of the masters, an Englishman named Christopher Penworth, forms an attachment for him, although Charles remains innocent of its homosexual implications. Meanwhile, Charles has formed a stronger, idyllically realised relationship with a girl, Margaret McLeod. The romance eventually excites Penworth's jealousy and leads to a cooling of his relationship with Charles. Penworth returns to England and at the same time Charles learns that Margaret is to leave for finishing school in Switzerland. The book ends with Charles back at school in the new year, a letter from Penworth in his hand, contemplating his past, irrevocable experiences.

Young Man of Talent, a novel by George Turner (q.v.), was published in London in 1959 and in New York the same year with the title *Scobie.* Set in New Guinea during the Second World War, it probes the fatally dissimilar personalities of three Australian soldiers: Scobie, a veteran New Guinea campaigner who has speedily risen to platoon commander and developed a taste for power; Payne, a rebel, who quickly accedes to total subservience to Scobie's superior intellect; and Tolley, a paranoid, insecure graduate from the Royal Military College, Duntroon, who arrives to take over Scobie's command. The story traces Scobie's moral deterioration as he effectively uses Payne to destroy Tolley, destroying his own humanity in the process.

Young Wife, The, a novel by David Martin (q.v.), was published in 1962. Anna Christofidou, a Cypriot girl, arrives in Sydney to marry a man she has never met, Yannis Joannides, a greengrocer. She is welcomed by Yannis, his successful but devious brother Alexis and his wife Elena, and by her future mother-in-law Maria, who has arranged the marriage. Yannis becomes friendly with a Cypriot artist, Criton, who has come to Australia to escape his terrorist past and is drawn to Anna by her special qualities of purity and deep feeling. He later paints a picture of Ariadne rising from the sea, based on his drawings of Anna, on the wall of Yannis's shop. Anna is drawn into amateur theatricals through her family's friendship with a Professor Peter Barwing and his wife Patricia, an association that ends abruptly when Peter Barwing attempts to make love to Anna. Yannis later beats Anna when he hears something of what has happened. Meanwhile Criton becomes unwittingly involved in the political feuds of the Greek community and in a love affair with Patricia Barwing that ends in her attempted suicide. Anna intercedes unavailingly on Patricia's behalf with Criton and Patricia leaves for an extended visit to India. On her return she contributes to false rumours about the now pregnant Anna and Criton, which are exacerbated by his enemies and by Yannis's insensitive reaction to his drawings of Anna. A fight ensues between Criton and Yannis in which Criton is killed. Martin also wrote a dramatised version of *The Young Wife*, which was staged in 1966.

YOUNG, William Blamire (1862–1935), painter and poster artist, was born in England and came to Australia in 1885, when he became friendly with Phil May, the illustrator. Young returned to England in 1912, served in the First World War and subsequently had several major exhibitions in London. In 1923 he returned to Melbourne, where he became art critic for the *Herald*. Two of Young's one-act plays, 'Art for Art's Sake' and *The Children's Bread* (1912), were produced in Melbourne in 1911. His painting was the subject of a special number of *Art in Australia* in 1921. Elly Fink has written *The Art of Blamire Young* (1983).

Z

ZABLE, Arnold (1947–), born Wellington, NZ, whither his parents (Polish Jews) had emigrated in the 1930s, grew up in the inner Melbourne suburb of Carlton. Educated at the University of Melbourne and Columbia University, he has travelled widely and worked in a variety of jobs in the USA, India, Papua New Guinea, Europe, South East Asia and China. In the 1970s a lecturer in the Arts Faculty (Social Sciences) at Melbourne University, he has, in recent years, been involved in migrant education, teaching English and adult literacy. Co-editor of the English-Yiddish periodical the *Melbourne Chronicle*, he has written two children's books, *Clown Boy* (1982) and *The River Man* (1982) and a film, *Glenn's Story* (1979). His most important work is the story of his journey back to the town in Poland where his parents had grown up, *Jewels and Ashes* (1991), which won the Ethnic Affairs Commission Award in the 1991 NSW State Literary Awards and the 1991 NBC Lysbeth Cohen Award. His father, Meier Zabludowski, leaves Poland in 1936 to join his wife Hoddes, who had gone to NZ several years before him. During boyhood Zable is a keen listener to the happy tales of pre-war Bialystock and the horror tales of the Holocaust. In response to the need to bear witness to the Holocaust, he travels to Bialystock in 1986 over the Trans-Siberian railway through Moscow and on to Poland. The journey, the people he meets, the ancestral ghosts that are laid, and the fearful reminiscences of the Holocaust as well as the joyous and happy moments that he experiences, are all recorded with great poignancy in *Jewels and Ashes*.

ZAVOS, Spiro (1937–), born Wellington, NZ, of Greek parents, arrived in Australia in 1977 after education at Victoria University, NZ, and at the Catholic University of America. After receiving the Katherine Mansfield Fellowship in 1978, he spent a year in France and has since worked as a journalist with the *Sydney Morning Herald*. He has published a biography of Sir Robert Muldoon, two books in the field of sociology and a collection of short fiction, *Faith of Our Fathers* (1982), which won the award for ethnic writing in the 1983 NSW Premier's Literary Awards.

ZILLMANN, John Herman Leopold (1842–1919), an Anglican minister, born Brisbane and resident in Queensland, published two novels which are mainly religious in tone, *In the Land of the Bunya: Or, the Convict and the Boy* (1899) and *From Old to New: Or, Mitre Versus Gown* (1901); four collections of religious verse and one of hymns; a prose meditation on the super-

natural, *Two Worlds Are Ours* (1885); and two works which mingle history, description and personal reminiscence, *Past and Present Australian Life* (1889) and *Career of a Cornstalk* (1914).

ZWICKY, Fay (1933–), born Melbourne, began writing as an undergraduate at the University of Melbourne and has published short stories and poems in anthologies and periodicals. A concert pianist for some years before teaching English at the University of WA 1972–87, she has published the collections of verse *Isaac Babel's Fiddle* (1975), *Kaddish and Other Poems* (1982, winner of the NSW Premier's Award), *Ask Me* (1990, winner of the 1991 WA Premier's Award for poetry), *A Touch of Ginger* (1991, with Dennis Haskell) and *Fay Zwicky: Poems 1970–1992* (1993). She has also edited *Quarry* (1981), a selection of contemporary WA poetry; *Journeys* (1982), an anthology of poems by Judith Wright, Rosemary Dobson, Gwen Harwood and Dorothy Hewett; and *Procession* (1987), a collection of poetry by members of the group known as the Young Street poets. Her first collection of short stories, *Hostages*, was published in 1983. A well-known critic, Zwicky has published a substantial collection of her essays, reviews and articles in *The Lyre in the Pawnshop* (1986).

Zwicky writes an individual, emotionally direct and densely textured poetry which is concerned with division, conflict and dispossession, the paradoxes of experience, the ambivalences of relationships and the relation between artist and art. One of the most marked characteristics of her poetry is a challenging of patriarchal myth and its implicit silencing of the language and experience of women. Resisting traditional values, structures and perceptions as they are represented both by myth and by linguistic convention, Zwicky's is an original, confident voice which can move easily from elegy to satire to parody. One of her most admired poems, 'Kaddish', is a lament for the death of her father, which is also a vivid, funny/sad evocation of life in a Melbourne Jewish family. Four of the stories of *Hostages* also draw on her youthful experience in Melbourne and evoke the pains, humiliations and enlightenments of growing up; others use a range of narrators to explore various aspects of contemporary Australian life. The essays in *The Lyre in the Pawnshop* range over Australian, American and English literature and probe what Zwicky describes as 'the interchange between a man's individual powers and the culture to which he belongs', working from the premise that the artist must find a way to balance the claims of individualism and community.